e v e r y D a y
with Jesus
BIBLE

A ONE-YEAR READING BIBLE

D1009231

With Devotions by
S E L W Y N   H U G H E S

HOLMAN
BIBLE PUBLISHERS

Nashville, Tennessee

TABLE OF CONTENTS

PLAN OF SALVATION

What do you understand it takes for a person to go to Heaven?
Consider how the Bible answers this question: It's a matter of FAITH

F is for FORGIVENESS
We cannot have eternal life and heaven without God's forgiveness.

—**Read Ephesians 1:7a.**

A is for AVAILABLE
Forgiveness is available. It is—
    Available for all.   —**Read John 3:16.**
    But not automatic.   —**Read Matthew 7:21a.**

I is for IMPOSSIBLE
It is impossible for God to allow sin into heaven.
Because of who He is:
    God is loving and just.
    His judgment is against sin.   —**Read James 2:13a.**
Because of who we are:
    Every person is a sinner.   —**Read Romans 3:23.**
But how can a sinful person enter heaven, when God allows no sin?

T is for TURN
Turn means to repent.
Turn from something—sin and self.   —**Read Luke 13:3b.**
Turn to Someone; trust Christ only.   —**Read Romans 10:9.**

H is for HEAVEN
Heaven is eternal life.
    Here   —**Read John 10:10b.**
    Hereafter   —**Read John 14:3.**
How can a person have God's forgiveness, heaven and eternal life, and Jesus as personal Savior and Lord? By trusting in Christ and asking Him for forgiveness. Take the step of faith described by another meaning of FAITH: Forsaking All I Trust Him.

Prayer:
    Lord Jesus, I know I am a sinner and have displeased You in many ways.
    I believe You died for my sin and only through faith in Your death and
    resurrection can I be forgiven.

    I want to turn from my sin and ask You to come into my life as my Savior
    and Lord. From this day on, I will follow You by living a life that pleases You.
    Thank You, Lord Jesus for saving me. Amen.

After you have received Jesus Christ into your life, tell a Christian friend about this important decision you have made. Follow Christ in believer's baptism and church membership. Grow in your faith and enjoy new friends in Christ by becoming part of His church. There, you'll find others who will love and support you.

INTRODUCTION TO THE
Holman Christian Standard Bible®

The Bible is God's revelation to man. It is the only book that gives us accurate information about God, man's need, and God's provision for that need. It provides us with guidance for life and tells us how to receive eternal life. The Bible can do these things because it is God's inspired Word, inerrant in the original manuscripts.

The Bible describes God's dealings with the ancient Jewish people and the early Christian church. It tells us about the great gift of God's Son, Jesus Christ, who fulfilled Jewish prophecies of the Messiah. It tells us about the salvation He accomplished through His death on the cross, His triumph over death in the resurrection, and His promised return to earth. It is the only book that gives us reliable information about the future, about what will happen to us when we die, and about where history is headed.

Bible translation is both a science and an art. It is a bridge that brings God's Word from the ancient world to the world today. In dependence on God to accomplish this sacred task, Holman Bible Publishers presents the Holman Christian Standard Bible, a new English translation of God's Word.

Textual base of the Holman CSB®

The textual base for the New Testament [NT] is the Nestle-Aland *Novum Testamentum Graece*, 27th edition, and the United Bible Societies' *Greek New Testament*, 4th corrected edition. The text for the Old Testament [OT] is the *Biblia Hebraica Stuttgartensia,* 5th edition. At times, however, the translators have followed an alternative manuscript tradition, disagreeing with the editors of these texts about the original reading.

Where there are significant differences among Hebrew [Hb] and Aramaic [Aram] manuscripts of the OT or among Greek [Gk] manuscripts of the NT, the translators have followed what they believe is the original reading and have indicated the main alternative(s) in footnotes. In a few places in the NT, large square brackets indicate texts that the translation team and most biblical scholars today believe were not part of the original text. However, these texts have been retained in brackets in the Holman CSB because of their undeniable antiquity and their value for tradition and the history of NT interpretation in the church. The Holman CSB uses traditional verse divisions found in most Protestant Bibles.

Goals of this translation

The goals of this translation are:

- to provide English-speaking people across the world with an accurate, readable Bible in contemporary English

- to equip serious Bible students with an accurate translation for personal study, private devotions, and memorization

- to give those who love God's Word a text that has numerous reader helps, is visually attractive on the page, and is appealing when heard

- to affirm the authority of Scripture as God's Word and to champion its absolute truth against social or cultural agendas that would compromise its accuracy

The name, Holman Christian Standard Bible, captures these goals: *Holman* Bible Publishers presents a new *Bible* translation, for *Christian* and English-speaking communities, which will be a *standard* in Bible translations for years to come.

Why is there a need for another English translation of the Bible?

There are several good reasons why Holman Bible publishers invested its resources in a modern language translation of the Bible:

1. Each generation needs a fresh translation of the Bible in its own anguage.

The Bible is the world's most important book, confronting each individual and each culture with issues that affect life, both now and forever. Since each new generation must be introduced to God's Word in its own language, there will always be a need for new translations such as the *Holman Christian Standard Bible*. The majority of Bible translations on the market today are revisions of translations from previous generations. The Holman CSB is a new translation for today's generation.

2. English, one of the world's greatest languages, is rapidly changing, and Bible translations must keep in step with those changes.

English is the first truly global language in history. It is the language of education, business, medicine, travel, research, and the Internet. More than 1.3 billion people around the world speak or read English as a primary or secondary language. The Holman CSB seeks to serve many of those people with a translation they can easily use and understand.

English is also the world's most rapidly changing language. The Holman CSB seeks to reflect recent changes in English by using modern punctuation, formatting, and vocabulary, while avoiding slang, regionalisms, or changes made specifically for the sake of political or social agendas. Modern linguistic and semantic advances have been incorporated into the Holman CSB, including modern grammar.

3. Rapid advances in biblical research provide new data for Bible translators.

This has been called the "information age," a term that accurately describes the field of biblical research. Never before in history has there been as much information about the Bible as there is today—from archaeological discoveries to analysis of ancient manuscripts to years of study and statistical research on individual Bible books. Translations made as recently as 10 or 20 years ago do not reflect many of these advances in biblical research. The translators have taken into consideration as much of this new data as possible.

4. Advances in computer technology have opened a new door for Bible translation.

The Holman CSB has used computer technology and telecommunications in its creation perhaps more than any Bible translation in history. Electronic mail was used daily and sometimes hourly for communication and transmission of manuscripts. An advanced Bible software program, Accordance®, was used to create and revise the translation at each step in its production. A developmental copy of the translation itself was used within Accordance to facilitate cross-checking during the translation process—something never done before with a Bible translation.

Translation Philosophy of the Holman CSB

Most discussions of Bible translations speak of two opposite approaches: formal equivalence and dynamic equivalence. Although this terminology is meaningful, Bible translations cannot be neatly sorted into these two categories any more than people can be neatly sorted into two categories according to height or weight. Holman Bible Publishers is convinced there is room for another category of translation philosophies that capitalizes on the strengths of the other two.

1. Formal Equivalence:

Often called "word-for-word" (or "literal") translation, the principle of formal equivalence seeks as nearly as possible to preserve the structure of the original language. It seeks to represent each word of the translated text with an exact equivalent word in the translation so that the reader can see word for word what the original human author wrote. The merits of this approach include its consistency with the conviction that the Holy Spirit did inspire the very words of Scripture in the original manuscripts. It also provides the English Bible student some access to the structure of the text in the original language. Formal equivalence can achieve accuracy to the degree that English has an exact equivalent for each word and that the grammatical patterns of the original language can be reproduced in understandable English. However, it can sometimes result in awkward, if not incomprehensible, English or in a misunderstanding of the author's intent. The literal rendering of ancient idioms is especially difficult.

2. Dynamic or Functional Equivalence:

Often called "thought-for-thought" translation, the principle of dynamic equivalence rejects as misguided the desire to preserve the structure of the original language. It proceeds by distinguishing the meaning of a text from its form and then translating the meaning so that it makes the same impact on modern readers that the ancient text made on its original readers. Strengths of this approach include a high degree of clarity and readability, especially in places where the original is difficult to render word for word. It also acknowledges that accurate and effective translation requires interpretation. However, the meaning of a text cannot always be neatly separated from its form, nor can it always be precisely determined. A biblical author may have intended multiple meanings. In striving for readability, dynamic equivalence also sometimes overlooks some of the less prominent elements of meaning. Furthermore, lack of formal correspondence to the original makes it difficult to verify accuracy and thus can affect the usefulness of the translation for in-depth Bible study.

3. Optimal Equivalence:

In practice, translations are seldom if ever purely formal or dynamic but favor one theory of Bible translation or the other to varying degrees. Optimal equivalence as a translation philosophy recognizes that form cannot be neatly separated from meaning and should not be changed (for example, nouns to verbs or third person "they" to second person "you") unless comprehension demands it. The primary goal of translation is to convey the sense of the original with as much clarity as the original text and the translation language permit. Optimal equivalence appreciates the goals of formal equivalence but also recognizes its limitations.

Optimal equivalence starts with an exhaustive analysis of the text at every level (word, phrase, clause, sentence, discourse) in the original language to determine its original meaning and intention (or purpose). Then relying on the latest and best language tools and experts, the nearest corresponding semantic and linguistic equivalents are used to convey as much of the information and intention of the original text with as much clarity and readability as possible. This process assures the maximum transfer of both the words and thoughts contained in the original.

The Holman CSB uses optimal equivalence as its translation philosophy. When a literal translation meets these criteria, it is used. When clarity and readability demand an idiomatic translation, the reader can still access the form of the original text by means of a footnote with the abbreviation "Lit."

The gender language policy in Bible translation

Some people today ignore the Bible's teachings on distinctive roles of men and women in family and church and have an agenda to eliminate those distinctions in every arena of life. These people have begun a program to engineer the removal of a perceived male bias in the English language. The targets of this program have been such traditional linguistic practices as the generic use of "man" or "men," as well as "he," "him," and "his."

A group of Bible scholars, translators, and other evangelical leaders met in 1997 to respond to this issue as it affects Bible translation. This group produced the "Guidelines for Translation of Gender-Related Language in Scripture" (adopted May 27, 1997 and revised Sept. 9, 1997). The Holman Christian Standard Bible was produced in accordance with these guidelines.

The goal of the translators has not been to promote a cultural ideology but to faithfully translate the Bible. While the Holman CSB avoids using "man" or "he" unnecessarily, the translation does not restructure sentences to avoid them when they are in the text. For example, the translators have not changed "him" to "you" or to "them," neither have they avoided other masculine words such as "father" or "son" by translating them in generic terms such as "parent" or "child."

History of the Holman Christian Standard Bible

After several years of preliminary development, Holman Bible Publishers, the oldest Bible publisher in America, assembled an international, interdenominational team of 100 scholars, editors, stylists, and proofreaders, all of whom were committed to biblical inerrancy. Outside consultants and reviewers contributed valuable suggestions from their areas of expertise. An executive team then edited, polished, and reviewed the final manuscripts.

Traditional features found in this edition of the Holman CSB

In keeping with a long line of Bible publications, the Holman Christian Standard Bible has retained these features found in traditional Bibles:

1. Traditional theological vocabulary (such as justification, sanctification, redemption, etc.) has been retained since such terms have no translation equivalent that adequately communicates their exact meaning.
2. Traditional spellings of names and places found in most Bibles have been used to make the Holman CSB compatible with most Bible study tools.
3. Nouns and personal pronouns that clearly refer to any person of the Trinity are capitalized.
4. Two common forms of punctuation are used in the Holman CSB to help with clarity and ease of reading: em dashes (a long dash —) are used to indicate sudden breaks in thought or to help clarify long or difficult sentences. Parentheses are used infrequently to indicate words that are parenthetical in the original languages.

How certain names and terms are translated

The names of God

The Holman Christian Standard Bible OT consistently translates the Hebrew names for God as follows:

Holman CSB English:	Hebrew original:
God	*Elohim*
LORD	*YHWH (Yahweh)*
Lord	*Adonai*
Lord GOD	*Adonai Yahweh*
LORD of Hosts	*Yahweh Sabaoth*
God Almighty	*El Shaddai*

However, the Holman CSB OT uses Yahweh, the personal name of God in Hebrew, when a biblical text emphasizes Yahweh as a name: "His name is Yahweh" (Ps 68:4). Yahweh is used more often in the Holman CSB than in most Bible translations because the word Lord in English is a title of God and does not accurately convey to modern readers the emphasis on God's name in the original Hebrew.

<u>The uses of Christ and Messiah</u>
The Holman CSB translates the Greek word Christos ("anointed one") as either "Christ" or "Messiah" based on its use in different NT contexts. Where the NT emphasizes Christos as a name of our Lord or has a Gentile context, "Christ" is used (Eph 1:1 "Paul, an apostle of Christ Jesus..."). Where the NT Christos has a Jewish context, the title "Messiah" is used (Eph 1:12 "...we who had already put our hope in the Messiah"). The first use of "Messiah" in each chapter is also marked with a bullet referring readers to the Bullet Note at the back of most editions.

<u>Place-names</u>
In the original text of the Bible, particularly in the OT, a number of well-known places have names different from the ones familiar to contemporary readers. For example, "the Euphrates" often appears in the original text simply as "the River." In cases like this, the Holman Christian Standard Bible uses the modern name, "the Euphrates River," in the text without a footnote or lower corner brackets.

<u>Substitution of words in sentences</u>
A literal translation of the biblical text sometimes violates standard rules of English grammar, such as the agreement of subject and verb or person and number. In order to conform to standard usage, the Holman CSB has often made these kinds of grammatical constructions agree in English without footnotes or lower corner brackets.
In addition, the Greek or Hebrew texts sometimes seem redundant or ambiguous by repeating nouns where modern writing substitutes pronouns or by using pronouns where we would supply nouns for clarity and good style. When a literal translation of the original would make the English unclear, the Holman CSB sometimes changes a pronoun to its corresponding noun or a noun to its corresponding pronoun without a footnote or lower corner brackets. For example, Jn 1:42 reads: "And he brought Simon to Jesus . . ." The original Greek of this sentence reads: "And he brought him to Jesus."

Formatting Features

This edition of the Holman CSB has several distinctive formatting features:

1. OT passages quoted in the NT are set in boldface type. OT quotes consisting of two or more lines are block indented.
2. In dialogue, a new paragraph is used for each new speaker as in most modern publications.

3. Many passages, such as 1 Co 13, have been formatted as dynamic prose (separate block-indented lines like poetry) for ease in reading and comprehension. Special block-indented formatting has also been used extensively in both the OT and NT to increase readability and clarity in lists, series, genealogies and other parallel or repetitive texts.

4. Almost every Bible breaks lines in poetry using automatic typesetting programs with the result that words are haphazardly turned over to the next line. In the Holman CSB, special attention has been given to break every line in poetry and dynamic prose so that awkward or unsightly word wraps are avoided and complete units of thought turn over to the next line. The result is a Bible page that is much more readable and pleasing to the eye.

5. Italics are used in the text for a transliteration of Greek and Hebrew words (*"Hosanna!"* in Jn 12:13) and in footnotes for direct quotations from the biblical text and for words in the original languages (the footnote at Jn 1:1 reads: "The Word (Gk *logos*) is a title for Jesus…").

6. Since the majority of English readers do not need to have numbers and fractions spelled out in the text, the Holman CSB uses a similar style to that of modern newspapers in using Arabic numerals for the numbers 10 and above and in fractions, except in a small number of cases, such as when a number begins a sentence.

JANUARY 1

GENESIS 1:1–2:25

1 In the beginning God created the heavens and the earth.

² Now the earth was formless and empty, darkness covered the surface of the watery depths, and the Spirit of God was hovering over the surface of the waters. ³ Then God said, "Let there be light," and there was light. ⁴ God saw that the light was good, and God separated the light from the darkness. ⁵ God called the light "day," and He called the darkness "night." Evening came, and then morning: the first day.

⁶ Then God said, "Let there be an expanse between the waters, separating water from water." ⁷ So God made the expanse and separated the water under the expanse from the water above the expanse. And it was so. ⁸ God called the expanse "sky." Evening came, and then morning: the second day.

⁹ Then God said, "Let the water under the sky be gathered into one place, and let the dry land appear." And it was so. ¹⁰ God called the dry land "earth," and He called the gathering of the water "seas." And God saw that it was good. ¹¹ Then God said, "Let the earth produce vegetation: seed-bearing plants, and fruit trees on the earth bearing fruit with seed in it, according to their kinds." And it was so. ¹² The earth brought forth vegetation: seed-bearing plants according to their kinds and trees bearing fruit with seed in it, according to their kinds. And God saw that it was good. ¹³ Evening came, and then morning: the third day.

¹⁴ Then God said, "Let there be lights in the expanse of the sky to separate the day from the night. They will serve as signs for festivals and for days and years. ¹⁵ They will be lights in the expanse of the sky to provide light on the earth." And it was so. ¹⁶ God made the two great lights—the greater light to have dominion over the day and the lesser light to have dominion over the night—as well as the stars. ¹⁷ God placed them in the expanse of the sky to provide light on the earth, ¹⁸ to dominate the day and the night, and to separate light from darkness. And God saw that it was good. ¹⁹ Evening came, and then morning: the fourth day.

²⁰ Then God said, "Let the water swarm with living creatures, and let birds fly above the earth across the expanse of the sky." ²¹ So God created the large sea-creatures and every living creature that moves and swarms in the water, according to their kinds. He also created every winged bird according to its kind. And God saw that it was good. ²² So God blessed them, "Be fruitful, multiply, and fill the waters of the seas, and let the birds multiply on the earth." ²³ Evening came, and then morning: the fifth day.

²⁴ Then God said, "Let the earth produce living creatures according to their kinds: livestock, creatures that crawl, and the wildlife of the earth according to their kinds." And it was so. ²⁵ So God made the wildlife of the earth according to their kinds, the livestock according to their kinds, and creatures that crawl on the ground according to their kinds. And God saw that it was good.

²⁶ Then God said, "Let Us make man in Our image, according to Our likeness. They will rule the fish of the sea, the birds of the sky, the animals, all the earth, and the creatures that crawl on the earth."

²⁷ So God created man in His own image;
     He created him in the image of God;
     He created them male and female.

[28] God blessed them, and God said to them, "Be fruitful, multiply, fill the earth, and subdue it. Rule the fish of the sea, the birds of the sky, and every creature that crawls on the earth." [29] God also said, "Look, I have given you every seed-bearing plant on the surface of the entire earth, and every tree whose fruit contains seed. This food will be for you, [30] for all the wildlife of the earth, for every bird of the sky, and for every creature that crawls on the earth—everything having the breath of life in it. I have given every green plant for food." And it was so. [31] God saw all that He had made, and it was very good. Evening came, and then morning: the sixth day.

2 So the heavens and the earth and everything in them were completed. [2] By the seventh day, God completed His work that He had done, and He rested on the seventh day from all His work that He had done. [3] God blessed the seventh day and declared it holy, for on it He rested from His work of creation.

[4] These are the records of the heavens and the earth, concerning their creation at the time that the LORD God made the earth and the heavens. [5] No shrub of the field had yet grown on the land, and no plant of the field had yet sprouted, for the LORD God had not made it rain on the land, and there was no man to work the ground. [6] But water would come out of the ground and water the entire surface of the land. [7] Then the LORD God formed the man out of the dust from the ground and breathed the breath of life into his nostrils, and the man became a living being.

[8] The LORD God planted a garden in Eden, in the east, and there He placed the man He had formed. [9] The LORD God caused to grow out of the ground every tree pleasing in appearance and good for food, including the tree of life in the midst of the garden, as well as the tree of the knowledge of good and evil.

[10] A river went out from Eden to water the garden. From there it divided and became the source of four rivers. [11] The name of the first is Pishon, which encircles the entire land of the Havilah, where there is gold. [12] Gold from that land is pure; bdellium and onyx are also there. [13] The name of the second river is Gihon, which encircles the entire land of Cush. [14] The name of the third river is the Tigris, which flows to the east of Assyria. And the fourth river is the Euphrates.

[15] The LORD God took the man and placed him in the garden of Eden to work it and watch over it. [16] And the LORD God commanded the man, "You are free to eat from any tree of the garden, [17] but you must not eat from the tree of the knowledge of good and evil, for on the day you eat from it, you will certainly die." [18] Then the LORD God said, "It is not good for the man to be alone. I will make a helper who is like him." [19] So the LORD God formed out of the ground each wild animal and each bird of the sky, and brought each to the man to see what he would call it. And whatever the man called a living creature, that was its name. [20] The man gave names to all the livestock, to the birds of the sky, and to every wild animal; but for the man no helper was found who was like him. [21] So the LORD God caused a deep sleep to come over the man, and he slept. God took one of his ribs and closed the flesh at that place. [22] Then the LORD God made the rib He had taken from the man into a woman and brought her to the man. [23] And the man said:

This one, at last, is bone of my
    bone,
and flesh of my flesh;
this one will be called woman,
for she was taken from man.

[24] This is why a man leaves his father and mother and bonds with his wife, and they become one flesh. [25] Both the man and his wife were naked, yet felt no shame.

PSALM 1:1-6

[1] How happy is the man
  who does not follow the advice of
    the wicked,

or take the path of sinners,
or join a group of mockers!
2 Instead, his delight is in the
LORD's instruction,
and he meditates on it day and
night.
3 He is like a tree planted beside
streams of water
that bears its fruit in season
and whose leaf does not wither.
Whatever he does prospers.

4 The wicked are not like this;
instead, they are like chaff that
the wind blows away.
5 Therefore the wicked will not
survive the judgment,
and sinners will not be in the
community of the righteous.

6 For the Lord watches over the way
of the righteous,
but the way of the wicked leads to
ruin.

*P*ROVERBS I:I-4

1 The Proverbs of Solomon son of
David, king of Israel:
2 For gaining wisdom and being
instructed;
for understanding insightful
sayings;
3 for receiving wise instruction
in righteousness, justice, and
integrity;
4 for teaching shrewdness to the
inexperienced,
knowledge and discretion to a
young man—

*M*ATTHEW I:I-25

1 The historical record of Jesus Christ,
the Son of David, the Son of Abraham:

2 Abraham fathered Isaac,
Isaac fathered Jacob,
Jacob fathered Judah and his
brothers,
3 Judah fathered Perez and Zerah
by Tamar,

Perez fathered Hezron,
Hezron fathered Aram,
4 Aram fathered Aminadab,
Aminadab fathered Nahshon,
Nahshon fathered Salmon,
5 Salmon fathered Boaz by Rahab,
Boaz fathered Obed by Ruth,
Obed fathered Jesse,
6 and Jesse fathered King David.

Then David fathered Solomon
by Uriah's wife,
7 Solomon fathered Rehoboam,
Rehoboam fathered Abijah,
Abijah fathered Asa,
8 Asa fathered Jehoshaphat,
Jehoshaphat fathered Joram,
Joram fathered Uzziah,
9 Uzziah fathered Jotham,
Jotham fathered Ahaz,
Ahaz fathered Hezekiah,
10 Hezekiah fathered Manasseh,
Manasseh fathered Amon,
Amon fathered Josiah,
11 and Josiah fathered Jechoniah
and his brothers
at the time of the exile
to Babylon.

12 Then after the exile to Babylon
Jechoniah fathered Salathiel,
Salathiel fathered Zerubbabel,
13 Zerubbabel fathered Abiud,
Abiud fathered Eliakim,
Eliakim fathered Azor,
14 Azor fathered Zadok,
Zadok fathered Achim,
Achim fathered Eliud,
15 Eliud fathered Eleazar,
Eleazar fathered Matthan,
Matthan fathered Jacob,
16 and Jacob fathered Joseph the
husband of Mary,
who gave birth to Jesus
who is called the Messiah.

17 So all the generations from Abraham to David were 14 generations; and
from David until the exile to Babylon,
14 generations; and from the exile to
Babylon until the Messiah, 14 generations.
18 The birth of Jesus Christ came
about this way: After His mother Mary

had been engaged to Joseph, it was discovered before they came together that she was pregnant by the Holy Spirit. [19] So her husband Joseph, being a righteous man, and not wanting to disgrace her publicly, decided to divorce her secretly.

[20] But after he had considered these things, an angel of the Lord suddenly appeared to him in a dream, saying, "Joseph, son of David, don't be afraid to take Mary as your wife, because what has been conceived in her is by the Holy Spirit. [21] She will give birth to a son, and you are to name Him Jesus, because He will save His people from their sins."

[22] Now all this took place to fulfill what was spoken by the Lord through the prophet:

[23]   See, the virgin will
       become pregnant
  and give birth to a son,
  and they will name Him
       Immanuel,

which is translated "God is with us." [24] When Joseph got up from sleeping, he did as the Lord's angel had commanded him. He married her [25] but did not know her intimately until she gave birth to a son. And he named Him Jesus.

The Primary Focus

In the beginning God.—GENESIS 1:1

We focus on what is without doubt the most noble and loftiest of themes: the nature and character of God. I have noticed that Christians, generally speaking, seem to be preoccupied with knowing more about themselves rather than knowing more about God. Ask any Christian bookshop manager: "What are the best-selling books?" Not those that unfold for us the nature of God, but those that direct us toward such things as how to get a better self-image, how to manage money, how to find inner healing, how to get more excitement out of life, and so on. Not that these subjects are unimportant, but they are explored in a self-absorbed way that gives the idea that the most important thing in life is knowing ourselves better. It isn't. The most important thing in life is knowing God better.

John Lancaster, a minister in Cardiff, South Wales, in an article entitled "Where on Earth Is God?" asks the question: "Given a choice between attending a seminar, say, on the 'Glory of God in Isaiah' and one on 'The Christian and Sex,' to which would you go?" He makes the point also that although the church often answers the questions that people are asking, the real problem may be that people are not asking the right questions. In today's church we are far too man-centered and not God-centered.

It is not by accident, I believe, that the Bible opens with the thunderous acclaim: "In the beginning God." I tell you with all the conviction of which I am capable: if God is not our primary focus, then everything else will soon get out of focus.

Prayer

O Father, from this day help me determine to make You my primary focus. And give me the grace and strength to maintain it, through all the vicissitudes and uncertainties of the days ahead. In Jesus' name I pray. Amen.

Further Study

Jn 1:1-5; Col 1:15-20; Heb 12:2; Rv 1:8
What did the Lord declare to John the revelator?
What did the apostle John declare?

JANUARY 2

GENESIS 3:1–4:26

3 Now the serpent was the most cunning of all the wild animals that the LORD God had made. He said to the woman, "Did God really say, 'You can't eat from any tree in the garden'?"

² The woman said to the serpent, "We may eat the fruit from the trees in the garden. ³ But about the fruit of the tree in the middle of the garden, God said, 'You must not eat it or touch it, or you will die.'"

⁴ "No! You will not die," the serpent said to the woman. ⁵ "In fact, God knows that when you eat it your eyes will be opened and you will be like God, knowing good and evil." ⁶ Then the woman saw that the tree was good for food and delightful to look at, and that it was desirable for obtaining wisdom. So she took some of its fruit and ate it; she also gave some to her husband, who was with her, and he ate it. ⁷ Then the eyes of both of them were opened, and they knew they were naked; so they sewed fig leaves together and made loincloths for themselves.

⁸ Then the man and his wife heard the sound of the LORD God walking in the garden at the time of the evening breeze, and they hid themselves from the LORD God among the trees of the garden. ⁹ So the LORD God called out to the man and said to him, "Where are you?"

¹⁰ And he said, "I heard You in the garden, and I was afraid because I was naked, so I hid."

¹¹ Then He asked, "Who told you that you were naked? Did you eat from the tree that I had commanded you not to eat from?"

¹² Then the man replied, "The woman You gave to be with me—she gave me some fruit from the tree, and I ate."

¹³ So the LORD God asked the woman, "What is this you have done?"

And the woman said, "It was the serpent. He deceived me, and I ate."

¹⁴ Then the LORD God said to the serpent:

Because you have done this,
you are cursed more than any
livestock
and more than any wild animal.
You will move on your belly
and eat dust all the days of your
life.
¹⁵ I will put hostility between you
and the woman,
and between your seed and her
seed.
He will strike your head,
and you will strike his heel.

¹⁶ He said to the woman:

I will intensify your labor pains;
you will bear children in anguish.
Your desire will be for your
husband,
yet he will dominate you.

5

¹⁷ And He said to Adam, "Because you listened to your wife's voice and ate from the tree about which I commanded you, 'Do not eat from it':

The ground is cursed because of you.
You will eat from it by means of painful labor
all the days of your life.
¹⁸ It will produce thorns and thistles for you,
and you will eat the plants of the field.
¹⁹ You will eat bread by the sweat of your brow
until you return to the ground,
since you were taken from it.
For you are dust,
and you will return to dust."

²⁰ Adam named his wife Eve because she was the mother of all the living. ²¹ The LORD God made clothing out of skins for Adam and his wife, and He clothed them. ²² The LORD God said, "Since man has become like one of Us, knowing good and evil, he must not reach out, and also take from the tree of life, and eat, and live forever." ²³ So the LORD God sent him away from the garden of Eden to work the ground from which he was taken. ²⁴ He drove man out, and east of the garden of Eden He stationed cherubim with a flaming, whirling sword to guard the way to the tree of life.

4 Adam knew his wife Eve intimately, and she conceived and gave birth to Cain. She said, "I have had a male child with the LORD's help." ² Then she also gave birth to his brother Abel. Now Abel became a shepherd of a flock, but Cain cultivated the land. ³ In the course of time Cain presented some of the land's produce as an offering to the LORD. ⁴ And Abel also presented an offering—some of the firstborn of his flock and their fat portions. The LORD had regard for Abel and his offering, ⁵ but He did not have regard for Cain and his offering. Cain was furious, and he was downcast.
⁶ Then the LORD said to Cain, "Why are you furious? And why are you downcast? ⁷ If you do right, won't you be accepted? But if you do not do right, sin is crouching at the door. Its desire is for you, but you must master it."
⁸ Cain said to his brother Abel, "Let's go out to the field." And while they were in the field, Cain attacked his brother Abel and killed him.
⁹ Then the LORD said to Cain, "Where is your brother Abel?"
"I don't know," he replied. "Am I my brother's guardian?"
¹⁰ Then He said, "What have you done? Your brother's blood cries out to Me from the ground! ¹¹ So now you are cursed with alienation from the ground that opened its mouth to receive your brother's blood you have shed. ¹² If you work the land, it will never again give you its yield. You will be a restless wanderer on the earth."
¹³ But Cain answered the LORD, "My punishment is too great to bear! ¹⁴ Since You are banishing me today from the soil, and I must hide myself from Your presence and become a restless wanderer on the earth, whoever finds me will kill me."
¹⁵ Then the LORD replied to him, "In that case, whoever kills Cain will suffer vengeance seven times over." And He placed a mark on Cain so that whoever found him would not kill him. ¹⁶ Then Cain went out from the LORD's presence and lived in the land of Nod, east of Eden.
¹⁷ Cain knew his wife intimately, and she conceived and gave birth to Enoch. Then Cain became the builder of a city, and he named the city Enoch after his son. ¹⁸ Irad was born to Enoch, Irad fathered Mehujael, Mehujael fathered Methushael, and Methushael fathered Lamech. ¹⁹ Lamech took two wives for himself, one named Adah and the other named Zillah. ²⁰ Adah bore Jabal; he was the father of the nomadic herdsmen. ²¹ His brother was named Jubal; he was the father of all who play the lyre and the flute. ²² Zillah bore Tubal-cain, who made all kinds of bronze and iron tools. Tubal-cain's sister was Naamah.
²³ Lamech said to his wives:

Adah and Zillah, hear my voice;
wives of Lamech, pay attention to
my words.
For I killed a man for wounding
me,
a boy for striking me.
24 If Cain is to be avenged seven
times over,
then for Lamech it will be
seventy-seven times!

25 Adam knew his wife intimately again, and she gave birth to a son and named him Seth, for she said, "God has given me another child in place of Abel, since Cain killed him." 26 A son was born to Seth also, and he named him Enosh. At that time people began to call on the name of the LORD.

PSALM 2:1-6

1 Why do the nations rebel
and the peoples plot in vain?
2 The kings of the earth take their
stand
and the rulers conspire together
against the LORD and His Anointed
One:
3 "Let us tear off their chains
and free ourselves from their
restraints."

4 The One enthroned in heaven
laughs;
the Lord ridicules them.
5 Then He speaks to them in His
anger
and terrifies them in His wrath:
6 "I have consecrated My King
on Zion, My holy mountain."

PROVERBS 1:5-6

5 a wise man will listen and
increase his learning,
and a discerning man will obtain
guidance—
6 for understanding a proverb or a
parable,
the words of the wise, and their
riddles.

MATTHEW 2:1-23

2 After Jesus was born in Bethlehem of Judea in the days of King Herod, wise men from the east arrived unexpectedly in Jerusalem, 2 saying, "Where is He who has been born King of the Jews? For we saw His star in the east and have come to worship Him."

3 When King Herod heard this, he was deeply disturbed, and all Jerusalem with him. 4 So he assembled all the chief priests and scribes of the people and asked them where the Messiah would be born.

5 "In Bethlehem of Judea," they told him, "because this is what was written by the prophet:

6 And you, Bethlehem, in the land
of Judah,
are by no means least
among the leaders of Judah:
because out of you will come
a leader
who will shepherd My people
Israel."

7 Then Herod secretly summoned the wise men and asked them the exact time the star appeared. 8 He sent them to Bethlehem and said, "Go and search carefully for the child. When you find Him, report back to me so that I too can go and worship Him." 9 After hearing the king, they went on their way. And there it was—the star they had seen in the east! It led them until it came and stopped above the place where the child was. 10 When they saw the star, they were overjoyed beyond measure. 11 Entering the house, they saw the child with Mary His mother, and falling to their knees, they worshiped Him. Then they opened their treasures and presented Him with gifts: gold, frankincense, and myrrh. 12 And being warned in a dream not to go back to Herod, they returned to their own country by another route.

13 After they were gone, an angel of the Lord suddenly appeared to Joseph in a dream, saying, "Get up! Take the child

7

and His mother, flee to Egypt, and stay there until I tell you. For Herod is about to search for the child to destroy Him." [14] So he got up, took the child and His mother during the night, and escaped to Egypt. [15] He stayed there until Herod's death, so that what was spoken by the Lord through the prophet might be fulfilled: Out of Egypt I called My Son. [16] Then Herod, when he saw that he had been outwitted by the wise men, flew into a rage. He gave orders to massacre all the male children in and around Bethlehem who were two years old and under, in keeping with the time he had learned from the wise men. [17] Then what was spoken through Jeremiah the prophet was fulfilled:

[18] A voice was heard in Ramah,
    weeping, and great mourning,

Rachel weeping for her children;
and she refused to be consoled,
because they were no more.

[19] After Herod died, an angel of the Lord suddenly appeared in a dream to Joseph in Egypt, [20] saying, "Get up! Take the child and His mother and go to the land of Israel, because those who sought the child's life are dead." [21] So he got up, took the child and His mother, and entered the land of Israel. [22] But when he heard that Archelaus was ruling over Judea in place of his father Herod, he was afraid to go there. And being warned in a dream, he withdrew to the region of Galilee. [23] Then he went and settled in a town called Nazareth to fulfill what was spoken through the prophets, that He will be called a Nazarene.

God's Great Intolerance

Then He speaks to them in His anger and terrifies them in His wrath.—PSALM 2:5

Wrath is not a defect in the divine character; rather, it would be a defect if wrath were absent from Him. Those who see God's wrath as petulance or retaliation, inflicting punishment just for the sake of it or in return for some injury received, do not really understand it. Divine wrath is not vindictiveness; it is divine perfection, issuing forth from God because it is right.

Human beings tend to make God in our own image. He made us in His image, but we want to return the compliment, and it is there that so often we go wrong. Instead of reasoning from the divine down to the human, recognizing that sin has marred the divine image within us, we reason from our fallen condition and project our own feelings and ideas onto God.

Thus, when thinking of the wrath of God, we tend to look at what happens in our own hearts when we get angry, and we imagine God to be the same. But divine anger must never be confused with human anger. Most of what goes on in our hearts whenever we are angry is a mixture of unpredictable petulance, retaliation, hostility, and self-concern. God's anger is always predictable, always steadfast, and always set against sin. We must never forget that God's nature is uncompromisingly set against sin. We may tolerate it; He never.

Sin has been defined as "God's one great intolerance," and for that we ought to be eternally grateful. As His children we ought to rejoice that He will not tolerate anything that is harmful to us.

Prayer

O Father, what a change comes over me when I realize that Your wrath is not so much directed at persons as at the sin that demeans and destroys them. You are not against me for my sin, but for me against my sin. I am deeply, deeply grateful. Amen.

Further Study

Ps 5:1-6; 11:5; Hab 1:12-13; Zch 8:16-17
How did the psalmist express God's great intolerance?
What does the Lord hate?

JANUARY 3

GENESIS 5:1–6:22

5 These are the family records of the descendants of Adam. On the day that God created man, He made him in the likeness of God; ² He created them male and female. When they were created, He blessed them and called them man.

³ Adam was 130 years old when he fathered a child in his likeness, according to his image, and named him Seth. ⁴ Adam lived 800 years after the birth of Seth, and he fathered sons and daughters. ⁵ So Adam's life lasted 930 years; then he died.

⁶ Seth was 105 years old when he fathered Enosh. ⁷ Seth lived 807 years after the birth of Enosh, and he fathered sons and daughters. ⁸ So Seth's life lasted 912 years; then he died.

⁹ Enosh was 90 years old when he fathered Kenan. ¹⁰ Enosh lived 815 years after the birth of Kenan, and he fathered sons and daughters. ¹¹ So Enosh's life lasted 905 years; then he died.

¹² Kenan was 70 years old when he fathered Mahalalel. ¹³ Kenan lived 840 years after the birth of Mahalalel, and he fathered sons and daughters. ¹⁴ So Kenan's life lasted 910 years; then he died.

¹⁵ Mahalalel was 65 years old when he fathered Jared. ¹⁶ Mahalalel lived 830 years after the birth of Jared, and he fathered sons and daughters. ¹⁷ So Mahalalel's life lasted 895 years; then he died.

¹⁸ Jared was 162 years old when he fathered Enoch. ¹⁹ Jared lived 800 years after the birth of Enoch, and he fathered sons and daughters. ²⁰ So Jared's life lasted 962 years; then he died.

²¹ Enoch was 65 years old when he fathered Methuselah. ²² And after the birth of Methuselah, Enoch walked with God 300 years and fathered sons and daughters. ²³ So Enoch's life lasted 365 years. ²⁴ Enoch walked with God, and he was not there, because God took him.

²⁵ Methuselah was 187 years old when he fathered Lamech. ²⁶ Methuselah lived 782 years after the birth of Lamech, and he fathered sons and daughters. ²⁷ So Methuselah's life lasted 969 years; then he died.

²⁸ Lamech was 182 years old when he fathered a son. ²⁹ And he named him

9

Noah, saying, "This one will bring us relief from the agonizing toil of our hands, caused by the ground the LORD has cursed." ³⁰ Lamech lived 595 years after Noah's birth, and he fathered sons and daughters. ³¹ So Lamech's life lasted 777 years; then he died.

³² Noah was 500 years old, and he fathered Shem, Ham, and Japheth.

6 When mankind began to multiply on the earth and daughters were born to them, ² the sons of God saw that the daughters of man were beautiful, and they took any they chose as wives for themselves. ³ And the LORD said, "My Spirit will not remain with mankind forever, because they are corrupt. Their days will be 120 years." ⁴ The Nephilim were on the earth both in those days and afterwards, when the sons of God came to the daughters of man, who bore children to them. They were the powerful men of old, the famous men.

⁵ When the LORD saw that man's wickedness was widespread on the earth and that every scheme his mind thought of was nothing but evil all the time, ⁶ the LORD regretted that He had made man on the earth, and He was grieved in His heart. ⁷ Then the LORD said, "I will wipe off the face of the earth: man, whom I created, together with the beasts, creatures that crawl, and birds of the sky—for I regret that I made them." ⁸ Noah, however, found favor in the eyes of the LORD.

⁹ These are the family records of Noah. Noah was a righteous man, blameless among his contemporaries; Noah walked with God. ¹⁰ And Noah fathered three sons: Shem, Ham, and Japheth.

¹¹ Now the earth was corrupt in God's sight, and the earth was filled with violence. ¹² God saw how corrupt the earth was, for all flesh had corrupted its way on the earth. ¹³ Then God said to Noah, "I have decided to put an end to all flesh, for the earth is filled with violence because of them; therefore I am going to destroy them along with the earth.

¹⁴ "Make yourself an ark of gofer wood. Make rooms in the ark, and cover it with pitch inside and outside. ¹⁵ This is how you are to make it: The ark will be 450 feet long, 75 feet wide, and 45 feet high. ¹⁶ You are to make a roof, finishing the sides of the ark to within 18 inches of the roof. You are to put a door in the side of the ark. Make it with lower, middle, and upper decks.

¹⁷ "Understand that I am bringing a deluge—floodwaters on the earth to destroy all flesh under heaven with the breath of life in it. Everything on earth will die. ¹⁸ But I will establish My covenant with you, and you will enter the ark with your sons, your wife, and your sons' wives. ¹⁹ You are also to bring into the ark two of every living thing of all flesh, male and female, to keep them alive with you. ²⁰ Two of everything—from the birds according to their kinds, from the livestock according to their kinds, and from every animal that crawls on the ground according to its kind—will come to you so that you can keep them alive. ²¹ Take with you every kind of food that is eaten; gather it as food for you and for them." ²² And Noah did this. He did everything that God had commanded him.

PSALM 2:7-12

⁷ I will declare the LORD's decree:
   He said to Me, "You are My Son;
   today I have become Your
      Father.

⁸ Ask of Me, and I will make the
   nations Your inheritance
   and the ends of the earth Your
      possession.

⁹ You will break them with a rod of
   iron;
   You will shatter them like pottery."

¹⁰ So now, kings, be wise;
   receive instruction, you judges of
      the earth.

¹¹ Serve the LORD with reverential
   awe,
   and rejoice with trembling.

¹² Pay homage to the Son, or He will
   be angry,

and you will perish in your
rebellion,
for His anger may ignite at any
moment.
All those who take refuge in Him
are happy.

PROVERBS 1:7

7 The fear of the LORD is the
beginning of knowledge;
fools despise wisdom and
instruction.

MATTHEW 3:1-17

3 In those days John the Baptist came, preaching in the Wilderness of Judea ² and saying, "Repent, because the kingdom of heaven has come near!" ³ For he is the one spoken of through the prophet Isaiah, who said:

A voice of one crying out
in the wilderness:
"Prepare the way for the Lord;
make His paths straight!"

⁴ John himself had a camel-hair garment with a leather belt around his waist, and his food was locusts and wild honey. ⁵ Then people from Jerusalem, all Judea, and all the vicinity of the Jordan were flocking to him, ⁶ and they were baptized by him in the Jordan River as they confessed their sins. ⁷ When he saw many of the Pharisees and Sadducees coming to the place of his baptism, he said to them, "Brood of vipers! Who warned you to flee from the coming wrath? ⁸ Therefore produce fruit consistent with repentance. ⁹ And don't presume to say to yourselves, 'We have Abraham as our father.' For I tell you that God is able to raise up children for Abraham from these stones! ¹⁰ Even now the ax is ready to strike the root of the trees! Therefore every tree that doesn't produce good fruit will be cut down and thrown into the fire.

¹¹ "I baptize you with water for repentance, but the One who is coming after me is more powerful than I. I am not worthy to take off His sandals. He Himself will baptize you with the Holy Spirit and fire. ¹² His winnowing shovel is in His hand, and He will clear His threshing floor and gather His wheat into the barn. But the chaff He will burn up with fire that never goes out."

¹³ Then Jesus came from Galilee to John at the Jordan, to be baptized by him. ¹⁴ But John tried to stop Him, saying, "I need to be baptized by You, and yet You come to me?"

¹⁵ Jesus answered him, "Allow it for now, because this is the way for us to fulfill all righteousness." Then he allowed Him to be baptized.

¹⁶ After Jesus was baptized, He went up immediately from the water. The heavens suddenly opened for Him, and He saw the Spirit of God descending like a dove and coming down on Him. ¹⁷ And there came a voice from heaven:

This is My beloved Son.
I take delight in Him!

On This Truth We Stand

[Jesus] . . . saw . . . the Spirit of God descending. . . . And there came a voice from heaven: "This is My beloved Son." —MATTHEW 3:16-17

Those who accept Scripture's teaching concerning God must be prepared to say that He is not only personal, but that He is a plurality of Persons—a Trinity. The doctrine of the Trinity, that God is one yet three separate Persons, is not easy to understand, but it is clear in Scripture. The term "Trinity" nowhere appears in the Bible (it was first used by Tertullian around A.D. 210), but its roots are deeply embedded in the Word of God. It is mainly a revelation of the New Testament, but there are glimpses of the truth to be seen in the Old Testament also.

"Let Us make man in Our image" (Gn 1:26). To whom was God speaking? Some say the angels, but nowhere in Scripture are angels seen as being involved in the act of creation or as being on the same level as God. Read Colossians 1:16 and it will become clear to whom God was speaking.

Other examples of the Trinity being mentioned in the Old Testament include these: "Man has become like one of Us" (Gn 3:22); and in Isaiah 6:8 God says: "Who should I send? Who will go for Us?"

"Go to the Jordan," wrote Augustine, "and you find the Trinity. There at the baptism of Jesus, the three Persons in the Godhead are simultaneously in evidence. The Father is heard speaking directly from heaven, the Son is seen being immersed in the river, and John the Baptist beholds the Spirit descending upon the Christ." Three in One and One in Three. On this truth we must stand, though we may not fully understand.

Prayer

Blessed Trinity, Three in One and One in Three, my spirit joins with Your Spirit this day to worship You in spirit and in truth. Though sometimes darkness to my intellect, Your truth is nevertheless sunshine to my heart. Amen.

Further Study

Mt 28:16-20; Jn 14:26-27; 15:26-27
How were the disciples to baptize new converts?
How did Jesus confirm the truth of the Trinity?

JANUARY 4

GENESIS 7:1–9:7

7 Then the LORD said to Noah, "Enter the ark, you and all your household, for I have seen that you alone are righteous before Me in this generation. ² You are to take with you seven pairs, a male and its female, of all the clean animals, and two of the animals that are not clean, a male and its female, ³ and seven pairs, male and female, of the birds of the sky—in order to keep offspring alive on the face of the whole earth. ⁴ Seven days from now I will make it rain on the earth 40 days and 40 nights, and I will wipe off the face of the earth every living thing I have made." ⁵ And Noah did everything that the LORD commanded him.

⁶ Noah was 600 years old when the

deluge came and water covered the earth. ⁷ So Noah, his sons, his wife, and his sons' wives entered the ark because of the waters of the deluge. ⁸ From the clean animals, unclean animals, birds, and every creature that crawls on the ground, ⁹ two of each, male and female, entered the ark with Noah, just as God had commanded him. ¹⁰ Seven days later the waters of the deluge came on the earth.

¹¹ In the six hundredth year of Noah's life, in the second month, on the seventeenth day of the month, on that day all the sources of the watery depths burst open, the floodgates of the sky were opened, ¹² and the rain fell on the earth 40 days and 40 nights. ¹³ On that same day Noah along with his sons Shem, Ham, and Japheth, Noah's wife, and his three sons' wives entered the ark with him. ¹⁴ They entered it with all the wildlife according to their kinds, all livestock according to their kinds, every creature that crawls on the earth according to its kind, all birds, every fowl, and everything with wings according to their kinds. ¹⁵ Two of all flesh that has the breath of life in it entered the ark with Noah. ¹⁶ Those that entered, male and female of all flesh, entered just as God had commanded him. Then the LORD shut him in.

¹⁷ The deluge continued 40 days on the earth; the waters increased and lifted up the ark so that it rose above the earth. ¹⁸ The waters surged and increased greatly on the earth, and the ark floated on the surface of the water. ¹⁹ Then the waters surged even higher on the earth, and all the high mountains under the whole sky were covered. ²⁰ The mountains were covered as the waters surged above them more than 20 feet. ²¹ All flesh perished—creatures that crawl on the earth, birds, livestock, wildlife, and all creatures that swarm on the earth, as well as all mankind. ²² Everything with the breath of the spirit of life in its nostrils—everything on dry land died. ²³ He wiped out every living thing that was on the surface of the ground, from mankind to livestock, to creatures that crawl, to the birds of

the sky, and they were wiped off the earth. Only Noah was left, and those that were with him in the ark. ²⁴ And the waters surged on the earth 150 days.

8 God remembered Noah, as well as all the wildlife and all the livestock that were with him in the ark. God caused a wind to pass over the earth, and the water began to subside. ² The sources of the watery depths and the floodgates of the sky were closed, and the rain from the sky stopped. ³ The water steadily receded from the earth, and by the end of 150 days the waters had decreased significantly. ⁴ The ark came to rest in the seventh month, on the seventeenth day of the month, on the mountains of Ararat.

⁵ The waters continued to recede until the tenth month; in the tenth month, on the first day of the month, the tops of the mountains were visible. ⁶ After 40 days Noah opened the window of the ark that he had made, ⁷ and he sent out a raven. It went back and forth until the waters had dried up from the earth. ⁸ Then he sent out a dove to see whether the water on the earth's surface had gone down, ⁹ but the dove found no resting place for her foot. She returned to him in the ark because water covered the surface of the whole earth. He reached out and brought her into the ark to himself. ¹⁰ So Noah waited seven more days and sent out the dove from the ark again. ¹¹ When the dove came to him at evening, there was a plucked olive leaf in her beak. So Noah knew that the water on the earth's surface had gone down. ¹² After he had waited another seven days, he sent out the dove, but she did not return to him again. ¹³ In the six hundred and first year, in the first month, on the first day of the month, the water that had covered the earth was dried up. Then Noah removed the ark's cover and saw that the surface of the ground was drying. ¹⁴ By the twenty-seventh day of the second month, the earth was dry.

¹⁵ Then God spoke to Noah, ¹⁶ "Come out of the ark, you, your wife, your sons, and your sons' wives with you.

[17] Bring out every living thing of all flesh that is with you—birds, livestock, creatures that crawl on the ground—and they will spread over the earth and be fruitful and multiply on the earth." [18] So Noah, along with his sons, his wife, and his sons' wives, came out. [19] All wildlife, all livestock, every bird, and every creature that crawls on the earth came out of the ark by their groups.

[20] Then Noah built an altar to the LORD. He took some of every kind of clean animal and every kind of clean bird and offered burnt offerings on the altar. [21] When the LORD smelled the pleasing aroma, He said to Himself, "I will never again curse the ground because of man, even though man's inclination is evil from his youth. And I will never again strike down every living thing as I have done.

[22]   As long as the earth endures,
    seedtime and harvest, cold and
        heat,
    summer and winter, and day and
        night
    will not cease."

9 God blessed Noah and his sons and said to them, "Be fruitful and multiply and fill the earth. [2] The fear and terror of you will be in every living creature on the earth, every bird of the sky, every creature that crawls on the ground, and all the fish of the sea. They are placed under your authority. [3] Every living creature will be food for you; as I gave the green plants, I have given you everything. [4] However, you must not eat meat with blood in it. [5] I will require the life of every animal and every man for your life and your blood. I will require the life of each man's brother for a man's life.

[6]   Whoever sheds man's blood,
    his blood will be shed by man,
    for God made man
    in His image.

[7] But you, be fruitful and multiply; spread out over the earth and multiply on it."

PSALM 3:1-8

[1] LORD, how my foes increase!
    There are many who attack me.
[2] Many say about me,
    "There is no help for him in God."
                        Selah

[3] But You, LORD, are a shield around
        me,
    my glory, and the One who lifts
        up my head.
[4] I cry aloud to the LORD,
    and He answers me from His holy
        mountain.   *Selah*

[5] I lie down and sleep;
    I wake again because the LORD
        sustains me.
[6] I am not afraid of the thousands of
        people
    who have taken their stand against
        me on every side.

[7] Rise up, LORD!
    Save me, my God!
    You strike all my enemies on the
        cheek;
    You break the teeth of the wicked.
[8] Salvation belongs to the Lord;
    may Your blessing be on Your
        people.   *Selah*

PROVERBS 1:8-9

[8] Listen, my son, to your father's
        instruction,
    and don't reject your mother's
        teaching,
[9] for they will be a garland of grace
        on your head
    and a gold chain around your
        neck.

MATTHEW 4:1-20

4 Then Jesus was led up by the Spirit into the wilderness to be tempted by the Devil. [2] After He had fasted 40 days and 40 nights, He was hungry. [3] Then the tempter approached Him and said, "If You are the Son of God, tell these stones to become bread."

⁴But He answered, "It is written:

Man must not live
on bread alone
but on every word that comes
from the mouth of God."

⁵Then the Devil took Him to the holy city, had Him stand on the pinnacle of the temple, ⁶and said to Him, "If You are the Son of God, throw Yourself down. For it is written:

He will give His angels orders
concerning you and,
they will support you
with their hands
so that you will not strike
your foot against a stone."

⁷Jesus told him, "It is also written: Do not test the Lord your God."
⁸Again, the Devil took Him to a very high mountain and showed Him all the kingdoms of the world and their splendor. ⁹And he said to Him, "I will give You all these things if You will fall down and worship me."
¹⁰Then Jesus told him, "Go away, Satan! For it is written:

Worship the Lord your God,
and serve only Him."

¹¹Then the Devil left Him, and immediately angels came and began to serve Him.
¹²When He heard that John had been arrested, He withdrew into Galilee. ¹³He left Nazareth behind and went to live in Capernaum by the sea, in the region of Zebulun and Naphtali. ¹⁴This was to fulfill what was spoken through the prophet Isaiah:

¹⁵ Land of Zebulun and land
of Naphtali,
along the sea road,
beyond the Jordan,
Galilee of the Gentiles!
¹⁶ The people who live in darkness
have seen a great light,
and for those living in the
shadowland of death,
light has dawned.

¹⁷From then on Jesus began to preach, "Repent, because the kingdom of heaven has come near!"
¹⁸As He was walking along the Sea of Galilee, He saw two brothers, Simon, who was called Peter, and his brother Andrew. They were casting a net into the sea, since they were fishermen. ¹⁹"Follow Me," He told them, "and I will make you fish for people!" ²⁰Immediately they left their nets and followed Him.

Influence or Intelligence?

Jesus told him,
"Go away, Satan! For it is written . . ."
—**MATTHEW 4:10**

Some of the names given to the devil in Scripture show him to be a real personality. In the passage that is before us today, Jesus is seen in direct confrontation with the devil, even engaging in conversation with him. Some liberal theologians explain this in these terms: Christ was having a conversation with the dark thoughts that arose within His nature, so any "devil" that was present was subjective, not objective.

If we allow the notion that Christ had dark thoughts within His nature, then the whole scheme of redemption tumbles like a pack of cards, for a Savior who is not perfect could never fully atone for our sins. As Dr. Handley Moule puts it: "A Savior who is not perfect is like a bridge broken at one end and is not a reliable passage of access." Once we try to get around Scripture, we create endless difficulties for ourselves and finish up looking foolish. Far better to accept the Bible as it stands and believe its testimony on everything.

It is actually to Satan's advantage to get us to believe that he is not a personal being, for if there is no personal devil, there can be no personal resistance. Don't allow yourself to be deceived into thinking that the term *devil* is a synonym for the evil influence that is in the world. The devil is more than an evil influence; he is an evil intelligence. Only when we recognize this fact will we be motivated to take effective steps to resist him.

Prayer

Father, help me see that the first step in spiritual warfare is to "know the enemy." For until I know and understand my enemy, I will not be able to defeat him. Deepen my knowledge of these important truths, I pray. In Jesus' name. Amen.

Further Study

1 Jn 3:1-8; Heb 2:14; Jn 12:30-31
Why was Jesus made manifest?
What did He declare?

JANUARY 5

GENESIS 9:8–10:32

⁸ Then God said to Noah and his sons with him, ⁹ "Understand that I am confirming My covenant with you and your descendants after you, ¹⁰ and with every living creature that is with you—birds, livestock, and all wildlife of the earth that are with you—all the animals of the earth that came out of the ark. ¹¹ I confirm My covenant with you that never again will all flesh be wiped out by the waters of a deluge; there will never again be a deluge to destroy the earth."

¹² And God said, "This is the sign of the covenant I am making between Me and you and every living creature with you, a covenant for all future genera-tions: ¹³ I have placed My bow in the clouds, and it will be a sign of the covenant between Me and the earth. ¹⁴ Whenever I form clouds over the earth and the bow appears in the clouds, ¹⁵ I will remember My covenant between Me and you and every living creature of all flesh: water will never again become a deluge to destroy all flesh. ¹⁶ The bow will be in the clouds, and I will look at it and remember the everlasting covenant between God and every living creature of all flesh on earth." ¹⁷ God said to Noah, "This is the sign of the covenant that I have confirmed between Me and all flesh on earth."

¹⁸ Noah's sons who came out of the

ark were Shem, Ham, and Japheth. Ham was the father of Canaan. ¹⁹ These three were Noah's sons, and from them the whole earth was populated.

²⁰ Noah, a man of the soil, was the first to plant a vineyard. ²¹ He drank some of the wine, became drunk, and uncovered himself inside his tent. ²² Ham, the father of Canaan, saw his father naked and told his two brothers outside. ²³ Then Shem and Japheth took a cloak and placed it over both their shoulders, and walking backwards, they covered their father's nakedness. Their faces were turned away, and they did not see their father naked.

²⁴ When Noah awoke from his drinking and learned what his youngest son had done to him, ²⁵ he said:

Canaan will be cursed.
He will be the lowest of slaves to his brothers.

²⁶ He also said:

Praise the LORD, the God of Shem;
Canaan will be his slave.
²⁷   God will extend Japheth;
he will dwell in the tents of Shem;
Canaan will be his slave.

²⁸ Now Noah lived 350 years after the flood. ²⁹ So Noah's life lasted 950 years; then he died.

10 These are the family records of Noah's sons, Shem, Ham, and Japheth. They also had sons after the deluge.

² Japheth's sons: Gomer, Magog, Madai, Javan, Tubal, Meshech, and Tiras. ³ Gomer's sons: Ashkenaz, Riphath, and Togarmah. ⁴ And Javan's sons: Elishah, Tarshish, Kittim, and Dodanim. ⁵ The coastland peoples spread out into their lands. These are Japheth's sons by their clans, in their nations. Each group had its own language.

⁶ Ham's sons: Cush, Egypt, Put, and Canaan. ⁷ Cush's sons: Seba, Havilah, Sabtah, Raamah, and Sabteca. And Raamah's sons: Sheba and Dedan. ⁸ Cush fathered Nimrod, who was the

first powerful man on earth. ⁹ He was a powerful hunter in the sight of the LORD. That is why it is said, "Like Nimrod, a powerful hunter in the sight of the LORD." ¹⁰ His kingdom started with Babylon, Erech, Accad, and Calneh, in the land of Shinar. ¹¹ From that land he went to Assyria and built Nineveh, Rehoboth-ir, Calah, ¹² and Resen, between Nineveh and the great city Calah.

¹³ Egypt fathered Ludim, Anamim, Lehabim, Naphtuhim, ¹⁴ Pathrusim, Casluhim (the Philistines came from them), and Caphtorim.

¹⁵ Canaan fathered Sidon his firstborn, and the Hittites, ¹⁶ the Jebusites, the Amorites, the Girgashites, ¹⁷ the Hivites, the Arkites, the Sinites, ¹⁸ the Arvadites, the Zemarites, and the Hamathites. Afterward the Canaanite clans scattered. ¹⁹ The Canaanite border went from Sidon going toward Gerar as far as Gaza, and going toward Sodom, Gomorrah, Admah, and Zeboiim, as far as Lasha.

²⁰ These are Ham's sons, by their clans, according to their languages, in their own lands and their nations.

²¹ And Shem, Japheth's older brother, also had children. Shem was the father of all the children of Eber. ²² Shem's sons were Elam, Asshur, Arpachshad, Lud, and Aram.

²³ Aram's sons: Uz, Hul, Gether, and Mash.

²⁴ Arpachshad fathered Shelah, and Shelah fathered Eber. ²⁵ Eber had two sons. One was named Peleg, for during his days the earth was divided; his brother was named Joktan. ²⁶ And Joktan fathered Almodad, Sheleph, Hazarmaveth, Jerah, ²⁷ Hadoram, Uzal, Diklah, ²⁸ Obal, Abimael, Sheba, ²⁹ Ophir, Havilah, and Jobab. All these were Joktan's sons. ³⁰ Their settlements extended from Mesha to Sephar, the eastern hill country.

³¹ These are Shem's sons by their clans, according to their languages, in their lands and their nations.

³² These are the clans of Noah's sons, according to their family records, in their nations. The nations on earth spread out from these after the flood.

PSALM 4:1-8

1 Answer me when I call,
   God, who vindicates me.
   You freed me from affliction;
   be gracious to me and hear my
      prayer.

2 How long, exalted men, will my
      honor be insulted?
   How long will you love what is
      worthless and pursue a lie?
                              Selah
3 Know that the LORD has set apart
      the faithful for Himself;
   the Lord will hear when I call to
      Him.
4 Be angry and do not sin;
   on your bed, reflect in your heart
      and be still.   *Selah*
5 Offer sacrifices in righteousness
   and trust in the LORD.

6 Many are saying, "Who can show
      us anything good?"
   Look on us with favor, LORD.

7 You have put more joy in my heart
   than they have when their grain
      and new wine abound.
8 I will both lie down and sleep in
      peace,
   for You alone, Lord, make me live
      in safety.

PROVERBS 1:10-14

10 My son, if sinners entice you,
      don't be persuaded.
11 If they say—"Come with us!
   Let's set an ambush and kill
      someone.
   Let's attack some innocent person
      just for fun!
12 Let's swallow them alive, like
      Sheol,
   still healthy as they go down to
      the Pit.
13 We'll find all kinds of valuable
      property
   and fill our houses with
      plunder.
14 Throw in your lot with us,

and we'll all share our
   money" —

MATTHEW 4:21–5:12

21 Going on from there, He saw two
other brothers, James the son of Zebedee, and his brother John. They were
in a boat with Zebedee their father,
mending their nets, and He called them.
22 Immediately they left the boat and
their father and followed Him.

23 Jesus was going all over Galilee,
teaching in their synagogues, preaching
the good news of the kingdom, and
healing every disease and sickness
among the people. 24 Then the news
about Him spread throughout Syria. So
they brought to Him all those who were
afflicted, those suffering from various
diseases and intense pains, the demon-
possessed, the epileptics, and the para-
lytics. And He healed them. 25 Large
crowds followed Him from Galilee, Decapolis, Jerusalem, Judea, and beyond
the Jordan.

5 When He saw the crowds, He went
   up on the mountain, and after He
sat down, His disciples came to Him.
2 Then He began to teach them, saying:

3 "Blessed are the poor in spirit,
      because the kingdom of heaven
         is theirs.
4 Blessed are those who mourn,
      because they will be comforted.
5 Blessed are the gentle,
      because they will inherit
         the earth.
6 Blessed are those who hunger
      and thirst for righteousness,
      because they will be filled.
7 Blessed are the merciful,
      because they will be shown
         mercy.
8 Blessed are the pure in heart,
      because they will see God.
9 Blessed are the peacemakers,
      because they will be called sons
         of God.
10 Blessed are those who are
      persecuted for righteousness,

because the kingdom of heaven is theirs.

[11] "Blessed are you when they insult you and persecute you and falsely say every kind of evil against you because of Me. [12] Be glad and rejoice, because your reward is great in heaven. For that is how they persecuted the prophets who were before you.

False Accusation

Blessed are you when they . . . falsely say every kind of evil against you because of Me.—MATTHEW 5:11

Today we examine a hurt that often arises within the human heart—false accusation. Has someone accused you of a wrong for which you were not responsible, and though you try to explain or defend yourself, no one seems to believe you? It hurts, doesn't it? I have known many Christians who, when faced with the hurt of false accusation, turned away from the Christian life altogether. How sad! I have a friend who was falsely accused by fellow Christians in a church, and although I and many others knew the accusation was not true and passionately defended him, he broke down and was placed in a mental institution.

People (even Christians) have their own ways of trying to cope with the feelings that arise when they are falsely accused. Some turn to liquor. They want to dull the pain inside them, and so they take what seems to them to be an easy way to that end. But it doesn't work, for there is always the morning after.

Some turn to books. That was the advice Edmund Gosse gave to his friend Robert Ross when he became involved in the Oscar Wilde scandal at the end of the nineteenth century. "Turn for consolation to books," he said. But it didn't work. Others might turn to nature, to art, or to music.

There is, however, a better way. If you are a Christian, and your heart is heavy because of a false accusation, then I assure you that the blessed Comforter is alongside you even now. Offer the hurt to Him. He delights to heal.

Prayer

Blessed Lord Jesus, You who knew the hurt of being falsely accused, draw near in the power of Your Spirit and heal me now. I take—and You undertake. Thank You, Savior. Amen.

Further Study

Jms 3; 1 Pt 3:16; 2:1; Lk 6:7
What is the hardest thing to tame?
For what should we use our tongues?

JANUARY 6

GENESIS 11:1–12:20

11 At one time the whole earth had the same language and vocabulary. ² As people migrated from the east, they found a valley in the land of Shinar and settled there. ³ They said to each other, "Come, let us make oven-fired bricks." They had brick for stone and asphalt for mortar. ⁴ And they said, "Come, let us build ourselves a city and a tower with its top in the sky. Let us make a name for ourselves; otherwise, we will be scattered over the face of the whole earth."

⁵ Then the LORD came down to look over the city and the tower that the men were building. ⁶ The LORD said, "If, as one people all having the same language, they have begun to do this, then nothing they plan to do will be impossible for them. ⁷ Come, let Us go down there and confuse their language so that they will not understand one another's speech." ⁸ So the LORD scattered them from there over the face of the whole earth, and they stopped building the city. ⁹ Therefore its name is called Babylon, for there the LORD confused the language of the whole earth, and from there the LORD scattered them over the face of the whole earth.

¹⁰ These are the family records of Shem. Shem lived 100 years and fathered Arpachshad two years after the deluge. ¹¹ After he fathered Arpachshad, Shem lived 500 years and fathered other sons and daughters. ¹² Arpachshad lived 35 years and fathered Shelah. ¹³ After he fathered Shelah, Arpachshad lived 403 years and fathered other sons and daughters. ¹⁴ Shelah lived 30 years and fathered Eber. ¹⁵ After he fathered Eber, Shelah lived 403 years and fathered other sons and daughters. ¹⁶ Eber lived 34 years and fathered Peleg. ¹⁷ After he fathered Peleg, Eber lived 430 years and fathered other sons and daughters. ¹⁸ Peleg lived 30 years and fathered Reu. ¹⁹ After he fathered Reu, Peleg lived 209 years and fathered other sons and daughters. ²⁰ Reu lived 32 years and fathered Serug. ²¹ After he fathered Serug, Reu lived 207 years and fathered other sons and daughters. ²² Serug lived 30 years and fathered Nahor. ²³ After he fathered Nahor, Serug lived 200 years and fathered other sons and daughters. ²⁴ Nahor lived 29 years and fathered Terah. ²⁵ After he fathered Terah, Nahor lived 119 years and fathered other sons and daughters. ²⁶ Terah lived 70 years and fathered Abram, Nahor, and Haran.

²⁷ These are the family records of Terah. Terah fathered Abram, Nahor, and Haran, and Haran fathered Lot. ²⁸ Haran died in his native land, in Ur of the Chaldeans, during his father Terah's lifetime. ²⁹ Abram and Nahor took wives: Abram's wife was named Sarai, and Nahor's wife was named Milcah. She was the daughter of Haran, the father of both Milcah and Iscah. ³⁰ Sarai was barren; she had no child.

³¹ Terah took his son Abram, his grandson Lot (Haran's son), and his daughter-in-law Sarai, his son Abram's wife, and they set out together from Ur of the Chaldeans to go to the land of Canaan. But when they came to Haran, they settled there. ³² Terah lived 205 years and died in Haran.

12 The LORD said to Abram:

Go out from your land,
your relatives,
and your father's house
to the land that I will show you.
² I will make you into a great
nation,
I will bless you,
I will make your name great,

and you will be a blessing. ³ I will bless those who bless you, I will curse those who treat you with contempt, and all the peoples on earth will be blessed through you.

⁴ So Abram went, as the LORD had told him, and Lot went with him. Abram was 75 years old when he left Haran. ⁵ He took his wife Sarai, his nephew Lot, all the possessions they had accumulated, and the people he had acquired in Haran, and they set out for the land of Canaan. When they came to the land of Canaan, ⁶ Abram passed through the land to the site of Shechem, at the oak of Moreh. At that time the Canaanites were in the land. ⁷ But the LORD appeared to Abram and said, "I will give this land to your offspring." So he built an altar there to the LORD who had appeared to him. ⁸ From there he moved on to the hill country east of Bethel and pitched his tent, with Bethel on the west and Ai on the east. There he built an altar to the LORD and worshiped Him. ⁹ Then Abram journeyed by stages to the Negev.

¹⁰ There was a famine in the land, so Abram went down to Egypt to live there for a while because the famine in the land was severe. ¹¹ When he was about to enter Egypt, he said to his wife Sarai, "Look, I know what a beautiful woman you are. ¹² When the Egyptians see you, they will say, 'This is his wife.' They will kill me but let you live. ¹³ Please say you're my sister so it will go well for me because of you, and my life will be spared on your account." ¹⁴ When Abram entered Egypt, the Egyptians saw that the woman was very beautiful. ¹⁵ Pharaoh's officials saw her and praised her to Pharaoh, so the woman was taken to Pharaoh's house. ¹⁶ He treated Abram well because of her, and Abram acquired flocks and herds, male and female donkeys, male and female slaves, and camels.

¹⁷ But the LORD struck Pharaoh and his house with severe plagues because of Abram's wife Sarai. ¹⁸ So Pharaoh sent for Abram and said, "What have you done to me? Why didn't you tell me she was your wife? ¹⁹ Why did you say, 'She's my sister,' so that I took her as my wife? Now, here's your wife. Take her and go!" ²⁰ Then Pharaoh gave his men orders about him, and they sent him away, with his wife and all he had.

PSALM 5:1-6

1 Listen to my words, LORD;
consider my sighing.
2 Pay attention to the sound of my cry,
my King and my God,
for I pray to You.

3 At daybreak, LORD, You hear my voice;
at daybreak I plead my case to You and watch expectantly.

4 For You are not a God who delights in wickedness;
evil cannot lodge with You.
5 The boastful cannot stand in Your presence;
You hate all evildoers.
6 You destroy those who tell lies;
the Lord abhors a man of bloodshed and treachery.

PROVERBS 1:15-16

15 my son, don't travel that road with them
or set foot on their path,
16 because their feet run toward trouble
and they hurry to commit murder.

MATTHEW 5:13-32

¹³ "You are the salt of the earth. But if the salt should lose its taste, how can it be made salty? It's no longer good for anything but to be thrown out and trampled on by men.

¹⁴ "You are the light of the world. A city situated on a hill cannot be hidden. ¹⁵ No one lights a lamp and puts it under a basket, but rather on a lampstand, and it gives light for all who are in the

house. [16] In the same way, let your light shine before men, so that they may see your good works and give glory to your Father in heaven.

[17] "Don't assume that I came to destroy the Law or the Prophets. I did not come to destroy but to fulfill. [18] For I assure you: Until heaven and earth pass away, not the smallest letter or one stroke of a letter will pass from the law until all things are accomplished. [19] Therefore, whoever breaks one of the least of these commandments and teaches people to do so will be called least in the kingdom of heaven. But whoever practices and teaches these commandments will be called great in the kingdom of heaven. [20] For I tell you, unless your righteousness surpasses that of the scribes and Pharisees, you will never enter the kingdom of heaven.

[21] "You have heard that it was said to our ancestors, **Do not murder**, and whoever murders will be subject to judgment. [22] But I tell you, everyone who is angry with his brother will be subject to judgment. And whoever says to his brother, 'Fool!' will be subject to the Sanhedrin. But whoever says, 'You moron!' will be subject to hellfire. [23] So if you are offering your gift on the altar, and there you remember that your brother has something against you, [24] leave your gift there in front of the altar. First go and be reconciled with your brother, and then come and offer your gift. [25] Reach a settlement quickly with your adversary while you're on the way with him, or your adversary will hand you over to the judge, the judge to the officer, and you will be thrown into prison. [26] I assure you: You will never get out of there until you have paid the last penny!

[27] "You have heard that it was said, **Do not commit adultery.** [28] But I tell you, everyone who looks at a woman to lust for her has already committed adultery with her in his heart. [29] If your right eye causes you to sin, gouge it out and throw it away. For it is better that you lose one of the parts of your body than for your whole body to be thrown into hell. [30] And if your right hand causes you to sin, cut it off and throw it away. For it is better that you lose one of the parts of your body than for your whole body to go into hell!

[31] "It was also said, **Whoever divorces his wife must give her a written notice of divorce.** [32] But I tell you, everyone who divorces his wife, except in a case of sexual immorality, causes her to commit adultery. And whoever marries a divorced woman commits adultery.

The Unyielding Judge

Reach a settlement quickly with your adversary . . . or your adversary will hand you over to the judge.—MATTHEW 5:25

"God's wrath," said George MacDonald, "is always judicial. It is always the wrath of the Judge administering justice. Cruelty is always immoral, but true justice—never." Those who experience the fullness of God's wrath get precisely what they deserve. This may sound hard, but it is true.

There is great wisdom in the words of our Lord in the passage before us today. Settle matters with an adversary, He says, before he drags you to court. Do at once what you must one day do anyway. There may be no escape from payment, but why not escape at least from the prison sentence that will enforce it?

The point our Lord is making is that we ought not to drive justice to extremities. God requires righteousness of us, does He not? It is utterly useless to think, then, that we can escape the eternal law. So yield yourself rather than be compelled.

To those whose hearts are true, the idea of judgment is right; to those whose hearts are untrue, the idea of judgment is wrong. Many people live under the illusion that perhaps it might be possible to find a way of escaping all that is required of us in this world. But there is no escape. A way to avoid the demands of righteousness, apart from the righteousness which God accounts to us at the Cross, would not be moral. When a man or woman accepts the payment God has made for them in Christ, the whole wealth of heaven is theirs; their debt is cleared. Those who deny that debt or who, acknowledging it, do nothing to avail themselves of the payment made for them on Calvary, face an unyielding Judge and an everlasting prison.

Prayer

O Father, how serious and solemn is all this, but yet how true. Sin must ultimately be punished. I am so grateful that in Christ my debt has been paid, and availing myself of Your offer I am eternally free. Blessed be Your name forever. Amen.

Further Study

Zph 3:1-5; Ps 103:6; Jn 5:30; Rm 2:2
What does God do morning by morning?
What is God's judgment based on?

JANUARY 7

GENESIS 13:1–15:6

13 Then Abram went up from Egypt to the Negev—he, his wife, and all he had, and Lot with him. ² Abram was very rich in livestock, silver, and gold. ³ He went by stages from the Negev to Bethel, to the place between Bethel and Ai where his tent had formerly been, ⁴ to the site where he had built the altar. And Abram worshiped the LORD there.

⁵ Now Lot, who was traveling with Abram, also had flocks, herds, and tents. ⁶ But the land was unable to support them as long as they stayed together, for they had so many possessions that they could not stay together, ⁷ and there was quarreling between the herdsmen of Abram's livestock and the herdsmen of Lot's livestock. At that time the Canaanites and the Perizzites were living in the land.

⁸ Then Abram said to Lot, "Please, let's not have quarreling between you and me, or between your herdsmen and my herdsmen, since we are relatives. ⁹ Isn't the whole land before you? Separate from me: if you go to the left, I will go to the right; if you go to the right, I will go to the left."

¹⁰ Lot looked out and saw that the entire Jordan Valley as far as Zoar was

23

well-watered everywhere like the LORD's garden and the land of Egypt. This was before God destroyed Sodom and Gomorrah. [11] So Lot chose the entire Jordan Valley for himself. Then Lot journeyed eastward, and they separated from each other. [12] Abram lived in the land of Canaan, but Lot lived in the cities of the valley and set up his tent near Sodom. [13] Now the men of Sodom were evil, sinning greatly against the LORD.

[14] After Lot had separated from him, the LORD said to Abram, "Look from the place where you are. Look north and south, east and west, [15] for I will give you and your offspring forever all the land that you see. [16] I will make your offspring like the dust of the earth, so that if one could count the dust of the earth, then your offspring could be counted. [17] Get up and walk from one end of the land to the other, for I will give it to you."

[18] So Abram moved his tent and went to live beside the oaks of Mamre at Hebron, where he built an altar to the LORD.

14 In those days Amraphel king of Shinar, Arioch king of Ellasar, Chedorlaomer king of Elam, and Tidal king of Goiim [2] waged war against Bera king of Sodom, Birsha king of Gomorrah, Shinab king of Admah, and Shemeber king of Zeboiim, as well as the king of Bela (that is, Zoar). [3] All of these came as allies to the Valley of Siddim (that is, the Dead Sea). [4] They were subject to Chedorlaomer for 12 years, but in the thirteenth year they rebelled. [5] In the fourteenth year Chedorlaomer and the kings who were with him came and defeated the Rephaim in Ashteroth-karnaim, the Zuzim in Ham, the Emim in Shaveh-kiriathaim, [6] and the Horites in the mountains of Seir, as far as El-paran by the wilderness. [7] Then they came back to invade En-mishpat (that is, Kadesh), and they defeated all the territory of the Amalekites, as well as the Amorites who lived in Hazazon-tamar.

[8] Then the king of Sodom, the king of Gomorrah, the king of Admah, the king of Zeboiim, and the king of Bela (that is,

Zoar) went out and lined up for battle in the Valley of Siddim [9] against Chedorlaomer king of Elam, Tidal king of Goiim, Amraphel king of Shinar, and Arioch king of Ellasar—four kings against five. [10] Now the Valley of Siddim contained many asphalt pits, and as the kings of Sodom and Gomorrah fled, some fell into them, but the rest fled to the mountains. [11] The four kings took all the goods of Sodom and Gomorrah and all their food and went on. [12] They also took Abram's nephew Lot and his possessions, for he was living in Sodom, and they went on.

[13] One of the survivors came and told Abram the Hebrew, who was at the oaks belonging to Mamre the Amorite, the brother of Eshcol and the brother of Aner. They were bound by a treaty with Abram. [14] When Abram heard that his relative had been taken prisoner, he assembled his 318 trained men, born in his household, and they went in pursuit as far as Dan. [15] And he and his servants deployed against them by night, attacked them, and pursued them as far as Hobah to the north of Damascus. [16] He brought back all the goods and also his relative Lot and his goods, as well as the women and the other people.

[17] After Abram returned from defeating Chedorlaomer and the kings who were with him, the king of Sodom went out to meet him in the Valley of Shaveh (that is, the King's Valley). [18] Then Melchizedek, king of Salem, brought out bread and wine; he was a priest to God Most High. [19] He blessed him and said:

> Abram is blessed by God Most
> High,
>   Creator of heaven and earth,
> [20] and give praise to God Most High
>   who has handed over your
>   enemies to you.

And Abram gave him a tenth of everything.
[21] Then the king of Sodom said to Abram, "Give me the people, but take the possessions for yourself."
[22] But Abram said to the king of Sodom, "I have raised my hand in an

oath to the LORD, God Most High, Creator of heaven and earth, ²³ that I will not take a thread or sandal strap or anything that belongs to you, so you can never say, 'I made Abram rich.' ²⁴ I will take nothing except what the servants have eaten. But as for the share of the men who came with me—Aner, Eshcol, and Mamre—they can take their share."

15 After these events, the word of the LORD came to Abram in a vision:

Do not be afraid, Abram.
I am your shield;
your reward will be very great.

² But Abram said, "Lord GOD, what can You give me, since I am childless and the heir of my house is Eliezer of Damascus?" ³ Abram continued, "Look, You have given me no offspring, so a slave born in my house will be my heir." ⁴ Now the word of the LORD came to him: "This one will not be your heir; instead, one who comes from your own body will be your heir." ⁵ He took him outside and said, "Look at the sky and count the stars, if you are able to count them." Then He said to him, "Your offspring will be that numerous." ⁶ Abram believed the LORD, and He credited it to him as righteousness.

PSALM 5:7-12

⁷ But I enter Your house by the
abundance of Your faithful
love;
I bow down toward Your holy
temple in reverential awe of
You.
⁸ LORD, lead me in Your
righteousness,
because of my adversaries;
make Your way straight before me.

⁹ For there is nothing reliable in
what they say;
destruction is within them;
their throat is an open grave;
they flatter with their tongues.

¹⁰ Punish them, God;
let them fall by their own
schemes.
Drive them out because of their
many crimes,
for they rebel against You.
¹¹ But let all who take refuge in You
rejoice;
let them shout for joy forever.
May You shelter them,
and may those who love Your
name boast about You.
¹² For You, LORD, bless the righteous
one;
You surround him with favor like a
shield.

PROVERBS 1:17-19

¹⁷ It is foolish to spread a net
where any bird can see it,
¹⁸ but they set an ambush to kill
themselves;
they attack their own lives.
¹⁹ Such are the paths of all who
pursue gain dishonestly;
it takes the lives of those who
profit from it.

MATTHEW 5:33–6:4

³³ "Again, you have heard that it was said to our ancestors, **You must not break your oath, but you must keep your oaths to the Lord.** ³⁴ But I tell you, don't take an oath at all: either by heaven, because it is God's throne; ³⁵ or by the earth, because it is His footstool; or by Jerusalem, because it is the city of the great King. ³⁶ Neither should you swear by your head, because you cannot make a single hair white or black. ³⁷ But let your word 'yes' be 'yes,' and your 'no' be 'no.' Anything more than this is from the evil one.

³⁸ "You have heard that it was said, **An eye for an eye** and **a tooth for a tooth.** ³⁹ But I tell you, don't resist an evildoer. On the contrary, if anyone slaps you on your right cheek, turn the other to him also. ⁴⁰ As for the one who wants to sue you and take away your shirt, let him

have your coat as well. ⁴¹ And if anyone forces you to go one mile, go with him two. ⁴² Give to the one who asks you, and don't turn away from the one who wants to borrow from you.

⁴³ "You have heard that it was said, **Love your neighbor** and hate your enemy. ⁴⁴ But I tell you, love your enemies and pray for those who persecute you, ⁴⁵ so that you may be sons of your Father in heaven. For He causes His sun to rise on the evil and the good, and sends rain on the righteous and the unrighteous. ⁴⁶ For if you love those who love you, what reward will you have? Don't even the tax collectors do the same? ⁴⁷ And if you greet only your brothers, what are you doing out of the ordinary? Don't

even the Gentiles do the same? ⁴⁸ Be perfect, therefore, as your heavenly Father is perfect.

6 "Be careful not to practice your righteousness in front of people, to be seen by them. Otherwise, you will have no reward from your Father in heaven. ² So whenever you give to the poor, don't sound a trumpet before you, as the hypocrites do in the synagogues and on the streets, to be applauded by people. I assure you: They've got their reward! ³ But when you give to the poor, don't let your left hand know what your right hand is doing, ⁴ so that your giving may be in secret. And your Father who sees in secret will reward you.

"I Am Your Shield"

Abram believed the LORD, and He credited it to him as righteousness.—GENESIS 15:6

It is no good saying you believe God is stronger than the devil if you do not act on that belief. Faith not only believes this but acts on it by quickly standing up to the devil and saying something similar to what David said when he stood before Goliath: "You come against me with a dagger, spear, and sword, but I come against you in the name of the LORD of Hosts" (1 Sm 17:45). You must never forget that God is much more powerful than the devil. Hold on to that, and quickly raise your shield whenever you experience an attack of Satan's "fiery darts."

The passage that introduces this devotion focuses on an incident in Abraham's life that took place when he was exhausted after making a great stand. Doubtless, Satan would have attacked him with thoughts like: "What is the point of all this action of God on your behalf and all these promises when you do not have an heir to carry on your line? God doesn't seem to have as much power as it would appear."

Abraham was fearful at this point until the Lord came to him and gave him these glorious words: "Do not be afraid, Abram. I am your shield; your reward will be very great" (Gn 15:1).

"I am your shield." Hold on to that great truth, my friend, and when under attack, quickly lift it up and remind the devil that you belong to One whose power is endless and eternal. His promises are ever sure. That is what it means to hold up the shield of faith.

Prayer

O God, how grateful I am for the sureness and certainty of Your Word. Once again I feel it entering into the core of my being. Help me to put these truths into practice the very moment I come under satanic attack. In Jesus' name I pray. Amen.

Further Study

Pr 30:1-5; Dt 33:29; Pss 33:20; 59:11; 84:9
Why was Israel blessed?
What was the psalmist's continual testimony?

JANUARY 8

GENESIS 15:7–17:27

⁷ He also said to him, "I am the LORD who brought you from Ur of the Chaldeans to give you this land to possess."
⁸ But he said, "Lord GOD, how can I know that I will possess it?"
⁹ He said to him, "Bring Me a three-year-old cow, a three-year-old female goat, a three-year-old ram, a turtledove, and a young pigeon."
¹⁰ So he brought all these to Him, split them down the middle, and laid the pieces opposite each other, but he did not cut up the birds. ¹¹ Birds of prey came down on the carcasses, but Abram drove them away. ¹² As the sun was setting, a deep sleep fell on Abram, and suddenly a terror and great darkness descended on him.
¹³ Then the LORD said to Abram, "Know this for certain: Your offspring will be strangers in a land that does not belong to them; they will be enslaved and oppressed 400 years. ¹⁴ However, I will judge the nation they serve, and afterward they will go out with many pos-

sessions. ¹⁵ But you will go to your fathers in peace and be buried at a ripe old age. ¹⁶ In the fourth generation they will return here, for the iniquity of the Amorites has not yet reached its full measure."
¹⁷ When the sun had set and it was dark, a smoking fire pot and a flaming torch appeared and passed between the divided animals. ¹⁸ On that day the LORD made a covenant with Abram, saying, "I give this land to your offspring, from the brook of Egypt to the Euphrates River: ¹⁹ the land of the Kenites, Kenizzites, Kadmonites, ²⁰ Hittites, Perizzites, Rephaim, ²¹ Amorites, Canaanites, Girgashites, and Jebusites."

16 Abram's wife Sarai had not borne him children. She owned an Egyptian slave named Hagar. ² Sarai said to Abram, "Since the LORD has prevented me from bearing children, go to my slave; perhaps I can have children by her." And Abram agreed to what Sarai said. ³ So Abram's wife Sarai took Hagar, her Egyptian slave, and gave her to her husband Abram as a wife for him. This

happened after Abram had lived in the land of Canaan 10 years. ⁴ He slept with Hagar, and she became pregnant. When she realized that she was pregnant, she looked down on her mistress. ⁵ Then Sarai said to Abram, "You are responsible for my suffering! I put my slave in your arms, and ever since she saw that she was pregnant, she has looked down on me. May the LORD judge between me and you."

⁶ Abram replied to Sarai, "Here, your slave is in your hands; do whatever you want with her." Then Sarai mistreated her so much that she ran away from her.

⁷ The Angel of the LORD found her by a spring of water in the wilderness, the spring on the way to Shur. ⁸ He said, "Hagar, slave of Sarai, where have you come from, and where are you going?"

She replied, "I'm running away from my mistress Sarai."

⁹ Then the Angel of the LORD said to her, "You must go back to your mistress and submit to her mistreatment." ¹⁰ The Angel of the LORD also said to her, "I will greatly multiply your offspring, and they will be too many to count."

¹¹ Then the Angel of the LORD said to her:

You have conceived and will have a son.
You will name him Ishmael,
for the LORD has heard your cry of affliction.
¹²   This man will be like a wild ass.
His hand will be against everyone, and everyone's hand will be against him;
he will live at odds with all his brothers.

¹³ So she named the LORD who spoke to her: The God Who Sees, for she said, "Have I really seen here the One who sees me?" ¹⁴ That is why she named the spring, "A Well of the Living One Who Sees Me." It is located between Kadesh and Bered.

¹⁵ So Hagar gave birth to Abram's son, and Abram gave the name Ishmael to the son Hagar had. ¹⁶ Abram was 86 years old when Hagar bore Ishmael to him.

17 When Abram was 99 years old, the LORD appeared to him, saying, "I am God Almighty. Live in My presence and be devout. ² I will establish My covenant between Me and you, and I will multiply you greatly."

³ Then Abram fell to the ground, and God spoke with him: ⁴ "As for Me, My covenant is with you, and you will become the father of many nations. ⁵ Your name will no longer be Abram, but your name will be Abraham, for I will make you the father of many nations. ⁶ I will make you extremely fruitful and will make nations and kings come from you. ⁷ I will keep My covenant between Me and you, and your offspring after you throughout their generations, as an everlasting covenant to be your God and the God of your offspring after you. ⁸ And to you and your offspring after you I will give the land where you are residing—all the land of Canaan—as an eternal possession, and I will be their God."

⁹ God also said to Abraham, "As for you, you and your offspring after you throughout their generations are to keep My covenant. ¹⁰ This is My covenant, which you are to keep, between Me and you and your offspring after you: Every one of your males must be circumcised. ¹¹ You must circumcise the flesh of your foreskin to serve as a sign of the covenant between Me and you. ¹² Throughout your generations, every male among you at eight days old is to be circumcised. This includes a slave born in your house and one purchased with money from any foreigner. The one who is not your offspring, ¹³ a slave born in your house, as well as one purchased with money, must be circumcised. My covenant will be in your flesh as an everlasting covenant. ¹⁴ If any male is not circumcised in the flesh of his foreskin, that man will be cut off from his people; he has broken My covenant."

¹⁵ God said to Abraham, "As for your wife Sarai, do not call her Sarai, for Sarah will be her name. ¹⁶ I will bless her; indeed, I will give you a son by her. I will bless her, and she will produce na-

tions; kings of peoples will come from her."

¹⁷ Abraham fell to the ground, laughed, and thought in his heart, "Can a child be born to a hundred-year-old man? Can Sarah, a ninety-year-old woman, give birth?" ¹⁸ So Abraham said to God, "If only Ishmael could live in Your presence!"

¹⁹ But God said, "No. Your wife Sarah will bear you a son, and you will name him Isaac. I will confirm My covenant with him as an everlasting covenant for his offspring after him. ²⁰ As for Ishmael, I have heard you. I will certainly bless him; I will make him fruitful and will multiply him greatly. He will father 12 tribal leaders, and I will make him into a great nation. ²¹ But I will confirm My covenant with Isaac, whom Sarah will bear to you at this time next year." ²² When He finished talking with him, God withdrew from Abraham.

²³ Then Abraham took his son Ishmael and all the slaves born in his house or purchased with his money—every male among the members of Abraham's household—and he circumcised the flesh of their foreskin on that very day, just as God had said to him. ²⁴ Abraham was 99 years old when the flesh of his foreskin was circumcised, ²⁵ and his son Ishmael was 13 years old when the flesh of his foreskin was circumcised. ²⁶ On that same day Abraham and his son Ishmael were circumcised. ²⁷ And all the men of his household—both slaves born in his house and those purchased with money from a foreigner—were circumcised with him.

PSALM 6:1-5

¹ LORD, do not rebuke me in Your anger;
  do not discipline me in Your wrath.
² Be gracious to me, LORD, for I am weak;
  heal me, LORD, for my bones are shaking;
³ my whole being is shaken with terror.

And You, LORD—how long?

⁴ Turn, LORD! Rescue me;
  save me because of Your faithful love.
⁵ For there is no remembrance of You in death;
  who can thank You in Sheol?

PROVERBS 1:20-23

²⁰ Wisdom calls out in the street;
  she raises her voice in the public squares.
²¹ She cries out above the commotion;
  she speaks at the entrance of the city gates:
²² "How long, foolish ones, will you love ignorance?
  How long will you mockers enjoy mocking
  and you fools hate knowledge?
²³ If you turn to my discipline,
  then I will pour out my spirit on you
  and teach you my words.

MATTHEW 6:5-24

⁵ "Whenever you pray, you must not be like the hypocrites, because they love to pray standing in the synagogues and on the street corners to be seen by people. I assure you: They've got their reward! ⁶ But when you pray, go into your private room, shut your door, and pray to your Father who is in secret. And your Father who sees in secret will reward you. ⁷ When you pray, don't babble like the idolaters, since they imagine they'll be heard for their many words. ⁸ Don't be like them, because your Father knows the things you need before you ask Him.

⁹ "Therefore, you should pray like this:
  Our Father in heaven,
  Your name be honored as holy.
¹⁰ Your kingdom come.
  Your will be done
  on earth as it is in heaven.

11 Give us today our daily bread.
12 And forgive us our debts,
as we also have forgiven
our debtors.
13 And do not bring us into
temptation,
but deliver us from the evil one.
[For Yours is the kingdom
and the power
and the glory forever. Amen.]

14 "For if you forgive people their wrongdoing, your heavenly Father will forgive you as well. 15 But if you don't forgive people, your Father will not forgive your wrongdoing.
16 "Whenever you fast, don't be sad-faced like the hypocrites. For they make their faces unattractive so their fasting is obvious to people. I assure you: They've got their reward! 17 But when you fast, put oil on your head, and wash your face, 18 so that you don't show your fasting to people but to your Father who is in secret. And your Father who sees in secret will reward you.

19 "Don't collect for yourselves treasures on earth, where moth and rust destroy and where thieves break in and steal. 20 But collect for yourselves treasures in heaven, where neither moth nor rust destroys, and where thieves don't break in and steal. 21 For where your treasure is, there your heart will be also.
22 "The eye is the lamp of the body. If your eye is good, your whole body will be full of light. 23 But if your eye is bad, your whole body will be full of darkness. So if the light within you is darkness—how deep is that darkness!
24 "No one can be a slave of two masters, since either he will hate one and love the other, or be devoted to one and despise the other. You cannot be slaves of God and of money.

Jesus' Pattern of Prayer

Therefore, you should pray like this: Our Father in heaven, Your name be honored as holy.—Matthew 6:9

One of the most precious passages in the whole of the New Testament is the Lord's Prayer. These words of Jesus, so seemingly simple, encompass every conceivable element in prayer and reduce it to a clearly understood pattern.

The Lord's Prayer (or, more correctly, The Disciples' Prayer) is, among other things, a miracle of condensation. In the short compass of sixty-six words, the Master presents a model of praying that touches on every major aspect of prayer. One writer says of it: "The Lord's Prayer sets the standard for all praying. Everything every man ever needed to understand about prayer is latent in the choice disclosure of these words." That might sound like an astonishing claim, but it is true. No set of theological volumes, no sermon, no series of writings could ever capture the fullness of everything prayer is, as does this simple yet profound model.

The more we understand this model, and the more we pray in line with it, the more powerful and productive our prayer life will become. Because this communication is so important, the enemy seeks to disrupt it. This is why we face the necessity to constantly refocus our thinking on the subject, and seek to deepen and enhance our prowess in the art of prayer. If the Lord's Prayer sets the standard for all praying, then we must lay our praying alongside His pattern in order that our prayers might become more and more like His.

Prayer

O God, as I begin this quest for a deeper and more effective prayer life, my heart cries out: "Lord, teach me to pray." For I know that when I learn to pray, I learn to live—vitally and victoriously. Amen.

Further Study

1 Tm 2:1-8; 1 Ch 16:11; Lk 18:1; 1 Th 5:17
What was Christ's injunction?
What is Paul's desire?

JANUARY 9

*G*ENESIS 18:1–19:22

18 Then the LORD appeared to Abraham at the oaks of Mamre while he was sitting in the entrance of his tent during the heat of the day. ² He looked up, and he saw three men standing near him. When he saw them, he ran from the entrance of the tent to meet them and bowed to the ground. ³ Then he said, "My lord, if I have found favor in your sight, please do not go on past your servant. ⁴ Let a little water be brought, that you may wash your feet and rest yourselves under the tree. ⁵ I will bring a bit of bread so that you may strengthen yourselves. This is why you have passed your servant's way. Later, you can continue on."

"Yes," they replied, "do as you have said."

⁶ So Abraham hurried into the tent and said to Sarah, "Quick! Knead three measures of fine flour and make bread." ⁷ Meanwhile, Abraham ran to the herd and got a tender, choice calf. He gave it to a young man, who hurried to prepare it. ⁸ Then Abraham took curds and milk,

and the calf that he had prepared, and set them before the men. He served them as they ate under the tree.

⁹ "Where is your wife Sarah?" they asked him.

"There, in the tent," he answered.

¹⁰ The LORD said, "I will certainly come back to you in about a year's time, and your wife Sarah will have a son!" Now Sarah was listening at the entrance of the tent behind him.

¹¹ Abraham and Sarah were old and getting on in years. Sarah had passed the age of childbearing. ¹² So she laughed to herself: "After I have become shriveled up and my lord is old, will I have delight?"

¹³ But the LORD asked Abraham, "Why did Sarah laugh, saying, 'Can I really have a baby when I'm old?' ¹⁴ Is anything impossible for the LORD? At the appointed time I will come back to you, and in about a year she will have a son."

¹⁵ Sarah denied it. "I did not laugh," she said, because she was afraid.

But He replied, "No, you did laugh."

¹⁶ The men got up from there and looked out over Sodom, and Abraham was walking with them to see them off.

31

[17] Then the LORD said, "Should I hide from Abraham what I am about to do? [18] Abraham is to become a great and powerful nation, and all the nations of the earth will be blessed through him. [19] For I have chosen him so that he will command his children and his house after him to keep the way of the LORD by doing what is right and just. This is how the LORD will fulfill to Abraham what He promised him." [20] Then the LORD said, "The outcry against Sodom and Gomorrah is immense, and their sin is extremely serious. [21] I will go down to see if what they have done justifies the cry that has come up to Me. If not, I will find out."

[22] The men turned from there and went toward Sodom while Abraham remained standing before the LORD. [23] Abraham stepped forward and said, "Will You really sweep away the righteous with the wicked? [24] What if there are 50 righteous people in the city? Will You really sweep it away instead of sparing the place for the sake of the 50 righteous people who are in it? [25] You could not possibly do such a thing: to kill the righteous with the wicked, treating the righteous and the wicked alike. You could not possibly do that! Won't the Judge of all the earth do what is just?"

[26] The LORD said, "If at Sodom I find 50 righteous people in the city, I will spare the whole place for their sake."

[27] Then Abraham answered, "Since I have ventured to speak to the Lord— even though I am dust and ashes— [28] suppose the 50 righteous lack five. Will you destroy the whole city for lack of five?"

He replied, "I will not destroy it if I find 45 there."

[29] Then he spoke to Him again, "Suppose 40 are found there?"

He answered, "I will not do it on account of 40."

[30] Then he said, "Let the Lord not be angry, and I will speak further. Suppose 30 are found there?"

He answered, "I will not do it if I find 30 there."

[31] Then he said, "Since I have ventured to speak to the Lord, suppose 20 are found there?"

He replied, "I will not destroy it on account of 20."

[32] Then he said, "Let the Lord not be angry, and I will speak one more time. Suppose 10 are found there?"

He answered, "I will not destroy it on account of 10." [33] When the LORD had finished speaking with Abraham, He departed, and Abraham returned to his place.

19

The two angels entered Sodom in the evening as Lot was sitting at Sodom's gate. When Lot saw them, he got up to meet them. He bowed with his face to the ground [2] and said, "My lords, turn aside to your servant's house, wash your feet, and spend the night. Then you can get up early and go on your way."

"No," they said. "We would rather spend the night in the square." [3] But he urged them so strongly that they followed him and went into his house. He prepared a feast and baked unleavened bread for them, and they ate.

[4] Before they went to bed, the men of the city of Sodom, both young and old, the whole population, surrounded the house. [5] They called out to Lot and said, "Where are the men who came to you tonight? Send them out to us so we can have sex with them!"

[6] Lot went out to them at the entrance and shut the door behind him. [7] He said, "Don't do this evil, my brothers. [8] Look, I've got two daughters who haven't had sexual relations with a man. I'll bring them out to you, and you can do whatever you want to them. However, don't do anything to these men, because they have come under the protection of my roof."

[9] "Get out of the way!" they said, adding, "This one came here as a foreigner, but he's acting like a judge! Now we'll do more harm to you than to them." They put pressure on Lot and came up to break down the door. [10] But the angels reached out, brought Lot into the house with them, and shut the door. [11] They struck the men who were at the door of the house, both young and old, with a blinding light so that they were unable to find the door.

[12] Then the angels said to Lot, "Do you have anyone else here: a son-in-law, your sons and daughters, or anyone else in the city who belongs to you? Get them out of this place, [13] for we are about to destroy this place because the outcry against its people is great before the LORD, and the LORD has sent us to destroy it." [14] So Lot went out and spoke to his sons-in-law, who were going to marry his daughters. "Get up," he said. "Get out of this place, for the LORD is about to destroy the city!" But his sons-in-law thought he was joking.

[15] At the crack of dawn the angels urged Lot on: "Get up! Take your wife and your two daughters who are here, or you will be swept away in the punishment of the city." [16] But he hesitated, so because of the LORD's compassion for him, the men grabbed his hand, his wife's hand, and the hands of his two daughters. And they brought him out and left him outside the city.

[17] As soon as the angels got them outside, one of them said, "Run for your lives! Don't look back and don't stop anywhere on the plain! Run to the mountains, or you will be swept away!" [18] But Lot said to them, "No, Lord— please. [19] Your servant has indeed found favor in Your sight, and You have shown me great kindness by saving my life. But I can't run to the mountains; the disaster will overtake me, and I will die. [20] Look, this town is close enough for me to run to. It is a small place. Please let me go there—it's only a small place, isn't it?—so that I can survive." [21] And he said to him, "All right, I'll grant your request about this matter, too, and will not overthrow the town you mentioned. [22] Hurry up! Run there, for I cannot do anything until you get there." Therefore the name of the city is Zoar.

𝒫SALM 6:6-10

[6] I am weary from my groaning;
with my tears I dampen my pillow
and drench my bed every night.
[7] My eyes are swollen from grief;

they grow old because of all my
enemies.

[8] Depart from me, all evildoers,
for the Lord has heard the sound
of my weeping.
[9] The LORD has heard my plea for
help;
the LORD accepts my prayer.
[10] All my enemies will be ashamed
and shake with terror;
they will turn back and suddenly
be disgraced.

𝒫ROVERBS 1:24-27

[24] Since I called out and you refused,
extended my hand and no one
paid attention,
[25] since you neglected all my counsel
and did not accept my correction,
[26] I, in turn, will laugh at your
calamity.
I will mock when terror strikes
you,
[27] when terror strikes you like a
storm
and your calamity comes like a
whirlwind,
when trouble and stress overcome
you.

𝑀ATTHEW 6:25–7:12

[25] "This is why I tell you: Don't worry about your life, what you will eat or what you will drink; or about your body, what you will wear. Isn't life more than food and the body more than clothing? [26] Look at the birds of the sky: they don't sow or reap or gather into barns, yet your heavenly Father feeds them. Aren't you worth more than they? [27] Can any of you add a single cubit to his height by worrying? [28] And why do you worry about clothes? Learn how the wildflowers of the field grow: they don't labor or spin thread. [29] Yet I tell you that not even Solomon in all his splendor was adorned like one of these! [30] If that's how God clothes the grass of the field, which is here today and thrown into the furnace tomorrow, won't He do

much more for you—you of little faith? [31] So don't worry, saying, 'What will we eat?' or 'What will we drink?' or 'What will we wear?' [32] For the idolaters eagerly seek all these things, and your heavenly Father knows that you need them. [33] But seek first the kingdom of God and His righteousness, and all these things will be provided for you. [34] Therefore don't worry about tomorrow, because tomorrow will worry about itself. Each day has enough trouble of its own.

7 "Do not judge, so that you won't be judged. [2] For with the judgment you use, you will be judged, and with the measure you use, it will be measured to you. [3] Why do you look at the speck in your brother's eye but don't notice the log in your own eye? [4] Or how can you say to your brother, 'Let me take the speck out of your eye,' and look, there's a log in your eye? [5] Hypocrite! First take the log out of your eye, and then you will see clearly to take the speck out of your brother's eye. [6] Don't give what is holy to dogs or toss your pearls before pigs, or they will trample them with their feet, turn, and tear you to pieces.

[7] "Keep asking, and it will be given to you. Keep searching, and you will find. Keep knocking, and the door will be opened to you. [8] For everyone who asks receives, and the one who searches finds, and to the one who knocks, the door will be opened. [9] What man among you, if his son asks him for bread, will give him a stone? [10] Or if he asks for a fish, will give him a snake? [11] If you then, who are evil, know how to give good gifts to your children, how much more will your Father in heaven give good things to those who ask Him! [12] Therefore, whatever you want others to do for you, do also the same for them—this is the Law and the Prophets.

"Your Kingdom Come"

But seek first the kingdom of God . . . and all these things will be provided for you.—MATTHEW 6:33

Let us examine the fourth phrase in the Lord's Prayer: "Your kingdom come." Jesus, after making clear that the first consideration in prayer is to focus on God's character, puts as the next issue the establishing of God's kingdom. Any pattern of praying that does not make the kingdom a priority is not Christian praying. Our text today tells us: "Seek first the kingdom of God and His righteousness, and all these things will be provided for you." If you seek something else first, then your life will be off balance.

A newspaper report tells of a small town in Alaska where all the electric clocks were showing the wrong time. The fault, it appears, was in the local power plant. It failed to run with systematic regularity, and thus all the electric clocks were "out." When your primary concern is for something other than the kingdom of God, then everything in your life will be "out," too. One of the sad things about church history is that the church has never really been gripped by the vision of the kingdom of God. There are notable exceptions, of course, but by and large the church has missed its way in this matter. One theologian points out that when the church drew up its creeds—the Apostle's, the Athanasian, the Nicene—it mentioned the kingdom once in all three of them, and then only marginally. The church will never move into the dimension God has planned for it until it puts the kingdom where Jesus put it in this prayer—in a place of primary consideration and primary allegiance.

Prayer

Gracious Father, I begin to see that there is something here that demands my thought and attention, and I don't want to miss it. Prepare me in mind and spirit for what You want to teach me in the days ahead. In Jesus' name. Amen.

Further Study

Lk 9:51-62; Mt 5:3; Jn 3:3; Jms 2:5
What did Jesus teach about the kingdom?
What did Jesus say to His would-be followers?

JANUARY 10

GENESIS 19:23–21:21

²³ The sun had risen over the land when Lot reached Zoar. ²⁴ Then the LORD rained burning sulfur on Sodom and Gomorrah from the LORD out of the sky. ²⁵ He overthrew these cities, the entire plain, all the inhabitants of the cities, and whatever grew on the ground. ²⁶ But his wife looked back and became a pillar of salt.

²⁷ Early in the morning Abraham went to the place where he had stood before the LORD. ²⁸ He looked down toward Sodom and Gomorrah and all the land of the plain, and he saw that smoke was going up from the land like the smoke of a furnace. ²⁹ So it was, when God destroyed the cities of the plain, He remembered Abraham and brought Lot out of the middle of the upheaval when He overthrew the cities where Lot had lived.

³⁰ Lot departed from Zoar and lived in the mountains along with his two daughters, because he was afraid to live in Zoar. Instead, he and his two daughters lived in a cave. ³¹ Then the firstborn said to the younger, "Our father is old, and there is no man in the land to sleep with us as is the custom of all the land. ³² Come, let's get our father to drink wine so that we can sleep with him and preserve our father's line." ³³ So they got their father to drink wine that night, and the firstborn came and slept with her father; he did not know when she lay down or when she got up.

³⁴ The next day the firstborn said to the younger, "Look, I slept with my father last night. Let's get him to drink wine again tonight so you can go sleep with him and we can preserve our father's line." ³⁵ That night they again got their father to drink wine, and the younger went and slept with him; he did not know when she lay down or when she got up.

³⁶ So both of Lot's daughters became pregnant by their father. ³⁷ The firstborn gave birth to a son and named him Moab. He is the father of the Moabites of today. ³⁸ The younger also gave birth to a son, and she named him Ben-ammi. He is the father of the Ammonites of today.

35

20 From there Abraham traveled to the region of the Negev and settled between Kadesh and Shur. While he lived in Gerar, ² Abraham said about his wife Sarah, "She is my sister." So Abimelech king of Gerar had Sarah brought to him.

³ But God came to Abimelech in a dream by night and said to him, "You are about to die because of the woman you have taken, for she is a married woman."

⁴ Now Abimelech had not approached her, so he said, "Lord, would you destroy a nation even though it is innocent? ⁵ Didn't he himself say to me, 'She is my sister'? And she herself said, 'He is my brother.' I did this with a clear conscience and clean hands."

⁶ Then God said to him in the dream, "Yes, I know that you did this with a clear conscience. I have also kept you from sinning against Me. Therefore I have not let you touch her. ⁷ Now return the man's wife, for he is a prophet, and he will pray for you and you will live. But if you do not return her, know that you will certainly die, you and all who are yours."

⁸ Early in the morning Abimelech got up, called all his servants together, and personally told them all these things; and the men were terrified.

⁹ Then Abimelech called Abraham in and said to him, "What have you done to us? How did I sin against you that you have brought such enormous guilt on me and on my kingdom? You have done things to me that should never be done." ¹⁰ Abimelech also said to Abraham, "What did you intend when you did this thing?"

¹¹ Abraham replied, "I thought, 'There is absolutely no fear of God in this place. They will kill me because of my wife.' ¹² Besides, she really is my sister, the daughter of my father though not the daughter of my mother, and she became my wife. ¹³ So when God had me wander from my father's house, I said to her: Show your loyalty to me wherever we go, and say about me: 'He's my brother.'"

¹⁴ Then Abimelech took sheep and cattle and male and female slaves, gave them to Abraham, and returned his wife Sarah to him. ¹⁵ Abimelech said, "Look, my land is before you. Settle wherever you want." ¹⁶ And to Sarah he said, "Look, I am giving your brother 1,000 pieces of silver. It is a verification of your honor to all who are with you. You are fully vindicated."

¹⁷ Then Abraham prayed to God, and God healed Abimelech, his wife, and his female slaves so that they could bear children, ¹⁸ for the LORD had completely closed all the wombs in Abimelech's household on account of Sarah, Abraham's wife.

21 The LORD came to Sarah as He had said, and the LORD did for Sarah what He had promised. ² Sarah became pregnant and bore a son to Abraham in his old age, at the appointed time God had told him. ³ Abraham named his son who was born to him— the one Sarah bore to him—Isaac. ⁴ When his son Isaac was eight days old, Abraham circumcised him, as God had commanded him. ⁵ Abraham was 100 years old when his son Isaac was born to him.

⁶ Sarah said, "God has made me laugh, and everyone who hears will laugh with me." ⁷ She also said, "Who would have told Abraham that Sarah would nurse children? Yet I have borne him a son in his old age."

⁸ The child grew and was weaned, and Abraham held a great feast on the day Isaac was weaned. ⁹ But Sarah saw the son mocking—the one Hagar the Egyptian had borne to Abraham. ¹⁰ So she said to Abraham, "Drive out this slave with her son, for the son of this slave will not be a co-heir with my son Isaac!"

¹¹ Now this was a very difficult thing for Abraham because of his son. ¹² But God said to Abraham, "Do not be concerned about the boy and your slave. Whatever Sarah says to you, listen to her, because your offspring will be traced through Isaac. ¹³ But I will also make a nation of the slave's son because he is your offspring."

¹⁴ Early in the morning Abraham got up, took bread and a waterskin, put them on Hagar's shoulders, and sent her and the boy away. She left and wandered in the Wilderness of Beer-sheba. ¹⁵ When the water in the skin was gone, she left the boy under one of the bushes. ¹⁶ Then she went and sat down nearby, about a bowshot away, for she said, "I can't bear to watch the boy die!" So as she sat nearby, she wept loudly.

¹⁷ God heard the voice of the boy, and the angel of God called to Hagar from heaven and said to her, "What's wrong, Hagar? Don't be afraid, for God has heard the voice of the boy from the place where he is. ¹⁸ Get up, help the boy up, and sustain him, for I will make him a great nation." ¹⁹ Then God opened her eyes, and she saw a well of water. So she went and filled the waterskin and gave the boy a drink. ²⁰ God was with the boy, and he grew; he settled in the wilderness and became an archer. ²¹ He settled in the Wilderness of Paran, and his mother got a wife for him from the land of Egypt.

*P*SALM 7:1-8

¹ Lord my God, I seek refuge in You;
    save me from all my pursuers and rescue me,
² or they will tear me like a lion,
    ripping me apart, with no one to rescue me.

³ Lord my God, if I have done this,
    if there is injustice on my hands,
⁴ if I have done harm to one at peace with me
    or have plundered my adversary without cause,
⁵ may an enemy pursue and overtake me;
    may he trample me to the ground
    and leave my honor in the dust.
        Selah

⁶ Rise up, Lord, in Your anger;
    lift Yourself up against the fury of my adversaries;

awake for me; You have ordained a judgment.
⁷ Let the assembly of peoples gather around You;
    take Your seat on high over it.
⁸ The Lord judges the peoples;
    vindicate me, Lord,
    according to my righteousness and my integrity.

*P*ROVERBS 1:28-31

²⁸ Then they will call me, but I won't answer;
    they will search for me, but won't find me.
²⁹ Because they hated knowledge,
    didn't choose to fear the Lord,
³⁰ were not interested in my counsel,
    and rejected all my correction,
³¹ they will eat the fruit of their way
    and be glutted with their own schemes.

*M*ATTHEW 7:13–8:4

¹³ "Enter through the narrow gate. For the gate is wide and the road is broad that leads to destruction, and there are many who go through it. ¹⁴ How narrow is the gate and difficult the road that leads to life, and few find it.

¹⁵ "Beware of false prophets who come to you in sheep's clothing but inwardly are ravaging wolves. ¹⁶ You'll recognize them by their fruit. Are grapes gathered from thornbushes or figs from thistles? ¹⁷ In the same way, every good tree produces good fruit, but a bad tree produces bad fruit. ¹⁸ A good tree can't produce bad fruit; neither can a bad tree produce good fruit. ¹⁹ Every tree that doesn't produce good fruit is cut down and thrown into the fire. ²⁰ So you'll recognize them by their fruit.

²¹ "Not everyone who says to Me, 'Lord, Lord!' will enter the kingdom of heaven, but only the one who does the will of My Father in heaven. ²² On that day many will say to Me, 'Lord, Lord, didn't we prophesy in Your name, drive out demons in Your name, and do

many miracles in Your name?' ²³ Then I will announce to them, 'I never knew you! **Depart from Me, you law-breakers!'**

²⁴ "Therefore, everyone who hears these words of Mine and acts on them will be like a sensible man who built his house on the rock. ²⁵ The rain fell, the rivers rose, and the winds blew and pounded that house. Yet it didn't collapse, because its foundation was on the rock. ²⁶ But everyone who hears these words of Mine and doesn't act on them will be like a foolish man who built his house on the sand. ²⁷ The rain fell, the rivers rose, the winds blew and pounded that house, and it collapsed. And its collapse was great!"

²⁸ When Jesus had finished this ser-

mon, the crowds were astonished at His teaching, ²⁹ because He was teaching them like one who had authority, and not like their scribes.

8 When He came down from the mountain, large crowds followed Him. ² Right away a man with a serious skin disease came up and knelt before Him, saying, "Lord, if You are willing, You can make me clean."

³ Reaching out His hand He touched him, saying, "I am willing; be made clean." Immediately his disease was healed. ⁴ Then Jesus told him, "See that you don't tell anyone; but go, show yourself to the priest, and offer the gift that Moses prescribed, as a testimony to them."

Sin Can Be Overcome

But put on the Lord Jesus Christ.
—ROMANS 13:14

Every sin can be overcome. Don't allow yourself to admit to any exception, for if you do, this exception will be the loose bolt that causes the bridge to fall down.

One of the sad things about certain sections of the modern-day church is the moral fatalism that says in regard to one's sin: "But what could I do? I am just a frail human being." The implication is that sin is an integral part of human nature, and as long as we remain human, we shall never be able to overcome sin. The clear message of the gospel is spelled out in this verse: "Sin will not rule over you" (Rm 6:14).

Today's text in *The Amplified Bible* reads: "But clothe yourself with the Lord Jesus Christ, the Messiah, and make no provision for indulging the flesh—put a stop to thinking about the evil cravings of your physical nature—to gratify its desires and lusts." Notice the phrase: "make no provision for indulging the flesh." In other words, do not provide for failure; provide for victory. There must be an absoluteness about the whole thing.

There are dangers in pretending we are winning the battle against sin when we are not, or in approaching the whole issue from self-effort. But these dangers, in my opinion, are not as great as mentally providing for sin in our lives. The tyranny of this fatalism—that as long as we are in the flesh, we must expect to sin—must be broken. The Christian life must be lived from the standpoint that we expect not to sin. I repeat: every sin can be overcome.

Prayer

My Father and my God, help me to lay hold on the fact that Your offer is not simply to help me realize what sin is, but to release me from it. May I enter more and more into that glorious deliverance day by day. Amen.

Further Study

Rm 7 & 8; 6:11; Jn 8:34
What set Paul free?
What is the obligation we have?

JANUARY 11

GENESIS 21:22–23:20

²² At that time Abimelech, with Phicol the commander of his army, said to Abraham, "God is with you in everything you do. ²³ Now swear to me here by God that you will not break an agreement with me or with my children and descendants. As I have kept faith with you, so you will keep faith with me and with the country where you are a resident alien."

²⁴ And Abraham said, "I swear it." ²⁵ But Abraham complained to Abimelech because of the water well that Abimelech's servants had seized.

²⁶ Abimelech replied, "I don't know who did this thing. You didn't report anything to me, so I hadn't heard about it until today."

²⁷ Then Abraham took sheep and cattle and gave them to Abimelech, and the two of them made a covenant. ²⁸ But Abraham had set apart seven ewe lambs from the flock. ²⁹ And Abimelech said to Abraham, "Why have you set apart these seven ewe lambs?"

³⁰ He replied, "You are to accept the seven ewe lambs from my hand so that this act will serve as my witness that I dug this well." ³¹ Therefore that place was called Beer-sheba because it was there that the two of them swore an oath. ³² After they had made a covenant at Beer-sheba, Abimelech and Phicol, the commander of his army, left and returned to the land of the Philistines.

³³ Abraham planted a tamarisk tree in Beer-sheba, and there he worshiped the LORD, the Everlasting God. ³⁴ And Abraham lived as a foreigner in the land of the Philistines for many days.

22 After these things God tested Abraham and said to him, "Abraham!"

"Here I am," he answered.

² "Take your son," He said, "your only son Isaac, whom you love, go to the land of Moriah, and offer him there as a burnt offering on one of the mountains I will tell you about."

³ So early in the morning Abraham got up, saddled his donkey, and took with him two of his young men and his son Isaac. He split wood for a burnt offering and set out to go to the place God had

told him about. ⁴ On the third day Abraham looked up and saw the place in the distance. ⁵ Then Abraham said to his young men, "Stay here with the donkey. The boy and I will go over there to worship; then we'll come back to you." ⁶ Abraham took the wood for the burnt offering and laid it on his son Isaac. In his hand he took the fire and the sacrificial knife, and the two of them walked on together.

⁷ Then Isaac spoke to his father Abraham and said, "My father."

And he replied, "Here I am, my son."

Isaac said, "The fire and the wood are here, but where is the lamb for the burnt offering?"

⁸ Abraham answered, "God Himself will provide the lamb for the burnt offering, my son." Then the two of them walked on together.

⁹ When they arrived at the place that God had told him about, Abraham built the altar there and arranged the wood. He bound his son Isaac and placed him on the altar, on top of the wood. ¹⁰ Then Abraham reached out and took the knife to slaughter his son.

¹¹ But the Angel of the LORD called to him from heaven and said, "Abraham, Abraham!"

He replied, "Here I am."

¹² Then He said, "Do not lay a hand on the boy or do anything to him. For now I know that you fear God, since you have not withheld your only son from Me." ¹³ Abraham looked up and saw a ram caught by its horns in the thicket. So Abraham went and took the ram and offered it as a burnt offering in place of his son. ¹⁴ And Abraham named that place The LORD Will Provide, so today it is said: "It will be provided on the LORD's mountain."

¹⁵ Then the Angel of the LORD called to Abraham a second time from heaven ¹⁶ and said, "By Myself I have sworn, says the LORD: Because you have done this thing and have not withheld your only son, ¹⁷ I will indeed bless you and make your offspring as numerous as the stars in the sky and the sand on the seashore. Your offspring will possess the gates of their enemies. ¹⁸ And all the

nations of the earth will be blessed by your offspring because you have obeyed My command."

¹⁹ Abraham went back to his young men, and they got up and went together to Beer-sheba. And Abraham settled in Beer-sheba.

²⁰ Now after these things Abraham was told, "Milcah also has borne sons to your brother Nahor: ²¹ Uz his firstborn, his brother Buz, Kemuel the father of Aram, ²² Chesed, Hazo, Pildash, Jidlaph, and Bethuel." ²³ And Bethuel fathered Rebekah. Milcah bore these eight to Nahor, Abraham's brother. ²⁴ His concubine, whose name was Reumah, also bore Tebah, Gaham, Tahash, and Maacah.

23

Now Sarah lived 127 years; these were all the years of her life. ² Sarah died in Kiriath-arba (that is, Hebron) in the land of Canaan, and Abraham went in to mourn for Sarah and to weep for her.

³ Then Abraham got up from beside his dead wife and spoke to the Hittites: ⁴ "I am a resident alien among you. Give me a burial site among you so that I can bury my dead."

⁵ The Hittites replied to Abraham, ⁶ "Listen to us, lord. You are God's chosen one among us. Bury your dead in our finest burial place. None of us will withhold from you his burial place for burying your dead."

⁷ Then Abraham rose and bowed down to the Hittites, the people of the land. ⁸ He said to them, "If you are willing for me to bury my dead, listen to me and ask Ephron son of Zohar on my behalf ⁹ to give me the cave of Machpelah that belongs to him; it is at the end of his field. Let him give it to me in your presence, for the full price, as a burial place."

¹⁰ Ephron was present with the Hittites. So in the presence of all the Hittites who came to the gate of his city, Ephron the Hittite answered Abraham: ¹¹ "No, my lord. Listen to me. I give you the field, and I give you the cave that is in it. I give it to you in the presence of my people. Bury your dead."

¹² Abraham bowed down to the peo-

ple of the land ¹³ and said to Ephron in the presence of the people of the land, "Please listen to me. Let me pay the price of the field. Accept it from me, and let me bury my dead there." ¹⁴ Ephron answered Abraham and said to him, ¹⁵ "My lord, listen to me. Land worth 400 shekels of silver—what is that between you and me? Bury your dead." ¹⁶ Abraham agreed with Ephron, and Abraham weighed out to Ephron the silver that he had agreed to in the hearing of the Hittites: 400 shekels of silver at the current commercial rate. ¹⁷ So Ephron's field at Machpelah near Mamre—the field with its cave and all the trees anywhere within the boundaries of the field—became ¹⁸ Abraham's possession in the presence of all the Hittites who came to the gate of his city. ¹⁹ After this, Abraham buried his wife Sarah in the cave of the field at Machpelah near Mamre (that is, Hebron) in the land of Canaan. ²⁰ The field with its cave passed from the Hittites to Abraham as a burial place.

PSALM 7:9-17

⁹ Let the evil of the wicked come to
   an end,
  but establish the righteous.
  The One who examines the
     thoughts and emotions
  is a righteous God.
¹⁰ My shield is with God,
  who saves the upright in heart.
¹¹ God is a righteous judge,
  and a God who executes justice
     every day.

¹² If anyone does not repent, God
     will sharpen His sword;
  He has strung His bow and made
     it ready.
¹³ He has prepared His deadly
     weapons;
  He tips His arrows with fire.

¹⁴ See, he is pregnant with evil,
  conceives trouble, and gives birth
     to deceit.
¹⁵ He dug a pit and hollowed it out,

but fell into the hole he had
   made.
¹⁶ His trouble comes back on his
     own head,
  and his violence falls on the top of
     his head.

¹⁷ I will thank the LORD for His
     righteousness;
  I will sing about the name of the
     LORD, the Most High.

PROVERBS 1:32-33

³² For the waywardness of the
     inexperienced will kill
     them,
  and the complacency of fools will
     destroy them.
³³ But whoever listens to me will live
     securely
  and be free from the fear of
     danger."

MATTHEW 8:5-27

⁵ When He entered Capernaum, a centurion came to Him, pleading with Him, ⁶ "Lord, my servant is lying at home paralyzed, in terrible agony!"
⁷ "I will come and heal him," He told him.
⁸ "Lord," the centurion replied, "I am not worthy to have You come under my roof. But only say the word, and my servant will be cured. ⁹ For I too am a man under authority, having soldiers under my command. I say to this one, 'Go!' and he goes; and to another, 'Come!' and he comes; and to my slave, 'Do this!' and he does it."
¹⁰ Hearing this, Jesus was amazed and said to those following Him, " I assure you: I have not found anyone in Israel with so great a faith! ¹¹ I tell you that many will come from east and west, and recline at the table with Abraham, Isaac, and Jacob in the kingdom of heaven. ¹² But the sons of the kingdom will be thrown into the outer darkness. In that place there will be weeping and gnashing of teeth." ¹³ Then Jesus told the centurion, "Go. As you have believed, let it

be done for you." And his servant was cured that very moment.

¹⁴ When Jesus went into Peter's house, He saw his mother-in-law lying in bed with a fever. ¹⁵ So He touched her hand, and the fever left her. Then she got up and began to serve Him. ¹⁶ When evening came, they brought to Him many who were demon-possessed. He drove out the spirits with a word and healed all who were sick, ¹⁷ so that what was spoken through the prophet Isaiah might be fulfilled:

He Himself took our weaknesses and carried our diseases.

¹⁸ When Jesus saw large crowds around Him, He gave the order to go to the other side of the sea. ¹⁹ A scribe approached Him and said, "Teacher, I will follow You wherever You go!"

²⁰ Jesus told him, "Foxes have dens and birds of the sky have nests, but the Son of Man has no place to lay His head."

²¹ "Lord," another of His disciples said, "first let me go bury my father."

²² But Jesus told him, "Follow Me, and let the dead bury their own dead."

²³ As He got into the boat, His disciples followed Him. ²⁴ Suddenly, a violent storm arose on the sea, so that the boat was being swamped by the waves. But He was sleeping. ²⁵ So the disciples came and woke Him up, saying, "Lord, save us! We're going to die!"

²⁶ But He said to them, "Why are you fearful, you of little faith?" Then He got up and rebuked the winds and the sea. And there was a great calm.

²⁷ The men were amazed and asked, "What kind of man is this?—even the winds and the sea obey Him!"

A Little-Known Sin

The One who examines the thoughts and emotions is a righteous God.—PSALM 7:9

Focusing only on correcting obvious sin (sins of behavior) without understanding what it means to deal with the issues of the heart will bring about a condition akin to that of the Pharisees—more smug than spiritual.

One of the things I have noticed about myself is that whenever I feel I am not pursuing God in the way I should, I tend to focus on the surface issues of my life—my above-the-waterline problems—and work at them all I can. But sin involves far more than what goes on above the surface; there is also something going on in the deep recesses of my heart.

As there is little need for me to discuss the sins that are obvious, I want to focus now on those that are not. I imagine that those of you who have been Christians for some time will expect me at this stage to identify the hidden sins of the heart under such categories as resentment, lukewarmness, impatience, jealousy, and so on. My concern, however, is with a category of sin that is not easily recognized and not very well-known. This sin is probably more deeply buried in our hearts than any other, and it acts, in my opinion, as a trigger to them.

The sin I refer to is—demandingness. You won't find the word in the Bible, but you will certainly see it illustrated there. Demandingness is insisting that our interests be served irrespective of others.

Clearly, if Christ is to live in us, then this has to die in us.

Prayer

Father, I see that again You are about to face me with a strong and serious challenge. Forgive me if I draw back when Your lance plunges deep. I have lived with demandingness for so long that I might not even be able to recognize it. Help me, Lord. Amen.

Further Study

Gl 2:15-21; Is 29:15; 30:1-2; 1 Co 10:24
How did Paul describe "demandingness"?
What were the children of Israel doing?

JANUARY 12

GENESIS 24:1-54

24 Abraham was now old, getting on in years, and the LORD had blessed him in everything. ² Abraham said to his servant, the elder of his household who managed all he owned, "Place your hand under my thigh, ³ and I will have you swear by the LORD, God of heaven and God of earth, that you will not take a wife for my son from the daughters of the Canaanites among whom I live, ⁴ but will go to my land and my family to take a wife for my son Isaac."

⁵ The servant said to him, "Suppose the woman is unwilling to follow me to this land? Should I have your son go back to the land you came from?"

⁶ Abraham answered him, "Make sure that you don't take my son back there. ⁷ The LORD, the God of heaven, who took me from my father's house and from my native land, who spoke to me and swore to me, 'I will give this land to your offspring'—He will send His angel before you, and you can take a wife for my son from there. ⁸ If the woman is un-

willing to follow you, then you are free from this oath to me, but don't let my son go back there." ⁹ So the servant placed his hand under his master Abraham's thigh and swore an oath to him concerning this matter.

¹⁰ The servant took 10 of his master's camels and departed with all kinds of his master's goods in hand. Then he set out for the town of Nahor, Aram-naharaim. ¹¹ He made the camels kneel beside a well of water outside the town at evening. This was the time when the women went out to draw water.

¹² "LORD, God of my master Abraham," he prayed, "grant me success today, and show kindness to my master Abraham. ¹³ I am standing here at the spring where the daughters of the men of the town are coming out to draw water. ¹⁴ Let the girl to whom I say, 'Please lower your water jug so that I may drink,' and who responds, 'Drink, and I'll water your camels also'—let her be the one You have appointed for Your servant Isaac. By this I will know that You have shown kindness to my master."

¹⁵ Before he had finished speaking, there was Rebekah—daughter of Bethuel

son of Milcah, the wife of Abraham's brother Nahor—coming with a jug on her shoulder. ¹⁶ Now the girl was very beautiful, a young woman who had not known a man intimately. She went down to the spring, filled her jug, and came up. ¹⁷ Then the servant ran to meet her and said, "Please let me have a little water from your jug."

¹⁸ She replied, "Drink, my lord." She quickly lowered her jug to her hand and gave him a drink. ¹⁹ When she had finished giving him a drink, she said, "I'll also draw water for your camels until they have had enough to drink." ²⁰ She quickly emptied her jug into the trough and hurried to the well again to draw water. She drew water for all his camels ²¹ while the man silently watched her to see whether or not the LORD had made his journey a success.

²² After the camels had finished drinking, the man took a gold ring weighing half a shekel, and for her wrists two bracelets weighing 10 shekels of gold. ²³ "Whose daughter are you?" he asked. "Please tell me, is there room in your father's house for us to spend the night?"

²⁴ She answered him, "I am the daughter of Bethuel son of Milcah, whom she bore to Nahor." ²⁵ She also said to him, "We have plenty of straw and feed, and a place to spend the night."

²⁶ Then the man bowed down, worshiped the LORD, ²⁷ and said, "Praise the LORD, the God of my master Abraham, who has not withheld His kindness and faithfulness from my master. As for me, the LORD has led me on the journey to the house of my master's relatives."

²⁸ The girl ran and told her mother's household about these things. ²⁹ Now Rebekah had a brother named Laban, and Laban ran out to the man at the spring. ³⁰ As soon as he had seen the ring, and the bracelets on his sister's wrists, and when he had heard his sister Rebekah's words—"The man said this to me!"—he went to the man. He was standing there by the camels at the spring.

³¹ Laban said, "Come, you who are blessed by the LORD. Why are you stand-ing out here? I have prepared the house and a place for the camels." ³² So the man came to the house, and the camels were unloaded. Straw and feed were given to the camels, and water was brought to wash his feet and the feet of the men with him.

³³ A meal was set before him, but he said, "I will not eat until I have said what I have to say."

So Laban said, "Speak on."

³⁴ "I am Abraham's servant," he said. ³⁵ "The LORD has greatly blessed my master, and he has become rich. He has given him sheep and cattle, silver and gold, male and female slaves, and camels and donkeys. ³⁶ Sarah, my master's wife, bore a son to my master in her old age, and he has given him everything he owns. ³⁷ My master put me under this oath: 'You will not take a wife for my son from the daughters of the Canaanites in whose land I live ³⁸ but will go to my father's household and to my family to take a wife for my son.' ³⁹ But I said to my master, 'Suppose the woman will not come back with me?' ⁴⁰ He said to me, 'The LORD before whom I have walked will send His angel with you and make your journey a success, and you will take a wife for my son from my family and from my father's household. ⁴¹ Then you will be free from my oath if you go to my family and they do not give her to you—you will be free from my oath.'

⁴² "Today when I came to the spring, I prayed: LORD, God of my master Abraham, if only You will make my journey successful! ⁴³ I am standing here at a spring. Let the virgin who comes out to draw water, and I say to her: Please let me drink a little water from your jug, ⁴⁴ and who responds to me, 'Drink, and I'll draw water for your camels also'— let her be the woman the LORD has appointed for my master's son.

⁴⁵ "Before I had finished praying in my heart, there was Rebekah coming with her jug on her shoulder, and she went down to the spring and drew water. So I said to her: Please let me have a drink. ⁴⁶ She quickly lowered her jug from her shoulder and said, 'Drink, and

I'll water your camels also.' So I drank, and she also watered the camels. [47] Then I asked her: Whose daughter are you? She responded, 'The daughter of Bethuel son of Nahor, whom Milcah bore to him.' So I put the ring on her nose and the bracelets on her wrists. [48] Then I bowed down, worshiped the LORD, and praised the LORD, the God of my master Abraham, who guided me on the right way to take the daughter of my master's brother for his son. [49] Now, if you are going to show kindness and faithfulness to my master, tell me; if not, tell me, and I will go elsewhere."

[50] Laban and Bethuel answered, "This is from the LORD; we have no choice in the matter. [51] Rebekah is here in front of you. Take her and go, and let her be a wife for your master's son, just as the LORD has spoken."

[52] When Abraham's servant heard their words, he bowed to the ground before the LORD. [53] Then he brought out objects of silver and gold, and garments, and gave them to Rebekah. He also gave precious gifts to her brother and her mother. [54] Then he and the men with him ate and drank and spent the night.

When they got up in the morning, he said, "Send me to my master."

$\mathcal{P}$SALM 8:1-9

[1] LORD, our Lord,
how magnificent is Your name
throughout the earth!

You have covered the heavens
with Your majesty.
[2] Because of Your adversaries, You
have established a stronghold
from the mouths of children and
nursing infants,
to silence the enemy and the
avenger.

[3] When I observe Your heavens, the
work of Your fingers,
the moon and the stars, which You
set in place,
[4] what is man that You remember
him,

the son of man that You look after
him?
[5] You made him little less than God
and crowned him with glory and
honor.
[6] You made him lord over the works
of Your hands;
You put everything under his feet:
[7] all the sheep and oxen,
as well as animals in the wild,
[8] birds of the sky,
and fish of the sea
passing through the currents of
the seas.

[9] O LORD, our Lord,
how magnificent is Your name
throughout the earth!

$\mathcal{P}$ROVERBS 2:1-5

2 My son, if you accept my words
and store up my commands within
you,
[2] listening closely to wisdom
and directing your heart to
understanding;
[3] furthermore, if you call out to
insight
and lift your voice to
understanding,
[4] if you seek it like silver
and search for it like hidden
treasure,
[5] then you will understand the
fear of the LORD
and discover the knowledge of God.

$\mathcal{M}$ATTHEW 8:28–9:17

[28] When He had come to the other side, to the region of the Gadarenes, two demon-possessed men met Him as they came out of the tombs. They were so violent that no one could pass that way. [29] Suddenly they shouted, "What do You have to do with us, Son of God? Have You come here to torment us before the time?"

[30] Now a long way off from them, a large herd of pigs was feeding. [31] "If You drive us out," the demons begged Him, "send us into the herd of pigs."

[32] "Go!" He told them. So when they had come out, they entered the pigs. And suddenly the whole herd rushed down the steep bank into the sea and perished in the water. [33] Then the men who tended them fled. They went into the city and reported everything—especially what had happened to those who were demon-possessed. [34] At that, the whole town went out to meet Jesus. When they saw Him, they begged Him to leave their region.

9 So He got into a boat, crossed over, and came to His own town. [2] Just then some men brought to Him a paralytic lying on a stretcher. Seeing their faith, Jesus told the paralytic, "Have courage, son, your sins are forgiven."

[3] At this, some of the scribes said among themselves, "He's blaspheming!"

[4] But perceiving their thoughts, Jesus said, "Why are you thinking evil things in your hearts? [5] For which is easier: to say, 'Your sins are forgiven,' or to say, 'Get up and walk'? [6] But so you may know that the Son of Man has authority on earth to forgive sins"—then He told the paralytic, "Get up, pick up your stretcher, and go home." [7] And he got up and went home. [8] When the crowds saw this, they were awestruck and gave glory to God who had given such authority to men.

[9] As Jesus went on from there, He saw a man named Matthew sitting at the tax office, and He said to him, "Follow Me!" So he got up and followed Him.

[10] While He was reclining at the table in the house, many tax collectors and sinners came as guests to eat with Jesus and His disciples. [11] When the Pharisees saw this, they asked His disciples, "Why does your Teacher eat with tax collectors and sinners?"

[12] But when He heard this, He said, "Those who are well don't need a doctor, but the sick do. [13] Go and learn what this means: **I desire mercy and not sacrifice.** For I didn't come to call the righteous, but sinners."

[14] Then John's disciples came to Him, saying, "Why do we and the Pharisees fast often, but Your disciples do not fast?"

[15] Jesus said to them, "Can the wedding guests be sad while the groom is with them? The days will come when the groom will be taken away from them, and then they will fast. [16] No one patches an old garment with unshrunk cloth, because the patch pulls away from the garment and makes the tear worse. [17] And no one puts new wine into old wineskins. Otherwise, the skins burst, the wine spills out, and the skins are ruined. But they put new wine into fresh wineskins, and both are preserved."

Who Can Forgive?

The Son of Man has authority on earth to forgive sins.—MATTHEW 9:6

Perhaps one of the most significant ways in which Jesus is unlike anyone else who has ever lived is that He has the ability to forgive sins. I am sure you will know the words of the famous hymn that refers to the forgiveness offered by Christ:

He breaks the power of cancelled sin,

He sets the prisoner free.

I know of no one else who can do that. Some psychoanalysts try to rid the soul of guilt, but though they may be successful with pseudo-guilt (guilt that is imagined rather than real), they are powerless to deal with the stain of sin that is deeply ingrained in every human soul. The secular therapist will examine the stuff of your dreams, invite you to answer a series of harmless questions, and then drag out from your forgotten past the source of all your trouble—some past transgression or sin. But even the most highly trained team of psychoanalysts cannot forgive. They may expose an old wound, but they cannot heal it. They may show you that your trouble is an ancient sin, but they cannot cleanse it from the system. And that is what our sick souls need most of all—forgiveness.

A man I talked to the other day said he went to a professional counselor, a non-Christian, who found the root of his trouble—an old and wicked sin. "Now," said the man, "tell me the cure." "Just forgive yourself," said the analyst. Forgive yourself? It's a lot easier to do that when you know that you yourself have been forgiven.

Prayer

Lord Jesus, not only have You forgiven me, but You keep on forgiving me. Help me realize, however, that though Your forgiveness is free, it is not cheap. For You had to die in order to bring me forgiveness. Help me never forget that. Amen.

Further Study

Mt 26:17-30; Ac 3:38; 13:38 Heb 9:22
Why is forgiveness available?
Seek forgiveness for your sin today.

JANUARY 13

GENESIS 24:55–26:11

⁵⁵ But her brother and mother said, "Let the girl stay with us for about 10 days. Then she can go."

⁵⁶ But he responded to them, "Do not delay me, since the LORD has made my journey a success. Send me away so that I may go to my master."

⁵⁷ So they said, "Let's call the girl and ask her opinion."

⁵⁸ They called Rebekah and said to her, "Will you go with this man?"

She replied, "I will go." ⁵⁹ So they sent away their sister Rebekah and her nurse, and Abraham's servant and his men. ⁶⁰ They blessed Rebekah, saying to her:

Our sister, may you become
thousands upon ten thousands.
May your offspring possess
the gates of their enemies.

⁶¹ Then Rebekah and her young women got up, mounted the camels, and followed the man. So the servant took Rebekah and left.

⁶² Now Isaac was returning from Beer-lahai-roi, for he was living in the Negev region. ⁶³ In the early evening, Isaac

went out to walk in the field, and looking up, he saw camels coming. [64] Rebekah looked up, and when she saw Isaac, she got down from her camel [65] and asked the servant, "Who is that man in the field coming to meet us?"

The servant answered, "It is my master." So she took her veil and covered herself. [66] Then the servant told Isaac everything he had done.

[67] And Isaac brought her into the tent of his mother Sarah and took Rebekah to be his wife. Isaac loved her, and he was comforted after his mother's death.

25 Now Abraham took another wife, whose name was Keturah, [2] and she bore him Zimran, Jokshan, Medan, Midian, Ishbak, and Shuah. [3] Jokshan fathered Sheba and Dedan. Dedan's sons were the Asshurim, Letushim, and Leummim. [4] And Midian's sons were Ephah, Epher, Hanoch, Abida, and Eldaah. All these were sons of Keturah. [5] Abraham gave everything he owned to Isaac. [6] And Abraham gave gifts to the sons of his concubines, but while he was still alive he sent them eastward, away from his son Isaac, to the land of the East.

[7] This is the length of Abraham's life: 175 years. [8] He took his last breath and died at a ripe old age, old and contented, and he was gathered to his people. [9] His sons Isaac and Ishmael buried him in the cave of Machpelah near Mamre, in the field of Ephron son of Zohar the Hittite. [10] This was the field that Abraham bought from the Hittites. Abraham was buried there with his wife Sarah. [11] After Abraham's death, God blessed his son Isaac, who lived near Beer-lahai-roi.

[12] These are the family records of Abraham's son Ishmael, whom Hagar the Egyptian, Sarah's slave, bore to Abraham. [13] These are the names of Ishmael's sons; their names according to the family records are: Nebaioth, Ishmael's firstborn, then Kedar, Adbeel, Mibsam, [14] Mishma, Dumah, Massa, [15] Hadad, Tema, Jetur, Naphish, and Kedemah. [16] These are Ishmael's sons, and these are their names by their villages and encampments: 12 leaders of their clans. [17] This is the length of Ishmael's life: 137 years. He took his last breath and died, and was gathered to his people. [18] And they settled from Havilah to Shur, which is opposite Egypt as you go toward Asshur. He lived in opposition to all his brothers.

[19] These are the family records of Isaac son of Abraham. Abraham fathered Isaac. [20] Isaac was 40 years old when he took as his wife Rebekah daughter of Bethuel the Aramean from Paddan-aram, and sister of Laban the Aramean. [21] Isaac prayed to the Lord on behalf of his wife because she was barren. The Lord heard his prayer, and his wife Rebekah conceived. [22] But the children inside her struggled with each other, and she said, "Why is this happening to me?" So she went to inquire of the Lord. [23] And the Lord said to her:

Two nations are in your womb;
two people will come from you
    and be separated.
One people will be stronger than
    the other,
and the older will serve the
    younger.

[24] When her time came to give birth, there were indeed twins in her womb. [25] The first one came out reddish, covered with hair like a fur coat, and they named him Esau. [26] After this, his brother came out grasping Esau's heel with his hand. So he was named Jacob. Isaac was 60 years old when they were born.

[27] When the boys grew up, Esau became an expert hunter, an outdoorsman, but Jacob was a quiet man who stayed at home. [28] Isaac loved Esau because he had a taste for wild game, but Rebekah loved Jacob.

[29] Once when Jacob was cooking a stew, Esau came in from the field, exhausted. [30] He said to Jacob, "Let me eat some of that red stuff, because I'm exhausted." That is why he was also named Edom.

[31] Jacob replied, "First sell me your birthright."

³² "Look," said Esau, "I'm about to die, so what good is a birthright to me?" ³³ Jacob said, "Swear to me first." So he swore to Jacob and sold his birthright to him. ³⁴ Then Jacob gave bread and lentil stew to Esau; he ate, drank, got up, and went away. So Esau despised his birthright.

26 There was another famine in the land in addition to the one that had occurred in Abraham's time. And Isaac went to Abimelech, king of the Philistines, at Gerar. ² The LORD appeared to him and said, "Do not go down to Egypt. Live in the land that I tell you about; ³ stay in this land as a foreigner, and I will be with you and bless you. For I will give all these lands to you and your offspring, and I will confirm the oath that I swore to your father Abraham. ⁴ I will make your offspring as numerous as the stars of the sky, I will give your offspring all these lands, and all the nations of the earth will be blessed by your offspring, ⁵ because Abraham listened to My voice and kept My mandate, My commands, My statutes, and My instructions." ⁶ So Isaac settled in Gerar.

⁷ When the men of the place asked about his wife, he said, "She is my sister," for he was afraid to say "my wife," thinking, "The men of the place will kill me on account of Rebekah, for she is a beautiful woman." ⁸ When Isaac had been there for some time, Abimelech king of the Philistines looked down from the window and was surprised to see Isaac caressing his wife Rebekah. ⁹ Abimelech sent for Isaac and said, "So she is really your wife! How could you say, 'She's my sister'?"

Isaac answered him, "Because I thought I might die on account of her." ¹⁰ Then Abimelech said, "What is this you've done to us? One of the people could easily have slept with your wife, and you would have brought guilt on us." ¹¹ So Abimelech warned all the people with these words: "Whoever harms this man or his wife will certainly die."

PSALM 9:1-6

¹ I will thank the LORD with all my heart;
I will declare all Your wonderful works.
² I will rejoice and boast about You;
I will sing about Your name, Most High.

³ When my enemies retreat,
they stumble and perish before You.
⁴ For You have upheld my just cause;
You are seated on Your throne as a righteous judge.
⁵ You have rebuked the nations; You have destroyed the wicked;
You have erased their name forever and ever.
⁶ The enemy has come to eternal ruin;
You have uprooted the cities,
and the very memory of them has perished.

PROVERBS 2:6-8

⁶ For the LORD gives wisdom;
from His mouth come knowledge and understanding.
⁷ He stores up success for the upright;
He is a shield for those who live with integrity
⁸ so that He may guard the paths of justice
and protect the way of His loyal followers.

MATTHEW 9:18-38

¹⁸ As He was telling them these things, suddenly one of the leaders came and knelt down before Him, saying, "My daughter is near death, but come and lay Your hand on her, and she will live." ¹⁹ So Jesus and His disciples got up and followed him.

²⁰ Just then, a woman who had suffered from bleeding for 12 years approached from behind and touched the

tassel on His robe, [21] for she said to herself, "If I can just touch His robe, I'll be made well!" [22] But Jesus turned and saw her. "Have courage, daughter," He said. "Your faith has made you well." And the woman was made well from that moment. [23] When Jesus came to the leader's house, He saw the flute players and a crowd lamenting loudly. [24] "Leave," He said, "because the girl isn't dead, but sleeping." And they started laughing at Him. [25] But when the crowd had been put outside, He went in and took her by the hand, and the girl got up. [26] And this news spread throughout that whole area.

[27] As Jesus went on from there, two blind men followed Him, shouting, "Have mercy on us, Son of David!" [28] When He entered the house, the blind men approached Him, and Jesus said to them, "Do you believe that I can do this?"

"Yes, Lord," they answered Him. [29] Then He touched their eyes, saying, "Let it be done for you according to your faith!" [30] And their eyes were opened. Then Jesus warned them sternly, "Be sure that no one finds out!" [31] But they went out and spread the news about Him throughout that whole area.

[32] Just as they were going out, a demon-possessed man who was unable to speak was brought to Him. [33] When the demon had been driven out, the man spoke. And the crowds were amazed, saying, "Nothing like this has ever been seen in Israel!"

[34] But the Pharisees said, "He drives out demons by the ruler of the demons!"

[35] Then Jesus went to all the towns and villages, teaching in their synagogues, preaching the good news of the kingdom, and healing every disease and every sickness. [36] When He saw the crowds, He felt compassion for them, because they were weary and worn out, like sheep without a shepherd. [37] Then He said to His disciples, "The harvest is abundant, but the workers are few. [38] Therefore, pray to the Lord of the harvest to send out workers into His harvest."

Another Kingdom

Then Jesus went to all the towns and villages, teaching in their synagogues, preaching the good news of the kingdom, and healing every disease and every sickness. —MATTHEW 9:35

While we focus our thoughts on the kingdom of God, we must not forget that there exists in the universe another kingdom—the kingdom of Satan. The Bible shows us that in ages past there was just one kingdom, the kingdom of God. But, through the rebellion of an angel named Lucifer (now known as Satan), another kingdom was established over which the Prince of Darkness rules.

Every person since Adam (with the single exception of Jesus Christ) comes under the dominion of Satan and is, in fact, classified as a citizen of the devil's kingdom (Eph 2:1-2). When, through conversion, we become followers of the Lord Jesus Christ, we become citizens of the kingdom of God (Col 1:13). Once we receive this new citizenship, whether we realize it or not, we are thrust into the front line of the age-long conflict which has existed between God and Satan, and we become participators in the Almighty's plan to bring about Satan's defeat and to bring the universe once again under the control of God and His kingdom.

Standing as we do on the cutting edge between the kingdom of God and the kingdom of

Satan, the Almighty has given us the most powerful weapon in all the armories of heaven. That weapon is prayer. Our citizenship in God's kingdom entitles and enables us to pray: "Thy kingdom come." And when said with sincerity and trust, those words spell out every time they are spoken the ultimate triumph of the kingdom of God.

Prayer

Father, I am utterly amazed when I realize You have not only taken me out of Satan's kingdom, but You are using my prayer, when it is in line with Your pattern, to demolish his kingdom and re-establish Yours. Help me participate with all my might. Amen.

Further Study

Eph 1:17-2:7; 6:1; 2 Co 4:4; 11:3
What is Christ's position?
What is our position?

JANUARY 14

GENESIS 26:12–27:29

¹² Isaac sowed seed in that land, and in that year he reaped a hundred times what was sown. The LORD blessed him, ¹³ and the man became rich and kept getting richer until he was very wealthy. ¹⁴ He had flocks of sheep, herds of cattle, and many slaves, and the Philistines were envious of him. ¹⁵ The Philistines stopped up all the wells that his father's slaves had dug in the days of his father Abraham, filling them with dirt. ¹⁶ And Abimelech said to Isaac, "Leave us, for you are much too powerful for us."

¹⁷ So Isaac left there, camped in the valley of Gerar, and lived there. ¹⁸ Isaac reopened the water wells that had been dug in the days of his father Abraham and that the Philistines had stopped up after Abraham died. He gave them the same names his father had given them. ¹⁹ Moreover, Isaac's slaves dug in the valley and found a well of spring water there. ²⁰ But the herdsmen of Gerar quarreled with Isaac's herdsmen and said, "The water is ours!" So he named the well Quarrel because they quarreled with him. ²¹ Then they dug another well and quarreled over that one also, so he named it Hostility. ²² He moved from there and dug another, and they did not quarrel over it. He named it Open Spaces and said, "For now the LORD has made room for us, and we will be fruitful in the land."

²³ From there he went up to Beersheba, ²⁴ and the LORD appeared to him that night and said, "I am the God of your father Abraham. Do not be afraid, for I am with you. I will bless you and

multiply your offspring because of My servant Abraham."

²⁵ So he built an altar there, worshiped the LORD, and pitched his tent there. Isaac's slaves also dug a well there.

²⁶ Then Abimelech came to him from Gerar with Ahuzzath his adviser and Phicol the commander of his army. ²⁷ Isaac said to them, "Why have you come to me? You hated me and sent me away from you."

²⁸ They replied, "We have clearly seen how the LORD has been with you. We think there should be an oath between two parties—between us and you. Let us make a covenant with you: ²⁹ You will not harm us, just as we have not harmed you but have only done good to you, sending you away in peace. You are now blessed by the LORD."

³⁰ So he prepared a banquet for them, and they ate and drank. ³¹ They got up early in the morning and swore an oath to each other. Then Isaac sent them on their way, and they left him in peace. ³² On that same day Isaac's slaves came to tell him about the well they had dug, saying to him, "We have found water!" ³³ He called it Oath. Therefore the name of the city is Beer-sheba to this day.

³⁴ When Esau was 40 years old, he took as his wives Judith daughter of Beeri the Hittite, and Basemath daughter of Elon the Hittite. ³⁵ They made life bitter for Isaac and Rebekah.

27 When Isaac was old and his eyes were so weak that he could not see, he called his older son Esau and said to him, "My son."

And he answered, "Here I am."

² He said, "Look, I am old and do not know the day of my death. ³ Take your hunting gear, your quiver and bow, and go out in the field to hunt some game for me. ⁴ Then make me the delicious food that I love and bring it to me to eat, so that I can bless you before I die."

⁵ Now Rebekah was listening to what Isaac said to his son Esau. So while Esau went to the field to hunt some game to bring in, ⁶ Rebekah said to her son Jacob, "Listen! I heard your father talking with your brother Esau. He said, ⁷ 'Bring me some game and make some delicious food for me to eat so that I can bless you in the LORD's presence before I die.' ⁸ Now obey every order I give you, my son. ⁹ Go to the flock and bring me two choice young goats, and I will make them into a delicious meal for your father—the kind he loves. ¹⁰ Then take it to your father to eat so that he may bless you before he dies."

¹¹ Jacob answered Rebekah his mother, "Look, my brother Esau is a hairy man, but I am a man with smooth skin. ¹² Suppose my father touches me. Then I will seem to be deceiving him, and I will bring a curse rather than a blessing on myself."

¹³ His mother said to him, "Your curse be on me, my son. Just obey me and go get them for me."

¹⁴ So he went and got them and brought them to his mother, and his mother made the delicious food his father loved. ¹⁵ Then Rebekah took the best clothes of her older son Esau, which were there at the house, and had her younger son Jacob wear them. ¹⁶ She put the goatskins on his hands and the smooth part of his neck. ¹⁷ Then she handed the delicious food and the bread she had made to her son Jacob.

¹⁸ When he came to his father, he said, "My father."

And he answered, "Here I am. Who are you, my son?"

¹⁹ Jacob replied to his father, "I am Esau, your firstborn. I have done as you told me. Please sit up and eat some of my game so that you may bless me."

²⁰ But Isaac said to his son, "How did you ever find it so quickly, my son?"

He replied, "Because the LORD your God worked it out for me."

²¹ Then Isaac said to Jacob, "Please come closer so I can touch you, my son. Are you really my son Esau, or not?"

²² So Jacob came closer to his father Isaac. When he touched him, he said, "The voice is the voice of Jacob, but the hands are the hands of Esau." ²³ He did not recognize him, because his hands were hairy like those of his brother

Esau; so he blessed him. ²⁴ Again he asked, "Are you really my son Esau?"

And he replied, "I am."

²⁵ Then he said, "Serve me, and let me eat some of my son's game so that I can bless you." Jacob brought it to him, and he ate; he brought him wine, and he drank.

²⁶ Then his father Isaac said to him, "Please come closer and kiss me, my son." ²⁷ So he came closer and kissed him. When Isaac smelled his clothes, he blessed him and said:

Ah, the smell of my son
is like the smell of a field
that the LORD has blessed.
²⁸ May God give to you—
from the dew of the sky
and from the richness of the land—
an abundance of grain and new wine.
²⁹ May peoples serve you
and nations bow down to you.
Be master over your brothers;
may your mother's sons bow down to you.
Those who curse you will be cursed,
and those who bless you will be blessed.

PSALM 9:7-12

⁷ But the LORD sits enthroned forever;
He has established His throne for judgment.
⁸ He judges the world with righteousness;
He executes judgment on the peoples with fairness.
⁹ The LORD is a refuge for the oppressed,
a refuge in times of trouble.
¹⁰ Those who know Your name trust in You
because You have not abandoned those who seek You, LORD.
¹¹ Sing to the LORD, who dwells in Zion;

proclaim His deeds among the peoples.
¹² For the One who seeks an accounting for bloodshed remembers them;
He does not forget the cry of the afflicted.

PROVERBS 2:9-10

⁹ Then you will understand righteousness, justice,
and integrity—every good path.
¹⁰ For wisdom will enter your mind,
and knowledge will delight your heart.

MATTHEW 10:1-20

10 Summoning His 12 disciples, He gave them authority over unclean spirits, to drive them out and to heal every disease and sickness. ² These are the names of the 12 apostles:

First, Simon, who is called Peter,
and Andrew his brother;
James the son of Zebedee,
and John his brother;
³ Philip and Bartholomew;
Thomas and Matthew the tax collector;
James the son of Alphaeus,
and Thaddaeus;
⁴ Simon the Zealot,
and Judas Iscariot,
who also betrayed Him.

⁵ Jesus sent out these 12 after giving them instructions: "Don't take the road leading to other nations, and don't enter any Samaritan town. ⁶ Instead, go to the lost sheep of the house of Israel. ⁷ As you go, announce this: 'The kingdom of heaven has come near.' ⁸ Heal the sick, raise the dead, cleanse those with skin diseases, drive out demons. You have received free of charge; give free of charge. ⁹ Don't take along gold, silver, or copper for your money-belts. ¹⁰ Don't take a traveling bag for the road, or an extra shirt, sandals, or a walking stick, for the worker is worthy of his food.

[11] "When you enter any town or village, find out who is worthy, and stay there until you leave. [12] Greet a household when you enter it, [13] and if the household is worthy, let your peace be on it. But if it is unworthy, let your peace return to you. [14] If anyone will not welcome you or listen to your words, shake the dust off your feet when you leave that house or town. [15] I assure you: It will be more tolerable on the day of judgment for the land of Sodom and Gomorrah than for that town.

[16] "Look, I'm sending you out like sheep among wolves. Therefore be as shrewd as serpents and as harmless as doves. [17] Because people will hand you over to sanhedrins and flog you in their synagogues, beware of them. [18] You will even be brought before governors and kings because of Me, to bear witness to them and to the nations. [19] But when they hand you over, don't worry about how or what you should speak. For you will be given what to say at that hour, [20] because you are not speaking, but the Spirit of your Father is speaking through you.

A Worldview for Reading and Meditation

*The LORD is a refuge for the oppressed,
a refuge in times of trouble.*—PSALM 9:9

Philosophers have said that if we are to live effectively and securely in this world, then we must have a worldview of things—a cosmic framework in which to live, think, and work. The Germans call it *weltanschauung*—the big picture. When we have a cosmic framework, it gives a sense of validity and meaning to all we do. It makes us feel we are a part of a universal purpose. Many modern thinkers believe that the reason there is so much insecurity in the hearts of men and women is that there is a breakdown of this world frame of reference. One writer says: "Modern man is homesick. He is going on a hand-to-mouth existence day by day, and what he does and thinks does not seem to be related to the Whole. This has made life empty and jittery because it is insecure."

The Chinese have a saying: "In a broken nest there are no whole eggs." The nest, the world in which we live and think and work, has been broken up by sin, and therefore our central unity has gone. This can be seen on a small scale when the home is broken. Nearly all the children in reform schools come from broken homes. Why? The framework in which they have lived has broken down and has left them inwardly disrupted and confused. As a consequence, morals break down.

Can you see now why Jesus taught us to have a worldview of things? With our eyes focused on the kingdom, we know that at the heart of things there is utter security.

Prayer

O God, I am so grateful that I am not an orphan in this universe. I have a homeland, the kingdom of God. And because nothing can hinder the establishing of that kingdom, I have a peace that nothing can disturb. I am so grateful. Amen.

JANUARY 15

GENESIS 27:30–29:12

³⁰ As soon as Isaac had finished blessing Jacob and Jacob had left the presence of his father Isaac, his brother Esau arrived from the hunt. ³¹ He had also made some delicious food and brought it to his father. Then he said to his father, "Let my father get up and eat some of his son's game, so that you may bless me."

³² But his father Isaac said to him, "Who are you?"

He answered, "I am Esau your firstborn son."

³³ Isaac began to tremble uncontrollably. "Who was it then," he said, "who hunted game and brought it to me? I ate it all before you came in, and I blessed him. Indeed, he will be blessed!"

³⁴ When Esau heard his father's words, he cried out with a loud and bitter cry and said to his father, "Bless me—me too, my father!"

³⁵ But he replied, "Your brother came deceitfully and took your blessing."

³⁶ So he said, "Isn't he rightly named Jacob? For he has cheated me twice now. He took my birthright, and look, now he has taken my blessing." Then he asked, "Haven't you saved a blessing for me?"

³⁷ But Isaac answered Esau: "Look, I have made him a master over you, have given him all of his relatives as his servants, and have sustained him with grain and new wine. What then can I do for you, my son?"

³⁸ Esau said to his father, "Do you only have one blessing, my father? Bless me—me too, my father!" And Esau wept loudly.

³⁹ Then his father Isaac answered him:

Look, your dwelling place will be
away from the richness of the
land,
away from the dew of the sky
above.
⁴⁰ You will live by your sword,
and you will serve your brother.
But when you rebel,
you will break his yoke from your
neck.

⁴¹ Esau held a grudge against Jacob because of the blessing his father had given him. And Esau determined in his heart: "The days of mourning for my father are approaching; then I will kill my brother Jacob."

⁴² When the words of her older son Esau were reported to Rebekah, she summoned her younger son Jacob and said to him, "Listen, your brother Esau is consoling himself by planning to kill you. ⁴³ So now, my son, listen to me. Flee at once to my brother Laban in Haran, ⁴⁴ and stay with him for a few days until your brother's anger subsides— ⁴⁵ until your brother's rage turns away from you and he forgets

what you have done to him. Then I will send for you and bring you back from there. Why should I lose you both in one day?"

⁴⁶ So Rebekah said to Isaac, "I'm sick of my life because of these Hittite women. If Jacob marries a Hittite woman like one of them, what good is my life?"

28 Isaac summoned Jacob, blessed him, and commanded him: "Don't take a wife from the Canaanite women. ² Go at once to Paddan-aram, to the house of Bethuel, your mother's father. Marry one of the daughters of Laban, your mother's brother. ³ May God Almighty bless you and make you fruitful and multiply you so that you become an assembly of peoples. ⁴ May God give you and your offspring the blessing of Abraham so that you may possess the land where you live as an alien, the land God gave to Abraham." ⁵ So Isaac sent Jacob to Paddan-aram, to Laban son of Bethuel the Aramean, the brother of Rebekah, the mother of Jacob and Esau.

⁶ Esau noticed that Isaac blessed Jacob and sent him to Paddan-aram to get a wife there. When he blessed him, Isaac commanded Jacob not to marry a Canaanite woman. ⁷ And Jacob listened to his father and mother and went to Paddan-aram. ⁸ Esau realized that his father Isaac disapproved of the Canaanite women, ⁹ so Esau went to Ishmael and married, in addition to his other wives, Mahalath daughter of Ishmael, Abraham's son. She was the sister of Nebaioth.

¹⁰ Jacob left Beer-sheba and went toward Haran. ¹¹ He reached a certain place and spent the night there because the sun had set. He took one of the stones from the place, put it there at his head, and lay down in that place. ¹² And he dreamed: A stairway was set on the ground with its top reaching heaven, and God's angels were going up and down on it. ¹³ The LORD was standing there beside him, saying, "I am the LORD, the God of your father Abraham and the God of Isaac. I will give you and your offspring the land that you are now sleeping on. ¹⁴ Your offspring will be like

the dust of the earth, and you will spread out toward the west, the east, the north, and the south. All the peoples on earth will be blessed through you and your offspring. ¹⁵ Look, I am with you and will watch over you wherever you go. I will bring you back to this land, for I will not leave you until I have done what I have promised you."

¹⁶ When Jacob awoke from his sleep, he said, "Surely the LORD is in this place, and I did not know it." ¹⁷ He was afraid and said, "What an awesome place this is! This is none other than the house of God. This is the gate of heaven."

¹⁸ Early in the morning Jacob took the stone that was near his head and set it up as a marker. He poured oil on top of it ¹⁹ and named the place Bethel, though previously the city was named Luz. ²⁰ Then Jacob made a vow: "If God will be with me and watch over me on this journey, if He provides me with food to eat and clothing to wear, ²¹ and if I return safely to my father's house, then the LORD will be my God. ²² This stone that I have set up as a marker will be God's house, and I will give to You a tenth of all that You give me."

29 Jacob resumed his journey and went to the eastern country. ² He looked and saw a well in a field. Three flocks of sheep were lying there beside it because the sheep were watered from this well. A large stone covered the opening of the well. ³ When all the flocks were gathered there, the shepherds would roll the stone from the opening of the well and water the sheep. The stone was then placed back on the well's opening.

⁴ Jacob asked the men at the well, "My brothers! Where are you from?"

"We're from Haran," they answered.

⁵ "Do you know Laban son of Nahor?" Jacob asked them.

They answered, "We know him."

⁶ "Is he well?" Jacob asked.

"Yes," they said, "and here is his daughter Rachel, coming with his sheep."

⁷ Then Jacob said, "Look, it is still

broad daylight. It's not time for the animals to be gathered. Water the flock, then go out and let them graze."

⁸ But they replied, "We can't, until all the flocks have been gathered and the stone is rolled from the well's opening. Then we will water the sheep."

⁹ While he was still speaking with them, Rachel came with her father's sheep, for she was a shepherdess. ¹⁰ As soon as Jacob saw his uncle Laban's daughter Rachel with his sheep, he went up and rolled the stone from the opening and watered his uncle Laban's sheep. ¹¹ Then Jacob kissed Rachel and wept loudly. ¹² He told Rachel that he was her father's relative, Rebekah's son. She ran and told her father.

ℙSALM 9:13-20

¹³ Be gracious to me, LORD;
consider my affliction at the hands
of those who hate me.
Lift me up from the gates of
death,
¹⁴ so that I may declare all Your
praises.
I will rejoice in Your salvation
within the gates of Daughter
Zion.

¹⁵ The nations have fallen into the
pit they made;
their foot is caught in the net they
have concealed.
¹⁶ The LORD has revealed Himself;
He has executed justice,
striking down the wicked by the
work of their hands.
Higgaion. Selah

¹⁷ The wicked will return to Sheol—
all the nations that forget God.
¹⁸ For the oppressed will not always
be forgotten;
the hope of the afflicted will not
perish forever.

¹⁹ Rise up, LORD! Do not let man
prevail;
let the nations be judged in Your
presence.

²⁰ Put terror in them, LORD;
let the nations know they are only
men. *Selah*

ℙROVERBS 2:11-15

¹¹ Discretion will watch over you,
and understanding will guard you,
¹² rescuing you from the way of
evil—
from the one who says perverse
things,
¹³ from those who abandon the right
paths
to walk in ways of darkness,
¹⁴ from those who enjoy doing evil
and celebrate perversity,
¹⁵ whose paths are crooked,
and whose ways are devious.

𝕄ATTHEW 10:21-42

²¹ "Brother will betray brother to death, and a father his child. Children will even rise up against their parents and have them put to death. ²² You will be hated by everyone because of My name. But the one who endures to the end will be delivered. ²³ When they persecute you in one town, escape to another. For I assure you: You will not have covered the towns of Israel before the Son of Man comes. ²⁴ A disciple is not above his teacher, or a slave above his master. ²⁵ It is enough for a disciple to become like his teacher and a slave like his master. If they called the head of the house ' Beelzebul,' how much more the members of his household!

²⁶ "Therefore, don't be afraid of them, since there is nothing covered that won't be uncovered, and nothing hidden that won't be made known. ²⁷ What I tell you in the dark, speak in the light. What you hear in a whisper, proclaim on the housetops. ²⁸ Don't fear those who kill the body but are not able to kill the soul; rather, fear Him who is able to destroy both soul and body in hell. ²⁹ Aren't two sparrows sold for a penny? Yet not one of them falls to the ground without your Father's consent. ³⁰ But even the hairs of your head have all been counted. ³¹ Don't

be afraid therefore; you are worth more than many sparrows. ³² "Therefore, everyone who will acknowledge Me before men, I will also acknowledge him before My Father in heaven. ³³ But whoever denies Me before men, I will also deny him before My Father in heaven. ³⁴ Don't assume that I came to bring peace on the earth. I did not come to bring peace, but a sword. ³⁵ For I came to turn

> a man against his father,
> a daughter against her
>   mother,
> a daughter-in-law against
>   her mother-in-law;
> ³⁶ and a man's enemies will be
>   the members of his
>   household.

³⁷ The person who loves father or mother more than Me is not worthy of Me; the person who loves son or daughter more than Me is not worthy of Me. ³⁸ And whoever doesn't take up his cross and follow Me is not worthy of Me. ³⁹ Anyone finding his life will lose it, and anyone losing his life because of Me will find it.

⁴⁰ "The one who welcomes you welcomes Me, and the one who welcomes Me welcomes Him who sent Me. ⁴¹ Anyone who welcomes a prophet because he is a prophet will receive a prophet's reward. And anyone who welcomes a righteous person because he's righteous will receive a righteous person's reward. ⁴² And whoever gives just a cup of cold water to one of these little ones because he is a disciple—I assure you: He will never lose his reward!"

The Example of Jacob

If God will . . . watch over me . . . and if I return safely . . .
then the LORD will be my God.—GENESIS 28:20-21

One of the things we discover about ourselves when we look deep into our hearts is a spirit of demandingness. We demand that people treat us in the way we believe they should. We demand that people support us in times of trouble. We demand that no one comes close to hurting us in the way that we might have been hurt in childhood. Wedged tightly in the recesses of our heart is this ugly splinter that, if not removed, will produce a poison that will infect every part of our lives.

Let there be no mistaking this issue—if we are to pursue God wholeheartedly, then the spirit of demandingness that resides in every human heart must be identified and removed.

Jacob is probably one of the clearest biblical illustrations of a demanding spirit. He insisted on having his father's blessing for himself and took advantage of his brother's hunger, buying his birthright for a plate of stew. Later, Jacob went through a kind of half conversion, making God his God and giving Him a tenth and so on, but deep in his heart there was still residing this spirit of demandingness.

It shows itself again at Paddan-aram where, after marrying Rachel, he worked out a scheme to make himself rich at his father-in-law's expense (Gn 30:41-43). He was still Jacob—the man who demanded to have his own way. He had talked about himself in terms of honesty—"my honesty will testify for me" (Gn 30:33)—but it was nothing more than above-the-waterline honesty. His mind was changed, but not his heart.

Prayer

O Father, I am so grateful that You have recorded in Scripture so many illustrations of the truths You want me to know. I see so much of myself in Jacob. Help me from this day forward to be less and less like him in this. In Jesus' name I pray. Amen.

Further Study

Lk 15:11-32; Mt 20:1-16
How did the prodigal's brother display demandingness?
How did Jesus illustrate it?

JANUARY 16

*G*ENESIS 29:13–30:43

¹³ When Laban heard the news about his sister's son Jacob, he ran to meet him, hugged him, and kissed him. Then he took him to his house, and Jacob told him all that had happened. ¹⁴ Laban said to him, "Yes, you are my own flesh and blood."

After Jacob had stayed with him a month, ¹⁵ Laban said to him, "Just because you're my relative, should you work for me for nothing? Tell me what your wages should be."

¹⁶ Now Laban had two daughters: the older was named Leah, and the younger was named Rachel. ¹⁷ Leah had delicate eyes, but Rachel was shapely and beautiful. ¹⁸ Jacob loved Rachel, so he answered Laban, "I'll work for you seven years for your younger daughter Rachel."

¹⁹ Laban replied, "Better that I give her to you than to some other man. Stay with me." ²⁰ So Jacob worked seven years for Rachel, and they seemed like only a few days to him because of his love for her.

²¹ Then Jacob said to Laban, "Give me my wife, for my time is completed. I want to sleep with her." ²² So Laban invited all the men of the place to a feast. ²³ That evening, Laban took his daughter Leah and gave her to Jacob, and he slept with her. ²⁴ And Laban gave his slave Zilpah to his daughter Leah as her slave.

²⁵ When morning came, there was Leah! So he said to Laban, "What is this you have done to me? Wasn't it for Rachel that I worked for you? Why have you deceived me?"

²⁶ Laban answered, "It is not the custom in this place to give the younger daughter in marriage before the first-born. ²⁷ Complete this week of wedding celebration, and we will also give you this younger one in return for working yet another seven years for me."

²⁸ And Jacob did just that. He finished the week of celebration, and Laban gave him his daughter Rachel as his wife. ²⁹ And Laban gave his slave Bilhah to his daughter Rachel as her slave. ³⁰ Jacob slept with Rachel also, and indeed, he loved Rachel more than Leah. And he worked for Laban another seven years. ³¹ When the LORD saw that Leah was

unloved, He opened her womb; but Rachel was barren. ³²Leah conceived, gave birth to a son, and named him Reuben, for she said, "The LORD has seen my affliction; surely my husband will love me now."

³³She conceived again, gave birth to a son, and said, "The LORD heard that I am unloved and has given me this son also." So she named him Simeon.

³⁴She conceived again, gave birth to a son, and said, "At last, my husband will become attached to me because I have borne him three sons." Therefore he was named Levi.

³⁵And she conceived again, gave birth to a son, and said, "This time I will praise the LORD." Therefore she named him Judah. Then Leah stopped having children.

30 When Rachel saw that she was not bearing Jacob any children, she envied her sister. "Give me sons, or I will die!" she said to Jacob.

²Jacob became angry with Rachel and said, "Am I in God's place, who has withheld children from you?"

³Then she said, "Here is my slave Bilhah. Go sleep with her, and she'll bear children for me so that through her I too can build a family." ⁴So Rachel gave her slave Bilhah to Jacob as a wife, and he slept with her. ⁵Bilhah conceived and bore Jacob a son. ⁶Rachel said, "God has vindicated me; yes, He has heard me and given me a son," and she named him Dan.

⁷Rachel's slave Bilhah conceived again and bore Jacob a second son. ⁸Rachel said, "In my wrestlings with God, I have wrestled with my sister and won," and she named him Naphtali.

⁹When Leah saw that she had stopped having children, she took her slave Zilpah and gave her to Jacob as a wife. ¹⁰Leah's slave Zilpah bore Jacob a son. ¹¹Then Leah said, "What good fortune!" and she named him Gad. ¹²When Leah's slave Zilpah bore Jacob a second son, ¹³Leah said, "I am happy that the women call me 'Happy'," so she named him Asher.

¹⁴Reuben went out during the wheat harvest and found some mandrakes in the field. When he brought them to his mother Leah, Rachel asked, "Please give me some of your son's mandrakes."

¹⁵But Leah replied to her, "Isn't it enough that you have taken my husband? Now you also want to take my son's mandrakes?"

"Well," Rachel said, "you can sleep with him tonight in exchange for your son's mandrakes."

¹⁶When Jacob came in from the field that evening, Leah went out to meet him and said, "You must come with me, for I have hired you with my son's mandrakes." So Jacob slept with her that night.

¹⁷God listened to Leah, and she conceived and bore Jacob a fifth son. ¹⁸Leah said, "God has rewarded me for giving my slave to my husband," and she named him Issachar.

¹⁹Then Leah conceived again and bore Jacob a sixth son. ²⁰"God has given me a good gift," Leah said. "This time my husband will honor me because I have borne him six sons," and she named him Zebulun. ²¹Later, Leah bore a daughter and named her Dinah.

²²Then God remembered Rachel. He listened to her and opened her womb. ²³She conceived and bore a son, and said, "God has taken away my shame." ²⁴She named him Joseph: "May the LORD add another son to me."

²⁵After Rachel gave birth to Joseph, Jacob said to Laban, "Send me on my way so that I can return to my homeland. ²⁶Give me my wives and my children that I have worked for, and let me go. You know how hard I have worked for you." ²⁷But Laban said to him, "If I have found favor in your sight, stay. I have learned by divination that the LORD has blessed me because of you." ²⁸Then Laban said, "Name your wages, and I will pay them."

²⁹So Jacob said to him, "You know what I have done for you and your herds. ³⁰For you had very little before I came, but now your wealth has increased. The LORD has blessed you because of me. And now, when will I also do something for my own family?"

³¹ Laban asked, "What should I give you?"

And Jacob said, "You don't need to give me anything. If you do this one thing for me, I will continue to shepherd and keep your flock. ³² Let me go through all your sheep today and remove every sheep that is speckled or spotted, every dark-colored sheep among the lambs, and the spotted and speckled among the female goats. Such will be my wages. ³³ In the future when you come to check on my wages, my honesty will testify for me. If I have any female goats that are not speckled or spotted, or any lambs that are not black, they will be considered stolen."

³⁴ "Good," said Laban. "Let it be as you have said."

³⁵ That day Laban removed the streaked and spotted male goats and all the speckled and spotted female goats— every one that had any white on it—and every dark-colored sheep among the lambs, and he placed his sons in charge of them. ³⁶ He put a three-day journey between himself and Jacob. Jacob, meanwhile, was shepherding the rest of Laban's flock.

³⁷ Jacob then took branches of fresh poplar, almond, and plane wood, and peeled the bark, exposing white stripes on the branches. ³⁸ He set the peeled branches in the troughs in front of the sheep—in the water channels where the sheep came to drink. And the sheep bred when they came to drink. ³⁹ The flocks bred in front of the branches and bore streaked, speckled, and spotted young. ⁴⁰ Jacob separated the lambs and made the flocks face the streaked and the completely dark sheep in Laban's flocks. Then he set his own stock apart and didn't put them with Laban's sheep. ⁴¹ Whenever the stronger of the flock were breeding, Jacob placed the branches in the troughs, in full view of the flocks, and they would breed in front of the branches. ⁴² As for the weaklings of the flocks, he did not put out the branches. So it turned out that the weak sheep belonged to Laban and the stronger ones to Jacob. ⁴³ And the man became very rich. He had many flocks, male and female slaves, and camels and donkeys.

PSALM 10:1-6

¹ LORD, why do You stand so far
    away?
  Why do You hide in times of
    trouble?
² In arrogance the wicked
    relentlessly pursue the
    afflicted;
  let them be caught in the schemes
    they have devised.

³ For the wicked one boasts about
    his own cravings;
  the one who is greedy curses and
    despises the LORD.
⁴ In all his scheming, the wicked
    arrogantly thinks:
  "There is no accountability, since
    God does not exist."
⁵ His ways are always secure;
  Your lofty judgments are beyond
    his sight;
  he scoffs at all his adversaries.
⁶ He says to himself, "I will never
    be moved—
  from generation to generation
    without calamity."

PROVERBS 2:16-19

¹⁶ It will rescue you from a
    forbidden woman,
  from a stranger with her
    flattering talk,
¹⁷ who abandons the companion of
    her youth
  and forgets the covenant of her
    God;
¹⁸ for her house sinks down to death
  and her ways to the land of the
    departed spirits.
¹⁹ None return who go to her;
  none reach the paths of life.

MATTHEW 11:1-19

11 When Jesus had finished giving orders to His 12 disciples, He moved on from there to teach and preach in their towns. [2] When John heard in prison what the Messiah was doing, he sent a message by his disciples [3] and asked Him, "Are You the One who is to come, or should we expect someone else?"

[4] Jesus replied to them, "Go and report to John what you hear and see: [5] the blind see, the lame walk, those with skin diseases are healed, the deaf hear, the dead are raised, and the poor are told the good news. [6] And if anyone is not offended because of Me, he is blessed."

[7] As these men went away, Jesus began to speak to the crowds about John: "What did you go out into the wilderness to see? A reed swaying in the wind? [8] What then did you go out to see? A man dressed in soft clothes? Look, those who wear soft clothes are in kings' palaces. [9] But what did you go out to see? A prophet? Yes, I tell you, and far more than a prophet. [10] This is the one it is written about:

Look, I am sending
My messenger ahead of You;
he will prepare Your way
before You.

[11] "I assure you: Among those born of women no one greater than John the Baptist has appeared, but the least in the kingdom of heaven is greater than he. [12] From the days of John the Baptist until now, the kingdom of heaven has been suffering violence, and the violent have been seizing it by force. [13] For all the prophets and the law prophesied until John; [14] if you're willing to accept it, he is the Elijah who is to come. [15] Anyone who has ears should listen!

[16] "To what should I compare this generation? It's like children sitting in the marketplaces who call out to each other:

[17] We played the flute for you,
but you didn't dance;
we sang a lament,
but you didn't mourn!

[18] For John did not come eating or drinking, and they say, 'He has a demon!' [19] The Son of Man came eating and drinking, and they say, 'Look, a glutton and a drunkard, a friend of tax collectors and sinners!' Yet wisdom is vindicated by her deeds."

Stop Arguing!

He says to himself, "I will never be moved—from generation to generation."—PSALM 10:6

"At life's core," says Dr. Larry Crabb, "the real issues are theological issues." When life is brought down to its irreducible minimum, the issue always is—God. What do we make of Him? How does He fit into our lives?

Have you not found that whenever you make sure God is in His place, everything around you falls into place too? You see things from a different perspective. God is sovereign, Solomon says in Ecclesiastes 6:10. Man "is not able to contend with the One stronger than he," and the sooner we recognize that the better. A purpose was written into the universe long before we arrived, and though at times it may look as if God is not in control, this is not so. And, he adds, because God is bigger than we are, it is useless to put ourselves in conflict with Him. C. S. Lewis put it well when he said in *The Problem of Pain*: "To argue with God is to argue with the very power that makes it possible to argue at all."

How different life would be for us if we would get hold of the fact that God is sovereign and that we are His subjects. God is the Potter; we are the clay. God is omnipotent; we are impotent—relatively speaking, anyway. God is consistent; we are inconsistent. God has a crystal-clear perspective on everything; we more often than not are confused. What is all this saying to us? Arguing against the divine purpose is a waste of time. Better to trust the Almighty; He always knows what He is doing.

Prayer

My Father and my God, I have gathered some wisdom on my journey through life, but now I pray for the kind of wisdom that is greater and sharper than all earthly wisdom—Your wisdom. Make me a wise person, my Father. In Jesus' name. Amen.

Further Study

Pr 2:1–3:35
What are we not to let out of our sight?
What do the wise inherit?

JANUARY 17

GENESIS 31:1-55

31 Now Jacob heard what Laban's sons were saying: "Jacob has taken all that was our father's and has built this wealth from what belonged to our father." ² And Jacob saw from Laban's face that his attitude toward him was not the same.

³ Then the LORD said to him, "Go back to the land of your fathers and to your family, and I will be with you."

⁴ Jacob had Rachel and Leah called to the field where his flocks were. ⁵ He said to them, "I can see from your father's face that his attitude toward me is not the same, but the God of my father has been with me. ⁶ You know that I've worked hard for your father ⁷ and that he has cheated me and changed my wages 10 times. But God has not let him harm me. ⁸ If he said, 'The spotted sheep will be your wages,' then all the sheep were born spotted. If he said, 'The streaked sheep will be your wages,' then all the sheep were born streaked. ⁹ God has taken your father's herds and given them to me.

¹⁰ "When the flocks were breeding, I saw in a dream that the streaked, spotted, and speckled males were mating with the females. ¹¹ In that dream the Angel of God said to me, 'Jacob!' and I said: Here I am. ¹² And He said, 'Look up and see: all the males that are mating with the flocks are streaked, spotted, and speckled, for I have seen all that Laban has been doing to you. ¹³ I am the

God of Bethel, where you poured oil on the stone marker and made a solemn vow to Me. Get up, leave this land, and return to your native land.'"

¹⁴ Then Rachel and Leah answered him, "Do we have any portion or inheritance in our father's household? ¹⁵ Are we not regarded by him as outsiders? For he has sold us and has certainly spent our money. ¹⁶ In fact, all the wealth that God has taken from our father belongs to us and to our children. So do whatever God has said to you."

¹⁷ Then Jacob got up and put his children and wives on the camels. ¹⁸ He took all the livestock and possessions he had acquired in Paddan-aram, and he drove his herds to go to the land of his father Isaac in Canaan. ¹⁹ When Laban had gone to shear his sheep, Rachel stole her father's household idols. ²⁰ And Jacob deceived Laban the Aramean, not telling him that he was fleeing. ²¹ He fled with all his possessions, crossed the Euphrates, and headed for the hill country of Gilead.

²² On the third day Laban was told that Jacob had fled. ²³ So he took his relatives with him, pursued Jacob for seven days, and overtook him at Mount Gilead. ²⁴ But God came to Laban the Aramean in a dream at night. "Watch yourself!" God warned him. "Don't say anything to Jacob, either good or bad."

²⁵ When Laban overtook Jacob, Jacob had pitched his tent in the hill country, and Laban and his brothers also pitched their tents in the hill country of Gilead. ²⁶ Then Laban said to Jacob, "What have you done? You have deceived me and taken my daughters away like prisoners of war! ²⁷ Why did you secretly flee from me, deceive me, and not tell me? I would have sent you away with joy and singing, with tambourines and lyres, ²⁸ but you didn't even let me kiss my grandchildren and my daughters. You have acted foolishly. ²⁹ I could do you great harm, but last night the God of your father said to me: 'Watch yourself. Don't say anything to Jacob, either good or bad.' ³⁰ Now you have gone off because you long for your father—but why have you stolen my gods?"

³¹ Jacob answered, "I was afraid, for I thought you would take your daughters from me by force. ³² If you find your gods with anyone here, he will not live! Before our relatives, point out anything that is yours and take it." Jacob did not know that Rachel had stolen the idols.

³³ So Laban went into Jacob's tent, then Leah's tent, and then the tents of the two female slaves, but he found nothing. Then he left Leah's tent and entered Rachel's. ³⁴ Now Rachel had taken Laban's household idols, put them in the saddlebag of the camel, and sat on them. Laban searched the whole tent but found nothing.

³⁵ She said to her father, "Sir, don't be angry that I cannot stand up in your presence; I am having my monthly period." So Laban searched, but could not find the household idols.

³⁶ Then Jacob became incensed and brought charges against Laban. "What is my crime?" he said to Laban. "What is my sin, that you have pursued me? ³⁷ You've searched all my possessions! Have you found anything of yours? Put it here before my relatives and yours, and let them decide between the two of us. ³⁸ I've been with you these 20 years. Your ewes and female goats have not miscarried, and I have not eaten the rams from your flock. ³⁹ I did not bring you any of the flock torn by wild beasts; I myself bore the loss. You demanded payment from me for what was stolen by day or by night. ⁴⁰ There I was—the heat consumed me by day and the frost by night, and sleep fled from my eyes. ⁴¹ For 20 years I have worked in your household—14 years for your two daughters and six years for your flocks—and you have changed my wages 10 times! ⁴² If the God of my father, the God of Abraham, the Fear of Isaac, had not been with me, certainly now you would have sent me off empty-handed. But God has seen my affliction and my hard work, and He issued His verdict last night."

⁴³ Then Laban answered Jacob, "The daughters are my daughters; the sons, my sons; and the flocks, my flocks! Everything you see is mine! But what

can I do today for these daughters of mine or for the children they have borne? ⁴⁴ Come now, let's make a covenant, you and I. Let it be a witness between the two of us."

⁴⁵ So Jacob picked out a stone and set it up as a marker. ⁴⁶ Then Jacob said to his relatives, "Gather stones." And they took stones and made a mound, then ate there by the mound. ⁴⁷ Laban named the mound Jegar-sahadutha, but Jacob named it Galeed.

⁴⁸ Then Laban said, "This mound is a witness between me and you today." Therefore the place was called Galeed, ⁴⁹ and also Mizpah, for he said, "May the LORD watch between you and me when we are out of each other's sight. ⁵⁰ If you mistreat my daughters or take other wives, though no one is with us, understand that God will be a witness between you and me." ⁵¹ Laban also said to Jacob, "Look at this mound and the marker I have set up between you and me. ⁵² This mound is a witness and the marker is a witness that I will not pass beyond this mound to you, and you will not pass beyond this mound and this marker to do me harm. ⁵³ The God of Abraham, and the gods of Nahor—the gods of their father—will judge between us." And Jacob swore by the Fear of his father Isaac. ⁵⁴ Then Jacob offered a sacrifice on the mountain and invited his relatives to eat a meal. So they ate a meal and spent the night on the mountain. ⁵⁵ Laban got up early in the morning, kissed his grandsons and daughters, and blessed them. Then Laban left to return home.

PSALM 10:7-12

⁷ Cursing, deceit, and violence fill
  his mouth;
  trouble and malice are under his
  tongue.
⁸ He waits in ambush near the
  villages;
  he kills the innocent in secret
  places;
  his eyes are on the lookout for the
  helpless.
⁹ He lurks in secret like a lion in a
  thicket.
  He lurks in order to seize the
  afflicted.
  He seizes the afflicted and drags
  him in his net.
¹⁰ He crouches and bends down;
  the helpless fall because of his
  strength.
¹¹ He says to himself, "God has
  forgotten;
  He hides His face and will never
  see."
¹² Rise up, LORD God! Lift up Your
  hand.
  Do not forget the afflicted.

PROVERBS 2:20-22

²⁰ So follow the way of good people,
  and keep to the paths of the
  righteous.
²¹ For the upright will inhabit the
  land,
  and those of integrity will remain
  in it;
²² but the wicked will be cut off
  from the land,
  and the treacherous uprooted
  from it.

MATTHEW 11:20–12:8

²⁰ Then He proceeded to denounce the towns where most of His miracles were done, because they did not repent: ²¹ "Woe to you, Chorazin! Woe to you, Bethsaida! For if the miracles that were done in you had been done in Tyre and Sidon, they would have repented in sackcloth and ashes long ago! ²² But I tell you, it will be more tolerable for Tyre and Sidon on the day of judgment than for you. ²³ And you, Capernaum, will you be exalted to heaven? You will go down to Hades. For if the miracles that were done in you had been done in Sodom, it would have remained until today. ²⁴ But I tell you, it will be more tolerable for the land of Sodom on the day of judgment than for you."

²⁵ At that time Jesus said, "I praise You, Father, Lord of heaven and earth, because You have hidden these things from the wise and learned and revealed them to infants. ²⁶ Yes, Father, because this was Your good pleasure. ²⁷ All things have been entrusted to Me by My Father. No one knows the Son except the Father, and no one knows the Father except the Son and anyone to whom the Son desires to reveal Him.

²⁸ "Come to Me, all of you who are weary and burdened, and I will give you rest. ²⁹ All of you, take up My yoke and learn from Me, because I am gentle and humble in heart, and you will find rest for yourselves. ³⁰ For My yoke is easy and My burden is light."

12 At that time Jesus passed through the grainfields on the Sabbath. His disciples were hungry and began to pick and eat some heads of grain. ² But when the Pharisees saw it, they said to Him, "Look, Your disciples are doing what is not lawful to do on the Sabbath!"

³ He said to them, "Haven't you read what David did when he and those who were with him were hungry— ⁴ how he entered the house of God, and they ate the sacred bread, which is not lawful for him or for those with him to eat, but only for the priests? ⁵ Or haven't you read in the Law that on Sabbath days the priests in the temple violate the Sabbath and are innocent? ⁶ But I tell you that something greater than the temple is here! ⁷ If you had known what this means: **I desire mercy and not sacrifice**, you would not have condemned the innocent. ⁸ For the Son of Man is Lord of the Sabbath."

An Island Within

I rise before dawn and cry out for help; I put my hope in Your word.—Psalm 119:147

Some Bible teachers say: "If you are filled with the Spirit, then you can draw from God's resources, not just at the beginning of the day, but every hour of the day. Better a fountain in the heart than a fountain by the way." This confuses two quite separate issues. It is perfectly true that by reason of the Spirit's indwelling, we can draw upon His resources moment by moment, but that does not do away with the need for a daily quiet time. One writer puts it like this: "Those who say they can live in a state of prayer without stated times for prayer will probably find themselves without both. It is as futile as thinking that you can live in a state of physical nourishment without stated times for nourishment." I believe with all my heart that the divine Shepherd seeks daily to lead His sheep to the "still waters" of His Word, and how sad it is that so many Christians prefer to drink from the polluted pools of the world. The poet says:

What a frail soul He gave me, and a heart
Lame and unlikely for the large events.

I wonder if, more often, we haven't given ourselves "a heart lame and unlikely for the large events." God has given us infinite resources through prayer and the reading of the Scriptures. They are ours for the asking and the taking. The quiet time creates an island of quiet within us, and that becomes the atmosphere of the day.

Prayer

O Father, help me come to the quiet time with quiet expectancy—expectancy that here my weakness shall become strength, my doubt become faith, my fears become courage, and my sin become redemption. I ask this for Your own dear name's sake. Amen.

Further Study

Jr 15:1-16; Dt 8:3; Jb 23:12; Ps 119:103
What was Jeremiah's experience?
What did the children of Israel have to learn?

JANUARY 18

GENESIS 32:1–33:20

32 Jacob went on his way, and God's angels met him. ² When he saw them, Jacob said, "This is God's camp." So he called that place Mahanaim.

³ Jacob sent messengers ahead of him to his brother Esau in the land of Seir, the country of Edom. ⁴ He commanded them, "You are to say to my lord Esau, 'This is what your servant Jacob says. I have been staying with Laban and have been delayed until now. ⁵ I have oxen, donkeys, flocks, male and female slaves. I have sent this message to inform my lord, in order to seek your favor.' "

⁶ When the messengers returned to Jacob, they said, "We went to your brother Esau; he is coming to meet you—and he has 400 men with him." ⁷ Jacob was greatly afraid and distressed; he divided the people with him into two camps, along with the flocks, cattle, and camels. ⁸ He thought, "If Esau comes to one camp and attacks it, the remaining one can escape."

⁹ Then Jacob said, "God of my father Abraham and God of my father Isaac, the LORD who said to me, 'Go back to your land and to your family, and I will cause you to prosper,' ¹⁰ I am unworthy of all the kindness and faithfulness You have shown Your servant. Indeed, I crossed over this Jordan with my staff, and now I have become two camps. ¹¹ Please rescue me from the hand of my brother Esau, for I am afraid of him; otherwise, he may come and attack me, the mothers, and their children. ¹² You have said, 'I will cause you to prosper, and I will make your offspring like the sand of the sea, which cannot be counted.' "

¹³ He spent the night there and took part of what he had brought with him as a gift for his brother Esau: ¹⁴ 200 female goats, 20 male goats, 200 ewes, 20 rams, ¹⁵ 30 milk camels with their young, 40 cows, 10 bulls, 20 female donkeys, and 10 male donkeys. ¹⁶ He entrusted them to his slaves as separate herds and said to them, "Go on ahead of me, and leave some distance between the herds."

¹⁷ And he told the first one: "When my brother Esau meets you and asks, 'Who do you belong to? Where are you

going? And whose animals are these ahead of you?' [18] then tell him, 'They belong to your servant Jacob. They are a gift sent to my lord Esau. And look, he is behind us.' "

[19] He also told the second one, the third, and everyone who was walking behind the animals, "Say the same thing to Esau when you find him. [20] You are to also say, 'Look, your servant Jacob is right behind us.' " For he thought, "I want to appease Esau with the gift that is going ahead of me. After that, I can face him, and perhaps he will forgive me."

[21] So the gift was sent on ahead of him while he remained in the camp that night. [22] During the night Jacob got up and took his two wives, his two female slaves, and his 11 sons, and crossed the ford of Jabbok. [23] He took them and brought them across the stream, along with all his possessions.

[24] Jacob was left alone, and a man wrestled with him until daybreak. [25] When the man saw that He could not defeat him, He struck Jacob's hip as they wrestled and dislocated his hip socket. [26] Then He said to Jacob, "Let Me go, for it is daybreak."

But Jacob said, "I will not let You go unless You bless me."

[27] "What is your name?" the man asked.

"Jacob!" he replied.

[28] "Your name will no longer be Jacob," He said. "It will be Israel because you have struggled with God and with men and have prevailed."

[29] Then Jacob asked Him, "Please tell me Your name."

But He answered, "Why do you ask My name?" And He blessed him there.

[30] Jacob then named the place Peniel, "For," he said, "I have seen God face to face, and I have been delivered." [31] The sun shone on him as he passed by Penuel—limping on his hip. [32] That is why, to this day, the Israelites don't eat the thigh muscle that is at the hip socket: because He struck Jacob's hip socket at the thigh muscle.

33 Now Jacob looked up and saw Esau coming toward him with 400 men. So he divided the children among Leah, Rachel, and the two female slaves. [2] He put the female slaves first, Leah and her sons next, and Rachel and Joseph last. [3] He himself went on ahead and bowed to the ground seven times until he approached his brother.

[4] But Esau ran to meet him, hugged him, threw his arms around him, and kissed him. Then they wept. [5] When Esau looked up and saw the women and children, he asked, "Who are these with you?"

He answered, "The children God has graciously given your servant." [6] Then the female slaves and their children approached him and bowed down. [7] Leah and her children also approached and bowed down, and then Joseph and Rachel approached and bowed down.

[8] So Esau said, "What do you mean by this whole procession I met?"

"To find favor with you, my lord," he answered.

[9] "I have enough, my brother," Esau replied. "Keep what you have."

[10] But Jacob said, "No, please! If I have found favor with you, take this gift from my hand. For indeed, I have seen your face, and it is like seeing God's face, since you have accepted me. [11] Please take my present that was brought to you, because God has been gracious to me and I have everything I need." So Jacob urged him until he accepted.

[12] Then Esau said, "Let's move on, and I'll go ahead of you."

[13] Jacob replied, "My lord knows that the children are weak, and I have nursing sheep and cattle. If they are driven hard for one day, the whole herd will die. [14] Let my lord go ahead of his servant. I will continue on slowly, at a pace suited to the livestock and the children, until I come to my lord at Seir."

[15] Esau said, "Let me leave some of my people with you."

But he replied, "Why do that? Please indulge me, my lord."

[16] On that day Esau started on his way

back to Seir, ¹⁷ but Jacob went on to Succoth. He built a house for himself and stalls for his cattle; that is why the place was called Succoth. ¹⁸ After Jacob came from Paddan-aram, he arrived safely at the Canaanite city of Shechem and camped in front of the city. ¹⁹ He purchased a section of the field from the sons of Hamor, Shechem's father, for 100 *qesitahs,* where he had pitched his tent. ²⁰ And he set up an altar there and called it "God, the God of Israel."

𝒫SALM 10:13-18

13 Why has the wicked despised God?
   He says to himself, "You will not demand an account."
14 But You Yourself have seen trouble and grief,
   observing it in order to take the matter into Your hands.
   The helpless entrusts himself to You;
   You are a helper of the fatherless.
15 Break the arm of the wicked and evil person;
   call his wickedness into account until nothing remains of it.

16 The LORD is King forever and ever;
   the nations will perish from His land.
17 LORD, You have heard the desire of the humble;
   You will strengthen their hearts.
   You will listen carefully,
18 doing justice for the fatherless and the oppressed,
   so that men of the earth may terrify them no more.

𝒫ROVERBS 3:1-2

3 My son, don't forget my teaching, but let your heart keep my commands;
2 for they will bring you many days, a full life, and well-being.

𝑀ATTHEW 12:9-37

⁹ Moving on from there, He entered their synagogue. ¹⁰ There He saw a man who had a paralyzed hand. And in order to accuse Him they asked Him, "Is it lawful to heal on the Sabbath?"
¹¹ But He said to them, "What man among you, if he had a sheep that fell into a pit on the Sabbath, wouldn't take hold of it and lift it out? ¹² A man is worth far more than a sheep, so it is lawful to do good on the Sabbath."
¹³ Then He told the man, "Stretch out your hand." So he stretched it out, and it was restored, as good as the other. ¹⁴ But the Pharisees went out and plotted against Him, how they might destroy Him.
¹⁵ When Jesus became aware of this, He withdrew from there. Huge crowds followed Him, and He healed them all. ¹⁶ He warned them not to make Him known, ¹⁷ so that what was spoken through the prophet Isaiah might be fulfilled:

18 Here is My Servant
   whom I have chosen,
   My beloved in whom
   My soul delights;
   I will put My Spirit on Him,
   and He will proclaim justice
      to the nations.
19 He will not argue or shout,
   and no one will hear His voice
      in the streets.
20 He will not break a bruised reed,
   and He will not put out
      a smoldering wick,
   until He has led justice
      to victory.
21 The nations will put their hope
      in His name.

²² Then a demon-possessed man who was blind and unable to speak was brought to Him. He healed him, so that the man could both speak and see. ²³ And all the crowds were astounded and said, "Perhaps this is the Son of David!"

²⁴ When the Pharisees heard this, they said, "The man drives out demons only by Beelzebul, the ruler of the demons." ²⁵ Knowing their thoughts, He told them: "Every kingdom divided against itself is headed for destruction, and no city or house divided against itself will stand. ²⁶ If Satan drives out Satan, he is divided against himself. How then will his kingdom stand? ²⁷ And if I drive out demons by Beelzebul, who is it your sons drive them out by? For this reason they will be your judges. ²⁸ If I drive out demons by the Spirit of God, then the kingdom of God has come to you. ²⁹ How can someone enter a strong man's house and steal his possessions unless he first ties up the strong man? Then he can rob his house. ³⁰ Anyone who is not with Me is against Me, and anyone who does not gather with Me scatters. ³¹ Because of this, I tell you, people will be forgiven every sin and blasphemy, but the blasphemy against the Spirit will not be forgiven. ³² Whoever speaks a word against the Son of Man, it will be forgiven him. But whoever speaks against the Holy Spirit, it will not be forgiven him, either in this age or in the one to come.

³³ "Either make the tree good and its fruit good, or make the tree bad and its fruit bad; for a tree is known by its fruit. ³⁴ Brood of vipers! How can you speak good things when you are evil? For the mouth speaks from the overflow of the heart. ³⁵ A good man produces good things from his storeroom of good, and an evil man produces evil things from his storeroom of evil. ³⁶ I tell you that on the day of judgment people will have to account for every careless word they speak. ³⁷ For by your words you will be acquitted, and by your words you will be condemned."

"What Is Your Name?"

Jacob was left alone, and a man wrestled with him until daybreak.—GENESIS 32:24

The way in which God helped Jacob to be rid of his spirit of demandingness is revealing—"a man wrestled with him until daybreak." Like the Hound of Heaven, the love of God pursued him down the years, awaiting the hour when he would be ready to admit that he was beaten.

This man (probably an angelic representative) wrestled with him until Jacob's strength was diminished, at which point he asked him: "What is your name?" To us it seems a simple question, but in those days one's name was the expression of one's character; if the character changed, the name was changed. So Jacob, after a tremendous struggle, made the crucial confession: "My name is Jacob—the supplanter," he sobbed. The depths were uncovered. Jacob's heart was naked before God. The real problem was identified.

If you have not reached this place in your spiritual experience, I suggest you stop everything and tell God your name. You might have to confess: "My name is Demandingness; I insist on having my own way in everything." This may be hard to say, but get it out no matter what the cost, for there will be no new name until you say the old name.

The saying of the old name is a confession, a catharsis. When Jacob said his name, the angel said: "Your name will no longer be Jacob . . . It will be Israel" (v. 28)—a striver with God. The new nation of Israel would be named for this crooked man made straight. Jacob was buried; Israel was alive forevermore.

Prayer

God, help me to tell You my name—my real name. Help me to dodge no longer; the game is up. Take out of me the spirit of demandingness. Change my name and change my character. Save me from myself. In Jesus' name I pray. Amen.

Further Study

1 Jn 1:1-9; Ezr 10:11; 2 Sm 12:13
What are we to do with our sin?
How did Nathan respond to David?

JANUARY 19

GENESIS 34:1–35:29

34 Dinah, Leah's daughter whom she bore to Jacob, went out to see some of the young women of the area. ² When Shechem son of Hamor the Hivite, a prince of the region, saw her, he took her and raped her. ³ He became infatuated with Dinah, daughter of Jacob. He loved the young girl and spoke tenderly to her. ⁴ "Get me this girl as a wife," he told his father Hamor.

⁵ Jacob heard that Shechem had defiled his daughter Dinah, but since his sons were with his cattle in the field, he remained silent until they returned. ⁶ Meanwhile, Shechem's father Hamor came to speak with Jacob. ⁷ Jacob's sons returned from the field when they heard about the incident and were deeply grieved and angry. For Shechem had committed an outrage against Israel by sleeping with Jacob's daughter, and such a thing should not be done.

⁸ Hamor said to Jacob's sons, "My son Shechem is strongly attracted to your daughter. Please give her to him as a wife. ⁹ Intermarry with us; give your daughters to us, and take our daughters for yourselves. ¹⁰ Live with us. The land is before you. Settle here, move about, and acquire property in it."

¹¹ Then Shechem said to Dinah's father and brothers, "Grant me this favor, and I'll give you whatever you say. ¹² Set for me the compensation and the gift; I'll give you whatever you ask me. Just give the girl to be my wife!"

¹³ But Jacob's sons answered Shechem and his father Hamor deceitfully because he had defiled their sister Dinah. ¹⁴ "We cannot do this thing," they said to them. "Giving our sister to an uncircumcised man is a disgrace to us. ¹⁵ We will agree with you only on this condition: if all your males are circumcised as we are. ¹⁶ Then we will give you our daughters, take your daughters for ourselves, live with you, and become one people. ¹⁷ But if you will not listen to us and be circumcised, then we will take our daughter and go."

¹⁸ Their words seemed good in the eyes of Hamor and his son Shechem. ¹⁹ The young man did not delay doing this, because he was delighted with Jacob's daughter. Now he was the most

important in all his father's house. ²⁰ So Hamor and his son Shechem went to the gate of their city and spoke to the men there.

²¹ "These men are peaceful toward us," they said. "Let them live in our land and move about in it, for indeed, the region is large enough for them. Let us take their daughters as our wives and give our daughters to them. ²² But the men will agree to live with us and be one people only on this condition: if all our men are circumcised as they are. ²³ Won't their herds, their possessions, and all their livestock become ours? Only let us agree with them, and they will live with us."

²⁴ All the able-bodied men listened to Hamor and his son Shechem, and all the able-bodied men were circumcised. ²⁵ On the third day, when they were still in pain, two of Jacob's sons, Simeon and Levi, Dinah's brothers, took their swords, went into the unsuspecting city, and killed every male. ²⁶ They killed Hamor and his son Shechem with their swords, took Dinah from Shechem's house, and went away. ²⁷ Jacob's other sons came to the slaughter and plundered the city because their sister had been defiled. ²⁸ They took their sheep, cattle, donkeys, and whatever was in the city and in the field. ²⁹ They captured all their possessions, children, and wives, and plundered everything in the houses.

³⁰ Then Jacob said to Simeon and Levi, "You have brought trouble on me, making me odious to the inhabitants of the land, the Canaanites and the Perizzites. We are few in number; if they unite against me and attack me, I and my household will be destroyed."

³¹ But they answered, "Should he have treated our sister like a prostitute?"

35 God said to Jacob, "Get up! Go to Bethel and settle there. Build an altar there to the God who appeared to you when you fled from your brother Esau."

² So Jacob said to his family and all who were with him, "Get rid of the for-

eign gods that are among you. Purify yourselves and change your clothes. ³ We must get up and go to Bethel. I will build an altar there to the God who answered me in my day of distress. He has been with me everywhere I have gone."

⁴ Then they gave Jacob all their foreign gods and their earrings, and Jacob hid them under the oak near Shechem. ⁵ When they set out, a terror from God came over the cities around them, and they did not pursue Jacob's sons. ⁶ So Jacob and all who were with him came to Luz (that is, Bethel) in the land of Canaan. ⁷ Jacob built an altar there and called the place God of Bethel because it was there that God had revealed Himself to him when he was fleeing from his brother.

⁸ Deborah, Rebekah's nurse, died and was buried under the oak south of Bethel. So Jacob named it Oak of Weeping.

⁹ God appeared to Jacob again after he returned from Paddan-aram, and He blessed him. ¹⁰ God said to him:

Your name is Jacob;
you will no longer be named Jacob,
but Israel will be your name.

So He named him Israel. ¹¹ God also said to him:

I am God Almighty.
Be fruitful and multiply.
A nation, indeed an assembly of nations, will come from you,
and kings will descend from you.
¹² The land that I gave to Abraham and Isaac
I will give to you.
And I will give the land to your descendants after you.

¹³ Then God withdrew from him at the place where He had spoken to him. ¹⁴ Jacob set up a marker at the place where He had spoken to him—a stone marker. He poured a drink offering on it and anointed it with oil. ¹⁵ Jacob named the place where God had spoken with him Bethel.

16 They set out from Bethel. When they were still some distance from Ephrath, Rachel began to give birth, and her labor was difficult. 17 During her difficult labor, the midwife said to her, "Don't be afraid, for this is another son for you." 18 With her last breath—for she was dying—she named him Benoni, but his father called him Benjamin. 19 So Rachel died and was buried on the way to Ephrath (that is, Bethlehem). 20 Jacob set up a marker on her grave; it is the marker at Rachel's grave to this day. 21 Israel set out again and pitched his tent beyond the tower at Eder. 22 While Israel was living in that region, Reuben went in and slept with his father's concubine Bilhah, and Israel heard about it.

Jacob had 12 sons:

23 Leah's sons were Reuben (Jacob's firstborn),
Simeon, Levi, Judah,
Issachar, and Zebulun.
24 Rachel's sons were
Joseph and Benjamin.
25 The sons of Rachel's slave Bilhah were Dan and Naphtali.
26 The sons of Leah's slave Zilpah were Gad and Asher.

These are the sons of Jacob, who were born to him in Paddan-aram.

27 Jacob came to his father Isaac at Mamre in Kiriath-arba (that is, Hebron), where Abraham and Isaac had stayed. 28 Isaac lived 180 years. 29 He took his last breath and died, and was gathered to his people, old and full of days. His sons Esau and Jacob buried him.

PSALM 11:1-3

1 I have taken refuge in the LORD.
How can you say to me,
"Escape to the mountain like a bird!
2 For look, the wicked string the bow;
they put the arrow on the bowstring
to shoot from the shadows at the upright in heart.
3 When the foundations are destroyed,
what can the righteous do?"

PROVERBS 3:3-4

3 Never let loyalty and faithfulness leave you.
Tie them around your neck;
write them on the tablet of your heart.
4 Then you will find favor and high regard
in the sight of God and man.

MATTHEW 12:38–13:9

38 Then some of the scribes and Pharisees said to Him, "Teacher, we want to see a sign from You."

39 But He answered them, "An evil and adulterous generation demands a sign, but no sign will be given to it except the sign of the prophet Jonah. 40 For as Jonah was in the belly of the great fish three days and three nights, so the Son of Man will be in the heart of the earth three days and three nights. 41 The men of Nineveh will stand up at the judgment with this generation and condemn it, because they repented at Jonah's proclamation; and look—something greater than Jonah is here! 42 The queen of the south will rise up at the judgment with this generation and condemn it, because she came from the ends of the earth to hear the wisdom of Solomon; and look—something greater than Solomon is here!

43 "When an unclean spirit comes out of a man, it roams through waterless places looking for rest but doesn't find any. 44 Then it says, 'I'll go back to my house that I came from.' And when it arrives, it finds the house vacant, swept, and put in order. 45 Then off it goes and brings with it seven other spirits more evil than itself, and they enter and settle down there. As a result, that man's last condition is worse than the first. That's how it will also be with this evil generation."

⁴⁶ He was still speaking to the crowds when suddenly His mother and brothers were standing outside wanting to speak to Him. ⁴⁷ Someone told Him, "Look, Your mother and Your brothers are standing outside, wanting to speak to You." ⁴⁸ But He replied to the one who told Him, "Who is My mother and who are My brothers?" ⁴⁹ And stretching out His hand toward His disciples, He said, "Here are My mother and My brothers! ⁵⁰ For whoever does the will of My Father in heaven, that person is My brother and sister and mother."

13 On that day Jesus went out of the house and was sitting by the sea. ² Such large crowds gathered around Him that He got into a boat and sat down, while the whole crowd stood on the shore. ³ Then He told them many things in parables, saying: "Consider the sower who went out to sow. ⁴ As he was sowing, some seeds fell along the path, and the birds came and ate them up. ⁵ Others fell on rocky ground, where there wasn't much soil, and they sprang up quickly since the soil wasn't deep. ⁶ But when the sun came up they were scorched, and since they had no root, they withered. ⁷ Others fell among thorns, and the thorns came up and choked them. ⁸ Still others fell on good ground, and produced a crop: some 100, some 60, and some 30 times what was sown. ⁹ Anyone who has ears should listen!"

The Mystery Rolled Back

O Death, where is your victory? O Death, where is your sting?—1 CORINTHIANS 15:55

Mark's observation "that the stone—which was very large—had been rolled away" (Mk 16:4) seems a simple statement, but behind it lies a truth that is positively staggering in its implications. One is that no longer can death be an intimidator. "Death," said someone, "is the great enigma of life; humanly speaking, it is the one secret of the universe which is kept, the silence of which is never broken." To the weary and despairing, death may come as a friend; the cynical and disillusioned may meet it with indifference; to the healthy and the happy it may appear as a foe; but it comes to all. Death is like a great stone that blocks the path of human aspiration. How certain can we be of the continuity of life beyond death? What modest person would find in himself anything worthy to endure for all eternity? Such questions have been asked down the centuries. Death is a mystery—"the undiscovered country from which no traveler returns." Then came the first Easter Day, and the stone was rolled away. One Traveler did return. Death is an abysmal cavern no longer but a tunnel with light at the farther end. If people have seen it as a blind alley, then they need think no longer in those terms. It is now a thoroughfare, a highway. " 'Tis death is dead, not He," said the hymnist. The mystery is a mystery no more. The stone that was rolled away the first Easter morn was not just the rock that sealed the tomb. Our Lord rolled back for us the mystery of death also.

74

Prayer

O Father, how can I ever sufficiently thank You that the work of salvation is complete? Nothing more needs to be done than has been done. Your Coronation spells it out in the clearest of terms. I am so deeply, deeply grateful. Amen.

Further Study

Heb 1:1-9; Lk 22:69; Col 1:18
What did God the Father say about the Son?
What did God the Father say to the Son?

JANUARY 20

GENESIS 36:1-43

36 These are the family records of Esau (that is, Edom). ² Esau took his wives from the Canaanite women: Adah daughter of Elon the Hittite, Oholibamah daughter of Anah and granddaughter of Zibeon the Hivite; ³ and Basemath daughter of Ishmael and sister of Nebaioth. ⁴ Adah bore Eliphaz to Esau, Basemath bore Reuel, ⁵ and Oholibamah bore Jeush, Jalam, and Korah. These were Esau's sons, who were born to him in the land of Canaan.

⁶ Esau took his wives, sons, daughters, and all the people of his household, as well as his herds, all his livestock, and all the property he had acquired in Canaan; he went to a land away from his brother Jacob. ⁷ For their possessions were too many for them to live together, and because of their herds, the land where they stayed could not support them. ⁸ So Esau (that is, Edom) lived in the mountains of Seir.

⁹ These are the family records of Esau, father of the Edomites in the mountains of Seir.

¹⁰ These are the names of Esau's sons:
Eliphaz son of Esau's wife Adah, and Reuel son of Esau's wife Basemath.
¹¹ The sons of Eliphaz were Teman, Omar, Zepho, Gatam, and Kenaz.
¹² Timna, a concubine of Esau's son Eliphaz,
bore Amalek to Eliphaz.
These were the sons of Esau's wife Adah.

¹³ These are Reuel's sons:
Nahath, Zerah, Shammah, and Mizzah.
These were the sons of Esau's wife Basemath.

¹⁴ These are the sons of Esau's wife Oholibamah
daughter of Anah and granddaughter of Zibeon:
She bore Jeush, Jalam, and Korah to Edom.

¹⁵ These are the chiefs of Esau's sons:

75

the sons of Eliphaz, Esau's firstborn:
Chiefs Teman, Omar, Zepho, Kenaz,
16 Korah, Gatam, and Amalek.
These are the chiefs of Eliphaz
in the land of Edom.
These are the sons of Adah.

17 These are the sons of Reuel,
Esau's son:
Chiefs Nahath, Zerah, Shammah,
and Mizzah.
These are the chiefs of Reuel
in the land of Edom.
These are the sons of Esau's wife
Basemath.

18 These are the sons of Esau's wife
Oholibamah:
Chiefs Jeush, Jalam, and Korah.
These are the chiefs of Esau's wife
Oholibamah
daughter of Anah.
19 These are the sons of Esau (that
is, Edom),
and these are their chiefs.

20 These are the sons of Seir the
Horite,
the inhabitants of the land:
Lotan, Shobal, Zibeon, Anah,
21 Dishon, Ezer, and Dishan.
These are the chiefs of the
Horites,
the sons of Seir, in the land of
Edom.
22 The sons of Lotan were Hori and
Heman.
Timna was Lotan's sister.
23 These are Shobal's sons:
Alvan, Manahath, Ebal, Shepho,
and Onam.
24 These are Zibeon's sons: Aiah and
Anah.
This was the Anah who found the
hot springs in the wilderness
while he was pasturing the
donkeys of his father Zibeon.
25 These are the children of Anah:
Dishon and Oholibamah daughter
of Anah.
26 These are Dishon's sons:
Hemdan, Eshban, Ithran, and
Cheran.

27 These are Ezer's sons:
Bilhan, Zaavan, and Akan.
28 These are Dishan's sons: Uz and
Aran.

29 These are the chiefs of the
Horites:
Chiefs Lotan, Shobal, Zibeon,
Anah,
30 Dishon, Ezer, and Dishan.
These are the chiefs of the
Horites,
according to their divisions, in the
land of Seir.

31 These are the kings who ruled in
the land of Edom
before any king ruled over the
Israelites:
32 Bela son of Beor ruled in Edom;
the name of his city was
Dinhabah.
33 When Bela died, Jobab son of
Zerah from Bozrah ruled in his
place.
34 When Jobab died, Husham from
the land of the Temanites ruled in
his place.
35 When Husham died, Hadad son of
Bedad ruled in his place.
He defeated Midian in the field of
Moab;
the name of his city was Avith.
36 When Hadad died, Samlah from
Masrekah ruled in his place.
37 When Samlah died, Shaul from
Rehoboth-on-the-River ruled in his
place.
38 When Shaul died, Baal-hanan son
of Achbor ruled in his place.
39 When Baal-hanan son of Achbor
died, Hadar ruled in his place.
His city was Pau, and his wife's
name was Mehetabel
daughter of Matred daughter of
Me-zahab.

40 These are the names of Esau's
chiefs,
according to their families and
their localities,
by their names:
Chiefs Timna, Alvah, Jetheth,
41 Oholibamah, Elah, Pinon,

42 Kenaz, Teman, Mibzar,
43 Magdiel, and Iram.
These are Edom's chiefs,
according to their settlements in
the land they possessed.
Esau was father of the Edomites.

PSALM 11:4-7

4 The LORD is in His holy temple;
the LORD's throne is in heaven.
His eyes watch; He examines
everyone.
5 The LORD examines the righteous
and the wicked.
He hates the lover of violence.
6 He will rain burning coals and
sulfur on the wicked;
a scorching wind will be their
portion.
7 For the LORD is righteous; He
loves righteous deeds.
The upright will see His face.

PROVERBS 3:5-6

5 Trust in the LORD with all your
heart,
and do not rely on your own
understanding;
6 think about Him in all your ways,
and He will guide you on the right
paths.

MATTHEW 13:10-35

10 Then the disciples came up and asked Him, "Why do You speak to them in parables?"
11 He answered them, "Because the secrets of the kingdom of heaven have been given for you to know, but it has not been given to them. 12 For whoever has, more will be given to him, and he will have more than enough. But whoever does not have, even what he has will be taken away from him. 13 For this reason I speak to them in parables, because looking they do not see, and hearing they do not listen or understand. 14 Isaiah's prophecy is fulfilled in them, which says:

You will listen and listen,
yet never understand;
and you will look and look,
yet never perceive.
15 For this people's heart
has grown callous;
their ears are hard of hearing,
and they have shut their eyes;
otherwise they might see
with their eyes
and hear with their ears,
understand with their hearts
and turn back—
and I would cure them.

16 "But your eyes are blessed because they do see, and your ears because they do hear! 17 For I assure you: Many prophets and righteous people longed to see the things you see yet didn't see them; to hear the things you hear yet didn't hear them.
18 "You, then, listen to the parable of the sower: 19 When anyone hears the word about the kingdom and doesn't understand it, the evil one comes and snatches away what was sown in his heart. This is the one sown along the path. 20 And the one sown on rocky ground—this is one who hears the word and immediately receives it with joy. 21 Yet he has no root in himself, but is short-lived. When pressure or persecution comes because of the word, immediately he stumbles. 22 Now the one sown among the thorns—this is one who hears the word, but the worries of this age and the seduction of wealth choke the word, and it becomes unfruitful. 23 But the one sown on the good ground—this is one who hears and understands the word, who does bear fruit and yields: some 100, some 60, some 30 times what was sown."
24 He presented another parable to them: "The kingdom of heaven may be compared to a man who sowed good seed in his field. 25 But while people were sleeping, his enemy came, sowed weeds among the wheat, and left. 26 When the plants sprouted and produced grain, then the weeds also appeared. 27 The landowner's slaves came to him and said, 'Master, didn't you sow

good seed in your field? Then where did the weeds come from?'

[28] " 'An enemy did this!' he told them. " 'So, do you want us to go and gather them up?' the slaves asked him.

[29] " 'No,' he said. 'When you gather up the weeds, you might also uproot the wheat with them. [30] Let both grow together until the harvest. At harvest time I'll tell the reapers: Gather the weeds first and tie them in bundles to burn them, but store the wheat in my barn.' "

[31] He presented another parable to them: "The kingdom of heaven is like a mustard seed that a man took and sowed in his field. [32] It's the smallest of all the seeds, but when grown, it's taller than the vegetables and becomes a tree, so that the birds of the sky come and nest in its branches."

[33] He told them another parable: "The kingdom of heaven is like yeast that a woman took and mixed into 50 pounds of flour until it spread through all of it."

[34] Jesus told the crowds all these things in parables, and He would not speak anything to them without a parable, [35] so that what was spoken through the prophet might be fulfilled:

I will open My mouth
in parables;
I will declare things kept
secret
from the foundation
of the world.

Heart of the Matter

*Trust in the LORD with all your heart,
and do not rely on your own understanding.*—PROVERBS 3:5

What is the essential difference between the heart and mind? Many believe there is no difference and that they are really the same thing. But I see a clear difference between the heart and the mind: the mind is the part of us that thinks and reasons; the heart is the part of us that contains our deep longings and desires. Although the mind is important, the heart is even more important because it is the engine room of our personality—the part from which come our drive and motivation. That is why our Lord says, "The mouth speaks from the overflow of the heart" (Mt 12:34).

Christ said that the words He spoke were the words given to Him by His Father (Jn 14:24). Does this mean the Father wrote out the words which He wanted Christ to say, and then Jesus had to learn them by heart? No—the heart of Jesus Christ was the very heart of God the Father; consequently, the words Christ spoke were the exact expression of God's thought. Jesus' tongue was always in its rightful place. He spoke not just from His head but from His heart; His heart and His mind were one.

Oswald Chambers put it like this: "The heart is the central altar and the mind the outer court. What we offer on the central altar will show itself in due course through the outer extremities of personality." In the search for unity of purpose and integration, there is no doubt that the heart of the matter is the matter of the heart.

Prayer

O God, help me to be like Jesus, to pass on to others not just the things that come into my head, but the things that flow out of my heart. Bring my heart in closer contact with Your heart, dear Father. In Jesus' name I pray. Amen.

Further Study

Mk 7:14-23; Pr 4:23; Rm 10:10
What comes from the heart?
What was Jesus' teaching?

JANUARY 21

GENESIS 37:1–38:30

37 Jacob lived in the land where his father had stayed, the land of Canaan. ² These are the family records of Jacob.

At 17 years of age, Joseph tended sheep with his brothers. The young man was working with the sons of Bilhah and Zilpah, his father's wives, and he brought a bad report about them to their father. ³ Now Israel loved Joseph more than his other sons because Joseph was a son born to him in his old age, and he made a robe of many colors for him. ⁴ When his brothers saw that their father loved him more than all his brothers, they hated him and could not bring themselves to speak peaceably to him.

⁵ Then Joseph had a dream. When he told it to his brothers, they hated him even more. ⁶ He said to them, "Listen to this dream I had: ⁷ There we were, binding sheaves of grain in the field. Suddenly my sheaf stood up, and your sheaves gathered around it and bowed down to my sheaf."

⁸ "Are you really going to reign over us?" his brothers asked him. "Are you really going to rule us?" So they hated him even more because of his dream and what he had said.

⁹ Then he had another dream and told it to his brothers. "Look," he said, "I had another dream, and this time the sun, moon, and 11 stars were bowing down to me."

¹⁰ He told his father and brothers, but his father rebuked him. "What kind of dream is this that you have had?" he said. "Are your mother and brothers and I going to bow down to the ground before you?" ¹¹ His brothers were jealous of him, but his father kept the matter in mind.

¹² His brothers had gone to pasture their father's flocks at Shechem. ¹³ Israel said to Joseph, "Your brothers, you know, are pasturing the flocks at Shechem. Get ready. I'm sending you to them."

"I'm ready," Joseph replied.

¹⁴ Then Israel said to him, "Go and see how your brothers and the flocks are doing, and bring word back to me." So he sent him from the valley of Hebron, and he went to Shechem.

¹⁵ A man found him there, wandering in the field, and asked him, "What are you looking for?" ¹⁶ "I'm looking for my brothers," Joseph said. "Can you tell me where they are pasturing their flocks?" ¹⁷ "They've moved on from here," the man said. "I heard them say, 'Let's go to Dothan.'" So Joseph set out after his brothers and found them at Dothan. ¹⁸ They saw him in the distance, and before he had reached them, they plotted to kill him. ¹⁹ They said to one another, "Here comes that dreamer! ²⁰ Come on, let's kill him and throw him into one of the pits. We can say that a vicious animal ate him. Then we'll see what becomes of his dreams!"

²¹ When Reuben heard this, he tried to save him from them. He said, "Let's not take his life." ²² Reuben also said to them, "Don't shed blood. Throw him into this pit in the wilderness, but don't lay a hand on him"—intending to rescue him from their hands and return him to his father.

²³ When Joseph came to his brothers, they stripped off his robe, the robe of many colors that he had on. ²⁴ Then they took him and threw him into the pit. The pit was empty; there was no water in it.

²⁵ Then they sat down to eat a meal. They looked up, and there was a caravan of Ishmaelites coming from Gilead. Their camels were carrying aromatic gum, balsam, and resin, going down to Egypt.

²⁶ Then Judah said to his brothers, "What do we gain if we kill our brother and cover up his blood? ²⁷ Come, let's sell him to the Ishmaelites and not lay a hand on him, for he is our brother, our own flesh." His brothers agreed. ²⁸ When Midianite traders passed by, they pulled Joseph out of the pit and sold him for 20 pieces of silver to the Ishmaelites, who took Joseph to Egypt.

²⁹ When Reuben returned to the pit and saw that Joseph was not there, he tore his clothes. ³⁰ He went back to his brothers and said, "The boy is gone! What am I going to do?" ³¹ So they took Joseph's robe, slaughtered a young goat, and dipped the robe in its blood. ³² They sent the robe of many colors to their father and said, "We found this. Examine it. Is it your son's robe or not?"

³³ His father recognized it. "It is my son's robe," he said. "A vicious animal has devoured him. Joseph has been torn to pieces!" ³⁴ Then Jacob tore his clothes, put sackcloth around his waist, and mourned for his son many days. ³⁵ All his sons and daughters tried to comfort him, but he refused to be comforted. "No," he said. "I will go down to Sheol to my son, mourning." And his father wept for him.

³⁶ Meanwhile, the Midianites sold Joseph in Egypt to Potiphar, an officer of Pharaoh and the captain of the guard.

38 At that time Judah left his brothers and settled near an Adullamite named Hirah. ² There Judah saw the daughter of a Canaanite named Shua; he took her as a wife and slept with her. ³ She conceived and gave birth to a son, and he named him Er. ⁴ She conceived again, gave birth to a son, and named him Onan. ⁵ She gave birth to another son and named him Shelah. It was at Chezib that she gave birth to him.

⁶ Judah got a wife for Er, his firstborn, and her name was Tamar. ⁷ Now Er, Judah's firstborn, was evil in the LORD's sight, and the LORD put him to death. ⁸ Then Judah said to Onan, "Sleep with your brother's wife. Perform your duty as her brother-in-law and produce offspring for your brother." ⁹ But Onan knew that the offspring would not be his; so whenever he slept with his brother's wife, he released his semen on the ground so that he would not produce offspring for his brother. ¹⁰ What he did was evil in the LORD's sight, so He put him to death also.

¹¹ Then Judah said to his daughter-in-law Tamar, "Remain a widow in your father's house until my son Shelah grows up." For he thought, "He might die too, like his brother." So Tamar went to live in her father's house.

¹² After a long time Judah's wife, the daughter of Shua, died. When Judah had finished mourning, he and his

friend Hirah the Adullamite went up to Timnah to the sheepshearers. ¹³ Tamar was told, "Your father-in-law is going up to Timnah to shear his sheep." ¹⁴ So she took off her widow's clothes, veiled her face, covered herself, and sat at the entrance to Enaim, which is on the way to Timnah. For she saw that, though Shelah had grown up, she had not been given to him as a wife. ¹⁵ When Judah saw her, he thought she was a prostitute, for she had covered her face.

¹⁶ He went over to her and said, "Come, let me sleep with you," for he did not know that she was his daughter-in-law.

She said, "What will you give me for sleeping with me?"

¹⁷ "I will send you a young goat from my flock," he replied.

But she said, "Only if you leave something with me until you send it."

¹⁸ "What should I give you?" he asked.

She answered, "Your signet ring, your cord, and the staff in your hand." So he gave them to her and slept with her, and she got pregnant by him. ¹⁹ She got up and left, then removed her veil and put her widow's clothes back on.

²⁰ When Judah sent the young goat by his friend the Adullamite in order to get back the items he had left with the woman, he could not find her. ²¹ He asked the men of the place, "Where is the cult prostitute who was beside the road at Enaim?"

"There has been no cult prostitute here," they answered.

²² So the Adullamite returned to Judah, saying, "I couldn't find her, and furthermore, the men of the place said, 'There has been no cult prostitute here.'"

²³ Judah replied, "Let her keep the items for herself; otherwise we will become a laughingstock. After all, I did send this young goat, but you couldn't find her."

²⁴ About three months later Judah was told, "Your daughter-in-law has been acting like a prostitute, and now she is pregnant."

"Bring her out!" Judah said. "Let her be burned to death!"

²⁵ As she was being brought out, she sent her father-in-law this message: "I am pregnant by the man to whom these items belong." And she added, "Examine them. Whose signet ring, cord, and staff are these?"

²⁶ Judah recognized them and said, "She is more in the right than I, since I did not give her to my son Shelah." And he did not know her intimately again.

²⁷ When the time came for her to give birth, there were twins in her womb. ²⁸ As she was giving birth, one of them put out his hand, and the midwife took it and tied a scarlet thread around it, announcing, "This one came out first." ²⁹ But then he pulled his hand back, and his brother came out. Then she said, "You have broken out first!" So he was named Perez. ³⁰ Then his brother, who had the scarlet thread tied to his hand, came out, and was named Zerah.

PSALM 12:1-5

¹ Help, LORD, for no faithful one remains;
the loyal have disappeared from the human race.

² They lie to one another;
they speak with flattering lips and deceptive hearts.

³ May the LORD cut off all flattering lips
and the tongue that speaks boastfully.

⁴ They say, "Through our tongues we have power;
our lips are our own—who can be our master?"

⁵ "Because of the oppression of the afflicted and the groaning of the poor,
I will now rise up," says the LORD.
"I will put in a safe place the one who longs for it."

PROVERBS 3:7-8

⁷ Don't consider yourself to be wise;
fear the LORD and turn away from evil.

8 This will be healing for your body and strengthening for your bones.

MATTHEW 13:36-58

36 Then He dismissed the crowds and went into the house. His disciples approached Him and said, "Explain the parable of the weeds in the field to us." 37 He replied: "The One who sows the good seed is the Son of Man; 38 the field is the world; and the good seed—these are the sons of the kingdom. The weeds are the sons of the evil one, and 39 the enemy who sowed them is the Devil. The harvest is the end of the age, and the harvesters are angels. 40 Therefore just as the weeds are gathered and burned in the fire, so it will be at the end of the age. 41 The Son of Man will send out His angels, and they will gather from His kingdom everything that causes sin and those guilty of lawlessness. 42 They will throw them into the blazing furnace where there will be weeping and gnashing of teeth. 43 Then the righteous will shine like the sun in their Father's kingdom. Anyone who has ears should listen!

44 "The kingdom of heaven is like treasure, buried in a field, that a man found and reburied. Then in his joy he goes and sells everything he has and buys that field.

45 "Again, the kingdom of heaven is like a merchant in search of fine pearls. 46 When he found one priceless pearl, he went and sold everything he had, and bought it.

47 "Again, the kingdom of heaven is like a large net thrown into the sea. It collected every kind of fish, 48 and when it was full, they dragged it ashore, sat down, and gathered the good fish into containers, but threw out the worthless ones. 49 So it will be at the end of the age. The angels will go out, separate the evil people from the righteous, 50 and throw them into the blazing furnace. In that place there will be weeping and gnashing of teeth.

51 "Have you understood all these things?"

"Yes," they told Him.

52 "Therefore," He said to them, "every student of Scripture instructed in the kingdom of heaven is like a landowner who brings out of his storeroom what is new and what is old." 53 When Jesus had finished these parables, He left there.

54 He went to His hometown and began to teach them in their synagogue, so that they were astonished and said, "How did this wisdom and these miracles come to Him? 55 Isn't this the carpenter's son? Isn't His mother called Mary, and His brothers James, Joseph, Simon, and Judas? 56 And His sisters, aren't they all with us? So where does He get all these things?" 57 And they were offended by Him.

But Jesus said to them, "A prophet is not without honor except in his hometown and in his household." 58 And He did not do many miracles there because of their unbelief.

Prevenient Grace

They pulled Joseph out of the pit and sold him for 20 pieces of silver to the Ishmaelites, who took Joseph to Egypt.—GENESIS 37:28

Therefore it was not you who sent me here, but God.—GENESIS 45:8

Sometimes God—the Divine Eagle—disturbs the nest to further His purposes. An illustration of this concerns that remarkable Old Testament character, Joseph. When Joseph's anxious and unenlightened brothers are ushered into his presence, they fall before him on their faces.

What a moment! Joseph must have seen in a flash the panorama of his strange and eventful life: his boyhood in Canaan, the dreams by which he had been haunted, the growing hostility of his brothers, the awful day when they fell upon him, cast him into a pit, and sold him to the Ishmaelites, the journey down into Egypt, and his life as a slave. He must have remembered, too, the extraordinary events that led to his becoming the Keeper of the Royal Seal with an authority second only to the throne.

But it is not the events, significant as they are, that interest me most, but the conclusions to which he comes as he ponders the past: "Don't be worried or angry with yourselves," he says, "for selling me here, because God sent me . . . " Three times he says it: "God sent me ahead of you . . . " and "It was not you who sent me here, but God . . . " The astonishing thing is that there was no anger or bitterness in his heart. And why? Because he recognized the work of the Divine Eagle who had pushed him out of the nest in Canaan in order that he might be the provider for his family in time of famine. God moved him into a position of greater usefulness. "You sold me," he said, "but God sent me."

Prayer

O Father, as I look back, the whole meaning of my life is made plain. Many times I have rebelled against the stirring of my own nest, but now I see it was for Your glory and my eternal good. I am so thankful. Amen.

Further Study

Gn 37; 47:11-12, 27; 50:15-21
How was Joseph used as an instrument in God's hand?
What was his final response to his brothers?

JANUARY 22

GENESIS 39:1–41:7

39 Now Joseph had been taken to Egypt. An Egyptian named Potiphar, an officer of Pharaoh and the captain of the guard, bought him from the Ishmaelites who had brought him there. ² The LORD was with Joseph, and he be- came a successful man, serving in the household of his Egyptian master. ³ When his master saw that the LORD was with him and that the LORD made everything he did successful, ⁴ Joseph found favor in his master's sight and be- came his personal attendant. Potiphar also put him in charge of his household and placed all that he owned under his authority. ⁵ From the time that he put him in charge of his household and of all that he owned, the LORD blessed the Egyptian's house because of Joseph. The LORD's blessing was on all that he owned, in his house and in his fields. ⁶ He left all that he owned under Joseph's authority; he did not concern himself with anything except the food he ate.

Now Joseph was well-built and handsome. ⁷ After some time his master's wife looked longingly at Joseph and said, "Sleep with me."

⁸ But he refused and said to his master's wife, "Look, my master does not concern himself with anything in his house, and he has put all that he owns under my authority. ⁹ No one in this house is greater than I am. He has withheld nothing from me except you, because you are his wife. So how could I do such a great evil and sin against God?"

¹⁰ Although she spoke to Joseph day after day, he refused to go to bed with her. ¹¹ Now one day he went into the house to do his work, and none of the household servants was there. ¹² She grabbed him by his garment and said, "Sleep with me!" But leaving his garment in her hand, he escaped and ran outside. ¹³ When she realized that he had left his garment with her and had run outside, ¹⁴ she called the household servants. "Look," she said to them, "my husband brought a Hebrew man to us to make fun of us. He came to me so he could sleep with me, and I screamed as loud as I could. ¹⁵ When he heard me screaming for help, he left his garment with me and ran outside."

¹⁶ She put Joseph's garment beside her until his master came home. ¹⁷ Then she told him the same story: "The Hebrew slave you brought to us came to me to make fun of me, ¹⁸ but when I screamed for help, he left his garment with me and ran outside."

¹⁹ When his master heard the story his wife told him—"These are the things your slave did to me"—he was furious ²⁰ and had him thrown into prison, where the king's prisoners were confined. So Joseph was there in prison.

²¹ But the LORD was with Joseph and extended kindness to him. He granted him favor in the eyes of the prison warden. ²² The warden put all the prisoners who were in the prison under Joseph's authority, and he was responsible for everything that was done there. ²³ The warden did not bother with anything under Joseph's authority, because the LORD was with him, and the LORD made everything that he did successful.

40 After this, the king of Egypt's cupbearer and his baker offended their master, the king of Egypt. ² Pharaoh was angry with his two officers, the chief cupbearer and the chief baker, ³ and put them in custody in the house of the captain of the guard, in the prison where Joseph was confined. ⁴ The captain of the guard assigned Joseph to them, and he became their personal attendant. And they were in custody for some time.

⁵ The cupbearer and the baker of the king of Egypt, who were confined in the prison, each had a dream. Both had a dream on the same night, and each dream had its own meaning. ⁶ When Joseph came to them in the morning, he saw that they looked distraught. ⁷ So he asked Pharaoh's officers who were in custody with him in his master's house, "Why are your faces sad today?"

⁸ "We had dreams," they said to him, "but there is no one to interpret them."

Then Joseph said to them, "Don't interpretations belong to God? Tell me your dreams."

⁹ So the chief cupbearer told his dream to Joseph: "In my dream there was a vine in front of me. ¹⁰ On the vine were three branches. As soon as it budded, its blossoms came out and its clusters ripened into grapes. ¹¹ Pharaoh's cup was in my hand, and I took the grapes, squeezed them into Pharaoh's cup, and placed the cup in Pharaoh's hand."

¹² "This is its interpretation," Joseph said to him. "The three branches are three days. ¹³ In just three days Pharaoh will lift up your head and restore you to

your position. You will put Pharaoh's cup in his hand the way you used to when you were his cupbearer. [14] But when all goes well for you, remember that I was with you. Please show kindness to me by mentioning me to Pharaoh, and get me out of this prison. [15] For I was kidnapped from the land of the Hebrews, and even here I have done nothing that they should put me in the dungeon."

[16] When the chief baker saw that the interpretation was positive, he said to Joseph, "I also had a dream. Three baskets of white bread were on my head. [17] In the top basket were all sorts of baked goods for Pharaoh, but the birds were eating them out of the basket on my head."

[18] "This is its interpretation," Joseph replied. "The three baskets are three days. [19] In just three days Pharaoh will lift up your head—from off you—and hang you on a tree. Then the birds will eat the flesh from your body."

[20] On the third day, which was Pharaoh's birthday, he gave a feast for all his servants. He lifted up the heads of the chief cupbearer and the chief baker: [21] he restored the chief cupbearer to his position as cupbearer, and he placed the cup in Pharaoh's hand; [22] but he hanged the chief baker, just as Joseph had explained to them. [23] Yet the chief cupbearer did not remember Joseph; he forgot him.

41 Two years later Pharaoh had a dream: He was standing beside the Nile, [2] when seven healthy-looking, well-fed cows came up from the Nile and began to graze among the reeds. [3] After them, seven other cows, sickly and thin, came up from the Nile and stood beside those cows along the bank of the Nile. [4] The sickly, thin cows ate the healthy, well-fed cows. Then Pharaoh woke up. [5] He fell asleep and dreamed a second time: Seven heads of grain, full and good, came up on one stalk. [6] After them, seven heads of grain, thin and scorched by the east wind, sprouted up. [7] The thin heads of grain swallowed up the seven full, good

ones. Then Pharaoh woke up, and it was only a dream.

PSALM 12:6-8

[6] The words of the LORD are pure words,
  like silver refined in an earthen furnace,
  purified seven times.

[7] You, LORD, will guard us;
  You will protect us from this generation forever.
[8] The wicked wander everywhere,
  and what is worthless is exalted by the human race.

PROVERBS 3:9-10

[9] Honor the LORD with your possessions
  and with the first produce your entire harvest;
[10] then your barns will be completely filled,
  and your vats will overflow with new wine.

MATTHEW 14:1-21

14 At that time Herod the tetrarch heard the report about Jesus. [2] "This is John the Baptist!" he told his servants. "He has been raised from the dead, and that's why supernatural powers are at work in him."

[3] For Herod had arrested John, chained him, and put him in prison on account of Herodias, his brother Philip's wife, [4] since John had been telling him, "It's not lawful for you to have her!" [5] Though he wanted to kill him, he feared the crowd, since they regarded him as a prophet.

[6] But when Herod's birthday celebration came, Herodias' daughter danced before them and pleased Herod. [7] So he promised with an oath to give her whatever she might ask. [8] And prompted by her mother, she answered, "Give me John the Baptist's head here on a platter!" [9] Although the king regretted it,

he commanded that it be granted because of his oaths and his guests. [10] So he sent orders and had John beheaded in the prison. [11] His head was brought on a platter and given to the girl, who carried it to her mother. [12] Then his disciples came, removed the corpse, buried it, and went and reported to Jesus.

[13] When Jesus heard about it, He withdrew from there by boat to a remote place to be alone. When the crowds heard this, they followed Him on foot from the towns. [14] As He stepped ashore, He saw a huge crowd, felt compassion for them, and healed their sick.

[15] When evening came, the disciples approached Him and said, "This place is a wilderness, and it is already late. Send the crowds away so they can go into the villages and buy food for themselves."

[16] "They don't need to go away," Jesus told them. "You give them something to eat."

[17] "But we only have five loaves and two fish here," they said to Him.

[18] "Bring them here to Me," He said. [19] Then He commanded the crowds to sit down on the grass. He took the five loaves and the two fish, and looking up to heaven, He blessed them. He broke the loaves and gave them to the disciples, and the disciples gave them to the crowds. [20] Everyone ate and was filled. Then they picked up 12 baskets full of leftover pieces! [21] Now those who ate were about 5,000 men, besides women and children.

Not the End—Beginning

Stay in the city until you are empowered from on high.—LUKE 24:49

Writing on the subject of the Holy Spirit has whetted my appetite for more of His fullness and His power. I can never be the same again. I hope something similar happens to you.

The Holy Spirit coordinates and unifies the conscious and the subconscious, He comforts and contributes, He clothes and convinces. There is much more that could be said, of course, about His ministry in our lives, but let me draw your attention to something else—God is willing to give you as much of His Spirit as you are willing to receive.

If you believe that you received all of the Spirit at conversion, then the question for you is this: How much is He ruling and reigning in your life at this present moment? If you believe that the Holy Spirit is given subsequent to conversion, then permit me to ask you this: What steps have you taken to open your entire being to Him in order that you might be filled with all His fullness? Don't, I beg you, remain stagnant because of some doctrinal position you might hold. Seek Him afresh today, that He might flow through your life in the fullness of His power.

And don't just focus on being filled for the blessing you might enjoy. Remember, the Holy Spirit is like electricity—He won't come in unless He can get out. Tell Him you want to be a channel, not just a consumer, and today will be not an end, but a beginning.

Prayer

O God, now as I take all barriers down, come in by Your Holy Spirit's power and flood my life with Your divine glory. May the receiving flow out in giving. This I ask for Your own dear name's sake. Amen.

Further Study

Jn 7:32-44; Mt 5:6; Is 55:1; Rv 22:17
What was the promise of Jesus?
How thirsty and hungry are you today?

JANUARY 23

GENESIS 41:8–42:4

⁸ When morning came, he was troubled, so he summoned all the magicians of Egypt and all its wise men. Pharaoh told them his dreams, but no one could interpret them for him.

⁹ Then the chief cupbearer said to Pharaoh, "Today I remember my faults. ¹⁰ Pharaoh had been angry with his servants, and he put me and the chief baker in the custody of the captain of the guard. ¹¹ He and I had dreams on the same night; each dream had its own meaning. ¹² Now a young Hebrew, a slave of the captain of the guards, was with us there. We told him our dreams, he interpreted our dreams for us, and each had its own interpretation. ¹³ It turned out just the way he interpreted them to us: I was restored to my position, and the other man was hanged."

¹⁴ Then Pharaoh sent for Joseph, and they quickly brought him from the dungeon. He shaved, changed his clothes, and went to Pharaoh.

¹⁵ Pharaoh said to Joseph, "I have had a dream, and no one can interpret it.

But I have heard it said about you that you can hear a dream and interpret it."

¹⁶ "I am not able to," Joseph answered Pharaoh. "It is God who will give Pharaoh a favorable answer."

¹⁷ So Pharaoh said to Joseph: "In my dream I was standing on the bank of the Nile, ¹⁸ when seven well-fed, healthy-looking cows came up from the Nile and began to graze among the reeds. ¹⁹ After them, seven other cows—ugly, very sickly, and thin—came up. I've never seen such ugly ones as these in all the land of Egypt. ²⁰ Then the thin, ugly cows ate the first seven well-fed cows. ²¹ When they had devoured them, you could not tell that they had devoured them; their appearance was as bad as it had been before. Then I woke up. ²² In my dream I had also seen seven heads of grain, full and good, coming up on one stalk. ²³ After them, seven heads of grain— withered, thin, and scorched by the east wind—sprouted up. ²⁴ The thin heads of grain swallowed the seven full ones. I told this to the magicians, but no one can tell me what it means."

²⁵ Then Joseph said to Pharaoh, "Pharaoh's dreams mean the same

87

thing. God has revealed to Pharaoh what He is about to do. ²⁶ The seven good cows are seven years, and the seven good heads are seven years. The dreams mean the same thing. ²⁷ The seven thin, ugly cows that came up after them are seven years, and the seven worthless, scorched heads of grain are seven years of famine.

²⁸ "It is just as I told Pharaoh: God has shown Pharaoh what He is about to do. ²⁹ Seven years of great abundance are coming throughout the land of Egypt. ³⁰ After them, seven years of famine will take place, and all the abundance in the land of Egypt will be forgotten. The famine will devastate the land. ³¹ The abundance in the land will not be remembered because of the famine that follows it, for the famine will be very severe. ³² Because the dream was given twice to Pharaoh, it means that the matter has been determined by God, and He will soon carry it out.

³³ "So now, let Pharaoh look for a discerning and wise man and set him over the land of Egypt. ³⁴ Let Pharaoh do this: Let him appoint overseers over the land and take one-fifth of the harvest of the land of Egypt during the seven years of abundance. ³⁵ Let them gather all the excess food during these good years that are coming, store the grain under Pharaoh's authority as food in the cities, and preserve it. ³⁶ The food will be a reserve for the land during the seven years of famine that will take place in the land of Egypt. Then the country will not be wiped out by the famine."

³⁷ The proposal pleased Pharaoh and all his servants. ³⁸ Then Pharaoh said to his servants, "Can we find anyone like this, a man who has the spirit of God in him?" ³⁹ So Pharaoh said to Joseph, "Since God has made all this known to you, there is no one as intelligent and wise as you. ⁴⁰ You will be over my house, and all my people will obey your commands. Only with regard to the throne will I be greater than you." ⁴¹ Pharaoh also said to Joseph, "See, I am placing you over all the land of Egypt." ⁴² Pharaoh removed his signet ring from his hand and put it on Joseph's hand, clothed him with fine linen garments, and placed a gold chain around his neck. ⁴³ He had Joseph ride in his second chariot, and servants called out before him, "*Abrek!*" So he placed him over all the land of Egypt. ⁴⁴ Pharaoh said to Joseph, "I am Pharaoh, but without your permission no one will be able to raise his hand or foot in all the land of Egypt." ⁴⁵ Pharaoh gave Joseph the name Zaphenath-paneah and gave him a wife, Asenath daughter of Potiphera, priest at On. And Joseph went throughout the land of Egypt.

⁴⁶ Joseph was 30 years old when he entered the service of Pharaoh king of Egypt. Joseph left Pharaoh's presence and traveled throughout the land of Egypt. ⁴⁷ During the seven years of abundance the land produced outstanding harvests. ⁴⁸ Joseph gathered all the excess food in the land of Egypt during the seven years and placed it in the cities. He placed the food in every city from the fields around it. ⁴⁹ So Joseph stored up grain in such abundance—like the sand of the sea—that he stopped measuring it because it was beyond measure.

⁵⁰ Two sons were born to Joseph before the years of famine arrived. Asenath daughter of Potiphera, priest at On, bore them to him. ⁵¹ Joseph named the firstborn Manasseh, meaning, "God has made me forget all my hardship in my father's house." ⁵² And the second son he named Ephraim, meaning, "God has made me fruitful in the land of my affliction."

⁵³ Then the seven years of abundance in the land of Egypt came to an end, ⁵⁴ and the seven years of famine began, just as Joseph had said. There was famine in every country, but throughout the land of Egypt there was food. ⁵⁵ Extreme hunger came to all the land of Egypt, and the people cried out to Pharaoh for food. Pharaoh told all Egypt, "Go to Joseph and do whatever he tells you." ⁵⁶ Because the famine had spread across the whole country, Joseph opened up all the storehouses and sold grain to the Egyptians, for the famine was severe in the land of Egypt. ⁵⁷ The

whole world came to Joseph in Egypt to buy grain, for the famine was severe all over the earth.

42 When Jacob learned that there was grain in Egypt, he said to his sons, "Why do you keep looking at each other? ² Listen," he went on, "I have heard there is grain in Egypt. Go down there and buy some for us so that we will live and not die." ³ So 10 of Joseph's brothers went down to buy grain from Egypt. ⁴ But Jacob did not send Joseph's brother Benjamin with his brothers, for he thought, "Something might happen to him."

PSALM 13:1-6

¹ LORD, how long will You
  continually forget me?
  How long will You hide Your face
  from me?
² How long will I store up anxious
  concerns within me,
  agony in my mind every day?
  How long will my enemy
  dominate me?

³ Consider me and answer, LORD,
  my God.
  Restore brightness to my eyes;
  otherwise, I will sleep in
  death,
⁴ my enemy will say, "I have
  triumphed over him,"
  and my foes will rejoice because I
  am defeated.

⁵ But I have trusted in Your faithful
  love;
  my heart will rejoice in Your
  deliverance.
⁶ I will sing to the LORD
  because He has treated me
  generously.

PROVERBS 3:11-12

¹¹ Do not despise the LORD's
   instruction, my son,
   and do not loathe His
   discipline;

¹² for the LORD disciplines the one
   He loves,
   just as a father, the son he
   delights in.

MATTHEW 14:22–15:9

²² Immediately He made the disciples get into the boat and go ahead of Him to the other side, while He dismissed the crowds. ²³ After dismissing the crowds, He went up on the mountain by Himself to pray. When evening came, He was there alone. ²⁴ But the boat was already over a mile from land, battered by the waves, because the wind was against them. ²⁵ Around three in the morning, He came toward them walking on the sea. ²⁶ When the disciples saw Him walking on the sea, they were terrified. "It's a ghost!" they said, and cried out in fear.

²⁷ Immediately Jesus spoke to them. "Have courage! It is I. Don't be afraid."

²⁸ "Lord, if it's You," Peter answered Him, "command me to come to You on the water."

²⁹ "Come!" He said.

And climbing out of the boat, Peter started walking on the water and came toward Jesus. ³⁰ But when he saw the strength of the wind, he was afraid. And beginning to sink he cried out, "Lord, save me!"

³¹ Immediately Jesus reached out His hand, caught hold of him, and said to him, "You of little faith, why did you doubt?" ³² When they got into the boat, the wind ceased. ³³ Then those in the boat worshiped Him and said, "Truly You are the Son of God!"

³⁴ Once they crossed over, they came to land at Gennesaret. ³⁵ When the men of that place recognized Him, they alerted the whole vicinity and brought to Him all who were sick. ³⁶ They were begging Him that they might only touch the tassel on His robe. And as many as touched it were made perfectly well.

15 Then Pharisees and scribes came from Jerusalem to Jesus and asked, ² "Why do Your disciples break

the tradition of the elders? For they don't wash their hands when they eat!"

³ He answered them, "And why do you break God's commandment because of your tradition? ⁴ For God said:

> Honor your father
> and your mother; and,
> The one who speaks evil of
> father or mother
> must be put to death.

⁵ But you say, 'Whoever tells his father or mother, "Whatever benefit you might have received from me is a gift committed to the temple"— ⁶ he does not have to honor his father.' In this way, you have revoked God's word because of your tradition. ⁷ Hypocrites! Isaiah prophesied correctly about you when he said:

> ⁸ These people honor Me
> with their lips,
> but their heart is far from
> Me.
> ⁹ They worship Me in vain,
> teaching as doctrines
> the commands of men."

Correcting Your Doubt

Jesus reached out His hand, caught hold of him, and said to him, "You of little faith, why did you doubt?"—MATTHEW 14:31

While it is possible for us to distinguish between doubt and unbelief in theory, it is not so easy in practice. Doubt can move in the direction of unbelief and cross the borderline, but when it does, it ceases to be doubt. The idea of "total" or "complete" doubt is a contradiction in terms, for doubt that is total can no longer be classified as doubt; it is unbelief.

Os Guinness points out that when we attempt to undertake a biblical analysis of doubt, we can come out with either a "hard" or "soft" view of the subject. Those who take a "soft" view of doubt point to how vastly different doubt is from unbelief, and those who take a "hard" view of doubt point out its similarities.

Both views can be drawn out of the Scriptures. Error is usually truth out of balance, and it is important, therefore, that we get a balanced view of what the Bible has to say about doubt. In my view it can be summarized like this—doubt is not the same as unbelief, but unless corrected, doubt can naturally lead to unbelief.

This view has helped me avoid what I consider to be the extremes of being too hard or too soft on doubt. It is a condition which must be regarded as serious, but it need not be fatal. Don't allow your doubts to bring you into condemnation, for when faced and brought into clear perspective, they can be the catalyst to a deeper pursuit of God.

Prayer

Father, when will I learn that in You all things serve—even doubt? Show me how to turn my doubts into stepping stones and use them to come into an even closer relationship with You. Amen.

Further Study

Mt 8:1-26; 6:30; 16:8
What phrase did Jesus often use?
What did He say of the centurion?

JANUARY 24

GENESIS 42:5–43:14

5 The sons of Israel were among those who came to buy grain, for the famine was in the land of Canaan. 6 Joseph was in charge of the country; he sold grain to all its people. His brothers came and bowed down before him with their faces to the ground. 7 When Joseph saw his brothers, he recognized them, but he treated them like strangers and spoke harshly to them.

"Where do you come from?" he asked.

"From the land of Canaan to buy food," they replied.

8 Although Joseph recognized his brothers, they did not recognize him. 9 Joseph remembered his dreams about them and said to them, "You are spies. You have come to see the weakness of the land."

10 "No, my lord. Your servants have come to buy food," they said. 11 "We are all sons of one man. We are honest; your servants are not spies."

12 "No," he said to them. "You have come to see the weakness of the land."

13 But they replied, "We, your servants, were 12 brothers, the sons of one man in the land of Canaan. The youngest is now with our father, and one is no longer living."

14 Then Joseph said to them, "I have spoken: 'You are spies!' 15 This is how you will be tested: As surely as Pharaoh lives, you will not leave this place unless your youngest brother comes here. 16 Send one of your number to get your brother. The rest of you will be imprisoned so that your words can be tested to see if they are true. If they are not, then as surely as Pharaoh lives, you are spies!" 17 So Joseph imprisoned them together for three days.

18 On the third day Joseph said to them, "I fear God—do this and you will live. 19 If you are honest men, let one of you be confined to the guardhouse, while the rest of you go and take grain to relieve the hunger of your households. 20 Bring your youngest brother to me so that your words can be confirmed; then you won't die." And they consented to this.

21 Then they said to each other, "It is plain that we are being punished for what we did to our brother. We saw his deep distress when he pleaded with us, but we would not listen. That is why this trouble has come to us."

22 But Reuben replied: "Didn't I tell you not to harm the boy? But you wouldn't listen. Now we must account for his blood!"

23 They did not realize that Joseph understood them, since there was an interpreter between them. 24 He turned away from them and wept. Then he turned back and spoke to them. He took Simeon from them and had him bound before their eyes. 25 Joseph then gave orders to fill their containers with grain,

return each man's money to his sack, and give them provisions for their journey. This order was carried out. ²⁶ They loaded the grain on their donkeys and left there.

²⁷ At the place where they lodged for the night, one of them opened his sack to get feed for his donkey, and he saw his money there at the top of the bag. ²⁸ He said to his brothers, "My money has been returned! It's here in my bag." Their hearts sank. Trembling, they turned to one another and said, "What is this that God has done to us?"

²⁹ When they reached their father Jacob in the land of Canaan, they told him all that had happened to them: ³⁰ "The man who is the lord of the country spoke harshly to us and accused us of spying on the country. ³¹ But we told him: We are honest men and not spies. ³² We were 12 brothers, sons of the same father. One is no longer living, and the youngest is now with our father in the land of Canaan. ³³ The man who is the lord of the country said to us, 'This is how I will know if you are honest men: Leave one brother with me, take food to relieve the hunger of your households, and go. ³⁴ Bring back your youngest brother to me, and I will know that you are not spies but honest men. I will then give your brother back to you, and you can trade in the country.'"

³⁵ As they began emptying their sacks, there in each man's sack was his bag of money! When they and their father saw their bags of money, they were afraid. ³⁶ Their father Jacob said to them, "You have deprived me of my sons. Joseph is gone and Simeon is gone. Now you want to take Benjamin. Everything happens to me!"

³⁷ Then Reuben said to his father, "You can kill my two sons if I don't bring him back to you. Put him in my care, and I will return him to you."

³⁸ But Jacob answered, "My son will not go down with you, for his brother is dead and he alone is left. If anything happens to him on your journey, you will bring my gray hairs down to Sheol in sorrow."

43 Now the famine in the land was severe. ² When they had used up the grain they had brought back from Egypt, their father said to them, "Go back and buy us some food."

³ But Judah said to him, "The man specifically warned us: 'You will not see me again unless your brother is with you.' ⁴ If you will send our brother with us, we will go down and buy food for you. ⁵ But if you will not send him, we will not go, for the man said to us, 'You will not see me again unless your brother is with you.'"

⁶ "Why did you cause me so much trouble?" Israel asked. "Why did you tell the man that you had another brother?"

⁷ They answered, "The man kept asking about us and our family: 'Is your father still alive? Do you have another brother?' And we answered him accordingly. How could we know that he would say, 'Bring your brother here'?"

⁸ Then Judah said to his father Israel, "Send the boy with me. We will be on our way so that we may live, and not die—neither we, nor you, nor our children. ⁹ I will be responsible for him. You can hold me personally accountable! If I do not bring him back to you and set him before you, I will be guilty before you forever. ¹⁰ If we had not wasted time, we could have come back twice by now."

¹¹ Then their father Israel said to them, "If it must be so, then do this: Put some of the best products of the land in your packs and take them down to the man as a gift—some balsam and some honey, aromatic gum and resin, pistachios and almonds. ¹² Take twice as much money with you. Return the money that was returned to you in the top of your bags. Perhaps it was a mistake. ¹³ Take your brother also, and go back at once to the man. ¹⁴ May God Almighty cause the man to be merciful to you so that he will release your other brother and Benjamin to you. As for me, if I am deprived of my sons, then I am deprived."

PSALM 14:1-7

1 The fool says in his heart, "God does not exist."
They are corrupt; their actions are revolting.
There is no one who does good.

2 The LORD looks down from heaven on the human race
to see if there is one who is wise, one who seeks God.

3 All have turned away; they have all become corrupt.
There is no one who does good, not even one.

4 Will evildoers never understand?
They consume my people as they consume bread;
they do not call on the LORD.

5 Then they will be filled with terror,
for God is with those who are righteous.

6 You sinners frustrate the plans of the afflicted,
but the LORD is his refuge.

7 Oh, that Israel's deliverance would come from Zion!
When the LORD restores His captive people,
Jacob will rejoice; Israel will be glad.

PROVERBS 3:13-14

13 Happy is a man who finds wisdom and who acquires understanding,
14 for she is more profitable than silver,
and her revenue is better than gold.

MATTHEW 15:10-39

10 Summoning the crowd, He told them, "Listen and understand: 11 It's not what goes into the mouth that defiles a man, but what comes out of the mouth, this defiles a man."

12 Then the disciples came up and told Him, "Do You know that the Pharisees took offense when they heard this statement?"

13 He replied, "Every plant that My heavenly Father didn't plant will be uprooted. 14 Leave them alone! They are blind guides. And if the blind guide the blind, both will fall into a pit."

15 Then Peter replied to Him, "Explain this parable to us."

16 "Are even you still lacking in understanding?" He asked. 17 "Don't you realize that whatever goes into the mouth passes into the stomach and is eliminated? 18 But what comes out of the mouth comes from the heart, and this defiles a man. 19 For from the heart come evil thoughts, murders, adulteries, sexual immoralities, thefts, false testimonies, blasphemies. 20 These are the things that defile a man, but eating with unwashed hands does not defile a man."

21 When Jesus left there, He withdrew to the area of Tyre and Sidon. 22 Just then a Canaanite woman from that region came and kept crying out, "Have mercy on me, Lord, Son of David! My daughter is cruelly tormented by a demon."

23 Yet He did not say a word to her. So His disciples approached Him and urged Him, "Send her away because she cries out after us."

24 He replied, "I was sent only to the lost sheep of the house of Israel."

25 But she came, knelt before Him, and said, "Lord, help me!"

26 He answered, "It isn't right to take the children's bread and throw it to their dogs."

27 "Yes, Lord," she said, "yet even the dogs eat the crumbs that fall from their masters' table!"

28 Then Jesus replied to her, "Woman, your faith is great. Let it be done for you as you want." And from that moment her daughter was cured.

29 Moving on from there, Jesus passed along the Sea of Galilee. He went up on a mountain and sat there, 30 and large crowds came to Him, having with them the lame, the blind, the deformed, those unable to speak, and

many others. They put them at His feet, and He healed them. [31] So the crowd was amazed when they saw those unable to speak talking, the deformed restored, the lame walking, and the blind seeing. And they gave glory to the God of Israel.

[32] Now Jesus summoned His disciples and said, "I have compassion on the crowd, because they've already stayed with Me three days and have nothing to eat. I don't want to send them away hungry; otherwise they might collapse on the way."

[33] The disciples said to Him, "Where could we get enough bread in this desolate place to fill such a crowd?"

[34] "How many loaves do you have?" Jesus asked them.

"Seven," they said, "and a few small fish."

[35] After commanding the crowd to sit down on the ground, [36] He took the seven loaves and the fish, and He gave thanks, broke them, and kept on giving them to the disciples, and the disciples gave them to the crowds. [37] They all ate and were filled. Then they collected the leftover pieces—seven large baskets full. [38] Now those who ate were 4,000 men, besides women and children. [39] After dismissing the crowds, He got into the boat and went to the region of Magadan.

The God Who Is There

The fool says in his heart, "God does not exist."—Psalm 14:1

The idea of a living, personal God gives men and women the jitters. They sense deep within that they are accountable to Him, but they don't know just what to do about it.

C. S. Lewis put it like this: "The Pantheist's God does nothing, demands nothing. He is there if you wish for Him, like a book on a shelf. He will not pursue you. There is no danger that at any time heaven and earth should feel awe at His glance. But Christ the Creator King is there. And His intervening presence is terribly startling to discover." Lewis goes on to compare the shock of discovering that there is a living, personal God in the universe to sitting alone in the dark and sensing someone breathing beside you. "It is always shocking," he says, "to meet life where we thought we were alone."

Listen to this paragraph by Lewis which I quote in full, as it puts the truth in a way that cannot be equaled: "There comes a moment when the children who have been playing at burglars hush suddenly; was that a real footstep in the hall? There comes a moment when people who have been dabbling in religion suddenly draw back. Supposing we really found Him! We never meant it to come to that! Worse still, supposing He has found us? So it is a sort of Rubicon. One goes across, or not. But if one does, there is no manner of security against miracles. One may be in for anything."

No one need worry about getting any shocks when they steadfastly resist believing in a personal God. No shocks, but no salvation either.

Prayer

Gracious God, how can I ever sufficiently thank You for bringing me to Yourself? The thought of a God who is alive, taking a personal interest in me, is more than I can comprehend. Yet I believe it. With all my heart. Thank You, dear Father. Amen.

Further Study

Pss 10:1-4; 36:1-4; 1 Jn 2:22
What is at the heart of the atheist?
How does John describe those who deny Christ?

JANUARY 25

GENESIS 43:15–44:34

¹⁵ The men took this gift, double the amount of money, and Benjamin. They made their way down to Egypt and stood before Joseph.

¹⁶ When Joseph saw Benjamin with them, he said to his steward, "Take the men to my house. Slaughter an animal and prepare it, for they will eat with me at noon." ¹⁷ The man did as Joseph had said and brought them to Joseph's house.

¹⁸ But the men were afraid because they were taken to Joseph's house. They said, "We have been brought here because of the money that was returned in our bags the first time. They intend to overpower us, seize us, make us slaves, and take our donkeys." ¹⁹ So they approached Joseph's steward and spoke to him at the doorway of the house.

²⁰ They said, "Sir, we really did come down here the first time only to buy food. ²¹ When we came to the place where we lodged for the night and opened our bags of grain, each one's money was at the top of his bag! It was the full amount of our money, and we have brought it back with us. ²² We have brought additional money with us to buy food. We don't know who put our money in the bags."

²³ Then the steward said, "May you be well. Don't be afraid. Your God and the God of your father must have put treasure in your bags. I received your money." Then he brought Simeon out to them. ²⁴ The man brought the men into Joseph's house, gave them water to wash their feet, and got feed for their donkeys. ²⁵ Since the men had heard that they were going to eat a meal there, they prepared their gift for Joseph's arrival at noon. ²⁶ When Joseph came home, they brought him the gift they had carried into the house, and they bowed to the ground before him.

²⁷ He asked if they were well, and he said, "How is your elderly father that you told me about? Is he still alive?" ²⁸ They answered, "Your servant our father is well. He is still alive." And they bowed down to honor him.

²⁹ When he looked up and saw his brother Benjamin, his mother's son, he asked, "Is this your youngest brother that you told me about?" Then he said, "May God be gracious to you, my son." ³⁰ Overcome with emotion for his brother, Joseph was about to weep. He went into an inner room to weep. ³¹ Then he washed his face and came

out. Regaining his composure, he said, "Serve the meal."

³² They served him by himself, his brothers by themselves, and the Egyptians who were eating with him by themselves, because Egyptians could not eat with Hebrews, since that is abhorrent to them. ³³ They were seated before him in order by age, from the firstborn to the youngest. The men looked at each other in astonishment. ³⁴ Portions were served to them from Joseph's table, and Benjamin's portion was five times larger than any of theirs. They drank, and they got drunk with Joseph.

44 Then Joseph commanded his steward: "Fill the men's bags with as much food as they can carry, and put each one's money at the top of his bag. ² Put my cup, the silver one, at the top of the youngest one's bag, along with his grain money." So he did as Joseph told him.

³ At morning light, the men were sent off with their donkeys. ⁴ They had not gone very far from the city when Joseph said to his steward, "Get up. Pursue the men, and when you overtake them, say to them, 'Why have you repaid evil for good? ⁵ Isn't this the cup that my master drinks from and uses for divination? What you have done is wrong!'"

⁶ When he overtook them, he said these words to them. ⁷ They said to him, "Why does my lord say these things? Your servants could not possibly do such a thing. ⁸ We even brought back to you from the land of Canaan the money we found at the top of our bags. How could we steal gold and silver from your master's house? ⁹ If any of us is found to have it, he must die, and we also will become my lord's slaves."

¹⁰ The steward replied, "What you have said is proper, but only the one who is found to have it will be my slave, and the rest of you will be blameless."

¹¹ So each one quickly lowered his sack to the ground and opened it. ¹² The steward searched, beginning with the oldest and ending with the youngest, and the cup was found in Benjamin's sack. ¹³ Then they tore their clothes, and each one loaded his donkey and returned to the city.

¹⁴ When Judah and his brothers reached Joseph's house, he was still there. They fell to the ground before him. ¹⁵ "What is this you have done?" Joseph said to them. "Didn't you know that a man like me could uncover the truth by divination?"

¹⁶ "What can we say to my lord?" Judah replied. "How can we plead? How can we justify ourselves? God has exposed your servants' iniquity. We are now my lord's slaves—both we and the one in whose possession the cup was found."

¹⁷ Then Joseph said, "I swear that I will not do this. The man in whose possession the cup was found will be my slave. The rest of you can go in peace to your father."

¹⁸ But Judah approached him and said, "Sir, please let your servant speak personally to my lord. Do not be angry with your servant, for you are like Pharaoh. ¹⁹ My lord asked his servants, 'Do you have a father or a brother?' ²⁰ and we answered my lord, 'We have an elderly father and a young brother, the child of his old age. The boy's brother is dead. He is the only one of his mother's sons left, and his father loves him.' ²¹ Then you said to your servants, 'Bring him to me so that I can see him.' ²² But we said to my lord, 'The boy cannot leave his father. If he were to leave, his father would die.' ²³ Then you said to your servants, 'If your younger brother does not come down with you, you will not see me again.'

²⁴ "This is what happened when we went back to your servant my father: We reported your words to him. ²⁵ But our father said, 'Go again, and buy us some food.' ²⁶ We told him, 'We cannot go down unless our younger brother goes with us. But if our younger brother isn't with us, we cannot see the man.' ²⁷ Your servant my father said to us, 'You know that my wife bore me two sons. ²⁸ One left—I said that he must have been torn to pieces—and I have never seen him again. ²⁹ If you also take this

one from me and anything happens to him, you will bring my gray hairs down to Sheol in sorrow.'

30 "So, if I come to your servant my father and the boy is not with us—his life is wrapped up with the boy's life— 31 when he sees that the boy is not with us, he will die. Then your servants will have brought the gray hairs of your servant our father down to Sheol in sorrow. 32 Your servant became accountable to my father for the boy, saying, 'If I do not return him to you, I will always bear the guilt for sinning against you, my father.' 33 Now please let your servant remain here as my lord's slave, in place of the boy. Let him go back with his brothers. 34 For how can I go back to my father without the boy? I could not bear to see the grief that would overwhelm my father."

PSALM 15:1-5

1 LORD, who can dwell in Your tent?
  Who can live on Your holy
    mountain?

2 The one who lives honestly,
    practices righteousness,
  and acknowledges the truth in his
    heart —
3 who does not slander with his
    tongue,
  who does not harm his friend
  or discredit his neighbor,
4 who despises the one rejected by
    the LORD,
  but honors those who fear the LORD,
  who keeps his word whatever the
    cost,
5 who does not lend his money at
    interest
  or take a bribe against the
    innocent—
  the one who does these things
    will never be moved.

PROVERBS 3:15-16

15 She is more precious than jewels;
  nothing you desire compares with
  her.

16 Long life is in her right hand;
  in her left, riches and honor.

MATTHEW 16:1-20

16 The Pharisees and Sadducees approached, and as a test, asked Him to show them a sign from heaven. 2 He answered them: "When evening comes you say, 'It will be good weather because the sky is red.' 3 And in the morning, 'Today will be stormy because the sky is red and threatening.' You know how to read the appearance of the sky, but you can't read the signs of the times. 4 An evil and adulterous generation wants a sign, but no sign will be given to it except the sign of Jonah." Then He left them and went away.

5 The disciples reached the other shore, and they had forgotten to take bread.

6 Then Jesus told them, "Watch out and beware of the yeast of the Pharisees and Sadducees."

7 And they discussed among themselves, "We didn't bring any bread."

8 Aware of this, Jesus said, "You of little faith! Why are you discussing among yourselves that you do not have bread? 9 Don't you understand yet? Don't you remember the five loaves for the 5,000 and how many baskets you collected? 10 Or the seven loaves for the 4,000 and how many large baskets you collected? 11 Why is it you don't understand that when I told you, 'Beware of the yeast of the Pharisees and Sadducees,' it wasn't about bread?" 12 Then they understood that He did not tell them to beware of the yeast in bread, but of the teaching of the Pharisees and Sadducees.

13 When Jesus came to the region of Caesarea Philippi, He asked His disciples, "Who do people say that the Son of Man is?"

14 And they said, "Some say John the Baptist; others, Elijah; still others, Jeremiah or one of the prophets."

15 "But you," He asked them, "who do you say that I am?"

¹⁶ Simon Peter answered, "You are the Messiah, the Son of the living God!"

¹⁷ And Jesus responded, "Simon son of Jonah, you are blessed because flesh and blood did not reveal this to you, but My Father in heaven. ¹⁸ And I also say to you that you are Peter, and on this rock I will build My church, and the forces of Hades will not overpower it. ¹⁹ I will give you the keys of the kingdom of heaven, and whatever you bind on earth is already bound in heaven, and whatever you loose on earth is already loosed in heaven."

²⁰ And He gave the disciples orders to tell no one that He was the Messiah.

A Test of Honesty

The one who lives honestly, practices righteousness, and acknowledges the truth in his heart.—Psalm 15:2

One of the steps toward producing a perfect coordination between our head and our heart involves facing this question: when I pray or seek the Lord, is my heart fully and enthusiastically behind what I am asking for with my lips? If not, we will fail to surmount the heights of God "with all four feet."

One of the things that used to puzzle me greatly in the early days of my pastoral ministry was to sit down with people who were not getting what they longed for spiritually and, after hours of counseling, sometimes to discover that although they were asking God for something with their lips, they were not really desiring it deep down in their hearts.

I am thinking specifically of a woman I knew who prayed earnestly (and loudly) in church for the conversion of her non-Christian husband. One day, however, in a moment of great openness and honesty (such as often occurs in counseling) she admitted that deep down in her heart she didn't really want her husband to be converted because she was afraid that if he was, the attention and sympathy she was getting from people in the church would no longer be there. Once she realized what was going on inside her, however, she was able to deal with it and became one of the most spiritually released women I have ever known. Her whole life (not just her prayer life) became one of deep, quiet conviction, and eventually—many years later—she had the joy of seeing her husband surrender to Christ.

Prayer

My Father, one thing is clear—such are the subterfuges of the human heart that without Your light and guidance, I can be self-deceived. Help me to apply the test of honesty and openness to my own spiritual life. In Jesus' name. Amen.

Further Study

Jr 17:1-10; 23:24; 1 Co 3:20
How does Jeremiah describe the heart?
How does the Lord view the thoughts of the worldly wise?

JANUARY 26

GENESIS 45:1–46:27

45 Joseph could no longer keep his composure in front of all his attendants, so he called out, "Send everyone away from me!" No one was with him when he revealed his identity to his brothers. ² But he wept so loudly that the Egyptians heard it, and also Pharaoh's household heard it. ³ Joseph said to his brothers, "I am Joseph! Is my father still living?" But his brothers were too terrified to answer him.

⁴ Then Joseph said to his brothers, "Please, come near me," and they came near. "I am Joseph, your brother," he said, "the one you sold into Egypt. ⁵ And now don't be worried or angry with yourselves for selling me here, because God sent me ahead of you to preserve life. ⁶ For the famine has been in the land these two years, and there will be five more years without plowing or harvesting. ⁷ God sent me ahead of you to establish you as a remnant within the land and to keep you alive by a great deliverance. ⁸ Therefore it was not you who sent me here, but God. He has made me a father to Pharaoh, lord of his entire household, and ruler over all the land of Egypt.

⁹ "Return quickly to my father and say to him, 'This is what your son Joseph says: "God has made me lord of all Egypt. Come down to me without delay. ¹⁰ You can settle in the land of Goshen and be near me—you, your children, and grandchildren, your sheep, cattle, and all you have. ¹¹ There I will sustain you, for there will be five more years of famine. Otherwise, you, your household, and everything you have will become destitute." ' ¹² Look! Your eyes and my brother Benjamin's eyes can see that it is I , Joseph, who am speaking to you. ¹³ Tell my father all about my glory in Egypt and about all you have seen. And bring my father here quickly."

¹⁴ Then Joseph threw his arms around Benjamin and wept, and Benjamin wept on his shoulder. ¹⁵ Joseph kissed each of his brothers as he wept, and afterward his brothers talked with him.

¹⁶ When the news reached Pharaoh's house, "Joseph's brothers have come," Pharaoh and his servants were pleased. ¹⁷ Pharaoh said to Joseph, "Tell your brothers, 'Do this: Load your animals and go on back to the land of Canaan. ¹⁸ Get your father and your households, and come back to me. I will give you the best of the land of Egypt, and you can eat from the richness of the land.' ¹⁹ You are also commanded, 'Do this: Take wagons from the land of Egypt for your young children, your wives, and bring your father here. ²⁰ Do not be concerned about your belongings, for the best of all the land of Egypt is yours.' "

²¹ The sons of Israel did this. Joseph gave them wagons as Pharaoh had commanded, and he gave them provisions for the journey. ²² He gave each of the brothers changes of clothes, but he gave Benjamin 300 pieces of silver and five changes of clothes. ²³ He sent his father the following: 10 donkeys carrying the best products of Egypt, and 10 female donkeys carrying grain, food, and provisions for his father on the journey. ²⁴ So Joseph sent his brothers on their way, and as they were leaving, he said to them, "Don't argue on the way."

²⁵ So they went up from Egypt and came to their father Jacob in the land of Canaan. ²⁶ They said, "Joseph is still alive, and he is ruler over all the land of Egypt!" Jacob was stunned, for he did not believe them. ²⁷ But when they told Jacob all that Joseph had said to them, and when he saw the wagons that Joseph had sent to transport him, the spirit of their father Jacob revived.

28 Then Israel said, "Enough! My son Joseph is still alive. I will go to see him before I die."

46 Israel set out with all that he had and came to Beer-sheba, and he offered sacrifices to the God of his father Isaac. 2 That night God spoke to Israel in a vision: "Jacob, Jacob!" He said.

And Jacob replied, "Here I am."

3 God said, "I am God, the God of your father. Do not be afraid to go down to Egypt, for I will make you a great nation there. 4 I will go down with you to Egypt, and I will also bring you back. Joseph will put his hands on your eyes."

5 Jacob left Beer-sheba. The sons of Israel took their father Jacob in the wagons Pharaoh had sent to carry him, along with their children and their wives. 6 They also took their cattle and possessions they had acquired in the land of Canaan. Then Jacob and all his children with him went to Egypt. 7 His sons and grandsons, his daughters and granddaughters, indeed all his offspring, he brought with him to Egypt.

8 These are the names of the Israelites, Jacob and his descendants, who went to Egypt:

Jacob's firstborn: Reuben.
9 Reuben's sons: Hanoch, Pallu, Hezron, and Carmi.
10 Simeon's sons: Jemuel, Jamin, Ohad, Jachin, Zohar, and Shaul, the son of a Canaanite woman.
11 Levi's sons: Gershon, Kohath, and Merari.
12 Judah's sons: Er, Onan, Shelah, Perez, and Zerah; but Er and Onan died in the land of Canaan. Perez's sons: Hezron and Hamul.
13 Issachar's sons: Tola, Puvah, Jashub, and Shimron.
14 Zebulun's sons: Sered, Elon, and Jahleel.
15 These were Leah's sons born to Jacob in Paddan-aram, as well as his daughter Dinah. The total number of persons: 33.
16 Gad's sons: Ziphion, Haggi, Shuni,

Ezbon, Eri, Arodi, and Areli.
17 Asher's sons: Imnah, Ishvah, Ishvi, Beriah, and their sister Serah. Beriah's sons were Heber and Malchiel.
18 These were the sons of Zilpah—whom Laban gave to his daughter Leah—that she bore to Jacob: 16 persons.
19 The sons of Jacob's wife Rachel: Joseph and Benjamin.
20 Manasseh and Ephraim were born to Joseph in the land of Egypt. They were born to him by Asenath daughter of Potiphera, a priest at On.
21 Benjamin's sons: Bela, Becher, Ashbel, Gera, Naaman, Ehi, Rosh, Muppim, Huppim, and Ard.
22 These were Rachel's sons who were born to Jacob: 14 persons.
23 Dan's son: Hashum.
24 Naphtali's sons: Jahzeel, Guni, Jezer, and Shillem.
25 These were the sons of Bilhah, whom Laban gave to his daughter Rachel. She bore to Jacob: seven persons.
26 The total number of persons belonging to Jacob—his direct descendants, not including the wives of Jacob's sons—who came to Egypt: 66.
27 And Joseph's sons who were born to him in Egypt: two persons. All those of Jacob's household who had come to Egypt: 70 persons.

PSALM 16:1-6

1 Protect me, God, for I take refuge in You.
2 I said to the LORD, "You are my Lord; I have no good besides You."
3 As for the holy people who are in the land, they are the noble ones in whom is all my delight.
4 The sorrows of those who take another god for themselves multiply;

I will not pour out their drink
offerings of blood,
and I will not speak their names
with my lips.

5 LORD, You are my portion and my
cup of blessing;
You hold my future.
6 The boundary lines have fallen for
me in pleasant places;
indeed, I have a beautiful
inheritance.

PROVERBS 3:17-18

17 Her ways are pleasant,
and all her paths, peaceful.
18 She is a tree of life to those who
embrace her,
and those who hold on to her are
happy.

MATTHEW 16:21–17:13

21 From then on Jesus began to point out to His disciples that He must go to Jerusalem and suffer many things from the elders, chief priests, and scribes, be killed, and be raised the third day. 22 Then Peter took Him aside and began to rebuke Him, "Oh no, Lord! This will never happen to You!"
23 But He turned and told Peter, "Get behind Me, Satan! You are an offense to Me because you're not thinking about God's concerns, but man's."
24 Then Jesus said to His disciples, "If anyone wants to come with Me, he must deny himself, take up his cross, and follow Me. 25 For whoever wants to save his life will lose it, but whoever loses his life because of Me will find it. 26 What will it benefit a man if he gains the whole world yet loses his life? Or what will a man give in exchange for his life? 27 For the Son of Man is going to come with His angels in the glory of His Father, and then He will reward each according to what he has done. 28 I assure

you: There are some standing here who will not taste death until they see the Son of Man coming in His kingdom."

17 After six days Jesus took Peter, James, and his brother John, and led them up on a high mountain by themselves. 2 He was transformed in front of them, and His face shone like the sun. Even His clothes became as white as the light. 3 Suddenly, Moses and Elijah appeared to them, talking with Him.
4 Then Peter said to Jesus, "Lord, it's good for us to be here! If You want, I will make three tabernacles here: one for You, one for Moses, and one for Elijah."
5 While he was still speaking, suddenly a bright cloud covered them, and a voice from the cloud said:

This is My beloved Son.
I take delight in Him.
Listen to Him!

6 When the disciples heard it, they fell facedown and were terrified. 7 Then Jesus came up, touched them, and said, "Get up; don't be afraid." 8 When they looked up they saw no one except Him—Jesus alone. 9 As they were coming down from the mountain, Jesus commanded them, "Don't tell anyone about the vision until the Son of Man is raised from the dead."
10 So the disciples questioned Him, "Why then do the scribes say that Elijah must come first?"
11 "Elijah is coming and will restore everything," He replied. 12 "But I tell you: Elijah has already come, and they didn't recognize him. On the contrary, they did whatever they pleased to him. In the same way the Son of Man is going to suffer at their hands." 13 Then the disciples understood that He spoke to them about John the Baptist.

"To Look at You"

They saw no one except Him—Jesus alone.
—MATTHEW 17:8

When we gaze at Christ's face and make Him the center of our attention and love, then we are gradually and continuously changed into the likeness of Christ. Thus we are transformed from one degree of glory to another, the Spirit within us being the silent Artist who makes us into His image. We become like Him in character and in countenance.

A young man was so much like his father in appearance that it prompted everyone who knew him to comment on the fact. The mother said: "It's strange, because when Andrew was a small child, he looked so much like me. Then, when he was about five, he became intrigued with being with his father. He used to go into his father's study and sit there until his father would say, 'Is there anything you want?' Andrew would reply, 'No, I don't want anything; I just want to look at you.' He would sit there and lovingly gaze into his father's face for such a long time that I honestly believe this is how he has come to look so much like him."

Just as there is a law in photography that says: "The angle of incidence equals the angle of reflection"—in other words, if you want a full-face reproduction, you must look full-face into the camera—so there is a law in life that causes us to become like that on which we gaze. If we look sideways on Christ, we get only a partial reflection. If we look fully at Him, we get a full reflection. We become like that on which we gaze.

Prayer

My Lord and my God, forgive me that so often I just give You a sideways glance when I ought to be continuously gazing into Your Face. Help me to behold You, so that I am transformed from what I am into what You are. Amen.

Further Study

Mk 5:1-20; Lk 23:44-49; Mt 27:55-56
What was the centurion's response?
What did the demoniac do when he saw Jesus?

JANUARY 27

GENESIS 46:28–48:22

²⁸ Now Jacob had sent Judah ahead of him to Joseph to prepare for his arrival at Goshen. When they came to the land of Goshen, ²⁹ Joseph hitched the horses to his chariot and went up to Goshen to meet his father Israel. Joseph presented himself to him, threw his arms around him, and wept for a long time. ³⁰ Then Israel said to Joseph, "At last I can die, now that I have seen your face and know you are still alive!"

³¹ Joseph said to his brothers and to his father's household, "I will go up and inform Pharaoh, telling him: My brothers and my father's household, who were in the land of Canaan, have come to me. ³² The men are shepherds; indeed they raise livestock. They have brought their sheep and cattle and all that they have. ³³ When Pharaoh addresses you and asks, 'What is your occupation?' ³⁴ you are to say, 'Your servants, both we and our fathers, have raised livestock from our youth until now.' Then you will be allowed to settle in the land of Goshen, since all shepherds are abhorrent to Egyptians."

47 So Joseph went and informed Pharaoh: "My father and my brothers, with their sheep and cattle and all that they have, have come from the land of Canaan and are now in the land of Goshen."

² He took five of his brothers and presented them before Pharaoh. ³ Then Pharaoh asked his brothers, "What is your occupation?"

And they said to Pharaoh, "Your servants, both we and our fathers, are shepherds." ⁴ Then they said to Pharaoh, "We have come to live in the land for a while because there is no grazing land for your servants' sheep, since the famine in the land of Canaan has been severe. So now, please let your servants settle in the land of Goshen."

⁵ Then Pharaoh said to Joseph, "Now that your father and brothers have come to you, ⁶ the land of Egypt is open before you; settle your father and brothers in the best part of the land. They can live in the land of Goshen. If you know of any capable men among them, put them in charge of my livestock."

⁷ Joseph then brought his father Jacob and presented him before Pharaoh, and Jacob blessed Pharaoh. ⁸ Then Pharaoh said to Jacob, "How many years have you lived?"

⁹ Jacob said to Pharaoh, "My pilgrimage has lasted 130 years. My years have been few and hard, and they have not surpassed the years of my fathers during their pilgrimages." ¹⁰ So Jacob blessed Pharaoh and departed from Pharaoh's presence.

¹¹ Then Joseph settled his father and brothers in the land of Egypt and gave them property in the best part of the land, the land of Rameses, as Pharaoh had commanded. ¹² And Joseph provided his father, his brothers, and all his father's household with food for their dependents.

¹³ But there was no food in that entire region, for the famine was very severe. The land of Egypt and the land of Canaan were exhausted by the famine. ¹⁴ Joseph collected all the money to be found in the land of Egypt and the land of Canaan in exchange for the grain they were purchasing, and he brought the money to Pharaoh's house. ¹⁵ When the money from the land of Egypt and the land of Canaan was gone, all the Egyptians came to Joseph and said, "Give us food. Why should we die here in front of you? The money is gone!"

¹⁶ But Joseph said, "Give me your livestock. Since the money is gone, I will give you food in exchange for your livestock."

[17] So they brought their livestock to Joseph, and he gave them food in exchange for the horses, the herds of sheep, the herds of cattle, and the donkeys. That year he provided them with food in exchange for all their livestock.

[18] When that year was over, they came the next year and said to him, "We cannot hide from our lord that the money is gone and that all our livestock belongs to our lord. There is nothing left for our lord except our bodies and our land. [19] Why should we perish here in front of you—both us and our land? Buy us and our land in exchange for food. Then we with our land will become Pharaoh's slaves. Give us seed so that we can live and not die, and so that the land won't become desolate."

[20] In this way, Joseph acquired all the land in Egypt for Pharaoh, because every Egyptian sold his field since the famine was so severe for them. The land became Pharaoh's, [21] and Joseph moved the people to the cities from one end of Egypt to the other. [22] The only land he didn't acquire was that of the priests, for it was their allotment from Pharaoh. They lived off the allotment Pharaoh had given them; therefore they did not sell their land.

[23] Then Joseph said to the people, "Understand today that I have acquired you and your land for Pharaoh. Here is seed for you. Sow it in the land. [24] At harvest, you are to give a fifth of it to Pharaoh, and four-fifths will be yours as seed for the field and as food for yourselves, your households, and your dependents."

[25] And they said, "You have saved our lives. We have found favor in our lord's eyes and will be Pharaoh's slaves." [26] So Joseph made it a law, still in effect today in the land of Egypt, that a fifth of the produce belongs to Pharaoh. Only the priests' land does not belong to Pharaoh.

[27] Israel settled in the land of Egypt, in the region of Goshen. They acquired property in it and became fruitful and very numerous. [28] Now Jacob lived in the land of Egypt 17 years, and his life span was 147 years. [29] When the time drew near for him to die, he called his son Joseph and said to him, "If I have found favor in your eyes, put your hand under my thigh and promise me that you will deal with me in faithful love. Do not bury me in Egypt. [30] When I lie down with my fathers, carry me away from Egypt and bury me in their burial place."

Joseph answered, "I will do what you have asked."

[31] And Jacob said, "Swear to me." So Joseph swore to him. Then Israel bowed in thanks at the head of his bed.

48 Some time after this, Joseph was told, "Your father is weaker." So he set out with his two sons, Manasseh and Ephraim. [2] When Jacob was told, "Your son Joseph has come to you," Israel summoned his strength and sat up in bed.

[3] Jacob said to Joseph, "God Almighty appeared to me at Luz in the land of Canaan and blessed me. [4] He said to me, 'I will make you fruitful and numerous; I will make many nations come from you, and I will give this land as an eternal possession to your descendants to come.' [5] Your two sons born to you in the land of Egypt before I came to you in Egypt are now mine. Ephraim and Manasseh belong to me just as Reuben and Simeon do. [6] Children born to you after them will be yours and will be recorded under the names of their brothers with regard to their inheritance. [7] When I was returning from Paddan, to my sorrow Rachel died along the way, some distance from Ephrath in the land of Canaan. I buried her there along the way to Ephrath," (that is, Bethlehem).

[8] When Israel saw Joseph's sons, he said, "Who are these?"

[9] And Joseph said to his father, "They are my sons God has given me here."

So Jacob said, "Bring them to me and I will bless them." [10] Now Jacob's eyesight was poor because of old age; he could hardly see. Joseph brought them to him, and he kissed and embraced them. [11] Israel said to Joseph, "I never expected to see your face again, but now God has even let me see your off-spring." [12] Then Joseph took them from his father's knees and bowed with his face to the ground.

[13] Then Joseph took them both—with his right hand Ephraim toward Israel's left, and with his left hand Manasseh toward Israel's right—and brought them to Israel. [14] But Israel stretched out his right hand and put it on the head of Ephraim, the younger, and crossing his hands, put his left on Manasseh's head, although Manasseh was the firstborn. [15] Then he blessed Joseph and said:

The God before whom my fathers
    Abraham and Isaac walked,
the God who has been my
    shepherd all my life to this
    day,
[16] the Angel who has redeemed me
    from all harm—
may He bless these boys.
And may they be called by my
    name
and the names of my fathers
    Abraham and Isaac,
and may they grow to be
    numerous within the land.

[17] When Joseph saw that his father had placed his right hand on Ephraim's head, he thought it was a mistake and took his father's hand to move it from Ephraim's head to Manasseh's. [18] Joseph said to his father, "Not that way, my father! This one is the firstborn. Put your right hand on his head." [19] But his father refused and said, "I know, my son, I know! He too will become a tribe, and he too will be great; nevertheless, his younger brother will be greater than he, and his offspring will become a populous nation." [20] So he blessed them that day with these words:

Israel will invoke blessings by you,
    saying,
"May God make you like Ephraim
    and Manasseh,"

putting Ephraim before Manasseh.
[21] Then Israel said to Joseph, "Look! I am about to die, but God will be with

you and will bring you back to the land of your fathers. [22] Over and above what I am giving your brothers, I am giving you the one mountain slope that I took from the hand of the Amorites with my sword and bow."

PSALM 16:7-11

7 I will praise the LORD who
    counsels me—
even at night my conscience
    instructs me.
8 I keep the LORD in mind always.
Because He is at my right hand,
    I will not be defeated.

9 Therefore my heart is glad, and
    my spirit rejoices;
my body also rests securely.
10 For You will not abandon me to
    Sheol;
You will not allow Your Faithful
    One to see the Pit.
11 You reveal the path of life to me;
in Your presence is abundant joy;
in Your right hand are eternal
    pleasures.

PROVERBS 3:19-20

19 The LORD founded the earth by
    wisdom
and established the heavens by
    understanding.
20 By His knowledge the watery
    depths broke open,
and the clouds dripped with dew.

MATTHEW 17:14–18:9

[14] When they reached the crowd, a man approached and knelt down before Him. [15] "Lord," he said, "have mercy on my son, because he has seizures and suffers severely. He often falls into the fire and often into the water. [16] I brought him to Your disciples, but they couldn't heal him."

[17] Jesus replied, "You unbelieving and rebellious generation! How long will I be with you? How long must I put up with you? Bring him here to Me."

¹⁸ Then Jesus rebuked the demon, and it came out of him, and from that moment the boy was healed.

¹⁹ Then the disciples approached Jesus privately and said, "Why couldn't we drive it out?"

²⁰ "Because of your little faith," He told them. "For I assure you: If you have faith the size of a mustard seed, you will tell this mountain, 'Move from here to there,' and it will move. Nothing will be impossible for you. [²¹ However, this kind does not come out except by prayer and fasting.]

²² As they were meeting in Galilee, Jesus told them, "The Son of Man is about to be betrayed into the hands of men. ²³ They will kill Him, and on the third day He will be raised up." And they were deeply distressed.

²⁴ When they came to Capernaum, those who collected the double-drachma tax approached Peter and said, "Doesn't your Teacher pay the double-drachma tax?"

²⁵ "Yes," he said.

When he went into the house, Jesus spoke to him first, "What do you think, Simon? Who do earthly kings collect tariffs or taxes from? From their sons or from strangers?"

²⁶ "From strangers," he said.

"Then the sons are free," Jesus told him. ²⁷ "But, so we won't offend them, go to the sea, cast in a fishhook, and catch the first fish that comes up. When you open its mouth you'll find a coin. Take it and give it to them for Me and you."

18 At that time the disciples came to Jesus and said, "Who is greatest in the kingdom of heaven?"

² Then He called a child to Him and had him stand among them. ³ " I assure you," He said, "unless you are converted and become like children, you will never enter the kingdom of heaven. ⁴ Therefore, whoever humbles himself like this child—this one is the greatest in the kingdom of heaven. ⁵ And whoever welcomes one child like this in My name welcomes Me.

⁶ "But whoever causes the downfall of one of these little ones who believe in Me—it would be better for him if a heavy millstone were hung around his neck and he were drowned in the depths of the sea! ⁷ Woe to the world because of offenses. For offenses must come, but woe to that man by whom the offense comes. ⁸ If your hand or your foot causes your downfall, cut it off and throw it away. It is better for you to enter life maimed or lame, than to have two hands or two feet and be thrown into the eternal fire. ⁹ And if your eye causes your downfall, gouge it out and throw it away. It is better for you to enter life with one eye, rather than to have two eyes and be thrown into hellfire!

Stirred, But Not Shaken

Because He is at my right hand,
I will not be shaken.—PSALM 16:8

Whenever I have the opportunity to address Christian counselors, I try to urge them to put the glory of God before their client's well-being. A good deal of "Christian counseling" today follows the client-centered approach, where the person is all-important. Thus more attention is paid to how the person has been hurt by others than how he or she may be hurting God by being unwilling to trust Him. This is a very sensitive issue, and I tell counselors in training that it must never be brought up until other issues have been explored and understood. But ultimately, however, this is the issue we must all face, whether we are in counseling or not.

Ask yourself this question now: Do I allow myself to be more overwhelmed by the wrong which people have done to me than the wrong I might have done (and may still be doing) to God by my unwillingness to trust Him? Putting the glory of God before our well-being does not go down well with some modern-day Christians brought up in the "me" generation. It means that we have to break away from the idea that life revolves around our desires, our ambitions, our self-image, our personal comfort, our hurts, and our problems, and embrace the fact that it revolves instead around the glory and the will of God. When we learn to apply the great text before us today to our lives, we will find, as did the psalmist, that when we set the Lord always before us, then no matter what happens, we will be stirred but not shaken.

Prayer

Father, thank You for reminding me that I cannot avoid my soul's being "stirred" by life's problems, but when I have set You ever before me, then I can avoid being "shaken." Drive this truth deep into my being this very day. In Jesus' name. Amen.

Further Study

1 Sm 4:1-22; Ex 33:12-18; Ps 29:1-2
Is there a parallel between this account and today's church?
What was Moses' request?

JANUARY 28

GENESIS 49:1–50:26

49 Then Jacob called his sons and said, "Gather around, and I will tell you what will happen to you in the days to come.

2 Come together and listen, sons of Jacob;
listen to your father Israel:

3 Reuben, you are my firstborn,
my strength and the firstfruits of my virility,
excelling in prominence, excelling in power.
4 Turbulent as water, you will no longer excel,
because you got into your father's bed
and you defiled it—he got into my bed.

5 Simeon and Levi are brothers;
   their knives are vicious weapons.
6 May I never enter their council;
   may I never join their assembly.
   For in their anger they kill men,
   and on a whim they hamstring
      oxen.
7 Their anger is cursed, for it is
      strong,
   and their fury, for it is cruel!
   I will disperse them throughout
      Jacob
   and scatter them throughout
      Israel.

8 Judah, your brothers will praise
      you.
   Your hand will be on the necks of
      your enemies;
   your father's sons will bow down
      to you.
9 Judah is a young lion—
   my son, you return from the kill—
   he crouches; he lies down like a
      lion
   and like a lioness—who wants to
      rouse him?
10 The scepter will not depart from
      Judah,
   or the staff from between his feet,
   until He whose right it is comes
   and the obedience of the peoples
      belongs to Him.
11 He ties his donkey to a vine,
   and the colt of his donkey to the
      choice vine.
   He washes his clothes in wine,
   and his robes in the blood of
      grapes.
12 His eyes are darker than wine,
   and his teeth are whiter than
      milk.

13 Zebulun will live by the seashore
   and will be a harbor for ships,
   and his territory will be next to
      Sidon.

14 Issachar is a strong donkey
   lying down between the
      saddlebags.
15 He saw that his resting place was
      good
   and that the land was pleasant,

so he leaned his shoulder to bear
   a load
and became a forced laborer.

16 Dan will judge his people
   as one of the tribes of Israel.
17 He will be a snake by the road,
   a viper beside the path,
   that bites the horses' heels
   so that its rider falls backwards.

18 I wait for Your salvation, LORD.

19 Gad will be attacked by marauding
      bands,
   but he will attack their heels.

20 Asher's food will be rich,
   and he will produce royal
      delicacies.

21 Naphtali is a doe set free
   that bears beautiful fawns.

22 Joseph is a fruitful vine,
   a fruitful vine beside a spring;
   its branches climb over the wall.
23 The archers attacked him,
   shot at him, and were hostile
      toward him.
24 Yet his bow remained steady,
   and his strong arms were made
      agile
   by the hands of the Mighty One
      of Jacob,
   by the name of the Shepherd, the
      Rock of Israel,
25 by the God of your father who
      helps you,
   and by the Almighty who blesses
      you
   with blessings of the heavens
      above,
   blessings of the deep that lies
      below,
   and blessings of the breasts and
      the womb.
26 The blessings of your father excel
   the blessings of my ancestors
   and the bounty of the eternal hills.
   May they rest on the head of
      Joseph,
   on the crown of the prince of his
      brothers.

27 Benjamin is a wolf; he tears his
prey.
In the morning he devours the
prey,
and in the evening he divides the
plunder."

28 These are the tribes of Israel, 12 in
all, and this was what their father said
to them. He blessed them, and he
blessed each one with a suitable blessing.
29 Then he commanded them: "I am
about to be gathered to my people. Bury
me with my fathers in the cave in the
field of Ephron the Hittite. 30 The cave is
in the field of Machpelah, near Mamre,
in the land of Canaan. This is the field
Abraham purchased from Ephron the
Hittite as a burial site. 31 Abraham and
his wife Sarah are buried there, Isaac
and his wife Rebekah are buried there,
and I buried Leah there. 32 The field and
the cave in it were purchased from the
Hittites." 33 When Jacob had finished instructing his sons, he drew his feet into
the bed and died. He was gathered to
his people.

50 Then Joseph, leaning over his father's face, wept and kissed him.
2 He commanded his servants who were
physicians to embalm his father. So they
embalmed Israel. 3 They took 40 days to
complete this, for embalming takes that
long, and the Egyptians mourned for
him 70 days.
4 When the days of mourning were
over, Joseph said to Pharaoh's household, "If I have found favor with you,
please tell Pharaoh that 5 my father
made me take an oath, saying, 'I am
about to die. You must bury me there in
the tomb that I hewed out for myself in
the land of Canaan.' Now let me go and
bury my father. Then I will return."
6 So Pharaoh said, "Go and bury your
father in keeping with your oath."
7 Then Joseph went to bury his father,
and all Pharaoh's servants, the elders of
his household, and all the elders of the
land of Egypt went with him, 8 along
with all Joseph's household, his brothers, and his father's household. Only

their children, their sheep, and their
cattle were left in the land of Goshen.
9 Horses and chariots went up with him;
it was a very impressive procession.
10 When they reached the threshing
floor of Atad, which is across the
Jordan, they lamented and wept loudly,
and Joseph mourned seven days for his
father. 11 When the Canaanite inhabitants of the land saw the mourning at
the threshing floor of Atad, they said,
"This is a solemn mourning on the part
of the Egyptians." Therefore the place is
named Abel-mizraim. It is across the
Jordan.
12 So Jacob's sons did for him what he
had commanded them. 13 They carried
him to the land of Canaan and buried
him in the cave at Machpelah in the
field near Mamre, which Abraham had
purchased as a burial site from Ephron
the Hittite. 14 After Joseph buried his father, he returned to Egypt with his
brothers and all who had gone with him
to bury his father.
15 When Joseph's brothers saw that
their father was dead, they said to one
another, "If Joseph is holding a grudge
against us, he will certainly repay us for
all the wrong we caused him."
16 So they sent this message to
Joseph, "Before he died your father
gave a command: 17 'Say this to Joseph:
Please forgive your brothers' transgression and their sin—the wrong they
caused you.' Therefore, please forgive
the transgression of the servants of the
God of your father." Joseph wept when
their message came to him. 18 Then his
brothers also came to him, bowed down
before him, and said, "We are your
slaves!"
19 But Joseph said to them, "Don't be
afraid. Am I in the place of God? 20 You
planned evil against me; God planned it
for good to bring about the present result—the survival of many people.
21 Therefore don't be afraid. I will take
care of you and your little ones." And he
comforted them and spoke kindly to
them.
22 Joseph and his father's household
remained in Egypt. Joseph lived 110
years. 23 He saw Ephraim's sons to the

third generation; the sons of Manasseh's son Machir were recognized by Joseph.

²⁴ Joseph said to his brothers, "I am about to die, but God will certainly come to your aid and bring you up from this land to the land He promised Abraham, Isaac, and Jacob." ²⁵ So Joseph made the Israelites take an oath: "When God comes to your aid, you are to carry my bones up from here."

²⁶ Joseph died at the age of 110. They embalmed him and placed him in a coffin in Egypt.

PSALM 17:1-5

¹ LORD, hear a just cause;
  pay attention to my cry;
  listen to my prayer—
  from lips free of deceit.
² Let my vindication come from
    You,
  for You see what is right.
³ You have tested my heart;
  You have visited by night;
  You have tried me and found
    nothing evil;
  I have determined that my mouth
    will not sin.
⁴ Concerning what people do: by
    the word of Your lips
  I have avoided the ways of the
    violent.
⁵ My steps are on Your paths;
  my feet have not slipped.

PROVERBS 3:21-24

²¹ Maintain your competence and
    discretion.
  My son, don't lose sight of them.
²² They will be life for you
  and adornment for your neck.
²³ Then you will go safely on your
    way;
  your foot will not stumble.
²⁴ When you lie down, you will not
    be afraid;
  you will lie down, and your sleep
    will be pleasant.

MATTHEW 18:10-35

¹⁰ "See that you don't look down on one of these little ones, because I tell you that in heaven their angels continually view the face of My Father in heaven. [¹¹ For the Son of Man has come to save the lost.] ¹² What do you think? If a man has 100 sheep, and one of them goes astray, won't he leave the 99 on the hillside and go and search for the stray? ¹³ And if he finds it, I assure you: He rejoices over that sheep more than over the 99 that did not go astray. ¹⁴ In the same way, it is not the will of your Father in heaven that one of these little ones perish.

¹⁵ "If your brother sins against you, go and rebuke him in private. If he listens to you, you have won your brother. ¹⁶ But if he won't listen, take one or two more with you, so that **by the testimony of two or three witnesses every fact may be established.** ¹⁷ If he pays no attention to them, tell the church. But if he doesn't pay attention even to the church, let him be like an unbeliever and a tax collector to you. ¹⁸ I assure you: Whatever you bind on earth is already bound in heaven, and whatever you loose on earth is already loosed in heaven. ¹⁹ Again, I assure you: If two of you on earth agree about any matter that you pray for, it will be done for you by My Father in heaven. ²⁰ For where two or three are gathered together in My name, I am there among them."

²¹ Then Peter came to Him and said, "Lord, how many times could my brother sin against me and I forgive him? As many as seven times?"

²² "I tell you, not as many as seven," Jesus said to him, "but 70 times seven. ²³ For this reason, the kingdom of heaven can be compared to a king who wanted to settle accounts with his slaves. ²⁴ When he began to settle accounts, one who owed 10,000 talents was brought before him. ²⁵ Since he had no way to pay it back, his master commanded that he, his wife, his children, and everything he had be sold to pay the debt.

²⁶ "At this, the slave fell facedown before him and said, 'Be patient with me, and I will pay you everything!' ²⁷ Then the master of that slave had compassion, released him, and forgave him the loan.

²⁸ "But that slave went out and found one of his fellow slaves who owed him 100 denarii. He grabbed him, started choking him, and said, 'Pay what you owe!'

²⁹ "At this, his fellow slave fell down and began begging him, 'Be patient with me, and I will pay you back.' ³⁰ But he wasn't willing. On the contrary, he went and threw him into prison until he could pay what was owed. ³¹ When the other slaves saw what had taken place, they were deeply distressed and went and reported to their master everything that had happened.

³² "Then, after he had summoned him, his master said to him, 'You wicked slave! I forgave you all that debt because you begged me. ³³ Shouldn't you also have had mercy on your fellow slave, as I had mercy on you?' ³⁴ And his master got angry and handed him over to the jailers until he could pay everything that was owed. ³⁵ So My heavenly Father will also do to you if each of you does not forgive his brother from his heart."

Sand in the Machinery

I forgave you all that debt because you begged me. Shouldn't you also have had mercy on your fellow slave, as I had mercy on you?—MATTHEW 18:32-33

If we are to maintain spiritual freshness, we must determine to forgive everyone who hurts us and refuse to nurse a grudge. Grudges become glooms.

A few years after World War II, a Christian Japanese boy at a public speaking contest announced that his subject would be "The Sacredness of Work." Some people smiled at his choice, but when they heard his story, their smiles turned to tears. His parents and home were burned to ashes in the atomic bomb explosion at Nagasaki. He was the eldest of three surviving children, and together they knelt in the ashes of their home and prayed to know what to do. One of them said: "I know—we can work." So they set to work, gathering bits of tin and boards, and soon they had built a little hut in which to live. They could have nursed their grudge and become gloomy; instead they forgave, forgot, and went to work.

No one who wants to maintain spiritual freshness can afford to nurse a grudge. It will poison both spirit and body. As one doctor put it: "Grudges put the whole physical and mental system on a war basis instead of on a peace basis."

Walter Alvarez, who is both a medical doctor and counselor, says: "I often tell patients they cannot afford to carry grudges or maintain hates. Such things can make them ill and tire them out. I once saw a man kill himself inch by inch, simply by thinking of nothing but hatred for a relative who had sued him. Within a year or two he was dead." A grudge or a resentment is sand in the machinery of living.

Prayer

O Father, teach me how to get the splinters of resentment out of my soul and also out of my body. Help me to decide that it is the oil of love, not the sand of resentments, that shall go into the machinery of my life day by day. Amen.

Further Study

Eph 4:21-32; Rm 3:14; Heb 12:15
What should not come out of our mouths?
What are we to do?

JANUARY 29

*E*XODUS 1:1–2:25

1 These are the names of the sons of Israel who came to Egypt with Jacob; each came with his family:

² Reuben, Simeon, Levi, and Judah;
³ Issachar, Zebulun, and Benjamin;
⁴ Dan and Naphtali; Gad and Asher.

⁵ The total number of Jacob's descendants was 70; Joseph was already in Egypt. ⁶ Then Joseph and all his brothers and all that generation died. ⁷ But the Israelites were fruitful, increased rapidly, multiplied, and became extremely numerous so that the land was filled with them.

⁸ A new king, who had not known Joseph, came to power in Egypt. ⁹ He said to his people, "Look, the Israelite people are more numerous and powerful than we are. ¹⁰ Let us deal shrewdly with them; otherwise they will multiply further, and if war breaks out, they may join our enemies, fight against us, and leave the country." ¹¹ So the Egyptians assigned taskmasters over the Israelites to oppress them with forced labor. They built Pithom and Rameses as supply cities for Pharaoh. ¹² But the more they oppressed them, the more they multiplied and spread so that the Egyptians came to dread the Israelites. ¹³ They worked the Israelites ruthlessly ¹⁴ and made their lives bitter with difficult labor in brick and mortar, and in all kinds of fieldwork. They ruthlessly imposed all this work on them.

¹⁵ Then the king of Egypt said to the Hebrew midwives, one of whom was named Shiphrah and the other Puah, ¹⁶ "When you help the Hebrew women give birth, observe them as they deliver. If the child is a son, kill him, but if it's a daughter, she may live." ¹⁷ The Hebrew midwives, however, feared God and did not do as the king of Egypt had told them; they let the boys live. ¹⁸ So the king of Egypt summoned the midwives and asked them, "Why have you done this and let the boys live?"

¹⁹ The midwives said to Pharaoh, "The Hebrew women are not like the Egyptian women, for they are vigorous and give birth before a midwife can get to them."

²⁰ So God was good to the midwives, and the people multiplied and became very numerous. ²¹ Since the midwives feared God, He gave them families. ²² Pharaoh then commanded all his people: "You must throw every son born to the Hebrews into the Nile, but let every daughter live."

2 Now a man from the family of Levi married a Levite woman. ² The woman became pregnant and gave birth to a son; when she saw that he was beautiful, she hid him for three months. ³ But when she could no longer hide him, she got a papyrus basket for him and coated it with asphalt and pitch.

She placed the child in it and set it among the reeds by the bank of the Nile. ⁴Then his sister stood at a distance in order to see what would happen to him.

⁵Pharaoh's daughter went down to bathe at the Nile while her servant girls walked along the riverbank. Seeing the basket among the reeds, she sent her slave girl to get it. ⁶When she opened it, she saw the child—a little boy, crying. She felt sorry for him and said, "This is one of the Hebrew boys."

⁷Then his sister said to Pharaoh's daughter, "Should I go and call a woman from the Hebrews to nurse the boy for you?"

⁸"Go." Pharaoh's daughter told her. So the girl went and called the boy's mother. ⁹Then Pharaoh's daughter said to her, "Take this child and nurse him for me, and I will pay your wages." So the woman took the boy and nursed him. ¹⁰When the child grew older, she brought him to Pharaoh's daughter, and he became her son. She named him Moses, "Because," she said, "I drew him out of the water."

¹¹Years later, after Moses had grown up, he went out to his own people and observed their forced labor. He saw an Egyptian beating a Hebrew, one of his people. ¹²Looking all around and seeing no one, he struck the Egyptian dead and hid him in the sand. ¹³The next day he went out and saw two Hebrews fighting. He asked the one in the wrong, "Why are you attacking your neighbor?"

¹⁴"Who made you a leader and judge over us?" the man replied. "Are you planning to kill me as you killed the Egyptian?"

Then Moses became afraid and thought: What I did is certainly known. ¹⁵When Pharaoh heard about this, he tried to kill Moses. But Moses fled from Pharaoh and went to live in the land of Midian, and sat down by a well.

¹⁶Now the priest of Midian had seven daughters. They came to draw water and filled the troughs to water their father's flock. ¹⁷Then some shepherds arrived and drove them away, but Moses came to their rescue and watered their flock. ¹⁸When they returned to their father Reuel he asked, "Why have you come back so quickly today?"

¹⁹They answered, "An Egyptian rescued us from the shepherds. He even drew water for us and watered the flock."

²⁰"So where is he?" he asked his daughters. "Why then did you leave the man behind? Invite him to eat dinner."

²¹Moses agreed to stay with the man, and he gave his daughter Zipporah to Moses in marriage. ²²She gave birth to a son whom he named Gershom, for he said, "I have become a stranger in a foreign land."

²³After a long time, the king of Egypt died. The Israelites groaned because of their difficult labor, and they cried out; and their cry for help ascended to God because of the difficult labor. ²⁴So God heard their groaning, and He remembered His covenant with Abraham, Isaac, and Jacob. ²⁵God saw the Israelites, and He took notice.

𝒫SALM 17:6-12

⁶ I call on You, God, because You
will answer me;
listen closely to me; hear what I
say.
⁷ Display the wonders of Your
faithful love, Savior of all who
seek refuge
from those who rebel against Your
right hand.
⁸ Guard me as the apple of Your
eye;
hide me in the shadow of Your
wings
⁹ from the wicked who treat me
violently,
my deadly enemies who surround
me.

¹⁰ They have become hardened;
their mouths speak arrogantly.
¹¹ They advance against me; now
they surround me.
They are determined to throw me
to the ground.
¹² They are like a lion eager to tear,

like a young lion lurking in ambush.

PROVERBS 3:25-26

25 Don't fear sudden danger
or the ruin of the wicked when it comes,
26 for the LORD will be your confidence
and will keep your foot from a snare.

MATTHEW 19:1-22

19 When Jesus had finished this instruction, He departed from Galilee and went to the region of Judea across the Jordan. ² Large crowds followed Him, and He healed them there. ³ Some Pharisees approached Him to test Him. They asked, "Is it lawful for a man to divorce his wife on any grounds?"
⁴ "Haven't you read," He replied, "that He who created them in the beginning **made them male and female,** ⁵ and He also said:

For this reason a man will leave his father and mother
and be joined to his wife,
and the two will become one flesh?

⁶ So they are no longer two, but one flesh. Therefore what God has joined together, man must not separate."
⁷ "Why then," they asked Him, "did Moses command us to give divorce papers and to send her away?"
⁸ He told them, "Moses permitted you to divorce your wives because of the hardness of your hearts. But it was not like that from the beginning. ⁹ And I tell you, whoever divorces his wife, except for sexual immorality, and marries another, commits adultery."
¹⁰ His disciples said to Him, "If the relationship of a man with his wife is like this, it's better not to marry!"

¹¹ But He told them, "Not everyone can accept this saying, but only those it has been given to. ¹² For there are eunuchs who were born that way from their mother's womb, there are eunuchs who were made by men, and there are eunuchs who have made themselves that way because of the kingdom of heaven. Let anyone accept this who can."
¹³ Then children were brought to Him so He might put His hands on them and pray. But the disciples rebuked them. ¹⁴ Then Jesus said, "Leave the children alone, and don't try to keep them from coming to Me, because the kingdom of heaven is made up of people like this." ¹⁵ After putting His hands on them, He went on from there.
¹⁶ Just then someone came up and asked Him, "Teacher, what good must I do to have eternal life?"
¹⁷ "Why do you ask Me about what is good?" He said to him. "There is only One who is good. If you want to enter into life, keep the commandments."
¹⁸ "Which ones?" he asked Him.
Jesus answered,

Do not murder;
do not commit adultery;
do not steal;
do not bear false witness;
¹⁹ honor your father and your mother;
and love your neighbor as yourself.

²⁰ "I have kept all these," the young man told Him. "What do I still lack?"
²¹ "If you want to be perfect," Jesus said to him, "go, sell your belongings and give to the poor, and you will have treasure in heaven. Then come, follow Me."
²² When the young man heard that command, he went away grieving, because he had many possessions.

114

Divine Re-parenting

I call on you, God, because You will answer me.

—PSALM 17:6

Using the Scriptures, we can build up a picture of God. So set up a canvas in your soul and allow the Holy Spirit to paint a picture for you of the Father using the palette of God's Word. As you read, let God re-parent you, and a fresh, clear and accurate picture of the Father will be drawn.

The first thing you need to know about your heavenly Father is: He is never too busy for you. Were your parents ever too busy for you? Were there occasions when you cried out for them and they were not there? Well, be assured that your heavenly Father is not like that. Even though He has a million and one things calling for His attention and a gigantic universe to run, He pays as much attention to you as if you were the only person on the face of the earth. Such is His relationship with you that it is as if there were not another soul in the universe. You don't have to share His attention with anyone—except, of course, when you are in prayer or fellowship with others. And even then He relates to you as if you were the only being in existence.

You may be too busy for your heavenly Father, but, take it from me, your heavenly Father is never too busy for you. Look once again at the text at the top of this page. It is written specially for you.

Prayer

O Father, burn this thought deep into my soul—I am Your special child. You relate to me as if I were the only one on the face of the earth. How wonderful. How truly wonderful. Thank You, Father. Amen.

Further Study

2 Sm 22:7; Ps 139:11-18; Mt 6:6-8; 1 Jn 3:21-22
Why can we pray with confidence?
Now pray confidently!

JANUARY 30

EXODUS 3:1–4:31

3 Meanwhile Moses was shepherding the flock of his father-in-law Jethro, the priest of Midian. He led the flock to the far side of the wilderness and came to Horeb, the mountain of God. ² Then the Angel of the LORD appeared to him in a flame of fire within a bush. As Moses looked, he saw that the bush was on fire but was not consumed. ³ So Moses thought: I must go over and look at this remarkable sight. Why isn't the bush burning up?

⁴ When the LORD saw that he had gone over to look, God called out to him from the bush, "Moses, Moses!"

"Here I am," he answered.

⁵ "Do not come closer," He said. "Take your sandals off your feet, for the place where you are standing is holy ground." ⁶ Then He continued, "I am the God of your father, the God of Abraham, the God of Isaac, and the God of Jacob." Moses hid his face because he was afraid to look at God.

⁷ Then the LORD said, "I have observed the misery of My people in Egypt, and have heard them crying out because of their oppressors, and I know about their sufferings. ⁸ I have come down to rescue them from the power of the Egyptians and to bring them from that land to a good and spacious land, a land flowing with milk and honey—the territory of the Canaanites, Hittites, Amorites, Perizzites, Hivites, and Jebusites. ⁹ The Israelites' cry for help has come to Me, and I have also seen the way the Egyptians are oppressing them. ¹⁰ Therefore, go. I am sending you to Pharaoh so that you may lead My people, the Israelites, out of Egypt."

¹¹ But Moses asked God, "Who am I that I should go to Pharaoh and that I should bring the Israelites out of Egypt?"

¹² He answered, "I will certainly be with you, and this will be the sign to you that I have sent you: when you bring the people out of Egypt, you will all worship God at this mountain."

¹³ Then Moses asked God, "If I go to the Israelites and say to them: The God of your fathers has sent me to you, and they ask me, 'What is His name?' what should I tell them?"

¹⁴ God replied to Moses, "I AM WHO I AM. This is what you are to say to the Israelites: I AM has sent me to you." ¹⁵ God also said to Moses, "Say this to the Israelites: Yahweh, the God of your fathers, the God of Abraham, the God of Isaac, and the God of Jacob, has sent me to you. This is My name forever; this is how I am to be remembered in every generation.

¹⁶ "Go and assemble the elders of Israel and say to them: Yahweh, the God of your fathers, the God of Abraham, Isaac, and Jacob, has appeared to me and said: I have paid close attention to you and to what has been done to you in Egypt. ¹⁷ And I have promised you that I will bring you up from the misery of Egypt to the land of the Canaanites, Hittites, Amorites, Perizzites, Hivites, and Jebusites—a land flowing with milk and honey. ¹⁸ They will listen to what you say. Then you, along with the elders of Israel, must go to the king of Egypt and say to him: The LORD, the God of the Hebrews, has met with us. Now please let us go on a three-day trip into the wilderness so that we may sacrifice to the LORD our God.

¹⁹ "However, I know that the king of Egypt will not allow you to go, unless he is forced by a strong hand. ²⁰ I will stretch out My hand and strike Egypt with all My miracles that I will perform in it. After that, he will let you go. ²¹ And I will give this people such favor in the sight of the Egyptians that when you go, you will not go empty-handed.

²² Each woman will ask her neighbor and any woman staying in her house for silver and gold jewelry, and clothing, and you will put them on your sons and daughters. So you will plunder the Egyptians."

4 Then Moses answered, "What if they won't believe me and will not obey me but say, 'The LORD did not appear to you'?" ² The LORD asked him, "What is that in your hand?"

"A staff," he replied.

³ Then He said, "Throw it on the ground." He threw it on the ground, and it became a snake. Moses ran from it, ⁴ but the LORD told him, "Stretch out your hand and grab it by the tail." So he stretched out his hand and caught it, and it became a staff in his hand. ⁵ "This will take place," He continued, "so they will believe that the LORD, the God of their fathers, the God of Abraham, the God of Isaac, and the God of Jacob, has appeared to you."

⁶ In addition the LORD said to him, "Put your hand inside your cloak." So he put his hand inside his cloak, and when he took it out, his hand was diseased, like snow. ⁷ Then He said, "Put your hand back inside your cloak." He put his hand back inside his cloak, and when he took it out, it had again become like the rest of his skin. ⁸ "If they will not believe you and will not respond to the evidence of the first sign, they may believe the evidence of the second sign. ⁹ And if they don't believe even these two signs or listen to what you say, take some water from the Nile and pour it on the dry ground. The water you take from the Nile will become blood on the ground."

¹⁰ But Moses replied to the LORD, "Please, Lord, I have never been eloquent—either in the past or recently or since You have been speaking to Your servant—because I am slow and hesitant in speech."

¹¹ The LORD said to him, "Who made the human mouth? Who makes him mute or deaf, seeing or blind? Is it not I, the LORD? ¹² Now go! I will help you speak and I will teach you what to say."

¹³ Moses said, "Please, Lord, send someone else."

¹⁴ Then the LORD's anger burned against Moses, and He said, "Isn't Aaron the Levite your brother? I know that he can speak well. And also, he is on his way now to meet you. When he sees you, his heart will rejoice. ¹⁵ You will speak with him and tell him what to say. I will help both you and him to speak, and will teach you both what to do. ¹⁶ He will speak to the people for you. He will be your spokesman, and you will serve as God to him. ¹⁷ And take this staff in your hand that you will perform the signs with."

¹⁸ Then Moses went back to his father-in-law Jethro and said to him, "Please let me return to my relatives in Egypt and see if they are still living."

Jethro said to Moses, "Go in peace."

¹⁹ Now in Midian the LORD told Moses, "Return to Egypt, for all the men who wanted to kill you are dead." ²⁰ So Moses took his wife and sons, put them on a donkey, and set out for the land of Egypt. And Moses took God's staff in his hand.

²¹ The LORD instructed Moses, "When you go back to Egypt, make sure you do in front of Pharaoh all the wonders I have put within your power. But I will harden his heart so that he won't let the people go. ²² Then you will say to Pharaoh: This is what the LORD says: Israel is My firstborn son. ²³ I told you: Let My son go so that he may worship Me, but you refused to let him go. Now I will kill your firstborn son!"

²⁴ On the trip, at an overnight campsite, it happened that the LORD confronted him and sought to put him to death. ²⁵ So Zipporah took a flint, cut off her son's foreskin, and threw it at Moses' feet. Then she said, "You are a bridegroom of blood to me!" ²⁶ So He let him alone. At that time she said, "You are a bridegroom of blood," referring to the circumcision.

²⁷ Now the LORD had said to Aaron, "Go and meet Moses in the wilderness." So he went and met him at the mountain of God and kissed him.

28 Moses told Aaron everything the LORD had sent him to say, and about all the signs He had commanded him to do. 29 Then Moses and Aaron went and assembled all the elders of the Israelites. 30 Aaron repeated everything the LORD had said to Moses and performed the signs before the people. 31 The people believed, and when they heard that the LORD had paid attention to them and that He had seen their misery, they bowed down and worshiped.

PSALM 17:13-15

13 Rise up, LORD!
    Confront him; bring him down.
    With Your sword, save me from
      the wicked.
14 With Your hand, LORD, save me
      from men,
    from men of the world, whose
      portion is in this life:
    You fill their bellies with what You
      have in store,
    their sons are satisfied,
    and they leave their surplus to
      their children.

15 But I will see Your face in
      righteousness;
    when I awake, I will be satisfied
      with Your presence.

PROVERBS 3:27-28

27 When it is in your power,
    don't withhold good from the one
      to whom it is due.
28 Don't say to your neighbor, "Go
      away! Come back later.
    I'll give it tomorrow"—when it is
      there with you.

MATTHEW 19:23–20:19

23 Then Jesus said to His disciples, " I assure you: It will be hard for a rich person to enter the kingdom of heaven! 24 Again I tell you, it is easier for a camel to go through the eye of a needle than for a rich person to enter the kingdom of God."

25 When the disciples heard this, they were utterly astonished and asked, "Then who can be saved?"

26 But Jesus looked at them and said, "With men this is impossible, but with God all things are possible."

27 Then Peter responded to Him, "Look, we have left everything and followed You. So what will there be for us?"

28 Jesus said to them, "I assure you: In the Messianic Age, when the Son of Man sits on His glorious throne, you who have followed Me will also sit on 12 thrones, judging the 12 tribes of Israel. 29 And everyone who has left houses, brothers or sisters, father or mother, children, or fields because of My name will receive 100 times more and will inherit eternal life. 30 But many who are first will be last, and the last first.

20 "For the kingdom of heaven is like a landowner who went out early in the morning to hire workers for his vineyard. 2 After agreeing with the workers on one denarius for the day, he sent them into his vineyard. 3 When he went out about nine in the morning, he saw others standing in the marketplace doing nothing. 4 To those men he said, 'You also go to my vineyard, and I'll give you whatever is right.' So off they went. 5 About noon and at three, he went out again and did the same thing. 6 Then about five he went and found others standing around, and said to them, 'Why have you been standing here all day doing nothing?'

7 " 'Because no one hired us,' they said to him.

" 'You also go to my vineyard,' he told them. 8 When evening came, the owner of the vineyard told his foreman, 'Call the workers and give them their pay, starting with the last and ending with the first.'

9 "When those who were hired about five came, they each received one denarius. 10 So when the first ones came, they assumed they would get more, but they also received a denarius each. 11 When they received it, they began to complain to the landowner: 12 'These last men put in one hour, and you made them equal

118

to us who bore the burden of the day and the burning heat!'

¹³ "He replied to one of them, 'Friend, I'm doing you no wrong. Didn't you agree with me on a denarius? ¹⁴ Take what's yours and go. I want to give this last man the same as I gave you. ¹⁵ Don't I have the right to do what I want with my business? Are you jealous because I'm generous?'

¹⁶ "So the last will be first, and the first last."

¹⁷ While going up to Jerusalem, Jesus took the 12 disciples aside privately and said to them on the way: ¹⁸ "Listen! We are going up to Jerusalem. The Son of Man will be handed over to the chief priests and scribes, and they will condemn Him to death. ¹⁹ Then they will hand Him over to the Gentiles to be mocked, flogged, and crucified, and He will be resurrected on the third day."

"Jehovah"—No Such Word

God replied to Moses, "I AM WHO I AM."—Exodus 3:14

Honoring the name of God is not just esteeming the letters in His name, nor speaking His name in hushed or quiet tones. The ancient Israelites attached such a sacredness to the name of God that they would not say it aloud. They thought that hallowing God's name meant hallowing the name itself. How utterly foolish and absurd! They paid honor to the actual letters of God's name, yet, on occasion, thought nothing about disobeying His Word and denying His truth.

One great Hebrew scholar points out that there is no such word as "Jehovah" in the Hebrew language, although it appears in English translations of the Old Testament. The name of God in Exodus 3:14, where the Almighty gave His name to Moses—("I AM WHO I AM")—is Yahweh, the English equivalent of which is "Jehovah." The Israelites would not say the word "Yahweh," and eventually the vowels were taken out and mixed with the consonants of another Hebrew word to form the word "Adonai." This was done as a device to avoid having to say the real word "Yahweh." How ridiculous can you get?

Let us be quite clear, then, about what Jesus meant when He taught us to pray, "Your name be honored as holy." God's name stands for who He is—His mercy, His compassion, His love, His power, His eternity, and so on. When, as God's children, we come to Him to honor His name, we do more than enter into a religious routine. We contemplate all that His name stands for and reverence Him for who He is.

Prayer

Father, I see that prayer, true prayer, is not just a technique; it is an art. Help me to learn this art and to implement what You are teaching me in my prayer life day by day. For Jesus' sake. Amen.

Further Study

Gn 15; 22:14; Ex 15:26; 17:15; Jdg 6:24; Ps 23:1; Jr 23:6; Ezk 48:35
List some of the names of God.
What do they mean?

JANUARY 31

EXODUS 5:1–6:30

5 Later, Moses and Aaron went in and said to Pharaoh, "This is what the Lord, the God of Israel, says: Let My people go, so that they may hold a festival for Me in the wilderness."

² But Pharaoh responded, "Who is the LORD that I should obey Him by letting Israel go? I do not know the LORD, and what's more, I will not let Israel go."

³ Then they answered, "The God of the Hebrews has met with us. Please let us go on a three-day trip into the wilderness so that we may sacrifice to the LORD our God, or else He may strike us with plague or sword."

⁴ The king of Egypt said to them, "Moses and Aaron, why are you causing the people to neglect their work? Get to your labors!" ⁵ Pharaoh also said, "Look, the people of the land are so numerous, and you would stop them from working."

⁶ That day Pharaoh commanded the overseers of the people as well as their foremen: ⁷ "Don't continue to supply the people with straw for making bricks, as before. They must go and gather straw for themselves. ⁸ But require the same quota of bricks from them as they were making before; do not reduce it. For they are slackers— that is why they are crying out, 'Let us go and sacrifice to our God.' ⁹ Impose heavier work on the men. Then they will be occupied with it and not pay attention to deceptive words."

¹⁰ So the overseers and foremen of the people went out and said to them, "This is what Pharaoh says: 'I am not giving you straw. ¹¹ Go get straw yourselves wherever you can find it, but there will be no reduction at all in your workload.'" ¹² So the people scattered throughout the land of Egypt to gather stubble for straw. ¹³ The overseers insisted, "Finish your assigned work each day, just as you did when straw was provided." ¹⁴ Then the Israelite foremen, whom Pharaoh's slave drivers had set over the people, were beaten and asked, "Why haven't you finished making your prescribed number of bricks yesterday or today, as you did before?"

¹⁵ So the Israelite foremen went in and cried for help to Pharaoh: "Why are you treating your servants this way? ¹⁶ No straw has been given to your servants, yet they say to us, 'Make bricks!' Look, your servants are being beaten, but it is your own people who are at fault."

¹⁷ But he said, "You are slackers. Slackers! That is why you are saying, 'Let us go sacrifice to the LORD.' ¹⁸ Now get to work. No straw will be given to you, but you must produce the same quantity of bricks."

¹⁹ The Israelite foremen saw that they were in trouble when they were told, "You cannot reduce your daily quota of

bricks." [20] When they left Pharaoh, they confronted Moses and Aaron, who stood waiting to meet them.

[21] "May the LORD take note of you and judge," they said to them, "because you have made us reek in front of Pharaoh and his officials—putting a sword in their hand to kill us!"

[22] So Moses went back to the LORD and asked, "Lord, why have You caused trouble for this people? And why did You ever send me? [23] Ever since I went in to Pharaoh to speak in Your name he has caused trouble for this people, and You haven't delivered Your people at all."

6 [1] But the LORD replied to Moses, "Now you are going to see what I will do to Pharaoh: he will let them go because of My strong hand; he will drive them out of his land because of My strong hand."

[2] Then God spoke to Moses, telling him, "I am Yahweh. [3] I appeared to Abraham, Isaac, and Jacob as God Almighty, but I did not make My name Yahweh known to them. [4] I also established My covenant with them to give them the land of Canaan, the land they lived in as foreigners. [5] Furthermore, I have heard the groaning of the Israelites, whom the Egyptians are forcing to work as slaves, and I have remembered My covenant.

[6] "Therefore tell the Israelites: I am Yahweh, and I will deliver you from the forced labor of the Egyptians and free you from slavery to them. I will redeem you with an outstretched arm and great acts of judgment. [7] I will take you as My people, and I will be your God. You will know that I am Yahweh your God, who delivered you from the forced labor of the Egyptians. [8] I will bring you to the land that I swore to give to Abraham, Isaac, and Jacob, and I will give it to you as a possession. I am the LORD." [9] Moses told this to the Israelites, but they did not listen to him because of their broken spirit and hard labor.

[10] Then the LORD spoke to Moses, [11] "Go and tell Pharaoh king of Egypt to let the Israelites go from his land."

[12] But Moses said in the LORD's presence: "If the Israelites will not listen to me, then how will Pharaoh listen to me, since I am such a poor speaker?" [13] Then the LORD spoke to Moses and Aaron and gave them commands concerning both the Israelites and Pharaoh king of Egypt to bring the Israelites out of the land of Egypt.

[14] These are the heads of their fathers' families:

The sons of Reuben, the firstborn of Israel:
Hanoch and Pallu, Hezron and Carmi.
These are the clans of Reuben.

[15] The sons of Simeon:
Jemuel, Jamin, Ohad, Jachin, Zohar, and Shaul, the son of a Canaanite woman.
These are the clans of Simeon.

[16] These are the names of the sons of Levi
according to their genealogy:
Gershon, Kohath, and Merari.
Levi lived 137 years.

[17] The sons of Gershon:
Libni and Shimei, by their clans.

[18] The sons of Kohath:
Amram, Izhar, Hebron, and Uzziel.
Kohath lived 133 years.

[19] The sons of Merari:
Mahli and Mushi.
These are the clans of the Levites according to their genealogy.

[20] Amram married his father's sister Jochebed,
and she bore him Aaron and Moses.
Amram lived 137 years.

[21] The sons of Izhar:
Korah, Nepheg, and Zichri.

[22] The sons of Uzziel:
Mishael, Elzaphan, and Sithri.

[23] Aaron married Elisheba, daughter of Amminadab and sister of Nahshon.
She bore him Nadab and Abihu, Eleazar and Ithamar.

[24] The sons of Korah:
Assir, Elkanah, and Abiasaph.

These are the clans of the Korahites.

²⁵ Aaron's son Eleazar married one of the daughters of Putiel and she bore him Phinehas.

These are the heads of the Levite families by their clans.

²⁶ It was this Aaron and Moses whom the LORD told, "Bring the Israelites out of the land of Egypt according to their divisions." ²⁷ Moses and Aaron were the ones who spoke to Pharaoh king of Egypt in order to bring the Israelites out of Egypt.

²⁸ On the day the LORD spoke to Moses in the land of Egypt, ²⁹ He said to him, "I am the LORD; tell Pharaoh king of Egypt everything I am telling you."

³⁰ But Moses replied in the LORD's presence, "Since I am such a poor speaker, how will Pharaoh listen to me?"

PSALM 18:1-6

¹ I love You, LORD, my strength.
² The LORD is my rock, my fortress, and my deliverer,
my God, my mountain where I seek refuge,
my shield and the horn of my salvation, my stronghold.
³ I called to the LORD, who is worthy of praise,
and I was saved from my enemies.

⁴ The ropes of death were wrapped around me;
the torrents of destruction terrified me.
⁵ The ropes of Sheol entangled me;
the snares of death confronted me.
⁶ I called to the LORD in my distress, and I cried to my God for help.
From His temple He heard my voice,
and my cry to Him reached His ears.

PROVERBS 3:29-32

²⁹ Don't plan any harm against your neighbor,

for he trusts you and lives near you.
³⁰ Don't accuse anyone without cause,
when he has done you no harm.
³¹ Don't envy a violent man or choose any of his ways;
³² for the devious are detestable to the LORD,
but He is a friend to the upright.

MATTHEW 20:20–21:11

²⁰ Then the mother of Zebedee's sons approached Him with her sons. She knelt down to ask Him for something. ²¹ "What do you want?" He asked her.

"Promise," she said to Him, "that these two sons of mine may sit, one on Your right and the other on Your left, in Your kingdom."

²² But Jesus answered, "You don't know what you're asking. Are you able to drink the cup that I am about to drink?"

"We are able," they said to Him.

²³ He told them, "You will indeed drink My cup. But to sit at My right and left is not Mine to give; instead, it belongs to those for whom it has been prepared by My Father." ²⁴ When the 10 disciples heard this, they became indignant with the two brothers. ²⁵ But Jesus called them over and said, "You know that the rulers of the Gentiles dominate them, and the men of high position exercise power over them. ²⁶ It must not be like that among you. On the contrary, whoever wants to become great among you must be your servant, ²⁷ and whoever wants to be first among you must be your slave; ²⁸ just as the Son of Man did not come to be served, but to serve, and to give His life—a ransom for many."

²⁹ As they were leaving Jericho, a large crowd followed Him. ³⁰ There were two blind men sitting by the road. When they heard that Jesus was passing by, they cried out, "Lord, have mercy on us, Son of David!" ³¹ The crowd told them to keep quiet, but they cried out

all the more, "Lord, have mercy on us, Son of David!" [32] Jesus stopped, called them, and said, "What do you want Me to do for you?" [33] "Lord," they said to Him, "open our eyes!" [34] Moved with compassion, Jesus touched their eyes. Immediately they could see, and they followed Him.

21 When they approached Jerusalem and came to Bethphage at the Mount of Olives, Jesus then sent two disciples, [2] telling them, "Go into the village ahead of you. At once you will find a donkey tied there, and a colt with her. Untie them and bring them to Me. [3] If anyone says anything to you, you should say that the Lord needs them, and immediately he will send them." [4] This took place so that what was spoken through the prophet might be fulfilled:

[5] Tell Daughter Zion,
"See, your King is coming to you,
gentle, and mounted on a
donkey,
even on a colt, the foal of a beast
of burden."

[6] The disciples went and did just as Jesus directed them. [7] They brought the donkey and the colt; then they laid their robes on them, and He sat on them. [8] A very large crowd spread their robes on the road; others were cutting branches from the trees and spreading them on the road. [9] Then the crowds who went ahead of Him and those who followed kept shouting:

Hosanna to the Son of David!
Blessed is He who comes
in the name of the Lord!
Hosanna in the highest
heaven!

[10] When He entered Jerusalem, the whole city was shaken, saying, "Who is this?" [11] And the crowds kept saying, "This is the prophet Jesus from Nazareth in Galilee!"

Ulterior Motives

You don't know what you're asking.—MATTHEW 20:22

There are many people in the Scriptures who appear to be spiritually minded but whose hearts harbor deeply unspiritual motives. Take the mother of the sons of Zebedee, for example, who according to Matthew 27:55 was one of the women who followed Jesus from Galilee in order to minister to Him.

Most commentators believe this small band of women to have been devotees of Christ, assisting Him and the disciples by preparing meals, washing and repairing clothes, and so on. Onlookers would have classified them as deeply spiritual, willing to give up their time to minister to Jesus—and of course, in the main, they were. In one place, however, the Scripture draws aside the veil from the heart of one of them, the mother of James and John, and shows her approaching Jesus with the request: "Promise . . . that these two sons of mine may sit, one on Your right and the other on Your left, in Your kingdom." . . . "You don't know what you're asking," Jesus said (Mt 20:21-22).

Yes, she served Jesus. Of that there can be no doubt. But she had a secret and selfish motive in her heart: a privileged position for her sons. It is easy to excuse her action, as many have done, on the grounds that she was doing only what any other concerned mother would have done—attempting to get the best for her children. But Jesus saw right into her heart and said: "You don't know what you're asking." How sad that her beautiful ministry to Jesus was spoiled by ulterior motives.

Prayer

My Father, help me to see that I cannot be a fully integrated person when I harbor within me two mutually exclusive loves. I cannot love You fully when I love my own interests fully. Set me free, dear Lord, to live only for You. Amen.

Further Study

Jms 2; Eph 2:3; 1 Jn 2:15-16
What motive was James exposing?
What did he say about the law?

FEBRUARY 1

EXODUS 7:1–8:32

7 The LORD answered Moses, "See, I have made you like God to Pharaoh, and Aaron your brother will be your prophet. ² You must say whatever I command you; then Aaron your brother must declare it to Pharaoh so that he will let the Israelites go from his land. ³ But I will harden Pharaoh's heart and multiply My signs and wonders in the land of Egypt. ⁴ Pharaoh will not listen to you, but I will put My hand on Egypt and bring out the ranks of My people the Israelites, out of the land of Egypt by great acts of judgment. ⁵ The Egyptians will know that I am the LORD when I stretch out My hand against Egypt, and bring out the Israelites from among them."

⁶ So Moses and Aaron did this, they did just as the LORD commanded them.

⁷ Moses was 80 years old and Aaron 83 when they spoke to Pharaoh.

⁸ The LORD said to Moses and Aaron, ⁹ "When Pharaoh tells you: Perform a miracle, tell Aaron: Take your staff and throw it down before Pharaoh. It will become a serpent." ¹⁰ So Moses and Aaron went in to Pharaoh and did just as the LORD had commanded. Aaron threw down his staff before Pharaoh and his officials, and it became a serpent. ¹¹ But then Pharaoh called the wise men and sorcerers—the magicians of Egypt, and they also did the same thing by their occult practices. ¹² Each one threw down his staff, and it became a serpent. But Aaron's staff swallowed their staffs. ¹³ However, Pharaoh's heart hardened, and he did not listen to them, as the LORD had said.

¹⁴ Then the LORD said to Moses, "Pharaoh is unresponsive: he refuses to let the people go. ¹⁵ Go to Pharaoh in

the morning. When you see him walking out to the water, stand ready to meet him by the bank of the Nile. Take in your hand the staff that turned into a snake. ¹⁶ Tell him: The LORD, the God of the Hebrews, has sent me to tell you: Let My people go, so that they may worship Me in the wilderness, but so far you have not listened. ¹⁷ This is what the LORD says: Here is how you will know that I am the LORD. Watch. I will strike the water in the Nile with the staff in my hand, and it will turn to blood. ¹⁸ The fish in the Nile will die, the river will stink, and the Egyptians will be unable to drink water from it."

¹⁹ So the LORD said to Moses, "Tell Aaron: Take your staff and stretch out your hand over the waters of Egypt— over their rivers, canals, ponds, and all their water reservoirs—and they will become blood. There will be blood throughout the land of Egypt, even in wooden and stone containers."

²⁰ Moses and Aaron did just as the LORD had commanded; in the sight of Pharaoh and his officials, he raised the staff and struck the water in the Nile, and all the water in the Nile was turned to blood. ²¹ The fish in the Nile died, and the river smelled so bad the Egyptians could not drink water from it. There was blood throughout the land of Egypt. ²² But the magicians of Egypt did the same thing by their occult practices. So Pharaoh's heart hardened, and he would not listen to them, as the LORD had said. ²³ Pharaoh turned around, went into his palace, and didn't even take this to heart. ²⁴ All the Egyptians dug around the Nile for water to drink because they could not drink the water from the river. ²⁵ Seven days passed after the LORD struck the Nile.

8 Then the LORD said to Moses, "Go in to Pharaoh and tell him: This is what the LORD says: Let My people go, so that they may worship Me. ² But if you refuse to let them go, then I will plague all your territory with frogs. ³ The Nile will swarm with frogs; they will come up and go into your palace, into your bed-

room and on your bed, into the houses of your officials and your people, and into your ovens and kneading bowls. ⁴ The frogs will come up on you, your people, and all your officials."

⁵ The LORD then said to Moses, "Tell Aaron: Stretch out your hand with your staff over the rivers, canals, and ponds, and cause the frogs to come up onto the land of Egypt." ⁶ When Aaron stretched out his hand over the waters of Egypt, the frogs came up and covered the land of Egypt. ⁷ But the magicians did the same thing by their occult practices and brought frogs up onto the land of Egypt.

⁸ Pharaoh summoned Moses and Aaron and said, "Ask the LORD that He remove the frogs from me and my people. Then I will let the people go and they can sacrifice to the LORD."

⁹ Moses said to Pharaoh, "Make the choice rather than me by saying when I should ask for you, your officials, and your people, that the frogs be taken away from you and your houses, and remain only in the Nile."

¹⁰ "Tomorrow," he answered.

Moses replied, "As you have said, so you may know there is no one like the LORD our God, ¹¹ the frogs will go away from you, your houses, your officials, and your people. The frogs will remain only in the Nile." ¹² After Moses and Aaron went out from Pharaoh, Moses cried out to the LORD for help concerning the frogs that He had brought against Pharaoh. ¹³ The LORD did as Moses had said: the frogs in the houses, courtyards, and fields died. ¹⁴ They piled them in countless heaps, and there was a terrible odor in the land. ¹⁵ But when Pharaoh saw there was relief, he hardened his heart and would not listen to them, as the LORD had said.

¹⁶ Then the LORD said to Moses, "Tell Aaron: Stretch out your staff and strike the dust of the earth, and it will become gnats throughout the land of Egypt." ¹⁷ And they did this. Aaron stretched out his hand with his staff, and when he struck the dust of the earth, gnats were on the people and animals. All the dust of the earth became gnats throughout the land of Egypt. ¹⁸ The magicians tried

to produce gnats using their occult practices, but they could not. The gnats remained on the people and animals.

¹⁹ "This is the finger of God," the magicians said to Pharaoh. But Pharaoh's heart hardened, and he would not listen to them, as the LORD had said.

²⁰ The LORD said to Moses, "Get up early in the morning and present yourself to Pharaoh when you see him going out to the water. Tell him: This is what the LORD says: Let My people go, so that they may worship Me. ²¹ But if you will not let My people go, then I will send swarms of flies against you, your officials, your people, and your houses. The Egyptians' houses will swarm with flies, and so will the land where they live. ²² But on that day I will give special treatment to the land of Goshen, where My people are living; no flies will be there. This way you will know that I, the LORD, am in the land. ²³ I will make a distinction between My people and your people. This sign will take place tomorrow."

²⁴ And the LORD did this. Thick swarms of flies went into Pharaoh's palace and his officials' houses. Throughout Egypt the land was ruined because of the swarms of flies. ²⁵ Then Pharaoh summoned Moses and Aaron and said, "Go sacrifice to your God within the country."

²⁶ But Moses said, "It would not be right to do that, because what we will sacrifice to the LORD our God is detestable to the Egyptians. If we sacrifice what the Egyptians detest in front of them, won't they stone us? ²⁷ We must go a distance of three days into the wilderness and sacrifice to the LORD our God as He instructs us."

²⁸ Pharaoh responded, "I will let you go and sacrifice to the LORD your God in the wilderness, but don't go very far. Make an appeal for me."

²⁹ "As soon as I leave you," Moses said, "I will appeal to the LORD, and tomorrow the swarms of flies will depart from Pharaoh, his officials, and his people. But Pharaoh must not act deceptively again by refusing to let the people go and sacrifice to the LORD." ³⁰ Then Moses left Pharaoh's presence and ap-

pealed to the LORD. ³¹ The LORD did as Moses had said: He removed the swarms of flies from Pharaoh, his officials, and his people; not one was left. ³² But Pharaoh hardened his heart this time also and did not let the people go.

PSALM 18:7-12

⁷ Then the earth shook and quaked;
   the foundations of the mountains
      trembled;
   they shook because He burned
      with anger.
⁸ Smoke rose from His nostrils,
   and consuming fire came from His
      mouth;
   coals were set ablaze by it.
⁹ He parted the heavens and came
      down,
   a dark cloud beneath His feet.
¹⁰ He rode on a cherub and flew,
   soaring on the wings of the wind.
¹¹ He made darkness His hiding
      place,
   dark storm clouds His canopy
      around Him.
¹² From the radiance of His
      presence,
   His clouds swept onward with hail
      and blazing coals.

PROVERBS 3:33-35

³³ The LORD's curse is on the
      household of the wicked,
   but He blesses the home of the
      righteous;
³⁴ He mocks those who mock,
   but gives grace to the humble.
³⁵ The wise will inherit honor,
   but He holds up fools to dishonor.

MATTHEW 21:12-27

¹² Jesus went into the temple complex and drove out all those buying and selling in the temple. He overturned the money changers' tables and the chairs of those selling doves. ¹³ And He said to them, "It is written, **My house will be called a house of prayer. But you are making it a den of thieves!**"

[14] The blind and the lame came to Him in the temple complex, and He healed them. [15] When the chief priests and the scribes saw the wonders that He did and the children in the temple complex cheering, "*Hosanna* to the Son of David!" they were indignant [16] and said to Him, "Do You hear what these children are saying?"

"Yes," Jesus told them. "Have you never read:

**You have prepared praise
from the mouths of children
and nursing infants?"**

[17] Then He left them, went out of the city to Bethany, and spent the night there.

[18] Early in the morning, as He was returning to the city, He was hungry. [19] Seeing a lone fig tree by the road, He went up to it and found nothing on it except leaves. And He said to it, "May no fruit ever come from you again!" At once the fig tree withered.

[20] When the disciples saw it, they were amazed and said, "How did the fig tree wither so quickly?"

[21] Jesus answered them, "I assure you: If you have faith and do not doubt, you will not only do what was done to the fig tree, but even if you tell this mountain, 'Be lifted up and thrown into the sea,' it will be done. [22] And if you believe, you will receive whatever you ask for in prayer."

[23] When He entered the temple complex, the chief priests and the elders of the people came up to Him as He was teaching and said, "By what authority are You doing these things? Who gave You this authority?"

[24] Jesus answered them, "I will also ask you one question, and if you answer it for Me, then I will tell you by what authority I do these things. [25] Where did John's baptism come from? From heaven or from men?"

They began to argue among themselves, "If we say, 'From heaven,' He will say to us, 'Then why didn't you believe him?' [26] But if we say, 'From men,' we're afraid of the crowd, because everyone thought John was a prophet." [27] So they answered Jesus, "We don't know."

And He said to them, "Neither will I tell you by what authority I do these things."

"Faith in Two Minds"

*If you have faith . . . even if you tell this mountain,
"Be lifted up and thrown into the sea," it will be done.*—MATTHEW 21:21

If we are to have feet like "hinds' feet," we must learn how to face and handle any doubts that may arise in our hearts.

Most of us have to face the problem of doubt at some time or another, and unless we have a clear understanding of what is involved when we doubt and how to deal with it, our pursuit of God can be greatly hindered. The English word doubt comes from the Latin *dubitare*, which is rooted in an Aryan word meaning "two." To doubt means to take two positions on something or to have a divided heart.

A major misconception concerning doubt—and one that has brought great anxiety to many a Christian's heart—is to view doubt as the opposite of faith, which clearly it is not. Unbelief is the opposite of faith.

Os Guinness puts it like this: "To believe is to be 'in one mind' about accepting something as true; to disbelieve is to be 'in one mind' about rejecting it. To doubt is to waver between the two, to believe and disbelieve all at once, and so to be 'in two minds.' "

Donald Bridge, in his book *When Christians Doubt*, refers to doubt as "faith asking questions." Some might think this definition elevates doubt to a position it does not deserve and masks its true nature—but not so. It is only when we understand what doubt really is that we can deal with it in the way we should. Doubt is, as Guinness puts it, "faith in two minds."

Prayer

My God and Father, I would be at my best—at Your best. But Your best cannot get across to me if doubt remains in my heart. Show me the steps I must take to overcome doubt. Amen.

Further Study

Mt 14:22-33; Lk 24:13-35
How does Peter illustrate being "in two minds"?
What did Jesus mean by slow to believe in your hearts?

FEBRUARY 2

*E*XODUS 9:1–10:20

9 Then the LORD said to Moses, "Go in to Pharaoh and say to him: This is what the LORD, the God of the Hebrews, says: Let My people go, so that they may worship Me. ²But if you refuse to let them go and keep holding them, ³then the LORD's hand will bring a severe plague against your livestock in the field—the horses, donkeys, camels, herds, and flocks. ⁴But the LORD will make a distinction between the livestock of Israel and the livestock of Egypt, so that nothing of all that the Israelites own will die." ⁵And the LORD set a time, saying, "Tomorrow the LORD will do this thing in the land." ⁶The LORD did this the next day. All the Egyptian livestock died, but none

among the Israelite livestock died. ⁷Pharaoh sent messengers who saw that not a single one of the Israelite livestock was dead. But Pharaoh's heart was hardened, and he did not let the people go.

⁸Then the LORD said to Moses and Aaron, "Take handfuls of furnace soot, and Moses is to throw it toward heaven in the sight of Pharaoh. ⁹It will become fine dust over the entire land of Egypt. It will become festering boils on people and animals throughout the land of Egypt." ¹⁰So they took furnace soot and stood before Pharaoh. Moses threw it toward heaven, and it became festering boils on man and beast. ¹¹The magicians could not stand before Moses because of the boils, for the boils were on the magicians as well as on all the Egyptians. ¹²But the LORD hardened

Pharaoh's heart and he did not listen to them, as the LORD had told Moses. [13] Then the LORD said to Moses, "Get up early in the morning and present yourself to Pharaoh. Tell him: This is what the LORD, the God of the Hebrews says: Let My people go, so that they may worship Me. [14] Otherwise, I am going to send all My plagues against you, your officials, and your people. Then you will know there is no one like Me in all the earth. [15] By now I could have stretched out My hand and struck you and your people with a plague, and you would have been obliterated from the earth. [16] However, I have let you live for this purpose: to show you My power and to make My name known in all the earth. [17] You are still acting arrogantly against My people by not letting them go. [18] Tomorrow at this time I will rain down the worst hail that has ever occurred in Egypt from the day it was founded until now. [19] Therefore give orders to bring your livestock and all that you have in the field into shelters. Every person and animal that is in the field and not brought inside will die when the hail falls on them." [20] Those among Pharaoh's officials who feared the word of the LORD made their servants and livestock flee to shelters, [21] but those who didn't take the LORD's word seriously left their servants and livestock in the field.

[22] Then the LORD said to Moses, "Stretch out your hand toward heaven and let there be hail throughout the land of Egypt—on man and beast and every plant of the field in the land of Egypt." [23] So Moses stretched out his staff toward heaven, and the LORD sent thunder and hail. Lightning struck the earth, and the LORD rained hail on the land of Egypt. [24] The hail, with lightning flashing through it, was so severe that nothing like it had occurred in the land of Egypt since it had become a nation. [25] Throughout the land of Egypt, the hail struck down everything in the field, both man and beast. The hail beat down every plant of the field and shattered every tree in the field. [26] The only place it didn't hail was in the land of Goshen where the Israelites were.

[27] Pharaoh sent for Moses and Aaron. "I have sinned this time," he said to them. "The LORD is the Righteous One, and I and my people are the guilty ones. [28] Make an appeal to the LORD. There has been enough of God's thunder and hail. I will let you go; you don't need to stay any longer."

[29] Moses said to him, "When I have left the city, I will extend my hands to the LORD. The thunder will cease, and there will be no more hail, so that you may know the earth is the LORD's. [30] But as for you and your officials, I know that you still do not fear the LORD God." [31] The flax and the barley were destroyed because the barley was ripe and the flax was budding, [32] but the wheat and the spelt were not destroyed since they are later crops.

[33] Moses went out from Pharaoh and the city, and extended his hands to the LORD. Then the thunder and hail ceased, and rain no longer poured down on the land. [34] When Pharaoh saw that the rain, hail, and thunder had ceased, he sinned again and hardened his heart, he and his officials. [35] So Pharaoh's heart hardened, and he did not let the Israelites go, as the LORD had said through Moses.

10 Then the LORD said to Moses, "Go to Pharaoh, for I have hardened his heart and the hearts of his officials so that I may do these miraculous signs of Mine among them, [2] and so that you may tell your son and grandson how severely I dealt with the Egyptians and performed miraculous signs among them, and you will know that I am the LORD."

[3] So Moses and Aaron went in to Pharaoh and told him, "This is what the LORD, the God of the Hebrews, says: How long will you refuse to humble yourself before Me? Let My people go, that they may worship Me. [4] But if you refuse to let My people go, then tomorrow I will bring locusts into your territory. [5] They will cover the surface of the land so that no one will be able to see the land. They will eat the remainder left to you that escaped the hail; they will eat every tree you have growing in

the fields. ⁶ They will fill your houses, all your officials' houses, and the houses of all the Egyptians—something your fathers and ancestors never saw since the time they occupied the land until today." Then he turned and left Pharaoh's presence.

⁷ Pharaoh's officials asked him, "How long must this man be a snare to us? Let the men go, so that they may worship the LORD their God. Don't you realize yet that Egypt is devastated?"

⁸ So Moses and Aaron were brought back to Pharaoh. "Go, worship the LORD your God," Pharaoh said. "But exactly who will be going?"

⁹ Moses replied, "We will go with our young and our old; we will go with our sons and daughters and with our flocks and herds because we must hold the LORD's festival."

¹⁰ He said to them, "May the LORD be with you if I ever let you and your families go! Look out—you are planning evil. ¹¹ No, only the men may go and worship the LORD, for that is what you have been asking for." And they were driven from Pharaoh's presence.

¹² The LORD then said to Moses, "Stretch out your hand over the land of Egypt and the locusts will come up over it and eat every plant in the land, everything that the hail left." ¹³ So Moses stretched out his staff over the land of Egypt, and the LORD sent an east wind over the land all that day and through the night. By morning the east wind had brought in the locusts. ¹⁴ The locusts went up over the entire land of Egypt and settled on the whole territory of Egypt. Never before had there been such a large number of locusts, and there will never be again. ¹⁵ They covered the surface of the whole land so that the land was black, and they consumed all the plants on the ground and all the fruit on the trees that the hail had left. Nothing green was left on the trees or the plants in the field throughout the land of Egypt.

¹⁶ Pharaoh urgently sent for Moses and Aaron and said, "I have sinned against the LORD your God and against you. ¹⁷ Please forgive my sin once more

and make an appeal to the LORD your God, so that He will take this death away from me." ¹⁸ Moses left Pharaoh's presence and appealed to the LORD. ¹⁹ Then the LORD changed the wind to a strong west wind, and it carried off the locusts and blew them into the Red Sea. Not a single locust was left in all the territory of Egypt. ²⁰ But the LORD hardened Pharaoh's heart, and he did not let the Israelites go.

PSALM 18:13-19

¹³ The LORD thundered from heaven;
   the Most High projected His
      voice.
¹⁴ He shot His arrows and scattered
      them;
   He hurled lightning bolts and
      routed them.
¹⁵ The depths of the sea became
      visible,
   the foundations of the world were
      exposed,
   at Your rebuke, LORD,
   at the blast of the breath of Your
      nostrils.

¹⁶ He reached down from on high
      and took hold of me;
   He pulled me out of deep waters.
¹⁷ He rescued me from my powerful
      enemy
   and from those who hated me, for
      they were too strong for me.
¹⁸ They confronted me in the day of
      my distress,
   but the LORD was my support.
¹⁹ He brought me out to a wide-open
      place;
   He rescued me because He
      delighted in me.

PROVERBS 4:1-2

4 Listen, my sons, to a father's
   discipline,
   and pay attention so that you may
      gain understanding,
² for I am giving you good
      instruction.
   Don't abandon my teaching.

$\mathcal{M}$ATTHEW 21:28-46

28 "But what do you think? A man had two sons. He went to the first and said, 'My son, go, work in the vineyard today.'

29 "He answered, 'I don't want to!' Yet later he changed his mind and went. 30 Then the man went to the other and said the same thing.

" 'I will, sir,' he answered. But he didn't go.

31 "Which of the two did his father's will?"

"The first," they said.

Jesus said to them, "I assure you: Tax collectors and prostitutes are entering the kingdom of God before you! 32 For John came to you in the way of righteousness, and you didn't believe him. Tax collectors and prostitutes did believe him, but you, when you saw it, didn't even change your minds then and believe him.

33 "Listen to another parable: There was a man, a landowner, who planted a vineyard, put a fence around it, dug a winepress in it, and built a watchtower. He leased it to tenant farmers and went away. 34 When the grape harvest drew near, he sent his slaves to the farmers to collect his fruit. 35 But the farmers took his slaves, beat one, killed another, and stoned a third. 36 Again, he sent other slaves, more than the first group, and they did the same to them. 37 Finally, he sent his son to them. 'They will respect my son,' he said.

38 "But when the tenant farmers saw the son, they said among themselves, 'This is the heir. Come, let's kill him and take his inheritance!' 39 So they seized him and threw him out of the vineyard, and killed him. 40 Therefore, when the owner of the vineyard comes, what will he do to those farmers?"

41 "He will completely destroy those terrible men," they told Him, "and lease his vineyard to other farmers who will give him his produce at the harvest."

42 Jesus said to them, "Have you never read in the Scriptures:

The stone that
    the builders rejected
has become the cornerstone.
This came from the Lord
and is wonderful in our eyes?

43 Therefore I tell you, the kingdom of God will be taken away from you and given to a nation producing its fruit. [44 Whoever falls on this stone will be broken to pieces; but on whomever it falls, it will grind him to powder!"]

45 When the chief priests and the Pharisees heard His parables, they knew He was speaking about them. 46 Although they were looking for a way to arrest Him, they feared the crowds, because they regarded Him as a prophet.

The Final Word

He pulled me out of deep waters. He rescued me from my powerful enemy.—PSALM 18:16-17

Once we become Christians, we are involved in a fight against Satan and his forces. God, however, has given us a defense against Satan and his tactics, which consists of six separate pieces of spiritual equipment.

First, He has given us the belt of truth—a willingness to let God's truth govern every part of our lives. Second, the breastplate of righteousness—seeing clearly that we are not saved by our own righteousness but Christ's. Third, we must have our feet sandaled with readiness for the gospel of peace—our determination to stand firmly in the faith. Fourth, we must raise the shield of faith—the quick action by which we act upon God's truth and refuse Satan's lies. Fifth, we must put on the helmet of salvation—the glorious hope that, one day, the Lord will right all wrongs and establish His eternal kingdom. And sixth, we must take up the sword of the Spirit, the Word of God, and wield the written Scriptures in the same way our Lord did in His wilderness temptations.

Having done all this, it is still possible to be defeated by the devil unless we know how to pray in the power of the Spirit. We must pray not only when things are going wrong but continuously, fervently, powerfully, and perseveringly. Our prayers must catch alight and burst into flame. Against such praying, the principalities and powers are helpless.

Prayer

My Father, now that I have seen the resources that are available to me in Christ, I realize that my responsibility to avail myself of these resources is greater than ever. Help me to put everything I have learned into action. For Your own dear name's sake. Amen.

Further Study

Ps 18:1-50; 65:6; Hab 3:19; Is 41:10
With what was David armed?
Have you put on your armor today?

FEBRUARY 3

*E*XODUS 10:21–12:36

²¹ Then the LORD said to Moses, "Stretch out your hand toward heaven, and there will be darkness over the land of Egypt, a darkness that can be felt." ²² So Moses stretched out his hand toward heaven, and there was thick darkness throughout the land of Egypt for three days. ²³ One person could not see another, and for three days they did not move from where they were. Yet all the Israelites had light where they lived. ²⁴ Pharaoh summoned Moses and

said, "Go, worship the LORD. Even your families may go with you; only your flocks and your herds must stay behind."

²⁵ Moses responded, "You must also let us have sacrifices and burnt offerings to prepare for the LORD our God. ²⁶ Even our livestock must go with us; not a hoof will be left behind because we will take some of them to worship the LORD our God. We will not know what we will use to worship the LORD until we get there."

²⁷ But the LORD hardened Pharaoh's

heart, and he was unwilling to let them go. ²⁸ Pharaoh said to him, "Leave me! Make sure you never see my face again, for on the day you see my face, you will die." ²⁹ "As you've said," Moses replied, "I will never see your face again."

11 The LORD said to Moses, "I will bring one more plague on Pharaoh and on Egypt. After that, he will let you go from here. When he lets you go, he will drive you out of here. ² Now announce to the people that both men and women should ask their neighbors for gold and silver jewelry." ³ The LORD gave the people favor in the sight of the Egyptians. And the man Moses was feared in the land of Egypt, by Pharaoh's officials and the people.

⁴ So Moses said, "This is what the LORD says: 'About midnight I will go throughout Egypt ⁵ and every firstborn male in the land of Egypt will die, from the firstborn of Pharaoh who sits on his throne to the firstborn of the servant girl who is behind the millstones, as well as every firstborn of the livestock. ⁶ Then there will be a great cry of anguish through all the land of Egypt such as never was before, or ever will be again. ⁷ But against all the Israelites, whether man or beast, not even a dog will snarl, so that you may know that the LORD makes a distinction between Egypt and Israel. ⁸ All these officials of yours will come down to me and bow before me, saying: Leave, you and all the people who follow you. After that, I will leave.' " And he left Pharaoh's presence in fierce anger.

⁹ The LORD said to Moses, "Pharaoh will not listen to you, so that My wonders may be multiplied in the land of Egypt." ¹⁰ Moses and Aaron did all these wonders before Pharaoh, but the LORD hardened Pharaoh's heart, and he would not let the Israelites go out of his land.

12 The LORD said to Moses and Aaron in the land of Egypt: ² "This month is to be the beginning of months for you; it is the first month of your year. ³ Tell the whole community of Israel that on the tenth day of this month they must each select an animal of the flock according to their fathers' households, one animal per household. ⁴ If the household is too small for a whole animal, that person and the neighbor nearest his house are to select one based on the combined number of people; you should apportion the animal according to what each person will eat. ⁵ You must have an unblemished animal, a year-old male; you may take it from either the sheep or the goats. ⁶ You are to keep it until the fourteenth day of this month; then the whole assembly of the community of Israel will slaughter the animals at twilight. ⁷ They must take some of the blood and put it on the two doorposts and the lintel of the houses in which they eat them. ⁸ They are to eat the meat that night; they should eat it, roasted over the fire along with unleavened bread and bitter herbs. ⁹ Do not eat any of it raw or cooked in boiling water, but only roasted over fire—its head as well as its legs and inner organs. ¹⁰ Do not let any of it remain until morning; you must burn up any part of it that does remain until morning. ¹¹ Here is how you must eat it: dressed for travel, your sandals on your feet, and your staff in your hand. You are to eat it in a hurry; it is the LORD's Passover.

¹² "I will pass through the land of Egypt on that night and strike every firstborn male in the land of Egypt, both man and beast. I am the LORD; I will execute judgments against all the gods of Egypt. ¹³ The blood on the houses where you are staying will be a distinguishing mark for you; when I see the blood, I will pass over you. No plague will be among you to destroy you when I strike the land of Egypt.

¹⁴ "This day is to be a memorial for you, and you must celebrate it as a festival to the LORD. You are to celebrate it throughout your generations as a permanent statute. ¹⁵ You must eat unleavened bread for seven days. On the first day you must remove yeast from your houses. Whoever eats what is leavened from the first day through the seventh day must be cut off from Israel. ¹⁶ You

are to hold a sacred assembly on the first day and another sacred assembly on the seventh day. No work may be done on those days except for preparing what people need to eat—you may do only that.

¹⁷ "You are to observe the Festival of Unleavened Bread because on this very day I brought your ranks out of the land of Egypt. You must observe this day throughout your generations as a permanent statute. ¹⁸ You are to eat unleavened bread in the first month, from the evening of the fourteenth day of the month until the evening of the twenty-first day. ¹⁹ Yeast must not be found in your houses for seven days. If anyone eats something leavened, that person, whether a foreign resident or native of the land, must be cut off from the community of Israel. ²⁰ Do not eat anything leavened; eat unleavened bread in all your homes."

²¹ Then Moses summoned all the elders of Israel and said to them, "Go, select an animal from the flock according to your families, and slaughter the Passover lamb. ²² Take a cluster of hyssop, dip it in the blood that is in the basin, and brush the lintel and the two doorposts with some of the blood in the basin. None of you may go out the door of his house until morning. ²³ When the Lord passes through to strike Egypt and sees the blood on the lintel and the two doorposts, He will pass over the door and not let the destroyer enter your houses to strike you. ²⁴ "Keep this command permanently as a statute for you and your descendants. ²⁵ When you enter the land that the Lord will give you as He promised, you are to observe this ritual. ²⁶ When your children ask you, 'What does this ritual mean to you?' ²⁷ you are to reply, 'It is the Passover sacrifice to the Lord, for He passed over the houses of the Israelites in Egypt when He struck the Egyptians and spared our homes.'" So the people bowed down and worshiped. ²⁸ Then the Israelites went and did this, they did just as the Lord had commanded Moses and Aaron.

²⁹ Now at midnight the Lord struck every firstborn male in the land of Egypt, from the firstborn of Pharaoh who sat on his throne to the firstborn of the prisoner who was in the dungeon, and every firstborn of the livestock. ³⁰ During the night Pharaoh got up, he along with all his officials and all the Egyptians, and there was a loud wailing throughout Egypt because there wasn't a house without someone dead. ³¹ He summoned Moses and Aaron during the night and said, "Get up, leave my people, both you and the Israelites, and go, worship the Lord as you have asked. ³² Take even your flocks and your herds as you asked, and leave, and this will also be a blessing to me."

³³ Now the Egyptians pressured the people in order to send them quickly out of the country, for they said, "We're all going to die!" ³⁴ So the people took their dough before it was leavened, with their kneading bowls wrapped up in their clothes on their shoulders. ³⁵ The Israelites acted on Moses' word and asked the Egyptians for silver and gold jewelry and for clothing. ³⁶ And the Lord gave the people such favor in the Egyptians' sight that they gave them what they requested. In this way they plundered the Egyptians.

PSALM 18:20-24

²⁰ The Lord rewarded me according
     to my righteousness;
   He repaid me according to the
     cleanness of my hands.
²¹ For I have kept the ways of the
     Lord
   and have not turned from my God
     to wickedness.
²² Indeed, I have kept all His
     ordinances in mind
   and have not disregarded His
     statutes.
²³ I was blameless toward Him
   and kept myself from sinning.
²⁴ So the Lord repaid me according
     to my righteousness,
   according to the cleanness of my
     hands in His sight.

PROVERBS 4:3-4

3 When I was a son with my father,
  tender and precious to my mother,
4 he taught me and said:
  "Your heart must hold on to my
    words.
Keep my commands and live.

MATTHEW 22:1-22

22 Once more Jesus spoke to them in parables: 2 "The kingdom of heaven may be compared to a king who gave a wedding banquet for his son. 3 He sent out his slaves to summon those invited to the banquet, but they didn't want to come. 4 Again, he sent out other slaves, and said, 'Tell those who are invited: Look, I've prepared my dinner; my oxen and fattened cattle have been slaughtered, and everything is ready. Come to the wedding banquet.'

5 "But they paid no attention and went away, one to his own farm, another to his business. 6 And the others seized his slaves, treated them outrageously and killed them. 7 The king was enraged, so he sent out his troops, destroyed those murderers, and burned down their city.

8 "Then he told his slaves, 'The banquet is ready, but those who were invited were not worthy. 9 Therefore, go to where the roads exit the city and invite everyone you find to the banquet.' 10 So those slaves went out on the roads and gathered everyone they found, both evil and good. The wedding banquet was filled with guests. 11 But when the king came in to view the guests, he saw a man there who was not dressed for a wedding. 12 So he said to him, 'Friend, how did you get in here without wedding clothes?' The man was speechless.

13 "Then the king told the attendants, 'Tie him up hand and foot, and throw him into the outer darkness, where there will be weeping and gnashing of teeth.'

14 "For many are invited, but few are chosen."

15 Then the Pharisees went and plotted how to trap Him by what He said. 16 They sent their disciples to Him, with the Herodians. "Teacher," they said, "we know that You are truthful and teach truthfully the way of God. You defer to no one, for You don't show partiality. 17 Tell us, therefore, what You think. Is it lawful to pay taxes to Caesar or not?"

18 But perceiving their malice, Jesus said, "Why are you testing Me, hypocrites? 19 Show Me the coin used for the tax." So they brought Him a denarius. 20 "Whose image and inscription is this?" He asked them.

21 "Caesar's," they said to Him.

Then He said to them, "Therefore, give back to Caesar the things that are Caesar's, and to God the things that are God's." 22 When they heard this, they were amazed. So they left Him and went away.

The Coal Miner

When I was a son with my father...he taught me and said:
"Your heart must hold on to my words."—PROVERBS 4:3-4

Some of you reading these lines may not have had the benefits of a good or extensive education. You may be deficient in your knowledge of many things. But here is the encouraging thing—none of these issues are important when it comes to the matter of defeating Satan.

I remember being present some years ago in a church in South Wales when a debate was held between a university professor and an ordinary coal miner. The subject was: "Is the Bible true?" The university professor presented his arguments in a clear fashion, and I remember feeling quite sorry for the miner as I envisaged some of the difficulties he might face when making his reply. After the professor had finished, the miner stood to his feet. And for over an hour, I witnessed one of the most amazing demonstrations of the Holy Spirit at work that I have ever seen in my life.

The miner began by asking everyone to bow their heads as he prayed a prayer which went something like this: "Lord, I have not had much education, but You know that I love Your Word and have spent my life searching its pages. Help me now to say something that will convince my friends here that Your Word is true." He then proceeded to demolish the arguments of the professor simply by quoting appropriate Scriptures without making even a simple comment.

When he finished, there was thunderous applause. The professor's well-articulated, highly intellectual arguments had been torn to pieces by the sharp edges of the sword of the Spirit— by that and by that alone.

Prayer

O Father, the more I hear, the more I want to hear. For I was created by Your Word, designed according to Your Word, and I can never remain content until I am indwelt with Your Word. Teach me even more. In Jesus' name. Amen.

Further Study

Jr 5:1-14; 23–29; Ps 119:105, 130; Heb 4:12
What was God's Word in Jeremiah's mouth?
What was it to the psalmist?

FEBRUARY 4

EXODUS 12:37–14:20

37 The Israelites traveled from Rameses to Succoth, about 600,000 soldiers on foot, besides their families. 38 An ethnically diverse crowd also went up with them, along with a huge number of livestock, both flocks and herds. 39 The people baked the dough they had brought out of Egypt into unleavened loaves, since it had no yeast; for when they had been driven out of Egypt they could not delay and had not prepared any provisions for themselves.

40 The time that the Israelites lived in Egypt was 430 years. 41 At the end of 430 years, on that same day, all the divisions of the LORD went out from the land of Egypt. 42 It was a night of vigil in honor of the LORD, because He would bring them out of the land of Egypt. This same night is in honor of the LORD, a night vigil for all the Israelites throughout their generations.

⁴³ The LORD said to Moses and Aaron, "This is the statute of the Passover: no foreigner may eat it. ⁴⁴ But any slave a man has purchased may eat it, after you have circumcised him. ⁴⁵ A temporary resident or hired hand may not eat the Passover. ⁴⁶ It is to be eaten in one house. You may not take any of the meat outside the house, and you may not break any of its bones. ⁴⁷ The whole community of Israel must celebrate it. ⁴⁸ If a foreigner resides with you and wants to celebrate the LORD's Passover, every male in his household must be circumcised, and then he may participate; he will become like a native of the land. But no uncircumcised person may eat it. ⁴⁹ The same law will apply to both the native and the foreigner who resides among you."

⁵⁰ Then all the Israelites did this, they did just as the LORD had commanded Moses and Aaron. ⁵¹ On that same day the LORD brought the Israelites out of the land of Egypt according to their military divisions.

13 The LORD spoke to Moses: ² "Consecrate every firstborn male to Me, the firstborn from every womb among the Israelites, both man and animal; it is Mine."

³ Then Moses said to the people, "Remember this day when you came out of Egypt, out of the place of slavery, for the LORD brought you out of here by the strength of His hand. Nothing leavened may be eaten. ⁴ Today, in the month of Abib, you are leaving. ⁵ When the LORD brings you into the land of the Canaanites, Hittites, Amorites, Hivites, and Jebusites, which He swore to your fathers that He would give you, a land flowing with milk and honey, you must carry out this ritual in this month. ⁶ For seven days you must eat unleavened bread, and on the seventh day there is to be a festival to the LORD. ⁷ Unleavened bread is to be eaten for those seven days. Nothing leavened may be found among you, and no yeast may be found among you in all your territory. ⁸ On that day explain to your son, 'This is because of what the LORD did for me

when I came out of Egypt.' ⁹ Let it serve as a sign for you on your hand and as a reminder on your forehead, so that the law of the LORD may be in your mouth; for the LORD brought you out of Egypt with a strong hand. ¹⁰ Keep this statute at its appointed time from year to year.

¹¹ "When the LORD brings you into the land of the Canaanites, as He swore to you and your fathers, and gives it to you, ¹² you are to present to the LORD every firstborn male of the womb. All firstborn offspring of the livestock you own that are males will be the LORD's. ¹³ You must redeem every firstborn of a donkey with a flock animal, but if you do not redeem it, break its neck. However, you must redeem every firstborn among your sons.

¹⁴ "In the future, when your son asks you, 'What does this mean?' say to him, 'By the strength of His hand the LORD brought us out of Egypt, out of the place of slavery. ¹⁵ When Pharaoh stubbornly refused to let us go, the LORD killed every firstborn male in the land of Egypt, from the firstborn of man to the firstborn of livestock. That is why I sacrifice to the LORD all the firstborn of the womb that are males, but I redeem all the firstborn of my sons.' ¹⁶ So let it be a sign on your hand and a symbol on your forehead, for the LORD brought us out of Egypt by the strength of His hand."

¹⁷ When Pharaoh let the people go, God did not lead them along the road to the land of the Philistines, even though it was nearby; for God said, "The people will change their minds and return to Egypt if they face war." ¹⁸ So He led the people around toward the Red Sea along the road of the wilderness. And the Israelites left the land of Egypt in battle formation.

¹⁹ Moses took the bones of Joseph with him, because Joseph had made the Israelites swear a solemn oath, saying, "God will certainly come to your aid; then you must take my bones with you from this place."

²⁰ They set out from Succoth and camped at Etham on the edge of the wilderness. ²¹ The LORD went ahead of

them in a pillar of cloud to lead them on their way during the day and in a pillar of fire to give them light at night, so that they could travel day or night. ²² The pillar of cloud by day and the pillar of fire by night never left its place in front of the people.

14 Then the LORD spoke to Moses: ² "Tell the Israelites to turn back and camp in front of Pi-hahiroth, between Migdol and the sea; you must camp in front of Baal-zephon, facing it by the sea. ³ Pharaoh will say of the Israelites: They are wandering around the land in confusion; the wilderness has boxed them in. ⁴ I will harden Pharaoh's heart so that he will pursue them. Then I will receive glory by means of Pharaoh and all his army, and the Egyptians will know that I am the LORD." So the Israelites did this.

⁵ When the king of Egypt was told that the people had fled, Pharaoh and his officials changed their minds about the people and said: "What have we done? We have released Israel from serving us." ⁶ So he got his chariot ready and took his troops with him; ⁷ he took 600 of the best chariots and all the rest of the chariots of Egypt, with officers in each one. ⁸ The LORD hardened the heart of Pharaoh king of Egypt, and he pursued the Israelites, who were going out triumphantly. ⁹ The Egyptians—all Pharaoh's horses and chariots, his horsemen, and his army—chased after them and caught up with them as they camped by the sea beside Pi-hahiroth, in front of Baal-zephon.

¹⁰ As Pharaoh approached, the Israelites looked up and saw the Egyptians coming after them. Then the Israelites were terrified and cried out to the LORD for help. ¹¹ They said to Moses: "Is it because there are no graves in Egypt that you took us to die in the wilderness? What have you done to us by bringing us out of Egypt? ¹² Isn't this what we told you in Egypt: Leave us alone so that we may serve the Egyptians? It would have been better for us to serve the Egyptians than to die in the wilderness."

¹³ But Moses said to the people, "Don't be afraid. Stand firm and see the LORD's salvation He will provide for you today; for the Egyptians you see today, you will never see again. ¹⁴ The LORD will fight for you; you must be quiet."

¹⁵ The LORD said to Moses, "Why are you crying out to Me? Tell the Israelites to break camp. ¹⁶ As for you, lift up your staff, stretch out your hand over the sea, and divide it so that the Israelites can go through the sea on dry ground. ¹⁷ I am going to harden the hearts of the Egyptians so that they will go in after them, and I will receive glory by means of Pharaoh, all his army, and his chariots and horsemen. ¹⁸ The Egyptians will know that I am the LORD when I receive glory through Pharaoh, his chariots, and his horsemen."

¹⁹ Then the Angel of God, who was going in front of the Israelite forces, moved and went behind them. The pillar of cloud moved from in front of them and stood behind them. ²⁰ It came between the Egyptian and Israelite forces. The cloud was there in the darkness, yet it lit up the night. So neither group came near the other all night long.

PSALM 18:25-29

²⁵ With the faithful You prove
    Yourself faithful;
  with the blameless man You prove
    Yourself blameless;
²⁶ with the pure You prove Yourself
    pure,
  but with the crooked You prove
    Yourself shrewd.
²⁷ For You rescue an afflicted
    people,
  but You humble those with
    haughty eyes.
²⁸ LORD, You light my lamp;
  my God illuminates my
    darkness.
²⁹ With You I can attack a barrier,
  and with my God I can leap over a
    wall.

PROVERBS 4:5-6

5 Get wisdom, get understanding;
don't forget or turn away from the
words of my mouth.
6 Don't abandon wisdom, and she
will watch over you;
love her, and she will guard you.

MATTHEW 22:23-46

23 The same day some Sadducees, who say there is no resurrection, came up to Him and questioned Him: 24 "Teacher, Moses said, **if a man dies, having no children, his brother is to marry his wife and raise up offspring for his brother.** 25 Now there were seven brothers among us. The first got married and died. Having no offspring, he left his wife to his brother. 26 The same happened to the second also, and the third, and so to all seven. 27 Then last of all the woman died. 28 Therefore, in the resurrection, whose wife will she be of the seven? For they all had married her."

29 Jesus answered them, "You are deceived, because you don't know the Scriptures or the power of God. 30 For in the resurrection they neither marry nor are given in marriage but are like angels in heaven. 31 Now concerning the resurrection of the dead, haven't you read what was spoken to you by God: 32 **I am the God of Abraham and the God of Isaac and the God of Jacob?** He is not the God of the dead, but of the living." 33 And when the crowds heard this, they were astonished at His teaching.

34 When the Pharisees heard that He had silenced the Sadducees, they came together in the same place. 35 And one of them, an expert in the law, asked a question to test Him: 36 "Teacher, which commandment in the law is the greatest?"

37 He said to him, "**Love the Lord your God with all your heart, with all your soul, and with all your mind.** 38 This is the greatest and most important commandment. 39 The second is like it: **Love your neighbor as yourself.** 40 All the Law and the Prophets depend on these two commandments."

41 While the Pharisees were together, Jesus questioned them, 42 "What do you think about the Messiah? Whose Son is He?"

"David's," they told Him.

43 He asked them, "How is it then that David, inspired by the Spirit, calls Him 'Lord':

44   The Lord declared to my Lord,
'Sit at My right hand
until I put Your enemies
under Your feet'?

45 "If David calls Him 'Lord,' how then can the Messiah be his Son" 46 No one was able to answer Him at all, and from that day no one dared to question Him any more.

The Need to Know

At the end of 430 years, on that same day, all the divisions of the LORD went out from the land of Egypt.—Exodus 12:41

The Bible is a veritable mine of information on the fact of God's faithfulness. More than 4,000 years ago He said: "As long as the earth endures, seedtime and harvest, cold and heat, summer and winter, and day and night will not cease" (Gn 8:22). Every year furnishes us with fresh evidence that He has not gone back on His Word.

In Genesis 15:13-14, God declared to Abram: "Know this for certain: Your offspring will be strangers in a land that does not belong to them; they will be enslaved and oppressed 400 years. However . . . afterwards they will go out with many possessions." Did that happen? Exodus 12:41 says: "At the end of 430 years, on that same day, all the divisions of the LORD went out from the land of Egypt."

The prophet Isaiah predicted that a virgin would conceive and bear a son whose name would be Immanuel (Is 7:14). Centuries later the prediction came to pass. In Galatians 4:4 we read: "But when the completion of the time came, God sent His Son, born of a woman."

I wish I had the space to take you through the pages of Scripture and show you how faithful God has been to His Word. But you have a Bible for yourself; study it. Read it to know God. This is the basis of our confidence in Him. And this is why the Bible fairly bulges with this great and gripping truth. The more of God's truth we pack into our souls, the better equipped we are for the road that lies ahead.

Prayer

Gracious and loving Father, the more I learn about Your nature and character, the more I want to know. Just these glimpses I am getting set my soul on fire to know You more intimately. Take me deeper, dear Lord. In Jesus' name. Amen.

Further Study

Mal 3:7; Ps 103:17; 102:27; Jms 1:1-17
What did the Lord declare to Israel?
How did James put it?

FEBRUARY 5

*E*XODUS 14:21–16:20

²¹ Then Moses stretched out his hand over the sea. The LORD drove the sea back with a powerful east wind all that night and turned the sea into dry land. So the waters were divided, ²² and the Israelites went through the sea on dry ground, with the waters like a wall to them on their right and their left.

²³ The Egyptians set out in pursuit—all Pharaoh's horses, his chariots, and his horsemen—and went into the sea after them. ²⁴ Then during the morning watch, the LORD looked down on the Egyptian forces from the pillar of fire and cloud, and threw them into confusion. ²⁵ He caused their chariot wheels to swerve and made them drive with difficulty. "Let's get away from Israel," the Egyptians said, "because the LORD is fighting for them against Egypt!"

²⁶ Then the LORD said to Moses, "Stretch out your hand over the sea so that the waters may come back on the Egyptians, on their chariots and horse-

men." ²⁷ So Moses stretched out his hand over the sea, and at daybreak the sea returned to its normal depth. While the Egyptians were trying to escape from it, the LORD overthrew them in the sea. ²⁸ The waters came back and covered the chariots and horsemen, the entire army of Pharaoh, that had gone after them into the sea. None of them survived.

²⁹ But the Israelites had walked through the sea on dry ground, with the waters like a wall to them on their right and their left. ³⁰ That day the LORD saved Israel from the power of the Egyptians, and Israel saw the Egyptians dead on the seashore. ³¹ When Israel saw the great power that the LORD used against the Egyptians, the people feared the LORD and believed in Him and in His servant Moses.

15 Then Moses and the Israelites sang this song to the LORD. They said:

I will sing to the LORD,
for He is highly exalted;
He has thrown the horse
and its rider into the sea.
² The LORD is my strength and my
song;
He has become my salvation.
This is my God, and I will praise
Him,
my father's God, and I will exalt
Him.
³ The LORD is a warrior;
Yahweh is His name.

⁴ He threw Pharaoh's chariots
and his army into the sea;
the elite of his officers
were drowned in the Red Sea.
⁵ The floods covered them;
they sank to the depths like a
stone.
⁶ LORD, Your right hand is glorious
in power.
LORD, Your right hand shattered
the enemy.
⁷ You overthrew Your adversaries
by Your great majesty.
You unleashed Your burning
wrath;

it consumed them like stubble.
⁸ The waters heaped up at the blast
of Your nostrils;
the currents stood firm like a
dam.
The watery depths congealed in
the heart of the sea.
⁹ The enemy said:
"I will pursue, I will overtake,
I will divide the spoil.
My desire will be gratified at their
expense.
I will unsheathe my sword;
my hand will destroy them."
¹⁰ But You blew with Your breath,
and the sea covered them.
They sank like lead
in the mighty waters.

¹¹ LORD, who is like You among the
gods?
Who is like You, glorious in
holiness,
revered with praises, performing
wonders?
¹² You stretched out Your right hand,
and the earth swallowed them.
¹³ You will lead the people
You have redeemed
with Your faithful love
You will guide them to Your holy
dwelling
with Your strength.

¹⁴ When the peoples hear, they will
shudder;
anguish will seize the inhabitants
of Philistia.
¹⁵ Then the chiefs of Edom will be
terrified;
trembling will seize the leaders of
Moab;
the inhabitants of Canaan will
panic;
¹⁶ and terror and dread will fall on
them.
They will be as still as a stone
because of Your powerful arm
until Your people pass by, LORD,
until the people whom You
purchased pass by.

¹⁷ You will bring them in and plant
them

on the mountain of Your
possession;
LORD, You have prepared the place
for Your dwelling;
Lord, Your hands have established
the sanctuary.
¹⁸ The LORD will reign forever and ever!

¹⁹ When Pharaoh's horses with his chariots and horsemen went into the sea, the LORD brought the waters of the sea back over them. But the Israelites walked through the sea on dry ground. ²⁰ Then Miriam the prophetess, Aaron's sister, took a tambourine in her hand, and all the women followed her with tambourines and dancing. ²¹ Miriam sang to them:

Sing to the LORD,
for He is highly exalted;
He has thrown the horse
and its rider into the sea.

²² Then Moses led Israel on from the Red Sea, and they went out to the Wilderness of Shur. They journeyed for three days in the wilderness without finding water. ²³ They came to Marah, but they could not drink the water at Marah because it was bitter—that is why it was named Marah. ²⁴ The people grumbled to Moses, "What are we going to drink?" ²⁵ So he cried out to the LORD, and the LORD showed him a tree. When he threw it into the water, the water became drinkable.

He made a statute and ordinance for them at Marah and He tested them there. ²⁶ He said, "If you will carefully obey the LORD your God, do what is right in His eyes, pay attention to His commands, and keep all His statutes, I will not inflict any illness on you I inflicted on the Egyptians. For I am the LORD who heals you."

²⁷ Then they came to Elim, where there were 12 springs of water and 70 date palms, and they camped there by the waters.

16 The entire Israelite community departed from Elim and came to the Wilderness of Sin, which is between Elim and Sinai, on the fifteenth day of the second month after they had left the land of Egypt. ² The entire Israelite community grumbled against Moses and Aaron in the wilderness. ³ The Israelites said to them, "If only we had died by the LORD's hand in the land of Egypt, when we sat by pots of meat and ate all the bread we wanted. Instead, you brought us into this wilderness to make this whole assembly die of hunger!"

⁴ Then the LORD said to Moses, "I am going to rain bread from heaven for you. The people are to go out each day and gather enough for that day. This way I will test them to see whether or not they will follow My instructions. ⁵ On the sixth day, when they prepare what they bring in, it will be twice as much as they gather on other days."

⁶ So Moses and Aaron said to all the Israelites: "This evening you will know that it was the LORD who brought you out of the land of Egypt; ⁷ in the morning you will see the LORD's glory because He has heard your complaints about Him. For who are we that you complain about us?" ⁸ Moses continued, "The LORD will give you meat to eat this evening and abundant bread in the morning, for He has heard the complaints that you are raising against Him. Who are we? Your complaints are not against us but against the LORD."

⁹ Then Moses told Aaron, "Say to the entire Israelite community, 'Come before the LORD, for He has heard your complaints.' " ¹⁰ As Aaron was speaking to the entire Israelite community, they turned toward the wilderness, and there, in a cloud, the LORD's glory appeared.

¹¹ The LORD spoke to Moses, ¹² "I have heard the complaints of the Israelites. Tell them: At twilight you will eat meat, and in the morning you will eat bread until you are full. Then you will know that I am the LORD your God."

¹³ So at evening quail came and covered the camp. In the morning there was a layer of dew all around the camp. ¹⁴ When the layer of dew evaporated, there on the desert surface were fine

flakes, as fine as frost on the ground. ¹⁵When the Israelites saw it, they asked one another, "What is it?" because they didn't know what it was.

Moses told them, "It is the bread the LORD has given you to eat. ¹⁶This is what the LORD has commanded: 'Gather as much of it as each person needs to eat. You may take two quarts per individual, according to the number of people each of you has in his tent.' "

¹⁷So the Israelites did this. Some gathered a lot, some a little. ¹⁸When they measured it by quarts, the person who gathered a lot had no surplus, and the person who gathered a little had no shortage. Each gathered as much as he needed to eat. ¹⁹Moses said to them, "No one is to let any of it remain until morning." ²⁰But they didn't listen to Moses; some people left part of it until morning, and it bred worms and smelled. Therefore Moses was angry with them.

*P*SALM 18:30-36

³⁰ God—His way is perfect;
the word of the LORD is pure.
He is a shield to all who take
refuge in Him.
³¹ For who is God besides the LORD?
And who is a rock? Only our God.
³² God—He clothes me with strength
and makes my way perfect.
³³ He makes my feet like the feet of
a deer
and sets me securely on the
heights.
³⁴ He trains my hands for war;
my arms can bend a bow of
bronze.
³⁵ You have given me the shield of
Your salvation;
Your right hand upholds me,
and Your humility exalts me.
³⁶ You widen a place beneath me for
my steps,
and my ankles do not give way.

*P*ROVERBS 4:7-9

⁷ Wisdom is supreme—so get
wisdom.

And whatever else you get, get
understanding.
⁸ Cherish her, and she will exalt
you;
if you embrace her, she will honor
you.
⁹ She will place a garland of grace
on your head;
she will give you a crown of
beauty."

*M*ATTHEW 23:1-22

23 Then Jesus spoke to the crowds and to His disciples: ²"The scribes and the Pharisees are seated in the chair of Moses. ³Therefore do whatever they tell you and observe it. But don't do what they do, because they don't practice what they teach. ⁴They tie up heavy loads that are hard to carry and put them on people's shoulders, but they themselves aren't willing to lift a finger to move them. ⁵They do everything to be observed by others: They enlarge their phylacteries and lengthen their tassels. ⁶They love the place of honor at banquets, the front seats in the synagogues, ⁷greetings in the marketplaces, and to be called 'Rabbi' by people.

⁸"But as for you, do not be called 'Rabbi,' because you have one Teacher, and you are all brothers. ⁹Do not call anyone on earth your father, because you have one Father, who is in heaven. ¹⁰And do not be called masters either, because you have one Master, the Messiah. ¹¹The greatest among you will be your servant. ¹²Whoever exalts himself will be humbled, and whoever humbles himself will be exalted.

¹³"But woe to you, scribes and Pharisees, hypocrites! You lock up the kingdom of heaven from people. For you don't go in, and you don't allow those entering to go in.

[¹⁴"Woe to you, scribes and Pharisees, hypocrites! You devour widows' houses and make long prayers just for show. This is why you will receive a harsher punishment.]

¹⁵"Woe to you, scribes and Pharisees,

hypocrites! You travel over land and sea to make one proselyte, and when he becomes one, you make him twice as fit for hell you are! ¹⁶ "Woe to you, blind guides, who say, 'Whoever takes an oath by the sanctuary, it means nothing. But whoever takes an oath by the gold of the sanctuary is bound by his oath.' ¹⁷ Blind fools! For which is greater, the gold or the sanctuary that sanctified the gold? ¹⁸ Also, 'Whoever takes an oath by the altar, it means nothing. But whoever takes an oath by the gift that is on it is bound by his oath.' ¹⁹ Blind people! For which is greater, the gift or the altar that sanctifies the gift? ²⁰ Therefore the one who takes an oath by the altar takes an oath by it and by everything on it. ²¹ The one who takes an oath by the sanctuary takes an oath by it and by Him who dwells in it. ²² And the one who takes an oath by heaven takes an oath by God's throne and by Him who sits on it.

Spiritually Sure-Footed

He makes my feet like the feet of a deer and sets me securely on the heights.—PSALM 18:33

In the book "Hinds' Feet on High Places", I read the story of a man who, while holidaying on a ranch in Wyoming, was given the use of one of its horses—the fastest he had ever ridden. One day a group of the ranch cowboys invited him to join them for a ride up into the mountains. As they climbed into the hills, they came to a dangerous ascent, at which point the foreman turned to the newcomer and said, "I think you would be well advised to take the longer but less dangerous trail to the top. Your horse is not dependable on the hills. Our horses are true climbers—their rear feet track exactly where their front feet are planted. Your horse has spent so many years on the plain that its rear feet could miss the track by inches, and one slip could mean serious injury—perhaps even death."

When I read those words, my thoughts turned immediately to the verse before us today, for no animal has such perfect correlation of its front and rear feet as the deer. When it leaps from rock to rock, its back feet land exactly where its front feet had been placed.

If we are to climb higher with God than we have ever gone before, then more is needed than just speed. We must know spiritual sure-footedness also. Let's determine we will let nothing stand in the way of making our feet like hinds' feet and climbing with God to the "high places."

Prayer

My Father and my God, hear my prayer as I begin perhaps a new chapter in my spiritual experience. Help me to climb higher with You than I have ever gone before, and do it not only with speed, but with sure-footedness also. In Jesus' name. Amen.

Further Study

Php 3:1-14; Is 54:2; Eph 3:17-19
What was the deep desire of Paul's heart?
What did he pray for the Ephesians?

FEBRUARY 6

EXODUS 16:21–18:27

²¹ They gathered it every morning. Each gathered as much as he needed to eat, but when the sun grew hot, it melted. ²² On the sixth day they gathered twice as much food, four quarts apiece, and all the leaders of the community came and reported this to Moses. ²³ He told them, "This is what the LORD has said: 'Tomorrow is a day of complete rest, a holy Sabbath to the LORD. Bake what you want to bake, and boil what you want to boil, and everything left over set aside to be kept until morning.' "

²⁴ So they set it aside until morning as Moses commanded, and it didn't smell or have any maggots in it. ²⁵ "Eat it today," Moses said, "because today is a Sabbath to the LORD. Today you won't find any in the field. ²⁶ For six days you may gather it, but on the seventh day, the Sabbath, there will be none."

²⁷ Yet on the seventh day some of the people went out to gather, but they did not find any. ²⁸ Then the LORD said to Moses, "How long will you refuse to keep My commands and instructions? ²⁹ Understand that the LORD has given you the Sabbath; therefore on the sixth day He will give you two days' worth of bread. Each of you stay where you are; no one is to leave his place on the seventh day." ³⁰ So the people rested on the seventh day.

³¹ The house of Israel named the substance manna. It resembled coriander seed, was white, and tasted like wafers made with honey. ³² Moses said, "This is what the LORD has commanded: 'Two quarts of it are to be preserved throughout your generations, so that they may see the bread I fed you in the wilderness when I brought you out of the land of Egypt.' "

³³ Moses told Aaron, "Take a container and put two quarts of manna in it. Then place it before the LORD to be preserved throughout your generations." ³⁴ As the LORD commanded Moses, Aaron placed it before the testimony to be preserved.

³⁵ The Israelites ate manna for 40 years, until they came to an inhabited land. They ate manna until they reached the border of the land of Canaan. ³⁶ (Two quarts are a tenth of an ephah.)

17 The entire Israelite community left the Wilderness of Sin, moving from one place to the next according to the LORD's command. They camped at Rephidim, but there was no water for the people to drink. ² So the people complained to Moses: "Give us water to drink."

"Why are you complaining to me?" Moses replied to them. "Why are you testing the LORD?"

³ But the people thirsted there for water, and grumbled against Moses. They said, "Why did you ever bring us out of Egypt to kill us and our children and our livestock with thirst?"

⁴Then Moses cried out to the LORD, "What should I do with these people? In a little while they will stone me!" ⁵The LORD answered Moses, "Go on ahead of the people and take some of the elders of Israel with you. Take the rod you struck the Nile with in your hand and go. ⁶I am going to stand there in front of you on the rock at Horeb; when you hit the rock, water will come out of it and the people will drink." Moses did this in the sight of the elders of Israel. ⁷He named the place Massah and Meribah because the Israelites complained, and because they tested the LORD, saying, "Is the LORD among us or not?"

⁸At Rephidim, Amalek came and fought against Israel. ⁹Moses said to Joshua, "Select some men for us, and go fight against Amalek. Tomorrow I will stand on the hilltop with God's staff in my hand." ¹⁰Joshua did as Moses had told him, and fought against Amalek, while Moses, Aaron, and Hur went up to the top of the hill. ¹¹While Moses held up his hand, Israel prevailed, but whenever he put his hand down, Amalek prevailed. ¹²When Moses' hands grew heavy, they took a stone and put it under him, and he sat down on it. Then Aaron and Hur supported his hands, one on one side and one on the other so that his hands remained steady until the sun went down. ¹³So Joshua defeated Amalek and his army with the sword.

¹⁴The LORD then said to Moses, "Write this down on a scroll as a reminder and recite it to Joshua: I will completely blot out the memory of Amalek under heaven." ¹⁵And Moses built an altar and named it, "The LORD Is My Banner." ¹⁶He said, "Indeed, my hand is lifted up toward the LORD's throne. The LORD will be at war with Amalek from generation to generation."

18 Moses' father-in-law Jethro, the priest of Midian, heard about everything that God had done for Moses and His people Israel, and how the LORD had brought Israel out of Egypt.

²Now Jethro, Moses' father-in-law, had taken in Zipporah, Moses' wife, after he had sent her back, ³along with her two sons, one of whom was named Gershom (because Moses had said, "I have been a stranger in a foreign land") ⁴and the other Eliezer (because he had said, "The God of my father was my helper and delivered me from Pharaoh's sword").

⁵Moses' father-in-law Jethro, along with Moses' wife and sons, came to him in the wilderness where he was camped at the mountain of God. ⁶He sent word to Moses, "I, your father-in-law Jethro, am coming to you with your wife and her two sons."

⁷So Moses went out to meet his father-in-law, bowed down, and then kissed him. They asked each other how they had been and went into the tent. ⁸Moses recounted to his father-in-law all that the LORD had done to Pharaoh and the Egyptians for Israel's sake, all the hardships that confronted them on the way, and how the LORD delivered them.

⁹Jethro rejoiced over all the good things the LORD had done for Israel when He rescued them from the Egyptians. ¹⁰"Blessed is the LORD," Jethro exclaimed, "who rescued you from Pharaoh and the power of the Egyptians, and snatched the people from the power of the Egyptians. ¹¹Now I know that the LORD is greater than all gods, because He did wonders at the time the Egyptians acted arrogantly against Israel."

¹²Then Jethro, Moses' father-in-law, brought a burnt offering and sacrifices to God, and Aaron came with all the elders of Israel to eat a meal with Moses' father-in-law in God's presence.

¹³The next day Moses sat down to judge the people, and they stood around Moses from morning until evening. ¹⁴When Moses' father-in-law saw everything he was doing for them he asked, "What is this thing you're doing for the people? Why are you alone sitting as judge, while all the people stand around you from morning until evening?" ¹⁵Moses replied to his father-in-law,

"Because the people come to me to inquire of God. ¹⁶Whenever they have a dispute, it comes to me, and I make a decision between one man and another. I teach them God's statutes and laws." ¹⁷"What you're doing is not good," Moses' father-in-law said to him. ¹⁸"You will certainly wear out both yourself and these people who are with you, because the task is too heavy for you. You can't do it alone. ¹⁹Now listen to me; I will give you some advice, and God be with you. You be the one to represent the people before God and bring their cases to Him. ²⁰Instruct them about the statutes and laws, and teach them the way to live and what they must do. ²¹But you should select from all the people able men, God-fearing, trustworthy, and hating bribes. Place them over the people as officials of thousands, hundreds, fifties, and tens. ²²They should judge the people at all times. Then they can bring you every important case but judge every minor case themselves. In this way you will lighten your load, and they will bear it with you. ²³If you do this, and God so directs you, you will be able to endure, and also all these people will be able to go home satisfied."

²⁴Moses listened to his father-in-law and did everything he said. ²⁵So Moses chose able men from all Israel and made them leaders over the people as officials of thousands, hundreds, fifties, and tens. ²⁶They judged the people at all times; the hard cases they would bring to Moses, but every minor case they would judge themselves.

²⁷Then Moses said goodbye to his father-in-law, and he journeyed to his own land.

PSALM 18:37-42

³⁷ I pursue my enemies and overtake them;
I do not turn back until they are wiped out.
³⁸ I crush them, and they cannot get up;
they fall beneath my feet.

³⁹ You have clothed me with strength for battle;
You subdue my adversaries beneath me.
⁴⁰ You have made my enemies retreat before me;
I annihilate those who hate me.
⁴¹ They cry for help, but there is no one to save them—
they cry to the LORD, but He does not answer them.
⁴² I pulverize them like dust before the wind;
I trample them like mud in the streets.

PROVERBS 4:10-13

¹⁰ Listen, my son. Accept my words, and you will live many years.
¹¹ I am teaching you the way of wisdom;
I am guiding you on straight paths.
¹² When you walk, your steps will not be hindered;
when you run, you will not stumble.
¹³ Hold on to instruction; don't let go.
Guard it, for it is your life.

MATTHEW 23:23-39

²³"Woe to you, scribes and Pharisees, hypocrites! You pay a tenth of mint, dill, and cumin, yet you have neglected the more important matters of the law—justice, mercy, and faith. These things should have been done without neglecting the others. ²⁴Blind guides! You strain out a gnat, yet gulp down a camel!

²⁵"Woe to you, scribes and Pharisees, hypocrites! You clean the outside of the cup and dish, but inside they are full of greed and self-indulgence! ²⁶Blind Pharisee! First clean the inside of the cup, so the outside of it may also become clean.

²⁷"Woe to you, scribes and Pharisees, hypocrites! You are like whitewashed tombs, which appear beautiful on the

outside, but inside are full of dead men's bones and every impurity. [28] In the same way, on the outside you seem righteous to people, but inside you are full of hypocrisy and lawlessness.

[29] "Woe to you, scribes and Pharisees, hypocrites! You build the tombs of the prophets and decorate the monuments of the righteous, [30] and you say, 'If we had lived in the days of our fathers, we wouldn't have taken part with them in shedding the prophets' blood.' [31] You therefore testify against yourselves that you are sons of those who murdered the prophets. [32] Fill up, then, the measure of your fathers' sins!

[33] "Snakes! Brood of vipers! How can you escape being condemned to hell? [34] This is why I am sending you prophets, sages, and scribes. Some of them you will kill and crucify, and some of them you will flog in your synagogues and hound from town to town. [35] So all the righteous blood shed on the earth will be charged to you, from the blood of righteous Abel to the blood of Zechariah, son of Berechiah, whom you murdered between the sanctuary and the altar. [36] I assure you: All these things will come on this generation!

[37] "Jerusalem, Jerusalem! The city who kills the prophets and stones those who are sent to her. How often I wanted to gather your children together, as a hen gathers her chicks under her wings, yet you were not willing! [38] See, your house is left to you desolate. [39] For I tell you, you will never see Me again until you say, **Blessed is He who comes in the name of the Lord!**"

No Pretense

You are like whitewashed tombs, which appear beautiful on the outside, but inside are full of dead men's bones and every impurity.—MATTHEW 23:27

The Pharisees of Jesus' day specialized in looking good. Sin was defined by them in terms of visible transgressions, and as long as they did nothing to violate the standards which they so carefully defined, they regarded themselves as being free from sin. And there can be little doubt about it—they were good performers. Their level of disciplined conformity to external expectations was very high. They impressed many by their performance, but there was someone they failed to impress—Jesus. He told them that they were nothing more than "whitewashed tombs" and called them "blind guides" (Mt 15:14).

In His rebuke to the Pharisees, our Lord established a principle that must guide us in our effort to become the people He wants us to be, and that principle is this—there must be no pretense. Christ's teaching seems to be that we can't make it as His followers unless we are willing to take an honest and straightforward look at what is going on beneath the surface of our lives. To look honestly at those parts of our being which we would rather not know about is not, as some would have it, a sign of morbid introspection but a sign of healthy spirituality.

Always remember, our Lord reserved His harshest criticism for those who, like the Pharisees, made pretense and denial into a trademark.

Prayer

O Father, You are boring deep—help me not to wriggle and squirm. Love me enough to overcome all my resistances, all my antipathies, and all my fears. For I don't just want to be a better person; I want to be a whole person. In Jesus' name. Amen.

Further Study

Col 2:1-20; Is 1:11-17; Gl 4:10
What did Paul bring to the Colossians' attention?
How similar was it to Isaiah's word centuries before?

FEBRUARY 7

Exodus 19:1–20:26

19 In the third month, on the same day of the month that the Israelites had left the land of Egypt, they entered the Wilderness of Sinai. ² After they departed from Rephidim, they entered the Wilderness of Sinai and camped in the wilderness, and Israel camped there in front of the mountain.

³ Moses went up the mountain to God, and the LORD called to him from the mountain: "This is what you must say to the house of Jacob, and explain to the Israelites: ⁴ You have seen what I did to the Egyptians and how I carried you on eagles' wings and brought you to Me. ⁵ Now if you will listen to Me and carefully keep My covenant, you will be My own possession out of all the peoples, although all the earth is Mine, ⁶ and you will be My kingdom of priests and My holy nation. These are the words that you are to say to the Israelites."

⁷ After Moses came back, He summoned the elders of the people, and put before them all these words that the LORD had commanded him. ⁸ Then all the people responded together, "We will do all that the LORD has spoken." So Moses brought the people's words back to the LORD.

⁹ The LORD said to Moses, "I am going to come to you in a dense cloud, so that the people will hear when I speak with you and will always believe you." Then Moses reported the people's words to the LORD. ¹⁰ And the LORD told Moses, "Go to the people and purify them today and tomorrow. They must wash their clothes ¹¹ and be prepared by the third day, for on the third day the LORD will come down on Mount Sinai in the sight of all the people. ¹² Put boundaries for the people all around the mountain and say: Be careful that you don't go up on the mountain or touch its base. Anyone who touches the mountain will be put to death. ¹³ No hand may touch him; instead he will be stoned or shot with arrows, neither animal or man will live. When the ram's horn sounds a long blast, they may go up the mountain."

¹⁴ Then Moses came down from the mountain to the people and consecrated them, and they washed their clothes.

¹⁵ He said to the people, "Be prepared by the third day. Do not have sexual relations with women."

¹⁶ On the third day, when morning came, there was thunder and lightning, a thick cloud on the mountain, and a loud trumpet sound, so that all the people in the camp shuddered. ¹⁷ Then Moses brought the people out of the camp to meet God, and they stood at the foot of the mountain. ¹⁸ Mount Sinai was completely enveloped in smoke because the LORD came down on it in fire. Its smoke went up like the smoke of a furnace, and the whole mountain shook violently. ¹⁹ As the sound of the trumpet grew louder and louder, Moses spoke and God answered him in the thunder.

²⁰ The LORD came down on Mount Sinai, at the top of the mountain. Then the LORD summoned Moses to the top of the mountain, and he went up. ²¹ The LORD directed Moses, "Go down and warn the people not to break through to see the LORD; otherwise many of them will die. ²² Even the priests who come near the LORD must purify themselves or the LORD will break out in anger against them."

²³ But Moses responded to the LORD, "The people cannot come up Mount Sinai, since You warned us: Put a boundary around the mountain and consider it holy." ²⁴ And the LORD replied to him, "Go down and come back with Aaron. But the priests and the people must not break through to come up to the LORD, or He will break out in anger against them." ²⁵ So Moses went down to the people and told them.

20 Then God spoke all these words:

² I am the LORD your God, who brought you out of the land of Egypt, out of the place of slavery. ³ Do not have other gods besides Me.

⁴ Do not make an idol for yourself, whether in the shape of anything in the heavens above or on the earth below or in the waters under the earth. ⁵ You must not bow down to them or worship them; for

I, the LORD your God, am a jealous God, punishing the children for the fathers' sin, to the third and fourth generations of those who hate Me, ⁶ but showing faithful love to a thousand generations of those who love Me and keep My commands.

⁷ Do not misuse the name of the LORD your God, because the LORD will punish anyone who misuses His name.

⁸ Remember to dedicate the Sabbath day: ⁹ You are to labor six days and do all your work, ¹⁰ but the seventh day is a Sabbath to the LORD your God. You must not do any work—you, your son or daughter, your male or female slave, your livestock, or the foreigner who is within your gates. ¹¹ For the LORD made the heavens and the earth, the sea, and everything in them in six days; then He rested on the seventh day. Therefore the LORD blessed the Sabbath day and declared it holy.

¹² Honor your father and your mother so that you may have a long life in the land that the LORD your God is giving you.

¹³ Do not murder.

¹⁴ Do not commit adultery.

¹⁵ Do not steal.

¹⁶ Do not give false testimony against your neighbor.

¹⁷ Do not covet your neighbor's house. Do not covet your neighbor's wife, his male or female slave, his ox or donkey, or anything that belongs to your neighbor.

¹⁸ All the people witnessed the thunder and lightning, the sound of the trumpet, and the mountain surrounded by smoke. When the people saw it they trembled and stood at a distance. ¹⁹ "You speak to us, and we will listen," they said to Moses, "but don't let God speak to us, or we will die."

²⁰ Moses responded to the people, "Don't be afraid, for God has come to test you, so that you will fear Him and will not sin." ²¹ And the people remained standing at a distance as Moses

approached the thick darkness where God was.

²² Then the LORD told Moses, "This is what you are to say to the Israelites: You have seen that I have spoken to you from heaven. ²³ You must not make gods of silver to rival Me; you must not make gods of gold for yourselves.

²⁴ "You must make an earthen altar for Me and sacrifice on it your burnt offerings and fellowship offerings, your sheep and goats, as well as your cattle. I will come to you and bless you in every place where I cause My name to be remembered. ²⁵ If you make a stone altar for Me, you must not build it out of cut stones. If you use your chisel on it, you will defile it. ²⁶ You must not go up to My altar on steps, so that your nakedness is not exposed on it.

PSALM 18:43-50

⁴³ You have freed me from the feuds
among the people;
You have appointed me the head
of nations;
a people I had not known serve
me.
⁴⁴ Foreigners submit to me
grudgingly;
as soon as they hear, they obey
me.
⁴⁵ Foreigners lose heart
and come trembling from their
fortifications.

⁴⁶ The LORD lives—may my rock be
praised!
The God of my salvation is
exalted.
⁴⁷ God—He gives me vengeance
and subdues peoples under me.
⁴⁸ He frees me from my enemies.
You exalt me above my
adversaries;
You rescue me from violent men.
⁴⁹ Therefore I will praise You, LORD,
among the nations;
I will sing about Your name.
⁵⁰ He gives great victories to His
king;
He shows loyalty to His anointed,

to David and his descendants
forever.

PROVERBS 4:14-17

¹⁴ Don't set foot on the path of the
wicked;
don't proceed in the way of evil
ones.
¹⁵ Avoid it; don't travel on it.
Turn away from it, and pass it by.
¹⁶ For they can't sleep unless they
have done evil;
they are robbed of sleep unless
they make someone stumble.
¹⁷ They eat the bread of wickedness
and drink the wine of violence.

MATTHEW 24:1-14

24 As Jesus left and was going out of the temple complex, His disciples came up and called His attention to the temple buildings. ² Then He replied to them, "Don't you see all these things? I assure you: Not one stone will be left here on another that will not be thrown down!"

³ While He was sitting on the Mount of Olives, the disciples approached Him privately and said, "Tell us, when will these things happen? And what is the sign of Your coming and of the end of the age?"

⁴ Then Jesus replied to them: "Watch out that no one deceives you. ⁵ For many will come in My name, saying, 'I am the Messiah,' and they will deceive many. ⁶ You are going to hear of wars and rumors of wars. See that you are not alarmed, because these things must take place, but the end is not yet. ⁷ For nation will rise up against nation, and kingdom against kingdom. There will be famines and earthquakes in various places. ⁸ All these events are the beginning of birth pains.

⁹ "Then they will hand you over for persecution, and they will kill you. You will be hated by all nations because of My name. ¹⁰ Then many will take offense, betray one another and hate one another. ¹¹ Many false prophets will rise

up and deceive many. ¹² Because lawlessness will multiply, the love of many will grow cold. ¹³ But the one who endures to the end will be delivered.

¹⁴ This good news of the kingdom will be proclaimed in all the world as a testimony to all nations. And then the end will come.

Three Forms of Dishonesty

Do not give false testimony against your neighbor.—EXODUS 20:16

The suggestion that even mature Christians can inwardly resist truth might shock some, but the real issue is—is it true?

Among the popular defenses we use to resist truth, the first is projection. This occurs when we are to blame for something, but we project the blame onto someone else so that we can feel more comfortable about ourselves. It may sound a simple thing, but all dishonesty is destructive—even simple dishonesty.

Then take the defense of denial. How many times do we refuse to face the fact that we may be angry about something, and when someone says: "Why are you angry?" we reply with bristling hostility: "I'm not angry!" We fail to recognize what others can plainly see. And denial, no matter how one looks at it, is a form of inner deceit.

Another dishonest defense is rationalization. We are guilty of this whenever we persuade ourselves that something is what it is not. C. S. Lewis points out that when our neighbor does something wrong, it is obviously because he or she is "bad," while if we do something wrong it is only because we did not get enough sleep, or someone gave us a rough time, or our blood chemistry is at fault, and so on.

All of these defense mechanisms deprive us of inner honesty, and apart from hindering our spiritual growth they also lower our defenses against Satan. This is why over and over again in Scripture, we are bidden to open up to honesty. The more honest we can be, the more spiritually powerful and effective we can be.

Prayer

Lord Jesus, help me open up to honesty. For I see that the more honest I am, the more authority I can wield over Satan. I want to be able to say, as You said: "The ruler of the world is coming. He has no power over me." (Jn 14:30 HCSB) I ask for Your name's sake. Amen.

Further Study

Rv 3:14-22; Jms 1:26; Gl 6:3
How did the Laodiceans see themselves?
How did God see them?

FEBRUARY 8

*E*XODUS 21:1–22:20

21 "These are the ordinances that you must set before them:
² "When you buy a Hebrew slave, he is to serve for six years; then in the seventh he is to leave as a free man without paying anything. ³ If he arrives alone, he is to leave alone; if he arrives with a wife, his wife is to leave with him. ⁴ If his master gives him a wife and she bears him sons or daughters, the wife and her children belong to her master, and the man must leave alone.

⁵ "But if the slave declares: 'I love my master, my wife, and my children,' I do not want to leave as a free man,' ⁶ his master is to bring him to the judges and then bring him to the door or doorpost. His master must pierce his ear with an awl, and he will serve his master for life.

⁷ "When a man sells his daughter as a slave, she is not to leave as the male slaves do. ⁸ If she is displeasing to her master, who chose her for himself, then he must let her be redeemed. He has no right to sell her to foreigners because he has acted treacherously toward her. ⁹ Or if he chooses her for his son, he must deal with her according to the customary treatment of daughters. ¹⁰ If he takes an additional wife, he must not reduce the food, clothing, or marital rights of the first wife. ¹¹ And if he does not do these three things for her, she may leave free of charge, without any exchange of money.

¹² "Whoever strikes a person so that he dies must be put to death. ¹³ But if he didn't intend any harm, and yet God caused it to happen by his hand, I will appoint a place for you where he may flee. ¹⁴ If a person willfully acts against his neighbor to murder him by scheming, you must take him from My altar to be put to death.

¹⁵ "Whoever strikes his father or his mother must be put to death.

¹⁶ "Whoever kidnaps a person must be put to death, whether he sells him or the person is found in his possession.

¹⁷ "Whoever curses his father or his mother must be put to death.

¹⁸ "When men quarrel and one strikes the other with a stone or fist, and the injured man does not die but is confined to bed, ¹⁹ if he can later get up and walk around outside leaning on his staff, then the one who struck him will be exempt from punishment. Nevertheless, he must pay for his lost work time and provide for his complete recovery.

²⁰ "When a man strikes his male or female slave with a rod, and the slave dies under his abuse, the owner must be punished. ²¹ However, if the slave can stand up after a day or two, the owner should not be punished because he is his owner's property.

²² "When men get in a fight, and hit a pregnant woman so that her children are born prematurely, but there is no injury, the one who hit her must be fined as the woman's husband demands from him, and he must pay according to judicial assessment. ²³ If there is an injury, then you must give life for life, ²⁴ eye for eye, tooth for tooth, hand for hand, foot for foot, ²⁵ burn for burn, bruise for bruise, wound for wound.

²⁶ "When a man strikes the eye of his male or female slave and destroys it, he must let the slave go free in compensation for his eye. ²⁷ If he knocks out the tooth of his male or female slave, he must let the slave go free in compensation for his tooth.

²⁸ "When an ox gores a man or a woman to death, the ox must be stoned, and its meat may not be eaten, but the ox's owner is innocent. ²⁹ However, if the ox was in the habit of goring, and its owner has been warned yet does not re-

strain it, and it kills a man or a woman, the ox must be stoned, and its owner must also be put to death. [30] If instead a ransom is demanded of him, he can pay a redemption price for his life in the full amount demanded from him. [31] If it gores a son or a daughter, he is to be dealt with according to this same law. [32] If the ox gores a male or female slave, he must give 30 shekels of silver to the slave's master, and the ox must be stoned.

[33] "When a man uncovers a pit or digs a pit, and does not cover it, and an ox or a donkey falls into it, [34] the owner of the pit must give compensation; he must pay money to its owner, but the dead animal will become his.

[35] "When a man's ox injures his neighbor's ox and it dies, they must sell the live ox and divide its proceeds; they must also divide the dead animal. [36] If, however, it is known that the ox was in the habit of goring, yet its owner has not restrained it, he must compensate fully, ox for ox; the dead animal will become his.

22 "When a man steals an ox or a sheep and butchers it or sells it, he must repay five cattle for the ox or four sheep for the sheep. [2] If a thief is caught in the act of breaking in, and he is beaten to death, no one is guilty of bloodshed. [3] But if this happens after sunrise, there is guilt of bloodshed. A thief must make full restitution. If he is unable, he is to be sold because of his theft. [4] If what was stolen—whether ox, donkey, or sheep—is actually found alive in his possession, he must repay double.

[5] "When a man lets a field or vineyard be grazed in, and then allows his animals to go and graze in someone else's field, he must repay with the best of his own field or vineyard.

[6] "When a fire gets out of control, spreads to thornbushes, and consumes stacks of cut grain, standing grain, or a field, the one who started the fire must make full restitution for what was burned.

[7] "When a man gives his neighbor money or goods to keep, but they are stolen from that person's house, the thief, if caught, must repay double. [8] If the thief is not caught, the owner of the house must present himself to the judges to determine whether or not he has taken his neighbor's property. [9] In any case of wrongdoing involving an ox, a donkey, a sheep, a garment, or anything else lost, and someone claims: That's mine, the case between the two parties is to come before the judges. The one the judges condemn must repay double to his neighbor.

[10] "When a man gives his neighbor a donkey, an ox, a sheep, or any other animal to care for, but it dies, is injured, or is stolen, while no one is watching, [11] there must be an oath before the LORD between the two of them to determine whether or not he has taken his neighbor's property. Its owner must accept the oath, and the other man does not have to make restitution. [12] But if, in fact, the animal was stolen from his custody, he must make restitution to its owner. [13] If it was actually torn apart by a wild animal, he is to bring it as evidence; he does not have to make restitution for the torn carcass.

[14] "When a man borrows an animal from his neighbor, and it is injured or dies while its owner is not there with it, the man must make full restitution. [15] If its owner is there with it, the man does not have to make restitution. If it was rented, the loss is covered by its rental price.

[16] "When a man seduces a virgin who was not promised in marriage, and he has sexual relations with her, he must certainly pay the bridal price for her to be his wife. [17] If her father absolutely refuses to give her to him, he must pay an amount in silver equal to the bridal price for virgins.

[18] "You must not allow a sorceress to live.

[19] "Whoever has sexual intercourse with an animal must be put to death.

[20] "Whoever sacrifices to any gods, except the LORD alone, is to be set apart for destruction.

PSALM 19:1-6

1 The heavens declare the glory of
God,
and the sky proclaims the work of
His hands.
2 Day after day they pour out
speech;
night after night they
communicate knowledge.
3 There is no speech; there are no
words;
their voice is not heard.
4 Their message has gone out to all
the earth,
and their words to the ends of the
inhabited world.

In the heavens He has pitched a
tent for the sun.
5 It is like a groom coming from the
bridal chamber;
it rejoices like an athlete running
a course.
6 It rises from one end of the
heavens
and circles to their other end;
nothing is hidden from its heat.

PROVERBS 4:18-19

18 The path of the righteous is like
the light of dawn,
shining brighter and brighter until
midday.
19 But the way of the wicked is like
the darkest gloom;
they don't know what makes them
stumble.

MATTHEW 24:15-35

15 "So when you see the abomination
that causes desolation, spoken of by
the prophet Daniel, standing in the
holy place" (let the reader understand),
16 "then those in Judea must flee to the
mountains! 17 A man on the housetop
must not come down to get things out
of his house. 18 And a man in the field
must not go back to get his clothes.
19 Woe to pregnant women and nursing
mothers in those days! 20 Pray that your
escape may not be in winter or on a
Sabbath. 21 For at that time there will be
great tribulation, the kind that hasn't
taken place from the beginning of the
world until now and never will again!
22 Unless those days were limited, no
one would survive. But those days will
be limited because of the elect.
23 "If anyone tells you then, 'Look,
here is the Messiah!' or, 'Over here!' do
not believe it! 24 False messiahs and
false prophets will arise and perform
great signs and wonders to lead astray, if
possible, even the elect. 25 Take note: I
have told you in advance. 26 So if they
tell you, 'Look, he's in the wilderness!'
don't go out; 'Look, he's in the inner
rooms!' do not believe it. 27 For as the
lightning comes from the east and
flashes as far as the west, so will be the
coming of the Son of Man. 28 Wherever
the carcass is, there the vultures will
gather.
29 "Immediately after the tribulation
of those days:

The sun will be darkened,
and the moon will not shed
its light;
the stars will fall from the sky,
and the celestial powers
will be shaken.

30 "Then the sign of the Son of Man will
appear in the sky, and then all the peoples of the earth will mourn; and they
will see the Son of Man coming on the
clouds of heaven with power and great
glory. 31 He will send out His angels
with a loud trumpet, and they will
gather His elect from the four winds,
from one end of the sky to the other.
32 "Now learn this parable from the
fig tree: As soon as its branch becomes
tender and sprouts leaves, you know
that summer is near. 33 In the same way,
when you see all these things, recognize
that He is near—at the door! 34 I assure
you: This generation will certainly not
pass away until all these things take
place. 35 Heaven and earth will pass
away, but My words will never pass
away.

The Universe Proclaims

The heavens declare the glory of God.

——PSALM 19:1

We must endeavor, in line with our Master's directive in the Lord's Prayer, to focus our gaze on the majesty of God. The greater the degree in which God becomes fixed in our gaze, the more realistically we will be able to evaluate the events that go on around us here on earth.

In today's passage the psalmist tells us that one way we can focus on the greatness of God is to consider His handiwork in creation. All around us in this wonderful world, we see evidences of His sublime sufficiency. Consider, for example, the vastness of the universe. Scientists tell us that in relation to the myriads of other celestial bodies in outer space, the planet we inhabit is like a tiny speck of dust in a huge railway station in relation to all the other specks of dust around it, or like a single grain of sand among all the sand on all the seashores of the world. They tell us also that if the earth were to fall out of its orbit and spin away into space, it would create no more disturbance than the dropping of a pea into the Pacific Ocean!

Such word pictures, inadequate as they are, do nevertheless help us form some idea of the greatness and power of our God. Who can meditate on the vastness of the universe without experiencing an expansion in their conception of the majesty of God? Why did God construct the universe on such a grand scale? My conclusion is: He did it to show us that He is gloriously sufficient, unchangingly adequate, and abidingly faithful. How wonderful to contemplate such creative enormity!

Prayer

God, what a fool I am to think that my resources might run dry. Help me to live in light of the fact that my demand will never exceed Your supply. You are the Enough. Amen.

Further Study

Mt 6:19-34; Lk 12:24; Ps 45:1-17
How did Jesus focus our attention on God's goodness?
Of whom does the psalmist give us a picture?

FEBRUARY 9

*E*XODUS 22:21–24:18

²¹ "You must not exploit a foreign resident or oppress him, since you were foreigners in the land of Egypt. ²² "You must not mistreat any widow or fatherless child. ²³ If you do mistreat them, they will no doubt cry to Me, and I will certainly hear their cry. ²⁴ My anger will burn, and I will kill you with the sword; then your wives will be widows and your children fatherless.

²⁵ "If you lend money to My people— to the poor person among you, you must not be like a moneylender to him; you must not charge him interest. ²⁶ "If you ever take your neighbor's cloak as collateral, return it to him before sunset. ²⁷ For it is his only covering; it is the clothing for his body. What will he sleep in? And if he cries out to Me, I will listen because I am compassionate.

²⁸ "You must not blaspheme God or curse a leader among your people.

²⁹ "You must not hold back offerings from your harvest or your vats. Give Me the firstborn of your sons. ³⁰ Do the same with your cattle and your flock. Let them stay with their mothers for seven days, but on the eighth day you are to give them to Me.

³¹ "Be My holy people. You must not eat the meat of a mauled animal found in the field; throw it to the dogs.

23 "You must not spread a false report. Do not join the wicked to be a malicious witness.

² "You must not follow a crowd in wrongdoing. Do not testify in a lawsuit and go along with a crowd to pervert justice. ³ Do not show favoritism to a poor person in his lawsuit.

⁴ "If you come across your enemy's stray ox or donkey, you must return it to him.

⁵ "If you see the donkey of someone who hates you lying helpless under its load, and you want to refrain from helping it, you must help with it.

⁶ "You must not deny justice to the poor among you in his lawsuit. ⁷ Stay far away from a false accusation. Do not kill the innocent and the just, because I will not justify the guilty. ⁸ You must not take a bribe, for a bribe blinds the clearsighted and corrupts the words of the righteous. ⁹ You must not oppress a foreign resident; you yourselves know how it feels to be a foreigner because you were foreigners in the land of Egypt.

¹⁰ "Sow your land for six years and gather its produce. ¹¹ But during the seventh year you are to let it rest and leave it uncultivated, so that the poor among your people may eat from it and the wild animals may consume what they leave. Do the same with your vineyard and your olive grove.

¹² "Do your work for six days but rest on the seventh day so that your ox and your donkey may rest, and the son of your female slave as well as the foreign resident may be refreshed.

¹³ "Pay strict attention to everything I have said to you. You must not invoke the names of other gods; they must not be heard on your lips.

¹⁴ "Celebrate a festival in My honor three times a year. ¹⁵ Observe the Festival of Unleavened Bread. As I commanded you, you are to eat unleavened bread for seven days at the appointed time in the month of Abib, because you came out of Egypt in that month. No one is to appear before Me empty-handed. ¹⁶ Also observe the Festival of Harvest with the firstfruits of your produce from what you sow in the field, and observe the Festival of Ingathering at the end of the year, when you gather your produce from the field. ¹⁷ Three times a year all your males are to appear before the Lord GOD.

[18] "You must not offer the blood of My sacrifices with anything leavened. The fat of My festival offering must not remain until morning.

[19] "Bring the best of the firstfruits of your land to the house of the LORD your God.

"You must not boil a young goat in its mother's milk.

[20] "I am going to send an Angel before you to protect you on the way and bring you to the place I have prepared. [21] Be attentive to Him and listen to His voice. Do not defy Him, because He will not forgive your acts of rebellion, for My name is in Him. [22] But if you will carefully obey Him and do everything I say, then I will be an enemy to your enemies and a foe to your foes. [23] For My Angel will go before you and bring you to the land of the Amorites, Hittites, Perizzites, Canaanites, Hivites, and Jebusites, and I will wipe them out. [24] You must not bow down to their gods or worship them. Do not imitate their practices. Instead, demolish them and smash their sacred pillars to pieces. [25] Worship the LORD your God, and He will bless your bread and your water. I will take away your illnesses. [26] No woman will miscarry or be barren in your land. I will give you the full number of your days.

[27] "I will cause the people ahead of you to feel terror and throw into confusion all the nations you come to. I will make all your enemies turn their backs to you in retreat. [28] I will send the hornet in front of you, and it will drive the Hivites, Canaanites, and Hittites away from you. [29] I will not drive them out ahead of you in a single year; otherwise, the land would become desolate, and wild animals would multiply against you. [30] I will drive them out little by little ahead of you until you have become numerous and take possession of the land. [31] I will set your borders from the Red Sea to the Mediterranean Sea, and from the wilderness to the Euphrates River. For I will place the inhabitants of the land under your control, and you will drive them out ahead of you. [32] You must not make a covenant with them or their gods. [33] They must not remain in your land, or else they will make you sin against Me. If you worship their gods, it will be a snare for you."

24 Then He said to Moses, "Go up to the LORD, you and Aaron, Nadab, and Abihu, and 70 of Israel's elders, and bow in worship at a distance. [2] Moses alone is to approach the LORD, but the others are not to approach, and the people are not to go up with him."

[3] Moses came and told the people all the commands of the LORD and all the ordinances. Then all the people responded with a single voice, "We will do everything that the LORD has commanded." [4] And Moses wrote down all the words of the LORD. He rose early the next morning and set up an altar and 12 pillars for the 12 tribes of Israel at the base of the mountain. [5] Then he sent out young Israelite men, and they offered burnt offerings and sacrificed bulls as fellowship offerings to the LORD. [6] Moses took half the blood and set it in basins; the other half of the blood he sprinkled on the altar. [7] He then took the covenant scroll and read it aloud to the people. They responded, "We will do and obey everything that the LORD has commanded."

[8] Moses took the blood, sprinkled it on the people, and said, "This is the blood of the covenant that the LORD has made with you concerning all these words."

[9] Then Moses went up with Aaron, Nadab, and Abihu, and 70 of Israel's elders, [10] and they saw the God of Israel. Beneath His feet was something like a pavement made of sapphire stone, as clear as the sky itself. [11] God did not harm the Israelite nobles; they saw Him, and they ate and drank.

[12] The LORD said to Moses, "Come up to Me on the mountain and stay there so that I may give you the stone tablets with the law and commands I have written for their instruction."

[13] So Moses arose with his assistant Joshua, and went up the mountain of God. [14] He told the elders, "Wait here

for us until we return to you. Aaron and Hur are here with you. Whoever has a dispute should go to them." ¹⁵ When Moses went up the mountain, the cloud covered it. ¹⁶ The glory of the LORD settled on Mount Sinai, and the cloud covered it for six days. On the seventh day He called to Moses from the cloud. ¹⁷ The appearance of the LORD's glory to the Israelites was like a consuming fire on the mountaintop. ¹⁸ Moses entered the cloud as he went up the mountain, and he remained on the mountain 40 days and 40 nights.

*P*SALM 19:7-14

⁷ The instruction of the LORD is
    perfect, reviving the soul;
  the testimony of the LORD is
    trustworthy, making the
    inexperienced wise.
⁸ The precepts of the LORD are
    right, making the heart glad;
  the commandment of the LORD is
    radiant, making the eyes light
    up.
⁹ The fear of the LORD is pure,
    enduring forever;
  the ordinances of the LORD are
    reliable and altogether
    righteous.
¹⁰ They are more desirable than
    gold—than an abundance of
    pure gold;
  and sweeter than honey—than
    honey dripping from the
    comb.
¹¹ In addition, Your servant is
    warned by them;
  there is great reward in keeping
    them.
¹² Who perceives his unintentional
    sins?
  Cleanse me from my hidden
    faults.
¹³ Moreover, keep Your servant from
    willful sins;
  do not let them rule over me.
  Then I will be innocent,
  and cleansed from blatant
    rebellion.

¹⁴ May the words of my mouth and
    the meditation of my heart
  be acceptable to You,
  LORD, my rock and my Redeemer.

*P*ROVERBS 4:20-22

²⁰ My son, pay attention to my
    words;
  listen closely to my sayings.
²¹ Don't lose sight of them;
  keep them within your heart.
²² For they are life to those who find
    them,
  and health to one's whole body.

*M*ATTHEW 24:36-51

³⁶ "Now concerning that day and hour no one knows—neither the angels in heaven, nor the Son—except the Father only. ³⁷ As the days of Noah were, so the coming of the Son of Man will be. ³⁸ For in those days before the flood they were eating and drinking, marrying and giving in marriage, until the day Noah boarded the ark. ³⁹ They didn't know until the flood came and swept them all away. So this is the way the coming of the Son of Man will be: ⁴⁰ Then two men will be in the field: one will be taken and one left. ⁴¹ Two women will be grinding at the mill: one will be taken and one left. ⁴² Therefore be alert, since you don't know what day your Lord is coming. ⁴³ But know this: If the homeowner had known what time the thief was coming, he would have stayed alert and not let his house be broken into. ⁴⁴ This is why you also must be ready, because the Son of Man is coming at an hour you do not expect.

⁴⁵ "Who then is a faithful and sensible slave, whom his master has put in charge of his household, to give them food at the proper time? ⁴⁶ That slave whose master finds him working when he comes will be rewarded. ⁴⁷ I assure you: He will put him in charge of all his possessions. ⁴⁸ But if that wicked slave says in his heart, 'My master is delayed,' ⁴⁹ and starts to beat his fellow slaves, and eats and drinks with drunkards,

⁵⁰ that slave's master will come on a day he does not expect and at an hour he does not know. ⁵¹ He will cut him to pieces and assign him a place with the hypocrites. In that place there will be weeping and gnashing of teeth.

"The Second Thought"

My son, pay attention to my words; listen closely to my sayings. Don't lose sight of them; keep them within your heart.—Proverbs 4:20-21

"To get the best out of life," said Pascal, "great matters have to be given a second thought." Meditation is just that—giving biblical truths a second thought. If you have been thinking that the way to get the best out of the Bible is by reading it, studying it, or memorizing it, then I urge you to think again. I have found that the way to get the best out of the Bible is by meditating on it.

Reading, studying, and memorizing the Bible are, in the main, intellectual exercises which bring spiritual results. Meditation is not primarily an intellectual exercise but a devotional exercise, a way by which the Word of God is carried into the spiritual digestive system so that it can be translated into spiritual nourishment and energy.

Be careful that you do not misunderstand me here. I am not saying that reading, studying, and memorizing the Bible are not important spiritual exercises. I strongly advocate them. But—it is possible to do all these things and yet fail to draw from the Scriptures the spiritual nourishment that God has put within them. This comes largely from meditation.

To ensure that this matter is crystal clear, let's go over it again: meditation is the process by which we take a text, thought, or phrase from the Word of God and roll it around in our mind, passing it backward and forward, letting it go out of conscious thought, bringing it back again into consciousness, prodding it, absorbing it, admiring it over and over again until its inherent power pervades our whole personality. God has gone into His Word, and God has to come out of it. Meditation is the way.

Prayer

O Father, if great matters need a second thought, then help me to slow down and take time to meditate on the truths that are contained in Your precious Word. For Jesus' sake. Amen.

Further Study

Col 3:1-16; Dt 6:6; Php 4:8; Jr 15:16
What does the word "dwell" mean?
How did Jeremiah put it?

FEBRUARY 10

EXODUS 25:1–26:14

25 The LORD spoke to Moses: [2] "Tell the Israelites to take an offering for Me. You are to take My offering from everyone whose heart stirs him to give. [3] This is the offering you are to receive from them: gold, silver, and bronze; [4] blue, purple, and scarlet yarn; fine linen and goat hair; [5] ram skins dyed red and manatee skins; acacia wood; [6] oil for the light; spices for the anointing oil and for the fragrant incense; [7] and onyx along with other gemstones for mounting on the ephod and breastpiece.

[8] "They are to make a sanctuary for Me so that I may dwell among them. [9] You must make it according to all that I show you—the design of the tabernacle as well as the design of all its furnishings."

[10] "They are to make an ark of acacia wood, 45 inches long, 27 inches wide, and 27 inches high. [11] Overlay it with pure gold; overlay it both inside and out. Also make a gold molding all around it. [12] Cast four gold rings for it and place them on its four feet, two rings on one side and two rings on the other side. [13] Make poles of acacia wood and overlay them with gold. [14] Insert the poles into the rings on the sides of the ark in order to carry the ark with them. [15] The poles are to remain in the rings of the ark; they must not be removed from it. [16] Put the tablets of the testimony that I will give you into the ark. [17] Make a mercy seat of pure gold, 45 inches long and 27 inches wide. [18] Make two cherubim of gold; make them of hammered work at the two ends of the mercy seat. [19] Make one cherub at one end and one cherub at the other end. Make the cherubim of one piece with the mercy seat at its two ends. [20] The cherubim are to have wings spread out above, covering the mercy seat with their wings, and are to face one another. The faces of the cherubim should be toward the mercy seat. [21] Set the mercy seat on top of the ark and put the testimony that I will give you into the ark. [22] I will meet with you there above the mercy seat, between the two cherubim that are over the ark of the testimony; I will speak with you from there about all that I command you regarding the Israelites.

[23] "You are to construct a table of acacia wood, 36 inches long, 18 inches wide, and 27 inches high. [24] Overlay it with pure gold and make a gold molding all around it. [25] Make a three-inch frame all around it and make a gold molding for it all around its frame. [26] Make four gold rings for it, and attach the rings to the four corners at its four legs. [27] The rings should be next to the frame as holders for the poles to carry the table. [28] Make the poles of acacia wood and overlay them with gold so that the table can be carried by them. [29] You are also to make its plates and cups, as well as its pitchers and bowls for pouring drink offerings. Make them out of pure gold. [30] Put the bread of the Presence on the table before Me at all times.

[31] "You are to make a lampstand out of pure, hammered gold. It is to be made of one piece: its base and shaft, its ornamental cups, and its calyxes and petals. [32] Six branches are to extend from its sides, three branches of the lampstand from one side and three branches of the lampstand from the other side. [33] There are to be three cups shaped like almond blossoms, each with a calyx and petals, on the first branch, and three cups shaped like almond blossoms, each with a calyx and petals, on the next branch. It is to be this way for the six branches that extend from the lampstand. [34] There are to be four cups shaped like almond blossoms on the

lampstand shaft along with its calyxes and petals. ³⁵ For the six branches that extend from the lampstand, a calyx must be under the first pair of branches from it, a calyx under the second pair of branches from it, and a calyx under the third pair of branches from it. ³⁶ Their calyxes and branches are to be of one piece. All of it is to be a single hammered piece of pure gold.

³⁷ "Make seven lamps on it. Its lamps are to be set up so they illuminate the area in front of it. ³⁸ Its snuffers and firepans must be of pure gold. ³⁹ The lampstand with all these utensils is to be made from 75 pounds of pure gold. ⁴⁰ Be careful to make everything according to the model of them you have been shown on the mountain.

26 "You are to construct the tabernacle itself with 10 curtains. You must make them of finely spun linen, and blue, purple, and scarlet yarn, with a design of cherubim worked into them. ² The length of each curtain should be 42 feet, and the width of each curtain six feet; all the curtains are to have the same measurements. ³ Five of the curtains should be joined together, and the other five curtains joined together. ⁴ Make loops of blue yarn on the edge of the last curtain in the first set, and do the same on the edge of the outermost curtain in the second set. ⁵ Make 50 loops on the one curtain and make 50 loops on the edge of the curtain in the second set, so that the loops line up together. ⁶ Also make 50 gold clasps and join the curtains together with the clasps, so that the tabernacle may be a single unit.

⁷ "You are to make curtains of goat hair for a tent over the tabernacle; make 11 of these curtains. ⁸ The length of each curtain should be 45 feet and the width of each curtain six feet. All 11 curtains are to have the same measurements. ⁹ Join five of the curtains by themselves, and the other six curtains by themselves. Then fold the sixth curtain double at the front of the tent. ¹⁰ Make 50 loops on the edge of the one curtain, the outermost in the first set,

and make 50 loops on the edge of the corresponding curtain of the second set. ¹¹ Make 50 bronze clasps; put the clasps through the loops and join the tent together so that it is a single unit. ¹² As for the flap that is left over from the tent curtains, the leftover half curtain is to hang down over the back of the tabernacle. ¹³ The half yard on one side and the half yard on the other of what is left over along the length of the tent curtains should be hanging down over the sides of the tabernacle on either side to cover it. ¹⁴ Make a covering for the tent from ram skins dyed red, and a covering of manatee skins on top of that.

𝒫SALM 20:1-9

¹ May the LORD answer you in a day
   of trouble;
  may the name of Jacob's God
   protect you.
² May He send you help from the
   sanctuary
  and sustain you from Zion.
³ May He remember all your
   offerings
  and accept your burnt offering.
                                    Selah

⁴ May He give you what your heart
   desires
  and fulfill your whole purpose.
⁵ Let us shout for joy at your victory
  and lift the banner in the name of
   our God.
  May the LORD fulfill all your
   requests.

⁶ Now I know that the LORD gives
   victory to His anointed;
  He will answer him from His holy
   heaven
  with mighty victories from His
   right hand.
⁷ Some take pride in a chariot, and
   others in horses,
  but we take pride in the name of
   the LORD our God.
⁸ They collapse and fall,
  but we rise and stand firm.

9 LORD, give victory to the king!
May He answer us on the day that
we call.

PROVERBS 4:23-24

23 Guard your heart above all else,
for it is the source of life.
24 Don't let your mouth speak
dishonestly,
and don't let your lips talk
deviously.

MATTHEW 25:1-13

25 "Then the kingdom of heaven will be like 10 virgins who took their lamps and went out to meet the groom. 2 Five of them were foolish and five were sensible. 3 When the foolish took their lamps, they didn't take oil with them. 4 But the sensible ones took oil in their flasks with their lamps. 5 Since the groom was delayed, they all became drowsy and fell asleep.

6 "In the middle of the night there was a shout: 'Here's the groom! Come out to meet him.'

7 "Then all those virgins got up and trimmed their lamps. 8 But the foolish ones said to the sensible ones, 'Give us some of your oil, because our lamps are going out.'

9 "The sensible ones answered, 'No, there won't be enough for us and for you. Go instead to those who sell, and buy oil for yourselves.'

10 "When they had gone to buy some, the groom arrived. Then those who were ready went in with him to the wedding banquet, and the door was shut.

11 "Later the rest of the virgins also came and said, 'Master, master, open up for us!'

12 "But he replied, 'I assure you: I do not know you!'

13 "Therefore be alert, because you don't know either the day or the hour.

Not Just What You Say

Guard your heart above all else, for it is the source of life.—PROVERBS 4:23

I am convinced that one of the major reasons why so many of us fail to receive from God the things which we ought to be receiving lies in the fact that our hearts and our minds are not properly correlated.

Do you find yourself continually praying for things you never receive? I don't mean things about which there may be some doubt, but things you definitely know the Almighty longs to give you—love, joy, peace, wisdom, patience, and so on. Maybe your mind is asking for one thing and your heart another. You see, it is possible to want something with the mind which is not supported by the heart. The mind is a much easier part of the personality to deal with than the heart, but, as our text for today states: "Guard your heart . . . for it is the source of life."

We can approach God with our minds and think that because we have a clear idea of what we want, God will give it to us, but the heart may contain hidden doubts which prevent us from being fully integrated people. We fail to receive because we are not asking out of a fully integrated personality. As someone has put it: "God does not just answer prayer—He answers you." Those who wish to receive from God the things He delights to give ought always to

remember that who we are is just as important (if not more so) than what we ask. God is not just listening to our words; He is listening to us.

Prayer

O Father, the more I meditate on the need for heart and mind to be in perfect coordination, the more I am set on fire to become a fully integrated person. I know You are eagerly reaching down to me; help me to be as eager to reach up to You. Amen.

Further Study

Mt 15:1-20; Pr 3:5; 23:7; Lk 8:45
What did Isaiah prophesy?
How did Jesus respond to Peter's request?

FEBRUARY 11

*E*XODUS 26:15–28:14

[15] "You are to make planks of acacia wood for the tabernacle. [16] The length of each plank is to be 15 feet, and the width of each plank 27 inches. [17] Each plank must be connected together with two tenons. Do the same for all the planks of the tabernacle. [18] Make the planks for the tabernacle as follows: 20 planks for the south side, [19] and make 40 silver bases under the 20 planks, two bases under the first plank for its two tenons, and two bases under the next plank for its two tenons; [20] 20 planks for the second side of the tabernacle, the north side, [21] along with their 40 silver bases, two bases under the first plank and two bases under each plank; [22] and make six planks for the west side of the tabernacle. [23] Make two additional planks for the two back corners of the tabernacle. [24] They are to be paired at the bottom, and joined together at the top in a single ring. So it should be for both of them; they will serve as the two corners. [25] There are to be eight planks with their silver bases: 16 bases; two bases under the first plank and two bases under each plank.

[26] "You are to make five crossbars of acacia wood for the planks on one side of the tabernacle, [27] five crossbars for the planks on the other side of the tabernacle, and five crossbars for the planks of the back side of the tabernacle on the west. [28] The central crossbar is to run through the middle of the planks from one end to the other. [29] Then overlay the planks with gold, and make their rings of gold as the holders for the crossbars. Also overlay the crossbars with gold. [30] You are to set up the tabernacle according to the plan for it that you have been shown on the mountain.

[31] "You are to make a veil of blue, purple, and scarlet yarn, and finely spun

linen with a design of cherubim worked into it. ³²Hang it on four gold-plated posts of acacia wood that have gold hooks and that stand on four silver bases. ³³Hang the veil under the clasps and bring the ark of the testimony there behind the veil, so the veil will make a separation for you between the holy place and the most holy place. ³⁴Put the mercy seat on the ark of the testimony in the holy place. ³⁵Place the table outside the veil and the lampstand on the south side of the tabernacle, opposite the table; put the table on the north side.

³⁶"For the entrance to the tent you are to make a screen embroidered with blue, purple, and scarlet yarn, and finely spun linen. ³⁷Make five posts of acacia wood for the screen and overlay them with gold; their hooks are to be gold, and you are to cast five bronze bases for them.

27 "You are to construct the altar of acacia wood. The altar must be square, seven and a half feet long, and seven and a half feet wide; it must be four and a half feet high. ²Make horns for it on its four corners; the horns are to be of one piece. Overlay it with bronze. ³Make its pots for removing ashes, and its shovels, basins, meat forks, and firepans; make all its utensils of bronze. ⁴Construct a grate for it of bronze mesh, and make four bronze rings on the mesh at its four corners. ⁵Set it below, under the altar's ledge, so that the mesh comes halfway up the altar. ⁶Then make poles for the altar, poles of acacia wood, and overlay them with bronze. ⁷The poles are to be inserted into the rings, so that the poles are on two sides of the altar when it is carried. ⁸Construct the altar with boards so that it is hollow. They are to make it just as it was shown to you on the mountain.

⁹"You are to make the courtyard for the tabernacle. Make the hangings on the south of the courtyard out of finely spun linen, 150 feet long on that side. ¹⁰There are to be 20 posts and 20 bronze bases. The hooks and bands of the posts must be silver. ¹¹Then make the hangings on the north side 150 feet long. There are to be 20 posts and 20 bronze bases. The hooks and bands of the posts must be silver. ¹²Make the hangings of the courtyard on the west side 75 feet long, including their 10 posts and 10 bases. ¹³Make the hangings of the courtyard on the east side toward the sunrise 75 feet. ¹⁴Make the hangings on one side of the gate 22 and a half feet, including their three posts and their three bases. ¹⁵And make the hangings on the other side 22 and a half feet, including their three posts and their three bases. ¹⁶The gate of the courtyard is to have a thirty-foot screen embroidered with blue, purple, and scarlet yarn, and finely spun linen. It is to have four posts including their four bases.

¹⁷"All the posts around the courtyard are to be banded with silver and have silver hooks and bronze bases. ¹⁸The length of the courtyard is to be 150 feet, the width 75 feet at each end, and the height seven and a half feet, all of it made of finely spun linen. The bases of the posts must be bronze. ¹⁹All the tools of the tabernacle for every use and all its tent pegs as well as all the tent pegs of the courtyard are to be made of bronze.

²⁰"You are to command the Israelites to bring you pure oil from crushed olives for the light, in order to keep the lamp burning continually. ²¹In the tent of meeting outside the veil that is in front of the testimony, Aaron and his sons are to tend the lamp from evening until morning before the LORD. This is to be a permanent statute for the Israelites throughout their generations.

28 "Have your brother Aaron, with his sons, come to you from the Israelites to serve Me as priest—Aaron, his sons Nadab and Abihu, Eleazar and Ithamar. ²Make holy garments for your brother Aaron, for glory and beauty. ³You are to instruct all the skilled craftsmen, whom I have filled with a spirit of wisdom, to make Aaron's garments for consecrating him to serve Me as priest. ⁴ These are the garments that they must make: a breastpiece, an ephod, a robe, a specially woven tunic, a turban, and a sash. They are to make holy garments for your brother Aaron and his sons so that they may serve Me as priests. ⁵ They should use gold; blue, purple, and scarlet yarn; and fine linen.

⁶ "They are to make the ephod of finely spun linen embroidered with gold, and with blue, purple, and scarlet yarn. ⁷ It must have two shoulder pieces attached to its two edges so that it can be joined together. ⁸ The artistically woven waistband that is on the ephod must be of one piece, according to the same workmanship of gold, of blue, purple, and scarlet yarn, and of finely spun linen.

⁹ "Take two onyx stones and engrave on them the names of Israel's sons: ¹⁰ six of their names on the first stone and the remaining six names on the second stone, in the order of their birth. ¹¹ Engrave the two stones with the names of Israel's sons as a gem cutter engraves a seal. Mount them, surrounded with gold filigree settings. ¹² Fasten both stones on the shoulder pieces of the ephod as memorial stones for the Israelites. Aaron will carry their names on his two shoulders before the LORD as a reminder. ¹³ Fashion gold filigree settings ¹⁴ and two chains of pure gold; you will make them of braided cord work, and attach the cord chains to the settings.

PSALM 21:1-7

¹ LORD, the king finds joy in Your
    strength.
  How greatly he rejoices in Your
    victory!
² You have given him his heart's
    desire
  and have not denied the request
    of his lips.   *Selah*
³ For You meet him with rich
    blessings;
  You place a crown of pure gold on
    his head.
⁴ He asked You for life, and You
    gave it to him—

length of days forever and ever.
⁵ His glory is great through Your
    victory;
  You confer majesty and splendor
    on him.
⁶ You give him blessings forever;
  You cheer him with joy in Your
    presence.
⁷ For the king relies on the LORD;
  through the faithful love of the
    Most High he is not shaken.

PROVERBS 4:25-27

²⁵ Let your eyes look forward;
   fix your gaze straight ahead.
²⁶ Carefully consider the path for
     your feet,
   and all your ways will be
     established.
²⁷ Don't turn to the right or to the
     left;
   keep your feet away from evil.

MATTHEW 25:14-30

¹⁴ "For it is just like a man going on a journey. He called his own slaves and turned over his possessions to them. ¹⁵ To one he gave five talents; to another, two; and to another, one—to each according to his own ability. Then he went on a journey. Immediately ¹⁶ the man who had received five talents went, put them to work, and earned five more. ¹⁷ In the same way the man with two earned two more. ¹⁸ But the man who had received one talent went off, dug a hole in the ground, and hid his master's money.

¹⁹ "After a long time the master of those slaves came and settled accounts with them. ²⁰ The man who had received five talents approached, presented five more talents, and said, 'Master, you gave me five talents. Look, I've earned five more talents.'

²¹ "His master said to him, 'Well done, good and faithful slave! You were faithful over a few things; I will put you in charge of many things. Share your master's joy!'

²² "Then the man with two talents

also approached. He said, 'Master, you gave me two talents. Look, I've earned two more talents.'

²³ "His master said to him, 'Well done, good and faithful slave! You were faithful over a few things; I will put you in charge of many things. Share your master's joy!'

²⁴ "Then the man who had received one talent also approached and said, 'Master, I know you. You're a difficult man, reaping where you haven't sown and gathering where you haven't scattered seed. ²⁵ So I was afraid and went off and hid your talent in the ground. Look, you have what is yours.'

²⁶ "But his master replied to him, 'You evil, lazy slave! If you knew that I reap where I haven't sown and gather where I haven't scattered, ²⁷ then you should have deposited my money with the bankers. And when I returned I would have received my money back with interest.

²⁸ " 'So take the talent from him and give it to the one who has 10 talents. ²⁹ For to everyone who has, more will be given, and he will have more than enough. But from the one who does not have, even what he has will be taken away from him. ³⁰ And throw this good-for-nothing slave into the outer darkness. In that place there will be weeping and gnashing of teeth.'

Don't Go on His Ground

Let your eyes look forward;
fix your gaze straight ahead.—Proverbs 4:25

Today we look at the issue of sexual experience and its need to be kept within marriage. Some temptations cannot be avoided; some, however, can. Anatole France has a story in which God and the devil are talking of a beautiful young girl. God asks: "How dare you tempt such a lovely creature as that?" The devil replies: "Well, she came on to my ground." R. W. Everrood tells this story: A young man seeking his fortune was traveling across an oasis at which a beautiful girl sat spinning on a loom. He asked for a drink and she said, "Certainly, providing you let me put these threads around you that I am spinning." He agreed, thinking he could easily brush away the thin gossamer threads as one would brush away a spider's web. After drinking the water, he fell asleep and awoke to find himself tied by thick, strong cords. And what was more, the beautiful young girl had changed into a disgusting and ugly hag.

The best way to deal with temptation is not to go toward it. Paul's advice to young Timothy was this: "Run from these things" (1 Tm 6:11). John Ruskin says: "No one can honestly ask to be delivered from temptation unless he has honestly and firmly determined to do the best he can to keep out of it." My advice to every unmarried man and woman reading these lines—and married people, too—is this: Keep out of the devil's territory. Don't go on to his ground.

Prayer

O God, make me alert to the dangers that beset my path, and when I move toward them unsuspectingly, grant that all the warning bells may ring within my heart. I know You will do Your part; help me do mine. In Jesus' name I ask it. Amen.

Further Study

1 Th 4:1-12; Heb 13:4; Eph 5:1-5
What instructions did Paul give concerning God's will?
What characteristics did Paul say are "proper for saints"?

FEBRUARY 12

EXODUS 28:15–29:25

¹⁵ "You are to make an embroidered breastpiece for decisions. Make it with the same workmanship as the ephod; make it of gold, of blue, purple, and scarlet yarn, and of finely spun linen. ¹⁶ It must be square and folded double, nine inches long and nine inches wide. ¹⁷ Place a setting of gemstones on it, four rows of stones:

The first row should be
a row of carnelian, topaz, and
emerald;
¹⁸ the second row,
a turquoise, a sapphire, and a diamond;
¹⁹ the third row,
a jacinth, an agate, and an
amethyst;
²⁰ and the fourth row,
a beryl, an onyx, and a jasper.

They should be adorned with gold filigree in their settings. ²¹ The 12 stones are to correspond to the names of Israel's sons. Each stone must be engraved like a seal, with one of the names of the 12 tribes.
²² "You are to make braided chains of pure gold cord work for the breastpiece.

²³ Fashion two gold rings for the breastpiece and attach them to its two corners. ²⁴ Then attach the two gold cords to the two gold rings at the corners of the breastpiece. ²⁵ Attach the other ends of the two cords to the two filigree settings and in this way attach them to the ephod's shoulder pieces in the front. ²⁶ Make two other gold rings and put them at the two other corners of the breastpiece on the edge that is next to the inner border of the ephod. ²⁷ Make two more gold rings and attach them to the bottom of the ephod's two shoulder pieces on its front, close to its seam, and above the ephod's woven waistband. ²⁸ The craftsmen are to tie the breastpiece from its rings to the rings of the ephod with a cord of blue yarn, so that the breastpiece is above the ephod's waistband and does not come loose from the ephod.
²⁹ "Whenever he enters the sanctuary, Aaron is to carry the names of Israel's sons over his heart on the breastpiece for decisions, as a continual reminder before the LORD. ³⁰ Place the Urim and Thummim in the breastpiece for decisions, so that they will also be over Aaron's heart whenever he comes before the LORD. Aaron will continually carry the means of decisions for the

Israelites over his heart before the LORD. ³¹ "You are to make the robe of the ephod entirely of blue yarn. ³² There should be an opening at its top in the center of it. Around the opening, there should be a woven collar with an opening like that for body armor so that it does not tear. ³³ Make pomegranates of blue, purple, and scarlet yarn on its lower hem and all around it. Put gold bells between them all the way around, ³⁴ so that gold bells and pomegranates alternate around the lower hem of the robe. ³⁵ The robe must be worn by Aaron whenever he ministers, and its sound will be heard when he enters the sanctuary before the LORD and when he exits, so that he does not die.

³⁶ "You are to make a plate of pure gold and engrave it, like the engraving of a seal:

HOLY TO THE LORD

³⁷ Fasten it to a cord of blue yarn so it can be placed on the turban; the plate is to be on the front of the turban. ³⁸ It will be on Aaron's forehead so that Aaron may bear the guilt connected with the holy offerings that the Israelites consecrate as all their holy gifts. It is always to be on his forehead, so that they may find acceptance with the LORD.

³⁹ "You are to weave the tunic from fine linen, make a turban of fine linen, and make an embroidered sash. ⁴⁰ Make tunics, sashes, and headbands for Aaron's sons to give them glory and beauty. ⁴¹ Put these on your brother Aaron and his sons; then anoint, ordain, and consecrate them, so that they may serve Me as priests. ⁴² Make them linen undergarments to cover their naked bodies; they must extend from the waist to the thighs. ⁴³ These must be worn by Aaron and his sons whenever they enter the tent of meeting or approach the altar to minister in the sanctuary area, so that they do not incur guilt and die. This is to be a permanent statute for Aaron and for his descendants after him.

29 "This is what you are to do for them to consecrate them to serve Me as priests. Take a young bull and two unblemished rams, ² with unleavened bread, unleavened cakes mixed with oil, and unleavened wafers coated with oil. Make them out of fine wheat flour, ³ put them in a basket, and bring them in the basket, along with the bull and two rams. ⁴ Bring Aaron and his sons to the entrance to the tent of meeting and wash them with water. ⁵ Then take the garments and clothe Aaron with the tunic, the robe for the ephod, the ephod itself, and the breastpiece; fasten the ephod on him with its woven waistband. ⁶ Put the turban on his head and place the holy diadem on the turban. ⁷ Take the anointing oil, pour it on his head, and anoint him. ⁸ You must also bring his sons, clothe them with tunics, ⁹ fasten headbands on them, and tie sashes around both Aaron and his sons. The priesthood is to be theirs by a permanent statute. This is the way you will ordain Aaron and his sons.

¹⁰ "You are to bring the bull to the front of the tent of meeting, and Aaron and his sons must lay their hands on the bull's head. ¹¹ Slaughter the bull before the LORD at the entrance to the tent of meeting. ¹² Take some of the bull's blood and apply it to the horns of the altar with your finger; then pour out all the rest of the blood at the base of the altar. ¹³ Take all the fat that covers the entrails, the fatty lobe of the liver, and the two kidneys with the fat on them, and burn them on the altar. ¹⁴ But burn up the bull's flesh, its hide, and its dung outside the camp; it is a sin offering.

¹⁵ "Take one ram, and Aaron and his sons are to lay their hands on the ram's head. ¹⁶ You are to slaughter the ram, take its blood, and sprinkle it on all sides of the altar. ¹⁷ Cut the ram into pieces. Wash its entrails and shanks, and place them with its head and its pieces on the altar. ¹⁸ Then burn the whole ram on the altar; it is a burnt offering to the LORD. It is a pleasing aroma, a fire offering to the LORD.

¹⁹ "You are to take the second ram, and Aaron and his sons must lay their

hands on the ram's head. ²⁰ Slaughter the ram, take some of its blood, and put it on Aaron's right earlobe, on his sons' right earlobes, on the thumbs of their right hands, and on the big toes of their right feet. Sprinkle the remaining blood on all sides of the altar. ²¹ Take some of the blood that is on the altar and some of the anointing oil, and sprinkle them on Aaron and his garments, as well as on his sons and their garments. In this way, he and his garments will become holy, as well as his sons and their garments.

²² "Take the fat from the ram, the fat tail, the fat covering the entrails, the fatty lobe of the liver, the two kidneys and the fat on them, and the right thigh (since this is a ram for ordination); ²³ take one loaf of bread, one cake of bread made with oil, and one wafer from the basket of unleavened bread that is before the LORD; ²⁴ and put all of them in the hands of Aaron and his sons and wave them as a presentation offering before the LORD. ²⁵ Take them from their hands and burn them on the altar on top of the burnt offering, as a pleasing aroma before the LORD; it is a fire offering to the LORD.

PSALM 21:8-13

8 Your hand will capture all your
      enemies;
    your right hand will seize those
      who hate you.
9 You will make them burn like a
      fiery furnace when you
      appear;
    the LORD will engulf them in His
      wrath,
    and fire will devour them.
10 You will wipe their descendants
      from the earth
    and their offspring from the
      human race.
11 Though they intend to harm you
    and devise a wicked plan, they
      will not prevail.
12 Instead, you will put them to flight
    when you aim your bow at their
      faces.

13 Be exalted, LORD, in Your strength;
    we will sing and praise Your
      might.

PROVERBS 5:1-2

5 My son, pay attention to my
    wisdom;
  listen closely to my understanding
2 so that you may maintain
      discretion
    and your lips safeguard
      knowledge.

MATTHEW 25:31–26:5

³¹ "When the Son of Man comes in His glory, and all the angels with Him, then He will sit on the throne of His glory. ³² All the nations will be gathered before Him, and He will separate them one from another, just as a shepherd separates the sheep from the goats. ³³ He will put the sheep on His right, and the goats on the left. ³⁴ Then the King will say to those on His right, 'Come, you who are blessed by My Father, inherit the kingdom prepared for you from the foundation of the world.

35 For I was hungry
      and you gave Me something
        to eat;
    I was thirsty
      and you gave Me something
        to drink;
    I was a stranger
      and you took Me in;
36 I was naked and you clothed Me;
    I was sick
      and you took care of Me;
    I was in prison
      and you visited Me.'

³⁷ "Then the righteous will answer Him, 'Lord, when did we see You hungry and feed You, or thirsty and give You something to drink? ³⁸ When did we see You a stranger and take You in, or without clothes and clothe You? ³⁹ When did we see You sick, or in prison, and visit You?'

[40] "And the King will answer them, 'I assure you: Whatever you did for one of the least of these brothers of Mine, you did for Me.' [41] Then He will also say to those on the left, 'Depart from Me, you who are cursed, into the eternal fire prepared for the Devil and his angels!

[42] For I was hungry
and you gave Me nothing to eat;
I was thirsty
and you gave Me nothing
      to drink;
[43] I was a stranger
and you didn't take Me in;
I was naked
and you didn't clothe Me,
sick and in prison
and you didn't take care of Me.'

[44] "Then they too will answer, 'Lord, when did we see You hungry, or thirsty, or a stranger, or without clothes, or sick, or in prison, and not help You?'

[45] "Then He will answer them, 'I assure you: Whatever you did not do for one of the least of these, you did not do for Me either.'

[46] "And they will go away into eternal punishment, but the righteous into eternal life."

26 When Jesus had finished saying all this, He told His disciples, [2] "You know that the Passover takes place after two days, and the Son of Man will be handed over to be crucified."

[3] Then the chief priests and the elders of the people assembled in the palace of the high priest, who was called Caiaphas, [4] and they conspired to arrest Jesus in a treacherous way and kill Him. [5] "Not during the festival," they said, "so there won't be rioting among the people."

The Great Peril of the Saints

Whatever you did for one of the least of these brothers of Mine, you did for Me.—MATTHEW 25:40

How does kindness grow in us? It depends on how deeply we live in God. Some Christians set out to be kind, but kindness which is the fruit of the Spirit is not the result of self-effort but comes from abiding in Christ. The Christian abides in Christ and the fruit grows and ripens of its own accord.

The kindest Christians are those who have no ambition to be kind and hold no such thought. This is not to say that they do not desire to be kind, but they do not try to manufacture their kindness. Consumed with a longing to be more like Jesus every day, their thought is not on their personal sanctity but on how they can reflect their Lord. They come across as people who were so self-forgetful that it could be said of them what was said of Samuel Barnett of Toynbee Hall: "He forgot himself even to the extent of forgetting that he had forgotten."

The great peril of the Christian life is that we may become selfish in our consuming longing to be unselfish. Only as our roots go down daily into God through prayer and meditation in His Word can we be kept secure from the temptation to focus on growth for its own sake—rather than for His sake. The person whose kindness is an appetite for praise gives up when the praise does not come. And they give up more quickly still if people say: "What are you getting out of this yourself?" The Christian whose kindness flows out of his relationship with God never gives up. He just can't help being kind.

Prayer

O Father, help me to spend time with You so that in the legislature of my heart You may write the law of kindness. Help me to come under its sway forever. Amen.

Further Study

2 Co 9:1-6; Dt 15:7-8; Ps 41:1; Ac 20:35
How are we to sow?
Of what did Paul remind the Ephesian elders?

FEBRUARY 13

EXODUS 29:26–30:38

26 "Take the breast from the ram of Aaron's ordination and wave it as a presentation offering before the LORD; it is to be your portion. 27 Consecrate for Aaron and his sons the breast of the presentation offering that is waved and the thigh of the contribution that is lifted up from the ram of ordination. 28 This will belong to Aaron and his sons as a regular portion from the Israelites, for it is a contribution. It will be the Israelites' contribution from their fellowship sacrifices, their contribution to the LORD.

29 "The holy garments that belong to Aaron are to belong to his sons after him, so that they can be anointed and ordained in them. 30 Any priest who is one of his sons and who succeeds him and enters the tent of meeting to minister in the sanctuary must wear them for seven days.

31 "You are to take the ram of ordination and boil its flesh in a holy place. 32 Aaron and his sons are to eat the meat of the ram and the bread that is in the basket at the entrance to the tent of meeting. 33 They must eat those things by which atonement was made at the time of their ordination and consecration. An unauthorized person must not eat them, for these things are holy. 34 If any of the meat of ordination or any of the bread is left until morning, burn up what is left over. It must not be eaten because it is holy.

35 "This is what you are to do for Aaron and his sons based on all I have commanded you. Ordain them for seven days. 36 Sacrifice a bull as a sin offering each day for atonement. Purify the altar when you make atonement for it, and anoint it in order to consecrate it. 37 For seven days you must make atonement for the altar and consecrate it. The altar will become especially holy; whatever touches the altar will become holy.

38 "This is what you are to offer regularly on the altar every day: two year-old lambs. 39 In the morning offer one lamb, and at twilight offer the other lamb. 40 With the first lamb offer two quarts of fine flour mixed with one quart of crushed olive oil, and a drink offering of one quart of wine. 41 You are to offer

the second lamb at twilight. Offer a grain offering and a drink offering with it, like the one in the morning, as a pleasing aroma, a fire offering to the LORD. ⁴²This will be a regular burnt offering throughout your generations at the entrance to the tent of meeting before the LORD, where I will meet you to speak with you. ⁴³I will also meet with the Israelites there, and that place will be consecrated by My glory. ⁴⁴I will consecrate the tent of meeting and the altar; I will also consecrate Aaron and his sons to serve Me as priests. ⁴⁵I will dwell among the Israelites and be their God. ⁴⁶And they will know that I am the LORD their God, who brought them out of the land of Egypt, so that I might dwell among them. I am the LORD their God.

30 "You are to make an altar for the burning of incense; make it of acacia wood. ²It must be square, 18 inches long and 18 inches wide; it must be 36 inches high. Its horns must be of one piece. ³Overlay its top, all around its sides, and its horns with pure gold; make a gold molding all around it. ⁴Make two gold rings for it under the molding on two of its sides; put these on opposite sides of it to be holders for the poles to carry it with. ⁵Make the poles of acacia wood and overlay them with gold.

⁶"You are to place the altar in front of the veil by the ark of the testimony—in front of the mercy seat that is over the testimony—where I will meet with you. ⁷Aaron must burn fragrant incense on it; he must burn it every morning when he tends the lamps. ⁸When Aaron sets up the lamps at twilight, he must burn incense. There is to be an incense offering before the LORD throughout your generations. ⁹You must not offer unauthorized incense on it, or a burnt or grain offering; you are not to pour a drink offering on it.

¹⁰"Once a year Aaron is to perform the purification rite on the horns of the altar. Throughout your generations he is to perform the purification rite for it once a year, with the blood of the sin offering for atonement. The altar is especially holy to the LORD."

¹¹The LORD spoke to Moses: ¹²"When you take a census of the Israelites to register them, each of the men must pay a ransom for himself to the LORD as they are registered. Then no plague will come on them as they are registered. ¹³Everyone who is registered must pay half a shekel according to the sanctuary shekel (20 gerahs to the shekel). This half shekel is a contribution to the LORD. ¹⁴Each man who is registered, 20 years old or more, must give this contribution to the LORD. ¹⁵The wealthy may not give more, and the poor may not give less, than half a shekel when giving the contribution to the LORD to atone for your lives. ¹⁶Take the atonement money from the Israelites and use it for the service of the tent of meeting. It will serve as a reminder for the Israelites before the LORD to atone for your lives."

¹⁷The LORD spoke to Moses: ¹⁸"Make a bronze basin for washing and a bronze stand for it. Set it between the tent of meeting and the altar, and put water in it. ¹⁹Aaron and his sons must wash their hands and feet from the basin. ²⁰Whenever they enter the tent of meeting or approach the altar to minister by burning up an offering to the LORD, they must wash with water so that they will not die. ²¹They must wash their hands and feet so that they will not die; this is to be a permanent statute for them, for Aaron and his descendants throughout their generations."

²²The LORD spoke to Moses: ²³"Take for yourself the finest spices: 12 and a half pounds of liquid myrrh, half as much (six and a quarter pounds) of fragrant cinnamon, six and a quarter pounds of fragrant cane, ²⁴12 and a half pounds of cassia (by the sanctuary shekel), and one gallon of olive oil. ²⁵Prepare from these a holy anointing oil, a scented blend, the work of a perfumer; it will be holy anointing oil. ²⁶"With it you are to anoint the tent of meeting, the ark of the testimony, ²⁷the table with all its utensils, the lampstand with its utensils, the altar of incense, ²⁸the altar of burnt offering

with all its utensils, and the basin with its stand. ²⁹ Consecrate them and they will be especially holy. Whatever touches them will be consecrated. ³⁰ Anoint Aaron and his sons and consecrate them to serve Me as priests.

³¹ "Tell the Israelites: This will be My holy anointing oil throughout your generations. ³² It must not be used for ordinary anointing on a person's body, and you must not make anything like it using its formula. It is holy, and it must be holy to you. ³³ Anyone who blends something like it or puts some of it on an unauthorized person must be cut off from his people."

³⁴ The LORD said to Moses: "Take fragrant spices: stacte, onycha, and galbanum; the spices and pure frankincense are to be in equal measures. ³⁵ Prepare expertly blended incense from these; it is to be seasoned with salt, pure and holy. ³⁶ Grind some of it into a fine powder and put some in front of the testimony in the tent of meeting, where I will meet with you. It must be especially holy to you. ³⁷ As for the incense you are making, you must not make any for yourselves using its formula. It is to be regarded by you as sacred to the LORD. ³⁸ Anyone who makes something like it to smell its fragrance must be cut off from his people."

*P*SALM 22:1-5

¹ My God, my God, why have You forsaken me?
  Why are You so far from my deliverance
  and from my words of groaning?
² My God, I cry by day, but You do not answer,
  by night, yet I have no rest.
³ But You are holy,
  enthroned on the praises of Israel.
⁴ Our fathers trusted in You;
  they trusted, and You rescued them.
⁵ They cried to You and were set free;
  they trusted in You and were not disgraced.

*P*ROVERBS 5:3-6

³ Though the lips of the forbidden woman drip honey
  and her words are smoother than oil,
⁴ in the end she's as bitter as wormwood
  and as sharp as a double-edged sword.
⁵ Her feet go down to death;
  her steps head straight for Sheol.
⁶ She doesn't consider the path of life;
  she doesn't know that her ways are unstable.

*M*ATTHEW 26:6-25

⁶ While Jesus was in Bethany at the house of Simon, a man who had a serious skin disease, ⁷ a woman approached Him with an alabaster jar of very expensive fragrant oil. She poured it on His head as He was reclining at the table. ⁸ When the disciples saw it, they were indignant. "Why this waste?" they asked. ⁹ "This might have been sold for a great deal and given to the poor."

¹⁰ But Jesus, aware of this, said to them, "Why are you bothering this woman? She has done a noble thing for Me. ¹¹ You always have the poor with you, but you do not always have Me. ¹² By pouring this fragrant oil on My body, she has prepared Me for burial. ¹³ I assure you: Wherever this gospel is proclaimed in the whole world, what this woman has done will also be told in memory of her."

¹⁴ Then one of the Twelve—the man called Judas Iscariot—went to the chief priests ¹⁵ and said, "What are you willing to give me if I hand Him over to you?" So they weighed out 30 pieces of silver for him. ¹⁶ And from that time he started looking for a good opportunity to betray Him.

¹⁷ On the first day of Unleavened Bread the disciples came to Jesus and asked, "Where do You want us to prepare the Passover so You may eat it?"

18 "Go into the city to a certain man," He said, "and tell him, 'The Teacher says: My time is near; I am celebrating the Passover at your place with My disciples.' " 19 So the disciples did as Jesus had directed them and prepared the Passover. 20 When evening came, He was reclining at the table with the Twelve. 21 While they were eating, He said, "I assure you: One of you will betray Me." 22 Deeply distressed, each one began to say to Him, "Surely not I, Lord?" 23 He replied, "The one who dipped his hand with Me in the bowl—he will betray Me. 24 The Son of Man will go just as it is written about Him, but woe to that man by whom the Son of Man is betrayed! It would have been better for that man if he had not been born." 25 Then Judas, His betrayer, replied, "Surely not I, Rabbi?"

"You have said it," He told him.

All Becomes "All"

My time is near; I am celebrating the Passover at your place with My disciples.—MATTHEW 26:18

The upper room was associated in the minds of the disciples with the Last Supper, for it was in this room that Jesus unfolded for them the meaning of redemption. As He broke bread with them, He said, "This is My body, which is given for you. Do this in remembrance of Me." In the same way He also took the cup after supper and said, "This cup is the new covenant established by My blood; it is shed for you" (Lk 22:19-20).

The upper room had a double content—the Cross and the Spirit. These are more closely connected than we might realize, for if we do not bear the spirit of the Cross we will not bear the Spirit of God. We are to be crucified followers of a crucified Lord.

Did that upper room stand in the minds of the disciples as a symbol of Christ's self-giving? And would the whole atmosphere of the place remind them that, just as He had offered His all, so must they offer their all? I cannot help but believe that the connection between the Last Supper and the promised descent of the Holy Spirit would be much upon their minds. In that room, God, in the person of His Son Jesus Christ, had offered His all. Now the 120 disciples were being confronted with the same challenge. Out of Christ's offering came power, for God answers self-giving by the giving of Himself. We can only conclude that something significant happened in the lives of those disciples in that ten-day waiting period, for out of that "all" offering came "all" power.

Prayer

O God, in this "upper room" where I am right now, I offer my little "all," and I take instead Your almighty "all." I exchange my poverty for Your riches, my emptiness for Your fullness, my weaknesses for Your strength. Amen.

FEBRUARY 14

EXODUS 31:1–32:35

31 The LORD also spoke to Moses: ² "Look, I have appointed by name Bezalel son of Uri, son of Hur, of the tribe of Judah. ³ I have filled him with God's Spirit, with wisdom, understanding, and ability in every craft ⁴ to design artistic works in gold, silver, and bronze, ⁵ to cut gemstones for mounting, and to carve wood for work in every craft. ⁶ I have also selected Oholiab son of Ahisamach, of the tribe of Dan, to be with him. I have placed wisdom within every skilled craftsman in order to make all that I have commanded you: ⁷ the tent of meeting, the ark of the testimony, the mercy seat that is on top of it, and all the other furnishings of the tent— ⁸ the table with its utensils, the pure gold lampstand with all its utensils, the altar of incense, ⁹ the altar of burnt offering with all its utensils, the basin with its stand— ¹⁰ the specially woven garments, both the holy garments for Aaron the priest and the garments for his sons to serve as priests, ¹¹ the anointing oil, and the fragrant incense for the sanctuary. They must make them according to all that I have commanded you."

¹² The LORD said to Moses: ¹³ "Tell the Israelites: You must observe My Sabbaths, for it is a sign between Me and you throughout your generations, so that you will know that I am the LORD who sets you apart. ¹⁴ Observe the Sabbath, for it is holy to you. Whoever profanes it must be put to death. If anyone does work on it, that person must be cut off from his people. ¹⁵ For six days work may be done, but on the seventh day there must be a Sabbath of complete rest, dedicated to the LORD. Anyone who does work on the Sabbath day must be put to death. ¹⁶ The Israelites must observe the Sabbath, celebrating it throughout their generations as a perpetual covenant. ¹⁷ It is a sign forever between Me and the Israelites, for in six days the LORD made the heavens and the earth, but on the seventh day He rested and was refreshed."

¹⁸ When He finished speaking with Moses on Mount Sinai, He gave him the two tablets of the testimony, stone tablets inscribed by the finger of God.

32 When the people saw that Moses delayed in coming down from the mountain, they gathered around Aaron and said to him, "Come, make us a god who will go before us because this Moses, the man who brought us up from the land of Egypt—we don't know what has happened to him!"

² Then Aaron replied to them, "Take off the gold rings that are on the ears of your wives, your sons, and your daughters and bring them to me." ³ So all the people took off the gold rings that were on their ears and brought them to Aaron. ⁴ He took the gold from their

hands, fashioned it with an engraving tool, and made it into an image of a calf.

Then they said, "Israel, this is your God, who brought you up from the land of Egypt!" ⁵ When Aaron saw this, he built an altar before it; then he made an announcement: "There will be a festival to the LORD tomorrow." ⁶ Early the next morning they arose, offered burnt offerings, and presented fellowship offerings. The people sat down to eat and drink, then got up to revel.

⁷ The LORD spoke to Moses: "Go down at once! For your people you brought up from the land of Egypt have acted corruptly. ⁸ They have quickly turned from the way I commanded them; they have made for themselves an image of a calf. They have bowed down to it, sacrificed to it, and said, 'Israel, this is your God, who brought you up from the land of Egypt.'" ⁹ The LORD also said to Moses: "I have seen this people, and they are indeed a stiff-necked people. ¹⁰ Now leave Me alone, so that My anger can burn against them and I can destroy them. Then I will make you into a great nation."

¹¹ But Moses interceded with the LORD his God: "LORD, why does Your anger burn against Your people You brought out of the land of Egypt with great power and a strong hand? ¹² Why should the Egyptians say, 'He brought them out with an evil intent to kill them in the mountains and wipe them off the face of the earth'? Turn from Your great anger and change Your mind about this disaster planned for Your people. ¹³ Remember that You swore to Your servants Abraham, Isaac, and Israel by Yourself and declared to them, 'I will make your offspring as numerous as the stars of the sky and will give your offspring all this land that I have promised, and they will inherit it forever.'" ¹⁴ So the LORD changed His mind about the disaster He said He would bring on His people.

¹⁵ Then Moses turned and went down the mountain with the two tablets of the testimony in his hands. They were inscribed on both sides—inscribed front and back. ¹⁶ The tablets were the work of God, and the writing was God's writing, engraved on the tablets.

¹⁷ When Joshua heard the sound of the people as they shouted, he said to Moses, "There is a sound of war in the camp."

¹⁸ But Moses replied:

It's not the sound of a victory cry
and not the sound of a cry of
    defeat;
I hear the sound of singing!

¹⁹ As he approached the camp and saw the calf and the dancing, Moses became enraged and threw the tablets out of his hands, smashing them at the base of the mountain. ²⁰ Then he took the calf they had made, burned it up, and ground it to powder. He scattered the powder over the surface of the water and forced the Israelites to drink the water.

²¹ Then Moses asked Aaron, "What did this people do to you that you have led them into such a grave sin?"

²² "Don't be enraged, my lord," Aaron replied. "You yourself know that the people are intent on evil. ²³ They said to me, 'Make us a god who will go before us because this Moses, the man who brought us up from the land of Egypt— we don't know what has happened to him!' ²⁴ So I said to them, 'Whoever has gold, take it off,' and they gave it to me. When I threw it into the fire, out came this calf!"

²⁵ Moses saw that the people were out of control, for Aaron had let them get out of control, so that they would be vulnerable to their enemies. ²⁶ And Moses stood at the camp's entrance and said, "Whoever is for the LORD, come to me." And all the Levites gathered around him. ²⁷ He told them, "This is what the LORD, the God of Israel, says, 'Every man fasten his sword to his side; go back and forth through the camp from entrance to entrance, and each of you kill his brother, his friend, and his neighbor.'" ²⁸ The Levites did as Moses commanded, and about 3,000 men fell dead that day among the people. ²⁹ Afterwards Moses said, "Today you have been dedicated to the LORD, since

each man went against his son and his brother. Therefore you have brought a blessing on yourselves today."

³⁰ The following day Moses said to the people, "You have committed a great sin. Now I will go up to the LORD; perhaps I will be able to pay for your sin."

³¹ So Moses returned to the LORD and said, "Oh, this people has committed a great sin; they have made for themselves a god of gold. ³² Now if You would only forgive their sin. But if not, please erase me from the book You have written."

³³ The LORD replied to Moses: "Whoever has sinned against Me I will erase from My book. ³⁴ Now go, lead the people to the place I told you about; see, My angel will go before you. But on the day I settle accounts, I will hold them accountable for their sin." ³⁵ And the LORD inflicted a plague on the people for what they did with the calf Aaron had made.

*P*SALM 22:6-10

⁶ But I am a worm and not a man,
    scorned by men and despised by
    people.
⁷ Everyone who sees me mocks me;
    they sneer and shake their heads:
⁸ "He relies on the LORD; let Him
    rescue him;
    let the LORD deliver him, since He
    takes pleasure in him."

⁹ You took me from the womb,
    making me secure while at my
    mother's breast.
¹⁰ I was given over to You at birth;
    You have been my God from my
    mother's womb.

*P*ROVERBS 5:7-8

⁷ So now, my sons, listen to me,
    and don't turn away from the
    words of my mouth.
⁸ Keep your way far from her.
    Don't go near the door of her
    house.

*M*ATTHEW 26:26-51

²⁶ As they were eating, Jesus took bread, blessed and broke it, gave it to the disciples, and said, "Take and eat it; this is My body." ²⁷ Then He took a cup, and after giving thanks, He gave it to them and said, "Drink from it, all of you. ²⁸ For this is My blood that establishes the covenant; it is shed for many for the forgiveness of sins. ²⁹ But I tell you, from this moment I will not drink of this fruit of the vine until that day when I drink it in a new way in My Father's kingdom with you." ³⁰ After singing psalms, they went out to the Mount of Olives.

³¹ Then Jesus said to them, "Tonight all of you will run away because of Me, for it is written:

I will strike the shepherd,
and the sheep of the flock
will be scattered.

³² But after I have been resurrected, I will go ahead of you to Galilee."

³³ Peter told Him, "Even if everyone runs away because of You, I will never run away!"

³⁴ "I assure you," Jesus said to him, "tonight—before the rooster crows, you will deny Me three times!"

³⁵ "Even if I have to die with You," Peter told Him, "I will never deny You!" And all the disciples said the same thing.

³⁶ Then Jesus came with them to a place called Gethsemane, and He told the disciples, "Sit here while I go over there and pray." ³⁷ Taking along Peter and the two sons of Zebedee, He began to be sorrowful and deeply distressed. ³⁸ Then He said to them, "My soul is swallowed up in sorrow—to the point of death. Remain here and stay awake with Me." ³⁹ Going a little farther, He fell facedown and prayed, "My Father! If it is possible, let this cup pass from Me. Yet not as I will, but as You will."

⁴⁰ Then He came to the disciples and found them sleeping. He asked Peter.

"So, couldn't you stay awake with Me one hour? [41] Stay awake and pray, so that you won't enter into temptation. The spirit is willing, but the flesh is weak."

[42] Again, a second time, He went away and prayed, "My Father, if this cannot pass unless I drink it, Your will be done." [43] And He came again and found them sleeping, because they could not keep their eyes open.

[44] After leaving them, He went away again and prayed a third time, saying the same thing once more. [45] Then He came to the disciples and said to them, "Are you still sleeping and resting? Look, the time is near. The Son of Man is being betrayed into the hands of sin-ners. [46] Get up; let's go! See—My betrayer is near."

[47] While He was still speaking, Judas, one of the Twelve, suddenly arrived. A large mob, with swords and clubs, was with him from the chief priests and elders of the people. [48] His betrayer had given them a sign: "The One I kiss, He's the One; arrest Him!" [49] So he went right up to Jesus and said, "Greetings, Rabbi!"—and kissed Him.

[50] "Friend," Jesus asked him, "why have you come?"

Then they came up, took hold of Jesus, and arrested Him. [51] At that moment one of those with Jesus reached out his hand and drew his sword. He struck the high priest's slave and cut off his ear.

Coping Through Christ

My soul is swallowed up in sorrow—to the point of death. Remain here and stay awake with Me.

—MATTHEW 26:38

It is better to face disappointment and feel it than to pretend it is not there. And when I say "feel it"—I mean exactly that. Most people, I find, just walk around the edges of their disappointment, in the way they would walk cautiously around the rim of a volcano, admitting they have been disappointed but working hard (often unconsciously) to blunt the feelings of disappointment with a "let's not stay here too long" attitude.

The usual response to what I am now saying is: "Surely there is no point in being willing to enter into all the pain of our disappointments. What is past is past; isn't it better to forget the hurts and disappointments of the past and get on with life?"

Sounds quite rational and sensible, doesn't it? However, it is not the best way to deal with life. The more deeply we are willing to face our disappointments, the readier we will be to turn to Christ and draw from Him the strength we need to cope with them.

The danger we face when we are unwilling to feel as openly as possible the disappointments that come our way is that we will come to depend on our own strategies to cope with them and turn only partially to Christ for strength. Facing and feeling disappointment is a sure way of coming to recognize that God is the only One who can help us cope. When we face and feel our disappointments, we will cling more closely to Christ.

Prayer

Gracious and loving heavenly Father, I want to live fully and frankly. Help me to face whatever goes on inside me with complete honesty. Save me from all self-deception and subterfuges, for I would be a fit instrument for You. In Jesus' name. Amen.

Further Study

1 Kg 19; Heb 4:15
What was Elijah's disappointment?
How did he respond to it?

FEBRUARY 15

EXODUS 33:1–34:35

33 The LORD spoke to Moses: "Go, leave here, you and the people you brought up from the land of Egypt, to the land I promised to Abraham, Isaac, and Jacob, saying: I will give it to your offspring. ² I will send an angel ahead of you and will drive out the Canaanites, Amorites, Hittites, Perizzites, Hivites, and Jebusites. ³ Go up to a land flowing with milk and honey. But I will not go with you because you are a stiff-necked people; otherwise, I might destroy you on the way." ⁴ When the people heard this bad news, they mourned and didn't put on their jewelry.

⁵ For the LORD said to Moses: "Tell the Israelites: You are a stiff-necked people. If I went with you for a single moment, I would destroy you. Now take off your jewelry, and I will decide what to do with you." ⁶ So the Israelites remained stripped of their jewelry from Mount Horeb onward.

⁷ Now Moses took a tent and set it up outside the camp, far away from the camp; he called it the tent of meeting.

Anyone who wanted to consult the LORD would go to the tent of meeting that was outside the camp. ⁸ Whenever Moses went out to the tent, all the people would stand up, each one at the door of his tent, and they would watch Moses until he entered the tent. ⁹ When Moses entered the tent, the pillar of cloud would come down and remain at the entrance to the tent, and the LORD would speak with Moses. ¹⁰ As all the people saw the pillar of cloud remaining at the entrance to the tent, they would stand up, then bow in worship, each one at the door of his tent. ¹¹ The LORD spoke with Moses face to face, just as a man speaks with his friend. Then Moses would return to the camp, but his assistant, the young man Joshua son of Nun, would not leave the inside of the tent.

¹² Moses said to the LORD, "Look, You have told me, 'Lead this people up,' but You have not let me know whom You will send with me. You said, 'I know you by name, and you have also found favor in My sight.' ¹³ Now if I have indeed found favor in Your sight, please teach me Your ways, and I will know You and

180

find favor in Your sight. Now consider that this nation is Your people." ¹⁴ Then He replied, "My presence will go with you, and I will give you rest." ¹⁵ "If Your presence does not go," Moses responded to Him, "don't make us go up from here. ¹⁶ How will it be known that I and Your people have found favor in Your sight unless You go with us? I and Your people will be distinguished by this from all the other people on the face of the earth." ¹⁷ The LORD answered Moses, "I will do this very thing you have asked, for you have found favor in My sight, and I know you by name." ¹⁸ Then Moses said, "Please, let me see Your glory."

¹⁹ He said, "I will cause all My goodness to pass in front of you, and I will proclaim the name Yahweh before you. I will be gracious to whom I will be gracious, and I will have compassion on whom I will have compassion." ²⁰ But He answered, "You cannot see My face, for no one can see Me and live." ²¹ The LORD said, "Here is a place near Me. You are to stand on the rock, ²² and when My glory passes by, I will put you in the crevice of the rock and cover you with My hand until I have passed by. ²³ Then I will take My hand away, and you will see My back, but My face will not be seen."

34 The LORD said to Moses, "Cut two stone tablets like the first ones, and I will write on them the words that were on the first tablets, which you broke. ² Be prepared by morning. Come up Mount Sinai in the morning and stand before Me on the mountaintop. ³ No one may go up with you; in fact, no one must be seen anywhere on the mountain. Even the flocks and herds are not to graze in front of that mountain."

⁴ Moses cut two stone tablets like the first ones. He got up early in the morning, and taking the two stone tablets in his hand, he climbed Mount Sinai, just as the LORD had commanded him.

⁵ The LORD came down in a cloud, stood with him there, and proclaimed

His name Yahweh. ⁶ Then the LORD passed in front of him and proclaimed:

Yahweh—Yahweh is a compassionate and gracious God, slow to anger and rich in faithful love and truth, ⁷ maintaining faithful love to a thousand generations, forgiving wrongdoing, rebellion, and sin. But He will not leave the guilty unpunished, bringing the consequences of the fathers' wrongdoing on the children and grandchildren to the third and fourth generation.

⁸ Moses immediately bowed down to the ground and worshiped. ⁹ Then he said, "My Lord, if I have indeed found favor in Your sight, my Lord, please go with us. Even though this is a stiff-necked people, forgive our wrongdoing and sin, and accept us as Your own possession."

¹⁰ And the LORD responded: "Look, I am making a covenant. I will perform wonders in the presence of all your people that have never been done in all the earth or in any nation. All the people you live among will see the LORD's work, for what I am doing with you is awe-inspiring. ¹¹ Observe what I command you today. I am going to drive out before you the Amorites, Canaanites, Hittites, Perizzites, Hivites, and Jebusites. ¹² Be careful not to make a treaty with the inhabitants of the land that you are going to enter; otherwise, they will become a snare among you. ¹³ Instead, you must tear down their altars, smash their sacred pillars, and chop down their Asherah poles. ¹⁴ You are to never bow down to another god because the LORD, being jealous by nature, is a jealous God.

¹⁵ "Do not make a treaty with the inhabitants of the land, or else when they prostitute themselves with their gods and sacrifice to their gods, they will invite you, and you will eat of their sacrifice. ¹⁶ Then you will take some of their daughters as brides for your sons. Their daughters will prostitute themselves with their gods and cause your sons to prostitute themselves with their gods.

MATTHEW 26:52-75

⁵²Then Jesus told him, "Put your sword back in place because all who take up a sword will perish by a sword. ⁵³Or do you think that I cannot call on My Father, and He will provide Me at once with more than 12 legions of angels? ⁵⁴How, then, would the Scriptures be fulfilled that say it must happen this way?"

⁵⁵At that time Jesus said to the crowds, "Have you come out with swords and clubs, as if I were a criminal, to capture Me? Every day I used to sit, teaching in the temple complex, and you didn't arrest Me. ⁵⁶But all this has happened so that the prophetic Scriptures would be fulfilled." Then all the disciples deserted Him and ran away.

⁵⁷Those who had arrested Jesus led Him away to Caiaphas the high priest, where the scribes and the elders had convened. ⁵⁸Meanwhile, Peter was following Him at a distance right to the high priest's courtyard. He went in and was sitting with the temple police to see the outcome.

⁵⁹The chief priests and the whole Sanhedrin were looking for false testimony against Jesus so they could put Him to death. ⁶⁰But they could not find any, even though many false witnesses came forward. Finally, two who came forward ⁶¹stated, "This man said, 'I can demolish God's sanctuary and rebuild it in three days.' "

⁶²The high priest then stood up and said to Him, "Don't You have an answer to what these men are testifying against You?" ⁶³But Jesus kept silent. Then the high priest said to Him, "By the living God I place You under oath: tell us if You are the Messiah, the Son of God!"

⁶⁴"You have said it," Jesus told him. "But I tell you, in the future you will see **the Son of Man seated at the right hand** of the Power and **coming on the clouds of heaven.**"

⁶⁵Then the high priest tore his robes and said, "He has blasphemed! Why do we still need witnesses? Look, now you've heard the blasphemy! ⁶⁶What is your decision?"

They answered, "He deserves death!" ⁶⁷Then they spit in His face and beat Him; others slapped Him ⁶⁸and said, "Prophesy to us, Messiah! Who hit You?"

⁶⁹Now Peter was sitting outside in the courtyard. A servant approached him and she said, "You were with Jesus the Galilean too."

⁷⁰But he denied it in front of everyone: "I don't know what you're talking about!"

⁷¹When he had gone out to the gateway, another woman saw him and told those who were there, "This man was with Jesus the Nazarene!"

⁷²And again he denied it with an oath, "I don't know the man!"

⁷³After a little while those standing there approached and said to Peter, "You certainly are one of them, since even your accent gives you away."

⁷⁴Then he started to curse and to swear with an oath, "I do not know the man!" Immediately a rooster crowed, ⁷⁵and Peter remembered the words Jesus had spoken, "Before the rooster crows, you will deny Me three times." And he went outside and wept bitterly.

The Father God

"If Your presence does not go," Moses responded to Him, "don't make us go up from here. How will it be known that I and Your people have found favor in Your sight unless You go with us?"—Exodus 33:15-16

Samuel Shoemaker, the American Episcopalian preacher who was instrumental in forming

Alcoholics Anonymous, pointed out that the whole principle of prayer depends on what kind of Being the Creator is. Listen to this statement made to a group of recovering alcoholics: "If He created the universe and gave everything a primeval push, and then retired beyond where we cannot get in contact with Him, prayer is a vain effort. But if He be a personal God as Christians believe He is, then He will have a concern for the people He made and will want to involve Himself with them in all their affairs." We are not alone in this universe; a personal God stands behind all things, waiting, longing that we might enter into a relationship with Him.

We said that one of the reasons why people desire an impersonal God is because this kind of God is easier to live with than one who is personal like themselves. It's rather nice to carry inside our hearts a subjective idea of a God of beauty, truth, and goodness. That kind of God demands nothing of us. Better still a formless life-force surging through all of us, a vast power we can tap and use to our advantage. This kind of God is extremely easy to live with.

But a living God who approaches us at infinite speed—the Hunter, the King, the Lover, the Husband—this is quite another matter. Yet whether we believe it or not, this is the kind of God He is.

Prayer

How thankful I am that You are not just a supernatural energy or a life-force, but a personal Being whom I can address as Father. Your personality engages with my personality, and we are one. In this my joy knows no bounds. Amen.

Further Study

Gn 3:1-8; Ex 33:14-17; Is 43:2; Lk 11:2
How did God present Himself as a personal Being?
What did He promise Moses?

FEBRUARY 16

EXODUS 35:1–36:19

35 Moses assembled the entire Israelite community and said to them, "These are the things that the LORD has commanded you to do: ² For six days work is to be done, but on the seventh day you are to have a holy day, a Sabbath of complete rest to the LORD. Anyone who does work on it must be executed. ³ Do not light a fire in any of your homes on the Sabbath day."

⁴ Then Moses said to the entire Israelite community, "This is what the LORD has commanded: ⁵ Take up an offering for the LORD among you. Let

everyone whose heart is willing bring this as the LORD's offering: gold, silver, and bronze; [6] blue, purple, and scarlet yarn; fine linen and goat hair; [7] ram skins dyed red and manatee skins; acacia wood; [8] oil for the light; spices for the anointing oil and for the fragrant incense; [9] and onyx with gemstones to mount on the ephod and breastpiece.

[10] "Let all the skilled craftsmen among you come and make everything that the LORD has commanded: [11] the tabernacle—its tent and covering, its clasps and planks, its crossbars, its posts and bases; [12] the ark with its poles, the mercy seat, and the veil for the screen; [13] the table with its poles, all its utensils, and the bread of the Presence; [14] the lampstand for light with its utensils and lamps as well as the oil for the light; [15] the altar of incense with its poles; the anointing oil and the fragrant incense; the entryway screen for the entrance to the tabernacle; [16] the altar of burnt offering with its bronze grate, its poles, and all its utensils; the basin with its stand; [17] the hangings of the courtyard, its posts and bases, and the screen for the gate of the courtyard; [18] the tent pegs for the tabernacle and the tent pegs for the courtyard, along with their ropes; [19] and the specially woven garments for ministering in the sanctuary—the holy garments for Aaron the priest and the garments for his sons to serve as priests."

[20] Then the entire Israelite community left Moses' presence. [21] Everyone whose heart was moved and whose spirit prompted him came and brought an offering to the LORD to construct the tent of meeting for every use, and to make the holy garments. [22] Both men and women came; all who had willing hearts brought brooches, earrings, rings, necklaces, and all kinds of gold jewelry—everyone who waved a presentation offering of gold to the LORD. [23] Everyone who had in his possession blue, purple, or scarlet yarn, fine linen or goat hair, ram skins dyed red or manatee skins, brought them. [24] Everyone who offered a contribution of silver or bronze brought it to the LORD. Everyone who possessed acacia wood useful for any task in the work brought it. [25] Every skilled woman spun yarn with her hands and brought it: blue, purple, and scarlet yarn, and fine linen. [26] And all the women whose hearts were moved spun the goat hair by virtue of their skill. [27] The leaders brought onyx and gemstones to mount on the ephod and breastpiece, [28] as well as the spice and oil for the light, for the anointing oil, and for the fragrant incense. [29] So the Israelites brought a freewill offering to the LORD, all the men and women whose hearts prompted them to bring something for all the work that the LORD, through Moses, had commanded to be done.

[30] Moses then said to the Israelites: "Look, the LORD has appointed by name Bezalel son of Uri, son of Hur, of the tribe of Judah. [31] He has filled him with God's Spirit, with wisdom, understanding, and ability in every kind of craft [32] to design artistic works in gold, silver, and bronze, [33] to cut gemstones for mounting, and to carve wood for work in every kind of artistic craft. [34] He has also given both him and Oholiab son of Ahisamach, of the tribe of Dan, the ability to teach others. [35] He has filled them with skill to do all the work of a gem cutter; a designer; an embroiderer in blue, purple, and scarlet yarn and fine linen; and a weaver. They can do every kind of craft and design artistic designs.

36 [1] Bezalel, Oholiab, and all the skilled people are to work based on everything the LORD has commanded. The LORD has given them wisdom and understanding to know how to do all the work of constructing the sanctuary."

[2] So Moses summoned Bezalel, Oholiab, and every skilled person in whose heart the LORD had placed wisdom, everyone whose heart moved him, to come to the work and do it. [3] They took from Moses' presence all the contributions that the Israelites had brought for the task of making the sanctuary. Meanwhile, the people continued to bring freewill offerings morning after morning.

⁴ Then all the craftsmen who were doing all the work for the sanctuary came one by one from the work they were doing ⁵ and said to Moses, "The people are bringing more than is needed for the construction of the work the LORD commanded to be done."

⁶ After Moses gave an order, they sent a proclamation throughout the camp: "Let no man or woman make anything else as an offering for the sanctuary." So the people stopped. ⁷ The materials were sufficient for them to do all the work. There was more than enough.

⁸ All the skilled craftsmen among those doing the work made the tabernacle with 10 curtains. Bezalel made them of finely spun linen, as well as blue, purple, and scarlet yarn, with a design of cherubim worked into them. ⁹ The length of each curtain was 42 feet, and the width of each curtain six feet; all the curtains had the same measurements. ¹⁰ He joined five of the curtains to each other, and the other five curtains he joined to each other. ¹¹ He made loops of blue yarn on the edge of the last curtain in the first set and did the same on the edge of the outermost curtain in the second set. ¹² He made 50 loops on the one curtain and 50 loops on the edge of the curtain in the second set, so that the loops lined up with each other. ¹³ He also made 50 gold clasps and joined the curtains to each other, so that the tabernacle became a single unit.

¹⁴ He made curtains of goat hair for a tent over the tabernacle; he also made 11 of them. ¹⁵ The length of each curtain was 45 feet, and the width of each curtain six feet. All 11 curtains had the same measurements. ¹⁶ He joined five of the curtains together, and the other six together. ¹⁷ He made 50 loops on the edge of the outermost curtain in the first set and 50 loops on the edge of the corresponding curtain in the second set. ¹⁸ He made 50 bronze clasps to join the tent together as a single unit. ¹⁹ He also made a covering for the tent from ram skins dyed red and a covering of manatee skins on top of it.

𝒫SALM 22:16-21

¹⁶ For dogs have surrounded me;
a gang of evildoers has closed in on me;
they pierced my hands and my feet.

¹⁷ I can count all my bones;
people look and stare at me.

¹⁸ They divided my garments among themselves,
and they cast lots for my clothing.

¹⁹ But You, LORD, don't be far away.
My strength, come quickly to help me.

²⁰ Deliver my life from the sword,
my very life from the power of the dog.

²¹ Save me from the mouth of the lion!
You have rescued me from the horns of the wild oxen.

𝒫ROVERBS 5:11-14

¹¹ At the end of your life, you will lament
when your physical body has been consumed,

¹² and you will say, "How I hated discipline,
and how my heart despised correction.

¹³ I didn't obey my teachers
or listen closely to my mentors.

¹⁴ I was on the verge of complete ruin
before the entire community."

𝓜ATTHEW 27:1-23

27 When daybreak came, all the chief priests and the elders of the people plotted against Jesus to put Him to death. ² After tying Him up, they led Him away and handed Him over to Pilate, the governor.

³ Then Judas, His betrayer, seeing that He had been condemned, was full of remorse and returned the 30 pieces of silver to the chief priests and elders.

⁴"I have sinned by betraying innocent blood," he said.

"What's that to us?" they said. "See to it yourself!"

⁵So he threw the silver into the sanctuary and departed. Then he went and hanged himself.

⁶The chief priests took the silver and said, "It's not lawful to put it into the temple treasury, since it is blood money." ⁷So they conferred together and bought the potter's field with it as a burial place for foreigners. ⁸Therefore that field has been called "Blood Field" to this day. ⁹Then what was spoken through the prophet Jeremiah was fulfilled:

They took the 30 pieces of silver, the price of Him whose price was set by the sons of Israel, ¹⁰and they gave them for the potter's field, as the Lord directed me.

¹¹Now Jesus stood before the governor. "Are You the King of the Jews?" the governor asked Him.

Jesus answered, "You have said it." ¹²And while He was being accused by the chief priests and elders, He didn't answer.

¹³Then Pilate said to Him, "Don't You hear how much they are testifying against You?" ¹⁴But He didn't answer him on even one charge, so that the governor was greatly amazed.

¹⁵At the festival the governor's custom was to release to the crowd a prisoner they wanted. ¹⁶At that time they had a notorious prisoner called Barabbas. ¹⁷So when they had gathered together, Pilate said to them, "Who is it you want me to release for you—Barabbas, or Jesus who is called Messiah?" ¹⁸For he knew they had handed Him over because of envy.

¹⁹While he was sitting on the judge's bench, his wife sent word to him, "Have nothing to do with that righteous man, for today I've suffered terribly in a dream because of Him!"

²⁰The chief priests and the elders, however, persuaded the crowds to ask for Barabbas and to execute Jesus. ²¹The governor asked them, "Which of the two do you want me to release for you?"

"Barabbas!" they answered.

²²Pilate asked them, "What should I do then with Jesus, who is called Messiah?"

They all answered, "Crucify Him!"

²³Then he said, "Why? What has He done wrong?"

But they kept shouting, "Crucify Him!" all the more.

The Way Is—Surrender

How I hated discipline, and how my heart despised correction.—PROVERBS 5:12

How do we go about controlling our strong urges? Do we push them under? No, for as Hadfield said, "Repressed instincts are like bad boys who, when put out of class, retaliate by throwing stones at the windows." It's better to keep the bad boys in class, and teach them to direct their energies to better ends.

If the answer is not to be found in repression, then is it to be found in expression? Shall we give free rein to the urges within us? No, for that would lead us into deeper bondage.

Shall we try to eliminate them? By no known process can these driving urges be eliminated. Put them out of the door and they will climb back in through the window, often in disguise. The philosophies of Buddhism are built on the idea that we can eliminate instincts and wipe out desire. A Buddhist monk was asked by a missionary: "What is your desire?" "Nothing." "Where are you going?" "Nowhere." "Where have you come from?" "Nowhere." He wanted to be a blank—but not quite. He ardently desired to be a blank, so desire was still there, turned toward the absence of desire.

If we can't eliminate the driving urges, and we shouldn't repress or suppress them, or express and release them, then what can we do?

We must allow the Holy Spirit to take them over. Our urges are properly fulfilled only when they are surrendered to the will of God. When we allow the Holy Spirit to get into the driving seat of our personalities, then we are in safe hands.

Prayer

O Father, help me to move over and let Your Holy Spirit do the steering. These urges that are within me are too strong for me to handle. From now on, You be the driver. Amen.

Further Study

Nm 11:1-9; Ec 6:7; 1 Co 10:6; Eph 2:3
What was the problem of the children of Israel?
What did they fail to see?

FEBRUARY 17

EXODUS 36:20–37:29

20 He made upright planks of acacia wood for the tabernacle. 21 The length of each plank was 15 feet, and the width of each was 27 inches. 22 There were two tenons connected to each other for each plank. He did the same for all the planks of the tabernacle. 23 He made planks for the tabernacle as follows: 20 for the south side, 24 and he made 40 silver bases to put under the 20 planks, two bases under the first plank for its two tenons, and two bases under each of the following planks for their two tenons; 25 for the second side of the tabernacle, the north side, he made 20 planks, 26 with their 40 silver bases, two bases under the first plank and two bases under each of the following ones; 27 and for the west side of the tabernacle he made six planks. 28 He also made two additional planks for the two back corners of the tabernacle. 29 They were paired at the bottom and joined together at the top in a single ring. This is what he did with both of them for the two corners. 30 So there were eight planks with their 16 silver bases, two bases under each one.

31 He made five crossbars of acacia wood for the planks on one side of the tabernacle, 32 five crossbars for the planks on the other side of the tabernacle, and five crossbars for those at the back of the tabernacle on the west.

33 He made the central crossbar run through the middle of the planks from one end to the other. 34 He overlaid them with gold and made their rings and holders for the crossbars out of gold. He also overlaid the crossbars with gold. 35 Then he made the veil with blue, purple, and scarlet yarn, and finely spun linen. He made it with a design of cherubim worked into it. 36 For it he made four posts of acacia wood and overlaid them with gold; their hooks were of gold. And he cast four silver bases for the posts.

37 He made a screen embroidered with blue, purple, and scarlet yarn, and finely spun linen for the entrance to the tent, 38 together with its five posts and their hooks. He overlaid the tops of the posts and their bands with gold, but their five bases were bronze.

37 Bezalel made the ark of acacia wood, 45 inches long, 27 inches wide, and 27 inches high. 2 He overlaid it with pure gold inside and out and made a gold molding all around it. 3 He cast four gold rings for it to be on its four feet, two rings on one side and two rings on the other side. 4 He made poles of acacia wood and overlaid them with gold. 5 He inserted the poles into the rings on the sides of the ark for carrying the ark.

6 He made a mercy seat of pure gold, 45 inches long and 27 inches wide. 7 He made two cherubim of gold; he made them of hammered work at the two ends of the mercy seat, 8 one cherub at one end and one cherub at the other end. He made the cherubim of one piece with the mercy seat, a cherub at each end. 9 They had wings spread out, covering the mercy seat with their wings and facing each other. The faces of the cherubim were looking toward the mercy seat.

10 He constructed the table of acacia wood, 36 inches long, 18 inches wide, and 27 inches high. 11 He overlaid it with pure gold and made a gold molding all around it. 12 He made a three-inch frame all around it and made a gold molding all around its frame. 13 He cast four gold rings for it and attached the rings to the four corners at its four legs. 14 The rings were next to the frame as holders for the poles to carry the table. 15 He made the poles for carrying the table from acacia wood and overlaid them with gold. 16 He also made the utensils that would be on the table out of pure gold: its plates and cups, as well as its bowls and pitchers for pouring drink offerings.

17 Then he made the lampstand out of pure hammered gold. He made it all of one piece: its base and shaft, its ornamental cups, and its calyxes and petals. 18 Six branches extended from its sides, three branches of the lampstand from one side and three branches of the lampstand from the other side. 19 There were three cups shaped like almond blossoms, each with a calyx and petals, on the first branch, and three cups shaped like almond blossoms, each with a calyx and petals, on the next branch. It was this way for the six branches that extended from the lampstand. 20 On the lampstand shaft there were four cups shaped like almond blossoms with its calyxes and petals. 21 For the six branches that extended from it, a calyx was under the first pair of branches from it, a calyx under the second pair of branches from it, and a calyx under the third pair of branches from it. 22 Their calyxes and branches were of one piece. All of it was a single hammered piece of pure gold. 23 He also made its seven lamps, snuffers, and firepans of pure gold. 24 He made it and all its utensils of 75 pounds of pure gold.

25 He made the altar of incense out of acacia wood. It was square, 18 inches long and 18 inches wide; it was 36 inches high. Its horns were of one piece. 26 He overlaid it, its top, all around its sides, and its horns with pure gold. Then he made a gold molding all around it. 27 He made two gold rings for it under the molding on two of its sides; he put these on opposite sides of it to be holders for the poles to carry it with. 28 He made the poles of acacia wood and overlaid them with gold.

²⁹ He also made the holy anointing oil and the pure, fragrant, and expertly blended incense.

PSALM 22:22-26

²² I will proclaim Your name to my brothers;
I will praise You in the congregation.
²³ You who fear the LORD, praise Him!
All you descendants of Jacob, honor Him!
All you descendants of Israel, revere Him!
²⁴ For He has not despised or detested the torment of the afflicted.
He did not hide His face from him,
but listened when he cried to Him for help.

²⁵ I will give praise in the great congregation because of You;
I will fulfill my vows before those who fear You.
²⁶ The humble will eat and be satisfied;
those who seek the LORD will praise Him.
May your hearts live forever!

PROVERBS 5:15-17

¹⁵ Drink water from your own cistern,
water flowing from your own well.
¹⁶ Should your springs flow in the streets,
streams of water in the public squares?
¹⁷ They should be for you alone and not for you to share with strangers.

MATTHEW 27:24-44

²⁴ When Pilate saw that he was getting nowhere, but that a riot was starting instead, he took some water, washed his hands in front of the crowd, and said, "I am innocent of this man's blood. See to it yourselves!"
²⁵ All the people answered, "His blood be on us and on our children!" ²⁶ Then he released Barabbas to them. But after having Jesus flogged, he handed Him over to be crucified.
²⁷ Then the governor's soldiers took Jesus into headquarters and gathered the whole company around Him. ²⁸ They stripped Him and dressed Him in a scarlet robe. ²⁹ They twisted together a crown of thorns, put it on His head, and placed a reed in His right hand. And they knelt down before Him and mocked Him: "Hail, King of the Jews!" ³⁰ Then they spit at Him, took the reed, and kept hitting Him on the head. ³¹ When they had mocked Him, they stripped Him of the robe, put His clothes on Him, and led Him away to crucify Him.
³² As they were going out, they found a Cyrenian man named Simon. They forced this man to carry His cross. ³³ When they came to a place called *Golgotha* (which means Skull Place), ³⁴ they gave Him wine mixed with gall to drink. But when He tasted it, He would not drink it. ³⁵ After crucifying Him they divided His clothes by casting lots. ³⁶ Then they sat down and were guarding Him there. ³⁷ Above His head they put up the charge against Him in writing:

> THIS IS JESUS
> THE KING OF THE JEWS

³⁸ Then two criminals were crucified with Him, one on the right and one on the left. ³⁹ Those who passed by were yelling insults at Him, shaking their heads ⁴⁰ and saying, "The One who would demolish the sanctuary and rebuild it in three days, save Yourself! If You are the Son of God, come down from the cross!" ⁴¹ In the same way the chief priests, with the scribes and elders, mocked Him and said, ⁴² "He saved others, but He cannot save Himself! He is the King of Israel! Let Him come down now from the cross, and we will

believe in Him. ⁴³ He has put His trust in God; let God rescue Him now—if He wants Him! For He said, 'I am God's Son.' " ⁴⁴ In the same way even the criminals who were crucified with Him kept taunting Him.

Self-Control

In the same way the chief priests, with the scribes and elders, mocked Him and said, "He saved others, but He cannot save Himself! He is the King of Israel! Let Him come down now from the cross, and we will believe in Him."

—MATTHEW 27: 41-42

The last of the nine fruits of the Spirit listed in Galatians 5 is self-control. It is interesting that Paul puts self-control last. Other religions would put it first. Confucianism taught that self-control would help produce the "superior" man. Hinduism thinks self-control will produce the "realized" man. Stoicism thought self-control produced the "detached" man. Modern cults believe self-control produces the "happy" man. They all go about it the wrong way. We do not gain Christ through self-control; we gain self-control through Christ.

"Self-control" is used here as a by-product of love. When you begin with love, you end up with self-control. If you attempt it the other way around, then you end up with a nervous breakdown. The self-control that comes by the Spirit is not a nervous, anxious self-control; it is a control that is unstrained, therefore beautiful. No wonder a great thinker said, "Love Christ and do what you like," for when you do, then you will like what He likes. That's the kind of self-control the Spirit gives. We delight to control what needs to be controlled because we desire to please Him.

Prayer

Blessed Holy Spirit, I am so thankful that You are working in me to produce the image of the Lord Jesus Christ. May the aspects of His nature show through me more and more every day. For His name's sake. Amen.

Further Study

Mt 27; Pr 16:32; Rm 6:12; 2 Pt 1:5-6
In what ways did Jesus display self-control?
In what ways do you show self-control?

FEBRUARY 18

*E*XODUS 38:1–39:31

38 Bezalel constructed the altar of burnt offering from acacia wood. It was square, seven and a half feet long and seven and a half feet wide, and was four and a half feet high. ² He made horns for it on its four corners; the horns were of one piece. Then he overlaid it with bronze.

³ He made all the altar's utensils: the pots, shovels, basins, meat forks, and firepans; he made all its utensils of bronze. ⁴ He constructed for the altar a grate of bronze mesh under its ledge, halfway up from the bottom. ⁵ At the four corners of the bronze grate he cast four rings as holders for the poles. ⁶ He also made the poles of acacia wood and overlaid them with bronze. ⁷ Then he inserted the poles into the rings on the sides of the altar in order to carry it with them. He constructed the altar with boards so that it was hollow.

⁸ He made the bronze basin and its stand from the bronze mirrors of the women who served at the entrance to the tent of meeting.

⁹ Then he made the courtyard. The hangings on the south side of the courtyard were of finely spun linen, 150 feet in length, ¹⁰ including their 20 posts and 20 bronze bases. The hooks and bands of the posts were silver. ¹¹ The hangings on the north side were also 150 feet in length, including their 20 posts and 20 bronze bases. The hooks and bands of the posts were silver. ¹² The hangings on the west side were 75 feet in length, including their 10 posts and 10 bases. The hooks and bands of the posts were silver. ¹³ The hangings on the east toward the sunrise were also 75 feet in length. ¹⁴ The hangings on one side of the gate were 22 and a half feet, including their three posts and three bases. ¹⁵ It was the same for the other side. The hangings were 22 and a half feet, including their three posts and three bases on both sides of the courtyard gate. ¹⁶ All the hangings around the courtyard were of finely spun linen. ¹⁷ The bases for the posts were bronze; the hooks and bands of the posts were silver; and the plating for the tops of the posts was silver. All the posts of the courtyard were banded with silver.

¹⁸ The screen for the gate of the courtyard was embroidered with blue, purple, and scarlet yarn, and finely spun linen. It was 30 feet long, and like the hangings of the courtyard, seven and a half feet high. ¹⁹ It had four posts, including their four bronze bases. Their hooks were silver, and the bands as well as the plating of their tops were silver. ²⁰ All the tent pegs for the tabernacle and for the surrounding courtyard were bronze.

²¹ This is the inventory for the tabernacle, the tabernacle of the testimony, that was recorded at Moses' command. It was the work of the Levites under the direction of Ithamar son of Aaron the priest. ²² Bezalel son of Uri, son of Hur, of the tribe of Judah, made everything that the LORD commanded Moses. ²³ With him was Oholiab son of Ahisamach, of the tribe of Dan, a gem cutter, a designer, and an embroiderer with blue, purple, and scarlet yarn, and fine linen.

²⁴ All the gold of the presentation offering that was used for the project in all the work on the sanctuary, was 2,193 pounds, according to the sanctuary shekel. ²⁵ The silver from those of the community who were registered was 7,544 pounds, according to the sanctuary shekel— ²⁶ two-fifths of an ounce per man, that is, half a shekel according to the sanctuary shekel, from everyone 20 years old or more who had crossed over to the registered group,

603,550 men. [27] There were 7,500 pounds of silver used to cast the bases of the sanctuary and the bases of the veil—100 bases from 7,500 pounds, 75 pounds for each base. [28] With the remaining 44 pounds he made the hooks for the posts, overlaid their tops, and supplied bands for them.

[29] The bronze of the presentation offering totaled 5,310 pounds. [30] He made with it the bases for the entrance to the tent of meeting, the bronze altar and its bronze grate, all the utensils for the altar, [31] the bases for the surrounding courtyard, the bases for the gate of the courtyard, all the tent pegs for the tabernacle, and all the tent pegs for the surrounding courtyard.

39 They made specially woven garments for ministry in the sanctuary, and the holy garments for Aaron from the blue, purple, and scarlet yarn, just as the LORD had commanded Moses. [2] Bezalel made the ephod of gold, of blue, purple, and scarlet yarn, and of finely spun linen. [3] They hammered out thin sheets of gold, and he cut threads from them to interweave with the blue, purple, and scarlet yarn, and the fine linen in a skillful design. [4] They made shoulder pieces for attaching it; it was joined together at its two edges. [5] The artistically woven waistband that was on the ephod was of one piece with the ephod, according to the same workmanship of gold, of blue, purple, and scarlet yarn, and of finely spun linen, just as the LORD had commanded Moses.

[6] Then they mounted the onyx stones surrounded with gold filigree settings, engraved with the names of Israel's sons as a gem cutter engraves a seal. [7] He fastened them on the shoulder pieces of the ephod as memorial stones for the Israelites, just as the LORD had commanded Moses.

[8] He also made the embroidered breastpiece with the same workmanship as the ephod of gold, of blue, purple, and scarlet yarn, and of finely spun linen. [9] They made the breastpiece square and folded double, nine inches

long and nine inches wide. [10] They mounted four rows of gemstones on it. The first row was a row of carnelian, topaz, and emerald; [11] the second row, a turquoise, a sapphire, and a diamond; [12] the third row, a jacinth, an agate, and an amethyst; [13] and the fourth row, a beryl, an onyx, and a jasper. They were surrounded with gold filigree in their settings.

[14] The 12 stones corresponded to the names of Israel's sons. Each stone was engraved like a seal with one of the names of the 12 tribes.

[15] They made braided chains of pure gold cord for the breastpiece. [16] They also fashioned two gold filigree settings and two gold rings and attached the two rings to its two corners. [17] Then they attached the two gold cords to the two gold rings on the corners of the breastpiece. [18] They attached the other ends of the two cords to the two filigree settings and, in this way, attached them to the ephod's shoulder pieces in front. [19] They made two other gold rings and put them at the two other corners of the breastpiece on the edge that is next to the inner border of the ephod. [20] They made two more gold rings and attached them to the bottom of the ephod's two shoulder pieces on its front, close to its seam, above the ephod's woven waistband. [21] Then they tied the breastpiece from its rings to the rings of the ephod with a cord of blue yarn, so that the breastpiece was above the ephod's waistband and did not come loose from the ephod. They did just as the LORD had commanded Moses.

[22] They made the woven robe of the ephod entirely of blue yarn. [23] There was an opening in the center of the robe like that for body armor with a collar around the opening so that it would not tear. [24] They made pomegranates of finely spun blue, purple, and scarlet yarn on the lower hem of the robe. [25] They made bells of pure gold and attached the bells between the pomegranates, all around the hem of the robe between the pomegranates, [26] a bell and a pomegranate alternating all around the lower hem of the robe. It is to be

used for ministry, just as the LORD had commanded Moses.

²⁷ They made the tunics of fine woven linen for Aaron and his sons. ²⁸ They also made the turban and the ornate headbands of fine linen, the undergarments, ²⁹ and the sash of finely spun linen of embroidered blue, purple, and scarlet yarn. They did just as the LORD had commanded Moses.

³⁰ They also made a plate, the holy diadem, out of pure gold, and wrote on it an inscription like the engraving on a seal:

HOLY TO THE LORD
---

³¹ Then they attached a cord of blue yarn to it in order to mount it on the turban, just as the LORD had commanded Moses.

PSALM 22:27-31

27 All the ends of the earth will
   remember and turn to the
   LORD.
   All the families of the nations will
   bow down before You,
28 for kingship belongs to the LORD;
   He rules over the nations.
29 All who prosper on earth will eat
   and bow down;
   all those who go down to the dust
   will kneel before Him—
   even the one who cannot preserve
   his life.
30 Descendants will serve Him;
   the next generation will be told
   about the Lord.
31 They will come and tell a people
   yet to be born
   about His righteousness—
   what He has done.

PROVERBS 5:18-20

18 Let your fountain be blessed,
   and take pleasure in the wife of
   your youth.
19 A loving doe, a graceful fawn—
   let her breasts always satisfy you;
   be lost in her love forever.

20 Why, my son, would you be
   infatuated with a forbidden
   woman
   or embrace the breast of a
   stranger?

MATTHEW 27:45-66

⁴⁵ From noon until three in the afternoon darkness came over the whole land. ⁴⁶ At about three in the afternoon Jesus cried out with a loud voice, *"Elì, Elì, lemá sabachtháni?"* that is, "My God, My God, why have You forsaken Me?"

⁴⁷ When some of those standing there heard this, they said, "He's calling for Elijah!"

⁴⁸ Immediately one of them ran and got a sponge, filled it with sour wine, fixed it on a reed, and offered Him a drink. ⁴⁹ But the rest said, "Let's see if Elijah comes to save Him!"

⁵⁰ Jesus shouted again with a loud voice and gave up His spirit. ⁵¹ Suddenly, the curtain of the sanctuary was split in two from top to bottom; the earth quaked and the rocks were split. ⁵² The tombs also were opened and many bodies of the saints who had gone to their rest were raised. ⁵³ And they came out of the tombs after His resurrection, entered the holy city, and appeared to many.

⁵⁴ When the centurion and those with him, who were guarding Jesus, saw the earthquake and the things that had happened, they were terrified and said, "This man really was God's Son!"

⁵⁵ Many women who had followed Jesus from Galilee and ministered to Him were there, looking on from a distance. ⁵⁶ Among them were Mary Magdalene, Mary the mother of James and Joseph, and the mother of Zebedee's sons.

⁵⁷ When it was evening, a rich man from Arimathea named Joseph came, who himself had also become a disciple of Jesus. ⁵⁸ He approached Pilate and asked for Jesus' body. Then Pilate ordered that it be released. ⁵⁹ So Joseph took the body, wrapped it in clean, fine

linen, [60] and placed it in his new tomb, which he had cut into the rock. He left after rolling a great stone against the entrance of the tomb. [61] Mary Magdalene and the other Mary were seated there, facing the tomb.

[62] The next day, which followed the preparation day, the chief priests and the Pharisees gathered before Pilate [63] and said, "Sir, we remember that while this deceiver was still alive, He said, 'After three days I will rise again.'

[64] Therefore give orders that the tomb be made secure until the third day. Otherwise, His disciples may come, steal Him, and tell the people, 'He has been raised from the dead.' Then the last deception will be worse than the first."

[65] "You have a guard of soldiers," Pilate told them. "Go and make it as secure as you know how." [66] Then they went and made the tomb secure by sealing the stone and setting the guard.

The Last Is the Best

Long ago God spoke to the fathers by the prophets at different times and in different ways. In these last days, He has spoken to us by His Son.—HEBREWS 1:1-2

The words of this text point out that though God spoke in times past through prophets and sages (referring to the religion of Judaism), His final Word to this world is in His Son. That is our claim as Christians. Not that the Jewish religion contains nothing of value. God forbid! But it is not God's last Word to the men and women of His creation.

No other world faith claims that its great teacher was God incarnate. Yet we claim for Christ just that—and also that as God He meets every human need. He comes to us where we are and He does the work. He can relieve any plight of the human soul, and He has the power to meet every human need. Every spiritually sensitive person is aware of the presence of guilt which arises from indwelling sin, and is aware too that he or she alone can do nothing to dissolve it. Christ atoned for sin and is able to forgive it. Every normal person also stands in awe of death, knowing it is impossible to escape it. But Christ has conquered death and has opened the way to eternal life.

Christ's call is to all humanity. He does not differentiate between groups of people or races. He abides no barriers of class or creed. "Whosoever will may come" is His constant message. Devotees of other faiths regard Christians as intolerant when they cannot concede even by implication that there are any "gods" or prophets equal to Him. He is unique in His Person, His mission, and in His finished work.

Prayer

O God, how can I express my gratitude that I have found the best, or rather that the Best has found me? May I lay hold of all that is in Jesus and reflect Him to the world, not in arrogance but in humility. Amen.

Further Study

Php 2:1-11; Eph 1:22; 1 Co 8:6; Heb 1:2
Why has God exalted Christ?
What does Paul acknowledge?

FEBRUARY 19

*E*XODUS 39:32–40:38

³² So all the work for the tabernacle, the tent of meeting, was finished. The Israelites did everything just as the LORD had commanded Moses. ³³ Then they brought the tabernacle to Moses: the tent with all its furnishings, its clasps, its planks, its crossbars, and its posts and bases; ³⁴ the covering of ram skins dyed red and the covering of manatee skins; the veil for the screen; ³⁵ the ark of the testimony with its poles and the mercy seat; ³⁶ the table, all its utensils, and the bread of the Presence; ³⁷ the pure gold lampstand, with its lamps arranged and all its utensils, as well as the oil for the light; ³⁸ the gold altar; the anointing oil; the fragrant incense; the screen for the entrance to the tent; ³⁹ the bronze altar with its bronze grate, its poles, and all its utensils; the basin with its stand; ⁴⁰ the hangings of the courtyard, its posts and bases, the screen for the gate of the courtyard, its ropes and tent pegs, and all the equipment for the service of the tabernacle, the tent of meeting; ⁴¹ and the specially woven garments for ministering in the sanctuary, the holy garments for Aaron the priest and the garments for his sons to serve as priests. ⁴² The Israelites had done all the work according to everything the LORD had commanded Moses. ⁴³ Moses inspected all the work they had accomplished. They had done just as the LORD commanded. Then Moses blessed them.

40 The LORD spoke to Moses: ² "You are to set up the tabernacle, the tent of meeting, on the first day of the first month. ³ Put the ark of the testimony there, and screen off the ark with the veil. ⁴ Then bring in the table and lay out its arrangement; also bring in the lampstand and set up its lamps. ⁵ Place the gold altar for incense in front of the ark of the testimony. Put up the screen for the entrance to the tabernacle. ⁶ Position the altar of burnt offering in front of the entrance to the tabernacle, the tent of meeting. ⁷ Place the basin between the tent of meeting and the altar, and put water in it. ⁸ Assemble the surrounding courtyard and hang the screen for the gate of the courtyard.

⁹ "Take the anointing oil, and anoint the tabernacle and everything in it; consecrate it along with all its furnishings so that it will be holy. ¹⁰ Anoint the altar of burnt offering and all its utensils; consecrate the altar so that it will be especially holy. ¹¹ Anoint the basin and its stand, and consecrate it.

¹² "Then bring Aaron and his sons to the entrance to the tent of meeting and wash them with water. ¹³ Clothe Aaron with the holy garments, anoint him, and consecrate him, so that he can serve Me as a priest. ¹⁴ Have his sons come forward and clothe them in tunics. ¹⁵ Anoint them just as you anointed

their father, so that they may also serve Me as priests. Their anointing will serve to inaugurate a permanent priesthood for them throughout their generations."

[16] Moses did everything just as the LORD had commanded him. [17] The tabernacle was set up in the first month of the second year, on the first day of the month. [18] Moses set up the tabernacle: he laid its bases, positioned its planks, inserted its crossbars, and set up its posts. [19] Then he spread the tent over the tabernacle and put the covering of the tent on top of it, just as the LORD had commanded Moses.

[20] Moses took the testimony and placed it in the ark, and attached the poles to the ark. He set the mercy seat on top of the ark. [21] He brought the ark into the tabernacle, put up the veil for the screen, and screened off the ark of the testimony, just as the LORD had commanded him.

[22] Moses placed the table in the tent of meeting on the north side of the tabernacle, outside the veil. [23] He arranged the bread on it before the LORD, just as the LORD had commanded him. [24] He also put the lampstand in the tent of meeting opposite the table on the south side of the tabernacle [25] and set up the lamps before the LORD, just as the LORD had commanded him.

[26] Moses also installed the gold altar in the tent of meeting, in front of the veil, [27] and burned fragrant incense on it, just as the LORD had commanded him. [28] He put up the screen at the entrance to the tabernacle. [29] Then he placed the altar of burnt offering at the entrance to the tabernacle, the tent of meeting, and offered the burnt offering and the grain offering on it, just as the LORD had commanded him.

[30] He set the basin between the tent of meeting and the altar and put water in it for washing. [31] Moses, Aaron, and his sons washed their hands and feet from it. [32] They washed whenever they came to the tent of meeting and approached the altar, just as the LORD had commanded Moses.

[33] Next Moses set up the surrounding courtyard for the tabernacle and the al-tar and hung a screen for the gate of the courtyard. So Moses finished the work.

[34] The cloud covered the tent of meeting, and the glory of the LORD filled the tabernacle. [35] Moses was unable to enter the tent of meeting because the cloud rested on it, and the glory of the LORD filled the tabernacle.

[36] The Israelites set out whenever the cloud was taken up from the tabernacle throughout all the stages of their journey. [37] If the cloud was not taken up, they did not set out until the day it was taken up. [38] For the cloud of the LORD was over the tabernacle by day, and there was a fire inside the cloud by night, visible to the entire house of Israel throughout all the stages of their journey.

PSALM 23:1-6

1 The LORD is my shepherd;
 there is nothing I lack.
2 He lets me lie down in green
  pastures;
 He leads me beside quiet waters.
3 He renews my life;
 He leads me along the right paths
  for His name's sake.
4 Even when I walk through the
  darkest valley,
 I fear no danger,
 for You are with me;
 Your rod and Your staff—they
  comfort me.

5 You prepare a table before me
 in the presence of my enemies;
 You anoint my head with oil;
 my cup overflows.
6 Only goodness and faithful love
  will pursue me all the days of
  my life,
 and I will dwell in the house of
  the LORD as long as I live.

PROVERBS 5:21-23

21 For a man's ways are before the
  LORD's eyes,
 and He considers all his paths.

22 A wicked man's iniquities entrap
him;
he is entangled in the ropes of his
own sin.
23 He will die because there is no
instruction,
and be lost because of his great
stupidity.

MATTHEW 28:1-20

28 After the Sabbath, as the first day of the week was dawning, Mary Magdalene and the other Mary went to view the tomb. 2 Suddenly there was a violent earthquake, because an angel of the Lord descended from heaven and approached the tomb. He rolled back the stone and was sitting on it. 3 His appearance was like lightning, and his robe was as white as snow. 4 The guards were so shaken from fear of him that they became like dead men.

5 But the angel told the women, "Don't be afraid, because I know you are looking for Jesus who was crucified. 6 He is not here! For He has been resurrected, just as He said. Come and see the place where He lay. 7 Then go quickly and tell His disciples, 'He has been raised from the dead. In fact, He is going ahead of you to Galilee; you will see Him there.' Listen, I have told you."

8 So, departing quickly from the tomb with fear and great joy, they ran to tell His disciples the news. 9 Just then Jesus met them and said, "Good morning!" They came up, took hold of His feet, and worshiped Him. 10 Then Jesus told them, "Do not be afraid. Go and tell My brothers to leave for Galilee, and they will see Me there."

11 As they were on their way, some of the guard came into the city and reported to the chief priests everything that had happened. 12 After the priests had assembled with the elders and agreed on a plan, they gave the soldiers a large sum of money 13 and told them, "Say this, 'His disciples came during the night and stole Him while we were sleeping.' 14 If this reaches the governor's ears, we will deal with him and keep you out of trouble." 15 So they took the money and did as they were instructed. And this story has been spread among Jewish people to this day.

16 The 11 disciples traveled to Galilee, to the mountain where Jesus had directed them. 17 When they saw Him, they worshiped, but some doubted. 18 Then Jesus came near and said to them, "All authority has been given to Me in heaven and on earth. 19 Go, therefore, and make disciples of all nations, baptizing them in the name of the Father and of the Son and of the Holy Spirit, 20 teaching them to observe everything I have commanded you. And remember, I am with you always, to the end of the age."

The Nature of Doubt

When they saw Him, they worshiped, but some doubted.

——MATTHEW 28:17

A man whom I regarded as truly converted said to me: "I am riddled with so many doubts that I sometimes feel I am not a Christian at all." When I pointed out to him the nature of doubt—that it is not the same as unbelief—I saw a new expression appear on his face. He grasped me by the hands and said: "How can I ever sufficiently thank you? You have released a pressure that has been building up inside me for years."

I met him years later, and he told me that the simple insight I had given him concerning the nature of doubt was all he needed to face his doubts and deal with them in a spiritual way. I say again, no misunderstanding causes more anxiety to the heart of a Christian than that which concerns the nature of doubt.

Let's put unbelief under the microscope for a moment, for by doing so we will see the nature of doubt still more clearly. Unbelief is a willful refusal to believe, resulting in a deliberate decision to disobey. It is a state of mind which is closed against God, an attitude of heart which disobeys God as much as it disbelieves the truth. It is the consequence of a settled choice.

Doubt is not a willful decision to disbelieve but a suspension between faith and unbelief. To believe is to be in one mind; to disbelieve is also to be in one mind, but to doubt is to be caught in the halfway stage between the two—suspended between the desire to affirm and the desire to negate.

Prayer

Father, while I am relieved to discover that doubt is not the same as unbelief, I nevertheless long to live a doubt-free existence. Break down any barriers within me that would hinder the flow of faith. In Christ's name I ask it. Amen.

Further Study

Jn 20:24-29; 11:16; 14:5; 21:2; Mt 10:3
How did Thomas display his total commitment?
Why then did he doubt?

FEBRUARY 20

LEVITICUS 1:1–3:17

1 Then the LORD summoned Moses and spoke to him from the tent of meeting: ² "Speak to the Israelites and tell them: When any of you brings an offering to the LORD from the livestock, you may bring your offering from the herd or the flock.

³ "If his gift is a burnt offering from the herd, he is to bring an unblemished male. He must bring it to the entrance to the tent of meeting so that he may be accepted by the LORD. ⁴ He is to lay his hand on the head of the burnt offering so it can be accepted on his behalf to make atonement for him. ⁵ He is to slaughter the bull before the LORD; Aaron's sons the priests are to present the blood and sprinkle it on all sides of the altar that is at the entrance to the tent of meeting. ⁶ Then he must skin the burnt offering and cut it into pieces. ⁷ The sons of Aaron the priest will prepare a fire on the altar and arrange wood on the fire. ⁸ Aaron's sons the priests are to arrange the pieces, the head, and the suet on top of the burning

wood on the altar. ⁹ The offerer must wash its entrails and shanks with water. Then the priest will burn all of it on the altar as a burnt offering, a fire offering of a pleasing aroma to the LORD.

¹⁰ "But if his gift for a burnt offering is from the flock, from sheep or goats, he is to present an unblemished male. ¹¹ He will slaughter it on the north side of the altar before the LORD. Aaron's sons the priests will sprinkle its blood against the altar on all sides. ¹² He will cut it into pieces with its head and its suet, and the priest will arrange them on top of the burning wood on the altar. ¹³ But he is to wash the entrails and shanks with water. The priest will then present all of it and burn it on the altar; it is a burnt offering, a fire offering of a pleasing aroma to the LORD.

¹⁴ "If his gift to the LORD is a burnt offering of birds, he is to present his offering from the turtledoves or young pigeons. ¹⁵ Then the priest must bring it to the altar, and must twist off its head and burn it on the altar; its blood should be drained at the side of the altar. ¹⁶ He will remove its digestive tract, cutting off the tail feathers, and throw it on the east side of the altar at the place for ashes. ¹⁷ He will tear it open by its wings without dividing the bird. Then the priest is to burn it on the altar on top of the burning wood. It is a burnt offering, a fire offering of a pleasing aroma to the LORD.

2 "When anyone presents a grain offering as a gift to the LORD, his gift must consist of fine flour. He is to pour olive oil on it, put frankincense on it, ² and bring it to Aaron's sons the priests. The priest will take a handful of fine flour and oil from it, along with all its frankincense, and will burn this memorial portion of it on the altar, a fire offering of a pleasing aroma to the LORD. ³ But the rest of the grain offering will belong to Aaron and his sons, the holiest part of the fire offerings to the LORD.

⁴ "When you present a grain offering baked in an oven, it must be made of fine flour, either unleavened cakes mixed with oil or unleavened wafers coated with oil. ⁵ If your gift is a grain offering prepared on the griddle, it must be unleavened bread made of fine flour mixed with oil. ⁶ Break it into pieces and pour oil on it; it is a grain offering. ⁷ If your gift is a grain offering prepared in a pan, it must be made of fine flour with oil. ⁸ When you bring to the LORD the grain offering made in any of these ways, it is to be presented to the priest, and he will take it to the altar. ⁹ The priest will remove the memorial portion from the grain offering and burn it on the altar, a fire offering of a pleasing aroma to the LORD. ¹⁰ But the rest of the grain offering will belong to Aaron and his sons, the holiest part of the fire offerings to the LORD.

¹¹ "No grain offering that you present to the LORD is to be made with yeast, for you are not to burn any yeast or honey as a fire offering to the LORD. ¹² You may present them to the LORD as an offering of firstfruits, but they are not to be offered on the altar as a pleasing aroma. ¹³ You are to season each of your grain offerings with salt; you must not omit from your grain offering the salt of the covenant with your God. You are to present salt with each of your offerings.

¹⁴ "If you present a grain offering of firstfruits to the LORD, you must present fresh heads of grain, crushed kernels, roasted on the fire, for your grain offering of firstfruits. ¹⁵ You are to put oil and frankincense on it; it is a grain offering. ¹⁶ The priest will then burn some of its crushed kernels and oil with all its frankincense as a fire offering to the LORD.

3 "If his offering is a fellowship sacrifice, and he is presenting an animal from the herd, whether male or female, he must present one without blemish before the LORD. ² He is to lay his hand on the head of his offering and slaughter it at the entrance to the tent of meeting. Then Aaron's sons the priests will sprinkle the blood on all sides of the altar. ³ He will present part of the fellowship sacrifice as a fire offering to the LORD: the fat surrounding the entrails, all the fat that is on the entrails,

4 and the two kidneys with the fat on them at the loins; he will also remove the fatty lobe of the liver with the kidneys. 5 Aaron's sons will burn it on the altar along with the burnt offering that is on the burning wood, a fire offering of a pleasing aroma to the LORD.

6 "If his offering as a fellowship sacrifice to the LORD is from the flock, he must present a male or female without blemish. 7 If he is presenting a lamb for his offering, he is to present it before the LORD. 8 He must lay his hand on the head of his offering, then slaughter it before the tent of meeting. Aaron's sons will sprinkle its blood on all sides of the altar. 9 He will then present part of the fellowship sacrifice as a fire offering to the LORD consisting of its fat and the entire fat tail, which he is to remove close to the backbone. He will also remove the fat surrounding the entrails, all the fat on the entrails, 10 the two kidneys with the fat on them at the loins, and the fatty lobe of the liver above the kidneys. 11 Then the priest will burn it on the altar as food, a fire offering to the LORD.

12 "If his offering is a goat, he is to present it before the LORD. 13 He must lay his hand on its head and slaughter it before the tent of meeting. Aaron's sons will sprinkle its blood on all sides of the altar. 14 He will present part of his offering as a fire offering to the LORD: the fat surrounding the entrails, all the fat that is on the entrails, 15 and the two kidneys with the fat on them at the loins; he will also remove the fatty lobe of the liver with the kidneys. 16 Then the priest will burn them on the altar as food, a fire offering for a pleasing aroma.

"All fat belongs to the LORD. 17 This is a permanent statute throughout your generations, wherever you live: you must not eat any fat or any blood."

PSALM 24:1-10

1 The earth and everything in it,
　the world and its inhabitants,
　belong to the LORD;

2 for He laid its foundation on the
　seas
　and established it on the rivers.

3 Who may ascend the mountain of
　the LORD?
　Who may stand in His holy place?

4 The one who has clean hands and
　a pure heart,
　who has not set his mind on what
　is false,
　and who has not sworn
　deceitfully.

5 He will receive blessing from the
　LORD,
　and righteousness from the God
　of his salvation.

6 Such is the generation of those
　who seek Him,
　who seek the face of the God of
　Jacob. *Selah*

7 Lift up your heads, you gates!
　Rise up, ancient doors!
　Then the King of glory will come
　in.

8 Who is this King of glory?
　The LORD, strong and mighty,
　the LORD, mighty in battle.

9 Lift up your heads, you gates!
　Rise up, ancient doors!
　Then the King of glory will come
　in.

10 Who is He, this King of glory?
　The LORD of Hosts,
　He is the King of glory. *Selah*

PROVERBS 6:1-3

6 My son, if you have put up security
　for your neighbor
　or entered into an agreement with
　a stranger,

2 you have been trapped by the
　words of your lips—
　ensnared by the words of your
　mouth.

3 Do this, then, my son, and free
　yourself,
　for you have put yourself in your
　neighbor's power:
　Go, humble yourself, and plead
　with your neighbor.

MARK 1:1-20

1 The beginning of the gospel of Jesus Christ, the Son of God. ² As it is written in Isaiah the prophet:

> Look, I am sending
> My messenger ahead of You,
> who will prepare Your way.
> ³ A voice of one crying out
> in the wilderness:
> "Prepare the way for the Lord;
> make His paths straight!"

⁴ John came baptizing in the wilderness and preaching a baptism of repentance for the forgiveness of sins. ⁵ The whole Judean countryside and all the people of Jerusalem were flocking to him, and they were baptized by him in the Jordan River as they confessed their sins. ⁶ John wore a camel-hair garment with a leather belt around his waist and ate locusts and wild honey. ⁷ He was preaching: "Someone more powerful than I will come after me. I am not worthy to stoop down and untie the strap of His sandals. ⁸ I have baptized you with water, but He will baptize you with the Holy Spirit."

⁹ In those days Jesus came from Nazareth in Galilee and was baptized in the Jordan by John. ¹⁰ As soon as He came up out of the water, He saw the heavens being torn open and the Spirit descending to Him like a dove. ¹¹ And a voice came from heaven:

> You are My beloved Son;
> I take delight in You!

¹² Immediately the Spirit drove Him into the wilderness. ¹³ He was in the wilderness 40 days, being tempted by Satan. He was with the wild animals, and the angels began to serve Him.

¹⁴ After John was arrested, Jesus went to Galilee, preaching the good news of God: ¹⁵ "The time is fulfilled, and the kingdom of God has come near. Repent and believe in the good news!"

¹⁶ As He was passing along by the Sea of Galilee, He saw Simon and Andrew, Simon's brother. They were casting a net into the sea, since they were fishermen. ¹⁷ "Follow Me," Jesus told them, "and I will make you fish for people!" ¹⁸ Immediately they left their nets and followed Him. ¹⁹ Going on a little farther, He saw James the son of Zebedee and his brother John. They were in their boat mending their nets. ²⁰ Immediately He called them, and they left their father Zebedee in the boat with the hired men and followed Him.

A Dip into the Depths

Who may ascend the mountain of the LORD? . . .
The one who has clean hands and a pure heart.

—PSALM 24:3-4

If we take an honest and straightforward look at what is going on inside us, we must be ready for a number of strong spiritual challenges. But we must not allow ourselves to be disheartened, for in looking at our hearts we become ready to move upwards into the mountains of God.

The suggestion I want to make to you is this—recognize the subtle and insidious nature of sin. There is a view in the Christian church that as long as we focus on the sins that are obvious (sins of behavior), then we can forget any hidden sins that may be in the heart, trusting God to deal with them in His own way. Dealing with obvious sin is extremely important—don't hear me minimizing this fact. Moral discipline is part of the Christian commitment. We are expected to resist the temptations that come our way and correct any spiritual violations that may occur. But to concern ourselves only with obvious sin and avoid facing the sins of the heart will cause us to miss our footing on the slopes of God.

Someone has put it like this: "The grime has been so embedded in the carpet that a simple vacuuming will not do the job. We need a scrubbing brush and a strong detergent." Diligence in putting right the things that are obviously wrong is good, but without a clear understanding of how sin has penetrated our hearts, we will be nothing more than surface-copers.

Prayer

Father, forgive me that I have been so content to live on the surface of life. Help me see that, in turning my gaze to what is going on inside me, You are not seeking to demean me but to develop me. Give me grace not to shrink from the task. Amen.

Further Study

Jr 17:1-11; Gn 3:8; Pr 28:13
What is the tendency of the human heart?
What is one condition for us to prosper spiritually?

FEBRUARY 21

LEVITICUS 4:1–5:19

4 Then the LORD spoke to Moses: ² "Tell the Israelites: When someone sins unintentionally against any of the LORD's commands and does anything prohibited by them—

³ "If the anointed priest sins, bringing guilt on the people, he is to present to the LORD a young, unblemished bull as a sin offering for the sin he has committed. ⁴ He must bring the bull to the entrance to the tent of meeting before the LORD, lay his hand on the bull's head, and slaughter it before the LORD. ⁵ The anointed priest must then take some of

the bull's blood and bring it into the tent of meeting. ⁶ The priest is to dip his finger in the blood and sprinkle some of it seven times before the LORD in front of the veil of the sanctuary. ⁷ The priest must apply some of the blood to the horns of the altar of fragrant incense that is before the LORD in the tent of meeting. He must pour out the rest of the bull's blood at the base of the altar of burnt offering that is at the entrance to the tent of meeting. ⁸ He is to remove all the fat from the bull of the sin offering: the fat surrounding the entrails; all the fat that is on the entrails; ⁹ and the two kidneys with the fat on them at the

203

loins. He will also remove the fatty lobe of the liver with the kidneys, [10] just as the fat is removed from the ox of the fellowship sacrifice. The priest is to burn them on the altar of burnt offering. [11] But the hide of the bull and all its flesh, with its head and shanks, and its entrails and dung— [12] all the rest of the bull—he must bring to a ceremonially clean place outside the camp to the ash heap, and must burn it on a wood fire. It is to be burned at the ash heap.

[13] "Now if the whole community of Israel errs, and the matter escapes the notice of the assembly, so that they violate any of the LORD's commands and incur guilt by doing what is prohibited, [14] then the assembly must present a young bull as a sin offering. When the sin they have committed in regard to the command becomes known, they are to bring it before the tent of meeting. [15] The elders of the assembly are to lay their hands on the bull's head before the LORD and it is to be slaughtered before the LORD. [16] The anointed priest will bring some of the bull's blood into the tent of meeting. [17] The priest is to dip his finger in the blood and sprinkle it seven times before the LORD in front of the veil. [18] He is to apply some of the blood to the horns of the altar that is before the LORD in the tent of meeting. He must pour out the rest of the blood at the base of the altar of burnt offering that is at the entrance to the tent of meeting. [19] He is to remove all the fat from it and burn it on the altar. [20] He is to offer this bull just as he did with the bull in the sin offering; he will offer it the same way. So the priest will make atonement on their behalf, and they will be forgiven. [21] Then he will bring the bull outside the camp and burn it just as he burned the first bull. It is the sin offering for the assembly.

[22] "When a leader sins and unintentionally violates any of the commands of the LORD his God by doing what is prohibited, and incurs guilt, [23] or someone informs him about the sin he has committed, he is to bring an unblemished male goat as his offering. [24] He is to lay his hand on the head of the goat and slaugh-

ter it at the place where the burnt offering is slaughtered before the LORD. It is a sin offering. [25] Then the priest must take some of the blood from the sin offering with his finger and apply it to the horns of the altar of burnt offering. The rest of its blood he must pour out at the base of the altar of burnt offering. [26] He must burn all its fat on the altar, like the fat of the fellowship sacrifice. In this way the priest will make atonement on his behalf for that person's sin, and he will be forgiven.

[27] "Now if any of the common people sins unintentionally by violating one of the LORD's commands, does what is prohibited, and incurs guilt, [28] or if someone informs him about the sin he has committed, then he is to bring an unblemished female goat as his offering for the sin that he has committed. [29] He is to lay his hand on the head of the sin offering and slaughter it at the place of the burnt offering. [30] Then the priest must take some of its blood with his finger and apply it to the horns of the altar of burnt offering. He must pour out the rest of its blood at the base of the altar. [31] He is to remove all its fat just as the fat is removed from the fellowship sacrifice. The priest is to burn it on the altar as a pleasing aroma to the LORD. In this way the priest will make atonement on his behalf, and he will be forgiven.

[32] "Or if the offering that he brings as a sin offering is a lamb, he is to bring an unblemished female. [33] He is to lay his hand on the head of the sin offering and slaughter it as a sin offering at the place where the burnt offering is slaughtered. [34] Then the priest must take some of the blood of the sin offering with his finger and apply it to the horns of the altar of burnt offering. He must pour out the rest of its blood at the base of the altar. [35] He is to remove all its fat just as the fat of the lamb is removed from the fellowship sacrifice. The priest will burn it on the altar along with the fire offerings to the LORD. In this way the priest will make atonement on his behalf for the sin he has committed, and he will be forgiven.

5 "When someone sins in any of these ways:

He has seen, heard, or known about something he has witnessed, and did not respond to a public call to testify, he is guilty. ² Or someone touches anything unclean—a carcass of an unclean wild animal, or unclean livestock, or an unclean swarming creature—without being aware of it, he is unclean and guilty. ³ Or he touches human uncleanness—any uncleanness by which one can become defiled—without being aware of it, but later recognizes it, he is guilty. ⁴ Or someone swears rashly to do good or evil—concerning anything a person may speak rashly in an oath—without being aware of it, but later recognizes it, he incurs guilt in such an instance.

⁵ If someone incurs guilt in one of these cases, he is to confess he has committed that sin. ⁶ He must bring his restitution for the sin he has committed to the LORD: a female lamb or goat from the flock as a sin offering. In this way the priest will make atonement on his behalf for his sin.

⁷ "But if he cannot afford an animal from the flock, then he may bring to the LORD two turtledoves or two young pigeons as restitution for his sin—one as a sin offering and the other as a burnt offering. ⁸ He is to bring them to the priest, who will first present the one for the sin offering. He must twist its head at the back of the neck without severing it. ⁹ Then he will sprinkle some of the blood of the sin offering on the side of the altar, while the rest of the blood is to be drained out at the base of the altar; it is a sin offering. ¹⁰ He must prepare the second bird as a burnt offering according to the regulation. In this way the priest will make atonement on his behalf for the sin he has committed, and he will be forgiven.

¹¹ "But if he cannot afford two turtledoves or two young pigeons, he may bring two quarts of fine flour as an offering for his sin. He must not put olive oil or frankincense on it, for it is a sin offering. ¹² He is to bring it to the priest, who will take a handful from it as its memorial portion and burn it on the altar along with the fire offerings to the LORD; it is a sin offering. ¹³ In this way the priest will make atonement on his behalf concerning the sin he has committed in any of these cases, and he will be forgiven. The rest will belong to the priest, like the grain offering."

¹⁴ Then the LORD spoke to Moses: ¹⁵ "If someone offends by sinning unintentionally in regard to any of the LORD's holy things, he must bring his restitution offering to the LORD: an unblemished ram from the flock by your valuation in silver shekels, according to the sanctuary shekel, as a restitution offering. ¹⁶ He must make restitution for his sin regarding any holy thing, adding a fifth of its value to it, and give it to the priest. Then the priest will make atonement on his behalf with the ram of the restitution offering, and he will be forgiven.

¹⁷ "If someone sins and without knowing it violates any of the LORD's commands concerning anything prohibited, he bears the consequences of his guilt. ¹⁸ He must bring an unblemished ram from the flock according to your valuation as a restitution offering to the priest. Then the priest will make atonement on his behalf for the error he has committed unintentionally, and he will be forgiven. ¹⁹ It is a restitution offering; he is indeed guilty before the LORD."

....

$\mathcal{P}$SALM 25:1-7

¹ LORD, I turn my hope to You.
² My God, I trust in You.
  Do not let me be disgraced;
  do not let my enemies gloat over
    me.
³ Not one person who waits for You
    will be disgraced;
  those who act treacherously
    without cause will be
    disgraced.

4 Make Your ways known to me,
   LORD;
   teach me Your paths.
5 Guide me in Your truth and teach
   me,
   for You are the God of my
   salvation;
   I wait for You all day long.
6 Remember, LORD, Your compassion
   and Your faithful love,
   for they have existed from
   antiquity.
7 Do not remember the sins of my
   youth or my acts of rebellion;
   in keeping with Your faithful love,
   remember me
   because of Your goodness, LORD.

PROVERBS 6:4-5

4 Don't give sleep to your eyes
   or slumber to your eyelids.
5 Escape like a gazelle from a
   hunter,
   like a bird from a fowler's trap.

MARK 1:21-45

21 Then they went into Capernaum,
and right away He entered the synagogue on the Sabbath and began to
teach. 22 They were astonished at His
teaching because, unlike the scribes, He
was teaching them as one having authority.
23 Just then a man with an unclean
spirit was in their synagogue. He cried
out, 24 "What do You have to do with us,
Jesus—Nazarene? Have You come to destroy us? I know who You are—the Holy
One of God!"
25 But Jesus rebuked him and said,
"Be quiet, and come out of him!" 26 And
the unclean spirit convulsed him, shouted with a loud voice, and came out of
him.
27 Then they were all amazed, so they
began to argue with one another, saying, "What is this? A new teaching with
authority! He commands even the unclean spirits, and they obey Him." 28 His
fame then spread throughout the entire
vicinity of Galilee.

29 As soon as they left the synagogue,
they went into Simon and Andrew's
house with James and John. 30 Simon's
mother-in-law was lying in bed with a
fever, and they told Him about her at
once. 31 So He went to her, took her by
the hand, and raised her up. The fever
left her, and she began to serve them.
32 When evening came, after the sun
had set, they began bringing to Him all
those who were sick and those who
were demon-possessed. 33 The whole
town was assembled at the door, 34 and
He healed many who were sick with
various diseases and drove out many
demons. But He would not permit the
demons to speak, because they knew
Him.
35 Very early in the morning, while it
was still dark, He got up, went out, and
made His way to a deserted place. And
He was praying there. 36 Simon and his
companions went searching for Him.
37 They found Him and said, "Everyone's looking for You!"
38 And He said to them, "Let's go on
to the neighboring villages so that I may
preach there too. This is why I have
come." 39 So He went into all of Galilee,
preaching in their synagogues and driving out demons.
40 Then a man with a serious skin disease came to Him and, on his knees,
begged Him: "If You are willing, You can
make me clean."
41 Moved with compassion, Jesus
reached out His hand and touched him.
"I am willing," He told him. "Be made
clean." 42 Immediately the disease left
him, and he was healed. 43 Then He
sternly warned him and sent him away
at once, 44 telling him, "See that you say
nothing to anyone; but go and show
yourself to the priest, and offer what
Moses prescribed for your cleansing, as
a testimony to them." 45 Yet he went out
and began to proclaim it widely and to
spread the news, with the result that
Jesus could no longer enter a town
openly. But He was out in deserted
places, and they would come to Him
from everywhere.

The Morning Watch

Very early in the morning . . . [Jesus] made His way to a deserted place. And He was praying there.—MARK 1:35

It is an exciting thought that spiritual staleness need not be so. Spiritual freshness is available to us all—and on a daily basis. Maintaining it, however, does not mean that we will be exempt from having to face occasional trials and difficulties. It means, rather, that no matter how dry and difficult our circumstances, our experience of God can remain fresh and vibrant.

What, then, is the first principle of maintaining spiritual freshness? Establish a daily quiet time with God in order to replenish your spiritual resources.

Some modern-day Christians balk at this idea. They say, "The Lord is with us all the time. Why do we need to fence off a particular part of the day to spend time with Him? A daily quiet time can soon bring one into legalism." I am well aware of this danger, but again I say—it need not be so. There have been periods in my own life when my quiet time was nothing more than a ritual, but that was more a consequence than a cause.

The best period for a quiet time, in my opinion, is in the morning, before the day starts. Some prefer the evening or perhaps—as in the case of busy mothers and wives—the late morning is better, when the family has left and the house is quiet. Each must establish the best time according to preference or convenience. I'm merely saying that a certain time of the day ought not to belong to the day, but to the getting of resources for the day. Start the day right and you will end it right.

Prayer

O God, help me to see that just as I need to take time out of the day to feed myself physically, so I need to take time out to feed myself spiritually. Help me not just to acknowledge this, but to act on it. In Christ's name I pray. Amen.

Further Study

Ps 119:137-148; 5:1-3; Gn 28:18; Dn 6:10
When did the psalmist pray?
When do you pray?

FEBRUARY 22

LEVITICUS 6:1–7:21

6 The LORD spoke to Moses: ² "When someone sins and offends the LORD by deceiving his neighbor in regard to a deposit, a security, or a robbery; or defrauds his neighbor; ³ or finds something lost and lies about it; or swears falsely about any of the sinful things a person may do— ⁴ once he has sinned and acknowledged his guilt—he must return what he stole or defrauded, or the deposit entrusted to him, or the lost item he found, ⁵ or anything else about which he swore falsely. He must make full restitution for it and add a fifth of its value to it. He is to pay it to its owner on the day he acknowledges his guilt. ⁶ Then he must bring his restitution offering to the LORD: an unblemished ram from the flock, according to your valuation, as a restitution offering to the priest. ⁷ In this way the priest will make atonement on his behalf before the LORD, and he will be forgiven for anything he may have done to incur guilt."

⁸ The LORD spoke to Moses: ⁹ "Command Aaron and his sons: This is the law of the burnt offering; the burnt offering itself must remain on the altar's hearth all night until morning, while the fire of the altar is kept burning on it. ¹⁰ The priest is to put on his linen robe and linen undergarments. He is to remove the ashes of the burnt offering the fire has consumed on the altar, and place them beside the altar. ¹¹ Then he must take off his garments, put on other clothes, and bring the ashes outside the camp to a ceremonially clean place. ¹² The fire on the altar is to be kept burning; it must not go out. Every morning the priest will burn wood on the fire. He is to arrange the burnt offering on the fire and burn the fat portions from the fellowship offerings on it. ¹³ Fire must be kept burning on the altar continually; it must not go out.

¹⁴ "Now this is the law of the grain offering: Aaron's sons will present it before the LORD in front of the altar. ¹⁵ The priest is to remove a handful of fine flour and olive oil from the grain offering, with all the frankincense that is on the offering, and burn its memorial portion on the altar as a pleasing aroma to the LORD. ¹⁶ Aaron and his sons may eat the rest of it. It is to be eaten as unleavened bread in a holy place; they are to eat it in the courtyard of the tent of meeting. ¹⁷ It must not be baked with yeast; I have assigned it as their portion from My fire offerings. It is especially holy, like the sin offering and the restitution offering. ¹⁸ Any male among Aaron's descendants may eat it. It is a permanent portion throughout your generations from the fire offerings to the LORD. Anything that touches the offerings will become holy."

¹⁹ The LORD spoke to Moses: ²⁰ "This is the offering that Aaron and his sons must present to the LORD on the day that he is anointed: two quarts of fine flour as a regular grain offering, half of it in the morning and half in the evening. ²¹ It is to be prepared with oil on a griddle; you are to bring it well-kneaded. You must present it as a grain offering of baked pieces, a pleasing aroma to the LORD. ²² The priest, who is of Aaron's sons and will be anointed to take his place, is to prepare it. It must be completely burned as a permanent portion for the LORD. ²³ Every grain offering for a priest will be a whole burnt offering; it is not to be eaten."

²⁴ The LORD spoke to Moses: ²⁵ "Tell Aaron and his sons: This is the law of the sin offering. The sin offering is most holy and must be slaughtered before the LORD at the place where the burnt offering is slaughtered. ²⁶ The priest

who offers it as a sin offering is to eat it. It must be eaten in a holy place, in the courtyard of the tent of meeting. ²⁷ Anything that touches its flesh will become holy, and if any of its blood spatters on a garment, then you must wash that garment in a holy place. ²⁸ A clay pot in which the sin offering is boiled must be broken; if it is boiled in a bronze vessel, it must be scoured and rinsed with water. ²⁹ Any male among the priests may eat it; it is especially holy. ³⁰ But no sin offering may be eaten if its blood has been brought into the tent of meeting to make atonement in the holy place; it must be burned up.

7 "Now this is the law of the restitution offering; it is especially holy. ² The restitution offering must be slaughtered at the place where the burnt offering is slaughtered, and the priest is to sprinkle its blood on all sides of the altar. ³ The offerer must present all the fat from it: the fat tail, the fat surrounding the entrails, ⁴ and the two kidneys with the fat on them at the loins; he will also remove the fatty lobe of the liver with the kidneys. ⁵ The priest will burn them on the altar as a fire offering to the LORD; it is a restitution offering. ⁶ Any male among the priests may eat it. It is to be eaten in a holy place; it is especially holy.

⁷ "The restitution offering is like the sin offering; the law is the same for both. It belongs to the priest who makes atonement with it. ⁸ As for the priest who presents someone's burnt offering, the hide of the burnt offering he has presented belongs to him; it is the priest's. ⁹ Any grain offering that is baked in an oven, or prepared in a pan or on a griddle, belongs to the priest who presents it; it is his. ¹⁰ But any grain offering, whether dry or mixed with oil, belongs equally to all of Aaron's sons.

¹¹ "Now this is the law of the fellowship sacrifice that someone may present to the LORD: ¹² If he presents it for thanksgiving, in addition to the thanksgiving sacrifice, he is to present unleavened cakes mixed with olive oil, unleavened wafers coated with oil, and well-kneaded cakes of fine flour mixed with oil. ¹³ He is to present as his offering cakes of leavened bread, with his thanksgiving sacrifice of fellowship. ¹⁴ From the cakes he must present one portion of each offering as a contribution to the LORD. It will belong to the priest who sprinkles the blood of the fellowship offering; it is his. ¹⁵ The meat of his thanksgiving sacrifice of fellowship must be eaten on the day he offers it; he may not leave any of it until morning.

¹⁶ "If the sacrifice he offers is a vow or a freewill offering, it is to be eaten on the day he presents his sacrifice, and what is left over may be eaten on the next day. ¹⁷ But what remains of the sacrificial meat by the third day must be burned up. ¹⁸ If any of the meat of his fellowship sacrifice is eaten on the third day, it will not be accepted. It will not be credited to the one who presents it; it is repulsive. The person who eats any of it will be guilty.

¹⁹ "Meat that touches anything unclean must not be eaten; it is to be burned up. Everyone who is clean may eat any other meat. ²⁰ But the one who eats meat from the LORD's fellowship sacrifice while he is unclean, that person must be cut off from his people. ²¹ If someone touches anything unclean, whether human uncleanness, an unclean animal, or any unclean, detestable creature, and eats meat from the LORD's fellowship sacrifice, that person must be cut off from his people."

······································

*P*SALM 25:8-15

⁸ The LORD is good and upright;
   therefore He shows sinners the
      way.
⁹ He leads the humble in what is
      right
   and teaches them His way.
¹⁰ All the LORD's ways show faithful
      love and truth
   to those who keep His covenant
      and decrees.
¹¹ Because of Your name, LORD,
   forgive my sin, for it is great.

12 Who is the person who fears the
      LORD?
   He will show him the way he
      should choose.
13 He will live a good life,
   and his descendants will inherit
      the land.
14 The secret counsel of the LORD is
      for those who fear Him,
   and He reveals His covenant to
      them.
15 My eyes are always on the LORD,
   for He will pull my feet out of the
      net.

PROVERBS 6:6-8

6 Go to the ant, you slacker!
   Observe its ways and become wise.
7 Without leader, administrator, or
      ruler,
8 it prepares its provisions in
      summer;
   it gathers its food during harvest.

MARK 2:1-22

2 When He entered Capernaum again
   after some days, it was reported that
He was at home. ² So many people gathered together that there was no more
room, not even in the doorway, and He
was speaking the message to them.
³ Then they came to Him bringing a paralytic, carried by four men. ⁴ Since they
were not able to bring him to Jesus because of the crowd, they removed the
roof above where He was. And when
they had broken through, they lowered
the stretcher on which the paralytic was
lying.
⁵ Seeing their faith, Jesus told the paralytic, "Son, your sins are forgiven."
⁶ But some of the scribes were sitting
there, thinking to themselves: ⁷ "Why
does He speak like this? He's blaspheming! Who can forgive sins but God
alone?"
⁸ Right away Jesus understood in His
spirit that they were reasoning like this
within themselves and said to them,
"Why are you reasoning these things in
your hearts? ⁹ Which is easier: to say to

the paralytic, 'Your sins are forgiven,' or
to say, 'Get up, pick up your stretcher,
and walk'? ¹⁰ But so you may know that
the Son of Man has authority on earth
to forgive sins," He told the paralytic,
¹¹ "I tell you: get up, pick up your
stretcher, and go home."
¹² Immediately he got up, picked up
the stretcher, and went out in front of
everyone. As a result, they were all astounded and gave glory to God, saying,
"We have never seen anything like
this!"
¹³ Then Jesus went out again beside
the sea. The whole crowd was coming
to Him, and He taught them. ¹⁴ Then,
moving on, He saw Levi the son of
Alphaeus sitting at the tax office, and
He said to him, "Follow Me!" So he got
up and followed Him.
¹⁵ While He was reclining at the table
in Levi's house, many tax collectors and
sinners were also guests with Jesus and
His disciples, because there were many
who were following Him. ¹⁶ When the
scribes of the Pharisees saw that He was
eating with sinners and tax collectors,
they asked His disciples, "Why does He
eat with tax collectors and sinners?"
¹⁷ When Jesus heard this, He told
them, "Those who are well don't need a
doctor, but the sick do need one. I
didn't come to call the righteous, but
sinners."
¹⁸ Now John's disciples and the Pharisees were fasting. People came and
asked Him, "Why do John's disciples
and the Pharisees' disciples fast, but
Your disciples do not fast?"
¹⁹ Jesus said to them, "The wedding
guests cannot fast while the groom is
with them, can they? As long as they
have the groom with them, they cannot
fast. ²⁰ But the time will come when the
groom is taken away from them, and
then they will fast in that day. ²¹ No one
sews a patch of unshrunk cloth on an
old garment. Otherwise, the new patch
pulls away from the old cloth, and a
worse tear is made. ²² And no one puts
new wine into old wineskins. Otherwise, the wine will burst the skins, and
the wine is lost as well as the skins. But
new wine is for fresh wineskins."

Prepare!

Go to the ant, you slacker! Observe its ways
and become wise.—PROVERBS 6:6

The vital principle of deferred satisfaction is brought out in the text that is before us today. We see it clearly in the animal kingdom: the ant doesn't spend all its time eating. It runs back and forth carrying food into the nest so that it may survive the winter when there will be no food.

Keep this picture of the ant continually in your mind. It is one of those images put into the Word of God to bring instruction to the heart. If you are young, prepare for the future in every way you can, not only by denying yourself to the things that God puts out of bounds, but also by giving yourself to the things you need to know about your chosen profession. Whatever you plan to do in life—prepare for it. Prepare by study and also by prayer.

Whatever your age—whenever you have to do anything in public, like speaking at a church meeting—prepare. Deny yourself pleasures, like watching television, and give yourself to the task at hand. There are not short cuts to success. I prepared myself for years by filling my heart and mind with the Word of God, and then, when the time came, God called me to launch these Bible notes that you are now reading. People say to me, "How can you continue to write year after year?" I know I would not be able to do so had I not, many years ago, denied myself many things so that I could prepare. Whatever God asks you to do, don't take His blessings for granted—prepare.

Prayer

Father, Your knife cuts deep, but Your cuts are always redemptive. Forgive me for taking so much for granted and for not giving myself to the task to which You have called me. Help me be a prepared person. In Jesus' name I ask it. Amen.

Further Study

Mt 16:21-28; Mk 8:34; Lk 9:23
What did Jesus say to His disciples?
Are there areas of your life in which you need to deny yourself?

FEBRUARY 23

LEVITICUS 7:22–8:36

²² The LORD spoke to Moses: ²³ "Tell the Israelites: You are not to eat any fat of an ox, a sheep, or a goat. ²⁴ The fat of an animal that dies naturally or is mauled by wild beasts may be used for any purpose, but you must not eat it. ²⁵ If anyone eats animal fat from a fire offering presented to the LORD, the person who eats it must be cut off from his people. ²⁶ Wherever you live, you must not eat the blood of any bird or animal. ²⁷ Whoever eats any blood, that person must be cut off from his people."

²⁸ The LORD spoke to Moses: ²⁹ "Tell the Israelites: The one who presents a fellowship sacrifice to the LORD must bring an offering to the LORD from his sacrifice. ³⁰ His own hands will bring the fire offerings to the LORD. He will bring the fat together with the breast. The breast is to be waved as a presentation offering before the LORD. ³¹ The priest is to burn the fat on the altar, but the breast belongs to Aaron and his sons. ³² You are to give the right thigh to the priest as a contribution from your fellowship sacrifices. ³³ The son of Aaron who presents the blood of the fellowship offering and the fat will have the right thigh as a portion. ³⁴ I have taken from the Israelites the breast of the presentation offering and the thigh of the contribution from their fellowship sacrifices, and have assigned them to Aaron the priest and his sons as a permanent portion from the Israelites."

³⁵ This is the portion from the fire offerings to the LORD for Aaron and his sons since the day they were presented to serve the LORD as priests. ³⁶ The LORD commanded this to be given to them by the Israelites on the day He anointed them. It is a permanent portion throughout their generations.

³⁷ This is the law for the burnt offering, the grain offering, the sin offering, the restitution offering, the ordination offering, and the fellowship sacrifice, ³⁸ which the LORD commanded Moses on Mount Sinai on the day He commanded the Israelites to present their offerings to the LORD in the Wilderness of Sinai.

8 The LORD spoke to Moses: ² "Take Aaron, his sons with him, the garments, the anointing oil, the bull of the sin offering, the two rams, and the basket of unleavened bread, ³ and assemble the whole community at the entrance to the tent of meeting." ⁴ So Moses did as the LORD commanded him, and the community assembled at the entrance to the tent of meeting. ⁵ Moses said to them, "This is what the LORD has commanded to be done."

⁶ Then Moses presented Aaron and his sons and washed them with water. ⁷ He put the tunic on Aaron, wrapped the sash around him, clothed him with the robe, and put the ephod on him. He put the woven band of the ephod around him and fastened it to him. ⁸ Then he put the breastpiece on him and placed the Urim and Thummim into the breastpiece. ⁹ He also put the turban on his head and placed the plate of gold, the holy diadem, on the front of the turban, as the LORD had commanded Moses.

¹⁰ Then Moses took the anointing oil and anointed the tabernacle and everything in it to consecrate them. ¹¹ He sprinkled some of the oil on the altar seven times, anointing the altar with all its utensils, and the basin with its stand, to consecrate them. ¹² He poured some of the anointing oil on Aaron's head and anointed and consecrated him. ¹³ Then Moses presented Aaron's sons, clothed them with tunics, wrapped sashes around them, and fastened headbands on them, as the LORD had commanded

Moses. ¹⁴ Then he brought the bull near for the sin offering, and Aaron and his sons laid their hands on the head of the bull for the sin offering. ¹⁵ Then Moses slaughtered it, took the blood, and applied it with his finger to the horns of the altar on all sides, purifying the altar. He poured out the blood at the base of the altar and consecrated it by making atonement for it. ¹⁶ Moses took all the fat that was on the entrails, the fatty lobe of the liver, and the two kidneys with their fat, and he burned them on the altar. ¹⁷ He burned up the bull with its hide, flesh, and dung outside the camp, as the LORD had commanded Moses. ¹⁸ Then he presented the ram for the burnt offering, and Aaron and his sons laid their hands on the head of the ram. ¹⁹ Moses slaughtered it and sprinkled the blood on all sides of the altar. ²⁰ Moses cut the ram into pieces and burned the head, the pieces, and the suet, ²¹ but he washed the entrails and shanks with water. He then burned the entire ram on the altar. It was a burnt offering for a pleasing aroma, a fire offering to the LORD as He had commanded Moses.

²² Next he presented the second ram, the ram of ordination, and Aaron and his sons laid their hands on the head of the ram. ²³ Moses slaughtered it, took some of its blood, and put it on Aaron's right earlobe, on the thumb of his right hand, and on the big toe of his right foot. ²⁴ Moses also presented Aaron's sons and put some of the blood on their right earlobes, on the thumbs of their right hands, and on the big toes of their right feet. Then Moses sprinkled the blood on all sides of the altar. ²⁵ He took the fat—the fat tail, all the fat that was on the entrails, the fatty lobe of the liver, and the two kidneys with their fat—as well as the right thigh. ²⁶ From the basket of unleavened bread that was before the LORD he took one cake of unleavened bread, one cake of bread made with oil, and one wafer, and placed them on the fat portions and the right thigh. ²⁷ He put all these in the hands of Aaron and his sons and waved them before the LORD as a presentation offering. ²⁸ Then Moses took them from their hands and burned them on the altar with the burnt offering. This was an ordination offering for a pleasing aroma, a fire offering to the LORD. ²⁹ He also took the breast and waved it before the LORD as a presentation offering; it was Moses' portion of the ordination ram as the LORD had commanded him.

³⁰ Then Moses took some of the anointing oil and some of the blood that was on the altar and sprinkled them on Aaron and his garments, as well as on his sons and their garments. In this way he consecrated Aaron and his garments, as well as his sons and their garments.

³¹ Moses said to Aaron and his sons, "Boil the meat at the entrance to the tent of meeting and eat it there with the bread that is in the basket for the ordination offering as I commanded: Aaron and his sons are to eat it. ³² You must burn up what remains of the meat and bread. ³³ You must not go outside the entrance to the tent of meeting for seven days, until the time your days of ordination are completed, because it will take seven days to ordain you. ³⁴ The LORD commanded what has been done today in order to make atonement for you. ³⁵ You must remain at the entrance to the tent of meeting day and night for seven days and keep the LORD's charge so that you will not die, for this is what I was commanded." ³⁶ So Aaron and his sons did everything the LORD had commanded through Moses.

....

PSALM 25:16-22

¹⁶ Turn to me and be gracious to me,
   for I am alone and afflicted.
¹⁷ The distresses of my heart
      increase;
   bring me out of my sufferings.
¹⁸ Consider my affliction and
      trouble,
   and take away all my sins.
¹⁹ Consider my enemies; they are
      numerous,
   and they hate me violently.

20 Guard me and deliver me;
do not let me be put to shame, for
I take refuge in You.
21 May integrity and uprightness
keep me,
for I wait for You.

22 God, redeem Israel, from all its
distresses.

PROVERBS 6:9-11

9 How long will you stay in bed, you
slacker?
When will you get up from your
sleep?
10 A little sleep, a little slumber,
a little folding of the arms to rest,
11 and your poverty will come like a
robber,
your need, like a bandit.

MARK 2:23–3:12

23 On the Sabbath He was going
through the grainfields, and His disciples began to make their way picking
some heads of grain. 24 The Pharisees
said to Him, "Look, why are they doing
what is not lawful on the Sabbath?"
25 He said to them, "Have you never
read what David and those who were
with him did when he was in need and
hungry— 26 how he entered the house
of God in the time of Abiathar the high
priest and ate the sacred bread—which
is not lawful for anyone to eat except
the priests—and also gave some to his
companions?" 27 Then He told them,
"The Sabbath was made for man and
not man for the Sabbath. 28 Therefore
the Son of Man is Lord even of the
Sabbath."

3 Now He entered the synagogue
again, and a man was there who had
a paralyzed hand. 2 In order to accuse
Him, they were watching Him closely to
see whether He would heal him on the
Sabbath. 3 He told the man with the paralyzed hand, "Stand before us." 4 Then
He said to them, "Is it lawful on the
Sabbath to do good or to do evil, to save
life or to kill?" But they were silent.
5 After looking around at them with
anger and sorrow at the hardness of
their hearts, He told the man, "Stretch
out your hand." So he stretched it out,
and his hand was restored. 6 Immediately the Pharisees went out and started
plotting with the Herodians against
Him, how they might destroy Him.
7 Jesus departed with His disciples to
the sea, and a great multitude followed
from Galilee, Judea, 8 Jerusalem, Idu-
mea, beyond the Jordan, and around
Tyre and Sidon. The great multitude
came to Him because they heard about
everything He was doing. 9 Then He told
His disciples to have a small boat ready
for Him, so the crowd would not crush
Him. 10 Since He had healed many, all
who had diseases were pressing toward
Him to touch Him. 11 Whenever the unclean spirits saw Him, those possessed
fell down before Him and cried out,
"You are the Son of God!" 12 And He
would strongly warn them not to make
Him known.

"God's Postal Address"?

*Guard me and deliver me; do not let me be put to
shame, for I take refuge in You.*—PSALM 25:20

Jesus, in the opening words of the Lord's Prayer, taught us to focus first on God before pre-
senting to Him our requests and petitions. Why did Jesus bid us pray, "Our Father in heaven"?
What is so important about the fact that God lives in heaven?
Someone has suggested that heaven is "God's postal address" and, therefore, the place to

which all prayers and petitions ought to be directed. I believe, however, that Jesus, in using the words "in heaven," sought to focus our minds not so much on God's location, but rather His elevation.

We are so used to living, as we say, "in a man's world," surrounded by limitations, that we are apt to forget that God exists in a realm where there are no shortages or restraints. Here on earth, we stagger from one crisis to another, face endless problems—such as economic recessions, strikes, political unrest—but in heaven, where God lives, such situations are nonexistent. There are no shortages in the factories of His grace, no disputes on His assembly lines and no faults in His communication system. Ring "Calvary" at any hour of the day or night, and you will be put into direct contact with the King of kings!

Can you now see what Jesus means when He bids us focus on God who is in heaven? He is telling us to elevate our spiritual vision until it breaks free of earth's gravitational pull and to remind ourselves constantly of the fact that, in our Father's presence, our greatest problems turn into possibilities.

Prayer

O Father, this phrase "in heaven" is like a rocket that launches me beyond earth's limitations into a realm where everything is blessedness and light. Help me never lose sight of this fact—today and every day. Amen.

Further Study

Rv 21; Is 66:1-2; Mt 5:34; Rv 4:2
What is the focal point of heaven?
How does this elevate our vision?

FEBRUARY 24

*L*EVITICUS 9:1–11:12

9 On the eighth day Moses summoned Aaron, his sons, and the elders of Israel. ² He said to Aaron, "Take a young bull for a sin offering and a ram for a burnt offering, both without blemish, and present them before the LORD. ³ And tell the Israelites: 'Take a male goat for a sin offering; a calf and a lamb, male yearlings without blemish, for a burnt offering; ⁴ an ox and a ram for a fellowship offering to sacrifice before the LORD; and a grain offering mixed with oil. For today the LORD is going to appear to you.' "

⁵ They brought what Moses had commanded to the front of the tent of meeting, and the whole community came forward and stood before the LORD. ⁶ Moses said, "This is what the LORD

215

commanded you to do, that the glory of the LORD may appear to you." [7] Then Moses said to Aaron, "Approach the altar and sacrifice your sin offering and your burnt offering; make atonement for yourself and the people. Sacrifice the people's offering and make atonement for them, as the LORD commanded."

[8] So Aaron approached the altar and slaughtered the calf as a sin offering for himself. [9] Aaron's sons brought the blood to him, and he dipped his finger in the blood and applied it to the horns of the altar. He poured out the blood at the base of the altar. [10] He burned the fat, the kidneys, and the fatty lobe of the liver from the sin offering on the altar, as the LORD had commanded Moses. [11] He burned up the flesh and the hide outside the camp.

[12] Then he slaughtered the burnt offering. Aaron's sons brought him the blood, and he sprinkled it on all sides of the altar. [13] They brought him the burnt offering piece by piece, along with the head, and he burned them on the altar. [14] He washed the entrails and the shanks and burned them with the burnt offering on the altar.

[15] Aaron presented the people's offering. He took the male goat for the people's sin offering, slaughtered it, and made a sin offering with it as he did before. [16] He presented the burnt offering and sacrificed it according to the regulation. [17] Next he presented the grain offering, took a handful of it, and burned it on the altar in addition to the morning burnt offering.

[18] Finally, he slaughtered the ox and the ram as the people's fellowship sacrifice. Aaron's sons brought him the blood, and he sprinkled it on all sides of the altar. [19] They also brought the fat portions from the ox and the ram—the fat tail, the fat surrounding the entrails, the kidneys, and the fatty lobe of the liver— [20] and placed these on the breasts. Aaron burned the fat portions on the altar, [21] but he waved the breasts and the right thigh as a presentation offering before the LORD, as Moses had commanded.

[22] Aaron lifted up his hands toward the people and blessed them. He came down after sacrificing the sin offering, the burnt offering, and the fellowship offering. [23] Moses and Aaron then entered the tent of meeting. When they came out, they blessed the people, and the glory of the LORD appeared to all the people. [24] Fire came out from the LORD and consumed the burnt offering and the fat portions on the altar. And when all the people saw it, they shouted and fell facedown on the ground.

10 Aaron's sons Nadab and Abihu each took his own firepan, put fire in it, placed incense on it, and presented unauthorized fire before the LORD, which He had not commanded them to do. [2] Then flames leaped from the LORD's presence and burned them to death before the LORD. [3] So Moses said to Aaron, "This is what the LORD meant when He said:

I will show My holiness
to those who are near Me,
and I will reveal My glory
before all the people."

But Aaron remained silent.

[4] Moses summoned Mishael and Elzaphan, sons of Aaron's uncle Uzziel, and said to them, "Come here and carry your relatives away from the front of the sanctuary to a place outside the camp." [5] So they came forward and carried them in their tunics outside the camp, as Moses had said.

[6] Then Moses said to Aaron and his sons Eleazar and Ithamar, "Do not let your hair hang loose and do not tear your garments, or else you will die, and the LORD will become angry with the whole community. However, your brothers, the whole house of Israel, may mourn over that tragedy when the LORD sent the fire. [7] You must not go outside the entrance to the tent of meeting or you will die, for the LORD's anointing oil is on you." So they did as Moses said.

[8] The LORD spoke to Aaron: [9] "You and your sons are not to drink wine or beer when you enter the tent of meeting, or

else you will die; this is a permanent statute throughout your generations. [10] You must distinguish between the holy and the common, and the clean and the unclean, [11] and teach the Israelites all the statutes that the LORD has given to them through Moses."

[12] Moses spoke to Aaron and his remaining sons, Eleazar and Ithamar: "Take the grain offering that is left over from the fire offerings to the LORD, and eat it prepared without yeast beside the altar, because it is especially holy. [13] You must eat it in a holy place because it is your portion and your sons' from the fire offerings to the LORD, for this is what I was commanded. [14] But you and your sons and your daughters may eat the breast of the presentation offering and the thigh of the contribution in any ceremonially clean place, because these portions have been assigned to you and your children from the Israelites' fellowship sacrifices. [15] They are to bring the thigh of the contribution and the breast of the presentation offering, together with the offerings of fat portions made by fire, to wave as a presentation offering before the LORD. It will belong permanently to you and your children, as the LORD commanded."

[16] Later, Moses inquired about the male goat of the sin offering, but it had already been burned up. He was angry with Eleazar and Ithamar, Aaron's surviving sons, and asked, [17] "Why didn't you eat the sin offering in the sanctuary area? For it is especially holy, and He has assigned it to you to take away the guilt of the community and make atonement for them before the LORD. [18] Since its blood was not brought inside the sanctuary, you should have eaten it in the sanctuary area, as I commanded."

[19] But Aaron replied to Moses, "See, today they presented their sin offering and their burnt offering before the LORD. Since these things have happened to me, if I had eaten the sin offering today, would it have been acceptable in the LORD's sight?" [20] When Moses heard this, it was acceptable to him.

11

The LORD spoke to Moses and Aaron: [2] "Tell the Israelites: You may eat all these kinds of land animals. [3] You may eat any animal with divided hooves and that chews the cud. [4] But among the ones that chew the cud or have hooves you are not to eat these:

the camel, though it chews the cud,
does not have hooves—it is unclean for you;
[5] the hyrax, though it chews the cud,
does not have hooves—it is unclean for you;
[6] the hare, though it chews the cud,
does not have hooves—it is unclean for you;
[7] the pig, though it has divided hooves,
does not chew the cud—it is unclean for you.

[8] Do not eat any of their meat or touch their carcasses—they are unclean for you.

[9] "This is what you may eat from all that is in the water: You may eat everything in the water that has fins and scales, whether in the seas or streams. [10] But these are to be detestable to you: everything that does not have fins and scales in the seas or streams, among all the swarming things and other living creatures in the water. [11] They are to remain detestable to you; you must not eat any of their meat, and you must detest their carcasses. [12] Everything in the water that does not have fins and scales will be detestable to you.

PSALM 26:1-7

[1] Vindicate me, LORD,
because I have lived with integrity
and have trusted in the LORD
without wavering.
[2] Test me, LORD, and try me;
examine my heart and mind.
[3] For Your faithful love is before my eyes,
and I live by Your truth.

⁴ I do not sit with the worthless
　or associate with hypocrites.
⁵ I hate a crowd of evildoers,
　and I do not sit with the wicked.
⁶ I wash my hands in innocence
　and go around Your altar, LORD,
⁷ raising my voice in thanksgiving
　and telling about Your wonderful
　works.

PROVERBS 6:12-15

¹² A worthless person, a wicked man,
　who goes around speaking
　dishonestly,
¹³ who winks his eyes, signals with
　his feet,
　and gestures with his fingers,
¹⁴ who plots evil with perversity in
　his heart—
　he stirs up trouble constantly.
¹⁵ Therefore calamity will strike him
　suddenly;
　he will be shattered instantly—
　beyond recovery.

MARK 3:13-35

¹³ Then He went up the mountain and
summoned those He wanted, and they
came to Him. ¹⁴ He also appointed 12—
He also named them apostles—to be
with Him, to send them out to preach,
¹⁵ and to have authority to drive out
demons.
¹⁶ He appointed the Twelve:

To Simon, He gave
the name Peter;
¹⁷ and to James the son of Zebedee,
and to his brother John,
He gave the name "Boanerges"
(that is, "Sons of Thunder");
¹⁸ Andrew;
Philip and Bartholomew;
Matthew and Thomas;
James the son of Alphaeus,

and Thaddaeus;
Simon the Zealot,
¹⁹ and Judas Iscariot,
who also betrayed Him.

²⁰ Then He went home, and the crowd
gathered again so that they were not
even able to eat. ²¹ When His family
heard this, they set out to restrain Him,
because they said, "He's out of His
mind."
²² The scribes who had come down
from Jerusalem said, "He has Beelzebul
in Him!" and, "He drives out demons by
the ruler of the demons!"
²³ So He summoned them and spoke
to them in parables: "How can Satan
drive out Satan? ²⁴ If a kingdom is divided against itself, that kingdom cannot stand. ²⁵ If a house is divided against
itself, that house cannot stand. ²⁶ And if
Satan rebels against himself and is divided, he cannot stand but is finished!
²⁷ "On the other hand, no one can enter a strong man's house and rob his
possessions unless he first ties up the
strong man. Then he will rob his house.
²⁸ I assure you: People will be forgiven
for all sins and whatever blasphemies
they may blaspheme. ²⁹ But whoever
blasphemes against the Holy Spirit
never has forgiveness, but is guilty of an
eternal sin"— ³⁰ because they were saying, "He has an unclean spirit."
³¹ Then His mother and His brothers
came, and standing outside, they sent
word to Him and called Him. ³² A crowd
was sitting around Him and told Him,
"Look, Your mother, Your brothers, and
Your sisters are outside asking for You."
³³ He replied to them, "Who are My
mother and My brothers?" ³⁴ And looking about at those who were sitting in a
circle around Him, He said, "Here are
My mother and My brothers! ³⁵ Whoever does the will of God is My brother
and sister and mother."

What Else Matters?

Whoever does the will of God is My brother and sister and mother.—MARK 3:35

Adoption is the highest privilege, and our entire Christian life must be understood in terms of it. Dr. Martyn Lloyd-Jones said: "The most wonderful thing of all is not that my sins have been forgiven, nor that I may enjoy certain experiences and blessings as a Christian. The thing that should astonish me . . . overwhelm me is that I am a child of God, one of God's people." The certainty that we are God's adopted children ought to be uppermost in our thoughts.

Almost every day since I became a Christian, I have reminded myself that I have been adopted into the family of God. It has become the dominant thought of my life. Some time ago, when I mentioned this fact to a fellow Christian, he looked at me blankly and said: "So what?" So what? So not only is Jesus my Savior, He is my Brother also. Following His resurrection our Lord said: "Go to My brothers and tell them that I am ascending to My Father and your Father—to My God and your God" (Jn 20:17). Then again, the writer to the Hebrews tells us that Jesus is not ashamed to call us brothers (Heb. 2:12).

When I was young I always wanted a brother. A sister came along twelve years after I was born, but I never had a brother. Not until I became a Christian, that is. Then, by virtue of the fact that I was adopted into the royal family of heaven, I found a Brother. And what a Brother! God is my Father, Jesus is my Brother . . . what else matters?

Prayer

Father God, forgive me that with such an inheritance as this I get taken up with trifling things. Help me make this the controlling thought of my life: I am a child of God. Nothing else matters. Amen.

Further Study

Rm 8:29; Eph 3:14-15; 1 Tm 5:1-2; 1 Jn 3:16-18
What are the privileges of being in the family of God?
What are the responsibilities?

FEBRUARY 25

LEVITICUS 11:13–13:17

13 "You are to detest these birds. They must not be eaten because they are detestable:

the eagle, the bearded vulture,
the black vulture, 14 the kite,
the various kinds of falcon,
15 every kind of raven, 16 the ostrich,
the short-eared owl, the gull,
the various kinds of hawk,
17 the little owl, the cormorant,
the long-eared owl,
18 the white owl, the desert owl,
the osprey, 19 the stork,
the various kinds of heron,
the hoopoe, and the bat.

20 "All winged insects that walk on all fours are to be detestable to you. 21 But you may eat these kinds of all the winged insects that walk on all fours: those that have jointed legs above their feet for hopping on the ground. 22 You may eat these:

the various kinds of locust,
the various kinds of katydid,
the various kinds of cricket,
and the various kinds of grasshopper.

23 All other winged insects that have four feet are to be detestable to you.
24 "These will make you unclean. Whoever touches their carcasses will be unclean until evening, 25 and whoever carries any of their carcasses must wash his clothes and will be unclean until evening. 26 All animals that have hooves but do not have a divided hoof and do not chew the cud are unclean for you. Whoever touches them becomes unclean. 27 All the four-footed animals that walk on their paws are unclean for you. Whoever touches their carcasses will be unclean until evening, 28 and anyone who carries their carcasses must wash his clothes and will be unclean until evening. They are unclean for you.
29 "These creatures that swarm on the ground are unclean for you:

the weasel, the mouse,
the various kinds of large lizard,
30 the gecko, the monitor lizard,
the common lizard, the skink,
and the chameleon.

31 These are unclean for you among all the swarming creatures. Whoever touches them when they are dead will be unclean until evening. 32 When any one of them dies and falls on anything it becomes unclean—any item of wood, clothing, leather, sackcloth, or any implement used for work. It is to be rinsed with water and will remain unclean until evening; then it will be clean. 33 If any of them falls into any clay pot, everything in it will become unclean; you must break it. 34 Any edible food coming into contact with that unclean water will become unclean, and any drinkable liquid in any container will become unclean. 35 Anything one of their carcasses falls on will become unclean. If it is an oven or stove, it must be smashed; it is unclean and will remain unclean for you. 36 A spring or cistern containing water will remain clean, but someone who touches a carcass in it will become unclean. 37 If one of their carcasses falls on any seed that is to be sown, it is clean; 38 but if water has been put on the seed and one of their carcasses falls on it, it is unclean for you. 39 "If one of the animals that you use for food dies, anyone who touches its carcass will be unclean until evening. 40 Anyone who eats some of its carcass must wash his clothes and will be unclean until evening. Anyone who carries

its carcass must wash his clothes and will be unclean until evening.

⁴¹ "All the creatures that swarm on the earth are detestable; they must not be eaten. ⁴² Do not eat any of the creatures that swarm on the earth, anything that moves on its belly or walks on all fours or on many feet, for they are detestable. ⁴³ Do not become contaminated by any creature that swarms; do not become unclean or defiled by them. ⁴⁴ For I am the LORD your God, so you must consecrate yourselves and be holy because I am holy. You must not defile yourselves by any swarming creature that crawls on the ground. ⁴⁵ For I am the LORD, who brought you up from the land of Egypt to be your God, so you must be holy because I am holy.

⁴⁶ "This is the law concerning animals, birds, all living creatures that move in the water, and all creatures that swarm on the ground, ⁴⁷ in order to distinguish between the unclean and the clean, between the animals that may be eaten and those that may not be eaten."

12 The LORD spoke to Moses: ² "Tell the Israelites: When a woman becomes pregnant and gives birth to a male child, she will be unclean seven days, as she is during the days of her menstrual impurity. ³ The flesh of his foreskin must be circumcised on the eighth day. ⁴ She will continue in purification from her bleeding for 33 days. She must not touch any holy thing or go into the sanctuary until completing her days of purification. ⁵ But if she gives birth to a female child, she will be unclean for two weeks as she is during her menstrual impurity. She will continue in purification from her bleeding for 66 days.

⁶ "When her days of purification are complete, whether for a son or daughter, she is to bring to the priest at the entrance to the tent of meeting a year-old male lamb for a burnt offering, and a young pigeon or a turtledove for a sin offering. ⁷ He will present them before the LORD and make atonement on her behalf; she will be clean from her discharge of blood. This is the law for a woman giving birth, whether to a male or female. ⁸ But if she doesn't have sufficient means for a sheep, she may take two turtledoves or two young pigeons, one for a burnt offering and the other for a sin offering. Then the priest will make atonement on her behalf, and she will be clean."

13 The LORD spoke to Moses and Aaron: ² "When a person has a swelling, scab, or spot on the skin of his body, and it becomes a disease on the skin of his body, he is to be brought to Aaron the priest or to one of his sons, the priests. ³ The priest will examine the infection on the skin of his body. If the hair in the infection has turned white and the infection appears to be deeper than the skin of his body, it is a skin disease. After the priest examines him, he must pronounce him unclean. ⁴ But if the spot on the skin of his body is white and does not appear to be deeper than the skin, and the hair in it has not turned white, the priest must quarantine the infected person for seven days. ⁵ The priest will then reexamine him on the seventh day. If the infection remains unchanged in his sight and has not spread on the skin, the priest must quarantine him for another seven days. ⁶ The priest will examine him again on the seventh day. If the infection has faded and has not spread on the skin, the priest is to pronounce him clean; it is a scab. The person is to wash his clothes and will become clean. ⁷ But if the scab spreads further on his skin after he has presented himself to the priest for his cleansing, he must present himself again to the priest. ⁸ The priest will examine him, and if the scab has spread on the skin, then the priest must pronounce him unclean; he has a skin disease.

⁹ "When a skin disease develops on a person, he is to be brought to the priest. ¹⁰ The priest will examine him. If there is a white swelling on the skin that has turned the hair white, and there is a patch of raw flesh in the swelling, ¹¹ it is a chronic disease on the skin of his body, and the priest must pronounce

him unclean. He need not quarantine him, for he is unclean. ¹²But if the skin disease breaks out completely over the skin so that it covers all the skin of the infected person from his head to his feet so far as the priest can see, ¹³the priest will look, and if the skin disease has covered his entire body, he is to pronounce the infected person clean. Since he has turned totally white, he is clean. ¹⁴But whenever raw flesh appears on him, he will be unclean. ¹⁵When the priest examines the raw flesh, he must pronounce him unclean. Raw flesh is unclean; it is a skin disease. ¹⁶But if the raw flesh changes and turns white, he must go to the priest. ¹⁷The priest will examine him, and if the infection has turned white, the priest must pronounce the infected person clean; he is clean.

𝒫SALM 26:8-12

⁸ LORD, I love the house where You dwell,
the place where Your glory resides.
⁹ Do not destroy me along with sinners,
or my life along with men of bloodshed
¹⁰ in whose hands are evil schemes,
and whose right hands are filled with bribes.

¹¹ But I live with integrity;
redeem me and be gracious to me.
¹² My foot stands on level ground;
I will praise the LORD in the assemblies.

𝒫ROVERBS 6:16-19

¹⁶ Six things the LORD hates;
in fact, seven are detestable to Him:
¹⁷ arrogant eyes, a lying tongue,
hands that shed innocent blood,
¹⁸ a heart that plots wicked schemes,
feet eager to run to evil,
¹⁹ a lying witness who gives false testimony,

and one who stirs up trouble among brothers.

𝑀ARK 4:1-20

4 Again He began to teach by the sea, and a very large crowd gathered around Him. So He got into a boat on the sea and sat down, while the whole crowd was on the shore facing the sea. ²He taught them many things in parables, and in His teaching He said to them: ³"Listen! Consider the sower who went out to sow. ⁴As he sowed, this occurred: Some seed fell along the path, and the birds came and ate it up. ⁵Other seed fell on rocky ground where it didn't have much soil, and it sprang up right away, since it didn't have deep soil. ⁶When the sun came up, it was scorched, and since it didn't have a root, it withered. ⁷Other seed fell among thorns, and the thorns came up and choked it, and it didn't produce a crop. ⁸Still others fell on good ground and produced a crop that increased 30, 60, and 100 times what was sown." ⁹Then He said, "Anyone who has ears to hear should listen!"

¹⁰When He was alone with the Twelve, those who were around Him asked Him about the parables. ¹¹He answered them, "The secret of the kingdom of God has been granted to you, but to those outside, everything comes in parables ¹²so that

they may look and look,
yet not perceive;
they may listen and listen,
yet not understand;
otherwise, they might
turn back—
and be forgiven."

¹³Then He said to them: "Do you not understand this parable? How then will you understand any of the parables? ¹⁴The sower sows the word. ¹⁵These are the ones along the path where the word is sown: when they hear, immediately Satan comes and takes away the word sown in them. ¹⁶And these are the

ones sown on rocky ground: when they hear the word, immediately they receive it with joy. [17] But they have no root in themselves; they are short-lived. When affliction or persecution comes because of the word, they immediately stumble. [18] Others are sown among thorns; these are the ones who hear the word, [19] but the worries of this age, the seduction of wealth, and the desires for other things enter in and choke the word, and it becomes unfruitful. [20] But the ones sown on good ground are those who hear the word, welcome it, and produce a crop: 30, 60, and 100 times what was sown."

The Key to Life

The secret of the kingdom of God has been granted to you.—MARK 4:11

Whenever I hear a person saying that all religions are the same, my mind runs immediately to the Cross. If what is found here is true (and I believe it is) and represents the meaning of life, then clearly all religions are not the same. No authentic note of divine self-sacrifice comes from other faiths. The Cross stands out in absolute uniqueness. As Toplady put it in his beautiful hymn:

> In the Cross of Christ I glory,
> Towering o'er the wrecks of time,
> All the light of sacred story
> Gathered round its head sublime.

For weeks and months after I became a Christian I wondered why anyone should preach anything except the Cross. The redemptive glowing mystery of it took hold of me in the early days of my conversion, and I think I can honestly say it has never ceased to magnetize my heart.

Among the ancient inscriptions and paintings on the tombs of Egyptian kings, so I am told, one finds everywhere the symbol of the key of life. Strangely enough, it is in the form of a cross. Christ's cross is the only true key to life. This and this alone unlocks the doors to some of life's greatest mysteries. Other religions try, sometimes with great sincerity, to unlock the doors to these profound mysteries, but they are unsuccessful because they do not have the right key. They do not have a cross.

Prayer

O Father, I see that if self-giving love is the meaning behind the Cross, and the meaning of the universe, then it must be the meaning behind my life too. May the Cross work itself out in all my relationships from this day forward. In Jesus' name. Amen.

Further Study

Jn 19:1-15; 1 Co 1:1-23; 2:2-8; Gl 6:14
What was central to Paul's message?
How was the message of Christ's crucifixion viewed?

FEBRUARY 26

LEVITICUS 13:18–14:14

¹⁸ "When a boil appears on the skin of one's body and it heals, ¹⁹ and a white swelling or a reddish-white spot develops where the boil was, the person must present himself to the priest. ²⁰ The priest will make an examination, and if the spot seems to be beneath the skin and the hair in it has turned white, the priest must pronounce him unclean; it is a skin disease that has broken out in the boil. ²¹ But when the priest examines it, if there is no white hair in it, and it is not beneath the skin but is faded, the priest must quarantine him seven days. ²² If it spreads further on the skin, the priest must pronounce him unclean; it is an infection. ²³ But if the spot remains where it is and does not spread, it is only the scar from the boil. The priest is to pronounce him clean.

²⁴ "When there is a burn on the skin of one's body produced by fire, and the patch made raw by the burn becomes a reddish-white or white spot, ²⁵ the priest is to examine it. If the hair in the spot has turned white and the spot appears to be deeper than the skin, it is a skin disease that has broken out in the burn. The priest must pronounce him unclean; it is a skin disease. ²⁶ But when the priest examines it, if there is no white hair in the spot and it is not beneath the skin but is faded, the priest must quarantine him seven days. ²⁷ The priest will reexamine him on the seventh day. If it has spread further on the skin, the priest must pronounce him unclean; it is a skin disease. ²⁸ But if the spot has remained where it was and has not spread on the skin but is faded, it is the swelling from the burn. The priest is to pronounce him clean, for it is only the scar from the burn.

²⁹ "When a man or woman has an infection on the head or chin, ³⁰ the priest must examine the infection. If it appears to be deeper than the skin, and the hair in it is yellow and sparse, the priest must pronounce the person unclean. It is a scaly outbreak, a skin disease of the head or chin. ³¹ When the priest examines the scaly infection, if it does not appear to be deeper than the skin, and there is no black hair in it, the priest must quarantine the person with the scaly infection for seven days. ³² The priest will reexamine the infection on the seventh day. If the scaly outbreak has not spread and there is no yellow hair in it and it does not appear to be deeper than the skin, ³³ the person must shave himself but not shave the scaly area. Then the priest must quarantine the person who has the scaly outbreak for another seven days. ³⁴ The priest will examine the scaly outbreak on the seventh day, and if it has not spread on the skin and does not appear to be deeper than the skin, the priest is to pronounce the person clean. He is to wash his clothes, and he will be clean. ³⁵ But if the scaly outbreak spreads further on the skin after his cleansing, ³⁶ the priest is to examine the person. If the scaly outbreak has spread on the skin, the priest does not need to look for yellow hair; the person is unclean. ³⁷ But if as far as he can see, the scaly outbreak remains unchanged and black hair has grown in it, then it has healed; he is clean. The priest is to pronounce the person clean.

³⁸ "When a man or a woman has white spots on the skin of the body, ³⁹ the priest is to make an examination. If the spots on the skin of the body are dull white, it is only a rash that has broken out on the skin; the person is clean.

⁴⁰ "If a man loses the hair of his head, he is bald, but he is clean. ⁴¹ Or if he loses the hair at his hairline, he is bald on his forehead, but he is clean. ⁴² But if

there is a reddish-white infection on the bald head or forehead, it is a skin disease breaking out on his head or forehead. [43] The priest is to examine him, and if the swelling of the infection on his bald head or forehead is reddish-white, like the appearance of a skin disease on his body, [44] the man is afflicted with a skin disease; he is unclean. The priest must pronounce him unclean; the infection is on his head.

[45] "The person afflicted with an infectious skin disease is to have his clothes torn and his hair hanging loose, and he must cover his mouth and cry out, 'Unclean, unclean!' [46] He will remain unclean as long as he has the infection; he is unclean. He must live alone in a place outside the camp.

[47] "If a fabric is contaminated with mildew—in wool or linen fabric, [48] in the warp or woof of linen or wool, or in leather or anything made of leather— [49] and if the contamination is green or red in the fabric, the leather, the warp, the woof, or any leather article, it is a mildew contamination and is to be shown to the priest. [50] The priest is to examine the contamination and quarantine the contaminated fabric for seven days. [51] The priest is to reexamine the contamination on the seventh day. If it has spread in the fabric, the warp, the woof, or the leather, regardless of how it is used, the contamination is harmful mildew; it is unclean. [52] He is to burn the fabric, the warp or woof in wool or linen, or any leather article, which is contaminated. Since it is harmful mildew it must be burned up.

[53] "When the priest examines it, if the contamination has not spread in the fabric, the warp or woof, or any leather article, [54] the priest is to order whatever is contaminated to be washed and quarantined for another seven days. [55] After it has been washed, the priest is to reexamine the contamination. If the appearance of the contaminated article has not changed, it is unclean. Even though the contamination has not spread, you must burn up the fabric. It is a fungus on the front or back of the fabric.

[56] "If the priest examines it, and the contamination has faded after it has been washed, he must cut the contaminated section out of the fabric, the leather, or the warp or woof. [57] But if it reappears in the fabric, the warp or woof, or any leather article, it has broken out again. You must burn up whatever is contaminated. [58] But if the contamination disappears from the fabric, the warp or woof, or any leather article, which have been washed, it is to be washed again, and it will be clean.

[59] "This is the law concerning a mildew contamination in wool or linen fabric, warp or woof, or any leather article, in order to pronounce it clean or unclean."

14 The LORD spoke to Moses: [2] "This is the law concerning the person afflicted with a skin disease on the day of his cleansing. He is to be brought to the priest, [3] who will go outside the camp and examine him. If the skin disease has disappeared from the afflicted person, [4] the priest will order that two live clean birds, cedar wood, scarlet yarn, and hyssop be brought for the one who is to be cleansed. [5] Then the priest will order that one of the birds be slaughtered over fresh water in a clay pot. [6] He is to take the live bird together with the cedar wood, scarlet yarn, and hyssop, and dip them all into the blood of the bird that was slaughtered over the fresh water. [7] He will then sprinkle the blood seven times on the one who is to be cleansed from the skin disease. He is to pronounce him clean and release the live bird over the open countryside. [8] The one who is to be cleansed must wash his clothes, shave off all his hair, and bathe with water; he is clean. Afterwards he may enter the camp, but he must remain outside his tent for seven days. [9] He is to shave off all his hair again on the seventh day: his head, his beard, his eyebrows, and the rest of his hair. He is to wash his clothes and bathe himself with water; he is clean. [10] "On the eighth day he must take two unblemished male lambs, an unblemished year-old ewe lamb, a grain

offering of three quarts of fine flour mixed with olive oil, and one-third of a quart of olive oil. [11] The priest who performs the cleansing will place the person who is to be cleansed, together with these offerings, before the LORD at the entrance to the tent of meeting. [12] The priest is to take one male lamb and present it as a restitution offering, along with the one-third quart of olive oil, and he must wave them as a presentation offering before the LORD. [13] He is to slaughter the male lamb at the place in the sanctuary area where the sin offering and burnt offering are slaughtered, for like the sin offering, the restitution offering belongs to the priest; it is especially holy. [14] The priest is to take some of the blood from the restitution offering and put it on the lobe of the right ear of the one to be cleansed, on the thumb of his right hand, and on the big toe of his right foot.

PSALM 27:1-6

[1] The LORD is my light and my
    salvation—
whom should I fear?
The LORD is the stronghold of my
    life—
of whom should I be afraid?
[2] When evildoers came against me
    to devour my flesh,
my foes and my enemies stumbled
    and fell.
[3] Though an army deploy against
    me,
my heart is not afraid;
though war break out against me,
    still I am confident.

[4] I have asked one thing from the
    LORD; it is what I desire:
to dwell in the house of the LORD
    all the days of my life,
gazing on the beauty of the LORD
    and seeking Him in His temple.
[5] For He will conceal me in His
    shelter in the day of
    adversity;
He will hide me under the cover
    of His tent;

He will set me high on a rock.
[6] Then my head will be high above
    my enemies around me;
I will offer sacrifices in His tent
    with shouts of joy.
I will sing and make music to the
    LORD.

PROVERBS 6:20-22

[20] My son, keep your father's
    command,
and don't reject your mother's
    teaching.
[21] Always bind them to your heart;
    tie them around your neck.
[22] When you walk here and there,
    they will guide you;
when you lie down, they will
    watch over you;
when you wake up, they will talk
    to you.

MARK 4:21-41

[21] He also said to them, "Is a lamp brought in to be put under a basket or under a bed? Isn't it to be put on a lampstand? [22] For nothing is concealed except to be revealed, and nothing hidden except to come to light. [23] If anyone has ears to hear, he should listen!" [24] Then He said to them, "Pay attention to what you hear. By the measure you use, it will be measured and added to you. [25] For to the one who has, it will be given, and from the one who does not have, even what he has will be taken away."

[26] "The kingdom of God is like this," He said. "A man scatters seed on the ground; [27] he sleeps and rises—night and day, and the seed sprouts and grows—he doesn't know how. [28] The soil produces a crop by itself—first the blade, then the head, and then the ripe grain on the head. [29] But as soon as the crop is ready, he sends for the sickle, because harvest has come."

[30] And He said: "How can we illustrate the kingdom of God, or what parable can we used to describe it? [31] It's like a mustard seed that, when sown in the soil, is smaller than all the seeds on

the ground. [32] And when sown, it comes up and grows taller than all the vegetables, and produces large branches, so that the birds of the sky can nest in its shade."

[33] He would speak the word to them with many parables like these, as they were able to understand. [34] And He did not speak to them without a parable. Privately, however, He would explain everything to His own disciples.

[35] On that day, when evening had come, He told them, "Let's cross over to the other side of the lake." [36] So they left the crowd and took Him along since He was already in the boat. And other boats were with Him. [37] A fierce windstorm arose, and the waves were breaking over the boat, so that the boat was already being swamped. [38] But He was in the stern, sleeping on the cushion. So they woke Him up and said to Him, "Teacher! Don't you care that we're going to die?"

[39] He got up, rebuked the wind, and said to the sea, "Silence! Be still!" The wind ceased, and there was a great calm. [40] Then He said to them, "Why are you fearful? Do you still have no faith?"

[41] And they were terrified and asked one another, "Who then is this? Even the wind and the sea obey Him!"

Homegrown Fears

He said to them, "Why are you fearful?
Do you still have no faith?" —MARK 4:40

Some social scientists maintain that there are no inherent fears except two; the rest are acquired. The two inherent fears, they say, are the fear of falling and the fear of loud noises.

I read of some psychologists who examined five hundred people and found that, between them, they had about seven thousand fears. The theory that we inherit just two fears, of course, is not a proven fact, but if that happens to be so, then those five hundred people were loading themselves down with hundreds of unnatural and useless fears!

Once when I was in India, I was told of a caste where the women on each of their birthdays add four rings of heavy brass—one on each ankle and one on each arm. By the time they are in middle age, they walk with great difficulty under this senseless burden. But this is no more senseless than weighting oneself down with useless fears: fear of failure, fear of rejection, fear of the future, fear of growing old, fear of what people might think, and so on. Most of our fears are homegrown—they come out of wrong home teaching and example. Parents who try to control their children by fear often succeed too well; their children grow up being controlled by the fears themselves.

A woman wrote to me and said: "All my life I have been a victim of fear. My nightly prayer was: 'Lord, thank You for not letting anything too bad happen to me today.' You said if I turned to Christ, He would rid me of all fear. Well, I have—and He did."

Prayer

Father, we have filled Your world and our hearts with fear—needless, devastating fears. Help us, we pray, to find release from these fears, for they are not our real selves—they are an importation. In Jesus' name I pray. Amen.

Further Study

Ps 34:1-22; 23:4; Pr 9:10; 19:23
What was David's testimony?
How can we find freedom from our fears?

FEBRUARY 27

LEVITICUS 14:15–15:12

15 Then the priest will take some of the one-third of a quart of olive oil and pour it into his left palm. 16 The priest will dip his right finger into the oil in his left palm and sprinkle some of the oil with his finger seven times before the LORD. 17 From the oil remaining in his palm the priest will put some on the lobe of the right ear of the one to be cleansed, on the thumb of his right hand, and on the big toe of his right foot, on top of the blood of the restitution offering. 18 What is left of the oil in the priest's palm he is to put on the head of the one to be cleansed. In this way the priest will make atonement for him before the LORD. 19 The priest must sacrifice the sin offering and make atonement for the one to be purified from his uncleanness. Afterwards he will slaughter the burnt offering. 20 The priest is to offer the burnt offering and the grain offering on the altar. The priest will make atonement for him, and he will be clean.

21 "But if he is poor and cannot afford these, he is to take one male lamb for a restitution offering to be waved in order to make atonement for him, along with two quarts of fine flour mixed with olive oil for a grain offering, one-third of a quart of olive oil, 22 and two turtledoves or two young pigeons, whatever he can afford, one to be a sin offering and the other a burnt offering.

23 On the eighth day he is to bring these things for his cleansing to the priest at the entrance to the tent of meeting before the LORD. 24 The priest will take the male lamb for the restitution offering and the one-third of a quart of olive oil, and wave them as a presentation offering before the LORD. 25 After he slaughters the male lamb for the restitution offering, the priest is to take some of the blood of the restitution offering and put it on the right earlobe of the one to be cleansed, on the thumb of his right hand, and on the big toe of his right foot. 26 Then the priest will pour some of the oil into his left palm. 27 With his right finger the priest will sprinkle some of the oil in his left palm seven times before the LORD. 28 The priest will also put some of the oil in his palm on the right earlobe of the one to be cleansed, on the thumb of his right hand, and on the big toe of his right foot, on the same place as the blood of the restitution offering. 29 What is left of the oil in the priest's palm he is to put on the head of the one to be cleansed to make atonement for him before the LORD. 30 He must then sacrifice one type of what he can afford, either the turtledoves or young pigeons, 31 one as a sin offering and the other as a burnt offering, sacrificing what he can afford together with the grain offering. In this way the priest will make atonement before the LORD for the one to be cleansed. 32 This is the law for

someone who has a skin disease and cannot afford the cost of his cleansing."

³³ The LORD spoke to Moses and Aaron: ³⁴ "When you enter the land of Canaan that I am giving you as a possession, and I place a mildew contamination in a house in the land you possess, ³⁵ the owner of the house is to come and tell the priest: Something like mildew contamination has appeared in my house. ³⁶ The priest must order them to clear the house before he enters to examine the contamination, so that nothing in the house becomes unclean. Afterwards the priest will come to examine the house. ³⁷ He will examine it, and if the contamination in the walls of the house consists of green or red indentations that appear to be beneath the surface of the wall, ³⁸ the priest is to go outside the house to its doorway and quarantine the house for seven days. ³⁹ The priest is to return on the seventh day and examine it. If the contamination has spread on the walls of the house, ⁴⁰ the priest must order that the stones with the contamination be pulled out and thrown into an unclean place outside the city. ⁴¹ He is to have the inside of the house completely scraped, and the plaster that is scraped off must be dumped in an unclean place outside the city. ⁴² Then they must take different stones to replace the former ones and take additional plaster to replaster the house.

⁴³ "If the contamination reappears in the house after the stones have been pulled out, and after the house has been scraped and replastered, ⁴⁴ the priest must come and examine it. If the contamination has spread in the house, it is harmful mildew; the house is unclean. ⁴⁵ It must be torn down with its stones, its beams, and all its plaster, and taken outside the city to an unclean place. ⁴⁶ Whoever enters the house during any of the days the priest quarantines it will be unclean until evening. ⁴⁷ Whoever lies down in the house is to wash his clothes, and whoever eats in it is to wash his clothes.

⁴⁸ "But when the priest comes and examines it, if the contamination has not spread in the house after it was replastered, he is to pronounce the house clean because the contamination has disappeared. ⁴⁹ He is to take two birds, cedar wood, scarlet yarn, and hyssop to purify the house, ⁵⁰ and he is to slaughter one of the birds over a clay pot containing fresh water. ⁵¹ He will take the cedar wood, the hyssop, the scarlet yarn, and the live bird, dip them in the blood of the slaughtered bird and the fresh water, and sprinkle the house seven times. ⁵² He will purify the house with the blood of the bird, the fresh water, the live bird, the cedar wood, the hyssop, and the scarlet yarn. ⁵³ Then he is to release the live bird into the open countryside outside the city. In this way he will make atonement for the house, and it will be clean.

⁵⁴ "This is the law for any skin disease or mildew, for a scaly outbreak, ⁵⁵ for mildew in clothing or on a house, ⁵⁶ and for a swelling, scab, or spot, ⁵⁷ to determine when something is unclean or clean. This is the law regarding skin disease and mildew."

15 The LORD spoke to Moses and Aaron: ² "Speak to the Israelites and tell them: When any man has a discharge from his body, he is unclean. ³ This is uncleanness of his discharge: Whether his body secretes the discharge or retains it, he is unclean. All the days that his body secretes or retains anything because of his discharge, he is unclean. ⁴ Any bed the man with the discharge lies on will be unclean, and any furniture he sits on will be unclean. ⁵ Anyone who touches his bed is to wash his clothes and bathe with water, and he will remain unclean until evening. ⁶ Whoever sits on furniture that the man with the discharge was sitting on is to wash his clothes and bathe with water, and he will remain unclean until evening. ⁷ Whoever touches the body of the man with a discharge is to wash his clothes and bathe with water, and he will remain unclean until evening. ⁸ If the man with the discharge spits on anyone who is clean, he is to

wash his clothes and bathe with water, and he will remain unclean until evening. ⁹ Any saddle the man with the discharge rides on will be unclean. ¹⁰ Whoever touches anything that was under him will be unclean until evening, and whoever carries such things is to wash his clothes and bathe with water, and he will remain unclean until evening. ¹¹ If the man with the discharge touches anyone without first rinsing his hands in water, the person who was touched is to wash his clothes and bathe with water, and he will remain unclean until evening. ¹² Any clay pot that the man with the discharge touches must be broken, while any wooden utensil must be rinsed with water.

℘SALM 27:7-14

⁷ LORD, hear my voice when I call;
  be gracious to me and answer
    me.
⁸ In Your behalf my heart says,
    "Seek My face."
  LORD, I will seek Your face.
⁹ Do not hide Your face from me;
  do not turn Your servant away in
    anger.
  You have been my help;
  do not leave me or abandon me,
    God of my salvation.
¹⁰ Even if my father and mother
    abandon me,
  the LORD cares for me.

¹¹ Because of my adversaries,
  show me Your way, LORD,
  and lead me on a level path.
¹² Do not give me over to the will of
    my foes,
  for false witnesses rise up against
    me, breathing violence.

¹³ I am certain that I will see the
    LORD's goodness
  in the land of the living.
¹⁴ Wait for the LORD;
  be courageous and let your heart
    be strong.
  Wait for the LORD.

℘ROVERBS 6:23-26

²³ For a commandment is a lamp,
    teaching is a light,
  and corrective instructions are the
    way to life.
²⁴ They will protect you from an evil
    woman,
  from the flattering tongue of a
    stranger.
²⁵ Don't lust in your heart for her
    beauty
  or let her captivate you with her
    eyelashes.
²⁶ For a prostitute's fee is only a loaf
    of bread,
  but an adulteress goes after your
    very life.

ℳARK 5:1-20

5 Then they came to the other side of the sea, to the region of the Gerasenes. ² As soon as He got out of the boat, a man with an unclean spirit came out of the tombs and met Him. ³ He lived in the tombs. No one was able to restrain him any more—even with chains— ⁴ because he often had been bound with shackles and chains, but had snapped off the chains and smashed the shackles. No one was strong enough to subdue him. ⁵ And always, night and day, he was crying out among the tombs and in the mountains and cutting himself with stones.

⁶ When he saw Jesus from a distance, he ran and knelt down before Him. ⁷ And he cried out with a loud voice, "What do You have to do with me, Jesus, Son of the Most High God? I beg You before God, don't torment me!" ⁸ For He had told him, "Come out of the man, you unclean spirit!" ⁹ "What is your name?" He asked him.

"My name is Legion," he answered Him, "because we are many." ¹⁰ And he kept begging Him not to send them out of the region. ¹¹ Now a large herd of pigs was there, feeding on the hillside. ¹² The demons begged Him, "Send us to the pigs, so we may enter them." ¹³ And He gave them permission. Then the unclean spirits came out and entered the pigs, and the herd of about 2,000 rushed down the steep bank into the sea and drowned there. ¹⁴ The men who tended them ran off and reported it in the town and the countryside, and people went to see what had happened. ¹⁵ They came to Jesus and saw the man who had been demon-possessed by the legion, sitting there, dressed and in his right mind; and they were afraid. ¹⁶ The eyewitnesses described to them what had happened to the demon-possessed man and told about the pigs. ¹⁷ Then they began to beg Him to leave their region.

¹⁸ As He was getting into the boat, the man who had been demon-possessed kept begging Him to be with Him. ¹⁹ But He would not let him; instead, He told him, "Go back home to your own people, and report to them how much the Lord has done for you and how He has had mercy on you." ²⁰ So he went out and began to proclaim in the Decapolis how much Jesus had done for him, and they were all amazed.

"Anyone Saved Lately?"

He told him, "Go back home to your own people, and report to them how much the Lord has done for you and how He has had mercy on you."—MARK 5:19

Christianity is not merely a conception but a contagion. And when the contagion is lost, the possibility is that the conception may also be lost.

An American pastor, an old friend of mine, says: "Christianity is catching, and if people are not catching it from us, then perhaps it's because we do not have a sufficiently virulent case of it." Once when he was in England, we visited Westminster Abbey. He looked around and asked in loud tones: "Has anyone been saved here lately?" I said I was not sure, to which he replied: "If a church is not evangelistic, then it is not evangelical." He was right, but that didn't stop me from getting him outside as quickly as possible!

"Nothing is really ours," said C. S. Lewis, "until we share it." The moment someone else shares our experience of Christ, then the faith means something more to us. *The Amplified Bible* translates Philippians 1:5 thus: "I thank my God for your fellowship—your sympathetic cooperation and contributions and partnership—in advancing the good news, the Gospel, from the first day you heard it until now." From the very first day they stepped into the kingdom of God, they began to contribute to it—to spread it. It was not something they learned; it was instinctive. It was as natural as a baby's cry at birth. Sharing Christ with others is not something we can take or leave; it is something which, if we don't take, we can easily lose. For the expression of the faith is the essence of the faith.

Prayer

O Father, help us to be like the converts in the church at Philippi who, from the moment they saw You, wanted to share You. We ask in Christ's precious and powerful name. Amen.

Further Study

Mk 5:15-20; Ac 1:8; 2 Tm 1:8
What did Jesus tell the man to do?
What was Paul's admonition to Timothy?

FEBRUARY 28

LEVITICUS 15:13–16:34

13 "When the man with the discharge has been cured of it, he is to count seven days for his cleansing, wash his clothes, and bathe his body in fresh water; he will be clean. 14 He must take two turtledoves or two young pigeons on the eighth day, come before the LORD at the entrance to the tent of meeting, and give them to the priest. 15 The priest is to sacrifice them, one as a sin offering and the other as a burnt offering. In this way the priest will make atonement for him before the LORD because of his discharge.

16 "When a man has an emission of semen, he is to bathe himself completely with water, and he will remain unclean until evening. 17 Any clothing or leather on which there is an emission of semen must be washed with water, and it will remain unclean until evening. 18 If a man sleeps with a woman and has an emission of semen, both of them are to bathe with water, and they will remain unclean until evening.

19 "When a woman has a discharge, and it consists of blood from her body, she will be unclean because of her menstruation for seven days. Everyone who touches her will be unclean until evening. 20 Anything she lies on during her menstruation will become unclean, and anything she sits on will become unclean. 21 Everyone who touches her bed is to wash his clothes and bathe with water, and he will remain unclean until evening. 22 Everyone who touches any furniture she was sitting on is to wash his clothes and bathe with water, and he will remain unclean until evening. 23 If discharge is on the bed or the furniture she was sitting on, when he touches it he will be unclean until evening. 24 If a man sleeps with her, and blood from her menstruation gets on him, he will be unclean for seven days, and every bed he lies on will become unclean.

25 "When a woman has a discharge of her blood for many days, though it is not the time of her menstruation, or if she has a discharge beyond her period, she will be unclean all the days of her unclean discharge, as she is during the days of her menstruation. 26 Any bed she lies on during the days of her discharge will be like her bed during menstrual impurity; any furniture she sits on will be unclean as in her menstrual period. 27 Everyone who touches them will be unclean; he must wash his clothes and bathe with water, and he will remain unclean until evening. 28 When she is cured of her discharge, she is to count seven days, and after that she will be clean. 29 On the eighth day she must take two turtledoves or two young pigeons and bring them to the priest at the entrance to the tent of meeting. 30 The priest is to sacrifice one as a sin offering and the other as a burnt offering. In this way the priest will

make atonement for her before the LORD because of her unclean discharge.
³¹ "You must keep the Israelites from their uncleanness, so that they do not die by defiling My tabernacle that is among them. ³² This is the law for someone with a discharge: a man who has an emission of semen, becoming unclean by it; ³³ a woman who is in her menstrual period; anyone who has a discharge, whether male or female; and a man who sleeps with an unclean woman."

16 The LORD spoke to Moses after the death of two of Aaron's sons when they approached the presence of the LORD and died. ² The LORD said to Moses: "Tell your brother Aaron that he may not come whenever he wants into the holy place behind the veil in front of the mercy seat on the ark or else he will die, because I appear in the cloud above the mercy seat.
³ "Aaron is to enter the most holy place in this way: with a young bull for a sin offering and a ram for a burnt offering. ⁴ He is to wear a holy linen tunic, and linen undergarments are to be on his body. He must tie a linen sash around him and wrap his head with a linen turban. These are holy garments; he must bathe his body with water before he wears them. ⁵ He is to take from the Israelite community two male goats for a sin offering and one ram for a burnt offering.
⁶ "Aaron will present the bull for his sin offering and make atonement for himself and his household. ⁷ Next he will take the two goats and place them before the LORD at the entrance to the tent of meeting. ⁸ After Aaron casts lots for the two goats, one lot for the LORD and the other for Azazel, ⁹ he is to present the goat chosen by lot for the LORD and sacrifice it as a sin offering. ¹⁰ But the goat chosen by lot for Azazel is to be presented alive before the LORD to make purification with it by sending it into the wilderness for Azazel.
¹¹ "When Aaron presents the bull for his sin offering and makes atonement for himself and his household, he will slaughter the bull for his sin offering.

¹² Then he must take a firepan full of fiery coals from the altar before the LORD and two handfuls of finely ground fragrant incense, and bring them inside the veil. ¹³ He is to put the incense on the fire before the LORD, so that the cloud of incense covers the mercy seat that is over the testimony, or else he will die. ¹⁴ He is to take some of the bull's blood and sprinkle it with his finger against the east side of the mercy seat; then he will sprinkle some of the blood with his finger before the mercy seat seven times.
¹⁵ "When he slaughters the male goat for the people's sin offering and brings its blood inside the veil, he must do the same with its blood as he did with the bull's blood: he is to sprinkle it against the mercy seat and in front of it. ¹⁶ He will purify the most holy place in this way for all their sins because of the Israelites' impurities and rebellious acts. He will do the same for the tent of meeting that remains among them, because it is surrounded by their impurities. ¹⁷ No one may be in the tent of meeting from the time he enters to make atonement in the most holy place until he leaves after he has made atonement for himself, his household, and the whole assembly of Israel. ¹⁸ Then he will go out to the altar that is before the LORD and make atonement for it. He is to take some of the bull's blood and some of the goat's blood and put it on the horns on all sides of the altar. ¹⁹ He is to sprinkle some of the blood on it with his finger seven times to cleanse and set it apart from the Israelites' impurities.
²⁰ "When he has finished purifying the most holy place, the tent of meeting, and the altar, he is to present the live male goat. ²¹ Aaron will lay both his hands on the head of the live goat and confess over it all the Israelites' wrongdoings and rebellious acts—all their sins. He is to put them on the goat's head and send it away into the wilderness by the man appointed for the task. ²² The goat will carry on it all their wrongdoings into a desolate land, and he will release it there.

23 "Then Aaron is to enter the tent of meeting, take off the linen garments he wore when he entered the most holy place, and leave them there. 24 He will bathe his body with water in a holy place and put on his clothes. Then he must go out and sacrifice his burnt offering and the people's burnt offering; he will make atonement for himself and for the people. 25 He is to burn the fat of the sin offering on the altar. 26 The man who released the goat for Azazel is to wash his clothes and bathe his body with water; afterwards he may reenter the camp. 27 The bull for the sin offering and the goat for the sin offering, whose blood was brought into the most holy place to make atonement, must be brought outside the camp and their hide, flesh, and dung burned up. 28 The one who burns them is to wash his clothes and bathe himself with water; afterwards he may reenter the camp.

29 "This is to be a permanent statute for you: In the seventh month, on the tenth day of the month you are to practice self-denial and do no work, both the native and the foreigner who resides among you. 30 Atonement will be made for you on this day to cleanse you, and you will be clean from all your sins before the LORD. 31 It is a Sabbath of complete rest for you, and you must practice self-denial; it is a permanent statute. 32 The priest who is anointed and ordained to serve as high priest in place of his father will make atonement. He will put on the linen garments, the holy garments, 33 and purify the most holy place. He will purify the tent of meeting and the altar and will make atonement for the priests and all the people of the assembly. 34 This is to be a permanent statute for you, to make atonement for the Israelites once a year because of all their sins." And all this was done as the LORD commanded Moses.

PSALM 28:1-5

1 LORD, I call to You;
  my rock, do not be deaf to me.

If You remain silent to me,
  I will be like those going down to
    the Pit.
2 Listen to the sound of my pleading
    when I cry to You for help,
  when I lift up my hands toward
    Your holy sanctuary.
3 Do not drag me away with the
    wicked,
  with the evildoers,
  who speak in friendly ways with
    their neighbors,
  while malice is in their hearts.
4 Repay them according to what
    they have done—
  according to the evil of their
    deeds.
  Repay them according to the work
    of their hands;
  give them back what they deserve.
5 Because they do not consider
    what the LORD has done
  or the work of His hands,
  He will tear them down and not
    rebuild them.

PROVERBS 6:27-29

27 Can a man embrace fire
  and his clothes not be burned?
28 Can a man walk on coals
  without scorching his feet?
29 So it is with the one who sleeps
    with another man's wife;
  no one who touches her will go
    unpunished.

MARK 5:21-43

21 When Jesus had crossed over again by boat to the other side, a large crowd gathered around Him while He was by the sea. 22 One of the synagogue leaders, named Jairus, came, and when he saw Jesus, he fell at His feet 23 and kept begging Him, "My little daughter is at death's door. Come and lay Your hands on her so she can get well and live." 24 So Jesus went with him, and a large crowd was following and pressing against Him. 25 A woman suffering from bleeding for 12 years 26 had endured

much under many doctors. She had spent everything she had and was not helped at all. On the contrary, she became worse. ²⁷ Having heard about Jesus, she came behind Him in the crowd and touched His robe. ²⁸ For she said, "If I can just touch His robes, I'll be made well!" ²⁹ Instantly her flow of blood ceased, and she sensed in her body that she was cured of her affliction.

³⁰ At once Jesus realized in Himself that power had gone out from Him. He turned around in the crowd and said, "Who touched My robes?"

³¹ His disciples said to Him, "You see the crowd pressing against You, and You say, 'Who touched Me?' "

³² So He was looking around to see who had done this. ³³ Then the woman, knowing what had happened to her, came with fear and trembling, fell down before Him, and told Him the whole truth. ³⁴ "Daughter," He said to her, "your faith has made you well. Go in peace and be free from your affliction."

³⁵ While He was still speaking, people came from the synagogue leader's house and said, "Your daughter is dead. Why bother the Teacher any more?"

³⁶ But when Jesus overheard what was said, He told the synagogue leader, "Don't be afraid. Only believe." ³⁷ He did not let anyone accompany Him except Peter, James, and John, James' brother. ³⁸ They came to the leader's house, and He saw a commotion—people weeping and wailing loudly. ³⁹ He went in and said to them, "Why are you making a commotion and weeping? The child is not dead but asleep."

⁴⁰ They started laughing at Him, but He put them all outside. He took the child's father, mother, and those who were with Him, and entered the place where the child was. ⁴¹ Then He took the child by the hand and said to her, *"Talitha koum!"* (which is translated, "Little girl, I say to you, get up!"). ⁴² Immediately the girl got up and began to walk. (She was 12 years old.) At this they were utterly astounded. ⁴³ Then He gave them strict orders that no one should know about this and said that she should be given something to eat.

Love Is Not Blind

I cry to You for help.—Psalm 28:2

If we draw back from facing and feeling our disappointments, then a part of us will experience spiritual deprivation. The more deeply we enter into our disappointment, then the more thoroughly we will see how committed we are to self-protection and turn from it in repentance to a more complete dependence on our Lord Jesus Christ.

Where have you been disappointed the most, I wonder? Most people to whom I address that question tell me: "My parents." It's surprising, though, how so many will not admit to being hurt or disappointed by their parents for fear they are failing to honor them or are being disloyal to them. Listen to what one writer has to say about this: "When someone appreciates his parents only because he overlooks the pain they caused him, his appreciation is not only superficial, it is self-protective. Love is never blind to others' faults. It sees them clearly and is not threatened. It admits disappointment but forgives and continues to be warmly involved."

Sadly, for far too many of us, love is not the bottom line—self-protection is. When we can look into the face of every disappointment and be willing to feel the pain it brings, there is no more powerful way of motivating our hearts to turn in full dependence toward the Lord. If we are unwilling to do this, then we might cling more to our own ways of handling disappointments than we do to His. And if we do, then in no way can we climb to higher and more distant spiritual peaks.

Prayer

Father, the more I become aware of what is involved in climbing higher with You, the easier it is to become discouraged. I am a dull, blundering disciple. Help me, dear Lord. Your grace works miracles. Work one in me today. In Jesus' name. Amen.

Further Study

2 Co 12:6-10; Php 4:11; Eph 3:16
What could have been a great disappointment to Paul?
What attitude did he take instead?

MARCH I

ℒEVITICUS 17:1–19:10

17 The LORD spoke to Moses: ² "Speak to Aaron, his sons, and all the Israelites and tell them: This is what the LORD has commanded: ³ Anyone from the house of Israel who slaughters an ox, sheep, or goat in the camp, or slaughters it outside the camp, ⁴ instead of bringing it to the entrance to the tent of meeting to present it as an offering to the LORD before His tabernacle—that person will be charged with murder. He has shed blood and must be cut off from his people. ⁵ This is so the Israelites will bring to the LORD the sacrifices they have been offering in the open country. They are to bring them to the priest at the entrance to the tent of meeting and offer them as fellowship sacrifices to the LORD. ⁶ The priest will then sprinkle the blood on the LORD's al-

tar at the entrance to the tent of meeting and burn the fat as a pleasing aroma to the LORD. ⁷ They must no longer offer their sacrifices to the goat-demons that they have prostituted themselves with. This will be a permanent statute for them throughout their generations.

⁸ "Say to them: Anyone from the house of Israel or from the foreigners who live among them who offers a burnt offering or a sacrifice ⁹ but does not bring it to the entrance to the tent of meeting to sacrifice it to the LORD, that person must be cut off from his people.

¹⁰ "Anyone from the house of Israel or from the foreigners who live among them who eats any blood, I will turn against that person who eats blood and cut him off from his people. ¹¹ For the life of a creature is in the blood, and I have appointed it to you to make atonement on the altar for your lives, since it

is the lifeblood that makes atonement. ¹² Therefore I say to the Israelites: None of you and no foreigner who lives among you may eat blood.

¹³ "Any Israelite or foreigner living among them, who hunts down a wild animal or bird that may be eaten must drain its blood and cover it with dirt. ¹⁴ Since the life of every creature is its blood, I have told the Israelites: You must not eat the blood of any creature, because the life of every creature is its blood; whoever eats it must be cut off.

¹⁵ "Every person, whether the native or the foreigner, who eats an animal that died a natural death or was mauled by wild beasts is to wash his clothes and bathe with water, and he will remain unclean until evening; he will be clean. ¹⁶ But if he does not wash his clothes and bathe himself, he will bear his punishment."

18 The LORD spoke to Moses: ² "Speak to the Israelites and tell them: I am the LORD your God. ³ Do not follow the practices of the land of Egypt, where you used to live, or follow the practices of the land of Canaan, where I am bringing you. You must not follow their customs. ⁴ You are to practice My ordinances and you are to keep My statutes by following them; I am the LORD your God. ⁵ Keep My statutes and ordinances; a person will live if he does them. I am the LORD.

⁶ "You are not to come near any close relative for sexual intercourse; I am the LORD. ⁷ You are not to shame your father by having sex with your mother. She is your mother; you must not have sexual intercourse with her. ⁸ You are not to have sex with your father's wife; it will shame your father. ⁹ You are not to have sexual intercourse with your sister, either your father's daughter or your mother's, whether born at home or born elsewhere. You are not to have sex with her. ¹⁰ You are not to have sexual intercourse with your son's daughter or your daughter's daughter, because it will shame your family. ¹¹ You are not to have sexual intercourse with your father's wife's daughter, who is adopted

by your father; she is your sister. ¹² You are not to have sexual intercourse with your father's sister; she is your father's close relative. ¹³ You are not to have sexual intercourse with your mother's sister, for she is your mother's close relative. ¹⁴ You are not to shame your father's brother by coming near his wife to have sexual intercourse; she is your aunt. ¹⁵ You are not to have sexual intercourse with your daughter-in-law. She is your son's wife; you are not to have sex with her. ¹⁶ You are not to have sexual intercourse with your brother's wife; it will shame your brother. ¹⁷ You are not to have sexual intercourse with a woman and her daughter. You are not to marry her son's daughter or her daughter's daughter and have sex with her. They are close relatives; it is depraved. ¹⁸ You are not to marry a woman as a rival to her sister and have sexual intercourse with her during her sister's lifetime.

¹⁹ "You are not to come near a woman during her menstrual impurity to have sexual intercourse with her. ²⁰ You are not to have sexual intercourse with your neighbor's wife, defiling yourself with her.

²¹ "You are not to make any of your children pass through the fire to Molech. Do not profane the name of your God; I am the LORD. ²² You are not to sleep with a man as with a woman; it is detestable. ²³ You are not to have sexual intercourse with any animal, defiling yourself with it; a woman is not to present herself to an animal to mate with it; it is a perversion.

²⁴ "Do not defile yourselves by any of these practices, for the nations I am driving out before you have defiled themselves by all these things. ²⁵ The land has become defiled, so I am punishing it for its sin, and the land will vomit out its inhabitants. ²⁶ But you are to keep My statutes and ordinances. You must not commit any of these abominations—not the native or the foreigner who lives among you. ²⁷ For the men who were in the land prior to you have committed all these abominations, and the land has become defiled. ²⁸ If you

defile the land, it will vomit you out as it has vomited out the nations that were before you. ²⁹ Any person who does any of these abominations must be cut off from his people. ³⁰ You must keep My instruction to not do any of the detestable customs that were practiced before you, so that you do not defile yourselves by them; I am the LORD your God."

19 The LORD spoke to Moses: ² "Speak to the entire Israelite community and tell them: Be holy because I, the LORD your God, am holy.

³ "Each of you is to respect his mother and father. You are to keep My Sabbaths; I am the LORD your God. ⁴ Do not turn to idols or make cast images of gods for yourselves; I am the LORD your God.

⁵ "When you offer a fellowship sacrifice to the LORD, sacrifice it that you may be accepted. ⁶ It is to be eaten on the day you sacrifice it or on the next day, but what remains on the third day must be burned up. ⁷ If any is eaten on the third day, it is a repulsive thing; it will not be accepted. ⁸ Anyone who eats it will bear his punishment, for he has profaned what is holy to the LORD. That person must be cut off from his people.

⁹ "When you reap the harvest of your land, you are not to reap to the very edge of your field or gather the gleanings of your harvest. ¹⁰ You must not strip your vineyard bare or gather its fallen grapes. Leave them for the poor and the foreign resident; I am the LORD your God.

PSALM 28:6-9

⁶ May the LORD be praised,
for He has heard the sound of my pleading.
⁷ The LORD is my strength and my shield;
my heart trusts in Him, and I am helped.
Therefore my heart rejoices,
and I praise Him with my song.

⁸ The LORD is the strength of His people;
He is a stronghold of salvation for His anointed.
⁹ Save Your people, bless Your possession,
shepherd them, and carry them forever.

PROVERBS 6:30-31

³⁰ People don't despise the thief if he steals
to satisfy himself when he is hungry.
³¹ Still, if caught, he must pay seven times as much;
he must give up all the wealth in his house.

MARK 6:1-20

6 He went away from there and came to His hometown, and His disciples followed Him. ² When the Sabbath came, He began to teach in the synagogue, and many who heard Him were astonished. "Where did this man get these things?" they said. "What is this wisdom given to Him, and how are these miracles performed by His hands? ³ Isn't this the carpenter, the son of Mary, and the brother of James, Joses, Judas, and Simon? And aren't His sisters here with us?" So they were offended by Him.

⁴ Then Jesus said to them, "A prophet is not without honor except in his hometown, among his relatives, and in his household." ⁵ So He was not able to do any miracles there, except that He laid His hands on a few sick people and healed them. ⁶ And He was amazed at their unbelief.

Now He was going around the villages in a circuit, teaching. ⁷ He summoned the Twelve and began to send them out in pairs and gave them authority over unclean spirits. ⁸ He instructed them to take nothing for the road except a walking stick: no bread, no traveling bag, no money in their belts. ⁹ They were to wear sandals, but not put on an extra shirt. ¹⁰ Then He said to them, "Whenever you enter a house, stay there until you leave that place. ¹¹ If any place does not welcome you and people refuse to listen to you, when you leave there, shake the dust off your feet as a testimony against them."

¹² So they went out and preached that people should repent. ¹³ And they were driving out many demons, anointing many sick people with oil, and healing.

¹⁴ King Herod heard of this, because Jesus' name had become well known. Some said, "John the Baptist has been raised from the dead, and that's why supernatural powers are at work in him." ¹⁵ But others said, "He's Elijah." Still others said, "He's a prophet—like one of the prophets."

¹⁶ When Herod heard of it, he said, "John, the one I beheaded, has been raised!" ¹⁷ For Herod himself had given orders to arrest John and to chain him in prison on account of Herodias, his brother Philip's wife, whom he had married. ¹⁸ John had been telling Herod, "It is not lawful for you to have your brother's wife!" ¹⁹ So Herodias held a grudge against him and wanted to kill him. But she could not, ²⁰ because Herod was in awe of John and was protecting him, knowing he was a righteous and holy man. When Herod heard him he would be very disturbed, yet would hear him gladly.

"Having" and "Taking"

The LORD is my strength and my shield; my heart trusts in Him, and I am helped.—PSALM 28:7

The first three pieces of the Christian armor should be worn at all times, while the last three should be taken up and used when and where it is necessary. Evidence for this can be seen when we look at Paul's use of the words "having" and "taking."

Listen to the passage: "Stand, therefore, [having] truth like a belt around your waist, righteousness like armor on your chest, and your feet sandaled with readiness for the gospel of peace" (Eph 6: 14-15). Then, in the second section, the word changes: "In every situation take the shield of faith . . . take the helmet of salvation, and the sword of the Spirit" (Eph 6:16-17). The difference between the first and last three pieces of equipment is the difference between "having" and "taking."

The "shield" referred to in Ephesians 6 was extremely large, about four feet long and about two and a half feet wide, designed to give as much protection as possible to the front of the body. More important, the front surface was covered with a sheet of fireproof metal so that the fiery darts of the enemy would have little or no effect. Clearly Paul thought that, in addition to the first three items, a further defense was needed to protect us from the devil's preliminary attacks.

When we consider the lengths to which God has gone in order to give us the protection we need against satanic attack, one wonders why we ever allow ourselves to be badgered and defeated by the devil.

Prayer

O Father, once again I want to record my gratitude for the way in which You have provided for my defense against satanic attack. Help me to see, however, that it will do me no good just to appreciate it; I must use it. In Christ's name I will use it. Amen.

Further Study

Heb 11:17-40; Rm 10:17; Php 3:8-9
How does faith come?
List some of the things accomplished through faith.

MARCH 2

*L*EVITICUS 19:11–20:27

11 "You must not steal. You must not act deceptively or lie to one another. 12 You must not swear falsely by My name, profaning the name of your God; I am the LORD.

13 "You must not oppress your neighbor or rob him. The wages due a hired hand must not remain with you until morning. 14 You must not curse the deaf or put a stumbling block in front of the blind, but you are to fear your God; I am the LORD.

15 "You must not act unjustly when rendering judgment. Do not be partial to the poor or give preference to the rich; judge your neighbor fairly. 16 You must not go about spreading slander among your people; you must not jeopardize your neighbor's life; I am the LORD.

17 "You must not hate your brother in your heart. Rebuke your neighbor directly, and you will not incur guilt because of him. 18 You must not take revenge or bear a grudge against members of your community, but you must love your neighbor as yourself, I am the LORD.

19 "You are to keep My statutes. You must not crossbreed two different kinds of your livestock, sow your fields with two kinds of seed, or put on a garment made of two kinds of material.

20 "If a man has sexual intercourse with a woman who is a slave designated for another man, but she has not been redeemed or given her freedom, there must be punishment. They are not to be put to death, because she had not been freed. 21 However, he must bring his ram as a restitution offering to the LORD at the entrance to the tent of meeting. 22 The priest will make atonement on his behalf before the LORD with the ram of the restitution offering for the sin he has committed, and he will be forgiven for the sin he committed.

23 "When you come into the land and plant any kind of tree for food, you are to consider the fruit forbidden. It will be forbidden to you for three years; it is not to be eaten. 24 In the fourth year all its fruit must be consecrated as a praise offering to the LORD. 25 But in the fifth

year you may eat its fruit. In this way its yield will increase for you; I am the LORD your God. ²⁶ "You are not to eat anything with blood in it. You are not to practice divination or sorcery. ²⁷ You are not to cut off the hair at the sides of your head or mar the edge of your beard. ²⁸ You are not to make gashes on your bodies for the dead or put tattoo marks on yourselves; I am the LORD.

²⁹ "Do not debase your daughter by making her a prostitute, or the land will be prostituted and filled with depravity. ³⁰ You must keep My Sabbaths and revere My sanctuary; I am the LORD.

³¹ "Do not turn to mediums or consult spiritists, or you will be defiled by them; I am the LORD your God.

³² "You are to rise in the presence of the elderly and honor the old. Fear your God; I am the LORD.

³³ "When a foreigner lives with you in your land, you must not oppress him. ³⁴ You must regard the foreigner who lives with you as the native-born among you. You are to love him as yourself, for you were foreigners in the land of Egypt; I am the LORD your God.

³⁵ "You must not act unfairly in measurements of length, weight, or volume. ³⁶ You are to have honest balances, honest weights, an honest dry measure, and an honest liquid measure; I am the LORD your God, who brought you out of the land of Egypt. ³⁷ You must keep all My statutes and all My ordinances and do them; I am the LORD."

20 The LORD spoke to Moses: ² "Say to the Israelites: Any Israelite or foreigner living in Israel who gives any of his children to Molech must be put to death; the people of the country are to stone him. ³ I will turn against that man and cut him off from his people, because he gave his offspring to Molech, defiling My sanctuary and profaning My holy name. ⁴ But if the people of the country look the other way when that man gives any of his children to Molech, and do not put him to death, ⁵ then I will turn against that man and his family, and cut off from their people

both him and all who follow him, prostituting themselves with Molech.

⁶ "Whoever turns to mediums or spiritists and prostitutes himself with them, I will turn against that person and cut him off from his people. ⁷ Consecrate yourselves and be holy, for I am the LORD your God. ⁸ Keep My statutes and do them; I am the LORD who sets you apart.

⁹ "If anyone curses his father or mother, he must be put to death. He has cursed his father or mother; his blood is on his own hands. ¹⁰ If a man commits adultery with a married woman—if he commits adultery with his neighbor's wife—both the adulterer and the adulteress must be put to death. ¹¹ If a man sleeps with his father's wife, he has shamed his father. Both of them must be put to death; their blood is on their own hands. ¹² If a man sleeps with his daughter-in-law, both of them must be put to death. They have acted perversely; their blood is on their own hands. ¹³ If a man sleeps with a man as with a woman, they have both committed an abomination. They must be put to death; their blood is on their own hands. ¹⁴ If a man marries a woman and her mother, it is depraved. Both he and they must be burned with fire, so that there will be no depravity among you. ¹⁵ If a man has sexual intercourse with an animal, he must be put to death; you are also to kill the animal. ¹⁶ If a woman comes near any animal and mates with it, you are to kill the woman and the animal. They must be put to death; their own blood is on them. ¹⁷ If a man marries his sister, whether his father's daughter or his mother's daughter, and they have sexual relations, it is a disgrace. They must be cut off publicly from their people. He has had sexual intercourse with his sister; he will bear his punishment. ¹⁸ If a man sleeps with a menstruating woman and has sexual intercourse with her, he has exposed the source of her flow, and she has uncovered the source of her blood. Both of them must be cut off from their people. ¹⁹ You must not have sexual intercourse with your mother's sister or your father's

sister, for it is exposing one's own blood relative; both people will bear their punishment. ²⁰ If a man sleeps with his aunt, he has shamed his uncle; they will bear their guilt and die childless. ²¹ If a man marries his brother's wife, it is impurity. He has shamed his brother; they will be childless.

²² "You are to keep all My statutes and all My ordinances, and do them, so that the land where I am bringing you to live will not vomit you out. ²³ You must not follow the statutes of the nations I am driving out before you, for they did all these things, and I abhorred them. ²⁴ And I promised you: You will inherit their land, since I will give it to you to possess, a land flowing with milk and honey. I am the LORD your God who set you apart from the peoples. ²⁵ Therefore you must distinguish the clean animal from the unclean one, and the unclean bird from the clean one. You are not to make yourselves detestable by any land animal, bird, or whatever crawls on the ground; I have set these apart as unclean for you. ²⁶ You are to be holy to Me because I, the LORD, am holy, and I have set you apart from the nations to be Mine. ²⁷ A man or a woman who is a medium or a spiritist must be put to death. They are to be stoned; their blood is on their own hands."

𝒫SALM 29:1-6

¹ Give the LORD—you heavenly
   beings—
   give the LORD glory and strength.
² Give the LORD the glory due His
   name;
   worship the LORD in the splendor
   of His holiness.
³ The voice of the LORD is above the
   waters.
   The God of glory thunders—
   the LORD, above vast waters,
⁴ the voice of the LORD in power,
   the voice of the LORD in
   splendor.
⁵ The voice of the LORD breaks the
   cedars;

the LORD shatters the cedars of
   Lebanon.
⁶ He makes Lebanon skip like a calf,
   and Sirion, like a young wild ox.

𝒫ROVERBS 6:32-33

³² The one who commits adultery
   lacks sense;
   whoever does so destroys himself.
³³ He will get a beating and
   dishonor,
   and his disgrace will never be
   removed.

𝓜ARK 6:21-46

²¹ Now an opportune time came on his birthday, when Herod gave a banquet for his nobles, military commanders, and the leading men of Galilee. ²² When Herodias' own daughter came in and danced, she pleased Herod and his guests. The king said to the girl, "Ask me whatever you want, and I'll give it to you." ²³ So he swore oaths to her: "Whatever you ask me I will give you, up to half my kingdom."

²⁴ Then she went out and said to her mother, "What should I ask for?"

"John the Baptist's head!" she said.

²⁵ Immediately she hurried to the king and said, "I want you to give me John the Baptist's head on a platter—right now!"

²⁶ Though the king was deeply distressed, because of his oaths and the guests he did not want to refuse her. ²⁷ The king immediately sent for an executioner and commanded him to bring John's head. So he went and beheaded him in prison, ²⁸ brought his head on a platter, and gave it to the girl. Then the girl gave it to her mother. ²⁹ When his disciples heard about it, they came and removed his corpse and placed it in a tomb.

³⁰ The apostles gathered around Jesus and reported to Him all that they had done and taught. ³¹ He said to them, "Come away by yourselves to a remote place and rest a while." For many people were coming and going, and they

did not even have time to eat. [32] So they went away in the boat by themselves to a remote place, [33] but many saw them leaving and recognized them. People ran there by land from all the towns and arrived ahead of them. [34] So as He stepped ashore, He saw a huge crowd and had compassion on them, because they were like sheep without a shepherd. Then He began to teach them many things.

[35] When it was already late, His disciples approached Him and said, "This place is a wilderness, and it is already late! [36] Send them away, so they can go into the surrounding countryside and villages to buy themselves something to eat."

[37] "You give them something to eat," He responded.

They said to Him, "Should we go and buy 200 denarii worth of bread and give them something to eat?"

[38] And He asked them, "How many loaves do you have? Go look."

When they found out they said, "Five, and two fish."

[39] Then He instructed them to have all the people sit down in groups on the green grass. [40] So they sat down in ranks of hundreds and fifties. [41] Then He took the five loaves and the two fish, and looking up to heaven, He blessed and broke the loaves. He kept giving them to His disciples to set before the people. He also divided the two fish among them all. [42] Everyone ate and was filled. [43] Then they picked up 12 baskets full of pieces of bread and fish. [44] Now those who ate the loaves were 5,000 men.

[45] Immediately He made His disciples get into the boat and go ahead of Him to the other side, to Bethsaida, while He dismissed the crowd. [46] After He said good-bye to them, He went away to the mountain to pray.

Be Selective

He said to them, "Come away by yourselves to a remote place and rest a while."—MARK 6:31

Disregard of our physical life may affect our spiritual well-being, for what goes on in the body greatly influences, though it does not control, what goes on in the soul and spirit.

My suggestion in relation to this physical aspect of our lives is this: discipline your times of rest and recreation. Some recreations do not recreate; rather, they exhaust one. They leave one morally and spiritually flabby and unfit. I find that after watching some television programs, I have been challenged or lifted, but others leave me feeling inwardly ravished. The delicacies of life seem somehow to have been invaded, the finest flowers of the spirit trampled on, and one comes out drooping. I am learning to be more selective in my recreations. One should never expose oneself to a film or television program that is likely to leave one spiritually or morally depleted—not if you value the higher values. It is like allowing pigs into your parlor.

The same can be said of other recreations. Some pieces of literature can leave you with a sense of moral and spiritual exhaustion. Don't fall for the idea that one has to read everything that comes to hand in order to understand life. This is where many of our Christian young people need help. Does one have to wallow in a mud-hole in order to understand filth? Does a doctor have to take germs into his own body in order to understand how they function? Recreation is extremely important to help us stay spiritually fresh, but we need to make sure our recreations really recreate.

Prayer

Father, You have made me for health and rhythm. Help me to be sensitive to all the things I need to do so that I am at my best spiritually and physically. I want to honor You in everything I do—even in my recreations. Amen.

Further Study

Heb 4:1-11; Ex 33:14; Mt 11:29
What are we invited to enter into?
What does this mean in practical terms?

MARCH 3

LEVITICUS 21:1–22:33

21 The LORD said to Moses: "Speak to Aaron's sons, the priests, and tell them: A priest is not to make himself ceremonially unclean for a dead person among his relatives, ² except for his immediate family: his mother, father, son, daughter, or brother. ³ He may make himself unclean for his young unmarried sister in his immediate family. ⁴ He is not to make himself unclean for those related to him by marriage and so defile himself.

⁵ "Priests may not make bald spots on their heads, shave the edge of their beards, or make gashes on their bodies. ⁶ They are to be holy to their God and not profane the name of their God, because they present the fire offerings to the LORD, the food of their God. They must be holy. ⁷ They are not to marry a woman defiled by prostitution or divorced by her husband, for the priest is holy to his God. ⁸ You are to consider him holy since he presents the food of your God. He will be holy to you because I, the LORD who sets you apart, am

holy. ⁹ If a priest's daughter defiles herself by promiscuity, she defiles her father; she must be burned up.

¹⁰ "The priest who is highest among his brothers, who has had the anointing oil poured on his head and has been ordained to wear the garments, must not dishevel his hair or tear his garments. ¹¹ He must not go near any dead person or make himself unclean even for his father or mother. ¹² He must not leave the sanctuary or he will desecrate the sanctuary of his God, for the consecration of the anointing oil of his God is on him; I am the LORD.

¹³ "He is to marry a woman who is a virgin. ¹⁴ He is not to marry a widow, a divorced woman, or one defiled by prostitution. He is to marry a virgin from his own people, ¹⁵ so that he does not corrupt his bloodline among his people, for I am the LORD who sets him apart."

¹⁶ The LORD spoke to Moses: ¹⁷ "Tell Aaron: None of your descendants throughout your generations who has a physical defect is to come near to present the food of his God. ¹⁸ No man who has any defect is to come near: no man who is blind, lame, facially disfigured,

or deformed; [19] no man who has a broken foot or hand, [20] or who is a hunchback or a dwarf, or who has an eye defect, a festering rash, scabs, or a crushed testicle. [21] No descendant of Aaron the priest who has a defect is to come near to present the fire offerings to the LORD. He has a defect and is not to come near to present the food of his God. [22] He may eat the food of his God from what is especially holy as well as from what is holy. [23] But because he has a defect, he must not go near the curtain or approach the altar. He is not to desecrate My sanctuaries, for I am the LORD who sets them apart." [24] Moses said this to Aaron and his sons and to all the Israelites.

22 The LORD spoke to Moses: [2] "Tell Aaron and his sons to deal respectfully with the holy offerings of the Israelites that they have consecrated to Me, so they do not profane My holy name; I am the LORD. [3] Say to them: If any man from any of your descendants throughout your generations is in a state of uncleanness yet approaches the holy offerings that the Israelites consecrate to the LORD, that person will be cut off from My presence; I am the LORD. [4] No man of Aaron's descendants who has a skin disease or a discharge is to eat from the holy offerings until he is clean. Whoever touches anything made unclean by a dead person or by a man who has an emission of semen, [5] or whoever touches any swarming creature that makes him unclean or any person who makes him unclean—whatever his uncleanness— [6] the man who touches any of these will remain unclean until evening and is not to eat from the holy offerings unless he has bathed his body with water. [7] When the sun has set, he will become clean, and then he may eat from the holy offerings, for that is his food. [8] He must not eat an animal that died naturally or was mauled by wild beasts, making himself unclean by it; I am the LORD. [9] They must keep My instruction, or they will be guilty and die because they profane it; I am the LORD who sets them apart.

[10] "No one outside a priest's family is to eat the holy offering. A foreigner staying with a priest or a hired hand is not to eat the holy offering. [11] But if a priest purchases someone with his money, that person may eat it, and those born in his house may eat his food. [12] If the priest's daughter is married to a man outside a priest's family, she is not to eat from the holy contributions. [13] But if the priest's daughter becomes widowed or divorced, has no children, and returns to her father's house as in her youth, she may share her father's food. But no outsider may share it. [14] If anyone eats a holy offering in error, he must add a fifth to its value and give the holy offering to the priest. [15] The priests must not profane the holy offerings the Israelites give to the LORD [16] and have them bear the penalty of restitution if the people eat their holy offerings. For I am the LORD who sets them apart."

[17] The LORD spoke to Moses: [18] "Speak to Aaron, his sons, and all the Israelites and tell them: Any man of the house of Israel or of the foreign residents in Israel who presents his offering—whether they present freewill gifts or payment of vows to the LORD as burnt offerings— [19] must offer an unblemished male from the cattle, sheep, or goats in order for you to be accepted. [20] You are not to present anything that has a defect, because it will not be accepted on your behalf.

[21] "When a man presents a fellowship sacrifice to the LORD to fulfill a vow or as a freewill offering from the herd or flock, it has to be unblemished to be acceptable; there must be no defect in it. [22] You are not to present any animal to the LORD that is blind, injured, maimed, or has a running sore, festering rash, or scabs; you may not put any of them on the altar as a fire offering to the LORD. [23] You may sacrifice as a freewill offering any animal from the herd or flock that has an elongated or stunted limb, but it is not acceptable as a vow offering. [24] You are not to present to the LORD anything that has bruised, crushed, torn, or severed testicles; you must not sacrifice them in your land. [25] Neither you nor a

foreigner are to present food to your God from any of these animals. They will not be accepted for you because they are deformed and have a defect."

²⁶ The LORD spoke to Moses: ²⁷ "When an ox, sheep, or goat is born, it must remain with its mother for seven days; from the eighth day on, it will be acceptable as a gift, a fire offering to the LORD. ²⁸ But you are not to slaughter an animal from the herd or flock on the same day as its young. ²⁹ When you sacrifice a thank offering to the LORD, sacrifice it so that you may be accepted. ³⁰ It is to be eaten on the same day. Do not let any of it remain until morning; I am the LORD.

³¹ "You are to keep My commands and do them; I am the LORD. ³² You must not profane My holy name; I must be treated as holy among the Israelites. I am the LORD who sets you apart, ³³ the One who brought you out of the land of Egypt to be your God; I am the LORD."

PSALM 29:7-11

⁷ The voice of the LORD flashes
   flames of fire.
⁸ The voice of the LORD shakes the
   wilderness;
   the LORD shakes the wilderness of
   Kadesh.
⁹ The voice of the LORD makes the
   deer give birth
   and strips the woodlands bare.

In His temple all cry, "Glory!"

¹⁰ The LORD sat enthroned at the
   flood;
   the LORD sits enthroned, King
   forever.
¹¹ The LORD gives His people
   strength;
   the LORD blesses His people with
   peace.

PROVERBS 6:34-35

³⁴ For jealousy enrages a husband,
   and he will show no mercy when
   he takes revenge.

³⁵ He will not be appeased by
   anything
   or be persuaded by lavish gifts.

MARK 6:47–7:16

⁴⁷ When evening came, the boat was in the middle of the sea, and He was alone on the land. ⁴⁸ He saw them being battered as they rowed, because the wind was against them. Around three in the morning He came toward them walking on the sea and wanted to pass by them. ⁴⁹ When they saw Him walking on the sea, they thought it was a ghost and cried out; ⁵⁰ for they all saw Him and were terrified. Immediately He spoke with them and said, "Have courage! It is I. Don't be afraid." ⁵¹ Then He got into the boat with them, and the wind ceased. They were completely astounded, ⁵² because they had not understood about the loaves. Instead, their hearts were hardened.

⁵³ When they had crossed over, they came to land at Gennesaret and beached the boat. ⁵⁴ As they got out of the boat, people immediately recognized Him. ⁵⁵ They hurried throughout that vicinity and began to carry the sick on stretchers to wherever they heard He was. ⁵⁶ Wherever He would go, into villages, towns, or the country, they laid the sick in the marketplaces and begged Him that they might touch just the tassel of His robe. And everyone who touched it was made well.

7 The Pharisees and some of the scribes who had come from Jerusalem gathered around Him. ² They observed that some of His disciples were eating their bread with unclean—that is, unwashed—hands. ³ (For the Pharisees, in fact all the Jews, will not eat unless they wash their hands ritually, keeping the tradition of the elders. ⁴ When they come from the marketplace, they do not eat unless they have washed. And there are many other customs they have received and keep, like the washing of cups, jugs, copper utensils, and dining couches.) ⁵ Then the Pharisees and the

scribes asked Him, "Why don't Your disciples live according to the tradition of the elders, instead of eating bread with ritually unclean hands?"

⁶He answered them, "Isaiah prophesied correctly about you hypocrites, as it is written:

> These people honor Me
>   with their lips,
> but their heart is far from Me.
> ⁷ They worship Me in vain,
>   teaching as doctrines
>   the commands of men.

⁸Disregarding the command of God, you keep the tradition of men." ⁹He also said to them, "You completely invalidate God's command in order to maintain your tradition! ¹⁰For Moses said:

> Honor your father
>   and your mother; and,
> Whoever speaks evil of father
>   or mother
> must be put to death.

¹¹But you say, 'If a man tells his father or mother: Whatever benefit you might have received from me is Corban'" (that is, a gift committed to the temple), ¹²"you no longer let him do anything for his father or mother. ¹³You revoke God's word by your tradition that you have handed down. And you do many other similar things." ¹⁴Summoning the crowd again, He told them, "Listen to Me, all of you, and understand: ¹⁵Nothing that goes into a person from outside can defile him, but the things that come out of a person are what defile him. ¹⁶If anyone has ears to hear, he should listen!"

Positive Thanksgiving

The LORD gives His people strength; the LORD blesses His people with peace.—PSALM 29:11

Here is a prescription for overcoming frustration. Look for something good to come out of everything that appears bad. How I wish I could hammer this thought into the mind of every Christian. Nowadays, it is almost second nature with me to look for a positive in every negative, but it was not always so. At one time, whenever anything bad happened to me, I used to say: "Oh no, not again! Just when everything seemed to be going right! Why should this happen to me?" I learned, however, to apply this principle, and I can honestly say it has transformed my life and ministry.

This also means learning to thank God for the good that is emerging, instead of brooding over any loss that has been sustained. This positive thanksgiving will make your heart receptive to God's power. He can do anything with a thankful heart, but He will usually do little or nothing with a complaining, self-pitying heart. It is closed to grace.

Also, find someone who is going through difficult circumstances, and help them find victory. Someone has said, "Sorrow expands the soul for joy." For joy? Yes—the joy of being useful and creative. God uses frustrating circumstances to prune you for fruit-bearing.

And the lessons you have learned will go even deeper as you share them with others. Expression deepens impression. If you incorporate your sorrows, they will multiply. And if you incorporate your blessings, they too will multiply. Learn this secret, and it will help you stay spiritually on top—no matter what.

Prayer

O God, help me not to be a whiner but a worshiper. Help me to cultivate an attitude of thanksgiving in all things—for I know that all things serve. I pray in Jesus' name. Amen.

Further Study

Rm 8:1-7; Col 3:15; Php 4:7
What brings life and peace?
What will the peace of God do?

MARCH 4

ℒEVITICUS 23:1–24:23

23 The LORD spoke to Moses: ² "Speak to the Israelites and tell them: These are My appointed times, the times of the LORD that you will proclaim as sacred assemblies.

³ "For six days work may be done, but on the seventh day there must be a Sabbath of complete rest, a sacred assembly. You are not to do any work; it is a Sabbath to the LORD wherever you live.

⁴ "These are the LORD's appointed times, the sacred assemblies you are to proclaim at their appointed times. ⁵ The Passover to the LORD comes in the first month, at twilight on the fourteenth day of the month. ⁶ The Festival of Unleavened Bread to the LORD is on the fifteenth day of the same month. For seven days you must eat unleavened bread. ⁷ On the first day you are to hold a sacred assembly; you are not to do any daily work. ⁸ You are to present a fire offering to the LORD for seven days. On the seventh day there will be a sacred assembly; you must not do any daily work."

⁹ The LORD spoke to Moses: ¹⁰ "Speak to the Israelites and tell them: When you enter the land I am giving you and reap its harvest, you are to bring the first sheaf of your harvest to the priest. ¹¹ He will wave the sheaf before the LORD so that you may be accepted; the priest is to wave it on the day after the Sabbath. ¹² On the day you wave the sheaf, you are to offer a year-old male lamb without blemish as a burnt offering to the LORD. ¹³ Its grain offering is to be four quarts of fine flour mixed with oil as a fire offering to the LORD, a pleasing aroma, and its drink offering will be one quart of wine. ¹⁴ You must not eat bread, roasted grain, or any new grain until this very day, and you have brought the offering of your God. This is to be a permanent statute throughout your generations wherever you live.

¹⁵ "You are to count seven complete weeks starting from the day after the Sabbath, the day you brought the sheaf of the presentation offering. ¹⁶ You are to count 50 days until the day after the seventh Sabbath and then present an offering of new grain to the LORD. ¹⁷ Bring two loaves of bread from your settle-

ments as a presentation offering, each of them made from four quarts of fine flour, baked with yeast, as firstfruits to the LORD. ¹⁸ You are to present with the bread seven unblemished male lambs a year old, one young bull, and two rams. They will be a burnt offering to the LORD, with their grain offerings and drink offerings, a fire offering of a pleasing aroma to the LORD. ¹⁹ You are also to prepare one male goat as a sin offering, and two male lambs a year old as a fellowship sacrifice. ²⁰ The priest will wave the lambs with the bread of firstfruits as a presentation offering before the LORD; the bread and the two lambs will be holy to the LORD for the priest. ²¹ On that same day you are to make a proclamation and hold a sacred assembly. You are not to do any daily work. This is to be a permanent statute wherever you live throughout your generations. ²² When you reap the harvest of your land, you are not to reap all the way to the edge of your field or gather the gleanings of your harvest. Leave them for the poor and the foreign resident; I am the LORD your God."

²³ The LORD spoke to Moses: ²⁴ "Tell the Israelites: In the seventh month, on the first day of the month, you are to have a day of complete rest, commemoration and jubilation—a sacred assembly. ²⁵ You must not do any daily work, but you must present a fire offering to the LORD."

²⁶ The LORD again spoke to Moses: ²⁷ "The tenth day of this seventh month is the Day of Atonement. You are to hold a sacred assembly and practice self-denial; you are to present a fire offering to the LORD. ²⁸ On this particular day you are not to do any work, for it is a Day of Atonement to make atonement for yourselves before the LORD your God. ²⁹ If any person does not practice self-denial on this particular day, he must be cut off from his people. ³⁰ I will destroy among his people anyone who does any work on this same day. ³¹ You are not to do any work. This is a permanent statute throughout your generations wherever you live. ³² It will be a Sabbath of complete rest for you, and

you must practice self-denial. You are to observe your Sabbath from the evening of the ninth day of the month until the following evening."

³³ The LORD spoke to Moses: ³⁴ "Tell the Israelites: The Festival of Booths to the LORD begins on the fifteenth day of this seventh month and continues for seven days. ³⁵ There is to be a sacred assembly on the first day; you are not to do any daily work. ³⁶ You are to present a fire offering to the LORD for seven days. On the eighth day you are to hold a sacred assembly and present a fire offering to the LORD. It is a solemn gathering; you are not to do any daily work.

³⁷ "These are the LORD's appointed times that you are to proclaim as sacred assemblies for presenting fire offerings to the LORD, burnt offerings and grain offerings, sacrifices and drink offerings, each on its designated day. ³⁸ These are in addition to the offerings for the LORD's Sabbaths, your gifts, all your vow offerings, and all your freewill offerings that you give to the LORD.

³⁹ "You are to celebrate the LORD's festival on the fifteenth day of the seventh month for seven days after you have gathered the produce of the land. There will be complete rest on the first day and complete rest on the eighth day. ⁴⁰ On the first day you are to take the product of majestic trees—palm fronds, boughs of leafy trees, and willows of the brook—and rejoice before the LORD your God for seven days. ⁴¹ You are to celebrate it as a festival to the LORD seven days each year. This is a permanent statute for you throughout your generations; you must celebrate it in the seventh month. ⁴² You are to live in booths for seven days. All the native-born of Israel must live in booths, ⁴³ so that your generations may know that I made the Israelites live in booths when I brought them out of the land of Egypt; I am the LORD your God." ⁴⁴ So Moses declared the LORD's appointed times to the Israelites.

24 The LORD spoke to Moses: ² "Command the Israelites to bring you pure oil of beaten olives for the light, so that the lamp will burn regularly. ³ Aaron is to tend it regularly from evening until morning before the LORD outside the veil of the testimony in the tent of meeting. This is a permanent statute throughout your generations. ⁴ He must regularly tend the lamps on the pure gold lampstand in the LORD's presence.

⁵ "Take fine flour and bake it into 12 loaves; each loaf is to be made with four quarts. ⁶ Arrange them in two rows, six to a row, on the pure gold table before the LORD. ⁷ Place pure frankincense near each row, so that it may serve as a memorial portion for the bread and a fire offering to the LORD. ⁸ The bread is to be set out before the LORD every Sabbath day as a perpetual covenant obligation on the part of the Israelites. ⁹ It belongs to Aaron and his sons, who are to eat it in a holy place, for it is the holiest portion for him from the fire offerings to the LORD; this is a permanent rule."

¹⁰ Now the son of an Israelite mother and an Egyptian father was among the Israelites. A fight broke out in the camp between the Israelite woman's son and an Israelite man. ¹¹ Her son cursed and blasphemed the Name, and they brought him to Moses. (His mother's name was Shelomith, a daughter of Dibri of the tribe of Dan.) ¹² They put him in custody until the LORD's decision could be made clear to them.

¹³ Then the LORD spoke to Moses: ¹⁴ "Bring the one who has cursed to the outside of the camp and have all who heard him lay their hands on his head; then have the whole community stone him. ¹⁵ And tell the Israelites: If anyone curses his God, he will bear the consequences of his sin. ¹⁶ Whoever blasphemes the name of the LORD is to be put to death; the whole community must stone him. If he blasphemes the Name, he is to be put to death, whether the foreign resident or the native. ¹⁷ "If a man kills anyone, he must be put to death. ¹⁸ Whoever kills an animal is to make restitution for it, life for life. ¹⁹ If any man inflicts a permanent injury on his neighbor, whatever he has done is to be done to him: ²⁰ fracture for fracture, eye for eye, tooth for tooth. Whatever injury he inflicted on the person, the same is to be inflicted on him. ²¹ Whoever kills an animal is to make restitution for it, but whoever kills a person is to be put to death. ²² You are to have the same law for the foreign resident and the native, because I am the LORD your God."

²³ After Moses spoke to the Israelites, they brought the one who had cursed to the outside of the camp and stoned him. So the Israelites did as the LORD had commanded Moses.

PSALM 30:1-6

¹ I will exalt You, LORD, because You
    have lifted me up
and have not allowed my enemies
    to triumph over me.
² LORD my God,
    I cried to You for help, and You
    healed me.
³ LORD, You brought me up from
    Sheol;
You spared me from among those
    going down to the Pit.

⁴ Sing to the LORD, you His faithful
    ones,
and praise His holy name.
⁵ For His anger lasts only a
    moment,
but His favor, a lifetime.
Weeping may spend the night,
but there is joy in the morning.

⁶ When I was secure, I said,
    "I will never be shaken."

PROVERBS 7:1-3

7 My son, obey my words,
    and treasure my commands.
² Keep my commands and live;
    protect my teachings as you would
    the pupil of your eye.
³ Tie them to your fingers;
    write them on the tablet of your
    heart.

MARK 7:17-37

¹⁷ When He went into the house away from the crowd, the disciples asked Him about the parable. ¹⁸ And He said to them, "Are you also as lacking in understanding? Don't you realize that nothing going into a man from the outside can defile him? ¹⁹ For it doesn't go into his heart but into the stomach and is eliminated." (As a result, He made all foods clean.) ²⁰ Then He said, "What comes out of a person—that defiles him. ²¹ For from within, out of people's hearts, come evil thoughts, sexual immoralities, thefts, murders, ²² adulteries, greed, evil actions, deceit, lewdness, stinginess, blasphemy, pride, and foolishness. ²³ All these evil things come from within and defile a person."

²⁴ He got up and departed from there to the region of Tyre and Sidon. He entered a house and did not want anyone to know it, but He could not escape notice. ²⁵ Instead, immediately after hearing about Him, a woman whose little daughter had an unclean spirit came and fell at His feet. ²⁶ Now the woman was Greek, a Syrophoenician by birth, and she kept asking Him to drive the demon out of her daughter. ²⁷ He said to her, "Allow the children to be satisfied first, because it isn't right to take the children's bread and throw it to the dogs."

²⁸ But she replied to Him, "Lord, even the dogs under the table eat the children's crumbs."

²⁹ Then He told her, "Because of this reply, you may go. The demon has gone out of your daughter." ³⁰ When she went back to her home, she found her child lying on the bed, and the demon was gone.

³¹ Again, leaving the region of Tyre, He went by way of Sidon to the Sea of Galilee, through the region of the Decapolis. ³² They brought to Him a deaf man who also had a speech difficulty, and begged Jesus to lay His hand on him. ³³ So He took him away from the crowd privately. After putting His fingers in the man's ears and spitting, He touched his tongue. ³⁴ Then, looking up to heaven, He sighed deeply and said to him, *"Ephphatha!"* (that is, "Be opened!"). ³⁵ Immediately his ears were opened, his speech difficulty was removed, and he began to speak clearly. ³⁶ Then He ordered them to tell no one, but the more He would order them, the more they would proclaim it.

³⁷ They were extremely astonished and said, "He has done everything well! He even makes deaf people hear, and people unable to speak, talk!"

"Surprised by Joy"

Weeping may spend the night, but there is joy in the morning.—Psalm 30:5

What a distinctive and intriguing difficulty it was for Jesus' disciples to struggle with disappointment, reluctant to believe in case what they were believing proved untrue. They were grown men whose lives had been far from sheltered and protected, yet the experience of the Crucifixion had been more harrowing than any of them ever cared to face again.

Over and over again during the days in which Jesus lay in the grave, they must have racked their brains to try to find some explanation for why His life had ended on a grisly cross. Doubtless, in the closing hours of that fateful weekend, their thoughts must have turned naturally toward how they might go about restructuring their lives. Then, suddenly, Jesus appeared to them. His appearance was everything they wanted, but such was the disappointment already in their hearts that they considered it too good to be true. Thus they protected themselves against the risk of being disappointed again.

This is the tragedy of disappointment—it can, unless looked at and dealt with, reverberate inside us and hinder us in our pursuit of God. When disappointment is put into its proper perspective and when faith comes into its own, far from being too good to be true, one discovers that there is nothing else so good and nothing else so true. God proves Himself to be not just better than our worst fears, but better than our greatest dreams. No longer believing in joy is quickly followed by being surprised by joy.

Prayer

Gracious and loving heavenly Father, give me insight into what I have been looking at today, and show me how to press through all disappointments in the knowledge that beyond the hurts, I shall be "surprised by joy." Amen.

Further Study

Jn 21:1-22; Ps 126:5; Is 35:10
How did Peter respond to his disappointment?
What were Jesus' words to him?

MARCH 5

LEVITICUS 25:1-55

25 The LORD spoke to Moses on Mount Sinai: ² "Speak to the Israelites and tell them: When you enter the land I am giving you, the land will observe a Sabbath to the LORD. ³ You may sow your field for six years, and you may prune your vineyard and gather its produce for six years. ⁴ But there will be a Sabbath of complete rest for the land in the seventh year, a Sabbath to the LORD: you are not to sow your field or prune your vineyard. ⁵ You are not to reap what grows by itself from your crop, or harvest the grapes of your un-tended vines. It must be a year of complete rest for the land. ⁶ Whatever the land produces during the Sabbath year can be food for you; for yourself, your male or female slave, and the hired hand or foreigner who stays with you. ⁷ All of its growth may serve as food for your livestock and the wild animals in your land.

⁸ "You are to count seven sabbatic years, seven times seven years, so that the time period of the seven sabbatic years amounts to 49. ⁹ Then you are to sound a trumpet loudly in the seventh month, on the tenth day of the month; you will sound it throughout your land on the Day of Atonement. ¹⁰ You are to

252

consecrate the fiftieth year and proclaim freedom in the land for all its inhabitants. It will be your Jubilee, when each of you is to return to his property and each of you to his clan. [11] The fiftieth year will be your Jubilee; you are not to sow, reap what grows by itself, or harvest its untended vines. [12] It is to be holy to you because it is the Jubilee; you may only eat its produce directly from the field. [13] "In this Year of Jubilee, each of you will return to his property. [14] If you make a sale to your neighbor or a purchase from him, do not cheat one another. [15] You are to make the purchase from your neighbor based on the number of years since the last Jubilee. He is to sell to you based on the number of remaining harvest years. [16] You are to increase its price in proportion to a greater amount of years, and decrease its price in proportion to a lesser amount of years, because what he is selling to you is a number of harvests. [17] You are not to cheat one another, but fear your God, for I am the LORD your God.

[18] "You are to observe My statutes and ordinances and carefully observe them, so that you may live securely in the land. [19] Then the land will yield its fruit, so that you can eat, be satisfied, and live securely in the land. [20] If you wonder: 'What will we eat in the seventh year if we don't sow or gather our produce?' [21] I will appoint My blessing for you in the sixth year, so that it will produce a crop sufficient for three years. [22] When you sow in the eighth year, you will be eating from the previous harvest. You will be eating this until the ninth year when its harvest comes in.

[23] "The land is not to be permanently sold because it is Mine, and you are only foreigners and temporary residents on My land. [24] You are to allow the redemption of any land you occupy. [25] If your brother becomes destitute and sells part of his property, his nearest relative may come and redeem what his brother has sold. [26] If a man has no family redeemer, but he prospers and obtains enough to redeem his land, [27] he

may calculate the years since its sale, repay the balance to the man he sold it to, and return to his property. [28] But if he cannot obtain enough to repay him, what he sold will remain in the possession of its purchaser until the Year of Jubilee. It is to be released at the Jubilee, so that he may return to his property.

[29] "If a man sells a residence in a walled city, his right of redemption will last until a year has passed after its sale; his right of redemption will last a year. [30] If it is not redeemed by the end of a full year, then the house in the walled city is permanently transferred to its purchaser throughout his generations. It is not to be released on the Jubilee. [31] But houses in villages that have no walls around them are to be classified as open fields. The right to redeem such houses stays in effect, and they are to be released at the Jubilee.

[32] "Concerning the Levitical cities, the Levites always have the right to redeem houses in the cities they possess. [33] Whatever property one of the Levites can redeem—a house sold in a city they possess—must be released at the Jubilee, because the houses in the Levitical cities are their possession among the Israelites. [34] The open pastureland around their cities may not be sold, for it is their permanent possession.

[35] "If your brother becomes destitute and cannot sustain himself among you, you are to support him as a foreigner or temporary resident, so that he can continue to live among you. [36] Do not profit or take interest from him, but fear your God and let your brother live among you. [37] You are not to lend him your silver with interest or sell him your food for profit. [38] I am the LORD your God, who brought you out of the land of Egypt to give you the land of Canaan and to be your God.

[39] "If your brother among you becomes destitute and sells himself to you, you must not force him to do slave labor. [40] Let him stay with you as a hired hand or temporary resident; he may work for you until the Year of Jubilee. [41] Then he and his children are to be

released from you, and he may return to his clan and his ancestral property. ⁴²They are not to be sold as slaves, because they are My slaves I brought out of the land of Egypt. ⁴³You are not to rule over them harshly but fear your God. ⁴⁴Your male and female slaves are to be from the nations around you; you may purchase male and female slaves. ⁴⁵You may also purchase them from the foreigners staying with you, or from their families living among you—those born in your land. These may become your property. ⁴⁶You may leave them to your sons after you to inherit as property; you can make them slaves for life. But concerning your brothers, the Israelites, you must not rule over one another harshly.

⁴⁷"If a foreigner or temporary resident living among you prospers, but your brother living near him becomes destitute and sells himself to the foreigner living among you, or to a member of the foreigner's clan, ⁴⁸he has the right of redemption after he has been sold. One of his brothers may redeem him. ⁴⁹His uncle or cousin may redeem him, or any of his close relatives from his clan may redeem him. If he prospers, he may redeem himself. ⁵⁰The one who purchased him is to calculate the time from the year he sold himself to him until the Year of Jubilee. The price of his sale will be determined by the number of years. It will be set for him like the daily wages of a hired hand. ⁵¹If many years are still left, he must pay his redemption price in proportion to them based on his purchase price. ⁵²If only a few years remain until the Year of Jubilee, he will calculate and pay the price of his redemption in proportion to his remaining years. ⁵³He will stay with him like a man hired year by year. A foreign owner is not to rule over him harshly in your sight. ⁵⁴If he is not redeemed in any of these ways, he and his children are to be released at the Year of Jubilee. ⁵⁵For the Israelites are My slaves. They are My slaves I brought out of the land of Egypt; I am the LORD your God.

PSALM 30:7-12

⁷ LORD, when You showed Your favor,
You made me stand like a strong mountain;
when You hid Your face, I was terrified.
⁸ LORD, I called to You;
I sought favor from my Lord:
⁹ "What gain is there in my death,
in my descending to the Pit?
Will the dust praise You?
Will it proclaim Your truth?
¹⁰ LORD, listen and be gracious to me;
LORD, be my helper."

¹¹ You turned my lament into dancing;
You removed my sackcloth and clothed me with gladness,
¹² so that I can sing to You and not be silent.
LORD my God, I will praise You forever.

PROVERBS 7:4-5

⁴ Say to wisdom, "You are my sister,"
and call understanding your relative.
⁵ She will keep you from a forbidden woman,
a stranger with her flattering talk.

MARK 8:1-21

8 In those days there was again a large crowd, and they had nothing to eat. He summoned the disciples and said to them, ²"I have compassion on the crowd, because they've already stayed with Me three days and have nothing to eat. ³If I send them home famished, they will collapse on the way, and some of them have come a long distance." ⁴His disciples answered Him, "Where can anyone get enough bread here in

this desolate place to fill these people?" ⁵ "How many loaves do you have?" He asked them.

"Seven," they said. ⁶ Then He commanded the crowd to sit down on the ground. Taking the seven loaves, He gave thanks, broke the loaves, and kept on giving them to His disciples to set before the people. So they served the loaves to the crowd. ⁷ They also had a few small fish, and when He had blessed them, He said these were to be served as well. ⁸ They ate and were filled. Then they collected seven large baskets of leftover pieces. ⁹ About 4,000 men were there. He dismissed them ¹⁰ and immediately got into the boat with His disciples and went to the district of Dalmanutha.

¹¹ The Pharisees came out and began to argue with Him, demanding of Him a sign from heaven to test Him. ¹² But sighing deeply in His spirit, He said, "Why does this generation demand a sign? I assure you: No sign will be given to this generation!" ¹³ Then He left them,

got on board the boat again, and went to the other side.

¹⁴ They had forgotten to take bread and had only one loaf with them in the boat. ¹⁵ Then he commanded them: "Watch out! Beware of the yeast of the Pharisees and the yeast of Herod."

¹⁶ They were discussing among themselves that they did not have any bread. ¹⁷ Aware of this, He said to them, "Why are you discussing that you do not have any bread? Do you not yet understand or comprehend? Is your heart hardened? ¹⁸ **Do you have eyes, and not see, and do you have ears, and not hear?** And do you not remember? ¹⁹ When I broke the five loaves for the 5,000, how many baskets full of pieces of bread did you collect?"

"Twelve," they told Him.

²⁰ "When I broke the seven loaves for the 4,000, how many large baskets full of pieces of bread did you collect?"

"Seven," they said.

²¹ And He said to them, "Don't you understand yet?"

Give Thanks

LORD, listen and be gracious to me; LORD, be my helper.
—PSALM 30:10

We pray because we have a need to tell God about our circumstances. To understand the truth of this statement, we must ask ourselves: what happens when we neglect to pray for our daily needs and thank God for providing them?

If we are honest about it and examine our lives over a period of time, we will discover a subtle change taking place in our feelings and in our thinking. If we neglect to pray for our needs, we will begin to take the blessings of life for granted, and gradually, without at first realizing it, we will succumb to the senseless notion that we can provide for the necessities of life and that we are perfectly capable of managing our own affairs without any help from God.

When we think this way, it is not long before pride steps in and a kind of spiritual blindness settles upon us—a blindness which blocks our vision in relation to God, others, and even ourselves. We need, therefore, to constantly remind ourselves that everything we have comes from His hand and that at any moment, should He choose to do so, He could turn off the supplies, and we would soon become beggared and bankrupt. The only way, therefore, that we can build a barricade against this awful blight of ingratitude is to pray daily, remembering, as the poet said:

Back of the bread is the snowy flour,
And back of the flour, the mill,
And back of the mill is the field of wheat,
The rain, and the Father's will.

Prayer

O Father, teach me the art of continual thankfulness, and help me never to become bored with acknowledging Your grace and goodness; otherwise life will begin to disintegrate. Help me, Lord Jesus. Amen.

Further Study

1 Kg 17; Ps 23:5; Is 41:10; Mal 3:10
How did God test Elijah's faith?
How did he respond?

MARCH 6

ℒEVITICUS 26:1-46

26 "Do not make idols for yourselves, set up a carved image or sacred pillar for yourselves, or place a sculpted stone in your land to bow down to it, for I am the LORD your God. ² You must keep My Sabbaths and honor My sanctuary; I am the LORD.

³ "If you follow My statutes and faithfully observe My commands, ⁴ I will give you rain at the right time, and the land will yield its produce, and the trees of the field will bear their fruit. ⁵ Your threshing will continue until grape harvest, and the grape harvest will continue until sowing time; you will have plenty of food to eat and live securely in your land. ⁶ I will give peace to the land, and you will lie down with nothing to frighten you. I will remove dangerous animals from the land, and no sword will pass through your land. ⁷ You will pursue your enemies, and they will fall before you by the sword. ⁸ Five of you will pursue 100, and 100 of you will pursue 10,000; your enemies will fall before you by the sword.

⁹ "I will turn to you, make you fruitful and multiply you, and confirm My covenant with you. ¹⁰ You will eat the old grain of the previous year and will clear out the old to make room for the new. ¹¹ I will place My residence among you, and I will not reject you. ¹² I will walk among you and be your God, and you will be My people. ¹³ I am the LORD your God, who brought you out of the land of Egypt, so that you would no longer be their slaves. I broke the bars of your yoke and enabled you to live in freedom.

¹⁴ "But if you do not obey Me and observe all these commands— ¹⁵ if you reject My statutes and despise My ordinances,

and do not observe all My commands—and break My covenant, [16] then I will do this to you: I will bring terror on you—wasting disease and fever that will cause your eyes to fail and your life to ebb away. You will sow your seed in vain because your enemies will eat it. [17] I will turn against you, so that you will be defeated by your enemies. Those who hate you will rule over you, and you will flee even though no one is pursuing you.

[18] "But if after these things you will not obey Me, I will proceed to discipline you seven times for your sins. [19] I will break down your strong pride. I will make your sky like iron and your land like bronze, [20] and your strength will be used up for nothing. Your land will not yield its produce, and the trees of the land will not bear their fruit.

[21] "If you act with hostility toward Me and are unwilling to obey Me, I will multiply your plagues seven times for your sins. [22] I will send wild animals against you that will deprive you of your children, ravage your livestock, and reduce your numbers until your roads are deserted.

[23] "If in spite of these things you do not accept My discipline, but act with hostility toward Me, [24] then I will act with hostility toward you; I also will strike you seven times for your sins. [25] I will bring a sword against you to execute the vengeance of the covenant. Though you withdraw into your cities, I will send a pestilence among you, and you will be delivered into enemy hands. [26] When I cut off your supply of bread, ten women will bake your bread in a single oven and ration out your bread by weight, so that you will eat but not be satisfied.

[27] "And if in spite of this you do not obey Me but act with hostility toward Me, [28] I will act with furious hostility toward you; I will also discipline you seven times for your sins. [29] You will eat the flesh of your sons; you will eat the flesh of your daughters. [30] I will destroy your high places, cut down your incense altars, and heap your dead bodies on the lifeless bodies of your idols; I will reject you. [31] I will reduce your cities to ruins

and devastate your sanctuaries. I will not smell the pleasing aroma of your sacrifices. [32] I also will devastate the land, so that your enemies who come to live there will be appalled by it. [33] But I will scatter you among the nations, and I will unsheathe a sword to chase after you. So your land will become desolate, and your cities will become ruins.

[34] "Then the land will make up for its Sabbath years during the time it lies desolate, while you are in the land of your enemies. At that time the land will rest and make up for its Sabbaths. [35] As long as it lies desolate, it will have the rest it did not have during your Sabbaths when you lived there.

[36] "I will put anxiety in the hearts of those of you who survive in the lands of their enemies. The sound of a wind-driven leaf will put them to flight, and they will flee as one flees from a sword, and fall though no one is pursuing them. [37] They will stumble over one another as if fleeing from a sword though no one is pursuing them. You will not be able to stand against your enemies. [38] You will perish among the nations; the land of your enemies will devour you. [39] Those who survive in the lands of your enemies will waste away because of their sin; they will also waste away because of their fathers' sins along with theirs.

[40] "But if they will confess their sin and the sin of their fathers—their unfaithfulness that they practiced against Me, and how they acted with hostility toward Me, [41] and I acted with hostility toward them and brought them into the land of their enemies—and if their uncircumcised hearts will be humbled, and if they will pay the penalty for their sin, [42] then I will remember My covenant with Jacob. I will also remember My covenant with Isaac and My covenant with Abraham, and I will remember the land. [43] For the land abandoned by them will make up for its Sabbaths by lying desolate without the people, while they pay the penalty for their sin, because they rejected My ordinances and abhorred My statutes. [44] Yet in spite of this, while they are in the land of

their enemies, I will not reject or abhor them so as to destroy them and break My covenant with them, since I am the LORD their God. ⁴⁵ For their sake I will remember the covenant with their fathers, whom I brought out of the land of Egypt in the sight of the nations to be their God; I am the LORD."

⁴⁶ These are the statutes, ordinances, and laws the LORD established between Himself and the Israelites through Moses on Mount Sinai.

PSALM 31:1-8

¹ LORD, I seek refuge in You;
let me never be disgraced.
Save me by Your righteousness.
² Listen closely to me; rescue me
quickly.
Be a rock of refuge for me,
a mountain fortress to save me.
³ For You are my rock and my
fortress;
You lead and guide me because of
Your name.
⁴ You will free me from the net that
is secretly set for me,
for You are my refuge.
⁵ Into Your hand I entrust my spirit;
You redeem me, LORD, God of
truth.

⁶ I hate those who are devoted to
worthless idols,
but I trust in the LORD.
⁷ I will rejoice and be glad in Your
faithful love
because You have seen my
affliction.
You have known the troubles of
my life
⁸ and have not handed me over to
the enemy.
You have set my feet in a spacious
place.

PROVERBS 7:6-8

⁶ At the window of my house
I looked through my lattice.
⁷ I saw among the inexperienced,
I noticed among the youths,

a young man lacking sense.
⁸ Crossing the street near her
corner,
he strolled down the road to her
house

MARK 8:22–9:1

²² Then they came to Bethsaida. They brought a blind man to Him and begged Him to touch him. ²³ He took the blind man by the hand and brought him out of the village. Spitting on his eyes and laying His hands on him, He asked him, "Do you see anything?"

²⁴ He looked up and said, "I see people—they look to me like trees walking."

²⁵ Again Jesus placed His hands on the man's eyes, and he saw distinctly. He was cured and could see everything clearly. ²⁶ Then He sent him home, saying, "Don't even go into the village."

²⁷ Jesus went out with His disciples to the villages of Caesarea Philippi. And on the road He asked His disciples, "Who do people say that I am?"

²⁸ They answered Him, "John the Baptist; others, Elijah; still others, one of the prophets."

²⁹ "But you," He asked them again, "who do you say that I am?"

Peter answered Him, "You are the Messiah!"

³⁰ And He strictly warned them to tell no one about Him.

³¹ Then He began to teach them that the Son of Man must suffer many things, and be rejected by the elders, the chief priests, and the scribes, be killed, and rise after three days. ³² He was openly talking about this. So Peter took Him aside and began to rebuke Him.

³³ But turning around and looking at His disciples, He rebuked Peter and said, "Get behind Me, Satan, because you're not thinking about God's concerns, but man's!"

³⁴ Summoning the crowd along with His disciples, He said to them, "If anyone wants to be My follower, he must deny himself, take up his cross, and follow Me. ³⁵ For whoever wants to save

his life will lose it, but whoever loses his life because of Me and the gospel will save it. ³⁶ For what does it benefit a man to gain the whole world yet lose his life? ³⁷ What can a man give in exchange for his life? ³⁸ For whoever is ashamed of Me and of My words in this adulterous and sinful generation, the Son of Man will also be ashamed of him when He comes in the glory of His Father with the holy angels."

9 Then He said to them, "I assure you: There are some standing here who will not taste death until they see the kingdom of God come in power."

Hallelujah—the Pressure's Off

For whoever wants to save his life will lose it, but whoever loses his life because of Me and the gospel will save it. For what does it benefit a man to gain the whole world yet lose his life?—Mark 8:35-36

Strive not so much to succeed as to do the right thing. I remember addressing a group of ministers in Atlanta, Georgia, on "Pitfalls in the Ministry." I told them the story of my own failures, which at that time amounted to a great many, and I said, "The lesson I have learned from my failures is that I don't have to succeed. I have to do the right thing under God's guidance and leave success or failure in His hands." One of the ministers came to me afterwards and said, "I am a pastor of one of the largest churches in this area and regarded by my peers as one of the most successful ministers in my denomination. But today you have helped me overcome the greatest pressure in my life—the pressure to succeed."

In the early years of my ministry, I was extremely success-oriented; when I succeeded, I felt good, and when I failed, I felt devastated. Then God said to me quite bluntly one day, "Are you willing to be a failure?" The question shook me rigid. It was a whole week later before I found sufficient grace to answer that question with a "Yes," and when I did, I was instantly released from the two things that had crippled my life and ministry—the pressure to succeed and the fear of failure. Now, what matters is not succeeding or failing, but being true to Him. Success and failure are in His hands. I am not on the way to success; I am on the Way. What a difference!

Prayer

Father, the more I think about this, the more excited I get. You have given me such security. I can stand anything because I can use everything. Oh glory! Amen.

Further Study

Jn 10:1-10; 2 Co 1:21, 9:8; Eph 3:20
What does the thief seek to do?
What does Christ bring us?

MARCH 7

LEVITICUS 27:1-34

27 The LORD spoke to Moses: [2] "Speak to the Israelites and tell them: When someone makes a special vow to the LORD that involves the valuation of people, [3] if the valuation concerns a male from 20 to 60 years old, your valuation is 50 silver shekels measured by the standard sanctuary shekel. [4] If the person is a female, your valuation is 30 shekels. [5] If the person is from five to 20 years old, your valuation for a male is 20 shekels and for a female 10 shekels. [6] If the person is from one month to five years old, your valuation for a male is five silver shekels, and for a female your valuation is three shekels of silver. [7] If the person is 60 years or more, your valuation is 15 shekels for a male and 10 shekels for a female. [8] But if one is too poor to pay the valuation, he must present the person before the priest and the priest will set a value for him. The priest will set a value for him according to what the one making the vow can afford.

[9] "If the vow involves one of the animals that may be brought as an offering to the LORD, any of these he gives to the LORD will be holy. [10] He may not replace it or make a substitution for it, either good for bad, or bad for good. But if he does substitute one animal for another, both that animal and its substitute will be holy.

[11] "If the vow involves any of the unclean animals that may not be brought as an offering to the LORD, the animal must be presented before the priest. [12] The priest will set its value, whether high or low; the price will be set as the priest makes the valuation for you. [13] If the one who brought it decides to redeem it, he must add a fifth to the valuation.

[14] "When a man consecrates his house as holy to the LORD, the priest will assess its value, whether high or low. The price will stand just as the priest assesses it. [15] But if the one who consecrated his house redeems it, he must add a fifth to the valuation price, and it will be his.

[16] "If a man consecrates to the LORD any part of a field that he possesses, your valuation will be proportional to the seed needed to sow it, at the rate of 50 silver shekels for every five bushels of barley seed. [17] If he consecrates his field during the Year of Jubilee, the price will stand according to your valuation. [18] But if he consecrates his field after the Jubilee, the priest will calculate the price for him in proportion to the years left until the next Year of Jubilee, so that your valuation will be reduced. [19] If the one who consecrated the field decides to redeem it, he must add a fifth to the valuation price, and the field will transfer back to him. [20] But if he does not redeem the field or if he has sold it to another man, it is no longer redeemable. [21] When the field is released in the Jubilee, it will be holy to the LORD like a field permanently set apart; it becomes the priest's property.

[22] "If a person consecrates to the LORD a field he has purchased that is not part of his inherited landholding, [23] then the priest will calculate for him the amount of the valuation up to the Year of Jubilee, and the person will pay the valuation on that day as a holy offering to the LORD. [24] In the Year of Jubilee the field will return to the one he bought it from, the original owner. [25] All your valuations will be measured by the standard sanctuary shekel, 20 gerahs to the shekel.

[26] "But no one can consecrate a firstborn of the livestock, whether an animal from the herd or flock, to the LORD, because a firstborn already belongs to the LORD. [27] If it is one of the unclean

livestock, it must be ransomed according to your valuation by adding a fifth of its value to it. If it is not redeemed, it can be sold according to your valuation. ²⁸ "Nothing that a man permanently sets apart to the LORD from all he owns, whether a person, an animal, or his inherited landholding, can be sold or redeemed; everything set apart is especially holy to the LORD. ²⁹ No person who has been set apart for destruction is to be ransomed; he must be put to death.

³⁰ "Every tenth of the land's produce, grain from the soil or fruit from the trees, belongs to the LORD; it is holy to the LORD. ³¹ If a man decides to redeem any part of this tenth, he must add onefifth to its value. ³² Every tenth animal from the herd or flock, which passes under the shepherd's rod, will be holy to the LORD. ³³ He is not to inspect whether it is good or bad, and he is not to make a substitution for it. But if he does make a substitution, both the animal and its substitute will be holy; they cannot be redeemed."

³⁴ These are the commands the LORD gave Moses for the Israelites on Mount Sinai.

PSALM 31:9-18

⁹ Be gracious to me, LORD, because I
  am in distress;
  my eyes are worn out from angry
  sorrow—
  my whole being as well.
¹⁰ Indeed, my life is consumed with
  grief,
  and my years with groaning;
  my strength has failed because of
  my sinfulness,
  and my bones waste away.
¹¹ I am ridiculed by all my
  adversaries
  and even by my neighbors.
  I am an object of dread to my
  acquaintances;
  those who see me in the street
  run from me.
¹² I am forgotten: gone from
  memory

like a dead person—like broken
  pottery.
¹³ I have heard the gossip of many;
  terror is on every side.
  When they conspired against me,
  they plotted to take my life.

¹⁴ But I trust in You, LORD;
  I say, "You are my God."
¹⁵ The course of my life is in Your
  power;
  deliver me from the power of my
  enemies and from my
  persecutors.
¹⁶ Show Your favor to Your servant;
  save me by Your faithful love.
¹⁷ LORD, do not let me be disgraced
  when I call on You.
  Let the wicked be disgraced;
  let them be silent in Sheol.
¹⁸ Let lying lips be quieted;
  they speak arrogantly against the
  righteous with pride and
  contempt.

PROVERBS 7:9-12

⁹ at twilight, in the evening,
  in the dark of the night.
¹⁰ A woman came to meet him,
  dressed like a prostitute, having a
  hidden agenda.
¹¹ She is loud and defiant;
  her feet do not stay at home.
¹² Now in the street, now in the
  squares,
  she lurks at every corner.

MARK 9:2-29

² After six days Jesus took Peter, James, and John and led them up on a high mountain by themselves to be alone. He was transformed in front of them, ³ and His clothes became dazzling—extremely white as no launderer on earth could whiten them. ⁴ Elijah appeared to them with Moses, and they were talking with Jesus.

⁵ Then Peter said to Jesus, "Rabbi, it is good for us to be here! Let us make three tabernacles: one for You, one for Moses, and one for Elijah"— ⁶ because

MARCH 7 ○ Leviticus 27:1-34 ○ Psalm 31:9-18 ○ Proverbs 7:9-12 ○ Mark 9:2-29

he did not know what he should say, since they were terrified. ⁷ A cloud appeared, overshadowing them, and a voice came from the cloud:

This is My beloved Son; listen to Him!

⁸ Then suddenly, looking around, they no longer saw anyone with them except Jesus alone.

⁹ As they were coming down from the mountain, He ordered them to tell no one what they had seen until the Son of Man had risen from the dead. ¹⁰ They kept this word to themselves, discussing what "rising from the dead" meant. ¹¹ Then they began to question Him, "Why do the scribes say that Elijah must come first?"

¹² "Elijah does come first and restores everything," He replied. "How then is it written about the Son of Man that He must suffer many things and be treated with contempt? ¹³ But I tell you that Elijah really has come, and they did to him whatever they wanted, just as it is written about him."

¹⁴ When they came to the disciples, they saw a large crowd around them and scribes disputing with them. ¹⁵ All of a sudden, when the whole crowd saw Him, they were amazed and ran to greet Him. ¹⁶ Then He asked them, "What are you arguing with them about?"

¹⁷ Out of the crowd, one man answered Him, "Teacher, I brought my son to You. He has a spirit that makes him unable to speak. ¹⁸ Wherever it seizes him, it throws him down, and he foams at the mouth, grinds his teeth, and becomes rigid. So I asked Your disciples to drive it out, but they couldn't."

¹⁹ He replied to them, "You unbelieving generation! How long will I be with you? How long must I put up with you? Bring him to Me." ²⁰ So they brought him to Him. When the spirit saw Him, it immediately convulsed the boy. He fell to the ground and rolled around, foaming at the mouth. ²¹ "How long has this been happening to him?" Jesus asked his father.

"From childhood," he said. ²² "And many times it has thrown him into fire or water to destroy him. But if You can do anything, have compassion on us and help us."

²³ Then Jesus said to him, " 'If You can?' Everything is possible to the one who believes."

²⁴ Immediately the father of the boy cried out, "I do believe! Help my unbelief."

²⁵ When Jesus saw that a crowd was rapidly coming together, He rebuked the unclean spirit, saying to it, "You mute and deaf spirit, I command you: come out of him and never enter him again!"

²⁶ Then it came out, shrieking and convulsing him violently. The boy became like a corpse, so that many said, "He's dead." ²⁷ But Jesus, taking him by the hand, raised him, and he stood up.

²⁸ After He went into a house, His disciples asked Him privately, "Why couldn't we drive it out?"

²⁹ And He told them, "This kind can come out by nothing but prayer [and fasting]."

Forced to Face Reality

How great is Your goodness that You have stored up for those who fear You.—PSALM 31:19

Whenever we pray, we are to pray in accordance with God's will. One Greek scholar says that the words "Your will be done on earth as it is in heaven" can be paraphrased in this way: "Your will, whatever You wish to happen, let it happen—as in heaven so in earth."

In other words: "God, do what You want." It's not easy to pray this way. If anyone thinks it is, then it is probably because they have never really sounded the true depths of self-interest within their own hearts. It's hard sometimes to pray, "Your will be done," when we know that if God has His way, we will not get our way.

Has this difficulty ever presented itself to you? The basic reason for this conflict is due to the major problem of the human heart—self-centeredness. Paul, when describing a self-centered life and its results in Romans 6:21, ends by asking this question: "What fruit was produced then from the things you are now ashamed of?" The end was zero. That is the inevitable end of a self-centered life—nothing. The major thing that stands in the way of God performing His will in our lives utterly and completely is just that—self-centeredness.

Jesus knew, as we now do, that if we are to become effective in prayer, then we must face up to the question: whose will comes first—mine or God's? I must be willing to say: "God, do what You want." That is the bottom line in prayer.

Prayer

Gracious Father, I am grateful for the gentle and loving way You are putting Your finger on the obstacles in my life. Give me the attitude that puts Your will first and my will second. For Jesus' sake. Amen.

Further Study

1 Jn 5:1-15; Jms 4:13-17; 1 Jn 2:17
What is the confidence we have?
What ought we to say?

MARCH 8

NUMBERS 1:1-54

1 The LORD spoke to Moses in the tent of meeting in the Wilderness of Sinai, on the first day of the second month of the second year after Israel's departure from the land of Egypt: ² "Take a census of the entire Israelite community by their clans and their ancestral houses, counting the names of every male one by one. ³ You and Aaron are to register those who are 20 years old or more by their military divisions—everyone who can serve in Israel's army. ⁴ A man from each tribe is to be with you, each one the head of his ancestral house. ⁵ These are the names of the men who are to assist you:

Elizur son of Shedeur from Reuben;

6 Shelumiel son of Zurishaddai from Simeon;
7 Nahshon son of Amminadab from Judah;
8 Nethanel son of Zuar from Issachar;
9 Eliab son of Helon from Zebulun;
10 from the sons of Joseph:
Elishama son of Ammihud from Ephraim,
Gamaliel son of Pedahzur from Manasseh;
11 Abidan son of Gideoni from Benjamin;
12 Ahiezer son of Ammishaddai from Dan;
13 Pagiel son of Ochran from Asher;
14 Eliasaph son of Deuel from Gad;
15 Ahira son of Enan from Naphtali.

16 These are the men called from the community; they are leaders of their ancestral tribes, the heads of Israel's clans."
17 So Moses and Aaron took these men who had been designated by name, 18 and they assembled the whole community on the first day of the second month. They recorded their ancestry by their clans and their ancestral houses, counting one by one the names of those 20 years old or more, 19 just as the LORD commanded Moses. He registered them in the Wilderness of Sinai:

20 The descendants of Reuben, the firstborn of Israel: according to their family records by their clans and their ancestral houses, counting one by one the names of every male 20 years old or more, everyone who could serve in the army, 21 those registered for the tribe of Reuben numbered 46,500.

22 The descendants of Simeon: according to their family records by their clans and their ancestral houses, those registered counting one by one the names of every male 20 years old or more, everyone who could serve in the army, 23 those registered for the tribe of Simeon numbered 59,300.

24 The descendants of Gad: according to their family records by their clans and their ancestral houses, counting the names of those 20 years old or more, everyone who could serve in the army, 25 those registered for the tribe of Gad numbered 45,650.

26 The descendants of Judah: according to their family records by their clans and their ancestral houses, counting the names of those 20 years old or more, everyone who could serve in the army, 27 those registered for the tribe of Judah numbered 74,600.

28 The descendants of Issachar: according to their family records by their clans and their ancestral houses, counting the names of those 20 years old or more, everyone who could serve in the army, 29 those registered for the tribe of Issachar numbered 54,400.

30 The descendants of Zebulun: according to their family records by their clans and their ancestral houses, counting the names of those 20 years old or more, everyone who could serve in the army, 31 those registered for the tribe of Zebulun numbered 57,400.

32 The descendants of Joseph:

The descendants of Ephraim: according to their family records by their clans and their ancestral houses, counting the names of those 20 years old or more, everyone who could serve in the army, 33 those registered for the tribe of Ephraim numbered 40,500.

34 The descendants of Manasseh: according to their family records by their clans and their ancestral houses, counting the names of those 20 years old or more, everyone who could serve in the army, 35 those registered for the tribe of Manasseh numbered 32,200.

³⁶ The descendants of Benjamin: according to their family records by their clans and their ancestral houses, counting the names of those 20 years old or more, everyone who could serve in the army, ³⁷ those registered for the tribe of Benjamin numbered 35,400.

³⁸ The descendants of Dan: according to their family records by their clans and their ancestral houses, counting the names of those 20 years old or more, everyone who could serve in the army, ³⁹ those registered for the tribe of Dan numbered 62,700.

⁴⁰ The descendants of Asher: according to their family records by their clans and their ancestral houses, counting the names of those 20 years old or more, everyone who could serve in the army, ⁴¹ those registered for the tribe of Asher numbered 41,500.

⁴² The descendants of Naphtali: according to their family records by their clans and their ancestral houses, counting the names of those 20 years old or more, everyone who could serve in the army, ⁴³ those registered for the tribe of Naphtali numbered 53,400.

⁴⁴ These are the men Moses and Aaron registered, with the assistance of the 12 leaders of Israel; each represented his ancestral house. ⁴⁵ So all the Israelites 20 years old or more, everyone who could serve in Israel's army, were registered by their ancestral houses. ⁴⁶ All those registered numbered 603,550.

⁴⁷ But the Levites were not registered with them by their ancestral tribe. ⁴⁸ For the LORD had told Moses: ⁴⁹ "Do not register or take a census of the tribe of Levi with the other Israelites. ⁵⁰ Appoint the Levites over the tabernacle of the testimony, all its furnishings, and everything in it. They are to transport the tabernacle and all its articles, take care of it,

and camp around it. ⁵¹ Whenever the tabernacle is to move, the Levites are to take it down, and whenever it is to stop at a campsite, the Levites are to set it up. Any unauthorized person who comes near it must be put to death. ⁵² "The Israelites are to camp by their military divisions, each man with his encampment and under his banner. ⁵³ The Levites are to camp around the tabernacle of the testimony and watch over it, so that no wrath will fall on the Israelite community." ⁵⁴ The Israelites did everything just as the LORD had commanded Moses.

ℙSALM 31:19-24

¹⁹ How great is Your goodness
   that You have stored up for those
      who fear You,
   and accomplished in the sight of
      everyone
   for those who take refuge in You.
²⁰ You hide them in the protection of
      Your presence;
   You conceal them in a shelter
   from the schemes of men,
   from quarrelsome tongues.
²¹ May the LORD be praised,
   for He has wonderfully shown His
      faithful love to me
   in a city under siege.
²² In my alarm I had said,
   "I am cut off from Your sight."
   But You heard the sound of my
      pleading
   when I cried to You for help.

²³ Love the LORD, all His faithful
      ones.
   The LORD protects the loyal,
   but fully repays the arrogant.
²⁴ Be strong and courageous,
   all you who hope in the LORD.

ℙROVERBS 7:13-17

¹³ She grabs him and kisses him;
   she brazenly says to him,
¹⁴ "I've made fellowship offerings;
   today I've fulfilled my vows.
¹⁵ So I came out to meet you,

to search for you, and I've found you.
¹⁶ I've spread coverings on my bed—richly colored linen from Egypt.
¹⁷ I've perfumed my bed with myrrh, aloes, and cinnamon.

MARK 9:30-50

³⁰ Then they left that place and made their way through Galilee, but He did not want anyone to know it. ³¹ For He was teaching His disciples and telling them, "The Son of Man is being betrayed into the hands of men. They will kill Him, and after He is killed, He will rise three days later." ³² But they did not understand this statement, and they were afraid to ask Him.
³³ Then they came to Capernaum. When He was in the house, He asked them, "What were you arguing about on the way?" ³⁴ But they were silent, because on the way they had been arguing with one another about who was the greatest. ³⁵ Sitting down, He called the Twelve and said to them, "If anyone wants to be first, he must be last of all and servant of all." ³⁶ Then He took a child, had him stand among them, and taking him in His arms, He said to them, ³⁷ "Whoever welcomes one little child such as this in My name welcomes Me. And whoever welcomes Me does not welcome Me, but Him who sent Me."
³⁸ John said to Him, "Teacher, we saw someone driving out demons in Your name, and we tried to stop him because he wasn't following us."
³⁹ "Don't stop him," said Jesus, "because there is no one who will perform a miracle in My name who can soon af-terwards speak evil of Me. ⁴⁰ For whoever is not against us is for us. ⁴¹ And whoever gives you a cup of water to drink because of My name, since you belong to the Messiah—I assure you: He will never lose his reward.

⁴² "But whoever causes the downfall of one of these little ones who believe in Me—it would be better for him if a heavy millstone were hung around his neck and he were thrown into the sea. ⁴³ And if your hand causes your downfall, cut it off. It is better for you to enter life maimed than to have two hands and go to hell—the unquenchable fire, [⁴⁴ where

Their worm does not die,
and the fire is not quenched.]

⁴⁵ And if your foot causes your downfall, cut it off. It is better for you to enter life lame than to have two feet and be thrown into hell—[the unquenchable fire, ⁴⁶ where

Their worm does not die,
and the fire is not quenched.]

⁴⁷ And if your eye causes your downfall, gouge it out. It is better for you to enter the kingdom of God with one eye than to have two eyes and be thrown into hell, ⁴⁸ where

Their worm does not die,
and the fire is not quenched.

⁴⁹ For everyone will be salted with fire. ⁵⁰ Salt is good, but if the salt should lose its flavor, how can you make it salty? Have salt among yourselves and be at peace with one another."

Get on the Offensive

If your hand causes your downfall, cut it off. . . .
And if your foot causes your downfall, cut it off. . . .
And if your eye causes your downfall, gouge it out.
—MARK 9:43, 45, 47

In spite of the importance of breaking decisively with everything of which Christ cannot approve, some Christians hide sins and are not willing to get rid of them. Let there be no illusion about this—no one can maintain their spiritual freshness as long as they allow known sin to remain and take root in their lives.

This matter of spiritual freshness is decided, not by living on the defensive, but by living on the offensive. It involves making definite decisions—decisions such as saying "Yes" to all that Christ offers and saying "No" to all that sin offers.

"Christianity," said someone, "is not a prohibition but a privilege." I would agree with that. But I would add that it does, however, have a prohibition in it. In our text for today, Jesus says that if your "hand" or your "eye" causes you to sin, then do something about it. In other words, do not tolerate anything that cuts across the central purpose of your life. From head to foot, you are to belong to Christ.

The order in these verses is important. The order is hand, foot, eye. The "hand" represents the doing of evil, the "foot" the approach toward evil, and the "eye" the seeing of evil with desire from afar.

What's the message in all this? Quite clearly, the message is that sin must be cut out at every stage. The place to begin, of course, is with the "eye"—the place of desire. Take care of that, and you won't have to worry too much about the "hand" and the "foot."

Prayer

O Father, teach me how to be a decisive and not a double-minded person—especially in relation to this matter of sin. Show me what things I need to break with in my life, and help me to do it. In Jesus' name. Amen.

Further Study

Mt 16:21-27; Lk 14:26-27; Mk 10:28
What does it mean to "take up our cross"?
What was Peter's declaration?

MARCH 9

NUMBERS 2:1–3:16

2 The LORD spoke to Moses and Aaron: ² "The Israelites are to camp under their respective banners beside the flags of their ancestral houses. They are to camp around the tent of meeting at a distance from it:

³ Judah's military divisions will camp on the east side toward the sunrise under their banner. The leader of the descendants of Judah is Nahshon son of Amminadab. ⁴ His military division numbers 74,600. ⁵ The tribe of Issachar will camp next to it. The leader of the

Issacharites is Nethanel son of Zuar. [6] His military division numbers 54,400. [7] The tribe of Zebulun will be next. The leader of the Zebulunites is Eliab son of Helon. [8] His military division numbers 57,400. [9] The total number in their military divisions who belong to Judah's encampment is 186,400; they will move out first.

[10] Reuben's military divisions will camp on the south side under their banner. The leader of the Reubenites is Elizur son of Shedeur. [11] His military division numbers 46,500. [12] The tribe of Simeon will camp next to it. The leader of the Simeonites is Shelumiel son of Zurishaddai. [13] His military division numbers 59,300. [14] The tribe of Gad will be next. The leader of the Gadites is Eliasaph son of Deuel. [15] His military division numbers 45,650. [16] The total number in their military divisions who belong to Reuben's encampment is 151,450; they will move out second.

[17] The tent of meeting is to move out with the Levites' camp, which is in the middle of the camps. They are to move out just as they camp, each in his place, with their banners.

[18] Ephraim's military divisions will camp on the west side under their banner. The leader of the Ephraimites is Elishama son of Ammihud. [19] His military division numbers 40,500. [20] The tribe of Manasseh will be next to it. The leader of the Manassites is Gamaliel son of Pedahzur. [21] His military division numbers 32,200. [22] The tribe of Benjamin will be next. The leader of the Benjaminites is Abidan son of Gideoni. [23] His military division numbers 35,400. [24] The total in their military divisions who belong to Ephraim's encampment number 108,100; they will move out third.

[25] Dan's military divisions will camp on the north side under their banner. The leader of the Danites is Ahiezer son of Ammishaddai. [26] His military division numbers 62,700. [27] The tribe of Asher will camp next to it. The leader of the Asherites is Pagiel son of Ochran. [28] His military division numbers 41,500. [29] The tribe of Naphtali will be next. The leader of the Naphtalites is Ahira son of Enan. [30] His military division numbers 53,400. [31] The total number who belong to Dan's encampment is 157,600; they are to move out last, with their banners."

[32] These are the Israelites registered by their ancestral houses. The total number in the camps by their military divisions is 603,550. [33] But the Levites were not registered among the Israelites, just as the LORD had commanded Moses.

[34] The Israelites did everything the LORD commanded Moses; they camped by their banners in this way and moved out the same way, each man by his clan and by his ancestral house.

3 These are the family records of Aaron and Moses at the time the LORD spoke with Moses on Mount Sinai. [2] These are the names of Aaron's sons: Nadab, the firstborn, and Abihu, Eleazar, and Ithamar. [3] These are the names of Aaron's sons, the anointed priests, who were ordained to serve as priests. [4] But Nadab and Abihu died in the LORD's presence when they presented unauthorized fire before the LORD in the Wilderness of Sinai, and they had no sons. So Eleazar and Ithamar served as priests under the direction of Aaron their father.

[5] The LORD spoke to Moses: [6] "Bring the tribe of Levi near and present them to Aaron the priest to assist him. [7] They are to perform duties for him and the entire community before the tent of meeting by attending to the service of the tabernacle. [8] They are to take care of all the furnishings of the tent of

meeting and perform duties for the Israelites by attending to the service of the tabernacle. ⁹Assign the Levites to Aaron and his sons; they have been assigned exclusively to him from the Israelites. ¹⁰ You are to appoint Aaron and his sons to carry out their priestly responsibilities, but any unauthorized person who comes near the sanctuary must be put to death."

¹¹ The LORD spoke to Moses: ¹² "See, I have taken the Levites from the Israelites in place of every firstborn Israelite from the womb. The Levites belong to Me, ¹³ because every firstborn belongs to Me. At the time I struck down every firstborn in the land of Egypt, I consecrated every firstborn in Israel to Myself, both man and animal; they are Mine; I am the LORD."

¹⁴ The LORD spoke to Moses in the Wilderness of Sinai: ¹⁵ "Register the Levites by their ancestral houses and their clans. You are to register every male one month old or more." ¹⁶ So Moses registered them in obedience to the LORD as he had been commanded:

𝒫SALM 32:1-7

1 How happy is the one whose
    transgression is forgiven,
    whose sin is covered!
2 How happy is the man
    the LORD does not charge
        with sin,
    and in whose spirit is no deceit!

3 When I kept silent, my bones
        became brittle
    from my groaning all day long.
4 For day and night Your hand was
        heavy on me;
    my strength was drained as in the
        summer's heat.   *Selah*
5 Then I acknowledged my sin to
        You
    and did not conceal my iniquity.
    I said, "I will confess my
        transgressions to the LORD,"
    and You took away the guilt of my
        sin.   *Selah*

6 Therefore let everyone who is
    faithful pray to You
    at a time that You may be found.
    When great floodwaters come,
    they will not reach him.
7 You are my hiding place;
    You protect me from trouble.
    You surround me with joyful
    shouts of deliverance.   *Selah*

𝒫ROVERBS 7:18-21

18 Come, let's drink deeply of
    lovemaking until morning.
    Let's feast on each other's love!
19 My husband isn't home;
    he went on a long journey.
20 He took a bag of money with
        him
    and will come home at the time of
        the full moon."
21 She seduces him with her
        persistent pleading;
    she lures with her flattering
        talk.

𝓜ARK 10:1-22

10 He set out from there and went to the region of Judea and across the Jordan. Then crowds converged on Him again and, as He usually did, He began teaching them once more. ²Some Pharisees approached Him to test Him. They asked, "Is it lawful for a man to divorce his wife?"

³ He replied to them, "What did Moses command you?"

⁴ They said, "Moses permitted us to write divorce papers and send her away."

⁵ But Jesus told them, "He wrote this commandment for you because of the hardness of your hearts. ⁶ But from the beginning of creation God **made them male and female.**

7   **For this reason a man will
        leave
    his father and mother
    [and be joined to his wife,]**
8   **and the two will become
        one flesh.**

So they are no longer two, but one flesh. ⁹ Therefore what God has joined together, man must not separate."

¹⁰ Now in the house the disciples questioned Him again about this matter. ¹¹ And He said to them, "Whoever divorces his wife and marries another commits adultery against her. ¹² Also, if she divorces her husband and marries another, she commits adultery."

¹³ Some people were bringing little children to Him so He might touch them, but His disciples rebuked them. ¹⁴ When Jesus saw it, He was indignant and said to them, "Let the little children come to Me. Don't stop them, for the kingdom of God belongs to such as these. ¹⁵ I assure you: Whoever does not welcome the kingdom of God like a little child will never enter it." ¹⁶ After taking them in His arms, He laid His hands on them and blessed them.

¹⁷ As He was setting out on a journey, a man ran up, knelt down before Him, and asked Him, "Good Teacher, what must I do to inherit eternal life?" ¹⁸ "Why do you call Me good?" Jesus asked him. "No one is good but One— God. ¹⁹ You know the commandments:

Do not murder;
do not commit adultery;
do not steal;
do not bear false witness;
do not defraud;
honor your father and
mother."

²⁰ He said to Him, "Teacher, I have kept all these from my youth."
²¹ Then, looking at him, Jesus loved him and said to him, "You lack one thing: Go, sell all you have and give to the poor, and you will have treasure in heaven. Then come, follow Me." ²² But he was stunned at this demand, and he went away grieving, because he had many possessions.

The Four "Alls"

Therefore let everyone who is faithful pray to You.—PSALM 32:6

If the effectiveness of our spiritual warfare depends not just on wearing the six pieces of armor (Eph 6:14-17), but also on constant, believing prayer, then we must ask ourselves: What can we do to make our prayer lives more effective?

The place given to prayer in both the Old and New Testaments is remarkable. All the great saints of the Old Testament knew how to pray—Abraham, David, Daniel, Jeremiah, Isaiah, to mention just a few. The same prowess in prayer can be seen also in the New Testament saints.

But of course the greatest Person of prayer was none other than our Lord Jesus Christ. Although He possessed great knowledge and wisdom, He found it essential to turn aside time and time again to pray. On certain occasions He would spend whole nights in prayer or rise long before dawn in order to pray and maintain His communion with God.

Is it surprising, therefore, that being so dependent on prayer, He should have told His disciples: "Pray always and [do] not become discouraged" (Lk 18:1). Praying is the only alternative to fainting—we must pray or else we faint.

Paul's teaching with regard to prayer in Ephesians 6:18 revolves around four "alls." We are to pray at all times, with all prayer, with all perseverance, and for all the saints. Most Christians, however, pray at some times, with some prayer, and some degree of perseverance for some of God's saints.

When we replace "some" by "all" in these expressions, we are on our way to effective praying.

Prayer

My Father and my God, I see that through prayer, You offer me the most breathtaking power. Help me humbly to take it and use it wisely. In Jesus' name I pray. Amen.

Further Study

1 Sm 7:1-10; 1:27; Ex 15:24-25; 1 Kg 18:37-38; Mt 14:23
List some prayers God answered.
List some answers to prayer you have received.

MARCH 10

NUMBERS 3:17–4:20

17 These were Levi's sons by name: Gershon, Kohath, and Merari. 18 These were the names of Gershon's sons by their clans: Libni and Shimei. 19 Kohath's sons by their clans were Amram, Izhar, Hebron, and Uzziel. 20 Merari's sons by their clans were Mahli and Mushi. These were the Levite clans by their ancestral houses.

21 The Libnite clan and the Shimeite clan came from Gershon; these were the Gershonite clans. 22 Those registered, counting every male one month old or more, numbered 7,500. 23 The Gershonite clans camped behind the tabernacle on the west side, 24 and the leader of the Gershonite family was Eliasaph son of Lael. 25 The Gershonites' duties at the tent of meeting involved the tabernacle, the tent, its covering, the screen for the entrance to the tent of meeting, 26 the hangings of the courtyard, the screen for the entrance to the courtyard that surrounds the tabernacle and the altar, and the tent ropes—all the work relating to these.

27 The Amramite clan, the Izharite clan, the Hebronite clan, and the Uzzielite clan came from Kohath; these were the Kohathites. 28 Counting every male one month old or more, there were 8,600 responsible for the duties of the sanctuary. 29 The clans of the Kohathites camped on the south side of the tabernacle, 30 and the leader of the family of the Kohathite clans was Elizaphan son of Uzziel. 31 Their duties involved the ark, the table, the lampstand, the altars, the sanctuary utensils that were used with these, and the screen—and all the work relating to them. 32 The chief of the Levite leaders was Eleazar son of Aaron the priest; he had oversight of those responsible for the duties of the sanctuary.

33 The Mahlite clan and the Mushite clan came from Merari; these

were the Merarite clans. [34] Those registered, counting every male one month old or more, numbered 6,200. [35] The leader of the family of the Merarite clans was Zuriel son of Abihail; they camped on the north side of the tabernacle. [36] The assigned duties of Merari's descendants involved the tabernacle's supports, crossbars, posts, bases, all its equipment, and all the work related to these, [37] in addition to the posts of the surrounding courtyard with their bases, tent pegs, and ropes.

[38] Moses, Aaron, and his sons, who performed the duties of the sanctuary as a service on behalf of the Israelites, camped in front of the tabernacle on the east, in front of the tent of meeting toward the sunrise. Any unauthorized person who came near it was to be put to death.

[39] The total number of all the Levite males one month old or more that Moses and Aaron registered by their clans at the LORD's command was 22,000.

[40] The LORD told Moses: "Register every firstborn male of the Israelites one month old or more, and list their names. [41] You are to take the Levites for Me—I am the LORD—in place of every firstborn among the Israelites, and the Levites' cattle in place of every firstborn among the Israelites' cattle." [42] So Moses registered every firstborn among the Israelites, as the LORD commanded him. [43] The total number of the firstborn males one month old or more listed by name was 22,273.

[44] The LORD spoke to Moses again: [45] "Take the Levites in place of every firstborn among the Israelites, and the Levites' cattle in place of their cattle. The Levites belong to Me; I am the LORD. [46] As the redemption price for the 273 firstborn Israelites who outnumber the Levites, [47] collect five shekels for each person, according to the standard sanctuary shekel—20 gerahs to the shekel. [48] Give the money to Aaron and his sons as the redemption price for those who are in excess among the Israelites."

[49] So Moses collected the redemption money from those in excess of the ones redeemed by the Levites. [50] He collected the money from the firstborn Israelites: 1,365 shekels measured by the standard sanctuary shekel. [51] He gave the redemption money to Aaron and his sons in obedience to the LORD, just as the LORD commanded Moses.

4 The LORD spoke to Moses and Aaron: [2] "Among the Levites, take a census of the Kohathites by their clans and their ancestral houses, [3] men from 30 years old to 50 years old—everyone who is qualified to do work at the tent of meeting.

[4] "The service of the Kohathites at the tent of meeting concerns the most holy objects. [5] Whenever the camp is about to move on, Aaron and his sons are to go in, take down the screening veil, and cover the ark of the testimony with it. [6] They are to place over this a covering made of manatee skin, spread a solid blue cloth on top, and insert its poles. [7] "They are to spread a blue cloth over the table of the Presence and place the plates and cups on it, as well as the bowls and pitchers for the drink offering. The regular bread offering is to be on it. [8] They are to spread a scarlet cloth over them, cover them with a covering made of manatee skin, and insert the poles in the table. [9] "They are to take a blue cloth and cover the lampstand used for light, with its lamps, snuffers, and firepans, as well as its jars of oil by which they service it. [10] Then they must place it with all its utensils inside a covering made of manatee skin and put them on the carrying frame. [11] "They are to spread a blue cloth over the gold altar, cover it with a covering made of manatee skin, and insert its poles. [12] They are to take all the serving utensils they use in the sanctuary, place them in a blue cloth, cover them with a covering made of manatee skin, and put them on a carrying frame.

[13] "They are to remove the ashes from the bronze altar, spread a purple cloth over it, [14] and place all the equipment on it that they use in serving: the firepans, meatforks, shovels, and basins—all the equipment of the altar. They are to spread a covering made of manatee skin over it and insert its poles.

[15] "Aaron and his sons are to finish covering the holy objects and all their equipment whenever the camp is to move on. The Kohathites will come and carry them, but they are not to touch the holy objects or they will die. These are the transportation duties of the Kohathites regarding the tent of meeting.

[16] "Eleazar, son of Aaron the priest, has oversight of the lamp oil, the fragrant incense, the daily grain offering, and the anointing oil. He has oversight of the entire tabernacle and everything in it, the holy objects and their utensils."

[17] Then the LORD spoke to Moses and Aaron: [18] "Do not allow the Kohathite tribal clans to be wiped out from the Levites. [19] Do this for them so that they may live and not die when they handle the most holy objects: Aaron and his sons are to go in and assign each man his task and transportation duty. [20] The Kohathites are not to go in and look at the holy objects, even for a moment, or they will die."

*P*SALM 32:8-11

[8] I will instruct you and show you
   the way to go;
   with My eye on you, I will give
   counsel.
[9] Do not be like a horse or mule,
   without understanding,
   that must be controlled with bit
   and bridle,
   or else it will not come near you.
[10] Many pains come to the wicked,
   but the one who trusts in the
   LORD
   will have faithful love surrounding
   him.

[11] Be glad in the LORD and rejoice,
   you righteous ones;
   shout for joy, all you upright in
   heart.

*P*ROVERBS 7:22-23

[22] He follows her impulsively
   like an ox going to the slaughter,
   like a deer bounding toward a trap
[23] until an arrow pierces its liver,
   like a bird darting into a snare—
   he doesn't know it will cost him
   his life.

*M*ARK 10:23-45

[23] Jesus looked around and said to His disciples, "How hard it is for those who have wealth to enter the kingdom of God!" [24] But the disciples were astonished at His words. Again Jesus said to them, "Children, how hard it is to enter the kingdom of God! [25] It is easier for a camel to go through the eye of a needle than for a rich person to enter the kingdom of God."

[26] So they were even more astonished, saying to one another, "Then who can be saved?"

[27] Looking at them, Jesus said, "With men it is impossible, but not with God, because all things are possible with God."

[28] Peter began to tell Him, "Look, we have left everything and followed You."

[29] "I assure you," Jesus said, "there is no one who has left house, brothers or sisters, mother or father, children, or fields because of Me and the gospel, [30] who will not receive 100 times more, now at this time—houses, brothers and sisters, mothers and children, and fields, with persecutions—and eternal life in the age to come. [31] But many who are first will be last, and the last first."

[32] They were on the road, going up to Jerusalem, and Jesus was walking ahead of them. They were astonished, but those who followed Him were afraid. Taking the Twelve aside again, He began to tell them the things that would happen to Him.

33 "Listen! We are going up to Jerusalem. The Son of Man will be handed over to the chief priests and the scribes, and they will condemn Him to death. Then they will hand Him over to the Gentiles, 34 and they will mock Him, spit on Him, flog Him, and kill Him, and He will rise after three days."

35 Then James and John, the sons of Zebedee, approached Him and said, "Teacher, we want You to do something for us if we ask You."

36 "What do you want Me to do for you?" He asked them.

37 They answered Him, "Allow us to sit at Your right and at Your left in Your glory."

38 But Jesus said to them, "You don't know what you're asking. Are you able to drink the cup I drink or to be baptized with the baptism I am baptized with?"

39 "We are able," they told Him.

Jesus said to them, "You will drink the cup I drink, and you will be baptized with the baptism I am baptized with. 40 But to sit at My right or left is not Mine to give; instead, it is for those it has been prepared for." 41 When the other 10 disciples heard this, they began to be indignant with James and John.

42 Jesus called them over and said to them, "You know that those who are regarded as rulers of the Gentiles dominate them, and their men of high positions exercise power over them. 43 But it must not be like that among you. On the contrary, whoever wants to become great among you must be your servant, 44 and whoever wants to be first among you must be a slave to all. 45 For even the Son of Man did not come to be served, but to serve, and to give His life—a ransom for many."

Suppose It Had Been "My"?

Whoever wants to become great among you must be your servant, and whoever wants to be first among you must be a slave to all. For even the Son of Man did not come to be served, but to serve.—MARK 10:43-45

The first word of the Lord's Prayer—"Our" (Mt 6:9)—determines the very nature of the Christian faith. Suppose it had been "My". That would have changed the whole nature of the Christian religion. Instead of our faith being "our"-centered it would have been "my"-centered—and that would have started us off wrong.

In the field of prayer, as in many other fields, to start wrong is to finish wrong. The word "our" involves a shifting of emphasis from me to the Father and to my brothers and sisters in the kingdom. It implies a renunciation—a renunciation of myself. We see something similar in the first words of the Beatitudes: "Blessed are the poor in spirit" (the renounced in spirit), "because the kingdom of heaven is theirs" (Mt 5:3). All the resources of God's kingdom belong to those who are renounced in spirit. So, in the first word of the Lord's Prayer, we find an implied demand that we adopt an attitude of self-surrender—to the Father and to His interests and the interests of others in His kingdom. If we do this, then everything opens to us. If not, then everything is closed. The rest of the Lord's Prayer has no meaning and dies if the "our" is not alive.

Furthermore, this "our" must stretch beyond our own fellowship, local church, or denomination to include the whole family of God—everywhere. We will never get very far in prayer unless we come to it prepared to sacrifice self-interest and willing to merge into God's greater plan for the whole.

Prayer

O Father, cleanse my heart from any limitations I might have in relation to the word "our." Help me to make it a true "our" with everybody included—those I like and those I don't like. For Jesus' sake. Amen.

Further Study

Lk 18:9-14; Mk 10:35-45; Mt 23:12
How did Jesus answer James and John?
What was wrong with the Pharisee's prayer?

MARCH 11

*N*UMBERS 4:21–5:31

21 The LORD spoke to Moses: 22 "Take a census of the Gershonites also, by their ancestral houses and their clans. 23 Register men from 30 years old to 50 years old, everyone who is qualified to perform service, to do work at the tent of meeting. 24 This is the service of the Gershonite clans regarding work and transportation duties: 25 They are to transport the tabernacle curtains, the tent of meeting with its covering and the covering made of manatee skin on top of it, the screen for the entrance to the tent of meeting, 26 the hangings of the courtyard, the screen for the entrance at the gate of the courtyard that surrounds the tabernacle and the altar, along with their ropes and all the equipment for their service. They will carry out everything that needs to be done with these items.

27 "All the service of the Gershonites, all their transportation duties and all their other work, is to be done at the command of Aaron and his sons; you are to assign to them all that they are re-

sponsible to carry. 28 This is the service of the Gershonite clans at the tent of meeting, and their duties will be under the direction of Ithamar son of Aaron the priest.

29 "As for the Merarites, you are to register them by their clans and their ancestral houses. 30 Register men from 30 years old to 50 years old, everyone who is qualified to do the work of the tent of meeting. 31 This is what they are responsible to carry as the whole of their service at the tent of meeting: the supports of the tabernacle, with its crossbars, posts, and bases, 32 the posts of the surrounding courtyard with their bases, tent pegs, and ropes, including all their equipment and all the work related to them. You are to assign by name the items that they are responsible to carry. 33 This is the service of the Merarite clans regarding all their work at the tent of meeting, under the direction of Ithamar son of Aaron the priest."

34 So Moses, Aaron, and the leaders of the community registered the Kohathites by their clans and their ancestral houses, 35 men from 30 years old to 50 years old, everyone who was

qualified for work at the tent of meeting. [36] The men registered by their clans numbered 2,750. [37] These were the registered men of the Kohathite clans, everyone who could serve at the tent of meeting. Moses and Aaron registered them at the LORD's command through Moses.

[38] The Gershonites were registered by their clans and their ancestral houses, [39] men from 30 years old to 50 years old, everyone who was qualified for work at the tent of meeting. [40] The men registered by their clans and their ancestral houses numbered 2,630. [41] These were the registered men of the Gershonite clans. At the LORD's command Moses and Aaron registered everyone who could serve at the tent of meeting.

[42] The men of the Merarite clans were registered by their clans and their ancestral houses, [43] those from 30 years old to 50 years old, everyone who was qualified for work at the tent of meeting. [44] The men registered by their clans numbered 3,200. [45] These were the registered men of the Merarite clans; Moses and Aaron registered them at the LORD's command through Moses.

[46] Moses, Aaron, and the leaders of Israel registered all the Levites by their clans and their ancestral houses, [47] from 30 years old to 50 years old, everyone who was qualified to do the work of serving at the tent of meeting and transporting it. [48] Their registered men numbered 8,580. [49] At the LORD's command they were registered under the direction of Moses, each one according to his work and transportation duty, and his assignment was as the LORD commanded Moses.

5 The LORD instructed Moses: [2] "Command the Israelites to send away anyone from the camp who is afflicted with a skin disease, anyone who has a bodily discharge, or anyone who is defiled because of a corpse. [3] You must send away both male or female; send them outside the camp, so that they will not defile their camps where I dwell among them." [4] The Israelites did this,

sending them outside the camp. The Israelites did as the LORD instructed Moses.

[5] The LORD spoke to Moses: [6] "Tell the Israelites: When a man or woman commits any sin against another, that person acts unfaithfully toward the LORD and is guilty. [7] The person is to confess the sin he has committed. He is to pay full compensation, add a fifth of its value to it, and give it to the individual he has wronged. [8] But if that individual has no relative to receive compensation, the compensation goes to the LORD for the priest, along with the atonement ram by which the priest will make atonement for the guilty person. [9] Every holy contribution the Israelites present to the priest will be his. [10] Each one's holy contribution is his to give; what each one gives to the priest will be his."

[11] The LORD spoke to Moses: [12] "Speak to the Israelites and tell them: If any man's wife goes astray, is unfaithful to him, [13] and sleeps with another, but it is concealed from her husband, and she is undetected, even though she has defiled herself, since there is no witness against her, and she wasn't caught in the act; [14] and if a feeling of jealousy comes over the husband and he becomes jealous because of his wife who has defiled herself—or if a feeling of jealousy comes over him and he becomes jealous of her though she has not defiled herself— [15] then the man is to bring his wife to the priest. He is also to bring an offering for her of two quarts of barley flour. He is not to pour oil over it or put frankincense on it because it is a grain offering of jealousy, a grain offering for remembrance that brings sin to mind.

[16] "The priest is to bring her forward and have her stand before the LORD. [17] Then the priest is to take holy water in a clay bowl, and take some of the dust from the tabernacle floor and put it in the water. [18] After the priest has the woman stand before the LORD, he is to let down her hair and place in her hands the grain offering for remembrance, which is the grain offering of jealousy. The priest is to hold the bitter water

that brings a curse. [19] The priest will require the woman to take an oath and will say to her, 'If no man has slept with you, if you have not gone astray and become defiled while under your husband's authority, be unaffected by this bitter water that brings a curse. [20] But if you have gone astray while under your husband's authority, if you have defiled yourself and a man other than your husband has slept with you'— [21] at this point the priest must make the woman take the oath with the sworn curse, and he is to say to her— 'May the LORD make you into an object of your people's cursing and swearing when He makes your thigh shrivel and your belly swell. [22] May this water that brings a curse enter your stomach, causing your belly to swell and your thigh to shrivel.'

"And the woman must reply, 'Amen, Amen.'

[23] "Then the priest is to write these curses on a scroll and wash them off into the bitter water. [24] He will require the woman to drink the bitter water that brings a curse, and it will enter her and cause bitter suffering. [25] The priest is to take the grain offering of jealousy from the woman's hand, wave the offering before the LORD, and bring it to the altar. [26] The priest is to take a handful of the grain offering as a memorial portion and burn it on the altar. Then he will require the woman to drink the water.

[27] "When he makes her drink the water, if she has defiled herself and been unfaithful to her husband, the water that brings a curse will enter her and cause bitter suffering; her belly will swell, and her thigh will shrivel. She will become a curse among her people. [28] But if the woman has not defiled herself and is pure, she will be unaffected and will be able to conceive children.

[29] "This is the law regarding jealousy when a wife goes astray and defiles herself while under her husband's authority, [30] or when a feeling of jealousy comes over a husband and he becomes jealous of his wife. He is to have the woman stand before the LORD, and the priest will apply this entire ritual to her. [31] The husband will be free of guilt, but that woman will bear the consequences of her guilt."

PSALM 33:1-9

[1] Rejoice in the LORD, you righteous ones;
praise from the upright is beautiful.
[2] Praise the LORD with the lyre;
make music to Him with a ten-stringed harp.
[3] Sing a new song to Him;
play skillfully on the strings, with a joyful shout.

[4] For the word of the LORD is right,
and all His work is trustworthy.
[5] He loves righteousness and justice;
the earth is full of the LORD's unfailing love.

[6] The heavens were made by the word of the LORD,
and all the stars, by the breath of His mouth.
[7] He gathers the waters of the sea into a heap;
He puts the depths into storehouses.
[8] Let the whole earth tremble before the LORD;
let all the inhabitants of the world stand in awe of Him.
[9] For He spoke, and it came into being;
He commanded, and it came into existence.

PROVERBS 7:24-27

[24] Now, my sons, listen to me,
and pay attention to the words of my mouth.
[25] Don't let your heart turn aside to her ways;
don't stray onto her paths.
[26] For she has brought many down to death;
her victims are countless.
[27] Her house is the road to Sheol,
descending to the chambers of death.

MARK 10:46–11:11

46 They came to Jericho. And as He was leaving Jericho with His disciples and a large crowd, Bartimaeus (the son of Timaeus), a blind beggar, was sitting by the road. 47 When he heard that it was Jesus the Nazarene, he began to cry out, "Son of David, Jesus, have mercy on me!" 48 Many people told him to keep quiet, but he was crying out all the more, "Have mercy on me, Son of David!"

49 Jesus stopped and said, "Call him." So they called the blind man and said to him, "Have courage! Get up; He's calling for you." 50 He threw off his coat, jumped up, and came to Jesus.

51 Then Jesus answered him, "What do you want Me to do for you?"

"Rabbouni," the blind man told Him, "I want to see!"

52 "Go your way," Jesus told him. "Your faith has healed you." Immediately he could see and began to follow Him on the road.

11 When they approached Jerusalem, at Bethphage and Bethany near the Mount of Olives, He sent two of His disciples 2 and told them, "Go into the village ahead of you. As soon as you enter it, you will find a young donkey tied there, on which no one has ever sat. Untie it and bring it here. 3 If anyone says to you, 'Why are you doing this?' say, 'The Lord needs it and will send it back here right away.' "

4 So they went and found a young donkey outside in the street, tied by a door. They untied it, 5 and some of those standing there said to them, "What are you doing, untying the donkey?" 6 They answered them just as Jesus had said, so they let them go. 7 Then they brought the donkey to Jesus and threw their robes on it, and He sat on it.

8 Many people spread their robes on the road, and others spread leafy branches cut from the fields. 9 Then those who went ahead and those who followed kept shouting:

Hosanna!
Blessed is He who comes in the name of the Lord!
10   Blessed is the coming kingdom of our father David!
Hosanna in the highest heaven!

11 And He went into Jerusalem and into the temple complex. After looking around at everything, since it was already late, He went out to Bethany with the Twelve.

"Not From Me!"

The heavens were made by the word of the LORD, and all the stars, by the breath of His mouth.—PSALM 33:6

Many modern astronomers probing into outer space with their gigantic telescopes favor two theories as to the origin of the universe. One is the so-called Big Bang Theory, according to which "the cosmos started with a titanic explosion, and as a consequence has been expanding ever since." The other is the Continuous Creation Theory, which maintains that "the universe is self-creating and is constantly making itself out of nothing and falling back into nothingness again."

What many scientists are not prepared to admit is that the ultimate energy behind the universe is not a Big Bang, but a Big Being—an intelligent Being of indescribable majesty and power who is able to do whatever He chooses. And because what He chooses is always good, He can be trusted to have the best interest of His creation at heart.

When Joseph Haydn, the famous Austrian composer, had finished his great oratorio *The Creation*, he is said to have cried: "Not from me! Not from me! From above it has all come!" Our text for today reminds us that by God's Word were the heavens made and by His breath the stars were formed.

I once heard my father describe the creation in this way: "It was no harder for God to create a world than it is for my son to blow soap bubbles into the air out of his clay pipe." I often go back to that lovely image. I find that when contemplating this awesome, mighty, all-powerful God, my soul instinctively cries: "How great Thou art." I hope yours does too!

Prayer

Yes Father, as I contemplate Your majesty and Your power, my soul cries out: "How great Thou art." It can do nothing else, for contemplation of You inevitably leads to adoration of You. Amen.

Further Study

Mt 19:16-26; 1 Ch 29:12; Ps 62:11; Is 43:12-13
What did Jesus declare?
What did God declare?

MARCH 12

NUMBERS 6:1–7:29

6 The LORD instructed Moses: 2 "Speak to the Israelites and tell them: When a man or woman makes a special vow, a Nazirite vow, to consecrate himself to the LORD, 3 he is to abstain from wine and beer. He must not drink vinegar made from wine or from beer. He must not drink any grape juice or eat fresh grapes or raisins. 4 He is not to eat anything produced by the grapevine, from seeds to skin, during his vow.

5 "You must not cut his hair throughout the time of his vow of consecration.

He must be holy until the time is completed during which he consecrates himself to the LORD; he is to let the hair of his head grow long. 6 He must not go near a dead body during the time he consecrates himself to the LORD. 7 He is not to defile himself for his father or mother, or his brother or sister, when they die, because the hair consecrated to his God is on his head. 8 He is holy to the LORD during the time of consecration.

9 "If someone suddenly dies near him, defiling his consecrated head of hair, he must shave his head on the day of his

purification; he is to shave it on the seventh day. ¹⁰ On the eighth day he is to bring two turtledoves or two young pigeons to the priest at the entrance to the tent of meeting. ¹¹ The priest is to offer one as a sin offering and the other as a burnt offering to make atonement on behalf of the Nazirite, since he sinned because of the corpse. On that day he must consecrate his head again. ¹² He is to rededicate his time of consecration to the LORD and to bring a year-old male lamb as a restitution offering. But do not count the previous period, because his consecrated hair became defiled.

¹³ "This is the law of the Nazirite: On the day his time of consecration is completed, he must be brought to the entrance to the tent of meeting. ¹⁴ He is to present an offering to the LORD of one unblemished year-old male lamb as a burnt offering, one unblemished year-old female lamb as a sin offering, one unblemished ram as a fellowship offering, ¹⁵ along with their grain offerings and drink offerings, and a basket of unleavened cakes made from fine flour mixed with oil, and unleavened wafers coated with oil. ¹⁶ "The priest is to present these before the LORD and sacrifice the Nazirite's sin offering and burnt offering. ¹⁷ He will also offer the ram as a fellowship sacrifice to the LORD, together with the basket of unleavened bread. Then the priest will offer the accompanying grain offering and drink offering. ¹⁸ "The Nazirite is to shave his consecrated head at the entrance to the tent of meeting, take the hair from his head, and put it on the fire under the fellowship sacrifice. ¹⁹ The priest is to take the boiled shoulder from the ram, one unleavened cake from the basket, and one unleavened wafer, and put them into the hands of the Nazirite after he has shaved his consecrated head. ²⁰ The priest is to wave them as a presentation offering before the LORD. It is a holy portion for the priest, in addition to the breast of the presentation offering and the thigh of the contribution. After that, the Nazirite may drink wine.

²¹ "This is the ritual of the Nazirite who vows his offering to the LORD for his consecration, in addition to whatever else he can afford; he must fulfill whatever vow he makes in keeping with the ritual for his consecration."

²² The LORD spoke to Moses: ²³ "Tell Aaron and his sons how you are to bless the Israelites. Say to them:

²⁴ The LORD bless you and protect
    you;
²⁵ the LORD make His face shine on
    you,
    and be gracious to you;
²⁶ the LORD look with favor on you
    and give you peace.

²⁷ In this way they will put My name on the Israelites, and I will bless them."

7 On the day Moses finished setting up the tabernacle, he anointed and consecrated it and all its furnishings, along with the altar and all its utensils. After he anointed and consecrated these things, ² the leaders of Israel, the heads of their ancestral houses, presented an offering. They were the tribal leaders who supervised the registration. ³ They brought as their offering before the LORD six covered carts and 12 oxen, a cart from every two leaders and an ox from each one, and presented them in front of the tabernacle.

⁴ The LORD said to Moses, ⁵ "Accept these from them to be used in the work of the tent of meeting, and give this offering to the Levites, to each division according to their service."

⁶ So Moses took the carts and oxen and gave them to the Levites. ⁷ He gave the Gershonites two carts and four oxen corresponding to their service, ⁸ and gave the Merarites four carts and eight oxen corresponding to their service, under the direction of Ithamar son of Aaron the priest. ⁹ But he did not give any to the Kohathites, since their responsibility was service related to the holy objects carried on their shoulders.

¹⁰ The leaders also presented the dedication gift for the altar when it was anointed. The leaders presented their

offerings in front of the altar. [11] The LORD told Moses, "Each day have one leader present his offering for the dedication of the altar."

[12] The one who presented his offering on the first day was Nahshon son of Amminadab from the tribe of Judah. [13] His offering was one silver dish weighing three and a quarter pounds and one silver basin weighing one and three-quarter pounds, measured by the standard sanctuary shekel, both of them full of fine flour mixed with oil for a grain offering; [14] one gold bowl weighing four ounces, full of incense; [15] one young bull, one ram, and one male lamb a year old, for a burnt offering; [16] one male goat for a sin offering; [17] and two bulls, five rams, five male breeding goats, and five male lambs a year old, for the fellowship sacrifice. This was the offering of Nahshon son of Amminadab.

[18] On the second day Nethanel son of Zuar, leader of Issachar, presented an offering. [19] As his offering, he presented one silver dish weighing three and a quarter pounds and one silver basin weighing one and three-quarter pounds, measured by the standard sanctuary shekel, both of them full of fine flour mixed with oil for a grain offering; [20] one gold bowl weighing four ounces, full of incense; [21] one young bull, one ram, and one male lamb a year old, for a burnt offering; [22] one male goat for a sin offering; [23] and two bulls, five rams, five male breeding goats, and five male lambs a year old, for the fellowship sacrifice. This was the offering of Nethanel son of Zuar.

[24] On the third day Eliab son of Helon, leader of the Zebulunites, presented an offering. [25] His offering was one silver dish weighing three and a quarter pounds and one silver basin weighing one and three-

quarter pounds, measured by the standard sanctuary shekel, both of them full of fine flour mixed with oil for a grain offering; [26] one gold bowl weighing four ounces, full of incense; [27] one young bull, one ram, and one male lamb a year old, for a burnt offering; [28] one male goat for a sin offering; [29] and two bulls, five rams, five male breeding goats, and five male lambs a year old, for the fellowship sacrifice. This was the offering of Eliab son of Helon.

PSALM 33:10-17

[10] The LORD frustrates the counsel of the nations;
He thwarts the plans of the peoples.
[11] The counsel of the LORD stands forever,
the plans of His heart from generation to generation.
[12] Happy is the nation whose God is the LORD—
the people He has chosen to be His own possession!

[13] The LORD looks down from heaven;
He observes everyone.
[14] He gazes on all the inhabitants of the earth
from His dwelling place.
[15] He alone crafts their hearts;
He considers all their works.
[16] A king is not saved by a large army;
a warrior will not be delivered by great strength.
[17] The horse is a false hope for safety;
it provides no escape by its great power.

PROVERBS 8:1-3

8 Doesn't Wisdom call out?
Doesn't Understanding make her voice heard?
[2] At the heights overlooking the road,

at the crossroads, she takes her
stand.
³ Beside the gates at the entry to
the city,
at the main entrance, she cries
out:

MARK 11:12-33

¹² The next day when they came out
from Bethany, He was hungry. ¹³ After
seeing in the distance a fig tree with
leaves, He went to find out if there was
anything on it. When He came to it, He
found nothing but leaves, because it
was not the season for figs. ¹⁴ He said to
it, "May no one ever eat fruit from you
again!" And His disciples heard it.

¹⁵ They came to Jerusalem, and He
went into the temple complex and began to throw out those buying and selling in the temple. He overturned the
money changers' tables and the chairs
of those selling doves, ¹⁶ and would not
permit anyone to carry goods through
the temple complex.

¹⁷ Then He began to teach them: "Is it
not written, **My house will be called a
house of prayer for all nations?** But
you have made it **a den of thieves!**"
¹⁸ Then the chief priests and the scribes
heard it and started looking for a way to
destroy Him. For they were afraid of
Him, because the whole crowd was astonished by His teaching.

¹⁹ And whenever evening came, they
would go out of the city.

²⁰ Early in the morning, as they were
passing by, they saw the fig tree withered
from the roots up. ²¹ Then Peter remembered and said to Him, "Rabbi, look! The
fig tree that You cursed is withered."

²² Jesus replied to them, "Have faith
in God. ²³ I assure you: If anyone says to
this mountain, 'Be lifted up and thrown
into the sea,' and does not doubt in his
heart, but believes that what he says
will happen, it will be done for him.
²⁴ Therefore, I tell you, all the things
you pray and ask for—believe that you
have received them, and you will have
them. ²⁵ And whenever you stand praying, if you have anything against anyone, forgive him, so that your Father in
heaven will also forgive you your wrongdoing. [²⁶ But if you don't forgive, neither will your Father in heaven forgive
your wrongdoing."]

²⁷ They came again to Jerusalem. As
He was walking in the temple complex,
the chief priests, the scribes, and the
elders came and asked Him, ²⁸ "By what
authority are You doing these things?
Who gave You this authority to do these
things?"

²⁹ Jesus said to them, "I will ask you
one question; then answer Me, and I
will tell you by what authority I am doing these things. ³⁰ Was John's baptism
from heaven or from men? Answer Me."

³¹ They began to argue among themselves: "If we say, 'From heaven,' He
will say, 'Then why didn't you believe
him?' ³² But if we say, 'From men' "—
they were afraid of the crowd, because
everyone thought that John was a genuine prophet. ³³ So they answered Jesus,
"We don't know."

And Jesus said to them, "Neither will
I tell you by what authority I do these
things."

Togetherness

*I assure you: If anyone says to this mountain, "Be lifted up
and thrown into the sea," and does not doubt in his heart,
but believes...it will be done for him.*—MARK 11:23

Just as the deer's perfect correlation between its front and rear feet allows it to make its way
swiftly and safely to the mountaintop, so the Christian who has perfect coordination between

the head and heart will rise to new heights with God. For you see, unless a person's head and heart are properly coordinated and move purposefully together, it is possible to miss one's step on the steep slopes of Christian experience and become a spiritual casualty.

I have known many Christians in my time who, because they lack coordination between what they ask for with their lips and what they want deep down in their hearts, stay in the same place spiritually year after year. They are not bad people; they just lack the spiritual coordination of the mature Christian, and thus they never know what it is to ascend into the mountain peaks with God.

Perhaps nowhere in Scripture is this truth more clearly portrayed than in the verse before us today. We are told that things happen in the spiritual realm when there is perfect coordination between what we ask for and what we believe. When our mind and our heart are in alignment, when they track together with the sure-footedness of a mountain deer, then nothing shall be impossible to us. How many of us, I wonder, miss our step on the slopes of the Christian life because our hearts and minds are not properly and perfectly coordinated?

Prayer

Gracious and loving Heavenly Father, slowly I am beginning to see the truth that underlies Your promise to make my feet like deers' feet. Show me how to be as coordinated in the spiritual realm as the deer is in the natural realm. Amen.

Further Study

Is 58:1-11; Mt 23
Why was the Lord displeased with Israel?
How did Jesus depict the Pharisees?

MARCH 13

NUMBERS 7:30-89

³⁰ On the fourth day Elizur son of Shedeur, leader of the Reubenites, presented an offering. ³¹ His offering was one silver dish weighing three and a quarter pounds and one silver basin weighing one and three-quarter pounds, measured by the standard sanctuary shekel, both of them full of fine flour mixed with oil for a grain offering; ³² one gold bowl weighing four ounces, full of incense; ³³ one young bull, one ram, and one male lamb a year old, for a burnt offering; ³⁴ one male goat for a sin offering; ³⁵ and two bulls, five rams, five male breeding

goats, and five male lambs a year old, for the fellowship sacrifice. This was the offering of Elizur son of Shedeur.

[36] On the fifth day Shelumiel son of Zurishaddai, leader of the Simeonites, presented an offering. [37] His offering was one silver dish weighing three and a quarter pounds and one silver basin weighing one and three-quarter pounds, measured by the standard sanctuary shekel, both of them full of fine flour mixed with oil for a grain offering; [38] one gold bowl weighing four ounces, full of incense; [39] one young bull, one ram, and one male lamb a year old, for a burnt offering; [40] one male goat for a sin offering; [41] and two bulls, five rams, five male breeding goats, and five male lambs a year old, for the fellowship sacrifice. This was the offering of Shelumiel son of Zurishaddai.

[42] On the sixth day Eliasaph son of Deuel, leader of the Gadites, presented an offering. [43] His offering was one silver dish weighing three and a quarter pounds and one silver basin weighing one and three-quarter pounds, measured by the standard sanctuary shekel, both of them full of fine flour mixed with oil for a grain offering; [44] one gold bowl weighing four ounces, full of incense; [45] one young bull, one ram, and one male lamb a year old, for a burnt offering; [46] one male goat for a sin offering; [47] and two bulls, five rams, five male breeding goats, and five male lambs a year old, for the fellowship sacrifice. This was the offering of Eliasaph son of Deuel.

[48] On the seventh day Elishama son of Ammihud, leader of the Ephraimites, presented an offering. [49] His offering was one silver dish weighing three and a quarter pounds and one silver basin weighing one and three-quarter pounds, measured by

the standard sanctuary shekel, both of them full of fine flour mixed with oil for a grain offering; [50] one gold bowl weighing four ounces, full of incense; [51] one young bull, one ram, and one male lamb a year old, for a burnt offering; [52] one male goat for a sin offering; [53] and two bulls, five rams, five male breeding goats, and five male lambs a year old, for the fellowship sacrifice. This was the offering of Elishama son of Ammihud.

[54] On the eighth day Gamaliel son of Pedahzur, leader of the Manassites, presented an offering. [55] His offering was one silver dish weighing three and a quarter pounds and one silver basin weighing one and three-quarter pounds, measured by the standard sanctuary shekel, both of them full of fine flour mixed with oil for a grain offering; [56] one gold bowl weighing four ounces, full of incense; [57] one young bull, one ram, and one male lamb a year old, for a burnt offering; [58] one male goat for a sin offering; [59] and two bulls, five rams, five male breeding goats, and five male lambs a year old, for the fellowship sacrifice. This was the offering of Gamaliel son of Pedahzur.

[60] On the ninth day Abidan son of Gideoni, leader of the Benjaminites, presented an offering. [61] His offering was one silver dish weighing three and a quarter pounds and one silver basin weighing one and three-quarter pounds, measured by the standard sanctuary shekel, both of them full of fine flour mixed with oil for a grain offering; [62] one gold bowl weighing four ounces, full of incense; [63] one young bull, one ram, and one male lamb a year old, for a burnt offering; [64] one male goat for a sin offering; [65] and two bulls, five rams, five male breeding goats, and five male lambs a year old, for the fellowship sacrifice. This was the offering of Abidan son of Gideoni.

⁶⁶ On the tenth day Ahiezer son of Ammishaddai, leader of the Danites, presented an offering. ⁶⁷ His offering was one silver dish weighing three and a quarter pounds and one silver basin weighing one and three-quarter pounds, measured by the standard sanctuary shekel, both of them full of fine flour mixed with oil for a grain offering; ⁶⁸ one gold bowl weighing four ounces, full of incense; ⁶⁹ one young bull, one ram, and one male lamb a year old, for a burnt offering; ⁷⁰ one male goat for a sin offering; ⁷¹ and two bulls, five rams, five male breeding goats, and five male lambs a year old, for the fellowship sacrifice. This was the offering of Ahiezer son of Ammishaddai.

⁷² On the eleventh day Pagiel son of Ochran, leader of the Asherites, presented an offering. ⁷³ His offering was one silver dish weighing three and a quarter pounds and one silver basin weighing one and three-quarter pounds, measured by the standard sanctuary shekel, both of them full of fine flour mixed with oil for a grain offering; ⁷⁴ one gold bowl weighing four ounces, full of incense; ⁷⁵ one young bull, one ram, and one male lamb a year old, for a burnt offering; ⁷⁶ one male goat for a sin offering; ⁷⁷ and two bulls, five rams, five male breeding goats, and five male lambs a year old, for the fellowship sacrifice. This was the offering of Pagiel son of Ochran.

⁷⁸ On the twelfth day Ahira son of Enan, leader of the Naphtalites, presented an offering. ⁷⁹ His offering was one silver dish weighing three and a quarter pounds and one silver basin weighing one and three-quarter pounds, measured by the standard sanctuary shekel, both of them full of fine flour mixed with oil for a grain offering; ⁸⁰ one gold bowl weighing four ounces, full of incense; ⁸¹ one young bull,

one ram, and one male lamb a year old, for a burnt offering; ⁸² one male goat for a sin offering; ⁸³ and two bulls, five rams, five male breeding goats, and five male lambs a year old, for the fellowship sacrifice. This was the offering of Ahira son of Enan.

⁸⁴ This was the dedication gift from the leaders of Israel for the altar when it was anointed: 12 silver dishes, 12 silver basins, and 12 gold bowls. ⁸⁵ Each silver dish weighed three and a quarter pounds, and each basin one and three-quarter pounds. The total weight of the silver articles was 60 pounds measured by the standard sanctuary shekel. ⁸⁶ The 12 gold bowls full of incense each weighed four ounces measured by the standard sanctuary shekel. The total weight of the gold bowls was three pounds. ⁸⁷ All the livestock for the burnt offering totaled 12 bulls, 12 rams, and 12 male lambs a year old, with their grain offerings, and 12 male goats for the sin offering. ⁸⁸ All the livestock for the fellowship sacrifice totaled 24 bulls, 60 rams, 60 male breeding goats, and 60 male lambs a year old. This was the dedication gift for the altar after it was anointed.

⁸⁹ When Moses entered the tent of meeting to speak with the LORD, he heard the voice speaking to him from above the mercy seat that was on the ark of the testimony, from between the two cherubim. He spoke to him that way.

𝒫SALM 33:18-22

¹⁸ Now the eye of the LORD is on
    those who fear Him—
    those who depend on His faithful
        love
¹⁹ to deliver them from death
    and to keep them alive in
        famine.

²⁰ We wait for the LORD;
    He is our help and shield.
²¹ For our hearts rejoice in Him,

because we trust in His holy
name.
22 May Your faithful love rest on us,
LORD,
for we hope in You.

PROVERBS 8:4-5

4 "People, I call out to you;
my cry is to mankind.
5 Learn to be shrewd, you who are
inexperienced;
develop common sense, you who
are foolish.

MARK 12:1-27

12 Then He began to speak to them in parables: "A man planted a vineyard, put a fence around it, dug out a pit for a winepress, and built a watchtower. Then he leased it to tenant farmers and went away. 2 At harvest time he sent a slave to the farmers to collect some of the fruit of the vineyard from the farmers. 3 But they took him, beat him, and sent him away empty-handed. 4 Again he sent another slave to them, and they hit him on the head and treated him shamefully. 5 Then he sent another, and they killed that one. He also sent many others; they beat some and they killed some.

6 "He still had one to send, a beloved son. Finally he sent him to them, saying, 'They will respect my son.'

7 "But those tenant farmers said among themselves, 'This is the heir. Come, let's kill him, and the inheritance will be ours!' 8 So they seized him, killed him, and threw him out of the vineyard.

9 "Therefore, what will the owner of the vineyard do? He will come and destroy the farmers and give the vineyard to others. 10 Haven't you read this Scripture:

The stone that the builders
rejected—
this has become the cornerstone.
11 This came from the Lord
and is wonderful in our eyes?"

12 Because they knew He had said this parable against them, they were looking for a way to arrest Him, but they were afraid of the crowd. So they left Him and went away.

13 Then they sent some of the Pharisees and the Herodians to Him to trap Him by what He said. 14 When they came, they said to Him, "Teacher, we know You are truthful and defer to no one, for You don't show partiality but teach truthfully the way of God. Is it lawful to pay taxes to Caesar or not? 15 Should we pay, or should we not pay?"

But knowing their hypocrisy, He said to them, "Why are you testing Me? Bring Me a denarius to look at." 16 So they brought one. "Whose image and inscription is this?" He asked them.

"Caesar's," they said.

17 Then Jesus told them, "Give back to Caesar the things that are Caesar's, and to God the things that are God's." And they were amazed at Him.

18 Some Sadducees, who say there is no resurrection, came to Him and questioned Him: 19 "Teacher, Moses wrote for us that **if a man's brother dies, leaves his wife behind, and leaves no child, his brother should take the wife and produce offspring for his brother.** 20 There were seven brothers. The first took a wife, and dying, left no offspring. 21 The second also took her, and he died, leaving no offspring. And the third likewise. 22 The seven also left no offspring. Last of all, the woman died too. 23 In the resurrection, when they rise, whose wife will she be, since the seven had married her?"

24 Jesus told them, "Are you not deceived because you don't know the Scriptures or the power of God? 25 For when they rise from the dead, they neither marry nor are given in marriage but are like angels in heaven. 26 Now concerning the dead being raised—haven't you read in the book of Moses, in the passage about the burning bush, how God spoke to him: **I am the God of Abraham and the God of Isaac and the God of Jacob?** 27 He is not God of the dead but of the living. You are badly deceived."

Overpopulation—A Myth

*Now the eye of the LORD is on those who fear Him—
those who depend on His faithful love.*
—Psalm 33:18

A modern writer tells how once he asked an old man how he managed to live alone in a single cottage, miles from anywhere. The old man answered cheerfully that he enjoyed it since, as he explained: "Providence is my next-door neighbor."

Despite what many politicians and scientists tell us, the problems of this earth are not physical but spiritual. It is not overpopulation that requires our attention, but spiritual ignorance. If people came into a knowledge of Jesus Christ as their Lord and Savior, then they would be given the wisdom to use the earth's resources rightly. Murray Norris in his book, *The Myth of Overpopulation,* says that only fifteen percent of the arable land on the globe is being farmed, and only half of that every year. It goes without saying, of course, that although God supplies the basic necessities, people have to put some effort into harvesting them; our problem is not lack of resources, nor too many people—it is our lack of dependency upon God.

Paul, in 1 Timothy 4:3, says that God has created all food "to be received with gratitude by those who believe and know the truth." Can you see what this verse is saying? God has provided us an incredible abundance of food so that we might express our thanks to Him.

The rest of the world indulges with little gratitude. Let's make sure that not one day passes without this prayer meaningfully crossing our lips: "Give us each day our daily bread."

Prayer

O Father, now that I understand the significance of Your words, "Give us each day our daily bread," help me, every time I utter them, to make them not just a recitation, but a realization. For Jesus' sake. Amen.

Further Study

Jms 2; Rm 12:11; Pr 13:11; 2 Th 3:10
How does James relate faith and works?
What is Paul's exhortation?

MARCH 14

NUMBERS 8:1–10:10

8 The LORD spoke to Moses: ² "Speak to Aaron and tell him: When you set up the lamps, the seven lamps are to give light in front of the lampstand." ³ So Aaron did this; he set up its lamps to give light in front of the lampstand just as the LORD had commanded Moses. ⁴ This is the way the lampstand was made: it was a hammered work of gold, hammered from its base to its flower petals. The lampstand was made according to the pattern the LORD had shown Moses.

⁵ The LORD spoke to Moses: ⁶ "Take the Levites from among the Israelites and ceremonially cleanse them. ⁷ This is what you must do to them for their purification: Sprinkle them with the purification water. Have them shave their entire bodies and wash their clothes, and so purify themselves.

⁸ "They are to take a young bull and its grain offering of fine flour mixed with oil, and you are to take a second young bull for a sin offering. ⁹ Bring the Levites before the tent of meeting and assemble the entire Israelite community. ¹⁰ Then present the Levites before the LORD, and have the Israelites lay their hands on them. ¹¹ Aaron is to present the Levites before the LORD as a presentation offering from the Israelites, so that they may perform the LORD's work. ¹² Next the Levites are to lay their hands on the heads of the bulls. Sacrifice one as a sin offering and the other as a burnt offering to the LORD, to make atonement for the Levites.

¹³ "You are to have the Levites stand before Aaron and his sons, and you are to present them before the LORD as a presentation offering. ¹⁴ In this way you are to separate the Levites from the rest of the Israelites so that the Levites will belong to Me. ¹⁵ After that the Levites may come to serve at the tent of meeting, once you have ceremonially cleansed them and presented them as a presentation offering. ¹⁶ For they have been exclusively assigned to Me from the Israelites. I have taken them for Myself in place of all who come first from the womb, every Israelite firstborn. ¹⁷ For every firstborn among the Israelites is Mine, both man and animal. I consecrated them to Myself on the day I struck down every firstborn in the land of Egypt. ¹⁸ But I have taken the Levites in place of every firstborn among the Israelites. ¹⁹ From the Israelites, I have given the Levites exclusively to Aaron and his sons to perform the work for the Israelites at the tent of meeting and to make atonement on their behalf, so that no plague will come against the Israelites when they approach the sanctuary."

²⁰ Moses, Aaron, and the entire Israelite community did this to the Levites. The Israelites did everything to them the LORD commanded Moses regarding the Levites. ²¹ The Levites purified themselves and washed their clothes; then Aaron presented them before the LORD as a presentation offering. Aaron also made atonement for them to ceremonially cleanse them. ²² After that, the Levites came to do their work at the tent of meeting in the presence of Aaron and his sons. So they did to them as the LORD had commanded Moses concerning the Levites.

²³ The LORD spoke to Moses: ²⁴ "In regard to the Levites: From 25 years old or more, a man enters the service in the work at the tent of meeting. ²⁵ But at 50 years old he is to retire from his service in the work and no longer serve. ²⁶ He may assist his brothers to fulfill responsibilities at the tent of meeting, but he must not do the work. This is how you are to deal with the Levites regarding their duties."

9 In the first month of the second year after their departure from the land of Egypt, the LORD told Moses in the Wilderness of Sinai: ² "The Israelites are to observe the Passover at its appointed time. ³ You must observe it at its appointed time on the fourteenth day of this month at twilight; you are to observe it according to all its statutes and ordinances." ⁴ So Moses told the Israelites to observe the Passover, ⁵ and they observed it in the first month on the fourteenth day at twilight in the Wilderness of Sinai. The Israelites did everything as the LORD had commanded Moses.

⁶ But there were some men who were unclean because of a human corpse, so they could not observe the Passover on that day. These men came before Moses and Aaron the same day ⁷ and said to him, "We are unclean because of a human corpse. Why should we be excluded from presenting the LORD's offering at its appointed time with the other Israelites?"

⁸ Moses replied to them, "Wait here until I hear what the LORD commands for you."

⁹ Then the LORD spoke to Moses: ¹⁰ "Tell the Israelites: When any one of you or your descendants is unclean because of a corpse or is on a distant journey, he may still observe the Passover to the LORD. ¹¹ Such people are to observe it in the second month, on the fourteenth day at twilight. They are to eat the animal with unleavened bread and bitter herbs; ¹² they may not leave any of it until morning or break any of its bones. They must observe the Passover according to all its statutes.

¹³ "But the man who is ceremonially clean, is not on a journey, and yet fails to observe the Passover is to be cut off from his people, because he did not present the LORD's offering at its appointed time. That man will bear the consequences of his sin.

¹⁴ "If a foreigner resides with you and wants to observe the Passover to the LORD, he is to do so according to the Passover statute and its ordinances. You are to apply the same statute to both the foreign resident and the native of the land."

¹⁵ On the day the tabernacle was set up, the cloud covered the tabernacle, the tent of the testimony, and it appeared like fire above the tabernacle from evening until morning. ¹⁶ It remained that way continuously: the cloud would cover it, appearing like fire at night. ¹⁷ Whenever the cloud was lifted up above the tent, the Israelites would set out; at the place where the cloud stopped, there the Israelites camped. ¹⁸ At the LORD's command the Israelites set out, and at the LORD's command they camped. As long as the cloud stayed over the tabernacle, they camped. ¹⁹ Even when the cloud stayed over the tabernacle many days, the Israelites carried out the LORD's requirement and did not set out. ²⁰ Sometimes the cloud remained over the tabernacle for only a few days. They would camp at the LORD's command and set out at the LORD's command. ²¹ Sometimes the cloud remained only from evening until morning; when the cloud lifted in the morning, they set out. Or if it remained a day and a night, they moved out when the cloud lifted. ²² Whether it was two days, a month, or longer, the Israelites camped and did not set out as long as the cloud stayed over the tabernacle. But when it was lifted, they set out. ²³ They camped at the LORD's command, and they set out at the LORD's command. They carried out the LORD's requirement according to His command through Moses.

10 The LORD spoke to Moses: ² "Make two trumpets of hammered silver to summon the community and have the camps set out. ³ When both are sounded in long blasts, the entire community is to gather before you at the entrance to the tent of meeting. ⁴ However, if one is sounded, only the leaders, the heads of Israel's clans, are to gather before you.

⁵ "When you sound short blasts, the camps pitched on the east are to set out. ⁶ When you sound short blasts a second time, the camps pitched on the

south are to set out. Short blasts are to be sounded for them to set out. ⁷ When calling the assembly together, you are to sound long blasts, not short ones. ⁸ The sons of Aaron, the priests, are to sound the trumpets. Your use of these is a permanent statute throughout your generations.

⁹ "When you enter into battle in your land against an adversary who is attacking you, sound short blasts on the trumpets, and you will be remembered before the LORD your God and be delivered from your enemies. ¹⁰ You are to sound the trumpets over your burnt offerings and your fellowship sacrifices and on your joyous occasions, your appointed festivals, and the beginning of each of your months. They will serve as a reminder for you before your God: I am the LORD your God."

PSALM 34:1-7

¹ I will praise the LORD at all times;
  His praise will always be on my
  lips.
² I will boast in the LORD;
  the humble will hear and be glad.
³ Proclaim with me the LORD's
  greatness;
  let us exalt His name together.

⁴ I sought the LORD, and He
  answered me
  and delivered me from all my
  fears.
⁵ Those who look to Him are
  radiant with joy;
  their faces will never be ashamed.
⁶ This poor man cried, and the LORD
  heard him
  and saved him from all his
  troubles.
⁷ The angel of the LORD encamps
  around those who fear Him, and
  rescues them.

PROVERBS 8:6-7

⁶ Listen, for I speak of noble things,
  and what my lips say is right.
⁷ For my mouth tells the truth,

and wickedness is detestable to
  my lips.

MARK 12:28-44

²⁸ One of the scribes approached. When he heard them debating and saw that Jesus answered them well, he asked Him, "Which commandment is the most important of all?"
²⁹ "This is the most important," Jesus answered:

Listen, Israel! The Lord our God, The Lord is One. ³⁰ Love the Lord your God with all your heart, with all your soul, with all your mind, and with all your strength.

³¹ "The second is: Love your neighbor as yourself. There is no other commandment greater than these."
³² Then the scribe said to Him, "You are right, Teacher! You have correctly said that He is One, and there is no one else except Him. ³³ And to love Him with all your heart, with all your understanding, and with all your strength, and to love your neighbor as yourself, is far more important than all the burnt offerings and sacrifices."
³⁴ When Jesus saw that he answered intelligently, He said to him, "You are not far from the kingdom of God." And no one dared to question Him any longer.
³⁵ So Jesus asked this question as He taught in the temple complex, "How can the scribes say that the Messiah is the Son of David? ³⁶ David himself says by the Holy Spirit:

The Lord declared to my Lord, 'Sit at My right hand until I put Your enemies under Your feet.'

³⁷ David himself calls Him 'Lord'; how then can the Messiah be his Son?" And the large crowd was listening to Him with delight.
³⁸ He also said in His teaching, "Beware of the scribes, who want to go

around in long robes, and who want greetings in the marketplaces, ³⁹ the front seats in the synagogues, and the places of honor at banquets. ⁴⁰ They devour widows' houses and say long prayers just for show. These will receive harsher punishment."

⁴¹ Sitting across from the temple treasury, He watched how the crowd dropped money into the treasury. Many rich people were putting in large sums. ⁴² And a poor widow came and dropped in two tiny coins worth very little. ⁴³ Summoning His disciples, He said to them, "I assure you: This poor widow has put in more than all those giving to the temple treasury. ⁴⁴ For they all gave out of their surplus, but she out of her poverty has put in everything she possessed—all she had to live on."

A Clear Perspective

Proclaim with me the LORD's greatness; let us exalt His name together.—PSALM 34:3

Honoring God's Name does not mean having some kind of fetish about pronouncing the word "God" in hushed or reverential tones. It is rather honoring all that God is, His qualities, character, and attributes—all the things embodied in His Name. When the psalmist said: "The nations will fear the name of the Lord" (Ps 102:15), did this mean they feared the letters in the word "Yahweh"? No, they feared the Lord God Himself.

At the risk of over-simplifying the opening clauses of the Lord's Prayer, what Jesus is teaching us is to come before the Father with this attitude: "Our Father, who cares for us with true tenderness, and who has in heaven the supplies to meet our every need; may Your attributes, Your nature, Your character, Your reputation, Your person, Your whole being itself be honored." Before we start asking for what we want from God, we need to have the right perspective of God.

I have just been reading some words of Gregory of Nyssa, who prayed: "May I become through Thy help blameless, just, and holy. May I abstain from every evil, speak the truth, and do justly. May I walk in the straight paths, sing with temperance adorned with incorruption, beautiful through wisdom and prudence. May I meditate upon the things that are above and despise what is earthly, for a man can hallow God's Name in no other way than by reflecting His character and bear witness to the fact that divine power is the cause of his goodness."

Prayer

Gracious Father, I see that if I am to become effective in prayer, then I must get all my values straight. Thank You for giving me a clear pattern to follow and for reminding me that when I honor Your Name, You will honor mine. Thank You, Father. Amen.

Further Study

Ps 111:1-10; 33:8; 34:9; 86:11
What is the beginning of wisdom?
What does it mean to fear the Lord?

MARCH 15

NUMBERS 10:11–11:35

¹¹ During the second year, in the second month on the twentieth day of the month, the cloud was lifted up above the tabernacle of the testimony. ¹² The Israelites traveled on from the Wilderness of Sinai, moving from one place to the next until the cloud stopped in the Wilderness of Paran. ¹³ They set out for the first time according to the LORD's command through Moses.

¹⁴ The military divisions of the camp of Judah with their banner set out first, and Nahshon son of Amminadab was over Judah's divisions. ¹⁵ Nethanel son of Zuar was over the division of the Issachar tribe, ¹⁶ and Eliab son of Helon was over the division of the Zebulun tribe. ¹⁷ The tabernacle was then taken down, and the Gershonites and the Merarites set out, transporting the tabernacle.

¹⁸ The military divisions of the camp of Reuben with their banner set out, and Elizur son of Shedeur was over Reuben's division. ¹⁹ Shelumiel son of Zurishaddai was over the division of Simeon's tribe, ²⁰ and Eliasaph son of Deuel was over the division of the tribe of Gad. ²¹ The Kohathites then set out, transporting the holy objects; the tabernacle was to be set up before their arrival.

²² Next the military divisions of the camp of Ephraim with their banner set out, and Elishama son of Ammihud was over Ephraim's division. ²³ Gamaliel son of Pedahzur was over the division of the tribe of Manasseh, ²⁴ and Abidan son of Gideoni was over the division of the tribe of Benjamin.

²⁵ The military divisions of the camp of Dan with their banner set out, serving as rear guard for all the camps, and Ahiezer son of Ammishaddai was over Dan's division. ²⁶ Pagiel son of Ochran was over the division of the tribe of Asher, ²⁷ and Ahira son of Enan was over the division of the tribe of Naphtali. ²⁸ This was the order of march for the Israelites by their military divisions as they set out.

²⁹ Moses said to Hobab, son of Moses' father-in-law Reuel the Midianite: "We're setting out for the place the LORD promised: 'I will give it to you.' Come with us, and we will treat you well, for the LORD has promised good things to Israel."

³⁰ But he replied to him, "I don't want to go. Instead, I will go to my own land and my relatives."

³¹ "Please don't leave us," Moses said, "since you know where we should camp in the wilderness, and you can serve as our eyes. ³² If you come with us, whatever good the LORD does for us we will do for you."

³³ They set out from the mountain of the LORD on a three-day journey to seek a resting place for them, with the ark of the LORD's covenant traveling ahead of them for the three days. ³⁴ Meanwhile,

the cloud of the LORD was over them by day when they set out from the camp. ³⁵ Whenever the ark set out, Moses would say:

Arise, LORD!
Let Your enemies be scattered,
and those who hate You flee from
Your presence.

³⁶ When it came to rest, he would say:

Return, LORD,
to the countless thousands of
Israel.

11 Now the people began complaining openly before the LORD about hardship. When the LORD heard, His anger burned, and the fire from the LORD blazed among them and consumed the outskirts of the camp. ² Then the people cried out to Moses, and he prayed to the LORD, and the fire died down. ³ So that place was named Taberah, because the LORD's fire had blazed among them.

⁴ Contemptible people among them had a strong craving for other food. The Israelites cried again and said, "Who will feed us meat? ⁵ We remember the free fish we ate in Egypt, along with the cucumbers, melons, leeks, onions, and garlic. ⁶ But now our appetite is gone; there's nothing to look at but this manna!"

⁷ The manna resembled coriander seed, and its appearance was like that of bdellium. ⁸ The people walked around and gathered it. They ground it on a pair of grinding stones or crushed it in a mortar, then boiled it in a cooking pot and shaped it into cakes. It tasted like a pastry cooked with the finest oil. ⁹ When the dew fell on the camp at night, the manna would fall with it.

¹⁰ Moses heard the people, family after family, crying at the entrance of their tents. The LORD was very angry; Moses was also provoked. ¹¹ So Moses asked the LORD, "Why have You brought such trouble on Your servant? Why are You angry with me, and why do You burden me with all these people? ¹² Did I con-

ceive all these people? Did I give them birth so You should tell me, 'Carry them at your breast, as a nursing woman carries a baby,' to the land that You swore to give their fathers? ¹³ Where can I get meat to give all these people? For they are crying to me: 'Give us meat to eat!' ¹⁴ "I can't carry all these people by myself. They are too much for me. ¹⁵ If You are going to treat me like this, please kill me right now. If You are pleased with me, don't let me see my misery any more."

¹⁶ The LORD answered Moses, "Bring Me 70 men from Israel known to you as elders and officers of the people. Take them to the tent of meeting and have them stand there with you. ¹⁷ Then I will come down and speak with you there. I will take some of the Spirit who is on you and put the Spirit on them. They will help you bear the burden of the people, so that you do not have to bear it by yourself.

¹⁸ "Tell the people: Purify yourselves in readiness for tomorrow, and you will eat meat because you cried before the LORD: 'Who will feed us meat? We really had it good in Egypt.' The LORD will give you meat and you will eat. ¹⁹ You will eat, not for one day, or two days, or five days, or 10 days, or 20 days, ²⁰ but for a whole month—until it comes out of your nostrils and becomes nauseating to you—because you have rejected the LORD who is among you, and cried to Him: 'Why did we ever leave Egypt?' "

²¹ But Moses replied, "I'm in the middle of a people with 600,000 foot soldiers, yet You say, 'I will give them meat, and they will eat for a month.' ²² If flocks and herds were slaughtered for them, would they have enough? Or if all the fish in the sea were caught for them, would they have enough?"

²³ The LORD answered Moses, "Is the LORD's power limited? You will see whether or not what I have promised will happen to you."

²⁴ Moses went out and told the people the words of the LORD. He brought 70 men from the elders of the people and had them stand around the tent. ²⁵ Then the LORD descended in the cloud and

spoke to him. He took some of the Spirit that was on Moses and placed the Spirit on the 70 elders. As the Spirit rested on them, they prophesied, but they never did it again. ²⁶ Two men had remained in the camp, one named Eldad and the other Medad; the Spirit rested on them—they were among those listed, but had not gone out to the tent—and they prophesied in the camp. ²⁷ A young man ran and reported to Moses, "Eldad and Medad are prophesying in the camp."

²⁸ Joshua son of Nun, assistant to Moses since his youth, responded, "Moses, my lord, stop them!"

²⁹ But Moses asked him, "Are you jealous on my account? If only all the LORD's people were prophets, and the LORD would place His Spirit on them." ³⁰ Then Moses returned to the camp along with the elders of Israel.

³¹ A wind sent by the LORD came up and blew quail in from the sea; it dropped them at the camp all around, three feet off the ground, about a day's journey in every direction. ³² The people were up all that day and night and all the next day gathering the quail—the one who took the least gathered 33 bushels—and they spread them out all around the camp. ³³ While the meat was still between their teeth, before it was chewed, the LORD's anger burned against the people, and the LORD struck them with a very severe plague. ³⁴ So they named that place Kibroth-hattaavah, because there they buried the people who had craved the meat. ³⁵ From Kibroth-hattaavah the people moved on to Hazeroth and remained there.

𝒫SALM 34:8-14

⁸ Taste and see that the LORD is good.
How happy is the man who takes refuge in Him!
⁹ Fear the LORD, you His saints, for those who fear Him lack nothing.

¹⁰ Young lions lack food and go hungry,
but those who seek the LORD will not lack any good thing.
¹¹ Come, children, listen to me; I will teach you the fear of the LORD.
¹² Who is the man who delights in life,
loving a long life to enjoy what is good?
¹³ Keep your tongue from evil and your lips from deceitful speech.
¹⁴ Turn away from evil and do good; seek peace and pursue it.

𝒫ROVERBS 8:8-9

⁸ All the words of my mouth are righteous;
none of them are deceptive or perverse.
⁹ All of them are clear to the perceptive,
and right to those who discover knowledge.

𝓜ARK 13:1-20

13 As He was going out of the temple complex, one of His disciples said to Him, "Teacher, look! What massive stones! What impressive buildings!"

² Jesus said to him, "Do you see these great buildings? Not one stone will be left here on another that will not be thrown down!"

³ While He was sitting on the Mount of Olives across from the temple complex, Peter, James, John, and Andrew asked Him privately, ⁴ "Tell us, when will these things happen? And what will be the sign when all these things are about to take place?"

⁵ Then Jesus began by telling them: "Watch out that no one deceives you. ⁶ Many will come in My name, saying, 'I am He,' and they will deceive many. ⁷ When you hear of wars and rumors of wars, don't be alarmed; these things

must take place, but the end is not yet. ⁸ For nation will rise up against nation, and kingdom against kingdom. There will be earthquakes in various places, and famines. These are the beginning of birth pains. ⁹ "But you, be on your guard! They will hand you over to sanhedrins, and you will be flogged in the synagogues. You will stand before governors and kings because of Me, as a witness to them. ¹⁰ And the good news must first be proclaimed to all nations. ¹¹ So when they arrest you and hand you over, don't worry beforehand what you will say. On the contrary, whatever is given to you in that hour—say it. For it isn't you speaking, but the Holy Spirit. ¹² Then brother will betray brother to death, and a father his child. Children will rise up against parents and put them to death. ¹³ And you will be hated by everyone because of My name. But the one who endures to the end will be delivered.

¹⁴ "When you see the **abomination that causes desolation** standing where it should not" (let the reader understand), "then those in Judea must flee to the mountains! ¹⁵ A man on the housetop must not come down or go in to get anything out of his house. ¹⁶ And a man in the field must not go back to get his clothes. ¹⁷ Woe to pregnant women and nursing mothers in those days! ¹⁸ Pray it won't happen in winter. ¹⁹ For those will be days of tribulation, the kind that hasn't been from the beginning of the world, which God created, until now and never will be again! ²⁰ Unless the Lord limited those days, no one would survive. But He limited those days because of the elect, whom He chose.

"But God"

They will hand you over to sanhedrins, and you will be flogged in the synagogues. You will stand before governors and kings because of Me, as a witness to them.—MARK 13:9

We must shape the powerful and transforming thought in our minds that the goodness and faithfulness of God follow hard on our heels to turn every tragedy into a triumph and every loss into a gain. It is easy to affirm this as we look back—the challenge is to affirm it with equal conviction as we look ahead.

If you can get hold of this truth and absorb it into your life as a working principle, then it will transform your attitude toward everything. Never again will you be at the mercy of circumstances. In Acts 5:40-41 we read an astonishing statement: "After they called in the apostles and had them flogged . . . Then they went out from the presence of the Sanhedrin, rejoicing . . ." Rejoicing? Over injustice? How is it possible to rejoice over an injustice? Because they believed, with David, that the last word was not with men, but with God—"goodness and faithfulness" would follow them and turn the situation to their advantage. When you can rejoice over injustice, you are indomitable.

Another verse from Acts that always intrigues me reads thus: "The patriarchs became jealous of Joseph and sold him into Egypt, but God . . ." (Ac 7:9). That phrase, "but God," is at the end of every injustice—He has the last word. And just as God used the injustice done to Joseph to feed the Egyptian people and his own family, so He transforms every sorrow, every bereavement, every tragedy. Christianity may not explain everything, but it most certainly transforms everything.

Prayer

O Father, I am so grateful that You are the center of my life. Can this life within me die? Never—for it is deathless and immortal. I rest in this glad and glorious assurance. Thank You, Father. Amen.

Further Study

2 Tm 1:1-12; Ps 27:1; Is 12:2; Rm 10:9
What was Paul's confession?
What are the two requirements for assurance of salvation?

MARCH 16

NUMBERS 12:1–14:4

12 Miriam and Aaron criticized Moses because of the Cushite woman he married (for he had married a Cushite woman). ² They said, "Does the LORD speak only through Moses? Does He not also speak through us?" And the LORD heard it. ³ Moses was a very humble man, more so than any man on the face of the earth.

⁴ Suddenly the LORD said to Moses, Aaron, and Miriam, "You three come out to the tent of meeting." So the three of them went out. ⁵ Then the LORD descended in a pillar of cloud, stood at the entrance to the tent, and summoned Aaron and Miriam. When the two of them came forward, ⁶ He said:

"Listen to what I say:
If there is a prophet among you
    from the LORD,
I make Myself known to him in a
    vision;
I speak with him in a dream.
⁷ Not so with My servant Moses;
he is faithful in all My household.
⁸ I speak with him directly,
openly, and not in riddles;
he sees the form of the LORD.

So why were you not afraid to speak against My servant Moses?" ⁹ The LORD's anger burned against them, and He left.

¹⁰ As the cloud moved away from the tent, Miriam's skin suddenly became diseased, as white as snow. When Aaron turned toward her, he saw that she was diseased ¹¹ and said to Moses, "My lord, please don't hold against us this sin we have so foolishly committed. ¹² Please don't let her be like a dead baby whose flesh is half eaten away when he comes out of his mother's womb."

¹³ Then Moses cried out to the LORD, "God, please heal her!"

¹⁴ The LORD answered Moses, "If her father had merely spit in her face, wouldn't she remain in disgrace for seven days? Let her be confined outside the camp for seven days; after that she may be brought back in." ¹⁵ So Miriam was confined outside the camp for seven days, and the people did not move on until Miriam was brought back

in. ¹⁶After that, the people set out from Hazeroth and camped in the Wilderness of Paran.

13 The LORD spoke to Moses: ² "Send men to scout out the land of Canaan I am giving to the Israelites. Send one man who is a leader among them from each of their ancestral tribes." ³ Moses sent them from the Wilderness of Paran at the LORD's command. All the men were leaders in Israel. ⁴ These were their names:

Shammua son of Zaccur from the tribe of Reuben;
⁵ Shaphat son of Hori from the tribe of Simeon;
⁶ Caleb son of Jephunneh from the tribe of Judah;
⁷ Igal son of Joseph from the tribe of Issachar;
⁸ Hoshea son of Nun from the tribe of Ephraim;
⁹ Palti son of Raphu from the tribe of Benjamin;
¹⁰ Gaddiel son of Sodi from the tribe of Zebulun;
¹¹ Gaddi son of Susi from the tribe of Manasseh (from the tribe of Joseph);
¹² Ammiel son of Gemalli from the tribe of Dan;
¹³ Sethur son of Michael from the tribe of Asher;
¹⁴ Nahbi son of Vophsi from the tribe of Naphtali;
¹⁵ Geuel son of Machi from the tribe of Gad.

¹⁶ These were the names of the men Moses sent to scout out the land, and Moses renamed Hoshea son of Nun, Joshua.

¹⁷ When Moses sent them to scout out the land of Canaan, he told them, "Go up this way to the Negev, then go up into the hill country. ¹⁸ See what the land is like, and whether the people who live there are strong or weak, few or many. ¹⁹ Is the land they live in good or bad? Are the cities they live in encampments or fortifications? ²⁰ Is the land fertile or unproductive? Are there

trees in it or not? Be courageous. Bring back some fruit from the land." It was the season for the first ripe grapes.

²¹ So they went up and scouted out the land from the Wilderness of Zin as far as Rehob near the entrance to Hamath. ²² They went up through the Negev and came to Hebron, where Ahiman, Sheshai, and Talmai, the descendants of Anak, were living. Hebron was built seven years before Zoan in Egypt. ²³ When they came to the Valley of Eshcol, they cut down a branch with a single cluster of grapes, which was carried on a pole by two men. They also took some pomegranates and figs. ²⁴ That place was called the Valley of Eshcol because of the cluster of grapes the Israelites cut there. ²⁵ At the end of 40 days they returned from scouting out the land.

²⁶ The men went back to Moses, Aaron, and the entire Israelite community in the Wilderness of Paran at Kadesh. They brought back a report for them and the whole community, and they showed them the fruit of the land. ²⁷ They reported to Moses: "We went into the land where you sent us. Indeed it is flowing with milk and honey, and here is some of its fruit. ²⁸ However, the people living in the land are strong, and the cities are large and fortified. We also saw the descendants of Anak there. ²⁹ The Amalekites are living in the land of the Negev; the Hittites, Jebusites, and Amorites live in the hill country; and the Canaanites live by the sea and along the Jordan."

³⁰ Then Caleb quieted the people in the presence of Moses and said, "We must go up and take possession of the land because we can certainly conquer it!"

³¹ But the men who had gone up with him responded, "We can't go up against the people because they are stronger than we are!" ³² So they gave a negative report to the Israelites about the land they had scouted: "The land we passed through to explore is one that devours its inhabitants, and all the people we saw in it are men of great size. ³³ We even saw the Nephilim there." (The offspring of Anak were descended from the

Nephilim.) "To ourselves we seemed like grasshoppers, and we must have seemed the same to them."

14 Then the whole community broke into loud cries, and the people wept that night. ² All the Israelites complained about Moses and Aaron, and the whole community told them, "If only we had died in the land of Egypt, or if only we had died in this wilderness! ³ Why is the LORD bringing us into this land to die by the sword? Our wives and little children will become plunder. Wouldn't it be better for us to go back to Egypt?" ⁴ So they said to one another, "Let's appoint a leader and go back to Egypt."

PSALM 34:15-22

¹⁵ The eyes of the LORD are on the
    righteous,
    and His ears are open to their cry
        for help.
¹⁶ The face of the LORD is set against
    those who do evil,
    to erase all memory of them from
        the earth.
¹⁷ The righteous cry out, and the
    LORD hears,
    and delivers them from all their
        troubles.
¹⁸ The LORD is near the brokenhearted;
    He saves those crushed in spirit.

¹⁹ Many adversities come to the one
    who is righteous,
    but the LORD delivers him from
        them all.
²⁰ He protects all his bones;
    not one of them is broken.
²¹ Evil brings death to the sinner,
    and those who hate the righteous
        will be punished.
²² The LORD redeems the life of His
    servants,
    and all who take refuge in Him
        will not be punished.

PROVERBS 8:10-13

¹⁰ Accept my instruction instead of
    silver,

and knowledge rather than pure
    gold.
¹¹ For wisdom is better than
    precious stones,
    and nothing desirable can
        compare with it.
¹² I, Wisdom, share a home with
    shrewdness
    and have knowledge and
        discretion.
¹³ To fear the LORD is to hate evil.
    I hate arrogant pride, evil conduct,
        and perverse speech.

MARK 13:21-37

²¹ "Then if anyone tells you, 'Look, here is the Messiah! Look—there!' do not believe it! ²² For false messiahs and false prophets will rise up and will perform signs and wonders to lead astray, if possible, the elect. ²³ And you must watch! I have told you everything in advance.

²⁴ "But in those days, after that tribulation:

    The sun will be darkened,
    and the moon will not shed
        its light;
²⁵ the stars will be falling
        from the sky,
    and the celestial powers
        will be shaken.

²⁶ Then they will see the Son of Man coming in clouds with great power and glory. ²⁷ He will send out the angels and gather His elect from the four winds, from the end of the earth to the end of the sky.

²⁸ "Learn this parable from the fig tree: As soon as its branch becomes tender and sprouts leaves, you know that summer is near. ²⁹ In the same way, when you see these things happening, know that He is near—at the door! ³⁰ I assure you: This generation will certainly not pass away until all these things take place. ³¹ Heaven and earth will pass away, but My words will never pass away.

³² "Now concerning that day or hour no one knows—neither the angels in

heaven nor the Son—except the Father. ³³Watch! Be alert! For you don't know when the time is coming. ³⁴It is like a man on a journey, who left his house, gave authority to his slaves, gave each one his work, and commanded the door-keeper to be alert. ³⁵Therefore be alert, since you don't know when the master of the house is coming—whether in the evening or at midnight or at the crowing of the rooster or early in the morning. ³⁶Otherwise, he might come suddenly and find you sleeping. ³⁷And what I say to you, I say to everyone: Be alert!"

The Fear of God

To fear the LORD is to hate evil.—PROVERBS 8:13

We are taught over and over again in Scripture that because God is uniquely and awesomely holy—pure, separated, and shining in His moral majesty—we are to draw near to Him with godly reverence and fear. The fear of the Lord, as we know, is the beginning of wisdom. Contemplation of His character, particularly His holiness, will lead to a reverential fear that prepares the soul (as it did for Isaiah) for more profitable service and activity.

But what does it mean to "fear" God? There are times in the Bible when we are told to fear and times when we are told not to fear. There is a fear that helps and a fear that hinders. How do we know the difference?

The fear that helps is the fear that expresses itself in reverence, veneration, awe, a sense of the grandeur and majesty of God. The fear that hinders is described for us in 2 Timothy 1:7: "For God has not given us a spirit of fearfulness, but one of power, love, and sound judgment."

The Greek word *deilia*, which is translated "fearfulness" or "timidity" in this verse, comes from a root that means "wretched, sorry, miserable" and implies someone lacking in courage. God is not to blame for attitudes of cowardice or timidity; they come from within our own hearts. Timid people are frightened people, and if you want to explore this thought still further, ask yourself: what kinds of things frighten me that are not related to the fear of God? If we fear them more than we fear God, then we are being ruled by the wrong kind of fear.

Prayer

O God, I bring to You all my unhealthy fears and lay them at Your feet. Help me develop such a reverential fear for You that all other fears are quickly swallowed up. In Jesus' name. Amen.

Further Study

Dt 10:1-12; Jos 24:14; Ec 12:13
What did the Lord require of Israel?
What did Joshua admonish Israel to do?

MARCH 17

NUMBERS 14:5-45

⁵ Then Moses and Aaron fell down with their faces to the ground in front of the whole assembly of the Israelite community. ⁶ Joshua son of Nun and Caleb son of Jephunneh, who were among those who scouted out the land, tore their clothes ⁷ and said to the entire Israelite community: "The land we passed through and explored is an extremely good land. ⁸ If the LORD is pleased with us, He will bring us into this land, a land flowing with milk and honey, and give it to us. ⁹ Only don't rebel against the LORD, and don't be afraid of the people of the land, for we will devour them. Their protection has been removed from them, and the LORD is with us. Don't be afraid of them!"

¹⁰ While the whole community threatened to stone them, the glory of the LORD appeared to all the Israelites at the tent of meeting.

¹¹ The LORD said to Moses, "How long will these people despise Me? How long will they not trust in Me despite all the signs I have performed among them? ¹² I will strike them with a plague and destroy them. Then I will make you into a greater and mightier nation than they are."

¹³ But Moses replied to the LORD, "The Egyptians will hear about it, for by Your strength You brought up this people from them. ¹⁴ They will tell it to the inhabitants of this land. They have heard that You, LORD, are among these people, how You, LORD, are seen face to face, how Your cloud stands over them, and how You go before them in a pillar of cloud by day and in a pillar of fire by night.¹⁵ If You kill this people with a single blow, the nations that have heard of Your fame will declare, ¹⁶ 'Since the LORD wasn't able to bring this people into the land He swore to give them, He

has slaughtered them in the wilderness.'

¹⁷ "So now, may My Lord's power be magnified just as You have spoken: ¹⁸ The LORD is slow to anger and rich in faithful love, forgiving wrongdoing and rebellion. But He will not leave the guilty unpunished, bringing the consequences of the fathers' wrongdoing on the children to the third and fourth generation. ¹⁹ Please pardon the wrongdoing of this people in keeping with the greatness of Your faithful love, just as You have forgiven them from Egypt until now."

²⁰ The LORD responded, "I have pardoned them as you requested. ²¹ Yet as surely as I live and as the whole earth is filled with the LORD's glory, ²² none of the men who have seen My glory and the signs I performed in Egypt and in the wilderness, and have tested Me these 10 times and did not obey Me, ²³ will ever see the land I swore to give their fathers. None of those who have despised Me will see it. ²⁴ But since My servant Caleb has a different spirit and has followed Me completely, I will bring him into the land where he has gone, and his descendants will inherit it. ²⁵ Since the Amalekites and Canaanites are living in the lowlands, turn back tomorrow and head for the wilderness in the direction of the Red Sea."

²⁶ Then the LORD spoke to Moses and Aaron: ²⁷ "How long must I endure this evil community that keeps complaining about Me? I have heard the Israelites' complaints that they make against Me. ²⁸ Tell them: As surely as I live, declares the LORD, I will do to you exactly as I heard you say. ²⁹ Your corpses will fall in this wilderness—all of you who were registered in the census, the entire number of you 20 years old or more — because you have complained about Me. ³⁰ I swear that none of you will en-

ter the land I promised to settle you in, except Caleb son of Jephunneh and Joshua son of Nun. ³¹ I will bring your children whom you said would become plunder into the land you rejected, and they will enjoy it. ³² But as for you, your corpses will fall in this wilderness. ³³ Your children will be shepherds in the wilderness for 40 years and bear the penalty for your acts of unfaithfulness until all your corpses lie scattered in the wilderness. ³⁴ You will bear the consequences of your sins 40 years based on the number of the 40 days that you scouted the land, a year for each day. You will know My displeasure. ³⁵ I, the LORD, have spoken. I swear that I will do this to the entire evil community that has conspired against Me. They will come to an end in the wilderness, and there they will die."

³⁶ So the men Moses sent to scout out the land, and who returned and incited the entire community to complain about him by spreading a bad report about the land— ³⁷ those men who spread the report about the land were struck down by the LORD. ³⁸ Only Joshua son of Nun and Caleb son of Jephunneh remained alive of those men who went to scout out the land.

³⁹ When Moses reported these words to all the Israelites, the people were overcome with grief. ⁴⁰ They got up early the next morning and went up the ridge of the hill country, saying, "Let's go to the place the LORD promised, for we were wrong."

⁴¹ But Moses responded, "Why are you going against the LORD's command? It won't succeed. ⁴² Don't go, because the LORD is not among you and you will be defeated by your enemies. ⁴³ The Amalekites and Canaanites are right in front of you, and you will fall by the sword. The LORD won't be with you, since you have turned from following Him."

⁴⁴ But they dared to go up the ridge of the hill country, even though the ark of the LORD's covenant and Moses did not leave the camp. ⁴⁵ Then the Amalekites and Canaanites who lived in that part of the hill country came down, attacked them, and routed them as far as Hormah.

PSALM 35:1-10

¹ Oppose my opponents, LORD;
  fight those who fight me.
² Take Your shields—large and
    small—
  and come to my aid.
³ Draw the spear and javelin against
    my pursuers,
  and assure me: "I am your
    deliverance."

⁴ Let those who seek to kill me
  be disgraced and humiliated;
  let those who plan to harm me
  be turned back and ashamed.
⁵ Let them be like husks in the
    wind,
  with the angel of the LORD driving
    them away.
⁶ Let their way be dark and
    slippery,
  with the angel of the LORD
    pursuing them.
⁷ They hid their net for me without
    cause;
  they dug a pit for me without
    cause.
⁸ Let ruin come on him
    unexpectedly,
  and let the net that he hid
    ensnare him;
  let him fall into it—to his ruin.

⁹ Then I will rejoice in the LORD;
  I will delight in His deliverance.
¹⁰ My very bones will say,
  "LORD, who is like You,
  rescuing the poor from one too
    strong for him,
  the poor or the needy from one
    who robs him?"

PROVERBS 8:14-17

¹⁴ I possess good advice and
    competence;
  I have understanding and
    strength.
¹⁵ It is by me that kings reign

and rulers enact just law;
16 by me, princes lead,
as do nobles and all righteous
judges.
17 I love those who love me,
and those who search for me find
me.

MARK 14:1-21

14 After two days it was the Passover and the Festival of Unleavened Bread. The chief priests and the scribes were looking for a treacherous way to arrest and kill Him. 2 "Not during the festival," they said, "or there may be rioting among the people."

3 While He was in Bethany at the house of Simon who had a serious skin disease, as He was reclining at the table, a woman came with an alabaster jar of pure and expensive fragrant oil of nard. She broke the jar and poured it on His head. 4 But some were expressing indignation to one another: "Why has this fragrant oil been wasted? 5 For this oil might have been sold for more than 300 denarii and given to the poor." And they began to scold her.

6 Then Jesus said, "Leave her alone. Why are you bothering her? She has done a noble thing for Me. 7 You always have the poor with you, and you can do good for them whenever you want, but you do not always have Me. 8 She has done what she could; she has anointed My body in advance for burial. 9 I assure you: Wherever the gospel is proclaimed in the whole world, what this woman has done will also be told in memory of her."

10 Then Judas Iscariot, one of the Twelve, went to the chief priests to hand Him over to them. 11 And when they heard this, they were glad and promised to give him silver. So he started looking for a good opportunity to betray Him.

12 On the first day of Unleavened Bread, when they sacrifice the Passover lamb, His disciples asked Him, "Where do You want us to go and prepare the Passover so You may eat it?"

13 So He sent two of His disciples and told them, "Go into the city, and a man carrying a water jug will meet you. Follow him. 14 Wherever he enters, tell the owner of the house, 'The Teacher says, "Where is the guest room for Me to eat the Passover with My disciples?"' 15 He will show you a large room upstairs, furnished and ready. Make the preparations for us there." 16 So the disciples went out, entered the city, and found it just as He had told them, and they prepared the Passover.

17 When evening came, He arrived with the Twelve. 18 While they were reclining and eating, Jesus said, "I assure you: One of you will betray Me—one who is eating with Me!"

19 They began to be distressed and to say to Him one by one, "Surely not I?"

20 He said to them, "It is one of the Twelve—the one who is dipping bread with Me in the bowl. 21 For the Son of Man will go just as it is written about Him, but woe to that man by whom the Son of Man is betrayed! It would have been better for that man if he had not been born."

The Safety of the Old

I love those who love me, and those who search for me find me.—PROVERBS 8:17

A Christian woman came to me who had an unconverted husband. She came to see that what she was asking for with her lips (his conversion) was not what she was desiring in her heart. After this revelation, she had the joy of seeing her husband become a Christian.

But this must not be taken to mean that we have a guaranteed formula for bringing a non-Christian spouse to the Lord. It is right to pray with passion for those in our families who are not converted, but we must remember that each man or woman must personally surrender his or her will to Christ in order to be converted. People are admitted into the family of God only as they give up their commitment to independence and say, in effect: "Heavenly Father, I can do nothing to save myself; save me, in Jesus' name."

A man came to me complaining that he was not getting what he wanted spiritually. He told me that he had a deep sense of unworthiness, and although he prayed desperately for God to take it away, it stayed with him.

After many hours of talking, praying, and heart-searching, he came to see that although in his head he was asking for God to take it away, deep down in his heart he was not desiring it. He had lived with it for so long that he was afraid of the new positive feelings he would have to face if the negative feelings were not there. He preferred the safety of the old to the adventure of the new.

Prayer

Father, day by day I see more clearly the subtle devices of the human heart. Give me the insight I need to probe my own heart, to track down those things that may be preventing me from climbing into the heights with You. In Jesus' name I pray. Amen.

Further Study

Lk 18:1-8; Dt 4:29; Mt 7:7
What characteristic did the woman display?
How can we be sure of finding God?

MARCH 18

NUMBERS 15:1-41

15 The LORD instructed Moses: ² "Speak to the Israelites and tell them: When you enter the land I am giving you to settle in, ³ and you make a fire offering to the LORD from the herd or flock—either a burnt offering or a sacrifice, to fulfill a vow, or as a freewill offering, or at your appointed festivals—to produce a pleasing aroma for the LORD, ⁴ the one presenting his offering to the LORD must also present a grain offering of two quarts of fine flour mixed with a quart of oil. ⁵ Prepare a quart of wine as a drink offering with the burnt offering or sacrifice of each lamb.

⁶ "If you prepare a grain offering with a ram, it must be four quarts of fine flour mixed with a third of a gallon of oil. ⁷ Also present a third of a gallon of wine for a drink offering as a pleasing aroma to the LORD.

⁸ "If you prepare a young bull as a burnt offering or as a sacrifice, to fulfill a vow, or as a fellowship offering to the LORD, ⁹ a grain offering of six quarts of fine flour mixed with two quarts of oil must be presented with the bull. ¹⁰ Also present two quarts of wine as a drink offering. It is a fire offering of pleasing aroma to the LORD. ¹¹ This is to be done for each ox, ram, lamb, or goat. ¹² This is how you must prepare each of them, no matter how many.

¹³ "Every Israelite is to prepare these things in this way when he presents a fire offering as a pleasing aroma to the LORD. ¹⁴ When a foreigner resides with you or someone else is among you and wants to prepare a fire offering as a pleasing aroma to the LORD, he is to do exactly as you do throughout your generations. ¹⁵ The assembly is to have the same statute for both you and the foreign resident as a permanent statute throughout your generations. You and the foreigner will be alike before the LORD. ¹⁶ The same law and the same ordinance will apply to both you and the foreigner who resides with you."

¹⁷ The LORD instructed Moses: ¹⁸ "Speak to the Israelites and tell them: After you enter the land where I am bringing you, ¹⁹ you are to offer a contribution to the LORD when you eat from the food of the land. ²⁰ You are to offer a loaf from your first batch of dough as a contribution; offer it just like a contribution from the threshing floor. ²¹ Throughout your generations, you are to give the LORD a contribution from the first batch of your dough.

²² "When you sin unintentionally and do not obey all these commands that the LORD spoke to Moses— ²³ all that the LORD has commanded you through Moses, from the day the LORD issued the commands and onward throughout your generations— ²⁴ and if it was done unintentionally without the commun-

ity's awareness, the entire community is to prepare one young bull for a burnt offering as a pleasing aroma to the LORD, with its grain offering and drink offering according to the regulation, and one male goat as a sin offering. ²⁵ The priest must then make atonement for the entire Israelite community so that they may be forgiven, for the sin was unintentional. They are to bring their offering, one made by fire to the LORD, and their sin offering before the LORD for their unintentional sin. ²⁶ The entire Israelite community and the foreigner who resides among them will be forgiven, since it happened to all the people unintentionally.

²⁷ "If one person sins unintentionally, he is to present a year-old female goat as a sin offering. ²⁸ The priest must then make atonement before the LORD on behalf of the person who acts in error sinning unintentionally, and when he makes atonement for him, he will be forgiven. ²⁹ You are to have the same law for the person who acts in error, whether he is an Israelite or a foreigner who lives among you.

³⁰ "But the person who acts defiantly, whether native or foreign resident, blasphemes the LORD. That person is to be cut off from his people. ³¹ He will certainly be cut off, because he has despised the LORD's word and broken His command; his guilt remains on him."

³² While the Israelites were in the wilderness, they found a man gathering wood on the Sabbath day. ³³ Those who found him gathering wood brought him to Moses, Aaron, and the entire community. ³⁴ They placed him in custody, because it had not been decided what should be done to him. ³⁵ Then the LORD told Moses, "The man is to be put to death. The entire community is to stone him outside the camp." ³⁶ So the entire community brought him outside the camp and stoned him to death, as the LORD had commanded Moses.

³⁷ The LORD said to Moses, ³⁸ "Speak to the Israelites and tell them that throughout their generations they are to make tassels for the corners of their garments, and put a blue cord on the tassel

at each corner. [39] These will serve as tassels for you to look at, so that you may remember all the LORD's commands and obey them and not become unfaithful by following your own heart and your own eyes. [40] This way you will remember and obey all My commands and be holy to your God. [41] I am the LORD your God who brought you out of the land of Egypt to be your God; I am the LORD your God."

$\mathcal{P}$SALM 35:11-16

[11] Malicious witnesses come forward;
  they question me about things I
  do not know.
[12] They repay me evil for good,
  making me desolate.
[13] Yet when they were sick,
  my clothing was sackcloth;
  I humbled myself with fasting,
  and my prayer was genuine.
[14] I went about grieving as if for my
  friend or brother;
  I was bowed down with grief, like
  one mourning a mother.
[15] But when I stumbled, they
  gathered in glee;
  they gathered against me.
  Assailants I did not know
  tore at me and did not stop.
[16] With godless mockery
  they gnashed their teeth at me.

$\mathcal{P}$ROVERBS 8:18-19

[18] With me are riches and honor,
  lasting wealth and righteousness.
[19] My fruit is better than solid gold,
  and my harvest than pure silver.

$\mathcal{M}$ARK 14:22-42

[22] As they were eating, He took bread, blessed and broke it, gave it to them, and said, "Take it; this is My body." [23] Then He took a cup, and after giving thanks, He gave it to them, and so they all drank from it. [24] He said to them, "This is My blood that establishes the covenant; it is shed for many. [25] I as-

sure you: I will no longer drink of the fruit of the vine until that day when I drink it in a new way in the kingdom of God." [26] After singing psalms, they went out to the Mount of Olives.
[27] Then Jesus said to them, "All of you will run away, because it is written:

I will strike the shepherd,
and the sheep will be scattered.

[28] But after I have been resurrected, I will go ahead of you to Galilee." [29] Peter told Him, "Even if everyone runs away, I will certainly not!" [30] "I assure you," Jesus said to him, "today, this very night, before the rooster crows twice, you will deny Me three times!" [31] But he kept insisting, "If I have to die with You, I will never deny You!" And they all said the same thing. [32] Then they came to a place named Gethsemane, and He told His disciples, "Sit here while I pray." [33] He took Peter, James, and John with Him, and He began to be deeply distressed and horrified. [34] Then He said to them, "My soul is swallowed up in sorrow—to the point of death. Remain here and stay awake." [35] Then He went a little farther, fell to the ground, and began to pray that if it were possible, the hour might pass from Him. [36] And He said, " *Abba*, Father! All things are possible for You. Take this cup away from Me. Nevertheless, not what I will, but what You will." [37] Then He came and found them sleeping. "Simon, are you sleeping?" He asked Peter. "Couldn't you stay awake one hour? [38] Stay awake and pray so that you won't enter into temptation. The spirit is willing, but the flesh is weak." [39] Once again He went away and prayed, saying the same thing. [40] And He came again and found them sleeping, because they could not keep their eyes open. They did not know what to say to Him. [41] Then He came a third time and said to them, "Are you still sleeping and resting? Enough! The time has come. Look, the Son of Man is being betrayed into the hands of sinners. [42] Get up; let's go! See—My betrayer is near."

Making Sadness Sing

They repay me evil for good, making me desolate. . . . I humbled myself with fasting, and my prayer was genuine.—Psalm 35:12-13

Expect God to supply you with the strength to transform everything that comes to you, making it contribute to the central purposes for which you live. "Expect God to supply you with strength." That is the secret.

In the Christian life, we get what we expect. You likely have heard the story of the woman who, having heard a sermon on the text, "If anyone says to this mounatin 'Be lifted up,' " decided to try out her faith on a mountain near her home. Prior to going to sleep, she looked out of her window and said to the mountain, "Be lifted up." In the morning, as soon as she awoke, she looked out, saw that the mountain was still there, and said woefully: "Just as I expected." Yes, in the Christian life, we get what we expect.

Notice the remainder of the phrase from this line of advice: ". . . strength to transform everything that comes . . ." This is what Jesus did. As the Gospel writer recorded, "Then He withdrew from them about a stone's throw, knelt down, and began to pray, 'Father, if You are willing, take this cup away from Me—nevertheless, not My will, but Yours, be done.' Then an angel from heaven appeared to Him, strengthening Him" (Lk 22:41-43). Here, God's answer was not to take away the cup but to supply the strength to turn that bitter cup into a cup of salvation, which He would put to the thirsty lips of humanity. In the midst of your trials, don't whine to be released. Ask rather for the strength to make every sadness sing.

Prayer

Father, don't ever let me forget this lesson—that if I cannot change my surroundings, I can change my soul. Help me see that if I am not saved from a situation, then I can be saved in the situation. I am deeply thankful. Amen.

Further Study

Is 40; 41:10; 2 Co 12:9
What is promised to those who wait on the Lord?
What was Paul's testimony?

MARCH 19

NUMBERS 16:1-50

16 Now Korah son of Izhar, son of Kohath, son of Levi, with Dathan and Abiram, sons of Eliab, and On son of Peleth, sons of Reuben, took ² 250 prominent Israelite men who were leaders of the community and representatives in the assembly, and they rebelled against Moses. ³ They came together against Moses and Aaron and told them, "You have gone too far! Everyone in the entire community is holy, and the LORD is among them. Why then do you exalt yourselves above the LORD's assembly?" ⁴ When Moses heard this, he fell facedown. ⁵ Then he said to Korah and all his followers, "Tomorrow morning the LORD will reveal who belongs to Him, who is set apart, and the one He will let come near Him. He will let the one He chooses come near Him. ⁶ Korah, you and all your followers are to do this: take firepans, and tomorrow ⁷ place fire in them and put incense on them before the LORD. Then the man the LORD chooses will be the one who is set apart. It is you Levites who have gone too far!"

⁸ Moses also told Korah, "Now listen, Levites! ⁹ Isn't it enough for you that the God of Israel has separated you from the Israelite community to bring you near to Himself, to perform the work at the LORD's tabernacle, and to stand before the community to minister to them? ¹⁰ He has brought you near, and all your fellow Levites who are with you, but you are seeking the priesthood as well. ¹¹ Therefore, it is you and all your followers who have conspired against the LORD! As for Aaron, who is he that you should complain about him?"

¹² Moses sent for Dathan and Abiram, the sons of Eliab, but they said, "We will not come! ¹³ Is it not enough that you brought us up from a land flowing with milk and honey to kill us in the wilderness? Do you also have to appoint yourself as ruler over us? ¹⁴ Furthermore, you didn't bring us to a land flowing with milk and honey or give us an inheritance of fields and vineyards. Will you gouge out the eyes of these men? We will not come!"

¹⁵ Then Moses became angry and said to the LORD, "Don't respect their offering. I have not taken one donkey from them or mistreated a single one of them." ¹⁶ So Moses told Korah, "You and all your followers are to appear before the LORD tomorrow—you, they, and Aaron. ¹⁷ Each of you is to take his firepan, place incense on it, and present his firepan before the LORD—250 firepans. You and Aaron are each to present your firepan also."

¹⁸ Each man took his firepan, placed fire in it, put incense on it, and stood at the entrance to the tent of meeting along with Moses and Aaron. ¹⁹ After Korah assembled the whole community against them at the entrance to the tent of meeting, the glory of the LORD appeared to the whole community. ²⁰ The LORD spoke to Moses and Aaron, ²¹ "Separate yourselves from this community so I may consume them instantly."

²² But Moses and Aaron fell facedown and said, "God, God of the spirits of all flesh, when one man sins, will you vent Your wrath on the whole community?"

²³ The LORD replied to Moses, ²⁴ "Tell the community: Get away from the dwellings of Korah, Dathan, and Abiram."

²⁵ Moses got up and went to Dathan and Abiram, and the elders of Israel followed him. ²⁶ He warned the community, "Get away now from the tents of these wicked men. Don't touch anything that belongs to them, or you will be swept away because of all their sins." ²⁷ So they got away from the dwellings of Korah, Dathan, and Abiram. Meanwhile, Dathan and Abiram came out and stood

at the entrance of their tents with their wives, children, and infants.

²⁸ Then Moses said, "This is how you will know that the LORD sent me to do all these things and that it was not of my own will: ²⁹ If these men die naturally as all people would, and suffer the fate of all, then the LORD has not sent me. ³⁰ But if the LORD brings about something unprecedented, and the ground opens its mouth and swallows them along with all that belongs to them so that they go down alive into Sheol, then you will know that these men have despised the LORD."

³¹ Just as he finished speaking all these words, the ground beneath them split open. ³² The earth opened its mouth and swallowed them and their households, all Korah's people, and all their possessions. ³³ They went down alive into Sheol with all that belonged to them. The earth closed over them, and they vanished from the assembly. ³⁴ At their cries, all the people of Israel who were around them fled because they thought, "The earth may swallow us too!" ³⁵ Fire also came out from the LORD and consumed the 250 men who were presenting the incense.

³⁶ Then the LORD spoke to Moses: ³⁷ "Tell Eleazar son of Aaron the priest to remove the firepans from the burning debris, because they are holy, and scatter the fire far away. ³⁸ As for the firepans of those who sinned at the cost of their own lives, make them into hammered sheets as plating for the altar, for they presented them before the LORD, and the firepans are holy. They will be a sign to the Israelites."

³⁹ So Eleazar the priest took the bronze firepans that those who were burned had presented, and they were hammered into plating for the altar, ⁴⁰ just as the LORD commanded him through Moses. It was to be a reminder for the Israelites that no unauthorized person outside the lineage of Aaron should approach to offer incense before the LORD and become like Korah and his followers.

⁴¹ The next day the entire Israelite community complained about Moses and Aaron, saying, "You have killed the LORD's people!" ⁴² When the community assembled against them, Moses and Aaron turned toward the tent of meeting, and suddenly the cloud covered it, and the LORD's glory appeared.

⁴³ Moses and Aaron went to the front of the tent of meeting, ⁴⁴ and the LORD said to Moses, ⁴⁵ "Get away from this community so that I may consume them instantly." But they fell facedown.

⁴⁶ Then Moses told Aaron, "Take your firepan, place fire from the altar in it, and add incense. Go quickly to the community and make atonement for them, because wrath has come from the LORD; the plague has begun." ⁴⁷ So Aaron took his firepan as Moses had ordered, ran into the middle of the assembly, and saw that the plague had begun among the people. After he added incense, he made atonement for the people. ⁴⁸ He stood between the dead and the living, and the plague was halted. ⁴⁹ But those who died from the plague numbered 14,700, in addition to those who died because of the Korah incident. ⁵⁰ Aaron then returned to Moses at the entrance to the tent of meeting, since the plague had been halted.

PSALM 35:17-21

¹⁷ Lord, how long will You look on?
Rescue my life from their ravages,
my very life from the young lions.
¹⁸ I will praise You in the great
congregation;
I will exalt You among many
people.
¹⁹ Do not let my deceitful enemies
rejoice over me;
do not let those who hate me
without cause look at me
maliciously.
²⁰ For they do not speak in friendly
ways,
but contrive deceitful schemes
against those who live peacefully
in the land.
²¹ They open their mouths wide
against me and say,
"Aha, aha! We saw it!"

PROVERBS 8:20-21

²⁰ I walk in the way of
righteousness,
along the paths of justice,
²¹ giving wealth as an inheritance to
those who love me,
and filling their treasuries.

MARK 14:43-72

⁴³ While He was still speaking, Judas, one of the Twelve, suddenly arrived. With him was a mob, with swords and clubs, from the chief priests, the scribes, and the elders. ⁴⁴ His betrayer had given them a signal. "The One I kiss," he said, "He's the One; arrest Him and take Him away under guard." ⁴⁵ So when he came, he went right up to Him and said, "Rabbi!"—and kissed Him. ⁴⁶ Then they took hold of Him and arrested Him. ⁴⁷ And one of those who stood by drew his sword, struck the high priest's slave, and cut off his ear.

⁴⁸ But Jesus said to them, "Have you come out with swords and clubs, as though I were a criminal, to capture Me? ⁴⁹ Every day I was among you, teaching in the temple complex, and you didn't arrest Me. But the Scriptures must be fulfilled." ⁵⁰ Then they all deserted Him and ran away.

⁵¹ Now a certain young man, having a linen cloth wrapped around his naked body, was following Him. They caught hold of him, ⁵² but he left the linen cloth behind and ran away naked.

⁵³ They led Jesus away to the high priest, and all the chief priests, the elders, and the scribes convened. ⁵⁴ Peter followed Him at a distance, right into the high priest's courtyard. He was sitting with the temple police, warming himself by the fire.

⁵⁵ The chief priests and the whole Sanhedrin were looking for testimony against Jesus to put Him to death, but they could find none. ⁵⁶ For many were giving false testimony against Him, but the testimonies did not agree. ⁵⁷ Some stood up and were giving false testimony against Him, stating, ⁵⁸ "We heard Him say, 'I will demolish this sanctuary made by human hands, and in three days I will build another not made by hands.' " ⁵⁹ Yet their testimony did not agree even on this.

⁶⁰ Then the high priest stood up before them all and questioned Jesus, "Don't You have an answer to what these men are testifying against You?" ⁶¹ But He kept silent and did not answer anything. Again the high priest questioned Him, "Are You the Messiah, the Son of the Blessed One?"

⁶² "I am," said Jesus, "and all of you will see **the Son of Man seated at the right hand** of the Power and **coming with the clouds of heaven.**"

⁶³ Then the high priest tore his robes and said, "Why do we still need witnesses? ⁶⁴ You have heard the blasphemy! What is your decision?"

And they all condemned Him to be deserving of death. ⁶⁵ Then some began to spit on Him, to blindfold Him, and to beat Him, saying, "Prophesy!" Even the temple police took Him and slapped Him.

⁶⁶ While Peter was in the courtyard below, one of the high priest's servants came. ⁶⁷ When she saw Peter warming himself, she looked at him and said, "You also were with that Nazarene, Jesus."

⁶⁸ But he denied it: "I don't know or understand what you're talking about!" Then he went out to the entryway, and a rooster crowed.

⁶⁹ When the servant saw him again she began to tell those standing nearby, "This man is one of them!"

⁷⁰ But again he denied it. After a little while those standing there said to Peter again, "You certainly are one of them, since you're also a Galilean!"

⁷¹ Then he started to curse and to swear with an oath, "I don't know this man you're talking about!"

⁷² Immediately a rooster crowed a second time, and Peter remembered when Jesus had spoken the word to him, "Before the rooster crows twice, you will deny Me three times." When he thought about it, he began to weep.

"Rise Up, O Men of God"

"I am," said Jesus, "and all of you will see the Son of Man seated at the right hand of the Power and coming with the clouds of heaven."—MARK **14:62**

Although the fullness of God's kingdom is yet to come, there is a sense in which the King is reigning now, and we can say with the utmost certainty, "Our God reigns!"

A lady once wrote to me indicating her intention to withdraw from life and await the day when God would finally establish His kingdom in power and glory on the earth. I replied with a parody of a hymn that apparently got her thinking. She wrote back in a few weeks and said, "You were right. I was waiting for God, but now I realize He is waiting for me." She ended her letter with the words of the hymn:

Rise up, O men of God!

Have done with lesser things;

Give heart and soul and mind and strength

To serve the King of kings.

This must indicate our line of action. Yes, of course, the final ushering in of God's kingdom is yet to take place, but that does not mean that He is taking a backseat in the world's affairs. God wants to reign through us!

We need not wait for the day when spectacularly the great God of the universe demonstrates His imperial power. As He sounds forth a rallying cry, even through these pages, respond to Him, I urge you, with a fresh consecration of purpose, and dedicate yourself to letting Him reign through you.

Prayer

God, I give myself wholly to You, not only just to live in me, but to reign through me. I gladly submit my whole being to You today. Live and reign in me. For Jesus' sake. Amen.

Further Study

Rm 13:1-14; 2 Co 10:4; 1 Tm 1:18; 6:12; 2 Tm 2:4

How can we overcome the works of darkness?

What was Paul's exhortation to Timothy?

MARCH 20

*N*UMBERS 17:1–19:8

17 The LORD instructed Moses: ² "Speak to the Israelites and take one staff from them for each ancestral house, 12 staffs from all the leaders of their ancestral houses. Write each man's name on his staff. ³ Write Aaron's name on Levi's staff, because there must be one staff for the head of each ancestral house. ⁴ Then place them in the tent of meeting in front of the testimony where I meet with you. ⁵ The staff of the man I choose will sprout, and I will rid Myself of the Israelites' complaints that they have been making about you."

⁶ So Moses spoke to the Israelites, and each of their leaders gave him a staff, one for each of the leaders of their ancestral houses, 12 staffs in all. Aaron's staff was among them. ⁷ Moses placed the staffs before the LORD in the tent of the testimony.

⁸ The next day Moses entered the tent of the testimony and saw that Aaron's staff, representing the house of Levi, had sprouted, formed buds, blossomed, and produced almonds! ⁹ Moses then brought out all the staffs from the LORD's presence to all the Israelites. They saw them, and each man took his own staff. ¹⁰ The LORD told Moses, "Put Aaron's rod back in front of the testimony to be kept as a sign for the rebels, so that you may put an end to their complaints before Me, or else they will die." ¹¹ So Moses did as the LORD commanded him.

¹² Then the Israelites declared to Moses, "Look, we're perishing! We're lost; we're all lost! ¹³ Anyone who comes near the LORD's tabernacle will die. Will we all perish?"

18 The LORD said to Aaron, "You, your sons, and your ancestral house will be responsible for sin against the sanctuary. You and your sons will be responsible for sin involving your priesthood. ² But also bring your brothers with you from the tribe of Levi, your ancestral tribe, so they may join you and serve with you and your sons in front of the tent of the testimony. ³ They are to perform duties for you and for the whole tent. They must not come near the sanctuary equipment or the altar; otherwise, both they and you will die. ⁴ They are to join you and guard the tent of meeting, doing all the work at the tent, but no unauthorized person may come near you.

⁵ "You are to guard the sanctuary and the altar so that wrath may not fall on the Israelites again. ⁶ Look, I have selected your fellow Levites from the Israelites as a gift for you, assigned by the LORD to work at the tent of meeting. ⁷ But you and your sons will carry out your priestly responsibilities for everything concerning the altar and for what is inside the veil, and you will do that work. I am giving you the work of the priesthood as a gift, but an unauthorized person who comes near the sanctuary will be put to death."

⁸ Then the LORD spoke to Aaron, "Look, I have put you in charge of the contributions brought to Me. As for all the holy offerings of the Israelites, I have given them to you and your sons as a portion and a perpetual statute. ⁹ A portion of the holiest offerings kept from the fire will be yours; every one of their offerings that they give Me, whether the grain offering, sin offering, or restitution offering will be most holy for you and your sons. ¹⁰ You are to eat it as a most holy offering. Every male may eat it; it is to be holy to you.

¹¹ "The contribution of their gifts also belongs to you. I have given all the Israelites' presentation offerings to you and to your sons and daughters as a

perpetual statute. Every ceremonially clean person in your house may eat it. ¹²I am giving you all the best of the fresh olive oil, new wine, and grain, which the Israelites give to the LORD as their firstfruits. ¹³The firstfruits of all that is in their land, which they bring to the LORD, belong to you. Every clean person in your house may eat them.
¹⁴"Everything in Israel that is permanently dedicated to the LORD belongs to you. ¹⁵The firstborn of every living thing, man or animal, presented to the LORD belongs to you. But you must certainly redeem the firstborn of man, and redeem the firstborn of an unclean animal. ¹⁶You will pay the redemption price for a month-old male according to your valuation: five shekels of silver by the standard sanctuary shekel, which is 20 gerahs.
¹⁷"However, you must not redeem the firstborn of an ox, a sheep, or a goat; they are holy. You are to sprinkle their blood on the altar and burn their fat as a fire offering for a pleasing aroma to the LORD. ¹⁸But their meat belongs to you. It belongs to you like the breast of the presentation offering and the right thigh.
¹⁹"I give to you and to your sons and daughters all the holy contributions that the Israelites present to the LORD as a perpetual statute. It is a perpetual covenant of salt before the LORD for you as well as your offspring."
²⁰The LORD told Aaron, "You will not have an inheritance in their land; there will be no portion among them for you. I am your portion and your inheritance among the Israelites.
²¹"Look, I have given the Levites every tenth in Israel as an inheritance in return for the work they do, the work of the tent of meeting. ²²The Israelites must never again come near the tent of meeting, or they will incur guilt and die. ²³The Levites will do the work of the tent of meeting, and they will bear the consequences of their sin. The Levites will not receive an inheritance among the Israelites; this is a perpetual statute throughout your generations. ²⁴For I have given them the tenth that

the Israelites present to the LORD as a contribution for their inheritance. That is why I told them that they would not receive an inheritance among Israelites."
²⁵The LORD instructed Moses, ²⁶"Speak to the Levites and tell them: When you receive from the Israelites the tenth that I have given you as your inheritance, you must present part of it as an offering to the LORD—a tenth of the tenth. ²⁷Your offering will be credited to you as if it were your grain from the threshing floor or the full harvest from the winepress. ²⁸You are to present an offering to the LORD from every tenth you receive from the Israelites. Give some of it to Aaron the priest as an offering to the LORD. ²⁹You must present the entire offering due the LORD from all your gifts. The best part of the tenth is to be consecrated.
³⁰"Tell them further: Once you have presented the best part of the tenth, and it is credited to you Levites as the produce of the threshing floor or the winepress, ³¹then you and your household may eat it anywhere. It is your wage in return for your work at the tent of meeting. ³²You will not incur guilt because of it once you have presented the best part of it, but you must not defile the Israelites' holy offerings, so that you will not die."

19 The LORD spoke to Moses and Aaron, ²"This is the legal statute that the LORD has commanded: Instruct the Israelites to bring you an unblemished red cow that has no defect and has never been yoked. ³Give it to Eleazar the priest, and he will have it brought outside the camp and slaughtered in his presence. ⁴Eleazar the priest is to take some of its blood with his finger and sprinkle it seven times toward the front of the tent of meeting. ⁵The cow must be burned in his sight. Its hide, flesh, and blood, are to be burned along with its dung. ⁶The priest is to take cedar wood, hyssop, and crimson yarn, and throw them onto the fire where the cow is burning. ⁷Then the priest must wash his clothes and bathe his body in water; after that he may enter the camp, but he will remain ceremonially unclean until evening. ⁸ The one who burned the cow must also wash his clothes and bathe his body in water, and he will remain unclean until evening.

𝒫SALM 35:22-28

²² You saw it, LORD; do not be silent.
  Lord, do not be far from me.
²³ Wake up and rise to my defense,
  to my cause, my God and my
    LORD!
²⁴ Vindicate me, LORD, my God,
  in keeping with Your
    righteousness,
  and do not let them rejoice over
    me.
²⁵ Do not let them say in their
    hearts,
  "Aha! Just what we wanted."
  Do not let them say,
  "We have swallowed him up!"
²⁶ Let those who rejoice at my
    misfortune
  be disgraced and humiliated;
  let those who exalt themselves
    over me
  be clothed with shame and
    reproach.

²⁷ Let those who want my
    vindication
  shout for joy and be glad;
  let them continually say,
  "The LORD be exalted,
  who wants His servant's well-
    being."
²⁸ And my tongue will proclaim Your
    righteousness,
  Your praise all day long.

𝒫ROVERBS 8:22-24

²² The LORD made me at the
  beginning of His creation,
  before His works of long ago.
²³ I was formed before ancient
    times,
  from the beginning, before the
    earth began.

²⁴ I was brought forth when there
  were no watery depths
  and no springs filled with water.

𝑀ARK 15:1-21

15 As soon as it was morning, the chief priests had a meeting with the elders, scribes, and the whole Sanhedrin. After tying Jesus up, they led Him away and handed Him over to Pilate. ² So Pilate asked Him, "Are You the King of the Jews?"

He answered him, "You have said it." ³ And the chief priests began to accuse Him of many things. ⁴ Then Pilate questioned Him again, "Are You not answering anything? Look how many things they are accusing You of!" ⁵ But Jesus still did not answer anything, so Pilate was amazed.

⁶ At the festival it was Pilate's custom to release for the people a prisoner they requested. ⁷ There was one named Barabbas, who was in prison with rebels who had committed murder during the rebellion. ⁸ The crowd came up and began to ask Pilate to do for them as was his custom. ⁹ So Pilate answered them, "Do you want me to release the King of the Jews for you?" ¹⁰ For he knew it was because of envy that the chief priests had handed Him over. ¹¹ But the chief priests stirred up the crowd so that he would release Barabbas to them instead. ¹² Pilate asked them again, "Then what do you want me to do with the One you call the King of the Jews?"

¹³ Again they shouted, "Crucify Him!" ¹⁴ Then Pilate said to them, "Why? What has He done wrong?"

But they shouted, "Crucify Him!" all the more.

¹⁵ Then, willing to gratify the crowd, Pilate released Barabbas to them. And after having Jesus flogged, he handed Him over to be crucified.

¹⁶ Then the soldiers led Him away into the courtyard (that is, headquarters) and called the whole company together. ¹⁷ They dressed Him in a purple robe, twisted together a crown of thorns, and

put it on Him. ¹⁸ And they began to salute Him, "Hail, King of the Jews!" ¹⁹ They kept hitting Him on the head with a reed and spitting on Him. Getting down on their knees, they were paying Him homage. ²⁰ When they had mocked Him, they stripped Him of the purple robe, put His clothes on Him, and led Him out to crucify Him.

²¹ They forced a man coming in from the country, who was passing by, to carry Jesus' cross. He was Simon, a Cyrenian, the father of Alexander and Rufus.

"Settling Down in God"

And my tongue will proclaim Your righteousness,
Your praise all day long.—PSALM 35:28

The words "Father in heaven" are intended to help us focus not only on God's location, but also on His elevation. The Savior (so I believe) encourages us, when we come to God in prayer, to get our perspective right and to look above "the ragged edges of time" to the heights of eternity where God has His royal throne.

The old Welsh preachers and theologians, such as Christmas Evans, Daniel Rowlands, and others, used to call this aspect of prayer "settling down in God." They taught that when we gain a right perspective of God and heavenly things, then and only then can we have a right perspective of man and earthly things. It was only when Isaiah saw the Lord "high and lofty" that he was able to put into focus the events that were happening around him. Our life here on earth can never be abundant until we realize that we have access to resources which are outside the realm of terrestrial things.

A good working translation of the term El-Shaddai (Gn 17:1) is "God—the Enough." Actually, of course, He is more than enough, but how comforting it is to know that He is at least that. So, when coming to God in prayer, learn to settle yourself down in God. Remind yourself that His resources so infinitely exceed your requirements; His sufficiency so immeasurably surpasses every demand you may make upon it. Get the divine perspective right, and earthly things will fall into their right and proper focus.

Prayer

My Father, gently and quietly I breathe the strength of Your Almightiness into every portion of my being. I realize that when I see You "high and lofty," then all of life is reduced to its proper proportions. I am so thankful. Amen.

Further Study

Mt 19:13-26; Eph 3:20; 2 Co 9:8; Php 4:19
What was the declaration of Jesus?
How did Paul describe "El-Shaddai"?

MARCH 21

$\mathcal{N}$UMBERS 19:9–21:9

⁹ "A man who is clean is to gather up the cow's ashes and deposit them outside the camp in a ceremonially clean place. The ashes must be kept by the Israelite community for preparing the water to remove impurity; it is a sin offering. ¹⁰ Then the one who gathers up the cow's ashes must wash his clothes, and he will remain unclean until evening. This is a perpetual statute for the Israelites and for the foreigner who resides among them.

¹¹ "The person who touches any human corpse will be unclean for seven days. ¹² He is to purify himself with the water on the third day and the seventh day; then he will be clean. But if he does not purify himself on the third and seventh days, he will not be clean. ¹³ Anyone who touches a body of a person who has died, and does not purify himself, defiles the tabernacle of the LORD. That person will be cut off from Israel. He remains unclean because the water for impurity has not been sprinkled on him, and his uncleanness is still on him.

¹⁴ "This is the law when a person dies in a tent: everyone who enters the tent and everyone who is already in the tent will be unclean for seven days, ¹⁵ and any open container without a lid tied on it is unclean. ¹⁶ Anyone in the open field who touches a person who has been killed by the sword or has died, or a human bone, or a grave, will be unclean for seven days. ¹⁷ For the purification of the unclean person, they are to take some of the ashes of the burnt sin offering, put them in a jar, and add fresh water to them. ¹⁸ A person who is clean is to take hyssop, dip it in the water, and sprinkle the tent, all the furnishings, and the people who were there. He is also to sprinkle the one who touched a bone, a grave, a corpse, or a person who had been killed.

¹⁹ "The one who is clean is to sprinkle the unclean person on the third day and the seventh day. After he purifies the unclean person on the seventh day, the one being purified must wash his clothes and bathe in water, and he will be clean by evening. ²⁰ But a person who is unclean and does not purify himself, that person will be cut off from the assembly because he has defiled the sanctuary of the LORD. The water for impurity has not been sprinkled on him; he is unclean. ²¹ This is a perpetual statute for them. The person who sprinkles the water for impurity is to wash his clothes, and whoever touches the water for impurity will be unclean until evening. ²² Anything the unclean person touches will become unclean, and anyone who touches it will be unclean until evening."

20 The entire Israelite community entered the Wilderness of Zin in the first month, and they settled in Kadesh. Miriam died and was buried there.

² There was no water for the community, so they assembled against Moses and Aaron. ³ The people quarreled with Moses and said, "If only we had perished when our brothers perished before the LORD. ⁴ Why have you brought the LORD's assembly into this wilderness for us and our livestock to die here? ⁵ Why have you led us up from Egypt to bring us to this evil place? It's not a place of grain, figs, vines, and pomegranates, and there is no water to drink!"

⁶ Then Moses and Aaron went from the presence of the assembly to the doorway of the tent of meeting. They fell down with their faces to the ground, and the glory of the LORD appeared to them. ⁷ The LORD spoke to Moses, ⁸ "Take

the staff and assemble the community. You and your brother Aaron are to speak to the rock while they watch, and it will yield its water. You will bring out water for them from the rock and provide drink for the community and their livestock."

⁹ So Moses took the staff from the LORD's presence just as He had commanded him. ¹⁰ Moses and Aaron summoned the assembly in front of the rock, and Moses said to them, "Listen, you rebels! Must we bring water out of this rock for you?" ¹¹ Then Moses raised his hand and struck the rock twice with his staff, so that a great amount of water gushed out, and the community and their livestock drank.

¹² But the LORD said to Moses and Aaron, "Because you did not trust Me to show My holiness in the sight of the Israelites, you will not bring this assembly into the land I have given them." ¹³ These are the waters of Meribah, where the Israelites quarreled with the LORD, and He showed His holiness to them.

¹⁴ Moses sent messengers from Kadesh to the king of Edom, "This is what your brother Israel says, 'You know all the hardships that have overtaken us. ¹⁵ Our fathers went down to Egypt, and we lived in Egypt many years, but the Egyptians treated us and our fathers badly. ¹⁶ When we cried out to the LORD, He heard our voice, sent an Angel, and brought us out of Egypt. Now look, we are in Kadesh, a city on the border of your territory. ¹⁷ Please let us travel through your land. We won't travel through any field or vineyard, or drink any well water. We will travel the King's Highway; we won't turn to the right or the left until we have traveled through your territory.' "

¹⁸ But Edom answered him, "You must not travel through our land, or we will come out and confront you with the sword."

¹⁹ "We will go on the main road," the Israelites replied to them, "and if we or our herds drink your water, we will pay its price. There will be no problem; only let us travel through on foot."

²⁰ Yet Edom insisted, "You must not travel through." And they came out to confront them with a large force of heavily-armed people. ²¹ Edom refused to allow Israel to travel through their territory, and Israel turned away from them.

²² After they set out from Kadesh, the entire Israelite community came to Mount Hor. ²³ The LORD said to Moses and Aaron at Mount Hor on the border of the land of Edom, ²⁴ "Aaron will be gathered to his people; he will not enter the land I have given the Israelites, because you both rebelled against My command at the waters of Meribah. ²⁵ Take Aaron and his son Eleazar and bring them up Mount Hor. ²⁶ Remove Aaron's garments and put them on his son Eleazar. Aaron will be gathered to his people and die there."

²⁷ So Moses did as the LORD commanded, and they climbed Mount Hor in the sight of the whole community. ²⁸ After Moses removed Aaron's garments and put them on his son Eleazar, Aaron died there on top of the mountain. Then Moses and Eleazar came down from the mountain. ²⁹ When the whole community saw that Aaron had passed away, the entire house of Israel mourned for him 30 days.

21 When the Canaanite king of Arad, who lived in the Negev, heard that Israel was coming on the Atharim road, he fought against Israel and captured some prisoners. ² Then Israel made a vow to the LORD, "If You will deliver this people into our hands, we will completely destroy their cities." ³ The LORD listened to Israel's request, the Canaanites were defeated, and Israel completely destroyed them and their cities. So they named the place Hormah.

⁴ Then they set out from Mount Hor by way of the Red Sea to bypass the land of Edom, but the people became impatient because of the journey. ⁵ The people spoke against God and Moses: "Why have you led us up from Egypt to die in the wilderness? There is no bread or water, and we detest this wretched

food!" ⁶ Then the LORD sent poisonous snakes among the people, and they bit them so that many Israelites died.

⁷ The people then came to Moses and said, "We have sinned by speaking against the LORD and against you. Intercede with the LORD so that He will take the snakes away from us." And Moses interceded for the people. ⁸ Then the LORD said to Moses, "Make a snake image and mount it on a pole. When anyone who is bitten looks at it, he will recover." ⁹ So Moses made a bronze snake and mounted it on a pole. Whenever someone was bitten, and he looked at the bronze snake, he recovered.

PSALM 36:1-6

¹ An oracle within my heart
concerning the transgression
of the wicked:
There is no dread of God before
his eyes,
² for in his own eyes he flatters
himself too much
to discover and hate his sin.
³ The words of his mouth are
malicious and deceptive;
he has stopped acting wisely and
doing good.
⁴ Even on his bed he makes
malicious plans.
He sets himself on a path that is
not good and does not reject
evil.

⁵ LORD, Your faithful love reaches to
heaven,
Your faithfulness to the skies.
⁶ Your righteousness is like the
highest mountain;
Your judgments, like the deepest
sea.
LORD, You preserve man and
beast.

PROVERBS 8:25-26

²⁵ I was brought forth
before the mountains and hills
were established,

²⁶ before He made the land, the
fields,
or the first soil on earth.

MARK 15:22-47

²² And they brought Jesus to the place called *Golgotha* (which means Skull Place). ²³ They tried to give Him wine mixed with myrrh, but He did not take it. ²⁴ Then they crucified Him and divided His clothes, casting lots for them to decide what each would get. ²⁵ Now it was nine in the morning when they crucified Him. ²⁶ The inscription of the charge written against Him was

THE KING OF THE JEWS

²⁷ They crucified two criminals with Him, one on His right and one on His left. [²⁸ So the Scripture was fulfilled that says: **And He was counted among outlaws.**] ²⁹ Those who passed by were yelling insults at Him, shaking their heads, and saying, "Ha! The One who would demolish the sanctuary and build it in three days, ³⁰ save Yourself by coming down from the cross!" ³¹ In the same way, the chief priests with the scribes were mocking Him to one another and saying, "He saved others; He cannot save Himself! ³² Let the Messiah, the King of Israel, come down now from the cross, so that we may see and believe." Even those who were crucified with Him were taunting Him.

³³ When it was noon, darkness came over the whole land until three in the afternoon. ³⁴ And at three Jesus cried out with a loud voice, ***"Eloi, Eloi, lemá sabachtháni?"*** which is translated, "My God, My God, why have You forsaken Me?"

³⁵ When some of those standing there heard this, they said, "Look, He's calling for Elijah!" ³⁶ Someone ran and filled a sponge with sour wine, fixed it on a reed, offered Him a drink, and said, "Let's see if Elijah comes to take Him down!"

³⁷ But Jesus let out a loud cry and

breathed His last. ³⁸ Then the curtain of the sanctuary was split in two from top to bottom. ³⁹ When the centurion, who was standing opposite Him, saw the way He breathed His last, he said, "This man really was God's Son!"

⁴⁰ There were also women looking on from a distance. Among them were Mary Magdalene, Mary the mother of James the younger and of Joses, and Salome. ⁴¹ When He was in Galilee, they would follow Him and help Him. Many other women had come up with Him to Jerusalem.

⁴² When it was already evening, because it was preparation day (that is, the day before the Sabbath), ⁴³ Joseph of Arimathea, a prominent member of the Sanhedrin who was himself looking forward to the kingdom of God, came and boldly went in to Pilate and asked for Jesus' body. ⁴⁴ Pilate was surprised that He was already dead. Summoning the centurion, he asked him whether He had already died. ⁴⁵ When he found out from the centurion, he gave the corpse to Joseph. ⁴⁶ After he bought some fine linen, he took Him down and wrapped Him in the linen. Then he placed Him in a tomb cut out of the rock, and rolled a stone against the entrance to the tomb. ⁴⁷ Now Mary Magdalene and Mary the mother of Joses were watching where He was placed.

Great Faithfulness

LORD, Your faithful love reaches to heaven,
Your faithfulness to the skies.—PSALM 36:5

How wonderful it is, in an age where unfaithfulness abounds, to focus our gaze on those Scriptures that point to the trustworthiness of our God. The one before us today is quite wonderful, but consider also these:

"LORD God of Hosts, who is strong like You, LORD? Your faithfulness surrounds You" (Ps 89:8).

"Righteousness and faithfulness will be a belt around His waist" (Is 11:5).

"If we are faithless, He remains faithful, for He cannot deny Himself" (2 Tm 2:13).

Can't you just feel the energy flowing from these Scriptures, buttressing your confidence in God? For God to be unfaithful would be to act contrary to His nature, and if He ever was (we are only speculating because He could never do so), then He would cease to be God. Focus again with me on the text at the top of the page. We are told God's faithfulness extends to the skies. This is the psalmist's picturesque way of expressing the fact that far above all finite comprehension is the unchanging faithfulness of God. Everything about God is vast and incomparable, including His faithfulness. He never forgets a thing, never makes a mistake, never fails to keep a promise, never falters over a decision, never retracts a statement He has made, and has never breached a contract. Every declaration He has made, every promise He has given, every covenant He has struck is bestowed by His faithful character.

Prayer

O God, how great Thou art. Great in power, great in majesty, great in love, great in mercy—great in so many things. But above all You are great in faithfulness. How I rejoice in that. Amen.

Further Study

1 Co 1:1-9; Heb 6:18; 1 Pt 4:19
What did Paul assure the Corinthians?
What is it impossible for God to do?

MARCH 22

NUMBERS 21:10–22:41

¹⁰ The Israelites set out and camped at Oboth. ¹¹ They set out from Oboth and camped at Iye-abarim in the wilderness that borders Moab on the east. ¹² From there they went and camped at Zered Valley. ¹³ They set out from there and camped on the other side of the Arnon River, in the wilderness that extends from the Amorite border, because the Arnon was the Moabite border between Moab and the Amorites. ¹⁴ Therefore it is stated in the Book of the LORD's Wars:

Waheb in Suphah
and the ravines of the Arnon,
¹⁵   even the slopes of the ravines
that extend to the site of Ar
and lie along the border of Moab.

¹⁶ From there they went to Beer, the well the LORD told Moses about, "Gather the people so I may give them water." ¹⁷ Then Israel sang this song:

Spring up, well—sing to it!
¹⁸   The princes dug the well;

The nobles of the people hollowed
it out
with a scepter and with their
staffs.

They went from the wilderness to Mattanah, ¹⁹ from Mattanah to Nahaliel, from Nahaliel to Bamoth, ²⁰ from Bamoth to the valley in the territory of Moab near the Pisgah highlands that overlook the wasteland. ²¹ Israel sent messengers to say to Sihon king of the Amorites: ²² "Let us travel through your land. We won't go into the fields or vineyards. We won't drink any well water. We will travel the King's Highway until we have traveled through your territory." ²³ But Sihon would not let Israel travel through his territory. Instead, he gathered his whole army and went out to confront Israel in the wilderness. When he came to Jahaz, he fought against Israel. ²⁴ Israel struck him with the sword and took possession of his land from the Arnon to the Jabbok, but only up to the Ammonite border, because it was fortified. ²⁵ Israel took all the cities and lived in all these Amorite cities, including Heshbon and all its villages. ²⁶ Heshbon was the city of Sihon king of the Amorites, who had fought against the former king of Moab and had taken control of all his land as far as the Arnon. ²⁷ Therefore the poets say:

Come to Heshbon, let it be
  rebuilt;
let the city of Sihon be restored.
²⁸ For fire came out of Heshbon,
a flame from the city of Sihon.
It consumed Ar of Moab,
the lords of Arnon's heights.
²⁹ Woe to you, Moab!
You have been destroyed, people
  of Chemosh!
He gave up his sons as refugees,
and his daughters into captivity
to Sihon the Amorite king.
³⁰ We threw them down;
Heshbon has been destroyed as
  far as Dibon.
We caused desolation as far as
  Nophah,
which reaches as far as Medeba.

³¹ So Israel lived in the Amorites' land. ³² After Moses sent spies to Jazer, Israel captured its villages and drove out the Amorites who were there.

³³ Then they turned and went up the road to Bashan, and Og king of Bashan came out against them with his whole army to do battle at Edrei. ³⁴ But the LORD said to Moses, "Do not fear him, for I have handed him over to you along with his whole army and his land. Do to him as you did to Sihon king of the Amorites, who lived in Heshbon." ³⁵ So they struck him, his sons, and his whole army until no one was left, and they took possession of his land.

22 The Israelites traveled on and camped in the plains of Moab near the Jordan across from Jericho. ² Now Balak son of Zippor saw all that Israel had done to the Amorites. ³ Moab was terrified of the people because they were numerous, and dreaded the Israelites. ⁴ So the Moabites said to the elders of Midian, "This horde will devour everything around us like an ox eats up the green plants in the field."

Since Balak son of Zippor was Moab's king at that time, ⁵ he sent messengers to Balaam son of Beor at Pethor, which is by the Euphrates in the land of his people. Balak said to him: "Look, a people has come out of Egypt; they cover the surface of the land and are living right across from me. ⁶ Please come and put a curse on these people for me because they are more powerful than I am. I may be able to defeat them and drive them out of the land, for I know that those you bless are blessed and those you curse are cursed."

⁷ The elders of Moab and Midian departed with fees for divination in hand. They came to Balaam and reported Balak's words to him. ⁸ He said to them, "Spend the night here, and I will give you the answer the LORD tells me." So the officials of Moab stayed with Balaam.

⁹ Then God came to Balaam and asked, "Who are these men with you?"

¹⁰ Balaam replied to God, "Balak son of Zippor, king of Moab, sent this message to me: ¹¹ 'Look, a people has come out of Egypt, and they cover the surface of the land. Now come and put a curse on them for me. I may be able to fight against them and drive them away.' "

¹² Then God said to Balaam, "You are not to go with them. You are not to curse this people, for they are blessed."

¹³ So Balaam got up the next morning and said to Balak's officials, "Go back to your land, because the LORD has refused to let me go with you."

¹⁴ The officials of Moab arose, returned to Balak, and reported, "Balaam refused to come with us."

¹⁵ Balak sent officials again who were more numerous and higher in rank than the others. ¹⁶ They came to Balaam and said to him, "This is what Balak son of Zippor says: 'Let nothing keep you from coming to me, ¹⁷ for I will greatly honor you and do whatever you ask me. So please come and put a curse on these people for me!' "

¹⁸ But Balaam responded to the servants of Balak, "If Balak were to give me his house full of silver and gold, I could

not go against the command of the LORD my God to do anything small or great. ¹⁹ Please stay here overnight as the others did, so that I may find out what else the LORD has to tell me."

²⁰ God came to Balaam at night and said to him, "Since these men have come to summon you, get up and go with them, but you must only do what I tell you." ²¹ When he got up in the morning, Balaam saddled his donkey and went with the officials of Moab.

²² But God was incensed that Balaam was going, and the Angel of the LORD took His stand on the path to oppose him. Balaam was riding his donkey, and his two servants were with him. ²³ When the donkey saw the Angel of the LORD standing on the path with a drawn sword in His hand, she turned off the path and went into the field. So Balaam hit her to return her to the path. ²⁴ Then the Angel of the LORD stood in a narrow passage between the vineyards, with a stone wall on either side. ²⁵ The donkey saw the Angel of the LORD and pressed herself against the wall, squeezing Balaam's foot against it. So he hit her once again. ²⁶ The Angel of the LORD went ahead and stood in a narrow place where there was no room to turn to the right or the left. ²⁷ When the donkey saw the Angel of the LORD, she crouched down under Balaam. So he became furious and beat the donkey with his stick.

²⁸ Then the LORD opened the donkey's mouth, and she asked Balaam, "What have I done to you that you have beaten me these three times?"

²⁹ Balaam answered the donkey, "You made me look like a fool. If I had a sword in my hand, I'd kill you now!"

³⁰ But the donkey said, "Am I not the donkey you've ridden all your life until today? Have I ever treated you this way before?"

"No," he replied.

³¹ Then the LORD opened Balaam's eyes, and he saw the Angel of the LORD standing in the path with a drawn sword in His hand. Balaam knelt and bowed with his face to the ground. ³² The Angel of the LORD asked him, "Why have you

beaten your donkey these three times? Look, I came out to oppose you, because what you are doing is evil in My sight. ³³ The donkey saw Me and turned away from Me these three times. If she had not turned away from Me, I would have killed you by now and let her live."

³⁴ Balaam said to the Angel of the LORD, "I have sinned, for I did not know that You were standing in the path to confront me. And now, if it is evil in Your sight, I will go back."

³⁵ Then the Angel of the LORD said to Balaam, "Go with the men, but you are to say only what I tell you." So Balaam went with Balak's officials.

³⁶ When Balak heard that Balaam was coming, he went out to meet him at the Moabite city on the Arnon border at the edge of his territory. ³⁷ Balak asked Balaam, "Did I not send you an urgent summons? Why didn't you come to me? Am I really not able to reward you?"

³⁸ Balaam said to him, "Look, I have come to you, but can I say anything I want? I must speak only the message God puts in my mouth." ³⁹ So Balaam went with Balak, and they came to Kiriath-huzoth. ⁴⁰ Balak sacrificed cattle and sheep, and sent for Balaam and the officials who were with him. ⁴¹ In the morning, Balak took Balaam and brought him to Bamoth-baal. From there he saw the outskirts of the people's camp.

PSALM 36:7-12

⁷ God, Your faithful love is so
    valuable
  that people take refuge in the
    shadow of Your wings.
⁸ They are filled from the
    abundance of Your house;
  You let them drink from Your
    refreshing stream,
⁹ for with You is life's fountain.
  In Your light we will see light.

¹⁰ Spread Your faithful love over
    those who know You,
  and Your righteousness over the
    upright in heart.

11 Do not let the foot of the arrogant
come near me
or the hand of the wicked drive
me away.
12 There the evildoers fall;
they have been thrown down and
cannot rise.

PROVERBS 8:27-29

27 I was there when He established
the heavens,
when He laid out the horizon on
the surface of the ocean,
28 when He placed the skies above,
when the fountains of the ocean
gushed forth,
29 when He set a limit for the sea
so that the waters would not
violate His command,
when He laid out the foundations
of the earth.

MARK 16:1-20

16 When the Sabbath was over,
Mary Magdalene, Mary the
mother of James, and Salome bought
spices, so they could go and anoint Him.
2 Very early in the morning, on the first
day of the week, they went to the tomb
at sunrise. 3 They were saying to one another, "Who will roll away the stone
from the entrance to the tomb for us?"
4 Looking up, they observed that the
stone—which was very large—had
been rolled away. 5 When they entered
the tomb, they saw a young man
dressed in a long white robe sitting on
the right side; they were amazed and
alarmed.
6 "Don't be alarmed," he told them.
"You are looking for Jesus the Nazarene,
who was crucified. He has been resurrected! He is not here! See the place
where they put Him. 7 But go, tell His

disciples and Peter, 'He is going ahead
of you to Galilee; you will see Him there
just as He told you.' "
8 So they went out and started running from the tomb, because trembling
and astonishment overwhelmed them.
And they said nothing to anyone, since
they were afraid.
[9 Early on the first day of the week,
after He had risen, He appeared first to
Mary Magdalene, out of whom He had
driven seven demons. 10 She went and
reported to those who had been with
Him, as they were mourning and weeping. 11 Yet, when they heard that He was
alive and had been seen by her, they did
not believe it. 12 Then after this, He appeared in a different form to two of
them walking on their way into the
country. 13 And they went and reported
it to the rest, who did not believe them
either.
14 Later, He appeared to the Eleven
themselves as they were reclining at the
table. He rebuked their unbelief and
hardness of heart, because they did not
believe those who saw Him after He had
been resurrected. 15 Then He said to
them, "Go into all the world and preach
the gospel to the whole creation.
16 Whoever believes and is baptized will
be saved, but whoever does not believe
will be condemned. 17 And these signs
will accompany those who believe: In
My name they will drive out demons;
they will speak in new languages; 18 they
will pick up snakes; if they should drink
anything deadly, it will never harm
them; they will lay hands on the sick,
and they will get well."
19 Then after speaking to them, the
Lord Jesus was taken up into heaven
and sat down at the right hand of God.
20 And they went out and preached
everywhere, the Lord working with
them and confirming the word by the
accompanying signs.]

Step Out in Faith

They will lay hands on the sick, and they will get well.
—MARK 16:18

Becoming intimately acquainted with the power aspect of the Holy Spirit's ministry is vital if we are to move out into the world and share with people the message of new life in Christ.

We have usually taken the words, "You will receive power when the Holy Spirit has come upon you" (Ac 1:8), as power to talk about Jesus. It is—but it is much more. It is power in general. Under that general power is the specific power to witness; but the power itself is for the total personality—the strengthening of faith, the heightening of expectancy, the flushing out of fear, the daring to believe. And one of the ways in which God seems to be leading His children to witness to their non-Christian friends in these days is by praying, in the power of the Spirit, for their physical as well as spiritual needs. Our aim in doing this should not be to try to convince those who have a "prove-it-to-me" mentality, as many of those who were eyewitnesses of Christ's healing ministry were not persuaded. It is rather to show them that Jesus Christ and the Christian faith are concerned about the physical as well as the spiritual needs of people.

If you have not yet experienced the empowering work of the Holy Spirit in your life, then be assured that such an experience awaits you as you take a step of faith toward what, up until now, has been a vast spiritual unknown. Just one more step—and you are there!

Prayer

Father, I've come too far to go back now. Take me in Your arms today, and empower me in such a way that my life of worship and witness will be entirely transformed. For Jesus' sake. Amen.

Further Study

Mt 8:1-13; 9:29-30; 17:20; Heb 11:1; Jn 6:28-29
How did the centurion show faith?
What did Jesus exclaim?

MARCH 23

*N*UMBERS 23:1–24:25

23 Then Balaam said to Balak, "Build me seven altars here and prepare seven bulls and seven rams for me." ² So Balak did as Balaam directed, and they offered a bull and a ram on each altar. ³ Balaam said to Balak, "Stay here by your burnt offering while I am gone. Maybe the LORD will meet with me. I will tell you whatever He reveals to me." So he went to a barren hill.

⁴ God met with him and Balaam said to Him, "I have arranged seven altars and offered a bull and a ram on each altar." ⁵ Then the LORD put a message in Balaam's mouth and said, "Return to Balak and say what I tell you."

⁶ So he returned to Balak, who was standing there by his burnt offering with all the officials of Moab.

⁷ Balaam proclaimed his poem:

Balak brought me from Aram;
the king of Moab, from the
eastern mountains:
"Come, put a curse on Jacob for
me;
come, denounce Israel!"
⁸ How can I curse someone God has
not cursed?
How can I denounce someone the
LORD has not denounced?
⁹ I see them from the top of rocky
cliffs,
and I watch them from the hills.
There is a people living alone;
it does not consider itself among
the nations.
¹⁰ Who has counted the dust of
Jacob
or numbered the dust clouds of
Israel?
Let me die the death of the
upright;
let the end of my life be like
theirs.

¹¹ "What have you done to me?" Balak asked Balaam. "I brought you to curse my enemies, but look, you have only blessed them!"

¹² He answered, "Shouldn't I say exactly what the LORD puts in my mouth?"

¹³ Then Balak said to him, "Please come with me to another place where you can see them. You will only see the outskirts of their camp; you won't see all of them. From there, put a curse on them for me." ¹⁴ So Balak took him to Lookout Field on top of Pisgah, built seven altars, and offered a bull and a ram on each altar.

¹⁵ Balaam said to Balak, "Stay here by your burnt offering while I seek the LORD over there."

¹⁶ The LORD met with Balaam and put a message in his mouth. Then He said, "Return to Balak and say what I tell you."

¹⁷ So he returned to Balak, who was standing there by his burnt offering with the officials of Moab. Balak asked him, "What did the LORD say?"

¹⁸ Balaam proclaimed his poem:

Balak, get up and listen;
son of Zippor, pay attention to
what I say!
¹⁹ God is not a man who lies,
or a son of man who changes His
mind.
Does He speak and not act,
or promise and not fulfill?
²⁰ I have indeed received a command
to bless;
since He has blessed, I cannot
change it.
²¹ He considers no disaster for
Jacob;
He sees no trouble for Israel.
The LORD their God is with them,
and there is rejoicing over the
King among them.
²² God brought them out of Egypt;

He is like the horns of a wild ox
for them.

23 There is no magic curse against
Jacob
and no divination against Israel.
It will now be said about Jacob
and Israel,
"What great things God has
done!"

24 A people rise up like a lioness;
They rouse themselves like a lion.
They will not lie down until they
devour the prey
and drink the blood of the slain.

25 Then Balak told Balaam, "Don't
curse them and don't bless them!"
26 But Balaam answered him, "Didn't I
tell you: Whatever the LORD says, I must
do?"
27 Again Balak said to Balaam, "Please
come. I will take you to another place.
Maybe it will be agreeable to God that
you can put a curse on them for me
there." 28 So Balak took Balaam to the
top of Peor, which overlooks the wasteland.
29 Balaam told Balak, "Build me seven
altars here and prepare seven bulls and
seven rams for me." 30 So Balak did as
Balaam said and offered a bull and a ram
on each altar.

24 Since Balaam saw that it pleased
the LORD to bless Israel, he did
not go to seek omens as on previous occasions, but turned toward the wilderness. 2 When Balaam looked up and saw
Israel encamped tribe by tribe, the
Spirit of God descended on him, 3 and
he proclaimed his poem:

The oracle of Balaam son of Beor,
the oracle of the man whose eyes
are opened,
4 the oracle of one who hears the
sayings of God,
who sees a vision from the
Almighty,
who falls into a trance with his
eyes uncovered:
5 How beautiful are your tents,
Jacob,
your dwellings, Israel.
6 they stretch out like river valleys,

like gardens beside a stream,
like aloes the LORD has planted,
like cedars beside the water.
7 Water will flow from his buckets,
and his seed will be by abundant
water.
His king will be greater than Agag,
and his kingdom will be exalted.
8 God brought him out of Egypt;
He is like the horns of a wild ox
for them.
He will feed on enemy nations
and gnaw their bones;
he will strike them with his
arrows.
9 He crouches, he lies down like a
lion
or a lioness—who dares to rouse
him?
Those who bless you will be
blessed,
and those who curse you will be
cursed.

10 Then Balak became furious with
Balaam, struck his hands together, and
said to him, "I summoned you to put a
curse on my enemies, but instead, you
have blessed them these three times.
11 Now go to your home! I said I would
reward you richly, but look, the LORD
has denied you a reward."
12 Balaam answered Balak, "Didn't I
previously tell the messengers you sent
me: 13 If Balak were to give me his
house full of silver and gold, I could not
go against the LORD's command, to do
anything good or bad of my own will? I
will say whatever the LORD says. 14 Now
I am going back to my people, but first,
let me warn you what these people will
do to your people in the future."
15 Then he proclaimed his poem:

The oracle of Balaam son of
Beor,
the oracle of the man whose eyes
are opened;
16 the oracle of one who hears the
sayings of God
and has knowledge from the Most
High,
who sees a vision from the
Almighty,

who falls into a trance with his
eyes uncovered:
17 I see him, but not now;
I perceive him, but not near.
A star will come from Jacob,
and a scepter will arise from
Israel.
He will smash the forehead of
Moab
and strike down all the Shethites.
18 Edom will become a possession;
Seir will become a possession of
its enemies,
but Israel will be triumphant.
19 One who comes from Jacob will
rule;
he will destroy the city's
survivors.

20 Then Balaam saw Amalek and proclaimed his poem:

Amalek was first among the
nations,
but his future is destruction.

21 Next he saw the Kenites and proclaimed his poem:

Your dwelling place is enduring;
your nest is set in the cliffs.
22 Kain will be destroyed
when Asshur takes you captive.

23 Once more he proclaimed his
poem:

Ah, who can live when God does
this?
24 Ships will come from the coast of
Kittim;
they will afflict Asshur and Eber,
but they too will come to
destruction.

25 Balaam then arose and went back to
his homeland, and Balak also went his
way.

PSALM 37:1-6

1 Do not be agitated by evildoers;
do not envy those who do wrong.

2 For they wither quickly like grass
and wilt like tender green plants.

3 Trust in the LORD and do good;
dwell in the land and live
securely.
4 Take delight in the LORD,
and He will give you your heart's
desires.

5 Commit your way to the LORD;
trust in Him, and He will act,
6 making your righteousness shine
like the dawn,
your justice like the noonday.

PROVERBS 8:30-31

30 I was a skilled craftsman beside
Him.
I was His delight every day,
always rejoicing before Him.
31 I was rejoicing in His inhabited
world,
delighting in the human race.

LUKE 1:1-23

1 Many have undertaken to compile a
narrative about the events that have
been fulfilled among us, 2 just as the
original eyewitnesses and servants of
the word handed them down to us. 3 It
also seemed good to me, since I have
carefully investigated everything from
the very first, to write to you in orderly
sequence, most honorable Theophilus,
4 so that you may know the certainty of
the things about which you have been
instructed.

5 In the days of King Herod of Judea,
there was a priest of Abijah's division
named Zechariah. His wife was from the
daughters of Aaron, and her name was
Elizabeth. 6 Both were righteous in
God's sight, living without blame according to all the commandments and
requirements of the Lord. 7 But they had
no children because Elizabeth could not
conceive, and both of them were well
along in years.

8 When his division was on duty and
he was serving as priest before God, 9 it

happened that he was chosen by lot, according to the custom of the priesthood, to enter the sanctuary of the Lord and burn incense. [10] At the hour of incense the whole assembly of the people was praying outside. [11] An angel of the Lord appeared to him, standing to the right of the altar of incense. [12] When Zechariah saw him, he was startled and overcome with fear. [13] But the angel said to him:

Do not be afraid, Zechariah,
because your prayer
has been heard.
Your wife Elizabeth will bear you
a son,
and you will name him John.
[14] There will be joy and delight
for you,
and many will rejoice at his birth.
[15] For he will be great in the sight
of the Lord
and will never drink wine or beer.
He will be filled
with the Holy Spirit
while still in his mother's womb.
[16] He will turn many
of the sons of Israel
to the Lord their God.
[17] And he will go before Him

in the spirit and power of Elijah,
to turn the hearts of fathers
to their children,
and the disobedient
to the understanding
of the righteous,
to make ready for the Lord
a prepared people.

[18] "How can I know this?" Zechariah asked the angel. "For I am an old man, and my wife is well along in years."
[19] The angel answered him, "I am Gabriel, who stands in the presence of God, and I was sent to speak to you and tell you this good news. [20] Now listen! You will become silent and unable to speak until the day these things take place, because you did not believe my words, which will be fulfilled in their proper time."
[21] Meanwhile, the people were waiting for Zechariah, amazed that he stayed so long in the sanctuary. [22] When he did come out, he could not speak to them. Then they realized that he had seen a vision in the sanctuary. He kept making signs to them and remained speechless. [23] When the days of his ministry were completed, he went back home.

Faithfulness, Meekness

Trust in the LORD and do what is good; dwell in the land and live securely.—PSALM 37:3

One of the fruits of the Spirit is faithfulness. A Christian in whom this fruit has developed will be completely dependable. Someone has said: "The ultimate test of a man's character is this: are there any circumstances under which he will not speak the truth? If so, the rest of his character is worthless, for basically he is unsound." Strong words. How many of us, I wonder, could pass this test? I knew a Christian worker who worked herself almost to a standstill in the cause of Christ, but she couldn't refrain from telling lies; those lies cancelled out a lot of her life's work.

Is it ever right to lie? "God is not a man who lies" (Nm 23:19). If God cannot lie, then He won't delegate to us the privilege of doing it for Him! Let's go over our lives today in the light of the Holy Spirit's presence and check to see if there are any loose ends, unfulfilled promises, or half-fulfilled tasks. If there are, let's decide to complete them.

Another fruit of the Spirit is gentleness or meekness. This word is greatly misunderstood in Christian circles, for meekness is seen by many as weakness. It brings to mind (for many) the cringing spirit of Uriah Heap, who said, "I am so very 'umble, Master Copperfield, so very 'umble." I once saw a powerful steam hammer come down so gently on an egg that it just cracked its top. That is meekness. It is divine strength and power projected in the gentlest manner.

Prayer

O Father, how I long for this quality to be seen in my life. Too often I am either too assertive or too unassertive. Give me, by the Spirit, a meekness that lets others know I am a follower of Yours. For Jesus' sake. Amen.

Further Study

Lk 19:1-28; Rv 2:10; Heb 10:23; 1 Pt 4:19; 1 Co 4:2; Jms 3:13
What was the master's response to the faithful steward?
How did he deal with the unfaithful one?

MARCH 24

*N*UMBERS 25:1–26:22

25 While Israel was staying in Acacia Grove, the people began to have sexual relations with the women of Moab. ² The women invited them to the sacrifices for their gods, and the people ate and bowed in worship to their gods. ³ So Israel aligned itself with Baal of Peor, and the LORD's anger burned against Israel. ⁴ The LORD said to Moses, "Take all the leaders of the people and execute them in broad daylight before the LORD so that His burning anger may turn away from Israel."

⁵ So Moses told Israel's judges, "Kill each of the men who aligned themselves with Baal of Peor."

⁶ An Israelite man came bringing a Midianite woman to his relatives in the sight of Moses and the whole Israelite community while they were weeping at the entrance to the tent of meeting. ⁷ When Phinehas son of Eleazar, son of Aaron the priest, saw this, he got up from the assembly, took a spear in his hand, ⁸ followed the Israelite man into the tent, and drove it through both the Israelite man and the woman—through her belly. Then the plague on the Israelites was stopped, ⁹ but those who died in the plague numbered 24,000.

¹⁰ The LORD spoke to Moses, ¹¹ "Phinehas son of Eleazar, son of Aaron the priest, has turned back My wrath from the Israelites because he was zealous among them with My zeal, so that I did not destroy the Israelites in My zeal. ¹² Therefore declare: I grant him My

covenant of peace. [13] It will be a covenant of perpetual priesthood for him and his descendants, because he was zealous for his God and made atonement for the Israelites."

[14] The name of the slain Israelite man, who was struck dead with the Midianite woman, was Zimri son of Salu, the leader of a Simeonite ancestral house. [15] The name of the slain Midianite woman was Cozbi, the daughter of Zur, a tribal head of an ancestral house in Midian.

[16] The LORD told Moses: [17] "Attack the Midianites and strike them dead. [18] For they attacked you with the treachery that they used against you in the Peor incident. They did the same in the case involving their sister Cozbi, daughter of the Midianite leader who was killed the day the plague came at Peor."

26 After the plague, the LORD said to Moses and Eleazar son of Aaron the priest, [2] "Take a census of the entire Israelite community by their ancestral houses of those 20 years old or more who can serve in Israel's army."

[3] So Moses and Eleazar the priest said to them in the plains of Moab by the Jordan across from Jericho, [4] "Take a census of those 20 years old or more, as the LORD had commanded Moses and the Israelites who came out of the land of Egypt."

[5] Reuben was the firstborn of Israel. Reuben's descendants:
the Hanochite clan from Hanoch;
the Palluite clan from Pallu;
[6] the Hezronite clan from Hezron;
the Carmite clan from Carmi.
[7] These were the Reubenite clans, and their registered men numbered 43,730.
[8] The son of Pallu was Eliab.
[9] The sons of Eliab were Nemuel, Dathan, and Abiram.
(It was Dathan and Abiram, chosen by the community, who fought against Moses and Aaron; they and Korah's followers fought against the LORD. [10] The earth opened its mouth and swallowed

them with Korah, when his followers died and the fire consumed 250 men. They serve as a warning sign. [11] The sons of Korah, however, did not die.)

[12] Simeon's descendants by their clans:
the Nemuelite clan from Nemuel;
the Jaminite clan from Jamin;
the Jachinite clan from Jachin;
[13] the Zerahite clan from Zerah;
the Shaulite clan from Shaul.
[14] These were the Simeonite clans, numbering 22,200 men.

[15] Gad's descendants by their clans:
the Zephonite clan from Zephon;
the Haggite clan from Haggi;
the Shunite clan from Shuni;
[16] the Oznite clan from Ozni;
the Erite clan from Eri;
[17] the Arodite clan from Arod;
the Arelite clan from Areli.
[18] These were the Gadite clans numbered by their registered men: 40,500.

[19] Judah's sons included Er and Onan, but they died in the land of Canaan. [20] Judah's descendants by their clans:
the Shelanite clan from Shelah;
the Perezite clan from Perez;
the Zerahite clan from Zerah.
[21] The descendants of Perez:
the Hezronite clan from Hezron;
the Hamulite clan from Hamul.
[22] These were Judah's clans numbered by their registered men: 76,500.

𝒫SALM 37:7-13

[7] Be silent before the LORD and wait expectantly for Him;
do not be agitated by one who prospers in his way,
by the man who carries out evil plans.

[8] Refrain from anger and give up your rage;

do not be agitated—it can only
bring harm.
9 For evildoers will be destroyed,
but those who hope in the LORD
will inherit the land.

10 A little while, and the wicked will
be no more;
though you look for him, he will
not be there.
11 But the humble will inherit the
land
and will enjoy abundant
prosperity.
12 The wicked schemes against the
righteous
and gnashes his teeth at him.
13 The Lord laughs at him
because He sees that his day is
coming.

PROVERBS 8:32-33

32 And now, my sons, listen to me;
those who keep my ways are
happy.
33 Listen to instruction and be wise;
don't ignore it.

LUKE 1:24-56

24 After these days his wife Elizabeth
conceived and kept herself in seclusion
for five months. She said, 25 "The Lord
has done this for me. He has looked
with favor in these days to take away my
disgrace among the people."
26 In the sixth month, the angel
Gabriel was sent by God to a town in
Galilee called Nazareth, 27 to a virgin engaged to a man named Joseph, of the
house of David. The virgin's name was
Mary. 28 And the angel came to her and
said, "Rejoice, favored woman! The
Lord is with you." 29 But she was deeply
troubled by this statement, wondering
what kind of greeting this could be.
30 Then the angel told her:

Do not be afraid, Mary,
for you have found favor
with God.

31 Now listen:
You will conceive and give birth to
a son,
and you will call His name JESUS.
32 He will be great
and will be called
the Son of the Most High,
and the Lord God will give Him
the throne of His father David.
33 He will reign over the house
of Jacob forever,
and His kingdom will have no end.

34 Mary asked the angel, "How can
this be, since I have not been intimate
with a man?"
35 The angel replied to her:

The Holy Spirit will come
upon you,
and the power of the Most High
will overshadow you.
Therefore the holy One to be born
will be called the Son of God.

36 And consider your relative Elizabeth—even she has conceived a son in
her old age, and this is the sixth month
for her who was called barren. 37 For
nothing will be impossible with God."
38 "I am the Lord's slave," said Mary.
"May it be done to me according to your
word." Then the angel left her.
39 In those days Mary set out and hurried to a town in the hill country of
Judah 40 where she entered Zechariah's
house and greeted Elizabeth. 41 When
Elizabeth heard Mary's greeting, the
baby leaped inside her, and Elizabeth
was filled with the Holy Spirit. 42 Then
she exclaimed with a loud cry:

You are the most blessed
of women,
and your child will be blessed!

43 How could this happen to me, that
the mother of my Lord should come to
me? 44 For you see, when the sound of
your greeting reached my ears, the baby
leaped for joy inside me! 45 She who has
believed is blessed because what was
spoken to her by the Lord will be fulfilled!"

⁴⁶ And Mary said:

My soul proclaims the greatness
of the Lord,
⁴⁷ and my spirit has rejoiced in God
my Savior,
⁴⁸ because He has looked with favor
on the humble condition
of His slave.
Surely, from now on
all generations
will call me blessed,
⁴⁹ because the Mighty One
has done great things for me,
and His name is holy.
⁵⁰ His mercy is from generation
to generation
on those who fear Him.
⁵¹ He has done a mighty deed
with His arm;

He has scattered the proud
because of the thoughts
of their hearts;
⁵² He has toppled the mighty
from their thrones
and exalted the lowly.
⁵³ He has satisfied the hungry
with good things
and sent the rich away empty.
⁵⁴ He has helped His servant
Israel,
mindful of His mercy,
⁵⁵ just as He spoke to our
ancestors,
to Abraham and his descendants
forever.

⁵⁶ And Mary stayed with her about three months; then she returned to her home.

"The Ground Is Level"

"I am the Lord's slave," said Mary. "May it be done to me according to your word."—LUKE 1:38

The coming of the Holy Spirit not only made all places and persons equal, but canceled out all distinctions based on blood or special privilege. Acts 1:14 says that among those who devoted themselves to prayer were "Mary the mother of Jesus, and His brothers." How easy it would have been to have established a privileged line through those who were closely related to the Lord. If the Holy Spirit had set these people aside in a certain way and had come to them and them alone, then Christianity would have merely followed the family line for all succeeding generations. However, Mary, blessed though she was, waited together with the others for the coming of the Holy Spirit. And when she received Him, she received Him on the same basis as the others—by faith in Christ as Savior and Lord. At the great moment of the Holy Spirit's coming, no one was singled out for special favor, no distinctions were made based on blood, and no one was identified as being superior or inferior. All were equal.

"At the foot of the cross," said Dr. Abernathy, when a judge and a Chinese laundryman stood before him to be received into the membership of his church, "the ground is level." In Islam, the descendants of the prophet Mohammed are greatly honored. In Christianity, no such hierarchy was ever attempted. Why? Because it was canceled out by the coming of the Spirit. A new hierarchy came into being. The blood of God's Son has made it possible for us all to become sons of God.

Prayer

O God, my Father, in giving Your Holy Spirit to me, You have opened the Highest to the lowest, the Greatest to the least. I belong to the twice-born nobility. Hallelujah!

Further Study

Lk 1:38-55; 2:51; Jn 2:3-5; 19-25
List some of the characteristics of Jesus' mother.
Does she have a special place within the church?

MARCH 25

NUMBERS 26:23-65

23 Issachar's descendants by their clans:
the Tolaite clan from Tola;
the Punite clan from Puvah;
24 the Jashubite clan from Jashub;
the Shimronite clan from Shimron.
25 These were Issachar's clans numbered by their registered men: 64,300.

26 Zebulun's descendants by their clans:
the Seredite clan from Sered;
the Elonite clan from Elon;
the Jahleelite clan from Jahleel.
27 These were the Zebulunite clans numbered by their registered men: 60,500.

28 Joseph's descendants by their clans from Manasseh and Ephraim:
29 Manasseh's descendants:
the Machirite clan from Machir. Machir fathered Gilead;
the Gileadite clan from Gilead.
30 These were Gilead's descendants:
the Iezerite clan from Iezer;
the Helekite clan from Helek;
31 The Asrielite clan from Asriel;
the Shechemite clan from Shechem;
32 the Shemidaite clan from Shemida;
the Hepherite clan from Hepher;
33 Zelophehad son of Hepher had no sons—only daughters. The names of Zelophehad's daughters were Mahlah, Noah, Hoglah, Milcah, and Tirzah.
34 These were Manasseh's clans, numbered by their registered men: 52,700.
35 These were Ephraim's descendants by their clans:
the Shuthelahite clan from Shuthelah;
the Becherite clan from Becher;
the Tahanite clan from Tahan.
36 These were Shuthelah's descendants:
the Eranite clan from Eran.
37 These were the Ephraimite clans numbered by their registered men: 32,500.

These were Joseph's descendants by their clans.

38 Benjamin's descendants by their clans:
the Belaite clan from Bela;
the Ashbelite clan from Ashbel;
the Ahiramite clan from Ahiram;
39 the Shuphamite clan from Shupham;
the Huphamite clan from Hupham.
40 Bela's descendants from Ard and Naaman:
the Ardite clan from Ard;
the Naamite clan from Naaman.
41 These were the Benjaminite clans numbered by their registered men: 45,600.

42 These were Dan's descendants by their clans:
the Shuhamite clan from Shuham.
These were the clans of Dan by their clans.
43 All the Shuhamite clans numbered by their registered men were 64,400.

44 Asher's descendants by their clans:
the Imnite clan from Imnah;
the Ishvite clan from Ishvi;
the Beriite clan from Beriah.
45 From Beriah's descendants:
the Heberite clan from Heber;
the Malchielite clan from Malchiel.
46 And the name of Asher's daughter was Serah.
47 These were the Asherite clans numbered by their registered men: 53,400.

48 Naphtali's descendants by their clans:
the Jahzeelite clan from Jahzeel;
the Gunite clan from Guni;
49 the Jezerite clan from Jezer;
the Shillemite clan from Shillem.
50 These were the Naphtali clans numbered by their registered men: 45,400.

51 These registered Israelite men numbered 601,730.

52 The LORD spoke to Moses, 53 "The land is to be divided among them as an inheritance based on the number of names. 54 Increase the inheritance for a large tribe, and decrease it for a small one. Each is to be given its inheritance according to those who were registered in it. 55 The land must be divided by lot; they will receive an inheritance according to the names of their ancestral tribes. 56 Each inheritance will be divided by lot among the larger and smaller tribes."

57 These were the Levites registered by their clans:
the Gershonite clan from Gershon;
the Kohathite clan from Kohath;
the Merarite clan from Merari.
58 These were the Levite family groups:
the Libnite clan,
the Hebronite clan,
the Mahlite clan,
the Mushite clan,
and the Korahite clan.

Kohath was the ancestor of Amram. 59 The name of Amram's wife was Jochebed, a descendant of Levi, born to Levi in Egypt. She bore to Amram: Aaron, Moses, and their sister Miriam. 60 Nadab, Abihu, Eleazar, and Ithamar were born to Aaron, 61 but Nadab and Abihu died when they presented unauthorized fire before the LORD. 62 Those registered were 23,000, every male one month old or more; they were not registered among the other Israelites, because no inheritance was given to them among the Israelites.

63 These were the ones registered by Moses and Eleazar the priest when they registered the Israelites on the plains of Moab by the Jordan across from Jericho. 64 But among them there was not one of those who had been registered by Moses and Aaron the priest when they registered the Israelites in the Wilderness of Sinai. 65 For the LORD had said to

them that they would all die in the wilderness. None of them was left except Caleb son of Jephunneh and Joshua son of Nun.

PSALM 37:14-20

14 The wicked have drawn the sword
    and strung the bow
  to bring down the afflicted and
    needy
  and to slaughter those whose way
    is upright.
15 Their swords will enter their own
    hearts,
  and their bows will be broken.

16 Better the little that the righteous
    man has
  than the abundance of many
    wicked people.
17 For the arms of the wicked will be
    broken,
  but the LORD supports the
    righteous.

18 The LORD watches over the
    blameless all their days,
  and their inheritance will last
    forever.
19 They will not be disgraced in
    times of adversity;
  they will be satisfied in days of
    hunger.

20 But the wicked will perish;
  the LORD's enemies, like the glory
    of the pastures, will fade
    away—
  they will fade away like smoke.

PROVERBS 8:34-36

34 Anyone who listens to me is happy,
  watching at my doors every day,
  waiting by the posts of my
    doorway.
35 For the one who finds me finds
    life
  and obtains favor from the LORD,
36 but the one who sins against me
    harms himself;
  all who hate me love death."

LUKE 1:57-80

57 Now the time had come for Elizabeth to give birth, and she had a son. 58 Then her neighbors and relatives heard that the Lord had shown her His great mercy, and they rejoiced with her.
59 When they came to circumcise the child on the eighth day, they were going to name him Zechariah, after his father. 60 But his mother responded, "No! He will be called John."
61 Then they said to her, "None of your relatives has that name." 62 So they motioned to his father to find out what he wanted him to be called. 63 He asked for a writing tablet and wrote:

HIS NAME IS JOHN

And they were all amazed. 64 Immediately his mouth was opened and his tongue set free, and he began to speak, praising God. 65 Fear came on all those who lived around them, and all these things were being talked about throughout the hill country of Judea. 66 All who heard about him took it to heart, saying, "What then will this child become?" For, indeed, the Lord's hand was with him.
67 Then his father Zechariah was filled with the Holy Spirit and prophesied:

68 Praise the Lord, the God of Israel,
  because He has visited
  and provided redemption
    for His people.
69 He has raised up a horn
    of salvation for us
  in the house of His servant David,
70 just as He spoke by the mouth
    of His holy prophets
    in ancient times;
71 salvation from our enemies
  and from the clutches of those
    who hate us.
72 He has dealt mercifully
    with our fathers
  and remembered
    His holy covenant—
73 the oath that He swore
    to our father Abraham.

He has given us the privilege,
74 since we have been rescued
from our enemies' clutches,
to serve Him without fear
75 in holiness and righteousness
in His presence all our days.
76 And child, you will be called
a prophet of the Most High,
for you will go before the Lord
to prepare His ways,
77 to give His people knowledge
of salvation
through the forgiveness
of their sins.

78 Because of our God's merciful
compassion,
the Dawn from on high will visit
us
79 to shine on those who live
in darkness
and the shadow of death,
to guide our feet into the way
of peace.

80 The child grew up and became
spiritually strong, and he was in the wilderness until the day of his public appearance to Israel.

They Will Be Satisfied

They will be satisfied in days of hunger.
—PSALM 37:19

Jesus directs us to ask God for our daily bread because we have a need to ask Him. It does us good to ask, for asking increases our awareness of our dependency upon God and builds a defense against ingratitude.

I find it greatly encouraging that the God of creation, who is infinitely holy and who holds the universe in His hand, cares that my physical needs are met. This implies that God regards our bodies as important. He designed them and is interested in the way they function.

Some Christians regard it as "unspiritual" to pray about the needs of the body, but, as Jesus pointed out, this is really where our personal petitions ought to begin. While Jesus endeavored to get His hearers to keep their values straight by saying that the spiritual was all important—"Seek first the kingdom of God" (Mt 6:33)—He nevertheless put the body in its rightful place, as being a matter of great concern. The Father, we are told, guarantees our physical needs if we seek first the kingdom of God.

Most of the promises in the Bible have to do with spiritual truth, but never to the exclusion of the physical. How much spiritual use would we be to our heavenly Father if He didn't meet our basic physical needs? This is why I do not fear the future. In whatever way people might mismanage the resources which God has placed in the earth, I have confidence in the truth of the verse before us today: "They will be satisfied in days of hunger."

Prayer

Father, help me not to get bogged down in wrong attitudes about the physical factors of my life, for they are a part of me. Teach me to live, physically and spiritually, as one. For Jesus' sake. Amen.

Further Study

Jn 6:1-15; Ps 37:25; Jl 2:24; Lk 6:38
What was the disciples' attitude?
How did Jesus show interest in physical needs?

MARCH 26

*N*UMBERS 27:1–28:31

27 The daughters of Zelophehad approached; Zelophehad was the son of Hepher, son of Gilead, son of Machir, son of Manasseh from the clans of Manasseh, the son of Joseph. These were the names of his daughters: Mahlah, Noah, Hoglah, Milcah, and Tirzah. ² They stood before Moses, Eleazar the priest, the leaders, and the entire community at the entrance to the tent of meeting and said, ³ "Our father died in the wilderness, but he was not among Korah's followers, who gathered together against the LORD. Instead, he died because of his own sin, and he had no sons. ⁴ Why should the name of our father be taken away from his clan? Since he had no son, give us property among our father's brothers."

⁵ Moses brought their case before the LORD, ⁶ and the LORD answered him, ⁷ "What Zelophehad's daughters say is correct. You are to give them hereditary property among their father's brothers and transfer their father's inheritance to them. ⁸ Tell the Israelites: When a man dies without having a son, transfer his inheritance to his daughter. ⁹ If he has no daughter, give his inheritance to his brothers. ¹⁰ If he has no brothers, give his inheritance to his father's brothers. ¹¹ If his father has no brothers, give his inheritance to the nearest relative of his clan, and he will take posses-

sion of it. This is to be a statutory ordinance for the Israelites as the LORD commanded Moses."

¹² Then the LORD said to Moses, "Go up this mountain of the Abarim range and see the land that I have given the Israelites. ¹³ After you have seen it, you will also be gathered to your people, as Aaron your brother was. ¹⁴ When the community quarreled in the Wilderness of Zin, both of you rebelled against My command to show My holiness in their sight at the waters." Those were the waters of Meribah of Kadesh in the Wilderness of Zin.

¹⁵ So Moses appealed to the LORD, ¹⁶ "May the LORD, the God of the spirits of all flesh, appoint a man over the community ¹⁷ who will go out before them and come back in before them, and who will bring them out and bring them in, so that the LORD's community won't be like sheep without a shepherd."

¹⁸ The LORD replied to Moses, "Take Joshua son of Nun, a man who has the Spirit in him, and lay your hands on him. ¹⁹ Have him stand before Eleazar the priest and the whole community, and commission him in their sight. ²⁰ Confer some of your authority on him so that the entire Israelite community will obey him. ²¹ He will stand before Eleazar who will consult the LORD for him with the decision of the Urim. He and all the Israelites with him, even the entire community, will go out and come back in at his command."

[22] Moses did as the LORD commanded him. He took Joshua, had him stand before Eleazar the priest and the entire community, [23] laid his hands on him, and commissioned him, as the LORD had spoken through Moses.

28 The LORD spoke to Moses, [2] "Command the Israelites and say to them: Be sure to present to Me at its appointed time My offering and My food as My fire offering, a pleasing aroma to Me. [3] And say to them: This is the fire offering you are to present to the LORD:

"Each day present two unblemished year-old male lambs as a regular burnt offering. [4] Offer one lamb in the morning and the other lamb at twilight, [5] along with two quarts of fine flour for a grain offering mixed with a quart of beaten olive oil. [6] It is a regular burnt offering established at Mount Sinai for a pleasing aroma, a fire offering to the LORD. [7] The drink offering is to be a quart with each lamb. Pour out the offering of beer to the LORD in the sanctuary area. [8] Offer the second lamb at twilight, along with the same kind of grain offering and drink offering as in the morning. It is a fire offering, a pleasing aroma to the LORD.

[9] "On the Sabbath day present two unblemished year-old male lambs, four quarts of fine flour mixed with oil as a grain offering, and its drink offering. [10] It is the burnt offering for every Sabbath, in addition to the regular burnt offering and its drink offering.

[11] "At the beginning of each of your months present a burnt offering to the LORD: two young bulls, one ram, seven male lambs a year old—all unblemished— [12] with six quarts of fine flour mixed with oil as a grain offering for each bull, four quarts of fine flour mixed with oil as a grain offering for the ram, [13] and two quarts of fine flour mixed with oil as a grain offering for each lamb. It is a burnt offering, a pleasing aroma, a fire offering to the LORD. [14] Their drink offerings are to be two quarts of wine with each bull, one and a third quarts with the ram, and one quart with each male lamb. This is the monthly burnt offering for all the months of the year. [15] And one male goat is to be offered as a sin offering to the LORD, in addition to the regular burnt offering with its drink offering.

[16] "The Passover to the LORD comes in the first month, on the fourteenth day of the month. [17] On the fifteenth day of this month there will be a festival; unleavened bread is to be eaten for seven days. [18] On the first day there is to be a sacred assembly; you are not to do any daily work. [19] Present a fire offering, a burnt offering to the LORD: two young bulls, one ram, and seven male lambs a year old. Your animals are to be unblemished. [20] The grain offering with them is to be of fine flour mixed with oil; offer six quarts with each bull and four quarts with the ram. [21] Offer two quarts with each of the seven lambs [22] and one male goat for a sin offering to make atonement for yourselves. [23] Offer these with the morning burnt offering that is part of the regular burnt offering. [24] You are to offer the same food each day for seven days as a fire offering, a pleasing aroma to the LORD. It is to be offered with its drink offering and the regular burnt offering. [25] On the seventh day you are to hold a sacred assembly; you are not to do any daily work.

[26] "On the day of firstfruits, you are to hold a sacred assembly when you present an offering of new grain to the LORD at your Festival of Weeks; you are not to do any daily work. [27] Present a burnt offering for a pleasing aroma to the LORD: two young bulls, one ram, and seven male lambs a year old, [28] with their grain offering of fine flour mixed with oil, six quarts with each bull, four quarts with the ram, [29] and two quarts with each of the seven lambs [30] and one male goat to make atonement for yourselves. [31] Offer them with their drink offerings in addition to the regular burnt offering and its grain offering. Your animals are to be unblemished.

*P*SALM 37:21-26

[21] The wicked borrows and does not repay,

but the righteous is gracious and
giving.
²² Those who are blessed by Him
will inherit the land,
but those cursed by Him will be
destroyed.
²³ A man's steps are established by
the LORD,
and He takes pleasure in his way.
²⁴ Though he falls, he will not be
overwhelmed,
because the LORD holds his hand.

²⁵ I have been young and now I am
old,
yet I have not seen the righteous
abandoned
or his children begging bread.
²⁶ He is always generous, always
lending,
and his children are a blessing.

PROVERBS 9:1-2

9 Wisdom has built her house;
she has carved out her seven
pillars.
² She has prepared her meat; she
has mixed her wine;
she has also set her table.

LUKE 2:1-20

2 In those days a decree went out
from Caesar Augustus that the
whole empire should be registered.
² This first registration took place while
Quirinius was governing Syria. ³ So
everyone went to be registered, each to
his own town.
⁴ And Joseph also went up from the
town of Nazareth in Galilee, to Judea, to
the city of David, which is called Bethlehem, because he was of the house and
family line of David, ⁵ to be registered
along with Mary, who was engaged to

him and was pregnant. ⁶ While they
were there, the time came for her to
give birth. ⁷ Then she gave birth to her
firstborn Son, and she wrapped Him
snugly in cloth and laid Him in a feeding
trough—because there was no room for
them at the inn.
⁸ In the same region, shepherds were
staying out in the fields and keeping
watch at night over their flock. ⁹ Then
an angel of the Lord stood before them,
and the glory of the Lord shone around
them, and they were terrified. ¹⁰ But the
angel said to them, "Don't be afraid, for
look, I proclaim to you good news of
great joy that will be for all the people:
¹¹ today a Savior, who is Messiah the
Lord, was born for you in the city of
David. ¹² This will be the sign for you:
you will find a baby wrapped snugly in
cloth and lying in a feeding trough."
¹³ Suddenly there was a multitude of
the heavenly host with the angel, praising God and saying:

¹⁴ Glory to God
in the highest heaven,
and peace on earth to people
He favors!

¹⁵ When the angels had left them and
returned to heaven, the shepherds said
to one another, "Let's go straight to
Bethlehem and see what has happened,
which the Lord has made known to us."
¹⁶ They hurried off and found both
Mary and Joseph, and the baby who was
lying in the feeding trough. ¹⁷ After seeing them, they reported the message
they were told about this child, ¹⁸ and all
who heard it were amazed at what the
shepherds said to them. ¹⁹ But Mary was
treasuring up all these things in her heart
and meditating on them. ²⁰ The shepherds returned, glorifying and praising
God for all they had seen and heard,
just as they had been told.

Come into My House

Wisdom has built her house;
she has carved out her seven pillars.

——PROVERBS 9:1

Our text for today tells us that wisdom is like a house built on seven pillars. There are two ways of interpreting this text. One view says that both wisdom and folly have a house to which humankind is invited. Wisdom has a much larger house than folly, being built upon "seven pillars"—a sign in ancient times of wealth, status and prestige. There is no doubt that this is one meaning of the text, but the other view is that wisdom has seven major aspects.

Never in the history of the human race have there been so many problems, so much confusion, and so many conflicting philosophies of how to live. Those who lack wisdom do not have the perspectives that enable them to discern the connection between cause and effect, and therefore they don't understand what they are stumbling over, or, if they do avoid problems, they don't understand why they avoid them. We need wisdom to live, and Proverbs shows us how.

Prayer

Gracious and loving heavenly Father, grant that as I expose myself day by day to the truths of Your Word, wisdom may be more deeply imprinted into my spirit. In Jesus' name I pray. Amen.

Further Study

Jb 28:1; Ps 119:169; Ec 1:13; 8:16-17
What question did Job ponder?
What conclusion did he come to?

MARCH 27

*N*UMBERS 29:1–30:16

29 "You are to hold a sacred assembly in the seventh month, on the first day of the month, and you are not to do any daily work. This will be a day of jubilation for you. ² Offer a burnt offering as a pleasing aroma to the LORD: one young bull, one ram, seven male lambs a year old—all unblemished— ³ with their grain offering of fine flour mixed with oil, six quarts with the bull, four quarts with the ram, ⁴ and two quarts with each of the seven male lambs. ⁵ Also offer one male goat as a sin offering to make atonement for yourselves. ⁶ These are in addition to the monthly and regular burnt offerings with their grain offerings and drink offerings. They are a pleasing aroma, a fire offering to the LORD.

⁷ "You are to hold a sacred assembly on the tenth day of this seventh month and practice self-denial; you must not do any work. ⁸ Present a burnt offering to the LORD, a pleasing aroma: one young bull, one ram, and seven male lambs a year old. All your animals are to be unblemished. ⁹ Their grain offering is to be of fine flour mixed with oil, six quarts with the bull, four quarts with the ram, ¹⁰ and two quarts with each of the seven lambs. ¹¹ Offer one male goat for a sin offering. The regular burnt offering with its grain offering and drink offerings are in addition to the sin offering of atonement.

¹² "You are to hold a sacred assembly on the fifteenth day of the seventh month; you must not do any daily work. You are to celebrate a seven-day festival for the LORD. ¹³ Present a burnt offering, a fire offering as a pleasing aroma to the LORD: 13 young bulls, two rams, and 14 male lambs a year old. They are to be unblemished. ¹⁴ Their grain offering is to be of fine flour mixed with oil, six

quarts with each of the 13 bulls, four quarts with each of the two rams, ¹⁵ and two quarts with each of the 14 lambs. ¹⁶ Also offer one male goat as a sin offering. These are in addition to the regular burnt offering with its grain and drink offerings.

¹⁷ "On the second day present 12 young bulls, two rams, and 14 male lambs a year old—all unblemished— ¹⁸ with their grain and drink offerings for the bulls, rams, and lambs, in proportion to their number. ¹⁹ Also offer one male goat as a sin offering. These are in addition to the regular burnt offering with its grain and drink offerings.

²⁰ "On the third day present 11 bulls, two rams, 14 male lambs a year old—all unblemished— ²¹ with their grain and drink offerings for the bulls, rams, and lambs, in proportion to their number. ²² Also offer one male goat as a sin offering. These are in addition to the regular burnt offering with its grain and drink offerings.

²³ "On the fourth day present 10 bulls, two rams, 14 male lambs a year old—all unblemished— ²⁴ with their grain and drink offerings for the bulls, rams, and lambs, in proportion to their number. ²⁵ Also offer one male goat as a sin offering. These are in addition to the regular burnt offering with its grain and drink offerings.

²⁶ "On the fifth day present nine bulls, two rams, 14 male lambs a year old—all unblemished— ²⁷ with their grain and drink offerings for the bulls, rams, and lambs, in proportion to their number. ²⁸ Also offer one male goat as a sin offering. These are in addition to the regular burnt offering with its grain and drink offerings.

²⁹ "On the sixth day present eight bulls, two rams, 14 male lambs a year old—all unblemished— ³⁰ with their grain and drink offerings for the bulls,

rams, and lambs, in proportion to their number. [31] Also offer one male goat as a sin offering. These are in addition to the regular burnt offering with its grain and drink offerings.

[32] "On the seventh day present seven bulls, two rams, and 14 male lambs a year old—all unblemished— [33] with their grain and drink offerings for the bulls, rams, and lambs, in proportion to their number. [34] Also offer one male goat as a sin offering. These are in addition to the regular burnt offering with its grain and drink offerings.

[35] "On the eighth day you are to hold a solemn assembly; you are not to do any daily work. [36] Present a burnt offering, a fire offering as a pleasing aroma to the LORD: one bull, one ram, seven male lambs a year old—all unblemished— [37] with their grain and drink offerings for the bulls, rams, and lambs, in proportion to their number. [38] Also offer one male goat as a sin offering. These are in addition to the regular burnt offering with its grain and drink offerings.

[39] "You must offer these to the LORD at your appointed times in addition to your vow and freewill offerings, whether burnt, grain, drink, or fellowship offerings." [40] So Moses told the Israelites everything the LORD had commanded him.

30 Moses told the leaders of the Israelite tribes, "This is what the LORD has commanded: [2] When a man makes a vow to the LORD or swears an oath to put himself under an obligation, he must not break his word; he must do whatever he has promised.

[3] "When a woman in her father's house during her youth makes a vow to the LORD or puts herself under an obligation, [4] and her father hears about her vow or the obligation she put herself under, and he says nothing to her, all her vows and every obligation she put herself under are binding. [5] But if her father prohibits her on the day he hears about it, none of her vows and none of the obligations she put herself under are binding. The LORD will absolve her because her father has prohibited her.

[6] "If a woman marries while her vows or the rash commitment she herself made are binding, [7] and her husband hears about it and says nothing to her when he finds out, her vows are binding, and the obligations she put herself under are binding. [8] But if her husband prohibits her when he hears about it, he will cancel her vow that is binding or the rash commitment she herself made, and the LORD will forgive her.

[9] "Every vow a widow or divorcée puts herself under is binding on her. [10] "If a woman in her husband's house has made a vow or put herself under an obligation with an oath, [11] and her husband hears about it, says nothing to her, and does not prohibit her, all her vows are binding, and every obligation she put herself under is binding. [12] But if her husband cancels them on the day he hears about it, nothing that came from her lips, whether her vows or her obligation, is binding. Her husband has canceled them, and the LORD will absolve her. [13] Her husband may confirm or cancel any vow or any sworn obligation to deny herself. [14] If her husband says nothing at all to her from day to day, he confirms all her vows and obligations, which are binding. He has confirmed them because he said nothing to her when he heard about them. [15] But if he cancels them after he hears about them, he will be responsible for her commitment."

[16] These are the statutes that the LORD commanded Moses concerning the relationship between a man and his wife, or between a father and his daughter in his house during her youth.

··

PSALM 37:27-33

[27] Turn away from evil and do good,
and dwell there forever.
[28] For the LORD loves justice
and will not abandon His faithful ones.
They are kept safe forever,
but the children of the wicked will be destroyed.
[29] The righteous will inherit the land
and dwell in it permanently.

30 The mouth of the righteous utters
wisdom;
his tongue speaks what is just.
31 The instruction of his God is in
his heart;
his steps do not falter.

32 The wicked lies in wait for the
righteous
and seeks to kill him;
33 the LORD will not leave him in his
hand
or allow him to be condemned
when he is judged.

PROVERBS 9:3-6

3 She has sent out her servants;
she calls out from the highest
points of the city:
4 "Whoever is inexperienced, enter
here!"
To the one who lacks sense, she
says,
5 "Come, eat my bread,
and drink the wine I have mixed.
6 Leave inexperience behind, and
you will live;
pursue the way of understanding.

LUKE 2:21-38

21 When the eight days were completed for His circumcision, He was named JESUS—the name given by the angel before He was conceived. 22 And when the days of their purification according to the law of Moses were finished, they brought Him up to Jerusalem to present Him to the Lord 23 (just as it is written in the law of the Lord: **Every firstborn male will be dedicated to the Lord**) 24 and to offer a sacrifice (according to what is stated in the law of the Lord: **a pair of turtledoves or two young pigeons**).

25 There was a man in Jerusalem whose name was Simeon. This man was righteous and devout, looking forward to Israel's consolation, and the Holy Spirit was on him. 26 It had been revealed to him by the Holy Spirit that he would not see death before he saw the Lord's Messiah. 27 Guided by the Spirit, he entered the temple complex. When the parents brought in the child Jesus to perform for Him what was customary under the law, 28 Simeon took Him up in his arms, praised God, and said:

29 Now, Master,
You can dismiss Your slave
in peace,
according to Your word.
30 For my eyes have seen
Your salvation.
31 You have prepared it
in the presence of all peoples—
32 a light for revelation
to the Gentiles
and glory to Your people Israel.

33 His father and mother were amazed at what was being said about Him. 34 Then Simeon blessed them and told His mother Mary: "Indeed, this child is destined to cause the fall and rise of many in Israel and to be a sign that will be opposed— 35 and a sword will pierce your own soul—that the thoughts of many hearts may be revealed."

36 There was also a prophetess, Anna, a daughter of Phanuel, of the tribe of Asher. She was well along in years, having lived with her husband seven years after her marriage, 37 and was a widow for 84 years. She did not leave the temple complex, serving God night and day with fastings and prayers. 38 At that very moment, she came up and began to thank God and to speak about Him to all who were looking forward to the redemption of Jerusalem.

The "Inner-Stances"

*For the LORD loves justice and will not abandon
His faithful ones. They are kept safe forever.*—PSALM 37:28

Why is it that while the same things can happen to us all, they may not have the same effect upon us all? The same thing happening to two different people may have entirely different effects. Why should this be so? It depends not so much on the circumstances, but on the "inner-stances"—or, in other words, our inner attitudes. As someone has said, "What life does to us in the long run depends on what life finds in us." Life's blows can make some people irritable and bitter; others they sweeten and refine—the same events, but with opposite effects.

The Gospels tell us that there were three crosses set up on Calvary on the first Good Friday. The same event happened to three different people, but look at the different results. One thief complained and blamed Jesus for not saving Himself and them; the other thief recognized his own unworthiness, repented of it, and found an open door to Paradise. Jesus, of course, saw it as the climax of His earthly achievements and made it the fulcrum on which He moved the world.

What counts, therefore, is not so much what happens to us, but what we do with it. The same sunshine falling on two different plants can cause one to wither and die, while the other will blossom and flourish. And why? It all depends on the response the plants make. Although, of course, they both need water, one plant is more suited to hot sunshine than the other and therefore responds with more life and growth, while the other shrivels up and dies.

Prayer

Gracious heavenly Father, write this precept upon my heart so that I shall never forget it: it's not so much what happens to me, but what I do with it that is important. Thank You, Father. Amen.

Further Study

2 Co 11:21-29; 2 Tm 4:7; Pr 2:8; 2 Co 8–9
What was Paul's testimony?
How did he sum up his life?

MARCH 28

NUMBERS 31:1-54

31 The LORD spoke to Moses, ² "Execute vengeance for the Israelites against the Midianites. After that, you will be gathered to your people."

³ So Moses spoke to the people, "Equip some of your men for war. They will go against Midian to inflict the LORD's vengeance on them. ⁴ Send 1,000 men to war from each Israelite tribe." ⁵ So 1,000 were recruited from each Israelite tribe out of the thousands in Israel—12,000 equipped for war. ⁶ Moses sent 1,000 from each tribe to war. They went with Phinehas son of Eleazar the priest, in whose care were the holy objects and signal trumpets.

⁷ They waged war against Midian, as the LORD had commanded Moses, and killed every male. ⁸ Along with the others slain by them, they killed the Midianite kings—Evi, Rekem, Zur, Hur, and Reba, the five kings of Midian. They also killed Balaam son of Beor with the sword. ⁹ The Israelites took the Midianite women and their children captive, and they plundered all their cattle, flocks, and property. ¹⁰ Then they burned all the cities where the Midianites lived, as well as all their encampments, ¹¹ and took away all the spoils of war and the captives, both human and animal. ¹² They brought the prisoners, animals, and spoils of war to Moses, Eleazar the priest, and the Israelite community at the camp on the plains of Moab by the Jordan across from Jericho.

¹³ Moses, Eleazar the priest, and all the leaders of the community went to meet them outside the camp. ¹⁴ But Moses became furious with the officers, the commanders of thousands and commanders of hundreds, who were returning from the military campaign. ¹⁵ "Have you let every female live?" he asked them. ¹⁶ "Yet they are the ones who, at Balaam's advice, incited the Israelites to unfaithfulness against the LORD in the Peor incident, so that the plague came against the LORD's community. ¹⁷ So now, kill all the male children and kill every woman who has had sexual relations with a man, ¹⁸ but keep alive for yourselves all the young females who have not had sexual relations.

¹⁹ "You are to remain outside the camp for seven days. All of you and your prisoners who have killed a person or touched the dead are to purify yourselves on the third day and the seventh day. ²⁰ Also purify everything: garments, leather goods, things made of goat hair, and every article of wood."

²¹ Then Eleazar the priest said to the soldiers who had gone to battle, "This is the legal statute the LORD commanded Moses: ²² Only the gold, silver, bronze, iron, tin, and lead— ²³ everything that can withstand fire—put through fire, and it will be clean. It must still be purified with the purification water. Anything that cannot withstand fire, put through the water. ²⁴ On the seventh day wash your clothes, and you will be clean. After that you may enter the camp."

²⁵ The LORD told Moses, ²⁶ "You, Eleazar the priest, and the family leaders of the community are to take a count of what was captured, human and animal. ²⁷ Then divide the captives between the troops who went out to war and the entire community. ²⁸ Set aside a tribute for the LORD from what belongs to the fighting men who went out to war: one out of every 500 humans, cattle, donkeys, sheep, and goats. ²⁹ Take the tribute from their half and give it to Eleazar the priest as a contribution to the LORD. ³⁰ From the Israelites' half, take one out of every 50 from the people, cattle, donkeys, sheep, and goats, all the livestock, and give them to the Levites who

perform the duties of the LORD's tabernacle."

[31] So Moses and Eleazar the priest did as the LORD commanded Moses. [32] The captives remaining from the plunder the army had taken totaled:

675,000 sheep and goats,
[33] 72,000 cattle,
[34] 61,000 donkeys,
[35] and 32,000 people, all the females who had not had sexual relations with a man.

[36] The half portion for those who went out to war numbered:

337,500 sheep and goats,
[37] and the tribute to the LORD was 675
from the sheep and goats;
[38] from the 36,000 cattle,
the tribute to the LORD was 72;
[39] from the 30,500 donkeys,
the tribute to the LORD was 61;
[40] and from the 16,000 people,
the tribute to the LORD was 32 people.

[41] Moses gave the tribute to Eleazar the priest as a contribution for the LORD, as the LORD had commanded Moses.
[42] From the Israelites' half, which Moses separated from the men who fought, [43] the community's half was:

337,500 sheep and goats,
[44] 36,000 cattle,
[45] 30,500 donkeys,
[46] and 16,000 people.

[47] Moses took one out of every 50, selected from the people and the livestock from the Israelites' half. He gave them to the Levites who perform the duties of the LORD's tabernacle, as the LORD had commanded him.
[48] The officers who were over the thousands of the army, the commanders of thousands and of hundreds, approached Moses [49] and told him, "Your servants have taken a census of the fighting men under our command, and not one of us is missing. [50] So we have

presented to the LORD an offering of the gold articles each man found—armlets, bracelets, rings, earrings, and necklaces—to make atonement for ourselves before the LORD."
[51] Moses and Eleazar the priest received from them all the articles made out of gold. [52] All the gold of the contribution they offered to the LORD, from the commanders of thousands and of hundreds, was 420 pounds. [53] Each of the soldiers had taken plunder for himself. [54] Moses and Eleazar the priest received the gold from the commanders of thousands and of hundreds and brought it into the tent of meeting as a memorial for the Israelites before the LORD.

PSALM 37:34-40

[34] Wait for the LORD and keep His way,
and He will exalt you to inherit the land.
You will watch when the wicked are destroyed.

[35] I have seen a wicked, violent man well-rooted like a flourishing native tree.
[36] Then I passed by and noticed he was gone;
I searched for him, but he could not be found.

[37] Watch the blameless and observe the upright,
for the man of peace will have a future.
[38] But transgressors will all be eliminated;
the future of the wicked will be destroyed.

[39] The salvation of the righteous is from the LORD,
their refuge in a time of distress.
[40] The LORD helps and delivers them;
He will deliver them from the wicked and will save them
because they take refuge in Him.

PROVERBS 9:7-9

7 The one who corrects a mocker
will bring dishonor on
himself;
the one who rebukes a wicked
man will get hurt.
8 Don't rebuke a mocker, or he will
hate you;
rebuke a wise man, and he will
love you.
9 Instruct a wise man, and he will
be wiser still;
teach a righteous man, and he will
learn more.

LUKE 2:39-52

39 When they had completed everything according to the law of the Lord,
they returned to Galilee, to their own
town of Nazareth. 40 The boy grew up
and became strong, filled with wisdom,
and God's grace was on Him.
41 Every year His parents traveled to
Jerusalem for the Passover Festival.
42 When He was 12 years old, they went
up according to the custom of the festival. 43 After those days were over, as
they were returning, the boy Jesus
stayed behind in Jerusalem, but His parents did not know it. 44 Assuming He
was in the traveling party, they went a
day's journey. Then they began looking
for Him among their relatives and
friends. 45 When they did not find Him,
they returned to Jerusalem to search for
Him. 46 After three days, they found
Him in the temple complex sitting
among the teachers, listening to them
and asking them questions. 47 And all
those who heard Him were astounded
at His understanding and His answers.
48 When His parents saw Him, they were
astonished, and His mother said to Him,
"Son, why have You treated us like this?
Your father and I have been anxiously
searching for You."
49 "Why were you searching for Me?"
He asked them. "Didn't you know that I
had to be in my Father's house?" 50 But
they did not understand what He said to
them.
51 Then He went down with them and
came to Nazareth and was obedient to
them. His mother kept all these things
in her heart. 52 And Jesus increased in
wisdom and stature, and in favor with
God and with people.

The Tenses of Salvation

*The salvation of the righteous is from the LORD,
their refuge in a time of distress.*—PSALM 37:39

Satan will take advantage of every situation that comes his way in order to disable a
Christian, and he will not hesitate to use chaotic world conditions and problems to oppose the
mind. But God's answer to this is the helmet of salvation.

In 1 Thessalonians 5:8, Paul is not talking about the salvation of the soul when he says, "We
must be sober and put the armor of faith and love on our chests, and put on a helmet of the
hope of salvation." He is not referring to salvation as regeneration or conversion. This is the mistake that many make when attempting to interpret this verse. They say: "Whenever the devil
attacks your mind and seeks to oppress it, remind yourself that you have been saved." Well,
there is nothing wrong with that, of course. This explanation is mistaken, however, not because
it is untrue, but because it does not go far enough.

The best way to interpret any verse of Scripture is with another verse of Scripture. Thus this
text from 1 Thessalonians throws a shaft of light on Paul's statement in Ephesians 6:17: "Take

the helmet of salvation," for it shows salvation, not just as something in the past, but something that is also a future "hope." He uses the word salvation the same way in Romans when he writes: "Our salvation is nearer than when we first believed" (Rm 13:11).

In the Bible, the word salvation has three distinct tenses—past, present, and future. At conversion, we are saved from the penalty of sin. At present, day by day, we are being saved from the power of sin. And one day in the future, we will be saved from the presence of sin. It is to the future Paul is looking when he invites us to put on the helmet of salvation.

Prayer

O Father, thank You for reminding me of the tenses of salvation. I see that in order to live effectively, I must view the present tense by the future tense. Help me lay hold on this. In Jesus' name. Amen.

Further Study

Ps 27:1-14; Is 12:2; 25:9
What was the psalmist's conviction?
What was the prophet proclaiming?

MARCH 29

NUMBERS 32:1-42

32 The Reubenites and Gadites had a very large number of livestock. When they surveyed the lands of Jazer and Gilead, they saw that the region was a good one for livestock. ² So the Gadites and Reubenites came to Moses, Eleazar the priest, and the leaders of the community and said: ³ "The territory of Ataroth, Dibon, Jazer, Nimrah, Heshbon, Elealeh, Sebam, Nebo, and Beon, ⁴ which the LORD struck down before the community of Israel, is good land for livestock, and your servants own livestock." ⁵ They said, "If we have found favor in your sight, let this land be given to your servants as a possession. Don't make us cross the Jordan."

⁶ But Moses asked the Gadites and Reubenites, "Should your brothers go to war while you stay here? ⁷ Why are you discouraging the Israelites from crossing into the land the LORD has given them? ⁸ That's what your fathers did when I sent them from Kadesh-barnea to see the land. ⁹ After they went up as far as Eshcol Valley and saw the land, they discouraged the Israelites from entering the land the LORD had given them. ¹⁰ So the LORD's anger burned that day, and He swore an oath: ¹¹ 'Because they did not follow Me completely, none of the men 20 years old or more who came up from Egypt will see the land I swore to give Abraham, Isaac, and Jacob— ¹² none except Caleb son of Jephunneh the Kenizzite and Joshua son of Nun, because they did follow the LORD completely.' ¹³ The LORD's anger

burned against Israel, and He made them wander in the wilderness 40 years until the whole generation that had done evil in the LORD's sight was gone. ¹⁴ And here you, a brood of sinners, stand in your fathers' place adding even more to the LORD's burning anger against Israel. ¹⁵ If you turn back from following Him, He will once again leave this people in the wilderness, and you will destroy all of them."

¹⁶ Then they approached him and said, "We want to build sheepfolds here for our livestock and cities for our dependents. ¹⁷ But we will arm ourselves and be ready to go ahead of the Israelites until we have brought them into their place. Meanwhile, our dependents will remain in the fortified cities because of the inhabitants of the land. ¹⁸ We will not return to our homes until each of the Israelites has taken possession of his inheritance. ¹⁹ Yet we will not have an inheritance with them across the Jordan and beyond, because our inheritance will be across the Jordan to the east."

²⁰ Moses replied to them, "If you do this—if you arm yourselves for battle before the LORD, ²¹ and every one of your armed men crosses the Jordan before the LORD until He has driven His enemies from His presence, ²² and the land is subdued before the LORD—afterwards you may return and be free from obligation to the LORD and to Israel. And this land will belong to you as a possession before the LORD. ²³ But if you don't do this, you will certainly sin against the LORD; be sure your sin will catch up with you. ²⁴ Build cities for your dependents and folds for your flocks, but do what you have promised."

²⁵ The Gadites and Reubenites answered Moses, "Your servants will do just as my lord commands. ²⁶ Our little children, wives, livestock, and all our animals will remain here in the cities of Gilead, ²⁷ but your servants are equipped for war before the LORD and will go across to the battle as my lord orders."

²⁸ So Moses gave orders about them to Eleazar the priest, Joshua son of Nun, and the family leaders of the Israelite tribes. ²⁹ Moses told them, "If the Gadites and Reubenites cross the Jordan with you, every man in battle formation before the LORD, and the land is subdued before you, you are to give them the land of Gilead as a possession. ³⁰ But if they don't go across with you in battle formation, they must accept land in Canaan with you."

³¹ The Gadites and Reubenites replied, "What the LORD has spoken to your servants is what we will do. ³² We will cross over in battle formation before the LORD into the land of Canaan, but we will keep our hereditary possession across the Jordan."

³³ So Moses gave them—the Gadites, Reubenites, and half the tribe of Manasseh son of Joseph—the kingdom of Sihon king of the Amorites and the kingdom of Og king of Bashan, the land including its cities with the territories surrounding them. ³⁴ The Gadites rebuilt Dibon, Ataroth, Aroer, ³⁵ Atroth-shophan, Jazer, Jogbehah, ³⁶ Beth-nimrah, and Beth-haran as fortified cities, and built sheepfolds. ³⁷ The Reubenites rebuilt Heshbon, Elealeh, Kiriathaim, ³⁸ as well as Nebo and Baal-meon (whose names were changed), and Sibmah. They gave names to the cities they rebuilt.

³⁹ The descendants of Machir son of Manasseh went to Gilead, captured it, and drove out the Amorites who were there. ⁴⁰ So Moses gave Gilead to the clan of Machir son of Manasseh, and they settled in it. ⁴¹ Jair, a descendant of Manasseh, went and captured their villages, which he renamed Jair's Villages. ⁴² Nobah went and captured Kenath with its villages and called it Nobah after his own name.

PSALM 38:1-8

¹ LORD, do not punish me in Your anger
or discipline me in Your wrath.
² For Your arrows have sunk into me,
and Your hand has pressed down on me.

3 There is no soundness in my body
   because of Your indignation;
 there is no health in my bones
   because of my sin.
4 For my sins have flooded over my
   head;
 they are a burden too heavy for
   me to bear.
5 My wounds are foul and festering
   because of my foolishness.
6 I am bent over and brought low;
   all day long I go around in
   mourning.
7 For my loins are full of burning
   pain,
 and there is no health in my body.
8 I am faint and severely crushed;
   I groan because of the anguish of
   my heart.

PROVERBS 9:10-12

10 The fear of the LORD is the
   beginning of wisdom,
 and the knowledge of the Holy
   One is understanding.
11 For by Wisdom your days will be
   many,
 and years will be added to your life.
12 If you are wise, you are wise for
   your own benefit;
 if you mock, you alone will bear
   the consequences."

LUKE 3:1-20

3 In the fifteenth year of the reign of
   Tiberius Caesar, while Pontius Pilate
was governor of Judea, Herod was tetrarch of Galilee, his brother Philip
tetrarch of the region of Iturea and
Trachonitis, and Lysanias tetrarch of
Abilene, ² during the high priesthood of
Annas and Caiaphas, God's word came
to John the son of Zechariah in the
wilderness. ³ He went into all the vicinity of the Jordan, preaching a baptism of
repentance for the forgiveness of sins,
⁴ as it is written in the book of the
words of the prophet Isaiah:

**A voice of one crying out
in the wilderness:**

**"Prepare the way for the Lord;
make His paths straight!**
5 **Every valley will be filled,
 and every mountain and hill
   will be made low;
 the crooked will become
   straight,
 the rough ways smooth,**
6 **and everyone will see
   the salvation of God."**

⁷ He then said to the crowds who
came out to be baptized by him, "Brood
of vipers! Who warned you to flee from
the coming wrath? ⁸ Therefore produce
fruit consistent with repentance. And
don't start saying to yourselves, 'We
have Abraham as our father,' for I tell
you that God is able to raise up children
for Abraham from these stones! ⁹ Even
now the ax is ready to strike the root of
the trees! Therefore every tree that
doesn't produce good fruit will be cut
down and thrown into the fire."
¹⁰ "What then should we do?" the
crowds were asking him.
¹¹ He replied to them, "The one who
has two shirts must share with someone
who has none, and the one who has
food must do the same."
¹² Tax collectors also came to be baptized, and they asked him, "Teacher,
what should we do?"
¹³ He told them, "Don't collect any
more than what you have been authorized."
¹⁴ Some soldiers also questioned him:
"What should we do?"
 He said to them, "Don't take money
from anyone by force or false accusation; be satisfied with your wages."
¹⁵ Now the people were waiting expectantly, and all of them were debating in their minds whether John might
be the Messiah. ¹⁶ John answered them
all, "I baptize you with water, but One
is coming who is more powerful than I.
I am not worthy to untie the strap of
His sandals. He will baptize you with
the Holy Spirit and fire. ¹⁷ His winnowing shovel is in His hand to clear His
threshing floor and gather the wheat
into His barn, but the chaff He will
burn up with a fire that never goes

out." [18] Then, along with many other exhortations, he proclaimed good news to the people. [19] But Herod the tetrarch, being rebuked by him about Herodias, his brother's wife, and about all the evil things Herod had done, [20] added this to everything else—he locked John up in prison.

The Place to Kill a Cobra

The fear of the LORD is the beginning of wisdom,
and the knowledge of the Holy One is understanding.
—PROVERBS 9:10

The most effective place to deal with sin is at the "eye" stage. That may mean the actual seeing of evil with the physical eye, or seeing it in imagination with the mental eye. "The best place to kill a cobra," runs an old Indian proverb, "is in its egg."

Most sin follows on from a failure to kill it at the place of desire—the "eye." Matthew 6:22 says, "The eye is the lamp of the body. If your eye is good, your whole body will be full of light." When an evil thought comes, try blinking your eyes very rapidly and you will discover that the thought is broken up. It is a voluntary act demanding the attention of the will, and thus draws attention away from the evil thought. Add to this action the simple prayer that Peter prayed when he was about to sink into the waters of the Sea of Galilee: "Lord, save me!"

Another thing you can do when a sinful thought or desire invades your mind is to change whatever you are doing in order to focus your attention elsewhere. An old Welsh miner I knew told me many years ago that when he was a young man, he was out walking one day and was attacked with an evil thought. He deliberately picked up a heavy stone and carried it back home. The attention necessary to carry the load made him forget the thought.

These ideas may not work for everyone, but they have certainly worked for some. Another way to deal with an evil thought or desire is to focus your attention on a mental picture of Christ on the cross. It is hard to think of evil and Him at the same time. They are incompatibilities.

Prayer

O Lord, help me to outmaneuver any sinful thoughts that come into my mind. Give me the kind of mind in which You can be at home. This I ask in Jesus' peerless and precious name. Amen.

Further Study

Is 33:10-17; Ps 119:59; Pr 15:26; Rm 8:6
What is the result of refusing to contemplate evil?
How will you guard your eyes today?

MARCH 30

NUMBERS 33:1-56

33 These were the stages of the Israelites' journey when they went out of the land of Egypt by their military divisions under the leadership of Moses and Aaron. ² At the LORD's command, Moses wrote down the starting points for the stages of their journey; these are the stages listed by their starting points:

³ They departed from Rameses in the first month, on the fifteenth day of the month. On the day after the Passover the Israelites went out triumphantly in the sight of all the Egyptians. ⁴ Meanwhile, the Egyptians were burying every firstborn male the LORD had struck down among them, for the LORD had executed judgment against their gods. ⁵ The Israelites departed from Rameses and camped at Succoth. ⁶ They departed from Succoth and camped at Etham, which is on the edge of the wilderness. ⁷ They departed from Etham and turned back to Pi-hahiroth, which faces Baal-zephon, and they camped before Migdol. ⁸ They departed from Pi-hahiroth and crossed through the middle of the sea into the wilderness. They took a three-day journey into the Wilderness of Etham and camped at Marah. ⁹ They departed from Marah and came to Elim. There were 12 springs of water and 70 date palms at Elim, so they camped there. ¹⁰ They departed from Elim and camped by the Red Sea. ¹¹ They departed from the Red Sea and camped in the Wilderness of Sin. ¹² They departed from the Wilder-

ness of Sin and camped in Dophkah. ¹³ They departed from Dophkah and camped at Alush. ¹⁴ They departed from Alush and camped at Rephidim, where there was no water for the people to drink. ¹⁵ They departed from Rephidim and camped in the Wilderness of Sinai. ¹⁶ They departed from the Wilderness of Sinai and camped at Kibroth-hattaavah. ¹⁷ They departed from Kibroth-hattaavah and camped at Hazeroth. ¹⁸ They departed from Hazeroth and camped at Rithmah. ¹⁹ They departed from Rithmah and camped at Rimmon-perez. ²⁰ They departed from Rimmon-perez and camped at Libnah. ²¹ They departed from Libnah and camped at Rissah. ²² They departed from Rissah and camped at Kehelathah. ²³ They departed from Kehelathah and camped at Mount Shepher. ²⁴ They departed from Mount Shepher and camped at Haradah. ²⁵ They departed from Haradah and camped at Makheloth. ²⁶ They departed from Makheloth and camped at Tahath. ²⁷ They departed from Tahath and camped at Terah. ²⁸ They departed from Terah and camped at Mithkah. ²⁹ They departed from Mithkah and camped at Hashmonah. ³⁰ They departed from Hashmonah and camped at Moseroth. ³¹ They departed from Moseroth and camped at Bene-jaakan. ³² They departed from Bene-jaakan and camped at Hor-haggidgad. ³³ They departed from Hor-haggidgad and camped at Jotbathah.

³⁴ They departed from Jotbathah and camped at Abronah. ³⁵ They departed from Abronah and camped at Ezion-geber. ³⁶ They departed from Ezion-geber and camped in the Wilderness of Zin (that is, Kadesh). ³⁷ They departed from Kadesh and camped at Mount Hor on the edge of the land of Edom. ³⁸ At the LORD's command, Aaron the priest climbed Mount Hor and died there on the first day of the fifth month in the fortieth year after the Israelites went out of the land of Egypt. ³⁹ Aaron was 123 years old when he died on Mount Hor. ⁴⁰ At that time the Canaanite king of Arad, who lived in the Negev in the land of Canaan, heard the Israelites were coming. ⁴¹ They departed from Mount Hor and camped at Zalmonah. ⁴² They departed from Zalmonah and camped at Punon. ⁴³ They departed from Punon and camped at Oboth. ⁴⁴ They departed from Oboth and camped at Iye-abarim on the border of Moab. ⁴⁵ They departed from Iyim and camped at Dibon-gad. ⁴⁶ They departed from Dibon-gad and camped at Almon-diblathaim. ⁴⁷ They departed from Almon-diblathaim and camped in the Abarim range facing Nebo. ⁴⁸ They departed from the Abarim range and camped on the plains of Moab by the Jordan across from Jericho. ⁴⁹ They camped by the Jordan from Beth-jeshimoth to Acacia Meadows on the plains of Moab.

⁵⁰ The LORD spoke to Moses in the plains of Moab by the Jordan across from Jericho, ⁵¹ "Tell the Israelites: When you cross the Jordan into the land of Canaan, ⁵² you must drive out all the inhabitants of the land before you, destroy all their stone images and cast images, and demolish all their high places. ⁵³ You are to take possession of the land and settle in it because I have given you the land to possess. ⁵⁴ You are to receive the land as an inheritance by lot according to your clans. Increase the inheritance for a large clan and decrease it for a small one. Whatever place the lot indicates for someone will be his. You will receive an inheritance according to your ancestral tribes. ⁵⁵ But if you don't drive out the inhabitants of the land before you, those you allow to remain will become thorns in your eyes and in your sides; they will harass you in the land where you will live. ⁵⁶ And what I had planned to do to them, I will do to you."

PSALM 38:9-14

⁹ LORD, my every desire is known to You;
my sighing is not hidden from You.
¹⁰ My heart races, my strength leaves me,
and even the light of my eyes has faded.
¹¹ My loved ones and friends stand back from my affliction,
and my relatives stand at a distance.
¹² Those who seek my life set traps,
and those who want to harm me threaten to destroy me;
they plot treachery all day long.

¹³ I am like a deaf person; I do not hear.
I am like a speechless person who does not open his mouth.
¹⁴ I am like a man who does not hear and has no arguments in his mouth.

PROVERBS 9:13-15

¹³ The woman Folly is rowdy;
she is gullible and knows nothing.
¹⁴ She sits by the doorway of her house,
on a seat at the highest point of the city,
¹⁵ calling to those who pass by,
who go straight ahead on their paths:

𝓛UKE 3:21-38

21 When all the people were baptized, Jesus also was baptized. As He was praying, heaven opened, 22 and the Holy Spirit descended on Him in a physical appearance like a dove. And a voice came from heaven:

You are My beloved Son.
I take delight in You!

23 As He began His ministry, Jesus was about 30 years old and was thought to be the

son of Joseph, son of Heli,
24 son of Matthat, son of Levi,
son of Melchi, son of Jannai,
son of Joseph, 25 son
of Mattathias,
son of Amos, son of Nahum,
son of Esli, son of Naggai,
26 son of Maath, son
of Mattathias,
son of Semein, son of Josech,
son of Joda, 27 son of Joanan,
son of Rhesa, son
of Zerubbabel,
son of Shealtiel, son of Neri,

28 son of Melchi, son of Addi,
son of Cosam, son of Elmadam,
son of Er, 29 son of Joshua,
son of Eliezer, son of Jorim,
son of Matthat, son of Levi,
30 son of Simeon, son of Judah,
son of Joseph, son of Jonam,
son of Eliakim, 31 son of Melea,
son of Menna, son of Mattatha,
son of Nathan, son of David,
32 son of Jesse, son of Obed,
son of Boaz, son of Salmon,
son of Nahshon, 33 son
of Amminadab,
son of Ram, son of Hezron,
son of Perez, son of Judah,
34 son of Jacob, son of Isaac,
son of Abraham, son of Terah,
son of Nahor, 35 son of Serug,
son of Reu, son of Peleg,
son of Eber, son of Shelah,
36 son of Cainan, son of Arphaxad,
son of Shem, son of Noah,
son of Lamech, 37 son
of Methuselah,
son of Enoch, son of Jared,
son of Mahalaleel, son of Cainan,
38 son of Enos, son of Seth,
son of Adam, son of God.

The Lyre Pine

*My heart races, my strength leaves me . . . My loved ones
and friends stand back from my affliction.*—PSALM 38:10-11

I want to share with you the lessons taught me by a radiant Christian woman on how to overcome frustration. In case of doubt, let me make clear that the woman concerned was not a thick-skinned individual who cared for nothing and nobody, but rather a highly sensitive person who knew how to turn every test into a testimony.

Here is her prescription for overcoming frustration.

First, realize that Christians aren't exempt from facing problems. It is true that Christians are exempted from many self-inflicted pains which non-Christians bring on themselves through wrong attitudes, wrong moral choices, wrong behavior, and so on. But apart from this, every Christian is as subject as a non-Christian to accidents, sickness, and even death. Some years ago a plane full of non-Christian Indian seamen crashed into the Alps; a few days later, fifty-eight Christians, fresh from a conference, crashed in the same Alps.

Secondly, fix in your mind that the Christian answer is along the line of using whatever comes—

justice or injustice, pain or pleasure, compliment or criticism. Ever heard of a lyre pine? The lyre pine is a pine tree whose top is shaped like a harp, with a number of branches forming the top, instead of one straight branch. It is produced, they say, by a calamity such as a storm or a lightning flash striking off the original top. Frustrated, it then puts up a whole series of tops stretched on a more or less horizontal bar. This, too, can happen to us—if we let it. Calamity can turn dullness into music, a lone top into a lyre.

Prayer

Father, let this truth sink deeply into my spirit so that I will be able to turn all my lone tops into lyres. Quicken within me today the sense that with You, I can overcome everything—including frustration. Amen.

Further Study

1 Pt 1:1-7; 4:12-13; Mt 5:45; Jn 16:33; 2 Co 4:17; Rm 5:3
What is the sequence of God's dealings in our lives?
How is this working out in your life?

MARCH 31

NUMBERS 34:1–35:34

34 The LORD spoke to Moses, ² "Command the Israelites and say to them: When you enter the land of Canaan, it will be allotted to you as an inheritance with these borders:

³ Your southern side will be from the Wilderness of Zin along the boundary of Edom. Your southern border on the east will begin at the east end of the Dead Sea. ⁴ Your border will turn south of the Ascent of Akrabbim, proceed to Zin, and end south of Kadesh-barnea. It will go to Hazar-addar and proceed to Azmon. ⁵ The border will turn from Azmon to the Brook of Egypt, where it will end at the Mediterranean Sea.

⁶ Your western border will be the coastline of the Mediterranean Sea; this will be your western border.

⁷ This will be your northern border: From the Mediterranean Sea draw a line to Mount Hor; ⁸ from Mount Hor draw a line to the entrance of Hamath, and the border will reach Zedad. ⁹ Then the border will go to Ziphron and end at Hazar-enan. This will be your northern border.

¹⁰ For your eastern border, draw a line from Hazar-enan to Shepham. ¹¹ The border will go down from Shepham to Riblah east of Ain. It will continue down and reach the eastern slope of the Sea of Chinnereth. ¹² Then the border will go

down to the Jordan and end at the Dead Sea. This will be your land defined by its borders on all sides."

¹³ So Moses commanded the Israelites, "This is the land you are to receive by lot as an inheritance, which the LORD commanded to be given to the nine and a half tribes. ¹⁴ For the tribe of the Reubenites and the tribe of the Gadites have received their inheritance according to their ancestral houses, and half the tribe of Manasseh has received its inheritance. ¹⁵ The two and a half tribes have received their inheritance across the Jordan from Jericho, eastward toward the sunrise."

¹⁶ The LORD spoke to Moses, ¹⁷ "These are the names of the men who are to distribute the land as an inheritance for you: Eleazar the priest and Joshua son of Nun. ¹⁸ Take one leader from each tribe to distribute the land. ¹⁹ These are the names of the men:

Caleb son of Jephunneh from the tribe of Judah;
20 Shemuel son of Ammihud from the tribe of Simeon;
21 Elidad son of Chislon from the tribe of Benjamin;
22 Bukki son of Jogli, a leader from the tribe of Dan;
23 from the sons of Joseph:
Hanniel son of Ephod, a leader from the tribe of Manasseh,
24 Kemuel son of Shiphtan, a leader from the tribe of Ephraim;
25 Eli-zaphan son of Parnach, a leader from the tribe of Zebulun;
26 Paltiel son of Azzan, a leader from the tribe of Issachar;
27 Ahihud son of Shelomi, a leader from the tribe of Asher;
28 Pedahel son of Ammihud, a leader from the tribe of Naphtali."

²⁹ These are the ones the LORD commanded to distribute the inheritance to the Israelites in the land of Canaan.

35 The LORD again spoke to Moses in the plains of Moab by the Jordan across from Jericho: ² "Command the Israelites to give cities out of their hereditary property for the Levites to live in and pastureland around the cities. ³ The cities will be for them to live in, and their pasturelands will be for their herds, flocks, and all their other animals. ⁴ The pasturelands of the cities you are to give the Levites will extend from the city wall 500 yards on every side. ⁵ Measure 1,000 yards outside the city for the east side, 1,000 yards for the south side, 1,000 yards for the west side, and 1,000 yards for the north side, with the city in the center. This will belong to them as pasturelands for the cities.

⁶ "The cities you give the Levites will include six cities of refuge, which you must provide so that the one who kills someone may flee there; in addition to these, give 42 other cities. ⁷ The total number of cities you give the Levites will be 48, along with their pasturelands. ⁸ Of the cities that you give from the Israelites' territory, you should take more from a larger tribe and less from a smaller one. Each tribe is to give some of its cities to the Levites in proportion to the inheritance it receives."

⁹ The LORD said to Moses, ¹⁰ "Speak to the Israelites and tell them: When you cross the Jordan into the land of Canaan, ¹¹ designate cities to serve as cities of refuge for you, so that a person who kills someone unintentionally may flee there. ¹² You will have the cities as a refuge from the avenger, so that the one who kills someone will not die until he stands trial before the assembly. ¹³ The cities you select will be your six cities of refuge. ¹⁴ Select three cities across the Jordan and three cities in the land of Canaan to be cities of refuge. ¹⁵ These six cities will serve as a refuge for the Israelites and for the foreigner or temporary resident among them, so that anyone who kills a person unintentionally may flee there.

¹⁶ "If anyone strikes a person with an iron object and death results, he is a murderer; the murderer must be put to death. ¹⁷ If a man has in his hand a stone capable of causing death and strikes another man and he dies, the murderer

must be put to death. ¹⁸ If a man has in his hand a wooden object capable of causing death and he dies, the murderer must be put to death. ¹⁹ The avenger of blood himself is to kill the murderer; when he finds him, he is to kill him. ²⁰ Likewise, if anyone in hatred pushes a person or throws an object at him with malicious intent and he dies, ²¹ or if in hostility he strikes him with his hand and he dies, the one who struck him must be put to death; he is a murderer. The avenger of blood is to kill the murderer when he finds him.

²² "But if anyone suddenly pushes a person without hostility or throws any object at him without malicious intent ²³ or drops a stone without looking that could kill a person and he dies, but he was not his enemy and wasn't trying to harm him, ²⁴ the assembly is to judge between the slayer and the avenger of blood according to these ordinances. ²⁵ The assembly is to protect the one who kills someone from the hand of the avenger of blood. Then the assembly will return him to the city of refuge he fled to, and he must live there until the death of the high priest who was anointed with the holy oil.

²⁶ "If the one who kills someone ever goes outside the border of the city of refuge he fled to, ²⁷ and the avenger of blood finds him outside the border of his city of refuge and kills him, the avenger will not be guilty of bloodshed, ²⁸ for the one who killed a person was supposed to live in his city of refuge until the death of the high priest. Only after the death of the high priest may the one who has killed a person return to the land he possesses. ²⁹ These instructions will be a statutory ordinance for you throughout your generations wherever you live.

³⁰ "If anyone kills a person, the murderer is to be put to death based on the word of witnesses. But no one is to be put to death based on the testimony of one witness. ³¹ You are not to accept a ransom for the life of a murderer who is guilty of killing someone; he must be put to death. ³² Neither should you accept a ransom for the person who flees

to his city of refuge, allowing him to return and live in the land before the death of the high priest.

³³ "Do not defile the land where you are, for bloodshed defiles the land, and there can be no atonement for the land because of the blood that is shed on it, except by the blood of the person who shed it. ³⁴ Do not make the land unclean where you live and where I reside; for I, the Lord, reside among the Israelites."

PSALM 38:15-22

¹⁵ I hope in You, Lord;
You will answer, Lord my God.
¹⁶ For I said, "Don't let them rejoice over me—
those who are arrogant toward me when I stumble."
¹⁷ For I am about to fall,
and my pain is constantly with me.
¹⁸ So I confess my guilt;
I am anxious because of my sin.
¹⁹ But my enemies are vigorous and powerful;
many hate me for no reason.
²⁰ Those who repay evil for good
attack me for pursuing good.

²¹ Lord, do not abandon me;
my God, do not be far from me.
²² Hurry to help me,
Lord, my Savior.

PROVERBS 9:16-18

¹⁶ "Whoever is inexperienced, enter here!"
To the one who lacks sense, she says,
¹⁷ "Stolen water is sweet,
and bread eaten secretly is tasty!"
¹⁸ But he doesn't know that the departed spirits are there,
that her guests are in the depths of Sheol.

LUKE 4:1-21

4 Then Jesus returned from the Jordan, full of the Holy Spirit, and was led by the Spirit in the wilderness

² for 40 days to be tempted by the Devil. He ate nothing during those days, and when they were over, He was hungry. ³ The Devil said to Him, "If You are the Son of God, tell this stone to become bread." ⁴ But Jesus answered him, "It is written: Man must not live on bread alone." ⁵ So he took Him up and showed Him all the kingdoms of the world in a moment of time. ⁶ The Devil said to Him, "I will give You their splendor and all this authority, because it has been given over to me, and I can give it to anyone I want. ⁷ If You, then, will worship me, all will be Yours." ⁸ And Jesus answered him, "It is written:

Worship the Lord your God,
and Him serve Him only."

⁹ So he took Him to Jerusalem, had Him stand on the pinnacle of the temple, and said to Him, "If You are the Son of God, throw Yourself down from here. ¹⁰ For it is written:

He will give His angels orders
    concerning you,
to protect you, ¹¹ and
they will support you
    with their hands,
so that you will not strike
your foot against a stone."

¹² And Jesus answered him, "It is said: Do not test the Lord your God." ¹³ After the Devil had finished every temptation, he departed from Him for a time.

¹⁴ Then Jesus returned to Galilee in the power of the Spirit, and news about Him spread throughout the entire vicinity. ¹⁵ He was teaching in their synagogues, being acclaimed by everyone. ¹⁶ He came to Nazareth, where He had been brought up. As usual, He entered the synagogue on the Sabbath day and stood up to read. ¹⁷ The scroll of the prophet Isaiah was given to Him, and unrolling the scroll, He found the place where it was written:

¹⁸ The Spirit of the Lord is on Me,
    because He has anointed Me
    to preach good news to the poor.
He has sent Me
    to proclaim freedom
        to the captives
    and recovery of sight
        to the blind,
    to set free the oppressed,
¹⁹ to proclaim the year
    of the Lord's favor.

²⁰ He then rolled up the scroll, gave it back to the attendant, and sat down. And the eyes of everyone in the synagogue were fixed on Him. ²¹ He began by saying to them, "Today as you listen, this Scripture has been fulfilled."

Leave Vengeance to God

*The Spirit of the Lord is on Me . . . to proclaim the
year of the Lord's favor.*—LUKE 4:18-19

Now and again I stress heavily this matter of grudges because I have found that this is the truth which always brings a positive response.

Following some remarks I made concerning an unforgiving spirit, a woman wrote: "I had often read in *Every Day with Jesus* your words about forgiveness, and I knew that one day I would have to face up to this challenge. Today's reading demolished all my defenses.

"Intellectually I had always accepted what you said about the need to forgive and that I could not be whole until I had completely forgiven those who had hurt me, but I wouldn't get down to actually putting it into words. I kept holding back my feelings, saying subconsciously: 'I will forgive some day, and then my troubles will be over—but not yet.'

"Your words today came like a bolt from the blue: 'There is usually a reason why we don't want to give up our grudges and resentments. One reason is that we use them to feel sorry for ourselves.' I certainly had done my share of that, but suddenly I let go. It was like a boil bursting. All the pent-up poisons gushed out of me, and I was a new person. I'm in the midst of a campaign now to overcome the misunderstandings of years." What happened to this woman can happen now, today, to you. No matter how wronged you have been—forgive.

When Jesus announced His mission in Nazareth, He read from Isaiah's prophecy until He came to the words, "the day of our God's vengeance." Then He closed the book. You do the same. Leave vengeance to God. Use only redemptive goodwill.

Prayer

Father, help me to realize that nothing anyone has ever done against me compares to what I have done against You. You have forgiven me—help me to forgive others. And not grudgingly, but graciously. In Jesus' name. Amen

Further Study

Mk 11:18-25; Lk 11:4; 17:4; Mt 18:21-22
What are we to do when we pray?
How many times should we forgive?

APRIL 1

NUMBERS 36:1– DEUTERONOMY 1:46

36 The family leaders from the clan of the descendants of Gilead—the son of Machir, son of Manasseh—one of the clans of the sons of Joseph approached and addressed Moses and the leaders who were over the Israelite families. ²They said, "The LORD commanded my lord to give the land as an inheritance by lot to the Israelites. My lord was further commanded by the LORD to give our brother Zelophehad's inheritance to his daughters. ³If they marry any of the men from the other Israelite tribes, their inheritance will be taken away from our fathers' inheritance and added to that of the tribe into which they marry. Therefore, part of our allotted inheritance would be taken away. ⁴When the Jubilee comes for the Israelites, their inheritance will be added to that of the tribe into which they marry, and their inheritance will be taken away from the inheritance of our ancestral tribe."

⁵ So Moses commanded the Israelites at the word of the LORD, "What the tribe of Joseph's descendants says is right. ⁶ This is what the LORD has commanded concerning Zelophehad's daughters: They may marry anyone they like provided they marry within a clan of their ancestral tribe. ⁷ An inheritance belonging to the Israelites must not transfer from tribe to tribe, because each of the Israelites is to retain the inheritance of his ancestral tribe. ⁸ Any daughter who possesses an inheritance from an Israelite tribe must marry someone from the clan of her ancestral tribe, so that each of the Israelites will possess the inheritance of his fathers. ⁹ No inheritance is to transfer from one tribe to another, because each of the Israelite tribes is to retain its inheritance."

¹⁰ The daughters of Zelophehad did as the LORD commanded Moses. ¹¹ Mahlah, Tirzah, Hoglah, Milcah, and Noah, the daughters of Zelophehad, married cousins on their father's side. ¹² They married men from the clans of the descendants of Manasseh son of Joseph, and their inheritance remained within the tribe of their father's clan.

¹³ These are the commands and ordinances the LORD commanded the Israelites through Moses in the plains of Moab by the Jordan across from Jericho.

1 These are the words Moses spoke to all Israel across the Jordan in the wilderness, in the Arabah opposite Suph, between Paran and Tophel, Laban, Hazeroth, and Di-zahab. ² It is an eleven-day journey from Horeb to Kadesh-barnea by way of Mount Seir. ³ In the fortieth year, in the eleventh month, on the first of the month, Moses told the Israelites everything the LORD had commanded him to say to them. ⁴ This was after he had defeated Sihon king of the Amorites, who lived in Heshbon, and Og king of Bashan, who lived in Ashtaroth, at Edrei. ⁵ Across the Jordan in the land of Moab, Moses began to explain this law, saying:

⁶ "The LORD our God spoke to us at Horeb, 'You have stayed at this mountain long enough. ⁷ Resume your journey and go to the hill country of the Amorites and their neighbors in the Arabah, the hill country, the lowlands, the Negev and the sea coast—to the land of the Canaanites and to Lebanon as far as the Euphrates River. ⁸ See, I have set the land before you. Enter and take possession of the land the LORD swore to give to your fathers Abraham, Isaac, and Jacob and their descendants after them.'

⁹ "I said to you at that time: I can't bear the responsibility for you on my own. ¹⁰ The LORD your God has so multiplied you that today you are as numerous as the stars of the sky. ¹¹ May the LORD, the God of your fathers, increase you a thousand times more, and bless you as He promised you. ¹² But how can I bear your troubles, burdens, and disputes by myself? ¹³ Appoint for yourselves wise, understanding, and respected men from each of your tribes, and I will make them your leaders.

¹⁴ "You replied to me, 'What you propose to do is good.'

¹⁵ "So I took the leaders of your tribes, wise and respected men, and set them over you as leaders: officials for thousands, hundreds, fifties, and tens, and officers for your tribes. ¹⁶ I commanded your judges at that time: Hear the cases between your brothers, and judge rightly between a man and his brother or a foreign resident. ¹⁷ Do not show partiality when rendering judgment; listen to small and great alike. Do not be intimidated by anyone, for judgment belongs to God. Bring me any case too difficult for you, and I will hear it. ¹⁸ At that time I commanded you about all the things you were to do.

¹⁹ "We then set out from Horeb and went across all the great and terrible wilderness you saw on the way to the hill country of the Amorites, just as the LORD our God had commanded us. When we reached Kadesh-barnea, ²⁰ I said to you: You have reached the hill country of the Amorites, which the LORD our God is giving us. ²¹ See, the LORD your God has set the land before you. Go up and take possession of it as the LORD, the God of your fathers, has

told you. Do not be afraid or discouraged.

²² "Then all of you approached me and said, 'Let's send men ahead of us, so that they may explore the land for us and bring us back a report about the route we should go up and the cities we will come to.' ²³ The plan seemed good to me, so I selected 12 men from among you, one man for each tribe. ²⁴ They left and went up into the hill country and came to the Valley of Eshcol, scouting the land. ²⁵ They took some of the fruit from the land in their hands, carried it down to us, and brought us back a report: 'The land the LORD our God is giving us is good.'

²⁶ "But you were not willing to go up, rebelling against the command of the LORD your God. ²⁷ You grumbled in your tents and said, 'The LORD brought us out of the land of Egypt to deliver us into the hands of the Amorites so they would destroy us, because He hated us. ²⁸ Where can we go? Our brothers have discouraged us, saying: The people are larger and taller than we are; the cities are large, fortified to the heavens. We also saw the descendants of the Anakim there.'

²⁹ "So I said to you: Don't be terrified or afraid of them! ³⁰ The LORD your God who goes before you will fight for you, just as you saw Him do for you in Egypt. ³¹ And you saw in the wilderness how the LORD your God carried you as a man carries his son all along the way you traveled until you reached this place. ³² But in spite of this you did not trust the LORD your God, ³³ who went before you on the journey to seek out a place for you to camp. He went in the fire by night and in the cloud by day to guide you on the road you were to travel.

³⁴ "When the LORD heard your words, He grew angry and swore an oath: ³⁵ 'None of these men in this evil generation will see the good land I swore to give your fathers, ³⁶ except Caleb the son of Jephunneh. He will see it, and I will give him and his descendants the land on which he has set foot, because he followed the LORD completely.' ³⁷ "The LORD was angry with me also

because of you and said: 'You will not enter there either. ³⁸ Joshua son of Nun, who attends you, will enter it. Encourage him, for he will enable Israel to inherit it. ³⁹ Your little children who you said would be plunder, your sons who don't know good from evil, will enter there. I will give them the land, and they will take possession of it. ⁴⁰ But you are to turn back and head for the wilderness by way of the Red Sea.'

⁴¹ "You answered me, 'We have sinned against the LORD. We will go up and fight just as the LORD our God commanded us.' Then each of you put on his weapons of war and thought it would be easy to go up into the hill country.

⁴² "But the LORD said to me, 'Tell them: Don't go up and fight, for I am not with you to keep you from being defeated by your enemies.' ⁴³ So I spoke to you, but you didn't listen. You rebelled against the LORD's command and defiantly went up into the hill country. ⁴⁴ Then the Amorites who lived there came out against you and chased you like a swarm of bees. They routed you from Seir as far as Hormah. ⁴⁵ When you returned, you wept before the LORD, but He didn't listen to your requests or pay attention to you. ⁴⁶ For this reason you stayed in Kadesh as long as you did.

PSALM 39:1-6

¹ I said, "I will guard my ways
  so that I may not sin with my
    tongue;
  I will guard my mouth with a
    muzzle
  as long as the wicked are in my
    presence."
² I was speechless and quiet;
  I kept silent, even from speaking
    good,
  and my pain intensified.
³ My heart grew hot within me;
  as I mused, a fire burned.
  I spoke with my tongue:

⁴ "LORD, reveal to me the end of my
    life
  and the number of my days.

Let me know how transitory I am.
5 You, indeed, have made my days
   short in length,
and my life span as nothing in
   Your sight.
Yes, every mortal man is only a
   vapor.   *Selah*
6 Certainly, man walks about like a
   mere shadow.
Indeed, they frantically rush
   around in vain,
gathering possessions without
   knowing who will get them.

*P*ROVERBS 10:1-2

10 Solomon's proverbs:

A wise son brings joy to his father,
but a foolish son, heartache to his
   mother.

2 Ill-gotten gains do not profit
   anyone,
but righteousness rescues from
   death.

*L*UKE 4:22-44

22 They were all speaking well of Him
and were amazed by the gracious words
that came from His mouth, yet they
said, "Isn't this Joseph's son?"
23 Then He said to them, "No doubt
you will quote this proverb to Me:
'Doctor, heal yourself.' 'All we've heard
that took place in Capernaum, do here
in Your hometown also.' "
24 He also said, "I assure you: No
prophet is accepted in his hometown.
25 But I say to you, there were certainly
many widows in Israel in Elijah's days,
when the sky was shut up for three
years and six months while a great
famine came over all the land. 26 Yet
Elijah was not sent to any of them—but
to a widow at Zarephath in Sidon. 27 And
in the prophet Elisha's time, there were
many in Israel who had serious skin diseases, yet not one of them was healed—
only Naaman the Syrian."
28 When they heard this, everyone in
the synagogue was enraged. 29 They got

up, drove Him out of town, and brought
Him to the edge of the hill their town
was built on, intending to hurl Him over
the cliff. 30 But He passed right through
the crowd and went on His way.
31 Then He went down to Capernaum,
a town in Galilee, and was teaching
them on the Sabbath. 32 They were astonished at His teaching because His
message had authority. 33 In the synagogue there was a man with an unclean
demonic spirit who cried out with a loud
voice, 34 "Leave us alone! What do You
have to do with us, Jesus—Nazarene?
Have You come to destroy us? I know
who You are—the Holy One of God!"
35 But Jesus rebuked him and said,
"Be quiet and come out of him!"
And throwing him down before them,
the demon came out of him without
hurting him at all. 36 They were all struck
with amazement and kept saying to one
another, "What is this message? For He
commands the unclean spirits with authority and power, and they come out!"
37 And news about Him began to go out
to every place in the vicinity.
38 After He left the synagogue, He entered Simon's house. Simon's mother-
in-law was suffering from a high fever,
and they asked Him about her. 39 So He
stood over her and rebuked the fever,
and it left her. She got up immediately
and began to serve them.
40 When the sun was setting, all those
who had anyone sick with various diseases brought them to Him. As He laid
His hands on each one of them, He
would heal them. 41 Also, demons were
coming out of many, shouting and saying, "You are the Son of God!" But He
rebuked them and would not allow
them to speak, because they knew He
was the Messiah.
42 When it was day, He went out and
made His way to a deserted place. But
the crowds were searching for Him.
They came to Him and tried to keep
Him from leaving them. 43 But He said to
them, "I must proclaim the good news
about the kingdom of God to the other
towns also, because I was sent for this
purpose." 44 And He was preaching in
the synagogues of Galilee.

"The Unseen Sculptor"

As I mused, a fire burned.—Psalm 39:3

What are the benefits of Scripture meditation? They are beyond telling. Here, however, are just some of the benefits the Bible offers to those of us who will take the time to meditate: (1) success—Joshua 1:8, (2) understanding—Psalm 119:99, (3) the ability to wisely discern between right and wrong—Psalm 119:11.

But the one that is most pivotal occurs in Psalm 1—spiritual freshness. This psalm makes it clear that one of the secrets of staying spiritually fresh is to send one's roots down into the Word of God by meditation.

In my teens I knew a man, a miner by trade, whose spiritual freshness and radiance were responsible for turning many people to Jesus Christ. Just before he died, and in the company of several other Christians, I asked him: "What is the secret of your spiritual freshness? You always seem to be on top of things, always radiant. Tell me how you maintain this inner poise and power." He replied in one word—meditation.

I pressed him for some further thoughts on the subject. This is not a verbatim quotation, but as far as I can remember, this is what he said: "Meditation is letting your heart become the workshop of the unseen Sculptor who chisels in its secret chambers the living forms that contribute to character development and an increasing likeness to Jesus Christ." That old man, now in heaven, was one of the greatest illustrations I have ever known of the spiritual freshness and fruitfulness that comes from meditating on God's Word. His experience can be ours—if we meditate.

Prayer

O Father, help me to master the art of Scripture meditation, so that through the written Word and by the meditated Word, those around me may see the Living Word. Amen.

Further Study

Rm 10:1-9; Dt 11:18; Pr 6:23; 2 Co 3:3
What happens when the Word is in our hearts?
What was Paul's testimony of the Corinthians?

APRIL 2

ᴅEUTERONOMY
2:1–3:29

2 "Then we turned back and headed for the wilderness by way of the Red Sea, as the Lᴏʀᴅ had told me, and we traveled around the hill country of Seir for many days. ² The Lᴏʀᴅ then said to me, ³ 'You've been traveling around this hill country long enough; turn north. ⁴ Command the people: You are about to travel through the territory of your brothers, the descendants of Esau, who live in Seir. They will be afraid of you, so you must be very careful. ⁵ Don't fight with them, for I will not give you any of their land, not even an inch of it, because I have given Esau the hill country of Seir as his possession. ⁶ You may purchase food from them with silver, so that you may eat, and buy water from them to drink. ⁷ For the Lᴏʀᴅ your God has blessed you in all the work of your hands. He has watched over your journey through this immense wilderness. The Lᴏʀᴅ your God has been with you this past 40 years, and you have lacked nothing.'

⁸ "So we bypassed our brothers, the descendants of Esau, who live in Seir. We turned away from the Arabah road and from Elath and Ezion-geber. We traveled along the road to the Wilderness of Moab. ⁹ The Lᴏʀᴅ said to me, 'Show no hostility toward Moab, and do not provoke them to battle, for I will not give you any of their land as a possession, since I have given Ar as a possession to the descendants of Lot.' "

¹⁰ The Emim, a great and numerous people as tall as the Anakim, had previously lived there. ¹¹ They were also regarded as Rephaim, like the Anakim, though the Moabites called them Emim. ¹² The Horites had previously lived in Seir, but the descendants of Esau drove them out, destroying them completely and settling in their place, just as Israel did in the land of its possession the Lᴏʀᴅ gave them.

¹³ "The Lᴏʀᴅ said, 'Now get up and cross the Zered Valley.' So we crossed the Zered Valley. ¹⁴ The time we spent traveling from Kadesh-barnea until we crossed the Zered Valley was 38 years until the entire generation of fighting men had perished from the camp, as the Lᴏʀᴅ had sworn to them. ¹⁵ Indeed, the Lᴏʀᴅ's hand was against them, to eliminate them from the camp until they had all perished.

¹⁶ "When all the fighting men had died among the people, ¹⁷ the Lᴏʀᴅ spoke to me, ¹⁸ 'Today you are going to cross the border of Moab at Ar. ¹⁹ When you get close to the Ammonites, don't show any hostility to them or fight with them, for I will not give you any of the Ammonites' land as a possession; I have given it as a possession to the descendants of Lot.' "

²⁰ This too used to be regarded as the land of the Rephaim. The Rephaim lived there previously, though the Ammonites called them Zamzummim, ²¹ a great and numerous people, tall as the Anakim. The Lᴏʀᴅ destroyed the Rephaim at the advance of the Ammonites, so that they drove them out and settled in their place. ²² This was just as He had done for the descendants of Esau who lived in Seir, when He destroyed the Horites before them; they drove them out and have lived in their place until now. ²³ The Caphtorim, who came from Caphtor, destroyed the Avvim, who lived in villages as far as Gaza, and settled in their place. ²⁴ "The Lᴏʀᴅ also said, 'Get up, move out, and cross the Arnon Valley. See, I have handed Sihon the Amorite, king of Heshbon, and his land over to you. Begin to take possession of it; engage

him in battle. ²⁵ Today I will begin to put the fear and dread of you on the peoples everywhere under heaven. They will hear the report about you, tremble, and be in anguish because of you.'

²⁶ "So I sent messengers with an offer of peace to Sihon king of Heshbon from the Wilderness of Kedemoth, saying, ²⁷ 'Let us travel through your land; we will keep strictly to the highway. We will not turn to the right or the left. ²⁸ You can sell us food in exchange for silver so we may eat, and give us water for silver so we may drink. Only let us travel through on foot, ²⁹ just as the descendants of Esau who live in Seir did for us, and the Moabites who live in Ar, until we cross the Jordan into the land the LORD our God is giving us.' ³⁰ But Sihon king of Heshbon would not let us travel through his land, for the LORD your God made his spirit stubborn and his heart obstinate in order to hand him over to you, as has now taken place.

³¹ "Then the LORD said to me, 'See, I have begun to give Sihon and his land to you. Begin to take possession of it.' ³² So Sihon and his whole army came out against us for battle at Jahaz. ³³ The LORD our God handed him over to us, and we defeated him, his sons, and his whole army. ³⁴ At that time we captured all his cities and completely destroyed the people of every city, including the women and children. We left no survivors. ³⁵ We took only the livestock and the spoil from the cities we captured as plunder for ourselves. ³⁶ There was no city that was inaccessible to us, from Aroer on the rim of the Arnon Valley, along with the city in the valley, even as far as Gilead. The LORD our God gave everything to us. ³⁷ But you did not go near the Ammonites' land, all along the bank of the Jabbok River and the cities of the hill country, everything that the LORD our God had commanded.

3 "Then we turned and went up the road to Bashan, and Og king of Bashan, with his whole army, came out against us for battle at Edrei. ² But the LORD said to me, 'Do not fear him, for I have handed him over to you, along with his whole army and his land. Do to him as you did to Sihon king of the Amorites, who lived in Heshbon.' ³ So the LORD our God also handed over Og king of Bashan and his whole army to us. We struck him until there was no survivor left. ⁴ We captured all his cities at that time. There wasn't a city that we didn't take from them: 60 cities, the entire region of Argob, the kingdom of Og in Bashan. ⁵ All these were fortified with high walls, gates, and bars, besides a large number of rural villages. ⁶ We completely destroyed them, as we had done to Sihon king of Heshbon, destroying the men, women, and children of every city. ⁷ But we took all the livestock and the spoil from the cities as plunder for ourselves.

⁸ "At that time we took the land from the two Amorite kings across the Jordan, from the Arnon Valley as far as Mount Hermon, ⁹ which the Sidonians call Sirion, but the Amorites call Senir, ¹⁰ all the cities of the plateau, Gilead, and Bashan as far as Salecah and Edrei, cities of Og's kingdom in Bashan. ¹¹ (Only Og king of Bashan was left of the remnant of the Rephaim. His bed was made of iron. Isn't it in Rabbah of the Ammonites? It is 13 feet six inches long and six feet wide by a standard measure.)

¹² "At that time we took possession of this land. I gave to the Reubenites and Gadites the area extending from Aroer by the Arnon Valley, and half the hill country of Gilead along with its cities. ¹³ I gave to half the tribe of Manasseh the rest of Gilead and all Bashan, the kingdom of Og. The entire region of Argob, the whole territory of Bashan, used to be called the land of the Rephaim. ¹⁴ Jair, a descendant of Manasseh, took over the entire region of Argob as far as the border of the Geshurites and Maacathites. He called Bashan by his own name, Jair's Villages, as it is today. ¹⁵ I gave Gilead to Machir, ¹⁶ and I gave to the Reubenites and Gadites the area extending from Gilead to the Arnon Valley (the middle of the valley was the border) and up to the Jabbok River, the border of the Ammonites. ¹⁷ The Arabah

and Jordan are also borders from Chinnereth as far as the Sea of the Arabah, the Dead Sea, under the slopes of Pisgah on the east. ¹⁸ "I commanded you at that time: The LORD your God has given you this land to possess. All your fighting men will cross over in battle formation ahead of your brothers the Israelites. ¹⁹ But your wives, young children, and livestock—I know that you have a lot of livestock—will remain in the cities I have given you ²⁰ until the LORD gives rest to your brothers as He has to you, and they also take possession of the land the LORD your God is giving them across the Jordan. Then each of you may return to his possession that I have given you.

²¹ "I commanded Joshua at that time: Your own eyes have seen everything the LORD your God has done to these two kings. The LORD will do the same to all the kingdoms you are about to enter. ²² Don't be afraid of them, for the LORD your God fights for you.

²³ "At that time I begged the LORD: ²⁴ Lord GOD, You have begun to show Your greatness and power to Your servant, for what god is there in heaven or on earth who can perform deeds and mighty acts like Yours? ²⁵ Please let me cross over and see the beautiful land on the other side of the Jordan, that good hill country and Lebanon.

²⁶ "But the LORD was angry with me on account of you and would not listen to me. The LORD said to me, 'That's enough! Do not speak to Me again about this matter. ²⁷ Go to the top of Pisgah and look to the west, north, south, and east, and see it with your own eyes, for you will not cross this Jordan. ²⁸ But commission Joshua and encourage and strengthen him, for he will cross over ahead of the people and enable them to inherit this land that you will see.' ²⁹ So we stayed in the valley facing Beth-peor.

𝒫SALM 39:7-13

⁷ "Now, Lord, what do I wait for?
My hope is in You.

⁸ Deliver me from all my
transgressions;
do not make me the taunt of fools.
⁹ I am speechless; I do not open my
mouth
because of what You have done.
¹⁰ Remove Your torment from me;
I fade away because of the force
of Your hand.
¹¹ You discipline a man with
punishment for sin,
consuming like a moth what is
precious to him;
every man is a mere vapor. *Selah*

¹² "Hear my prayer, LORD,
and listen to my cry for help;
do not be silent at my tears.
For I am a foreigner residing with
You,
a sojourner like all my fathers.
¹³ Turn Your angry gaze from me so
that I may be cheered up
before I die and am gone."

𝒫ROVERBS 10:3-5

³ The LORD will not let the
righteous go hungry,
but He denies the wicked what
they crave.

⁴ Idle hands make one poor,
but diligent hands bring riches.

⁵ The son who gathers during
summer is prudent;
the son who sleeps during harvest
is disgraceful.

𝓛UKE 5:1-20

5 As the crowd was pressing in on Jesus to hear God's word, He was standing by Lake Gennesaret. ² He saw two boats at the edge of the lake; the fishermen had left them and were washing their nets. ³ He got into one of the boats, which belonged to Simon, and asked him to put out a little from the land. Then He sat down and was teaching the crowds from the boat.

⁴When He had finished speaking, He said to Simon, "Put out into deep water and let down your nets for a catch."

⁵"Master," Simon replied, "we've worked hard all night long and caught nothing! But at Your word, I'll let down the nets."

⁶When they did this, they caught a great number of fish, and their nets began to tear. ⁷So they signaled to their partners in the other boat to come and help them; they came and filled both boats so full that they began to sink.

⁸When Simon Peter saw this, he fell at Jesus' knees and said, "Go away from me, because I'm a sinful man, Lord!" ⁹For he and all those with him were amazed at the catch of fish they took, ¹⁰and so were James and John, Zebedee's sons, who were Simon's partners.

"Don't be afraid," Jesus told Simon. "From now on you will be catching people!" ¹¹Then they brought the boats to land, left everything, and followed Him.

¹²While He was in one of the towns, a man was there who had a serious skin disease all over him. He saw Jesus, fell facedown, and begged Him: "Lord, if You are willing, You can make me clean."

¹³Reaching out His hand, He touched him, saying, "I am willing; be made clean," and immediately the disease left him. ¹⁴Then He ordered him to tell no one: "But go and show yourself to the priest, and offer what Moses prescribed for your cleansing as a testimony to them."

¹⁵But the news about Him spread even more, and large crowds would come together to hear Him and to be healed of their sicknesses. ¹⁶Yet He often withdrew to deserted places and prayed.

¹⁷On one of those days while He was teaching, Pharisees and teachers of the law were sitting there who had come from every village of Galilee and Judea, and also from Jerusalem. And the Lord's power to heal was in Him. ¹⁸Just then some men came, carrying on a stretcher a man who was paralyzed. They tried to bring him in and set him down before Him. ¹⁹Since they could not find a way to bring him in because of the crowd, they went up on the roof and lowered him on the stretcher through the roof tiles into the middle of the crowd before Jesus.

²⁰Seeing their faith He said, "Friend, your sins are forgiven you."

First Principles

Put out into deep water.

—LUKE 5:4

I find myself compelled to discuss Paul's pregnant phrase: "praying in the Spirit."

There are times in my own life, as I am sure there are in yours, when I struggle in prayer and find it difficult to concentrate, only to discover that suddenly I am taken out of myself and given a freedom that transforms my prayer time from that point on. When this happens, I know I have been praying in the Spirit. This is the kind of thing about which the apostle Paul is exhorting us in Ephesians 6:18. Formal prayer is fine and has its place, but oh, how we need to experience more times of praying in the Spirit.

But how do we attain these times? Is it the Spirit's responsibility to bring us there, or do we have some responsibility in the matter, too? I believe we can learn to pray in the Spirit.

Some first principles are these: (1) Come to God in an attitude of dependence. This means recognizing that your greatest need in prayer is not an ability to put words together or form fine phrases, but the Holy Spirit's empowerment. (2) Yield yourself totally to the Spirit, letting Him guide and direct your praying. Be continually aware that He wants to have the bigger part in your prayer life. Start with these two principles, learning to depend less and less on your own experience or ability and more and more on the Spirit's enabling. Once you experience what it means to "pray in the Spirit," you will long to experience it more and more.

Prayer

O Father, my appetite is being whetted. Help me "launch out into the deep" and give myself to You in the way that You are willing to give Yourself to me. In Christ's name I ask it. Amen.

Further Study

Jn 3:22-27; 2 Ch 20:12; 2 Co 3:3-5
What was John's declaration?
How did Paul express his dependence on God?

APRIL 3

DEUTERONOMY 4:1-49

4 "Now, Israel, listen to the statutes and ordinances I am teaching you to follow, so that you may live, enter, and take possession of the land the LORD, the God of your fathers, is giving you. ² You must not add anything to what I command you or take anything away from it, so that you may keep the commands of the LORD your God I am giving you. ³ Your eyes have seen what the LORD did at Baal-peor, for the LORD your God destroyed every one of you who followed Baal of Peor. ⁴ But you who have remained faithful to the LORD your God are all alive today. ⁵ Look, I have taught you statutes and ordinances as the LORD my God has commanded me, so that you may follow them in the land you are entering to possess. ⁶ Carefully follow them, for this will show your wisdom and understanding in the eyes of the peoples. When they hear about all these statutes, they will say, 'This great nation is indeed a wise and understanding people.' ⁷ For what great nation is there that has a god near to it as the LORD our God is to us whenever we call to Him? ⁸ And what great nation has righteous statutes and ordinances like this entire law I set before you today?

⁹ "Only be on your guard and diligently watch yourselves, so that you don't forget the things your eyes have seen and so that they don't slip from your mind as long as you live. Teach them to

your children and your grandchildren. ¹⁰ The day you stood before the LORD your God at Horeb, the LORD said to me, 'Assemble the people before Me, and I will let them hear My words, so that they may learn to fear Me all the days they live on the earth and may instruct their children.' ¹¹ You came near and stood at the base of the mountain, a mountain blazing with fire into the heavens and enveloped in a dense, black cloud. ¹² Then the LORD spoke to you from the fire. You kept hearing the sound of the words, but didn't see a form; there was only a voice. ¹³ He declared His covenant to you. He commanded you to follow the Ten Commandments, which He wrote on two stone tablets. ¹⁴ At that time the LORD commanded me to teach you statutes and ordinances for you to follow in the land you are about to cross into and possess.

¹⁵ "Be extremely careful for your own good—because you did not see any form on the day the LORD spoke to you at Horeb out of the fire— ¹⁶ not to act corruptly and make an idol for yourselves in the shape of any figure: a male or female form, ¹⁷ or the form of any beast on the earth, any winged creature that flies in the sky, ¹⁸ any creature that crawls on the ground, or any fish in the waters under the earth. ¹⁹ When you look to the heavens and see the sun, moon, and stars—all the array of heaven—do not be led astray to bow down and worship them. The LORD your God has provided them for all people everywhere under heaven. ²⁰ But the LORD selected you and brought you out of Egypt's iron furnace to be a people for His inheritance, as you are today.

²¹ "The LORD was angry with me on your account. He swore that I would not cross the Jordan and enter the good land the LORD your God is giving you as an inheritance. ²² I won't be crossing the Jordan because I am going to die in this land. But you are about to cross over and take possession of this good land. ²³ Be careful not to forget the covenant of the LORD your God that He made with you, and make an idol for yourselves in the shape of anything He has forbidden you. ²⁴ For the LORD your God is a consuming fire, a jealous God.

²⁵ "When you have children and grandchildren and have been in the land a long time, and if you act corruptly, make an idol in the form of anything, and do what is evil in the sight of the LORD your God, provoking Him to anger, ²⁶ I call heaven and earth as witnesses against you today that you will quickly perish from the land you are about to cross the Jordan to possess. You will not live long there, but you will certainly be destroyed. ²⁷ The LORD will scatter you among the peoples, and you will be reduced to a few survivors among the nations where the LORD your God will drive you. ²⁸ There you will worship man-made gods of wood and stone, which cannot see, hear, eat, or smell. ²⁹ But from there, you will search for the LORD your God, and you will find Him when you seek Him with all your heart and all your soul. ³⁰ When you are in distress and all these things have happened to you, you will return to the LORD your God in later days and obey Him. ³¹ He will not leave you, destroy you, or forget the covenant with your fathers that He swore to them by oath, because the LORD your God is a compassionate God.

³² "Indeed, ask about the earlier days that preceded you, from the day God created man on the earth and from one end of the heavens to the other: Has anything like this great event ever happened, or has anything like it been heard of? ³³ Has a people ever heard God's voice speaking from the fire as you have, and lived? ³⁴ Or has a god ever attempted to go and take a nation as his own out of another nation, by trials, signs, wonders, and war, by a strong hand and an outstretched arm, by great terrors, as the LORD your God did for you in Egypt before your eyes? ³⁵ You were shown these things so that you would know that the LORD is God; there is no other besides Him. ³⁶ He let you hear His voice from heaven to instruct you. He showed you His great fire on earth, and you heard His words from the fire. ³⁷ Because He loved your fa-

thers, He chose their descendants after them and brought you out of Egypt by His presence and great power, [38] to drive out before you nations greater and stronger than you and to bring you in and give you their land as an inheritance, as is now taking place. [39] Today, recognize and keep in mind that the LORD is God in heaven above and on earth below; there is no other. [40] Keep His statutes and commands, which I am giving you today, so that you and your children after you may prosper and so that you may live long in the land the LORD your God is giving you for all time."

[41] Then Moses set apart three cities across the Jordan to the east, [42] where one could flee who committed manslaughter and killed his neighbor accidentally without previously hating him. He could flee to one of these cities and stay alive: [43] Bezer in the wilderness on the plateau land, belonging to the Reubenites; Ramoth in Gilead, belonging to the Gadites; or Golan in Bashan, belonging to the Manassites.

[44] This is the law Moses gave the Israelites. [45] These are the decrees, statutes, and ordinances Moses proclaimed to them after they came out of Egypt, [46] across the Jordan in the valley facing Beth-peor in the land of Sihon king of the Amorites. He lived in Heshbon, and Moses and the Israelites defeated him after they came out of Egypt. [47] They took possession of his land and the land of Og king of Bashan, the two Amorite kings who were across the Jordan to the east, [48] from Aroer on the rim of the Arnon Valley as far as Mount Sion (that is, Hermon) [49] and all the Arabah on the east side of the Jordan as far as the Dead Sea below the slopes of Pisgah.

*P*SALM 40:1-5

[1] I waited patiently for the LORD,
and He turned to me and heard
my cry for help.
[2] He brought me up from a desolate
pit,
out of the muddy clay,

and set my feet on a rock,
making my steps secure.
[3] He put a new song in my mouth,
a hymn of praise to our God.
Many will see and fear,
and put their trust in the LORD.

[4] How happy is the man
who has put his trust in the LORD
and has not turned to the proud
or to those who run after lies!
[5] LORD my God, You have done
many things—
Your wonderful works and Your
plans for us;
none can compare with You.
If I were to report and speak of
them
they are more than can be told.

*P*ROVERBS 10:6-8

[6] Blessings are on the head of the
righteous,
but the mouth of the wicked
conceals violence.

[7] The remembrance of the
righteous is a blessing,
but the name of the wicked will
rot.

[8] A wise heart accepts commands,
but foolish lips will be destroyed.

*L*UKE 5:21–6:11

[21] Then the scribes and the Pharisees began to reason: "Who is this man who speaks blasphemies? Who can forgive sins but God alone?"

[22] But perceiving their thoughts, Jesus replied to them, "Why are you reasoning this in your hearts? [23] Which is easier: to say, 'Your sins are forgiven you,' or to say, 'Get up and walk'? [24] But so you may know that the Son of Man has authority on earth to forgive sins"—He told the paralyzed man, "I tell you: get up, pick up your stretcher, and go home."

[25] Immediately he got up before them, picked up what he had been lying on,

and went home glorifying God. ²⁶ Then everyone was astounded, and they were giving glory to God. And they were filled with awe and said, "We have seen incredible things today!"

²⁷ After this, Jesus went out and saw a tax collector named Levi sitting at the tax office, and He said to him, "Follow Me!" ²⁸ So, leaving everything behind, he got up and began to follow Him.

²⁹ Then Levi hosted a grand banquet for Him at his house. Now there was a large crowd of tax collectors and others who were guests with them. ³⁰ But the Pharisees and their scribes were complaining to His disciples, "Why do you eat and drink with tax collectors and sinners?"

³¹ Jesus replied to them, "The healthy don't need a doctor, but the sick do. ³² I have not come to call the righteous, but sinners to repentance."

³³ Then they said to Him, "John's disciples fast often and say prayers, and those of the Pharisees do the same, but Yours eat and drink."

³⁴ Jesus said to them, "You can't make the wedding guests fast while the groom is with them, can you? ³⁵ But the days will come when the groom will be taken away from them—then they will fast in those days."

³⁶ He also told them a parable: "No one tears a patch from a new garment and puts it on an old garment. Otherwise, not only will he tear the new, but also the piece from the new garment will not match the old. ³⁷ And no one puts new wine into old wineskins. Otherwise, the new wine will burst the skins, it will spill, and the skins will be ruined. ³⁸ But new wine should be put into fresh wineskins. ³⁹ And no one, after drinking old wine, wants new, because he says, 'The old is better.' "

6 On a Sabbath, He passed through the grainfields. His disciples were picking heads of grain, rubbing them in their hands, and eating them. ² But some of the Pharisees said, "Why are you doing what is not lawful on the Sabbath?"

³ Jesus answered them, "Haven't you read what David and those who were with him did when he was hungry— ⁴ how he entered the house of God, and took and ate the sacred bread, which is not lawful for any but the priests to eat? He even gave some to those who were with him." ⁵ Then He told them, "The Son of Man is Lord of the Sabbath."

⁶ On another Sabbath He entered the synagogue and was teaching. A man was there whose right hand was paralyzed. ⁷ The scribes and Pharisees were watching Him closely, to see if He would heal on the Sabbath, so that they could find a charge against Him. ⁸ But He knew their thoughts and told the man with the paralyzed hand, "Get up and stand here." So he got up and stood there. ⁹ Then Jesus said to them, "I ask you: is it lawful on the Sabbath to do good or to do evil, to save life or to destroy it?" ¹⁰ After looking around at them all, He told him, "Stretch out your hand." He did so, and his hand was restored. ¹¹ They, however, were filled with rage and started discussing with one another what they might do to Jesus.

God Has the Biggest Part

He . . . set my feet on a rock, making my steps secure.
—PSALM 40:2

The more we are acquainted with the way a deer functions in its natural habitat, the more clearly we can see the spiritual lessons that God wants us to learn. While the male deer, the hart, is a wonderful example of sure-footedness, still more wonderful is the female, the hind.

Those who have watched it leading its young into the hidden fastnesses of the mountain peaks say it is the most perfect example of physical coordination that God ever made.

Why is this physical coordination so important?

When a deer moves upwards over a steep mountain slope, it proceeds by leaping from one spot to another. So it needs to be certain that its back feet will land on something solid. By positioning its front feet on something secure, it instinctively knows that if its rear feet land there also, it will proceed upwards in safety. If this were not so, and the deer's back feet were to land on a loose rock, then it would slip and meet with serious injury—perhaps even death. This sense of perfect coordination is not something the deer learns; it is an instinctive ability given to it by its Creator.

And what God has done for the deer in the natural realm, He is able to do for us in the spiritual realm. Listen to the words of the psalmist: "He makes my feet like the feet of a deer" (Ps 18:33). Note the word "makes." I find that deeply encouraging. It is not something I have to achieve on my own; He has a part in it too. And, may I add—the biggest part.

Prayer

O Father, help me understand that although You have the biggest part in making my feet like hinds' feet, it cannot be accomplished unless I, too, do my part. Thus I willingly surrender to Your divine purposes. In Jesus' name I pray. Amen.

Further Study

Is 26:1-4; Ps 92:15; 61:2; Mt 7:24-29
What did Isaiah declare?
What was Jesus teaching?

APRIL 4

DEUTERONOMY 5:1–6:25

5 Moses summoned all Israel and said to them, "Israel, listen to the statutes and ordinances I am proclaiming as you hear them today. Learn and follow them carefully. ² The LORD our God made a covenant with us at Horeb. ³ He did not make this covenant with our fathers, but with all of us who are alive here today. ⁴ The LORD spoke to you face to face from the fire on the mountain. ⁵ At that time I was standing between the LORD and you to report the word of the LORD to you, because you were afraid of the fire and did not go up the mountain. And He said:

⁶ I am the LORD your God, who brought you out of the land of Egypt, out of the place of slavery. ⁷ Do not have other gods besides Me. ⁸ Do not make an idol for yourself in the shape of anything in the heavens above or on the earth below or in the waters under the earth. ⁹ You must not bow down to them or worship them, because I, the LORD your God, am a jealous God, punishing the children for the fathers' sin to the third and fourth generations of those who hate Me, ¹⁰ but showing faithful love to a thousand generations of those who love Me and keep My commands.

¹¹ Do not misuse the name of the LORD your God, because the LORD will punish anyone who misuses His name.

¹² Be careful to dedicate the Sabbath day, as the LORD your God has commanded you. ¹³ You are to labor six days and do all your work, ¹⁴ but the seventh day is a Sabbath to the LORD your God. You must not do any work—you, your son or daughter, your male or female slave, your ox or donkey, any of your livestock, or the foreigner who lives within your gates, so that your male and female slaves may rest as you do. ¹⁵ Remember that you were a slave in the land of Egypt, and the LORD your God brought you out of there with a strong hand and an outstretched arm. That is why the LORD your God has commanded you to keep the Sabbath day.

¹⁶ Honor your father and your mother, as the LORD your God has commanded you, so that you may live long and so that you may prosper in the land the LORD your God is giving you.

¹⁷ Do not murder.

¹⁸ Do not commit adultery.

¹⁹ Do not steal.

²⁰ Do not give dishonest testimony against your neighbor.

²¹ Do not desire your neighbor's wife or covet your neighbor's house, his field, his male or female slave, his ox or donkey, or anything that belongs to your neighbor.

²² "The LORD spoke these commands in a loud voice to your entire assembly from the fire, cloud, and thick darkness on the mountain; He added nothing more. He wrote them on two stone tablets and gave them to me. ²³ All of you approached me with your tribal leaders and elders when you heard the voice from the darkness and while the mountain was blazing with fire. ²⁴ You said, 'Look, the LORD our God has shown us His glory and greatness, and we have heard His voice from the fire. Today we have seen that God speaks with a person, yet he still lives. ²⁵ But now, why should we die? This great fire will consume us and we will die if we hear the voice of the LORD our God any longer. ²⁶ For who out of all mankind has heard the voice of the living God speaking from the fire, as we have, and lived? ²⁷ Go near and listen to everything the LORD our God says. Then you can tell us everything the LORD our God tells you; we will listen and obey.'

²⁸ "The LORD heard your words when you spoke to me. He said to me, 'I have heard the words that these people have spoken to you. Everything they have said is right. ²⁹ If only they had such a heart to fear Me and keep all My commands, so that they and their children will prosper forever. ³⁰ Go and tell them: Return to your tents. ³¹ But you stand here with Me, and I will tell you every command—the statutes and ordinances—you are to teach them, so that they may follow them in the land I am giving them to possess.'

³² "Be careful to do as the LORD your God has commanded you; you are not to turn aside to the right or the left. ³³ Follow the whole instruction the LORD your God has commanded you, so that you may live, prosper, and have a long life in the land you will possess.

6 "This is the command—the statutes and ordinances—the LORD your God has instructed me to teach you, so that

you may follow them in the land you are about to enter and possess. ² Do this so that you may fear the LORD your God all the days of your life by keeping all His statutes and commands I am giving you, your son, and your grandson, so that you may have a long life. ³ Listen, Israel, and be careful to follow them, so that you may prosper and multiply greatly, because the LORD, the God of your fathers, has promised you a land flowing with milk and honey.

⁴ "Listen, Israel: The LORD our God, the LORD is One. ⁵ Love the LORD your God with all your heart, with all your soul, and with all your strength. ⁶ These words that I am giving you today are to be in your heart. ⁷ Repeat them to your children. Talk about them when you sit in your house and when you walk along the road, when you lie down and when you get up. ⁸ Bind them as a sign on your hand and let them be a symbol on your forehead. ⁹ Write them on the doorposts of your house and on your gates.

¹⁰ "When the LORD your God brings you into the land He swore to your fathers Abraham, Isaac, and Jacob that He would give you—a land with large and beautiful cities that you did not build, ¹¹ houses full of every good thing that you did not fill them with, wells dug that you did not dig, and vineyards and olive groves that you did not plant—and when you eat and are satisfied, ¹² be careful not to forget the LORD who brought you out of the land of Egypt, out of the place of slavery. ¹³ Fear the LORD your God, worship Him, and take your oaths in His name. ¹⁴ Do not follow other gods, the gods of the peoples around you, ¹⁵ for the LORD your God, who is among you, is a jealous God. Otherwise, the LORD your God will become angry with you and wipe you off the face of the earth. ¹⁶ Do not test the LORD your God as you tested Him at Massah. ¹⁷ Carefully observe the commands of the LORD your God, the decrees and statutes He has commanded you. ¹⁸ Do what is right and good in the LORD's sight, so that you may prosper and so that you may enter and possess the good land the LORD your God swore

to give your fathers, ¹⁹ by driving out all your enemies before you, as the LORD has said.

²⁰ "When your son asks you in the future, 'What is the meaning of the decrees, statutes, and ordinances, which the LORD our God has commanded you?' ²¹ tell him, 'We were slaves of Pharaoh in Egypt, but the LORD brought us out of Egypt with a strong hand. ²² Before our eyes the LORD inflicted great and devastating signs and wonders on Egypt, on Pharaoh and all his household, ²³ but He brought us from there in order to lead us in and give us the land that He swore to our fathers. ²⁴ The LORD commanded us to follow all these statutes and to fear the LORD our God for our prosperity always and for our preservation, as it is today. ²⁵ Righteousness will be ours if we are careful to follow every one of these commands before the LORD our God, as He has commanded us.'

PSALM 40:6-10

⁶ You do not delight in sacrifice and offering;
  You open my ears to listen.
  You do not ask for a whole burnt offering or a sin offering.
⁷ Then I said, "See, I have come;
  it is written about me in the volume of the scroll.
⁸ I delight to do Your will, my God;
  Your instruction resides within me."

⁹ I proclaim righteousness in the great assembly;
  see, I do not keep my mouth closed—as You know, LORD.
¹⁰ I did not hide Your righteousness in my heart;
  I spoke about Your faithfulness and salvation;
  I did not conceal Your constant love and truth from the great assembly.

PROVERBS 10:9-11

⁹ The one who lives with integrity lives securely,

but whoever perverts his ways
will be found out.

10 A sly wink of the eye causes grief,
and foolish lips will be destroyed.

11 The mouth of the righteous is a
fountain of life,
but the mouth of the wicked
conceals violence.

ℒUKE 6:12-36

12 During those days He went out to
the mountain to pray and spent all night
in prayer to God. 13 When daylight
came, He summoned His disciples, and
He chose 12 of them—He also named
them apostles:

14 Simon, whom He also
named Peter,
and Andrew his brother;
James and John;
Philip and Bartholomew;
15 Matthew and Thomas;
James the son of Alphaeus,
and Simon called the Zealot;
16 Judas the son of James,
and Judas Iscariot, who became
a traitor.

17 After coming down with them, He
stood on a level place with a large crowd
of His disciples and a great multitude of
people from all Judea and Jerusalem and
from the seacoast of Tyre and Sidon.
18 They came to hear Him and to be
healed of their diseases; and those tormented by unclean spirits were made
well. 19 The whole crowd was trying to
touch Him, because power was coming
out from Him and healing them all.
20 Then looking up at His disciples, He
said:

Blessed are you who are poor,
because the kingdom of God
is yours.
21 Blessed are you
who are hungry now,
because you will be filled.
Blessed are you who weep now,

because you will laugh.
22 Blessed are you when people
hate you,
when they exclude you,
insult you,
and slander your name as evil,
because of the Son of Man.

23 "Rejoice in that day and leap for
joy! Take note—your reward is great in
heaven, because this is the way their
ancestors used to treat the prophets.

24 But woe to you who are rich,
because you have received
your comfort.
25 Woe to you who are full now,
because you will be hungry.
Woe to you who are laughing now,
because you will mourn and weep.
26 Woe to you
when all people speak well of you,
because this is the way
their ancestors
used to treat the false prophets.

27 "But I say to you who listen: Love
your enemies, do good to those who
hate you, 28 bless those who curse you,
pray for those who mistreat you. 29 If
anyone hits you on the cheek, offer the
other also. And if anyone takes away
your coat, don't hold back your shirt either. 30 Give to everyone who asks from
you, and from one who takes away your
things, don't ask for them back. 31 Just
as you want others to do for you, do the
same for them. 32 If you love those who
love you, what credit is that to you?
Even sinners love those who love them.
33 If you do what is good to those who
are good to you, what credit is that to
you? Even sinners do that. 34 And if you
lend to those from whom you expect to
receive, what credit is that to you? Even
sinners lend to sinners to be repaid in
full. 35 But love your enemies, do what is
good, and lend, expecting nothing in return. Then your reward will be great,
and you will be sons of the Most High.
For He is gracious to the ungrateful and
evil. 36 Be merciful, just as your Father
also is merciful.

Louder Than "Amen"

I delight to do Your will, my God; Your instruction resides within me.—PSALM 40:8

To pray the words "Your will be done" sometimes creates a conflict in us, particularly when we know that God's will is the opposite of what we ourselves want. We must consider whose will is to have precedence—ours or God's.

There are some Christians who pray, "Your will be done," but they do it with an attitude of rebellion and resentment. They believe that they cannot escape the inevitable, and they become angry about it. They say the words "Your will be done" almost through clenched teeth. Other people say the words with an attitude of passive resignation. They say, "Your will be done," but what they mean is something like this: "Lord, I'm not very happy about the way things are turning out, but I suppose You know best. So I'll go along with it, and I'll try hard to believe it's for the best."

The proper attitude to the will of God, and the goal for which we should aim, is one of rejoicing. It's not easy to arrive at such an attitude, I know, but nevertheless we must have it before us as the desired end.

David, as we see in the passage before us today, prayed this way. If we can cultivate this attitude as our normal and characteristic reaction to everything that happens around us—sorrow, disappointment, disillusionment, frustration, disaster, loss, bereavement—then such a spirit is more than a match for anything. As someone has said: "The Hallelujah of triumph is louder than the Amen of resignation." It is!

Prayer

God, help me drop my anchor into the depths of Your eternal love and ride out my storms in the assurance that You are willing my highest good. Help me to accept it joyously. For Jesus' sake. Amen.

Further Study

Ps 100; Jn 5:30; Eph 6:6; Heb 13:21
What is the psalmist's exhortation?
What should be our heart attitude?

APRIL 5

*D*EUTERONOMY
7:1–8:20

7 "When the LORD your God brings you into the land you are entering to possess, and He drives out many nations before you—the Hittites, Girgashites, Amorites, Canaanites, Perizzites, Hivites and Jebusites, seven nations more numerous and powerful than you— ² and when the LORD your God delivers them over to you and you defeat them, you must completely destroy them. Make no treaty with them and show them no mercy. ³ Do not intermarry with them. Do not give your daughters to their sons or take their daughters for your sons, ⁴ because they will turn your sons away from Me to worship other gods. Then the LORD's anger will burn against you, and He will swiftly destroy you. ⁵ Instead, this is what you are to do to them: tear down their altars, smash their standing pillars, cut down their Asherah poles, and burn up their carved images. ⁶ For you are a holy people belonging to the LORD your God. The LORD your God has chosen you to be His own possession out of all the peoples on the face of the earth.

⁷ "The LORD was devoted to you and chose you, not because you were more numerous than all peoples, for you were the fewest of all peoples. ⁸ But because the LORD loved you and kept the oath He swore to your fathers, He brought you out with a strong hand and redeemed you from the place of slavery, from the power of Pharaoh king of Egypt. ⁹ Know that Yahweh your God is God, the faithful God who keeps His gracious covenant loyalty for a thousand generations with those who love Him and keep His commands. ¹⁰ But He directly pays back and destroys those who hate Him. He will not hesitate to directly pay back the one who hates Him. ¹¹ So keep the command—the statutes and ordinances—that I am giving you to follow today.

¹² "If you listen to and are careful to keep these ordinances, the LORD your God will keep His covenant loyalty with you, as He swore to your fathers. ¹³ He will love you, bless you, and multiply you. He will bless your descendants, and the produce of your soil—your grain, new wine, and oil—the young of your herds, and the newborn of your flocks, in the land He swore to your fathers that He would give you. ¹⁴ You will be blessed above all peoples; there will be no infertile male or female among you or your livestock. ¹⁵ The LORD will remove all sickness from you; He will not put on you all the terrible diseases of Egypt that you know about, but He will inflict them on all who hate you. ¹⁶ You must destroy all the peoples the LORD your God is delivering over to you and not look on them with pity. Do not worship their gods, for that will be a snare to you.

¹⁷ "If you say to yourself, 'These nations are greater than I; how can I drive them out?' ¹⁸ do not be afraid of them. Be sure to remember what the LORD your God did to Pharaoh and all Egypt: ¹⁹ the great trials that you saw, the signs and wonders, the strong hand and outstretched arm, by which the LORD your God brought you out. The LORD your God will do the same to all the peoples you fear. ²⁰ The LORD your God will also send the hornet against them until all the survivors and those hiding from you perish. ²¹ Don't be terrified of them, for the LORD your God, a great and awesome God, is among you. ²² The LORD your God will drive out these nations before you little by little. You will not be able to destroy them all at once; otherwise, the wild animals will become too numerous for you. ²³ The LORD your God

will give them over to you and throw them into great confusion until they are destroyed. ²⁴ He will hand their kings over to you, and you will wipe out their names under heaven. No one will be able to stand against you; you will annihilate them. ²⁵ You must burn up the carved images of their gods. Don't covet the silver and gold on the images and take it for yourself, or else you will be ensnared by it, for it is abhorrent to the LORD your God. ²⁶ You must not bring any abhorrent thing into your house, or you will be set apart for destruction like it. You are to utterly detest and abhor it, because it is set apart for destruction.

8 "You must carefully follow every command I am giving you today, so that you may live and increase, and may enter and take possession of the land the LORD swore to your fathers. ² Remember that the LORD your God led you on the entire journey these 40 years in the wilderness, so that He might humble you and test you to know what was in your heart, whether or not you would keep His commands. ³ He humbled you by letting you go hungry; then He gave you manna to eat, which you and your fathers had not known, so that you might learn that man does not live on bread alone but on every word that comes from the mouth of the LORD. ⁴ Your clothing did not wear out, and your feet did not swell these 40 years. ⁵ Keep in mind that the LORD your God has been disciplining you just as a man disciplines his son. ⁶ So keep the commands of the LORD your God by walking in His ways and fearing Him. ⁷ For the LORD your God is bringing you into a good land, a land with streams of water, springs, and deep water sources, flowing in both valleys and hills; ⁸ a land of wheat, barley, vines, figs, and pomegranates; a land of olive oil and honey; ⁹ a land where you will eat food without shortage, where you will lack nothing; a land whose rocks are iron and from whose hills you will mine copper. ¹⁰ When you eat and are full, you will praise the LORD your God for the good land He has given you.

¹¹ "Be careful that you don't forget the LORD your God by failing to keep His command—the ordinances and statutes—I am giving you today. ¹² When you eat and are full, and build beautiful houses to live in, ¹³ and your herds and flocks grow large, and your silver and gold multiply, and everything else you have increases, ¹⁴ be careful that your heart doesn't become proud and you forget the LORD your God who brought you out of the land of Egypt, out of the place of slavery. ¹⁵ He led you through the great and terrible wilderness with its poisonous snakes and scorpions, a thirsty land where there was no water. He brought water out of the flintlike rock for you. ¹⁶ He fed you in the wilderness with manna that your fathers had not known, in order to humble and test you, so that in the end He might cause you to prosper. ¹⁷ You may say to yourself, 'My power and my own ability have gained this wealth for me,' ¹⁸ but remember that the LORD your God gives you the power to gain wealth, in order to confirm His covenant He swore to your fathers, as it is today. ¹⁹ If you ever forget the LORD your God and go after other gods to worship and bow down to them, I testify against you today that you will perish. ²⁰ Like the nations the LORD is about to destroy before you, you will perish if you do not obey the LORD your God.

*P*SALM 40:11-17

¹¹ LORD, do not withhold Your
     compassion from me;
   Your constant love and truth will
     always guard me.
¹² For troubles without number have
     surrounded me;
   my sins have overtaken me; I am
     unable to see.
   They are more than the hairs of
     my head,
   and my courage leaves me.
¹³ LORD, be pleased to deliver me;
   hurry to help me, LORD.

¹⁴ Let those who seek to take my life
   be disgraced and confounded.

Let those who wish me harm
be driven back and humiliated.
¹⁵ Let those who say to me, "Aha,
aha!"
be horrified because of their
shame.

¹⁶ Let all who seek You rejoice and
be glad in You;
let those who love Your salvation
continually say,
"The LORD is great!"
¹⁷ I am afflicted and needy;
the Lord thinks of me.
You are my help and my deliverer;
my God, do not delay.

PROVERBS 10:12-14

¹² Hatred stirs up conflicts,
but love covers all offenses.

¹³ Wisdom is found on the lips of the
discerning,
but a rod is for the back of the
one who lacks sense.

¹⁴ The wise store up knowledge,
but the mouth of the fool hastens
destruction.

LUKE 6:37–7:10

³⁷ "Do not judge, and you will not be judged. Do not condemn, and you will not be condemned. Forgive, and you will be forgiven. ³⁸ Give, and it will be given to you; a good measure—pressed down, shaken together, and running over—will be poured into your lap. For with the measure you use, it will be measured back to you."

³⁹ He also told them a parable: "Can the blind guide the blind? Won't they both fall into a pit? ⁴⁰ A disciple is not above his teacher, but everyone who is fully trained will be like his teacher. ⁴¹ "Why do you look at the speck in your brother's eye, but don't notice the log in your own eye? ⁴² Or how can you say to your brother, 'Brother, let me take out the speck that is in your eye,' when you yourself don't see the log in

your eye? Hypocrite! First take the log out of your eye, and then you will see clearly to take out the speck in your brother's eye.

⁴³ "A good tree doesn't produce bad fruit; on the other hand, a bad tree doesn't produce good fruit. ⁴⁴ For each tree is known by its own fruit. Figs aren't gathered from thornbushes, or grapes picked from a bramble bush. ⁴⁵ A good man produces good out of the good storeroom of his heart. An evil man produces evil out of the evil storeroom, for his mouth speaks from the overflow of the heart.

⁴⁶ "Why do you call Me 'Lord, Lord,' and don't do the things I say? ⁴⁷ I will show you what someone is like who comes to Me, hears My words, and acts on them: ⁴⁸ He is like a man building a house, who dug deep and laid the foundation on the rock. When the flood came, the river crashed against that house and couldn't shake it, because it was well built. ⁴⁹ But the one who hears and does not act is like a man who built a house on the ground without a foundation. The river crashed against it, and immediately it collapsed. And the destruction of that house was great!"

⁷ When He had concluded all His sayings in the hearing of the people, He entered Capernaum. ² A centurion's slave, who was highly valued by him, was sick and about to die. ³ When the centurion heard about Jesus, he sent some Jewish elders to Him, requesting Him to come and save the life of his slave. ⁴ When they reached Jesus, they pleaded with Him earnestly, saying, "He is worthy for You to grant this, ⁵ because he loves our nation and has built us a synagogue." ⁶ Jesus went with them, and when He was not far from the house, the centurion sent friends to tell Him, "Lord, don't trouble Yourself, since I am not worthy to have You come under my roof. ⁷ That is why I didn't even consider myself worthy to come to You. But say the word, and my servant will be cured. ⁸ For I too am a man placed under authority, having soldiers under my command. I say to this one,

'Go!' and he goes; and to another, 'Come!' and he comes; and to my slave, 'Do this!' and he does it."

⁹ Jesus heard this and was amazed at him, and turning to the crowd following Him, He said, "I tell you, I have not found so great a faith even in Israel!" ¹⁰ When those who had been sent returned to the house, they found the slave in good health.

Amazing Love!

The LORD . . . chose you,
not because you were more numerous. . . .
But because the LORD loved you.—Deuteronomy 7:7-8

When the Bible says God is love, it is saying more than the fact that God loves, or that God is loving, or even that God is lovely; it is saying that love is the power behind everything He does. Love is not merely one of His attributes but His whole nature. God is not only the Author of loving acts; He is love in the very core of His being. Our thoughts of God's love must be built on God's revelation about Himself in the Scriptures, not by projecting our own ideas about love onto Him. Let's focus, therefore, on what the Bible has to say about the God who is love.

First, God's love is uninfluenced. By this I mean that nothing in us can give rise to it and nothing in us can extinguish it. It is "love for nothing," as someone once put it.

The love which we humans have for one another is drawn out of us by something in the object of our love. But God's love is not like that; His love is free, spontaneous, and uncaused. The passage before us today makes clear that there is no reason behind the love of God for His people. If you look for a reason, you just won't find one. He loves because . . . He loves.

No man or woman can ever explain why God loves us. To explain it would require that He loves us for something outside of Himself. And as we have seen, He loves us for ourselves alone. His love has its beginning not in us but in Himself. He is love's source, as well as its river.

Prayer

O God, what security this gives me to know that Your love for me will never be diminished and never be taken away. Help me reflect on this and draw from it the inspiration I need to walk tall and strong through every day. In Jesus' name. Amen.

Further Study

Eph 2:1-10; 1 Jn 3:1
How does Paul describe God's reason for saving us?
How does John put it?

APRIL 6

DEUTERONOMY
9:1–10:22

9 "Listen, Israel: Today you are about to cross the Jordan to go and drive out nations greater and stronger than you with large cities fortified to the heavens. ² The people are strong and tall, the descendants of the Anakim. You know about them and you have heard it said about them, 'Who can stand up to the sons of Anak?' ³ But understand that today the LORD your God will cross over ahead of you as a consuming fire; He will devastate and subdue them before you. You will drive them out and destroy them swiftly, as the LORD has told you. ⁴When the LORD your God drives them out before you, do not say to yourself, 'The LORD brought me in to take possession of this land because of my righteousness.' Instead, the LORD will drive out these nations before you because of their wickedness. ⁵ You are not going to take possession of their land because of your righteousness or your integrity. Instead, the LORD your God will drive out these nations before you because of their wickedness, in order to keep the promise He swore to your fathers, Abraham, Isaac, and Jacob. ⁶ Understand that the LORD your God is not giving you this good land to possess because of your righteousness, for you are a stiff-necked people.

⁷ "Remember and do not forget how you provoked the LORD your God in the wilderness. You have been rebelling against the LORD from the day you left the land of Egypt until you reached this place. ⁸ You provoked the LORD at Horeb, and He was angry enough with you to destroy you. ⁹ When I went up the mountain to receive the stone tablets, the tablets of the covenant the LORD made with you, I stayed on the mountain 40 days and 40 nights. I did not eat bread or drink water. ¹⁰ On the day of the assembly the LORD gave me the two stone tablets, inscribed by God's finger. The exact words were on them, which the LORD spoke to you from the fire on the mountain. ¹¹ The LORD gave me the two stone tablets, the tablets of the covenant, at the end of the 40 days and 40 nights.

¹² "The LORD said to me, 'Get up and go down immediately from here. For your people you brought out of Egypt have acted corruptly. They have quickly turned from the way that I commanded them; they have made a cast image for themselves.' ¹³ The LORD also said to me, 'I have seen this people, and indeed, they are a stiff-necked people. ¹⁴ Leave Me alone, and I will destroy them and blot out their name under heaven. Then I will make you into a nation stronger and more numerous than they.'

¹⁵ "So I went back down the mountain, while it was blazing with fire, and the two tablets of the covenant were in my hands. ¹⁶ I saw how you had sinned against the LORD your God; you had made a calf image for yourselves. You had quickly turned from the way the LORD had commanded for you. ¹⁷ So I took hold of the tablets and threw them from my hands, shattering them before your eyes. ¹⁸ Then I fell down like the first time in the presence of the LORD for 40 days and 40 nights; I did not eat bread or drink water because of all the sin you committed, doing what was evil in the LORD's sight and provoking Him to anger. ¹⁹ I was afraid of the fierce anger the LORD had directed against you, because He was about to destroy you. But again, the LORD listened to me on that occasion. ²⁰ The LORD was angry enough with Aaron to destroy him. But I prayed for Aaron at that time also. ²¹ I took the sinful calf you had made,

burned it up, and crushed it, thoroughly grinding it to powder as fine as dust. Then I threw it into the stream that came down from the mountain.

²² "You continued to provoke the LORD at Taberah, Massah, and Kibroth-hattaavah. ²³ When the LORD sent you from Kadesh-barnea, He said, 'Go up and possess the land I have given you'; you rebelled against the command of the LORD your God. You did not believe or obey Him. ²⁴ You have been rebelling against the LORD ever since I have known you.

²⁵ "I fell down in the presence of the LORD 40 days and 40 nights because the LORD had threatened to destroy you. ²⁶ I prayed to the LORD:

Lord GOD, do not annihilate Your people, Your inheritance, whom You redeemed through Your greatness and brought out of Egypt with a strong hand. ²⁷ Remember Your servants Abraham, Isaac, and Jacob. Disregard this people's stubbornness, and their wickedness and sin. ²⁸ Otherwise, those in the land you brought us from will say, 'Because the LORD wasn't able to bring them into the land He had promised them, and because He hated them, He brought them out to kill them in the wilderness.' ²⁹ But they are Your people, Your inheritance, whom You brought out by Your great power and outstretched arm.

10 "The LORD said to me at that time, 'Cut two stone tablets like the first ones and come to Me on the mountain and make a wooden ark. ² I will write on the tablets the words that were on the first tablets you broke, and you are to place them in the ark.' ³ So I made an ark of acacia wood, cut two stone tablets like the first ones, and climbed the mountain with the two tablets in my hand. ⁴ Then, on the day of the assembly, the LORD wrote on the tablets what had been written previously, the Ten Commandments that He had spoken to you on the mountain from the

fire. The LORD gave them to me, ⁵ and I went back down the mountain and placed the tablets in the ark I had made. And they have remained there, as the LORD commanded me."

⁶ The Israelites traveled from Beeroth Bene-jaakan to Moserah. Aaron died and was buried there, and Eleazar his son became priest in his place. ⁷ They traveled from there to Gudgodah, and from Gudgodah to Jotbathah, a land with streams of water.

⁸ "At that time the LORD set apart the tribe of Levi to carry the ark of the LORD's covenant, to stand before the LORD to serve Him, and to bless in His name, as it is today. ⁹ For this reason, Levi does not have a portion or inheritance like his brothers; the LORD is his inheritance, as the LORD your God told him.

¹⁰ "I stayed on the mountain 40 days and 40 nights like the first time. The LORD also listened to me on this occasion; He agreed not to annihilate you. ¹¹ Then the LORD said to me, 'Get up. Continue your journey ahead of the people, so that they may enter and possess the land I swore to give their fathers.'

¹² "And now, Israel, what does the LORD your God ask of you except to fear the LORD your God by walking in all His ways, to love Him, and to worship the LORD your God with all your heart and all your soul? ¹³ Keep the LORD's commands and statutes I am giving you today, for your own good. ¹⁴ The heavens, indeed the highest heavens, belong to the LORD your God, as does the earth and everything in it. ¹⁵ Yet the LORD was devoted to your fathers and loved them. He chose their descendants after them— He chose you out of all the peoples, as it is today. ¹⁶ Therefore, circumcise your hearts and don't be stiff-necked any longer. ¹⁷ For the LORD your God is the God of gods and Lord of lords, the great, mighty, and awesome God, showing no partiality and taking no bribe. ¹⁸ He executes justice for the fatherless and the widow, and loves the foreign resident, giving him food and clothing. ¹⁹ You also must love the foreigner, since you were foreigners in the land of Egypt. ²⁰ You

are to fear the Lord your God and worship Him. Remain faithful to Him and take oaths in His name. ²¹ He is your praise and He is your God, who has done for you these great and awesome works your eyes have seen. ²² Your fathers went down to Egypt, 70 people in all, and now the Lord your God has made you as numerous as the stars of the sky.

Psalm 41:1-6

¹ Happy is one who cares for the
    poor;
  the Lord will save him in a day of
    adversity.
² The Lord will keep him and
    preserve him;
  he will be blessed in the land.
  You will not give him over to the
    desire of his enemies.
³ The Lord will sustain him on his
    sickbed;
  You will heal him on the bed
    where he lies.

⁴ I said, "Lord, be gracious to me;
  heal me, for I have sinned against
    You."
⁵ My enemies speak maliciously
    about me:
  "When will he die and be
    forgotten?"
⁶ When one of them comes to visit,
  he speaks deceitfully;
  he stores up evil in his heart;
  he goes out and talks.

Proverbs 10:15-17

¹⁵ A rich man's wealth is his fortified
    city;
  the poverty of the poor is their
    destruction.

¹⁶ The labor of the righteous leads to
    life;
  the activity of the wicked leads to
    sin.

¹⁷ The one who follows instruction is
    on the path to life,

but the one who rejects correction
  goes astray.

Luke 7:11-35

¹¹ Soon afterwards He was on His way to a town called Nain. His disciples and a large crowd were traveling with Him. ¹² Just as He neared the gate of the town, a dead man was being carried out. He was his mother's only son, and she was a widow. A large crowd from the city was also with her. ¹³ When the Lord saw her, He had compassion on her and said, "Don't cry." ¹⁴ Then He came up and touched the open coffin, and the pallbearers stopped. And He said, "Young man, I tell you, get up!"

¹⁵ The dead man sat up and began to speak, and Jesus gave him to his mother. ¹⁶ Then fear came over everyone, and they glorified God, saying, "A great prophet has risen among us," and "God has visited His people." ¹⁷ This report about Him went throughout Judea and all the vicinity.

¹⁸ Then John's disciples told him about all these things. So John summoned two of his disciples ¹⁹ and sent them to the Lord, asking, "Are You the One who is to come, or should we look for someone else?"

²⁰ When the men reached Him, they said, "John the Baptist sent us to ask You, 'Are You the One who is to come, or should we look for someone else?' "

²¹ At that time Jesus healed many people of diseases, plagues, and evil spirits, and He granted sight to many blind people. ²² He replied to them, "Go and report to John the things you have seen and heard: The blind receive their sight, the lame walk, those with skin diseases are healed, the deaf hear, the dead are raised, and the poor have the good news preached to them. ²³ And anyone who is not offended because of Me is blessed." ²⁴ After John's messengers left, He began to speak to the crowds about John: "What did you go out into the wilderness to see? A reed swaying in the wind? ²⁵ What then did you go out to see? A man dressed in soft robes? Look,

those who are splendidly dressed and live in luxury are in royal palaces. ²⁶ What then did you go out to see? A prophet? Yes, I tell you, and far more than a prophet. ²⁷ This is the one it is written about:

Look, I am sending
My messenger
ahead of You;
he will prepare Your way
before You.

²⁸ I tell you, among those born of women no one is greater than John, but the least in the kingdom of God is greater than he."

²⁹ (And when all the people, including the tax collectors, heard this, they acknowledged God's way of righteousness, because they had been baptized with John's baptism. ³⁰ But since the Pharisees and experts in the law had not been baptized by him, they rejected the plan of God for themselves.)

³¹ "To what then should I compare the people of this generation, and what are they like? ³² They are like children sitting in the marketplace and calling to each other:

We played the flute for you,
but you didn't dance;
we sang a lament,
but you didn't weep!

³³ For John the Baptist did not come eating bread or drinking wine, and you say, 'He has a demon!' ³⁴ The Son of Man has come eating and drinking, and you say, 'Look, a glutton and a drunkard, a friend of tax collectors and sinners!' ³⁵ Yet wisdom is vindicated by all her children."

Toward Perfection

What does the LORD your God ask of you except to fear the LORD your God?

—DEUTERONOMY 10:12

The first thing God called Israel to do—when He announced that they were to be His special people and to live the way He wanted them to live—was to fear Him. Loving Him, serving Him, and keeping His laws were of great importance, of course, but the very first things God asked of them were reverence and fear.

How does all this relate to the love of God? When thinking about God, it is wise to see love and holiness as intertwined; not to do so can sometimes lead to serious error.

Many in today's church present the love of God in such a way that it has given rise to the saying "God loves me as I am." The idea in many minds is: "God loves me as I am, and whether I go on from here or whether I stay the same, it makes no difference to His love for me." This is entirely true, but it is not the entire truth. Because God is love, He loves us as we are, but because He is holy love, He loves us too much to let us stay as we are. Yes, we can be secure in the fact that God loves us just the way we are, but the holy love of God calls us to move ever closer to Him. It cries out: "Be holy as I am holy."

Error is truth out of balance. We need to rejoice in the fact that we are loved because of who we are and not for what we do, but we must see also that God's love is a holy love and thus will inevitably prod us toward perfection.

Prayer

O Father, help me keep these two things in balance—both Your love and Your holiness. Don't let the security I feel as I rest in Your love turn to smugness and complacency. Show me that though I am accepted "in the Beloved," that does not mean You don't want me to come closer. Amen.

Further Study

1 Sm 6:1-21; Rv 15:4
What question did the men of Beth-shemesh ask?
What truth was revealed to John in the song of the Lamb?

APRIL 7

DEUTERONOMY 11:1–12:19

11 "Therefore, love the LORD your God and always keep His mandate and His statutes, ordinances, and commands. ² You must understand today that it is not your children who experienced or saw the discipline of the LORD your God:

His greatness, strong hand, and outstretched arm; ³ His signs and the works He did in Egypt to Pharaoh king of Egypt and all his land; ⁴ what He did to Egypt's army, its horses and chariots, when He made the waters of the Red Sea flow over them as they pursued you, and He destroyed them completely; ⁵ what He did to you in the wilderness until you reached this place; ⁶ and what He did to Dathan and Abiram, the sons of Eliab the Reubenite, when in the middle of the whole Israelite camp the earth opened its mouth and swallowed them, their households,

their tents, and every living thing with them.

⁷ Your own eyes have seen every great work the LORD has done.

⁸ "Keep every command I am giving you today, so that you may have the strength to cross into and possess the land you are to inherit, ⁹ and so that you may live long in the land the LORD swore to your fathers to give them and their descendants, a land flowing with milk and honey. ¹⁰ For the land you are entering to possess is not like the land of Egypt, from which you have come, where you sowed your seed and irrigated by hand as in a vegetable garden. ¹¹ But the land you are entering to possess is a land of mountains and valleys, watered by rain from the sky. ¹² It is a land the LORD your God cares for. He is always watching over it from the beginning to the end of the year.

¹³ "If you carefully obey My commands I am giving you today, to love the LORD your God and worship Him with all your heart and all your soul, ¹⁴ I will provide rain for your land in season, the early and late rains, and you will harvest

your grain, new wine, and oil. ¹⁵ I will provide grass in your fields for your livestock. You will eat and be satisfied. ¹⁶ Be careful that you are not enticed to turn aside, worship, and bow down to other gods. ¹⁷ Then the LORD's anger will burn against you. He will close the sky, and there will be no rain; the land will not yield its produce, and you will perish quickly from the good land the LORD is giving you.

¹⁸ "Impress these words of Mine on your hearts and souls, bind them as a sign on your hands, and let them be a symbol on your foreheads. ¹⁹ Teach them to your children, talking about them when you sit in your house and when you walk along the road, when you lie down and when you get up. ²⁰ Write them on the doorposts of your house and on your gates, ²¹ so that as long as the heavens are above the earth, your days and those of your children may be many in the land the LORD swore to give your fathers. ²² For if you carefully observe every one of these commands I am giving you to follow—to love the LORD your God, walk in all His ways, and remain faithful to Him— ²³ the LORD will drive out all these nations before you, and you will drive out nations greater and stronger than you are. ²⁴ Every place the sole of your foot treads will be yours. Your territory will extend from the wilderness to Lebanon and from the Euphrates River to the Mediterranean Sea. ²⁵ No one will be able to stand against you; the LORD your God will put fear and dread of you in all the land where you set foot, as He has promised you.

²⁶ "Look, today I set before you a blessing and a curse: ²⁷ there will be a blessing, if you obey the commands of the LORD your God I am giving you today, ²⁸ and a curse, if you do not obey the commands of the LORD your God, and you turn aside from the path I command you today by following other gods you have not known. ²⁹ When the LORD your God brings you into the land you are entering to possess, you are to proclaim the blessing at Mount Gerizim and the curse at Mount Ebal. ³⁰ Aren't these mountains across the Jordan, beyond the western road in the land of the Canaanites, who live in the Arabah, opposite Gilgal, near the oaks of Moreh? ³¹ For you are about to cross the Jordan to enter and take possession of the land the LORD your God is giving you. When you possess it and settle in it, ³² be careful to follow all the statutes and ordinances I set before you today.

12 "Be careful to follow these statutes and ordinances in the land that the LORD, the God of your fathers, has given you to possess all the days you live on the earth. ² Destroy completely all the places where the nations you are driving out worship their gods—on the high mountains, on the hills, and under every flourishing tree. ³ Tear down their altars, smash their sacred pillars, burn up their Asherah poles, cut down the carved images of their gods, and wipe out their names from every place. ⁴ Don't worship the LORD your God this way. ⁵ Instead, you must go to the place the LORD your God chooses from all your tribes to put His name for His dwelling. ⁶ You are to bring there your burnt offerings and sacrifices, your tenths and personal contributions, your vow offerings and freewill offerings, and the firstborn of your herds and flocks. ⁷ You will eat there in the presence of the LORD your God and rejoice with your household in everything you do, because the LORD your God has blessed you.

⁸ "You are not to do as we are doing here today; everyone is doing whatever seems right in his own eyes. ⁹ Indeed, you have not yet come into the resting place and the inheritance the LORD your God is giving you. ¹⁰ When you cross the Jordan and live in the land the LORD your God is giving you to inherit, and He gives you rest from all the enemies around you and you live in security, ¹¹ then the LORD your God will choose the place to have His name dwell. Bring there everything I command you: your burnt offerings, sacrifices, offerings of the tenth, personal contributions, and all your choice offerings you vow to the

LORD. ¹² You will rejoice before the LORD your God—you, your sons and daughters, your male and female slaves, and the Levite who is within your gates, since he has no portion or inheritance among you. ¹³ Be careful not to offer your burnt offerings in all the sacred places you see. ¹⁴ You must offer your burnt offerings only in the place the LORD chooses in one of your tribes, and there you must do everything I command you.

¹⁵ "But whenever you want, you may slaughter and eat meat within any of your gates, according to the blessing the LORD your God has given you. Those who are clean or unclean may eat it, as they would a gazelle or deer, ¹⁶ but you must not eat the blood; pour it on the ground like water. ¹⁷ Within your gates you may not eat: the tenth of your grain, new wine, or oil; the firstborn of your herd or flock; any of your vow offerings that you pledge; your freewill offerings; or your personal contributions. ¹⁸ You must eat them in the presence of the LORD your God at the place the LORD your God chooses—you, your son and daughter, your male and female slave, and the Levite who is within your gates. Rejoice before the LORD your God in everything you do, ¹⁹ and be careful not to neglect the Levite, as long as you live in your land.

PSALM 41:7-13

⁷ All who hate me whisper together
about me;
they plan to harm me.
⁸ "Lethal poison has been poured
into him,
and he won't rise again from
where he lies!"
⁹ Even my friend in whom I trusted,
one who ate my bread,
has lifted up his heel against me.

¹⁰ But You, LORD, be gracious to me
and raise me up;
then I will repay them.
¹¹ By this I know that You delight in
me:

my enemy does not shout in
triumph over me.
¹² You supported me because of my
integrity
and set me in Your presence
forever.

¹³ May the LORD, the God of Israel,
be praised
from everlasting to everlasting.
Amen and amen.

PROVERBS 10:18-21

¹⁸ The one who conceals hatred has
lying lips,
and whoever spreads slander is a
fool.

¹⁹ When there are many words, sin
is unavoidable,
but the one who controls his lips
is wise.

²⁰ The tongue of the righteous is
pure silver;
the heart of the wicked is of little
value.

²¹ The lips of the righteous feed
many,
but fools die for lack of sense.

LUKE 7:36–8:3

³⁶ Then one of the Pharisees invited Him to eat with him. He entered the Pharisee's house and reclined at the table. ³⁷ And a woman in the town who was a sinner found out that Jesus was reclining at the table in the Pharisee's house. She brought an alabaster flask of fragrant oil ³⁸ and stood behind Him at His feet, weeping, and began to wash His feet with her tears. She wiped His feet with the hair of her head, kissing them and anointing them with the fragrant oil.

³⁹ When the Pharisee who had invited Him saw this, he said to himself, "This man, if He were a prophet, would know who and what kind of woman this is who is touching Him—she's a sinner!"

⁴⁰ Jesus replied to him, "Simon, I have something to say to you."

"Teacher," he said, "say it."

⁴¹ "A creditor had two debtors. One owed 500 denarii, and the other 50. ⁴² Since they could not pay it back, he graciously forgave them both. So, which of them will love him more?"

⁴³ Simon answered, "I suppose the one he forgave more."

"You have judged correctly," He told him. ⁴⁴ Turning to the woman, He said to Simon, "Do you see this woman? I entered your house; you gave Me no water for My feet, but she, with her tears, has washed My feet and wiped them with her hair. ⁴⁵ You gave Me no kiss, but she hasn't stopped kissing My feet since I came in. ⁴⁶ You didn't anoint My head with oil, but she has anointed My feet with fragrant oil. ⁴⁷ Therefore I tell you, her many sins have been for-given; that's why she loved much. But the one who is forgiven little, loves lit-tle." ⁴⁸ Then He said to her, "Your sins are forgiven."

⁴⁹ Those who were at the table with Him began to say among themselves, "Who is this man who even forgives sins?"

⁵⁰ And He said to the woman, "Your faith has saved you. Go in peace."

8 Soon afterwards He was traveling from one town and village to anoth-er, preaching and telling the good news of the kingdom of God. The Twelve were with Him, ² and also some women who had been healed of evil spirits and sick-nesses: Mary, called Magdalene (seven demons had come out of her); ³ Joanna the wife of Chuza, Herod's steward; Sus-anna; and many others who were sup-porting them from their possessions.

An Inspired Book

Impress these words of Mine on your hearts and souls, bind them as a sign on your hands, and let them be a symbol on your foreheads.—DEUTERONOMY 11:18

Why are the Scriptures described as a sword provided by the Holy Spirit? Quite simply, it is the Holy Spirit who has given us the Scriptures. They come altogether from Him.

It was the Holy Spirit who inspired men to write them: "Moved by the Holy Spirit, men spoke from God" (2 Pt 1:21). Again in 2 Timothy 3:16 we read: "All Scripture is inspired by God"—a statement which assures us that the Scriptures come from the Holy Spirit.

The Bible is not a mere human document. The Holy Spirit breathed into men and inspired them to write the way they did. This does not mean that the people who wrote the Scriptures did so mechanically, in the way that a dictating machine would record someone's dictation. The Holy Spirit used their natural way of expression but gave them an additional ability to write without error.

It is vital, if you are to win the battle against Satan, that you not only see this truth but be-lieve it. When you consider how powerful Satan is, you need something that is even more pow-erful. The Bible, the inspired Word of God, is your strength.

One step further—only the Holy Spirit can enable us truly to understand God's Word: "We have not received the spirit of the world, but the Spirit who is from God, in order to know what has been freely given to us by God" (1 Co 2:12). Without the Holy Spirit, we would be no more able to understand the Scriptures than a blind man could judge a beauty contest.

Prayer

Gracious Holy Spirit, just as You breathed into the Bible to give it its life and power, breathe also into my heart today so that I might know and understand its truth. I ask this in Jesus' name. Amen.

Further Study

Col 3:1-16; Dt 6:6; Heb 10:15-16
What does the word "dwell" mean?
Where must God's Word be written?

APRIL 8

DEUTERONOMY
12:20–14:21

20 "When the LORD your God enlarges your territory as He has promised you, and you say, 'I want to eat meat' because you have a strong desire to eat meat, you may eat it whenever you want. 21 If the place where the LORD your God chooses to put His name is too far from you, you may slaughter any of your herd or flock He has given you, as I have commanded you, and you may eat it within your gates whenever you want. 22 Indeed, you may eat it as the gazelle and deer are eaten; both the clean and the unclean may eat it. 23 But don't eat the blood, since the blood is the life, and you must not eat the life with the meat. 24 Do not eat blood; pour it on the ground like water. 25 Do not eat it, so that you and your children after you will prosper, because you will be doing what is right in the LORD's sight.

26 "But you are to take the holy offerings you have and your vow offerings and go to the place the LORD chooses. 27 Present the meat and blood of your burnt offerings on the altar of the LORD your God. The blood of your other sacrifices is to be poured out beside the altar of the LORD your God, but you may eat the meat. 28 Be careful to obey all these things I command you, so that you and your children after you may prosper forever, because you will be doing what is good and right in the sight of the LORD your God.

29 "When the LORD your God annihilates the nations before you, which you are entering to take possession of, and you drive them out and live in their land, 30 be careful not to be ensnared by their ways after they have been destroyed before you. Do not inquire about their gods, asking, 'How did these nations worship their gods? I'll also do the same.' 31 You must not do the same to the LORD your God, because they practice for their gods every detestable thing the LORD hates. They even burn their sons and daughters in the fire to their gods. 32 You must be careful to do everything I command you; do not add anything to it or take anything away from it.

13 "If a prophet or someone who has dreams arises among you and proclaims a sign or wonder to you, ² and that sign or wonder he has promised you comes about, but he says, 'Let us follow other gods,' which you have not known, 'and let us worship them,' ³ do not listen to that prophet's words or to that dreamer. For the LORD your God is testing you to know whether you love the LORD your God with all your heart and all your soul. ⁴ You must follow the LORD your God and fear Him. You must keep His commands and listen to His voice; you must worship Him and remain faithful to Him. ⁵ That prophet or dreamer must be put to death, because he has urged rebellion against the LORD your God who brought you out of the land of Egypt and redeemed you from the place of slavery, to turn you from the way the LORD your God has commanded you to walk. You must purge the evil from you.

⁶ "If your brother, the son of your mother, or your son or daughter, or the wife you embrace, or your closest friend secretly entices you, saying, 'Let us go and worship other gods'—which neither you nor your fathers have known, ⁷ any of the gods of the peoples around you, near you or far from you, from one end of the earth to the other— ⁸ you must not yield to him or listen to him. Show him no pity, and do not spare him or shield him. ⁹ Instead, you must kill him. Your hand is to be the first against him to put him to death, and then the hands of all the people. ¹⁰ Stone him to death for trying to turn you away from the LORD your God who brought you out of the land of Egypt, out of the place of slavery. ¹¹ All Israel will hear and be afraid, and they will no longer do anything evil like this among you.

¹² "If you hear it said about one of your cities the LORD your God is giving you to live in, ¹³ that wicked men have sprung up among you, led the inhabitants of their city astray, and said, 'Let us go and worship other gods,' which you have not known, ¹⁴ you are to inquire, investigate, and interrogate thoroughly. If the report turns out to be true

that this detestable thing has happened among you, ¹⁵ you must strike down the inhabitants of that city with the sword. Completely destroy everyone in it as well as its livestock with the sword. ¹⁶ You are to gather all its spoil in the middle of the city square and completely burn up the city and all its spoil for the LORD your God. The city must remain a mound of ruins forever; it is not to be rebuilt. ¹⁷ Nothing set apart for destruction is to remain in your hand, so that the LORD will turn from His burning anger and grant you mercy, show you compassion, and multiply you as He swore to your fathers. ¹⁸ This will occur if you obey the LORD your God, keeping all His commands I am giving you today, doing what is right in the sight of the LORD your God.

14 "You are sons of the LORD your God; do not cut yourselves or make a bald spot on your head on behalf of the dead, ² for you are a holy people belonging to the LORD your God. The LORD has chosen you to be His special people out of all the peoples on the face of the earth.

³ "You must not eat any detestable thing. ⁴ These are the animals you may eat:

the ox, the sheep, the goat,
⁵ the deer, the gazelle, the roedeer, the wild goat, the ibex, the antelope,
and the mountain sheep.

⁶ You may eat any animal that has hooves divided in two and chews the cud. ⁷ But among the ones that chew the cud or have divided hooves, you are not to eat these:

the camel, the hare, and the hyrax,
though they chew the cud, they do not have hooves—
they are unclean for you;
⁸ and the pig, though it has hooves, it does not chew the cud—
it is unclean for you.

You must not eat their meat or touch their carcasses.

⁹ "You may eat everything from the water that has fins and scales, ¹⁰ but you may not eat anything that does not have fins and scales—it is unclean for you. ¹¹ "You may eat every clean bird, ¹² but these are the ones you may not eat:

> the eagle, the bearded vulture,
> the black vulture, ¹³ the kite,
> the various kinds of falcon,
> ¹⁴ every kind of raven, ¹⁵ the ostrich,
> the short-eared owl, the gull,
> the various kinds of hawk,
> ¹⁶ the little owl, the long-eared owl,
> the white owl, ¹⁷ the desert owl,
> the osprey, the cormorant, ¹⁸ the
> stork,
> the various kinds of heron,
> the hoopoe, and the bat.

¹⁹ All winged insects are unclean for you; they may not be eaten. ²⁰ But you may eat every clean flying creature.

²¹ "You are not to eat any carcass; you may give it to a resident alien within your gates, and he may eat it, or you may sell it to a foreigner. For you are a holy people belonging to the LORD your God. You must not boil a young goat in its mother's milk.

PSALM 42:1-11

¹ As a deer longs for streams of
   water,
   so I long for You, God.
² I thirst for God, the living God.
   When can I come and appear
     before God?
³ My tears have been my food day
     and night,
   while all day long people say to
     me,
   "Where is your God?"
⁴ I remember this as I pour out my
     heart:
   how I walked with many,
   leading the festive procession to
     the house of God,
   with joyful and thankful shouts.

⁵ Why am I so depressed?
   Why this turmoil within me?
   Hope in God, for I will still praise
     Him,
   my Savior and my God.
⁶ I am deeply depressed;
   therefore I remember You from
     the land of Jordan
   and the peaks of Hermon,
   from Mount Mizar.
⁷ Deep calls to deep in the roar of
     Your waterfalls;
   all Your breakers and Your billows
     have swept over me.
⁸ The LORD will send His faithful
     love by day;
   His song will be with me in the
     night—
   a prayer to the God of my life.

⁹ I will say to God, my rock,
   "Why have You forgotten me?
   Why must I go about in sorrow
   because of the enemy's
     oppression?"
¹⁰ My adversaries taunt me,
   as if crushing my bones,
   while all day long they say to
     me,
   "Where is your God?"
¹¹ Why am I so depressed?
   Why this turmoil within me?
   Hope in God, for I will still praise
     Him,
   my Savior and my God.

PROVERBS 10:22-25

²² The LORD's blessing enriches,
   and toil adds nothing to it.

²³ As shameful conduct is pleasure
     for a fool,
   so wisdom is for a man of
     understanding.

²⁴ What the wicked dreads will come
     to him,
   but what the righteous desires
     will be given to him.

²⁵ When the whirlwind passes, the
     wicked are no more,

but the righteous are secure forever.

ᒪUKE 8:4-25

⁴ As a large crowd was gathering, and people were flocking to Him from every town, He said in a parable: ⁵ "A sower went out to sow his seed. As he was sowing, some fell along the path; it was trampled on, and the birds of the sky ate it up. ⁶ Other seed fell on the rock; when it sprang up, it withered, since it lacked moisture. ⁷ Other seed fell among thorns; the thorns sprang up with it and choked it. ⁸ Still other seed fell on good ground; when it sprang up, it produced a crop: 100 times what was sown." As He said this, He called out, "Anyone who has ears to hear should listen!"

⁹ Then His disciples asked Him, "What does this parable mean?" ¹⁰ So He said, "The secrets of the kingdom of God have been given for you to know, but to the rest it is in parables, so that

Looking they may not see,
and hearing they may not
understand.

¹¹ "This is the meaning of the parable: The seed is the word of God. ¹² The seeds along the path are those who have heard. Then the Devil comes and takes away the word from their hearts, so that they may not believe and be saved. ¹³ And the seeds on the rock are those who, when they hear, welcome the word with joy. Having no root, these believe for a while and depart in a time of testing. ¹⁴ As for the seed that fell among thorns, these are the ones who, when they have heard, go on their way

and are choked with worries, riches, and pleasures of life, and produce no mature fruit. ¹⁵ But the seed in the good ground—these are the ones who, having heard the word with an honest and good heart, hold on to it and by enduring, bear fruit.

¹⁶ "No one, after lighting a lamp, covers it with a basket or puts it under a bed, but puts it on a lampstand so that those who come in may see the light. ¹⁷ For nothing is concealed that won't be revealed, and nothing hidden that won't be made known and come to light. ¹⁸ Therefore, take care how you listen. For whoever has, more will be given to him; and whoever does not have, even what he thinks he has will be taken away from him."

¹⁹ Then His mother and brothers came to Him, but they could not meet with Him because of the crowd. ²⁰ He was told, "Your mother and Your brothers are standing outside, wanting to see You." ²¹ But He replied to them, "My mother and My brothers are those who hear and do the word of God."

²² One day He and His disciples got into a boat, and He told them, "Let's cross over to the other side of the lake." So they set out, ²³ and as they were sailing He fell asleep. Then a fierce windstorm came down on the lake; they were being swamped and were in danger. ²⁴ They came and woke Him up, saying, "Master, Master, we're going to die!" Then He got up and rebuked the wind and the raging waves. So they ceased, and there was a calm. ²⁵ He said to them, "Where is your faith?"

They were fearful and amazed, asking one another, "Who can this be? He commands even the winds and the waves, and they obey Him!"

A Heart Panting for God

As a deer longs for streams of water, so I long for You, God.
—PSALM 42:1

If we are to be able to pursue God with a coordinated heart and mind, we must be willing to get in touch with the deep thirst for God which resides at the core of our being. You will never pursue God "with all four feet" until you become intensely aware of this deep inner thirst.

The thought underlying the word picture in our text today is that of a deer craving for water during a prolonged drought or after having been chased. The psalmist said his heart longed, or panted, for God, and the strong Hebrew word used here suggests a desire so intense that it is audible.

Do you pant after God in the way the psalmist described? Do you pursue Him in such a way that everything else in your life takes second place? I have to confess that I don't. Oh yes, I long after God. But I know I don't pant after Him in the way the psalmist described. And neither, I am convinced, do most other Christians.

Now don't react defensively and say: "Whatever does he mean? My heart pants after God, and I will not let anyone try to tell me differently." Let me ask you to reserve any judgment you have on the statement I have just made, and I think I will be able to show you in some of the following readings that although you have a deep desire to know God, you still might not have gotten to the place where your heart pants after Him in the way the psalmist described. But take heart—you can.

Prayer

God my Father, I would be rid of all that hinders my pursuit of You. Help me to see clearly into my heart, for I am so prone to defend myself. If there is something here that I need to know, then help me to look at it—openly and honestly. Amen.

Further Study

Ps 73:15-28; 27:4; 2 Ch 15:15
What was the psalmist's confession?
What happened when Israel sought the Lord wholeheartedly?

APRIL 9

*D*EUTERONOMY
14:22–16:22

22 "Each year you are to set aside a tenth of all the produce grown in your fields. 23 You are to eat a tenth of your grain, new wine, and oil, and the firstborn of your herd and flock, in the presence of the LORD your God at the place where He chooses to have His name dwell, so that you will always learn to fear the LORD your God. 24 But if the distance is too great for you to carry it, since the place where the LORD your God chooses to put His name is too far away from you and since the LORD your God has blessed you, 25 then exchange it for money, take the money in your hand, and go to the place the LORD your God chooses. 26 You may spend the money on anything you want: cattle, sheep, wine, beer, or anything you desire. You are to feast there in the presence of the LORD your God and rejoice with your family. 27 Do not forget the Levite within your gates, since he has no portion or inheritance among you.

28 "At the end of every three years, bring a tenth of all your produce for that year and store it within your gates. 29 Then the Levite, who has no portion or inheritance among you, the foreign resident, fatherless, and widow within your gates may come, eat, and be satisfied. And the LORD your God will bless you in all the work of your hands that you do.

15 "At the end of every seven years you must cancel debts. 2 This is how to cancel debt: Every creditor is to cancel what he has lent his neighbor. He is not to collect anything from his neighbor or brother, because the LORD's release of debts has been proclaimed. 3 You may collect something from a for-eigner, but you must forgive whatever your brother owes you.

4 "There will be no poor among you, however, because the LORD is certain to bless you in the land the LORD your God is giving you to possess as an inheritance— 5 if only you obey the LORD your God and are careful to follow every one of these commands I am giving you today. 6 When the LORD your God blesses you as He has promised you, you will lend to many nations but not borrow; you will rule over many nations, but they will not rule over you.

7 "If there is a poor person among you, one of your brothers within any of your gates in the land the LORD your God is giving you, you must not be hardhearted or tightfisted toward your poor brother. 8 Instead, you are to open your hand to him and freely loan him enough for whatever need he has. 9 Be careful that there isn't this wicked thought in your heart, 'The seventh year, the year of canceling debts, is near,' and you are stingy toward your poor brother and give him nothing. He will cry out to the LORD against you, and you will be guilty. 10 Give to him, and don't have a stingy heart when you give, and because of this the LORD your God will bless you in all your work and in everything you do. 11 For there will never cease to be poor people in the land; that is why I am commanding you, 'You must willingly open your hand to your afflicted and poor brother in your land.'

12 "If your fellow Hebrew, a man or woman, is sold to you and serves you six years, you must set him free in the seventh year. 13 When you set him free, do not send him away empty-handed. 14 Give generously to him from your flock, your threshing floor, and your winepress. You are to give him whatever the LORD your God has blessed you with. 15 Remember that you were a slave

in the land of Egypt and the LORD your God redeemed you; that is why I am giving you this command today. ¹⁶ But if your slave says to you, 'I don't want to leave you,' because he loves you and your family, and is well off with you, ¹⁷ take an awl and pierce through his ear into the door, and he will become your slave for life. Also treat your female slave the same way. ¹⁸ Do not regard it as a hardship when you set him free, because he worked for you six years—worth twice the wages of a hired hand. Then the LORD your God will bless you in everything you do.

¹⁹ "You must consecrate to the LORD your God every firstborn male produced by your herd and flock. You are not to put the firstborn of your oxen to work or shear the firstborn of your flock. ²⁰ Each year you and your family are to eat it before the LORD your God in the place the LORD chooses. ²¹ But if there is a defect in the animal, if it is lame or blind or has any serious defect, you must not sacrifice it to the LORD your God. ²² Eat it within your gates; both the unclean person and the clean may eat it, as though it were a gazelle or deer. ²³ But you must not eat its blood; pour it on the ground like water.

16 "Observe the month of Abib and celebrate the Passover to the LORD your God, because the LORD your God brought you out of Egypt by night in the month of Abib. ² Sacrifice to the LORD your God a Passover animal from the herd or flock in the place where the LORD chooses to have His name dwell. ³ You must not eat leavened bread with it. For seven days you are to eat unleavened bread with it, the bread of hardship—because you left the land of Egypt in a hurry—so that you may remember for the rest of your life the day you left the land of Egypt. ⁴ No yeast is to be found anywhere in your territory for seven days, and none of the meat you sacrifice in the evening of the first day is to remain until morning. ⁵ You are not to sacrifice the Passover animal in any of the towns the LORD your God is giving you. ⁶ You must only sacrifice the

Passover animal at the place where the LORD your God chooses to have His name dwell. Do this in the evening as the sun sets at the same time of day you departed from Egypt. ⁷ You are to cook and eat it in the place the LORD your God chooses, and you are to return to your tents in the morning. ⁸ You must eat unleavened bread for six days. On the seventh day there is to be a solemn assembly to the LORD your God, and you must not do any work.

⁹ "You are to count seven weeks, counting the weeks from the time the sickle is first put to the standing grain. ¹⁰ You are to celebrate the Festival of Weeks to the LORD your God with a freewill offering that you give in proportion to how the LORD your God has blessed you. ¹¹ Rejoice before the LORD your God in the place where He chooses to have His name dwell—you, your son and daughter, your male and female slave, the Levite within your gates, as well as the foreign resident, the fatherless, and the widow among you. ¹² Remember that you were slaves in Egypt; carefully follow these statutes.

¹³ "You are to celebrate the Festival of Booths for seven days when you have gathered in everything from your threshing floor and winepress. ¹⁴ Rejoice during your festival—you, your son and daughter, your male and female slave, as well as the Levite, the foreign resident, the fatherless, and the widow within your gates. ¹⁵ You are to hold a seven-day festival for the LORD your God in the place He chooses, because the LORD your God will bless you in all your produce and in all the work of your hands, and you will have abundant joy.

¹⁶ "All your males are to appear three times a year before the LORD your God in the place He chooses: at the Festival of Unleavened Bread, the Festival of Weeks, and the Festival of Booths. No one is to appear before the LORD empty-handed. ¹⁷ Everyone must appear with a gift suited to his means, according to the blessing the LORD your God has given you.

¹⁸ "Appoint judges and officials for your tribes in all your towns the LORD

your God is giving you. They are to judge the people with righteous judgment. ¹⁹ Do not deny justice or show partiality to anyone. Do not accept a bribe, for it blinds the eyes of the wise and twists the words of the righteous. ²⁰ Pursue justice and justice alone, so that you will live and possess the land the LORD your God is giving you.

²¹ "Do not set up an Asherah of any kind of wood next to the altar you will build for the LORD your God, ²² and do not set up a sacred pillar; the LORD your God hates them.

$\mathcal{P}$SALM 43:1-5

¹ Vindicate me, God, and defend my cause
against an ungodly nation;
rescue me from the deceitful and unjust man.
² For You are the God of my refuge.
Why have You rejected me?
Why must I go about in sorrow because of the enemy's oppression?

³ Send Your light and Your truth; let them lead me.
Let them bring me to Your holy mountain,
to Your dwelling place.
⁴ Then I will come to the altar of God,
to God, my greatest joy.
I will praise You with the lyre, God, my God.

⁵ Why am I so depressed?
Why this turmoil within me?
Hope in God, for I will still praise Him,
my Savior and my God.

$\mathcal{P}$ROVERBS 10:26-27

²⁶ Like vinegar to the teeth and smoke to the eyes,
so the slacker is to the one who sends him on an errand.

²⁷ The fear of the LORD prolongs life,
but the years of the wicked are cut short.

$\mathcal{L}$UKE 8:26-56

²⁶ Then they sailed to the region of the Gerasenes, which is opposite Galilee. ²⁷ When He got out on land, a demon-possessed man from the town met Him. For a long time he had worn no clothes and did not stay in a house but in the tombs. ²⁸ When he saw Jesus, he cried out, fell down before Him, and said in a loud voice, "What do You have to do with me, Jesus, You Son of the Most High God? I beg You, don't torment me!" ²⁹ For He had commanded the unclean spirit to come out of the man. Many times it had seized him, and although he was guarded, bound by chains and shackles, he would snap the restraints and be driven by the demon into deserted places.

³⁰ "What is your name?" Jesus asked him.

"Legion," he said—because many demons had entered him. ³¹ And they begged Him not to banish them to the abyss.

³² A large herd of pigs was there, feeding on the hillside. The demons begged Him to permit them to enter the pigs, and He gave them permission. ³³ The demons came out of the man and entered the pigs, and the herd rushed down the steep bank into the lake and drowned. ³⁴ When the men who tended them saw what had happened, they ran off and reported it in the town and in the countryside. ³⁵ Then people went out to see what had happened. They came to Jesus and found the man the demons had daparted from, sitting at Jesus' feet, dressed and in his right mind. And they were afraid. ³⁶ Meanwhile the eyewitnesses reported to them how the demon-possessed man was delivered. ³⁷ Then all the people of the Gerasene region asked Him to leave them, because they were gripped by great fear. So getting into the boat, He returned.

38 The man from whom the demons had departed kept begging Him to be with Him. But He sent him away and said, 39 "Go back to your home, and tell all that God has done for you." And off he went, proclaiming throughout the town all that Jesus had done for him.

40 When Jesus returned, the crowd welcomed Him, for they were all expecting Him. 41 Just then, a man named Jairus came. He was a leader of the synagogue. He fell down at Jesus' feet and pleaded with Him to come to his house, 42 because he had an only daughter about 12 years old, and she was at death's door.

While He was going, the crowds were nearly crushing Him. 43 A woman suffering from bleeding for 12 years, who had spent all she had on doctors yet could not be healed by any, 44 approached from behind and touched the tassel of His robe. Instantly her bleeding stopped.

45 "Who touched Me?" Jesus asked.

When they all denied it, Peter said, "Master, the crowds are hemming You in and pressing against You."

46 "Somebody did touch Me," said Jesus. "I know that power has gone out from Me." 47 When the woman saw that she was discovered, she came trembling and fell down before Him. In the presence of all the people, she declared the reason she had touched Him and how she was instantly cured. 48 "Daughter," He said to her, "your faith has made you well. Go in peace."

49 While He was still speaking, someone came from the synagogue leader's house, saying, "Your daughter is dead. Don't bother the Teacher anymore." 50 When Jesus heard it, He answered him, "Don't be afraid. Only believe, and she will be made well." 51 After He came to the house, He let no one enter with Him except Peter, John, James, and the child's father and mother. 52 Everyone was crying and mourning for her. But He said, "Stop crying, for she is not dead but asleep." 53 They started laughing at Him, because they knew she was dead. 54 So He took her by the hand and called out, "Child, get up!" 55 Her spirit returned, and she got up at once. Then He gave orders that she be given something to eat. 56 Her parents were astounded, but He instructed them to tell no one what had happened.

Disappointment

For You are the God of my refuge. Why have You rejected me?—Psalm 43:2

A deep hurt that may come is disappointment. We expect things to happen in a certain way, and when they don't, then we feel let down. We can be disappointed by people, or even by God if He chooses to direct our lives in a way other than we had hoped.

A woman wrote to me that during a meeting where I spoke on "The Healing of Life's Hurts," the Lord had ministered to her deep feelings of disappointment. Her disappointment was with God (as she put it) for "not healing my husband and for taking him to be with Himself." On the way home from the meeting, she narrowly missed being involved in a serious accident, and the Lord whispered to her heart: "And you have been doubting My love for you?" Within hours the bitter pain she had been carrying for a number of years was healed.

Are you in the throes of disappointment at this moment? Have others let you down? Or perhaps you feel God has let you down, and, because He is God, you feel you ought not to feel that way; therefore, you are repressing your disappointment and pushing it down into your subconscious. Bring it to Him now. God is not going to get mad at you for telling Him that you are disappointed with Him. If you feel upset with God, then confess the hurt; tell Him exactly how you feel. Then, when it is all out and you admit you were wrong—and not He—surrender the hurt into His hands and experience the healing that the divine Comforter brings.

Prayer

Father, I am thankful that I can bring all my disappointments to You. Some earthly fathers won't permit their children to be upset with them, but You accept me as I am. I am so grateful. Heal every disappointment in me now. For Jesus' sake. Amen.

Further Study

Jn 11:6-22; Ps 13:1-6; 69:3; 2 Pt 3:9
How did David express his disappointment?
What did Martha do about her disappointment?

APRIL 10

DEUTERONOMY 17:1–19:13

17 "You must not sacrifice to the LORD your God an ox or sheep with a defect or any serious flaw, for that is detestable to the LORD your God. ² "If a man or woman among you in one of your towns that the LORD your God will give you is discovered doing evil in the sight of the LORD your God and violating His covenant ³ and has gone to worship other gods by bowing down to the sun, moon, or all the stars in the sky—which I have forbidden— ⁴ and if you are told or hear about it, you must investigate it thoroughly. If the report turns out to be true that this detestable thing has happened in Israel, ⁵ you must bring out to your gates that man or woman who has done this evil thing and stone them to death. ⁶ The one condemned to die is to be executed on the testimony of two or three witnesses. No one is to be executed on the testimony of a single witness. ⁷ The witnesses' hands are to be the first in putting him to death, and after that, the hands of all the people. You must purge the evil from you.

⁸ "If a case is too difficult for you—concerning bloodshed, lawsuits, or assaults—cases disputed at your gates, you must go up to the place the LORD your God chooses. ⁹ You are to go up to the Levitical priests and to the judge who presides at that time. Ask, and they will give you a verdict in the case. ¹⁰ You must abide by the verdict they give you at the place the LORD chooses. Be careful

to do exactly as they instruct you. ¹¹ You must abide by the instruction they give you and the verdict they announce to you. Do not turn to the right or the left from the decision they declare to you. ¹² The person who acts arrogantly, refusing to listen either to the priest who stands there serving the LORD your God or to the judge, must die. You must purge the evil from Israel. ¹³ Then all the people will hear about it, be afraid, and no longer behave arrogantly.

¹⁴ "When you enter the land the LORD your God is giving you, take possession of it, live in it, and say, 'We want to appoint a king over us like all the nations around us,' ¹⁵ you are to appoint over you the king the LORD your God chooses. Appoint a king from your brothers. You are not to set a foreigner over you, or one who is not of your people. ¹⁶ However, he must not acquire many horses for himself or send the people back to Egypt to acquire many horses, for the LORD has told you, 'You are never to go back that way again.' ¹⁷ He must not acquire many wives for himself so that his heart won't go astray. He must not acquire very large amounts of silver and gold for himself. ¹⁸ When he is seated on his royal throne, he is to write a copy of this instruction for himself on a scroll in the presence of the Levitical priests. ¹⁹ It is to remain with him, and he is to read from it all the days of his life, so that he may learn to fear the LORD his God, to observe all the words of this instruction, and to do these statutes. ²⁰ Then his heart will not be exalted above his countrymen, he will not turn from this command to the right or the left, and he and his sons will continue ruling many years over Israel.

18 "The Levitical priests, the whole tribe of Levi, will have no portion or inheritance with Israel. They will eat the LORD's fire offerings; that is their inheritance. ² Although Levi has no inheritance among his brothers, the LORD is his inheritance, as He promised him. ³ This is the priests' share from the people who offer a sacrifice, whether it is an ox, a sheep, or a goat; the priests are to be given the shoulder, jaws, and stomach. ⁴ You are to give him the firstfruits of your grain, new wine, and oil, and the first sheared wool of your flock. ⁵ For the LORD your God has chosen him and his sons from all your tribes to stand and minister in the LORD's name from now on. ⁶ When a Levite leaves one of your towns where he lives in Israel and wants to go to the place the LORD chooses, ⁷ he may serve in the name of the LORD his God like all his fellow Levites who minister there in the presence of the LORD. ⁸ They will eat equal portions besides what he has received from the sale of the family estate.

⁹ "When you enter the land the LORD your God is giving you, do not imitate the detestable customs of those nations. ¹⁰ No one among you is to make his son or daughter pass through the fire, practice divination, tell fortunes, interpret omens, practice sorcery, ¹¹ cast spells, consult a medium or a familiar spirit, or inquire of the dead. ¹² Everyone who does these things is detestable to the LORD, and the LORD your God is driving out the nations before you because of these detestable things. ¹³ You must be blameless before the LORD your God. ¹⁴ Though these nations you are about to drive out listen to fortune-tellers and diviners, the LORD your God has not permitted you to do this.

¹⁵ "The LORD your God will raise up for you a prophet like me from among your own brothers. You must listen to him. ¹⁶ This is what you requested from the LORD your God at Horeb on the day of the assembly when you said, 'Let us not continue to hear the voice of the LORD our God or see this great fire any longer, so that we will not die!' ¹⁷ Then the LORD said to me, 'They have spoken well. ¹⁸ I will raise up for them a prophet like you from among their brothers. I will put My words in his mouth, and he will tell them everything I command him. ¹⁹ I will hold accountable whoever does not listen to My words that he speaks in My name. ²⁰ But the prophet who dares to speak in My name a message I have not commanded him to

speak, or who speaks in the name of other gods—that prophet must die.' ²¹ You may say to yourself, 'How can we recognize a message the LORD has not spoken?' ²² When a prophet speaks in the LORD's name, and the message does not come true or is not fulfilled, that is a message the LORD has not spoken. The prophet has spoken it presumptuously. Do not be afraid of him.

19 "When the LORD your God annihilates the nations whose land He is giving you, so that you drive them out and live in their cities and houses, ² you are to set apart three cities for yourselves within the land the LORD your God is giving you to possess. ³ You are to determine the distances and divide the land the LORD your God is granting you as an inheritance into three regions, so that anyone who commits manslaughter can flee to these cities.

⁴ "Here is the law concerning a case of someone who kills a person and flees there to save his life, having killed his neighbor accidentally without previously hating him: ⁵ If he goes into the forest with his neighbor to cut timber, and his hand swings the ax to chop down a tree, but the blade flies off the handle and strikes his neighbor so that he dies, that person may flee to one of these cities and live. ⁶ Otherwise, the avenger of blood in the heat of his anger might pursue the one who committed manslaughter, overtake him because the distance is great, and strike him dead. Yet he did not deserve to die, since he did not previously hate his neighbor. ⁷ This is why I am commanding you to set apart three cities for yourselves. ⁸ If the LORD your God enlarges your territory as He swore to your fathers, and gives you all the land He promised to give them— ⁹ provided you keep every one of these commands I am giving you today and follow them, loving the LORD your God and walking in His ways at all times—you are to add three more cities to these three. ¹⁰ In this way, innocent blood will not be shed, and you will not become guilty of bloodshed in the land the LORD your God is giving you as an inheri-

tance. ¹¹ But if someone hates his neighbor, lies in ambush for him, attacks him, and strikes him fatally, and flees to one of these cities, ¹² the elders of his city must send for him, take him from there, and hand him over to the avenger of blood and he will die. ¹³ You must not look on him with pity but purge from Israel the guilt of shedding innocent blood, and you will prosper.

𝒫SALM 44:1-8

¹ God, we have heard with our
    ears—
our forefathers have told us—
the work You accomplished in
    their days,
in days long ago:
² to plant them, You drove out the
    nations with Your hand;
to settle them, You crushed the
    peoples.
³ For they did not take the land by
    their sword—
their arm did not bring them
    victory—
but by Your right hand, Your arm,
    and the light of Your face,
for You were pleased with them.

⁴ You are my King, my God,
who ordains victories for Jacob.
⁵ Through You we drive back our
    foes;
through Your name we trample
    our enemies.
⁶ For I do not trust in my bow,
and my sword does not bring me
    victory.
⁷ But You give us victory over our
    foes
and let those who hate us be
    disgraced.
⁸ We boast in God all day long;
we will praise Your name forever.
Selah

𝒫ROVERBS 10:28-30

²⁸ The hope of the righteous is joy,
but the expectation of the wicked
    comes to nothing.

²⁹ The way of the LORD is a
stronghold for the honorable,
but destruction awaits the
malicious.

³⁰ The righteous will never be
shaken,
but the wicked will not remain on
the earth.

LUKE 9:1-22

9 Summoning the Twelve, He gave
them power and authority over all
the demons, and power to heal dis-
eases. ² Then He sent them to proclaim
the kingdom of God and to heal the
sick.

³ "Take nothing for the road," He told
them, "no walking stick, no traveling
bag, no bread, no money; and don't take
an extra shirt. ⁴ Whatever house you enter, stay there and leave from there. ⁵ If
they do not welcome you, when you
leave that town, shake off the dust from
your feet as a testimony against them."
⁶ So they went out and traveled from vil-
lage to village, proclaiming the good
news and healing everywhere.

⁷ Herod the tetrarch heard about
everything that was going on. He was
perplexed, because some said that John
had been raised from the dead, ⁸ some
that Elijah had appeared, and others
that one of the ancient prophets had
risen. ⁹ "I beheaded John," Herod said,
"but who is this I hear such things
about?" And he wanted to see Him.

¹⁰ When the apostles returned, they
reported to Jesus all that they had done.
He took them along and withdrew pri-
vately to a town called Bethsaida. ¹¹ When

the crowds found out, they followed
Him. He welcomed them, spoke to
them about the kingdom of God, and
cured those who needed healing.

¹² Late in the day, the Twelve ap-
proached and said to Him, "Send the
crowd away, so they can go into the surrounding villages and countryside to
find food and lodging, because we are in
a deserted place here."

¹³ "You give them something to eat,"
He told them.

"We have no more than five loaves
and two fish," they said, "unless we go
and buy food for all these people."
¹⁴ (For about 5,000 men were there.)

Then He told His disciples, "Have
them sit down in groups of about 50
each." ¹⁵ They did so, and had them all
sit down. ¹⁶ Then He took the five loaves
and the two fish, and looking up to
heaven, He blessed and broke them. He
kept giving them to the disciples to set
before the crowd. ¹⁷ Everyone ate and
was filled. Then they picked up 12 baskets of leftover pieces.

¹⁸ While He was praying in private and
His disciples were with Him, He asked
them, "Who do the crowds say that I
am?"

¹⁹ They answered, "John the Baptist;
others, Elijah; still others, that one of
the ancient prophets has come back."

²⁰ "But you," He asked them, "who do
you say that I am?"

Peter answered, "God's Messiah!"

²¹ But He strictly warned and in-
structed them to tell this to no one,
²² saying, "The Son of Man must suffer
many things and be rejected by the elders, chief priests, and scribes, be killed,
and be raised the third day."

Christ's Righteousness

*For I do not trust in my bow, and my sword does not bring me victory.
But You give us victory over our foes.*—PSALM 44:6-7

When Paul talks about the "righteousness like armor on your chest" in Ephesians 6:14, is he
talking about our righteousness or Christ's righteousness?

I believe he is talking about Christ's righteousness. That is not to say, of course, that our own righteousness (our moral uprightness) is unimportant, for as Paul points out in 2 Corinthians 6:7, our righteousness can be a definite defense against Satan. In Ephesians 6, however, the emphasis is not on our righteousness in Christ, but Christ's righteousness in us.

So how does putting on the breastplate of righteousness act as a spiritual defense against the wiles of the devil? Take, for example, those people who have definitely surrendered their lives to Christ but whom Satan afflicts with a feeling that they are not good enough to be saved. Why do they have such feelings? The answer is simple—they have taken their eyes off Christ and His righteousness and have focused on themselves and their righteousness. And in doing that, they have played right into the Devil's hands.

You see, the Devil can find all kinds of flaws and blemishes in your righteousness, but he can find nothing wrong with the righteousness of Christ. The way to withstand an attack like this, then, is to put on the breastplate of righteousness. In other words, remind yourself and Satan that you stand not on your own merits but on Christ's. This may sound simple, even simplistic to some, but I have lived long enough to see people latch on to it and come from the depths of emotional distress to the heights of spiritual exaltation.

Prayer

Lord Jesus, help me to latch onto it. Make it crystal clear to my spirit that although the Devil can find many flaws in my righteousness, he cannot find a single flaw in Yours. I rest my case—on You. Thank You, dear Lord. Amen.

Further Study

1 Co 1:19-31; Is 64:6; Rm 8:34; Php 3:9
What is our righteousness like?
What was Paul's declaration?

APRIL 11

DEUTERONOMY 19:14–21:23

14 "You must not move your neighbor's boundary marker, established at the start in the inheritance you will receive in the land the LORD your God is giving you to possess.

15 "One witness cannot establish any wrongdoing or sin against a person, whatever that person has done. A fact must be established by the testimony of two or three witnesses.

16 "If a malicious witness testifies against someone accusing him of a crime, 17 the two people in the dispute

401

must stand in the presence of the LORD before the priests and judges in authority at the time. [18] The judges are to make a careful investigation, and if the witness turns out to be a liar who has falsely accused his brother, [19] you must do to him as he intended to do to his brother. You must purge the evil from you. [20] Then everyone else will hear and be afraid, and they will never again do anything evil like this among you. [21] You must not show pity: life for life, eye for eye, tooth for tooth, hand for hand, and foot for foot.

20 "When you go out to war against your enemies and see horses, chariots, and an army larger than yours, do not be afraid of them, for the LORD your God, who brought you out of the land of Egypt, is with you. [2] When you are about to engage in battle, the priest is to come forward and address the army. [3] He is to say to them: 'Listen, Israel: Today you are about to engage in battle with your enemies. Do not be fainthearted. Do not be afraid, alarmed, or terrified because of them. [4] For the LORD your God is the One who goes with you to fight for you against your enemies to give you victory.'

[5] "The officers are to address the army, 'Has any man built a new house and not dedicated it? Let him leave and return home. Otherwise, he may die in battle and another man dedicate it. [6] Has any man planted a vineyard and not begun to enjoy its fruit? Let him leave and return home. Otherwise he may die in battle and another man enjoy its fruit. [7] Has any man become engaged to a woman and not married her? Let him leave and return home. Otherwise he may die in battle and another man marry her.' [8] The officers will continue to address the army and say, 'Is there any man who is afraid or fainthearted? Let him leave and return home, so that his brothers' hearts won't melt like his own.' [9] When the officers have finished addressing the army, they will appoint military commanders to lead it.

[10] "When you approach a city to fight against it, you must make an offer of peace. [11] If it accepts your offer of peace and opens its gates to you, all the people found in it will become forced laborers for you and serve you. [12] However, if it does not make peace with you but wages war against you, lay siege to it. [13] When the LORD your God hands it over to you, you must strike down all its males with the sword. [14] But you may take the women, children, animals, and whatever else is in the city—all its spoil—as plunder. You may enjoy the spoil of your enemies that the LORD your God has given you. [15] This is how you are to treat all the cities that are far away from you and are not among the cities of these nations. [16] However, you must not let any living thing survive among the cities of these people the LORD your God is giving you as an inheritance. [17] You must completely destroy them—the Hittite, Amorite, Canaanite, Perizzite, Hivite, and Jebusite—as the LORD your God has commanded you, [18] so that they won't teach you to do all the detestable things they do for their gods, and you sin against the LORD your God.

[19] "When you lay siege to a city for a long time, fighting against it in order to capture it, you must not destroy its trees by putting an ax to them, because you can get food from them. You must not cut them down. Are trees of the field human, to come under siege by you? [20] But you may destroy the trees that you know do not produce food. You may cut them down to build siege works against the city that is waging war with you, until it falls.

21 "If a murder victim is found lying in a field in the land the LORD your God is giving you to possess, and it is not known who killed him, [2] your elders and judges must come out and measure the distance from the victim to the nearby cities. [3] The elders of the city nearest to the victim are to get a cow that has not been yoked or used for work. [4] The elders of that city will bring the cow down to a continually flowing stream, to a place not tilled or sown, and they will break the cow's neck there by the stream. ⁵ Then the priests, the sons of Levi, will come forward, for the LORD your God has chosen them to serve Him and pronounce blessings in the LORD's name, and they are to give a ruling in every dispute and case of assault. ⁶ All the elders of the city nearest to the victim will wash their hands by the stream over the heifer whose neck has been broken. ⁷ They will declare, 'Our hands did not shed this blood; our eyes did not see it. ⁸ LORD, forgive Your people Israel You redeemed, and do not hold the shedding of innocent blood against them.' Then they will be absolved of responsibility for bloodshed. ⁹ You must purge from yourselves the guilt of shedding innocent blood, for you will be doing what is right in the LORD's sight.

¹⁰ "When you go to war against your enemies and the LORD your God hands them over to you and you take some of them prisoner, and ¹¹ if you see a beautiful woman among the captives, desire her, and want to take her as your wife, ¹² you are to bring her into your house. She must shave her head, trim her nails, ¹³ remove the clothes she was wearing when she was taken prisoner, live in your house, and mourn for her father and mother a full month. After that, you may have sexual relations with her and be her husband, and she will be your wife. ¹⁴ Then if you are not satisfied with her, you are to let her go where she wants, but you must not sell her for money or treat her as merchandise, because you have humiliated her.

¹⁵ "If a man has two wives, one loved and the other unloved, and both the loved and the unloved bear him sons, and if the unloved wife has the firstborn son, ¹⁶ when that man gives what he has to his sons as an inheritance, he is not to show favoritism to the son of the loved wife as his firstborn over the firstborn of the unloved wife. ¹⁷ He must acknowledge the firstborn, the son of the unloved wife, by giving him a double portion of everything that belongs to him, for he is the firstfruits of his virility; he has the rights of the firstborn.

¹⁸ "If a man has a stubborn and rebellious son who does not obey his father or mother and doesn't listen to them even after they discipline him, ¹⁹ his father and mother must take hold of him and bring him to the elders of his city, to the gate of his hometown. ²⁰ They will say to the elders of his city, 'This son of ours is stubborn and rebellious; he doesn't obey us. He's a glutton and a drunkard.' ²¹ Then all the men of his city will stone him to death. You must purge the evil from you, and all Israel will hear and be afraid.

²² "If anyone is found guilty of an offense deserving the death penalty and is executed, and you hang his body on a tree, ²³ you are not to leave his corpse on the tree overnight but are to bury him that day, for anyone hung on a tree is under God's curse. You must not defile the land the LORD your God is giving you as an inheritance.

PSALM 44:9-16

⁹ But You have rejected and
   humiliated us;
   You do not march out with our
      armies.
¹⁰ You make us retreat from the foe,
   and those who hate us have taken
      plunder for themselves.
¹¹ You hand us over to be eaten like
      sheep
   and scatter us among the nations.
¹² You sell Your people for nothing;
   You make no profit from selling
      them.
¹³ You make us an object of reproach
      to our neighbors,
   a source of mockery and ridicule
      to those around us.
¹⁴ You make us a joke among the
      nations,
   a laughingstock among the
      peoples.
¹⁵ My disgrace is before me all day
      long,
   and shame has covered my face,
¹⁶ because of the voice of the
      scorner and reviler,
   because of the enemy and
      avenger.

*P*ROVERBS 10:31-32

31 The mouth of the righteous
produces wisdom,
but a perverse tongue will be cut
out.

32 The lips of the righteous know
what is appropriate,
but the mouth of the wicked, only
what is perverse.

*L*UKE 9:23-45

23 Then He said to them all, "If any-one wants to come with Me, he must deny himself, take up his cross daily, and follow Me. 24 For whoever wants to save his life will lose it, but whoever loses his life because of Me will save it. 25 What is a man benefited if he gains the whole world, yet loses or forfeits himself? 26 For whoever is ashamed of Me and My words, the Son of Man will be ashamed of him when He comes in His glory and that of the Father and the holy angels. 27 I tell you the truth: there are some standing here who will not taste death until they see the kingdom of God."

28 About eight days after these words, He took along Peter, John, and James, and went up on the mountain to pray. 29 As He was praying, the appearance of His face changed, and His clothes be-came dazzling white. 30 Suddenly, two men were talking with Him—Moses and Elijah. 31 They appeared in glory and were speaking of His death, which He was about to accomplish in Jerusalem. 32 Peter and those with him were in a deep sleep, and when they became ful-ly awake, they saw His glory and the two men who were standing with Him. 33 As the two men were departing from Him, Peter said to Jesus, "Master, it's good for us to be here! Let us make

three tabernacles: one for You, one for Moses, and one for Elijah"—not know-ing what he said. 34 While he was saying this, a cloud appeared and overshadowed them. They became afraid as they entered the cloud. 35 Then a voice came from the cloud, saying:

This is My Son, the Chosen One;
listen to Him!

36 After the voice had spoken, only Jesus was found. They kept silent, and in those days told no one what they had seen.

37 The next day, when they came down from the mountain, a large crowd met Him. 38 Just then a man from the crowd cried out, "Teacher, I beg You to look at my son, because he's my only child. 39 Often a spirit seizes him; sud-denly he shrieks, and it throws him into convulsions until he foams at the mouth; wounding him, it hardly ever leaves him. 40 I begged Your disciples to drive it out, but they couldn't."

41 Jesus replied, "You unbelieving and rebellious generation! How long will I be with you and put up with you? Bring your son here."

42 As the boy was still approaching, the demon knocked him down and threw him into severe convulsions. But Jesus rebuked the unclean spirit, cured the boy, and gave him back to his father. 43 And they were all astonished at the greatness of God.

While everyone was amazed at all the things He was doing, He told His disci-ples, 44 "Let these words sink in: the Son of Man is about to be betrayed into the hands of men."

45 But they did not understand this statement; it was concealed from them so that they could not grasp it, and they were afraid to ask Him about it.

God Speaks

Then a voice came from the cloud, saying:
"This is My Son, the Chosen One; listen to Him!"—LUKE 9:35

Peter's Jewish heart is divided—wanting to keep Moses, representing the Law; Elijah, representing the Prophets; and Jesus, representing the new revelation, all on the same level. He said: "Let us make three tabernacles." This was serious, for the whole future was bound up with the question of whether Jesus was final and whether supreme allegiance should be given to Him. It is significant that immediately following this statement, a cloud descended and "they became afraid as they entered the cloud."

Where there is division, there will always be clouds. There are clouds over our churches, and we fear as we enter those clouds. Why are we afraid? The answer is simple—division. Each denomination is thinking in terms of itself, is losing a sense of the collective unity. But out of the cloud comes a Voice. God speaks! The voice is one of evaluation and invitation: "This is my Son, the Chosen One; listen to Him!" (Lk 9:35). The clouds will never lift and the fears will never depart until we listen to Christ. And what is He saying? This: "May they all be one, as You, Father, are in Me and I am in You" (Jn 17:21). Christ must be first, and the unity of His Body must take priority over any denominational allegiance.

As the Divine Eagle nudges His Church toward the edge of the nest in an effort to cause it to soar above denominational divides, I pray that it will not be long before we who share Christ's Name truly become one.

Prayer

O Father, I am so thankful that I am part of Your glorious Family. Make me a good member of that Family. May the Family spirit be in all I do and say, for I want others to come into this Family. In Jesus' name. Amen.

Further Study

Mt 5:21-26; Is 11:13; 52:7; Jn 10:16
What steps will you take to build Christian unity?
Is there anyone you need to be reconciled to?

APRIL 12

DEUTERONOMY
22:1–23:25

22 "If you see your brother's ox or sheep straying, you must not ignore it; make sure you return it to your brother. [2] If your brother does not live near you or you don't know him, you are to bring the animal to your home to remain with you until your brother comes looking for it; then you can return it to him. [3] Do the same for his donkey, his garment, or anything your brother has lost and you have found. You must not ignore it. [4] If you see your brother's donkey or ox fallen down on the road, you must not ignore it; you must help him lift it up.

[5] "A woman is not to wear male clothing, and a man is not to put on a woman's garment, for everyone who does these things is detestable to the LORD your God.

[6] "If you come across a bird's nest with chicks or eggs, either in a tree or on the ground along the road, and the mother is sitting on the chicks or eggs, you must not take the mother along with the young. [7] You may take the young for yourself, but be sure to let the mother go free, so that you may prosper and live long. [8] If you build a new house, make a railing around your roof, so that you don't bring bloodguilt on your house if someone falls from it. [9] Do not plant your vineyard with two types of seed; otherwise, the entire harvest, both the crop you plant and the produce of the vineyard, will be defiled. [10] Do not plow with an ox and a donkey together. [11] Do not wear clothes made of both wool and linen. [12] Make tassels on the four corners of the outer garment you wear.

[13] "If a man marries a woman, has sexual relations with her, and comes to hate her, [14] and accuses her of shameful conduct, and gives her a bad name, saying, 'I married this woman and was intimate with her, but I didn't find any evidence of her virginity,' [15] the young woman's father and mother will take the evidence of her virginity and bring it to the city elders at the gate. [16] The young woman's father will say to the elders, 'I gave my daughter to this man as a wife, but he hates her. [17] He has accused her of shameful conduct, saying: "I didn't find any evidence of your daughter's virginity, but here is the evidence of my daughter's virginity." They will spread out the cloth before the city elders. [18] Then the elders of that city will take the man and punish him. [19] They will also fine him 100 silver shekels and give them to the young woman's father, because that man gave an Israelite virgin a bad name. She will remain his wife; he cannot divorce her as long as he lives. [20] But if this accusation is true and no evidence of the young woman's virginity is found, [21] they will bring the woman to the door of her father's house, and the men of her city will stone her to death. For she has committed an outrage in Israel by being promiscuous in her father's house. You must purge the evil from you.

[22] "If a man is discovered having sexual relations with another man's wife, both the man who had sex with the woman and the woman must die. You must purge the evil from Israel. [23] If there is a young woman who is a virgin engaged to a man, and another man encounters her in the city and has sex with her, [24] you must take the two of them out to the gate of that city and stone them to death—the young woman because she did not cry out in the city and the man because he has violated his neighbor's fiancée. You must

purge the evil from you. ²⁵ But if the man encounters the engaged woman in the open country, and he seizes and rapes her, only the man who raped her must die. ²⁶ Do nothing to the young woman, because she is not guilty of an offense deserving death. This case is just like one in which a man attacks his neighbor and murders him. ²⁷ When he found her in the field, the engaged woman cried out, but there was no one to rescue her. ²⁸ If a man encounters a young woman, a virgin who is not engaged, takes hold of her and rapes her, and they are discovered, ²⁹ the man who raped her must give the young woman's father 50 silver shekels, and she must become his wife because he violated her. He cannot divorce her as long as he lives.

³⁰ "A man is not to marry his father's wife; he must not violate his father's marriage bed.

23 "No man whose testicles have been crushed or whose penis has been cut off may enter the LORD's assembly. ² No one of illegitimate birth may enter the LORD's assembly; none of his descendants, even to the tenth generation, may enter the LORD's assembly. ³ No Ammonite or Moabite may enter the LORD's assembly; none of their descendants, even to the tenth generation, may ever enter the LORD's assembly. ⁴ This is because they did not meet you with food and water on the journey after you came out of Egypt, and because Balaam son of Beor from Pethor in Aram-naharaim was hired to curse you. ⁵ Yet the LORD your God would not listen to Balaam, but He turned the curse into a blessing for you because the LORD your God loves you. ⁶ Never seek peace or friendship with them as long as you live. ⁷ Do not despise an Edomite, because he is your brother. Do not despise an Egyptian, because you were a foreign resident in his land. ⁸ The children born to them in the third generation may enter the LORD's assembly.

⁹ "When you are encamped against your enemies, be careful to avoid anything offensive. ¹⁰ If there is a man among you who is unclean because of a bodily emission during the night, he must go outside the camp; he may not come anywhere inside the camp. ¹¹ When evening approaches, he must wash with water, and when the sun sets he may come inside the camp. ¹² You must have a place outside the camp and go there to relieve yourself. ¹³ You must have a digging tool in your equipment; when you relieve yourself, dig a hole with it and cover up your excrement. ¹⁴ For the LORD your God walks throughout your camp to protect you and deliver your enemies to you; so your encampments must be holy. He must not see anything improper among you or He will turn away from you.

¹⁵ "Do not return a slave to his master when he has escaped from his master to you. ¹⁶ Let him live among you wherever he wants within your gates. Do not mistreat him.

¹⁷ "No Israelite woman is to be a cult prostitute, and no Israelite man is to be a cult prostitute. ¹⁸ Do not bring a female prostitute's wages or a male prostitute's earnings into the house of the LORD your God to fulfill any vow, because both are detestable to the LORD your God.

¹⁹ "Do not charge your brother interest on money, food, or anything that can earn interest. ²⁰ You may charge a foreigner interest, but you must not charge your brother interest, so that the LORD your God may bless you in everything you do in the land you are entering to possess.

²¹ "If you make a vow to the LORD your God, do not be slow to keep it, because He will require it of you, and it will be counted against you as sin. ²² But if you refrain from making a vow, it will not be counted against you as sin. ²³ Be careful to do whatever comes from your lips, because you have freely vowed what you promised to the LORD your God.

²⁴ "When you enter your neighbor's vineyard, you may eat as many grapes as you want until you are full, but you must not put any in your container. ²⁵ When you enter your neighbor's standing grain, you may pluck heads of

grain with your hand, but you must not put a sickle to your neighbor's grain.

PSALM 44:17-26

17 All this has happened to us, but
we have not forgotten You
or betrayed Your covenant.
18 Our hearts have not turned
back;
our steps have not strayed from
Your path.
19 But You have crushed us in a
haunt of jackals
and have covered us with deepest
darkness.
20 If we had forgotten the name of
our God
and spread out our hands to a
foreign god,
21 wouldn't God have found this
out,
since He knows the secrets of the
heart?
22 Because of You we are slain all day
long;
we are counted as sheep to be
slaughtered.
23 Wake up, LORD! Why are You
sleeping?
Get up! Don't reject us forever!
24 Why do You hide Yourself
and forget our affliction and
oppression?
25 For we have sunk down to the
dust;
our bodies cling to the ground.
26 Rise up! Help us!
Redeem us because of Your
faithful love.

PROVERBS 11:1-4

11 Dishonest scales are detestable
to the LORD,
but an accurate weight is His
delight.

2 When pride comes, disgrace
follows,
but with humility comes wisdom.

3 The integrity of the upright guides
them,
but the perversity of the
treacherous destroys them.

4 Wealth is not profitable on a day
of wrath,
but righteousness rescues from
death.

LUKE 9:46-62

46 Then an argument started among them about who would be the greatest of them. 47 But Jesus, knowing the thoughts of their hearts, took a little child and had him stand next to Him. 48 He told them, "Whoever welcomes this little child in My name welcomes Me. And whoever welcomes Me welcomes Him who sent Me. For whoever is least among you—this one is great."

49 John responded, "Master, we saw someone driving out demons in Your name, and we tried to stop him because he does not follow us."

50 "Don't stop him," Jesus told him, "because whoever is not against you is for you."

51 When the days were coming to a close for Him to be taken up, He determined to journey to Jerusalem. 52 He sent messengers ahead of Him, and on the way they entered a village of the Samaritans to make preparations for Him. 53 But they did not welcome Him, because He determined to journey to Jerusalem. 54 When the disciples James and John saw this, they said, "Lord, do You want us to call down fire from heaven to consume them?"

55 But He turned and rebuked them, 56 and they went to another village.

57 As they were traveling on the road someone said to Him, "I will follow You wherever You go!"

58 Jesus told him, "Foxes have dens, and birds of the sky have nests, but the Son of Man has no place to lay His head." 59 Then He said to another, "Follow Me."

"Lord," he said, "first let me go bury my father."

⁶⁰ But He told him, "Let the dead bury their own dead, but you go and spread the news of the kingdom of God."

⁶¹ Another also said, "I will follow You, Lord, but first let me go and say good-bye to those at my house."

⁶² But Jesus said to him, "No one who puts his hand to the plow and looks back is fit for the kingdom of God."

The Measure of Maturity

We saw someone driving out demons in Your name, and we tried to stop him because he does not follow us.—LUKE 9:49

Our fellowship with other Christians heightens our understanding of God and helps us stay spiritually fresh. I have no doubt that my fellowship with other Christians has helped more than words can convey in keeping me spiritually alert and topped up. When for some reason I am not able to fellowship with other Christians, my spiritual life tends to sag. This is one of the laws of the Christian life, and we ignore it to our peril.

Dr. E. Stanley Jones said, "The measure of our spiritual maturity can be and is measured by the breadth and depth of our capacity and willingness for fellowship." Note the words "capacity" and "willingness." This doesn't mean working at enlarging our circle of fellowship— though for some it may mean that—but that we have the capacity and willingness to do it if God should so lead.

I know there are Christians in churches, fellowships, and denominations whom I will never meet down here on earth, but I have the capacity and willingness to fellowship with them if God were to make it possible. We are only as mature as our willingness and capacity for fellowship. Therefore, if we cannot or do not want to fellowship with others who are truly Christ's, then we are immature Christians. Churches and denominations have different rules and guidelines in relation to mixing with others of different groups, but as far as individual fellowship is concerned, our basis ought to be this: everyone who belongs to Christ should belong to everyone else who belongs to Christ.

Prayer

Father, I see that if I shut out my brother, I shut out You, and my life will soon become stale. Help me deepen all the areas of my fellowship—my fellowship with You and my fellowship with others. In Jesus' name. Amen.

Further Study

Jn 13:31-35; Rm 12:5; 1 Co 10:17; Gl 3:28
What is the greatest testimony of Christ to the world?
To what does Paul liken the body of Christ?

APRIL 13

DEUTERONOMY
24:1–26:19

24 "If a man marries a woman, but she becomes displeasing to him because he finds something improper about her, he may write her a divorce certificate, hand it to her, and send her away from his house. ² If after leaving his house she goes and becomes another man's wife, ³ and the second man hates her, writes her a divorce certificate, hands it to her, and sends her away from his house or if he dies, ⁴ the first husband who sent her away may not marry her again after she has been defiled, because that would be detestable to the LORD. You must not bring guilt on the land the LORD your God is giving you as an inheritance.

⁵ "When a man takes a bride, he must not go out with the army or be liable for any duty. He is free to stay at home for one year, so that he can bring joy to the wife he has married.

⁶ "Do not take a pair of millstones or an upper millstone as security for a debt, because that is like taking a life as security.

⁷ "If a man is discovered kidnapping one of his Israelite brothers, whether he treats him as a slave or sells him, the kidnapper must die. You must purge the evil from you.

⁸ "Be careful in a case of infectious skin disease, following carefully everything the Levitical priests instruct you to do. Be careful to do as I have commanded them. ⁹ Remember what the LORD your God did to Miriam on the journey after you left Egypt.

¹⁰ "When you make a loan of any kind to your neighbor, do not enter his house to collect what he offers as security. ¹¹ You must stand outside while the man you are making the loan to brings the security out to you. ¹² If he is a poor man, you must not sleep in the garment he has given as security. ¹³ Be sure to return it to him at sunset. Then he will sleep in it and bless you, and this will be counted as righteousness to you before the LORD your God.

¹⁴ "Do not oppress a hired hand who is poor and needy, whether one of your brothers or one of the foreigners residing within a town in your land. ¹⁵ You are to pay him his wages each day before the sun sets, because he is poor and depends on them. Otherwise he will cry out to the LORD against you, and you will be held guilty.

¹⁶ "Fathers are not to be put to death for their children or children for their fathers; each person will be put to death for his own sin. ¹⁷ Do not deny justice to a foreign resident or fatherless child, and do not take a widow's garment as security. ¹⁸ Remember that you were a slave in Egypt, and the LORD your God redeemed you from there. Therefore I am commanding you to do this.

¹⁹ "When you reap the harvest in your field, and you forget a sheaf in the field, do not go back to get it. It is to be left for the foreign resident, the fatherless, and the widow, so that the LORD your God may bless you in all the work of your hands. ²⁰ When you knock down the fruit from your olive tree, you must not go over the branches again. What remains will be for the foreign resident, the fatherless, and the widow. ²¹ When you gather the grapes of your vineyard, you must not glean what is left. What remains will be for the foreign resident, the fatherless, and the widow. ²² Remember that you were a slave in the land of Egypt. Therefore I am commanding you to do this.

25 "If there is a dispute between men, they are to go to court, and the judges will hear their case. They will clear the innocent and condemn the guilty. ² If the guilty party deserves to be flogged, the judge will make him lie down and be flogged in his presence with the number of lashes appropriate for his crime. ³ He may be flogged with 40 lashes, but no more. Otherwise, if he is flogged with more lashes than these, your brother will be degraded in your sight.

⁴ "Do not muzzle an ox while it treads out grain.

⁵ "When brothers live on the same property and one of them dies without a son, the wife of the dead man may not marry a stranger outside the family. Her brother-in-law is to take her as his wife, have sexual relations with her, and perform the duty of a brother-in-law for her. ⁶ The first son she bears will carry on the name of the dead brother, so his name will not be blotted out from Israel. ⁷ But if the man doesn't want to marry his sister-in-law, she must go to the elders at the city gate and say, 'My brother-in-law refuses to preserve his brother's name in Israel. He isn't willing to perform the duty of a brother-in-law for me.' ⁸ The elders of his city will summon him and speak with him. If he persists and says, 'I don't want to marry her,' ⁹ then his sister-in-law will go up to him in the sight of the elders, remove his sandal from his foot, and spit in his face. Then she will declare, 'This is what is done to a man who will not build up his brother's house.' ¹⁰ And his family name in Israel will be called 'The house of the man whose sandal was removed.'

¹¹ "If two men are fighting with each other, and the wife of one steps in to rescue her husband from the one striking him, and she puts out her hand and grabs his genitals, ¹² you are to cut off her hand. You must not show pity.

¹³ "You must not have two different weights in your bag, one heavy and one light. ¹⁴ You must not have two differing dry measures in your house, a larger and a smaller. ¹⁵ You must have a full and honest weight, a full and honest dry measure, so that you may live long in

the land the LORD your God is giving you. ¹⁶ For everyone who does such things and acts unfairly is detestable to the LORD your God.

¹⁷ "Remember what the Amalekites did to you on the journey after you left Egypt. ¹⁸ They met you along the way and attacked all your stragglers from behind when you were tired and weary. They did not fear God. ¹⁹ When the LORD your God gives you rest from all the enemies around you in the land the LORD your God is giving you to possess as an inheritance, blot out the memory of Amalek from under heaven. Do not forget.

26 "When you enter the land the LORD your God is giving you as an inheritance, and you take possession of it and live in it, ² you must take some of the first of all the soil's produce that you harvest from the land the LORD your God is giving you and put it in a container. Then go to the place where the LORD your God chooses to have His name dwell. ³ When you come before the priest who is serving at that time, you must say to him, 'Today I acknowledge to the LORD your God that I have entered the land the LORD swore to our fathers to give us.'

⁴ "Then the priest will take the container from your hand and place it before the altar of the LORD your God. ⁵ You are to respond by saying in the presence of the LORD your God:

My father was a wandering Aramean. He went down to Egypt with a few people and lived there. There he became a great, powerful, and populous nation. ⁶ But the Egyptians mistreated and afflicted us, and forced us to do hard labor. ⁷ So we called out to the LORD, the God of our fathers, and the LORD heard our cry and saw our misery, hardship, and oppression. ⁸ Then the LORD brought us out of Egypt with a strong hand and an outstretched arm, with terrifying power, and with signs and wonders. ⁹ He led us to this place and gave us this land, a land flowing with milk and honey. ¹⁰ I have now brought the first of the land's produce that You, LORD, have given me.

You will then place the container before the LORD your God and bow down to Him. ¹¹ You, the Levite, and the foreign resident among you will rejoice in all the good things the LORD your God has given you and your household.

¹² "When you have finished paying all the tenth of your produce in the third year, the year of the tenth, you are to give it to the Levite, the foreign resident, the fatherless, and the widow, so that they may eat in your towns and be satisfied. ¹³ Then you will say in the presence of the LORD your God:

I have taken the consecrated portion out of my house; I have also given it to the Levite, the foreign resident, the fatherless, and the widow, according to all the commands You gave me. I have not violated or forgotten Your commands. ¹⁴ I have not eaten any of it while in mourning, or removed any of it while unclean, or offered any of it for the dead. I have obeyed the LORD my God; I have done all You commanded me. ¹⁵ Look down from Your holy dwelling, from heaven, and bless Your people Israel and the land You have given us as You swore to our fathers, a land flowing with milk and honey.

¹⁶ "The LORD your God is commanding you this day to follow these statutes and ordinances. You must be careful to follow them with all your heart and all your soul. ¹⁷ Today you have affirmed that the LORD is your God and that you will walk in His ways, keep His statutes, commands, and ordinances, and obey Him. ¹⁸ And today the LORD has affirmed that you are His special people as He promised you, that you are to keep all His commands, ¹⁹ that He will put you far above all the nations He has made in praise, fame, and glory, and that you will be a holy people to the LORD your God as He promised."

PSALM 45:1-5

¹ My heart is moved by a noble theme
as I recite my verses to the king;
my tongue is the pen of a skillful writer.
² You are the most handsome of men;
grace flows from your lips.
Therefore God has blessed you forever.

³ Mighty warrior, strap your sword at your side.
In your majesty and splendor—
⁴ in your splendor ride triumphantly in the cause of truth, humility, and justice.
May your right hand show your awe-inspiring deeds.
⁵ Your arrows pierce the hearts of the king's enemies;
the peoples fall under you.

PROVERBS 11:5-6

⁵ The righteousness of the blameless clears his path,
but the wicked person will fall because of his wickedness.

⁶ The righteousness of the upright rescues them,
but the treacherous are trapped by their own desires.

LUKE 10:1-24

10 After this, the Lord appointed 70 others, and He sent them ahead of Him in pairs to every town and place where He Himself was about to go. ² He told them: "The harvest is abundant, but the workers are few. Therefore, pray to the Lord of the harvest to send out workers into His harvest. ³ Now go; I'm sending you out like lambs among wolves. ⁴ Don't carry a money-bag, traveling bag, or sandals; don't greet anyone along the road. ⁵ Whatever house you enter, first say, 'Peace to this household.' ⁶ If a son of peace is there, your

peace will rest on him; but if not, it will return to you. [7] Remain in the same house, eating and drinking what they offer, for the worker is worthy of his wages. Don't be moving from house to house. [8] When you enter any town, and they welcome you, eat the things set before you. [9] Heal the sick who are there, and tell them, 'The kingdom of God has come near you.' [10] When you enter any town, and they don't welcome you, go out into its streets and say, [11] 'We are wiping off as a witness against you even the dust of your town that clings to our feet. Know this for certain: the kingdom of God has come near.' [12] I tell you, on that day it will be more tolerable for Sodom than for that town.

[13] "Woe to you, Chorazin! Woe to you, Bethsaida! For if the miracles that were done in you had been done in Tyre and Sidon, they would have repented long ago, sitting in sackcloth and ashes! [14] But it will be more tolerable for Tyre and Sidon at the judgment than for you. [15] And you, Capernaum, will you be exalted to heaven? No, you will go down to Hades! [16] Whoever listens to you listens to Me. Whoever rejects you rejects Me. And whoever rejects Me rejects the One who sent Me."

[17] The Seventy returned with joy, saying, "Lord, even the demons submit to us in Your name." [18] He said to them, "I watched Satan fall from heaven like a lightning flash. [19] Look, I have given you the authority to trample on snakes and scorpions and over all the power of the enemy; nothing will ever harm you. [20] However, don't rejoice that the spirits submit to you, but rejoice that your names are written in heaven."

[21] In that same hour He rejoiced in the Holy Spirit and said, "I praise You, Father, Lord of heaven and earth, because You have hidden these things from the wise and the learned and have revealed them to infants. Yes, Father, because this was Your good pleasure. [22] All things have been entrusted to Me by My Father. No one knows who the Son is except the Father, and who the Father is except the Son, and anyone to whom the Son desires to reveal Him."

[23] Then turning to His disciples He said privately, "The eyes that see the things you see are blessed! [24] For I tell you that many prophets and kings wanted to see the things you see yet didn't see them; to hear the things you hear yet didn't hear them."

The Sword of the Spirit

I'm sending you out like lambs among wolves.

—LUKE 10:3

The last of the six pieces of the Christian's armor listed in Ephesians 6 is "the sword of the Spirit, which is God's word" (Eph 6:17). John Stott points out that "of all the six pieces of armor or weaponry listed, the sword is the only one which can clearly be used for attack as well as defense." And the kind of attack envisaged here is one that involves a close encounter, for the word used for sword is *machaira*, meaning a short sword or dagger.

There is much more to spiritual warfare than standing up to the Devil. We possess, according to James 4:7, the potential to make him "flee": "Resist the Devil, and he will flee from you." The word "flee" is a very strong word in the original Greek. It means much more than just a strategic withdrawal; it means beating a swift retreat. What an amazing truth! It is possible for a Christian so to resist the Devil that he races away as fast as he can.

This truth must not be seen in any way as limiting the Devil's power, for he is a strong and determined foe. It means rather that a Christian able to wield the sword of the Spirit can ensure that Satan is overpowered. We are right to develop a healthy respect for the Devil's wiles, but we are wrong when we allow him to terrorize us.

We must have the assurance, given everywhere in the New Testament, that to engage in conflict with the Devil is not a hopeless task. We are not to indulge in overconfidence, but, at the same time, we are not to be frightened by him.

Prayer

O Father, the thought that I, a sinner saved by grace, am able to send Satan into retreat almost overwhelms me. Yet I must believe it, for Your Word tells me so. Help me understand even more clearly the authority I have in Christ. In His name I ask it. Amen.

Further Study

Lk 10:1-20; Ac 3:6-8; 16:16-18; 1 Pt 5:8-9
How much authority over Satan have we been given?
How did the early church exercise this authority?

APRIL 14

DEUTERONOMY
27:1–28:14

27 Moses and the elders of Israel commanded the people, "Keep every command I am giving you today. ² At the time you cross the Jordan into the land the LORD your God is giving you, you must set up large stones and cover them with plaster. ³ Write all the words of this law on the stones after you cross to enter the land the LORD your God is giving you, a land flowing with milk and honey, as the LORD, the God of your fathers, has promised you. ⁴ When you have crossed the Jordan, you are to set up these stones on Mount Ebal, as I am commanding you today,

and you are to cover them with plaster. ⁵ Build an altar of stones there to the LORD your God—you must not use any iron tool on them. ⁶ Use uncut stones to build the altar of the LORD your God and offer burnt offerings to the LORD your God on it. ⁷ There you are to sacrifice fellowship offerings, eat, and rejoice in the presence of the LORD your God. ⁸ Write clearly all the words of this law on the plastered stones."

⁹ Moses and the Levitical priests spoke to all Israel, "Be silent, Israel, and listen! This day you have become the people of the LORD your God. ¹⁰ Obey the LORD your God and follow His commands and statutes I am giving you today."

¹¹ On that day Moses commanded the

people, ¹² "When you have crossed the Jordan, these tribes will stand on Mount Gerizim to bless the people: Simeon, Levi, Judah, Issachar, Joseph, and Benjamin. ¹³ And these tribes will stand on Mount Ebal to deliver the curse: Reuben, Gad, Asher, Zebulun, Dan, and Naphtali: ¹⁴ The Levites will proclaim in a loud voice to every Israelite:

¹⁵ "Cursed is the person who makes a carved idol or cast image, which is detestable to the Lord, the work of a craftsman, and sets it up in secret."
And all the people will reply, "Amen!"
¹⁶ "Cursed is the one who dishonors his father or mother."
And all the people will say, "Amen!"
¹⁷ "Cursed is the one who moves his neighbor's boundary marker."
And all the people will say, "Amen!"
¹⁸ "Cursed is the one who leads a blind person astray on the road."
And all the people will say, "Amen!"
¹⁹ "Cursed is the one who denies justice to a foreign resident, a fatherless child, or a widow."
And all the people will say, "Amen!"
²⁰ "Cursed is the one who sleeps with his father's wife, for he has violated his father's marriage bed."
And all the people will say, "Amen!"
²¹ "Cursed is the one who has sexual intercourse with any animal."
And all the people will say "Amen!"
²² "Cursed is the one who sleeps with his sister, whether his father's daughter or his mother's daughter."
And all the people will say, "Amen!"
²³ "Cursed is the one who sleeps with his mother-in-law."
And all the people will say, "Amen!"
²⁴ "Cursed is the one who kills his neighbor in secret."

And all the people will say, "Amen!"
²⁵ "Cursed is the one who accepts a bribe to kill an innocent person."
And all the people will say, "Amen!"
²⁶ "Cursed is anyone who does not put the words of this law into practice."
And all the people will say, "Amen!"

28 "Now if you faithfully obey the Lord your God and are careful to follow all His commands I am giving you today, the Lord your God will put you far above all the nations of the earth. ² All these blessings will come and overtake you, because you obey the Lord your God:

³ You will be blessed in the city
and blessed in the country.
⁴ Your descendants will be blessed,
and your soil's produce,
and the offspring of your livestock,
including the young of your herds
and the newborn of your flocks.
⁵ Your basket and kneading bowl
will be blessed.
⁶ You will be blessed when you come in
and blessed when you go out.

⁷ "The Lord will cause the enemies who rise up against you to be defeated before you. They will march out against you from one direction but flee from you in seven directions. ⁸ The Lord will grant you a blessing on your storehouses and on everything you do; He will bless you in the land the Lord your God is giving you. ⁹ The Lord will establish you as His holy people, as He swore to you, if you obey the commands of the Lord your God and walk in His ways. ¹⁰ Then all the peoples of the earth will see that you are called by the Lord's name, and they will stand in awe of you. ¹¹ The Lord will make you prosper abundantly with children, the offspring of your livestock, and your soil's produce in the land the Lord swore to your

fathers to give you. ¹²The LORD will open for you His abundant storehouse, the sky, to give your land rain in its season and to bless all the work of your hands. You will lend to many nations, but you will not borrow. ¹³The LORD will make you the head and not the tail; you will only move upward and never downward if you listen to the LORD your God's commands I am giving you today and are careful to follow them. ¹⁴Do not turn aside to the right or the left from all the things I am commanding you today, and do not go after other gods to worship them.

PSALM 45:6-12

⁶ Your throne, God, is forever and
  ever;
   the scepter of Your kingdom is a
   scepter of justice.
⁷ You love righteousness and hate
  wickedness;
   therefore God, your God, has
   anointed you,
   more than your companions, with
   the oil of joy.
⁸ Myrrh, aloes, and cassia perfume
  all your garments;
   from ivory palaces harps bring you
   joy.
⁹ Kings' daughters are among your
  honored women;
   the queen, adorned with gold from
   Ophir, stands at your right hand.

¹⁰ Listen, daughter, pay attention and
   consider:
    forget your people and your
    father's house,
¹¹ and the king will desire your
   beauty.
    Bow down to him, for he is your
    lord.
¹² The daughter of Tyre, the wealthy
   people,
    will seek your favor with gifts.

PROVERBS 11:7-8

⁷ When the wicked dies, his
  expectation comes to nothing,

and hope placed in wealth
vanishes.

⁸ The righteous is rescued from
  trouble;
   in his place, the wicked goes in.

LUKE 10:25–11:4

²⁵Just then an expert in the law stood up to test Him, saying, "Teacher, what must I do to inherit eternal life?"
²⁶"What is written in the law?" He asked him. "How do you read it?"
²⁷He answered:

Love the Lord your God with all your heart, with all your soul, with all your strength, and with all your mind; and your neighbor as yourself.

²⁸"You've answered correctly," He told him. "Do this and you will live."
²⁹But wanting to justify himself, he asked Jesus, "And who is my neighbor?"
³⁰Jesus took up the question and said: "A man was going down from Jerusalem to Jericho and fell into the hands of robbers. They stripped him, beat him up, and fled, leaving him half dead. ³¹A priest happened to be going down that road. When he saw him, he passed by on the other side. ³²In the same way, a Levite, when he arrived at the place and saw him, passed by on the other side. ³³But a Samaritan on his journey came up to him, and when he saw the man, he had compassion. ³⁴He went over to him and bandaged his wounds, pouring on oil and wine. Then he put him on his own animal, brought him to an inn, and took care of him. ³⁵The next day he took out two denarii, gave them to the innkeeper, and said, 'Take care of him. When I come back I'll reimburse you for whatever extra you spend.'
³⁶"Which of these three do you think proved to be a neighbor to the man who fell into the hands of the robbers?"
³⁷"The one who showed mercy to him," he said.

Then Jesus told him, "Go and do the same."

³⁸ While they were traveling, He entered a village, and a woman named Martha welcomed Him into her home. ³⁹ She had a sister named Mary, who also sat at the Lord's feet and was listening to what He said. ⁴⁰ But Martha was distracted by her many tasks, and she came up and asked, "Lord, don't You care that my sister has left me to serve alone? So tell her to give me a hand."

⁴¹ The Lord answered her, "Martha, Martha, you are worried and upset about many things, ⁴² but one thing is necessary. Mary has made the right choice, and it will not be taken away from her."

11 He was praying in a certain place, and when He finished, one of His disciples said to Him, "Lord, teach us to pray, just as John also taught his disciples."

² He said to them, "Whenever you pray, say:

Father,
Your name be honored as holy.
Your kingdom come.
³ Give us each day our daily bread.
⁴ And forgive us our sins,
for we ourselves also
forgive everyone
in debt to us.
And do not bring us
into temptation."

The Purpose of Living

Love the Lord your God . . . and your neighbor as yourself.
—LUKE 10:27

The energy behind most of our behavior (particularly strange or abnormal behavior) is an independent attempt to satiate the deep longings which God—and God alone—can satisfy. If you want to know a biblical reason why people do the things they do, then keep these thoughts in mind.

A man said to me some time ago: "Why do I browbeat my wife and make demands on her which I know are not loving? And why, despite my best efforts to change, do I fall back into my usual patterns?" I told him: "Your legitimate longings for impact and respect are not being met by God, and as you can't function very well when these longings go unmet, you set about trying to get your wife to meet them." He saw the point, asked God to forgive him for drinking at the wrong well, and turned in a fresh way to Christ for life and power and reality.

But what about the person who goes in the other direction and withdraws from others, manifesting such symptoms as extreme shyness and some forms of depression? This person is someone who has little awareness of their thirst being quenched by God—hence a degree of inner emptiness—and is motivated to avoid moving toward involvement with others for fear he or she might be rejected.

Self-enhancement (a selfish attempt to quench our own thirst) or self-rejection—these are the two styles of relationship which characterize many Christians' lives. And both are a violation of the law of love.

Prayer

Loving Lord, Your Word is crystal clear—the purpose of living is simply to love as I am loved. If I am not loving others, then quite simply I am not allowing You to love me. I am sinning in both directions. Help me, my Savior. Amen.

Further Study

Jn 13:1-35; 15:12; Mt 22:39; 1 Th 3:12
How do we show that we belong to Jesus?
What was Paul's desire for the Thessalonians?

APRIL 15

DEUTERONOMY 28:15-68

¹⁵ "But if you do not obey the LORD your God by carefully following all His commands and statutes I am giving you today, all these curses will come and overtake you:

¹⁶ You will be cursed in the city
and cursed in the country.
¹⁷ Your basket and kneading bowl
will be cursed.
¹⁸ Your descendants will be cursed,
and your soil's produce,
the young of your herds,
and the newborn of your flocks.
¹⁹ You will be cursed when you come in
and cursed when you go out.

²⁰ The LORD will send against you curses, confusion, and rebuke in everything you do until you are destroyed and quickly perish, because of the wickedness of your actions in abandoning Me. ²¹ The LORD will make pestilence cling to you until He has exterminated you from the land you are entering to possess. ²² The LORD will afflict you with wasting disease, fever, inflammation, burning heat, drought, blight, and mildew; these will pursue you until you perish. ²³ The sky above you will be bronze, and the earth beneath you iron. ²⁴ The LORD will turn the rain of your land into falling dust; it will descend on you from the sky until you are destroyed. ²⁵ The LORD will cause you to be defeated before your enemies. You will march out against them from one direction but flee from them in seven directions. You will be an object of horror to all the kingdoms of the earth. ²⁶ Your corpses will be food for all the birds of the sky and the wild animals of the land, and no one will scare them away.

²⁷ "The LORD will afflict you with the boils of Egypt, tumors, a festering rash, and scabies, from which you cannot be cured. ²⁸ The LORD will afflict you with madness, blindness, and mental confusion, ²⁹ so that at noon you will grope as a blind man gropes in the dark. You will not be successful in anything you do. You will only be oppressed and robbed

continually, and no one will help you. ³⁰ You will become engaged to a woman, but another man will rape her. You will build a house but not live in it. You will plant a vineyard but not enjoy its fruit. ³¹ Your ox will be slaughtered before your eyes, but you will not eat any of it. Your donkey will be taken away from you and not returned to you. Your flock will be given to your enemies, and no one will help you. ³² Your sons and daughters will be given to another people, while your eyes grow weary looking for them every day. But you will be powerless to do anything. ³³ A people you don't know will eat your soil's produce and everything you have labored for. You will only be oppressed and crushed continually. ³⁴ You will be driven mad by what you see. ³⁵ The LORD will afflict you on your knees and thighs with painful and incurable boils from the sole of your foot to the top of your head.

³⁶ "The LORD will bring you and your king that you have appointed to a nation neither you nor your fathers have known, and there you will worship other gods, of wood and stone. ³⁷ You will become an object of horror, scorn, and ridicule among all the peoples where the LORD will drive you.

³⁸ "You will sow much seed in the field but harvest little, because locusts will devour it. ³⁹ You will plant and cultivate vineyards but not drink the wine or gather the grapes, because worms will eat them. ⁴⁰ You will have olive trees throughout your territory but not anoint yourself with oil, because your olives will drop off. ⁴¹ You will father sons and daughters, but they will not remain yours, because they will be taken prisoner. ⁴² Whirring insects will take possession of all your trees and your land's produce. ⁴³ The foreign resident among you will rise higher and higher above you, while you sink lower and lower. ⁴⁴ He will lend to you, but you won't lend to him. He will be the head, and you will be the tail.

⁴⁵ "All these curses will come, pursue, and overtake you until you are destroyed, since you did not obey the LORD your God and keep the commands and statutes He gave you. ⁴⁶ These curses will be a sign and a wonder against you and your descendants forever. ⁴⁷ Because you didn't serve the LORD your God with joy and a cheerful heart, even though you had an abundance of everything, ⁴⁸ you will serve your enemies the LORD will send against you, in famine, thirst, nakedness, and a lack of everything. He will place an iron yoke on your neck until He has destroyed you. ⁴⁹ The LORD will bring a nation from far away, from the ends of the earth, to swoop down on you like an eagle, a nation whose language you don't understand, ⁵⁰ a ruthless nation, showing no respect for the old and not sparing the young. ⁵¹ They will eat the offspring of your livestock and your soil's produce until you are destroyed. They will leave you no grain, new wine, oil, young of your herds, or newborn of your flocks until they cause you to perish. ⁵² They will besiege you within all your gates until your high and fortified walls, that you trust in, come down throughout your land. They will besiege you within all your gates throughout the land the LORD your God has given you.

⁵³ "You will eat your children, the flesh of your sons and daughters the LORD your God has given you during the siege and hardship your enemy imposes on you. ⁵⁴ The most sensitive and refined man among you will look grudgingly at his brother, the wife he embraces, and the rest of his children, ⁵⁵ refusing to share with any of them his children's flesh that he will eat because he has nothing left during the siege and hardship your enemy imposes on you in all your towns. ⁵⁶ The most sensitive and refined woman among you, who would not venture to set the sole of her foot on the ground because of her refinement and sensitivity, will begrudge the husband she embraces, her son, and her daughter, ⁵⁷ the afterbirth that comes out from between her legs and the children she bears, because she will secretly eat them for lack of anything else during the siege and hardship your enemy imposes on you within your gates.

⁵⁸ "If you are not careful to obey all

the words of this law, which are written in this scroll, by fearing this glorious and awesome name—Yahweh, your God— [59] He will bring extraordinary plagues on you and your descendants, severe and lasting plagues, and terrible and chronic sicknesses. [60] He will afflict you again with all the diseases of Egypt, which you dreaded, and they will cling to you. [61] The LORD will also inflict you with every sickness and plague not recorded in the book of this law, until you are destroyed. [62] Though you were as numerous as the stars of the sky, you will be left with only a few people, because you did not obey the LORD your God. [63] Just as the LORD was glad to cause you to prosper and to multiply you, so He will also be glad to cause you to perish and to destroy you. You will be deported from the land you are entering to possess. [64] Then the LORD will scatter you among all peoples from one end of the earth to the other, and there you will worship other gods of wood and stone, which neither you nor your fathers have known. [65] You will find no peace among those nations, and there will be no resting place for the sole of your foot. There the LORD will give you a trembling heart, failing eyes, and a despondent spirit. [66] Your life will hang in doubt before you. You will be in dread night and day, never certain of survival. [67] In the morning you will say, 'If only it were evening!' and in the evening you will say, 'If only it were morning!'—because of the dread you will have in your heart and because of what you will see. [68] The LORD will take you back in ships to Egypt by a route that I said you would never see again. There you will sell yourselves to your enemies as male and female slaves, but no one will buy you."

PSALM 45:13-17

[13] In her chamber, the royal daughter is all glorious,
her clothing embroidered with gold.
[14] In colorful garments she is led to the king;

after her, the virgins, her companions, are brought to you.
[15] They are led in with gladness and rejoicing;
they enter the king's palace.

[16] Your sons will succeed your ancestors;
you will make them princes throughout the land.
[17] I will cause your name to be remembered for all generations;
therefore the peoples will praise you forever and ever.

PROVERBS 11:9-11

[9] With his mouth the ungodly destroys his neighbor,
but through knowledge the righteous are rescued.

[10] When the righteous thrive, a city rejoices,
and when the wicked die, there is joyful shouting.

[11] A city is built up by the blessing of the upright,
but it is torn down by the mouth of the wicked.

LUKE 11:5-28

[5] He also said to them: "Suppose one of you has a friend and goes to him at midnight and says to him, 'Friend, lend me three loaves of bread, [6] because a friend of mine on a journey has come to me, and I don't have anything to offer him.' [7] Then he will answer from inside and say, 'Don't bother me! The door is already locked, and my children and I have gone to bed. I can't get up to give you anything.' [8] I tell you, even though he won't get up and give him anything because he is his friend, yet because of his persistence, he will get up and give him as much as he needs.
[9] "So I say to you, keep asking, and it will be given to you. Keep searching,

and you will find. Keep knocking, and the door will be opened to you. [10] For everyone who asks receives, and the one who searches finds, and to the one who knocks, the door will be opened. [11] What father among you, if his son asks for a fish, will give him a snake instead of a fish? [12] Or if he asks for an egg, will give him a scorpion? [13] If you then, who are evil, know how to give good gifts to your children, how much more will the heavenly Father give the Holy Spirit to those who ask Him?"

[14] Now He was driving out a demon that was mute. When the demon came out, the man who had been mute, spoke, and the crowds were amazed. [15] But some of them said, "He drives out demons by Beelzebul, the ruler of the demons!" [16] And others, as a test, were demanding of Him a sign from heaven.

[17] Knowing their thoughts, He told them: "Every kingdom divided against itself is headed for destruction, and a house divided against itself falls. [18] If Satan also is divided against himself, how will his kingdom stand? For you say I drive out demons by Beelzebul. [19] And if I drive out demons by Beelzebul, who is it your sons drive them out by? For this reason they will be your judges. [20] If I drive out demons by the finger of God, then the kingdom of God has come to you. [21] When a strong man, fully armed, guards his estate, his possessions are secure. [22] But when one stronger than he attacks and overpowers him, he takes from him all his weapons he trusted in, and divides up his plunder. [23] Anyone who is not with Me is against Me, and anyone who does not gather with Me scatters.

[24] "When an unclean spirit comes out of a man, it roams through waterless places looking for rest, and not finding rest, it then says, 'I'll go back to my house where I came from.' [25] And returning, it finds the house swept and put in order. [26] Then it goes and brings seven other spirits more evil than itself, and they enter and settle down there. As a result, that man's last condition is worse than the first."

[27] As He was saying these things, a woman from the crowd raised her voice and said to Him, "The womb that bore You and the one who nursed You are blessed!"

[28] He said, "Even more, those who hear the word of God and keep it are blessed!"

Proper Priorities

How much more will the heavenly Father give the Holy Spirit to those who ask Him?—LUKE 11:13

In the passage before us today, Jesus spends some time sharing with His hearers that God is both a Father and a Friend. It is vitally important that we realize that God wants to give us the Holy Spirit, for if we are not absolutely sure of this, then our asking will be shot through with indecision and uncertainty.

The great Archbishop Temple said, "We ask for the Holy Spirit, yet in the depth of our hearts we are not sure whether He wants to give it to us, and this one single doubt negates the object of the exercise." So stop wishing to receive the Spirit in all His fullness and start expecting. You can be positive in asking because God is positive in giving.

Bring the whole matter to a crisis. One great preacher said that "the soul grows by a series of crises." Make it a matter of priority to spend some time in prayer to receive more of His Spirit and become desperate over the issue. Treat it as if God dropped a letter into your mailbox this morning that said, "I would like to see you as soon as possible over a matter of a very important gift I want to give you."

If that happened, I wonder how you would handle your schedule over the next few days? Things you thought were top priority would become of secondary importance. When you decide to give God top priority in your plans, then, believe me, God will give you His top priority—the Holy Spirit.

Prayer

Lord, I wonder, am I thirsty or desperate enough to make this matter of being filled with the Spirit my top priority? Help me to face up to the challenge—now. For Jesus' sake. Amen.

Further Study

Mt 6:1-15; 14:23; 2 Kg 4:33; Lk 6:12
What did Jesus teach about prayer?
What was His example?

APRIL 16

DEUTERONOMY 29:1–30:20

29 These are the words of the covenant the LORD commanded Moses to make with the Israelites in the land of Moab, in addition to the covenant He had made with them at Horeb. ² Moses summoned all Israel and said to them, "You have seen with your own eyes everything the LORD did in Egypt to Pharaoh, to all his officials, and to his entire land. ³ You saw with your own eyes the great trials and those great signs and wonders. ⁴ Yet to this day the LORD has not given you a mind to understand, eyes to see, or ears to hear. ⁵ I led you 40 years in the wilderness; your clothes and the sandals on your feet did not wear out; ⁶ you did not eat bread or drink wine or beer—so that you might know that I am the LORD your God. ⁷ When you reached this place, Sihon king of Heshbon and Og king of Bashan came out against us in battle, but we defeated them. ⁸ We took their land and gave it as an inheritance to the Reubenites, the Gadites, and half the tribe of Manasseh. ⁹ Therefore, observe the words of this covenant and follow them, so that you will succeed in everything you do.

¹⁰ "All of you are standing today before the LORD your God—your leaders, tribes, elders, officials, all the men of Israel, ¹¹ your children, your wives, and the foreigners in your camps who cut

your wood and draw your water— ¹²so that you may enter into the covenant of the Lord your God, which He is making with you today, so that you may enter into His oath ¹³and so that He may establish you today as His people and He may be your God as He promised you and as He swore to your fathers Abraham, Isaac, and Jacob. ¹⁴I am making this covenant and this oath not only with you, ¹⁵but also with those who are standing here with us today in the presence of the Lord our God and with those who are not here today.

¹⁶"Indeed, you know how we lived in the land of Egypt and passed through the nations where you traveled. ¹⁷You saw their detestable images and idols made of wood, stone, silver, and gold, which were among them. ¹⁸Be sure there is no man, woman, clan, or tribe among you today whose heart turns away from the Lord our God to go and worship the gods of those nations. Be sure there is no root among you bearing poisonous and bitter fruit. ¹⁹When someone hears the words of this oath, he may bless himself in his mind, thinking, 'I will have peace even though I follow my own stubborn heart.' This will lead to the destruction of the well-watered land as well as the dry land. ²⁰The Lord will not be willing to forgive him. Instead, His anger and jealousy will burn against that person, and every curse written in this scroll will descend on him. The Lord will blot out his name under heaven, ²¹and single him out for harm from all the tribes of Israel, according to all the curses of the covenant written in this book of the law.

²²"Future generations of your children who follow you and the foreigner who comes from a distant country will see the plagues of the land and the sicknesses the Lord has inflicted on it. ²³All its soil will be a burning waste of sulfur and salt, unsown, producing nothing, with no plant growing on it, just like the fall of Sodom and Gomorrah, Admah and Zeboiim, which the Lord demolished in His fierce anger. ²⁴All the nations will ask, 'Why has the Lord done this to this land? Why this great outburst of anger?' ²⁵Then people will answer, 'It is because they abandoned the covenant of the Lord, the God of their fathers, which He had made with them when He brought them out of the land of Egypt. ²⁶They began to worship other gods, bowing down to gods they had not known—gods that the Lord had not permitted them to worship. ²⁷Therefore the Lord's anger burned against this land, and He brought every curse written in this book on it. ²⁸The Lord uprooted them from their land in His anger, fury, and great wrath, and threw them into another land where they are today.' ²⁹The hidden things belong to the Lord our God, but the revealed things belong to us and our children forever, so that we may follow all the words of this law.

30 "When all these things happen to you—the blessings and curses I have set before you—and you come to your senses while you are in all the nations where the Lord your God has driven you, ²and you and your children return to the Lord your God and obey Him with all your heart and all your soul by doing everything I am giving you today, ³then He will restore your fortunes, have compassion on you, and gather you again from all the peoples where the Lord your God has scattered you. ⁴Even if your exiles are at the ends of the earth, He will gather you and bring you back from there. ⁵The Lord your God will bring you into the land your fathers possessed, and you will take possession of it. He will cause you to prosper and multiply you more than He did your fathers. ⁶The Lord your God will circumcise your heart and the hearts of your descendants, and you will love Him with all your heart and all your soul, so that you will live. ⁷The Lord your God will put all these curses on your enemies who hate and persecute you. ⁸Then you will again obey Him and follow all His commands I am giving you today. ⁹The Lord your God will make you prosper abundantly in all the work of your hands with children, the offspring of your livestock, and your soil's

produce. Indeed, the LORD will again delight in your prosperity, as He delighted in that of your fathers, ¹⁰ when you obey the LORD your God by keeping His commands and statutes that are written in this book of the law and return to Him with all your heart and all your soul. ¹¹ "This command that I give you today is certainly not too difficult or beyond your reach. ¹² It is not in heaven, so that you have to ask, 'Who will go up to heaven, get it for us, and proclaim it to us so that we may follow it?' ¹³ And it is not across the sea, so that you have to ask, 'Who will cross the sea, get it for us, and proclaim it to us so that we may follow it?' ¹⁴ But the message is very near you, in your mouth and in your heart, so that you may follow it. ¹⁵ See, today I have set before you life and prosperity, death and adversity. ¹⁶ For I am commanding you today to love the LORD your God, to walk in His ways, and to keep His commands, statutes, and ordinances, so that you may live and multiply, and the LORD your God may bless you in the land you are entering to possess. ¹⁷ But if your heart turns away and you do not listen and you are led astray to bow down to other gods and worship them, ¹⁸ I tell you today that you will certainly perish and will not live long in the land you are entering to possess across the Jordan. ¹⁹ I call heaven and earth as witnesses against you today that I have set before you life and death, blessing and curse. Choose life so that you and your descendants may live, ²⁰ love the LORD your God, obey Him, and remain faithful to Him. For He is your life, and He will prolong your life in the land the LORD swore to give to your fathers Abraham, Isaac, and Jacob."

𝒫SALM 46:1-11

¹ God is our refuge and strength,
   a helper who is always found in
      times of trouble.
² Therefore we will not be afraid,
      though the earth trembles
   and the mountains topple into the
      depths of the seas,

³ though its waters roar and foam
   and the mountains quake with its
      turmoil.   *Selah*

⁴ There is a river—its streams
      delight the city of God,
   the holy dwelling place of the
      Most High.
⁵ God is within her; she will not be
      toppled.
   God will help her when the
      morning dawns.
⁶ Nations rage, kingdoms topple;
   the earth melts when He lifts His
      voice.
⁷ The LORD of Hosts is with us;
   the God of Jacob is our
      stronghold.   *Selah*

⁸ Come, see the works of the LORD,
   who brings devastation on the
      earth.
⁹ He makes wars cease throughout
      the earth.
   He shatters bows and cuts spears
      to pieces;
   He burns up the chariots.
¹⁰ "Stop your fighting—and know
      that I am God,
   exalted among the nations, exalted
      on the earth."
¹¹ The LORD of Hosts is with us;
   the God of Jacob is our
      stronghold.   *Selah*

𝒫ROVERBS 11:12-13

¹² Whoever shows contempt for his
      neighbor lacks sense,
   but a man with understanding
      keeps silent.

¹³ A gossip goes around revealing a
      secret,
   but the trustworthy keeps a
      confidence.

ℒUKE 11:29-54

²⁹ As the crowds were increasing, He began saying: "This generation is an evil generation. It demands a sign, but no sign will be given to it except the sign of

Jonah. [30] For just as Jonah became a sign to the people of Nineveh, so also the Son of Man will be to this generation. [31] The queen of the south will rise up at the judgment with the men of this generation and condemn them, because she came from the ends of the earth to hear the wisdom of Solomon, and look—something greater than Solomon is here! [32] The men of Nineveh will rise up at the judgment with this generation and condemn it, because they repented at Jonah's proclamation, and look—something greater than Jonah is here!

[33] "No one lights a lamp and puts it in the cellar or under a basket, but on a lampstand, so that those who come in may see its light. [34] Your eye is the lamp of the body. When your eye is good, your whole body is also full of light. But when it is bad, your body is also full of darkness. [35] Take care then, that the light in you is not darkness. [36] If therefore your whole body is full of light, with no part of it in darkness, the whole body will be full of light, as when a lamp shines its light on you."

[37] As He was speaking, a Pharisee asked Him to dine with him. So He went in and reclined at the table. [38] When the Pharisee saw this, he was amazed that He did not first perform the ritual washing before dinner. [39] But the Lord said to him: "Now you Pharisees clean the outside of the cup and dish, but inside you are full of greed and evil. [40] Fools! Didn't He who made the outside make the inside too? [41] But give to charity what is within, and then everything is clean for you.

[42] "But woe to you Pharisees! You give a tenth of mint, rue, and every kind of herb, and you bypass justice and love for God. These things you should have done without neglecting the others.

[43] "Woe to you Pharisees! You love the front seat in the synagogues and greetings in the marketplaces.

[44] "Woe to you! You are like unmarked graves; the people who walk over them don't know it."

[45] One of the experts in the law answered Him, "Teacher, when You say these things You insult us too."

[46] Then He said: "Woe also to you experts in the law! You load people with burdens that are hard to carry, yet you yourselves don't touch these burdens with one of your fingers.

[47] "Woe to you! You build monuments to the prophets, and your fathers killed them. [48] Therefore you are witnesses that you approve the deeds of your fathers, for they killed them, and you build their monuments. [49] Because of this, the wisdom of God said, 'I will send them prophets and apostles, and some of them they will kill and persecute,' [50] so that this generation may be held responsible for the blood of all the prophets shed since the foundation of the world— [51] from the blood of Abel to the blood of Zechariah, who perished between the altar and the sanctuary.

"Yes, I tell you, this generation will be held responsible.

[52] "Woe to you experts in the law! You have taken away the key of knowledge! You didn't go in yourselves, and you hindered those who were going in."

[53] When He left there, the scribes and the Pharisees began to oppose Him fiercely and to cross-examine Him about many things; [54] they were lying in wait for Him to trap Him in something He said.

Why Fear to Meditate?

Stop your fighting—and know that I am God.—Psalm 46:10

In our age of increasing uncertainty, one sure way of staying on top is by the continuous activity of Scripture meditation. Many Christians, however, are afraid of the word "meditation." They view it as something to be practiced by gurus, mystics, or the devotees of Eastern religions. They look askance at those who advocate its usefulness and power in the Christian life.

Scripture meditation in the Christian's life, however, is as different from that practiced in Eastern religions as chalk is from cheese. Those who practice these other faiths advocate emptying the mind, while the Bible advocates filling it—with the truths of God's holy Word.

David Ray, an American author and pastor of a large church, says: "I, for one, looked with suspicion on any Christian who advocated the practice of meditation. I thought to myself: 'They are out of touch with reality. Give me action and work, lots of work. Let somebody else waste his time by staring at the end of his nose.'" Then somebody introduced him to the principles of Scripture meditation. He was shown how to place a verse of Scripture on the tip of his spiritual tongue and slowly suck from it the refreshment it contained.

The verse he chose as the focus of his meditation was the one before us today: "Stop your fighting—and know that I am God." Take this text now and begin to focus on it. Place it on the tip of your spiritual tongue and draw from it hour by hour the spiritual refreshment that it contains. In your spare moments, pull it to the center of your mind and begin to experience the joy of drawing from God's Word the power He has placed within it.

Prayer

Father, I sense that here I am at the crux of the matter of spiritual freshness. Help me not to miss out on any of the lessons You are trying to teach me at this moment in my life. In Jesus' name. Amen.

Further Study

1 Pt 3:1-4; Jb 37:14; Ps 131:2; Is 32:17
What is of great worth?
What advice was given to Job?

APRIL 17

DEUTERONOMY 31:1-29

31 Then Moses continued to speak these words to all Israel, ² saying, "I am now 120 years old; I can no longer act as your leader. The LORD has told me, 'You will not cross this Jordan.'

³ The LORD your God is the One who will cross ahead of you. He will destroy these nations before you, and you will drive them out. Joshua is the one who will cross ahead of you, as the LORD has said. ⁴ The LORD will deal with them as He did Sihon and Og, the kings of the Amorites, and their land when He de-

stroyed them. ⁵ The LORD will deliver them over to you, and you must do to them exactly as I have commanded you. ⁶ Be strong and courageous; don't be terrified or afraid of them. For it is the LORD your God who goes with you; He will not leave you or forsake you."

⁷ Moses then summoned Joshua and said to him in the sight of all Israel, "Be strong and courageous, for you will go with this people into the land the LORD swore to give to their fathers. You will enable them to take possession of it. ⁸ The LORD is the One who will go before you. He will be with you; He will not leave you or forsake you. Do not be afraid or discouraged."

⁹ Moses wrote down this law and gave it to the priests, the sons of Levi, who carried the ark of the LORD's covenant, and to all the elders of Israel. ¹⁰ Moses commanded them, "At the end of every seven years, at the appointed time in the year of debt cancellation, during the Festival of Booths, ¹¹ when all Israel assembles in the presence of the LORD your God at the place He chooses, you are to read this law aloud before all Israel. ¹² Gather the people—men, women, children, and foreigners living within your gates—so that they may listen and learn to fear the LORD your God and be careful to follow all the words of this law. ¹³ Then their children who do not know the law will listen and learn to fear the LORD your God as long as you live in the land you are crossing the Jordan to possess."

¹⁴ The LORD said to Moses, "The time of your death is now approaching. Call Joshua and present yourselves at the tent of meeting, so that I may commission him." When Moses and Joshua went and presented themselves at the tent of meeting, ¹⁵ the LORD appeared at the tent in a pillar of cloud, and the cloud stood at the entrance to the tent.

¹⁶ The LORD said to Moses, "You are about to rest with your fathers, and this people will soon commit adultery with the foreign gods of the land they are entering. They will abandon Me and break the covenant I have made with them. ¹⁷ My anger will burn against them on that day; I will abandon them and hide My face from them so that they will become easy prey. Many troubles and afflictions will come to them. On that day they will say, 'Haven't these troubles come to us because our God is no longer with us?' ¹⁸ I will certainly hide My face on that day because of all the evil they have done by turning to other gods. ¹⁹ Therefore write down this song for yourselves and teach it to the Israelites; have them recite it, so that this song may be a witness for Me against the Israelites. ²⁰ When I bring them into the land I swore to give their fathers, a land flowing with milk and honey, they will eat their fill and prosper. They will turn to other gods and worship them, despising Me and breaking My covenant. ²¹ And when many troubles and afflictions come to them, this song will testify against them, because their descendants will not have forgotten it. For I know what they are prone to do, even before I bring them into the land I swore to give them." ²² So Moses wrote down this song on that day and taught it to the Israelites.

²³ The LORD commissioned Joshua son of Nun, "Be strong and courageous, for you will bring the Israelites into the land I swore to them, and I will be with you."

²⁴ When Moses had finished writing down on a scroll every single word of this law, ²⁵ he commanded the Levites who carried the ark of the LORD's covenant, ²⁶ "Take this book of the law and place it beside the ark of the covenant of the LORD your God, so that it may remain there as a witness against you. ²⁷ For I know how rebellious and stiffnecked you are. If you are rebelling against the LORD now, while I am still alive, how much more will you rebel after I am dead! ²⁸ Assemble all your tribal elders and officers before me, so that I may speak these words directly to them and call heaven and earth as witnesses against them. ²⁹ For I know that after my death you will become completely corrupt and turn from the path I have commanded you. Disaster will come to you in the future, because you

will do what is evil in the LORD's sight, infuriating Him with what your hands have made."

PSALM 47:1-9

1 Clap your hands, all you peoples; shout to God with a jubilant cry.
2 For the LORD Most High is awe-inspiring,
a great King over all the earth.
3 He subdues peoples under us and nations under our feet.
4 He chooses for us our inheritance—
the pride of Jacob, whom He loves. *Selah*

5 God ascends amid shouts of joy, the LORD, amid the sound of trumpets.
6 Sing praise to God, sing praise; sing praise to our King, sing praise!
7 Sing a song of instruction, for God is King of all the earth.

8 God reigns over the nations; God is seated on His holy throne.
9 The nobles of the peoples have assembled
with the people of the God of Abraham.
For the leaders of the earth belong to God;
He is greatly exalted.

PROVERBS 11:14-15

14 Without guidance, people fall, but with many counselors there is deliverance.

15 If someone puts up security for a stranger, he will suffer for it, but the one who hates such agreements is protected.

LUKE 12:1-21

12 In these circumstances, a crowd of many thousands came together, so that they were trampling on one another. He began to say to His disciples first: "Be on your guard against the yeast of the Pharisees, which is hypocrisy. 2 There is nothing covered that won't be uncovered, nothing hidden that won't be made known. 3 Therefore whatever you have said in the dark will be heard in the light, and what you have whispered in an ear in private rooms will be proclaimed on the housetops.

4 "And I say to you, My friends, don't fear those who kill the body, and after that can do nothing more. 5 But I will show you the One to fear: Fear Him who has authority to throw people into hell after death. Yes, I say to you, this is the One to fear! 6 Aren't five sparrows sold for two pennies? Yet not one of them is forgotten in God's sight. 7 Indeed, the hairs of your head are all counted. Don't be afraid; you are worth more than many sparrows!

8 "And I say to you, anyone who acknowledges Me before men, the Son of Man will also acknowledge him before the angels of God, 9 but whoever denies Me before men will be denied before the angels of God. 10 Anyone who speaks a word against the Son of Man will be forgiven, but the one who blasphemes against the Holy Spirit will not be forgiven. 11 Whenever they bring you before synagogues and rulers and authorities, don't worry about how you should defend yourselves or what you should say. 12 For the Holy Spirit will teach you at that very hour what must be said."

13 Someone from the crowd said to Him, "Teacher, tell my brother to divide the inheritance with me."

14 "Friend," He said to him, "who appointed Me a judge or arbitrator over you?" 15 He then told them, "Watch out and be on guard against all greed because one's life is not in the abundance of his possessions."

16 Then He told them a parable: "A rich man's land was very productive. 17 He thought to himself, 'What should I do, since I don't have anywhere to store my crops? 18 I will do this,' he said. 'I'll tear down my barns and build bigger

ones, and store all my grain and my goods there. ¹⁹ Then I'll say to myself, "You have many goods stored up for many years. Take it easy; eat, drink, and enjoy yourself." '

²⁰ "But God said to him, 'You fool!

This very night your life is demanded of you. And the things you have prepared—whose will they be?'

²¹ "That's how it is with the one who stores up treasure for himself and is not rich toward God."

Jittery Theologians

But God said . . . "You fool!
This very night your life is demanded of you."—Luke 12:20

Why is it that so many in our day and age are attracted to the notion of a God who is impersonal? New Age theories seem to be infiltrating all parts of society in almost every country of the world.

I think there is a very subtle reason why men and women prefer to think of God as a power rather than as a person. If God is merely a power, or a formless life-force flowing through the universe, He can make no demands. One is not challenged to relate to an energy in the same way that one is challenged to relate to a person. When we believe God is a Person, the next question we have to face is: "How do I relate to Him?" It is the idea of meeting a personal God which causes men and women to tremble.

But deep down in every human heart, placed there by the Almighty, is a conviction that a personal God exists. We have all been made in His image, and His stamp is upon us whether we like it or not. In reality there are very few atheists; most people believe in some kind of God.

Someone has described an atheist as "a theologian with the jitters." A good way of dealing with those jitters is to expunge from the heart the idea that God may be personal and that one might be accountable to Him. Better a life-force or a celestial energy—a power that can be tapped—rather than a Person one might some day have to meet. How foolish it all is— settling for short-term comfort but facing eternal loss.

Prayer

Father, I am saddened when I realize how so many want to run from You when their best interests lie in running to You. Draw many to You this very day, dear Lord. In Jesus' name. Amen.

Further Study

Gn 1:26-30; 5:1; 1 Co 11:7; Jms 3:9; Ec 3:11
What are the implications of being created in God's image?
What has God set within us?

APRIL 18

DEUTERONOMY 31:30–32:52

³⁰ Then Moses recited aloud every single word of this song to the entire assembly of Israel:

32 Pay attention, heavens, and I will speak;
listen, earth, to the words of my mouth.
² Let my teaching fall like rain
and my word settle like dew,
like gentle rain on new grass
and showers on tender plants.
³ For I will proclaim the LORD's name.
Declare the greatness of our God!
⁴ The Rock—His work is perfect;
all His ways are entirely just.
A faithful God, without prejudice,
He is righteous and true.

⁵ His people have acted corruptly toward Him;
this is their defect—they are not His children
but a devious and crooked generation.
⁶ Is this how you repay the LORD,
you foolish and senseless people?
Isn't He your Father and Creator?
Didn't He make you and sustain you?
⁷ Remember the days of old;
consider the years long past.
Ask your father, and he will tell you,
your elders, and they will teach you.
⁸ When the Most High gave the nations their inheritance
and divided the human race,
He set the boundaries of the peoples

according to the number of the people of Israel.
⁹ But the LORD's portion is His people,
Jacob, His own inheritance.

¹⁰ He found him in a desolate land,
in a barren, howling wilderness;
He surrounded him, cared for him,
and guarded him as the pupil of His eye.
¹¹ He watches over His nest like an eagle
and hovers over His young;
He spreads His wings, catches him,
and lifts him up on His pinions.
¹² The LORD alone led him,
with no help from a foreign god.
¹³ He made him ride on the heights of the land
and eat the produce of the field.
He nourished him with honey from the rock
and oil from flintlike rock,
¹⁴ cream from the herd and milk from the flock,
with the fat of lambs,
rams from Bashan, and goats,
with the choicest grains of wheat;
you drank wine from the finest grapes.

¹⁵ Then Jeshurun became fat and rebelled—
you became fat, bloated, and gorged.
He abandoned the God who made him
and scorned the Rock of his salvation.
¹⁶ They provoked His jealousy with foreign gods;
they enraged Him with detestable practices.
¹⁷ They sacrificed to demons, not God,

to gods they had not known,
new gods that had just arrived,
which your fathers did not fear.
18 You ignored the Rock who gave
  you birth;
you forgot the God who brought
  you forth.

19 When the LORD saw this, He
  despised them,
provoked to anger by His sons and
  daughters.
20 He said: "I will hide My face from
  them;
I will see what will become of
  them,
for they are a perverse
  generation—
unfaithful children.
21 They have provoked My jealousy
  with their so-called gods;
they have enraged Me with their
  worthless idols.
So I will provoke their jealousy
  with an inferior people;
I will enrage them with a foolish
  nation.
22 For fire has been kindled because
  of My anger
and burns to the depths of Sheol;
it devours the land and its
  produce,
and scorches the foundations of
  the mountains.

23 I will pile disasters on them;
I will use up My arrows against
  them.
24 They will be weak from hunger,
  ravaged by pestilence and bitter
  plague;
I will unleash on them wild beasts
  with fangs,
as well as venomous snakes that
  slither in the dust.
25 Outside, the sword will take their
  children,
and inside, there will be terror;
the young man and the virgin will
  be killed,
the infant and the gray-haired man.

26 I would have said: I will cut them
  to pieces

and blot out the memory of them
  from mankind,
27 if I had not feared insult from the
  enemy,
or feared that these foes might
  misunderstand
and say: Our own hand has
  prevailed;
it wasn't the LORD who did all
  this."

28 Israel is a nation lacking sense
  with no understanding at all.
29 If only they were wise, they would
  figure it out;
they would understand their fate.
30 How could one man pursue a
  thousand,
or two put ten thousand to flight,
unless their Rock had sold them,
unless the LORD had given them
  up?
31 But their "rock" is not like our
  Rock;
even our enemies concede.
32 For their vine is from the vine of
  Sodom
and from the fields of Gomorrah.
Their grapes are poisonous;
their clusters are bitter.
33 Their wine is serpents' venom,
the deadly poison of cobras.

34 "Is it not stored up with Me,
sealed up in My vaults?
35 Vengeance belongs to Me; I will
  repay.
In time their foot will slip,
for their day of disaster is near,
and their doom is coming
  quickly."
36 The LORD will indeed vindicate His
  people
and have compassion on His
  servants
when He sees that their strength
  is gone
and no one is left—slave or free.
37 He will say: "Where are their
  gods,
the 'rock' they found refuge in?
38 Who ate the fat of their sacrifices
and drank the wine of their drink
  offerings?

431

Let them rise up and help you;
let it be a shelter for you.
39 See now that I alone am He;
there is no God but Me.
I bring death and I give life;
I wound and I heal.
No one can rescue anyone from
My hand.
40 I raise My hand to heaven and
declare:
As surely as I live forever,
41 when I sharpen My flashing sword,
and My hand takes hold of
judgment,
I will take vengeance on My
adversaries
and repay those who hate Me.
42 I will make My arrows drunk with
blood
while My sword devours flesh—
the blood of the slain and the
captives,
the heads of the enemy leaders."

43 Rejoice, you nations, over His
people,
for He will avenge the blood of
His servants.
He will take vengeance on His
adversaries;
He will purify His land and His
people.

44 Moses came with Joshua son of Nun and recited all the words of this song in the presence of the people. 45 After Moses finished reciting all these words to all Israel, 46 he said to them, "Take to heart all these words I am giving as a warning to you today, so that you may command your children to carefully follow all the words of this law. 47 For they are not meaningless words to you but they are your life, and by them you will live long in the land you are crossing the Jordan to possess." 48 On that same day the LORD spoke to Moses, 49 "Go up Mount Nebo in the Abarim range in the land of Moab, across from Jericho, and view the land of Canaan I am giving the Israelites as a possession. 50 Then you will die on the mountain that you go up, and you will be gathered to your people, just as your brother Aaron died on Mount Hor and was gathered to his people. 51 For both of you broke faith with Me among the Israelites at the waters of Meribath-kadesh in the Wilderness of Zin by failing to treat Me as holy in their presence. 52 Although you will view the land from a distance, which I am giving the Israelites, you will not go there."

*P*SALM 48:1-7

1 The LORD is great and is highly
praised
in the city of our God.
His holy mountain, 2 rising
splendidly,
is the joy of the whole earth.
Mount Zion on the slopes of the
north
is the city of the great King.
3 God is known as a stronghold
in its citadels.

4 Look! The kings assembled;
they advanced together.
5 They looked, and froze with fear;
they fled in terror.
6 Trembling seized them there,
agony like that of a woman in
labor,
7 as You wrecked the ships of
Tarshish
with the east wind.

*P*ROVERBS 11:16-18

16 A gracious woman gains honor,
but violent men gain only riches.

17 A kind man benefits himself,
but a cruel man brings disaster on
himself.

18 The wicked man earns an empty
wage,
but the one who sows
righteousness, a true reward.

*L*UKE 12:22-40

22 Then He said to His disciples: "Therefore I tell you, don't worry about

your life, what you will eat; or about the body, what you will wear. ²³ For life is more than food and the body more than clothing. ²⁴ Consider the ravens: they don't sow or reap; they don't have a storeroom or a barn; yet God feeds them. Aren't you worth much more than the birds? ²⁵ Can any of you add a cubit to his height by worrying? ²⁶ If then you're not able to do even a little thing, why worry about the rest?

²⁷ "Consider how the wildflowers grow: they don't labor or spin thread. Yet I tell you, not even Solomon in all his splendor was adorned like one of these! ²⁸ If that's how God clothes the grass, which is in the field today and is thrown into the furnace tomorrow, how much more will He do for you— you of little faith? ²⁹ Don't keep striving for what you should eat and what you should drink, and don't be anxious. ³⁰ For the Gentile world eagerly seeks all these things, and your Father knows that you need them.

³¹ "But seek His kingdom, and these things will be provided for you. ³² Don't be afraid, little flock, because your Father delights to give you the kingdom. ³³ Sell your possessions and give to the poor. Make money-bags for yourselves that won't grow old, an inexhaustible treasure in heaven, where no thief comes near and no moth destroys. ³⁴ For where your treasure is, there your heart will be also.

³⁵ "Be ready for service and have your lamps lit. ³⁶ You must be like people waiting for their master to return from the wedding banquet so that when he comes and knocks, they can open the door for him at once. ³⁷ Those slaves the master will find alert when he comes will be blessed. I assure you: He will get ready, have them recline at the table, then come and serve them. ³⁸ If he comes in the middle of the night, or even near dawn, and finds them alert, those slaves are blessed. ³⁹ But know this: if the homeowner had known at what hour the thief was coming, he would not have let his house be broken into. ⁴⁰ You also be ready, because the Son of Man is coming at an hour that you do not expect."

No Blemish in God

I will take vengeance on My adversaries and repay those who hate Me.—Deuteronomy 32:41

There is one aspect of God's character that for some reason many see as a blotch or blemish in the divine nature. I refer to the matter of God's wrath. Though the subject may be missing from many modern-day pulpits, it is not missing from the Bible. If you look up in a Bible concordance all the texts that refer to the wrath, anger, or the severity of God, you will find that there are more references to these than there are to His love, graciousness, or tenderness. A proper study of God can never be complete unless consideration is given to the fact that God is not only a God of love but a God of wrath and anger also.

I remember in the early days of my Christian experience that whenever I heard any reference to the wrath of God, I would feel a deep resentment arise within me, and instead of regarding this aspect of God's nature with delight, I looked upon it with disdain. Later, however, when I came to understand it and saw it in its proper light—as something to rejoice in rather than to be resented—I found my love for God and my awe of God swell to new proportions.

Arthur W. Pink describes the wrath of God as the "eternal detestation of all unrighteousness

. . . the displeasure and indignation of divine equity against evil . . . the holiness of God stirred into activity against sin." Never view the wrath of God as a moral blemish or a blotch on His character. It would be a blemish if wrath were absent from Him.

Prayer

Father, I would face all reality—even those aspects that do not fit into my preconceived ideas. Help me not to balk at the idea that You are a God of wrath as well as a God of wonder. In Jesus' name I pray. Amen.

Further Study

2 Kg 22:1-13; Ps 90:11
Why did God's anger burn?
What did the psalmist say about God's wrath?

APRIL 19

DEUTERONOMY
33:1–34:12

33 This is the blessing that Moses, the man of God, gave the Israelites before his death. ² He said:

The LORD came from Sinai
and appeared to them from Seir;
He shone on them from Mount
    Paran
and came with ten thousand holy
    ones,
with lightning from His right hand
    for them.
³ Indeed He loves the people.
All Your holy ones are in Your
    hand,
and they assemble at Your feet.
Each receives Your words.
⁴ Moses gave us instruction,

a possession for the assembly of
    Jacob.
⁵ So He became King in Jeshurun
when the leaders of the people
    gathered
with the tribes of Israel.

⁶ Let Reuben live and not die
though his people become few.

⁷ He said this about Judah:

LORD, hear Judah's cry and bring
    him to his people.
He fights for his cause with his
    own hands,
but may You be a help against his
    foes.

⁸ He said about Levi:

Your Thummim and Urim belong
    to Your faithful one;

You tested him at Massah
and contended with him at the
waters of Meribah.
⁹ He said about his father and
mother,
"I do not regard them."
He disregarded his brothers
and didn't acknowledge his sons,
for they kept Your word
and maintained Your covenant.
¹⁰ They will teach Your ordinances to
Jacob
and Your instruction to Israel;
they will set incense before You
and whole burnt offerings on Your
altar.
¹¹ LORD, bless his possessions,
and accept the work of his hands.
Smash the loins of his adversaries
and enemies,
so that they cannot rise again.

¹² He said about Benjamin:

The LORD's beloved rests securely
on Him.
He shields him all day long,
and he rests on His shoulders.

¹³ He said about Joseph:

May his land be blessed by the
LORD
with the dew of heaven's bounty
and the watery depths that lie
beneath;
¹⁴ with the bountiful harvest from
the sun
and the abundant yield of the
seasons;
¹⁵ with the best products of the
ancient mountains
and the bounty of the eternal
hills;
¹⁶ with the choice gifts of the land
and everything in it;
and with the favor of Him
who appeared in the burning bush.
May these rest on the head of
Joseph,
on the crown of the prince of his
brothers.
¹⁷ His firstborn bull has splendor,
and horns like those of a wild ox;

he gores all the peoples with them
to the ends of the earth.
Such are the ten thousands of
Ephraim,
and such are the thousands of
Manasseh.

¹⁸ He said about Zebulun:

Rejoice, Zebulun, in your
journeys,
and Issachar, in your tents.
¹⁹ They summon the peoples to a
mountain;
there they offer acceptable
sacrifices.
For they draw from the wealth of
the seas
and the hidden treasures of the
sand.

²⁰ He said about Gad:

The one who enlarges Gad's
territory
will be blessed.
He lies down like a lion
and tears off an arm or even a
head.
²¹ He chose the best part for
himself,
because a ruler's portion was
assigned there for him.
He came with the leaders of the
people;
he carried out the LORD's justice
and His ordinances for Israel.

²² He said about Dan:

Dan is a young lion,
leaping out of Bashan.

²³ He said about Naphtali:

Naphtali, enjoying approval,
full of the LORD's blessing,
take possession to the west and
the south.

²⁴ He said about Asher:

May Asher be the most blessed of
the sons;

may he be the most favored
among his brothers
and dip his foot in olive oil.
²⁵ May the bolts of your gate be iron
and bronze,
and your strength last as long as
you live.

²⁶ There is none like the God of
Jeshurun,
who rides the heavens to your aid
on the clouds in His majesty.
²⁷ The God of old is your dwelling
place,
and underneath are the
everlasting arms.
He drives out the enemy before
you,
and commands, "Destroy!"
²⁸ So Israel dwells securely;
Jacob lives untroubled
in a land of grain and new wine;
even his skies drip with dew.
²⁹ How happy you are, Israel!
Who is like you,
a people saved by the LORD?
He is the shield that protects you,
the sword you boast in.
Your enemies will cringe before
you,
and you will tread on their backs.

34 Then Moses went up from the
plains of Moab to Mount Nebo,
to the top of Pisgah, which faces
Jericho, and the LORD showed him all
the land: Gilead as far as Dan, ²all of
Naphtali, the land of Ephraim and
Manasseh, all the land of Judah as far as
the Mediterranean Sea, ³the Negev,
and the region from the Valley of
Jericho, the City of Palms, as far as Zoar.
⁴The LORD then said to him, "This is the
land I promised Abraham, Isaac, and
Jacob, 'I will give it to your descendants.' I have let you see it with your
own eyes, but you will not cross into it."
⁵So Moses the servant of the LORD
died there in the land of Moab, as the
LORD had said. ⁶He buried him in the
valley in the land of Moab facing Beth-
peor, and no one to this day knows
where his grave is. ⁷Moses was 120
years old when he died; his eyes were

not weak, and his vitality had not left
him. ⁸The Israelites wept for Moses in
the plains of Moab 30 days. Then the
days of weeping and mourning for
Moses came to an end.
⁹Joshua son of Nun was filled with
the spirit of wisdom, because Moses
had laid his hands on him. So the
Israelites obeyed him and did as the
LORD had commanded Moses. ¹⁰No
prophet has arisen again in Israel like
Moses, whom the LORD knew face to
face. ¹¹He was unparalleled for all the
signs and wonders the LORD sent him to
do against the land of Egypt—to Pharaoh, to all his officials, and to all his
land, ¹²and for all the mighty acts of
power and terrifying deeds that Moses
performed in the sight of all Israel.

PSALM 48:8-14

⁸ Just as we heard, so we have seen
in the city of the LORD of Hosts,
in the city of our God;
God will establish it forever. *Selah*

⁹ God, within Your temple,
we contemplate Your faithful love.
¹⁰ Your name, God, like Your praise,
reaches to the ends of the earth;
Your right hand is filled with
justice.
¹¹ Mount Zion is glad.
The towns of Judah rejoice
because of Your judgments.

¹² Go around Zion, encircle it;
count its towers,
¹³ note its ramparts; tour its
citadels
so that you can tell a future
generation:
¹⁴ "This God, our God forever and
ever—
He will lead us eternally."

PROVERBS 11:19-21

¹⁹ Genuine righteousness leads to
life,
but pursuing evil leads to death.

20 Those with twisted minds are
detestable to the LORD,
but those with blameless conduct
are His delight.

21 Be assured that the wicked will
not go unpunished,
but the offspring of the righteous
will escape.

LUKE 12:41-59

41 "Lord," Peter asked, "are You telling this parable to us or to everyone?" 42 The Lord said: "Who then is the faithful and sensible manager his master will put in charge of his household servants to give them their allotted food at the proper time? 43 That slave whose master finds him working when he comes will be rewarded. 44 I tell you the truth: he will put him in charge of all his possessions. 45 But if that slave says in his heart, 'My master is delaying his coming,' and starts to beat the male and female slaves, and to eat and drink and get drunk, 46 that slave's master will come on a day he does not expect him and at an hour he does not know. He will cut him to pieces and assign him a place with the unbelievers. 47 And that slave who knew his master's will and didn't prepare himself or do it will be severely beaten. 48 But the one who did not know and did things deserving of blows will be beaten lightly. Much will be required of everyone who has been given much. And even more will be expected of the one who has been entrusted with more.

49 "I came to bring fire on the earth, and how I wish it were already set ablaze! 50 But I have a baptism to be baptized with, and how it consumes Me until it is finished! 51 Do you think that I came here to give peace to the earth? No, I tell you, but rather division! 52 From now on, five in one household will be divided: three against two, and two against three.

53 They will be divided,
father against son,
son against father,
mother against daughter,
daughter against mother,
mother-in-law against
her daughter-in-law,
and daughter-in-law against
mother-in-law."

54 He also said to the crowds: "When you see a cloud rising in the west, right away you say, 'A storm is coming,' and so it does. 55 And when the south wind is blowing, you say, 'It's going to be a scorcher!' and it is. 56 Hypocrites! You know how to interpret the appearance of the earth and the sky, but why don't you know how to interpret this time? 57 "Why don't you judge for yourselves what is right? 58 As you are going with your adversary to the ruler, make an effort to settle with him on the way. Then he won't drag you before the judge, the judge hand you over to the bailiff, and the bailiff throw you into prison. 59 I tell you, you will never get out of there until you have paid the last cent."

Pluralism's Persuasiveness

*This God, our God forever and ever—
He will lead us eternally.*—PSALM 48:14

The argument presented by pluralists that Christians must view their religion as one among many, and Jesus as only one Savior among others, must be firmly resisted. It may sound arrogant to say so but it is nevertheless a fact that Christianity is unique, absolute, definitive, ultimate, and final.

Critics of the uniqueness of Christianity can be very persuasive. "The world is under great threat," they tell us, "because of environmental pollution, economic injustice, and many other problems. Nothing that divides us, including our religions, should be considered as important as the need to live together in harmony." Another emphasis is on the need to study comparative faiths. There is a sense in which understanding what other people believe is useful, but not until the claims of Christianity are seen to be definitive and final. Christianity is not a comparative religion; it reveals God's one and only way of entering into a personal relationship with Him.

Galatians 2:20 in the *Amplified Bible* reads: "The life I now live . . . I live by faith—by adherence to and reliance on and [complete] trust—in the Son of God, Who loved me and gave Himself up for me." Bishop Leslie Newbigin put it well: "If it is really true, as it is, that 'the Son of God loved me and gave Himself up for me,' how can I agree that this amazing act of matchless grace should merely become part of a syllabus for the 'comparative study of religions'?" Christ is not first in a class; He occupies the category all by Himself.

Prayer

My Father and my God, may the Person of Your Son become as real and as precious to me as He is to You. And teach me more about Him so that I can make clear to others why He is a Savior beyond compare. For His own dear name's sake. Amen.

Further Study

Ac 4:1-12; 1 Tm 2:1-6; 1 Co 3:11
What did Peter declare to the Sanhedrin?
What did Paul declare to Timothy?

APRIL 20

JOSHUA 1:1–3:17

1 After the death of Moses the LORD's servant, the LORD spoke to Joshua son of Nun, who had served Moses: ² "Moses My servant is dead. Now you and all the people prepare to cross over the Jordan to the land I am giving the Israelites. ³ I have given you every place where the sole of your foot treads, just as I promised Moses. ⁴ Your territory will be from the wilderness and Lebanon to the great Euphrates River—all the land of the Hittites—and west to the Mediterranean Sea. ⁵ No one will be able to stand against you as long as you live. I will be with you, just as I was with Moses. I will not leave you or forsake you.

⁶ "Be strong and courageous, for you

will distribute the land I swore to their fathers to give them as an inheritance. ⁷ Above all, be strong and very courageous to carefully observe the whole instruction My servant Moses commanded you. Do not turn from it to the right or the left, so that you will have success wherever you go. ⁸ This book of instruction must not depart from your mouth; you are to recite it day and night, so that you may carefully observe everything written in it. For then you will prosper and succeed in whatever you do. ⁹ Haven't I commanded you: be strong and courageous? Do not be afraid or discouraged, for the LORD your God is with you wherever you go."

¹⁰ Then Joshua commanded the officers of the people: ¹¹ "Go through the camp and tell the people, 'Get provisions ready for yourselves, for within three days you will be crossing the Jordan to go in and take possession of the land the LORD your God is giving you to inherit.' "

¹² Joshua said to the Reubenites, the Gadites, and half the tribe of Manasseh: ¹³ "Remember what Moses the LORD's servant commanded you when he said, 'The LORD your God will give you rest, and He will give you this land.' ¹⁴ Your wives, young children, and livestock may remain in the land Moses gave you on this side of the Jordan. But your fighting men must cross over in battle formation ahead of your brothers and help them ¹⁵ until the LORD gives our brothers rest, as He has given you, and they too possess the land the LORD your God is giving them. You may then return to the land of your inheritance and take possession of what Moses the LORD's servant gave you on the east side of the Jordan."

¹⁶ They answered Joshua, "Everything you have commanded us we will do, and everywhere you send us we will go. ¹⁷ We will obey you, just as we obeyed Moses in everything. And may the LORD your God be with you, as He was with Moses. ¹⁸ Anyone who rebels against your order and does not obey your words in all that you command him, will be put to death. Above all, be strong and courageous!"

2 Joshua son of Nun secretly sent two men as spies from Acacia Grove, saying, "Go and scout the land, especially Jericho." So they left, and they came to the house of a woman, a prostitute named Rahab, and stayed there.

² The king of Jericho was told, "Look, some of the Israelite men have come here tonight to investigate the land." ³ Then the king of Jericho sent word to Rahab and said, "Bring out the men who came to you and entered your house, for they came to investigate the entire land."

⁴ But the woman had taken the two men and hidden them. So she said, "Yes, the men did come to me, but I didn't know where they were from. ⁵ At nightfall, when the gate was about to close, the men went out, and I don't know where they were going. Chase after them quickly, and you can catch up with them!" ⁶ But she had taken them up to the roof and hidden them among the stalks of flax that she had arranged on the roof. ⁷ The men pursued them along the road to the fords of the Jordan, and as soon as they left to pursue them, the gate was shut.

⁸ Before the men fell asleep, she went up on the roof ⁹ and said to them, "I know that the LORD has given you this land and that dread of you has fallen on us, and everyone who lives in the land is panicking because of you. ¹⁰ For we have heard how the LORD dried up the waters of the Red Sea before you when you came out of Egypt, and what you did to Sihon and Og, the two Amorite kings you completely destroyed across the Jordan. ¹¹ When we heard this, we lost heart, and everyone's courage failed because of you, for the LORD your God is God in heaven above and on earth below. ¹² Now please swear to me by the LORD that you will also show kindness to my family, because I showed kindness to you. Give me a sure sign ¹³ that you will spare the lives of my father, mother, brothers, sisters, and all who belong to them, and save us from death."

¹⁴ The men answered her, "We will give our lives for yours. If you don't report

our mission, we will show kindness and faithfulness to you when the LORD gives us the land."

¹⁵ Then she let them down by a rope through the window, since she lived in a house that was built into the wall of the city. ¹⁶ "Go to the hill country so that the men pursuing you won't find you," she said to them. "Hide yourselves there for three days until they return; afterwards, go on your way."

¹⁷ The men said to her, "We will be free from this oath you made us swear, ¹⁸ unless, when we enter the land, you tie this scarlet cord to the window through which you let us down. Bring your father, mother, brothers, and all your father's family into your house. ¹⁹ If anyone goes out the doors of your house, his blood will be on his own head, and we will be innocent. But if anyone with you in the house should be harmed, his blood will be on our heads. ²⁰ And if you report our mission, we are free from the oath you made us swear."

²¹ "Let it be as you say," she replied, and she sent them away. After they had gone, she tied the scarlet cord to the window.

²² So the two men went into the hill country and stayed there three days until the pursuers had returned. They searched all along the way, but did not find them. ²³ Then the men returned, came down from the hill country, and crossed the Jordan. They went to Joshua son of Nun and reported everything that had happened to them. ²⁴ They told Joshua, "The LORD has handed over the entire land to us. Everyone who lives in the land is also panicking because of us."

3 Joshua started early the next morning and left Acacia Grove with all the Israelites. They went as far as the Jordan and stayed there before crossing. ² After three days the officers went through the camp ³ and commanded the people: "When you see the ark of the covenant of the LORD your God carried by the Levitical priests, you must break camp and follow it. ⁴ But keep a distance of about 1,000 yards between your-

selves and the ark. Don't go near it, so that you can see the way to go, for you haven't traveled this way before."

⁵ Joshua told the people, "Consecrate yourselves, because the LORD will do wonders among you tomorrow." ⁶ Then he said to the priests, "Take the ark of the covenant and go on ahead of the people." So they carried the ark of the covenant and went ahead of them.

⁷ The LORD spoke to Joshua: "Today I will begin to exalt you in the sight of all Israel, so they will know that I will be with you just as I was with Moses. ⁸ Command the priests carrying the ark of the covenant: 'When you reach the edge of the waters, stand in the Jordan.' "

⁹ Then Joshua told the Israelites, "Come closer and listen to the words of the LORD your God." ¹⁰ He said, "You will know that the living God is among you and that He will certainly dispossess before you the Canaanites, Hittites, Hivites, Perizzites, Girgashites, Amorites, and Jebusites ¹¹ when the ark of the covenant of the Lord of all the earth goes ahead of you into the Jordan. ¹² Now choose 12 men from the tribes of Israel, one man for each tribe. ¹³ When the feet of the priests who carry the ark of the LORD, the Lord of all the earth, come to rest in the Jordan's waters, its waters will be cut off. The water flowing downstream will stand up in a mass."

¹⁴ When the people broke camp to cross the Jordan, the priests carried the ark of the covenant ahead of the people. ¹⁵ Now the Jordan overflows its banks throughout the harvest season. But as soon as the priests carrying the ark reached the Jordan, their feet touched the water at its edge ¹⁶ and the water flowing downstream stood still, rising up in a mass that extended as far as Adam, a city next to Zarethan. The water flowing downstream into the Sea of the Arabah (the Dead Sea) was completely cut off, and the people crossed opposite Jericho. ¹⁷ The priests carrying the ark of the LORD's covenant stood firmly on dry ground in the middle of the Jordan, while all Israel crossed on

dry ground until the entire nation had finished crossing the Jordan.

PSALM 49:1-9

1 Hear this, all you peoples;
  listen, all who inhabit the world,
2 both low and high,
  rich and poor together.
3 My mouth speaks wisdom;
  my heart's meditation brings understanding.
4 I turn my ear to a proverb;
  I explain my riddle with a lyre.

5 Why should I fear in times of trouble?
  The iniquity of my foes surrounds me.
6 They trust in their wealth
  and boast of their abundant riches.
7 Yet these cannot redeem a person
  or pay his ransom to God—
8 since the price of redeeming him is too costly,
  one should forever stop trying—
9 so that he may live forever
  and not see the Pit.

PROVERBS 11:22-23

22 A beautiful woman who rejects good sense
   is like a gold ring in a pig's snout.

23 The desire of the righteous turns out well,
   but the hope of the wicked leads to wrath.

LUKE 13:1-21

13 At that time, some people came and reported to Him about the Galileans whose blood Pilate had mixed with their sacrifices. 2 And He responded to them, "Do you think that these Galileans were more sinful than all Galileans because they suffered these things? 3 No, I tell you; but unless you repent, you will all perish as well! 4 Or those 18 that the tower in Siloam fell on and killed—do you think they were more sinful than all the people who live in Jerusalem? 5 No, I tell you; but unless you repent, you will all perish as well!"

6 And He told this parable: "A man had a fig tree that was planted in his vineyard. He came looking for fruit on it and found none. 7 He told the vineyard worker, 'Listen, for three years I have come looking for fruit on this fig tree and haven't found any. Cut it down! Why should it even waste the soil?' 8 "But he replied to him, 'Sir, leave it this year also, until I dig around it and fertilize it. 9 Perhaps it will bear fruit next year, but if not, you can cut it down.' "

10 As He was teaching in one of the synagogues on the Sabbath, 11 a woman was there who had been disabled by a spirit for over 18 years. She was bent over and could not straighten up at all. 12 When Jesus saw her, He called out to her, "Woman, you are free of your disability." 13 Then He laid His hands on her, and instantly she was restored and began to glorify God.

14 But the leader of the synagogue, indignant because Jesus had healed on the Sabbath, responded by telling the crowd, "There are six days when work should be done; therefore come on those days and be healed and not on the Sabbath day." 15 But the Lord answered him and said, "Hypocrites! Doesn't each one of you untie his ox or donkey from the feeding trough on the Sabbath, and lead it to water? 16 Satan has bound this woman, a daughter of Abraham, for 18 years—shouldn't she be untied from this bondage on the Sabbath day?" 17 When He had said these things, all His adversaries were humiliated, but the whole crowd was rejoicing over all the glorious things He was doing.

18 He said therefore, "What is the kingdom of God like, and what can I compare it to? 19 It's like a mustard seed that a man took and sowed in his garden. It grew and became a tree, and the birds of the sky nested in its branches." 20 Again He said, "What can I compare the kingdom of God to? 21 It's like yeast that a woman took and mixed into 50 pounds of flour until it spread through the entire mixture."

The Mantle of Power

Above all, be strong and very courageous.
—Joshua 1:7

The Holy Spirit clothes His people with supernatural power. It is one thing to be unified on the inside; it is another to be fortified to meet whatever happens on the outside. The Holy Spirit—if we let Him—can do both. Jesus, when speaking of the Holy Spirit in John's Gospel (14:17), used two different prepositions to describe His work. He said, "He remains *with* you and will be *in* you" (italics added). In Acts 1:8 he uses a different preposition: "the Holy Spirit has come *upon* you"(italics added). The word "upon" gives us a picture of the Holy Spirit wrapping a mantle of divine omnipotence around the shoulders of His disciples, which would enable them to do great exploits in His Name.

The story of Elijah and Elisha in the Old Testament illustrates this particular aspect. Elijah, you remember, wore a mantle that was invested with supernatural power. Elijah's servant Elisha no doubt greatly coveted that supernatural mantle. Elijah promised him that if he saw him when he returned to heaven, the mantle (the double share of his spirit) would be his. On the day of Elijah's departure to heaven, Elisha fulfilled the condition and received the desired mantle. He then went out and performed twice as many miracles as his master.

The mantle of power Jesus used when He was here on earth, He has now given to us. Now, hold your breath, for this is what Jesus said of those who have faith in Him: "He will do even greater works than these" (Jn 14:12).

Prayer

O Father, what a challenge this puts before me and everyone else in the church today. We are hardly performing a tenth of what You did, let alone twice as much. Something is wrong. Show me how to put it right in my life. In Jesus' name. Amen.

Further Study

2 Kg 2; Zch 4:6; Lk 4:14; Ac 19:11-12
What characteristics did Elisha show in obtaining the mantle?
What is said of Jesus when He returned from the wilderness?

APRIL 21

JOSHUA 4:1–6:27

4 After the entire nation had finished crossing the Jordan, the LORD spoke to Joshua, ² "Choose 12 men from the people, one man for each tribe, ³ and command them, 'Take 12 stones from this place in the middle of the Jordan where the priests' feet are standing, carry them with you, and set them down at the place where you spend the night.' "

⁴ So Joshua summoned the 12 men selected from the Israelites, one man for each tribe, ⁵ and said to them, "Go across to the ark of the LORD your God in the middle of the Jordan. Each of you lift a stone onto his shoulder, one for each of the Israelite tribes, ⁶ so that this will be a sign among you. In the future, when your children ask you, 'What do these stones mean to you?' ⁷ you should tell them, 'The waters of the Jordan were cut off in front of the ark of the LORD's covenant. When it crossed the Jordan, the Jordan's waters were cut off.' Therefore these stones will always be a memorial for the Israelites."

⁸ The Israelites did just as Joshua had commanded them. The 12 men took stones from the middle of the Jordan, one for each of the Israelite tribes, just as the LORD had told Joshua. They carried them to the camp and set them down there. ⁹ Joshua also set up 12 stones in the middle of the Jordan where the priests who carried the ark of the covenant were standing. The stones are there to this day.

¹⁰ The priests carrying the ark continued standing in the middle of the Jordan until everything was completed that the LORD had commanded Joshua to tell the people, in keeping with all that Moses had commanded Joshua. The people hurried across, ¹¹ and after everyone had finished crossing, the priests with the ark of the LORD crossed in the sight of the people. ¹² The Reubenites, Gadites, and half the tribe of Manasseh went in battle formation in front of the Israelites, as Moses had instructed them. ¹³ About 40,000 equipped for war crossed to the plains of Jericho in the LORD's presence.

¹⁴ On that day the LORD exalted Joshua in the sight of all Israel, and they revered him throughout his life, as they had revered Moses. ¹⁵ The LORD told Joshua, ¹⁶ "Command the priests who carry the ark of the testimony to come up from the Jordan."

¹⁷ So Joshua commanded the priests, "Come up from the Jordan." ¹⁸ When the priests carrying the ark of the LORD's covenant came up from the middle of the Jordan, and their feet stepped out on solid ground, the waters of the Jordan resumed their course, flowing over all the banks as before.

¹⁹ The people came up from the Jordan on the tenth day of the first month, and camped at Gilgal on the eastern limits of Jericho. ²⁰ Then Joshua set up in Gilgal the 12 stones they had taken from the Jordan, ²¹ and he said to the Israelites, "When your children ask their fathers in the future, 'What is the meaning of these stones?' ²² you should tell your children, 'Israel crossed the Jordan on dry ground.' ²³ For the LORD your God dried up the waters of the Jordan before you until you had crossed over, just as the LORD your God did to the Red Sea, which He dried up before us until we had crossed over. ²⁴ This is so that all the people of the earth may know that the LORD's hand is mighty, and so that you may always fear the LORD your God."

5 When all the Amorite kings across the Jordan to the west and all the Canaanite kings near the sea heard how the LORD had dried up the waters of the

Jordan before the Israelites until they had crossed over, they lost heart and their courage failed because of the Israelites.

² At that time the LORD said to Joshua, "Make flint knives and circumcise the Israelite men again." ³ So Joshua made flint knives and circumcised the Israelite men at Gibeath-haaraloth. ⁴ This is the reason Joshua circumcised them: All the people who came out of Egypt who were males—all the men of war—had died in the wilderness along the way after they had come out of Egypt. ⁵ Though all the people who came out were circumcised, none of the people born in the wilderness along the way were circumcised after they had come out of Egypt. ⁶ For the Israelites wandered in the wilderness 40 years until all the nation's men of war who came out of Egypt had died off because they did not obey the LORD. So the LORD vowed never to let them see the land He had sworn to their fathers to give us, a land flowing with milk and honey. ⁷ Joshua raised up their sons in their place; it was these he circumcised. They were still uncircumcised, since they had not been circumcised along the way. ⁸ After the entire nation had been circumcised, they stayed where they were in the camp until they recovered. ⁹ The LORD then said to Joshua, "Today I have rolled away the disgrace of Egypt from you." Therefore, that place has been called Gilgal to this day.

¹⁰ While the Israelites camped at Gilgal on the plains of Jericho, they kept the Passover on the evening of the fourteenth day of the month. ¹¹ The day after Passover they ate unleavened bread and roasted grain from the produce of the land. ¹² And the day after they ate from the produce of the land, the manna ceased. Since there was no more manna for the Israelites, they ate from the crops of the land of Canaan that year.

¹³ When Joshua was near Jericho, he looked up and saw a man standing in front of him with a drawn sword in His hand. Joshua approached Him and asked, "Are You for us or for our enemies?"

¹⁴ "Neither," He replied. "I have now come as commander of the LORD's army."

Then Joshua bowed with his face to the ground in worship and asked Him, "What does my Lord want to say to His servant?"

¹⁵ The commander of the Lord's army said to Joshua, "Remove the sandals from your feet, for the place where you are standing is holy." And Joshua did so.

6 Now Jericho was strongly fortified because of the Israelites—no one leaving or entering. ² The LORD said to Joshua, "Look, I have handed Jericho, its king, and its fighting men over to you. ³ March around the city with all the men of war, circling the city one time. Do this for six days. ⁴ Have seven priests carry seven ram's-horn trumpets in front of the ark. But on the seventh day, march around the city seven times, while the priests blow the trumpets. ⁵ When there is a prolonged blast of the horn and you hear its sound, have all the people give a mighty shout. Then the city wall will collapse, and the people will advance, each man straight ahead."

⁶ So Joshua son of Nun summoned the priests and said to them, "Take up the ark of the covenant and have seven priests carry seven trumpets in front of the ark of the LORD." ⁷ He said to the people, "Move forward, march around the city, and have the armed troops go ahead of the ark of the LORD."

⁸ After Joshua had spoken to the people, seven priests carrying seven trumpets before the LORD moved forward and blew the trumpets; the ark of the LORD's covenant followed them. ⁹ While the trumpets were blowing, the armed troops went in front of the priests who blew the trumpets, and the rear guard went behind the ark. ¹⁰ But Joshua had commanded the people: "Do not shout or let your voice be heard. Don't let one word come out of your mouth until the time I say, 'Shout!' Then you are to shout." ¹¹ So the ark of the LORD was carried around the city, circling it once. They returned to the camp and spent the night there.

¹²Joshua got up early the next morning. The priests took the ark of the LORD, ¹³and the seven priests carrying seven trumpets marched in front of the ark of the LORD. While the trumpets were blowing, the armed troops went in front of them, and the rear guard went behind the ark of the LORD. ¹⁴On the second day they marched around the city once and returned to the camp. They did this for six days.

¹⁵Early on the seventh day, they started at dawn and marched around the city seven times in the same way. That was the only day they marched around the city seven times. ¹⁶After the seventh time, the priests blew the trumpets, and Joshua said to the people, "Shout! For the LORD has given you the city. ¹⁷But the city and everything in it are set apart to the LORD for destruction. Only Rahab the prostitute and everyone with her in the house will live, because she hid the men we sent. ¹⁸But keep yourselves from the things set apart, or you will be set apart for destruction. If you take any of those things, you will set apart the camp of Israel for destruction and bring disaster on it. ¹⁹For all the silver and gold, and the articles of bronze and iron, are dedicated to the LORD and must go into the LORD's treasury."

²⁰So the people shouted, and the trumpets sounded. When they heard the blast of the trumpet, the people gave a great shout, and the wall collapsed. The people advanced into the city, each man straight ahead, and they captured the city. ²¹They completely destroyed everything in the city with the sword—every man and woman, both young and old, and every ox, sheep, and donkey.

²²Joshua said to the two men who had scouted the land, "Go to the prostitute's house and bring the woman out of there, and all who are with her, just as you promised her." ²³So the young men who had scouted went in and brought out Rahab and her father, mother, brothers, and all who belonged to her. They brought out her whole family and settled them outside the camp of Israel.

²⁴They burned up the city and everything in it, but they put the silver and gold and the articles of bronze and iron into the treasury of the LORD's house. ²⁵But Joshua spared Rahab the prostitute, her father's household, and all who belonged to her, because she hid the men Joshua had sent to spy on Jericho, and she lives in Israel to this day.

²⁶At that time Joshua imposed this curse:

Cursed before the LORD is the man
who undertakes the rebuilding
of this city, Jericho.
He will lay its foundation
at the cost of his firstborn;
He will set up its gates
at the cost of his youngest.

²⁷And the LORD was with Joshua, and his fame spread throughout the land.

𝒫SALM 49:10-15

¹⁰ For one can see that wise men
die;
the foolish and the senseless also
pass away.
Then they leave their wealth to
others.
¹¹ Their graves are their eternal
homes,
their homes from generation to
generation,
though they have named estates
after themselves.
¹² But despite his assets, man will
not last;
he is like the animals that perish.

¹³ This is the way of those who are
arrogant,
and of their followers, who
approve of their words. *Selah*
¹⁴ Like sheep they are headed for
Sheol;
Death will shepherd them.
The upright will rule over them in
the morning,
and their form will waste away in
Sheol, far from their lofty
abode.

15 But God will redeem my life from
the power of Sheol,
for He will take me.   *Selah*

PROVERBS 11:24-26

24 One person gives freely, yet gains
more;
another withholds what is right,
only to become poor.

25 A generous person will be
enriched,
and the one who gives a drink of
water will receive water.

26 People will curse anyone who
hoards grain,
but a blessing will come to the
one who sells it.

LUKE 13:22–14:6

22 He went through one town and village after another, teaching and making
His way to Jerusalem. 23 "Lord," someone asked Him, "are there few being
saved?"

He said to them, 24 "Make every effort
to enter through the narrow door, because I tell you, many will try to enter
and won't be able 25 once the homeowner gets up and shuts the door. Then
you will stand outside and knock on the
door, saying, 'Lord, open up for us!' He
will answer you, 'I don't know you or
where you're from.' 26 Then you will say,
'We ate and drank in Your presence, and
You taught in our streets!' 27 But He will
say, 'I tell you, I don't know you or
where you're from. Get away from Me,
all you workers of unrighteousness!'
28 There will be weeping and gnashing
of teeth in that place, when you see

Abraham, Isaac, Jacob, and all the
prophets in the kingdom of God but
yourselves thrown out. 29 They will
come from east and west, from north
and south, and recline at the table in
the kingdom of God. 30 Note this: some
are last who will be first, and some are
first who will be last."

31 At that time some Pharisees came
and told Him, "Go, get out of here!
Herod wants to kill You!"

32 He said to them, "Go tell that fox,
'Look! I'm driving out demons and performing healings today and tomorrow,
and on the third day I will complete My
work.' 33 Yet I must travel today, tomorrow, and the next day, because it is not
possible for a prophet to perish outside
of Jerusalem!

34 "Jerusalem, Jerusalem! The city
who kills the prophets and stones those
who are sent to her. How often I wanted to gather your children together, as a
hen gathers her chicks under her wings,
but you were not willing! 35 See, your
house is abandoned to you. And I tell
you, you will not see Me until the time
comes when you say, **Blessed is He
who comes in the name of the Lord!**"

14 One Sabbath, when He went to
eat at the house of one of the
leading Pharisees, they were watching
Him closely. 2 There in front of Him was
a man whose body was swollen with flu-
id. 3 In response, Jesus asked the law experts and the Pharisees, "Is it lawful to
heal on the Sabbath or not?" 4 But they
kept silent. He took the man, healed
him, and sent him away. 5 And to them,
He said, "Which of you whose son or ox
falls into a well, will not immediately
pull him out on the Sabbath day?" 6 To
this they could find no answer.

Divine Mathematics

*One person gives freely, yet gains more; another with-
holds what is right, only to become poor.*—PROVERBS 11:24

What all the passages in Proverbs which talk about generosity are really teaching us is that selfishness short-circuits human happiness and that the route to joy is liberality—liberality with our talents, our treasure, and our time.

Today's text is, of course, difficult for some to accept because it violates all the rules of mathematics. How can it be that the more you give away, the more you have? It doesn't seem logical! Well, let Lord Bertrand Russell, one of the greatest mathematicians of the century, comment on that: "Mathematics and logic have nothing to do with reality." David Rivett, a chartered accountant and one of the directors of CWR—Crusade for World Revival—says that since he has been with the organization he has found that God has a quite different arithmetic from what he as an accountant has been used to. For example—what do five and two make? Seven? Yes, in man's arithmetic, but not in God's. In God's arithmetic five and two make five thousand. How come? Well, five loaves and two fish—the little lunch which a boy once gave to Jesus—were taken by Him and turned into enough food to feed five thousand. And just to add to the point—twelve baskets of fragments were gathered up after everyone had eaten their fill!

Nature, we are told, abhors a vacuum; it is the same in the spiritual realm. Liberality and generosity create a vacuum into which God flows, enabling us to give and to go on giving. I cannot explain it, but I have seen it happen again and again.

Prayer

O God, You who are always reaching out to me in generosity and love, help me this day to do the same. May You use my generosity to touch the lives of others. For Your own dear name's sake. Amen.

Further Study

Mt 26:1-13; 25:34-40; Ec 5:13
How did the disciples view this extravagant act?
How did Jesus view it?

APRIL 22

JOSHUA 7:1–8:35

7 The Israelites, however, were unfaithful regarding the things set apart for destruction. Achan son of Carmi, son of Zabdi, son of Zerah, of the tribe of Judah, took some of what was set apart, and the LORD's anger burned against the Israelites.

² Joshua sent men from Jericho to Ai, which is near Beth-aven, east of Bethel, and told them, "Go up and scout the land." So the men went up and scouted Ai. ³ After returning to Joshua they reported to him, "Don't send all the people, but send about 2,000 or 3,000 men to attack Ai. Since the people of Ai are so few, don't wear out all our people there." ⁴ So about 3,000 men went up there, but they fled from the men of Ai. ⁵ The men of Ai struck down about 36 of them and chased them from outside the gate to the quarries, striking them down on the descent. As a result, the people's hearts melted and became like water.

⁶ Then Joshua tore his clothes and fell before the ark of the LORD with his face to the ground until evening, as did the elders of Israel; they all put dust on their heads. ⁷ "Oh, Lord GOD," Joshua said, "why did You ever bring these people across the Jordan to hand us over to the Amorites for our destruction? If only we had been content to remain on the other side of the Jordan! ⁸ What can I say, Lord, now that Israel has turned its back and run from its enemies? ⁹ When the Canaanites and all who live in the land hear about this, they will surround us and wipe out our name from the earth. Then what will You do about Your great name?"

¹⁰ The LORD then said to Joshua, "Stand up! Why are you on the ground? ¹¹ Israel has sinned. They have violated My covenant that I appointed for them.

They have taken some of what was set apart. They have stolen, deceived, and put the things with their own belongings. ¹² This is why the Israelites cannot stand against their enemies. They will turn their backs and run from their enemies, because they have been set apart for destruction. I will no longer be with you unless you remove from you what is set apart.

¹³ "Go and consecrate the people. Tell them to consecrate themselves tomorrow, for this is what the LORD, the God of Israel, says, 'There are among you, Israel, things set apart. You will not be able to stand against your enemies until you remove what is set apart. ¹⁴ In the morning you must present yourselves tribe by tribe. The tribe the LORD selects is to come forward clan by clan. The clan the LORD selects is to come forward family by family. The family the LORD selects is to come forward man by man. ¹⁵ The one who is caught with the things set apart must be burned, along with everything he has, because he has violated the LORD's covenant and committed an outrage in Israel.' "

¹⁶ Joshua got up early the next morning. He had Israel come forward tribe by tribe, and the tribe of Judah was selected. ¹⁷ He had the clans of Judah come forward, and the Zerahite clan was selected. He had the Zerahite clan come forward by heads of families, and Zabdi was selected. ¹⁸ He then had Zabdi's family come forward man by man, and Achan son of Carmi, son of Zabdi, son of Zerah, of the tribe of Judah, was selected.

¹⁹ So Joshua said to Achan, "My son, give glory to the LORD, the God of Israel, and make a confession to Him. I urge you, tell me what you have done. Don't hide anything from me."

²⁰ Achan replied to Joshua, "It is true. I have sinned against the LORD, the God

of Israel. This is what I did: ²¹ When I saw among the spoils a beautiful cloak from Babylon, 200 silver shekels, and a bar of gold weighing 50 shekels, I coveted them and took them. You can see for yourself. They are concealed in the ground inside my tent, with the money under the cloak." ²² So Joshua sent messengers who ran to the tent, and there was the cloak, concealed in his tent, with the money underneath. ²³ They took the things from inside the tent, brought them to Joshua and all the Israelites, and spread them out in the LORD's presence.

²⁴ Then Joshua and all Israel with him took Achan son of Zerah, the silver, the cloak, and the bar of gold, his sons and daughters, his ox, donkey, and sheep, his tent, and all that he had, and brought them up to the Valley of Achor. ²⁵ Joshua said, "Why have you troubled us? Today the LORD will trouble you!" So all Israel stoned him to death. They burned their bodies, threw stones on them, ²⁶ and raised over him a large pile of rocks that remains to this day. Then the LORD turned from His burning anger. Therefore that place has been called the Valley of Achor to this day.

8 The LORD said to Joshua, "Do not be afraid or discouraged. Take the whole military force with you and go attack Ai. Look, I have handed over to you the king of Ai, his people, city, and land. ² Treat Ai and its king as you did Jericho and its king; you may plunder its spoil and livestock for yourselves. Set an ambush behind the city."

³ So Joshua and the whole military force set out to attack Ai. Joshua selected 30,000 fighting men and sent them out at night. ⁴ He commanded them: "Pay attention. Lie in ambush behind the city, not too far from it, and all of you be ready. ⁵ Then I and all the people who are with me will approach the city. When they come out against us as they did the first time, we will flee from them. ⁶ They will come after us until we have drawn them away from the city, for they will say, 'They are fleeing from us as before.' While we are fleeing from

them, ⁷ you are to come out of your ambush and seize the city, for the LORD your God has handed it over to you. ⁸ After taking the city, set it on fire. Follow the LORD's command—see that you do as I have ordered you." ⁹ So Joshua sent them out, and they went to the ambush site and waited between Bethel and Ai, to the west of Ai. But he spent that night with the troops.

¹⁰ Joshua started early the next morning and mobilized them. Then he and the elders of Israel led the troops up to Ai. ¹¹ All those who were with him went up and approached the city, arriving opposite Ai, and camped to the north of it, with a valley between them and the city. ¹² Now Joshua had taken about 5,000 men and set them in ambush between Bethel and Ai, to the west of the city. ¹³ The military force was stationed in this way: the main camp to the north of the city and its rear guard to the west of the city. And that night Joshua went into the valley.

¹⁴ When the king of Ai saw the Israelites, the men of the city hurried and went out early in the morning, so that he and all his people could engage Israel in battle at a suitable place facing the plain of the Jordan. But he did not know there was an ambush waiting for him behind the city. ¹⁵ Joshua and all Israel pretended to be beaten back by them and fled toward the wilderness. ¹⁶ Then all the troops of Ai were summoned to pursue them, and they pursued Joshua and were drawn away from the city. ¹⁷ Not a man was left in Ai or Bethel who did not go out after Israel, leaving the city exposed while they pursued Israel.

¹⁸ Then the LORD said to Joshua, "Hold out the sword in your hand toward Ai, for I will hand the city over to you." So Joshua held out his sword toward it. ¹⁹ When he held out his hand, the men in ambush rose quickly from their position. They ran, entered the city, captured it, and immediately set it on fire.

²⁰ The men of Ai turned and looked back, and smoke from the city was rising to the sky! They could not escape in any direction, and the troops who had

fled to the wilderness now became the pursuers. ²¹ When Joshua and all Israel saw that the men in ambush had captured the city and that smoke was rising from it, they turned back and struck down the men of Ai. ²² The men in the ambush came out of the city against them, and the men of Ai were trapped between the Israelite forces, some on one side and some on the other. They struck them down until no survivor or fugitive remained, ²³ but they captured the king of Ai alive and brought him to Joshua.

²⁴ When Israel had finished killing everyone living in Ai who had pursued them into the open country, and when every last one of them had fallen by the sword, all Israel returned to Ai and struck it down with the sword. ²⁵ The total of those who fell that day, both men and women, was 12,000—all the people of Ai. ²⁶ Joshua did not draw back his hand that was holding the sword until all the inhabitants of Ai were completely destroyed. ²⁷ Israel plundered only the cattle and spoil of that city for themselves, according to the Lord's command that He had given Joshua.

²⁸ Joshua burned Ai and left it a permanent ruin, desolate to this day. ²⁹ He hung the body of the king of Ai on a tree until evening, and at sunset Joshua commanded that they take his body down from the tree. They threw it down at the entrance of the city gate and put a large pile of rocks over it, which remains to this day.

³⁰ At that time Joshua built an altar on Mount Ebal to the Lord, the God of Israel, ³¹ just as Moses the Lord's servant had commanded the Israelites. He built it according to what is written in the book of the law of Moses: an altar of uncut stones on which no iron tool has been used. Then they offered burnt offerings to the Lord and sacrificed fellowship offerings on it. ³² There on the stones, Joshua copied the law of Moses, which he had written in the presence of the Israelites. ³³ All Israel, foreigner and citizen alike, with their elders, officers, and judges, stood on either side of the ark of the Lord's covenant facing the

Levitical priests who carried it. As Moses the Lord's servant had commanded earlier, half of them were in front of Mount Gerizim and half in front of Mount Ebal, to bless the people of Israel. ³⁴ Afterwards, Joshua read aloud all the words of the law—the blessings as well as the curses—according to all that is written in the book of the law. ³⁵ There was not a word of all that Moses had commanded that Joshua did not read before the entire assembly of Israel, including the women, little children, and foreigners who were with them.

PSALM 49:16-20

¹⁶ Do not be afraid when a man gets rich,
    when the wealth of his house increases.
¹⁷ For when he dies, he will take nothing at all;
    his wealth will not follow him down.
¹⁸ Though he praises himself during his lifetime—
    and people praise you when you do well for yourself—
¹⁹ he will go to the generation of his fathers;
    they will never see the light.
²⁰ A man with valuable possessions but without understanding
    is like the animals that perish.

PROVERBS 11:27-29

²⁷ The one who searches for what is good finds favor,
    but if someone looks for trouble, it will come to him.
²⁸ Anyone trusting in his riches will fall,
    but the righteous will flourish like foliage.
²⁹ The one who brings ruin on his household will inherit the wind,
    and a fool will be a slave to someone whose heart is wise.

*L*UKE 14:7-24

⁷ He told a parable to those who were invited, when He noticed how they would choose the best places for themselves: ⁸ "When you are invited by someone to a wedding banquet, don't recline at the best place, because a more distinguished person than you may have been invited by your host. ⁹ The one who invited both of you may come and say to you, 'Give your place to this man,' and then in humiliation, you will proceed to take the lowest place. ¹⁰ "But when you are invited, go and recline in the lowest place, so that when the one who invited you comes, he will say to you, 'Friend, move up higher.' You will then be honored in the presence of all the other guests. ¹¹ For everyone who exalts himself will be humbled, and the one who humbles himself will be exalted."

¹² He also said to the one who had invited Him, "When you give a lunch or a dinner, don't invite your friends, your brothers, your relatives, or your rich neighbors, because they might invite you back, and you would be repaid. ¹³ On the contrary, when you host a banquet, invite those who are poor, maimed, lame, or blind. ¹⁴ And you will be blessed, because they cannot repay you; for you will be repaid at the resurrection of the righteous."

¹⁵ When one of those who reclined at the table with Him heard these things, he said to Him, "The one who will eat bread in the kingdom of God is blessed!"

¹⁶ Then He told him: "A man was giving a large banquet and invited many. ¹⁷ At the time of the banquet, he sent his slave to tell those who were invited, 'Come, because everything is now ready.'

¹⁸ "But without exception they all began to make excuses. The first one said to him, 'I have bought a field, and I must go out and see it. I ask you to excuse me.'

¹⁹ "Another said, 'I have bought five yoke of oxen, and I'm going to try them out. I ask you to excuse me.'

²⁰ "And another said, 'I just got married, and therefore I'm unable to come.'

²¹ "So the slave came back and reported these things to his master. Then in anger, the master of the house told his slave, 'Go out quickly into the streets and alleys of the city, and bring in here the poor, maimed, blind, and lame!'

²² " 'Master,' the slave said, 'what you ordered has been done, and there's still room.'

²³ "Then the master told the slave, 'Go out into the highways and lanes and make them come in, so that my house may be filled. ²⁴ For I tell you, not one of those men who were invited will enjoy my banquet!' "

A Little of Eternity

For everyone who exalts himself will be humbled, and the one who humbles himself will be exalted.—LUKE 14:11

Why does Jesus insist that our first consideration in prayer should be the honor of God's Name? Is this a device (as some have suggested) to appeal to the vanity and egotism of the Almighty? Can it be that our loving heavenly Father wants us to give Him what He wants (admiration and praise) before He gives us what we want?

No, of course not! God encourages us to focus on Himself because He knows that in contemplating Him, we complete ourselves and bring all parts of our personality to health. To admire, appreciate, respect, and venerate the character of God is to awaken ourselves to reality. Not to do so is to deprive ourselves and bring about a depletion of spiritual power. We are designed for the worship and contemplation of God, and when, therefore, we stand before Him and gaze at His majesty and glory, the machinery of our inner being whirs into activity, and our characters take on the features of His character.

God, therefore, has our interests at heart more than His own when He asks us to venerate Him. We "hallow" His Name, and our own name (our character) is hallowed. We gaze at His character, and our own character is made better for the gazing. A shop assistant put it this way: "I just go quiet and empty into His presence, gaze at His glory and loveliness, and give myself time for His disposition to get through to mine."

Yes, that's the secret. Give God a little of your time, and He will give you a little of eternity.

Prayer

O Father, forgive me for the times I rush into Your presence intent only on getting my needs met. Slow me down and make me a more contemplative person. Then Your character can rub off on mine. In Jesus' name I pray. Amen.

Further Study

2 Pt 1; Rm 8:29; Php 3:21; 1 Jn 3:2
How do we become partakers of the divine nature?
List some of these characteristics.

APRIL 23

JOSHUA 9:1–10:28

9 When all the kings heard about Jericho and Ai, those who were west of the Jordan in the hill country, in the Judean foothills, and all along the coast of the Mediterranean Sea toward Lebanon—the Hittites, Amorites, Canaanites, Perizzites, Hivites, and Jebusites— ²they formed a unified alliance to fight against Joshua and Israel.

³When the inhabitants of Gibeon heard what Joshua had done to Jericho and Ai, ⁴they acted deceptively. They gathered provisions and took worn-out sacks on their donkeys and old wineskins, cracked and mended. ⁵They wore old, patched sandals on their feet and threadbare clothing on their bodies. Their entire provision of bread was dry and crumbly. ⁶They went to Joshua in the camp at Gilgal and said to him and the men of Israel, "We have come from a distant land. Please make a treaty with us."

⁷The men of Israel replied to the Hivites, "Perhaps you live among us. How can we make a treaty with you?"

[8] They said to Joshua, "We are your servants."

Then Joshua asked them, "Who are you and where do you come from?" [9] They replied to him, "Your servants have come from a far away land because of the reputation of the LORD your God. For we have heard of His fame, and all that He did in Egypt, [10] and all that He did to the two Amorite kings beyond the Jordan—Sihon king of Heshbon and Og king of Bashan, who was in Ashtaroth. [11] So our elders and all the inhabitants of our land told us, 'Take provisions with you for the journey; go and meet them and say, "We are your servants. Please make a treaty with us." ' [12] This bread of ours was warm when we took it from our houses as food on the day we left to come to you. But take a look, it is now dry and crumbly. [13] These wineskins were new when we filled them, but look, they are cracked. And these clothes and sandals of ours are worn out from the extremely long journey." [14] Then the men of Israel took some of their provisions, but did not seek the LORD's counsel. [15] So Joshua established peace with them and made a treaty to let them live, and the leaders of the community swore an oath to them.

[16] Three days after making the treaty with them, they heard that the Gibeonites were their neighbors, living among them. [17] So the Israelites set out and reached the Gibeonite cities on the third day. Now their cities were Gibeon, Chephirah, Beeroth, and Kiriath-jearim. [18] But the Israelites did not attack them, because the leaders of the community had sworn an oath to them by the LORD, the God of Israel. Then the whole community grumbled against the leaders. [19] All the leaders answered them, "We have sworn an oath to them by the LORD, the God of Israel, and now we cannot touch them. [20] This is how we will treat them: we will let them live, so that no wrath will fall on us because of the oath we swore to them." [21] They also said, "Let them live." So the Gibeonites became woodcutters and water carriers for the whole community, as the leaders had promised them.

[22] Joshua summoned the Gibeonites and said to them, "Why did you deceive us by telling us you live far away from us, when in fact you live among us? [23] Therefore you are cursed and will always be slaves—woodcutters and water carriers for the house of my God." [24] The Gibeonites answered him, "It was clearly reported to your servants that the LORD your God had commanded His servant Moses to give you all the land and to destroy all the inhabitants of the land before you. We greatly feared for our lives because of you, and that is why we did this. [25] Now we are in your hands. Do to us whatever you think is right." [26] This is what Joshua did to them: he delivered them from the hands of the Israelites, and they did not kill them. [27] On that day he made them woodcutters and water carriers—as they are today—for the community and for the LORD's altar at the place He would choose.

10 Now Adoni-zedek king of Jerusalem heard that Joshua had captured Ai and completely destroyed it, doing to Ai and its king as he had done to Jericho and its king, and that the inhabitants of Gibeon had made peace with Israel and were living among them. [2] So Adoni-zedek and his people were greatly alarmed because Gibeon was a large city like one of the royal cities; it was larger than Ai, and all its men were warriors. [3] Therefore Adoni-zedek king of Jerusalem sent word to Hoham king of Hebron, Piram king of Jarmuth, Japhia king of Lachish, and Debir king of Eglon, saying, [4] "Come up and help me. We will attack Gibeon, because they have made peace with Joshua and the Israelites." [5] So the five Amorite kings—the kings of Jerusalem, Hebron, Jarmuth, Lachish, and Eglon—joined forces, advanced with all their armies, besieged Gibeon, and fought against it.

[6] Then the men of Gibeon sent word to Joshua in the camp at Gilgal: "Don't abandon your servants. Come quickly and save us! Help us, for all the Amorite

kings living in the hill country have joined forces against us." [7] So Joshua and his whole military force, including all the fighting men, came from Gilgal.

[8] The LORD said to Joshua, "Do not be afraid of them, for I have handed them over to you. Not one of them will be able to stand against you."

[9] So Joshua caught them by surprise, after marching all night from Gilgal. [10] The LORD threw them into confusion before Israel. He defeated them in a great slaughter at Gibeon, chased them through the ascent of Beth-horon, and struck them down as far as Azekah and Makkedah. [11] As they fled before Israel, the LORD threw large hailstones on them from the sky along the descent of Beth-horon all the way to Azekah, and they died. More of them died from the hail than the Israelites killed with the sword.

[12] On the day the LORD gave the Amorites over to the Israelites, Joshua spoke to the LORD in the presence of Israel:

> "Sun, stand still over Gibeon,
> and moon, over the valley
> of Aijalon."
> [13] And the sun stood still
> and the moon stopped,
> until the nation took vengeance
> on its enemies.

Isn't this written in the Book of Jashar?

> So the sun stopped
> in the middle of the sky
> and delayed its setting
> almost a full day.

[14] There has been no day like it before or since, when the LORD listened to the voice of a man, because the LORD fought for Israel. [15] Then Joshua and all Israel with him returned to the camp at Gilgal.

[16] Now the five defeated kings had fled and hidden themselves in the cave at Makkedah. [17] It was reported to Joshua: "The five kings have been found; they are hiding in the cave at Makkedah."

[18] Joshua said, "Roll large stones against the mouth of the cave, and sta-tion men by it to guard the kings. [19] But as for the rest of you, don't stay there. Pursue your enemies and attack them from behind. Don't let them enter their cities, for the LORD your God has handed them over to you." [20] So Joshua and the Israelites finished inflicting a terrible slaughter on them until they were destroyed, although a few survivors ran away to the fortified cities. [21] The people returned safely to Joshua in the camp at Makkedah. No one could say a thing against the Israelites.

[22] Then Joshua said, "Open the mouth of the cave, and bring those five kings to me out of there." [23] That is what they did. They brought the five kings of Jerusalem, Hebron, Jarmuth, Lachish, and Eglon to Joshua out of the cave. [24] When they had brought the kings to him, Joshua summoned all the men of Israel and said to the military commanders who had accompanied him, "Come here and put your feet on the necks of these kings." So the commanders came forward and put their feet on their necks. [25] Joshua said to them, "Do not be afraid or discouraged. Be strong and courageous, for the LORD will do this to all the enemies you fight."

[26] After this, Joshua struck them down and executed them. He hung their bodies on five trees and they were there until evening. [27] At sunset Joshua commanded that they be taken down from the trees and thrown into the cave where they had hidden. Then large stones were placed against the mouth of the cave, and the stones are there to this day.

[28] On that day Joshua captured Makkedah and struck it down with the sword, including its king. He completely destroyed it and everyone in it, leaving no survivors. So he treated the king of Makkedah as he had the king of Jericho.

PSALM 50:1-6

[1] God, the LORD God speaks;
    He summons the earth from east
      to west.

² From Zion, the perfection of beauty,
God appears in radiance.
³ Our God is coming; He will not be silent!
Devouring fire precedes Him,
and a storm rages around Him.
⁴ On high, He summons heaven and earth
in order to judge His people.
⁵ "Gather My faithful ones to Me,
those who made a covenant with Me by sacrifice."
⁶ The heavens proclaim His righteousness,
for God is the judge. _Selah_

PROVERBS 11:30-31

³⁰ The fruit of the righteous is a tree of life,
but violence takes lives.

³¹ If the righteous will be repaid on earth,
how much more the wicked and sinful.

LUKE 14:25–15:10

²⁵ Now great crowds were traveling with Him. So He turned and said to them: ²⁶ "If anyone comes to Me and does not hate his own father and mother, wife and children, brothers and sisters—yes, and even his own life—he cannot be My disciple. ²⁷ Whoever does not bear his own cross and come after Me cannot be My disciple. ²⁸ "For which of you, wanting to build a tower, doesn't first sit down and calculate the cost to see if he has enough to complete it? ²⁹ Otherwise, after he has laid the foundation and cannot finish it, all the onlookers will begin to make fun of him, ³⁰ saying, 'This man started to build and wasn't able to finish.'

³¹ "Or what king, going to war against another king, will not first sit down and decide if he is able with 10,000 to oppose the one who comes against him with 20,000? ³² If not, while the other is still far off, he sends a delegation and asks for terms of peace. ³³ In the same way, therefore, every one of you who does not say good-bye to all his possessions cannot be My disciple.

³⁴ "Now, salt is good, but if salt should lose its taste, how will it be made salty? ³⁵ It isn't fit for the soil or for the manure pile; they throw it out. Anyone who has ears to hear should listen!"

15 All the tax collectors and sinners were approaching to listen to Him. ² And the Pharisees and scribes were complaining, "This man welcomes sinners and eats with them!"

³ So He told them this parable: ⁴ "What man among you, who has 100 sheep and loses one of them, does not leave the 99 in the open field and go after the lost one until he finds it? ⁵ When he has found it, he joyfully puts it on his shoulders, ⁶ and coming home, he calls his friends and neighbors together, saying to them, 'Rejoice with me, because I have found my lost sheep!' ⁷ I tell you, in the same way, there will be more joy in heaven over one sinner who repents than over 99 righteous people who don't need repentance.

⁸ "Or what woman who has 10 silver coins, if she loses one coin, does not light a lamp, sweep the house, and search carefully until she finds it? ⁹ When she finds it, she calls her women friends and neighbors together, saying, 'Rejoice with me, because I have found the silver coin I lost!' ¹⁰ I tell you, in the same way, there is joy in the presence of God's angels over one sinner who repents."

The God Who Seeks

'Rejoice with me, because I have found my lost sheep!
—LUKE 15:6

One of the aspects that makes Christianity unique is the issue of personal salvation. The vocabulary of salvation is distasteful to those of other religions, and many insist we should give it up. They say, "It smacks of spiritual smugness and arrogance."

But before we answer this criticism we must realize what Christianity is all about. Christianity is essentially a rescue religion; it is the announcement of the good news that God has come in the Person of His Son to save us from the power of sin, the penalty of sin, and one day in the future, the presence of sin. In the passage before us today we see that God likens Himself to a shepherd who leaves the rest of the sheep in order to go after one sheep that is lost. The Divine Shepherd, far from abandoning the sheep in the hope that, bleating and stumbling, it may find its own way home, puts His own life on the line to search it out.

Judaism denies that Jesus is the Messiah and that His sin-bearing death is the only ground on which divine forgiveness can be offered. One Jewish scholar, C. G. Montefiore, goes so far as to generously refer to the "greatness and originality" of Jesus in His attitude to sinners that "instead of avoiding them he actively sought them out." However, though Orthodox Jewish teaching recognizes that God receives sinners who return to Him, it fails to see that He also seeks them out. How utterly amazing. The One who *seeks* and saves is God.

Prayer

O Father, what a thought: You did not send an angel to seek us out and save us. You came Yourself in the Person of Your Son. I can never put my gratitude into mere words. Help me show it by my life. In Jesus' name. Amen.

Further Study

Lk 19:1-10; Mt 18:10-14; Jn 1:43; 5:14; 9:35
What was Jesus' message to Zacchaeus?
How did Jesus illustrate the heart of the shepherd?

APRIL 24

JOSHUA 10:29–12:24

²⁹ Joshua and all Israel with him crossed from Makkedah to Libnah and fought against Libnah. ³⁰ The LORD also handed it and its king over to Israel. He struck it down, putting everyone in it to the sword, and left no survivors in it. He treated Libnah's king as he had the king of Jericho.

³¹ From Libnah, Joshua and all Israel with him crossed to Lachish. They laid siege to it and attacked it. ³² The LORD handed Lachish over to Israel, and Joshua captured it on the second day. He struck it down, putting everyone in it to the sword, just as he had done to Libnah. ³³ At that time Horam king of Gezer went to help Lachish, but Joshua struck him down along with his people, leaving no survivors in it.

³⁴ Then Joshua crossed from Lachish to Eglon and all Israel with him. They laid siege to it and attacked it. ³⁵ On that day they captured it and struck it down, putting everyone in it to the sword. He completely destroyed it that day, just as he had done to Lachish.

³⁶ Next, Joshua and all Israel with him went up from Eglon to Hebron and attacked it. ³⁷ They captured it and struck down its king, all its villages, and everyone in it with the sword. Just as he had done at Eglon, he left no survivors. He completely destroyed Hebron and everyone in it.

³⁸ Finally, Joshua turned toward Debir and attacked it. And all Israel was with him. ³⁹ He captured it—its king and all its villages. They struck them down with the sword and completely destroyed everyone in it, leaving no survivors. He treated Debir and its king as he had treated Hebron and as he had treated Libnah and its king.

⁴⁰ So Joshua conquered the whole region—the hill country, the Negev, the Judean foothills, and the slopes—with all their kings, leaving no survivors. He completely destroyed every living being, as the LORD, the God of Israel, had commanded. ⁴¹ Joshua conquered everyone from Kadesh-barnea to Gaza, and all the land of Goshen as far as Gibeon. ⁴² Joshua captured all these kings and their land in one campaign, because the LORD, the God of Israel, fought for Israel. ⁴³ Then Joshua returned with all Israel to the camp at Gilgal.

11 When Jabin king of Hazor heard this news, he sent a message to:

Jobab king of Madon,
the kings of Shimron
    and Achshaph,
² and the kings of the north
    in the hill country,
the plain south of Chinnereth,
the Judean foothills,
and the Slopes of Dor to the west,
³ the Canaanites in the east
    and west,
the Amorites, Hittites,
    Perizzites,
and Jebusites in the hill country,
and the Hivites at the foot
    of Hermon
    in the land of Mizpah.

⁴ They went out with all their armies— a multitude as numerous as the sand on the seashore—along with a vast number of horses and chariots. ⁵ All these kings joined forces; they came together and camped at the waters of Merom to attack Israel.

⁶ The LORD said to Joshua, "Do not be afraid of them, for at this time tomorrow I will hand all of them over dead to Israel. You are to hamstring their horses and burn up their chariots." ⁷ So Joshua and his whole military force surprised them at the waters of

Merom and attacked them. [8] The LORD handed them over to Israel, and they struck them down, pursuing them as far as Great Sidon and Misrephoth-maim, and to the east as far as the valley of Mizpeh. They struck them down, leaving no survivors. [9] Joshua treated them as the LORD had told him; he hamstrung their horses and burned up their chariots.

[10] At that time Joshua turned back, captured Hazor, and struck down its king with the sword, because Hazor had formerly been the leader of all these kingdoms. [11] They struck down everyone in it with the sword, completely destroying them; he left no one alive. Then he burned down Hazor.

[12] Joshua captured all these kings and their cities and struck them down with the sword. He completely destroyed them, as Moses the LORD's servant had commanded. [13] However, Israel did not burn any of the cities that stood on their mounds except Hazor, which Joshua burned. [14] The Israelites plundered all the spoils and cattle of these cities for themselves. But they struck down every person with the sword until they had annihilated them, leaving no one alive. [15] Just as the LORD had commanded His servant Moses, Moses commanded Joshua. That is what Joshua did, leaving nothing undone of all that the LORD had commanded Moses.

[16] So Joshua took all this land—the hill country, all the Negev, all the land of Goshen, the Judean foothills, the plain, and the hill country of Israel with its Judean foothills— [17] from Mount Halak, which ascends to Seir, as far as Baal-gad in the Valley of Lebanon at the foot of Mount Hermon. He captured all their kings and struck them down, putting them to death. [18] Joshua waged war with all these kings for a long time. [19] No city made peace with the Israelites except the Hivites who inhabited Gibeon; all of them were taken in battle. [20] For it was the LORD's intention to harden their hearts, so that they would engage Israel in battle, be completely destroyed without mercy, and be annihilated, just as the LORD had commanded Moses.

[21] At that time Joshua proceeded to exterminate the Anakim from the hill country—Hebron, Debir, Anab—all the hill country of Judah and of Israel. Joshua completely destroyed them with their cities. [22] No Anakim were left in the land of the Israelites, except for some remaining in Gaza, Gath, and Ashdod.

[23] So Joshua took the entire land, in keeping with all that the LORD had told Moses. Joshua then gave it as an inheritance to Israel according to their tribal allotments. After this, the land had rest from war.

12 The Israelites struck down the following kings of the land and took possession of their land beyond the Jordan to the east and from the Arnon Valley to Mount Hermon, including all the Arabah eastward:

[2] Sihon king of the Amorites lived in Heshbon. He ruled over the territory from Aroer on the rim of the Arnon Valley, along the middle of the valley, and half of Gilead up to the Jabbok River (the border of the Ammonites), [3] the Arabah east of the Sea of Chinnereth to the Sea of the Arabah (that is, the Dead Sea), eastward through Beth-jeshimoth and southward below the slopes of Pisgah.

[4] Og king of Bashan, of the remnant of the Rephaim, lived in Ashtaroth and Edrei. [5] He ruled over Mount Hermon, Salecah, all Bashan up to the Geshurite and Maacathite border, and half of Gilead to the border of Sihon, king of Heshbon.

[6] Moses the LORD's servant and the Israelites struck them down. And Moses the LORD's servant gave their land as an inheritance to the Reubenites, Gadites, and half the tribe of Manasseh.

[7] Joshua and the Israelites struck down the following kings of the land beyond the Jordan to the west, from Baalgad in the valley of Lebanon to Mount Halak, which ascends toward Seir

(Joshua gave their land as an inheritance to the tribes of Israel according to their allotments: ⁸ the hill country, the Judean foothills, the plain, the slopes, the desert, and the Negev of the Hittites, Amorites, Canaanites, Perizzites, Hivites, and Jebusites):

⁹	the king of Jericho	one
	the king of Ai, which is next to Bethel	one
¹⁰	the king of Jerusalem	one
	the king of Hebron	one
¹¹	the king of Jarmuth	one
	the king of Lachish	one
¹²	the king of Eglon	one
	the king of Gezer	one
¹³	the king of Debir	one
	the king of Geder	one
¹⁴	the king of Hormah	one
	the king of Arad	one
¹⁵	the king of Libnah	one
	the king of Adullam	one
¹⁶	the king of Makkedah	one
	the king of Bethel	one
¹⁷	the king of Tappuah	one
	the king of Hepher	one
¹⁸	the king of Aphek	one
	the king of Lasharon	one
¹⁹	the king of Madon	one
	the king of Hazor	one
²⁰	the king of Shimron-meron	one
	the king of Achshaph	one
²¹	the king of Taanach	one
	the king of Megiddo	one
²²	the king of Kedesh	one
	the king of Jokneam in Carmel	one
²³	the king of Dor in Naphoth-dor	one
	the king of Goiim in Gilgal	one
²⁴	the king of Tirzah	one
	the total number of all kings:	31

PSALM 50:7-15

⁷ "Listen, My people, and I will speak;
I will testify against you, Israel.
I am God, your God.
⁸ I do not rebuke you for your sacrifices
or for your burnt offerings, which
are continually before Me.
⁹ I will not accept a bull from your household
or male goats from your pens,
¹⁰ for every animal of the forest is Mine,
the cattle on a thousand hills.
¹¹ I know every bird of the mountains,
and the creatures of the field are Mine.
¹² If I were hungry, I would not tell you,
for the world and everything in it is Mine.
¹³ Do I eat the flesh of bulls
or drink the blood of goats?
¹⁴ Sacrifice a thank offering to God,
and pay your vows to the Most High.
¹⁵ Call on Me in a day of trouble;
I will rescue you, and you will honor Me."

PROVERBS 12:1-3

12 Whoever loves instruction loves knowledge,
but one who hates correction is stupid.

² The good obtain favor from the LORD,
but He condemns a man who schemes.

³ Man cannot be made secure by wickedness,
but the root of the righteous is immovable.

LUKE 15:11-32

¹¹ He also said: "A man had two sons. ¹² The younger of them said to his father, 'Father, give me the share of the estate I have coming to me.' So he distributed the assets to them. ¹³ Not many days later, the younger son gathered together all he had and traveled to a distant country, where he squandered his estate in foolish living. ¹⁴ After he had

459

spent everything, a severe famine struck that country, and he had nothing. [15] Then he went to work for one of the citizens of that country, who sent him into his fields to feed pigs. [16] He longed to eat his fill from the carob pods the pigs were eating, but no one would give him any. [17] When he came to his senses, he said, 'How many of my father's hired hands have more than enough food, and here I am dying of hunger! [18] I'll get up, go to my father, and say to him, Father, I have sinned against heaven and in your sight. [19] I'm no longer worthy to be called your son. Make me like one of your hired hands.' [20] So he got up and went to his father. But while the son was still a long way off, his father saw him and was filled with compassion. He ran, threw his arms around his neck, and kissed him. [21] The son said to him, 'Father, I have sinned against heaven and in your sight. I'm no longer worthy to be called your son.'

[22] "But the father told his slaves, 'Quick! Bring out the best robe and put it on him; put a ring on his finger and sandals on his feet. [23] Then bring the fattened calf and slaughter it, and let's celebrate with a feast, [24] because this son of mine was dead and is alive again; he was lost and is found!' So they began to celebrate.

[25] "Now his older son was in the field; as he came near the house, he heard music and dancing. [26] So he summoned one of the servants and asked what these things meant. [27] 'Your brother is here,' he told him, 'and your father has slaughtered the fattened calf because he has him back safe and sound.'

[28] "Then he became angry and didn't want to go in. So his father came out and pleaded with him. [29] But he replied to his father, 'Look, I have been slaving many years for you, and I have never disobeyed your orders, yet you never gave me a young goat so I could celebrate with my friends. [30] But when this son of yours came, who has devoured your assets with prostitutes, you slaughtered the fattened calf for him.'

[31] " 'Son,' he said to him, 'you are always with me, and everything I have is yours. [32] But we had to celebrate and rejoice, because this brother of yours was dead and is alive again; he was lost and is found.' "

The Hurt of Rejection

The younger [son] said to his father, "Father, give me the share of the estate I have coming to me." So he distributed the assets to them. . . . The younger son gathered together all he had and traveled to a distant country.

—LUKE 15:12-13

One of the greatest, most encouraging ministries of the Holy Spirit within our lives is that of a Comforter.

During my ministry, I have observed that there are five main hurts which people experience in life. The first is the hurt of rejection. Can the Holy Spirit comfort us when we feel rejected? He most certainly can. Sooner or later in this mixed-up world, everyone feels rejected. Indeed, some go through so much rejection, they cease to expect anything else.

Rejection often happens in childhood: the child may have been unwanted by his parents, or may have been the wrong sex, or for some reason doesn't please her parents. These feelings of rejection are recorded in our system on a kind of tape recorder, and later in life, whenever we feel rejected, we not only experience the present rejection, but in some strange way it triggers the "tape recorder" inside us, and we play back all the feelings of rejection we felt in earlier years.

Past feelings of rejection that have never been healed may put a weight on the personality that is too heavy for it to bear, and this is why, as we say, a person breaks down. People rarely break down because of one event; it is usually the one event that becomes the last straw.

Have you deep feelings of rejection within you that you are carrying from the past? Or have you been rejected in recent days or weeks? Then draw near to God. The Spirit is with you to heal your hurts—right now.

Prayer

Gracious Holy Spirit, I am so thankful that You come alongside to help in my hour of need. I offer You every feeling of rejection and hurt that lies within my heart. Heal me now in Jesus' name. Thank You, Father. It's done. Amen.

Further Study

Lk 15:11-32; Eph 1:6; 2 Co 5:9; Ac 10:35
What is the message of the parable?
What three things did the younger son receive to verify this?

APRIL 25

JOSHUA 13:1–14:15

13 Joshua was now old, advanced in years, and the LORD said to him, "You have become old, advanced in years, but a great deal of the land remains to be possessed. ² This is the land that remains:

All the districts of the Philistines and the Geshurites: ³ from the Shihor east of Egypt to the border of Ekron on the north (considered to be Canaanite territory)—the five Philistine rulers of Gaza, Ashdod, Ashkelon, Gath, and Ekron, as well as the Avvites ⁴ in the south; all the land of the Canaanites: from Arah of the Sidonians to Aphek and as far as the border of the Amorites; ⁵ the land of the Gebalites; and all

Lebanon east from Baal-gad below Mount Hermon to the entrance of Hamath—⁶ all the inhabitants of the hill country from Lebanon to Misrephoth-maim, all the Sidonians.

I will drive them out before the Israelites, only distribute the land as an inheritance for Israel, as I have commanded you. ⁷ Therefore, divide this land as an inheritance to the nine tribes and half the tribe of Manasseh."

⁸ With the other half of the tribe, the Reubenites and Gadites had received the inheritance Moses gave them beyond the Jordan to the east, just as Moses the LORD's servant had given them:

⁹ From Aroer on the rim of the Arnon Valley, along with the city in

the middle of the valley, all the Medeba plateau as far as Dibon, [10] and all the cities of Sihon king of the Amorites, who reigned in Heshbon, to the border of the Ammonites; [11] also Gilead and the territory of the Geshurites and Maacathites, all Mount Hermon, and all Bashan to Salecah— [12] the whole kingdom of Og in Bashan, who reigned in Ashtaroth and Edrei; he was one of the remaining Rephaim.

Moses struck them down and drove them out, [13] but the Israelites did not drive out the Geshurites and Maacathites. So Geshur and Maacath live in Israel to this day.

[14] He did not give any inheritance to the tribe of Levi. This was its inheritance, just as He had promised: the offerings made by fire to the LORD, the God of Israel.

[15] To the tribe of the Reubenites by their clans, Moses gave [16] this as their territory:

From Aroer on the rim of the Arnon Valley, along with the city in the middle of the valley, to the whole plateau as far as Medeba, [17] with Heshbon and all its cities on the plateau—Dibon, Bamoth-baal, Beth-baal-meon, [18] Jahaz, Kedemoth, Mephaath, [19] Kiriathaim, Sibmah, Zereth-shahar on the hill in the valley, [20] Beth-peor, the slopes of Pisgah, and Beth-jeshimoth— [21] all the cities of the plateau, and all the kingdom of Sihon king of the Amorites, who reigned in Heshbon. Moses had killed him and the chiefs of Midian—Evi, Rekem, Zur, Hur, and Reba—the princes of Sihon who lived in the land. [22] Along with those the Israelites put to death, they also killed the diviner, Balaam son of Beor, with the sword.

[23] The border of the Reubenites was the Jordan and its plain. This was the inheritance of the Reubenites by their clans, with the cities and their villages.

[24] To the tribe of the Gadites by their clans, Moses gave [25] this as their territory:

Jazer and all the cities of Gilead, and half the land of the Ammonites to Aroer, near Rabbah; [26] from Heshbon to Ramath-mizpeh and Betonim, and from Mahanaim to the border of Debir; [27] in the valley: Beth-haram, Beth-nimrah, Succoth, and Zaphon—the rest of the kingdom of Sihon king of Heshbon. Their land also included the Jordan and its territory as far as the edge of the Sea of Chinnereth on the east side of the Jordan.

[28] This was the inheritance of the Gadites by their clans, with the cities and their villages.

[29] And to half the tribe of Manasseh, that is, to half the tribe of Manasseh's descendants by their clans, Moses gave [30] this as their territory:

From Mahanaim through all Bashan—all the kingdom of Og king of Bashan, including all of Jair's Villages that are in Bashan—60 cities. [31] But half of Gilead, and Og's royal cities in Bashan— Ashtaroth and Edrei—are for the descendants of Machir son of Manasseh, that is, half the descendants of Machir by their clans.

[32] These were the portions Moses gave them on the plains of Moab beyond the Jordan east of Jericho. [33] But Moses did not give a portion to the tribe of Levi. The LORD, the God of Israel, was their inheritance, just as He had promised them.

14 The Israelites received these portions that Eleazar the priest, Joshua son of Nun, and the heads of the families of the Israelite tribes gave them in the land of Canaan. [2] Their inheritance was by lot as the LORD commanded through Moses for the nine and a half tribes, [3] because Moses had given the inheritance to the two and a half tribes beyond the Jordan. But he gave no inheritance among them to the Levites. ⁴The descendants of Joseph became two tribes, Manasseh and Ephraim. No portion of the land was given to the Levites except cities to live in, along with pasturelands for their cattle and livestock. ⁵So the Israelites did as the LORD commanded Moses, and they divided the land.

⁶The descendants of Judah approached Joshua at Gilgal, and Caleb son of Jephunneh the Kenizzite said to him, "You know what the LORD promised Moses the man of God at Kadesh-barnea about you and me. ⁷I was 40 years old when Moses the LORD's servant sent me from Kadesh-barnea to scout the land, and I brought back an honest report. ⁸My brothers who went with me caused the people's hearts to melt with fear, but I remained loyal to the LORD my God. ⁹On that day Moses promised me, 'The land where you have set foot will be an inheritance for you and your descendants forever, because you have remained loyal to the LORD my God.'

¹⁰"As you see, the LORD has kept me alive these 45 years as He promised, since the LORD spoke this word to Moses while Israel was journeying in the wilderness. Here I am today, 85 years old. ¹¹I am still as strong today as I was the day Moses sent me out. My strength for battle and for daily tasks is now as it was then. ¹²Now give me this hill country the LORD promised me on that day, because you heard then that the Anakim are there, as well as large fortified cities. Perhaps the LORD will be with me and I will drive them out as the LORD promised."

¹³Then Joshua blessed Caleb son of Jephunneh and gave him Hebron as an inheritance. ¹⁴Therefore, Hebron has belonged to Caleb son of Jephunneh the Kenizzite as an inheritance to this day, because he remained loyal to the LORD, the God of Israel. ¹⁵Hebron's name used to be Kiriath-arba; Arba was the greatest man among the Anakim. After this, the land had rest from war.

PSALM 50:16-23

16 But God says to the wicked:
"What right do you have to recite My statutes
and to take My covenant on your lips?
17 You hate instruction
and turn your back on My words.
18 When you see a thief, you make friends with him,
and you associate with adulterers.
19 You unleash your mouth for evil
and harness your tongue for deceit.
20 You sit, maligning your brother,
slandering your mother's son.
21 You have done these things, and I kept silent;
you thought I was just like you.
But I will rebuke you and lay out the case before you.

22 "Understand this, you who forget God,
or I will tear you apart, and there will be no rescuer.
23 Whoever sacrifices a thank offering honors Me,
and whoever orders his conduct, I will show him the salvation of God."

PROVERBS 12:4-5

4 A capable wife is her husband's crown,
but a wife who causes shame is like rottenness in his bones.

5 The thoughts of the righteous are just,
but guidance from the wicked leads to deceit.

LUKE 16:1-18

16 He also said to the disciples: "There was a rich man who received an accusation that his manager was squandering his possessions. ²So he called the manager in and asked, 'What is this I hear about you? Give an

account of your management, because you can no longer be my manager.'

³ "Then the manager said to himself, 'What should I do, since my master is taking the management away from me? I'm not strong enough to dig; I'm ashamed to beg. ⁴ I know what I'll do so that when I'm removed from management, people will welcome me into their homes.'

⁵ "So he summoned each one of his master's debtors. 'How much do you owe my master?' he asked the first one.

⁶ " 'A hundred measures of oil,' he said.

" 'Take your invoice,' he told him, 'sit down quickly, and write 50.'

⁷ "Next he asked another, 'How much do you owe?'

" 'A hundred measures of wheat,' he said.

" 'Take your invoice,' he told him, 'and write 80.'

⁸ "The master praised the unrighteous manager because he had acted astutely. For the sons of this age are more astute than the sons of light in dealing with their own people. ⁹ And I tell you, make friends for yourselves by means of the unrighteous money so that when it fails, they may welcome you into eternal dwellings. ¹⁰ Whoever is faithful in very little is also faithful in much, and who-ever is unrighteous in very little is also unrighteous in much. ¹¹ So if you have not been faithful with the unrighteous money, who will trust you with what is genuine? ¹² And if you have not been faithful with what belongs to someone else, who will give you what is your own? ¹³ No household slave can be the slave of two masters, since either he will hate one and love the other, or he will be devoted to one and despise the other. You can't be slaves to both God and money."

¹⁴ The Pharisees, who were lovers of money, were listening to all these things and scoffing at Him. ¹⁵ And He told them: "You are the ones who justify yourselves in the sight of others, but God knows your hearts. For what is highly admired by people is revolting in God's sight.

¹⁶ "The Law and the Prophets were until John; since then, the good news of the kingdom of God has been proclaimed, and everyone is strongly urged to enter it. ¹⁷ But it is easier for heaven and earth to pass away than for one stroke of a letter in the law to drop out.

¹⁸ "Everyone who divorces his wife and marries another woman commits adultery, and everyone who marries a woman divorced from her husband commits adultery.

The Choice Facing Us

Whoever is faithful in very little is also faithful in much.
—Luke 16:10

What is denial? It is the attitude that avoids looking realistically at issues and pretends that things are not the way they are.

Most Christians (myself included) are to varying degrees held together by denial. Deep down we sense that if we were to face the realities of life openly and honestly, we might not be able to cope, and so we pretend things are not what they are.

I know Christians who pretend that what they have in life satisfies more than it does, or pretend they haven't been hurt as badly as they have. They refuse to face and feel what is going on inside them, due to the strange belief that it is lack of faith on their part to admit to anything that is negative.

This faulty teaching—that we ought to ignore what is going on inside us instead of facing it and dealing with it—is responsible for more casualties in the Christian life than anything I know. A Christian psychologist says: "I am convinced that much of what we admire as spiritual maturity is a fragile adjustment to life based on the foundation of denial." I would agree. My own observation would lead me to say that I have found some non-Christians to be more open and honest in facing what is going on inside them than some Christians.

Is denial a wise plan for life? Absolutely not. The choice, then, is stark: either to deny and live comfortably or to face every painful issue—and go on to climb the heights with God.

Prayer

Father, help me to see that I need never be afraid to face anything, for in You I have the resources to resolve all problems, not just skirt them. Show me how to blast denial right out of my life—once and for all. In Jesus' name. Amen.

Further Study

Ec 5:1-7; Is 29:13; Mt 15:1-9
What do fools do?
What prophecy was fulfilled by the Pharisees?

APRIL 26

JOSHUA 15:1-63

15 Now the allotment for the tribe of the descendants of Judah by their clans was in the southernmost region, south of the Wilderness of Zin to the border of Edom.

2 Their southern border began at the tip of the Dead Sea on the south bay 3 and went south of the ascent of Akrabbim, proceeded to Zin, ascended to the south of Kadesh-barnea, passed Hezron, ascended to Addar, and turned to Karka. 4 It proceeded to Azmon and to the Brook of Egypt and so the border ended at the Mediterranean Sea. This is your southern border.

5 Now the eastern border was along the Dead Sea to the mouth of the Jordan.

The border on the north side was from the bay of the sea at the mouth of the Jordan. 6 It ascended to Beth-hoglah, proceeded north of Beth-arabah, and ascended to the stone of Bohan son of Reuben. 7 Then the border ascended to Debir from the Valley of Achor, turning north to the Gilgal that is opposite the ascent of Adummim, which is south of the ravine. The border proceeded to the waters of En-shemesh and ended at En-rogel. [8] From there the border ascended the Valley of Hinnom to the southern Jebusite slope (that is, Jerusalem) and ascended to the top of the hill that faces the Valley of Hinnom on the west, at the northern end of the Valley of Rephaim. [9] From the top of the hill the border curved to the spring of the Waters of Nephtoah, went to the cities of Mount Ephron, and then curved to Baalah (that is, Kiriath-jearim). [10] The border turned westward from Baalah to Mount Seir, went to the northern slope of Mount Jearim (that is, Chesalon), descended to Beth-shemesh, and proceeded to Timnah. [11] Then the border reached to the slope north of Ekron, curved to Shikkeron, proceeded to Mount Baalah, went to Jabneel, and ended at the Mediterranean Sea.

[12] Now the western border was the coastline of the Mediterranean Sea.

This was the boundary of the descendants of Judah around their clans.
[13] He gave Caleb son of Jephunneh the following portion among the descendants of Judah based on the LORD's instruction to Joshua: Kiriath-arba (that is, Hebron; Arba was the father of Anak). [14] Caleb drove out from there the three sons of Anak: Sheshai, Ahiman, and Talmai, descendants of Anak. [15] From there he marched against the inhabitants of Debir whose name used to be Kiriath-sepher, [16] and Caleb said, "I will give my daughter Achsah as a wife to the one who strikes down and captures Kiriath-sepher." [17] So Othniel son of Caleb's brother, Kenaz, captured it, and Caleb gave his daughter Achsah to him as a wife. [18] When she arrived, she persuaded Othniel to ask her father for a field. As she got off her donkey, Caleb asked her, "What do you want?" [19] She replied, "Give me a blessing. Since you have given me land in the Negev, give me the springs of water also." So he gave her the upper and lower springs.

[20] This was the inheritance of the tribe of the descendants of Judah by their clans.

[21] These were the outermost cities of the tribe of the descendants of Judah toward the border of Edom in the Negev: Kabzeel, Eder, Jagur, [22] Kinah, Dimonah, Adadah, [23] Kedesh, Hazor, Ithnan, [24] Ziph, Telem, Bealoth, [25] Hazor-hadattah, Kerioth-hezron (that is, Hazor), [26] Amam, Shema, Moladah, [27] Hazar-gaddah, Heshmon, Beth-pelet, [28] Hazar-shual, Beer-sheba, Biziothiah, [29] Baalah, Iim, Ezem, [30] Eltolad, Chesil, Hormah, [31] Ziklag, Madmannah, Sansannah, [32] Lebaoth, Shilhim, Ain, and Rimmon—29 cities in all, with their villages.
[33] In the Judean foothills: Eshtaol, Zorah, Ashnah, [34] Zanoah, En-gannim, Tappuah, Enam, [35] Jarmuth, Adullam, Socoh, Azekah, [36] Shaaraim, Adithaim, Gederah, and Gederothaim—14 cities, with their villages; [37] Zenan, Hadashah, Migdal-gad, [38] Dilan, Mizpeh, Jokthe-el, [39] Lachish, Bozkath, Eglon, [40] Cabbon, Lahmam, Chitlish, [41] Gederoth, Beth-dagon, Naamah, and Makkedah—16 cities, with their villages; [42] Libnah, Ether, Ashan, [43] Iphtah, Ashnah, Nezib, [44] Keilah, Achzib, and Mareshah—nine cities, with their villages; [45] Ekron, with its towns and villages; [46] from Ekron to the sea, all the cities near Ashdod, with their villages; [47] Ashdod, with its towns and villages; Gaza, with its towns and villages, to the Brook of Egypt and the coastline of the Mediterranean Sea.

[48] In the hill country: Shamir, Jattir, Socoh, [49] Dannah, Kiriath-sannah (that is, Debir), [50] Anab, Eshtemoh, Anim, [51] Goshen, Holon, and Giloh—11 cities, with their villages; [52] Arab, Dumah, Eshan, [53] Janim, Beth-tappuah, Aphekah,

⁵⁴Humtah, Kiriath-arba (that is, Hebron), and Zior—nine cities, with their villages; ⁵⁵Maon, Carmel, Ziph, Juttah, ⁵⁶Jezreel, Jokdeam, Zanoah, ⁵⁷Kain, Gibeah, and Timnah—10 cities, with their villages; ⁵⁸Halhul, Beth-zur, Gedor, ⁵⁹Maarath, Beth-anoth, and Eltekon—six cities, with their villages; ⁶⁰Kiriath-baal (that is, Kiriath-jearim), and Rabbah—two cities, with their villages.

⁶¹In the wilderness: Beth-arabah, Middin, Secacah, ⁶²Nibshan, the City of Salt, and En-gedi—six cities, with their villages.

⁶³But the descendants of Judah could not drive out the Jebusites who lived in Jerusalem. So the Jebusites live in Jerusalem among the descendants of Judah to this day.

PSALM 51:1-5

¹ Be gracious to me, God, according
   to Your faithful love;
   according to Your abundant
   compassion, blot out my
   rebellion.
² Wash away my guilt,
   and cleanse me from my sin.
³ For I am conscious of my
   rebellion,
   and my sin is always before me.
⁴ Against You—You alone—I have
   sinned
   and done this evil in Your sight.
   So You are right when You pass
   sentence;
   You are blameless when You judge.
⁵ Indeed, I was guilty when I was
   born;
   I was sinful when my mother
   conceived me.

PROVERBS 12:6-7

⁶ The words of the wicked are a
   deadly ambush,
   but the speech of the upright
   rescues them.

⁷ The wicked are overthrown and
   perish,
   but the house of the righteous
   will stand.

LUKE 16:19–17:10

¹⁹ "There was a rich man who would dress in purple and fine linen, feasting lavishly every day. ²⁰ But a poor man named Lazarus, covered with sores, was left at his gate. ²¹ He longed to be filled with what fell from the rich man's table, but instead the dogs would come and lick his sores. ²² One day the poor man died and was carried away by the angels to Abraham's side. The rich man also died and was buried. ²³ And being in torment in Hades, he looked up and saw Abraham a long way off, with Lazarus at his side. ²⁴ 'Father Abraham!' he called out, 'Have mercy on me and send Lazarus to dip the tip of his finger in water and cool my tongue, because I am in agony in this flame!'

²⁵ " 'Son,' Abraham said, 'remember that during your life you received your good things, just as Lazarus received bad things, but now he is comforted here, while you are in agony. ²⁶ Besides all this, a great chasm has been fixed between us and you, so that those who want to pass over from here to you cannot; neither can those from there cross over to us.'

²⁷ " 'Father,' he said, 'then I beg you to send him to my father's house— ²⁸ because I have five brothers—to warn them, so they won't also come to this place of torment.'

²⁹ "But Abraham said, 'They have Moses and the prophets; they should listen to them.'

³⁰ " 'No, father Abraham,' he said. 'But if someone from the dead goes to them, they will repent.'

³¹ "But he told him, 'If they don't listen to Moses and the prophets, they will not be persuaded if someone rises from the dead.' "

17 He said to His disciples, "Offenses will certainly come, but woe to the one they come through! ² It would be better for him if a millstone were hung around his neck and he were thrown into the sea than for him to cause one of these little ones to stumble. ³Be on your guard. If your brother sins, rebuke him, and if he repents, forgive him. ⁴And if he sins against you seven times in a day, and comes back to you seven times, saying, 'I repent,' you must forgive him."

⁵The apostles said to the Lord, "Increase our faith."

⁶"If you have faith the size of a mustard seed," the Lord said, "you can say to this mulberry tree, 'Be uprooted and planted in the sea,' and it will obey you. ⁷"Which one of you having a slave plowing or tending sheep, will say to him when he comes in from the field, 'Come at once and sit down to eat'? ⁸Instead, will he not tell him, 'Prepare something for me to eat, get ready, and serve me while I eat and drink; later you can eat and drink'? ⁹Does he thank that slave because he did what was commanded? ¹⁰In the same way, when you have done all that you were commanded, you should say, 'We are good-for-nothing slaves; we've only done our duty.' "

Heaven or Hell

And being in torment in Hades, he looked up and saw Abraham a long way off.—LUKE 16:23

The final state of those who die without availing themselves of God's freely offered forgiveness is eternal banishment from God's presence. The Bible calls this "hell." "There is no heaven with a little hell in it," said George MacDonald, meaning that the God who is passionately for righteousness and implacably against sin must ensure that the two are finally separated.

However, hell is always something that people choose for themselves. It is a state for which men and women opt. Before hell is experienced as eternal, it is always experienced as something temporary in the sense that, as men and women retreat from the light God shines into their hearts to lead them to Himself, they experience in a small way what they will experience in full when they are banished into "outer darkness" (Mt 25:30). Dorothy Sayers described hell as "the enjoyment of one's own way forever." God says to those who die impenitent: "You preferred your own way to mine; you shall have it—forever." In the last analysis, all that God does in consigning people to hell is to allow them to face the full consequences of the choice they have made. God is resolute in punishing sin, and hell is the final consequence of this.

I know most of my readers are Christians, but I know also some are not. Those of you reading these lines who have never surrendered your lives to Christ, I urge you to surrender your hearts to Him today. Christ has died to save you from hell. Pray this prayer with me now.

Prayer

Father God, I come to You now through Your Son, the Lord Jesus Christ. I repent of my sin, ask Your forgiveness, and receive You into my life as Savior and Lord. Thank You, dear Lord. Amen.

Further Study

Mt 5:27-30; 18:7-9; 25:34-43
How did Jesus illustrate the importance of avoiding hell?
How can we be sure of avoiding hell?

APRIL 27

JOSHUA 16:1–18:28

16 The allotment for the descendants of Joseph went from the Jordan at Jericho to the waters of Jericho on the east, through the wilderness ascending from Jericho into the hill country of Bethel. ² From Bethel it went to Luz and proceeded to the border of the Archites by Ataroth. ³ It then descended westward to the border of the Japhletites as far as the border of lower Beth-horon, then to Gezer, and ended at the Mediterranean Sea. ⁴ So Ephraim and Manasseh, the sons of Joseph, received their inheritance.

⁵ This was the territory of the descendants of Ephraim by their clans:

The border of their inheritance went from Ataroth-addar on the east of Upper Beth-horon. ⁶ In the north the border went westward from Michmethath; it turned eastward from Taanath-shiloh and passed it east of Janoah. ⁷ From Janoah it descended to Ataroth and Naarah, and then reached Jericho and went to the Jordan. ⁸ From Tappuah the border went westward along the Brook of Kanah and ended at the Mediterranean Sea.

This was the inheritance of the tribe of the descendants of Ephraim by their clans, together with ⁹ the cities set apart for the descendants of Ephraim within the inheritance of the descendants of Manasseh—all these cities with their villages. ¹⁰ But, they did not drive out the Canaanites who lived in Gezer. So the Canaanites live in Ephraim to this day, but they are forced laborers.

17 This was the allotment for the tribe of Manasseh as Joseph's firstborn. Gilead and Bashan came to Machir, the firstborn of Manasseh and the father of Gilead, who was a man of war. ² So the allotment was for the rest of Manasseh's descendants by their clans, for the sons of Abiezer, Helek, Asriel, Shechem, Hepher, and Shemida. These are the male descendants of Manasseh son of Joseph, by their clans.

³ Now Zelophehad son of Hepher, son of Gilead, son of Machir, son of Manasseh, had no sons, only daughters. These are the names of his daughters: Mahlah, Noah, Hoglah, Milcah, and Tirzah. ⁴ They came before Eleazar the priest, Joshua son of Nun, and the leaders, saying, "The LORD commanded Moses to give us an inheritance among our male relatives." So they gave them an inheritance among their father's brothers, in keeping with the LORD's instruction. ⁵ As a result, 10 tracts fell to Manasseh, besides the land of Gilead and Bashan, which are beyond the Jordan, ⁶ because

Manasseh's daughters received an inheritance among his sons. The land of Gilead belonged to the rest of Manasseh's sons.

[7] The border of Manasseh went from Asher to Michmethath near Shechem. It then went southward toward the inhabitants of Entappuah. [8] The region of Tappuah belonged to Manasseh, but Tappuah itself on Manasseh's border belonged to the descendants of Ephraim. [9] From there the border descended to the Brook of Kanah; south of the brook, cities belonged to Ephraim among Manasseh's cities. Manasseh's border was on the north side of the brook and ended at the Mediterranean Sea. [10] Ephraim's territory was to the south and Manasseh's to the north, with the Sea as its border. They reached Asher on the north and Issachar on the east. [11] Within Issachar and Asher, Manasseh had Beth-shean with its towns, Ibleam with its towns, and the inhabitants of Dor with its towns; the inhabitants of En-dor with its towns, the inhabitants of Taanach with its towns, and the inhabitants of Megiddo with its towns—the three cities of Naphath.

[12] The descendants of Manasseh could not possess these cities, because the Canaanites were determined to stay in this land. [13] However, when the Israelites grew stronger, they imposed forced labor on the Canaanites but did not drive them out completely.

[14] Joseph's descendants said to Joshua: "Why did you give us only one tribal allotment as an inheritance? We have many people, because the LORD has greatly blessed us."

[15] "If you have so many people," Joshua replied to them, "go to the forest and clear an area for yourselves there in the land of the Perizzites and the Rephaim, because Ephraim's hill country is too small for you."

[16] But the descendants of Joseph said,

"The hill country is not enough for us, and all the Canaanites who inhabit the valley area have iron chariots, both at Beth-shean with its towns and in the Jezreel Valley."

[17] So Joshua replied to Joseph's family (that is, Ephraim and Manasseh), "You have many people and great strength. You will not have just one lot, [18] because the hill country will be yours also. It is a forest; clear it and its outlying areas will be yours. You can also drive out the Canaanites, even though they have iron chariots and are strong."

18 The entire Israelite community assembled at Shiloh where it set up the tent of meeting there; the land had been subdued by them. [2] Seven tribes among the Israelites were left who had not divided up their inheritance. [3] So Joshua said to the Israelites, "How long will you delay going out to take possession of the land that the LORD, the God of your fathers, gave you? [4] Appoint for yourselves three men from each tribe, and I will send them out. They are to go and survey the land, write a description of it for the purpose of their inheritance, and return to me. [5] Then they are to divide it into seven portions. Judah is to remain in its territory in the south, and Joseph's family in their territory in the north. [6] When you have written a description of the seven portions of land and brought it to me, I will cast lots for you here in the presence of the LORD our God. [7] But the Levites among you do not get a portion, because their inheritance is the priesthood of the LORD. Gad, Reuben, and half the tribe of Manasseh have taken their inheritance beyond the Jordan to the east, which Moses the LORD's servant gave them."

[8] As the men prepared to go, Joshua commanded them to write down a description of the land, saying, "Go and survey the land, write a description of it, and return to me. I will then cast lots for you here in Shiloh in the presence of the LORD." [9] So the men left, went through the land, and described it by towns in a document of seven sections.

They returned to Joshua at the camp in Shiloh. ¹⁰ Joshua cast lots for them at Shiloh in the presence of the LORD where he distributed the land to the Israelites according to their divisions. ¹¹ The lot came up for the tribe of Benjamin's descendants by their clans, and their allotted territory lay between Judah's descendants and Joseph's descendants.

¹² Their border on the north side began at the Jordan, ascended to the slope of Jericho on the north, through the hill country westward, and ended at the wilderness of Beth-aven. ¹³ From there the border went toward Luz, to the southern slope of Luz (that is, Bethel); it then went down by Ataroth-addar, over the hill south of Lower Beth-horon.

¹⁴ On the west side, from the hill facing Beth-horon on the south, the border curved, turning southward, and ended at Kiriath-baal (that is, Kiriath-jearim), a city of the descendants of Judah. This was the west side of their border.

¹⁵ The south side began at the edge of Kiriath-jearim, and the border extended westward; it went to the spring at the Waters of Nephtoah. ¹⁶ The border descended to the foot of the hill that faces the Valley of Hinnom at the northern end of the Valley of Rephaim. It ran down the Valley of Hinnom toward the south Jebusite slope and downward to En-rogel. ¹⁷ It curved northward and went to En-shemesh and on to Geliloth, which is opposite the ascent of Adummim, and continued down to the Stone of Bohan, Reuben's son. ¹⁸ Then it went north to the slope opposite the Jordan Valley and proceeded into the valley. ¹⁹ The border continued to the north slope of Beth-hoglah and ended at the northern bay of the Dead Sea, at the southern end of the Jordan. This was the southern border.

²⁰ The Jordan formed the border on the east side.

This was the inheritance of Benjamin's descendants, by their clans, according to its surrounding borders. ²¹ These were the cities of the tribe of Benjamin's descendants by their clans:

Jericho, Beth-hoglah, Emek-keziz, ²² Beth-arabah, Zemaraim, Bethel, ²³ Avvim, Parah, Ophrah, ²⁴ Chephar-ammoni, Ophni, and Geba—12 cities, with their villages; ²⁵ Gibeon, Ramah, Beeroth, ²⁶ Mizpeh, Chephirah, Mozah, ²⁷ Rekem, Irpeel, Taralah, ²⁸ Zela, Haeleph, Jebus (that is, Jerusalem), Gibeah, and Kiriath—14 cities, with their villages.

This was the inheritance for Benjamin's descendants by their clans.

PSALM 51:6-9

⁶ Surely You desire integrity in the inner self,
and You teach me wisdom deep within.
⁷ Purify me with hyssop, and I will be clean;
wash me, and I will be whiter than snow.
⁸ Let me hear joy and gladness;
let the bones You have crushed rejoice.
⁹ Turn Your face away from my sins and blot out all my guilt.

PROVERBS 12:8-10

⁸ A man is praised for his insight,
but a twisted mind is despised.

⁹ Better to be dishonored, yet have a servant,
than to act important but have no food.

¹⁰ A righteous man cares about his animal's health,
but even the merciful acts of the wicked are cruel.

LUKE 17:11-37

¹¹ While traveling to Jerusalem, He passed between Samaria and Galilee. ¹² As He entered a village, 10 men with serious skin diseases met Him. They stood at a distance ¹³ and raised their voices, saying, "Jesus, Master, have mercy on us!"

¹⁴ When He saw them, He told them, "Go and show yourselves to the priests." And while they were going, they were healed.

¹⁵ But one of them, seeing that he was healed, returned and, with a loud voice, gave glory to God. ¹⁶ He fell facedown at His feet, thanking Him. And he was a Samaritan.

¹⁷ Then Jesus said, "Were not 10 cleansed? Where are the nine? ¹⁸ Didn't any return to give glory to God except this foreigner?" ¹⁹ And He told him, "Get up and go on your way. Your faith has made you well."

²⁰ Being asked by the Pharisees when the kingdom of God will come, He answered them, "The kingdom of God is not coming with something observable; ²¹ no one will say, 'Look here!' or 'There!' For you see, the kingdom of God is among you."

²² Then He told the disciples: "The days are coming when you will long to see one of the days of the Son of Man, but you won't see it. ²³ They will say to you, 'Look there!' or 'Look here!' Don't follow or run after them. ²⁴ For as the lightning flashes from horizon to horizon and lights up the sky, so the Son of Man will be in His day. ²⁵ But first He must suffer many things and be rejected by this generation.

²⁶ "Just as it was in the days of Noah, so it will be in the days of the Son of Man: ²⁷ people went on eating, drinking, marrying and giving in marriage until the day Noah boarded the ark, and the flood came and destroyed them all. ²⁸ It will be the same as it was in the days of Lot: people went on eating, drinking, buying, selling, planting, building. ²⁹ But on the day Lot left Sodom, fire and sulfur rained from heaven and destroyed them all. ³⁰ It will be like that on the day the Son of Man is revealed. ³¹ On that day, a man on the housetop, whose belongings are in the house, must not come down to get them. Likewise the man who is in the field must not turn back. ³² Remember Lot's wife! ³³ Whoever tries to make his life secure will lose it, and whoever loses his life will preserve it. ³⁴ I tell you, on that night two will be in one bed: one will be taken and the other will be left. ³⁵ Two women will be grinding grain together: one will be taken and the other left. [³⁶ Two will be in a field: one will be taken, and the other will be left."]

³⁷ "Where, Lord?" they asked Him.

He said to them, "Where the corpse is, there also the vultures will be gathered."

Below the Waterline

Surely You desire integrity in the inner self.—Psalm 51:6

When considering the proposition that a balanced, honest look at what is going on beneath the surface of your life can contribute greatly to your spiritual health, think of your life as an iceberg.

We are told that the visible part of an iceberg—that is, the part we see above the water—is about one-tenth of its total size. Its bulk lies beneath the surface and is revealed only to those who are equipped to go down below the waterline. Our lives are like that; there is much more to them than we see on the surface.

Think of the visible part above the waterline as representing the things you do, the thoughts you consciously think, and the feelings you sense going on within you. Let the mass below the waterline represent the things that go on inside you that cannot be clearly seen or understood, such as motives, attitudes, impulses, and so on. Facing what goes on above the waterline—our visible behaviors and actions—is a whole lot easier than delving below the surface, and this is why many Christians (not all, of course) concern themselves only with what they can see, know, and understand.

These people can be described as "surface copers," who cope with life by dealing with whatever they can see and ignoring all the rest. If, however, we are to enjoy a deeper relationship with God, then we will do so only as we come to grips with the tough issues that lie beneath the surface of our lives.

Prayer

God, help me this day to stand before You in complete and utter honesty. Save me from becoming a "surface coper," and give me the grace I need to face the things that I would normally avoid. In Jesus' name I pray. Amen.

Further Study

Is 11; 1 Kg 3:1-10; Jn 5:30
How does Jesus judge and reprove?
What did Solomon ask for?

APRIL 28

JOSHUA 19:1-51

19 The second lot came out for Simeon, for the tribe of his descendants by their clans, but their inheritance was within the portion of Judah's descendants. ² Their inheritance included:

Beer-sheba (or Sheba), Moladah, ³ Hazar-shual, Balah, Ezem, ⁴ Eltolad, Bethul, Hormah, ⁵ Ziklag, Beth-marcaboth, Hazar-susah, ⁶ Beth-lebaoth, and Sharuhen—13 cities, with their villages; ⁷ Ain, Rimmon, Ether, and Ashan—four cities, with their villages; ⁸ and all the villages surrounding these cities as far as Baalath-beer (Ramah of the south).

This was the inheritance of the tribe of Simeon's descendants by their clans. ⁹ The inheritance of Simeon's descendants was within the territory of Judah's descendants, because the share for Judah's descendants was too large for them. So Simeon's descendants received an inheritance within Judah's portion.

[10] The third lot came up for Zebulun's descendants by their clans.

The territory of their inheritance stretched as far as Sarid; [11] their border went up westward to Maralah, reached Dabbesheth, and met the brook east of Jokneam. [12] From Sarid, it turned east toward the sunrise along the border of Chisloth-tabor, went to Daberath, and went up to Japhia. [13] From there, it went east toward the sunrise to Gath-hepher and to Eth-kazin; it extended to Rimmon, curving around to Neah. [14] The border then circled around Neah on the north to Hannathon and ended at the valley of Iphtah-el, [15] along with Kattath, Nahalal, Shimron, Idalah, and Bethlehem—12 cities, with their villages.

[16] This was the inheritance of Zebulun's descendants by their clans, these cities, with their villages.

[17] The fourth lot came out for the tribe of Issachar's descendants by their clans.

[18] Their territory went to Jezreel, and included Chesulloth, Shunem, [19] Hapharaim, Shion, Anaharath, [20] Rabbith, Kishion, Ebez, [21] Remeth, En-gannim, En-haddah, Beth-pazzez. [22] The border reached Tabor, Shahazumah, and Beth-shemesh, and ended at the Jordan—16 cities, with their villages.

[23] This was the inheritance of the tribe of Issachar's descendants by their clans, the cities, with their villages.

[24] The fifth lot came out for the tribe of Asher's descendants by their clans.

[25] Their boundary included Helkath, Hali, Beten, Achshaph, [26] Allammelech, Amad, and Mishal and reached westward to Carmel and Shihor-libnath. [27] It turned eastward to Beth-dagon, passed Zebulun and the valley of Iphtah-el, north toward Beth-emek and Neiel, and went north to Cabul, [28] Ebron, Rehob, Hammon, and Kanah, as far as Great Sidon. [29] The boundary then turned to Ramah as far as the fortified city of Tyre; it turned back to Hosah and ended at the sea, including Mahalab, Achzib, [30] Ummah, Aphek, and Rehob—22 cities, with their villages.

[31] This was the inheritance of the tribe of Asher's descendants by their clans, these cities with their villages.

[32] The sixth lot came out for Naphtali's descendants by their clans.

[33] Their boundary went from Heleph and from the oak in Zaanannim, including Adami-nekeb and Jabneel, as far as Lakkum, and ended at the Jordan. [34] To the west, the boundary turned to Aznoth-tabor and went from there to Hukkok, reaching Zebulun on the south, Asher on the west, and Judah at the Jordan on the east. [35] The fortified cities were Ziddim, Zer, Hammath, Rakkath, Chinnereth, [36] Adamah, Ramah, Hazor, [37] Kedesh, Edrei, En-hazor, [38] Iron, Migdal-el, Horem, Beth-anath, and Beth-shemesh—19 cities, with their villages.

[39] This was the inheritance of the tribe of Naphtali's descendants by their clans, the cities with their villages.

[40] The seventh lot came out for the Danite tribe by its clans.

[41] The territory of their inheritance included Zorah, Eshtaol, Ir-shemesh, [42] Shaalabbin, Aijalon, Ithlah, [43] Elon, Timnah, Ekron, [44] Eltekeh, Gibbethon, Baalath, [45] Jehud, Bene-berak, Gath-rimmon, [46] Me-jarkon, and Rakkon, with the territory facing Joppa.

[47] When the territory of the Danites slipped out of their control, they went

up and fought against Leshem, captured it, and struck it down with the sword. So they took possession of it, lived there, and renamed Leshem after their ancestor Dan. ⁴⁸This was the inheritance of the Danite tribe by its clans, these cities with their villages.

⁴⁹When they had finished distributing the land into its territories, the Israelites gave Joshua son of Nun an inheritance among them. ⁵⁰By the LORD's command, they gave him the city Timnath-serah in the hill country of Ephraim, which he requested. He rebuilt the city and lived in it.

⁵¹These were the portions that Eleazar the priest, Joshua son of Nun, and the heads of the families distributed to the Israelite tribes by lot at Shiloh in the LORD's presence at the entrance to the tent of meeting. So they finished dividing up the land.

PSALM 51:10-13

¹⁰ God, create a clean heart for me
and renew a steadfast spirit within me.
¹¹ Do not banish me from Your presence
or take Your Holy Spirit from me.
¹² Restore the joy of Your salvation to me,
and give me a willing spirit.
¹³ Then I will teach the rebellious Your ways,
and sinners will return to You.

PROVERBS 12:11-12

¹¹ The one who works his land will have plenty of food,
but whoever chases fantasies lacks sense.

¹² The wicked desire what evil men have,
but the root of the righteous produces fruit.

LUKE 18:1-23

18 He then told them a parable on the need for them to pray always and not become discouraged: ²"There was a judge in one town who didn't fear God or respect man. ³And a widow in that town kept coming to him, saying, 'Give me justice against my adversary.'

⁴"For a while he was unwilling, but later he said to himself, 'Even though I don't fear God or respect man, ⁵yet because this widow keeps pestering me, I will give her justice, so she doesn't wear me out by her persistent coming.'"

⁶Then the Lord said, "Listen to what the unjust judge says. ⁷Will not God grant justice to His elect who cry out to Him day and night? Will He delay to help them? ⁸I tell you that He will swiftly grant them justice. Nevertheless, when the Son of Man comes, will He find that faith on earth?"

⁹He also told this parable to some who trusted in themselves that they were righteous and looked down on everyone else: ¹⁰"Two men went up to the temple complex to pray, one a Pharisee and the other a tax collector. ¹¹The Pharisee took his stand and was praying like this: 'God, I thank You that I'm not like other people—greedy, unrighteous, adulterers, or even like this tax collector. ¹²I fast twice a week; I give a tenth of everything I get.'

¹³"But the tax collector, standing far off, would not even raise his eyes to heaven but kept striking his chest and saying, 'God, turn Your wrath from me—a sinner!' ¹⁴I tell you, this one went down to his house justified rather than the other; because everyone who exalts himself will be humbled, but the one who humbles himself will be exalted."

¹⁵Some people were even bringing infants to Him so He might touch them, but when the disciples saw it, they rebuked them. ¹⁶Jesus, however, invited them: "Let the little children come to Me, and don't stop them, because the kingdom of God belongs to such as

these. ¹⁷ I assure you: Whoever does not welcome the kingdom of God like a little child will never enter it."

¹⁸ A ruler asked Him, "Good Teacher, what must I do to inherit eternal life?"

¹⁹ "Why do you call Me good?" Jesus asked him. "No one is good but One—God. ²⁰ You know the commandments:

Do not commit adultery;
do not murder;
do not steal;
do not bear false witness;
honor your father and mother."

²¹ "I have kept all these from my youth," he said.

²² When Jesus heard this, He told him, "You still lack one thing: sell all that you have and distribute it to the poor, and you will have treasure in heaven. Then come, follow Me."

²³ After he heard this, he became extremely sad, because he was very rich.

Our Biggest Problem

God, create a clean heart for me and renew a steadfast spirit within me.—PSALM 51:10

What is the biggest problem we face? Some would say ill health; others, lack of money; still others, uncertainty about the future or fear of dying. My own view is that the biggest problem with which human beings have to grapple is the problem of guilt. It is the most powerfully destructive force in the personality. We cannot live with guilt—that is, truly live.

When I was a young Christian, I heard some great preaching in my native Wales, most of which focused on how God was able to release us from the guilt of inbred sin. Nowadays, apart from a few exceptions, that message is hardly heard in the pulpits of the Principality, nor for that matter in many other pulpits. The emphasis ceased to appeal to the modern mind and so was discarded. However, it is now coming back to us through the science of psychology. Someone said that the point at which psychology and religion meet is at the point of guilt. Christianity and the social sciences underline what the human heart knows so well: it cannot live comfortably with guilt.

In this simple prayer of Jesus, however, we have an adequate answer: "Forgive us our debts, as we also have forgiven our debtors." If we have fully accepted the forgiveness of God and we know that our sins have been forgiven, then the result is a pervading sense of peace. The human heart cannot be put off by subterfuge; it needs reconciliation, forgiveness, and assurance.

Prayer

O God, my Father, I see that within the ways of men, You have a way—a way that is written into the nature of reality. And that way is the way of forgiveness. May I ever walk in it. For Jesus' sake. Amen.

Further Study

Jn 8:1-11; Ps 40:12; 38:4; 73:21
What made the Pharisees leave?
How did Jesus respond to the woman?

APRIL 29

JOSHUA 20:1–21:45

20 Then the LORD spoke to Joshua, ² "Tell the Israelites: 'Select your cities of refuge, as I instructed you through Moses, ³ so that a person who kills someone unintentionally or accidentally may flee there. These will be your refuge from the avenger of blood. ⁴ When someone flees to one of these cities, stands at the entrance of the city gate, and states his case before the elders of that city, they are to bring him into the city and give him a place to live among them. ⁵ And if the avenger of blood pursues him, they must not hand the one who committed manslaughter over to him, for he killed his neighbor accidentally and did not hate him beforehand. ⁶ He is to stay in that city until he stands trial before the assembly and until the death of the high priest serving at that time. Then the one who committed manslaughter may return home to his own city from which he fled.' "

⁷ So they designated Kedesh in the hill country of Naphtali in Galilee, Shechem in the hill country of Ephraim, and Kiriath-arba (that is, Hebron) in the hill country of Judah. ⁸ Across the Jordan east of Jericho, they selected Bezer on the wilderness plateau from Reuben's tribe, Ramoth in Gilead from Gad's tribe, and Golan in Bashan from Manasseh's tribe. ⁹ These are the cities appointed for all the Israelites and foreigners among them, so that anyone who kills a person unintentionally may flee there and not die at the hand of the avenger of blood until he stands before the assembly.

21 The heads of the Levite families approached Eleazar the priest, Joshua son of Nun, and the heads of the families of the Israelite tribes. ² They told them at Shiloh in the land of Canaan: "The LORD commanded through Moses that we be given cities to live in, with their pasturelands for our livestock." ³ So the Israelites, by the LORD's command, gave the Levites these cities with their pasturelands from their inheritance.

⁴ The lot came out for the Kohathite clans: The Levites who were the descendants of Aaron the priest received 13 cities by lot from the tribes of Judah, Simeon, and Benjamin. ⁵ The remaining descendants of Kohath received 10 cities by lot from the clans of the tribes of Ephraim, Dan, and half the tribe of Manasseh.

⁶ Gershon's descendants received 13 cities by lot from the clans of the tribes of Issachar, Asher, Naphtali, and half the tribe of Manasseh in Bashan.

⁷ Merari's descendants received 12 cities for their clans from the tribes of Reuben, Gad, and Zebulun.

[8] The Israelites gave these cities with their pasturelands around them to the Levites by lot, as the LORD had commanded through Moses.

[9] The Israelites gave these cities by name from the tribes of the descendants of Judah and Simeon [10] to the descendants of Aaron from the Kohathite clans of the Levites, because they received the first lot. [11] They gave them Kiriath-arba (that is, Hebron) with its surrounding pasturelands in the hill country of Judah. Arba was the father of Anak. [12] But they gave the fields and villages of the city to Caleb son of Jephunneh as his possession.

[13] They gave to the descendants of Aaron the priest:

Hebron, the city of refuge for the one who commits manslaughter, with its pasturelands, Libnah with its pasturelands, [14] Jattir with its pasturelands, Eshtemoa with its pasturelands, [15] Holon with its pasturelands, Debir with its pasturelands, [16] Ain with its pasturelands, Juttah with its pasturelands, and Beth-shemesh with its pasturelands—nine cities from these two tribes.

[17] From the tribe of Benjamin they gave:

Gibeon with its pasturelands, Geba with its pasturelands, [18] Anathoth with its pasturelands, and Almon with its pasturelands—four cities. [19] All 13 cities with their pasturelands were for the priests, the descendants of Aaron.

[20] The allotted cities to the remaining clans of Kohath's descendants, who were Levites, came from the tribe of Ephraim. [21] The Israelites gave them:

Shechem, the city of refuge for the one who commits manslaughter, with its pasturelands in the hill country of Ephraim, Gezer with its pasturelands, [22] Kibzaim with its pasturelands, and Beth-horon with its pasturelands—four cities.

[23] From the tribe of Dan they gave:

Elteke with its pasturelands, Gibbethon with its pasturelands, [24] Aijalon with its pasturelands, and Gath-rimmon with its pasturelands—four cities.

[25] From half the tribe of Manasseh they gave:

Taanach with its pasturelands and Gath-rimmon with its pasturelands—two cities.

[26] All 10 cities with their pasturelands were for the clans of Kohath's other descendants.

[27] From half the tribe of Manasseh, they gave to the descendants of Gershon, who were one of the Levite clans:

Golan, the city of refuge for the one who commits manslaughter, with its pasturelands in Bashan, and Beeshterah with its pasturelands—two cities.

[28] From the tribe of Issachar they gave:

Kishion with its pasturelands, Daberath with its pasturelands, [29] Jarmuth with its pasturelands, and En-gannim with its pasturelands—four cities.

[30] From the tribe of Asher they gave:

Mishal with its pasturelands, Abdon with its pasturelands, [31] Helkath with its pasturelands, and Rehob with its pasturelands—four cities.

[32] From the tribe of Naphtali they gave:

Kedesh in Galilee, the city of refuge for the one who commits manslaughter, with its pasturelands, Hammoth-dor with its pasturelands, and Kartan with its pasturelands—three cities.

³³ All 13 cities with their pasturelands were for the Gershonites by their clans.

³⁴ From the tribe of Zebulun, they gave to the clans of the descendants of Merari, who were the remaining Levites:

Jokneam with its pasturelands, Kartah with its pasturelands, ³⁵ Dimnah with its pasturelands, and Nahalal with its pasturelands—four cities.

³⁶ From the tribe of Reuben, they gave:

Bezer with its pasturelands, Jahzah with its pasturelands, ³⁷ Kedemoth with its pasturelands, and Mephaath with its pasturelands—four cities.

³⁸ From the tribe of Gad, they gave:

Ramoth in Gilead, the city of refuge for the one who commits manslaughter, with its pasturelands, Mahanaim with its pasturelands, ³⁹ Heshbon with its pasturelands, and Jazer with its pasturelands—four cities in all. ⁴⁰ All 12 cities were allotted to the clans of Merari's descendants, the remaining Levite clans.

⁴¹ Within the Israelite possession there were 48 cities in all with their pasturelands for the Levites. ⁴² Each of these cities had its own surrounding pasturelands; this was true for all the cities.

⁴³ So the LORD gave Israel all the land He had sworn to give their fathers, and they took possession of it and settled there. ⁴⁴ The LORD gave them rest on every side according to all He had sworn to their fathers. None of their enemies were able to stand against them, for the LORD handed over all their enemies to them. ⁴⁵ None of the good promises the LORD had made to the house of Israel failed. Everything was fulfilled.

PSALM 51:14-19

¹⁴ Save me from the guilt of
  bloodshed, God, the God of
  my salvation,
and my tongue will sing of Your
  righteousness.
¹⁵ Lord, open my lips,
and my mouth will declare Your
  praise.
¹⁶ You do not want a sacrifice, or I
  would give it;
You are not pleased with a burnt
  offering.
¹⁷ The sacrifice pleasing to God is a
  broken spirit.
God, You will not despise a broken
  and humbled heart.
¹⁸ In Your good pleasure, cause Zion
  to prosper;
build the walls of Jerusalem.
¹⁹ Then You will delight in righteous
  sacrifices, whole burnt
  offerings;
then bulls will be offered on Your
  altar.

PROVERBS 12:13-14

¹³ An evil man is trapped by his
  rebellious speech,
but the righteous escapes from
  trouble.

¹⁴ A man will be satisfied with good
  by the words of his mouth,
and the work of a man's hands
  will reward him.

LUKE 18:24-43

²⁴ Seeing that he became sad, Jesus said, "How hard it is for those who have wealth to enter the kingdom of God! ²⁵ For it is easier for a camel to go through the eye of a needle than for a rich person to enter the kingdom of God."

²⁶ Those who heard this asked, "Then who can be saved?"

²⁷ He replied, "What is impossible with men is possible with God."

²⁸ Then Peter said, "Look, we have left what we had and followed You."

²⁹ So He said to them, "I assure you: There is no one who has left a house, wife or brothers, parents or children because of the kingdom of God, ³⁰ who will not receive many times more at this time, and eternal life in the age to come."

³¹ Then He took the Twelve aside and told them, "Listen! We are going up to Jerusalem. Everything that is written through the prophets about the Son of Man will be accomplished. ³² For He will be handed over to the Gentiles, and He will be mocked, insulted, spit on; ³³ and after they flog Him, they will kill Him, and He will rise on the third day."

³⁴ They understood none of these things. This saying was hidden from them, and they did not grasp what was said.

³⁵ As He drew near Jericho, a blind man was sitting by the road begging. ³⁶ Hearing a crowd passing by, he inquired what this meant. ³⁷ "Jesus the Nazarene is passing by," they told him. ³⁸ So he called out, "Jesus, Son of David, have mercy on me!" ³⁹ Then those in front told him to keep quiet, but he kept crying out all the more, "Son of David, have mercy on me!"

⁴⁰ Jesus stopped and commanded that he be brought to Him. When he drew near, He asked him, ⁴¹ "What do you want Me to do for you?"

"Lord," he said, "I want to see!"

⁴² "Receive your sight!" Jesus told him. "Your faith has healed you." ⁴³ Instantly he could see, and he began to follow Him, glorifying God. All the people, when they saw it, gave praise to God.

The Spirit of Holiness

The sacrifice pleasing to God is a broken spirit. God, You will not despise a broken and humbled heart.

——PSALM 51:17

Here are two important steps toward greater openness to the work of the Holy Spirit in your life:

(1) Ask yourself: "Is there any unresolved conflict, unrepented sin, or anything I must put right in order that God can flood my life with His Holy Spirit?" We must not forget that the Spirit of God is called the Holy Spirit. Holy symbolizes purity; Spirit symbolizes power. The Holy Spirit is completely holy, searching, convicting, cleansing, yet at the same time immensely powerful to support, strengthen, and sustain. If there is anything in your life that needs to be put right, then talk to God about it now. Remember at this point that you are not just reading a page—you are ridding yourself of a plague. You cannot have the Holy Spirit flowing through your life and hold onto unrepented sin. One or the other must go.

(2) Remind yourself that God is more eager to give you His Holy Spirit than you are to receive. Jesus called the giving of the Spirit "the Father's promise" (Ac 1:4). This is the promise of promises. For God to go back on a promise would be the very reverse of His nature; it is impossible. The character of God is behind this promise. You can bank on it. If you could part the clouds for a moment and look into heaven, you would see in the heart of God such an intense longing and yearning for you to be filled with His Spirit that it would completely overwhelm and overawe you. He aches to give you the fullness of His Spirit—He really does.

480

Prayer

O Father, what You want for my life, I want too—for my will and Your will to coincide. Make me as eager to be filled as You are to fill me. For Jesus' sake. Amen.

Further Study

Ac 2:14-38; Ps 34:18; Is 66:2; Eph 4:24
How did Peter exhort the people to receive the Spirit?
What was the result?

APRIL 30

JOSHUA 22:1–23:16

22 Joshua summoned the Reubenites, Gadites, and half the tribe of Manasseh, ² and told them, "You have done everything Moses the LORD's servant commanded you and have obeyed me in everything I commanded you. ³ You have not deserted your brothers even once this whole time but have carried out the requirement of the command of the LORD your God. ⁴ Now that He has given your brothers rest, just as He promised them, return to your homes in your own land that Moses the LORD's servant gave you across the Jordan. ⁵ Only carefully obey the command and instruction that Moses the LORD's servant gave you: to love the LORD your God, walk in all His ways, keep His commands, remain faithful to Him, and serve Him with all your heart and all your soul."

⁶ Joshua blessed them and sent them on their way, and they went to their homes. ⁷ Moses had given territory to half the tribe of Manasseh in Bashan, but Joshua had given territory to the other half, with their brothers, on the west side of the Jordan. When Joshua sent them to their homes and blessed them, ⁸ he said, "Return to your homes with great wealth: a huge number of cattle, and silver, gold, bronze, iron, and a large quantity of clothing. Share the spoil of your enemies with your brothers."

⁹ The Reubenites, Gadites, and half the tribe of Manasseh left the Israelites at Shiloh in the land of Canaan to go to their own land of Gilead, which they took possession of according to the LORD's command through Moses. ¹⁰ When they came to the region of the Jordan in the land of Canaan, the Reubenites, Gadites, and half the tribe of Manasseh built a large, impressive altar there by the Jordan.

¹¹ Then the Israelites heard it said, "Look, the Reubenites, Gadites, and half the tribe of Manasseh have built an altar on the frontier of the land of Canaan at the region of the Jordan, on the Israelite side." ¹² When the Israelites heard this, the entire Israelite community assembled at Shiloh to go to war against them.

¹³ The Israelites sent Phinehas son of

Eleazar the priest to the Reubenites, Gadites, and half the tribe of Manasseh, in the land of Gilead. ¹⁴ They sent 10 leaders with him—one family leader for each tribe of Israel. All of them were heads of their families among the clans of Israel. ¹⁵ They went to the Reubenites, Gadites, and half the tribe of Manasseh, in the land of Gilead, and told them, ¹⁶ "This is what the LORD's entire community says: 'What is this treachery you have committed today against the God of Israel by turning away from the LORD and building an altar for yourselves, so that you are in rebellion against the LORD today? ¹⁷ Wasn't the sin of Peor, which brought a plague on the LORD's community, enough for us, so that we have not cleansed ourselves from it even to this day, ¹⁸ and now, you would turn away from the LORD? If you rebel against the LORD today, tomorrow He will be angry with the entire community of Israel. ¹⁹ But if the land you possess is defiled, cross over to the land the LORD possesses where the LORD's tabernacle stands, and take possession of it among us. But don't rebel against the LORD or against us by building for yourselves an altar other than the altar of the LORD our God. ²⁰ Wasn't Achan son of Zerah unfaithful regarding what was set apart for destruction, bringing wrath on the entire community of Israel? He was not the only one who perished because of his sin.' "

²¹ The Reubenites, Gadites, and half the tribe of Manasseh answered the leaders of the Israelite clans, ²² "The LORD is the God of gods! The LORD is the God of gods! He knows, and may Israel also know. Do not spare us today, if it was in rebellion or treachery against the LORD ²³ that we have built for ourselves an altar to turn away from Him. May the LORD Himself hold us accountable if we intended to offer burnt offerings and grain offerings on it, or to sacrifice fellowship offerings on it. ²⁴ We actually did this from a specific concern that in the future your descendants might say to our descendants, 'What relationship do you have with the LORD, the God of Israel? ²⁵ For the LORD has made the

Jordan a border between us and you descendants of Reuben and Gad. You have no share in the LORD!' So your descendants may cause our descendants to stop fearing the LORD.

²⁶ "Therefore we said: Let us take action and build an altar for ourselves, but not for burnt offering or sacrifice. ²⁷ Instead, it is to be a witness between us and you, and between the generations after us, so that we may carry out the worship of the LORD in His presence with our burnt offerings, sacrifices, and fellowship offerings. Then in the future, your descendants will not be able to say to our descendants, 'You have no share in the LORD!' ²⁸ We thought that if they said this to us or to our generations in the future, we would reply: Look at the replica of the LORD's altar that our fathers made, not for burnt offering or sacrifice, but as a witness between us and you. ²⁹ We would never rebel against the LORD or turn away from Him today by building an altar for burnt offering, grain offering, or sacrifice, other than the altar of the LORD our God, which is in front of His tabernacle."

³⁰ When Phinehas the priest and the community leaders, the heads of Israel's clans who were with him, heard what the descendants of Reuben, Gad, and Manasseh had to say, they were pleased. ³¹ Phinehas son of Eleazar the priest said to the descendants of Reuben, Gad, and Manasseh, "Today we know that the LORD is among us, because you have not committed this treachery against Him. As a result, you have delivered the Israelites from the LORD's power."

³² Then Phinehas son of Eleazar the priest and the leaders returned from the Reubenites and Gadites in the land of Gilead to the Israelites in the land of Canaan and brought back a report to them. ³³ The Israelites were pleased with the report, and they praised God. They spoke no more about going to war against them to ravage the land where the Reubenites and Gadites lived. ³⁴ So the Reubenites and Gadites named the altar: It is a witness between us that the LORD is God.

23 A long time after the LORD had given Israel rest from all the enemies around them, Joshua was old, getting on in years. ² So Joshua summoned all Israel, including its elders, leaders, judges, and officers, and said to them, "I am old, getting on in years, ³ and you have seen for yourselves everything the LORD your God did to all these nations on your account, because it was the LORD your God who was fighting for you. ⁴ See, I have allotted these remaining nations to you as an inheritance for your tribes, including all the nations I have destroyed, from the Jordan westward to the Mediterranean Sea. ⁵ The LORD your God will force them back on your account and drive them out before you, so that you can take possession of their land, as the LORD your God promised you.

⁶ "Be very strong, and continue obeying all that is written in the book of the law of Moses, so that you do not turn from it to the right or left ⁷ and so that you do not associate with these nations remaining among you. Do not call on the names of their gods or make an oath to them; do not worship them or bow down to them. ⁸ Instead, remain faithful to the LORD your God, as you have done to this day.

⁹ "The LORD has driven out great and powerful nations before you, and no one has been able to stand against you to this day. ¹⁰ One of you routed a thousand, because the LORD your God was fighting for you, as He promised. ¹¹ So be very diligent to love the LORD your God for your own well-being. ¹² For if you turn away and cling to the rest of these nations remaining among you, and if you intermarry or associate with them and they with you, ¹³ know for certain that the LORD your God will not continue to drive these nations out before you. They will become a snare and a trap for you, a scourge for your sides and thorns in your eyes, until you disappear from this good land the LORD your God has given you.

¹⁴ "I am now going the way of all the earth, and you know with all your heart and all your soul that none of the good promises the LORD your God made to you has failed. Everything was fulfilled for you; not one promise has failed. ¹⁵ Since every good thing the LORD your God promised you has come about, so He will bring on you every bad thing until He has annihilated you from this good land the LORD your God has given you. ¹⁶ If you break the covenant of the LORD your God, which He commanded you, and go and worship other gods, and bow down to them, the LORD's anger will burn against you, and you will quickly disappear from this good land He has given you."

𝒫SALM 52:1-9

¹ Why brag about evil, you hero!
  God's faithful love is constant.
² Like a sharpened razor,
  your tongue devises destruction,
  working treachery.
³ You love evil instead of good,
  lying instead of speaking
        truthfully.   *Selah*
⁴ You love any words that destroy,
  you treacherous tongue!

⁵ This is why God will bring you
        down forever.
  He will take you, ripping you out
        of your tent;
  He will uproot you from the land
        of the living.   *Selah*
⁶ The righteous will look on with
        awe
  and will ridicule him:
⁷ "Here is the man who would not
        make God his refuge,
  but trusted in the abundance of
        his riches,
  taking refuge in his destructive
        behavior."

⁸ But I am like a flourishing olive
        tree in the house of God;
  I trust in God's faithful love
        forever and ever.
⁹ I will praise You forever for what
        You have done.
  In the presence of Your faithful
        people,

I will put my hope in Your name,
  for it is good.

PROVERBS 12:15-16

15 A fool's way is right in his own
    eyes,
  but whoever listens to counsel is
    wise.

16 A fool's displeasure is known at
    once,
  but whoever ignores an insult is
    sensible.

LUKE 19:1-27

19 He entered Jericho and was passing through. ² There was a man named Zacchaeus who was a chief tax collector, and he was rich. ³ He was trying to see who Jesus was, but he was not able because of the crowd, since he was a short man. ⁴ So running ahead, he climbed up a sycamore tree to see Jesus, since He was about to pass that way. ⁵ When Jesus came to the place, He looked up and said to him, "Zacchaeus, hurry and come down, because today I must stay at your house."

⁶ So he quickly came down and welcomed Him joyfully. ⁷ All who saw it began to complain, "He's gone to lodge with a sinful man!"

⁸ But Zacchaeus stood there and said to the Lord, "Look, I'll give half of my possessions to the poor, Lord! And if I have extorted anything from anyone, I'll pay back four times as much!"

⁹ "Today salvation has come to this house," Jesus told him, "because he too is a son of Abraham. ¹⁰ For the Son of Man has come to seek and to save the lost."

¹¹ As they were listening to this, He went on to tell a parable because He was near Jerusalem, and they thought the kingdom of God was going to appear right away.

¹² Therefore He said: "A nobleman traveled to a far country to receive for himself authority to be king and then return. ¹³ He called 10 of his slaves, gave them 10 minas, and told them, 'Engage in business until I come back.'

¹⁴ "But his subjects hated him and sent a delegation after him, saying, 'We don't want this man to rule over us!'

¹⁵ "At his return, having received the authority to be king, he summoned those slaves he had given the money to so he could find out how much they had made in business. ¹⁶ The first came forward and said, 'Master, your mina has earned 10 more minas.'

¹⁷ " 'Well done, good slave!' he told him. 'Because you have been faithful in a very small matter, have authority over 10 towns.'

¹⁸ "The second came and said, 'Master, your mina has made five minas.'

¹⁹ "So he said to him, 'You will be over five towns.'

²⁰ "And another came and said, 'Master, here is your mina. I have kept it hidden away in a cloth ²¹ because I was afraid of you, for you're a tough man: you collect what you didn't deposit and reap what you didn't sow.'

²² "He told him, 'I will judge you by what you have said, you evil slave! If you knew I was a tough man, collecting what I didn't deposit and reaping what I didn't sow, ²³ why didn't you put my money in the bank? And when I returned, I would have collected it with interest!' ²⁴ So he said to those standing there, 'Take the mina away from him and give it to the one who has 10 minas.'

²⁵ "But they said to him, 'Master, he has 10 minas.'

²⁶ " 'I tell you, that to everyone who has, more will be given; and from the one who does not have, even what he does have will be taken away. ²⁷ But bring here these enemies of mine, who did not want me to rule over them, and slaughter them in my presence.' "

No Matter What . . .

But I am like a flourishing olive tree in the house of God;
I trust in God's faithful love forever and ever.—PSALM 52:8

As he encourages himself in God, David utters: "The LORD is my shepherd; there is nothing I lack" (Ps 23:1). What a bold and positive statement to make! At first glance, however, the words seem quite absurd. Here is David in the midst of intense privation, hunted and hounded by hostile enemy forces, deserted by many of his former supporters—yet quietly affirming, "there is nothing I lack." In the past I have known many Christians who have had great difficulty in understanding this phrase. They have said, "How can I recite this verse with any meaning when I want so many things? I want a happy family/better living conditions/an adequate supply of money/employment/a wife/a husband" and so on.

David's meaning becomes clear when we dig a little deeper into the original Hebrew words that are used. Our translation says: "There is nothing I lack." Another puts it like this: "I shall not lack any good thing." "The main thought," says one commentator, "is that of not lacking—not being deficient—in proper care, management or husbandry."

So what David is really saying is this: no matter what hardships or privations come my way, I am confident of this one thing—that I shall not lack the expert care and tender supervision of my Master and my Shepherd. There were many things that David lacked—he lacked the comforts of life, family affection, physical security, and so on. What he did not lack, however, was the assurance that God was with him in his difficulties, managing his affairs and turning all his stumbling blocks into stepping-stones.

Prayer

Dear Lord Jesus, You who took everything that men threw at You and made it work toward Your ends—teach me how to do the same. Impress this truth deeply upon my spirit: that it is not what happens to me, but what I do with it, that determines the result. Amen.

Further Study

Is 40:11; 41:1-10; Dt 33:27; Ps 18:35-36
What was God's assurance to the children of Israel?
What was the psalmist's affirmation?

MAY I

JOSHUA 24:1-33

24 Joshua assembled all the tribes of Israel at Shechem and summoned Israel's elders, leaders, judges, and officers, and they presented themselves before God. ²Joshua said to all the people, "This is what the LORD, the God of Israel, says: 'Long ago your ancestors, including Terah, the father of Abraham and Nahor, lived beyond the Euphrates River and worshiped other gods. ³But I took your father Abraham from the region beyond the Euphrates River, led him throughout the land of Canaan, and multiplied his descendants. I gave him Isaac, ⁴and to Isaac I gave Jacob and Esau. I gave the hill country of Seir to Esau as a possession, but Jacob and his sons went down to Egypt.

⁵" 'Then I sent Moses and Aaron, I plagued Egypt by what I did there, and afterwards I brought you out. ⁶When I brought your fathers out of Egypt and you reached the Red Sea, the Egyptians pursued your fathers with chariots and horsemen as far as the sea. ⁷Your fathers cried out to the LORD, so He put darkness between you and the Egyptians, and brought the sea over them, engulfing them. Your own eyes saw what I did to Egypt. After that, you lived in the wilderness a long time.

⁸" 'Later, I brought you to the land of the Amorites who lived beyond the Jordan. They fought against you, but I handed them over to you. You possessed their land, and I annihilated them before you. ⁹Balak son of Zippor, king of Moab, set out to fight against Israel. He sent for Balaam son of Beor to curse you, ¹⁰but I would not listen to Balaam. Instead, he repeatedly blessed you, and I delivered you from his hand. ¹¹" 'You then crossed the Jordan and came to Jericho. The people of Jericho—as well as the Amorites, Perizzites, Canaanites, Hittites, Girgashites, Hivites, and Jebusites—fought against you, but I handed them over to you. ¹²I sent the hornet ahead of you, and it drove out the two Amorite kings before you. It was not by your sword or bow. ¹³I gave you a land you did not labor for, and cities you did not build, though you live in them; you are eating from vineyards and olive groves you did not plant.'

¹⁴"Therefore, fear the LORD and worship Him in sincerity and truth. Get rid of the gods your ancestors worshiped beyond the Euphrates River and in Egypt, and worship the LORD. ¹⁵But if it doesn't please you to worship the LORD, choose for yourselves today the one you will worship: the gods your fathers worshiped beyond the Euphrates River, or the gods of the Amorites in whose land you are living. As for me and my family, we will worship the LORD."

¹⁶The people replied, "We will certainly not abandon the LORD to worship other gods! ¹⁷For the LORD our God brought us and our fathers out of the land of Egypt, the place of slavery and performed these great signs before our eyes. He also protected us all along the way we went and among all the peoples whose lands we traveled through. ¹⁸The LORD drove out before us all the peoples, including the Amorites who lived in the land. We too will worship the LORD, because He is our God."

¹⁹But Joshua told the people, "You will not be able to worship the LORD, because He is a holy God. He is a jealous God; He will not remove your transgressions and sins. ²⁰If you abandon the LORD and worship foreign gods, He will turn against you, harm you, and completely destroy you, after He has been good to you."

²¹"No!" the people answered Joshua. "We will worship the LORD."

486

²²Joshua then told the people, "You are witnesses against yourselves that you yourselves have chosen to worship the LORD."

"We are witnesses," they said.

²³"Then get rid of the foreign gods that are among you and offer your hearts to the LORD, the God of Israel."

²⁴So the people said to Joshua, "We will worship the LORD our God and obey Him."

²⁵On that day Joshua made a covenant for the people at Shechem and established a statute and ordinance for them. ²⁶Joshua recorded these things in the book of the law of God; he also took a large stone and set it up there under the oak next to the sanctuary of the LORD. ²⁷And Joshua said to all the people, "You see this stone—it will be a witness against us, for it has heard all the words the LORD said to us, and it will be a witness against you, so that you will not deny your God." ²⁸Then Joshua sent the people away, each to his own inheritance.

²⁹After these things, the LORD's servant, Joshua son of Nun, died at the age of 110. ³⁰They buried him in his allotted territory at Timnath-serah, in the hill country of Ephraim north of Mount Gaash. ³¹Israel worshiped the LORD throughout Joshua's lifetime and during the lifetimes of the elders who outlived Joshua, and who had experienced all the works the LORD had done for Israel.

³²Joseph's bones, which the Israelites had brought up from Egypt, were buried at Shechem in the parcel of land Jacob had purchased from the sons of Hamor, Shechem's father, for 100 *qesitahs*. It was an inheritance for Joseph's descendants.

³³And Eleazar son of Aaron died, and they buried him at Gibeah, which had been given to his son Phinehas in the hill country of Ephraim.

𝒫SALM 53:1-6

¹ The fool says in his heart, "God does not exist."
They are corrupt, and they do vile deeds.
There is no one who does good.
² God looks down from heaven on the human race
to see if there is anyone who is wise
and who seeks God.
³ Everyone has turned aside;
they have all become corrupt.
There is no one who does good,
not even one.

⁴ Will those who practice sin never understand?
They consume My people as they consume bread;
they do not call on God.
⁵ Then they will be filled with terror—
terror like no other—
because God will scatter the bones of those who besiege you.
You will put them to shame, for God has rejected them.

⁶ Oh, that Israel's deliverance would come from Zion!
When God restores His captive people,
Jacob will rejoice; Israel will be glad.

𝒫ROVERBS 12:17-18

¹⁷ Whoever speaks the truth declares what is right,
but a false witness, deceit.

¹⁸ There is one who speaks rashly, like a piercing sword;
but the tongue of the wise brings healing.

ℒUKE 19:28-48

²⁸When He had said these things, He went on ahead, going up to Jerusalem. ²⁹As He approached Bethphage and Bethany, at the place called the Mount of Olives, He sent two of the disciples ³⁰and said, "Go into the village ahead of you. As you enter it, you will find a young donkey tied there, on which no

one has ever sat. Untie it and bring it here. ³¹ If anyone asks you, 'Why are you untying it?' say this: 'The Lord needs it.' "

³² So those who were sent left and found it just as He had told them. ³³ As they were untying the young donkey, its owners said to them, "Why are you untying the donkey?"

³⁴ "The Lord needs it," they said. ³⁵ Then they brought it to Jesus, and after throwing their robes on the donkey, they helped Jesus get on it. ³⁶ As He was going along, they were spreading their robes on the road. ³⁷ Now He came near the path down the Mount of Olives, and the whole crowd of the disciples began to praise God joyfully with a loud voice for all the miracles they had seen:

³⁸ **Blessed is the King
who comes in the name
of the Lord.**
Peace in heaven
and glory in the highest heaven!

³⁹ Some of the Pharisees from the crowd told Him, "Teacher, rebuke Your disciples."

⁴⁰ He answered, "I tell you, if they were to keep silent, the stones would cry out!"

⁴¹ As He approached and saw the city, He wept over it, ⁴² saying, "If you knew this day what would bring peace—but now it is hidden from your eyes. ⁴³ For the days will come on you when your enemies will build an embankment against you, surround you, and hem you in on every side. ⁴⁴ They will crush you and your children within you to the ground, and they will not leave one stone on another in you, because you did not recognize the time of your visitation."

⁴⁵ He went into the temple complex and began to throw out those who were selling, ⁴⁶ and He said, "It is written, **My house will be a house of prayer,** but you have made it **a den of thieves!"**

⁴⁷ Every day He was teaching in the temple complex. The chief priests, the scribes, and the leaders of the people were looking for a way to destroy Him, ⁴⁸ but they could not find a way to do it, because all the people were captivated by what they heard.

The Worst Thing . . .

Whoever speaks the truth declares what is right, but a false witness, deceit.—PROVERBS 12:17

Both we and the universe are made for integrity, and both the universe and we are alien to untruth and dishonesty. The whole thrust of the universe which God designed and created is simple, uncomplicated, and built on truth. There are great mysteries, of course, but no lies. Scientific laws are upheld by truth. Gravity, for example, will not lie; it is as true in one country as it is in another, as reliable in Jerusalem as it is in Japan.

It has often been pointed out that the word "evil" is the word "live" spelled backwards. Satan delights to take what God does and try to reverse it—to move life in the opposite way to that in which it was designed to go. Satan is a liar (Jn 8:44), and lies are always roundabout, complicated, and deceiving.

The fact that the universe is built on truth can be verified by the simple device known as a "lie detector." The lie detector test works on the basis that people who tell lies and know they are telling lies become extremely anxious and uncomfortable, and this anxiety is then picked up by the machine. But why does telling a lie make a person anxious? Because we are built for truth, and any departure from it registers on the inside in a way that can be picked up on the outside. A lie detector is not infallible and can sometimes (though not often) be fooled. But what cannot be fooled is the soul of the person who is lying. The worst thing about being a liar is to be the person telling the lie.

Prayer

Father, help me lay hold of the fact that a lie demeans me, but the truth develops me. I cannot live successfully by a lie any more than I can fling myself out of the window and defy gravity. May I be a person of truth. In Jesus' name I pray. Amen.

Further Study

Ps 10:1-8; Mt 17:17; 1 Tm 6:3-10; Pr 28:18-28
List some of the aspects of integrity to which David committed himself.
What did Paul highlight as one area where integrity is compromised?

MAY 2

JUDGES 1:1–2:23

1 After the death of Joshua, the Israelites inquired of the LORD, "Who will be the first to fight for us against the Canaanites?"

² The LORD answered, "Judah is to go. I have handed the land over to him."

³ Judah said to his brother Simeon, "Come with me to my territory, and let us fight against the Canaanites. I will also go with you to your territory." So Simeon went with him.

⁴ When Judah attacked, the LORD handed the Canaanites and Perizzites over to them. They struck down 10,000 men in Bezek. ⁵ They found Adoni-bezek in Bezek, fought against him, and struck down the Canaanites and Perizzites.

⁶ When Adoni-bezek fled, they pursued him, seized him, and cut off his thumbs and big toes. ⁷ Adoni-bezek said, "Seventy kings with their thumbs and big toes cut off used to pick up scraps under my table. God has repaid me for what I have done." They brought him to Jerusalem, and he died there.

⁸ The men of Judah fought against Jerusalem and captured it. They put the city to the sword and set it on fire. ⁹ Afterwards, the men of Judah marched down to fight against the Canaanites who were living in the hill country, the Negev, and the Judean foothills. ¹⁰ Judah also marched against the Canaanites who were living in Hebron (Hebron was formerly named Kiriath-arba). They struck down Sheshai, Ahiman, and Talmai. ¹¹ From there they marched against the residents of Debir (Debir was formerly named Kiriath-sepher).

¹² Caleb said, "Whoever strikes down and captures Kiriath-sepher, I will give my daughter Achsah to him as a wife." ¹³ So Othniel son of Kenaz, Caleb's youngest brother, captured it, and Caleb gave his daughter Achsah to him as his wife.
¹⁴ When she arrived, she persuaded Othniel to ask her father for a field. As she got off her donkey, Caleb asked her, "What do you want?" ¹⁵ She answered him, "Give me a blessing. Since you have given me land in the Negev, give me springs of water also." So Caleb gave her both the upper and lower springs.
¹⁶ The descendants of the Kenite, Moses' father-in-law, had gone up with the men of Judah from the City of Palms to the Wilderness of Judah, which was in the Negev of Arad. They went to live among the people.
¹⁷ Judah went with his brother Simeon, struck the Canaanites who were living in Zephath, and completely destroyed the town. So they named the town Hormah. ¹⁸ Judah captured Gaza and its territory, Ashkelon and its territory, and Ekron and its territory. ¹⁹ The LORD was with Judah and enabled them to take possession of the hill country, but they could not drive out the people who were living in the valley because those people had iron chariots.
²⁰ Judah gave Hebron to Caleb, just as Moses had promised. Then Caleb drove out the three sons of Anak who lived there.
²¹ At the same time the Benjaminites did not drive out the Jebusites who were living in Jerusalem. The Jebusites have lived among the Benjaminites in Jerusalem to this day.
²² The house of Joseph also attacked Bethel, and the LORD was with them. ²³ They sent spies to Bethel (the town was formerly named Luz). ²⁴ The spies saw a man coming out of the town and said to him, "Please show us how to get into town, and we will treat you well." ²⁵ When he showed them the way into the town, they put the town to the sword but released the man and his entire family. ²⁶ Then the man went to the land of the Hittites, built a town, and

named it Luz. That is its name to this day.
²⁷ At that time Manasseh failed to take possession of Beth-shean and its villages, or Taanach and its villages, or the residents of Dor and its villages, or the residents of Ibleam and its villages, or the residents of Megiddo and its villages. But the Canaanites refused to leave this land. ²⁸ When Israel became stronger, they made the Canaanites serve as forced labor but never drove them out completely.
²⁹ At that time Ephraim failed to drive out the Canaanites who were living in Gezer, so the Canaanites have lived among them in Gezer.
³⁰ Zebulun failed to drive out the residents of Kitron or the residents of Nahalol, so the Canaanites lived among them and served as forced labor.
³¹ Asher failed to drive out the residents of Acco or of Sidon, or Ahlab, Achzib, Helbah, Aphik, or Rehob. ³² The Asherites lived among the Canaanites who were living in the land, because they failed to drive them out.
³³ Naphtali did not drive out the residents of Beth-shemesh or the residents of Beth-anath. They lived among the Canaanites who were living in the land, but the residents of Beth-shemesh and Beth-anath served as their forced labor.
³⁴ The Amorites forced the Danites into the hill country and did not allow them to go down into the valley. ³⁵ The Amorites refused to leave Har-heres, Aijalon, and Shaalbim. When the house of Joseph got the upper hand, the Amorites were made to serve as forced labor. ³⁶ The territory of the Amorites extended from the ascent of Akrabbim, that is from Sela upward.

2 The Angel of the LORD went up from Gilgal to Bochim and said, "I brought you out of Egypt and led you into the land I had promised to your fathers. I also said: I will never break My covenant with you. ² You are not to make a covenant with the people who are living in this land, and you are to tear down their altars. But you have not obeyed Me. What is this you have done?

³ Therefore, I now say: I will not drive out these people before you. They will be thorns in your sides, and their gods will be a trap to you." ⁴ When the Angel of the LORD had spoken these words to all the Israelites, the people wept loudly. ⁵ So they named that place Bochim and offered sacrifices there to the LORD.

⁶ Joshua sent the people away, and the Israelites went to take possession of the land, each to his own inheritance. ⁷ The people worshiped the LORD throughout Joshua's lifetime and during the lifetimes of the elders who outlived Joshua. They had seen all the LORD's great works He had done for Israel.

⁸ Joshua son of Nun, the servant of the LORD, died at the age of 110. ⁹ They buried him in the territory of his inheritance, in Timnath-heres, in the hill country of Ephraim, north of Mount Gaash. ¹⁰ That whole generation was also gathered to their ancestors. After them another generation rose up who did not know the LORD or the works He had done for Israel.

¹¹ The Israelites did what was evil in the LORD's sight. They worshiped the Baals ¹² and abandoned the LORD, the God of their fathers, who had brought them out of Egypt. They went after other gods from the surrounding peoples and bowed down to them. They infuriated the LORD, ¹³ for they abandoned Him and worshiped Baal and the Ashtoreths.

¹⁴ The LORD's anger burned against Israel, and He handed them over to marauders who raided them. He sold them to the enemies around them, so that they could no longer resist their enemies. ¹⁵ Whenever the Israelites went out, the LORD was against them and brought disaster on them, just as He had promised and sworn to them. So they suffered greatly.

¹⁶ The LORD raised up judges, who saved them from the power of their marauders, ¹⁷ but they did not listen to their judges. Instead, they prostituted themselves with other gods, bowing down to them. They quickly turned from the way of their fathers, who had walked in obedience to the LORD's commands. They did not do as their fathers did. ¹⁸ Whenever the LORD raised up a judge for the Israelites, the LORD was with him and saved the people from the power of their enemies while the judge was still alive. The LORD was moved to pity whenever they groaned because of those who were oppressing and afflicting them. ¹⁹ Whenever the judge died, the Israelites would act even more corruptly than their fathers, going after other gods to worship and bow down to them. They did not turn from their evil practices or their obstinate ways.

²⁰ The LORD's anger burned against Israel, and He declared, "Because this nation has violated My covenant that I made with their fathers and disobeyed Me, ²¹ I will no longer drive out before them any of the nations Joshua left when he died. ²² I did this to test Israel and to see whether they would keep the LORD's way by walking in it, as their fathers had." ²³ The LORD left these nations and did not drive them out immediately. He did not hand them over to Joshua.

𝒫SALM 54:1-7

¹ God, save me by Your name,
    and vindicate me by Your might!
² God, hear my prayer;
    listen to the words of my mouth.
³ For strangers rise up against me,
    and violent men seek my life.
    They have no regard for God.
                        Selah

⁴ God is my helper;
    the Lord is the sustainer of my
    life.
⁵ He will repay my adversaries for
    their evil.
  Because of Your faithfulness,
    annihilate them.

⁶ I will sacrifice a freewill offering
    to You.
  I will praise Your name, LORD,
    because it is good.
⁷ For He has delivered me from
    every trouble,

and my eye has looked down on
my enemies.

PROVERBS 12:19-22

19 Truthful lips endure forever,
but a lying tongue, only a
moment.

20 Deceit is in the hearts of those
who plot evil,
but those who promote peace
have joy.

21 No disaster overcomes the
righteous,
but the wicked are full of misery.

22 Lying lips are detestable to the
LORD,
but faithful people are His delight.

LUKE 20:1-19

20 One day as He was teaching the
people in the temple complex and
proclaiming the good news, the chief
priests and the scribes, with the elders,
came up ² and said to Him: "Tell us, by
what authority are You doing these
things? Who is it who gave You this authority?"

³ He answered them, "I will also ask
you a question. Tell Me, ⁴ was the baptism of John from heaven or from men?"

⁵ They discussed it among themselves: "If we say, 'From heaven,' He
will say, 'Why didn't you believe him?'
⁶ But if we say, 'From men,' all the people will stone us, because they are convinced that John was a prophet."

⁷ So they answered that they did not
know its origin.

⁸ And Jesus said to them, "Neither
will I tell you by what authority I do
these things."

⁹ Then He began to tell the people
this parable: "A man planted a vineyard,
leased it to tenant farmers, and went
away for a long time. ¹⁰ At harvest time
he sent a slave to the farmers so that
they might give him some fruit from the
vineyard. But the farmers beat him and
sent him away empty-handed. ¹¹ He sent
yet another slave, but they beat that one
too, treated him shamefully, and sent
him away empty-handed. ¹² And he sent
yet a third, but they wounded this one
too and threw him out.

¹³ "Then the owner of the vineyard
said, 'What should I do? I will send my
beloved son. Perhaps they will respect
him.'

¹⁴ "But when the tenant farmers saw
him, they discussed it among themselves and said, 'This is the heir. Let's
kill him, so the inheritance will be
ours!' ¹⁵ So they threw him out of the
vineyard and killed him.

"Therefore, what will the owner of
the vineyard do to them? ¹⁶ He will
come and destroy those farmers and
give the vineyard to others."

But when they heard this they said,
"No—never!"

¹⁷ But He looked at them and said,
"Then what is the meaning of this Scripture:

The stone that the builders
rejected—
this has become
the cornerstone?

¹⁸ Everyone who falls on that stone will
be broken to pieces, and if it falls on
anyone, it will grind him to powder!"

¹⁹ Then the scribes and the chief
priests looked for a way to get their
hands on Him that very hour, because
they knew He had told this parable
against them, but they feared the people.

Before You Can Say "Yes"

God, save me by Your name…For strangers rise up
against me…They have no regard for God.
—PSALM 54:1, 3

The more disillusioned we are with the world, the more motivated we will be to pursue the Christian way. If we are not willing to face the reality that we live in a fallen world, that the latest invention is not going to bring us Utopia, that possessions fail to give any lasting happiness, then we are not going to move along the rugged road of faith with a steady tread.

My favorite word to summarize the message of this, the first of the Songs of Ascents, is renunciation. The psalmist seems to have made a decision to move away from the lies he has heard, and we too must make a similar decision. We must renounce lies such as that human beings are basically good, we are not responsible for the way we are, we can find happiness independently of God. The truth of God does not begin to dawn upon us until we realize that what we have assumed was the truth—that we are the masters of our fate—is in fact a lie. It is painful to admit that we have been taken in by the world's lies, but until we accept that we have and confess it, we are not ready to move on into all that God has for us.

If the psalmist were writing today, he might have worded his prayer like this: "Save me, O Lord, from the lies of those who think they know the answer to life but don't." We must discover that before we can say "yes" to God we must first learn to say "no" to the world.

Prayer

Father, I would make the prayer of the psalmist my prayer also. Rescue me from those who would represent the world to me in terms that are not entirely true. I turn from the untrue to the True. Help me dear Lord. In Jesus' name. Amen.

Further Study

Lk 21:29-36; Rm 12:1-2; Col 3:2
How does Paul admonish the Romans?
What did he encourage the Colossians to do?

MAY 3

JUDGES 3:1–4:24

3 These are the nations the LORD left in order to test Israel, since none of these Israelites had fought in any of the wars with Canaan. ² This was to teach the future generations of the Israelites how to fight in battle, especially those who had not fought before. ³ These nations included: the five rulers of the Philistines and all of the Canaanites, the Sidonians, and the Hivites who lived in the Lebanese mountains from Mount Baal-hermon as far as the entrance to Hamath. ⁴ The LORD left them to test Israel, to determine if they would keep the LORD's commands He had given their fathers through Moses. ⁵ But they settled among the Canaanites, Hittites, Amorites, Perizzites, Hivites, and Jebusites. ⁶ The Israelites took their daughters as wives for themselves, gave their own daughters to their sons, and worshiped their gods.

⁷ The Israelites did what was evil in the LORD's sight; they forgot the LORD their God and worshiped the Baals and the Asherahs. ⁸ The LORD's anger burned against Israel, and He sold them to Cushan-rishathaim king of Aram of the Two Rivers, and the Israelites served him eight years.

⁹ The Israelites cried out to the LORD. So the LORD raised up Othniel son of Kenaz, Caleb's youngest brother as a deliverer to save the Israelites. ¹⁰ The Spirit of the LORD was on him, and he judged Israel. Othniel went out to battle, and the LORD handed over Cushan-rishathaim king of Aram to him, so that Othniel overpowered him. ¹¹ Then the land was peaceful 40 years, and Othniel son of Kenaz died.

¹² The Israelites again did what was evil in the LORD's sight. He gave Eglon king of Moab power over Israel, because they had done what was evil in the LORD's sight. ¹³ After Eglon convinced the Ammonites and the Amalekites to join forces with him, he attacked and defeated Israel and took possession of the City of Palms. ¹⁴ The Israelites served Eglon king of Moab 18 years.

¹⁵ Then the Israelites cried out to the LORD, and He raised up Ehud son of Gera, a left-handed Benjaminite, as a deliverer for them. The Israelites sent him to Eglon king of Moab with tribute money.

¹⁶ Ehud made himself a double-edged sword 18 inches long. He strapped it to his right thigh under his clothes ¹⁷ and brought the tribute to Eglon king of Moab, who was an extremely fat man. ¹⁸ When Ehud had finished presenting the tribute, he dismissed the people who had carried it. ¹⁹ At the carved images near Gilgal he returned and said, "King Eglon, I have a secret message for you." The king called for silence, and all his attendants left him. ²⁰ Then Ehud approached him while he was sitting alone in his room upstairs where it was cool. Ehud said, "I have a word from God for you," and the king stood up from his throne. ²¹ Ehud reached with his left hand, took the sword from his right thigh, and plunged it into Eglon's belly. ²² Even the handle went in after the blade, and Eglon's fat closed in over it, so that Ehud did not withdraw the sword from his belly. And Eglon's insides came out. ²³ Ehud escaped by way of the porch, closing and locking the doors of the upstairs room behind him.

²⁴ Ehud was gone when Eglon's servants came in. They looked and found the doors of the upstairs room locked and thought he was relieving himself in the cool room. ²⁵ The servants waited until they became worried and saw that he had still not opened the doors of the upstairs room. So they took the key and

opened the doors—and there was their lord lying dead on the floor! ²⁶ Ehud escaped while the servants waited. He crossed over the Jordan near the carved images and reached Seirah. ²⁷ After he arrived, he sounded the ram's horn throughout the hill country of Ephraim. The Israelites came down with him from the hill country, and he became their leader. ²⁸ He told them, "Follow me, because the LORD has handed over your enemies, the Moabites, to you." So they followed him, captured the fords of the Jordan leading to Moab, and did not allow anyone to cross over. ²⁹ At that time they struck down about 10,000 Moabites, all strong and able-bodied men. Not one of them escaped. ³⁰ Moab became subject to Israel that day, and the land was peaceful 80 years.

³¹ After Ehud, Shamgar son of Anath became judge. He delivered Israel by striking down 600 Philistines with an oxgoad.

4 The Israelites again did what was evil in the sight of the LORD after Ehud had died. ² So the LORD sold them into the hand of Jabin king of Canaan, who reigned in Hazor. The commander of his forces was Sisera who lived in Harosheth of the Nations. ³ Then the Israelites cried out to the LORD, because Jabin had 900 iron chariots, and he harshly oppressed them 20 years.

⁴ Deborah, a woman who was a prophet and the wife of Lappidoth, was judging Israel at that time. ⁵ It was her custom to sit under the palm tree of Deborah between Ramah and Bethel in the hill country of Ephraim, and the Israelites went up to her for judgment. ⁶ She summoned Barak son of Abinoam from Kedesh in Naphtali and said to him, "Hasn't the LORD, the God of Israel, commanded you: 'Go, deploy the troops on Mount Tabor, and take with you 10,000 men from the Naphtalites and Zebulunites? ⁷ Then I will lure Sisera commander of Jabin's forces, his chariots, and his army at the Wadi Kishon to fight against you, and I will hand him over to you.' "

⁸ Barak said to her, "If you will go with me, I will go. But if you will not go with me, I will not go."

⁹ "I will go with you," she said, "but you will receive no honor on the road you are about to take, because the LORD will sell Sisera into a woman's hand." So Deborah got up and went with Barak to Kedesh. ¹⁰ Barak summoned Zebulun and Naphtali to Kedesh; 10,000 men followed him, and Deborah also went with him.

¹¹ Now Heber the Kenite had moved away from the Kenites, the sons of Hobab, Moses' father-in-law, and pitched his tent beside the oak tree of Zaanannim, which was near Kedesh.

¹² It was reported to Sisera that Barak son of Abinoam had gone up Mount Tabor. ¹³ Sisera summoned all his 900 iron chariots and all the people who were with him from Harosheth of the Nations to the Wadi Kishon. ¹⁴ Then Deborah said to Barak, "Move on, for this is the day the LORD has handed Sisera over to you. Hasn't the LORD gone before you?" So Barak came down from Mount Tabor with 10,000 men following him.

¹⁵ The LORD threw Sisera, all his charioteers, and all his army into confusion with the sword before Barak. Sisera left his chariot and fled on foot. ¹⁶ Barak pursued the chariots and the army as far as Harosheth of the Nations, and the whole army of Sisera fell by the sword; not a single man was left.

¹⁷ Meanwhile, Sisera had fled on foot to the tent of Jael, the wife of Heber the Kenite, because there was peace between Jabin king of Hazor and the family of Heber the Kenite. ¹⁸ Jael went out to greet Sisera and said to him, "Come in, my lord. Come in with me. Don't be afraid." So he went into her tent, and she covered him with a rug. ¹⁹ He said to her, "Please give me a little water to drink for I am thirsty." She opened a container of milk, gave him a drink, and covered him again. ²⁰ Then he said to her, "Stand at the entrance to the tent. If a man comes and asks you, 'Is there a man here?' say, 'No.' " ²¹ While he was sleeping from exhaustion, Heber's wife

Jael took a tent peg, grabbed a hammer, and went silently to Sisera. She hammered the peg into his temple and drove it into the ground, and he died. ²² When Barak arrived in pursuit of Sisera, Jael went out to greet him and said to him, "Come and I will show you the man you are looking for." So he went in with her, and there was Sisera lying dead with a tent peg through his temple! ²³ That day God subdued Jabin king of Canaan before the Israelites. ²⁴ The power of the Israelites continued to increase against Jabin king of Canaan until they destroyed him.

PSALM 55:1-8

¹ God, listen to my prayer
and do not ignore my plea for help.
² Pay attention to me and answer me.
I am restless and in turmoil with my complaint,
³ because of the enemy's voice,
because of the pressure of the wicked.
For they bring down disaster on me
and harass me in anger.

⁴ My heart shudders within me;
terrors of death sweep over me.
⁵ Fear and trembling grip me;
horror has overwhelmed me.
⁶ I said, "If only I had wings like a dove!
I would fly away and find rest.
⁷ How far away I would flee;
I would stay in the wilderness.
Selah
⁸ I would hurry to my shelter
from the raging wind and the storm."

PROVERBS 12:23-24

²³ A shrewd person conceals knowledge,
but a foolish heart publicizes stupidity.

²⁴ The diligent hand will rule,
but laziness will lead to forced labor.

LUKE 20:20-40

²⁰ They watched closely and sent spies who pretended to be righteous, so they could catch Him in what He said, to hand Him over to the governor's rule and authority. ²¹ They questioned Him, "Teacher, we know that You speak and teach correctly, and You don't show partiality, but teach truthfully the way of God. ²² Is it lawful for us to pay taxes to Caesar or not?"

²³ But detecting their craftiness, He said to them, ²⁴ "Show Me a denarius. Whose image and inscription does it have?"

"Caesar's," they said.

²⁵ "Well then," He told them, "give back to Caesar the things that are Caesar's and to God the things that are God's."

²⁶ They were not able to catch Him in what He said in public, and being amazed at His answer, they became silent.

²⁷ Some of the Sadducees, who say there is no resurrection, came up and questioned Him: ²⁸ "Teacher, Moses wrote for us that **if a man's brother** has a wife, and **dies childless, his brother should take the wife and produce offspring for his brother.** ²⁹ Now there were seven brothers. The first took a wife and died without children. ³⁰ Also the second ³¹ and the third took her. In the same way, all seven died and left no children. ³² Finally, the woman died too. ³³ Therefore, in the resurrection, whose wife will the woman be? For all seven had married her."

³⁴ Jesus told them, "The sons of this age marry and are given in marriage. ³⁵ But those who are counted worthy to take part in that age and in the resurrection from the dead neither marry nor are given in marriage. ³⁶ For they cannot die anymore, because they are like angels and are sons of God, since they are sons of the resurrection. ³⁷ Moses even

indicated in the passage about the burning bush that the dead are raised, where he calls the Lord **the God of Abraham and the God of Isaac and the God of Jacob.** ³⁸ He is not God of the dead but of the living, because all are living to Him."

³⁹ Some of the scribes answered, "Teacher, You have spoken well." ⁴⁰ And they no longer dared to ask Him anything.

The Secret of Survival

The diligent hand will rule, but laziness will lead to forced labor.—PROVERBS 12:24

We need to make clear the difference between diligence and obstinacy. I know people who have experienced spiritual shipwreck because they didn't know the difference between these two things. When asked to clarify the difference between perseverance and obstinacy, a student wrote: "One is a strong will and the other is a strong won't." Diligence is dogged perseverance; obstinacy is dogged inflexibility and self-will.

A man whose life was full of promise as far as the Christian ministry was concerned now spends his days in depression because he did not know the difference between these two things. He set out on a project that he thought was God's will for him, and when things started to go wrong, instead of checking his guidance, he continued to press on and ended up in failure. Those who loved him, and were more objective, urged him to give up as what he was doing was clearly not the will of God. However, he did not have the wisdom to realize that what he was doing was not being diligent but obstinate. Now he lives in perpetual disillusionment.

When Jesus came to Calvary, He said, "I have glorified You on the earth by completing the work You gave Me to do" (Jn 17:4). Note the word "You." There were many who would have liked Jesus to do this and that, to go here and go there, but He did only what the Father required Him to do. Saying "yes" to God's will and pursuing it is diligence. Saying "yes" to a thing that is not God's will and pursuing that is obstinacy. We had better learn the difference.

Prayer

Father, I see how important it is to be clear about these two issues. Help me differentiate between diligence and obstinacy so that at the end of my time here on earth I, too, will be able to say, "I have finished the work which You have given me to do." Amen.

Further Study

Mt 25:14-30; 7:26; Jms 2:14
What was Jesus' teaching in the parable of the talents?
Why were the two who multiplied the talents successful?

MAY 4

JUDGES 5:1–6:10

5 On that day Deborah and Barak son of Abinoam sang:

2 When the leaders lead in Israel,
when the people volunteer,
praise the LORD.
3 Listen, kings! Pay attention,
princes!
I will sing to the LORD;
I will sing praise to the LORD God
of Israel.
4 LORD, when You came from Seir,
when You marched from the fields
of Edom,
the earth trembled,
the heavens poured rain,
the clouds poured water.
5 The mountains melted
before the LORD,
even Sinai before the LORD,
the God of Israel.

6 In the days of Shamgar
son of Anath,
in the days of Jael,
the main ways were deserted,
because travelers kept
to the side roads.
7 Villages were deserted,
they were deserted in Israel,
until I, Deborah,
I arose, a mother in Israel.
8 Israel chose new gods,
then war was in the gates.
Not a shield or spear was seen
among 40,000 in Israel.
9 My heart is with the leaders
of Israel,
with the volunteers of the
people.
Praise the LORD!
10 You who ride on white donkeys,
who sit on saddle blankets,
and who travel on the road,
give praise!

11 Let them tell the righteous acts
of the LORD,
the righteous deeds
of His warriors in Israel,
with the voices of the singers
at the watering places.

Then the LORD's people went
down to the gates.
12 "Awake! Awake, Deborah!
Awake! Awake, sing a song!
Arise Barak,
and take hold of your captives,
son of Abinoam!"
13 The survivors came down
to the nobles;
the LORD's people came down
to me with the warriors.
14 Those with their roots in Amalek
came from Ephraim;
Benjamin came with your people
after you.
The leaders came down
from Machir,
and those who carry
a marshal's staff came
from Zebulun.
15 The princes of Issachar were
with Deborah;
Issachar was with Barak.
They set out at his heels
in the valley.
There was great searching
of heart
among the clans of Reuben.
16 Why did you sit
among the sheepfolds
listening to the playing of pipes
for the flocks?
There was great searching
of heart
among the clans of Reuben.
17 Gilead remained
beyond the Jordan.
Dan, why did you linger
at the ships?
Asher remained at the seashore

and stayed in his harbors.
¹⁸ Zebulun was a people risking
their lives,
Naphtali also, on the heights
of the battlefield.
¹⁹ Kings came and fought.
Then the kings of Canaan fought
at Taanach by the waters
of Megiddo,
but they took no spoil of silver.
²⁰ The stars fought
from the heavens;
the stars fought with Sisera
from their courses.
²¹ The river Kishon swept them
away,
the ancient river, the river Kishon.
March on, my soul, in strength!
²² The horses' hooves then
hammered—
the galloping, galloping of his
stallions.
²³ "Curse Meroz," says the Angel
of the LORD,
"Bitterly curse her inhabitants,
for they did not come to help
the LORD,
to help the LORD against
the mighty warriors."
²⁴ Jael is most blessed of women,
the wife of Heber the Kenite;
she is most blessed among
tent-dwelling women.
²⁵ He asked for water; she gave him
milk.
She brought him curdled milk
in a majestic bowl.
²⁶ She reached for a tent peg,
her right hand,
for a workman's mallet.
Then she hammered Sisera—
she crushed his head;
she shattered and pierced
his temple.
²⁷ He collapsed, he fell, he lay down
at her feet;
he collapsed, he fell at her feet;
where he collapsed,
there he fell—dead.
²⁸ Sisera's mother looked
through the window;

she peered the lattice,
crying out:
"Why is his chariot so long
in coming?
Why don't I hear the hoofbeats
of his horses?"
²⁹ Her wisest princesses answer
her;
she even answers herself:
³⁰ "Are they not finding and dividing
the spoil—
a girl or two for each warrior,
the spoil of colored garments
for Sisera,
the spoil of an embroidered garment
or two for my neck?"

³¹ LORD, may all your enemies perish
as Sisera did.
But may those who love Him
be like the rising of the sun
in its strength.
And the land was peaceful 40 years.

6 The Israelites did what was evil in
the sight of the LORD. So the LORD
handed them over to Midian seven
years, ² and they oppressed Israel. Because of Midian, the Israelites made hiding places for themselves in the
mountains, caves, and strongholds.
³ Whenever the Israelites planted crops,
the Midianites, Amalekites, and the
eastern peoples came and attacked
them. ⁴ They encamped against them
and destroyed the produce of the land,
even as far as Gaza. They left nothing for
Israel to eat, as well as no sheep, ox or
donkey. ⁵ For the Midianites came with
their cattle and their tents like a great
swarm of locusts. They and their camels
were without number, and they entered
the land to waste it. ⁶ So Israel became
poverty-stricken because of Midian, and
the Israelites cried out to the LORD.
⁷ When the Israelites cried out to Him
because of Midian, ⁸ the LORD sent a
prophet to them. He said to them, "This
is what the LORD God of Israel says: 'I
brought you out of Egypt and out of the
place of slavery. ⁹ I delivered you from
the power of Egypt and the power of
all who oppressed you. I drove them
out before you and gave you their land.

10 I said to you: I am the LORD your God. Do not fear the gods of the Amorites whose land you live in. But you did not obey Me.' "

PSALM 55:9-14

9 Lord, confuse and confound their
  speech,
  for I see violence and strife in the
  city;
10 day and night they make the
  rounds on its walls.
  Crime and trouble are within it;
11 destruction is inside it;
  oppression and deceit never leave
  its marketplace.

12 Now, it is not an enemy who
  insults me—
  otherwise I could bear it;
  it is not a foe who rises up against
  me—
  otherwise I could hide from him.
13 But it is you, a man who is my
  peer,
  my companion and good friend!
14 We used to have close fellowship;
  we walked with the crowd into
  the house of God.

PROVERBS 12:25-26

25 Anxiety in a man's heart weighs it
  down,
  but a good word cheers it up.

26 A righteous man is careful in
  dealing with his neighbor,
  but the ways of wicked men lead
  them astray.

LUKE 20:41–21:19

41 Then He said to them, "How can they say that the Messiah is the Son of David? 42 For David himself says in the Book of Psalms:

The Lord declared to my Lord,
  'Sit at My right hand
43 until I make Your enemies
  Your footstool.'

44 David calls Him 'Lord'; how then can the Messiah be his Son?"

45 While all the people were listening, He said to His disciples, 46 "Beware of the scribes, who want to go around in long robes and who love greetings in the marketplaces, the front seats in the synagogues, and the places of honor at banquets. 47 They devour widows' houses and say long prayers just for show. These will receive greater punishment."

21 He looked up and saw the rich dropping their offerings into the temple treasury. 2 He also saw a poor widow dropping in two tiny coins. 3 "I tell you the truth," He said. "This poor widow has put in more than all of them. 4 For all these people have put in gifts out of their surplus, but she out of her poverty has put in all she had to live on."

5 As some were talking about the temple complex, how it was adorned with beautiful stones and gifts dedicated to God, He said, 6 "These things that you see—the days will come when not one stone will be left on another that will not be thrown down!"

7 "Teacher," they asked Him, "so when will these things be? And what will be the sign when these things are about to take place?"

8 Then He said, "Watch out that you are not deceived. For many will come in My name, saying, 'I am He,' and, 'The time is near.' Don't follow them. 9 When you hear of wars and rebellions, don't be alarmed. Indeed, these things must take place first, but the end won't come right away."

10 Then He told them: "Nation will be raised up against nation, and kingdom against kingdom. 11 There will be violent earthquakes, and famines and plagues in various places, and there will be terrifying sights and great signs from heaven. 12 But before all these things, they will lay their hands on you and persecute you. They will hand you over to the synagogues and prisons, and you will be brought before kings and governors because of My name. 13 It will lead to an opportunity for you to witness. 14 Therefore make up your minds not to

prepare your defense ahead of time, ¹⁵ for I will give you such words and a wisdom that none of your adversaries will be able to resist or contradict. ¹⁶ You will even be betrayed by parents, broth-ers, relatives, and friends. They will kill some of you. ¹⁷ You will be hated by everyone because of My name, ¹⁸ but not a hair of your head will be lost. ¹⁹ By your endurance gain your lives.

"Clinging to His Creeks"

Asher remained at the seashore and stayed in his harbors.

——Judges 5:17

One of the greatest mistakes we can make in life is to block the efforts of the Divine Eagle when He attempts to push us out of the nest of the accustomed into the world of the adventurous. Asher did this—the account in the Moffatt translation reads: "Asher sat still by the seaboard clinging to his creeks." Although the metaphor is changed, the principle is still the same. There was Asher sitting by the seaboard, clinging to his creeks, when he could have launched out into the ocean and experienced the joy of a great adventure. In the face of the big, he settled for the little. They were "his" creeks and he wasn't going to let the accustomed go to venture into the unaccustomed no matter how great the possibilities.

Asher is a type of the Christian who wants to stay by the safe and secure and finishes up by doing nothing and getting nowhere. I am not advocating spiritual recklessness, nor am I arguing for an unmindful approach to the Christian life; I am simply saying that we ought to be ocean-minded and not creek-minded Christians. The people who try to find inner security by clinging to the creeks are invariably unfulfilled, for we are inwardly made for growth and creativity.

A turtle doesn't get anywhere until he sticks his neck out! To cling to our creeks for safety and security is to be upset at every call of the big. We are made for the big and are restless in our littleness. We cannot be content this side of God's purpose.

Prayer

O Father, You are calling and I must come. I come from my littleness and watch it sink into the bigness of Your purpose for me. The great calls and I must come—at any price. Amen.

Further Study

1 Sm 17; Mt 21:22; Mk 11:24; 1 Jn 5:14-15
In what ways was David adventurous?
On what was his adventurous spirit based?

MAY 5

JUDGES 6:11–7:25

¹¹ The Angel of the LORD came, and He sat under the oak that was in Ophrah, which belonged to Joash, the Abiezrite. His son Gideon was threshing wheat in the wine vat in order to hide it from the Midianites. ¹² Then the Angel of the LORD appeared to him and said: "The LORD is with you, mighty warrior." ¹³ Gideon said to Him, "Please Sir, if the LORD is with us, why has all this happened? And where are all His wonders that our fathers told us about? They said, 'Hasn't the LORD brought us out of Egypt?' But now the LORD has abandoned us and handed us over to Midian." ¹⁴ The LORD turned to him and said, "Go in the strength you have and deliver Israel from the power of Midian. Am I not sending you?" ¹⁵ He said to Him, "Please, Lord, how can I deliver Israel? Look, my family is the weakest in Manasseh, and I am the youngest in my father's house." ¹⁶ "But I will be with you," the LORD said to him. "You will strike Midian down as if it were one man." ¹⁷ Then he said to Him, "If I have found favor in Your sight, give me a sign that You are speaking with me. ¹⁸ Please do not leave this place until I return to You. Let me bring my gift and set it before You."

And He said, "I will stay until you return."

¹⁹ So Gideon went and prepared a young goat and unleavened bread from a half bushel of flour. He placed the meat in a basket and the broth in a pot. He brought them out and offered them to Him under the oak. ²⁰ The Angel of God said to him, "Take the meat with the unleavened bread, put it on this stone, and pour the broth on it." And he did so. ²¹ The Angel of the LORD extended the tip of the staff that was in His hand and touched the meat and the unleavened bread. Fire came up from the rock and consumed the meat and the unleavened bread. Then the Angel of the LORD vanished from his sight. ²² When Gideon realized that He was the Angel of the LORD, he said, "Oh no, Lord GOD! I have seen the Angel of the LORD face to face!" ²³ But the LORD said to him, "Peace to you. Don't be afraid, for you will not die." ²⁴ So Gideon built an altar to the LORD there and called it Yahweh Shalom. It is in Ophrah of the Abiezrites until today.

²⁵ On that very night the LORD said to him, "Take your father's young bull and a second bull seven years old. Then tear down the altar of Baal that belongs to your father and cut down the Asherah pole beside it. ²⁶ Build a well-constructed altar to the LORD your God on the top of this rock. Take the second bull and offer it as a burnt offering with the wood of the Asherah pole you cut down." ²⁷ So Gideon took 10 of his male servants and did as the LORD had told him. But because he was too afraid of his father's household and the men of the city to do it in the daytime, he did it at night. ²⁸ When the men of the city got up in the morning, they found Baal's altar torn down, the Asherah pole beside it cut down, and the second bull offered up on the altar that had been built. ²⁹ They said to each other, "Who did this?" After they made a thorough investigation, they said, "Gideon son of Joash did it." ³⁰ Then the men of the city said to Joash, "Bring out your son. He must die, because he tore down Baal's altar and cut down the Asherah pole beside it." ³¹ But Joash said to all who stood against him, "Would you plead Baal's

case for him? Would you save him? Whoever pleads his case will be put to death by morning! If he is a god, let him plead his own case, because someone tore down his altar." ³²That day, Gideon's father called him Jerubbaal, saying, "Let Baal plead his case with him," because he tore down his altar.

³³All the Midianites, Amalekites, and Qedemites gathered together, crossed over the Jordan, and camped in the Valley of Jezreel.

³⁴The Spirit of the LORD enveloped Gideon, and he blew the ram's horn and the Abiezrites rallied behind him. ³⁵He sent messengers throughout all of Manasseh, who rallied behind him. He also sent messengers throughout Asher, Zebulun, and Naphtali, who also came to meet him.

³⁶Then Gideon said to God, "If You will deliver Israel by my hand, as You said, ³⁷I will put a fleece of wool here on the threshing floor. If dew is only on the fleece, and all the ground is dry, I will know that You will deliver Israel by my strength, as You said." ³⁸And that is what happened. When he got up early in the morning, he squeezed the fleece and wrung dew out of it, filling a bowl with water.

³⁹Gideon then said to God, "Don't be angry with me; let me speak one more time. Please allow me to make one more test with the fleece. Let it remain dry, and the dew be all over the ground." ⁴⁰That night God did as Gideon requested: only the fleece was dry, and dew was all over the ground.

7 Jerubbaal (that is, Gideon) and everyone who was with him, got up early and camped beside the spring of Harod. The camp of Midian was north of them, below the hill of Moreh, in the valley. ²The LORD said to Gideon, "You have too many people for Me to hand the Midianites over to you, or else Israel might brag: 'I did it myself.' ³Now announce in the presence of the people: 'Whoever is fearful and trembling may turn back and leave Mount Gilead.' " So 22,000 of the people turned back, but 10,000 remained.

⁴Then the LORD said to Gideon, "There are still too many people. Take them down to the water, and I will test them for you there. If I say to you, 'This one can go with you,' he can go. But if I say about anyone, 'This one cannot go with you,' he cannot go." ⁵So he brought the people down to the water, and the LORD said to Gideon, "Separate everyone who laps water with his tongue like a dog. Do the same with everyone who kneels to drink." ⁶The number of those who lapped with their hands to their mouths was 300 men, and all the rest of the people knelt to drink water. ⁷The LORD said to Gideon, "I will deliver you with the 300 men who lapped and hand the Midianites over to you. But everyone else is to go home." ⁸So Gideon sent all the Israelites to their tents, but kept the 300 who took the people's provisions and their trumpets. The camp of Midian was below him in the valley.

⁹That night the LORD said to him, "Get up and go into the camp, for I have given it into your hand. ¹⁰But if you are afraid to go to the camp, go with Purah your servant. ¹¹Listen to what they say, and then you will be strengthened to go to the camp." So he went with Purah his servant to the outpost of the troops who were in the camp.

¹²Now the Midianites, Amalekites, and all the Qedemites had settled down in the valley like a swarm of locusts, and their camels were as innumerable as the sand on the seashore. ¹³When Gideon arrived, there was a man telling his friend about a dream. He said, "Listen, I had a dream: a loaf of barley bread came tumbling into the Midianite camp, struck a tent, and it fell. The loaf turned the tent upside down so that it collapsed."

¹⁴His friend answered: "This is nothing less than the sword of Gideon son of Joash, the Israelite. God has handed the entire Midianite camp over to him."

¹⁵When Gideon heard the account of the dream and its interpretation, he bowed in worship. He returned to Israel's camp and said, "Get up, for the LORD has handed the Midianite camp

over to you." ¹⁶ Then he divided the 300 men into three companies and gave each of the men a trumpet in one hand and an empty pitcher with a torch inside it in the other. ¹⁷ "Watch me," he said, "and do the same. When I come to the outpost of the camp, do as I do. ¹⁸ When I and everyone with me blow our trumpets, you are also to blow your trumpets all around the camp. Then you will say, 'The sword of the LORD and of Gideon!' "

¹⁹ Gideon and the 100 men who were with him went to the outpost of the camp at the beginning of the middle watch after the sentries had been stationed. They blew their trumpets and broke the pitchers that were in their hands. ²⁰ The three companies blew their trumpets and shattered their pitchers. They held their torches in their left hands, their trumpets in their right hands, and shouted, "The sword of the LORD and of Gideon!" ²¹ Each Israelite took his position around the camp, and the entire Midianite army fled, and cried out as they ran. ²² When Gideon's men blew their 300 trumpets, the LORD set the swords of each man in the army against each other. They fled to Beth-shittah in the direction of Zererah as far as the border of Abel-meholah near Tabbath. ²³ Then the men of Israel were called from Naphtali, Asher, and Manasseh, and they pursued the Midianites.

²⁴ Gideon sent messengers throughout the hill country of Ephraim with this message: "Come down to intercept the Midianites and take control of the watercourses ahead of them as far as Beth-barah and the Jordan." So all the men of Ephraim were called out, and they took control of the watercourses as far as Beth-barah and the Jordan. ²⁵ They captured Oreb and Zeeb, the two princes of Midian; they killed Oreb at the rock of Oreb and Zeeb at the winepress of Zeeb, while they were pursuing the Midianites. They brought the heads of Oreb and Zeeb to Gideon across the Jordan.

PSALM 55:15-23

¹⁵ Let death take them by surprise;
   let them go down to Sheol alive,
   because evil is in their homes and
      within them.
¹⁶ But I call to God,
   and the LORD will save me.
¹⁷ I complain and groan morning,
      noon, and night,
   and He hears my voice.
¹⁸ Though many are against me,
   He will redeem me from my battle
      unharmed.
¹⁹ God, the One enthroned from
      long ago,
   will hear, and will humiliate them
                              Selah
   because they do not change
   and do not fear God.

²⁰ He acts violently against those at
      peace with him;
   he violates his covenant.
²¹ His buttery words are smooth,
   but war is in his heart.
   His words are softer than oil,
   but they are drawn swords.

²² Cast your burden on the LORD,
   and He will support you;
   He will never allow the righteous
      to be shaken.

²³ You, God, will bring them down to
      the pit of destruction;
   men of bloodshed and treachery
      will not live out half their
      days.
   But I will trust in You.

PROVERBS 12:27-28

²⁷ A lazy man doesn't roast his game,
   but to a diligent man, his wealth
      is precious.

²⁸ There is life in the path of
      righteousness,
   but another path leads to death.

$\mathcal{L}$UKE 21:20-38

20 "When you see Jerusalem surrounded by armies, then recognize that its desolation has come near. 21 Then those in Judea must flee to the mountains! Those inside the city must leave it, and those who are in the country must not enter it, 22 because these are days of vengeance to fulfill all the things that are written. 23 Woe to pregnant women and nursing mothers in those days, for there will be great distress in the land and wrath against this people. 24 They will fall by the edge of the sword and be led captive into all the nations, and Jerusalem will be trampled by the Gentiles until the times of the Gentiles are fulfilled.

25 "Then there will be signs in the sun, moon, and stars; and there will be anguish on the earth among nations bewildered by the roaring sea and waves. 26 People will faint from fear and expectation of the things that are coming on the world, because the celestial powers will be shaken. 27 Then they will see the Son of Man coming in a cloud with power and great glory. 28 But when these things begin to take place, stand up and lift up your heads, because your redemption is near!"

29 Then He told them a parable: "Look at the fig tree, and all the trees. 30 As soon as they put out leaves you can see for yourselves and recognize that summer is already near. 31 In the same way, when you see these things happening, recognize that the kingdom of God is near. 32 I assure you: This generation will certainly not pass away until all things take place. 33 Heaven and earth will pass away, but My words will never pass away.

34 "Be on your guard, so that your minds are not dulled from carousing, drunkenness, and worries of life, or that day will come on you unexpectedly 35 like a trap. For it will come on all who live on the face of the whole earth. 36 But be alert at all times, praying that you may have strength to escape all these things that are going to take place and to stand before the Son of Man."

37 During the day, He was teaching in the temple complex, but in the evening He would go out and spend the night on what is called the Mount of Olives. 38 Then all the people would come early in the morning to hear Him in the temple complex.

A Spiritual Adventure

The LORD said to Gideon, "I will deliver you with the 300 men who lapped."—JUDGES 7:7

This passage illustrates an important point: God is looking for people who will "stand." When the hosts of Midian came against the Israelites, Gideon gathered together a large army of 32,000 men. Then God reduced them to a mere handful. Of the 32,000, there were only three hundred whom God could trust. He saw that they were men who would stand and never quit, so He dismissed the rest. And with just a small army of three hundred, He proceeded to discomfit and rout the Midianites.

God has always done His greatest work in and through a comparatively small number of people. This is why, when it comes to spiritual victories, we forget the idea of numbers. What God wants is men and women who are prepared to "stand," whose feet are "shod with the preparation of the gospel of peace." He will not entrust great responsibility to people whom He knows will not "stand," for that would be an exercise in fruitlessness.

Are you standing for God—in the environment in which God has put you? Or are you ready to stand? You cannot stand until you are prepared to stand. It begins with a firm attitude which then issues into resolute action. As in Gideon's day, the Lord is looking for people who will take their stand on His Word, come what may, and commit themselves to doing what He asks even though they may not feel like it or see the sense of it. Are you such a one? If you are, then I predict that ahead of you is an exciting spiritual adventure.

Prayer

O God, help me not to miss the highest because of my spiritual unpreparedness. Help me to be ready for all that You have for me—even before I see it. In Jesus' name. Amen.

Further Study

Gl 6:1-9; 1 Co 15:58; Eph 4:15
What is the result of remaining steadfast?
What can hinder our spiritual success?

MAY 6

JUDGES 8:1–9:21

8 The men of Ephraim said to him, "Why have you done this to us, not calling us when you went to fight against the Midianites?" And they argued with him violently.

² So he said to them, "What have I done now compared to you? Is not the gleaning of Ephraim better than the vintage of Abiezer? ³ God handed over to you Oreb and Zeeb, the two princes of Midian. What was I able to do compared to you?" When he said this, their anger against him subsided.

⁴ Gideon and the 300 men came to the Jordan and crossed it. They were exhausted, but still in pursuit. ⁵ He said to the men of Succoth, "Please give some loaves of bread to the people who are following me, because they are exhausted, for I am pursuing Zebah and Zalmunna, the kings of Midian."

⁶ But the princes of Succoth asked, "Are Zebah and Zalmunna now in your hands that we should give bread to your army?"

⁷ Gideon replied, "Very well, when the LORD has handed Zebah and Zalmunna over to me, I will trample your flesh on thorns and briers from the wilderness!" ⁸ He went from there to Penuel and asked the same thing from them. The men of Penuel answered just as the men of Succoth had answered. ⁹ He also told the men of Penuel, "When I return in peace, I will tear down this tower!"

¹⁰ Now Zebah and Zalmunna were in Karkor, and with them was their army of about 15,000 men, who were all those left of the entire army of the Qedemites. Those who had been killed were 120,000 warriors. ¹¹ Gideon traveled on the caravan route, east of Nobah and Jogbehah, and attacked their army while the army was unsuspecting. ¹² Zebah and Zalmunna fled, and he pursued them. He captured these two kings of Midian and routed the entire army. ¹³ Gideon son of Joash returned from the battle by the ascent of Heres. ¹⁴ He captured a youth from the men of Succoth and interrogated him. The youth wrote down for him the names of the 77 princes and elders of Succoth. ¹⁵ Then he went to the men of Succoth and said, "Here are Zebah and Zalmunna. You taunted me about them, saying, 'Are Zebah and Zalmunna now in your power that we should give bread to your exhausted men?' " ¹⁶ So he took the elders of the city, as well as some thorns and briers from the wilderness, and he disciplined the men of Succoth with them. ¹⁷ He also tore down the tower of Penuel and killed the men of the city.

¹⁸ He asked Zebah and Zalmunna, "What kind of men did you kill at Tabor?"

"They were like you," they said. "Each resembled the son of a king."

¹⁹ So he said, "They were my brothers, the sons of my mother! As the LORD lives, if you had let them live, I would not kill you." ²⁰ Then he said to Jether, his firstborn, "Get up and kill them." The youth did not draw his sword, because he was afraid, for he was still a youth.

²¹ Zebah and Zalmunna said, "Get up and kill us yourself, for a man is judged by his strength." So Gideon got up, killed Zebah and Zalmunna, and took the crescent ornaments that were on the necks of their camels.

²² Then the Israelites said to Gideon, "Rule over us, you as well as your sons and your grandsons, for you delivered us from the power of Midian."

²³ But Gideon said to them, "I will not rule over you, and my son will not rule over you; the LORD will rule over you."

²⁴ Then he said to them, "Let me make a request of you: Everyone give me an earring from his plunder." Now the enemy had gold earrings because they were Ishmaelites.

²⁵ They said, "We agree to give them." So they spread out a mantle, and everyone threw an earring from his plunder on it. ²⁶ The weight of the gold earrings he requested was about 43 pounds of gold, in addition to the crescent ornaments and ear pendants, the purple garments on the kings of Midian, and the chains on the necks of their camels. ²⁷ Gideon made an ephod from all this and put it in Ophrah, his hometown. Then all Israel prostituted themselves with it there, and it became a snare to Gideon and his household.

²⁸ So Midian was subdued before the Israelites, and they were no longer a threat. The land was peaceful 40 years during the days of Gideon. ²⁹ Jerubbaal (that is, Gideon) son of Joash went back to live at his house.

³⁰ Gideon had 70 sons, his own offspring, since he had many wives. ³¹ His concubine who was in Shechem also bore him a son, and he named him Abimelech. ³² Then Gideon son of Joash died at a ripe old age and was buried in the tomb of his father Joash in Ophrah of the Abiezrites.

³³ When Gideon died, the Israelites turned and prostituted themselves with the Baals and made Baal-berith their god. ³⁴ The Israelites did not remember the LORD their God who had delivered them from the power of the enemies around them. ³⁵ They did not show kindness to the house of Jerubbaal (that is, Gideon) for all the good he had done for Israel.

9 Abimelech son of Jerubbaal went to his mother's brothers at Shechem and spoke to them and to all his maternal grandfather's clan, saying, ² "Please speak in the presence of all the lords of Shechem, 'Is it better for you that 70 men, all the sons of Jerubbaal, rule over you or that one man rule over you?' Remember that I am your own flesh and blood."

³ His mother's relatives spoke all these words about him in the presence of all the lords of Shechem, and they were favorable to Abimelech, for they said, "He is our brother." ⁴ So they gave him 70 pieces of silver from the temple of Baal-berith. Abimelech hired worthless and reckless men with this money, and they followed him. ⁵ He went to his father's house in Ophrah and killed his 70 brothers, the sons of Jerubbaal, on top of a large stone. But Jotham, the youngest son of Jerubbaal, survived, because he hid himself. ⁶ Then all the lords of Shechem and of Beth-millo gathered together and proceeded to make Abimelech king at the oak of the pillar in Shechem.

⁷ When they told Jotham, he climbed to the top of Mount Gerizim, raised his voice, and called to them:

Listen to me, lords of Shechem,
and may God listen to you:

⁸ The trees set out
to anoint a king over themselves.
They said to the olive tree,
"Reign over us."

⁹ But the olive tree said to them,
"Should I stop giving my oil
that honors both God and man,
and rule over the trees?"

¹⁰ Then the trees said to the fig tree,
"Come and reign over us."

¹¹ But the fig tree said to them,
"Should I stop giving
my sweetness and my good fruit,
and rule over trees?"

¹² Later, the trees said
to the grapevine,
"Come and reign over us."

¹³ But the grapevine said to them,
"Should I stop giving my wine
that cheers both God and man,
and rule over trees?"

¹⁴ Finally, all the trees said
to the bramble,
"Come and reign over us."

¹⁵ The bramble said to the trees,
"If you really are anointing me

as king over you,
come and find refuge in my shade.
But if not,
may fire come out
from the bramble
and consume the cedars
of Lebanon."

¹⁶ "Now if you have acted faithfully and honestly in making Abimelech king, if you have done well by Jerubbaal and his family, and if you have rewarded him appropriately for what he did— ¹⁷ for my father fought for you, risked his life, and delivered you from the hand of Midian, ¹⁸ and now you have attacked my father's house today, killed his 70 sons on top of a large stone, and made Abimelech, the son of his slave, king over the lords of Shechem 'because he is your brother'— ¹⁹ if then, you have acted faithfully and honestly with Jerubbaal and his house this day, rejoice in Abimelech and may he also rejoice in you. ²⁰ But if not, may fire come from Abimelech and consume the lords of Shechem and Beth-millo, and may fire come from the lords of Shechem and Beth-millo and consume Abimelech." ²¹ Then Jotham fled, escaping to Beer, and lived there because of his brother Abimelech.

*P*SALM 56:1-7

¹ Be gracious to me, God, for man
tramples me;
he fights and oppresses me all day
long.

² My adversaries trample me all day,
for many arrogantly fight against
me.

³ When I am afraid,
I will trust in You.

⁴ In God, whose word I praise,
in God I trust; I will not fear.
What can man do to me?

⁵ They twist my words all day long;
all their thoughts are against me
for evil.

⁶ They stir up strife, they lurk;

they watch my steps
while they wait to take my life.
7 Will they escape in spite of such
sin?
God, bring down the nations in
wrath.

PROVERBS 13:1-2

13 A wise son hears his father's
instruction,
but a mocker doesn't listen to
rebuke.

2 From the words of his mouth, a
man will enjoy good things,
but treacherous people have an
appetite for violence.

LUKE 22:1-23

22 The Festival of Unleavened Bread,
which is called Passover, was
drawing near. 2 The chief priests and the
scribes were looking for a way to put
Him to death, because they were afraid
of the people. 3 Then Satan entered Judas, called
Iscariot, who was numbered among the
Twelve. 4 He went away and discussed
with the chief priests and temple police
how he could hand Him over to them.
5 They were glad and agreed to give him
silver. 6 So he accepted the offer and
started looking for a good opportunity
to betray Him to them when the crowd
was not present. 7 Then the Day of Unleavened Bread
came when the Passover lamb had to be
sacrificed. 8 Jesus sent Peter and John,
saying, "Go and prepare the Passover
meal for us, so we can eat it."

9 "Where do You want us to prepare
it?" they asked Him. 10 "Listen," He said to them, "when
you've entered the city, a man carrying
a water jug will meet you. Follow him
into the house he enters. 11 Tell the
owner of the house, 'The Teacher asks
you, "Where is the guest room where I
can eat the Passover with My disciples?" ' 12 Then he will show you a large,
furnished room upstairs. Make the
preparations there." 13 So they went and found it just as
He had told them, and they prepared
the Passover. 14 When the hour came, He reclined
at the table, and the apostles with Him.
15 Then He said to them, "I have fervently desired to eat this Passover with
you before I suffer. 16 For I tell you, I
will not eat it again until it is fulfilled in
the kingdom of God." 17 Then He took a
cup, and after giving thanks, He said,
"Take this and share it among yourselves. 18 For I tell you, from now on I
will not drink of the fruit of the vine until the kingdom of God comes." 19 And He took bread, gave thanks,
broke it, gave it to them, and said, "This
is My body, which is given for you. Do
this in remembrance of Me." 20 In the same way He also took the
cup after supper and said, "This cup is
the new covenant established by My
blood; it is shed for you. 21 But look, the
hand of the one betraying Me is at the
table with Me! 22 For the Son of Man
will go away as it has been determined,
but woe to that man by whom He is betrayed!" 23 So they began to argue among
themselves which of them it could be
who was going to do this thing.

The Three Elements of Fear

In God I trust; I will not fear. What can man do to me?
—PSALM 56:4

Many people, some Christians included, see death as an intruder. Gandhi, the great Indian
leader and politician, said that he started his Swaraj movement to help people overcome the

fear of death. Politics was only a minor part of his purpose. "My aim," he said, "was the abandonment of the fear of death. So long as we let ourselves be influenced by the fear of death, we can never attain freedom."

When we come to analyze the fear of death, three elements can be seen to be present: the fear of the physical act of dying, the fear of finality, and the fear of judgment. Let's look first at the fear of the physical act of dying. This is very real to some people. Perhaps they have suffered and know, through bitter experience, how pain lacerates and hurts.

Doctors assure us that what people normally call "the agony of death" is felt much more by those who are watching than by the one who is passing away. Sir Frederick Treves, the eminent surgeon, said: "A last illness may be long, wearisome and painful, but the closing moments of it are, as a rule, free from suffering. There may appear to be a terrible struggle at the end, but of this struggle the subject is unconscious. It is the onlooker who bears the misery of it." Add to this natural phenomenon the supporting power of God's never-failing grace, and it is possible to look even this physical aspect of death quietly in the face and say, "My enemy—you are not really the terror that you seem."

Prayer

Lord Jesus, You who are Master of life and death, I am so grateful that in You I see the death of death and the defeat of defeat. In You everything is alive—alive with meaning, destiny, goal—alive forevermore. Hallelujah!

Further Study

Is 43:2-3; 1 Co 15:1-21; Jn 11:11; Ac 13:36
Of what is Christ the firstfruits?
What is the difference between sleep and death?

MAY 7

JUDGES 9:22–10:18

²² When Abimelech had ruled over Israel three years, ²³ God sent an evil spirit between Abimelech and the lords of Shechem. They treated Abimelech deceitfully, ²⁴ so that the crime against the 70 sons of Jerubbaal might come to justice and their blood would be avenged on their brother Abimelech, who killed them, and on the lords of Shechem, who had helped him kill his brothers. ²⁵ The lords of Shechem rebelled against him by putting people on

the tops of the mountains to ambush and rob everyone who passed by them on the road. So this was reported to Abimelech. ²⁶ Gaal son of Ebed came with his brothers and crossed into Shechem, and the lords of Shechem trusted him. ²⁷ So they went out to the countryside and harvested grapes from their vineyards. They trod the grapes and held a celebration. Then they went to the house of their god, and as they ate and drank, they cursed Abimelech. ²⁸ Gaal son of Ebed said, "Who is Abimelech and who is Shechem that we should serve him? Isn't he the son of Jerubbaal, and isn't Zebul his officer? You are to serve the men of Hamor, the father of Shechem. Why should we serve Abimelech? ²⁹ If only these people were in my power, I would remove Abimelech." So he said to Abimelech, "Gather your army and come out."

³⁰ When Zebul, the ruler of the city, heard the words of Gaal son of Ebed, he was angry. ³¹ So he sent messengers secretly to Abimelech, saying, "Look, Gaal son of Ebed, with his brothers, have come to Shechem and are turning the city against you. ³² Now tonight, you and the people with you are to come wait in ambush in the countryside. ³³ Then get up early and at sunrise, charge the city. When he and the people who are with him come out against you, do to him whatever you can." ³⁴ So Abimelech and all the people with him got up at night and waited in ambush for Shechem in four units.

³⁵ Gaal son of Ebed went out and stood at the entrance of the city gate. Then Abimelech and the people who were with him got up from their ambush. ³⁶ When Gaal saw the people, he said to Zebul, "Look, people are coming down from the mountaintops!" But Zebul said to him, "The shadows of the mountains look like men to you."

³⁷ Then Gaal spoke again: "Look, people are coming down from the central part of the land, and one unit is coming from the direction of the Diviners' Oak." ³⁸ Zebul replied, "Where is your mouthing off now? You said, 'Who is

Abimelech that we should serve him?' Aren't these the people you despised? Now go and fight them!"

³⁹ So Gaal went out leading the lords of Shechem and fought against Abimelech, ⁴⁰ but Abimelech pursued him, and Gaal fled before him. Many wounded died as far as the entrance of the gate. ⁴¹ Abimelech stayed in Arumah, and Zebul drove Gaal and his brothers from Shechem.

⁴² The next day when the people went into the countryside, this was reported to Abimelech. ⁴³ He took the people, divided them into three companies, and waited in ambush in the countryside. He looked, and the people were coming out of the city, so he arose against them and struck them down. ⁴⁴ Then Abimelech and the units that were with him rushed forward and took their stand at the entrance of the city gate. The other two units rushed against all who were in the countryside and struck them down. ⁴⁵ So Abimelech fought against the city that entire day, captured it, and killed the people who were in it. Then he tore down the city and sowed it with salt.

⁴⁶ When all the lords of the Tower of Shechem heard, they entered the inner chamber of the temple of El-berith. ⁴⁷ Then it was reported to Abimelech that all the lords of the Tower of Shechem had gathered together. ⁴⁸ So Abimelech and all the people who were with him went up to Mount Zalmon. Abimelech took his ax in his hand and cut a branch from the trees. He picked up the branch, put it on his shoulder, and said to the people who were with him, "Hurry and do what you have seen me do." ⁴⁹ Each person also cut his own branch and followed Abimelech. They put the branches against the inner chamber and set it on fire around the people, and all the people in the Tower of Shechem died—about 1,000 men and women.

⁵⁰ Abimelech went to Thebez, camped against it, and captured it. ⁵¹ There was a strong tower inside the city, and all the men, women, and lords of the city fled there. They locked themselves in

and went up to the roof of the tower. ⁵² When Abimelech came to attack the tower, he approached its entrance to set it on fire. ⁵³ But a woman threw the upper portion of a millstone on Abimelech's head and fractured his skull. ⁵⁴ He quickly called his armor-bearer and said to him, "Draw your sword and kill me, or they'll say about me, 'A woman killed him.' " So his armor-bearer thrust him through, and he died. ⁵⁵ When the Israelites saw that Abimelech was dead, they all went home.

⁵⁶ In this way, the evil that Abimelech had done against his father, by killing his 70 brothers, God turned back on him. ⁵⁷ And God also returned all the evil of the men of Shechem on their heads. So the curse of Jotham son of Jerubbaal came on them.

10 After Abimelech, Tola son of Puah, son of Dodo became judge and began to deliver Israel. He was from Issachar and lived in Shamir in the hill country of Ephraim. ² Tola judged Israel 23 years, and when he died, was buried in Shamir.

³ After him came Jair the Gileadite, who judged Israel 22 years. ⁴ He had 30 sons who rode on 30 young donkeys. They had 30 towns in Gilead, which are called Jair's Villages to this day. ⁵ When Jair died, he was buried in Kamon.

⁶ Then the Israelites again did what was evil in the sight of the LORD. They worshiped the Baals and the Ashtoreths, the gods of Aram, Sidon, and Moab, and the gods of the Ammonites and the Philistines. They abandoned the LORD and did not worship Him. ⁷ So the LORD's anger burned against Israel, and He sold them to the Philistines and the Ammonites. ⁸ They shattered and crushed the Israelites that year, and for 18 years they did the same to all the Israelites who were on the other side of the Jordan in the land of the Amorites in Gilead. ⁹ The Ammonites also crossed the Jordan to fight against Judah, Benjamin, and the house of Ephraim. Israel was greatly oppressed, ¹⁰ so they cried out to the LORD, saying, "We have sinned against You. We have aban-

doned our God and worshiped the Baals."

¹¹ The LORD said to the Israelites, "When the Egyptians, Amorites, Ammonites, Philistines, ¹² Sidonians, Amalekites, and Maonites oppressed you, and you cried out to Me, did I not deliver you from their power? ¹³ But you have abandoned Me and worshiped other gods. Therefore, I will not deliver you again. ¹⁴ Go and cry out to the gods you have chosen. Let them deliver you in the time of your oppression."

¹⁵ But the Israelites said, "We have sinned. Deal with us as You see fit; only deliver us today!" ¹⁶ So they got rid of the foreign gods among them and worshiped the LORD, but He became weary of Israel's misery.

¹⁷ The Ammonites were called together, and they camped in Gilead. So the Israelites assembled and camped at Mizpah. ¹⁸ The rulers of Gilead said to one another, "Which man will lead the fight against the Ammonites? He will be the leader of all the inhabitants of Gilead."

PSALM 56:8-13

⁸ You Yourself have recorded my wanderings.
Put my tears in Your bottle.
Are they not in Your records?
⁹ Then my enemies will retreat on the day when I call.
This I know: God is for me.

¹⁰ In God, whose word I praise,
in the LORD, whose word I praise,
¹¹ in God I trust; I will not fear.
What can man do to me?

¹² I am obligated by vows to You, God;
I will make my thank offerings to You.
¹³ For You delivered me from death,
even my feet from stumbling,
to walk before God in the light of life.

PROVERBS 13:3-4

³ The one who guards his mouth protects his life;

the one who opens his lips invites his own ruin.

4 The slacker craves, yet has nothing,
but the diligent is fully satisfied.

....

LUKE 22:24-46

24 Then a dispute also arose among them about who should be considered the greatest. 25 But He said to them, "The kings of the Gentiles dominate them, and those who have authority over them are called 'Benefactors.' 26 But it must not be like that among you. On the contrary, whoever is greatest among you must become like the youngest, and whoever leads, like the one serving. 27 For who is greater, the one at the table or the one serving? Isn't it the one at the table? But I am among you as the One who serves. 28 You are the ones who stood by Me in My trials. 29 I bestow on you a kingdom, just as My Father bestowed one on Me, 30 so that you may eat and drink at My table in My kingdom. And you will sit on thrones judging the 12 tribes of Israel.

31 "Simon, Simon, look out! Satan has asked to sift you like wheat. 32 But I have prayed for you that your faith may not fail. And you, when you have turned back, strengthen your brothers."

33 "Lord," he told Him, "I'm ready to go with You both to prison and to death!"

34 "I tell you, Peter," He said, "the rooster will not crow today until you deny three times that you know Me!"

35 He also said to them, "When I sent you out without money-bag, traveling bag, or sandals, did you lack anything?"

"Not a thing," they said.

36 Then He said to them, "But now, whoever has a money-bag should take it, and also a traveling bag. And whoever doesn't have a sword should sell his robe and buy one. 37 For I tell you, what is written must be fulfilled in Me: **And He was counted among the outlaws.** Yes, what is written about Me is coming to its fulfillment."

38 "Lord," they said, "look, here are two swords."

"Enough of that!" He told them.

39 He went out and made His way as usual to the Mount of Olives, and the disciples followed Him. 40 When He reached the place, He told them, "Pray that you may not enter into temptation." 41 Then He withdrew from them about a stone's throw, knelt down, and began to pray, 42 "Father, if You are willing, take this cup away from Me—nevertheless, not My will, but Yours, be done."

[43 Then an angel from heaven appeared to Him, strengthening Him. 44 Being in anguish, He prayed more fervently, and His sweat became like drops of blood falling to the ground.] 45 When He got up from prayer and came to the disciples, He found them sleeping, exhausted from their grief. 46 "Why are you sleeping?" He asked them. "Get up and pray, so that you won't enter into temptation."

Satan's Pincer Movement

Simon, Simon, look out! Satan has asked to sift you like wheat. But I have prayed for you that your faith may not fail.—Luke 22:31-32

One of the reasons the Apostle Paul bids us pray for one another is this: the failure of any one of us is going to have some effect upon the spiritual campaign which God is waging against the Devil through the church.

All those who have committed themselves to Jesus Christ should know that the forces of two kingdoms—the kingdoms of God and of the Devil—are locked together in mortal combat. And Christians, whether they like it or not, are thrust right onto the cutting edge of this conflict.

The battle line between the forces of God and the forces of Satan is the church—and that means you and me. What is Satan's best tactic in attempting to bring about the church's spiritual defeat? He probes at every point he can, looking for the weakest part. When he finds a weak Christian (or a group of weak Christians), he calls for reinforcements. Then, using what military strategists call "a pincer movement," he attempts to break through at that point. And when one Christian fails, all of us to some extent are affected, for we are all part of the one line of defense.

How the Devil rejoices when an individual Christian falls—especially a church leader. Therefore, we are called to a ministry of prayer—not just for ourselves but for one another also—that we might stand perfect and complete in the will of God and that our faith will not fail when under attack by the Devil.

Prayer

Father, I am encouraged as I think that today, millions of Christians around the world will be praying for me. Help me never to fail in my responsibility to pray for them. In Christ's peerless and precious name. Amen.

Further Study

Gl 6:1-10; 1 Co 9:27; Php 3:12; Jms 5:16
What are we to carry in prayer?
Of what was Paul conscious?

MAY 8

JUDGES 11:1–12:15

11 Jephthah the Gileadite was a great warrior, but he was the son of a prostitute, and Gilead was his father. ² Gilead's wife bore him sons, and when they grew up, they drove Jephthah out and said to him, "You will have no inheritance in our father's house, because you are the son of another woman." ³ So

Jephthah fled from his brothers and lived in the land of Tob. Then some lawless men joined Jephthah and traveled with him.

⁴ Some time later, the Ammonites fought against Israel. ⁵ When the Ammonites made war with Israel, the elders of Gilead went to get Jephthah from the land of Tob. ⁶ They said to him, "Come, be our commander, and let's fight against the Ammonites."

⁷Jephthah replied to the elders of Gilead, "Didn't you hate me and drive me from my father's house? Why then have you come to me now when you're in trouble?" ⁸They answered Jephthah, "Since that's true, we now turn to you. Come with us, fight the Ammonites, and you will become leader of all the inhabitants of Gilead." ⁹So Jephthah said to them, "If you are bringing me back to fight the Ammonites and the Lord gives them to me, I will be your leader." ¹⁰The elders of Gilead said to Jephthah, "The Lord is our witness if we don't do as you say." ¹¹So Jephthah went with the elders of Gilead. The people put him over themselves as leader and commander, and Jephthah repeated all his terms in the presence of the Lord at Mizpah.

¹²Jephthah sent messengers to the king of the Ammonites, saying, "What do you have against me that you have come to fight against me in my land?" ¹³The king of the Ammonites said to Jephthah's messengers, "When Israel came from Egypt, they seized my land from the Arnon to the Jabbok and the Jordan. Now restore it peaceably." ¹⁴Jephthah again sent messengers to the king of the Ammonites ¹⁵to tell him, "This is what Jephthah says: Israel did not take away the land of Moab or the land of the Ammonites. ¹⁶But when they came from Egypt, Israel traveled through the wilderness to the Red Sea and came to Kadesh. ¹⁷Israel sent messengers to the king of Edom, saying, 'Please let us travel through your land,' but the king of Edom would not listen. They also sent messengers to the king of Moab, but he refused. So Israel stayed in Kadesh. ¹⁸"Then they traveled through the wilderness and around the lands of Edom and Moab. They came to the east side of the land of Moab and camped on the other side of the Arnon but did not enter into the territory of Moab, for the Arnon was the boundary of Moab. ¹⁹"Then Israel sent messengers to Sihon king of the Amorites, king of

Heshbon. Israel said to him, 'Please let us travel through your land to our country,' ²⁰but Sihon did not trust Israel. Instead, Sihon gathered all his people, camped at Jahaz, and fought with Israel. ²¹Then the Lord God of Israel handed over Sihon and all his people to Israel, and they defeated them. So Israel took possession of the entire land of the Amorites who lived in that country. ²²They took possession of all the territory of the Amorites from the Arnon to the Jabbok and from the wilderness to the Jordan.

²³"The Lord God of Israel has now driven out the Amorites before His people Israel, but will you drive us out? ²⁴Isn't it true that you may possess whatever your god Chemosh drives out for you, and we may possess everything the Lord our God drives out before us? ²⁵Now are you any better than Balak son of Zippor, king of Moab? Did he ever contend with Israel or fight against them? ²⁶While Israel lived 300 years in Heshbon and its villages, in Aroer and its villages, and in all the cities that are on the banks of the Arnon, why didn't you take them back at that time? ²⁷I have not sinned against you, but you have wronged me by fighting against me. Let the Lord who is the Judge decide today between the Israelites and the Ammonites." ²⁸But the king of the Ammonites would not listen to Jephthah's message that he sent him.

²⁹The Spirit of the Lord came on Jephthah, who traveled through Gilead and Manasseh, and then through Mizpah of Gilead. He crossed over to the Ammonites from Mizpah of Gilead. ³⁰Jephthah made this vow to the Lord: "If You will hand over the Ammonites to me, ³¹whatever comes out of the doors of my house to greet me when I return in peace from the Ammonites will belong to the Lord, and I will offer it as a burnt offering." ³²Jephthah crossed over to the Ammonites to fight against them, and the Lord handed them over to him. ³³He defeated 20 of their cities with a great slaughter from Aroer all the way to the entrance of Minnith and to Abel-keramim.

So the Ammonites were subdued before the Israelites.

³⁴ When Jephthah went to his home in Mizpah, there was his daughter, coming out to meet him with tambourines and dancing! She was his only child; he had no other son or daughter besides her. ³⁵ When he saw her, he tore his clothes and said, "No! Not my daughter! You have devastated me! You have brought great misery on me. I have given my word to the LORD and cannot take it back."

³⁶ Then she said to him, "My father, you have given your word to the LORD. Do to me as you have said, for the LORD brought vengeance on your enemies, the Ammonites." ³⁷ She also said to her father, "Let me do this one thing: Let me wander two months through the mountains with my friends and mourn my virginity."

³⁸ "Go," he said. And he sent her away two months. So she left with her friends and mourned her virginity as she wandered through the mountains. ³⁹ At the end of two months, she returned to her father, and he kept the vow he had made about her. And she had never been intimate with a man. Now it became a custom in Israel ⁴⁰ that four days each year the young women of Israel would commemorate the daughter of Jephthah the Gileadite.

12 The men of Ephraim were called together and crossed the Jordan to Zaphon. They said to Jephthah, "Why have you crossed over to fight against the Ammonites but didn't call us to go with you? We will burn your house down with you in it!"

² Then Jephthah said to them, "My people and I had a serious conflict with the Ammonites. So I called for you, but you didn't deliver me from their power. ³ When I saw that you weren't going to deliver me, I took my life in my own hands and crossed over to the Ammonites, and the LORD handed them over to me. Why then have you come today to fight against me?"

⁴ Then Jephthah gathered all of the men of Gilead. They fought and defeated

Ephraim, because Ephraim had said, "You Gileadites are Ephraimite fugitives in the territories of Ephraim and Manasseh." ⁵ The Gileadites captured the fords of the Jordan leading to Ephraim. Whenever a fugitive from Ephraim said, "Let me cross over," the Gileadites asked him, "Are you an Ephraimite?" If he answered, "No," ⁶ they told him, "Please say Shibboleth." If he said, "Sibboleth," because he could not pronounce it correctly, they seized him and killed him at the fords of the Jordan. At that time, 42,000 from Ephraim died.

⁷ Jephthah judged Israel six years, and when he died, he was buried in one of the cities of Gilead.

⁸ Ibzan, who was from Bethlehem, judged Israel after Jephthah ⁹ and had 30 sons. He gave his 30 daughters in marriage to men outside the tribe and brought back 30 wives for his sons from outside the tribe. Ibzan judged Israel seven years, ¹⁰ and when he died, he was buried in Bethlehem.

¹¹ Elon, who was from Zebulun, judged Israel after Ibzan. He judged Israel 10 years, ¹² and when he died, he was buried in Aijalon in the land of Zebulun.

¹³ After Elon, Abdon son of Hillel, who was from Pirathon, judged Israel. ¹⁴ He had 40 sons and 30 grandsons, who rode on 70 donkeys. Abdon judged Israel eight years, ¹⁵ and when he died, he was buried in Pirathon in the land of Ephraim, in the hill country of the Amalekites.

PSALM 57:1-6

¹   Be gracious to me, God, be
        gracious to me,
    for I take refuge in You.
    I will seek refuge in the shadow of
        Your wings
    until danger passes.
²   I call to God Most High,
    to God who fulfills His purpose
        for me.
³   He reaches down from heaven and
        saves me,

challenging the one who tramples
me.   *Selah*
God sends His faithful love and
truth.
4 I am in the midst of lions;
I lie down with those who devour
men.
Their teeth are spears and
arrows;
their tongues are sharp swords.
5 God, be exalted above the
heavens;
let Your glory be above the whole
earth.
6 They prepared a net for my steps;
I was downcast.
They dug a pit ahead of me,
but they fell into it!   *Selah*

*P*ROVERBS 13:5-6

5 The righteous hate lying,
but the wicked act disgustingly
and disgracefully.

6 Righteousness guards people of
integrity,
but wickedness undermines the
sinner.

*L*UKE 22:47-71

47 While He was still speaking, suddenly a mob was there, and one of the
Twelve named Judas was leading them.
He came near Jesus to kiss Him, 48 but
Jesus said to him, "Judas, are you betraying the Son of Man with a kiss?"
49 When those around Him saw what
was going to happen, they asked, "Lord,
should we strike with the sword?"
50 Then one of them struck the high
priest's slave and cut off his right ear.
51 But Jesus responded, "No more of
this!" And touching his ear, He healed
him. 52 Then Jesus said to the chief
priests, temple police, and the elders
who had come for Him, "Have you come
out with swords and clubs as if I were a
criminal? 53 Every day while I was with
you in the temple complex, you never

laid a hand on Me. But this is your
hour—and the dominion of darkness."
54 They seized Him, led Him away,
and brought Him into the high priest's
house. Meanwhile Peter was following
at a distance. 55 They lit a fire in the
middle of the courtyard and sat down
together, and Peter sat among them.
56 When a servant saw him sitting in the
firelight, and looked closely at him, she
said, "This man was with Him too."
57 But he denied it: "Woman, I don't
know Him!"
58 After a little while, someone else
saw him and said, "You're one of them
too!"
"Man, I am not!" Peter said.
59 About an hour later, another kept
insisting, "This man was certainly with
Him, since he's also a Galilean."
60 But Peter said, "Man, I don't know
what you're talking about!" Immediately, while he was still speaking, a rooster crowed. 61 Then the Lord turned and
looked at Peter. So Peter remembered
the word of the Lord, how He had said
to him, "Before the rooster crows today,
you will deny Me three times." 62 And
he went outside and wept bitterly.
63 The men who were holding Jesus
started mocking and beating Him.
64 After blindfolding Him, they kept asking, "Prophesy! Who hit You?" 65 And
they were saying many other blasphemous things against Him.
66 When daylight came, the elders of
the people, both the chief priests and
the scribes, convened and brought Him
before their Sanhedrin. 67 They said, "If
You are the Messiah, tell us."
But He said to them, "If I do tell you,
you will not believe. 68 And if I ask you,
you will not answer. 69 But from now on,
the Son of Man will be seated at the
right hand of the Power of God."
70 They all asked, "Are You, then, the
Son of God?"
And He said to them, "You say that I
am."
71 "Why do we need any more testimony," they said, "since we've heard it
ourselves from His mouth?"

"Stupid"

Peter said, "Man, I don't know what you're talking about!"
—LUKE 22:60

Today we look at a game called "Stupid." Simon Peter played this game. Picture the scene. Peter, the big fisherman, strong, resolute, determined, firm in his declaration of love for Christ, denies all knowledge of the Master. Why? He had walked with the Master for three whole years, heard Him speak the most wonderful words, saw Him heal the sick, raise the dead, cleanse the lepers, and work other amazing miracles. Yet when he is asked if he knows Jesus, his response is one of withdrawal. In other words, he plays stupid.

Eric Berne claims that whenever we play games, it is always for a reward. What was Peter's reward? It was the reinforcement of his fear. Why should the reinforcement of his fear be a reward? Well, the more deeply he believed that he was afraid and the more he did to reinforce that fear, the easier it would be to excuse himself for his failure to stand up for Jesus when confronted. The final pay-off was to be protected from danger.

A Christian schoolteacher told me that at an educational conference, someone happened to remark that the Bible was a fable. The man then turned to the schoolteacher and said: "What do you think?" He told me that his first impulse was to play stupid and say: "I am not sure," or "I don't know." He caught himself just about to play the game but instead accepted the challenge of the situation and responded with some positive comments. To play the game of "Stupid" may bring temporary benefits, but the dishonesty involved greatly upsets one's spiritual balance.

Prayer

O Father, help me to be an honest person. Help me to absorb Your love in such a measure that it will dissolve every fear. Then strengthen me to face life—fearless and unafraid. Amen.

Further Study

Ac 5:1-10; Ps 63:11; Pr 19:5; Jr 9:5
When we play "Stupid," what are we really doing?
How serious is it?

MAY 9

JUDGES 13:1–15:8

13 The Israelites again did what was evil in the LORD's sight, so the LORD handed them over to the Philistines 40 years. ² There was a certain man from Zorah, from the family of Dan, whose name was Manoah; his wife was barren and had no children. ³ The Angel of the LORD appeared to the woman and said to her, "It is true that you are barren and have no children, but you will conceive and give birth to a son. ⁴ Now please be careful not to drink wine or other alcoholic beverages, or to eat anything unclean; ⁵ for indeed, you will conceive and give birth to a son. You must never cut his hair, because the boy will be a Nazirite to God from birth, and he will begin to save Israel from the power of the Philistines."

⁶ Then the woman went and told her husband, "A man of God came to me. He looked like the awe-inspiring Angel of God. I didn't ask Him where He came from, and He didn't tell me His name. ⁷ He said to me, 'You will conceive and give birth to a son. Therefore, do not drink wine or other alcoholic beverages, and do not eat anything unclean, because the boy will be a Nazirite to God from birth until the day of his death.' "

⁸ Manoah prayed to the LORD and said, "Please Lord, let the man of God you sent come again to us and teach us what we should do for the boy who will be born."

⁹ God listened to Manoah, and the Angel of GOD came again to the woman. She was sitting in the field, and her husband Manoah was not with her. ¹⁰ The woman ran quickly to her husband and told him, "The man who came to me today has just come back!"

¹¹ So Manoah got up and followed his wife. When he came to the man, he asked, "Are You the man who spoke to my wife?"

"I am," He said.

¹² Then Manoah asked, "When Your words come true, what will the boy's responsibilities and mission be?"

¹³ The Angel of the LORD answered Manoah, "Your wife needs to do everything I told her. ¹⁴ She must not eat anything that comes from the grapevine or drink wine or other alcoholic beverages. And she must not eat anything unclean. Your wife must do everything I have commanded her."

¹⁵ "Please stay here," Manoah told Him, "and we will prepare a young goat for You."

¹⁶ The Angel of the LORD said to him, "If I stay, I won't eat your food. But if you want to prepare a burnt offering, offer it to the LORD." For Manoah did not know He was the Angel of the LORD.

¹⁷ Then Manoah said to Him, "What is Your name, so that we may honor You when Your words come true?"

¹⁸ "Why do you ask My name," the Angel of the LORD asked him, "since it is wonderful."

¹⁹ Manoah took a young goat and a grain offering and offered them on a rock to the LORD, and He did a wonderful thing while Manoah and his wife were watching. ²⁰ When the flame went up from the altar to the sky, the Angel of the LORD went up in its flame. When Manoah and his wife saw this, they fell facedown on the ground. ²¹ The Angel of the LORD did not appear again to Manoah and his wife. Then Manoah realized that it was the Angel of the LORD.

²² "We're going to die," he said to his wife, "because we have seen God!"

²³ But his wife said to him, "If the LORD had intended to kill us, He wouldn't have accepted the burnt offering and the grain offering from us, and

He would not have shown us all these things or spoken to us now like this."

²⁴ So the woman gave birth to a son and named him Samson. The boy grew, and the LORD blessed him. ²⁵ Then the Spirit of the LORD began to direct him in the Camp of Dan, between Zorah and Eshtaol.

14 Samson went down to Timnah and saw a young Philistine woman there. ² He went back and told his father and his mother: "I have seen a young Philistine woman in Timnah. Now get her for me as a wife."

³ But his father and mother said to him, "Can't you find a young woman among your relatives or among any of our people? Must you go to the uncircumcised Philistines for a wife?"

But Samson told his father, "Get her for me, because I want her." ⁴ Now his father and mother did not know this was from the LORD, who was seeking an occasion against the Philistines. At that time, the Philistines were ruling over Israel.

⁵ Samson went down to Timnah with his father and mother and came to the vineyards of Timnah. Suddenly a young lion came roaring at him, ⁶ the Spirit of the LORD took control of him, and he tore the lion apart with his bare hands as he might have torn a young goat. But he did not tell his father or mother what he had done. ⁷ Then he went and spoke to the woman, because Samson wanted her.

⁸ After some time, when he returned to get her, he left the road to see the lion's carcass, and there was a swarm of bees with honey in the carcass. ⁹ He scooped some honey into his hands and ate it as he went along. When he returned to his father and mother, he gave some to them and they ate it. But he did not tell them that he had scooped the honey from the lion's carcass.

¹⁰ His father went to visit the woman, and Samson prepared a feast there, as young men were accustomed to do. ¹¹ When the Philistines saw him, they brought 30 men to accompany him.

¹² "Let me tell you a riddle," Samson said to them. "If you can explain it to me during the seven days of the feast and figure it out, I will give you 30 linen garments and 30 changes of clothes. ¹³ But if you can't explain it to me, you must give me 30 linen garments and 30 changes of clothes."

"Tell us your riddle," they replied. "Let's hear it."

¹⁴ So he said to them:

Out of the eater came something
    to eat,
and out of the strong came
    something sweet.

After three days, they were unable to explain the riddle. ¹⁵ On the fourth day they said to Samson's wife, "Persuade your husband to explain the riddle to us, or we will burn you and your father's household to death. Did you invite us here to rob us?"

¹⁶ So Samson's wife came to him, weeping, and said, "You hate me and don't love me! You told my people the riddle, but haven't explained it to me."

"Look," he said, "I haven't even explained it to my father or mother, so why should I explain it to you?"

¹⁷ She wept the whole seven days of the feast, and at last, on the seventh day, he explained it to her, because she had nagged him so much. Then she explained it to her people. ¹⁸ On the seventh day before sunset, the men of the city said to him:

What is sweeter than honey?
What is stronger than a lion?

So he said to them:

If you hadn't plowed with
    my young cow,
you wouldn't know
    my riddle now!

¹⁹ The Spirit of the LORD took control of him, and he went down to Ashkelon and killed 30 of their men. He stripped them and gave their clothes to those who had explained the riddle. In a rage,

Samson returned to his father's house, ²⁰ and his wife was given to one of the men who had accompanied him.

15 Later on, during the wheat harvest, Samson took a young goat as a gift and visited his wife. "I want to go to my wife in her room," he said. But her father would not let him enter.

² "I was sure you hated her," her father said, "so I gave her to one of the men who accompanied you. Isn't her younger sister more beautiful than she is? Why not take her instead?"

³ Samson said to them, "This time I won't be responsible when I harm the Philistines." ⁴ So he went out and caught 300 foxes. He took torches, turned the foxes tail-to-tail, and put a torch between each pair of tails. ⁵ Then he ignited the torches and released the foxes into the standing grain of the Philistines. He burned up the piles of grain and the standing grain as well as the vineyards and olive groves.

⁶ Then the Philistines asked, "Who did this?"

They were told, "It was Samson, the Timnite's son-in-law, because he has taken Samson's wife and given her to another man." So the Philistines went to her and her father and burned them to death.

⁷ Then Samson told them, "Because you did this, I swear that I won't rest until I have taken vengeance on you." ⁸ He tore them limb from limb with a great slaughter, and he went down and stayed in the cave at the rock of Etam.

PSALM 57:7-11

⁷ My heart is confident, God, my heart is confident.
I will sing; I will sing praises.
⁸ Wake up, my soul!
Wake up, harp and lyre!
I will wake up the dawn.
⁹ I will praise You, Lord, among the peoples;
I will sing praises to You among the nations.

¹⁰ For Your faithful love is as high as the heavens;
Your faithfulness reaches to the clouds.
¹¹ God, be exalted above the heavens;
let Your glory be over the whole earth.

PROVERBS 13:7-8

⁷ One man pretends to be rich but has nothing;
another pretends to be poor but has great wealth.

⁸ Riches are a ransom for a man's life,
but a poor man hears no threat.

LUKE 23:1-19

23 Then their whole assembly rose up and brought Him before Pilate. ² They began to accuse Him, saying, "We found this man subverting our nation, opposing payment of taxes to Caesar, and saying that He Himself is the Messiah, a King."

³ So Pilate asked Him, "Are You the King of the Jews?"

He answered him, "You have said it."

⁴ Pilate then told the chief priests and the crowds, "I find no grounds for charging this man."

⁵ But they kept insisting, "He stirs up the people, teaching throughout all Judea, from Galilee where He started even to here."

⁶ When Pilate heard this, he asked if the man was a Galilean. ⁷ Finding that He was under Herod's jurisdiction, he sent Him to Herod, who was also in Jerusalem during those days. ⁸ Herod was very glad to see Jesus; for a long time he had wanted to see Him, because he had heard about Him and was hoping to see some miracle performed by Him. ⁹ So he kept asking Him questions, but Jesus did not answer him. ¹⁰ The chief priests and the scribes stood by, vehemently accusing Him. ¹¹ Then Herod, with his soldiers, treated Him

with contempt, mocked Him, dressed Him in a brilliant robe, and sent Him back to Pilate. ¹²That very day Herod and Pilate became friends. Previously, they had been hostile toward each other.
¹³Pilate called together the chief priests, the leaders, and the people, ¹⁴and said to them, "You have brought me this man as one who subverts the people. But in fact, after examining Him in your presence, I have found no grounds to charge this man with those things you accuse Him of. ¹⁵Neither has Herod, because he sent Him back to us. Clearly, He has done nothing to deserve death. ¹⁶Therefore I will have Him whipped and then release Him." [¹⁷For according to the festival he had to release someone to them.]
¹⁸Then they all cried out together, "Take this man away! Release Barabbas to us!" ¹⁹(He had been thrown into prison for a rebellion that had taken place in the city, and for murder.)

The High-Water Mark

For Your faithful love is as high as the heavens; Your faithfulness reaches to the clouds.—PSALM 57:10

Let us consider an important aspect of God's nature and character—love. There are at least three things that are told us in Scripture concerning the nature of God.

First, "God is spirit" (Jn 4:24), which means He has no visible substance.

Second, "God is light" (1 Jn 1:5), which means no darkness can dwell in Him. In Scripture darkness stands for sin, death, and so on.

Third, "God is love" (1 Jn 4:16), which means that the energy which flows out from His being is that of infinite, eternal beneficence.

When John wrote the words "God is love," it was no slick statement, since it was the first time in history that the phrase had been used in that way. People had believed God was love and had speculated about His benevolence, but now the categorical statement was laid down for all to behold. These words, in my judgment, are the high-water mark of divine revelation; nothing more needs to be said, for nothing greater can be said.

I often create a mental picture for myself of the angels peering over the battlements of heaven as John wrote these words. And then, when they had been written down, I imagine them breaking into rapturous applause and saying to each other: "They've got it. They've got it! At last they see that God is love." A sigh of deep satisfaction and great joy would have filled the portals of heaven in the knowledge that the greatest truth about God was now finally made crystal clear. The implied was now inscribed.

Prayer

Father, I am so thankful that You have demonstrated categorically that the greatest thing about You is love. My heart gladly rests upon that glorious fact. I look forward to exploring it forever. In Jesus' name. Amen.

Further Study

Jr 31:1-4; Jn 3:16; Rm 5:8
What did the Lord appear and say?
How did He demonstrate this?

MAY 10

JUDGES 15:9–17:13

⁹ The Philistines went up, camped in Judah, and raided Lehi. ¹⁰ So the men of Judah said, "Why have you attacked us?"

They replied, "We have come to arrest Samson and pay him back for what he did to us."

¹¹ Then 3,000 men of Judah went to the cave at the rock of Etam, and they asked Samson, "Don't you realize that the Philistines rule over us? What have you done to us?"

"I have done to them what they did to me," he answered.

¹² They said to him, "We've come to arrest you and hand you over to the Philistines."

Then Samson told them, "Swear to me that you yourselves won't kill me."

¹³ "No," they said, "we won't kill you, but we will tie you up securely and hand you over to them." So they tied him up with two new ropes and led him away from the rock.

¹⁴ When he came to Lehi, the Philistines came to meet him shouting. The Spirit of the LORD took control of him, and the ropes that were on his arms became like burnt flax and his bonds fell off his wrists. ¹⁵ He found a fresh jawbone of a donkey, reached out his hand, took it, and killed 1,000 men with it. ¹⁶ Then Samson said:

With the jawbone of a donkey
I have piled them in a heap.
With the jawbone of a donkey
I have killed 1,000 men.

¹⁷ When he finished speaking, he threw away the jawbone and named that place Ramath-lehi. ¹⁸ He became very thirsty and called out to the LORD: "You have accomplished this great victory through Your servant. Must I now die of thirst and fall into the hands of the uncircumcised?" ¹⁹ So God split a hollow place in the ground at Lehi, and water came out of it. After Samson drank, his strength returned, and he revived. That is why he named it En-hakkore, which is in Lehi to this day. ²⁰ And he judged Israel 20 years in the days of the Philistines.

16 Samson went to Gaza, where he saw a prostitute and went to bed with her. ² When the Gazites heard that Samson was there, they surrounded the place and waited in ambush for him all that night at the city gate. While they were waiting quietly, they said, "Let us wait until dawn; then we will kill him." ³ But Samson stayed in bed until midnight when he got up, took hold of the doors of the city gate along with the two gateposts, and pulled them out, bar and all. He put them on his shoulders and took them to the top of the mountain overlooking Hebron.

⁴ Some time later, he fell in love with a woman named Delilah, who lived in

the Sorek Valley. ⁵ The Philistine leaders went to her and said, "Persuade him to tell you where his great strength comes from, so we can overpower him, tie him up, and make him helpless. Each of us will then give you 1,100 pieces of silver."

⁶ So Delilah said to Samson, "Please tell me, where does your great strength come from? How could someone tie you up and make you helpless?"

⁷ Samson told her, "If they tie me up with seven fresh bowstrings that have not been dried, I will become weak and be like any other man."

⁸ The Philistine leaders brought her seven fresh bowstrings that had not been dried, and she tied him up with them. ⁹ While the men in ambush were waiting in her room, she called out to him, "Samson, the Philistines are here!" But he snapped the bowstrings as a strand of yarn snaps when it touches fire. The secret of his strength remained unknown.

¹⁰ Then Delilah said to Samson, "You have mocked me and told me lies! Won't you please tell me how you can be tied up?"

¹¹ He told her, "If they tie me up with new ropes that have never been used, I will become weak and be like any other man."

¹² Delilah took new ropes, tied him up with them, and shouted, "Samson, the Philistines are here!" But while the men in ambush were waiting in her room, he snapped the ropes off his arms like a thread.

¹³ Then Delilah said to Samson, "You have mocked me all along and told me lies! Tell me how you can be tied up."

He told her, "If you weave the seven braids on my head with the web of a loom—"

¹⁴ She fastened the braids with a pin and called to him, "Samson, the Philistines are here!" He awoke from his sleep and pulled out the pin, with the loom and the web.

¹⁵ "How can you say, 'I love you,'" she told him, "when your heart is not with me? This is the third time you have mocked me and not told me what makes your strength so great!"

¹⁶ Because she nagged him day after day and pled with him until she wore him out, ¹⁷ he told her the whole truth and said to her, "My hair has never been cut, because I am a Nazirite to God from birth. If I am shaved, my strength will leave me, and I will become weak and be like any other man."

¹⁸ When Delilah realized that he had told her the whole truth, she sent this message to the Philistine leaders: "Come one more time, for he has told me the whole truth." The Philistine leaders came to her and brought the money with them.

¹⁹ Then she let him fall asleep on her lap and called a man to shave off the seven braids on his head. In this way, she rendered him helpless, and his strength left him. ²⁰ Then she cried, "Samson, the Philistines are here!" When he awoke from his sleep, he said, "I will escape as I did before and shake myself free." But he did not know that the LORD had left him.

²¹ The Philistines seized him and gouged out his eyes. They brought him down to Gaza and bound him with bronze shackles, and he was forced to grind grain in the prison. ²² But his hair began to grow back after it had been shaved.

²³ Now the Philistine leaders gathered together to offer a great sacrifice to their god Dagon. They rejoiced and said:

Our god has handed over
our enemy Samson to us.

²⁴ When the people saw him, they praised their god and said:

Our god has handed over to us
our enemy who destroyed
our land
and who multiplied our dead.

²⁵ When they were drunk, they said, "Bring Samson here to entertain us." So they brought Samson from prison, and he entertained them. They had him stand between the pillars.

²⁶ Samson said to the young man who was leading him by the hand, "Lead me

where I can feel the pillars supporting the temple, so I can lean against them." ²⁷ The temple was full of men and women; all the leaders of the Philistines were there, and about 3,000 men and women were on the roof watching Samson entertain them. ²⁸ He called out to the LORD: "Lord GOD, please remember me. Strengthen me, God, just once more. With one act of vengeance, let me pay back the Philistines for my two eyes." ²⁹ Samson took hold of the two middle pillars supporting the temple and leaned against them, one on his right hand and the other on his left. ³⁰ Samson said, "Let me die with the Philistines." He pushed with all his might, and the temple fell on the leaders and all the people in it. And the dead he killed at his death were more than those he had killed in his life.

³¹ Then his brothers and his father's family came down, carried him back, and buried him between Zorah and Eshtaol in the tomb of his father Manoah. So he judged Israel 20 years.

17 There was a man from the hill country of Ephraim named Micah. ² He said to his mother, "The 1,100 pieces of silver taken from you, and that I heard you utter a curse about—here, I have the silver with me. I took it. So now I return it to you."

Then his mother said, "My son, you are blessed by the LORD!"

³ He returned the 1,100 pieces of silver to his mother, and his mother said, "I personally consecrate the silver to the LORD for my son's benefit to make a carved image overlaid with silver." ⁴ So he returned the silver to his mother, and she took five pounds of silver and gave it to a silversmith. He made it into a carved image overlaid with silver, and it was in Micah's house.

⁵ This man Micah had a shrine, and he made an ephod and household idols, and installed one of his sons to be his priest. ⁶ In those days there was no king in Israel; everyone did whatever he wanted.

⁷ There was a young man, a Levite, from Bethlehem in Judah, who resided within the clan of Judah. ⁸ The man left the town of Bethlehem in Judah to settle wherever he could find a place. On his way he came to Micah's home in the hill country of Ephraim.

⁹ "Where do you come from?" Micah asked him.

He answered him, "I am a Levite from Bethlehem in Judah, and I'm going to settle wherever I can find a place."

¹⁰ Micah replied, "Stay with me and be my father and priest, and I will give you four ounces of silver a year, along with your clothing and provisions." So the Levite went in ¹¹ and agreed to stay with the man, and the young man became like one of his sons. ¹² Micah consecrated the Levite, and the young man became his priest and lived in Micah's house. ¹³ Then Micah said, "Now I know that the LORD will be good to me, because a Levite has become my priest."

℘SALM 58:1-5

¹ Do you really speak righteously,
   you mighty ones?
   Do you judge people fairly?
² No, you practice injustice in your
   hearts;
   with your hands you weigh out
   violence in the land.

³ The wicked go astray from the
   womb;
   liars err from birth.
⁴ They have venom like the venom
   of a snake,
   like the deaf cobra that stops up
   its ears,
⁵ that does not listen to the sound
   of the charmers
   who skillfully weave spells.

℘ROVERBS 13:9-10

⁹ The light of the righteous shines
   brightly,
   but the lamp of the wicked is
   extinguished.
¹⁰ Arrogance leads to nothing but
   strife,

but wisdom is gained by those who take advice.

ＬUKE 23:20-38

²⁰ Pilate, wanting to release Jesus, addressed them again, ²¹ but they kept shouting, "Crucify! Crucify Him!" ²² A third time he said to them, "Why? What has this man done wrong? I have found in Him no grounds for the death penalty. Therefore I will have Him whipped and then release Him." ²³ But they kept up the pressure, demanding with loud voices that He be crucified. And their voices won out. ²⁴ So Pilate decided to grant their demand ²⁵ and released the one they were asking for, who had been thrown into prison for rebellion and murder. But he handed Jesus over to their will.

²⁶ As they led Him away, they seized Simon, a Cyrenian, who was coming in from the country, and laid the cross on him to carry behind Jesus. ²⁷ A great multitude of the people followed Him, including women who were mourning and lamenting Him. ²⁸ But turning to them, Jesus said, "Daughters of Jerusalem, do not weep for Me, but weep for yourselves and your children. ²⁹ Look,

the days are coming when they will say, 'Blessed are the barren, the wombs that never bore, and the breasts that never nursed!' ³⁰ Then they will begin to say to the mountains, 'Fall on us!' and to the hills, 'Cover us!' ³¹ For if they do these things when the wood is green, what will happen when it is dry?"

³² Two others—criminals—were also led away to be executed with Him. ³³ When they arrived at the place called The Skull, they crucified Him there, along with the criminals, one on the right and one on the left. [³⁴ Then Jesus said, "Father, forgive them, because they do not know what they are doing."] And they divided His clothes and cast lots.

³⁵ The people stood watching, and even the leaders kept scoffing: "He saved others; let Him save Himself if this is God's Messiah, the Chosen One!" ³⁶ The soldiers also mocked Him. They came offering Him sour wine ³⁷ and said, "If You are the King of the Jews, save Yourself!"

³⁸ An inscription was above Him:

> THIS IS
> THE KING OF THE JEWS

The Divine Example

Jesus said, "Father, forgive them,
because they do not know what they are doing."

—LUKE 23:34

We can only ask God to forgive us our sins when we are willing to forgive those who have sinned against us.

Does this mean that before we can be converted to Christ and have our sins forgiven, we have to search our hearts in order to make sure that we hold no bitterness or resentment against anyone? No. There is nothing in the Scripture that states that a non-Christian receives forgiveness from God on the basis of claiming to forgive everyone else. Jesus is referring here, so I believe, to those who are already His followers. They have been forgiven for their sins, but they now need a principle by which they can deal with guilt that arises, subsequent to conversion, through the violation of some biblical standard. Paul says in Ephesians 1:7: "In Him we have redemption through His blood, the forgiveness of our trespasses, according to the riches of His grace." Grace—that's the basis of our forgiveness when we first come to Christ. But although we have received that forgiveness, we can never enjoy freedom from defilement in our Christian walk unless we are ready to extend the forgiveness God has given us to those who have hurt us.

This is an extremely important issue, for if we fail to forgive those who have offended us, we break the bridge over which God's forgiveness flows into us.

Prayer

Blessed Lord Jesus, You who hung upon a cross, tortured in every nerve, yet prayed, "Father, forgive them," help me this day to forgive all those who have wronged me in a lesser way. For Your own dear name's sake. Amen.

Further Study

Lk 17:1-10; Mk 11:25; Col 3:13; Eph 4:32
What did Jesus teach on forgiveness?
What was the disciples' response?

MAY 11

JUDGES 18:1-31

18 In those days, there was no king in Israel, and the Danite tribe was looking for territory to occupy. Up to that time no territory had been captured by them among the tribes of Israel. ² So the Danites sent out five brave men from all their clans, from Zorah and Eshtaol, to spy out the land and explore it. They told them, "Go and explore the land."

They came to the hill country of Ephraim as far as the home of Micah and spent the night there. ³ While they were near Micah's home, they recognized the speech of the young Levite. So they went over to him and asked,

"Who brought you here? What are you doing in this place? What is keeping you here?" ⁴ He told them what Micah had done for him and that he had hired him as his priest.

⁵ Then they said to him, "Please inquire of God so we will know if we will have a successful journey."

⁶ The priest told them, "Go in peace. The LORD is watching over the journey you are going on."

⁷ The five men left and came to Laish. They saw that the people who were there were living securely, in the same way as the Sidonians, quiet and unsuspecting. There was nothing lacking in the land and no oppressive ruler. They were far from the Sidonians, having no alliance with anyone.

⁸ When the men went back to their clans at Zorah and Eshtaol, their people asked them, "What did you find out?" ⁹ They answered, "Come on, let's go up against them, for we have seen the land, and it is very good. Why wait? Don't hesitate to go and invade and take possession of the land! ¹⁰ When you get there, you will come to an unsuspecting people and a wide-open land, for God has handed it over to you. It is a place where nothing on earth is lacking." ¹¹ Six hundred Danites departed from Zorah and Eshtaol armed with weapons of war. ¹² They went up and camped at Kiriath-jearim in Judah. This is why the place is called the Camp of Dan to this day; it is west of Kiriath-jearim. ¹³ From there they traveled to the hill country of Ephraim and arrived at Micah's house.

¹⁴ The five men who had gone to spy out the land of Laish told their brothers, "Did you know that there are an ephod, household gods, and a carved image overlaid with silver in these houses? Now think about what you should do." ¹⁵ So they detoured there and went to the house of the young Levite at the home of Micah and greeted him. ¹⁶ The 600 Danite men were standing by the entrance of the gate, armed with their weapons of war. ¹⁷ Then the five men who had gone to spy out the land went in and took the carved image overlaid with silver, the ephod, and the household idols, while the priest was standing by the entrance of the gate with the 600 men armed with weapons of war.

¹⁸ When they entered Micah's house and took the carved image overlaid with silver, the ephod, and the household idols, the priest said to them, "What are you doing?"

¹⁹ They told him, "Be quiet. Keep your mouth shut. Come with us and be a father and a priest to us. Is it better for you to be a priest for the house of one person or for you to be a priest for a tribe and family in Israel?" ²⁰ So the priest was pleased and took his ephod, household idols, and carved image, and went with the people. ²¹ They prepared to leave, putting their small children, livestock, and possessions in front of them.

²² After they were some distance from Micah's house, the men who were in the houses near it mobilized and caught up with the Danites. ²³ They called to the Danites, who turned to face them, and said to Micah, "What's the matter with you that you mobilized the men?"

²⁴ He said, "You took the gods I had made and the priest, and went away. What do I have left? How can you say to me, 'What's the matter with you?' "

²⁵ The Danites said to him, "Don't raise your voice against us, or angry men will attack you, and you and your family will lose your lives." ²⁶ The Danites went on their way, and Micah turned to go back home, because he saw that they were stronger than he was.

²⁷ After they had taken the gods Micah had made and the priest that belonged to him, they went to Laish, to a quiet and unsuspecting people. They killed them with their swords and burned down the city. ²⁸ There was no one to save them, because it was far from Sidon and they had no alliance with anyone. It was in a valley that belonged to Beth-rehob. They rebuilt the city and lived in it. ²⁹ They named the city Dan, after the name of their ancestor Dan, who was born to Israel. The city was formerly named Laish.

³⁰ The Danites set up the carved image for themselves. Jonathan son of Gershom, son of Moses, and his sons were priests for the Danite tribe until the time of the exile from the land. ³¹ So they set up for themselves Micah's carved image that he had made, and it was there as long as the house of God was in Shiloh.

PSALM 58:6-11

⁶ God, knock the teeth out of their
  mouths;
  Lord, tear out the young lions'
  fangs.
⁷ They will vanish like water that
  flows by;
  they will aim their useless arrows.
⁸ Like a slug that moves along in
  slime,

like a woman's miscarried child,
they will not see the sun.

⁹ Before your pots can feel the heat
of the thorns—
whether green or burning—He
will sweep them away.

¹⁰ The righteous will rejoice when
he sees the retribution;
he will wash his feet in the blood
of the wicked.

¹¹ Then people will say, "Yes, there
is a reward for the righteous!
There is a God who judges on
earth!"

PROVERBS 13:11-12

¹¹ Wealth obtained by fraud will
dwindle,
but whoever earns it through
labor will multiply it.

¹² Delayed hope makes the heart
sick,
but fulfilled desire is a tree of life.

LUKE 23:39-56

³⁹ Then one of the criminals hanging
there began to yell insults at Him:
"Aren't You the Messiah? Save Yourself
and us!"
⁴⁰ But the other answered, rebuking
him: "Don't you even fear God, since
you are undergoing the same punishment? ⁴¹ We are punished justly, because we're getting back what we
deserve for the things we did, but this
man has done nothing wrong." ⁴² Then

he said, "Jesus, remember me when You
come into Your kingdom!"
⁴³ And He said to him, "I assure you:
Today you will be with Me in paradise."
⁴⁴ It was now about noon, and darkness came over the whole land until
three, ⁴⁵ because the sun's light failed.
The curtain of the sanctuary was split
down the middle. ⁴⁶ And Jesus called
out with a loud voice, "Father, **into Your
hands I entrust My spirit.**" Saying this,
He breathed His last.
⁴⁷ When the centurion saw what happened, he began to glorify God, saying,
"This man really was righteous!" ⁴⁸ All
the crowds that had gathered for this
spectacle, when they saw what had
taken place, went home, striking their
chests. ⁴⁹ But all who knew Him, including the women who had followed Him
from Galilee, stood at a distance, watching these things.
⁵⁰ There was a good and righteous
man named Joseph, a member of the
Sanhedrin, ⁵¹ who had not agreed with
their plan and action. He was from Arimathea, a Judean town, and was looking
forward to the kingdom of God. ⁵² He
approached Pilate and asked for Jesus'
body. ⁵³ Taking it down, he wrapped it in
fine linen and placed it in a tomb cut
into the rock, where no one had ever
been placed. ⁵⁴ It was preparation day,
and the Sabbath was about to begin.
⁵⁵ The women who had come with Him
from Galilee followed along and observed the tomb and how His body was
placed. ⁵⁶ Then they returned and prepared spices and perfumes. And they
rested on the Sabbath according to the
commandment.

The Patience of God

*The righteous will rejoice when he sees the retribution. . . .
Then people will say, "Yes, there is a reward for the righteous!
There is a God who judges on earth!"* —PSALM 58:10-11

Ever found yourself feeling frustrated because of the way in which wickedness seems to win
over justice? Then you know something of how Solomon felt when he said, "God will judge the

righteous and the wicked" (Ec 3:17). Every generation, throughout time, has had to face this problem. James Russell Lowell put it this way:

Truth forever on the scaffold,
Wrong forever on the throne.

Solomon struggles, as no doubt you have done (and perhaps still do), with the fact that in the very place where you would expect to see justice, you find wickedness and corruption prevailing. In the days when I was a pastor, I sometimes went to court with people who had a genuine case to be heard, only to see it broken down by tactics that were dishonest and unjust. I have seen enough injustice in my time to share something of Solomon's cynicism.

Are you at this moment a victim of judicial injustice? Then don't allow yourself to become cynical, for, as Solomon said: "God will judge the righteous and the wicked." Wrong will not continue forever. The day is coming when all corruption and injustice will be called to judgment before the throne of God's truth. But of course, being human, we wish the injustices we have received could be put right—now. God seems to be much more patient than we are, and what we must do is to ask for grace to be patient with the patience of God.

Prayer

O God my Father, give me the divine perspective on things so that present injustices may be swallowed up in the long-term purposes. Help me see that I will have my day in court—Your court. In Jesus' name I ask it. Amen.

Further Study

Ps 58:1-11; Gn 18:25; Ps 96:13
What was the view of the psalmist?
How does God judge?

MAY 12

JUDGES 19:1–20:25

19 In those days, when there was no king in Israel, a Levite living in a remote part of the hill country of Ephraim acquired a woman from Bethlehem in Judah as his concubine. ² But she was unfaithful to him and left him for her father's house in Bethlehem in Judah. She was there for a period of four months. ³ Then her husband got up and went after her to speak kindly to her and bring her back. His servant and a couple of donkeys were with him. So she brought him to her father's house, and when the girl's father saw him, he gladly welcomed him. ⁴ His father-in-law, the girl's father, detained him, and he stayed with him for three days. They ate, drank, and spent the nights there.

⁵ On the fourth day, they got up early in the morning and prepared to go, but the girl's father said to his son-in-law, "Have something to eat to keep up your strength and then you can go." ⁶ So they sat down and the two of them ate and drank together. Then the girl's father said to the man, "Please agree to stay overnight and enjoy yourself." ⁷ The man got up to go, but his father-in-law persuaded him, so he stayed and spent the night there again. ⁸ He got up early in the morning of the fifth day to leave, but the girl's father said to him, "Please keep up your strength." So they waited until late afternoon and the two of them ate. ⁹ The man got up to go with his concubine and his servant, when his father-in-law, the girl's father, said to him, "Look, night is coming. Please spend the night. See, the day is almost over. Spend the night here, enjoy yourself, then you can get up early tomorrow for your journey and go home."

¹⁰ But the man was unwilling to spend the night. He got up, departed, and arrived opposite Jebus (that is, Jerusalem). The man had his two saddled donkeys and his concubine with him. ¹¹ When they were near Jebus and the day was almost gone, the servant said to his master, "Please, why not let us stop at this Jebusite city and spend the night here?"

¹² But his master replied to him, "We will not stop at a foreign city where there are no Israelites. Let's move on to Gibeah." ¹³ "Come on," he said, "let's try to reach one of these places and spend the night in Gibeah or Ramah." ¹⁴ So they continued on their journey, and the sun set as they neared Gibeah in Benjamin. ¹⁵ They stopped to go in and spend the night in Gibeah. The Levite went in and sat down in the city square, but no one took them into their home to spend the night.

¹⁶ In the evening, an old man came in from his work in the field. He was from the hill country of Ephraim but was residing in Gibeah, and the men of that place were Benjaminites. ¹⁷ When he

looked up and saw the traveler in the city square, the old man asked, "Where are you going, and where do you come from?"

¹⁸ He answered him, "We're traveling from Bethlehem in Judah to the remote hill country of Ephraim, where I am from. I went to Bethlehem in Judah, and now I'm going to the house of the LORD. No one has taken me into his home, ¹⁹ although we have both straw and feed for our donkeys, and bread and wine for me, your female servant, and the young man with your servant. There is nothing we lack."

²⁰ "Peace to you," said the old man. "I'll take care of everything you need. Only don't spend the night in the square." ²¹ So he brought him to his house and fed the donkeys. Then they washed their feet and ate and drank. ²² While they were enjoying themselves, all of a sudden, perverted men of the city surrounded the house and beat on the door. They said to the old man who was the owner of the house, "Bring out the man who came to your house so we can have sex with him!"

²³ The owner of the house went out and said to them, "No, don't do this evil, my brothers. After all, this man has come into my house. Don't do this horrible thing. ²⁴ Here, let me bring out my virgin daughter and the man's concubine now. Use them and do whatever you want to them. But don't do this horrible thing to this man."

²⁵ But the men would not listen to him, so the man seized his concubine and took her outside to them. They raped her and abused her all night until morning. At daybreak they let her go. ²⁶ Early that morning, the woman made her way back, and as it was getting light, she collapsed at the doorway of the man's house where her master was.

²⁷ When her master got up in the morning, opened the doors of the house, and went out to leave on his journey, there was the woman, his concubine, collapsed near the doorway of the house with her hands on the threshold. ²⁸ "Get up," he told her. "Let's go." But there was no response. So the man put

her on his donkey and set out for home. ²⁹When he entered his house, he picked up a knife, took hold of his concubine, cut her into 12 pieces, limb by limb, and sent her throughout the territory of Israel. ³⁰Everyone who saw it said, "Nothing like this has ever happened or been seen since the day the Israelites came out of the land of Egypt to this day. Think it over, discuss it, and speak up!"

20 All the Israelites from Dan to Beer-sheba and from the land of Gilead came out, and the community assembled as one body before the LORD at Mizpah. ²The leaders of all the people and of all the tribes of Israel presented themselves in the assembly of God's people: 400,000 armed foot soldiers. ³The Benjaminites heard that the Israelites had gone up to Mizpah.

The Israelites asked, "Tell us, how did this outrage occur?"

⁴The Levite, the husband of the murdered woman, answered: "I went to Gibeah in Benjamin with my concubine to spend the night. ⁵Citizens of Gibeah ganged up on me and surrounded the house at night. They intended to kill me, but they raped my concubine, and she died. ⁶Then I took my concubine and cut her in pieces, and sent her throughout Israel's territory, because they committed a horrible shame in Israel. ⁷Look, all of you are Israelites. Give your judgment and verdict here and now."

⁸Then all the people stood united and said, "None of us will go to his tent or return to his house. ⁹Now this is what we will do to Gibeah: we will go against it by lot. ¹⁰We will take 10 men out of every 100 from all the tribes of Israel, and 100 out of every 1,000, and 1,000 out of every 10,000 to get provisions for the people when they go to Gibeah in Benjamin to punish them for all the horror they did in Israel."

¹¹So all the men of Israel gathered united against the city. ¹²Then the tribes of Israel sent men throughout the tribe of Benjamin, saying, "What is this outrage that has occurred among you?

¹³Hand over the perverted men in Gibeah so we can put them to death and eradicate evil from Israel." But the Benjaminites would not obey their fellow Israelites. ¹⁴Instead, the Benjaminites gathered together from their cities to Gibeah to go out and fight against the Israelites. ¹⁵On that day the Benjaminites rallied 26,000 armed men from their cities, besides 700 choice men rallied by the inhabitants of Gibeah. ¹⁶There were 700 choice men who were left-handed among all these people; all could sling a stone at a hair and not miss.

¹⁷The Israelites, apart from Benjamin, rallied 400,000 armed men, every one an experienced warrior. ¹⁸They set out, went to Bethel, and inquired of God. The Israelites asked, "Who is to go first to fight for us against the Benjaminites?"

And the LORD answered, "Judah will be first."

¹⁹In the morning, the Israelites set out and camped near Gibeah. ²⁰The men of Israel went out to fight against Benjamin and took their battle positions against Gibeah. ²¹The Benjaminites came out of Gibeah and slaughtered 22,000 men of Israel on the field that day. ²²But the Israelite army rallied and again took their battle positions in the same place where they positioned themselves on the first day. ²³They went up, wept before the LORD until evening, and inquired of Him: "Should we again fight against our brothers the Benjaminites?"

And the LORD answered: "Fight against them."

²⁴On the second day the Israelites advanced against the Benjaminites. ²⁵That same day the Benjaminites came out from Gibeah to meet them and slaughtered an additional 18,000 Israelites on the field; all were armed men.

*P*SALM 59:1-10

¹ Deliver me from my enemies, my God;

protect me from those who rise
up against me.
² Deliver me from those who
practice sin,
and save me from men of
bloodshed.
³ LORD, look! They set an ambush
for me.
Powerful men attack me,
but not because of any sin or
rebellion of mine.
⁴ For no fault of mine, they run and
take up a position.
Awake to help me, and take
notice.
⁵ You, LORD God of Hosts, God of
Israel,
rise up to punish all the nations;
do not show grace to any wicked
traitors.   *Selah*

⁶ They return at evening, snarling
like dogs
and prowling around the city.
⁷ Look, they spew from their
mouths—
sharp words from their lips.
"For who," they say, "will hear?"
⁸ But You laugh at them, LORD;
You ridicule all the nations.
⁹ I will keep watch for You, my
strength,
because God is my stronghold.
¹⁰ My faithful God will come to meet
me;
God will let me look down on my
adversaries.

PROVERBS 13:13

¹³ The one who has contempt for
instruction will pay the
penalty,
but the one who respects a
command will be rewarded.

LUKE 24:1-24

24 On the first day of the week,
very early in the morning, they
came to the tomb, bringing the spices
they had prepared. ² They found the
stone rolled away from the tomb. ³ They

went in but did not find the body of the
Lord Jesus. ⁴ While they were perplexed
about this, suddenly two men stood by
them in dazzling clothes. ⁵ So the
women were terrified and bowed down
to the ground.
"Why are you looking for the living
among the dead?" asked the men. ⁶ "He
is not here, but He has been resurrected! Remember how He spoke to you
when He was still in Galilee, ⁷ saying,
'The Son of Man must be betrayed into
the hands of sinful men, be crucified,
and rise on the third day'?" ⁸ And they
remembered His words.
⁹ Returning from the tomb, they reported all these things to the Eleven and
to all the rest. ¹⁰ Mary Magdalene,
Joanna, Mary the mother of James, and
the other women with them were
telling the apostles these things. ¹¹ But
these words seemed like nonsense to
them, and they did not believe the
women. ¹² Peter, however, got up and
ran to the tomb. When he stooped to
look in, he saw only the linen cloths. So
he went home, amazed at what had happened.
¹³ Now that same day two of them
were on their way to a village called
Emmaus, which was about seven miles
from Jerusalem. ¹⁴ Together they were
discussing everything that had taken
place. ¹⁵ And while they were discussing
and arguing, Jesus Himself came near
and began to walk along with them.
¹⁶ But they were prevented from recognizing Him. ¹⁷ Then He asked them,
"What is this dispute that you're having
with each other as you are walking?"
And they stopped walking and looked
discouraged.
¹⁸ The one named Cleopas answered
Him, "Are You the only visitor in
Jerusalem who doesn't know the things
that happened there in these days?"
¹⁹ "What things?" He asked them.
So they said to Him, "The things concerning Jesus the Nazarene, who was a
Prophet powerful in action and speech
before God and all the people, ²⁰ and
how our chief priests and leaders
handed Him over to be sentenced to
death, and they crucified Him. ²¹ But we

were hoping that He was the One who was about to redeem Israel. Besides all this, it's the third day since these things happened. [22] Moreover, some women from our group astounded us. They arrived early at the tomb, [23] and when they didn't find His body, they came and reported that they had seen a vision of angels who said He was alive. [24] Some of those who were with us went to the tomb and found it just as the women had said, but they didn't see Him."

Worship Is Central

*I will keep watch for You, my strength, because God is my stronghold.
My faithful God will come to meet me.*

—PSALM 59:9-10

If we are to go deeper with God, then we must understand both the importance and meaning of worship. Dr. Dick Averby, professor of the Old Testament at Dallas Seminary, claims that the antidote to every human problem is worship. I am sure he is thinking of personality problems, not physical problems, and allowing for this caveat, I would agree with him. Dr. Larry Crabb, professor of counseling at Colorado Christian University, says something similar: "Worship means, in the middle of life as it is experienced, that you find some way to be caught up in God's character and purpose so that His will becomes central."

Mature Christians are people who think of themselves first and foremost as worshipers. They will see their other roles in life—as fathers, mothers, factory workers, business people, farmers, doctors, evangelists, pastors, and so on—as secondary.

Some worship the servants of God more than they worship God Himself. A story is told of an occasion when Christmas Evans, the great Welsh preacher of a past century, was due to preach. Prior to the service the church was packed with people eager to hear the great orator. As the service was about to begin, it was announced that Christmas Evans was unable to keep the engagement and a lesser-known preacher would take his place. People began to show signs of leaving until the moderator said: "All those who have come to worship Christmas Evans may leave. All those who have come to worship God may stay." No one left.

Prayer

O God, my soul is too big to be satisfied with the writings of a mere man. I can be inspired by human words, but I can be fed only by Your words. May I continually seek You. Amen.

Further Study

Jn 6:25-58; Ps 132:7; Is 55:2; 1 Co 10:3-4
What did Jesus declare?
Why did the Jews stumble over it?

MAY 13

JUDGES 20:26–21:25

²⁶ The whole Israelite army went to Bethel where they wept and sat before the LORD. They fasted that day until evening and offered burnt offerings and fellowship offerings to the LORD. ²⁷ Then the Israelites inquired of the LORD. In those days, the ark of the covenant of God was there, ²⁸ and Phinehas son of Eleazar, son of Aaron, was serving before it. The Israelites asked: "Should we again fight against our brothers the Benjaminites or should we stop?"

The LORD answered: "Fight, because I will hand them over to you tomorrow." ²⁹ So Israel set up an ambush around Gibeah. ³⁰ On the third day the Israelites fought against the Benjaminites and took their battle positions against Gibeah as before. ³¹ Then the Benjaminites came out against the people and were drawn away from the city. They began to attack the people as before, killing about 30 men of Israel on the highways, one of which goes up to Bethel and the other to Gibeah through the open country. ³² The Benjaminites said, "We are defeating them as before."

But the Israelites said, "Let's flee and draw them away from the city to the highways." ³³ So all the men of Israel got up from their places and took their battle positions at Baal-tamar, while the Israelites in ambush charged out of their places west of Geba. ³⁴ Then 10,000 choice men from all Israel made a frontal assault against Gibeah, and the battle was fierce, but the Benjaminites did not know that disaster was about to strike them. ³⁵ The LORD defeated Benjamin in the presence of Israel, and on that day the Israelites slaughtered 25,100 men of Benjamin; all were armed men. ³⁶ Then the Benjaminites realized they had been defeated.

The men of Israel had retreated before Benjamin, because they were confident in the ambush they had set against Gibeah. ³⁷ The men in ambush had rushed quickly against Gibeah; they advanced and put the whole city to the sword. ³⁸ The men of Israel had a prearranged signal with the men in ambush: when they sent up a great cloud of smoke from the city, ³⁹ the men of Israel would return to the battle. When Benjamin had begun to strike them down, killing about 30 men of Israel, they said, "They're defeated before us, just as they were in the first battle." ⁴⁰ But when the column of smoke began to go up from the city, Benjamin looked behind them, and the whole city was going up in smoke. ⁴¹ Then the men of Israel returned, and the men of Benjamin were terrified when they realized that disaster had struck them. ⁴² They retreated before the men of Israel toward the wilderness, but the battle overtook them, and those who came out of the cities slaughtered those between them. ⁴³ They surrounded the Benjaminites, pursued them, and easily overtook them near Gibeah toward the east. ⁴⁴ There were 18,000 men who died from Benjamin; all were warriors. ⁴⁵ Then Benjamin turned and fled toward the wilderness to the rock of Rimmon, and Israel killed 5,000 men on the highways. They overtook them at Gidom and struck 2,000 more dead.

⁴⁶ All the Benjaminites who died that day were 25,000 armed men; all were warriors. ⁴⁷ But 600 men escaped into the wilderness to the rock of Rimmon and stayed there four months. ⁴⁸ The men of Israel turned back against the other Benjaminites and killed them with their swords—the entire city, the animals, and everything that remained. They also burned down all the cities that remained.

535

21 The men of Israel had sworn an oath at Mizpah: "None of us will give his daughter to a Benjaminite in marriage." ² So the people went to Bethel and sat there before God until evening. They wept loudly and bitterly, ³ and cried out, "Why, LORD God of Israel, has it occurred that one tribe is missing in Israel today?" ⁴ The next day the people got up early, built an altar there, and offered burnt offerings and fellowship offerings. ⁵ The Israelites asked, "Who of all the tribes of Israel didn't come to the LORD with the assembly?" For a great oath had been taken that anyone who had not come to the LORD at Mizpah would certainly be put to death.

⁶ But the Israelites had compassion on their brothers, the Benjaminites, and said, "Today a tribe has been cut off from Israel. ⁷ What should we do about wives for the survivors? We've sworn to the LORD not to give them any of our daughters as wives." ⁸ They asked, "Which city among the tribes of Israel didn't come to the LORD at Mizpah?" It turned out that no one from Jabesh-gilead had come to the camp and the assembly. ⁹ For when the people were counted, no one was there from the inhabitants of Jabesh-gilead.

¹⁰ The congregation sent 12,000 brave warriors there and commanded them: "Go and kill the inhabitants of Jabesh-gilead with the sword, including women and children. ¹¹ This is what you should do: Completely destroy every male, as well as every female who has slept with a man." ¹² They found among the inhabitants of Jabesh-gilead 400 young virgins, who had not had sexual relations with a man, and they brought them to the camp at Shiloh in the land of Canaan.

¹³ The whole congregation sent a message of peace to the Benjaminites who were at the rock of Rimmon. ¹⁴ Benjamin returned at that time, and Israel gave them the women they had kept alive from Jabesh-gilead. But there were not enough for them.

¹⁵ The people had compassion on Benjamin, because the LORD had made this gap in the tribes of Israel. ¹⁶ The elders of the congregation said, "What should we do about wives for those who are left, since the women of Benjamin have been destroyed?" ¹⁷ They said, "There must be heirs for the survivors of Benjamin, so that a tribe of Israel will not be wiped out. ¹⁸ But we can't give them our daughters as wives." For the Israelites had sworn: "Anyone who gives a wife to a Benjaminite is cursed." ¹⁹ They also said, "Look, there's an annual festival to the LORD in Shiloh, which is north of Bethel, east of the highway that goes up from Bethel to Shechem, and south of Lebonah."

²⁰ Then they commanded the Benjaminites: "Go and hide in the vineyards. ²¹ Watch, and when you see the young women of Shiloh come out to perform the dances, each of you leave the vineyards and catch a wife for yourself from the young women of Shiloh, and go to the land of Benjamin. ²² When their fathers or brothers come to us and protest, we will tell them, 'Show favor to them, since we did not get enough wives for each of them in the battle. You didn't actually give the women to them, so you are not guilty of breaking your oath.'"

²³ The Benjaminites did this and took the number of women they needed from the dancers they caught. They went back to their own inheritance, rebuilt their cities, and lived in them. ²⁴ At that time, each of the Israelites returned from there to his own tribe and family. Each returned from there to his own inheritance.

²⁵ In those days there was no king in Israel; everyone did whatever he wanted.

PSALM 59:11-17

¹¹ Do not kill them; otherwise, my
   people will forget.
By Your power, make them
   homeless wanderers and
   bring them down,
Lord, our shield.
¹² The sin of their mouths is the
   word of their lips,

so let them be caught in their
pride.
They utter curses and lies.
¹³ Consume them in rage;
consume them until they are
gone.
Then they will know to the ends
of the earth
that God rules over Jacob. *Selah*

¹⁴ And they return at evening,
snarling like dogs
and prowling around the city.
¹⁵ They scavenge for food;
they growl if they are not
satisfied.

¹⁶ But I will sing of Your strength
and will joyfully proclaim Your
faithful love in the morning.
For You have been a stronghold
for me,
a refuge in my day of trouble.
¹⁷ To You, my strength, I sing praises,
because God is my stronghold—
my faithful God.

PROVERBS 13:14-15

¹⁴ A wise man's instruction is a
fountain of life,
turning people away from the
snares of death.

¹⁵ Good sense wins favor,
but the way of the treacherous
never changes.

LUKE 24:25-53

²⁵ He said to them, "How unwise and
slow you are to believe in your hearts all
that the prophets have spoken! ²⁶ Didn't
the Messiah have to suffer these things
and enter into His glory?" ²⁷ Then beginning with Moses and all the Prophets, He interpreted for them the things
concerning Himself in all the Scriptures.
²⁸ They came near the village where
they were going, and He gave the impression that He was going farther.
²⁹ But they urged Him: "Stay with us,

because it's almost evening, and now
the day is almost over." So He went in
to stay with them.
³⁰ It was as He reclined at the table
with them that He took the bread,
blessed and broke it, and gave it to
them. ³¹ Then their eyes were opened,
and they recognized Him, but He disappeared from their sight. ³² So they
said to each other, "Weren't our hearts
ablaze within us while He was talking
with us on the road and explaining the
Scriptures to us?" ³³ That very hour they
got up and returned to Jerusalem. They
found the Eleven and those with them
gathered together, ³⁴ who said, "The
Lord has certainly been raised, and has
appeared to Simon!" ³⁵ Then they began
to describe what had happened on the
road and how He was made known to
them in the breaking of the bread.
³⁶ And as they were saying these
things, He Himself stood among them.
He said to them, "Peace to you!" ³⁷ But
they were startled and terrified and
thought they were seeing a ghost.
³⁸ "Why are you troubled?" He asked
them. "And why do doubts arise in your
hearts? ³⁹ Look at My hands and My
feet, that it is I Myself! Touch Me and
see, because a ghost does not have flesh
and bones as you can see I have."
⁴⁰ Having said this, He showed them His
hands and feet. ⁴¹ But while they still
could not believe because of their joy
and were amazed, He asked them, "Do
you have anything here to eat?" ⁴² So
they gave Him a piece of a broiled fish,
⁴³ and He took it and ate in their presence.
⁴⁴ Then He told them, "These are My
words that I spoke to you while I was
still with you—that everything written
about Me in the Law of Moses, the
Prophets, and the Psalms must be fulfilled." ⁴⁵ Then He opened their minds
to understand the Scriptures. ⁴⁶ He also
said to them, "This is what is written:
the Messiah would suffer and rise from
the dead the third day, ⁴⁷ and repentance for forgiveness of sins would be
proclaimed in His name to all the nations, beginning at Jerusalem. ⁴⁸ You are
witnesses of these things. ⁴⁹ And look, I

am sending you what My Father promised. As for you, stay in the city until
you are empowered from on high."
⁵⁰ Then He led them out as far as
Bethany, and lifting up His hands He
blessed them. ⁵¹ And while He was

blessing them, He left them and was
carried up into heaven. ⁵² After worshiping Him, they returned to Jerusalem with great joy. ⁵³ And they were
continually in the temple complex
blessing God.

"Too Good to Be True"

While they still could not believe because of their joy and were amazed,
He asked them, "Do you have anything here to eat?"
—LUKE 24:41

If we are to let nothing stand between us and the making of our feet into "hinds' feet," we
must understand the nature of disappointment and how it hinders our pursuit of God.

All of us have been disappointed. Living in a fallen world means we have been subjected to
experiences where we have been let down by others, even our loved ones at times. But this is
not the problem—the problem occurs when we allow the hurts of the past to prevent us from
reaching out to God and to others in an attitude of love.

A dramatic illustration of this is found in the passage before us today. It is the evening of the
day of the Resurrection, and, without warning, Jesus suddenly enters the room where His disciples are assembled and makes Himself known to them. How did they respond? "They were still
unconvinced, still wondering, for it seemed too good to be true" (v. 41, NEB). It was obvious
that the disappointment of Christ's crucifixion and death still reverberated within them. And
now, faced with the reality of the Resurrection, they did not want to believe it in case it was
not true—and they would be disappointed again.

They wanted to believe, but they had difficulty in doing so because they knew they could
not cope with what would happen in their hearts if it turned out to be untrue. Rather than take
the risk of faith, they preferred—for a little while at least—to withdraw into the safety of disappointment.

Prayer

God, forgive me that so often I allow the disappointments of life to deter me from moving
toward You—in case something might happen that would disappoint me again. Help me to
put everything I am and have in Your hands—with nothing held back. Amen.

Further Study

Lk 24:13-35; Jb 30:26
How did the disciples express their disappointment?
How did Jesus deal with them?

MAY 14

RUTH 1:1–2:23

1 During the time of the judges, there was a famine in the land. A man left Bethlehem in Judah with his wife and two sons to live in the land of Moab for a while. ² The man's name was Elimelech, and his wife's name was Naomi. The names of his two sons were Mahlon and Chilion. They were Ephrathites from Bethlehem in Judah. They entered the land of Moab and settled there. ³ Naomi's husband Elimelech died, and she was left with her two sons. ⁴ Her sons took Moabite women as their wives: one was named Orpah and the second was named Ruth. After they lived in Moab about 10 years, ⁵ both Mahlon and Chilion also died, and Naomi was left without her two children and without her husband.

⁶ She and her daughters-in-law prepared to leave the land of Moab, because she had heard in Moab that the Lord had paid attention to His people's need by providing them food. ⁷ She left the place where she had been living, accompanied by her two daughters-in-law, and traveled along the road leading back to the land of Judah.

⁸ She said to them, "Each of you go back to your mother's home. May the Lord show faithful love to you as you have shown to the dead and to me. ⁹ May the Lord enable each of you to find security in the house of your new husband." She kissed them, and they wept loudly.

¹⁰ "No," they said to her. "We will go with you to your people."

¹¹ But Naomi replied, "Return home, my daughters. Why do you want to go with me? Am I able to have any more sons who could become your husbands? ¹² Return home, my daughters. Go on, for I am too old to have another husband. Even if I thought there was still hope for me to have a husband tonight and to bear sons, ¹³ would you be willing to wait for them to grow up? Would you restrain yourselves from remarrying? No, my daughters, my life is much too bitter for you to share, because the Lord's hand has turned against me."

¹⁴ Again they wept loudly, and Orpah kissed her mother-in-law, but Ruth clung to her. ¹⁵ Naomi said, "Look, your sister-in-law has gone back to her people and to her god. Follow your sister-in-law."

¹⁶ But Ruth replied:

> Do not persuade me to leave you
> or go back and not follow you.
> For wherever you go, I will go,
> and wherever you live, I will live;
> your people will be my people,
> and your God will be my God.
> ¹⁷ Where you die, I will die,
> and there I will be buried.
> May the Lord do this to me,
> and even more,
> if anything but death
> separates you and me.

¹⁸ When Naomi saw that Ruth was determined to go with her, she stopped trying to persuade her.

¹⁹ The two of them traveled until they came to Bethlehem. When they entered Bethlehem, the whole town was excited about their arrival and the local women exclaimed, "Can this be Naomi?"

²⁰ "Don't call me Naomi. Call me Mara," she answered, "for the Almighty has made me very bitter. ²¹ I left full, but the Lord has brought me back empty. Why do you call me Naomi, since the Lord has pronounced judgment on me, and the Almighty has afflicted me?"

²² So Naomi came back from the land of Moab with her daughter-in-law Ruth the Moabitess. They arrived in Bethlehem at the beginning of the barley harvest.

2 Now Naomi had a relative on her husband's side named Boaz. He was a prominent man of noble character from Elimelech's family.

² Ruth the Moabitess asked Naomi, "Will you let me go into the fields and gather fallen grain behind someone who allows me to?"

Naomi answered her, "Go ahead, my daughter." ³ So Ruth left and entered the field to gather grain behind the harvesters. She happened to be in the portion of land belonging to Boaz, who was from Elimelech's family.

⁴ Later, when Boaz arrived from Bethlehem, he said to the harvesters, "The LORD be with you."

"The LORD bless you," they replied.

⁵ Boaz asked his servant who was in charge of the harvesters, "Whose young woman is this?"

⁶ The servant answered, "She is the young Moabite woman who returned with Naomi from the land of Moab. ⁷ She asked, 'Will you let me gather fallen grain among the bundles behind the harvesters?' She came and has remained from early morning until now, except that she rested a little in the shelter."

⁸ Then Boaz said to Ruth, "Listen, my daughter. Don't go and gather grain in another field, and don't leave this one, but stay here close to my young women. ⁹ See which field they are harvesting, and follow them. Haven't I ordered the young men not to touch you? When you are thirsty, go and drink from the jars the young men have filled."

¹⁰ She bowed with her face to the ground and said to him, "Why are you so kind to notice me, although I am a foreigner?"

¹¹ Boaz answered her, "Everything you have done for your mother-in-law since your husband's death has been fully reported to me: how you left your father and mother, and the land of your birth, and how you came to a people you didn't previously know. ¹² May the LORD reward you for what you have done, and may you receive a full reward from the LORD God of Israel, under whose wings you have come for refuge."

¹³ "My lord," she said, "you have been so kind to me, for you have comforted and encouraged your slave, although I am not like one of your female servants."

¹⁴ At mealtime Boaz told her, "Come over here and have some bread and dip it in the vinegar sauce." So she sat beside the harvesters, and he offered her roasted grain. She ate and was satisfied and had some left over.

¹⁵ When she got up to gather grain, Boaz ordered his young men, "Be sure to let her gather grain among the bundles, and don't humiliate her. ¹⁶ Pull out some stalks from the bundles for her and leave them for her to gather. Don't rebuke her." ¹⁷ So Ruth gathered grain in the field until evening. She beat out what she had gathered, and it was about 26 quarts of barley. ¹⁸ She picked up the grain and went into the city, where her mother-in-law saw what she had gleaned. Then she brought out what she had left over from her meal and gave it to her.

¹⁹ Then her mother-in-law said to her, "Where did you gather barley today, and where did you work? May the LORD bless the man who noticed you."

Ruth told her mother-in-law about the men she had worked with and said, "The name of the man I worked with today is Boaz."

²⁰ Then Naomi said to her daughter-in-law, "May he be blessed by the LORD, who has not forsaken his kindness to the living or the dead." Naomi continued, "The man is a close relative. He is one of our family redeemers."

²¹ Ruth the Moabitess said, "He also told me, 'Stay with my young men until they have finished all of my harvest.'"

²² So Naomi said to her daughter-in-law Ruth, "My daughter, it is good for you to work with his young women, so that nothing will happen to you in another field." ²³ Ruth stayed close to Boaz's young women and gathered grain until the barley and the wheat harvests were finished. And she lived with her mother-in-law.

PSALM 60:1-5

1 God, You have rejected us; You
   have broken out against us;
   You have been angry. Restore us!
2 You have shaken the land and split
   it open.
   Heal its fissures, for it shudders.
3 You have made Your people suffer
   hardship;
   You have given us a wine to drink
   that made us stagger.
4 You have given a signal flag to
   those who fear You,
   so that they can flee before the
   archers. *Selah*
5 Save with Your right hand, and
   answer me,
   so that those You love may be
   rescued.

PROVERBS 13:16-17

16 Every sensible person acts
   knowledgeably,
   but a fool displays his stupidity.

17 A wicked messenger falls into
   trouble,
   but a trustworthy courier brings
   healing.

JOHN 1:1-23

1 In the beginning was the Word,
   and the Word was with God,
   and the Word was God.
2 He was with God
   in the beginning.
3 All things were created
   through Him,
   and apart from Him not one thing
   was created
   that has been created.
4 Life was in Him,
   and that life was the light of men.
5 That light shines in the darkness,
   yet the darkness did not
   overcome it.

6 There was a man named John
   who was sent from God.
7 He came as a witness
   to testify about the light,
   so that all might believe
   through him.
8 He was not the light,
   but he came to testify
   about the light.
9 The true light, who gives light
   to everyone,
   was coming into the world.

10 He was in the world,
   and the world was created
   through Him,
   yet the world did not recognize
   Him.
11 He came to His own,
   and His own people
   did not receive Him.
12 But to all who did receive Him,
   He gave them the right to be
   children of God,
   to those who believe in His name,
13 who were born,
   not of blood,
   or of the will of the flesh,
   or of the will of man,
   but of God.

14 The Word became flesh
   and took up residence among us.
   We observed His glory,
   the glory as the
   One and Only Son
   from the Father,
   full of grace and truth.
15 (John testified concerning Him
   and exclaimed,
   "This was the One of whom
   I said,
   'The One coming after me
   has surpassed me,
   because He existed before me.' ")
16 Indeed, we have all received grace
   after grace
   from His fullness,
17 for although the law was given
   through Moses,
   grace and truth came
   through Jesus Christ.
18 No one has ever seen God.
   The One and Only Son—
   the One who is
   at the Father's side—
   He has revealed Him.

¹⁹ This is John's testimony when the Jews from Jerusalem sent priests and Levites to ask him, "Who are you?" ²⁰ He did not refuse to answer, but he declared: "I am not the Messiah." ²¹ "What then?" they asked him. "Are you Elijah?"

"I am not," he said.

"Are you the Prophet?"

"No," he answered.

²² "Who are you, then?" they asked. "We need to give an answer to those who sent us. What can you tell us about yourself?"

²³ He said, "I am a **voice of one crying out in the wilderness: Make straight the way of the Lord**—just as Isaiah the prophet said."

The Great Triune God

The Word became flesh and took up residence among us.—John 1:14

Dr. W. E. Sangster tells the story of following three children out of church. One remarked to the others: "I can't understand all this 'Three in One and One in Three' business."

"I can't either," said another child, "but I think of it like this: my mother is Mummy to me, she is Mabel to Daddy, and Mrs. Douglas to lots of other people."

Is that the answer? Is it just a question of names? Are we right in finding the doctrine of the Trinity in the text of Matthew 28:19, where the word "name" is singular, but three names are given—Father, Son, and Holy Spirit?

No, that is just part of it; there is much more to it than that. God, we know, is one God. But there stepped into the world someone who claimed also to be God. His name was Jesus. He forgave sins, claimed to have existence before Abraham, and accepted worship as His right. Worship, remember, is for God alone. After Jesus was resurrected and returned to heaven, He sent back the Holy Spirit, who was also seen as God (2 Co 13:13). He—the Holy Spirit—came into the disciples and brought with Him the resources of the Godhead, breaking the sin in their nature, pleading in prayer, and exalting the Savior.

Thus we see God is One but also Three in One: God above us, God among us, God within us. The Father in majesty, the Son in suffering, the Spirit in striving. This is the central mystery of our most holy faith. Together, and with all our hearts, let us adore the great triune God.

Prayer

Father, Son, and Holy Spirit, though I cannot comprehend Your essential oneness and unity, I can worship You nevertheless. This I do now, in humble adoration. Glory, honor, and power be unto Your name forever and ever. Amen.

Further Study

Jn 1:1-14; 8:58; 10:30; 17:5
How did John describe Jesus?
What did Jesus declare of Himself?

MAY 15

RUTH 3:1–4:22

3 Ruth's mother-in-law Naomi said to her, "My daughter, shouldn't I find security for you, so that you will be taken care of? ² Now isn't Boaz our relative? Haven't you been working with his young women? This evening he will be winnowing barley on the threshing floor. ³ Wash, put on perfumed oil, and wear your best clothes. Go down to the threshing floor, but don't let the man know you are there until he has finished eating and drinking. ⁴ When he lies down, notice the place where he's lying, go in and uncover his feet, and lie down. Then he will explain to you what you should do."

⁵ So Ruth said to her, "I will do everything you say." ⁶ She went down to the threshing floor and did everything her mother-in-law had instructed her. ⁷ After Boaz ate, drank, and was in good spirits, he went to lie down at the end of the pile of barley. Then she went in secretly, uncovered his feet, and lay down.

⁸ At midnight, Boaz was startled, turned over, and there lying at his feet was a woman! ⁹ So he asked, "Who are you?"

"I am Ruth, your slave," she replied. "Spread your cloak over me, for you are a family redeemer."

¹⁰ Then he said, "May the LORD bless you, my daughter. You have shown more kindness now than before, because you have not pursued younger men, whether rich or poor. ¹¹ Now don't be afraid, my daughter. I will do for you whatever you say, since all the people in my town know that you are a woman of noble character. ¹² Yes, it is true that I am a family redeemer, but there is a redeemer closer than I am. ¹³ Stay here tonight, and in the morning, if he wants to redeem you, that's good. Let him re-deem you. But if he doesn't want to re-deem you, as the LORD lives, I will. Now, lie down until morning."

¹⁴ So she lay down at his feet until morning but got up while it was still dark. Then Boaz said, "Don't let it be known that a woman came to the threshing floor." ¹⁵ And he told Ruth, "Bring the shawl you're wearing and hold it out." When she held it out, he shoveled six measures of barley into her shawl, and she went into the city.

¹⁶ She went to her mother-in-law, Naomi, who asked her, "How did it go, my daughter?"

Then Ruth told her everything the man had done for her. ¹⁷ She said, "He gave me these six measures of barley, because he said, 'Don't go back to your mother-in-law empty-handed.' "

¹⁸ "Wait, my daughter," she said, "until you find out how things go, for he won't rest unless he resolves this to-day."

4 Boaz went to the gate of the town and sat down there. Soon, the family redeemer Boaz had spoken about came by. Boaz called him by name and said, "Come over here and sit down." So he went over and sat down. ² Then Boaz took 10 men of the city's elders and said, "Sit here." And they sat down. ³ He said to the redeemer, "Naomi, who has returned from the land of Moab, is sell-ing a piece of land that belonged to our brother Elimelech. ⁴ I thought I should inform you: Buy it back in the presence of those seated here and in the pres-ence of the elders of my people. If you want to redeem it, do so. But if you do not want to redeem it, tell me, so that I will know, because there isn't anyone other than you to redeem it, and I am next after you."

"I want to redeem it," he answered.

⁵ Then Boaz said, "On the day you buy

the land from Naomi, you will also acquire Ruth the Moabitess, the wife of the deceased man, to perpetuate the man's name on his property."

⁶ The redeemer replied, "I can't redeem it myself, or I will ruin my own inheritance. Take my right of redemption, because I can't redeem it."

⁷ At an earlier period in Israel, a man removed his sandal and gave it to the other party in order to make any matter legally binding concerning the right of redemption or the exchange of property. This was the method of legally binding a transaction in Israel.

⁸ So the redeemer removed his sandal and said to Boaz, "Buy back the property yourself."

⁹ Boaz said to the elders and all the people, "You are witnesses today that I am buying from Naomi everything that belonged to Elimelech, Chilion, and Mahlon. ¹⁰ I will also acquire Ruth the Moabitess, Mahlon's widow, as my wife, to perpetuate the deceased man's name on his property, so that his name will not disappear among his relatives or from the gate of his home. You are witnesses today."

¹¹ The elders and all the people who were at the gate said, "We are witnesses. May the LORD make the woman who is entering your house like Rachel and Leah, who together built the house of Israel. May you be powerful in Ephrathah and famous in Bethlehem. ¹² May your house become like the house of Perez, the son Tamar bore to Judah, because of the offspring the LORD will give you by this young woman."

¹³ Boaz took Ruth and she became his wife. When he was intimate with her, the LORD enabled her to conceive, and she gave birth to a son. ¹⁴ Then the women said to Naomi, "Praise the LORD, who has not left you without a family redeemer today. May his name be famous in Israel. ¹⁵ He will renew your life and sustain you in your old age. Indeed, your daughter-in-law, who loves you and is better to you than seven sons, has given birth to him." ¹⁶ Naomi took the child, placed him on her lap, and took care of him. ¹⁷ The neighbor women

said, "A son has been born to Naomi," and they named him Obed. He was the father of Jesse, the father of David.

¹⁸ Now this is the genealogy of Perez:

Perez fathered Hezron.
¹⁹ Hezron fathered Ram,
who fathered Amminadab.
²⁰ Amminadab fathered Nahshon,
who fathered Salmon.
²¹ Salmon fathered Boaz,
who fathered Obed.
²² And Obed fathered Jesse,
who fathered David.

PSALM 60:6-12

⁶ God has spoken in His sanctuary:
"I will triumph! I will divide up Shechem.
I will apportion the Valley of Succoth.
⁷ Gilead is Mine, Manasseh is Mine,
and Ephraim is My helmet;
Judah is My scepter.
⁸ Moab is My washbasin;
on Edom I throw My sandal.
Over Philistia I shout in triumph."

⁹ Who will bring me to the fortified city?
Who will lead me to Edom?
¹⁰ Is it not You, God, who have rejected us?
God, You do not march out with our armies.
¹¹ Give us aid against the foe,
for human help is worthless.
¹² With God we will perform valiantly;
He will trample our foes.

PROVERBS 13:18-20

¹⁸ Poverty and disgrace come to those who ignore instruction,
but the one who accepts rebuke will be honored.

¹⁹ Desire fulfilled is sweet to the taste,
but fools hate to turn from evil.

20 The one who walks with the wise
will become wise,
but a companion of fools will
suffer harm.

JOHN 1:24-51

24 Now they had been sent from the
Pharisees. 25 So they asked him, "Why
then do you baptize if you aren't the
Messiah, or Elijah, or the Prophet?"
26 "I baptize with water," John answered them. "Someone stands among
you, but you don't know Him. 27 He is
the One coming after me, whose sandal
strap I'm not worthy to untie."
28 All this happened in Bethany across
the Jordan, where John was baptizing.
29 The next day John saw Jesus coming toward him and said, "Here is the
Lamb of God, who takes away the sin of
the world! 30 This is the One I told you
about: 'After me comes a man who has
surpassed me, because He existed before me.' 31 I didn't know Him, but I
came baptizing with water so He might
be revealed to Israel."
32 And John testified, "I watched the
Spirit descending from heaven like a
dove, and He rested on Him. 33 I didn't
know Him, but He who sent me to baptize with water told me, 'The One you
see the Spirit descending and resting
on—He is the One who baptizes with
the Holy Spirit.' 34 I have seen and testified that He is the Son of God!"
35 Again the next day, John was standing with two of his disciples. 36 When he
saw Jesus passing by, he said, "Look!
The Lamb of God!"
37 The two disciples heard him say
this and followed Jesus. 38 When Jesus
turned and noticed them following
Him, He asked them, "What are you
looking for?"
They said to Him, "Rabbi" (which

means "Teacher"), "where are You staying?"
39 "Come and you'll see," He replied.
So they went and saw where He was
staying, and they stayed with Him that
day. It was about 10 in the morning.
40 Andrew, Simon Peter's brother, was
one of the two who heard John and
followed Him. 41 He first found his own
brother Simon and told him, "We have
found the Messiah!" (which means
"Anointed One"), 42 and he brought
Simon to Jesus.
When Jesus saw him, He said, "You
are Simon, son of John. You will be
called Cephas" (which means "Rock").
43 The next day He decided to leave
for Galilee. Jesus found Philip and told
him, "Follow Me!"
44 Now Philip was from Bethsaida, the
hometown of Andrew and Peter.
45 Philip found Nathanael and told him,
"We have found the One Moses wrote
about in the law (and so did the
prophets): Jesus the son of Joseph, from
Nazareth!"
46 "Can anything good come out of
Nazareth?" Nathanael asked him.
"Come and see," Philip answered.
47 Then Jesus saw Nathanael coming
toward Him and said about him, "Here
is a true Israelite; no deceit is in him."
48 "How do you know me?" Nathanael
asked.
"Before Philip called you, when you
were under the fig tree, I saw you,"
Jesus answered.
49 "Rabbi," Nathanael replied, "You
are the Son of God! You are the King of
Israel!"
50 Jesus responded to him, "Do you
believe only because I told you I saw
you under the fig tree? You will see
greater things than this." 51 Then He
said, "I assure you: You will see heaven
opened and the angels of God ascending
and descending on the Son of Man."

He Reigns—Now

With God we will perform valiantly.—Psalm 60:12

The final part of the Lord's Prayer, which is really a doxology, contains a categorical assertion that God reigns through His kingdom—now. It manifestly requires a measure of faith and courage to affirm this truth in our modern society, when so many things seem positively to shout against it—so many wrongs that clamor for redress, so many problems that demand a solution, and so many social evils whose existence appears utterly incompatible with the reign of God. Yet affirm it we must.

A dear Christian, in a letter to me some time ago, said, "I look around the world and am appalled. My only comfort is the hymn 'Jesus Shall Reign Where'er the Sun.' I, therefore, sit back and watch and wait the day." I told her that her letter reminded me of some words I heard someone put together in a conference once:

> Sit down, O men of God!
> His kingdom He will bring.
> Whenever it shall please His will.
> You need not do a thing!

In my reply I said, "Yes, it's true that one day the kingdom of God shall 'stretch from shore to shore,' but let us not ignore the fact that God is reigning now. Given our cooperation, the Almighty can greatly affect the world through our committed lives. If we fail to see this, then it is possible that we struggle and stumble through life, waiting for Him, while all the time He is waiting for us."

Prayer

O God, deliver me from a view of life that says, "Look what the world is coming to." Help me to look at You; then I can say: "Look what has come to the world." Thank You, Father. Amen.

Further Study

Rv 7:9-17; Ex 24:17; 40:34; Ps 19:1; Jn 1:14; Rm 11:36
How can we behold His glory?
How is our vision of God enlarged?

MAY 16

I SAMUEL 1:1–2:36

1 There was a man from Ramathaim-zophim in the hill country of Ephraim. His name was Elkanah son of Jeroham, son of Elihu, son of Tohu, son of Zuph, an Ephraimite. ² He had two wives, the first named Hannah and the second Peninnah. Peninnah had children, but Hannah was childless. ³ This man would go up from his town every year to worship and to sacrifice to the LORD of Hosts at Shiloh, where Eli's two sons, Hophni and Phinehas, were the LORD's priests.

⁴ Whenever Elkanah offered a sacrifice, he always gave portions of the meat to his wife Peninnah and to each of her sons and daughters. ⁵ But he gave a double portion to Hannah, for he loved her even though the LORD had kept her from conceiving. ⁶ Her rival would taunt her severely just to provoke her, because the LORD had kept Hannah from conceiving. ⁷ Whenever she went up to the LORD's house, her rival taunted her in this way every year. Hannah wept and would not eat. ⁸ "Hannah, why are you crying?" her husband Elkanah asked. "Why won't you eat? Why are you troubled? Am I not better to you than 10 sons?"

⁹ Hannah got up after they ate and drank at Shiloh. Eli the priest was sitting on a chair by the doorpost of the LORD's tabernacle. ¹⁰ Deeply hurt, Hannah prayed to the LORD and wept with many tears. ¹¹ Making a vow, she pleaded, "LORD of Hosts, if You will take notice of Your servant's affliction, remember and not forget me, and give Your servant a son, I will give him to the LORD all the days of his life, and his hair will never be cut."

¹² While she was praying in the LORD's presence, Eli watched her lips. ¹³ Hannah was speaking to herself, and although her lips were moving, her voice could not be heard. Eli thought she was drunk ¹⁴ and scolded her, "How long are you going to be drunk? Get rid of your wine!"

¹⁵ "No, my lord," Hannah replied. "I am a woman with a broken heart. I haven't had any wine or beer; I've been pouring out my heart before the LORD. ¹⁶ Don't think of me as a wicked woman; I've been praying from the depth of my anguish and resentment."

¹⁷ Eli responded, "Go in peace, and may the God of Israel grant the petition you've requested from Him."

¹⁸ "May your servant find favor with you," she replied. Then Hannah went on her way; she ate and no longer appeared downcast.

¹⁹ The next morning Elkanah and Hannah got up early to bow and to worship the LORD. Afterwards, they returned home to Ramah. Then Elkanah was intimate with his wife Hannah, and the LORD remembered her. ²⁰ After some time, Hannah conceived and gave birth to a son. She named him Samuel, because she said, "I requested him from the LORD."

²¹ When Elkanah and all his household went up to make the annual sacrifice and his vow offering to the LORD, ²² Hannah did not go and explained to her husband, "After the child is weaned, I'll take him to appear in the LORD's presence and to stay there permanently."

²³ Her husband Elkanah replied, "Do what you think is best, and stay here until you've weaned him. May the LORD confirm your word." So Hannah stayed there and nursed her son until she weaned him. ²⁴ When she had weaned him, she took him with her to Shiloh, as well as a three-year-old bull, two and one-half gallons of flour, and a jar of wine. Though the boy was still young,

she took him to the LORD's house at
Shiloh. [25] Then they slaughtered the
bull and brought the boy to Eli.

[26] "Please, my lord," she said, "as sure
as you live, my lord, I am the woman
who stood here beside you praying to
the LORD. [27] I prayed for this boy, and
since the LORD gave me what I asked
Him for, [28] I now give the boy to the
LORD. For as long as he lives, he is given
to the LORD." Then he bowed and worshiped the LORD there.

2 Hannah prayed:

My heart rejoices in the LORD;
my horn is lifted up by the LORD.
My mouth boasts
over my enemies,
because I rejoice in Your salvation.
[2] There is no one holy
like the LORD.
There is no one besides You!
And there is no rock like our God.
[3] Do not boast so proudly,
or let arrogant words come out of
your mouth,
for the LORD is a God
of knowledge,
and actions are weighed by Him.
[4] The bows of the warriors
are broken,
but the feeble are clothed
with strength.
[5] Those who are full hire
themselves out for food,
but those who are starving hunger
no more.
The barren woman gives birth
to seven,
but the woman with many sons
pines away.
[6] The LORD brings death and gives
life;
He sends some to Sheol,
and He raises others up.
[7] The LORD brings poverty and gives
wealth;
He humbles and He exalts.
[8] He raises the poor from the dust
and lifts the needy
from the garbage pile.
He seats them with noblemen
and gives them a throne of honor.

For the foundations of the earth
are the LORD's;
He has set the world on them.
[9] He guards the steps
of His faithful ones,
but the wicked are silenced
in darkness,
for a man does not prevail by
his own strength.
[10] Those who oppose the LORD
will be shattered;
He will thunder in the heavens
against them.
The LORD will judge the ends
of the earth.
He will give power to His king;
He will lift up the horn
of His anointed.

[11] Elkanah went home to Ramah, but
the boy served the LORD in the presence
of Eli the priest.

[12] Eli's sons were wicked men; they
had no regard for the LORD [13] or for the
priests' share of the sacrifices from the
people. When any man offered a sacrifice, the priest's servant would come
with a three-pronged meat fork while
the meat was boiling [14] and plunge it
into the container or kettle or caldron or
cooking pot. The priest would claim for
himself whatever the meat fork brought
up. This is the way they treated all the
Israelites who came there to Shiloh.
[15] Even before the fat was burned, the
priest's servant would come and say to
the man who was sacrificing, "Give the
priest some meat to roast, because he
won't accept boiled meat from you—
only raw." [16] If that man said to him,
"The fat must be burned first; then you
can take whatever you want for yourself," the servant would reply, "No, I insist that you hand it over right now. If
you don't, I'll take it by force!" [17] So the
servants' sin was very severe in the
presence of the LORD, because they
treated the LORD's offering with contempt.

[18] The boy Samuel served in the
LORD's presence and wore a linen
ephod. [19] Each year his mother made
him a little robe and took it to him
when she went with her husband to of-

fer the annual sacrifice. ²⁰ Eli would bless Elkanah and his wife: "May the LORD give you children by this woman in place of the one she has given to the LORD." Then they would go home.

²¹ The LORD paid attention to Hannah's need, and she conceived and gave birth to three sons and two daughters. Meanwhile, the boy Samuel grew up in the presence of the LORD.

²² Now Eli was very old. He heard about everything his sons were doing to all Israel and how they were sleeping with the women who served at the entrance to the tent of meeting. ²³ He said to them, "Why are you doing these things? I have heard about your evil actions from all these people. ²⁴ No, my sons, the report I hear from the LORD's people is not good. ²⁵ If a man sins against another man, God can intercede for him, but if a man sins against the LORD, who can intercede for him?" But they would not listen to their father, since the LORD intended to kill them. ²⁶ By contrast, the boy Samuel grew in stature and in favor with the LORD and with men.

²⁷ A man of God came to Eli and said to him, "This is what the LORD says: 'Didn't I reveal Myself to your ancestral house when it was in Egypt and belonged to Pharaoh's palace? ²⁸ I selected your house from the tribes of Israel to be priests, to offer sacrifices on My altar, to burn incense, and to wear an ephod in My presence. I also gave your house all the Israelite fire offerings. ²⁹ Why, then, do all of you despise My sacrifices and offerings that I require at the place of worship? You have honored your sons more than Me, by making yourselves fat with the best part of all of the offerings of My people Israel.'

³⁰ "Therefore, the LORD, the God of Israel, says:

'Although I said
your family and
    your ancestral house
would walk before Me forever,
the LORD now says, "No longer!"
I will honor those who honor
    Me,

but those who despise Me
    will be disgraced.

³¹ " 'Look, the days are coming when I will cut off your strength and the strength of your ancestral family, so that none in your family will reach old age. ³² You will see distress in the place of worship, in spite of all that is good in Israel, and no one in your family will ever again reach old age. ³³ Any man from your family I do not cut off from My altar will bring grief and sadness to you. All your descendants will die violently. ³⁴ This will be the sign that will come to you concerning your two sons Hophni and Phinehas: both of them will die on the same day.

³⁵ " 'Then I will raise up a faithful priest for Myself. He will do whatever is in My heart and mind. I will establish a lasting dynasty for him, and he will walk before My anointed one for all time. ³⁶ Anyone who is left in your family will come and bow down to him for a piece of silver or a loaf of bread. He will say: Please appoint me to some priestly office so I can have a piece of bread to eat.' "

PSALM 61:1-8

¹ God, hear my cry;
    pay attention to my prayer.
² I call to You from the ends of the
        earth when my heart is
        without strength.
Lead me to a rock that is high
        above me,
³ for You have been a refuge for me,
    a strong tower in the face of the
        enemy.
⁴ I will live in Your tent forever
    and take refuge under the shelter
        of Your wings.   *Selah*

⁵ God, You have heard my vows;
    You have given a heritage to those
        who fear Your name.
⁶ Add days to the king's life;
    may his years span many
        generations.
⁷ May he sit enthroned before God
        forever;

appoint faithful love and truth to
guard him.
⁸ Then I will continually sing of
Your name,
fulfilling my vows day by day.

PROVERBS 13:21-22

²¹ Disaster pursues sinners,
but good rewards the righteous.

²² A good man leaves an inheritance
to his grandchildren,
but the sinner's wealth is stored
up for the righteous.

JOHN 2:1-25

2 On the third day a wedding took
place in Cana of Galilee. Jesus'
mother was there, and ² Jesus and His
disciples were invited to the wedding
as well. ³ When the wine ran out, Jesus'
mother told Him, "They don't have any
wine."
⁴ "What has this concern of yours to
do with Me, woman?" Jesus asked. "My
hour has not yet come."
⁵ "Do whatever He tells you," His
mother told the servants.
⁶ Now six stone water jars had been
set there for Jewish purification. Each
contained 20 or 30 gallons.
⁷ "Fill the jars with water," Jesus told
them. So they filled them to the brim.
⁸ Then He said to them, "Now draw
some out and take it to the chief servant." And they did.
⁹ When the chief servant tasted the
water (after it had become wine), he did
not know where it came from—though
the servants who had drawn the water
knew. He called the groom ¹⁰ and told
him, "Everybody sets out the fine wine
first, then, after people have drunk
freely, the inferior. But you have kept
the fine wine until now."

¹¹ Jesus performed this first sign in
Cana of Galilee. He displayed His glory,
and His disciples believed in Him.
¹² After this, He went down to
Capernaum, together with His mother,
His brothers, and His disciples, and they
stayed there only a few days.
¹³ The Jewish Passover was near, so
Jesus went up to Jerusalem. ¹⁴ In the
temple complex He found people selling oxen, sheep, and doves, and He also
found the money changers sitting there.
¹⁵ After making a whip out of cords, He
drove everyone out of the temple complex with their sheep and oxen. He also
poured out the money changers' coins
and overturned the tables. ¹⁶ He told
those who were selling doves, "Get
these things out of here! Stop turning
My Father's house into a marketplace!"
¹⁷ And His disciples remembered that
it is written: **Zeal for Your house will
consume Me.**
¹⁸ So the Jews replied to Him, "What
sign of authority will You show us for
doing these things?"
¹⁹ Jesus answered, "Destroy this sanctuary, and I will raise it up in three
days."
²⁰ Therefore the Jews said, "This sanctuary took 46 years to build, and will
You raise it up in three days?"
²¹ But He was speaking about the
sanctuary of His body. ²² So when He
was raised from the dead, His disciples
remembered that He had said this. And
they believed the Scripture and the
statement Jesus had made.
²³ While He was in Jerusalem at the
Passover Festival, many trusted in His
name when they saw the signs He was
doing. ²⁴ Jesus, however, would not entrust Himself to them, since He knew
them all ²⁵ and because He did not need
anyone to testify about man; for He
Himself knew what was in man.

Have a Great Childhood

'Disaster pursues sinners, but good rewards the righteous.

——PROVERBS 13:21

Solomon's comments in Ecclesiastes 11:9 are aimed at the young: "Let your heart be glad in the days of your youth." Enjoy your days one by one, he is saying, because before you know it, you will be an adult.

The words that come next have sent some Christians into apoplexy: "Walk in the ways of your heart and in the sights of your eyes" (v. 9). I remember a youth leader in a church I pastored who set out to teach the Book of Ecclesiastes to the young people. But he deliberately left out these words. When I asked him why, he said: "That's bad advice for young people. They are inclined that way already so I thought it best not to draw attention to it." I drew his attention to the words that follow: "but know that for all of these things God will bring you to judgment." This is what Solomon is really saying: "Relax and have a super time when you are young. There will be many impulses and many things that appeal to your eyes. Follow them, but keep in mind there will be a day of accountability. So don't let your impulses go wild."

Some believe that warning takes the joy out of living, but it shouldn't. If we ignore the God to whom we must all answer, then we leave ourselves open to experiencing not life but unrestricted liberty. And that kind of freedom is bad for us. So banish all worries, Solomon tells the young, and avoid those things that bring pain to your body. Young person, you are only young once. Stay close to God and you'll get the most out of it.

Prayer

O God my Father, while I am thankful for all the books that help me learn of You and know about You, help me never to put these ahead of Your Word, the Bible, but always behind it. Make me a person of the Book. In Jesus' name. Amen.

Further Study

Jos 1:1-8; 2 Kg 22:1-20
What was God's command to Joshua?
Why did the king tear his robes?

MAY 17

I SAMUEL 3:1–5:12

3 The boy Samuel served the LORD in Eli's presence. In those days the word of the LORD was rare and prophetic visions were not widespread.

² One day Eli, whose eyesight was failing, was lying in his room. ³ Before the lamp of God had gone out, Samuel was lying down in the tabernacle of the LORD where the ark of God was located. ⁴ Then the LORD called Samuel, and he answered, "Here I am." ⁵ He ran to Eli and said, "Here I am; you called me."

"I didn't call," Eli replied. "Go and lie down." So he went and lay down.

⁶ Once again the LORD called, "Samuel!"

Samuel got up, went to Eli, and said, "Here I am; you called me."

"I didn't call, my son," he replied. "Go and lie down."

⁷ Now Samuel had not yet experienced the LORD, because the word of the LORD had not yet been revealed to him. ⁸ Once again, for the third time, the LORD called Samuel. He got up, went to Eli, and said, "Here I am; you called me."

Then Eli understood that the LORD was calling the boy. ⁹ He told Samuel, "Go and lie down. If He calls you, say, 'Speak, LORD, for Your servant is listening.'" So Samuel went and lay down in his place.

¹⁰ The LORD came, stood there, and called as before, "Samuel, Samuel!"

Samuel responded, "Speak, for Your servant is listening."

¹¹ The LORD said to Samuel, "I am about to do something in Israel that everyone who hears about it will shudder. ¹² On that day I will carry out against Eli everything I said about his family, from beginning to end. ¹³ I told him that I am going to judge his family forever because of the iniquity he

knows about: his sons are defiling the sanctuary, and he has not stopped them. ¹⁴ Therefore, I have sworn to Eli's family: The iniquity of Eli's family will never be wiped out by either sacrifice or offering."

¹⁵ Samuel lay down until the morning; then he opened the doors of the LORD's house. He was afraid to tell Eli the vision, ¹⁶ but Eli called him and said, "Samuel, my son."

"Here I am," answered Samuel.

¹⁷ "What was the message He gave you?" Eli asked. "Don't hide it from me. May God punish you and do so severely if you hide anything from me that He told you." ¹⁸ So Samuel told him everything and did not hide anything from him. Eli responded, "He is the LORD. He will do what He thinks is good."

¹⁹ Samuel grew, and the LORD was with him and let nothing he said prove false. ²⁰ All Israel from Dan to Beersheba knew that Samuel was a confirmed prophet of the LORD. ²¹ The LORD continued to appear in Shiloh, because there He revealed Himself to Samuel by **4** His word. ¹ And Samuel's words came to all Israel.

Israel went out to meet the Philistines in battle and camped at Ebenezer while the Philistines camped at Aphek. ² The Philistines lined up in battle formation against Israel, and as the battle intensified, Israel was defeated by the Philistines, who struck down about 4,000 men on the battlefield.

³ When the troops returned to the camp, the elders of Israel asked, "Why did the LORD let us be defeated today by the Philistines? Let's bring the ark of the LORD's covenant from Shiloh. Then it will go with us and save us from the hand of our enemies." ⁴ So the people sent men to Shiloh to bring back the ark of the covenant of the LORD of Hosts, who dwells between the cherubim. Eli's

two sons, Hophni and Phinehas, were there with the ark of the covenant of God. ⁵ When the ark of the covenant of the Lord entered the camp, all the Israelites raised such a loud shout that the ground shook. ⁶ The Philistines heard the sound of the war cry and asked, "What's this loud shout in the Hebrews' camp?" When the Philistines discovered that the ark of the Lord had entered the camp, ⁷ they panicked. "The gods have entered their camp!" they said. "Woe to us, nothing like this has happened before. ⁸ Woe to us, who will rescue us from the hand of these magnificent gods? These are the gods that slaughtered the Egyptians with all kinds of plagues in the wilderness. ⁹ Show some courage and be men, Philistines! Otherwise, you'll serve the Hebrews just like they served you. Now be men and fight!"

¹⁰ So the Philistines fought, and Israel was defeated, and each man fled to his tent. The slaughter was severe—30,000 of the Israelite foot soldiers fell. ¹¹ The ark of God was captured, and Eli's two sons, Hophni and Phinehas, died.

¹² That same day, a Benjaminite man ran from the battle and came to Shiloh. His clothes were torn, and there was dirt on his head. ¹³ When he arrived, there was Eli sitting on his chair beside the road watching, because he was anxious about the ark of God. When the man entered the city to give a report, the entire city cried out.

¹⁴ Eli heard the outcry and asked, "Why this commotion?" The man quickly came and reported to Eli. ¹⁵ At that time Eli was 98 years old, and his gaze was fixed because he couldn't see. ¹⁶ The man said to Eli, "I'm the one who came from the battle. I fled from there today."

"What happened, my son?" Eli asked.

¹⁷ The messenger answered, "Israel has fled from the Philistines, and also there was a great slaughter among the people. Your two sons, Hophni and Phinehas, are both dead, and the ark of God has been captured." ¹⁸ When he mentioned the ark of God, Eli fell backwards off the chair by the city gate, and

since he was old and heavy, his neck broke and he died. Eli had judged Israel 40 years.

¹⁹ Eli's daughter-in-law, the wife of Phinehas, was pregnant and about to give birth. When she heard the news about the capture of God's ark and the deaths of her father-in-law and her husband, she collapsed and gave birth because her labor pains came on her. ²⁰ As she was dying, the women taking care of her said, "Don't be afraid. You've given birth to a son!" But she did not respond, and did not pay attention. ²¹ She named the boy Ichabod, saying, "The glory has departed from Israel," referring to the capture of the ark of God and to the deaths of her father-in-law and her husband. ²² "The glory has departed from Israel," she said, "because the ark of God has been captured."

5 After the Philistines had captured the ark of God, they took it from Ebenezer to Ashdod, ² brought it into the temple of Dagon and placed it next to his statue. ³ When the people of Ashdod got up early the next morning, there was Dagon, fallen with his face to the ground before the ark of the Lord. So they took Dagon and returned him to his place. ⁴ But when they got up early the next morning, there was Dagon, fallen with his face to the ground before the ark of the Lord. This time, both Dagon's head and the palms of his hands were broken off and lying on the threshold. Only Dagon's torso remained. ⁵ That is why, to this day, the priests of Dagon and everyone who enters the temple of Dagon in Ashdod do not step on Dagon's threshold.

⁶ The Lord severely oppressed the people of Ashdod, terrorizing and afflicting the people of Ashdod and its territory with tumors. ⁷ When the men of Ashdod saw what was happening, they said, "The ark of Israel's God must not stay here with us, because His hand is severe against us and our god Dagon." ⁸ So they called all the Philistine rulers together and asked, "What should we do with the ark of Israel's God?"

"The ark of Israel's God should be moved to Gath," they replied. So the men of Ashdod moved the ark. ⁹ After they had moved it, the LORD's hand was against the city of Gath, causing a great panic. He afflicted the men of the city, from the youngest to the oldest, with an outbreak of tumors.

¹⁰ The Gathites then sent the ark of God to Ekron, but when it got there, the Ekronites cried out, "They've moved the ark of Israel's God to us to kill us and our people!"

¹¹ The Ekronites called all the Philistine rulers together. They said, "Send the ark of Israel's God away. It must return to its place so it won't kill us and our people!" For the fear of death pervaded the city; God's hand was very heavy there. ¹² The men who did not die were afflicted with tumors, and the outcry of the city went up to heaven.

PSALM 62:1-8

¹ I am at rest in God alone;
   my salvation comes from Him.
² He alone is my rock and my
      salvation,
   my stronghold; I will never be
      shaken.

³ How long will you threaten a
      man?
   Will all of you attack
   as if he were a leaning wall
   or a tottering stone fence?
⁴ They only plan to bring him down
      from his high position.
   They take pleasure in lying;
   they bless with their mouths,
   but they curse inwardly.   *Selah*

⁵ Rest in God alone, my soul,
   for my hope comes from Him.
⁶ He alone is my rock and my
      salvation,
   my stronghold; I will not be
      shaken.
⁷ My salvation and glory depend on
      God;
   my strong rock, my refuge, is in
      God.

⁸ Trust in Him at all times, you
      people;
   pour out your hearts before Him.
   God is our refuge.   *Selah*

PROVERBS 13:23-25

²³ The field of the poor yields
      abundant food,
   but without justice, it is swept
      away.

²⁴ The one who will not use the rod
      hates his son,
   but the one who loves him
      disciplines him diligently.

²⁵ A righteous man eats until he is
      satisfied,
   but the stomach of the wicked is
      empty.

JOHN 3:1-21

3 There was a man from the Pharisees named Nicodemus, a ruler of the Jews. ² This man came to Him at night and said, "Rabbi, we know that You have come from God as a teacher, for no one could perform these signs You do unless God were with him."

³ Jesus replied, "I assure you: Unless someone is born again, he cannot see the kingdom of God."

⁴ "But how can anyone be born when he is old?" Nicodemus asked Him. "Can he enter his mother's womb a second time and be born?"

⁵ Jesus answered, "I assure you: Unless someone is born of water and the Spirit, he cannot enter the kingdom of God. ⁶ Whatever is born of the flesh is flesh, and whatever is born of the Spirit is spirit. ⁷ Do not be amazed that I told you that you must be born again. ⁸ The wind blows where it pleases, and you hear its sound, but you don't know where it comes from or where it is going. So it is with everyone born of the Spirit."

⁹ "How can these things be?" asked Nicodemus.

¹⁰ "Are you a teacher of Israel and

don't know these things?" Jesus replied. ¹¹ "I assure you: We speak what We know and We testify to what We have seen, but you do not accept Our testimony. ¹² If I have told you about things that happen on earth and you don't believe, how will you believe if I tell you about things of heaven? ¹³ No one has ascended into heaven except the One who descended from heaven—the Son of Man. ¹⁴ Just as Moses lifted up the snake in the wilderness, so the Son of Man must be lifted up, ¹⁵ so that everyone who believes in Him will have eternal life.

¹⁶ "For God loved the world in this way: He gave His One and Only Son, so that everyone who believes in Him will not perish but have eternal life. ¹⁷ For God did not send His Son into the world that He might judge the world, but that the world might be saved through Him. ¹⁸ Anyone who believes in Him is not judged, but anyone who does not believe is already judged, because he has not believed in the name of the One and Only Son of God.

¹⁹ "This, then, is the judgment: the light has come into the world, and people loved darkness rather than the light because their deeds were evil. ²⁰ For everyone who practices wicked things hates the light and avoids it, so that his deeds may not be exposed. ²¹ But anyone who lives by the truth comes to the light, so that his works may be shown to be accomplished by God."

The Birth of the Spirit

Unless someone is born of water and the Spirit, he cannot enter the kingdom of God.
—John 3:5

Jesus prepared His disciples for the reception of the Holy Spirit. This course of training is best revealed in John's Gospel.

It is through the ministry of the Holy Spirit that we are born again into the kingdom of God. John makes clear what the new birth is not: "[Children] born not of blood, or of the will of the flesh, or of the will of man, but of God" (1:13). The new birth is brought about by the Holy Spirit, and unless He is involved in it, then it is not a new birth at all.

Someone has described the new birth as "the change, gradual or sudden, by which we, who are the children of the first birth, through a physical birth into a physical world, become children of the second birth, through a spiritual birth into a spiritual world." Just as you have to have brains to enter the kingdom of knowledge, an aesthetic nature to enter the kingdom of beauty, a musical sensitivity to enter the kingdom of music, an emotional nature to enter the kingdom of love, so you have to have a spiritual birth to enter the kingdom of God.

Jesus, in His first reference to the Holy Spirit in John's Gospel, put His finger on the first step of the Spirit's ministry in human life—the birth of the Spirit. Jesus said these words, not to a down-and-out, but to a member of the Jewish ruling council, a Pharisee. If Nicodemus, a morally upright religious leader, needed the Spirit, then we all need Him.

Prayer

O Father, I am grateful for this new life within—the new birth—and now I want more. This that I have experienced sets my heart on fire for life in all its fullness. Amen.

Further Study

Gl 5; Jn 1:13; Ti 3:5; 1 Pt 1:23
What are the characteristics of those born of the Spirit?
What does it mean to "walk in the Spirit"?

MAY 18

1 SAMUEL 6:1–8:22

6 When the ark of the LORD had been in the land of the Philistines for seven months, ² the Philistines summoned the priests and the diviners and pleaded, "What should we do with the ark of the LORD? Tell us how we can send it back to its place."

³ They replied, "If you send the ark of Israel's God away, you must not send it without an offering. You must return it with a guilt offering, and you will be healed. Then the reason His hand hasn't been removed from you will be revealed."

⁴ They asked, "What guilt offering should we send back to Him?"

And they answered, "Five gold tumors and five gold mice corresponding to the number of Philistine rulers, since there was one plague for both you and your rulers. ⁵ Make images of your tumors and of your mice that are destroying the land. Give glory to Israel's God, and perhaps He will stop oppressing you, your gods, and your land. ⁶ Why harden your hearts as the Egyptians and

Pharaoh hardened theirs? When He afflicted them, didn't they send Israel away, and Israel left?

⁷ "Now then, prepare one new cart and two milk cows that have never been yoked. Hitch the cows to the cart, but take their calves away and pen them up. ⁸ Take the ark of the LORD, place it on the cart, and put the gold objects in a box beside it, which you're sending Him as a guilt offering. Send it off and let it go its way. ⁹ Then watch: If it goes up the road to its homeland toward Bethshemesh, it is the LORD who has made this terrible trouble for us. However, if it doesn't, we will know that it was not His hand that punished us—it was just something that happened to us by chance."

¹⁰ The men did this: They took two milk cows, hitched them to the cart, and confined their calves in the pen. ¹¹ Then they put the ark of the LORD on the cart, along with the box containing the gold mice and the images of the tumors. ¹² The cows went straight up the road to Beth-shemesh. They stayed on that one highway, lowing as they went; they never strayed to the right or to the

left. The Philistine rulers were walking behind them to the territory of Beth-shemesh.

¹³ The people of Beth-shemesh were harvesting wheat in the valley, and when they looked up and saw the ark, they were overjoyed to see it. ¹⁴ The cart came to the field of Joshua of Beth-shemesh and stopped there near a large rock. The people of the city chopped up the cart and offered the cows as a burnt offering to the LORD. ¹⁵ The Levites removed the ark of the LORD, along with the box containing the gold objects, and placed them on the large rock. That day the men of Beth-shemesh offered burnt offerings and made sacrifices to the LORD. ¹⁶ When the five Philistine rulers observed this, they returned to Ekron that same day.

¹⁷ As a guilt offering to the LORD, the Philistines had sent back one gold tumor for each city: Ashdod, Gaza, Ashkelon, Gath, and Ekron. ¹⁸ The number of gold mice also corresponded to the number of Philistine cities of the five rulers, the fortified cities and the outlying villages. The large rock on which the ark of the LORD was placed is in the field of Joshua of Beth-shemesh to this day.

¹⁹ God struck down the men of Beth-shemesh because they looked inside the ark of the LORD. He struck down 70 men out of 50,000 men. The people wept because the LORD struck them with a great slaughter. ²⁰ The men of Beth-shemesh asked, "Who is able to stand in the presence of this holy LORD God? Who should the ark go to from here?"

²¹ They sent messengers to the residents of Kiriath-jearim, saying, "The Philistines have returned the ark of the LORD. Come down and get it."

7 So the men of Kiriath-jearim came for the ark of the LORD and took it to Abinadab's house on the hill. They consecrated his son Eleazar to take care of it. ² Time went by until 20 years had passed since the ark had been taken to Kiriath-jearim. Then the whole house of Israel began to seek the LORD. ³ Samuel told them, "If you are returning to the LORD with all your heart, get rid of the foreign gods and the Ashtoreths that are among you, dedicate yourselves to the LORD, and worship only Him. Then He will rescue you from the hand of the Philistines." ⁴ So the Israelites removed the Baals and the Ashtoreths and only worshiped the LORD.

⁵ Samuel said, "Gather all Israel at Mizpah, and I will pray to the LORD on your behalf." ⁶ When they gathered at Mizpah, they drew water and poured it out in the LORD's presence. They fasted that day, and there they confessed, "We have sinned against the LORD." And Samuel began to lead the Israelites at Mizpah as their judge.

⁷ When the Philistines heard that the Israelites had gathered at Mizpah, their rulers marched up toward Israel. When the Israelites heard about it, they were afraid because of the Philistines. ⁸ The Israelites said to Samuel, "Don't stop crying out to the LORD our God for us, so that He will save us from the hand of the Philistines."

⁹ Then Samuel took a young lamb and offered it as a whole burnt offering to the LORD. He cried out to the LORD on behalf of Israel, and the LORD answered him. ¹⁰ Samuel was offering the burnt offering as the Philistines drew near to fight against Israel. The LORD thundered loudly against the Philistines that day and threw them into such confusion that they fled before Israel. ¹¹ Then the men of Israel charged out of Mizpah and pursued the Philistines striking them down all the way to a place below Beth-car.

¹² Afterwards, Samuel took a stone and set it upright between Mizpah and Shen. He named it Ebenezer, explaining, "The LORD has helped us to this point." ¹³ So the Philistines were subdued and did not invade Israel's territory again. The LORD's hand was against the Philistines all of Samuel's life. ¹⁴ The cities from Ekron to Gath, which they had taken from Israel, were restored; Israel even rescued their surrounding territories from Philistine control. There was also peace between Israel and the Amorites.

¹⁵ Samuel judged Israel throughout his life. ¹⁶ Every year he would go on a circuit to Bethel, Gilgal, and Mizpah and would judge Israel at all these locations. ¹⁷ Then he would return to Ramah because his home was there, he judged Israel there, and he had built an altar to the LORD there.

8 When Samuel grew old, he appointed his sons as judges over Israel. ² His firstborn son's name was Joel and his second was Abijah. They were judges in Beer-sheba. ³ However, his sons did not walk in his ways—they turned toward dishonest gain, took bribes, and perverted justice.

⁴ So all the elders of Israel gathered together and went to Samuel at Ramah. ⁵ They said to him, "Look, you are old, and your sons do not follow your example. Therefore, appoint a king to judge us the same as all the other nations have."

⁶ When they said, "Give us a king to judge us," Samuel considered their demand sinful, so he prayed to the LORD. ⁷ But the LORD told him, "Listen to the people and everything they say to you. They have not rejected you; they have rejected Me as their king. ⁸ They are doing the same thing to you that they have done to Me, since the day I brought them out of Egypt until this day, abandoning Me and worshiping other gods. ⁹ Listen to them, but you must solemnly warn them and tell them about the rights of the king who will rule over them."

¹⁰ Samuel told all the LORD's words to the people who were asking him for a king. ¹¹ He said, "These are the rights of the king who will rule over you: He can take your sons and put them to his use in his chariots, on his horses, or running in front of his chariots. ¹² He can appoint them for his use as commanders of thousands or commanders of fifties, to plow his ground or reap his harvest, or to make his weapons of war or the equipment for his chariots. ¹³ He can take your daughters to become perfumers, cooks, and bakers. ¹⁴ He can take your best fields, vineyards, and olive orchards and give them to his servants. ¹⁵ He can take a tenth of your grain and your vineyards and give them to his officials and servants. ¹⁶ He can take your male servants, your female servants, your best young men, and your donkeys and use them for his work. ¹⁷ He can take a tenth of your flocks, and you yourselves can become his servants. ¹⁸ When that day comes, you will cry out because of the king you've chosen for yourselves, but the LORD won't answer you on that day."

¹⁹ The people refused to listen to Samuel. "No!" they said. "We must have a king over us. ²⁰ Then we'll be like all the other nations: our king will judge us, go out before us, and fight our battles."

²¹ Samuel listened to all the people's words and then repeated them to the LORD. ²² "Listen to them," the LORD told Samuel. "Appoint a king for them."

Then Samuel told the men of Israel, "Each of you, go back to your city."

PSALM 62:9-12

⁹ Men are only a vapor;
 exalted men, an illusion.
 On a balance scale, they go up;
 together they weigh less than a
 vapor.
¹⁰ Place no trust in oppression,
 or false hope in robbery.
 If wealth increases,
 pay no attention to it.

¹¹ God has spoken once;
 I have heard this twice:
 strength belongs to God,
¹² and faithful love belongs to You,
 LORD.
 For You repay each according to
 his works.

PROVERBS 14:1-2

14 Every wise woman builds her house,
 but a foolish one tears it down
 with her own hands.

² Whoever lives with integrity fears
the LORD,
but the one who is devious in his
ways despises Him.

JOHN 3:22–4:6

²² After this, Jesus and His disciples
went to the Judean countryside, where
He spent time with them and baptized.
²³ John also was baptizing in Aenon near
Salim, because there was plenty of water there. People were coming and being baptized, ²⁴ since John had not yet
been thrown into prison.
²⁵ Then a dispute arose between
John's disciples and a Jew about purification. ²⁶ So they came to John and told
him, "Rabbi, the One you testified
about, and who was with you across the
Jordan, is baptizing—and everyone is
flocking to Him."
²⁷ John responded, "No one can receive a single thing unless it's given to
him from heaven. ²⁸ You yourselves can
testify that I said, 'I am not the Messiah,
but I've been sent ahead of Him.' ²⁹ He
who has the bride is the groom. But
the groom's friend, who stands by and
listens for him, rejoices greatly at
the groom's voice. So this joy of mine is
complete. ³⁰ He must increase, but I
must decrease."

³¹ The One who comes from above is
above all. The one who is from the earth
is earthly and speaks in earthly terms.
The One who comes from heaven is
above all. ³² He testifies to what He has
seen and heard, yet no one accepts His
testimony. ³³ The one who has accepted
His testimony has affirmed that God is
true. ³⁴ For God sent Him, and He
speaks God' words, since He gives the
Spirit without measure. ³⁵ The Father
loves the Son and has given all things
into His hands. ³⁶ The one who believes
in the Son has eternal life, but the one
who refuses to believe in the Son will
not see life; instead, the wrath of God
remains on him.

4 When Jesus knew that the Pharisees
heard He was making and baptizing
more disciples than John ² (though
Jesus Himself was not baptizing, but
His disciples were), ³ He left Judea and
went again to Galilee. ⁴ He had to travel
through Samaria, ⁵ so He came to a
town of Samaria called Sychar near the
property that Jacob had given his son
Joseph. ⁶ Jacob's well was there, and
Jesus, worn out from His journey, sat
down at the well. It was about six in the
evening.

"A Time Exposure to God"

I have heard this twice: strength belongs to God.
—PSALM 62:11

It is futile to present our requests to God before pausing to reflect on His unchanging
adequacy and sufficiency. One reason why Jesus directed us to use the words "Our Father in
heaven" was to encourage us to focus our gaze on a God who is unaffected by the restrictions
and limitations of earth and who dwells in a place where the resources never run dry. Those
who plunge into the areas of petition and intercession before reflecting on the abundant resources that lie in God will find their praying ineffective. They are praying contrary to God's pattern. As the poet says:

What a frail soul he gave me, and a heart
Lame, and unlikely for the large events.

However, I wonder if, more often than not, we haven't given ourselves "a heart lame, and unlikely for the large events" because we rush into God's presence to present our petitions before taking stock of our spiritual resources.

God offers us infinite resources for the asking and the taking—Himself. The first moments of prayer should, therefore, be contemplative, reflective, meditative. As we gaze upon God and His infinite resources, we take, as someone put it, "a time exposure to God." His adequacy and sufficiency are printed indelibly upon us. No matter, then, what difficulties and problems face us—He is more than a match for them. The vision of His greatness puts the whole of life into its proper perspective. "We kneel, how weak—we rise, how full of power."

Prayer

O Father, I am so thankful that Your resources are so near at hand. I reflect on Your greatness and Your wonder in the depths of my heart, and my praying takes on new strength and power. I am so grateful. Amen.

Further Study

Eph 1; Ps 5:3; 65:5-7; 1 Ch 29:12
What was Paul's prayer for the Ephesians?
Ask God to enlarge your vision in this way.

MAY 19

1 SAMUEL 9:1–10:27

9 There was an influential man of Benjamin named Kish son of Abiel, son of Zeror, son of Becorath, son of Aphiah, son of a Benjaminite. ²He had a son named Saul, an impressive young man. There was no one more impressive among the Israelites than he. He stood a head taller than anyone else.

³One day the donkeys of Saul's father Kish wandered off. Kish said to his son Saul, "Take one of the attendants with you and go look for the donkeys." ⁴Saul and his attendant went through the hill country of Ephraim and then through the region of Shalishah, but they didn't find them. They went through the region of Shaalim—nothing. Then they went through the Benjaminite region but still didn't find them.

⁵When they came to the land of Zuph, Saul said to the attendant who was with him, "Come on, let's go back, or my father will stop worrying about the donkeys and start worrying about us."

⁶"Look," the attendant said, "there's a man of God in this city who is highly respected; everything he says is sure to come true. Let's go there now. Maybe he'll tell us which way we should go."

⁷"Suppose we do go," Saul said to his attendant, "what do we take the man? The food from our packs is gone, and there's no gift to take to the man of God. What do we have?"

⁸The attendant answered Saul: "Here, I have a piece of silver. I'll give it to the

560

man of God, and he will tell us our way."

⁹ Formerly in Israel, a man who was going to inquire of God would say, "Come, let's go to the seer," for the prophet of today was formerly called the seer. ¹⁰ "Good," Saul replied to his attendant. "Come on, let's go." So they went to the city where the man of God was. ¹¹ As they were climbing the hill to the city, they found some young women coming out to draw water and asked, "Is the seer here?"

¹² The women answered, "Yes, he is ahead of you. Hurry, he just now came to the city, because there's a sacrifice for the people at the high place today. ¹³ If you go quickly, you can catch up with him before he goes to the high place to eat. The people won't eat until he comes because he must bless the sacrifice; after that, the guests can eat. Go up immediately—you can find him now." ¹⁴ So they went up toward the city.

Saul and his attendant were entering the city when they saw Samuel coming toward them on his way to the high place. ¹⁵ Now the day before Saul's arrival, the LORD had informed Samuel, ¹⁶ "At this time tomorrow I will send you a man from the land of Benjamin. Anoint him ruler over My people Israel. He will save them from the hand of the Philistines because I have seen the affliction of My people, for their cry has come to Me." ¹⁷ When Samuel saw Saul, the LORD told him, "Here is the man I told you about; he will rule over My people."

¹⁸ Saul approached Samuel in the gate area and asked, "Would you please tell me where the seer's house is?"

¹⁹ "I am the seer," Samuel answered. "Go up ahead of me to the high place and eat with me today. When I send you off in the morning, I'll tell you everything that's in your heart. ²⁰ As for the donkeys that wandered away from you three days ago, don't worry about them because they've been found. And who does all Israel desire but you and all your father's family?"

²¹ Saul responded, "Am I not a Benja-minite from the smallest of Israel's tribes and isn't my clan the least important of all the clans of the Benjaminite tribe? So why have you said something like this to me?"

²² Samuel took Saul and his attendant, brought them a place at the banquet hall, and gave them a place at the head of the 30 or so men who had been invited. ²³ Then Samuel said to the cook, "Get the portion of meat that I gave you and told you to set aside."

²⁴ The cook picked up the thigh and what was attached to it and set it before Saul. Then Samuel said, "Notice that the reserved piece is set before you. Eat it because it was saved for you for this solemn event at the time I said, 'I've invited the people.' " So Saul ate with Samuel that day. ²⁵ Afterwards, they went down from the high place to the city, and Samuel spoke with Saul on the roof.

²⁶ They got up early, and just before dawn, Samuel called to Saul on the roof, "Get up, and I'll send you on your way!" Saul got up, and both he and Samuel went outside. ²⁷ As they were going down to the edge of the city, Samuel said to Saul, "Tell the attendant to go on ahead of us, but you stay for awhile, and I'll reveal the word of God to you." So the attendant went on.

10 Samuel took the flask of oil, poured it out on Saul's head, kissed him, and said, "Hasn't the LORD anointed you ruler over His inheritance? ² Today when you leave me, you'll find two men at Rachel's Grave at Zelzah in the land of Benjamin. They will say to you, 'The donkeys you went looking for have been found, and now your father has stopped being concerned about the donkeys and is worried about you, asking: What should I do about my son?'

³ "You will proceed from there until you come to the oak of Tabor. Three men going up to God at Bethel will meet you there, one bringing three goats, one bringing three loaves of bread, and one bringing a skin of wine. ⁴ They will ask how you are and give you

two loaves of bread, which you will accept from them.

5 "After that you will come to the Hill of God where there are Philistine garrisons. When you arrive at the city, you will meet a group of prophets coming down from the high place prophesying. They will be preceded by harps, tambourines, flutes, and lyres. 6 The Spirit of the LORD will control you, you will prophesy with them, and you will be transformed into a different person. 7 When these signs have happened to you, do whatever your circumstances require because God is with you. 8 Afterwards, go ahead of me to Gilgal. I will come to you to offer burnt offerings and to sacrifice fellowship offerings. Wait seven days until I come to you and show you what to do."

9 When Saul turned around to leave Samuel, God changed his heart, and all the signs came about that day. 10 When Saul and his attendant arrived at Gibeah, a group of prophets met him. Then the Spirit of God took control of him, and he prophesied along with them.

11 Everyone who knew him previously and saw him prophesy with the prophets asked each other, "What has happened to the son of Kish? Is Saul also among the prophets?"

12 Then a man who was from there asked, "And who is their father?"

As a result, "Is Saul also among the prophets?" became a popular saying.

13 Then Saul finished prophesying and went to the high place.

14 Saul's uncle asked him and his attendant, "Where did you go?"

"To look for the donkeys," Saul answered. "When we saw they weren't there, we went to Samuel."

15 "Tell me," Saul's uncle asked, "what did Samuel say to you?"

16 Saul told him, "He assured us the donkeys had been found." However, Saul did not tell him what Samuel had said about the matter of kingship.

17 Samuel summoned the people to the LORD at Mizpah 18 and said to the Israelites, "This is what the LORD, the God of Israel, says: 'I brought Israel out of Egypt, and I rescued you from the power of the Egyptians and all the kingdoms that were oppressing you.' 19 But today you have rejected your God, who saves you from all your troubles and afflictions. You said to Him, 'You must set a king over us.' Now therefore present yourselves before the LORD by your tribes and clans."

20 Samuel had all the tribes of Israel come forward, and the tribe of Benjamin was selected. 21 Then he had the tribe of Benjamin come forward by its clans, and the Matrite clan was selected. Finally, Saul son of Kish was selected. But when they searched for him, they could not find him. 22 They again inquired of the LORD, "Has the man come here yet?"

The LORD replied, "There he is, hidden among the supplies."

23 They ran and got him from there. When he stood among the people, he stood a head taller than anyone else. 24 Samuel said to all the people, "Do you see the one the LORD has chosen? There is no one like him among the entire population."

And all the people shouted, "Long live the king!"

25 Samuel proclaimed to the people the rights of kingship. He wrote them on a scroll, which he placed in the presence of the LORD. Then, Samuel sent all the people away, each to his home.

26 Saul also went to his home in Gibeah, and brave men whose hearts God had touched went with him. 27 But some wicked men said, "How can this guy save us?" They despised him and did not bring him a gift, but Saul said nothing.

*P*SALM 63:1-5

1 God, You are my God; I eagerly
    seek You.
  I thirst for You;
  my body faints for You
  in a land that is dry, desolate, and
    without water.
2 So I gaze on You in the
    sanctuary

to see Your strength and Your
glory.

3 My lips will glorify You
because Your faithful love is better
than life.
4 So I will praise You as long as I
live;
at Your name, I will lift up my
hands.
5 You satisfy me as with rich
food;
my mouth will praise You with
joyful lips.

PROVERBS 14:3

3 The proud speech of a fool brings
a rod of discipline,
but the lips of the wise protect
them.

JOHN 4:7-26

7 A woman of Samaria came to draw
water.
"Give Me a drink," Jesus said to her,
8 for His disciples had gone into town to
buy food.
9 "How is it that You, a Jew, ask for a
drink from me, a Samaritan woman?"
she asked Him. For Jews do not associate with Samaritans.
10 Jesus answered, "If you knew the
gift of God, and who is saying to you,
'Give Me a drink,' you would ask Him,
and He would give you living water."
11 "Sir," said the woman, "You don't
even have a bucket, and the well is
deep. So where do you get this 'living
water'? 12 You aren't greater than our father Jacob, are you? He gave us the well
and drank from it himself, as did his
sons and livestock."

13 Jesus said, "Everyone who drinks
from this water will get thirsty again.
14 But whoever drinks from the water
that I will give him will never get thirsty
again—ever! In fact, the water I will
give him will become a well of water
springing up within him for eternal
life."
15 "Sir," the woman said to Him, "give
me this water so I won't get thirsty and
come here to draw water."
16 "Go call your husband," He told
her, "and come back here."
17 "I don't have a husband," she answered.
"You have correctly said, 'I don't have
a husband,' " Jesus said. 18 "For you've
had five husbands, and the man you
now have is not your husband. What
you have said is true."
19 "Sir," the woman replied, "I see
that You are a prophet. 20 Our fathers
worshiped on this mountain, yet you
Jews say that the place to worship is in
Jerusalem."
21 Jesus told her, "Believe Me,
woman, an hour is coming when you
will worship the Father neither on this
mountain nor in Jerusalem. 22 You Samaritans worship what you do not
know. We worship what we do know,
because salvation is from the Jews.
23 But an hour is coming, and is now
here, when the true worshipers will
worship the Father in spirit and truth.
Yes, the Father wants such people to
worship Him. 24 God is spirit, and those
who worship Him must worship in spirit
and truth."
25 The woman said to Him, "I know
that Messiah is coming" (who is called
Christ). "When He comes, He will explain everything to us."
26 "I am He," Jesus told her, "the One
speaking to you."

Living Water

Whoever drinks from the water that I will give him will never get thirsty again . . . the water I will give him will become a well of water springing up within him for eternal life.—John 4:14

John 7:38 says, "The one who believes in Me...will have streams of living water flow from deep within him." *The Amplified Bible* translates this passage: "He who believes in Me . . . From his innermost being shall flow continuously springs and rivers of living water. But He was speaking here of the Spirit, whom those who believe in Him were afterward to receive."

Are our lives truly like this? Do fresh springs flow out of us day after day? If not, why not? The answer is simple—there can be no outflow unless there is an inflow. This is the rhythm of the Holy Spirit—intake and outflow. If there is more intake than outflow, then the intake stops; if there is more outflow than intake, then the outflow stops. The doors open inward to receive, only to open outward to give.

When we come to talk about life in the Spirit, we are not to think in terms of a reservoir which has only limited resources. Life is a channel, attached to infinite resources. The more we draw on these resources, the more we have. There is no danger of exhausting one's resources. We do not have to hold back—for the more we give, the more we have.

Living on the overflow is what many of us lack today. A sign could be put up over our individual and collective lives saying, "Life Limited." According to Jesus' promise, however, when the Spirit comes, life is unlimited: "From his innermost being shall flow rivers of living water." Not rivulets, not trickles, not brooks, not streams—but rivers. Rivers!

Prayer

O God, help me to link my channel to Your infinite resources. Flow through me until I become a flowing river—no, an overflowing river. In Jesus' name. Amen.

Further Study

Ac 10:34-38; 1 Co 3:16; 6:19; 2 Tm 1:14
How did Peter link Christ's work with that of the Spirit?
What has God made us to be?

MAY 20

1 SAMUEL 11:1–13:22

11 Nahash the Ammonite came up and laid siege to Jabesh-gilead. All the men of Jabesh said to him, "Make a treaty with us, and we will serve you."

² Nahash the Ammonite replied, "I'll make one with you on this condition: that I gouge out everyone's right eye and humiliate all Israel."

³ "Don't do anything to us for seven days," the elders of Jabesh said to him, "and let us send messengers throughout the territory of Israel. If no one saves us, we will surrender to you."

⁴ When the messengers came to Gibeah, Saul's hometown, and told the terms to the people, all wept aloud. ⁵ Just then Saul was coming in from the field behind his oxen. "What's the matter with the people? Why are they weeping?" Saul inquired, and they repeated to him the words of the men from Jabesh.

⁶ When Saul heard these words, the Spirit of God suddenly took control of him, and his anger burned furiously. ⁷ He took a team of oxen, cut them in pieces, and sent them throughout the land of Israel by messengers who said, "This is what will be done to the ox of anyone who doesn't march behind Saul and Samuel." As a result, the terror of the LORD fell on the people, and they went out united.

⁸ Saul counted them at Bezek. There were 300,000 Israelites and 30,000 men from Judah. ⁹ He told the messengers who had come, "Tell this to the men of Jabesh-gilead: 'Deliverance will be yours tomorrow by the time the sun is hot.' " So the messengers told the men of Jabesh, and they rejoiced.

¹⁰ Then the men of Jabesh said to Nahash, "Tomorrow we will come out, and you can do whatever you want to us."
¹¹ The next day Saul organized the troops into three divisions. During the morning watch, they invaded the Ammonite camp and slaughtered them until the heat of the day. There were survivors, but they were so scattered that no two of them were left together.

¹² Afterwards, the people said to Samuel, "Who said that Saul should not reign over us? Give us those men so we can kill them!"

¹³ But Saul ordered, "No one will be executed this day, for today the LORD has provided deliverance in Israel."

¹⁴ Then Samuel said to the people, "Come, let's go to Gilgal, so we can renew the kingship there." ¹⁵ So all the people went to Gilgal, and there in the LORD's presence they made Saul king. There they sacrificed fellowship offerings in the LORD's presence, and Saul and all the men of Israel greatly rejoiced.

12 Then Samuel said to all Israel, "I have carefully listened to everything you said to me and placed a king over you. ² But now, you can see that the king is leading you. As for me, I'm old and gray, and my sons are here with you. I have led you from my youth until today. ³ Here I am. Bring charges against me before the LORD and His anointed: Whose ox or donkey have I taken? Whom have I wronged or mistreated? From whose hand have I taken a bribe to overlook something? I will return it to you."

⁴ "You haven't wronged us, you haven't mistreated us, and you haven't taken anything from anyone's hand," they responded.

⁵ He said to them, "The LORD is a witness against you, and His anointed is a witness today that you haven't found anything in my hand."

"He is a witness," they said.

⁶ Then Samuel said to the people,

"The LORD, who appointed Moses and Aaron and who brought your ancestors up from the land of Egypt, is a witness. [7] Now present yourselves, so I may judge you before the LORD about all the righteous acts He has done for you and your ancestors.

[8] "When Jacob went to Egypt, your ancestors cried out to the LORD, and He sent them Moses and Aaron, who led your ancestors out of Egypt and settled them in this place. [9] But they forgot the LORD their God, so He handed them over to Sisera commander of the army of Hazor, to the Philistines, and to the king of Moab. These enemies fought against them. [10] Then they cried out to the LORD and said, 'We have sinned, for we abandoned the LORD and worshiped the Baals and the Ashtoreths. Now deliver us from the power of our enemies, and we will serve You.' [11] So the LORD sent Jerubbaal, Barak, Jephthah, and Samuel. He rescued you from the power of the enemies around you, and you lived securely. [12] But when you saw that Nahash king of the Ammonites was coming against you, you said to me, 'No, we must have a king rule over us'—even though the LORD your God is your king.

[13] "Now here is the king you've chosen, the one you requested. Look, this is the king the LORD has placed over you. [14] If you fear the LORD, worship and obey Him, and if you don't rebel against the LORD's command, then both you and the king who rules over you will follow the LORD your God. [15] However, if you disobey the LORD and rebel against His command, the LORD's hand will be against you and against your ancestors.

[16] "Now, therefore, present yourselves and see this great thing that the LORD will do before your eyes. [17] Isn't the wheat harvest today? I will call on the LORD and He will send thunder and rain, so that you will know and see what a great evil you committed in the LORD's sight by requesting a king for yourselves." [18] Samuel called on the LORD, and on that day the LORD sent thunder and rain. As a result, all the people greatly feared the LORD and Samuel.

[19] They pleaded with Samuel, "Pray to the LORD your God for your servants, so we won't die! For we have added to all our sins the evil of requesting a king for ourselves."

[20] Samuel replied, "Don't be afraid. Even though you have committed all this evil, don't turn away from following the LORD. Instead, worship the LORD with all your heart. [21] Don't turn away to follow worthless things that can't profit or deliver you; they are worthless. [22] The LORD will not abandon His people, because of His great name and because He has determined to make you His own people.

[23] "As for me, I vow that I will not sin against the LORD by ceasing to pray for you. I will teach you the good and right way. [24] Above all, fear the LORD and worship Him faithfully with all your heart, considering the great things He has done for you. [25] However, if you continue to do what is evil, both you and your king will be swept away."

13 Saul was 30 years old when he became king, and he reigned 42 years over Israel. [2] He chose 3,000 men from Israel for himself: 2,000 were with Saul at Michmash and in Bethel's hill country, and 1,000 were with Jonathan in Gibeah of Benjamin. He sent the rest of the troops away, each to his own tent.

[3] Jonathan attacked the Philistine garrison that was in Geba, and the Philistines heard about it. So Saul blew the ram's horn throughout the land saying, "Let the Hebrews hear!" [4] And all Israel heard the news, "Saul has attacked the Philistine garrison, and Israel is now repulsive to the Philistines." Then the troops were summoned to join Saul at Gilgal.

[5] The Philistines also gathered to fight against Israel: 3,000 chariots, 6,000 horsemen, and troops as numerous as the sand on the seashore. They went up and camped at Michmash, east of Beth-aven.

[6] The men of Israel saw that they were in trouble because the troops were in a difficult situation. They hid in caves, thickets, among rocks, and in

holes and cisterns. ⁷ Some Hebrews even crossed the Jordan to the land of Gad and Gilead.

Saul, however, was still at Gilgal, and all his troops were gripped with fear. ⁸ He waited seven days for the appointed time that Samuel had set, but Samuel didn't come to Gilgal, and the troops were deserting him. ⁹ So Saul said, "Bring me the burnt offering and the fellowship offerings." Then he offered the burnt offering.

¹⁰ Just as he finished offering the burnt offering, Samuel arrived. So Saul went out to greet him, ¹¹ and Samuel asked, "What have you done?"

Saul answered, "When I saw that the troops were deserting me and you didn't come within the appointed days and the Philistines were gathering at Michmash, ¹² I thought: The Philistines will now descend on me at Gilgal, and I haven't sought the LORD's favor. So I forced myself to offer the burnt offering."

¹³ Samuel said to Saul, "You have been foolish. You have not kept the command which the LORD your God gave you. It was at this time that the LORD would have permanently established your reign over Israel, ¹⁴ but now your reign will not endure. The LORD has found a man loyal to Him, and the LORD has appointed him as ruler over His people, because you have not done what the LORD commanded." ¹⁵ Then Samuel went from Gilgal to Gibeah in Benjamin. Saul registered the troops who were with him, about 600 men.

¹⁶ Saul, his son Jonathan, and the troops who were with them were staying in Geba of Benjamin, and the Philistines were camped at Michmash. ¹⁷ Raiding parties went out from the Philistine camp in three divisions. One division headed toward the Ophrah road leading to the land of Shual. ¹⁸ The next division headed toward the Bethhoron road, and the last division headed down the border road that looks out over the valley of Zeboim toward the wilderness.

¹⁹ No blacksmith could be found in all the land of Israel, because the Phil-istines had said, "Otherwise, the Hebrews will make swords or spears." ²⁰ So all the Israelites went to the Philistines to sharpen their plowshares, mattocks, axes, and sickles. ²¹ The price was two-thirds of a shekel for plowshares and mattocks, and one-third of a shekel for pitchforks and axes, and for putting a point on an oxgoad. ²² So on the day of battle not a sword or spear could be found in the hand of any of the troops who were with Saul and Jonathan; only Saul and his son Jonathan had weapons.

ᛈSALM 63:6-11

⁶ When, on my bed, I think of You,
   I meditate on You during the night watches
⁷ because You are my help;
   I will rejoice in the shadow of Your wings.
⁸ I follow close to You;
   Your right hand holds on to me.

⁹ But those who seek to destroy my life
   will go into the depths of the earth.
¹⁰ They will be given over to the power of the sword;
   they will become the jackals' prey.
¹¹ But the king will rejoice in God;
   all who swear by Him will boast,
   for the mouths of liars will be shut.

ᛈROVERBS 14:4

⁴ Where there are no oxen, the feeding-trough is empty,
   but an abundant harvest comes through the strength of an ox.

ᒍOHN 4:27-54

²⁷ Just then His disciples arrived, and they were amazed that He was talking with a woman. Yet no one said, "What do You want?" or "Why are You talking with her?"

²⁸ Then the woman left her water jar,

went into town, and told the men, ²⁹"Come, see a man who told me everything I ever did! Could this be the Messiah?" ³⁰They left the town and made their way to Him.

³¹In the meantime the disciples kept urging Him, "Rabbi, eat something." ³²But He said, "I have food to eat that you don't know about."

³³The disciples said to one another, "Could someone have brought Him something to eat?"

³⁴"My food is to do the will of Him who sent Me and to finish His work," Jesus told them. ³⁵"Don't you say, 'There are still four more months, then comes the harvest'? Listen to what I'm telling you: Open your eyes and look at the fields, for they are ready for harvest. ³⁶The reaper is already receiving pay and gathering fruit for eternal life, so the sower and reaper can rejoice together. ³⁷For in this case the saying is true: 'One sows and another reaps.' ³⁸I sent you to reap what you didn't labor for; others have labored, and you have benefited from their labor."

³⁹Now many Samaritans from that town believed in Him because of what the woman said when she testified, "He told me everything I ever did." ⁴⁰Therefore, when the Samaritans came to Him, they asked Him to stay with them, and He stayed there two days. ⁴¹Many more believed because of what He said. ⁴²And they told the woman, "We no longer believe because of what you said, for we have heard for ourselves and know that this really is the Savior of the world."

⁴³After two days He left there for Galilee. ⁴⁴Jesus Himself testified that a prophet has no honor in his own country. ⁴⁵When they entered Galilee, the Galileans welcomed Him because they had seen everything He did in Jerusalem during the festival. For they also had gone to the festival.

⁴⁶Then He went again to Cana of Galilee, where He had turned the water into wine. There was a certain royal official whose son was ill at Capernaum. ⁴⁷When this man heard that Jesus had come from Judea into Galilee, he went to Him and pleaded with Him to come down and heal his son, for he was about to die.

⁴⁸Jesus told him, "Unless you people see signs and wonders, you will not believe."

⁴⁹"Sir," the official said to Him, "come down before my boy dies!"

⁵⁰"Go," Jesus told him, "your son will live." The man believed what Jesus said to him and departed.

⁵¹While he was still going down, his slaves met him saying that his boy was alive. ⁵²He asked them at what time he got better. "Yesterday at seven in the morning the fever left him," they answered. ⁵³The father realized this was the very hour at which Jesus had told him, "Your son will live." Then he himself believed, along with his whole household.

⁵⁴This therefore was the second sign Jesus performed after He came from Judea to Galilee.

Four Simple Words

The woman ...went into town, and told the men, "Come, see a man who told me everything I ever did!"
—JOHN 4:28-29

In the true Christian heart, sharing is instinctive. What was the instinct of the woman at the well as soon as she had received salvation? It was to share what she had found with others.

What I am saying will cause some people to feel guilty, especially those who do not find it easy to share their faith. It is not that we should go out and accost everyone we meet with the message of salvation, but we do need to be alert for every opportunity and to take advantage of it. The four words which most succinctly summarize the gospel are each found in the Scripture passage before us today. They are these: "come . . . see . . . went . . . told." We get a firsthand knowledge—"come and see"—and then the instinctive impulse takes over—"go and tell." And if there is no "go and tell" impulse, then perhaps the "come and see" impulse is not ours, or at least it has ceased to hold a commanding place in our lives.

A woman once wrote to me following something I had written in *Every Day with Jesus* and said: "I had a real experience of God and refused to share it with anyone, so it died." How sad. J. B. Phillips' translation of 2 Corinthians 9:10 is luminous: "He who gives the seed to the sower . . ." See the inference? He gives seed only to the one who uses it—the sower. If we won't use the seed, then we won't get it. Our powers are either dead or dedicated. If they are dedicated, they are alive with God. If they are saved up or conserved, they die.

Prayer

O Father, I ask not for an experience of You—I already have that. I ask rather for the courage to share it with others. Give me some seed today, and help me to sow it in prepared hearts. For Your own dear name's sake. Amen.

Further Study

1 Pt 3:1-16; Ps 66:16; Is 63:7
What must we always be prepared to do?
How did Isaiah and the psalmist do this?

MAY 21

1 SAMUEL 13:23–14:52

²³ Now a Philistine garrison took control **14** of the pass at Michmash. ¹ That same day Saul's son Jonathan said to the attendant who carried his weapons, "Come on, let's cross over to the Philistine garrison on the other side." However, he did not tell his father.

² Saul was staying under the pomegranate tree in Migron on the outskirts of Gibeah. The troops with him numbered about 600. ³ Ahijah, who was wearing an ephod, was also there. He was the son of Ahitub, the brother of Ichabod son of Phinehas, son of Eli the LORD's priest at Shiloh. But the troops did not know that Jonathan had left.

⁴ There were sharp columns of rock on both sides of the pass that Jonathan intended to cross to reach the Philistine garrison. One was named Bozez and the other Seneh; ⁵ one stood to the north in

front of Michmash and the other to the south in front of Geba. ⁶ Jonathan said to the attendant who carried his weapons, "Come on, let's cross over to the garrison of these uncircumcised men. Perhaps the LORD will help us. Nothing can keep the LORD from saving, whether by many or by few." ⁷ His armor-bearer responded, "Do what is in your heart. You choose. I'm right here with you whatever you decide."

⁸ "All right," Jonathan replied, "we'll cross over to the men and then let them see us. ⁹ If they say, 'Wait until we reach you,' then we will stay where we are and not go up to them. ¹⁰ But if they say, 'Come on up,' then we'll go up, because the LORD has handed them over to us— that will be our sign."

¹¹ They let themselves be seen by the Philistine garrison, and the Philistines said, "Look, the Hebrews are coming out of the holes where they've been hiding!" ¹² The men of the garrison called to Jonathan and his armor-bearer. "Come on up, and we'll teach you a lesson!" they said.

"Follow me," Jonathan told his armor-bearer, "for the LORD has handed them over to Israel." ¹³ Jonathan went up using his hands and feet, with his armor-bearer behind him. Jonathan cut them down, and his armor-bearer followed and finished them off. ¹⁴ In that first assault Jonathan and his armor-bearer struck down about 20 men in a half-acre field.

¹⁵ Terror spread through the Philistine camp and the open fields to all the troops. Even the garrison and the raiding parties were terrified. The earth shook, and terror from God spread. ¹⁶ When Saul's watchmen in Gibeah of Benjamin looked, they saw the panicking troops scattering in every direction. ¹⁷ So Saul said to the troops with him, "Call the roll and determine who has left us." They called the roll and saw that Jonathan and his armor-bearer were gone.

¹⁸ Saul told Ahijah, "Bring the ark of God," for it was with the Israelites at that time. ¹⁹ While Saul spoke to the priest, the panic in the Philistine camp increased in intensity. So Saul said to the priest, "Stop what you're doing."

²⁰ Saul and all the troops with him assembled and marched to the battle, and there, the Philistines were fighting against each other in great confusion! ²¹ There were Hebrews from the area who had gone earlier into the camp to join the Philistines, but even they joined the Israelites who were with Saul and Jonathan. ²² When all the Israelite men who had been hiding in the hill country of Ephraim heard that the Philistines were fleeing, they also joined Saul and Jonathan in the battle. ²³ So the LORD saved Israel that day.

The battle extended beyond Beth-aven, ²⁴ and the men of Israel were worn out that day, for Saul had placed the troops under an oath: "Cursed is the man who eats food before evening, before I have taken vengeance on my enemies." So none of the troops tasted any food.

²⁵ Everyone went into the forest, and there was honey on the ground. ²⁶ When the troops entered the forest, they saw the flow of honey, but none of them ate any of it because they feared the oath. ²⁷ However, Jonathan had not heard his father make the troops swear the oath. He reached out with the end of the staff he was carrying and dipped it into the honeycomb. When he ate the honey, he had renewed energy. ²⁸ Then, one of the troops said, "Your father made the troops solemnly swear, 'Cursed is the man who eats food today,' and the troops are exhausted."

²⁹ Jonathan replied, "My father has brought trouble to the land. Just look at how I have renewed energy because I tasted a little honey. ³⁰ How much better if the troops had eaten freely today from the plunder they took from their enemies! Then the slaughter of the Philistines would have been much greater."

³¹ The Israelites struck down the Philistines that day from Michmash all the way to Aijalon. Since the Israelites were completely exhausted, ³² they rushed to the plunder, took sheep, cattle, and calves, slaughtered them on the

ground, and ate meat with the blood still in it. ³³ Some reported to Saul: "Look, the troops are sinning against the LORD by eating meat with the blood still in it."

Saul said, "You have been unfaithful. Roll a large stone over here at once." ³⁴ He then said, "Go among the troops and say to them, 'Each man must bring me his ox or his sheep. Do the slaughtering here and then you can eat. Don't sin against the LORD by eating meat with the blood in it.' " So every one of the troops brought his ox that night and slaughtered it there. ³⁵ Then Saul built an altar to the LORD; it was the first time he had built an altar to the LORD.

³⁶ Saul said, "Let's go down after the Philistines tonight and plunder them until morning. Don't let even one remain!"

"Do whatever you want," the troops replied.

But the priest said, "We must consult God here."

³⁷ So Saul inquired of God, "Should I go after the Philistines? Will You hand them over to Israel?" But God did not answer him that day.

³⁸ Saul said, "All you leaders of the troops, come here. Let us investigate how this sin has occurred today. ³⁹ As surely as the LORD lives who saves Israel, even if it is because of my son Jonathan, he must die!" Not one of the troops answered him.

⁴⁰ So he said to all Israel, "You will be on one side, and I and my son Jonathan will be on the other side."

And the troops replied, "Do whatever you want."

⁴¹ So Saul said to the LORD, "God of Israel, give us the right decision." Jonathan and Saul were selected, and the troops were cleared of the charge.

⁴² Then Saul said, "Cast the lot between me and my son Jonathan," and Jonathan was selected. ⁴³ Saul commanded him, "Tell me what you did."

Jonathan told him, "I tasted a little honey with the end of the staff I was carrying. I am ready to die!"

⁴⁴ Saul declared to him, "May God punish me severely if you do not die, Jonathan!"

⁴⁵ But the people said to Saul, "Must Jonathan die, who accomplished such a great deliverance for Israel? No, as the LORD lives, not a hair of his head will fall to the ground, for he worked with God's help today." So the people rescued Jonathan, and he did not die. ⁴⁶ Then Saul gave up the pursuit of the Philistines, and the Philistines returned to their own territory.

⁴⁷ When Saul assumed the kingship over Israel, he fought against all his enemies in every direction: against Moab, the Ammonites, Edom, the kings of Zobah, and the Philistines. Wherever he turned, he caused havoc. ⁴⁸ He fought bravely, defeated the Amalekites, and delivered Israel from the hand of those who plundered them.

⁴⁹ Saul's sons were Jonathan, Ishvi, and Malchishua. The names of his two daughters were: Merab, his firstborn, and Michal, the younger. ⁵⁰ The name of Saul's wife was Ahinoam daughter of Ahimaaz. The name of the commander of his army was Abner son of Saul's uncle Ner. ⁵¹ Saul's father was Kish. Abner's father was Ner son of Abiel.

⁵² The conflict with the Philistines was fierce all of Saul's days, so whenever Saul noticed any strong or brave man, he enlisted him.

*P*SALM 64:1-6

1 God, hear my voice when I
     complain.
   Protect my life from the terror of
     the enemy.
2 Hide me from the scheming of the
     wicked,
   from the mob of evildoers,
3 who sharpen their tongues like
     swords
   and aim bitter words like arrows,
4 shooting from concealed places at
     the innocent.
   They shoot at him suddenly and
     are not afraid.
5 They encourage each other in an
     evil plan;
   they talk about hiding traps and
     say,

"Who will see them?"

6 They devise crimes and say,
"We have perfected a secret plan."
The inner man and the heart are
mysterious.

PROVERBS 14:5-7

5 An honest witness does not
deceive,
but a dishonest witness utters lies.

6 A mocker seeks wisdom and
doesn't find it,
but knowledge comes easily to the
perceptive.

7 Stay away from a foolish man;
you will gain no knowledge from
his speech.

JOHN 5:1-23

5 After this, a Jewish festival took
place, and Jesus went up to Jerusalem. 2 By the Sheep Gate in Jerusalem
there is a pool, called Bethesda in
Hebrew, which has five colonnades.
3 Within these lay a multitude of the
sick—blind, lame, and paralyzed [wait-
ing for the moving of the water, 4 because an angel would go down into
the pool from time to time and stir up
the water. Then the first one who got in
after the water was stirred up recovered
from whatever ailment he had].
5 One man was there who had been
sick for 38 years. 6 When Jesus saw him
lying there and knew he had already
been there a long time, He said to him,
"Do you want to get well?"
7 "Sir," the sick man answered, "I
don't have a man to put me into the
pool when the water is stirred up, but
while I'm coming, someone goes down
ahead of me."
8 "Get up," Jesus told him, "pick up
your bedroll and walk!" 9 Instantly the

man got well, picked up his bedroll, and
started to walk.
Now that day was the Sabbath, 10 so
the Jews said to the man who had been
healed, "This is the Sabbath! It's illegal
for you to pick up your bedroll."
11 He replied, "The man who made
me well told me, 'Pick up your bedroll
and walk.'"
12 "Who is this man who told you,
'Pick up your bedroll and walk?'" they
asked. 13 But the man who was cured did
not know who it was, because Jesus had
slipped away into the crowd that was
there.
14 After this, Jesus found him in the
temple complex and said to him, "See,
you are well. Do not sin any more, so
that something worse doesn't happen
to you." 15 The man went and reported
to the Jews that it was Jesus who had
made him well.
16 Therefore, the Jews began persecuting Jesus because He was doing
these things on the Sabbath. 17 But Jesus
responded to them, "My Father is still
working, and I am working also." 18 This
is why the Jews began trying all the
more to kill Him: not only was He
breaking the Sabbath, but He was even
calling God His own Father, making
Himself equal with God.
19 Then Jesus replied, "I assure you:
The Son is not able to do anything on
His own, but only what He sees the
Father doing. For whatever the Father
does, the Son also does these things in
the same way. 20 For the Father loves the
Son and shows Him everything He is
doing, and He will show Him greater
works than these so that you will be
amazed. 21 And just as the Father raises
the dead and gives them life, so the Son
also gives life to anyone He wants to.
22 The Father, in fact, judges no one but
has given all judgment to the Son, 23 so
that all people will honor the Son just as
they honor the Father. Anyone who
does not honor the Son does not honor
the Father who sent Him."

Safe and Sealed

He will show Him greater works than these
so that you will be amazed.—John 5:20

In Ephesians 1:13-14, we see that those who "heard" were "sealed": "In Him you also, when you heard the word...were sealed with the promised Holy Spirit." Does the "sealing" take place at conversion or at some point beyond it? I believe it takes place at conversion. A seal is a mark of ownership, and when the Holy Spirit comes in to regenerate our beings at conversion, He produces the assurance in our hearts that we are heirs of God and joint heirs with Christ.

I know that some believe that the "sealing" takes place subsequent to conversion, such as at one's baptism by total immersion, or at a crisis point of sanctification, or, as some would describe it, when we are baptized in the Holy Spirit. But how insecure life would be if we had to wait for "this" or "that" experience in order to know that we are safe in Christ.

One historian says that it was customary in Ephesus for certain traders to send their slaves into the marketplace to make purchases for them and, once the transaction was complete, the slaves would mark the item with their master's seal, whereupon it was delivered to the master's home. In something of the same way, the Holy Spirit in our own hearts seals, once and for all, the question of His ownership over our lives, and also acts as a pledge, or guarantee, that one day we will be safely delivered to our Father's home in glory. In Wales, many years ago, I heard a frail old Christian say: "The envelope (meaning his body) may be a bit tattered, but the letter inside is quite safe." It is!

Prayer

O Father, what endless blessings follow the coming of Your Spirit into my life. I am saved by grace, sealed by the Spirit, and supported by eternal love. What more could I ask for this side of glory! Amen.

Further Study

Jn 5; Rm 8:16; Gl 4:6; 1 Jn 4:13
How does the Holy Spirit "bear witness"?
What confidence does this give us?

MAY 22

1 SAMUEL 15:1–16:23

15 Samuel told Saul, "The LORD sent me to anoint you as king over His people Israel. Now, listen to the words of the LORD. ² This is what the LORD of Hosts says: 'I witnessed what the Amalekites did to the Israelites when they opposed them along the way as they were coming out of Egypt. ³ Now go and attack the Amalekites and completely destroy everything they have. Do not spare them. Kill men and women, children and infants, oxen and sheep, camels and donkeys.' "

⁴ Then Saul summoned the troops and counted them at Telaim: 200,000 foot soldiers and 10,000 men from Judah. ⁵ Saul came to the city of Amalek and set up an ambush in the wadi. ⁶ He warned the Kenites, "Since you showed kindness to all the Israelites when they came out of Egypt, go on and leave! Get away from the Amalekites, or I'll sweep you away with them." So the Kenites withdrew from the Amalekites.

⁷ Then Saul struck down the Amalekites from Havilah all the way to Shur, which is next to Egypt. ⁸ He captured Agag king of Amalek alive, but he completely destroyed all the rest of the people with the sword. ⁹ Saul and the troops spared Agag, and the best of the sheep, cattle, and fatlings, as well as the young rams and the best of everything else. They were not willing to destroy them, but they did destroy all the worthless and unwanted things.

¹⁰ Then the word of the LORD came to Samuel: ¹¹ "I regret that I made Saul king, for he has turned away from following Me and has not carried out My instructions." So Samuel became angry and cried out to the LORD all night. ¹² Early in the morning Samuel got up to confront Saul, but it was reported to Samuel, "Saul went to Carmel where he set up a monument for himself. Then he turned around and went down to Gilgal." ¹³ When Samuel came to him, Saul said, "May the LORD bless you. I have carried out the LORD's instructions."

¹⁴ Samuel replied, "Then what is this sound of sheep and cattle I hear?"

¹⁵ Saul answered, "The troops brought them from the Amalekites and spared the best sheep and cattle in order to offer a sacrifice to the LORD your God, but the rest we destroyed."

¹⁶ "Stop!" exclaimed Samuel. "Let me tell you what the LORD said to me last night."

"Tell me," he replied.

¹⁷ Samuel continued, "Although you once considered yourself unimportant, have you not become the leader of the tribes of Israel? The LORD anointed you king over Israel ¹⁸ and then sent you on a mission and said: 'Go and completely destroy the sinful Amalekites. Fight against them until you have annihilated them.' ¹⁹ So why didn't you obey the LORD? Why did you rush on the plunder and do what was evil in the LORD's sight?"

²⁰ "But I did obey the LORD!" Saul answered. "I went on the mission the LORD gave me: I brought back Agag, king of Amalek, and I completely destroyed the Amalekites. ²¹ The troops took sheep and cattle from the plunder—the best of what was set apart for destruction—to sacrifice to the LORD your God at Gilgal."

²² Then Samuel said:

> Does the LORD take pleasure in
>   burnt offerings and sacrifices
> as much as in obeying the LORD?
>
> Look: to obey is better
>   than sacrifice,
> to pay attention is better
>   than the fat of rams.

23 For rebellion is like the sin of
divination,
and defiance is like wickedness
and idolatry.
Because you have rejected
the word of the LORD,
He has rejected you as king.

24 Saul answered Samuel, "I have
sinned. I have transgressed the LORD's
command and your words. Because I
was afraid of the people, I obeyed them.
25 Now therefore, please forgive my sin
and return with me so I can worship the
LORD."
26 Samuel replied to Saul, "I will not
return with you. Because you rejected
the word of the LORD, the LORD has rejected you from being king over Israel."
27 When Samuel turned to go, Saul
grabbed the hem of his robe, and it tore.
28 Samuel said to him, "The LORD has
torn the kingship of Israel away from
you today and has given it to your neighbor who is better than you. 29 Furthermore, the Eternal One of Israel does not
lie or change His mind, for He is not
man who changes his mind."
30 Saul said, "I have sinned. Please
honor me now before the elders of my
people and before Israel. Come back
with me so I can bow and worship the
LORD your God." 31 Then Samuel went
back, following Saul, and Saul bowed
down to the LORD.
32 Samuel said, "Bring me Agag king
of Amalek."
Agag came to him trembling, for he
thought, "Certainly the bitterness of
death has come."
33 Samuel declared:

As your sword has made women
childless,
so your mother will be childless
among women.

Then he hacked Agag to pieces before
the LORD at Gilgal.
34 Samuel went to Ramah, and Saul
went up to his home in Gibeah of
Saul. 35 Even to the day of his death,
Samuel never again visited Saul. Samuel mourned for Saul, and the LORD re-

gretted He had made Saul king over
Israel.

16 The LORD said to Samuel, "How
long are you going to mourn for
Saul, since I have rejected him as king
over Israel? Fill your horn with oil and
go. I am sending you to Jesse of Bethlehem because I have selected a king
from his sons."
2 Samuel asked, "How can I go? Saul
will hear about it and kill me!"
The LORD answered, "Take a young
cow with you and say, 'I have come to
sacrifice to the LORD.' 3 Then invite
Jesse to the sacrifice, and I will let you
know what you are to do. You are to
anoint for Me the one I indicate to
you."
4 Samuel did what the LORD directed
and went to Bethlehem. When the elders of the town met him, they trembled
and asked, "Do you come in peace?"
5 "In peace," he replied. "I've come to
sacrifice to the LORD. Consecrate yourselves and come with me to the sacrifice." Then he consecrated Jesse and his
sons and invited them to the sacrifice.
6 When they arrived, Samuel saw Eliab
and said, "Certainly the LORD's anointed
one is here before Him."
7 But the LORD said to Samuel, "Do
not look at his appearance or his
stature, because I have rejected him.
Man does not see what the LORD sees,
for man sees what is visible, but the
LORD sees the heart."
8 Jesse called Abinadab and presented
him to Samuel. "The LORD hasn't chosen this one either," Samuel said. 9 Then
Jesse presented Shammah, but Samuel
said, "The LORD hasn't chosen this one
either." 10 After Jesse presented seven
of his sons to him, Samuel told Jesse,
"The LORD hasn't chosen any of these."
11 Samuel asked him, "Are these all the
sons you have?"
"There is still the youngest," he answered, "but right now he's tending the
sheep." Samuel told Jesse, "Send for
him. We won't sit down to eat until he
gets here." 12 So Jesse sent for him. He
had beautiful eyes and a healthy, handsome appearance.

Then the LORD said, "Anoint him, for he is the one." ¹³ So Samuel took the horn of oil, anointed him in the presence of his brothers, and the Spirit of the LORD took control of David from that day forward. Then Samuel set out and went to Ramah.

¹⁴ Now the Spirit of the LORD had left Saul, and an evil spirit from the LORD began to torment him, ¹⁵ so Saul's servants said to him, "You see that an evil spirit from God is tormenting you. ¹⁶ Let our lord command your servants here in your presence to look for someone who knows how to play the harp. Whenever the evil spirit from God troubles you, that person can play the harp, and you will feel better."

¹⁷ Then Saul commanded his servants, "Find me someone who plays well and bring him to me."

¹⁸ One of the young men answered, "I have seen a son of Jesse of Bethlehem who knows how to play the harp. He is also a valiant man, a warrior, eloquent, handsome, and the LORD is with him."

¹⁹ Then Saul dispatched messengers to Jesse and said, "Send me your son David, who is with the sheep." ²⁰ So Jesse took a donkey loaded with bread, a skin of wine, and one young goat and sent them by his son David to Saul. ²¹ When David came to Saul and entered his service, Saul admired him greatly, and David became his armor-bearer. ²² Then Saul sent word to Jesse: "Let David remain in my service, for I am pleased with him." ²³ Whenever the spirit from God troubled Saul, David would pick up his harp and play, and Saul would then be relieved, feel better, and the evil spirit would leave him.

PSALM 64:7-10

⁷ But God will shoot them with arrows;
  suddenly, they will be wounded.
⁸ They will be made to stumble;
  their own tongues work against them.
  All who see them will shake their heads.

⁹ Then everyone will fear
  and will tell about God's work,
  for they will understand what He has done.

¹⁰ The righteous rejoice in the LORD
  and take refuge in Him;
  all the upright in heart offer praise.

PROVERBS 14:8-9

⁸ The sensible man's wisdom is to consider his way,
  but the stupidity of fools deceives them.

⁹ Fools mock at making restitution,
  but there is goodwill among the upright.

JOHN 5:24-47

²⁴ "I assure you: Anyone who hears My word and believes Him who sent Me has eternal life and will not come under judgment but has passed from death to life. ²⁵ "I assure you: An hour is coming, and is now here, when the dead will hear the voice of the Son of God, and those who hear will live. ²⁶ For just as the Father has life in Himself, so also He has granted to the Son to have life in Himself. ²⁷ And He has granted Him the right to pass judgment, because He is the Son of Man. ²⁸ Do not be amazed at this, because a time is coming when all who are in the graves will hear His voice ²⁹ and come out—those who have done good things, to the resurrection of life, but those who have done wicked things, to the resurrection of judgment.

³⁰ "I can do nothing on My own. I judge only as I hear, and My judgment is righteous, because I do not seek My own will, but the will of Him who sent Me. ³¹ "If I testify about Myself, My testimony is not valid. ³² There is Another who testifies about Me, and I know that the testimony He gives about Me is valid. ³³ You have sent messengers to

John, and he has testified to the truth. [34] I don't receive man's testimony, but I say these things so that you may be saved. [35] John was a burning and shining lamp, and for a time you were willing to enjoy his light.

[36] "But I have a greater testimony than John's because of the works that the Father has given Me to accomplish. These very works I am doing testify about Me that the Father has sent Me. [37] The Father who sent Me has Himself testified about Me. You have not heard His voice at any time, and you haven't seen His form. [38] You don't have His word living in you, because you don't believe the One He sent. [39] You pore over the Scriptures because you think you have eternal life in them, yet they testify about Me. [40] And you are not willing to come to Me that you may have life.

[41] "I do not accept glory from men, [42] but I know you—that you have no love for God within you. [43] I have come in My Father's name, yet you don't accept Me. If someone else comes in his own name, you will accept him. [44] How can you believe? While accepting glory from one another, you don't seek the glory that comes from the only God. [45] Do not think that I will accuse you to the Father. Your accuser is Moses, on whom you have set your hope. [46] For if you believed Moses, you would believe Me, because he wrote about Me. [47] But if you don't believe his writings, how will you believe My words?"

Easier to Pretend

You are not willing to come to Me that you may have life.

——JOHN 5:40

In Psalm 42:1, the psalmist states, "As a deer longs for streams of water, so I long for You, God." Why do most Christians not long for God in this way? Because to long for God means we must get in touch with the deep thirst that is at the center of our being and acknowledge our basic helplessness—a feeling which our fallen human nature deeply dislikes.

Most of us instinctively draw back from dealing with this stubborn commitment to independence, pretending we are all right as we are. It is much easier to pretend we are thirsting after God than it is to face the challenge of giving up our commitment to independence.

I am conscious that the challenge I am putting before you is one I want to deny in my own life. There is something in me that would like to think—and would like you to think—that I have a heart that thirsts for God. But I know that if I stop short of identifying my independent strategies for finding life on my own and giving them up, I will never get in touch with the deep thirst for God that exists at the core of my being.

What is the answer? I must ask God to search my heart, expose my self-centered motivations, and help me see just where it is that I stop short of panting after Him.

You see, the more deeply we sense our thirst, the more passionately we will pursue water. But we will never sense that thirst until we are willing to face the fact that we may be drinking more from our own self-constructed wells than from the wells of God.

Prayer

Father, I tremble as I recognize this tendency within me to walk right past the fountain of living water and drink from a well of my own making. But help me to recognize it for what it really is—not just a terrible tendency, but a terrible sin. Amen.

Further Study

Ex 32:1-9; Is 28:12; 30:15; 2 Ch 24:19
How did God describe the children of Israel?
What is said of them time and time again?

MAY 23

I SAMUEL 17:1-58

17 The Philistines gathered their forces for war at Socoh in Judah and camped between Socoh and Azekah in Ephes-dammim. ² Saul and the men of Israel gathered and camped in the Valley of Elah; then they lined up in battle formation to face the Philistines.

³ The Philistines were standing on one hill, and the Israelites were standing on another hill with a ravine between them. ⁴ Then a champion named Goliath, from Gath, came out from the Philistine camp. He was nine feet, nine inches tall ⁵ and wore a bronze helmet and bronze scale armor that weighed 125 pounds. ⁶ There was bronze armor on his shins, and a bronze sword was slung between his shoulders. ⁷ His spear shaft was like a weaver's beam, and the iron point of his spear weighed 15 pounds. In addition, a shield-bearer was walking in front of him.

⁸ He stood and shouted to the Israelite battle formations: "Why do you come out to line up in battle formation?" He asked them, "Am I not a Phil-istine and are you not servants of Saul? Choose one of your men and have him come down against me. ⁹ If he wins in a fight against me and kills me, we will be your servants. But if I win against him and kill him, then you will be our servants and serve us." ¹⁰ Then the Philistine said, "I defy the ranks of Israel today. Send me a man so we can fight each other!" ¹¹ When Saul and all Israel heard these words from the Philistine, they lost their courage and were terrified.

¹² Now David was the son of the Ephrathite from Bethlehem of Judah named Jesse. Jesse had eight sons, and during Saul's reign was already an old man. ¹³ Jesse's three oldest sons had followed Saul to the war, and their names were Eliab, the firstborn, Abinadab, the next, and Shammah, the third, ¹⁴ and David was the youngest. The three oldest had followed Saul, ¹⁵ but David kept going back and forth from Saul to tend his father's flock in Bethlehem.

¹⁶ Every morning and evening for 40 days the Philistine came forward and took his stand. ¹⁷ One day, Jesse had told his son David, "Take this half-bushel of

roasted grain along with these loaves of bread for your brothers and hurry to their camp. ¹⁸ Also, take these 10 portions of cheese to the field commander. Check on the welfare of your brothers and bring a confirmation from them. ¹⁹ They are with Saul and all the men of Israel are in the Valley of Elah fighting with the Philistines."

²⁰ So David got up early in the morning, left the flock with someone to keep it, loaded up, and set out as Jesse had instructed him.

He arrived at the perimeter of the camp as the army was marching out to its battle formation shouting their battle cry. ²¹ Israel and the Philistines lined up in battle formation facing each other. ²² David left his supplies in the care of the quartermaster and ran to the battle line. When he arrived, he asked his brothers how they were. ²³ While he was speaking with them, suddenly the champion named Goliath, the Philistine from Gath, came forward from the Philistine battle line and shouted his usual words, which David heard. ²⁴ When all the Israelite men saw Goliath, they retreated from him terrified.

²⁵ Previously, an Israelite man had declared, "Do you see this man who keeps coming out? He comes to defy Israel. The king will make the man who kills him very rich and will give him his daughter. The king will also make the household of that man's father exempt from paying taxes in Israel."

²⁶ David spoke to the men who were standing with him: "What will be done for the man who kills that Philistine and removes this disgrace from Israel? Just who is this uncircumcised Philistine that he should defy the armies of the living God?"

²⁷ The people told him about the offer, concluding, "That is what will be done for the man who kills him."

²⁸ David's oldest brother Eliab listened as he spoke to the men, and became angry with him. "Why did you come down here?" he asked. "Who did you leave those few sheep with in the wilderness? I know your arrogance and your evil heart—you came down to see the battle!"

²⁹ "What have I done now?" protested David. "It was just a question." ³⁰ Then he turned from those beside him to others in front of him and asked about the offer. The people gave him the same answer as before.

³¹ What David said was overheard and reported to Saul, so he had David brought to him. ³² David said to Saul, "Don't let anyone be discouraged by him; your servant will go and fight this Philistine!"

³³ But Saul replied, "You can't go fight this Philistine. You're just a youth, and he's been a warrior since he was young."

³⁴ David answered Saul, "Your servant has been tending his father's sheep. Whenever a lion or a bear came and carried off a lamb from the flock, ³⁵ I went after it, struck it down, and rescued the lamb from its mouth. If it reared up against me, I would grab it by its fur, strike it down, and kill it. ³⁶ Your servant has killed lions and bears; this uncircumcised Philistine will be like one of them, for he has defied the armies of the living God." ³⁷ Then David said, "The LORD who rescued me from the paw of the lion and the paw of the bear will rescue me from the hand of this Philistine."

Saul said to David, "Go, and may the LORD be with you."

³⁸ Then Saul had his own military clothes put on David. He put a bronze helmet on David's head and had him put on armor. ³⁹ David strapped his sword on over the military clothes and tried to walk, but he was not used to them. "I can't walk in these," David said to Saul, "I'm not used to them." So David took them off. ⁴⁰ Instead, he took his staff in his hand and chose five smooth stones from the wadi and put them in the pouch, in his shepherd's bag. Then, with his sling in his hand, he approached the Philistine.

⁴¹ The Philistine came closer and closer to David, with the shield-bearer in front of him. ⁴² When the Philistine looked and saw David, he despised him because he was just a youth, healthy and handsome. ⁴³ He said to David, "Am

I a dog that you come against me with sticks?" Then he cursed David by his gods. ⁴⁴ "Come here," the Philistine called to David, "and I'll give your flesh to the birds of the sky and the wild beasts!"

⁴⁵ David said to the Philistine, "You come against me with a dagger, spear, and sword, but I come against you in the name of the LORD of Hosts, the God of Israel's armies—you have defied Him. ⁴⁶ Today, the LORD will hand you over to me. Today, I'll strike you down, cut your head off, and give the corpses of the Philistine camp to the birds of the sky and the creatures of the earth. Then all the world will know that Israel has a God, ⁴⁷ and this whole assembly will know that it is not by sword or by spear that the LORD saves, for the battle is the LORD's. He will hand you over to us."

⁴⁸ When the Philistine started forward to attack him, David ran quickly to the battle line to meet the Philistine. ⁴⁹ David put his hand in the bag, took out a stone, slung it, and hit the Philistine on his forehead. The stone sank into his forehead, and he fell on his face to the ground. ⁵⁰ David defeated the Philistine with a sling and a stone. Even though David had no sword, he struck down the Philistine and killed him. ⁵¹ David ran and stood over him. He grabbed the Philistine's sword, pulled it from its sheath, and used it to kill him. Then he cut off his head. When the Philistines saw that their hero was dead, they ran. ⁵² The men of Israel and Judah rallied, shouting their battle cry, and chased the Philistines to the entrance of the valley and to the gates of Ekron. Philistine bodies were strewn all along the Shaaraim road to Gath and Ekron.

⁵³ When the Israelites returned from the pursuit of the Philistines, they plundered their camps. ⁵⁴ David took Goliath's head and brought it to Jerusalem, but he put Goliath's weapons in his own tent.

⁵⁵ When Saul had seen David going out to confront the Philistine, he asked Abner the commander of the army, "Whose son is this youth, Abner?"

"My king, as surely as you live, I don't know," Abner replied.

⁵⁶ The king said, "Find out whose son this young man is!"

⁵⁷ When David returned from killing the Philistine, Abner took him and brought him before Saul with the Philistine's head still in his hand. ⁵⁸ Saul said to him, "Whose son are you, young man?"

"The son of your servant Jesse of Bethlehem," David answered.

PSALM 65:1-8

¹ Praise is rightfully Yours,
God, in Zion;
vows to You will be fulfilled.
² All humanity will come to You,
the One who hears prayer.
³ Iniquities overwhelm me;
only You can atone for our
rebellions.
⁴ How happy is the one You
choose
and bring near to live in Your
courts!
We will be satisfied with the
goodness of Your house,
the holiness of Your temple.

⁵ You answer us in righteousness,
with awe-inspiring works,
God of our salvation,
the hope of all the ends of the
earth and of the distant seas;
⁶ You establish the mountains by
Your power,
robed with strength;
⁷ You silence the roar of the seas,
the roar of their waves,
and the tumult of the nations.
⁸ Those who live far away are awed
by Your signs;
You make east and west shout for
joy.

PROVERBS 14:10-12

¹⁰ The heart knows its own
bitterness,
and no outsider shares in its joy.

11 The house of the wicked will be
   destroyed,
   but the tent of the upright will
   stand.

12 There is a way that seems right to
   a man,
   but its end is the way to death.

JOHN 6:1-21

6 After this, Jesus crossed the Sea of Galilee (or Tiberias). ² And a huge crowd was following Him because they saw the signs that He was performing on the sick. ³ So Jesus went up a mountain and sat down there with His disciples.

⁴ Now the Passover, a Jewish festival, was near. ⁵ Therefore, when Jesus looked up and noticed a huge crowd coming toward Him, He asked Philip, "Where will we buy bread so these people can eat?" ⁶ He asked this to test him, for He Himself knew what He was going to do.

⁷ Philip answered, "Two hundred denarii worth of bread wouldn't be enough for each of them to have a little."

⁸ One of His disciples, Andrew, Simon Peter's brother, said to Him, ⁹ "There's a boy here who has five barley loaves and two fish—but what are they for so many?"

¹⁰ Then Jesus said, "Have the people sit down."

There was plenty of grass in that place, so they sat down. The men numbered about 5,000. ¹¹ Then Jesus took the loaves, and after giving thanks He distributed them to those who were seated—so also with the fish, as much as they wanted.

¹² When they were full, He told His disciples, "Collect the leftovers so that nothing is wasted." ¹³ So they collected them and filled 12 baskets with the pieces from the five barley loaves that were left over by those who had eaten.

¹⁴ When the people saw the sign He had done, they said, "This really is the Prophet who was to come into the world!" ¹⁵ Therefore, when Jesus knew that they were about to come and take Him by force to make Him king, He withdrew again to the mountain by Himself.

¹⁶ When evening came, His disciples went down to the sea, ¹⁷ got into a boat, and started across the sea to Capernaum. Darkness had already set in, but Jesus had not yet come to them. ¹⁸ Then a high wind arose, and the sea began to churn. ¹⁹ After they had rowed about three or four miles, they saw Jesus walking on the sea. He was coming near the boat, and they were afraid. ²⁰ But He said to them, "It is I. Don't be afraid!" ²¹ Then they were willing to take Him on board, and at once the boat was at the shore where they were heading.

Two Opposite Pairs

There is a way that seems right to a man, but its end is the way to death.
—PROVERBS 14:12

I have met many people who have experienced such deep hurt in their early relationships that they cannot rid themselves of negative ideas about having God as their Father, and by God's grace I have been able to help some of them. But the route to healing is not an easy one and involves walking a path that is quite different from the one a secular counselor might suggest.

The route which the world usually advises victims of parental abuse to take consists of three steps: self-discovery, self-expression, and self-protection. Self-discovery is where the victim is encouraged to get in touch with his or her repressed emotions. Self-expression is the release and expression of those emotions. Self-protection is the establishment of boundaries around one's life so that one will never have to endure or experience serious hurt again.

The biblical route to healing, while recognizing some truth in these ideas, starts from a different base and leads to a different goal. It begins with the question: Do I believe that a God who allowed me to be as deeply hurt as I was is good? And it ends with the question: Am I willing to give myself to those I am called to love and to be more interested in loving well than in protecting myself against hurt?

Which sounds like the easier path of these two? Undoubtedly, the way of the world. The way of Christ may seem as if it is the route to death, but really it is the route to life. To live we must be willing to die; to find we must be willing to lose.

Prayer

Father, help me take Your way in everything I pray. I don't want symptom relief; I want a complete cure. And if I don't need help on this particular issue, help me learn how to be of help to others. Amen.

Further Study

Mt 5:43-48; 7:13-14; 16:24-25; Jn 12:24-25
What is the biblical way to life?
What makes the narrow way narrow?

MAY 24

I SAMUEL 18:1–19:24

18 When David had finished speaking with Saul, Jonathan committed himself to David, and loved him as much as he loved himself. ² Saul kept David with him from that day on and did not let him return to his father's house.

³ Jonathan made a covenant with David because he loved him as much as himself. ⁴ Then Jonathan removed the robe he was wearing and gave it to

David, along with his military tunic, his sword, his bow, and his belt.

⁵ David marched out with the army, and was successful in everything Saul sent him to do. Saul put him in command of the soldiers, which pleased all the people and Saul's servants as well.

⁶ As David was returning from killing the Philistine, the women came out from all the cities of Israel to meet King Saul, singing and dancing with tambourines, with shouts of joy, and with

three-stringed instruments. ⁷As they celebrated, the women sang:

Saul has killed his thousands,
but David his tens of thousands.

⁸Saul was furious and resented this song. "They credited tens of thousands to David," he complained, "but they only credited me with thousands. What more can he have but the kingdom?" ⁹So Saul watched David jealously from that day forward.

¹⁰The next day an evil spirit from God took control of Saul, and he began to rave inside the palace. David was playing the harp as usual, but Saul was holding a spear, ¹¹and he threw it, thinking, "I'll pin David to the wall." But David got away from him twice.

¹²Saul was afraid of David, because the LORD was with David but had left from Saul. ¹³Therefore, Saul reassigned David and made him commander over 1,000 men. David led the troops ¹⁴and continued to be successful in all his activities because the LORD was with him. ¹⁵When Saul observed that David was very successful, he dreaded him. ¹⁶But all Israel and Judah loved David because he was leading their troops. ¹⁷Saul told David, "Here is my oldest daughter Merab. I'll give her to you as a wife, if you will be a warrior for me and fight the LORD's battles." But Saul was thinking, "My hand doesn't need to be against him; let the hand of the Philistines be against him."

¹⁸Then David responded, "Who am I, and what is my family or my father's clan in Israel that I should become the king's son-in-law?" ¹⁹When it was time to give Saul's daughter Merab to David, she was given to Adriel the Meholathite as a wife.

²⁰Now Saul's daughter Michal loved David, and when it was reported to Saul, it pleased him. ²¹"I'll give her to him," Saul thought. "She'll be a trap for him, and the hand of the Philistines will be against him." So Saul said to David a second time, "You can now be my son-in-law."

²²Saul then ordered his servants,

"Speak to David in private and tell him, 'Look, the king is pleased with you, and all his servants love you. Therefore, you should become the king's son-in-law.'" ²³Saul's servants reported these words directly to David, but he replied, "Is it trivial in your sight to become the king's son-in-law? I am a poor man who is common."

²⁴The servants reported back to Saul, "These are the words David spoke." ²⁵Then Saul replied, "Say this to David: 'The king desires no other brideprice except 100 Philistine foreskins, to take revenge on his enemies.'" Actually, Saul intended to cause David's death at the hands of the Philistines.

²⁶When the servants reported these terms to David, he was pleased to become the king's son-in-law. Before the wedding day arrived, ²⁷David and his men went out and killed 200 Philistines. He brought their foreskins and presented them as full payment to the king to become his son-in-law. Then Saul gave his daughter Michal to David as his wife. ²⁸Saul realized that the LORD was with David and that his daughter Michal loved him, ²⁹and he became even more afraid of David. As a result, Saul was David's enemy from then on.

³⁰Every time the Philistine commanders came out to fight, David was more successful than all of Saul's officers. So his name became very famous.

19 Saul ordered his son Jonathan and all his servants to kill David. But Saul's son Jonathan liked David very much, ²so he told him: "My father Saul intends to kill you. Be on your guard in the morning and hide in a secret place and stay there. ³I'll go out and stand beside my father in the field where you are and talk to him about you. When I see what he says, I'll tell you."

⁴Jonathan spoke well of David to his father Saul. He said to him: "The king should not sin against his servant David. He hasn't sinned against you; in fact, his actions have been a great advantage to you. ⁵He took his life in his hands when he struck down the Philistine, and the LORD brought about a great victory for

all Israel. You saw it and rejoiced, so why would you sin against innocent blood by killing David for no reason?"

⁶ Saul listened to Jonathan's advice and swore an oath: "As surely as the LORD lives, David will not be killed." ⁷ So Jonathan summoned David and told him all these words. Then Jonathan brought David to Saul, and he served him as he did before.

⁸ When war broke out again, David went out and fought against the Philistines. He defeated them with such a great force that they fled from him.

⁹ Now an evil spirit from the LORD came on Saul as he was sitting in his palace holding a spear. David was playing the harp, ¹⁰ and Saul tried to pin David to the wall with the spear. As the spear struck the wall, David eluded Saul and escaped. That night he ran away. ¹¹ Saul sent agents to David's house to watch for him and kill him in the morning. But his wife Michal warned David: "If you don't escape tonight, you will be dead tomorrow!" ¹² So she lowered David from the window, and he fled and escaped. ¹³ Then Michal took the household idol and put it on the bed, placed some goats' hair on its head, and covered it with a garment. ¹⁴ When Saul sent agents to seize David, Michal said, "He's sick."

¹⁵ Saul sent the agents back to see David and said, "Bring him on his bed so I can kill him." ¹⁶ When the messengers arrived, to their surprise, the household idol was on the bed with some goats' hair on its head.

¹⁷ Saul asked Michal, "Why did you deceive me like this? You sent my enemy away, and he has escaped!"

She answered him, "He said to me, 'Let me go! Why should I kill you?' "

¹⁸ So David fled and escaped and went to Samuel at Ramah and told him everything Saul had done to him. Then he and Samuel left and stayed at Naioth.

¹⁹ When it was reported to Saul that David was at Naioth in Ramah, ²⁰ Saul sent agents to seize David. However, when they saw the group of prophets prophesying with Samuel leading them, the Spirit of God came on Saul's agents,

and they also started prophesying. ²¹ When they reported to Saul, he sent other agents, and they also began prophesying. So Saul tried again and sent a third group of agents, and even they began prophesying. ²² Then Saul himself went to Ramah. He came to the large cistern at Secu, looked around, and asked, "Where are Samuel and David?"

"At Naioth in Ramah," someone said.

²³ So he went to Naioth in Ramah. The Spirit of God also came on him, and as he walked along, he prophesied until he entered Naioth in Ramah. ²⁴ Saul then removed his clothes and also prophesied before Samuel; he collapsed and lay naked all that day and all that night. That is why they say, "Is Saul also among the prophets?"

PSALM 65:9-13

⁹ You visit the earth and water it
　　abundantly, enriching it
　　greatly.
　God's stream is filled with water,
　for You prepare the earth in this
　　way, providing people with
　　grain.
¹⁰ You soften it with showers and
　　bless its growth,
　soaking its furrows and leveling its
　　ridges.
¹¹ You crown the year with Your
　　goodness;
　Your ways overflow with plenty.
¹² The wilderness pastures overflow,
　and the hills are robed with joy.
¹³ The pastures are clothed with
　　flocks,
　and the valleys covered with grain.
　They shout in triumph; indeed,
　　they sing.

PROVERBS 14:13-14

¹³ Even in laughter a heart may be
　　sad,
　and joy may end in grief.

¹⁴ The disloyal will get what their
　　conduct deserves,

and a good man, what his deeds deserve.

JOHN 6:22-40

²² The next day, the crowd that had stayed on the other side of the sea knew there had been only one boat. They also knew that Jesus had not boarded the boat with His disciples, but that His disciples had gone off alone. ²³ Some boats from Tiberias came near the place where they ate the bread after the Lord gave thanks. ²⁴ When the crowd saw that neither Jesus nor His disciples were there, they got into the boats and went to Capernaum looking for Jesus. ²⁵ When they found Him on the other side of the sea, they said to Him, "Rabbi, when did You get here?"

²⁶ Jesus answered, "I assure you: You are looking for Me, not because you saw the signs, but because you ate the loaves and were filled. ²⁷ Don't work for the food that perishes but for the food that lasts for eternal life, which the Son of Man will give you, because God the Father has set His seal of approval on Him."

²⁸ "What can we do to perform the works of God?" they asked.

²⁹ Jesus replied, "This is the work of God: that you believe in the One He has sent."

³⁰ "What sign then are You going to do so we may see and believe You?" they asked. "What are You going to perform? ³¹ Our fathers ate the manna in the wilderness, just as it is written: **He gave them bread from heaven to eat.**"

³² Jesus said to them, "I assure you: Moses didn't give you the bread from heaven, but My Father gives you the real bread from heaven. ³³ For the bread of God is the One who comes down from heaven and gives life to the world."

³⁴ Then they said, "Sir, give us this bread always!"

³⁵ "I am the bread of life," Jesus told them. "No one who comes to Me will ever be hungry, and no one who believes in Me will ever be thirsty again. ³⁶ But as I told you, you've seen Me, and yet you do not believe. ³⁷ Everyone the Father gives Me will come to Me, and the one who comes to Me I will never cast out. ³⁸ For I have come down from heaven, not to do My will, but the will of Him who sent Me. ³⁹ This is the will of Him who sent Me: that I should lose none of those He has given Me but should raise them up on the last day. ⁴⁰ For this is the will of My Father: that everyone who sees the Son and believes in Him may have eternal life, and I will raise him up on the last day."

He Can't Forget!

Jesus replied, "This is the work of God: that you believe in the One He has sent."—JOHN 6:29

In this passage, our Lord is asked: "What can we do to perform the works of God?" (v. 28). His answer was entirely different from that which you would receive if you posed the question to adherents of different religious systems today. A Buddhist would answer: "We must follow the eightfold path of Buddhism." A Muslim would answer: "We must fast and pray and make a trip to Mecca." Some followers of the Christian way might answer "We must engage in regular Bible study, prayer, tithing, and Christian fellowship." But the answer Jesus gave was: "This is the work of God: that you believe . . ."

George Watson, a devotional writer, said: "To trust the Origin of our existence is the fundamental grace of life. There is one virtue [in God] that stands out forever more conspiculously than friendship, or love, or knowledge, or wisdom. It is fidelity. God's fidelity is in Him what trust is in us."

Understanding that God is utterly trustworthy will deliver us from such incapacitating emotions as worry, anxiety, and fear. To be overwhelmed by the concerns of this life reflects poorly upon the faithfulness of God.

An old saint who was dying became concerned that he couldn't remember any of God's promises. His pastor said: "Do you think God will forget any of them?" A smile came over the face of the dying Christian as he exclaimed joyfully: "No, no, He won't." This, too, is our confidence. He won't forget, because being God, He can't forget.

Prayer

O God my Father, if fidelity in You is what trust is in us, then help us come to a place where our trust matches Your fidelity. We confess we are not there yet, but we long to arrive. Help us, dear Father. In Jesus' name. Amen.

Further Study

2 Tm 2:1-13; Heb 2:17; 10:23
What did Paul assure Timothy?
Why was Jesus made like His brothers?

MAY 25

I SAMUEL 20:1–21:15

20 David fled from Naioth in Ramah and came to Jonathan and asked, "What have I done? What did I do wrong? How have I sinned against your father so that he wants to take my life?"

² Jonathan said to him, "No, you won't die. Listen, my father doesn't do anything, great or small, without telling me. So why would he hide this matter from me? This can't be true."

³ But David said, "Your father certainly knows that you have come to look favorably on me. He has said, 'Jonathan

must not know of this, or else he will be grieved.'" David also swore, "As surely as the LORD lives and as you yourself live, there is but a step between me and death."

⁴ Jonathan said to David, "Whatever you say, I will do for you."

⁵ So David told him, "Look, tomorrow is the New Moon, and I'm supposed to sit down and eat with the king. Instead, let me go, and I'll hide in the field until the third night. ⁶ If your father misses me at all, say, 'David urgently requested my permission to quickly go to his town Bethlehem for an annual sacrifice there

involving the whole clan.' ⁷ If he says, 'Good,' then your servant is safe, but if he becomes angry, you will know he has evil intentions. ⁸ Deal faithfully with your servant, for you have brought me into a covenant before the LORD with you. If I have done anything wrong, then kill me yourself; why take me to your father?"

⁹ "No!" Jonathan responded. "If I ever find out my father has evil intentions against you, wouldn't I tell you about it?"

¹⁰ So David asked Jonathan, "Who will tell me if your father answers you harshly?"

¹¹ He answered David, "Come on, let's go out to the field." So both of them went out to the field. ¹² "By the LORD, the God of Israel, if I sound out my father by this time tomorrow or the next day and I find out that he is favorable toward you, and if I do not send for you and tell you, ¹³ then may God punish Jonathan and do so severely. If my father intends to bring evil on you, then I will tell you, and I will send you away, and you will go in peace. May the LORD be with you, just as He was with my father. ¹⁴ If I continue to live, treat me with the LORD's faithful love, but if I die, ¹⁵ don't ever withdraw your faithful love from my household—not even when the LORD cuts off every one of David's enemies from the face of the earth." ¹⁶ Then Jonathan made a covenant with the house of David, saying, "May the LORD hold David's enemies accountable." ¹⁷ Jonathan once again swore to David in his love for him, because he loved him as he loved himself.

¹⁸ Then Jonathan said to him, "Tomorrow is the New Moon; you'll be missed because your seat will be empty. ¹⁹ The following day hurry down and go to the place where you hid on the day this incident began and stay beside the rock Ezel. ²⁰ I will shoot three arrows beside it as if I'm aiming at a target. ²¹ Then I will send the young man and say, 'Go and find the arrows!' Now, if I expressly say to the young man, 'Look, the arrows are on this side of you—get them,' then come, because as the LORD lives, it is safe for you and there is no problem.

²² But if I say this to the youth: 'Look, the arrows are beyond you!' then go, for the LORD is sending you away. ²³ As for the matter you and I have spoken about, the LORD will be a witness between you and me forever." ²⁴ So David hid in the field.

At the New Moon, the king sat down to eat the meal. ²⁵ He sat at his usual place on the seat by the wall. Jonathan sat facing him and Abner took his place beside Saul, but David's place was empty. ²⁶ Saul did not say anything that day because he thought, "Something unexpected has happened; he must be ceremonially unclean—yes, that's it, he is unclean."

²⁷ However, the day after the New Moon, the second day, David's place was still empty, and Saul asked his son Jonathan, "Why didn't Jesse's son come to the meal either yesterday or today?"

²⁸ Jonathan answered, "David asked for my permission to go to Bethlehem. ²⁹ He said, 'Please let me go because our clan is holding a sacrifice in the town, and my brother has told me to be there. So now, if you are pleased with me, let me go so I can see my brothers.' That's why he didn't come to the king's table."

³⁰ Then Saul became angry with Jonathan and shouted, "You son of a perverse and rebellious woman! Don't I know that you are siding with Jesse's son to your own shame and to the disgrace of your mother? ³¹ Every day Jesse's son lives on earth you and your kingship are not secure. Now send for him and bring him to me—he deserves to die."

³² Jonathan answered his father back: "Why is he to be killed? What has he done?"

³³ Then Saul threw his spear at Jonathan to kill him, so he knew that his father was determined to kill David. ³⁴ He got up from the table in fierce anger and did not eat any food that second day of the New Moon, for he was grieved because of his father's shameful behavior toward David.

³⁵ In the morning Jonathan went out to the field for the appointed meeting with David. A small young man was with

him. ³⁶ He said to the young man, "Run and find the arrows I'm shooting." As the young man ran, Jonathan shot an arrow beyond him. ³⁷ He came to the location of the arrow that Jonathan had shot, but Jonathan called to him and said, "The arrow is beyond you, isn't it?" ³⁸ Then Jonathan called to him, "Hurry up and don't stop!" Jonathan's young man picked up the arrow and returned to his master. ³⁹ He did not know anything; only Jonathan and David knew the arrangement. ⁴⁰ Then Jonathan gave his equipment to the young man who was with him and said, "Go, take it back to the city."

⁴¹ When the young man had gone, David got up from the south side of the stone Ezel, fell with his face to the ground, and bowed three times. Then he and Jonathan kissed each other and wept with each other, though David wept more.

⁴² Jonathan then said to David, "Go in the assurance the two of us pledged in the name of the LORD when we said: The LORD will be a witness between you and me and between my offspring and your offspring forever." Then David left, and Jonathan went into the city.

21 David went to Ahimelech the priest at Nob. Ahimelech was afraid to meet David, so he said to him, "Why are you alone and no one is with you?"

² David answered Ahimelech the priest, "The king gave me a mission, but he told me, 'Don't let anyone know anything about the mission I'm sending you on or what I have ordered you to do.' I have stationed my young men at a certain place. ³ Now what do you have on hand? Give me five loaves of bread or whatever can be found."

⁴ The priest told him, "There is no ordinary bread on hand. However, there is consecrated bread, but the young men may eat it only if they have kept themselves from women."

⁵ David answered him, "I swear that women are being kept from us, as always when I go out to battle. The young men's bodies are consecrated even on

an ordinary mission, so of course their bodies are consecrated today." ⁶ So the priest gave him the consecrated bread, for there was no bread there except the bread of the Presence that had been removed from before the LORD. When the bread was removed, it had been replaced with warm bread.

⁷ One of Saul's servants, detained before the LORD, was there that day. His name was Doeg the Edomite, chief of Saul's shepherds.

⁸ David said to Ahimelech, "Do you have a spear or sword on hand? I didn't even bring my sword or my weapons since the king's mission was urgent."

⁹ The priest replied, "The sword of Goliath the Philistine, whom you killed in the valley of Elah, is here, wrapped in a cloth behind the ephod. If you want to take it for yourself, then take it, for there isn't another one here."

"There's none like it!" David said. "Give it to me."

¹⁰ David fled that day from Saul's presence and went to King Achish of Gath. ¹¹ But Achish's servants said to him, "Isn't this David, the king of the land? Don't they sing about him during their dances:

Saul has killed his thousands,
but David his tens of thousands?"

¹² David took this to heart and became very afraid of King Achish of Gath, ¹³ so he pretended to be insane in their presence. He acted like a madman around them, scribbling on the doors of the gate and letting saliva run down his beard.

¹⁴ "Look! You can see the man is crazy," Achish said to his servants. "Why did you bring him to me? ¹⁵ Do I have such a shortage of crazy people that you brought this one to act crazy around me? Is this one going to come into my house?"

....

$\mathcal{P}$ SALM 66:1-7

¹ Shout joyfully to God, all the earth!

2 Sing the glory of His name;
make His praise glorious.
3 Say to God, "How awe-inspiring
are Your works!
Your enemies will cringe before
You
because of Your great strength.
4 All the earth will worship You and
sing praise to You.
They will sing praise to Your
name."   *Selah*

5 Come and see the works of God;
His acts toward mankind are awe-
inspiring.
6 He turned the sea into dry land,
and they crossed the river on foot.
There we rejoiced in Him.
7 He rules forever by His might;
He keeps His eye on the nations.
The rebellious should not exalt
themselves.   *Selah*

*P*ROVERBS 14:15-16

15 The inexperienced believe
anything,
but the sensible watch their steps.

16 A wise man is cautious and turns
from evil,
but a fool is easily angered and is
careless.

*J*OHN 6:41-59

41 Therefore the Jews started complaining about Him, because He said, "I
am the bread that came down from
heaven." 42 They were saying, "Isn't this
Jesus the son of Joseph, whose father
and mother we know? How can He now
say, 'I have come down from heaven'?"

43 Jesus answered them, "Stop complaining among yourselves. 44 No one
can come to Me unless the Father who
sent Me draws him, and I will raise him
up on the last day. 45 It is written in the
Prophets: **And they will all be taught
by God.** Everyone who has listened to
and learned from the Father comes to
Me— 46 not that anyone has seen the
Father except the One who is from God.
He has seen the Father.
47 "I assure you: Anyone who believes
has eternal life. 48 I am the bread of life.
49 Your fathers ate the manna in the
wilderness, and they died. 50 This is the
bread that comes down from heaven so
that anyone may eat of it and not die.
51 I am the living bread that came down
from heaven. If anyone eats of this
bread he will live forever. The bread
that I will give for the life of the world
is My flesh."
52 At that, the Jews argued among
themselves, "How can this man give us
His flesh to eat?"
53 So Jesus said to them, "I assure
you: Unless you eat the flesh of the Son
of Man and drink His blood, you do not
have life in yourselves. 54 Anyone who
eats My flesh and drinks My blood has
eternal life, and I will raise him up on
the last day, 55 because My flesh is real
food and My blood is real drink. 56 The
one who eats My flesh and drinks My
blood lives in Me, and I in him. 57 Just as
the living Father sent Me and I live because of the Father, so the one who
feeds on Me will live because of Me.
58 This is the bread that came down from
heaven; it is not like the manna your fathers ate—and they died. The one who
eats this bread will live forever."
59 He said these things while teaching
in the synagogue in Capernaum.

"As Good as Your Book"

I am the living bread that came down from heaven.
If anyone eats of this bread he will live forever.—JOHN 6:51

A Hindu said to a missionary in India: "Sir, I do not want to appear presumptuous, but have you found out what the Acts of the Apostles records? I see there a strange power, making weak, ineffective men into strong, effective, radiant men. That seems new and central—have you found that?" And that is the central question we must ask ourselves. We are taken up with so many little and marginal things in church life that we miss the central power.

A group of children, on the way to see the ocean, got occupied with a pond that one of them had made by blocking the flow of a tiny stream. One little fellow, seeing the ocean in the distance, said, "Come on, Billy, that ain't the ocean—that's only a pond!"

Sometimes I feel like calling to the thousands of Christians who are gathered around their little denominational pools, thinking them to be the ocean: "Come on, brothers and sisters, that isn't the whole thing. Look over there. The ocean awaits us—God's ocean of power and plenty. I'll race you to it!"

A Christian who gave a Bible to an acquaintance asked him some time later if he had read it. "Yes," said the man, "and what is more, I have found you out. You are not as good as your Book! The Book says there is power for human weakness, joy instead of sorrow, victory instead of defeat—but I see little of this in you." What an indictment! Could the same be said of you and me?

Prayer

O Father, help me to be as good as the Book. Show me the way to power and poise, so that I will represent the highest qualities of life to those I live with or work with. For Jesus' sake. Amen.

Further Study

Jn 6:44-71; Rv 2:4, 3:16; Mt 24:12; Ac 5:13
How did some of Jesus' disciples respond?
What did Simon Peter say?

MAY 26

1 SAMUEL 22:1–23:29

22 So David left Gath and took refuge in the cave of Adullam. When David's brothers and his father's whole family heard, they went down and joined him there. ² In addition, every man who was desperate, in debt, or discontented rallied around him, and he became their leader. About 400 men were with him.

³ From there David went to Mizpeh of Moab where he said to the king of Moab, "Please let my father and mother stay with you until I know what God will do for me." ⁴ So he left them in the care of the king of Moab, and they stayed with him the whole time David was in the stronghold.

⁵ Then the prophet Gad said to David, "Don't stay in the stronghold. Leave and return to the land of Judah." So David left and went to the forest of Hereth.

⁶ Saul heard that David and his men had been discovered. At that time Saul was in Gibeah, sitting under the tamarisk tree at the high place. His spear was in his hand, and all his servants were standing around him. ⁷ Saul said to his servants, "Listen, men of Benjamin: Is Jesse's son going to give all of you fields and vineyards? Do you think he'll make all of you commanders of thousands and commanders of hundreds? ⁸ That's why all of you have conspired against me! Nobody tells me when my own son makes a covenant with Jesse's son. None of you cares about me or tells me that my son has stirred up my own servant to wait in ambush for me, as is the case today."

⁹ Then Doeg the Edomite, who was in charge of Saul's servants, answered: "I saw Jesse's son come to Ahimelech son of Ahitub at Nob. ¹⁰ Ahimelech inquired of the LORD for him and gave him provi-sions. He also gave him the sword of Goliath the Philistine."

¹¹ The king sent messengers to summon Ahimelech the priest, son of Ahitub, and his father's whole family, who were priests in Nob. All of them came to the king. ¹² Then Saul said, "Listen, son of Ahitub!"

"I'm at your service, my lord," he said.

¹³ Saul asked him, "Why did you and Jesse's son conspire against me? You gave him bread and a sword and inquired of God for him, so he could rise up against me and wait in ambush, as is the case today."

¹⁴ Ahimelech replied to the king: "Who among all your servants is as faithful as David? He is the king's son-in-law, captain of your bodyguard, and honored in your house. ¹⁵ Was today the first time I inquired of God for him? Of course not! Please don't let the king make an accusation against your servant or any of my father's household, for your servant didn't have any idea about all this."

¹⁶ But the king said, "You will die, Ahimelech—you and your father's whole family!"

¹⁷ Then the king ordered the guards standing by him, "Turn and kill the priests of the LORD because they sided with David. For they knew he was fleeing, but they didn't tell me." But the king's servants would not lift a hand to execute the priests of the LORD.

¹⁸ So the king said to Doeg, "Go and execute the priests!" So Doeg the Edomite went and executed the priests himself. On that day, he killed 85 men who wore linen ephods. ¹⁹ He also struck down Nob, the city of the priests, with the sword—both men and women, children and infants, oxen, donkeys, and sheep.

²⁰ However, one of the sons of Ahimelech son of Ahitub escaped. His name

was Abiathar, and he fled to David. ²¹ Abiathar told David that Saul had killed the priests of the LORD. ²² Then David said to Abiathar, "I knew that Doeg the Edomite was there that day and that he was sure to report to Saul. I myself am responsible for the lives of everyone in your father's family. ²³ Stay with me. Don't be afraid, for the one who wants to take my life wants to take your life. You will be safe with me."

23 It was reported to David: "Look, the Philistines are fighting against Keilah and raiding the threshing floors."
² So David inquired of the LORD: "Should I launch an attack against these Philistines?"

The LORD answered David, "Launch an attack against the Philistines and rescue Keilah."
³ But David's men said to him, "Look, we're afraid here in Judah; how much more if we go to Keilah against the Philistine forces!"
⁴ Once again, David inquired of the LORD, and the LORD answered him: "Go at once to Keilah, for I will hand the Philistines over to you." ⁵ Then David and his men went to Keilah, fought against the Philistines, drove their livestock away, and inflicted heavy losses on them. So David rescued the inhabitants of Keilah. ⁶ Abiathar son of Ahimelech fled to David at Keilah, and he brought an ephod with him.
⁷ When it was reported to Saul that David had gone to Keilah, he said, "God has handed him over to me, for he has trapped himself by entering a town with barred gates." ⁸ Then Saul summoned all the troops to go to war at Keilah and besiege David and his men.
⁹ When David learned that Saul was plotting evil against him, he said to Abiathar the priest, "Bring the ephod."
¹⁰ Then David said, "LORD God of Israel, Your servant has heard that Saul intends to come to Keilah and destroy the town because of me. ¹¹ Will the citizens of Keilah hand me over to him? Will Saul come down as Your servant has heard? LORD God of Israel, please tell Your servant."

The LORD answered, "He will come down."
¹² Then David asked, "Will the citizens of Keilah hand me and my men over to Saul?"
"They will," the LORD responded.
¹³ So David and his men, numbering about 600, left Keilah at once and moved from place to place. When it was reported to Saul that David had escaped from Keilah, he called off the expedition. ¹⁴ David then stayed in the wilderness strongholds and in the hill country of the Wilderness of Ziph. Saul searched for him every day, but God did not hand David over to him.
¹⁵ David was in the Wilderness of Ziph in Horesh when he saw that Saul had come out to take his life. ¹⁶ Then Saul's son Jonathan came to David in Horesh and encouraged him in his faith in God, ¹⁷ saying, "Don't be afraid, for my father Saul will never lay a hand on you. You yourself will be king over Israel, and I'll be your second-in-command. Even my father Saul knows it is true." ¹⁸ Then the two of them made a covenant in the LORD's presence. Afterwards, David remained in Horesh, while Jonathan went home.
¹⁹ Some Ziphites came up to Saul at Gibeah and said, "David is hiding among us in the strongholds in Horesh on the hill of Hachilah south of Jeshimon. ²⁰ Now, whenever the king wants to come down, let him come down. Our part will be to hand him over to the king."
²¹ "May you be blessed by the LORD," replied Saul, "for you have taken pity on me. ²² Go and check again. Investigate and watch carefully where he goes and who has seen him there; they tell me he is extremely cunning. ²³ Look and find out all the places where he hides. Then come back to me with accurate information, and I'll go with you. If it turns out he really is in the region, I'll search for him among all the clans of Judah." ²⁴ So they went to Ziph ahead of Saul.

Now David and his men were in the wilderness near Maon in the Arabah south of Jeshimon, ²⁵ and Saul and his men went to look for him. When David was told about it, he went down to the rock and stayed in the Wilderness of Maon. Saul heard of this and pursued David there. ²⁶ Saul went along one side of the mountain and David and his men went along the other side. Even though David was hurrying to get away from Saul, Saul and his men were closing in on David and his men to capture them. ²⁷ Then a messenger came to Saul saying, "Come quickly, because the Philistines have raided the land!" ²⁸ So Saul broke off his pursuit of David and went to engage the Philistines. Therefore, that place was named the Rock of Separation. ²⁹ From there David went up and stayed in the strongholds of En-gedi.

PSALM 66:8-15

⁸ Praise our God, you peoples;
let the sound of His praise be
heard.
⁹ He keeps us alive
and does not allow our feet to slip.

¹⁰ For You, God, tested us;
You refined us as silver is refined.
¹¹ You lured us into a trap;
You placed burdens on our backs.
¹² You let men ride over our heads;
we went through fire and water,
but You brought us out to
abundance.

¹³ I will enter Your house with burnt
offerings;
I will pay You my vows
¹⁴ that my lips promised
and my mouth spoke during my
distress.
¹⁵ I will offer You fattened sheep as
burnt offerings,
with the fragrant smoke of rams;
I will sacrifice oxen with goats.
Selah

PROVERBS 14:17-19

¹⁷ A quick-tempered man acts
foolishly,

and a man who schemes is
hated.
¹⁸ The gullible inherit foolishness,
but the sensible are crowned with
knowledge.
¹⁹ The evil bow before those who are
good,
the wicked, at the gates of the
righteous.

JOHN 6:60–7:9

⁶⁰ Therefore, when many of His disciples heard this, they said, "This teaching is hard! Who can accept it?" ⁶¹ Jesus, knowing in Himself that His disciples were complaining about this, asked them, "Does this offend you? ⁶² Then what if you were to observe the Son of Man ascending to where He was before? ⁶³ The Spirit is the One who gives life. The flesh doesn't help at all. The words that I have spoken to you are spirit and are life. ⁶⁴ But there are some among you who don't believe." (For Jesus knew from the beginning those who would not believe and the one who would betray Him.) ⁶⁵ He said, "This is why I told you that no one can come to Me unless it is granted to him by the Father."

⁶⁶ From that moment many of His disciples turned back and no longer accompanied Him. ⁶⁷ Therefore Jesus said to the Twelve, "You don't want to go away too, do you?"

⁶⁸ Simon Peter answered, "Lord, who will we go to? You have the words of eternal life. ⁶⁹ We have come to believe and know that You are the Holy One of God!"

⁷⁰ Jesus replied to them, "Didn't I choose you, the Twelve? Yet one of you is the Devil!" ⁷¹ He was referring to Judas, Simon Iscariot's son, one of the Twelve, because he was going to betray Him.

7 After this, Jesus traveled in Galilee, since He did not want to travel in Judea because the Jews were trying to

kill Him. ² The Jewish Festival of Tabernacles was near, ³ so His brothers said to Him, "Leave here and go to Judea so Your disciples can see Your works that You are doing. ⁴ For no one does anything in secret while he's seeking public recognition. If You do these things, show Yourself to the world." ⁵ (For not even His brothers believed in Him.)

⁶ Jesus told them, "My time has not yet arrived, but your time is always at hand. ⁷ The world cannot hate you, but it does hate Me because I testify about it—that its deeds are evil. ⁸ Go up to the festival yourselves. I'm not going up to the festival yet, because My time has not yet fully come." ⁹ After He had said these things, He stayed in Galilee.

Spirit-Aided Praying

The Spirit is the One who gives life.—JOHN 6:63

The more I consider "praying in the Spirit," the more convinced I am that the majority of Christians do not know what it means to pray in this particular way. Many are content to recite prayers and know nothing of the thrill of entering a dimension of prayer in which the Holy Spirit has full control.

Not that there is anything wrong with liturgical or written prayers—they can be a wonderful primer for one's spiritual pump. Many people tell me that the prayers I frame at the end of each devotion in *Every Day with Jesus* have sometimes helped them more than the actual notes I have written. Using written prayers can be helpful, but we must heed the apostle's exhortation to move on into that dimension which he calls "praying in the Spirit." The best description of this I have ever heard is that given by some of the old Welsh preachers, like Daniel Rowlands, Christmas Evans, and others. They describe it as "praying with unusual liberty and freedom."

There is hardly anything more wonderful in the Christian life than to experience this "liberty and freedom" in prayer. I can remember the minister and elders of the church in which I was converted in South Wales saying after a prayer meeting in which there had been great liberty and power: "Tonight we have prayed in the Spirit."

Have you not experienced moments when, after struggling and halting in prayer, you were suddenly taken out of yourself and words just poured out of you? At that moment, you were "praying in the Spirit."

Prayer

O Father, forgive me that I try to do so much in my own strength instead of learning how to let You do it in me. Teach me how to let go and let You take over in everything—particularly my praying. In Jesus' name. Amen.

MAY 27

1 SAMUEL 24:1–25:44

24 When Saul returned from pursuing the Philistines, he was told, "David is in the wilderness near Engedi." ² So Saul took 3,000 of Israel's choice men and went to look for David and his men in front of the Rocks of the Wild Goats. ³ When Saul came to the sheep pens along the road, a cave was there, and he went in to relieve himself. David and his men were staying in the back of the cave, ⁴ so they said to him, "Look, this is the day the LORD told you about: 'I will hand your enemy over to you so you can do to him whatever you desire.'" Then David got up and secretly cut off the corner of Saul's robe.

⁵ Afterwards, David's conscience bothered him because he had cut off the corner of Saul's robe. ⁶ He said to his men, "I swear before the LORD: I would never do such a thing to my lord, the LORD's anointed. I will never lift my hand against him, since he is the LORD's anointed." ⁷ With these words David persuaded his men, and he did not let them rise up against Saul.

Then Saul left the cave and went on his way. ⁸ After that, David got up, went out of the cave, and called to Saul, "My lord the king!" When Saul looked behind him, David bowed to the ground in homage. ⁹ David said to Saul, "Why do you listen to the words of people who say, 'Look, David intends to harm you'? ¹⁰ You can see with your own eyes that the LORD handed you over to me today in the cave. Someone advised me to kill you, but I took pity on you and said: I won't lift my hand against my lord, since he is the LORD's anointed. ¹¹ See, my father! Look at the corner of your robe in my hand, for I cut it off, but I didn't kill you. Look and recognize that there is no evil or rebellion in me. I haven't sinned against you even though you are hunting me down to take my life.

¹² "May the LORD judge between you and me, and may the LORD take vengeance on you for me, but my hand will never be against you. ¹³ As the old proverb says, 'Wickedness comes from wicked people.' My hand will never be against you. ¹⁴ Who has the king of Israel come after? What are you chasing after? A dead dog? A flea? ¹⁵ May the LORD be judge and decide between you and me. May He take notice and plead my case and deliver me from you."

¹⁶ When David finished saying these things to him, Saul replied, "Is that your voice, David my son?" Then Saul wept aloud ¹⁷ and said to David, "You are more righteous than I, for you have done what is good to me though I have done what is evil to you. ¹⁸ You yourself have told me today what good you did for me: when the LORD handed me over to you, you didn't kill me. ¹⁹ When a man finds his enemy, does he let him go unharmed? May the LORD repay you with good for what you've done for me today.

20 "Now I know for certain you will be king, and the kingdom of Israel will be established in your hand. 21 Therefore swear to me by the LORD that you will not cut off my descendants or wipe out my name from my father's family." 22 So David swore to Saul. Then Saul went back home, and David and his men went up to the stronghold.

25 Samuel died, and all Israel assembled to mourn for him, and they buried him by his home in Ramah. David then went down to the Wilderness of Paran.

2 A man in Maon had a business in Carmel; he was a very rich man with 3,000 sheep and 1,000 goats and was shearing his sheep in Carmel. 3 The man's name was Nabal, and his wife's name, Abigail. The woman was intelligent and beautiful, but the man, a Calebite, was harsh and evil in his dealings.

4 While David was in the wilderness, he heard that Nabal was shearing sheep, 5 so David sent 10 young men instructing them, "Go up to Carmel, and when you come to Nabal, greet him in my name. 6 Then say this: 'Long life to you, and peace to you, to your family, and to all that is yours. 7 I hear that you are shearing. When your shepherds were with us, we did not harass them, and nothing of theirs was missing the whole time they were in Carmel. 8 Ask your young men, and they will tell you. So let my young men find favor with you, for we have come on a feast day. Please give whatever you can afford to your servants and to your son David.' "

9 David's young men went and said all these things to Nabal on David's behalf, and they waited. 10 Nabal asked them, "Who is David? Who is Jesse's son? Many slaves these days are running away from their masters. 11 Am I supposed to take my bread, my water, and my meat that I butchered for my shearers and give them to men who are from I don't know where?"

12 David's men retraced their steps. When they returned to him, they reported all these words. 13 He said to his men, "All of you, put on your swords!" So David and all his men put on their swords. About 400 men followed David while 200 stayed with the supplies.

14 One of Nabal's young men informed Abigail, Nabal's wife: "Look, David sent messengers from the wilderness to greet our master, but he yelled at them. 15 The men treated us well. When we were in the field, we weren't harassed and nothing of ours was missing the whole time we were living among them. 16 They were a wall around us, both day and night, the entire time we were herding the sheep. 17 Now consider carefully what you must do, because there is certain to be trouble for our master and his entire family. He is such a worthless fool nobody can talk to him!"

18 Abigail hurried, taking 200 loaves of bread, two skins of wine, five butchered sheep, a bushel of roasted grain, 100 clusters of raisins, and 200 cakes of pressed figs, and loaded them on donkeys. 19 Then she said to her male servants, "Go ahead of me. I will be right behind you." But she did not tell her husband Nabal.

20 As she rode the donkey down a mountain pass hidden from view, she saw David and his men coming toward her and met them. 21 David had just said, "I guarded everything that belonged to this man in the wilderness for nothing. He was not missing anything, yet he paid me back evil for good. 22 May God punish me, and even more if I let any of his men survive until morning."

23 When Abigail saw David, she quickly got off the donkey and fell with her face to the ground in front of David. 24 She fell at his feet and said, "The guilt is mine, my lord, but please let your servant speak to you directly. Listen to the words of your servant. 25 My lord should pay no attention to this worthless man Nabal, for he lives up to his name: His name is Nabal, and stupidity is all he knows. I, your servant, didn't see my lord's young men whom you sent. 26 Now my lord, as surely as the LORD lives and as you yourself live, it is the

LORD who kept you from participating in bloodshed and avenging yourself by your own hand. May your enemies and those who want trouble for my lord be like Nabal. [27] Accept this gift your servant has brought to my lord, and let it be given to the young men who follow my lord. [28] Please forgive your servant's offense, for the LORD is certain to make a lasting dynasty for my lord because he fights the LORD's battles. Throughout your life, may evil not be found in you.

[29] "When someone pursues you and attempts to take your life, my lord's life will be tucked safely in the place where the LORD your God protects the living. However, He will fling away your enemies' lives like stones from a sling. [30] When the LORD does for my lord all the good He promised and appoints you ruler over Israel, [31] there will not be remorse or a troubled conscience for my lord because of needless bloodshed or my lord's revenge. And when the LORD does good things for my lord, may you remember me your servant."

[32] Then David said to Abigail, "Praise to the LORD God of Israel, who sent you to meet me today! [33] Blessed is your discernment, and blessed are you. Today you kept me from participating in bloodshed and avenging myself by my own hand. [34] Otherwise, as surely as the LORD God of Israel lives, who prevented me from harming you, if you had not come quickly to meet me, Nabal wouldn't have had any men left by morning light." [35] Then David accepted what she had brought him and said, "Go home in peace. See, I have heard what you said and have granted your request."

[36] Then Abigail went to Nabal, and there he was in his house, feasting like a king. Nabal was in a good mood and very drunk, so she didn't say anything to him until morning light. [37] In the morning when Nabal sobered up, his wife told him about these events. Then he had a seizure and became paralyzed. [38] About 10 days later, the LORD struck Nabal dead. [39] When David heard that Nabal was dead, he said, "Praise the LORD who championed my cause against Nabal's

insults and restrained His servant from doing evil. The LORD brought Nabal's evil deeds back on his own head."

Then David sent messengers to speak to Abigail about marrying him. [40] When David's servants came to Abigail at Carmel, they said to her, "David sent us to bring you to him as a wife."

[41] She bowed her face to the ground and said, "Here I am, your servant, to wash the feet of my lord's servants." [42] Then Abigail got up quickly, and with her five female servants accompanying her, rode on the donkey following David's messengers. And so she became his wife.

[43] David also married Ahinoam of Jezreel, and the two of them became his wives. [44] But Saul gave his daughter Michal, David's wife, to Palti son of Laish, who was from Gallim.

$\mathcal{P}$SALM 66:16-20

[16] Come and listen, all who fear
     God,
   and I will tell what He has done
     for me.
[17] I cried out to Him with my mouth,
   and praise was on my tongue.
[18] If I had been aware of malice in
     my heart,
   the Lord would not have listened.
[19] However, God has listened;
   He has paid attention to the sound
     of my prayer.
[20] May God be praised!
   He has not turned away my prayer
   or turned His faithful love from
     me.

$\mathcal{P}$ROVERBS 14:20-22

[20] A poor man is hated even by his
     neighbor,
   but there are many who love the
     rich.

[21] The one who despises his
     neighbor sins,
   but whoever shows kindness to
     the poor will be happy.

²² Don't those who plan evil go astray?
But those who plan good find loyalty and faithfulness.

JOHN 7:10-29

¹⁰ After His brothers had gone up to the festival, then He also went up, not openly but secretly. ¹¹ The Jews were looking for Him at the festival and saying, "Where is He?" ¹² And there was a lot of discussion about Him among the crowds. Some were saying, "He's a good man." Others were saying, "No, on the contrary, He's deceiving the people." ¹³ Still, nobody was talking publicly about Him because they feared the Jews.

¹⁴ When the festival was already half over, Jesus went up into the temple complex and began to teach. ¹⁵ Then the Jews were amazed and said, "How does He know the Scriptures, since He hasn't been trained?"

¹⁶ Jesus answered them, "My teaching isn't Mine but is from the One who sent Me. ¹⁷ If anyone wants to do His will, he will understand whether the teaching is from God or if I am speaking on My own. ¹⁸ The one who speaks for himself seeks his own glory. But He who seeks the glory of the One who sent Him is true, and there is no unrighteousness in

Him. ¹⁹ Didn't Moses give you the law? Yet none of you keeps the law! Why do you want to kill Me?"

²⁰ "You have a demon!" the crowd responded. "Who wants to kill You?"

²¹ "I did one work, and you are all amazed," Jesus answered. ²² "Consider this: Moses has given you circumcision—not that it comes from Moses but from the fathers—and you circumcise a man on the Sabbath. ²³ If a man receives circumcision on the Sabbath so that the law of Moses won't be broken, are you angry at Me because I made a man entirely well on the Sabbath? ²⁴ Stop judging according to outward appearances; rather judge according to righteous judgment."

²⁵ Some of the people of Jerusalem were saying, "Isn't this the man they want to kill? ²⁶ Yet, look! He's speaking publicly and they're saying nothing to Him. Can it be true that the authorities know He is the Messiah? ²⁷ But we know where this man is from. When the Messiah comes, nobody will know where He is from."

²⁸ As He was teaching in the temple complex, Jesus cried out, "You know Me and you know where I am from. Yet I have not come on My own, but the One who sent Me is true. You don't know Him; ²⁹ I know Him because I am from Him, and He sent Me."

Why Many Slip and Fail

If I had been aware of malice in my heart,
the Lord would not have listened.—PSALM 66:18

A Christian woman begged God to deliver her from an unforgiving spirit, yet deep down in her heart, she held onto it because of the way in which it served her unconscious purposes.

I want to suggest that you read the next sentence carefully, for in it lies the secret of the failure of many Christians to walk with "hinds' feet" to the high places which God has prepared for them.

If you harbor resentment or hatred toward just one individual in the world, by that much you are separated from God Himself.

By just that much do your rear feet fail to track with your front feet and, in the pursuit of God, you are in danger of slipping over the edge to spiritual failure. Let me put it even more clearly—if anyone has sinned against you and you have not forgiven them from the depths of your heart, then your attitude of unwillingness is a sin against God.

Listen to what the Apostle John says about this: "If anyone says, 'I love God,' yet hates his brother, he is a liar. For the person who does not love his brother whom he has seen cannot love God whom he has not seen" (1 Jn 4:20).

The very first thing we must do if we are to climb higher with God is make sure there is no bitterness or resentment lingering in our hearts. If you have not done so before, turn now in thought to all those who have trespassed against you, and forgive them—fully and completely.

Prayer

God, once again I plead for the insight and courage to see myself truly, for I may be cloaking my resentments with garments of piety. I would harbor no dangerous Trojan horses within me. Help me to be free of all resentment. In Jesus' name. Amen.

Further Study

1 Jn 4; 3:14-24; Jn 15:12
What was Christ's commandment?
Try memorizing 1 John 3:16 today.

MAY 28

I SAMUEL 26:1–28:25

26 Then the Ziphites came to Saul at Gibeah saying, "David is hiding on the hill of Hachilah opposite Jeshimon." ² So Saul, accompanied by 3,000 of the choice men of Israel, went to the Wilderness of Ziph to search for David there. ³ Saul camped beside the road at the hill of Hachilah opposite Jeshimon. David was living in the wilderness and discovered Saul had come there after him. ⁴ So David sent out spies and knew for certain that Saul had come. ⁵ Immediately, David went to the place where Saul had camped. He saw the place where Saul and Abner son of Ner, the general of his army, had lain down. Saul was lying inside the inner circle of the camp with the troops camped around him. ⁶ Then David asked Ahimelech the Hittite and Joab's brother Abishai son of Zeruiah, "Who will go with me into the camp to Saul?"

"I'll go with you," answered Abishai.

⁷ That night, David and Abishai came to the troops, and Saul was lying there asleep in the inner circle of the camp with his spear stuck in the ground by his head. Abner and the troops were lying around him. ⁸ Then Abishai said to David, "Today God has handed your enemy over to you. Let me thrust

the spear through him into the ground just once. I won't have to strike him twice!"

⁹ But David said to Abishai, "Don't destroy him, for who can lift a hand against the LORD's anointed and be blameless?" ¹⁰ David added, "As the LORD lives, the LORD will certainly strike him down: either his day will come and he will die, or he will go into battle and perish. ¹¹ However, because of the LORD, I will never lift my hand against the LORD's anointed. Instead, take the spear and the water jug by his head, and let's go."

¹² So David took the spear and the water jug by Saul's head, and they went their way. No one saw them, no one knew, and no one woke up; they all remained asleep because a deep sleep from the LORD came over them. ¹³ David crossed to the other side and stood on top of the mountain at a distance; there was a considerable space between them. ¹⁴ Then David shouted to the troops and to Abner son of Ner: "Aren't you going to answer, Abner?"

"Who are you who calls to the king?" Abner asked.

¹⁵ David called to Abner, "You're a man, aren't you? Who in Israel is your equal? So why didn't you protect your lord the king when one of the people came to destroy him? ¹⁶ What you have done is not good. As the LORD lives, all of you deserve to die since you didn't protect your lord, the LORD's anointed. Now look around; where are the king's spear and water jug that were by his head?"

¹⁷ Saul recognized David's voice and asked, "Is that your voice, my son David?"

"It is my voice, my lord and king," David said. ¹⁸ Then he continued, "Why is my lord pursuing his servant? What have I done? What evil is in my hand? ¹⁹ Now, may my lord the king please hear the words of his servant: If it is the LORD who has incited you against me, then may He accept an offering. But if it is people, may they be cursed in the presence of the LORD, for today they have driven me away from sharing in the inheritance of the LORD saying, 'Go

and worship other gods.' ²⁰ So don't let my blood fall to the ground far from the LORD's presence, for the king of Israel has come out to search for a flea, like one who pursues a partridge in the mountains."

²¹ Saul responded, "I have sinned. Come back, my son David, I will never harm you again because today you considered my life precious. I have been a fool! I've committed a grave error."

²² David answered, "Here is the king's spear; have one of the young men come over and get it. ²³ May the LORD repay every man for his righteousness and his loyalty. I wasn't willing to lift my hand against the LORD's anointed, even though the LORD handed you over to me today. ²⁴ Just as I considered your life valuable today, so may the LORD consider my life valuable and rescue me from all trouble."

²⁵ Saul said to him, "You are blessed, my son David. You will certainly do great things and will also prevail." Then David went on his way, and Saul returned home.

27 David said to himself, "One of these days I'll be swept away by Saul. There is nothing better for me than to escape immediately to the land of the Philistines. Then Saul will stop searching for me everywhere in Israel, and I'll escape from him." ² So David set out with his 600 men and went to Achish son of Maoch, the king of Gath. ³ David and his men stayed with Achish in Gath. Each man had his family with him, and David had his two wives: Ahinoam of Jezreel and Abigail of Carmel, Nabal's widow. ⁴ When it was reported to Saul that David had fled to Gath, he no longer searched for him.

⁵ Now David said to Achish, "If I have found favor with you, let me be given a place in one of the outlying towns, so I can live there. Why should your servant live in the royal city with you?" ⁶ That day Achish gave Ziklag to him, and it still belongs to the kings of Judah today. ⁷ The time that David stayed in the Philistine territory amounted to a year and four months.

⁸ David and his men went up and raided the Geshurites, the Girzites, and the Amalekites. From ancient times they had been the inhabitants of the region through Shur as far as the land of Egypt. ⁹ Whenever David attacked the land, he did not leave a single person alive, either man or woman, but he took flocks, herds, donkeys, camels, and clothing. Then he came back to Achish, ¹⁰ who inquired, "Where did you raid today?"

David replied, "The south country of Judah," "The south country of the Jerahmeelites," or "Against the south country of the Kenites."

¹¹ David did not let a man or woman live to be brought to Gath, for he said, "Or they will inform on us and say, 'This is what David did.'" This was David's custom during the whole time he stayed in the Philistine territory. ¹² So Achish trusted David, thinking, "Since he has made himself detestable to his people Israel, he will be my servant forever."

28 At that time, the Philistines brought their military units together into one army to fight against Israel. So Achish said to David, "You know, of course, that you and your men must march out in the army with me."

² David replied to Achish, "Good, you will find out what your servant can do."

So Achish said to David, "Very well, I will appoint you as my permanent bodyguard."

³ By this time Samuel had died, and all Israel had mourned for him and buried him in Ramah, his city, and Saul had removed the mediums and spiritists from the land. ⁴ The Philistines came together and camped at Shunem. So Saul gathered all Israel, and they camped at Gilboa. ⁵ When Saul saw the Philistine camp, he was afraid and trembled violently. ⁶ He inquired of the LORD, but the LORD did not answer him in dreams or by the Urim or by the prophets. ⁷ Saul then said to his servants, "Find me a woman who is a medium, so I can go and consult her."

His servants replied, "There is a woman at Endor who is a medium."

⁸ Saul disguised himself by putting on different clothes and set out with two of his men. They came to the woman at night, and Saul said, "Consult a spirit for me. Bring up for me the one I tell you."

⁹ But the woman said to him, "You surely know what Saul has done, how he has killed the mediums and spiritists in the land. Why are you setting a trap for me to get me killed?"

¹⁰ Then Saul swore to her by the LORD: "As surely as the LORD lives, nothing bad will happen to you because of this."

¹¹ "Who is it that you want me to bring up for you?" the woman asked.

"Bring up Samuel for me," he answered.

¹² When the woman saw Samuel, she screamed, and then she asked Saul, "Why did you deceive me? You are Saul!"

¹³ But the king said to her, "Don't be afraid. What do you see?"

"I see a spirit form coming up out of the earth," the woman answered.

¹⁴ Then Saul asked her, "What does he look like?"

"An old man is coming up," she replied. "He's wearing a robe." Then Saul knew that it was Samuel, and he bowed his face to the ground and paid homage.

¹⁵ "Why have you disturbed me by bringing me up?" Samuel asked Saul.

"I'm in serious trouble," replied Saul. "The Philistines are fighting against me and God has turned away from me. He doesn't answer me any more, either through the prophets or in dreams. So I've called on you to tell me what I should do."

¹⁶ Samuel answered, "Since the LORD has turned away from you and has become your enemy, why are you asking me? ¹⁷ The LORD has done exactly what He said through me: The LORD has torn the kingship out of your hand and given it to your neighbor David. ¹⁸ You did not obey the LORD and did not carry out His wrath against Amalek; therefore the LORD has done this to you today. ¹⁹ The LORD will also hand Israel over to the Philistines along with you. Tomorrow you and your sons will be with me,

and the LORD will hand Israel's army over to the Philistines."

²⁰ Immediately, Saul fell flat on the ground. He was terrified by Samuel's words and was also weak because he hadn't had any food all day and all night. ²¹ The woman came over to Saul, and she saw that he was terrified and said to him, "Look, your servant has obeyed you. I took my life in my hands and did what you told me to do. ²² Now please listen to your servant. Let me set some food in front of you. Eat and it will give you strength so you can go on your way."

²³ He refused, saying, "I won't eat," but when his servants and the woman urged him, he listened to them. He got up off the ground and sat on the bed. ²⁴ The woman had a fattened calf at her house, and she quickly slaughtered it. She also took flour, kneaded it, and baked unleavened bread. ²⁵ She served it to Saul and his servants, and they ate. Afterwards, they got up and left that night.

*P*SALM 67:1-7

¹ May God be gracious to us and
      bless us;
   look on us with favor   *Selah*
² so that Your way may be known
      on earth,
   Your salvation among all nations.

³ Let the peoples praise You, God;
   let all the peoples praise You.
⁴ Let the nations rejoice and shout
      for joy,
   for You judge the peoples with
      fairness
   and lead the nations on earth.
                                    Selah
⁵ Let the peoples praise You, God,
   let all the peoples praise You.

⁶ The earth has produced its
      harvest;
   God, our God, blesses us.
⁷ God will bless us,
   and all the ends of the earth will
      fear Him.

*P*ROVERBS 14:23-25

²³ There is profit in all hard work,
   but endless talk leads only to
      poverty.

²⁴ The crown of the wise is their
      wealth,
   but the foolishness of fools
      produces foolishness.

²⁵ A truthful witness rescues lives,
   but one who utters lies is
      deceitful.

*J*OHN 7:30-53

³⁰ Then they tried to seize Him. Yet no one laid a hand on Him because His hour had not yet come. ³¹ However, many from the crowd believed in Him and said, "When the Messiah comes, He won't perform more signs than this man has done, will He?"

³² The Pharisees heard the crowd muttering these things about Him, so the chief priests and the Pharisees sent temple police to arrest Him. ³³ Then Jesus said, "I am only with you for a short time. Then I'm going to the One who sent Me. ³⁴ You will look for Me, but you will not find Me; and where I am, you cannot come."

³⁵ Then the Jews said to one another, "Where does He intend to go so we won't find Him? He doesn't intend to go to the Dispersion among the Greeks and teach the Greeks, does He? ³⁶ What is this remark He made: 'You will look for Me, and you will not find Me; and where I am, you cannot come'?"

³⁷ On the last and most important day of the festival, Jesus stood up and cried out, "If anyone is thirsty, he should come to Me and drink! ³⁸ The one who believes in Me, as the Scripture has said, will have streams of living water flow from deep within him." ³⁹ He said this about the Spirit, whom those who believed in Him were going to receive, for the Spirit had not yet been received, because Jesus had not yet been glorified.

⁴⁰ When some from the crowd heard these words, they said, "This really is the Prophet!" ⁴¹ Others said, "This is the Messiah!" But some said, "Surely the Messiah doesn't come from Galilee, does He? ⁴² Doesn't the Scripture say that the Messiah comes from David's offspring and from the town of Bethlehem, where David once lived?" ⁴³ So a division occurred among the crowd because of Him. ⁴⁴ Some of them wanted to seize Him, but no one laid hands on Him.

⁴⁵ Then the temple police came to the chief priests and Pharisees, who asked them, "Why haven't you brought Him?"

⁴⁶ The police answered, "No man ever spoke like this!"

⁴⁷ Then the Pharisees responded to them: "Are you fooled too? ⁴⁸ Have any of the rulers believed in Him? Or any of the Pharisees? ⁴⁹ But this crowd, which doesn't know the law, is accursed!"

⁵⁰ Nicodemus—the one who came to Him previously, being one of them—said to them, ⁵¹ "Our law doesn't judge a man before it hears from him and knows what he's doing, does it?"

⁵² "You aren't from Galilee too, are you?" they replied. "Investigate and you will see that no prophet arises from Galilee." [⁵³ So each one went to his house.

How Problems Occur

If anyone is thirsty, he should come to Me and drink!
—JOHN 7:37

In my opinion, the biggest single preventative to us having feet like "hinds' feet" is a stubborn commitment to independence. This reflects itself in the lives of every one of us—even those who have been on the Way for several decades. In the garden of Eden, Adam and Eve, who were designed to experience fulfillment by being dependent on God, decided to act independently of Him. Sin can be summed up as a "Declaration of Independence"—an attempt to do for ourselves what only God can do for us.

What happened in the garden of Eden is duplicated millions of times daily, not only in the lives of unbelievers but in the lives of Christians also—Christians who use self-centered strategies to satisfy the deep thirst that is in their heart for God. Almost every spiritual or psychological problem has at its roots this condition—the person is failing in some way to let God satisfy his deep inner thirst.

This might sound simplistic to some, but after many years of experience working in the field of counseling, I am convinced that this is what underlies such conditions as anorexia, sexual perversions, worry, hostility, depression, homosexuality, and so on. You see, if we are not conscious that God is meeting the deep thirst we have for Him on the inside of our being, then the inner emptiness will move us in one of two directions—to fill the emptiness in any way we can or to withdraw and protect ourselves from the possibility of any further pain.

Prayer

Father, I see yet again that until and unless my deep thirst for You is being quenched, I am in deep trouble and vulnerable to all kinds of problems. I simply must get this issue straightened out. Help me, dear Father. In Jesus' name. Amen.

Further Study

Mt 5:1-6; Jn 4:1-42
What was the message of Jesus to the woman?
How was this reinforced through the Sermon on the Mount?

MAY 29

1 SAMUEL 29:1–31:13

29 The Philistines brought all their military units together at Aphek while Israel was camped by the spring in Jezreel. ² As the Philistine leaders were passing in review with their units of hundreds and thousands, David and his men were passing in review behind them with Achish. ³ Then the Philistine commanders asked, "What are these Hebrews doing here?"

Achish answered the Philistine commanders, "That is David, servant of King Saul of Israel. He has been with me a considerable period of time. From the day he defected until today, I've found no fault with him."

⁴ The Philistine commanders, however, were enraged with Achish and told him, "Send that man back and let him return to the place you assigned him. He must not go down with us into battle only to become our adversary during the battle. What better way could he regain his master's favor than with the heads of our men? ⁵ Isn't this the David they sing about during their dances:

Saul has killed his thousands,
but David his tens of thousands?"

⁶ So Achish summoned David and told him, "As the LORD lives, you are an honorable man. I think it is good to have you working with me in the camp, because I have found no fault in you from the day you came to me until today. But the leaders don't think you are reliable. ⁷ Now go back quietly and you won't be doing anything the Philistine leaders think is wrong."

⁸ "But what have I done?" David replied to Achish. "From the first day I was with you until today, what have you found against your servant to keep me from going along to fight against the enemies of my lord the king?"

⁹ Achish answered David, "I'm convinced that you are as reliable as an angel of God. But the Philistine commanders have said, 'He must not go into battle with us.' ¹⁰ So get up early in the morning, you and your masters' servants who came with you. When you've all gotten up early, go as soon as it's light." ¹¹ So David and his men got up early in the morning to return to the land of the Philistines. And the Philistines went up to Jezreel.

30 David and his men arrived in Ziklag on the third day. The Amalekites had raided the Negev and attacked and burned down Ziklag. ² They also had kidnapped the women and everyone in it from the youngest to the oldest. They had killed no one but had carried them off as they went on their way.

³ When David and his men arrived at the town, they found it burned down. Their wives, sons, and daughters had been kidnapped. ⁴ David and the troops

with him wept loudly until they had no strength left to weep. ⁵ David's two wives, Ahinoam the Jezreelite and Abigail the widow of Nabal the Carmelite, had also been kidnapped. ⁶ David was in a difficult position because the troops talked about stoning him, for they were all very bitter over the loss of their sons and daughters. But David found strength in the LORD his God.

⁷ David said to Abiathar the priest, son of Ahimelech, "Bring me the ephod." So Abiathar brought it to him, ⁸ and David asked the LORD: "Should I pursue these raiders? Will I overtake them?"

The LORD replied to him, "Pursue them, for you will certainly overtake them and rescue the people."

⁹ David and the 600 men with him went as far as the Wadi Besor, where 200 men who were to remain behind would stop. ¹⁰ They stopped because they were too exhausted to cross the Wadi Besor. David and 400 of the men continued in pursuit.

¹¹ They found an Egyptian in the open country and brought him to David. They gave him some bread to eat and water to drink. ¹² Then they gave him some pressed figs and two clusters of raisins. After he ate he revived, for he hadn't eaten food or drunk water for three days and three nights.

¹³ Then David said to him, "Who do you belong to? Where are you from?"

"I'm an Egyptian, the slave of an Amalekite man," he said. "My master abandoned me when I got sick three days ago. ¹⁴ We raided the south country of the Cherethites, the territory of Judah, and the south country of Caleb, and we burned down Ziklag."

¹⁵ David then asked him, "Will you lead me to these raiders?"

He said, "Swear to me by God that you won't kill me or turn me over to my master, and I will lead you to them."

¹⁶ So he led him, and there were the Amalekites, spread out over the entire area, eating, drinking, and celebrating because of the great amount of plunder they had taken from the land of the Philistines and the land of Judah. ¹⁷ David slaughtered them from twilight until the evening of the next day. None of them escaped, except 400 young men who got on camels and fled.

¹⁸ David recovered everything the Amalekites had taken; he also rescued his two wives. ¹⁹ Nothing of theirs was missing from the youngest to the oldest, including the sons and daughters, of all the plunder the Amalekites had taken. David got everything back. ²⁰ He took all the sheep and cattle, which were driven ahead of the other livestock, and the people shouted, "This is David's plunder!"

²¹ When David came to the 200 men who had been too exhausted to go with him and had been left at the Wadi Besor, they came out to meet him and to meet the troops with him. When David approached the men, he greeted them, ²² but all the worthless men among those who had gone with David retorted, "Because they didn't go with us, we will not give any of the plunder we recovered to them except for each man's wife and children. They may take them and go."

²³ But David said, "My brothers, you must not do this with what the LORD has given us. He protected us and handed over to us the raiders who came against us. ²⁴ Who can agree to your proposal? The share of the one who goes into battle is to be the same as the share of the one who remains with the supplies. They will share equally." ²⁵ And it has been so from that day forward. David established this policy as a law and an ordinance for Israel and it continues to this very day.

²⁶ When David came to Ziklag, he sent some of the plunder to his friends, the elders of Judah, saying, "Here is a gift for you from the plunder of the LORD's enemies." ²⁷ He sent gifts to those in Bethel, in Ramoth of the Negev, and in Jattir; ²⁸ to those in Aroer, in Siphmoth, and in Eshtemoa; ²⁹ to those in Racal, in the towns of the Jerahmeelites, and in the towns of the Kenites; ³⁰ to those in Hormah, in Bor-ashan, and in Athach; ³¹ to those in Hebron, and to those in all the places where David and his men had roamed.

31 The Philistines fought against Israel, and Israel's men fled from them. Many were killed on Mount Gilboa. ² The Philistines overtook Saul and his sons and killed his sons, Jonathan, Abinadab, and Malchishua. ³ When the battle intensified against Saul, the archers caught up with him and severely wounded him. ⁴ Then Saul said to his armor-bearer, "Draw your sword and run me through with it, or these uncircumcised men will come and run me through and torture me." But his armor-bearer would not do it because he was terrified. Then Saul took his sword and fell on it. ⁵ When his armor-bearer saw that Saul was dead, he also fell on his own sword and died with him. ⁶ So on that day, Saul died together with his three sons, his armor-bearer, and all his men.

⁷ When the men of Israel on the other side of the valley and on the other side of the Jordan saw that Israel's men had run away and that Saul and his sons were dead, they abandoned the cities and fled. So the Philistines came and settled in them.

⁸ The next day when the Philistines came to strip the slain, they found Saul and his three sons dead on Mount Gilboa. ⁹ They cut off Saul's head, stripped off his armor, and sent messengers throughout the land of the Philistines to spread the good news in the temples of their idols and among the people. ¹⁰ Then they put his armor in the temple of the Ashtoreths and hung his body on the wall of Beth-shan.

¹¹ When the residents of Jabesh-gilead heard what the Philistines had done to Saul, ¹² all their brave men set out, journeyed all night, and retrieved the body of Saul and the bodies of his sons from the wall of Beth-shan. When they arrived at Jabesh, they burned the bodies there. ¹³ Afterwards, they took their bones and buried them under the tamarisk tree in Jabesh and fasted seven days.

PSALM 68:1-6

¹ God arises. His enemies scatter,
  and those who hate Him flee from
  His presence.

² As smoke is blown away,
  so You blow them away.
  As wax melts before the fire,
  so the wicked are destroyed
    before God.
³ But the righteous are glad;
  they rejoice before God and
    celebrate with joy.

⁴ Sing to God! Sing praises to His
    name.
  Exalt Him who rides
    on the clouds—
  His name is Yahweh—and rejoice
    before Him.
⁵ A father of the fatherless and a
    champion of widows
  is God in His holy dwelling.
⁶ God provides homes for those
    who are deserted.
  He leads out the prisoners to
    prosperity,
  but the rebellious live in a
    scorched land.

PROVERBS 14:26-28

²⁶ In the fear of the LORD one has
    strong confidence
  and his children have a refuge.

²⁷ The fear of the LORD is a fountain
    of life,
  turning people from the snares of
    death.

²⁸ A large population is a king's
    splendor,
  but a shortage of people is a
    ruler's devastation.

JOHN 8:1-20

8 ¹ But Jesus went to the Mount of Olives.

² At dawn He went to the temple complex again, and all the people were coming to Him. He sat down and began to teach them.

³ Then the scribes and the Pharisees brought a woman caught in adultery, making her stand in the center. ⁴ "Teacher," they said to Him, "this woman was

caught in the act of committing adultery. [5] In the law Moses commanded us to stone such women. So what do You say?" [6] They asked this to trap Him, in order that they might have evidence to accuse Him.

Jesus stooped down and started writing on the ground with His finger. [7] When they persisted in questioning Him, He stood up and said to them, "The one without sin among you should be the first to throw a stone at her." [8] Then He stooped down again and continued writing on the ground. [9] When they heard this, they left one by one, starting with the older men. Only He was left, with the woman in the center. [10] When Jesus stood up, He said to her, "Woman, where are they? Has no one condemned you?"

[11] "No one, Lord," she answered.

"Neither do I condemn you," said Jesus. "Go, and from now on do not sin any more."]

[12] Then Jesus spoke to them again: "I am the light of the world. Anyone who follows Me will never walk in the darkness but will have the light of life."

[13] So the Pharisees said to Him, "You are testifying about Yourself. Your testimony is not valid."

[14] "Even if I testify about Myself," Jesus replied, "My testimony is valid, because I know where I came from and where I'm going. But you don't know where I come from or where I'm going. [15] You judge by human standards. I judge no one. [16] And if I do judge, My judgment is true, because I am not alone, but I and the Father who sent Me judge together. [17] Even in your law it is written that the witness of two men is valid. [18] I am the One who testifies about Myself, and the Father who sent Me testifies about Me."

[19] Then they asked Him, "Where is Your Father?"

"You know neither Me nor My Father," Jesus answered. "If you knew Me, you would also know My Father." [20] He spoke these words by the treasury, while teaching in the temple complex. But no one seized Him, because His hour had not come.

Family Within a Family

A father of the fatherless and a champion of widows is God in His holy dwelling.—PSALM 68:5

The second word in our Master's model of prayer is "Father." In Christian circles the term "Father" is probably the most common term used when addressing God, and rightly so, for this is the pattern Jesus set when teaching His disciples the art of effective praying.

This raises the much debated question: Is God a Father to all men and women everywhere or only to those who are committed members of the Christian church? For many years now liberally minded theologians have taught that God is everyone's Father, so we are all His children and thus all brothers and sisters. This teaching, known as the universal brotherhood of man, makes conversion unnecessary and puts to one side the redemptive sufferings of Christ on the cross.

The Bible teaches that God is a Father in two senses. Firstly, He is the Father of the human family by virtue of creation. Malachi 2:10 says: "Don't all of us have one Father? Didn't one God create us?" In Acts 17:28 Paul said: "We are...His offspring." In the sense of creation, yes, God is our Father.

In the sense of a familial relationship, He is not. Jesus said to the Jewish leaders: "You are of your father the Devil" (John 8:44). Quite clearly, the fatherhood of God is seen in the Bible in two senses. He is the Father of all as their Creator, but He has another family—a family within a family—consisting of those who have committed themselves to Jesus Christ, the Son.

Prayer

O God, I am so grateful that I know You as my Father—not only in the creative sense, but in the familial sense. May the wonder of this closer relationship grow within me hour by hour and day by day. For Jesus' sake. Amen.

Further Study

Rm 8:1-17; Is 64:8; Jn 1:12
How have we "received the Spirit of adoption"?
What is our cry?

MAY 30

2 SAMUEL 1:1–2:32

1 After the death of Saul, David returned from defeating the Amalekites and stayed at Ziklag two days. ² On the third day a man with torn clothes and dust on his head came from Saul's camp. When he came to David, he fell to the ground and paid homage. ³ David asked him, "Where have you come from?"

He replied to him, "I've escaped from the Israelite camp."

⁴ "What was the outcome? Tell me," David asked him.

"The troops fled from the battle," he answered. "Many of the troops have fallen and are dead. Also, Saul and his son Jonathan are dead."

⁵ David asked the young man who had brought him the report, "How do you know Saul and his son Jonathan are dead?"

⁶ "I happened to be on Mount Gil-

boa," he replied, "and there was Saul, leaning on his spear. At that very moment the chariots and the cavalry were closing in on him. ⁷ When he turned around and saw me, he called out to me, so I answered: I'm at your service. ⁸ He asked me, 'Who are you?' I told him: I'm an Amalekite. ⁹ Then he begged me, 'Stand over me and kill me, for I'm mortally wounded, but my life still lingers.' ¹⁰ So I stood over him and killed him because I knew that after he had fallen he couldn't survive. I took the crown that was on his head and the armband that was on his arm, and I've brought them here to my lord."

¹¹ Then David took hold of his clothes and tore them, and all the men with him did the same. ¹² They mourned, wept, and fasted until the evening for those who died by the sword—for Saul, his son Jonathan, the LORD's people, and the house of Israel.

¹³ David inquired of the young man

who had brought him the report, "Where are you from?"

"I'm the son of a foreigner" he said. "I'm an Amalekite."

¹⁴ David questioned him, "How is it that you were not afraid to lift your hand to destroy the LORD's anointed?" ¹⁵ Then David summoned one of his servants and said, "Come here and kill him!" The servant struck him, and he died. ¹⁶ For David had said to the Amalekite, "Your blood is on your own head because your own mouth testified against you by saying, 'I killed the LORD's anointed.' "

¹⁷ David sang the following lament for Saul and his son Jonathan, ¹⁸ and he ordered that the Judahites be taught The Song of the Bow. It is written in the Book of Jashar:

¹⁹ The splendor of Israel lies slain
　　on your heights.
　How the mighty have fallen!
²⁰ Do not tell it in Gath,
　　don't announce it in the streets
　　　of Ashkelon,
　　or the daughters of the Philistines
　　　will rejoice,
　　and the daughters
　　　of the uncircumcised will gloat.
²¹ Mountains of Gilboa,
　　let no dew or rain be on you,
　　or fields of offerings,
　　for there the shield of the mighty
　　　was defiled—
　　the shield of Saul, no longer
　　　anointed with oil.
²² Jonathan's bow never retreated,
　　Saul's sword never returned
　　　unstained,
　　from the blood of the slain,
　　from the bodies of the mighty.
²³ Saul and Jonathan,
　　loved and delightful,
　　they were not parted in life
　　　or in death.
　　They were swifter than eagles,
　　　stronger than lions.
²⁴ Daughters of Israel,
　　weep for Saul,
　　who clothed you in scarlet,
　　　with luxurious things,
　　who decked your garments
　　　with gold ornaments.

²⁵ How the mighty have fallen
　　in the thick of battle!
　Jonathan lies slain
　　on your heights.
²⁶ I grieve for you, Jonathan
　　my brother.
　You were such a friend to me.
　Your love for me was
　　more wonderful
　than the love of a woman for me.
²⁷ How the mighty have fallen
　　and the weapons of war
　　　have perished!

2 Some time later, David inquired of the LORD: "Should I go to one of the towns of Judah?"

The LORD answered him, "Go."

Then David asked, "Where should I go?"

"To Hebron," the LORD replied.

² So David went there with his two wives, Ahinoam the Jezreelite and Abigail, the widow of Nabal the Carmelite. ³ In addition, David brought the men who were with him, each one with his household, and they settled in the towns near Hebron. ⁴ Then the men of Judah came, and there they anointed David king over the house of Judah. They told David: "It was the men of Jabesh-gilead who buried Saul."

⁵ David sent messengers to the men of Jabesh-gilead and said to them, "The LORD bless you, because you have shown this special kindness to Saul your lord when you buried him. ⁶ Now, may the LORD show special kindness and faithfulness to you, and I will also show the same goodness to you because you have done this deed. ⁷ Therefore, be strong and courageous, for though Saul your lord is dead, the house of Judah has anointed me king over them."

⁸ Abner son of Ner, commander of Saul's army, took Saul's son Ish-bosheth and moved him to Mahanaim. ⁹ He made him king over Gilead, Asher, Jezreel, Ephraim, Benjamin—over all Israel. ¹⁰ Saul's son Ish-bosheth was 40 years old when he began his reign over Israel; he ruled for two years. The house of Judah, however, followed David. ¹¹ The length of time that David

was king in Hebron over the house of Judah was seven years and six months.

¹²Abner son of Ner and soldiers of Ish-bosheth son of Saul marched out from Mahanaim to Gibeon. ¹³So Joab son of Zeruiah and David's soldiers marched out and met them by the pool of Gibeon. The two groups took up positions on opposite sides of the pool.

¹⁴Then Abner said to Joab, "Let's have the young men get up and compete in front of us."

"Let them get up," Joab replied.

¹⁵So they got up and were counted off—12 for Benjamin and Ish-bosheth son of Saul, and 12 from David's soldiers. ¹⁶Then each man grabbed his opponent by the head and thrust his sword into his opponent's side so that they all died together. So this place, which is in Gibeon, is named Field of Blades.

¹⁷The battle that day was extremely fierce, and Abner and the men of Israel were defeated by David's soldiers. ¹⁸The three sons of Zeruiah were there: Joab, Abishai, and Asahel. Asahel was a fast runner, like one of the wild gazelles. ¹⁹He chased Abner and did not turn to the right or the left in his pursuit of him. ²⁰Abner glanced back and said, "Is that you, Asahel?"

"Yes it is," Asahel replied.

²¹Abner said to him, "Turn to your right or left, seize one of the young soldiers, and take whatever you can get from him." But Asahel would not stop chasing him. ²²Once again, Abner warned Asahel, "Stop chasing me. Why should I strike you to the ground? How could I ever look your brother Joab in the face?"

²³But Asahel refused to turn away, so Abner hit him in the stomach with the end of his spear. The spear went through his body, and he fell and died right there. When all who came to the place where Asahel had fallen and died, they stopped, ²⁴but Joab and Abishai pursued Abner. By sunset, they had gone as far as the hill of Ammah, which is opposite Giah on the way to the wilderness of Gibeon.

²⁵The Benjaminites rallied to Abner; they formed a single unit and took their stand on top of a hill. ²⁶Then Abner called out to Joab: "Must the sword devour forever? Don't you realize this will only end in bitterness? How long before you tell the troops to stop pursuing their brothers?"

²⁷"As God lives," Joab replied, "if you had not spoken up, the troops wouldn't have stopped pursuing their brothers until morning." ²⁸Then Joab blew the ram's horn, and all the troops stopped; they no longer pursued Israel or continued to fight. ²⁹So Abner and his men marched through the Arabah all that night. They crossed the Jordan, marched all morning, and arrived at Mahanaim.

³⁰When Joab had turned back from pursuing Abner, he gathered all the troops. In addition to Asahel, 19 of David's soldiers were missing, ³¹but they had killed 360 of the Benjaminites and Abner's men. ³²Afterwards, they carried Asahel to his father's tomb in Bethlehem and buried him. Then Joab and his men marched all night and reached Hebron at dawn.

PSALM 68:7-14

⁷ God, when You went out before
Your people,
when You marched through the
desert,   *Selah*
⁸ the earth trembled, and the skies
poured down rain
before God, the God of Sinai,
before God, the God of Israel.
⁹ You, God, showered abundant
rain;
You revived Your inheritance when
it languished.
¹⁰ Your people settled in it;
by Your goodness You provided for
the poor, God.

¹¹ The Lord gave the command;
a great company of women
brought the good news:
¹² "The kings of the armies flee—
they flee!"
She who stays at home divides the
spoil.

13 While you lie among the
    sheepfolds,
  the wings of a dove are covered
    with silver,
  and its feathers with glistening
    gold.
14 When the Almighty scattered
    kings in the land,
  it snowed on Zalmon.

PROVERBS 14:29-30

29 A patient person shows great
    understanding,
  but a quick-tempered one
    promotes foolishness.

30 A tranquil heart is life to the body,
  but jealousy is rottenness to the
    bones.

JOHN 8:21-41

21 Then He said to them again, "I'm
going away; you will look for Me, and
you will die in your sin. Where I'm going, you cannot come."
22 So the Jews said again, "He won't
kill Himself, will He, since He says,
'Where I'm going, you cannot come'?"
23 "You are from below," He told
them, "I am from above. You are of this
world; I am not of this world. 24 Therefore I told you that you will die in your
sins. For if you do not believe that I am
He, you will die in your sins."
25 "Who are You?" they questioned.
"Precisely what I've been telling you
from the very beginning," Jesus told
them. 26 "I have many things to say
and to judge about you, but the One
who sent Me is true, and what I have
heard from Him—these things I tell the
world."

27 They did not know He was speaking
to them about the Father. 28 So Jesus
said to them, "When you lift up the Son
of Man, then you will know that I am
He, and that I do nothing on My own.
But just as the Father taught Me, I say
these things. 29 The One who sent Me is
with Me. He has not left Me alone, because I always do what pleases Him."
30 As He was saying these things,
many believed in Him. 31 So Jesus said
to the Jews who had believed Him, "If
you continue in My word, you really are
My disciples. 32 You will know the truth,
and the truth will set you free."
33 "We are descendants of Abraham,"
they answered Him, "and we have never
been enslaved to anyone. How can You
say, 'You will become free'?"
34 Jesus responded, "I assure you:
Everyone who commits sin is a slave of
sin. 35 A slave does not remain in the
household forever, but a son does remain forever. 36 Therefore if the Son
sets you free, you really will be free.
37 I know you are descendants of Abraham, but you are trying to kill Me because My word is not welcome among
you. 38 I speak what I have seen in the
presence of the Father, and therefore
you do what you have heard from your
father."
39 "Our father is Abraham!" they
replied.
"If you were Abraham's children,"
Jesus told them, "you would do what
Abraham did. 40 But now you are trying
to kill Me, a man who has told you the
truth that I heard from God. Abraham
did not do this! 41 You're doing what
your father does."
"We weren't born of sexual immorality," they said. "We have one Father—
God."

The Danger of Denial

You will know the truth, and the truth will set you free.
——JOHN 8:32

It may be difficult for you to admit that perhaps your heart and your head are not spiritually coordinated. Many Christians are content to live above the waterline and insist that it is quite unnecessary to wrestle and struggle with the things that go on deep inside us. Their motto is: just trust, persevere, and obey. This is fine as far as it goes, but in my opinion it does not go far enough.

The effect of this teaching is to blunt the painful reality of what the Bible says about the condition of the human heart: "The heart is more deceitful than anything else and desperately sick—who can understand it? I, the Lord, examine the mind" (Jr 17:9-10). It is possible for even mature Christians to be self-deceived, to not really know their own hearts. This is why we must live in constant dependence on God, inviting Him from time to time, as did the psalmist, to "search me, God, and know my heart" (Ps 139:23).

There is a word to describe the attitude of those who ignore what may be going on deep inside them and concentrate only on what they can see above the waterline, and that word is denial. In many Christian circles, maintaining a comfortable distance from what may be going on deep down inside is strongly encouraged. But nothing can be gained from denial. In fact, I would say it is one of the major reasons why our feet are not like "hinds' feet" and why we slip and slide on the slopes that lead upward to a deeper understanding and knowledge of God.

Prayer

God, I realize I am dealing with something too devastating to pass over quickly or lightly. Help me be aware of the tendency that is in me to deny that I deny. Stay close to me at this moment, dear Father, for without You I can do nothing. Amen.

Further Study

Gl 6; Rm 6:16-23
What was Paul's word to the Galatians?
How are we to walk?

MAY 31

2 SAMUEL 3:1–4:12

3 The war between the house of Saul and the house of David was long and drawn out, with David growing stronger and the house of Saul becoming weaker. ² Sons were born to David in Hebron:

his firstborn was Amnon,
  by Ahinoam the Jezreelite;
³ his second was Chileab,
  by Abigail, the widow of Nabal
    the Carmelite;
  the third was Absalom,
  son of Maacah the daughter
    of King Talmai of Geshur;
⁴ the fourth was Adonijah,
  son of Haggith;
  the fifth was Shephatiah,
  son of Abital;
⁵ the sixth was Ithream,
  by David's wife Eglah.

These were born to David in Hebron.

⁶ During the war between the house of Saul and the house of David, Abner kept acquiring more power in the house of Saul. ⁷ Now Saul had a concubine whose name was Rizpah daughter of Aiah, and Ish-bosheth questioned Abner, "Why did you sleep with my father's concubine?"

⁸ Abner was very angry about Ish-bosheth's accusation. "Am I a dog's head who belongs to Judah?" he asked. "All this time I've been loyal to the house of your father Saul, to his brothers, and to his friends and haven't handed you over to David, but now you accuse me of wrongdoing with this woman! ⁹ May God punish Abner and do so severely if I don't do for David what the LORD swore to him: ¹⁰ to transfer the kingdom from the house of Saul and establish the throne of David over Israel and Judah from Dan to Beersheba." ¹¹ Ish-bosheth could not answer Abner because he was afraid of him.

¹² Abner sent messengers as his representatives to say to David, "Whose land is it? Make your covenant with me, and you can be certain I am on your side to hand all Israel over to you."

¹³ David replied, "Good, I will make a covenant with you. However, there's one thing I require of you: Do not appear before me unless you bring Saul's daughter Michal here when you come to see me."

¹⁴ Then David sent messengers to say to Ish-bosheth son of Saul, "Give me back my wife, Michal. I was engaged to her for the price of 100 Philistine foreskins."

¹⁵ So Ish-bosheth sent someone to take her away from her husband, Paltiel son of Laish. ¹⁶ Her husband followed her, weeping all the way to Bahurim. Abner said to him, "Go back." So he went back.

¹⁷ Abner conferred with the elders of Israel: "In the past you wanted David to be king over you. ¹⁸ Now take action, because the LORD has spoken concerning David: 'Through My servant David I will save My people Israel from the power of the Philistines and the power of all Israel's enemies.' "

¹⁹ Abner also informed the Benjaminites and went to Hebron to inform David about all that was agreed on by Israel and the whole house of Benjamin. ²⁰ When Abner and 20 men came to David at Hebron, David held a banquet for him and his men.

²¹ Abner said to David, "Let me now go and I will gather all Israel to my lord the king. They will make a covenant with you, and you will rule over all you desire." So David dismissed Abner, and he went in peace.

²² Just then David's soldiers and Joab returned from a raid and brought a large amount of plundered goods with them. Abner was not with David in Hebron

because David had dismissed him, and he had gone in peace. ²³ When Joab and all his army arrived, Joab was informed, "Abner son of Ner came to see the king, the king dismissed him, and he went in peace."

²⁴ Joab went to the king and said, "What have you done? Look here, Abner came to you. Why did you dismiss him? Now he's getting away. ²⁵ You know that Abner son of Ner came to deceive you and to find out about your activities and everything you're doing." ²⁶ Then Joab left David and sent messengers after Abner. They brought him back from the well of Sirah, but David was unaware of it. ²⁷ When Abner returned to Hebron, Joab pulled him aside to the middle of the gateway, as if to speak to him privately, and there Joab stabbed him in the stomach. So Abner died in revenge for the death of Asahel, Joab's brother.

²⁸ David heard about it later and said: "I and my kingdom are forever innocent before the LORD concerning the blood of Abner son of Ner. ²⁹ May it hang over Joab's head and his father's whole house, and may the house of Joab never be without someone who has an infection or leprosy or a man who can only work a spindle or someone who falls by the sword or starves." ³⁰ Joab and his brother Abishai killed Abner because he had put their brother Asahel to death in the battle at Gibeon.

³¹ David then ordered Joab and all the people who were with him, "Tear your clothes, put on sackcloth, and mourn over Abner." And King David walked behind the funeral procession. ³² When they buried Abner in Hebron, the king wept aloud at Abner's tomb. All the people wept, ³³ and the king sang a lament for Abner:

> Should Abner die as a fool dies?
> ³⁴ Your hands were not bound,
>   your feet not placed
>   in bronze shackles.
> You fell like one who falls victim
>   to criminals.

And all the people wept over him even more.

³⁵ Then they came to urge David to eat bread while it was still day, but David took an oath: "May God punish me and do so severely if I taste bread or anything else before sunset!" ³⁶ All the people took note of this, and it pleased them. In fact, everything the king did pleased them. ³⁷ On that day all the troops and all Israel were convinced that the king had no part in the killing of Abner son of Ner.

³⁸ Then the king said to his soldiers, "You must know that a great leader has fallen in Israel today. ³⁹ As for me, even though I am the anointed king, I have little power today. These men, the sons of Zeruiah, are too fierce for me. May the LORD repay the evildoer according to his evil!"

4 When Saul's son Ish-bosheth heard that Abner had died in Hebron, his courage failed, and all Israel was dismayed. ² Saul's son had two men who were leaders of raiding parties: one named Baanah and the other Rechab, sons of Rimmon the Beerothite of the Benjaminites. Beeroth is also considered part of Benjamin, ³ and the Beerothites fled to Gittaim and still live there as aliens to this very day.

⁴ Saul's son Jonathan had a son whose feet were crippled. He was five years old when the report about Saul and Jonathan came from Jezreel. His nurse picked him up and fled, but as she was hurrying to flee, he fell and became lame. His name was Mephibosheth.

⁵ Rechab and Baanah, the sons of Rimmon the Beerothite, set out and arrived at Ish-bosheth's house during the heat of the day while the king was taking his midday nap. ⁶ They entered the interior of the house as if to get wheat and stabbed him in the stomach. Then Rechab and his brother Baanah escaped. ⁷ They had entered the house while Ish-bosheth was lying on his bed in his bedroom and stabbed and killed him. Then they beheaded him, took his head, and traveled by way of the Arabah all night. ⁸ They brought Ish-bosheth's head to

David at Hebron and said to the king, "Here's the head of Ish-bosheth son of Saul, your enemy who intended to take your life. Today the LORD has granted vengeance to my lord the king against Saul and his offspring."

⁹ But David answered Rechab and his brother Baanah, sons of Rimmon the Beerothite, "As surely as the LORD lives, the One who has redeemed my life from every distress, ¹⁰ when the person told me, 'Look, Saul is dead,' he thought he was a bearer of good news, but I seized him and put him to death at Ziklag. That was my reward to him for his news! ¹¹ How much more when wicked men kill a righteous man in his own house on his own bed! So now, should I not require his blood from your hands and wipe you off the earth?" ¹² So David gave orders to the young men, and they killed Rechab and Baanah. They cut off their hands and feet and hung their bodies by the pool in Hebron, but they took Ish-bosheth's head and buried it in Abner's tomb in Hebron.

𝒫SALM 68:15-19

¹⁵ Mount Bashan is God's towering mountain;
Mount Bashan is a mountain of many peaks.
¹⁶ Why gaze with envy, you mountain peaks,
at the mountain God desired for His dwelling?
The LORD will live there forever!
¹⁷ God's chariots are tens of thousands, thousands and thousands;
the Lord is among them in the sanctuary as He was at Sinai.
¹⁸ You ascended to the heights, taking away captives;
You received gifts from people, even from the rebellious,
so that the LORD God might live there.

¹⁹ May the Lord be praised!
Day after day He bears our burdens;
God is our salvation.   *Selah*

𝒫ROVERBS 14:31-32

³¹ The one who oppresses the poor insults their Maker,
but one who is kind to the needy honors Him.

³² The wicked are thrown down by their own sin,
but the righteous have a refuge when they die.

𝒥OHN 8:42–9:7

⁴² Jesus said to them, "If God were your Father, you would love Me, because I came from God and I am here. For I didn't come on My own, but He sent Me. ⁴³ Why don't you understand what I say? Because you cannot listen to My word. ⁴⁴ You are of your father the Devil, and you want to carry out your father's desires. He was a murderer from the beginning and has not stood in the truth, because there is no truth in him. When he tells a lie, he speaks from his own nature, because he is a liar and the father of liars. ⁴⁵ Yet because I tell the truth, you do not believe Me. ⁴⁶ Who among you can convict Me of sin? If I tell the truth, why don't you believe Me? ⁴⁷ The one who is from God listens to God's words. This is why you don't listen, because you are not from God."

⁴⁸ The Jews responded to Him, "Aren't we right in saying that You're a Samaritan and have a demon?"

⁴⁹ "I do not have a demon," Jesus answered. "On the contrary, I honor My Father and you dishonor Me. ⁵⁰ I do not seek My glory; the One who seeks it also judges. ⁵¹ I assure you: If anyone keeps My word, he will never see death—ever!"

⁵² Then the Jews said, "Now we know You have a demon. Abraham died and so did the prophets. You say, 'If anyone keeps My word, he will never taste death—

ever!' ⁵³ Are You greater than our father Abraham who died? Even the prophets died. Who do You pretend to be?"

⁵⁴ "If I glorify Myself," Jesus answered, "My glory is nothing. My Father—you say about Him, 'He is our God'—He is the One who glorifies Me. ⁵⁵ You've never known Him, but I know Him. If I were to say I don't know Him, I would be a liar like you. But I do know Him, and I keep His word. ⁵⁶ Your father Abraham was overjoyed that he would see My day; he saw it and rejoiced."

⁵⁷ The Jews replied, "You aren't 50 years old yet, and You've seen Abraham?"

⁵⁸ Jesus said to them, "I assure you: Before Abraham was, I am."

⁵⁹ At that, they picked up stones to throw at Him. But Jesus was hidden and went out of the temple complex.

9 As He was passing by, He saw a man blind from birth. ² His disciples questioned Him: "Rabbi, who sinned, this man or his parents, that he was born blind?"

³ "Neither this man nor his parents sinned," Jesus answered. "This came about so that God's works might be displayed in him. ⁴ We must do the works of Him who sent Me while it is day. Night is coming when no one can work. ⁵ As long as I am in the world, I am the light of the world."

⁶ After He said these things He spit on the ground, made some mud from the saliva, and spread the mud on his eyes. ⁷ "Go," He told him, "wash in the pool of Siloam" (which means "Sent"). So he left, washed, and came back seeing.

Keeping Our Faith Trim

He is a liar and the father of liars.

—JOHN 8:44

There are many things in life that at first glance appear to have no point. Fear is one such thing; doubt is another. I have heard it argued that all fear is of the Devil and can serve no useful purpose in human life—but this is not true. Fear of being burned, for example, helps us avoid coming in contact with hot metals. Fear can have a positive purpose—and so can doubt.

Doubt, for one, can be used to help us detect error. We live in a world of which Satan is temporarily "prince," and he tries his utmost to get us to believe his lies. Jesus was not merely being poetic when He described Satan as the "father of liars." Half-truths and half-lies that masquerade as the whole truth are the Devil's stock-in-trade. So because all things are not true, not everything should be believed. Some things clearly ought to be doubted.

One writer says: "The inescapable presence of doubt is a constant reminder of our responsibility to truth in a twilight world of truth and half-truth." It acts like a spur to challenge us to find out the truth about a situation. It is precisely because all is not certain that we have to make certain.

Francis Bacon put it like this: "If a man will begin with certainties, he shall end in doubts; but if he will be content to begin with doubts, he shall end in certainties." Doubt can act as a sparring partner both to truth and error; it keeps faith trim and assists us in shedding the paunchiness of false ideas.

Prayer

Gracious and loving Father, thank You for reminding me yet again that I can take anything that comes and use it to positive ends—even doubt. Help me to use my doubts as a sparring partner to keep my faith trim. In Jesus' name I pray. Amen.

Further Study

2 Pt 2:1-10; Ti 1:9-11; 2 Tm 4:1-5
What will come in the last days?
How did Paul exhort Timothy?

JUNE I

2 SAMUEL 5:1–6:23

5 All the tribes of Israel came to David at Hebron and said, "Here we are, your own flesh and blood. ² Even while Saul was king over us, you were the one who led us out to battle and brought us back. The LORD also said to you, 'You will shepherd My people Israel and be ruler over Israel.' "

³ So all the elders of Israel came to the king at Hebron. King David made a covenant with them at Hebron in the LORD's presence, and they anointed David king over Israel.

⁴ David was 30 years old when he began his reign; he reigned 40 years. ⁵ In Hebron he reigned over Judah seven years and six months, and in Jerusalem he reigned 33 years over all Israel and Judah.

⁶ The king and his men marched to Jerusalem against the Jebusites who inhabited the land. The Jebusites had said to David: "You will never get in here. Even the blind and lame can repel you," thinking, "David can't get in here."

⁷ Yet David did capture the stronghold of Zion, the city of David. ⁸ He said that day, "Whoever attacks the Jebusites must go through the water shaft to reach the lame and the blind who are despised by David." For this reason it is said, "The blind and the lame will never enter the house."

⁹ David took up residence in the stronghold, which he named the city of David. He built it up all the way around from the supporting terraces inward. ¹⁰ David became more and more powerful, and the LORD God of Hosts was with him. ¹¹ King Hiram of Tyre sent envoys to David; he also sent cedar logs, carpenters, and stonemasons, and they built a palace for David. ¹² Then David knew that the LORD had established him as king over Israel and had exalted his kingdom for the sake of His people Israel.

¹³ After he arrived from Hebron, David took more concubines and wives in Jerusalem, and more sons and daughters were born to him. ¹⁴ These are the names of those born to him in Jerusalem: Shammua, Shobab, Nathan, Solomon, ¹⁵ Ibhar, Elishua, Nepheg, Japhia, ¹⁶ Elishama, Eliada, and Eliphelet.

17 When the Philistines heard that David had been anointed king over Israel, they all went in search of David, but he heard about it and went down to the stronghold. 18 So the Philistines came and spread out in the Valley of Rephaim.

19 Then David inquired of the LORD: "Should I go to war against the Philistines? Will you hand them over to me?"

The LORD replied to David, "Go, for I will certainly hand the Philistines over to you."

20 So David went to Baal-perazim and defeated them there and said, "Like a bursting flood, the LORD has burst out against my enemies before me." Therefore, he named that place the Lord Bursts Out. 21 The Philistines abandoned their idols there, and David and his men carried them off.

22 The Philistines came up again and spread out in the Valley of Rephaim. 23 So David inquired of the LORD, and He answered, "Do not make a frontal assault. Circle around behind them and attack them opposite the balsam trees. 24 When you hear the sound of marching in the tops of the balsam trees, act decisively, for then the LORD will have marched out ahead of you to attack the camp of the Philistines." 25 So David did exactly as the LORD commanded him, and he struck down the Philistines all the way from Geba to Gezer.

6 David again assembled all the choice men in Israel, 30,000. 2 He and all his troops set out to bring the ark of God from Baale-judah. The ark is called by the Name, the name of the LORD of Hosts who dwells between the cherubim. 3 They set the ark of God on a new cart and transported it from Abinadab's house, which was on the hill. Uzzah and Ahio, sons of Abinadab, were guiding the cart 4 and brought it with the ark of God from Abinadab's house on the hill. Ahio walked in front of the ark. 5 David and the whole house of Israel were celebrating before the LORD with all kinds of fir wood instruments, lyres, harps, tambourines, sistrums, and cymbals.

6 When they came to Nacon's threshing floor, Uzzah reached out to the ark of God and took hold of it, because the oxen had stumbled. 7 Then the LORD's anger burned against Uzzah, and God struck him dead on the spot for his irreverence, and he died there next to the ark of God. 8 David was angry because of the LORD's outburst against Uzzah, so he named that place an Outburst Against Uzzah, as it is today. 9 David feared the LORD that day and said, "How can the ark of the LORD ever come to me?" 10 So he was not willing to move the ark of the LORD to the city of David; instead, he took it to the house of Obed-edom the Gittite. 11 The ark of the LORD remained in his house three months, and the LORD blessed Obed-edom and his whole family.

12 It was reported to King David: "The LORD has blessed Obed-edom's family and all that belongs to him because of the ark of God." So David went and had the ark of God brought up from Obed-edom's house to the city of David with rejoicing. 13 When those carrying the ark of the LORD advanced six steps, he sacrificed an ox and a fattened calf. 14 David was dancing with all his might before the LORD wearing a linen ephod. 15 He and the whole house of Israel were bringing up the ark of the LORD with shouts and the sound of the ram's horn. 16 As the ark of the LORD was entering the city of David, Saul's daughter Michal looked down from the window and saw King David leaping and dancing before the LORD, and she despised him in her heart.

17 They brought the ark of the LORD and set it in its place inside the tent David had set up for it. Then David offered burnt offerings and fellowship offerings in the LORD's presence. 18 When David had finished offering the burnt offering and the fellowship offerings, he blessed the people in the name of the LORD of Hosts. 19 Then he distributed a loaf of bread, a date cake, and a raisin cake to each one of the whole multitude of the people of Israel, both men and women. Then all the people left, each to his own home.

[20] When David returned home to bless his household, Saul's daughter Michal came out to meet him. "How the king of Israel honored himself today!" she said. "He exposed himself today in the sight of the slave girls of his subjects like a vulgar person would expose himself." [21] David replied to Michal, "I was dancing before the LORD who chose me over your father and his whole family to appoint me ruler over the LORD's people Israel. I will celebrate before the LORD, [22] and I will humble myself even more and humiliate myself. I will be honored by the slave girls you spoke about." [23] And Saul's daughter Michal had no child to the day of her death.

*P*SALM 68:20-27

20 Our God is a God of salvation,
and escape from death belongs to the Lord GOD.
21 Surely God crushes the heads of His enemies,
the hairy head of one who goes on in his guilty acts.
22 The Lord said, "I will bring them back from Bashan;
I will bring them back from the depths of the sea
23 so that your foot may wade in blood
and your dogs' tongues may have their share from the enemies."
24 People have seen Your procession, God,
the procession of my God, my King, in the sanctuary.
25 Singers lead the way, with musicians following;
among them are young women playing tambourines.
26 Praise God in the assemblies;
praise the LORD from the fountain of Israel.
27 There is Benjamin, the youngest, leading them,
the rulers of Judah in their assembly,
the rulers of Zebulun, the rulers of Naphtali.

*P*ROVERBS 14:33-35

33 Wisdom resides in the heart of the discerning;
she is known even among fools.

34 Righteousness exalts a nation,
but sin is a disgrace to any people.

35 A king favors a wise servant,
but his anger falls on a disgraceful one.

*J*OHN 9:8-27

[8] His neighbors and those who formerly had seen him as a beggar said, "Isn't this the man who sat begging?" [9] Some said, "He's the one." "No," others were saying, "but he looks like him." He kept saying, "I'm the one!" [10] Therefore they asked him, "Then how were your eyes opened?" [11] He answered, "The man called Jesus made mud, spread it on my eyes, and told me, 'Go to Siloam and wash.' So when I went and washed I received my sight." [12] "Where is He?" they asked. "I don't know," he said. [13] They brought the man who used to be blind to the Pharisees. [14] The day that Jesus made the mud and opened his eyes was a Sabbath. [15] So again the Pharisees asked him how he received his sight. "He put mud on my eyes," he told them. "I washed and I can see." [16] Therefore some of the Pharisees said, "This man is not from God, for He doesn't keep the Sabbath!" But others were saying, "How can a sinful man perform such signs?" And there was a division among them. [17] Again they asked the blind man, "What do you say about Him, since He opened your eyes?" "He's a prophet," he said. [18] The Jews did not believe this about him—that he was blind and received sight—until they summoned the parents of the one who had received his sight.

[19] They asked them, "Is this your son, the one you say was born blind? How then does he now see?" [20] "We know this is our son and that he was born blind," his parents answered. [21] "But we don't know how he now sees, and we don't know who opened his eyes. Ask him; he's of age. He will speak for himself." [22] His parents said these things because they were afraid of the Jews, since the Jews had already agreed that if anyone confessed Him as Messiah, he would be banned from the synagogue. [23] This is why his parents said, "He's of age; ask him."

[24] So a second time they summoned the man who had been blind and told him, "Give glory to God. We know that this man is a sinner!" [25] He answered, "Whether or not He's a sinner, I don't know. One thing I do know: I was blind, and now I can see!" [26] Then they asked him, "What did He do to you? How did He open your eyes?" [27] "I already told you," he said, "and you didn't listen. Why do you want to hear it again? You don't want to become His disciples too, do you?"

Completing the Framework

Wisdom resides in the heart of the discerning; she is known even among fools.—PROVERBS 14:33

It is important to build a biblical framework for generosity. First, give at least a tithe of your earnings to the Lord's work. The giving of a tithe is seen by many as legalistic, but the tithe is really a symbol of acknowledgment that the nine-tenths belongs to God. The Hebrews waved the firstfruits of the harvest before the Lord as an acknowledgment that the coming harvest belonged to Him. Some will be able to give far more than a tithe, but the tithe is a good place to begin.

Next, make your will under God's direction and maintain a balance between responsibility for your family and the continuing work of God. Make sure your relatives don't waste what God has given you to invest in His kingdom. You might need advice here from a wise Christian.

Also, remember that the principle of generosity applies not only to your treasure but also to your talents and your time. Each day ask God to show you ways of using your talents and time for Him. John Wesley's advice is worth repeating: "Make all you can; save all you can; give all you can."

Finally, accept the smallest opportunity to be generous as a proving ground for faithfulness. "You were faithful over a few things; I will put you in charge of many things" (Mt 25:21). Don't wait for the big opportunities to be generous but start with the next opportunity that comes your way—no matter how small it may be. Get ready for the bigger by doing the little well. Why does the Bible make much of generosity? Because the truly generous are the truly wise.

Prayer

Father, just like Simon Peter, who gave Your Son his boat from which to preach, I give You my treasure, my talents, and my time for You to use as Your pulpit—today and every day. In Christ's name. Amen.

Further Study

Gn 14:20; Lv 27:30; 2 Ch 31:5; Mt 3:1-10
What principle did Abram follow?
What is your response to the biblical principle expressed by the tithe?

JUNE 2

2 SAMUEL 7:1–9:13

7 When the king had settled into his palace and the LORD had given him rest on every side from all his enemies, ²the king said to Nathan the prophet, "Look, I am living in a cedar house while the ark of God sits inside tent curtains."

³So Nathan told the king, "Go and do all that is on your heart, for the LORD is with you."

⁴But that night the word of the LORD came to Nathan: ⁵"Go to My servant David and say, 'This is what the LORD says: Are you to build a house for Me to live in? ⁶From the time I brought the Israelites out of Egypt until today I have not lived in a house; instead, I have been moving around with the tabernacle tent. ⁷In all My journeys with all the Israelites, have I ever asked anyone among the tribes of Israel, whom I commanded to shepherd My people Israel: Why haven't you built Me a house of cedar?'

⁸"Now this is what you are to say to My servant David: 'This is what the LORD of Hosts says: I took you from the pasture and from following the sheep to be ruler over My people Israel. ⁹I have been with you wherever you have gone, and I have destroyed all your enemies before you. I will make a name for you like that of the greatest in the land. ¹⁰I will establish a place for My people Israel and plant them, so that they may live there and not be disturbed again. Evildoers will not afflict them as they have done ¹¹ever since the day I ordered judges to be over My people Israel. I will give you rest from all your enemies.

" 'The LORD declares to you: The LORD Himself will make a house for you. ¹²When your time comes and you rest with your fathers, I will raise up after you your descendant, who will come from your body, and I will establish his kingdom. ¹³He will build a house for My name, and I will establish the throne of his kingdom forever. ¹⁴I will be a father to him, and he will be a son to Me. When he does wrong, I will discipline him with a human rod and with blows from others. ¹⁵But My faithful love will never leave him as I removed it from Saul; I removed him from your way. ¹⁶Your house and kingdom will endure before Me forever, and your throne will be established forever.' "

¹⁷Nathan spoke all these words and this entire vision to David.

¹⁸Then King David went in, sat in the LORD's presence, and said, "Who am I, Lord GOD, and what is my house that You have brought me this far? ¹⁹What You have done so far was a little thing to You, Lord GOD, for You have also spoken about Your servant's house in the distant future. And this is a revelation for mankind, Lord GOD. ²⁰What more can David say to You? You know Your servant, Lord GOD. ²¹Because of Your

word and according to Your will, You have revealed all these great things to Your servant. [22] "This is why You are great, Lord GOD. There is no one like You, and there is no God besides You, as all we have heard confirms. [23] And who is like Your people Israel? God came to one nation on earth in order to redeem a people for Himself, to make a name for Himself, and to perform for them great and awesome acts, driving out nations and their gods before Your people You redeemed for Yourself from Egypt. [24] You established Your people Israel Your own people forever, and You, LORD, have become their God.

[25] "Now, LORD God, fulfill the promise forever that You have made to Your servant and his house. Do as You have promised, [26] so that Your name will be exalted forever, when it is said, 'The LORD of Hosts is God over Israel.' The house of Your servant David will be established before You [27] since You, LORD of Hosts, God of Israel, have revealed this to Your servant when You said, 'I will build a house for you.' Therefore, Your servant has found the courage to pray this prayer to You. [28] Lord GOD, You are God; Your words are true, and You have promised this grace to Your servant. [29] Now, please bless Your servant's house so that it will continue before You forever. For You, Lord GOD, have spoken, and with Your blessing Your servant's house will be blessed forever."

8 After this, David defeated the Philistines, subdued them, and took Metheg-ammah from Philistine control. [2] He also defeated the Moabites, and after making them lie down on the ground, he measured them off with a cord. He measured every two cord lengths of those to be put to death and one length of those to be kept alive. So the Moabites became David's subjects and brought tribute.

[3] David also defeated Hadadezer son of Rehob, king of Zobah, who went to restore his control at the Euphrates River. [4] David captured 1,700 horsemen and 20,000 foot soldiers from him, and

he hamstrung all the horses, and he kept 100 chariots.

[5] When the Arameans of Damascus came to assist King Hadadezer of Zobah, David struck down 22,000 Aramean men. [6] Then he placed garrisons in Aram of Damascus, and the Arameans became David's subjects and brought tribute. The LORD made David victorious wherever he went. [7] David took the gold shields of Hadadezer's officers and brought them to Jerusalem. [8] King David also took huge quantities of bronze from Betah and Berothai, Hadadezer's cities.

[9] When King Toi of Hamath heard that David had defeated the entire army of Hadadezer, [10] he sent his son Joram to King David to greet him and to congratulate him because David had fought against Hadadezer and defeated him, for Toi and Hadadezer had fought many wars. Joram had items of silver, gold, and bronze with him. [11] King David also dedicated these to the LORD, along with the silver and gold he had dedicated from all the nations he had subdued— [12] from Edom, Moab, the Ammonites, the Philistines, the Amalekites, and the spoil of Hadadezer son of Rehob, king of Zobah.

[13] David made a reputation for himself when he returned from striking down 18,000 Edomites in the Valley of Salt. [14] He placed garrisons throughout Edom, and all the Edomites were subject to David. The LORD made David victorious wherever he went.

[15] So David reigned over all Israel, administering justice and righteousness for all his people.

[16] Joab son of Zeruiah was
over the army;
Jehoshaphat son of Ahilud was
court historian;
[17] Zadok son of Ahitub
and Ahimelech son of Abiathar
were priests;
Seraiah was court secretary;
[18] Benaiah son of Jehoiada was over
the Cherethites
and the Pelethites;
and David's sons were chief officials.

9 David asked, "Is there anyone remaining from Saul's family I can show kindness to because of Jonathan?" ² There was a servant of Saul's family named Ziba. They summoned him to David, and the king said to him, "Are you Ziba?"

"I am your servant," he replied.

³ So the king asked, "Is there anyone left of Saul's family I can show the kindness of God to?"

Ziba said to the king, "There is still Jonathan's son who is lame in both feet."

⁴ The king asked him, "Where is he?"

Ziba answered the king, "You'll find him in Lo-debar at the house of Machir son of Ammiel." ⁵ So King David had him brought from the house of Machir son of Ammiel in Lo-debar.

⁶ Mephibosheth son of Jonathan son of Saul came to David, bowed down to the ground and paid homage. David said, "Mephibosheth!"

"I am your servant," he replied.

⁷ "Don't be afraid," David said to him, "since I intend to show you kindness because of your father Jonathan. I will restore to you all your grandfather Saul's fields, and you will always eat meals at my table."

⁸ Mephibosheth bowed down and said, "What is your servant that you take an interest in a dead dog like me?"

⁹ Then the king summoned Saul's attendant Ziba and said to him, "I have given to your master's grandson all that belonged to Saul and his family. ¹⁰ You, your sons, and your servants are to work the ground for him, and you are to bring in the crops so your master's grandson will have food to eat. But Mephibosheth, your master's grandson, is always to eat at my table." Now Ziba had 15 sons and 20 servants.

¹¹ Ziba said to the king, "Your servant will do all my lord the king commands."

So Mephibosheth ate at David's table just like one of the king's sons. ¹² Mephibosheth had a young son whose name was Mica. All those living in Ziba's house were Mephibosheth's servants. ¹³ However, Mephibosheth lived in Jerusalem because he always ate at the king's table. He was lame in both feet.

PSALM 68:28-31

28 Your God has decreed your
    strength.
Show Your strength, God,
You who have acted on our behalf.
29 Because of Your temple at
    Jerusalem,
kings will bring tribute to You.
30 Rebuke the beast in the reeds,
the herd of bulls with the calves
    of the peoples.
Trample underfoot those with bars
    of silver.
Scatter the peoples who take
    pleasure in war.
31 Ambassadors will come from
    Egypt;
Cush will stretch out its hands to
    God.

PROVERBS 15:1-3

15 A gentle answer turns away
    anger,
but a harsh word stirs up wrath.

2 The tongue of the wise makes
    knowledge attractive,
but the mouth of fools blurts out
    foolishness.

3 The eyes of the LORD are
    everywhere,
observing the wicked and the
    good.

JOHN 9:28–10:6

²⁸ They ridiculed him: "You're that man's disciple, but we're Moses' disciples. ²⁹ We know that God has spoken to Moses. But this man—we don't know where He's from!"

³⁰ "This is an amazing thing," the man told them. "You don't know where He is from, yet He opened my eyes! ³¹ We know that God doesn't listen to sinners, but if anyone is God-fearing and does His will, He listens to him. ³² Throughout

history no one has ever heard of someone opening the eyes of a person born blind. [33] If this man were not from God, He wouldn't be able to do anything."

[34] "You were born entirely in sin," they replied, "and are you trying to teach us?" Then they threw him out.

[35] When Jesus heard that they had thrown the man out, He found him and asked, "Do you believe in the Son of Man?"

[36] "Who is He, Sir, that I may believe in Him?" he asked.

[37] Jesus answered, "You have seen Him; in fact, He is the One speaking with you."

[38] "I believe, Lord!" he said, and he worshiped Him.

[39] Jesus said, "I came into this world for judgment, in order that those who do not see will see and those who do see will become blind."

[40] Some of the Pharisees who were with Him heard these things and asked Him, "We aren't blind too, are we?"

[41] "If you were blind," Jesus told them, "you wouldn't have sin. But now that you say, 'We see'—your sin remains.

10 "I assure you: Anyone who doesn't enter the sheep pen by the door but climbs in some other way, is a thief and a robber. [2] The one who enters by the door is the shepherd of the sheep. [3] The doorkeeper opens it for him, and the sheep hear his voice. He calls his own sheep by name and leads them out. [4] When he has brought all his own outside, he goes ahead of them. The sheep follow him because they recognize his voice. [5] They will never follow a stranger; instead they will run away from him, because they don't recognize the voice of strangers."

[6] Jesus gave them this illustration, but they did not understand what He was telling them.

We Become What We Say

The tongue of the wise makes knowledge attractive, but the mouth of fools blurts out foolishness.
—**Proverbs 15:2**

Why is the tongue so important? Because the expression of a thing deepens the impression. A word uttered becomes a word made flesh—in us. We become the incarnation of what we express. Jesus said, "For by your words you will be acquitted, and by your words you will be condemned" (Mt 12:37). After I saw that a person becomes what he says, I have looked at this verse in a different light. If you tell a lie, you become a lie. The deepest punishment of a lie is to be the one who tells the lie. That person has to live with someone he cannot trust.

Now look at what I am saying from the opposite perspective. When we express good things, positive things, loving things, scriptural things, these things go deeper into us. Clear expression deepens impression. A brilliant young physicist tells how he often discusses complex issues relating to physics with his wife who doesn't know the first thing about the subject. He told a friend, "I describe in detail what I am doing and she doesn't understand a word. But sometimes when I'm through—I do."

If it is true—and I believe it is—that we become the incarnation of what we express, then how careful we ought to be to ensure that what we say is guarded and governed by truth, integrity, and kindness. Always remember: every word you utter becomes flesh—in you.

Prayer

O Father, how awesome is this thought—I become the incarnation of what I express. Cleanse me deep within so that I may be pure in soul as well as speech. I would be a clarified person. Grant it please, dear Father. In Jesus' name. Amen.

Further Study

1 Tm 4:1-12; Ps 34:13; Php 4:8; Pr 21:16-31
In what areas was Timothy to set a good example?
What should our thoughts be focused on?

JUNE 3

2 SAMUEL 10:1–11:27

10 Some time later the king of the Ammonites died, and his son Hanun became king in his place. ² Then David said, "I'll show kindness to Hanun son of Nahash, just as his father showed kindness to me."

So David sent his emissaries to console Hanun concerning his father. However, when they arrived in the land of the Ammonites, ³ the Ammonite leaders said to Hanun their lord, "Just because David has sent men with condolences for you, do you really believe he's showing respect for your father? Instead, hasn't David sent his emissaries in order to scout out the city, spy on it, and overthrow it?" ⁴ So Hanun took David's emissaries, shaved off half their beards, cut their clothes in half at the hips, and sent them away.

⁵ When this was reported to David, he sent someone to meet them, since they were deeply humiliated. The king said, "Stay in Jericho until your beards grow back; then return."

⁶ When the Ammonites realized they had become repulsive to David, they hired 20,000 foot soldiers from the Arameans of Beth-rehob and Zobah, 1,000 men from the king of Maacah, and 12,000 men from Tob.

⁷ David heard about it and sent Joab and all the fighting men. ⁸ The Ammonites marched out and lined up in battle formation at the entrance to the city gate while the Arameans of Zobah and Rehob and the men of Tob and Maacah were in the field by themselves. ⁹ When Joab saw that there was a battle line in front of him and another behind him, he chose some men out of all the elite troops of Israel and lined up in battle formation to engage the Arameans. ¹⁰ He placed the rest of the forces under the command of his brother Abishai who lined up in battle formation to engage the Ammonites.

¹¹ "If the Arameans are too strong for me," Joab said, "then you will be my help. However, if the Ammonites are too strong for you, I'll come to help you. ¹² Be strong! We must prove ourselves strong for our people and for the cities of our God. May the LORD's will be done."

¹³ Joab and his troops advanced to

fight against the Arameans, and they fled before him. [14] When the Ammonites saw that the Arameans had fled, they too fled before Abishai and entered the city. So Joab withdrew from the attack against the Ammonites and went to Jerusalem.

[15] When the Arameans saw that they had been defeated by Israel, they regrouped. [16] Hadadezer sent messengers to bring the Arameans who were across the Euphrates River, and they came to Helam with Shobach, commander of Hadadezer's army, leading them.

[17] When this was reported to David, he gathered all Israel, crossed the Jordan, and went to Helam. Then the Arameans lined up in formation to engage David in battle and fought against him. [18] But the Arameans fled before Israel, and David killed 700 of their charioteers and 40,000 foot soldiers. He also struck down Shobach commander of their army, who died there. [19] When all the kings who were Hadadezer's subjects saw that they had been defeated by Israel, they made peace with Israel and became their subjects. After this, the Arameans were afraid to ever help the Ammonites again.

11 In the spring when kings march out to war, David sent Joab with his officers and all Israel. They destroyed the Ammonites and besieged Rabbah, but David remained in Jerusalem.

[2] One evening David got up from his bed and strolled around on the roof of the palace. From the roof he saw a woman bathing—a very beautiful woman. [3] So David sent someone to inquire about her, and he reported, "This is Bathsheba, daughter of Eliam and wife of Uriah the Hittite." [4] David sent messengers to get her, and when she came to him, he slept with her. Now she had just been purifying herself from her uncleanness. Afterwards, she returned home. [5] The woman conceived and sent word to inform David: "I am pregnant."

[6] David sent orders to Joab: "Send me Uriah the Hittite." So Joab sent Uriah to David. [7] When Uriah came to him, David asked how Joab and the troops were doing and how the war was going. [8] Then he said to Uriah, "Go down to your house and wash your feet." So Uriah left the palace, and a gift from the king followed him. [9] But Uriah slept at the door of the palace with all his master's servants; he did not go down to his house.

[10] When it was reported to David, "Uriah didn't go home," David questioned Uriah, "Haven't you just come from a journey? Why didn't you go home?"

[11] Uriah answered David, "The ark, Israel, and Judah are dwelling in tents, and my master Joab and his soldiers are camping in the open field. How can I enter my house to eat and drink and sleep with my wife? As surely as you live and by your life, I will not do this!"

[12] "Stay here today also," David said to Uriah, "and tomorrow I will send you back." So Uriah stayed in Jerusalem that day and the next. [13] Then David invited Uriah to eat and drink with him, and David got him drunk. He went out in the evening to lie down on his cot with his master's servants, but he did not go home.

[14] The next morning David wrote a letter to Joab and sent it with Uriah. [15] In the letter he wrote:

Put Uriah at the front of the fiercest fighting, then withdraw from him so that he is struck down and dies.

[16] When Joab was besieging the city, he put Uriah in the place where he knew the best enemy soldiers were. [17] Then the men of the city came out and attacked Joab, and some of the men from David's soldiers fell in battle; Uriah the Hittite also died.

[18] Joab sent someone to report to David all the details of the battle. [19] He commanded the messenger, "When you've finished telling the king all the details of the battle— [20] if the king's anger gets stirred up and he asks you, 'Why did you get so close to the city to fight? Didn't you realize they would shoot from the top of the wall? [21] At

Thebez, who struck Abimelech son of Jerubbesheth? Didn't a woman drop an upper millstone on him from the top of the wall so that he died? Why did you get so close to the wall?'—then say, 'Your servant Uriah the Hittite is dead also.' " [22] Then the messenger left. When he arrived, he reported to David all that Joab had sent him to tell. [23] The messenger reported to David, "The men gained the advantage over us and came out against us in the field, but we counterattacked right up to the entrance of the gate. [24] However, the archers shot down on your soldiers from the top of the wall, and some of the king's soldiers died. Your servant Uriah the Hittite is also dead."

[25] David told the messenger, "Say this to Joab: 'Don't let this matter upset you because the sword devours all alike. Intensify your fight against the city and demolish it.' Encourage him."

[26] When Uriah's wife heard that her husband Uriah had died, she mourned for him. [27] When the time of mourning ended, David had her brought to his house. She became his wife and bore him a son. However, the LORD considered what David had done to be evil.

PSALM 68:32-35

[32] Sing to God, you kingdoms of the earth;
    sing praise to the Lord,   *Selah*
[33] to Him who rides in the ancient, highest heavens.
    Look, He thunders with His powerful voice!
[34] Ascribe power to God.
    His majesty is over Israel,
    His power among the clouds.
[35] God, You are awe-inspiring in Your sanctuaries.
    The God of Israel gives power and strength to His people.
    May God be praised!

PROVERBS 15:4-5

[4] The tongue that heals is a tree of life,

but a devious tongue breaks the spirit.
[5] A fool despises his father's instruction,
    but a person who heeds correction is sensible.

JOHN 10:7-30

[7] So Jesus said again, "I assure you: I am the door of the sheep. [8] All who came before Me are thieves and robbers, but the sheep didn't listen to them. [9] I am the door. If anyone enters by Me, he will be saved and will come in and go out and find pasture. [10] A thief comes only to steal and to kill and to destroy. I have come that they may have life and have it in abundance.

[11] "I am the good shepherd. The good shepherd lays down his life for the sheep. [12] The hired man, since he is not the shepherd and doesn't own the sheep, leaves them and runs away when he sees a wolf coming. The wolf then snatches and scatters them. [13] This happens because he is a hired man and doesn't care about the sheep.

[14] "I am the good shepherd. I know My own sheep, and they know Me, [15] as the Father knows Me, and I know the Father. I lay down My life for the sheep. [16] But I have other sheep that are not of this fold; I must bring them also, and they will listen to My voice. Then there will be one flock, one shepherd. [17] This is why the Father loves Me, because I am laying down My life so I may take it up again. [18] No one takes it from Me, but I lay it down on My own. I have the right to lay it down, and I have the right to take it up again. I have received this command from My Father."

[19] Again a division took place among the Jews because of these words. [20] Many of them were saying, "He has a demon and He's crazy! Why do you listen to Him?" [21] Others were saying, "These aren't the words of someone demon-possessed. Can a demon open the eyes of the blind?"

[22] Then the Festival of Dedication

took place in Jerusalem, and it was winter. ²³ Jesus was walking in the temple complex in Solomon's Colonnade. ²⁴ Then the Jews surrounded Him and asked, "How long are You going to keep us in suspense? If You are the Messiah, tell us plainly."

²⁵ "I did tell you and you don't believe," Jesus answered them. "The works that I do in My Father's name testify about Me. ²⁶ But you don't believe because you are not My sheep. ²⁷ My sheep hear My voice, I know them, and they follow Me. ²⁸ I give them eternal life, and they will never perish—ever! No one will snatch them out of My hand. ²⁹ My Father, who has given them to Me, is greater than all. No one is able to snatch them out of the Father's hand. ³⁰ The Father and I are one."

Life to its Fullest

*I have come that they may have life
and have it in abundance.*

—John 10:10

A nest which God seeks to overturn in our lives is spiritual complacency. Many Christians are content to live at a level far below the best. It might be comfortable in the nest, but it is far better to expand one's wings, launch out into the clear, blue sky, and live life to its fullest potential. God's desire is to get you out of the nest and up into the air.

I am thinking particularly of those Christians who, although soundly saved and fully committed to Jesus Christ, have never experienced all the fullness of the Holy Spirit. Although every Christian has the Holy Spirit (1 Co 12:3), the Holy Spirit does not have every Christian. When you surrendered your life to Jesus Christ, the Holy Spirit came in to regenerate you, give you a new birth, but now you need to experience another encounter with the Spirit that lifts you clean out of the nest and up into the air.

The text before us today claims that Jesus came not merely to give us life but to give it—abundantly. One writer says of this verse: "At conversion, Christ gives us life, but when we experience the fullness of the Spirit, we encounter not merely life but life that is abundant. In conversion, God's life is imparted to us. In the fullness of the Spirit, God's life inundates us." A sign over a shop read: "Life Ltd." A sign could be put over our individual and collectives lives: "Life Ltd." And yet Jesus said that the purpose of His coming was to give life more abundantly.

Prayer

O Father, take me from life limited to Life Unlimited. I have lived far too long in the nest. Now I want to get up into the air. Amen.

Further Study

Ac 1-2; Jn 7:38-39; 1 Co 3:16; Rm 8:11
What caused the disciples to soar to new heights?
What does the word "quicken" (KJV) mean?

JUNE 4

2 SAMUEL 12:1–13:39

12 So the LORD sent Nathan to David. When he arrived, he said to him:

There were two men in a certain city, one rich and the other poor. ² The rich man had a large number of sheep and cattle, ³ but the poor man had nothing except one small ewe lamb that he had bought. It lived and grew up with him and his children. It shared his meager food and drank from his cup; it slept in his arms, and it was like a daughter to him. ⁴ Now a traveler came to the rich man, but the rich man could not bring himself to take one of his own sheep or cattle to prepare for the traveler who had come to him. Instead, he took the poor man's lamb and prepared it for his guest.

⁵ David was infuriated with the man and said to Nathan: "As surely as the LORD lives, the man who did this deserves to die! ⁶ Because he has done this thing and shown no pity, he must pay four lambs for that lamb."

⁷ Nathan replied to David, "You are the man! This is what the LORD God of Israel says: 'I anointed you king over Israel, and I delivered you from the hand of Saul. ⁸ I gave your master's house to you and your master's wives into your arms, and I gave you the house of Israel and Judah, and if that was not enough, I would have given you even more. ⁹ Why then have you despised the command of the LORD by doing what I consider evil? You struck down Uriah the Hittite with the sword and took his wife as your own wife—you murdered him with the Ammonite's sword. ¹⁰ Now therefore, the sword will never leave your house because you despised Me and took the wife of Uriah the Hittite to be your own wife.'

¹¹ "This is what the LORD says, 'I am going to bring disaster on you from your own family: I will take your wives and give them to another before your very eyes, and he will sleep with them publicly. ¹² You acted in secret, but I will do this before all Israel and in broad daylight.' "

¹³ David responded to Nathan, "I have sinned against the LORD."

Then Nathan replied to David, "The LORD has taken away your sin; you will not die. ¹⁴ However, because you treated the LORD with such contempt in this matter, the son born to you will die." ¹⁵ Then Nathan went home.

The LORD struck the baby that Uriah's wife had borne to David, and he became ill. ¹⁶ David pleaded with God for the boy. He fasted, went home, and spent the night lying on the ground. ¹⁷ The elders of his house stood beside him to get him up from the ground, but he was unwilling and would not eat anything with them.

¹⁸ On the seventh day the baby died. But David's servants were afraid to tell him the baby was dead. They said, "Look, while the baby was alive, we spoke to him, and he wouldn't listen to us. So how can we tell him the baby is dead? He may do something desperate." ¹⁹ When David saw that his servants were whispering to each other, he guessed that the baby was dead. So he asked his servants, "Is the baby dead?"

"He is dead," they replied.

²⁰ Then David got up from the ground. He washed, anointed himself, changed his clothes, went to the LORD's house, and worshiped. Then he went home and requested something to eat. So they served him food, and he ate. ²¹ His servants asked him, "What did you just do? While the baby was alive, you fasted and wept, but when he died, you got up and ate food."

²² He answered, "While the baby was alive, I fasted and wept because I thought, 'Who knows? The LORD may be gracious to me and let him live.' ²³ But now that he is dead, why should I fast? Can I bring him back again? I'll go to him, but he will never return to me."

²⁴ Then David comforted his wife Bathsheba; he went and slept with her. She gave birth to a son and named him Solomon. The LORD loved him, ²⁵ and He sent a message through Nathan the prophet, who named him Jedidiah, because of the LORD.

²⁶ Joab fought against Rabbah of the Ammonites and captured the royal fortress. ²⁷ Then Joab sent messengers to David to say, "I have fought against Rabbah and have also captured the water supply. ²⁸ Now therefore, assemble the rest of the troops, lay siege to the city, and capture it. Otherwise I will be the one to capture the city, and it will be named after me. ²⁹ So David assembled all the troops and went to Rabbah; he fought against it and captured it. ³⁰ He took the crown from the head of their king, and it was placed on David's head. The crown weighed 75 pounds of gold, and it had a precious stone in it. In addition, David took away a large quantity of plunder from the city. ³¹ He re-

moved the people who were in the city and put them to work with saws, iron picks, and iron axes, and to labor at brickmaking. He did the same to all the Ammonite cities. Then he and all his troops returned to Jerusalem.

13 Some time passed. David's son Absalom had a beautiful sister named Tamar, and David's son Amnon was infatuated with her. ² Amnon was frustrated to the point of making himself sick over his sister Tamar because she was a virgin, but it seemed impossible to do anything to her. ³ Amnon had a friend named Jonadab, a son of David's brother Shimeah. Jonadab was a very shrewd man, ⁴ and he asked Amnon, "Why are you, the king's son, so miserable every morning? Won't you tell me?"

Amnon replied, "I'm in love with Tamar, my brother Absalom's sister."

⁵ Jonadab said to him, "Lie down on your bed and pretend you're sick. When your father comes to see you, say to him, 'Please let my sister Tamar come and give me something to eat. Let her prepare food in my presence so I can watch and eat from her hand.' "

⁶ So Amnon lay down and pretended to be sick. When the king came to see him, Amnon said to him, "Please let my sister Tamar come and make a couple of cakes in my presence so I can eat from her hand."

⁷ David sent word to Tamar at the palace: "Please go to your brother Amnon's house and prepare a meal for him."

⁸ Then Tamar went to his house while Amnon was lying down. She took dough, kneaded it, made cakes in his presence, and baked them. ⁹ She brought the pan and set it down in front of him, but he refused to eat. Amnon said, "Everyone leave me!" And everyone left him. ¹⁰ "Bring the meal to the bedroom," Amnon told Tamar, "so I can eat from your hand." Tamar took the cakes she had made and went to her brother Amnon's bedroom. ¹¹ When she brought them to him to eat, he grabbed her and said, "Come sleep with me, my sister!" ¹² "Don't, my brother!" she cried.

"Don't humiliate me, for such a thing should never be done in Israel. Don't do this horrible thing! [13] Where could I ever go with my disgrace? And you—you would be like one of the immoral men in Israel! Please, speak to the king, for he won't keep me from you." [14] But he refused to listen to her, and because he was stronger than she was, he raped her.

[15] After this, Amnon hated Tamar with such intensity that the hatred he hated her with was greater than the love he had loved her with. "Get out of here!" he said.

[16] "No," she cried, "sending me away is much worse than the great wrong you've already done to me!" But he refused to listen to her. [17] Instead, he called to the servant who waited on him: "Throw this woman out and bolt the door behind her!" [18] Amnon's servant threw her out and bolted the door behind her. Now Tamar was wearing a long-sleeved garment, because this is what the king's virgin daughters wore. [19] Tamar put ashes on her head and tore the long-sleeved garment she was wearing. She put her hand on her head and went away weeping.

[20] Her brother Absalom said to her: "Has your brother Amnon been with you? Be quiet for now, my sister. He is your brother. Don't take this thing to heart." So Tamar lived as a desolate woman in the house of her brother Absalom.

[21] When King David heard about all these things, he was furious. [22] Absalom didn't say anything to Amnon, either good or bad, because he hated Amnon since he disgraced his sister Tamar.

[23] Two years later, Absalom's sheep-shearers were at Baal-hazor near Ephraim, and Absalom invited all the king's sons. [24] Then he went to the king and said, "Your servant has just hired sheepshearers. Will the king and his servants please come with your servant?" [25] The king replied to Absalom, "No, my son, we should not all go, or we would be a burden to you." Although Absalom urged him, he wasn't willing to go, though he did bless him.

[26] "If not," Absalom said, "please let my brother Amnon go with us."

The king asked him, "Why should he go with you?" [27] But Absalom urged him, so he sent Amnon and all the king's sons.

[28] Now Absalom commanded his young men, "Watch Amnon until he is in a good mood from the wine. When I order you to strike Amnon, then kill him. Don't be afraid. Am I not the one who has commanded you? Be strong and courageous!" [29] So Absalom's young men did to Amnon just as Absalom had commanded. Then all the rest of the king's sons got up, and each fled on his mule.

[30] While they were on the way, a report reached David: "Absalom struck down all the king's sons; not even one of them survived!" [31] In response the king stood up, tore his clothes, and lay down on the ground, and all his servants stood by with their clothes torn.

[32] But Jonadab, son of David's brother Shimeah, spoke up: "My lord must not think they have killed all the young men, the king's sons, because only Amnon is dead. In fact, Absalom has planned this ever since the day Amnon disgraced his sister Tamar. [33] So now, my lord the king, don't take seriously the report that says all the king's sons are dead. Only Amnon is dead."

[34] Meanwhile, Absalom had fled. When the young man who was standing watch looked up, there were many people coming from the road west of him from the side of the mountain. [35] Jonadab said to the king, "Look, the king's sons have come! It's exactly like your servant said." [36] Just as he finished speaking, the king's sons entered and wept loudly. Then the king and all his servants also wept bitterly.

[37] Now Absalom fled and went to Talmai son of Ammihud, king of Geshur. And David mourned for his son every day. [38] Absalom had fled and gone to Geshur where he stayed three years. [39] Then King David longed to go to Absalom, for David had finished grieving over Amnon's death.

PSALM 69:1-4

1 Save me, God,
for the water has risen to my neck.
2 I have sunk in deep mud, and there is no footing;
I have come into deep waters, and a flood sweeps over me.
3 I am weary from my crying; my throat is parched.
My eyes fail, looking for my God.
4 Those who hate me without cause are more numerous than the hairs of my head;
my deceitful enemies, who would destroy me, are powerful.
Though I did not steal, I must repay.

PROVERBS 15:6-7

6 The house of the righteous has great wealth,
but trouble accompanies the income of the wicked.
7 The lips of the wise broadcast knowledge,
but not so the heart of fools.

JOHN 10:31–11:6

31 Again the Jews picked up rocks to stone Him.
32 Jesus replied, "I have shown you many good works from the Father. Which of these works are you stoning Me for?"
33 "We aren't stoning You for a good work," the Jews answered, "but for blasphemy, because You—being a man—make Yourself God."
34 Jesus answered them, "Isn't it written in your law, I said, you are gods? 35 If He called those whom the word of God came to 'gods'—and the Scripture cannot be broken— 36 do you say, 'You are blaspheming' to the One the Father set apart and sent into the world, because I said: I am the Son of God? 37 If I am not doing My Father's works, don't believe Me. 38 But if I am doing them and you don't believe Me, believe the works. This way you will know and understand that the Father is in Me and I in Father." 39 Then they were trying again to seize Him, yet He eluded their grasp.
40 So He departed again across the Jordan to the place where John had been baptizing earlier, and He remained there. 41 Many came to Him and said, "John never did a sign, but everything John said about this man was true." 42 And many believed in Him there.

11 Now a man was sick, Lazarus, from Bethany, the village of Mary and her sister Martha. 2 Mary was the one who anointed the Lord with fragrant oil and wiped His feet with her hair, and it was her brother Lazarus who was sick. 3 So the sisters sent a message to Him: "Lord, the one You love is sick." 4 When Jesus heard it, He said, "This sickness will not end in death but is for the glory of God, so that the Son of God may be glorified through it." 5 (Jesus loved Martha, her sister, and Lazarus.) 6 So when He heard that he was sick, He stayed two more days in the place where He was.

God's Great Masterpiece

And the Scripture cannot be broken.—JOHN 10:35

I subscribe to the supervisal inspiration of the Bible. I believe God led the minds and hearts of the writers of Scripture to go to the right sources for information, to come up with the required data, and in the process protected them from exposure to error, deceit, or imposture. He supervised them in their research, in their reporting, and when He spoke directly to them, He was there also to make sure that they received clearly the message He wanted to convey. Ian Macpherson puts this truth most powerfully in his book *The Faith Once Delivered* when he says: "As in the mystery of the Incarnation, God linked Himself to humanity, so in the mystery of the inspiration of the Holy Scripture, God made use of human channels, yet He never surrendered His Divine authorship or permitted the Book to become the word of man rather than the word of God."

Another writer, H. O. Mackey, put it like this: "Who built St. Paul's Cathedral? So many masons, carpenters, iron-workers, carvers, painters—and then there was Wren. He was not a mason, or a carpenter . . . and never laid a stone. What did he do? He did it all. He planned it, inspired it with his thought." Mackey does not intend to dishonor the workmen who toiled hard and long, but simply to make the point that in the final analysis St. Paul's Cathedral is Sir Christopher Wren's masterpiece.

Who wrote the Bible? Moses, David, Isaiah, Jeremiah, John, Peter, Paul, and many others. But whose book is it really? It is God's.

Prayer

O God, it is the entrance of Your Word that brings light, and the neglect of Your Word that brings darkness. Help me to expose myself more and more to that light, so that I may walk through life with a sure and steady tread. In Jesus' name. Amen.

Further Study

Rv 22:12-21; Dt 4:2; 12:32; Pr 30:5-6
What was the conclusion of the writer of Proverbs?
What was John's warning?

JUNE 5

2 SAMUEL 14:1–15:37

14 Joab son of Zeruiah observed that the king's mind was on Absalom. ² So Joab sent someone to Tekoa to bring a clever woman from there. He told her, "Pretend to be in mourning: dress in mourning clothes and don't put on any oil. Act like a woman who has been mourning for the dead for a long time. ³ Go to the king and speak these words to him." Then Joab told her exactly what to say.

⁴ When the woman from Tekoa came to the king, she fell with her face to the ground in homage and said, "Help me, my king!"

⁵ "What's the matter?" the king asked her.

"To tell the truth, I am a widow; my husband died," she said. [6] "Your servant had two sons. They were fighting in the field with no one to separate them, and one struck the other and killed him. [7] Now the whole clan has risen up against your servant and said, 'Hand over the one who killed his brother so we may put him to death for the life of the brother he murdered. We will destroy the heir!' They would extinguish my one remaining ember by not preserving my husband's name or posterity on earth."

[8] The king told the woman, "Go home. I will issue a command on your behalf."

[9] Then the woman of Tekoa said to the king, "My lord the king, may any blame be on me and my father's house, and may the king and his throne be innocent."

[10] "Whoever speaks to you," the king said, "bring him to me. He will not trouble you again!"

[11] She replied, "Please, may the king invoke the LORD your God, so that the avenger of blood will not increase the loss, and they will not eliminate my son!"

"As the LORD lives," he vowed, "not a hair of your son will fall to the ground."

[12] Then the woman said, "Please, may your servant speak a word to my lord the king?"

"Speak," he replied.

[13] The woman asked, "Why have you devised something similar against the people of God? When the king spoke as he did about this matter, he has pronounced his own guilt. The king has not brought back his own banished one. [14] For we will certainly die and be like water poured out on the ground, which can't be recovered. But God would not take away a life; He would devise plans so that the one banished from Him does not remain banished.

[15] "Now therefore, I've come to present this matter to my lord the king because the people have made me afraid. Your servant thought: I must speak to the king. Perhaps the king will grant his servant's request. [16] The king will surely listen in order to rescue his servant from the hand of this man who would eliminate both me and my son from God's inheritance. [17] Your servant thought: May the word of my lord the king bring relief, for my lord the king is able to discern the good and the bad like the Angel of God. May the LORD your God be with you."

[18] Then the king answered the woman, "I'm going to ask you something; don't conceal it from me!"

"Let my lord the king speak," the woman replied.

[19] The king asked, "Did Joab put you up to all this?"

The woman answered. "As surely as you live, my lord the king, no one can turn to the right or left from all my lord the king says. Yes, your servant Joab is the one who gave orders to me; he told your servant exactly what to say. [20] Joab your servant has done this to address the issue indirectly, but my lord has wisdom like the wisdom of the Angel of God, knowing everything on earth."

[21] Then the king said to Joab, "I hereby grant this request. Go, bring back the young man Absalom."

[22] Joab fell with his face to the ground in homage and praised the king. "Today," Joab said, "your servant knows I have found favor with you, my lord the king, because the king has granted the request of your servant."

[23] So Joab got up, went to Geshur, and brought Absalom to Jerusalem. [24] However, the king added, "He may return to his house, but he may not see my face." So Absalom returned to his house, but he did not see the king.

[25] No man in all Israel was as handsome and highly praised as Absalom. From the sole of his foot to the top of his head, he did not have a single flaw. [26] When he shaved his head—he shaved it every year because his hair got so heavy for him that he had to shave it off—he would weigh the hair from his head and it would be five pounds according to the royal standard.

[27] Three sons were born to Absalom, and a daughter named Tamar, who was a beautiful woman. [28] Absalom resided in Jerusalem two years but never saw

the king. ²⁹ Then Absalom sent for Joab in order to send him to the king, but Joab was unwilling to come. So he sent again, a second time, but he still wouldn't come. ³⁰ Then Absalom said to his servants, "See, Joab has a field right next to mine, and he has barley there. Go and set fire to it!" So Absalom's servants set the field on fire.

³¹ Then Joab came to Absalom's house and demanded, "Why did your servants set my field on fire?"

³² "Look," Absalom explained to Joab, "I sent for you and said, 'Come here. I want to send you to the king to ask: Why have I come back from Geshur? I'd be better off if I were still there.' So now, let me see the king. If I am guilty, let him kill me."

³³ Joab went to the king and told him. So David summoned Absalom, who came to the king and bowed down with his face to the ground before the king. Then the king kissed Absalom.

15 After this, Absalom got himself a chariot, horses, and 50 men to run before him. ² He would get up early and stand beside the road leading to the city gate. Whenever anyone had a grievance to bring before the king for settlement, Absalom called out to him and asked, "What city are you from?" If he replied, "Your servant is from one of the tribes of Israel," ³ Absalom said to him, "Look, your claims are good and right, but the king does not have anyone to listen to you." ⁴ He added, "If only someone would appoint me judge in the land. Then anyone who had a grievance or dispute could come to me, and I would make sure he received justice." ⁵ When a person approached to bow down to him, Absalom reached out his hand, took hold of him, and kissed him. ⁶ Absalom did this to all the Israelites who came to the king for a settlement. So Absalom stole the hearts of the men of Israel.

⁷ When four years had passed, Absalom said to the king, "Please let me go to Hebron to fulfill a vow I made to the Lord. ⁸ For your servant made a vow when I lived in Geshur of Aram, saying:

If the Lord really brings me back to Jerusalem, I will worship the Lord in Hebron."

⁹ "Go in peace," the king said to him. So he went to Hebron.

¹⁰ Then Absalom sent messengers throughout the tribes of Israel with this message: "When you hear the sound of the ram's horn, you are to say, 'Absalom has become king in Hebron!' "

¹¹ Two hundred men from Jerusalem went with Absalom. They had been invited and were going innocently, for they knew nothing about the whole matter. ¹² While he was offering the sacrifices, Absalom sent for David's adviser Ahithophel the Gilonite, from his city of Giloh. So the conspiracy grew strong, and the people supporting Absalom continued to increase.

¹³ Then an informer came to David and reported, "The hearts of the men of Israel are with Absalom."

¹⁴ David said to all the servants with him in Jerusalem, "Get up. We have to flee, or we will not escape from Absalom! Leave quickly, or he will overtake us, heap disaster on us, and strike the city with the edge of the sword."

¹⁵ The king's servants said to him, "Whatever my lord the king decides, we are your servants." ¹⁶ Then the king set out, and his entire household followed him. But he left behind 10 concubines to take care of the palace. ¹⁷ So the king set out, and all the people followed him. They stopped at the last house ¹⁸ while all his servants marched past him. Then all the Cherethites, the Pelethites, and the Gittites—600 men who came with him from Gath—marched past the king.

¹⁹ The king said to Ittai the Gittite, "Why are you also going with us? Go back and stay with the king since you're both a foreigner and an exile from your homeland. ²⁰ Besides, you only arrived yesterday; should I make you wander around with us today while I go wherever I can? Go back and take your brothers with you. May the Lord show you kindness and faithfulness."

²¹ But in response, Ittai vowed to the king, "As surely as the Lord lives and as

my lord the king lives, wherever my lord the king is, whether it means life or death, your servant will be there!"

²² "March on," David replied to Ittai. So Ittai the Gittite marched past with all his men and the children who were with him. ²³ Everyone in the countryside was weeping loudly while all the people were marching past. As the king was crossing the Kidron Valley, all the people were marching past on the road that leads to the desert.

²⁴ Zadok was also there, and all the Levites with him were carrying the ark of the covenant of God. They set the ark of God down, and Abiathar offered sacrifices until the people had finished marching past. ²⁵ Then the king instructed Zadok, "Return the ark of God to the city. If I find favor in the LORD's eyes, He will bring me back and allow me to see both it and its dwelling place. ²⁶ However, if He should say, 'I do not delight in you,' then here I am—He can do with me whatever pleases Him."

²⁷ The king also said to Zadok the priest, "Look, return to the city in peace and your two sons with you: your son Ahimaaz and Abiathar's son Jonathan. ²⁸ Remember, I'll wait at the fords of the wilderness until word comes from you to inform me." ²⁹ So Zadok and Abiathar returned the ark of God to Jerusalem and stayed there.

³⁰ David was climbing the slope of the Mount of Olives, weeping as he ascended. His head was covered, and he was walking barefoot. Each of the people with him covered their heads and went up, weeping as they ascended. ³¹ Then someone reported to David: "Ahithophel is among the conspirators with Absalom."

"LORD," David pleaded, "please turn the counsel of Ahithophel into foolishness!"

³² When David came to the summit where he used to worship God, there to meet him was Hushai the Archite with his robe torn and dust on his head. ³³ David said to him, "If you go away with me, you'll be a burden to me, ³⁴ but if you return to the city and tell Absalom, 'I will be your servant, my king! Previously, I was your father's servant, but now I will be your servant,' then you can counteract Ahithophel's counsel for me. ³⁵ Won't Zadok and Abiathar the priests be there with you? Report everything you hear from the king's palace to Zadok and Abiathar the priests. ³⁶ Take note: their two sons, Zadok's son Ahimaaz and Abiathar's son Jonathan, are there with them. Send me everything you hear through them." ³⁷ So Hushai, David's personal adviser, entered Jerusalem just as Absalom was entering the city.

*P*SALM 69:5-12

⁵ God, You know my foolishness,
  and my guilty acts are not hidden
    from You.
⁶ Do not let those who hope in You
    be disgraced because of me,
  Lord GOD of Hosts;
  do not let those who seek You be
    humiliated because of me,
  God of Israel.
⁷ For I have endured insults
    because of You,
  and shame has covered my face.
⁸ I have become a stranger to my
    brothers
  and a foreigner to my mother's
    sons
⁹ because zeal for Your house has
    consumed me,
  and the insults of those who insult
    You have fallen on me.
¹⁰ I mourned and fasted,
  but it brought me insults.
¹¹ I wore sackcloth as my clothing,
  and I was a joke to them.
¹² Those who sit at the city gate talk
    about me,
  and drunkards make up songs
    about me.

*P*ROVERBS 15:8-9

⁸ The sacrifice of the wicked is
    detestable to the LORD,
  but the prayer of the upright is
    His delight.

⁹ The LORD detests the way of the wicked,
but He loves the one who pursues righteousness.

JOHN 11:7-20

⁷ Then after that, He said to the disciples, "Let's go to Judea again."

⁸ "Rabbi," the disciples told Him, "just now the Jews tried to stone You, and You're going there again?"

⁹ "Aren't there 12 hours in a day?" Jesus answered. "If anyone walks during the day, he doesn't stumble, because he sees the light of this world. ¹⁰ If anyone walks during the night, he does stumble, because the light is not in him." ¹¹ He said this, and then He told them, "Our friend Lazarus has fallen asleep, but I'm on My way to wake him up."

¹² Then the disciples said to Him, "Lord, if he has fallen asleep, he will get well."

¹³ Jesus, however, was speaking about his death, but they thought He was speaking about natural sleep. ¹⁴ So Jesus then told them plainly, "Lazarus has died. ¹⁵ I'm glad for you that I wasn't there so that you may believe. But let's go to him."

¹⁶ Then Thomas (called "Twin") said to his fellow disciples, "Let's go so that we may die with Him."

¹⁷ When Jesus arrived, He found that Lazarus had already been in the tomb four days. ¹⁸ Bethany was near Jerusalem (about two miles away). ¹⁹ Many of the Jews had come to Martha and Mary to comfort them about their brother. ²⁰ As soon as Martha heard that Jesus was coming, she went to meet Him. But Mary remained seated in the house.

Worship—Expected of All

The prayer of the upright is His delight.
—PROVERBS 15:8

When you can stop in the midst of life's most pressing problems and give yourself eagerly to worshiping God, then you are moving along the road to knowing God more intimately. Sometimes when I have had the occasion to talk face to face with people who were going through difficult circumstances, I have asked them: "How does all this affect your ability to worship God?" Most have responded something like this: "I find it very difficult to give my heart in worship as I struggle with these problems." And some have said: "I find it utterly impossible."

Are we justified in refusing to worship God because life has dealt us some hard blows? Those who are at a standstill spiritually might react like this: "Yes, how can God expect me to worship Him when He has allowed these troubles to weigh me down?" Those moving slowly along the road of discipleship might say: "I know I should worship Him, but my preoccupation with my problems makes it almost impossible to do so." The spiritually mature will affirm: "Nothing is more important than the worship of the One who holds my life in His hands. Because He is God then I know that no matter how things might look to the contrary, all will be well. Thus my heart delights to worship Him."

Christian counseling ought to be seen (though in some parts of the church it isn't) as restoring people to worship. This may be hard for some to accept, but it is true nevertheless—nothing that ever happens to us can justify a Christian's refusal to worship God.

Prayer

My Father and my God, may this emphasis on worship remain undiminished as I turn to other things. I see it is so central. Help me not only to remember it but to apply it. In Jesus' name. Amen.

Further Study

1 Co 1:1-17; Ac 3:11-16; 14:11-15
What was a problem in the early church?
How did Peter and John deal with this problem?

JUNE 6

2 SAMUEL 16:1–17:29

16 When David had gone a little beyond the summit, Ziba, Mephibosheth's servant, was right there to meet him. He had a pair of saddled donkeys loaded with 200 loaves of bread, 100 clusters of raisins, 100 bunches of summer fruit, and a skin of wine. ²The king said to Ziba, "Why do you have these?"

Ziba answered, "The donkeys are for the king's household to ride, the bread and summer fruit are for the young men to eat, and the wine is for those who become exhausted to drink in the desert."

³"Where is your master's son?" the king asked.

"Why, he's staying in Jerusalem," Ziba replied to the king, "for he said, 'Today, the house of Israel will restore my father's kingdom to me.'"

⁴The king said to Ziba, "All that belongs to Mephibosheth is now yours!"

"I bow before you," Ziba said. "May you look favorably on me, my lord the king!"

⁵When King David got to Bahurim, a man belonging to the family of the house of Saul was just coming out. His name was Shimei son of Gera, and he was yelling curses as he approached. ⁶He threw stones at David and at all the royal servants, the people and the warriors on David's right and left. ⁷Shimei said as he cursed: "Get out, get out, you worthless murderer! ⁸The LORD has paid you back for all the blood of the house of Saul in whose place you rule, and the LORD has handed the kingdom over to your son Absalom. Look, you are in trouble because you're a murderer!"

⁹Then Abishai son of Zeruiah said to the king, "Why should this dead dog curse my lord the king? Let me go over and cut his head off!"

¹⁰The king replied, "Sons of Zeruiah, do we agree on anything? He curses me this way because the LORD told him, 'Curse David!' Therefore, who can say, 'Why did you do that?' " ¹¹Then David said to Abishai and all his servants, "Look, my own son, my own flesh and blood, intends to take my life—how much more now this Benjaminite! Leave him alone and let him curse me; the LORD has told him to. ¹²Perhaps the LORD will see my affliction and restore

goodness to me instead of Shimei's curses today." [13] So David and his men proceeded along the road as Shimei was going along the ridge of the hill opposite him. As Shimei went, he cursed David, and threw stones and dirt at him. [14] Finally, the king and all the people with him arrived exhausted, so they rested there.

[15] Now Absalom and all the Israelites came to Jerusalem. Ahithophel was also with him. [16] When David's friend Hushai the Archite came to Absalom, Hushai said to Absalom, "Long live the king! Long live the king!"

[17] "Is this your loyalty to your friend?" Absalom asked Hushai. "Why didn't you go with your friend?"

[18] "Not at all," Hushai answered Absalom. "I am on the side of the one that the LORD, the people, and all the men of Israel have chosen. I will stay with him. [19] Furthermore, whom will I serve if not his son? As I served in your father's presence, I will also serve in yours."

[20] Then Absalom said to Ahithophel, "Give me your advice. What should we do?"

[21] Ahithophel replied to Absalom, "Sleep with your father's concubines he left to take care of the palace. When all Israel hears that you have become repulsive to your father, everyone with you will be encouraged." [22] So they pitched a tent for Absalom on the roof, and he slept with his father's concubines in the sight of all Israel.

[23] Now the advice Ahithophel gave in those days was like someone asking about a word from God—such was the regard that both David and Absalom had **17** for Ahithophel's advice. [1] Ahithophel said to Absalom, "Let me choose 12,000 men, and I will set out in pursuit of David tonight. [2] I will attack him while he is weak and weary, throw him into a panic, and all the people with him will scatter. I will strike down only the king [3] and bring all the people back to you. When everyone returns except the man you're seeking, all the people will be at peace." [4] This proposal seemed good to Absalom and all the elders of Israel.

[5] Then Absalom said, "Summon Hushai the Archite also. Let's hear what he has to say as well."

[6] So Hushai came to Absalom, and Absalom told him: "Ahithophel offered this proposal. Should we carry out his proposal? If not, what do you say?"

[7] Hushai replied to Absalom, "The advice Ahithophel has given this time is not good." [8] Hushai continued, "You know your father and his men. They are warriors and are desperate like a wild bear robbed of her cubs. Your father is an experienced soldier who won't spend the night with the people. [9] He's probably already hiding in one of the caves or some other place. If some of our troops fall first, someone is sure to hear and say, 'There's been a slaughter among the people who follow Absalom.' [10] Then, even a brave man with the heart of a lion will melt because all Israel knows that your father and the valiant men with him are warriors. [11] Instead, I advise that all Israel from Dan to Beersheba—as numerous as the sand by the sea—be gathered to you and that you personally go into battle. [12] Then we will attack David wherever we find him, and we will descend on him like dew on the ground. Not even one will be left of all the men with him. [13] If he retreats to some city, all Israel will bring ropes to that city, and we will drag its stones into the valley until not even a pebble can be found there." [14] Since the LORD had decreed that Ahithophel's good advice be undermined in order to bring about Absalom's ruin, Absalom and all the men of Israel said, "The advice of Hushai the Archite is better than Ahithophel's advice."

[15] Hushai then told the priests Zadok and Abiathar, "This is what Ahithophel advised Absalom and the elders of Israel, and this is what I advised. [16] Now send someone quickly and tell David, 'Don't spend the night at the wilderness ford of the Jordan, but be sure to cross over, or the king and all the people with him will be destroyed.' "

[17] Jonathan and Ahimaaz were staying at En-rogel, where a servant girl would come and pass along information to

them. They in turn would go and inform King David, because they dared not be seen entering the city. [18] However, a young man did see them and informed Absalom. So the two left quickly and came to the house of a man in Bahurim. He had a well in his courtyard, and they climbed down into it. [19] Then his wife took the cover, placed it over the mouth of the well, and scattered grain on it so nobody would know anything.

[20] Absalom's servants came to the woman at the house and asked, "Where are Ahimaaz and Jonathan?"

"They passed by toward the water," the woman replied to them. The men searched but did not find them, so they returned to Jerusalem.

[21] After they had gone, Ahimaaz and Jonathan climbed out of the well and went and informed King David. They told him, "Get up and immediately ford the river, for Ahithophel has given this advice against you." [22] So David and all the people with him got up and crossed the Jordan. By daybreak, there was no one who had not crossed the Jordan. [23] When Ahithophel realized that his advice had not been followed, he saddled his donkey and set out for his house in his hometown. He set his affairs in order and hanged himself. So he died and was buried in his father's tomb.

[24] David had arrived at Mahanaim by the time Absalom crossed the Jordan with all the men of Israel. [25] Now Absalom had appointed Amasa over the army in Joab's place. Amasa was the son of a man named Ithra the Israelite; Ithra had married Abigail daughter of Nahash. Abigail was a sister to Zeruiah, Joab's mother. [26] And Israel and Absalom camped in the land of Gilead. [27] When David came to Mahanaim, Shobi son of Nahash from Rabbah of the Ammonites, Machir son of Ammiel from Lo-debar, and Barzillai the Gileadite from Rogelim [28] brought beds, basins, and pottery items. They also brought wheat, barley, flour, roasted grain, beans, lentils, [29] honey, curds, sheep, and cheese from the herd for David and the people with him to eat. They had reasoned, "The people must be hungry, exhausted, and thirsty in the desert."

PSALM 69:13-18

[13] But as for me, Lord, my prayer to
You is for a time of favor.
In Your abundant, faithful love,
God,
answer me with Your sure
salvation.
[14] Rescue me from the miry mud;
don't let me sink.
Let me be rescued from those
who hate me,
and from the deep waters.
[15] Don't let the floodwaters sweep
over me
or the deep swallow me up;
don't let the Pit close its mouth
over me.
[16] Answer me, Lord, for Your faithful
love is good;
in keeping with Your great
compassion, turn to me.
[17] Don't hide Your face from Your
servant,
for I am in distress.
Answer me quickly!
[18] Draw near to me and redeem me;
ransom me because of my
enemies.

PROVERBS 15:10-11

[10] Discipline is harsh for the one
who leaves the path;
the one who hates correction will
die.

[11] Sheol and Abaddon lie open
before the Lord—
how much more, human hearts.

JOHN 11:21-44

[21] Then Martha said to Jesus, "Lord, if You had been here, my brother wouldn't have died. [22] Yet even now I know that whatever You ask from God, God will give You."

[23] "Your brother will rise again," Jesus told her.

²⁴ Martha said, "I know that he will rise again in the resurrection at the last day."

²⁵ Jesus said to her, "I am the resurrection and the life. The one who believes in Me, even if he dies, will live. ²⁶ Everyone who lives and believes in Me will never die—ever. Do you believe this?"

²⁷ "Yes, Lord," she told Him, "I believe You are the Messiah, the Son of God, who was to come into the world."

²⁸ Having said this, she went back and called her sister Mary, saying in private, "The Teacher is here and is calling for you."

²⁹ As soon as she heard this, she got up quickly and went to Him. ³⁰ Jesus had not yet come into the village but was still in the place where Martha had met Him. ³¹ The Jews who were with her in the house consoling her saw that Mary got up quickly and went out. So they followed her, supposing that she was going to the tomb to cry there.

³² When Mary came to where Jesus was and saw Him, she fell at His feet and told Him, "Lord, if You had been here, my brother would not have died!"

³³ When Jesus saw her crying, and the Jews who had come with her crying, He was angry in His spirit and deeply moved. ³⁴ "Where have you put him?" He asked.

"Lord," they told Him, "come and see."

³⁵ Jesus wept.

³⁶ So the Jews said, "See how He loved him!" ³⁷ But some of them said, "Couldn't He who opened the blind man's eyes also have kept this man from dying?"

³⁸ Then Jesus, angry in Himself again, came to the tomb. It was a cave, and a stone was lying against it. ³⁹ "Remove the stone," Jesus said.

Martha, the dead man's sister, told Him, "Lord, he already stinks. It's been four days."

⁴⁰ Jesus said to her, "Didn't I tell you that if you believed you would see the glory of God?"

⁴¹ So they removed the stone. Then Jesus raised His eyes and said, "Father, I thank You that You heard Me. ⁴² I know that You always hear Me, but because of the crowd standing here I said this, so they may believe You sent Me." ⁴³ After He said this, He shouted with a loud voice, "Lazarus, come out!" ⁴⁴ The dead man came out bound hand and foot with linen strips and with his face wrapped in a cloth. Jesus said to them, "Loose him and let him go."

Blessings—Not Just for Now

They also brought wheat, barley, flour, roasted grain, beans, lentils, honey, curds, sheep, and cheese from the herd for David and the people with him to eat.—2 SAMUEL 17:28-29

Some commentators believe that when David wrote the words, "You prepare a table before me in the presence of my enemies" (Ps 23:5), he had in mind the events about which we read in today's passage. Driven into the wilderness by his son Absalom's rebellion, David and his followers became desperately hungry, thirsty, and weary. God came to his aid, however, and directed to him three men who "brought beds [and] basins" (so that David could wash and refresh himself) as well as "pottery items . . . wheat, barley, flour, roasted grain, beans, lentils, honey, curds, sheep, and cheese."

How David must have rubbed his eyes in astonishment as he saw God provide for him a table "in the presence of [his] enemies." Can you cast your mind back at this moment to something "special" that God did for you to demonstrate His tender love and care? I can. Every Christian has these times—how sad that we forget them so soon.

God never does anything "special" in our lives just for the sake of the passing hour—it is done also as a pledge for the future. It is as though God is saying: "I'll do this for you now, not only to meet your need, but also that you might *always* know you are the object of My love."

If new dangers startle us with fear, we have forgotten the past mercies. I believe that David's confidence in God was due to the fact that whenever he faced a new problem, he remembered vividly the past hour of deliverance.

Prayer

O Father, forgive me for taking so much for granted—rather than taking it with gratitude. I recall the words of Your servant John Newton and make them my own this day: "His love in time past forbids me to think, He'll leave me at last in trouble to sink." Thank You, Father—thank You. Amen.

Further Study

1 Kg 17; Ezk 34:14; Is 25:6; Jn 6:51
How did Elijah experience God's provision?
What are we to feed on?

JUNE 7

2 SAMUEL 18:1–19:23

18 David reviewed his troops and appointed commanders of hundreds and of thousands over them. ² He then sent out the troops, one third under Joab, one third under Joab's brother Abishai son of Zeruiah, and one third under Ittai the Gittite. The king said to the troops, "I will also march out with you."

³ "You must not go!" the people pleaded. "If we have to flee, they will not pay any attention to us. Even if half of us die, they will not pay any attention to us because you are worth 10,000 of us. Therefore, it is better if you support us from the city."

⁴ "I will do whatever you think is best," the king replied to them. So he stood beside the gate while all the troops marched out by hundreds and thousands. ⁵ The king commanded Joab, Abishai, and Ittai, "Treat the young man Absalom gently for my sake." All the people heard the king's orders to all the commanders about Absalom.

⁶ Then David's forces marched into the field to engage Israel in battle, which took place in the forest of Ephraim. ⁷ The people of Israel were defeated by David's soldiers, and the slaughter there was vast that day—20,000 casualties. ⁸ The battle spread over the entire region, and that day the forest claimed more people than the sword.

⁹ Absalom was riding on his mule

when he happened to meet David's soldiers. When the mule went under the tangled branches of a large oak tree, Absalom's head was caught fast in the tree. The mule under him kept going, so he was suspended in midair. ¹⁰ One of the men saw him and informed Joab. He said, "I just saw Absalom hanging in an oak tree!"

¹¹ "You just saw him!" Joab exclaimed. "Why didn't you strike him to the ground right there? I would have given you 10 silver pieces and a belt!"

¹² The man replied to Joab, "Even if I had the weight of 1,000 pieces of silver in my hand, I would not raise my hand against the king's son. For we heard the king command you, Abishai, and Ittai, 'Protect the young man Absalom for me.' ¹³ If I had jeopardized my own life—and nothing is hidden from the king—you would have abandoned me."

¹⁴ Joab said, "I'm not going to waste time with you!" He then took three spears in his hand and thrust them into Absalom's heart while he was still alive in the oak tree, ¹⁵ and 10 young men who were Joab's armor-bearers surrounded Absalom, struck him, and killed him.

¹⁶ Afterwards, Joab blew the ram's horn, and the troops broke off their pursuit of Israel because Joab restrained them. ¹⁷ They took Absalom, threw him into a large pit in the forest, and piled a huge mound of stones over him. And all Israel fled, each to his tent.

¹⁸ When he was alive, Absalom had erected for himself a pillar in the King's Valley, for he had said, "I have no son to preserve the memory of my name." So he gave the pillar his name. It is still called Absalom's Monument today.

¹⁹ Ahimaaz son of Zadok said, "Please let me run and tell the king the good news that the LORD has delivered him from his enemies."

²⁰ Joab replied to him, "You are not the man to take good news today. You may do it another day, but today you aren't taking good news, because the king's son is dead." ²¹ Joab then said to the Cushite, "Go tell the king what you have seen." The Cushite bowed to Joab and took off running.

²² However, Ahimaaz son of Zadok persisted and said to Joab, "No matter what, please let me run too behind the Cushite!"

Joab replied, "My son, why do you want to run since you won't get a reward?"

²³ "No matter what I want to run!"

"Then run!" Joab said to him. So Ahimaaz ran by way of the plain and outran the Cushite.

²⁴ David was sitting between the two gates when the watchman went up to the roof of the gate and over to the wall. The watchman looked out and saw a man running alone. ²⁵ He called out and told the king.

The king said, "If he's alone, he bears good news."

As the first runner came closer, ²⁶ the watchman saw another man running. He called out to the gatekeeper, "Look! Another man is running alone!"

"This one is also bringing good news," said the king.

²⁷ The watchman said, "The way the first man runs looks to me like the way Ahimaaz son of Zadok runs."

"This is a good man; he comes with good news," the king commented.

²⁸ Ahimaaz called out to the king, "All is well," and then bowed down to the king with his face to the ground. He continued, "May the LORD your God be praised! He delivered up the men who rebelled against my lord the king."

²⁹ The king asked, "Is the young man Absalom all right?"

Ahimaaz replied, "When Joab sent the king's servant and your servant, I saw a big disturbance, but I don't know what it was."

³⁰ The king said, "Move aside and stand here." So he stood to one side.

³¹ Just then the Cushite came and said, "May my lord the king hear the good news: today the LORD has delivered you from all those rising up against you!"

³² The king asked the Cushite, "Is the young man Absalom all right?"

The Cushite replied, "May what has become of the young man happen to the enemies of my lord the king and to all who rise up against you with evil intent."

³³ The king was deeply moved and went up to the gate chamber and wept. As he walked, he cried, "My son Absalom! My son, my son Absalom! If only I had died instead of you, Absalom, my son, my son!"

19 It was reported to Joab, "The king is weeping. He's mourning over Absalom." ² That day's victory was turned into mourning for all the troops because on that day the troops heard, "The king is grieving over his son." ³ So they returned to the city quietly that day like people come in when they are humiliated after fleeing in battle. ⁴ But the king hid his face and cried out at the top of his voice, "My son Absalom! Absalom, my son, my son!"

⁵ Then Joab went into the house to the king and said, "Today you have shamed all your soldiers—those who rescued your life and the lives of your sons and daughters, your wives, and your concubines. ⁶ You love your enemies and hate those who love you! Today you have made it clear that the commanders and soldiers mean nothing to you. In fact, today I know that if Absalom were alive and all of us were dead, it would be fine with you!

⁷ "Now get up! Go out and encourage your soldiers, for I swear by the LORD that if you don't go out, not a man will remain with you tonight. This will be worse for you than all the trouble that has come to you from your youth until now!"

⁸ So the king got up and sat in the gate, and all the people were told: "Look, the king is sitting in the gate." Then they all came into the king's presence.

Meanwhile, each Israelite had fled to his tent. ⁹ All the people among all the tribes of Israel were arguing: "The king delivered us from the grasp of our enemies, and he rescued us from the grasp of the Philistines, but now he has fled from the land because of Absalom. ¹⁰ But Absalom, the man we anointed over us, has died in battle. So why do you say nothing about restoring the king?"

¹¹ King David sent word to the priests, Zadok and Abiathar: "Say to the elders of Judah, 'Why should you be the last to restore the king to his palace? The talk of all Israel has reached the king at his house. ¹² You are my brothers, my flesh and blood. So why should you be the last to restore the king?' ¹³ And tell Amasa, 'Aren't you my flesh and blood? May God punish me and do so severely if you don't become commander of the army from now on instead of Joab!' "

¹⁴ So he won over all the men of Judah, and they sent word to the king: "Come back, you and all your servants." ¹⁵ Then the king returned. When he arrived at the Jordan, Judah came to Gilgal to meet the king and escort him across the Jordan.

¹⁶ Shimei son of Gera, a Benjaminite from Bahurim, hurried down with the men of Judah to meet King David. ¹⁷ There were 1,000 men from Benjamin with him. Ziba, an attendant from the house of Saul, with his 15 sons and 20 servants also rushed down to the Jordan ahead of the king. ¹⁸ They forded the Jordan to bring the king's household across and do whatever the king desired.

When Shimei son of Gera crossed the Jordan, he fell down before the king ¹⁹ and said to him, "My lord, don't hold me guilty, and don't remember your servant's wrongdoing on the day my lord the king left Jerusalem. May the king not take it to heart. ²⁰ For your servant knows that I have sinned. But look! Today I am the first one of the entire house of Joseph to come down to meet my lord the king."

²¹ Abishai son of Zeruiah asked, "Shouldn't Shimei be put to death for this, because he ridiculed the LORD's anointed?"

²² David answered, "Sons of Zeruiah, do we agree on anything? Have you become my adversary today? Should any man be killed in Israel today? Am I not aware that today I'm king over Israel?" ²³ So the king said to Shimei, "You will not die." Then the king gave him his oath.

PSALM 69:19-28

19 You know the insults I endure—
   my shame and disgrace.
   You are aware of all my
   adversaries.
20 Insults have broken my heart, and
   I am in despair.
   I waited for sympathy, but there
   was none;
   for comforters, but found no one.
21 Instead, they gave me gall for my
   food,
   and for my thirst they gave me
   vinegar to drink.

22 Let their table set before them be
   a snare,
   and let it be a trap for their allies.
23 Let their eyes grow too dim to
   see,
   and let their loins continually
   shake.
24 Pour out Your rage on them,
   and let Your burning anger
   overtake them.
25 Make their fortification
   desolate;
   may no one live in their tents.
26 For they persecute the one You
   struck
   and talk about the pain of those
   You wounded.
27 Add guilt to their guilt;
   do not let them share in Your
   righteousness.
28 Let them be erased from the book
   of life
   and not be recorded with the
   righteous.

PROVERBS 15:12-13

12 A mocker doesn't love one who
   corrects him;
   he will not consult the wise.

13 A joyful heart makes a face
   cheerful,
   but a sad heart produces a broken
   spirit.

JOHN 11:45–12:11

45 Therefore many of the Jews who came to Mary and saw what He did believed in Him. 46 But some of them went to the Pharisees and told them what Jesus had done.

47 So the chief priests and the Pharisees convened the Sanhedrin and said, "What are we going to do since this man does many signs? 48 If we let Him continue in this way, everybody will believe in Him! Then the Romans will come and remove both our place and our nation."

49 One of them, Caiaphas, who was high priest that year, said to them, "You know nothing at all! 50 You're not considering that it is to your advantage that one man should die for the people rather than the whole nation perish." 51 He did not say this on his own, but being high priest that year he prophesied that Jesus was going to die for the nation, 52 and not for the nation only, but also to unite the scattered children of God. 53 So from that day on they plotted to kill Him. 54 Therefore Jesus no longer walked openly among the Jews but departed from there to the countryside near the wilderness, to a town called Ephraim. And He stayed there with the disciples.

55 The Jewish Passover was near, and many went up to Jerusalem from the country to purify themselves before the Passover. 56 They were looking for Jesus and asking one another as they stood in the temple complex: "What do you think? He won't come to the festival, will He?" 57 The chief priests and the Pharisees had given orders that if anyone knew where He was, he should report it so they could arrest Him.

12 Six days before the Passover, Jesus came to Bethany where Lazarus was, the one Jesus had raised from the dead. 2 So they gave a dinner for Him there; Martha was serving them, and Lazarus was one of those reclining at the table with Him. 3 Then Mary took a pound of fragrant oil—pure and expensive nard—anointed

Jesus' feet, and wiped His feet with her hair. So the house was filled with the fragrance of the oil.

⁴Then one of His disciples, Judas Iscariot (who was about to betray Him), said, ⁵ "Why wasn't this fragrant oil sold for 300 denarii and given to the poor?" ⁶He didn't say this because he cared about the poor but because he was a thief. He was in charge of the money-bag and would steal part of what was put in it.

⁷Jesus answered, "Leave her alone; she has kept it for the day of My burial. ⁸For you always have the poor with you, but you do not always have Me."

⁹Then a large crowd of the Jews learned He was there. They came not only because of Jesus, but also to see Lazarus the one He had raised from the dead. ¹⁰Therefore the chief priests decided to also kill Lazarus, ¹¹because he was the reason many of the Jews were deserting them and believing in Jesus.

Joy—Always There

*A joyful heart makes a face cheerful,
but a sad heart produces a broken spirit.*
—Proverbs 15:13

Joy is a central characteristic of the Christian—and yet so many know nothing of it. They are under the lash of duty and not unabashed delight. They are artificial, not artesian. Someone once described such Christians as "creaking in body and soul as they limp along the highway toward glory." They walk the road to glory, but they are certainly not walking the glory road.

The word "joy" (Greek: *chara*) is a strong and robust word. It is not resignation wearing a wan smile. It means a joy that is exuberant and overflowing. The summons to rejoice is sounded no less than seventy times in the New Testament, and the word *chara* occurs close to sixty times. The New Testament is a book of joy. Dr. William Barclay says that joy is the distinguishing atmosphere of the Christian life. He wrote: "We may put it this way—whatever the ingredients of Christian experience and in whatever proportions they are mixed together, joy is one of them."

Even in the first year after the death of my wife, I was wonderfully conscious of Christ's joy quietly breaking through the layers of my sadness and grief. Joy is always present in the heart of a Christian. It may not always be felt or recognized—but it is always there. And eventually it will break the surface, no matter what our situation or our circumstances. I have always maintained that joy is an inevitable part of the Christian life. Now I am sure. Oh, so very sure.

Prayer

Father, thank You for reminding me that when joy has its roots in You, then its fruits will eventually appear—no matter what happens. Eternal honor and praise be to Your wonderful name. Amen.

Further Study

Pss 16:11; 30:1-12; 126:1-6; Neh 8:10
What does joy bring to our beings?
How are tears linked with joy?

JUNE 8

2 SAMUEL 19:24–21:22

²⁴ Mephibosheth, Saul's grandson, also went down to meet the king. He had not taken care of his feet, trimmed his moustache, or washed his clothes from the day the king left until the day he returned safely. ²⁵ When he came from Jerusalem to meet the king, the king asked him, "Mephibosheth, why didn't you come with me?"

²⁶ "My lord the king," he replied, "my servant Ziba betrayed me. Actually your servant said: 'I'll saddle the donkey for myself so that I may ride it and go with the king'—for your servant is lame. ²⁷ Ziba slandered your servant to my lord the king. But my lord the king is like the Angel of God, so do whatever you think best. ²⁸ For my grandfather's entire family deserves death from my lord the king, but you set your servant among those who eat at your table. So what further right do I have to keep on making appeals to the king?"

²⁹ The king said to him, "Why keep on speaking about these matters of yours? I hereby declare: you and Ziba are to divide the land."

³⁰ Mephibosheth said to the king, "Instead, since my lord the king has come to his palace safely, let Ziba take it all!"

³¹ Barzillai the Gileadite had come down from Rogelim and accompanied the king to the Jordan River to see him off at the Jordan. ³² Barzillai was a very old man—80 years old—and since he was a very wealthy man, he had provided for the needs of the king while he stayed in Mahanaim.

³³ The king said to Barzillai, "Cross over with me, and I'll provide for you at my side in Jerusalem."

³⁴ Barzillai replied to the king, "How many years of my life are left that I should go up to Jerusalem with the king? ³⁵ I'm now 80 years old. Can I discern what is pleasant and what is not? Can your servant taste what he eats or drinks? Can I still hear the voice of male and female singers? Why should your servant be an added burden to my lord the king? ³⁶ Since your servant is only going with the king a little way across the Jordan, why should the king repay me with such a reward? ³⁷ Please let your servant return so that I may die in my own city near the tomb of my father and mother. But here is your servant Chimham: let him cross over with my lord the king. Do for him what seems good to you."

³⁸ The king replied, "Chimham will cross over with me, and I will do for him what seems good to you, and whatever you desire from me I will do for you." ³⁹ So all the people crossed the Jordan, and then the king crossed. The king kissed Barzillai and blessed him, and Barzillai returned to his home.

⁴⁰ The king went on to Gilgal, and Chimham went with him. All the troops

of Judah and half of Israel's escorted the king. ⁴¹ Suddenly, all the men of Israel came to the king. They asked him, "Why did our brothers, the men of Judah, take you away secretly and transport the king and his household across the Jordan, along with all of David's men?"

⁴² All the men of Judah responded to the men of Israel, "Because the king is our relative. Why does this make you angry? Have we ever eaten anything of the king's or been honored at all?"

⁴³ The men of Israel answered the men of Judah: "We have 10 shares in the king, so we have a greater claim to David than you. Why then do you despise us? Weren't we the first to speak of restoring our king?" But the words of the men of Judah were harsher than those of the men of Israel.

20 Now a wicked man, a Benjaminite named Sheba son of Bichri, happened to be there. He blew the ram's horn and shouted:

We have no portion in David,
no inheritance in Jesse's son.
Each man to his tent, Israel!

² So all the men of Israel deserted David and followed Sheba son of Bichri, but the men of Judah from the Jordan all the way to Jerusalem remained loyal to their king.

³ When David came to his palace in Jerusalem, he took the 10 concubines he had left to take care of the palace and placed them under guard. He provided for them, but he was not intimate with them. They were confined until the day of their death, living as widows.

⁴ The king said to Amasa, "Summon the men of Judah to me within three days and be here yourself." ⁵ Amasa went to summon Judah, but he took longer than the time allotted him. ⁶ So David said to Abishai, "Sheba son of Bichri will do more harm to us than Absalom. Take your lord's soldiers and pursue him, or he will find fortified cities and elude us."

⁷ So Joab's men, the Cherethites, the Pelethites, and all the warriors marched out under Abishai's command; they left Jerusalem to pursue Sheba son of Bichri. ⁸ They were at the great stone in Gibeon when Amasa joined them. Joab was wearing his uniform and over it was a belt around his waist with a sword in its sheath. As he approached, the sword fell out. ⁹ Joab asked Amasa, "Are you well, my brother?" Then with his right hand Joab grabbed Amasa by the beard to kiss him. ¹⁰ Amasa was not on guard against the sword in Joab's hand, and Joab stabbed him in the stomach with it and spilled his intestines out on the ground. Joab did not stab him again for Amasa was dead. Joab and his brother Abishai pursued Sheba son of Bichri.

¹¹ One of Joab's young men had stood over Amasa saying, "Whoever favors Joab and whoever is for David, follow Joab!" ¹² Now Amasa was writhing in his blood in the middle of the highway, and the man had seen that all the people stopped. So he moved Amasa from the highway to the field and threw a garment over him because he realized that all those who encountered Amasa were stopping. ¹³ When he was removed from the highway, all the men passed by and followed Joab to pursue Sheba son of Bichri.

¹⁴ Sheba passed through all the tribes of Israel to Abel of Beth-maacah. All the Berites came together and followed him. ¹⁵ Joab's troops came and besieged Sheba in Abel of Beth-maacah. They built an assault ramp against the outer wall of the city. While all the troops with Joab were battering the wall to make it collapse, ¹⁶ a wise woman called out from the city, "Listen! Listen! Please tell Joab to come here and let me speak with him."

¹⁷ When he had come near her, the woman asked, "Are you Joab?"

"I am," he replied.

"Listen to the words of your servant," she said to him.

He answered, "I'm listening."

¹⁸ She said, "In the past they used to say, 'Seek counsel in Abel,' and that's how they settled disputes. ¹⁹ I am a peaceful person, one of the faithful in

Israel, but you're trying to destroy a city that is like a mother in Israel. Why would you devour the LORD's inheritance?"

²⁰ Joab protested: "Never! I do not want to destroy! ²¹ That is not my intention. There is a man named Sheba son of Bichri, from the hill country of Ephraim, who has rebelled against King David. Deliver this one man, and I will withdraw from the city."

The woman replied to Joab, "All right. His head will be thrown over the wall to you." ²² The woman went to all the people with her wise counsel, and they cut off the head of Sheba son of Bichri and threw it to Joab. So he blew the ram's horn, and they dispersed from the city, each to his own tent. Joab returned to the king in Jerusalem.

²³ Joab commanded the whole army of Israel; Benaiah son of Jehoiada was over the Cherethites and Pelethites; ²⁴ Adoram was in charge of forced labor; Jehoshaphat son of Ahilud was court historian; ²⁵ Sheva was court secretary; Zadok and Abiathar were priests; ²⁶ and in addition, Ira the Jairite was David's priest.

21 During David's reign there was a famine for three successive years, so David inquired of the LORD. The LORD answered, "It is because of the blood shed by Saul and his family when he killed the Gibeonites."

² The Gibeonites were not Israelites but rather a remnant of the Amorites. The Israelites had taken an oath concerning them, but Saul had tried to kill them in his zeal for the Israelites and Judah. So David summoned the Gibeonites and spoke to them. ³ He asked the Gibeonites, "What should I do for you? How can I wipe out this guilt so that you will bring a blessing on the LORD's inheritance?"

⁴ The Gibeonites said to him, "We are not asking for money from Saul or his family, and we cannot put anyone to death in Israel."

"Whatever you say, I will do for you," he said.

⁵ They replied to the king, "As for the man who annihilated us and plotted to exterminate us so we would not exist within the whole territory of Israel, ⁶ let seven of his male descendants be handed over to us so we may hang them in the presence of the LORD at Gibeah of Saul, the LORD's chosen."

The king answered, "I will hand them over."

⁷ David spared Mephibosheth, the son of Saul's son Jonathan, because of the oath of the LORD that was between David and Jonathan, Saul's son. ⁸ But the king took Armoni and Mephibosheth, who were the two sons whom Rizpah daughter of Aiah had borne to Saul, and the five sons whom Merab daughter of Saul had borne to Adriel son of Barzillai the Meholathite ⁹ and handed them over to the Gibeonites. They hanged them on the hill in the presence of the LORD; the seven of them died together. They were executed in the first days of the harvest at the beginning of the barley harvest.

¹⁰ Rizpah, Aiah's daughter, took sackcloth and spread it out for herself on the rock from the beginning of the harvest until the rain poured down from heaven on the bodies. She kept the birds of the sky from them by day and the wild animals by night.

¹¹ When it was reported to David what Saul's concubine Rizpah, daughter of Aiah, had done, ¹² he went and got the bones of Saul and his son Jonathan from the leaders of Jabesh-gilead. They had stolen them from the public square of Beth-shan where the Philistines had hung them the day the Philistines killed Saul at Gilboa. ¹³ David had the bones brought from there. They also gathered up the bones of Saul's family who had been hung. ¹⁴ They also buried the bones of Saul and his son Jonathan at Zela in the land of Benjamin in the tomb of Saul's father Kish. They did everything the king commanded. After this, God answered prayer for the land.

¹⁵ The Philistines again waged war against Israel. David went down with his soldiers, and they fought the Philistines, but David became exhausted. ¹⁶ Then Ishbi-benob, one of the descendants of

the giant, whose bronze spear weighed about eight pounds and who wore new armor, intended to kill David. [17] But Abishai son of Zeruiah came to his aid, struck the Philistine, and killed him. Then David's men swore to him: "You must never again go out with us to battle. You must not extinguish the lamp of Israel."

[18] After this, there was another battle with the Philistines at Gob. At that time Sibbecai the Hushathite killed Saph, who was one of the descendants of the giant.

[19] Once again there was a battle with the Philistines at Gob, and Elhanan son of Jaare-oregim the Bethlehemite killed Goliath the Gittite. The shaft of his spear was like a weaver's beam.

[20] At Gath there was still another battle. A huge man was there with six fingers on each hand and six toes on each foot—24 in all. He, too, was descended from the giant. [21] When he taunted Israel, Jonathan, son of David's brother Shimei, killed him.

[22] These four were descended from the giant in Gath and were killed by David and his soldiers.

PSALM 69:29-36

[29] But as for me—poor and in pain—
let Your salvation protect me, God.
[30] I will praise God's name with song
and exalt Him with thanksgiving.
[31] That will please the LORD more
than an ox,
more than a bull with horns and hooves.
[32] The humble will see it and rejoice.
You who seek God, take heart!
[33] For the LORD listens to the needy
and does not despise His own who are prisoners.
[34] Let heaven and earth praise Him,
the seas and everything that moves in them,
[35] for God will save Zion
and build up the cities of Judah.
They will live there and possess it.
[36] The descendants of His servants will inherit it,
and those who love His name will live in it.

PROVERBS 15:14-15

[14] A discerning mind seeks knowledge,
but the mouth of fools feeds on foolishness.

[15] All the days of the oppressed are miserable,
but a cheerful heart has a continual feast.

JOHN 12:12-33

[12] The next day, when the large crowd that had come to the festival heard that Jesus was coming to Jerusalem, [13] they took palm branches and went out to meet Him. They kept shouting:
"*Hosanna!* Blessed is He who comes in the name of the Lord—the King of Israel!"

[14] Jesus found a young donkey and sat on it, just as it is written: [15] Fear no more, Daughter Zion; look! your King is coming, sitting on a donkey's colt.

[16] His disciples did not understand these things at first. However, when Jesus was glorified, then they remembered that these things had been written about Him and that they had done these things to Him. [17] Meanwhile the crowd, which had been with Him when He called Lazarus out of the tomb and raised him from the dead, continued to testify. [18] This is also why the crowd met Him, because they heard He had done this sign.

[19] Then the Pharisees said to one another, "You see? You've accomplished nothing. Look—the world has gone after Him!"

[20] Now some Greeks were among those who went up to worship at the festival. [21] So they came to Philip, who was from Bethsaida in Galilee, and requested of him, "Sir, we want to see Jesus."

22 Philip went and told Andrew; then Andrew and Philip went and told Jesus. 23 Jesus replied to them, "The hour has come for the Son of Man to be glorified. 24 "I assure you: Unless a grain of wheat falls into the ground and dies, it remains by itself. But if it dies, it produces a large crop. 25 The one who loves his life will lose it, and the one who hates his life in this world will keep it for eternal life. 26 If anyone serves Me, he must follow Me. Where I am, there My servant also will be. If anyone serves Me, the Father will honor him. 27 "Now My soul is troubled. What should I say—Father, save Me from this hour? But that is why I came to this hour. 28 Father, glorify Your name!"

Then a voice came from heaven: "I have glorified it, and I will glorify it again!" 29 The crowd standing there heard it and said it was thunder. Others said, "An angel has spoken to Him!" 30 Jesus responded, "This voice came, not for Me, but for you. 31 Now is the judgment of this world. Now the ruler of this world will be cast out. 32 As for Me, if I am lifted up from the earth I will draw people to Myself." 33 He said this to signify what kind of death He was about to die.

The Cross's Magnetism

As for Me, if I am lifted up from the earth I will draw people to Myself.

—John 12:32

The love for God that burns in our hearts must never be seen as the fruit of our labor, as if it is something we manufacture. Seeing the love of God for us, our own hearts respond with love. We give love for love. We cannot help it. Let's be done with the idea that love for God is something we work at. It issues forth in good works, of course, but it begins in contemplation of how much we are loved.

I often tell my students that they cannot love until they have been loved. By this I mean that love is a response. Our souls must receive love before we can give out love. Those who did not receive much love from their parents complain at this stage: "I can't love God because my soul was never properly prepared to love; my parents didn't love me."

This is a problem, I agree, but it must never be seen as an insoluble problem. No one who stands at Calvary and sees God dying for them on that tree can ever argue that because they were not loved by their parents, they cannot now receive God's love. If they really believe that, then they are saying that God's love is balked by the adverse influence of human conditioning.

God's love will only flow into us if we let it and if we really want it. To desire it is like the touch of the hand on a spring blind: the blind is released and the sunlight flows in. Just to want His love is enough; He will do the rest.

Prayer

O God, forgive me if I have used excuses to barricade my heart against Your love. I gaze once more on Calvary and open my heart to allow its mighty magnetism to draw my soul toward You in a way it has never been drawn before. Amen.

Further Study

2 Th 3:1-5; Jd 21; Eph 3:17-19
What was Paul's desire for the Thessalonians?
What was Paul's prayer for the Ephesians?

JUNE 9

2 SAMUEL 22:1–23:7

22 David spoke the words of this song to the LORD on the day the LORD rescued him from the hand of all his enemies and from the hand of Saul. ² He said:

The LORD is my rock, my fortress,
and my deliverer,
³ my God, my mountain where
I seek refuge.
My shield, the horn
of my salvation,
my stronghold, my refuge,
and my Savior, You save me
from violence.
⁴ I called to the LORD,
who is worthy of praise,
and I was saved from my enemies.
⁵ For the waves of death
engulfed me;
the torrents of destruction
terrified me.
⁶ The ropes of Sheol entangled me;
the snares of death
confronted me.

⁷ I called to the LORD in my distress;
I called to my God.
From His temple He heard
my voice,
and my cry for help reached
His ears.
⁸ Then the earth shook and quaked;
the foundations of the heavens
trembled;

they shook because He burned
with anger.
⁹ Smoke rose from His nostrils,
and consuming fire came
from His mouth;
coals were set ablaze by it.
¹⁰ He parted the heavens
and came down,
a dark cloud beneath His feet.
¹¹ He rode on a cherub and flew,
soaring on the wings of the wind.
¹² He made darkness a canopy
around Him,
a gathering of water
and thick clouds.
¹³ From the radiance
of His presence,
flaming coals were ignited.
¹⁴ The LORD thundered from
heaven;
the Most High projected
His voice.
¹⁵ He shot arrows
and scattered them;
He hurled lightning bolts
and routed them.
¹⁶ The depths of the sea
became visible,
the foundations of the world
were exposed
at the rebuke of the LORD,
at the blast of the breath
of His nostrils.

¹⁷ He reached down from on high
and took hold of me;
He pulled me out of deep waters.

18 He rescued me
    from my powerful enemy
and from those who hated me,
    for they were too strong for me.
19 They confronted me in the day
    of my distress,
but the LORD was my support.
20 He brought me out
    to a wide-open place;
He rescued me because
    He delighted in me.

21 The LORD rewarded me
    according to my righteousness;
He repaid me
    according to the cleanness
    of my hands.
22 For I have kept the ways
    of the LORD
and have not turned from my God
    to wickedness.
23 Indeed, I have kept
    all His ordinances in mind
and have not disregarded
    His statutes.
24 I was blameless before Him
    and kept myself from sinning.
25 So the LORD repaid me
    according to my righteousness,
according to my cleanness
    in His sight.

26 With the faithful
    You prove Yourself faithful;
with the blameless man
    You prove Yourself blameless;
27 with the pure
    You prove Yourself pure,
but with the crooked
    You prove Yourself shrewd.
28 You rescue an afflicted people,
    but Your eyes are set
      against the proud—
You humble them.
29 LORD, You are my lamp;
    the LORD illuminates my darkness.
30 With You I can attack a barrier,
    and with my God I can leap
      over a wall.
31 God—His way is perfect;
    the word of the LORD is pure.
He is a shield to all
    who take refuge in Him.

32 For who is God besides the LORD?
    And who is a rock? Only our God.
33 God is my strong refuge;
    He makes my way perfect.
34 He makes my feet like the feet of
    a deer
and sets me securely on the
    heights.
35 He trains my hands for war;
    my arms can bend a bow
    of bronze.
36 You have given me the shield
    of Your salvation;
Your help exalts me.
37 You widen a place beneath me
    for my steps,
and my ankles do not give way.
38 I pursue my enemies
    and destroy them;
I do not turn back until they are
    wiped out.
39 I wipe them out and crush them,
    and they do not rise;
they fall beneath my feet.
40 You have clothed me with strength
    for battle;
You subdue my adversaries
    beneath me.
41 You have made my enemies
    retreat before me;
I annihilate those who hated me.
42 They look, but there is no one
    to save them—
they look to the LORD,
    but He does not answer them.
43 I pulverize them like dust
    of the earth;
I crush them and trample them
    like mud in the streets.

44 You have freed me from the feuds
    among my people;
You have appointed me the head
    of nations;
a people I had not known
    serve me.
45 Foreigners submit to me
    grudgingly;
as soon as they hear,
    they obey me.
46 Foreigners lose heart
    and come trembling
    from their fortifications.

47 The LORD lives—may my rock
be praised!
God, the rock of my salvation,
is exalted.
48 God—He gives me vengeance
and casts down peoples under me.
49 He frees me from my enemies.
You exalt me
above my adversaries;
You rescue me from violent men.

50 Therefore I will praise You, LORD,
among the nations;
I will sing about Your name.
51 He is a tower of salvation for
His king;
He shows loyalty to His anointed,
to David and his descendants
forever.

23 These are the last words of
David:

The proclamation of David
son of Jesse,
the proclamation of the man
raised on high,
the one anointed by the God
of Jacob,
the favorite singer of Israel:
2 The Spirit of the LORD spoke
through me,
His word was on my tongue.
3 The God of Israel spoke;
the Rock of Israel said to me,
"The one who rules the people
with justice,
who rules in the fear of God,
4 is like the morning light
when the sun rises
on a cloudless morning,
the glisten of rain
on sprouting grass."

5 Is it not true my house is
with God?
For He has established
an everlasting covenant
with me,
ordered and secured
in every detail.
Will He not bring about
my whole salvation and my
every desire?

6 But all the wicked are like thorns
raked aside;
they can never be picked up
by hand.
7 The man who touches them
must be armed with iron
and the shaft of a spear.
They will be completely
burned up on the spot.

PSALM 70:1-5

1 God, deliver me.
Hurry to help me, LORD!

2 Let those who seek my life
be disgraced and confounded;
let those who wish me harm
be driven back and humiliated.
3 Let those who say, "Aha, aha!"
retreat because of their shame.

4 Let all who seek You rejoice and
be glad in You;
let those who love Your salvation
continually say,
"God is great!"
5 I am afflicted and needy;
hurry to me, God.
You are my help and my deliverer;
LORD, do not delay.

PROVERBS 15:16-17

16 Better a little with the fear of the
LORD
than great treasure with turmoil.

17 Better a meal of vegetables where
there is love
than a fattened calf with hatred.

JOHN 12:34–13:11

34 Then the crowd replied to Him,
"We have heard from the law that the
Messiah will remain forever. So how
can You say, 'The Son of Man must be
lifted up'? Who is this Son of Man?"
35 Jesus answered, "The light will be
with you only a little longer. Walk while
you have the light so that darkness
doesn't overtake you. The one who walks

in darkness doesn't know where he's going. [36] While you have the light, believe in the light so that you may become sons of light." Jesus said this, then went away and hid from them.

[37] Even though He had performed so many signs in their presence, they did not believe in Him. [38] But this was to fulfill the word of Isaiah the prophet, who said:

> Lord, who has believed
> our message?
> And who has the arm
> of the Lord been
> revealed to?

[39] This is why they were unable to believe, because Isaiah also said:

> [40] He has blinded their eyes
> and hardened their hearts,
> so that they would not see
> with their eyes
> or understand with their hearts,
> and be converted,
> and I would heal them.

[41] Isaiah said these things because he saw His glory and spoke about Him.

[42] Nevertheless, many did believe in Him even among the rulers, but because of the Pharisees they did not confess Him, so they would not be banned from the synagogue. [43] For they loved praise from men more than praise from God.

[44] Then Jesus cried out, "The one who believes in Me believes not in Me, but in Him who sent Me. [45] And the one who sees Me sees Him who sent Me. [46] I have come as a light into the world, so that everyone who believes in Me would not remain in darkness. [47] If anyone hears My words and doesn't keep them, I do not judge him; for I did not come to judge the world but to save the world. [48] The one who rejects Me and doesn't accept My sayings has this as his judge: the word I have spoken will judge him on the last day. [49] For I have not spoken on My own, but the Father Himself who sent Me has given Me a command as to what I should say and what I should speak. [50] I know that His command is eternal life. So the things that I speak, I speak just as the Father has told Me."

13 Before the Passover Festival, Jesus knew that His hour had come to depart from this world to the Father. Having loved His own who were in the world, He loved them to the end. [2] Now by the time of supper, the Devil had already put it into the heart of Judas, Simon Iscariot's son, to betray Him. [3] Jesus knew that the Father had given everything into His hands, that He had come from God, and that He was going back to God. [4] So He got up from supper, laid aside His robe, took a towel, and tied it around Himself. [5] Next, He poured water into a basin and began to wash His disciples' feet and to dry them with the towel tied around Him.

[6] He came to Simon Peter, who asked Him, "Lord, are You going to wash my feet?"

[7] Jesus answered him, "What I'm doing you don't understand now, but afterwards you will know."

[8] "You will never wash my feet—ever!" Peter said.

Jesus replied, "If I don't wash you, you have no part with Me."

[9] Simon Peter said to Him, "Lord, not only my feet, but also my hands and my head."

[10] "One who has bathed," Jesus told him, "doesn't need to wash anything except his feet, but he is completely clean. You are clean, but not all of you." [11] For He knew who would betray Him. This is why He said, "You are not all clean."

The Satanic Strategy

The Devil had already put it into the heart of Judas . . . to betray Him.—JOHN 13:2

The "fiery darts" of the Devil are quite different from the thoughts that are generated by our carnal nature. These "fiery darts" come at us rather than from within us. A satanic attack can usually be differentiated from something that arises within by the force with which the thought hits us. Thoughts that arise out of the carnal nature are offensive, but the thoughts that come as "fiery darts" from the Devil burn.

Many Christians have told me that they often experience these attacks when they go to read their Bibles or to pray. When they read a newspaper, nothing seems to happen. But when they turn their attention to something spiritual, they find it almost impossible to concentrate, by reason of the shameful thoughts that occupy their minds.

The other thing one notices about these attacks is that they seem to come in cycles. They are not there permanently, but they come at certain times and seasons. I once counseled a man for one hour a week over a period of a whole year and got him to write down in his diary the times and dates when he felt under satanic attack. When we looked through his diary together at the end of the year, we discovered an amazing thing—every single attack took place immediately prior to his doing something special for the Lord, like leading a Bible study, conducting a service, visiting the sick, or giving a public testimony. I shall never forget the expression on his face as he looked at me and said: "Who says that Satan isn't a strategist?"

Prayer

My Father and my God, I realize that even though Satan is a strategist, he is no match for You. You know how to outmaneuver his every move. Help me to stay close to You, that I might experience Your strategy and not his. Amen.

Further Study

Gn 3; Mt 4:1-10
How did Satan seek to penetrate Eve's mind?
How does this correlate with the temptation of Christ?

JUNE 10

2 SAMUEL 23:8–24:25

⁸ These are the names of David's warriors:

Josheb-basshebeth the Tahchemonite was chief of the officers. He wielded his spear against 800 men he killed at one time.

⁹ After him, Eleazar son of Dodo son of Ahohi was among the three warriors with David when they defied the Philistines. The men of Israel retreated in the place they had gathered for battle, ¹⁰ but Eleazar stood his ground and attacked the Philistines until his hand was tired and stuck to his sword. The LORD brought about a great victory that day. Then the troops came back to him, but only to plunder the dead.

¹¹ After him was Shammah son of Agee the Hararite. The Philistines had assembled in formation where there was a field full of lentils. The troops fled from the Philistines, ¹² but Shammah took his stand in the middle of the field, defended it, and struck down the Philistines. So the LORD brought about a great victory.

¹³ Three of the 30 leading warriors went down at harvest time and came to David at the cave of Adullam, while a company of Philistines was camping in the Valley of Rephaim. ¹⁴ At that time David was in the stronghold, and a Philistine garrison was at Bethlehem. ¹⁵ David was extremely thirsty and said, "If only someone would bring me water to drink from the well at the city gate of Bethlehem!" ¹⁶ So three of the warriors broke through the Philistine camp and drew water from the well at the gate of Bethlehem. They brought it back to David, but he refused to drink it. Instead, he poured it out to the LORD. ¹⁷ David said, "LORD, I would never do such a thing! Is this not the blood of men who risked their lives?" So he re-

fused to drink it. Such were the exploits of the three warriors.

¹⁸ Abishai, Joab's brother and son of Zeruiah, was leader of the Three. He raised his spear against 300 men and killed them, gaining a reputation among the Three. ¹⁹ Was he not the most honored of the Three? He became their commander even though he did not become one of the Three.

²⁰ Benaiah son of Jehoiada was the son of a brave man from Kabzeel, a man of many exploits. Benaiah killed two sons of Ariel of Moab, and he went down into a pit on a snowy day and killed a lion. ²¹ He also killed an Egyptian, a huge man. Even though the Egyptian had a spear in his hand, Benaiah went down to him with a club, snatched the spear out of the Egyptian's hand, and then killed him with his own spear. ²² These were the exploits of Benaiah son of Jehoiada, who had a reputation among the three warriors. ²³ He was the most honored of the Thirty, but he did not become one of the Three. David put him in charge of his bodyguard.

²⁴ Among the Thirty were:

Joab's brother Asahel,
Elhanan son of Dodo
    of Bethlehem,
25 Shammah the Harodite,
    Elika the Harodite,
26 Helez the Paltite,
    Ira son of Ikkesh the Tekoite,
27 Abiezer the Anathothite,
    Mebunnai the Hushathite,
28 Zalmon the Ahohite,
    Maharai the Netophathite,
29 Heleb son of Baanah
    the Netophahite,
    Ittai son of Ribai from Gibeah
    of the Benjaminites,
30 Benaiah the Pirathonite,
    Hiddai from the Wadis of Gaash,
31 Abi-albon the Arbathite,

Azmaveth the Barhumite,
³² Eliahba the Shaalbonite,
the sons of Jashen,
Jonathan son of ³³ Shammah
the Hararite,
Ahiam son of Sharar the Hararite,
³⁴ Eliphelet son of Ahasbai
son of the Maacathite,
Eliam son of Ahithophel
the Gilonite,
³⁵ Hezro the Carmelite,
Paarai the Arbite,
³⁶ Igal son of Nathan from Zobah,
Bani the Gadite,
³⁷ Zelek the Ammonite,
Naharai the Beerothite, the armor-
bearer for Joab son of Zeruiah,
³⁸ Ira the Ithrite,
Gareb the Ithrite,
³⁹ and Uriah the Hittite.

There were 37 in all.

24 The LORD's anger burned against Israel again, and it stirred up David against them to say: "Go, count the people of Israel and Judah."
² So the king said to Joab, the commander of his army, "Go through all the tribes of Israel from Dan to Beer-sheba and register the troops so I can know their number."
³ Joab replied to the king, "May the LORD your God multiply the troops 100 times more than they are—while my lord the king looks on! But why does my lord the king want to do this?"
⁴ Yet the king's order prevailed over Joab and the commanders of the army. So Joab and the commanders of the army left the king's presence to register the troops of Israel.
⁵ They crossed the Jordan and camped in Aroer, south of the town in the middle of the valley, and then proceeded toward Gad and Jazer. ⁶ They went to Gilead and to the land of the Hittites and continued on to Dan-jaan and around to Sidon. ⁷ They went to the fortress of Tyre and all the cities of the Hivites and Canaanites. Afterwards, they went to the Negev of Judah at Beer-sheba.
⁸ When they had gone through the whole land, they returned to Jerusalem

at the end of nine months and 20 days. ⁹ Joab gave the king the total of the registration of the troops. There were 800,000 fighting men from Israel and 500,000 men from Judah.
¹⁰ David's conscience troubled him after he had taken a census of the troops. He said to the LORD, "I have sinned greatly in what I've done. Now, LORD, because I've been very foolish, please take away Your servant's guilt."
¹¹ When David got up in the morning, a revelation from the LORD had come to the prophet Gad, David's seer: ¹² "Go and say to David, 'This is what the LORD says: I am offering you three choices. Choose one of them, and I will do it to you.' "
¹³ So Gad went to David, told him the choices, and asked him, "Do you want three years of famine to come on your land, to flee from your foes three months while they pursue you, or to have a plague in your land three days? Now, think it over and decide what answer I should take back to the One who sent me."
¹⁴ David answered Gad, "I have great anxiety. Please, let us fall into the LORD's hands because His mercies are great, but don't let me fall into human hands."
¹⁵ So the LORD sent a plague on Israel from that morning until the appointed time, and from Dan to Beer-sheba 70,000 men died. ¹⁶ Then the angel extended his hand toward Jerusalem to destroy it, but the LORD relented concerning the destruction and said to the angel who was destroying the people, "Enough, withdraw your hand now!" The angel of the LORD was then at the threshing floor of Araunah the Jebusite.
¹⁷ When David saw the angel striking the people, he said to the LORD, "Look, I am the one who has sinned; I am the one who has done wrong. But these sheep, what have they done? Please, let Your hand be against me and my father's family."
¹⁸ Gad came to David that day and said to him, "Go up and set up an altar to the LORD on the threshing floor of Araunah the Jebusite." ¹⁹ David went up

in obedience to Gad's command, just as the LORD had commanded. ²⁰ Araunah looked down and saw the king and his servants coming toward him, so he went out and bowed to the king with his face to the ground.

²¹ Araunah said, "Why has my lord the king come to his servant?"

David replied, "To buy the threshing floor from you in order to build an altar to the LORD, so the plague on the people may be halted."

²² Araunah said to David, "My lord the king may take whatever he wants and offer it. Here are the oxen for a burnt offering and the threshing sledges and ox yokes for the wood. ²³ My king, Araunah gives everything here to the king." Then he said to the king, "May the LORD your God accept you."

²⁴ The king answered Araunah, "No, I insist on buying it from you for a price, for I will not offer to the LORD my God burnt offerings that cost me nothing." David bought the threshing floor and the oxen for 50 ounces of silver. ²⁵ He built an altar to the LORD there and offered burnt offerings and fellowship offerings. Then the LORD answered prayer on behalf of the land, and the plague on Israel ended.

PSALM 71:1-8

1 LORD, I seek refuge in You;
 never let me be disgraced.
2 In Your justice, rescue and deliver me;
 listen closely to me and save me.
3 Be a rock of refuge for me,
 where I can always go.
 Give the command to save me,
 for You are my rock and fortress.
4 Deliver me, My God, from the hand of the wicked,
 from the grasp of the unjust and oppressive.
5 For You are my hope, Lord GOD,
 my confidence from my youth.
6 I have leaned on You from birth;
 You took me from my mother's womb.
 My praise is always about You.

7 I have become an ominous sign to many,
 but You are my strong refuge.
8 My mouth is full of praise
 and honor to You all day long.

PROVERBS 15:18-19

18 A hot-tempered man stirs up conflict,
 but a man slow to anger calms strife.

19 A slacker's way is like a thorny hedge,
 but the path of the upright is a highway.

JOHN 13:12-38

¹² When Jesus had washed their feet and put on His robe, He reclined again and said to them, "Do you know what I have done for you? ¹³ You call Me Teacher and Lord. This is well said, for I am. ¹⁴ So if I, your Lord and Teacher, have washed your feet, you also ought to wash one another's feet. ¹⁵ For I have given you an example that you also should do just as I have done for you.

¹⁶ "I assure you: A slave is not greater than his master, and a messenger is not greater than the one who sent him. ¹⁷ If you know these things, you are blessed if you do them. ¹⁸ I'm not speaking about all of you; I know those I have chosen. But the Scripture must be fulfilled: **The one who eats My bread has raised his heel against Me.**

¹⁹ "I am telling you now before it happens, so that when it does happen you will believe that I am He. ²⁰ I assure you: The one who receives whomever I send receives Me, and the one who receives Me receives Him who sent Me."

²¹ When Jesus had said this, He was troubled in His spirit and testified, "I assure you: One of you will betray Me!"

²² The disciples started looking at one another—uncertain which one He was speaking about. ²³ One of His disciples, the one Jesus loved, was reclining close beside Jesus. ²⁴ Simon Peter motioned

to him to find out who it was He was talking about. ²⁵ So he leaned back against Jesus and asked Him, "Lord, who is it?"

²⁶ Jesus replied, "He's the one I give the piece of bread to after I have dipped it." When He had dipped the bread, He gave it to Judas, Simon Iscariot's son. ²⁷ After Judas ate the piece of bread, Satan entered him. Therefore Jesus told him, "What you're doing, do quickly."

²⁸ None of those reclining at the table knew why He told him this. ²⁹ Since Judas kept the money-bag, some thought that Jesus was telling him, "Buy what we need for the festival," or that he should give something to the poor. ³⁰ After receiving the piece of bread, he went out immediately. And it was night.

³¹ When he had gone out, Jesus said, "Now the Son of Man is glorified, and God is glorified in Him. ³² If God is glorified in Him, God will also glorify Him

in Himself and will glorify Him at once.

³³ "Children, I am with you a little while longer. You will look for Me, and just as I told the Jews, 'Where I am going you cannot come,' so now I tell you. ³⁴ "I give you a new commandment: love one another. Just as I have loved you, you must also love one another. ³⁵ By this all people will know that you are My disciples, if you have love for one another."

³⁶ "Lord," Simon Peter said to Him, "where are You going?"

Jesus answered, "Where I am going you cannot follow Me now, but you will follow later."

³⁷ "Lord," Peter asked, "why can't I follow You now? I will lay down my life for You!"

³⁸ Jesus replied, "Will you lay down your life for Me? I assure you: A rooster will not crow until you have denied Me three times."

Our Code Is a Character

I give you a new commandment: love one another. Just as I have loved you, you must also love one another.—JOHN 13:34

What other teacher has taken the Ten Commandments and had the right to add another commandment to them? But this is precisely what Jesus did, as we see from our text today. "I give you a new commandment," He says. "Love one another. Just as I have loved you, you must also love one another."

The Old Testament and other religious writings enjoined loving one another. What was new was this: "As I have loved you." Our Lord's conduct—"as I have loved you"—produced a new code for the human race. Paul, writing to the Philippians, catches the spirit of it when he says: "Treat one another with the same spirit as you experience in Christ Jesus" (Php 2:5, Moffatt). Here morality reaches its high-water mark. From the moment Jesus uttered the words that are occupying our attention, there came into human life something more than a code—there came a Character. Now, therefore, our code is a Character—the Character of Jesus.

When someone asks me if I believe in the Ten Commandments, I say: "Yes, and very much more besides. I believe in Jesus." The Ten Commandments are an injunction—and a God-given one. But Jesus is an injunction plus an inspiration. To follow an injunction is to obey imposed morality, but to follow a Person and do the things He does is an inspired morality. One is legalism, the other love. One binds you, the other frees you. One makes you feel trammeled, the other relaxed and spontaneous. Our code is not a commandment but a Character. One greater than the commandments is here.

Prayer

O Christ, Your law lays upon me an injunction, but Your life entering into my life inspires me to live up to that injunction. It is this that makes Your yoke so easy. I am deeply, deeply grateful. Amen.

Further Study

Jn 15:1-17; Jms 2:8; Mt 7:12
What was the basis of Christ's love?
What is the basis of our being able to fulfill the Royal Law?

JUNE 11

1 KINGS 1:1-53

1 Now King David was old and getting on in years. Although they covered him with bedclothes, he could not get warm. ² So his servants said to him: "Let us search for a young virgin for my lord the king. She is to attend the king and be his caregiver. She is to lie by your side so that my lord the king will get warm." ³ They searched for a beautiful girl throughout the territory of Israel; they found Abishag the Shunammite and brought her to the king. ⁴ The girl was of unsurpassed beauty, and she became the king's caregiver. She served him, but he was not intimate with her.

⁵ Adonijah son of Haggith kept exalting himself, saying, "I will be king!" He also assembled chariots, cavalry, and 50 men to run ahead of him. ⁶ But his father had never once reprimanded him by saying, "Why do you act this way?" In addition, he was quite handsome and was born after Absalom. ⁷ He conspired with Joab son of Zeruiah and with Abiathar the priest. They supported Adonijah, ⁸ but Zadok the priest, Benaiah

son of Jehoiada, Nathan the prophet, Shimei, Rei, and David's warriors did not side with Adonijah.

⁹ Adonijah sacrificed sheep, oxen, and fattened cattle near the stone of Zoheleth, which is next to En-rogel. He invited all his royal brothers and all the men of Judah, the servants of the king, ¹⁰ but he did not invite Nathan the prophet, Benaiah, the warriors, or his brother Solomon.

¹¹ Then Nathan said to Bathsheba, Solomon's mother, "Have you not heard that Adonijah son of Haggith has become king and our lord David does not know it? ¹² Now please come and let me advise you. Save your life and the life of your son Solomon. ¹³ Go, approach King David and say to him, 'My lord king, did you not swear to your servant: Your son Solomon is to become king after me, and he is the one who is to sit on my throne? So why has Adonijah become king?' ¹⁴ At that moment, while you are still there speaking with the king, I'll come in after you and confirm your words."

¹⁵ So Bathsheba went to the king in his bedroom. Since the king was very

old, Abishag the Shunammite was serving him. [16] Bathsheba bowed down and paid homage to the king, and he asked, "What do you want?"

[17] She replied, "My lord, you swore to your servant by the LORD your God, 'Your son Solomon is to become king after me, and he is the one who is to sit on my throne.' [18] Now look, Adonijah has become king. And, my lord king, you didn't know it. [19] He has lavishly sacrificed oxen, fattened cattle, and sheep. He invited all the king's sons, Abiathar the priest, and Joab the commander of the army, but he did not invite your servant Solomon. [20] Now, my lord king, the eyes of all Israel are on you to tell them who will sit on the throne of my lord the king after him. [21] Otherwise, when my lord the king rests with his fathers, I and my son Solomon will be regarded as criminals."

[22] At that moment, while she was still speaking with the king, Nathan the prophet arrived, [23] and it was announced to the king, "Nathan the prophet is here." He came into the king's presence and bowed to him with his face to the ground.

[24] "My lord king," Nathan said, "did you say, 'Adonijah is to become king after me, and he is the one who is to sit on my throne?' [25] For today he went down and lavishly sacrificed oxen, fattened cattle, and sheep. He invited all the sons of the king, the commanders of the army, and Abiathar the priest. And look! They're eating and drinking in his presence, and they're saying, 'Long live King Adonijah!' [26] But he did not invite me—me, your servant—or Zadok the priest or Benaiah son of Jehoiada or your servant Solomon. [27] I'm certain my lord the king would not have let this happen without letting your servant know who will sit on my lord the king's throne after him."

[28] King David responded by saying, "Call in Bathsheba for me." So she came into the king's presence and stood before him. [29] The king swore an oath and said, "As the LORD lives, who has redeemed my life from every difficulty, [30] just as I swore to you by the LORD God of Israel: Your son Solomon is to become king after me, and he is the one who is to sit on my throne in my place, that is exactly what I will do this very day."

[31] Bathsheba bowed with her face to the ground, paying homage to the king, and said, "May my lord King David live forever!"

[32] King David then said, "Call in Zadok the priest, Nathan the prophet, and Benaiah son of Jehoiada for me." So they came into the king's presence. [33] The king said to them, "Take my servants with you, have my son Solomon ride on my own mule, and take him down to Gihon. [34] There, Zadok the priest and Nathan the prophet are to anoint him as king over Israel. You are to blow the ram's horn and say, 'Long live King Solomon!' [35] You are to come up after him, and he is to come in and sit on my throne. He is the one who is to become king in my place; he is the one I have commanded to be ruler over Israel and Judah."

[36] "Amen," Benaiah son of Jehoiada replied to the king. "May the LORD, the God of my lord the king, so affirm it. [37] Just as the LORD was with my lord the king, so may He be with Solomon and make his throne greater than the throne of my lord King David."

[38] Then Zadok the priest, Nathan the prophet, Benaiah son of Jehoiada, the Cherethites, and the Pelethites went down, had Solomon ride on King David's mule, and took him to Gihon. [39] Zadok the priest took the horn of oil from the tabernacle and anointed Solomon. Then they blew the ram's horn, and all the people proclaimed, "Long live King Solomon!" [40] All the people followed him, playing flutes and rejoicing with such a great joy that the earth split open from the sound.

[41] Adonijah and all the invited guests who were with him heard the noise as they finished eating. Joab heard the sound of the ram's horn and said, "Why is the town in such an uproar?" [42] He was still speaking when Jonathan son of Abiathar the priest, suddenly arrived. Adonijah said, "Come in, for you are an

excellent man, and you must be bringing good news."

⁴³ "Unfortunately not," Jonathan answered him. "Our lord King David has made Solomon king. ⁴⁴ And with Solomon, the king has sent Zadok the priest, Nathan the prophet, Benaiah son of Jehoiada, the Cherethites, and the Pelethites, and they have had him ride on the king's mule. ⁴⁵ Zadok the priest and Nathan the prophet have anointed him king in Gihon. They have gone from there rejoicing. The town has been in an uproar; that's the noise you heard. ⁴⁶ Solomon has even taken his seat on the royal throne.

⁴⁷ "The king's servants have also gone to congratulate our lord King David, saying, 'May your God make the name of Solomon more famous than your name, and may He make his throne greater than your throne.' Then the king bowed in worship on his bed. ⁴⁸ And the king went on to say this: 'May the LORD God of Israel be praised! Today He has provided one to sit on my throne, and I am a witness.' "

⁴⁹ Then all of Adonijah's guests got up trembling and went their separate ways. ⁵⁰ Adonijah was afraid of Solomon, so he got up and went to take hold of the horns of the altar.

⁵¹ It was reported to Solomon: "Look, Adonijah fears King Solomon, and he has taken hold of the horns of the altar, saying, 'Let King Solomon first swear to me that he will not kill his servant with the sword.' "

⁵² Then Solomon said, "If he is a man of character, then not a single hair of his will fall to the ground, but if evil is found in him, then he dies." ⁵³ So King Solomon sent for him, and they took him down from the altar. He came and paid homage to King Solomon, and Solomon said to him, "Go to your home."

𝒫SALM 71:9-16

⁹ Don't discard me in my old age;
    as my strength fails, do not
      abandon me.
¹⁰ For my enemies talk about me,

and those who spy on me plot
      together,
¹¹ saying, "God has abandoned him;
    chase him and catch him,
    for there is no one to rescue him"
¹² God, do not be far from me;
    my God, hurry to help me.
¹³ May my adversaries be disgraced
      and confounded;
    may those who seek my harm
    be covered with disgrace and
      humiliation.
¹⁴ But I will hope continually
    and will praise You more and
      more.
¹⁵ My mouth will tell about Your
      righteousness
    and Your salvation all day long,
    though I cannot sum them up.
¹⁶ I come because of the mighty acts
      of the Lord GOD;
    I will proclaim Your righteousness,
      Yours alone.

𝒫ROVERBS 15:20-21

²⁰ A wise son brings joy to his father,
    but a foolish one despises his
      mother.

²¹ Foolishness brings joy to one
      without sense,
    but a man with understanding
      walks a straight path.

𝒥OHN 14:1-21

14 "Your heart must not be troubled. Believe in God; believe also in Me. ² In My Father's house are many dwelling places; if not, I would have told you. I am going away to prepare a place for you. ³ If I go away and prepare a place for you, I will come back and receive you to Myself, so that where I am you may be also. ⁴ You know the way where I am going."

⁵ "Lord," Thomas said, "we don't know where You're going. How can we know the way?"

⁶ Jesus told him, "I am the way, the truth, and the life. No one comes to the Father except through Me.

⁷"If you know Me, you will also know My Father. From now on you do know Him and have seen Him."

⁸"Lord," said Philip, "show us the Father, and that's enough for us."

⁹Jesus said to him, "Have I been among you all this time without your knowing Me, Philip? The one who has seen Me has seen the Father. How can you say, 'Show us the Father'? ¹⁰Don't you believe that I am in the Father and the Father is in Me? The words I speak to you I do not speak on My own. The Father who lives in Me does His works. ¹¹Believe Me that I am in the Father and the Father is in Me. Otherwise, believe because of the works themselves.

¹²"I assure you: The one who believes in Me will also do the works that I do. And he will do even greater works than these, because I am going to the Father. ¹³Whatever you ask in My name, I will do it so that the Father may be glorified in the Son. ¹⁴If you ask Me anything in My name, I will do it.

¹⁵"If you love Me, you will keep My commandments. ¹⁶And I will ask the Father, and He will give you another Counselor to be with you forever. ¹⁷He is the Spirit of truth. The world is unable to receive Him because it doesn't see Him or know Him. But you do know Him, because He remains with you and will be in you. ¹⁸I will not leave you as orphans; I am coming to you.

¹⁹"In a little while the world will see Me no longer, but you will see Me. Because I live, you will live too. ²⁰In that day you will know that I am in My Father, you are in Me, and I am in you. ²¹The one who has My commands and keeps them is the one who loves Me. And the one who loves Me will be loved by My Father. I also will love him and will reveal Myself to him."

A Permanent Guest

He will give you another Counselor to be with you forever . . . the Spirit of truth.—John 14:16-17

One of the lessons Jesus gave His disciples when preparing them to receive the Holy Spirit was that the Spirit's coming would not be a temporary visitation—He would abide in them forever. In the Old Testament, the Holy Spirit provided temporary supplies of power to individual people for certain tasks. When these purposes were accomplished, He returned to heaven. The disciples were no doubt aware of this aspect of the Spirit's ministry, but now Jesus gives them the breathtaking news that the Holy Spirit's coming would be permanent: "He will abide in you and be with you forever." What a revelation this must have been to the disciples! The occasional would give place to the permanent; the special would give way to the general. Jesus was saying, in effect, that the Holy Spirit would not come and go—a kind of "hide-and-seek" experience—but He would move within the inner recesses of their beings and abide with them forever.

This is probably one of the most important truths we can grasp from the Scripture, for there are many Christians who think of the possession of the Holy Spirit as tentative and momentary. However, that would defeat the very point and purpose of redemption, for as someone said: "The Holy Spirit is the applied point of redemption." His coming into our lives must be permanent, or our redemption (at least its application) will be temporary. The Holy Ghost becomes a Holy Guest! And, thank God, a permanent guest!

Prayer

Blessed Holy Spirit, I am so grateful that You are willing to take up a permanent abode within my heart. With You abiding in me, I want for nothing and am equipped for every task. I am so thankful. Amen.

Further Study

Gn 1; Ezk 36:27; 1 Jn 3:24; Heb 9:14; Rv 22:17
What was the Holy Spirit's ministry in the beginning?
What is His ministry since Pentecost?

JUNE 12

1 KINGS 2:1-46

2 As the time approached for David to die, he instructed his son Solomon, ² "As for me, I am going the way of all of the earth. Be strong and brave, ³ and keep your obligation to the LORD your God to walk in His ways and to keep His statutes, commandments, judgments, and testimonies. This is written in the law of Moses, so that you will have success in everything you do and wherever you turn, ⁴ and so that the LORD will carry out His promise that He made to me: 'If your sons are careful to walk faithfully before Me with their whole mind and heart, you will never fail to have a man on the throne of Israel.'

⁵ "You also know what Joab son of Zeruiah did to me and what he did to the two commanders of Israel's army, Abner son of Ner and Amasa son of Jether. He murdered them in a time of peace to avenge blood shed in war. He spilled that blood on his own waistband and on the sandals of his feet. ⁶ Act according to your wisdom, and do not let his gray head descend to Sheol in peace.

⁷ "Show loyalty to the sons of Barzillai the Gileadite and let them be among those who eat at your table because they supported me when I fled from your brother Absalom.

⁸ "Keep an eye on Shimei son of Gera, the Benjaminite from Bahurim who is with you. He uttered malicious curses against me the day I went to Mahanaim. But he came down to meet me at the Jordan River, and I swore to him by the LORD: 'I will never kill you with the sword.' ⁹ So don't let him go unpunished, for you are a wise man. You know how to deal with him to bring his gray head down to Sheol with blood."

¹⁰ Then David rested with his fathers and was buried in the city of David. ¹¹ The length of time David reigned over Israel was 40 years: he reigned seven years in Hebron and 33 years in Jerusalem. ¹² Solomon sat on the throne of his father David, and his kingship was firmly established.

¹³ Now Adonijah son of Haggith came to Bathsheba, Solomon's mother. She asked, "Do you come peacefully?"

"Peacefully," he replied, ¹⁴ and then asked, "May I talk with you?"

"Go ahead," she answered.

¹⁵ "You know the kingship was mine," he said. "All Israel expected me to be king, but then the kingship was turned over to my brother, for the LORD gave it to him. ¹⁶ So now I have just one request of you; don't turn me down."

She said to him, "Go on."

¹⁷ He replied, "Please speak to King Solomon since he won't turn you down. Let him give me Abishag the Shunammite as a wife."

¹⁸ "Very well," Bathsheba replied. "I will speak to the king for you."

¹⁹ So Bathsheba went to King Solomon to speak to him about Adonijah. The king stood up to greet her, bowed to her, sat down on his throne, and had a throne placed for the king's mother. So she sat down at his right hand.

²⁰ Then she said, "I have just one small request of you. Don't turn me down."

"Go ahead and ask, mother," the king replied, "for I won't turn you down."

²¹ So she said, "Let Abishag the Shunammite be given to your brother Adonijah as a wife."

²² King Solomon answered his mother, "Why are you requesting Abishag the Shunammite for Adonijah? Since he is my elder brother, you might as well ask the kingship for him, for Abiathar the priest, and for Joab son of Zeruiah."

²³ Then Solomon took an oath by the LORD: "May God punish me and do so severely if Adonijah has not made this request at the cost of his life. ²⁴ And now, as the LORD lives, the One who established me, seated me on the throne of my father David, and made me a dynasty as He promised—I swear Adonijah will be put to death today!" ²⁵ Then King Solomon gave the order to Benaiah son of Jehoiada, who struck down Adonijah, and he died.

²⁶ The king said to Abiathar the priest, "Go to your fields in Anathoth. Even though you deserve to die, I will not put you to death today, since you carried the ark of the Lord GOD in the presence of my father David and you suffered through all that my father suffered."

²⁷ So Solomon banished Abiathar from being the LORD's priest, and it fulfilled the LORD's prophecy He had spoken at Shiloh against Eli's family.

²⁸ The news reached Joab. Since he had supported Adonijah but not Absalom, Joab fled to the LORD's tabernacle and took hold of the horns of the altar.

²⁹ It was reported to King Solomon: "Joab has fled to the LORD's tabernacle and is now beside the altar." Then Solomon sent Benaiah son of Jehoiada and told him, "Go and strike him down!"

³⁰ So Benaiah went to the tabernacle and said to Joab, "This is what the king says: 'Come out!' "

But Joab said, "No, for I will die here."

So Benaiah took a message back to the king, "This is what Joab said, and this is how he answered me."

³¹ The king said to him, "Do just as he says. Strike him down and bury him in order to remove from me and from my father's house the blood that Joab shed without just cause. ³² The LORD will bring back his own blood on his own head because he struck down two men more righteous and better than he, without my father David's knowledge. With his sword, Joab murdered Abner son of Ner, commander of Israel's army, and Amasa son of Jether, commander of Judah's army. ³³ Their blood will come back on Joab's head and on the head of his descendants forever, but for David, his descendants, his dynasty, and his throne, there will be peace from the LORD forever."

³⁴ Benaiah son of Jehoiada went up, struck down Joab, and put him to death. He was buried at his house in the wilderness. ³⁵ Then the king appointed Benaiah son of Jehoiada in Joab's place over the army, and he appointed Zadok the priest in Abiathar's place.

³⁶ Then the king summoned Shimei and said to him, "Build a house for yourself in Jerusalem and live there, but don't leave there and go anywhere else. ³⁷ On the day you do leave and cross the Kidron Valley, know for sure that you will certainly die. Your blood will be on your own head."

³⁸ Shimei said to the king, "The sentence is fair; your servant will do as my lord the king has spoken." And Shimei lived in Jerusalem for a long time.

³⁹ But then, at the end of three years, two of Shimei's slaves ran away to Achish son of Maacah, king of Gath. Shimei was informed, "Look, your slaves are in Gath." ⁴⁰ So Shimei saddled his donkey and set out to Achish at Gath to search for his slaves. He went and brought them back from Gath.

⁴¹ It was reported to Solomon that Shimei had gone from Jerusalem to Gath and had returned. ⁴² So the king summoned Shimei and said to him, "Didn't I make you swear by the LORD and warn you, saying, 'On the day you leave and go anywhere else, know for sure that you will certainly die'? And you said to me, 'The sentence is fair; I will obey.' ⁴³ So why have you not kept the LORD's oath and the command that I gave you?" ⁴⁴ The king also said, "You yourself know all the evil that you did to my father David. Therefore, the LORD has brought back your evil on your head, ⁴⁵ but King Solomon will be blessed, and David's throne will remain established before the LORD forever."

⁴⁶ Then the king commanded Benaiah son of Jehoiada, and he went out and struck Shimei down, and he died. So the kingdom was established in Solomon's hand.

PSALM 71:17-24

¹⁷ God, You have taught me from my youth,
and I still proclaim Your wonderful works.
¹⁸ Even when I am old and gray, God, do not abandon me.
Then I will proclaim Your power to another generation,
Your strength to all who are to come.
¹⁹ Your righteousness reaches heaven, God,
You who have done great things; God, who is like You?
²⁰ You caused me to experience many troubles and misfortunes,

but You will revive me again.
You will bring me up again, even from the depths of the earth.
²¹ You will increase my honor and comfort me once again.
²² Therefore, with a lute I will praise You
for Your faithfulness, my God;
I will sing to You with a harp, Holy One of Israel.
²³ My lips will shout for joy when I sing praise to You,
because You have redeemed me.
²⁴ Therefore, my tongue will proclaim Your righteousness all day long,
for those who seek my harm will be disgraced and confounded.

PROVERBS 15:22-23

²² Plans fail when there is no counsel,
but with many advisers they succeed.

²³ A man takes joy in giving an answer;
and a timely word—how good that is!

JOHN 14:22–15:10

²² Judas (not Iscariot) said to Him, "Lord, how is it You're going to reveal Yourself to us and not to the world?"

²³ Jesus answered, "If anyone loves Me, he will keep My word. My Father will love him, and We will come to him and make Our home with him. ²⁴ The one who doesn't love Me will not keep My words. The word that you hear is not Mine but is from the Father who sent Me.

²⁵ "I have spoken these things to you while I remain with you. ²⁶ But the Counselor, the Holy Spirit—the Father will send Him in My name—will teach you all things and remind you of everything I have told you. ²⁷ "Peace I leave with you. My peace I give to you. I do not give to you as the world gives. Your heart must not be

troubled or fearful. [28] You have heard Me tell you, 'I am going away and I am coming to you.' If you loved Me, you would have rejoiced that I am going to the Father, because the Father is greater than I. [29] I have told you now before it happens so that when it does happen you may believe. [30] I will not talk with you much longer, because the ruler of the world is coming. He has no power over Me. [31] On the contrary, I am going away so that the world may know that I love the Father. Just as the Father commanded Me, so I do.

"Get up; let's leave this place.

15 "I am the true vine, and My Father is the vineyard keeper. [2] Every branch in Me that does not produce fruit He removes, and He prunes every branch that produces fruit so that it will produce more fruit. [3] You are already clean because of the word I have spoken to you. [4] Remain in Me, and I in you. Just as a branch is unable to produce fruit by itself unless it remains on the vine, so neither can you unless you remain in Me.

[5] "I am the vine; you are the branches. The one who remains in Me and I in him produces much fruit, because you can do nothing without Me. [6] If anyone does not remain in Me, he is thrown aside like a branch and he withers. They gather them, throw them into the fire, and they are burned. [7] If you remain in Me and My words remain in you, ask whatever you want and it will be done for you. [8] My Father is glorified by this: that you produce much fruit and prove to be My disciples.

[9] "As the Father has loved Me, I have also loved you. Remain in My love. [10] If you keep My commands you will remain in My love, just as I have kept My Father's commands and remain in His love.

The Whole Truth

The Holy Spirit . . . will teach you all things and remind you of everything I have told you.—JOHN 14:26

Another lesson given by Jesus to His disciples when preparing them to receive the Holy Spirit was that the Holy Spirit would teach them and remind them of all that Jesus had said. A famous agnostic once said that the irreconcilable conflict between science and religion is that science is never fixed—it is open and progressive: religion, on the other hand, is fixed on absolutes and dogmas.

Well, it is true that Christianity is fixed, but it also provides for a continuing revelation: "The Holy Spirit . . . will teach you all things." Jesus is God's final and complete revelation, but because of the limitations in us, this revelation must be gradually unfolding. Notice, however, that the teaching of the Spirit is according to a fixed pattern: "[He] will . . . remind you of everything I have told you" (v. 26). He will teach us more than Jesus taught but not other than Jesus taught. Someone said of this approach that it is both conservative and radical because it conserves all that Jesus taught and because it applies to new areas of life the universal aspect of Jesus.

"[He] will . . . remind you of everything I have told you." Note that word "everything." When we are not under the Holy Spirit's tutelage, we tend to focus on just one thing Jesus said and neglect the "everything." Then what happens? We produce a lopsided type of Christianity, with an overemphasis on one thing and an underemphasis on another. Christian communities who concentrate on one truth can easily miss the whole truth. Christians under the Spirit's control give heed to the "everything."

JUNE 13

1 KINGS 3:1–4:34

3 Solomon made an alliance with Pharaoh king of Egypt by marrying Pharaoh's daughter. Solomon brought her to the city of David until he finished building his palace, the LORD's temple, and the wall surrounding Jerusalem. ² However, the people were sacrificing on the high places, because until that time a temple for the LORD's name had not been built. ³ Solomon loved the LORD by walking in the statutes of his father David, but he also sacrificed and burned incense on the high places.

⁴ The king went to Gibeon to sacrifice there because it was the most famous high place. He offered 1,000 burnt offerings on that altar. ⁵ At Gibeon the LORD appeared to Solomon in a dream at night. God said, "Ask. What should I give you?"

⁶ And Solomon replied, "You have shown great and faithful love to Your servant, my father David, because he walked before You in faithfulness, righteousness, and integrity. You have continued this great and faithful love for

him by giving him a son to sit on his throne, as it is today.

⁷ "LORD my God, You have now made Your servant king in my father David's place. Yet I am just a youth with no experience in leadership. ⁸ Your servant is among Your people You have chosen, a people too numerous to be numbered or counted. ⁹ So give Your servant an obedient heart to judge Your people and to discern between good and evil. For who is able to judge this great people of Yours?"

¹⁰ Now it pleased the Lord that Solomon had requested this. ¹¹ So God said to him, "Because you have requested this and did not ask for long life or riches for yourself, or the death of your enemies, but you asked discernment for yourself to understand justice, ¹² I will therefore do what you have asked. I will give you a wise and understanding heart, so that there has never been anyone like you before and never will be again. ¹³ In addition, I will give you what you did not ask for: both riches and honor, so that no man in any kingdom will be your equal during your entire life. ¹⁴ If you walk in My ways and keep

My statutes and commandments just as your father David did, I will give you a long life."

¹⁵ Then Solomon woke up and realized it had been a dream. He went to Jerusalem, stood before the ark of the Lord's covenant, and offered burnt offerings and fellowship offerings. Then he held a feast for all his servants.

¹⁶ Then two women who were prostitutes came to the king and stood before him. ¹⁷ One woman said, "Please my lord, this woman and I live in the same house, and I had a baby while she was in the house. ¹⁸ On the third day after I gave birth, she also had a baby and we were alone. No one else was with us in the house; just the two of us were there. ¹⁹ During the night this woman's son died because she lay on him. ²⁰ She got up in the middle of the night and took my son from my side while your servant was asleep. She laid him at her breast, and she put her dead son in my arms. ²¹ When I got up in the morning to nurse my son, I discovered he was dead. That morning, when I looked closely at him I realized that he was not the son I gave birth to."

²² "No," the other woman said. "My son is the living one; your son is the dead one."

The first woman said, "No, your son is the dead one; my son is the living one." So they argued before the king.

²³ The king replied, "This woman says, 'This is my son who is alive, and your son is dead,' but that woman says, 'No, your son is dead, and my son is alive.' " ²⁴ The king continued, "Bring me a sword." So they brought the sword to the king. ²⁵ Solomon said, "Cut the living boy in two and give half to one and half to the other."

²⁶ The woman whose son was alive spoke to the king because she felt great compassion for her son. "My lord, give her the living baby," she said, "but please don't have him killed!"

But the other one said, "He will not be mine or yours. Cut him in two!"

²⁷ The king responded, "Give the living baby to the first woman, and don't kill him. She is his mother." ²⁸ All Israel heard about the judgment the king had given, and they stood in awe of the king because they saw that God's wisdom was in him to carry out justice.

4 King Solomon ruled over Israel, ² and these were his officials:

Azariah son of Zadok, priest;
³ Elihoreph and Ahijah the sons of Shisha, secretaries;
Jehoshaphat son of Ahilud, historian;
⁴ Benaiah son of Jehoiada, in charge of the army;
Zadok and Abiathar, priests;
⁵ Azariah son of Nathan, in charge of the deputies;
Zabud son of Nathan, a priest and adviser to the king;
⁶ Ahishar, in charge of the palace; and Adoniram son of Abda, in charge of forced labor.

⁷ Solomon had 12 deputies for all Israel. They provided food for the king and his household; each one made provision for one month out of the year. ⁸ These were their names:

Ben-hur, in the hill country of Ephraim;
⁹ Ben-deker, in Makaz, Shaalbim, Beth-shemesh, and Elon-beth-hanan;
¹⁰ Ben-hesed, in Arubboth (he had Socoh and the whole land of Hepher);
¹¹ Ben-abinadab, in all Naphath-dor (Taphath daughter of Solomon was his wife);
¹² Baana son of Ahilud, in Taanach, Megiddo, and all Beth-shean which is beside Zarethan below Jezreel, from Beth-shean to Abel-meholah, as far as the other side of Jokmeam;
¹³ Ben-geber, in Ramoth-gilead (he had the villages of Jair son of Manasseh, which are in Gilead, and he had the region of Argob, which is in Bashan, 60 great cities with walls and bronze bars);
¹⁴ Ahinadab son of Iddo, in Mahanaim;

¹⁵ Ahimaaz, in Naphtali (he also had married a daughter of Solomon—Basemath); ¹⁶ Baana son of Hushai, in Asher and Bealoth; ¹⁷ Jehoshaphat son of Paruah, in Issachar; ¹⁸ Shimei son of Ela, in Benjamin; ¹⁹ Geber son of Uri, in the land of Gilead, the country of Sihon king of the Amorites and of Og king of Bashan.

There was one deputy in the land of Judah. ²⁰ Judah and Israel were as numerous as the sand by the sea; they were eating, drinking, and rejoicing. ²¹ Solomon ruled over all the kingdoms from the Euphrates River to the land of the Philistines and as far as the border of Egypt. They offered tribute and served Solomon all the days of his life.

²² Solomon's provisions for one day were 150 bushels of fine flour and 300 bushels of meal, ²³ 10 fattened oxen, 20 range oxen, and 100 sheep, besides deer, gazelles, roebucks, and pen-fed poultry, ²⁴ for he had dominion over everything west of the Euphrates from Tiphsah to Gaza and over all the kings west of the Euphrates. He had peace on all his surrounding borders. ²⁵ Throughout Solomon's reign, Judah and Israel lived in safety from Dan to Beer-sheba, each man under his own vine and his own fig tree. ²⁶ Solomon had 40,000 stalls of horses for his chariots, and 12,000 horsemen. ²⁷ Each of those deputies for a month in turn provided food for King Solomon and for everyone who came to King Solomon's table. They neglected nothing. ²⁸ Each man brought the barley and the straw for the chariot teams and the other horses to the required place according to his assignment.

²⁹ God gave Solomon wisdom, very great insight, and understanding as vast as the sand on the seashore. ³⁰ Solomon's wisdom was greater than the wisdom of all the people of the East, greater than all the wisdom of Egypt. ³¹ He was wiser than anyone—wiser than Ethan the Ezrahite, and Heman, Calcol, and Darda, sons of Mahol. His reputation extended to all the surrounding nations. ³² Solomon composed 3,000 proverbs, and his songs numbered 1,005. ³³ He described trees, from the cedar in Lebanon to the hyssop growing out of the wall. He also taught about animals, birds, reptiles, and fish. ³⁴ People came from everywhere, sent by every king on earth who had heard of his wisdom, to listen to Solomon's wisdom.

*P*SALM 72:1-7

¹ God, give Your justice to the king
and Your righteousness to the
king's son.
² He will judge Your people with
righteousness
and Your afflicted ones with
justice.
³ May the mountains bring
prosperity to the people,
and the hills, righteousness.
⁴ May he vindicate the afflicted
among the people,
help the poor,
and crush the oppressor.
⁵ May he continue while the sun
endures,
and as long as the moon,
throughout all generations.
⁶ May he be like rain that falls on
the cut grass,
like spring showers that water the
earth.
⁷ May the righteous flourish in his
days,
and prosperity abound until the
moon is no more.

*P*ROVERBS 15:24-25

²⁴ For the discerning the path of life
leads upward,
so that he may avoid going down
to Sheol.

²⁵ The LORD destroys the house of
the proud,

but He protects the widow's territory.

JOHN 15:11–16:4

¹¹ "I have spoken these things to you so that My joy may be in you and your joy may be complete. ¹² This is My command: love one another as I have loved you. ¹³ No one has greater love than this, that someone would lay down his life for his friends. ¹⁴ You are My friends if you do what I command you. ¹⁵ I do not call you slaves anymore, because a slave doesn't know what his master is doing. I have called you friends, because I have made known to you everything I have heard from My Father. ¹⁶ You did not choose Me, but I chose you. I appointed you that you should go out and produce fruit and that your fruit should remain, so that whatever you ask the Father in My name, He will give you. ¹⁷ This is what I command you: love one another.

¹⁸ "If the world hates you, understand that it hated Me before it hated you. ¹⁹ If you were of the world, the world would love you as its own. However, because you are not of the world, but I have chosen you out of it, the world hates you. ²⁰ Remember the word I spoke to you: 'A slave is not greater than his master.' If they persecuted Me, they will also persecute you. If they kept My word, they will also keep yours. ²¹ But they will do all these things to you on account of My name, because they don't know the One who sent Me. ²² If I had not come and spoken to them, they would not have sin. Now they have no excuse for their sin. ²³ The one who hates Me also hates My Father. ²⁴ If I had not done the works among them that no one else has done, they would not have sin. Now they have seen and hated both Me and My Father. ²⁵ But this happened so that the statement written in their law might be fulfilled: **They hated Me for no reason.**

²⁶ "When the Counselor comes, the One I will send to you from the Father—the Spirit of truth who proceeds from the Father—He will testify about Me. ²⁷ You also will testify, because you have been with Me from the beginning.

16 "I have told you these things to keep you from stumbling. ² They will ban you from the synagogues. In fact, a time is coming when anyone who kills you will think he is offering service to God. ³ They will do these things because they haven't known the Father or Me. ⁴ But I have told you these things so that when their time comes you may remember I told them to you. I didn't tell you these things from the beginning, because I was with you.

Believing—We Receive

Whatever you ask the Father in My name, He will give you.—JOHN 15:16

An important step to help you access the power of the Spirit is to reach out in faith and receive the fullness of all that God has for you. We enter into all God's blessing by faith. As a child of God, you are heir to all that the Father has—Himself. So reach out and take Him now. Jesus said, "If anyone is thirsty, he should come to Me and drink" (Jn 7:37).

Are you thirsty? Then drink. "Now this is the confidence we have before Him: whenever we ask anything according to His will, He hears us. And if we know that He hears whatever we ask, we know that we have what we have asked Him for" (1 Jn 5:14-15). Here are the principles:

Confidence—"the confidence we have before Him."
Conversing—"we ask anything."

Condition—"according to His will."
Conviction—"we know that He hears whatever we ask."
Consequence—"we know that we have."
Follow the principles one by one. Have confidence in the character of God. Converse with Him and tell Him your need—to be filled to overflowing with His Holy Spirit. Believe that the condition is met and your asking is in harmony with His will. Remind yourself that He hears your request and that He is flooding your whole being with His power. Have the boldness to take what is there. Faith will turn it to fact; fact will turn it to feeling. Welcome His coming in whatever manner He comes. You are thirsty—so drink . . . and drink . . . and drink.

Prayer

O Father, how can I thank You enough for bringing me to this moment? It is an end, yet it is a beginning. I know that life is ahead of me, for life is within me. I am grateful beyond words. Amen.

Further Study

Ac 7:42-56; Jn 20:22; Eph 5:18; 3:19
What was said of Stephen?
What is Paul's exhortation?

JUNE 14

1 KINGS 5:1–6:38

5 Hiram king of Tyre sent his servants to Solomon when he heard that he had been anointed king in his father's place, for Hiram had always been friends with David.

² Solomon sent this message to Hiram: ³ "You know my father David was not able to build a temple for the name of the LORD his God. This was because of the warfare all around him until the LORD put his enemies under his feet. ⁴ The LORD my God has now given me rest all around; there is no enemy or crisis. ⁵ So I plan to build a temple for the name of the LORD my God, according to what the LORD promised my father David: 'I will put your son on your throne in your place, and he will build the temple for My name.'

⁶ "Therefore, command that cedars from Lebanon be cut down for me. My servants will be with your servants, and I will pay your servants' wages according to whatever you say, for you know that not a man among us knows how to cut timber like the Sidonians."

⁷ When Hiram heard Solomon's words, he greatly rejoiced and said, "May the

LORD be praised today! He has given David a wise son to be over this great people!" ⁸ Then Hiram sent a reply to Solomon, saying, "I have heard your message; I will do everything you want regarding the cedar and cypress timber. ⁹ My servants will bring the logs down from Lebanon to the sea, and I will make them into rafts to go by sea to the place you indicate. I will break them apart there, and you can take them away. You then can meet my needs by providing my household with food."

¹⁰ So Hiram provided Solomon with all the cedar and cypress timber he wanted, ¹¹ and Solomon provided Hiram with 100,000 bushels of wheat as food for his household and 110,000 gallons of beaten oil. Solomon did this for Hiram year after year.

¹² The LORD gave Solomon wisdom, as He had promised him. There was peace between Hiram and Solomon, and the two of them made a treaty.

¹³ Then King Solomon drafted forced laborers from all Israel; the labor force numbered 30,000 men. ¹⁴ He sent 10,000 to Lebanon each month in shifts; one month they were in Lebanon, two months they were at home. Adoniram was in charge of the forced labor. ¹⁵ Solomon had 70,000 porters and 80,000 stonecutters in the mountains, ¹⁶ not including his 3,300 deputies in charge of the work. They ruled over the people doing the work. ¹⁷ The king commanded them to quarry large, costly stones to lay the foundation of the temple with dressed stones. ¹⁸ So Solomon's builders and Hiram's builders, along with the Gebalites, quarried the stone and prepared the timber and stone for the temple's construction.

6 Solomon began to build the temple for the LORD in the four hundred eightieth year after the Israelites came out from the land of Egypt, in the fourth year of his reign over Israel, in the second month, in the month of Ziv. ² The temple that King Solomon built for the LORD was 90 feet long, 30 feet wide, and 45 feet high. ³ The portico in front of the temple sanctuary was 30 feet long extending across the temple's width, and 15 feet deep in front of the temple. ⁴ He also made windows with beveled frames for the temple.

⁵ He then built a chambered structure along the temple wall, encircling the walls of the temple, that is, the sanctuary and the inner sanctuary. And he made side chambers all around. ⁶ The lowest chamber was seven and a half feet wide, the middle was nine feet wide, and the third was 10 and a half feet wide. He also provided offset ledges for the temple all around the outside so that nothing would be inserted into the temple walls. ⁷ The temple's construction used finished stones cut at the quarry so that no hammer, chisel, or any iron tool was heard in the temple while it was being built.

⁸ The door for the lowest side chamber was on the right side of the temple. They went up a stairway to the middle chamber, and from the middle to the third. ⁹ When he finished building the temple, he paneled it with boards and planks of cedar. ¹⁰ He built the chambers along the entire temple, joined to the temple with cedar beams; each story was seven and a half feet high.

¹¹ The word of the LORD came to Solomon: ¹² "As for this temple you are building—if you walk in My statutes, execute My ordinances, and keep all My commandments by walking in them, I will fulfill My promise to you, which I made to your father David. ¹³ I will live among the Israelites and not abandon My people Israel."

¹⁴ When Solomon finished building the temple, ¹⁵ he paneled the interior temple walls with cedar boards; from the temple floor to the surface of the ceiling he overlaid the interior with wood. He also overlaid the floor with cypress boards. ¹⁶ Then he lined 30 feet of the rear of the temple with cedar boards from the floor to the surface of the ceiling, and he built the interior as an inner sanctuary, the most holy place. ¹⁷ The temple, that is, the sanctuary in front of the most holy place, was 60 feet long. ¹⁸ The cedar paneling inside the temple was carved with ornamental gourds and

flower blossoms. Everything was cedar; not a stone could be seen.

¹⁹ He prepared the inner sanctuary inside the temple to put the ark of the LORD's covenant there. ²⁰ The interior of the sanctuary was 30 feet long, 30 feet wide, and 30 feet high; he overlaid it with pure gold. He also overlaid the cedar altar. ²¹ Next, Solomon overlaid the interior of the temple with pure gold, and he hung gold chains across the front of the inner sanctuary and overlaid it with gold. ²² So he added the gold overlay to the entire temple until everything was completely finished, including the entire altar that belongs in the inner sanctuary.

²³ In the inner sanctuary he made two cherubim 15 feet high out of olive wood. ²⁴ One wing of the first cherub was seven and a half feet long, and the other wing was seven and a half feet long. The wingspan was 15 feet from tip to tip. ²⁵ The second cherub also was 15 feet; both cherubim had the same size and shape. ²⁶ The first cherub's height was 15 feet and so was the second cherub's. ²⁷ Then he put the cherubim inside the inner temple. Since their wings were spread out, the first one's wing touched one wall while the second cherub's wing touched the other wall, and in the middle of the temple their wings were touching wing to wing. ²⁸ He also overlaid the cherubim with gold.

²⁹ He carved all the surrounding temple walls with carved engravings—cherubim, palm trees and flower blossoms—in both the inner and outer sanctuaries. ³⁰ He overlaid the temple floor with gold in both the inner and outer sanctuaries.

³¹ For the entrance of the inner sanctuary, he made olive wood doors. The pillars of the doorposts were five-sided. ³² The two doors were made of olive wood. He carved cherubim, palm trees and flower blossoms on them and overlaid them with gold, hammering gold over the cherubim and palm trees. ³³ In the same way, he made four-sided olive wood doorposts for the sanctuary entrance. ³⁴ The two doors were made of

cypress wood; the first door had two folding sides, and the second door had two folding panels. ³⁵ He carved cherubim, palm trees and flower blossoms on them and overlaid them with gold applied evenly over the carving. ³⁶ He built the inner courtyard with three rows of dressed stone and a row of trimmed cedar beams.

³⁷ The foundation of the LORD's temple was laid in Solomon's fourth year in the month of Ziv. ³⁸ In his eleventh year in the eighth month, in the month of Bul, the temple was completed in every detail and according to every specification. So he built it in seven years.

PSALM 72:8-14

⁸ And may he rule from sea to sea
and from the Euphrates to the
ends of the earth.
⁹ May desert tribes kneel before
him
and his enemies lick the dust.
¹⁰ May the kings of Tarshish and the
coasts and islands bring
tribute,
the kings of Sheba and Seba offer
gifts.
¹¹ And let all kings bow down to
him,
all nations serve him.

¹² For he will rescue the poor who
cry out
and the afflicted who have no
helper.
¹³ He will have pity on the poor and
helpless
and save the lives of the poor.
¹⁴ He will redeem them from
oppression and violence,
for their lives are precious in his
sight.

PROVERBS 15:26-27

²⁶ The LORD detests the plans of an
evil man,
but pleasant words are pure.

27 The one who profits dishonestly
troubles his household,
but the one who hates bribes will
live.

JOHN 16:5-33

5 "But now I am going away to Him
who sent Me, and not one of you asks
Me, 'Where are You going?' 6 Yet, because I have spoken these things to you,
sorrow has filled your heart. 7 Nevertheless, I am telling you the truth. It is
for your benefit that I go away, because
if I don't go away the Counselor will not
come to you. If I go, I will send Him to
you. 8 When He comes, He will convict
the world about sin, righteousness, and
judgment: 9 about sin, because they do
not believe in Me; 10 about righteousness, because I am going to the Father
and you will no longer see Me; 11 and
about judgment, because the ruler of
this world has been judged.

12 "I still have many things to tell you,
but you can't bear them now. 13 When
the Spirit of truth comes, He will guide
you into all the truth. For He will not
speak on His own, but He will speak
whatever He hears. He will also declare
to you what is to come. 14 He will glorify Me, because He will take from what
is Mine and declare it to you. 15 Everything the Father has is Mine. This is
why I told you that He takes from what
is Mine and will declare it to you.

16 "A little while and you will no
longer see Me; again a little while and
you will see Me."

17 Therefore some of His disciples
said to one another, "What is this He
tells us: 'A little while and you will not
see Me; again a little while and you will
see Me'; and, 'because I am going to the
Father'?" 18 They said, "What is this He
is saying, 'A little while'? We don't know
what He's talking about!"

19 Jesus knew they wanted to question Him, so He said to them, "Are you
asking one another about what I said, 'A

little while and you will not see Me;
again a little while and you will see
Me'?

20 "I assure you: You will weep and
wail, but the world will rejoice. You will
become sorrowful, but your sorrow will
turn to joy. 21 When a woman is in labor
she has pain because her time has
come. But when she has given birth to a
child, she no longer remembers the suffering because of the joy that a person
has been born into the world. 22 So you
also have sorrow now. But I will see you
again. Your hearts will rejoice, and no
one will rob you of your joy. 23 In that
day you will not ask Me anything.

"I assure you: Anything you ask the
Father in My name, He will give you.
24 Until now you have asked for nothing
in My name. Ask and you will receive,
that your joy may be complete.

25 "I have spoken these things to you
in figures of speech. A time is coming
when I will no longer speak to you in
figures, but I will tell you plainly about
the Father. 26 In that day you will ask in
My name. I am not telling you that I will
make requests to the Father on your behalf. 27 For the Father Himself loves you,
because you have loved Me and have
believed that I came from God. 28 I came
from the Father and have come into the
world. Again, I am leaving the world and
going to the Father."

29 "Ah!" His disciples said. "Now
You're speaking plainly and not using
any figurative language. 30 Now we
know that You know everything and
don't need anyone to question You.
By this we believe that You came from
God."

31 Jesus responded to them, "Do you
now believe? 32 Look: An hour is coming, and has come, when each of you
will be scattered to his own home, and
you will leave Me alone. Yet I am not
alone, because the Father is with Me.
33 I have told you these things so that in
Me you may have peace. You will have
suffering in this world. Be courageous! I
have conquered the world."

Who Is the Holy Spirit?

He will guide you into all the truth.
For He will not speak on His own.

—JOHN 16:13

The Christian faith is a religion of the Spirit, and unless we are continually filled with His divine resources, then our lives are largely ineffective. If the Scripture places so much emphasis on being possessed by the Holy Spirit, then it follows that we ought to find out everything we can about the One who seeks to indwell us.

I say "who," for the Holy Spirit is not just an impersonal influence, nor is He just a sense of fellowship when we get together, nor an enthusiasm over ideas or causes. It is evident from the personal pronouns used of Him in the Scriptures that the writers viewed Him as a member of the Trinity, equal in honor and status to the Father and the Son. However, the Holy Spirit does not like to draw attention to Himself. In the Old Testament, the Spirit turns the spotlight fully upon the face of the Father. In the New Testament, He turns it fully upon the face of the Son. Never does He focus attention on Himself.

We owe a great deal of our understanding of the Holy Spirit to what Christ said of Him in the Gospels, for there Jesus returns the compliment and occasionally turns the spotlight upon the Holy Spirit, revealing His nature and His ministry. Jesus, in fact, put His disciples through a deliberate course of mental and spiritual training to prepare them for the reception of the Spirit. If we are to understand the Spirit's ministry in our lives, then we must enroll in this course, too.

Prayer

Gracious Father, as I seek to understand who the Holy Spirit is and what He wants to do in my life, give me an eager mind and a receptive spirit. In Jesus' name I pray. Amen.

Further Study

Jn 14:16-31; 15:26-27; Lk 24:49; 11:13
What did Jesus teach about the Holy Spirit?
What does the word "comforter" mean?

JUNE 15

1 KINGS 7:1-51

7 Solomon completed his entire palace-complex after 13 years of construction. ² He built the House of the Forest of Lebanon. It was 150 feet long, 75 feet wide, and 45 feet high on four rows of cedar pillars, with cedar beams on top of the pillars. ³ It was paneled above with cedar at the top of the chambers that rested on 45 pillars, fifteen per row. ⁴ There were three rows of window frames, facing each other in three tiers. ⁵ All the doors and doorposts had rectangular frames, the openings facing each other in three tiers. ⁶ He made the hall of pillars 75 feet long and 45 feet wide. A portico was in front of the pillars, and a canopy with pillars was in front of them. ⁷ He made the Hall of the Throne where he would judge—the Hall of Judgment. It was paneled with cedar from the floor to the rafters. ⁸ Solomon's own palace where he would live, in the other courtyard behind the hall, was of similar construction. And he made a house like this hall for Pharaoh's daughter, his wife.

⁹ All of these buildings were of costly stones, cut to size and sawed with saws on the inner and outer surfaces, from foundation to coping and from the outside to the great courtyard. ¹⁰ The foundation was made of large, costly stones 12 and 15 feet long. ¹¹ Above were also costly stones, cut to size, as well as cedar wood. ¹² Around the great courtyard, as well as the inner courtyard of the LORD's temple and the portico of the temple, were three rows of dressed stone and a row of trimmed cedar beams.

¹³ King Solomon had Hiram brought from Tyre. ¹⁴ He was a widow's son from the tribe of Naphtali, and his father was a man of Tyre, a bronze craftsman. Hiram had great skill, understanding, and knowledge to do every kind of bronze work. So he came to King Solomon and carried out all his work.

¹⁵ He cast two hollow bronze pillars: each 27 feet high and 18 feet in circumference. ¹⁶ He also made two capitals of cast bronze to set on top of the pillars; seven and a half feet was the height of the first capital, and seven and a half feet was also the height of the second capital. ¹⁷ The capitals on top of the pillars had gratings of latticework, wreaths made of chainwork—seven for the first capital and seven for the second.

¹⁸ He made the pillars with two encircling rows of pomegranates on the one grating to cover the capital on top; he did the same for the second capital. ¹⁹ And the capitals on top of the pillars in the portico were shaped like lilies, six feet high. ²⁰ The capitals on the two pillars were also immediately above the rounded surface next to the grating, and 200 pomegranates were in rows encircling each capital. ²¹ He set up the pillars at the portico of the sanctuary: he set up the right pillar and named it Jachin; then he set up the left pillar and named it Boaz. ²² The tops of the pillars were shaped like lilies. Then the work of the pillars was completed.

²³ He made the cast metal reservoir, 15 feet from brim to brim, perfectly round. It was seven and a half feet high and 45 feet in circumference. ²⁴ Ornamental gourds encircled it below the brim, 10 every half yard, completely encircling the reservoir. The gourds were cast in two rows when the reservoir was cast. ²⁵ It stood on 12 oxen, three facing north, three facing west, three facing south, and three facing east. The reservoir was on top of them and all their hindquarters were toward the center. ²⁶ The reservoir was three inches thick, and its rim was fashioned like the brim

of a cup or of a lily blossom. It held 11,000 gallons. ²⁷ Then he made 10 bronze water carts. Each water cart was six feet long, six feet wide, and four and a half feet high. ²⁸ This was the design of the carts: They had frames; the frames were between the cross-pieces, ²⁹ and on the frames between the cross-pieces were lions, oxen, and cherubim. On the cross-pieces there was a pedestal above, and below the lions and oxen were wreaths of hanging work. ³⁰ Each cart had four bronze wheels with bronze axles. Underneath the four corners of the basin were cast supports, each next to a wreath. ³¹ And the water cart's opening inside the crown on top was 18 inches wide. The opening was round, made as a pedestal 27 inches wide. On it were carvings, but their frames were square, not round. ³² There were four wheels under the frames, and the wheel axles were part of the water cart; each wheel was 27 inches tall. ³³ The wheels' design was similar to that of chariot wheels: their axles, rims, spokes, and hubs were all of cast metal. ³⁴ Four supports were at the four corners of each water cart; each support was one piece with the water cart. ³⁵ At the top of the cart was a band nine inches high encircling it; also, at the top of the cart, its braces and its frames were one piece with it. ³⁶ He engraved cherubim, lions, and palm trees on the plates of its braces and on its frames, wherever each had space, with encircling wreaths. ³⁷ In this way he made the 10 water carts using the same casting, dimensions, and shape for all of them.

³⁸ Then he made 10 bronze basins—each basin holding 220 gallons and each was six feet wide—one basin for each of the 10 water carts. ³⁹ He set five water carts on the right side of the temple and five on the left side. He put the reservoir near the right side of the temple toward the southeast. ⁴⁰ Then Hiram made the basins, the shovels, and the sprinkling basins.

So Hiram finished all the work that he was doing for King Solomon on the LORD's temple: ⁴¹ two pillars; bowls for the capitals that were on top of the two pillars; the two gratings for covering both bowls of the capitals that were on top of the pillars; ⁴² the 400 pomegranates for the two gratings (two rows of pomegranates for each grating covering both capitals' bowls on top of the pillars); ⁴³ the 10 water carts; the 10 basins on the water carts; ⁴⁴ the reservoir; the 12 oxen underneath the reservoir; ⁴⁵ and the pots, shovels, and sprinkling basins. All the utensils that Hiram made for King Solomon at the LORD's temple were made of burnished bronze. ⁴⁶ The king had them cast in clay molds in the Jordan Valley between Succoth and Zarethan. ⁴⁷ Solomon left all the utensils unweighed because there were so many; the weight of the bronze was not determined.

⁴⁸ Solomon also made all the equipment in the LORD's temple: the gold altar; the gold table that the bread of the Presence was placed on; ⁴⁹ the pure gold lampstands in front of the inner sanctuary, five on the right and five on the left; the gold flowers, lamps, and tongs; ⁵⁰ the pure gold ceremonial bowls, wick trimmers, sprinkling basins, ladles, and firepans; and the gold hinges for the doors of the inner temple (that is, the most holy place) and for the doors of the temple sanctuary.

⁵¹ So all the work King Solomon did in the LORD's temple was completed. Then Solomon brought in the consecrated things of his father David—the silver, the gold, and the utensils—and put them in the treasuries of the LORD's temple.

....

P SALM 72:15-20

¹⁵ May he live long!
May gold from Sheba be given to him.
May prayer be offered for him continually,
and may he be blessed all day long.
¹⁶ May there be plenty of grain in the land;
may it wave on the tops of the mountains.

May its crops be like Lebanon.
May people flourish in the cities
like the grass of the field.
¹⁷ May his name endure forever;
as long as the sun shines, may his
fame increase.
May all nations be blessed by him
and call him blessed.

¹⁸ May the LORD God, the God of
Israel, be praised,
who alone does wonders.
¹⁹ May His glorious name be praised
forever;
the whole earth is filled with His
glory.
Amen and amen.
²⁰ The prayers of David son of Jesse
are concluded.

PROVERBS 15:28-29

²⁸ The mind of the righteous person
thinks before answering,
but the mouth of the wicked
blurts out evil things.

²⁹ The LORD is far from the wicked,
but He hears the prayer of the
righteous.

JOHN 17:1-26

17 Jesus spoke these things, looked
up to heaven, and said:

Father,
the hour has come.
Glorify Your Son
so that the Son may glorify You,
² for You gave Him authority
over all flesh;
so He may give eternal life
to all You have given Him.
³ This is eternal life:
that they may know You,
the only true God,
and the One You have sent—
Jesus Christ.
⁴ I have glorified You on the earth
by completing the work
You gave Me to do.
⁵ Now, Father, glorify Me

in Your presence
with that glory I had with You
before the world existed.

⁶ I have revealed Your name
to the men You gave Me
from the world.
They were Yours, You gave them
to Me,
and they have kept Your word.
⁷ Now they know that all things
You have given to Me are
from You,
⁸ because the words that You
gave Me,
I have given them.
They have received them
and have known for certain
that I came from You.
They have believed
that You sent Me.
⁹ I pray for them.
I am not praying for the world
but for those You have given Me,
because they are Yours.
¹⁰ All My things are Yours,
and Yours are Mine,
and I have been glorified in them.
¹¹ I am no longer in the world,
but they are in the world,
and I am coming to You.
Holy Father,
protect them by Your name
that You have given Me,
so that they may be one
as We are one.
¹² While I was with them,
I was protecting them
by Your name
that You have given Me.
I guarded them and not one
of them is lost,
except the son of destruction,
so that the Scripture may be
fulfilled.
¹³ Now I am coming to You,
and I speak these things
in the world
so that they may have My joy
completed in them.
¹⁴ I have given them Your word.
The world hated them
because they are not of the world,
as I am not of the world.

15 I am not praying
   that You take them
      out of the world
   but that You protect them
      from the evil one.
16 They are not of the world,
   as I am not of the world.
17 Sanctify them by the truth;
   Your word is truth.
18 As You sent Me into the world,
   I also have sent them
      into the world.
19 I sanctify Myself for them,
   so they also may be sanctified
      by the truth.

20 I pray not only for these,
   but also for those who believe
      in Me
   through their message.
21 May they all be one,
   as You, Father, are in Me and I am
      in You.
   May they also be one in Us,
   so the world may believe
      You sent Me.
22 I have given them the glory
   You have given Me.

   May they be one as We are one.
23 I am in them and You are in Me.
   May they be made
      completely one,
   so the world may know You have
      sent Me
   and have loved them as
      You have loved Me.
24 Father,
   I desire those You have given Me
   to be with Me where I am.
   Then they will see My glory,
   which You have given Me
   because You loved Me
      before the world's
      foundation.
25 Righteous Father!
   The world has not known You.
   However, I have known You,
   and these have known
      that You sent Me.
26 I made Your name known to
      them
   and will make it known,
   so the love
      You have loved Me with
   may be in them and I may be
      in them.

Not Just a "Father"

Holy Father, protect them by Your name.

—JOHN 17:11

John Calvin said: "That God's name should be hallowed is to say that God should have His own honor of which He is so worthy, so that men should never think or speak of Him without the greatest veneration."

One of the things that saddens me about the contemporary Christian church is the way that some believers refer to the Almighty in terms that drag Him down to a "good buddy" relationship. They refer to the great God of creation as "The Man Upstairs" or "My Partner in the Sky." When people talk about God in such low-level terms, they do Him an injustice. And it's not so much the terms but the image of God that lies behind those terms which is the real problem.

We must, of course, strike a balanced note on this issue, for Paul himself teaches us that the Holy Spirit in our hearts prompts us to call God not merely "Father," but "Daddy" (Rm 8:15). Too much of the "Daddy," however, can lead us, if we are not careful, into sloppy sentimentalism. I believe this is why, after the phrase "Our Father," Jesus introduces us to another aspect of God—hallowed, holy, reverenced be His Name. It is right that we think of God in familiar terms such as "Daddy," but it is right also that we remember that our heavenly Father is a God of majestic holiness and unsullied purity. A. W. Tozer was right when he said, "No religion has been greater than its idea of God." Jesus put it into proper focus when He addressed God, not only as Father, but Holy Father.

Prayer

My Father and my God, help me gain a healthy and balanced view of Your person, so that while I enjoy the familiarity of Your Fatherhood, I am exceedingly conscious also of Your holiness. In Jesus' name. Amen.

Further Study

Heb 12:1-14; Ex 15:11; 1 Sm 6:20; Is 6:3; Rv 15:4
Where are we to look?
How do we become holy?

JUNE 16

1 KINGS 8:1-66

8 At that time Solomon assembled the elders of Israel, all the tribal heads and the ancestral leaders of the Israelites before him at Jerusalem in order to bring the ark of the LORD's covenant from Zion, the city of David. ² So all the men of Israel were assembled in the presence of King Solomon in the seventh month, the month of Ethanim at the festival.

³ All the elders of Israel came, and the priests picked up the ark. ⁴ The priests and the Levites brought the ark of the LORD, the tent of meeting, and the holy utensils that were in the tent. ⁵ King Solomon and the entire congregation of Israel, who had gathered around him and were with him in front of the ark, were sacrificing sheep and cattle that could not be counted or numbered, be-

cause there were so many. ⁶ The priests brought the ark of the LORD's covenant to its place, into the inner sanctuary of the temple, to the most holy place beneath the wings of the cherubim. ⁷ For the cherubim were spreading their wings over the place of the ark, so that the cherubim covered the ark and its poles from above. ⁸ The poles were so long that their ends were seen from the holy place in front of the inner sanctuary, but they were not seen from outside the sanctuary; they are there to this day. ⁹ Nothing was in the ark except the two stone tablets that Moses had put there at Horeb, where the LORD made a covenant with the Israelites when they came out of the land of Egypt.

¹⁰ When the priests came out of the holy place, the cloud filled the LORD's temple, ¹¹ and because of the cloud, the priests were not able to continue minis-

tering, for the glory of the LORD filled the temple.

¹² Then Solomon said:

The LORD said that
He would dwell
in thick darkness,
¹³ but I have indeed built
an exalted temple for You,
a place for Your dwelling forever.

¹⁴ The king turned around and blessed the entire congregation of Israel while they were standing. ¹⁵ He said:

May the LORD God of Israel
be praised!
He spoke directly
to my father David,
and He has fulfilled the promise
by His power.
He said,
¹⁶ "Since the day I brought
My people Israel out of Egypt,
I have not chosen a city to build
a temple in
among any of the tribes of Israel,
so that My name would be there.
But I have chosen David to rule
My people Israel."
¹⁷ It was in the desire
of my father David
to build a temple for the name
of the LORD God of Israel.
¹⁸ But the LORD said
to my father David,
"Since it was your desire to build
a temple for My name,
you have done well to have
this desire.
¹⁹ Yet you are not the one
to build it;
instead, your son,
your own offspring,
will build it for My name."
²⁰ The LORD has fulfilled
what He promised.
I have taken the place
of my father David,
and I sit on the throne of Israel,
as the LORD promised.
I have built the temple
for the name of the LORD God
of Israel.

²¹ I have provided a place there
for the ark,
where the LORD's covenant is
that He made with our ancestors
when He brought them out
of the land of Egypt.

²² Then Solomon stood before the altar of the LORD in front of the entire congregation of Israel and spread out his hands toward heaven. ²³ He said:

LORD God of Israel,
there is no God like You
in heaven above or on earth
below,
keeping the gracious covenant
with Your servants who walk
before You
with their whole heart.
²⁴ You have kept what You promised
to Your servant, my father David.
You spoke directly to him
and You fulfilled Your promise
by Your power
as it is today.
²⁵ Therefore, LORD God of Israel,
keep what You promised
to Your servant, my father David:
You will never fail to have a man
to sit before Me on the throne
of Israel,
if only your sons guard their walk
before Me
as you have walked before Me.
²⁶ Now LORD God of Israel,
please confirm what You promised
to Your servant, my father David.

²⁷ But will God indeed live on earth?
Even heaven, the highest heaven,
cannot contain You,
much less this temple I have built.
²⁸ Listen to Your servant's prayer
and his petition,
LORD my God,
so that You may hear the cry
and the prayer
that Your servant prays
before You today,
²⁹ so that Your eyes may watch over
this temple night and day,
toward the place where You said:
My name will be there,

and so that You may hear
the prayer
that Your servant prays
toward this place.
³⁰ Hear the petition of Your servant
and Your people Israel,
which they pray toward this place.
May You hear
in Your dwelling place
in heaven.
May You hear and forgive.

³¹ When a man sins
against his neighbor
and is forced to take an oath,
and he comes to take an oath
before Your altar in this temple,
³² may You hear in heaven and act.
May You judge Your servants,
condemning the wicked
by bringing
what he has done on his own head
and providing justice
for the righteous
by rewarding him according to
his righteousness.

³³ When Your people Israel are de-
feated before an enemy,
because they have sinned
against You,
and they return to You and praise
Your name,
and they pray and plead with You
for mercy in this temple,
³⁴ may You hear in heaven
and forgive the sin
of Your people Israel.
May You restore them
to the land
You gave their ancestors.

³⁵ When the skies are shut
and there is no rain,
because they have sinned
against You,
and they pray toward this place
and praise Your name,
and they turn from their sins
because You are afflicting them,
³⁶ may You hear in heaven
and forgive the sin
of Your servants
and Your people Israel,

so that You may teach them
the good way
they should walk in.
May You send rain on Your land
that You gave Your people
for an inheritance.

³⁷ When there is famine
on the earth,
when there is pestilence,
when there is blight, mildew,
locust, or grasshopper,
when their enemy besieges them
in the region
of their fortified cities,
when there is any plague
or illness,
³⁸ whatever prayer or petition
anyone from Your people Israel
might have—
each man knowing
his own afflictions
and spreading out his hands
toward this temple—
³⁹ may You hear in heaven,
Your dwelling place,
and may You forgive, act,
and repay the man,
according to all his ways,
since You know his heart,
for You alone know
every human heart,
⁴⁰ so that they may fear You
all the days they live on the land
You gave our ancestors.

⁴¹ Even for the foreigner who is not
of Your people Israel
but has come from a distant land
because of Your name—
⁴² for they will hear
of Your great name,
mighty hand,
and outstretched arm,
and will come and pray
toward this temple—
⁴³ may You hear in heaven,
Your dwelling place,
and do according to
all the foreigner asks You for.
Then all the people on earth
will know Your name,
to fear You
as Your people Israel do

and know that this temple
I have built
is called by Your name.

⁴⁴ When Your people go out to fight
against their enemies,
wherever You send them,
and they pray to the LORD
in the direction of the city
You have chosen
and the temple I have built
for Your name,
⁴⁵ may You hear their prayer
and petition in heaven
and uphold their cause.

⁴⁶ When they sin against You—
for there is no one
who does not sin—
and You are angry with them
and hand them over to the enemy,
and their captors deport them
to the enemy's country—
whether distant or nearby—
⁴⁷ and when they come
to their senses
in the land where
they were deported
and repent and petition You
in their captors' land:
"We have sinned and done wrong;
we have been wicked,"
⁴⁸ and when they return to You
with their whole mind
and heart
in the land of their enemies
who took them captive,
and when they pray to You
in the direction of their land
that You gave their ancestors,
the city You have chosen,
and the temple I have built
for Your name,
⁴⁹ may You hear in heaven,
Your dwelling place,
their prayer and petition
and uphold their cause.
⁵⁰ May You forgive Your people
who sinned against You
and all their rebellions
against You,
and may You give
them compassion
in the eyes of their captors,

so that they may be
compassionate to them.
⁵¹ For they are Your people
and Your inheritance;
You brought them out of Egypt,
out of the middle
of an iron furnace.
⁵² May Your eyes be open
to Your servant's petition
and to the petition
of Your people Israel,
listening to them whenever
they call to You.
⁵³ For You, Lord GOD, have set them
apart as Your inheritance
from all the people on earth,
as You spoke
through Your servant Moses
when You brought their ancestors
out of Egypt.

⁵⁴ When Solomon finished praying this entire prayer and petition to the LORD, he got up from kneeling before the altar of the LORD, with his hands spread out toward heaven, ⁵⁵ and he stood and blessed the whole congregation of Israel with a loud voice: ⁵⁶ "May the LORD be praised! He has given rest to His people Israel according to all He has said. Not one of all the good promises He made through His servant Moses has failed. ⁵⁷ May the LORD our God be with us as He was with our ancestors. May He not abandon us or leave us. ⁵⁸ May He incline our hearts toward Him to walk in all His ways and to keep His commands, ordinances, and judgments, which He commanded our ancestors. ⁵⁹ May my words I have made my petition with before the LORD be near the LORD our God day and night, so that He may uphold His servant's cause and the cause of His people Israel, as each day requires, ⁶⁰ and so that all the peoples of the earth may know that the LORD is God. There is no other! ⁶¹ Let your heart be completely devoted to the LORD our God to walk in His ordinances and to keep His commands, as it is today."

⁶² The king and all Israel with him were offering sacrifices in the LORD's presence. ⁶³ Solomon offered a sacrifice

of fellowship offerings to the LORD: 22,000 cattle and 120,000 sheep. In this manner the king and all the Israelites dedicated the LORD's temple.

⁶⁴ On the same day, the king consecrated the middle of the courtyard that was in front of the LORD's temple because that was where he offered the burnt offering, the grain offering, and the fat of the fellowship offerings since the bronze altar before the LORD was too small to accommodate the burnt offerings, the grain offerings, and the fat of the fellowship offerings.

⁶⁵ Solomon and all Israel with him—a great assembly, from the entrance of Hamath to the Brook of Egypt—observed the festival at that time in the presence of the LORD our God, seven days, and seven more days—14 days. ⁶⁶ On the fifteenth day he sent the people away. So they blessed the king and went home to their tents rejoicing and with joyful hearts for all the goodness that the LORD had done for His servant David and for His people Israel.

*P*SALM 73:1-6

¹ God is indeed good to Israel,
    to the pure in heart.
² But as for me, my feet almost
       slipped;
    my steps nearly went astray.
³ For I envied the arrogant;
    I saw the prosperity of the wicked.

⁴ They have an easy time until they
       die,
    and their bodies are well-fed.
⁵ They are not in trouble like
       others;
    they are not afflicted like most
       people.
⁶ Therefore, pride is their necklace,
    and violence covers them like a
       garment.

*P*ROVERBS 15:30-31

³⁰ Bright eyes cheer the heart;
    good news strengthens the bones.

³¹ An ear that listens to life-giving
       rebukes
    will be at home among the wise.

*J*OHN 18:1-24

18 After Jesus had said these things, He went out with His disciples across the Kidron Valley, where there was a garden, and He and His disciples went into it. ² Judas, who betrayed Him, also knew the place, because Jesus often met there with His disciples. ³ So Judas took a company of soldiers and some temple police from the chief priests and the Pharisees and came there with lanterns, torches, and weapons.

⁴ Then Jesus, knowing everything that was about to happen to Him, went out and said to them, "Who is it you're looking for?"

⁵ "Jesus the Nazarene," they answered.

"I am He," Jesus told them.

Judas, who betrayed Him, was also standing with them. ⁶ When He told them, "I am He," they stepped back and fell to the ground.

⁷ Then He asked them again, "Who is it you're looking for?"

"Jesus the Nazarene," they said.

⁸ "I told you I am He," Jesus replied. "So if you're looking for Me, let these men go." ⁹ This was to fulfill the words He had said: "I have not lost one of those You have given Me."

¹⁰ Then Simon Peter, who had a sword, drew it, struck the high priest's slave, and cut off his right ear. (The slave's name was Malchus.)

¹¹ At that, Jesus said to Peter, "Sheathe your sword! Am I not to drink the cup the Father has given Me?"

¹² Then the company of soldiers, the commander, and the Jewish temple police arrested Jesus and tied Him up. ¹³ First they led Him to Annas, for he was the father-in-law of Caiaphas, who was high priest that year. ¹⁴ Caiaphas was the one who had advised the Jews that it was advantageous that one man should die for the people.

¹⁵ Meanwhile Simon Peter was following Jesus, as was another disciple. That

disciple was an acquaintance of the high priest; so he went with Jesus into the high priest's courtyard. ¹⁶ But Peter remained standing outside by the door. So the other disciple, the one known to the high priest, went out and spoke to the girl who was the doorkeeper and brought Peter in.

¹⁷ Then the slave girl who was the doorkeeper said to Peter, "You aren't one of this man's disciples too, are you?"

"I am not!" he said. ¹⁸ Now the slaves and the temple police had made a charcoal fire, because it was cold. They were standing there warming themselves, and Peter was standing with them, warming himself.

¹⁹ The high priest questioned Jesus about His disciples and about His teaching.

²⁰ "I have spoken openly to the world," Jesus answered him. "I have always taught in the synagogue and in the temple complex, where all the Jews congregate, and I haven't spoken anything in secret. ²¹ Why do you question Me? Question those who heard what I told them. Look, they know what I said."

²² When He had said these things, one of the temple police standing by slapped Jesus, saying, "Is this the way you answer the high priest?"

²³ "If I have spoken wrongly," Jesus answered him, "give evidence about the wrong; but if rightly, why do you hit Me?"

²⁴ Then Annas sent Him bound to Caiaphas the high priest.

Paul's Breastplate

"I told you I am He," Jesus replied.
—JOHN 18:8

A feeling, which Satan can arouse in a heart that is unprotected by a spiritual breastplate, is that of a subtle form of discouragement, in which he draws our attention to what other Christians may be saying or thinking about us.

The Apostle Paul was a particular target of Satan in this respect, but see how he used the breastplate of righteousness as his spiritual defense. Paul's background was anti-Christian, and he could never get completely away from that. He had been the most hostile persecutor of the church, and he must therefore have constantly run across families whose loved ones he had put to death. Perhaps there were many who doubted his claim to be an apostle. Some commentators claim that in 1 Corinthians 15:10, he was replying to such an accusation.

How does Paul react to this criticism? Does he succumb to discouragement? Does he say: "What's the use of working my fingers to the bone for these unappreciative people? They don't do anything but hurl recriminations in my face!" This is what the Devil would have liked him to do. But look at what he does. He says: "By God's grace I am what I am" (1 Co 15:10). Can you see what he is doing? He is using the breastplate of righteousness. He is saying, in other words: "I don't need to do anything to protect myself; what I am is what Christ has made me. I am not standing in my own righteousness, I am standing in His."

What a lesson this is in how to use the spiritual breastplate. You and I need to learn this lesson, too.

Prayer

O God, day by day I am catching little glimpses of what You are trying to teach me—that the more I depend on Your righteousness and the less I depend on my own, the better off I will be. Help me to learn it—and learn it completely. Amen.

Further Study

Ps 73:1-28; 2 Co 5:7-21
What brought discouragement to the psalmist?
How did Paul encourage the Corinthians?

JUNE 17

1 KINGS 9:1–10:29

9 When Solomon finished building the temple of the LORD, the royal palace, and all that Solomon desired to do, ²the LORD appeared to Solomon a second time just as He had appeared to him at Gibeon. ³The LORD said to him:

I have heard your prayer and petition you have made before Me. I have consecrated this temple you have built, to put My name there forever; My eyes and My heart will be there at all times.

⁴As for you, if you walk before Me as your father David walked, with integrity of heart and uprightness, doing everything I have commanded you, and if you keep My statutes and ordinances, ⁵I will establish your royal throne over Israel forever, as I promised your father David: You will never fail to have a man on the throne of Israel.

⁶If you or your sons turn away from following Me and do not keep My commands—My statutes that I have set before you—and if you go and serve other gods and worship them, ⁷I will cut off Israel from the land I gave them, and I will reject the temple I have sanctified for My name. Israel will become an object of scorn and ridicule among all the peoples. ⁸Though this temple is now exalted, every passerby will be appalled and will hiss. They will say: Why did the LORD do this to this land and this temple? ⁹Then they will say: Because they abandoned the LORD their God who brought their ancestors out of the land of Egypt. They clung to other gods and worshiped and served them. Because of this, the LORD brought all this ruin on them.

¹⁰At the end of 20 years during which Solomon had built the two houses, the LORD's temple and the royal palace—¹¹Hiram king of Tyre having supplied him with cedar and cypress logs and gold for his every wish—King Solomon gave Hiram 20 towns in the land of Galilee. ¹²So Hiram went out from Tyre to look over the towns that Solomon

688

had given him, but he was not pleased with them. ¹³ So he said, "What are these towns you've given me, my brother?" So he called them the Land of Cabul, as they are still called today. ¹⁴ Now Hiram had sent the king 9,000 pounds of gold.

¹⁵ This is the account of the forced labor that King Solomon had imposed to build the Lord's temple, his own palace, the supporting terraces, the wall of Jerusalem, and Hazor, Megiddo, and Gezer. ¹⁶ Pharaoh king of Egypt had attacked and captured Gezer. He then burned it down, killed the Canaanites who lived in the city, and gave it as a dowry to his daughter, Solomon's wife. ¹⁷ Then Solomon rebuilt Gezer, Lower Beth-horon, ¹⁸ Baalath, Tamar in the Wilderness of Judah, ¹⁹ all the storage cities that belonged to Solomon, the chariot cities, the cavalry cities, and whatever Solomon desired to build in Jerusalem, Lebanon, or anywhere else in the land of his dominion.

²⁰ As for all the peoples who remained of the Amorites, Hittites, Perizzites, Hivites, and Jebusites, who were not Israelites— ²¹ their descendants who remained in the land after them, those whom the Israelites were unable to annihilate—Solomon imposed forced labor on them; it is this way until today. ²² But Solomon did not consign the Israelites to slavery; they were soldiers, his servants, his commanders, his captains, and commanders of his chariots and his cavalry. ²³ These were the deputies who were over Solomon's work: 550 who ruled over the people doing the work.

²⁴ Pharaoh's daughter moved from the city of David to the house that Solomon had built for her; he then built the terraces.

²⁵ Three times a year Solomon offered burnt offerings and fellowship offerings on the altar he had built for the Lord, and he burned incense with them in the Lord's presence. So he completed the temple.

²⁶ King Solomon put together a fleet of ships at Ezion-geber, which is near Eloth on the shore of the Red Sea in the land of Edom. ²⁷ With the fleet, Hiram sent his servants, experienced seamen, along with Solomon's servants. ²⁸ They went to Ophir and acquired gold there—16 tons—and delivered it to Solomon.

10 The queen of Sheba heard about Solomon's fame connected with the name of the Lord and came to test him with difficult questions. ² She came to Jerusalem with a very large retinue, with camels bearing spices, gold in great abundance, and precious stones. She came to Solomon and spoke to him about everything that was on her mind. ³ So Solomon answered all her questions; nothing was too difficult for the king to explain to her. ⁴ When the queen of Sheba observed all of Solomon's wisdom, the palace he had built, ⁵ the food at his table, his servants' residence, his attendants' service and their attire, his cupbearers, and the burnt offerings he offered at the Lord's temple, it took her breath away.

⁶ She said to the king, "The report I heard in my own country about your words and about your wisdom is true. ⁷ But I didn't believe the reports until I came and saw with my own eyes. Indeed, I was not even told half. Your wisdom and prosperity far exceed the report I heard. ⁸ How happy are your men. How happy are these servants of yours, who always stand in your presence hearing your wisdom. ⁹ May the Lord your God be praised! He delighted in you and put you on the throne of Israel, because of the Lord's eternal love for Israel. He has made you king to carry out justice and righteousness."

¹⁰ Then she gave the king four and a half tons of gold, a great quantity of spices, and precious stones. Never again did such a quantity of spices arrive as those the queen of Sheba gave to King Solomon.

¹¹ In addition, Hiram's fleet that carried gold from Ophir brought from Ophir a large quantity of almug wood and precious stones. ¹² The king made the almug wood into steps for the Lord's temple and the king's palace and

into harps and lyres for the singers. Never before had such almug wood come, and the like has not been seen again even to this very day.

[13] King Solomon gave the queen of Sheba her every desire—whatever she asked—besides what he had given her out of his royal bounty. Then she, along with her servants, returned to her own country.

[14] The weight of gold that came to Solomon annually was 25 tons, [15] besides what came from merchants, traders' merchandise, and all the Arabian kings and governors of the land.

[16] King Solomon made 200 large shields of hammered gold; 15 pounds of gold went into each shield. [17] He made 300 small shields of hammered gold; about four pounds of gold went into each shield. The king put them in the House of the Forest of Lebanon.

[18] The king also made a large ivory throne and overlaid it with fine gold. [19] The throne had six steps; there was a rounded top at the back of the throne, armrests on either side of the seat, and two lions standing beside the armrests. [20] Twelve lions were standing there on the six steps, one at each end. Nothing like it had ever been made in any other kingdom.

[21] All of King Solomon's drinking cups were gold, and all the utensils of the House of the Forest of Lebanon were pure gold. There was no silver, since it was considered as nothing in Solomon's time, [22] for the king had ships of Tarshish at sea with Hiram's fleet, and once every three years the ships of Tarshish would arrive bearing gold, silver, ivory, apes, and peacocks.

[23] King Solomon surpassed all the kings of the world in riches and in wisdom. [24] The whole world wanted an audience with Solomon to hear the wisdom that God had put in his heart. [25] Every man would bring his annual tribute: items of silver and gold, clothing, weapons, spices, and horses and mules.

[26] Solomon accumulated 1,400 chariots and 12,000 horsemen and stationed them in the chariot cities and with the king in Jerusalem. [27] The king made sil-ver as common in Jerusalem as stones, and he made cedar as abundant as sycamore in the Judean foothills. [28] Solomon's horses were imported from Egypt and Kue. The king's traders bought them from Kue at the going price. [29] A chariot was imported from Egypt for 15 pounds of silver, and a horse for about four pounds. In the same way, they exported them to all the kings of the Hittites and to the kings of Aram through their agents.

PSALM 73:7-12

7 Their eyes bulge out from fatness;
the imaginations of their hearts
run wild.
8 They mock, and they speak
maliciously;
they arrogantly threaten
oppression.
9 They set their mouths against
heaven,
and their tongues strut across the
earth.
10 Therefore His people turn to them
and drink in their overflowing
waters.
11 They say, "How can God know?
Does the Most High know
everything?"
12 Look at them—the wicked!
They are always at ease, and they
increase their wealth.

PROVERBS 15:32-33

32 Anyone who ignores instruction
despises himself,
but whoever listens to correction
acquires good sense.

33 The fear of the LORD is wisdom's
instruction,
and humility comes before honor.

JOHN 18:25–19:4

[25] Now Simon Peter was standing and warming himself. They said to him, "You aren't one of His disciples too, are you?"

He denied it and said, "I am not!"

²⁶ One of the high priest's slaves, a relative of the man whose ear Peter had cut off, said, "Didn't I see you with Him in the garden?"

²⁷ Peter then denied it again. Immediately a rooster crowed.

²⁸ Then they took Jesus from Caiaphas to the governor's headquarters. It was early morning. They did not enter the headquarters themselves; otherwise they would be defiled and unable to eat the Passover.

²⁹ Then Pilate came out to them and said, "What charge do you bring against this man?"

³⁰ They answered him, "If this man weren't a criminal, we wouldn't have handed Him over to you."

³¹ So Pilate told them, "Take Him yourselves and judge Him according to your law."

"It's not legal for us to put anyone to death," the Jews declared. ³² They said this so that Jesus' words might be fulfilled signifying what sort of death He was going to die.

³³ Then Pilate went back into the headquarters, summoned Jesus, and said to Him, "Are You the King of the Jews?"

³⁴ Jesus answered, "Are you asking this on your own, or have others told you about Me?"

³⁵ "I'm not a Jew, am I?" Pilate replied. "Your own nation and the chief priests handed You over to me. What have You done?"

³⁶ "My kingdom is not of this world," said Jesus. "If My kingdom were of this world, My servants would fight, so that I wouldn't be handed over to the Jews. As it is, My kingdom does not have its origin here."

³⁷ "You are a king then?" Pilate asked.

"You say that I'm a king," Jesus replied. "I was born for this, and I have come into the world for this: to testify to the truth. Everyone who is of the truth listens to My voice."

³⁸ "What is truth?" said Pilate.

After he had said this, he went out to the Jews again and told them, "I find no grounds for charging Him. ³⁹ You have a custom that I release one prisoner to you at the Passover. So, do you want me to release to you the King of the Jews?"

⁴⁰ They shouted back, "Not this man, but Barabbas!" Now Barabbas was a revolutionary.

19 Then Pilate took Jesus and had Him flogged. ² The soldiers also twisted together a crown of thorns, put it on His head, and threw a purple robe around Him. ³ And they repeatedly came up to Him and said, "Hail, King of the Jews!" and were slapping His face.

⁴ Pilate went outside again and said to them, "Look, I'm bringing Him outside to you to let you know I find no grounds for charging Him."

Our God Reigns

"My kingdom is not of this world," said Jesus.
—JOHN 18:36

The kingdom of God was the motif running through everything Jesus taught. However, I pick up many Christian books and magazines today and find that, with one or two exceptions, the kingdom of God is not mentioned. Yet Jesus made it the central note of His preaching and also His praying.

It is time now to ask ourselves: What exactly does Jesus mean when He uses the word "kingdom"? The word for kingdom (*basileia* in the Greek) means "rule" or "reign." The kingdom of God, then, is the rule or reign of God, His sovereignty, for which we are to pray. Jesus spoke of the kingdom as being in the present as well as in the future. In Luke 17:21 He said, "The kingdom of God is among you." Wherever there is a heart that is surrendered to the claims and demands of Jesus Christ, there the kingdom exists. But there is a day coming, says Jesus in Matthew 8:11, when both small and great will sit side by side in the kingdom and realize that in God's order of things there are no favorites.

The Scripture tells us also that God has a kingdom that is established in the heavens (Heb 12:22-28), and the phrase from the Lord's Prayer "Your kingdom come" is a petition for God to let that kingdom extend to every area of the universe where His rule is resisted. We are thus introduced to another great purpose of prayer—transporting to all parts of the universe, across the bridge of prayer, the power that overcomes all sin, all rebellion, and all evil.

Prayer

Father, what can I say? When I see that You have given me the privilege of helping You usher in Your kingdom through prayer, my heart is overwhelmed. What confidence You place in Your redeemed children. May we be worthy of it. For Jesus' sake. Amen.

Further Study

Ps 93; 47:8; Ex 15:18; Mc 4:7; Rm 5:17
What does the psalmist conclude?
What is Paul's expectation?

JUNE 18

1 KINGS 11:1–12:11

11 King Solomon loved many foreign women in addition to Pharaoh's daughter: Moabite, Ammonite, Edomite, Sidonian, and Hittite women ² from the nations that the LORD had told the Israelites about, "Do not intermarry with them, and they must not intermarry with you, because they will turn you away from Me to their gods." Solomon was deeply attached to these women and loved them. ³ He had 700 wives who were princesses and 300 concubines, and they turned his heart away from the LORD.

⁴ When Solomon was old, his wives seduced him to follow other gods. His heart was not completely with the LORD his God, as his father David's heart had been. ⁵ Solomon followed Ashtoreth, the goddess of the Sidonians, and Milcom, the detestable idol of the Ammonites. ⁶ Solomon did what was evil in the LORD's sight, and unlike his father David, he did not completely follow the LORD.

⁷ At that time, Solomon built a high

place for Chemosh, the detestable idol of Moab, and for Milcom, the detestable idol of the Ammonites on the hill across from Jerusalem. [8] He did the same for all his foreign wives, who were burning incense and offering sacrifices to their gods.

[9] The LORD was angry with Solomon, because his heart had turned away from the LORD God of Israel, who had appeared to him twice. [10] He had commanded him about this, so that he would not follow other gods, but Solomon did not do what the LORD had commanded.

[11] Then the LORD said to Solomon, "Since you have done this and did not keep My covenant and My statutes, which I commanded you, I will tear the kingdom away from you and give it to your servant. [12] However, I will not do it during your lifetime because of your father David; I will tear it out of your son's hand. [13] Yet, I will not tear the entire kingdom away from him. I will give one tribe to your son because of my servant David and because of Jerusalem that I chose."

[14] So the LORD raised up Hadad the Edomite as an enemy against Solomon. He was of the royal family in Edom. [15] Earlier, when David was in Edom, Joab, the commander of the army, had gone to bury the dead and had struck down every male in Edom. [16] For Joab and all Israel had remained there six months, until he had killed every male in Edom. [17] Hadad fled to Egypt, along with some Edomites from his father's servants. At the time Hadad was a small boy. [18] Hadad and his men set out from Midian and went to Paran. They took men with them from Paran and went to Egypt, to Pharaoh king of Egypt, who gave Hadad a house, ordered that he be given food, and gave him land. [19] Pharaoh liked Hadad so much that he gave him a wife, the sister of his own wife, Queen Tahpenes. [20] Tahpenes' sister gave birth to Hadad's son Genubath. Tahpenes herself weaned him in Pharaoh's palace, and Genubath lived there along with Pharaoh's sons.

[21] When Hadad heard in Egypt that David rested with his fathers and that Joab, the commander of the army, was dead, Hadad said to Pharaoh, "Let me leave, so I can go to my own country." [22] But Pharaoh asked him, "What do you lack here with me for you to want to go back to your own country?"

"Nothing," he replied, "but please let me leave."

[23] God raised up Rezon son of Eliada as an enemy against Solomon. Rezon had fled from his master Hadadezer king of Zobah [24] and gathered men to himself. He became captain of a raiding party when David killed the Zobaites. He went to Damascus, lived there, and became king in Damascus. [25] Rezon was Israel's enemy throughout Solomon's reign, adding to the trouble Hadad had caused. He ruled over Aram, but he loathed Israel.

[26] Now Solomon's servant, Jeroboam son of Nebat, was an Ephraimite from Zeredah. His widowed mother's name was Zeruah. Jeroboam rebelled against Solomon, [27] and this is the reason he rebelled against the king: Solomon had built the supporting terraces and repaired the opening in the wall of the city of his father David. [28] Now the man Jeroboam was capable, and Solomon noticed the young man because he was getting things done. So he appointed him over the entire labor force of the house of Joseph.

[29] During that time, the prophet Ahijah the Shilonite met Jeroboam on the road as Jeroboam came out of Jerusalem. Now Ahijah had wrapped himself with a new cloak, and the two of them were alone in the open field. [30] Then Ahijah took hold of the new cloak he had on, tore it into 12 pieces, [31] and said to Jeroboam, "Take 10 pieces for yourself, for this is what the LORD God of Israel says: 'I am about to tear the kingdom out of Solomon's hand. I will give you 10 tribes, [32] but one tribe will remain his because of my servant David and because of Jerusalem, the city I chose out of all the tribes of Israel. [33] For they have abandoned Me; they have bowed the knee to Ashtoreth, the goddess of the Sidonians, to Chemosh,

the god of Moab, and to Milcom, the god of the Ammonites. They have not walked in My ways to do right in My eyes and to carry out My statutes and My judgments as his father David did. 34 " 'However, I will not take the whole kingdom from his hand but will let him be ruler all the days of his life because of My servant David, whom I chose and who kept My commandments and My statutes. 35 I will take 10 tribes of the kingdom from his son's hand and give them to you. 36 I will give one tribe to his son, so that My servant David will always have a lamp before Me in Jerusalem, the city I chose for Myself to put My name there. 37 I will appoint you, and you will reign as king over all you want, and you will be king over Israel.

38 " 'After that, if you obey all I command you, walk in My ways, and do what is right in My sight in order to keep My statutes and My commandments as My servant David did, I will be with you. I will build you a lasting dynasty just as I built for David, and I will give you Israel. 39 I will humble David's descendants, because of their unfaithfulness, but not forever.' "

40 Therefore, Solomon tried to kill Jeroboam, but he fled to Egypt, to Shishak king of Egypt, where he remained until Solomon's death.

41 The rest of the events of Solomon's reign, along with all his accomplishments and his wisdom, are written about in the Book of Solomon's Events. 42 The length of Solomon's reign in Jerusalem over all Israel totaled 40 years. 43 Solomon rested with his fathers and was buried in the city of his father David. His son Rehoboam became king in his place.

12 Then Rehoboam went to Shechem, for all Israel had gone to Shechem to make him king. 2 When Jeroboam son of Nebat heard about it, for he was still in Egypt where he had fled from King Solomon's presence, Jeroboam stayed in Egypt. 3 They summoned him, and Jeroboam and the whole assembly of Israel came and spoke to Rehoboam: 4 "Your father made

our yoke harsh. You, therefore, lighten your father's harsh service and the heavy yoke he put on us, and we will serve you."

5 Rehoboam replied, "Go home for three days and then return to me." So the people left. 6 Then King Rehoboam consulted with the elders who had served his father Solomon when he was alive, asking, "How do you advise me to respond to these people?"

7 They replied, "Today if you will be a servant to these people and serve them, and if you respond to them by speaking kind words to them, they will be your servants forever."

8 But he rejected the advice of the elders who had advised him and consulted with the young men who had grown up with him and served him. 9 He asked them, "What message do you advise that we send back to these people who said to me, 'Lighten the yoke your father put on us'?"

10 Then the young men who had grown up with him told him, "This is what you should say to these people who said to you, 'Your father made our yoke heavy, but you, make it lighter on us!' This is what you should tell them: 'My little finger is thicker than my father's loins! 11 Although my father burdened you with a heavy yoke, I will add to your yoke; my father disciplined you with whips, but I will discipline you with barbed whips.' "

𝒫SALM 73:13-20

13 Did I purify my heart
   and wash my hands in innocence
      for nothing?
14 For I am afflicted all day long,
   and punished every morning.
15 If I had decided to say these
      things aloud,
   I would have betrayed Your
      people.
16 When I tried to understand all
      this,
   it seemed hopeless
17 until I entered God's sanctuary.
   Then I understood their destiny.

18 Indeed You put them in slippery
places;
You make them fall into ruin.
19 How suddenly they become a
desolation!
They come to an end, swept away
by terrors.
20 Like one waking from a dream,
Lord, when arising, You will
despise their image.

PROVERBS 16:1-2

16 The reflections of the heart
belong to man,
but the answer of the tongue is
from the LORD.

2 All a man's ways seem right in his
own eyes,
but the LORD weighs the motives.

JOHN 19:5-24

5 Then Jesus came out wearing the
crown of thorns and the purple robe.
Pilate said to them, "Here is the man!"
6 When the chief priests and the temple police saw Him, they shouted,
"Crucify! Crucify!"
Pilate responded, "Take Him and crucify Him yourselves, for I find no
grounds for charging Him."
7 "We have a law," the Jews replied to
him, "and according to that law He must
die, because He made Himself the Son
of God."
8 When Pilate heard this statement,
he was more afraid than ever. 9 He went
back into the headquarters and asked
Jesus, "Where are You from?" But Jesus
did not give him an answer. 10 So Pilate
said to Him, "You're not talking to me?
Don't You know that I have the authority to release You and the authority to
crucify You?"
11 "You would have no authority over
Me at all," Jesus answered him, "if it
hadn't been given you from above. This
is why the one who handed Me over to
you has the greater sin."
12 From that moment Pilate made
every effort to release Him. But the Jews
shouted, "If you release this man, you
are not Caesar's friend. Anyone who
makes himself a king opposes Caesar!"
13 When Pilate heard these words, he
brought Jesus outside. He sat down on
the judge's bench in a place called the
Stone Pavement (but in Hebrew *Gab-
batha*). 14 It was the preparation day for
the Passover, and it was about six in the
morning. Then he told the Jews, "Here
is your king!"
15 But they shouted, "Take Him away!
Take Him away! Crucify Him!"
Pilate said to them, "Should I crucify
your king?"
"We have no king but Caesar!" the
chief priests answered.
16 So then, because of them, he handed Him over to be crucified.
Therefore they took Jesus away.
17 Carrying His own cross, He went out
to what is called Skull Place, which in
Hebrew is called *Golgotha*. 18 There
they crucified Him and two others with
Him, one on either side, with Jesus in
the middle. 19 Pilate also had a sign let-
tered and put on the cross. The inscription was:

> **JESUS THE NAZARENE
> THE KING OF THE JEWS**

20 Many of the Jews read this sign, because the place where Jesus was crucified was near the city, and it was
written in Hebrew, Latin, and Greek.
21 So the chief priests of the Jews said to
Pilate, "Don't write, 'The King of the
Jews,' but that He said, 'I am the King of
the Jews.' "
22 Pilate replied, "What I have written, I have written."
23 When the soldiers crucified Jesus,
they took His clothes and divided them
into four parts, a part for each soldier.
They also took the tunic, which was
seamless, woven in one piece from the
top. 24 So they said to one another,
"Let's not tear it, but toss for it, to see
who gets it." They did this to fulfill the
Scripture that says: **They divided My
clothes among themselves, and they
cast lots for My clothing.** And this is
what the soldiers did.

Love Creating Love

Carrying His own cross, He went out to what
is called Skull Place....There they crucified Him.
—JOHN 19:17-18

Although the love of God is clearly laid out in the Old Testament, why did humankind have to wait so long to have the message spelled out in such clear terms as John uses: "God is love" (1 Jn 4:8)? People could not see this sufficiently clearly until they had looked into the face of Jesus. In the life of Jesus is the clearest revelation that God is love.

So few of us open ourselves to the love of God. We have more fear of Him than we have love for Him. There is, of course, a godly fear (or reverence), but that is not what I mean. If we fail to comprehend how much we are loved by God, then there will be no energy to turn the machinery of our lives in the way they were meant to turn.

Whenever I doubted the love of God as a young Christian, I was told I should go to Calvary. I never quite understood what that meant until one day I complained to God that He could not really love me; if He did, He wouldn't let such things happen as were befalling me. He gave me no answer but showed me the Cross. And as I saw His Son dying there for me, the scales fell from my eyes and I found love for Him flowing out of His love for me. I discovered what 1 John 4:19 means: "We love because He first loved us."

Love for God is not the fruit of labor but the response of our hearts to being loved. It is not something we manufacture; it is something we receive.

Prayer

O God my Father, save me from believing that my problem is "I don't love You enough," when the real problem is "I don't know how much I am loved by You." Let the scales fall from my eyes right now and let me see—really see. In Jesus' name. Amen.

Further Study

Jn 19:16-30; Eph 2:15-16; Col 1:19-22
What is the result of the Cross?
Spend some moments in prayer contemplating the Cross.

JUNE 19

1 KINGS 12:12–13:34

¹² So Jeroboam and all the people came to Rehoboam on the third day, as the king had ordered: "Return to me on the third day." ¹³ Then the king answered the people harshly. He rejected the advice the elders had given him ¹⁴ and spoke to them according to the young men's advice: "My father made your yoke heavy, but I will add to your yoke; my father disciplined you with whips, but I will discipline you with barbed whips."

¹⁵ The king did not listen to the people, because the turn of events came from the LORD to carry out His word, which the LORD had spoken through Ahijah the Shilonite to Jeroboam son of Nebat. ¹⁶ When all Israel saw that the king had not listened to them, the people answered him:

What portion do we have
in David?
We have no inheritance in the son
of Jesse.
Israel, return to your tents;
David, now look
after your own house!

So Israel went to their tents, ¹⁷ but Rehoboam reigned over the Israelites living in the cities of Judah.

¹⁸ Then King Rehoboam sent Adoram, who was in charge of forced labor, but all Israel stoned him to death. King Rehoboam managed to get into the chariot and flee to Jerusalem. ¹⁹ Israel is in rebellion against the house of David until today.

²⁰ When all Israel heard that Jeroboam had come back, they summoned him to the assembly and made him king over all Israel. No one followed the house of David except the tribe of Judah alone. ²¹ When Rehoboam arrived in Jeru-salem, he mobilized 180,000 choice warriors from the entire house of Judah and the tribe of Benjamin to fight against the house of Israel to restore the kingdom to Rehoboam son of Solomon. ²² But a revelation from God came to Shemaiah, the man of God: ²³ "Say to Rehoboam son of Solomon, king of Judah, to the whole house of Judah and Benjamin, and to the rest of the people, ²⁴ 'This is what the LORD says: You are not to march up and fight against your brothers, the Israelites. Each of you must return home, for I have done this.' "

So they listened to what the LORD said and went back as He had told them.

²⁵ Jeroboam built Shechem in the hill country of Ephraim and lived there. From there he went out and built Penuel. ²⁶ Jeroboam said to himself, "The way things are going now, the kingdom might return to the house of David. ²⁷ If these people regularly go to offer sacrifices in the LORD's temple in Jerusalem, the heart of these people will return to their lord, Rehoboam king of Judah. They will murder me and go back to the king of Judah." ²⁸ So the king sought advice.

Then he made two gold calves, and he said to the people, "Going to Jerusalem is too difficult for you. Israel, here is your God who brought you out of the land of Egypt." ²⁹ He set up one in Bethel, and put the other in Dan. ³⁰ This led to sin; the people walked in procession before one of the calves all the way to Dan.

³¹ Jeroboam also built shrines on the high places and set up priests from every class of people who were not Levites. ³² Jeroboam made a festival in the eighth month on the fifteenth day of the month, like the festival in Judah. He offered sacrifices on the altar; he made this offering in Bethel to sacrifice to the calves he had set up. He also stationed

in Bethel the priests for the high places he had set up. ³³ He offered sacrifices on the altar he had set up in Bethel on the fifteenth day of the eighth month, the month he had decided on his own. He made a festival for the Israelites, offered sacrifices on the altar, and burned incense.

13 A man of God came from Judah to Bethel by a revelation from the LORD while Jeroboam was standing beside the altar to burn incense. ² The man of God cried out against the altar by a revelation from the LORD: "Altar, altar, this is what the LORD says, 'A son will be born to the house of David, named Josiah, and he will sacrifice on you the priests of the high places who are burning incense on you. Human bones will be burned on you.' " ³ He gave a sign that day. He said, "This is the sign that the LORD has spoken: 'The altar will now be ripped apart, and the ashes that are on it will be spilled out.' "

⁴ When the king heard the word that the man of God had cried out against the altar at Bethel, Jeroboam stretched out his hand from the altar and said, "Arrest him!" But the hand he stretched out against him withered, and he could not pull it back to himself. ⁵ The altar was ripped apart, and the ashes spilled off the altar, according to the sign that the man of God had given by the word of the LORD.

⁶ Then the king responded to the man of God, "Please plead for the favor of the LORD your God and pray for me so that my hand may be restored to me." So the man of God pleaded for the favor of the LORD, and the king's hand was restored to him and became as it had been at first.

⁷ Then the king declared to the man of God, "Come home with me, refresh yourself, and I'll give you a reward."

⁸ But the man of God replied, "If you were to give me half your house, I still wouldn't go with you, and I wouldn't eat bread or drink water in this place, ⁹ for this is what I was commanded by the word of the LORD: 'You must not eat bread or drink water or go back the way you came.' " ¹⁰ So he went another way; he did not go back by the way he had come to Bethel.

¹¹ Now a certain old prophet was living in Bethel. His son came and told him all the deeds that the man of God had done that day in Bethel. His sons also told their father the words that he had spoken to the king. ¹² Then their father said to them, "Which way did he go?" His sons had seen the way taken by the man of God who had come from Judah. ¹³ Then he said to his sons, "Saddle the donkey for me." So they saddled the donkey for him, and he got on it. ¹⁴ He followed the man of God and found him sitting under an oak tree. He asked him, "Are you the man of God who came from Judah?"

"I am," he said.

¹⁵ Then he said to him, "Come home with me and eat bread."

¹⁶ But he answered, "I cannot go back with you, eat bread, or drink water with you in this place, ¹⁷ for a message came to me by the word of the LORD: 'You must not eat bread or drink water there or go back by the way you came.' "

¹⁸ He said to him, "I am also a prophet like you. An angel spoke to me by the word of the LORD: 'Bring him back with you to your house so that he may eat bread and drink water.' " The old prophet deceived him, ¹⁹ and the man of God went back with him, ate bread in his house, and drank water.

²⁰ While they were sitting at the table, the word of the LORD came to the prophet who had brought him back, ²¹ and the prophet cried out to the man of God who had come from Judah, "This is what the LORD says: 'Because you rebelled against the command of the LORD and did not keep the commandment that the LORD your God commanded you, ²² but you went back and ate bread and drank water in the place that He said to you: Do not eat bread and do not drink water, your corpse will never reach the grave of your fathers.' "

²³ So after he had eaten bread and after he had drunk, the old prophet saddled the donkey for the prophet he had brought back. ²⁴ When he left, a lion

met him along the way and killed him. His corpse was thrown on the road, and the donkey was standing beside it; the lion was standing beside the corpse too. ²⁵ There were men passing by who saw the corpse thrown on the road and the lion standing beside it, and they went and spoke about it in the city where the old prophet lived. ²⁶ When the prophet who had brought him back from his way heard about it, he said, "He is the man of God who disobeyed the command of the Lord. The Lord has given him to the lion, and it has mauled him and killed him, according to the word of the Lord that He spoke to him." ²⁷ Then the old prophet instructed his sons, "Saddle the donkey for me." They saddled it, ²⁸ and he went and found the corpse of the man of God thrown on the road with the donkey and the lion standing beside the corpse. The lion had not eaten the corpse or mauled the donkey. ²⁹ So the prophet lifted the corpse of the man of God and laid it on the donkey and brought it back. The old prophet came into the city to mourn and to bury him. ³⁰ Then he laid the corpse in his own grave, and they mourned over him: "Oh, my brother!" ³¹ After he had buried him, he said to his sons, "When I die, you must bury me in the grave where the man of God is buried; lay my bones beside his bones, ³² for the word that he cried out by a revelation from the Lord against the altar in Bethel and against all the shrines of the high places in the cities of Samaria is certain to happen." ³³ After all this Jeroboam did not repent of his evil way but again set up priests from every class of people for the high places. Whoever so desired it, he ordained, and they became priests of the high places. ³⁴ For the house of Jeroboam, this was the sin that caused it to be wiped out and annihilated from the face of the earth.

*P*SALM 73:21-28

21 When I became embittered
    and my innermost being was
        wounded,

22 I was a fool and didn't understand;
    I was an unthinking animal toward
        You.
23 Yet I am always with You;
    You hold my right hand.
24 You guide me with Your counsel,
    and afterward You will take me up
        in glory.
25 Whom do I have in heaven but
        You?
    And I desire nothing on earth but
        You.
26 My flesh and my heart may fail,
    but God is the strength of my
        heart, my portion forever.
27 Those far from You will certainly
        perish;
    You destroy all who are unfaithful
        to You.
28 But as for me, God's presence is
        my good.
    I have made the Lord God my
        refuge,
    so I can tell about all You do.

*P*ROVERBS 16:3-4

3 Commit your activities to the Lord
   and your plans will be achieved.

4 The Lord has prepared everything
       for His purpose—
   even the wicked for the day of
       disaster.

*J*OHN 19:25-42

²⁵ Standing by the cross of Jesus were His mother, His mother's sister, Mary the wife of Clopas, and Mary Magdalene. ²⁶ When Jesus saw His mother and the disciple He loved standing there, He said to His mother, "Woman, here is your son." ²⁷ Then He said to the disciple, "Here is your mother." And from that hour the disciple took her into his home. ²⁸ After this, when Jesus knew that everything was now accomplished that the Scripture might be fulfilled, He said, "I'm thirsty!" ²⁹ A jar full of sour wine was sitting there; so they fixed a sponge full of sour wine on hyssop and held it up to His mouth.

³⁰ When Jesus had received the sour wine, He said, "It is finished!" Then bowing His head, He gave up His spirit. ³¹ Since it was the preparation day, the Jews did not want the bodies to remain on the cross on the Sabbath (for that Sabbath was a special day). They requested that Pilate have the men's legs broken and that their bodies be taken away. ³² So the soldiers came and broke the legs of the first man and of the other one who had been crucified with Him. ³³ When they came to Jesus, they did not break His legs since they saw that He was already dead. ³⁴ But one of the soldiers pierced His side with a spear, and at once blood and water came out. ³⁵ He who saw this has testified so that you also may believe. His testimony is true, and he knows he is telling the truth. ³⁶ For these things happened so that the Scripture would be fulfilled:

Not one of His bones will be broken. ³⁷ Also, another Scripture says: They will look at the One they pierced.

³⁸ After this, Joseph of Arimathea, who was a disciple of Jesus—but secretly because of his fear of the Jews—asked Pilate that he might remove Jesus' body. Pilate gave him permission, so he came and took His body away. ³⁹ Nicodemus (who had previously come to Him at night) also came, bringing a mixture of about 75 pounds of myrrh and aloes. ⁴⁰ Then they took Jesus' body and wrapped it in linen cloths with the aromatic spices, according to the burial custom of the Jews. ⁴¹ There was a garden in the place where He was crucified. A new tomb was in the garden; no one had yet been placed in it. ⁴² They placed Jesus there because of the Jewish preparation and since the tomb was nearby.

Is There an Answer?

Yet I am always with You; You hold my right hand. You guide me with Your counsel.—PSALM 73:23-24

A devoted Christian man I knew married a widow who had a teenage son. The son was deeply rebellious, and the man, now his stepfather, grew very resentful toward him. One night, while the mother was away, they shared the same bedroom, and the man woke up in the middle of the night, finding himself trying to push the young man out of the bedroom window. Another push, and he would have fallen and been seriously injured. What had happened? The man told me that he had gone to sleep that night with a great bitterness in his heart toward his stepson. The subconscious mind is very receptive at the moment one drops into sleep, and the resentment his subconscious mind received precipitated an act which would have horrified him when conscious.

A little girl said, "I want to be good, but I don't want to be obedient." Her conscious mind wanted her to be known as good, but her subconscious mind, where self-centeredness was the driving urge, did not want to obey anything except itself. The minister who preaches full surrender to God yet yearns to be praised and complimented is suffering from a division between the conscious and the subconscious mind. The person who works hard at helping others but does it to meet some inner need rather than truly giving himself to the needs of others is inwardly divided. The question is: can the subconscious be reached by the Holy Spirit? With all my heart, I say it can. In the Holy Spirit, we are provided with a divine presence that redeems and unifies the whole personality.

Prayer

Father, I am tired of inward division that threatens to tear me apart. Tame these wild horses within me that I might know Your perfect peace in every part of my being. For Jesus' sake. Amen.

Further Study

Jms 1; Rm 7:22-23, 8:6; Is 26:3; Php 4:8
What makes a man unstable?
What brings stability and peace?

JUNE 20

I KINGS 14:1–15:34

14 At that time Abijah son of Jeroboam became sick. ² Jeroboam said to his wife, "Go disguise yourself, so they won't know that you're Jeroboam's wife, and go to Shiloh. Ahijah the prophet is there; it was he who told about me becoming king over this people. ³ Take with you 10 loaves of bread, some cakes, and a jar of honey, and go to him. He will tell you what will happen to the boy."

⁴ Jeroboam's wife did that: she went to Shiloh and arrived at Ahijah's house. Ahijah could not see; his gaze was fixed due to his age. ⁵ But the LORD had said to Ahijah, "Jeroboam's wife is coming soon to ask you about her son, for he is sick. You are to say such and such to her. When she arrives, she will be disguised."

⁶ When Ahijah heard the sound of her feet entering the door, he said, "Come in, wife of Jeroboam! Why are you disguised? I have bad news for you. ⁷ Go tell Jeroboam, 'This is what the LORD God of Israel says: I raised you up from among the people, appointed you ruler over My people Israel, ⁸ tore the kingdom away from the house of David, and gave it to you. But you were not like My servant David, who kept My commandments and followed Me with all of his heart, doing only what is right in My eyes. ⁹ You behaved more wickedly than all who were before you. In order to provoke Me, you have proceeded to make for yourself other gods and cast images, but you have flung Me behind your back. ¹⁰ Because of all this, I am about to bring disaster on the house of Jeroboam:

I will eliminate all of
    Jeroboam's males,
both slave and free, in Israel;
I will sweep away the house
    of Jeroboam
as one sweeps away dung
    until it is all gone!
¹¹ Anyone who belongs to Jeroboam
    and dies in the city,
the dogs will eat,
and anyone who dies in the field,
the birds of the sky will eat,
for the LORD has said it!'

[12] "As for you, get up and go to your house. When your feet enter the city, the boy will die. [13] All Israel will mourn for him and bury him, for this one alone out of Jeroboam's sons will come to the grave, because in him alone out of the house of Jeroboam something was found pleasing to the LORD God of Israel. [14] The LORD will raise up for Himself a king over Israel, who will eliminate the house of Jeroboam. This is the day, yes, even today! [15] For the LORD will strike Israel and the people will shake as a reed shakes in water. He will uproot Israel from this good soil that He gave to their forefathers. He will scatter them beyond the Euphrates because they made their Asherah poles, provoking the LORD. [16] He will give up Israel, because of Jeroboam's sins that he committed and caused Israel to commit."

[17] Then Jeroboam's wife got up and left and went to Tirzah. As she was crossing the threshold of the house, the boy died. [18] He was buried, and all Israel mourned for him, according to the word of the LORD He had spoken through His servant Ahijah the prophet. [19] As for the rest of the events of Jeroboam's reign, how he waged war and how he reigned, note that they are written about in the Historical Record of Israel's Kings. [20] The length of Jeroboam's reign was 22 years. He rested with his fathers, and his son Nadab became king in his place.

[21] Now Rehoboam, Solomon's son, reigned in Judah. Rehoboam was 41 years old when he became king; he reigned 17 years in Jerusalem, the city the LORD had chosen from all the tribes of Israel to put His name. Rehoboam's mother's name was Naamah the Ammonite. [22] Judah did what was evil in the LORD's eyes. They provoked Him to jealous anger more than all that their ancestors had done with the sins they committed. [23] They also built for themselves high places, sacred pillars, and Asherah poles on every high hill and under every green tree; [24] there were even male shrine prostitutes in the land. They imitated all the abominations of the nations the LORD had dispossessed before the Israelites.

[25] In the fifth year of King Rehoboam, Shishak king of Egypt went to war against Jerusalem. [26] He seized the treasuries of the LORD's temple and the treasuries of the royal palace. He took everything. He took all the gold shields that Solomon had made. [27] King Rehoboam made bronze shields in their place and committed them into the care of the captains of the royal escorts who guarded the entrance to the king's palace. [28] Whenever the king entered the LORD's temple, the royal escorts would carry the shields, then they would take them back to the royal escorts' armory.

[29] The rest of the events of Rehoboam's reign, along with all his accomplishments, are written about in the Historical Record of Judah's Kings. [30] There was war between Rehoboam and Jeroboam throughout their reigns. [31] Rehoboam rested with his fathers and was buried with his fathers in the city of David. His mother's name was Naamah the Ammonite. His son Abijam became king in his place.

15 In the eighteenth year of Israel's King Jeroboam son of Nebat, Abijam became king over Judah; [2] he reigned three years in Jerusalem. His mother's name was Maacah daughter of Abishalom.

[3] Abijam walked in all the sins his father had done before him, and he was not completely devoted to the LORD his God as his ancestor David had been. [4] But because of David, the LORD his God gave him a lamp in Jerusalem to raise up his son after him and to establish Jerusalem [5] because David did what was right in the LORD's eyes, and he did not turn aside from anything He had commanded him all the days of his life, except in the matter of Uriah the Hittite.

[6] There had been war between Rehoboam and Jeroboam all the days of Rehoboam's life. [7] The rest of the events of Abijam's reign, along with all his accomplishments, are written about in the Historical Record of Judah's Kings.

There was also war between Abijam and Jeroboam. ⁸ Abijam rested with his fathers and was buried in the city of David. His son Asa became king in his place.

⁹ In the twentieth year of Israel's King Jeroboam, Asa became king of Judah; ¹⁰ he reigned 41 years in Jerusalem. His grandmother's name was Maacah daughter of Abishalom.

¹¹ Asa did what was right in the LORD's eyes, as his ancestor David had done. ¹² He banished the male shrine prostitutes from the land and removed all of the idols that his fathers had made. ¹³ He also removed his grandmother Maacah from being queen mother because she had made an obscene image of Asherah. Asa chopped down her obscene image and burned it in the Kidron Valley. ¹⁴ The high places were not taken away; but Asa's heart was completely with the LORD his entire life. ¹⁵ He brought his father's consecrated gifts and his own consecrated gifts into the LORD's temple: silver, gold, and utensils.

¹⁶ There was war between Asa and Baasha king of Israel throughout their reigns. ¹⁷ Israel's King Baasha went to war against Judah. He built Ramah in order to deny anyone access to Judah's King Asa. ¹⁸ So Asa withdrew all the silver and gold that remained in the treasuries of the LORD's temple and the treasuries of the royal palace and put it into the hands of his servants. Then King Asa sent them to Ben-hadad son of Tabrimmon son of Hezion king of Aram who lived in Damascus, saying, ¹⁹ "There is a treaty between me and you, between my father and your father. Look, I have sent you a gift of silver and gold. Go and break your treaty with Baasha king of Israel so that he will withdraw from me."

²⁰ Ben-hadad listened to King Asa and sent the commanders of his armies against the cities of Israel. He attacked Ijon, Dan, Abel-beth-maacah, all Chinneroth, and the whole land of Naphtali. ²¹ When Baasha heard about it, he quit building Ramah and stayed in Tirzah. ²² Then King Asa gave a command to everyone without exception in Judah,

and they carried away the stones of Ramah and the timbers Baasha had built it with. Then King Asa built Geba of Benjamin and Mizpah with them.

²³ The rest of all the events of Asa's reign, along with all his might, all his accomplishments, and the cities he built, are written about in the Historical Record of Judah's Kings. But in his old age he developed a disease in his feet. ²⁴ Then Asa rested with his fathers and was buried in the city of his forefather David. His son Jehoshaphat became king in his place.

²⁵ Nadab son of Jeroboam became king over Israel in the second year of Judah's King Asa; he reigned over Israel two years. ²⁶ Nadab did what was evil in the LORD's sight and followed the example of his father and the sin he had caused Israel to commit.

²⁷ Then Baasha son of Ahijah of the house of Issachar conspired against Nadab, and Baasha struck him down at Gibbethon of the Philistines while Nadab and all Israel were besieging Gibbethon. ²⁸ In the third year of Judah's King Asa, Baasha killed Nadab and reigned in his place.

²⁹ When Baasha became king, he struck down the entire house of Jeroboam. He did not leave Jeroboam anyone alive until he had destroyed his family according to the word of the LORD He had spoken through His servant Ahijah the Shilonite. ³⁰ This was because of Jeroboam's sins he had committed and had caused Israel to commit in the provocation he had provoked the LORD God of Israel with.

³¹ The rest of the events of Nadab's reign, along with all his accomplishments, are written about in the Historical Record of Israel's Kings. ³² There was war between Asa and Baasha king of Israel throughout their reigns.

³³ In the third year of Judah's King Asa, Baasha son of Ahijah became king over all Israel at Tirzah; he reigned 24 years. ³⁴ He did what was evil in the LORD's sight and followed the example of Jeroboam and the sin he had caused Israel to commit.

PSALM 74:1-6

1 Why have You rejected us forever,
God?
Why does Your anger burn against
the sheep of Your pasture?
2 Remember Your congregation,
which You purchased long ago
and redeemed as the tribe for
Your own possession.
Remember Mount Zion where You
dwell.
3 Make Your way to the everlasting
ruins,
to all that the enemy has
destroyed in the sanctuary.
4 Your adversaries roared in the
meeting place where You met
with us.
They set up their emblems as
signs.
5 It was like men in a thicket of
trees,
wielding axes,
6 then smashing all the carvings
with hatchets and picks.

PROVERBS 16:5-7

5 Everyone with a proud heart is
detestable to the LORD;
be assured, he will not go
unpunished.

6 Wickedness is atoned for by
loyalty and faithfulness,
and one turns from evil by the
fear of the LORD.

7 When a man's ways please the
LORD,
He makes even his enemies to be
at peace with him.

JOHN 20:1-20

20 On the first day of the week
Mary Magdalene came to the
tomb early, while it was still dark. She
saw that the stone had been removed
from the tomb. 2 So she ran to Simon
Peter and to the other disciple, the one

Jesus loved, and said to them, "They
have taken the Lord out of the tomb,
and we don't know where they have put
Him!"
3 At that, Peter and the other disciple
went out, heading for the tomb. 4 The
two were running together, but the
other disciple outran Peter and got to
the tomb first. 5 Stooping down, he saw
the linen cloths lying there, yet he did
not go in. 6 Then, following him, Simon
Peter came also. He entered the tomb
and saw the linen cloths lying there.
7 The wrapping that had been on His
head was not lying with the linen cloths
but was folded up in a separate place by
itself. 8 The other disciple, who had
reached the tomb first, then entered
the tomb, saw, and believed. 9 For they
still did not understand the Scripture
that He must rise from the dead. 10 Then
the disciples went home again.
11 But Mary stood outside facing the
tomb, crying. As she was crying, she
stooped to look into the tomb. 12 She
saw two angels in white sitting there,
one at the head and one at the feet,
where Jesus' body had been lying.
13 They said to her, "Woman, why are
you crying?"
"Because they've taken away my
Lord," she told them, "and I don't know
where they've put Him." 14 Having said
this, she turned around and saw Jesus
standing there, though she did not
know it was Jesus.
15 "Woman," Jesus said to her, "why
are you crying? Who is it you are looking for?"
Supposing He was the gardener, she
replied, "Sir, if you've removed Him,
tell me where you've put Him, and I will
take Him away."
16 Jesus said, "Mary."
Turning around, she said to Him in
Hebrew, *"Rabbouni!"*—which means
"Teacher."
17 "Don't cling to Me," Jesus told her,
"for I have not yet ascended to the
Father. But go to My brothers and tell
them that I am ascending to My Father
and your Father—to My God and your
God."
18 Mary Magdalene went and an-

nounced to the disciples, "I have seen the Lord!" And she told them what He had said to her.

¹⁹ In the evening of that first day of the week, the disciples were gathered together with the doors locked because of their fear of the Jews. Then Jesus came, stood among them, and said to them, "Peace to you!"

²⁰ Having said this, He showed them His hands and His side. So the disciples rejoiced when they saw the Lord.

The Forgotten Father

I am ascending to My Father and your Father—
to My God and your God.
—JOHN 20:17

The theme in this verse—My Father and your Father—is one that I view as among the greatest I have ever tackled, and I approach it with the earnest prayer that as the Father revealed Himself through the "Word made flesh" (God's most perfect self-revelation), so He might reveal Himself also through the words that are being written about Him here.

It has been said that the Christian faith is essentially a Father movement. Yet theologian Tom Smail suggested that in today's church the Father is forgotten in precisely the same way that the Spirit was forgotten before the growth of the Pentecostal and charismatic movements. Can this be true? Are we in danger of focusing so much on the work of the Holy Spirit that we forget the Father? I think that in some sections of the church there are evidences that this is the case. We hear much about the Son and much about the Spirit, but how much do we hear about the Father? When our Lord Jesus Christ lived on this earth, He fulfilled many roles—Savior, Shepherd, Deliverer, Healer, Prophet, Life-giver—but the overall purpose of His being here was to restore us to relationship with the Father. Some of the greatest words He ever uttered are the words of our text for today: "I am ascending to My Father and your Father." Your Father.

Let those words sing their way into your consciousness. Through our Lord's redemptive work on the cross, God is not just the Father of Jesus. He is our Father too.

Prayer

O God my Father, over these coming weeks give me a new understanding of what it means to have You as my Father. I am standing on the shore of a great and wondrous truth. Help me launch out into the deep. In Jesus' name. Amen.

Further Study

Ac 17:22-30; Dt 32:18; Ps 44:20-21; Is 17:10-11
In what way is God unknown today?
What are our modern-day idol substitutes?

JUNE 21

I KINGS 16:1–17:24

16 Now the word of the LORD came to Jehu son of Hanani against Baasha: ² "Because I raised you up from the dust and made you ruler over My people Israel, but you have walked in the way of Jeroboam and have caused My people Israel to sin, provoking Me with their sins, ³ take note: I will sweep away Baasha and his house, and I will make your house like the house of Jeroboam son of Nebat:

⁴ Anyone who belongs to Baasha
   and dies in the city,
 the dogs will eat,
 and anyone who is his and dies
   in the field,
 the birds of the sky will eat.

⁵ The rest of the events of Baasha's reign, along with all his accomplishments and might, are written about in the Historical Record of Israel's Kings. ⁶ Baasha rested with his fathers and was buried in Tirzah. His son Elah became king in his place. ⁷ Through the prophet Jehu son of Hanani the word of the LORD also came against Baasha and against his house because of all the evil he had done in the LORD's sight, provoking Him with the work of his hands and being like the house of Jeroboam, and because Baasha had struck down the house of Jeroboam.

⁸ In the twenty-sixth year of Judah's King Asa, Elah son of Baasha became king over Israel in Tirzah; he reigned two years. ⁹ His servant Zimri, commander of half his chariots, conspired against him while Elah was in Tirzah drinking himself drunk in the house of Arza, who was in charge of the household at Tirzah. ¹⁰ In the twenty-seventh year of Judah's King Asa, Zimri went in, struck Elah down, and killed him. Then Zimri became king in his place.

¹¹ When he became king, as soon as he was seated on his throne, Zimri struck down the entire house of Baasha. He did not leave him a single male, whether of his kinsmen or his friends. ¹² So Zimri exterminated the entire house of Baasha, according to the word of the LORD He had spoken against Baasha through Jehu the prophet, ¹³ because of all the sins of Baasha and the sins of his son Elah, which they committed and caused Israel to commit, provoking the LORD God of Israel with their worthless idols. ¹⁴ The rest of the events of Elah's reign, along with all his accomplishments, are written about in the Historical Record of Israel's Kings.

¹⁵ In the twenty-seventh year of Judah's King Asa, Zimri became king for seven days in Tirzah. Now the troops were encamped against Gibbethon of the Philistines. ¹⁶ When the encamped troops heard that Zimri had not only conspired but had also struck down the king, then all Israel made Omri, the army commander, king over Israel that very day in the camp. ¹⁷ Omri along with all Israel marched up from Gibbethon and besieged Tirzah. ¹⁸ When Zimri saw that the city was captured, he entered the citadel of the royal palace and burned down the royal palace over himself. He died ¹⁹ because of his sin he committed by doing what was evil in the LORD's sight and by following the example of Jeroboam and the sin he caused Israel to commit.

²⁰ The rest of the events of Zimri's reign, along with the conspiracy that he instigated, are written about in the Historical Record of Israel's Kings. ²¹ At that time the people of Israel were split in half: half the people followed Tibni son of Ginath, to make him king, and

706

half followed Omri. ²² However, the people who followed Omri proved stronger than those who followed Tibni son of Ginath. So Tibni died and Omri became king.

²³ In the thirty-first year of Judah's King Asa, Omri became king over Israel; he reigned 12 years. He reigned six years in Tirzah, ²⁴ then he bought the hill of Samaria from Shemer for 150 pounds of silver, and he built up the hill. He named the city he built Samaria based on the name Shemer, the owner of the hill.

²⁵ Omri did what was evil in the LORD's sight; he did more evil than all who were before him. ²⁶ He followed the example of Jeroboam son of Nebat and the sins he caused Israel to commit, provoking the LORD God of Israel with their worthless idols. ²⁷ The rest of the events of Omri's reign, along with his accomplishments and the might he exercised, are written about in the Historical Record of Israel's Kings. ²⁸ Omri rested with his fathers and was buried in Samaria. His son Ahab became king in his place.

²⁹ Ahab son of Omri became king over Israel in the thirty-eighth year of Judah's King Asa; Ahab son of Omri reigned over Israel in Samaria 22 years. ³⁰ But Ahab son of Omri did what was evil in the LORD's sight more than all who were before him. ³¹ Then, as if following the sin of Jeroboam son of Nebat were a trivial matter, he married Jezebel, the daughter of Ethbaal king of the Sidonians, and then proceeded to serve Baal and worship him. ³² He set up an altar for Baal in the temple of Baal that he had built in Samaria. ³³ Ahab also made an Asherah pole. Ahab did more to provoke the LORD God of Israel than all the kings of Israel who were before him.

³⁴ During his reign, Hiel the Bethelite built Jericho. At the cost of Abiram his firstborn, he laid its foundation, and at the cost of Segub his youngest, he set up its gates, according to the word of the LORD He had spoken through Joshua son of Nun.

17 Now Elijah the Tishbite, from the Gilead settlers, said to Ahab, "As the LORD God of Israel lives, I stand before Him, and there will be no dew or rain during these years except by my command!"

² Then a revelation from the LORD came to him: ³ "Leave here, turn eastward, and hide yourself at the Wadi Cherith where it enters the Jordan. ⁴ You are to drink from the wadi. I have commanded the ravens to provide for you there."

⁵ So he did what the LORD commanded. Elijah left and lived by the Wadi Cherith where it enters the Jordan. ⁶ The ravens kept bringing him bread and meat in the morning and in the evening, and he drank from the wadi. ⁷ After a while, the wadi dried up because there had been no rain in the land.

⁸ Then the word of the LORD came to him: ⁹ "Get up, go to Zarephath that belongs to Sidon, and stay there. Look, I have commanded a woman who is a widow to provide for you there." ¹⁰ So Elijah got up and went to Zarephath. When he arrived at the city gate, there was a widow woman gathering wood. Elijah called to her and said, "Please bring me a little water in a cup and let me drink." ¹¹ As she went to get it, he called to her and said, "Please bring me a piece of bread in your hand."

¹² But she said, "As the LORD your God lives, I don't have anything baked—only a handful of flour in the jar and a bit of oil in the jug. Just now, I am gathering a couple of sticks in order to go prepare it for myself and my son so we can eat it and die."

¹³ Then Elijah said to her, "Don't be afraid; go and do as you have said. Only make me a small loaf from it and bring it out to me. Afterwards, you may make some for yourself and your son, ¹⁴ for this is what the LORD God of Israel says: 'The flour jar will not become empty and the oil jug will not run dry until the day the LORD sends rain on the surface of the land.' "

¹⁵ So she proceeded to do according to the word of Elijah. She and he and

her household ate for many days. ¹⁶ The flour jar did not become empty, and the oil jug did not run dry, according to the word of the LORD He had spoken through Elijah.

¹⁷ After this, the son of the woman who owned the house became ill. His illness became very severe until no breath remained in him. ¹⁸ She said to Elijah, "Man of God, what do we have in common? Have you come to remind me of my guilt and to kill my son?"

¹⁹ But Elijah said to her, "Give me your son." So he took him from her arms, brought him up to the upper room where he was staying, and laid him on his own bed. ²⁰ Then he cried out to the LORD and said, "My LORD God, have You also brought tragedy on the widow I am staying with by killing her son?" ²¹ Then he stretched himself out over the boy three times. He cried out to the LORD and said, "My LORD God, please let this boy's life return to him!"

²² So the LORD listened to Elijah's voice, and the boy's life returned to him, and he lived. ²³ Then Elijah took the boy, brought him down from the upper room into the house, and gave him to his mother. Elijah said, "Look, your son is alive."

²⁴ Then the woman said to Elijah, "Now I know you are a man of God and the LORD's word in your mouth is the truth."

PSALM 74:7-11

⁷ They set Your sanctuary on fire;
    they utterly desecrated the
        dwelling place of Your name.
⁸ They said in their hearts, "Let us
        oppress them relentlessly."
    They burned down every place
        throughout the land where
        God met with us.
⁹ We don't see any signs for us.
    There is no longer a prophet.
    And none of us knows how long
        this will last.
¹⁰ God, how long will the foe
        mock?

Will the enemy insult Your name
        forever?
¹¹ Why do You hold back Your hand?
    Stretch out Your right hand and
        destroy them!

PROVERBS 16:8-10

⁸ Better a little with righteousness
    than great income with injustice.

⁹ A man's heart plans his way,
    but the LORD determines his steps.

¹⁰ God's verdict is on the lips of a
        king;
    his mouth should not err in
        judgment.

JOHN 20:21–21:9

²¹ Jesus said to them again, "Peace to you! As the Father has sent Me, I also send you." ²² After saying this, He breathed on them and said, "Receive the Holy Spirit. ²³ If you forgive the sins of any, they are forgiven them; if you retain the sins of any, they are retained."

²⁴ But one of the Twelve, Thomas (called "Twin"), was not with them when Jesus came. ²⁵ So the other disciples kept telling him, "We have seen the Lord!"

But he said to them, "If I don't see the mark of the nails in His hands, put my finger into the mark of the nails, and put my hand into His side, I will never believe!"

²⁶ After eight days His disciples were indoors again, and Thomas was with them. Even though the doors were locked, Jesus came and stood among them. He said, "Peace to you!"

²⁷ Then He said to Thomas, "Put your finger here and observe My hands. Reach out your hand and put it into My side. Don't be an unbeliever, but a believer."

²⁸ Thomas responded to Him, "My Lord and my God!"

²⁹ Jesus said, "Because you have seen Me, you have believed. Those who believe without seeing are blessed."

[30] Jesus performed many other signs in the presence of His disciples that are not written in this book. [31] But these are written so that you may believe Jesus is the Messiah, the Son of God, and by believing you may have life in His name.

21 After this, Jesus revealed Himself again to His disciples by the Sea of Tiberias. He revealed Himself in this way: [2] Simon Peter, Thomas (called "Twin"), Nathanael from Cana of Galilee, Zebedee's sons, and two others of His disciples were together. [3] "I'm going fishing," Simon Peter said to them.

"We're coming with you," they told him. They went out and got into the boat, but that night they caught nothing. [4] When daybreak came, Jesus stood on the shore. However, the disciples did not know it was Jesus.

[5] "Men," Jesus called to them, "you don't have any fish, do you?"

"No," they answered.

[6] "Cast the net on the right side of the boat," He told them, "and you'll find some." So they did, and they were unable to haul it in because of the large number of fish. [7] Therefore the disciple, the one Jesus loved, said to Peter, "It is the Lord!"

When Simon Peter heard that it was the Lord, he tied his outer garment around him (for he was stripped) and plunged into the sea. [8] But since they were not far from land (about 100 yards away), the other disciples came in the boat, dragging the net full of fish. [9] When they got out on land, they saw a charcoal fire there, with fish lying on it, and bread.

"The Doubter's Prayer"

Don't be an unbeliever, but a believer.

—JOHN 20:27

If your doubts still persist after facing them, praying about them, and developing the habit of talking to yourself with a Scripture passage that refutes them, then seek the help of a minister or a Christian counselor. God has given us three resources to help us whenever we get into spiritual difficulties: the Word of God, the Spirit of God, and the people of God. The final answer to doubt may come as you share with an experienced Christian the things that are going on in your heart.

If you are not able to get the kind of help I am suggesting, then get in touch with your nearest Christian bookshop and ask them to recommend some helpful reading on the subject. Whatever you do, don't allow yourself to settle down into a complacent attitude about your doubts. Adopt a positive approach and determine to do something about resolving them. This will ensure that even though your doubts may take a certain amount of time to be cleared away, they will not be able to degenerate into unbelief.

Let me remind you of "The Doubter's Prayer" compiled by Martin Luther:

Dear Lord, although I am sure of my position,

I am unable to sustain it without Thee.

Help me or I am lost.

If the only thing you are able to do is pray, then that by itself will prevent doubt from becoming unbelief. If you also adopt the principle of "talking to yourself" from the Word of God, then you have in your hands the strategy for overcoming doubt.

Prayer

Father, help me, whenever I don't know what to do, to turn naturally to prayer. Then no moment will be empty or fruitless. But help me also to utilize the power of Your Word, the Bible. Let these two things become my central strategy. Amen.

Further Study

Mk 9:14-29; Mt 9:29-30; 21:21
What was the father's request?
Do you need to pray that prayer today?

JUNE 22

1 KINGS 18:1-46

18 After a long time, the word of the LORD came to Elijah in the third year: "Go and present yourself to Ahab. I will send rain on the surface of the land." ² So Elijah went to present himself to Ahab.

The famine was severe in Samaria. ³ Ahab called for Obadiah, who was in charge of the palace. Obadiah was a man who greatly feared the LORD ⁴ and took 100 prophets and hid them, 50 men to a cave, and provided them with food and water when Jezebel slaughtered the LORD's prophets. ⁵ Ahab said to Obadiah, "Go throughout the land to every spring of water and to every wadi. Perhaps we'll find grass so we can keep the horses and mules alive and not have to destroy any cattle." ⁶ They divided the land between them in order to cover it. Ahab went one way by himself, and Obadiah went the other way by himself.

⁷ While Obadiah was walking along the road, Elijah suddenly met him. When Obadiah recognized him, he fell with his face to the ground and said, "Is it you, my lord Elijah?"

⁸ "It is I," he replied. "Go tell your lord, 'Elijah is here!' "

⁹ But Obadiah said, "What sin have I committed, that you are handing your servant over to Ahab to put me to death? ¹⁰ As the LORD your God lives, there is no nation or kingdom where my lord has not sent someone to search for you. When they said, 'He is not here,' he made that kingdom or nation swear they had not found you.

¹¹ "Now you say, 'Go tell your lord, "Elijah is here!" ' ¹² But when I leave you, the Spirit of the LORD may carry you off to some place I don't know. Then when I go report to Ahab and he doesn't find you, he will kill me. But I, your servant, have feared the LORD from my youth. ¹³ Wasn't it reported to my lord what I did when Jezebel slaughtered the LORD's prophets? I hid 100 of the prophets of the LORD, 50 men to a cave, and I provided them with food and water. ¹⁴ Now you say, 'Go tell your lord, "Elijah is here!" ' He will kill me!"

¹⁵ Then Elijah said, "As the LORD of

Hosts lives, before whom I stand, today I will present myself to Ahab."

16 Obadiah went to meet Ahab and report to him. Then Ahab went to meet Elijah. 17 When Ahab saw Elijah, Ahab said to him, "Is that you, you destroyer of Israel?"

18 He replied, "I have not destroyed Israel, but you and your father's house have, because you have abandoned the LORD's commandments and followed the Baals. 19 Now summon all Israel to meet me at Mount Carmel, along with the 450 prophets of Baal and the 400 prophets of Asherah who eat at Jezebel's table."

20 So Ahab summoned all the Israelites and gathered the prophets at Mount Carmel. 21 Then Elijah approached all the people and said, "How long will you hesitate between two opinions? If Yahweh is God, follow Him. But if Baal, follow him." But the people didn't answer him a word.

22 Then Elijah said to the people, "I am the only remaining prophet of the LORD, but Baal's prophets are 450 men. 23 Let two bulls be given to us. They are to choose one bull for themselves, cut it in pieces, and place it on the wood but not light the fire. I will prepare the other bull and place it on the wood but not light the fire. 24 Then you call on the name of your god, and I will call on the name of Yahweh. The God who answers with fire, He is God."

All the people answered, "That sounds good."

25 Then Elijah said to the prophets of Baal, "Since you are so numerous, choose for yourselves one bull and prepare it first. Then call on the name of your god but don't light the fire."

26 So they took the bull that he gave them, prepared it, and called on the name of Baal from morning until noon, saying, "Baal, answer us!" But there was no sound; no one answered. Then they did their lame dance around the altar they had made.

27 At noon Elijah mocked them. He said, "Shout loudly, for he's a god! Maybe he's thinking it over; maybe he has wandered away; or maybe he's on the road. Perhaps he's sleeping and will wake up!" 28 They shouted loudly, and cut themselves with knives and spears, according to their custom, until blood gushed out on them. 29 All afternoon, they kept on raving until the offering of the evening sacrifice, but there was no sound, no one answered, no one paid attention.

30 Then Elijah said to all the people, "Come near me." So all the people approached him. Then he repaired the LORD's altar that had been torn down: 31 Elijah took 12 stones—according to the number of the tribes of the sons of Jacob, to whom the word of the LORD had come, saying, "Israel will be your name"— 32 and he built an altar with the stones in the name of Yahweh. Then he made a trench around the altar large enough to hold about four gallons. 33 Next, he arranged the wood, cut up the bull, and placed it on the wood. He said, "Fill four water pots with water and pour it on the offering to be burned and on the wood." 34 Then he said, "A second time!" and they did it a second time. And then he said, "A third time!" and they did it a third time. 35 So the water ran all around the altar; he even filled the trench with water.

36 At the time for offering the evening sacrifice, Elijah the prophet approached the altar and said, "LORD God of Abraham, Isaac, and Israel, today let it be known that You are God in Israel and I am Your servant, and that at Your word I have done all these things. 37 Answer me, LORD! Answer me so that this people will know that You, Yahweh, are God and that You have turned their hearts back."

38 Then Yahweh's fire fell and consumed the burnt offering, the wood, the stones, and the dust, and it licked up the water that was in the trench. 39 When all the people saw it, they fell facedown and said, "Yahweh, He is God! Yahweh, He is God!"

40 Then Elijah ordered them, "Seize the prophets of Baal! Do not let even one of them escape." So they seized them, and Elijah brought them down to the Wadi Kishon and slaughtered them there. 41 Elijah said to Ahab, "Go up, eat

and drink, for there is the sound of a rainstorm."

⁴² So Ahab went to eat and drink, but Elijah went up to the summit of Carmel. He bowed down to the ground and put his face between his knees. ⁴³ Then he said to his servant, "Go up and look toward the sea."

So he went up, looked, and said, "There's nothing."

Seven times Elijah said, "Go back." ⁴⁴ On the seventh time, he reported, "There's a cloud as small as a man's hand coming from the sea."

Then Elijah said, "Go and tell Ahab, 'Get your chariot ready and go down so the rain doesn't stop you.' "

⁴⁵ In a little while, the sky grew dark with clouds and wind, and there was a downpour. So Ahab got in his chariot and went to Jezreel. ⁴⁶ The power of the LORD was on Elijah, and he tucked his mantle under his belt and ran ahead of Ahab to the entrance of Jezreel.

PSALM 74:12-17

12 God my king is from ancient times,
      performing saving acts on the earth.
13 You divided the sea with Your strength;
      You smashed the heads of the sea monsters in the waters;
14 You crushed the heads of Leviathan;
      You fed him to the creatures of the desert.
15 You opened up springs and streams;
      You dried up ever-flowing rivers.
16 The day is Yours, also the night; You established the moon and the sun.
17 You set all the boundaries of the earth;
      You made summer and winter.

PROVERBS 16:11-12

11 Honest balances and scales are the LORD's;

all the weights in the bag are His concern.
12 Wicked behavior is detestable to kings,
      since a throne is established through righteousness.

JOHN 21:10-25

¹⁰ "Bring some of the fish you've just caught," Jesus told them. ¹¹ So Simon Peter got up and hauled the net ashore, full of large fish—153 of them. Even though there were so many, the net was not torn.

¹² "Come and have breakfast," Jesus told them. None of the disciples dared ask Him, "Who are You?" because they knew it was the Lord. ¹³ Jesus came, took the bread, and gave it to them. He did the same with the fish.

¹⁴ This was now the third time Jesus appeared to the disciples after He was raised from the dead.

¹⁵ When they had eaten breakfast, Jesus asked Simon Peter, "Simon, son of John, do you love Me more than these?"

"Yes, Lord," he said to Him, "You know that I love You."

"Feed My lambs," He told him.

¹⁶ A second time He asked him, "Simon, son of John, do you love Me?"

"Yes, Lord," he said to Him, "You know that I love You."

"Shepherd My sheep," He told him.

¹⁷ He asked him the third time, "Simon, son of John, do you love Me?"

Peter was grieved that He asked him the third time, "Do you love Me?" He said, "Lord, You know everything! You know that I love You."

"Feed My sheep," Jesus said. ¹⁸ "I assure you: When you were young, you would tie your belt and walk wherever you wanted. But when you grow old, you will stretch out your hands and someone else will tie you and carry you where you don't want to go." ¹⁹ He said this to signify by what kind of death he would glorify God. After saying this, He told him, "Follow Me!"

²⁰ So Peter turned around and saw the

disciple Jesus loved following them. That disciple was the one who had leaned back against Jesus at the supper and asked, "Lord, who is the one that's going to betray You?" 21 When Peter saw him, he said to Jesus, "Lord—what about him?"

22 "If I want him to remain until I come," Jesus answered, "what is that to you? As for you, follow Me."

23 So this report spread to the brothers that this disciple would not die. Yet Jesus did not tell him that he would not die, but, "If I want him to remain until I come, what is that to you?"

24 This is the disciple who testifies to these things and who wrote them down. We know that his testimony is true.

25 And there are also many other things that Jesus did, which, if they were written one by one, I suppose not even the world itself could contain the books that would be written.

Devout Realists

Wicked behavior is detestable to kings, since a throne is established through righteousness.—PROVERBS 16:12

The confession and acknowledgement of God's goodness is evident when we consider the time when the Israelites first settled in Canaan—the period of the judges—and the monarchy. Throughout these years the same pattern repeated itself over and over again—disobedience led to warnings, repentance, and appeals to God for mercy. The words "You" and "them" draw attention to the interaction between God and His people in Nehemiah 9:31: "You did not destroy them or abandon them."

This review of their national history provides every one of the Jews listening with encouraging evidences of what God has done in the past, the awesome consequences of ingratitude, and the inevitability of punishment if sin goes unconfessed. But most important of all, there is hope for the future. And that hope is based on the unchanging character of God. They see in the present a product of the past and the seed of the future. Their anticipation now is that the knowledge of past events will help them avoid the evil and follow the good, which is Paul's message in 1 Corinthians 10:6 and 11.

One person has said: "We have no light to illuminate the pathway of the future save that which falls over our shoulder from the past." Reflecting on what God has done for us in the past enables us to have a clearer perspective on the present and the future. A biblical approach to history makes us neither wide-eyed optimists nor downhearted pessimists. We become devout realists, for we see God at work in all things and triumphing over everything.

Prayer

O God, help me build into my life times for reflection on the way in which Your goodness has been with me in the past. For I see that by contemplating this I draw hope and encouragement for the future. Answer my prayer. In Jesus' name. Amen.

Further Study

Ps 23:1-6; Lk 22:35-38; Neh 9:26-31
As you read the psalm, reflect on God's dealings with you.
How will devout realists react to different situations?

JUNE 23

1 KINGS 19:1–20:43

19 Ahab told Jezebel everything that Elijah had done and how he had killed all the prophets with the sword. ² So Jezebel sent a messenger to Elijah, saying, "May the gods punish me and do so severely if I don't make your life like the life of one of them by this time tomorrow!"

³ Then Elijah became afraid and immediately ran for his life. When he came to Beer-sheba that belonged to Judah, he left his servant there, ⁴ but he went on a day's journey into the wilderness. He sat down under a broom tree and prayed that he might die. He said, "I have had enough! LORD, take my life, for I'm no better than my fathers." ⁵ Then he lay down and slept under the broom tree.

Suddenly, an angel touched him. The angel told him, "Get up and eat." ⁶ Then he looked, and there at his head was a loaf of bread baked over hot stones and a jug of water. So he ate and drank and lay down again. ⁷ Then the angel of the LORD returned a second time and touched him. He said, "Get up and eat, or the journey will be too much for you." ⁸ So he got up, ate, and drank. Then on the strength from that food, he walked 40 days and 40 nights to Horeb, the mountain of God. ⁹ He entered a cave there and spent the night.

Then the word of the LORD came to him, and He said to him, "What are you doing here, Elijah?"

¹⁰ He replied, "I have been very zealous for the LORD God of Hosts, but the Israelites have abandoned Your covenant, torn down Your altars, and killed Your prophets with the sword. I alone am left, and they are looking for me to take my life."

¹¹ Then He said, "Go out and stand on the mountain in the LORD's presence."

At that moment, the LORD passed by. A great and mighty wind was tearing at the mountains and was shattering cliffs before the LORD, but the LORD was not in the wind. After the wind there was an earthquake, but the LORD was not in the earthquake. ¹² After the earthquake there was a fire, but the LORD was not in the fire. And after the fire there was a voice, a soft whisper. ¹³ When Elijah heard it, he wrapped his face in his mantle and went out and stood at the entrance of the cave.

Suddenly, a voice came to him and said, "What are you doing here, Elijah?"

¹⁴ "I have been very zealous for the LORD God of Hosts," he replied, "but the Israelites have abandoned Your covenant, torn down Your altars, and killed Your prophets with the sword. I alone am left, and they're looking for me to take my life."

¹⁵ Then the LORD said to him, "Go and return by the way you came to the Wilderness of Damascus. When you ar-

rive, you are to anoint Hazael as king over Aram. ¹⁶ You are to anoint Jehu son of Nimshi as king over Israel and Elisha son of Shaphat from Abel-meholah as prophet in your place. ¹⁷ Then Jehu will put to death whoever escapes the sword of Hazael, and Elisha will put to death whoever escapes the sword of Jehu. ¹⁸ But I will leave 7,000 in Israel—every knee that has not bowed to Baal and every mouth that has not kissed him."

¹⁹ Elijah left there and found Elisha son of Shaphat as he was plowing. Twelve teams of oxen were in front of him, and he was with the twelfth team. Elijah walked by him and threw his mantle over him. ²⁰ Elisha left the oxen, ran to follow Elijah, and said, "Please let me kiss my father and mother, and then I will follow you."

"Go on back," he replied, "for what have I done to you?"

²¹ So he turned back from following him, took the team of oxen, and slaughtered them. With the oxen's wooden yoke and plow, he cooked the meat and gave it to the people, and they ate. Then he left, followed Elijah, and served him.

20 Now Ben-hadad king of Aram assembled his entire army. Thirty-two kings, along with horses and chariotry, were with him. He marched up, besieged Samaria, and fought against it. ² He sent messengers into the city to Ahab king of Israel and said to him, "This is what Ben-hadad says: ³ 'Your silver and your gold are mine! And your best wives and children are mine as well!' "

⁴ Then the king of Israel answered, "Just as you say, my lord king: I am yours, along with all that I have."

⁵ The messengers then returned and said, "This is what Ben-hadad says: 'I have sent messengers to you, saying: Your silver, your gold, your wives, and your children you are to give to me. ⁶ But at this time tomorrow I will send my servants to you, and they will search your palace and your servants' houses. Whatever is precious to you, they will lay their hands on and take away.' "

⁷ Then the king of Israel called for all the elders of the land and said, "Think it over and you will see that this one is only looking for trouble, for he demanded my wives, my children, my silver, and my gold, and I didn't turn him down."

⁸ All the elders and all the people said to him, "Don't listen or agree."

⁹ So he said to Ben-hadad's messengers, "Say to my lord the king, 'Everything you demanded of your servant the first time, I will do, but this thing I cannot do.' " So the messengers left and took word back to him.

¹⁰ Then Ben-hadad sent messengers to him and said, "May the gods punish me and do so severely if Samaria's dust amounts to a handful for each of the people who follow me."

¹¹ The king of Israel answered, "Say this: 'Let not him who puts on his armor boast like the one who takes it off.' "

¹² When Ben-hadad heard this response, while he and the kings were drinking in the tents, he said to his servants, "Take your positions." So they took their positions against the city.

¹³ A prophet came to Ahab king of Israel and said, "This is what the LORD says: 'Do you see this entire immense horde? Watch, I am handing it over to you today so that you may know that I am the LORD.' "

¹⁴ Ahab asked, "By whom?"

And the prophet said, "This is what the LORD says: 'By the young men of the provincial leaders.' "

Then he asked, "Who is to start the battle?"

He said, "You."

¹⁵ So Ahab counted the young men of the provincial leaders, and there were 232. After them he counted all the Israelite troops: 7,000. ¹⁶ They marched out at noon while Ben-hadad and the 32 kings who were helping him were getting drunk in the tents. ¹⁷ The young men of the provincial leaders marched out first. Then Ben-hadad sent out scouts, and they reported to him, saying, "Men are marching out of Samaria."

¹⁸ So he said, "If they have marched out in peace, take them alive, and if they have marched out for battle, take them alive."

¹⁹ The young men of the provincial leaders and the army behind them marched out from the city, ²⁰ and each one struck down his opponent. So the Arameans fled and Israel pursued them, but Ben-hadad king of Aram escaped on a horse with the cavalry. ²¹ Then the king of Israel marched out and attacked the cavalry and the chariotry. He inflicted a great slaughter on Aram.

²² The prophet approached the king of Israel and said to him, "Go and strengthen yourself, then consider what you should do, for in the spring the king of Aram will march up against you."

²³ Now the king of Aram's servants said to him, "Their gods are gods of the hill country. That's why they were stronger than we. Instead, we should fight with them on the plain; then we will certainly be stronger than they. ²⁴ Also do this: remove each king from his position and appoint captains in their place. ²⁵ Raise another army for yourself like the army you lost—horse for horse, chariot for chariot—and let's fight with them on the plain; and we will certainly be stronger than they." The king listened to them and did so.

²⁶ In the spring, Ben-hadad mobilized the Arameans and went up to Aphek to battle Israel. ²⁷ The Israelites mobilized, gathered supplies, and went to fight them. The Israelites camped in front of them like two little flocks of goats, while the Arameans filled the landscape.

²⁸ Then the man of God approached and said to the king of Israel, "This is what the LORD says: 'Because the Arameans have said: The LORD is a god of the mountains and not a god of the valleys, I will hand over this entire immense horde to you. Then you will know that I am the LORD.' "

²⁹ They camped opposite each other for seven days. On the seventh day, the battle took place, and the Israelites struck down the Arameans—100,000 foot soldiers in one day. ³⁰ The ones who remained fled into the city of Aphek, and the wall fell on those 27,000 remaining men.

Ben-hadad also fled and went into an inner room in the city. ³¹ His servants said to him, "Consider this: we have heard that the kings of the house of Israel are kings who show special kindness. So let's put sackcloth around our waists and ropes around our heads, and let's go out to the king of Israel. Perhaps he will spare your life."

³² So they dressed with sackcloth around their waists and ropes around their heads, went to the king of Israel, and said, "Your servant Ben-hadad says, 'Please spare my life.' "

So he said, "Is he still alive? He is my brother."

³³ Now the men were looking for a sign of hope, so they quickly latched onto the hint and said, "Yes, your brother Ben-hadad."

Then he said, "Go and bring him."

So Ben-hadad came out to him, and Ahab had him come up into the chariot. ³⁴ Then Ben-hadad said to him, "The cities that my father took from your father I restore to you, and you may set up marketplaces for yourself in Damascus, like my father set up in Samaria."

Ahab responded, "On the basis of this treaty, I release you." So he made a treaty with him and released him.

³⁵ One of the sons of the prophets said to his fellow prophet by the word of the LORD, "Strike me!" But the man refused to strike him.

³⁶ He told him, "Because you did not listen to the voice of the LORD, mark my words: When you leave me, a lion will kill you." When he left him, a lion found him and killed him.

³⁷ The prophet found another man and said to him, "Strike me!" So the man struck him, inflicting a wound. ³⁸ Then the prophet went and waited for the king on the road. He disguised himself with a bandage over his eyes. ³⁹ As the king was passing by, he cried out to the king and said, "Your servant marched out into the midst of the battle. Suddenly, a man turned aside and brought someone to me and said, 'Guard this man! If he is ever missing, it will be your life in place of his life, or you will weigh out 75 pounds of silver.' ⁴⁰ But while your servant was busy here and there, he disappeared."

The king of Israel said to him, "That will be your sentence; you yourself have decided it." [41] He quickly removed the bandage from his eyes. The king of Israel recognized that he was one of the prophets. [42] The prophet said to him, "This is what the LORD says: 'Because you released from your hand the man I had devoted to destruction, it will be your life in place of his life and your people in place of his people.' " [43] The king of Israel left for home resentful and angry, and he entered Samaria.

PSALM 74:18-23

[18] Remember this: the enemy has mocked the LORD,
and a foolish people has insulted Your name.
[19] Do not give the life of Your dove to beasts;
do not forget the lives of Your poor people forever.
[20] Consider the covenant,
for the dark places of the land are full of violence.
[21] Do not let the oppressed turn away in shame;
let the poor and needy praise Your name.
[22] Arise, God, defend Your cause!
Remember the insults that fools bring against You all day long.
[23] Do not forget the clamor of Your adversaries,
the tumult of Your opponents that goes up constantly.

PROVERBS 16:13-15

[13] Righteous lips are a king's delight,
and he loves one who speaks honestly.

[14] A king's fury is a messenger of death,
but a wise man appeases it.

[15] When a king's face lights up, there is life;

his favor is like a cloud with spring rain.

ACTS 1:1-26

[1] I wrote the first narrative, Theophilus, about all that Jesus began to do and teach [2] until the day He was taken up, after He had given orders through the Holy Spirit to the apostles whom He had chosen. [3] After He had suffered, He also presented Himself alive to them by many convincing proofs, appearing to them during 40 days and speaking about the kingdom of God.

[4] While He was together with them, He commanded them not to leave Jerusalem, but to wait for the Father's promise. "This," He said, "is what you heard from Me; [5] for John baptized with water, but you will be baptized with the Holy Spirit not many days from now."

[6] So when they had come together, they asked Him, "Lord, at this time are You restoring the kingdom to Israel?"

[7] He said to them, "It is not for you to know times or periods that the Father has set by His own authority. [8] But you will receive power when the Holy Spirit has come upon you, and you will be My witnesses in Jerusalem, in all Judea and Samaria, and to the ends of the earth."

[9] After He had said this, He was taken up as they were watching, and a cloud received Him out of their sight. [10] While He was going, they were gazing into heaven, and suddenly two men in white clothes stood by them. [11] They said, "Men of Galilee, why do you stand looking up into heaven? This Jesus, who has been taken from you into heaven, will come in the same way that you have seen Him going into heaven."

[12] Then they returned to Jerusalem from the mount called Olive Grove, which is near Jerusalem—a Sabbath day's journey away. [13] When they arrived, they went to the room upstairs where they were staying:

Peter, John,
James, Andrew,

Philip, Thomas,
Bartholomew, Matthew,
James the son of Alphaeus,
Simon the Zealot, and Judas
the son of James.

[14] All these were continually united in prayer, along with the women, including Mary the mother of Jesus, and His brothers.

[15] During these days Peter stood up among the brothers—the number of people who were together was about 120—and said: [16] "Brothers, the Scripture had to be fulfilled that the Holy Spirit through the mouth of David spoke in advance about Judas, who became a guide to those who arrested Jesus. [17] For he was one of our number and was allotted a share in this ministry." [18] Now this man acquired a field with his unrighteous wages; and falling headfirst, he burst open in the middle, and all his insides spilled out. [19] This became known to all the residents of Jerusalem, so that in their own language that field is called *Hakeldama*, that is, Field of Blood. [20] "For it is written in the Book of Psalms:

Let his dwelling become
   desolate;
let no one live in it; and
Let someone else take
   his position.

[21] "Therefore, from among the men who have accompanied us during the whole time the Lord Jesus went in and out among us— [22] beginning from the baptism of John until the day He was taken up from us—from among these, it is necessary that one become a witness with us of His resurrection."

[23] So they proposed two: Joseph, called Barsabbas, who was also known as Justus, and Matthias. [24] Then they prayed, "You, Lord, know the hearts of all; show which of these two You have chosen [25] to take the place in this apostolic service that Judas left to go to his own place." [26] Then they cast lots for them, and the lot fell to Matthias. So he was numbered with the 11 apostles.

"With"—or "In" and "Upon"

You will receive power when the Holy Spirit has come upon you.—Acts 1:8

The Holy Spirit is a resident counselor. The Greek word here is interesting: *parakletos—para* (beside), *kletos* (call)—one who is called alongside to help. There isn't a single thing needed in the Christian life that He isn't there to provide. Note the difference in the prepositions that are found in these passages: "He remains with you and will be in you" (Jn 14:17) and "You will receive power when the Holy Spirit has come upon you" (Ac 1:8). Jesus said that the Spirit was "with" them, but later would be "in" them and "upon" them. I take these prepositions to mean that the Holy Spirit was "with" them prior to Pentecost but was "in" them and "upon" them subsequent to Pentecost. Prior to Pentecost their lives lacked character and consistency. They cast out devils, but, on other occasions, they seemed to be somewhat influenced by them.

Simon Peter is a case in point (Mt 16:23). The disciples were loud in their assertions of loyalty and loud in their blunderings and misunderstandings. The Spirit was most certainly "with" them—helping, encouraging, and revealing—but He was most certainly not "in" them or "upon" them. When the Spirit came "in" and "upon" them at a later date, then fitful living became faithful living; erratic loyalty became everlasting loyalty.

Today, in the lives of many Christians, the Holy Spirit seems to be working on the outside rather than on the inside. Actually, of course, the Holy Spirit is resident "in" every Christian, but

He wants to be more than just resident—He wants also to be president! How is it in your life and experience? Is the Spirit a passing guest or a permanent guest?

Prayer

God, forgive me for not utilizing the resources of the Holy Spirit You have placed within me. Help me see that the Spirit within makes for adequacy without if I avail myself of Him. Amen.

Further Study

1 Co 2; Neh 9:20; Lk 12:12; 1 Jn 2:27
What has God revealed to us by His Spirit?
What does the Holy Spirit bring to us?

JUNE 24

1 KINGS 21:1–22:23

21 Some time passed after these events. Naboth the Jezreelite had a vineyard; it was in Jezreel next to the palace of Ahab king of Samaria. ² So Ahab spoke to Naboth, saying, "Give me your vineyard so I can have it for a vegetable garden, since it is right next to my palace. I will give you a better vineyard in its place, or if you prefer, I will give you its value in silver."

³ But Naboth said to Ahab, "I will never give my fathers' inheritance to you."

⁴ So Ahab went to his palace resentful and angry, because of what Naboth the Jezreelite had told him. He had said, "I will not give you my fathers' inheritance." He lay down on his bed, turned his face away, and didn't eat any food.

⁵ Then his wife Jezebel came to him and said to him, "Why are you so upset that you refuse to eat?"

⁶ "Because I spoke to Naboth the Jezreelite," he replied. "I told him: Give me your vineyard for silver, or if you wish, I will give you a vineyard in its place. But he said, 'I won't give you my vineyard!' "

⁷ Then his wife Jezebel said to him, "Now, exercise your royal power over Israel. Get up, eat some food, and be happy. For I will give you the vineyard of Naboth the Jezreelite." ⁸ So she wrote letters in Ahab's name and sealed them with his seal. She sent the letters to the elders and nobles who lived with Naboth in his city. ⁹ In the letters, she wrote:

Proclaim a fast and seat Naboth at the head of the people. ¹⁰ Then seat two wicked men opposite him and have them testify against him, saying, "You have cursed God and king!" Then take him out and stone him to death.

[11] The men of his city, the elders and nobles who lived in his city, did as Jezebel had commanded them, as was written in the letters she had sent them. [12] They proclaimed a fast and seated Naboth at the head of the people. [13] The two wicked men came in and sat opposite him. Then the wicked men testified against Naboth in the presence of the people, saying, "Naboth has cursed God and king!" So they took him outside the city and stoned him to death with stones. [14] Then they sent word to Jezebel, "Naboth has been stoned to death."

[15] When Jezebel heard that Naboth had been stoned to death, she said to Ahab, "Get up and take possession of the vineyard of Naboth the Jezreelite who refused to give it to you for silver, since Naboth isn't alive, but dead." [16] When Ahab heard that Naboth was dead, he got up to go down to the vineyard of Naboth the Jezreelite to take possession of it.

[17] Then the word of the LORD came to Elijah the Tishbite: [18] "Get up and go to meet Ahab king of Israel, who is in Samaria. You'll find him in Naboth's vineyard, where he has gone to take possession of it. [19] Tell him, 'This is what the LORD says: Have you murdered and also taken possession?' Then tell him, 'This is what the LORD says: In the place where the dogs licked Naboth's blood, the dogs will also lick your blood!' "

[20] Ahab said to Elijah, "So, you have caught me, my enemy."

He replied, "I have caught you because you devoted yourself to do what is evil in the LORD's sight. [21] This is what the LORD says: 'I am about to bring disaster on you and will sweep away your descendants:

> I will eliminate all of
> Ahab's males,
> both slave and free, in Israel;

[22] I will make your house like the house of Jeroboam son of Nebat and like the house of Baasha son of Ahijah, because you have provoked My anger and caused Israel to sin. [23] The LORD also speaks of Jezebel: The dogs will eat Jezebel in the plot of land at Jezreel:

> [24]   He who belongs to Ahab and dies
>   in the city, the dogs will eat,
>   and he who dies in the field,
>   the birds of the sky
>   will eat.' "

[25] Still, there was no one like Ahab, who devoted himself to do what was evil in the LORD's sight, because his wife Jezebel incited him. [26] He committed the most detestable acts by going after idols as the Amorites had, whom the LORD had dispossessed before the Israelites.

[27] When Ahab heard these words, he tore his clothes, put sackcloth over his body, and fasted. He lay down in sackcloth and walked around subdued. [28] Then the word of the LORD came to Elijah the Tishbite: [29] "Have you seen how Ahab has humbled himself before Me? I will not bring the disaster during his lifetime, because he has humbled himself before Me. I will bring the disaster on his house during his son's lifetime."

22 There was a lull of three years without war between Aram and Israel. [2] However, in the third year, Jehoshaphat king of Judah went to visit the king of Israel. [3] The king of Israel had said to his servants, "Don't you know that Ramoth-gilead is ours, but we have failed to take it from the hand of the king of Aram?" [4] So he asked Jehoshaphat, "Will you go with me to fight Ramoth-gilead?"

Jehoshaphat replied to the king of Israel, "I am as you are, my people as your people, my horses as your horses." [5] But Jehoshaphat said to the king of Israel, "First, please ask what the LORD's will is."

[6] So the king of Israel gathered the prophets, about 400 men, and asked them, "Should I go against Ramoth-gilead for war or should I refrain?"

They replied, "March up, and the Lord will hand it over to the king."

[7] But Jehoshaphat asked, "Isn't there a

prophet of Yahweh here any more? Let's ask him."

⁸ The king of Israel said to Jehoshaphat, "There is still one man who can ask the LORD, but I hate him because he never prophesies good about me, but only disaster. He is Micaiah son of Imlah."

"The king shouldn't say that!" Jehoshaphat replied.

⁹ So the king of Israel called an officer and said, "Hurry and get Micaiah son of Imlah!"

¹⁰ Now the king of Israel and Jehoshaphat king of Judah, clothed in royal attire, were each sitting on his own throne. They were on the threshing floor at the entrance to Samaria's gate, and all the prophets were prophesying in front of them. ¹¹ Then Zedekiah son of Chenaanah made iron horns and said, "This is what the LORD says: 'You will gore the Arameans with these until they are finished off.' " ¹² And all the prophets were prophesying the same: "March up to Ramoth-gilead and succeed, for the LORD will hand it over to the king."

¹³ The messenger who went to call Micaiah instructed him, "Look, the words of the prophets are unanimously favorable for the king. So let your words be like theirs, and speak favorably."

¹⁴ But Micaiah said, "As the LORD lives, I will say whatever the LORD says to me."

¹⁵ So he went to the king, and the king asked him, "Micaiah, should we go to Ramoth-gilead for war, or should we refrain?"

Micaiah told him, "March up and succeed. The LORD will hand it over to the king."

¹⁶ But the king said to him, "How many times must I make you swear not to tell me anything but the truth in the name of the LORD?"

¹⁷ So Micaiah said:

I saw all Israel scattered
    on the hills
like sheep without a shepherd.
And the LORD said,
'They have no master;
let everyone return home
    in peace.'

¹⁸ So the king of Israel said to Jehoshaphat, "Didn't I tell you he never prophesies good about me, but only disaster?"

¹⁹ Then Micaiah said, "Therefore, hear the word of the LORD: I saw the LORD sitting on His throne, and the whole heavenly host was standing by Him at His right hand and at His left hand. ²⁰ And the LORD said, 'Who will entice Ahab to march up and fall at Ramoth-gilead?' So one was saying this and another was saying that.

²¹ "Then a spirit came forward, stood before the LORD, and said, 'I will entice him.'

²² "The LORD asked him, 'How?'

"He said, 'I will go and become a lying spirit in the mouth of all his prophets.'

"Then He said, 'You will certainly entice him and prevail. Go and do that.'

²³ "You see, the LORD has put a lying spirit into the mouth of all these prophets of yours, and the LORD has pronounced disaster against you."

*P*SALM 75:1-10

¹ We give thanks to You, God;
    we give thanks to You, for Your
        name is near.
People tell about Your wonderful
        works.

² "When I choose a time,
    I will judge fairly.
³ When the earth and all its
        inhabitants shake,
    I am the One who steadies its
        pillars.   *Selah*
⁴ I say to the boastful, 'Do not
        boast,'
    and to the wicked, 'Do not lift up
        your horn.
⁵ Do not lift up your horn against
        heaven
    or speak arrogantly.' "

⁶ Exaltation does not come
    from the east, the west, or the
        desert,
⁷ for God is the judge:

He brings down one and exalts
another.
8 For there is a cup in the LORD's
hand,
full of wine blended with spices,
and He pours from it.
All the wicked of the earth will
drink,
draining it to the dregs.

9 As for me, I will tell about Him
forever;
I will sing praise to the God of
Jacob.

10 "I will cut off all the horns of the
wicked,
but the horns of the righteous will
be lifted up."

Proverbs 16:16-17

16 Acquire wisdom—how much
better it is than gold!
And acquire understanding—it is
preferable to silver.

17 The highway of the upright avoids
evil;
the one who guards his way
protects his life.

Acts 2:1-21

2 When the day of Pentecost had arrived, they were all together in one
place. ² Suddenly a sound like that of a
violent rushing wind came from heaven,
and it filled the whole house where
they were staying. ³ And tongues, like
flames of fire that were divided, appeared to them and rested on each one
of them. ⁴ Then they were all filled with
the Holy Spirit and began to speak in different languages, as the Spirit gave them
ability for speech.

⁵ There were Jews living in Jerusalem,
devout men from every nation under
heaven. ⁶ When this sound occurred,
the multitude came together and was
confused because each one heard them
speaking in his own language. ⁷ And

they were astounded and amazed, saying, "Look, aren't all these who are
speaking Galileans? ⁸ How is it that we
hear, each of us, in our own native language? ⁹ Parthians, Medes, Elamites;
those who live in Mesopotamia, in
Judea and Cappadocia, Pontus and Asia,
¹⁰ Phrygia and Pamphylia, Egypt and the
parts of Libya near Cyrene; visitors from
Rome, both Jews and proselytes, ¹¹ Cretans and Arabs—we hear them speaking
in our own languages the magnificent
acts of God." ¹² And they were all astounded and perplexed, saying to one
another, "What could this be?" ¹³ But
some sneered and said, "They're full of
new wine!"

¹⁴ But Peter stood up with the Eleven,
raised his voice, and proclaimed to
them: "Jewish men and all you residents of Jerusalem, let this be known to
you and pay attention to my words.
¹⁵ For these people are not drunk, as
you suppose, since it's only nine in the
morning. ¹⁶ On the contrary, this is what
was spoken through the prophet Joel:

17 **And it will be** in the last days,
says God,
that **I will pour out My Spirit
on all humanity;
then your sons
and your daughters
will prophesy,
your young men will see
visions,
and your old men will dream
dreams.**
18 **I will even pour out My Spirit
on My male and female slaves
in those days,**
and they will prophesy.
19 **I will display wonders
in the heaven** above
and signs on the earth below:
**blood and fire and a cloud
of smoke.**
20 **The sun will be turned
to darkness,
and the moon to blood,
before the great and remarkable
day of the Lord comes;**
21 **then whoever calls on the name
of the Lord will be saved.**

The Young and the Old

I will pour out My Spirit on all humanity; then your sons and your daughters will prophesy, your young men will see visions, and your old men will dream dreams.—Acts 2:17

A barrier that went down in the upper room was that between the young and the old. Peter pointed out that what had happened in the upper room was the fulfillment of Joel's prophecy, in which the prophet had declared that the day would come when young and old alike would receive the gift of the Holy Spirit. "This is the day the prophet spoke about!" said Peter. "It's arrived!"

"There has always been a sacred age," said someone, "—old age." In almost all religions, power and sanctity have been associated with the old. This is why many religions tend to be backward-looking rather than forward-looking. In the upper room there were young men (I think we can assume this) who received the gift of the Holy Spirit in the same way as their elders. What a dynamic this produced. Young and old, moving together in the power of the Spirit. The old would naturally want to conserve the values and good things they had come to love and respect, while the young would want to move these values into greater realms and make them more widely operative.

One writer said, "The Christian faith demands radicalism as well as conservatism to fully express itself." Young and old combine to fully express the nature of the Christian faith, for conservatism or radicalism on their own are weak. Together, however, they become strong and powerful.

Prayer

Heavenly Father, I am thankful that both young and old can be used in the kingdom. Blend the conservatism of the old with the radicalism of the young, so that this generation might see a new Pentecost. For Jesus' sake. Amen.

Further Study

1 Tm 5; 4:12; 1 Jn 2:13-14; 1 Pt 5:5; Rm 12:10
What was Paul teaching Timothy?
What does Paul mean: "Out do one another in showing honor"?

JUNE 25

1 KINGS 22:24– 2 KINGS 1:18

²⁴ Then Zedekiah son of Chenaanah came up, hit Micaiah in the face, and demanded, "Did the Spirit of the LORD leave me to speak to you?"

²⁵ Micaiah replied, "You will soon see when you go to hide yourself in an inner chamber on that day."

²⁶ Then the king of Israel ordered, "Take Micaiah and return him to Amon, the governor of the city, and to Joash, the king's son, ²⁷ and say, 'This is what the king says: Put this guy in prison and feed him only bread and water until I come back safely.' "

²⁸ But Micaiah said, "If you ever return safely, the LORD has not spoken through me." Then he said, "Listen, all you people!"

²⁹ Then the king of Israel and Judah's King Jehoshaphat went up to Ramoth-gilead. ³⁰ But the king of Israel said to Jehoshaphat, "I will disguise myself and go into battle, but you wear your royal attire." So the king of Israel disguised himself and went into battle.

³¹ Now the king of Aram had ordered his 32 chariot commanders, "Do not fight with anyone at all except the king of Israel."

³² When the chariot commanders saw Jehoshaphat, they shouted, "He must be the king of Israel!" So they turned to fight against him, but Jehoshaphat cried out. ³³ When the chariot commanders saw that he was not the king of Israel, they turned back from pursuing him.

³⁴ But a man drew his bow without taking special aim and struck the king of Israel through the joints of his armor. So he said to his charioteer, "Turn around and take me out of the battle, for I am badly wounded!" ³⁵ The battle raged throughout that day, and the king was propped up in his chariot facing the Arameans. He died that evening, and blood from his wound flowed into the bottom of the chariot. ³⁶ Then the cry rang out in the army as the sun set, declaring:

Each man to his own city,
and each man to his own land!

³⁷ So the king died and was brought to Samaria. They buried the king in Samaria. ³⁸ Then someone washed the chariot at the pool of Samaria. The dogs licked up his blood, and the prostitutes bathed in it, according to the word of the LORD that He had spoken.

³⁹ The rest of the events of Ahab's reign, along with all his accomplishments, the ivory palace he built, and all the cities he built, are written about in the Historical Record of Israel's Kings. ⁴⁰ Ahab rested with his fathers, and his son Ahaziah became king in his place.

⁴¹ Jehoshaphat son of Asa became king over Judah in the fourth year of Israel's King Ahab. ⁴² Jehoshaphat was 35 years old when he became king; he reigned 25 years in Jerusalem. His mother's name was Azubah daughter of Shilhi. ⁴³ He walked in all the ways of his father Asa; he did not turn away from them but did what was right in the LORD's sight. However, the high places were not taken away; the people still sacrificed and burned incense on the high places. ⁴⁴ Jehoshaphat also made peace with the king of Israel.

⁴⁵ The rest of the events of Jehoshaphat's reign, along with the might he exercised and how he waged war, are written about in the Historical Record of Judah's Kings. ⁴⁶ He removed from the land the rest of the male shrine prostitutes who were left from the days of his father Asa. ⁴⁷ There was no king in Edom; a deputy served as king.

⁴⁸ Jehoshaphat made ships of Tarshish to go to Ophir for gold, but they did not go because the ships were wrecked at Ezion-geber. ⁴⁹ At that time, Ahaziah son of Ahab said to Jehoshaphat, "Let my servants go with your servants in the ships," but Jehoshaphat was not willing. ⁵⁰ Jehoshaphat rested with his fathers and was buried with his fathers in the city of his forefather David. His son Jehoram became king in his place.

⁵¹ Ahaziah son of Ahab became king over Israel in Samaria in the seventeenth year of Judah's King Jehoshaphat; he reigned over Israel two years. ⁵² He did what was evil in the LORD's sight. He walked in the way of his father, in the way of his mother, and in the way of Jeroboam son of Nebat, who had caused Israel to sin. ⁵³ He served Baal and worshiped him. He provoked the LORD God of Israel just as his father had done.

1 After the death of Ahab, Moab rebelled against Israel. ² Ahaziah had fallen through the latticed window of his upper room in Samaria and was injured. So he sent messengers instructing them: "Go inquire of Baal-zebub, the god of Ekron, if I will recover from this injury."

³ But the angel of the LORD said to Elijah the Tishbite, "Go and meet the messengers of the king of Samaria and ask them, 'Is it because there is no God in Israel that you are going to inquire of Baal-zebub, the god of Ekron?' ⁴ Therefore, this is what the LORD says: 'You will not get up from your sickbed—you will certainly die.' " Then Elijah left.

⁵ The messengers returned to the king, who asked them, "Why have you come back?"

⁶ They replied, "A man came to meet us and said, 'Go back to the king who sent you and declare to him: This is what the LORD says: Is it because there is no God in Israel that you're sending these men to inquire of Baal-zebub, the god of Ekron? Therefore, you will not get up from your sickbed—you will certainly die.' "

⁷ The king asked them: "What sort of man came up to meet you and spoke those words to you?"

⁸ They replied, "A hairy man with a leather belt around his waist."

He said, "It's Elijah the Tishbite."

⁹ So King Ahaziah sent a captain of 50 with his 50 men to Elijah. When the captain went up to him, he was sitting on top of the hill. He announced, "Man of God, the king declares, 'Come down!' "

¹⁰ Elijah responded to the captain of the 50, "If I am a man of God, may fire come down from heaven and consume you and your 50 men." Then fire came down from heaven and consumed him and his 50 men.

¹¹ So the king sent another captain of 50 with his 50 men to Elijah. He took in the situation and announced, "Man of God, this is what the king says: 'Come down immediately!' "

¹² Elijah responded, "If I am a man of God, may fire come down from heaven and consume you and your 50 men." So a divine fire came down from heaven and consumed him and his 50 men.

¹³ Then the king sent a third captain of 50 with his 50 men. The third captain of 50 went up and fell on his knees in front of Elijah and begged him, "Man of God, please let my life and the lives of these 50 servants of yours be precious in your sight. ¹⁴ Already fire has come down from heaven and consumed the first two captains of 50 with their fifties, but this time let my life be precious in your sight."

¹⁵ The angel of the LORD said to Elijah, "Go down with him. Don't be afraid of him." So he got up and went down with him to the king.

¹⁶ Then Elijah said to King Ahaziah, "This is what the LORD says: 'Because you have sent messengers to inquire of Baal-zebub, the god of Ekron—is it because there is no God in Israel for you to inquire of His will? You will not get up from your sickbed; you will certainly die.' "

¹⁷ Ahaziah died according to the word of the LORD that Elijah had spoken. Since he had no son, Joram became king in his place. This happened in the

second year of Judah's King Jehoram son of Jehoshaphat. ¹⁸ The rest of the events of Ahaziah's reign, along with his accomplishments, are written about in the Historical Record of Israel's Kings.

PSALM 76:1-6

¹ God is known in Judah;
  His name is great in Israel.
² His tent is in Salem,
  His dwelling place in Zion.
³ There He shatters the bow's
    flaming arrows,
  the shield, the sword, and the
    weapons of war.   *Selah*

⁴ You are resplendent and majestic
    coming down from the mountains
    of prey.
⁵ The brave-hearted have been
    plundered;
  they have slipped into their final
    sleep.
  None of the warriors was able to
    lift a hand.
⁶ At Your rebuke, God of Jacob,
  both chariot and horse lay still.

PROVERBS 16:18-19

¹⁸ Pride comes before destruction,
   and an arrogant spirit before a
   fall.

¹⁹ Better to be lowly of spirit with
   the humble
   than to divide plunder with the
   proud.

ACTS 2:22-47

²² "Men of Israel, listen to these words: This Jesus the Nazarene was a man pointed out to you by God with miracles, wonders, and signs that God did among you through Him, just as you yourselves know. ²³ Though He was delivered up according to God's determined plan and foreknowledge, you used lawless people to nail Him to a cross and kill Him. ²⁴ God raised Him up, ending the pains of death, because

it was not possible for Him to be held by it. ²⁵ For David says of Him:

  I saw the Lord ever before me;
  because He is at my right hand,
  I will not be shaken.
²⁶ Therefore my heart was glad,
  and my tongue rejoiced.
  Moreover my flesh will rest
    in hope,
²⁷ because You will not leave
    my soul in Hades,
  or allow Your Holy One
    to see decay.
²⁸ You have revealed
    the paths of life to me;
  You will fill me with gladness
    in Your presence.

²⁹ "Brothers, I can confidently speak to you about the patriarch David: he is both dead and buried, and his tomb is with us to this day. ³⁰ Since he was a prophet, he knew that God had sworn an oath to him to seat one of his descendants on his throne. ³¹ Seeing this in advance, he spoke concerning the resurrection of the Messiah:

  He was not left in Hades,
  and His flesh did not experience
    decay.

³² "God has resurrected this Jesus. We are all witnesses of this. ³³ Therefore, since He has been exalted to the right hand of God and has received from the Father the promised Holy Spirit, He has poured out what you both see and hear. ³⁴ For it was not David who ascended into the heavens, but he himself says:

  The Lord said to my Lord,
  'Sit at My right hand
³⁵ until I make Your enemies
    Your footstool.'

³⁶ "Therefore let all the house of Israel know with certainty that God has made this Jesus, whom you crucified, both Lord and Messiah!"
³⁷ When they heard this, they were pierced to the heart and said to Peter and the rest of the apostles: "Brothers,

what must we do?"

[38] "Repent," Peter said to them, "and be baptized, each of you, in the name of Jesus the Messiah for the forgiveness of your sins, and you will receive the gift of the Holy Spirit. [39] For the promise is for you and for your children, and for all who are far off, as many as the Lord our God will call." [40] And with many other words he testified and strongly urged them, saying, "Be saved from this corrupt generation!"

[41] So those who accepted his message were baptized, and that day about 3,000 people were added to them. [42] And they devoted themselves to the apostles' teaching, to fellowship, to the breaking of bread, and to prayers.

[43] Then fear came over everyone, and many wonders and signs were being performed through the apostles. [44] Now all the believers were together and had everything in common. [45] So they sold their possessions and property and distributed the proceeds to all, as anyone had a need. [46] And every day they devoted themselves to meeting together in the temple complex, and broke bread from house to house. They ate their food with gladness and simplicity of heart, [47] praising God and having favor with all the people. And every day the Lord added to them those who were being saved.

Made for Fellowship

They devoted themselves to the apostles' teaching, to fellowship.—Acts 2:42

I read a passage in a book that said: "We can only get to know ourselves and others to the extent that we tune in to the heartbeat of the universe."

Here is a psychologist, a non-Christian, attempting to put into words one of the greatest truths of Scripture—namely, that it is only as we have fellowship with God that we can experience fellowship with ourselves and others. What a pity he could not see that what he calls "the heartbeat of the universe" is the heart that was broken on the cross.

Isn't it sad that so many philosophers and scientists come so close to seeing the reality that lies behind the universe and yet, for some reason, sidestep the great issue of entering into a personal relationship with God? They struggle to know the secrets of the cosmos, and yet miss the "open secret" of God's revelation through Christ which He laid bare at Calvary. Instead, they try to achieve fellowship through psychological processes that leave the heart estranged.

The astonishing rise in our day of the "group therapy movement" testifies to the need of the human heart for fellowship. Almost every country in the world reports a rapid rise of small groups meeting together to encourage, confront, and stimulate one another toward good emotional health and maturity. The world is waking up to the fact that we are made for fellowship. Oh, if only they could see that fellowship which does not begin with God, does not begin.

Prayer

Father, I am so thankful for the discovery that fellowship cannot be produced by trying but by trusting. It begins and ends with You. Take me deeper into Your heart that I might take others deeper into mine. For Jesus' sake. Amen.

Further Study

1 Jn 1:1-7; Rm 1:11-12; 12:5
What is the purpose of fellowship?
Who do you have fellowship with?

JUNE 26

2 KINGS 2:1–3:27

2 The time had come for the LORD to take Elijah up to heaven in a whirlwind. Elijah and Elisha were traveling from Gilgal, ² and Elijah said to Elisha, "Stay here; the LORD is sending me on to Bethel."

But Elisha replied, "As the LORD lives and as you yourself live, I will not leave you." So they went down to Bethel.

³ Then the sons of the prophets who were at Bethel came out to Elisha and said, "Do you know that today the LORD will take your master away from you?"

He said, "Yes, I know. Be quiet."

⁴ Elijah said to him, "Elisha, stay here; the LORD is sending me to Jericho."

But Elisha said, "As the LORD lives and as you yourself live, I will not leave you." So they went to Jericho.

⁵ Then the sons of the prophets who were in Jericho came up to Elisha and said, "Do you know that today the LORD will take your master away from you?"

He said, "Yes, I know. Be quiet."

⁶ Elijah said to him, "Stay here; the LORD is sending me to the Jordan."

But Elisha said, "As the LORD lives and as you yourself live, I will not leave you." So the two of them went on.

⁷ Fifty men from the sons of the prophets came and stood facing them from a distance while the two of them stood by the Jordan. ⁸ Elijah took his mantle, rolled it up, and struck the waters, which parted to the right and left.

Then the two of them crossed over on dry ground. ⁹ After they had crossed over, Elijah said to Elisha, "Tell me what I can do for you before I am taken from you."

So Elisha answered, "Please, let there be a double portion of your spirit on me."

¹⁰ Elijah replied, "You have asked for something difficult. If you see me being taken from you, you will have it. If not, you won't."

¹¹ As they continued walking and talking, a chariot of fire with horses of fire suddenly appeared and separated the two of them. Then Elijah went up into heaven in the whirlwind. ¹² As Elisha watched, he kept crying out, "My father, my father, the chariots and horsemen of Israel!" Then he saw Elijah no more. He took hold of his own clothes and tore them into two pieces.

¹³ Elisha picked up the mantle that had fallen off Elijah and went back and stood on the bank of the Jordan. ¹⁴ Then he took the mantle Elijah had dropped and struck the waters. "Where is the LORD God of Elijah?" he asked. He struck the waters himself, and they parted to the right and the left, and Elisha crossed over.

¹⁵ When the sons of the prophets from Jericho, who were facing him, saw him, they said, "The spirit of Elijah rests on Elisha." They came to meet him and bowed down to the ground in front of him.

¹⁶ Then the sons of the prophets said to Elisha, "Since there are 50 strong men here with your servants, please let them go and search for your master. Maybe the Spirit of the LORD has carried him away and put him on one of the mountains or into one of the valleys." He answered, "Don't send them." ¹⁷ However, they urged him to the point of embarrassment, so he said, "Send them." They sent 50 men, who looked for three days but did not find him. ¹⁸ When they returned to him in Jericho where he was staying, he said to them, "Didn't I tell you not to go?"

¹⁹ Then the men of the city said to Elisha, "Even though our lord can see that the city's location is good, the water is bad and the land unfruitful." ²⁰ He replied, "Bring me a new bowl and put salt in it."

After they had brought him one, ²¹ Elisha went out to the spring of water, threw salt in it, and said, "This is what the LORD says: 'I have healed this water. No longer will death or unfruitfulness result from it.' " ²² Therefore, the water remains healthy to this very day according to the word that Elisha spoke.

²³ From there Elisha went up to Bethel. As he was walking up the path, some small boys came out of the city and harassed him, chanting, "Go up, baldy! Go up, baldy!" ²⁴ He turned around, looked at them, and cursed them in the name of the LORD. Then two female bears came out of the woods and mauled 42 of the youths. ²⁵ From there Elisha went to Mount Carmel, and then he returned to Samaria.

3 Joram son of Ahab became king over Israel in Samaria during the eighteenth year of Judah's King Jehoshaphat; he reigned 12 years. ² He did what was evil in the LORD's sight, but not like his father and mother, for he removed the sacred pillar of Baal his father had made. ³ Nevertheless, Joram clung to the sins that Jeroboam son of Nebat had caused Israel to commit. He did not turn away from them.

⁴ King Mesha of Moab was a sheep breeder. He used to pay the king of Israel 100,000 lambs and the wool of 100,000 rams, ⁵ but when Ahab died, the king of Moab rebelled against the king of Israel. ⁶ So King Joram marched out from Samaria at that time and mobilized all Israel. ⁷ Then he sent a message to King Jehoshaphat of Judah: "The king of Moab has rebelled against me. Will you go with me to fight against Moab?"

Jehoshaphat said, "I will go. I am as you are, my people as your people, my horses as your horses." ⁸ Then he asked, "Which route should we take?"

Joram replied, "The route of the wilderness of Edom."

⁹ So the king of Israel, the king of Judah, and the king of Edom set out. After they had traveled their indirect route for seven days, they had no water for the army or their animals. ¹⁰ Then the king of Israel said, "Oh no, the LORD has summoned us three kings, only to hand us over to Moab." ¹¹ But Jehoshaphat said, "Isn't there a prophet of the LORD here? Let's inquire of the LORD through him."

One of the servants of the king of Israel answered, "Elisha son of Shaphat, who used to pour water on Elijah's hands, is here." ¹² Jehoshaphat affirmed, "The LORD's words are with him." So the king of Israel and Jehoshaphat and the king of Edom went to him.

¹³ However, Elisha said to King Joram of Israel, "We have nothing in common. Go to the prophets of your father and your mother!"

But the king of Israel replied, "No, because it is the LORD who has summoned us three kings to hand us over to Moab."

¹⁴ Elisha responded, "As the LORD of Hosts lives, I stand before Him. If I did not have respect for King Jehoshaphat of Judah, I would not look at you; I wouldn't take notice of you. ¹⁵ Now, bring me a musician."

While the musician played, the LORD's hand came on Elisha. ¹⁶ Then he said, "This is what the LORD says: 'Dig ditch after ditch in this wadi.' ¹⁷ For the LORD says, 'You will not see wind or rain, but the wadi will be filled with water, and you will drink—you and your cattle and your animals.' [18] This is easy in the LORD's sight. He will also hand Moab over to you. [19] Then you must attack every fortified city and every choice city. You must cut down every good tree and stop up every spring of water. You must ruin every good piece of land with stones."

[20] About the time for the grain offering the next morning, water suddenly came from the direction of Edom and filled the land.

[21] All Moab had heard that the kings had come up to fight against them. So all who could bear arms, from the youngest to the oldest, were summoned and took their stand at the border. [22] When they got up early in the morning, the sun was shining on the water, and the Moabites saw that the water across from them was red like blood. [23] "This is blood!" they exclaimed. "The kings have clashed swords and killed each other. So, to the spoil, Moab!"

[24] However, when the Moabites came to Israel's camp, the Israelites attacked them, and they fled from them. So Israel went into the land and struck down the Moabites. [25] They destroyed the cities, and each of them threw stones to cover every good piece of land. They stopped up every spring of water and cut down every good tree. In the end, only the buildings of Kir-hareseth were left. Then men with slings surrounded the city and attacked it.

[26] When the king of Moab saw that the battle was too fierce for him, he took 700 swordsmen with him to try to break through to the king of Edom, but they could not do it. [27] So he took his firstborn son, who was to become king in his place, and offered him as a burnt offering on the city wall. Great wrath was on the Israelites, and they withdrew from him and returned to their land.

PSALM 76:7-12

[7] And You—You are to be feared. When You are angry, who can stand before You?

[8] From heaven You pronounced judgment.
The earth feared and grew quiet
[9] when God rose up to judge
and to save all the lowly of the earth. *Selah*
[10] Even human wrath will praise You;
You will clothe Yourself with their remaining wrath.
[11] Make and keep your vows to the LORD your God;
let all who are around Him bring tribute to the awe-inspiring One.
[12] He humbles the spirit of leaders;
He is feared by the kings of the earth.

PROVERBS 16:20

[20] The one who understands a matter finds success,
and the one who trusts in the LORD will be happy.

ACTS 3:1-26

3 Now Peter and John were going up together to the temple complex at the hour of prayer at three in the afternoon. [2] And a man who was lame from his mother's womb was carried there and placed every day at the temple gate called Beautiful, so he could beg from those entering the temple complex. [3] When he saw Peter and John about to enter the temple complex, he asked for help. [4] Peter, along with John, looked at him intently and said, "Look at us." [5] So he turned to them, expecting to get something from them. [6] But Peter said, "I have neither silver nor gold, but what I have, I give to you: In the name of Jesus Christ the Nazarene, get up and walk!" [7] Then, taking him by the right hand he raised him up, and at once his feet and ankles became strong. [8] So he jumped up, stood, and started to walk, and he entered the temple complex with them—walking, leaping, and praising God. [9] All the people saw him walking and praising God, [10] and they

recognized that he was the one who used to sit and beg at the Beautiful Gate of the temple complex. So they were filled with awe and astonishment at what had happened to him.

[11] While he was holding on to Peter and John, all the people, greatly amazed, ran toward them in what is called Solomon's Colonnade. [12] When Peter saw this, he addressed the people: "Men of Israel, why are you amazed at this? Or why do you stare at us, as though by our own power or godliness we had made him walk? [13] The God of Abraham, Isaac, and Jacob, the God of our fathers, has glorified His Servant Jesus, whom you handed over and denied in the presence of Pilate, when he had decided to release Him. [14] But you denied the Holy and Righteous One, and asked to have a murderer given to you. [15] And you killed the source of life, whom God raised from the dead; we are witnesses of this. [16] By faith in His name, His name has made this man strong, whom you see and know. So the faith that comes through Him has given him this perfect health in front of all of you.

[17] "And now, brothers, I know that you did it in ignorance, just as your leaders also did. [18] But what God predicted through the mouth of all the prophets—

that His Messiah would suffer—He has fulfilled in this way. [19] Therefore repent and turn back, that your sins may be wiped out so that seasons of refreshing may come from the presence of the Lord, [20] and He may send Jesus, who has been appointed Messiah for you. [21] Heaven must welcome Him until the times of the restoration of all things, which God spoke about by the mouth of His holy prophets from the beginning. [22] Moses said:

The Lord your God will raise up for you a Prophet like me from among your brothers. You must listen to Him in everything He will say to you. [23] And it will be that everyone who will not listen to that Prophet will be completely cut off from the people.

[24] "In addition, all the prophets who have spoken, from Samuel and those after him, have also announced these days. [25] You are the sons of the prophets and of the covenant that God made with your forefathers, saying to Abraham, And in your seed all the families of the earth will be blessed. [26] God raised up His Servant and sent Him first to you to bless you by turning each of you from your evil ways."

"But Your Head Is Gone"

Therefore repent and turn back, that your sins may be wiped out so that seasons of refreshing may come from the presence of the Lord.—Acts 3:19

One of the things we must do if we are to stay spiritually fresh is to break decisively with everything that Christ cannot approve.

When we are fighting sin and evil, we are fighting a defeated foe, because Jesus met and conquered every sin on the cross. You will never meet a single sin that has not been defeated by Christ. So if sin is bullying you, do what E. Stanley Jones advised. He said: "When sin intimidates me, I quietly ask it to bend its neck. When it does, I joyfully point to the footprints of the Son of God on its neck. My inferiority complex is gone. I am on the winning side." This language may be picturesque, but the truth is powerful—because of what Christ has accomplished on Calvary, we walk the earth amid conquered foes.

A far-fetched but illustrative story from the ancient battles of Africa tells how a warrior was beheaded during a skirmish, but he fought on even though his head was gone. He succeeded in killing many until someone said, "But your head has gone! You're dead," whereupon he fell down and died. When sin comes against you, point and say: "Look, your head has gone. My Master conquered you on the cross. Begone! You are headless." Evil fights on, but it is brainless. It depends on prejudices, old habits, and perhaps above all on our lack of decisiveness. So if there are still any sins in your life that need to be dealt with, face them in the assurance that they are conquered foes, and break decisively with everything that Christ cannot approve.

Prayer

O God, thank You for reminding me that I need not develop an inferiority complex in relation to sin—it is a conquered foe. Help me to accept and enter into the great victory of Calvary. In Christ's powerful name. Amen.

Further Study

1 Jn 1; Pr 28:13; Col 2:14
What prevents us from prospering?
How are we to deal with sin?

JUNE 27

2 KINGS 4:1–5:14

4 One of the wives of the sons of the prophets cried out to Elisha, "Your servant, my husband, has died. You know that your servant feared the Lord. Now the creditor is coming to take my two children as his slaves."

² Elisha asked her, "What can I do for you? Tell me, what do you have in the house?"

She said, "Your servant has nothing in the house except a jar of oil."

³ Then he said, "Go and borrow empty containers from everyone—from all your neighbors. Do not get just a few. ⁴ Then go in and shut the door behind you and your sons, and pour oil into all these containers. Set the full ones to one side." ⁵ So she left.

After she had shut the door behind her and her sons, they kept bringing her containers, and she kept pouring. ⁶ When they were full, she said to her son, "Bring me another container."

But he replied, "There aren't any more." Then the oil stopped.

⁷ She went and told the man of God, and he said, "Go sell the oil and pay your debt; you and your sons can live on the rest."

⁸ One day Elisha went to Shunem. A prominent woman who lived there persuaded him to eat some food. So whenever he passed by, he stopped there to

eat. ⁹ Then she said to her husband, "I know that the one who often passes by here is a holy man of God, ¹⁰ so let's make a small room upstairs and put a bed, a table, a chair, and a lamp there for him. Whenever he comes, he can stay there."

¹¹ One day he came there and stopped and went to the room upstairs to lie down. ¹² He ordered his attendant Gehazi, "Call this Shunammite woman." So he called her and she stood before him. ¹³ Then he said to Gehazi, "Say to her, 'Look, you've gone to all this trouble for us. What can we do for you? Can we speak on your behalf to the king or to the commander of the army?' "

She answered, "I am living among my own people."

¹⁴ So he asked, "Then what should be done for her?"

Gehazi answered, "Well, she has no son, and her husband is old."

¹⁵ "Call her," Elisha said. So Gehazi called her, and she stood in the doorway. ¹⁶ Elisha said, "At this time next year you will have a son in your arms."

Then she said, "No, my lord. Man of God, do not deceive your servant."

¹⁷ The woman conceived and gave birth to a son at the same time the following year, as Elisha had promised her.

¹⁸ The child grew and one day went out to his father and the harvesters. ¹⁹ Suddenly, he complained to his father, "My head! My head!"

His father told his servant, "Carry him to his mother." ²⁰ So he picked him up and took him to his mother. The child sat on her lap until noon and then died. ²¹ Then she went up and laid him on the bed of the man of God, shut him in, and left.

²² She summoned her husband and said, "Please send me one of the servants and one of the donkeys, so I can hurry to the man of God and then come back."

²³ But he said, "Why go to him today? It's neither New Moon or Sabbath."

She replied, "Everything is all right."

²⁴ Then she saddled the donkey and said to her servant, "Hurry, don't slow the pace for me unless I tell you." ²⁵ So she set out and went to the man of God at Mount Carmel.

When the man of God saw her at a distance, he said to his attendant Gehazi, "Look, there's the Shunammite woman. ²⁶ Run out to meet her and ask, 'Are you all right? Is your husband all right? Is your son all right?' "

And she answered, "Everything's all right."

²⁷ When she came up to the man of God at the mountain, she clung to his feet. Gehazi came to push her away, but the man of God said, "Leave her alone—she is in severe anguish, and the LORD has hidden it from me. He hasn't told me."

²⁸ Then she said, "Did I ask my lord for a son? Didn't I say, 'Do not deceive me?' "

²⁹ So Elisha said to Gehazi, "Tuck your mantle under your belt, take my staff with you, and go. If you meet anyone, don't stop to greet him, and if a man greets you, don't answer him. Then place my staff on the boy's face."

³⁰ The boy's mother said to Elisha, "As the LORD lives and as you yourself live, I will not leave you." So he got up and followed her.

³¹ Gehazi went ahead of them and placed the staff on the boy's face, but there was no sound or sign of life, so he went back to meet Elisha and told him, "The boy didn't wake up."

³² When Elisha got to the house, he discovered the boy lying dead on his bed. ³³ So he went in, closed the door behind the two of them, and prayed to the LORD. ³⁴ Then he went up and lay on the boy: he put mouth to mouth, eye to eye, hand to hand. While he bent down over him, the boy's flesh became warm. ³⁵ Elisha got up, went into the house, and paced back and forth. Then he went up and bent down over him again. The boy sneezed seven times and opened his eyes.

³⁶ Elisha called Gehazi and said, "Call the Shunammite woman." He called her and she came. Then Elisha said, "Pick up your son." ³⁷ She came, fell at his feet, and bowed to the ground; she picked up her son and left.

³⁸ When Elisha returned to Gilgal, there was a famine in the land. The sons of the prophets were sitting at his feet. He said to his attendant, "Put on the large pot and make stew for the sons of the prophets."

³⁹ One went out to the field to gather herbs and found a wild vine from which he gathered as many wild gourds as his garment would hold. Then he came back and cut them up into the pot of stew, but they were unaware of what they were.

⁴⁰ They served some for the men to eat, but when they ate the stew they cried out, "There's death in the pot, man of God!" And they were unable to eat it.

⁴¹ Then Elisha said, "Get some meal." He threw it into the pot and said, "Serve it for the people to eat." And there was nothing bad in the pot.

⁴² A man from Baal-shalishah came to the man of God with his sack full of 20 loaves of barley bread from the first bread of the harvest. Elisha said, "Give it to the people to eat."

⁴³ But Elisha's attendant asked, "What? Am I to set 20 loaves before 100 men?"

"Give it to the people to eat," Elisha said, "for this is what the LORD says: 'They will eat, and they will have some left over.' " ⁴⁴ So he gave it to them, and as the LORD had promised, they ate and had some left over.

5 Naaman, commander of the army for the king of Aram, was a great man in his master's sight and highly regarded because through him, the LORD had given victory to Aram. The man was a brave warrior, but he had a skin disease.

² Aram had gone on raids and brought back from the land of Israel a young girl who served Naaman's wife. ³ She said to her mistress, "If only my master would go to the prophet who is in Samaria, he would cure him of his skin disease."

⁴ So Naaman went and told his master what the girl from the land of Israel had said. 5 Therefore, the king of Aram said, "Go and I will send a letter with you to the king of Israel."

So he went and took with him 750 pounds of silver, 150 pounds of gold, and 10 changes of clothes. ⁶ He brought the letter to the king of Israel, and it read:

When this letter comes to you, note that I have sent you my servant Naaman for you to cure him of his skin disease.

⁷ When the king of Israel read the letter, he tore his clothes and asked, "Am I God, killing and giving life that this man expects me to cure a man of his skin disease? Think it over and you will see that he is only picking a fight with me."

⁸ When Elisha the man of God heard that the king of Israel tore his clothes, he sent a message to the king, "Why have you torn your clothes? Have him come to me, and he will know there is a prophet in Israel." ⁹ So Naaman came with his horses and chariots and stood at the door of Elisha's house.

¹⁰ Then Elisha sent him a messenger, who said, "Go wash seven times in the Jordan and your flesh will be restored and you will be clean."

¹¹ But Naaman got angry and left, saying, "I was telling myself: He will surely come out, stand and call on the name of Yahweh his God, and will wave his hand over the spot and cure the skin disease. ¹² Aren't Abana and Pharpar, the rivers of Damascus, better than all the waters of Israel? Could I not wash in them and be clean?" So he turned and left in a rage.

¹³ But his servants approached and said to him, "My father, if the prophet had told you to do some great thing, would you not have done it? How much more should you do it when he tells you, 'Wash and be clean'?" ¹⁴ So Naaman went down and dipped himself in the Jordan seven times, according to the command of the man of God. Then his skin was restored and became like the skin of a small boy, and he was clean.

PSALM 77:1-6

¹ I cry aloud to God,
  aloud to God, and He will hear me.

2 In my day of trouble I sought the
   Lord.
My hands were lifted up all night
   long;
I refused to be comforted.
3 I think of God; I groan;
I meditate; my spirit becomes
   weak.   *Selah*

4 You have kept me from closing my
   eyes;
I am troubled and cannot speak.
5 I consider days of old,
years long past.
6 At night I remember my music;
I meditate in my heart, and my
   spirit ponders.

*P*ROVERBS 16:21-22

21 Anyone with a wise heart is called
   discerning,
and pleasant speech increases
   learning.

22 Insight is a fountain of life for its
   possessor,
but folly is the instruction of fools.

*A*CTS 4:1-22

4 Now as they were speaking to the
people, the priests, the commander
of the temple guard, and the Sadducees
confronted them, 2 because they were
provoked that they were teaching the
people and proclaiming in the person of
Jesus the resurrection from the dead.
3 So they seized them and put them in
custody until the next day, since it was
already evening. 4 But many of those
who heard the message believed, and
the number of the men came to about
5,000.

5 The next day, their rulers, elders,
and scribes assembled in Jerusalem
6 with Annas the high priest, Caiaphas,
John and Alexander, and all the members of the high-priestly family. 7 After
they had Peter and John stand before
them, they asked the question: "By
what power or in what name have you
done this?"

8 Then Peter was filled with the Holy
Spirit and said to them, "Rulers of the
people and elders: 9 If we are being examined today about a good deed done
to a disabled man—by what means he
was healed— 10 let it be known to all of
you and to all the people of Israel, that
by the name of Jesus Christ the Nazarene—whom you crucified and whom
God raised from the dead—by Him this
man is standing here before you
healthy. 11 This Jesus is

**The stone despised by you
   builders,
who has become the cornerstone.**

12 There is salvation in no one else, for
there is no other name under heaven
given to people by which we must be
saved."
13 When they observed the boldness
of Peter and John and realized that they
were uneducated and untrained men,
they were amazed and knew that they
had been with Jesus. 14 And since they
saw the man who had been healed
standing with them, they had nothing to
say in response. 15 After they had ordered them to leave the Sanhedrin, they
conferred among themselves, 16 saying,
"What should we do with these men?
For an obvious sign, evident to all who
live in Jerusalem, has been done through
them, and we cannot deny it! 17 But so
this does not spread any further among
the people, let's threaten them against
speaking to anyone in this name again."
18 So they called for them and ordered
them not to preach or teach at all in the
name of Jesus.
19 But Peter and John answered them,
"Whether it's right in the sight of God
for us to listen to you rather than to
God, you decide; 20 for we are unable to
stop speaking about what we have seen
and heard."
21 After threatening them further,
they released them. They found no way
to punish them, because the people
were all giving glory to God over what
had been done; 22 for the man was over
40 years old on whom this sign of healing had been performed.

No Other Name

There is salvation in no one else.
—ACTS 4:12

We must continually watch out for statements that assert that all religions are the same, for when they are repeated over and over again, and by seemingly sincere people, we can be brainwashed into accepting them.

In 1966, when the first multi-faith service was held in an Anglican church in London, in which Hindus, Buddhists, Muslims, and Christians took part on equal terms, some Christian newspapers described it as a "betrayal of the faith." Nowadays there is hardly a mention of such services although they take place regularly in different parts of our nation and also in other countries. People seem to have given up the idea of syncretism—the idea that all religions can be fused into one—and are focusing more on pluralism—the recognition of each faith as being of equal value. I take my stand with Dr. Visser't Hooft, who said: "It is high time that Christians should rediscover that Jesus Christ did not come to make a contribution to the religious storehouse of mankind, but that in Him God reconciled the world unto Himself."

The words of our text for today were displayed outside a church in London until the minister was told by the local authority to take the poster down as it offended some local inhabitants who were adherents of other faiths. "It is not the best way to love one's neighbor as oneself" was how one critic put it. But how can we love our neighbor as ourselves if we make no attempt to share with them the knowledge of salvation in Jesus Christ?

Prayer

O Father, in an age when the faith once delivered to the saints is being watered down, deepen my understanding of it so that I may contend for it without being contentious. In Christ's name I pray. Amen.

Further Study

Jn 3:1-17; 6:35; 14:6
What Old Testament example shows there is only one way to salvation?
What did Jesus declare about Himself?

JUNE 28

2 KINGS 5:15–7:9

[15] Then Naaman and his whole company went back to the man of God, stood before him, and declared, "I know there's no God in the whole world except in Israel. Therefore, please accept a gift from your servant." [16] But Elisha said, "As the LORD lives, I stand before Him. I will not accept it." Naaman urged him to accept it, but he refused.

[17] Naaman responded, "If not, please let two mule-loads of dirt be given to your servant, for your servant will no longer offer a burnt offering or a sacrifice to any other god but Yahweh. [18] However, in a particular matter may the LORD pardon your servant: When my master, the king of Aram, goes into the temple of Rimmon to worship and I, as his right-hand man, bow in the temple of Rimmon—when I bow in the temple of Rimmon, may the LORD pardon your servant in this matter."

[19] So he said to him, "Go in peace."

After Naaman had traveled a short distance from Elisha, [20] Gehazi, the attendant of Elisha the man of God, thought: My master has let this Aramean Naaman off lightly by not accepting from him what he brought. As the LORD lives, I will run after him and get something from him.

[21] So Gehazi pursued Naaman. When Naaman saw someone running after him, he got down from the chariot to meet him and asked, "Is everything all right?"

[22] Gehazi said, "It's all right. My master has sent me to say, 'I have just now discovered that two young men from the sons of the prophets have come to me from the hill country of Ephraim. Please give them 75 pounds of silver and two changes of clothes.' "

[23] But Naaman insisted, "Please, accept 150 pounds." He urged Gehazi and then packed 150 pounds of silver in two bags with two changes of clothes. Naaman gave them to two of his young men who carried them ahead of Gehazi. [24] When Gehazi came to the hill, he took the gifts from them and stored them in the house. Then he dismissed the men, and they left.

[25] Gehazi came and stood by his master. "Where did you go, Gehazi?" Elisha asked him.

"Your servant didn't go anywhere," he replied.

[26] But Elisha questioned him, "Wasn't my spirit there when the man got down from his chariot to meet you? Is it a time to accept money and clothes, olive orchards and vineyards, sheep and oxen, and male and female slaves? 27 Therefore, Naaman's skin disease will cling to you and your descendants forever." So Gehazi went out from his presence diseased—white as snow.

6 The sons of the prophets said to Elisha, "Please notice that the place where we live under your supervision is too small for us. [2] Please let us go to the Jordan where we can each get a log and can build ourselves a place to live there."

"Go," he said.

[3] Then one said, "Please come with your servants."

"I'll come," he answered.

[4] So he went with them, and when they came to the Jordan, they cut down trees. [5] As one of them was cutting down a tree, the iron ax head fell into the water, and he cried out: "Oh, my master, it was borrowed!"

[6] Then the man of God asked, "Where did it fall?"

When he showed him the place, the man of God cut a stick, threw it there, and made the iron float. [7] Then he said,

"Pick it up." So he reached out and took it.

⁸ When the king of Aram was waging war against Israel, he conferred with his servants, "My camp will be at such and such a place."

⁹ But the man of God sent word to the king of Israel: "Be careful passing by this place, for the Arameans are going down there." ¹⁰ Consequently, the king of Israel sent word to the place the man of God had told him about. The man of God repeatedly warned the king, so the king would be on his guard.

¹¹ The king of Aram was enraged because of this matter, and he called his servants and demanded of them, "Tell me, which one of us is for the king of Israel?"

¹² One of his servants said, "No one, my lord the king. Elisha, the prophet in Israel, tells the king of Israel even the words you speak in your bedroom."

¹³ So the king said, "Go and see where he is, so I can send men to capture him."

When he was told, "Elisha is in Dothan," ¹⁴ he sent horses, chariots, and a massive army there. They went by night and surrounded the city.

¹⁵ When the servant of the man of God got up early and went out, he discovered an army with horses and chariots surrounding the city. So he asked Elisha, "Oh, my master, what are we to do?"

¹⁶ Elisha said, "Don't be afraid, for those who are with us outnumber those who are with them."

¹⁷ Then Elisha prayed, "LORD, please open his eyes and let him see." So the LORD opened the servant's eyes. He looked and saw that the mountain was covered with horses and chariots of fire all around Elisha.

¹⁸ When the Arameans came against him, Elisha prayed to the LORD, "Please strike this nation with blindness." So He struck them with blindness, according to Elisha's word. ¹⁹ Then Elisha said to them, "This is not the way, and this is not the city. Follow me, and I will take you to the man you're looking for." And he led them to Samaria. ²⁰ When they

entered Samaria, Elisha said, "LORD, open these men's eyes and let them see." So the LORD opened their eyes. They looked and discovered they were in Samaria.

²¹ When the king of Israel saw them, he said to Elisha, "My father, should I kill them? I will kill them."

²² Elisha replied, "Don't kill them. Do you kill those you have captured with your sword or your bow? Set food and water in front of them so they can eat and drink and go to their master."

²³ So he prepared a great feast for them. When they had eaten and drunk, he sent them away, and they went to their master. The Aramean raiders did not come into Israel's land again.

²⁴ Some time later, King Ben-hadad of Aram brought all his military units together and marched up to besiege Samaria. ²⁵ So there was a great famine in Samaria, and they continued the siege against it until a donkey's head sold for 80 silver shekels, and a cup of dove's dung sold for five silver shekels.

²⁶ As the king of Israel was passing by on the wall, a woman cried out to him, "My lord the king, help!"

²⁷ He answered, "If the LORD doesn't help you, where can I get help for you? From the threshing floor or the winepress?" ²⁸ Then the king asked her, "What's the matter?"

She said, "This woman said to me, 'Give up your son, and we will eat him today. Then we will eat my son tomorrow.' ²⁹ So we boiled my son and ate him, and I said to her the next day, 'Give up your son, and we will eat him,' but she has hidden her son."

³⁰ When the king heard the woman's words, he tore his clothes. Then, as he was passing by on the wall, the people saw that there was sackcloth under his clothes next to his skin. ³¹ He announced, "May God punish me and do so severely if the head of Elisha son of Shaphat remains on his shoulders today."

³² Elisha was sitting in his house, and the elders were sitting with him. The king sent a man ahead of him, but be-

fore the messenger got to him, Elisha said to the elders, "Do you see how this murderer has sent someone to cut off my head? Look, when the messenger comes, shut the door to keep him out. Isn't the sound of his master's feet behind him?" [33] While Elisha was still speaking with them, the messenger came down to him. Then he said, "This disaster is from the LORD. Why should I trust the LORD any longer?"

7 Elisha said, "Hear the word of the LORD! This is what the LORD says: 'About this time tomorrow at the gate of Samaria, six quarts of fine meal will sell for a shekel and 12 quarts of barley will sell for a shekel.' " [2] Then the captain, the king's right-hand man, responded to the man of God, "Look, even if the LORD were to make windows in heaven, could this really happen?" Elisha announced, "You will in fact see it with your own eyes, but you won't eat any of it." [3] Four men with skin diseases were at the entrance to the gate. They said to each other, "Why just sit here until we die? [4] If we say, 'Let's go into the city,' we will die there because the famine is in the city, but if we sit here, we will also die. So now, come on. Let's go to the Arameans' camp. If they let us live, we will live; if they kill us, we will die." [5] So the diseased men got up at twilight to go to the Arameans' camp. When they came to the camp's edge, they discovered that there was not a single man there, [6] for the Lord had caused the Aramean camp to hear the sound of chariots, horses, and a great army. The Arameans had said to each other, "The king of Israel must have hired the kings of the Hittites and the kings of Egypt to attack us." [7] So they had gotten up and fled at twilight abandoning their tents, horses, and donkeys. The camp was intact, and they had fled for their lives. [8] When these men came to the edge of the camp, they went into a tent to eat

and drink. Then they picked up the silver, gold, and clothing and went off and hid them. They came back and entered another tent, picked things up, and hid them. [9] Then they said to each other, "We're not doing what is right. Today is a day of good news. If we are silent and wait until morning light, we will be punished. Let's go tell the king's household."

PSALM 77:7-12

[7] "Will the Lord reject forever and never again show favor?
[8] Has His faithful love ceased forever?
Is His promise at an end for all generations?
[9] Has God forgotten to be gracious? Has He in anger withheld His compassion?" *Selah*
[10] So I say, "It is my sorrow that the right hand of the Most High has changed."
[11] I will remember the LORD's works; yes, I will remember Your ancient wonders.
[12] I will reflect on all You have done and meditate on Your actions.

PROVERBS 16:23-24

[23] A wise heart instructs its mouth and increases learning with its speech.
[24] Pleasant words are a honeycomb: sweet to the taste and health to the body.

ACTS 4:23–5:11

[23] After they were released, they went to their own fellowship and reported all that the chief priests and the elders had said to them. [24] When they heard this, they raised their voices to God unanimously and said, "Master, You are the One who made the heaven, the earth, and the sea, and everything in them. [25] You said through the Holy

Spirit, by the mouth of our father David Your servant:

Why did the Gentiles rage,
and the peoples plot futile things?
26 The kings of the earth
took their stand,
and the rulers assembled
together
against the Lord and against His
Messiah.

27 "For, in fact, in this city both Herod and Pontius Pilate, with the Gentiles and the peoples of Israel, assembled together against Your holy Servant Jesus, whom You anointed, 28 to do whatever Your hand and Your plan had predestined to take place. 29 And now, Lord, consider their threats, and grant that Your slaves may speak Your message with complete boldness, 30 while You stretch out Your hand for healing, signs, and wonders to be performed through the name of Your holy Servant Jesus." 31 When they had prayed, the place where they were assembled was shaken, and they were all filled with the Holy Spirit and began to speak God's message with boldness.

32 Now the multitude of those who believed were of one heart and soul, and no one said that any of his possessions was his own, but instead they held everything in common. 33 And with great power the apostles were giving testimony to the resurrection of the Lord Jesus, and great grace was on all of them. 34 For there was not a needy person among them, because all those who owned lands or houses sold them, brought the proceeds of the things that were sold, 35 and laid them at the apostles' feet. This was then distributed

to each person as anyone had a need. 36 Joseph, a Levite and a Cypriot by birth, whom the apostles named Barnabas, which is translated Son of Encouragement, 37 sold a field he owned, brought the money, and laid it at the apostles' feet.

5 But a man named Ananias, with Sapphira his wife, sold a piece of property. 2 However, he kept back part of the proceeds with his wife's knowledge, and brought a portion of it and laid it at the apostles' feet.

3 Then Peter said, "Ananias, why has Satan filled your heart to lie to the Holy Spirit and keep back part of the proceeds from the field? 4 Wasn't it yours while you possessed it? And after it was sold, wasn't it at your disposal? Why is it that you planned this thing in your heart? You have not lied to men but to God!" 5 When he heard these words, Ananias dropped dead, and a great fear came on all who heard. 6 The young men got up, wrapped his body, carried him out, and buried him.

7 There was an interval of about three hours; then his wife came in, not knowing what had happened. 8 "Tell me," Peter asked her, "did you sell the field for this price?"

"Yes," she said, "for that price."

9 Then Peter said to her, "Why did you agree to test the Spirit of the Lord? Look! The feet of those who have buried your husband are at the door, and they will carry you out!" 10 Instantly she dropped dead at his feet. When the young men came in, they found her dead, carried her out, and buried her beside her husband. 11 Then great fear came on the whole church and on all who heard these things.

Pretense, Consequence

When he heard these words, Ananias dropped dead,
and a great fear came on all who heard.—Acts 5:5

Consider this story about a couple from the Bible who forfeited their lives because they pretended to be more spiritual than they really were.

Ananias and Sapphira were highly respected members of the early church and appeared on the surface to be deeply committed disciples of the Lord Jesus Christ. Doubtless, they had a fairly high degree of dedication, and they easily went along with the idea of selling their possessions and putting the proceeds into the treasury of the church. Their mistake, of course, was in pretending they had given their all when in reality they hadn't, and the consequences that fell to them because of their pretenses were swift and dramatic.

God deals harshly with dishonesty, but He is compassionate to those who see themselves as they really are, who confess this to Him, and who request His help in becoming the people they know He wants them to be.

I have known people who have stood up in front of a Christian audience and talked about how wonderful it is to live a victorious Christian life, when in reality they were inwardly messed up. And I have known of others getting up before their brothers and sisters, confessing that though they love the Lord, they are experiencing great struggles and difficulties in seeking to live for Him. Who do you think is the closer to God? I will tell you—it is the one who is honest and open. Pretense repels God; openness and honesty draw Him quickly to our side.

Prayer

Father, help me to be a sincere and transparent person. Save me, I pray, from adopting an air of pretense and masquerading as someone I am not. You delight in openness and honesty. Help me to delight in them too. Amen.

Further Study

Ac 19; Eph 1; Rv 2:1-5
Why did the word of the Lord spread rapidly in Ephesus?
What words did Christ bring to them some years later?

JUNE 29

2 KINGS 7:10–9:13

¹⁰ The diseased men went and called to the city's gatekeepers and told them, "We went to the Aramean camp and no one was there—no human sounds. There was nothing but tethered horses and donkeys, and the tents were intact." ¹¹ The gatekeepers called out, and the news was reported to the king's household.

¹² So the king got up in the night and said to his servants, "Let me tell you what the Arameans have done to us. They know we are starving, so they have left the camp to hide in the open country, thinking, 'When they come out of the city, we will take them alive and go into the city.' "

¹³ But one of his servants responded, "Please, let messengers take five of the horses that are left in the city. The messengers are like the whole multitude of Israelites who will die, so let's send them and see."

¹⁴ The messengers took two chariots with horses, and the king sent them after the Aramean army, saying, "Go and see." ¹⁵ So they followed them as far as the Jordan. They saw that the whole way was littered with clothes and equipment the Arameans had thrown off in their haste. The messengers returned and told the king. ¹⁶ Then the people went out and plundered the Aramean camp.

It was then that six quarts of fine meal sold for a shekel and 12 quarts of barley sold for a shekel, according to the word of the LORD. ¹⁷ The king had appointed the captain, his right-hand man, to be in charge of the gate, but the people trampled him in the gateway. He died, just as the man of God had predicted when the king came to him. ¹⁸ When the man of God had said to the king, "About this time tomorrow 12 quarts of barley will sell for a shekel and six quarts of fine meal will sell for a shekel at the gate of Samaria," ¹⁹ this captain had answered the man of God, "Look, even if the LORD were to make windows in heaven, could this really happen?" Elisha had said, "You will in fact see it with your own eyes, but you won't eat any of it." ²⁰ This is what happened to him: the people trampled him in the gateway, and he died.

8 Elisha said to the woman whose son he had restored to life, "Get ready, you and your household, and go and live as a foreigner wherever you can. For the LORD has announced a seven-year famine, and it has already come to the land."

² So the woman got ready and did what the man of God said. She and her household lived as foreigners in the land of the Philistines for seven years. ³ When the woman returned from the land of the Philistines at the end of seven years, she went to appeal to the king for her house and field.

⁴ The king had been speaking to Gehazi, the servant of the man of God, saying, "Tell me all the great things Elisha has done." ⁵ While he was telling the king how Elisha restored the dead son to life, the woman whose son he had restored to life came to appeal to the king for her house and field. So Gehazi said, "My lord the king, this is the woman and this is the son Elisha restored to life."

⁶ When the king asked the woman, she told him the story. So the king appointed a court official for her, saying, "Restore all that was hers, along with all the income from the field from the day she left the country until now."

⁷ Elisha came to Damascus while Ben-hadad king of Aram was sick, and the king was told, "The man of God has

come here." [8] So the king said to Hazael, "Take a gift with you and go meet the man of God. Inquire of the LORD through him, 'Will I recover from this sickness?' "

[9] Hazael went to meet Elisha, taking with him a gift: 40 camel-loads of all kinds of goods from Damascus. When he came and stood before him, he said, "Your son, Ben-hadad king of Aram, has sent me to ask you, 'Will I recover from this sickness?' "

[10] Elisha told him, "Go say to him, 'You are sure to recover.' But the LORD has shown me that he is sure to die." [11] Then Elisha stared steadily at him until Hazael was ashamed.

The man of God wept, [12] and Hazael asked, "Why is my lord weeping?"

He replied, "Because I know the evil you will do to the people of Israel. You will set their fortresses on fire. You will kill their young men with the sword. You will dash their little ones to pieces. You will rip open their pregnant women."

[13] Hazael said, "How could your servant, a mere dog, do this monstrous thing?"

Elisha answered, "The LORD has shown me that you will be king over Aram."

[14] Hazael left Elisha and went to his master, who asked him, "What did Elisha say to you?"

He responded, "He told me you are sure to recover." [15] The next day Hazael took a heavy cloth, dipped it in water, and spread it over the king's face. Ben-hadad died, and Hazael reigned instead of him.

[16] In the fifth year of Israel's King Joram son of Ahab, Jehoram son of Jehoshaphat became king of Judah, replacing his father. [17] He was 32 years old when he became king; he reigned eight years in Jerusalem. [18] He walked in the way of the kings of Israel, as the house of Ahab had done, for Ahab's daughter was his wife. He did what was evil in the LORD's sight. [19] The LORD was unwilling to destroy Judah because of His servant David, since He had promised to give a lamp to David and to his sons forever.

[20] During Jehoram's reign, Edom rebelled against Judah's control and appointed their own king. [21] So Jehoram crossed over to Zair with all his chariots. Then at night he set out to attack the Edomites who had surrounded him and the chariot commanders, but his troops fled to their tents. [22] So Edom is still in rebellion against Judah's control today. Libnah also rebelled at that time.

[23] The rest of the events of Jehoram's reign, along with all his accomplishments, are written about in the Historical Record of Israel's Kings. [24] Jehoram rested with his fathers and was buried with his fathers in the city of David, and his son Ahaziah became king in his place.

[25] In the twelfth year of Israel's King Joram son of Ahab, Ahaziah son of Jehoram became king of Judah. [26] Ahaziah was 22 years old when he became king; he reigned one year in Jerusalem. His mother's name was Athaliah, granddaughter of Israel's King Omri. [27] He walked in the way of the house of Ahab and did what was evil in the LORD's sight like the house of Ahab, for he was a son-in-law to Ahab's family.

[28] Ahaziah went with Joram son of Ahab to fight against Hazael king of Aram in Ramoth-gilead, and the Arameans wounded Joram. [29] So King Joram returned to Jezreel to recover from the wounds that the Arameans had inflicted on him in Ramoth-gilead when he fought against Aram's King Hazael. Then Judah's King Ahaziah son of Jehoram went down to Jezreel to visit Joram son of Ahab since Joram was ill.

9 The prophet Elisha called one of the sons of the prophets and said, "Tuck your mantle under your belt, take this flask of oil with you, and go to Ramoth-gilead. [2] When you get there, look for Jehu son of Jehoshaphat, son of Nimshi. Go in, get him away from his colleagues, and take him to an inner room. [3] Then, take the flask of oil, pour it on his head, and say, 'This is what the LORD says: "I anoint you king over Israel." ' Open the door and escape. Don't wait." [4] So the young prophet went to Ramoth-gilead.

⁵ When he arrived, the army commanders were sitting there, so he said, "I have a message for you, commander." Jehu asked, "For which one of us?" He answered, "For you, commander." ⁶ So Jehu got up and went into the house. The young prophet poured the oil on his head and said, "This is what the LORD God of Israel says: 'I anoint you king over the LORD's people, Israel. ⁷ You are to strike down the house of your master Ahab so that I may avenge the blood shed by the hand of Jezebel— the blood of My servants the prophets and of all the servants of the LORD. ⁸ The whole house of Ahab will perish, and I will eliminate all of Ahab's males, both slave and free, in Israel. ⁹ I will make the house of Ahab like the house of Jeroboam son of Nebat and like the house of Baasha son of Ahijah. ¹⁰ The dogs will eat Jezebel in the plot of land at Jezreel—no one will bury her.' " Then the young prophet opened the door and escaped.

¹¹ When Jehu came out to his master's servants, they asked, "Is everything all right? Why did this crazy person come to you?"

Then he said to them, "You know the sort and their ranting."

¹² But they replied, "That's a lie! Tell us!"

So Jehu said, "He talked to me about this and that and said, 'This is what the LORD says: I anoint you king over Israel.' "

¹³ Each man quickly took his garment and put it under Jehu on the bare steps. They blew the ram's horn and proclaimed, "Jehu is king!"

PSALM 77:13-20

¹³   God, Your way is holy.
     What god is great like God?
¹⁴   You are the God who works
     wonders;
     You revealed Your strength among
     the peoples.
¹⁵   With power You redeemed Your
     people,
     the descendants of Jacob and
     Joseph.   Selah

¹⁶   The waters saw You, God.
     The waters saw You; they
     trembled.
     Even the depths shook.
¹⁷   The clouds poured down water.
     The storm clouds thundered;
     Your arrows flashed back and
     forth.
¹⁸   The sound of Your thunder was in
     the whirlwind;
     lightning lit up the world.
     The earth shook and quaked.
¹⁹   Your way went through the sea,
     and Your path through the great
     waters,
     but Your footprints were unseen.
²⁰   You led Your people like a flock
     by the hand of Moses and Aaron.

PROVERBS 16:25-26

²⁵   There is a way that seems right to
     a man,
     but in the end it is the way of
     death.

²⁶   A worker's appetite works for him
     because his hunger urges him on.

ACTS 5:12-32

¹² Many signs and wonders were being done among the people through the hands of the apostles. By common consent they would all meet in Solomon's Colonnade. ¹³ None of the rest dared to join them, but the people praised them highly. ¹⁴ Believers were added to the Lord in increasing numbers—crowds of both men and women. ¹⁵ As a result, they would carry the sick out into the streets and lay them on beds and pallets so that when Peter came by, at least his shadow might fall on some of them. ¹⁶ In addition, a multitude came together from the towns surrounding Jerusalem, bringing sick people and those who were tormented by unclean spirits, and they were all healed.

¹⁷ Then the high priest took action. He and all his colleagues, those who belonged to the party of the Sadducees, were filled with jealousy. ¹⁸ So they ar-

rested the apostles and put them in the city jail. ¹⁹ But an angel of the Lord opened the doors of the jail during the night, brought them out, and said, ²⁰ "Go and stand in the temple complex, and tell the people all about this life." ²¹ In obedience to this, they entered the temple complex at daybreak and began to teach.

When the high priest and those who were with him arrived, they convened the Sanhedrin—the full Senate of the sons of Israel—and sent orders to the jail to have them brought. ²² But when the temple police got there, they did not find them in the jail, so they returned and reported, ²³ "We found the jail securely locked, with the guards standing in front of the doors; but when we opened them, we found no one inside!" ²⁴ As the captain of the temple police and the chief priests heard these things, they were baffled about them, as to what could come of this.

²⁵ Someone came and reported to them, "Look! The men you put in jail are standing in the temple complex and teaching the people." ²⁶ Then the captain went with the temple police and brought them in without force, because they were afraid the people might stone them. ²⁷ When they had brought them in, they had them stand before the Sanhedrin, and the high priest asked, ²⁸ "Didn't we strictly order you not to teach in this name? And look, you have filled Jerusalem with your teaching and are determined to bring this man's blood on us!"

²⁹ But Peter and the apostles replied, "We must obey God rather than men. ³⁰ The God of our fathers raised up Jesus, whom you had murdered by hanging Him on a tree. ³¹ God exalted this man to His right hand as ruler and Savior, to grant repentance to Israel, and forgiveness of sins. ³² We are witnesses of these things, and so is the Holy Spirit whom God has given to those who obey Him."

The Final Emphasis—Jesus

We are witnesses of these things, and so is the Holy Spirit whom God has given to those who obey Him.—Acts 5:32

The Holy Spirit will glorify Jesus. The promise of John 16:14—"He will glorify Me"—was fulfilled after the Holy Spirit came on the disciples at Pentecost, for we read: "We are witnesses of these things, and so is the Holy Spirit whom God has given to those who obey Him" (Ac 5:32). This shows that the divine Spirit and human spirits were working together for the same end—the glorification of Jesus.

The statement that the Holy Spirit would glorify Jesus was one of the most important lessons in the process of spiritual education. The whole purpose of the Spirit's coming was not to glorify Himself or the person who receives Him, but to glorify Jesus. That puts the emphasis in the proper place. If the Holy Spirit glorified the person who received Him, then that would make Christianity an eccentric religion—off center. If He glorified Himself, then it would make Christianity Spirit-centered rather than Christ-centered. Christianity that is not linked to the Incarnation can have no fixed idea as to what God is really like. Spirit-centered Christianity would leave us going off on a tangent into all kinds of weird areas of subjectivity.

There are some Christians who are more Spirit-oriented than Christ-oriented. They hear what they describe as the "voice of the Spirit" telling them to do strange and unseemly things. Every "voice" we hear must be tested against the character of Jesus, and if it doesn't come up to His standard, then it has to be rejected. The Holy Spirit will always glorify Jesus.

Prayer

O God, my Father, I am conscious that I am thinking through a delicate issue here. Give me such a clear vision of Jesus that I shall always decide according to Him. Amen.

Further Study

Mt 3; Is 11:2; 42:1; 61:1; Jn 1:32, 16:14; Ac 10:38
What did Isaiah prophesy?
How was this fulfilled?

JUNE 30

2 KINGS 9:14–10:36

¹⁴ Then Jehu son of Jehoshaphat, son of Nimshi, conspired against Joram. Joram and all Israel had been at Ramoth-gilead on guard against Hazael king of Aram. ¹⁵ But King Joram had returned to Jezreel to recover from the wounds that the Arameans had inflicted on him when he fought against Aram's King Hazael. Jehu said, "If you commanders wish to make me king, then don't let anyone escape from the city to go tell about it in Jezreel."

¹⁶ Jehu got into his chariot and went to Jezreel since Joram was laid up there and Ahaziah king of Judah had gone down to visit Joram. ¹⁷ Now the watchman was standing on the tower in Jezreel. He saw Jehu's troops approaching and shouted, "I see troops!"

Joram responded, "Choose a rider and send him to meet them and have him ask, 'Do you come in peace?' "

¹⁸ So a horseman went to meet Jehu and said, "This is what the king asks: 'Do you come in peace?' "

Jehu replied, "What do you have to do with peace? Fall in behind me."

The watchman reported, "The messenger reached them but hasn't started back."

¹⁹ So he sent out a second horseman, who went to them and said, "This is what the king asks: 'Do you come in peace?' "

Jehu answered, "What do you have to do with peace? Fall in behind me."

²⁰ Again the watchman reported, "He reached them but hasn't started back. Also, the driving is like that of Jehu son of Nimshi—he drives like a madman."

²¹ "Harness!" Joram shouted, and they harnessed his chariot. Then Joram king of Israel and Ahaziah king of Judah set out, each in his own chariot, and met Jehu at the plot of land of Naboth the Jezreelite. ²² When Joram saw Jehu he asked, "Do you come in peace, Jehu?"

He answered, "What peace can there be as long as there is so much prostitution and witchcraft from your mother Jezebel?"

²³ Joram turned around and fled, shouting to Ahaziah, "It's treachery, Ahaziah!"

²⁴ Then Jehu drew his bow and shot Joram between the shoulders. The ar-

row went through his heart, and he slumped down in his chariot. ²⁵ Jehu said to Bidkar his aide, "Pick him up and throw him on the plot of ground belonging to Naboth the Jezreelite. For remember when you and I were riding side by side behind his father Ahab, and the LORD uttered this oracle against him: ²⁶ 'As surely as I saw the blood of Naboth and the blood of his sons yesterday,' this is the LORD's message, 'so will I repay you on this plot of land,' this is the LORD's message. So now, according to the word of the LORD, pick him up and throw him on the plot of land."

²⁷ When King Ahaziah of Judah saw what was happening, he fled up the road toward Beth-haggan. Jehu pursued him, shouting, "Shoot him too!" So they shot him in his chariot at Gur Pass near Ibleam, but he fled to Megiddo and died there. ²⁸ Then his servants carried him to Jerusalem in a chariot and buried him in his fathers' tomb in the city of David. ²⁹ It was in the eleventh year of Joram son of Ahab that Ahaziah had become king over Judah.

³⁰ When Jehu came to Jezreel, Jezebel heard about it, so she painted her eyes, adorned her head, and looked down from the window. ³¹ As Jehu entered the gate, she said, "Do you come in peace, Zimri, killer of your master?" ³² He looked up toward the window and said, "Who is on my side? Who?" Two or three eunuchs looked down at him, ³³ and he said, "Throw her down!" So they threw her down, and some of her blood splattered on the wall and on the horses, and Jehu rode over her. ³⁴ Then he went in, ate and drank, and said, "Take care of this cursed woman and bury her, since she's a king's daughter." ³⁵ But when they went out to bury her, they did not find anything but her skull, her feet, and the palms of her hands. ³⁶ So they went back and told him, and he said, "This fulfills the LORD's word that He spoke through His servant Elijah the Tishbite: 'In the plot of land at Jezreel, the dogs will eat Jezebel's flesh. ³⁷ Jezebel's corpse will be like manure on the surface of the field in the plot of land at Jezreel so that no one will be able to say: This is Jezebel.' "

10 Since Ahab had 70 sons in Samaria, Jehu wrote letters and sent them to Samaria to the rulers of Jezreel, to the elders, and to the guardians of Ahab's sons, saying:

² When this letter arrives, since your master's sons are with you and you have chariots, horses, a fortified city, and weaponry, ³ select the most qualified of your master's sons, set him on his father's throne, and fight for your master's house.

⁴ However, they were terrified and reasoned, "Look, two kings couldn't stand against him; how can we?" ⁵ So the overseer of the palace, the overseer of the city, the elders, and the guardians sent a message to Jehu: "We are your servants, and we will do whatever you tell us. We will not make anyone king. Do whatever you think is right."

⁶ Then Jehu wrote them a second letter, saying:

If you are on my side, and if you will obey me, bring me the heads of your master's sons at this time tomorrow at Jezreel.

All 70 of the king's sons were being cared for by the city's prominent men. ⁷ When the letter came to them, they took the king's sons and slaughtered all 70, put their heads in baskets, and sent them to Jehu at Jezreel. ⁸ When the messenger came and told him, "They have brought the heads of the king's sons," the king said, "Pile them in two heaps at the entrance of the gate until morning."

⁹ The next morning when he went out and stood at the gate, he said to all the people, "You are innocent. It was I who conspired against my master and killed him. But who struck down all these? ¹⁰ Know, then, that not a word the LORD spoke against the house of Ahab will

fail, for the LORD has done what He promised through His servant Elijah." [11] So Jehu killed all who remained of the house of Ahab in Jezreel—all his great men, close friends, and priests—leaving him no survivors.

[12] Then he set out and went on his way to Samaria. On the way, while he was at Beth-eked of the Shepherds, [13] Jehu met the relatives of Ahaziah king of Judah and asked, "Who are you?"

They answered, "We're Ahaziah's relatives. We've come down to greet the king's sons and the queen mother's sons."

[14] Then Jehu ordered, "Take them alive." So they took them alive and then slaughtered them at the pit of Beth-eked—42 men. He didn't spare any of them.

[15] When he left there, he found Jehonadab son of Rechab coming to meet him. He greeted him and then asked, "Is your heart one with mine?"

"It is," Jehonadab replied.

Jehu said, "If it is, give me your hand."

So he gave him his hand, and Jehu pulled him up into the chariot with him. [16] Then he said, "Come with me and see my zeal for the LORD!" So he let him ride with him in his chariot. [17] When Jehu came to Samaria, he struck down all who remained from the house of Ahab in Samaria until he had annihilated his house, according to the word of the LORD spoken to Elijah.

[18] Then Jehu brought all the people together and said to them, "Ahab served Baal a little, but Jehu will serve him a lot. [19] Now, therefore, summon to me all the prophets of Baal, all his servants, and all his priests. None must be missing, for I have a great sacrifice for Baal. Whoever is missing will not live." However, Jehu was acting deceptively in order to destroy the servants of Baal. [20] Jehu commanded, "Consecrate a solemn assembly for Baal." So they called one.

[21] Then Jehu sent messengers throughout all Israel, and all the servants of Baal came; there was not a man left who did not come. They entered the temple of Baal, and it was filled from one end to the other. [22] Then he said to the custodian of the wardrobe, "Bring out the garments for all the servants of Baal." So he brought out their garments.

[23] Then Jehu and Jehonadab son of Rechab entered the temple of Baal, and Jehu said to the servants of Baal, "Look carefully to see that there are no servants of the LORD here among you—only servants of Baal." [24] Then they went in to offer sacrifices and burnt offerings.

Now Jehu had stationed 80 men outside, and he warned them, "Whoever allows any of the men I am delivering into your hands to escape will forfeit his life for theirs." [25] When he finished offering the burnt offering, Jehu said to the guards and officers, "Go in and kill them. Don't let anyone out." So they struck them down with the sword. Then the guards and officers threw the bodies out and went into the inner room of the temple of Baal. [26] They brought out the pillars of the temple of Baal and burned them [27] and tore down the pillar of Baal. Then they tore down the temple of Baal and made it a latrine—which it is to this day.

[28] Jehu eliminated Baal worship from Israel, [29] but he did not turn away from the sins that Jeroboam son of Nebat had caused Israel to commit—worshiping the golden calves that were in Bethel and Dan. [30] Nevertheless, the LORD said to Jehu, "Because you have done well in carrying out what is right in My sight and have done to the house of Ahab all that was in My heart, four generations of your sons will sit on the throne of Israel."

[31] Yet, Jehu was not careful to follow with all his heart the law of the LORD God of Israel. He did not turn from the sins that Jeroboam had caused Israel to commit.

[32] In those days the LORD began to reduce the size of Israel. Hazael defeated the Israelites throughout their territory: [33] from the Jordan eastward, all the land of Gilead—the Gadites, the Reubenites, and the Manassites—from Aroer which

is by the Arnon Valley through Gilead to Bashan.

³⁴ Now the rest of the events of Jehu's reign, along with all his accomplishments and all his might, are written about in the Historical Record of Israel's Kings. ³⁵ Jehu rested with his fathers, and he was buried in Samaria. His son Jehoahaz became king in his place. ³⁶ The length of Jehu's reign over Israel in Samaria was 28 years.

*P*SALM 78:1-8

¹ My people, hear my instruction;
  listen to what I say.
² I will declare wise sayings;
  I will speak mysteries from the
    past—
³ things we have heard and known
  and that our fathers have passed
    down to us.
⁴ We must not hide them from their
    children,
  but must tell a future generation
    the praises of the LORD,
  His might, and the wonderful
    works He has performed.
⁵ He established a testimony in
    Jacob
  and set up a law in Israel,
  which He commanded our
    fathers
  to teach to their children
⁶ so that a future generation—
    children yet to be born—
    might know.
  They were to rise and tell their
    children
⁷ so that they might put their
    confidence in God
  and not forget God's works,
  but keep His commandments.
⁸ Then they would not be like their
    fathers,
  a stubborn and rebellious
    generation,
  a generation whose heart was not
    loyal
  and whose spirit was not faithful
    to God.

*P*ROVERBS 16:27-28

²⁷ A worthless man digs up evil,
  and his speech is like a scorching
    fire.

²⁸ A contrary man spreads conflict,
  and a gossip separates friends.

*A*CTS 5:33–6:15

³³ When they heard this, they were enraged and wanted to kill them. ³⁴ A Pharisee named Gamaliel, a teacher of the law who was respected by all the people, stood up in the Sanhedrin and ordered the men to be taken outside for a little while. ³⁵ He said to them, "Men of Israel, be careful about what you're going to do to these men. ³⁶ Not long ago Theudas rose up, claiming to be somebody, and a group of about 400 men rallied to him. He was killed, and all his partisans were dispersed and came to nothing. ³⁷ After this man, Judas the Galilean rose up in the days of the census and attracted a following. That man also perished, and all his partisans were scattered. ³⁸ And now, I tell you, stay away from these men and leave them alone. For if this plan or this work is of men, it will be overthrown; ³⁹ but if it is of God, you will not be able to overthrow them. You may even be found fighting against God." So they were persuaded by him. ⁴⁰ After they called in the apostles and had them flogged, they ordered them not to speak in the name of Jesus and released them. ⁴¹ Then they went out from the presence of the Sanhedrin, rejoicing that they were counted worthy to be dishonored on behalf of the name. ⁴² Every day in the temple complex, and in various homes, they continued teaching and proclaiming the good news that the Messiah is Jesus.

6 In those days, as the number of the disciples was multiplying, there arose a complaint by the Hellenistic Jews against the Hebraic Jews that their widows were being overlooked in the

daily distribution. ²Then the Twelve summoned the whole company of the disciples and said, "It would not be right for us to give up preaching about God to wait on tables. ³Therefore, brothers, select from among you seven men of good reputation, full of the Spirit and wisdom, whom we can appoint to this duty. ⁴But we will devote ourselves to prayer and to the preaching ministry." ⁵The proposal pleased the whole company. So they chose Stephen, a man full of faith and the Holy Spirit, and Philip, Prochorus, Nicanor, Timon, Parmenas, and Nicolaus, a proselyte from Antioch. ⁶They had them stand before the apostles, who prayed and laid their hands on them.

⁷So the preaching about God flourished, the number of the disciples in Jerusalem multiplied greatly, and a large group of priests became obedient to the faith.

⁸Stephen, full of grace and power, was performing great wonders and signs among the people. ⁹Then some from what is called the Freedmen's Synagogue, composed of both Cyrenians and Alexandrians, and some from Cilicia and Asia, came forward and disputed with Stephen. ¹⁰But they were unable to stand up against the wisdom and the Spirit by whom he spoke.

¹¹Then they induced men to say, "We heard him speaking blasphemous words against Moses and God!" ¹²They stirred up the people, the elders, and the scribes; so they came up, dragged him off, and took him to the Sanhedrin. ¹³They also presented false witnesses who said, "This man does not stop speaking blasphemous words against this holy place and the law. ¹⁴For we heard him say that Jesus, this Nazarene, will destroy this place and change the customs that Moses handed down to us." ¹⁵And all who were sitting in the Sanhedrin looked intently at him and saw that his face was like the face of an angel.

Creative Commonplace

They chose Stephen, a man full of faith and the Holy Spirit, and Philip.—Acts 6:5

No matter what happens to you or when it happens to you, it is never too late to become creative. Pray as one man did who was on the verge of going insane: "O Jesus, come into my soul, my mind, my body, into every brain cell, and help me to be a contributive person." Jesus did come into every brain cell, and that man is now well and contributing to the kingdom of God in an astonishing way.

I wonder, am I talking today to someone who feels they are caught up in so many routines that they are in the rut? Routines often become (if I might coin a word) "rut"-ines. They make us into grooved, non-creative individuals unless—and this is the point—unless we make the commonplace a creative place. And how do we do that? By the creative spirit we bring to it.

Someone has described Philip the evangelist as "a third-rate man in a second-rate task who did a first-rate job." He was quite different from the Philip who was one of Christ's group of twelve disciples. He didn't have the privilege of having been chosen as one of the apostolic band. He was instead one of "the seven" whose task was "to wait on tables." He might have folded up under these limitations and said: "I am in a rut." Instead, he accepted the commonplace as a consecrated place and gently pushed against the barriers until they broke. His creativity marks him out as one of the greatest characters of the New Testament.

Prayer

O God, help me to turn all common places into creative places. Give me the attitude of Your servant Philip, who turned a routine task into a redemptive one. In Jesus' name I pray this. Amen.

Further Study

Col 3:1-10; 2 Co 5:17; Rm 12:2
In what image is the new self made?
What are you creating at present?

JULY 1

2 KINGS 11:1–13:9

11 When Athaliah, Ahaziah's mother, saw that her son was dead, she proceeded to annihilate all the royal heirs. ² Jehosheba, who was King Jehoram's daughter and Ahaziah's sister, secretly rescued Joash son of Ahaziah from the king's sons who were being killed and put him and his nurse in a bedroom. So he was hidden from Athaliah and was not killed. ³ Joash was in hiding with Jehosheba in the LORD's temple six years while Athaliah ruled over the land.

⁴ Then, in the seventh year, Jehoiada sent messengers and brought in the commanders of hundreds, the Carites, and the guards. He had them come to him in the LORD's temple, where he made a covenant with them and put them under oath. He showed them the king's son ⁵ and commanded them, "This is what you are to do: one third of you who come on duty on the Sabbath are to provide protection for the king's palace. ⁶ A third are to be at the Sur gate and a third at the gate behind the guards. You are to take turns providing protection for the palace.

⁷ Your two divisions that go off duty on the Sabbath are to provide protection for the LORD's temple. ⁸ You must completely surround the king with weapons in hand. Anyone who approaches the ranks is to be put to death. You must be with the king in all his daily tasks."

⁹ So the commanders of hundreds did everything Jehoiada the priest commanded. They each brought their men—those coming on duty on the Sabbath and those going off duty—and went to Jehoiada the priest. ¹⁰ The priest gave to the commanders of hundreds King David's spears and shields that were in the LORD's temple. ¹¹ Then the guards stood with their weapons in hand surrounding the king—from the right side of the temple to the left side, by the altar and by the temple.

¹² He brought out the king's son, put the crown on him, gave him the testimony, and made him king. They anointed him and clapped their hands and cried, "Long live the king!"

¹³ When Athaliah heard the noise

from the guard and the crowd, she went out to the people at the LORD's temple. [14] As she looked, there was the king standing by the pillar according to the custom. The commanders and the trumpeters were by the king, and all the people of the land were rejoicing and blowing trumpets. Athaliah tore her clothes and screamed "Treason! Treason!"

[15] Then Jehoiada the priest ordered the commanders of hundreds in charge of the army, "Take her out between the ranks, and put anyone who follows her to death by the sword," for the priest had said, "She is not to be put to death in the LORD's temple." [16] So they arrested her, and she went out by way of the Horses' Entrance to the king's palace, where she was put to death.

[17] Then Jehoiada made a covenant between the LORD, the king, and the people that they would be the LORD's people and another one between the king and the people. [18] So all the people of the land went to the temple of Baal and tore it down. They broke its altars and images into pieces, and they killed Mattan, the priest of Baal, at the altars.

Then Jehoiada the priest appointed guards for the LORD's temple. [19] He took with him the commanders of hundreds, the Carites, the guards, and all the people of the land, and they brought the king from the LORD's temple. They entered the king's palace by way of the guards' gate. Then Joash sat on the throne of the kings. [20] All the people of the land rejoiced, and the city was quiet, for they had put Athaliah to death by the sword in the king's palace.

[21] Joash was seven years old when he **12** became king. [1] In the seventh year of Jehu, Joash became king; he reigned 40 years in Jerusalem. His mother's name was Zibiah, who was from Beer-sheba. [2] Throughout the time Jehoiada the priest instructed him, Joash did what was right in the LORD's sight. [3] Yet the high places were not taken away; the people continued sacrificing and burning incense on the high places.

[4] Then Joash said to the priests, "All the dedicated money brought to the LORD's temple, census money, money from vows, and all money voluntarily given for the LORD's temple, [5] each priest is to take from his assessor and repair whatever damage to the temple is found.

[6] But by the twenty-third year of the reign of King Joash, the priests had not repaired the damage to the temple. [7] So King Joash called Jehoiada the priest and the other priests and said, "Why haven't you repaired the temple's damage? Since you haven't, don't take any money from your assessors; instead, hand it over for the repair of the temple." [8] So the priests agreed they would not take money from the people and they would not repair the temple's damage.

[9] Then Jehoiada the priest took a chest, bored a hole in its lid, and set it beside the altar on the right side as one enters the LORD's temple; in it the priests who guarded the threshold put all the money brought into the LORD's temple. [10] Whenever they saw there was a large amount of money in the chest, the king's secretary and the high priest would go to the LORD's temple and count the money found there and tie it up in bags. [11] Then they would put the counted money into the hands of those doing the work—those who oversaw the LORD's temple. They in turn would pay it out to those working on the LORD's temple—the carpenters, the builders, [12] the masons, and the stonecutters—and would use it to buy timber and quarried stone to repair the damage to the LORD's temple and for all spending for temple repairs.

[13] However, no silver bowls, wick trimmers, sprinkling basins, trumpets, or any articles of gold or silver were made for the LORD's temple from the money brought into the temple. [14] Instead, it was given to those doing the work, and they repaired the LORD's temple with it. [15] No accounting was required from the men who received the money to pay those doing the work, since they worked with integrity. [16] The money from the compensation offering

and the sin offering was not brought to the LORD's temple since it belonged to the priests. ¹⁷ At that time Hazael king of Aram marched up and fought against Gath and captured it. Then he planned to attack Jerusalem. ¹⁸ So King Joash of Judah took all the consecrated items that his ancestors—Judah's kings Jehoshaphat, Jehoram, and Ahaziah—had consecrated, along with his own consecrated items and all the gold found in the treasuries of the LORD's temple and in the king's palace, and he sent them to Hazael king of Aram. Then Hazael withdrew from Jerusalem.

¹⁹ The rest of the events of Joash's reign, along with all his accomplishments, are written about in the Historical Record of Judah's Kings. ²⁰ Joash's servants conspired against him and killed him at Beth-millo on the road that goes down to Silla. ²¹ His servants Jozabad son of Shimeath and Jehozabad son of Shomer struck him down, and he died. Then they buried him with his fathers in the city of David, and his son Amaziah became king in his place.

13 In the twenty-third year of Judah's King Joash son of Ahaziah, Jehoahaz son of Jehu became king over Israel in Samaria; he reigned 17 years. ² He did what was evil in the LORD's sight and followed the sins that Jeroboam son of Nebat had caused Israel to commit; he did not turn away from them. ³ So the LORD's anger burned against Israel, and He surrendered them to the power of Hazael king of Aram and his son Ben-hadad during their reigns. ⁴ Then Jehoahaz sought the LORD's favor, and the LORD heard him, for He saw the oppression the king of Aram inflicted on Israel. ⁵ Therefore, the LORD gave Israel a deliverer, and they escaped from the power of the Arameans. Then the people of Israel dwelt in their tents as before, ⁶ but they didn't turn away from the sins that the house of Jeroboam had caused Israel to commit. Jehoahaz walked in them, and the Asherah pole also remained standing in

Samaria. ⁷ Jehoahaz did not have an army left, except for 50 horsemen, 10 chariots, and 10,000 foot soldiers, because the king of Aram had destroyed them, making them like dust at threshing. ⁸ The rest of the events of Jehoahaz's reign, along with all his accomplishments and his might, are written about in the Historical Record of Israel's Kings. ⁹ Jehoahaz rested with his fathers, and he was buried in Samaria. His son Jehoash became king in his place.

𝒫SALM 78:9-16

⁹ The Ephraimite archers turned back
on the day of battle.
¹⁰ They did not keep God's covenant
and refused to live by His law.
¹¹ They forgot what He had done,
the wonderful works He had
shown them.
¹² He worked wonders in the sight of
their fathers,
in the land of Egypt, the region of
Zoan.
¹³ He split the sea and brought them
across;
the water stood firm like a wall.
¹⁴ He led them with a cloud by day
and with a fiery light throughout
the night.
¹⁵ He split rocks in the wilderness
and gave them drink as abundant
as the deep.
¹⁶ He brought streams out of the
stone
and made water flow down like
rivers.

𝒫ROVERBS 16:29-30

²⁹ A violent man lures his neighbor,
leading him in a way that is not
good.

³⁰ The one who narrows his eyes is
planning deceptions;
the one who compresses his lips
brings about evil.

$\mathcal{A}$CTS 7:1-22

7 "Is this true?" the high priest asked. ² "Brothers and fathers," he said, "listen: The God of glory appeared to our father Abraham when he was in Mesopotamia, before he settled in Haran, ³ and said to him:

> Get out of your country
> and away from
> your relatives,
> and come to the land
> that I will show you.

⁴ "Then he came out of the land of the Chaldeans and settled in Haran. And from there, after his father died, God had him move to this land in which you now live. ⁵ He didn't give him an inheritance in it, not even a foot of ground, but He promised to give it to him as a possession, and to his descendants after him, even though he was childless. ⁶ God spoke in this way:

> His descendants would be aliens
> in a foreign country,
> and they would enslave
> and oppress them
> for 400 years.
> ⁷ I will judge the nation
> that they will serve
> as slaves, God said.
> After this, they will come out
> and worship Me
> in this place.

⁸ Then He gave him the covenant of circumcision. This being so, he fathered Isaac and circumcised him on the eighth day; Isaac did the same with Jacob, and Jacob with the 12 patriarchs.

⁹ "The patriarchs became jealous of Joseph and sold him into Egypt, but God was with him ¹⁰ and rescued him out of all his troubles. He gave him favor and wisdom in the sight of Pharaoh, king of Egypt, who appointed him governor over Egypt and over his whole household. ¹¹ Then a famine came over all of Egypt and Canaan, with great suffering, and our forefathers could find no food. ¹² When Jacob heard there was grain in Egypt, he sent our forefathers the first time. ¹³ The second time, Joseph was revealed to his brothers, and Joseph's family became known to Pharaoh. ¹⁴ Joseph then invited his father Jacob and all his relatives, 75 people in all, ¹⁵ and Jacob went down to Egypt. He and our forefathers died there, ¹⁶ were carried back to Shechem, and were placed in the tomb that Abraham had bought for a sum of silver from the sons of Hamor in Shechem.

¹⁷ "As the time was drawing near to fulfill the promise that God had made to Abraham, the people flourished and multiplied in Egypt ¹⁸ until a different king ruled over Egypt who did not know Joseph. ¹⁹ He dealt deceitfully with our race and oppressed our forefathers by making them leave their infants outside so they wouldn't survive. ²⁰ At this time Moses was born, and he was beautiful before God. He was nursed in his father's home three months, ²¹ and when he was left outside, Pharaoh's daughter adopted and raised him as her own son. ²² So Moses was educated in all the wisdom of the Egyptians, and was powerful in his speech and actions.

The Original Quitters

They forgot what He had done,
the wonderful works He had shown them.—PSALM 78:11

The psalm before us today begins by commanding us to listen: "My people, hear my instruction; listen to what I say" (Ps 78:1). You have only to read a few verses of this psalm to see that the psalmist Asaph is recalling the disobedience that characterized the Jews during their forty years' wandering in the wilderness. Then a strange verse appears: "The Ephraimite archers turned back on the day of battle" (v. 9).

These Ephraimites were equipped with all they needed for warfare, but on the day of battle—that is, the first day of the fray—they "turned back." Although well armed, in the moment of testing they were overcome by fear. Doubtless they paraded well and looked fine as they marched out to battle, but when they came face to face with the enemy, the only weapon they used was a cloud of dust as they retreated *en masse*—and in a hurry.

A preacher I once heard referred to the Ephraimites in this verse as "the original quitters." What an indictment. The Ephraimites live on, you know; they are to be found in the rank and file of many a modern-day congregation. They look fine in church on Sunday mornings with a hymn book and a Bible in their hands, but let the hot rays of temptation beat upon them— and they run. They surrender to temptation because they have never learned how to surrender to God. When we surrender to God, then we need not surrender to anything else.

Prayer

Lord Jesus, help me clarify to myself whether I am surrendered or not. For I see that if I do not fall at Your feet, then I fall at the feet of things and circumstances. Show me at whose feet I am lying. For Your own name's sake. Amen.

Further Study

Dn 1:1-21; Rm 6:13; Eph 6:13
How did Daniel resist the temptation to compromise?
What are the results of resisting temptation?

JULY 2

2 KINGS 13:10–15:15

¹⁰ In the thirty-seventh year of Judah's King Joash, Jehoash son of Jehoahaz became king over Israel in Samaria; he reigned 16 years. ¹¹ He did what was evil in the LORD's sight. He did not turn away from all the sins that Jeroboam son of Nebat had caused Israel to commit, but he walked in them.

¹² The rest of the events of Jehoash's reign, along with all his accomplishments and the power he had to wage war against Judah's King Amaziah, are written about in the Historical Record of Israel's Kings. ¹³ Jehoash rested with

his fathers, and Jeroboam sat on his throne. Jehoash was buried in Samaria with the kings of Israel.

¹⁴ When Elisha became sick with the illness that he died from, Jehoash king of Israel went down and wept over him and said, "My father, my father, the chariots and horsemen of Israel!" ¹⁵ Elisha responded, "Take a bow and arrows." So he got a bow and arrows. ¹⁶ Then Elisha said to the king of Israel, "Put your hand on the bow." So the king put his hand on it, and Elisha put his hands on the king's hands. ¹⁷ Elisha said, "Open the east window." So he opened it. Elisha said, "Shoot!" So he shot. Then Elisha said, "The LORD's arrow of victory, yes, the arrow of victory over Aram. You are to strike down the Arameans in Aphek until you have put an end to them." ¹⁸ Then Elisha said, "Take the arrows!" So he took them, and he said to the king of Israel, "Strike the ground!" So he struck the ground three times and stopped. ¹⁹ The man of God was angry with him and said, "You should have struck the ground five or six times. Then you would have struck down Aram until you had put an end to them, but now you will only strike down Aram three times." ²⁰ Then Elisha died and was buried.

Now marauding bands of Moabites used to come into the land in the spring of the year. ²¹ Once, as the Israelites were burying a man, suddenly they saw a marauding band, so they threw the man into Elisha's tomb. When he touched Elisha's bones, the man revived and stood up!

²² Hazael king of Aram oppressed Israel throughout the reign of Jehoahaz, ²³ but the LORD was gracious to them and had compassion on them and turned toward them because of His covenant with Abraham, Isaac, and Jacob. He was not willing to destroy them. Even now He has not banished them from His presence.

²⁴ King Hazael of Aram died, and his son Ben-hadad became king in his place. ²⁵ Then Jehoash son of Jehoahaz took back from Ben-hadad son of Hazael the cities that Hazael had taken in war from Jehoash's father Jehoahaz. Jehoash defeated Ben-hadad three times and recovered the cities of Israel.

14 In the second year of Israel's King Jehoash son of Jehoahaz, Amaziah son of Joash became king of Judah. ² He was 25 years old when he became king; he reigned 29 years in Jerusalem. His mother's name was Jehoaddan and was from Jerusalem. ³ He did what was right in the LORD's sight, but not like his ancestor David. He did everything his father Joash had done. ⁴ Yet, the high places were not taken away, and the people continued sacrificing and burning incense on the high places.

⁵ As soon as the kingdom was firmly in his grasp, Amaziah killed his servants who had murdered his father the king. ⁶ However, he did not put the children of the murderers to death, as it is written in the book of the law of Moses where the LORD commanded, "Fathers must not be put to death because of children, and children must not be put to death because of fathers; instead, each one will be put to death for his own sin."

⁷ Amaziah killed 10,000 Edomites in the Valley of Salt. He took Sela in battle and called it Joktheel, which is its name to this very day. ⁸ Amaziah then sent messengers to Jehoash son of Jehoahaz, son of Jehu, king of Israel, saying, "Come, let us meet face to face."

⁹ King Jehoash of Israel sent word to Amaziah king of Judah, saying, "The thistle that was in Lebanon once sent a message to the cedar that was in Lebanon, saying, 'Give your daughter to my son as a wife.' Then a wild animal that was in Lebanon passed by and trampled the thistle. ¹⁰ You have indeed defeated Edom, and you have become overconfident. Enjoy your glory and stay at home. Why should you stir up such trouble that you fall—you and Judah with you?"

¹¹ But Amaziah would not listen, so King Jehoash of Israel advanced. He and

King Amaziah of Judah faced off at Beth-shemesh that belongs to Judah. [12] Judah was routed before Israel, and Judah's men fled, each to his own tent. [13] King Jehoash of Israel captured Judah's King Amaziah son of Joash, son of Ahaziah, at Beth-shemesh. Then Jehoash went to Jerusalem and broke down 200 yards of Jerusalem's wall from the Ephraim Gate to the Corner Gate. [14] He took all the gold and silver and all the utensils found in the LORD's temple and in the treasuries of the king's palace, and the hostages. Then he returned to Samaria.

[15] The rest of the events of Jehoash's reign, along with his accomplishments, his might, and how he waged war against Amaziah king of Judah, are written about in the Historical Record of Israel's Kings. [16] Jehoash rested with his fathers, and he was buried in Samaria with the kings of Israel. His son Jeroboam became king in his place.

[17] Judah's King Amaziah son of Joash lived 15 years after the death of Israel's King Jehoash son of Jehoahaz. [18] The rest of the events of Amaziah's reign are written about in the Historical Record of Judah's Kings. [19] A conspiracy was formed against him in Jerusalem, and he fled to Lachish. However, men were sent after him to Lachish, and they put him to death there. [20] They carried him back on horses, and he was buried in Jerusalem with his fathers in the city of David.

[21] Then all the people of Judah took Azariah, who was 16 years old, and made him king in place of his father Amaziah. [22] He rebuilt Elath and restored it to Judah after Amaziah the king rested with his fathers.

[23] In the fifteenth year of Judah's King Amaziah son of Joash, Jeroboam son of Jehoash became king of Israel in Samaria; he reigned 41 years. [24] He did what was evil in the LORD's sight. He did not turn away from all the sins Jeroboam son of Nebat had caused Israel to commit.

[25] It was he who restored Israel's border from Lebo-hamath as far as the Sea of the Arabah, according to the word the LORD, the God of Israel, had spoken through His servant, the prophet Jonah son of Amittai from Gath-hepher. [26] For the LORD saw that the affliction of Israel was very bitter. There was no one to help Israel, neither bond nor free. [27] However, the LORD had not said He would blot out the name of Israel from under heaven, so He delivered them by the hand of Jeroboam son of Jehoash.

[28] The rest of the events of Jeroboam's reign—along with all his accomplishments and the power he had to wage war and how he recovered for Israel Damascus and Hamath, which had belonged to Judah—are written about in the Historical Record of Israel's Kings. [29] Jeroboam rested with his fathers, the kings of Israel. His son Zechariah became king in his place.

15 In the twenty-seventh year of Israel's King Jeroboam, Azariah son of Amaziah became king of Judah. [2] He was 16 years old when he became king; he reigned 52 years in Jerusalem. His mother's name was Jecoliah; she was from Jerusalem. [3] Azariah did what was right in the LORD's sight just as his father Amaziah had done. [4] Yet, the high places were not taken away; the people continued sacrificing and burning incense on the high places.

[5] The LORD afflicted the king, and he had a serious skin disease until the day of his death. He lived in a separate house, while Jotham, the king's son, was over the household governing the people of the land.

[6] The rest of the events of Azariah's reign, along with all his accomplishments, are written about in the Historical Record of Judah's Kings. [7] Azariah rested with his fathers, and he was buried with his fathers in the city of David. His son Jotham became king in his place.

[8] In the thirty-eighth year of Judah's King Azariah, Zechariah son of Jeroboam became king over Israel in Samaria for six months. [9] He did what was evil in the LORD's sight as his fathers had done. He did not turn away from the sins Jeroboam son of Nebat had caused Israel to commit.

¹⁰ Shallum son of Jabesh conspired against Zechariah. He struck him down publicly, killed him, and became king in his place. ¹¹ As for the rest of the events of Zechariah's reign, they are written about in the Historical Record of Israel's Kings. ¹² The word of the LORD that He spoke to Jehu was, "Four generations of your sons will sit on the throne of Israel." And it was so.

¹³ In the thirty-ninth year of Judah's King Uzziah, Shallum son of Jabesh became king; he reigned in Samaria a full month. ¹⁴ Then Menahem son of Gadi came up from Tirzah to Samaria and struck down Shallum son of Jabesh there. He killed him and became king in his place. ¹⁵ As for the rest of the events of Shallum's reign, along with the conspiracy that he formed, they are written about in the Historical Record of Israel's Kings.

PSALM 78:17-22

¹⁷ But they continued to sin against Him,
rebelling in the desert against the Most High.
¹⁸ They deliberately tested God,
demanding the food they craved.
¹⁹ They spoke against God,
saying, "Is God able to provide food in the wilderness?
²⁰ Look! He struck the rock and water gushed out;
torrents overflowed.
But can He also provide bread or furnish meat for His people?"
²¹ Therefore, the LORD heard and became furious;
then fire broke out against Jacob,
and anger flared up against Israel
²² because they did not believe God or rely on His salvation.

PROVERBS 16:31-33

³¹ Gray hair is a glorious crown;
it is found in the way of righteousness.
³² Patience is better than power,
and controlling one's temper, than capturing a city.
³³ The lot is cast into the lap,
but its every decision is from the LORD.

ACTS 7:23-43

²³ "As he was approaching the age of 40, he decided to visit his brothers, the sons of Israel. ²⁴ When he saw one of them being mistreated, he came to his rescue and avenged the oppressed man by striking down the Egyptian. ²⁵ He assumed his brothers would understand that God would give them deliverance through him, but they did not understand. ²⁶ The next day he showed up while they were fighting and tried to reconcile them peacefully, saying, 'Men, you are brothers. Why are you mistreating each other?'
²⁷ "But the one who was mistreating his neighbor pushed him away, saying:

Who appointed you a ruler and a judge over us? ²⁸ Do you want to kill me, the same way you killed the Egyptian yesterday?

²⁹ "At this disclosure, Moses fled and became an exile in the land of Midian, where he fathered two sons. ³⁰ After 40 years had passed, an angel appeared to him in the desert of Mount Sinai, in the flame of a burning bush. ³¹ When Moses saw it, he was amazed at the sight. As he was approaching to look at it, the voice of the Lord came: ³² **I am the God of your forefathers—the God of Abraham, of Isaac, and of Jacob.** So Moses began to tremble and did not dare to look.
³³ "Then the Lord said to him:

Take the sandals off your feet, because the place where you are standing is holy ground. ³⁴ I have certainly seen the oppression of My people in Egypt; I have heard their groaning and have come

down to rescue them. And now, come, I will send you to Egypt.

35 "This Moses, whom they rejected when they said, **Who appointed you a ruler and a judge?**—this one God sent as a ruler and a redeemer by means of the angel who appeared to him in the bush. 36 This man led them out and performed wonders and signs in the land of Egypt, at the Red Sea, and in the desert for 40 years. 37 "This is the Moses who said to the sons of Israel, **God will raise up for you a Prophet like me from among your brothers.** 38 He is the one who was in the congregation in the desert together with the angel who spoke to him on Mount Sinai, and with our forefathers. He received living oracles to give to us. 39 Our forefathers were unwilling to obey him, but pushed him away, and in their hearts turned back to Egypt. 40 They told Aaron:

Make us gods who will go before us. As for this Moses who brought us out of the land of Egypt, we don't know what's become of him.

41 They even made a calf in those days, offered sacrifice to the idol, and were celebrating what their hands had made. 42 Then God turned away and gave them up to worship the host of heaven, as it is written in the book of the prophets:

Did you bring Me offerings
    and sacrifices
for 40 years in the desert,
    O house of Israel?
43 No, you took up
    the tent of Moloch
and the star of your god Rephan,
the images that you made
    to worship.
So I will deport you
    beyond Babylon!

Good Temper

Patience is better than power, and controlling one's temper, than capturing a city.—PROVERBS 16:32

One of the fruits of the Spirit is patience. The central meaning of this word (Greek: *makrothumia*) is "good temper." It denotes a person who does not easily "fly off the handle." He maintains good temper amid the flux and flow of human events.

One commentator says of this word: "This . . . fruit of the Spirit expresses the attitude to people which never loses patience with them, however unlovely and unteachable they may be." Archbishop Trench defined the word as "a long holding out of the mind before it gives room to action or to passion, the self-restraint which does not hastily retaliate a wrong." And Moffatt describes it as "the tenacity with which faith holds out."

Good temper must not, however, be confused with apathy. In the days of the early church, the group called the Stoics made indifference a virtue. They said: "Nothing is worth suffering for, so build a wall around your heart and keep out all sense of feeling." The early Christians did not share that view, however, for Christians care—and because they care, they suffered. Through the ministry of the Spirit in their lives, they found poise and good temper amidst their sufferings. The more we care, the more sensitive we will be to things that tend to block our goal of caring—that is why the quality of patience is so essential. An evangelist addressing a meeting was subjected to persistent heckling. Unfortunately, he lost his temper—and also his audience. They saw he had little to offer except words.

Prayer

O Father, help me to become a person of good temper. Dwell deep in me so that I shall be the peaceful exception amid the disturbed surroundings that I encounter day by day. Amen.

Further Study

Ec 7:1-12; Nm 20:1-13; Lk 21:19; Rm 12:12
What was the result of Moses' impatience?
What will be the result of our impatience?

JULY 3

2 KINGS 15:16–16:20

¹⁶ At that time, starting from Tirzah, Menahem attacked Tiphsah, all who were in it, and its territory. Because they wouldn't surrender, he attacked it and ripped open all the pregnant women.

¹⁷ In the thirty-ninth year of Judah's King Azariah, Menahem son of Gadi became king over Israel; he reigned 10 years in Samaria. ¹⁸ He did what was evil in the LORD's sight. Throughout his reign, he did not turn away from the sins Jeroboam son of Nebat had caused Israel to commit.

¹⁹ Pul king of Assyria invaded the land, so Menahem gave Pul 75,000 pounds of silver so that Pul would support him to strengthen his grip on the kingdom. ²⁰ Then Menahem exacted 20 ounces of silver from each of the wealthy men of Israel to give to the king of Assyria. So the king of Assyria withdrew and did not stay there in the land.

²¹ The rest of the events of Menahem's reign, along with all his accomplishments, are written about in the Historical Record of Israel's Kings.

²² Menahem rested with his fathers, and his son Pekahiah became king in his place.

²³ In the fiftieth year of Judah's King Azariah, Pekahiah son of Menahem became king over Israel in Samaria; he reigned two years. ²⁴ He did what was evil in the LORD's sight and did not turn away from the sins Jeroboam son of Nebat had caused Israel to commit.

²⁵ Then his officer, Pekah son of Remaliah, conspired against him and struck him down, as well as Argob and Arieh, in Samaria at the citadel of the king's palace. There were 50 Gileadite men with Pekah. He killed Pekahiah and became king in his place.

²⁶ As for the rest of the events of Pekahiah's reign, along with all his accomplishments, they are written about in the Historical Record of Israel's Kings.

²⁷ In the fifty-second year of Judah's King Azariah, Pekah son of Remaliah became king over Israel in Samaria; he reigned 20 years. ²⁸ He did what was evil in the LORD's sight. He did not turn away from the sins Jeroboam son of Nebat had caused Israel to commit.

²⁹ In the days of Pekah king of Israel, Tiglath-pileser king of Assyria came and captured Ijon, Abel-beth-maacah, Janoah, Kedesh, Hazor, Gilead, and Galilee—all the land of Naphtali—and deported the people to Assyria. ³⁰ Then Hoshea son of Elah organized a conspiracy against Pekah son of Remaliah. He attacked him, killed him, and became king in his place in the twentieth year of Jotham son of Uzziah. ³¹ As for the rest of the events of Pekah's reign, along with all his accomplishments, they are written about in the Historical Record of Israel's Kings.

³² In the second year of Israel's King Pekah son of Remaliah, Jotham son of Uzziah became king of Judah. ³³ He was 25 years old when he became king; he reigned 16 years in Jerusalem. His mother's name was Jerusha daughter of Zadok. ³⁴ He did what was right in the LORD's sight just as his father Uzziah had done. ³⁵ Yet, the high places were not taken away; the people continued sacrificing and burning incense on the high places.

It was Jotham who built the Upper Gate of the LORD's temple. ³⁶ The rest of the events of Jotham's reign, along with all his accomplishments, are written about in the Historical Record of Judah's Kings. ³⁷ In those days the LORD began sending Rezin king of Aram and Pekah son of Remaliah against Judah. ³⁸ Jotham rested with his fathers, and he was buried with his fathers in the city of his ancestor David. His son Ahaz became king in his place.

16 In the seventeenth year of Pekah son of Remaliah, Ahaz son of Jotham became king of Judah. ² Ahaz was 20 years old when he became king; he reigned 16 years in Jerusalem. He did not do what was right in the sight of the LORD his God like his ancestor David ³ but walked in the way of the kings of Israel. He even made his son pass through the fire, imitating the abominations of the nations the LORD had dispossessed before the Israelites. ⁴ He sacrificed and burned incense on the

high places, on the hills, and under every green tree.

⁵ Then Aram's King Rezin and Israel's King Pekah son of Remaliah came to wage war against Jerusalem. They besieged Ahaz but were not able to conquer him. ⁶ At that time Rezin king of Aram recovered Elath for Aram and expelled the Judahites from Elath. Then the Arameans came to Elath, and they live there until today.

⁷ So Ahaz sent messengers to Tiglath-pileser king of Assyria, saying, "I am your servant and your son. March up and save me from the power of the king of Aram and of the king of Israel, who are rising up against me." ⁸ Ahaz also took the silver and gold found in the LORD's temple and in the treasuries of the king's palace and sent them to the king of Assyria as a gift. ⁹ So the king of Assyria listened to him and marched up to Damascus and captured it. He deported its people to Kir but put Rezin to death.

¹⁰ King Ahaz went to Damascus to meet Tiglath-pileser king of Assyria. When he saw the altar that was in Damascus, King Ahaz sent a model of the altar and complete plans for its construction to Uriah the priest. ¹¹ Uriah built the altar according to all the instructions King Ahaz sent from Damascus. Therefore, by the time King Ahaz came back from Damascus, Uriah the priest had made it. ¹² When the king came back from Damascus, he saw the altar. Then he approached the altar and ascended it. ¹³ He offered his burnt offering and his grain offering, poured out his drink offering, and sprinkled the blood of his fellowship offerings on the altar. ¹⁴ He took the bronze altar that was before the LORD in front of the temple between his altar and the LORD's temple, and put it on the north side of his altar.

¹⁵ Then King Ahaz commanded Uriah the priest, "Offer on the great altar the morning burnt offering, the evening grain offering, and the king's burnt offering and his grain offering. Also offer the burnt offering of all the people of the land, their grain offering, and their

drink offerings. Sprinkle on the altar all the blood of the burnt offering and all the blood of sacrifice. The bronze altar will be for me to seek guidance." ¹⁶ Uriah the priest did everything King Ahaz commanded.

¹⁷ Then King Ahaz cut off the frames of the water carts and removed the bronze basin from each of them. He took the reservoir from the bronze oxen that were under it and put it on a stone pavement. ¹⁸ To satisfy the king of Assyria, he removed from the LORD's temple the Sabbath canopy they had built in the palace, and he closed the outer entrance for the king.

¹⁹ The rest of the events of Ahaz's reign, along with his accomplishments, are written about in the Historical Record of Judah's Kings. ²⁰ Ahaz rested with his fathers and was buried with his fathers in the city of David, and his son Hezekiah became king in his place.

PSALM 78:23-31

²³ He gave a command to the clouds above
and opened the doors of heaven.
²⁴ He rained manna for them to eat;
He gave them grain from heaven.
²⁵ People ate the bread of angels.
He sent them an abundant supply of food.
²⁶ He made the east wind blow in the skies
and drove the south wind by His might.
²⁷ He rained meat on them like dust,
and winged birds like the sand of the seas.
²⁸ He made them fall in His camp,
all around His tent.
²⁹ They ate and were completely satisfied,
for He gave them what they craved.
³⁰ Before they had satisfied their desire,
while the food was still in their mouths,

³¹ God's anger flared up against them,
and He killed some of their best men.
He struck down Israel's choice young men.

PROVERBS 17:1-2

17 Better a dry crust with peace than a house full of feasting with strife.

² A wise servant will rule over a disgraceful son
and share an inheritance among brothers.

ACTS 7:44–8:3

⁴⁴ "Our forefathers had the tabernacle of the testimony in the desert, just as He who spoke to Moses commanded him to make it according to the pattern he had seen. ⁴⁵ Our forefathers in turn received it and with Joshua brought it in when they dispossessed the nations that God drove out before our fathers, until the days of David. ⁴⁶ He found favor in God's sight and asked that he might provide a dwelling place for the God of Jacob. ⁴⁷ But it was Solomon who built Him a house. ⁴⁸ However, the Most High does not dwell in sanctuaries made with hands, as the prophet says:

⁴⁹ **Heaven is My throne,
and earth My footstool.
What sort of house
will you build for Me?
says the Lord,
or what is My resting place?**
⁵⁰ **Did not My hand make all
these things?**

⁵¹ "You stiff-necked people with uncircumcised hearts and ears! You are always resisting the Holy Spirit; as your forefathers did, so do you. ⁵² Which of the prophets did your fathers not persecute? They even killed those who announced beforehand the coming of the Righteous One, whose betrayers and

murderers you have now become. ⁵³ You received the law under the direction of angels and yet have not kept it."

⁵⁴ When they heard these things, they were enraged in their hearts and gnashed their teeth at him. ⁵⁵ But Stephen, filled by the Holy Spirit, gazed into heaven. He saw God's glory, with Jesus standing at the right hand of God, and he said, ⁵⁶ "Look! I see the heavens opened and the Son of Man standing at the right hand of God!"

⁵⁷ Then they screamed at the top of their voices, stopped their ears, and rushed together against him. ⁵⁸ They threw him out of the city and began to stone him. And the witnesses laid their robes at the feet of a young man named Saul. ⁵⁹ They were stoning Stephen as he called out: "Lord Jesus, receive my spirit!" ⁶⁰ Then he knelt down and cried out with a loud voice, "Lord, do not charge them with this sin!" And saying this, he fell asleep.

8 Saul agreed with putting him to death. On that day a severe persecution broke out against the church in Jerusalem, and all except the apostles were scattered throughout the land of Judea and Samaria. ² But devout men buried Stephen and mourned deeply over him. ³ Saul, however, was ravaging the church, and he would enter house after house, drag off men and women, and put them in prison.

The First Christian Martyr

Lord, do not charge them with this sin!

—ACTS 7:60

If Christ lives in you then He can love in you. You too can forgive injuries, pray for your enemies, and make every allowance for their wickedness.

The first man ever to die for Christ was Stephen. Our reading makes it clear that he was unjustly murdered. But Christ lived in him. His last words were a magnificent echo of Calvary: "Lord, do not charge them with this sin." Remember Stephen was stoned to death. Imagine how painful that must have been. It was almost as cruel as crucifixion. One by one the stones pounded the life from his body, but though they battered the life out of him they could not batter the love out of him. Like his Lord he kept on loving to the end. Christ was in his mind up until his last moments. "Lord," he said, "do not charge them with this sin."

The chapter ends with a lovely sentence: "And saying this, he fell asleep." But don't let these words lead you to think there was no hurt, no pain, no physical agony. He would have felt it all; you can be certain of that. But the love of Christ poured into him and through him, and, taken up with Him in his heart and mind, his soul was taken up to be with Him. Some words ring in my mind as I write—words spoken by one who stood holding the coats of those who threw the stones: "Make your own attitude that of Christ Jesus" (Php 2:5).

Prayer

Heavenly Father, I must not perpetuate the treatment people give to me. I must echo Your words and treat people as You do. But I can't do this except by Your grace. May Your love melt all my resentments and heal all my hurts. Amen.

Further Study

1 Sm 24:1-25; Ac 22:19-21; Rm 12:14-21
How did David have the mind of Christ?
How are we to treat those who treat us badly?

JULY 4

2 KINGS 17:1-41

17 In the twelfth year of Judah's King Ahaz, Hoshea son of Elah became king over Israel in Samaria; he reigned nine years. ² He did what was evil in the LORD's sight, but not like the kings of Israel who preceded him.

³ Shalmaneser king of Assyria attacked him, and Hoshea became his vassal and paid him tribute money. ⁴ But the king of Assyria discovered a conspiracy by Hoshea—he had sent envoys to So king of Egypt and had not paid tribute money to the king of Assyria as in previous years. Therefore, the king of Assyria arrested him and put him in prison. ⁵ Then the king of Assyria invaded the whole land, marched up to Samaria, and besieged it for three years.

⁶ In the ninth year of Hoshea, the king of Assyria captured Samaria. He deported the Israelites to Assyria and settled them in Halah and by the Habor, Gozan's river, and in the cities of the Medes.

⁷ This disaster happened because the people of Israel had sinned against the LORD their God who had brought them out of the land of Egypt from the power of Pharaoh king of Egypt and because they had worshiped other gods. ⁸ They had lived according to the customs of the nations that the LORD had dispossessed before the Israelites and the customs the kings of Israel had introduced. ⁹ The Israelites secretly did what was not right against the LORD their God. They built high places in all their towns from watchtower to fortified city. ¹⁰ They set up for themselves sacred pillars and Asherah poles on every high hill and under every green tree. ¹¹ They burned incense on all the high places just like those nations that the LORD had driven out before them. They did evil things, provoking the LORD. ¹² They served idols, although the LORD had told them, "You must not do this." ¹³ Still, the LORD warned Israel and Judah through every prophet and every seer, saying, "Turn from your evil ways and keep My commandments and statutes according to all the law I commanded your ancestors and sent to you through My servants the prophets."

¹⁴ But they would not listen. Instead,

they became obstinate like their ancestors who did not believe the LORD their God. ¹⁵ They rejected His statutes and His covenant He had made with their ancestors and the warnings He had given them. They pursued worthless idols and became worthless themselves, following the surrounding nations the LORD had commanded them not to imitate.

¹⁶ They abandoned all the commandments of the LORD their God. They made for themselves molded images—even two calves—and an Asherah pole. They worshiped the whole heavenly host and served Baal. ¹⁷ They made their sons and daughters pass through the fire and practiced divination and interpreted omens. They devoted themselves to do what was evil in the LORD's sight and provoked Him.

¹⁸ Therefore, the LORD was very angry with Israel, and He removed them from His presence. Only the tribe of Judah remained. ¹⁹ Even Judah did not keep the commandments of the LORD their God but lived according to the customs Israel had introduced. ²⁰ So the LORD rejected all the descendants of Israel, afflicted them, and handed them over to plunderers until He had banished them from His presence.

²¹ When the LORD tore Israel from the house of David, Israel made Jeroboam son of Nebat king. Then Jeroboam led Israel away from following the LORD and caused them to commit great sin. ²² The Israelites persisted in all the sins that Jeroboam committed and did not turn away from them. ²³ Finally, the LORD removed Israel from His presence just as He had declared through all His servants the prophets. So Israel has been exiled to Assyria from their homeland until today.

²⁴ Then the king of Assyria brought people from Babylon, Cuthah, Avva, Hamath, and Sepharvaim and settled them in place of the Israelites in the cities of Samaria. The settlers took possession of Samaria and lived in its cities. ²⁵ When they first lived there, they did not fear the LORD. So the LORD sent lions among them, which killed some of them. ²⁶ The settlers spoke to the king of Assyria, saying, "The nations that you have deported and placed in the cities of Samaria do not know the custom of the God of the land. Therefore, He has sent lions among them, which are killing them because the people don't know the custom of the God of the land."

²⁷ Then the king of Assyria issued a command: "Send back one of the priests you deported. Have him go and live there so he can teach them the custom of the God of the land." ²⁸ So one of the priests they had deported came and lived in Bethel, and he began to teach them how they should fear the LORD.

²⁹ But the people of each nation, in the cities where they lived, were still making their own gods and putting them in the shrines of the high places that the Samaritans had made. ³⁰ The men of Babylon made Succoth-benoth, the men of Cuth made Nergal, the men of Hamath made Ashima, ³¹ the Avvites made Nibhaz and Tartak, and the Sepharvites burned their children in the fire to Adrammelech and Anammelech, the gods of the Sepharvaim. ³² So they feared the LORD, but they also appointed from their number, priests to serve them in the shrines of the high places. ³³ They feared the LORD, but they also worshiped their own gods according to the custom of the nations where they had been deported from.

³⁴ They are still practicing the former customs to this day. None of them fear the LORD or observe their statutes and ordinances, the law and commandments the LORD commanded the descendants of Jacob; He renamed him Israel. ³⁵ The LORD made a covenant with them and commanded them, "Do not fear other gods; do not bow down to them; do not serve them; do not sacrifice to them. ³⁶ Instead, fear the LORD, who brought you from the land of Egypt with great power and an outstretched arm. You are to bow down to Him, and you are to sacrifice to Him. ³⁷ You are to be careful always to observe the statutes, the ordinances, the laws, and the commandment He wrote for you; do

not fear other gods. [38] Do not forget the covenant that I have made with you. Do not fear other gods, [39] but fear the LORD your God, and He will deliver you from the hand of all your enemies."

[40] However, they would not listen but continued practicing their former custom. [41] These nations feared the LORD but also served their idols. Their children and grandchildren continue doing as their fathers did until today.

PSALM 78:32-39

[32] Despite all this, they kept sinning
and did not believe His wonderful works.
[33] He made their days end in futility,
their years in sudden disaster.
[34] When He killed some of them, the rest began to seek Him;
they repented and searched for God.
[35] They remembered that God was their rock,
the Most High God, their Redeemer.
[36] But they deceived Him with their mouths,
they lied to Him with their tongues,
[37] their hearts were insincere toward Him,
and they were unfaithful to His covenant.
[38] Yet He was compassionate;
He atoned for their guilt
and did not destroy them.
He often turned His anger aside
and did not unleash all His wrath.
[39] He remembered that they were only flesh,
a wind that passes and does not return.

PROVERBS 17:3-4

[3] A crucible is for silver and a smelter for gold,
but the LORD is a tester of hearts.

[4] A wicked person listens to malicious talk;
a liar pays attention to a destructive tongue.

ACTS 8:4-40

[4] So those who were scattered went on their way proclaiming the message of good news. [5] Philip went down to a city in Samaria and preached the Messiah to them. [6] The crowds paid attention with one mind to what Philip said, as they heard and saw the signs he was performing. [7] For unclean spirits, crying out with a loud voice, came out of many who were possessed, and many who were paralyzed and lame were healed. [8] So there was great joy in that city.

[9] A man named Simon had previously practiced sorcery in that city and astounded the Samaritan people, while claiming to be somebody great. [10] They all paid attention to him, from the least of them to the greatest, and they said, "This man is called the Great Power of God!" [11] They were attentive to him because he had astounded them with his sorceries for a long time. [12] But when they believed Philip, as he proclaimed the good news about the kingdom of God and the name of Jesus Christ, both men and women were baptized. [13] Then even Simon himself believed. And after he was baptized, he went around constantly with Philip and was astounded as he observed the signs and great miracles that were being performed.

[14] When the apostles who were at Jerusalem heard that Samaria had welcomed God's message, they sent Peter and John to them. [15] After they went down there, they prayed for them, that they might receive the Holy Spirit. [16] For He had not yet come down on any of them; they had only been baptized in the name of the Lord Jesus. [17] Then Peter and John laid their hands on them, and they received the Holy Spirit.

[18] When Simon saw that the Holy Spirit was given through the laying on of the apostles' hands, he offered them money, [19] saying, "Give me this power

too, so that anyone I lay hands on may receive the Holy Spirit."

²⁰ But Peter told him, "May your silver be destroyed with you, because you thought the gift of God could be obtained with money! ²¹ You have no part or share in this matter, because your heart is not right before God. ²²Therefore repent of this wickedness of yours, and pray to the Lord that the intent of your heart may be forgiven you. ²³ For I see you are poisoned by bitterness and bound by iniquity."

²⁴ "Please pray to the Lord for me," Simon replied, "so that nothing you have said may happen to me."

²⁵ Then, after they had testified and spoken the message of the Lord, they traveled back to Jerusalem, evangelizing many villages of the Samaritans.

²⁶ An angel of the Lord spoke to Philip: "Get up and go south to the road that goes down from Jerusalem to desert Gaza." ²⁷ So he got up and went. There was an Ethiopian man, a eunuch and high official of Candace, queen of the Ethiopians, who was in charge of her entire treasury. He had come to worship in Jerusalem ²⁸ and was sitting in his chariot on his way home, reading the prophet Isaiah aloud.

²⁹ The Spirit told Philip, "Go and join that chariot."

³⁰ When Philip ran up to it, he heard him reading the prophet Isaiah, and said, "Do you understand what you're reading?"

³¹ "How can I," he said, "unless someone guides me?" So he invited Philip to come up and sit with him. ³² Now the Scripture passage he was reading was this:

He was led like a sheep
    to the slaughter,
and as a lamb is silent
    before its shearer,
so He does not open His
    mouth.
³³ In His humiliation justice
    was denied Him.
Who will describe
    His generation?
For His life is taken
    from the earth.

³⁴ The eunuch replied to Philip, "I ask you, who is the prophet saying this about—himself or another person?" ³⁵ So Philip proceeded to tell him the good news about Jesus, beginning from that Scripture.

³⁶ As they were traveling down the road, they came to some water. The eunuch said, "Look, there's water! What would keep me from being baptized?" [³⁷ And Philip said, "If you believe with all your heart you may." And he replied, "I believe that Jesus Christ is the Son of God."] ³⁸ Then he ordered the chariot to stop, and both Philip and the eunuch went down into the water, and he baptized him. ³⁹ When they came up out of the water, the Spirit of the Lord carried Philip away, and the eunuch did not see him any longer. But he went on his way rejoicing. ⁴⁰ Philip appeared in Azotus, and passing through, he was evangelizing all the towns until he came to Caesarea.

Amazing!

Yet He was compassionate; He atoned for their guilt.
—Psalm 78:38

If we are to go deeper with God, we need to know how to avail ourselves of God's grace. Romans 5:17 talks about "those who receive the overflow of grace." Though God's grace may be abundant, it is only effective in our lives if it is received. But what do we mean by "grace"? Grace is spoken of in both the Old and New Testaments, and the root meaning of the word is that of kindness and favor. In the New Testament it is used chiefly in connection with God's un-deserved mercy in redeeming humankind. Grace, as undeserved favor, is a term still used in business—especially the world of insurance. Sometimes a representative of a firm will write to a client and say something like this: "In the circumstances you have no claim, we will give you a certain sum as an act of grace." They acknowledge no indebtedness, but out of their kindness (and in hope of business to come) they give the client something to which he has no legal right.

A definition of grace I like very much is this: "Grace is the strength God gives us to obey His commands." Grace is not just a kindly attitude but an impartation of power, too. We can be sure that the people who seem to know God in a much deeper way than we do have received more of that power that God imparts "unmerited and free." It is by grace that they leap over all the impediments on their onward way. Grace truly is amazing!

Prayer

O God, help me look at the values of earth in the light of heaven. Show me the folly of accu-mulating riches, the absurdity of heaping together the treasures of earth. May I come to recog-nize what has the highest value of all—Your matchless grace. Amen.

Further Study

2 Co 8:9; 12:9; 2 Tm 2:1-10
How did Paul describe grace at work?
What was Paul's admonition to Timothy?

JULY 5

2 KINGS 18:1–19:19

18 In the third year of Israel's King Hoshea son of Elah, Hezekiah son of Ahaz became king of Judah. ² He was 25 years old when he became king; he reigned 29 years in Jerusalem. His mother's name was Abi daughter of Zechariah. ³ He did what was right in the LORD's sight just as his ancestor David had done. ⁴ He removed the high places and shattered the sacred pillars and cut down the Asherah poles. He broke into pieces the bronze serpent that Moses made, for the Israelites burned incense to it up to that time. He called it Nehushtan.

⁵ Hezekiah trusted in the LORD God of Israel; not one of the kings of Judah was like him, either before him or after him. ⁶ He held fast to the LORD and did not turn from following Him but kept the

commandments the LORD had commanded Moses. ⁷The LORD was with him, and wherever he went, he prospered. He rebelled against the king of Assyria and did not serve him. ⁸He defeated the Philistines as far as Gaza and its borders, from watchtower to fortified city. ⁹In the fourth year of King Hezekiah, which was the seventh year of Israel's King Hoshea son of Elah, Shalmaneser king of Assyria marched against Samaria and besieged it. ¹⁰The Assyrians captured it at the end of three years. In the sixth year of Hezekiah, which was the ninth year of Israel's King Hoshea, Samaria was captured. ¹¹The king of Assyria deported the Israelites to Assyria and put them in Halah and by the Habor, Gozan's river, and in the cities of the Medes, ¹²because they did not listen to the voice of the LORD their God but violated His covenant—all He had commanded Moses the servant of the LORD. They did not listen, and they did not obey.

¹³In the fourteenth year of King Hezekiah, Sennacherib king of Assyria attacked all the fortified cities of Judah and captured them. ¹⁴So Hezekiah king of Judah sent word to the king of Assyria at Lachish, saying, "I have done wrong. Withdraw from me. Whatever you demand from me, I will pay." The king of Assyria demanded from King Hezekiah of Judah 11 tons of silver and one ton of gold. ¹⁵So Hezekiah gave him all the silver found in the LORD's temple and in the treasuries of the king's palace.

¹⁶At that time Hezekiah stripped the gold from the doors of the LORD's sanctuary and from the doorposts he had overlaid and gave it to the king of Assyria.

¹⁷Then the king of Assyria sent the Tartan, the Rab-saris, and the Rabshakeh, along with a massive army, from Lachish to King Hezekiah at Jerusalem. They advanced and came to Jerusalem, and they took their position by the aqueduct of the upper pool, which is by the highway to the Fuller's Field. ¹⁸Then they called for the king, but

Eliakim son of Hilkiah, who was in charge of the palace, Shebnah the court secretary, and Joah son of Asaph, the court historian, came out to them.

¹⁹Then the Rabshakeh said to them, "Tell Hezekiah this is what the great king, the king of Assyria, says: 'What are you relying on? ²⁰You think mere words are strategy and strength for war. What are you now relying on so that you have rebelled against me? ²¹Look, you now trust in Egypt, the stalk of this splintered reed, which if a man leans on it will go into his palm and pierce it. This is how Pharaoh king of Egypt is to all who trust in him. ²²Suppose you say to me: We trust in the LORD our God. Isn't He the One whose high places and altars Hezekiah has removed, saying to Judah and to Jerusalem: You must worship at this altar in Jerusalem?'

²³"So now make a bargain with my master the king of Assyria. I'll give you 2,000 horses if you're able to supply riders for them! ²⁴How then can you drive back a single officer among the least of my master's servants and trust in Egypt for chariots and for horsemen? ²⁵Have I attacked this place to destroy it without the LORD's approval? The LORD said to me, 'Attack this land and destroy it.' "

²⁶Then Eliakim son of Hilkiah, Shebnah, and Joah said to the Rabshakeh, "Please speak to your servants in Aramaic, since we understand it. Don't speak with us in Hebrew within earshot of the people on the wall."

²⁷But the Rabshakeh said to them, "Has my master sent me only to your master and to you to speak these words? Hasn't he also sent me to the men who sit on the wall, destined with you to eat their own excrement and drink their own urine?"

²⁸The Rabshakeh stood and called out loudly in Hebrew. Then he spoke: "Hear the word of the great king, the king of Assyria. ²⁹This is what the king says: 'Don't let Hezekiah deceive you; he can't deliver you from my hand. ³⁰Don't let Hezekiah persuade you to trust in the LORD by saying: Certainly the LORD will deliver us! This city will not be handed over to the king of Assyria.'

[31] "Don't listen to Hezekiah, for this is what the king of Assyria says: 'Make peace with me and surrender to me. Then every one of you may eat from his own vine and his own fig tree, and every one may drink water from his own cistern [32] until I come and take you away to a land like your own land—a land of grain and new wine, a land of bread and vineyards, a land of olive trees and honey—so that you may live and not die. But don't listen to Hezekiah when he misleads you, saying: The LORD will deliver us. [33] Has any of the gods of the nations ever delivered his land from the power of the king of Assyria? [34] Where are the gods of Hamath and Arpad? Where are the gods of Sepharvaim, Hena, and Ivvah? Have they delivered Samaria from my hand? [35] Who among all the gods of the lands has delivered his land from my power? So how is the LORD to deliver Jerusalem?' "

[36] But the people kept silent; they answered him not a word, for the king's command was, "Don't answer him." [37] Then Eliakim son of Hilkiah, who was in charge of the palace, Shebna the court secretary, and Joah son of Asaph, the court historian, came to Hezekiah with their clothes torn and reported to him the words of the Rabshakeh.

19 When King Hezekiah heard their report, he tore his clothes, covered himself with sackcloth, and went into the LORD's temple. [2] Then he sent Eliakim, who was in charge of the palace, Shebna the court secretary, and the elders of the priests, covered with sackcloth, to the prophet Isaiah son of Amoz. [3] They said to him, "This is what Hezekiah says: 'Today is a day of distress, rebuke, and disgrace, for children have come to the point of birth, but there is no strength to deliver them. [4] Perhaps the LORD your God will hear all the words of the Rabshakeh, whom his master the king of Assyria sent to mock the living God, and will rebuke him for the words that the LORD your God has heard. Therefore, offer a prayer for the surviving remnant.' "

[5] So the servants of King Hezekiah went to Isaiah, [6] who said to them, "Tell your master this, 'The LORD says: Don't be afraid because of the words you have heard, that the king of Assyria's attendants have blasphemed Me with. [7] I am about to put a spirit in him, and he will hear a rumor and return to his own land where I will cause him to fall by the sword.' "

[8] When the Rabshakeh heard that the king of Assyria had left Lachish, he returned and found him fighting against Libnah. [9] The king had heard this about Tirhakah king of Cush: "Look, he has set out to fight against you." So he again sent messengers to Hezekiah, saying, [10] "Say this to Hezekiah king of Judah: 'Don't let your God, whom you trust, deceive you by promising that Jerusalem will not be handed over to the king of Assyria. [11] Look, you have heard what the kings of Assyria have done to all the countries: they destroyed them completely. Will you be rescued? [12] Did the gods of the nations that my predecessors destroyed rescue them—nations such as Gozan, Haran, Rezeph, and the Edenites in Telassar? [13] Where is the king of Hamath, the king of Arpad, the king of the city of Sepharvaim, Hena, or Ivvah?' "

[14] Hezekiah took the letter from the hand of the messengers, read it, then went up to the LORD's temple, and spread it out before the LORD. [15] Then Hezekiah prayed before the LORD: "LORD God of Israel who is enthroned above the cherubim, You are God—You alone—of all the kingdoms of the earth. You made the heavens and the earth. [16] Listen closely, LORD, and hear; open Your eyes, LORD, and see; hear the words that Sennacherib has sent to mock the living God. [17] LORD, it is true that the kings of Assyria have devastated the nations and their lands. [18] They have thrown their gods into the fire, for they were not gods but made by human hands—wood and stone. So they have destroyed them. [19] Now, LORD our God, please save us from his hand so that all the kingdoms of the earth may know that You are the LORD God—You alone."

PSALM 78:40-47

40 How often they rebelled against
   Him in the wilderness
   and grieved Him in the desert.
41 They constantly tested God
   and provoked the Holy One of
   Israel.
42 They did not remember His power
   shown
   on the day He redeemed them
   from the foe,
43 when He performed His
   miraculous signs in Egypt
   and His marvels in the region of
   Zoan.
44 He turned their rivers into blood,
   and they could not drink from
   their streams.
45 He sent among them swarms of
   flies, which fed on them,
   and frogs, which devastated them.
46 He gave their crops to the
   caterpillar
   and the fruit of their labor to the
   locust.
47 He killed their vines with hail
   and their sycamore-fig trees with a
   flood.

PROVERBS 17:5-6

5 The one who mocks the poor
   insults his Maker,
   and one who rejoices over disaster
   will not go unpunished.

6 Grandchildren are the crown of
   the elderly,
   and the pride of sons is their
   fathers.

ACTS 9:1-22

9 Meanwhile Saul, still breathing
threats and murder against the disciples of the Lord, went to the high priest
2 and requested letters from him to the synagogues in Damascus, so that if he found any who belonged to the Way, either men or women, he might bring them as prisoners to Jerusalem. 3 As he traveled and was nearing Damascus, a light from heaven suddenly flashed around him. 4 Falling to the ground, he heard a voice saying to him, "Saul, Saul, why are you persecuting Me?"

5 "Who are You, Lord?" he said.

"I am Jesus, whom you are persecuting," He replied. 6 "But get up and go into the city, and you will be told what you must do."

7 The men who were traveling with him stood speechless, hearing the sound but seeing no one. 8 Then Saul got up from the ground, and though his eyes were open, he could see nothing. So they took him by the hand and led him into Damascus. 9 He was unable to see for three days, and did not eat or drink.

10 Now in Damascus there was a disciple named Ananias. And the Lord said to him in a vision, "Ananias!"

"Here I am, Lord!" he said.

11 "Get up and go to the street called Straight," the Lord said to him, "to the house of Judas, and ask for a man from Tarsus named Saul, since he is praying there. 12 In a vision he has seen a man named Ananias coming in and placing his hands on him so he may regain his sight."

13 "Lord," Ananias answered, "I have heard from many people about this man, how much harm he has done to Your saints in Jerusalem. 14 And he has authority here from the chief priests to arrest all who call on Your name."

15 But the Lord said to him, "Go! For this man is My chosen instrument to carry My name before Gentiles, kings, and the sons of Israel. 16 I will certainly show him how much he must suffer for My name!"

17 So Ananias left and entered the house. Then he placed his hands on him and said, "Brother Saul, the Lord Jesus, who appeared to you on the road you were traveling, has sent me so you may regain your sight and be filled with the Holy Spirit."

18 At once something like scales fell from his eyes, and he regained his sight. Then he got up and was baptized. 19 And after taking some food, he regained his strength.

Saul was with the disciples in Damascus for some days. [20] Immediately he began proclaiming Jesus in the synagogues: "He is the Son of God."

[21] But all who heard him were astounded and said, "Isn't this the man who, in Jerusalem, was destroying those who called on this name, and then came here for the purpose of taking them as prisoners to the chief priests?"

[22] But Saul grew more capable, and kept confounding the Jews who lived in Damascus by proving that this One is the Messiah.

Nothing!

Who are You, Lord?
——ACTS 9:5

Max Muller, a writer on religious issues, once made this arresting statement: "You do not know the worth of your Christian faith until you have compared it to others." The first article of belief we look at is the fact that God has appeared in this world in the Person of His eternal Son. Our faith is not the word of a prophet but the Word of the Son Himself. No other world faith even attempts to represent its great teacher as God incarnate. Yet we claim for Christ just that. As God, He comes to us from the highest, and He comes all the way.

I remember hearing a missionary to India say that he was forced to rethink his faith in the light of other faiths and other ways of life. "All the old shibboleths and modes of expression and accepted outlooks on life are challenged," he said, "and one begins to see where the relevant lies." He started discussions with Hindu, Buddhist, and Muslim leaders, as well as representatives of India's many other religions. The gatherings were called "Round Table" discussions to suggest that everyone could present what they considered to be the distinctives of their faith. One could see scintillations of truth, the missionary recalled, as people spoke from experience or from their sacred books. But whenever a Christian spoke and unfolded the truth of the Incarnation, the meeting would lapse into silence. Sometimes the silence would last for many minutes, only to be broken with the remark: "We have nothing in our faith that compares to that. Nothing!"

Prayer

Dear God and Father, if You hadn't come down to us, how could we have ever come up to You? What humiliation this must have meant for You. Yet what love. Our hearts sing with gratitude. Blessed be Your name forever. Amen.

Further Study

Ac 1:1-5; 1 Co 15:1-8; Ac 9:1-6; 1 Tm 3:16
What was Paul's testimony?
How did he substantiate it?

JULY 6

2 KINGS 19:20–21:26

²⁰ Then Isaiah son of Amoz sent a message to Hezekiah: "The LORD, the God of Israel says: 'I have heard your prayer to Me about Sennacherib king of Assyria.' ²¹ This is the word the LORD has spoken against him:

The young woman, Daughter Zion,
despises you and scorns you:
Daughter Jerusalem
shakes her head behind your
back.
²² Who is it you mocked and
blasphemed?
Against whom have you raised
your voice
and lifted your eyes in pride?
Against the Holy One of Israel!
²³ You have mocked the Lord
through your messengers.
You have said:

With my many chariots
I have gone up to the heights of
the mountains,
to the far recesses of Lebanon.
I cut down its tallest cedars,
its choice cypress trees.
I came to its farthest outpost,
its densest forest.
²⁴ I dug wells,
and I drank foreign waters.
I dried up all the streams of Egypt
with the soles of my feet.

²⁵ Have you not heard?
I designed it long ago;
I planned it in days gone by.
I have now brought it to pass,
and you have crushed fortified
cities
into piles of rubble.
²⁶ Their inhabitants have become
powerless,
dismayed, and ashamed.

They are plants of the field,
tender grass,
grass on the rooftops,
blasted by the east wind.

²⁷ But I know your sitting down,
your going out and your coming
in,
and your raging against Me.
²⁸ Because your raging against Me
and your arrogance have reached
My ears,
I will put My hook in your nose
and My bit in your mouth;
I will make you go back
the way you came.

²⁹ This will be the sign for you: This year you will eat what grows on its own, and in the second year what grows from that. But in the third year sow and reap, plant vineyards and eat their fruit. ³⁰ The surviving remnant of the house of Israel will again take root downward and bear fruit upward. ³¹ For a remnant will go out from Jerusalem, and survivors from Mount Zion. The zeal of the LORD of Hosts will accomplish this.

³² Therefore, this is what the LORD
says about the king of Assyria:
He will not enter this city
or shoot an arrow there
or come before it with a shield
or build up an assault ramp
against it.
³³ He will go back
on the road that he came
and he will not enter this city,
declares the LORD.
³⁴ I will defend this city and
rescue it
for My sake and for the sake of
My servant David.

³⁵ That night the angel of the LORD went out and struck down 185,000 in

the camp of the Assyrians. When the people got up the next morning—there were all the dead bodies! [36] So Sennacherib king of Assyria broke camp and left. He returned home and lived in Nineveh.

[37] One day, while he was worshiping in the temple of his god Nisroch, his sons Adrammelech and Sharezer struck him down with the sword and escaped to the land of Ararat. Then his son Esarhaddon became king in his place.

20 In those days Hezekiah became terminally ill. The prophet Isaiah son of Amoz came and said to him, "This is what the LORD says: 'Put your affairs in order, for you are about to die; you will not recover.' "

[2] Then Hezekiah turned his face to the wall and prayed to the LORD, [3] "Please LORD, remember how I have walked before You faithfully and wholeheartedly and have done what is good in Your sight." And Hezekiah wept bitterly.

[4] Isaiah had not yet gone out of the inner courtyard when the word of the LORD came to him: [5] "Go back and tell Hezekiah, the leader of My people, 'This is what the LORD God of your ancestor David says: I have heard your prayer; I have seen your tears. Look, I will heal you. On the third day from now you will go up to the LORD's temple. [6] I will add 15 years to your life. I will deliver you and this city from the hand of the king of Assyria. I will defend this city for My sake and for the sake of My servant David.' "

[7] Then Isaiah said, "Bring a lump of pressed figs." So they brought it and applied it to his infected skin, and he recovered.

[8] Hezekiah had asked Isaiah, "What is the sign that the LORD will heal me and that I will go up to the LORD's temple on the third day?"

[9] Isaiah said, "This is the sign to you from the LORD that He will do what He has promised: Should the shadow go ahead 10 steps or go back 10 steps?"

[10] Then Hezekiah answered, "It's easy for the shadow to lengthen 10 steps. No, let the shadow go back 10 steps."

[11] So Isaiah the prophet called out to the LORD, and He brought the shadow back the 10 steps it had descended on Ahaz's stairway.

[12] At that time Merodach-baladan son of Baladan, king of Babylon, sent letters and a gift to Hezekiah since he heard that Hezekiah had been sick. [13] Hezekiah gave them a hearing and showed them his whole treasure house—the silver, the gold, the spices, and the precious oil—and his armory, and everything that was found in his treasuries. There was nothing in his palace and in all his realm that Hezekiah did not show them.

[14] Then the prophet Isaiah came to King Hezekiah and asked him, "What did these men say, and where did they come to you from?"

Hezekiah replied, "They came from a distant country, from Babylon."

[15] Isaiah asked, "What have they seen in your palace?"

Hezekiah answered, "They have seen everything in my palace. There isn't anything in my treasuries that I didn't show them."

[16] Then Isaiah said to Hezekiah, "Hear the word of the LORD: [17] 'The time will certainly come when everything in your palace and all that your fathers have stored up until this day will be carried off to Babylon; nothing will be left,' says the LORD. [18] 'Some of your descendants who come from you will be taken away, and they will become eunuchs in the palace of the king of Babylon.' "

[19] Then Hezekiah said to Isaiah, "The word of the LORD that you have spoken is good," for he thought: Why not, if there will be peace and security during my lifetime?

[20] The rest of the events of Hezekiah's reign, along with all his might and how he made the pool and the tunnel and brought water into the city, are written about in the Historical Record of Judah's Kings. [21] Hezekiah rested with his fathers, and his son Manasseh became king in his place.

21 Manasseh was 12 years old when he became king; he reigned 55 years in Jerusalem. His mother's name was Hephzibah. ² He did what was evil in the LORD's sight, imitating the abominations of the nations that the LORD had dispossessed before the Israelites. ³ He rebuilt the high places that his father Hezekiah had destroyed and re-established the altars for Baal. He made an Asherah, as King Ahab of Israel had done; he also worshiped the whole heavenly host and served them. ⁴ He would build altars in the LORD's temple, where the LORD had said, "Jerusalem is where I will put My name." ⁵ He built altars to the whole heavenly host in both courtyards of the LORD's temple. ⁶ He made his son pass through the fire, practiced witchcraft and divination, and consulted mediums and spiritists. He did a great amount of evil in the LORD's sight, provoking Him.

⁷ Manasseh set up the carved image of Asherah he made in the temple that the LORD had spoken about to David and his son Solomon, "I will establish My name forever in this temple and in Jerusalem, which I have chosen out of all the tribes of Israel. ⁸ I will never again cause the feet of the Israelites to wander from the land I gave to their ancestors if only they will be careful to do all I have commanded them—the whole law that My servant Moses commanded them." ⁹ But they did not listen; Manasseh caused them to stray so that they did greater evil than the nations the LORD had destroyed before the Israelites.

¹⁰ The LORD spoke through His servants the prophets, saying, ¹¹ "Since Manasseh king of Judah has committed all these abominations—greater evil than the Amorites who preceded him had done—and by means of his idols has also caused Judah to sin, ¹² this is what the LORD God of Israel says: 'I am about to bring such disaster on Jerusalem and Judah that everyone who hears about it will shudder. ¹³ I will stretch over Jerusalem the measuring line used on Samaria and the mason's level used on the house of Ahab, and I will wipe Jerusalem clean as one wipes a bowl—wiping it and turning it upside down. ¹⁴ I will abandon the remnant of My inheritance and hand them over to their enemies. They will become plunder and spoil to all their enemies, ¹⁵ because they have done what is evil in My sight and have provoked Me from the day their ancestors came out of Egypt until today.' "

¹⁶ Manasseh also shed so much innocent blood that he filled Jerusalem with it from one end to another. This was in addition to his sin he caused Judah to commit so that they did what was evil in the LORD's sight.

¹⁷ The rest of the events of Manasseh's reign, along with all his accomplishments and the sin that he committed, are written about in the Historical Record of Judah's Kings. ¹⁸ Manasseh rested with his fathers and was buried in the garden of his own house, the garden of Uzza. His son Amon became king in his place.

¹⁹ Amon was 22 years old when he became king; he reigned two years in Jerusalem. His mother's name was Meshullemeth daughter of Haruz; she was from Jotbah. ²⁰ He did what was evil in the LORD's sight as his father Manasseh had done. ²¹ He walked in all the ways his father had walked; he served the idols his father had served, and he worshiped them. ²² He abandoned the LORD God of his ancestors and did not walk in the way of the LORD.

²³ Amon's servants conspired against the king and killed him in his own house. ²⁴ Then the common people executed all those who had conspired against King Amon and made his son Josiah king in his place.

²⁵ The rest of the events of Amon's reign, along with his accomplishments, are written about in the Historical Record of Judah's Kings. ²⁶ He was buried in his tomb in the garden of Uzza, and his son Josiah became king in his place.

PSALM 78:48-55

⁴⁸ He handed over their livestock to hail

and their cattle to lightning bolts.
49 He sent His burning anger against
    them:
    fury, indignation, and calamity—
    a band of deadly messengers.
50 He cleared a path for His anger.
    He did not spare them from death,
    but delivered their lives to the
        plague.
51 He struck all the firstborn in Egypt,
    the first progeny of the tents of
        Ham.
52 He led His people out like sheep
    and guided them like a flock in
        the wilderness.
53 He led them safely, and they were
        not afraid;
    but the sea covered their enemies.
54 He brought them to His holy land,
    to the mountain His right hand
        acquired.
55 He drove out nations before them.
    He apportioned their inheritance
        by lot
    and settled the tribes of Israel in
        their tents.

PROVERBS 17:7-8

7 Excessive speech is not
        appropriate on a fool's lips;
    how much worse are lies for a
        ruler.

8 A bribe seems like a magic stone
        to its owner;
    wherever he turns, he succeeds.

ACTS 9:23-43

23 After many days had passed, the
Jews conspired to kill him, 24 but their
plot became known to Saul. So they
were watching the gates day and night
intending to kill him, 25 but his disciples
took him by night and lowered him in a
large basket through an opening in the
wall.
26 When he arrived in Jerusalem, he
tried to associate with the disciples, but
they were all afraid of him, since they
did not believe he was a disciple. 27 Barnabas, however, took him and brought

him to the apostles and explained to
them how, on the road, Saul had seen
the Lord, and that He had talked to him,
and how in Damascus he had spoken
boldly in the name of Jesus. 28 Saul was
coming and going with them in Jerusalem, speaking boldly in the name of
the Lord. 29 He conversed and debated
with the Hellenistic Jews, but they attempted to kill him. 30 When the brothers found out, they took him down to
Caesarea and sent him off to Tarsus.
31 So the church throughout all Judea,
Galilee, and Samaria had peace, being
built up and walking in the fear of the
Lord and in the encouragement of the
Holy Spirit, and it increased in numbers.
32 As Peter was traveling from place to
place, he also came down to the saints
who lived in Lydda. 33 There he found a
man named Aeneas, who was paralyzed
and had been bedridden for eight years.
34 Peter said to him, "Aeneas, Jesus
Christ heals you. Get up and make your
own bed," and immediately he got up.
35 So all who lived in Lydda and Sharon
saw him and turned to the Lord.
36 In Joppa there was a disciple named
Tabitha, which is translated Dorcas. She
was always doing good works and acts
of charity. 37 In those days she became
sick and died. After washing her, they
placed her in a room upstairs. 38 Since
Lydda was near Joppa, the disciples
heard that Peter was there and sent two
men to him who begged him, "Don't delay in coming with us." 39 So Peter got
up and went with them. When he arrived, they led him to the room upstairs.
And all the widows approached him,
weeping and showing him the robes and
clothes that Dorcas had made while she
was with them. 40 Then Peter sent them
all out of the room. He knelt down,
prayed, and turning toward the body
said, "Tabitha, get up!" She opened her
eyes, saw Peter, and sat up. 41 He gave
her his hand and helped her stand up.
Then he called the saints and widows
and presented her alive. 42 This became
known throughout all Joppa, and many
believed in the Lord. 43 And Peter stayed
on many days in Joppa with Simon, a
leather tanner.

Righteous Indignation

He sent His burning anger against them: fury,
indignation, and calamity.—PSALM 78:49

For many of us, "wrath" conjures up the idea of being out of control, an outburst of "seeing red," a sense of wounded pride or just downright petulance. But it is quite wrong to take these ideas or feelings and impose them on God. God's wrath is never out of control, never capricious, never self-indulgent, never irritable, and never ignoble. These may be indicative of human anger but never of the divine. God is angry only when anger is called for.

Even among men and women, there is such a thing as righteous indignation, though (in my opinion) it is more rare than we think.

I used to believe the difference between righteous indignation and carnal hostility was this: when someone was angry with me, that was carnal hostility; when I was angry with someone else, that was righteous indignation! I have "grown out" of that opinion now, I hasten to add.

All God's indignation is righteous. It is grief at what is happening to others, not a grudge because of what is happening to Him. Would a God who took as much pleasure in evil as He did in good be a God we could love? Would a God who did not react adversely to evil be morally perfect? Of course not. It is precisely this adverse reaction to evil that the Bible has in mind when it talks about God's wrath. God cannot treat good and evil alike. He can look over it—look over it to the Cross where it can be forgiven—but He cannot overlook it.

Prayer

O God, the more I see the reason behind Your wrath and the more I consider the purity of its motive, the more praise and adoration I want to give. What a great and wonderful God You are. And how glad I am You looked over my sin. Amen.

Further Study

Is 13:1-22; Ps 78:40-55; Is 30:27; Rm 1:18
How does the psalmist describe God's wrath?
How did Isaiah depict God's anger toward Babylon?

JULY 7

2 KINGS 22:1–23:37

22 Josiah was eight years old when he became king; he reigned 31 years in Jerusalem. His mother's name was Jedidah the daughter of Adaiah; she was from Bozkath. ² He did what was right in the LORD's sight and walked in all the ways of his ancestor David; he did not turn to the right or the left.

³ In the eighteenth year of King Josiah, the king sent the court secretary Shaphan son of Azaliah, son of Meshullam, to the LORD's temple, saying, ⁴ "Go up to Hilkiah the high priest so that he may total up the money brought into the LORD's temple—the money the doorkeepers have collected from the people. ⁵ It is to be put into the hands of those doing the work—those who oversee the LORD's temple. They in turn are to give it to the workmen in the LORD's temple to repair the damage. ⁶ They are to give it to the carpenters, builders, and masons to buy timber and quarried stone to repair the temple. ⁷ But no accounting is to be required from them for the money put into their hands since they work with integrity."

⁸ Hilkiah the high priest told Shaphan the court secretary, "I have found the book of the law in the LORD's temple," and he gave the book to Shaphan, who read it.

⁹ Then Shaphan the court secretary went to the king and reported, "Your servants have emptied out the money that was found in the temple and have put it into the hand of those doing the work—those who oversee the LORD's temple." ¹⁰ Then Shaphan the court secretary told the king, "Hilkiah the priest has given me a book," and Shaphan read it in the presence of the king.

¹¹ When the king heard the words of the book of the law, he tore his clothes. ¹² Then he commanded Hilkiah the priest, Ahikam son of Shaphan, Achbor son of Micaiah, Shaphan the court secretary, and the king's servant Asaiah: ¹³ "Go and inquire of the LORD for me, the people, and all Judah about the instruction in this book that has been found. For great is the LORD's wrath that is kindled against us because our ancestors have not obeyed the words of this book in order to do everything written about us."

¹⁴ So Hilkiah the priest, Ahikam, Achbor, Shaphan, and Asaiah went to the prophetess Huldah, wife of Shallum son of Tikvah, son of Harhas, keeper of the wardrobe. She lived in Jerusalem in the Second District. They spoke with her.

¹⁵ She said to them, "This is what the LORD God of Israel says, 'Say to the man who sent you to Me: ¹⁶ This is what the LORD says: I am about to bring disaster on this place and on its inhabitants, fulfilling all the words of the book that the king of Judah has read, ¹⁷ because they have abandoned Me and burned incense to other gods in order to provoke Me with all the work of their hands. My wrath will be kindled against this place, and it will not be quenched. ¹⁸ Say this to the king of Judah who sent you to inquire of the LORD: This is what the LORD God of Israel says: As for the words that you heard, ¹⁹ because your heart was tender and you humbled yourself before the LORD when you heard what I spoke against this place and against its inhabitants, that they would become a desolation and a curse, and because you have torn your clothes and wept before Me, I Myself have heard you—declares the LORD. ²⁰ Therefore, I will indeed gather you to your fathers, and you will be gathered to your grave in peace. Your eyes will not see all the disaster that I am bringing on this place.'"

Then they reported to the king.

23 So the king sent messengers, and they gathered to him all the elders of Jerusalem and Judah. [2] Then the king went to the LORD's temple with all the men of Judah and all the inhabitants of Jerusalem, as well as the priests and the prophets—all the people from the youngest to the oldest. As they listened, he read all the words of the book of the covenant that had been found in the LORD's temple. [3] Next, the king stood by the pillar and made a covenant in the presence of the LORD to follow the LORD and to keep His commandments, His decrees, and His statutes with all his mind and with all his heart, and to carry out the words of this covenant that were written in this book; all the people agreed to the covenant.

[4] Then the king commanded Hilkiah the high priest and the priests of the second rank and the doorkeepers to bring out of the LORD's temple all the articles made for Baal, Asherah, and the whole heavenly host. He burned them outside Jerusalem in the fields of the Kidron and carried their ashes to Bethel. [5] Then he did away with the idolatrous priests the kings of Judah had appointed to burn incense at the high places in the cities of Judah and in the areas surrounding Jerusalem. They had burned incense to Baal, and to the sun, moon, constellations, and the whole heavenly host. [6] He brought out the Asherah pole from the LORD's temple to the Kidron Valley outside Jerusalem. He burned it at the Kidron Valley, beat it to dust, and threw its dust on the graves of the common people. [7] He also tore down the houses of the male shrine prostitutes that were in the LORD's temple, in which the women were weaving tapestries for Asherah.

[8] Then Josiah brought all the priests from the cities of Judah, and he defiled the high places from Geba to Beersheba, where the priests had burned incense. He tore down the high places of the gates at the entrance of the gate of Joshua the governor of the city (on the left at the city gate). [9] The priests of the high places, however, did not come up to the altar of the LORD in Jerusalem;

instead, they ate unleavened bread with their fellow priests.

[10] He defiled Topheth, which is in the Valley of Hinnom, so that no one could make his son or his daughter pass through the fire to Molech. [11] He did away with the horses that the kings of Judah had dedicated to the sun. They had been at the entrance of the LORD's temple in the precincts by the chamber of Nathan-melech the court official, and he burned up the chariots of the sun. [12] The king tore down the altars that were on the roof—Ahaz's upper chamber that the kings of Judah had made—and the altars that Manasseh had made in the two courtyards of the LORD's temple. Then he smashed them there and threw their dust into the Kidron Valley. [13] The king also defiled the high places that were across from Jerusalem, to the south of the Mount of Destruction, which Solomon king of Israel had built for Ashtoreth, the detestable idol of the Sidonians; for Chemosh, the detestable idol of Moab; and for Milcom, the abomination of the Ammonites. [14] He broke the sacred pillars into pieces, cut down the Asherah poles, then filled their places with human bones.

[15] He even tore down the altar at Bethel and the high place that Jeroboam son of Nebat, who caused Israel to sin, had made. Then he burned the high place, crushed it to dust, and burned the Asherah. [16] As Josiah turned, he saw the tombs there on the mountain. He sent someone to take the bones out of the tombs, and he burned them on the altar. He defiled it according to the word of the LORD proclaimed by the man of God who proclaimed these things. [17] Then he said, "What is this monument I see?"

The men of the city told him, "It is the tomb of the man of God who came from Judah and proclaimed these things that you have done to the altar at Bethel."

[18] So he said, "Let him rest. Don't let anyone disturb his bones." So they left his bones undisturbed with the bones of the prophet who came from Samaria.

[19] Josiah also removed all the shrines

of the high places that were in the cities of Samaria, which the kings of Israel had made to provoke the LORD. Josiah did the same things to them that he had done at Bethel. 20 He slaughtered on the altars all the priests of the high places who were there, and he burned human bones on the altars. Then he returned to Jerusalem.

21 The king commanded all the people, "Keep the Passover of the LORD your God as written in the book of the covenant." 22 No such Passover had ever been kept from the time of the judges who judged Israel through the entire time of the kings of Israel and Judah. 23 But in the eighteenth year of King Josiah, this Passover was observed to the LORD in Jerusalem.

24 In addition, Josiah removed the mediums, the spiritists, household idols, images, and all the detestable things that were seen in the land of Judah and in Jerusalem. He did this in order to carry out the words of the law that were written in the book that Hilkiah the priest found in the LORD's temple. 25 Before him there was no king like him who turned to the LORD with all his mind and with all his heart and with all his strength according to all the law of Moses, and no one like him arose after him.

26 In spite of all that, the LORD did not turn from the fierceness of His great wrath and anger, which burned against Judah because of all the provocations Manasseh had provoked Him with. 27 For the LORD had said, "I will also remove Judah from My sight just as I have removed Israel. I will reject this city Jerusalem, that I have chosen, and the temple about which I said, 'My name will be there.' "

28 The rest of the events of Josiah's reign, along with all his accomplishments, are written about in the Historical Record of Judah's Kings. 29 During his reign, Pharaoh Neco king of Egypt marched up to the king of Assyria at the Euphrates river. King Josiah went to confront him, and at Megiddo when Neco saw him he killed him. 30 From Megiddo his servants carried his dead

body in a chariot, brought him into Jerusalem, and buried him in his own tomb. Then the common people took Jehoahaz son of Josiah, anointed him, and made him king in place of his father.

31 Jehoahaz was 23 years old when he became king; he reigned three months in Jerusalem. His mother's name was Hamutal daughter of Jeremiah; she was from Libnah. 32 He did what was evil in the LORD's sight just as his ancestors had done. 33 Pharaoh Neco imprisoned him at Riblah in the land of Hamath to keep him from reigning in Jerusalem, and he imposed on the land a fine of 7,500 pounds of silver and 75 pounds of gold.

34 Then Pharaoh Neco made Eliakim son of Josiah king in place of his father Josiah and changed Eliakim's name to Jehoiakim. But Neco took Jehoahaz and went to Egypt, and he died there. 35 So Jehoiakim gave the silver and the gold to Pharaoh, but at Pharaoh's command he taxed the land to give the money. He exacted the silver and the gold from the people of the land, each man according to his valuation, to give it to Pharaoh Neco.

36 Jehoiakim was 25 years old when he became king; he reigned 11 years in Jerusalem. His mother's name was Zebidah daughter of Pedaiah; she was from Rumah. 37 He did what was evil in the LORD's sight just as his ancestors had done.

𝒫SALM 78:56-64

56 But they rebelliously tested the
    Most High God,
    for they did not keep His decrees.
57 They treacherously turned away
    like their fathers;
    they became warped like a faulty
    bow.
58 They enraged Him with their high
    places
    and provoked His jealousy with
    their carved images.
59 God heard and became furious;
    He completely rejected Israel.

60 He abandoned the tabernacle at
   Shiloh,
   the tent where He resided among
   men.
61 He gave up His strength to
   captivity
   and His splendor to the hand of a
   foe.
62 He surrendered His people to the
   sword
   because He was enraged with His
   heritage.
63 Fire consumed His chosen young
   men,
   and His young women had no
   wedding songs.
64 His priests fell by the sword,
   but the widows could not lament.

PROVERBS 17:9-10

9 Whoever conceals an offense
   promotes love,
   but whoever gossips about it
   separates friends.

10 A rebuke cuts into a perceptive
   person
   more than a hundred lashes into a
   fool.

ACTS 10:1-23

10 There was a man in Caesarea
named Cornelius, a centurion of
what was called the Italian Regiment.
2 He was a devout man and feared God
along with his whole household. He did
many charitable deeds for the Jewish
people and always prayed to God. 3 At
about three in the afternoon he distinctly saw in a vision an angel of God who
came in and said to him, "Cornelius!"
4 Looking intently at him, he became
afraid and said, "What is it, Lord?"
   And he told him, "Your prayers and
your acts of charity have come up as a
memorial offering before God. 5 Now
send men to Joppa and call for Simon,
who is also named Peter. 6 He is lodging
with Simon, a tanner, whose house is by
the sea."
   7 When the angel who spoke to him

had gone, he called two of his household servants and a devout soldier, who
was one of those who attended him.
8 After explaining everything to them,
he sent them to Joppa.
   9 The next day, as they were traveling
and nearing the city, Peter went up to
pray on the housetop at about noon.
10 Then he became hungry and wanted
to eat, but while they were preparing
something he went into a visionary
state. 11 He saw heaven opened and an
object coming down that resembled a
large sheet being lowered to the earth
by its four corners. 12 In it were all the
four-footed animals and reptiles of the
earth, and the birds of the sky. 13 Then a
voice said to him, "Get up, Peter; kill
and eat!"
   14 "No, Lord!" Peter said. "For I have
never eaten anything common and unclean!"
   15 Again, a second time, a voice said to
him, "What God has made clean, you
must not call common." 16 This happened three times, and then the object
was taken up into heaven.
   17 While Peter was deeply perplexed
about what the vision he had seen might
mean, the men who had been sent by
Cornelius, having asked directions to
Simon's house, stood at the gate. 18 They
called out, asking if Simon, who was also
named Peter, was lodging there.
   19 While Peter was thinking about the
vision, the Spirit told him, "Three men
are here looking for you. 20 Get up, go
downstairs, and accompany them with
no doubts at all, because I have sent
them."
   21 Then Peter went down to the men
and said, "Here I am, the one you're
looking for. What is the reason you're
here?"
   22 They said, "Cornelius, a centurion,
an upright and God-fearing man, who
has a good reputation with the whole
Jewish nation, was divinely directed by a
holy angel to call you to his house and to
hear a message from you." 23 Peter then
invited them in and gave them lodging.
   The next day he got up and set out
with them, and some of the brothers
from Joppa went with him.

Choose to Forgive

*Whoever conceals an offense promotes love, but
whoever gossips about it separates friends.*—Proverbs 17:9

Jesus gives us stern and uncompromising warnings about forgiveness. But if forgiveness is so important and yet so difficult, how do we go about it? We must do several things.

First, we must not try to minimize or dismiss the offense as if it never happened. If it hurts, then we must face it and feel it. A common misconception that keeps people from forgiving is that they think in order to forgive they must come to the place where they look upon the things done to them as being really not that bad. That is excusing, not forgiving. C. S. Lewis says: "Real forgiveness means looking steadily at the sin, the sin that is left over without any excuse after all allowances have been made, and seeing it in all its horror, dirt, meanness and malice, and nevertheless being wholly reconciled to the man who has done it. That, and only that, is forgiveness."

Second, we must see that forgiveness is not an emotional thing (though it can affect the emotions), but a matter of the will. It is making the decision that the wrong done against you will not count or cause a separation. In making that decision, remember you have all the re-sources of God available to you. This applies not just to minor matters like snubs, but major matters like divorce.

The task of forgiving must be more than a match for the magnitude of the pain involved. A choice has to be made. No matter how we are wronged, we can choose out of a desire for love to forgive.

Prayer

Lord Jesus Christ, You looked into the eyes of those who hammered You to a cross and cried: "Father, forgive them!" Help me do the same when I am confronted with lesser injury or hurt. For Your own dear name's sake. Amen.

Further Study

Mc 6:1-8; 7:18; Is 43:25
What does God delight to do?
What are we to love?

JULY 8

2 KINGS 24:1–25:30

24 During his reign, Nebuchadnezzar king of Babylon attacked, and Jehoiakim became his vassal for three years. Then he turned and rebelled against him. ² The LORD sent Chaldean, Aramean, Moabite, and Ammonite raiders against Jehoiakim. He sent them against Judah to destroy it, according to the word of the LORD He had spoken through His servants the prophets. ³ This happened to Judah only at the LORD's command to remove them from His sight. It was because of the sins of Manasseh, according to all he had done, ⁴ and also because of all the innocent blood he had shed. He had filled Jerusalem with innocent blood, and the LORD would not forgive.

⁵ The rest of the events of Jehoiakim's reign, along with all his accomplishments, are written about in the Historical Record of Judah's Kings. ⁶ Jehoiakim rested with his fathers, and his son Jehoiachin became king in his place.

⁷ Now the king of Egypt did not march out of his land again, for the king of Babylon took everything that belonged to the king of Egypt, from the Brook of Egypt to the Euphrates River.

⁸ Jehoiachin was 18 years old when he became king; he reigned three months in Jerusalem. His mother's name was Nehushta daughter of Elnathan; she was from Jerusalem. ⁹ He did what was evil in the LORD's sight as his father had done.

¹⁰ At that time the servants of Nebuchadnezzar king of Babylon marched up to Jerusalem, and the city came under siege. ¹¹ Then King Nebuchadnezzar of Babylon came to the city while his servants were besieging it. ¹² Jehoiachin king of Judah, along with his mother, his servants, his commanders, and his officials, surrendered to the king of Babylon.

So the king of Babylon took him captive in the eighth year of his reign. ¹³ He also carried off from there all the treasures of the LORD's temple and the treasures of the king's palace, and he cut into pieces all the gold articles that Solomon king of Israel had made for the LORD's sanctuary, just as God had predicted. ¹⁴ Then he deported all Jerusalem and all the commanders and all the fighting men, 10,000 captives, and all the craftsmen and metal smiths. Except for the poorest people of the land, nobody remained.

¹⁵ Nebuchadnezzar deported Jehoiachin to Babylon. Also, he took the king's mother, the king's wives, his officials, and the leading men of the land into exile from Jerusalem to Babylon. ¹⁶ The king of Babylon also brought captive into Babylon all 7,000 fighting men and 1,000 craftsmen and metal smiths—all strong and fit for war. 17 Then the king of Babylon made Mattaniah, Jehoiachin's uncle, king in his place and changed his name to Zedekiah.

¹⁸ Zedekiah was 21 years old when he became king; he reigned 11 years in Jerusalem. His mother's name was Hamutal daughter of Jeremiah; she was from Libnah. ¹⁹ Zedekiah did what was evil in the LORD's sight just as Jehoiakim had done. ²⁰ Because of the LORD's anger, it came to the point in Jerusalem and Judah that He finally banished them from His presence. Then, Zedekiah rebelled against the king of Babylon.

25 In the ninth year of Zedekiah's reign, on the tenth day of the tenth month, King Nebuchadnezzar of Babylon advanced against Jerusalem with his entire army. They laid siege to the city and built a siege wall against it all around. ² The city was under siege until King Zedekiah's eleventh year.

³ By the ninth day of the fourth month the famine was so severe in the city that the people of the land had no food. ⁴ Then the city was broken into, and all the warriors fled by night by way of the gate between the two walls near the king's garden, even though the Chaldeans surrounded the city. As the king made his way along the route to the Arabah, ⁵ the Chaldean army pursued him and overtook him in the plains of Jericho. Zedekiah's entire army was scattered from him. ⁶ The Chaldeans seized the king and brought him up to the king of Babylon at Riblah, and they passed sentence on him. ⁷ They slaughtered Zedekiah's sons before his eyes. Finally, the king of Babylon blinded Zedekiah, bound him in bronze chains, and took him to Babylon.

⁸ On the seventh day of the fifth month, which was the nineteenth year of King Nebuchadnezzar, king of Babylon, Nebuzaradan, the commander of the guards, a servant of the king of Babylon, entered Jerusalem. ⁹ He burned the LORD's temple, the king's palace, and all the houses of Jerusalem; he burned down all the great houses. ¹⁰ The whole Chaldean army with the commander of the guards tore down the walls surrounding Jerusalem. ¹¹ Nebuzaradan, the commander of the guards, deported the rest of the people who were left in the city, the deserters who had defected to the king of Babylon, and the rest of the population. ¹² But the commander of the guards left some of the poorest of the land to be vinedressers and farmers.

¹³ Now the Chaldeans broke into pieces the bronze pillars of the LORD's temple, the water carts, and the bronze reservoir, which were in the LORD's temple, and carried the bronze to Babylon. ¹⁴ They also took the pots, the shovels, the wick trimmers, the dishes, and all the bronze articles used in temple service. ¹⁵ The commander of the guards took away the firepans and the sprinkling basins—whatever was gold or silver.

¹⁶ As for the two pillars, the one reservoir, and the water carts that Solomon had made for the LORD's temple, the weight of the bronze of all these articles was beyond measure. ¹⁷ One pillar was 27 feet tall and had a bronze capital on top of it. The capital, encircled by a grating and pomegranates of bronze, stood five feet high. The second pillar was the same, with its own grating.

¹⁸ The commander of the guards also took away Seraiah the chief priest, Zephaniah the priest of the second rank, and the three doorkeepers. ¹⁹ From the city he took a court official who had been appointed over the warriors; five trusted royal aides found in the city; the secretary of the commander of the army, who enlisted the people of the land for military duty; and 60 men from the common people who were found within the city. ²⁰ Nebuzaradan, the commander of the guards, took them and brought them to the king of Babylon at Riblah. ²¹ The king of Babylon put them to death at Riblah in the land of Hamath. So Judah went into exile from its land.

²² Nebuchadnezzar king of Babylon appointed Gedaliah son of Ahikam, son of Shaphan, over the rest of the people he left in the land of Judah. ²³ When all the commanders of the armies—they and their men—heard that the king of Babylon had appointed Gedaliah, they came to Gedaliah at Mizpah. The commanders included Ishmael son of Nethaniah, Johanan son of Kareah, Seraiah son of Tanhumeth the Netophathite, and Jaazaniah son of the Maacathite—they and their men. ²⁴ Gedaliah swore an oath to them and their men, assuring them, "Don't be afraid of the servants of the Chaldeans. Live in the land and serve the king of Babylon, and it will go well for you."

²⁵ In the seventh month, however, Ishmael son of Nethaniah, son of Elishama, of the royal family, came with 10 men and struck down Gedaliah, and he died. Also, they killed the Jews and the Chaldeans who were with him at Mizpah. ²⁶ Then all the people, from the youngest to the oldest, and the commanders of the army, left and went to

Egypt, for they were afraid of the Chaldeans.

²⁷ On the twenty-seventh day of the twelfth month of the thirty-seventh year of the exile of Judah's King Jehoiachin, Evil-merodach king of Babylon, in the year he became king, pardoned King Jehoiachin of Judah and released him from prison. ²⁸ He spoke kindly to him and set his throne over the thrones of the kings who were with him in Babylon. ²⁹ So Jehoiachin changed his prison clothes, and he dined regularly in the presence of the king of Babylon for the rest of his life. ³⁰ As for his allowance, a regular allowance was given to him by the king, a portion for each day, for the rest of his life.

℘SALM 78:65-72

⁶⁵ Then the Lord awoke as if from sleep,
   like a warrior from the effects of wine.
⁶⁶ He beat back His foes;
   He gave them lasting shame.
⁶⁷ He rejected the tent of Joseph
   and did not choose the tribe of Ephraim.
⁶⁸ He chose instead the tribe of Judah,
   Mount Zion, which He loved.
⁶⁹ He built His sanctuary like the heights,
   like the earth that He established forever.
⁷⁰ He chose David His servant
   and took him from the sheepfolds;
⁷¹ He brought him from tending ewes
   to be shepherd over His people Jacob—
   over Israel, His inheritance.
⁷² He shepherded them with a pure heart
   and guided them with his skillful hands.

℘ROVERBS 17:11-12

¹¹ An evil man seeks only rebellion;
   a cruel messenger will be sent against him.

¹² Better for a man to meet a bear robbed of her cubs
   than a fool in his foolishness.

℘CTS 10:24-48

²⁴ The following day he entered Caesarea. Now Cornelius was expecting them and had called together his relatives and close friends. ²⁵ When Peter entered, Cornelius met him, fell at his feet, and worshiped him. ²⁶ But Peter helped him up and said, "Stand up! I myself am also a man." ²⁷ While talking with him, he went on in and found that many had come together there. ²⁸ Peter said to them, "You know it's forbidden for a Jewish man to associate with or visit a foreigner. But God has shown me that I must not call any person common or unclean. ²⁹ That's why I came without any objection when I was sent for. So I ask, 'Why did you send for me?' "

³⁰ Cornelius replied, "Four days ago at this hour, at three in the afternoon, I was praying in my house. Just then a man in a dazzling robe stood before me ³¹ and said, 'Cornelius, your prayer has been heard, and your acts of charity have been remembered in God's sight. ³² Therefore send someone to Joppa and invite Simon here, who is also named Peter. He is lodging in Simon the tanner's house by the sea.' ³³ Therefore I immediately sent for you, and you did the right thing in coming. So we are all present before God, to hear everything you have been commanded by the Lord."

³⁴ Then Peter began to speak: "In truth, I understand that God doesn't show favoritism, ³⁵ but in every nation the person who fears Him and does righteousness is acceptable to Him. ³⁶ He sent the message to the sons of Israel, proclaiming the good news of peace through Jesus Christ—He is Lord of all. ³⁷ You know the events that took place throughout all Judea, beginning from Galilee after the baptism that John preached: ³⁸ how God anointed Jesus of Nazareth with the Holy Spirit and with

power, and how He went about doing good and curing all who were under the tyranny of the Devil, because God was with Him. ³⁹ We ourselves are witnesses of everything He did in both the Judean country and in Jerusalem; yet they killed Him by hanging Him on a tree. ⁴⁰ God raised up this man on the third day and permitted Him to be seen, ⁴¹ not by all the people, but by us, witnesses appointed beforehand by God, who ate and drank with Him after He rose from the dead. ⁴² He commanded us to preach to the people, and to solemnly testify that He is the One appointed by God to be the Judge of the living and the dead. ⁴³ All the prophets testify about Him that through His

name everyone who believes in Him will receive forgiveness of sins."

⁴⁴ While Peter was still speaking these words, the Holy Spirit came down on all those who heard the message. ⁴⁵ The circumcised believers who had come with Peter were astounded, because the gift of the Holy Spirit had been poured out on the Gentiles also. ⁴⁶ For they heard them speaking in other languages and declaring the greatness of God.

Then Peter responded, ⁴⁷ "Can anyone withhold water and prevent these from being baptized, who have received the Holy Spirit just as we have?" ⁴⁸ And he commanded them to be baptized in the name of Jesus Christ. Then they asked him to stay for a few days.

Channels of Blessing

God anointed Jesus of Nazareth with the Holy Spirit and with power, and…He went about doing good and curing all who were under the tyranny of the Devil.

—Acts 10:38

How much spiritual power is projected from our lives into a lost and dying world? If we are honest, we will be compelled to say, "Very little."

A sign on the door of the electricity company stated: "The electric bell is not working—please knock." All our signs, making great claims for the gospel, are cancelled out if power is not apparent in our everyday lives. The Holy Spirit's power is not confined to delighting the saints with manifestations of the gifts of the Spirit in our church gatherings, but in empowering them for effective witness in the world. We must watch that we do not degenerate into being simply consumers of blessing rather than channels of blessing.

Recently I have had a stream of letters telling me how God has been leading people to pray for healing from sickness for their non-Christian friends—and remarkable things have happened as a result. Some would regard it as doctrinally incorrect to pray for a person's healing if that person is not a Christian. Jesus did it, and so did Paul. I feel that the Holy Spirit is nudging me to say that, in the future, one of the ways by which we will see multitudes won to Christ is by allowing the Holy Spirit to work through us in supernatural signs and wonders. God is calling us to launch out into the deep.

Prayer

O Father, something within me seems to draw back at the borders of the supernatural. Give me the faith and expectancy, however, to step over that line and demonstrate to others that I am not just a consumer, but a channel of Your blessings. Amen.

Further Study

Ac 3:1-13; Is 53:5; Lk 4:18; 1 Co 12:9
What were Peter and John doing after the Spirit's coming?
How did they respond to the lame man?

JULY 9

1 CHRONICLES 1:1–2:2

1 Adam, Seth, Enosh,
² Kenan, Mahalalel, Jared,
³ Enoch, Methuselah, Lamech,
⁴ Noah, Noah's sons:
Shem, Ham, and Japheth.

⁵ Japheth's sons: Gomer, Magog, Madai, Javan, Tubal, Meshech, and Tiras.
⁶ Gomer's sons: Ashkenaz, Riphath, and Togarmah.
⁷ Javan's sons: Elishah, Tarshish, Kittim, and Rodanim.

⁸ Ham's sons: Cush, Mizraim, Put, and Canaan.
⁹ Cush's sons: Seba, Havilah, Sabta, Raama, and Sabteca.
Raama's sons: Sheba and Dedan.
¹⁰ Cush fathered Nimrod, who was the first to become a great warrior on earth.
¹¹ Mizraim fathered Ludim, Anamim, Lehabim, Naphtuhim,
¹² Pathrusim, Casluhim (the Philistines came from them), and Caphtorim.

¹³ Canaan fathered Sidon, his first-born, and Heth, ¹⁴ the Jebusites, Amorites, Girgashites, ¹⁵ Hivites, Arkites, Sinites, ¹⁶ Arvadites, Zemarites, and Hamathites.

¹⁷ Shem's sons: Elam, Asshur, Arpachshad, Lud, Aram, Uz, Hul, Gether, and Meshech.
¹⁸ Arpachshad fathered Shelah, and Shelah fathered Eber. ¹⁹ Two sons were born to Eber. One of them was named Peleg, because the earth was divided during his lifetime, and the name of his brother was Joktan. ²⁰ Joktan fathered Almodad, Sheleph, Hazarmaveth, Jerah, ²¹ Hadoram, Uzal, Diklah, ²² Ebal, Abimael, Sheba, ²³ Ophir, Havilah, and Jobab.
All of these were Joktan's sons.

²⁴ Shem, Arpachshad, Shelah,
²⁵ Eber, Peleg, Reu,
²⁶ Serug, Nahor, Terah,
²⁷ and Abram (that is, Abraham).

²⁸ Abraham's sons: Isaac and Ishmael.

29 These are their family records:
Nebaioth, Ishmael's firstborn,
Kedar, Adbeel, Mibsam,
30 Mishma, Dumah, Massa, Hadad,
Tema, 31 Jetur, Naphish,
and Kedemah.
These were Ishmael's sons.

32 The sons born to Keturah,
Abraham's concubine: Zimran,
Jokshan, Medan, Midian, Ishbak,
and Shuah.
Jokshan's sons: Sheba and Dedan.
33 Midian's sons: Ephah, Epher,
Hanoch, Abida, and Eldaah.
All of these were Keturah's sons.

34 Abraham fathered Isaac.
Isaac's sons: Esau and Israel.

35 Esau's sons: Eliphaz, Reuel,
Jeush, Jalam, and Korah.
36 Eliphaz's sons: Teman, Omar,
Zephi, Gatam, and Kenaz; and by
Timna, Amalek. 37 Reuel's sons:
Nahath, Zerah, Shammah,
and Mizzah.

38 Seir's sons: Lotan, Shobal,
Zibeon, Anah, Dishon, Ezer,
and Dishan.
39 Lotan's sons: Hori and Homam.
Timna was Lotan's sister.
40 Shobal's sons: Alian, Manahath,
Ebal, Shephi, and Onam.
Zibeon's sons: Aiah and Anah.
41 Anah's son: Dishon.
Dishon's sons: Hamran, Eshban,
Ithran, and Cheran.
42 Ezer's sons: Bilhan, Zaavan,
and Jaakan.
Dishan's sons: Uz and Aran.

43 These were the kings who ruled in
the land of Edom before any king ruled
over the Israelites: Bela son of Beor.
Bela's town was named Dinhabah.
44 When Bela died, Jobab son of Zerah
from Bozrah ruled in his place. 45 When
Jobab died, Husham from the land of the
Temanites ruled in his place. 46 When
Husham died, Hadad son of Bedad, who
defeated Midian in the country of
Moab, ruled in his place. Hadad's town

was named Avith. 47 When Hadad died,
Samlah from Masrekah ruled in his
place. 48 When Samlah died, Shaul from
Rehoboth on the Euphrates River ruled
in his place. 49 When Shaul died, Baal-
hanan son of Achbor ruled in his place.
50 When Baal-hanan died, Hadad ruled
in his place. Hadad's city was named
Pai, and his wife's name was Mehetabel
daughter of Matred, daughter of Me-
zahab. 51 Then Hadad died.

Edom's chiefs: Timna, Alvah,
Jetheth, 52 Oholibamah, Elah,
Pinon, 53 Kenaz, Teman, Mibzar,
54 Magdiel, and Iram.
These were Edom's chiefs.

2 These were Israel's sons:
Reuben, Simeon, Levi,
Judah, Issachar, Zebulun,
2 Dan, Joseph, Benjamin,
Naphtali, Gad, and Asher.

PSALM 79:1-8

1 God, the nations have invaded
Your inheritance,
desecrated Your holy temple,
and turned Jerusalem into ruins.
2 They gave the corpses of Your
servants
to the birds of the sky for food,
the flesh of Your godly ones to the
beasts of the earth.
3 They poured out their blood like
water all around Jerusalem,
and there was no one to bury
them.
4 We have become an object of
reproach to our neighbors,
a source of mockery and ridicule
to those around us.

5 How long, LORD? Will You be
angry forever?
Will Your jealousy keep burning
like fire?
6 Pour out Your wrath on the
nations that don't
acknowledge You,
on the kingdoms that don't call on
Your name,
7 for they have devoured Jacob

and devastated his homeland.
⁸ Do not hold past sins against us;
let Your compassion come to us
quickly,
for we have become weak.

PROVERBS 17:13-14

¹³ If anyone returns evil for good,
evil will never depart from his
house.

¹⁴ To start a conflict is to release a
flood;
stop the dispute before it breaks
out.

ACTS 11:1-30

11 The apostles and the brothers
who were throughout Judea
heard that the Gentiles had welcomed
God's message also. ² When Peter went
up to Jerusalem, those who stressed circumcision argued with him, ³ saying,
"You visited uncircumcised men and ate
with them!"
⁴ Peter began to explain to them in an
orderly sequence, saying: ⁵ "I was in the
town of Joppa praying, and I saw, in a visionary state, an object coming down
that resembled a large sheet being lowered from heaven by its four corners,
and it came to me. ⁶ When I looked
closely and considered it, I saw the four-
footed animals of the earth, the wild
beasts, the reptiles, and the birds of the
sky. ⁷ Then I also heard a voice telling
me, 'Get up, Peter; kill and eat!'
⁸ " 'No, Lord!' I said. 'For nothing
common or unclean has ever entered
my mouth!' ⁹ But a voice answered from
heaven a second time, 'What God has
made clean, you must not call common.'
¹⁰ "Now this happened three times,
and then everything was drawn up
again into heaven. ¹¹ At that very moment, three men who had been sent to
me from Caesarea arrived at the house
where we were. ¹² Then the Spirit told
me to go with them with no doubts at
all. These six brothers accompanied me,
and we went into the man's house. ¹³ He

reported to us how he had seen the angel standing in his house and saying,
'Send to Joppa, and call for Simon, who
is also named Peter. ¹⁴ He will speak
words to you by which you and all your
household will be saved.'
¹⁵ "As I began to speak, the Holy Spirit
came down on them, just as on us at the
beginning. ¹⁶ Then I remembered the
word of the Lord, how He said, 'John
baptized with water, but you will be
baptized with the Holy Spirit.' ¹⁷ Therefore, if God gave them the same gift
that He also gave to us when we believed on the Lord Jesus Christ, how
could I possibly hinder God?"
¹⁸ When they heard this they became
silent. Then they glorified God, saying,
"So God has granted repentance resulting in life to even the Gentiles!"
¹⁹ Those who had been scattered as a
result of the persecution that started
because of Stephen made their way as
far as Phoenicia, Cyprus, and Antioch,
speaking the message to no one except
Jews. ²⁰ But there were some of them,
Cypriot and Cyrenian men, who came
to Antioch and began speaking to the
Hellenists, proclaiming the good news
about the Lord Jesus. ²¹ The Lord's hand
was with them, and a large number who
believed turned to the Lord. ²² Then the
report about them reached the ears of
the church in Jerusalem, and they sent
out Barnabas to travel as far as Antioch.
²³ When he arrived and saw the grace of
God, he was glad, and he encouraged all
of them to remain true to the Lord with
a firm resolve of the heart— ²⁴ for he
was a good man, full of the Holy Spirit
and of faith—and large numbers of people were added to the Lord. ²⁵ Then he
went to Tarsus to search for Saul, ²⁶ and
when he found him he brought him to
Antioch. For a whole year they met with
the church and taught large numbers,
and the disciples were first called
Christians in Antioch.
²⁷ In those days some prophets came
down from Jerusalem to Antioch.
²⁸ Then one of them, named Agabus,
stood up and predicted by the Spirit
that there would be a severe famine
throughout the Roman world. This took

place during the time of Claudius. ²⁹ So each of the disciples, according to his ability, determined to send relief to the brothers who lived in Judea. ³⁰ This they did, sending it to the elders by means of Barnabas and Saul.

All Persons Sacred

The Holy Spirit came down on them,
just as on us at the beginning.

—Acts 11:15

An interesting thing to notice about the upper room is that the Holy Spirit came, not just on the Twelve, but on the one hundred and twenty.

Suppose the Spirit had come on the Twelve and had bypassed the others who were waiting in that room—what would that have done to Christianity? It would have limited the Spirit's power and presence to special people, called to a specially sacred task. Someone has remarked that the addition of a zero to the twelve, making 120, is one of the greatest additions in history. It is! The coming of the Holy Spirit on the 120 meant that all distinctions based on a special class or group were gone. Some have different gifts, of course, such as are described in Romans 12, 1 Corinthians 12, and Ephesians 4:11. As far as receiving the gift of the Holy Spirit is concerned, however, all who are redeemed are eligible.

If we think this through carefully, it might enable us to regain a sense of mission in life. Some occupations are considered sacred and some secular. This produces a sag in every so-called secular occupation—the layman is in a secular occupation and so is excused if he lives a second-rate Christian life. This impoverishes life because it removes any sense of divine calling. A minister can be holy and a layman can be holy—all on the same conditions with no special favors. Sacredness is found in character, not in a collar; in values, not in vestments.

Prayer

O Father, I am grateful that I, as a person, can receive the greatest gift of all—the Holy Spirit—and live out my life where You have placed me, with a sense of divine vocation. Thank You, dear Father. Amen.

Further Study

Ac 11:5-10; 16-18
What problem did some of the early Christians have?
How did God overcome this?

JULY 10

1 CHRONICLES 2:3-55

³ Judah's sons: Er, Onan, and Shelah. These three were born to him by Bath-shua the Canaanite woman. Er, Judah's firstborn, was evil in the LORD's sight, so He put him to death. ⁴ Judah's daughter-in-law Tamar bore him Perez and Zerah. Judah had five sons in all.

⁵ Perez's sons: Hezron and Hamul. ⁶ Zerah's sons: Zimri, Ethan, Heman, Calcol, and Dara—five in all.
⁷ Carmi's son: Achar, who brought trouble on Israel when he was unfaithful by taking what was devoted to destruction.
⁸ Ethan's son: Azariah.
⁹ Hezron's sons, who were born to him: Jerahmeel, Ram, and Chelubai.

¹⁰ Ram fathered Amminadab, and Amminadab fathered Nahshon, a leader of Judah's descendants.
¹¹ Nahshon fathered Salma, and Salma fathered Boaz.
¹² Boaz fathered Obed, and Obed fathered Jesse.
¹³ Jesse fathered Eliab, his firstborn; Abinadab was born second, Shimea third, ¹⁴ Nethanel fourth, Raddai fifth, ¹⁵ Ozem sixth, and David seventh.
¹⁶ Their sisters were Zeruiah and Abigail. Zeruiah's three sons: Abishai, Joab, and Asahel.
¹⁷ Amasa's mother was Abigail, and his father was Jether the Ishmaelite.

¹⁸ Caleb son of Hezron had children by his wife Azubah and by Jerioth. These were Azubah's sons: Jesher, Shobab, and Ardon. ¹⁹ When Azubah died, Caleb married Ephrath, and she bore him Hur. ²⁰ Hur fathered Uri, and Uri fathered Bezalel. ²¹ After this, Hezron slept with the daughter of Machir the father of Gilead. Hezron had married her when he was 60 years old, and she bore him Segub. ²² Segub fathered Jair, who possessed 23 towns in the land of Gilead. ²³ But Geshur and Aram captured Jair's Villages along with Kenath and its villages—60 towns. All these were the sons of Machir father of Gilead. ²⁴ After Hezron's death in Caleb-ephrathah, his wife Abijah bore him Ashhur the father of Tekoa.

²⁵ The sons of Jerahmeel, Hezron's firstborn: Ram, his firstborn, Bunah, Oren, Ozem, and Ahijah.
²⁶ Jerahmeel had another wife named Atarah, who was the mother of Onam.
²⁷ The sons of Ram, Jerahmeel's firstborn: Maaz, Jamin, and Eker.
²⁸ Onam's sons: Shammai and Jada. Shammai's sons: Nadab and Abishur. ²⁹ Abishur's wife was named Abihail, who bore him Ahban and Molid.
³⁰ Nadab's sons: Seled and Appaim. Seled died without children.
³¹ Appaim's son: Ishi. Ishi's son: Sheshan. Sheshan's descendant: Ahlai.
³² The sons of Jada brother of Shammai: Jether and Jonathan. Jether died without children.
³³ Jonathan's sons: Peleth and Zaza. These were the descendants of Jerahmeel.
³⁴ Sheshan had no sons, only daughters, but he did have an Egyptian servant whose name was

Jarha. ³⁵ Sheshan gave his daughter in marriage to his servant Jarha, and she bore him Attai.

³⁶ Attai fathered Nathan,
and Nathan fathered Zabad.
³⁷ Zabad fathered Ephlal,
and Ephlal fathered Obed.
³⁸ Obed fathered Jehu,
and Jehu fathered Azariah.
³⁹ Azariah fathered Helez,
and Helez fathered Eleasah.
⁴⁰ Eleasah fathered Sismai,
and Sismai fathered Shallum.
⁴¹ Shallum fathered Jekamiah,
and Jekamiah fathered Elishama.

⁴² The sons of Caleb brother of Jerahmeel:
Mesha, his firstborn, fathered Ziph,
and Mareshah, his second son, fathered Hebron.
⁴³ Hebron's sons: Korah, Tappuah, Rekem, and Shema.
⁴⁴ Shema fathered Raham, who fathered Jorkeam,
and Rekem fathered Shammai.
⁴⁵ Shammai's son was Maon,
and Maon fathered Beth-zur.
⁴⁶ Caleb's concubine Ephah was the mother of Haran, Moza, and Gazez.
Haran fathered Gazez.
⁴⁷ Jahdai's sons: Regem, Jotham, Geshan, Pelet, Ephah, and Shaaph.
⁴⁸ Caleb's concubine Maacah was the mother of Sheber and Tirhanah. ⁴⁹ She was also the mother of Shaaph, Madmannah's father, and of Sheva, the father of Machbenah and Gibea. Caleb's daughter was Achsah.
⁵⁰ These were Caleb's descendants.

The sons of Hur, Ephrathah's firstborn:
Shobal fathered Kiriath-jearim;
⁵¹ Salma fathered Bethlehem,
and Hareph fathered Beth-gader.

⁵² These were the descendants of Shobal the father of Kiriath-jearim:

Haroeh, half of the Manahathites, ⁵³ and the families of Kiriath-jearim—the Ithrites, Puthites, Shumathites, and Mishraites. The Zorathites and Eshtaolites descended from these.

⁵⁴ Salma's sons: Bethlehem, the Netophathites, Atroth-beth-joab, and half of the Manahathites, the Zorites, ⁵⁵ and the families of scribes who lived in Jabez—the Tirathites, Shimeathites, and Sucathites. These are the Kenites who came from Hammath, the father of Rechab's family.

PSALM 79:9-13

⁹ God of our salvation, help us—
for the glory of Your name.
Deliver us and atone for our sins,
Because of Your name.
¹⁰ Why should the nations ask,
"Where is their God?"
Before our eyes, let vengeance for the shed blood of Your servants
be known among the nations.
¹¹ Let the groans of the prisoners reach You;
according to Your great power,
preserve those condemned to die.

¹² Pay back sevenfold to our neighbors
the reproach they have hurled at You, Lord.
¹³ Then we, Your people, the sheep of Your pasture,
will thank You forever;
we will declare Your praise to generation after generation.

PROVERBS 17:15-16

¹⁵ Acquitting the guilty and condemning the just—
both are detestable to the LORD.

¹⁶ Why does a fool have money in his hand
with no intention of buying wisdom?

ᏇCTS 12:1-25

12 About that time King Herod cruelly attacked some who belonged to the church, ² and he killed James, John's brother, with the sword. ³ When he saw that it pleased the Jews, he proceeded to arrest Peter too, during the days of Unleavened Bread. ⁴ After the arrest, he put him in prison and assigned four squads of four soldiers each to guard him, intending to bring him out to the people after the Passover. ⁵ So Peter was kept in prison, but prayer was being made earnestly to God for him by the church.

⁶ On the night before Herod was to bring him out for execution, Peter was sleeping between two soldiers, bound with two chains, while the sentries in front of the door guarded the prison. ⁷ Suddenly an angel of the Lord appeared, and a light shone in the cell. Striking Peter on the side, he woke him up and said, "Quick, get up!" Then the chains fell off his wrists. ⁸ "Get dressed," the angel told him, "and put on your sandals." And he did so. "Wrap your cloak around you," he told him, "and follow me." ⁹ So he went out and followed, and he did not know that what took place through the angel was real, but thought he was seeing a vision. ¹⁰ After they passed the first and second guard posts, they came to the iron gate that leads into the city, which opened to them by itself. They went outside and passed one street, and immediately the angel left him.

¹¹ Then Peter came to himself and said, "Now I know for certain that the Lord has sent His angel and rescued me from Herod's grasp and from all that the Jewish people expected." ¹² When he realized this, he went to the house of Mary, the mother of John Mark, where many had assembled and were praying.

¹³ He knocked at the door in the gateway, and a servant named Rhoda came to answer. ¹⁴ She recognized Peter's voice, and because of her joy she did not open the gate, but ran in and announced that Peter was standing at the gateway. ¹⁵ "You're crazy!" they told her. But she kept insisting that it was true. Then they said, "It's his angel!" ¹⁶ Peter, however, kept on knocking, and when they opened the door and saw him, they were astounded.

¹⁷ Motioning to them with his hand to be silent, he explained to them how the Lord had brought him out of the prison. "Report these things to James and the brothers," he said. Then he departed and went to a different place.

¹⁸ At daylight, there was a great commotion among the soldiers as to what could have become of Peter. ¹⁹ After Herod had searched and did not find him, he interrogated the guards and ordered their execution. Then Herod went down from Judea to Caesarea and stayed there.

²⁰ He had been very angry with the Tyrians and Sidonians. Together they presented themselves before him, and having won over Blastus, who was in charge of the king's bedroom, they asked for peace, because their country was supplied with food from the king's country. ²¹ So on an appointed day, dressed in royal robes and seated on the throne, Herod delivered a public address to them. ²² The populace began to shout, "It's the voice of a god and not of a man!" ²³ At once an angel of the Lord struck him because he did not give the glory to God, and he became infected with worms and died. ²⁴ Then God's message flourished and multiplied. ²⁵ And Barnabas and Saul returned to Jerusalem after they had completed their relief mission, on which they took John Mark.

Our Only Protection

God of our salvation, help us—for the glory of Your name. Deliver us.—PSALM 79:9

The armor of God is our only protection against the wiles of Satan, but it will do us no good unless we avail ourselves of it in its entirety.

In considering this matter, we must constantly keep before us the fact that such is the might and power of Satan that nothing apart from the armor of God will protect us from his onslaughts. Mark this and mark it well, for there are many Christians who have tried to stand against Satan in their own strength and have found themselves not victors but victims. One of the "wiles" of Satan is to get us to believe that we can resist him in our own strength. But the moment we think this—we are finished!

In my time I have seen many believers lulled by Satan into thinking that their long experience in the faith and their understanding of Christian doctrine were all they needed in order to be protected from satanic attack. But they found to their great cost that this was inadequate and insufficient. We never live more dangerously than when we depend on our spiritual experience and understanding to protect us from the flaming arrows of the enemy.

One thing and one thing only can protect us from the attacks of Satan, and that is the spiritual armor that God has provided to His people. In the Devil, you see, we are dealing with a foe who is inferior in power only to the Almighty Himself. Therefore, nothing less than the protection that God provides is adequate for our need.

Prayer

O Father, I need to get this matter straight, for I see that if my dependence is on anything other than You, then I am sunk. Drive this truth deep into my spirit this day. In Jesus' name. Amen.

Further Study

Rm 13:1-12; 1 Th 5:8; 2 Tm 2:4; Eph 6:11
What are we to put aside?
What are we to put on?

JULY 11

1 CHRONICLES 3:1–4:43

3 These were David's sons who were born to him in Hebron:
Amnon was the firstborn, by Ahinoam of Jezreel;
Daniel was born second, by Abigail of Carmel;
² Absalom son of Maacah, daughter of King Talmai of Geshur, was third;
Adonijah son of Haggith was fourth;
³ Shephatiah, by Abital, was fifth; and Ithream, by David's wife Eglah, was sixth.
⁴ Six sons were born to David in Hebron, where he ruled seven years and six months, and he ruled in Jerusalem 33 years.
⁵ These sons were born to him in Jerusalem:
Shimea, Shobab, Nathan, and Solomon. These four were born to him by Bath-shua daughter of Ammiel.
⁶ David's other sons: Ibhar, Elishua, Eliphelet, ⁷ Nogah, Nepheg, Japhia, ⁸ Elishama, Eliada, and Eliphelet—nine sons.
⁹ These were all David's sons, with their sister Tamar, in addition to the sons by his concubines.

¹⁰ Solomon's son was Rehoboam;
his son was Abijah, his son Asa, his son Jehoshaphat, ¹¹ his son Jehoram,
his son Ahaziah, his son Joash, ¹² his son Amaziah, his son Azariah, his son Jotham, ¹³ his son Ahaz, his son Hezekiah, his son Manasseh,
¹⁴ his son Amon, and his son Josiah.
¹⁵ Josiah's sons:
Johanan was the firstborn, Jehoiakim second,

Zedekiah third, and Shallum fourth.
¹⁶ Jehoiakim's sons:
his sons Jeconiah and Zedekiah.

¹⁷ The sons of Jeconiah the captive:
his sons Shealtiel, ¹⁸ Malchiram, Pedaiah, Shenazzar, Jekamiah, Hoshama, and Nedabiah.
¹⁹ Pedaiah's sons: Zerubbabel and Shimei.
Zerubbabel's sons: Meshullam and Hananiah, with their sister Shelomith; ²⁰ and five others—Hashubah, Ohel, Berechiah, Hasadiah, and Jushab-hesed.
²¹ Hananiah's descendants:
Pelatiah, Jeshaiah, and the sons of Rephaiah, Arnan, Obadiah, and Shecaniah.
²² The son of Shecaniah:
Shemaiah.
Shemaiah's sons: Hattush, Igal, Bariah, Neariah, and Shaphat—six.
²³ Neariah's sons: Elioenai, Hizkiah, and Azrikam—three.
²⁴ Elioenai's sons: Hodaviah, Eliashib, Pelaiah, Akkub, Johanan, Delaiah, and Anani—seven.

4 Judah's sons: Perez, Hezron, Carmi, Hur, and Shobal.
² Reaiah son of Shobal fathered Jahath,
and Jahath fathered Ahumai and Lahad.
These were the families of the Zorathites.
³ These were Etam's sons: Jezreel, Ishma, and Idbash, and their sister was named Hazzelelponi.
⁴ Penuel fathered Gedor, and Ezer fathered Hushah.
These were the sons of Hur, Ephrathah's firstborn and the father of Bethlehem:

795

⁵ Ashhur fathered Tekoa and had two wives, Helah and Naarah. ⁶ Naarah bore him Ahuzzam, Hepher, Temeni, and Haahashtari. These were Naarah's sons. ⁷ Helah's sons: Zereth, Zohar, and Ethnan. ⁸ Koz fathered Anub, Zobebah, and the families of Aharhel son of Harum.

⁹ Jabez was more honorable than his brothers. His mother named him Jabez and said, "I gave birth to him in pain." ¹⁰ Jabez called out to the God of Israel: "If only You would bless me, extend my border, let Your hand be with me, and keep me from harm, so that I will not cause any pain." And God granted his request.

¹¹ Chelub brother of Shuhah fathered Mehir, who was the father of Eshton. ¹² Eshton fathered Bethrapha, Paseah, and Tehinnah the father of Irnahash. These were the men of Recah. ¹³ Kenaz's sons: Othniel and Seraiah.
Othniel's sons: Hathath and Meonothai. ¹⁴ Meonothai fathered Ophrah, and Seraiah fathered Joab, the ancestor of those in the Valley of Craftsmen, for they were craftsmen. ¹⁵ The sons of Caleb son of Jephunneh: Iru, Elah, and Naam. Elah's son: Kenaz. ¹⁶ Jehallelel's sons: Ziph, Ziphah, Tiria, and Asarel. ¹⁷ Ezrah's sons: Jether, Mered, Epher, and Jalon. Mered's wife Bithiah gave birth to Miriam, Shammai, and Ishbah the father of Eshtemoa. ¹⁸ These were the sons of Pharaoh's daughter Bithiah; Mered had married her. His Judean wife gave birth to Jered the father of Gedor, Heber the father of Soco, and Jekuthiel the father of Zanoah. ¹⁹ The sons of Hodiah's wife, the sister of Naham: the father of Keilah the Garmite and the father of Eshtemoa the Maacathite.

²⁰ Shimon's sons: Amnon, Rinnah, Ben-hanan, and Tilon. Ishi's sons: Zoheth and Ben-zoheth.

²¹ The sons of Shelah son of Judah: Er the father of Lecah, Laadah the father of Mareshah, the families of the guild of linen workers at Beth-ashbea, ²² Jokim, the men of Cozeba; and Joash and Saraph, who married Moabites and returned to Lehem. These names are from ancient records. ²³ They were the potters and residents of Netaim and Gederah. They lived there in the service of the king.

²⁴ Simeon's sons: Nemuel, Jamin, Jarib, Zerah, and Shaul; ²⁵ Shaul's sons: his son Shallum, his son Mibsam, and his son Mishma. ²⁶ Mishma's sons: his son Hammuel, his son Zaccur, and his son Shimei.

²⁷ Shimei had 16 sons and six daughters, but his brothers did not have many children, so their whole family did not become as numerous as the Judeans. ²⁸ They lived in Beer-sheba, Moladah, Hazar-shual, ²⁹ Bilhah, Ezem, Tolad, ³⁰ Bethuel, Hormah, Ziklag, ³¹ Bethmarcaboth, Hazar-susim, Beth-biri, and Shaaraim. These were their cities until David became king. ³² Their villages were Etam, Ain, Rimmon, Tochen, and Ashan—five cities, ³³ and all their surrounding villages as far as Baal. These were their settlements, and they kept a genealogical record for themselves.

³⁴ Meshobab, Jamlech, Joshah son of Amaziah, ³⁵ Joel, Jehu son of Joshibiah, son of Seraiah, son of Asiel, ³⁶ Elioenai, Jaakobah, Jeshohaiah, Asaiah, Adiel, Jesimiel, Benaiah, ³⁷ and Ziza son of Shiphi, son of Allon, son of Jedaiah, son of Shimri, son of Shemaiah—

³⁸ these mentioned by name were leaders in their families. Their ancestral

houses increased greatly. ³⁹ They went to the entrance of Gedor, to the east side of the valley to seek pasture for their flocks. ⁴⁰ They found rich, good pasture, and the land was broad, peaceful, and quiet, for some Hamites had lived there previously.

⁴¹ These who were recorded by name came in the days of King Hezekiah of Judah, attacked the Hamites' tents and the Meunim who were found there, and set them apart for destruction, as they are today. Then they settled in their place because there was pasture for their flocks. ⁴² Now 500 men from these sons of Simeon went with Pelatiah, Neariah, Rephaiah, and Uzziel, the sons of Ishi, as their leaders to Mount Seir. ⁴³ They struck down the remnant of the Amalekites who had escaped and still live there today.

PSALM 80:1-7

¹ Listen, Shepherd of Israel,
who guides Joseph like a flock;
You who sit enthroned on the
cherubim, rise up
² at the head of Ephraim, Benjamin,
and Manasseh.
Rally Your power and come to save
us.
³ Restore us, God;
look on us with favor, and we will
be saved.

⁴ LORD God of Hosts,
how long will You be angry with
Your people's prayers?
⁵ You fed them the bread of tears
and gave them a full measure of
tears to drink.
⁶ You set us at strife with our
neighbors;
our enemies make fun of us.
⁷ Restore us, God of Hosts;
look on us with favor, and we will
be saved.

PROVERBS 17:17

¹⁷ A friend loves at all times,
and a brother is born for a
difficult time.

ACTS 13:1-22

13 In the local church at Antioch there were prophets and teachers: Barnabas, Simeon who was called Niger, Lucius the Cyrenian, Manaen, a close friend of Herod the tetrarch, and Saul.

² As they were ministering to the Lord and fasting, the Holy Spirit said, "Set apart for Me Barnabas and Saul for the work that I have called them to." ³ Then, after they had fasted, prayed, and laid hands on them, they sent them off.

⁴ Being sent out by the Holy Spirit, they came down to Seleucia, and from there they sailed to Cyprus. ⁵ Arriving in Salamis, they proclaimed God's message in the Jewish synagogues. They also had John as their assistant. ⁶ When they had gone through the whole island as far as Paphos, they came across a sorcerer, a Jewish false prophet named Bar-Jesus. ⁷ He was with the proconsul, Sergius Paulus, an intelligent man. This man summoned Barnabas and Saul and desired to hear God's message. ⁸ But Elymas, the sorcerer, which is how his name is translated, opposed them and tried to turn the proconsul away from the faith.

⁹ Then Saul—also called Paul—filled with the Holy Spirit, stared straight at the sorcerer ¹⁰ and said, "You son of the Devil, full of all deceit and all fraud, enemy of all righteousness! Won't you ever stop perverting the straight paths of the Lord? ¹¹ Now, look! The Lord's hand is against you: you are going to be blind, and will not see the sun for a time." Suddenly a mist and darkness fell on him, and he went around seeking someone to lead him by the hand.

¹² Then the proconsul, seeing what happened, believed and was astonished at the teaching about the Lord.

¹³ Paul and his companions set sail from Paphos and came to Perga in Pamphylia. John, however, left them and went back to Jerusalem. ¹⁴ They continued their journey from Perga and reached Antioch in Pisidia. On the Sabbath day they went into the synagogue and sat

down. ¹⁵ After the reading of the Law and the Prophets, the leaders of the synagogue sent word to them, saying, "Brothers, if you have any message of encouragement for the people, you can speak."

¹⁶ Then standing up, Paul motioned with his hand and spoke: "Men of Israel, and you who fear God, listen! ¹⁷ The God of this people Israel chose our forefathers, exalted the people during their stay in the land of Egypt, and led them out of it with a mighty arm. ¹⁸ And for about 40 years He put up with them in the desert; ¹⁹ then after destroying seven nations in the land of Canaan, He gave their land to them as an inheritance. ²⁰ This all took about 450 years. After this, He gave them judges until Samuel the prophet. ²¹ Then they asked for a king, so God gave them Saul the son of Kish, a man of the tribe of Benjamin, for 40 years. ²² After removing him, He raised up David as their king, of whom He testified: 'I have found David the son of Jesse, a man after My heart, who will carry out all My will.'

Our Primary View of Him

Listen, Shepherd of Israel, who guides Joseph like a flock.

—PSALM 80:1

Why did David choose to think of God as his Shepherd? The picture of God we carry deep in our hearts is the one we relate to whenever we find ourselves surrounded by trouble or difficulties. But perhaps what is more important is this—we will interpret every event of our lives in accordance with the inner picture that we have of Him.

When I have asked people during counseling to describe to me their *primary* view of God, I have been surprised that so often they see Him not as a loving Shepherd but as an austere and stern Judge. God *is* a Judge, of course—as David discovered when he committed adultery with Bathsheba—but that is not His *primary* relationship to His children. Someone has pointed out that the two most beautiful illustrations of God's relationship to His people given in Scripture are those of a Father and a Shepherd. It is interesting also that the two best-known passages in the whole of God's Word—the Lord's Prayer and Psalm 23—use these analogies.

What kind of picture of God, I wonder, do you carry deep down in your heart? If your *primary* view of God is as a Judge, then you will tend to interpret your problems as God's judgment upon you, rather than an opportunity to experience in your troubles His tender love and care. Make no mistake about it—the image of God that you carry deep in your heart is the one that you will relate to in a moment of crisis.

Prayer

O Father, help me develop a true image of You in my heart: a picture that is exposed, not from my own feelings and ideas about You, but from the principles that lie hidden in Your precious Word. In Jesus' name I ask it. Amen.

Further Study

Col 1:1-15; 2:9; Jn 1:1-2
How has God revealed Himself to us?
What is your picture of God?

JULY 12

1 CHRONICLES 5:1–6:32

5 These were the sons of Reuben the firstborn of Israel. He was the firstborn, but his birthright was given to the sons of Joseph son of Israel, because Reuben defiled his father's bed. He is not listed in the genealogy according to birthright. ² Although Judah became strong among his brothers and a ruler came from him, the birthright was given to Joseph.

³ The sons of Reuben, Israel's firstborn:
Hanoch, Pallu, Hezron, and Carmi.
⁴ Joel's sons: his son Shemaiah,
his son Gog, his son Shimei,
⁵ his son Micah, his son Reaiah,
his son Baal, ⁶ and his son Beerah.

Beerah was a leader of the Reubenites, and Tiglath-pileser king of Assyria took him into exile. ⁷ His relatives by their families as they are recorded in their genealogy: Jeiel the chief, Zechariah, ⁸ and Bela son of Azaz, son of Shema, son of Joel. They settled in Aroer as far as Nebo and Baal-meon. ⁹ They also settled in the east as far as the edge of the desert that extends to the Euphrates River, because their herds had increased in the land of Gilead. ¹⁰ During Saul's reign they waged war against the Hagrites, who were defeated by their power. And they lived in their tents throughout the region east of Gilead.

¹¹ The sons of Gad lived next to them in the land of Bashan as far as Salecah:
¹² Joel the chief, Shapham the second in command, Janai, and Shaphat in Bashan.
¹³ Their relatives according to their ancestral houses: Michael, Meshullam, Sheba, Jorai, Jacan, Zia, and Eber—seven.
¹⁴ These were the sons of Abihail son of Huri,
son of Jaroah, son of Gilead,
son of Michael, son of Jeshishai,
son of Jahdo, son of Buz.
¹⁵ Ahi son of Abdiel, son of Guni, was head of their ancestral houses. ¹⁶ They lived in Gilead, in Bashan and its towns, and throughout the pasturelands of Sharon. ¹⁷ All of them were registered in the genealogies during the reigns of Judah's King Jotham and Israel's King Jeroboam.

¹⁸ The sons of Reuben and Gad and half the tribe of Manasseh had 44,760 warriors who could serve in the army—men who carried shield and sword, drew the bow, and were trained for war. ¹⁹ They waged war against the Hagrites, Jetur, Naphish, and Nodab. ²⁰ They received help against these enemies, and the Hagrites and all their allies were

handed over to them, because they cried out to God in battle. He granted their request because they trusted in Him. ²¹ They captured the Hagrites' livestock—50,000 of their camels, 250,000 sheep, and 2,000 donkeys—as well as 100,000 people. ²² Many of the Hagrites were killed because it was God's battle. And they lived there in the Hagrites' place until the exile.

²³ The sons of half the tribe of Manasseh settled in the land from Bashan to Baal-hermon (that is, Senir or Mount Hermon). They were numerous. ²⁴ These were the heads of their ancestral houses: Epher, Ishi, Eliel, Azriel, Jeremiah, Hodaviah, and Jahdiel. They were brave warriors, famous men, and heads of their patriarchal families. ²⁵ But they were unfaithful to the God of their ancestors. They prostituted themselves with the gods of the nations God had destroyed before them. ²⁶ So the God of Israel put it into the mind of Pul (that is, Tiglath-pileser) king of Assyria to take the Reubenites, Gadites, and half the tribe of Manasseh into exile. He took them to Halah, Habor, Hara, and Gozan's river, where they are until today.

6 Levi's sons: Gershom, Kohath, and Merari.
² Kohath's sons: Amram, Izhar, Hebron, and Uzziel.
³ Amram's children: Aaron, Moses, and Miriam.
Aaron's sons: Nadab, Abihu, Eleazar, and Ithamar.
⁴ Eleazar fathered Phinehas; Phinehas fathered Abishua;
⁵ Abishua fathered Bukki; Bukki fathered Uzzi;
⁶ Uzzi fathered Zerahiah; Zerahiah fathered Meraioth;
⁷ Meraioth fathered Amariah; Amariah fathered Ahitub;
⁸ Ahitub fathered Zadok; Zadok fathered Ahimaaz;
⁹ Ahimaaz fathered Azariah; Azariah fathered Johanan;
¹⁰ Johanan fathered Azariah, who served as priest in the temple that Solomon built in Jerusalem;

¹¹ Azariah fathered Amariah; Amariah fathered Ahitub;
¹² Ahitub fathered Zadok; Zadok fathered Shallum;
¹³ Shallum fathered Hilkiah; Hilkiah fathered Azariah;
¹⁴ Azariah fathered Seraiah; and Seraiah fathered Jehozadak.
¹⁵ Jehozadak went into exile when the LORD sent Judah and Jerusalem into exile at the hands of Nebuchadnezzar.

¹⁶ Levi's sons: Gershom, Kohath, and Merari.
¹⁷ These are the names of Gershom's sons: Libni and Shimei.
¹⁸ Kohath's sons: Amram, Izhar, Hebron and Uzziel.
¹⁹ Merari's sons: Mahli and Mushi. These are the Levites' families according to their fathers:
²⁰ Of Gershom: his son Libni, his son Jahath, his son Zimmah,
²¹ his son Joah, his son Iddo, his son Zerah, and his son Jeatherai.
²² Kohath's sons: his son Amminadab, his son Korah, his son Assir,
²³ his son Elkanah, his son Ebiasaph, his son Assir, ²⁴ his son Tahath, his son Uriel, his son Uzziah, and his son Shaul.
²⁵ Elkanah's sons: Amasai and Ahimoth,
²⁶ his son Elkanah, his son Zophai, his son Nahath, ²⁷ his son Eliab, his son Jeroham, and his son Elkanah.
²⁸ Samuel's sons: his firstborn Joel, and his second son Abijah.
²⁹ Merari's sons: Mahli, his son Libni,
his son Shimei, his son Uzzah,
³⁰ his son Shimea, his son Haggiah, and his son Asaiah.

³¹ These are the men David put in charge of the music in the LORD's temple after the ark came to rest there. ³² They ministered with song in front of the tabernacle, the tent of meeting, un-

til Solomon built the LORD's temple in Jerusalem, and they performed their task according to the regulations given to them.

*P*SALM 80:8-13

⁸ You uprooted a vine from Egypt;
  You drove out the nations and
    planted it.
⁹ You cleared a place for it;
  it took root and filled the land.
¹⁰ The mountains were covered by
    its shade,
  and the mighty cedars with its
    branches.
¹¹ It sent out sprouts toward the Sea
  and shoots toward the River.

¹² Why have You broken down its
    walls
  so that all who pass by pick its
    fruit?
¹³ The boar from the forest
    gnaws at it,
  and creatures of the field
    feed on it.

*P*ROVERBS 17:18-19

¹⁸ One without sense enters an
    agreement
  and puts up security for his friend.

¹⁹ One who loves to offend loves
    strife;
  one who builds a high threshold
    invites injury.

*A*CTS 13:23-41

²³ "From this man's descendants, according to the promise, God brought the Savior, Jesus, to Israel. ²⁴ Before He came to public attention, John had previously proclaimed a baptism of repentance to all the people of Israel. ²⁵ Then as John was completing his life work, he said, 'Who do you think I am? I am not the One. But look! Someone is coming after me, and I am not worthy to untie the sandals on His feet.' ²⁶ "Brothers, sons of Abraham's race, and those among you who fear God, the

message of this salvation has been sent to us. ²⁷ For the residents of Jerusalem and their rulers, since they did not recognize Him or the voices of the prophets that are read every Sabbath, have fulfilled their words by condemning Him. ²⁸ Though they found no grounds for the death penalty, they asked Pilate to have Him killed. ²⁹ When they had fulfilled all that had been written about Him, they took Him down from the tree and put Him in a tomb. ³⁰ But God raised Him from the dead, ³¹ and He appeared for many days to those who came up with Him from Galilee to Jerusalem, who are now His witnesses to the people. ³² And we ourselves proclaim to you the good news of the promise that was made to our forefathers. ³³ God has fulfilled this to us their children by raising up Jesus, as it is written in the second Psalm:

You are My Son;
today I have become Your Father.

³⁴ Since He raised Him from the dead, never to return to decay, He has spoken in this way, I will grant you the faithful covenant blessings made to David. ³⁵ Therefore He also says in another passage, You will not allow Your Holy One to see decay. ³⁶ For David, after serving his own generation in God's plan, fell asleep, was buried with his fathers, and decayed. ³⁷ But the One whom God raised up did not decay. ³⁸ Therefore, let it be known to you, brothers, that through this man forgiveness of sins is being proclaimed to you, ³⁹ and everyone who believes in Him is justified from everything, which you could not be justified from through the law of Moses. ⁴⁰ So beware that what is said in the prophets does not happen to you:

⁴¹ Look, you scoffers,
  marvel and vanish away,
  because I am doing a work
    in your days,
  a work that you will
    never believe,
  even if someone were
    to explain it to you."

Rejected by God?

*Let it be known…that through this man forgiveness of sins
is being proclaimed to you, and everyone who believes in Him
is justified from everything.*—ACTS 13:38

A feeling that the Devil likes to arouse in an unguarded heart is the feeling that when we have committed a sin, we will be rejected by God and have to forfeit our salvation. The Hebrew name "Satan" means "adversary," and the Greek name for "devil" means "slanderer." This gives us a pretty good idea of the nature of the evil one. He is never happier than when he is engaged in pointing the finger of scorn at us whenever we have failed.

It is part of the doctrine of the church that a Christian may sometimes fall into sin. We are saved, but we are still fallible. God forbid that we should fall into sin, but when we do, we must remember that we have "an advocate with the Father—Jesus Christ the righteous One" (1 Jn 2:1).

You can be sure, however, that when you fall into sin, the Devil will come to you and say: "You were forgiven when you became a Christian because you sinned in ignorance, but now that you are a Christian, you have sinned against the light. There can be no forgiveness for you now because of what you have done. You are lost—forever!"

The answer to this, as with all of Satan's accusations, is to put on the "armor of righteousness." You must remind him that God's righteousness not only covers us at our salvation but continues to cover us for time and eternity. Never allow the Devil to use a particular sin to call into question your whole standing before God. This is something that has been settled in heaven, not in the debating chamber of the Devil.

Prayer

My Father and my God, my heart overflows at the revelation of Your full and free forgiveness. Help me not to take it for granted but to take it with gratitude. In Jesus' name I pray. Amen.

Further Study

Is 55:1-7; 43:25; Eph 1:7-8; Ac 13:38; 1 Jn 1:9
What does God do when He blots out our sin?
How does the Lord respond when we return to Him?

JULY 13

1 CHRONICLES 6:33-81

33 These are the men who served with their sons.

From the Kohathites:
Heman the singer,
son of Joel, son of Samuel,
34 son of Elkanah, son of Jeroham,
son of Eliel, son of Toah,
35 son of Zuph, son of Elkanah,
son of Mahath, son of Amasai,
36 son of Elkanah, son of Joel,
son of Azariah, son of Zephaniah,
37 son of Tahath, son of Assir,
son of Ebiasaph, son of Korah,
38 son of Izhar, son of Kohath,
son of Levi, son of Israel.

39 Heman's relative was Asaph,
who stood at his right hand:
Asaph son of Berechiah,
son of Shimea,
40 son of Michael, son of Baaseiah,
son of Malchijah, 41 son of Ethni,
son of Zerah, son of Adaiah,
42 son of Ethan, son of Zimmah,
son of Shimei, 43 son of Jahath,
son of Gershom, son of Levi.

44 On the left, their relatives were
Merari's sons:
Ethan son of Kishi, son of Abdi,
son of Malluch,
45 son of Hashabiah,
son of Amaziah, son of Hilkiah,
46 son of Amzi, son of Bani,
son of Shemer, 47 son of Mahli,
son of Mushi, son of Merari,
son of Levi.

48 Their relatives the Levites were assigned to all the service of the tabernacle, God's temple. 49 But Aaron and his sons did all the work of the most holy place. They presented the offerings on the altar of burnt offerings and on the altar of incense to make atonement for Israel according to all that Moses the servant of God had commanded.

50 These are Aaron's sons: his son
Eleazar,
his son Phinehas, his son Abishua,
51 his son Bukki, his son Uzzi,
his son Zerahiah, 52 his son
Meraioth,
his son Amariah, his son Ahitub,
53 his son Zadok, and his son
Ahimaaz.

54 These were the places assigned to Aaron's sons from the Kohathite family for their settlements in their territory, because the first; lot was for them. 55 They were given Hebron in the land of Judah and its surrounding pasturelands, 56 but the fields and villages around the city were given to Caleb son of Jephunneh. 57 Aaron's sons were given:

Hebron (a city of refuge), Libnah and its pasturelands, Jattir, Eshtemoa and its pasturelands, 58 Hilen and its pasturelands, Debir and its pasturelands, 59 Ashan and its pasturelands, and Beth-shemesh and its pasturelands. 60 From the tribe of Benjamin they were given Geba and its pasturelands, Alemeth and its pasturelands, and Anathoth and its pasturelands. They had 13 towns in all among their families.

61 To the rest of the Kohathites, 10 towns from the half tribe of Manasseh were assigned by lot. 62 The Gershomites were assigned 13 towns from the tribes of Issachar, Asher, Naphtali, and Manasseh in Bashan according to their families. 63 The Merarites were assigned by lot 12 towns from the tribes of Reuben,

Gad, and Zebulun according to their families. ⁶⁴ So the Israelites gave these towns and their pasturelands to the Levites. ⁶⁵ They assigned by lot the towns named above from the tribes of the Judahites, Simeonites, and Benjaminites.

⁶⁶ Some of the families of the Kohathites were given towns from the tribe of Ephraim for their territory:

⁶⁷ Shechem (a city of refuge) with its pasturelands in the hill country of Ephraim, Gezer and its pasturelands, ⁶⁸ Jokmeam and its pasturelands, Beth-horon and its pasturelands, ⁶⁹ Aijalon and its pasturelands, and Gath-rimmon and its pasturelands. ⁷⁰ From half the tribe of Manasseh, Aner and its pasturelands, and Bileam and its pasturelands were given to the rest of the families of the Kohathites.

⁷¹ The Gershomites received:

Golan in Bashan and its pasturelands, and Ashtaroth and its pasturelands from the families of half the tribe of Manasseh. ⁷² From the tribe of Issachar they received Kedesh and its pasturelands, Daberath and its pasturelands, ⁷³ Ramoth and its pasturelands, and Anem and its pasturelands. ⁷⁴ From the tribe of Asher they received Mashal and its pasturelands, Abdon and its pasturelands, ⁷⁵ Hukok and its pasturelands, and Rehob and its pasturelands. ⁷⁶ From the tribe of Naphtali they received Kedesh in Galilee and its pasturelands, Hammon and its pasturelands, and Kiriathaim and its pasturelands.

⁷⁷ The rest of the Merarites received:

From the tribe of Zebulun, they received Rimmono and its pasturelands and Tabor and its pasturelands. ⁷⁸ From the tribe of Reuben across the Jordan at Jericho, to the east of the Jordan, they received Bezer in the desert and its pasture-

lands, Jahzah and its pasturelands, ⁷⁹ Kedemoth and its pasturelands, and Mephaath and its pasturelands. ⁸⁰ From the tribe of Gad they received Ramoth in Gilead and its pasturelands, Mahanaim and its pasturelands, ⁸¹ Heshbon and its pasturelands, and Jazer and its pasturelands.

PSALM 80:14-19

14　Return, God of Hosts.
　　Look down from heaven and see;
　　take care of this vine,
15　the root Your right hand has planted,
　　the shoot that You made strong for Yourself.
16　It was cut down and burned up;
　　they perish at the rebuke of Your countenance.
17　Let Your hand be with the man at Your right hand,
　　with the son of man You have made strong for Yourself.
18　Then we will not turn away from You;
　　revive us, and we will call on Your name.
19　Restore us, LORD God of Hosts;
　　look on us with favor, and we will be saved.

PROVERBS 17:20-21

20　One with a twisted mind will not succeed,
　　and one with deceitful speech will fall into ruin.

21　A man fathers a fool to his own sorrow;
　　the father of a fool has no joy.

ACTS 13:42–14:7

⁴² As they were leaving, they begged that these matters be presented to them the following Sabbath. ⁴³ After the synagogue had been dismissed, many of the Jews and devout proselytes followed Paul and Barnabas, who were speaking

with them and persuading them to continue in the grace of God.

⁴⁴ The following Sabbath almost the whole town assembled to hear the message of the Lord. ⁴⁵ But when the Jews saw the crowds, they were filled with jealousy and began to oppose what Paul was saying by insulting him.

⁴⁶ Then Paul and Barnabas boldly said: "It was necessary that God's message be spoken to you first. But since you reject it, and consider yourselves unworthy of eternal life, we now turn to the Gentiles! ⁴⁷ For this is what the Lord has commanded us:

> I have appointed you as a light
> for the Gentiles,
> to bring salvation to the ends
> of the earth."

⁴⁸ When the Gentiles heard this, they rejoiced and glorified the message of the Lord, and all who had been appointed to eternal life believed. ⁴⁹ So the message of the Lord spread through the whole region. ⁵⁰ But the Jews incited the religious women of high standing and the leading men of the city. They stirred up persecution against Paul and Barnabas and expelled them from their district. ⁵¹ But shaking the dust off their feet against them, they proceeded to Iconium. ⁵² And the disciples were filled with joy and the Holy Spirit.

14 The same thing happened in Iconium; they entered the Jewish synagogue and spoke in such a way that a great number of both Jews and Greeks believed. ² But the Jews who refused to believe stirred up and poisoned the minds of the Gentiles against the brothers. ³ So they stayed there for some time and spoke boldly, in reliance on the Lord, who testified to the message of His grace by granting that signs and wonders be performed through them. ⁴ But the people of the city were divided, some siding with the Jews and some with the apostles. ⁵ When an attempt was made by both the Gentiles and Jews, with their rulers, to assault and stone them, ⁶ they found out about it and fled to the Lycaonian towns called Lystra and Derbe, and to the surrounding countryside. ⁷ And there they kept evangelizing.

"Lies Have Short Legs"

One with a twisted mind will not succeed, and one with deceitful speech will fall into ruin.—Proverbs 17:20

Both the universe and ourselves are made for truth and honesty, and both the universe and ourselves are alien to untruth and dishonesty. The universe is made for the same thing as we are—namely, righteousness. Not only the face of the Lord but the face of the universe is set against those who live below its standards.

I know that this may sound somewhat hollow in an age that appears to thrive on dishonesty and corruption, but I stand by it nevertheless. The universe is not built for the success of dishonesty and corruption. A lie breaks itself upon the moral universe, perhaps not today, not tomorrow—but certainly at some point in the future. The Tamils of South India have a saying: "The life of the cleverest lie is only eight days." The Germans have a saying: "Lies have short legs." During the Second World War, they adapted that saying to, "Lies have one leg." That was because Goebbels, the Propaganda Minister, had one short leg.

A passionate antagonist of Communism is reported to have said: "In our fight against Communism we are handicapped by our decency and honesty." Since when were honesty and decency handicaps? Rather, Indecency and dishonesty are handicaps; they bring us into bondage—inwardly and outwardly. Governments, organizations, and institutions that practice dishonesty will be broken from within. History has proved that. The Roman Empire collapsed not from without but from within—broken upon the rock of its own corruption. Believe me, no one gets away with anything in a moral universe. No one.

Prayer

Gracious Father, I don't want my moral joints to creak with dishonesty, so dwell deeply within me by Your Spirit and lubricate them with the oil of Your honesty. In Jesus' name I ask it. Amen.

Further Study

Lk 12:1-12; 1 Co 4:1-5; Nm 32:23; Ec 12:14
What will happen when the Lord comes?
What can we be sure of?

JULY 14

1 CHRONICLES 7:1–8:28

7 Issachar's sons: Tola, Puah, Jashub, and Shimron—four.
² Tola's sons: Uzzi, Rephaiah, Jeriel, Jahmai, Ibsam, and Shemuel, the heads of their ancestral houses. During David's reign, 22,600 descendants of Tola were recorded as warriors in their genealogies.
³ Uzzi's son: Izrahiah.
Izrahiah's sons: Michael, Obadiah, Joel, Isshiah. All five of them were chiefs. ⁴ Along with them, they had 36,000 troops for battle according to the genealogical records of their ancestral houses, for they had many wives and children. ⁵ Their tribesmen who were

warriors belonging to all the families of Issachar totalled 87,000 in their genealogies.

⁶ Three of Benjamin's sons: Bela, Becher, and Jediael.
⁷ Bela's sons: Ezbon, Uzzi, Uzziel, Jerimoth, and Iri—five. They were warriors and heads of their ancestral houses; 22,034 were listed in their genealogies.
⁸ Becher's sons: Zemirah, Joash, Eliezer, Elioenai, Omri, Jeremoth, Abijah, Anathoth, and Alemeth; all these were Becher's sons. ⁹ Their genealogies were recorded according to the heads of their ancestral houses—20,200 warriors.
¹⁰ Jediael's son: Bilhan.
Bilhan's sons: Jeush, Benjamin,

Ehud, Chenaanah, Zethan, Tarshish, and Ahishahar. [11] All these sons of Jediael listed by heads of families were warriors; there were 17,200 who could serve in the army. [12] Shuppim and Huppim were sons of Ir, and the Hushim were the sons of Aher.

[13] Naphtali's sons: Jahziel, Guni, Jezer, and Shallum—Bilhah's sons.

[14] Manasseh's sons through his Aramean concubine: Asriel and Machir the father of Gilead. [15] Machir took wives from Huppim and Shuppim. The name of his sister was Maacah. Another descendant was named Zelophehad, but he had only daughters. [16] Machir's wife Maacah gave birth to a son, and she named him Peresh. His brother was named Sheresh, and his sons were Ulam and Rekem. [17] Ulam's son: Bedan. These were the sons of Gilead son of Machir, son of Manasseh. [18] His sister Hammolecheth gave birth to Ishhod, Abiezer, and Mahlah. [19] Shemida's sons: Ahian, Shechem, Likhi, and Aniam.

[20] Ephraim's sons: Shuthelah, and his son Bered, his son Tahath, his son Eleadah, his son Tahath, [21] his son Zabad, his son Shuthelah, Ezer, and Elead. The men of Gath who were born in the land killed Ezer and Elead because they went down to raid their cattle. [22] Their father Ephraim mourned a long time, and his relatives came to comfort him. [23] He slept with his wife, and she conceived and gave birth to a son. So he named him Beriah, because there had been misfortune in his home. [24] His daughter was Sheerah, who built Lower and Upper Beth-horon and Uzzen-sheerah, [25] his son Rephah, his son Resheph,

his son Telah, his son Tahan, [26] his son Ladan, his son Ammihud, his son Elishama, [27] his son Nun, and his son Joshua.

[28] Their holdings and settlements were Bethel and its villages; Naaran to the east, Gezer and its villages to the west, and Shechem and its villages as far as Ayyah and its villages, [29] and along the borders of the sons of Manasseh, Beth-shean and its villages, Taanach and its villages, Megiddo and its villages, and Dor and its villages. The sons of Joseph son of Israel lived in these towns.

[30] Asher's sons: Imnah, Ishvah, Ishvi, and Beriah, with their sister Serah. [31] Beriah's sons: Heber, and Malchiel, who fathered Birzaith. [32] Heber fathered Japhlet, Shomer, and Hotham, with their sister Shua. [33] Japhlet's sons: Pasach, Bimhal, and Ashvath. These were Japhlet's sons. [34] Shemer's sons: Ahi, Rohgah, Hubbah, and Aram. [35] His brother Helem's sons: Zophah, Imna, Shelesh, and Amal. [36] Zophah's sons: Suah, Harnepher, Shual, Beri, Imrah, [37] Bezer, Hod, Shamma, Shilshah, Ithran, and Beera. [38] Jether's sons: Jephunneh, Pispa, and Ara. [39] Ulla's sons: Arah, Hanniel, and Rizia. [40] All these were Asher's sons. They were the heads of their ancestral houses, chosen men, warriors, and chiefs among the leaders. The number of men listed in their genealogies for military service was 26,000.

8 Benjamin fathered Bela, his firstborn;

Ashbel was born second,
Aharah third,
[2] Nohah fourth, and Rapha fifth.
[3] Bela's sons: Addar, Gera, Abihud,
[4] Abishua, Naaman, Ahoah,
[5] Gera, Shephuphan, and Huram.
[6] These were Ehud's sons, who were the heads of the families living in Geba and who were deported to Manahath: [7] Naaman, Ahijah, and Gera. Gera deported them and was the father of Uzza and Ahihud.
[8] Shaharaim had sons in the country of Moab after he had divorced his wives Hushim and Baara. [9] His sons by his wife Hodesh: Jobab, Zibia, Mesha, Malcam, [10] Jeuz, Sachia, and Mirmah. These were his sons, heads of families. [11] He also had sons by Hushim: Abitub and Elpaal.
[12] Elpaal's sons: Eber, Misham, and Shemed who built Ono and Lod and its villages, [13] Beriah and Shema, who were the heads of families of Aijalon's residents and who drove out the residents of Gath, [14] Ahio, Shashak, and Jeremoth.
[15] Zebadiah, Arad, Eder, [16] Michael, Ishpah, and Joha were Beriah's sons.
[17] Zebadiah, Meshullam, Hizki, Heber, [18] Ishmerai, Izliah, and Jobab were Elpaal's sons.
[19] Jakim, Zichri, Zabdi, [20] Elienai, Zillethai, Eliel, [21] Adaiah, Beraiah, and Shimrath were Shimei's sons.
[22] Ishpan, Eber, Eliel, [23] Abdon, Zichri, Hanan, [24] Hananiah, Elam, Anthothijah, [25] Iphdeiah, and Penuel were Shashak's sons.
[26] Shamsherai, Shehariah, Athaliah, [27] Jaareshiah, Elijah, and Zichri were Jeroham's sons.
[28] These were heads of families, chiefs according to their genealogies, and lived in Jerusalem.

PSALM 81:1-7

[1] Sing for joy to God our strength;
shout in triumph to the God of Jacob.
[2] Lift up a song—play the tambourine,
the melodious lyre, and the harp.
[3] Blow the horn during the new moon
and during the full moon, on the day of our feast.
[4] For this is a statute for Israel,
a judgment of the God of Jacob.
[5] He set it up as an ordinance for Joseph
when He went throughout the land of Egypt.

I heard an unfamiliar language:
[6] "I relieved his shoulder from the burden;
his hands were freed from carrying the basket.
[7] You called out in distress, and I rescued you;
I answered you from the thundercloud.
I tested you at the waters of Meribah.   *Selah*

PROVERBS 17:22-23

[22] A joyful heart is good medicine,
but a broken spirit dries up the bones.

[23] A wicked man secretly takes a bribe
to subvert the course of justice.

ACTS 14:8-28

[8] In Lystra a man without strength in his feet, lame from birth, and who had never walked, sat [9] and heard Paul speaking. After observing him closely and seeing that he had faith to be healed, [10] Paul said in a loud voice, "Stand up straight on your feet!" And he jumped up and started to walk around.
[11] When the crowds saw what Paul had done, they raised their voices, saying in the Lycaonian language, "The gods have come down to us in the form of men!" [12] And they started to call Barnabas, Zeus, and Paul, Hermes, because he was the main speaker. [13] Then

the priest of Zeus, whose temple was just outside the town, brought oxen and garlands to the gates. He, with the crowds, intended to offer sacrifice. ¹⁴ The apostles Barnabas and Paul tore their robes when they heard this and rushed into the crowd, shouting: ¹⁵ "Men! Why are you doing these things? We are men also, with the same nature as you, and we are proclaiming good news to you, that you should turn from these worthless things to the living God, **who made the heaven, the earth, the sea, and everything in them.** ¹⁶ In past generations He allowed all the nations to go their own way, ¹⁷ although He did not leave Himself without a witness, since He did good: giving you rain from heaven and fruitful seasons, and satisfying your hearts with food and happiness." ¹⁸ Even though they said these things, they barely stopped the crowds from sacrificing to them.

¹⁹ Then some Jews came from Antioch and Iconium, and when they had won over the crowds and stoned Paul, they dragged him out of the city, thinking he was dead. ²⁰ After the disciples sur-rounded him, he got up and went into the town. The next day he left with Barnabas for Derbe.

²¹ After they had evangelized that town and made many disciples, they returned to Lystra, to Iconium, and to Antioch, ²² strengthening the hearts of the disciples by encouraging them to continue in the faith, and by telling them, "It is necessary to pass through many troubles on our way into the kingdom of God."

²³ When they had appointed elders in every church and prayed with fasting, they committed them to the Lord in whom they had believed. ²⁴ Then they passed through Pisidia and came to Pamphylia. ²⁵ After they spoke the message in Perga, they went down to Attalia. ²⁶ From there they sailed back to Antioch where they had been entrusted to the grace of God for the work they had completed. ²⁷ After they arrived and gathered the church together, they reported everything God had done with them, and that He had opened the door of faith to the Gentiles. ²⁸ And they spent a considerable time with the disciples.

"No Reason to Smile"

A joyful heart is good medicine,
but a broken spirit dries up the bones.—PROVERBS 17:22

A surprising thing takes place in those whose temper is tempered by the Holy Spirit—bad temper is replaced by a growing sense of humor. God has given us the power of humor, not only to laugh at things, but to laugh off things. I am not suggesting that we ought to use laughter to deny realities, but humor often reduces things to their proper size.

I once heard a preacher say: "There is no good in a movement or a person where there is no good humor, for goodness has laughter as a corollary." There is something basically wrong with a person who, at appropriate times, cannot break out into hearty laughter. I heard recently of a member of the Irish Republican Army who was wonderfully converted. He spent the first month after his conversion in the home of a minister who said of him: "It was two weeks before I saw him smile, and when I spoke to him about this, he said: 'I have been in a grim business, plotting against people—and the way I was living, there was just no reason to smile.'"

How tragic—"just no reason to smile." Depend on it, where you cannot smile, you cannot live—you just exist.

Over the years, I have watched many groups come to the CWS Institutes in Christian Counseling. Many are tied up with fears, guilt, and apprehension. We invite them to share their fears and get them up and out. They do. Then the laughter begins. They grow progressively happier as the week goes on. By the end of the week, they are ready to laugh at anything—themselves included.

Prayer

Lord Jesus, it is said of You that You were anointed "more than your companions, with the oil of joy." Let that same anointing rest and remain upon me today—and every day. For Your own dear name's sake. Amen.

Further study

Pr 15:1-15; Jms 5:13; Ps 126:2
What does a happy heart enjoy?
How is this expressed?

JULY 15

1 CHRONICLES 8:29–9:44

²⁹ Jeiel, fathered Gibeon and lived in Gibeon. His wife's name was Maacah. ³⁰ Abdon was his firstborn son, then Zur, Kish, Baal, Nadab, ³¹ Gedor, Ahio, Zecher, ³² and Mikloth who fathered Shimeah. These also lived opposite their relatives in Jerusalem, with their other relatives.

³³ Ner fathered Kish, Kish fathered Saul, and Saul fathered Jonathan, Malchishua, Abinadab, and Esh-baal.

³⁴ Jonathan's son was Merib-baal, and Merib-baal fathered Micah.

³⁵ Micah's sons: Pithon, Melech, Tarea, and Ahaz.

³⁶ Ahaz fathered Jehoaddah, Jehoaddah fathered Alemeth, Azmaveth, and Zimri, and Zimri fathered Moza.

³⁷ Moza fathered Binea. His son was Raphah, his son Eleasah, and his son Azel.

³⁸ Azel had six sons, and these were their names: Azrikam, Bocheru, Ishmael, Sheariah, Obadiah, and Hanan. All these were Azel's sons.

³⁹ His brother Eshek's sons: Ulam was his firstborn, Jeush second, and Eliphelet third.

⁴⁰ Ulam's sons were warriors and archers. They had many sons and grandsons—150 of them.

All these were among Benjamin's sons.

9 All Israel was registered in the genealogies that are written about in the Book of the Kings of Israel. But Judah was exiled to Babylon because of their unfaithfulness. ² The first to live in their towns on their own property again were Israelites, priests, Levites, and temple servants.

³ These people from the descendants of Judah, Benjamin, Ephraim, and Manasseh settled in Jerusalem:
⁴ Uthai son of Ammihud,
son of Omri,
son of Imri, son of Bani,
a descendant of Perez
son of Judah;
⁵ from the Shilonites:
Asaiah the firstborn and his sons;
⁶ and from the sons of Zerah:
Jeuel and 690 of their relatives.

⁷ The Benjaminites: Sallu son of Meshullam,
son of Hodaviah,
son of Hassenuah;
⁸ Ibneiah son of Jeroham;
Elah son of Uzzi, son of Michri;
Meshullam son of Shephatiah,
son of Reuel, son of Ibnijah;
⁹ and 956 of their relatives according to their genealogical records. All these men were heads of their ancestral houses.

¹⁰ The priests: Jedaiah; Jehoiarib; Jachin;
¹¹ Azariah son of Hilkiah,
son of Meshullam,
son of Zadok, son of Meraioth,
son of Ahitub, the chief official of God's temple;
¹² Adaiah son of Jeroham,
son of Pashhur,
son of Malchijah; Maasai
son of Adiel,
son of Jahzerah,
son of Meshullam,
son of Meshillemith,
son of Immer;
¹³ and 1,760 of their relatives, the heads of households. They were capable men employed in the ministry of God's temple.

¹⁴ The Levites: Shemaiah
son of Hasshub,
son of Azrikam, son of Hashabiah of the Merarites;
¹⁵ Bakbakkar, Heresh, Galal,
and Mattaniah,
son of Mica, son of Zichri,
son of Asaph;
¹⁶ Obadiah son of Shemaiah,
son of Galal,
son of Jeduthun; and Berechiah
son of Asa,
son of Elkanah who lived
in the villages
of the Netophathites.

¹⁷ The gatekeepers: Shallum,
Akkub, Talmon, Ahiman,
and their relatives.
Shallum was their chief; ¹⁸ he was previously stationed at the King's Gate on the east side. These were the gatekeepers from the camp of the Levites. ¹⁹ Shallum son of Kore, son of Ebiasaph, son of Korah and his relatives from his household, the Korahites, were assigned to guard the thresholds of the tent. Their ancestors had been assigned to the LORD's camp as guardians of the entrance. ²⁰ In earlier times Phinehas son of Eleazar had been their leader, and the LORD was with him. ²¹ Zechariah son of Meshelemiah was the gatekeeper at the entrance to the tent of meeting.

²² The total number of those chosen to be gatekeepers at the thresholds was 212. They were registered by genealogy in their villages. David and Samuel the seer had appointed them to their trusted positions. ²³ So they and their sons were assigned to the gates of the LORD's house, the house of the tent. ²⁴ The gatekeepers were on the four sides: east, west, north, and south. ²⁵ Their relatives came from their villages at fixed times to be with them seven days, ²⁶ but

the four chief gatekeepers, who were Levites, were entrusted with the rooms and the treasuries of God's temple. ²⁷ They spent the night in the vicinity of God's temple, because they had guard duty and were in charge of opening it every morning. ²⁸ Some of them were in charge of the utensils used in worship. They would count them when they brought them in and when they took them out. ²⁹ Others were put in charge of the furnishings and all the utensils of the sanctuary, as well as the fine flour, wine, oil, incense, and spices. ³⁰ But some of the priests' sons mixed the spices. ³¹ A Levite called Mattithiah, the firstborn of Shallum the Korahite, was entrusted with baking the bread. ³² Some of the Kohathites' relatives were responsible for preparing the rows of the bread of the Presence every Sabbath.

³³ The singers, the heads of Levite families, stayed in the temple chambers and were exempt from other tasks because they were on duty day and night. ³⁴ These were the heads of Levite families, chiefs according to their genealogies, and lived in Jerusalem.

³⁵ Jeiel fathered Gibeon and lived in Gibeon. His wife's name was Maacah. ³⁶ Abdon was his firstborn son, then Zur, Kish, Baal, Ner, Nadab, ³⁷ Gedor, Ahio, Zechariah, and Mikloth. ³⁸ Mikloth fathered Shimeam. These also lived opposite their relatives in Jerusalem with their other relatives. ³⁹ Ner fathered Kish, Kish fathered Saul, and Saul fathered Jonathan, Malchishua, Abinadab, and Esh-baal. ⁴⁰ Jonathan's son was Merib-baal, and Merib-baal fathered Micah. ⁴¹ Micah's sons: Pithon, Melech, Tahrea, and Ahaz. ⁴² Ahaz fathered Jarah; Jarah fathered Alemeth, Azmaveth, and Zimri; Zimri fathered Moza. ⁴³ Moza fathered Binea. His son was Rephaiah, his son Eleasah, and his son Azel.

⁴⁴ Azel had six sons, and these were their names: Azrikam, Bocheru, Ishmael, Sheariah, Obadiah, and Hanan. These were Azel's sons.

PSALM 81:8-16

⁸ Listen, My people, and I will admonish you.
Israel, if you would only listen to Me!
⁹ There must not be a strange god among you;
you must not bow down to a foreign god.
¹⁰ I am Yahweh your God, who brought you up from the land of Egypt.
Open your mouth wide, and I will fill it.

¹¹ "But My people did not listen to Me;
Israel did not obey Me.
¹² So I gave them over to their stubborn hearts
to follow their own plans.
¹³ If only My people would listen to Me
and Israel would follow My ways,
¹⁴ I would quickly subdue their enemies
and turn My hand against their foes."
¹⁵ Those who hate the LORD would pretend submission to Him;
their doom would last forever.
¹⁶ But He would feed Israel with the best wheat.
"I would satisfy you with honey from the rock."

PROVERBS 17:24-25

²⁴ Wisdom is the focus of the perceptive,
but a fool's eyes roam to the ends of the earth.

²⁵ A foolish son is grief to his father and bitterness to the one who bore him.

ACTS 15:1-21

15 Some men came down from Judea and began to teach the brothers: "Unless you are circumcised according to the custom prescribed by Moses, you cannot be saved!" [2] But after Paul and Barnabas had engaged them in serious argument and debate, they arranged for Paul and Barnabas and some others of them to go up to the apostles and elders in Jerusalem concerning this controversy. [3] When they had been sent on their way by the church, they passed through both Phoenicia and Samaria, explaining in detail the conversion of the Gentiles, and they created great joy among all the brothers.

[4] When they arrived at Jerusalem, they were welcomed by the church, the apostles, and the elders, and they reported all that God had done with them. [5] But some of the believers from the party of the Pharisees stood up and said, "It is necessary to circumcise them and to command them to keep the law of Moses!"

[6] Then the apostles and the elders assembled to consider this matter. [7] After there had been much debate, Peter stood up and said to them: "Brothers, you are aware that in the early days God made a choice among you, that by my mouth the Gentiles would hear the gospel message and believe. [8] And God, who knows the heart, testified to them by giving the Holy Spirit, just as He also did to us. [9] He made no distinction between us and them, cleansing their hearts by faith. [10] Why, then, are you now testing God by putting on the disciples' necks a yoke that neither our forefathers nor we have been able to bear? [11] On the contrary, we believe we are saved through the grace of the Lord Jesus, in the same way they are."

[12] Then the whole assembly fell silent and listened to Barnabas and Paul describing all the signs and wonders God had done through them among the Gentiles. [13] After they stopped speaking, James responded: "Brothers, listen to me! [14] Simeon has reported how God first intervened to take from the Gentiles a people for His name. [15] And the words of the prophets agree with this, as it is written:

[16] After these things I will return
and will rebuild David's tent,
which has fallen down.
I will rebuild its ruins
and will set it up again,
[17] so that those who are left
of mankind
may seek the Lord—
even all the Gentiles
who are called by My name,
says the Lord who does
these things,
[18] which have been known
from long ago.

[19] Therefore, in my judgment, we should not cause difficulties for those who turn to God from among the Gentiles, [20] but instead we should write to them to abstain from things polluted by idols, from sexual immorality, from eating anything that has been strangled, and from blood. [21] For since ancient times, Moses has had in every city those who proclaim him, and he is read aloud in the synagogues every Sabbath day."

Purity—Not a Popular Thought

*He made no distinction between us and them,
cleansing their hearts by faith.* —Acts 15:9

Now that we understand what Scripture means by the term "heart"—the core of our being—we ask ourselves another important question: what does our Lord mean when He uses the word "pure"? "Blessed are the pure in heart, because they will see God" (Mt 5:8). The word "pure" (Greek: *katharos*) means a heart that is clean or clear. Unfortunately, purity does not seem to be popular in contemporary Christianity. The emphasis nowadays seems to be more on power than on purity. Most Christians I talk to want to know how they can possess and develop spiritual gifts. Few, generally speaking, want to know how to experience the blessing of what our text today calls a heart purified by faith.

Sixteen hundred years ago St. Augustine expressed a sentiment in words which might well sum up the thoughts of many—thankfully, not all—in today's church: "Lord, make me pure . . . but not just yet." Most of us would be willing to identify ourselves with the conditions laid down in the first five of our Lord's Beatitudes, but how do we feel about the condition of being pure in heart? Are we ready and willing to pray:

I want, dear Lord, a heart that's true and clean
A sunlit heart, with not a cloud between.
A heart like Thine, a heart divine.
A heart as white as snow.
On me, dear Lord, a heart like this bestow.

Prayer

O yes, dear Father, from the depths of my being I cry out make me clean. I have come so far with You—how can I turn back now? I'm a candidate for both power and purity. Give me the deep inner cleansing I need—today. For Jesus' sake. Amen.

Further Study

Jn 13:1-17; 2 Co 7:1; Jms 4:8; 1 Jn 3:3
What was Peter's request?
Make your request today.

JULY 16

1 CHRONICLES
10:1–11:47

10 The Philistines fought against Israel, and Israel's men fled from them and were killed on Mount Gilboa.

[2] The Philistines pursued Saul and his sons and killed Saul's sons Jonathan, Abinadab, and Malchishua. [3] When the battle intensified against Saul, the archers found him and severely wounded him. [4] Then Saul said to his armorbearer, "Draw your sword and run me

through with it, or these uncircumcised men will come and torture me!" But his armor-bearer wouldn't do it because he was terrified. Then Saul took his sword and fell on it. ⁵ When his armor-bearer saw that Saul was dead, he also fell on his own sword and died. ⁶ So Saul and his three sons died—his whole house died together.

⁷ When all the men of Israel in the valley saw that the army had run away and that Saul and his sons were dead, they abandoned their cities and fled. So the Philistines came and settled in them.

⁸ The next day when the Philistines came to strip the slain, they found Saul and his sons dead on Mount Gilboa. ⁹ They stripped Saul, cut off his head, took his armor, and sent messengers throughout the land of the Philistines to spread the good news to their idols and their people. ¹⁰ Then they put his armor in the temple of their gods and hung his skull in the temple of Dagon.

¹¹ When all Jabesh-gilead heard of everything the Philistines had done to Saul, ¹² all their brave men set out and retrieved the body of Saul and the bodies of his sons and brought them to Jabesh. They buried their bones under the oak in Jabesh and fasted seven days. ¹³ Saul died for his unfaithfulness to the LORD because he did not keep the LORD's word. He even consulted a medium for guidance, ¹⁴ but he did not inquire of the LORD. So the LORD put him to death and turned the kingdom over to David son of Jesse.

11 All Israel came together to David at Hebron and said, "Here we are, your own flesh and blood. ² Even when Saul was king, you led us out to battle and brought us back. The LORD your God also said to you, 'You will shepherd My people Israel and be ruler over My people Israel.' "

³ So all the elders of Israel came to the king at Hebron. David made a covenant with them at Hebron in the LORD's presence, and they anointed David king over Israel, in keeping with the LORD's word through Samuel.

⁴ David and all Israel marched to Jerusalem (that is, Jebus); the Jebusites who inhabited the land were there. ⁵ The inhabitants of Jebus said to David, "You will never get in here." Yet David did capture the stronghold of Zion (that is, the city of David).

⁶ David said, "Whoever is the first to kill a Jebusite will become commander-in-chief." Joab son of Zeruiah went up first, so he became the chief.

⁷ Then David took up residence in the stronghold; therefore, it was called the city of David. ⁸ He built up the city all the way around, from the supporting terraces to the surrounding parts, and Joab restored the rest of the city. ⁹ David steadily grew more powerful, and the LORD of Hosts was with him.

¹⁰ The following were the chiefs of David's warriors who, together with all Israel, strongly supported him in his reign to make him king according to the LORD's word about Israel. ¹¹ This is the list of David's warriors:

Jashobeam son of Hachmoni was chief of the Thirty; he wielded his spear against 300 and killed them at one time.

¹² After him, Eleazar son of Dodo the Ahohite was one of the three warriors. ¹³ He was with David at Pas-dammim when the Philistines had gathered there for battle. A plot of ground full of barley was there, where the troops had fled from the Philistines. ¹⁴ But Eleazar and David took their stand in the middle of the plot and defended it. They killed the Philistines, and the LORD gave them a great victory.

¹⁵ Three of the 30 chief men went down to David, to the rock at the cave of Adullam, while the Philistine army was encamped in the Valley of Rephaim. ¹⁶ At that time David was in the stronghold, and a Philistine garrison was at Bethlehem. ¹⁷ David was extremely thirsty and said, "If only someone would bring me water from the well at the city gate of Bethlehem!" ¹⁸ So the Three broke through the Philistine camp and drew water from the well at the gate of Bethlehem. They brought it back to David, but he refused to drink it. Instead, he poured it out to the LORD. ¹⁹ David said, "I would never do such a

thing in the presence of God! How can I drink the blood of these men who risked their lives?" For they brought it at the risk of their lives. So he would not drink it. Such were the exploits of the three warriors.

20 Abishai, Joab's brother, was the leader of the Three. He raised his spear against 300 men and killed them, gaining a reputation among the Three. 21 He was the most honored of the Three and became their commander even though he did not become one of the Three.

22 Benaiah son of Jehoiada was the son of a brave man from Kabzeel, a man of many exploits. Benaiah killed two sons of Ariel of Moab, and he went down into a pit on a snowy day and killed a lion. 23 He also killed an Egyptian who was seven and a half feet tall. Even though the Egyptian had a spear in his hand like a weaver's beam, Benaiah went down to him with a club, snatched the spear out of the Egyptian's hand, and then killed him with his own spear. 24 These were the exploits of Benaiah son of Jehoiada, who had a reputation among the three warriors. 25 He was the most honored of the Thirty, but he did not become one of the Three. David put him in charge of his bodyguard.

26 The fighting men were:

Joab's brother Asahel,
Elhanan son of Dodo of Bethlehem,
27 Shammoth the Harorite,
Helez the Pelonite,
28 Ira son of Ikkesh the Tekoite,
Abiezer the Anathothite,
29 Sibbecai the Hushathite,
Ilai the Ahohite,
30 Maharai the Netophathite,
Heled son of Baanah
the Netophathite,
31 Ithai son of Ribai from Gibeah
of the Benjaminites,
Benaiah the Pirathonite,
32 Hurai from the wadis of Gaash,
Abiel the Arbathite,
33 Azmaveth the Baharumite,
Eliahba the Shaalbonite,
34 the sons of Hashem the Gizonite,
Jonathan son of Shagee
the Hararite,

35 Ahiam son of Sachar the Hararite,
Eliphal son of Ur,
36 Hepher the Mecherathite,
Ahijah the Pelonite,
37 Hezro the Carmelite,
Naarai son of Ezbai,
38 Joel the brother of Nathan,
Mibhar son of Hagri,
39 Zelek the Ammonite,
Naharai the Beerothite, the armorbearer for Joab son of Zeruiah,
40 Ira the Ithrite,
Gareb the Ithrite,
41 Uriah the Hittite,
Zabad son of Ahlai,
42 Adina son of Shiza the Reubenite,
chief of the Reubenites,
and 30 with him,
43 Hanan son of Maacah,
Joshaphat the Mithnite,
44 Uzzia the Ashterathite,
Shama and Jeiel the sons
of Hotham the Aroerite,
45 Jediael son of Shimri
and his brother Joha
the Tizite,
46 Eliel the Mahavite,
Jeribai and Joshaviah, the sons
of Elnaam,
Ithmah the Moabite,
47 Eliel, Obed, and Jaasiel
the Mezobaite.

PSALM 82:1-8

1 God has taken His place in the
divine assembly;
He judges among the gods:
2 "How long will you judge unjustly
and show partiality to the wicked?
Selah
3 Provide justice for the needy and
the fatherless;
uphold the rights of the oppressed
and the destitute.
4 Rescue the poor and needy;
save them from the hand of the
wicked."

5 They do not know or understand;
they wander in darkness.
All the foundations of the earth
are shaken.

⁶ I said, "You are gods;
   you are all sons of the Most High.
⁷ However, you will die like men
   and fall like any other ruler."

⁸ Rise up, God, judge the earth,
   for all the nations belong to You.

ᏢROVERBS 17:26

²⁶ It is certainly not good to fine an
   innocent person,
   or to beat a noble for his honesty.

ᏗCTS 15:22-41

²² Then the apostles and the elders, with the whole church, decided to select men from among them and to send them to Antioch with Paul and Barnabas: Judas, called Barsabbas, and Silas, both leading men among the brothers. ²³ They wrote this letter to be delivered by them:

From the apostles and the elders, your brothers,
To the brothers from among the Gentiles in Antioch, Syria, and Cilicia:
Greetings.
²⁴ Because we have heard that some to whom we gave no authorization went out from us and troubled you with their words and unsettled your hearts, ²⁵ we have unanimously decided to select men and send them to you along with our beloved Barnabas and Paul, ²⁶ who have risked their lives for the name of our Lord Jesus Christ. ²⁷ Therefore we have sent Judas and Silas, who will personally report the same things by word of mouth. ²⁸ For it

was the Holy Spirit's decision—and ours—to put no greater burden on you than these necessary things: ²⁹ that you abstain from food offered to idols, from blood, from eating anything that has been strangled, and from sexual immorality. If you keep yourselves from these things, you will do well.
Farewell.

³⁰ Then, being sent off, they went down to Antioch, and after gathering the assembly, they delivered the letter. ³¹ When they read it, they rejoiced because of its encouragement. ³² Both Judas and Silas, who were also prophets themselves, encouraged the brothers and strengthened them with a long message. ³³ After spending some time there, they were sent back in peace by the brothers to those who had sent them. ³⁵ But Paul and Barnabas, along with many others, remained in Antioch teaching and proclaiming the message of the Lord.

³⁶ After some time had passed, Paul said to Barnabas, "Let's go back and visit the brothers in every town where we have preached the message of the Lord, and see how they're doing." ³⁷ Barnabas wanted to take along John Mark. ³⁸ But Paul did not think it appropriate to take along this man who had deserted them in Pamphylia and had not gone on with them to the work. ³⁹ There was such a sharp disagreement that they parted company, and Barnabas took Mark with him and sailed off to Cyprus. ⁴⁰ Then Paul chose Silas and departed, after being commended to the grace of the Lord by the brothers. ⁴¹ He traveled through Syria and Cilicia, strengthening the churches.

It's All Under Control

Rise up, God, judge the earth,
for all the nations belong to You.—Psalm 82:8

The salvation spoken of in the phrase "the helmet of salvation" is the salvation we are going to enjoy when God works out His eternal purposes.

The Christian has a hope for the future. He has an understanding that God is working out His purposes in history, and therefore we need not be disturbed when human programs appear to be going wrong. We hear about "new deals" and "fair deals" and "better deals," yet they end up in disappointment for all concerned.

The Christian expects the world to get worse and worse, for this is what the Bible tells us will happen. He expects false teachings to abound. He expects the world's systems to fail, for anything that is not built on Christ has no guarantee of success. The Christian knows that wars and international tension are unavoidable, even though every effort is made to avoid them. The world is in such a state and such a condition that the more attention we give it, the more weary our minds become.

What is a Christian to do in such a world as ours? How are we to react when the Devil takes advantage of our sensitivities to world conditions and focuses our thoughts upon them? Shall we give up? Shall we withdraw from life?

No, we put on the helmet of salvation and remind ourselves that in the face of everything that appears contrary, God is working out His eternal plan and purpose. History remains His story! Almighty God is at work in the very events that appear to be filled with darkness and confusion.

Prayer

O God, help me see that although You are apart from the events of history, You are also in the events of history. Ultimately all things are going to glorify You. Thank You, Father. Amen.

Further Study

Heb 6; 1 Pt 1:3; 1 Jn 3:3; Eph 1:11
What does this hope provide for us?
How does Peter describe our hope?

JULY 17

1 CHRONICLES
12:1–13:14

12 The following were the men who came to David at Ziklag while he was still banned from the presence of Saul son of Kish. They were among the warriors who helped him in battle. ² They were archers who, using either their right or left hand, could throw stones with a sling or shoot arrows with a bow. They were Saul's relatives from Benjamin:

³ Their chief was Ahiezer son of Shemaah the Gibeathite. Then there was his brother Joash; Jeziel and Pelet sons of Azmaveth; Beracah, Jehu the Anathothite; ⁴ Ishmaiah the Gibeonite, a warrior among the Thirty and a leader over the Thirty; Jeremiah, Jahaziel, Johanan, Jozabad the Gederathite; ⁵ Eluzai, Jerimoth, Bealiah, Shemariah, Shephatiah the Haruphite; ⁶ Elkanah, Isshiah, Azarel, Joezer, and Jashobeam, the Korahites; ⁷ and Joelah and Zebadiah, the sons of Jeroham from Gedor.

⁸ Some Gadites defected to David at his stronghold in the desert. They were fighting men, trained for battle, expert with shield and spear. Their faces were like the faces of lions, and they were as swift as gazelles on the mountains.

⁹ Ezer was the chief, Obadiah second, Eliab third, ¹⁰ Mishmannah fourth, Jeremiah fifth, ¹¹ Attai sixth, Eliel seventh, ¹² Johanan eighth, Elzabad ninth, ¹³ Jeremiah tenth, and Machbannai eleventh.

¹⁴ These Gadites were army commanders; the least of them was a match for a hundred, and the greatest of them for a thousand. ¹⁵ These are the men who crossed the Jordan in the first month when it was overflowing all its banks, and put to flight all those in the valleys to the east and to the west.

¹⁶ Other Benjaminites and men from Judah also went to David at the stronghold. ¹⁷ David went out to meet them and said to them, "If you have come in peace to help me, my heart will be united with you, but if you have come to betray me to my enemies even though my hands have done no wrong, may the God of our ancestors look on it and judge."

¹⁸ Then the Spirit took control of Amasai, chief of the Thirty, and he said:

We are yours, David,
we are with you, son of Jesse!
Peace, peace to you,
and peace to him who helps you,
for your God helps you.

So David received them and made them leaders of his troops. ¹⁹ Some Manassites defected to David when he went with the Philistines to fight against Saul. However, they did not help the Philistines because the Philistine rulers, following consultation, sent David away. They said, "It will be our heads if he defects to his master Saul." ²⁰ When David went to Ziklag, some men from Manasseh defected to him: Adnah, Jozabad, Jediael, Michael, Jozabad, Elihu, and Zillethai, chiefs of thousands in Manasseh. ²¹ They helped David against the marauders, for they were all brave warriors and commanders in the army. [22] At that time, men came day after day to help David until there was a great army, like an army of God.

[23] The numbers of the armed troops who came to David at Hebron to turn Saul's kingdom over to him, according to the LORD's word, were as follows:

[24] From the Judahites: 6,800 armed troops bearing shields and spears.

[25] From the Simeonites: 7,100 brave warriors ready for war.

[26] From the Levites: 4,600 [27] in addition to Jehoiada, leader of the house of Aaron, with 3,700 men; [28] and Zadok, a young brave warrior, with 22 commanders from his own ancestral house.

[29] From the Benjaminites, the relatives of Saul: 3,000 (up to that time the majority of the Benjaminites maintained their allegiance to the house of Saul).

[30] From the Ephraimites: 20,800 brave warriors who were famous men in their ancestral houses.

[31] From half the tribe of Manasseh: 18,000 designated by name to come and make David king.

[32] From the Issacharites, who understood the times and knew what Israel should do: 200 chiefs with all their relatives under their command.

[33] From Zebulun: 50,000 who could serve in the army, trained for battle with all kinds of weapons of war, with singleness of purpose to help David.

[34] From Naphtali: 1,000 commanders accompanied by 37,000 men with shield and spear.

[35] From the Danites: 28,600 trained for battle.

[36] From Asher: 40,000 who could serve in the army, trained for battle.

[37] From across the Jordan—from the Reubenites, Gadites, and half the tribe of Manasseh: 120,000 men equipped with all the military weapons of war.

[38] All these warriors, lined up in battle formation, came to Hebron with wholehearted determination to make David king over all Israel. All the rest of Israel was also of one mind to make David king. [39] They were there with David for three days, eating and drinking, for their relatives had provided for them. [40] In addition, their neighbors from as far away as Issachar, Zebulun, and Naphtali came bringing food on donkeys, camels, mules, and oxen—abundant provisions of flour, fig cakes, raisins, wine and oil, oxen, and sheep. Indeed, there was joy in Israel.

13 David consulted with all his leaders, the commanders of hundreds and of thousands. [2] Then he said to the whole assembly of Israel, "If it seems good to you, and if this is from the LORD our God, let us spread out and send the message to the rest of our relatives in all the districts of Israel, including the priests and Levites in their cities with pasturelands, that they should gather together with us. [3] Then let us bring back the ark of our God, for we did not inquire of Him in Saul's days." [4] Since the proposal seemed right to all the people, the whole assembly agreed to do it.

[5] So David assembled all Israel, from the Shihor of Egypt to the entrance of Hamath, to bring the ark of God from Kiriath-jearim. [6] David and all Israel went to Baalah (that is, Kiriath-jearim), which belongs to Judah, to take from there the ark of God, which is called by the name of the LORD who dwells between the cherubim. [7] At Abinadab's house, they set the ark of God on a new cart. Uzzah and Ahio were guiding the cart.

[8] David and all Israel were celebrating with all their might before God with songs and with lyres, harps, tambourines, cymbals, and trumpets. [9] When they came to Chidon's threshing floor, Uzzah reached out to hold the

ark, because the oxen had stumbled. [10] Then the LORD's anger burned against Uzzah, and He struck him dead because he had reached out to the ark. So he died there in the presence of God.

[11] David was angry because of the LORD's outburst against Uzzah, so he named that place Outburst Against Uzzah, as it is still named today. [12] David feared God that day, and said, "How can I ever bring the ark of God to me?" [13] So David did not move the ark of God home to the city of David; instead, he took it to the house of Obed-edom the Gittite. [14] The ark of God remained with Obed-edom's family in his house for three months, and the LORD blessed his family and all that he had.

PSALM 83:1-8

[1] God, do not keep silent.
  Do not be deaf, God; do not be
    idle.
[2] See how Your enemies make an
    uproar;
  those who hate You have acted
    arrogantly.
[3] They devise clever schemes
    against Your people;
  they conspire against Your
    treasured ones.
[4] They say, "Come, let us wipe
    them out as a nation
  so that Israel's name will no
    longer be remembered."
[5] For they have conspired with one
    mind;
  they form an alliance against
    You—
[6] the tents of Edom and the
    Ishmaelites,
  Moab and the Hagrites,
[7] Gebal, Ammon, and Amalek,
  Philistia with the inhabitants of
    Tyre.
[8] Even Assyria has joined them;
  they lend support to the sons of
    Lot.   *Selah*

PROVERBS 17:27-28

[27] The intelligent person restrains
    his words,

and one who keeps a cool head is
  a man of understanding.

[28] Even a fool is considered wise
    when he keeps silent,
  discerning, when he seals his lips.

ACTS 16:1-24

16 Then he went on to Derbe and Lystra, where there was a disciple named Timothy, the son of a believing Jewish woman, but his father was a Greek. [2] The brothers at Lystra and Iconium spoke highly of him. [3] Paul wanted Timothy to go with him, so he took him and circumcised him because of the Jews who were in those places, since they all knew that his father was a Greek. [4] As they traveled through the towns, they delivered to them the decisions reached by the apostles and elders at Jerusalem. [5] So the churches were strengthened in the faith and were increased in number daily.

[6] They went through the region of Phrygia and Galatia and were prevented by the Holy Spirit from speaking the message in the province of Asia. [7] When they came to Mysia, they tried to go into Bithynia, but the Spirit of Jesus did not allow them. [8] So, bypassing Mysia, they came down to Troas. [9] During the night a vision appeared to Paul: a Macedonian man was standing and pleading with him, "Cross over to Macedonia and help us!" [10] After he had seen the vision, we immediately made efforts to set out for Macedonia, concluding that God had called us to evangelize them.

[11] Then, setting sail from Troas, we ran a straight course to Samothrace, the next day to Neapolis, [12] and from there to Philippi, a Roman colony, which is a leading city of that district of Macedonia. We stayed in that city for a number of days. [13] On the Sabbath day we went outside the city gate by the river, where we thought there was a place of prayer. We sat down and spoke to the women gathered there. [14] A woman named Lydia, a dealer in purple cloth from the city of Thyatira, who worshiped

God, was listening. The Lord opened her heart to pay attention to what was spoken by Paul. ¹⁵ After she and her household were baptized, she urged us, "If you consider me a believer in the Lord, come and stay at my house." And she persuaded us.

¹⁶ Once, as we were on our way to prayer, a slave girl met us who had a spirit of prediction and made a large profit for her owners by fortune-telling. ¹⁷ As she followed Paul and us she cried out, "These men are the slaves of the Most High God, who are proclaiming to you the way of salvation." ¹⁸ And she did this for many days.

But Paul was greatly aggravated, and turning to the spirit, said, "I command you in the name of Jesus Christ to come out of her!" And it came out right away.

¹⁹ When her owners saw that their hope of profit was gone, they seized Paul and Silas and dragged them into the marketplace to the authorities. ²⁰ And bringing them before the chief magistrates, they said, "These men are seriously disturbing our city. They are Jews, ²¹ and are promoting customs that are not legal for us as Romans to adopt or practice."

²² Then the mob joined in the attack against them, and the chief magistrates stripped off their clothes and ordered them to be beaten with rods. ²³ After they had inflicted many blows on them, they threw them in jail, ordering the jailer to keep them securely guarded. ²⁴ Receiving such an order, he put them into the inner prison and secured their feet in the stocks.

The Spirit Guides

When they came to Mysia, they tried to go into Bithynia, but the Spirit of Jesus did not allow them.

—Acts 16:7

The Holy Spirit seeks to bring us around to accepting God's guidance for our lives. "All those led by God's Spirit are God's sons" (Rm 8:14).

This is a stage in life which many Christians never attain—they are not Spirit-led Christians. They are led by self-interest, physical impulses, or by the opinions of others. They have not put themselves at the disposal of the Spirit to be led of Him in the details of their lives. Hence they lack direction and, therefore, a goal.

When Christians say to me, "The Spirit never seems to guide me," I usually reply, "How well do you listen?" The problem we face over guidance is not because the Spirit fails to lead us, but because we are not listening. We must be prepared to stop talking and wait before Him so that He can talk to us.

In this frenzied age many Christians have lost the art of listening. They are willing to spend time in prayer talking to God, but are not willing to spend very much of the time listening to God. We must stop, wait, and tune ourselves in to the Holy Spirit's wavelength if we are to hear His voice in our hearts and feel His gentle impressions.

A Quaker woman inquired of a young man, "Hast thou heard God speak lately?" "No," said the young man. "Then thou hast forgotten to be still," said the woman. "Stop . . . and know . . ." says the Scripture (Ps 46:10). Be restless and you will not know. God guides everyone who wants to be guided.

Prayer

O Spirit of the living God, help me tune my heart so that I can hear Your voice, for without Your guidance my life lacks mission and direction. Take the reins of my life and guide me. For Jesus' sake, I pray. Amen.

Further Study

Ac 16; 10:19-20; 13:2; Jn 16:13
How did the Holy Spirit guide Paul?
What was the result?

JULY 18

1 CHRONICLES
14:1–16:6

14 King Hiram of Tyre sent envoys to David, along with cedar logs, stonemasons, and carpenters to build a palace for him. ² Then David knew that the LORD had established him as king over Israel and that his kingdom had been exalted for the sake of His people Israel.

³ David took more wives in Jerusalem, and he became the father of more sons and daughters. ⁴ These are the names of the children born to him in Jerusalem: Shammua, Shobab, Nathan, Solomon, ⁵ Ibhar, Elishua, Elpelet, ⁶ Nogah, Nepheg, Japhia, ⁷ Elishama, Beeliada, and Eliphelet.

⁸ When the Philistines heard that David had been anointed king over all Israel, they all went in search of David; when David heard of this, he went out to face them. ⁹ Now the Philistines had come and made a raid in the Valley of Rephaim, ¹⁰ so David inquired of God, "Should I go to war against the Philistines? Will You hand them over to me?"

The LORD replied, "Go, and I will hand them over to you."

¹¹ So the Israelites went up to Baal-perazim, and David defeated the Philistines there. Then David said, "Like a bursting flood, God has used me to burst out against my enemies." Therefore, they named that place the Lord Bursts Out. ¹² The Philistines abandoned their idols there, and David ordered that they be burned in the fire.

¹³ Once again the Philistines made a raid in the valley. ¹⁴ So David again inquired of God, and God answered him, "Do not pursue them directly. Circle down away from them and attack them opposite the balsam trees. ¹⁵ When you hear the sound of marching in the tops of the balsam trees, then march out to battle, for God will have marched out ahead of you to attack the camp of the Philistines." ¹⁶ So David did exactly as God commanded him, and they struck down the Philistine army from Gibeon to Gezer. ¹⁷ Then David's fame spread throughout the lands, and the LORD caused all the nations to be terrified of him.

15 David built houses for himself in the city of David, and he prepared a place for the ark of God and pitched a tent for it. ² Then David said, "No one but the Levites may carry the ark of God, because the LORD has chosen them to carry the ark of the LORD and to minister before Him forever."

³ David assembled all Israel at Jerusalem to bring the ark of the LORD to the place he had prepared for it. ⁴ Then he gathered together the descendants of Aaron and the Levites:

⁵ From the Kohathites, Uriel the leader and 120 of his relatives; ⁶ from the Merarites, Asaiah the leader and 220 of his relatives; ⁷ from the Gershomites, Joel the leader and 130 of his relatives; ⁸ from the Elizaphanites, Shemaiah the leader and 200 of his relatives; ⁹ from the Hebronites, Eliel the leader and 80 of his relatives; ¹⁰ from the Uzzielites, Amminadab the leader and 112 of his relatives.

¹¹ David summoned the priests Zadok and Abiathar and the Levites Uriel, Asaiah, Joel, Shemaiah, Eliel, and Amminadab. ¹² He said to them, "You are the heads of the Levite families. You and your relatives must consecrate yourselves so that you may bring the ark of the LORD God of Israel to the place I have prepared for it. ¹³ For the LORD our God burst out in anger against us because you Levites were not with us the first time, for we didn't inquire of Him about the proper procedures." ¹⁴ So the priests and the Levites consecrated themselves to bring up the ark of the LORD God of Israel. ¹⁵ Then the Levites carried the ark of God the way Moses had commanded according to the word of the LORD: on their shoulders with the poles.

¹⁶ Then David told the leaders of the Levites to appoint their relatives as singers and to have them raise their voices with joy accompanied by musical instruments—harps, lyres, and cymbals. ¹⁷ So the Levites appointed Heman son of Joel; from his relatives, Asaph son of Berechiah; and from their relatives the Merarites, Ethan son of Kushaiah. ¹⁸ With them were their relatives second in rank: Zechariah, Jaaziel, Shemiramoth, Jehiel, Unni, Eliab, Benaiah, Maaseiah, Mattithiah, Eliphelehu, Mikneiah, and the gatekeepers Obed-edom and Jeiel. ¹⁹ The singers Heman, Asaph, and Ethan were to sound the bronze cymbals; ²⁰ Zechariah, Aziel, Shemiramoth, Jehiel, Unni, Eliab, Maaseiah, and Benaiah were to play harps according to *Alamoth*; ²¹ and Mattithiah, Eliphelehu, Mikneiah, Obed-edom, Jeiel, and Azaziah were to lead the music with lyres according to the *Sheminith*. ²² Chenaniah, the leader of the Levites in music, was to direct the music because he was skillful. ²³ Berechiah and Elkanah were to be gatekeepers for the ark. ²⁴ The priests, Shebaniah, Joshaphat, Nethanel, Amasai, Zechariah, Benaiah, and Eliezer, were to blow trumpets before the ark of God. Obed-edom and Jehiah were also to be gatekeepers for the ark.

²⁵ David, the elders of Israel, and the commanders of the thousands went with rejoicing to bring the ark of the covenant of the LORD from the house of Obed-edom. ²⁶ And because God helped the Levites who were carrying the ark of the covenant of the LORD, they sacrificed seven bulls and seven rams.

²⁷ Now David was dressed in a robe of fine linen, as were all the Levites who were carrying the ark, as well as the singers and Chenaniah, the music leader of the singers. David also wore a linen ephod. ²⁸ So all Israel was bringing the ark of the covenant of the LORD up with shouts, the sound of the ram's horn, trumpets, and cymbals, and the playing of harps and lyres. ²⁹ As the ark of the covenant of the LORD was entering the city of David, Saul's daughter Michal looked down from the window and saw King David dancing and celebrating, and she despised him in her heart.

16 They brought the ark of God and placed it inside the tent David had pitched for it. Then they offered burnt offerings and fellowship offerings in God's presence. ² When David had finished offering the burnt offerings and the fellowship offerings, he blessed the people in the name of the LORD. ³ Then he distributed to each and every Israelite, both men and women, a loaf of bread, a date cake, and a raisin cake.

⁴ David appointed some of the Levites to be ministers before the ark of the LORD, to celebrate the LORD God of Israel, and to give thanks and praise to Him. ⁵ Asaph was the chief and Zechariah was second to him. Jeiel, Shemiramoth, Jehiel, Mattithiah, Eliab, Benaiah, Obed-edom, and Jeiel played the harps and lyres, while Asaph sounded the cymbals ⁶ and the priests Benaiah and Jahaziel blew the trumpets regularly before the ark of the covenant of God.

PSALM 83:9-18

⁹ Deal with them as You did with Midian,
 as You did with Sisera and Jabin at the Kishon River.
¹⁰ They were destroyed at En-dor;
 they became manure for the ground.
¹¹ Make their nobles like Oreb and Zeeb,
 and all their tribal leaders like Zebah and Zalmunna,
¹² who said, "Let us seize God's pastures for ourselves."

¹³ Make them like tumbleweed, my God,
 like straw before the wind.
¹⁴ As fire burns a forest,
 as a flame blazes through mountains,
¹⁵ so pursue them with Your tempest and terrify them with Your storm.
¹⁶ Cover their faces with shame
 so that they will seek Your name, LORD.
¹⁷ Let them be put to shame and terrified forever;
 let them perish in disgrace.
¹⁸ May they know that You alone—
 whose name is Yahweh—
 are the Most High over all the earth.

PROVERBS 18:1-3

18 One who isolates himself pursues selfish desires;
he rebels against all sound judgment.

² A fool does not delight in understanding,
 but only wants to show off his opinions.

³ When a wicked man comes, shame does also,
 and along with dishonor, disgrace.

ACTS 16:25–17:9

²⁵ About midnight Paul and Silas were praying and singing hymns to God, and the prisoners were listening to them. ²⁶ Suddenly there was such a violent earthquake that the foundations of the jail were shaken, and immediately all the doors were opened, and everyone's chains came loose. ²⁷ When the jailer woke up and saw the doors of the prison open, he drew his sword and was going to kill himself, since he thought the prisoners had escaped.

²⁸ But Paul called out in a loud voice, "Don't harm yourself, because all of us are here!"

²⁹ Then the jailer called for lights, rushed in, and fell down trembling before Paul and Silas. ³⁰ Then he escorted them out and said, "Sirs, what must I do to be saved?"

³¹ So they said, "Believe on the Lord Jesus, and you will be saved—you and your household." ³² Then they spoke the message of the Lord to him along with everyone in his house. ³³ He took them the same hour of the night and washed their wounds. Right away he and all his family were baptized. ³⁴ He brought them up into his house, set a meal before them, and rejoiced because he had believed God with his entire household.

³⁵ When daylight came, the chief magistrates sent the police to say, "Release those men!"

³⁶ The jailer reported these words to

Paul: "The magistrates have sent orders for you to be released. So come out now and go in peace."

[37] But Paul said to them, "They beat us in public without a trial, although we are Roman citizens, and threw us in jail. And now are they going to smuggle us out secretly? Certainly not! On the contrary, let them come themselves and escort us out!"

[38] Then the police reported these words to the magistrates. And they were afraid when they heard that Paul and Silas were Roman citizens. [39] So they came and apologized to them, and escorting them out, they urged them to leave town. [40] After leaving the jail, they came to Lydia's house where they saw and encouraged the brothers, and departed.

17 Then they traveled through Amphipolis and Apollonia and came to Thessalonica, where there was a Jewish synagogue. [2] As usual, Paul went to them, and on three Sabbath days reasoned with them from the Scriptures,

[3] explaining and showing that the Messiah had to suffer and rise from the dead, and saying: "This is the Messiah, Jesus, whom I am proclaiming to you." [4] Then some of them were persuaded and joined Paul and Silas, including a great number of God-fearing Greeks, as well as a number of the leading women.

[5] But the Jews became jealous, and when they had brought together some scoundrels from the marketplace and formed a mob, they set the city in an uproar. Attacking Jason's house, they searched for them to bring them out to the public assembly. [6] When they did not find them, they dragged Jason and some of the brothers before the city officials, shouting, "These men who have turned the world upside down have come here too, [7] and Jason has received them as guests! They are all acting contrary to Caesar's decrees, saying that there is another king—Jesus!" [8] The Jews stirred up the crowd and the city officials who heard these things. [9] So taking a security bond from Jason and the others, they released them.

The Cement of Society

When a wicked man comes, shame does also, and along with dishonor, disgrace.

—PROVERBS 18:3

Nobody gets away with anything in a moral universe if that "anything" is dishonest and untrue. The whole history of humanity is a commentary on this. Remember the first lie uttered by Satan—"You will not die"? He keeps on repeating that well-worn but discredited lie to every member of Adam's race. Something dies in us the moment we are dishonest—not the least, our self-respect. Death eats away at our hearts the moment dishonesty is let in. We are not so much punished for sin as by sin. I came across a statement in a book in which the writer said, "There are two major principles for getting and keeping political power: (1) let nothing, least of all truth and honor, interfere with success; (2) be honest and trustworthy in the little things, but boldly dishonest in the large ones." What would be the result of someone getting political power by following those two principles? I will tell you. Like blind Samson, they would pull down the pillars of society around their heads and the heads of others also.

It is the ten righteous men who spare the Sodoms of this world. Fidelity is the cement that holds society together; take it away and it destroys itself. I may be stretching imagination too far by saying this, but in my opinion the Christian presence, especially as it represents fidelity, holds the world on its course. Civilization would have disintegrated long ago were it not for the moral and Christian character that flows out of the church into the world.

Prayer

Father, help me to be one who holds the world together by my character. And let the hallmark of my character be fidelity to truth and righteousness. In Jesus' name I ask it. Amen.

Further Study

Mt 5:13-30; Mk 9:38-50; 1 Th 1:8; Heb 11:4
When is salt useless?
For what did Paul commend the Thessalonians?

JULY 19

1 CHRONICLES
16:7–17:15

⁷ On that day David decreed for the first time that thanks be given to the LORD by Asaph and his relatives:

⁸ Give thanks to the LORD; call on
　　His name;
　proclaim His deeds among
　　the peoples.
⁹ Sing to Him; sing praise to Him;
　tell about all His wonderful works!
¹⁰ Honor His holy name;
　let the hearts of those who seek
　　the LORD rejoice.
¹¹ Search for the LORD and for
　　His strength;
　seek His face always.
¹² Remember the wonderful works
　　He has done,
　His wonders, and the judgments
　　He has pronounced,
¹³ you offspring of Israel His servant,

Jacob's descendants—
　His chosen ones.

¹⁴ He is the LORD our God;
　His judgments govern
　　the whole earth.
¹⁵ Remember His covenant forever—
　the promise He ordained
　　for a thousand generations,
¹⁶ the covenant He made
　　with Abraham,
　swore to Isaac,
¹⁷ and confirmed to Jacob
　　as a decree,
　and to Israel
　　as an everlasting covenant:
¹⁸ "I will give the land of Canaan
　　to you
　as your inherited portion."

¹⁹ When they were few in number,
　very few indeed,
　　and temporary residents
　　in Canaan

²⁰ wandering from nation to nation
and from one kingdom to another,
²¹ He allowed no one to oppress
them;
He rebuked kings on their behalf:
²² "Do not touch My anointed ones
or harm My prophets."

²³ Sing to the LORD, all the earth.
Proclaim His salvation from day
to day.
²⁴ Declare His glory
among the nations,
His wonderful works
among all peoples.

²⁵ For the LORD is great
and is highly praised;
He is feared above all gods.
²⁶ For all the gods of the peoples
are idols,
but the LORD made the heavens.
²⁷ Splendor and majesty are
before Him;
strength and joy are in His place.
²⁸ Ascribe to the LORD, families
of the peoples,
ascribe to the LORD glory
and strength.
²⁹ Ascribe to the LORD the glory
of His name;
bring an offering and come
before Him.
Worship the LORD
in the splendor of His
holiness;
³⁰ tremble before Him, all the earth.

The world is firmly established;
it cannot be shaken.
³¹ Let the heavens be glad
and the earth rejoice,
and let them say
among the nations, "The LORD
is King!"
³² Let the sea and everything in it
resound;
let the fields and all that is
in them exult.
³³ Then the trees of the forest
will shout for joy
before the LORD,
for He is coming to judge
the earth.

³⁴ Give thanks to the LORD,
for He is good;
His faithful love endures forever.
³⁵ And say: "Save us,
God of our salvation;
gather us and rescue us from
the nations
so that we may give thanks to
Your holy name
and rejoice in Your praise.
³⁶ May the LORD, the God of Israel,
be praised
from everlasting to everlasting."

Then all the people said, "Amen" and
"Praise the LORD."
³⁷ So David left Asaph and his relatives there before the ark of the LORD's
covenant to minister regularly before
the ark according to the daily requirements. ³⁸ He also left Obed-edom and
his 68 relatives. Obed-edom son of
Jeduthun and Hosah were to be gatekeepers. ³⁹ David left Zadok the priest
and his fellow priests before the tabernacle of the LORD at the high place in
Gibeon ⁴⁰ to offer burnt offerings regularly, morning and evening, to the LORD
on the altar of burnt offerings and to do
everything that was written in the law
of the LORD, which He had commanded
Israel to keep. ⁴¹ With them were
Heman, Jeduthun, and the rest who
were chosen and designated by name to
give thanks to the LORD—for His faithful
love endures forever. ⁴² Heman and
Jeduthun had with them trumpets and
cymbals to play and musical instruments of God. Jeduthun's sons were at
the gate.
⁴³ Then all the people left for their
homes, and David returned home to
bless his household.

17 When David had settled into his
palace, he said to Nathan the
prophet, "Look! I am living in a cedar
house while the ark of the LORD's
covenant is under tent curtains."
² So Nathan told David, "Do all that is
on your heart, for God is with you."
³ But that night the word of God came
to Nathan: ⁴ "Go to David My servant
and say, 'This is what the LORD says: You

are not the one to build Me a house to dwell in. [5] From the time I brought Israel out of Egypt until today I have not lived in a house; instead, I have moved from tent to tent and from tabernacle to tabernacle. [6] In all My travels throughout Israel, have I ever spoken a word to even one of the judges of Israel, whom I commanded to shepherd My people, asking: Why haven't you built Me a house of cedar?'

[7] "Now this is what you will say to My servant David: 'This is what the LORD of Hosts says: I took you from the pasture and from following the sheep, to be ruler over My people Israel. [8] I have been with you wherever you have gone, and I have destroyed all your enemies before you. I will make a name for you like that of the greatest in the land. [9] I will establish a place for My people Israel and plant them, so that they may live there and not be disturbed again. Evildoers will not continue to oppress them as they formerly have [10] ever since the day I ordered judges to be over My people Israel. I will also subdue all your enemies.

" 'Furthermore, I declare to you that the LORD Himself will build a house for you. [11] When your time comes to be with your fathers, I will raise up after you your descendant, who is one of your own sons, and I will establish his kingdom. [12] He will build a house for Me, and I will establish his throne forever. [13] I will be a father to him, and he will be a son to Me. I will not take away My faithful love from him as I took it from the one who was before you. [14] I will appoint him over My house and My kingdom forever, and his throne will be established forever.' "

[15] Nathan recounted all these words and this entire vision to David.

PSALM 84:1-12

[1] How lovely is Your dwelling place,
LORD of Hosts.
[2] I long and yearn for
the courts of the LORD;
my heart and flesh cry out for the
living God.

[3] Even a sparrow finds a home,
and a swallow, a nest for herself
where she places her young—
near Your altars, LORD of Hosts,
my King and my God.
[4] How happy are those who reside
in Your house,
who praise You continually. Selah

[5] Happy are the people whose
strength is in You,
whose hearts are set on
pilgrimage.
[6] As they pass through the Valley of
Baca,
they make it a source of
springwater;
even the autumn rain will cover it
with blessings.
[7] They go from strength to strength;
each appears before God in Zion.

[8] LORD God of Hosts, hear my
prayer;
listen, God of Jacob. Selah
[9] Consider our shield, God;
look on the face of Your anointed
one.

[10] Better a day in Your courts than a
thousand anywhere else.
I would rather be at the door of
the house of my God
than to live in the tents of the
wicked.
[11] For the LORD God is a sun and
shield.
The LORD gives grace and glory;
He does not withhold the good
from those who live with
integrity.
[12] LORD of Hosts,
happy is the person who trusts in
You!

PROVERBS 18:4-5

[4] The words of a man's mouth are
deep waters,
a flowing river, a fountain of
wisdom.

[5] It is not good to show partiality to
the guilty

Go Still Deeper

*They welcomed the message with eagerness
and examined the Scriptures daily
to see if these things were so.*
—Acts 17:11

Christians who do not accept the authority of the Scriptures have no effective weapon with which to overcome Satan. It is as simple as that. If you are not certain that the Bible is the Word of God, if you do not believe that it is without error in all that it affirms, then you are like a soldier with a broken sword.

To use the sword of the Spirit effectively, we need to have as wide a knowledge of the Bible as possible. Let me take you back to Christ's encounter with Satan in the wilderness of temptation. When Satan advanced, Jesus took up the sword of the Spirit and knew exactly which particular Scriptures to use to rebut each of the three separate temptations of the Devil.

If we are to conquer Satan in the same way that Jesus conquered him, then we must know the Bible in its entirety. It is no good saying to the Devil: "The verse I want to use against you is somewhere in the Bible." You must quote it to him and quote it precisely.

You need a deep, intensive program of study if you are to become proficient in the use of the Scriptures against Satan. Decide right now to commit yourself to exploring the Bible more deeply and thoroughly than you have ever done before.

Prayer

O Father, I see that the more I know of Your Word, the more effective I will be in resisting Satan. Show me how to go more deeply into the Scriptures than I have ever done before. In Jesus' name I pray. Amen.

Further Study

Ezk 37:1-10; Jn 17:17; Rm 10:8
What was the result of the spoken Word through Ezekiel?
What did Paul say of the Bereans?

JULY 20

1 CHRONICLES
17:16–20:8

¹⁶ Then King David went in, sat in the LORD's presence, and said, "Who am I, LORD God, and what is my house that You have brought me this far? ¹⁷ This was a little thing to You, God, for You have spoken about Your servant's house in the distant future. You regard me as a man of distinction, LORD God. ¹⁸ What more can David say to You for honoring Your servant? You know Your servant. ¹⁹ LORD, You have done all this greatness, making known all these great promises because of Your servant and according to Your will. ²⁰ LORD, there is no one like You, and there is no God besides You, as all we have heard confirms. ²¹ And who is like Your people Israel? God, You came to one nation on earth to redeem a people for Yourself, to make a name for Yourself through great and awesome deeds by driving out nations before Your people You redeemed from Egypt. ²² You made Your people Israel Your own people forever, and You, LORD, have become their God.

²³ "Now, LORD, let the word that You have spoken concerning Your servant and his house be confirmed forever, and do as You have promised. ²⁴ Let your name be confirmed and magnified forever in the saying, 'The LORD of Hosts, the God of Israel, is God over Israel.' May the house of Your servant David be established before You. ²⁵ Since You, my God, have revealed to Your servant that You will build him a house, Your servant has found courage to pray in Your presence. ²⁶ LORD, You indeed are God, and You have promised this good thing to Your servant. ²⁷ So now, You have been pleased to bless Your servant's house that it may continue before You forever.

For You, LORD, have blessed it, and it is blessed forever."

18 After this, David defeated the Philistines, subdued them, and took Gath and its villages from Philistine control. ² He also defeated the Moabites, and they became David's subjects and brought tribute.

³ David also defeated King Hadadezer of Zobah at Hamath when he went to establish his control at the Euphrates River. ⁴ David captured 1,000 chariots, 7,000 horsemen, and 20,000 foot soldiers from him and hamstrung all the horses, and he kept 100 chariots. ⁵ When the Arameans of Damascus came to assist King Hadadezer of Zobah, David struck down 22,000 Aramean men. ⁶ Then he placed garrisons in Aram of Damascus, and the Arameans became David's subjects and brought tribute. The LORD made David victorious wherever he went.

⁷ David took the gold shields carried by Hadadezer's officers and brought them to Jerusalem. ⁸ From Tibhath and Cun, Hadadezer's cities, David also took huge quantities of bronze, from which Solomon made the bronze reservoir, the pillars, and the bronze articles.

⁹ When King Tou of Hamath heard that David had defeated the entire army of King Hadadezer of Zobah, ¹⁰ he sent his son Hadoram to King David to greet him and to congratulate him because David had fought against Hadadezer and defeated him, for Tou and Hadadezer had fought many wars. Hadoram brought all kinds of items of gold, silver, and bronze. ¹¹ King David also dedicated these to the LORD, along with the silver and gold he had carried off from all the nations—from Edom, Moab, the Ammonites, the Philistines, and the Amalekites. ¹² Abishai son of Zeruiah struck down

18,000 Edomites in the Valley of Salt. [13] He put garrisons in Edom, and all the Edomites were subject to David. The LORD made David victorious wherever he went. [14] So David reigned over all Israel, administering justice and righteousness for all his people.

[15] Joab son of Zeruiah was
   over the army;
   Jehoshaphat son of Ahilud was
   court historian;
[16] Zadok son of Ahitub
   and Ahimelech son of Abiathar
   were priests;
   Shavsha was court secretary;
[17] Benaiah son of Jehoiada was over
   the Cherethites
   and the Pelethites;
   and David's sons were
   the chief officials
   at the king's side.

19 Some time later, King Nahash of the Ammonites died, and his son became king in his place. [2] Then David said, "I'll show kindness to Hanun son of Nahash, because his father showed kindness to me."

So David sent messengers to console him concerning his father. However, when David's emissaries arrived in the land of the Ammonites to console him, [3] the Ammonite leaders said to Hanun, "Just because David has sent men with condolences for you, do you really believe he's showing respect for your father? Instead, hasn't David sent his emissaries in order to scout out, overthrow, and spy on the land?" [4] So Hanun took David's emissaries, shaved them, cut their clothes in half at the hips, and sent them away.

[5] Someone came and reported to David about his men, so he sent someone to meet them, since the men were deeply humiliated. The king said, "Stay in Jericho until your beards grow back; then return."

[6] When the Ammonites realized they had made themselves repulsive to David, Hanun and the Ammonites sent 38 tons of silver to hire chariots and horsemen from Aram-naharaim, Aram-maacah, and Zobah. [7] They hired 32,000 chariots and the king of Maacah with his army, who came and camped near Medeba. The Ammonites also gathered from their cities and came for the battle. [8] David heard about this and sent Joab and the entire army of warriors. [9] The Ammonites marched out and lined up in battle formation at the entrance of the city while the kings who had come were in the field by themselves. [10] When Joab saw that there was a battle line in front of him and another behind him, he chose some men out of all the elite troops of Israel and lined up in battle formation to engage the Arameans. [11] He placed the rest of the forces under the command of his brother Abishai, and they lined up in battle formation to engage the Ammonites. [12] "If the Arameans are too strong for me," Joab said, "then you'll be my help. However, if the Ammonites are too strong for you, I'll help you. [13] Be strong! We must prove ourselves strong for our people and for the cities of our God. May the LORD's will be done." [14] Joab and the people with him approached the Arameans for battle, and they fled before him. [15] When the Ammonites saw that the Arameans had fled, they likewise fled before Joab's brother Abishai and entered the city. Then Joab went to Jerusalem.

[16] When the Arameans realized that they had been defeated by Israel, they sent messengers to bring out the Arameans who were across the Euphrates with Shophach, commander of Hadadezer's army, leading them. [17] When this was reported to David, he gathered all Israel and crossed the Jordan. He came up to them and lined up in battle formation against them. When David lined up to engage the Arameans in battle, they fought against him. [18] But the Arameans fled before Israel, and David killed 7,000 of their charioteers and 40,000 foot soldiers. He also killed Shophach, commander of the army. [19] When Hadadezer's subjects saw that they had been defeated by Israel,

they made peace with David and became his subjects. After this, the Arameans were never willing to help the Ammonites again.

20 In the spring when kings march out to war, Joab led the army and destroyed the Ammonites' land. He came to Rabbah and besieged it, but David remained in Jerusalem. Joab attacked Rabbah and demolished it. ² Then David took the crown from the head of their king, and it was placed on David's head. He discovered the crown weighed 75 pounds of gold, and there was a precious stone in it. In addition, David took away a large quantity of plunder from the city. ³ He brought out the people who were in it and put them to work with saws, iron picks, and axes. David did the same to all the Ammonite cities. Then he and all his troops returned to Jerusalem.

⁴ After this, a war broke out with the Philistines at Gezer. At that time Sibbecai the Hushathite killed Sippai, a descendant of the giants, and the Philistines were subdued.

⁵ Once again there was a battle with the Philistines, and Elhanan son of Jair killed Lahmi the brother of Goliath the Gittite. The shaft of his spear was like a weaver's beam.

⁶ There was still another battle at Gath where there was a man of extraordinary stature with six fingers on each hand and six toes on each foot— 24 in all. He, too, was descended from the giant. ⁷ When he taunted Israel, Jonathan, son of David's brother Shimei, killed him.

⁸ These were the descendants of the giant in Gath killed by David and his soldiers.

𝒫SALM 85:1-7

¹ LORD, You showed favor to Your land;
  You restored Jacob's prosperity.
² You took away Your people's guilt;
  You covered all their sin. *Selah*
³ You withdrew all Your fury;

You turned from Your burning anger.
⁴ Return to us, God of our salvation,
  and abandon Your displeasure with us.
⁵ Will You be angry with us forever?
  Will You prolong Your anger for all generations?
⁶ Will You not revive us again
  so that Your people may rejoice in You?
⁷ Show us Your faithful love, LORD,
  and give us Your salvation.

𝒫ROVERBS 18:6-8

⁶ A fool's lips lead to strife,
  and his mouth provokes a beating.

⁷ A fool's mouth is his devastation,
  and his lips are a trap for his life.

⁸ A gossip's words are like choice food
  that goes down to one's innermost being.

𝒜CTS 18:1-23

18 After this, he left from Athens and went to Corinth, ² where he found a Jewish man named Aquila, a native of Pontus, who had recently come from Italy with his wife Priscilla because Claudius had ordered all the Jews to leave Rome. Paul came to them, ³ and being of the same occupation, stayed with them and worked, for they were tentmakers by trade. ⁴ He reasoned in the synagogue every Sabbath and tried to persuade both Jews and Greeks.

⁵ When Silas and Timothy came down from Macedonia, Paul was occupied with preaching the message and solemnly testified to the Jews that the Messiah is Jesus. ⁶ But when they resisted and blasphemed, he shook out his clothes and told them, "Your blood is on your own heads! I am clean. From now on I will go to the Gentiles." ⁷ So he left there and went to the house of a man named Titius Justus, a worshiper of

God, whose house was next door to the synagogue. [8] Crispus, the leader of the synagogue, believed the Lord, along with his whole household; and many of the Corinthians, when they heard, believed and were baptized.

[9] Then the Lord said to Paul in a night vision, "Don't be afraid, but keep on speaking and don't be silent. [10] For I am with you, and no one will lay a hand on you to hurt you, because I have many people in this city." [11] And he stayed there a year and six months, teaching the word of God among them.

[12] While Gallio was proconsul of Achaia, the Jews made a united attack against Paul and brought him to the judge's bench. [13] "This man," they said, "persuades people to worship God contrary to the law!"

[14] And as Paul was about to open his mouth, Gallio said to the Jews, "If it were a matter of a crime or of moral evil, it would be reasonable for me to put up with you Jews. [15] But if these are questions about words, names, and your own law, see to it yourselves. I don't want to be a judge of such things." [16] So he drove them from the judge's bench. [17] Then they all seized Sosthenes, the leader of the synagogue, and beat him in front of the judge's bench. But none of these things concerned Gallio.

[18] So Paul, having stayed on for many days, said good-bye to the brothers and sailed away to Syria. Priscilla and Aquila were with him. He shaved his head at Cenchreae, because he had taken a vow. [19] When they reached Ephesus he left them there, but he himself entered the synagogue and engaged in discussion with the Jews. [20] And though they asked him to stay for a longer time, he declined, [21] but said good-bye and stated, "I'll come back to you again, if God wills." Then he set sail from Ephesus.

[22] On landing at Caesarea, he went up and greeted the church, and went down to Antioch. [23] He set out, traveling through one place after another in the Galatian territory and Phrygia, strengthening all the disciples.

Build on the Rock

LORD, there is no one like You, and there is no God besides You, as all we have heard confirms.—1 CHRONICLES 17:20

"The biggest problem we face in the Christian life," said Dr. Cynddylan Jones, a famous Welsh preacher, "is distance." He continued, "The only way that distance can be overcome is by having the perspective of Job who said: 'Though He slay me yet will I trust Him.'"

When I talk to counselors in training I tell them that what they should be listening for as a counselee tells his or her story is distance. That's what underlies most problems that bring people into counseling. This does not mean we should ignore or make light of the surface problems with which people may be struggling. But the plain fact is this—when we are close to God and have a deep and intimate relationship with Him, we may feel downcast but not destroyed. Therefore, every Christian counselor's ultimate goal should be to close any distance there may be between the person and God and to develop spiritual oneness. Counseling is not effective or complete until this is accomplished.

How does distance come between ourselves and God? There are many causes—bitterness and resentment against another, persistent sin, failure to establish a devotional life—but largely it arises through a lack of trust. If you cut your way through the maze of human problems, that's what you find—an inability to trust. That's what happened in the garden of Eden, and that's what happens in our personal garden of Eden also. To try to develop a close relationship with God and fail to deal with this most basic issue is about as effective as building a skyscraper on an acre of sand.

Prayer

O God, bring us closer day by day to that place of deep confidence and absolute trust. May we know You so deeply that nothing we see around us will shake or shatter our belief in Your unchanging goodness. In our Lord's name we pray. Amen.

Further Study

Dn 3:13-30; Hab 3:16-18; Ps 46:2; Mt 7:26
How did the Hebrew youths demonstrate faith in God?
What does Habakkuk declare?

JULY 21

1 CHRONICLES
21:1–23:13

21 Satan stood up against Israel and incited David to count the people of Israel. ² So David said to Joab and the commanders of the troops, "Go and count Israel from Beer-sheba to Dan and bring a report to me so I can know their number."

³ Joab replied, "May the LORD multiply the number of His people a hundred times over! My lord the king, aren't they all my lord's servants? Why does my lord want to do this? Why should he bring guilt on Israel?"

⁴ Yet the king's order prevailed over Joab. So Joab left and traveled throughout Israel and then returned to Jerusalem. ⁵ Joab gave David the total of the registration of the troops. In all Israel there were 1,100,000 swordsmen and in Judah itself 470,000 swordsmen. ⁶ But he did not include Levi and Benjamin in the count because the king's command was detestable to him. ⁷ This command was also evil in God's sight, so He afflicted Israel.

⁸ David said to God, "I have sinned greatly because I have done this thing. Now, because I've been very foolish, please take away Your servant's guilt."

⁹ Then the LORD instructed Gad, David's seer, ¹⁰ "Go and say to David, 'This is what the LORD says: I am offering you three choices. Choose one of them for yourself, and I will do it to you.'"

¹¹ So Gad went to David and said to him, "This is what the LORD says: 'Take your choice—¹² either three years of famine, three months of devastation by your foes with the sword of your enemy overtaking you, or three days of the sword of the LORD—a plague on the land, the angel of the LORD bringing destruction to the whole territory of Israel.' Now decide what answer I should take back to the One who sent me."

¹³ David answered Gad, "I have great anxiety. Please, let me fall into the LORD's hands because His mercies are very great, but don't let me fall into human hands."

¹⁴ So the LORD sent a plague on Israel, and 70,000 Israelite men died. ¹⁵ Then

God sent an angel to Jerusalem to destroy it, but when the angel was about to destroy the city, the LORD looked, relented concerning the destruction, and said to the angel who was destroying the people, "Enough, withdraw your hand now!" The angel of the LORD was then standing at the threshing floor of Ornan the Jebusite.

¹⁶ When David looked up and saw the angel of the LORD standing between earth and heaven, with his drawn sword in his hand stretched out over Jerusalem, David and the elders, clothed in sackcloth, fell down with their faces to the ground. ¹⁷ David said to God, "Wasn't I the one who gave the order to count the people? I am the one who has sinned and acted very wickedly. But these sheep, what have they done? My LORD God, please let Your hand be against me and against my father's family, but don't let the plague be against Your people."

¹⁸ So the angel of the LORD ordered Gad to tell David to go and set up an altar to the LORD on the threshing floor of Ornan the Jebusite. ¹⁹ David went up at Gad's command spoken in the name of the LORD.

²⁰ Ornan was threshing wheat when he turned and saw the angel. His four sons, who were with him, hid themselves. ²¹ David came to Ornan, and when Ornan looked and saw David, he left the threshing floor and bowed to David with his face to the ground. ²² Then David said to Ornan, "Give me this threshing-floor plot so that I may build an altar to the LORD on it. Give it to me for the full price, so the plague on the people may be halted." ²³ Ornan said to David, "Take it! My lord the king may do whatever he wants. See, I give the oxen for the burnt offerings, the threshing sledges for the wood, and the wheat for the grain offering—I give it all." ²⁴ King David answered Ornan, "No, I insist on paying the full price, for I will not take for the LORD what belongs to you or offer burnt offerings that cost me nothing." ²⁵ So David gave Ornan 15 pounds of gold for the plot. ²⁶ He built an altar to the LORD there and offered burnt offerings and fellowship offerings. He called on the LORD, and He answered him with fire from heaven on the altar of burnt offering.

²⁷ Then the LORD spoke to the angel, and he put his sword back into its sheath. ²⁸ At that time, when David saw that the LORD answered him at the threshing floor of Ornan the Jebusite, he offered sacrifices there. ²⁹ At that time the tabernacle of the LORD, which Moses made in the desert, and the altar of burnt offering were at the high place in Gibeon, ³⁰ but David could not go before it to inquire of God, because he was terrified of the sword of the LORD's angel. ¹ Then David said, "This is the house of the LORD God, and this is the altar of burnt offering for Israel."

²² So David gave orders to gather the foreigners that were in the land of Israel, and he appointed stonemasons to cut finished stones for building God's house. ³ David supplied a great deal of iron to make the nails for the doors of the gateways and for the fittings, together with an immeasurable quantity of bronze, ⁴ and innumerable cedar logs, because the Sidonians and Tyrians had brought a large quantity of cedar logs to David. ⁵ David said, "My son Solomon is young and inexperienced, and the house that is to be built for the LORD must be exceedingly great and famous and glorious in all the lands. Therefore, I must make provision for it." So David made lavish preparations for it before his death.

⁶ Then he summoned his son Solomon and instructed him to build a house for the LORD God of Israel. ⁷ "My son," David said to Solomon, "It was in my heart to build a house for the name of the LORD my God, ⁸ but the word of the LORD came to me: 'You have shed much blood and waged great wars. You are not to build a house for My name because you have shed so much blood on the ground before Me. ⁹ But a son will be born to you; he will be a man of rest. I will give him rest from all his

surrounding enemies, for his name will be Solomon, and I will give peace and quiet to Israel during his reign. ¹⁰ He is the one who will build a house for My name. He will be My son, and I will be his father. I will establish the throne of his kingdom over Israel forever.'

¹¹ "Now, my son, may the LORD be with you, and may you succeed in building the house of the LORD your God, as He said about you. ¹² Above all, may the LORD give you insight and understanding when He puts you in charge of Israel so that you may keep the law of the LORD your God. ¹³ Then you will succeed if you carefully follow the statutes and ordinances the LORD commanded Moses for Israel. Be strong and courageous. Don't be afraid or discouraged.

¹⁴ "Notice I have taken great pains to provide for the house of the LORD— 3,775 tons of gold, 37,750 tons of silver, and bronze and iron that can't be weighed because there is so much of it. I have also provided timber and stone, but you will need to add more to them. ¹⁵ You also have many workers: stonecutters, masons, carpenters, and people skilled in every kind of work ¹⁶ in gold, silver, bronze, and iron—beyond number. Now begin the work, and may the LORD be with you."

¹⁷ Then David ordered all the leaders of Israel to help his son Solomon: ¹⁸ "The LORD your God is with you, isn't He? And hasn't He given you rest on every side? For He has handed the land's inhabitants over to me, and the land has been subdued before the LORD and His people. ¹⁹ Now determine in your mind and heart to seek the LORD your God. Get started building the LORD God's sanctuary so that you may bring the ark of the LORD's covenant and the holy articles of God to the temple that is to be built for the name of the LORD."

23 When David was old and full of days, he installed his son Solomon as king over Israel. ² Then he gathered all the leaders of Israel, the priests, and the Levites. ³ The Levites 30 years old and above were counted; the total number of men was 38,000 by

headcount. ⁴ "Of these," David said, "24,000 are to be in charge of the work on the LORD's temple, 6,000 are to be officers and judges, ⁵ 4,000 are to be gatekeepers, and 4,000 are to praise the LORD with the instruments that I have made for worship."

⁶ Then David divided them into divisions according to Levi's sons: Gershom, Kohath, and Merari.

⁷ The Gershomites: Ladan and Shimei.
⁸ Ladan's sons: Jehiel was the first, then Zetham, and Joel—three.
⁹ Shimei's sons: Shelomoth, Haziel, and Haran—three. Those were the heads of the families of Ladan.
¹⁰ Shimei's sons: Jahath, Zizah, Jeush, and Beriah. Those were Shimei's sons—four. ¹¹ Jahath was the first and Zizah was the second; however, Jeush and Beriah did not have many sons, so they became an ancestral house and received a single assignment.
¹² Kohath's sons: Amram, Izhar, Hebron, and Uzziel—four.
¹³ Amram's sons: Aaron and Moses.

Aaron, along with his descendants, was set apart forever to consecrate the most holy things, to burn incense in the presence of the LORD, to minister to Him, and to pronounce blessings in His name forever.

PSALM 85:8-13

⁸ I will listen to what God will say;
surely the LORD will declare peace
to His people, His godly ones,
and not let them go back to
foolish ways.
⁹ His salvation is very near those
who fear Him,
so that glory may dwell in our
land.

¹⁰ Faithful love and truth will join
together;

righteousness and peace will
embrace.

11 Truth will spring up from the
earth,
and righteousness will look down
from heaven.

12 Also, the LORD will provide what is
good,
and our land will yield its crops.

13 Righteousness will go before Him
to prepare the way for His steps.

PROVERBS 18:9-11

9 The one who is truly lazy in his
work
is brother to a vandal.

10 The name of the LORD is a strong
tower;
the righteous run to it and are
protected.

11 A rich man's wealth is his fortified
city;
in his imagination it is like a high
wall.

ACTS 18:24–19:20

24 A Jew named Apollos, a native
Alexandrian, an eloquent man who was
powerful in the Scriptures, arrived in
Ephesus. 25 This man had been instructed in the way of the Lord; and being fervent in spirit, he spoke and taught the
things about Jesus accurately, although
he knew only John's baptism. 26 He began to speak boldly in the synagogue.
After Priscilla and Aquila heard him,
they took him home and explained the
way of God to him more accurately.
27 When he wanted to cross over to
Achaia, the brothers wrote to the disciples urging them to welcome him. After
he arrived, he greatly helped those who
had believed through grace. 28 For he
vigorously refuted the Jews in public,
demonstrating through the Scriptures
that Jesus is the Messiah.

19 While Apollos was in Corinth,
Paul traveled through the interior regions and came to Ephesus. He
found some disciples 2 and asked them,
"Did you receive the Holy Spirit when
you believed?"

"No," they told him, "we haven't
even heard that there is a Holy Spirit."

3 "Then with what baptism were you
baptized?" he asked them.

"With John's baptism," they replied.

4 Paul said, "John baptized with a baptism of repentance, telling the people
that they should believe in the One who
would come after him, that is, in Jesus."
5 On hearing this, they were baptized
in the name of the Lord Jesus. 6 And
when Paul had laid his hands on them,
the Holy Spirit came on them, and they
began to speak with other languages
and to prophesy. 7 Now there were
about 12 men in all.

8 Then he entered the synagogue and
spoke boldly over a period of three
months, engaging in discussion and trying to persuade them about the things related to the kingdom of God. 9 But when
some became hardened and would not
believe, slandering the Way in front of
the crowd, he withdrew from them and
met separately with the disciples, conducting discussions every day in the lec-
ture hall of Tyrannus. 10 And this went
on for two years, so that all the inhabitants of the province of Asia, both Jews
and Greeks, heard the word of the Lord.

11 God was performing extraordinary
miracles by Paul's hands, 12 so that even
facecloths or work aprons that had
touched his skin were brought to the
sick, and the diseases left them, and the
evil spirits came out of them.

13 Then some of the itinerant Jewish
exorcists attempted to pronounce the
name of the Lord Jesus over those who
had evil spirits, saying, "I command you
by the Jesus whom Paul preaches!"
14 Seven sons of Sceva, a Jewish chief
priest, were doing this. 15 The evil spirit
answered them, "Jesus I know, and Paul
I recognize—but who are you?" 16 Then
the man who had the evil spirit leaped
on them, overpowered them all, and
prevailed against them, so that they ran
out of that house naked and wounded.
17 This became known to everyone who

lived in Ephesus, both Jews and Greeks. Then fear fell on all of them, and the name of the Lord Jesus was magnified. [18] And many who had become believers came confessing and disclosing their practices, [19] while many of those who had practiced magic collected their books and burned them in front of everyone. So they calculated their value, and found it to be 50,000 pieces of silver. [20] In this way the Lord's message flourished and prevailed.

Having Your Own Way

I will listen to what God will say;
surely the LORD will . . . not let them go back
to foolish ways.—PSALM 85:8

Although our divine Shepherd seeks to lead us in the paths that are right, often we are so stubborn and self-centered that we decline to follow. We prefer our own way even though it may lead us straight into trouble.

When challenged about this issue, many of us, of course, strongly deny it. Yet in actual fact, comparatively few of God's people follow continually in His path. We say: "I want to do God's will and be led by Him in all that I do"—and then promptly proceed to follow our own self-determined desires. We sing beautiful hymns and choruses that contain such words as: "The Lord knows the way through the wilderness, all I have to do is follow"—then take the path that we think is best.

This is an issue that we must come to grips with right now, for unless we learn how to give up our self-centeredness, we will fall into serious trouble—no matter how loving and concerned is our Shepherd. I recognize that this is a difficult issue for many Christians, for our civilization teaches us self-interest as the primary motivating force in life— "every man for himself and the Devil take the hindmost." Actually if self-interest is primary, then the result is self-destruction, for the self-centered soon become the self-disrupted. They are making themselves God, and they are not God, so the universe won't back their way of life.

Prayer

Blessed Lord Jesus, You show me how to truly live—help me to live Your way. I want to abound, not drag leaden feet to dead tasks. Purge me of self and make me a committed follower of Your Way. For Your own name's sake. Amen.

Further Study

Pr 14:12; Col 3; Gl 2:20; Rm 6:11
What was Paul's confession?
List some characteristics of the unselfish life.

JULY 22

1 CHRONICLES
23:14–24:31

¹⁴ As for Moses the man of God, his sons were named among the tribe of Levi.

¹⁵ Moses' sons: Gershom and Eliezer.
¹⁶ Gershom's sons: Shebuel first.
¹⁷ Eliezer's sons were Rehabiah, first; Eliezer did not have any other sons, but Rehabiah's sons were very numerous.
¹⁸ Izhar's sons: Shelomith was first.
¹⁹ Hebron's sons: Jeriah was first, Amariah second, Jahaziel third, and Jekameam fourth.
²⁰ Uzziel's sons: Micah was first, and Isshiah second.
²¹ Merari's sons: Mahli and Mushi. Mahli's sons: Eleazar and Kish.
²² Eleazar died having no sons, only daughters. Their cousins, the sons of Kish, married them.
²³ Mushi's sons: Mahli, Eder, and Jeremoth—three.

²⁴ These were the sons of Levi by their ancestral houses—the heads of families, according to their registration by name in the headcount—20 years old or more, who worked in the service of the LORD's temple. ²⁵ For David said, "The LORD God of Israel has given rest to His people, and He has come to stay in Jerusalem forever. ²⁶ Also, the Levites no longer need to carry the tabernacle or any of the equipment for its service"— ²⁷ for according to the last words of David, the Levites 20 years old or more were to be counted— ²⁸ "but their duty will be to assist the sons of Aaron with the service of the LORD's temple, being responsible for the courts and the chambers, the purification of all the holy things, and the work of the service of God's temple— ²⁹ as well as the rows of the bread of the Presence, the fine flour for the grain offering, the wafers of unleavened bread, the baking, the mixing, and all measurements of volume and length. ³⁰ They are also to stand every morning to give thanks and praise to the LORD, and likewise in the evening. ³¹ Whenever burnt offerings are offered to the LORD on the Sabbaths, New Moons, and appointed festivals, they are to do so regularly in the LORD's presence according to the number prescribed for them. ³² They are to carry out their responsibilities to the tent of meeting, to the holy place, and to their relatives, the sons of Aaron, in the service of the LORD's temple."

24 The divisions of the descendants of Aaron were as follows: Aaron's sons were Nadab, Abihu, Eleazar, and Ithamar. ² But Nadab and Abihu died before their father, and they had no sons, so Eleazar and Ithamar served as priests. ³ Together with Zadok from the sons of Eleazar and Ahimelech from the sons of Ithamar, David divided them according to the assigned duties of their service. ⁴ Since more leaders were found among Eleazar's descendants than Ithamar's, they were divided accordingly: 16 heads of ancestral houses were from Eleazar's descendants, and eight heads of ancestral houses were from Ithamar's. ⁵ They were divided impartially by lot, for there were officers of the sanctuary and officers of God among both Eleazar's and Ithamar's descendants.

⁶ The secretary, Shemaiah son of Nethanel, a Levite, recorded them in the presence of the king and the officers, Zadok the priest, Ahimelech son of Abiathar, and the heads of families of the priests and the Levites. One

ancestral house was taken for Eleazar, and then one for Ithamar.

7 The first lot fell to Jehoiarib,
the second to Jedaiah,
8 the third to Harim, the fourth
to Seorim,
9 the fifth to Malchijah, the sixth
to Mijamin,
10 the seventh to Hakkoz, the eighth
to Abijah,
11 the ninth to Jeshua, the tenth
to Shecaniah,
12 the eleventh to Eliashib,
the twelfth to Jakim,
13 the thirteenth to Huppah,
the fourteenth to Jeshebeab,
14 the fifteenth to Bilgah, the sixteenth to Immer,
15 the seventeenth to Hezir, the eighteenth to Happizzez,
16 the nineteenth to Pethahiah,
the twentieth to Jehezkel,
17 the twenty-first to Jachin,
the twenty-second to Gamul,
18 the twenty-third to Delaiah,
and the twenty-fourth to Maaziah.

19 These had their assigned duties for service when they entered the LORD's temple, according to their regulations, which they received from their ancestor Aaron, as the LORD God of Israel had commanded him.

20 As for the rest of Levi's sons:
from Amram's sons: Shubael;
from Shubael's sons: Jehdeiah.
21 From Rehabiah:
from Rehabiah's sons: Isshiah was the first.
22 From the Izharites: Shelomoth;
from Shelomoth's sons: Jahath.
23 Hebron's sons:
Jeriah the first, Amariah the second,
Jahaziel the third, and Jekameam the fourth.
24 From Uzziel's sons: Micah;
from Micah's sons: Shamir.
25 Micah's brother: Isshiah;
from Isshiah's sons: Zechariah.
26 Merari's sons: Mahli and Mushi,
and from his sons, Jaaziah his son.

27 Merari's sons, by his son Jaaziah:
Shoham, Zaccur, and Ibri.
28 From Mahli: Eleazar, who had no sons.
29 From Kish, from Kish's sons: Jerahmeel.
30 Mushi's sons: Mahli, Eder, and Jerimoth.

Those were the sons of the Levites according to their ancestral houses. 31 They also cast lots the same way as their relatives, the sons of Aaron did in the presence of King David, Zadok, Ahimelech, and the heads of the families of the priests and Levites—the family heads and their younger brothers alike.

PSALM 86:1-10

1 Listen, LORD, and answer me,
for I am poor and needy.
2 Protect my life, for I am faithful.
You are my God; save Your servant
who trusts in You.
3 Be gracious to me, Lord,
for I call to You all day long.
4 Bring joy to Your servant's life,
since I set my hope on You, Lord.

5 For You, Lord, are kind and ready
to forgive,
abundant in faithful love to all
who call on You.
6 LORD, hear my prayer;
listen to my plea for mercy.
7 I call on You in the day of my
distress,
for You will answer me.

8 Lord, there is no one like You
among the gods,
and there are no works like Yours.
9 All the nations You have made
will come and bow down before
You, Lord,
and will honor Your name.
10 For You are great and perform
wonders;
You alone are God.

PROVERBS 18:12-13

12 Before his downfall a man's heart
is proud,
but before honor comes humility.

13 The one who gives an answer
before he listens—
this is foolishness and disgrace for
him.

ACTS 19:21-41

21 When these events were over, Paul
resolved in the Spirit to pass through
Macedonia and Achaia and go to Jerusalem. "After I've been there," he said,
"I must see Rome as well!" 22 So after
sending two of those who assisted him,
Timothy and Erastus, to Macedonia, he
himself stayed in the province of Asia
for a while.

23 During that time there was a major
disturbance about the Way. 24 For a person named Demetrius, a silversmith
who made silver shrines of Artemis,
provided a great deal of business for the
craftsmen. 25 When he had assembled
them, as well as the workers engaged in
this type of business, he said: "Men,
you know that our prosperity is derived
from this business. 26 You both see and
hear that not only in Ephesus, but in almost the whole province of Asia, this
man Paul has persuaded and misled a
considerable number of people by saying that gods made by hand are not
gods! 27 So not only do we run a risk that
our business may be discredited, but
also that the temple of the great goddess Artemis may be despised and her
magnificence come to the verge of
ruin—the very one whom the whole
province of Asia and the world adore."
28 When they had heard this, they
were filled with rage and began to cry
out, "Great is Artemis of the Ephe-

sians!" 29 So the city was filled with confusion; and they rushed all together into
the amphitheater, dragging along Gaius
and Aristarchus, Macedonians who were
Paul's traveling companions. 30 Though
Paul wanted to go in before the people,
the disciples did not let him. 31 Even
some of the provincial officials of Asia,
who were his friends, sent word to him,
pleading with him not to take a chance
by going into the amphitheater. 32 Meanwhile, some were shouting one thing
and some another, because the assembly was in confusion, and most of them
did not know why they had come together. 33 Then some of the crowd gave
Alexander advice when the Jews pushed
him to the front. So motioning with his
hand, Alexander wanted to make his defense to the people. 34 But when they
recognized that he was a Jew, a united
cry went up from all of them for about
two hours: "Great is Artemis of the
Ephesians!"

35 However, when the city clerk had
calmed the crowd down, he said, "Men
of Ephesus! What man is there who
doesn't know that the city of the Ephesians is the temple guardian of the great
Artemis, and of the image that fell from
heaven? 36 Therefore, since these things
are undeniable, you must keep calm
and not do anything rash. 37 For you
have brought these men here who are
not temple robbers or blasphemers of
our goddess. 38 So if Demetrius and the
craftsmen who are with him have a case
against anyone, the courts are in session, and there are proconsuls. Let
them bring charges against one another.
39 But if you want something else, it
must be decided in a legal assembly.
40 In fact, we run a risk of being charged
with rioting for what happened today,
since there is no justification that we
can give as a reason for this disorderly
gathering." 41 After saying this, he dismissed the assembly.

The Wonder of Forgiveness

*For You, Lord, are kind and ready to forgive,
abundant in faithful love to all who call on You.*—PSALM 86:5

Psalm 130:3 says, "LORD, if You considered sins . . . who could stand?" The psalmist is conscious of a great gulf that divides people from God, particularly himself, and he makes the assertion that if God kept a strict tally of mankind's sins, there would be no hope for anyone. But then come the most beautiful and wondrous words in the Old Testament: "But with You there is forgiveness, so that You may be revered" (Psalm 130:4). The Living Bible paraphrases the verse like this: "But you forgive! What an awesome thing this is!"

Eight times the divine name "LORD" is used in this psalm, and as we observe how God is addressed we see what a difference knowing Him makes whatever plight we find ourselves in. He is addressed in the first couple of verses as the God who hears, and then, in verses 3 to 4, as the God who forgives. What a wonderful thing it is that God forgives. It is, as the Living Bible puts it, awesome.

As Christians we are so used to hearing about God's forgiveness that we are in danger of taking it for granted. Heinrich Hein, when lying on his deathbed, was asked by a friend: "Do you think God has forgiven you?" Hein replied: "Of course God will forgive me. That's His job." I hope none of my readers will approach the subject of divine forgiveness with such cynicism. The fact that God forgives and forgets is something we will never fully understand, but it must never be taken for granted.

Prayer

O Father, forgive me if I have thought that divine forgiveness is just the result of Your doing Your job. Grant that my reaction to being forgiven will not be one of complacency but of constant reverence and holy awe. In Jesus' name I ask it. Amen.

Further Study

Ps 104:1-35; Eph 1:7; 1 Jn 1:9
Why was the psalmist filled with praise?
How did he describe the removal of sins?

JULY 23

I CHRONICLES
25:1–26:32

25 David and the officers of the army also set apart some of the sons of Asaph, Heman, and Jeduthun, who were to prophesy accompanied by lyres, harps, and cymbals. This is the list of the men who performed their service:

² From Asaph's sons:
Zaccur, Joseph, Nethaniah,
and Asarelah, sons of Asaph,
under Asaph's authority, who
prophesied under the authority
of the king.
³ From Jeduthun: Jeduthun's sons:
Gedaliah, Zeri, Jeshaiah, Shimei,
Hashabiah, and Mattithiah—six—
under the authority of their father
Jeduthun, prophesying to the ac-
companiment of lyres, giving
thanks and praise to the LORD.
⁴ From Heman: Heman's sons:
Bukkiah, Mattaniah, Uzziel,
Shebuel, Jerimoth, Hananiah,
Hanani, Eliathah, Giddalti,
Romamti-ezer, Joshbekashah,
Mallothi, Hothir, and Mahazioth.
⁵ All these sons of Heman, the
king's seer, were given by the
promises of God to exalt him, for
God had given Heman fourteen
sons and three daughters.

⁶ All these men were under their own fathers' authority for the music in the LORD's temple, with cymbals, harps, and lyres for the service of God's temple. Asaph, Jeduthun, and Heman were under the king's authority. ⁷ Together with their relatives who were all trained and skillful in music for the LORD, they numbered 288. ⁸ They cast lots impartially for their duties, the young and old alike, the teacher along with the pupil.

⁹ The first lot for Asaph fell
to Joseph, his sons,
and his brothers—   12
to Gedaliah the second: him,
his brothers,
and his sons—   12
¹⁰ the third to Zaccur, his sons,
and his brothers—   12
¹¹ the fourth to Izri, his sons,
and his brothers—   12
¹² the fifth to Nethaniah,
his sons,
and his brothers—   12
¹³ the sixth to Bukkiah, his sons,
and his brothers—   12
¹⁴ the seventh to Jesarelah,
his sons,
and his brothers—   12
¹⁵ the eighth to Jeshaiah,
his sons,
and his brothers—   12
¹⁶ the ninth to Mattaniah,
his sons,
and his brothers—   12
¹⁷ the tenth to Shimei, his sons,
and his brothers—   12
¹⁸ the eleventh to Azarel,
his sons,
and his brothers—   12
¹⁹ the twelfth to Hashabiah,
his sons,
and his brothers—   12
²⁰ the thirteenth to Shubael,
his sons,
and his brothers—   12
²¹ the fourteenth to Mattithiah,
his sons,
and his brothers—   12
²² the fifteenth to Jeremoth,
his sons,
and his brothers—   12
²³ the sixteenth to Hananiah,
his sons,
and his brothers—   12
²⁴ the seventeenth to Joshbekashah,
his sons,
and his brothers—   12

²⁵ the eighteenth to Hanani,
his sons,
and his brothers—   12
²⁶ the nineteenth to Mallothi,
his sons,
and his brothers—   12
²⁷ the twentieth to Eliathah,
his sons,
and his brothers—   12
²⁸ the twenty-first to Hothir,
his sons,
and his brothers—   12
²⁹ the twenty-second to Giddalti,
his sons,
and his brothers—   12
³⁰ the twenty-third to Mahazioth,
his sons,
and his brothers—   12
³¹ and the twenty-fourth
to Romamti-ezer, his sons,
and his brothers—   12.

26 The following were the divisions of the gatekeepers:

From the Korahites: Meshelemiah son of Kore, one of the sons of Asaph.
² Meshelemiah had sons:
Zechariah the firstborn, Jediael the second,
Zebadiah the third, Jathniel the fourth,
³ Elam the fifth, Jehohanan the sixth,
and Eliehoenai the seventh.
⁴ Obed-edom also had sons:
Shemaiah the firstborn, Jehozabad the second,
Joah the third, Sachar the fourth,
Nethanel the fifth, ⁵ Ammiel the sixth,
Issachar the seventh,
and Peullethai the eighth,
for God blessed him.
⁶ Also, to his son Shemaiah were born sons who ruled over their ancestral houses because they were strong, capable men.
⁷ Shemaiah's sons: Othni, Rephael, Obed, and Elzabad; his brothers Elihu and Semachiah were also capable men. ⁸ All of these were among the sons of Obed-edom with their sons and brothers; they were capable men with strength for the work—62 from Obed-edom.

⁹ Meshelemiah also had sons and brothers who were capable men—18.

¹⁰ Hosah, from the Merarites, also had sons: Shimri the first (although he was not the firstborn, his father had appointed him as the first), ¹¹ Hilkiah the second, Tebaliah the third, and Zechariah the fourth. The sons and brothers of Hosah were 13 in all.

¹² These divisions of the gatekeepers, under their leading men, had duties for ministering in the LORD's temple, just as their brothers did. ¹³ They cast lots according to their ancestral houses, young and old alike, for each gate.

¹⁴ The lot for the east gate fell to Shelemiah. They also cast lots for his son Zechariah, an insightful counselor, and his lot came out for the north gate. ¹⁵ Obed-edom's was the south gate, and his sons' lot was the storehouses; ¹⁶ for Shuppim and Hosah it was the west gate and the gate of Shallecheth on the ascending highway.

There were guards stationed at every watch. ¹⁷ There were six Levites each day on the east, four each day on the north, four each day on the south, and two pair at the storehouses. ¹⁸ As for the court on the west, there were four at the highway and two at the court. ¹⁹ Those were the divisions of the gatekeepers from the sons of the Korahites and Merarites.

²⁰ From the Levites, Ahijah was in charge of the treasuries of God's temple and the treasuries for what had been dedicated. ²¹ From the sons of Ladan, who were the sons of the Gershonites through Ladan and were the heads of families belonging to Ladan the Gershonite: Jehieli. ²² The sons of Jehieli, Zetham and his brother Joel, were in charge of the treasuries of the LORD's temple.

²³ From the Amramites, the Izharites, the Hebronites, and the Uzzielites:

²⁴ Shebuel, a descendant of Moses' son Gershom, was the officer in charge of the treasuries. ²⁵ His relative through Eliezer: his son Rehabiah, his son Jeshaiah, his son Joram, his son Zichri, and his son Shelomith. ²⁶ This Shelomith and his brothers were in charge of all the treasuries for what had been dedicated by King David, by the heads of families who were the commanders of the thousands and of the hundreds, and by the army commanders. ²⁷ They dedicated part of the plunder from their battles for the repair of the LORD's temple. ²⁸ All that Samuel the seer, Saul son of Kish, Abner son of Ner, and Joab son of Zeruiah had dedicated, along with everything else that had been dedicated, were in the care of Shelomith and his brothers.

²⁹ From the Izrahites: Chenaniah and his sons had the outside duties as officers and judges over Israel. ³⁰ From the Hebronites: Hashabiah and his relatives, 1,700 capable men, had assigned duties in Israel west of the Jordan for all the work of the LORD and for the service of the king. ³¹ From the Hebronites: Jerijah was the head of the Hebronites, according to the genealogical records of his ancestors. In the fortieth year of David's reign a search was made, and strong, capable men were found among them at Jazer in Gilead. ³² There were among Jerijah's relatives, 2,700 capable men who were heads of families. King David appointed them over the Reubenites, the Gadites, and half the tribe of Manasseh as overseers in every matter relating to God and the king.

PSALM 86:11-17

¹¹ Teach me Your way, LORD,
and I will live by Your truth.
Give me an undivided mind to
fear Your name.
¹² I will praise You with all my heart,
Lord my God,
and will honor Your name forever.
¹³ For Your faithful love for me is
great,
and You deliver my life from the
depths of Sheol.

¹⁴ God, arrogant people have
attacked me;
a gang of ruthless men seeks my
life.
They have no regard for You.
¹⁵ But You, Lord, are a
compassionate and gracious
God,
slow to anger and abundant in
faithful love and truth.
¹⁶ Turn to me and be gracious to me.
Give Your strength to Your
servant;
save the son of Your female
servant.
¹⁷ Show me a sign of Your goodness;
my enemies will see and be put to
shame
because You, LORD, have helped
and comforted me.

PROVERBS 18:14-15

¹⁴ A man's spirit can endure
sickness,
but who can survive a broken
spirit?

¹⁵ The mind of the discerning
acquires knowledge,
and the ear of the wise seeks it.

ACTS 20:1-21

20 After the uproar was over, Paul sent for the disciples, encouraged them, and after saying good-bye, departed to go to Macedonia. ² And when he had passed through those areas and exhorted them at length, he came to Greece ³ and stayed three months. When he was about to set sail for Syria, a plot was devised against him by the Jews, so a decision was made to go back through Macedonia. ⁴ He was accompanied by Sopater, son of Pyrrhus, from Beroea, Aristarchus and Secundus from Thessalonica, Gaius from Derbe, Timothy, and Tychicus and Trophimus from Asia. ⁵ These men went on ahead and waited for us in Troas, ⁶ but we sailed away from Philippi after the days of Unleavened Bread. In five

days we reached them at Troas, where we spent seven days.

⁷ On the first day of the week, we assembled to break bread. Paul spoke to them, and since he was about to depart the next day, he extended his message until midnight. ⁸ There were many lamps in the room upstairs where we were assembled, ⁹ and a young man named Eutychus was sitting on a window sill and sank into a deep sleep as Paul kept on speaking. When he was overcome by sleep he fell down from the third story, and was picked up dead. ¹⁰ But Paul went down, threw himself on him, embraced him, and said, "Don't be alarmed, for his life is in him!" ¹¹ After going upstairs, breaking the bread, and eating, he conversed a considerable time until dawn. Then he left. ¹² They brought the boy home alive and were greatly comforted.

¹³ Then we went on ahead to the ship and sailed for Assos, from there intending to take Paul on board. For these were his instructions, since he himself was going by land. ¹⁴ When he met us at Assos, we took him on board and came to Mitylene. ¹⁵ Sailing from there, the next day we arrived off Chios. The following day we crossed over to Samos, and the day after, we came to Miletus. ¹⁶ For Paul had decided to sail past Ephesus so he would not have to spend time in the province of Asia, because he was hurrying to be in Jerusalem, if possible, for the day of Pentecost.

¹⁷ Now from Miletus, he sent to Ephesus and called for the elders of the church. ¹⁸ And when they came to him, he said to them: "You know, from the first day I set foot in Asia, how I was with you the whole time— ¹⁹ serving the Lord with all humility, with tears, and with the trials that came to me through the plots of the Jews— ²⁰ and that I did not shrink back from proclaiming to you anything that was profitable, or from teaching it to you in public and from house to house. ²¹ I testified to both Jews and Greeks about repentance toward God and faith in our Lord Jesus.

Clinging to Unforgiveness

Give me an undivided mind to fear Your name.

—PSALM 86:11

A friend of mine who is a minister and Christian counselor shared with me about a woman who told him that she spent thirty to forty-five minutes every day asking God to take away from her an unforgiving spirit. She told Him that what she wanted more than anything in the world was the ability to forgive those in her family who had brought her hurt.

The minister joined her in prayer, but the Holy Spirit spoke to his heart and showed him that deep down, the woman did not want a forgiving spirit. The minister waited for the Spirit to show more, but nothing came. Realizing that he had enough information to pursue the matter, the minister invited the woman to explore the possibility that what she was asking for with her lips was not what she was asking for in her heart.

At first the woman seemed annoyed and upset by the suggestion that deep down she might not really want what she was asking for, but gradually she agreed to take an inside look. In the hour or two that followed, this came out—despite her claim that she wanted to forgive, deep down in her heart she clung to an unforgiving spirit. This gave her the justification she felt she needed when she was the cause of hurt to someone else. In other words, she was saying to herself: "Other people have hurt me, so it won't matter so much when I hurt them." When she saw what she was doing, however, she immediately surrendered it to God and found inner release and freedom.

Prayer

God, I am deeply challenged by this yet deeply relieved to know that whatever might elude me can never elude You. I open up my heart right now for inspection and examination. Search me and make me whole. In Jesus' name. Amen.

Further Study

Lk 17:1-5; Mk 11:25; Eph 4:32
How did the apostles respond to Christ's challenge?
How did Paul admonish the Ephesians?

JULY 24

1 CHRONICLES
27:1–28:21

27 This is the list of the Israelites, the heads of families, the commanders of thousands and the commanders of hundreds, and their officers who served the king in every matter to do with the divisions that were on rotated military duty each month throughout the year. There were 24,000 in each division:

² Jashobeam son of Zabdiel was in charge of the first division, for the first month; 24,000 were in his division. ³ He was a descendant of Perez and chief of all the army commanders for the first month. ⁴ Dodai the Ahohite was in charge of the division for the second month, and Mikloth was the leader; 24,000 were in his division.

⁵ The third army commander, as chief for the third month, was Benaiah son of Jehoiada the priest; 24,000 were in his division. ⁶ This Benaiah was a mighty man among the Thirty and over the Thirty, and his son Ammizabad was in charge of his division.

⁷ The fourth commander, for the fourth month, was Joab's brother Asahel, and his son Zebadiah was commander after him; 24,000 were in his division.

⁸ The fifth, for the fifth month, was the commander Shamhuth the Izrahite; 24,000 were in his division.

⁹ The sixth, for the sixth month, was Ira son of Ikkesh the Tekoite; 24,000 were in his division.

¹⁰ The seventh, for the seventh

month, was Helez the Pelonite from the sons of Ephraim; 24,000 were in his division. ¹¹ The eighth, for the eighth month, was Sibbecai the Hushathite, a Zerahite; 24,000 were in his division. ¹² The ninth, for the ninth month, was Abiezer the Anathothite, a Benjaminite; 24,000 were in his division. ¹³ The tenth, for the tenth month, was Maharai the Netophathite, a Zerahite; 24,000 were in his division. ¹⁴ The eleventh, for the eleventh month, was Benaiah the Pirathonite from the sons of Ephraim; 24,000 were in his division. ¹⁵ The twelfth, for the twelfth month, was Heldai the Netophathite, of Othniel's family; 24,000 were in his division.

¹⁶ The following were in charge of the tribes of Israel:
For the Reubenites, Eliezer son of Zichri was the chief official;
for the Simeonites, Shephatiah son of Maacah;
¹⁷ for the Levites, Hashabiah son of Kemuel; for Aaron, Zadok;
¹⁸ for Judah, Elihu, one of David's brothers; for Issachar, Omri son of Michael;
¹⁹ for Zebulun, Ishmaiah son of Obadiah;
for Naphtali, Jerimoth son of Azriel;
²⁰ for the Ephraimites, Hoshea son of Azaziah;
for half the tribe of Manasseh, Joel son of Pedaiah;
²¹ for half the tribe of Manasseh in Gilead, Iddo son of Zechariah;
for Benjamin, Jaasiel son of Abner;
²² for Dan, Azarel son of Jeroham.
Those were the leaders of the tribes of Israel.

²³ David didn't count the men aged 20 or under, for the LORD had said He would make Israel as numerous as the stars of heaven. ²⁴ Joab son of Zeruiah began to count them, but he didn't complete it. There was wrath against Israel because of this census, and the number was not entered in the Historical Record of King David.

²⁵ Azmaveth son of Adiel was in charge of the king's storehouses. Jonathan son of Uzziah was in charge of the storehouses in the country, in the cities, in the villages, and in the fortresses. ²⁶ Ezri son of Chelub was in charge of those who worked in the fields tilling the soil. ²⁷ Shimei the Ramathite was in charge of the vineyards. Zabdi the Shiphmite was in charge of the produce of the vineyards for the wine cellars. ²⁸ Baal-hanan the Gederite was in charge of the olive and sycamore trees in the Shephelah. Joash was in charge of the stores of olive oil. ²⁹ Shitrai the Sharonite was in charge of the herds that grazed in Sharon, while Shaphat son of Adlai was in charge of the herds in the valleys. ³⁰ Obil the Ishmaelite was in charge of the camels. Jehdeiah the Meronothite was in charge of the donkeys. ³¹ Jaziz the Hagrite was in charge of the flocks. All these were officials in charge of King David's property.

³² David's uncle Jonathan was a counselor; he was a man of understanding and a scribe. Jehiel son of Hachmoni attended the king's sons. ³³ Ahithophel was the king's counselor. Hushai the Archite was the king's friend. ³⁴ After Ahithophel came Jehoiada son of Benaiah, then Abiathar. Joab was the commander of the king's army.

28 David assembled in Jerusalem all the leaders of Israel: the leaders of the tribes, the leaders of the divisions in the king's service, the commanders of thousands and the commanders of hundreds, and the officials in charge of all the property and cattle of the king and his sons, along with the court officials, the fighting men, and all the brave warriors. ² Then King David rose to his feet and said, "Listen to me, my brothers and my people. It was in my heart to build a house as a resting place for the ark of the LORD's covenant and as a footstool for our God. I had made preparations to build, ³ but God said to me, 'You are not to build a house for My name because you are a man of war and have shed blood.'

⁴ "Yet the LORD God of Israel chose me out of all my father's household to be king over Israel forever. For He chose Judah as leader, and from the house of Judah, my father's household, and from my father's sons, He was pleased to make me king over all Israel. ⁵ And out of all my sons—for the LORD has given me many sons—He has chosen my son Solomon to sit on the throne of the LORD's kingdom over Israel. ⁶ He said to me, 'Your son Solomon is the one who is to build My house and My courts, for I have chosen him to be My son, and I will be his father. ⁷ I will establish his kingdom forever if he perseveres in keeping My commandments and My ordinances as he is today.'

⁸ "So now in the sight of all Israel, the assembly of the LORD, and in the hearing of our God, observe and seek after all the commandments of the LORD your God so that you may possess this good land and leave it as an inheritance to your descendants forever.

⁹ "As for you, Solomon my son, know the God of your father, and serve Him with a whole heart and a willing mind, for the LORD searches every heart and understands the intention of every thought. If you seek Him, He will be found by you, but if you forsake Him, He will reject you forever. ¹⁰ Realize now that the LORD has chosen you to build a house for the sanctuary. Be strong, and do it."

¹¹ Then David gave his son Solomon the plans for the vestibule of the temple and its buildings, treasuries, upper rooms, inner rooms, and the room for the place of atonement. ¹² The plans contained everything he had in mind for the courts of the LORD's house, all the surrounding chambers, the treasuries of God's house, and the treasuries for what is dedicated. ¹³ Also included were plans for the divisions of the priests and the Levites; all the work of service in the LORD's house; all the articles of service of the LORD's house; ¹⁴ the weight of gold for all the articles for every kind of service; the weight of all the silver articles for every kind of service; ¹⁵ the weight of the gold lampstands and their gold lamps, including the weight of each lampstand and its lamps; the weight of each silver lampstand and its lamps, according to the service of each lampstand; ¹⁶ the weight of gold for each table for the rows of the bread of the Presence and the silver for the silver tables; ¹⁷ the pure gold for the forks, sprinkling basins, and pitchers; the weight of each gold dish; the weight of each silver bowl; ¹⁸ the weight of refined gold for the altar of incense; and the plans for the chariot of the gold cherubim that spread out their wings and cover the ark of the LORD's covenant.

¹⁹ David concluded, "By the LORD's hand on me, He enabled me to understand everything in writing, all the details of the plan."

²⁰ Then David said to his son Solomon, "Be strong and courageous, and do the work. Don't be afraid or discouraged, for the LORD God, my God, is with you. He won't leave you or forsake you until all the work for the service of the LORD's house is finished. ²¹ Here are the divisions of the priests and the Levites for all the service of God's house. Every willing man of any skill will be at your disposal for the work, and the leaders and all the people are at your every command."

$\mathcal{P}$SALM 87:1-7

¹ His foundation is on the holy mountains.

2 The LORD loves the gates of Zion
more than all the dwellings of
Jacob.
3 Glorious things are said about you,
city of God.   *Selah*

4 "I will mention those who know
Me:
Rahab, Babylon, Philistia, Tyre,
and Cush—
each one was born there."
5 And it will be said of Zion,
"This one and that one were born
in her."
The Most High Himself will
establish her.
6 When He registers the peoples,
the LORD will record,
"This one was born there."   *Selah*
7 Singers and dancers alike will say,
"All my springs are in you."

PROVERBS 18:16-17

16 A gift opens doors for a man
and brings him before the great.

17 The first to state his case seems
right
until another comes and cross-
examines him.

ACTS 20:22–21:6

22 "And now I am on my way to Jerusalem, bound in my spirit, not knowing
what I will encounter there, 23 except
that in town after town the Holy Spirit
testifies to me that chains and afflictions are waiting for me. 24 But I count
my life of no value to myself, so that I
may finish my course and the ministry I
received from the Lord Jesus, to testify
to the gospel of God's grace.

25 "And now I know that none of you,
among whom I went about preaching
the kingdom, will ever see my face
again. 26 Therefore I testify to you this
day that I am innocent of everyone's
blood, 27 for I did not shrink back from
declaring to you the whole plan of God.
28 Be on guard for yourselves and for all
the flock, among whom the Holy Spirit
has appointed you as overseers, to shepherd the church of God, which He purchased with His own blood. 29 I know
that after my departure savage wolves
will come in among you, not sparing the
flock. 30 And men from among yourselves will rise up with deviant doctrines
to lure the disciples into following them.
31 Therefore be on the alert, remembering that night and day for three years I
did not stop warning each one of you
with tears.

32 "And now I commit you to God and
to the message of His grace, which is
able to build you up and to give you an
inheritance among all who are sanctified. 33 I have not coveted anyone's silver or gold or clothing. 34 You yourselves
know that these hands have provided
for my needs, and for those who were
with me. 35 In every way I've shown you
that by laboring like this, it is necessary
to help the weak and to keep in mind
the words of the Lord Jesus, for He said,
'It is more blessed to give than to receive.' "

36 After he said this, he knelt down
and prayed with all of them. 37 There was
a great deal of weeping by everyone.
And embracing Paul, they kissed him,
38 grieving most of all over his statement
that they would never see his face
again. Then they escorted him to the
ship.

21 After we tore ourselves away
from them and set sail, we came
by a direct route to Cos, the next day to
Rhodes, and from there to Patara. 2 Finding a ship crossing over to Phoenicia, we
boarded and set sail. 3 After we sighted
Cyprus, leaving it on the left, we sailed
on to Syria and arrived at Tyre, because
the ship was to unload its cargo there.
4 So we found some disciples and stayed
there seven days. They said to Paul
through the Spirit not to go to Jerusalem. 5 When our days there were over,
we left to continue our journey, while
all of them, with their wives and children, escorted us out of the city. After
kneeling down on the beach to pray,
6 we said good-bye to one another. Then
we boarded the ship, and they returned
home.

Deliverance from Fear

Be strong and courageous. . . . Don't be afraid or discouraged,
for the LORD God, my God, is with you.

—1 CHRONICLES 28:20

If we are to have feet like "hinds' feet," we must ask God to rid our hearts of all and every fear. I am convinced that perhaps millions of Christians are held back from pursuing God by fear.

Not all fears are harmful. When fear is spelled with a small "f," it can have useful, biological ends. It makes the frightened deer alert and fleet of foot; it makes the surgeon skillful, for he sees the dangers that beset him if he does the wrong thing. Fear harnessed to constructive ends may be constructive. When we use fear and control it, then it is good.

But when fear uses and controls us, it is bad. When fear becomes Fear with a capital "F," it becomes fearsome. I am sure that you have known times, as I have, when God beckons to you, as He did with John in the Revelation, to "come up here" (Rv 4:1), only to find that as your mind got ready to begin the journey, your heart suddenly became gripped with fear. You wanted to move upward, but your progress was halted because you could not mount "with all four feet."

Overcoming fear ought to be one of our greatest objectives. The first spoken word of Luke's Gospel was the voice of the angel: "Do not be afraid" (Lk 1:13). The first word of Jesus after His resurrection was: "Do not be afraid" (Mt 28:10). Between that first word and the last, the constant endeavor of Jesus was to help us get rid of fear. We must learn His secret.

Prayer

O God, give me deliverance from every harmful and unproductive fear. I know this is a prayer that You delight to answer, for You have fashioned me for faith, not for fear. Help me, then, to surrender to what I am made for. Amen.

Further Study

1 Ch 28:20; Mt 14:22-33; 17:1-8
What caused Peter to sink?
What did Jesus say to the disciples on the mountain?

JULY 25

1 CHRONICLES 29:1– 2 CHRONICLES 1:17

29 Then King David said to all the assembly, "My son Solomon—God has chosen him alone—is young and inexperienced. The task is great, for the temple will not be for man, but for the LORD God. ² So to the best of my ability I've made provision for the house of my God: gold for the gold articles, silver for the silver, bronze for the bronze, iron for the iron, and wood for the wood, as well as onyx, stones for mounting, antimony, stones of various colors, all kinds of precious stones, and a great quantity of marble. ³ Moreover, because of my delight in the house of my God, I now give my personal treasures of gold and silver for the house of my God over and above all that I've provided for the holy house: ⁴ 100 tons of gold (gold of Ophir) and 250 tons of refined silver for overlaying the walls of the buildings, ⁵ the gold for the gold work and the silver for the silver, for all the work to be done by the craftsmen. Now, who will volunteer to consecrate himself to the LORD today?"

⁶ Then the leaders of the households, the leaders of the tribes of Israel, the commanders of thousands and of hundreds, and the officials in charge of the king's work gave willingly. ⁷ For the service of God's house they gave 185 tons of gold and 10,000 gold drachmas, 375 tons of silver, 675 tons of bronze, and 4,000 tons of iron. ⁸ Whoever had precious stones gave them to the treasury of the LORD's house under the care of Jehiel the Gershonite. ⁹ Then the people rejoiced because of their leaders' willingness to give, for they had given to the LORD with a whole heart. King David also rejoiced greatly.

¹⁰ Then David praised the LORD in the sight of all the assembly. David said, "May You be praised, LORD God of our father Israel, from eternity to eternity. ¹¹ Yours, LORD, is the greatness and the power and the glory and the splendor and the majesty, for everything in the heavens and on earth belongs to You. Yours, LORD, is the kingdom, and You are exalted as head over all. ¹² Riches and honor come from You, and You are the ruler of everything. In Your hand are power and might, and it is in Your hand to make great and to give strength to all. ¹³ Now therefore, our God, we give You thanks and praise Your glorious name.

¹⁴ "But who am I, and who are my people, that we should be able to give as generously as this? For everything comes from You, and we have given You only what comes from Your own hand. ¹⁵ For we are foreigners and sojourners in Your presence as were all our ancestors. Our days on earth are like a shadow, without hope. ¹⁶ LORD our God, all this wealth that we've provided for building You a house for Your holy name comes from Your hand; everything belongs to You. ¹⁷ I know, my God, that You test the heart and that You are pleased with uprightness. I have willingly given all these things with an upright heart, and now I have seen Your people who are present here giving joyfully and willingly to You. ¹⁸ LORD God of Abraham, Isaac, and Israel, our ancestors, keep this desire forever in the thoughts of the hearts of Your people, and confirm their hearts toward You. ¹⁹ Give my son Solomon a whole heart to keep and to carry out all Your commandments, Your decrees, and Your statutes, and to build the temple for which I have made provision."

²⁰ Then David said to the whole assembly, "Praise the LORD your God." So the whole assembly praised the LORD God of their ancestors. They bowed

down and paid homage to the LORD and the king.

²¹ The following day they offered sacrifices to the LORD and burnt offerings to the LORD: 1,000 bulls, 1,000 rams, and 1,000 lambs, along with their drink offerings, and sacrifices in abundance for all Israel. ²² They ate and drank with great joy in the LORD's presence that day.

Then, for a second time, they made David's son Solomon king; they anointed him as the LORD's ruler, and Zadok as the priest. ²³ Solomon sat on the LORD's throne as king in place of his father David. He prospered, and all Israel obeyed him. ²⁴ All the leaders and the mighty men, and all of King David's sons as well, pledged their allegiance to King Solomon. ²⁵ The LORD highly exalted Solomon in the sight of all Israel and bestowed on him such royal majesty as had not been bestowed on any king over Israel before him.

²⁶ David son of Jesse was king over all Israel. ²⁷ The length of his reign over Israel was 40 years; he reigned in Hebron for seven years and in Jerusalem for 33. ²⁸ He died at a good old age, full of days, riches, and honor, and his son Solomon became king in his place. ²⁹ As for the events of King David's reign, from beginning to end, note that they are written about in the Events of Samuel the Seer, the Events of Nathan the Prophet, and the Events of Gad the Seer, ³⁰ along with all his reign, his might, and the incidents that affected him and Israel and all the kingdoms of the surrounding lands.

1 Solomon son of David strengthened his hold on his kingdom. The LORD his God was with him and highly exalted him. ² Then Solomon spoke to all Israel, to the commanders of thousands and of hundreds, to the judges, and to every leader in all Israel—the heads of the families. ³ Solomon and the whole assembly with him went to the high place that was in Gibeon because God's tent of meeting, which the LORD's servant Moses had made in the wilderness, was there. ⁴ Now, David had brought the ark of God from Kiriath-jearim to the place he had set up for it, because he had pitched a tent for it in Jerusalem, ⁵ but he put the bronze altar, which Bezalel son of Uri, son of Hur, had made, in front of the LORD's tabernacle. Solomon and the assembly inquired of Him there. ⁶ Solomon offered sacrifices there in the LORD's presence on the bronze altar at the tent of meeting; he offered 1,000 burnt offerings on it.

⁷ That night God appeared to Solomon and said to him: "Ask. What should I give you?"

⁸ And Solomon said to God: "You have shown great faithful love to my father David, and You have made me king in his place. ⁹ LORD God, let Your promise to my father David now come true. For You have made me king over a people as numerous as the dust of the earth. ¹⁰ Now, grant me wisdom and knowledge so that I may lead these people, for who can judge this great people of Yours?"

¹¹ God said to Solomon, "Because this was in your heart, and you have not requested riches, wealth, or glory, or for the life of those who hate you, and you have not even requested long life, but you have requested for yourself wisdom and knowledge that you may judge My people over whom I have made you king, ¹² wisdom and knowledge are given to you. I will also give you riches, wealth, and glory, such that it was not like this for the kings who were before you, nor will it be like this for those after you." ¹³ So Solomon went to Jerusalem from the high place that was in Gibeon in front of the tent of meeting, and he reigned over Israel.

¹⁴ Solomon accumulated 1,400 chariots and 12,000 horsemen, which he stationed in the chariot cities and with the king in Jerusalem. ¹⁵ The king made silver and gold as common in Jerusalem as stones, and he made cedar as abundant as sycamore in the Judean foothills. ¹⁶ Solomon's horses came from Egypt and Kue. The king's traders would get them from Kue at the going price. ¹⁷ A chariot could be imported from Egypt for 15 pounds of silver and a horse for

about four pounds. In the same way, they exported them to all the kings of the Hittites and to the kings of Aram through their agents.

PSALM 88:1-9

1 LORD, God of my salvation,
   I cry out before You day and
      night.
2 May my prayer reach Your
      presence;
   listen to my cry.

3 For I have had enough troubles,
   and my life is near Sheol.
4 I am counted among those going
      down to the Pit.
   I am like a man without strength,
5 abandoned among the dead.
   I am like the slain lying in the
      grave,
   whom You no longer remember,
   and who are cut off from Your
      care.

6 You have put me in the lowest
      part of the Pit,
   in the darkest places, in the
      depths.
7 Your wrath weighs heavily on me;
   You have overwhelmed me with
      all Your waves.   *Selah*
8 You have distanced my friends
      from me;
   You have made me repulsive to
      them.
   I am shut in and cannot go out.
9 My eyes are worn out from
      crying.
   LORD, I cry out to You all day long;
   I spread out my hands to You.

PROVERBS 18:18-19

18 Casting the lot ends quarrels
   and separates powerful
      opponents.

19 An offended brother is harder to
      reach than a fortified city,
   and quarrels are like the bars of a
      fortress.

ACTS 21:7-29

7 When we completed our voyage from Tyre, we reached Ptolemais, where we greeted the brothers and stayed with them one day. 8 The next day we left and came to Caesarea, where we entered the house of Philip the evangelist, who was one of the Seven, and stayed with him. 9 This man had four virgin daughters who prophesied.

10 While we were staying there many days, a prophet named Agabus came down from Judea. 11 He came to us, took Paul's belt, tied his own feet and hands, and said, "This is what the Holy Spirit says: 'In this way the Jews in Jerusalem will bind the man who owns this belt, and deliver him into Gentile hands.' " 12 When we heard this, both we and the local people begged him not to go up to Jerusalem.

13 Then Paul replied, "What are you doing, weeping and breaking my heart? For I am ready not only to be bound, but also to die in Jerusalem for the name of the Lord Jesus."

14 Since he would not be persuaded, we stopped talking and simply said, "The Lord's will be done!"

15 After these days we got ready and went up to Jerusalem. 16 Some of the disciples from Caesarea also went with us and brought us to Mnason, a Cypriot and an early disciple, with whom we were to stay.

17 When we reached Jerusalem, the brothers welcomed us gladly. 18 The following day Paul went in with us to James, and all the elders were present. 19 After greeting them, he related one by one what God did among the Gentiles through his ministry.

20 When they heard it, they glorified God and said, "You see, brother, how many thousands of Jews there are who have believed, and they are all zealous for the law. 21 But they have been told about you that you teach all the Jews who are among the Gentiles to abandon Moses, by telling them not to circumcise their children or to walk in our customs. 22 So what is to be done? They will

certainly hear that you've come. ²³ Therefore do what we tell you: We have four men who have obligated themselves with a vow. ²⁴ Take these men, purify yourself along with them, and pay for them to get their heads shaved. Then everyone will know that what they were told about you amounts to nothing, but that you yourself are also careful about observing the law. ²⁵ With regard to the Gentiles who have believed, we have written a letter containing our decision that they should keep themselves from food sacrificed to idols, from blood, from what is strangled, and from sexual immorality."

²⁶ Then the next day, Paul took the men, having purified himself along with them, and entered the temple, announcing the completion of the purification days when the offering for each of them would be made. ²⁷ As the seven days were about to end, the Jews from the province of Asia saw him in the temple complex, stirred up the whole crowd, and seized him, ²⁸ shouting, "Men of Israel, help! This is the man who teaches everyone everywhere against our people, our law, and this place. What's more, he also brought Greeks into the temple and has profaned this holy place." ²⁹ For they had previously seen Trophimus the Ephesian in the city with him, and they supposed that Paul had brought him into the temple complex.

Creativity Is Contagious

This man had four virgin daughters who prophesied.

—Acts 21:9

Philip's creative spirit heightened everything he touched. We find no evidence of spiritual staleness in his life. He was spiritually alert, spiritually alive, and spiritually creative.

Our text today tells us that he had four unmarried daughters who prophesied. We must not, of course, ignore the evident work of the Holy Spirit in the lives of these four women, but we must also recognize their father Philip's creative influence in their lives. We often say, "Like father, like son." Here it was a case of "Like father, like daughters." Creativity is contagious.

When you consider that the society in which these daughters were born and brought up was a male-dominated one, the statement that Philip had "four daughters who prophesied" comes as a surprise. What caused these unmarried women to break the mold in which they found themselves and exercise their prophetic gifts? Popular opinion at the time said that women should remain in the background and take no part in public ministry. It was the Holy Spirit, of course, who inspired them to prophesy, but I think I see some of the marks of Philip's creativity rubbing off on them also.

These young women did not stay at home and lament the fact that they were not married. If they could not be creative on a physical level, they could be creative on a spiritual level. Some of the greatest work in the kingdom of God has been done by the spiritual descendants of the daughters of Philip—single women who have had their creativity blocked on one level but have released it on another level.

Prayer

Father, I want to thank You today for the ministry of those in Your kingdom who, while remaining single, have produced great and creative achievements. We appreciate them, but as You have taught us, we give all the honor to You. Amen.

Further Study

1 Co 7; Mt 19:12
What does Jesus teach about singleness?
How did Paul reinforce this?

JULY 26

2 CHRONICLES 2:1–4:22

2 Solomon decided to build a temple for the name of the LORD and a royal palace for himself, ² so he assigned 70,000 men as porters, 80,000 men as stonecutters in the mountains, and 3,600 as supervisors over them.

³ Then Solomon sent word to King Hiram of Tyre:

Do for me what you did for my father David. You sent him cedars to build him a house to live in. ⁴ Now I myself am building a temple for the name of the LORD my God in order to dedicate it to Him for burning sweet incense before Him, for displaying the rows of the bread of the Presence continuously, and for sacrificing burnt offerings for the evening and the morning, the Sabbaths and the New Moons, and the appointed festivals of the LORD our God. This is ordained for Israel forever. ⁵ The temple that I am building will be great, for our God is greater than any of the gods. ⁶ But who is able to build a temple for Him, since even heaven and the highest heaven cannot contain Him? Who am I then that I should build a house for Him except as a place to burn incense before Him? ⁷ Therefore, send me a craftsman who is skilled in engraving to work with gold, silver, bronze, and iron, and with purple, crimson, and blue yarn. He will work with the craftsmen who are with me in Judah and Jerusalem, appointed by my father David. ⁸ Also, send me cedar, cypress, and algum logs from Lebanon, for I know that your servants know how to cut the trees of Lebanon. Note that my servants will be with your servants ⁹ to prepare logs for me in abundance because the temple I am building will be great and wonderful. ¹⁰ I will give your servants, the woodcutters who cut the trees, 100,000 bushels of wheat flour, 100,000 bushels of barley, 110,000 gallons of wine, and 110,000 gallons of oil.

¹¹ Then King Hiram of Tyre wrote a letter and sent it to Solomon:

Because the LORD loves His people,
He set you over them as king.

¹² Hiram also said:

May the LORD God of Israel, who
made the heavens and the earth, be
praised! He gave King David a wise
son with insight and understanding, who will build a temple for the
LORD and a royal palace for himself.
¹³ I have now sent Huram-abi, a
skillful man who has understanding. ¹⁴ He is the son of a woman
from the daughters of Dan. His father is a man of Tyre. He knows
how to work with gold, silver,
bronze, iron, stone, and wood, with
purple, blue, crimson yarn, and
fine linen. He knows how to do all
kinds of engraving and to execute
any design that may be given him. I
have sent him to be with your
craftsmen and the craftsmen of my
lord, your father David. ¹⁵ Now, let
my lord send the wheat, barley, oil,
and wine to his servants as promised. ¹⁶ We will cut logs from
Lebanon, as many as you need, and
bring them to you as rafts by sea to
Joppa. You can then take them up
to Jerusalem.

¹⁷ Solomon took a census of all the
foreign men in the land of Israel, after
the census that his father David had
conducted, and the total was 153,600.
¹⁸ Solomon made 70,000 of them porters, 80,000 stonecutters in the mountains, and 3,600 supervisors to make
the people work.

3 Then Solomon began to build the
LORD's temple in Jerusalem on
Mount Moriah where the LORD had appeared to his father David, at the site
David had prepared on the threshing
floor of Ornan the Jebusite. ² He began
to build on the second day of the second
month in the fourth year of his reign.
³ These are Solomon's foundations for
building God's temple: the length was
90 feet, and the width 30 feet. ⁴ The
portico, which was across the front

extending across the width of the temple, was 30 feet wide; its height was
30 feet; he overlaid its inner surface
with pure gold. ⁵ The larger room he
paneled with cypress wood, overlaid
with fine gold, and decorated with palm
trees and chains. ⁶ He adorned the temple with precious stones for beauty, and
the gold was the gold of Parvaim. ⁷ He
overlaid the temple—the beams, the
thresholds, its walls and doors—with
gold, and he carved cherubim on the
walls.

⁸ Then he made the most holy place;
its length corresponded to the width of
the temple, 30 feet, and its width was
30 feet. He overlaid it with 45,000
pounds of fine gold. ⁹ The weight of the
nails was 20 ounces of gold, and he
overlaid the ceiling with gold.

¹⁰ He made two cherubim of sculp-
tured work, for the most holy place, and
he overlaid them with gold. ¹¹ The overall length of the wings of the cherubim
was 30 feet: the wing of one was seven
and a half feet, touching the wall of the
room; its other wing was seven and a
half feet, touching the wing of the other
cherub. ¹² The wing of the other cherub
was seven and a half feet, touching the
wall of the room; its other wing was
seven and a half feet, reaching the wing
of the other cherub. ¹³ The wingspan of
these cherubim was 30 feet. They stood
on their feet and faced the larger room.

¹⁴ He made the veil of blue, purple,
and crimson yarn and fine linen, and he
wove cherubim into it.

¹⁵ In front of the temple he made two
pillars, each 27 feet high. The capital on
top of each was seven and half feet
high. ¹⁶ He had made chainwork in the
inner sanctuary and also put it on top of
the pillars. He made 100 pomegranates
and fastened them into the chainwork.
¹⁷ Then he set up the pillars in front of
the sanctuary, one on the right and one
on the left. He named the one on the
right Jachin and the one on the left
Boaz.

4 He made a bronze altar 30 feet long,
30 feet wide, and 15 feet high.
² Then he made the cast metal

reservoir, 15 feet from brim to brim, perfectly round. It was seven and a half feet high, and 45 feet in circumference. ³ The likeness of oxen was below it, completely encircling it, 10 every half yard, completely surrounding the reservoir. The oxen were cast in two rows when the reservoir was cast. ⁴ It stood on 12 oxen, three facing north, three facing west, three facing south, and three facing east. The reservoir was on top of them and all their hindquarters were toward the center. ⁵ The reservoir was three inches thick, and its rim was fashioned like the brim of a cup or a lily blossom. It could hold 11,000 gallons.

⁶ He made 10 basins for washing and he put five on the right and five on the left. The parts of the burnt offering were rinsed in them, but the reservoir was used by the priests for washing.

⁷ He made the 10 gold lampstands according to their specifications and put them in the sanctuary, five on the right and five on the left. ⁸ He made 10 tables and placed them in the sanctuary, five on the right and five on the left. He also made 100 gold bowls.

⁹ He made the courtyard of the priests and the large court, and doors for the court. He overlaid the doors with bronze. ¹⁰ He put the reservoir on the right side, toward the southeast. ¹¹ Then Huram made the pots, the shovels, and the bowls.

So Huram finished doing the work that he was doing for King Solomon in God's temple: ¹² two pillars; the bowls and the capitals on top of the two pillars; the two gratings for covering both bowls of the capitals that were on top of the pillars; ¹³ the 400 pomegranates for the two gratings (two rows of pomegranates for each grating covering both capitals' bowls on top of the pillars). ¹⁴ He also made the water carts and the basins on the water carts. ¹⁵ The one reservoir and the 12 oxen underneath it, ¹⁶ the pots, the shovels, the forks, and all their utensils—Huram-abi made them for King Solomon for the Lord's temple. All these were made of polished bronze. ¹⁷ The king had them cast in clay molds in the Jordan Valley between

Succoth and Zeredah. ¹⁸ Solomon made all these utensils in such great abundance that the weight of the bronze was not determined.

¹⁹ Solomon also made all the equipment in God's temple: the gold altar; the tables on which to put the bread of the Presence; ²⁰ the lampstands and their lamps of pure gold to burn in front of the inner sanctuary according to specifications; ²¹ the flowers, lamps, and gold tongs—of purest gold; ²² the wick trimmers, sprinkling basins, ladles, and firepans—of purest gold; and the entryway to the temple, its inner doors to the most holy place, and the doors of the temple sanctuary—of gold.

*P*SALM 88:10-18

10 Do You work wonders for the
dead?
Do departed spirits rise up to
praise You? *Selah*
11 Will Your faithful love be declared
in the grave,
Your faithfulness in Abaddon?
12 Will Your wonders be known in
the darkness,
or Your righteousness in the land
of oblivion?

13 But I call to You for help, Lord;
in the morning my prayer meets
You.
14 Lord, why do You reject me?
Why do You hide Your face from
me?
15 From my youth, I have been
afflicted and near death.
I suffer Your horrors; I am
desperate.
16 Your wrath sweeps over me;
Your terrors destroy me.
17 They surround me like water all
day long;
they close in on me from every
side.
18 You have distanced loved one and
neighbor from me;
darkness is my only friend.

PROVERBS 18:20-21

20 From the fruit of his mouth a
   man's stomach is satisfied;
   he is filled with the product of his
   lips.

21 Life and death are in the power of
   the tongue,
   and those who love it will eat its
   fruit.

....

ACTS 21:30–22:10

30 The whole city was stirred up, and
the people rushed together. They seized
Paul, dragged him out of the temple
complex, and at once the gates were
shut. 31 As they were trying to kill him,
word went up to the commander of the
regiment that all Jerusalem was in
chaos. 32 Taking along soldiers and centurions, he immediately ran down to
them. Seeing the commander and the
soldiers, they stopped beating Paul.
33 Then the commander came up, took
him into custody, and ordered him to be
bound with two chains. He asked who
he was and what he had done. 34 Some
in the mob were shouting one thing and
some another. Since he was not able to
get reliable information because of the
uproar, he ordered him to be taken into
the barracks. 35 When Paul got to the
steps, he had to be carried by the soldiers because of the mob's violence,
36 for the mass of people were following
and yelling, "Kill him!"
37 As he was about to be brought into
the barracks, Paul said to the commander,
"Am I allowed to say something to you?"
He replied, "Do you know Greek?
38 Aren't you the Egyptian who raised a
rebellion some time ago and led 4,000
Assassins into the desert?"

39 Paul said, "I am a Jewish man from
Tarsus of Cilicia, a citizen of an important city. Now I ask you, let me speak to
the people."
40 After he had given permission, Paul
stood on the steps and motioned with
his hand to the people. When there was
a great hush, he addressed them in the
22 Hebrew language: 1 "Brothers
and fathers, listen now to my defense before you." 2 When they heard
that he was addressing them in the
Hebrew language, they became even
quieter. 3 He continued, "I am a Jewish
man, born in Tarsus of Cilicia, but
brought up in this city at the feet of
Gamaliel, and educated according to
the strict view of our patriarchal law.
Being zealous for God, just as all of
you are today, 4 I persecuted this Way to
the death, binding and putting both
men and women in jail, 5 as both the
high priest and the whole council of
elders can testify about me. Having received letters from them to the brothers, I was traveling to Damascus to
bring those who were prisoners there to
be punished in Jerusalem.
6 "As I was traveling and near Damascus, about noon an intense light
from heaven suddenly flashed around
me. 7 I fell to the ground and heard a
voice saying to me, 'Saul, Saul, why are
you persecuting Me?'
8 "I answered, 'Who are You, Lord?'
"He said to me, 'I am Jesus the Nazarene, whom you are persecuting!' 9 Now
those who were with me saw the light,
but they did not hear the voice of the
One who was speaking to me.
10 "Then I said, 'What should I do,
Lord?'
"And the Lord told me, 'Get up and go
into Damascus, and there you will be
told about everything that is assigned
for you to do.'

Children of the Dawn

But I call to You for help, LORD; in the morning
my prayer meets You.—PSALM 88:13

Those who do not provide for a set-aside time during the day—preferably in the morning, when they can replenish their spiritual resources—may find that they have to provide a time at the end of the day for regret, for repentance, and for eating humble pie.

A traveler in the Himalayas told how he arose very early one morning to watch the sun rise on the towering peaks. He said: "There, as the day began to dawn, we saw arise before our enraptured gaze, within a complete semicircle, twenty peaks each above twenty thousand feet in height, snow-capped with virgin snow. For half an hour the curtain was lifted and we inwardly worshiped. Then the mists began to fill the valleys between, and the view was gone. Gone? No, not really—it was forever laid up in our green and grateful memories."

That is what a quiet time in the early part of the day does for you. Before the mists of worldly happenings blot out your view of God, you can take a time-exposure of Him which is indelibly imprinted on your mind. Then, after the mists close in, the vision is still there within. You live in two worlds at once—drawing physical strength from the world around you while drawing spiritual sustenance from the world above you.

Pascal, the great French philosopher and Christian, once said: "Nearly all the ills of life spring from this simple source: that we are not able to sit still in a room." But what if in the stillness, we were to meet with God? How healing that would be! We would arise with what Stevenson calls "happy morning faces." We would become children of the dawn.

Prayer

Heavenly Father, give me the wisdom to be able to take "the pause that refreshes," to drink every day from the living Fountain, the Eternal spring. In Jesus' name I pray. Amen.

Further Study

Lm 3:22-26; Ps 40:1; Is 26:8; 33:2
What was the psalmist's testimony?
What did the psalmist say he would do?

JULY 27

2 CHRONICLES 5:1–6:42

5 So all the work Solomon did for the LORD's temple was completed. Then Solomon brought the consecrated things of his father David—the silver, the gold, and all the utensils—and put them in the treasuries of God's temple.

² At that time Solomon assembled at Jerusalem the elders of Israel—all the tribal heads, the ancestral chiefs of the Israelites—in order to bring the ark of the covenant of the LORD up from the city of David, that is, Zion. ³ So all the men of Israel were assembled in the king's presence at the festival; this was in the seventh month.

⁴ All the elders of Israel came, and the Levites picked up the ark. ⁵ They brought up the ark, the tent of meeting, and the holy utensils that were in the tent. The priests and the Levites brought them up. ⁶ King Solomon and the entire congregation of Israel who had gathered around him were in front of the ark sacrificing sheep and cattle that could not be counted or numbered because there were so many. ⁷ The priests brought the ark of the LORD's covenant to its place, into the inner sanctuary of the temple, to the most holy place, beneath the wings of the cherubim. ⁸ And the cherubim spread their wings over the place of the ark so that the cherubim formed a cover above the ark and its poles. ⁹ The poles were so long that their ends were seen from the holy place in front of the inner sanctuary, but they were not seen from outside; they are there to this very day. ¹⁰ Nothing was in the ark except the two tablets that Moses had put in it at Horeb, where the LORD had made a covenant with the Israelites when they came out of Egypt.

¹¹ When the priests came out of the holy place—for all the priests who were present had consecrated themselves regardless of their tour of duty— ¹² the Levitical singers of Asaph, of Heman, of Jeduthun, and of their sons and their relatives, dressed in fine linen, with cymbals, harps and lyres, were standing east of the altar, and with them were 120 priests blowing trumpets. ¹³ The trumpeters and singers joined together to praise and thank the LORD with one voice. They raised their voices, accompanied by trumpets, cymbals, and musical instruments, in praise to the LORD:

> For He is good;
> His faithful love endures forever;

the temple, the LORD's temple, was filled with a cloud. ¹⁴ And because of the cloud, the priests were not able to continue ministering, for the glory of the LORD filled God's temple.

6 Then Solomon said:

> The LORD said He would dwell
>   in thick darkness,
> ² but I have built an exalted temple
>   for You,
> a place for Your residence forever.

³ Then the king turned and blessed the entire congregation of Israel while they were standing. ⁴ He said:

> May the LORD God of Israel
>   be praised!
> He spoke directly
>   to my father David,
> and He has fulfilled the promise
>   by His power.
> He said,
> ⁵ "Since the day I brought My people Israel
>   out of the land of Egypt,
> I have not chosen a city to build
>   a temple in

among any of the tribes of Israel,
so that My name would be there,
and I have not chosen a man
to be ruler over My people Israel.
6 But I have chosen Jerusalem
so that My name will be there,
and I have chosen David
to be over My people Israel."

7 Now it was in the heart of my
father David
to build a temple for the name
of the LORD God of Israel.
8 However, the LORD said
to my father David,
"Since it was your desire to build
a temple for My name,
you have done well to have
this desire.
9 Yet, you are not the one to build
the temple,
but your son,
your own offspring,
will build the temple
for My name."
10 So the LORD has fulfilled
what He promised.
I have taken the place
of my father David
and I sit on the throne of Israel,
as the LORD promised.
I have built the temple
for the name of the LORD God
of Israel.
11 I have put the ark there,
where the LORD's covenant is
that He made with the Israelites.

12 Then Solomon stood before the altar of the LORD in front of the entire congregation of Israel and spread out his hands. 13 For Solomon had made a bronze platform seven and a half feet long, seven and a half feet wide, and four and a half feet high and put it in the court. He stood on it, knelt down in front of the entire congregation of Israel, and spread out his hands toward heaven. 14 He said:

LORD God of Israel,
there is no God like You
in heaven or on earth,
keeping His gracious covenant

with Your servants who walk
before You
with their whole heart.
15 You have kept what You promised
to Your servant, my father David.
You spoke directly to him,
and You fulfilled Your promise
by Your power,
as it is today.
16 Therefore, LORD God of Israel,
keep what You promised
to Your servant, my father David:
You will never fail to have a man
to sit before Me on the throne
of Israel,
if only your sons guard their way
to walk in My Law
as you have walked before Me.
17 Now, LORD God of Israel,
please confirm
what You promised
to Your servant David.

18 But will God indeed live on earth
with man?
Even heaven, the highest heaven,
cannot contain You,
much less this temple I have built.
19 Listen to Your servant's prayer
and his petition,
LORD my God,
so that You may hear the cry
and the prayer
that Your servant prays
before You,
20 so that Your eyes watch over
this temple
day and night,
toward the place where You said
You would put Your name;
and so that You may hear
the prayer
Your servant prays
toward this place.
21 Hear the petitions of Your servant
and Your people Israel,
which they pray toward this place.
May You hear
in Your dwelling place
in heaven.
May You hear and forgive.

22 If a man sins against his neighbor
and is forced to take an oath

and he comes to take an oath
before Your altar in this temple,
²³ may You hear in heaven and act.
May You judge Your servants,
condemning the wicked
by bringing
what he has done on his own head
and providing justice
for the righteous
by rewarding him according to
his righteousness.

²⁴ If Your people Israel are defeated
before an enemy,
because they have sinned
against You,
and they return to You and praise
Your name,
and they pray and plead for mercy
before You in this temple,
²⁵ may You hear in heaven
and forgive the sin
of Your people Israel.
May You restore them to the land
You gave them
and their ancestors.

²⁶ When the skies are shut
and there is no rain
because they have sinned
against You,
and they pray toward this place
and praise Your name,
and they turn from their sins
because You are afflicting them,
²⁷ may You hear in heaven
and forgive the sin
of Your servants
and Your people Israel,
so that You may teach them
the good way
they should walk in. May You send
rain on Your land
that You gave Your people
for an inheritance.

²⁸ When there is famine
on the earth,
when there is pestilence,
when there is blight, mildew,
locust, or grasshopper,
when their enemies besiege them
in the region
of their fortified cities,

when there is any plague
or illness,
²⁹ whatever prayer or petition
anyone from your people Israel
might have—
each man knowing
his own affliction
and suffering,
and spreading out his hands
toward this temple—
³⁰ may You hear in heaven,
Your dwelling place,
and may You forgive
and repay the man
according to all his ways,
since You know his heart,
for You alone know
the human heart,
³¹ so that they may fear You
and walk in Your ways
all the days they live on the land
You gave our ancestors.

³² Even for the foreigner who is not
of Your people Israel
but has come from a distant land
because of Your great name
and Your mighty hand
and outstretched arm:
when he comes and prays
toward this temple,
³³ may You hear in heaven
in Your dwelling place,
and do all the foreigner
asks You for.
Then all the peoples of the earth
will know Your name,
to fear You
as Your people Israel do
and know that this temple
I have built
is called by Your name.

³⁴ When Your people go out to fight
against their enemies,
wherever You send them,
and they pray to You
in the direction of this city
You have chosen
and the temple that I have built
for Your name,
³⁵ may You hear their prayer
and petition in heaven
and uphold their cause.

36 When they sin against You—
for there is no one
who does not sin—
and You are angry with them
and hand them over to the enemy,
and their captors deport them
to a distant or nearby country,
37 and when they come
to their senses
in the land where they
were deported
and repent and petition You
in their captors' land,
saying: "We have sinned
and done wrong;
we have been wicked,"
38 and when they return to You
with their whole mind
and heart
in the land of their captivity
where they were taken captive,
and when they pray
in the direction of their land
that You gave their ancestors,
and the city You have chosen,
and toward the temple I have built
for Your name,
39 may You hear in heaven,
in Your dwelling place,
their prayer and petitions
and uphold their cause.
May You forgive Your people
who sinned against You.

40 Now, my God,
please let Your eyes be open
and Your ears attentive
to the prayer of this place.
41 Now therefore:

Arise, Lord God, come
to Your resting place,
You and the ark that shows
Your strength.
May Your priests, Lord God,
be clothed with salvation,
and may Your godly people rejoice
in goodness.
42 Lord God, do not reject
Your anointed one;
remember the loyalty
of Your servant David.

PSALM 89:1-10

1 I will sing about the Lord's
faithful love forever;
with my mouth I will proclaim
Your faithfulness to all
generations.
2 For I will declare, "Faithful love is
built up forever;
You establish Your faithfulness in
the heavens."

3 The Lord said, "I have made a
covenant with My chosen
one;
I have sworn an oath to David My
servant:
4 'I will establish your offspring
forever
and build up your throne for all
generations.' " *Selah*

5 Lord, the heavens praise Your
wonders—
Your faithfulness also—in the
assembly of the holy ones.
6 For who in the skies can compare
with the Lord?
Who among the heavenly beings is
like the Lord?
7 God is greatly feared in the
council of the holy ones,
more awe-inspiring than all who
surround Him.
8 Lord God of Hosts,
who is strong like You, Lord?
Your faithfulness surrounds You.
9 You rule the raging sea;
when its waves surge, You still
them.
10 You crushed Rahab like one who is
slain;
You scattered Your enemies with
Your powerful arm.

PROVERBS 18:22

22 A man who finds a wife finds a
good thing
and obtains favor from the
Lord.

$\mathcal{A}$CTS 22:11-30

¹¹ "Since I couldn't see because of the brightness of that light, I was led by the hand by those who were with me, and came into Damascus. ¹² Someone named Ananias, a devout man according to the law, having a good reputation with all the Jews residing there, ¹³ came to me, stood by me, and said, 'Brother Saul, regain your sight.' And in that very hour I looked up and saw him. ¹⁴ Then he said, 'The God of our fathers has appointed you to know His will, to see the Righteous One, and to hear the sound of His voice. ¹⁵ For you will be a witness for Him to all people of what you have seen and heard. ¹⁶ And now, why delay? Get up and be baptized, and wash away your sins by calling on His name.'

¹⁷ "After I came back to Jerusalem and was praying in the temple complex, I went into a visionary state ¹⁸ and saw Him telling me, 'Hurry and get out of Jerusalem quickly, because they will not accept your testimony about Me!'

¹⁹ "But I said, 'Lord, they know that in synagogue after synagogue I had those who believed in You imprisoned and beaten. ²⁰ And when the blood of Your witness Stephen was being shed, I myself was standing by and approving, and I guarded the clothes of those who killed him.'

²¹ "Then He said to me, 'Go, because I will send you far away to the Gentiles.' "

²² They listened to him up to this word. Then they raised their voices, shouting, "Wipe this person off the earth—it's a disgrace for him to live!"

²³ As they were yelling and flinging aside their robes and throwing dust into the air, ²⁴ the commander ordered him to be brought into the barracks, directing that he be examined with the scourge, so he could discover the reason they were shouting against him like this. ²⁵ As they stretched him out for the lash, Paul said to the centurion standing by, "Is it legal for you to scourge a man who is a Roman citizen and is uncondemned?"

²⁶ When the centurion heard this, he went and reported to the commander, saying, "What are you going to do? For this man is a Roman citizen."

²⁷ The commander came and said to him, "Tell me—are you a Roman citizen?"

"Yes," he said.

²⁸ The commander replied, "I bought this citizenship for a large amount of money."

"But I myself was born a citizen," Paul said.

²⁹ Therefore, those who were about to examine him withdrew from him at once. The commander too was alarmed when he realized Paul was a Roman citizen and he had bound him.

³⁰ The next day, since he wanted to find out exactly why Paul was being accused by the Jews, he released him and instructed the chief priests and all the Sanhedrin to convene. Then he brought Paul down and placed him before them.

Our Trustworthy God

I will sing about the LORD's faithful love forever; with my mouth I will proclaim Your faithfulness to all generations.—PSALM 89:1

God is utterly trustworthy in all He says and does, and this is the rock-bottom reality on which everything in the universe depends. In an age when so much unfaithfulness abounds, how good it is to realize that we have One who will never let us down, never have to apologize for failing us, and never go back on His Word.

Am I speaking to someone who has just discovered unfaithfulness in a marriage partner, or experienced the break-up of a relationship because a person you trusted did not keep their word? It's a sad moment when we get a revelation of the inconsistency of the human heart. But we need to look into our own hearts also, for none of us can claim complete immunity to the sin of unfaithfulness. We may not have broken a contract or violated the marriage covenant, but we have been unfaithful to Christ in other ways—to the light and privileges that God has entrusted to us, perhaps.

How refreshing it is, then, to read today's text and focus our gaze on the One who is faithful at all times and in all things. We may let Him down, but He will never let us down.

A chorus I learned as a young Christian comes back to me when I am tempted to doubt the faithfulness of God:

> He cannot fail for He is God,
> He cannot fail, He pledged His Word,
> He cannot fail, He'll see you through,
> He cannot fail, He'll answer you.

Prayer

Gracious and loving God, what inspiration it brings to my soul to realize that of all the things You can do, the one thing You can't do is fail. May the reality of this be the pavement on which I tread this day and every day. In Jesus' name. Amen.

Further Study

Dt 7:9; 1 Kg 8:54-61; Ps 89:1-8
What did Solomon testify?
What did the psalmist promise to do?

JULY 28

2 CHRONICLES 7:1–8:18

7 When Solomon finished praying, fire descended from heaven and consumed the burnt offering and the sacrifices, and the glory of the LORD filled the temple. ² The priests were not able to enter the LORD's temple because the glory of the LORD filled the temple of the LORD. ³ All the Israelites were watching when the fire descended and

the glory of the LORD came on the temple. They bowed down with their faces to the ground on the pavement. They worshiped and praised the LORD:

> For He is good,
> for His faithful love
> endures forever.

⁴ The king and all the people were offering sacrifices in the LORD's presence. ⁵ King Solomon offered a sacrifice of

22,000 cattle and 120,000 sheep. In this manner the king and all the people dedicated God's temple. ⁶ The priests were standing at their stations, as were the Levites with the musical instruments of the LORD, which King David had made to praise the LORD—"for His faithful love endures forever"—when David offered praise with them. Across from them, the priests were blowing trumpets, and all the people were standing. ⁷ Solomon consecrated the middle of the courtyard that was in front of the LORD's temple because that was where he offered the burnt offerings and the fat of the fellowship offerings since the bronze altar that Solomon had made could not accommodate the burnt offering, the grain offering, and the fat of the fellowship offerings.

⁸ So Solomon and all Israel with him—a very great assembly, from the entrance to Hamath to the Brook of Egypt—observed the festival at that time for seven days. ⁹ On the eighth day they held a sacred assembly, for the dedication of the altar lasted seven days and the festival seven days. ¹⁰ On the twenty-third day of the seventh month he sent the people away to their tents, rejoicing and with happy hearts for the goodness the LORD had done for David, for Solomon, and for His people Israel.

¹¹ So Solomon finished the LORD's temple and the royal palace. Everything that had entered Solomon's heart to do for the LORD's temple and for his own palace succeeded. ¹² Then the LORD appeared to Solomon at night and said to him:

I have heard your prayer and have chosen this place for Myself as a temple of sacrifice. ¹³ If I close the sky so there is no rain, or if I command the grasshopper to consume the land, or if I send pestilence on My people, ¹⁴ and My people who are called by My name humble themselves, pray and seek My face, and turn from their evil ways, then I will hear from heaven, forgive their sin, and heal their land. ¹⁵ My eyes will now be open and My ears

attentive to prayer from this place. ¹⁶ And I have now chosen and consecrated this temple so that My name may be there forever; My eyes and My heart will be there at all times.

¹⁷ As for you, if you walk before Me as your father David walked, doing everything I have commanded you, and if you keep My statutes and ordinances, ¹⁸ I will establish your royal throne, as I promised your father David: You will never fail to have a man on the throne of Israel.

¹⁹ However, if you turn away and abandon My statutes and My commands that I have set before you and if you go and serve other gods and worship them, ²⁰ then I will uproot Israel from the soil that I gave them, and this temple that I have sanctified for My name I will banish from My presence; I will make it an object of scorn and ridicule among all the peoples. ²¹ As for this temple, which was exalted, every passerby will be appalled and will say: Why did the LORD do this to this land and this temple? ²² Then they will say: Because they abandoned the LORD God of their ancestors who brought them out of the land of Egypt. They clung to other gods and worshiped and served them. Because of this, He brought all this ruin on them.

8 At the end of 20 years during which Solomon had built the LORD's temple and his own palace— ² Solomon having rebuilt the cities Hiram gave him and having settled the Israelites there— ³ Solomon went to Hamath-zobah and seized it. ⁴ He built Tadmor in the wilderness along with all the storage cities that he built in Hamath. ⁵ He built Upper Beth-horon and Lower Beth-horon—fortified cities with walls, gates, and bars— ⁶ Baalath, all the storage cities that belonged to Solomon, all the chariot cities, the cavalry cities, and everything Solomon desired to build in

Jerusalem, Lebanon, or anywhere else in the land of his dominion.

⁷ As for all the peoples who remained of the Hittites, Amorites, Perizzites, Hivites, and Jebusites, who were not from Israel— ⁸ their descendants who remained in the land after them, those whom the Israelites had not completely destroyed—Solomon imposed forced labor on them; it is this way today. ⁹ But Solomon did not consign the Israelites to be slaves for his work; they were soldiers, commanders of his captains, and commanders of his chariots and his cavalry. ¹⁰ These were King Solomon's deputies: 250 who ruled over the people.

¹¹ Solomon brought the daughter of Pharaoh from the city of David to the house he had built for her, for he said, "My wife must not live in the house of David king of Israel because the places to which the ark of the LORD has come are holy."

¹² At that time Solomon offered burnt offerings to the LORD on the LORD's altar he had made in front of the vestibule ¹³ following the daily requirement for offerings according to the commandment of Moses for Sabbaths, New Moons, and the three annual appointed festivals: the Festival of Unleavened Bread, the Festival of Weeks, and the Festival of Booths. ¹⁴ According to the ordinances of his father David, he appointed the divisions of the priests over their service, of the Levites over their responsibilities to offer praise and to minister before the priests following the daily requirement, and of the gatekeepers by their divisions with respect to each gate, for this had been the command of David, the man of God. ¹⁵ They did not turn aside from the king's command regarding the priests and the Levites concerning any matter or concerning the treasuries. ¹⁶ All of Solomon's work was carried out from the day the foundation was laid for the LORD's temple until it was finished. So the LORD's temple was completed.

¹⁷ At that time Solomon went to Ezion-geber and to Eloth on the seashore in the land of Edom. ¹⁸ So through his servants, Hiram sent him ships with crews of experienced seamen. They went with Solomon's servants to Ophir, took from there 17 tons of gold, and delivered it to King Solomon.

PSALM 89:11-18

¹¹ The heavens are Yours; the earth
    also is Yours.
The world and everything in it—
    You founded them.
¹² North and south—You created
    them.
Tabor and Hermon shout for joy at
    Your name.
¹³ You have a mighty arm;
Your hand is powerful; Your right
    hand is lifted high.
¹⁴ Righteousness and justice are the
    foundation of Your throne;
faithful love and truth go before
    You.
¹⁵ Happy are the people who know
    the joyful shout;
LORD, they walk in the light of
    Your presence.
¹⁶ They rejoice in Your name all day
    long,
and they are exalted by Your
    righteousness.
¹⁷ For You are their magnificent
    strength;
by Your favor our horn is exalted.
¹⁸ Surely our shield belongs to the
    LORD,
our king to the Holy One of Israel.

PROVERBS 18:23-24

²³ The poor man pleads,
    but the rich one answers roughly.

²⁴ A man with many friends may be
    harmed,
but there is a friend who stays
    closer than a brother.

ACTS 23:1-22

23 ¹ Paul looked intently at the Sanhedrin and said, "Brothers, I have lived my life before God in all good conscience until this day." ² But the high priest Ananias ordered those who were standing next to him to strike him on the mouth. ³ Then Paul said to him, "God is going to strike you, you whitewashed wall! You are sitting there judging me according to the law, and in violation of the law are you ordering me to be struck?"

⁴ And those standing nearby said, "Do you dare revile God's high priest?"

⁵ "I did not know, brothers," Paul said, "that it was the high priest. For it is written, **You must not speak evil of a ruler of your people.**" ⁶ When Paul realized that one part of them were Sadducees and the other part were Pharisees, he cried out in the Sanhedrin, "Brothers, I am a Pharisee, a son of Pharisees! I am being judged because of the hope of the resurrection of the dead!" ⁷ When he said this, a dispute broke out between the Pharisees and the Sadducees, and the assembly was divided. ⁸ For the Sadducees say there is no resurrection, and no angel or spirit, but the Pharisees affirm them all.

⁹ The shouting grew loud, and some of the scribes of the Pharisees' party got up and argued vehemently: "We find nothing evil in this man. What if a spirit or an angel has spoken to him?" ¹⁰ When the dispute became violent, the commander feared that Paul might be torn apart by them and ordered the troops to go down, rescue him from them, and bring him into the barracks.

¹¹ The following night, the Lord stood by him and said, "Have courage! For as you have testified about Me in Jerusalem, so you must also testify in Rome."

¹² When it was day, the Jews formed a conspiracy and bound themselves under a curse: neither to eat nor to drink until they had killed Paul. ¹³ There were more than 40 who had formed this plot. ¹⁴ These men went to the chief priests and elders and said, "We have bound ourselves under a solemn curse that we won't eat anything until we have killed Paul. ¹⁵ So now you, along with the Sanhedrin, make a request to the commander that he bring him down to you as if you were going to investigate his case more thoroughly. However, before he gets near, we are ready to kill him."

¹⁶ But the son of Paul's sister, hearing about their ambush, came and entered the barracks and reported it to Paul. ¹⁷ Then Paul called one of the centurions and said, "Take this young man to the commander, because he has something to report to him."

¹⁸ So he took him, brought him to the commander, and said, "The prisoner Paul called me and asked me to bring this young man to you, because he has something to tell you."

¹⁹ Then the commander took him by the hand, led him aside, and inquired privately, "What is it you have to report to me?"

²⁰ "The Jews," he said, "have agreed to ask you to bring Paul down to the Sanhedrin tomorrow, as though they are going to hold a somewhat more careful inquiry about him. ²¹ Don't let them persuade you, because there are more than 40 of them arranging to ambush him, men who have bound themselves under a curse not to eat or drink until they kill him. Now they are ready, waiting for a commitment from you."

²² So the commander dismissed the young man and instructed him, "Don't tell anyone that you have informed me about this."

The Word That Irritates

[If] my people . . . humble themselves . . . and turn from their evil ways, then I will . . . forgive their sin, and heal their land.—2 CHRONICLES 7:14

Most Christians never allow themselves to come too close to the deep thirst for God that exists at the core of their being, for if they did, they would be compelled to get in touch with their basic helplessness.

Why would we want to deny this? Because to recognize our helplessness puts us in a position where we have to repent of it—and that is something our fallen human nature pulls back from doing. Believe me, the one word that grates and irritates our carnal nature is the word "repent." It is much easier to be given advice like: "Read more of the Bible every day," "Add extra minutes to your prayer time," or "Seize more opportunities to share your faith," than to be told to repent. All these things I have just mentioned may be excellent in themselves, but more is required if we are to get in touch with our deep thirst for God.

We must repent!

But repent of what? Our stubborn commitment to independence, as well as the awful desire and practice of choosing to dig our own wells.

A passionate pursuit of God demands this. Believe me, no matter what we say with our lips, we will never begin to pant after God until we repent of the self-sufficiency that has made its home deep within our hearts. This, in my opinion, is the biggest single step we can take in our pursuit of God and the experience of having feet like "hinds' feet."

Prayer

Gracious and loving heavenly Father, help me to repent deeply. May I know at this moment a turning from self-dependence to God-dependence. I give You my willingness—now give me Your power. In Jesus' name I ask it. Amen.

Further Study

Ps 34:1-18; Jl 2:12; Lk 13:1-3
What was the central message of Jesus?
How does the psalmist express it?

JULY 29

2 CHRONICLES
9:1–10:19

9 The queen of Sheba heard of Solomon's fame, so she came to test Solomon with difficult questions at Jerusalem with a very large retinue, with camels bearing spices, gold in abundance, and precious stones. She came to Solomon and spoke with him about everything that was on her mind. ² So Solomon answered all her questions; nothing was too difficult for Solomon to explain to her. ³ When the queen of Sheba observed Solomon's wisdom, the palace he had built, ⁴ the food at his table, his servants' residence, his attendants' service and their attire, his cupbearers and their attire, and the burnt offerings he offered at the LORD's temple, it took her breath away.

⁵ She said to the king, "The report I heard in my own country about your words and about your wisdom is true. ⁶ But I didn't believe their reports until I came and saw with my own eyes. Indeed, I was not even told half of your great wisdom! You far exceed the report I heard. ⁷ How happy are your men. How happy are these servants of yours, who always stand in your presence hearing your wisdom. ⁸ May the LORD your God be praised! He delighted in you and put you on his throne as king for the LORD your God. Because Your God loved Israel enough to establish them forever, He has set you over them as king to carry out justice and righteousness."

⁹ Then she gave the king four and a half tons of gold, a great quantity of spices, and precious stones. There never were such spices as those the queen of Sheba gave to King Solomon. ¹⁰ In addition, Hiram's servants and Solomon's servants who brought gold from Ophir also brought algum wood and precious stones. ¹¹ The king made the algum wood into walkways for the LORD's temple and for the king's palace and into harps and lyres for the singers. Never before had anything like them been seen in the land of Judah.

¹² King Solomon gave the queen of Sheba her every desire, whatever she asked—far more than she had brought the king. Then she, along with her servants, returned to her own country.

¹³ The weight of gold that came to Solomon annually was 25 tons, ¹⁴ besides what was brought by the merchants and traders. All the Arabian kings and governors of the land also brought gold and silver to Solomon.

¹⁵ King Solomon made 200 large shields of hammered gold; 15 pounds of hammered gold went into each shield. ¹⁶ He made 300 small shields of hammered gold; about eight pounds of gold went into each shield. The king put them in the House of the Forest of Lebanon.

¹⁷ The king also made a large ivory throne and overlaid it with pure gold. ¹⁸ The throne had six steps; there was a footstool covered in gold for the throne, armrests on either side of the seat, and two lions standing beside the armrests. ¹⁹ Twelve lions were standing there on the six steps, one at each end. Nothing like it had ever been made in any other kingdom.

²⁰ All of King Solomon's drinking cups were gold, and all the utensils of the House of the Forest of Lebanon were pure gold. There was no silver, since it was considered as nothing in Solomon's time, ²¹ for the king's ships kept going to Tarshish with Hiram's servants, and once every three years the ships of Tarshish would arrive bearing gold, silver, ivory, apes, and peacocks.

²² King Solomon surpassed all the kings of the world in riches and wisdom. ²³ All the kings of the world wanted an audience with Solomon to hear the wisdom God had put in his heart. ²⁴ Each of them would bring his own gift—items of silver and gold, clothing, weapons, spices, and horses and mules—as an annual tribute. ²⁵ Solomon had 4,000 stalls for horses and chariots, and 12,000 horsemen. He stationed them in the chariot cities and with the king in Jerusalem. ²⁶ He ruled over all the kings from the Euphrates River to the land of the Philistines and as far as the border of Egypt. ²⁷ The king made silver as common in Jerusalem as stones, and he made cedar as abundant as sycamore in the Judean foothills. ²⁸ They were bringing horses for Solomon from Egypt and from all the countries.

²⁹ The remaining events of Solomon's reign, from beginning to end, are written about in the Events of Nathan the Prophet, the Prophecy of Ahijah the Shilonite, and the Visions of Iddo the Seer concerning Jeroboam son of Nebat. ³⁰ Solomon reigned in Jerusalem over all Israel for 40 years. ³¹ Solomon rested with his fathers and was buried in the city of his father David. His son Rehoboam became king in his place.

10 Then Rehoboam went to Shechem, for all Israel had gone to Shechem to make him king. ² When Jeroboam son of Nebat heard about it—for he was in Egypt where he had fled from King Solomon's presence—Jeroboam returned from Egypt. ³ So they summoned him. Then Jeroboam and all Israel came and spoke to Rehoboam: ⁴ "Your father made our yoke harsh. Therefore, lighten your father's harsh service and the heavy yoke he put on us, and we will serve you."

⁵ Rehoboam replied, "Return to me in three days." So the people left.

⁶ Then King Rehoboam consulted with the elders who had served his father Solomon when he was alive, asking, "How do you advise me to respond to this people?"

⁷ They replied, "If you will be kind to these people and please them by speaking kind words to them, they will be your servants forever."

⁸ But he rejected the advice of the elders who had advised him and consulted with the young men who had grown up with him, the ones serving him. ⁹ He asked them, "What message do you advise we send back to this people who said to me, 'Lighten the yoke your father put on us'?"

¹⁰ Then the young men who had grown up with him told him, "This is what you should say to the people who said to you, 'Your father made our yoke heavy, but you, make it lighter on us!' This is what you should say to them: 'My little finger is thicker than my father's loins. ¹¹ Now therefore, my father burdened you with a heavy yoke, but I will add to your yoke; my father disciplined you with whips, but I, with barbed whips.' "

¹² So Jeroboam and all the people came to Rehoboam on the third day, just as the king had ordered, saying, "Return to me on the third day." ¹³ Then the king answered them harshly. King Rehoboam rejected the elders' advice ¹⁴ and spoke to them according to the young men's advice, saying, "My father made your yoke heavy, but I will add to it; my father disciplined you with whips, but I, with barbed whips."

¹⁵ The king did not listen to the people because the turn of events came from God, in order that the LORD might carry out His word that He had spoken through Ahijah the Shilonite to Jeroboam son of Nebat.

¹⁶ When all Israel saw that the king had not listened to them, the people answered the king:

> What portion do we have in David?
> We have no inheritance in the son
> of Jesse.
> Israel, each man to your tent;
> David, look after
> your own house now!

So all Israel went to their tents. ¹⁷ But as for the Israelites living in the cities of

Judah, Rehoboam reigned over them. [18] Then King Rehoboam sent Hadoram, who was in charge of the forced labor, but the Israelites stoned him to death. However, King Rehoboam managed to get up into the chariot to flee to Jerusalem. [19] Israel is in rebellion against the house of David until today.

PSALM 89:19-29

[19] You once spoke in a vision to Your
loyal ones and said:
"I have granted help to a warrior;
I have exalted one chosen from
the people.
[20] I have found David My servant;
I have anointed him with My
sacred oil.
[21] My hand will always be with him,
and My arm will strengthen him.
[22] The enemy will not afflict him;
no wicked man will oppress him.
[23] I will crush his foes before him
and strike those who hate him.
[24] My faithfulness and love will be
with him,
and through My name his horn
will be exalted.
[25] I will extend his power to the sea
and his right hand to the rivers.
[26] He will call to Me, 'You are my
Father,
my God, the rock of my salvation.'
[27] I will also make him My firstborn,
greatest of the kings of the earth.
[28] I will always preserve My faithful
love for him,
and My covenant with him will
endure.
[29] I will establish his line forever,
his throne as long as heaven lasts.

PROVERBS 19:1-3

19 Better a poor man who walks
in integrity
than someone who has deceitful
lips and is a fool.

[2] Even zeal is not good without
knowledge,
and the one who acts hastily sins.

[3] A man's own foolishness leads
him astray,
yet his heart rages against the
LORD.

ACTS 23:23–24:9

[23] He summoned two of his centurions and said, "Get 200 soldiers ready with 70 cavalry and 200 spearmen to go to Caesarea at nine tonight. [24] Also provide mounts so they can put Paul on them and bring him safely to Felix the governor." [25] He wrote a letter of this kind:

[26] Claudius Lysias,
To the most excellent governor
Felix:
Greetings.
[27] When this man had been seized by the Jews and was about to be killed by them, I arrived with my troops and rescued him because I learned that he is a Roman citizen. [28] Wanting to know the charge for which they were accusing him, I brought him down before their Sanhedrin. [29] I found out that the accusations were about disputed matters in their law, and that there was no charge that merited death or chains. [30] When I was informed that there was a plot against the man, I sent him to you right away. I also ordered his accusers to state their case against him in your presence.

[31] Therefore, during the night, the soldiers took Paul and brought him to Antipatris as they were ordered. [32] The next day, they returned to the barracks, allowing the cavalry to go on with him. [33] When these men entered Caesarea and delivered the letter to the governor, they also presented Paul to him. [34] After he read it, he asked what province he was from. So when he learned he was from Cilicia, [35] he said, "I will give you a hearing whenever your accusers get here too." And he ordered that he be kept under guard in Herod's palace.

24 After five days Ananias the high priest came down with some elders and a lawyer named Tertullus. These men presented their case against Paul to the governor. ² When he was called in, Tertullus began to accuse him and said: "Since we enjoy great peace because of you, and reforms are taking place for the benefit of this nation by your foresight, ³ we gratefully receive them always and in all places, most excellent Felix, with all thankfulness. ⁴ However, so that I will not burden you any further, I beg you in your graciousness to give us a brief hearing.

⁵ For we have found this man to be a plague, an agitator among all the Jews throughout the Roman world, and a ringleader of the sect of the Nazarenes! ⁶ He even tried to desecrate the temple, so we apprehended him [and wanted to judge him according to our law. ⁷ But Lysias the commander came and took him from our hands, commanding his accusers to come to you.] ⁸ By examining him yourself you will be able to discern all these things of which we accuse him." ⁹ The Jews also joined in the attack, alleging that these things were so.

Satan—Angel of Light

My faithfulness and love will be with him.

—PSALM 89:24

A feeling that the Devil delights to arouse in an unguarded heart is the feeling that God does not love us. He usually times his attack to coincide with those moments when everything is going wrong and we are beset by all kinds of difficulties. Then he whispers in our ear: "Do you still believe that God is love?"

When you respond by saying that you do, he transforms himself into an angel of light and tries another of his deceitful tactics. "Well," he says, "it is obvious that He does not love you, for if He did, then He would not allow you to go through these difficult situations."

There is only one protection against such an assault; it is to put firmly in place the "armor of righteousness." Nothing else will avail at this point. You must point him to the truth of Romans 8:28—"We know that all things work together for the good of those who love God." Paul does not say "we understand," but "we know."

This brings you directly to the theme of justification by faith, which is in fact the righteousness of Christ. You rest on this established truth, and that is all you need. You must say to yourself: "He would never have clothed me with His righteousness if He had not also set His love upon me and saved me. I will have courage. I do not know what is happening to me now. I cannot fathom it. But if He has begun His work in me, then I know He will go on to complete it."

Prayer

O God, what wondrous power there is in Your Word. I can feel it doing me good even as I read and ponder it. Give me a greater knowledge of Your Word, for only through its truth can I maintain an advantage over the Devil. Amen.

Further Study

Jr 31:1-3; Eph 2:1-7; 3:16-19; Php 1:6; Rm 5:8
How has God demonstrated His love?
What was Paul's desire for the Ephesians?

JULY 30

2 CHRONICLES
11:1–13:22

11 When Rehoboam arrived in Jerusalem, he mobilized the house of Judah and Benjamin—180,000 choice warriors—to fight against Israel to restore the reign to Rehoboam. ² But the word of the LORD came to Shemaiah, the man of God: ³ "Say to Rehoboam son of Solomon, king of Judah, to all Israel in Judah and Benjamin, and to the rest of the people: ⁴ 'This is what the LORD says: You are not to march up and fight against your brothers. Each of you must return home, for this incident has come from Me.'"

So they listened to what the LORD said and turned back from going against Jeroboam.

⁵ Rehoboam stayed in Jerusalem, and he fortified cities in Judah. ⁶ He built up Bethlehem, Etam, Tekoa, ⁷ Beth-zur, Soco, Adullam, ⁸ Gath, Mareshah, Ziph, ⁹ Adoraim, Lachish, Azekah, ¹⁰ Zorah, Aijalon, and Hebron, which are fortified cities in Judah and in Benjamin. ¹¹ He strengthened their fortifications and put leaders in them with supplies of food, oil, and wine. ¹² He also put large shields and spears in each and every city to make them very strong. So Judah and Benjamin were his.

¹³ The priests and Levites from all their regions throughout Israel took their stand with Rehoboam, ¹⁴ for the Levites left their pasturelands and their possessions and went to Judah and Jerusalem, because Jeroboam and his sons refused to let them serve as priests of the LORD. ¹⁵ Jeroboam appointed his own priests for the high places, the goat-demons, and the gold calves he had made. ¹⁶ Those from every tribe of Israel who had determined in their hearts to seek the LORD their God followed the Levites to Jerusalem to sacrifice to the LORD God of their ancestors. ¹⁷ So they strengthened the kingdom of Judah and supported Rehoboam son of Solomon for three years, because they walked in the way of David and Solomon for three years.

¹⁸ Rehoboam married Mahalath, daughter of David's son Jerimoth and of Abihail daughter of Jesse's son Eliab. ¹⁹ She bore him sons: Jeush, Shemariah, and Zaham. ²⁰ After her, he married Maacah daughter of Absalom. She bore him Abijah, Attai, Ziza, and Shelomith. ²¹ Rehoboam loved Maacah daughter of Absalom more than all his wives and concubines. He acquired 18 wives and 60 concubines and was the father of 28 sons and 60 daughters.

²² Rehoboam appointed Abijah son of Maacah as chief, leader among his brothers, intending to make him king. ²³ Rehoboam also showed discernment by dispersing some of his sons to all the regions of Judah and Benjamin and to all the fortified cities. He gave them plenty of provisions and sought many wives for them.

12 When Rehoboam had established his sovereignty and royal power, he abandoned the law of the LORD—he and all Israel with him. ² Because they were unfaithful to the LORD, in the fifth year of King Rehoboam, Shishak king of Egypt went to war against Jerusalem ³ with 1,200 chariots, 60,000 cavalrymen, and countless people who came with him from Egypt—Libyans, Sukkiim, and Ethiopians. ⁴ He captured the fortified cities of Judah and came as far as Jerusalem.

⁵ Then Shemaiah the prophet went to Rehoboam and the leaders of Judah who were gathered at Jerusalem because of Shishak. He said to them: "This is what the LORD says: 'You have abandoned Me; therefore, I have abandoned you into the hand of Shishak.' "

⁶ So the leaders of Israel and the king humbled themselves and said, "The LORD is righteous."

⁷ When the LORD saw that they had humbled themselves, the LORD's message came to Shemaiah: "They have humbled themselves; I will not destroy them but will grant them a little deliverance. My wrath will not be poured out on Jerusalem through Shishak. ⁸ However, they will become his servants so that they may recognize the difference between serving Me and serving the kingdoms of the land."

⁹ So King Shishak of Egypt went to war against Jerusalem. He seized the treasuries of the LORD's temple and the treasuries of the royal palace. He took everything. He took the gold shields that Solomon had made. ¹⁰ King Rehoboam made bronze shields in their place and committed them into the care of the captains of the royal escorts who guarded the entrance to the king's palace. ¹¹ Whenever the king entered the LORD's temple, the royal escorts would carry the shields and take them back to the royal escorts' armory. ¹² When Rehoboam humbled himself, the LORD's anger turned away from him, and He did not destroy him completely. Besides that, conditions were good in Judah.

¹³ King Rehoboam established his royal power in Jerusalem. Rehoboam was 41 years old when he became king; he reigned 17 years in Jerusalem, the city the LORD had chosen from all the tribes of Israel to put His name. Rehoboam's mother's name was Naamah the Ammonite. ¹⁴ Rehoboam did what was evil, because he did not determine in his heart to seek the LORD.

¹⁵ The events of Rehoboam's reign, from beginning to end, are written about in the Events of Shemaiah the Prophet and of Iddo the Seer concerning genealogies. There was war between Rehoboam and Jeroboam throughout their reigns. ¹⁶ Rehoboam rested with his fathers and was buried in the city of David. His son Abijah became king in his place.

13 In the eighteenth year of Israel's King Jeroboam, Abijah became king over Judah; ² he reigned three years in Jerusalem. His mother's name was Micaiah daughter of Uriel; she was from Gibeah.

There was war between Abijah and Jeroboam. ³ Abijah set his army of warriors in order with 400,000 choice men. Jeroboam arranged his mighty army of 800,000 choice men in battle formation against him. ⁴ Then Abijah stood on Mount Zemaraim, which is in the hill country of Ephraim, and said, "Jeroboam and all Israel, hear me. ⁵ Don't you know that the LORD God of Israel gave the kingship over Israel to David and his descendants forever by a covenant of salt? ⁶ But Jeroboam son of Nebat, a servant of Solomon son of David, rose up and rebelled against his lord. ⁷ Then worthless and wicked men gathered around him to resist Rehoboam son of Solomon when Rehoboam was young, inexperienced, and unable to assert himself against them.

⁸ "And now you are saying you can assert yourselves against the LORD's kingdom in the hand of one of David's sons. You are a vast multitude and have with you the golden calves that Jeroboam made for you as gods. ⁹ Didn't you banish the priests of the LORD, the descendants of Aaron and the Levites, and

make your own priests like the peoples of other lands do? Whoever comes to ordain himself with a young bull and seven rams may become a priest of what are not gods. ¹⁰ "But as for us, the LORD is our God. We have not abandoned Him; the priests ministering to the LORD are descendants of Aaron, and the Levites serve at their tasks. ¹¹ They offer a burnt offering and fragrant incense to the LORD every morning and every evening, and they set the rows of the bread of the Presence on the ceremonially clean table. They light the lamps of the gold lampstand every evening. We are carrying out the requirements of the LORD our God, while you have abandoned Him. ¹² Look, God and His priests are with us at our head. The trumpets are ready to sound the charge against you. Israelites, don't fight against the LORD God of your ancestors, for you will not succeed."

¹³ Now Jeroboam had sent an ambush around to advance from behind them. So they were in front of Judah, and the ambush was behind them. ¹⁴ Judah turned and discovered that the battle was in front of them and behind them, so they cried out to the LORD. Then the priests blew the trumpets, ¹⁵ and the men of Judah raised the battle cry. When the men of Judah raised the battle cry, God routed Jeroboam and all Israel before Abijah and Judah. ¹⁶ So the Israelites fled before Judah, and God handed them over to them. ¹⁷ Then Abijah and his people struck them with a mighty blow, and 500,000 choice men of Israel were killed. ¹⁸ The Israelites were subdued at that time. The Judahites succeeded because they depended on the LORD, the God of their ancestors. ¹⁹ Abijah pursued Jeroboam and captured some cities from him: Bethel and its villages, Jeshanah and its villages, and Ephron and its villages. ²⁰ Jeroboam no longer retained his power during Abijah's reign; ultimately, the LORD struck him and he died. ²¹ However, Abijah grew strong, acquired 14 wives, and fathered 22 sons and 16 daughters. ²² The rest of the

events of Abijah's reign, along with his ways and his sayings, are written about in the Writing of the Prophet Iddo.

𝒫SALM 89:30-37

³⁰ If his sons forsake My instruction
  and do not live by My ordinances,
³¹ if they dishonor My statutes
  and do not keep My
    commandments,
³² then I will call their rebellion to
    account with the rod,
  their sin with blows.
³³ But I will not withdraw My
    faithful love from him
  or betray My faithfulness.
³⁴ I will not violate My covenant
  or change what My lips have said.
³⁵ Once and for all I have sworn an
    oath by My holiness;
  I will not lie to David.
³⁶ His offspring will continue
    forever,
  his throne like the sun before Me,
³⁷ like the moon, established forever,
  a faithful witness in the sky."
                                    Selah

𝒫ROVERBS 19:4-5

⁴ Wealth attracts many friends,
  but a poor man is separated from
    his friend.

⁵ A false witness will not go
    unpunished,
  and one who utters lies will not
    escape.

𝒜CTS 24:10-27

¹⁰ When the governor motioned to him to speak, Paul replied: "Because I know you have been a judge of this nation for many years, I am glad to offer my defense in what concerns me. ¹¹ You are able to determine that it is no more than 12 days since I went up to worship in Jerusalem. ¹² And they didn't find me disputing with anyone or causing a disturbance among the crowd, either in the temple complex or in the syna-

gogues, or anywhere in the city. ¹³ Neither can they provide evidence to you of what they now bring against me. ¹⁴ But I confess this to you: that according to the Way, which they call a sect, so I worship my fathers' God, believing all the things that are written in the Law and in the Prophets. ¹⁵ And I have a hope in God, which these men themselves also accept, that there is going to be a resurrection, both of the righteous and the unrighteous. ¹⁶ I always do my best to have a clear conscience toward God and men. ¹⁷ After many years, I came to bring charitable gifts and offerings to my nation, ¹⁸ and while I was doing this, some Jews from the province of Asia found me ritually purified in the temple, without a crowd and without any uproar. ¹⁹ It is they who ought to be here before you to bring charges, if they have anything against me. ²⁰ Either let these men here state what wrongdoing they found in me when I stood before the Sanhedrin, ²¹ or about this one statement I cried out while standing among them, 'Today I am being judged before

you concerning the resurrection of the dead.' " ²² Since Felix was accurately informed about the Way, he adjourned the hearing, saying, "When Lysias the commander comes down, I will decide your case." ²³ He ordered that the centurion keep Paul under guard, though he could have some freedom, and that he should not prevent any of his friends from serving him.

²⁴ After some days, when Felix came with his wife Drusilla, who was Jewish, he sent for Paul and listened to him on the subject of faith in Christ Jesus. ²⁵ Now as he spoke about righteousness, self-control, and the judgment to come, Felix became afraid and replied, "Leave for now, but when I find time I'll call for you." ²⁶ At the same time he was also hoping that money would be given to him by Paul. For this reason he sent for him quite often and conversed with him. ²⁷ After two years had passed, Felix received a successor, Porcius Festus, and because he wished to do a favor for the Jews, Felix left Paul in prison.

Can a Lie Be Justified?

A false witness will not go unpunished, and one who utters lies will not escape.—PROVERBS 19:5

Will the universe sustain a lie? Today the church is being inundated with a philosophy called "situational ethics," which would have us believe that sometimes a lie can be right. I think that is a deadly and diabolical doctrine. A lie is never right—no matter what attempts we might make to justify it. "God is not a man who lies," says the Scripture in Numbers 23:19, and in 1 John 2:21 we read, "No lie comes from the truth." God cannot lie, and He will never delegate to you the task of lying for Him. When we take dishonesties into our lives we take fire into our lives—here and hereafter: "All liars—their share will be in the lake that burns with fire and sulfur" (Rv 21:8).

"Situational ethics" proponents come up with all kinds of possible scenarios, such as: "What if someone came to your house to murder a member of your family and asked if that person was in. Would it not be right to lie in those circumstances?" Can you see the thrust of this question? It is the argument, "This is what we ought to do because it makes sense." But once we view sin as an "ought," it is magically turned into something that is "good."

The Bible does not teach that anyone in any situation ought to sin. First Corinthians 10:13 teaches that because God is faithful, we will never find ourselves in a situation where we must sin, but there will always be a way of escape. God never calls upon us to break one of His laws in order to keep another.

Prayer

O Father, in a world that seems to be always looking for excuses and exceptions, help me to steer my life by the clear statements of Your revealed will. I don't want to measure up to exceptions; I want to conform to the rules—Your rules. In Jesus' name. Amen.

Further Study

Jn 8:31-47; Col 3:9; Rv 21:8
Who did Jesus say is the source of lies?
What was Paul's exhortation to the Colossians?

JULY 31

2 CHRONICLES
14:1–16:14

14 ¹ Abijah rested with his fathers and was buried in the city of David. His son Asa became king in his place. During his reign the land experienced peace for 10 years.

² Asa did what was good and right in the sight of the LORD his God. ³ He removed the pagan altars and the high places. He shattered their sacred pillars and chopped down their Asherah poles. ⁴ He told the people of Judah to seek the LORD God of their ancestors and to carry out the instruction and the command. ⁵ He also removed the high places and the incense altars from all the cities of Judah, and the kingdom experienced peace under him.

⁶ Because the land experienced peace, Asa built fortified cities in Judah. No one made war with him in those days

because the LORD gave him rest. ⁷ So he said to the people of Judah, "Let's build these cities and surround them with walls and towers, with doors and bars. The land is still ours because we sought the LORD our God. We sought Him and He gave us rest on every side." So they built and succeeded.

⁸ Asa had an army of 300,000 from Judah bearing large shields and spears, and 280,000 from Benjamin bearing regular shields and drawing the bow. All these were brave warriors. ⁹ Then Zerah the Cushite came against them with an army of one million men and 300 chariots. They came as far as Mareshah. ¹⁰ So Asa marched out against him and lined up in battle formation in the Valley of Zephathah at Mareshah. ¹¹ Then Asa cried out to the LORD his God: "LORD, there is no one besides You to help the mighty and those without strength. Help us, LORD our God, for we depend on You, and in Your name we

have come against this multitude. LORD, You are our God. Do not let a mere mortal hinder You."

[12] So the LORD routed the Cushites before Asa and before Judah, and the Cushites fled. [13] Then Asa and the people who were with him pursued them as far as Gerar. The Cushites fell until they had no survivors, for they were crushed before the LORD and before His army. So the people of Judah carried off a great supply of loot. [14] Then they attacked all the cities around Gerar because the terror of the LORD was on them. They also plundered all the cities, since there was a great deal of plunder in them. [15] They also attacked the tents of the herdsmen and captured many sheep and camels. Then they returned to Jerusalem.

15 The Spirit of God came on Azariah son of Oded. [2] So he went out to meet Asa and said to him, "Asa and all Judah and Benjamin, hear me. The LORD is with you when you are with Him. If you seek Him, He will be found by you, but if you abandon Him, He will abandon you. [3] For many years Israel has been without the true God, without a teaching priest, and without law, [4] but when they turned to the LORD God of Israel in their distress and sought Him, He was found by them. [5] In those times there was no peace for those who went about their daily activities because the residents of the lands had many conflicts. [6] Nation was crushed by nation and city by city, for God troubled them with every possible distress. [7] But as for you, be strong; don't be discouraged, for your work has a reward."

[8] When Asa heard these words and the prophecy of Azariah son of Oded the prophet, he took courage and removed the detestable idols from the whole land of Judah and Benjamin and from the cities he had captured in the hill country of Ephraim. He renovated the altar of the LORD that was in front of the vestibule of the LORD's temple. [9] Then he gathered all Judah and Benjamin, as well as those from the tribes of Ephraim, Manasseh, and Simeon who had settled among them, for they had defected to him from Israel in great numbers when they saw that the LORD his God was with him.

[10] They were gathered in Jerusalem in the third month of the fifteenth year of Asa's reign. [11] At that time they sacrificed to the LORD 700 cattle and 7,000 sheep from all the plunder they had brought. [12] Then they entered into a covenant to seek the LORD God of their ancestors with all their mind and all their heart. [13] Whoever would not seek the LORD God of Israel would be put to death, young or old, man or woman. [14] They took an oath to the LORD in a loud voice, with shouting, with trumpets, and with rams' horns. [15] All Judah rejoiced over the oath, for they had sworn it with all their mind. They had sought Him with all their heart, and He was found by them. So the LORD gave them rest on every side.

[16] King Asa also removed Maacah, his grandmother, from being queen mother because she had made an obscene image of Asherah. Asa chopped down her obscene image, then crushed it and burned it in the Kidron Valley. [17] The high places were not taken away from Israel; nevertheless, Asa was wholehearted his entire life. [18] He brought his father's consecrated gifts and his own consecrated gifts into God's temple: silver, gold, and utensils.

[19] There was no war until the thirty-fifth year of Asa's reign.

16 In the thirty-sixth year of Asa, Israel's King Baasha went to war against Judah. He built Ramah in order to deny anyone's access—going or coming—to Judah's King Asa. [2] So Asa brought out the silver and gold from the treasuries of the LORD's temple and the royal palace and sent it to Aram's King Ben-hadad, who lived in Damascus, saying, [3] "There's a treaty between me and you, between my father and your father. Look, I have sent you silver and gold. Go break your treaty with Israel's King Baasha so that he will withdraw from me."

[4] Ben-hadad listened to King Asa and sent the commanders of his armies to

the cities of Israel. They attacked Ijon, Dan, Abel-maim, and all the storage cities of Naphtali. ⁵ When Baasha heard about it, he quit building Ramah and stopped his work. ⁶ Then King Asa brought all Judah, and they carried away the stones of Ramah and the timbers Baasha had built it with. Then he built Geba and Mizpah with them.

⁷ At that time, Hanani the seer came to King Asa of Judah and said to him, "Because you depended on the king of Aram and have not depended on the Lord your God, the army of the king of Aram has escaped from your hand. ⁸ Were not the Cushites and Libyans a vast army with very many chariots and horsemen? When you depended on the Lord, He handed them over to you. ⁹ For the eyes of the Lord range throughout the earth to show Himself strong for those whose hearts are completely His. You have been foolish in this matter, for from now on, you will have wars." ¹⁰ Asa was angry with the seer and put him in prison because of his anger over this. And Asa mistreated some of the people at that time.

¹¹ Note that the events of Asa's reign, from beginning to end, are written about in the Book of the Kings of Judah and Israel. ¹² In the thirty-ninth year of his reign, Asa developed a disease in his feet, and his disease became increasingly severe. Yet even in his disease he didn't seek the Lord but the physicians. ¹³ Asa died in the forty-first year of his reign and rested with his fathers. ¹⁴ He was buried in his own tomb that he had hewn out for himself in the city of David. They laid him out in a coffin that was full of spices and various mixtures of prepared ointments; then they made a great fire in his honor.

𝒫SALM 89:38-45

³⁸ But You have spurned and rejected him;
 You have become enraged with Your anointed.
³⁹ You have repudiated the covenant with Your servant;

You have completely dishonored his crown.
⁴⁰ You have broken down all his walls;
 You have reduced his fortified cities to ruins.
⁴¹ All who pass by plunder him;
 he has become a joke to his neighbors.
⁴² You have lifted high the right hand of his foes;
 You have made all his enemies rejoice.
⁴³ You have also turned back his sharp sword
 and have not let him stand in battle.
⁴⁴ You have made his splendor cease
 and have overturned his throne.
⁴⁵ You have shortened the days of his youth;
 You have covered him with shame.
 Selah

𝒫ROVERBS 19:6-7

⁶ Many seek the favor of a ruler,
 and everyone is a friend of one who gives gifts.

⁷ All the brothers of a poor man hate him;
 how much more do his friends keep their distance from him!
He may pursue them with words, but they are not there.

𝒜CTS 25:1-22

25 Three days after Festus arrived in the province, he went up to Jerusalem from Caesarea. ² Then the chief priests and the leaders of the Jews presented their case against Paul to him; and they appealed, ³ asking him to do them a favor against Paul, that he might summon him to Jerusalem. They were preparing an ambush along the road to kill him. ⁴ However, Festus answered that Paul should be kept at Caesarea, and that he himself was about to go there shortly. ⁵ "Therefore," he said, "let the men of authority among

you go down with me and accuse him, if there is any wrong in this man."

⁶ When he had spent not more than eight or 10 days among them, he went down to Caesarea. The next day, seated at the judge's bench, he commanded Paul to be brought in. ⁷ When he arrived, the Jews who had come down from Jerusalem stood around him and brought many serious charges that they were not able to prove, ⁸ while Paul made the defense that, "Neither against the Jewish law, nor against the temple, nor against Caesar have I sinned at all."

⁹ Then Festus, wanting to do a favor for the Jews, replied to Paul, "Are you willing to go up to Jerusalem, there to be tried before me on these charges?"

¹⁰ But Paul said: "I am standing at Caesar's tribunal, where I ought to be tried. I have done no wrong to the Jews, as even you can see very well. ¹¹ If then I am doing wrong, or have done anything deserving of death, I do not refuse to die, but if there is nothing to what these men accuse me of, no one can give me up to them. I appeal to Caesar!"

¹² After Festus conferred with his council, he replied, "You have appealed to Caesar; to Caesar you will go!"

¹³ After some days had passed, King Agrippa and Bernice arrived in Caesarea and paid a courtesy call on Festus.

¹⁴ Since they stayed there many days, Festus presented Paul's case to the king, saying, "There's a man who was left as a prisoner by Felix. ¹⁵ When I was in Jerusalem, the chief priests and the elders of the Jews presented their case and asked for a judgment against him. ¹⁶ I answered them that it's not the Romans' custom to give any man up before the accused confronts the accusers face to face and has an opportunity to give a defense concerning the charge. ¹⁷ Therefore, when they had assembled here, I did not delay. The next day I sat at the judge's bench and ordered the man to be brought in. ¹⁸ Concerning him, the accusers stood up and brought no charge of the sort I was expecting. ¹⁹ Instead they had some disagreements with him about their own religion and about a certain Jesus, a dead man whom Paul claimed to be alive. ²⁰ Since I was at a loss in a dispute over such things, I asked him if he wished to go to Jerusalem and be tried there concerning these matters. ²¹ But when Paul appealed to be held for trial by the Emperor, I ordered him to be kept in custody until I could send him to Caesar."

²² Then Agrippa said to Festus, "I would like to hear the man myself."

"Tomorrow," he said, "you will hear him."

Where Is Our Trust?

You have become enraged with Your anointed.—PSALM 89:38

God's glory is more important than our own well-being. The serious problem is not the pain that others have inflicted upon us, but the pain we have inflicted (and continue to inflict) upon God. Let me spell out as clearly as I can exactly what I mean.

Many Christians are far more interested in focusing on how they can get God to comfort them when they have been hurt than considering how much they have hurt Him. Not that it is wrong to seek His comfort—Scripture encourages us to do this—but it is only one side of the picture. The most popular books in our bookshops today are titles such as these: *How to Be Healed of Life's Hurts* or *How to Overcome the Pains of the Past*. I repeat that this is a legitimate emphasis, but we must not lose sight of the fact that the important issue is not how badly people have behaved toward us, but how badly we have behaved (and continue to behave) toward God.

Take this for example: Someone hurts us or upsets us, and we decide to become the architects of their judgment. But what does God say? "Friends, do not avenge yourselves; instead, leave room for His wrath. For it is written: Vengeance belongs to Me; I will repay" (Rm 12:19). Don't you think God is hurt when He sees us ignoring His Word? We may have been sinned against, but is that any justification for sinning against God? Let's not mince words here, for any violation of a divine principle must be called by its rightful name—sin. And no sin ought to be treated lightly—especially a sin against God.

Prayer

O God, forgive me that so often I am more concerned about how others have treated me than the way I treat You. I see that a failure to trust You is a failure in love. I say, "I love You," but only so far. Forgive me and help me. In Jesus' name. Amen.

Further Study

Ps 62:1-12; Mt 21:12-13; 23:37-39; Lk 19:41
What pain was inflicted on Jesus as He observed the Temple area?
What pain did Jesus feel as He approached the city?

AUGUST I

2 CHRONICLES
17:1–18:34

17 His son Jehoshaphat became king in his place and strengthened himself against Israel. ² He stationed troops in every fortified city of Judah and set garrisons in the land of Judah and in the cities of Ephraim that his father Asa had captured.

³ Now the LORD was with Jehoshaphat because he walked in the former ways of his father David. He did not seek the Baals ⁴ but sought the God of his father and walked by His commands, not according to the practices of Israel. ⁵ So the LORD established the kingdom in his hand. Then all Judah brought him tribute, and he had riches and honor in abundance. ⁶ His mind rejoiced in the LORD's ways, and he again removed the high places and Asherah poles from Judah.

⁷ In the third year of his reign, Jehoshaphat sent his officials—Ben-hail, Obadiah, Zechariah, Nethanel, and Micaiah—to teach in the cities of Judah. ⁸ The Levites with them were Shemaiah, Nethaniah, Zebadiah, Asahel, Shemiramoth, Jehonathan, Adonijah, Tobijah, and Tob-adonijah; the priests, Elishama and Jehoram, were with these Levites. ⁹ They taught throughout Judah, having the book of the LORD's instruction with them. They went throughout the towns of Judah and taught the people.

¹⁰ The terror of the LORD was on all the kingdoms of the lands that surrounded Judah, so they didn't fight against Jehoshaphat. ¹¹ Some of the Philistines also brought gifts and silver as tribute to Jehoshaphat, and the Arabs brought him flocks: 7,700 rams and 7,700 male goats.

¹² Jehoshaphat grew stronger and stronger. He built fortresses and storage cities in Judah ¹³ and carried out great works in the towns of Judah. He had fighting men, brave warriors, in Jerusalem. ¹⁴ These are their numbers according to their ancestral families. For Judah, the commanders of thousands:

Adnah the commander and
300,000 brave warriors with him;
¹⁵ next to him, Jehohanan the commander and 280,000 with him;
¹⁶ next to him, Amasiah son of Zichri, the volunteer of the LORD, and 200,000 brave warriors with him;
¹⁷ from Benjamin, Eliada, a brave warrior, and 200,000 with him armed with bow and shield;
¹⁸ next to him, Jehozabad and 180,000 with him equipped for war.

¹⁹ These were the ones who served the king, besides those he stationed in the fortified cities throughout all Judah.

18 Now Jehoshaphat had riches and honor in abundance, and he made an alliance with Ahab through marriage. ² Then after some years, he went down to visit Ahab in Samaria. Ahab sacrificed many sheep and cattle for him and for the people who were with him. Then he persuaded him to march up to Ramoth-gilead, ³ for Israel's King Ahab asked Judah's King Jehoshaphat, "Will you go with me to Ramoth-gilead?"

He replied to him, "I am as you are, my people as your people; we will be with you in the battle." ⁴ But Jehoshaphat said to the king of Israel, "First, please ask what the LORD's will is."

⁵ So the king of Israel gathered the prophets, 400 men, and asked them, "Should we go to Ramoth-gilead for war or should I refrain?"

They replied, "March up, and God will hand it over to the king."

⁶ But Jehoshaphat asked, "Isn't there a prophet of Yahweh here any more? Let's ask him."

⁷ The king of Israel said to Jehoshaphat, "There is still one man who can ask the LORD, but I hate him because he never prophesies good about me, but only disaster. He is Micaiah son of Imlah."

"The king shouldn't say that," Jehoshaphat replied.

⁸ So the king of Israel called an officer and said, "Hurry and get Micaiah son of Imlah!"

⁹ Now the king of Israel and King Jehoshaphat of Judah, clothed in royal attire, were each sitting on his own throne. They were sitting on the threshing floor at the entrance to Samaria's gate, and all the prophets were prophesying in front of them. ¹⁰ Then Zedekiah son of Chenaanah made iron horns and said, "This is what the LORD says: 'You will gore the Arameans with these until they are finished off.'" ¹¹ And all the prophets were prophesying the same, saying, "March up to Ramoth-gilead and succeed, for the LORD will hand it over to the king."

¹² The messenger who went to call Micaiah instructed him, "Look, the words of the prophets are unanimously favorable for the king. So let your words be like theirs, and speak favorably."

¹³ But Micaiah said, "As the LORD lives, I will say whatever my God says."

¹⁴ So he went to the king, and the king asked him, "Micaiah, should we go to Ramoth-gilead for war, or should I refrain?"

Micaiah said, "March up and succeed, for they will be handed over to you."

¹⁵ But the king said to him, "How many times must I make you swear not to tell me anything but the truth in the name of the LORD?"

¹⁶ So Micaiah said:

I saw all Israel scattered
on the hills
like sheep without a shepherd.
And the LORD said,
'They have no master;
let each return home in peace.'

¹⁷ So the king of Israel said to Jehoshaphat, "Didn't I tell you he never prophesies good about me, but only disaster?"
¹⁸ Then Micaiah said, "Therefore, hear the word of the LORD. I saw the LORD sitting on His throne, and the whole heavenly host was standing at His right hand and at His left hand. ¹⁹ And the LORD said, 'Who will entice Ahab king of Israel to march up and fall at Ramoth-gilead?' So one was saying this and another was saying that.
²⁰ "Then a spirit came forward, stood before the LORD, and said, 'I will entice him.'
"The LORD asked him, 'How?'
²¹ "So he said, 'I will go and become a lying spirit in the mouth of all his prophets.'
"Then He said, 'You will entice him and also prevail. Go and do that.'
²² "Now, you see, the LORD has put a lying spirit into the mouth of these prophets of yours, and the LORD has pronounced disaster against you."
²³ Then Zedekiah son of Chenaanah came up, hit Micaiah in the face, and demanded, "Did the Spirit of the LORD leave me to speak to you?"
²⁴ Micaiah replied, "You will soon see when you go to hide yourself in an inner chamber on that day."
²⁵ Then the king of Israel ordered, "Take Micaiah and return him to Amon, the governor of the city, and to Joash, the king's son, ²⁶ and say, 'This is what the king says: Put this guy in prison and feed him only bread and water until I come back safely.' "
²⁷ But Micaiah said, "If you ever return safely, the LORD has not spoken through me." Then he said, "Listen, all you people!"
²⁸ Then the king of Israel and Judah's King Jehoshaphat went up to Ramoth-gilead. ²⁹ But the king of Israel said to

Jehoshaphat, "I will disguise myself and go into battle, but you wear your royal attire." So the king of Israel disguised himself, and they went into battle.
³⁰ Now the king of Aram had ordered his chariot commanders, "Do not fight with anyone, small or great, except the king of Israel."
³¹ When the chariot commanders saw Jehoshaphat, they shouted, "He must be the king of Israel!" So they turned to attack him, but Jehoshaphat cried out and the LORD helped him. God drew them away from him. ³² When the chariot commanders saw that he was not the king of Israel, they turned back from pursuing him.
³³ But a man drew his bow without taking special aim and struck the king of Israel through the joints of his armor. So he said to the charioteer, "Turn around and take me out of the battle, for I am badly wounded!" ³⁴ The battle raged throughout that day, and the king of Israel propped himself up in his chariot facing the Arameans until evening. Then he died at sunset.

𝒫SALM 89:46-52

⁴⁶ How long, LORD? Will You hide
Yourself forever?
Will Your anger keep burning like
fire?
⁴⁷ Remember how short my life is.
Have You created everyone for
nothing?
⁴⁸ What man can live and never see
death?
Who can save himself from the
power of Sheol?   Selah
⁴⁹ Lord, where are the former acts of
Your faithful love
that You swore to David in Your
faithfulness?
⁵⁰ Remember, Lord, the ridicule
against Your servants—
in my heart I carry abuse from all
the peoples—
⁵¹ how Your enemies have ridiculed,
LORD,
how they have ridiculed every
step of Your anointed.

52 May the LORD be praised forever.
Amen and amen.

PROVERBS 19:8-9

8 The one who acquires good sense
loves himself;
one who safeguards understanding
finds success.

9 A false witness will not go
unpunished,
and one who utters lies perishes.

ACTS 25:23–26:18

23 So the next day, Agrippa and Bernice came with great pomp and entered the auditorium with the commanders and prominent men of the city. When Festus gave the command, Paul was brought in. 24 Then Festus said: "King Agrippa and all men present with us, you see this man about whom the whole Jewish community has appealed to me, both in Jerusalem and here, shouting that he should not live any longer. 25 Now I realized that he had not done anything deserving of death, but when he himself appealed to the Emperor, I decided to send him. 26 I have nothing definite to write to the Emperor about him. Therefore, I have brought him before all of you, and especially before you, King Agrippa, so that after this examination is over, I may have something to write. 27 For it seems unreasonable to me to send a prisoner and not to indicate the charges against him."

26 Agrippa said to Paul, "It is permitted for you to speak for yourself."

Then Paul stretched out his hand and began his defense: 2 "I consider myself fortunate, King Agrippa, that today I am going to make a defense before you about everything I am accused of by the Jews, 3 especially since you are an expert in all the Jewish customs and controversies. Therefore I beg you to listen to me patiently.

4 "All the Jews know my way of life from my youth, which was spent from the beginning among my own nation and in Jerusalem. 5 They had previously known me for quite some time, if they were willing to testify, that according to the strictest party of our religion I lived as a Pharisee. 6 And now I stand on trial for the hope of the promise made by God to our fathers, 7 the promise our 12 tribes hope to attain as they earnestly serve Him night and day. Because of this hope I am being accused by the Jews, O king! 8 Why is it considered incredible by any of you that God raises the dead? 9 In fact, I myself supposed it was necessary to do many things in opposition to the name of Jesus the Nazarene. 10 This I actually did in Jerusalem, and I locked up many of the saints in prison, since I had received authority for that from the chief priests. When they were put to death, I cast my vote against them. 11 In all the synagogues I often tried to make them blaspheme by punishing them. Being greatly enraged at them, I even pursued them to foreign cities.

12 "Under these circumstances I was traveling to Damascus with authority and a commission from the chief priests. 13 At midday, while on the road, O king, I saw a light from heaven brighter than the sun, shining around me and those traveling with me. 14 When we had all fallen to the ground, I heard a voice speaking to me in the Hebrew language, 'Saul, Saul, why are you persecuting Me? It is hard for you to kick against the goads.'

15 "But I said, 'Who are You, Lord?'

"And the Lord replied: 'I am Jesus, whom you are persecuting. 16 But get up and stand on your feet. For I have appeared to you for this purpose, to appoint you as a servant and a witness of things you have seen, and of things in which I will appear to you. 17 I will rescue you from the people and from the Gentiles, to whom I now send you, 18 to open their eyes that they may turn from darkness to light and from the power of Satan to God, that they may receive forgiveness of sins and a share among those who are sanctified by faith in Me.'

No Need for Dead Reckoning

*In fact, I myself supposed it was necessary to do many things
in opposition to the name of Jesus the Nazarene.*

—Acts 26:9

The place where we can see life as a whole is in the sanctuary of God, or, if you prefer, in the presence of God. There we are reminded of things we have forgotten or ignored. See how the Good News Bible translates Acts 26:9: "I myself thought that I should do everything I could against the cause of Jesus of Nazareth." Here you see the root of Paul's problem: "I myself thought." And is not that the underlying cause of many of our problems too? We say, "I myself thought . . ." instead of asking: "What does God think?"

Sometimes sailors will attempt to establish the position of their ships by estimating the distance and direction they have traveled, rather than by astronomical observation. This is called "dead reckoning." It is sometimes necessary in foul weather, but it is fraught with peril. One mariner has said: "Undue trust in the dead reckoning has produced more disastrous shipwrecks of seaworthy ships than all other causes put together."

There are people who attempt the voyage of life by dead reckoning, but there is no need. God has charted the map for us with loving care in the Scriptures, and our plain duty is to study the chart so that we might become better acquainted with His purposes and His ways. For the better we know the Scriptures, the better we will know God. We cannot ignore the facts of history or science—they help—but if our perspective is not drawn from the Scriptures it will lead us astray. We must not rely on dead reckoning but on divine reckoning.

Prayer

O Father, just as the art of navigation requires definite and fixed points from which to take a bearing, so does my voyage through life. I am grateful, dear Father, that in You I have all the fixed points I need. Amen.

Further Study

Jdg 17:1-6; 21:25
What was said of the children of Israel?
Can the same be said of us?

AUGUST 2

2 CHRONICLES
19:1–21:11

19 Jehoshaphat king of Judah returned to his home in Jerusalem in peace. ² Then Jehu son of Hanani the seer went out to confront him and said to King Jehoshaphat, "Do you help the wicked and love those who hate the LORD? Because of this, the LORD's wrath is on you. ³ However, some good is found in you, for you have removed the Asherah poles from the land and have decided to seek God."

⁴ Jehoshaphat lived in Jerusalem, and once again he went out among the people from Beer-sheba to the hill country of Ephraim and brought them back to the LORD God of their ancestors. ⁵ He appointed judges in all the fortified cities of the land of Judah, city by city. ⁶ Then he said to the judges, "Consider what you are doing, for you do not judge for man, but for the LORD, who is with you in the matter of judgment. ⁷ And now, may the terror of the LORD be on you. Watch what you do, for there is no injustice or partiality or taking bribes with the LORD our God."

⁸ Jehoshaphat also appointed in Jerusalem some of the Levites and priests and some of the heads of the Israelite families for rendering the LORD's judgments and for settling disputes of the residents of Jerusalem. ⁹ He commanded them, saying, "In the fear of the LORD, with integrity, and with a whole heart, you are to do the following: ¹⁰ for every dispute that comes to you from your brothers who dwell in their cities—whether it regards differences of bloodguilt, law, commandment, statutes, or judgments—you are to warn them, so they will not incur guilt before the LORD and wrath will not come on you and your brothers. Do this, and you will not incur guilt.

¹¹ "Note that Amariah, the chief priest, is over you in all matters related to the LORD, and Zebadiah son of Ishmael, the ruler of the house of Judah, in all matters related to the king, and the Levites are officers in your presence. Be strong; may the LORD be with those who do what is good."

20 After this, the Moabites and Ammonites, together with some of the Meunites, came to fight against Jehoshaphat. ² People came and told Jehoshaphat, "A vast multitude from beyond the Dead Sea and from Edom has come to fight against you; they are already in Hazazon-tamar" (that is, Engedi). ³ Jehoshaphat was afraid, so he resolved to seek the LORD. So he proclaimed a fast for all Judah, ⁴ who gathered to seek the LORD. They even came from all the cities of Judah to seek Him.

⁵ Then Jehoshaphat stood in the assembly of Judah and Jerusalem in the LORD's temple before the new courtyard. ⁶ He said:

LORD God of our ancestors, are You not the God who is in heaven, and do You not rule over all the kingdoms of the nations? Power and might are in Your hand, and no one can stand against You. ⁷ Are You not our God who drove out the inhabitants of this land before Your people Israel and who gave it forever to the descendants of Abraham Your friend? ⁸ They have lived in the land and have built You a sanctuary in it for Your name and have said, ⁹ "If disaster comes on us— sword or judgment, pestilence or famine—we will stand before this temple and before You, for Your name is in this temple. We will cry out to You because of our distress, and You will hear and deliver."

¹⁰ Now here are the Ammonites, Moabites, and the inhabitants of Mount Seir. You did not let Israel invade them when Israel came out of the land of Egypt, but Israel turned away from them and did not destroy them. ¹¹ Look how they repay us by coming to drive us out of Your possession that You gave us as an inheritance. ¹² Our God, will You not judge them? For we are powerless before this vast multitude that comes to fight against us. We do not know what to do, but we look to You.

¹³ All Judah was standing before the LORD with their infants, their wives, and their children. ¹⁴ In the midst of the congregation, the Spirit of the LORD came on Jahaziel (son of Zechariah, son of Benaiah, son of Jeiel, son of Mattaniah, a Levite from Asaph's descendants), ¹⁵ and he said, "Listen carefully, all Judah and you inhabitants of Jerusalem, and King Jehoshaphat. This is what the LORD says: 'Do not be afraid or discouraged because of this vast multitude, for the battle is not yours, but God's. ¹⁶ Tomorrow, go down against them. You will see them coming up the ascent of Ziz, and you will find them at the end of the valley facing the Wilderness of Jeruel. ¹⁷ You do not have to fight this battle. Position yourselves, stand still, and see the salvation of the LORD. He is with you, Judah and Jerusalem. Do not be afraid or discouraged. Tomorrow, go out to face them, for the LORD is with you.' "

¹⁸ Then Jehoshaphat bowed with his face to the ground, and all Judah and the inhabitants of Jerusalem fell down before the LORD to worship Him. ¹⁹ Then the Levites from the sons of the Kohathites and the Korahites stood up to praise the LORD God of Israel shouting in a loud voice.

²⁰ In the morning they got up early and went out to the wilderness of Tekoa. As they were about to go out, Jehoshaphat stood and said, "Hear me, Judah and you inhabitants of Jerusalem. Believe in the LORD your God, and you will be established; believe in His prophets, and you will succeed." ²¹ Then he consulted with the people and appointed some to sing for the LORD and some to praise the splendor of His holiness. When they went out in front of the armed forces, they kept singing:

Give thanks to the LORD,
for His faithful love
    endures forever.

²² The moment they began their shouts and praises, the LORD set an ambush against the Ammonites, Moabites, and the inhabitants of Mount Seir who came to fight against Judah, and they were defeated. ²³ The Ammonites and Moabites turned against the inhabitants of Mount Seir and completely annihilated them. When they had finished with the inhabitants of Seir, they helped destroy each other.

²⁴ When Judah came to a place overlooking the wilderness, they looked toward the multitude, and there were corpses lying on the ground; nobody had escaped. ²⁵ Then Jehoshaphat and his people went to gather the plunder. They found among them an abundance of goods on the bodies and valuable items. So they stripped them until nobody could carry any more. They were gathering the plunder for three days because there was so much. ²⁶ They assembled in the Valley of Beracah on the fourth day, for there they praised the LORD. Therefore, that place is still called the Valley of Beracah today.

²⁷ Then all the men of Judah and Jerusalem turned back with Jehoshaphat at their head, returning joyfully to Jerusalem, for the LORD enabled them to rejoice over their enemies. ²⁸ So they came into Jerusalem to the LORD's temple with harps, lyres, and trumpets.

²⁹ The terror of God was on all the kingdoms of the lands when they heard that the LORD had fought against the enemies of Israel. ³⁰ Then Jehoshaphat's kingdom was quiet, for his God gave him rest on every side.

³¹ Jehoshaphat became king over Judah. He was 35 years old when he

became king; he reigned 25 years in Jerusalem. His mother's name was Azubah daughter of Shilhi. ³² He walked in the way of Asa his father; he did not turn away from it but did what was right in the LORD's sight. ³³ However, the high places were not taken away; the people had not yet determined in their hearts to worship the God of their ancestors.

³⁴ The rest of the events of Jehoshaphat's reign from beginning to end are written about in the Events of Jehu son of Hanani, which is recorded in the Book of Israel's Kings.

³⁵ After this, Judah's King Jehoshaphat made an alliance with Israel's King Ahaziah, who was guilty of wrongdoing. ³⁶ Jehoshaphat formed an alliance with him to make ships to go to Tarshish, and they made the ships in Ezion-geber. ³⁷ Then Eliezer son of Dodavahu of Mareshah prophesied against Jehoshaphat, saying, "Because you formed an alliance with Ahaziah, the LORD has broken up what you have made." So the ships were wrecked and were not able to go to Tarshish.

21 Jehoshaphat rested with his fathers and was buried with his fathers in the city of David. His son Jehoram became king in his place. ² He had brothers, sons of Jehoshaphat: Azariah, Jehiel, Zechariah, Azariah, Michael, and Shephatiah; all these were the sons of Jehoshaphat, king of Judah. ³ Their father had given them many gifts of silver, gold, and valuable things, along with fortified cities in Judah, but he gave the kingdom to Jehoram because he was the firstborn. ⁴ When Jehoram had established himself over his father's kingdom, he strengthened his position by killing with the sword all his brothers as well as some of the princes of Israel.

⁵ Jehoram was 32 years old when he became king; he reigned eight years in Jerusalem. ⁶ He walked in the way of the kings of Israel, as the house of Ahab had done, for Ahab's daughter was his wife. He did what was evil in the LORD's sight, ⁷ but because of the covenant the LORD had made with David, He was unwilling

to destroy the house of David since the LORD had promised to give a lamp to David and to his sons forever.

⁸ During Jehoram's reign, Edom rebelled against Judah's domination and appointed their own king. ⁹ So Jehoram crossed into Edom with his commanders and all his chariots. Then at night he set out to attack the Edomites who had surrounded him and the chariot commanders. ¹⁰ So Edom is still in rebellion against Judah's domination today. Libnah also rebelled at that time against his domination because he had abandoned the LORD God of his ancestors. ¹¹ Jehoram also built high places in the hills of Judah, and he caused the inhabitants of Jerusalem to prostitute themselves, and he led Judah astray.

PSALM 90:1-12

1 Lord, You have been our refuge
 in every generation.
2 Before the mountains were born,
 before You gave birth to the earth
 and the world,
 from eternity to eternity, You are
 God.

3 You return mankind to the dust,
 saying, "Return, descendants of
 Adam."
4 For in Your sight a thousand
 years
 are like yesterday that passes by,
 like a few hours of the night.
5 You end their life; they sleep.
 They are like grass that grows in
 the morning—
6 in the morning it sprouts and
 grows;
 by evening it withers and dries up.

7 For we are consumed by Your
 anger;
 we are terrified by Your wrath.
8 You have set our unjust ways
 before You,
 our secret sins in the light of Your
 presence.
9 For all our days ebb away under
 Your wrath;

we end our years like a sigh.
10 Our lives last seventy years
or, if we are strong, eighty
years.
Even the best of them are toil and
sorrow;
indeed, they pass quickly and we
fly away.
11 Who understands the power of
Your anger?
Your wrath matches the fear that
is due You.
12 Teach us to number our days
carefully
so that we may develop wisdom in
our hearts.

PROVERBS 19:10-12

10 Luxury is not appropriate for a
fool—
how much less for a slave to rule
over princes!

11 A person's insight gives him
patience,
and his virtue is to overlook an
offense.

12 A king's rage is like a lion's roar,
but his favor is like dew on the
grass.

ACTS 26:19–27:8

19 "Therefore, King Agrippa, I was not
disobedient to the heavenly vision.
20 Instead, I preached to those in Damascus first, and to those in Jerusalem and
in all the region of Judea, and to the
Gentiles, that they should repent and
turn to God, and do works worthy of repentance. 21 For this reason the Jews
seized me in the temple complex and
were trying to kill me. 22 Since I have
obtained help that comes from God, to
this day I stand and testify to both small
and great, saying nothing else than what
the prophets and Moses said would take
place— 23 that the Messiah must suffer,
and that as the first to rise from the
dead, He would proclaim light to our
people and to the Gentiles."

24 As he was making his defense this
way, Festus exclaimed in a loud voice,
"You're out of your mind, Paul! Too
much study is driving you mad!"
25 But Paul replied, "I'm not out of my
mind, most excellent Festus. On the
contrary, I'm speaking words of truth
and good judgment. 26 For the king
knows about these matters. It is to him
I am actually speaking boldly. For I'm
not convinced that any of these things
escapes his notice, since this was not
done in a corner! 27 King Agrippa, do
you believe the prophets? I know you
believe."
28 Then Agrippa said to Paul, "Are
you going to persuade me to become a
Christian so easily?"
29 "I wish before God," replied Paul,
"that whether easily or with difficulty,
not only you but all who listen to me today might become as I am—except for
these chains."
30 So the king, the governor, Bernice,
and those sitting with them got up,
31 and when they had left they talked
with each other and said, "This man is
doing nothing that deserves death or
chains."
32 Then Agrippa said to Festus, "This
man could have been released if he had
not appealed to Caesar."

27 When it was decided that we
were to sail to Italy, they handed
over Paul and some other prisoners to a
centurion named Julius, of the Imperial
Regiment. 2 So when we had boarded a
ship of Adramyttium, we put to sea,
intending to sail to ports along the
coast of the Province of Asia. Aristarchus, a Macedonian of Thessalonica,
was with us. 3 The next day we put in at
Sidon, and Julius treated Paul kindly
and allowed him to go to his friends to
receive their care. 4 When we had put
out to sea from there, we sailed along
the northern coast of Cyprus because
the winds were against us. 5 After sailing through the open sea off Cilicia and
Pamphylia, we reached Myra in Lycia.
6 There the centurion found an Alexandrian ship sailing for Italy and put
us on board. 7 Sailing slowly for many

days, we came with difficulty as far as Cnidus. But since the wind did not allow us to approach it, we sailed along the south side of Crete off Salmone. [8] With yet more difficulty we sailed along the coast, and came to a place called Fair Havens near the city of Lasea.

Not a Private Fight

Do not be afraid or discouraged . . . for the battle is yours, but God's.—2 CHRONICLES 20:15

The spiritual application of the helmet of salvation is not so much the enjoyment of our present salvation (though it includes that) as it is the assurance that a sure salvation is coming—and is even now at work.

This is what we need to know if we are to prevent the Devil from bringing us into a state of mental distress—not merely that things will finally end right, but that God's plan is being worked out now. "History," writes Ray Stedman, an American Bible teacher, "is not a meaningless jumble but a controlled pattern, and the Lord Jesus Christ is the one who is directing these events."

The attack of Satan on the mind proceeds differently. He says to us: "Just look around you at the state of the world. God seems powerless to put things right. He has given lots of promises that things will one day get better, but none has come to pass. Hadn't you better give up this foolish idea that it's all going to work out right?"

If you were to let your mind dwell on that kind of satanic argument, you would soon find yourself in distress. The answer is to put on the helmet, the hope of salvation. You must remind yourself that things are not as they appear. The battle is not ours, but the Lord's. We may be individual soldiers fighting in the army of God, but the ultimate cause is sure and the end is certain. We need not be unduly troubled by what is happening in the world, for our commander is not just winning—He has already won!

Prayer

Lord Jesus, I am grateful that the Cross is the guarantee that neither sin nor Satan will ever defeat You. Your victory at Calvary has settled forever the question of who has the final word in the universe. I am so deeply, deeply thankful. Amen.

Further Study

Lk 21:10-28; Jn 14:1-4; 16:33
How did Jesus describe the world?
What did He say to His disciples?

AUGUST 3

2 CHRONICLES 21:12–24:16

¹² Then a letter came to Jehoram from Elijah the prophet, saying:

This is what the LORD God of your ancestor David says: "Because you have not walked in the ways of your father Jehoshaphat or in the ways of Asa king of Judah ¹³ but have walked in the way of the kings of Israel, have caused Judah and the inhabitants of Jerusalem to prostitute themselves like the house of Ahab prostituted itself, and also have killed your brothers, your father's family, who were better than you, ¹⁴ the LORD is now about to strike your people, your sons, your wives, and all your possessions with a horrible affliction. ¹⁵ You yourself will be struck with many illnesses, including a disease of the intestines, until your intestines come out day after day because of the disease."

¹⁶ The LORD put it into the mind of the Philistines and the Arabs who live near the Cushites to attack Jehoram. ¹⁷ So they went to war against Judah and invaded it. They carried off all the possessions found in the king's palace and also his sons and wives; not a son was left to him except Jehoahaz, his youngest son. ¹⁸ After all these things, the LORD afflicted him in his intestines with an incurable disease. ¹⁹ This continued day after day until two full years passed. Then his intestines came out because of his disease, and he died from severe illnesses. But his people did not hold a fire in his honor like the fire in honor of his fathers.

²⁰ Jehoram was 32 years old when he became king; he reigned eight years in Jerusalem. He died to no one's regret and was buried in the city of David but not in the tombs of the kings.

22 Then the inhabitants of Jerusalem made Ahaziah, his youngest son, king in his place, because the troops that had come with the Arabs to the camp had killed all the older sons. So Ahaziah son of Jehoram became king of Judah. ² Ahaziah was 22 years old when he became king; he reigned one year in Jerusalem. His mother's name was Athaliah, granddaughter of Omri.

³ He walked in the ways of the house of Ahab, for his mother gave him evil advice. ⁴ So he did what was evil in the LORD's sight like the house of Ahab, for they were his advisers after the death of his father, to his destruction. ⁵ He also followed their advice and went with Joram son of Israel's King Ahab to fight against Hazael, king of Aram, in Ramoth-gilead. The Arameans wounded Joram, ⁶ so he returned to Jezreel to recover from the wounds they inflicted on him in Ramoth-gilead when he fought against Aram's King Hazael. Then Judah's King Ahaziah son of Jehoram went down to Jezreel to visit Joram son of Ahab since Joram was ill.

⁷ With his going to Joram, Ahaziah's downfall was from God, for when Ahaziah went, he went out with Joram to meet Jehu son of Nimshi, whom the LORD had anointed to destroy the house of Ahab. ⁸ So it happened when Jehu executed judgment on the house of Ahab, he found the rulers of Judah and the sons of Ahaziah's brothers who were serving Ahaziah, and he killed them. ⁹ Then Jehu looked for Ahaziah, and Jehu's soldiers captured him (he was hiding in Samaria). Then they brought him to Jehu, and they killed him. They buried him, for they said, "He is the

grandson of Jehoshaphat who sought the LORD with all his heart." So the house of Ahaziah had no one to exercise power over the kingdom.

¹⁰When Athaliah, Ahaziah's mother, saw that her son was dead, she proceeded to annihilate all the royal heirs of the house of Judah. ¹¹Jehoshabeath, the king's daughter, rescued Joash son of Ahaziah from the king's sons who were being killed and put him and his nurse in a bedroom. Now Jehoshabeath was the daughter of King Jehoram and the wife of Jehoiada the priest. Since she was Ahaziah's sister, she hid Joash from Athaliah so that she did not kill him. ¹²While Athaliah ruled over the land, he was hiding with them in God's temple six years.

23 Then, in the seventh year, Jehoiada summoned his courage and took the commanders of hundreds into a covenant with him: Azariah son of Jeroham, Ishmael son of Jehohanan, Azariah son of Obed, Maaseiah son of Adaiah, and Elishaphat son of Zichri. ²They made a circuit throughout Judah. They gathered the Levites from all the cities of Judah and the heads of the families of Israel, and they came to Jerusalem. ³Then the whole assembly made a covenant with the king in God's temple. Jehoiada said to them, "Here is the king's son! He must reign, just as the LORD promised concerning David's sons. ⁴This is what you are to do: one third of you, priests and Levites who are coming on duty on the Sabbath, are to be gatekeepers. ⁵A third are to be at the king's palace, and a third are to be at the Foundation Gate, and all the troops will be in the courtyards of the LORD's temple. ⁶No one is to enter the LORD's temple but the priests and those Levites who serve; they may enter because they are holy, but all the people are to obey the requirement of the LORD. ⁷You must completely surround the king with weapons in hand. Anyone who enters the temple is to be put to death. You must be with the king in all his daily tasks."

⁸So the commanders of hundreds did everything Jehoiada the priest commanded. They each brought their men—those coming on duty on the Sabbath and those going off duty on the Sabbath—for Jehoiada the priest did not release the divisions. ⁹Jehoiada the priest gave to the commanders of hundreds King David's spears, shields, and quivers that were in God's temple. ¹⁰Then he stationed all the troops with their weapons in hand surrounding the king—from the right side of the temple to the left side, by the altar and by the temple.

¹¹They brought out the king's son, put the crown on him, gave him the testimony, and made him king. Jehoiada and his sons anointed him and cried, "Long live the king!"

¹²When Athaliah heard the noise from the troops, the guards, and those praising the king, she went to the troops in the LORD's temple. ¹³As she looked, there was the king standing by his pillar at the entrance. The commanders and the trumpeters were by the king, and all the people of the land were rejoicing and blowing trumpets while the singers with musical instruments were leading the praise. Athaliah tore her clothes and screamed, "Treason, treason!"

¹⁴Then Jehoiada the priest sent out the commanders of hundreds, those in charge of the army, saying, "Take her out between the ranks, and put anyone who follows her to death by the sword," for the priest had said, "Don't put her to death in the LORD's temple." ¹⁵So they arrested her, and she went by the entrance of the Horses' Gate to the king's palace, where they put her to death.

¹⁶Then Jehoiada made a covenant between himself, the king, and the people that they would be the LORD's people. ¹⁷So all the people went to the temple of Baal and tore it down. They broke its altars and images into pieces and killed Mattan, the priest of Baal, at the altars. ¹⁸Then Jehoiada put the oversight of the LORD's temple into the hands of the Levitical priests, whom David had appointed over the LORD's temple, to offer

burnt offerings to the LORD as it is written in the law of Moses, with rejoicing and song ordained by David. ¹⁹ He stationed gatekeepers at the gates of the LORD's temple so that nothing unclean could enter for any reason. ²⁰ Then he took with him the commanders of hundreds, the nobles, the governors of the people, and all the people of the land and brought the king down from the LORD's temple. They entered the king's palace through the upper gate and seated the king on the throne of the kingdom. ²¹ All the people of the land rejoiced, and the city was quiet, for they had put Athaliah to death by the sword.

24 Joash was seven years old when he became king; he reigned 40 years in Jerusalem. His mother's name was Zibiah; she was from Beer-sheba. ² Throughout the time of Jehoiada the priest, Joash did what was right in the LORD's sight. ³ Jehoiada acquired two wives for him, and he was the father of sons and daughters.

⁴ Afterwards, Joash took it to heart to renovate the LORD's temple. ⁵ So he gathered the priests and Levites and said, "Go out to the cities of Judah and collect money from all Israel to repair the temple of your God as needed year by year, and do it quickly."

However, the Levites did not hurry. ⁶ So the king called Jehoiada the high priest and said, "Why haven't you required the Levites to bring from Judah and Jerusalem the tax imposed by the LORD's servant Moses and the assembly of Israel for the tent of the testimony? ⁷ For the sons of that wicked Athaliah broke into the LORD's temple and even used the sacred things of the LORD's temple for the Baals."

⁸ At the king's command a chest was made and placed outside the gate of the LORD's temple. ⁹ Then a proclamation was issued in Judah and Jerusalem that the tax God's servant Moses imposed on Israel in the wilderness be brought to the LORD. ¹⁰ All the leaders and all the people rejoiced, brought the tax, and put it in the chest until it was full. ¹¹ Whenever the chest was brought by the Levites to the king's overseers, and when they saw that there was a large amount of money, the king's secretary and the high priest's deputy came and emptied the chest, picked it up, and returned it to its place. They did this daily and gathered the money in abundance. ¹² Then the king and Jehoiada gave it to those in charge of the labor on the LORD's temple, who were hiring masons and carpenters to renovate the LORD's temple, also blacksmiths and coppersmiths to repair the LORD's temple.

¹³ The workmen did their work, and through them the repairs progressed. They restored God's temple to its specifications and reinforced it. ¹⁴ When they finished, they presented the rest of the money to the king and Jehoiada, who made articles for the LORD's temple with it—articles for ministry and for making burnt offerings, and ladles and articles of gold and silver. They regularly offered burnt offerings in the LORD's temple throughout Jehoiada's life.

¹⁵ Jehoiada died when he was old and full of days; he was 130 years old at his death. ¹⁶ He was buried in the city of David with the kings because he had done what was good in Israel with respect to God and His temple.

··

PSALM 90:13-17

¹³ LORD—how long?
Turn and have compassion on Your
    servants.
¹⁴ Satisfy us in the morning with
    Your faithful love
so that we may shout with joy and
    be glad all our days.
¹⁵ Make us rejoice for as many days
    as You have humbled us,
for as many years as we have seen
    adversity.
¹⁶ Let Your work be seen by Your
    servants,
and Your splendor by their
    children.
¹⁷ Let the favor of the Lord our God
    be on us;
establish for us the work of our
    hands—

establish the work of our
hands!

PROVERBS 19:13-14

13 A foolish son is his father's ruin,
and a wife's nagging is an endless
dripping.

14 A house and wealth are inherited
from fathers,
but a sensible wife is from the
LORD.

ACTS 27:9-29

9 By now much time had passed, and
the voyage was already dangerous.
Since the Fast was already over, Paul
gave his advice 10 and told them, "Men,
I can see that this voyage is headed toward damage and heavy loss, not only of
the cargo and the ship, but also of our
lives." 11 But the centurion paid attention to the captain and the owner of the
ship rather than to what Paul said.
12 Since the harbor was unsuitable to
winter in, the majority decided to set
sail from there, hoping somehow to
reach Phoenix, a harbor on Crete open
to the southwest and northwest, and to
winter there.

13 When a gentle south wind sprang
up, they thought they had achieved
their purpose; they weighed anchor and
sailed along the shore of Crete. 14 But
not long afterwards, a fierce wind called
the "northeaster" rushed down from
the island. 15 Since the ship was caught
and was unable to head into the wind,
we gave way to it and were driven
along. 16 After running under the shelter of a little island called Cauda, we

were barely able to get control of the
skiff. 17 After hoisting it up, they used
ropes and tackle and girded the ship.
Then, fearing they would run aground
on the Syrtis, they lowered the drift-
anchor, and in this way they were driven
along. 18 Because we were being severely battered by the storm, they began to
jettison the cargo the next day. 19 On the
third day, they threw the ship's gear
overboard with their own hands.

20 For many days neither sun nor stars
appeared, and the severe storm kept
raging; finally all hope that we would be
saved was disappearing. 21 Since many
were going without food, Paul stood up
among them and said, "You men should
have followed my advice not to sail from
Crete and sustain this damage and loss.
22 Now I urge you to take courage, because there will be no loss of any of
your lives, but only of the ship. 23 For
this night an angel of the God I belong
to and serve stood by me, 24 saying,
'Don't be afraid, Paul. You must stand
before Caesar. And, look! God has
graciously given you all those who are
sailing with you.' 25 Therefore, take
courage, men, because I believe God
that it will be just the way it was told to
me. 26 However, we must run aground
on a certain island."

27 When the fourteenth night came,
we were drifting in the Adriatic Sea,
and in the middle of the night the
sailors thought they were approaching
land. 28 They took a sounding and found
it to be 120 feet deep; when they had
sailed a little farther and sounded again,
they found it to be 90 feet deep.
29 Then, fearing we might run aground
in some rocky place, they dropped four
anchors from the stern and prayed for
daylight to come.

Joy—More Than Pleasure

Satisfy us in the morning with Your faithful love
so that we may shout with joy and be glad all our days.
—Psalm 90:14

One of the reasons why so many Christians do not experience the delights of spiritual joy is that they do not expect to. A woman who came into the experience of Christian conversion said: "Strange, but I never associated joy with God before." How sad that many do not expect their faith to make them basically and fully joyful now. They think that joy is reserved for the hereafter. Our Lord pointed out to the disciples that it was for the present.

We can better understand this supernatural joy if we distinguish it from the pleasures of life with which it is sometimes confused. Spiritual or supernatural joy is quite different from pleasure or happiness. A worldling can experience pleasure and happiness, but he cannot experience supernatural joy. Indeed, worldly people often pride themselves in knowing how to experience pleasure.

Yet pleasure and Christian joy cannot be equated. Look with me at some of the differences. Pleasure depends on circumstances. It requires a measure of health and wealth. It demands that the life conditions be kindly, and thus it can be stolen from us by things like lack of money—or even a toothache. Christian joy is completely independent of circumstances. It is there in the believer even when "strength and health and friends" are gone; when circumstances are not only unkind but savage. Out of all the miracles I have witnessed in my life, none is more wonderful than the miracle of seeing Christ's exuberant joy burst forth in those who are caught up in pain or persecution. The springs of Christian joy are deep within and can exist, no matter what the circumstances.

Prayer

O Father, how can I thank You enough for imparting into my sadness Your unconquerable gladness? No matter what happens—all is well with my soul. I am so grateful. Amen.

Further Study

Jn 16:17-33; Ac 5:12-42; 15:23-25; 2 Co 6:10
How did the apostles respond to persecution?
How did Paul express it?

AUGUST 4

2 CHRONICLES
24:17–26:23

¹⁷ However, after Jehoiada died, the rulers of Judah came and paid homage to the king. Then the king listened to them, ¹⁸ and they abandoned the temple of the LORD God of their ancestors and served the Asherah poles and the idols. So there was wrath against Judah and Jerusalem for this guilt of theirs. ¹⁹ Nevertheless, He sent them prophets to bring them back to the LORD; they admonished them, but they would not listen.

²⁰ The Spirit of God took control of Zechariah son of Jehoiada the priest. He stood above the people and said to them, "This is what God says: 'Why are you transgressing the LORD's commands and you do not prosper? Because you have abandoned the LORD, He has abandoned you.'" ²¹ But they conspired against him and stoned him at the king's command in the courtyard of the LORD's temple. ²² King Joash didn't remember the kindness that Zechariah's father Jehoiada had extended to him, but killed his son. While he was dying, he said, "May the LORD see and demand an account."

²³ At the turn of the year, an Aramean army went to war against Joash. They entered Judah and Jerusalem and destroyed all the leaders of the people among them and sent all the plunder to the king of Damascus. ²⁴ Although the Aramean army came with only a few men, the LORD handed over a vast army to them because the people of Judah had abandoned the LORD God of their ancestors. So they executed judgment on Joash.

²⁵ When the Arameans saw that Joash had many wounds, they left him. His servants conspired against him, and killed him on his bed, because he had shed the blood of the sons of Jehoiada the priest. So he died, and they buried him in the city of David, but they did not bury him in the tombs of the kings.

²⁶ Those who conspired against him were Zabad, son of the Ammonite woman Shimeath, and Jehozabad, son of the Moabite woman Shimrith. ²⁷ Concerning his sons, the many oracles about him, and the restoration of the LORD's temple, they are recorded in the Writing of the Book of the Kings. His son Amaziah became king in his place.

25 Amaziah became king when he was 25 years old; he reigned 29 years in Jerusalem. His mother's name was Jehoaddan; she was from Jerusalem. ² He did what was right in the LORD's sight but not completely.

³ As soon as the kingdom was firmly in his grasp, he executed his servants who had murdered his father the king. ⁴ However, he did not put their children to death, because—as it is written in the Law, in the book of Moses, where the LORD commanded—"Fathers must not die because of children, and children must not die because of fathers, but each one will die for his own sin."

⁵ Then Amaziah gathered Judah and assembled them according to patriarchal family, according to commanders of thousands, and according to commanders of hundreds. He numbered those 20 years old or more for all Judah and Benjamin. He found there to be 300,000 choice men who could serve in the army, bearing spear and shield. ⁶ Then for 7,500 pounds of silver he hired 100,000 brave warriors from Israel.

⁷ However, a man of God came to him and said, "King, do not let Israel's army go with you, for the LORD is not with

Israel—all the Ephraimites. ⁸ But if you go with them, do it! Be strong for battle! But God will make you stumble before the enemy, for God has the power to help or to make one stumble.

⁹ Then Amaziah said to the man of God, "What should I do about the 7,500 pounds of silver I gave to Israel's division?"

The man of God replied, "The LORD is able to give you much more than this."

¹⁰ So Amaziah released the division that came to him from Ephraim to go home. But they got very angry with Judah and returned home in a fierce rage.

¹¹ Amaziah strengthened his position and led his people to the Valley of Salt. He struck down 10,000 Seirites, ¹² and the Judahites captured 10,000 alive. They took them to the top of a cliff where they threw them off, and all of them were dashed to pieces.

¹³ As for the men of the division that Amaziah sent back so they would not go with him into battle, they raided the cities of Judah from Samaria to Beth-horon, struck down 3,000 of their people, and took a great deal of plunder.

¹⁴ After Amaziah came from the attack on the Edomites, he brought the gods of the Seirites and set them up as his gods. He worshiped before them and burned incense to them. ¹⁵ So the LORD's anger was against Amaziah, and He sent a prophet to him, who said, "Why have you sought a people's gods that could not deliver their own people from your hand?"

¹⁶ While he was still speaking to him, the king asked, "Have we made you the king's counselor? Stop, why should you lose your life?"

So the prophet stopped, but he said, "I know that God intends to destroy you, because you have done this and have not listened to my advice."

¹⁷ King Amaziah of Judah took counsel and sent word to Jehoash son of Jehoahaz, son of Jehu, king of Israel, saying, "Come, let us meet face to face."

¹⁸ King Jehoash of Israel sent word to King Amaziah of Judah, saying, "The thistle that was in Lebanon sent a message to the cedar that was in Lebanon, saying, 'Give your daughter to my son as a wife.' Then a wild animal that was in Lebanon passed by and trampled the thistle. ¹⁹ You have said, 'Look, I have defeated Edom,' and you have become overconfident that you will get glory. Now stay at home. Why stir up such trouble so that you fall and Judah with you?"

²⁰ But Amaziah would not listen, for this turn of events was from God in order to hand them over to their enemies because they went after the gods of Edom. ²¹ So King Jehoash of Israel advanced. He and King Amaziah of Judah faced off at Beth-shemesh in Judah. ²² Judah was routed before Israel, and each fled to his own tent. ²³ King Jehoash of Israel captured Judah's King Amaziah son of Joash, son of Jehoahaz, at Beth-shemesh. Then Jehoash took him to Jerusalem and broke down 200 yards of Jerusalem's wall from the Ephraim Gate to the Corner Gate. ²⁴ He took all the gold, silver, all the utensils that were found with Obed-edom in God's temple, the treasures of the king's palace, and the hostages. Then he returned to Samaria.

²⁵ Judah's King Amaziah son of Joash lived 15 years after the death of Israel's King Jehoash son of Jehoahaz. ²⁶ The rest of the events of Amaziah's reign, from beginning to end, are written about in the Book of the Kings of Judah and Israel.

²⁷ From the time Amaziah turned from following the LORD, a conspiracy was formed against him in Jerusalem, and he fled to Lachish. However, men were sent after him to Lachish, and they put him to death there. ²⁸ They carried him back on horses and buried him with his fathers in the city of Judah.

26 All the people of Judah took Uzziah, who was 16 years old, and made him king in place of his father Amaziah. ² He rebuilt Eloth and restored it to Judah after Amaziah the king rested with his fathers.

³ Uzziah was 16 years old when he be-

came king; he reigned 52 years in Jerusalem. His mother's name was Jecoliah; she was from Jerusalem. ⁴He did what was right in the LORD's sight as his father Amaziah had done. ⁵He sought God throughout the lifetime of Zechariah, the teacher of the fear of God. During the time that he sought the LORD, God gave him success.

⁶Uzziah went out to wage war against the Philistines, and he tore down the wall of Gath, the wall of Jabneh, and the wall of Ashdod. Then he built cities in the vicinity of Ashdod and among the Philistines. ⁷God helped him against the Philistines, the Arabs that live in Gur-baal, and the Meunites. ⁸The Ammonites gave Uzziah tribute money, and his fame spread as far as the entrance of Egypt, for God made him very powerful. ⁹Uzziah built towers in Jerusalem at the Corner Gate, the Valley Gate, and the corner buttress, and he fortified them. ¹⁰Since he had many cattle both in the lowlands and the plain, he built towers in the desert and dug many wells. And since he was a lover of the soil, he had farmers and vinedressers in the hills and in the fertile lands.

¹¹Uzziah had an army equipped for combat that went out to war by division according to their assignments, as recorded by Jeiel the court secretary and Maaseiah the officer under the authority of Hananiah, one of the king's commanders. ¹²The total number of heads of families was 2,600 brave warriors. ¹³Under their authority was an army of 307,500 equipped for combat, a powerful force to help the king against the enemy. ¹⁴Uzziah provided the entire army with shields, spears, helmets, armor, bows and slingstones. ¹⁵He made skillfully designed devices in Jerusalem to shoot arrows and catapult large stones for use on the towers and on the corners. So his fame spread even to distant places, for he was marvelously helped until he became strong.

¹⁶But when he became strong, he grew arrogant and it led to his own destruction. He acted unfaithfully against the LORD his God by going into the LORD's sanctuary to burn incense on the incense altar. ¹⁷Azariah the priest, along with 80 brave priests of the LORD, went in after him. ¹⁸They took their stand against King Uzziah and said, "Uzziah, you have no right to offer incense to the LORD—only the consecrated priests, the descendants of Aaron, have the right to offer incense. Leave the sanctuary, for you have acted unfaithfully! You will not receive honor from the LORD God."

¹⁹Uzziah, with a censer in his hand to offer incense, was enraged. But when he became enraged with the priests, in the presence of the priests in the LORD's temple beside the altar of incense, a skin disease broke out on his forehead. ²⁰Then Azariah the chief priest and all the priests turned to him and saw that he was diseased on his forehead. They rushed him out of there. He himself also hurried to get out because the LORD had afflicted him. ²¹So King Uzziah was diseased to the time of his death. He lived in quarantine with a serious skin disease and was excluded from access to the LORD's temple, while his son Jotham was over the king's household governing the people of the land.

²²Now the prophet Isaiah son of Amoz wrote about the rest of the events of Uzziah's reign, from beginning to end. ²³Uzziah rested with his fathers, and he was buried with his fathers in the burial ground of the kings' cemetery, for they said, "He has a skin disease." His son Jotham became king in his place.

....

𝒫SALM 91:1-8

¹ The one who lives under the
    protection of the Most High
    dwells in the shadow of the
    Almighty.

² I will say to the LORD, "My refuge
    and my fortress,
    my God, in whom I trust."

³ He Himself will deliver you from
    the hunter's net,
    from the destructive plague.

⁴ He will cover you with His
feathers;
you will take refuge under His
wings.
His faithfulness will be a
protective shield.
⁵ You will not fear the terror of the
night,
the arrow that flies by day,
⁶ the plague that stalks in darkness,
or the pestilence that ravages at
noon.
⁷ Though a thousand fall at your
side
and ten thousand at your right
hand,
the pestilence will not reach you.
⁸ You will only see it with your eyes
and witness the punishment of
the wicked.

₱ROVERBS 19:15-16

¹⁵ Laziness induces deep sleep,
and a lazy person will go hungry.

¹⁶ The one who keeps commands
preserves himself;
one who disregards his ways will
die.

₳CTS 27:30–28:10

³⁰ Some sailors tried to escape from
the ship; they had let down the skiff
into the sea, pretending that they were
going to put out anchors from the bow.
³¹ Paul said to the centurion and the soldiers, "Unless these men stay in the
ship, you cannot be saved." ³² Then the
soldiers cut the ropes holding the skiff
and let it drop away.
³³ When it was just about daylight,
Paul urged them all to take food, saying,
"Today is the fourteenth day that you
have been waiting and going without
food, having eaten nothing. ³⁴ Therefore
I urge you to take some food. For this
has to do with your survival, since not a
hair will be lost from the head of any of
you." ³⁵ After he said these things and
had taken some bread, he gave thanks
to God in the presence of them all, and

when he had broken it, he began to eat.
³⁶ They all became encouraged and took
food themselves. ³⁷ In all there were
276 of us on the ship. ³⁸ And having eat-
en enough food, they began to lighten
the ship by throwing the grain overboard into the sea.
³⁹ When daylight came, they did not
recognize the land, but sighted a bay
with a beach. They planned to run the
ship ashore if they could. ⁴⁰ After casting off the anchors, they left them in
the sea, at the same time loosening the
ropes that held the rudders. Then they
hoisted the foresail to the wind and
headed for the beach. ⁴¹ But they struck
a sandbar and ran the ship aground. The
bow jammed fast and remained immovable, but the stern began to break up
with the pounding of the waves.
⁴² The soldiers' plan was to kill the
prisoners so that no one could swim off
and escape. ⁴³ But the centurion kept
them from carrying out their plan because he wanted to save Paul, so he ordered those who could swim to jump
overboard first and get to land. ⁴⁴ The
rest were to follow, some on planks and
some on debris from the ship. In this
way, all got safely to land.

28 Safely ashore, we then learned
that the island was called Malta.
² The local people showed us extraordinary kindness, for they lit a fire and
took us all in, since rain was falling and
it was cold. ³ As Paul gathered a bundle
of brushwood and put it on the fire, a
viper came out because of the heat and
fastened itself to his hand. ⁴ When the
local people saw the creature hanging
from his hand, they said to one another,
"This man is probably a murderer, and
though he has escaped the sea, Justice
does not allow him to live!" ⁵ However,
he shook the creature off into the fire
and suffered no harm. ⁶ They expected
that he would swell up or suddenly drop
dead. But after they waited a long time
and saw nothing unusual happen to
him, they changed their minds and said
he was a god.
⁷ Now in the area around that place
was an estate belonging to the leading

man of the island, named Publius, who welcomed us and entertained us hospitably for three days. ⁸ It happened that Publius' father was in bed suffering from fever and dysentery. Paul went to him, and praying and laying his hands on him, he healed him. ⁹ After this, the rest of those on the island who had diseases also came and were cured. ¹⁰ So they heaped many honors on us, and when we sailed, they gave us what we needed.

Inner Cohesion

He did what was right in the LORD's sight but not completely.

—2 CHRONICLES 25:2

One scriptural example that illustrates the need for a proper correlation between heart and mind is the Old Testament character, Amaziah. Second Chronicles 25:2 tells us: "He did what was right in the LORD's sight but not completely." His mind gave itself to doing right in the sight of the Lord, but his heart did not support his actions.

This lack of coordination proved to be his undoing: "After Amaziah came from the attack on the Edomites, he brought the gods of the Seirites and set them up as his gods. He worshiped before them and burned incense to them" (25:14). Now look at how the life of Amaziah ends: "From the time Amaziah turned from following the LORD, a conspiracy was formed against him . . . men were sent after him to Lachish, and they put him to death there." (25:27). Notice the steps:

(1) He was outwardly correct but inwardly uncoordinated.
(2) His inner disunity showed itself in outer disloyalty.
(3) This disunity resulted in his failure and death.

At the beginning, Amaziah does not appear to be a particularly bad individual—he just failed to be wholehearted in his commitment. He did all the right things outwardly, but his heart was not in them—hence, his spiritual ruin. We could say he missed his step by inches, but his fall was one of the worst ever recorded. If we are not held together by a single-minded devotion, our spiritual life can quickly go to pieces. Commitment to God demands cohesion—the cohesion of heart and mind.

Prayer

O God my Father, help me to live a life of single purpose, with heart and mind moving together as one. Let me will the highest with all my being. In Jesus' name I ask this. Amen.

Further Study

Jms 1:1-8; 4:8; Heb 13:9; Lk 11:17
What makes us unstable?
What was the Word of the Lord to the Hebrews?

AUGUST 5

2 CHRONICLES
27:1–29:17

27 Jotham was 25 years old when he became king; he reigned 16 years in Jerusalem. His mother's name was Jerushah daughter of Zadok. ² He did what was right in the LORD's sight as his father Uzziah had done, except that he didn't enter the LORD's sanctuary. However, the people still behaved corruptly.

³ Jotham built the Upper Gate of the LORD's temple, and he built extensively on the wall of Ophel. ⁴ He also built cities in the hill country of Judah and fortresses and towers in the forests. ⁵ He waged war against the king of the Ammonites. He overpowered the Ammonites, and that year they gave him 7,500 pounds of silver, 50,000 bushels of wheat, and 50,000 bushels of barley. They paid him the same in the second and third years. ⁶ So Jotham strengthened himself because he did not waver in obeying the LORD his God.

⁷ As for the rest of the events of Jotham's reign, along with all his wars and his ways, note that they are written about in the Book of the Kings of Israel and Judah. ⁸ He was 25 years old when he became king; he reigned 16 years in Jerusalem. ⁹ Jotham rested with his fathers and was buried in the city of David. His son Ahaz became king in his place.

28 Ahaz was 20 years old when he became king; he reigned 16 years in Jerusalem. He did not do what was right in the LORD's sight like his forefather David, ² for he walked in the ways of the kings of Israel and made cast images of the Baals. ³ He burned incense in the Valley of Hinnom and burned his children in the fire, imitating the detestable practices of the nations the LORD had dispossessed before the Israelites. ⁴ He sacrificed and burned incense on the high places, on the hills, and under every green tree.

⁵ So the LORD his God handed Ahaz over to the king of Aram. He attacked him and took many captives to Damascus.

Ahaz was also handed over to the king of Israel, who struck him with great force: ⁶ Pekah son of Remaliah killed 120,000 in Judah in one day—all brave men—because they had abandoned the LORD God of their ancestors. ⁷ An Ephraimite warrior named Zichri killed the king's son Maaseiah, Azrikam governor of the palace, and Elkanah who was second to the king. ⁸ Then the Israelites took 200,000 captives from their brothers—women, sons, and daughters. They also took a great deal of plunder from them and brought it to Samaria.

⁹ A prophet of the LORD named Oded was there. He went out to meet the army that came to Samaria and said to them, "Look, the LORD God of your ancestors handed them over to you because of His wrath against Judah, but you slaughtered them in a rage that has reached heaven. ¹⁰ Now you plan to reduce the people of Judah and Jerusalem, male and female, to slavery. Are you not also guilty before the LORD your God? ¹¹ Listen to me and return the captives you took from your brothers, for the LORD's fierce wrath is on you."

¹² So some men who were leaders of the Ephraimites—Azariah son of Johanan, Berechiah son of Meshillemoth, Jehizkiah son of Shallum, and Amasa son of Hadlai—stood in opposition to those coming from the war. ¹³ They said to them, "You must not bring the captives here, for you plan to bring guilt on us from the LORD to add to our sins and

our guilt. For we have much guilt, and fierce wrath is on Israel."

¹⁴ The army left the captives and the plunder in the presence of the officers and the congregation. ¹⁵ Then the men who were designated by name took charge of the captives and provided clothes for their naked ones from the plunder. They clothed them, gave them sandals, food and drink, dressed their wounds, and provided donkeys for all the feeble. The Israelites brought them to Jericho, the City of Palms, among their brothers. Then they returned to Samaria.

¹⁶ At that time King Ahaz asked the king of Assyria for help. ¹⁷ The Edomites came again, attacked Judah, and took captives. ¹⁸ The Philistines also raided the cities of the Judean foothills and the Negev of Judah and captured Beth-shemesh, Aijalon, Gederoth, Soco and its villages, Timnah and its villages, Gimzo and its villages, and they lived there. ¹⁹ For the LORD humbled Judah because of King Ahaz of Judah, who threw off restraint in Judah and was unfaithful to the LORD. ²⁰ Then Tiglath-pileser king of Assyria came against Ahaz; he oppressed him and did not give him support. ²¹ Although Ahaz plundered the LORD's temple and the palace of the king and of the rulers and gave the plunder to the king of Assyria, it did not help him.

²² At the time of his distress, King Ahaz himself became more unfaithful to the LORD. ²³ He sacrificed to the gods of Damascus which had defeated him; he said, "Since the gods of the kings of Aram are helping them, I will sacrifice to them so that they will help me." But they were the downfall of him and of all Israel.

²⁴ Then Ahaz gathered up the utensils of God's temple, cut them into pieces, shut the doors of the LORD's temple, and made himself altars on every street corner in Jerusalem. ²⁵ He made high places in every city of Judah to offer incense to other gods, and he provoked the God of his ancestors.

²⁶ As for the rest of his deeds and all his ways, from beginning to end, they are written about in the Book of the Kings of Judah and Israel. ²⁷ Ahaz rested with his fathers and was buried in the city, in Jerusalem, and his son Hezekiah became king in his place.

29 Hezekiah was 25 years old when he became king; he reigned 29 years in Jerusalem. His mother's name was Abijah daughter of Zechariah. ² He did what was right in the LORD's sight just as his ancestor David had done.

³ In the first year of his reign, in the first month, he opened the doors of the LORD's temple and repaired them. ⁴ Then he brought in the priests and Levites and gathered them in the eastern public square. ⁵ He said to them, "Hear me, Levites. Consecrate yourselves now and consecrate the temple of the LORD God of your ancestors. Remove everything detestable from the holy place. ⁶ For our fathers were unfaithful and did what is evil in the sight of the LORD our God. They abandoned Him, turned their faces away from the LORD's tabernacle, and turned their backs on Him. ⁷ They also closed the doors of the vestibule, extinguished the lamps, did not burn incense, and did not offer burnt offerings in the holy place of the God of Israel. ⁸ Therefore, the wrath of the LORD was on Judah and Jerusalem, and He made them an object of terror, horror, and hissing, as you see with your own eyes. ⁹ Our fathers fell by the sword, and our sons, our daughters, and our wives are in captivity because of this. ¹⁰ It is in my heart now to make a covenant with the LORD God of Israel so that His fierce wrath may turn away from us. ¹¹ My sons, don't be negligent now, for the LORD has chosen you to stand in His presence, to serve Him, and to be His ministers and burners of incense."

¹² Then the Levites stood up:

Mahath son of Amasai and Joel son of Azariah from the Kohathites; Kish son of Abdi and Azariah son of Jehallelel from the Merarites;

Joah son of Zimmah and Eden
son of Joah from the Gershonites;
¹³ Shimri and Jeuel
from the Elizaphanites;
Zechariah and Mattaniah
from the Asaphites;
¹⁴ Jehiel and Shimei
from the Hemanites;
Shemaiah and Uzziel
from the Jeduthunites.

¹⁵ They gathered their brothers together, consecrated themselves, and went
according to the king's command by the
words of the LORD to cleanse the LORD's
temple. ¹⁶ The priests went to the entrance of
the LORD's temple to cleanse it. They
took all the detestable things they
found in the LORD's sanctuary to the
courtyard of the LORD's temple. Then
the Levites received them and took
them outside to the Kidron Valley.
¹⁷ They began the consecration on the
first day of the first month, and on the
eighth day of the month they came to
the vestibule of the LORD's temple. They
consecrated the LORD's temple for eight
days, and on the sixteenth day of the
first month they finished.

𝓟SALM 91:9-16

⁹ Because you have made the
LORD—my refuge,
the Most High—your dwelling
place,
¹⁰ no harm will come to you;
no plague will come near your
tent.
¹¹ For He will give His angels orders
concerning you,
to protect you in all your ways.
¹² They will support you with their
hands
so that you will not strike your
foot against a stone.
¹³ You will tread on the lion and the
cobra;
you will trample the young lion
and the serpent.

¹⁴ Because he is lovingly devoted to
Me, I will deliver him;

I will exalt him because he knows
My name.
¹⁵ When he calls out to Me, I will
answer him;
I will be with him in trouble.
I will rescue him and give him
honor.
¹⁶ I will satisfy him with a long life
and show him My salvation.

𝓟ROVERBS 19:17

¹⁷ Kindness to the poor is a loan to
the LORD,
and He will give a reward to the
lender.

𝓐CTS 28:11-31

¹¹ After three months we set sail in an
Alexandrian ship that had wintered at
the island, with the Twin Brothers as its
figurehead. ¹² Putting in at Syracuse, we
stayed three days. ¹³ From there, after
making a circuit along the coast, we
reached Rhegium. After one day a south
wind sprang up, and the second day we
came to Puteoli. ¹⁴ There we found believers and were invited to stay with
them for seven days.

And so we came to Rome. ¹⁵ Now the
believers from there had heard the
news about us and had come to meet us
as far as Forum of Appius and Three
Taverns. When Paul saw them, he
thanked God and took courage. ¹⁶ And
when we entered Rome, Paul was permitted to stay by himself with the soldier who guarded him.

¹⁷ After three days he called together
the leaders of the Jews. And when they
had gathered he said to them: "Brothers,
although I have done nothing against
our people or the customs of our forefathers, I was delivered as a prisoner
from Jerusalem into the hands of the
Romans ¹⁸ who, after examining me,
wanted to release me, since I had not
committed a capital offense. ¹⁹ Because
the Jews objected, I was compelled to
appeal to Caesar; it was not as though I
had any accusation against my nation.
²⁰ So, for this reason I've asked to see

you and speak to you. In fact, it is for the hope of Israel that I'm wearing this chain."

²¹ And they said to him, "We haven't received any letters about you from Judea; none of the brothers has come and reported or spoken anything evil about you. ²² But we consider it suitable to hear from you what you think. For concerning this sect, we are aware that it is spoken against everywhere."

²³ After arranging a day with him, many came to him at his lodging. From dawn to dusk he expounded and witnessed about the kingdom of God. He persuaded them concerning Jesus from both the Law of Moses and the Prophets. ²⁴ Some were persuaded by what he said, but others did not believe.

²⁵ Disagreeing among themselves, they began to leave after Paul made one statement: "The Holy Spirit correctly spoke through the prophet Isaiah to your forefathers ²⁶ when He said,

Go to this people and say:
'You will listen and listen,
  yet never understand;

and you will look and look,
  yet never perceive.
²⁷ For this people's heart
  has grown callous,
  their ears are hard
  of hearing,
and they have shut their eyes;
  otherwise they might see
  with their eyes
and hear with their ears,
  understand with their heart,
and be converted—
  and I would heal them.'

²⁸ Therefore, let it be known to you that this saving work of God has been sent to the Gentiles; they will listen!" [²⁹ After he said these things, the Jews departed, while engaging in a prolonged debate among themselves.]

³⁰ Then he stayed two whole years in his own rented house. And he welcomed all who visited him, ³¹ proclaiming the kingdom of God and teaching the things concerning the Lord Jesus Christ with full boldness and without hindrance.

Generosity Generates

Kindness to the poor is a loan to the LORD, and He will give a reward to the lender.—PROVERBS 19:17

One of God's purposes for money is to bless and enrich other Christians. One of the characteristics which God wants to develop in us is that of generosity, for our generosity will determine how much spiritual light we have in our being. Take this verse: "The eye is the lamp of the body. If your eye is good, your whole body will be full of light" (Mt 6:22). If your "eye"—your outlook on life, your whole way of looking at things and people—is generous, then your whole personality is illuminated. If you have a greedy or selfish "eye," your whole being will be filled with darkness.

In Acts 11:27-30 we read about a severe famine that caused suffering to many Jewish Christians. The church at Antioch—made up mostly of Gentiles—sent an offering to their fellow believers in Jerusalem, and that offering was an important means of tearing down national and cultural barriers between them and building bonds of genuine Christian love. God likens generous giving to reaping a harvest: "The person who sows sparingly will also reap sparingly, and the person who sows generously will also reap generously" (2 Co 9:6).

Perhaps the greatest benefit of generous giving to other Christians, however, is this—it results in "overflowing in many acts of thanksgiving to God" (2 Co 9:12). Yes, God will give you much so that you can give away much, and when you take your gifts to those who need them, they will break out in thanksgiving and praise of God for your help. Giving to the needs of fellow Christians means that many will thank God and fill His church with praise.

Prayer

O God, help me to become a truly generous person, for I see that when I am generous, then my generosity generates generosity in others. I ask this in the peerless and exalted name of the Lord Jesus. Amen.

Further Study

Rm 12:9-21; 1 Kg 17:8-16; Pr 25:21; 11:25; Ec 11:1
What is the lesson of the widow of Zarephath?
How will you be generous today?

AUGUST 6

2 CHRONICLES 29:18–31:10

18 Then they went inside to King Hezekiah and said, "We have cleansed the whole temple of the LORD, the altar of burnt offering and all its utensils, and the table for the rows of the bread of the Presence and all its utensils. 19 All the utensils that King Ahaz rejected during his reign when he became unfaithful we have set up and consecrated. They are in front of the altar of the LORD."

20 King Hezekiah got up early, gathered the city officials, and went up to the LORD's temple. 21 They brought seven bulls, seven rams, seven lambs, and seven male goats as a sin offering for the kingdom, for the sanctuary, and for Judah. Then he told the descendants of Aaron, the priests, to offer them on the altar of the LORD. 22 So they slaughtered the bulls, and the priests received the blood and sprinkled it on the altar. They slaughtered the rams and sprinkled the blood on the altar. They slaughtered the lambs and sprinkled the blood on the altar. 23 Then they brought the sin offering goats right into the presence of the king and the congregation, who laid their hands on them. 24 The priests slaughtered the goats and put their blood on the altar for a sin offering, to make atonement for all Israel, for the king said that the burnt offering and sin offering were for all Israel.

25 Hezekiah stationed the Levites in the LORD's temple with cymbals, harps, and lyres according to the command of David, Gad the king's seer, and Nathan the prophet. For the command was from the LORD through His prophets. 26 The Levites stood with the instruments of

David, and the priests with the trumpets.

²⁷ Then Hezekiah ordered that the burnt offering be offered on the altar. When the burnt offerings began, the song of the LORD and the trumpets began, accompanied by the instruments of David king of Israel. ²⁸ The whole assembly was worshiping, singing the song, and blowing the trumpets—all of this continued until the burnt offering was completed. ²⁹ When the burnt offerings were completed, the king and all those present with him bowed down and worshiped. ³⁰ Then King Hezekiah and the officials told the Levites to sing praise to the LORD in the words of David and of Asaph the seer. So they sang praises with rejoicing and bowed down and worshiped.

³¹ Hezekiah concluded, "Now you are consecrated to the LORD. Come near and bring sacrifices and thank offerings to the LORD's temple." So the congregation brought sacrifices and thank offerings, and all those with willing hearts brought burnt offerings. ³² The number of burnt offerings the congregation brought was 70 bulls, 100 rams, and 200 lambs; all these were for a burnt offering to the LORD. ³³ Six hundred bulls and 3,000 sheep were consecrated.

³⁴ However, since there were not enough priests, they weren't able to skin all the burnt offerings, so their Levite brothers helped them until the work was finished and until the priests consecrated themselves. For the Levites were more conscientious to consecrate themselves than the priests were. ³⁵ Furthermore, the burnt offerings were abundant, along with the fat of the fellowship offerings and with the drink offerings for the burnt offering.

So the service of the LORD's temple was established. ³⁶ Then Hezekiah and all the people rejoiced over how God had prepared the people, for it had come about suddenly.

30 Then Hezekiah sent word throughout all Israel and Judah, and he also wrote letters to Ephraim and Manasseh to come to the LORD's temple in Jerusalem to observe the Passover of the LORD God of Israel. ² For the king and his officials and the entire congregation in Jerusalem decided to observe the Passover of the LORD in the second month ³ because they were not able to observe it at the appropriate time, since not enough of the priests had consecrated themselves and the people hadn't been gathered together in Jerusalem. ⁴ The proposal pleased the king and the congregation, ⁵ so they affirmed the proposal and spread the message throughout all Israel, from Beer-sheba to Dan, to come to observe the Passover of the LORD God of Israel in Jerusalem, for they hadn't observed it often, as prescribed.

⁶ So the couriers went throughout Israel and Judah with letters from the hand of the king and his officials, and according to the king's command, saying, "Israelites, return to the LORD God of Abraham, Isaac, and Israel so that He may return to those of you who remain, who have escaped from the grasp of the kings of Assyria. ⁷ Don't be like your fathers and your brothers who were unfaithful to the LORD God of their ancestors so that He made them an object of horror as you yourselves see. ⁸ Don't become obstinate now like your fathers did. Give your allegiance to the LORD, and come to His sanctuary that He has consecrated forever. Serve the LORD your God so that He may turn His fierce wrath away from you, ⁹ for when you return to the LORD, your brothers and your sons will receive mercy in the presence of their captors and will return to this land. For the LORD your God is gracious and merciful; He will not turn His face away from you if you return to Him."

¹⁰ The couriers traveled from city to city in the land of Ephraim and Manasseh as far as Zebulun, but the inhabitants laughed at them and mocked them. ¹¹ But some from Asher, Manasseh, and Zebulun humbled themselves and came to Jerusalem. ¹² Also, the hand of God was in Judah to give them one heart to carry out the command of the king and his officials by the word of the LORD.

¹³ A very large assembly of people was gathered in Jerusalem to observe the Festival of Unleavened Bread in the second month. ¹⁴ They proceeded to take away the altars that were in Jerusalem, and they took away the incense altars and threw them into the Kidron Valley. ¹⁵ They slaughtered the Passover lamb on the fourteenth day of the second month. The priests and Levites were ashamed, and they consecrated themselves and brought burnt offerings to the Lord's temple. ¹⁶ They stood at their prescribed posts, according to the law of Moses the man of God. The priests sprinkled the blood received from the hand of the Levites, ¹⁷ for there were many in the assembly who had not consecrated themselves, and so the Levites were in charge of slaughtering the Passover lambs for every unclean person to consecrate the lambs to the Lord. ¹⁸ For a large number of the people— many from Ephraim, Manasseh, Issachar, and Zebulun—were unclean, yet they had eaten the Passover contrary to what was written. But Hezekiah had interceded for them, saying, "May the good Lord provide atonement on behalf of ¹⁹ whoever sets his whole heart on seeking God, the Lord God of his ancestors, even though not according to the purification rules of the sanctuary." ²⁰ So the Lord heard Hezekiah and healed the people. ²¹ The Israelites who were present in Jerusalem observed the Festival of Unleavened Bread seven days with great joy, and the Levites and the priests praised the Lord day after day with loud instruments. ²² Then Hezekiah encouraged all the Levites who performed skillfully before the Lord. They ate the appointed feast for seven days, sacrificing fellowship offerings and giving thanks to the Lord God of their ancestors.

²³ The whole congregation decided to observe seven more days, so they observed seven days with joy, ²⁴ for Hezekiah king of Judah contributed 1,000 bulls and 7,000 sheep for the congregation. Also, the officials contributed 1,000 bulls and 10,000 sheep for the congregation, and many priests conse-

crated themselves. ²⁵ Then the whole assembly of Judah with the priests and Levites, the whole assembly that came from Israel, the foreigners who came from the land of Israel, and those who were living in Judah, rejoiced. ²⁶ Such rejoicing had not been seen in Jerusalem since the days of Solomon son of David, the king of Israel. ²⁷ Then the priests and the Levites stood to bless the people, and God heard their voice, and their prayer came into His holy dwelling place in heaven.

31 When all this was completed, all Israel who had attended went out to the cities of Judah and broke up the sacred pillars, chopped down the Asherah poles, and tore down the high places and altars throughout Judah and Benjamin, as well as in Ephraim and Manasseh, to the last one. Then all the Israelites returned to their cities, each to his own possession.

² Hezekiah reestablished the divisions of the priests and Levites for the burnt offerings and fellowship offerings, for ministry, for giving thanks, and for praise in the gates of the camp of the Lord, each division corresponding to his service among the priests and Levites. ³ The king contributed from his own possessions for the regular morning and evening burnt offerings, the burnt offerings of the Sabbaths, of the New Moons, and of the appointed feasts, as written in the law of the Lord. ⁴ He told the people who lived in Jerusalem to give a contribution for the priests and Levites so that they could devote their energy to the law of the Lord. ⁵ When the word spread, the Israelites gave liberally of the best of the grain, wine, oil, honey, and of all the produce of the field, and they brought an abundant tenth of everything. ⁶ As for the Israelites and Judahites who lived in the cities of Judah, they also brought a tenth of the cattle and sheep, and a tenth of the dedicated things that were consecrated to the Lord their God. They gathered them into large piles. ⁷ In the third month they began building up the piles, and they finished in the seventh

month. [8] When Hezekiah and his officials came and viewed the piles, they praised the LORD and His people Israel. [9] Hezekiah asked the priests and Levites about the piles. [10] Azariah, the chief priest of the household of Zadok, answered him, "Since they began bringing the offering to the LORD's temple, we eat and are satisfied and there is plenty left over because the LORD has blessed His people; this abundance is what is left over."

PSALM 92:1-7

[1] It is good to praise the LORD,
to sing praise to Your name,
Most High,
[2] to declare Your faithful love in the
morning
and Your faithfulness at night,
[3] with a ten-stringed harp
and the music of a lyre.

[4] For You have made me rejoice,
LORD, by what You have done;
I will shout for joy because of the
works of Your hands.
[5] How magnificent are Your works,
LORD,
how profound Your thoughts!
[6] A stupid person does not know,
a fool does not understand this:
[7] though the wicked sprout like
grass
and all evildoers flourish,
they will be eternally destroyed.

PROVERBS 19:18-19

[18] Discipline your son while there is
hope;
don't be intent on killing him.

[19] A person with great anger bears
the penalty;
if you rescue him, you'll have to
do it again.

ROMANS 1:1-23

1 Paul, a slave of Christ Jesus, called as an apostle and singled out for God's good news— [2] which He promised long ago through His prophets in the Holy Scriptures— [3] concerning His Son, Jesus Christ our Lord, who was a descendant of David according to the flesh [4] and was established as the powerful Son of God by the resurrection from the dead according to the Spirit of holiness. [5] We have received grace and apostleship through Him to bring about the obedience of faith among all the nations, on behalf of His name, [6] including yourselves who are also Jesus Christ's by calling:

[7] To all who are in Rome, loved by God, called as saints.

Grace to you and peace from God our Father and the Lord Jesus Christ.

[8] First, I thank my God through Jesus Christ for all of you because the news of your faith is being reported in all the world. [9] For God, whom I serve with my spirit in telling the good news about His Son, is my witness that I constantly mention you, [10] always asking in my prayers that if it is somehow in God's will, I may now at last succeed in coming to you. [11] For I want very much to see you, that I may impart to you some spiritual gift to strengthen you, [12] that is, to be mutually encouraged by each other's faith, both yours and mine.

[13] Now I want you to know, brothers, that I often planned to come to you (but was prevented until now) in order that I might have a fruitful ministry among you, just as among the rest of the Gentiles. [14] I am obligated both to Greeks and barbarians, both to the wise and the foolish. [15] So I am eager to preach the good news to you also who are in Roman.

[16] For I am not ashamed of the gospel, because it is God's power for salvation to everyone who believes, first to the Jew, and also to the Greek. [17] For in it God's righteousness is revealed from faith to faith, just as it is written: **The righteous will live by faith.**

[18] For God's wrath is revealed from heaven against all godlessness and unrighteousness of people who by their unrighteousness suppress the truth, [19] since what can be known about God

is evident among them, because God has shown it to them. [20] From the creation of the world His invisible attributes, that is, His eternal power and divine nature, have been clearly seen, being understood through what He has made. As a result, people are without excuse. [21] For though they knew God, they did not glorify Him as God or show gratitude. Instead, their thinking became nonsense, and their senseless minds were darkened. [22] Claiming to be wise, they became fools [23] and exchanged the glory of the immortal God for images resembling mortal man, birds, four-footed animals, and reptiles.

Quiet Contemplation

You have made me rejoice, LORD, by what You have done.—PSALM 92:4

The contemplation of God humbles the mind, expands the soul, and consoles the heart.

How does it expand the soul? "The soul," says one theologian, "is at home only when it is in God." He meant, of course, that as the soul was made for God, it can only function effectively when indwelt by God. Contemplation of God is like breath to the soul; it inflates it and causes it to be fully actualized. "My body and my whole physiology functions better when God is in it," said a doctor to me some years ago. I replied: "And so it is also with the soul, dear doctor, so it is also with the soul."

Another benefit of contemplating God is that it consoles the heart. But how? It does so by focusing the heart's attention on the greatness and goodness of the Eternal and also on His tender mercies and compassion. The more we know of God, the more we realize that when He permits us to pass through deep and dark waters, it is not because He is powerless to deliver us, but because a beneficent and eternal purpose is being worked out in that process. And what is more, we discover that God is not interested merely in working out His purposes in us, but in imparting to us a richer sense of His presence. In God there is a balm for every wound, a comfort for every sorrow, and healing for every heartache.

All kinds of nostrums are on offer in today's church to help the hurting (some of them more secular than sacred), but I know of nothing that calms the swelling billows of sorrow and grief as does the quiet contemplation of the Godhead.

Prayer

My Father and my God, forgive me if in times of trial and distress I look for comfort in the wrong places. You and You alone are able to meet my soul's deepest needs. Help me to see this not merely as an opinion but as a conviction. In Jesus' name. Amen.

Further Study

Ps 145:1-21; Dt 32:1-4; 1 Ch 29:10-13
How did David express the feelings of his soul?
How did Moses put it?

AUGUST 7

2 CHRONICLES
31:11–33:13

¹¹ Hezekiah told them to prepare chambers in the LORD's temple, and they prepared them. ¹² The offering, the tenth, and the dedicated things were brought faithfully. Conaniah the Levite was the officer in charge of them, and his brother Shimei was second. ¹³ Jehiel, Azaziah, Nahath, Asahel, Jerimoth, Jozabad, Eliel, Ismachiah, Mahath, and Benaiah were deputies under the authority of Conaniah and his brother Shimei by appointment of King Hezekiah and of Azariah the ruler of God's temple.

¹⁴ Kore son of Imnah the Levite, the keeper of the East Gate, was over the freewill offerings to God to distribute the contribution to the LORD and the consecrated things. ¹⁵ Eden, Miniamin, Jeshua, Shemaiah, Amariah, and Shecaniah in the cities of the priests were to faithfully distribute it under his authority to their brothers by divisions, whether large or small. ¹⁶ In addition, they distributed it to males registered by genealogy three years old and above; to all who would enter the LORD's temple for their daily duty, for their service in their responsibilities according to their divisions. ¹⁷ They distributed also to those recorded by genealogy of the priests by their ancestral families and the Levites 20 years old and above, by their responsibilities in their divisions; ¹⁸ to those registered by genealogy—with all their infants, wives, sons, and daughters—of the whole assembly (for they had faithfully consecrated themselves as holy); ¹⁹ and to the descendants of Aaron, the priests, in the common fields of their cities, in each and every city. There were men who were registered by name to distribute a portion to every male among the priests and to every Levite recorded by genealogy.

²⁰ Hezekiah did this throughout all Judah. He did what was good and upright and true before the LORD his God. ²¹ He was diligent in every deed that he began in the service of God's temple, in the law and in the commandment, in order to seek his God, and he prospered.

32 After these faithful deeds, Sennacherib king of Assyria came and entered Judah. He laid siege to the fortified cities and intended to break into them. ² Hezekiah saw that Sennacherib had come and that he planned war on Jerusalem, ³ so he consulted with his officials and his warriors about stopping up the waters of the springs that were outside the city, and they helped him. ⁴ Many people gathered and stopped up all the springs and the stream that flowed through the land; they said, "Why should the kings of Assyria come and find plenty of water?" ⁵ Then Hezekiah strengthened his position by rebuilding the entire broken-down wall and heightening the towers and the other outside wall. He repaired the supporting terraces of the city of David, and made an abundance of weapons and shields.

⁶ He set military commanders over the people and gathered the people in the square of the city gate. Then he encouraged them, saying, ⁷ "Be strong and courageous! Don't be afraid or discouraged before the king of Assyria or before all the multitude with him, for there are more with us than with him. ⁸ He has only human strength, but we have the LORD our God to help us and to fight our battles." So the people relied on the words of King Hezekiah of Judah.

⁹ After this, while Sennacherib king of Assyria with all his armed forces be-

sieged Lachish, he sent his servants to Jerusalem against King Hezekiah of Judah and against all those of Judah who were in Jerusalem, saying, ¹⁰ "This is what King Sennacherib of Assyria says: 'What are you trusting in, you who remain under the siege of Jerusalem? ¹¹ Isn't Hezekiah misleading you to give you over to death by famine and thirst when he says, "The LORD our God will deliver us from the power of the king of Assyria"? ¹² Didn't Hezekiah himself remove His high places and His altars and say to Judah and Jerusalem: "You must worship before one altar, and you must burn incense on it"?

¹³ " 'Don't you know what I and my fathers have done to all the peoples of the lands? Have any of the national gods of the lands been able to deliver their land from my power? ¹⁴ Who among all the gods of these nations that my fathers utterly destroyed was able to deliver his people from my power, that your God should be able to do the same for you? ¹⁵ So now, don't let Hezekiah deceive you, and don't let him mislead you like this. Don't believe him, for no god of any nation or kingdom has been able to deliver his people from my power or the power of my fathers. How much less will your gods deliver you from my power!' "

¹⁶ His servants said more against the LORD God and against His servant Hezekiah. ¹⁷ He also wrote letters to mock the LORD God of Israel, saying against Him:

Just like the national gods of the lands that did not deliver their people from my power, so Hezekiah's God will not deliver His people from my power.

¹⁸ Then they called out loudly in Hebrew to the people of Jerusalem who were on the wall to frighten and discourage them in order that he might capture the city. ¹⁹ They spoke against the God of Jerusalem like they had spoken against the gods of the peoples of the land, which were made by human hands.

²⁰ King Hezekiah and the prophet Isaiah son of Amoz prayed about this and cried out to heaven, ²¹ and the LORD sent an angel who annihilated every brave warrior, leader, and commander in the camp of the king of Assyria. So the king of Assyria returned with shame to his land. He went to the temple of his god, and there some of his own children cut him down with the sword.

²² So the LORD saved Hezekiah and the inhabitants of Jerusalem from the power of King Sennacherib of Assyria and from the power of all others. He gave them rest on every side. ²³ Many were bringing an offering to the LORD to Jerusalem and valuable gifts to King Hezekiah of Judah, and he was exalted in the eyes of all the nations after that.

²⁴ In those days Hezekiah became sick to the point of death, so he prayed to the LORD, and He spoke to him and gave him a miraculous sign. ²⁵ However, because his heart was proud, Hezekiah didn't respond according to the benefit that had come to him. So there was wrath upon him, upon Judah, and upon Jerusalem. ²⁶ Then Hezekiah humbled himself for the pride of his heart—he and the inhabitants of Jerusalem—so the LORD's wrath didn't come on them during Hezekiah's lifetime.

²⁷ Hezekiah had abundant riches and glory, and he made himself treasuries for silver, gold, precious stones, spices, shields, and every desirable item. ²⁸ He made warehouses for the harvest of grain, wine, and oil, and stalls for all kinds of cattle, and pens for flocks. ²⁹ He made cities for himself, and he acquired herds of sheep and cattle in abundance, for God gave him abundant possessions. ³⁰ This same Hezekiah blocked the outlet of the water of the Upper Gihon and channeled it smoothly downward and westward to the city of David. Hezekiah succeeded in everything he did. ³¹ When the ambassadors of Babylon's rulers were sent to him to inquire about the miraculous sign that happened in the land, God left him to test him and discover what was in his heart.

³² As for the rest of the events of Hezekiah's reign and his deeds of faithful

love, note that they are written about in the Visions of the Prophet Isaiah son of Amoz, and in the Book of the Kings of Judah and Israel. [33] Hezekiah rested with his fathers and was buried on the ascent to the tombs of David's descendants. All Judah and the inhabitants of Jerusalem paid him honor at his death. His son Manasseh became king in his place.

33

Manasseh was 12 years old when he became king; he reigned 55 years in Jerusalem. [2] He did what was evil in the LORD's sight, imitating the detestable practices of the nations that the LORD had dispossessed before the Israelites. [3] He rebuilt the high places that his father Hezekiah had torn down and reestablished the altars for the Baals. He made Asherah poles, and he worshiped the whole heavenly host and served them. [4] He built altars in the LORD's temple, where the LORD had said: "Jerusalem is where My name will remain forever." [5] He built altars to the whole heavenly host in both courtyards of the LORD's temple. [6] He passed his sons through the fire in the Valley of Hinnom. He practiced witchcraft, divination, and sorcery, and consulted mediums and spiritists. He did a great deal of evil in the LORD's sight, provoking Him.

[7] Manasseh set up a carved image of the idol he had made, in God's temple, about which God had said to David and his son Solomon: "I will establish My name forever in this temple and in Jerusalem, which I have chosen out of all the tribes of Israel. [8] I will never again remove the feet of the Israelites from upon the land where I stationed your ancestors, if only they will be careful to do all that I have commanded them through Moses—all the law, statutes, and judgments." [9] So Manasseh caused Judah and the inhabitants of Jerusalem to stray so that they did worse evil than the nations the LORD had destroyed before the Israelites.

[10] The LORD spoke to Manasseh and his people, but they didn't listen. [11] So He brought against them the military commanders of the king of Assyria. They captured Manasseh with hooks, bound him with bronze shackles, and took him to Babylon. [12] When he was in distress, he sought the favor of the LORD his God and earnestly humbled himself before the God of his ancestors. [13] He prayed to Him, so He heard his petition and granted his request, and brought him back to Jerusalem, to his kingdom. So Manasseh came to know that the LORD is God.

PSALM 92:8-15

[8] But You, LORD, are exalted forever.
[9] For indeed, LORD, Your enemies—
indeed, Your enemies will perish;
all evildoers will be scattered.
[10] You have lifted up my horn like
that of a wild ox;
I have been anointed with oil.
[11] My eyes look down on my
enemies;
my ears hear evildoers when they
attack me.
[12] The righteous thrive like a palm
tree
and grow like a cedar tree in
Lebanon.
[13] Planted in the house of the LORD,
they thrive in the courtyards of
our God.
[14] They will still bear fruit in old
age,
healthy and green,
[15] to declare: "The LORD is just;
He is my rock, and there is no
unrighteousness in Him."

PROVERBS 19:20-21

[20] Listen to counsel and receive
instruction
so that you may be wise in later
life.

[21] Many plans are in a man's heart,
but the LORD's decree will prevail.

ROMANS 1:24–2:16

²⁴ Therefore God delivered them over in the cravings of their hearts to sexual impurity, so that their bodies were degraded among themselves. ²⁵ They exchanged the truth of God for a lie, and worshiped and served something created instead of the Creator, who is blessed forever. Amen. ²⁶ This is why God delivered them over to degrading passions. For even their females exchanged natural sexual intercourse for what is unnatural. ²⁷ The males in the same way also left natural sexual intercourse with females and were inflamed in their lust for one another. Males committed shameless acts with males and received in their own persons the appropriate penalty for their perversion.

²⁸ And because they did not think it worthwhile to have God in their knowledge, God delivered them over to a worthless mind to do what is morally wrong. ²⁹ They are filled with all unrighteousness, evil, greed, and wickedness. They are full of envy, murder, disputes, deceit, and malice. They are gossips, ³⁰ slanderers, God-haters, arrogant, proud, boastful, inventors of evil, disobedient to parents, ³¹ undiscerning, untrustworthy, unloving, and unmerciful. ³² Although they know full well God's just sentence—that those who practice such things deserve to die—they not only do them, but even applaud others who practice them.

2 Therefore, anyone of you who judges is without excuse. For when you judge another, you condemn yourself, since you, the judge, do the same things. ² We know that God's judgment on those who do such things is based on the truth. ³ Do you really think—anyone of you who judges those who do such things yet do the same—that you will escape God's judgment? ⁴ Or do you despise the riches of His kindness, restraint, and patience, not recognizing that God's kindness is intended to lead you to repentance? ⁵ But because of your hardness and unrepentant heart you are storing up wrath for yourself in the day of wrath, when God's righteous judgment is revealed. ⁶ He will repay each one according to his works: ⁷ eternal life to those who by patiently doing good seek for glory, honor, and immortality; ⁸ but wrath and indignation to those who are self-seeking and disobey the truth, but are obeying unrighteousness; ⁹ affliction and distress for every human being who does evil, first to the Jew, and also to the Greek; ¹⁰ but glory, honor, and peace for everyone who does good, first to the Jew, and also to the Greek. ¹¹ There is no favoritism with God.

¹² All those who sinned without the law will also perish without the law, and all those who sinned under the law will be judged by the law. ¹³ For the hearers of the law are not righteous before God, but the doers of the law will be declared righteous. ¹⁴ So, when Gentiles, who do not have the law, instinctively do what the law demands, they are a law to themselves even though they do not have the law. ¹⁵ They show that the work of the law is written on their hearts. Their consciences testify in support of this, and their competing thoughts either accuse or excuse them ¹⁶ on the day when God judges what people have kept secret, according to my gospel through Christ Jesus.

Too Close to the Ground

But You, LORD, are exalted forever.

—PSALM 92:8

The reason our personal problems and difficulties seem so large and ominous is due mainly to the fact that we have not brought God into proper focus. When we are able to see Him as He really is—"high and lofty"—then all our troubles and anxieties are reduced to their proper proportions.

A minister looked through his study window one day into the garden next door. He saw a little boy there, holding in his hand two pieces of wood, each about eighteen inches long. He heard him ask his mother if he could make a weathercock. After getting her permission, he proceeded to nail one piece of wood upright on the low garden wall, then nailed the other piece loosely on top. Soon the loosely nailed piece of wood turned and twisted, first this way and then that, and the little boy danced with delight. He thought he had made a weathercock that registered the winds, but all it did was register the draughts. "It turned half a circle," said the minister, "when the back door banged."

From where the minister sat in his study, he could see a real weathercock on the church steeple. It was as steady as a rock in the constant winds that blew in from the sea. There are many Christians, however, who are like the little boy's weathercock, always living at the mercy of every gust of circumstance, their thoughts of God fluctuating with their personal experiences. They take their direction from a weathercock that is too close to the ground.

Prayer

O God, my Father, forgive me that my life is taken up more with the immediate than the ultimate. I have been glancing at You and gazing at my circumstances. From today it will be different—I will glance at my circumstances and gaze at You. Amen.

Further Study

Ps 8:1-9; 1 Co 13:12; 2 Co 3:18
How did the psalmist focus his gaze on God?
How did Paul describe it?

AUGUST 8

2 CHRONICLES
33:14–35:15

¹⁴ After this, he built the outer wall of the city of David from west of Gihon in the valley to the entrance of the Fish Gate; he brought it around the Ophel, and he heightened it considerably. He also placed military commanders in all the fortified cities of Judah.

¹⁵ He removed the foreign gods and the idol from the LORD's temple, along with all the altars that he had built on the mountain of the LORD's temple and in Jerusalem, and he threw them outside the city. ¹⁶ He built the altar of the LORD and offered fellowship and thank offerings on it. Then he told Judah to serve the LORD God of Israel. ¹⁷ However, the people still sacrificed at the high places, but only to the LORD their God.

¹⁸ The rest of the events of Manasseh's reign, along with his prayer to his God and the words of the seers who spoke to him in the name of the LORD God of Israel, are written about in the Events of Israel's Kings. ¹⁹ His prayer and how God granted his request, and all his sin and unfaithfulness and the sites where he built high places and set up Asherah poles and carved images before he humbled himself, they are written about in the Records of Hozai. ²⁰ Manasseh rested with his fathers, and he was buried in his own house. His son Amon became king in his place.

²¹ Amon was 22 years old when he became king; he reigned two years in Jerusalem. ²² He did what was evil in the LORD's sight just as his father Manasseh had done. Amon sacrificed to all the carved images that his father Manasseh had made, and he served them. ²³ But he did not humble himself before the LORD like his father Manasseh humbled himself; instead, Amon increased his guilt. ²⁴ So his servants conspired against him and put him to death in his own house. ²⁵ Then the common people executed all those who conspired against King Amon and made his son Josiah king in his place.

34 Josiah was eight years old when he became king; he reigned 31 years in Jerusalem. ² He did what was right in the LORD's sight and walked in the ways of his ancestor David; he did not turn aside to the right or the left.

³ In the eighth year of his reign, while he was still a youth, Josiah began to seek the God of his ancestor David, and in the twelfth year he began to cleanse Judah and Jerusalem of the high places, the Asherah poles, the carved images, and the cast images. ⁴ Then in his presence the altars of the Baals were torn down, and the incense altars that were above them he chopped down. The Asherah poles, the carved images, and the cast images he shattered, crushed to dust, and scattered over the graves of those who had sacrificed to them. ⁵ He burned the bones of the priests on their altars. So he cleansed Judah and Jerusalem. ⁶ He did the same in the cities of Manasseh, Ephraim, and Simeon, and as far as Naphtali and on their surrounding mountain shrines. ⁷ He tore down the altars, and he smashed the Asherah poles and the carved images to powder. He chopped down all the incense altars throughout the land of Israel and returned to Jerusalem.

⁸ In the eighteenth year of his reign, in order to cleanse the land and the temple, Josiah sent Shaphan son of Azaliah, along with Maaseiah the governor of the city and the recorder Joah son of Joahaz, to repair the temple of the LORD his God.

⁹ So they went to Hilkiah the high priest, and gave him the money brought into God's temple. The Levites and the doorkeepers had collected money from Manasseh, Ephraim, and from the entire remnant of Israel, and from all Judah, Benjamin, and the inhabitants of Jerusalem. ¹⁰ They put it into the hands of those doing the work—those who oversaw the LORD's temple. They in turn gave it to the workmen who were working in the LORD's temple, to repair and restore the temple; ¹¹ they gave it to the carpenters and builders and also used it to buy quarried stone and timbers—for joining and to make beams—for the buildings that Judah's Kings had destroyed.

¹² The men were doing the work with integrity. Their overseers were Jahath and Obadiah the Levites from the Merarites, and Zechariah and Meshullam from the Kohathites as supervisors. The Levites were all skilled on musical instruments. ¹³ They were also over the porters and were supervising all those doing the work task by task. Some of the Levites were secretaries, officers, and gatekeepers.

¹⁴ When they brought out the money that had been deposited in the LORD's temple, Hilkiah the priest found the book of the law of the LORD written by the hand of Moses. ¹⁵ Consequently, Hilkiah told Shaphan the court secretary, "I have found the book of the law in the LORD's temple," and he gave the book to Shaphan.

¹⁶ Shaphan took the book to the king, and also reported, "Your servants are doing all that was placed in their hands. ¹⁷ They have emptied out the money that was found in the LORD's temple and have put it into the hand of the overseers and the hand of those doing the work." ¹⁸ Then Shaphan the court secretary told the king, "Hilkiah the priest gave me a book," and Shaphan read it in the presence of the king.

¹⁹ When the king heard the words of the law, he tore his clothes. ²⁰ Then he commanded Hilkiah, Ahikam son of Shaphan, Abdon son of Micah, Shaphan the court secretary, and the king's servant Asaiah, ²¹ "Go. Inquire of the LORD for me and for those remaining in Israel and Judah, concerning the words of the book that was found. For great is the LORD's wrath that is poured out on us because our fathers have not kept the word of the LORD in order to do everything written in this book."

²² So Hilkiah and those the king had designated went to the prophetess Huldah, the wife of Shallum son of Tokhath, son of Hasrah, keeper of the wardrobe. She lived in Jerusalem in the Second District. They spoke with her about this.

²³ She said to them, "This is what the LORD God of Israel says: Say to the man who sent you to Me, ²⁴ 'This is what the LORD says: I am about to bring disaster on this place and on its inhabitants, fulfilling all the curses written in the book that they read in the presence of the king of Judah, ²⁵ because they have abandoned Me and burned incense to other gods in order to provoke Me with all the works of their hands. My wrath will be poured out on this place, and it will not be quenched.' ²⁶ Say this to the king of Judah who sent you to inquire of the LORD: 'This is what the LORD God of Israel says: As for the words that you heard, ²⁷ because your heart was tender and you humbled yourself before God when you heard His words against this place and against its inhabitants, and because you humbled yourself before Me, and you tore your clothes and wept before Me, I Myself have heard'—this is the LORD speaking. ²⁸ 'I will indeed gather you to your fathers, and you will be gathered to your grave in peace. Your eyes will not see all the disaster that I am bringing on this place and on its inhabitants.' "

Then they reported to the king.

²⁹ So the king sent messengers and gathered all the elders of Judah and Jerusalem. ³⁰ Then the king went up to the LORD's temple with all the men of Judah and the inhabitants of Jerusalem, as well as the priests and the Levites—all the people from great to small. He read in their hearing all the words of the book of the covenant that had been

found in the LORD's temple. ³¹ Next the king stood at his post and made a covenant in the LORD's presence to follow the LORD and to keep His commandments, His decrees, and His statutes with all his heart and with all his soul in order to carry out the words of the covenant written in this book. ³² Then he had all those present in Jerusalem and Benjamin enter the covenant. So all the inhabitants of Jerusalem carried out the covenant of God, the God of their ancestors.

³³ So Josiah removed everything that was detestable from all the lands belonging to the Israelites, and he required all who were present in Israel to serve the LORD their God. Throughout his reign they did not turn aside from following the LORD God of their ancestors.

35 Josiah observed the LORD's Passover and slaughtered the Passover lambs on the fourteenth day of the first month. ² He appointed the priests to their responsibilities and encouraged them to serve in the LORD's temple. ³ He said to the Levites who taught all Israel the holy things of the LORD, "Put the holy ark in the temple built by Solomon son of David king of Israel. Since you do not have to carry it on your shoulders, now serve the LORD your God and His people Israel.

⁴ "Organize your ancestral houses by your divisions according to the written instruction of David king of Israel and that of his son Solomon. ⁵ Serve in the holy place by the divisions of the ancestral houses for your brothers, the lay people, and the distribution of the tribal household of the Levites. ⁶ Slaughter the Passover lambs, consecrate yourselves, and make preparations for your brothers to carry out the word of the LORD through Moses."

⁷ Then Josiah donated 30,000 sheep, lambs, and kid goats, plus 3,000 bulls from his own possessions, for the Passover sacrifices for all the lay people who were present.

⁸ His officials also donated willingly for the people, the priests, and the Levites. Hilkiah, Zechariah, and Jehiel, leaders of God's temple, gave 2,600 Passover sacrifices and 300 bulls for the priests. ⁹ Conaniah and his brothers Shemaiah and Nethanel, and Hashabiah, Jeiel, and Jozabad, officers of the Levites, donated 5,000 Passover sacrifices for the Levites, plus 500 bulls.

¹⁰ So the service was established; the priests stood at their posts and the Levites in their divisions according to the king's command. ¹¹ Then they slaughtered the Passover lambs, and while the Levites were skinning the animals, the priests sprinkled the blood they had been given. ¹² They removed the burnt offerings so that they might be given to the divisions of the ancestral houses of the lay people to offer to the LORD, according to what is written in the book of Moses; they did the same with the bulls. ¹³ They roasted the Passover lambs with fire according to regulation. They boiled the holy sacrifices in pots, in kettles, and in bowls; and they quickly brought them to the lay people. ¹⁴ Afterwards, they made preparations for themselves and for the priests, since the priests, the descendants of Aaron, were busy offering up burnt offerings and fat until night. So the Levites made preparations for themselves and for the priests, the descendants of Aaron.

¹⁵ The singers, the descendants of Asaph, were at their stations according to the command of David, Asaph, Heman, and Jeduthun the king's seer. Also, the gatekeepers were at each gate. Because their Levite brothers had made preparations for them, none of them left their tasks.

....

PSALM 93:1-5

¹ The LORD reigns! He is robed in
majesty;
The LORD is robed, enveloped in
strength.
The world is firmly established; it
cannot be shaken.
² Your throne has been established
from the beginning;

You are from eternity.
3 The floods have lifted up, LORD,
the floods have lifted up their
voice;
the floods lift up their pounding
waves.
4 Greater than the roar of many
waters—
the mighty breakers of the sea—
the LORD on high is majestic.

5 LORD, Your testimonies are
completely reliable;
holiness is the beauty of Your
house
for all the days to come.

PROVERBS 19:22-23

22 A man's desire should be loyalty
to the covenant;
better to be a poor man than a
perjurer.

23 The fear of the LORD leads to life;
one will sleep at night without
danger.

ROMANS 2:17–3:8

17 Now if you call yourself a Jew, and
rest in the law, and boast in God, 18 and
know His will, and approve the things
that are superior, being instructed from
the law, 19 and are convinced that you
are a guide for the blind, a light to those
in darkness, 20 an instructor of the ignorant, a teacher of the immature, having
in the law the full expression of knowledge and truth— 21 you then, who teach
another, do you not teach yourself? You
who preach, "You must not steal"—do
you steal? 22 You who say, "You must not
commit adultery"—do you commit
adultery? You who detest idols, do you
rob their temples? 23 You who boast in
the law, do you dishonor God by break-

ing the law? 24 For, as it is written: **The
name of God is blasphemed among
the Gentiles because of you.**

25 For circumcision benefits you if you
observe the law, but if you are a lawbreaker, your circumcision has become
uncircumcision. 26 Therefore if an uncircumcised man keeps the law's requirements, will his uncircumcision not be
counted as circumcision? 27 A man who
is physically uncircumcised, but who
fulfills the law, will judge you who are a
lawbreaker in spite of having the letter
of the law and circumcision. 28 For a person is not a Jew who is one outwardly,
and true circumcision is not something
visible in the flesh. 29 On the contrary, a
person is a Jew who is one inwardly, and
circumcision is of the heart—by the
Spirit, not the letter. His praise is not
from men but from God.

3 So what advantage does the Jew
have? Or what is the benefit of circumcision? 2 Considerable in every way.
First, they were entrusted with the spoken words of God. 3 What then? If some
did not believe, will their unbelief cancel God's faithfulness? 4 Absolutely not!
God must be true, but everyone is a liar,
as it is written:

That You may be justified
in Your words
and triumph when You judge.

5 But if our unrighteousness highlights
God's righteousness, what are we to
say? I use a human argument: Is God
unrighteous to inflict wrath? 6 Absolutely not! Otherwise, how will God
judge the world? 7 But if by my lie God's
truth is amplified to His glory, why am I
also still judged as a sinner? 8 And why
not say, just as some people slanderous-
ly claim we say, "Let us do evil so that
good may come"? Their condemnation
is deserved!

Unassailable—but Accessible

The LORD reigns! He is robed in majesty . . .
Your throne has been established from the beginning.

—PSALM 93:1-2

Ultimate authority rests with God who sits upon His throne. Years ago congregations frequently sang a chorus that goes like this:

God is still on the throne,
And He will remember His own;
Though trials may press us
And burdens distress us
He never will leave us alone.

The story is told of a little boy who, when introduced to this chorus for the first time in his Sunday school, came home and told his mother: "We learned a new song in Sunday school today." "Oh yes," said his mother, "what was it?" "God is still on the phone," said the little lad. Well that wasn't exactly what he had been taught, but the thought contained in those words was equally true. Though God reigns from a majestic throne, He is accessible to us at all times of day and night. The lines of communication that lead from us to Him are never blocked and never "down." When a man or woman, boy or girl says, "God be merciful to me a sinner," the message goes straight through to the throne, and they receive His personal reply: "You are forgiven, redeemed, and set free from your sin."

The throne of God, you see, is not only a throne of righteousness but a throne of grace! Righteousness says: "Stay back until you are good enough to approach." Grace says: "I will put on you the robes of righteousness that are provided for you by Christ—now you are good enough." Too good to be true? Too good not to be true!

Prayer

Father, I draw near again today to Your throne of grace and with the redeemed all around the world sing: "How marvelous, how wonderful, this my song shall ever be; how marvelous, how wonderful is my Savior's love to me." Amen.

Further Study

Heb 4:1-6; Eph 1:1-7; 2:7; Php 4:19; 1 Tm 1:14
What will God meet according to His riches?
What was Paul's testimony?

AUGUST 9

2 CHRONICLES 35:16– EZRA 1:11

16 So all the service of the LORD was established that day for observing the Passover and for offering burnt offerings on the altar of the LORD, according to the command of King Josiah. 17 The Israelites who were present in Judah also observed the Passover at that time and the Festival of Unleavened Bread for seven days. 18 No Passover had been observed like it in Israel since the days of Samuel the prophet. None of the kings of Israel ever observed a Passover like the one that Josiah observed with the priests, the Levites, all Judah, the Israelites who were present in Judah, and the inhabitants of Jerusalem. 19 In the eighteenth year of Josiah's reign, this Passover was observed.

20 After all this that Josiah had prepared for the temple, Neco king of Egypt marched up to fight at Carchemish by the Euphrates, and Josiah went out to confront him. 21 But Neco sent messengers to him, saying, "What is the issue between you and me, king of Judah? I have not come against you today but to the dynasty I am fighting. God told me to hurry. Stop opposing God who is with me; don't make Him destroy you!"

22 But Josiah did not turn away from him; instead, in order to fight with him he disguised himself. He did not listen to Neco's words from the mouth of God, but went to the Valley of Megiddo to fight. 23 The archers shot King Josiah, and he said to his servants, "Take me away, for I am severely wounded!" 24 So his servants took him out of the war chariot, carried him in his second chariot, and brought him to Jerusalem. Then he died, and they buried him in the tomb of his fathers. All Judah and Jerusalem mourned for Josiah. 25 Jeremiah chanted a dirge over Josiah, and all the singing men and singing women still speak of Josiah in their dirges to this very day. They established them as a statute for Israel, and indeed they are written in the Dirges.

26 The rest of the events of Josiah's reign, along with his deeds of faithful love according to what is written in the law of the LORD, 27 and his words, from beginning to end, are written about in the Book of the Kings of Israel and Judah.

36 Then the common people took Jehoahaz son of Josiah and made him king in Jerusalem in place of his father.

2 Jehoahaz was 23 years old when he became king; he reigned three months in Jerusalem. 3 The king of Egypt deposed him in Jerusalem and fined the land 7,500 pounds of silver and 75 pounds of gold.

4 Then Neco king of Egypt made Jehoahaz's brother Eliakim king over Judah and Jerusalem and changed Eliakim's name to Jehoiakim. But Neco took his brother Jehoahaz and brought him to Egypt.

5 Jehoiakim was 25 years old when he became king; he reigned 11 years in Jerusalem. He did what was evil in the sight of the LORD his God. 6 Now Nebuchadnezzar king of Babylon attacked him and bound him in bronze shackles to take him to Babylon. 7 Also Nebuchadnezzar took some of the utensils of the LORD's temple to Babylon and put them in his temple in Babylon.

8 The rest of the deeds of Jehoiakim, the detestable things he did, and what was found against him, are written about in the Book of Israel's Kings. His brother Jehoiachin became king in his place.

⁹ Jehoiachin was 18 years old when he became king; he reigned three months and 10 days in Jerusalem. He did what was evil in the LORD's sight. ¹⁰ In the spring Nebuchadnezzar sent for him and brought him to Babylon along with the valuable utensils of the LORD's temple. Then he made Jehoiachin's brother Zedekiah king over Judah and Jerusalem.

¹¹ Zedekiah was 21 years old when he became king; he reigned 11 years in Jerusalem. ¹² He did what was evil in the sight of the LORD his God and did not humble himself before Jeremiah the prophet at the LORD's command. ¹³ He also rebelled against King Nebuchadnezzar who had made him swear allegiance by God. He became obstinate and hardened his heart against returning to the LORD God of Israel. ¹⁴ All the leaders of the priests and the people multiplied their unfaithful deeds, imitating all the detestable practices of the nations, and they defiled the LORD's temple that He had consecrated in Jerusalem.

¹⁵ But the LORD God of their ancestors sent word against them by the hand of his messengers, sending them time and time again, for He had compassion on His people and on His dwelling place. ¹⁶ But they kept ridiculing God's messengers, despising His words, and scoffing at His prophets, until the LORD's wrath was so stirred up against His people that there was no remedy. ¹⁷ So He brought up against them the king of the Chaldeans, who killed their choice young men with the sword in the house of their sanctuary. He had no pity on young man and virgin or elderly and aged; He handed them all over to him. ¹⁸ He took everything to Babylon—all the articles of God's temple, large and small, the treasures of the LORD's temple, and the treasures of the king and his officials. ¹⁹ Then the Chaldeans burned God's temple. They tore down Jerusalem's wall, burned down all its palaces, and destroyed all its valuable utensils.

²⁰ Those who escaped from the sword he deported to Babylon, and they became servants to him and his sons until the rise of the Persian kingdom. ²¹ This fulfilled the word of the LORD through Jeremiah and the land enjoyed its Sabbath rest all the days of the desolation until 70 years were fulfilled.

²² In the first year of Cyrus king of Persia, the word of the LORD spoken through Jeremiah was fulfilled. The LORD put it into the mind of King Cyrus of Persia to issue a proclamation throughout his entire kingdom and also to put it in writing:

²³ This is what King Cyrus of Persia says: The LORD, the God of heaven, has given me all the kingdoms of the earth and has appointed me to build Him a temple at Jerusalem in Judah. Whoever among you of His people may go up, and may the LORD his God be with him.

1 In the first year of Cyrus king of Persia, the word of the LORD spoken through Jeremiah was fulfilled. The LORD put it into the mind of King Cyrus to issue a proclamation throughout his entire kingdom and to put it in writing:

² This is what King Cyrus of Persia says: "The LORD, the God of heaven, has given me all the kingdoms of the earth and has appointed me to build Him a house at Jerusalem in Judah. ³ Whoever is among His people, may his God be with him, and may he go to Jerusalem in Judah and build the house of the LORD, the God of Israel, the God who is in Jerusalem. ⁴ Let every survivor, wherever he lives, be assisted by the men of that region with silver, gold, goods, and livestock, along with a freewill offering for the house of God in Jerusalem."

⁵ So the family leaders of Judah and Benjamin, along with the priests and Levites—everyone God had motivated—prepared to go up and rebuild the LORD's house in Jerusalem. ⁶ All their neighbors supported them with silver articles, gold, goods, livestock,

and valuables, in addition to all that was given as a freewill offering. [7] King Cyrus also brought out the articles of the LORD's house that Nebuchadnezzar had taken from Jerusalem and had placed in the house of his gods. [8] King Cyrus of Persia had them brought out under the supervision of Mithredath the treasurer, who counted them out to Sheshbazzar the prince of Judah. [9] This was the inventory:

> 30 gold basins,
> 1,000 silver basins,
> 29 silver knives, [10] 30 gold bowls,
> 410 various silver bowls,
> and 1,000 other articles.

[11] The gold and silver articles totaled 5,400. Sheshbazzar brought all of them when the exiles went up from Babylon to Jerusalem.

PSALM 94:1-11

1 LORD, God of vengeance—
  God of vengeance, appear.
2 Rise up, Judge of the earth;
  repay the proud what they
    deserve.
3 LORD, how long will the wicked—
  how long will the wicked gloat?

4 They pour out arrogant words;
  all the evildoers boast.
5 LORD, they crush Your people;
  they afflict Your heritage.
6 They kill the widow and the
    foreigner
  and murder the fatherless.
7 They say, "The LORD doesn't see it.
  The God of Jacob doesn't pay
    attention."

8 Pay attention, you stupid people!
  Fools, when will you be wise?
9 Can the One who shaped the ear
    not hear,
  the One who formed the eye not
    see?
10 The One who instructs nations,
   the One who teaches man
     knowledge—

does He not discipline?
11 The LORD knows man's thoughts;
   they are meaningless.

PROVERBS 19:24-25

24 The slacker buries his hand in the
     bowl;
   he doesn't even bring it back to
     his mouth.

25 Strike a mocker, and the
     inexperienced learn a lesson;
   rebuke the discerning, and he
     gains knowledge.

ROMANS 3:9-31

9 What then? Are we any better? Not at all! For we have previously charged that both Jews and Gentiles are all under sin, [10] as it is written:

> There is no one righteous,
>   not even one;
> 11 there is no one
>   who understands,
>   there is no one who seeks God.
> 12 All have turned away,
>   together they have become
>   useless;
>   there is no one who does good,
>   there is not even one.
> 13 Their throat is an open grave;
>   they deceive with their tongues.
>   Vipers' venom is
>   under their lips.
> 14 Their mouth is full of cursing
>   and bitterness.
> 15 Their feet are swift
>   to shed blood;
> 16 ruin and wretchedness are
>   in their paths,
> 17 and the path of peace
>   they have not known.
> 18 There is no fear of God
>   before their eyes.

[19] Now we know that whatever the law says speaks to those who are subject to the law, so that every mouth may be shut and the whole world may become subject to God's judgment. [20] For

no flesh will be justified in His sight by the works of the law, for through the law comes the knowledge of sin. ²¹ But now, apart from the law, God's righteousness has been revealed—attested by the Law and the Prophets ²² —that is, God's righteousness through faith in Jesus Christ, to all who believe, since there is no distinction. ²³ For all have sinned and fall short of the glory of God. ²⁴ They are justified freely by His grace through the redemption that is in Christ Jesus. ²⁵ God presented Him as a propitiation through faith in His blood, to demonstrate His righteousness, because in His restraint God passed over the sins previously committed. ²⁶ He presented Him to demonstrate His righteousness at the present time, so that He would be righteous and declare righteous the one who has faith in Jesus. ²⁷ Where then is boasting? It is excluded. By what kind of law? By one of works? No, on the contrary, by a law of faith. ²⁸ For we conclude that a man is justified by faith apart from works of law. ²⁹ Or is God for Jews only? Is He not also for Gentiles? Yes, for Gentiles too, ³⁰ since there is one God who will justify the circumcised by faith and the uncircumcised through faith. ³¹ Do we then cancel the law through faith? Absolutely not! On the contrary, we uphold the law.

God's Thorn Hedges

In His restraint God passed over the sins previously committed.

—ROMANS 3:25

There are some psychiatrists who take the attitude that guilt is dangerous to the personality, and so they persuade their clients that there is no basis for their guilt feelings, that conscience and the moral universe are man-made concepts and must be eliminated. There is nothing, they say, to feel guilty about, so, as some put it: "Let bygones be bygones, and wave goodbye to guilt."

It must be acknowledged that some ideas regarding guilt have to be dealt with in that way, for some guilt is false and needlessly torments many sincere people. However, I am not talking here about false guilt. I am talking about real guilt—the guilt that the human heart carries because it has offended a holy God. You cannot get rid of that by waving your hand and saying, "Let bygones be bygones." Nor can you get away from sin by joking about it. Oscar Wilde said, "The only way to get rid of a temptation is to yield to it." But you do not get rid of temptation by yielding to it. It becomes an act, and then a habit, and then part of you.

No, we are hedged in—thorn hedges on either side. The only open door is the mercy of God. And these thorn hedges are His provision, too. They are God's creation enabling us not to live comfortably with evil, for evil is bad for us. God has so arranged the universe that we can only be truly comfortable with that which is good for us. Guilt cannot be banished by subterfuge. Only God can redeem our wickedness.

Prayer

O God, I know that although men might be able to help me with my false guilt, only You can help me with my real guilt. I bring my guilty heart to You for cleansing, forgiveness, and reconciliation. In Jesus' name. Amen.

Further Study

Ps 32; Ac 2:37; Ezr 9:6; Jn 16:8
What was the result of guilt?
What did confession produce?

AUGUST 10

EZRA 2:1-70

2 These now are the people of the province who came from those captive exiles King Nebuchadnezzar of Babylon had deported to Babylon. Each of them returned to his hometown Jerusalem and Judah. ² They came with Zerubbabel, Jeshua, Nehemiah, Seraiah, Reelaiah, Mordecai, Bilshan, Mispar, Bigvai, Rehum, and Baanah.

The number of the Israelite men included:

³ Parosh's descendants   2,172
⁴ Shephatiah's descendants   372
⁵ Arah's descendants   775
⁶ Pahath-moab's descendants:
   Jeshua's and Joab's
   descendants   2,812
⁷ Elam's descendants   1,254
⁸ Zattu's descendants   945
⁹ Zaccai's descendants   760
¹⁰ Bani's descendants   642
¹¹ Bebai's descendants   623
¹² Azgad's descendants   1,222
¹³ Adonikam's descendants   666

¹⁴ Bigvai's descendants   2,056
¹⁵ Adin's descendants   454
¹⁶ Ater's descendants: Hezekiah's 98
¹⁷ Bezai's descendants   323
¹⁸ Jorah's descendants   112
¹⁹ Hashum's descendants   223
²⁰ Gibbar's descendants   95
²¹ Bethlehem's people   123
²² Netophah's men   56
²³ Anathoth's men   128
²⁴ Azmaveth's people   42
²⁵ Kiriatharim's, Chephirah's,
   and Beeroth's people   743
²⁶ Ramah's and Geba's people   621
²⁷ Michmas's men   122
²⁸ Bethel's and Ai's men   223
²⁹ Nebo's people   52
³⁰ Magbish's people   156
³¹ the other Elam's people   1,254
³² Harim's people   320
³³ Lod's, Hadid's, and Ono's
   people   725
³⁴ Jericho's people   345
³⁵ Senaah's people   3,630

³⁶ The priests included:

Jedaiah's descendants
   of the house of Jeshua   973

928

³⁷ Immer's descendants   1,052
³⁸ Pashhur's descendants   1,247
³⁹ and Harim's descendants   1,017

⁴⁰ The Levites included:

Jeshua's and Kadmiel's
descendants
from Hodaviah's descendants   74

⁴¹ The singers included:

Asaph's descendants   128

⁴² The gatekeepers' descendants included:

Shallum's descendants,
Ater's descendants,
Talmon's descendants,
Akkub's descendants,
Hatita's descendants, Shobai's
descendants, in all   139

⁴³ The temple servants included:

Ziha's descendants, Hasupha's
descendants,
Tabbaoth's descendants,
⁴⁴ Keros's descendants,
Siaha's descendants, Padon's
descendants,
⁴⁵ Lebanah's descendants,
Hagabah's descendants,
Akkub's descendants,
⁴⁶ Hagab's descendants,
Shalmai's descendants,
Hanan's descendants,
⁴⁷ Giddel's descendants, Gahar's
descendants,
Reaiah's descendants,
⁴⁸ Rezin's descendants,
Nekoda's descendants,
Gazzam's descendants,
⁴⁹ Uzza's descendants,
Paseah's descendants,
Besai's descendants,
⁵⁰ Asnah's descendants,
Meunim's descendants,
Nephusim's descendants,
⁵¹ Bakbuk's descendants,
Hakupha's descendants,
Harhur's descendants,
⁵² Bazluth's descendants,

Mehida's descendants,
Harsha's descendants,
⁵³ Barkos's descendants,
Sisera's descendants,
Temah's descendants,
⁵⁴ Neziah's descendants,
and Hatipha's descendants.

⁵⁵ The descendants of Solomon's servants included:

Sotai's descendants,
Hassophereth's descendants,
Peruda's descendants,
⁵⁶ Jaalah's descendants,
Darkon's descendants, Giddel's descendants,
⁵⁷ Shephatiah's descendants,
Hattil's descendants,
Pochereth-
hazzebaim's descendants,
and Ami's descendants.
⁵⁸ All the temple servants
and the descendants
of Solomon's servants   392

⁵⁹ The following are those who came from Tel-melah, Tel-harsha, Cherub, Addan, and Immer but were unable to prove that their families and ancestry were Israelite:

⁶⁰ Delaiah's descendants,
Tobiah's descendants,
Nekoda's descendants   652

⁶¹ and from the descendants of the priests: the descendants of Habaiah, the descendants of Hakkoz, the descendants of Barzillai—who had taken a wife from the daughters of Barzillai the Gileadite and was called by their name. ⁶² These searched for their entries in the genealogical records, but they could not be found, so they were disqualified from the priesthood. ⁶³ The governor ordered them not to eat the most holy things until there was a priest who could consult the Urim and Thummim.

⁶⁴ The whole combined assembly
numbered   42,360
⁶⁵ not including their 7,337 male
and female slaves,

and their 200 male
and female singers.
⁶⁶ They had 736 horses, 245 mules,
⁶⁷ 435 camels, and 6,720 donkeys.

⁶⁸ After they arrived at the LORD's
house in Jerusalem, some of the family
leaders gave freewill offerings for the
house of God in order to have it rebuilt
on its original site. ⁶⁹ Based on what
they could give, they gave 61,000 gold
coins, 6,250 pounds of silver, and 100
priestly garments to the treasury for the
project. ⁷⁰ The priests, Levites, singers,
gatekeepers, temple servants, and some
of the people settled in their towns, and
the rest of Israel settled in their towns.

PSALM 94:12-23

¹² LORD, happy is the man You
discipline
and teach from Your law
¹³ to give him relief from troubled
times
until a pit is dug for the wicked.
¹⁴ The LORD will not forsake His
people
or abandon His heritage,
¹⁵ for justice will again be righteous,
and all the upright in heart will
follow it.
¹⁶ Who stands up for me against the
wicked?
Who takes a stand for me against
evildoers?
¹⁷ If the LORD had not been my help,
I would soon rest in the silence of
death.
¹⁸ If I say, "My foot is slipping,"
Your faithful love will support me,
LORD.
¹⁹ When I am filled with cares,
Your comfort brings me joy.
²⁰ Can a corrupt throne—
one that creates trouble by law—
become Your ally?
²¹ They band together against the
life of the righteous
and condemn the innocent to
death.

²² But the LORD is my refuge;
my God is the rock of my
protection.
²³ He will pay them back for their
sins
and destroy them for their evil.
The LORD our God will destroy
them.

PROVERBS 19:26-27

²⁶ The one who assaults his father
and evicts his mother
is a disgraceful and shameful
son.

²⁷ If you stop listening to
instruction, my son,
you will stray from the words of
knowledge.

ROMANS 4:1-25

4 What then can we say that Abraham, our forefather according to the
flesh, has found? ² If Abraham was justified by works, then he has something to
brag about—but not before God. ³ For
what does the Scripture say?

**Abraham believed God,
and it was credited to him
for righteousness.**

⁴ Now to the one who works, pay is not
considered as a gift, but as something
owed. ⁵ But to the one who does not
work, but believes on Him who declares
righteous the ungodly, his faith is credited for righteousness.
⁶ Likewise, David also speaks of the
blessing of the man to whom God cred-
its righteousness apart from works:

⁷ **How happy those whose lawless
acts are forgiven
and whose sins are covered!**
⁸ **How happy the man whom
the Lord will never charge
with sin!**

⁹ Is this blessing only for the circumcised, then? Or is it also for the uncir-

cumcised? For we say, **Faith was credited to Abraham for righteousness.** ¹⁰ How then was it credited—while he was circumcised, or uncircumcised? Not while he was circumcised, but uncircumcised. ¹¹ And he received the sign of circumcision as a seal of the righteousness that he had by faith while still uncircumcised. This was to make him the father of all who believe but are not circumcised, so that righteousness may be credited to them also. ¹² And he became the father of the circumcised, not only to those who are circumcised, but also to those who follow in the footsteps of the faith our father Abraham had while still uncircumcised.

¹³ For the promise to Abraham or to his descendants that he would inherit the world was not through the law, but through the righteousness that comes by faith. ¹⁴ If those who are of the law are heirs, faith is made empty and the promise is canceled. ¹⁵ For the law produces wrath; but where there is no law, there is no transgression.

¹⁶ This is why the promise is by faith, so that it may be according to grace, to guarantee it to all the descendants—not only to those who are of the law, but also to those who are of Abraham's faith. He is the father of us all ¹⁷ in God's sight. As it is written: **I have made you the father of many nations.** He believed in God, who gives life to the dead and calls things into existence that do not exist. ¹⁸ Against hope, with hope he believed, so that he became **the father of many nations,** according to what had been spoken: **So will your descendants be.** ¹⁹ He considered his own body to be already dead (since he was about a hundred years old), and the deadness of Sarah's womb, without weakening in the faith. ²⁰ He did not waver in unbelief at God's promise, but was strengthened in his faith and gave glory to God, ²¹ because he was fully convinced that what He had promised He was also able to perform. ²² Therefore, **it was credited to him for righteousness.** ²³ Now **it was credited to him** was not written for Abraham alone, ²⁴ but also for us. It will be credited to us who believe in Him who raised Jesus our Lord from the dead. ²⁵ He was delivered up for our trespasses and raised for our justification.

The Elements of Prophecy

Because he was fully convinced that what He had promised He was also able to perform.—ROMANS 4:21

Prophecy is a revelation of God to humankind. It will take place at exactly the right time: "For the vision is yet for the appointed time; it testifies about the end and will not lie" (Hab 2:3). The time for the fulfillment is fixed by God, and it will come to pass at the exact moment that God foreordains.

Yet another element is that of foretelling the future. Here again, some Bible teachers object to this and say that prophecy is forth-telling rather foretelling. It is quite true, of course, that prophecy is a form of teaching and therefore contains an element of forth-telling (speaking out the truth), but the true nature of prophecy lies in the fact that it is predictive. God told Habakkuk things that would happen long before they came to pass.

The last element of prophecy is that it will be fulfilled: "Write down this vision; clearly inscribe it on tablets . . . For the vision is yet for the appointed time" (vv. 2-3). The events God foretells are certain to take place—and in God's time. The revelation may seem to be delayed, but nothing can prevent or frustrate its fulfillment.

How does all this relate to the more practical aspects of daily Christian living? Let me put the answer in the form of two questions: Has God given you a word or promise that is yet to be fulfilled? And does the delay cause you to wonder whether or not He has forgotten His promise? Then take heart—there are trains on His line until 11:59. What God has promised, He will most certainly perform.

Prayer

O God, I bring to You my doubts and uncertainties for You to put them to rest—forever. Today I want You to burn deep into me the conviction that nothing can ever stop Your Word from being fulfilled. Nothing. I am so thankful. Amen.

Further Study

Mt 5:1-18; 1 Kg 8:56; Ps 111:7-8; Ezk 12:25
What did Christ promise concerning God's Word?
Reaffirm your trust in His ability to fulfill His promise to you.

AUGUST 11

*E*ZRA 3:1–5:17

3 By the seventh month, the Israelites had settled in their towns, and the people gathered together in Jerusalem. ² Jeshua son of Jozadak and his brothers the priests along with Zerubbabel son of Shealtiel and his brothers began to build the altar of Israel's God in order to offer burnt offerings on it, as it is written in the law of Moses the man of God. ³ They set up the altar on its foundation and offered burnt offerings for the morning and evening on it to the LORD even though they feared the surrounding peoples. ⁴ They celebrated the Festival of Booths as prescribed, and offered burnt offerings each day, based on the number specified by ordinance for each festival day. ⁵ After that, they offered the regular burnt offering and the offerings for the beginning of each month and for all the LORD's appointed holy occasions, as well as the freewill offerings brought to the LORD.

⁶ On the first day of the seventh month they began to offer burnt offerings to the LORD, even though the foundation of the LORD's temple had not yet been laid. ⁷ They gave money to the stonecutters and artisans, and gave food, drink, and oil to the people of Sidon and Tyre, so they could bring cedar wood from Lebanon to Joppa by sea, according to the authorization given them by King Cyrus of Persia.

⁸ In the second month of the second year after they arrived at God's house in Jerusalem, Zerubbabel son of Shealtiel, Jeshua son of Jozadak, and the rest of their brothers, including the priests, the Levites, and all who had returned to

Jerusalem from the captivity, began to build. They appointed the Levites who were 20 years old or more to supervise the work on the LORD's house. ⁹ Jeshua with his sons and brothers, Kadmiel with his sons, and the sons of Judah and of Henadad, with their sons and brothers, the Levites, joined together to supervise those working on the house of God.

¹⁰ When the builders had laid the foundation of the LORD's temple, the priests, dressed in their robes and holding trumpets, and the Levites descended from Asaph, holding cymbals, took their positions to praise the LORD, as King David of Israel had instructed. ¹¹ They sang with praise and thanksgiving to the LORD: "For He is good; His faithful love to Israel endures forever." Then all the people gave a great shout of praise to the LORD because the foundation of the LORD's house had been laid.

¹² But many of the older priests, Levites, and family leaders, who had seen the first temple, wept loudly when they saw the foundation of this house, but many others shouted joyfully. ¹³ The people could not distinguish the sound of the joyful shouting from that of the weeping, because the people were shouting so loudly. And the sound was heard far away.

4 When the enemies of Judah and Benjamin heard that the returned exiles were building a temple for the LORD, the God of Israel, ² they approached Zerubbabel and the leaders of the families and said to them, "Let us build with you, for we also worship your God and have been sacrificing to Him since the time King Esar-haddon of Assyria brought us here."

³ But Zerubbabel, Jeshua, and the other leaders of Israel's families answered them, "You may have no part with us in building a house for our God, since we alone must build it for the LORD, the God of Israel, as King Cyrus, the king of Persia has commanded us." ⁴ Then the people who were already in the land discouraged the people of Judah and

made them afraid to build. ⁵ They also bribed officials to act against them to frustrate their plans throughout the reign of King Cyrus of Persia and until the reign of King Darius of Persia.

⁶ At the beginning of the reign of Ahasuerus, the people who were already in the land wrote an accusation against the residents of Judah and Jerusalem. ⁷ During the time of King Artaxerxes of Persia, Bishlam, Mithredath, Tabeel and the rest of his colleagues wrote to King Artaxerxes. The letter was written in Aramaic and translated.

⁸ Rehum the chief deputy and Shimshai the scribe wrote a letter to King Artaxerxes concerning Jerusalem as follows:

⁹ From Rehum the chief deputy, Shimshai the scribe, and the rest of their colleagues—the judges and magistrates from Tripolis, Persia, Erech, Babylon, Susa (that is, the people of Elam), ¹⁰ and the rest of the peoples whom the great and illustrious Ashurbanipal deported and settled in the cities of Samaria and the region west of the Euphrates River.

¹¹ This is the text of the letter they sent to him:

To King Artaxerxes from your servants, the men from the region west of the Euphrates River:

¹² Let it be known to the king that the Jews who came from you have returned to us at Jerusalem. They are rebuilding that rebellious and evil city, finishing its walls, and repairing its foundations. ¹³ Let it now be known to the king that if that city is rebuilt and its walls are finished, they will not pay tribute, duty, or land tax, and the royal revenue will suffer. ¹⁴ Since we have taken an oath of loyalty to the king, and it is not right for us to witness his dishonor, we have sent to inform the king ¹⁵ that a search

should be made in your fathers' record books. In these record books you will discover and verify that the city is a rebellious city, harmful to kings and provinces. There have been revolts in it since ancient times. That is why this city was destroyed. [16] We advise the king that if this city is rebuilt and its walls are finished, you will not have any possession west of the Euphrates.

[17] The king sent a reply to his chief deputy Rehum, Shimshai the scribe, and the rest of their colleagues living in Samaria and elsewhere in the region west of the Euphrates River:

Greetings.

[18] The letter you sent us has been translated and read in my presence. [19] I issued a decree and a search was conducted. It was discovered that this city has had uprisings against kings since ancient times, and there have been rebellions and revolts in it. [20] Powerful kings have also ruled over Jerusalem and exercised authority over the whole region, and tribute, duty, and land tax were paid to them. [21] Therefore, issue an order for these men to stop, so that this city will not be rebuilt until a further decree has been pronounced by me. [22] See that you not neglect this matter. Otherwise, the damage will increase and the royal interests will suffer.

[23] As soon as the text of King Artaxerxes' letter was read to Rehum, Shimshai the scribe, and their colleagues, they immediately went to the Jews in Jerusalem and forcibly stopped them.
[24] Now the construction of God's house in Jerusalem had stopped and remained at a standstill until the second year of the reign of King Darius of

5 Persia. [1] But when the prophets Haggai and Zechariah son of Iddo prophesied to the Jews who were in

Judah and Jerusalem, in the name of the God of Israel who was over them, [2] Zerubbabel son of Shealtiel and Jeshua son of Jozadak began to rebuild God's house in Jerusalem. The prophets of God were with them, helping them.

[3] At that time Tattenai the governor of the region west of the Euphrates River, Shethar-bozenai, and their colleagues came to the Jews and asked, "Who gave you the order to rebuild this temple and finish this structure?" [4] They also asked them, "What are the names of the workers who are constructing this building?" [5] But God was watching over the Jewish elders. These men wouldn't stop them until a report was sent to Darius, so that they could receive written instructions about this matter.

[6] This is the text of the letter that Tattenai the governor of the region west of the Euphrates River, Shethar-bozenai, and their colleagues, the officials in the region, sent to King Darius. [7] They sent him a report, written as follows:

To King Darius:

All greetings.

[8] Let it be known to the king that we went to the house of the great God in the province of Judah. It is being built with cut stones, and its beams are being set in the walls. This work is being done diligently and succeeding through the people's efforts. [9] So we questioned the elders and asked, "Who gave you the order to rebuild this temple and finish this structure?" [10] We also asked them for their names, so that we could write down the names of their leaders for your information.

[11] This is the reply they gave us:

We are the servants of the God of heaven and earth and are rebuilding the temple that was built many years ago, which a great king of Israel built and finished. [12] But since our fathers angered the God of heaven, He handed them over to King Nebuchadnezzar of Babylon, the Chaldean, who destroyed this temple and deported the people to Babylon. [13] However, in the first year of Cyrus king of Babylon, he issued a decree to rebuild this house of God. [14] He also took from the temple in Babylon the gold and silver articles of God's house that Nebuchadnezzar had taken from the temple in Jerusalem and carried them to the temple in Babylon. He released them from the temple in Babylon to a man named Sheshbazzar, the governor by the appointment of King Cyrus. [15] He told him, 'Take these articles, put them in the temple in Jerusalem, and let the house of God be rebuilt on its original site.' [16] Then this same Sheshbazzar came and laid the foundation of God's house in Jerusalem. It has been under construction from that time until now, yet it has not been completed.

[17] So if it pleases the king, let a search of the royal archives in Babylon be conducted to see if it is true that a decree was issued by King Cyrus to rebuild this house of God in Jerusalem. Let the king's decision regarding this matter be sent to us.

PSALM 95:1-11

[1] Come, let us shout joyfully to the LORD,
shout triumphantly to the rock of our salvation!
[2] Let us enter His presence with thanksgiving;
let us shout triumphantly to Him in song.

[3] For the LORD is a great God,
a great King above all gods.
[4] The depths of the earth are in His hand,
and the mountain peaks are His.

[5] The sea is His; He made it.
His hands formed the dry land.

[6] Come, let us worship and bow down;
let us kneel before the LORD our Maker.
[7] For He is our God,
and we are the people of His pasture, the sheep under His care.

Today, if you hear His voice:
[8] "Do not harden your hearts as at Meribah,
as on that day at Massah in the wilderness
[9] where your fathers tested Me;
they tried Me, though they had seen what I did.
[10] For 40 years I was disgusted with that generation;
I said, 'They are a people whose hearts go astray;
they do not know My ways.'
[11] So I swore in My anger,
'They will not enter My rest.' "

PROVERBS 19:28-29

[28] A worthless witness mocks justice,
and a wicked mouth swallows iniquity.

[29] Judgments are prepared for mockers,
and beatings for the backs of fools.

ROMANS 5:1-21

5 Therefore, since we have been declared righteous by faith, we have peace with God through our Lord Jesus Christ. [2] Also through Him, we have obtained access by faith into this grace in which we stand, and we rejoice in the hope of the glory of God. [3] And not only that, but we also rejoice in our afflictions, because we know that affliction produces endurance, [4] endurance produces proven character, and proven

character produces hope. ⁵ This hope does not disappoint, because God's love has been poured out in our hearts through the Holy Spirit who was given to us.

⁶ For while we were still helpless, at the appointed moment, Christ died for the ungodly. ⁷ For rarely will someone die for a just person—though for a good person perhaps someone might even dare to die. ⁸ But God proves His own love for us in that while we were still sinners Christ died for us! ⁹ Much more then, since we have now been declared righteous by His blood, we will be saved through Him from wrath. ¹⁰ For if, while we were enemies, we were reconciled to God through the death of His Son, then how much more, having been reconciled, will we be saved by His life! ¹¹ And not only that, but we also rejoice in God through our Lord Jesus Christ, through whom we have now received reconciliation.

¹² Therefore, just as sin entered the world through one man, and death through sin, in this way death spread to all men, because all sinned. ¹³ In fact, sin was in the world before the law, but sin is not charged to one's account when there is no law. ¹⁴ Nevertheless, death reigned from Adam to Moses, even over those who did not sin in the likeness of Adam's transgression. He is a prototype of the Coming One.

¹⁵ But the gift is not like the trespass. For if by the one man's trespass the many died, how much more have the grace of God and the gift overflowed to the many by the grace of the one man, Jesus Christ. ¹⁶ And the gift is not like the one man's sin, because from one sin came the judgment, resulting in condemnation, but from many trespasses came the gift, resulting in justification. ¹⁷ Since by the one man's trespass, death reigned through that one man, how much more will those who receive the overflow of grace and the gift of righteousness reign in life through the one man, Jesus Christ.

¹⁸ So then, as through one trespass there is condemnation for everyone, so also through one righteous act there is life-giving justification for everyone. ¹⁹ For just as through one man's disobedience the many were made sinners, so also through the one man's obedience the many will be made righteous. ²⁰ The law came along to multiply the trespass. But where sin multiplied, grace multiplied even more, ²¹ so that, just as sin reigned in death, so also grace will reign through righteousness, resulting in eternal life through Jesus Christ our Lord.

Tyranny of the Oughts

Therefore, since we have been declared righteous by faith, we have peace with God through our Lord Jesus Christ.—ROMANS 5:1

The breastplate of righteousness protects us from the feeling that we are not good enough to be saved. We now look at a feeling which Satan delights to whip up in the heart of a Christian—the feeling that we are only accepted by God when we are doing everything perfectly. The feeling gives rise to *perfectionism*—a condition which afflicts multitudes of Christians.

The chief characteristic of perfectionism is a constant overall feeling of never doing enough to be thought well of by God. Karen Horney describes it as "the tyranny of the oughts." Here are some typical statements of those who are afflicted in this way: "I ought to do better," "I ought to have done better," "I ought to be able to do better." There is nothing wrong with wanting to do better, but in the twisted thinking of a perfectionist, a person believes that because he or she could or ought to have done better, they will not be accepted or thought well of by God. They come to believe that their acceptance by God depends on their performance. They constantly try to develop a righteousness of their own rather than resting in the righteousness that Christ has provided for them.

If you suffer from this condition, then it's time to put on your spiritual breastplate. You need to remind yourself that the way you came into the Christian life is the same way you are enabled to go on in it—by depending on Christ and His righteousness, not on yourself and your righteousness. You are not working to be saved; you are working because you are saved.

Prayer

Lord Jesus, I see that when I stand in Your righteousness, I stand in God's smile. But when I stand in my own righteousness, I stand in God's frown. Help me move over from frown to smile. In Your dear name. Amen.

Further Study

Gl 3; Gn 15:6; Ac 13:39
What was the purpose of the law?
What does it mean to be "justified"?

AUGUST 12

EZRA 6:1–7:28

6 King Darius gave the order, and they searched in the library of Babylon in the archives. ² But it was in the fortress of Ecbatana in the province of Media that a scroll was found with this record written on it:

³ In the first year of King Cyrus, he issued a decree concerning the house of God in Jerusalem:

Let the house be rebuilt as a place for offering sacrifices, and let its original foundations be retained. Its height is to be 90 feet and its width 90 feet, ⁴ with three layers of cut stones and one of timber. The cost is to be paid from the royal treasury. ⁵ The gold and silver articles of God's house that Nebuchadnezzar took from the temple in Jerusalem and carried to Babylon must also be returned. They are to be brought to the temple in Jerusalem, where they belong, and put into the house of God.

⁶ Therefore, you must stay away from that place, Tattenai governor of the region west of the Euphrates River, Shethar-bozenai, and your colleagues, the officials in the region. ⁷ Leave the construction of this house of God alone. Let the governor and elders of the Jews

rebuild this house of God on its original site.

[8] I hereby issue a decree concerning what you must do, so that the elders of the Jews can rebuild this house of God:

The cost is to be paid in full to these men out of the royal revenues from the taxes of the region west of the Euphrates River, so that the work will not stop. [9] Whatever is needed—young bulls, rams, and lambs for burnt offerings to the God of heaven, or wheat, salt, wine, and oil, as requested by the priests in Jerusalem—let it be given to them every day without fail, [10] so that they can offer sacrifices of pleasing aroma to the God of heaven and pray for the life of the king and his sons.

[11] I also issue a decree concerning any man who interferes with this directive:

Let a beam be torn from his house and raised up; he will be impaled on it, and his house will be made into a garbage dump because of this offense. [12] May the God who caused His name to dwell there overthrow any king or people who dares to harm or interfere with this house of God in Jerusalem. I, Darius, have issued the decree. Let it be carried out diligently.

[13] Then Tattenai governor of the region west of the Euphrates River, Shethar-bozenai, and their colleagues diligently carried out what King Darius had decreed. [14] So the Jewish elders continued successfully with the building under the prophesying of Haggai the prophet and Zechariah son of Iddo. They finished the building according to the command of the God of Israel and the decrees of Cyrus, Darius, and King Artaxerxes of Persia. [15] This house was completed on the third day of the month of Adar in the sixth year of the reign of King Darius.

[16] Then the Israelites, including the priests, the Levites, and the rest of the exiles, celebrated the dedication of this house of God with joy. [17] For the dedication of God's house they offered 100 bulls, 200 rams, and 400 lambs, as well as 12 male goats as a sin offering for all Israel—one for each Israelite tribe. [18] They also appointed the priests by their divisions and the Levites by their groups to the service of God in Jerusalem, according to what is written in the book of Moses.

[19] The exiles observed the Passover on the fourteenth day of the first month. [20] All of the priests and Levites were ceremonially clean, because they had purified themselves. They killed the Passover lamb for themselves, their priestly brothers, and all the exiles. [21] The Israelites who had returned from exile ate it, together with all who had separated themselves from the uncleanness of the Gentiles of the land in order to worship the LORD, the God of Israel. [22] They observed the Festival of Unleavened Bread for seven days with joy, because the LORD had made them joyful, having changed the Assyrian king's attitude toward them, so that he supported them in the work on the house of the God of Israel.

7 After these events, during the reign of King Artaxerxes of Persia, Ezra—

Seraiah's son, Azariah's son, Hilkiah's son, [2] Shallum's son, Zadok's son, Ahitub's son,
[3] Amariah's son, Azariah's son, Meraioth's son, [4] Zerahiah's son, Uzzi's son, Bukki's son,
[5] Abishua's son, Phinehas's son, Eleazar's son, Aaron the chief priest's son

[6] —came up from Babylon. He was a scribe skilled in the law of Moses, which the LORD, the God of Israel, had given. The king had granted him everything he requested because the hand of the LORD his God was on him. [7] Some of the Israelites, priests, Levites, singers, gatekeepers, and temple servants ac-

companied him to Jerusalem in the seventh year of King Artaxerxes.

[8] Ezra came to Jerusalem in the fifth month, during the seventh year of the king. [9] He began the journey from Babylon on the first day of the first month and arrived in Jerusalem on the first day of the fifth month. The gracious hand of his God was on him, [10] because Ezra had determined in his heart to study the law of the LORD, obey it, and teach its statutes and ordinances in Israel.

[11] This is the text of the letter King Artaxerxes gave to Ezra the priest and scribe, an expert in matters of the LORD's commandments and statutes for Israel:

[12] Artaxerxes, king of kings, to Ezra the priest, an expert in the law of the God of heaven:

Greetings to you.

[13] I issue a decree that any of the Israelites in my kingdom, including their priests and Levites, who want to go to Jerusalem, may go with you. [14] You are sent by the king and his seven counselors to evaluate Judah and Jerusalem according to the law of your God, which is in your possession. [15] You are also to bring the silver and gold the king and his counselors have willingly given to the God of Israel, whose dwelling is in Jerusalem, [16] and all the silver and gold you receive throughout the province of Babylon, together with the freewill offerings given by the people and the priests to the house of their God in Jerusalem. [17] Then, you are to buy with this money as many bulls, rams, and lambs as needed, along with their grain and drink offerings, and offer them on the altar at the house of your God in Jerusalem. [18] You may do whatever seems best to you and your brothers with the rest of the silver and gold, according to the will of your God. [19] You must deliver to the God of Jerusalem all the articles given to you for the service of the house of your God. [20] You may use the royal treasury to pay for anything else you have to supply to meet the needs of the house of your God.

[21] I, King Artaxerxes, issue a decree to all the treasurers in the region west of the Euphrates River:

Whatever Ezra the priest and expert in the law of the God of heaven asks of you must be provided promptly, [22] up to 7,500 pounds of silver, 500 bushels of wheat, 550 gallons of wine, 550 gallons of oil, and salt without limit. [23] Whatever is commanded by the God of heaven must be done diligently for the house of the God of heaven, so that wrath will not fall on the realm of the king and his sons. [24] Be advised that tribute, duty, and land tax must not be imposed on any priests, Levites, singers, doorkeepers, temple servants, or other servants of this house of God.

[25] And you, Ezra, according to God's wisdom that you possess, appoint magistrates and judges to judge all the people in the region west of the Euphrates who know the laws of your God and to teach anyone who does not know them. [26] Anyone who does not keep the law of your God and the law of the king, let a fair judgment be executed against him, whether death, banishment, confiscation of property, or imprisonment.

[27] Praise the LORD God of our fathers, who has put it into the king's mind to glorify the house of the LORD in Jerusalem, [28] and who has shown favor to me before the king, his counselors, and all his powerful officers. So I took courage because I was strengthened by the LORD my God, and I gathered Israelite leaders to return with me.

PSALM 96:1-9

1 Sing a new song to the LORD;
  sing to the LORD, all the earth.
2 Sing to the LORD, praise His name;
  proclaim His salvation from day to
    day.
3 Declare His glory among the
    nations,
  His wonderful works among all
    peoples.

4 For the LORD is great and is highly
    praised;
  He is feared above all gods.
5 For all the gods of the peoples are
    idols,
  but the LORD made the heavens.
6 Splendor and majesty are before
    Him;
  strength and beauty are in His
    sanctuary.

7 Ascribe to the LORD, you families
    of the peoples,
  ascribe to the LORD glory and
    strength.
8 Ascribe to the LORD the glory of
    His name;
  bring an offering and enter His
    courts.
9 Worship the LORD in the splendor
    of His holiness;
  tremble before Him, all the earth.

PROVERBS 20:1

20 Wine is a mocker, beer is a
    brawler,
  and whoever staggers because of
    them is not wise.

ROMANS 6:1-23

6 What should we say then? Should
  we continue in sin in order that
grace may multiply? 2 Absolutely not!
How can we who died to sin still live in
it? 3 Or are you unaware that all of us
who were baptized into Christ Jesus
were baptized into His death? 4 Therefore we were buried with Him by baptism into death, in order that, just as
Christ was raised from the dead by the
glory of the Father, so we too may walk
in a new way of life. 5 For if we have
been joined with Him in the likeness of
His death, we will certainly also be in
the likeness of His resurrection. 6 For
we know that our old self was crucified
with Him in order that sin's dominion
over the body may be abolished, so that
we may no longer be enslaved to sin,
7 since a person who has died is freed
from sin's claims. 8 Now if we died with
Christ, we believe that we will also live
with Him, 9 because we know that
Christ, having been raised from the
dead, no longer dies. Death no longer
rules over Him. 10 For in that He died,
He died to sin once for all; but in that
He lives, He lives to God. 11 So, you too
consider yourselves dead to sin, but
alive to God in Christ Jesus.
12 Therefore do not let sin reign in
your mortal body, so that you obey its
desires. 13 And do not offer any parts of
it to sin as weapons for unrighteousness. But as those who are alive from
the dead, offer yourselves to God, and
all the parts of yourselves to God as
weapons for righteousness. 14 For sin
will not rule over you, because you are
not under law but under grace.
15 What then? Should we sin because
we are not under law but under grace?
Absolutely not! 16 Do you not know that
if you offer yourselves to someone as
obedient slaves, you are slaves of that
one you obey—either of sin leading to
death or of obedience leading to righteousness? 17 But thank God that, although you used to be slaves of sin, you
obeyed from the heart that pattern of
teaching you were entrusted to, 18 and
having been liberated from sin, you became enslaved to righteousness. 19 I am
using a human analogy because of the
weakness of your flesh. For just as you
offered the parts of yourselves as slaves
to moral impurity, and to greater and
greater lawlessness, so now offer them
as slaves to righteousness, which results in sanctification. 20 For when you
were slaves of sin, you were free from
allegiance to righteousness. 21 And what
fruit was produced then from the
things you are now ashamed of? For the

end of those things is death. ²² But now, since you have been liberated from sin and become enslaved to God, you have your fruit, which results in sanctifica-tion—and the end is eternal life! ²³ For the wages of sin is death, but the gift of God is eternal life in Christ Jesus our Lord.

Leave Nothing Behind

How can we who died to sin still live in it?

—ROMANS 6:2

If we are to stay spiritually fresh we must break decisively with everything of which Christ cannot approve. We must get rid of everything that mars our relationship with the Master. This means that we must make up our minds that anything the Lord speaks to us about must go. There is to be no trifling with Him.

A gardener who works in an evangelical conference center tells how, during the first two or three days of a conference, Christians are keen to obey the signs that say, "Do not litter." They go out of their way to carry unwanted paper to the litter bins. After four or five days have passed, however, he finds that people grow tired of looking for the bins and hide their unwanted paper under the bushes. They have enough conscience to hide the paper, but not enough to get rid of it.

Do not let this matter of getting rid of the things of which Christ disapproves end in a compromise or a stalemate. Look down into the hidden recesses where your sins may have been tucked away, and bring them all out—every one. They will plead to be left alone, but bring them all out. Not a thing must be left behind. Don't be content with a conscience that will hide sins but not get rid of sins. If I had to put into one word the biggest single barrier to maintaining spiritual freshness, it would be procrastination. So be decisive—beginning today.

Prayer

Father, I have put my hand to the plow, and I do not intend to look back. This shall be no halfway business. Help me to bring to You everything that needs to be dealt with today. Amen.

Further Study

Ac 24:1-25; Jr 8:20; Heb 3:7-15
What was Felix's mistake?
What lesson must we learn from the children of Israel?

AUGUST 13

*E*ZRA 8:1–9:15

8 These are the family leaders and the genealogical records of those who returned with me from Babylon during the reign of King Artaxerxes:

2 Gershom, from Phinehas's
  descendants;
  Daniel, from Ithamar's
  descendants;
  Hattush, from David's
  descendants,
3 who was of Shecaniah's
  descendants;
  Zechariah, from Parosh's
  descendants,
  and 150 men with him
  who were registered
  by genealogy;
4 Eliehoenai son of Zerahiah
  from Pahath-moab's descendants,
  and 200 men with him;
5 Shecaniah son of Jahaziel
  from Zattu's descendants,
  and 300 men with him;
6 Ebed son of Jonathan
  from Adin's descendants,
  and 50 men with him;
7 Jeshaiah son of Athaliah
  from Elam's descendants,
  and 70 men with him;
8 Zebadiah son of Michael
  from Shephatiah's descendants,
  and 80 men with him;
9 Obadiah son of Jehiel
  from Joab's descendants,
  and 218 men with him;
10 Shelomith son of Josiphiah
  from Bani's descendants,
  and 160 men with him;
11 Zechariah son of Bebai
  from Bebai's descendants,
  and 28 men with him;
12 Johanan son of Hakkatan
  from Azgad's descendants,
  and 110 men with him;
13 these are the last ones,
  from Adonikam's descendants,
  and their names are:
  Eliphelet, Jeuel, and Shemaiah,
  and 60 men with them;
14 Uthai and Zaccur
  from Bigvai's descendants,
  and 70 men with them.

15 I gathered them at the river that flows to Ahava, and we camped there for three days. I searched among the people and priests, but found no Levites there. 16 Then I summoned the leaders: Eliezer, Ariel, Shemaiah, Elnathan, Jarib, Elnathan, Nathan, Zechariah, and Meshullam, as well as the teachers Joiarib and Elnathan. 17 I sent them to Iddo, the leader at Casiphia, with a message for him and his brothers, the temple servants at Casiphia, that they should bring us ministers for the house of our God. 18 Since the gracious hand of our God was on us, they brought us Sherebiah—a man of insight from the descendants of Mahli, a descendant of Levi son of Israel—along with his sons and brothers, 18 men, 19 plus Hashabiah, along with Jeshaiah, from the descendants of Merari, and his brothers and their sons, 20 men. 20 There were also 220 of the temple servants, who had been appointed by David and the leaders for the work of the Levites. All were identified by name.

21 I proclaimed a fast by the Ahava River, so that we might humble ourselves before our God and ask Him for a safe journey for us, our children, and all our possessions. 22 I did this because I was ashamed to ask the king for infantry and cavalry to protect us from enemies during the journey, since we had told him, "The hand of our God is gracious to all who seek Him, but His great anger is against all who abandon Him." 23 So we fasted and pleaded with

our God about this, and He granted our request.

²⁴ I selected 12 of the leading priests, along with Sherebiah, Hashabiah, and 10 of their brothers. ²⁵ I weighed out to them the silver, the gold, and the articles—the contribution for the house of our God that the king, his counselors, his leaders, and all the Israelites who were present had offered. ²⁶ I weighed out to them 24 tons of silver, silver articles weighing 7,500 pounds, 7,500 pounds of gold, ²⁷ 20 gold bowls worth 1,000 gold coins, and two articles of fine gleaming bronze, as valuable as gold. ²⁸ Then I said to them, "You are holy to the LORD, and the articles are holy. The silver and gold are a freewill offering to the LORD God of your fathers. ²⁹ Guard them carefully until you weigh them out in the chambers of the LORD's house before the leading priests, Levites, and heads of the Israelite families in Jerusalem." ³⁰ So the priests and Levites took charge of the silver, the gold, and the articles that had been weighed out, to bring them to the house of our God in Jerusalem.

³¹ We set out from the Ahava River on the twelfth day of the first month to go to Jerusalem. We were strengthened by our God, and He protected us from the power of the enemy and from ambush along the way. ³² So we arrived at Jerusalem and rested there for three days. ³³ On the fourth day the silver, the gold, and the articles were weighed out in the house of our God into the care of Meremoth the priest, son of Uriah. Eleazar son of Phinehas was with him. The Levites Jozabad son of Jeshua and Noadiah son of Binnui were also with them. ³⁴ Everything was verified by number and weight, and the total weight was recorded at that time.

³⁵ The exiles who had returned from the captivity offered burnt offerings to the God of Israel: 12 bulls for all Israel, 96 rams, and 77 lambs, along with 12 male goats as a sin offering. All this was a burnt offering for the LORD. ³⁶ They also delivered the king's edicts to the royal satraps and governors of the region west of the Euphrates, so that they would support the people and the house of God.

9 After these things had been done, the leaders approached me and said: "The people of Israel, the priests, and the Levites have not separated themselves from the surrounding peoples whose detestable practices are like those of the Canaanites, Hittites, Perizzites, Jebusites, Ammonites, Moabites, Egyptians, and Amorites. ² Indeed, they have taken some of their daughters as wives for themselves and their sons, so that the holy people has become mixed with the surrounding peoples. The leaders and officials have taken the lead in this unfaithfulness!" ³ When I heard this report, I tore my tunic and robe, pulled out some of the hair from my head and beard, and sat down devastated.

⁴ Everyone who trembled at the words of the God of Israel gathered around me, because of the unfaithfulness of the exiles, while I sat devastated until the evening offering. ⁵ At the evening offering, I got up from my humiliation, with my tunic and robe torn. Then I fell on my knees and spread out my hands to the LORD my God. ⁶ And I said:

My God, I am ashamed and embarrassed to lift my face toward You, my God, because our iniquities are higher than our heads and our guilt is as high as the heavens. ⁷ Our guilt has been terrible from the days of our fathers until the present. Because of our iniquities we have been handed over, along with our kings and priests, to the surrounding kings, and to the sword, captivity, plundering, and open shame, as it is today. ⁸ But now, for a brief moment, grace has come from the LORD our God to preserve a remnant for us and give us a stake in His holy place. Even in our slavery, God has given us new life and light to our eyes. ⁹ Though we are slaves, our God has not abandoned us in our slavery. He has extended grace to us in the presence of the Persian kings, giving us new life, so that we can rebuild the house of our God and repair its ruins, to give us a wall in Judah and Jerusalem.

[10] Now, our God, what can we say in light of this? For we have abandoned the commandments [11] You gave through Your servants the prophets, saying: "The land you are entering to possess is an impure land. The surrounding peoples have filled it from end to end with their uncleanness by their impurity and detestable practices. [12] So do not give your daughters to their sons in marriage or take their daughters for your sons. Never seek their peace or prosperity, so that you will be strong, eat the good things of the land, and leave it as an inheritance to your sons forever." [13] After all that has happened to us because of our evil deeds and terrible guilt—though You, our God, have punished us less than our sins deserve and have allowed us to survive— [14] should we break Your commandments again and intermarry with the peoples who commit these detestable practices? Wouldn't You become so angry with us that You would destroy us, leaving no survivors? [15] LORD God of Israel, You are righteous, for we survive as a remnant today. Here we are before You with our guilt, though no one can stand in Your presence because of this.

PSALM 96:10-13

[10] Say among the nations: "The LORD reigns.
The world is firmly established; it cannot be shaken.
He judges the peoples fairly."
[11] Let the heavens be glad and the earth rejoice;
let the sea and all that fills it resound.

[12] Let the fields and everything in them exult.
Then all the trees of the forest will shout for joy
[13] before the LORD, for He is coming—
for He is coming to judge the earth.
He will judge the world with righteousness
and the peoples with His faithfulness.

PROVERBS 20:2-3

[2] A king's terrible wrath is like the roaring of a lion;
anyone who provokes him endangers himself.

[3] It is honorable for a man to resolve a dispute,
but any fool can get himself into a quarrel.

ROMANS 7:1-25

7 Since I am speaking to those who understand law, brothers, are you unaware that the law has authority over someone as long as he lives? [2] For example, a married woman is legally bound to her husband while he lives. But if her husband dies, she is released from the law regarding the husband. [3] So then, if she gives herself to another man while her husband is living, she will be called an adulteress. But if her husband dies, she is free from that law. Then, if she gives herself to another man, she is not an adulteress.

[4] Therefore, my brothers, you also were put to death in relation to the law through the crucified body of the Messiah, so that you may belong to another—to Him who was raised from the dead—that we may bear fruit for God. [5] For when we were in the flesh, the sinful passions operated through the law in every part of us and bore fruit for death. [6] But now we have been released from the law, since we have died to what held us, so that we may serve in the new way

of the Spirit and not in the old letter of the law. ⁷What should we say then? Is the law sin? Absolutely not! On the contrary, I would not have known sin if it were not for the law. For example, I would not have known what it is to covet if the law had not said, **Do not covet.** ⁸And sin, seizing an opportunity through the commandment, produced in me coveting of every kind. For apart from the law sin is dead. ⁹Once I was alive apart from the law, but when the commandment came, sin sprang to life ¹⁰and I died. The commandment that was meant for life resulted in death for me. ¹¹For sin, seizing an opportunity through the commandment, deceived me, and through it killed me. ¹²So then, the law is holy, and the commandment is holy and just and good.

¹³Therefore, did what is good cause my death? Absolutely not! On the contrary, sin, in order to be recognized as sin, was producing death in me through what is good, so that through the commandment sin might become sinful beyond measure. ¹⁴For we know that the law is spiritual; but I am made out of flesh, sold into sin's power. ¹⁵For I do not understand what I am doing, because I do not practice what I want to do, but I do what I hate. ¹⁶And if I do what I do not want to do, I agree with the law that it is good. ¹⁷So now I am no longer the one doing it, but it is sin living in me. ¹⁸For I know that nothing good lives in me, that is, in my flesh. For the desire to do what is good is with me, but there is no ability to do it. ¹⁹For I do not do the good that I want to do, but I practice the evil that I do not want to do. ²⁰Now if I do what I do not want, I am no longer the one doing it, but it is the sin that lives in me. ²¹So I discover this principle: when I want to do good, evil is with me. ²²For in my inner self I joyfully agree with God's law. ²³But I see a different law in the parts of my body, waging war against the law of my mind and taking me prisoner to the law of sin in the parts of my body. ²⁴What a wretched man I am! Who will rescue me from this body of death? ²⁵I thank God through Jesus Christ our Lord! So then, with my mind I myself am a slave to the law of God, but with my flesh, to the law of sin.

Two Ways to Honk a Horn

It is honorable for a man to resolve a dispute, but any fool can get himself into a quarrel.—PROVERBS 20:3

"Temper," someone has said, "turns to bad or good according to what is behind it." Remember that the word "temper" simply means "a disposition of mind" and really requires the words "good" or "bad" to be prefixed to it if it is to be clearly identified.

Dr. Stanley Jones says that there are two ways to honk a horn—the Christian way and the non-Christian way. The Christian way calls attention to a situation; the non-Christian way not only calls attention to the situation but it also calls attention to what the honker feels about it. In the USA I once saw a sign on a car that said: "Honk away—it's your ulcer." Ulcers are usually visible signs of an ulcerated spirit—ulcerated by irritation and bad temper.

Whenever we lose our temper and take it out on people around us, we do the utmost harm, not to them, but to ourselves. The one who is out of sorts with someone else is usually out of sorts with himself. He projects his inner problems onto others and fails to see the cause and remedy are in himself. I once witnessed a Sunday School superintendent lose his temper in a committee meeting, and when reprimanded by another for his bad spirit, he said: "I have to lose my temper in order to get anything done around here." James 1:20 contradicts that view: "For man's anger does not accomplish God's righteousness." Listen to it again, this time in the Phillips translation: "For man's temper is never the means of achieving God's true goodness." Wrong means lead to wrong ends—inevitably.

Prayer

O Father, help me to meet all impatience with patience, all hate with love, all grumpiness with joy, and all bad temper with good temper. In Jesus' name I ask it. Amen.

Further Study

Mt 5:1-26; Ps 37:8; Pr 14:17
What did Jesus teach about anger?
Are you angry with anyone?

AUGUST 14

EZRA 10:1– NEHEMIAH 1:11

10 While Ezra prayed and confessed, weeping and falling facedown before the house of God, an extremely large assembly of Israelite men, women, and children gathered around him. The people also wept bitterly. ² Then Shecaniah son of Jehiel, an Elamite, responded to Ezra: "We have been unfaithful to our God by marrying foreign women from the surrounding peoples, but there is still hope for Israel in spite of this. ³ Let us therefore make a covenant before our God to send away all the foreign wives and their children, according to the counsel of my lord and of those who tremble at the commandment of our God. Let it be done according to the law. ⁴ Get up, for this matter is your re-

sponsibility, and we support you. Be strong and take action!"

⁵ Then Ezra got up and made the leading priests, Levites, and all Israel take an oath to do what had been said; so they took the oath. ⁶ Ezra then went from the house of God, walked to the chamber of Jehohanan son of Eliashib, where he spent the night. He did not eat food or drink water, because he was mourning over the unfaithfulness of the exiles.

⁷ They circulated a proclamation throughout Judah and Jerusalem that all the exiles should gather at Jerusalem. ⁸ Whoever did not come within three days would forfeit all his possessions, according to the decision of the leaders and elders, and would be excluded from the assembly of the exiles.

⁹ So all the men of Judah and Ben-

jamin gathered in Jerusalem within the three days. On the twentieth day of the ninth month, all the people sat in the square at the house of God, trembling because of this matter and because of the heavy rain. ¹⁰ Then Ezra the priest stood up and said to them, "You have been unfaithful by marrying foreign women, adding to Israel's guilt. ¹¹ Therefore, make a confession to the LORD God of your fathers and do His will. Separate yourselves from the surrounding peoples and your foreign wives."

¹² Then all the assembly responded with a loud voice: "Yes, we will do as you say! ¹³ But there are many people, and it is the rainy season. We don't have the stamina to stay out in the open. This isn't something that can be done in a day or two, for we have rebelled terribly in this matter. ¹⁴ Let our leaders represent the entire assembly. Then let all those in our towns who have married foreign women come at appointed times, together with the elders and judges of each town, in order to avert the fierce anger of our God concerning this matter." ¹⁵ Only Jonathan son of Asahel and Jahzeiah son of Tikvah opposed this, with Meshullam and Shabbethai the Levite supporting them.

¹⁶ The exiles did what had been proposed. Ezra the priest selected men who were family leaders, all identified by name, to represent their ancestral houses. They convened on the first day of the tenth month to investigate the matter, ¹⁷ and by the first day of the first month they had dealt with all the men who had married foreign women.

¹⁸ The following were found to have married foreign women from the descendants of the priests:

from the descendants of Jeshua son of Jozadak and his brothers: Maaseiah, Eliezer, Jarib, and Gedaliah. ¹⁹ They pledged to send their wives away, and being guilty, they offered a ram from the flock for their guilt;

²⁰ Hanani and Zebadiah from Immer's descendants;

²¹ Maaseiah, Elijah, Shemaiah, Jehiel, and Uzziah from Harim's descendants;

²² Elioenai, Maaseiah, Ishmael, Nethanel, Jozabad, and Elasah from Pashhur's descendants.

²³ The Levites:

Jozabad, Shimei, Kelaiah (that is Kelita), Pethahiah, Judah, and Eliezer.

²⁴ The singers:

Eliashib.

The gatekeepers:

Shallum, Telem, and Uri.

²⁵ The Israelites:

Parosh's descendants: Ramiah, Izziah, Malchijah, Mijamin, Eleazar, Malchijah, and Benaiah;

²⁶ Elam's descendants: Mattaniah, Zechariah, Jehiel, Abdi, Jeremoth, and Elijah;

²⁷ Zattu's descendants: Elioenai, Eliashib, Mattaniah, Jeremoth, Zabad, and Aziza;

²⁸ Bebai's descendants: Jehohanan, Hananiah, Zabbai, and Athlai;

²⁹ Bani's descendants: Meshullam, Malluch, Adaiah, Jashub, Sheal, and Jeremoth;

³⁰ Pahath-moab's descendants: Adna, Chelal, Benaiah, Maaseiah, Mattaniah, Bezalel, Binnui, and Manasseh;

³¹ Harim's descendants: Eliezer, Isshijah, Malchijah, Shemaiah, Shimeon,

³² Benjamin, Malluch, and Shemariah;

³³ Hashum's descendants: Mattenai, Mattattah, Zabad, Eliphelet, Jeremai, Manasseh, and Shimei;

³⁴ Bani's descendants: Maadai, Amram, Uel,

³⁵ Benaiah, Bedeiah, Cheluhi,
³⁶ Vaniah, Meremoth, Eliashib,
³⁷ Mattaniah, Mattenai, Jaasu,
³⁸ Bani, Binnui, Shimei,
³⁹ Shelemiah, Nathan, Adaiah,
⁴⁰ Machnadebai, Shashai, Sharai,
⁴¹ Azarel, Shelemiah, Shemariah,
⁴² Shallum, Amariah, and Joseph;
⁴³ Nebo's descendants: Jeiel,
    Mattithiah, Zabad, Zebina,
    Jaddai, Joel, and Benaiah.

⁴⁴ All of these had married foreign women, and some of the wives had borne children.

1 The words of Nehemiah son of Hacaliah:

During the month of Chislev in the twentieth year, when I was in the fortress city of Susa, ² Hanani, one of my brothers, arrived with men from Judah, and I questioned them about Jerusalem and the Jewish remnant that had returned from exile. ³ They said to me, "The survivors in the province, who returned from the exile, are in great trouble and disgrace. Jerusalem's wall has been broken down, and its gates have been burned down."

⁴ When I heard these words, I sat down and wept. I mourned for a number of days, fasting and praying before the God of heaven. ⁵ I said,

LORD God of heaven, the great and awe-inspiring God who keeps His gracious covenant with those who love Him and keep His commands, ⁶ let Your eyes be open and Your ears be attentive to hear Your servant's prayer that I now pray to You day and night for Your servants, the Israelites. I confess the sins we have committed against You. Both I and my father's house have sinned. ⁷ We have acted corruptly toward You and have not kept the commands, statutes, and ordinances You gave Your servant Moses. ⁸ Please remember what You commanded Your servant Moses: "If you are unfaithful, I will scatter you among the peoples. ⁹ But if you

return to Me and carefully observe My commands, even though your exiles were banished to the ends of the earth, I will gather them from there and bring them to the place where I chose to have My name dwell." ¹⁰ They are Your servants and Your people. You redeemed them by Your great power and strong hand. ¹¹ Please, Lord, let Your ear be attentive to the prayer of Your servant and to that of Your servants who delight to revere Your name. Give Your servant success today, and have compassion on him in the presence of this man.

At the time, I was the king's cupbearer.

PSALM 97:1-6

¹ The LORD reigns! Let the earth rejoice;
   let the many coasts and islands be glad.

² Clouds and thick darkness surround Him;
   righteousness and justice are the foundation of His throne.

³ Fire goes before Him
   and burns up His foes on every side.

⁴ His lightning lights up the world;
   the earth sees and trembles.

⁵ The mountains melt like wax at the presence of the LORD—
   at the presence of the Lord of all the earth.

⁶ The heavens proclaim His righteousness;
   all the peoples see His glory.

PROVERBS 20:4-6

⁴ The slacker does not plow during planting season;
   at harvest time he looks, and there is nothing.

⁵ Counsel in a man's heart is deep water;

but a man of understanding draws
it up.

6 Many a man proclaims his own
loyalty,
but who can find a trustworthy
man?

ROMANS 8:1-25

8 Therefore, no condemnation now exists for those in Christ Jesus, ² because the Spirit's law of life in Christ Jesus has set you free from the law of sin and of death. ³ What the law could not do since it was limited by the flesh, God did. He condemned sin in the flesh by sending His own Son in flesh like ours under sin's domain, and as a sin offering, ⁴ in order that the law's requirement would be accomplished in us who do not walk according to the flesh but according to the Spirit. ⁵ For those whose lives are according to the flesh think about the things of the flesh, but those whose lives are according to the Spirit, about the things of the Spirit. ⁶ For the mind-set of the flesh is death, but the mind-set of the Spirit is life and peace. ⁷ For the mind-set of the flesh is hostile to God because it does not submit itself to God's law, for it is unable to do so. ⁸ Those whose lives are in the flesh are unable to please God. ⁹ You, however, are not in the flesh, but in the Spirit, since the Spirit of God lives in you. But if anyone does not have the Spirit of Christ, he does not belong to Him. ¹⁰ Now if Christ is in you, the body is dead because of sin, but the Spirit is life because of righteousness. ¹¹ And if the Spirit of Him who raised Jesus from the dead lives in you, then He who

raised Christ from the dead will also bring your mortal bodies to life through His Spirit who lives in you.

¹² So then, brothers, we are not obligated to the flesh to live according to the flesh, ¹³ for if you live according to the flesh, you are going to die. But if by the Spirit you put to death the deeds of the body, you will live. ¹⁴ All those led by God's Spirit are God's sons. ¹⁵ For you did not receive a spirit of slavery to fall back into fear, but you received the Spirit of adoption, by whom we cry out, "*Abba*, Father!" ¹⁶ The Spirit Himself testifies together with our spirit that we are God's children, ¹⁷ and if children, also heirs—heirs of God and co-heirs with Christ—seeing that we suffer with Him so that we may also be glorified with Him.

¹⁸ For I consider that the sufferings of this present time are not worth comparing with the glory that is going to be revealed to us. ¹⁹ For the creation eagerly waits with anticipation for God's sons to be revealed. ²⁰ For the creation was subjected to futility—not willingly, but because of Him who subjected it—in the hope ²¹ that the creation itself will also be set free from the bondage of corruption into the glorious freedom of God's children. ²² For we know that the whole creation has been groaning together with labor pains until now. ²³ And not only that, but we ourselves who have the Spirit as the firstfruits— we also groan within ourselves, eagerly waiting for adoption, the redemption of our bodies. ²⁴ Now in this hope we were saved, yet hope that is seen is not hope, because who hopes for what he sees? ²⁵ But if we hope for what we do not see, we eagerly wait for it with patience.

It's OK to Feel It

When I heard these words, I sat down and wept.
—NEHEMIAH 1:4

Why is it necessary to know how to cope with disappointment? Because if it is allowed to reverberate in our hearts, however much we pretend with our minds that we do not care, our true feelings will prevent us from moving upward toward the peaks of God "with all four feet." Our back feet will not track where our front feet have been positioned, and thus we will miss our step on the steep slopes that lead us upward to closer fellowship with God.

The first thing we should learn about disappointment is this—it's OK to feel it. The worst possible thing we can do with any problem that arises in our lives is to refuse to face it and feel it. Yet this is a typical response made by many Christians to life's problems.

I once counseled a young, unmarried woman who had gone through some bitter disappointments both in her childhood and in her adolescent years. Such was the pain these disappointments brought that the only way she could cope with them was to turn her mind to something else. She toyed with the idea of drink, sensual pleasures, and several other things, but because she possessed a deep commitment to Christ, she decided to enroll in a Bible correspondence course. As we talked, it became clear to me that in doing this, her primary goal was not to learn more about Scripture but to relieve the pain of disappointment that was reverberating in her heart. Bible study became a way to escape from her problems rather than what it should have been—a way to confront them.

Prayer

Father, help me to see that You have made me in such a way that I function best when I go through problems rather than around them. Show me that maturity means being in charge of my feelings, not my feelings being in charge of me. Amen.

Further Study

Jnh 1–4; Pr 16:32; Ec 7:9
Why was Jonah disappointed?
How did demandingness come into it?

AUGUST 15

NEHEMIAH 2:1–3:32

2 During the month of Nisan in the twentieth year of King Artaxerxes, when wine was set before him, I took the wine and gave it to the king. I had never been sad in his presence, ² so the king said to me, "Why are you sad, when you aren't sick? This is nothing but sadness of heart."

I was overwhelmed with fear ³ and replied to the king, "May the king live forever! Why should I not be sad when the city where my ancestors are buried lies in ruins and its gates have been destroyed by fire?"

⁴ Then the king asked me, "What is your request?"

So I prayed to the God of heaven ⁵ and answered the king, "If it pleases the king, and if your servant has found favor with you, send me to Judah and to the city where my ancestors are buried, so that I may rebuild it."

⁶ The king, with the queen seated beside him, asked me, "How long will your journey take, and when will you return?" So I gave him a definite time, and it pleased the king to send me.

⁷ I also said to the king: "If it pleases the king, let me have letters written to the governors of the region west of the Euphrates River, so that they will grant me safe passage until I reach Judah. ⁸ And let me have a letter written to Asaph, keeper of the king's forest, so that he will give me timber to rebuild the gates of the temple's fortress, the city wall, and the home where I will live." The king granted my requests, for I was graciously strengthened by my God.

⁹ I went to the governors of the region west of the Euphrates and gave them the king's letters. The king had also sent officers of the infantry and cavalry with me. ¹⁰ When Sanballat the Horonite and Tobiah the Ammonite official heard that someone had come to seek the well-being of the Israelites, they were greatly displeased.

¹¹ After I arrived in Jerusalem and had been there three days, ¹² I got up at night and took a few men with me. I didn't tell anyone what my God had laid on my heart to do for Jerusalem. The only animal I took was the one I was riding. ¹³ I went out at night through the Valley Gate toward the Serpent's Well and the Dung Gate, and I inspected the walls of Jerusalem that had been broken down and its gates that had been destroyed by fire. ¹⁴ I went on to the Fountain Gate and the King's Pool, but farther down it became too narrow for my animal to go through. ¹⁵ So I went up at night by way of the valley and inspected the wall. Then heading back, I entered through the Valley Gate and returned. ¹⁶ The officials did not know where I had gone or what I was doing, for I had not yet told the Jews, priests, nobles, officials, or the rest of those who would be doing the work. ¹⁷ So I said to them, "You see the trouble we are in. Jerusalem lies in ruins and its gates have been burned down. Come, let's rebuild Jerusalem's wall, so that we will no longer be a disgrace." ¹⁸ I told them how the gracious hand of my God had been on me, and what the king had said to me.

They said, "Let's start rebuilding," and they were encouraged to do this good work.

¹⁹ When Sanballat the Horonite, Tobiah the Ammonite official, and Geshem the Arab heard about this, they mocked and despised us, and said, "What is this you're doing? Are you rebelling against the king?"

²⁰ I gave them this reply, "The God of heaven is the One who will grant us success. We, His servants, will start

building, but you have no share, right, or historic claim in Jerusalem."

3 Eliashib the high priest and his fellow priests began rebuilding the Sheep Gate. They dedicated it and installed its doors. After building the wall to the Tower of the Hundred and the Tower of Hananel, they dedicated it. ² The men of Jericho built next to Eliashib, and next to them Zaccur son of Imri built.

³ The sons of Hassenaah built the Fish Gate. They built it with beams and installed its doors, bolts, and bars. ⁴ Next to them Meremoth son of Uriah, son of Hakkoz, made repairs. Beside them Meshullam son of Berechiah, son of Meshezabel, made repairs. Next to them Zadok son of Baana made repairs. ⁵ Beside them the Tekoites made repairs, but their nobles did not lift a finger to help their supervisors.

⁶ Joiada son of Paseah and Meshullam son of Besodeiah repaired the Old Gate. They built it with beams and installed its doors, bolts, and bars. ⁷ Next to them Melatiah the Gibeonite, Jadon the Meronothite, and the men of Gibeon and Mizpah, who were under the authority of the governor of the region west of the Euphrates River. ⁸ After him Uzziel son of Harhaiah, the goldsmith, made repairs, and next to him Hananiah son of the perfumer made repairs. They restored Jerusalem as far as the Broad Wall.

⁹ Next to them Rephaiah son of Hur, ruler over half the district of Jerusalem, made repairs. ¹⁰ After them Jedaiah son of Harumaph made repairs across from his house. Next to him Hattush the son of Hashabneiah made repairs. ¹¹ Malchijah son of Harim and Hasshub son of Pahath-moab made repairs to another section, as well as to the Tower of the Ovens. ¹² Beside him Shallum son of Hallohesh, ruler over half the district of Jerusalem, made repairs—he and his daughters.

¹³ Hanun and the inhabitants of Zanoah repaired the Valley Gate. They rebuilt it and installed its doors, bolts, and bars, and repaired 500 yards of the wall to the Dung Gate. ¹⁴ Malchijah son of Rechab, ruler over the district of Beth-haccherem, repaired the Dung Gate. He rebuilt it and installed its doors, bolts, and bars.

¹⁵ Shallun son of Col-hozeh, ruler over the district of Mizpah, repaired the Fountain Gate. He rebuilt it and roofed it. Then he installed its doors, bolts, and bars. He also made repairs to the wall of the Pool of Shelah near the king's garden, as far as the stairs that descend from the city of David.

¹⁶ After him Nehemiah son of Azbuk, ruler over half the district of Beth-zur, made repairs up to a point opposite the tombs of David, as far as the artificial pool and the House of the Warriors. ¹⁷ Next to him the Levites made repairs under Rehum son of Bani. Beside him Hashabiah, ruler over half the district of Keilah, made repairs for his district. ¹⁸ After him their fellow Levites made repairs under Binnui son of Henadad, ruler over half the district of Keilah. ¹⁹ Next to him Ezer son of Jeshua, ruler over Mizpah, made repairs to another section opposite the ascent to the armory at the Angle.

²⁰ After him Baruch son of Zabbai diligently repaired another section, from the Angle to the door of the house of Eliashib the high priest. ²¹ Beside him Meremoth son of Uriah, son of Hakkoz, made repairs to another section, from the door of Eliashib's house to the end of his house. ²² And next to him the priests from the surrounding area made repairs.

²³ After them Benjamin and Hasshub made repairs opposite their house. Beside them Azariah son of Maaseiah, son of Ananiah, made repairs beside his house. ²⁴ After him Binnui son of Henadad made repairs to another section, from the house of Azariah to the Angle and the corner. ²⁵ Palal son of Uzai made repairs opposite the Angle and tower that juts out from the upper palace of the king, by the courtyard of the guard. Beside him Pedaiah son of Parosh, ²⁶ and the temple servants living on Ophel made repairs opposite the Water Gate toward the east and the

tower that juts out. ²⁷ Next to him the Tekoites made repairs to another section from a point opposite the great tower that juts out, as far as the wall of Ophel.

²⁸ Each of the priests made repairs above the Horse Gate, each opposite his own house. ²⁹ After them Zadok son of Immer made repairs opposite his house. And beside him Shemaiah son of Shecaniah, guard of the East Gate, made repairs. ³⁰ Next to him Hananiah son of Shelemiah and Hanun the sixth son of Zalaph made repairs to another section.

After them Meshullam son of Berechiah made repairs opposite his room. ³¹ Next to him Malchijah, one of the goldsmiths, made repairs to the house of the temple servants and the merchants, opposite the Inspection Gate, and as far as the upper room of the corner. ³² The goldsmiths and merchants made repairs between the upper room of the corner and the Sheep Gate.

PSALM 97:7-12

⁷ All who serve carved images,
those who boast in idols, will be
put to shame.
All the gods must worship Him.

⁸ Zion hears and is glad,
and the towns of Judah rejoice
because of Your judgments, LORD.
⁹ For You, LORD, are the Most High
over all the earth;
You are exalted above all the gods.

¹⁰ You who love the LORD, hate evil!
He protects the lives of His godly
ones;
He rescues them from the hand of
the wicked.
¹¹ Light dawns for the righteous,
gladness for the upright in heart.
¹² Be glad in the LORD, you righteous
ones,
and praise His holy name.

PROVERBS 20:7-9

⁷ The one who lives with integrity is
righteous;

his children who come after him
will be happy.

⁸ A king sitting on a throne to judge
sifts out all evil with his eyes.

⁹ Who can say, "I have kept my
heart pure;
I am cleansed from my sin"?

ROMANS 8:26–9:5

²⁶ In the same way the Spirit also joins to help in our weakness, because we do not know what to pray for as we should, but the Spirit Himself intercedes for us with unspoken groanings. ²⁷ And He who searches the hearts knows the Spirit's mind-set, because He intercedes for the saints according to the will of God.

²⁸ We know that all things work together for the good of those who love God: those who are called according to His purpose. ²⁹ For those He foreknew He also predestined to be conformed to the image of His Son, so that He would be the firstborn among many brothers. ³⁰ And those He predestined, He also called; and those He called, He also justified; and those He justified, He also glorified.

³¹ What then are we to say
about these things?
If God is for us, who is against us?
³² He did not even spare
His own Son,
but offered Him up for us all;
how will He not also with Him
grant us everything?
³³ Who can bring an accusation
against God's elect?
God is the One who justifies.
³⁴ Who is the one who condemns?
Christ Jesus is the One who died,
but even more,
has been raised;
He also is at the right hand of God
and intercedes for us.
³⁵ Who can separate us
from the love of Christ?
Can affliction or anguish
or persecution

or famine or nakedness or danger or sword?

36 As it is written:

Because of You we are being put to death all day long; we are counted as sheep to be slaughtered.

37 No, in all these things we are more than victorious through Him who loved us.

38 For I am persuaded that neither death nor life, nor angels nor rulers, nor things present, nor things to come, nor powers,

39 nor height, nor depth, nor any other created thing will have the power to separate us from the love of God that is in Christ Jesus our Lord!

9 I speak the truth in Christ—I am not lying; my conscience is testifying to me with the Holy Spirit— 2 that I have intense sorrow and continual anguish in my heart. 3 For I could wish that I myself were cursed and cut off from the Messiah for the benefit of my brothers, my countrymen by physical descent. 4 They are Israelites, and to them belong the adoption, the glory, the covenants, the giving of the law, the temple service, and the promises. 5 The forefathers are theirs, and from them, by physical descent, came the Messiah, who is God over all, blessed forever. Amen.

God's One Great Goal

For those He foreknew He also predestined to be conformed to the image of His Son.—ROMANS 8:29

What is God's great goal in the universe to which His energies are devoted? We have it in our text for today. The Living Bible puts this best, and I have no hesitation in saying that although it is not regarded as a true translation (it is, rather, a paraphrase), its rendering of Romans 8:29 is one of the most exciting things I have ever read. This is what it says: "For from the very beginning God decided that those who came to him . . . should become like his Son." God's great energy and wisdom, working on behalf of all Christians, is directed to making us like His Son Jesus Christ. Of course this purpose will only be fully realized in the world to come, but while we are here, He is pursuing this same purpose nevertheless.

It is only when we comprehend this that we will be able to understand the purpose that lies behind all our trials and difficulties. Romans 8:28—"We know that all things work together for the good of those who love God"—must be read in connection with Romans 8:29. Because God is committed to making us like His Son, His wisdom goes to work on every trial that comes our way in order to bring from it something that will enrich our character and make us more like Jesus Christ.

Infinite power is ruled by infinite wisdom. He could deliver us and make our lives comfortable, but in a fallen world this is not the best purpose. Understanding this is crucial if we are to live our lives the way God desires.

Prayer

Father, forgive me that so often my goals are diametrically opposed to Yours. Help me bring my goals in line with Your goals. I shall need Your help to adjust. Whatever happens, keep me ever moving toward becoming more and more like Jesus. Amen.

Further Study

1 Co 1:1-31; Col 2:3
How does Paul describe the foolishness of God?
What is hidden in Christ?

AUGUST 16

NEHEMIAH 4:1–6:19

4 When Sanballat heard that we were rebuilding the wall, he became furious. He mocked the Jews ² before his colleagues and the powerful men of Samaria, and said, "What are these pathetic Jews doing? Can they restore it by themselves? Will they offer sacrifices? Will they ever finish it? Can they bring these burnt stones back to life from the mounds of rubble?" ³ Then Tobiah the Ammonite, who was beside him, said, "Indeed, even if a fox climbed up what they are building, he would break down their stone wall!"

⁴ Listen, our God, for we are despised. Make their insults return on their own heads and let them be taken as plunder to a land of captivity. ⁵ Do not cover their guilt or let their sin be erased from Your sight, because they have provoked the builders.

⁶ So we rebuilt the wall until the entire wall was joined together up to half its height, for the people had the will to keep working.

⁷ When Sanballat, Tobiah, and the Arabs, Ammonites, and Ashdodites heard that the repair to the walls of Jerusalem was progressing and that the gaps were being closed, they became furious. ⁸ They all plotted together to come and fight against Jerusalem and throw it into confusion. ⁹ So we prayed to our God and stationed a guard because of them day and night.

¹⁰ In Judah, it was said:

The strength of the laborer fails,
since there is so much rubble.
We will never be able
to rebuild the wall.

¹¹ And our enemies said, "They won't know or see anything until we're among them and can kill them and stop the work." ¹² When the Jews who lived nearby arrived, they said to us time and again, "Everywhere you turn, they attack us." ¹³ So I stationed people behind the lowest sections of the wall, at the vulnerable areas. I stationed them by families with their swords, spears, and bows. ¹⁴ After I made an inspection, I stood up and said to the nobles, the officials, and the rest of the people,

"Don't be afraid of them. Remember the great and awe-inspiring Lord, and fight for your countrymen, your sons and daughters, your wives and homes."

¹⁵ When our enemies realized that we knew their scheme and that God had frustrated it, every one of us returned to his own work on the wall. ¹⁶ From that day on, half of my men did the work while the other half held spears, shields, bows, and armor. The officers supported all the people of Judah, ¹⁷ who were rebuilding the wall. The laborers who carried the loads worked with one hand and held a weapon with the other. ¹⁸ Each of the builders had his sword strapped around his waist while he was building, and the trumpeter was beside me. ¹⁹ Then I said to the nobles, the officials, and the rest of the people: "The work is enormous and spread out, and we are separated far from one another along the wall. ²⁰ Wherever you hear the trumpet sound, rally to us there. Our God will fight for us!" ²¹ So we continued the work, while half of the men were holding spears from daybreak until the stars came out. ²² At that time, I also said to the people, "Let everyone and his servant spend the night inside Jerusalem, so that they can stand guard by night and work by day." ²³ And I, my brothers, my men, and the guards with me never took off our clothes. Each carried his weapon, even when washing.

5 There was a widespread outcry from the people and their wives against their Jewish countrymen. ² Some were saying, "We, our sons, and our daughters are numerous. Let us get grain so that we can eat and live." ³ Others were saying, "We are mortgaging our fields, vineyards, and homes to get grain during the famine." ⁴ Still others were saying, "We have borrowed money to pay the king's tax on our fields and vineyards. ⁵ We and our children are just like our countrymen and their children, yet we are subjecting our sons and daughters to slavery. Some of our daughters are already enslaved, but we are powerless because our fields and vineyards belong to others."

⁶ I became extremely angry when I heard their outcry and these complaints. ⁷ After seriously considering the matter, I accused the nobles and officials, saying to them, "Each of you is charging his countrymen interest." So I called a large assembly against them ⁸ and said, "We have done our best to buy back our Jewish countrymen who were sold to foreigners, but now you sell your own countrymen, and we have to buy them back." They remained silent and could not say a word. ⁹ Then I said, "What you are doing isn't right. Shouldn't you walk in the fear of our God and not invite the reproach of our foreign enemies? ¹⁰ Even I, as well as my brothers and my servants, have been lending them money and grain. Please, let us stop charging this interest. ¹¹ Return their fields, vineyards, olive groves, and houses to them immediately, along with the percentage of the money, grain, new wine, and olive oil that you have been assessing them."

¹² They responded: "We will return these things and require nothing more from them. We will do as you say."

So I summoned the priests and made everyone take an oath to do this. ¹³ I also shook the folds of my robe and said, "May God likewise shake from his house and property everyone who doesn't keep this promise. May he be shaken out and have nothing!"

The whole assembly said, "Amen," and they praised the Lord. Then the people did as they had promised.

¹⁴ Furthermore, from the day King Artaxerxes appointed me to be their governor in the land of Judah—from the twentieth year until his thirty-second year, 12 years—I and my associates never ate from the food allotted to the governor. ¹⁵ The governors who preceded me had heavily burdened the people, taking food and wine from them, as well as a pound of silver. Their subordinates also oppressed the people, but I didn't do this, because of the fear of God. ¹⁶ Instead, I devoted myself to the construction of the wall, and all my subordinates were gathered there for the work. We didn't buy any land.

¹⁷ There were 150 Jews and officials, as well as guests from the surrounding nations at my table. ¹⁸ Each day, one ox, six choice sheep, and some fowl were prepared for me. An abundance of all kinds of wine was provided every 10 days. But I didn't demand the food allotted to the governor, because the burden on the people was so heavy. ¹⁹ Remember me favorably, my God, for all that I have done for this people.

6 When Sanballat, Tobiah, Geshem the Arab, and the rest of our enemies heard that I had rebuilt the wall and that no gap was left in it—though at that time I had not installed the doors in the gates— ² Sanballat and Geshem sent me a message: "Come, let's meet together in the villages of the Ono Valley." But they were planning to harm me. ³ So I sent messengers to them, saying, "I am doing a great work and cannot come down. Why should the work cease while I leave it and go down to you?" ⁴ Four times they sent me the same proposal, and I gave them the same reply. ⁵ Sanballat sent me this same message a fifth time by his aide, who had an open letter in his hand. ⁶ In it was written:

It is reported among the nations—and Geshem agrees—that you and the Jews plan to rebel. This is the reason you are building the wall. According to these reports, you are to become their king ⁷ and have even set up the prophets in Jerusalem to proclaim on your behalf: "There is a king in Judah." These rumors will be heard by the king. So come, let's confer together.

⁸ Then I replied to him, "There is nothing to these rumors you are spreading; you are inventing them in your own mind." ⁹ For they were all trying to intimidate us, saying, "They will become discouraged in the work, and it will never be finished."

But now, my God, strengthen me. ¹⁰ I went to the house of Shemaiah son of Delaiah, son of Mehetabel, who was restricted to his house. He said:

Let us meet at the house of God
inside the temple.
Let us shut the temple doors
because they are coming to kill
you.
They are coming to kill you
tonight!

¹¹ But I said, "Should a man like me run away? How can I enter the temple and live? I will not go." ¹² I realized that God had not sent him, because of the prophecy he spoke against me. Tobiah and Sanballat had hired him. ¹³ He was hired, so that I would be intimidated, do as he suggested, sin, and get a bad reputation, in order that they could discredit me.

¹⁴ My God, remember Tobiah and Sanballat for what they have done, and also Noadiah the prophetess and the other prophets who wanted to intimidate me.

¹⁵ The wall was completed in 52 days, on the twenty-fifth day of the month Elul. ¹⁶ When all our enemies heard this, all the surrounding nations were intimidated and lost their confidence, for they realized that this task had been accomplished by our God.

¹⁷ During those days, the nobles of Judah sent many letters to Tobiah, and Tobiah's letters came to them. ¹⁸ For many in Judah were bound by oath to him, since he was a son-in-law of Shecaniah son of Arah, and his son Jehohanan had married the daughter of Meshullam son of Berechiah. ¹⁹ These nobles kept mentioning Tobiah's good deeds to me, and they reported my words to him. And Tobiah sent letters to intimidate me.

PSALM 98:1-9

¹ Sing a new song to the LORD,
for He has performed wonders;
His right hand and holy arm have
won Him victory.
² The LORD has made His victory
known;

He has revealed His righteousness
in the sight of the nations.
³ He has remembered His love and
faithfulness to the house of
Israel;
all the ends of the earth have seen
our God's victory.

⁴ Shout to the Lᴏʀᴅ, all the earth;
be jubilant, shout for joy, and sing.
⁵ Sing to the Lᴏʀᴅ with the lyre,
with the lyre and melodious song.
⁶ With trumpets and the blast of the
ram's horn
shout triumphantly in the
presence of the Lᴏʀᴅ, our King.

⁷ Let the sea and all that fills it,
the world and those who live in it,
resound.
⁸ Let the rivers clap their hands;
let the mountains shout together
for joy
⁹ before the Lᴏʀᴅ, for He is coming
to judge the earth.
He will judge the world
righteously
and the peoples fairly.

Pʀᴏᴠᴇʀʙs 20:10-12

¹⁰ Differing weights and varying
measures —
both are detestable to the Lᴏʀᴅ.

¹¹ Even a young man is known by his
actions—
by whether his behavior is pure
and upright.

¹² The hearing ear and the seeing
eye—
the Lᴏʀᴅ made them both.

Rᴏᴍᴀɴs 9:6-26

⁶ But it is not as though the word of
God has failed. For not all who are descended from Israel are Israel. ⁷ Neither
are they all children because they are
Abraham's descendants. On the contrary, in Isaac your seed will be called.
⁸ That is, it is not the children by physi-

cal descent who are God's children, but
the children of the promise are considered seed. ⁹ For this is the statement of
the promise: At this time I will come,
and Sarah will have a son. ¹⁰ And not
only that, but also when Rebekah became pregnant by Isaac our forefather
¹¹ (for though they had not been born
yet or done anything good or bad, so
that God's purpose according to election might stand, ¹² not from works but
from the One who calls) she was told:
The older will serve the younger. ¹³ As
it is written: Jacob I have loved, but
Esau I have hated.

¹⁴ What should we say then? Is there
injustice with God? Absolutely not!
¹⁵ For He tells Moses:

I will show mercy to whom
I show mercy,
and I will have compassion
on whom I have compassion.

¹⁶ So then it does not depend on human
will or effort, but on God who shows
mercy. ¹⁷ For the Scripture tells Pharaoh:

For this reason I raised you up:
so that I may display
My power in you,
and that My name
may be proclaimed
in all the earth.

¹⁸ So then, He shows mercy to whom He
wills, and He hardens whom He wills.
¹⁹ You will say to me, therefore, "Why
then does He still find fault? For who
can resist His will?" ²⁰ But who are
you—anyone who talks back to God?
Will what is formed say to the one who
formed it, "Why did you make me like
this?" ²¹ Or has the potter no right over
His clay, to make from the same lump
one piece of pottery for honor and another for dishonor? ²² And what if God,
desiring to display His wrath and to
make His power known, endured with
much patience objects of wrath ready
for destruction? ²³ And what if He did
this to make known the riches of His
glory on objects of mercy that He pre-

pared beforehand for glory— [24] on us whom He also called, not only from the Jews but also from the Gentiles? [25] As He also says in Hosea:

I will call "Not-My-People," "My-People,"

and she who is "Unloved," "Beloved."
[26] And it will be in the place where they were told,
you are not My people,
there they will be called
sons of the living God.

The Conscience Corrected

Even a young man is known by his actions—by whether his behavior is pure and upright.—PROVERBS 20:11

One way that the Holy Spirit exercises His convincing ministry in our lives is by addressing our consciences, prevailing upon them to take the way of Christ in every issue. Romans 9:1 brings together the objective standard, "the truth in Christ," and the subjective standard, "my conscience is testifying to me with the Holy Spirit."

Some people say, "I'm living in accordance with my conscience—isn't that enough?" No, for conscience by itself is not a safe guide. Conscience is the capacity to distinguish between right and wrong—according to the standards you uphold. It can be taught to approve directly opposite things.

For example, a missionary intervened to stop an Indian woman from throwing her child into the Ganges River as a human sacrifice. "But my conscience tells me to do it," she said. "Yes," said the missionary, "and my conscience tells me to stop you from doing it."

Conscience is not an infallible guide unless it has in it the highest content possible—the Holy Spirit. He can be relied upon to act as Jesus would act in every situation, for the Spirit is a Christlike Spirit. I am bold to say that there is not one of you reading these lines (if you are a Christian) who, by the mercy of God, doesn't know something in your conscience of the work of the Holy Spirit as Convincer. He pleads in you and with you to bring your conscience to the highest place possible, "a clear conscience toward God and men" (Ac 24:16).

Prayer

O Father, I surrender myself and my standards to You for cleansing and correction. Teach me the standards of Christ so that my conscience may bear a true witness. For Jesus' sake. Amen.

Further Study

Rm 14; 15:1-13; Ac 24:16; 2 Co 1:12; 1 Tm 1:5
What is Paul teaching about our conscience?
How does he relate it to the ministry of the Holy Spirit?

AUGUST 17

*N*EHEMIAH 7:1-60

7 When the wall had been rebuilt and I had the doors installed, the gatekeepers, singers, and Levites were appointed. ² Then I put my brother Hanani in charge of Jerusalem, along with Hananiah, commander of the fortress, because he was a faithful man who feared God more than most. ³ I said to them, "Do not open the gates of Jerusalem until the sun is hot, and let the doors be shut and securely fastened while the guards are on duty. Station the citizens of Jerusalem as guards, some at their posts and some at their homes."

⁴ The city was large and spacious, but there were few people in it, and no houses had been built yet. ⁵ Then my God put it into my mind to assemble the nobles, the officials, and the people to be registered by genealogy. I found the genealogical record of those who came back first, and I found the following written in it:

⁶ These are the people of the province who went up from among the captive exiles deported by King Nebuchadnezzar of Babylon. Each of them returned to his own town in Jerusalem and Judah. ⁷ They came with Zerubbabel, Jeshua, Nehemiah, Azariah, Raamiah, Nahamani, Mordecai, Bilshan, Mispereth, Bigvai, Nehum, and Baanah.

The number of the Israelite men included:

⁸	Parosh's descendants	2,172
⁹	Shephatiah's descendants	372
¹⁰	Arah's descendants	652
¹¹	Pahath-moab's descendants: Jeshua's and Joab's descendants	2,818
¹²	Elam's descendants	1,254
¹³	Zattu's descendants	845
¹⁴	Zaccai's descendants	760
¹⁵	Binnui's descendants	648
¹⁶	Bebai's descendants	628
¹⁷	Azgad's descendants	2,322
¹⁸	Adonikam's descendants	667
¹⁹	Bigvai's descendants	2,067
²⁰	Adin's descendants	655
²¹	Ater's descendants: of Hezekiah	98
²²	Hashum's descendants	328
²³	Bezai's descendants	324
²⁴	Hariph's descendants	112
²⁵	Gibeon's descendants	95
²⁶	Bethlehem's and Netophah's men	188
²⁷	Anathoth's men	128
²⁸	Beth-azmaveth's men	42
²⁹	Kiriath-jearim's, Chephirah's, and Beeroth's men	743
³⁰	Ramah's and Geba's men	621
³¹	Michmas's men	122
³²	Bethel's and Ai's men	123
³³	the other Nebo's men	52
³⁴	the other Elam's people	1,254
³⁵	Harim's people	320
³⁶	Jericho's people	345
³⁷	Lod's, Hadid's, and Ono's people	721
³⁸	Senaah's people	3,930

³⁹ The priests included:

	Jedaiah's descendants of the house of Jeshua	973
⁴⁰	Immer's descendants	1,052
⁴¹	Pashhur's descendants	1,247
⁴²	Harim's descendants	1,017

⁴³ The Levites included:

	Jeshua's descendants: of Kadmiel Hodevah's descendants	74

⁴⁴ The singers included:

	Asaph's descendants	148

⁴⁵ The gatekeepers included:

Shallum's descendants,
Ater's descendants,
Talmon's descendants,
Akkub's descendants,
Hatita's descendants,
Shobai's descendants   138

46 The temple servants included:

Ziha's descendants,
Hasupha's descendants,
Tabbaoth's descendants,
47 Keros's descendants,
Sia's descendants,
Padon's descendants,
48 Lebana's descendants,
Hagaba's descendants,
Shalmai's descendants,
49 Hanan's descendants,
Giddel's descendants,
Gahar's descendants,
50 Reaiah's descendants,
Rezin's descendants,
Nekoda's descendants,
51 Gazzam's descendants,
Uzza's descendants,
Paseah's descendants,
52 Besai's descendants,
Meunim's descendants,
Nephishesim's descendants,
53 Bakbuk's descendants,
Hakupha's descendants,
Harhur's descendants,
54 Bazlith's descendants,
Mehida's descendants,
Harsha's descendants,
55 Barkos's descendants,
Sisera's descendants,
Temah's descendants,
56 Neziah's descendants,
Hatipha's descendants.

57 The descendants of Solomon's servants included:

Sotai's descendants,
Sophereth's descendants,
Perida's descendants,
58 Jaala's descendants,
Darkon's descendants,
Giddel's descendants,
59 Shephatiah's descendants,
Hattil's descendants,

Pochereth-hazzebaim's
descendants,
Amon's descendants.

60 All the temple servants
and the descendants
of Solomon's servants   392

PSALM 99:1-9

1 The LORD reigns! Let the peoples
tremble.
He is enthroned above the
cherubim.
Let the earth quake.
2 The LORD is great in Zion;
He is exalted above all the
peoples.
3 Let them praise Your great and
awe-inspiring name.
He is holy.

4 The mighty King loves justice.
You have established fairness;
You have administered justice and
righteousness in Jacob.
5 Exalt the LORD our God;
bow in worship at His footstool.
He is holy.

6 Moses and Aaron were among His
priests;
Samuel also was among those
calling on His name.
They called to the LORD, and He
answered them.
7 He spoke to them in a pillar of
cloud;
they kept His decrees and the
statutes He gave them.
8 LORD our God, You answered them.
You were a God who forgave
them,
but punished their misdeeds.

9 Exalt the LORD our God;
bow in worship at His holy
mountain,
for the LORD our God is holy.

PROVERBS 20:13-15

13 Don't love sleep, or you will
become poor;

open your eyes, and you'll have enough to eat.

14 "It's worthless, it's worthless!" the buyer says,
but after he is on his way, he gloats.

15 There is gold and a multitude of jewels,
but knowledgeable lips are a rare treasure.

ROMANS 9:27–10:15

27 But Isaiah cries out concerning Israel:

Though the number
of Israel's sons is like
the sand of the sea,
only the remnant will be saved;
28 for the Lord will execute
His sentence
completely and decisively
on the earth.

29 And just as Isaiah predicted:

If the Lord of Hosts had not left
us a seed,
we would have become
like Sodom,
and we would have been made
like Gomorrah.

30 What should we say then? Gentiles, who did not pursue righteousness, have obtained righteousness—namely the righteousness that comes from faith. 31 But Israel, pursuing the law for righteousness, has not achieved the law. 32 Why is that? Because they did not pursue it by faith, but as if it were by works. They stumbled over the stumbling stone. 33 As it is written:

Look! I am putting
a stone in Zion
to stumble over,

and a rock to trip over,
yet the one who believes on Him
will not be put to shame.

10 Brothers, my heart's desire and prayer to God concerning them is for their salvation! 2 I can testify about them that they have zeal for God, but not according to knowledge. 3 Because they disregarded the righteousness from God and attempted to establish their own righteousness, they have not submitted to God's righteousness. 4 For Christ is the end of the law for righteousness to everyone who believes. 5 For Moses writes about the righteousness that is from the law: The one who does these things will live by them. 6 But the righteousness that comes from faith speaks like this: Do not say in your heart, "Who will go up to heaven?" that is, to bring Christ down 7 or, "Who will go down into the abyss?" that is, to bring Christ up from the dead. 8 On the contrary, what does it say? The message is near you, in your mouth and in your heart. This is the message of faith that we proclaim: 9 if you confess with your mouth, "Jesus is Lord," and believe in your heart that God raised Him from the dead, you will be saved. 10 With the heart one believes, resulting in righteousness, and with the mouth one confesses, resulting in salvation. 11 Now the Scripture says, No one who believes on Him will be put to shame, 12 for there is no distinction between Jew and Greek, since the same Lord of all is rich to all who call on Him. 13 For everyone who calls on the name of the Lord will be saved.

14 But how can they call on Him in whom they have not believed? And how can they believe without hearing about Him? And how can they hear without a preacher? 15 And how can they preach unless they are sent? As it is written: How welcome are the feet of those who announce the gospel of good things!

The Power of Holiness

*Exalt the LORD our God; bow in worship
at His footstool. He is holy.*—PSALM 99:5

"No one can know the true grace of God," said the great Bible teacher A. W. Tozer, "who has not first known the fear of God." He continued: "Always there was about any manifestation of God something that dismayed the onlookers, that daunted and overawed them. . . . I do not believe any lasting good can come from religious activities that are not rooted in this fear. Until we have been gripped by that nameless terror that results when an unholy creature is suddenly confronted by the One who is holiest of all, we are not likely to be affected by the doctrine of love and grace."

There was a time when the nature and character of God was a constant theme in Christian pulpits, but not any more. Generally speaking, today's preachers (and writers) tend to give people what they want rather than what they need. This is why we must stop every time we come across a reference to God's character in our Bibles and pause to consider it. No one has done anything mighty for God without a new vision of God's holiness. Ezekiel tells us of the "rims" in his vision that were "large and frightening" (Ezk 1:18), and Jacob, rising from his sleep, said: "What an awesome place this is!" (Gn 28:17).

We will be of little use to God unless we know how to tremble before Him, for otherwise our own ideas and feelings of self-sufficiency will soon take over. Have we lost the sense of awe when we come into God's presence which seemed to characterize the saints of the past? I am afraid we have.

Prayer

O God, I am afraid as I draw near to You, but I draw near because I am afraid. Nothing or no one can dissolve the fears that hinder me but You. Draw me closer, for in You and You alone lie both my salvation and sanctification. Amen.

Further Study

Ex 3:1-5; Jos 5:15; Ps 33:8; 89:7
What was Moses and Joshua's experience?
What did the psalmist admonish?

AUGUST 18

*N*EHEMIAH 7:61–9:38

⁶¹ The following are those who came from Tel-melah, Tel-harsha, Cherub, Addon, and Immer, but were unable to prove that their families and ancestry were Israelite:

⁶²   Delaiah's descendants,
     Tobiah's descendants,
     and Nekoda's descendants   642

⁶³ and from the priests: the descendants of Hobaiah, the descendants of Hakkoz, and the descendants of Barzillai—who had taken a wife from the daughters of Barzillai the Gileadite and was called by their name. ⁶⁴ These searched for their entries in the genealogical records, but they could not be found, so they were disqualified from the priesthood. ⁶⁵ The governor ordered them not to eat the most holy things until there was a priest who could consult the Urim and Thummim.

⁶⁶ The whole combined assembly
     numbered   42,360
⁶⁷   not including their 7,337 male
     and female slaves,
     as well as their 245 male
     and female singers.
⁶⁸   They had 736 horses,
     245 mules,
⁶⁹   435 camels, and 6,720 donkeys.

⁷⁰ Some of the family leaders gave to the project. The governor gave 1,000 gold drachmas, 50 bowls, and 530 priestly garments to the treasury. ⁷¹ Some of the family leaders gave 20,000 gold drachmas and 2,200 silver minas to the treasury for the project. ⁷² The rest of the people gave 20,000 gold drachmas, 2,000 silver minas, and 67 priestly garments. ⁷³ So the priests, Levites, gatekeepers, temple singers, some of the people, temple servants, and all Israel settled in their towns.

8 When the seventh month came and the Israelites had settled in their towns, ¹ all the people gathered together at the square in front of the Water Gate. They asked Ezra the scribe to bring the book of the law of Moses that the LORD had given Israel. ² On the first day of the seventh month, Ezra the priest brought the law before the assembly of men, women, and all who could listen with understanding. ³ While he was facing the square in front of the Water Gate, he read out of it from daybreak until noon before the men, women, and those who could understand. All the people listened attentively to the book of the law. ⁴ Ezra the scribe stood on a high wooden platform made for this purpose. Mattithiah, Shema, Anaiah, Uriah, Hilkiah, and Maaseiah stood beside him on his right; to his left were Pedaiah, Mishael, Malchijah, Hashum, Hash-baddanah, Zechariah, and Meshullam. ⁵ Ezra opened the book in full view of all the people, since he was elevated above everyone. As he opened it, all the people stood up. ⁶ Ezra blessed the LORD, the great God, and with their hands uplifted all the people said, "Amen, Amen!" Then they bowed down and worshiped the LORD with their faces to the ground.

⁷ Jeshua, Bani, Sherebiah, Jamin, Akkub, Shabbethai, Hodiah, Maaseiah, Kelita, Azariah, Jozabad, Hanan, and Pelaiah, who were Levites, explained the law to the people as they stood in their places. ⁸ They read the book of law of God, translating and giving the meaning so that the people could understand what was read. ⁹ Nehemiah the governor, Ezra the priest and scribe, and the Levites who were instructing

the people said to all of them, "This day is holy to the LORD your God. Do not mourn or weep." For all the people were weeping as they heard the words of the law. ¹⁰ Then he said to them, "Go and eat what is rich, drink what is sweet, and send portions to those who have nothing prepared, since today is holy to our Lord. Do not grieve, because your strength comes from rejoicing in the LORD." ¹¹ And the Levites quieted all the people, saying, "Be still, since today is holy. Do not grieve." ¹² Then all the people began to eat and drink, send portions, and have a great celebration, because they had understood the words that were explained to them.

¹³ On the second day, the family leaders of all the people, along with the priests and Levites, assembled before Ezra the scribe to study the words of the law. ¹⁴ They found written in the law how the LORD had commanded through Moses that the Israelites should dwell in booths during the festival of the seventh month. ¹⁵ So they proclaimed and spread this news throughout all their towns and in Jerusalem, saying, "Go out to the hill country and bring back branches of olive, wild olive, myrtle, palm, and other leafy trees to make booths, just as it is written." ¹⁶ The people went out, brought back branches, and made booths for themselves on each of their rooftops, and courtyards, the court of the house of God, the square by the Water Gate, and the square by the Gate of Ephraim. ¹⁷ The whole community that had returned from exile made booths and lived in them. They had not celebrated like this from the days of Joshua son of Nun until that day. And there was tremendous joy. ¹⁸ Ezra read out of the book of the law of God every day, from the first day to the last. The Israelites celebrated the feast for seven days, and on the eighth day there was an assembly, according to the ordinance.

9 On the twenty-fourth day of this month the Israelites assembled; they were fasting, wearing sackcloth, and had put dust on their heads. ² Those of Israelite descent separated themselves from all foreigners, and they stood and confessed their sins and the guilt of their fathers. ³ While they stood in their places, they read from the book of the law of the LORD their God for a fourth of the day and spent another fourth of the day in confession and worship of the LORD their God. ⁴ Jeshua, Bani, Kadmiel, Shebaniah, Bunni, Sherebiah, Bani, and Chenani stood on the raised platform built for the Levites and cried out loudly to the LORD their God. ⁵ Then the Levites—Jeshua, Kadmiel, Bani, Hashabneiah, Sherebiah, Hodiah, Shebaniah, and Pethahiah—said:

Stand up. Bless the LORD your God
from everlasting to everlasting.
Praise Your glorious name,
and may it be exalted above
all blessing and praise.
⁶ You alone are the LORD.
You created the heavens,
the highest heavens with all
their host,
the earth and all that is on it,
the seas and all that is in them.
You give life to all of them,
and the heavenly host worships
You.
⁷ You are the LORD God
who chose Abram
and brought him out of Ur
of the Chaldeans,
and changed his name
to Abraham.
⁸ You found his heart faithful
in Your sight,
and made a covenant with him
to give the land of the Canaanites,
Hittites, Amorites, Perizzites,
Jebusites, and Girgashites—
to give it to his descendants.
You have kept Your promise,
for You are righteous.
⁹ You saw the oppression
of our ancestors in Egypt
and heard their cry at the Red Sea.
¹⁰ You performed signs and wonders
against Pharaoh,
all his officials, and all the people
of his land,

for You knew how arrogantly
    they treated our ancestors.
You made a name for Yourself
    that endures to this day.
11 You divided the sea before them,
    and they crossed through it
        on dry ground.
You hurled their pursuers
        into the depths
    like a stone into churning waters.
12 You led them with a pillar of cloud
        by day,
    and with a pillar of fire by night,
    to illuminate the way
        they should go.
13 You came down on Mount Sinai,
    and spoke to them from heaven.
You gave them
        impartial ordinances,
        reliable instructions,
    and good decrees
        and commandments.
14 You revealed Your holy Sabbath
        to them,
    and gave them commandments,
        statutes, and a law
    through Your servant Moses.
15 You provided bread from heaven
        for their hunger;
You brought them water
        from the rock for their thirst.
You told them to go in and possess
        the land
You had sworn to give them.

16 But our ancestors
        acted arrogantly;
    they became stiff-necked
        and did not listen
        to Your commands.
17 They refused to listen
    and did not remember
        Your wonders
    You performed among them.
They became stiff-necked
        and appointed a leader
    to return to their slavery in Egypt.
But You are a forgiving God,
        gracious and compassionate,
    slow to anger and rich
        in faithful love,
    and You did not abandon them.
18 Even after they had cast an image
        of a calf

for themselves and said,
    "This is your God who brought you
        out of Egypt,"
    and they had committed
        terrible blasphemies,
19 You did not abandon them
        in the wilderness
    because of Your great compassion.
During the day the pillar of cloud
        never turned away from them,
    guiding them on their journey.
And during the night the pillar
        of fire
    illuminated the way
        they should go.
20 You sent Your good Spirit
        to instruct them.
You did not withhold Your manna
        from their mouths,
    and You gave them water
        for their thirst.
21 You provided for them
        in the wilderness 40 years
    and they lacked nothing.
Their clothes did not wear out,
    and their feet did not swell.

22 You gave them kingdoms
        and peoples
    and assigned them to be
        a boundary.
They took possession
        of the land of Sihon
        king of Heshbon
    and of the land of Og
        king of Bashan.
23 You multiplied their descendants
        like the stars of heaven
    and brought them to the land
You told their ancestors to go in
        and take possession of it.
24 So their descendants went in
        and possessed the land:
You subdued the Canaanites
        who inhabited the land
        before them
    and handed their kings
        and the surrounding peoples
        over to them,
    to do as they pleased with them.
25 They captured fortified cities
        and fertile land
    and took possession of
        well-supplied houses,

rock-hewn cisterns, vineyards,
olive groves, and fruit trees
in abundance.
They ate, were filled,
became prosperous, and delighted
in Your great goodness.
²⁶ But they were disobedient
and rebelled against You.
They flung Your law
behind their backs
and killed Your prophets
who warned them to turn them
back to You.
They committed
terrible blasphemies.
²⁷ So You handed them over
to their enemies,
who oppressed them.
In their time of distress,
they cried out to You,
and You heard from heaven.
In Your abundant compassion
You gave them deliverers,
who rescued them
from the power of their enemies.
²⁸ But as soon as they had relief,
they again did what was evil
in Your sight.
So You abandoned them
to the power
of their enemies,
who dominated them.
When they cried out to You again,
You heard from heaven
and rescued them
many times in Your compassion.
²⁹ You warned them to turn back
to Your law,
but they acted arrogantly
and would not obey
Your commandments.
They sinned against
Your ordinances,
by which a person will live
if he does them.
They stubbornly resisted,
stiffened their necks,
and would not obey.
³⁰ You were patient with them
for many years,
and Your Spirit warned them
through Your prophets,
but they would not listen.

Therefore, You handed them over
to the surrounding peoples.
³¹ However,
in Your abundant compassion,
You did not destroy them
or abandon them,
for You are a gracious
and compassionate God.
³² So now, our God—the great,
mighty,
and awe-inspiring God who keeps
His gracious covenant—
do not view lightly
all the hardships
that have afflicted us,
our kings and leaders,
our priests and prophets,
our ancestors and all Your people,
from the days
of the Assyrian kings
until today.
³³ You are righteous concerning all
that has come on us,
because You have acted faithfully,
while we have acted wickedly.
³⁴ Our kings, leaders, priests,
and ancestors
did not obey Your law
or listen to Your commandments
and warnings You gave them.
³⁵ When they were
in their kingdom,
with Your abundant goodness
You gave them,
and in the spacious
and fertile land You set
before them,
they would not serve You or turn
from their wicked ways.

³⁶ Here we are today,
slaves in the land You gave
our ancestors
so that they could enjoy its fruit
and its goodness.
Here we are—slaves in it!
³⁷ Its abundant harvest goes
to the kings
You have set over us,
because of our sins.
They rule over our bodies
and our livestock as they please.
We are in great distress.

³⁸ In view of all this, we are making a binding agreement in writing on a sealed document containing the names of our leaders, Levites, and priests.

PSALM 100:1-5

¹ Shout triumphantly to the LORD, all the earth.
² Serve the LORD with gladness; come before Him with joyful songs.
³ Acknowledge that the LORD is God. He made us, and we are His— His people, the sheep of His pasture.
⁴ Enter His gates with thanksgiving and His courts with praise. Give thanks to Him and praise His name.
⁵ For the LORD is good, and His love is eternal; His faithfulness endures through all generations.

PROVERBS 20:16-18

¹⁶ Take his garment, for he has put up security for a stranger; get collateral if it is for foreigners.

¹⁷ Food gained by fraud is sweet to a man, but afterward his mouth is full of gravel.

¹⁸ Finalize plans through counsel, and wage war with sound guidance.

ROMANS 10:16–11:10

¹⁶ But all did not obey the gospel. For Isaiah says, **Lord, who has believed our message?** ¹⁷ So faith comes from what is heard, and what is heard comes through the message about Christ. ¹⁸ But I ask, "Did they not hear?" Yes, they did:

Their voice has gone out to all the earth, and their words to the ends of the inhabited world.

¹⁹ But I ask, "Did Israel not understand?" First, Moses said:

I will make you jealous of those who are not a nation; I will make you angry by a nation that lacks understanding.

²⁰ And Isaiah says boldly:

I was found by those who were not looking for Me; I revealed Myself to those who were not asking for Me.

²¹ But to Israel he says: **All day long I have spread out My hands to a disobedient and defiant people.**

11 I ask, then, has God rejected His people? Absolutely not! For I too am an Israelite, a descendant of Abraham, from the tribe of Benjamin. ² God has not rejected His people whom He foreknew. Or do you not know what the Scripture says in the Elijah section— how he pleads with God against Israel?

³ Lord, they have killed Your prophets, torn down Your altars; and I am the only one left, and they are trying to take my life!

⁴ But what was God's reply to him? **I have left 7,000 men for Myself who have not bowed down to Baal.** ⁵ In the same way, then, there is also at the present time a remnant chosen by grace. ⁶ Now if by grace, then it is not by works; otherwise grace ceases to be grace.

⁷ What then? Israel did not find what it was looking for, but the elect did find it. The rest were hardened, ⁸ as it is written:

God gave them a spirit of stupor, eyes that cannot see and ears that cannot hear, to this day.

⁹ And David says:

Let their feasting become
a snare and a trap,
a pitfall and a retribution
to them.

¹⁰ Let their eyes be darkened
so they cannot see,
and their backs be bent
continually.

Prompt Action

So faith comes from what is heard, and what is heard comes through the message about Christ.—ROMANS 10:17

In Ephesians 6:16, Paul refers to "the shield of faith." Prayerfully, we must ask ourselves this question: How does faith act as a protective shield? First of all, we must understand what faith is and how the word is being used here by Paul.

A little boy, when asked to give a definition of faith, said: "Faith is believing something you know isn't true." Well, that is precisely what faith is not! Faith is believing what you know to be true! But it is even more than that—it is acting on what you know to be true.

Some people see faith as something vague and mysterious, but faith is one of the Christian's most practical commodities. Take this verse, for example: ". . . faith without works is dead" (Jms 2:26). There is always the element of activity in faith; it prompts us to action. "Now faith is the reality of what is hoped for, the proof of what is not seen" (Heb 11:1).

Taking the shield of faith, then, is responding to the things the Devil hurls at us by the quick application of what we believe about God and His Word, the Bible. When Satan sends his "flaming arrows" in our direction, we can either stand and lament the fact that we are being attacked, or quickly raise the shield of faith and remind ourselves that the Devil is a liar from the very beginning. We affirm that because we are redeemed by the blood of Christ, the Devil has no legal or moral right to taunt us. But believing this is not enough; it must be acted on—and acted on quickly.

Prayer

Father, I see that when Satan throws his "flaming arrows" at me, I must act and act quickly. Help my faith to be so strong that it will not need a "jump start" to get it going. This I ask in Jesus' name. Amen.

Further Study

Jms 2:14-26; Heb 11:1; 1 Jn 5:4
How are we justified?
Write out your definition of faith.

AUGUST 19

NEHEMIAH 10:1–11:19

10 Those whose seals were on the document were:

Nehemiah the governor,
    son of Hacaliah, and Zedekiah,
2 Seraiah, Azariah, Jeremiah,
3 Pashhur, Amariah, Malchijah,
4 Hattush, Shebaniah, Malluch,
5 Harim, Meremoth, Obadiah,
6 Daniel, Ginnethon, Baruch,
7 Meshullam, Abijah, Mijamin,
8 Maaziah, Bilgai, and Shemaiah.
These were the priests.

9 The Levites were:
Jeshua son of Azaniah,
Binnui of the sons of Henadad,
    Kadmiel,
10 and their brothers
Shebaniah, Hodiah, Kelita, Pelaiah,
    Hanan,
11 Mica, Rehob, Hashabiah,
12 Zaccur, Sherebiah, Shebaniah,
13 Hodiah, Bani, and Beninu.

14 The leaders of the people were:
Parosh, Pahath-moab, Elam, Zattu,
    Bani,
15 Bunni, Azgad, Bebai,
16 Adonijah, Bigvai, Adin,
17 Ater, Hezekiah, Azzur,
18 Hodiah, Hashum, Bezai,
19 Hariph, Anathoth, Nebai,
20 Magpiash, Meshullam, Hezir,
21 Meshezabel, Zadok, Jaddua,
22 Pelatiah, Hanan, Anaiah,
23 Hoshea, Hananiah, Hasshub,
24 Hallohesh, Pilha, Shobek,
25 Rehum, Hashabnah, Maaseiah,
26 Ahiah, Hanan, Anan,
27 Malluch, Harim, Baanah.

28 The rest of the people—the priests, Levites, singers, gatekeepers, and temple servants, along with their wives, sons, and daughters, everyone who is able to understand and who has separated themselves from the surrounding peoples to obey the law of God— 29 join with their noble brothers and commit themselves with a sworn oath to follow the law of God given through God's servant Moses and to carefully obey all the commands, ordinances, and statutes of the LORD our Lord.

30 We will not give our daughters in marriage to the surrounding peoples and will not take their daughters as wives for our sons.

31 When the surrounding peoples bring merchandise or any kind of grain to sell on the Sabbath day, we will not buy from them on the Sabbath or a holy day. We will also leave the land uncultivated in the seventh year and will cancel every debt.

32 We will impose the following commandments on ourselves:

To give an eighth of an ounce of silver yearly for the service of the house of our God: 33 the bread displayed before the LORD, the daily grain offering, the regular burnt offering, the Sabbath and New Moon offerings, the appointed festivals, the holy things, the sin offerings to atone for Israel, and for all the work of the house of our God.

34 We have cast lots among the priests, Levites, and people for the donation of wood by our ancestral houses at the appointed times each year. They are to bring the wood to our God's house to burn on the altar of the LORD our God, as it is written in the law.

³⁵ We will bring the firstfruits of our land and of every fruit tree to the LORD's house year by year. ³⁶ We will also bring the firstborn of our sons and our livestock, as prescribed by the law, and will bring the firstborn of our herds and flocks to the house of our God, to the priests who serve in our God's house. ³⁷ We will bring a loaf from our first batch of dough to the priests at the storerooms of the house of our God. We will also bring the firstfruits of our grain offerings, of every fruit tree, and of the new wine and oil. A tenth of our land's produce from our lands belongs to the Levites, for the Levites are to collect the one-tenth offering in all our agricultural towns. ³⁸ A priest of Aaronic descent must accompany the Levites when they collect the tenth, and the Levites must take a tenth of this offering to the storerooms of the treasury in the house of our God. ³⁹ For the Israelites and the Levites are to bring the contributions of grain, new wine, and oil to the storerooms where the articles of the sanctuary are kept and where the priests, gatekeepers, and singers serve. We will not neglect the house of our God.

11 Now the leaders of the people stayed in Jerusalem, and the rest of the people cast lots for one out of ten to come and live in Jerusalem, the holy city, while the other nine-tenths remained in their towns. ² The people praised all the men who volunteered to live in Jerusalem.

³ These are the heads of the province who stayed in Jerusalem (but in the villages of Judah each lived on his own property in their towns—the Israelites, priests, Levites, temple servants, and descendants of Solomon's servants— ⁴ while some of the descendants of Judah and Benjamin settled in Jerusalem):

Judah's descendants:

Athaiah son of Uzziah, son of Zechariah, son of Amariah, son of Shephatiah, son of Mahalalel, of Perez's descendants; ⁵ and Maaseiah son of Baruch, son of Col-hozeh, son of Hazaiah, son of Adaiah, son of Joiarib, son of Zechariah, a descendant of the Shilonite. ⁶ The total number of Perez's descendants, who settled in Jerusalem, was 468 capable men.

⁷ These were Benjamin's descendants:

Sallu son of Meshullam, son of Joed, son of Pedaiah, son of Kolaiah, son of Maaseiah, son of Ithiel, son of Jeshaiah, ⁸ and after him Gabbai and Sallai: 928. ⁹ Joel son of Zichri was the officer over them, and Judah son of Hassenuah was second in command over the city.

¹⁰ The priests:

Jedaiah son of Joiarib, Jachin, and ¹¹ Seraiah son of Hilkiah, son of Meshullam, son of Zadok, son of Meraioth, son of Ahitub, the chief official of God's house, ¹² and their relatives who did the work at the temple: 822. Adaiah son of Jeroham, son of Pelaliah, son of Amzi, son of Zechariah, son of Pashhur, son of Malchijah ¹³ and his relatives, the leaders of families: 242. Amashsai son of Azarel, son of Ahzai, son of Meshillemoth, son of Immer, ¹⁴ and their relatives, capable men: 128. Zabdiel son of Haggedolim, was their chief.

¹⁵ The Levites:

Shemaiah son of Hasshub, son of Azrikam, son of Hashabiah, son of Bunni; ¹⁶ and Shabbethai and Jozabad, from the leaders of the Levites, who supervised the work outside the house of God; ¹⁷ Mattaniah son of Mica, son of Zabdi, son of Asaph, the leader who began the thanksgiving in prayer;

Bakbukiah, second among his relatives; and Abda son of Shammua, son of Galal, son of Jeduthun. [18] All the Levites in the holy city: 284.

[19] The gatekeepers:

Akkub, Talmon, and their relatives, who guarded the gates: 172.

PSALM 101:1-8

1 I will sing of faithful love and
    justice;
  I will sing praise to You, LORD.
2 I will pay attention to the way of
    integrity.
  When will You come to me?
  I will live with integrity of heart in
    my house.
3 I will not set anything godless
    before my eyes.
  I hate the doing of transgression;
  it will not cling to me.
4 A devious heart will be far from
    me;
  I will not be involved with evil.

5 I will destroy anyone who secretly
    slanders his neighbor;
  I cannot tolerate anyone with
    haughty eyes or an arrogant
    heart.
6 My eyes favor the faithful of the
    land
  so that they may sit down with
    me.
  The one who follows the way of
    integrity may serve me.
7 No one who acts deceitfully will
    live in my palace;
  no one who tells lies will remain
    in my presence.
8 Every morning I will destroy all
    the wicked of the land,
  eliminating all evildoers from the
    LORD's city.

PROVERBS 20:19-21

19 The one who reveals secrets is a
    constant gossip;
  avoid someone with a big mouth.

20 Whoever curses his father or
    mother—
  his lamp will go out in deep
    darkness.

21 An inheritance gained prematurely
  will not be blessed ultimately.

ROMANS 11:11-36

[11] I ask, then, have they stumbled so as to fall? Absolutely not! On the contrary, by their stumbling, salvation has come to the Gentiles to make Israel jealous. [12] Now if their stumbling brings riches for the world, and their failure riches for the Gentiles, how much more will their full number bring!

[13] Now I am speaking to you Gentiles. In view of the fact that I am an apostle to the Gentiles, I magnify my ministry, [14] if I can somehow make my own people jealous and save some of them. [15] For if their being rejected is world reconciliation, what will their acceptance mean but life from the dead? [16] Now if the firstfruits offered up are holy, so is the whole batch. And if the root is holy, so are the branches.

[17] Now if some of the branches were broken off, and you, though a wild olive branch, were grafted in among them, and have come to share in the rich root of the cultivated olive tree, [18] do not brag that you are better than those branches. But if you do brag—you do not sustain the root, but the root sustains you. [19] Then you will say, "Branches were broken off so that I might be grafted in." [20] True enough; they were broken off by unbelief, but you stand by faith. Do not be arrogant, but be afraid. [21] For if God did not spare the natural branches, He will not spare you either. [22] Therefore, consider God's kindness and severity: severity toward those who have fallen, but God's kindness toward you—if you remain in His kindness. Otherwise you too will be cut off. [23] And even they, if they do not remain in unbelief, will be grafted in, because God has the power to graft them in again. [24] For if you were cut off from your native wild olive, and

against nature were grafted into a cultivated olive tree, how much more will these—the natural branches—be grafted into their own olive tree?

²⁵ So that you will not be conceited, brothers, I do not want you to be unaware of this mystery: a partial hardening has come to Israel until the full number of the Gentiles has come in. ²⁶ And in this way all Israel will be saved, as it is written:

The Liberator will come
 from Zion;
He will turn away godlessness
 from Jacob.
²⁷ And this will be My covenant
 with them,
when I take away their sins.

²⁸ Regarding the gospel, they are enemies for your advantage, but regarding election, they are loved because of their forefathers, ²⁹ since God's gracious gifts and calling are irrevocable. ³⁰ As you once disobeyed God, but now have received mercy through their disobedience, ³¹ so they too have now disobeyed, resulting in mercy to you, so that they also now may receive mercy. ³² For God has imprisoned all in disobedience, so that He may have mercy on all.

³³ Oh, the depth of the riches
 both of the wisdom
  and the knowledge of God!
How unsearchable His judgments
 and untraceable His ways!
³⁴ For who has known the mind
  of the Lord?
Or who has been His counselor?
³⁵ Or who has ever first given
  to Him,
and has to be repaid?
³⁶ For from Him and through Him
  and to Him are all things.
To Him be the glory forever.
 Amen.

A Lost Art

For who has known the mind of the Lord?
Or who has been His counselor?—ROMANS 11:34

A subject which is of great interest to many today is anthropology: the study of man. Although this subject is of great importance, for a Christian there is something far more important: the study of God. The great preacher C. H. Spurgeon said: "The highest science, the loftiest speculation, the mightiest philosophy that can ever engage the attention of a child of God is the name, the nature, the person, the work, the doings, and the existence of the great God whom he calls his Father."

The contemplation of God seems to be a lost art today. We appear to be more concerned about subjects such as church growth, the end times, signs, wonders, and miracles. I am not suggesting these issues are unimportant, but they must not be allowed to replace the supremely important matter of the constant, earnest, and continued investigation of the great subject of the Deity. The more we know of God, the more effective will be our lives here on earth. Those who have given themselves to the study of God tell us that it humbles the mind, expands the soul, and consoles the heart.

It humbles the mind. When our minds grapple with other subjects, we feel a degree of self-content and come away thinking: "Behold, I am wise." But when our minds engage with thoughts of God, we discover that there is no plumb line that can sound His depth, and we come away thinking: "Behold, I know nothing." In an age that stresses the supremacy of the human ego, it is no bad thing to learn that there is something far greater.

Prayer

Gracious and loving heavenly Father, teach me how to focus on You and contemplate You so that all vanity and pride dies within me, and I go on my way no longer caught up with how wise I am but how wonderful You are. In Jesus' name. Amen.

Further Study

Is 40:18-26; Jb 11:7-9
What probing question does Isaiah ask?
What conclusion had Zophar come to?

AUGUST 20

*N*EHEMIAH 11:20–12:47

²⁰ The rest of Israel, the priests, and the Levites were in all the villages of Judah, each on his own inherited property. ²¹ The temple servants lived on Ophel; Ziha and Gishpa supervised the temple servants.

²² The leader of the Levites in Jerusalem was Uzzi son of Bani, son of Hashabiah, son of Mattaniah, son of Mica, of the descendants of Asaph, who were singers for the service of God's house. ²³ For there was a command of the king regarding them, and an ordinance regulating the singers' daily tasks. ²⁴ Pethahiah son of Meshezabel, of the descendants of Zerah son of Judah, was the king's agent in every matter concerning the people.

²⁵ As for the farming settlements with their fields:

Some of Judah's descendants lived
     in Kiriath-arba and its villages,
Dibon and its villages,
     and Jekabzeel and its villages,
²⁶   in Jeshua, Moladah, Beth-pelet,

²⁷   Hazar-shual, and Beer-sheba
     and its villages;
²⁸   in Ziklag and Meconah
     and its villages,
²⁹   in En-rimmon, Zorah, Jarmuth,
     and
³⁰   Zanoah and Adullam
     with their villages;
in Lachish with its fields
     and Azekah and its villages.
So they settled from Beer-sheba
     to the Valley of Hinnom.
³¹   Benjamin's descendants:
     from Geba, Michmash, Aija,
     and Bethel—and its villages,
³²   Anathoth, Nob, Ananiah,
³³   Hazor, Ramah, Gittaim,
³⁴   Hadid, Zeboim, Neballat,
³⁵   Lod, and Ono, the valley
     of the craftsmen.
³⁶   Some of the Judean divisions
     of Levites were in Benjamin.

12 These are the priests and Levites who went up with Zerubbabel son of Shealtiel and with Jeshua:

Seraiah, Jeremiah, Ezra,
²   Amariah, Malluch, Hattush,

³ Shecaniah, Rehum, Meremoth,
⁴ Iddo, Ginnethoi, Abijah,
⁵ Mijamin, Maadiah, Bilgah,
⁶ Shemaiah, Joiarib, Jedaiah,
⁷ Sallu, Amok, Hilkiah, Jedaiah.

These were the leaders of the priests and their relatives in the days of Jeshua.
⁸ The Levites:

Jeshua, Binnui, Kadmiel,
Sherebiah, Judah,
and Mattaniah—
he and his relatives were
in charge of the praise songs.
⁹ Bakbukiah, Unni, and their relatives
stood opposite them
in the services.
¹⁰ Jeshua fathered Joiakim,
Joiakim fathered Eliashib,
Eliashib fathered Joiada,
¹¹ Joiada fathered Jonathan,
and Jonathan fathered Jaddua.

¹² In the days of Joiakim, the leaders of the priestly families were:

Meraiah	of Seraiah,
Hananiah	of Jeremiah,
¹³ Meshullam	of Ezra,
Jehohanan	of Amariah,
¹⁴ Jonathan	of Malluchi,
Joseph	of Shebaniah,
¹⁵ Adna	of Harim,
Helkai	of Meraioth,
¹⁶ Zechariah	of Iddo,
Meshullam	of Ginnethon,
¹⁷ Zichri	of Abijah,
Piltai	of Moadiah, of Miniamin,
¹⁸ Shammua	of Bilgah,
Jehonathan	of Shemaiah,
¹⁹ Mattenai	of Joiarib,
Uzzi	of Jedaiah,
²⁰ Kallai	of Sallai,
Eber	of Amok,
²¹ Hashabiah	of Hilkiah,
and Nethanel	of Jedaiah.

²² In the days of Eliashib, Joiada, Johanan, and Jaddua, the leaders of the families of the Levites and priests were recorded while Darius the Persian ruled. ²³ Levi's descendants, the leaders of families, were recorded in the Book of the

Historical Records during the days of Johanan son of Eliashib. ²⁴ The leaders of the Levites—Hashabiah, Sherebiah, and Jeshua son of Kadmiel, along with their relatives opposite them—gave praise and thanks, division by division, as David the man of God had prescribed. ²⁵ This included Mattaniah, Bakbukiah, and Obadiah. Meshullam, Talmon, and Akkub were gatekeepers who guarded the storerooms at the gates. ²⁶ These served in the days of Joiakim son of Jeshua, son of Jozadak, and in the days of Nehemiah the governor and Ezra the priest and scribe.

²⁷ At the dedication of the wall of Jerusalem, they sent for the Levites wherever they lived and brought them to Jerusalem to celebrate the joyous dedication with thanksgiving and singing accompanied by cymbals, harps, and lyres. ²⁸ The singers gathered from the region around Jerusalem, from the villages of the Netophathites, ²⁹ from Beth-gilgal, and from the fields of Geba and Azmaveth, for they had built villages for themselves around Jerusalem. ³⁰ After the priests and Levites had purified themselves, they purified the people, the gates, and the wall.

³¹ Then I brought the leaders of Judah up on top of the wall, and I appointed two large processions that gave thanks. One went to the right on the wall, toward the Dung Gate. ³² Hoshaiah and half the leaders of Judah followed:

³³ Azariah, Ezra, Meshullam,
³⁴ Judah, Benjamin, Shemaiah,
and Jeremiah.

³⁵ Some of the priests' sons had trumpets:

Zechariah son of Jonathan,
son of Shemaiah,
son of Mattaniah, son of Micaiah,
son of Zaccur, son of Asaph,
³⁶ and his relatives:
Shemaiah, Azarel, Milalai,
Gilalai, Maai, Nethanel,
Judah, and Hanani,
with the musical instruments
of David, the man of God.

Ezra the scribe went in front of them.

³⁷ At the Fountain Gate they climbed the steps of the city of David on the ascent of the wall and went above the house of David to the Water Gate on the east.

³⁸ The second thanksgiving procession went to the left, and I followed it with half the people along the top of the wall, past the Tower of the Ovens to the Broad Wall, ³⁹ above the Gate of Ephraim, and by the Old Gate, the Fish Gate, the Tower of Hananel, and the Tower of the Hundred, to the Sheep Gate. They stopped at the Gate of the Guard. ⁴⁰ The two thanksgiving processions stood in the house of God. So did I and half of the officials accompanying me, as well as ⁴¹ the priests:

Eliakim, Maaseiah, Miniamin, Micaiah, Elioenai, Zechariah, and Hananiah, with trumpets;
⁴² and Maaseiah, Shemaiah, Eleazar, Uzzi, Jehohanan, Malchijah, Elam, and Ezer.

Then the singers sang, with Jezrahiah as the leader. ⁴³ On that day they offered great sacrifices and rejoiced because God had given them great joy. The women and children also celebrated, and Jerusalem's rejoicing was heard far away.

⁴⁴ On that same day men were placed in charge of the rooms that housed the supplies, contributions, firstfruits, and tenths. The legally required portions for the priests and Levites were gathered from the village fields, because Judah was grateful to the priests and Levites who were serving. ⁴⁵ They performed the service of their God and the service of purification, along with the singers and gatekeepers, as David and his son Solomon had prescribed. ⁴⁶ For long ago, in the days of David and Asaph, there were leaders of the singers and songs of praise and thanksgiving to God. ⁴⁷ So in the days of Zerubbabel and Nehemiah, all Israel contributed the daily portions for the singers and gatekeepers. They also set aside daily portions for the Levites, and the Levites set aside daily portions for the descendants of Aaron.

PSALM 102:1-11

¹ LORD, hear my prayer;
let my cry for help come before You.
² Do not hide Your face from me in my day of trouble.
Listen closely to me;
answer me quickly when I call.

³ For my days vanish like smoke,
and my bones burn like a furnace.
⁴ My heart is afflicted, withered like grass;
I even forget to eat my food.
⁵ Because of the sound of my groaning,
my flesh sticks to my bones.
⁶ I am like a desert owl,
like an owl among the ruins.
⁷ I stay awake;
I am like a solitary bird on a roof.
⁸ My enemies taunt me all day long;
they ridicule and curse me.
⁹ I eat ashes like bread
and mingle my drinks with tears
¹⁰ because of Your indignation and wrath;
for You have picked me up and thrown me aside.
¹¹ My days are like a lengthening shadow,
and I wither away like grass.

PROVERBS 20:22-23

²² Don't say, "I will avenge this evil!"
Wait on the LORD, and He will rescue you.

²³ Differing weights are detestable to the LORD,
and dishonest scales are unfair.

ROMANS 12:1-21

12 Therefore, brothers, by the mercies of God, I urge you to present your bodies as a living sacrifice, holy and pleasing to God; this is your spiritual worship. [2] Do not be conformed to this age, but be transformed by the renewing of your mind, so that you may discern what is the good, pleasing, and perfect will of God.

[3] For by the grace given to me, I tell everyone among you not to think of himself more highly than he should think. Instead, think sensibly, as God has distributed a measure of faith to each one. [4] Now as we have many parts in one body, and all the parts do not have the same function, [5] in the same way we who are many are one body in Christ and individually members of one another. [6] According to the grace given to us, we have different gifts:

If prophecy, use it according to
     the standard of faith;
[7] if service, in service; if teaching,
     in teaching;
[8] if exhorting, in exhortation;
giving, with generosity;
leading, with diligence;
showing mercy,
     with cheerfulness.

[9] Love must be without hypocrisy. Detest evil; cling to what is good. [10] Show family affection to one another with brotherly love. Outdo one another in showing honor. [11] Do not lack diligence; be fervent in spirit; serve the Lord. [12] Rejoice in hope; be patient in affliction; be persistent in prayer. [13] Share with the saints in their needs; pursue hospitality. [14] Bless those who persecute you; bless and do not curse. [15] Rejoice with those who rejoice; weep with those who weep. [16] Be in agreement with one another. Do not be proud; instead, associate with the humble. Do not be wise in your own estimation. [17] Do not repay anyone evil for evil. Try to do what is honorable in everyone's eyes. [18] If possible, on your part, live at peace with everyone. [19] Friends, do not avenge yourselves; instead, leave room for His wrath. For it is written: **Vengeance belongs to Me; I will repay,** says the Lord. [20] But

If your enemy is hungry,
     feed him.
If he is thirsty, give him
     something to drink.
For in so doing you will be
     heaping fiery coals
     on his head.

[21] Do not be conquered by evil, but conquer evil with good.

Evil Is Bad for Us

Love must be without hypocrisy. Detest evil; cling to what is good.

—Romans 12:9

In considering the words "Do not bring us into temptation, but deliver us from the evil one," here we concentrate on "deliver us from the evil one." Notice it is not a prayer for deliverance from this or that type of evil, but from evil itself. To Jesus, evil was evil in whatever form it came—whether in the evil of the flesh or the evil of the disposition, whether in the individual will or in the corporate will. Evil was never good, and good was never evil.

Someone has pointed out that the word "evil" is the word "live" spelled backwards. Evil, then, could be said to be anti-life. Non-Christians are finding out how not to live the hard way. They think they know better than God and follow a way of their own choosing, only to find, like the rats in the scientific experiments who go down the wrong path, that there are wires at the end which carry electric shocks. These shocks are of various kinds: neuroses, inner conflicts, as well as some forms of physical illness.

Society is concerned about a disease called sexual herpes which is spread through sexual permissiveness. God has made it impossible for us to live against His design or harm ourselves without His protest. And He protests because He loves us.

We can decide to have done with evil. The best way to deal with evil is to keep away from it, hence the prayer "Lead us not into temptation, but deliver us from evil." I say again, evil is bad for us, and good is good for us.

Prayer

My Father, You who made me for good, because goodness is good for me, help me to abstain, not only from evil, but from the very appearance of it. For Your own dear name's sake. Amen.

Further Study

Gn 39; 1 Co 10:6; 1 Th 5:22; 1 Pt 3:11; 2 Tm 2:22
How did Joseph resist temptation?
What did Paul advise Timothy?

AUGUST 21

NEHEMIAH 13:1– ESTHER 1:22

13 At that time the book of Moses was read publicly to the people. The command was found written in it that no Ammonite or Moabite should ever enter the assembly of God, ²because they did not meet the Israelites with food and water. Instead, they hired Balaam against them to curse them, but our God turned the curse into a blessing. ³When they heard the law, they separated all those of mixed descent from Israel.

⁴Now before this, Eliashib the priest had been put in charge of the store-rooms of the house of our God. He was a relative of Tobiah ⁵and had prepared a large room for him where they had previously stored the grain offerings, the frankincense, the articles, and the tenths of grain, new wine, and oil prescribed for the Levites, singers, and gatekeepers, along with the contributions for the priests.

⁶While all this was happening, I was not in Jerusalem, because I had returned to King Artaxerxes of Babylon in the thirty-second year of his reign. It was only later that I asked the king for a leave of absence ⁷so I could return to Jerusalem. Then I discovered the evil that Eliashib had done on behalf of Tobiah by providing him a room in the

courts of God's house. [8] I was greatly displeased and threw all of Tobiah's household possessions out of the room. [9] I ordered that the rooms be purified, and I had the articles of the house of God restored there, along with the grain offering and frankincense. [10] I also found out that because the portions for the Levites had not been given, each of the Levites and the singers performing the service had gone back to his own field. [11] Therefore, I rebuked the officials, saying, "Why has the house of God been neglected?" I gathered the Levites and singers together and stationed them at their posts. [12] Then all Judah brought a tenth of the grain, new wine, and oil into the storehouses. [13] I appointed as treasurers over the storehouses Shelemiah the priest, Zadok the scribe, and Pedaiah of the Levites, with Hanan son of Zaccur, son of Mattaniah to assist them, because they were considered trustworthy. They were responsible for the distribution to their colleagues.

[14] Remember me for this, my God, and don't erase the good deeds I have done for the house of my God and for its services.

[15] At that time I saw people in Judah treading wine presses on the Sabbath. They were also bringing in stores of grain and loading them on donkeys, along with wine, grapes, and figs. All kinds of goods were being brought to Jerusalem on the Sabbath day. So I warned them against selling food on that day. [16] The Tyrians living there were importing fish and all kinds of merchandise and selling them on the Sabbath to the people of Judah in Jerusalem. [17] I rebuked the nobles of Judah and said to them: "What is this evil you are doing—profaning the Sabbath day? [18] Didn't your ancestors do the same, so that our God brought all this disaster on us and on this city? And now you are rekindling His anger against Israel by profaning the Sabbath!"

[19] When shadows began to fall on the gates of Jerusalem just before the Sabbath, I gave orders that the gates be closed and not opened until after the Sabbath. I posted some of my men at the gates, so that no goods could enter during the Sabbath day. [20] Once or twice the merchants and those who sell all kinds of goods camped outside Jerusalem, [21] but I warned them, "Why are you camping in front of the wall? If you do it again, I'll use force against you." After that they did not come again on the Sabbath. [22] Then I instructed the Levites to purify themselves and guard the gates in order to keep the Sabbath day holy.

Remember me for this also, my God, and look on me with compassion in keeping with Your abundant, faithful love.

[23] In those days I also saw Jews who had married women from Ashdod, Ammon, and Moab. [24] Half of their children spoke the language of Ashdod or of one of the other peoples but could not speak Hebrew. [25] I rebuked them, cursed them, beat some of their men, and pulled out their hair. I forced them to take an oath before God and said: "You must not give your daughters in marriage to their sons or take their daughters as wives for your sons or yourselves! [26] Didn't King Solomon of Israel sin in matters like this? There was not a king like him among many nations. He was loved by his God and God made him king over all Israel, yet foreign women drew him into sin. [27] Why then should we hear about you doing all this terrible evil and acting unfaithfully against our God by marrying foreign women?"

[28] Even one of the sons of Jehoiada, son of Eliashib the high priest, had become a son-in-law to Sanballat the Horonite. So I drove him away from me. [29] Remember them, my God, for defiling the priesthood as well as the covenant of the priesthood and the Levites.

[30] So I purified them from everything foreign and assigned specific duties to each of the priests and Levites. [31] I also arranged for the donation of wood at the appointed times and for the firstfruits.

Remember me, my God, with favor.

1 These events took place during the days of Ahasuerus, who ruled 127 provinces from India to Cush. ² In those days King Ahasuerus reigned from his royal throne in the fortress at Susa. ³ He held a feast in the third year of his reign for all his officials and staff, the army of Persia and Media, the nobles, and the officials from the provinces. ⁴ He displayed the glorious wealth of his kingdom and the magnificent splendor of his greatness for a total of 180 days.

⁵ At the end of this time, the king held a week-long banquet in the garden courtyard of the royal palace for all the people, from the greatest to the least, who were present in the fortress of Susa. ⁶ White and violet linen hangings were fastened with fine white and purple linen cords to silver rods on marble columns. Gold and silver couches were arranged on a mosaic pavement of red feldspar, marble, mother-of-pearl, and precious stones.

⁷ Beverages were served in an array of gold goblets, each with a different design. Royal wine flowed freely, according to the king's bounty ⁸ and no restraint was placed on the drinking. The king had ordered every wine steward in his household to serve as much as each person wanted. ⁹ Queen Vashti also gave a feast for the women of King Ahasuerus' palace.

¹⁰ On the seventh day, when the king was feeling good from the wine, Ahasuerus commanded Mehuman, Biztha, Harbona, Bigtha, Abagtha, Zethar, and Carkas, the seven eunuchs who personally served him, ¹¹ to bring Queen Vashti before him with her royal crown. He wanted to show off her beauty to the people and the officials, because she was very beautiful. ¹² But Queen Vashti refused to come at the king's command that was delivered by his eunuchs. The king became furious and his anger burned within him.

¹³ The king consulted the wise men who understood the times, for it was his normal procedure to confer with experts in law and justice. ¹⁴ The most trusted ones were Carshena, Shethar, Admatha, Tarshish, Meres, Marsena,

and Memucan. They were the seven officials of Persia and Media who had personal access to the king and occupied the highest positions in the kingdom. ¹⁵ The king asked, "According to the law, what should be done with Queen Vashti, since she refused to obey King Ahasuerus' command that was delivered by the eunuchs?"

¹⁶ Memucan said in the presence of the king and his officials, "Queen Vashti has defied not only the king, but all the officials and the peoples who are in every one of King Ahasuerus' provinces. ¹⁷ For the queen's action will become public knowledge to all the women and cause them to despise their husbands and say, 'King Ahasuerus ordered Queen Vashti brought before him, but she did not come.' ¹⁸ Before this day is over, the noble women of Persia and Media who hear about the queen's act will say the same thing to all the king's officials, resulting in more contempt and fury.

¹⁹ "If it meets the king's approval, he should personally issue a royal decree. Let it be recorded in the laws of Persia and Media, so that it cannot be revoked: Vashti is not to enter King Ahasuerus' presence, and her royal position is to be given to another woman who is more worthy than she. ²⁰ The decree the king issues will be heard throughout his vast kingdom, so all women will honor their husbands, from the least to the greatest."

²¹ The king and his counselors approved the proposal, and he followed Memucan's advice. ²² He sent letters to all the royal provinces, to each province in its own script and to each ethnic group in its own language, that every man should be master of his own house and speak in the language of his own people.

℘SALM 102:12-17

¹² But You, LORD, are enthroned
   forever;
   Your fame endures to all
   generations.

13 You will arise and have
   compassion on Zion,
   for it is time to show favor to
   her—
   the appointed time has come.
14 For Your servants take delight in
   its stones
   and favor its dust.
15 Then the nations will fear the
   name of the LORD,
   and all the kings of the earth Your
   glory,
16 for the LORD will rebuild Zion;
   He will appear in His glory.
17 He will pay attention to the prayer
   of the destitute
   and will not despise their prayer.

PROVERBS 20:24-25

24 A man's steps are determined by
   the LORD,
   so how can anyone understand his
   own way?

25 It is a trap for anyone to dedicate
   something rashly
   and later to reconsider his vows.

ROMANS 13:1–14:12

13 Everyone must submit to the
governing authorities, for there
is no authority except from God, and
those that exist are instituted by God.
² So then, the one who resists the authority is opposing God's command, and
those who oppose it will bring judgment
on themselves. ³ For rulers are not a terror to good conduct, but to bad. Do you
want to be unafraid of the authority? Do
good and you will have its approval.
⁴ For government is God's servant to
you for good. But if you do wrong, be
afraid, because it does not carry the
sword for no reason. For government is
God's servant, an avenger that brings
wrath on the one who does wrong.
⁵ Therefore, you must submit, not only
because of wrath, but also because of
your conscience. ⁶ And for this reason
you pay taxes, since the authorities are

God's public servants, continually attending to these tasks. ⁷ Pay your obligations to everyone: taxes to those you
owe taxes, tolls to those you owe tolls,
respect to those you owe respect, and
honor to those you owe honor.
⁸ Do not owe anyone anything, except
to love one another, for the one who
loves another has fulfilled the law. ⁹ The
commandments:

**Do not commit adultery,
do not murder,
do not steal,
do not covet,**

and if there is any other commandment—all are summed up by this: **Love
your neighbor as yourself.**
¹⁰ Love does no wrong to a neighbor.
Love, therefore, is the fulfillment of the
law.
¹¹ Besides this, knowing the time, it is
already the hour for you to wake up
from sleep, for now our salvation is
nearer than when we first believed.
¹² The night is nearly over, and the daylight is near, so let us discard the deeds
of darkness and put on the armor of
light. ¹³ Let us walk with decency, as in
the daylight: not in carousing and
drunkenness; not in sexual impurity and
promiscuity; not in quarreling and jealousy. ¹⁴ But put on the Lord Jesus
Christ, and make no plans to satisfy the
fleshly desires.

14 Accept anyone who is weak in
faith, but don't argue about
doubtful issues. ² One person believes
he may eat anything, but one who is
weak eats only vegetables. ³ One who
eats must not look down on one who
does not eat; and one who does not eat
must not criticize one who does, because God has accepted him. ⁴ Who are
you to criticize another's household
slave? Before his own Lord he stands or
falls. And stand he will! For the Lord is
able to make him stand.
⁵ One person considers one day to be
above another day. Someone else considers every day to be the same. Each
one must be fully convinced in his own

mind. ⁶Whoever observes the day, observes it to the Lord. Whoever eats, eats to the Lord, since he gives thanks to God; and whoever does not eat, it is to the Lord that he does not eat, yet he thanks God. ⁷For none of us lives to himself, and no one dies to himself. ⁸If we live, we live to the Lord; and if we die, we die to the Lord. Therefore, whether we live or die, we belong to the Lord. ⁹Christ died and came to life for this: that He might rule over both the dead and the living. ¹⁰But you, why

do you criticize your brother? Or you, why do you look down on your brother? For we will all stand before the judgment seat of God. ¹¹For it is written:

As I live, says the Lord,
every knee will bow to Me,
and every tongue will give praise
to God.

¹²So then, each of us will give an account of himself to God.

"Wobbly Christians"

*So let us discard the deeds of the darkness
and put on the armor of light.*
—ROMANS 13:12

The armor of God will not do us any good unless it is worn in its entirety. We must put on the whole armor of God, not just a few of the pieces we think are most suitable for us.

This again is something of crucial importance. If we are to be steadfast soldiers in the Lord's army, if we are to avoid becoming what John Stott calls "wobbly Christians who have no firm foothold in Christ," then we must put on the entire equipment which God provides for us. We cannot—we dare not—select parts of the armor and say: "I don't really like the helmet of salvation, but I don't mind wearing the breastplate of righteousness." You can do that, of course, but if you do, then you must know exactly what will happen to you—you will be overcome by Satan. The moment you say: "I need the breastplate, but I don't need the helmet," you are defeated. You need it all—the whole armor of God.

You see, our understanding of what is involved in spiritual defense against Satan is extremely inadequate. We just don't have sufficient knowledge of what is involved. It is God alone who knows our enemy, and it is God alone who knows exactly how to protect us so that we remain firm and steadfast when Satan and his forces hurl themselves against us. So learn this lesson now before going any further—every single piece of God's armor is essential, and to select some and leave out the others is to take the route to failure and defeat.

Prayer

O God, deliver me from the attitude of pride that seeks to put my ideas ahead of Your ideas. You know more about what I need to protect me from the enemy than I do. Help me ever to trust Your judgment. In Jesus' name I ask it. Amen.

Further Study

2 Co 6:1-10; Php 1:27; 1 Pt 5:9
What was a necessary requirement for Paul's ministry?
What are we called to do?

AUGUST 22

ESTHER 2:1–4:17

2 Some time later, when King Aha-suerus' rage had cooled down, he remembered Vashti, what she had done, and what was decided against her. ² The king's personal attendants suggested, "Let a search be made for beautiful young virgins for the king. ³ Let the king appoint commissioners in each province of his kingdom, so that they may assemble all the beautiful young virgins to the harem at the fortress of Susa. Put them under the care of Hegai, the king's eunuch, who is in charge of the women, and give them the required beauty treatments. ⁴ Then the young woman who pleases the king will reign in place of Vashti." This suggestion pleased the king, and he did accordingly.

⁵ A Jewish man was in the fortress of Susa named Mordecai son of Jair, son of Shimei, son of Kish, a Benjaminite. ⁶ He had been taken into exile from Jeru-salem with the other captives when King Nebuchadnezzar of Babylon took King Jeconiah of Judah into exile. ⁷ Mor-decai was the legal guardian of his cousin Hadassah (that is, Esther), be-cause she didn't have a father or moth-er. The young woman had a beautiful figure and was extremely good-looking. When her father and mother died, Mordecai had adopted her as his own daughter.

⁸ When the king's command and edict became public knowledge, many young women gathered at the fortress of Susa under Hegai's care. Esther was also taken to the palace and placed under the care of Hegai, who was in charge of the women. ⁹ The young woman pleased him and gained his favor so that he ac-celerated the process of the beauty treatments and the special diet that she received. He assigned seven hand-picked female servants to her from the palace and transferred her and her ser-vants to the harem's best quarters.

¹⁰ Esther did not reveal her ethnic background or her birthplace, because Mordecai had ordered her not to. ¹¹ Every day Mordecai took a walk in front of the harem's courtyard to learn how Esther was doing and to see what was happening to her.

¹² During the year before each young woman's turn to go to King Ahasuerus, the harem regulation required her to re-ceive beauty treatments with oil of myrrh for six months and then with per-fumes and cosmetics for another six months. ¹³ When the young woman would go to the king, she was given whatever she requested to take with her from the harem to the palace. ¹⁴ She would go in the evening, and in the morning she would return to a second harem under the supervision of Shaash-gaz, the king's eunuch in charge of the concubines. She never went to the king again, unless he desired her and sum-moned her by name.

¹⁵ Esther was the daughter of Abihail,

the uncle of Mordecai who had adopted her as his own daughter. When her turn came to go to the king, she did not ask for anything except what Hegai, the king's trusted official in charge of the harem, suggested. Esther won approval in the sight of everyone who saw her.

¹⁶ Esther was taken to King Ahasuerus in the royal palace in the tenth month, the month Tebeth, in the seventh year of his reign. ¹⁷ The king loved Esther more than all the other women. She won more favor and approval from him than did any of the other virgins. He placed the royal crown on her head and made her queen in place of Vashti. ¹⁸ The king held a great banquet for all his officials and staff. It was Esther's banquet. He freed his provinces from tax payments and gave gifts worthy of the king's bounty.

¹⁹ When the young women were assembled together for a second time, Mordecai was sitting at the King's Gate. ²⁰ Esther still had not revealed her birthplace or her ethnic background, as Mordecai had directed. She obeyed Mordecai's orders, as she always had while he raised her.

²¹ During those days while Mordecai was sitting at the King's Gate, Bigthan and Teresh, two eunuchs who guarded the king's entrance, became infuriated and tried to assassinate King Ahasuerus. ²² When Mordecai learned of the plot, he reported it to Queen Esther, and she told the king on Mordecai's behalf. ²³ When the report was investigated and verified, both men were hanged on the gallows. This event was recorded in the court records of daily events in the king's presence.

3 After all this took place, King Ahasuerus honored Haman, son of Hammedatha the Agagite. He promoted him in rank and gave him a higher position than all the other officials. ² The entire royal staff at the King's Gate bowed down and paid homage to Haman, because the king had commanded this to be done for him. But Mordecai would not bow down or pay homage. ³ The members of the royal staff at the King's Gate asked Mordecai, "Why are you disobeying the king's command?" ⁴ When they had warned him day after day and he still would not listen to them, they told Haman to see if Mordecai's actions would be tolerated, since he had told them he was a Jew.

⁵ When Haman saw that Mordecai was not bowing down or paying him homage, he was filled with rage. ⁶ And when he learned of Mordecai's ethnic identity, Haman decided not to do away with Mordecai alone. He set out to destroy all of Mordecai's people, the Jews, throughout Ahasuerus' kingdom.

⁷ In the first month, the month of Nisan, in King Ahasuerus' twelfth year, Pur (that is, the lot) was cast before Haman for each day in each month, and it fell on the twelfth month, the month Adar. ⁸ Then Haman informed King Ahasuerus, "There is one ethnic group, scattered throughout the peoples in every province of your kingdom, yet living in isolation. Their laws are different from everyone else's, so that they defy the king's laws. It is not in the king's best interest to tolerate them. ⁹ If the king approves, let an order be drawn up authorizing their destruction, and I will pay 375 tons of silver to the accountants for deposit in the royal treasury."

¹⁰ The king removed his signet ring from his finger and gave it to Haman son of Hammedatha the Agagite, the enemy of the Jewish people. ¹¹ Then the king told Haman, "The money and people are given to you to do with as you see fit."

¹² The royal scribes were summoned on the thirteenth day of the first month, and the order was written exactly as Haman commanded. It was intended for the royal satraps, the governors of each of the provinces, and the officials of each ethnic group and written for each province in its own script and to each ethnic group in its own language. It was written in the name of King Ahasuerus and sealed with the royal signet ring. ¹³ Letters were sent by couriers to each of the royal provinces telling the officials to destroy, kill, and annihilate all the Jewish people—young and

old, women and children—and plunder their possessions on a single day, the thirteenth day of Adar, the twelfth month. ¹⁴ A copy of the text, issued as law throughout every province, was distributed to all the peoples so that they might get ready for that day. ¹⁵ The couriers left, spurred on by royal command, and the law was issued in the fortress of Susa. The king and Haman sat down to drink, while the city of Susa was in confusion.

4 When Mordecai learned all that had occurred, he tore his clothes, put on sackcloth and ashes, went into the middle of the city, and cried loudly and bitterly. ² He only went as far as the King's Gate, since the law prohibited anyone wearing sackcloth from entering the King's Gate. ³ There was great mourning among the Jewish people in every province where the king's command and edict came. They fasted, wept, and lamented, and many lay on sackcloth and ashes.

⁴ Esther's female servants and her eunuchs came and reported the news to her, and the queen was overcome with fear. She sent clothes for Mordecai to wear so he could take off his sackcloth, but he did not accept them. ⁵ Esther summoned Hathach, one of the king's eunuchs assigned to her, and dispatched him to Mordecai to learn what he was doing and why. ⁶ So Hathach went out to Mordecai in the city square in front of the King's Gate. ⁷ Mordecai told him everything that had happened as well as the exact amount of money Haman had promised to pay the royal treasury for the slaughter of the Jews.

⁸ Mordecai also gave him a copy of the written decree issued in Susa ordering their destruction, so that Hathach might show it to Esther, explain it to her, and instruct her to approach the king, implore his favor, and plead with him personally for her people. ⁹ Hathach came and repeated Mordecai's response to Esther.

¹⁰ Esther spoke to Hathach and commanded him to tell Mordecai, ¹¹ "All the royal officials and the people of the royal provinces know that one law applies to every man or woman who approaches the king in the inner courtyard and who has not been summoned—the death penalty. Only if the king extends the golden scepter will that person live. I have not been summoned to appear before the king for the last 30 days." ¹² Esther's response was reported to Mordecai.

¹³ Mordecai told the messenger to reply to Esther, "Don't think that you will escape the fate of all the Jews because you are in the king's palace. ¹⁴ If you keep silent at this time, liberation and deliverance will come to the Jewish people from another place, but you and your father's house will be destroyed. Who knows, perhaps you have come to the kingdom for such a time as this."

¹⁵ Esther sent this reply to Mordecai: ¹⁶ "Go and assemble all the Jews who can be found in Susa and fast for me. Don't eat or drink for three days, night and day. I and my female servants will also fast in the same way. After that, I will go to the king even if it is against the law. If I perish, I perish." ¹⁷ So Mordecai went and did everything Esther had ordered him.

PSALM 102:18-22

¹⁸ This will be written for a later
generation,
and a newly created people will
praise the LORD:
¹⁹ He looked down from His holy
heights—
the LORD gazed out from heaven
to earth—
²⁰ to hear a prisoner's groaning,
to set free those condemned to
die,
²¹ so that they might declare the
name of the LORD in Zion
and His praise in Jerusalem,
²² when peoples and kingdoms are
assembled
to serve the LORD.

PROVERBS 20:26-27

26 A wise king separates out the
wicked
and drives the threshing wheel
over them.

27 A person's breath is the lamp of
the LORD,
searching the innermost parts.

ROMANS 14:13–15:13

13 Therefore, let us no longer criticize one another, but instead decide not to put a stumbling block or pitfall in your brother's way. 14 (I know and am persuaded by the Lord Jesus that nothing is unclean in itself. Still, to someone who considers a thing to be unclean, to that one it is unclean.) 15 For if your brother is hurt by what you eat, you are no longer walking according to love. By what you eat, do not destroy that one for whom Christ died. 16 Therefore, do not let your good be slandered, 17 for the kingdom of God is not eating and drinking, but righteousness, peace, and joy in the Holy Spirit. 18 Whoever serves the Messiah in this way is acceptable to God and approved by men.

19 So then, we must pursue what promotes peace and what builds up one another. 20 Do not tear down God's work because of food. Everything is clean, but it is wrong for a man to cause stumbling by what he eats. 21 It is a noble thing not to eat meat, or drink wine, or do anything that makes your brother stumble. 22 Do you have faith? Keep it to yourself before God. Blessed is the man who does not condemn himself by what he approves. 23 But whoever doubts stands condemned if he eats, because his eating is not from faith, and everything that is not from faith is sin.

15 Now we who are strong have an obligation to bear the weaknesses of those without strength, and not to please ourselves. 2 Each one of us must please his neighbor for his good, in order to build him up. 3 For even the Messiah did not please Himself. On the contrary, as it is written, **The insults of those who insult You have fallen on Me.** 4 For whatever was written before was written for our instruction, so that through our endurance and through the encouragement of the Scriptures we may have hope. 5 Now may the God of endurance and encouragement grant you agreement with one another, according to Christ Jesus, 6 so that you may glorify the God and Father of our Lord Jesus Christ with a united mind and voice.

7 Therefore accept one another, just as the Messiah also accepted you, to the glory of God. 8 Now I say that Christ has become a servant of the circumcised on behalf of the truth of God, to confirm the promises to the fathers, 9 and so that Gentiles may glorify God for His mercy. As it is written:

Therefore I will praise You
among the Gentiles,
and I will sing psalms
to Your name.

10 Again it says: **Rejoice, you Gentiles, with His people!** 11 And again:

Praise the Lord, all you Gentiles;
all the peoples should praise
Him!

12 And again, Isaiah says:

The root of Jesse will appear,
the One who rises to rule
the Gentiles;
in Him the Gentiles will hope.

13 Now may the God of hope fill you with all joy and peace in believing, so that you may overflow with hope by the power of the Holy Spirit.

Ostrich Christians

*A person's breath is the lamp of the LORD,
searching the innermost parts.*—PROVERBS 20:27

Most of us (myself included) are not good at observing ourselves and reflecting honestly on what goes on beneath the surface of our lives. Why is this so? I think one of the reasons is fear—fear of the unknown, fear of losing control, fear of spoiling a comfortable existence, or fear of having to face some unpleasant discoveries about ourselves. I have met many Christians in my time who adopt this attitude: however things are, good or bad, they could be worse, so it is better to leave well enough alone.

When we read the Bible, however, we discover texts like the one before us today, showing us that God has designed us with the ability to explore our deepest parts. We also hear men like the psalmist crying out to God: "Search me, God, and know my heart; test me and know my concerns. See if there is any offensive way in me; lead me in the everlasting way" (Ps 139:23-24).

I want to stress that too much introspection is unhealthy, but occasionally and in proper doses it is "good medicine." Those who resist this and pretend everything is well when it isn't are what a friend of mine calls "ostrich Christians." They have peace, but it is a peace built on unreality. When they lift their heads out of the sand, the peace they possess somehow falls to pieces. God's peace can keep our hearts and minds intact while we face whatever is true—outside and inside.

Prayer

Father, save me from becoming an "ostrich Christian"—someone who pretends everything is well when it isn't. Nothing must be allowed to hinder the work that You want to do in my heart. Corner my soul and make me what You want me to be. Amen.

Further Study

Mk 2:1-8; Mt 12:25; Lk 6:8; Jn 2:25
How deeply did Jesus see into people's lives?
How deeply do you let Him penetrate into your life?

AUGUST 23

*E*STHER 5:1–7:10

5 On the third day, Esther dressed up in her royal clothing and stood in the inner courtyard of the palace facing it. The king was sitting on his royal throne in the royal courtroom, facing its entrance. ² As soon as the king saw Queen Esther standing in the courtyard, she won his approval. The king extended the golden scepter in his hand toward Esther, and she approached and touched the tip of the scepter.

³ "What is it, Queen Esther?" the king asked her. "Whatever you want, even to half the kingdom, will be given to you."

⁴ "If it pleases the king," Esther replied, "may the king and Haman come today to the banquet I have prepared for them."

⁵ The king commanded, "Hurry, and get Haman so we can do as Esther has requested." So the king and Haman went to the banquet Esther had prepared.

⁶ While drinking the wine, the king asked Esther, "Whatever you ask will be given to you. Whatever you want, even to half the kingdom, will be done."

⁷ Esther answered, "This is my petition and my request: ⁸ If the king approves of me and if it pleases the king to grant my petition and perform my request, may the king and Haman come to the banquet I will prepare for them. Tomorrow I will do what the king has asked."

⁹ That day Haman left full of joy and in good spirits. But when Haman saw Mordecai at the King's Gate, and Mordecai didn't rise or tremble in fear at his presence, Haman was filled with rage toward Mordecai. ¹⁰ Yet Haman controlled himself and went home. He sent for his friends and his wife Zeresh to join him. ¹¹ Then Haman described for them his glorious wealth and his many sons. He told them all how the king had promoted him in rank and given him a high position over the other officials and the royal staff. ¹² "What's more," Haman added, "Queen Esther invited no one but me to join the king at the banquet she had prepared. I am invited again tomorrow to join her with the king. ¹³ Still, none of this satisfies me since I see Mordecai the Jew sitting at the King's Gate all the time."

¹⁴ His wife Zeresh and all his friends told him, "Have them build a gallows 75 feet high. Ask the king in the morning to hang Mordecai on it. Then go to the banquet with the king and enjoy yourself." The advice pleased Haman, so he had the gallows constructed.

6 That night sleep escaped the king, so he ordered the book recording daily events to be brought and read to the king. ² They found the written report of how Mordecai had informed on Bigthana and Teresh, two eunuchs who guarded the king's entrance, when they planned to assassinate King Ahasuerus. ³ The king inquired, "What honor and special recognition have been given to Mordecai for this act?"

The king's personal attendants replied, "Nothing has been done for him."

⁴ The king asked, "Who's in the court?" Now Haman was just entering the outer court of the palace to ask the king to hang Mordecai on the gallows he had prepared for him.

⁵ The king's attendants answered him, "See, Haman is standing in the court."

"Have him enter," the king ordered.

⁶ Haman entered, and the king asked him, "What should be done for the man the king wants to honor?"

Haman thought to himself, "Who is it the king would want to honor more than me?" [7] Haman told the king, "For the man the king wants to honor: [8] Have them bring a royal garment that the king himself has worn and a horse the king himself has ridden, which has a royal diadem on its head. [9] Put the garment and the horse under the charge of one of the king's most noble officials. Have them clothe the man the king wants to honor, parade him on the horse through the city square, and proclaim before him, 'This is what is done for the man the king wants to honor.' "

[10] The king told Haman, "Hurry, and do just as you proposed. Take a garment and a horse for Mordecai the Jew, who is sitting at the King's Gate. Do not leave out anything you have suggested." [11] So Haman took the garment and the horse. He clothed Mordecai and paraded him through the city square, crying out before him, "This is what is done for the man the king wants to honor."

[12] Then Mordecai returned to the King's Gate, but Haman, overwhelmed, hurried off for home with his head covered. [13] Haman told his wife Zeresh and all his friends everything that had happened. His advisers and his wife Zeresh said to him, "If Mordecai, before whom you have begun to fall, is Jewish, you won't overcome him, because your downfall is certain." [14] While they were still speaking with him, the eunuchs of the king arrived and rushed Haman to the banquet Esther had prepared.

7 The king and Haman came to feast with Esther the queen. [2] Once again, on the second day while drinking wine, the king asked Esther, "Queen Esther, whatever you ask will be given to you. Whatever you seek, even to half the kingdom, will be done."

[3] Queen Esther answered, "If I have obtained your approval, my king, and if the king is pleased, spare my life—[this is] my request; and [spare] my people—[this is] my desire. [4] For my people and I have been sold out to destruction, death, and extermination. If we had merely been sold as male and female slaves, I would have kept silent. Indeed,

the trouble wouldn't be worth burdening the king."

[5] King Ahasuerus spoke up and asked Queen Esther, "Who is this, and where is the one who would devise such a scheme?"

[6] Esther answered, "The adversary and enemy is this evil Haman."

Haman stood terrified before the king and queen. [7] Angered by this, the king arose from where they were drinking wine and went to the palace garden. Haman remained to beg Queen Esther for his life because he realized the king was planning something terrible for him. [8] Just as the king returned from the palace garden to the house of wine drinking, Haman was falling on the couch where Esther was reclining. The king exclaimed, "Would he actually violate the queen while I am in the palace?" As soon as the statement left the king's mouth, Haman's face was covered.

[9] Harbona, one of the royal eunuchs, said: "There is a gallows 75 feet tall at Haman's house that he made for Mordecai, who gave the report that saved the king."

The king commanded, "Hang him on it."

[10] They hanged Haman on the gallows he had prepared for Mordecai. Then the king's anger subsided.

𝒫SALM 102:23-28

[23] He has broken my strength in midcourse;
He has shortened my days.
[24] I say: "My God, do not take me in the middle of my life!
Your years continue through all generations.
[25] Long ago You established the earth, and the heavens are the work of Your hands.
[26] They will perish, but You will endure;
all of them will wear out like clothing.
You will change them like a garment, and they will pass away.

27 But You are the same,
and Your years will never end.
28 Your servants' children will dwell
securely,
and their offspring will be
established before You."

PROVERBS 20:28-30

28 Loyalty and faithfulness deliver a
king;
through loyalty he maintains his
throne.

29 The glory of young men is their
strength,
and the splendor of old men is
gray hair.

30 Lashes and wounds purge away
evil,
and beatings cleanse the
innermost parts.

ROMANS 15:14-33

14 Now, my brothers, I myself am convinced about you that you also are full of goodness, filled with all knowledge, and able to instruct one another. 15 Nevertheless, to remind you, I have written to you more boldly on some points because of the grace given me by God 16 to be a minister of Christ Jesus to the Gentiles, serving as a priest of God's good news. My purpose is that the offering of the Gentiles may be acceptable, sanctified by the Holy Spirit. 17 Therefore I have reason to boast in Christ Jesus regarding what pertains to God. 18 For I would not dare say anything except what Christ has accomplished through me to make the Gentiles obedient by word and deed, 19 by the power of miraculous signs and wonders, and by the power of God's Spirit. As a result, I have fully proclaimed the good news about the Messiah from Jerusalem all the way around to Illyricum. 20 So my aim is to evangelize where Christ has not been named, in order that I will not be building on someone else's foundation, 21 but, as it is written:

Those who had no report of Him
will see,
and those who have not heard
will understand.

22 That is why I have been prevented many times from coming to you. 23 But now I no longer have any work to do in these provinces, and I have strongly desired for many years to come to you 24 whenever I travel to Spain. For I do hope to see you when I pass through, and to be sent on my way there by you, once I have first enjoyed your company for a while. 25 Now, however, I am traveling to Jerusalem to serve the saints; 26 for Macedonia and Achaia were pleased to make a contribution to the poor among the saints in Jerusalem. 27 Yes, they were pleased, and they are indebted to them. For if the Gentiles have shared in their spiritual benefits, then they are obligated to minister to Jews in material needs. 28 So when I have finished this and safely delivered the funds to them, I will go by way of you to Spain. 29 But I know that when I come to you, I will come in the fullness of the blessing of Christ.

30 Now I implore you, brothers, through the Lord Jesus Christ and through the love of the Spirit, to agonize together with me in your prayers to God on my behalf: 31 that I may be rescued from the unbelievers in Judea, that my service for Jerusalem may be acceptable to the saints, 32 and that, by God's will, I may come to you with joy and be refreshed together with you.

33 The God of peace be with all of you. Amen.

Three Great Errors

*I implore you . . . through the Lord Jesus Christ and through the love
of the Spirit, to agonize together with me in your prayers to God.*
——Romans 15:30

"God is One, yet God is Three. How can such a strange thing be?" These are the lines of a ditty
that supposedly was sung by troops on the march in World War I. Theologians down the ages
have tried to illuminate this doctrine for us, but it is an issue that will never be fully clarified
until we arrive in heaven (1 Co 13:12). Basically the doctrine of the Trinity is God is One but
with three distinct centers of consciousness. Around this truth a number of errors have been
propounded.

The first was the teaching that there are three gods. The Jehovah's Witnesses accuse present-
day Christians of believing this and say that we conceive of God as a body with three heads.
That might be true of ancient heresy, but it is not true of classic Trinitarianism. The second
heresy taught that God is unipersonal and the other two Persons in the Trinity are simply manifestations of the one God. The third main error denied the equality of the divine Persons and
regarded them as being of different rank.

The historic church formulated the Athanasian Creed, which states that we worship one God
in Trinity and Trinity in unity. What we must see, however, is that no words can fully explain the
truth of the Trinity. "The creed is a safety net to keep us from falling into error," says one preacher,
"rather than a verbal net in which to trap the truth." We use the term "Trinity" expecting not so
much that in that one word the truth may be spoken, but that it may not be left unspoken.

Prayer

Father, I see that life often presents me with facts which seem irreconcilable at one stage of
knowledge, though better understood at another. Perhaps one day this great mystery of the
Trinity may be cleared up. Meanwhile I simply worship and adore. Amen.

Further Study

1 Pt 1:1-6; 1 Tm 2:5
How did Peter distinguish the members of the Trinity?
What did Paul confirm to Timothy?

AUGUST 24

ESTHER 8:1–10:3

8 That same day King Ahasuerus awarded Queen Esther the estate of Haman, the enemy of the Jews. Mordecai entered the king's presence because Esther had revealed her relationship to Mordecai. ² The king removed his signet ring he had recovered from Haman and gave it to Mordecai, and Esther put him in charge of Haman's estate.

³ Then Esther addressed the king again. She fell at his feet, wept, and begged him to revoke the evil of Haman the Agagite, and his plot he had devised against the Jews. ⁴ The king extended the golden scepter toward Esther, so she got up and stood before the king.

⁵ She said, "If it pleases the king, and I have found approval before him, if the matter seems right to the king and I am pleasing in his sight, let a royal edict be written. Let it revoke the documents the scheming Haman son of Hammedatha the Agagite, wrote to destroy the Jews who reside in all the king's provinces. ⁶ For how could I bear to see the evil that would come on my people? How could I bear to see the destruction of my relatives?"

⁷ King Ahasuerus said to Esther the Queen and to Mordecai the Jew, "Look, I have given Haman's estate to Esther, and he was hanged on the gallows because he attacked the Jews. ⁸ You may write in the king's name whatever pleases you concerning the Jews, and seal it with the royal signet ring. A document written in the king's name and sealed with the royal signet ring cannot be revoked."

⁹ On the twenty-third day of the third month (that is, the month Sivan), the royal scribes were summoned. Everything was written exactly as Mordecai ordered for the Jews, to the satraps, the governors, and the officials of the 127 provinces from India to Cush. The edict was written for each province in its own script, for each ethnic group in its own language, and to the Jews in their own script and language.

¹⁰ Mordecai wrote in King Ahasuerus' name and sealed the edicts with the royal signet ring. He sent the documents by mounted couriers, who rode fast horses bred from the royal racing mares.

¹¹ The king's edict gave the Jews in each and every city the right to assemble and defend themselves, to destroy, kill, and annihilate every ethnic and provincial army hostile to them, including women and children, and to take their possessions as spoils of war. ¹² This would take place on a single day throughout all the provinces of King Ahasuerus, on the thirteenth day of the twelfth month, the month Adar.

¹³ A copy of the document was to be issued as law in every province. It was to be published for every ethnic group so the Jews could be ready to avenge themselves against their enemies on that day. ¹⁴ On their royal horses, the couriers rode out in haste, at the king's urgent command. The law was also issued in the fortress of Susa.

¹⁵ Mordecai went out from the king's presence clothed in royal purple and white, with a great golden crown and a purple robe of fine linen. The city of Susa shouted and rejoiced, ¹⁶ and the Jews celebrated with gladness, joy and honor. ¹⁷ In every province and every city, wherever the king's command and his law reached, rejoicing and jubilation took place among the Jews. There was a celebration and a holiday. And, many of the ethnic groups of the land professed themselves to be Jews because fear of the Jews had overcome them.

9 The king's command and law went into effect on the thirteenth day of the twelfth month, the month Adar. On the day when the Jews' enemies had hoped to overpower them, just the opposite happened. The Jews overpowered those who hated them. ²In each of King Ahasuerus' provinces the Jews assembled in their cities to attack those who intended to harm them. Not a single person could withstand them; terror of them fell on every nationality.

³All the officials of the provinces, the satraps, the governors, and the royal civil administrators aided the Jews because they were afraid of Mordecai. ⁴For Mordecai exercised great power in the palace, and his fame spread throughout the provinces as he became more and more powerful.

⁵The Jews put all their enemies to the sword, killing and destroying them. They did what they pleased to those who hated them. ⁶In the fortress of Susa the Jews killed and destroyed 500 men, ⁷including Parshandatha, Dalphon, Aspatha, ⁸Poratha, Adalia, Aridatha, ⁹Parmashta, Arisai, Aridai, and Vaizatha. ¹⁰They killed these 10 sons of Haman son of Hammedatha, the enemy of the Jews. However, they did not seize any plunder.

¹¹On that day the number of people killed in the fortress of Susa was reported to the king. ¹²The king said to Queen Esther, "In the fortress of Susa the Jews have killed and destroyed 500 men, including Haman's 10 sons. What have they done in the rest of the royal provinces? Whatever you ask will be given to you. Whatever you seek will also be done."

¹³Esther answered, "If it pleases the king, may the Jews who are in Susa also have tomorrow to carry out today's law, and may the bodies of Haman's 10 sons be hung on the gallows." ¹⁴The king gave the orders for this to be done, so a law was announced in Susa, and they hung the bodies of Haman's 10 sons. ¹⁵The Jews in Susa assembled again on the fourteenth day of the month of Adar and killed 300 men in Susa, but they did not seize any plunder.

¹⁶The rest of the Jews in the royal provinces assembled, defended themselves, and got rid of their enemies. They killed 75,000 of those who hated them, but they did not seize any plunder. ¹⁷They fought on the thirteenth day of the month of Adar and rested on the fourteenth, and it became a day of feasting and rejoicing.

¹⁸But the Jews in Susa had assembled on the thirteenth and the fourteenth days of the month. They rested on the fifteenth day of the month, and it became a day of feasting and rejoicing. ¹⁹This explains why the rural Jews who live in villages observe the fourteenth day of the month of Adar as a time of rejoicing and feasting. It is a holiday when they send gifts to one another.

²⁰Mordecai recorded these events and sent letters to all the Jews in all of King Ahasuerus' provinces, both near and far. ²¹He ordered them to celebrate the fourteenth and fifteenth days of the month Adar every year ²²because during those days the Jews got rid of their enemies. That was the month when their sorrow was turned into rejoicing and their mourning into a holiday. They were to be days of feasting, rejoicing, and of sending gifts to one another and the poor.

²³So the Jews agreed to continue the practice they had begun, as Mordecai had written them to do. ²⁴For Haman son of Hammedatha the Agagite, the enemy of all the Jews, had plotted against the Jews to destroy them. He cast the Pur (that is, the lot) to crush and destroy them. ²⁵But when the matter was brought before the king, he commanded by letter that the evil plan Haman had devised against the Jews return on his own head and that he should be hanged with his sons on the gallows. ²⁶For this reason these days are called Purim, from the word Pur.

Because of all the instructions in this letter as well as what they had witnessed and what had happened to them, ²⁷the Jews bound themselves, their descendants, and all who joined with them to a commitment that they would not fail to celebrate these two days each and every year according to the written instructions and according to the time appointed. ²⁸ These days are remembered and celebrated by every generation, family, province, and city, so that these days of Purim will not lose their significance in Jewish life and their memory will not fade from their descendants.

²⁹ Queen Esther daughter of Abihail, along with Mordecai the Jew, wrote this second letter with full authority to confirm the letter about Purim. ³⁰ He sent letters with messages of peace and faithfulness to all the Jews who were in the 127 provinces of the kingdom of Ahasuerus, ³¹ in order to confirm these days of Purim at their proper time just as Mordecai the Jew and Queen Esther had established them and just as they had committed themselves and their descendants to the practices of fasting and lamentation. ³² So Esther's command confirmed these customs of Purim, which were then written into the record.

10 King Ahasuerus imposed a tax throughout the land even to the farthest shores. ² All of his powerful and magnificent accomplishments and the detailed account of Mordecai's great rank to which the king had promoted him, have they not been written in the court record of daily events of the kings of Media and Persia? ³ Mordecai the Jew was second only to King Ahasuerus, famous among the Jews, and highly popular with many of his relatives. He continued to seek good for his people and to speak for the welfare of all his kindred.

PSALM 103:1-5

¹ My soul, praise the LORD,
  and all that is within me, praise
  His holy name.
² My soul, praise the LORD,
  and do not forget all His benefits.

³ He forgives all your sin;
  He heals all your diseases.

⁴ He redeems your life from the Pit;
  He crowns you with faithful love
  and compassion.
⁵ He satisfies you with goodness;
  your youth is renewed like the
  eagle.

PROVERBS 21:1-3

21 A king's heart is a water channel
  in the LORD's hand:
  He directs it wherever He
  chooses.

² All the ways of a man seem right
  to him,
  but the LORD evaluates the
  motives.

³ Doing what is righteous and just
  is more acceptable to the LORD
  than sacrifice.

ROMANS 16:1-27

16 I commend to you our sister Phoebe, who is a servant of the church in Cenchreae. ² So you should welcome her in the Lord in a manner worthy of the saints, and assist her in whatever matter she may require your help. For indeed she has been a benefactor of many—and of me also.

³ Give my greetings to Prisca and
  Aquila, my co-workers in
  Christ Jesus, ⁴ who risked
  their own necks for my life.
  Not only do I thank them, but
  so do all the Gentile
  churches.
⁵ Greet also the church that meets
  in their home.
  Greet my dear friend Epaenetus,
  who is the first convert to
  Christ from Asia.
⁶ Greet Mary, who has worked very
  hard for you.
⁷ Greet Andronicus and Junia, my
  fellow countrymen and fellow
  prisoners. They are outstanding among the apostles, and
  they were also in Christ
  before me.

8 Greet Ampliatus, my dear friend in the Lord.
9 Greet Urbanus, our co-worker in Christ, and my dear friend Stachys.
10 Greet Apelles, who is approved in Christ.
Greet those who belong to the household of Aristobulus.
11 Greet Herodion, my fellow countryman.
Greet those who belong to the household of Narcissus who are in the Lord.
12 Greet Tryphaena and Tryphosa, who have worked hard in the Lord.
Greet my dear friend Persis, who has worked very hard in the Lord.
13 Greet Rufus, chosen in the Lord; also his mother—and mine.
14 Greet Asyncritus, Phlegon, Hermes, Patrobas, Hermas, and the brothers who are with them.
15 Greet Philologus and Julia, Nereus and his sister, and Olympas, and all the saints who are with them.
16 Greet one another with a holy kiss. All the churches of Christ send you greetings.

17 Now I implore you, brothers, watch out for those who cause dissensions and pitfalls contrary to the doctrine you have learned. Avoid them; 18 for such people do not serve our Lord Christ but their own appetites, and by smooth talk and flattering words they deceive the hearts of the unsuspecting.

19 The report of your obedience has reached everyone. Therefore I rejoice over you. But I want you to be wise about what is good, yet innocent about what is evil. 20 The God of peace will soon crush Satan under your feet. The grace of our Lord Jesus be with you.

21 Timothy, my co-worker, and Lucius, Jason, and Sosipater, my fellow countrymen, greet you.

22 I Tertius, who penned this epistle in the Lord, greet you.

23 Gaius, who is host to me and to the whole church, greets you. Erastus, the city treasurer, and our brother Quartus greet you.

[24 The grace of our Lord Jesus Christ be with you all.]

25 Now to Him who has power to strengthen you according to my gospel and the proclamation of Jesus Christ, according to the revelation of the sacred secret kept silent for long ages, 26 but now revealed and made known through the prophetic Scriptures, according to the command of the eternal God, to advance the obedience of faith among all nations— 27 to the only wise God, through Jesus Christ—to Him be the glory forever! Amen.

Fullness—Only in God

To the only wise God, through Jesus Christ—to Him be the glory forever!—ROMANS 16:27

The subject of God's knowledge must be linked to His wisdom, and it is this aspect of the divine nature that we consider now. What does the Bible mean when it describes God as wise? Wisdom is the ability to use knowledge to the best possible ends. This ability is found in its fullness only in God. God is never other than wise in everything He does. Knowledge without wisdom would be pathetic, a broken reed. Wisdom without knowledge would be inoperative and quite frightening. God's boundless knowledge and wisdom are perfect in every way, and it is this that makes Him utterly worthy of our trust.

One of the great difficulties we have in the Christian life is trusting the divine wisdom. We can recognize wisdom only when we see the end to which it is moving. Yet God often calls us to trust Him when we can't see the end that He is pursuing. And then in such times we have to ask ourselves: "How much do I trust Him?"

Before I began speaking to a Christian youth group once, I asked if someone could offer a definition of God's wisdom. One young man said: "God's wisdom is the ability to get us through scrapes and difficulties without getting hurt." I gave the young man full marks for attempting a definition, but I had to show him that this was not what divine wisdom is all about. The goal behind divine wisdom is not to make us happy but to make us holy. And sometimes pursuing that goal may involve us in considerable pain.

Prayer

Father, here I am again—at the road less traveled. Help me tread the road ahead knowing that whatever pain You allow me to feel is for my good. I do not welcome it, but I do not run from it either, as long as You stay with me. Amen.

Further Study

Ps 104:1-24; Pr 3:19; Rm 11:33
Where is God's wisdom evidenced?
What was Paul's conclusion?

AUGUST 25

JOB 1:1–3:26

1 There was a man in the country of Uz named Job. He was a man of perfect integrity, who feared God and turned away from evil. ² He had seven sons and three daughters. ³ His estate included 7,000 sheep, 3,000 camels, 500 yoke of oxen, 500 female donkeys, and a very large number of servants. Job was the greatest man among all the people of the east.

⁴ His sons used to have banquets, each at his house in turn. They would send an invitation to their three sisters to eat and drink with them. ⁵ Whenever a round of banqueting was over, Job would send for his children and purify them, rising early in the morning to offer burnt offerings for all of them. For Job thought: Perhaps my children have sinned, having cursed God in their hearts. This was Job's regular practice.

⁶ One day the sons of God came to present themselves before the LORD, and Satan also came with them. ⁷ The LORD asked Satan, "Where have you come from?"

"From roaming through the earth," Satan answered Him, "and walking around on it."

⁸ Then the LORD said to Satan, "Have you considered My servant Job? No one else on earth is like him, a man of perfect integrity, who fears God and turns away from evil." ⁹ Satan answered the LORD, "Does Job fear God for nothing? ¹⁰ Haven't You placed a hedge around him, his household, and everything he owns? You have blessed the work of his hands, and his possessions are spread out in the land. ¹¹ But stretch out Your hand and strike everything he owns, and he will surely curse You to Your face."

¹² "Very well," the LORD told Satan, "everything he owns is in your power. However, you must not lay a hand on Job himself." So Satan went out from the LORD's presence.

¹³ One day when Job's sons and daughters were eating and drinking wine in their oldest brother's house, ¹⁴ a messenger came to Job and reported: "While the oxen were plowing and the donkeys grazing nearby, ¹⁵ the Sabeans swooped down and took them away. They struck down the servants with the sword, and I alone have escaped to tell you!"

¹⁶ He was still speaking when another messenger came and reported: "A lightning storm struck from heaven. It burned up the sheep and the servants, and devoured them, and I alone have escaped to tell you!"

¹⁷ That messenger was still speaking when yet another came and reported: "The Chaldeans formed three bands, made a raid on the camels, and took them away. They struck down the servants with the sword, and I alone have escaped to tell you!"

¹⁸ He was still speaking when another messenger came and reported: "Your sons and daughters were eating and drinking wine in their oldest brother's house. ¹⁹ Suddenly a powerful wind swept in from the desert and struck the four corners of the house. It collapsed on the young people so that they died, and I alone have escaped to tell you!"

²⁰ Then Job stood up, tore his robe and shaved his head. He fell to the ground and worshiped, ²¹ saying:

Naked I came
from my mother's womb,
and naked I will leave this life.
The LORD gives, and the LORD
takes away.
Praise the name of the LORD.

²² Throughout all this Job did not sin or blame God for anything.

2 One day the sons of God came again to present themselves before the LORD, and Satan also came with them to present himself before the LORD. ² The LORD asked Satan, "Where have you come from?"

"From roaming through the earth," Satan answered Him, "and walking around on it."

³ Then the LORD said to Satan, "Have you considered My servant Job? No one else on earth is like him, a man of perfect integrity, who fears God and turns away from evil. He still retains his integrity, even though you incited Me against him, to destroy him without just cause."

⁴ "Skin for skin!" Satan answered the LORD. "A man will give up everything he owns in exchange for his life. ⁵ But stretch out Your hand and strike his flesh and bones, and he will surely curse You to Your face."

⁶ "Very well," the LORD told Satan, "he is in your power; only spare his life." ⁷ So Satan left the LORD's presence and infected Job with incurable boils from the sole of his foot to the top of his head. ⁸ Then Job took a piece of broken pottery to scrape himself while he sat among the ashes.

⁹ His wife said to him, "Do you still retain your integrity? Curse God and die!"

¹⁰ "You speak as a foolish woman speaks," he told her. "Should we accept only good from God and not adversity?" Throughout all this Job did not sin in what he said.

¹¹ Now when Job's three friends— Eliphaz the Temanite, Bildad the

Shuhite, and Zophar the Naamathite—heard about all this adversity that had happened to him, each of them came from his home. They met together to go and offer sympathy and comfort to him. [12] When they looked from a distance, they could barely recognize him. They wept aloud, and each man tore his robe and threw dust into the air and on his head. [13] Then they sat on the ground with him seven days and nights, but no one spoke a word to him because they saw that his suffering was very intense.

3 After this Job began to speak and cursed the day he was born. [2] He said:

[3]   May the day I was born perish,
and the night when they said,
    "A boy is conceived."
[4]   If only that day had turned
    to darkness!
May God above not care about it,
or light shine on it.
[5]   May darkness and gloom
    reclaim it,
and a cloud settle over it.
May an eclipse of the sun
    terrify it.
[6]   If only darkness had taken
    that night away!
May it not appear among the days
    of the year
or be listed in the calendar.
[7]   Yes, may that night be barren;
may no joyful shout be heard in it.
[8]   Let those who curse certain days
cast a spell on it,
those who are skilled
    in rousing Leviathan.
[9]   May its morning stars grow dark.
May it wait for daylight
    but have none;
may it not see the breaking
    of dawn.
[10]   For that night did not shut
the doors of my mother's womb,
and hide sorrow from my eyes.

[11]   Why was I not stillborn;
why didn't I die as I came
    from the womb?
[12]   Why did the knees receive me,

and why were there breasts
    for me to nurse?
[13]   For then I would have laid down
    in peace;
I would be asleep.
Then I would be at rest
[14]   with the kings and counselors
    of the earth,
who rebuilt ruined cities
    for themselves,
[15]   or with princes who had gold,
who filled their houses with silver.
[16]   Or why was I not hidden
    like a miscarried child,
like infants who never
    see daylight?
[17]   There the wicked cease
    to make trouble,
and there the weary find rest.
[18]   The captives are completely
    at ease;
they do not hear the voice of their
    oppressor.
[19]   Both the small and the great
    are there,
and the slave is set free
    from his master.

[20]   Why is light given
    to one burdened with grief,
and life to those whose existence
    is bitter,
[21]   who wait for death,
    but it does not come,
and search for it more than
    for hidden treasure,
[22]   who are filled with much joy
and are glad when they reach
    the grave?
[23]   Why is life given to a man
    whose path is hidden,
whom God has hedged in?
[24]   I sigh when food is put
    before me,
and my groans pour out
    like water.
[25]   For the thing I feared
    has overtaken me,
and what I dreaded has happened
    to me.
[26]   I cannot relax or be still;
I have no rest, for trouble comes.

PSALM 103:6-14

6 The LORD executes acts of
    righteousness
    and justice for all the oppressed.
7 He revealed His ways to Moses,
    His deeds to the people of Israel.
8 The LORD is compassionate and
    gracious,
    slow to anger and full of faithful
    love.
9 He will not always accuse us
    or be angry forever.
10 He has not dealt with us as our
    sins deserve
    or repaid us according to our
    offenses.

11 For as high as the heavens are
    above the earth,
    so great is His faithful love toward
    those who fear Him.
12 As far as the east is from the west,
    so far has He removed our
    transgressions from us.
13 As a father has compassion on his
    children,
    so the LORD has compassion on
    those who fear Him.
14 For He knows what we are made
    of,
    remembering that we are dust.

PROVERBS 21:4-5

4 The lamp that guides the
    wicked—
    haughty eyes and an arrogant
    heart—is sin.

5 The plans of the diligent certainly
    lead to profit,
    but anyone who is reckless only
    becomes poor.

1 CORINTHIANS 1:1-19

1 Paul, called as an apostle of Christ
    Jesus by God's will, and our brother
Sosthenes:
2 To God's church at Corinth, to those
who are sanctified in Christ Jesus and
called as saints, with all those in every
place who call on the name of Jesus
Christ our Lord—theirs and ours.
3 Grace to you and peace from God
our Father and the Lord Jesus Christ.
4 I always thank my God for you because of God's grace given to you in
Christ Jesus, 5 that by Him you were
made rich in everything—in all speaking and all knowledge— 6 as the testimony about Christ was confirmed
among you, 7 so that you do not lack any
spiritual gift as you eagerly wait for the
revelation of our Lord Jesus Christ. 8 He
will also confirm you to the end, blameless in the day of our Lord Jesus Christ.
9 God is faithful; by Him you were called
into fellowship with His Son, Jesus
Christ our Lord.
10 Now I urge you, brothers, in the
name of our Lord Jesus Christ, that you
all say the same thing, that there be no
divisions among you, and that you be
united with the same understanding
and the same conviction. 11 For it has
been reported to me about you, my
brothers, by members of Chloe's household, that there are quarrels among you.
12 What I am saying is this: each of you
says, "I'm with Paul," or "I'm with
Apollos," or "I'm with Cephas," or "I'm
with Christ." 13 Is Christ divided? Was it
Paul who was crucified for you? Or
were you baptized in Paul's name? 14 I
thank God that I baptized none of you
except Crispus and Gaius, 15 so that no
one can say you had been baptized in
my name. 16 I did, in fact, baptize the
household of Stephanas; beyond that, I
don't know if I baptized anyone else.
17 For Christ did not send me to baptize,
but to preach the gospel—not with
clever words, so that the cross of Christ
will not be emptied of its effect.
18 For to those who are perishing the
message of the cross is foolishness, but
to us who are being saved it is God's
power. 19 For it is written:

I will destroy the wisdom
    of the wise,
and I will set aside
    the understanding
    of the experts.

Fellowship

God is faithful; by Him you were called into fellowship
with His Son, Jesus Christ our Lord.

—1 CORINTHIANS 1:9

Seek fellowship with other Christians. Daniel Rowlands, a famous Welsh revivalist of a past century, said: "The whole purpose of the Christian message can be summarized in a single word—fellowship."

What did he mean? First John 1:3 spells it out clearly: "And indeed our fellowship is with the Father and with His Son Jesus Christ." Listen to it as it appears in *The Amplified Bible*: "What we have seen and ourselves heard, we are also telling you, so that you too may realize and enjoy fellowship as partners and partakers with us. And this fellowship that we have . . . is with the Father and with His Son Jesus Christ, the Messiah." At first, John seems to say that the fellowship is "with us," but he hastens to add that our fellowship "is with the Father and with His Son, Jesus Christ."

Follow me carefully now, for what I am about to say can be easily misunderstood: the person who does not know fellowship with God can never know fellowship with anyone else. It must be noted that I am here using the word "fellowship" in its highest possible sense. The one who does not know fellowship with God will feel, consciously or unconsciously, that he is cut off from the very roots of his being. He will feel like a spiritual orphan. This is why our horizontal relationships—that is, our relationship with ourselves and with others—can never be fully realized until we experience a vertical relationship, a relationship with God. Only when we are reconciled with God do we have the potential for experiencing true fellowship with ourselves and with others.

Prayer

Father, I see that I cannot experience true fellowship with myself or with others until I have known it with You. Help me to deepen my fellowship with You so that I might deepen it with others. In Jesus' name. Amen.

Further Study

Ex 19:1-22; 20:21; 24:2; 25:22; 33:9
What was the key to Moses' ministry?
What was the effect?

AUGUST 26

JOB 4:1–6:10

4 Then Eliphaz the Temanite replied:

2 Should anyone try to speak
    with you
when you are exhausted?
Yet who can keep from speaking?
3 Look! You have instructed many
and have strengthened
    weak hands.
4 Your words have steadied the one
    who was stumbling,
and braced the knees
    that were buckling.
5 But now that this has happened
    to you,
you have become exhausted.
It strikes you, and you
    are dismayed.
6 Isn't your piety your confidence,
and the integrity of your life
    your hope?
7 Consider: who has perished
    when he was innocent?
Where have the honest
    been destroyed?
8 In my experience,
    those who plow injustice
and those who sow trouble reap
    the same.
9 They perish at a single blast
    from God
and come to an end by the breath
    of His nostrils.
10 The lion may roar
    and the fierce lion growl,
but the fangs of young lions
    are broken.
11 The strong lion dies if it catches
    no prey,
and the cubs of the lioness
    are scattered.
12 A word was brought to me
    in secret;
my ears caught a whisper of it.

13 Among unsettling thoughts
    from visions in the night,
when deep sleep descends
    on men,
14 fear and trembling came over me
and made all my bones shake.
15 A wind passed by me,
and I shuddered with fear.
16 A figure stood there,
    but I could not recognize
    its appearance;
a form loomed before my eyes.
I heard a quiet voice:
17 "Can a person be more righteous
    than God,
or a man more pure
    than his Maker?"
18 If God puts no trust in His servants
and He charges His angels
    with foolishness,
19 how much more those who dwell
    in clay houses,
whose foundation is in the dust,
who are crushed like a moth!
20 They are smashed to pieces
    from dawn to dusk;
they perish forever while no one
    notices.
21 Are their tent cords not pulled up?
They die without wisdom.

5 Call out if you please. Will anyone
    answer you?
Which of the holy ones will you
    turn to?
2 For anger kills a fool,
and jealousy slays the gullible.
3 I have seen a fool taking root,
but I immediately pronounced
    a curse on his home.
4 His children are far from safety.
They are crushed at the city gate,
with no one to defend them.
5 The hungry consume his harvest,
even taking it out of the thorns.
The thirsty pant
    for his children's wealth.

6 For distress does not grow
   out of the soil,
and trouble does not sprout
   from the ground.
7 But mankind is born for trouble
as surely as sparks fly upward.

8 However, if I were you,
   I would appeal to God
and would present my case to Him.
9 He does great
   and unsearchable things,
wonders without number.
10 He gives rain to the earth
and sends water to the fields.
11 He sets the lowly on high,
and mourners are lifted to safety.
12 He frustrates the schemes
   of the crafty
so that they achieve no success.
13 He traps the wise
   in their craftiness
so that the plans of the deceptive
are quickly brought to an end.
14 They encounter darkness by day,
and they grope at noon
   as if it were night.
15 He saves the needy
   from their sharp words
and from the clutches
   of the powerful.
16 So the poor have hope,
and injustice shuts its mouth.
17 See how happy the man is
   God corrects;
so do not reject the discipline
   of the Almighty.
18 For He crushes but also binds up;
He strikes, but His hands
   also heal.
19 He will rescue you
   from six calamities;
no harm will touch you in seven.
20 In famine He will redeem you
   from death,
and in battle, from the power
   of the sword.
21 You will be safe from slander
and not fear destruction
   when it comes.
22 You will laugh at destruction
   and hunger
and not fear the animals
   of the earth.

23 For you will have a covenant
   with the stones of the field,
and the wild animals will be
   at peace with you.
24 You will know that your tent
   is secure,
and nothing will be missing
   when you inspect your home.
25 You will also know
   that your offspring
   will be many
and your descendants
   like the grass of the earth.
26 You will approach the grave
   in full vigor,
as a stack of sheaves is gathered
   in its season.

27 We have investigated this,
   and it is true!
Hear it and understand it
   for yourself.

6 Then Job answered:

2 If only my grief could be weighed
and my devastation placed with it
   on a scale.
3 For then it would outweigh
   the sand of the seas!
That is why my words are rash.
4 Surely the arrows of the Almighty
   have pierced me;
my spirit drinks their poison.
God's terrors are arrayed
   against me.
5 Does a wild donkey bray
   over fresh grass
or an ox low over its fodder?
6 Is bland food eaten without salt?
Is there flavor in an egg white?
7 I refuse to touch them;
they are like contaminated food.

8 If only my request
   would be granted
and God would provide what
   I hope for:
9 that He would decide to crush me,
to unleash His power
   and cut me off!
10 It would still bring me comfort,
and I would leap for joy
   in unrelenting pain

that I have not denied the words of the Holy One.

PSALM 103:15-22

15 As for man, his days are like grass—
he blooms like a flower of the field;
16 when the wind passes over it, it vanishes,
and its place is no longer known.
17 But from eternity to eternity the LORD's faithful love is toward those who fear Him,
and His righteousness toward the grandchildren
18 of those who keep His covenant, who remember to observe His instructions.
19 The LORD has established His throne in heaven,
and His kingdom rules over all.

20 Praise the LORD, all His angels of great strength,
who do His word,
obedient to His command.
21 Praise the LORD, all His armies, His servants who do His will.
22 Praise the LORD, all His works in all the places where He rules.
My soul, praise the LORD!

PROVERBS 21:6-7

6 Making a fortune through a lying tongue
is a vanishing mist, a pursuit of death.

7 The violence of the wicked sweeps them away
because they refuse to act justly.

1 CORINTHIANS 1:20–2:9

20 Where is the philosopher? Where is the scholar? Where is the debater of this age? Hasn't God made the world's wisdom foolish? 21 For since, in God's

wisdom, the world did not know God through wisdom, God was pleased to save those who believe through the foolishness of the message preached. 22 For the Jews ask for signs and the Greeks seek wisdom, 23 but we preach Christ crucified, a stumbling block to the Jews and foolishness to the Gentiles. 24 Yet to those who are called, both Jews and Greeks, Christ is God's power and God's wisdom, 25 because God's foolishness is wiser than human wisdom, and God's weakness is stronger than human strength.

26 Brothers, consider your calling: not many are wise from a human perspective, not many powerful, not many of noble birth. 27 Instead, God has chosen the world's foolish things to shame the wise, and God has chosen the world's weak things to shame the strong. 28 God has chosen the world's insignificant and despised things—the things viewed as nothing—so He might bring to nothing the things that are viewed as something, 29 so that no one can boast in His presence. 30 But from Him you are in Christ Jesus, who for us became wisdom from God, as well as righteousness, sanctification, and redemption, 31 in order that, as it is written: **The one who boasts must boast in the Lord.**

2 When I came to you, brothers, announcing the testimony of God to you, I did not come with brilliance of speech or wisdom. 2 For I determined to know nothing among you except Jesus Christ and Him crucified. 3 And I was with you in weakness, in fear, and in much trembling. 4 My speech and my proclamation were not with persuasive words of wisdom, but with a demonstration of the Spirit and power, 5 so that your faith might not be based on men's wisdom but on God's power.

6 However, among the mature we do speak a wisdom, but not a wisdom of this age, or of the rulers of this age, who are coming to nothing. 7 On the contrary, we speak God's hidden wisdom in a mystery, which God predestined before the ages for our glory. 8 None of the rulers of this age knew it, for if they had

known it, they would not have crucified the Lord of glory. ⁹ But as it is written:

What no eye has seen and no ear has heard,

and what has never come into a man's heart, is what God has prepared for those who love Him.

It Lacks That

My speech and my proclamation were not with persuasive words of wisdom, but with a demonstration of the Spirit and power.

—1 Corinthians 2:4

Much of modern-day Christianity is lacking power and conviction because it lacks a close encounter with this aspect of the Spirit's resources. If we are to experience the fullness of the Spirit in our lives, then we must open ourselves to everything He wants to give us. We must not pick and choose and say, "I'll take this but not that," for in order to be God's true representatives in this world, we must know Him in all His fullness.

I watched a man on television one day examine a beautiful painting. He studied it for a few moments and said, "Its perspective is good, the coloring is fine, the tones are excellent, the idea behind it is to be commended, but it lacks . . . that."

The same can be said of a lot of Christian activity in this generation. Our preaching is correct, our worship services are well-structured, our music is fine, our organization is superb, but it lacks one thing—the throbbing power of the Holy Spirit. Without the power of the Spirit in our midst, we are preaching unquickened truth—truth that doesn't fall upon the soul with convicting, sobering, awakening, converting power. Our Christianity is not bad—it is just dull. The Holy Spirit, when accepted and obeyed, turns insipidity into inspiration, dullness into dancing, and mediocrity into magnificence. If we are not careful, we may find ourselves in court one of these days accused of contravening the Trade Descriptions Act!

Prayer

Ouch, Lord, this hurts! But I know from experience that You hurt me in order to heal me. Begin with me today, and set me on fire that others may catch it, too! Amen.

Further Study

Ac 19:21-41; Eph 5:18; 3:19
How did the Holy Spirit give Paul holy boldness?
What was Paul's exhortation to the Ephesian church?

AUGUST 27

JOB 6:11–8:22

11 What strength do I have
    that I should continue
      to hope?
  What is my future, that I should
    be patient?
12 Is my strength that of stone,
  or my flesh made of bronze?
13 Since I cannot help myself,
  the hope for success
      has been banished from me.

14 A despairing man should receive
    loyalty from his friends,
  even if he abandons the fear
    of the Almighty.
15 My brothers are as treacherous
    as a wadi,
  as seasonal streams that overflow
16 and become darkened
    because of ice,
  and the snow melts into them.
17 The wadis evaporate
    in warm weather;
  they disappear
    from their channels
      in hot weather.
18 Caravans turn away
    from their routes,
  go up into the desert,
    and perish.
19 The caravans of Tema look
    for these streams.
  The traveling merchants of Sheba
    hope for them.
20 They are ashamed because they
    had been confident
    of finding water.
  When they arrive there,
    they are frustrated.
21 So this is what you have
    now become to me.
  When you see something dreadful,
    you are afraid.
22 Have I ever said:
    Give me something

    or Pay a bribe for me
      from your wealth
23 or Deliver me
    from the enemy's power
  or Redeem me from the grasp
    of the ruthless?

24 Teach me, and I will be silent.
  Help me understand
    what I did wrong.
25 How painful honest words can be!
  But what does your rebuke prove?
26 Do you think that you
    can disprove my words
  or that a despairing man's words
    are mere wind?
27 No doubt you would cast lots
    for a fatherless child
  and negotiate a price to sell
    your friend.

28 But now, please look at me;
  would I lie to your face?
29 Reconsider; don't be unjust.
  Reconsider; my righteousness
    is still the issue.
30 Am I lying,
  or can I not recognize lies?

7 Isn't mankind consigned
    to forced labor on earth?
  Are not his days like those
    of a hired hand?
2 Like a slave he longs for shade;
  like a hired man he waits
    for his pay.
3 So I have been made to inherit
    months of futility,
  and troubled nights
    have been assigned to me.
4 When I lie down I think:
  When will I get up?
  But the evening drags
    on endlessly,
  and I toss and turn until dawn.
5 My flesh is clothed with maggots
    and encrusted with dirt.

My skin forms scabs
and then oozes.

6 My days pass more swiftly
than a weaver's shuttle;
they come to an end
without hope.
7 Remember that my life is but
a breath.
My eye will never again see
anything good.
8 The eye of anyone who looks
on me
will no longer see me.
Your eyes will look for me, but I
will be gone.
9 As a cloud fades away
and vanishes,
so the one who goes down
to Sheol will never rise again.
10 He will never return to his house;
his hometown will no longer
remember him.

11 Therefore I will not restrain
my mouth.
I will speak in the anguish
of my spirit;
I will complain in the bitterness
of my soul.
12 Am I the sea or a sea monster,
that You keep me under guard?
13 When I say: My bed
will comfort me,
and my couch will ease
my complaint,
14 then You frighten me
with dreams,
and terrify me with visions,
15 so that I prefer strangling,
death rather than life in this body.
16 I give up! I will not live forever.
Leave me alone, for my days are
a breath.

17 What is man, that You think
so highly of him
and pay so much attention to him?
18 You inspect him every morning,
and put him to the test
every moment.
19 Will You ever look away from me,
or leave me alone until I swallow
my saliva?

20 If I have sinned, what have I done
to You,
Watcher of mankind?
Why have You made me
Your target,
so that I have become a burden
to You?
21 Why not forgive my sin
and pardon my transgression?
For soon I will lie down
in the grave.
You will eagerly seek me, but I
will be gone.

8 Then Bildad the Shuhite replied:

2 How long will you go on saying
these things?
Your words are a blast of wind.
3 Does God pervert justice?
Does the Almighty pervert
what is right?
4 Since your children sinned
against Him,
He gave them over
to their rebellion.
5 But if you earnestly seek God
and ask the Almighty for mercy,
6 if you are pure and upright,
then He will move even now
on your behalf
and restore the home where
your righteousness dwells.
7 Then, even if your beginnings
were modest,
your final days will be
full of prosperity.

8 For ask the previous generation,
and pay attention to what
their fathers discovered,
9 since we were born only yesterday
and know nothing.
Our days on earth are
but a shadow.
10 Will they not teach you and tell you
and speak from
their understanding?
11 Does papyrus grow where there is
no marsh?
Do reeds flourish without water?
12 While still uncut shoots,
they would dry up quicker than
any other plant.

13 Such is the destiny of all
who forget God;
the hope of the godless
will perish.
14 His source of confidence is fragile;
what he trusts in is
a spider's web.
15 He leans on his web,
but it doesn't stand firm.
He grabs it, but it does not
hold up.
16 He is an amply watered plant
in the sunshine;
his shoots spread out
over his garden.
17 His roots are intertwined
around a pile of rocks.
He looks for a home
among the stones.
18 If he is uprooted from his place,
it will deny knowing him, saying,
"I never saw you."
19 Surely this is the joy of his way
of life;
yet others will sprout
from the dust.
20 Look, God does not reject
a person of integrity,
and He will not support evildoers.
21 He will yet fill your mouth
with laughter
and your lips with a shout of joy.
22 Your enemies will be clothed
with shame;
the tent of the wicked will exist
no longer.

PSALM 104:1-9

1 My soul, praise the LORD!
LORD my God, You are very great;
You are clothed with majesty and
splendor.
2 He wraps Himself in light as if it
were a robe,
spreading out the sky like a
canopy,
3 laying the beams of His palace on
the waters above,
making the clouds His chariot,
walking on the wings of the wind,
4 and making the winds His
messengers,
flames of fire His servants.

5 He established the earth on its
foundations;
it will never be shaken.
6 You covered it with the deep as if
it were a garment;
the waters stood above the
mountains.
7 At Your rebuke the waters fled;
at the sound of Your thunder they
hurried away—
8 mountains rose and valleys
sank —
to the place You established for
them.
9 You set a boundary they cannot
cross;
they will never cover the earth
again.

PROVERBS 21:8-9

8 A guilty man's conduct is crooked,
but the behavior of the innocent
is upright.

9 Better to live on the corner of a
roof
than to share a house with a
nagging wife.

1 CORINTHIANS 2:10–3:15

10 Now God has revealed them to us by the Spirit, for the Spirit searches everything, even the deep things of God. 11 For who among men knows the concerns of a man except the spirit of the man that is in him? In the same way, no one knows the concerns of God except the Spirit of God. 12 Now we have not received the spirit of the world, but the Spirit who is from God, in order to know what has been freely given to us by God. 13 We also speak these things, not in words taught by human wisdom, but in those taught by the Spirit, explaining spiritual things to spiritual people. 14 But the natural man does not welcome what comes from God's Spirit, because it is foolishness to him; he is not able to know it since it is evaluated spiritually. 15 The spiritual person,

however, can evaluate everything, yet he himself cannot be evaluated by anyone. ¹⁶ For:

who has known the Lord's mind, that he may instruct Him?

But we have the mind of Christ.

3 Brothers, I was not able to speak to you as spiritual people but as people of the flesh, as babies in Christ. ² I fed you milk, not solid food, because you were not yet able to receive it. In fact, you are still not able, ³ because you are still fleshly. For since there is envy and strife among you, are you not fleshly and living like ordinary people? ⁴ For whenever someone says, "I'm with Paul," and another, "I'm with Apollos," are you not typical men?

⁵ So, what is Apollos? And what is Paul? They are servants through whom you believed, and each has the role the Lord has given. ⁶ I planted, Apollos watered, but God gave the growth. ⁷ So then neither the one who plants nor the one who waters is anything, but only God who gives the growth. ⁸ Now the one who plants and the one who waters are equal, and each will receive his own reward according to his own labor. ⁹ For we are God's co-workers. You are God's field, God's building. ¹⁰ According to God's grace that was given to me, as a skilled master builder I have laid a foundation, and another builds on it. But each one must be careful how he builds on it, ¹¹ because no one can lay any other foundation than what has been laid—that is, Jesus Christ. ¹² If anyone builds on the foundation with gold, silver, costly stones, wood, hay, or straw, ¹³ each one's work will become obvious, for the day will disclose it, because it will be revealed by fire; the fire will test the quality of each one's work. ¹⁴ If anyone's work that he has built survives, he will receive a reward. ¹⁵ If anyone's work is burned up, it will be lost, but he will be saved; yet it will be like an escape through fire.

Divide and Conquer

What comes from God's Spirit . . . is evaluated spiritually.
—1 Corinthians 2:14

Only the Holy Spirit can help us properly to interpret the Word of God. A person may have a fine mind, a good seminary training, even a theological degree, but none of these is a sufficient foundation on which to attempt to interpret the Word of God. Truth, as the above text tells us, is "evaluated spiritually."

But there is one more thing we need to understand—only the Holy Spirit can show us how to use it aright. Doubtless, this was the consideration in the mind of the apostle when he penned this statement: "the sword of the Spirit . . . is God's word." It is one thing to know the contents of Scripture; it is another thing to know how to use those contents in a way that defeats the devil. Only the Holy Spirit can enable us to do this.

The relationship between the Holy Spirit and the Word of God is an important one. Some tend to put the emphasis on one side or the other. But the moment we separate the Spirit and the Word, we are in trouble. The late Donald Gee once said: "All Spirit and no Word, you blow up. All Word and no Spirit, you dry up. Word and Spirit—you grow up."

Without the Spirit, the Word is a dead letter; with the Spirit, it is a living and powerful force. The devil has a policy of "divide and conquer." And if he can get us to separate the Word from the Spirit, then he has us just where he wants us.

Prayer

My Father, I see that when I separate the Spirit from the Word and the Word from the Spirit, I am in trouble. Help me to be as open to the Spirit as I am to the Bible, and as open to the Bible as I am to the Spirit. In Jesus' name. Amen.

Further Study

2 Co 3:1-6; Jn 6:63; 1 Pt 3:18
What "gives life"?
What made Paul an able minister of truth?

AUGUST 28

JOB 9:1–10:22

9 Then Job answered:

2 Yes, I know what you've said
   is true,
   but how can a person be justified
   before God?
3 If one wanted to take Him to court,
   he could not answer God once
   in a thousand times.
4 God is wise and all-powerful.
   Who has opposed Him
   and come out unharmed?
5 He removes mountains
   without their knowledge,
   overturning them in His anger.
6 He shakes the earth from its place
   so that its pillars tremble.
7 He commands the sun
   not to shine
   and seals off the stars.
8 He alone stretches out
   the heavens
   and treads on the waves
   of the sea.
9 He makes the stars: the Bear,
   Orion,

the Pleiades,
   and the constellations
   of the southern sky.
10 He performs great
    and unsearchable things,
   wonders without number.
11 If He passes by me,
    I wouldn't see Him;
   if He goes right by,
    I wouldn't recognize Him.
12 If He snatches something,
    who can stop Him?
   Who can ask Him, "What are
    You doing?"
13 God does not hold back His anger;
   Rahab's assistants cringe in fear
    beneath Him!

14 How then can I answer Him
   or choose my arguments
    against Him?
15 Even if I were in the right,
    I could not answer.
   I could only beg my judge
    for mercy.
16 If I summoned Him
    and He answered me,
   I do not believe He would
    pay attention to what I said.

17 He batters me with a whirlwind
    and multiplies my wounds
        without cause.
18 He doesn't let me catch my breath
    but soaks me
        with bitter experiences.
19 If it is a matter of strength, look,
        He is the Mighty One!
    If it is a matter of justice, who can
        summon Him?
20 Even if I were in the right,
        my own mouth would
        condemn me;
    if I were blameless, my mouth
        would declare me guilty.

21 Though I am blameless,
    I no longer care about myself;
    I renounce my life.
22 It is all the same. Therefore I say,
    "He destroys both the blameless
        and the wicked."
23 When disaster brings
        sudden death,
    He mocks the despair
        of the innocent.
24 The earth is handed over
        to the wicked;
    He blindfolds its judges.
    If it isn't He, then who is it?

25 My days fly by faster
        than a runner;
    they flee without seeing any good.
26 They sweep by like boats made
        of papyrus,
    like an eagle swooping down
        on its prey.
27 If I said, "I will forget
        my complaint,
    change my expression, and smile,"
28 I would still live in terror of all
        my pains.
    I know You will not acquit me.
29 Since I will be found guilty,
    why should I labor in vain?
30 If I wash myself with snow,
    and cleanse my hands with lye,
31 then You dip me in a pit
        of mud,
    and my own clothes despise me!

32 For He is not a man like me,
        that I can answer Him,

that we can take each other
        to court.
33 There is no one to judge
        between us,
    to lay his hand on both of us.
34 Let Him take His rod away
        from me
    so His terror will no longer
        frighten me.
35 Then I would speak and not
        fear Him.
    But that is not the case; I am
        on my own.

10 I am disgusted with my life.
    I will express my complaint
    and speak in the bitterness
        of my soul.
2 I will say to God:
    Do not declare me guilty!
    Let me know why
        You prosecute me.
3 Is it good for You to oppress,
    to reject the work of Your hands,
    and favor the plans of the wicked?
4 Do You have eyes of flesh,
    or do You see as a human sees?
5 Are Your days like those
        of a human,
    or Your years like those of a man,
6 that You look for my wrongdoing
    and search for my sin,
7 even though You know that
        I am not wicked
    and that there is no one
        who can deliver
        from Your hand?

8 Your hands shaped me
        and formed me.
    Will You now turn around
        and destroy me?
9 Please remember that You
        formed me like clay.
    Will You now return me to dust?
10 Did You not pour me out like milk
    and curdle me like cheese?
11 You clothed me with skin
        and flesh,
    and wove me together with bones
        and tendons.
12 You gave me life and faithful love,
    and Your care has guarded my life.

13 Yet You concealed these thoughts
in Your heart;
I know that this was
Your hidden plan:
14 if I sin, You would notice,
and would not acquit me
of my wrongdoing.
15 If I am wicked, woe to me!
And even if I am righteous,
I cannot lift up my head.
I am filled with shame
and aware of my affliction.
16 If I am proud, You hunt me
like a lion
and again display
Your miraculous power
against me.
17 You produce new witnesses
against me
and multiply Your anger
toward me.
Hardships assault me,
wave after wave.

18 Why did You bring me out of
the womb?
I should have died and never
been seen.
19 I wish I had never existed
but had been carried
from the womb to the grave.
20 Are my days not few? Stop it!
Leave me alone, so that
I can smile a little
21 before I go to a land of darkness
and gloom,
never to return.
22 It is a land of blackness
like the deepest darkness,
gloomy and chaotic,
where even the light is like
the darkness.

₱SALM 104:10-15

10 He causes the springs to gush into
the valleys;
they flow between the mountains.
11 They supply water for every wild
beast;
the wild donkeys quench their
thirst.
12 The birds of the sky live beside
the springs;

they sing among the foliage.
13 He waters the mountains from His
palace;
the earth is satisfied by the fruit
of Your labor.

14 He causes grass to grow for the
livestock
and provides crops for man to
cultivate,
producing food from the earth,
15 wine that makes man's heart
glad—
making his face shine with oil—
and bread that sustains man's
heart.

₱ROVERBS 21:10-11

10 A wicked person desires evil;
he has no consideration for his
neighbor.

11 When a mocker is punished, the
inexperienced become wiser;
when one teaches a wise man, he
acquires knowledge.

1 CORINTHIANS 3:16–4:13

16 Don't you know that you are God's
sanctuary and that the Spirit of God
lives in you? 17 If anyone ruins God's
sanctuary, God will ruin him; for God's
sanctuary is holy, and that is what you
are.
18 No one should deceive himself. If
anyone among you thinks he is wise
in this age, he must become foolish so
that he can become wise. 19 For the wisdom of this world is foolishness with
God, since it is written: **He catches the
wise in their craftiness**— 20 and again,
**The Lord knows the reasonings of the
wise, that they are futile.** 21 So no one
should boast in men, for all things are
yours: 22 whether Paul or Apollos or Cephas or the world or life or death or
things present or things to come—all
are yours, 23 and you belong to Christ,
and Christ to God.

4 A person should consider us in this way: as servants of Christ and managers of God's mysteries. ² In this regard, it is expected of managers that each one be found faithful. ³ It is of little importance that I should be evaluated by you or by a human court. In fact, I don't even evaluate myself. ⁴ For I am not conscious of anything against myself, but I am not justified by this. The One who evaluates me is the Lord. ⁵ Therefore don't judge anything prematurely, before the Lord comes, who will both bring to light what is hidden in darkness and reveal the intentions of the hearts. And then praise will come to each one from God.

⁶ Now, brothers, I have applied these things to myself and Apollos for your benefit, so that you may learn from us the saying: "Nothing beyond what is written." The purpose is that none of you will be inflated with pride in favor of one person over another. ⁷ For who makes you so superior? What do you have that you didn't receive? If, in fact, you did receive it, why do you boast as if you hadn't received it? ⁸ Already you are full! Already you are rich! You have begun to reign as kings without us—and I wish you did reign, so that we also could reign with you! ⁹ For I think God has displayed us, the apostles, in last place, like men condemned to die: we have become a spectacle to the world and to angels and to men. ¹⁰ We are fools for Christ, but you are wise in Christ! We are weak, but you are strong! You are distinguished, but we are dishonored! ¹¹ Up to the present hour we are both hungry and thirsty; we are poorly clothed, roughly treated, homeless; ¹² we labor, working with our own hands. When we are reviled, we bless; when we are persecuted, we endure it; ¹³ when we are slandered, we entreat. We are, even now, like the world's garbage, like the filth of all things.

Body and Soul—United

Don't you know that you are God's sanctuary and that the Spirit of God lives in you? . . . God's sanctuary is holy, and that is what you are.
—1 CORINTHIANS 3:16-17

Many centuries of misunderstanding have brought about a division between body and soul. This division is in evidence in some parts of the church today. Jesus, however, did not see His body as something to be ignored but as something to be used. As He said, "You prepared a body for Me" (Heb 10:5).

His body and soul were attuned. He neither neglected His body nor pampered it, but offered it as the vehicle of God's will and purpose. And He kept it fit for God. There is no mention of His ever being sick. Tired, yes, but never ill.

It is accepted today that body and soul are a unity, that a sick soul can produce a sick body, just as a healthy spirit contributes to a healthy body. It also works the other way around—a healthy body can contribute to good emotional and mental health. We Christians tend to overemphasize the spiritual side of life while underestimating the importance of physical facts like body chemistry, weather, water, air pollution, and nutrition. But through ignorance of the way in which body and soul are related, we succeed only in tearing them apart. I believe what is said about husband and wife in the marriage service can also be applied to the body and the soul: "Therefore what God has joined together, man must not separate" (Mt 19:6).

A good pianist may be able to get a lot out of a poor instrument, but he cannot give full expression to the music if the piano is out of tune. You cannot ignore the physical if you want to stay spiritually fresh.

Prayer

O Father, help me see that my body is not something over which to be offended, but something to be offered. Give me a balanced understanding of this matter so that I can be at my best for You—spirit, soul, and body. Amen.

Further Study

1 Kg 19; Rm 8:11; 1 Co 3:16
What was part of Elijah's problem?
How did the angel minister to Elijah?

AUGUST 29

JOB 11:1–13:12

11 Then Zophar the Naamathite replied:

2 Should this stream of words
    go unanswered
    and such a talker be acquitted?
3 Should your babbling put others
    to silence,
    so that you can keep on ridiculing
    with no one to humiliate you?
4 You have said, "My teaching
    is sound,
    and I am pure in Your sight."
5 But if only God would speak
    and declare His case against you,
6 He would show you the secrets
    of wisdom,
    for true wisdom has two sides.
    Know then that God has chosen
    to overlook some of your sin.

7 Can you fathom the depths of God
    or discover the limits
    of the Almighty?
8 They are higher
    than the heavens—what can
    you do?

They are deeper than Sheol—
    what can you know?
9 Their measure is longer
    than the earth
    and wider than the sea.
10 If He passes by and throws
    someone in prison
    or convenes a court, who can
    stop Him?
11 Surely He knows which people
    are worthless.
    If He sees iniquity, will He not
    take note of it?
12 But a stupid man
    will gain understanding
    as soon as a wild donkey is born
    a man!

13 As for you, if you redirect
    your heart
    and lift up your hands to Him
    in prayer—
14 if there is iniquity in your hand,
    remove it,
    and don't allow injustice to dwell
    in your tents—
15 then you will hold your head high,
    free from fault.

You will be firmly established
and unafraid.
16 For you will forget your suffering,
recalling it only as waters
that have flowed by.
17 Your life will be brighter
than noonday;
its darkness will be
like the morning.
18 You will be confident, because
there is hope.
You will look carefully about
and lie down in safety.

19 You will lie down without fear,
and many will seek your favor.
20 But the sight of the wicked
will fail.
Their way of escape will be
cut off,
and their only hope will be
to die.

12 Then Job answered:

2 No doubt you are the people,
and wisdom will die with you!
3 But I also have a mind;
I am not inferior to you.
Who doesn't know the things
you are talking about?

4 I am a laughingstock to my
friends,
by calling on God,
who answers me.
The righteous and upright man is
a laughingstock.
5 The one who is at ease
holds calamity in contempt
and thinks it is prepared
for those whose feet
are slipping.
6 The tents of robbers are safe,
and those who provoke God
are secure;
God's power provides this.

7 But ask the animals, and they will
instruct you;
ask the birds of the sky,
and they will tell you.
8 Or speak to the earth, and it will
instruct you;

let the fish of the sea inform you.
9 Which of all these does not know
that the hand of the LORD
has done this?
10 The life of every living thing is
in His hand,
as well as the breath
of all mankind.
11 Doesn't the ear test words
as the palate tastes food?
12 Wisdom is found with the elderly,
and understanding comes
with long life.

13 Wisdom and strength belong
to God;
counsel and understanding
are His.
14 Whatever He tears down cannot
be rebuilt;
whoever He imprisons cannot
be released.
15 When He withholds the waters,
everything dries up,
and when He releases them,
they destroy the land.
16 True wisdom and power belong
to Him.
The deceived and the deceiver
are His.
17 He leads counselors away barefoot
and makes judges go mad.
18 He releases the bonds put on
by kings
and ties a cloth
around their waists.
19 He leads priests away barefoot
and overthrows
established leaders.
20 He deprives trusted advisers
of speech
and takes away the elders'
good judgment.
21 He pours out contempt on
nobles
and disarms the strong.
22 He reveals mysteries
from the darkness
and brings the deepest darkness
into the light.
23 He makes nations great,
then destroys them;
He enlarges nations,
then leads them away.

24 He deprives the world's leaders
of reason,
and makes them wander
in a trackless wasteland.
25 They grope around in darkness
without light;
He makes them stagger
like drunken men.

13 Look, my eyes have seen
all this;
my ears have heard
and understood it.
2 Everything you know, I also know;
I am not inferior to you.
3 Yet I prefer to speak
to the Almighty
and argue my case before God.
4 But you coat the truth with lies;
you are all worthless doctors.
5 If only you would shut up
and let that be your wisdom!

6 Hear now my argument,
and listen to my defense.
7 Would you testify unjustly
on God's behalf
or speak deceitfully for Him?
8 Would you show partiality to Him
or argue the case in His defense?
9 Would it go well
if He examined you?
Could you deceive Him
as you would deceive a man?
10 Surely He would rebuke you
if you secretly showed partiality.
11 Would God's majesty
not terrify you?
Would His dread not fall on you?
12 Your memorable sayings
are proverbs of ash;
your defenses are made of clay.

*P*SALM 104:16-23

16 The trees of the LORD flourish,
the cedars of Lebanon that He
planted.
17 There the birds make their nests;
the stork makes its home in the
pine trees.
18 The high mountains are for the
wild goats;
the cliffs are a refuge for hyraxes.

19 He made the moon to mark the
seasons;
the sun knows when to set.
20 You bring darkness, and it
becomes night,
when all the forest animals stir.
21 The young lions roar for their prey
and seek their food from God.
22 The sun rises; they go back
and lie down in their dens.
23 Man goes out to his work
and to his labor until evening.

*P*ROVERBS 21:12-14

12 The Righteous One considers the
house of the wicked;
He brings the wicked to ruin.

13 The one who shuts his ears to the
cry of the poor
will himself also call out and not
be answered.

14 A secret gift soothes anger,
and a covert bribe, fierce rage.

1 *C*ORINTHIANS 4:14–5:13

14 I'm not writing this to shame you,
but to warn you as my dear children.
15 For you can have 10,000 instructors
in Christ, but you can't have many fathers. Now I have fathered you in Christ
Jesus through the gospel. 16 Therefore I
urge you, be imitators of me. 17 This is
why I have sent to you Timothy, who is
my beloved and faithful child in the
Lord. He will remind you about my ways
in Christ Jesus, just as I teach everywhere in every church. 18 Now some are
inflated with pride, as though I were
not coming to you. 19 But I will come to
you soon, if the Lord wills, and I will
know not the talk but the power of
those who are inflated with pride. 20 For
the kingdom of God is not in talk but in
power. 21 What do you want? Should I
come to you with a rod, or in love and a
spirit of gentleness?

5 It is widely reported that there is sexual immorality among you, and the kind of sexual immorality that is not even condoned among the Gentiles—a man is living with his father's wife. ² And you are inflated with pride, instead of filled with grief so that he who has committed this act might be removed from among you. ³ For though absent in body but present in spirit, I have already decided about him who has done this thing as though I were present. ⁴ In the name of our Lord Jesus, when you are assembled, along with my spirit and with the power of our Lord Jesus, ⁵ turn that one over to Satan for the destruction of the flesh, so that his spirit may be saved in the Day of the Lord.

⁶ Your boasting is not good. Don't you know that a little yeast permeates the whole batch of dough? ⁷ Clean out the old yeast so that you may be a new batch, since you are unleavened. For Christ our Passover has been sacrificed. ⁸ Therefore, let us observe the feast, not with old yeast, or with the yeast of malice and evil, but with the unleavened bread of sincerity and truth.

⁹ I wrote to you in a letter not to associate with sexually immoral people— ¹⁰ by no means referring to this world's immoral people, or to the greedy and swindlers, or to idolaters; otherwise you would have to leave the world. ¹¹ But now I am writing you not to associate with anyone who bears the name of brother who is sexually immoral or greedy, an idolater or a reviler, a drunkard or a swindler. Do not even eat with such a person. ¹² For what is it to me to judge outsiders? Do you not judge those who are inside? ¹³ But God judges outsiders. **Put away the evil person from among yourselves.**

He Burns Me Up

Therefore, let us observe the feast, not with…malice and evil, but with the unleavened bread of sincerity and truth.—1 CORINTHIANS 5:8

Is it true that nursing a grudge can cause physical illness? A man I knew became enraged over something another Christian had done to him. I advised him to forgive and forget. He replied: "But every time I see him, he burns me up." I said: "That's because you want to burn him up, and all you succeed in doing is burning yourself up." I told him about the sadistic farmer who tied a stick of dynamite to a hawk, lit the fuse, and then turned the bird loose, expecting it to blow itself up in mid-air. Instead, the hawk flew into the man's barn, and the explosion wrecked not only the barn but part of his house also.

He listened, but I could see my words had not gone in. He could think and talk of nothing else but getting even with his fellow Christian. His wife told me that his breath became foul, his appetite left him, his digestion became bad, he suffered loss of sleep and, after a few months, he dropped down dead.

In case someone says, "But there could have been other reasons for his death," I can tell you that I talked to his doctor, who was a close personal friend of mine, and he told me that the man had died of an "undrained grudge." Of course, you can't put that on a death certificate, but many doctors know that "undrained grudges" play a major role in creating physical disorders. A missionary suffered a breakdown because of a grudge he had held against his ministry organization for not supplying him with enough money. Apparently, grudges are just as deadly in the godly as the ungodly.

Prayer

Father, I see so clearly that my hurts harm me even more when I harbor them. Help me not to hold on stubbornly to my wounded pride, but consent for You to lance my inner boils, no matter how much it may hurt. In Jesus' name. Amen.

Further Study

1 Jn 2:1-11; Pr 10:12; Is 59:9-10
What brings us back into darkness?
What is the result of walking in darkness?

AUGUST 30

JOB 13:13–15:13

13 Be quiet, and I will speak.
Let whatever comes happen
to me.
14 Why do I put myself at risk
and take my life in my own hands?
15 Even if He kills me, I will hope
in Him.
I will still defend my ways
before Him.
16 Yes, this will result
in my deliverance,
for no godless person can appear
before Him.
17 Pay close attention to my words;
let my declaration ring
in your ears.
18 Now then, I have prepared my
case;
I know that I am right.
19 Can anyone indict me?
If so, I will be silent and die.

20 Only grant these two things
to me, God,
so that I will not have to hide
from Your presence:

21 remove Your hand from me,
and do not let Your terror
frighten me.
22 Then call, and I will answer,
or I will speak, and You
can respond to me.
23 How many iniquities and sins
have I committed?
Reveal to me my transgression
and sin.
24 Why do You hide Your face
and consider me Your enemy?
25 Will You frighten
a wind-driven leaf?
Will You chase after dry straw?
26 For You record bitter accusations
against me
and make me inherit the iniquities
of my youth.
27 You put my feet in the stocks
and stand watch over all
my paths,
setting a limit for the soles
of my feet.

28 Man wears out
like something rotten,
like a moth-eaten garment.

14 Man born of woman
is short of days and full
of trouble.
2 He blossoms like a flower,
then withers;
he flees like a shadow
and does not last.
3 Do You really take notice of one
like this?
Will You bring me into judgment
against You?
4 Who can produce something pure
from what is impure?
No one!
5 Since man's days are determined
and the number of his months
depends on You,
and since You have set limits
he cannot pass,
6 look away from him
and let him rest
so that he can enjoy his day
like a hired hand.

7 There is hope for a tree:
If it is cut down, it will
sprout again,
and its shoots will not die.
8 If its roots grow old in the ground
and its stump starts to die
in the soil,
9 the smell of water makes it thrive
and produce twigs like a sapling.
10 But a man dies and fades away;
he breathes his last—where is he?
11 As water disappears from the sea
and a wadi becomes parched
and dry,
12 so man lies down never
to rise again.
They will not wake up
until the heavens are
no more;
they will not stir from their sleep.

13 If only You would hide me
in Sheol
and conceal me
until Your anger passes,
that You would appoint a time
for me
and then remember me.
14 When a man dies, will he
come back to life?

If so, I would wait all the days
of my struggle
until my relief comes.
15 You would call, and I would
answer You.
You would long for the work
of Your hands.
16 For then You would count
my steps
but would not take note of my sin.
17 My rebellion would be sealed up
in a bag,
and You would cover over
my iniquity.

18 But as a mountain collapses
and crumbles
and a rock is dislodged
from its place,
19 as water wears away stones
and torrents wash away the soil
from the land,
so You destroy a man's hope.
20 You completely overpower him,
and he passes on;
You change his appearance
and send him away.
21 If his sons receive honor,
he does not know it;
if they become insignificant,
he is unaware of it.
22 He feels only the pain
of his own body
and mourns only for himself.

15 Then Eliphaz the Temanite replied:
2 Does a wise man answer
with empty counsel
or fill himself
with the hot east wind?
3 Should he argue with useless talk
or with words that serve
no good purpose?
4 But you even undermine the fear
of God
and hinder meditation
before Him.
5 Your iniquity teaches you
what to say,
and you choose the language
of the crafty.
6 Your own mouth condemns you,
not I;

your own lips testify
against you.

7 Were you the first person
ever born,
or were you brought forth
before the hills?
8 Do you listen in on the council
of God,
or have a monopoly on wisdom?
9 What do you know that we don't?
What do you understand that
is not clear to us?
10 Both the gray-haired
and the elderly are with us,
men older than your father.
11 Are God's consolations
not enough for you,
even the words that deal gently
with you?
12 Why has your heart misled you,
and why do your eyes flash
13 as you turn your anger
against God
and allow such words to leave
your mouth?

*P*SALM 104:24-30

24 How countless are Your works,
LORD!
In wisdom You have made them
all;
the earth is full of Your creatures.
25 Here is the sea, vast and wide,
teeming with creatures beyond
number—
living things both large and small.
26 There the ships move about,
and Leviathan, which You formed
to play there.
27 All of them wait for You
to give them their food at the
right time.
28 When You give it to them, they
gather it;
when You open Your hand, they
are satisfied with good things.
29 When You hide Your face, they are
terrified;
when You take away their breath,
they die and return to the
dust.

30 When You send Your breath, they
are created,
and You renew the face of the
earth.

*P*ROVERBS 21:15-16

15 Justice executed is a joy to the
righteous
but a terror to those who practice
iniquity.

16 The man who strays from the way
of wisdom
will come to rest in the assembly
of the departed spirits.

I *C*ORINTHIANS 6:1-20

6 Does any of you who has a complaint against someone dare go to
law before the unrighteous, and not before the saints? 2 Or do you not know
that the saints will judge the world? And
if the world is judged by you, are you
unworthy to judge the smallest cases?
3 Do you not know that we will judge angels—not to speak of things pertaining
to this life? 4 So if you have cases pertaining to this life, do you select those
who have no standing in the church to
judge? 5 I say this to your shame! Can it
be that there is not one wise person
among you who will be able to arbitrate
between his brothers? 6 Instead, brother
goes to law against brother, and that before unbelievers!

7 Therefore, it is already a total defeat
for you that you have lawsuits against
one another. Why not rather put up with
injustice? Why not rather be cheated?
8 Instead, you act unjustly and cheat—
and this to brothers! 9 Do you not know
that the unjust will not inherit God's
kingdom? Do not be deceived: no sexually immoral people, idolaters, adulterers, male prostitutes, homosexuals,
10 thieves, greedy people, drunkards, re-
vilers, or swindlers will inherit God's
kingdom. 11 Some of you were like this;
but you were washed, you were sanctified, you were justified in the name of
the Lord Jesus Christ and by the Spirit
of our God.

¹² "Everything is permissible for me," but not everything is helpful. "Everything is permissible for me," but I will not be brought under the control of anything. ¹³ "Foods for the stomach and the stomach for foods," but God will do away with both of them. The body is not for sexual immorality but for the Lord, and the Lord for the body. ¹⁴ God raised up the Lord and will also raise us up by His power. ¹⁵ Do you not know that your bodies are the members of Christ? So should I take the members of Christ and make them members of a prostitute?

Absolutely not! ¹⁶ Do you not know that anyone joined to a prostitute is one body with her? For it says, **The two will become one flesh.** ¹⁷ But anyone joined to the Lord is one spirit with Him.

¹⁸ Flee from sexual immorality! "Every sin a person can commit is outside the body," but the person who is sexually immoral sins against his own body. ¹⁹ Do you not know that your body is a sanctuary of the Holy Spirit who is in you, whom you have from God? You are not your own, ²⁰ for you were bought at a price; therefore glorify God in your body.

Sustained and Secure

All of them wait for You to give them their food at the right time.—PSALM 104:27

No creature has the power to preserve itself. "Does papyrus grow where there is no marsh?" asked Job (Jb 8:11). Both man and beast would perish if there were no food, and there would be no food if the earth were not refreshed with fruitful showers. As one preacher put it: "We came from God's hand, and we remain in His hand."

Think of the marvel of life in the womb. How an infant can live for so many months in such a cramped environment—and without breathing—is unaccountable except for the power of God in preservation. It was divine preservation Daniel was thinking of when he said to the godless Belshazzar: "But you have not glorified the God who holds your life-breath in His hand and who controls the whole course of your life" (Dn 5:23). Everywhere in the Scriptures God is presented not only as the Creator of the world but as its Sustainer and Preserver also. God has not wound up the universe like a clock and then separated Himself from it; rather, He is active in sustaining it, and were He to remove Himself from it, it would cease to exist.

The writer to the Hebrews reminds us that "He sustains all things by His powerful word" (1:3). If the maker of some artifact were to die, his death would make no difference to it. It would continue to exist just as it did before. Not so with God and His world, however. If God were to die, the universe would fall to pieces. But don't worry—God cannot die. The universe is quite secure.

Prayer

O God, when I consider how You are my Sustainer and my Preserver, my heart is humbled before You. You cannot die, and because I am linked to You, I cannot die. I know my body will die, but my soul is Yours forever. Thank You, dear Father. Amen.

Further Study

Is 46:1-13; Ps 18:35; 147:6
What did the Lord underline to the children of Israel?
What did the psalmist testify?

AUGUST 31

JOB 15:14–17:16

14 What is man, that he
  should be pure,
or one born of woman, that he
  should be righteous?
15 If God puts no trust
  in His holy ones
and the heavens are not pure
  in His sight,
16 how much less one
  who is revolting and corrupt,
who drinks injustice like water?

17 Listen to me and I will inform you.
I will describe what I have seen,
18 what was declared by wise men
and was not suppressed
  by their ancestors,
19 the land was given to them alone
when no foreigner passed
  among them.
20 A wicked man writhes in pain
  all his days;
few years are stored up
  for the ruthless.
21 Dreadful sounds fill his ears;
when he is at peace, a robber
  attacks him.
22 He doesn't believe he will return
  from darkness;
he is destined for the sword.
23 He wanders about for food,
  saying, "Where is it?"
He knows the day of darkness is
  at hand.
24 Trouble and distress terrify him,

overwhelming him like a king
  prepared for battle.
25 For he has stretched out his hand
  against God
and has arrogantly opposed
  the Almighty.
26 He rushes headlong at Him
with his thick, studded shields.
27 Though his face is covered
  with fat
and his waistline bulges with it,
28 he will dwell in ruined cities,
in abandoned houses destined
  to become piles of rubble.
29 He will no longer be rich;
  his wealth will not endure.
His possessions will not spread
  over the land.
30 He will not escape
  from the darkness;
flames will wither his shoots,
and he will depart by the breath
  of God's mouth.
31 Let him not put trust
  in worthless things, being
  led astray,
for what he gets in exchange
  will prove worthless.
32 It will be accomplished
  before his time,
and his branch will not flourish.
33 He will be like a vine that drops
  its unripe grapes
and like an olive tree that sheds
  its blossoms.
34 For the company of the godless
  will be barren,

and fire will consume the tents
of those who offer bribes.
35 They conceive trouble
and give birth to evil;
their womb prepares deception.

16 Then Job answered:

2 I have heard many things
like these.
You are all miserable comforters.
3 Is there no end to your empty
words?
What provokes you that you
continue testifying?
4 If you were in my place I could
also talk like you.
I could string words together
against you
and shake my head at you,
but I wouldn't.
5 I would encourage you
with my mouth,
and the consolation from my lips
would bring relief.

6 Even if I speak, my suffering
is not relieved,
and if I hold back, what have I lost?
7 Surely He has now exhausted me.
You have devastated
my entire family.
8 You have shriveled me up—
it has become a witness;
My frailty rises up against me
and testifies to my face.
9 His anger tears at me,
and He harasses me.
He gnashes His teeth at me.
My enemy pierces me
with His eyes.
10 They open their mouths
against me
and strike my cheeks
with contempt;
they join themselves together
against me.
11 God hands me over to unjust men;
He throws me into the hands
of the wicked.
12 I was at ease,
but He shattered me;
He seized me by the scruff
of the neck

and smashed me to pieces.
He set me up as His target;
13 His archers surround me.
He pierces my kidneys
without mercy
and pours my bile on the ground.
14 He breaks through my defenses
again and again;
He charges at me like a warrior.

15 I have sewn sackcloth
over my skin;
I have buried my strength
in the dust.
16 My face has grown red
with weeping,
and the shadow of death covers
my eyes,
17 although my hands are free
from violence
and my prayer is pure.

18 Earth, do not cover my blood;
may my cry for help find
no resting place.
19 Even now my witness is
in heaven,
and my advocate is in the heights!
20 My friends scoff at me
as I weep before God.
21 I wish that someone
might arbitrate
between a man and God
just as a man pleads for his friend.
22 For only a few years will pass
before I go the way of no return.

17 My spirit is broken.
My days are extinguished.
A graveyard awaits me.
2 Surely mockers surround me
and my eyes must gaze
at their rebellion.

3 Make arrangements! Put up
security for me.
Who else will be my sponsor?
4 You have closed their minds
to understanding,
therefore You will not honor them.
5 If a man informs on his friends
for a price,
the eyes of his children will fail.

6 He has made me an object
   of scorn to the people;
   I have become a man people
      spit at.
7 My eyes have grown dim
      from grief,
   and my whole body has become
      but a shadow.
8 The upright are appalled at this,
   and the innocent are roused
      against the godless.
9 Yet the righteous person will hold
      to his way,
   and the one whose hands
      are clean will grow stronger.
10 But come back and try again,
      all of you.
   I will not find a wise man
      among you.
11 My days have slipped by;
   my plans have been ruined,
   even the things dear to my heart.
12 They turned night into day
   and made light seem near
      in the face of darkness.
13 If I await Sheol as my home,
   spread out my bed in darkness,
14 and say to the Pit: You are
      my father,
   and to the worm: My mother
      or my sister,
15 where then is my hope?
   Who can see any hope for me?
16 Will it go down to the gates
      of Sheol,
   or will we descend together
      to the dust?

PSALM 104:31-35

31 May the glory of the LORD endure
      forever;
   may the LORD rejoice in His works.
32 He looks at the earth, and it
      trembles;
   He touches the mountains, and
      they pour out smoke.
33 I will sing to the LORD all my life;
   I will sing praise to my God while
      I live.
34 May my meditation be pleasing to
      Him;

I will rejoice in the LORD.
35 May sinners vanish from the earth
   and the wicked be no more.
   My soul, praise the LORD!
   Hallelujah!

PROVERBS 21:17-19

17 The one who loves pleasure will
      become a poor man;
   whoever loves wine and oil will
      not get rich.

18 The wicked are a ransom for the
      righteous,
   and the treacherous, for the
      upright.

19 Better to live in a wilderness
   than with a nagging and hot-
      tempered wife.

1 CORINTHIANS 7:1-24

7 About the things you wrote: "It is
good for a man not to have relations
with a woman." 2 But because of sexual
immorality, each man should have his
own wife, and each woman should have
her own husband. 3 A husband should
fulfill his marital duty to his wife, and
likewise a wife to her husband. 4 A wife
does not have authority over her own
body, but her husband does. Equally, a
husband does not have authority over
his own body, but his wife does. 5 Do
not deprive one another—except when
you agree, for a time, to devote yourselves to prayer. Then come together
again; otherwise, Satan may tempt you
because of your lack of self-control. 6 I
say this as a concession, not as a command. 7 I wish that all people were just
like me. But each has his own gift from
God, one this and another that.

8 I say to the unmarried and to widows: It is good for them if they remain
as I am. 9 But if they do not have self-
control, they should marry, for it is better to marry than to burn with desire.

10 I command the married—not I, but
the Lord—a wife is not to leave her
husband. 11 But if she does leave, she

must remain unmarried or be reconciled to her husband—and a husband is not to leave his wife. [12] But to the rest I, not the Lord, say: If any brother has an unbelieving wife, and she is willing to live with him, he must not leave her. [13] Also, if any woman has an unbelieving husband, and he is willing to live with her, she must not leave her husband. [14] For the unbelieving husband is sanctified by the wife, and the unbelieving wife is sanctified by the Christian husband. Otherwise your children would be unclean, but now they are holy. [15] But if the unbeliever leaves, let him leave. A brother or a sister is not bound in such cases. God has called you to peace. [16] For you, wife, how do you know whether you will save your husband? Or you, husband, how do you know whether you will save your wife? [17] However, each one must live his life in the situation the Lord assigned when God called him. This is what I command in all the churches. [18] Was anyone already circumcised when he was called? He should not undo his circumcision. Was anyone called while uncircumcised? He should not get circumcised. [19] Circumcision does not matter and uncircumcision does not matter, but keeping God's commandments does. [20] Each person should remain in the life situation in which he was called. [21] Were you called while a slave? It should not be a concern to you. But if you can become free, by all means take the opportunity. [22] For he who is called by the Lord as a slave is the Lord's freedman. Likewise he who is called as a free man is Christ's slave. [23] You were bought at a price; do not become slaves of men. [24] Brothers, each person should remain with God in whatever situation he was called.

The Ceaseless Creator

May my meditation be pleasing to Him;
I will rejoice in the LORD.
—PSALM 104:34

Dr. Douglas Speere says that with advancing years, "Our greatest danger is not hardening of the arteries but hardening of the attitudes." We harden our viewpoint, refusing to look at anything beyond it. We groove our thinking and acting, and the grooves get deeper until they become graves that bury us. As someone put it: "You don't grow old; you get old by not growing." Some people are dead at 40, although their funerals are postponed until they are 60. For many Christians, life has settled into ruts—mental, physical, and spiritual ruts. "And a rut," said someone, "is a grave with ends knocked out." In Canada I saw a dirt road leading off the main highway which had a sign on it that read: "Choose your rut—you will be in it for the next 20 miles." When New Year's Day comes, many could say to themselves: "I'd better choose my rut, for I'll be in it for the next 365 days." Life for them is not an adventure. It holds no surprises, offers no excitement, and is uncreative. My friend, I beg you, open your mind to God today and don't resist the Divine Eagle as He prepares to push you out into a more creative way of thinking, acting, and living. Someone has said that the last words of the church when it is taken up to heaven will be these: "It has never been done like this before." Focus your mind once again on today's psalm, and keep in mind that the God who created all things desires to live, move, and think in you.

Prayer

O Father, You who are a ceaseless Creator, make me a ceaseless creator. Break the molds of my thinking patterns, and give me new ones. In Jesus' name. Amen.

Further Study

Col 2; Is 11:2; Mt 13:15; 1 Co 1:25; Rm 11:33
What are the characteristics of Christ's thoughts?
How are they opposed to human philosophy and tradition?

SEPTEMBER I

JOB 18:1–20:11

18 Then Bildad the Shuhite replied:

2 How long until you stop talking?
 Show some sense, and then
  we can talk.
3 Why are we regarded as cattle,
 as stupid in your sight?
4 You who tear yourself in anger—
 should the earth be abandoned
  on your account,
 or a rock be removed
  from its place?

5 Yes, the light of the wicked
  is extinguished;
 the flame of his fire does
  not glow.
6 The light in his tent grows dark,
 and the lamp beside him
  is put out.
7 His powerful stride is shortened,
 and his own schemes trip him up.
8 For his own feet lead him
  into a net,
 and he strays into its mesh.
9 A trap catches him by the heel;

a noose seizes him.
10 A rope lies hidden for him
  on the ground,
 and a snare waits for him
  along the path.
11 Terrors frighten him on every side
 and harass him at every step.
12 His strength is depleted;
 disaster lies ready for him
  to stumble.
13 Parts of his skin are eaten away;
 death's firstborn consumes
  his limbs.
14 He is ripped from the security
  of his tent
 and marched away to the king
  of terrors.
15 Nothing he owned remains
  in his tent.
 Burning sulfur is scattered
  over his home.
16 His roots below dry up,
 and his branches above
  wither away.
17 All memory of him perishes
  from the earth;
 he has no name abroad.
18 He is driven from light
  to darkness

and chased
from the inhabited world.
19 He has no children or descendants
among his people,
no survivor where he used to live.
20 Those in the west are appalled
at his fate,
while those in the east tremble
in horror.
21 Indeed, such is the dwelling
of the wicked,
and this is the place of the one
who does not know God.

19 Then Job answered:

2 How long will you torment me
and crush me with words?
3 You have humiliated me ten times
now,
and you mistreat me
without shame.
4 Even if it is true that
I have sinned,
my mistake concerns only me.
5 If you really want to appear
superior to me
and would use my disgrace
as evidence against me,
6 then understand that it is God
who has wronged me
and caught me in His net.

7 I cry out: Violence!
but get no response;
I call for help, but there is
no justice.
8 He has blocked my way so that
I cannot pass through;
He has veiled my paths
with darkness.
9 He has stripped me of my honor
and removed the crown
from my head.
10 He tears me down on every side
so that I am ruined.
He uproots my hope like a tree.
11 His anger burns against me,
and He regards me as one of
His enemies.
12 His troops advance together;
they construct a ramp
against me
and camp around my tent.

13 He has removed my brothers
from me;
my acquaintances
have abandoned me.
14 My relatives stop coming by,
and my close friends
have forgotten me.
15 My house guests
and female servants
regard me as a stranger;
I am a foreigner in their sight.
16 I call for my servant, but he
does not answer,
even if I beg him
with my own mouth.
17 My breath is offensive to my wife,
and my own children
find me repulsive.
18 Even young boys scorn me.
When I stand up, they mock me.
19 All of my best friends despise me,
and those I love have turned
against me.
20 My skin and my flesh cling
to my bones;
I have escaped by the skin
of my teeth.

21 Have mercy on me, my friends,
have mercy,
for God's hand has struck me.
22 Why do you persecute me
as God does?
Will you never get enough
of my flesh?

23 I wish that my words
were written down,
that they were recorded on a scroll
24 or were inscribed in stone forever
by an iron stylus and lead!
25 But I know my living Redeemer,
and He will stand on the dust
at last.
26 Even after my skin
has been destroyed,
yet I will see God in my flesh.
27 I will see Him myself;
my eyes will look at Him, and not
as a stranger.
My heart longs within me.

28 If you say, "How will
we pursue him,

since the root of the problem lies with him?"

29 be afraid of the sword,
because wrath brings punishment by the sword,
so that you may know there is a judgment.

20 Then Zophar the Naamathite replied:

2 This is why
my unsettling thoughts compel me to answer,
because I am upset!
3 I have heard a rebuke
that insults me,
and my understanding makes me reply.
4 Don't you know that
ever since antiquity,
from the time man was placed on earth,
5 the joy of the wicked has been brief
and the happiness of the godless has lasted only a moment?
6 Though his arrogance reaches heaven,
and his head touches the clouds,
7 he will vanish forever like his own dung.
Those who know him will ask, "Where is he?"
8 He will fly away like a dream and never be found;
he will be chased away like a vision in the night.
9 The eye that saw him will see him no more,
and his household will no longer see him.
10 His children will beg from the poor,
for his own hands must give back his wealth.
11 His bones may be full of youthful vigor,
but it will lie down with him in the grave.

PSALM 105:1-6

1 Give thanks to the LORD, call on His name;
proclaim His deeds among the peoples.
2 Sing to Him, sing praise to Him;
tell about all His wonderful works!
3 Honor His holy name;
let the hearts of those who seek the LORD rejoice.
4 Search for the LORD and for His strength;
seek His face always.
5 Remember the wonderful works He has done,
His wonders, and the judgments He has pronounced,
6 you offspring of Abraham His servant,
Jacob's descendants—
His chosen ones.

PROVERBS 21:20-21

20 Precious treasure and oil are in the dwelling of the wise,
but a foolish man consumes them.

21 The one who pursues righteousness and faithful love
will find life, righteousness, and honor.

1 CORINTHIANS 7:25-40

25 About virgins: I have no command from the Lord, but I do give an opinion as one who by the Lord's mercy is trustworthy. 26 Therefore I consider this to be good because of the present distress: it is fine for a man to stay as he is. 27 Are you bound to a wife? Do not seek to be loosed. Are you loosed from a wife? Do not seek a wife. 28 However, if you do get married, you have not sinned, and if a virgin marries, she has not sinned. But such people will have trouble in this life, and I am trying to spare you. 29 And I say this, brothers: the time is limited, so from now on those who have wives

should be as though they had none, [30] those who weep as though they did not weep, those who rejoice as though they did not rejoice, those who buy as though they did not possess, [31] and those who use the world as though they did not make full use of it. For this world in its current form is passing away.

[32] I want you to be without concerns. An unmarried man is concerned about the things of the Lord—how he may please the Lord. [33] But a married man is concerned about the things of the world—how he may please his wife— [34] and he is divided. An unmarried woman or a virgin is concerned about the things of the Lord, so that she may be holy both in body and in spirit. But a married woman is concerned about the things of the world—how she may please her husband. [35] Now I am saying this for your own benefit, not to put a restraint on you, but because of what is proper, and so that you may be devoted to the Lord without distraction.

[36] But if any man thinks he is acting improperly toward his virgin, if she is past marriageable age, and so it must be, he can do what he wants. He is not sinning; they can get married. [37] But he who stands firm in his heart (who is under no compulsion, but has control over his own will) and has decided in his heart to keep his own virgin, will do well. [38] So then he who marries his virgin does well, but he who does not marry will do better.

[39] A wife is bound as long as her husband is living. But if her husband dies, she is free to be married to anyone she wants—only in the Lord. [40] But she is happier if she remains as she is, in my opinion. And I think that I also have the Spirit of God.

Always a Reason to Rejoice

Honor His holy name; let the hearts of those who seek the LORD rejoice.—PSALM 105:3

The second fruit of the Spirit listed by Paul is joy (Gl 5:22). It is no mere accident that "joy" follows the first, love. Joy is a byproduct of love. If you concentrate on getting joy, it will elude you. But if you concentrate on getting love, then joy will seek you out—you will be automatically joyful.

The nine qualities of the fruit of the Spirit are not natural attributes, but supernatural ones. You cannot manufacture them—they just appear in our lives as we allow the Holy Spirit to have His way within us. I know many Christians who find it difficult to embrace the fact that the fruit of the Spirit is joy. They not only don't expect joy—they don't want it. One grim Christian said to me once: "At the heart of our faith is a cross. This means we ought to be spending our time weeping, not laughing."

Well, it is true that there is a cross at the heart of the Christian faith and that following Christ involves some rigorous self-denials, but it does not alter—and cannot alter—the fact that the fruit of the Spirit is joy. We cannot deny that there is a good deal of suffering in Christianity, but beneath the suffering is a joy that will, if we allow it, burst upward through everything. I am bound to say that if there is no joy, there is no Christianity, for Christianity is inherent joy. The empty tomb takes away our empty gloom. We have an Easter morning in our faith, and that means there is always a reason to rejoice.

Prayer

Father, I am so thankful that Your Holy Spirit applies redemption right to the roots of my being. Thus I can be glad even when I am sad. Thank You, dear Father. Amen.

Further Study

Lk 10:17-22; 15:4-6; Heb 12:2
How did Christ relate joy to the Cross?
What brings joy to His heart?

SEPTEMBER 2

JOB 20:12–21:34

12 Though evil tastes sweet
      in his mouth
   and he conceals it
      under his tongue,
13 though he cherishes it
      and will not let it go
   but keeps it in his mouth,
14 yet the food in his stomach turns
   into cobras' venom inside him.
15 He swallows wealth but must
      vomit it up;
   God will force it
      from his stomach.
16 He will suck the poison of cobras;
   a viper's fangs will kill him.
17 He will not enjoy the streams,
   the rivers flowing with honey
      and cream.
18 He must return the fruit
      of his labor
      without consuming it;
   he doesn't enjoy the profits
      from his trading.
19 For he oppressed and abandoned
      the poor;
   he seized a house he did not build.

20 Because his appetite
      is never satisfied,
   he does not escape his desires.
21 Nothing is left for him to consume;
   therefore, his prosperity
      will not last.
22 At the height of his success
      distress will come to him;
   the full weight of misery
      will crush him.
23 When he fills his stomach,
   God will send His burning anger
      against him,
   raining it down on him
      while he is eating.
24 If he flees from an iron weapon,
   an arrow from a bronze bow
      will pierce him.
25 He pulls it out of his back,
   the flashing tip out of his liver.
   Terrors come over him.
26 Total darkness is reserved
      for his treasures.
   A fire unfanned by human hands
      will consume him;
   it will feed on what is left
      in his tent.
27 The heavens will expose
      his iniquity,

and the earth will rise up
against him.

28 The possessions in his house
will be removed,
flowing away on the day
of God's anger.

29 This is the wicked man's lot
from God,
the inheritance God ordained
for him.

21 Then Job answered:

2 Pay close attention to my words;
let this be the consolation
you offer.

3 Bear with me while I speak;
then after I have spoken, you may
continue mocking.

4 As for me, is my complaint
against a man?
Then why shouldn't I be impatient?

5 Look at me and shudder;
put your hand over your mouth.

6 When I think about it,
I am terrified
and my body trembles in horror.

7 Why do the wicked continue
to live,
growing old and becoming
powerful?

8 Their children are established
while they are still alive,
and their descendants,
before their eyes.

9 Their homes are secure
and free of fear;
no rod from God strikes them.

10 Their bulls breed without fail;
their cows calve
and do not miscarry.

11 They let their little ones run
around like lambs;
their children skip about,

12 singing to the tambourine and lyre
and rejoicing at the sound
of the flute.

13 They spend their days
in prosperity
and go down to Sheol in peace.

14 Yet they say to God:
"Leave us alone!
We don't want to know Your ways.

15 Who is the Almighty, that we
should serve Him,
and what will we gain by pleading
with Him?"

16 But their prosperity is not
of their own doing.
The counsel of the wicked is far
from me!

17 How often is the lamp
of the wicked put out?
Does disaster come on them?
Does He apportion destruction
in His anger?

18 Are they like straw
before the wind,
like chaff a storm sweeps away?

19 God reserves
a person's punishment
for his children.
Let God repay the person himself,
so that he may know it.

20 Let his own eyes see his demise;
let him drink from
the Almighty's wrath!

21 For what does he care
about his family once
he is dead,
when the number of his months
has run out?

22 Can anyone teach God knowledge,
since He judges the exalted ones?

23 One person dies
in excellent health,
completely secure and at ease.

24 His body is well-fed,
and his bones are full of marrow.

25 Yet another person dies
with a bitter soul,
having never tasted prosperity.

26 But they both lie in the dust,
and worms cover them.

27 Look, I know your thoughts,
the schemes you would
wrong me with.

28 For you say, "Where now is
the nobleman's house?"
and "Where are the tents
the wicked lived in?"

29 Have you never consulted
those who travel the roads?
Don't you accept their reports?

30 Indeed, the evil man is spared
from the day of disaster,
rescued from the day of wrath.
31 Who would denounce his behavior
to his face?
Who would repay him for what
he has done?
32 He is carried to the grave,
and someone keeps watch over his
tomb.
33 The dirt on his grave is sweet
to him.
Everyone follows behind him,
and those who go before him are
without number.

34 So how can you offer me
such futile comfort?
Your answers are deceptive.

PSALM 105:7-15

7 He is the LORD our God;
His judgments govern the whole
earth.
8 He forever remembers His
covenant,
the promise He ordained for a
thousand generations—
9 the covenant He made with
Abraham,
swore to Isaac,
10 and confirmed to Jacob as a decree
and to Israel as an everlasting
covenant:
11 "To you I will give the land of
Canaan
as your inherited portion."

12 When they were few in number,
very few indeed, and temporary
residents in Canaan,
13 wandering from nation to nation
and from one kingdom to another,
14 He allowed no one to oppress
them;
He rebuked kings on their behalf:
15 "Do not touch My anointed ones,
or harm My prophets."

PROVERBS 21:22-24

22 The wise conquer a city of
warriors

and bring down its mighty
fortress.

23 The one who guards his mouth
and tongue
keeps himself out of trouble.

24 The proud and arrogant person,
named "Mocker,"
acts with excessive pride.

1 CORINTHIANS 8:1–9:12

8 About food offered to idols: We
know that "we all have knowledge."
Knowledge inflates with pride, but love
builds up. ² If anyone thinks he knows
anything, he does not yet know it as he
ought to know it. ³ But if anyone loves
God, he is known by Him.
⁴ About eating food offered to idols,
then, we know that "an idol is nothing
in the world," and that "there is no God
but one." ⁵ For even if there are so-
called gods, whether in heaven or on
earth—as there are many "gods" and
many "lords"—

6 yet for us there is one God,
the Father,
from whom are all things, and we
for Him;
and one Lord, Jesus Christ,
through whom are all things,
and we through Him.

⁷ However, not everyone has this
knowledge. In fact, some have been so
used to idolatry up until now, that when
they eat food offered to an idol, their
conscience, being weak, is defiled.
⁸ Food will not make us acceptable to
God. We are not inferior if we don't eat,
and we are not better if we do eat. ⁹ But
be careful that this right of yours in no
way becomes a stumbling block to the
weak. ¹⁰ For if somebody sees you, the
one who has this knowledge, dining in
an idol's temple, won't his weak conscience be encouraged to eat food offered to idols? ¹¹ Then the weak person,
the brother for whom Christ died, is

ruined by your knowledge. ¹²Now when you sin like this against the brothers and wound their weak conscience, you are sinning against Christ. ¹³Therefore, if food causes my brother to fall, I will never again eat meat, so that I won't cause my brother to fall.

9 Am I not free? Am I not an apostle? Have I not seen Jesus our Lord? Are you not my work in the Lord? ²If I am not an apostle to others, at least I am to you, for you are the seal of my apostleship in the Lord. ³My defense to those who examine me is this: ⁴Don't we have the right to eat and drink? ⁵Don't we have the right to be accompanied by a Christian wife, like the other apostles, the Lord's brothers, and Cephas? ⁶Or is it only Barnabas and I who have no right to refrain from working? ⁷Who ever goes to war at his own expense?

Who plants a vineyard and does not eat its fruit? Or who shepherds a flock and does not drink the milk from the flock? ⁸Am I saying this from a human perspective? Doesn't the law also say the same thing? ⁹For it is written in the law of Moses, **Do not muzzle an ox while it treads out the grain.** Is God really concerned with oxen? ¹⁰Or isn't He really saying it for us? Yes, this is written for us, because he who plows ought to plow in hope, and he who threshes should do so in hope of sharing the crop. ¹¹If we have sown spiritual things for you, is it too much if we reap material things from you? ¹²If others share this authority over you, don't we even more?

However, we have not used this authority; instead we endure everything so that we will not hinder the gospel of Christ.

The Great Stimulator

*There is one God, the Father, from whom are all things . . .
and one Lord, Jesus Christ, through whom are all things.*

—1 CORINTHIANS 8:6

In order to remain spiritually vibrant we must strive to be creative and outgoing. It is never too late to acquire this characteristic. We are made in the image of our Creator, and when we cease to be creative, we cease to be.

Kagawa, the famous Japanese Christian, used to refer to Jesus as "the great Stimulator." One day some students asked him why he was so fond of this phrase, and he replied: "Because He stimulates the creative center in each one of us, making us first aware of God, and then aware of the infinite possibilities in God."

When I was at school, I struggled with my studies, and although I passed all my examinations and went to college, my passes were always on the borderline. Then I found Christ as the great Stimulator—and what a change. He stimulated the creative center within me, and He so transformed my attitude toward work that within months I had moved from near the bottom of my classes to near the top.

When taking a seminar in Birmingham, I met a friend who had recently come to live there. "What do you think of Birmingham?" I asked. His reply was: "I have lived here for three months, and every day I keep seeing new horizons." This is what happens when we stay close to Jesus—every day we keep seeing new horizons. In His company we begin to see farther, feel for people on a wider scale, act more decisively, and live on the growing edge of adventure. Why? Because a creative God gives to His creation the same creative impulses.

Prayer

O God, stimulate my whole being, I pray, so that every day I shall see new horizons. Help me never to walk with my eyes focused on the ground, but with my eyes fixed on You. For Your own dear name's sake I ask it. Amen.

Further Study

Jn 1:1-18; Col 1:16; Php 2:1
Who is at the center of creation?
What happens if He is the center of our lives?

SEPTEMBER 3

JOB 22:1–24:12

22 Then Eliphaz the Temanite replied:

2 Can a man be of any use to God?
Can even a wise man be of use
to Him?
3 Does it delight the Almighty if you
are righteous?
Does He profit if you perfect
your behavior?

4 Does He correct you and take you
to court
because of your piety?
5 Isn't your wickedness abundant
and aren't your iniquities endless?
6 For you took collateral
from your brothers
without cause,
stripping off their clothes
and leaving them naked.
7 You gave no water to the thirsty
and withheld food
from the famished,
8 while the land belonged
to a powerful man

and an influential man lived on it.
9 You sent widows away
empty-handed,
and the strength of the fatherless
was crushed.
10 Therefore snares surround you,
and sudden dread terrifies you,
11 or darkness, so you cannot see,
and a flood of water covers you.

12 Isn't God as high as the heavens?
And look at the highest stars—
how lofty they are!
13 Yet you say: "What does God know?
Can He judge
through thick darkness?
14 Clouds veil Him so that
He cannot see,
as He walks on the circle
of the sky."
15 Will you continue
on the ancient path
that wicked men have walked?
16 They were snatched away
before their time,
and their foundations
were washed away by a river.
17 They were the ones who said
to God, "Leave us alone!"

and "What can the Almighty do
to us?"
18 But it was He who filled
their houses with good things.
The counsel of the wicked is
far from me!
19 The righteous see this
and rejoice;
the innocent mock them, saying,
20 "Surely our opponents
are destroyed,
and fire has consumed
what they left behind."

21 Come to terms with God and be
at peace;
in this way good will come to you.
22 Receive instruction
from His mouth,
and place His sayings
in your heart.
23 If you return to the Almighty,
you will be renewed.
If you banish injustice
from your tent
24 and consign your gold to the dust,
the gold of Ophir to the stones
in the wadis,
25 the Almighty will be your gold
and your finest silver.
26 Then you will delight in
the Almighty
and lift up your face to God.
27 You will pray to Him, and He will
hear you,
and you will fulfill your vows.
28 When you make a decision,
it will be carried out,
and light will shine on your ways.
29 When others are humiliated
and you say, "Lift them up,"
God will save the humble.
30 He will even rescue
the guilty one,
who will be rescued by the purity
of your hands.

23 Then Job answered:
2 Today also my complaint is bitter.
His hand is heavy
despite my groaning.
3 If only I knew how to find Him,
so that I could go to His throne.

4 I would plead my case before Him
and fill my mouth with arguments.
5 I would learn how He would
answer me;
and understand what
He would say to me.
6 Would He prosecute
me forcefully?
No, He will certainly pay attention
to me.
7 There an upright man
could reason with Him,
and I would escape from my Judge
forever.

8 If I go east, He is not there,
and if I go west, I cannot
perceive Him.
9 When He is at work to the north,
I cannot see Him;
when He turns south, I cannot
find Him.
10 Yet He knows the way
I have taken;
when He has tested me,
I will emerge as pure gold.
11 My feet have followed
in His tracks;
I have kept to His way and not
turned aside.
12 I have not departed
from the commands
of His lips;
I have treasured the words
of His mouth
more than my daily food.

13 But He is unchangeable; who can
oppose Him?
He does what He desires.
14 He will certainly accomplish
what He has decreed for me,
and He has many more things
like these in mind.
15 Therefore I am terrified
in His presence;
when I consider this, I am afraid
of Him.
16 God has made my heart faint;
the Almighty has terrified me.
17 Yet I am not destroyed
by the darkness,
by the thick darkness that covers
my face.

24

Why does the Almighty
not reserve times
for judgment?
Why do those who know Him
never see His days?
2 The wicked displace
boundary markers.
They steal a flock and provide
pasture for it.
3 They drive away the donkeys
owned by the fatherless
and take the widow's ox
as collateral.
4 They push the needy off the road;
the poor of the land are forced
into hiding.
5 Like wild donkeys in the desert,
the poor go out to their task
of foraging for food;
the wilderness provides
nourishment
for their children.
6 They gather their fodder
in the field
and glean the vineyards
of the wicked.
7 Without clothing, they spend
the night naked,
having no covering
against the cold.
8 Drenched by mountain rains,
they huddle against the rocks,
shelterless.
9 The fatherless infant is snatched
from the breast;
the nursing child of the poor
is seized as collateral.
10 Without clothing,
they wander about naked.
They carry sheaves but go hungry.
11 They crush olives in their presses;
they tread the winepresses,
but go thirsty.
12 From the city, men groan;
the mortally wounded cry
for help,
yet God pays no attention
to this crime.

PSALM 105:16-27

16 He called down famine against the
land

and destroyed the entire food
supply.
17 He had sent a man ahead of
them—
Joseph, who was sold as a slave.
18 They hurt his feet with shackles;
his neck was put in an iron collar.
19 Until the time his prediction came
true,
the word of the LORD tested him.
20 The king sent for him and
released him;
the ruler of peoples set him free.
21 He made him master of his
household,
ruler over all his possessions—
22 binding his officials at will
and instructing his elders.
23 Then Israel went to Egypt;
Jacob lived as a foreigner in the
land of Ham.
24 The LORD made His people very
fruitful;
He made them more numerous
than their foes,
25 whose hearts He turned to hate
His people
and to deal deceptively with His
servants.
26 He sent Moses His servant,
and Aaron, whom He had chosen.
27 They performed His miraculous
signs among them,
and wonders in the land of Ham.

PROVERBS 21:25-26

25 A slacker's craving will kill him
because his hands refuse to work.
26 He is filled with craving all day
long,
but the righteous give and don't
hold back.

1 CORINTHIANS 9:13–10:5

13 Do you not know that those who
perform the temple services eat the
food from the temple, and those who
serve at the altar share in the offerings
of the altar? 14 In the same way, the Lord

1035

has commanded that those who preach the gospel should earn their living by the gospel. [15] But I have used none of these rights, and I have not written this to make it happen that way for me. For it would be better for me to die than for anyone to deprive me of my boast! [16] For if I preach the gospel, I have no reason to boast, because an obligation is placed on me. And woe to me if I do not preach the gospel! [17] For if I do this willingly, I have a reward; but if unwillingly, I am entrusted with a stewardship. [18] What then is my reward? To preach the gospel and offer it free of charge, and not make full use of my authority in the gospel.

[19] For although I am free from all people, I have made myself a slave to all, in order to win more people. [20] To the Jews I became like a Jew, to win Jews; to those under the law, like one under the law—though I myself am not under the law—to win those under the law. [21] To those who are outside the law, like one outside the law—not being outside God's law, but under the law of Christ—to win those outside the law. [22] To the weak I became weak, in order to win the weak. I have become all things to all people, so that I may by all means save some. [23] Now I do all this because of the gospel, that I may become a partner in its benefits.

[24] Do you not know that the runners in a stadium all race, but only one receives the prize? Run in such a way that you may win. [25] Now everyone who competes exercises self-control in everything. However, they do it to receive a perishable crown, but we an imperishable one. [26] Therefore I do not run like one who runs aimlessly, or box like one who beats the air. [27] Instead, I discipline my body and bring it under strict control, so that after preaching to others, I myself will not be disqualified.

10 Now I want you to know, brothers, that our fathers were all under the cloud, all passed through the sea, [2] and all were baptized into Moses in the cloud and in the sea. [3] They all ate the same spiritual food, [4] and all drank the same spiritual drink. For they drank from a spiritual rock that followed them, and that rock was Christ. [5] But God was not pleased with most of them, for they were struck down in the desert.

Like a Fine-Tuned Violin

Do you not know that the runners in a stadium all race, but only one receives the prize? Run in such a way that you may win.—1 CORINTHIANS 9:24

What and how much we eat can greatly affect the way we feel. If the nerves are starved on account of a lack of vitamins, they will kick back in physical depression—exactly the same way that a starved soul or spirit will kick back in psychological depression. So discipline yourself to eat correctly and nutritionally.

Next, discipline yourself to take appropriate physical exercise. God designed our bodies for movement, and if they don't move, they get sluggish. Then what happens? A sluggish body contributes to a sluggish spirit.

Time and time again, when counseling people who are suffering with depression, I have recommended (along with other suggestions) that they take up physical exercise. One should not, of course, embark upon vigorous exercise, like playing racket ball or jogging, without having a medical check-up. But I have been surprised at how even a short, brisk walk can do wonders for the soul.

I feel a word of caution may be needed here, because many people in our culture are fast becoming exercise "freaks." It is possible to regulate the body too much! You should get enough exercise to remain fit, but also keep in mind that too much attention to exercise or sports may drain higher interests. Everything must be kept in balance: just enough food to keep you fit and not enough to make you fat; just enough sleep to keep you fresh and a little less than that which would make you lazy. We must keep our bodies like a fine-tuned violin, and then the music of God will come out from every fiber of our being.

Prayer

O God of my mind and my body, I come to You to have both of these brought under the control of Your redemption and Your guidance. May I pass on the health of my mind to my body and the health of my body to my mind. Amen.

Further Study

1 Kg 19:8; Php 3:1-16; Gl 2:2; Heb 12:1
What picture did Paul use in illustrating truth?
How much exercise do you take?

SEPTEMBER 4

JOB 24:13–27:23

13 The wicked are those who rebel
  against the light.
  They do not recognize its ways
  or stay on its paths.
14 The murderer rises at dawn
  to kill the poor and needy,
  and by night he becomes a thief.
15 The adulterer's eye watches
    for twilight,
  thinking: No eye will see me,
  he covers his face.
16 In the dark they break into houses;
  by day they lock themselves in,
  never experiencing the light.
17 For the morning is
    like death's shadow to them.
  Surely they are familiar
    with the terrors
    of death's shadow!

18 They float on the surface
    of the water.
  Their section of the land is cursed,
  so that they never go to their
    vineyards.
19 As dry ground and heat
    snatch away the melted snow,
  so Sheol steals those
    who have sinned.
20 The womb forgets them;
  worms feed on them;
  they are remembered no more.
  So injustice is broken like a tree.
21 They prey on the barren,
    childless woman
  and do not deal kindly
    with the widow.
22 Yet God drags away the mighty
    by His power;
  when He rises up, they have
    no assurance of life.

23 He gives them a sense of security,
　　so they can rely on it,
but His eyes watch
　　over their ways.
24 They are exalted for a moment,
　　then they are gone;
they are brought low and shrivel up
　　like everything else.
They wither like heads of grain.

25 If this is not true, then who
　　can prove me a liar
and show that my speech
　　is worthless?

25 Then Bildad the Shuhite replied:

2 Dominion and dread belong
　　to Him,
the One who establishes harmony
　　in the heavens.
3 Can His troops be numbered?
Does His light not shine
　　on everyone?
4 How can a person be justified
　　before God?
How can one born of woman
　　be pure?
5 If even the moon does not shine
and the stars are not pure
　　in His sight,
6 how much less man, who is
　　a maggot,
and the son of man, who is
　　a worm!

26 Then Job answered:

2 How you have helped
　　the powerless
and delivered the arm
　　that is weak!
3 How you have counseled
　　the unwise
and thoroughly explained
　　the path to success!
4 Who did you speak
　　these words to?
Whose breath came out of
　　your mouth?

5 The departed spirits tremble
beneath the waters and all that
　　inhabit them.

6 Sheol is naked before God,
and Abaddon has no covering.
7 He stretches the northern skies
　　over empty space;
He hangs the earth on nothing.
8 He enfolds the waters
　　in His clouds,
yet the clouds do not burst
　　beneath their weight.
9 He obscures the view of His
　　throne,
spreading His cloud over it.
10 He laid out the horizon
　　on the surface of the waters
at the boundary between light
　　and darkness.
11 The pillars that hold up
　　the sky tremble,
astounded at His rebuke.
12 By His power He stirred the sea,
and by His understanding
　　He crushed Rahab.
13 By His breath the heavens gained
　　their beauty;
His hand pierced
　　the fleeing serpent.
14 These are but the fringes
　　of His ways;
how faint is the word we hear
　　of Him!
Who can understand
　　His mighty thunder?

27 Job continued his discourse, saying:

2 As God lives, who has
　　deprived me of justice,
and the Almighty who has
　　made me bitter,
3 as long as my breath is still in me
and the breath from God remains
　　in my nostrils,
4 my lips will not speak unjustly,
and my tongue will not
　　utter deceit.
5 I will never affirm that you
　　are right.
I will maintain my integrity
　　until I die.
6 I will cling to my righteousness
　　and never let it go.
My conscience will not accuse me
　　as long as I live!

7 May my enemy be like the wicked
and my opponent like the unjust.
8 For what hope does
the godless man have when
he is cut off,
when God takes away his life?
9 Will God hear his cry
when distress comes on him?
10 Will he delight in the Almighty?
Will he call on God at all times?
11 I will teach you
about God's power.
I will not conceal
what the Almighty
has planned.
12 All of you have seen this
for yourselves,
why do you keep up
this empty talk?

13 This is a wicked man's lot
from God,
the inheritance the ruthless
receive from the Almighty.
14 Even if his children increase,
they are destined
for the sword;
his descendants will never
have enough food.
15 Those who survive him
will be buried by the plague,
yet their widows will not weep
for them.
16 Though he piles up silver like dust
and heaps up a wardrobe
like clay—
17 he may heap it up,
but the righteous will wear it,
and the innocent will divide up
his silver.
18 The house he built is
like a moth's cocoon
or a booth set up by a watchman.
19 He lies down wealthy, but will
do so no more;
when he opens his eyes,
it is gone.
20 Terrors overtake him like a flood;
a storm wind sweeps him away
at night.
21 An east wind picks him up,
and he is gone;
it carries him away from his place.
22 It blasts at him without mercy,

while he flees desperately
from its grasp.
23 It claps its hands at him
and scorns him from its place.

PSALM 105:28-36

28 He sent darkness, and it became
dark—
for did they not defy His
commands?
29 He turned their waters into blood
and caused their fish to die.
30 Their land was overrun with frogs,
even in their kings' chambers.
31 He spoke, and insects came—
gnats throughout their country.
32 He gave them hail for rain,
and lightning throughout their
land.
33 He struck their vines and fig trees
and shattered the trees of their
territory.
34 He spoke and locusts came—
young locusts without number.
35 They devoured all the vegetation
in their land
and consumed the produce of
their soil.
36 He struck all the firstborn in their
land,
all their first progeny.

PROVERBS 21:27-28

27 The sacrifice of a wicked person is
detestable—
how much more so when he
brings it with ulterior
motives!

28 A lying witness will perish,
but the one who listens will speak
successfully.

1 CORINTHIANS 10:6-24

6 Now these things became examples
for us, so that we will not desire evil as
they did. 7 Don't become idolaters as
some of them were; as it is written, **The
people sat down to eat and drink, and
got up to play.** 8 Let us not commit sex-

ual immorality as some of them did, and in a single day 23,000 people fell dead. [9] Let us not tempt Christ as some of them did, and were destroyed by snakes. [10] Nor should we complain as some of them did, and were killed by the destroyer. [11] Now these things happened to them as examples, and they were written as a warning to us, on whom the ends of the ages have come. [12] Therefore, whoever thinks he stands must be careful not to fall! [13] No temptation has overtaken you except what is common to humanity. God is faithful and He will not allow you to be tempted beyond what you are able, but with the temptation He will also provide a way of escape, so that you are able to bear it.

[14] Therefore, my dear friends, flee from idolatry. [15] I am speaking as to wise people. Judge for yourselves what I say. [16] The cup of blessing that we bless, is it not a sharing in the blood of Christ?

The bread that we break, is it not a sharing in the body of Christ? [17] Because there is one bread, we who are many are one body, for all of us share that one bread. [18] Look at the people of Israel. Are not those who eat the sacrifices partners in the altar? [19] What am I saying then? That food offered to idols is anything, or that an idol is anything? [20] No, but I do say that what they sacrifice, they sacrifice to demons and not to God. I do not want you to be partners with demons! [21] You cannot drink the cup of the Lord and the cup of demons. You cannot share in the Lord's table and the table of demons. [22] Or are we provoking the Lord to jealousy? Are we stronger than He?

[23] "Everything is permissible," but not everything is helpful. "Everything is permissible," but not everything builds up. [24] No one should seek his own good, but the good of the other person.

"Lord, Help Me"

God is faithful and He will not allow you to be tempted beyond what you are able.—1 CORINTHIANS **10:13**

One perspective on the phrase "Do not bring us into temptation" tells us that if we pray for the ability to recognize temptation when it comes our way, then we will be able to confront it and turn it to advantage.

Another interpretation explains that this is a prayer for us to be kept back from more temptation than we can cope with. It's like saying: "Lord, help us not to get involved in more temptation than we can handle." This view, as I am sure you can see at once, makes good sense and could well be what Jesus meant.

One of the biographers of an intrepid missionary tells how, in his early days in China, Hudson Taylor met with several great disappointments. One day, after a spate of troubles, he took hold of a guide who had demanded an outrageous fee from him, and shook him violently. A few hours later, he realized he had denied his Lord by this action, and after searching his heart for the reason why he had succumbed to anger and violence, he realized that he had been so preoccupied with his problems that he had failed to commit his ways to the Lord. His biographer says: "If Hudson Taylor had prayed the prayer, 'Lead us not into temptation,' and committed his ways to the Lord, then perhaps the Spirit would have been able to direct his path so that he would not have faced more temptation than he could bear."

It is an intriguing thought.

Prayer

Father, though the meaning of this phrase is not yet clear, one thing is—I need Your help at every stage of my earthly pilgrimage, for I cannot face temptation alone. So stay with me, every day and every hour. For Jesus' sake. Amen.

Further Study

Ac 5:1-11; Pr 1:10; 4:14; Rm 6:13
Why did Ananias and Sapphira yield to temptation?
What is Paul's antidote?

SEPTEMBER 5

JOB 28:1–30:8

28 Surely there is a mine for silver
and a place where gold
is refined.
2 Iron is taken from the ground,
and copper is smelted from ore.
3 A miner puts an end
to the darkness;
he probes the deepest recesses
for ore in the gloomy darkness.
4 He cuts a shaft far
from human habitation,
in places unknown to those
who walk above ground.
Suspended far away from people,
the miners swing back and forth.
5 Food may come from the earth,
but below the surface the earth
is transformed as by fire.
6 Its rocks are a source of sapphire,
containing flecks of gold.
7 No bird of prey knows that path;
no falcon's eye has seen it.
8 Proud beasts have never walked
on it;
no lion has ever prowled over it.
9 The miner strikes the flint

and transforms the mountains
at their foundations.
10 He cuts out channels in the rocks,
and his eyes spot every treasure.
11 He dams up the streams
from flowing
so that he may bring to light
what is hidden.

12 But where can wisdom be found,
and where is understanding
located?
13 No man can know its value,
since it cannot be found
in the land of the living.
14 The ocean depths say, "It's not
in me,"
while the sea declares, "I don't
have it."
15 Gold cannot be exchanged for it,
and silver cannot be weighed out
for its price.
16 Wisdom cannot be valued
in the gold of Ophir,
in precious onyx or sapphire.
17 Gold and glass do not compare
with it,
and articles of fine gold
cannot be exchanged for it.

1041

¹⁸ Coral and quartz are not
        worth mentioning.
     The price of wisdom
        is beyond pearls.
¹⁹ Topaz from Cush cannot compare
        with it,
     and it cannot be valued
        in pure gold.

²⁰ Where then does wisdom
        come from,
     and where is understanding
        located?
²¹ It is hidden from the eyes
        of every living thing
     and concealed from the birds
        of the sky.
²² Abaddon and Death say,
     "We have heard news of it
        with our ears."
²³ But God understands the way
        to wisdom,
     and He knows its location.
²⁴ For He looks to the ends
        of the earth
     and sees everything
        under the heavens.
²⁵ When God fixed the weight
        of the wind
     and limited the water by measure,
²⁶ when He established a limit
        for the rain
     and a path for the lightning,
²⁷ He considered wisdom
        and evaluated it;
     He established it
        and examined it.
²⁸ He said to mankind,
     "Look! The fear of the Lord—
        that is wisdom,
     and to turn from evil
        is understanding."

29 Job continued his discourse,
        saying:

² If only I could be as in months
        gone by,
     in the days when God
        watched over me,
³ when His lamp shone
        above my head,
     and I walked through darkness
        by His light!

⁴ I would be as I was in the days
        of my youth
     when God's friendship rested
        on my tent,
⁵ when the Almighty was still
        with me
     and my children were around me,
⁶ when my feet were bathed
        in cream
     and the rock poured out streams
        of oil for me!

⁷ When I went out to the city gate
     and took my seat
        in the town square,
⁸ the young men saw me
        and withdrew,
     while older men stood
        to their feet.
⁹ City officials stopped talking
     and covered their mouths
        with their hands.
¹⁰ The noblemen's voices
        were hushed,
     and their tongues stuck
        to the roof of their mouths.
¹¹ When they heard me,
        they blessed me,
     and when they saw me,
        they spoke well of me.
¹² For I rescued the poor man
        who cried out for help,
     and the fatherless child who had
        no one to support him.
¹³ The dying man blessed me,
     and I made the widow's heart
        rejoice.
¹⁴ I clothed myself in righteousness,
        and it enveloped me;
     my just decisions were like a robe
        and a turban.
¹⁵ I was eyes to the blind
     and feet to the lame.
¹⁶ I was a father to the needy,
     and I examined the case
        of the stranger.
¹⁷ I shattered the fangs of the unjust
     and snatched the prey
        from his teeth.

¹⁸ So I thought: I will die
     in my own nest
     and multiply my days
        as the sand.

¹⁹ My roots will have access
to water,
and the dew will rest
on my branches all night.
²⁰ My strength will be refreshed
within me,
and my bow will be renewed
in my hand.
²¹ Men listened to me
with expectation,
waiting silently for my advice.
²² After a word from me they did not
speak again;
my speech settled on them
like dew.
²³ They waited for me as for the rain
and opened their mouths as for
spring showers.
²⁴ If I smiled at them, they couldn't
believe it;
they were thrilled at the light
of my countenance.
²⁵ I directed their course
and presided as chief.
I lived as a king among his troops,
like one who comforts
those who mourn.

30 But now they mock me,
men younger than I am,
whose fathers I would have
refused to put
with my sheep dogs.
² What use to me was the strength
of their hands?
Their vigor had left them.
³ Emaciated from poverty
and hunger,
they gnawed the dry land,
the desolate wasteland by night.
⁴ They plucked mallow
among the shrubs,
and the roots of the broom tree
were their food.
⁵ They were expelled
from human society;
people shouted at them
as if they were thieves.
⁶ They are living on the slopes
of the wadis,
among the rocks and in holes
in the ground.
⁷ They bray among the shrubs;

they huddle beneath the thistles.
⁸ Foolish men,
without even a name!
They were forced to leave
the land.

PSALM 105:37-45

³⁷ Then He brought Israel out with
silver and gold,
and no one among His tribes
stumbled.
³⁸ Egypt was glad when they left,
for dread of Israel had fallen on
them.
³⁹ He spread a cloud as a covering
and gave a fire to light up the
night.
⁴⁰ They asked, and He brought quail
and satisfied them with bread
from heaven.
⁴¹ He opened a rock, and water
gushed out;
it flowed like a stream in the
desert.
⁴² For He remembered His holy
promise
to Abraham His servant.
⁴³ He brought His people out with
rejoicing,
His chosen ones with shouts of
joy.
⁴⁴ He gave them the lands of the
nations,
and they inherited what other
peoples had worked for.

⁴⁵ All this happened so that they
might keep His statutes
and obey His laws.
Hallelujah!

PROVERBS 21:29-31

²⁹ A wicked man puts on a bold face,
but the upright man considers his
way.

³⁰ No wisdom, no understanding,
and no counsel
will prevail against the LORD.

³¹ A horse is prepared for the day of
battle,

but victory comes from the LORD.

1 CORINTHIANS 10:25–11:16

²⁵ Eat everything that is sold in the meat market, asking no questions for conscience' sake, for ²⁶ **the earth is the Lord's, and all that is in it.** ²⁷ If one of the unbelievers invites you over and you want to go, eat everything that is set before you, without raising questions of conscience. ²⁸ But if someone says to you, "This is food offered to an idol," do not eat it, out of consideration for the one who told you, and for conscience' sake. ²⁹ I do not mean your own conscience, but the other person's. For why is my freedom judged by another person's conscience? ³⁰ If I partake with thanks, why am I slandered because of something for which I give thanks?

³¹ Therefore, whether you eat or drink, or whatever you do, do everything for God's glory. ³² Give no offense to the Jews or the Greeks or the church of God, ³³ just as I also try to please all people in all things, not seeking my own profit, but the profit of many, that they 11 may be saved. ¹ Be imitators of me, as I also am of Christ.

² Now I praise you because you remember me in all things and keep the traditions just as I delivered them to you. ³ But I want you to know that Christ is the head of every man, and the man is the head of the woman, and God is the head of Christ. ⁴ Every man who prays or prophesies with something on his head dishonors his head. ⁵ But every woman who prays or prophesies with her head uncovered dishonors her head, since that is one and the same as having her head shaved. ⁶ So if a woman's head is not covered, her hair should be cut off. But if it is disgraceful for a woman to have her hair cut off or her head shaved, she should be covered.

⁷ A man, in fact, should not cover his head, because he is God's image and glory, but woman is man's glory. ⁸ For man did not come from woman, but woman came from man; ⁹ and man was not created for woman, but woman for man. ¹⁰ This is why a woman should have a symbol of authority on her head: because of the angels. ¹¹ However, in the Lord, woman is not independent of man, and man is not independent of woman. ¹² For just as woman came from man, so man comes through woman, and all things come from God.

¹³ Judge for yourselves: Is it proper for a woman to pray to God with her head uncovered? ¹⁴ Does not even nature itself teach you that if a man has long hair it is a disgrace to him, ¹⁵ but that if a woman has long hair, it is her glory? For her hair is given to her as a covering. ¹⁶ But if anyone wants to argue about this, we have no other custom, nor do the churches of God.

Deadly Weapons

Whether you eat or drink, or whatever you do, do everything for God's glory.—1 CORINTHIANS **10:31**

Disregard for the physical aspect of life can greatly contribute to spiritual dryness. This means that a certain amount of discipline must be introduced into our lives. But what kind of discipline?

Firstly, we need discipline in what and how much we eat. Every meal should be a sacrament offered on the altar of fitter and finer living. Doctors tell us that excess food—as well as too little food—destroys brain power. What is in the stomach often determines what is in the head. Scripture says, "the kingdom of God is not eating and drinking" (Rm 14:17). But it is not a contradiction of that verse to say that often our food and drink determine our fitness for the kingdom of God.

Seneca, in an exaggerated statement made for the sake of emphasis, said, "Man does not die: he kills himself." Dr. R. L. Greene, a professor of chemistry and a specialist in nutrition, says, "The most deadly weapons used by man in committing suicide are the knife, fork, and spoon." You may be repelled at the idea of committing suicide—and so you should be—but you may well be contributing to your death by choosing wrong ways of eating.

We need discipline also to ensure that we get at least the minimum amount of vitamins. Vitamins are necessary to vitality; they are God's gift to us. The divine Chemist has designed our bodies to work in a certain way. And if we ignore His prescription for health, we reduce our physical effectiveness, which can also reduce our spiritual effectiveness.

Prayer

O Father, help me recognize that physical vitality contributes to spiritual vitality. May I respect the body You have given me and pay attention to the laws of health that You have built into the universe. In Jesus' name I pray. Amen.

Further Study

Pr 23:1-21; Ec 6:7; Php 3:19
How does the Scripture regard gluttony?
What is gluttony?

SEPTEMBER 6

JOB 30:9–31:40

9 Now I am mocked by their songs;
  I have become an object of scorn
    to them.
10 They despise me and keep
      their distance from me;
   they do not hesitate to spit
     in my face.
11 Because God has loosened my
      bowstring and oppressed me,
   they have cast off restraint
     in my presence.

12 The rabble rise up at my right;
     they trap my feet
   and construct their siege ramp
       against me.
13 They tear up my path;
   they contribute to my destruction,
     without anyone to help them.
14 They advance as through
      a gaping breach;
   they keep rolling in through
       the ruins.
15 Terrors are turned loose against me;
     they chase my dignity away
         like the wind,

and my prosperity has passed by
    like a cloud.

16 Now my life is poured out
    before my eyes,
and days of suffering
    have seized me.
17 Night pierces my bones,
and my gnawing pains never abate.
18 My clothing is distorted
    with great force;
He chokes me by the neck
    of my garment.
19 He throws me into the mud,
and I have become like dust
    and ashes.

20 I cry out to You for help, but You
    do not answer me;
when I stand up, You merely look
    at me.
21 You have turned against me
    with cruelty;
You harass me
    with Your strong hand.
22 You lift me up on the wind
    and make me ride it;
You scatter me in the storm.
23 Yes, I know that You will lead me
    to death—
the place appointed for all
    who live.

24 Yet no one would stretch out his
    hand
against a ruined man
when he cries out to him for help
because of his distress.
25 Have I not wept for those
    who have fallen
    on hard times?
Has my soul not grieved
    for the needy?
26 But when I hoped for good,
    evil came;
when I looked for light,
    darkness came.
27 I am churning within
    and cannot rest;
days of suffering confront me.
28 I walk about blackened, but not
    by the sun.
I stood in the assembly
    and cried out for help.

29 I have become a brother to jackals
and a companion of ostriches.
30 My skin blackens and flakes off,
and my bones burn with fever.
31 My lyre is used for mourning
and my flute for the sound
    of weeping.

31 I have made a covenant
    with my eyes.
How then could I look
    at a young woman?
2 For what portion would I have
    from God above,
or what inheritance
    from the Almighty on high?
3 Doesn't disaster come
    to the wicked
and misfortune to evildoers?
4 Does He not see my ways
and number all my steps?

5 If I have walked in falsehood
or my foot has rushed to deceit,
6 let God weigh me
    with an accurate balance,
and He will recognize
    my integrity.

7 If my step has turned
    from the way,
my heart has followed my eyes,
or impurity has stained my hands,
8 let someone else eat
    what I have sown,
and let my crops be uprooted.

9 If my heart has been seduced by
    my neighbor's wife
or I have lurked at his door,
10 let my own wife grind grain
    for another man,
and let other men sleep with her.
11 For that would be a disgrace;
it would be a crime
    deserving punishment.
12 For it is a fire that consumes
    down to Abaddon;
it would destroy my entire harvest.

13 If I have dismissed the case
    of my male or female servants
when they made a complaint
    against me,

14 what could I do when God
stands up to judge?
How should I answer Him
when He calls me
to account?
15 Did not the One who made me
in the womb also make them?
Did not the same God
form us both in the womb?

16 If I have refused the wishes
of the poor
or let the widow's eyes go blind,
17 if I have eaten
my few crumbs alone
without letting the fatherless
eat any of it—
18 for from my youth, I raised him
as his father,
and since the day I was born
I guided the widow—
19 if I have seen anyone dying
for lack of clothing
or a needy person without a cloak,
20 if he did not bless me
while warming himself
with the fleece
from my sheep,
21 if I ever cast my vote
against a fatherless child
when I saw that I had support
in the city gate,
22 then let my shoulder blade fall
from my back,
and my arm be pulled
from its socket.
23 For disaster from God
terrifies me,
and because of His majesty
I could not do these things.

24 If I placed my confidence in gold
or called fine gold my trust,
25 if I have rejoiced because
my wealth is great
or because my own hand
has acquired so much,
26 if I have gazed at the sun
when it was shining
or at the moon moving
in splendor,
27 so that my heart
was secretly enticed
and I threw them a kiss,

28 this would also be a crime
deserving punishment,
for I would have denied God above.
29 Have I rejoiced over
my enemy's distress,
or become excited when trouble
came his way?
30 I have not allowed my mouth
to sin
by asking for his life with a curse.
31 Haven't the members
of my household said,
"Who is there who has not
had enough to eat
at Job's table?"
32 No stranger had to spend
the night on the street,
for I opened my door
to the traveler.
33 Have I covered my transgressions
as others do
by hiding my guilt in my heart,
34 because I greatly feared
the crowds,
and the contempt of the clans
terrified me,
so I grew silent and would not
go outside?

35 If only I had someone to hear
my case!
Here is my signature;
let the Almighty answer me.
Let my Opponent compose His
indictment.
36 I would surely carry it
on my shoulder
and wear it like a crown.
37 I would give Him an account of all
my steps;
I would approach Him
like a prince.

38 If my land cries out against me
and its furrows join in weeping,
39 if I have consumed its produce
without payment
or shown contempt for its tenants,
40 then let thorns grow
instead of wheat
and stinkweed instead of barley.

The words of Job are concluded.

PSALM 106:1-12

1 Hallelujah!
Give thanks to the LORD, for He is good;
His faithful love endures forever.
2 Who can declare the LORD's mighty acts
or proclaim all the praise due Him?
3 How happy are those who uphold justice,
who practice righteousness at all times.

4 Remember me, LORD, when You show favor to Your people.
Come to me with Your salvation
5 so that I may enjoy the prosperity of Your chosen ones,
rejoice in the joy of Your nation,
and boast about Your heritage.

6 Both we and our fathers have sinned;
we have gone astray and have acted wickedly.
7 Our fathers in Egypt did not grasp the significance of Your wonderful works
or remember Your many acts of faithful love;
instead, they rebelled by the sea—the Red Sea.
8 Yet He saved them because of His name,
to make His power known.
9 He rebuked the Red Sea, and it dried up;
He led them through the depths as through a desert.
10 He saved them from the hand of the adversary;
He redeemed them from the hand of the enemy.
11 Water covered their foes;
not one of them remained.
12 Then they believed His promises
and sang His praise.

PROVERBS 22:1-2

22 A good name is to be chosen over great wealth;
favor is better than silver and gold.

2 The rich and the poor have this in common:
the LORD made them both.

1 CORINTHIANS 11:17-34

17 Now in giving the following instruction I do not praise you, since you come together not for the better but for the worse. 18 For, to begin with, I hear that when you come together as a church there are divisions among you, and in part I believe it. 19 There must, indeed, be factions among you, so that the approved among you may be recognized. 20 Therefore when you come together in one place, it is not really to eat the Lord's Supper. 21 For in eating, each one takes his own supper ahead of others, and one person is hungry while another is drunk! 22 Don't you have houses to eat and drink in? Or do you look down on the church of God and embarrass those who have nothing? What should I say to you? Should I praise you? I do not praise you for this!

23 For I received from the Lord what I also passed on to you: on the night when He was betrayed, the Lord Jesus took bread, 24 gave thanks, broke it, and said, "This is My body, which is for you. Do this in remembrance of Me."

25 In the same way He also took the cup, after supper, and said, "This cup is the new covenant in My blood. Do this, as often as you drink it, in remembrance of Me." 26 For as often as you eat this bread and drink the cup, you proclaim the Lord's death until He comes.

27 Therefore, whoever eats the bread or drinks the cup of the Lord in an unworthy way will be guilty of sin against the body and blood of the Lord. 28 So a man should examine himself; in this way he should eat of the bread and drink of the cup. 29 For whoever

eats and drinks without recognizing the body, eats and drinks judgment on himself. [30] This is why many are sick and ill among you, and many have fallen asleep. [31] If we were properly evaluating ourselves, we would not be judged, [32] but when we are judged, we are disciplined by the Lord, so that we may not be condemned with the world. [33] Therefore, my brothers, when you come together to eat, wait for one another. [34] If anyone is hungry, he should eat at home, so that you can come together and not cause judgment. And I will give instructions about the other matters whenever I come.

An Honest Look

So a man should examine himself.

—1 CORINTHIANS 11:28

An important step in bringing about a more perfect coordination between heart and mind is to take an honest, straightforward look at what is going on beneath the surface of your life.

I have often invited my readers to spend a few days taking an honest look at themselves. The reactions I have gotten to this suggestion have been quite interesting. Some Christians hear in my words a call to self-preoccupation and become concerned that I am pushing them toward becoming engrossed with their aches and pains.

One of my readers put it like this: "What people need is to forget about themselves and concentrate on reaching out to others; then their personal problems will quickly be forgotten." Others have taken an opposite position and said, "We need more of this, for our hearts are so self-deceived that unless we are constantly challenged in this way, we will never get through to a close relationship with God." I am unhappy about both those reactions, for both are unbalanced positions.

The first one fears that taking a look beneath the surface of our lives leads to unhealthy self-preoccupation. And the second opinion assumes that constant self-examination is the only way forward. But I believe an occasional, honest, straightforward look at what is going on beneath the surface of our lives contributes greatly to our spiritual progress , providing it is done in a proper and balanced way.

Prayer

O God, help me to see that in inviting me to examine myself, You are not seeking to demean me but to develop me; not to take away from my spiritual stature but to add to it. Make me an honest person—with You, with myself, with others. Amen.

Further Study

Lk 8:1-15; Ps 51:1-6; 15:1-2; Rm 8:27
Where does God require truth?
What must we allow God to do?

SEPTEMBER 7

JOB 32:1–33:33

32 So these three men quit answering Job, because he was righteous in his own eyes. ² Then Elihu son of Barachel the Buzite from the family of Ram became angry. He was angry at Job because he had justified himself rather than God. ³ He was also angry at Job's three friends because they had failed to refute him, and yet had condemned him.

⁴ Now Elihu had waited to speak to Job because they were all older than he. ⁵ But when he saw that the three men could not answer Job, he became angry.

⁶ So Elihu son of Barachel the Buzite replied:

I am young in years,
while you are old;
therefore I was timid and afraid
to tell you what I know.
⁷ I thought that age should speak
and maturity should teach
wisdom.
⁸ But it is a spirit in man
and the breath of the Almighty
that give him understanding.
⁹ It is not only the old
who are wise
or the elderly who understand
how to judge.
¹⁰ Therefore I say, "Listen to me.
I too will declare what I know."
¹¹ Look, I waited
for your conclusions;
I listened to your insights
as you sought for words.
¹² I paid close attention to you.
Yet no one proved Job wrong;
not one of you refuted
his arguments.
¹³ So do not claim,
"We have found wisdom;
let God deal with him, not man."

¹⁴ But Job has not directed
his argument to me,
and I will not respond to him
with your arguments.

¹⁵ Job's friends are dismayed and can
no longer answer;
words have left them.
¹⁶ Should I continue to wait
now that they are silent,
now that they stand there
and no longer answer?
¹⁷ I too will answer;
yes, I will tell what I know.
¹⁸ For I am full of words,
and my spirit compels me
to speak.
¹⁹ My heart is like unvented wine;
it is about to burst
like new wineskins.
²⁰ I must speak so that
I can find relief;
I must open my lips and respond.
²¹ I will be partial to no one,
and I will not give anyone
an undeserved title.
²² For I do not know how to give
such titles;
otherwise, my Maker
would remove me in an instant.

33 But now, Job, pay attention
to my speech,
and listen to all my words.
² I am going to open my mouth;
my tongue will form words
on my palate.
³ My words come from
my upright heart,
and my lips speak what they know
with sincerity.
⁴ The Spirit of God has made me,
and the breath of the Almighty
gives me life.
⁵ Refute me if you can.
Prepare your case against me;
take your stand.

6 I am just like you before God;
I was also pinched off
from a piece of clay.
7 Fear of me should not terrify you;
the pressure I exert against you
will be light.

8 Surely you have spoken
in my hearing,
and I have heard these very
words:
9 "I am pure, without transgression;
I am clean and have no guilt.
10 But He finds reasons
to oppose me;
He regards me as his enemy.
11 He puts my feet in the stocks;
He stands watch over
all my paths."

12 But I tell you that you are wrong
in this matter,
since God is greater than man.
13 Why do you take Him to court
for not answering anything
a person asks?
14 For God speaks time and again,
but a person may not notice it.
15 In a dream, a vision in the night,
when deep sleep falls on people
as they slumber on their beds,
16 He uncovers their ears
at that time
and terrifies them with warnings,
17 in order to turn a person from his
actions
and suppress his pride.
18 God spares his soul from the Pit,
his life from crossing the river
of death.
19 A person may be disciplined
on his bed with pain
and constant distress in his bones,
20 so that he detests bread,
and his soul despises his
favorite food.
21 His flesh wastes away to nothing,
and his unseen bones stick out.
22 He draws near the Pit,
and his life to the executioners.
23 If there is an angel on his side,
one mediator out of a thousand,
to tell a person what is right
for him

24 and to be gracious to him and say,
"Spare him from going down
to the Pit;
I have found a ransom,"
25 then his flesh will be healthier
than in his youth,
and he will return to the days
of his youthful vigor.
26 He will pray to God, and God
will delight in him.
That man will behold His face
with a shout of joy,
and God will restore
his righteousness to him.
27 He will look at men and say,
"I have sinned and perverted
what was right;
yet I did not get what I deserved.
28 He redeemed my soul
from going down to the Pit,
and I will continue to see
the light."
29 God certainly does all these things
two or three times to a man
30 in order to turn him back
from the Pit,
so he may shine with the light
of life.
31 Pay attention, Job, and listen
to me.
Be quiet, and I will speak.
32 But if you have something to say,
answer me;
speak, for I would like
to justify you.
33 If not, then listen to me;
be quiet, and I will teach
you wisdom.

PSALM 106:13-23

13 They soon forgot His works
and would not wait for His
counsel.
14 They were seized with craving in
the wilderness
and tested God in the desert.
15 He gave them what they asked for,
but sent a wasting disease among
them.

16 In the camp they were envious of
Moses

and of Aaron, the LORD's holy one.
¹⁷ The earth opened up and
swallowed Dathan;
it covered the assembly of Abiram.
¹⁸ Fire blazed throughout their
assembly;
flames consumed the wicked.

¹⁹ At Horeb they made a calf
and worshiped the cast metal
image.
²⁰ They exchanged their glory
for the image of a grass-eating ox.
²¹ They forgot God their Savior,
who did great things in Egypt,
²² wonderful works in the land of
Ham,
awe-inspiring deeds at the Red
Sea.
²³ So He said He would have
destroyed them—
if Moses His chosen one had not
stood before Him in the breach
to turn His wrath away from
destroying them.

PROVERBS 22:3-4

³ A sensible person sees danger and
takes cover,
but the inexperienced keep going
and are punished.

⁴ The result of humility is fear of
the LORD,
along with wealth, honor, and life.

I CORINTHIANS 12:1-20

12 About matters of the spirit: brothers, I do not want you to be unaware. ² You know how, when you were pagans, you were led to dumb idols—being led astray. ³ Therefore I am informing you that no one speaking by the Spirit of God says, "Jesus is cursed," and no one can say, "Jesus is Lord," except by the Holy Spirit.

⁴ Now there are different gifts, but the same Spirit. ⁵ There are different ministries, but the same Lord. ⁶ And there are different activities, but the same God is active in everyone and everything. ⁷ A manifestation of the Spirit is given to each person to produce what is beneficial:

⁸ to one is given a message
of wisdom through the Spirit,
to another, a message
of knowledge
by the same Spirit,
⁹ to another, faith
by the same Spirit,
to another, gifts of healing
by the one Spirit,
¹⁰ to another, the performing
of miracles,
to another, prophecy,
to another, distinguishing
between spirits,
to another, different kinds
of languages,
to another, interpretation
of languages.

¹¹ But one and the same Spirit is active in all these, distributing to each one as He wills.

¹² For as the body is one and has many parts, and all the parts of that body, though many, are one body—so also is Christ. ¹³ For we were all baptized by one Spirit into one body—whether Jews or Greeks, whether slaves or free—and we were all made to drink of one Spirit. ¹⁴ So the body is not one part but many. ¹⁵ If the foot should say, "Because I'm not a hand, I don't belong to the body," in spite of this it still belongs to the body. ¹⁶ And if the ear should say, "Because I'm not an eye, I don't belong to the body," in spite of this it still belongs to the body. ¹⁷ If the whole body were an eye, where would the hearing be? If the whole were an ear, where would be the sense of smell? ¹⁸ But now God has placed the parts, each one of them, in the body just as He wanted. ¹⁹ And if they were all the same part, where would the body be? ²⁰ Now there are many parts, yet one body.

Purity and Power

A manifestation of the Spirit is given to each person to produce what is beneficial.

—1 CORINTHIANS 12:7

Although Jesus told us that through the Holy Spirit's power, we would do greater works than He had performed, the truth is that we are just not availing ourselves of the divine resources. There are notable exceptions to what I am saying, but, by and large, this is the way it is in today's church. Paul says in 1 Thessalonians 1:5: "Our gospel [came] to you . . . in power, in the Holy Spirit, and with much assurance." At the center of that "power" and "assurance" was the Holy Spirit. These traits are largely lacking in much of modern Christianity, because too many of us lack a full encounter with the Holy Spirit.

Some years ago, when I was a pastor in the north of England, another minister in the town (a good friend of mine) said, "You preach about the Spirit's power, and I'll preach about the Spirit's purity. That way we will keep a balance in the lives of Christians in this town." I pondered what he said and came to the conclusion that such a procedure would produce lopsided Christians, for both congregations needed to hear of the Spirit's purity and power.

Today's churches can be divided into two camps—those where the purity aspect is emphasized and those where the power aspect is emphasized. If every church focused with equal emphasis on both these characteristics of the Spirit, we would witness a healthier body of believers. Purity is essential, but so is power. The Holy Spirit supplies both.

Prayer

O Spirit of purity and power, live in Your church as both. For I need purity to see my destiny and power to follow it. Give me equal measure. In Jesus' name. Amen.

Further Study

Ac 5:1-16; 1 Co 12; Gl 5:22-26
How did the early church learn about this power and purity?
What was the result?

SEPTEMBER 8

JOB 34:1–35:16

34 Then Elihu continued, saying:

2 Hear my words, you wise men,
and listen to me,
you knowledgeable ones.
3 Doesn't the ear test words
as the palate tastes food?
4 Let us judge for ourselves
what is right;
let us decide together
what is good.
5 For Job has declared,
"I am righteous,
yet God has deprived me
of justice.
6 Would I lie about my case?
My wound is incurable,
though I am
without transgression."
7 What man is like Job?
He drinks derision like water.
8 He keeps company with evildoers
and walks with wicked men.
9 For he has said,
"A man gains nothing
when he becomes God's friend."

10 Therefore listen to me, you men
of understanding.
It is impossible for God to do
wrong,
and for the Almighty to act
unjustly.
11 For He repays a person
according to his deeds,
and He bring his ways on him.
12 Indeed, it is true that God
does not act wickedly
and the Almighty does not
pervert justice.
13 Who gave Him authority
over the earth?
Who put Him in charge of
the entire world?
14 If He put His mind to it

and withdrew the spirit
and breath He gave,
15 every living thing would perish
together
and mankind would return
to the dust.

16 If you have understanding,
hear this;
listen to what I have to say.
17 Could one who hates justice
govern the world?
Will you condemn the mighty
Righteous One,
18 who says to a king,
"Worthless man!"
and to nobles, "Wicked men!"?
19 God is not partial to princes
and does not favor the rich
over the poor,
for they are all the work
of His hands.
20 They die suddenly in the middle
of the night;
people shudder, then pass away.
Even the mighty are removed
without effort.

21 For His eyes watch over
a man's ways,
and He observes all his steps.
22 There is no darkness,
no deep darkness,
where evildoers
can hide themselves.
23 God does not need to examine
a person further,
that one should approach Him
in court.
24 He shatters the mighty
without an investigation
and sets others in their place.
25 Therefore, He recognizes
their deeds
and overthrows them by night,
and they are crushed.
26 In full view of the public,

He strikes them
for their wickedness,

27 because they turned aside
from following Him
and did not understand any
of His ways

28 but caused the poor to cry out
to Him,
and He heard the outcry
of the afflicted.

29 But when God is silent,
who can declare Him guilty?
When He hides His face, who can
see Him?
Yet He watches over both
individuals and nations,

30 so that godless men
should not rule
or ensnare the people.

31 Suppose someone says to God,
"I have endured my punishment;
I will no longer act wickedly.

32 Teach me what I cannot see;
if I have done wrong, I won't
do it again."

33 Should God repay you
on your terms
when you have rejected His?
You must choose, not I!
So declare what you know.

34 Reasonable men will say to me,
along with the wise men
who hear me,

35 "Job speaks without knowledge;
his words are without insight."

36 If only Job were tested
to the limit,
because his answers are like those
of wicked men.

37 For he adds rebellion to his sin;
he scornfully claps
in our presence,
while multiplying his words
against God.

35 Then Elihu continued, saying:

2 Do you think it is just when you say,
"I am righteous before God"?

3 For you ask, "What does
it profit You,
and what benefit comes to me,
if I do not sin?"

4 I will answer you
and your friends with you.

5 Look at the heavens and see;
gaze at the clouds high above you.

6 If you sin, how does it affect God?
If you multiply your transgressions,
what does it do to Him?

7 If you are righteous, what do you
give Him,
or what does He receive
from your hand?

8 Your wickedness affects a person
like yourself,
and your righteousness another
human being.

9 People cry out because of
severe oppression;
they shout for help from the arm
of the mighty.

10 But no one asks, "Where is God
my Maker,
who provides us with songs
in the night,

11 who gives us more understanding
than the animals of the earth
and makes us wiser than the birds
of the sky?"

12 There they cry out,
but He does not answer,
because of the pride of evil men.

13 Indeed, God does not listen
to empty cries,
and the Almighty does not
take note of it—

14 how much less when
you complain
that you do not see Him,
that your case is before Him
and you are waiting for Him.

15 But now, because God's anger
does not punish
and He does not pay attention
to transgression,

16 Job opens his mouth in vain
and multiplies words
without knowledge.

*P*SALM 106:24-31

24 They despised the pleasant land
and did not believe His promise.

25 They grumbled in their tents
and did not listen to the LORD's
voice.

26 So He raised His hand against
    them with an oath
that He would make them fall in
    the desert
27 and would disperse their
    descendants among the
    nations,
scattering them throughout the
    lands.

28 They aligned themselves with Baal
    of Peor
and ate sacrifices offered to
    lifeless gods.
29 They provoked the LORD with their
    deeds,
and a plague broke out against
    them.
30 But Phinehas stood up and
    intervened,
and the plague was stopped.
31 It was credited to him as
    righteousness
throughout all generations to
    come.

*P*ROVERBS 22:5-6

5 There are thorns and snares on
    the path of the crooked;
the one who guards himself stays
    far from them.

6 Teach a youth about the way he
    should go;
even when he is old he will not
    depart from it.

I *C*ORINTHIANS
12:21–13:13

21 So the eye cannot say to the hand,
"I don't need you!" nor again the head
to the feet, "I don't need you!" 22 On the
contrary, all the more, those parts of the
body that seem to be weaker are necessary. 23 And those parts of the body that
we think to be less honorable, we
clothe these with greater honor, and our
unpresentable parts have a better presentation. 24 But our presentable parts
have no need of clothing. Instead, God
has put the body together, giving

greater honor to the less honorable,
25 so that there would be no division in
the body, but that the members would
have the same concern for each other.
26 So if one member suffers, all the
members suffer with it; if one member
is honored, all the members rejoice
with it.
27 Now you are the body of Christ,
and individual members of it. 28 And
God has placed these in the church:

    first apostles, second prophets,
        third teachers, next, miracles,
    then gifts of healing, helping,
        managing, various kinds
        of languages.
29 Are all apostles? Are all prophets?
    Are all teachers?
        Do all do miracles?
30 Do all have gifts of healing?
    Do all speak in languages?
    Do all interpret?

31 But desire the greater gifts. And I will
show you an even better way.

13 If I speak the languages of men
    and of angels,
        but do not have love,
    I am a sounding gong
        or a clanging cymbal.
2 If I have the gift of prophecy,
    and understand all mysteries
        and all knowledge,
    and if I have all faith,
        so that I can move mountains,
    but do not have love,
        I am nothing.
3 And if I donate all my goods
        to feed the poor,
    and if I give my body
        to be burned,
    but do not have love,
        I gain nothing.
4 Love is patient; love is kind.
    Love does not envy;
    is not boastful; is not conceited;
5 does not act improperly;
        is not selfish;
    is not provoked; does not keep
        a record of wrongs;
6 finds no joy in unrighteousness,
        but rejoices in the truth;

⁷ bears all things,
    believes all things,
   hopes all things, endures all things.

⁸ Love never ends.
   But as for prophecies,
    they will come to an end;
   as for languages, they will cease;
   as for knowledge, it will come
    to an end.

⁹ For we know in part,
   and we prophesy in part.

¹⁰ But when the perfect comes,
   the partial will come
    to an end.

¹¹ When I was a child, I spoke
    like a child,
   I thought like a child,
    I reasoned like a child.
   When I became a man, I put aside
    childish things.

¹² For now we see indistinctly,
    as in a mirror, but then
    face to face.
   Now I know in part, but then
    I will know fully,
    as I am fully known.

¹³ Now these three remain:
    faith, hope, and love.
   But the greatest of these is love.

Katargeo

When I was a child . . . I thought like a child, I reasoned like a child.
When I became a man, I put aside childish things.

—1 CORINTHAINS 13:11

Today we ask ourselves: how do we deal with those pushes from our past which tend to influence and control our present attitudes and reactions?

We must find how and where they began. They come especially from the early formative years of childhood. There we were subjected to influences, ideas, and experiences that helped to shape our expectations and attitudes to life. Many of these influences, ideas, and experiences were good—and this point must not be overlooked—but by the same token, many were bad. These negative things sometimes stay inside us and can become dictating forces in our lives. We need the help of the Holy Spirit to track down some of these hidden agendas, and we then need to deal with them in a mature and adult manner.

How do we do this? Look once again at the verse before us today: "When I became a man, I put aside childish things." The Greek word for "put away" is *katargeo*. It is an extremely strong word, meaning "to put away, to break a hold, finish it off, have done with, render inoperative."

Childhood agendas don't just fall away like the leaves fall off the trees in the autumn; we have to "put them away"—we have to *katargeo* them—and be finished with childish things. If the Holy Spirit has identified any hidden agendas in your life, then bring them to Him now and lay them at His feet. Decide to have done with them. Get out of the passenger seat and into the driving seat. Remember—with God, all things are possible.

Prayer

O Father, give me the victory over all the enemies that may be within me. *Katargeo* them—render them inoperative—once and for all. In Jesus' name. Amen.

SEPTEMBER 9

JOB 36:1–37:24

36 Then Elihu continued, saying:

2 Be patient with me a little longer,
    and I will inform you,
  for there is still more to be said
    on God's behalf.
3 I will get my knowledge from afar
  and ascribe righteousness
    to my Maker.
4 For my arguments are
    without flaw;
  one who has perfect knowledge is
    with you.

5 Yes, God is mighty,
    but He despises no one;
  He understands all things.
6 He does not keep
    the wicked alive,
  but He gives justice
    to the afflicted.
7 He does not remove His gaze
    from the righteous,
  but He seats them forever
    with enthroned kings,
  and they are exalted.

8 If people are bound with chains
  and trapped by the cords
    of affliction,
9 God tells them
    what they have done
  and how arrogantly
    they have transgressed.
10 He opens their ears to correction

and insists they repent
    from iniquity.
11 If they serve Him obediently,
  they will end their days
    in prosperity
  and their years in happiness.
12 But if they do not obey,
  they will cross the river of death
  and die without knowledge.

13 Those who have a godless heart
    harbor anger;
  even when God binds them,
    they do not cry for help.
14 They die in their youth;
  their life ends among
    male cult prostitutes.
15 God rescues the afflicted
    by afflicting them;
  He instructs them by means of
    their torment.

16 Indeed, He lured you
    from the jaws of distress
  to a spacious
    and unconfined place.
  Your table was spread
    with choice food.
17 Yet now you are obsessed
    with the judgment due
    the wicked;
  judgment and justice
    have seized you.
18 Be careful that no one lures you
    with riches;
  do not let a large ransom
    lead you astray.

19 Can your wealth or all your
physical exertion
keep you from distress?
20 Do not long for the night
when nations will disappear
from their places.
21 Be careful that you do not turn
to iniquity,
for that is why you
have been tested by affliction.
22 Look, God shows Himself exalted
by His power.
Who is a teacher like Him?
23 Who has appointed His way
for Him,
and who has declared, "You have
done wrong"?
24 Remember that you should praise
His work,
which people have sung about.
25 All mankind has seen it;
people have looked at it
from a distance.
26 Look, God is exalted
beyond our knowledge;
the number of His years
cannot be counted.
27 For He makes waterdrops
evaporate;
they distill the rain into its mist,
28 which the clouds pour out
and shower abundantly
on mankind.
29 Can anyone understand
how the clouds spread out
or how the thunder roars
from God's pavilion?
30 Look, He spreads His lightning
around Him
and covers the depths of the sea.
31 For He judges the nations
with these;
He gives food in abundance.
32 He covers His hands
with lightning
and commands it to hit its mark.
33 The thunder declares
His presence;
the cattle also,
the approaching storm.

37 My heart pounds at this
and leaps from my chest.

2 Just listen to His thunderous voice
and the rumbling that comes
from His mouth.
3 He lets it loose beneath
the entire sky;
His lightning to the ends
of the earth.
4 Then there comes
a roaring sound;
God thunders
with His majestic voice.
He does not restrain the lightning
when His rumbling voice
is heard.
5 God thunders marvelously
with His voice;
He does great things that
we cannot comprehend.
6 For He says to the snow,
"Fall to the earth,"
and the torrential rains,
His mighty torrential rains,
7 serve as His signature
to all mankind,
so that all men may know
His work.
8 The wild animals enter their lairs
and stay in their dens.
9 The windstorm comes
from its chamber,
and the cold
from the driving north winds.
10 Ice is formed by the breath
of God,
and watery expanses are frozen.
11 He saturates clouds
with moisture;
He scatters His lightning
through them.
12 They swirl about,
turning round and round
at His direction,
accomplishing everything
He commands them
over the surface
of the inhabited world.
13 He causes this to happen
for punishment,
for His land,
or for His faithful love.
14 Listen to this, Job.
Stop and consider God's wonders.

15 Do you know how God directs
His clouds
or makes their lightning flash?
16 Do you understand
how the clouds float,
those wonderful works of Him
who has perfect knowledge?
17 You whose clothes get hot
when the south wind brings calm
to the land,
18 can you help God spread out
the skies
as hard as a cast metal mirror?
19 Teach us what we should say
to Him;
we cannot prepare our case
because of our darkness.
20 Should He be told that I want
to speak?
Can a man speak
when he is confused?
21 Now men cannot even look
at the sun
when it is in the skies,
after a wind has swept through
and cleared them away.
22 Yet out of the north He comes,
shrouded in a golden glow;
awesome majesty surrounds Him.
23 The Almighty—we cannot
reach Him—
He is exalted in power!
In His justice and righteousness,
He will not oppress.
24 Therefore, men fear Him.
He does not look favorably on any
who are wise in heart.

PSALM 106:32-39

32 They angered the LORD at the
waters of Meribah,
and Moses suffered because of
them;
33 for they embittered his spirit,
and he spoke rashly with his lips.
34 They did not destroy the peoples
as the LORD had commanded
them,
35 but mingled with the nations
and adopted their ways.
36 They served their idols,

which became a snare to them.
37 They sacrificed their sons and
daughters to demons.
38 They shed innocent blood—
the blood of their sons and
daughters
whom they sacrificed to the idols
of Canaan;
so the land became polluted with
blood.
39 They defiled themselves by their
actions
and prostituted themselves by
their deeds.

PROVERBS 22:7-8

7 The rich rule over the poor,
and the borrower is a slave to the
lender.
8 The one who sows injustice will
reap disaster,
and the rod of his fury will be
destroyed.

I CORINTHIANS 14:1-25

14 Pursue love and desire spiritual
gifts, and above all that you may
prophesy. 2 For the person who speaks
in another language is not speaking to
men but to God, since no one understands him; however, he speaks mysteries in the Spirit. 3 But the person who
prophesies speaks to people for edification, encouragement, and consolation.
4 The person who speaks in another language builds himself up, but he who
prophesies builds up the church. 5 I
wish all of you spoke in other languages,
but even more that you prophesied. The
person who prophesies is greater than
the person who speaks in languages, unless he interprets so that the church
may be built up.
6 But now, brothers, if I come to you
speaking in other languages, how will I
benefit you unless I speak to you with a
revelation or knowledge or prophecy or
teaching? 7 Even inanimate things
producing sounds—whether flute or
harp—if they don't make a distinction
in the notes, how will what is played on

the flute or harp be recognized? [8] In fact, if the trumpet makes an unclear sound, who will prepare for battle? [9] In the same way, unless you use your tongue for intelligible speech, how will what is spoken be known? For you will be speaking into the air. [10] There are doubtless many different kinds of languages in the world, and all have meaning. [11] Therefore, if I do not know the meaning of the language, I will be a foreigner to the speaker, and the speaker will be a foreigner to me. [12] So also you—since you are zealous in matters of the spirit, seek to excel in building up the church.

[13] Therefore the person who speaks in another language should pray that he can interpret. [14] For if I pray in another language, my spirit prays, but my understanding is unfruitful. [15] What then? I will pray with the spirit, and I will also pray with my understanding. I will sing with the spirit, and I will also sing with my understanding. [16] Otherwise, if you bless with the spirit, how will the uninformed person say "Amen" at your giving of thanks, since he does not know what you are saying? [17] For you may very well be giving thanks, but the other person is not being built up. [18] I thank God that I speak in other languages more than all of you; [19] yet in the church I would rather speak five words with my understanding, in order to teach others also, than 10,000 words in another language.

[20] Brothers, don't be childish in your thinking, but be infants in evil and adult in your thinking. [21] It is written in the law:

By people of other languages
and by the lips of foreigners,
I will speak to this people;
and even then, they will not
listen to Me,

says the Lord. [22] It follows that speaking in other languages is intended as a sign, not to believers but to unbelievers. But prophecy is not for unbelievers but for believers. [23] Therefore if the whole church assembles together, and all are speaking in other languages, and people who are uninformed or unbelievers come in, will they not say that you are out of your minds? [24] But if all are prophesying, and some unbeliever or uninformed person comes in, he is convicted by all and is judged by all. [25] The secrets of his heart will be revealed, and as a result he will fall down on his face and worship God, proclaiming, "God is really among you."

"Praying in the Spirit"

I will pray with the spirit,
and I will also pray with my understanding.
—1 CORINTHIANS 14:15

What does it mean to pray "in the Spirit"? Here again, there is a good deal of misunderstanding among Christians as to the true meaning of this phrase.

There are times when one feels deeply affected emotionally as one prays, but this is not the meaning of the phrase "praying in the Spirit." It has no relationship to the emotions that we feel in prayer. I am not saying that feelings are unimportant in prayer; I am simply saying that I do not believe this is what Paul had in mind when he used the phrase "praying in the Spirit."

The "spirit" spoken of here is not the human spirit but the Holy Spirit. Some believe that "praying in the Spirit" takes place when we pray in other tongues, and although it can include that, I believe it is much more than that.

Prayer that is "in the Spirit" is prayer that is prompted and guided by the Spirit. One commentator puts it this way: "It means that the Holy Spirit directs the prayer, creates the prayer within us, and empowers us to offer it and to pray it."

Dr. Martyn Lloyd-Jones calls praying in the Spirit "the secret of true prayer" and goes on to say: "If we do not pray in the Spirit, we do not really pray." I would hesitate to make such a sweeping statement myself, but I would go so far as to say that if we do not know what it means to pray in the Spirit, our prayers will have little impact upon Satan and his forces.

Prayer

Dear Father, I have so much to learn about prayer that unless You take my hand and guide me, I can soon lose my way. Teach me how to enter the deeper levels of prayer. In Jesus' name. Amen.

Further Study

Rm 8:1-17, 26; Lk 11:13; 24:49
To what does the Spirit bear witness?
What was Christ's promise to His disciples?

SEPTEMBER 10

JOB 38:1–39:12

38 Then the LORD answered Job from the whirlwind. He said:

2 Who is this who obscures My counsel
    with ignorant words?
3 Get ready to answer Me like a man;
    when I question you,
        you will inform Me.
4 Where were you
        when I established the earth?
    Tell Me, if you have
        understanding.
5 Who fixed its dimensions?
        Certainly you know!
    Who stretched a measuring line
        across it?
6 What supports its foundations?
    Or who laid its cornerstone
7 while the morning stars
        sang together
    and all the sons of God shouted
        for joy?

8 Who enclosed the sea
        behind doors
    when it burst from the womb,
9 when I made the clouds
        its garment
    and thick darkness its blanket,
10 when I determined its boundaries
    and put its bars and doors
        in place,

11 when I declared: "You may come
this far, but no farther;
your proud waves stop here"?

12 Have you ever in your life
commanded the morning
or assigned the dawn its place,
13 so it may seize the edges
of the earth
and shake the wicked out of it?
14 The earth is changed as clay is
by a seal;
its hills stand out like the folds of
a garment.
15 Light is withheld from the wicked,
and the arm raised in violence
is broken.

16 Have you traveled to the sources
of the sea
or walked in the depths
of the oceans?
17 Have the gates of death
been revealed to you?
Have you seen the gates
of death's shadow?
18 Have you comprehended
the extent of the earth?
Tell Me, if you know all this.

19 Where is the road to the home
of light?
Do you know
where darkness lives,
20 so you can lead it back
to its border?
Are you familiar with the paths
to its home?
21 Don't you know? You were
already born;
you have lived so long!
22 Have you entered the place
where the snow is stored?
Or have you seen the storehouses
of hail,
23 which I hold in reserve for times
of trouble,
for the day of warfare and battle?
24 What road leads to the place
where light is dispersed?
Where is the source of
the east wind that spreads
across the earth?

25 Who cuts a channel
for the flooding rain
or clears the way for lightning,
26 to bring rain
on an uninhabited land,
on a desert with no human life,
27 to satisfy the parched wasteland
and cause the grass to sprout?
28 Does the rain have a father?
Who fathered the drops of dew?
29 Whose womb did the ice
come from?
Who gave birth to the frost
of heaven
30 when water becomes as hard
as stone,
and the surface
of the watery depths
is frozen?

31 Can you fasten the chains
of the Pleiades
or loosen the belt of Orion?
32 Can you bring out
the constellations
in their season
and lead the Bear and her cubs?
33 Do you know the laws of heaven?
Can you impose its authority
on earth?
34 Can you command the clouds
so that a flood of water
covers you?
35 Can you send out lightning bolts,
and they go?
Do they report to you:
"Here we are"?

36 Who put wisdom in the heart
or gave the mind understanding?
37 Who has the wisdom to number
the clouds?
Or who can tilt the water jars
of heaven
38 when the dust hardens
like cast metal
and the clods of dirt
stick together?

39 Can you hunt prey for a lioness
or satisfy the appetite
of young lions
40 when they crouch in their dens
and lie in wait within their lairs?

41 Who provides the raven's food
   when its young cry out to God
   and wander about for lack
      of food?

39 Do you know when
      mountain goats give birth?
   Have you watched the deer
      in labor?
2 Can you count the months
   they are pregnant
   so you can know the time
   they give birth?
3 They crouch down to give birth
   to their young;
   they deliver their newborn.
4 Their offspring are healthy
   and grow up
   in the open field.
   They leave and do not return.

5 Who set the wild donkey free?
   Who released the swift donkey
   from its harness?
6 I made the wilderness its home,
   and the salty wasteland
      its dwelling.
7 It scoffs at the noise of the village
   and never hears the shouts
      of a driver.
8 It roams the mountains
   for its pastureland,
   searching for anything green.
9 Would the wild ox be willing
   to serve you?
   Would it spend the night
      by your feeding trough?
10 Can you hold the wild ox
   by its harness to the furrow?
   Will it plow the valleys
      behind you?
11 Can you depend on it because of
   its strength?
   Would you leave it to do
      your hard work?
12 Can you trust the wild ox
   to harvest your grain
   and bring it
      to your threshing floor?

PSALM 106:40-48

40 Therefore the LORD's anger
   burned against His people,

and He abhorred His own
      inheritance.
41 He handed them over to the
      nations;
   those who hated them ruled
      them.
42 Their enemies oppressed them,
   and they were subdued under
      their power.
43 He rescued them many times,
   but they continued to rebel
      deliberately
   and were beaten down by their
      sin.

44 When He heard their cry,
   He took note of their distress,
45 remembered His covenant with
      them,
   and relented according to the
      abundance of His faithful
      love.
46 He caused them to be pitied
   before all their captors.

47 Save us, LORD our God,
   and gather us from the nations,
   so that we may give thanks to
      Your holy name
   and rejoice in Your praise.

48 May the LORD, the God of Israel,
   be praised
   from everlasting to everlasting.
   Let all the people say, "Amen!"
   Hallelujah!

PROVERBS 22:9-10

9 A generous person will be blessed,
   for he shares his food with the
      poor.

10 Drive out a mocker, and conflict
      goes too;
   then lawsuits and dishonor will
      cease.

1 CORINTHIANS 14:26–15:11

26 How is it then, brothers? Whenever you come together, each one has a

psalm, a teaching, a revelation, another language, or an interpretation. All things must be done for edification. ²⁷ If any person speaks in another language, there should be only two, or at the most three, each in turn, and someone must interpret. ²⁸ But if there is no interpreter, that person should keep silent in the church and speak to himself and to God. ²⁹ Two or three prophets should speak, and the others should evaluate. ³⁰ But if something has been revealed to another person sitting there, the first prophet should be silent. ³¹ For you can all prophesy one by one, so that everyone may learn and everyone may be encouraged. ³² And the prophets' spirits are under the control of the prophets, ³³ since God is not a God of disorder but of peace.

As in all the churches of the saints, ³⁴ the women should be silent in the churches, for they are not permitted to speak, but should be submissive, as the law also says. ³⁵ And if they want to learn something, they should ask their own husbands at home, for it is disgraceful for a woman to speak in the church meeting. ³⁶ Did the word of God originate from you, or did it come to you only?

³⁷ If anyone thinks he is a prophet or spiritual, he should recognize that what I write to you is the Lord's command. ³⁸ But if anyone ignores this, he will be ignored. ³⁹ Therefore, my brothers, be eager to prophesy, and do not forbid speaking in other languages. ⁴⁰ But everything must be done decently and in order.

15 Now brothers, I want to clarify for you the gospel I proclaimed to you; you received it and have taken your stand on it. ² You are also saved by it, if you hold to the message I proclaimed to you—unless you believed to no purpose. ³ For I passed on to you as most important what I also received:

that Christ died for our sins
    according to the Scriptures,
⁴ that He was buried,
    that He was raised
    on the third day
    according to the Scriptures,
⁵ and that He appeared to Cephas,
    then to the Twelve.
⁶ Then He appeared to
    over 500 brothers
    at one time,
    most of whom remain
    to the present,
    but some have fallen asleep.
⁷ Then He appeared to James,
    then to all the apostles.
⁸ Last of all, as to one
    abnormally born,
    He also appeared to me.

⁹ For I am the least of the apostles, unworthy to be called an apostle, because I persecuted the church of God. ¹⁰ But by God's grace I am what I am, and His grace toward me was not ineffective. However, I worked more than any of them, yet not I, but God's grace that was with me. ¹¹ Therefore, whether it is I or they, so we preach and so you have believed.

The God of All Grace

But by God's grace I am what I am.—1 CORINTHIANS 15:10

Is it any wonder that throughout the history of the Christian church, men and women have found the thought of grace so overwhelmingly wonderful that they seemed unable to get over it? Grace was the constant theme of their prayers, their preaching, their writing—and their hymns. Take this for example:

Great God of wonders, all Thy ways
Display the attributes divine;

But countless acts of pardoning grace
Beyond Thine other wonders shine;
Who is a pardoning God like Thee?
Or who has grace so rich and free?

Many have fought to uphold the truth of God's grace, accepting ridicule and loss of privilege as the price of their stand. Paul waged war against the legalists in the Galatian churches over this matter, and the battle to uphold this great truth has gone on ever since. Augustine fought it in the fourth and fifth centuries, as did the Reformers in the sixteenth.

I sense that the church once again is in danger of losing out to legalism as more and more Christians get caught up with doing rather than being. Talk to people about what they are doing, and they are with you at once; talk to them about who they are being (who they really are), and their attitude is one of deferential blankness.

The church of Jesus Christ is in a sad state when it can't say with conviction and meaning, as did the apostle Paul: "By the grace of God I am what I am."

Prayer

God of all grace, give me grace to feel my need of grace. And give me grace to ask for grace. Then give me grace to receive grace. And when grace is given to me, give me grace to use that grace. In Jesus' name I pray. Amen.

Further Study

2 Co 1:1-12; 6:1; Gl 2:21
Where was Paul's boast rooted?
What was Paul's warning to the Corinthians?

SEPTEMBER 11

JOB 39:13–40:24

13 The wings of the ostrich
flap joyfully,
but are her feathers and plumage
like the stork's?
14 She abandons her eggs
on the ground
and lets them be warmed
in the sand.
15 She forgets that a foot
may crush them

or that some wild animal
may trample them.
16 She treats her young harshly, as if
they were not her own,
with no fear that her labor
may have been in vain.
17 For God has deprived her
of wisdom;
He has not endowed her
with understanding.
18 When she proudly spreads
her wings,

she laughs at the horse
and its rider.

¹⁹ Do you give strength to the horse?
Do you adorn his neck
with a mane?
²⁰ Do you make him leap
like a locust?
His proud snorting fills one with
terror.
²¹ He paws in the valley and rejoices
in his strength;
He charges into battle.
²² He laughs at fear,
since he is afraid of nothing;
he does not run from the sword.
²³ A quiver rattles at his side,
along with a flashing spear
and a lance.
²⁴ He charges ahead
with trembling rage;
he cannot stand still
at the trumpet's sound.
²⁵ When the trumpet blasts,
he snorts defiantly.
He smells the battle
from a distance;
he hears the officers' shouts
and the battle cry.

²⁶ Does the hawk take flight
by your understanding
and spread its wings to the south?
²⁷ Does the eagle soar
at your command
and make its nest on high?
²⁸ It lives on a cliff where it spends
the night;
its stronghold is on a rocky crag.
²⁹ From there it searches for prey;
its eyes penetrate the distance.
³⁰ Its brood gulps down blood,
and wherever corpses lie,
it is there.

40 The LORD answered Job:

² Will the one who contends
with the Almighty
correct Him?
Let him who argues with God
give an answer.
³ Then Job answered the LORD:

⁴ I am so insignificant. How can I
answer You?
I place my hand over my mouth.
⁵ I have spoken once,
and I will not reply;
twice, but now
I can add nothing.

⁶ Then the LORD answered Job from
the whirlwind:

⁷ Get ready to answer Me
like a man;
When I question you, you will
inform Me.
⁸ Would you really challenge
My justice?
Would you declare Me guilty
to justify yourself?
⁹ Do you have an arm like God's?
Can you thunder with a voice
like His?

¹⁰ Adorn yourself with majesty
and splendor,
and clothe yourself with honor
and glory.
¹¹ Unleash your raging anger;
look on every proud person
and humiliate him.
¹² Look on every proud person
and humble him;
trample the wicked
where they stand.
¹³ Hide them together in the dust;
imprison them in the grave.
¹⁴ Then I will confess to you
that your own right hand
can deliver you.

¹⁵ Look at Behemoth,
which I made along with you.
He eats grass like an ox.
¹⁶ Look at the strength of his loins
and the power in the muscles
of his belly.
¹⁷ He stiffens his tail
like a cedar tree;
the tendons of his thighs
are woven firmly together.
¹⁸ His bones are bronze tubes;
his limbs are like iron rods.
¹⁹ He is the foremost
of God's works;

only his Maker can draw
the sword against him.
20 The hills yield food for him,
while all sorts of wild animals
play there.
21 He lies under the lotus plants,
hiding in the protection
of marshy reeds.
22 Lotus plants cover him
with their shade;
the willows by the brook
surround him.
23 Though the river rages,
Behemoth is unafraid;
he remains confident, even if
the Jordan surges up
to his mouth.
24 Can anyone capture him
while he looks on,
or pierce his nose with snares?

PSALM 107:1-9

1 Give thanks to the LORD, for He is
good;
His faithful love endures forever.
2 Let the redeemed of the LORD
proclaim
that He has redeemed them from
the hand of the foe
3 and has gathered them from the
lands—
from the east and the west,
from the north and the south.

4 Some wandered in the desolate
wilderness,
finding no way to a city where
they could live.
5 They were hungry and thirsty;
their spirits failed within them.
6 Then they cried out to the LORD in
their trouble;
He rescued them from their
distress.
7 He led them by the right path
to go to a city where they could
live.
8 Let them give thanks to the LORD
for His faithful love
and His wonderful works for the
human race.
9 For He has satisfied the thirsty

and filled the hungry with good
things.

PROVERBS 22:11-12

11 The one who loves a pure heart
and gracious lips—the king is his
friend.

12 The LORD's eyes keep watch over
knowledge,
but He overthrows the words of
the treacherous.

1 CORINTHIANS 15:12-34

12 Now if Christ is preached as raised
from the dead, how can some of you say,
"There is no resurrection of the dead"?
13 But if there is no resurrection of the
dead, then Christ has not been raised;
14 and if Christ has not been raised, then
our preaching is without foundation,
and so is your faith. 15 In addition, we are
found to be false witnesses about God,
because we have testified about God
that He raised up Christ—whom He did
not raise up if in fact the dead are not
raised. 16 For if the dead are not raised,
Christ has not been raised. 17 And if
Christ has not been raised, your faith is
worthless; you are still in your sins.
18 Therefore those who have fallen
asleep in Christ have also perished. 19 If
we have placed our hope in Christ for
this life only, we should be pitied more
than anyone.
20 But now Christ has been raised
from the dead, the firstfruits of those
who have fallen asleep. 21 For since
death came through a man, the resurrection of the dead also comes through
a man. 22 For just as in Adam all die, so
also in Christ all will be made alive.
23 But each in his own order: Christ, the
firstfruits; afterward, at His coming, the
people of Christ. 24 Then comes the end,
when He hands over the kingdom to
God the Father, when He abolishes all
rule and all authority and power. 25 For
He must reign until He puts all His enemies under His feet. 26 The last enemy

to be abolished is death. ²⁷ For **He has put everything under His feet.** But when it says "everything" is put under Him, it is obvious that He who puts everything under Him is the exception. ²⁸ And when everything is subject to Him, then the Son Himself will also be subject to Him who subjected everything to Him, so that God may be all in all.

²⁹ Otherwise what will they do who are being baptized for the dead? If the dead are not raised at all, then why are people baptized for them? ³⁰ Why are we in danger every hour? ³¹ I affirm by the pride in you that I have in Christ Jesus our Lord: I die every day! ³² If I fought wild animals in Ephesus with only human hope, what good does that do me? If the dead are not raised, **Let us eat and drink, for tomorrow we die.** ³³ Do not be deceived: "Bad company corrupts good morals." ³⁴ Become right-minded and stop sinning, because some people are ignorant about God. I say this to your shame.

A Position of Strength

Then comes the end, when He hands over the kingdom to God the Father, when He abolishes all rule and all authority and power.—1 Corinthians 15:24

If people are to live securely in this world, then they must cultivate a worldview. They must see the "big picture." Is this why Jesus, when laying down a pattern for prayer, taught His disciples to focus on the "big picture" of the kingdom of God? Whether it is or not, one thing is certain—when we start off in prayer, gripped by the certainty of God's coming kingdom, our prayers are launched from a position of strength.

Just as I was about to begin this page, a sales bulletin came in the mail, and on it were the words: "Get the idea—and all else follows." I thought to myself: When the idea is God's idea (the kingdom) then, indeed, all else follows. What if we were to begin our prayers, however, by focusing, not on the kingdom of God, but on the kingdoms of this world? We would receive very little motivation from such an action. Man-made empires come and go. Egypt came and went. Syria came and went. Babylon came and went. Greece came and went. Historians tell us that at least twenty-one former great civilizations are extinct. Earthly kingdoms go the way of all flesh.

The kingdom of God, however, unlike earthly kingdoms, is destined for success. Call it triumphalism if you like, but the eventual accomplishment of God's kingdom has more reliability about it than tomorrow's dawn. When our minds are permitted to focus on such a tremendous truth, it will not be long before the heart leaps up in confident, believing prayer.

Prayer

Father, I think I get the idea. When I focus my mind on the glory of Your coming kingdom, then, against such a wonderful backdrop, my prayers take on a new boldness and authority. "Get the idea, then all else follows." Thank You, Father. Amen.

Further Study

Ps 115:1-18; Php 2:10; Heb 1:8; Rv 11:15
How does the psalmist relate heaven and earth?
How can we help to bring the kingdom of heaven to earth?

SEPTEMBER 12

JOB 41:1–42:17

41 Can you pull in Leviathan
with a hook
or tie his tongue down
with a rope?
² Can you put a cord
through his nose
or pierce his jaw with a hook?
³ Will he beg you for mercy
or speak softly to you?
⁴ Will he make a covenant with you
so that you can take him as a slave
forever?
⁵ Can you play with him like a bird
or put him on a leash
for your girls?
⁶ Will traders bargain for him
or divide him
among the merchants?
⁷ Can you fill his hide
with harpoons
or his head with fishing spears?
⁸ Lay a hand on him.
You will remember the battle
and never repeat it!
⁹ Any hope of capturing him
proves false.
Does a person not collapse
at the very sight of him?
¹⁰ No one is ferocious enough
to rouse Leviathan;
who then can stand against Me?
¹¹ Who confronted Me, that I
should repay him?
Everything under heaven belongs
to Me.

¹² I cannot be silent about his limbs,
his power,
and his graceful proportions.
¹³ Who can strip off
his outer covering?
Who can penetrate
his double layer of armor?
¹⁴ Who can open his jaws,
surrounded by
those terrifying teeth?
¹⁵ His pride is in his rows
of scales,
closely sealed together.
¹⁶ One scale is so close to another
that no air can pass
between them.
¹⁷ They are joined to one another,
so closely connected they cannot
be separated.
¹⁸ His snorting flashes with light,
while his eyes are like the rays
of dawn.
¹⁹ Flaming torches shoot
from his mouth;
fiery sparks fly out!
²⁰ Smoke billows from his nostrils
as from a boiling pot
or burning reeds.
²¹ His breath sets coals ablaze,
and flames pour out of his mouth.
²² Strength resides in his neck,
and dismay dances before him.
²³ The folds of his flesh
are joined together,
solid as metal and immovable.
²⁴ His heart is as hard as a rock,
as hard as a lower millstone!

25 When Leviathan rises, the mighty
are terrified;
they withdraw because of his
thrashing.
26 The sword that reaches him
will have no effect,
nor will a spear, dart, or arrow.
27 He regards iron as straw,
and bronze as rotten wood.
28 No arrow can make him flee;
slingstones become like stubble
to him.
29 A club is regarded as stubble,
and he laughs at the whirring
of a javelin.
30 His undersides are
jagged potsherds,
spreading the mud
like a threshing sledge.
31 He makes the depths seethe
like a caldron;
he makes the sea
like an ointment jar.
32 He leaves a shining wake
behind him;
one would think the deep had
white hair!
33 He has no equal on earth—
a creature devoid of fear!
34 He surveys everything
that is haughty;
he is king over all
the proud beasts.

42 Then Job replied to the LORD:

2 I know that You can do anything
and no plan of Yours
can be thwarted.
3 You asked, "Who is this
who conceals My counsel
with ignorance?"
Surely I spoke about things
I did not understand,
things too wonderful for me to
know.
4 You said, "Listen now,
and I will speak.
When I question you, you will
inform Me."
5 I had heard rumors about You,
but now my eyes have seen You.
6 Therefore I take back my words
and repent in dust and ashes.

7 After the LORD had finished speaking to Job, He said to Eliphaz the Temanite: "I am angry with you and your two friends, for you have not spoken the truth about Me, as My servant Job has. 8 Now take seven bulls and seven rams, go to My servant Job, and offer a burnt offering for yourselves. Then My servant Job will pray for you. I will surely accept his prayer and not deal with you as your folly deserves. For you have not spoken the truth about Me, as My servant Job has." 9 Then Eliphaz the Temanite, Bildad the Shuhite, and Zophar the Naamathite went and did as the LORD had told them, and the LORD accepted Job's prayer.

10 After Job had prayed for his friends, the LORD restored his prosperity and doubled his previous possessions. 11 All his brothers, sisters, and former acquaintances came to his house and dined with him in his house. They offered him sympathy and comfort concerning all the adversity the LORD had brought on him. Each one gave him a *qesitah*, and a gold earring.

12 So the LORD blessed the latter part of Job's life more than the earlier. He owned 14,000 sheep, 6,000 camels, 1,000 yoke of oxen, and 1,000 female donkeys. 13 He also had seven sons and three daughters. 14 He named his first daughter Jemimah, his second Keziah, and his third Keren-happuch. 15 No women as beautiful as Job's daughters could be found in all the land, and their father granted them an inheritance with their brothers.

16 Job lived 140 years after this and saw his children and their children to the fourth generation. 17 Then Job died, old and full of days.

*P*SALM 107:10-16

10 Others sat in darkness
and gloom—
prisoners in cruel chains—
11 because they rebelled against
God's commands
and despised the counsel of the
Most High.

12 He broke their spirits with hard
labor;
they stumbled, and there was no
one to help.
13 Then they cried out to the LORD in
their trouble;
He saved them from their distress.
14 He brought them out of darkness
and gloom
and broke their chains apart.
15 Let them give thanks to the LORD
for His faithful love
and His wonderful works for the
human race.
16 For He has broken down the
bronze gates
and cut through the iron bars.

PROVERBS 22:13-14

13 The slacker says, "There's a lion
outside!
I'll be killed in the streets!"

14 The mouth of the forbidden
woman is a deep pit;
a man cursed by the LORD will fall
into it.

1 CORINTHIANS
15:35-58

35 But someone will say, "How are the
dead raised? What kind of body will
they have when they come?" 36 Foolish
one! What you sow does not come to
life unless it dies. 37 And as for what you
sow—you are not sowing the future
body, but only a seed, perhaps of wheat
or another grain. 38 But God gives it a
body as He wants, and to each of the
seeds its own body. 39 Not all flesh is
the same flesh; there is one flesh for
humans, another for animals, another
for birds, and another for fish. 40 There
are heavenly bodies and earthly bodies,
but the splendor of the heavenly bodies
is different from that of the earthly
ones. 41 There is a splendor of the sun,
another of the moon, and another of the
stars; for star differs from star in splendor. 42 So it is with the resurrection of
the dead:

Sown in corruption, raised in incorruption;
43 sown in dishonor, raised in glory;
sown in weakness,
raised in power;
44 sown a natural body,
raised a spiritual body.

If there is a natural body, there is also a
spiritual body. 45 So it is written: **The
first man Adam became a living being**; the last Adam became a life-giving
Spirit. 46 However, the spiritual is not
first, but the natural; then the spiritual.

47 The first man was from the earth
and made of dust;
the second man is from heaven.
48 Like the man made of dust,
so are those who are made
of dust;
like the heavenly man,
so are those
who are heavenly.
49 And just as we have borne
the image of the man
made of dust,
we will also bear the image
of the heavenly man.

50 Brothers, I tell you this: flesh and
blood cannot inherit the kingdom of
God, and corruption cannot inherit incorruption. 51 Listen! I am telling you a
mystery:

We will not all fall asleep,
but we will all be changed,
52 in a moment, in the twinkling
of an eye, at the last trumpet.
For the trumpet will sound,
and the dead will be raised
incorruptible,
and we will be changed.
53 Because this corruptible
must be clothed
with incorruptibility,
and this mortal must be clothed
with immortality.
54 Now when this corruptible
is clothed
with incorruptibility,
and this mortal is clothed
with immortality,

then the saying that is written
will take place:
**Death has been swallowed up
in victory.**
55 **O Death, where is your victory?
O Death, where is your sting?**
56 Now the sting of death is sin, and
the power of sin is the law.

57 But thanks be to God,
who gives us the victory
through our Lord Jesus Christ!

58 Therefore, my dear brothers, be steadfast, immovable, always excelling in the
Lord's work, knowing that your labor in
the Lord is not in vain.

Deep Trauma

*So the LORD blessed the latter part of Job's life
more than the earlier.*

—JOB 42:12

There are many "walking wounded" in the Christian church who have experienced some deep horror, such as physical beating, sexual abuse, or serious injury. The Holy Spirit yearns to heal you of these hurts, but He can only do so when you let Him.

For the Holy Spirit to be able to heal our deep hurts, we must be willing to part with the resentment that is often mixed up in them. When something traumatic happens to us, more often than not, we respond to it with a measure of self-pity and say, "Why should that have happened to me?" In whatever way you might justify the bitterness at the time, there must be a willingness to abandon all resentment before there can be a deep healing.

This is what I mean when I say that the Holy Spirit will heal your hurts—if you let Him. He can't bring healing where there is bitterness. That would be like healing over a boil. When you truly part with the bitterness, however, then I assure you, a deep healing will begin.

Have you heard the story of Joni Eareckson Tada? Young, beautiful, vivacious, she had a diving accident that resulted in paralysis. She is now a quadriplegic. She paints pictures with a brush held between her teeth. Her witness has become worldwide. At first she was angry and bitter, but one day she let go of the bitterness and experienced inner healing. Outside she remained the same, but inside she was made anew.

Prayer

Blessed Holy Spirit, I see that when I hold onto bitterness and resentment, I succeed only in blocking Your healing power. I surrender every resentment, every ounce of self-pity, into Your hands, and receive in its place complete healing. Amen.

Further Study

Gn 41:51; Jb 42; Heb 12:15; Eph 4:31; Dt 32:32; Ac 8:23
What was Job's confession?
When did God bring good out of Job's calamity?

SEPTEMBER 13

ECCLESIASTES 1:1–3:8

1 The words of the Teacher, son of David, king in Jerusalem.

2 "Absolute futility,"
   says the Teacher.
"Absolute futility. Everything
   is futile."
3 What does a man gain for all
   his efforts
he labors at under the sun?
4 A generation goes
   and a generation comes,
but the earth remains forever.
5 The sun rises and the sun sets;
panting, it returns to its place
where it rises.
6 Gusting to the south,
turning to the north,
turning, turning, goes the wind,
and the wind returns in its cycles.
7 All the streams flow to the sea,
yet the sea is never full.
The streams are flowing
   to the place,
and they flow there again.
8 All things are wearisome;
man is unable to speak.
The eye is not satisfied by seeing
or the ear filled with hearing.
9 What has been is what will be,
and what has been done is
   what will be done;
there is nothing new under the sun.
10 Can one say about anything,
"Look, this is new"?
It has already existed in the ages
   before us.
11 There is no memory of those who
   came before;
and of those who will come after
there will also be no memory
among those who follow them.

12 I, the Teacher, have been king over Israel in Jerusalem. 13 I applied my mind to seek and explore through wisdom all that is done under heaven. God has given people this miserable task to keep them occupied. 14 I have seen all the things that are done under the sun and have found everything to be futile, a pursuit of the wind.

15 What is crooked cannot
      be straightened;
   what is lacking cannot be counted.

16 I said to myself, "Look, I have amassed wisdom far beyond all those who were over Jerusalem before me, and my mind has thoroughly grasped wisdom and knowledge." 17 I applied my mind to know wisdom and knowledge, madness and folly; I learned that this too is a pursuit of the wind.

18 For with much wisdom is
      much sorrow;
   as knowledge increases,
      grief increases.

2 I said to myself, "Go ahead, I will test you with pleasure and enjoy what is good." But it turned out to be futile. 2 I said about laughter, "It is madness," and about pleasure, "What does this accomplish?" 3 I explored with my mind how to let my body enjoy life with wine and how to grasp folly—my mind still guiding me with wisdom—until I could see what is good for people to do under heaven during the few days of their lives.

4 I increased my achievements. I built houses and planted vineyards for myself. 5 I made gardens and parks for myself and planted every kind of fruit tree in them. 6 I constructed reservoirs of water for myself from which to irrigate a grove of flourishing trees. 7 I acquired male and female servants and had slaves who were born in my house. I also owned

many herds of cattle and flocks, more than all who were before me in Jerusalem. [8] I also amassed silver and gold for myself, and the treasure of kings and provinces. I gathered male and female singers for myself, and many concubines, the delights of men. [9] Thus, I became great and surpassed all who were before me in Jerusalem; my wisdom also remained with me. [10] All that my eyes desired, I did not deny them. I did not refuse myself any pleasure, for I took pleasure in all my struggles. This was my reward for all my struggles. [11] When I considered all that I had accomplished and what I had labored to achieve, I found everything to be futile and a pursuit of the wind. There was nothing to be gained under the sun.

[12] Then I turned to consider wisdom, madness, and folly, for what will the man be like who comes after the king? He will do what has already been done. [13] And I realized that there is an advantage to wisdom over folly, like the advantage of light over darkness.

[14] The wise man has eyes
          in his head,
      but the fool walks in darkness.

Yet I also knew that one fate comes to them both. [15] So I said to myself, "What happens to the fool will also happen to me. Why then have I been overly wise?" And I said to myself that this is also futile. [16] For, just like the fool, there is no lasting remembrance of the wise man, since in the days to come both will be forgotten. How is it that the wise man dies just like the fool? [17] Therefore, I hated life because the work that was done under the sun was distressing to me. For everything is futile and a pursuit of the wind.

[18] I hated all my work at which I labored under the sun because I must leave it to the man who comes after me. [19] And who knows whether he will be a wise man or a fool? Yet he will take over all my work that I labored at skillfully under the sun. This too is futile. [20] So I began to give myself over to despair concerning all my work I had labored at

under the sun. [21] For there is a man whose work was done with wisdom, knowledge, and skill, but he must give his portion to a man who has not worked for it. This too is futile and a great wrong. [22] For what does a man get with all his work and all his efforts that he labors with under the sun? [23] For all his days are filled with grief, and his occupation is sorrowful; even at night, his mind does not rest. This too is futile.

[24] There is nothing better for man than to eat, drink, and to enjoy his work. I have seen that even this is from God's hand. [25] For who can eat and who can enjoy life apart from Him? [26] For to the man who is pleasing in His sight, He gives wisdom, knowledge, and joy, but to the sinner He gives the task of gathering and accumulating in order to give to the one who is pleasing in God's sight. This too is futile and a pursuit of the wind.

3 There is an occasion for everything, and a time for every activity
          under heaven:
[2] a time to give birth and a time
          to die;
      a time to plant and a time
          to uproot;
[3] a time to kill and a time to heal;
      a time to tear down and a time
          to build;
[4] a time to weep and a time
          to laugh;
      a time to mourn and a time
          to dance;
[5] a time to throw stones and a time
          to gather stones;
      a time to embrace and a time
          to avoid embracing;
[6] a time to search and a time
          to count as lost;
      a time to keep and a time
          to throw away;
[7] a time to tear and a time
          to sew;
      a time to be silent and a time
          to speak;
[8] a time to love and a time
          to hate;
      a time for war and a time
          for peace.

PSALM 107:17-22

17 Fools suffered affliction
because of their rebellious ways
and their sins.
18 They loathed all food
and came near the gates of death.
19 Then they cried out to the LORD in
their trouble;
He saved them from their distress.
20 He sent His word and healed
them;
He rescued them from the Pit.
21 Let them give thanks to the LORD
for His faithful love
and His wonderful works for the
human race.
22 Let them offer sacrifices of
thanksgiving
and announce His works with
shouts of joy.

PROVERBS 22:15-16

15 Foolishness is tangled up in the
heart of a youth;
the rod of discipline will drive it
away from him.

16 Oppressing the poor to enrich
oneself,
and giving to the rich—both lead
only to poverty.

1 CORINTHIANS 16:1-24

16 Now about the collection for the
saints: you should do the same as
I instructed the Galatian churches. 2 On
the first day of the week, each of you is
to set something aside and save to the
extent that he prospers, so that no collections will need to be made when I
come. 3 And when I arrive, I will send
those whom you recommend by letter
to carry your gracious gift to Jerusalem.
4 If it is also suitable for me to go, they
will travel with me.
5 I will come to you after I pass
through Macedonia—for I will be traveling through Macedonia— 6 and perhaps
I will remain with you, or even spend
the winter, that you may send me on my
way wherever I go. 7 I don't want to see
you now just in passing, for I hope to
spend some time with you, if the Lord
allows. 8 But I will stay in Ephesus until
Pentecost, 9 because a wide door for effective ministry has opened for me—yet
many oppose me. 10 If Timothy comes,
see that he has nothing to fear from you,
because he is doing the Lord's work, just
as I am. 11 Therefore no one should look
down on him; but you should send him
on his way in peace so he can come to
me, for I am expecting him with the
brothers.
12 About our brother Apollos: I strongly urged him to come to you with the
brothers, but he was not at all willing to
come now. However, when he has time,
he will come.
13 Be alert, stand firm in the faith, be
brave and strong. 14 Your every action
must be done with love.
15 Brothers, you know the household
of Stephanas: they are the firstfruits of
Achaia and have devoted themselves
to serving the saints. I urge you 16 also
to submit to such people, and to everyone who works and labors with them.
17 I am delighted over the presence of
Stephanas, Fortunatus, and Achaicus,
because these men have made up for
your absence. 18 For they have refreshed
my spirit and yours. Therefore recognize such people.
19 The churches of the Asian province
greet you. Aquila and Priscilla greet you
heartily in the Lord, along with the
church that meets in their home. 20 All
the brothers greet you. Greet one another with a holy kiss.
21 This greeting is in my own hand—
Paul. 22 If anyone does not love the Lord,
a curse be on him. *Maranatha!* 23 The
grace of our Lord Jesus be with you.
24 My love be with all of you in Christ
Jesus.

"Don't Adjust Your Life"

There is nothing new under the sun.

—ECCLESIASTES 1:9

It is surprising how many Christians have never read the book of Ecclesiastes. One woman told me that Ecclesiastes was the one book in the Bible she could not read. "I am put off by all that pessimism and gloom," she explained. There is, however a purpose behind this pessimism and gloom. Dr. Cynddylan Jones, a famous Welsh preacher, put it like this: "No Christian will be ready to open himself up to God until he has been gripped, as Ecclesiastes was gripped, by the emptiness and pointlessness of life. It is only when we see, and see clearly, that life is not to be found in the world that we will be ready to move closer toward God."

It is interesting to observe that most philosophers, when they look reality in the face, come to the same conclusion as Solomon. Malcolm Muggeridge, for example, in the days before he found God, saw the world as "an interminable soap opera." Some graffiti found on the walls of Bath University was even more to the point: "Do not adjust your life, the fault lies in reality."

One of the reasons, I believe, that Solomon used such vivid illustrations is in order to break through our defensive attempts to avoid reality. Life "under the sun," he has told us, can be boring, fleeting, repetitive, and empty. Life will never be meaningful "under the sun" until we make contact with the One who is above the sun. Those who try to find meaning without living their lives to the Creator inevitably see life as an "interminable soap opera." Is it any wonder?

Prayer

Gracious and loving Father, wean me off any idea I may have that life can be found "under the sun." Grant that I might be gripped by the truth that life, real life, is never found in the horizontal but in the vertical. In You. Amen.

Further Study

Is 55:1-13; Jn 4:13-14
What question does Isaiah ask?
What remedy does he advocate?

SEPTEMBER 14

*E*CCLESIASTES 3:9–6:12

⁹ What does the worker gain from his struggles? ¹⁰ I have seen the task that God has given people to keep them occupied. ¹¹ He has made everything appropriate in its time. He has also put eternity in their hearts, but man cannot discover the work God has done from beginning to end. ¹² I know that there is nothing better for them than to rejoice and enjoy the good life. ¹³ It is also the gift of God whenever anyone eats, drinks, and enjoys all his efforts. ¹⁴ I know that all God does will last forever; there is no adding to it or taking from it. God works so that people will be in awe of Him. ¹⁵ Whatever is, has already been, and whatever will be, already is. God repeats what has passed.

¹⁶ I also observed under the sun: there is wickedness at the place of judgment and there is wickedness at the place of righteousness. ¹⁷ I said to myself, "God will judge the righteous and the wicked, since there is a time for every activity and every work." ¹⁸ I said to myself, "This happens concerning people, so that God may test them and they may see for themselves that they are like animals." ¹⁹ For the fate of people and the fate of animals is the same. As one dies, so dies the other; they all have the same breath. People have no advantage over animals, for everything is futile. ²⁰ All are going to the same place; all come from dust, and all return to dust. ²¹ Who knows if the spirit of people rises upward and the spirit of animals goes downward to the earth? ²² I have seen that there is nothing better than for a person to enjoy his activities, because that is his reward. For who can enable him to see what will happen after he dies?

4 Again, I observed all the acts of oppression being done under the sun.

Look at the tears of those who are oppressed; they have no one to comfort them. Power is with those who oppress them; they have no one to comfort them. ² So I admired the dead, who have already died, more than the living, who are still alive. ³ But better than either of them is the one who has not yet existed, who has not seen the evil activity that is done under the sun.

⁴ I saw that all labor and all skillful work is due to a man's jealousy of his friend. This too is futile and a pursuit of the wind.

⁵ The fool folds his arms
  and consumes his own flesh.
⁶ Better one handful with rest,
  than two handfuls with effort
    and pursuit of the wind.

⁷ Again, I saw futility under the sun: ⁸ There is a person without a companion, without even a son or brother, and though there is no end to all his struggles, his eyes are still not content with riches. "So who am I struggling for," he asks, "and depriving myself from good?" This too is futile and a miserable task.

⁹ Two are better than one because they have a good reward for their efforts. ¹⁰ For if either falls, his companion can lift him up; but pity the one who falls without another to lift him up. ¹¹ Also, if two lie down together, they can keep warm; but how can one person alone keep warm? ¹² And if somebody overpowers one person, two can resist him. A cord of three strands is not easily broken.

¹³ Better is a poor but wise youth than an old but foolish king who no longer pays attention to warnings. ¹⁴ For he came from prison to be king, even though he was born poor in his kingdom. ¹⁵ I saw all the living who move

about under the sun follow a second youth who succeeds him. ¹⁶There is no limit to all the people who were before them, yet those who come later will not rejoice in him. This too is futile and a pursuit of the wind.

5 Guard your step when you go to the house of God. Better to draw near in obedience than to offer the sacrifice as fools do, for they are ignorant and do wrong. ²Do not be hasty to speak, and do not be impulsive to make a speech before God. God is in heaven and you are on earth, so let your words be few. ³For dreams result from much work and a fool's voice from many words. ⁴When you make a vow to God, don't delay fulfilling it, because He does not delight in fools. Fulfill what you vow. ⁵Better that you do not vow than that you vow and not fulfill it. ⁶Do not let your mouth bring guilt on you, and do not say in the presence of the messenger that it was a mistake. Why should God be angry with your words and destroy the work of your hands? ⁷For many dreams bring futility, also many words. So, fear God.

⁸If you see oppression of the poor and perversion of justice and righteousness in the province, don't be astonished at the situation, because one official protects another official, and higher officials protect them. ⁹The profit from the land is taken by all; the king is served by the field.

¹⁰The one who loves money is never satisfied with money, and whoever loves wealth is never satisfied with income. This too is futile. ¹¹When good things increase, the ones who consume them multiply; what, then, is the profit to the owner, except to gaze at them with his eyes? ¹²The sleep of the worker is sweet, whether he eats little or much; but the abundance of the rich permits him no sleep.

¹³There is a sickening tragedy I have seen under the sun: wealth kept by its owner to his harm. ¹⁴That wealth was lost in a bad venture, so when he fathered a son, he was empty-handed. ¹⁵As he came from his mother's womb, so he will go again, naked as he came;

he will take nothing for his efforts that he can carry in his hands. ¹⁶This too is a sickening tragedy: exactly as he comes, so he will go. What does he gain who struggles for the wind? ¹⁷What is more, he eats in darkness all his days, with much sorrow, sickness, and anger.

¹⁸Here is what I have seen to be good: it is appropriate to eat, drink, and experience good in all the labor one does under the sun during the few days of his life God has given him, because that is his reward. ¹⁹God has also given riches and wealth to every man, and He has allowed him to enjoy them, take his reward, and rejoice in his labor. This is a gift of God, ²⁰for he does not often consider the days of his life because God keeps him occupied with the joy of his heart.

6 Here is a tragedy I have observed under the sun, and it weighs heavily on humanity: ²God gives a man riches, wealth, and honor so that he lacks nothing of all he desires for himself, but God does not allow him to enjoy them. Instead, a stranger will enjoy them. This is futile and a sickening tragedy. ³A man may father a hundred children and live many years. No matter how long he lives, if he is not satisfied by good things and does not even have a proper burial, I say that a stillborn child is better off than he. ⁴For he comes in futility and he goes in darkness, and his name is shrouded in darkness. ⁵Though a stillborn child does not see the sun and is not conscious, it has more rest than he. ⁶And if he lives a thousand years twice, but does not experience happiness, do not both go to the same place?

⁷　All man's labor is for his stomach,
　　yet the appetite is never satisfied.

⁸What advantage then does the wise man have over the fool? What advantage is there for the poor person who knows how to conduct himself before others? ⁹Better what the eyes see than wandering desire. This too is futile and a pursuit of the wind.

[10] Whatever exists was given its name long ago, and who man is, is known. But he is not able to contend with the One stronger than he. [11] For when there are many words, they increase futility. What is the advantage for man? [12] For who knows what is good for man in life, in the few days of his futile life that he spends like a shadow? Who can tell man what will happen after him under the sun?

PSALM 107:23-32

[23] Others went to sea in ships,
conducting trade on the vast
waters.
[24] They saw the LORD's works,
His wonderful works in the deep.
[25] He spoke and raised a tempest
that stirred up the waves of the
sea.
[26] Rising up to the sky, sinking down
to the depths,
their courage melting away in
anguish,
[27] they reeled and staggered like
drunken men,
and all their skill was useless.
[28] Then they cried out to the LORD in
their trouble,
and He brought them out of their
distress.
[29] He stilled the storm to a murmur,
and the waves of the sea were
hushed.
[30] They rejoiced when the waves
grew quiet.
Then He guided them to the
harbor they longed for.
[31] Let them give thanks to the LORD
for His faithful love
and His wonderful works for the
human race.
[32] Let them exalt Him in the
assembly of the people
and praise Him in the council of
the elders.

PROVERBS 22:17-19

[17] Listen closely, pay attention to the
words of the wise,

and apply your mind to my
knowledge.
[18] For it is pleasing if you keep them
within you
and if they are constantly on your
lips.
[19] I have instructed you today—even
you—
so that your confidence may be in
the LORD.

2 CORINTHIANS 1:1-22

[1] Paul, an apostle of Christ Jesus by God's will, and Timothy our brother:
To God's church at Corinth, with all the saints who are throughout Achaia. [2] Grace to you and peace from God our Father and the Lord Jesus Christ.

[3] Blessed be the God and Father of our Lord Jesus Christ, the Father of mercies and the God of all comfort. [4] He comforts us in all our affliction, so that we may be able to comfort those who are in any kind of affliction, through the comfort we ourselves receive from God. [5] For as the sufferings of Christ overflow to us, so our comfort overflows through Christ. [6] If we are afflicted, it is for your comfort and salvation; if we are comforted, it is for your comfort, which is experienced in the endurance of the same sufferings that we suffer. [7] And our hope for you is firm, because we know that as you share in the sufferings, so you will share in the comfort.

[8] For we don't want you to be unaware, brothers, of our affliction that took place in the province of Asia: we were completely overwhelmed—beyond our strength—so that we even despaired of life. [9] However, we personally had a death sentence within ourselves so that we would not trust in ourselves, but in God who raises the dead. [10] He has delivered us from such a terrible death, and He will deliver us; we have placed our hope in Him that He will deliver us again. [11] And you can join in helping with prayer for us, so that thanks may be given by many on our behalf for the gift that came to us through the prayers of many.

¹² For our boast is this: the testimony of our conscience that we have conducted ourselves in the world, and especially toward you, with God-given sincerity and purity, not by fleshly wisdom but by God's grace. ¹³ Now we are writing you nothing other than what you can read and also understand. I hope you will understand completely— ¹⁴ as you have partially understood us—that we are your reason for pride, as you are ours, in the day of our Lord Jesus.

¹⁵ In this confidence, I planned to come to you first, so you could have a double benefit, ¹⁶ and to go on to Macedonia with your help, then come to you again from Macedonia and be given a start by you on my journey to Judea. ¹⁷ So when I planned this, was I irresponsible? Or what I plan, do I plan in a purely human way so that I say "Yes, yes" and "No, no" simultaneously? ¹⁸ As God is faithful, our message to you is not "Yes and no." ¹⁹ For the Son of God, Jesus Christ, who was preached among you by us—by me and Silvanus and Timothy—did not become "Yes and no"; on the contrary, "Yes" has come about in Him. ²⁰ For every one of God's promises is "Yes" in Him. Therefore the "Amen" is also through Him for God's glory through us. ²¹ Now the One who confirms us with you in Christ, and has anointed us, is God; ²² He has also sealed us and given us the Spirit as a down payment in our hearts.

The Irreducible Minimum

For every one of God's promises is "Yes" in Him.
—2 Corinthians 1:20

It is time to face some very personal and pointed questions. Do you believe the Bible is the Word of God, divinely and uniquely inspired and reliable in all it affirms? Do you believe that Jesus Christ is the Son of God, born of a virgin, and the only way to God? Do you believe that He was crucified for your sins, raised again on the third day, and is now sitting on the right hand of God?

I could go on raising more questions, but the ones I have mentioned are what I consider to be the irreducible minimum of Christianity. In other words, these are the basic truths of the gospel, and if you don't take your stand on these truths, then you cannot call yourself a Christian.

This is what is meant by having your feet shod with the preparation of the gospel of peace—that you are ready to stand for the authority of Scripture, the deity of Christ, His substitutionary death, His resurrection from the dead, and His return to earth in power and glory.

Do you know where you stand on these matters? Are you sure of your spiritual position? How can you fight the enemy if you do not know what you believe? As I write, some of the daily newspapers here in Britain are calling on church leaders to give a spiritual lead. But many of our leaders do not have a high view of Scripture. How can they give a lead when they don't know where they are going? They don't know where they stand, and no one else knows either.

Prayer

O Father, Your Word promises to be a lamp to our feet and a light for our path. Bring those whose feet are slipping and sliding in the faith back to an unshakable confidence in Your gospel. In Jesus' name I ask it. Amen.

Further Study

2 Pt 1; Col 2:7; 1 Co 3:11
Why are we given so many great and precious promises?
What should our foundation be?

SEPTEMBER 15

ECCLESIASTES 7:1–9:10

7 A good name is better than
    fine perfume,
and the day of one's death than
    the day of one's birth.
² It is better to go to a house
    of mourning
than to go to a house of feasting,
since that is the end
    of all mankind,
and the living should take it to heart.
³ Grief is better than laughter,
for when a face is sad, a heart
    may be glad.
⁴ The heart of the wise is in a house
    of mourning,
but the heart of fools is in a house
    of pleasure.
⁵ It is better to listen to rebuke
    from a wise person
than to listen to the song of fools.
⁶ For like the crackling of burning
    thorns under the pot,
so is the laughter of the fool.
This too is futile.
⁷ Surely, the practice of extortion
    turns a wise person
    into a fool,

and a bribe destroys the mind.
⁸ The end of a matter is better
    than its beginning;
a patient spirit is better
    than a proud spirit.
⁹ Don't let your spirit rush
    to be angry,
for anger abides in the heart
    of fools.
¹⁰ Don't say, "Why were
    the former days better
    than these?"
For it is not wise of you
    to ask this.
¹¹ Wisdom is as good
    as an inheritance,
and an advantage to those
    who see the sun.
¹² For wisdom is protection
    as money is protection,
and the advantage of knowledge is
    that wisdom preserves the life
    of its owner.
¹³ Consider the work of God;
for who can straighten out what
    He has made crooked?

¹⁴ In the day of prosperity be joyful,
but in the day of adversity, consider:

without question, God has made the one as well as the other, so that man cannot discover anything that will come after him.

¹⁵ In my futile life I have seen everything: there is a righteous man who perishes in spite of his righteousness, and there is a wicked man who lives long in spite of his evil. ¹⁶ Don't be excessively righteous, and don't be overly wise. Why should you destroy yourself? ¹⁷ Don't be excessively wicked, and don't be foolish. Why should you die before your time? ¹⁸ It is good that you grasp the one and do not let the other slip from your hand. For the one who fears God will end up with both of them.

¹⁹ Wisdom makes the wise man
       stronger
          than ten rulers of a city.
²⁰ There is certainly
       no righteous man
          on the earth
       who does good and never sins.

²¹ Don't pay attention to everything people say, or you may hear your servant cursing you; ²² for you know that many times you yourself have cursed others.

²³ I have tested all this by wisdom. I resolved, "I will be wise," but it was beyond me. ²⁴ What exists is beyond reach and very deep. Who can discover it? ²⁵ I turned my thoughts to know, explore, and seek wisdom and an explanation for things, and to know that wickedness is stupidity and folly is madness. ²⁶ And I find more bitter than death the woman who is a trap, her heart a net, and her hands chains. The one who pleases God will escape her, but the sinner will be captured by her. ²⁷ "Look," says the Teacher, "this I have discovered, by adding one thing to another to find out the explanation, ²⁸ which my soul continually searches for but does not find: among a thousand people I have found one true man, but among all these I have not found a true woman. ²⁹ Only see this: I have discovered that God made people upright, but they pursued many schemes."

8 Who is like the wise person, and who knows the interpretation of a matter? A man's wisdom brightens his face, and the sternness of his face is changed.

² Keep the king's command. Concerning an oath by God, ³ do not be in a hurry. Leave his presence, and don't persist in a bad cause, since he will do whatever he wants. ⁴ For the king's word is authoritative, and who can say to him, "What are you doing?" ⁵ The one who keeps a command will not experience anything harmful, and a wise heart knows the right time and procedure. ⁶ For every activity there is a right time and procedure, even though man's troubles are heavy on him. ⁷ Yet no one knows what will happen, because who can tell him what will happen? ⁸ No one has authority over the wind to restrain it, and there is no authority over the day of death; there is no furlough in battle, and wickedness will not allow those who practice it to escape. ⁹ All this I have seen, applying my mind to all the work that is done under the sun, at a time when one man has authority over another to his harm.

¹⁰ In such circumstances, I saw the wicked buried. They came and went from the holy place, and they were praised in the city where they did so. This too is futile. ¹¹ Because the sentence against a criminal act is not carried out quickly, therefore the heart of people is filled with the desire to commit crime. ¹² Although a sinner commits crime a hundred times and prolongs his life, yet I also know that it will go well with God-fearing people, for they are reverent before Him. ¹³ However, it will not go well with the wicked, and they will not lengthen their days like a shadow, for they are not reverent before God.

¹⁴ There is a futility that is done on the earth: there are righteous people who get what the actions of the wicked deserve, and there are wicked people who get what the actions of the righteous deserve. I say that this too is futile. ¹⁵ So I commended enjoyment, because there is nothing better for man under the sun except to eat, drink, and enjoy

himself, for this will accompany him in his labor during the years of his days that God gives him under the sun. [16] When I applied my mind to know wisdom and to observe the activity that is done on the earth (even though one's eyes do not close in sleep day or night), [17] I observed all the work of God and concluded that man is unable to discover the work that is done under the sun. Even though a man labors hard to explore it, he cannot find it; even if the wise man claims to know it, he is unable to discover it.

9 Indeed, I took all this to heart and explained it all: the righteous, the wise, and their works are in God's hands. People don't know whether to expect love or hate. Everything lies ahead of them. [2] Everything is the same for everyone: there is one fate for the righteous and the wicked, for the good and the bad, for the clean and the unclean, for the one who sacrifices and the one who does not sacrifice. As it is for the good, so it is for the sinner, as for the one who takes an oath, so for the one who fears an oath. [3] This is an evil in all that is done under the sun: there is one fate for everyone. In addition, the hearts of people are full of evil, and madness is in their hearts while they live—after that they go to the dead. [4] But there is hope for whoever is joined with all the living, since a live dog is better than a dead lion. [5] For the living know that they will die, but the dead don't know anything. There is no longer a reward for them because the memory of them is forgotten. [6] Their love, their hate, and their envy have already disappeared, and there is no longer a portion for them in all that is done under the sun.

[7] Go, eat your bread with pleasure, and drink your wine with a cheerful heart, for God has already accepted your works. [8] Let your clothes be white all the time, and never let oil be lacking on your head. [9] Enjoy life with the wife you love all the days of your fleeting life, which has been given to you under the sun, all your fleeting days. For that

is your portion in life and in your struggle under the sun. [10] Whatever your hands find to do, do with all your strength, because there is no work, planning, knowledge, or wisdom in Sheol where you are going.

PSALM 107:33-38

33 He turns rivers into desert,
   springs of water into thirsty
      ground,
34 and fruitful land into salty
      wasteland,
   because of the wickedness of its
      inhabitants.
35 He turns a desert into a pool of
      water,
   dry land into springs of water.
36 He causes the hungry to settle
      there,
   and they establish a city where
      they can live.
37 They sow fields and plant
      vineyards
   that yield a fruitful harvest.
38 He blesses them, and they
      multiply greatly;
   He does not let their livestock
      decrease.

PROVERBS 22:20-21

20 Haven't I written for you thirty
      sayings
   about counsel and knowledge,
21 in order to teach you true and
      reliable words,
   so that you may give a dependable
      report to those who sent you?

2 CORINTHIANS 1:23–3:3

[23] I call on God as a witness against me: it was to spare you that I did not come to Corinth. [24] Not that we have control of your faith, but we are workers with you for your joy, because you 2 stand by faith. [1] In fact, I made up my mind about this: not to come to you on another painful visit. [2] For if I cause you pain, then who will cheer me

other than the one hurt? ³ I wrote this very thing so that when I came I wouldn't have pain from those who ought to give me joy, because I am confident about all of you that my joy is yours. ⁴ For out of an extremely troubled and anguished heart I wrote to you with many tears—not that you should be hurt, but that you should know the abundant love I have for you.

⁵ If anyone has caused pain, he has not caused pain to me, but in some degree—not to exaggerate—to all of you. ⁶ The punishment by the majority is sufficient for such a person, ⁷ so now you should forgive and comfort him instead; otherwise, this one may be overwhelmed by excessive grief. ⁸ Therefore I urge you to confirm your love to him. ⁹ It was for this purpose I wrote: so I may know your proven character, if you are obedient in everything. ¹⁰ Now to whom you forgive anything, I do too. For what I have forgiven, if I have forgiven anything, it is for you in the presence of Christ, ¹¹ so that we may not be taken advantage of by Satan; for we are not ignorant of his intentions.

¹² When I came to Troas for the gospel of Christ, a door was opened to me by the Lord. ¹³ I had no rest in my spirit because I did not find my brother Titus, but I said good-bye to them and left for Macedonia.

¹⁴ But thanks be to God, who always puts us on display in Christ, and spreads through us in every place the scent of knowing Him. ¹⁵ For to God we are the fragrance of Christ among those who are being saved and among those who are perishing. ¹⁶ To some we are a scent of death leading to death, but to others, a scent of life leading to life. And who is competent for this? ¹⁷ For we are not like the many who make a trade in God's message for profit, but as those with sincerity, we speak in Christ, as from God and before God.

3 Are we beginning to commend ourselves again? Or like some, do we need letters of recommendation to you or from you? ² You yourselves are our letter, written on our hearts, recognized and read by everyone, ³ since it is plain that you are Christ's letter, produced by us, not written with ink but with the Spirit of the living God; not on stone tablets but on tablets that are hearts of flesh.

Blasphemous Thoughts

For we are not ignorant of [Satan's] intentions.—2 CORINTHIANS 2:11

The form of satanic attack that is probably the most difficult of all to endure is having blasphemous thoughts. Dr. Martyn Lloyd-Jones said on this: "The devil has often plagued some of the noblest saints with blasphemous thoughts—blasphemous thoughts about God, blasphemous thoughts about the Lord Jesus Christ, and blasphemous thoughts about the Holy Spirit."

How horrible and terrifying such thoughts can be. Sometimes the Devil hurls the most awful words and phrases into the mind; but again, it is important to see that these do not arise from within the heart of the believer—they come from the Devil, who is trying to confuse and demoralize you.

How grateful we should be to the saints down the ages who have recorded these satanic attacks, for otherwise we would be tempted when experiencing them to believe that they have never happened to anyone else. Many masters of the spiritual life have described these satanic attacks in great detail—John Bunyan and Martin Luther being the two best examples.

But how do we deal with these "flaming arrows" of Satan? What action must we take to repel these devilish attacks? There is only one answer—we must take and use the shield of faith. Faith alone enables us to meet and overcome this particular type of attack. What we must not do is expose our chests, expecting the breastplate of righteousness to deal with this problem. Each piece of the equipment is designed to deal with a particular attack. And the answer here is—faith.

Prayer

Heavenly Father, I understand the problem—now show me how to apply the answer. The answer, I see, is faith. But how does it work? How can I apply it? Teach me more. In Jesus' name. Amen.

Further Study

2 Co 10:1-5; Mt 22:37-38; Eph 1:22-23; Jms 4:7-8
In what ways does Satan attack the mind?
What is the scriptural antidote?

SEPTEMBER 16

ECCLESIASTES
9:11–12:14

¹¹ Again I saw under the sun that the race is not to the swift, or the battle to the strong, or bread to the wise, or riches to the discerning, or favor to the skillful; rather, time and chance happen to all of them. ¹² For man certainly does not know his time: like fish caught in a cruel net, or like birds caught in a trap, so people are trapped in an evil time, as it suddenly falls on them.

¹³ I have observed that this also is wisdom under the sun, and it is significant to me: ¹⁴ There was a small city with few men in it. A great king came against it, surrounded it, and built large siege works against it. ¹⁵ Now a poor wise man

was found in the city, and he delivered the city by his wisdom. Yet no one remembered that poor man. ¹⁶ And I said, "Wisdom is better than strength, but the wisdom of the poor man is despised, and his words are not heeded."

¹⁷ The calm words of the wise
    are heeded
more than the shouts of a ruler
    over fools.
¹⁸ Wisdom is better than weapons
    of war,
but one sinner can destroy
    much good.

10 Dead flies make a perfumer's oil
    ferment and stink;
so a little folly outweighs wisdom
    and honor.

2 A wise man's heart goes to the
    right,
  but a fool's heart to the left.
3 Even when the fool walks
    along the road, his heart
    lacks sense,
  and he shows everyone he is
    a fool.
4 If the ruler's anger rises
    against you, don't leave
    your place,
  for calmness puts great offenses
    to rest.

5 There is an evil I have seen under
the sun, an error proceeding from the
presence of the ruler:

6 The fool is appointed
    to great heights,
  but the rich remain
    in lowly positions.
7 I have seen slaves on horses,
  but princes walking on the ground
    like slaves.

8 The one who digs a pit may fall
    into it,
  and the one who breaks
    through a wall may be bitten
    by a snake.
9 The one who quarries stones
    may be hurt by them;
  the one who splits trees
    may be endangered by them.
10 If the axe is dull, and one
    does not sharpen its edge,
  then one must exert
    more strength;
  however, the advantage of wisdom
    is that it brings success.
11 If the snake bites before
    it is charmed,
  then there is no advantage
    for the charmer.
12 The words from the mouth
    of a wise man are gracious,
  but the lips of a fool
    consume him.
13 The beginning of the words
    of his mouth is folly,
  but the end of his speaking
    is evil madness.
14 Yet the fool multiplies words.

No one knows what will happen,
  and who can tell anyone
    what will happen after him?
15 The struggles of fools
    weary them,
  for they don't know how to go
    to the city.
16 Woe to you, land, when your king
    is a household servant,
  and your princes feast
    in the morning.
17 Blessed are you, land,
    when your king is a son
    of nobles
  and your princes feast
    at the proper time—
  for strength and not
    for drunkenness.
18 Because of laziness the roof
    caves in,
  and because of negligent hands
    the house leaks.
19 A feast is prepared for laughter,
  and wine makes life happy,
  and money is the answer
    for everything.
20 Do not curse the king
    even in your thoughts,
  and do not curse a rich person
    even in your bedroom,
  for a bird of the sky may carry
    the message,
  and a winged creature may report
    the matter.

11 Send your bread on the surface
    of the waters,
  for after many days
    you may find it.
2 Give a portion to seven or even
    to eight,
  for you don't know what disaster
    may happen on earth.
3 If the clouds are full,
    they will pour out rain
    on the earth;
  whether a tree falls to the south
    or the north,
  the place where the tree falls,
    there it will lie.
4 One who watches the wind
    will not sow,
  and the one who looks
    at the clouds will not reap.

5 Just as you don't know the path
of the wind,
or how bones develop in
the womb
of a pregnant woman,
so you don't know the work
of God who makes
everything.
6 In the morning sow your seed,
and at evening do not let
your hand rest,
because you don't know
which will succeed,
whether one or the other,
or if both of them will be
equally good.
7 Light is sweet,
and it is pleasing for the eyes
to see the sun.
8 For if a man should live
many years,
let him rejoice in them all,
and let him remember the days
of darkness, since they
will be many.
All that comes is futile.
9 Rejoice, young man,
while you are young,
and let your heart be glad
in the days of your youth.
And walk in the ways
of your heart
and in the sights of your eyes;
but know that for all
of these things God will bring
you to judgment.
10 Remove sorrow from your heart,
and put away pain
from your flesh,
because youth and the prime
of life are fleeting.

12 So remember your Creator in the
days of your youth:

Before the days of adversity come,
and the years approach
when you will say,
"I have no delight in them";
2 before the sun and the light
are darkened,
and the moon and the stars,
and the clouds return after
the rain;

3 on the day when the guardians
of the house tremble,
and the strong men stoop,
the women who grind cease
because they are few,
and the ones who watch
through the windows
see dimly,
4 and the doors at the street
are shut
while the sound of the mill fades;
when one rises at the sound
of a bird,
and all the daughters of song
grow faint.
5 Also, they are afraid of heights
and dangers on the road;
the almond tree blossoms,
the grasshopper loses its spring,
and the caper berry has no effect;
for man is headed
to his eternal home,
and mourners will walk around
in the street;
6 before the silver cord is snapped,
and the golden bowl is broken,
and the jar is shattered
at the spring,
and the wheel is broken
into the well;
7 and the dust returns to the earth
as it once was,
and the spirit returns to God
who gave it.

8 "Absolute futility," says the Teacher.
"Everything is futile."

9 In addition to the Teacher being a
wise man, he constantly taught the people knowledge; he weighed, explored,
and arranged many proverbs. 10 The
Teacher sought to find delightful sayings
and to accurately write words of truth.
11 The sayings of the wise are like goads,
and those from masters of collections
are like firmly embedded nails. The sayings are given by one Shepherd.
12 But beyond these, my son, be
warned: there is no end to the making
of many books, and much study wearies
the body. 13 When all has been heard,
the conclusion of the matter is: fear
God and keep His commands, because
this is for all humanity. 14 For God will

bring every act to judgment, including every hidden thing, whether good or evil.

PSALM 107:39-43

39 When they are diminished and are humbled
by cruel oppression and sorrow,
40 He pours contempt on nobles
and makes them wander in trackless wastelands.
41 But He lifts the needy out of their suffering
and makes their families multiply like flocks.
42 The upright see it and rejoice,
and all injustice shuts its mouth.

43 Let whoever is wise pay attention to these things
and consider the LORD's acts of faithful love.

PROVERBS 22:22-23

22 Don't rob a poor man because he is poor,
and don't crush the oppressed at the gate,
23 for the LORD will take up their case
and will plunder those who plunder them.

2 CORINTHIANS 3:4–4:6

4 We have this kind of confidence toward God through Christ: 5 not that we are competent in ourselves to consider anything as coming from ourselves, but our competence is from God. 6 He has made us competent to be ministers of a new covenant, not of the letter, but of the Spirit; for the letter kills, but the Spirit produces life.

7 Now if the ministry of death, chiseled in letters on stones, came with glory, so that the sons of Israel were not able to look directly at Moses' face because of the glory from his face—a fad-

ing glory— 8 how will the ministry of the Spirit not be more glorious? 9 For if the ministry of condemnation had glory, the ministry of righteousness overflows with even more glory. 10 In fact, what had been glorious is not glorious in this case because of the glory that surpasses it. 11 For if what was fading away was glorious, what endures will be even more glorious.

12 Therefore having such a hope, we use great boldness— 13 not like Moses, who used to put a veil over his face so that the sons of Israel could not look at the end of what was fading away. 14 But their minds were closed. For to this day, at the reading of the old covenant, the same veil remains; it is not lifted, because it is set aside only in Christ. 15 However, to this day, whenever Moses is read, a veil lies over their hearts, 16 but whenever a person turns to the Lord, the veil is removed. 17 Now the Lord is the Spirit; and where the Spirit of the Lord is, there is freedom. 18 We all, with unveiled faces, are reflecting the glory of the Lord and are being transformed into the same image from glory to glory; this is from the Lord who is the Spirit.

4 Therefore, since we have this ministry, as we have received mercy, we do not give up. 2 Instead, we have renounced shameful secret things, not walking in deceit or distorting God's message, but in God's sight we commend ourselves to every person's conscience by an open display of the truth. 3 But if, in fact, our gospel is veiled, it is veiled to those who are perishing. 4 Regarding them: the god of this age has blinded the minds of the unbelievers so they cannot see the light of the gospel of the glory of Christ, who is the image of God. 5 For we are not proclaiming ourselves but Jesus Christ as Lord, and ourselves as your slaves because of Jesus. 6 For God, who said, "Light shall shine out of darkness"—He has shone in our hearts to give the light of the knowledge of God's glory in the face of Jesus Christ.

Full Surrender

Now the Lord is the Spirit; and where the Spirit of the Lord is, there is freedom.—2 CORINTHIANS 3:17

Modern approaches to the subconscious can do no more than throw the pale light of information into it. The message of the Bible, however, is not merely information but transformation: "Where the Spirit of the Lord is, there is freedom." So if the Spirit of the Lord is within us, there is freedom from the conflict between the conscious and the subconscious.

If such a freedom is possible, why do so many live out their lives in conflict? Because they have never appropriated the power and presence of the Spirit available to them and channeled Him into the deeper regions of their personality through self-surrender. God, Christ, or the Holy Spirit will never barge their way into any area of the personality. They come in when we put up the white flag of surrender and, by a conscious act, agree to their residing and presiding within us.

It's surprising how many Christians say with the conscious mind, "I surrender all," and yet with the subconscious say, "I want some areas for myself." We must take ourselves in hand and decide whether or not we want the Holy Spirit simply to evangelize certain areas of our personality, or whether we want Him to occupy our entire being. If you haven't properly settled this issue, then ask yourself today: "Am I just kidding myself when I say I want to be filled with God? Is there a part of me that says, 'Come in,' while another part of me says at the same time, 'Keep out'?" The Holy Spirit only comes into the areas where He is freely admitted.

Prayer

O Father, I think You have put Your finger right on my problem. Perhaps the reason I have never felt the Holy Spirit's full control is because deep down I never wanted it. But now I do. My whole being cries out for its rightful Lord. I surrender now. Amen.

Further Study

Jms 4; Gl 2:20; Rm 6:6; 2 Tm 2:11
Where does strife come from?
What was Paul's testimony?

SEPTEMBER 17

SONG OF SONGS
1:1–4:16

1 Solomon's Finest Song

2 Oh, that he would kiss me
with the kisses of his mouth!
For your love is more delightful
than wine.
3 The fragrance of your perfume
is intoxicating;
your name is perfume poured out.
No wonder young women adore
you.
4 Take me with you—let us hurry.
Oh, that the king would bring me
to his chambers.

We will rejoice and be glad
for you;
we will praise your love
more than wine.

It is only right that they adore you.

5 Daughters of Jerusalem,
I am dark like the tents of Kedar,
yet lovely like the curtains
of Solomon.
6 Do not stare at me because
I am dark,
for the sun has gazed on me.
My mother's sons were angry
with me;
they made me a keeper
of the vineyards.
I have not kept my own vineyard.

7 Tell me, you, the one I love:
Where do you pasture your sheep?
Where do you let them rest
at noon?
Why should I be like one
who veils herself
beside the flocks
of your companions?

8 If you do not know,
most beautiful of women,
follow the tracks of the flock,
and pasture your young goats
near the shepherds' tents.

9 I compare you, my darling,
to a mare
among Pharaoh's chariots.
10 Your cheeks are beautiful
with jewelry,
your neck with its necklace.
11 We will make gold jewelry
for you,
accented with silver.

12 While the king is on his couch,
my perfume releases
its fragrance.
13 My love is a sachet of myrrh
to me,
spending the night
between my breasts.
14 My love is a cluster
of henna blossoms to me,
in the vineyards of En-gedi.

15 How beautiful you are,
my darling.
How very beautiful!
Your eyes are doves.

16 How handsome you are, my love.
How delightful!
Our bed is lush with foliage;
17 the beams of our house
are cedars,
and our rafters are cypresses.

2 I am a rose of Sharon,
a lily of the valleys.

2 Like a lily among thorns,
so is my darling
among the young women.

3 Like an apricot tree
among the trees of the forest,

so is my love among the young men.
I delight to sit in his shade,
and his fruit is sweet to my taste.
4 He brought me to the banquet hall,
and he looked on me with love.
5 Sustain me with raisins;
refresh me with apricots,
for I am lovesick.
6 His left hand is under my head,
and his right hand embraces me.
7 Young women of Jerusalem,
    I charge you,
by the gazelles and the wild does
    of the field:
do not stir up or awaken love
until the appropriate time.
8 Listen! My love is approaching.
Look! Here he comes,
leaping over the mountains,
bounding over the hills.
9 My love is like a gazelle
or a young stag.
Look, he is standing
    behind our wall,
gazing through the windows,
peering through the lattice.
10 My love calls to me:

Arise, my darling.
Come away, my beautiful one.
11 For now the winter is past;
the rain has ended and gone away.
12 The blossoms appear
    in the countryside.
The time of singing has come,
and the turtledove's cooing
    is heard in our land.
13 The fig tree ripens its figs;
the blossoming vines give off
    their fragrance.
Arise, my darling.
Come away, my beautiful one.

14 My dove, in the clefts of the rock,
in the crevices of the cliff,
let me see your face,
let me hear your voice;
for your voice is sweet,
and your face is lovely.

15 Catch the foxes for us—
the little foxes that ruin
    the vineyards—
for our vineyards are in bloom.

16 My love is mine and I am his;
he feeds among the lilies.
17 Before the day breaks
and the shadows flee,
turn to me, my love, and be
    like a gazelle
or a young stag
    on the divided mountains.

3 In my bed at night
I sought the one I love;
I sought him, but did not
    find him.
2 I will arise now and go
    about the city,
through the streets and the plazas.
I will seek the one I love.
I sought him, but did not
    find him.
3 The guards who go about the city
    found me.
"Have you seen the one I love?"
    I asked them.
4 I had just passed them
when I found the one I love.
I held on to him and would not
    let him go
until I brought him
    to my mother's house—
to the chamber of the one
    who conceived me.
5 Young women of Jerusalem,
    I charge you,
by the gazelles and the wild does
    of the field:
do not stir up or awaken love
until the appropriate time.

6 What is this coming up
    from the wilderness
like columns of smoke,
scented with myrrh
    and frankincense
from every fragrant powder
    of the merchant?
7 It is Solomon's royal litter
surrounded by 60 warriors
from the mighty of Israel.
8 All of them are skilled
    with swords
and trained in warfare.
Each has his sword at his side
to guard against the terror
    of the night.

9 King Solomon made a sedan chair
    for himself
with wood from Lebanon.
10 He made its posts of silver,
    its back of gold,
    and its seat of purple.
Its interior is inlaid with love
    by the young women
        of Jerusalem.
11 Come out, young women of Zion,
    and gaze at King Solomon,
    wearing the crown
        his mother placed on him
    the day of his wedding—
    the day of his heart's rejoicing.

4 How beautiful you are, my darling.
    How very beautiful!
Behind your veil,
    your eyes are doves.
Your hair is like a flock of goats
    streaming down Mount Gilead.
2 Your teeth are like a flock
    of newly shorn sheep
coming up from washing,
    each one having a twin,
    and not one missing.
3 Your lips are like a scarlet cord,
    and your mouth is lovely.
Behind your veil,
    your brow is like a slice
        of pomegranate.
4 Your neck is like the tower
        of David,
constructed in layers.
A thousand bucklers are hung
        on it—
all of them shields of warriors.
5 Your breasts are like two fawns,
    twins of a gazelle, that feed
        among the lilies.
6 Before the day breaks
    and the shadows flee,
I will make my way
    to the mountain of myrrh
    and the hill of frankincense.
7 You are absolutely beautiful,
        my darling,
with no imperfection in you.

8 Come with me from Lebanon,
        my bride—
with me from Lebanon!
Descend from the peak of Amana,

from the summit of Senir
    and Hermon,
from the dens of the lions,
from the mountains
    of the leopards.
9 You have captured my heart,
    my sister, my bride.
You have captured my heart
    with one glance of your eyes,
with one jewel of your necklace.
10 How delightful your love is,
    my sister, my bride.
Your love is much better
    than wine,
and the fragrance of your perfume
    than any balsam.
11 Your lips drip sweetness like
    the honeycomb, my bride.
Honey and milk are
    under your tongue.
The fragrance of your garments is
    like the fragrance of Lebanon.

12 My sister, my bride, you are
    a locked garden—
a locked garden
    and a sealed spring.
13 Your branches are a paradise
    of pomegranates
with choicest fruits,
    henna with nard—
14 nard and saffron, calamus
    and cinnamon,
with all the trees of frankincense,
    myrrh and aloes,
with all the best spices.
15 You are a garden spring,
    a well of flowing water
streaming from Lebanon.

16 Awaken, north wind—
    come, south wind.
Blow on my garden,
    and spread the fragrance
        of its spices.
Let my love come to his garden
    and eat its choicest fruits.

....

PSALM 108:1-6

1 My heart is confident, God;
    I will sing; I will sing praises with
        the whole of my being.

2 Wake up, harp and lyre!
I will wake up the dawn.
3 I will praise You, LORD, among the
peoples;
I will sing praises to You among
the nations.
4 For Your faithful love is higher
than the heavens;
Your faithfulness reaches the
clouds.
5 God, be exalted above the
heavens;
let Your glory be over the whole
earth.
6 Save with Your right hand and
answer me
so that those You love may be
rescued.

PROVERBS 22:24-25

24 Don't make friends with an angry
man,
and don't be a companion of a
hot-tempered man,
25 or you will learn his ways
and entangle yourself in a snare.

2 CORINTHIANS 4:7–5:10

7 Now we have this treasure in clay
jars, so that this extraordinary power
may be from God and not from us. 8 We
are pressured in every way but not
crushed; we are perplexed but not in
despair; 9 we are persecuted but not
abandoned; we are struck down but not
destroyed. 10 We always carry the death
of Jesus in our body, so that the life of
Jesus may also be revealed in our body.
11 For we who live are always given over
to death because of Jesus, so that Jesus'
life may also be revealed in our mortal
flesh. 12 So death works in us, but life
in you. 13 And since we have the same
spirit of faith in accordance with what is
written, **I believed, therefore I spoke,**
we also believe, and therefore speak,
14 knowing that the One who raised the
Lord Jesus will raise us also with Jesus,
and present us with you. 15 For all this is
because of you, so that grace, extended
through more and more people, may
cause thanksgiving to overflow to God's
glory.

16 Therefore we do not give up; even
though our outer person is being destroyed, our inner person is being renewed day by day. 17 For our momentary
light affliction is producing for us an
absolutely incomparable eternal weight
of glory. 18 So we do not focus on what
is seen, but on what is unseen; for
what is seen is temporary, but what is
unseen is eternal.

5 For we know that if our earthly
house, a tent, is destroyed, we have
a building from God, a house not made
with hands, eternal in the heavens.
2 And, in fact, we groan in this one,
longing to put on our house from
heaven, 3 since, when we are clothed,
we will not be found naked. 4 Indeed,
we who are in this tent groan, burdened
as we are, because we do not want to be
unclothed but clothed, so that mortality
may be swallowed up by life. 5 And the
One who prepared us for this very thing
is God, who gave us the Spirit as a down
payment.

6 Therefore, though we are always
confident and know that while we are at
home in the body we are away from the
Lord— 7 for we walk by faith, not by
sight— 8 yet we are confident and satisfied to be out of the body and at home
with the Lord. 9 Therefore, whether we
are at home or away, we make it our aim
to be pleasing to Him. 10 For we must all
appear before the judgment seat of
Christ, so that each may be repaid for
what he has done in the body, whether
good or bad.

Overcoming Frustration

We are pressured in every way but not crushed;
we are perplexed but not in despair. . . .
Therefore we do not give up; even though our outer person is being destroyed,
our inner person is being renewed day by day.
—2 CORINTHIANS 4:8,16

Learn how to deal with frustration. Time and time again, I have sat with people who have said: "What's wrong with me? I feel so low spiritually. I am not involved in sin. Why does my Christian life feel so stale?" On many of these occasions, I have observed that the problem contributing to their feelings of spiritual staleness was an inability to cope with frustration.

One of the most radiant Christians I have ever met was a seed salesman in West Wales whose name was Mordecai Price. Crippled in both his lower limbs by poliomyelitis, he drove a hand-controlled car and would make his way to outlying farms to sell seed to the farmers. Sometimes it would take him an hour just to get out of his car and open a farm gate—but he persevered nevertheless.

One day I said to him: "Don't you get frustrated by your condition? How do you keep going like this when many others would have settled for a lifetime of invalidism and inactivity?" My friend has gone to be with the Lord now, but his reply has lived on in my heart for over thirty years: "I take every project prisoner to make it obey Christ—even the project of poliomyelitis." He had learned how to make his frustration fruitful. When you and I can learn how to turn the ugly into the beautiful, and the evil into the good, then frustration will never get a hold on us. The secret of living is the secret of using. Learn this, and you will never be frustrated again.

Prayer

O Father, teach me how to turn the ugly into the beautiful, the evil into the good, and take every project prisoner for Christ. I ask this for Your own dear name's sake. Amen.

Further Study

2 Co 4:1-10; 10:5; Ps 44:5; Rm 8:35-37
What was Paul's testimony?
What does it mean to be "more than a conqueror"?

SEPTEMBER 18

SONGS OF SONGS
5:1–8:14

5 I have come to my garden—
my sister, my bride.
I gather my myrrh with my spices.
I eat my honeycomb
with my honey.
I drink my wine with my milk.

Eat, friends!
Drink, be intoxicated with love!

² I sleep, but my heart is awake.
A sound! My love is knocking!

Open to me, my sister, my darling,
my dove, my perfect one.
For my head is drenched
with dew,
my hair with droplets of the night.

³ I have taken off my clothing.
How can I put it back on?
I have washed my feet.
How can I get them dirty?
⁴ My love thrust his hand
through the opening,
and my feelings were stirred
for him.
⁵ I rose to open for my love.
My hands dripped with myrrh,
my fingers with flowing myrrh
on the handles of the bolt.
⁶ I opened to my love,
but my love had turned
and gone away.
I was crushed that he had left.
I sought him, but did not find
him.
I called him, but he did not
answer.
⁷ The guards who go about the city
found me.
They beat and wounded me;
they took my cloak from me—

the guardians of the walls.
⁸ Young women of Jerusalem,
I charge you:
if you find my love,
tell him that I am lovesick.

⁹ What makes the one you love
better than another,
most beautiful of women?
What makes him better than
another,
that you would give us this charge?

¹⁰ My love is fit and strong,
notable among ten thousand.
¹¹ His head is purest gold.
His hair is wavy
and black as a raven.
¹² His eyes are like doves
beside streams of water,
washed in milk
and set like jewels.
¹³ His cheeks are like beds of spice,
towers of perfume.
His lips are lilies,
dripping with flowing myrrh.
¹⁴ His arms are rods of gold
set with topaz.
His body is an ivory panel
covered with sapphires.
¹⁵ His legs are alabaster pillars
set on pedestals of pure gold.
His presence is like Lebanon,
as majestic as the cedars.
¹⁶ His mouth is sweetness.
He is absolutely desirable.
This is my love, and this is
my friend,
young women of Jerusalem.

6 Where has your love gone,
most beautiful of women?
Which way has he turned?
We will seek him with you.

² My love has gone down
to his garden,

to beds of spice,
to feed in the gardens
and gather lilies.
3 I am my love's and my love is mine;
he feeds among the lilies.

4 You are as beautiful as Tirzah,
my darling,
lovely as Jerusalem,
awe-inspiring as an army
with banners.
5 Turn your eyes away from me,
for they captivate me.
Your hair is like a flock of goats
streaming down from Gilead.
6 Your teeth are like a flock of ewes
coming up from washing,
each one having a twin,
and not one missing.
7 Behind your veil,
your brow is like a slice
of pomegranate.
8 There are 60 queens
and 80 concubines
and young women
without number.
9 But my dove, my virtuous one,
is unique;
she is the favorite of her mother,
perfect to the one who gave
her birth.
Women see her and declare
her fortunate;
queens and concubines also,
and they sing her praises:

10 Who is this who shines
like the dawn—
as beautiful as the moon,
bright as the sun,
awe-inspiring as an army
with banners?

11 I came down to the walnut grove
to see the blossoms of the valley,
to see if the vines were budding
and the pomegranates blooming.
12 Before I knew it,
my desire put me
among the chariots
of my noble people.

13 Come back, come back,
Shulammite!

Come back, come back, that
we may look at you!

Why are you looking
at the Shulammite,
as you look at the dance
of the two camps?

7 How beautiful are
your sandaled feet, princess!
The curves of your thighs are
like jewelry,
the handiwork of a master.
2 Your navel is a rounded bowl;
it never lacks mixed wine.
Your waist is a mound of wheat
surrounded by lilies.
3 Your breasts are like two fawns,
twins of a gazelle.
4 Your neck is like a tower of ivory,
your eyes like pools in Heshbon
by the gate of Bath-rabbim.
Your nose is like the tower
of Lebanon
looking toward Damascus.
5 Your head crowns you
like Mount Carmel,
the hair of your head
like purple cloth—
a king could be held captive
in your tresses.
6 How beautiful you are
and how pleasant,
my love, with such delights!
7 Your stature is like a palm tree;
your breasts are clusters of fruit.
8 I said, "I will climb the palm tree
and take hold of its fruit."
May your breasts be like clusters
of grapes,
and the fragrance of your breath
like apricots.
9 Your mouth is like fine wine—

flowing smoothly for my love
gliding past my lips and teeth!
10 I belong to my love,
and his desire is for me.
11 Come, my love,
let's go to the field;
let's spend the night
among the henna blossoms.
12 Let's go early to the vineyards;
let's see if the vine has budded,
if the blossom has opened,

if the pomegranates are in bloom.
There I will give you my love.
13 The mandrakes give off a fragrance,
and at our doors is
every delicacy—
new as well as old.
I have treasured them up for you,
my love.

8 If only I could treat you
like my brother,
one who nursed
at my mother's breasts,
I would find you in public
and kiss you,
and no one would scorn me.
2 I would lead you, I would take you,
to the house of my mother
who taught me.
I would give you spiced wine
to drink
from my pomegranate juice.

3 His left hand is under my head,
and his right hand embraces me.
4 Young women of Jerusalem,
I charge you:
do not stir up or awaken love
until the appropriate time.

5 Who is this coming up
from the wilderness,
leaning on the one she loves?
I awakened you under
the apricot tree.
There your mother conceived you;
there she conceived and gave you
birth.
6 Set me as a seal on your heart,
as a seal on your arm.
For love is as strong as death;
ardent love is as unrelenting as
Sheol.
Love's flames are fiery flames—
the fiercest of all.
7 Mighty waters cannot extinguish
love;
rivers cannot sweep it away.
If a man were to give all
his wealth for love,
it would be utterly scorned.

8 Our sister is young;
she has no breasts.
What will we do for our sister

on the day she is spoken for?
9 If she is a wall,
we will build a silver parapet on it.
If she is a door,
we will enclose it
with cedar planks.
10 I am a wall
and my breasts like towers.
So in his eyes I have become
like one who finds peace.
11 Solomon owned a vineyard
in Baal-hamon.
He leased the vineyard to tenants.
Each was to bring for his fruit
1,000 pieces of silver.
12 I have my own vineyard.
The 1,000 are for you, Solomon,
but 200 for those who guard
its fruits.

13 You who dwell in the gardens—
companions are listening
for your voice—
let me hear you!

14 Hurry to me, my love,
and be like a gazelle
or a young stag
on the mountains of spices.

*P*SALM 108:7-13

7 God has spoken in His sanctuary:
"I will triumph!
I will divide up Shechem.
I will apportion the Valley of
Succoth.
8 Gilead is Mine, Manasseh is
Mine,
and Ephraim is My helmet;
Judah is My scepter.
9 Moab is My washbasin;
on Edom I throw My sandal.
Over Philistia I shout in triumph."

10 Who will bring me to the fortified
city?
Who will lead me to Edom?
11 Have You not rejected us, God?
God, You do not march out with
our armies.

¹² Give us aid against the foe,
for human help is worthless.
¹³ With God we will perform
valiantly;
He will trample our foes.

ℙROVERBS 22:26-27

²⁶ Don't be one of those who enter
agreements,
who put up security for loans.
²⁷ If you have no money to pay,
even your bed will be taken from
under you.

2 ℂORINTHIANS 5:11–6:13

¹¹ Knowing, then, the fear of the Lord, we persuade people. We are completely open before God, and I hope we are completely open to your consciences as well. ¹² We are not commending ourselves to you again, but giving you an opportunity to be proud of us, so that you may have a reply for those who take pride in the outward appearance rather than in the heart. ¹³ For if we are out of our mind, it is for God; if we have a sound mind, it is for you. ¹⁴ For Christ's love compels us, since we have reached this conclusion: if One died for all, then all died. ¹⁵ And He died for all so that those who live should no longer live for themselves, but for the One who died for them and was raised.

¹⁶ From now on, then, we do not know anyone in a purely human way. Even if we have known Christ in a purely human way, yet now we no longer know Him like that. ¹⁷ Therefore if anyone is in Christ, there is a new creation; old things have passed away, and look, new things have come. ¹⁸ Now everything is from God, who reconciled us to Himself through Christ and gave us the ministry of reconciliation: ¹⁹ that is, in Christ, God was reconciling the world to Himself, not counting their trespasses against them, and He has committed the message of reconciliation to us. ²⁰ Therefore, we are ambassadors for Christ; certain that God is appealing through us, we plead on Christ's behalf, "Be reconciled to God." ²¹ He made the One who did not know sin to be sin for us, so that we might become the righteousness of God in Him.

6 Working together with Him, we also appeal to you: "Don't receive God's grace in vain." ² For He says:

In an acceptable time,
I heard you,
and in the day of salvation,
I helped you.

Look, now is the acceptable time; look, now is the day of salvation. ³ We give no opportunity for stumbling to anyone, so that the ministry will not be blamed. ⁴ But in everything, as God's ministers, we commend ourselves:

by great endurance, by afflictions,
by hardship, by pressures,
⁵ by beatings, by imprisonments,
by riots, by labors,
by sleepless nights,
by times of hunger,
⁶ by purity, by knowledge,
by patience, by kindness,
by the Holy Spirit, by sincere love,
⁷ by the message of truth,
by the power of God;
through weapons of righteousness
on the right hand and the left,
⁸ through glory and dishonor,
through slander
and good report;
as deceivers yet true;
⁹ as unknown yet recognized;
as dying and look—we live;
as being chastened yet not killed;
¹⁰ as grieving yet always rejoicing;
as poor yet enriching many;
as having nothing
yet possessing everything.

¹¹ We have spoken openly to you, Corinthians; our heart has been opened wide. ¹² You are not limited by us, but are limited by your own affections. ¹³ Now in like response—I speak as to children—you also should be open to us.

When God's People Share

Therefore, we are ambassadors for Christ; certain that
God is appealing through us.—2 CORINTHIANS 5:20

The aspects of experience and expression are extremely important in the Christian life: if experience gets low, then expression gets low; if expression gets low, then experience gets low.

We focus now on expression. If this side of the Christian life is not transformed from a bottled-up, non-contagious type of outflowing, then spiritual staleness is the inevitable result.

Two young men, both fairly new converts, had been listening to a sermon on evangelism. Afterwards, they approached their pastor and said: "We have never shared with anyone the experience we have had in Christ. How do we do it?" He suggested that they could go out, knock on a few doors, and just begin to share their experience of Christ. The next night, in fear and trembling, they knocked on the first door of the street that they had decided to evangelize and found it to be the home of a well-known lawyer. They were a little nonplussed when they discovered this and blurted out: "We have come to invite you to join our church." The lawyer said: "A lot of people have asked me to join the church over the years. Haven't you anything better than that to say to me?" They said: "Well, how about committing your life to Jesus Christ?"

The lawyer invited them in, and within an hour had surrendered to Christ. "Now, where are you going next," he said, "because I want to go with you." Before the end of the evening, the lawyer had the joy of witnessing another conversion like his own. Things happen when people share.

Prayer

O Father, help me to come to such a place in my Christian life that in every situation where You want someone to pass on a special word from You, You will hear me say, "Here am I, Lord—send me." Amen.

Further Study

Ac 2; 5:20; 18:9; 22:15
What was the hallmark of the early church?
Witness to someone today.

SEPTEMBER 19

*I*SAIAH 1:1–2:22

1 The vision concerning Judah and Jerusalem that Isaiah son of Amoz saw during the reigns of Uzziah, Jotham, Ahaz, and Hezekiah, kings of Judah.

² Listen, heavens,
and pay attention, earth,
for the LORD has spoken:
"I have raised children
and brought them up,
but they have rebelled against Me.
³ The ox knows its owner,
and the donkey
its master's feeding-trough,
but Israel does not know;
My people do not understand."

⁴ Oh—sinful nation,
people weighed down
with iniquity,
brood of evildoers,
depraved children!
They have abandoned the LORD;
they have despised the Holy One
of Israel;
they have turned their backs
on Him.

⁵ Why do you want more beatings?
Why do you keep on rebelling?
The whole head is hurt,
and the whole heart is sick.
⁶ From the sole of the foot
even to the head,
no spot is uninjured—
wounds, welts, and festering sores
not cleansed, bandaged,
or soothed with oil.

⁷ Your land is desolate,
your cities burned with fire;
before your very eyes
foreigners devour your fields—
a desolation overthrown
by foreigners.

⁸ Daughter Zion is abandoned
like a shelter in a vineyard,
like a shack in a cucumber field,
like a besieged city.
⁹ If the LORD of Hosts
had not left us a few survivors,
we would be like Sodom,
we would resemble Gomorrah.

¹⁰ Hear the word of the LORD,
you rulers of Sodom!
Listen to the instruction
of our God,
you people of Gomorrah!
¹¹ "What are all your sacrifices
to Me?"
asks the LORD.
"I have had enough of
burnt offerings and rams
and the fat of well-fed cattle;
I have no desire for the blood
of bulls,
lambs, or male goats.
¹² When you come to appear
before Me,
who requires this from you—
this trampling of My courts?
¹³ Stop bringing useless offerings.
I despise your incense.
New Moons and Sabbaths,
and the calling
of solemn assemblies—
I cannot stand iniquity
with a festival.
¹⁴ I hate your New Moons
and prescribed festivals.
They have become a burden
to Me;
I am tired of putting up
with them.
¹⁵ When you lift up your hands
in prayer,
I will refuse to look at you;
even if you offer
countless prayers,
I will not listen.
Your hands are covered with blood.

16 "Wash yourselves.
    Cleanse yourselves.
    Remove your evil deeds
      from My sight.
    Stop doing evil.
17 Learn to do what is good.
    Seek justice.
    Correct the oppressor.
    Defend the rights
      of the fatherless.
    Plead the widow's cause.

18 "Come, let us discuss this,"
    says the LORD.
    "Though your sins are like scarlet,
    they will be as white as snow;
    though they are as red as crimson,
    they will be like wool.
19 If you are willing and obedient,
    you will eat the good things
      of the land.
20 But if you refuse and rebel,
    you will be devoured
      by the sword."
    For the mouth of the LORD
      has spoken.

21 The faithful city—
    what an adulteress
      she has become!
    She was once full of justice.
    Righteousness once dwelt in her—
    but now, murderers!
22 Your silver has become dross,
    your beer is diluted with water.
23 Your rulers are rebels,
    friends of thieves.
    They all love graft
    and chase after bribes.
    They do not defend the rights
      of the fatherless,
    and the widow's case never comes
      before them."

24 Therefore the Lord GOD of Hosts,
    the Mighty One
      of Israel, declares:
    "Ah, I will gain satisfaction
      against My foes;
    I will take revenge
      against My enemies.
25 I will turn My hand against you
    and will burn away your dross
      completely;

    I will remove all your impurities.
26 I will restore your judges to what
      they once were,
    and your advisers
      to their former state.
    Afterwards you will be called
      the Righteous City,
    a Faithful City."

27 Zion will be redeemed by justice,
    her repentant ones
      by righteousness.
28 But both rebels and sinners
      will be destroyed,
    and those who abandon the LORD
      will perish.
29 Indeed, they will be ashamed
    of the sacred trees
    you desired,
    and you will be embarrassed
      because of the gardens
    you have chosen.
30 For you will become like an oak
    whose leaves are withered,
    and like a garden without water.
31 The strong one
      will become tinder,
    and his work a spark;
    both will burn together,
    with no one to quench
      the flames.

2 The vision that Isaiah son of Amoz saw concerning Judah and Jerusalem:

2 In the last days
    the mountain of the LORD's house
      will be established
    at the top of the mountains
    and will be raised above the hills.
    All nations will stream to it,
3 and many peoples will come
      and say,
    "Come, let us go up
      to the mountain of the LORD,
    to the house of the God of Jacob.
    He will teach us about His ways
    so that we may walk in His paths."
    For instruction will go out of Zion
    and the word of the LORD
      from Jerusalem.
4 He will settle disputes
    among the nations

and provide arbitration
for many peoples.
They will turn their swords
into plows
and their spears
into pruning knives.
Nations will not take up the sword
against other nations,
and they will never again train
for war.

⁵ House of Jacob,
come and let us walk
in the LORD's light.
⁶ For You have abandoned
Your people,
the house of Jacob,
because they are full of divination
from the East
and of fortune-tellers
like the Philistines.
They are in league
with foreigners.
⁷ Their land is full of silver
and gold,
and there is no limit
to their treasures;
their land is full of horses,
and there is no limit
to their chariots.
⁸ Their land is full of idols;
they bow down to the work
of their hands,
to what their fingers have made.
⁹ So humanity is brought low,
and man is humbled.
Do not forgive them!
¹⁰ Go into the rocks
and hide in the dust
from the terror of the LORD
and from His majestic splendor.
¹¹ Human pride will be humbled,
and the loftiness of men
will be brought low;
the LORD alone will be exalted
on that day.

¹² For a day belonging to the LORD of
Hosts is coming
against all that is proud and lofty,
against all that is lifted up—it will
be humbled—
¹³ against all the cedars of Lebanon,
lofty and lifted up,

against all the oaks of Bashan,
¹⁴ against all the high mountains,
against all the lofty hills,
¹⁵ against every high tower,
against every fortified wall,
¹⁶ against every ship of Tarshish,
and against every splendid
sea vessel.
¹⁷ So human pride will be
brought low,
and the loftiness of men
will be humbled;
the LORD alone will be exalted
on that day.
¹⁸ The idols will vanish completely.

¹⁹ People will go into caves
in the rocks
and holes in the ground,
away from the terror of the LORD
and from His majestic splendor,
when He rises to terrify the earth.
²⁰ On that day people will throw
their silver and gold idols,
which they made to worship,
to the moles and the bats.
²¹ They will go into the caves
of the rocks
and the crevices in the cliffs,
away from the terror of the LORD
and from His majestic splendor,
when He rises to terrify the earth.
²² Put no more trust in man,
who has only the breath
in his nostrils.
What is he really worth?

PSALM 109:1-7

¹ God of my praise, do not be silent.

² For wicked and deceitful mouths
open against me;
they speak against me with lying
tongues.
³ They surround me with hateful
words
and attack me without cause.
⁴ In return for my love they accuse
me,
but I continue to pray.
⁵ They repay me evil for good,
and hatred for my love.

⁶ Set a wicked person over him;
let an accuser stand at his right
hand.
⁷ When he is judged, let him be
found guilty,
and let his prayer be counted as
sin.

PROVERBS 22:28-29

²⁸ Don't move an ancient property
line
that your fathers set up.

²⁹ Do you see a man skilled in his
work?
He will stand in the presence of
kings.
He will not stand in the presence
of unknown men.

2 CORINTHIANS 6:14–7:16

¹⁴ Do not be mismatched with unbelievers. For what partnership is there
between righteousness and lawlessness? Or what fellowship does light
have with darkness? ¹⁵ What agreement
does Christ have with Belial? Or what
does a believer have in common with an
unbeliever? ¹⁶ And what agreement does
God's sanctuary have with idols? For we
are the sanctuary of the living God, as
God said:

I will dwell among them
and walk among them,
and I will be their God,
and they will be My people.
¹⁷ Therefore, come out
from among them
and be separate, says the Lord;
do not touch any unclean thing,
and I will welcome you.
¹⁸ I will be a Father to you,
and you will be sons
and daughters to Me,
says the Lord Almighty.

7 Therefore dear friends, since we
have such promises, we should
wash ourselves clean from every impurity of the flesh and spirit, making our
sanctification complete in the fear of
God.
² Take us into your hearts. We have
wronged no one, corrupted no one, defrauded no one. ³ I don't say this to condemn you, for I have already said that
you are in our hearts, to die together
and to live together. ⁴ I have great confidence in you; I have great pride in you.
I am filled with encouragement; I am
overcome with joy in all our afflictions.
⁵ In fact, when we came into Macedonia, we had no rest. Instead, we were
afflicted in every way: struggles on the
outside, fears inside. ⁶ But God, who
comforts the humble, comforted us by
the coming of Titus, ⁷ and not only
by his coming, but also by the comfort
he received from you. He announced to
us your deep longing, your sorrow, your
zeal for me, so that I rejoiced even
more. ⁸ For although I grieved you with
my letter, I do not regret it—even
though I did regret it since I saw that
the letter grieved you, though only for
a little while. ⁹ Now I am rejoicing, not
because you were grieved, but because
your grief led to repentance. For you
were grieved as God willed, so that you
didn't experience any loss from us.
¹⁰ For godly grief produces a repentance
not to be regretted and leading to salvation, but worldly grief produces death.
¹¹ For consider how much diligence this
very thing—this grieving as God wills—
has produced in you: what a desire to
clear yourselves, what indignation, what
fear, what deep longing, what zeal, what
justice! In every way you have commended yourselves to be pure in this
matter. ¹² So even though I wrote to
you, it was not because of the one who
did wrong, or because of the one who
was wronged, but in order that your diligence for us might be made plain to you
in the sight of God. ¹³ For this reason we
have been comforted.
In addition to our comfort, we were
made to rejoice even more over the joy
Titus had, because his spirit was refreshed by all of you. ¹⁴ For if I have
made any boast to him about you, I
have not been embarrassed; but as I

have spoken everything to you in truth, so our boasting to Titus has also turned out to be the truth. ¹⁵ And his affection toward you is even greater as he re-

members the obedience of all of you, and how you received him with fear and trembling. ¹⁶ I rejoice that I have complete confidence in you.

Holiness Is Healthiness

We should wash ourselves clean from every impurity of the flesh, making our sanctification complete in the fear of God.

—2 Corinthians 7:1

When we study the Scriptures, particularly the Old Testament, we find that those who got closest to God thought more of His holiness than any other thing. Why should this be? I think in the nature of things it cannot be any other way because, more than anything else, God wants us to be holy. Over and over again in the Bible we are told: "Be holy even as I am holy." We are not directed to be omnipotent (all-powerful) or omniscient (all-wise) as God is, but we are to be holy. This is the prime way of honoring God. We do not glorify Him by eloquent expressions of pompous service but by aspiring to converse with Him with unstained spirits and live to Him in living *like* Him.

Are you seeking to be holy? God has made holiness the moral condition necessary to the health of His universe. Sin's temporary presence in the world only accentuates this. Whatever is holy is healthy, and evil is a moral sickness that must ultimately end in death. The formation of the language itself suggest this, the English word "holy" deriving from the Anglo-Saxon *halig*, meaning "well" or "whole". To be whole in Christian terms means to be holy. Can you say "I am holy—truly holy"? I am afraid I can't. I don't think any honest Christian would say "yes" to that question. But neither would any honest Christian ignore these solemn words: "Pursue peace with everyone, and holiness—without it no one will see the Lord" (Heb 12:14).

Prayer

O Father, help me to be as concerned for the moral health of the universe as You are. But more, help me to focus first on my own moral health and to be rid of all in my life that is contrary to You and Your nature. In Jesus' name I ask it. Amen.

Further Study

Lk 1:67-80; 2 Pt 3:11; 2 Co 7:1
Why has God raised up a horn of salvation?
What kind of people ought we to be?

SEPTEMBER 20

ISAIAH 3:1–5:23

3 Observe this: The Lord GOD of
Hosts
is about to remove from Jerusalem
and from Judah
every kind of security:
the entire supply of bread
and water,
2 the hero and warrior,
the judge and prophet,
the fortune-teller and elder,
3 the commander of 50
and the dignitary,
the counselor, cunning magician,
and necromancer.
4 "I will make youths their leaders,
and the unstable
will govern them."
5 The people will oppress
one another,
man against man, neighbor
against neighbor;
the youth will act arrogantly
toward the elder,
and the worthless
toward the honorable.
6 A man will even seize his brother
in his father's house, saying:
"You have a cloak—you be
our leader!
This heap of rubble will be
under your control."
7 On that day
he will cry out, saying:
"I'm not a healer.
I don't even have food or clothing
in my house.
Don't make me the leader
of the people!"
8 For Jerusalem has stumbled
and Judah has fallen
because they have spoken
and acted against the LORD,
defying His glorious presence.
9 The look on their faces testifies
against them,

and like Sodom, they flaunt
their sin.
They do not conceal it.
Woe to them!
For they have brought evil
on themselves.
10 Tell the righteous that
it will go well for them,
for they will eat the fruit
of their deeds.
11 Woe to the wicked—it will go
badly for them,
for what they have done
will be done to them.
12 Youths oppress My people,
and women rule over them.
My people, your leaders
mislead you;
they confuse the direction
of your paths.

13 The LORD rises to argue the case
and stands to judge the people.
14 The LORD brings this charge
against the elders and leaders
of His people:
"You have devastated
the vineyard.
The plunder from the poor is
in your houses.
15 Why do you crush My people
and grind the faces of the poor?"
says the Lord GOD of Hosts.

16 The LORD also says:

Because the daughters of Zion
are haughty,
walking with heads held high
and seductive eyes,
going along with prancing steps,
jingling their ankle bracelets,
17 the Lord will put scabs
on the heads
of the daughters of Zion,
and the LORD will shave
their foreheads bare.

¹⁸ On that day the Lord will strip their finery: ankle bracelets, headbands, crescents, ¹⁹ pendants, bracelets, veils, ²⁰ headdresses, ankle jewelry, sashes, perfume bottles, amulets, ²¹ signet rings, nose rings, ²² festive robes, capes, cloaks, purses, ²³ garments, linen clothes, turbans, and veils.

²⁴ Instead of perfume there will be
a stench;
instead of a belt, a rope;
instead of beautifully styled hair,
baldness;
instead of fine clothes, sackcloth;
instead of beauty, branding.
²⁵ Your men will fall by the sword,
your warriors in battle.
²⁶ Then her gates will lament
and mourn;
deserted, she will sit
on the ground.
4 On that day seven women
will seize one man, saying,
"We will eat our own bread
and provide our own clothing.
Just let us be called by your name.
Take away our disgrace."

² On that day the branch of the LORD will be beautiful and glorious, and the fruit of the land will be the pride and glory of Israel's survivors. ³ Whoever remains in Zion and whoever is left in Jerusalem will be called holy—all in Jerusalem who are destined to live— ⁴ when the Lord has washed away the filth of the daughters of Zion and cleansed the bloodguilt from the heart of Jerusalem by a spirit of judgment and a spirit of burning. ⁵ Then the LORD will create a cloud of smoke by day and a glowing flame of fire by night over the entire site of Mount Zion and over its assemblies. For there will be a canopy over all the glory, ⁶ and there will be a booth for shade from heat by day, and a refuge and shelter from storm and rain.

5 I will sing about the one I love,
a song about my loved one's
vineyard:
The one I love had a vineyard
on a very fertile hill.

² He broke up the soil, cleared it
of stones,
and planted it
with the finest vines.
He built a tower in the middle
of it
and even hewed
out a winepress there.
He expected it to yield
good grapes,
but it yielded worthless grapes.

³ So now, residents of Jerusalem
and men of Judah,
please judge between Me
and My vineyard.
⁴ What more could I have done
for My vineyard
than I did?
Why, when I expected a yield
of good grapes,
did it yield worthless grapes?
⁵ Now I will tell you
what I am about to do
to My vineyard:
I will remove its hedge,
and it will be consumed;
I will tear down its wall,
and it will be trampled.
⁶ I will make it a wasteland.
It will not be pruned or weeded;
thorns and briers will grow up.
I will also give orders
to the clouds
that rain should not fall on it.
⁷ For the vineyard of the LORD of
Hosts
is the house of Israel,
and the men of Judah,
the plant He delighted in.
He looked for justice
but saw injustice,
for righteousness,
but heard cries of wretchedness.

⁸ Woe to those who add house
to house
and join field to field
until there is no more room
and you alone are left in the land.

⁹ In my hearing the LORD of Hosts has taken an oath:

Indeed, many houses
will become desolate,
grand and lovely ones
without inhabitants.
¹⁰ For a ten-acre vineyard will yield
only six gallons,
and 10 bushels of seed will yield
only one bushel.

¹¹ Woe to those who rise early
in the morning
in pursuit of beer,
who linger into the evening,
inflamed by wine.
¹² At their feasts they have
lyre, harp,
tambourine, flute, and wine.
They do not perceive
the LORD's actions,
and they do not see the work
of His hands.

¹³ Therefore My people go into exile
because they lack knowledge;
the dignitaries are starving,
and the masses are parched
with thirst.
¹⁴ Therefore Sheol enlarges its throat
and opens wide
its enormous jaws,
and down go Zion's dignitaries,
her masses,
her crowds, and those
who carouse in her!
¹⁵ Humanity is brought low,
man is humbled,
and haughty eyes are humbled.
¹⁶ But the LORD of Hosts is exalted
by His justice,
and the holy God is distinguished
by righteousness.
¹⁷ Lambs will graze
as if in their own pastures,
and strangers will eat
among the ruins of the rich.

¹⁸ Woe to those
who drag wickedness
with cords of deceit
and pull sin along
with cart ropes,
¹⁹ to those who say:
"Let Him hurry up and do
His work quickly

so that we can see it!
Let the plan of the Holy One
of Israel take place
so that we can know it!"
²⁰ Woe to those who call evil good
and good evil,
who substitute darkness for light
and light for darkness,
who substitute bitter for sweet
and sweet for bitter.
²¹ Woe to those who are wise
in their own opinion
and clever in their own sight.
²² Woe to those who are heroes
at drinking wine,
who are fearless at mixing beer,
²³ who acquit the guilty for a bribe
and deprive the innocent
of justice.

PSALM 109:8-15

⁸ Let his days be few;
let another take over his position.
⁹ Let his children be fatherless
and his wife a widow.
¹⁰ Let his children wander as
beggars,
searching for food far from their
demolished homes.
¹¹ Let a creditor seize all he has;
let strangers plunder what he has
worked for.
¹² Let no one show him kindness,
and let no one be gracious to his
fatherless children.
¹³ Let the line of his descendants be
cut off;
let their name be blotted out in
the next generation.
¹⁴ Let his forefathers' guilt be
remembered before the LORD,
and do not let his mother's sin be
blotted out.
¹⁵ Let their sins always remain
before the LORD,
and let Him cut off all memory of
them from the earth.

PROVERBS 23:1-3

23 When you sit down to dine with
a ruler,

consider carefully what is before
you,
2 and stick a knife in your throat
if you have a big appetite;
3 don't desire his choice food,
for that food is deceptive.

2 CORINTHIANS
8:1-24

8 We want you to know, brothers,
about the grace of God granted to
the churches of Macedonia: 2 during a
severe testing by affliction, their abundance of joy and their deep poverty
overflowed into the wealth of their generosity. 3 I testify that, on their own, according to their ability and beyond their
ability, 4 they begged us insistently for
the privilege of sharing in the ministry
to the saints, 5 and not just as we had
hoped. Instead, they gave themselves
especially to the Lord, then to us by
God's will. 6 So we urged Titus that, just
as he had begun, so he should also complete this grace to you. 7 Now as you excel in everything—in faith, in speech,
in knowledge, in all diligence, and in
your love for us—excel also in this
grace.
8 I am not saying this as a command.
Rather, by means of the diligence of others, I am testing the genuineness of
your love. 9 For you know the grace of
our Lord Jesus Christ: although He was
rich, for your sake He became poor, so
that by His poverty you might become
rich. 10 Now I am giving an opinion on
this because it is profitable for you, who
a year ago began not only to do something but also to desire it. 11 But now
finish the task as well, that just as there
was eagerness to desire it, so there may
also be a completion from what you
have. 12 For if the eagerness is there, it

is acceptable according to what one has,
not according to what he does not have.
13 It is not that there may be relief for
others and hardship for you, but it is a
question of equality— 14 at the present
time your surplus is available for their
need, so that their abundance may also
become available for your need, that
there may be equality. 15 As it has been
written:

> The person who gathered much
> did not have too much,
> and the person who gathered
> little did not have too little.

16 Thanks be to God who put the same
diligence for you into the heart of Titus.
17 For he accepted our urging and, being
very diligent, went out to you by his
own choice. 18 With him we have sent
the brother who is praised throughout
the churches for his gospel ministry.
19 And not only that, but he was also appointed by the churches to accompany
us with this gift that is being administered by us for the glory of the Lord
Himself and to show our eagerness to
help. 20 We are taking this precaution so
no one can find fault with us concerning this large sum administered by us.
21 For we are making provision for what
is honorable, not only before the Lord
but also before men. 22 We have also
sent with them our brother whom we
have often tested, in many circumstances, and found diligent—and now
even more diligent because of his great
confidence in you. 23 As for Titus, he
is my partner and co-worker serving
you; as for our brothers, they are the
messengers of the churches, the glory
of Christ. 24 Therefore, before the
churches, show them the proof of your
love and of our boasting about you.

Some Things Bitter to Digest

Woe to them! For they have brought evil on themselves.—Isaiah 3:9

The fifth Beatitude, when practiced, engenders within us good mental and spiritual health. Psychologists have shown that those who lack the qualities of mercy and compassion are more likely to develop physical problems. Harsh, judgmental attitudes may bring a sense of satisfaction to the person who does not know the meaning of mercy, but it is a false sense of satisfaction.

A verse that, strictly speaking, does not apply to what I am saying here, but nevertheless has some application is this: "It was as sweet as honey in my mouth, but when I ate it, my stomach became bitter" (Rv 10:10). That is what happens whenever we adopt any attitude that is not in harmony with Jesus Christ. At first it is "as sweet as honey"—its beginnings are apparently sweet—but it "[becomes] bitter"—it cannot be assimilated. Our human constitution is not made to function effectively on any attitude that is foreign to the spirit of Jesus Christ.

A Christian doctor says: "We are allergic to wrong attitudes just as some people are allergic to shrimps." I am physically allergic to red and green peppers. I have tried them scores of times, but the result has always been the same—I get sick. I am just as allergic to harsh, judgmental attitudes. I can't assimilate them. They disrupt me—body, soul and spirit. And what goes for me goes also for you. When we fail to practice the principles which our Lord outlined for us in the Beatitudes, then our sense of well-being is lowered, depleted, and poisoned. Goodness is good for us—spiritually, mentally, and physically.

Prayer

Father, something is being burned into my consciousness: there is only one healthy way to live—Your Way. When I break with You, I break with life. Help me always to maintain a close connection with You. In Jesus' name. Amen.

Further Study

Ps 23:1-6; 31:9; Ex 34:6; Gl 5:22; Eph 5:9
Of what is goodness a characteristic?
Can you make the same declaration as the psalmist?

SEPTEMBER 21

ISAIAH 5:24–7:25

24 Therefore, as a tongue of fire
consumes straw
and as dry grass shrivels
in the flame,
so their roots will become
like something rotten
and their blossoms will blow away
like dust,
for they have rejected
the instruction of the LORD
of Hosts,
and they have despised
the word of the Holy One
of Israel.
25 Therefore the LORD's anger burns
against His people.
He raised His hand against them
and struck them;
the mountains quaked,
and their corpses were
like garbage in the streets.
In all this, His anger is
not removed,
and His hand is still raised
to strike.

26 He raises a signal flag
for the distant nations
and whistles for them
from the ends of the earth.
Look—how quickly and swiftly
they come!
27 None of them grows weary
or stumbles;
no one slumbers or sleeps.
No belt is loose,
and no sandal strap broken.
28 Their arrows are sharpened,
and all their bows strung.
Their horses' hooves are like flint;
their chariot wheels are
like a whirlwind.
29 Their roaring is like a lion's;
they roar like young lions;
they growl and seize their prey

and carry it off,
and no one can rescue it.
30 On that day they will roar over it,
like the roaring of the sea.
When one looks at the land,
there will be darkness
and distress;
light will be obscured by clouds.

6 In the year that King Uzziah died, I
saw the Lord seated on a high and
lofty throne, and His robe filled the
temple. 2 Seraphim were standing above
Him; each one had six wings: with two
he covered his face, with two he covered his feet, and with two he flew.
3 And one called to another:

Holy, holy, holy is the LORD of
Hosts;
His glory fills the whole earth.

4 The foundations of the doorways
shook at the sound of their voices, and
the temple was filled with smoke.
5 Then I said:

Woe is me, for I am ruined,
because I am a man
of unclean lips
and live among a people
of unclean lips,
and because my eyes have seen
the King,
the LORD of Hosts.

6 Then one of the seraphim flew to
me, and in his hand was a glowing coal
that he had taken from the altar with
tongs. 7 He touched my mouth with it
and said:

Now that this has touched
your lips,
your wickedness is removed,
and your sin is atoned for.

[8] Then I heard the voice of the Lord saying:

Who should I send?
Who will go for Us?

I said:

Here I am. Send me.

[9] And He replied:

Go! Say to these people:
Keep listening,
    but do not understand;
keep looking, but do not perceive.
[10] Dull the minds of these people;
    deafen their ears and blind
        their eyes;
    otherwise they might see
        with their eyes
    and hear with their ears,
    understand with their minds,
    turn back, and be healed.

[11] Then I said, "Until when, Lord?"
And He replied:

Until cities lie in ruins
    without inhabitants,
houses are without people,
    the land is ruined and desolate,
[12]   and the LORD drives the people
        far away,
    leaving great emptiness
        in the land.
[13] Though a tenth will remain
        in the land,
    it will be burned again.
Like the terebinth or the oak,
    which leaves a stump when felled,
    the holy seed is the stump.

7 This took place during the reign of Ahaz, son of Jotham, son of Uzziah king of Judah: Rezin king of Aram, along with Pekah, son of Remaliah, king of Israel, waged war against Jerusalem, but he could not succeed. [2] When it became known to the house of David that Aram had occupied Ephraim, the heart of Ahaz and the hearts of his people trembled like trees of a forest shaking in a wind.

[3] Then the LORD said to Isaiah, "Go out with your son Shear-jashub to meet Ahaz at the end of the conduit of the upper pool, by the road to the Fuller's Field. [4] Say to him: Calm down and be quiet. Don't be afraid or fainthearted because of these two smoldering stubs of firebrands, Rezin of Aram, and the son of Remaliah. [5] For Aram, along with Ephraim and the son of Remaliah, has plotted harm against you. They say: [6] Let us go up against Judah, terrorize it, and conquer it for ourselves. Then we can install Tabeel's son as king in it." [7] This is what the Lord GOD says:

It will not happen;
    it will not occur.
[8] The head of Aram is Damascus,
    the head of Damascus is Rezin
    (within 65 years
    Ephraim will be too shattered
        to be a people),
[9] the head of Ephraim is Samaria,
    and the head of Samaria is the son
        of Remaliah.
If you do not stand firm
    in your faith,
then you will not stand at all.

[10] Then the LORD spoke again to Ahaz: [11] "Ask for a sign from the LORD your God—from the depths of Sheol to the heights of heaven." [12] But Ahaz replied, "I will not ask. I will not test the LORD." [13] Isaiah said, "Listen, house of David! Is it not enough for you to try the patience of men? Will you also try the patience of my God? [14] Therefore, the Lord Himself will give you a sign: The virgin will conceive, have a son, and name him Immanuel. [15] By the time he learns to reject what is bad and choose what is good, he will be eating butter and honey. [16] For before the boy knows to reject what is bad and choose what is good, the land of the two kings you dread will be abandoned. [17] The LORD will bring on you, your people, and the house of your father, such a time as has never been since Ephraim separated from Judah—the king of Assyria is coming.

[18] On that day
the LORD will whistle to the fly
that is at the farthest streams
of the Nile
and to the bee that is in the land
of Assyria.
[19] All of them will come and settle
in the steep ravines, in the clefts
of the rocks,
in all the thornbushes, and in all
the water holes.

[20] On that day the Lord will use a razor hired from beyond the Euphrates River—the king of Assyria—to shave the head, the hair on the legs, and to remove the beard as well.

[21] On that day
a man will raise a young cow
and two sheep,
[22] and from the abundant milk
they give
he will eat butter,
for every survivor in the land
will eat butter and honey.

[23] And on that day
every place where there were
1,000 vines,
worth 1,000 pieces of silver,
will become thorns and briers.
[24] A man will go there with bow
and arrows
because the whole land
will be thorns and briers.
[25] You will not go to all the hills
that were once tilled with a hoe,
for fear of the thorns and briers.
Those hills will be places for oxen
to graze
and for sheep to trample.

*P*SALM 109:16-25

[16] For he did not think to show
kindness,
but pursued the wretched poor
and the brokenhearted
in order to put them to death.
[17] He loved cursing—let it fall on him;
he took no delight in blessing—let
it be far from him.

[18] He wore cursing like his coat—
let it enter his body like water
and go into his bones like oil.
[19] Let it be like a robe he wraps
around himself,
like a belt he always wears.
[20] Let this be the LORD's payment to
my accusers,
to those who speak evil against me.

[21] But You, GOD my Lord,
deal kindly with me because of
Your name;
deliver me because of the
goodness of Your faithful love.
[22] For I am poor and needy;
my heart is wounded within me.
[23] I fade away like a lengthening
shadow;
I am shaken off like a locust.
[24] My knees are weak from fasting,
and my body is emaciated.
[25] I have become an object of
ridicule to my accusers;
when they see me, they shake
their heads in scorn.

*P*ROVERBS 23:4-5

[4] Don't wear yourself out to get
rich;
stop giving your attention to it.
[5] As soon as your eyes fly to it, it
disappears,
for it makes wings for itself
and flies like an eagle to the sky.

2 *C*ORINTHIANS
9:1–10:11

[9] Now concerning the ministry to the saints, it is unnecessary for me to write to you. [2] For I know your eagerness, and I brag about you to the Macedonians: "Achaia has been prepared since last year," and your zeal has stirred up most of them. [3] But I sent the brothers so our boasting about you in the matter would not prove empty, and so you would be prepared just as I said. [4] For if any Macedonians should come with me and find you unprepared, we, not to mention you, would be embarrassed in

that situation. [5] Therefore I considered it necessary to urge the brothers to go on ahead to you and arrange in advance the generous gift you promised, so that it will be ready as a gift and not an extortion.

[6] Remember this: the person who sows sparingly will also reap sparingly, and the person who sows generously will also reap generously. [7] Each person should do as he has decided in his heart—not out of regret or out of necessity, for God loves a cheerful giver. [8] And God is able to make every grace overflow to you, so that in every way, always having everything you need, you may excel in every good work. [9] As it is written:

> He has scattered;
> He has given to the poor;
> His righteousness endures forever.

[10] Now the One who provides seed for the sower and bread for food will provide and multiply your seed and increase the harvest of your righteousness, [11] as you are enriched in every way for all generosity, which produces thanksgiving to God through us. [12] For the ministry of this service is not only supplying the needs of the saints, but is also overflowing in many acts of thanksgiving to God. [13] Through the proof of this service, they will glorify God for your obedience to the confession of the gospel of Christ, and for your generosity in sharing with them and with others. [14] And in their prayers for you they will have deep affection for you because of the surpassing grace of God on you. [15] Thanks be to God for His indescribable gift.

10 Now I, Paul, make a personal appeal to you by the gentleness and graciousness of Christ—I who am humble among you in person, but bold toward you when absent. [2] I beg you that when I am present I will not need to be bold with the confidence by which I plan to challenge certain people who think we are walking in a fleshly way. [3] For although we are walking in the flesh, we do not wage war in a fleshly way, [4] since the weapons of our warfare are not fleshly, but are powerful through God for the demolition of strongholds. We demolish arguments [5] and every high-minded thing that is raised up against the knowledge of God, taking every thought captive to the obedience of Christ. [6] And we are ready to punish any disobedience, once your obedience is complete.

[7] Look at what is obvious. If anyone is confident that he belongs to Christ, he should remind himself of this: just as he belongs to Christ, so do we. [8] For if I boast some more about our authority, which the Lord gave for building you up and not for tearing you down, I am not ashamed. [9] I don't want to seem as though I am trying to terrify you with my letters. [10] For it is said, "His letters are weighty and powerful, but his physical presence is weak, and his public speaking is despicable." [11] Such a person should consider this: what we are in the words of our letters when absent, we will be in actions when present.

Quality Par Excellence

*Holy, holy, holy is the L*ORD *of Hosts.*—Isaiah 6:3

Even the most casual reader of the Scriptures cannot help but notice that God is portrayed in the Bible as uniquely and awesomely holy. In fact, there are more references to the holiness of God in Scripture than to any other aspect of His character. This ought to give us some indication of how important it is.

But what do we mean when we say God is "holy"? There are three thoughts underlying the word "holy."

First, the idea of separation, being withdrawn or apart.
Second, brightness or brilliance.
Third, moral majesty, purity, or cleanliness.

It is interesting that those who came into direct contact with the Almighty in the Old Testament were inevitably overwhelmed by His moral majesty.

Isaiah went into the temple to pray at a time when his people were in grave difficulties. Uzziah, the king who had ruled for half a century, was dying, and Assyria, a terrible and evil force, stood threateningly to the north. Whatever answer Isaiah thought he would get as he opened up his heart to God, it was not the one he received. He was given instead a vision of a holy God that shook him to the core of his being.

Why should this be? I think it was because the concept of God's holiness is the main lesson in His school, the divine prerequisite for admission to the inner heart of God, the most important qualification for learning from the Lord.

Prayer

Father, I must search my heart this day and ask myself: Do I know what it is to serve a holy God? Have I ever received a vision of the moral majesty and purity of the divine? Deepen my understanding of all this I pray. In Jesus' name. Amen.

Further Study

Ex 15:1-11; Ps 99:9
What question did Moses pose?
What did the psalmist affirm?

SEPTEMBER 22

*I*SAIAH 8:1–10:11

8 Then the LORD said to me, "Take a large piece of parchment and write on it with an ordinary pen: Maher-shalal-hash-baz. ² I have appointed trustworthy witnesses—Uriah the priest and Zechariah son of Jeberechiah."

³ I was then intimate with the prophetess, and she conceived and gave birth to a son. The LORD said to me, "Name him Maher-shalal-hash-baz, ⁴ for before the boy knows how to call out father or mother, the wealth of Damascus and the spoils of Samaria will be carried off to the king of Assyria."

⁵ The LORD spoke to me again:

⁶   Because these people rejected
     the slowly flowing waters
         of Shiloah

and rejoiced with Rezin
and the son of Remaliah,
7 the Lord will certainly bring
against them
the mighty rushing waters
of the Euphrates River—
the king of Assyria
and all his glory.
It will overflow its channels
and spill over all its banks.
8 It will pour into Judah,
flood over it, and sweep through,
reaching up to the neck;
and its spreading streams
will fill your entire land,
Immanuel!

9 Band together, peoples,
and be broken;
pay attention,
all you distant lands;
prepare for war, and be broken;
prepare for war, and be broken.
10 Devise a plan; it will fail.
Make a prediction;
it will not happen.
For God is with us.

11 For this is what the LORD said to me
with great power, to keep me from going the way of this people:

12 Do not call everything an alliance
these people say is an alliance.
Do not fear what they fear;
do not be terrified.
13 You are to regard only the LORD of
Hosts as holy.
Only He should be feared;
only He should be held in awe.
14 He will be a sanctuary;
but for the two houses of Israel,
He will be a stone to stumble over
and a rock to trip over,
and a trap and a snare
to the inhabitants
of Jerusalem.
15 Many will stumble over these;
they will fall and be broken;
they will be snared and captured.

16 Bind up the testimony.
Seal up the instruction
among my disciples.

17 I will wait for the LORD,
who is hiding His face
from the house of Jacob.
I will wait for Him.

18 Here I am with the children the
LORD has given me to be signs and wonders in Israel from the LORD of Hosts
who dwells on Mount Zion. 19 When
they say to you, "Consult the spirits of
the dead and the spiritists who chirp
and mutter," shouldn't a people consult
their God? Should they consult the dead
on behalf of the living? 20 To the law and
to the testimony! If they do not speak
according to this word, there will be no
dawn for them. 21 They will wander through the land,
dejected and hungry. When they are
famished, they will become enraged,
and, looking upward, will curse their
king and their God. 22 They will look toward the earth and see only distress,
darkness, and the gloom of affliction,
and they will be driven into thick darkness.

9 Nevertheless, the gloom of the distressed land will not be like that of
the former times when He humbled the
land of Zebulun and the land of
Naphtali. But in the future He will bring
honor to the Way of the Sea, to the land
east of the Jordan, and to Galilee of the
nations.

2 The people walking in darkness
have seen a great light;
on those living in the land
of darkness,
a light has dawned.
3 You have enlarged the nation
and increased its joy.
The people have rejoiced
before You
as they rejoice at harvest time
and as they rejoice
when dividing spoils.
4 For You have shattered
their burdensome yoke
and the rod on their shoulders,
the staff of their oppressor,
just as You did on the day
of Midian.

5 For the trampling boot of battle
and the bloodied garments of war
will be burned as fuel for the fire.
6 For a child will be born for us,
a son will be given to us,
and the government will be
on His shoulders.
He will be named
Wonderful Counselor,
Mighty God,
Eternal Father, Prince of Peace.
7 The dominion will be vast,
and its prosperity will never end.
He will reign on the throne
of David
and over his kingdom,
to establish and sustain it
with justice and righteousness
from now on and forever.
The zeal of the LORD of Hosts
will accomplish this.

8 The Lord sent a message
against Jacob;
it came against Israel.
9 All the people—
Ephraim and the inhabitants
of Samaria—will know it.
They will say with pride
and arrogance:
10 "The bricks have fallen,
but we will rebuild with cut stones;
the sycamores have been cut down,
but we will replace them
with cedars."
11 The LORD has raised up
Rezin's adversaries
against him
and stirred up his enemies.
12 Aram from the east and Philistia
from the west
have consumed Israel
with open mouths.
In all this, His anger
is not removed,
and His hand is still raised
to strike.
13 The people did not turn to Him
who struck them;
they did not seek the LORD
of Hosts.
14 So the LORD cut off Israel's head
and tail,

palm branch and reed
in a single day.
15 The head is the elder,
the honored one;
the tail is the prophet,
the lying teacher.
16 The leaders of the people
mislead them,
and those they mislead
are swallowed up.
17 Therefore the Lord does not
rejoice over
Israel's young men
and has no compassion
on its fatherless and widows,
for everyone is a godless evildoer,
and every mouth speaks folly.
In all this, His anger
is not removed,
and His hand is still raised
to strike.

18 For wickedness burns like a fire
that consumes thorns and briers
and kindles the forest thickets
so that they go up in a column
of smoke.
19 The land is scorched
by the wrath of the LORD of Hosts,
and the people are like fuel
for the fire.
No one has compassion
on his brother.
20 They carve meat on the right,
but they are still hungry;
they have eaten on the left,
but they are still not satisfied.
Each one eats the flesh
of his own arm.
21 Manasseh is with Ephraim,
and Ephraim with Manasseh;
together, both are against Judah.
In all this, His anger is
not removed,
and His hand is still raised
to strike.

10 Woe to those enacting
crooked statutes
and writing oppressive laws
2 to keep the poor from getting
a fair trial
and to deprive the afflicted
among my people of justice,

so that widows can be their spoil
and they can plunder the fatherless.
3 What will you do on the day
of punishment
when devastation comes
from far away?
Who will you run to for help?
Where will you leave your wealth?
4 There will be nothing to do
except crouch
among the prisoners
or fall among the slain.
In all this, His anger
is not removed,
and His hand is still raised
to strike.

5 Woe to Assyria, the rod
of My anger—
the staff in their hands is
My wrath.
6 I will send him against
a godless nation;
I will command him to go
against a people destined
for My rage,
to take spoils, to plunder,
and to trample them down
like clay in the streets.
7 But this is not what he intends;
this is not what he plans.
It is his intent to destroy
and to cut off many nations.
8 For he says:
Aren't all my commanders kings?
9 Isn't Calno like Carchemish?
Isn't Hamath like Arpad?
Isn't Samaria like Damascus?
10 As my hand seized
the idolatrous kingdoms,
whose idols exceeded
those of Jerusalem
and Samaria,
11 and as I did to Samaria
and its idols
will I not also do to Jerusalem
and its idols?

𝒫SALM 109:26-31

26 Help me, LORD my God;
save me according to Your faithful
love

27 so they may know that this is Your
hand
and that You, LORD, have done it.
28 Though they curse, You will bless.
When they rise up, they will be
put to shame,
but Your servant will rejoice.
29 My accusers will be clothed with
disgrace;
they will wear their shame like a
cloak.
30 I will fervently thank the LORD
with my mouth;
I will praise Him in the presence
of many.
31 For He stands at the right hand of
the needy,
to save him from those who would
condemn him.

𝒫ROVERBS 23:6-8

6 Don't eat a stingy person's bread,
and don't desire his choice food,
7 for as he thinks within himself, so
he is.
"Eat and drink," he says to you,
but his heart is not with you.
8 You will vomit the little you've
eaten
and waste your pleasant words.

2 CORINTHIANS 10:12–11:15

¹² For we don't dare classify or compare ourselves with some who commend themselves. But in measuring
themselves by themselves and comparing themselves to themselves, they lack
understanding. ¹³ We, however, will not
boast beyond measure, but according to
the measure of the area of ministry that
God has assigned to us, which reaches
even to you. ¹⁴ For we are not overex-
tending ourselves, as if we had not
reached you, since we have come
to you with the gospel of Christ. ¹⁵ We
are not bragging beyond measure about
other people's labors. But we have the
hope that as your faith increases,
our area of ministry will be greatly enlarged, ¹⁶ so that we may preach the

gospel to the regions beyond you, not boasting about what has already been done in someone else's area of ministry. ¹⁷ So the one who boasts must boast in the Lord. ¹⁸ For it is not the one commending himself who is approved, but the one the Lord commends.

11 I wish you would put up with a little foolishness from me. Yes, do put up with me. ² For I am jealous over you with a godly jealousy, because I have promised you in marriage to one husband—to present a pure virgin to Christ. ³ But I fear that, as the serpent deceived Eve by his cunning, your minds may be corrupted from a complete and pure devotion to Christ. ⁴ For if a person comes and preaches another Jesus, whom we did not preach, or you receive a different spirit, which you had not received, or a different gospel, which you had not accepted, you put up with it splendidly! ⁵ Now I consider myself in no way inferior to the "super-apostles." ⁶ Though untrained in public speaking, I am certainly not untrained in knowledge.

Indeed, we have always made that clear to you in everything. ⁷ Or did I commit a sin by humbling myself so that you might be exalted, because I preached the gospel of God to you free of charge? ⁸ I robbed other churches by taking pay from them to minister to you. ⁹ When I was present with you and in need, I did not burden anyone, for the brothers who came from Macedonia supplied my needs. I have kept myself, and will keep myself, from burdening you in any way. ¹⁰ As the truth of Christ is in me, this boasting of mine will not be stopped in the regions of Achaia. ¹¹ Why? Because I don't love you? God knows I do!

¹² But I will continue to do what I am doing, in order to cut off the opportunity of those who want an opportunity to be regarded just as we are in what they are boasting about. ¹³ For such people are false apostles, deceitful workers, disguising themselves as apostles of Christ. ¹⁴ And no wonder! For Satan himself is disguised as an angel of light. ¹⁵ So it is no great thing if his servants also disguise themselves as servants of righteousness. Their destiny will be according to their works.

The Helmet of Salvation

I fear that, as the serpent deceived Eve by his cunning, your minds may be corrupted from a complete and pure devotion to Christ.

—2 Corinthians 11:3

The second piece of armor that is not tied or fixed to the body but that a Christian soldier has to take up and put on is "the helmet of salvation" (Eph 6:17). The helmet worn by a Roman soldier was usually made of bronze or iron with an inside lining of felt or sponge. In some cases a hinged visor added frontal protection. When a Roman soldier saw an enemy coming, he would take hold of his shield, put on his helmet, take his sword in hand, and stand alert and ready to do battle.

The figure of a helmet immediately suggests to us that this is something designed to protect the mind, the intelligence, the ability to think and reason. Just as the breastplate of righteousness protects us from emotional distress, the helmet of salvation protects us from mental distress. This helmet can help us keep our thinking straight and preserve us from mental confusion.

Has there ever been a time in history when we needed something to keep our thinking straight more than we do now? Politicians vacillate and oscillate between despairing pessimism and unrealistic optimism. Just think of the staggering complexities of the issues we face in our current generation—AIDS, violence, nuclear missiles, international tensions, economic instability, inner-city slums, and so on. The intelligentsia of our day confess to being utterly baffled in dealing with the problems with which human society is confronted. Where can we turn to ease the pressure on our minds? The only answer is God—in the helmet of salvation that He provides.

Prayer

O Father, I am so grateful that You have provided freedom from that most terrifying of human problems—mental distress. Teach me all I need to know in applying Your truth to the important area of my mind. In Jesus' name. Amen.

Further Study

Eph 4:1-17; Rm 8:7; Col 1:21
How were the Ephesians not to live?
How powerful is the influence of the mind?

SEPTEMBER 23

ISAIAH 10:12–12:6

¹² But when the Lord finishes all His work against Mount Zion and Jerusalem, He will say, "I will punish the king of Assyria for his arrogant acts and the proud look in his eyes." ¹³ For he said:

I have done this
  by my own strength
and wisdom, for I am clever.
I abolished the borders of nations
and plundered their treasures;
like a mighty warrior, I subjugated
  the inhabitants.
¹⁴ My hand has reached out, as if
  into a nest,
to seize the wealth of the nations.
Like one gathering
  abandoned eggs,

I gathered the whole earth.
No wing fluttered;
no beak opened or chirped.

¹⁵ Does an ax exalt itself
above the one who chops with it?
Does a saw magnify itself
above the one who saws with it?
As if a staff could wave
  those who lift it!
As if a rod could lift
  what isn't wood!
¹⁶ Therefore the Lord GOD of Hosts
will inflict an emaciating disease
on the well-fed of Assyria,
and He will kindle a burning fire
under its glory.
¹⁷ Israel's Light will become a fire,
and its Holy One, a flame.
In one day it will burn up
  Assyria's thorns and thistles.
¹⁸ He will completely destroy

the glory of its forests
and orchards
as a sickness consumes a person.
¹⁹ The remaining trees of its forest
will be so few in number
that a child could count them.

²⁰ On that day the remnant of Israel and the survivors of the house of Jacob will no longer depend on the one who struck them, but they will faithfully depend on the Lᴏʀᴅ, the Holy One of Israel.

²¹ The remnant will return,
the remnant of Jacob,
to the Mighty God.
²² Israel, even if your people were
as numerous
as the sand of the sea,
only a remnant of them
will return.
Destruction has been decreed;
justice overflows.
²³ For throughout the land
the Lord Gᴏᴅ of Hosts
is carrying out a destruction
that was decreed.

²⁴ Therefore, the Lord Gᴏᴅ of Hosts says this: "My people who dwell in Zion, do not fear Assyria, though he strikes you with a rod and raises his staff over you as the Egyptians did. ²⁵ In just a little while My wrath will be spent and My anger will turn to their destruction." ²⁶ And the Lᴏʀᴅ of Hosts will brandish a whip against him as He did when He struck Midian at the rock of Oreb; and He will raise His staff over the sea as He did in Egypt.

²⁷ On that day
his burden will fall
from your shoulders,
and his yoke from your neck.
The yoke will be broken
because of his fatness.
²⁸ Assyria has come to Aiath
and has gone through Migron,
storing his equipment
at Michmash.
²⁹ They crossed over
at the ford, saying,

"We will spend the night
at Geba."
The people of Ramah
are trembling;
those at Gibeah of Saul have fled.
³⁰ Cry aloud, daughter of Gallim!
Listen, Laishah!
Anathoth is miserable.
³¹ Madmenah has fled.
The inhabitants of Gebim
have sought refuge.
³² Today he will stand at Nob,
shaking his fist at the mountain
of Daughter Zion,
the hill of Jerusalem.
³³ Look, the Lord Gᴏᴅ of Hosts
will chop off the branches
with terrifying power,
and the tall trees will be
cut down,
the high trees felled.
³⁴ He is clearing the thickets
of the forest with an ax,
and Lebanon with its majesty
will fall.

11 Then a shoot will grow
from the stump of Jesse,
and a branch from his roots
will bear fruit.
² The Spirit of the Lᴏʀᴅ will rest
on Him—
a Spirit of wisdom
and understanding,
a Spirit of counsel and strength,
a Spirit of knowledge and of the
fear of the Lᴏʀᴅ.
³ His delight will be in the fear
of the Lᴏʀᴅ.
He will not judge
by what He sees with His eyes,
He will not execute justice
by what He hears with His ears,
⁴ but He will judge
the poor righteously
and execute justice
for the oppressed of the land.
He will strike the land
with discipline from His mouth,
and He will kill the wicked
with a command from His lips.
⁵ Righteousness and faithfulness
will be a belt around His waist.
⁶ The wolf will live with the lamb,

and the leopard will lie down
    with the goat.
The calf, the young lion,
    and the fatling
    will be together,
and a child will lead them.
7 The cow and the bear will graze,
    their young ones
        will lie down together,
and the lion will eat straw
        like an ox.
8 An infant will play
        beside the cobra's pit,
and a toddler will put his hand
        into a snake's den.
9 No one will harm or destroy
    on My entire holy mountain,
for the land will be as full
    of the knowledge of the LORD
    as the sea is filled with water.

10 On that day the root of Jesse
    will stand as a banner
        for the peoples.
The nations will seek Him,
    and His resting place
        will be glorious.

11 On that day the Lord will extend
His hand a second time to recover—
from Assyria, Egypt, Pathros, Cush,
Elam, Shinar, Hamath, and the coasts
and islands of the west—the remnant of
His people who survive.

12 He will lift up a banner
        for the nations
    and gather the dispersed of Israel;
He will collect the scattered
        of Judah
    from the four corners of the earth.
13 Ephraim's envy will cease;
    Judah's harassment will end.
Ephraim will no longer be envious
        of Judah,
    and Judah will not harass Ephraim.
14 But they will swoop down
    on the Philistine flank to the west.
Together they will plunder
        the people of the east.
They will extend their power
        over Edom and Moab,
and the Ammonites will be
        their subjects.

15 The LORD will divide the Gulf
        of Suez.
He will wave His hand
        over the Euphrates
    with His mighty wind
    and will split it
        into seven streams,
letting people walk through
    on foot.
16 There will be a highway
    for the remnant of His people
who will survive from Assyria,
    as there was for Israel
    when they came up from the land
        of Egypt.

12 On that day you will say:
    "I will praise You, LORD,
although You were angry with me.
Your anger has turned away,
and You have had compassion
        on me.
2 Indeed, God is my salvation.
    I will trust Him and not
        be afraid.
Because Yah, the LORD,
    is my strength and my song,
He has become my salvation."
3 You will joyfully draw water
    from the springs of salvation,
4 and on that day you will say:
"Give thanks to the LORD;
    proclaim His name!
Celebrate His deeds
    among the peoples.
Declare that His name is exalted.
5 Sing to the LORD, for He has done
        glorious things.
Let this be known
    throughout the earth.
6 Cry out and sing, citizen of Zion,
for the Holy One of Israel is
        among you
in His greatness."

PSALM 110:1-7

1 The LORD declared to my Lord:
"Sit at My right hand
until I make Your enemies Your
        footstool."
2 The LORD will extend Your mighty
    scepter from Zion.

1122

Rule over Your surrounding
enemies.
3 Your people will volunteer
on Your day of battle.
In holy splendor, from the womb
of the dawn,
the dew of Your youth belongs to
You.
4 The LORD has sworn an oath and
will not take it back:
"Forever, You are a priest
like Melchizedek."

5 The Lord is at Your right hand;
He will crush kings on the day of
His anger.
6 He will judge the nations, heaping
up corpses;
He will crush leaders over the
entire world.
7 He will drink from the brook by
the road;
therefore, He will lift up His head.

PROVERBS 23:9-11

9 Don't speak to a fool,
for he will despise the insight of
your words.

10 Don't move an ancient property
line,
and don't encroach on the fields
of the fatherless,
11 for their Redeemer is strong,
and He will take up their case
against you.

2 CORINTHIANS
11:16–12:10

16 I repeat: no one should consider me
a fool. But if you do, at least accept me
as a fool, so I too may boast a little.
17 What I say in this matter of boasting,
I don't speak as the Lord would, but
foolishly. 18 Since many boast from a human perspective, I will also boast. 19 For
you gladly put up with fools since you
are so smart! 20 In fact, you put up with
it if someone enslaves you, if someone
devours you, if someone captures you,
if someone dominates you, or if some-

one hits you in the face. 21 I say this to
our shame: we have been weak.
But in whatever anyone dares to
boast—I am talking foolishly—I also
dare:

22 Are they Hebrews? So am I.
Are they Israelites? So am I.
Are they the seed of Abraham?
So am I.
23 Are they servants of Christ?
I'm talking like a madman—
I'm a better one:
with far more labors,
many more imprisonments,
far worse beatings, near death
many times.
24 Five times I received
from the Jews 40 lashes
minus one.
25 Three times I was beaten with rods.
Once I was stoned.
Three times I was shipwrecked.
I have spent a night and a day
in the depths of the sea.
26 On frequent journeys, I faced
dangers from rivers,
dangers from robbers,
dangers from my own people,
dangers from the Gentiles,
dangers in the city,
dangers in the open country,
dangers on the sea, and dangers
among false brothers;
27 labor and hardship,
many sleepless nights,
hunger and thirst,
often without food, cold,
and lacking clothing.

28 Not to mention other things, there is
the daily pressure on me: my care for all
the churches. 29 Who is weak, and I am
not weak? Who is made to stumble, and
I do not burn with indignation? 30 If
boasting is necessary, I will boast about
my weaknesses. 31 The eternally blessed
One, the God and Father of the Lord
Jesus, knows I am not lying. 32 In Damascus, the governor under King Aretas
guarded the city of the Damascenes in
order to arrest me, 33 so I was let down
in a basket through a window in the
wall and escaped his hands.

12 It is necessary to boast; it is not helpful, but I will move on to visions and revelations of the Lord. ² I know a man in Christ who was caught up into the third heaven 14 years ago. Whether he was in the body or out of the body, I don't know; God knows. ³ I know that this man—whether in the body or out of the body I do not know, God knows— ⁴ was caught up into paradise. He heard inexpressible words, which a man is not allowed to speak. ⁵ I will boast about this person, but not about myself, except of my weaknesses. ⁶ For if I want to boast, I will not be a fool, because I will be telling the truth. But I will spare you, so that no one can credit me with something beyond what

he sees in me or hears from me, ⁷ especially because of the extraordinary revelations. Therefore, so that I would not exalt myself, a thorn in the flesh was given to me, a messenger of Satan to torment me so I would not exalt myself. ⁸ Concerning this, I pleaded with the Lord three times to take it away from me. ⁹ But He said to me, "My grace is sufficient for you, for power is perfected in weakness." Therefore, I will most gladly boast all the more about my weaknesses, so that Christ's power may reside in me. ¹⁰ So because of Christ, I am pleased in weaknesses, in insults, in catastrophes, in persecutions, and in pressures. For when I am weak, then I am strong.

"Keep Your Eyes on the Tide"

Your people will volunteer on Your day of battle.
——PSALM 110:3

Has God something bigger for us than we are at present seeing? I hope I have convinced you that He has! How can we be open to receiving it? It comes at the precise moment God appoints but it is carried down from heaven on the wings of fervent, believing prayer. Dr. A. T. Pierson said: "From the Day of Pentecost until now, there has not been one great spiritual awakening in any land which has not begun in a union of prayer though only among two or three, and no such outward or upward movement has continued after such prayer meetings have declined." Revivals are born in prayer and sustained by prayer.

Just as there are signs concerning the second coming, so there are signs that the Lord is not far from reviving His whole church. In the early days of the Salvation Army in France, the eldest daughter of General Booth, known by her French rank as the "Marechale," found herself at one point in an extremely discouraging situation. She wrote to General Booth asking for his advice, which came in these words: "Take your eyes off the waves and fix them on the tide."

I give you now that same advice. Don't let your eyes become focused on the waves, with their advances and retreats. Keep your eyes on the tide and ask yourself: is it rising? If you look with the eye of faith I think you will see that it is. When it breaks I pray that it will not find you or me unprepared but that we shall be a people who are willing in the day of God's power.

Prayer

Father, I don't know whether I will live to see a world-wide revival, but I want to live to experience a personal revival. Take me on from this point to know You in a much greater way. In Christ's name I ask it. Amen.

Further Study

Ezk 37:1-14; 2 Kg 3:16-17; Is 40:3-5; Rv 22:1
What was God's message to Ezekiel?
What will you do to bring about revival?

SEPTEMBER 24

ISAIAH 13:1–14:32

13 An oracle against Babylon that Isaiah son of Amoz saw:

2 Lift up a banner
on a barren mountain.
Call out to them.
Wave your hand, and they will go
through the gates of the nobles.
3 I have commanded
My chosen ones;
I have also called My warriors,
who exult in My triumph,
to execute My wrath.
4 Listen, a tumult on the mountains,
like that of a mighty people!
Listen, an uproar
among the kingdoms,
like nations being
gathered together!
The LORD of Hosts is mobilizing
an army for war.
5 They are coming from a far land,
from the distant horizon—
the LORD and the weapons
of His wrath—
to destroy the whole country.

6 Wail! For the day of the LORD
is near.
It will come like destruction
from the Almighty.
7 Therefore everyone's hands
will become weak,
and every man's heart will melt.
8 They will be horrified;
pain and agony will seize them;
they will be in anguish
like a woman in labor.
They will look at each other,
their faces flushed with fear.
9 Look, the day of the LORD
is coming—
cruel, with rage
and burning anger—
to make the earth a desolation
and to destroy the sinners on it.
10 Indeed, the stars of the sky
and its constellations
will not give their light.
The sun will be dark when it rises,
and the moon will not shine.
11 I will bring disaster on the world,
and their own iniquity,
on the wicked.
I will put an end to the pride
of the arrogant

1125

and humiliate the insolence
of tyrants.
¹² I will make man scarcer than gold,
and mankind more rare
than the gold of Ophir.
¹³ Therefore I will make
the heavens tremble,
and the earth will shake
from its foundations
at the wrath of the LORD of Hosts,
on the day of His burning anger.
¹⁴ Like wandering gazelles
and like sheep
without a shepherd,
each one will turn
to his own people,
each one will flee to his own land.
¹⁵ Whoever is found will be stabbed,
and whoever is caught will die
by the sword.
¹⁶ Their children will be smashed
to death before their eyes;
their houses will be looted,
and their wives raped.
¹⁷ Look! I am stirring up the Medes
against them,
who cannot be bought off with
silver
and who have no desire for gold.
¹⁸ Their bows will cut young men
to pieces.
They will have no compassion
on little ones;
they will not look with pity
on children.
¹⁹ And Babylon, the jewel
of the kingdoms,
the glory of the pride
of the Chaldeans,
will be like Sodom and Gomorrah
when God overthrew them.
²⁰ It will never be inhabited
or lived in from generation
to generation;
a nomad will not pitch
his tent there,
and shepherds will not let
their flocks rest there.
²¹ But wild animals
will lie down there,
and owls will fill the houses.
Ostriches will dwell there,
and wild goats will leap about.

²² Hyenas will howl in the fortresses,
and jackals,
in the luxurious palaces.
Babylon's time is almost up;
her days are almost over.

14 For the LORD will have compassion on Jacob and will choose Israel again. He will settle them on their own land. The foreigner will join them and be united with the house of Jacob. ² The nations will escort Israel and bring it to its homeland. Then the house of Israel will possess them as male and female slaves in the LORD's land. They will make captives of their captors and will rule over their oppressors.
³ When the LORD gives you rest from your pain, torment, and the hard labor you were forced to do, ⁴ you will sing this song of contempt about the king of Babylon and say:

How the oppressor
has quieted down,
and how the raging
has become quiet!
⁵ The LORD has broken the staff
of the wicked,
the scepter of the rulers.
⁶ It struck the peoples in anger
with unceasing blows.
It subdued the nations in rage
with relentless persecution.
⁷ All the earth is calm and at rest;
people shout with a ringing cry.
⁸ Even the cypresses and the cedars
of Lebanon
rejoice over you:
"Since you have been laid low,
no woodcutter has come
against us."

⁹ Sheol below is eager to greet
your coming.
He stirs up the spirits
of the departed for you—
all the rulers of the earth.
He makes all the kings
of the nations
rise from their thrones.
¹⁰ They all respond to you, saying:
"You too have become as weak
as we are;

you have become like us!
¹¹ Your splendor has been
brought down to Sheol,
along with the music
of your harps.
Maggots are spread out
under you,
and worms cover you."

¹² Shining morning star,
how you have fallen
from the heavens!
You destroyer of nations,
you have been cut down
to the ground.
¹³ You said to yourself:
"I will ascend to the heavens;
I will set up my throne
above the stars of God.
I will sit on the mount
of the gods' assembly,
in the remotest parts
of the North.
¹⁴ I will ascend above
the highest clouds;
I will make myself like the
Most High."
¹⁵ But you will be brought down
to Sheol
into the deepest regions of the
Pit.

¹⁶ Those who see you will stare
at you;
they will look closely at you:
"Is this the man who caused
the earth to tremble,
who shook the kingdoms,
¹⁷ who turned the world
into a wilderness,
who trampled its cities
and would not release
the prisoners
to return home?"
¹⁸ All the kings of the nations
lie in splendor,
each in his own tomb.
¹⁹ But you are thrown out
without a grave,
like a worthless branch,
covered by those slain
with the sword
and dumped into a rocky pit
like a trampled corpse.

²⁰ You will not join them in burial,
because you destroyed your land
and slaughtered your own people.
The offspring of evildoers
will never be remembered.
²¹ Prepare a place of slaughter
for his sons,
because of the iniquity
of their fathers.
They never rise up to possess
a land
or fill the surface of the earth
with cities.

²² "I will rise up against them"—the declaration of the LORD of Hosts—"and I will cut off from Babylon her reputation, remnant, offspring, and posterity"—the LORD's declaration. ²³ "I will make her a swampland and a region for wild animals, and I will sweep her away with a broom of destruction."
This is the declaration
of the LORD of Hosts.

²⁴ The LORD of Hosts has sworn:

As I have planned, so it will be;
as I have purposed it,
so it will happen.
²⁵ I will break Assyria in My land;
I will tread him down
on My mountain.
Then his yoke will be taken
from them,
and his burden will be removed
from their shoulders.
²⁶ This is the plan prepared
for the whole earth,
and this is the hand stretched out
against all the nations.
²⁷ The LORD of Hosts Himself
has planned it;
therefore, who can stand
in its way?
It is His hand that is outstretched,
so who can turn it back?
²⁸ In the year that King Ahaz died, this oracle came:

²⁹ Don't rejoice, all of you in
Philistia,
because the rod of the one
who struck you is broken.

For a viper will come out
of the root of a snake,
and from its egg comes
a flying serpent.
30 Then the firstborn of the poor
will be well fed,
and the impoverished
will lie down in safety,
but I will kill your root
with hunger,
and your remnant will be slain.
31 Wail, you gates! Cry out, city!
Tremble with fear, all Philistia!
For a cloud of dust is coming
from the north,
and there is no one missing from
the invader's ranks.
32 What answer will be given
to the messengers
from that nation?
The LORD has founded Zion,
and His afflicted people
find refuge in her.

PSALM 111:1-5

1 Hallelujah!
I will praise the LORD with all my
heart
in the assembly of the upright and
in the congregation.

2 The LORD's works are great,
studied by all who delight in them.
3 All that He does is splendid and
majestic;
His righteousness endures forever.
4 He has caused His wonderful
works to be remembered.
The LORD is gracious and
compassionate.
5 He has provided food for those
who fear Him;
He remembers His covenant
forever.

PROVERBS 23:12-14

12 Apply yourself to instruction
and listen to words of knowledge.

13 Don't withhold correction from a
youth;

if you beat him with a rod, he will
not die.
14 Strike him with a rod,
and you will rescue his life from
Sheol.

2 CORINTHIANS 12:11–13:13

11 I have become a fool; you forced it on me. I ought to have been recommended by you, since I am in no way inferior to the "super-apostles," even though I am nothing. 12 The signs of an apostle were performed among you in all endurance—not only signs but also wonders and miracles. 13 So in what way were you treated worse than the other churches, except that I personally did not burden you? Forgive me this wrong!

14 Look! I am ready to come to you this third time. I will not burden you, for I am not seeking what is yours, but you. For children are not obligated to save up for their parents, but parents for their children. 15 I will most gladly spend and be spent for you. If I love you more, am I to be loved less? 16 Now granted, I have not burdened you; yet sly as I am, I took you in by deceit! 17 Did I take advantage of you by anyone I sent you? 18 I urged Titus to come, and I sent the brother with him. Did Titus take advantage of you? Didn't we walk in the same spirit and in the same footsteps?

19 You have thought all along that we were defending ourselves to you. No, in the sight of God we are speaking in Christ, and everything, dear friends, is for building you up. 20 For I fear that perhaps when I come I will not find you to be what I want, and I may not be found by you to be what you want; there may be quarreling, jealousy, outbursts of anger, selfish ambitions, slander, gossip, arrogance, and disorder. 21 I fear that when I come my God will again humiliate me in your presence, and I will grieve for many who sinned before and have not repented of the uncleanness, sexual immorality, and promiscuity they practiced.

13 This is the third time I am coming to you. **On the testimony of two or three witnesses every word will be confirmed.** ²I gave warning, and I give warning—as when I was present the second time, so now while I am absent—to those who sinned before and to all the rest: if I come again, I will not be lenient, ³since you seek proof of Christ speaking in me. He is not weak toward you, but powerful among you. ⁴In fact, He was crucified in weakness, but He lives by God's power. For we also are weak in Him, yet toward you we will live with Him by God's power.

⁵Test yourselves to see if you are in the faith. Examine yourselves. Or do you not recognize for yourselves that Jesus Christ is in you?—unless you fail the test. ⁶And I hope you will recognize that we are not failing the test. ⁷Now we pray to God that you do nothing wrong, not that we may appear to pass the test, but that you may do what is right, even though we may appear to fail. ⁸For we are not able to do anything against the truth, but only for the truth. ⁹In fact, we rejoice when we are weak and you are strong. We also pray for this: your maturity. ¹⁰This is why I am writing these things while absent, that when I am there I will not use severity, in keeping with the authority the Lord gave me for building up and not for tearing down.

¹¹Finally, brothers, rejoice. Be restored, be encouraged, be of the same mind, be at peace, and the God of love and peace will be with you. ¹²Greet one another with a holy kiss. All the saints greet you.

¹³The grace of the Lord Jesus Christ, and the love of God, and the fellowship of the Holy Spirit be with all of you.

A Watershed Truth

The grace of the Lord Jesus Christ, and the love of God, and the fellowship of the Holy Spirit be with all of you.
—2 CORINTHIANS 13:13

That great Christian, Francis Schaeffer, said that he would have remained an agnostic if it weren't for the doctrine of the Trinity. It was this, he claimed, that gave him the answer—the only answer—to the theme of unity and diversity.

The question I have been asked most often about the Trinity is this: Why did not God make clear the truth of the Trinity in the Old Testament, rather than leaving it as something to be deduced in the New Testament? I usually answer like this: Before God could entrust His people with the knowledge of His essential Threeness, He had to lay deep in their minds a piercing conviction of His Oneness. The Bible begins in monotheism (belief in one God), but soon after the Fall comes polytheism (belief in many gods). Which god is the real God? Not until belief in one God was laid deep in the consciousness of the Jewish nation was God ready to reveal more clearly to mankind the sublime truth of the Trinity.

Dr. George Smeaton says: "The biblical idea of the Trinity is the heart of the unique message of Christianity. To explain this mystery is not our province. Ours is simply to conserve the mystery." Those who call themselves Christians yet reject the doctrine of the Trinity will soon latch onto some other error. It is a strange thing, but I have observed it as a fact of the Christian life that when this truth is modified or pushed aside, it is as if the door is opened to the inrush of all kinds of absurd ideas, bizarre theories, and half-truths.

Prayer

Father, help me hold fast to this sublime truth, and enable me to see that though something is above reason, it is not necessarily against reason. Blessed Trinity—Father, Son, and Holy Spirit—I worship You. Amen.

Further Study

Jn 14:8-21; 17:22
How did Jesus depict the Trinity?
What did Jesus confirm?

SEPTEMBER 25

ISAIAH 15:1–18:7

15 An oracle against Moab:

Ar in Moab is devastated,
destroyed in a night.
Kir in Moab is devastated,
destroyed in a night.
2 Dibon went up to its temple
to weep at its high places.
Moab wails on Nebo and at
Medeba.
Every head is shaved;
every beard is cut off.
3 In its streets they wear sackcloth;
on its rooftops
and in its public squares
everyone wails,
falling down and weeping.
4 Heshbon and Elealeh cry out;
their voices are heard as far away
as Jahaz.
Therefore the soldiers of Moab
cry out,
and they tremble.
5 My heart cries out over Moab,
whose fugitives flee
as far as Zoar,

to Eglath-shelishiyah;
they go up the slope
of Luhith weeping;
they raise a cry of destruction
on the road to Horonaim.
6 The waters of Nimrim
are desolate;
the grass is withered, the foliage
is gone,
and the vegetation has vanished.
7 So they carry their wealth
and belongings
over the Wadi of the Willows.
8 For their cry echoes
throughout the territory of Moab.
Their wailing reaches Eglaim;
their wailing reaches Beer-elim.
9 The waters of Dibon are full
of blood,
but I will bring on Dibon
even more than this—
a lion for those who escape
from Moab,
and for the survivors in the land.

16 Send lambs to the ruler
of the land,
from Sela in the desert
to the mountain of Daughter Zion.

² Like a bird fleeing,
forced from the nest,
the daughters of Moab
will be at the fords of the Arnon.

³ Give us counsel and make
a decision.
Shelter us at noonday
with shade that is as dark as night.
Hide the refugee;
do not betray the one who flees.
⁴ Let my refugees stay with you;
be a refuge for Moab
from the aggressor.

When the oppressor has gone,
destruction has ended,
and marauders have vanished
from the land.
⁵ Then in the tent of David
a throne will be established
by faithful love.
A judge who seeks what is right
and is quick to execute justice
will sit on the throne forever.

⁶ We have heard of Moab's pride—
how very proud he is—
his haughtiness, his pride,
his arrogance,
and his empty boasting.
⁷ Therefore let Moab wail;
let every one of them wail
for Moab.
Mourn, you who are
completely devastated,
for the raisin cakes of Kir-haresheth.
⁸ For Heshbon's terraced vineyards
and the grapevines of Sibmah
have withered.
The rulers of the nations
have trampled its choice vines
that reached as far as Jazer
and spread to the desert.
Their shoots spread out
and reached the Dead Sea.
⁹ So I join with Jazer
to weep for the vines of Sibmah;
I drench Heshbon and Elealeh
with my tears.
Triumphant shouts
have fallen silent
over your summer fruit
and your harvest.

¹⁰ Joy and rejoicing
have been removed
from the orchard;
no one is singing or shouting
for joy in the vineyards.
No one tramples grapes
in the winepresses.
I have put an end to the shouting.
¹¹ Therefore I moan like
the sound of a lyre
for Moab,
as does my innermost being
for Kir-heres.
¹² When Moab appears on the
high place,
when he tires himself out
and comes to his sanctuary to pray,
it will do him no good.

¹³ This is the message that the LORD previously announced about Moab. ¹⁴ And now the LORD says, "In three years, as a hired worker counts years, Moab's splendor will become an object of contempt, in spite of a very large population. And those who are left will be few and weak."

17 An oracle against Damascus:
Look, Damascus is no longer
a city.
It has become a ruined heap.
² The cities of Aroer are forsaken;
they will be places for flocks.
They will lie down without fear.
³ The fortress disappears
from Ephraim,
and a kingdom from Damascus.
The remnant of Aram will be
like the splendor of the Israelites.
This is the declaration
of the LORD of Hosts.

⁴ On that day
the splendor of Jacob will fade,
and his healthy body
will become emaciated.
⁵ It will be as if a reaper
had gathered standing grain—
his arm harvesting the heads
of grain—
and as if one had gleaned heads
of grain

in the valley of Rephaim.

⁶ Only gleanings will be left in Israel,
  as if an olive tree
    had been beaten—
two or three berries
  at the very top of the tree,
four or five
  on its fruitful branches.
      This is the declaration
          of the LORD,
      the God of Israel.

⁷ On that day people will look to their Maker and will turn their eyes to the Holy One of Israel. ⁸ They will not look to the altars they made with their hands or to the Asherahs and incense altars they made with their fingers.

⁹ On that day their strong cities
    will be
  like the abandoned woods
    and mountaintops
  that were abandoned because of
    the Israelites;
  there will be desolation.
¹⁰ For you have forgotten the God
    of your salvation,
  and you have failed to remember
  the rock of your strength;
    therefore you will plant
      beautiful plants
  and set out cuttings
    from exotic vines.
¹¹ On the day that you plant,
  you will help them to grow,
  and in the morning
  you will help your seed to sprout,
  but the harvest will vanish
  on the day of disease
    and incurable pain.
¹² Ah! The roar of many peoples—
  they roar like the roaring
    of the seas.
  The raging of the nations—
  they rage like the raging
    of mighty waters.
¹³ The nations rage like the raging
    of many waters.
  He rebukes them, and they flee
    far away,
  driven before the wind like chaff
    on the hills

and like dead thistles
    before a gale.
¹⁴ In the evening—sudden terror!
  Before morning—it is gone!
  This is the fate of those
    who plunder us
  and the lot of those who ravage us.

18 Ah! The land
    of buzzing insect wings
  beyond the rivers of Cush
² sends envoys by sea,
  in reed vessels on the waters.

Go, swift messengers,
  to a nation tall and smooth-skinned,
  to a people feared near and far,
  a powerful nation
    with a strange language,
  whose land is divided by rivers.
³ All you inhabitants of the world
  and you who live on the earth,
  when a banner is raised
    on the mountains, look!
  When a trumpet sounds, listen!

⁴ For, the LORD said to me:

I will quietly look out
    from My place,
  like shimmering heat in sunshine,
  like a rain cloud in harvest heat.
⁵ For before the harvest,
    when the blossoming is over
  and the blossom becomes
    a ripening grape,
  He will cut off the shoots
    with a pruning knife,
  and tear away and remove
    the branches.
⁶ They will all be left for the birds
    of prey on the hills
  and for the wild animals
    of the land.
  The birds will spend the summer
    on them,
  and all the animals, the winter
    on them.

⁷ At that time a gift will be brought to the LORD of Hosts from a people tall and smooth-skinned, a people feared near and far, a powerful nation with a strange language, whose land is divided

by rivers—to Mount Zion, the place of the name of the LORD of Hosts.

PSALM 111:6-10

6 He has shown His people the
power of His works
by giving them the inheritance of
the nations.
7 The works of His hands are truth
and justice;
all His instructions are
trustworthy.
8 They are established forever and
ever,
enacted in truth and uprightness.
9 He has sent redemption to His
people.
He has ordained His covenant
forever.
His name is holy and awe-inspiring.

10 The fear of the LORD is the
beginning of wisdom;
all who follow His instructions
have good insight.
His praise endures forever.

PROVERBS 23:15-16

15 My son, if your heart is wise,
my heart will indeed rejoice.
16 My innermost being will cheer
when your lips say what is right.

GALATIANS 1:1-24

1 Paul, an apostle—not from men or by man, but by Jesus Christ and God the Father who raised Him from the dead— 2 and all the brothers who are with me:

To the churches of Galatia.

3 Grace to you and peace from God the Father and our Lord Jesus Christ, 4 who gave Himself for our sins to rescue us from this present evil age, according to the will of our God and Father, 5 to whom be the glory forever and ever. Amen.

6 I am amazed that you are so quickly turning away from Him who called you by the grace of Christ, and are turning to a different gospel— 7 not that there is another gospel, but there are some who are troubling you and want to change the gospel of Christ. 8 But even if we or an angel from heaven should preach to you a gospel other than what we have preached to you, a curse be on him! 9 As we have said before, I now say again: if anyone preaches to you a gospel contrary to what you received, a curse be on him!

10 For am I now trying to win the favor of people, or God? Or am I striving to please people? If I were still trying to please people, I would not be a slave of Christ.

11 Now I want you to know, brothers, that the gospel preached by me is not based on a human point of view. 12 For I did not receive it from a human source and I was not taught it, but it came by a revelation from Jesus Christ.

13 For you have heard about my former way of life in Judaism: I persecuted God's church to an extreme degree and tried to destroy it; 14 and I advanced in Judaism beyond many contemporaries among my people, because I was extremely zealous for the traditions of my ancestors. 15 But when God, who from my mother's womb set me apart and called me by His grace, was pleased 16 to reveal His Son in me, so that I could preach Him among the Gentiles, I did not immediately consult with anyone. 17 I did not go up to Jerusalem to those who had become apostles before me; instead I went to Arabia and came back to Damascus.

18 Then after three years I did go up to Jerusalem to get to know Cephas, and I stayed with him 15 days. 19 But I didn't see any of the other apostles except James, the Lord's brother. 20 Now in what I write to you, I'm not lying. God is my witness.

21 Afterwards, I went to the regions of Syria and Cilicia. 22 I remained personally unknown to the Judean churches in Christ; 23 they simply kept hearing: "He who formerly persecuted us now preaches the faith he once tried to destroy." 24 And they glorified God because of me.

What Is Faith?

My son, if your heart is wise, my heart will indeed rejoice.
—PROVERBS 23:15

"A man's belief," says Dr Albert Ellis, a well-known modern-day psychologist, "determines both his conduct and his character." Proverbs 23:7, written almost 3,000 years before Ellis, puts the truth in an even more succinct form: "For as he thinks within himself, so he is."

There are two possibilities before each of us as we look at life: we can base our conclusions about the meaning of life on what the humanistic philosophers, poets, and historians tell us, or we can base them on what God tells us in His Word. Either we take the Word of God and live by it—or we do not. If we take the attitude that the prophets didn't know what they were talking about and there are no such things as miracles in the universe, then we do what the writer to the Hebrews tells us—we draw back from the godly way of life (Heb 10:39). The biblical way is living by faith.

Listen to the word given to Habakkuk: "The righteous one will live by his faith" (Hab 2:4). Faith is taking the Word of God and relying on it. It involves believing what God says, simply and solely because He said it. The heroes of faith listed in Hebrews 11 did just that—they had no real reason for believing what God told them, other than the fact that He had spoken. Why did Abraham take his son Isaac to Mount Moriah? Why did he prepare to offer him as a sacrifice? Simply because God had spoken. A little boy, when invited to comment on the statement, "Faith is having confidence in what God has spoken," said: "God has confidence in what He has said—so must we."

Prayer

O Father, forgive my doubts and hesitancies—and help me to have an unshakable confidence in the truth and power of Your Word. Show me how to link my littleness to Your greatness. In Jesus' name I ask it. Amen.

Further Study

Heb 11:1-40; Gl 3:6; Php 3:8-9
How does this chapter describe faith?
Write out your definition of faith.

SEPTEMBER 26

ISAIAH 19:1–22:8

19 An oracle against Egypt:

Look, the LORD rides
    on a swift cloud
and is coming to Egypt.
Egypt's idols will tremble
    before Him,
and Egypt's heart will melt
    within it.

2 I will provoke Egypt against Egypt;
each will fight against his brother
    and each against his friend,
city against city,
    kingdom against kingdom.

3 Egypt's spirit will be disturbed
    within it,
and I will frustrate its plans.
Then they will seek idols, ghosts,
    spirits of the dead, and spiritists.

4 I will deliver Egypt into the hands
    of harsh masters,
and a strong king will rule it.
            This is the declaration
    of the Lord GOD of Hosts.

5 The waters of the sea will dry up,
and the river will be parched
    and dry.

6 The channels will stink;
they will dwindle, and Egypt's canals
    will be parched.
Reed and rush will die.

7 The reeds by the Nile,
    by the mouth of the river,
and all the cultivated areas
    of the Nile
will wither, blow away,
    and vanish.

8 Then the fishermen will mourn.
All those who cast hooks
    into the Nile will lament,
and those who spread nets
    on the water will shrivel up.

9 Those who work with flax
    will be dismayed;
the combers and weavers
    will turn pale.

10 Egypt's weavers will be dejected;
all her wage earners
    will be demoralized.

11 The princes of Zoan
    are complete fools;
Pharaoh's wisest advisers
    give stupid advice!
How can you say to Pharaoh,
"I am one of the wise,
    a student of eastern kings."

12 Where then are your wise men?
Let them tell you and reveal
what the LORD of Hosts
    has planned against Egypt.

13 The princes of Zoan
    have been fools;
the princes of Memphis
    are deceived.
Her tribal chieftains have led
    Egypt astray.

14 The LORD has mixed within her
    a spirit of confusion.
The leaders have made Egypt
    stagger in all she does,
as a drunkard staggers
    in his vomit.

15 No head or tail, palm or reed,
will be able to do anything
    for Egypt.

16 On that day Egypt will be like
women. She will tremble with fear because of the threatening hand of the LORD
of Hosts when He raises it against her.
17 The land of Judah will terrify Egypt;
whenever Judah is mentioned, Egypt
will tremble because of what the LORD
of Hosts has planned against it.

18 On that day five cities in the land of
Egypt will speak the language of Canaan
and swear loyalty to the LORD of Hosts.
One of the cities will be called the City
of the Sun.

19 On that day there will be an altar to

the LORD in the center of the land of Egypt and a pillar to the LORD near her border. ²⁰ It will be a sign and witness to the LORD of Hosts in the land of Egypt. When they cry out to the LORD because of their oppressors, He will send them a savior and leader, and he will rescue them. ²¹ The LORD will make Himself known to Egypt, and Egypt will know the LORD on that day. They will offer sacrifices and offerings; they will make vows to the LORD and fulfill them. ²² The LORD will strike Egypt, striking and healing. Then they will return to the LORD and He will hear their prayers and heal them.

²³ On that day there will be a highway from Egypt to Assyria. Assyria will go to Egypt, Egypt to Assyria, and Egypt will worship with Assyria.

²⁴ On that day Israel will form a triple alliance with Egypt and Assyria—a blessing within the land. ²⁵ The LORD of Hosts will bless them, saying, "Blessed be Egypt My people, Assyria My handiwork, and Israel My inheritance."

20 In the year that the commander-in-chief, sent by Sargon king of Assyria, came to Ashdod and attacked and captured it— ² during that time the LORD had spoken through Isaiah son of Amoz, saying, "Go, take off your sackcloth and remove the sandals from your feet," and he did so, going naked and barefoot— ³ the LORD said, "As My servant Isaiah has gone naked and barefoot three years as a sign and omen against Egypt and Cush, ⁴ so the king of Assyria will lead the captives of Egypt and the exiles of Cush, young and old alike, naked and barefoot, with bared buttocks, to Egypt's shame. ⁵ Those who made Cush their hope and Egypt their boast will be dismayed and ashamed. ⁶ And the inhabitants of this coastland will say on that day: Look, this is what has happened to those we relied on and fled to for help to rescue us from the king of Assyria! Now, how will we escape?"

21 An oracle against the desert by the sea:

Like storms that pass over the Negev, it comes from the desert, from the land of terror.
² A troubling vision is declared to me:
"The treacherous one acts treacherously, and the destroyer destroys. Advance, Elam! Lay siege, you Medes! I will put an end to all her groaning."

³ Therefore I am filled with anguish. Pain grips me, like the pain of a woman in labor. I am too perplexed to hear, too dismayed to see.
⁴ My heart staggers; horror terrifies me. He has turned my last glimmer of hope into sheer terror.
⁵ Prepare a table, and spread out a carpet! Eat and drink! Rise up, you princes, and oil the shields!

⁶ For the Lord has said to me, "Go, post a lookout; let him report what he sees.
⁷ When he sees riders— pairs of horsemen, riders on donkeys, riders on camels— pay close attention."
⁸ Then the lookout reported, "Lord, I stand on the watchtower all day, and I stay at my post all night.
⁹ Look, riders come— horsemen in pairs." And he answered, saying, "Babylon has fallen, has fallen. All the idols of her gods have been shattered on the ground."

¹⁰ My downtrodden and threshed people, I have declared to you

what I have heard from the LORD
of Hosts,
the God of Israel.

¹¹ An oracle against Dumah:

One calls to me from Seir,
"Watchman, what is left
of the night?
Watchman, what is left
of the night?"
¹² The watchman said,
"Morning has come,
and also night.
If you want to ask, ask!
Come back again."

¹³ An oracle against Arabia:

You will camp for the night
in the scrublands of the desert,
you caravans of Dedanites.
¹⁴ Bring water for the thirsty.
The inhabitants of the land
of Tema
meet the refugees with food.
¹⁵ For they have fled from swords,
from the drawn sword,
and from the bent bow,
from the stress of battle.

¹⁶ For the Lord said this to me:
"Within one year, as a hired worker
counts years, all the glory of Kedar will
be gone. ¹⁷ The remaining Kedarite
archers will be few in number." For the
LORD, the God of Israel, has spoken.

22 An oracle against the Valley of
Vision:

What's the matter with you?
Why have all of you gone up
to the rooftops?
² The noisy city, the jubilant town,
is filled with revelry.
Your dead did not die
by the sword;
they were not killed in battle.
³ All your rulers have fled together,
captured without a bow.
All your fugitives
were captured together;
they had fled far away.

⁴ Therefore I said,
"Look away from me!
Let me weep bitterly!
Do not try to comfort me
about the destruction of my dear
people."
⁵ For the Lord GOD of Hosts
had a day of tumult, trampling,
and bewilderment
in the Valley of Vision—
people shouting and crying
to the mountains;
⁶ Elam took up a quiver
with chariots and horsemen,
and Kir uncovered the shield.
⁷ Your best valleys were full
of chariots,
and horsemen were positioned
at the gates.
⁸ He removed the defenses
of Judah.

On that day you looked to the
weapons in the House of the Forest.

PSALM 112:1-5

¹ Hallelujah!
Happy is the man who fears the
LORD,
taking great delight in His
commandments.

² His descendants will be powerful
in the land;
the generation of the upright will
be blessed.
³ Wealth and riches are in his
house,
and his righteousness endures
forever.
⁴ Light shines in the darkness for
the upright.
He is gracious, compassionate, and
righteous.
⁵ Good will come to a man who
lends generously
and conducts his business fairly.

PROVERBS 23:17-18

¹⁷ Don't be jealous of sinners;
instead, always fear the LORD.

¹⁸ For then you will have a future,
and your hope will never fade.

....

GALATIANS 2:1-21

2 Then after 14 years I went up again to Jerusalem with Barnabas, taking Titus along also. ² I went up because of a revelation and presented to them the gospel I preach among the Gentiles— but privately to those recognized as leaders—so that I might not be running, or have run, in vain. ³ But not even Titus who was with me, though he was a Greek, was compelled to be circumcised. ⁴ This issue arose because of false brothers smuggled in, who came in secretly to spy on our freedom that we have in Christ Jesus, in order to enslave us. ⁵ But we did not yield in submission to these people for even an hour, so that the truth of the gospel would remain for you.

⁶ But from those recognized as important (what they really were makes no difference to me; God does not show favoritism)—those recognized as important added nothing to me. ⁷ On the contrary, they saw that I had been entrusted with the gospel for the uncircumcised, just as Peter was for the circumcised. ⁸ For He who was at work with Peter in the apostleship to the circumcised was also at work with me among the Gentiles. ⁹ When James, Cephas, and John, recognized as pillars, acknowledged the grace that had been given to me, they gave the right hand of fellowship to me and Barnabas, agreeing that we should go to the Gentiles and they to the circumcised. ¹⁰ They asked only that we would remember the poor, which I made every effort to do.

¹¹ But when Cephas came to Antioch, I opposed him to his face because he stood condemned. ¹² For he used to eat with the Gentiles before certain men came from James. However, when they came, he withdrew and separated himself, because he feared those from the circumcision party. ¹³ Then the rest of the Jews joined his hypocrisy, so that even Barnabas was carried away by their hypocrisy. ¹⁴ But when I saw that they were deviating from the truth of the gospel, I told Cephas in front of everyone, "If you, who are a Jew, live like a Gentile and not like a Jew, how can you compel Gentiles to live like Jews?"

¹⁵ We are Jews by birth and not "Gentile sinners"; ¹⁶ yet we know that no one is justified by the works of the law but by faith in Jesus Christ. And we have believed in Christ Jesus, so that we might be justified by faith in Christ and not by the works of the law, because by the works of the law no human being will be justified. ¹⁷ But if, while seeking to be justified by Christ, we ourselves are also found to be sinners, is Christ then a promoter of sin? Absolutely not! ¹⁸ If I rebuild those things that I tore down, I show myself to be a lawbreaker. ¹⁹ For through the law I have died to the law, that I might live to God. I have been crucified with Christ; ²⁰ and I no longer live, but Christ lives in me. The life I now live in the flesh, I live by faith in the Son of God, who loved me and gave Himself for me. ²¹ I do not set aside the grace of God; for if righteousness comes through the law, then Christ died for nothing.

Touching the Intangible

When James, Cephas, and John . . . acknowledged the grace that had been given to me, they gave the right hand of fellowship to me and Barnabas, agreeing that we should go to the Gentiles and they to the circumcised.

—GALATIANS 2:9

Truly, in making an effort to go outside of ourselves and relate to others, we receive a wider awareness and a deeper understanding of God. This has been one of the greatest and most exciting discoveries of my life. The more I have given myself to my brothers and sisters in Christ, the greater has been my awareness and understanding of God.

I am not saying that in order to know God, we first have to get to know each other. That would be blatant error. We can know *about* Him through such means as creation, providence, and so on, but we can only know Him through His Son Jesus Christ. "No one has ever seen God. The One and Only Son—the One who is at the Father's side—He has revealed Him" (Jn 1:18). However, once we know Him in this way, our fellowship with Him and our understanding of Him can be deepened by our relationship with others who know Him.

How does this work? The more I have focused on learning to listen—really listen—to my brothers and sisters in Christ, the more I have found that the effort I have made to do this has resulted in a heightening of my ability to listen to God. And the more I have sought to understand the mystery of His dealings in their lives, the more I have come to know the depth and beauty of His character. Although down the years I have come to know Him intimately in prayer, I believe I can say that I know Him even better because I have met Him in others.

Prayer

O Father, how can I sufficiently thank You for the fellowship we have with one another in Christ. In the tangible I see the Intangible, and through the visible I see the Invisible. I am eternally grateful. Amen.

Further Study

Jn 14:20; Gl 2:1-20; Col 1:27; 1 Jn 3:24
How does God make His riches known?
Are those riches being made known to others through you?

SEPTEMBER 27

ISAIAH 22:9–24:23

⁹ You saw that there were many breaches in the walls of the city of David. You collected water from the lower pool. ¹⁰ You counted the houses of Jerusalem so that you could tear them down to fortify the wall. ¹¹ You made a reservoir between the walls for the waters of the ancient pool, but you did not look to the One who made it, or consider the One who created it long ago.

¹² On that day the Lord God of Hosts
    called for weeping, for wailing,
    for shaven heads,

1139

and for the wearing of sackcloth.
¹³ But look: joy and gladness,
butchering of cattle,
slaughtering of sheep,
eating of meat, and drinking
of wine—
"Let us eat and drink,
for tomorrow we die!"
¹⁴ The LORD of Hosts has revealed
this in my hearing:
"This sin of yours will never be
wiped out."
The Lord GOD of Hosts
has spoken.

¹⁵ The Lord GOD of Hosts said: "Go to Shebna, that steward who is in charge of the palace, and say to him: ¹⁶ What are you doing here? Who authorized you to carve out a tomb for yourself here, carving your tomb on the height and cutting a crypt for yourself out of rock? ¹⁷ Look, young man! The LORD is about to shake you violently. He will take hold of you, ¹⁸ wind you up into a ball, and sling you into a wide land. There you will die, and there your glorious chariots will be—a disgrace to the house of your lord. ¹⁹ I will remove you from your office; you will be ousted from your position.

²⁰ "On that day I will call for my servant, Eliakim son of Hilkiah. ²¹ I will clothe him with your robe and tie your sash around him. I will put your authority into his hand, and he will be like a father to the inhabitants of Jerusalem and to the House of Judah. ²² I will place the key of the House of David on his shoulder; what he opens, no one can close; what he closes, no one can open. ²³ I will drive him, like a peg, into a firm place. He will be a throne of honor for his father's house. ²⁴ They will hang on him the whole burden of his father's house: the descendants and the offshoots—all the small vessels, from bowls to every kind of jar. ²⁵ On that day"—the declaration of the LORD of Hosts—"the peg that was driven into a firm place will give way, be cut off, and fall, and the load on it will be destroyed." Indeed, the LORD has spoken.

23 An oracle against Tyre:

Wail, ships of Tarshish,
for your haven
has been destroyed.
Word has reached them
from the land of Cyprus.
² Mourn, inhabitants
of the coastland,
you merchants of Sidon;
your agents have crossed the sea
³ on many waters.
Tyre's revenue was the grain
from Shihor—
the harvest of the Nile.
She was the merchant
among the nations.
⁴ Be ashamed Sidon, the stronghold
of the sea,
for the sea has spoken:
"I have not been in labor
or given birth.
I have not raised young men
or brought up young women."
⁵ When the news reaches Egypt,
they will be in anguish
over the news about Tyre.
⁶ Cross over to Tarshish;
wail, inhabitants of the coastland!
⁷ Is this your jubilant city,
whose origin was in ancient times,
whose feet have taken her
to settle far away?
⁸ Who planned this against Tyre,
the bestower of crowns,
whose traders are princes,
whose merchants are
the honored ones
of the earth?
⁹ The LORD of Hosts planned it,
to desecrate all its
glorious beauty,
to disgrace all the honored ones
of the earth.
¹⁰ Overflow your land like the Nile,
daughter of Tarshish;
there is no longer anything
to restrain you.
¹¹ He stretched out His hand
over the sea;
He made kingdoms tremble.
The LORD has commanded
that the Canaanite fortresses
be destroyed.

¹² He said,
"You will not rejoice any more,
ravished young woman,
    daughter of Sidon.
Get up and cross over to Cyprus—
even there you will have
    no rest!"
¹³ Look at the land of Chaldeans—
a people who no longer exist.
Assyria destined it for wild beasts.
They set up their siege towers
and stripped its palaces.
They made it a ruin.
¹⁴ Wail, ships of Tarshish,
because your fortress is destroyed!

¹⁵ On that day Tyre will be forgotten
for 70 years—the life span of one king.
At the end of 70 years, what the song
says about the prostitute will happen to
Tyre:

¹⁶ Pick up your harp,
    stroll through the city,
    prostitute forgotten by men.
Play skillfully,
    sing many a song,
    and you will be thought of again.

¹⁷ And at the end of the 70 years, the
LORD will restore Tyre and she will go
back into business, prostituting herself
with all the kingdoms of the world on
the face of the earth. ¹⁸ But her profits
and wages will be dedicated to the
LORD. They will not be stored or saved,
for her profit will go to those who live
in the LORD's presence, to provide them
with ample food and sacred clothing.

24 Look, the LORD is stripping
    the earth bare
    and making it desolate.
He will twist its surface
    and scatter its inhabitants:
² people and priest alike,
    servant and master,
    female servant and mistress,
    buyer and seller,
    lender and borrower,
    creditor and debtor.
³ The earth will be stripped
    completely bare
    and will be totally plundered,

for the LORD has spoken
    this message.

⁴ The earth mourns and withers;
the world wastes away
    and withers;
the exalted people of the earth
    waste away.
⁵ The earth is polluted
    by its inhabitants,
for they have transgressed
    teachings,
overstepped decrees,
and broken
    the everlasting covenant.
⁶ Therefore a curse has consumed
    the earth,
and its inhabitants
    have become guilty;
the earth's inhabitants
    have been burned,
and only a few survive.
⁷ The new wine mourns;
    the vine withers.
All the carousers now groan.
⁸ The joyful tambourines
    have ceased.
The noise of the jubilant
    has stopped.
The joyful lyre has ceased.
⁹ They no longer sing
    and drink wine;
beer is bitter to those
    who drink it.
¹⁰ The city of chaos is shattered;
every house is closed to entry.
¹¹ In the streets they cry for wine.
All joy grows dark;
    earth's rejoicing goes into exile.
¹² Only desolation remains
    in the city;
its gate has collapsed in ruins.
¹³ For this is how it will be on earth
among the nations:
like a harvested olive tree,
like a gleaning after
    a grape harvest.

¹⁴ They raise their voices,
    they sing out;
they proclaim in the west
    the majesty of the LORD.
¹⁵ Therefore in the east honor
    the LORD!

In the islands of the west honor
the name of the LORD, the God
of Israel.
16 From the ends of the earth
we hear songs:
The Splendor
of the Righteous One.

But I said, "I waste away!
I waste away!
Woe is me."
The treacherous act treacherously;
the treacherous deal
very treacherously.

17 Terror, pit, and snare await you
who dwell on the earth.
18 Whoever flees at the sound
of terror
will fall into a pit,
and whoever escapes
from the pit
will be caught in a snare.
For the windows are opened
from above,
and the foundations of the earth
are shaken.
19 The earth is
completely devastated;
the earth is split open;
the earth is violently shaken.
20 The earth staggers
like a drunkard
and sways like a hut.
Earth's rebellion weighs it down,
and it falls, never to rise again.
21 On that day the LORD
will punish
the host of heaven above
and kings of the earth below.
22 They will be gathered together
like prisoners in a pit.
They will be confined
to a dungeon;
after many days
they will be punished.
23 The moon will be put to shame
and the sun disgraced,
because the LORD of Hosts
will reign as king
on Mount Zion in Jerusalem,
and He will display His glory
in the presence of His elders.

PSALM 112:6-10

6 He will never be shaken.
The righteous will be remembered
forever.
7 He will not fear bad news;
his heart is confident, trusting in
the LORD.
8 His heart is assured; he will not
fear.
In the end he will look in triumph
on his foes.
9 He distributes freely to the poor;
his righteousness endures forever.
His horn will be exalted in honor.

10 The wicked man will see it and be
angry;
he will gnash his teeth in despair.
The desire of the wicked will
come to nothing.

PROVERBS 23:19-21

19 Listen, my son, and be wise;
keep your mind on the right
course.
20 Don't associate with those who
drink too much wine,
or with those who gorge
themselves on meat.
21 For the drunkard and the glutton
will become poor,
and grogginess will clothe them in
rags.

GALATIANS 3:1-18

3 You foolish Galatians! Who has hyp-
notized you, before whose eyes
Jesus Christ was vividly portrayed as
crucified? 2 I only want to learn this
from you: Did you receive the Spirit by
the works of the law or by hearing with
faith? 3 Are you so foolish? After beginning with the Spirit, are you now going
to be made complete by the flesh? 4 Did
you suffer so much for nothing—if in
fact it was for nothing? 5 So then, does
God supply you with the Spirit and
work miracles among you by the works
of the law or by hearing with faith?

⁶ Just as Abraham **believed God, and it was credited to him for righteousness,** ⁷ so understand that those who have faith are Abraham's sons. ⁸ Now the Scripture foresaw that God would justify the Gentiles by faith and foretold the good news to Abraham, saying, **All the nations will be blessed in you.** ⁹ So those who have faith are blessed with Abraham, who had faith.

¹⁰ For all who rely on the works of the law are under a curse, because it is written: **Cursed is everyone who does not continue doing everything written in the book of the law.** ¹¹ Now it is clear that no one is justified before God by the law, because **the righteous will live by faith.** ¹² But the law is not based on faith; instead, **the one who does these things will live by them.** ¹³ Christ has redeemed us from the curse of the law by becoming a curse for us, because it is written: **Cursed is everyone who is hung on a tree.** ¹⁴ The purpose was that the blessing of Abraham would come to the Gentiles in Christ Jesus, so that we could receive the promise of the Spirit through faith.

¹⁵ Brothers, I'm using a human illustration. No one sets aside even a human covenant that has been ratified, or makes additions to it. ¹⁶ Now the promises were spoken to Abraham and to his seed. He does not say "and to seeds," as though referring to many, but **and to your seed,** referring to one, who is Christ. ¹⁷ And I say this: the law, which came 430 years later, does not revoke a covenant that was previously ratified by God, so as to cancel the promise. ¹⁸ For if the inheritance is from the law, it is no longer from the promise; but God granted it to Abraham through the promise.

Balanced Christianity

After beginning with the Spirit, are you now going to be made complete by the flesh?—GALATIANS 3:3

The Christian church has always struggled to get the balance right between faith and works. Romans is the great book on "faith," while James is the great book on "works." I know some Christians who never read the book of James, taking sides with Martin Luther who called it a "book of straw." Martin Luther may have been right about many things, but he was wrong when he referred to the Epistle of James in this way. We need to study both Romans and James if we want to be properly balanced Christians.

The difficulty with faith and works is this: we come into the Christian life by depending on Jesus' innocent sufferings on Calvary as sufficient ground for our acceptance with God, and then when we learn the principles of Christian living, we turn from dependency on Christ to dependency on them. This was the great problem in the Galatian churches, and it is still a problem here in the church of the current century. Bringing forth the fruit of repentance by good works is terribly important, but we are not to depend on works for our salvation.

We tend to focus more on works than faith because it is something visible and tangible. We can see what we are doing and assess it or measure it. Faith is different. It requires of us a degree of helplessness (something the carnal nature detests), but if we are to know God better and avoid falling into the trap of pursuing godliness more keenly than pursuing God, then faith must be seen as the primary virtue.

Prayer

O Father, help me get this right. I am saved to good works, but I am not saved by good works. Prevent me from falling into the trap of being more preoccupied with Your principles than with You Yourself. In Jesus' name. Amen.

Further Study

Eph 2:1-9; Gl 2:16: Rm 9:32
What did Paul remind the Ephesians?
What did he emphasize to the Galatians?

SEPTEMBER 28

ISAIAH 25:1–27:13

25 LORD, You are my God;
I will exalt You. I will praise
Your name,
for You have accomplished
wonders,
plans formed long ago,
with perfect faithfulness.
² For You have turned the city
into a pile of rubble,
a fortified city, into a ruin;
the fortress of barbarians is
no longer a city;
it will never be rebuilt.
³ Therefore, a strong people
will honor You.
A city of violent people will
fear You.
⁴ For You have been a stronghold
for the poor,
a stronghold
for the humble person
in his distress,
a refuge from the rain, a shade
from the heat.
When the breath of the violent
is like rain against a wall,

⁵ like heat in a dry land,
You subdue the uproar
of barbarians.
As the shade of a cloud cools
the heat of the day,
so He stills the song
of the violent.

⁶ The LORD of Hosts will prepare
a feast
for all the peoples
on this mountain—
a feast of aged wine, choice meat,
finely aged wine.
⁷ On this mountain
He will destroy the burial
shroud,
the shroud over all the peoples,
the sheet covering all the nations;
⁸ He will destroy death forever.
The Lord GOD will wipe away
the tears
from every face
and remove His people's disgrace
from the whole earth,
for the LORD has spoken.

⁹ On that day it will be said,
"Look, this is our God;

we have waited for Him,
and He has saved us.
This is the LORD; we have waited
for Him.
Let us rejoice and be glad
in His salvation."
¹⁰ For the LORD's power will rest
on this mountain.

But Moab will be trampled
in his place
as straw is trampled in a dung pile.
¹¹ He will spread out his arms
in the middle of it,
as a swimmer spreads out
his arms to swim.
His pride will be brought low,
along with the trickery
of his hands.
¹² The high-walled fortress
will be brought down,
thrown to the ground, to the dust.

26 On that day this song will be
sung in the land of Judah:

We have a strong city.
Salvation is established as walls
and ramparts.
² Open the gates
so a righteous nation
can come in—
one that remains faithful.
³ You will keep in perfect peace
the mind that is dependent
on You,
for it is trusting in You.
⁴ Trust in the LORD forever,
because in Yah, the LORD, is
an everlasting rock!
⁵ For He has humbled those who live
in lofty places—
an inaccessible city.
He brings it down;
He brings it down
to the ground;
He throws it to the dust.
⁶ Feet trample it,
the feet of the humble,
the steps of the poor.

⁷ The path of the righteous is level;
You clear a straight path
for the righteous.

⁸ Yes, LORD, we wait for You
in the path of Your judgments.
Our desire is for Your name
and renown.
⁹ I long for You in the night;
yes, my spirit within me
diligently seeks You,
for when Your judgments are in
the land,
the inhabitants of the world
will learn righteousness.
¹⁰ But if the wicked is shown favor,
he does not learn righteousness.
In a righteous land he acts unjustly
and does not see the majesty
of the LORD.

¹¹ LORD, Your hand is lifted up
to take action,
but they do not see it.
They will see Your zeal for Your
people,
and they will be put to shame.
The fire for Your adversaries
will consume them!
¹² LORD, You will establish peace
for us,
for You have also done
all our work for us.
¹³ LORD, our God, other lords
than You have ruled over us,
but we remember
Your name alone.

¹⁴ The dead do not live;
departed spirits do not rise up.
Indeed, You have visited
and destroyed them;
You have wiped out all memory
of them.
¹⁵ You have added
to the nation, LORD.
You have added to the nation;
You are honored.
You have expanded all the borders
of the land.
¹⁶ LORD, they went to You
in their distress;
they poured out
whispered prayers
because Your discipline fell
on them.
¹⁷ As a pregnant woman
about to give birth

writhes and cries out in her pains,
so we were before You, LORD.

¹⁸ We became pregnant, we writhed
in pain;
we gave birth to wind.
We have won no victories on earth,
and the earth's inhabitants
have not fallen.

¹⁹ Your dead will live; their bodies
will rise.
Awake and sing, you who dwell
in the dust!
For you will be covered
with the morning dew,
and the earth will bring forth
the departed spirits.

²⁰ Go, my people, enter your rooms
and close your doors behind you.
Hide for a little while
until the wrath has passed.

²¹ For look, the LORD is coming
from His place
to punish the inhabitants
of the earth for their iniquity.
The earth will reveal the blood
shed on it
and will no longer conceal
her slain.

27 On that day the LORD with His
harsh, great, and strong sword,
will bring judgment on Leviathan, the
fleeing serpent—Leviathan, the twisting serpent. He will slay the monster
that is in the sea.

² On that day
sing about a desirable vineyard:

³ I, the LORD, watch over it;
I water it regularly.
I guard it night and day
so that no one disturbs it.

⁴ I am not angry,
but if it produces thorns
and briers for Me,
I will fight against it, trample it,
and burn it to the ground.

⁵ Or let it take hold of My strength;
let it make peace with Me—
make peace with Me.

⁶ In days to come,
Jacob will take root.

Israel will blossom and bloom
and fill the whole world
with fruit.

⁷ Did the LORD strike Israel
as He struck the one
who struck Israel?
Was he killed like those killed
by Him?

⁸ You disputed with her
by banishing and driving her away.
He removed her
with His severe storm
on the day of the east wind.

⁹ Therefore Jacob's iniquity
will be purged in this way,
and the result of the removal
of his sin will be this:
when he makes all the altar stones
like crushed bits of chalk,
no Asherah poles or incense altars
will remain standing.

¹⁰ For the fortified city
will be deserted,
pastures abandoned and forsaken
like a wilderness.
Calves will graze there,
and there they will spread out
and strip its branches.

¹¹ When its branches dry out,
they will be broken off.
Women will come and make fires
with them,
for they are not a people
with understanding.
Therefore their Maker will not
have compassion on them,
and their Creator will not
be gracious to them.

¹² On that day
the LORD will thresh grain
from the Euphrates River
as far as the Wadi of Egypt,
and you Israelites will be gathered
one by one.

¹³ On that day
a great trumpet will be blown,
and those lost in the land
of Assyria will come,
as well as those dispersed
in the land of Egypt;
and they will worship the LORD
at Jerusalem on the holy mountain.

PSALM 113:1-9

1 Hallelujah!
Give praise, servants of the LORD;
praise the name of the LORD.
2 Let the name of the LORD be
praised
both now and forever.
3 From the rising of the sun to its
setting,
let the name of the LORD be
praised.

4 The LORD is exalted above all the
nations,
His glory above the heavens.
5 Who is like the LORD our God—
the One enthroned on high,
6 who stoops down to look
on the heavens and the earth?
7 He raises the poor from the dust
and lifts the needy from the
garbage pile
8 in order to seat them with
nobles—
with the nobles of His people.
9 He gives the childless woman a
household,
making her the joyful mother of
children.
Hallelujah!

PROVERBS 23:22-23

22 Listen to your father who gave you
life,
and don't despise your mother
when she is old.
23 Buy—and do not sell—truth,
wisdom, instruction, and
understanding.

GALATIANS 3:19–4:11

19 Why the law then? It was added because of transgressions until the Seed to
whom the promise was made would
come. The law was ordered through angels by means of a mediator. 20 Now a
mediator is not for just one person, but
God is one. 21 Is the law therefore contrary to God's promises? Absolutely not!
For if a law had been given that was able
to give life, then righteousness would
certainly be by the law. 22 But the
Scripture has imprisoned everything
under sin's power, so that the promise
by faith in Jesus Christ might be given
to those who believe. 23 Before this faith
came, we were confined under the law,
imprisoned until the coming faith was
revealed. 24 The law, then, was our
guardian until Christ, so that we could
be justified by faith. 25 But since that
faith has come, we are no longer under
a guardian, 26 for you are all sons of God
through faith in Christ Jesus.

27 For as many of you as have been
baptized into Christ have put on Christ.
28 There is no Jew or Greek, slave or
free, male or female; for you are all one
in Christ Jesus. 29 And if you are Christ's,
then you are Abraham's seed, heirs
4 according to the promise. 1 Now I
say that as long as the heir is a child,
he differs in no way from a slave,
though he is the owner of everything.
2 Instead, he is under guardians and
stewards until the time set by his father.
3 In the same way we also, when we
were children, were in slavery under
the elemental forces of the world. 4 But
when the completion of the time came,
God sent His Son, born of a woman,
born under the law, 5 to redeem those
under the law, so that we might receive
adoption as sons. 6 And because you are
sons, God has sent the Spirit of His Son
into our hearts, crying, "Abba, Father!"
7 So you are no longer a slave, but a son;
and if a son, then an heir through God.

8 But in the past, when you didn't
know God, you were enslaved to things
that by nature are not gods. 9 But now,
since you know God, or rather have become known by God, how can you turn
back again to the weak and bankrupt elemental forces? Do you want to be enslaved to them all over again? 10 You
observe special days, months, seasons,
and years. 11 I am fearful for you, that
perhaps my labor for you has been
wasted.

"Imagineering"

You will keep in perfect peace the mind that is dependent on You.

—ISAIAH 26:3

How many times, when making an approach to God in prayer, have we gone immediately into a series of petitions that have to do with our problems, our difficulties, our circumstances? And so, by focusing our attention on what is troubling us, we end up wondering whether or not God is big enough or strong enough to help us.

In the first six words of the Lord's Prayer, Jesus shows us a better way. He tells us to take a slow, calm, reassuring gaze at God—at His tenderness, His eagerness to give, His unwearying patience and untiring love. The result of this, of course, is that we develop a calmness and tranquility in our spirit which means we will find it no longer necessary to plunge into a panicky flood of words.

In some parts of the world one can enroll in courses called "Imagineering"—courses that are designed to stimulate creative imagination. Most of our problems begin in the imagination—hence the instruction in the words of our text for today. "One can never become proficient in prayer," said one great writer, "until the imagination has been redeemed." He meant that when the imagination is redeemed from self-concentration, sex-concentration, and sin-concentration, and makes God its primary focus, then it becomes creative-conscious, since its attention is concentrated on the Creator and the Re-Creator. And when the imagination is redeemed, all the doors of the personality fly open.

Prayer

O God, how can I be calm and tranquil when my imagination is more self-centered than God-centered? Help me to be a God-focused person, not only at prayer times, but at all times. Amen.

Further Study

1 Co 2:1-16; Gn 6:5; Rm 1:21; 2 Co 10:5
How can we "cast down imaginations"?
What has God given to us?

SEPTEMBER 29

ISAIAH 28:1–29:24

28 Woe to the majestic crown
of Ephraim's drunkards,
and to the fading flower
of its beautiful splendor,
which is on the summit above
the rich valley.
Woe to those overcome
with wine.
2 Look, the Lord has a strong
and mighty one—
like a devastating hail storm,
like a storm with strong
flooding waters.
He will bring it across the land
with His hand.
3 The majestic crown
of Ephraim's drunkards
will be trampled underfoot.
4 The fading flower
of his beautiful splendor,
which is on the summit
above the rich valley,
will be like a ripe fig
before the summer harvest.
Whoever sees it will swallow it
while it is still in his hand.
5 On that day
the LORD of Hosts will become
a crown of beauty
and a diadem of splendor
to the remnant of His people,
6 a spirit of justice
to the one who sits in judgment,
and strength
to those who turn back the battle
at the gate.

7 These also stagger
because of wine
and stumble under the influence
of beer:
priest and prophet stagger
because of beer,
they are confused by wine.
They stumble because of beer,

they are muddled in their
visions,
they stumble in their judgments.
8 Indeed, all their tables are covered
with vomit;
there is no place without a stench.
9 Who is he trying to teach?
Who is he trying to instruct?
Infants just weaned from milk?
Babies removed from the breast?
10 For he says: "Law after law,
law after law,
line after line, line after line,
a little here, a little there."
11 So He will speak to this people
with stammering speech
and in a foreign language.
12 He had said to them:
"This is the place of rest,
let the weary rest;
this is the place of repose."
But they would not listen.

13 Then the word of the LORD came
to them:
"Law after law, law after law,
line after line, line after line,
a little here, a little there,"
so they go stumbling backwards,
to be broken, trapped,
and captured.

14 Therefore hear the word
of the LORD, you mockers
who rule this people in Jerusalem.
15 For you said, "We have cut a deal
with Death,
and we have made an agreement
with Sheol;
when the overwhelming scourge
passes through,
it will not touch us,
because we have made falsehood
our refuge
and have hidden
behind treachery."
16 Therefore the Lord GOD said:

"Look, I have laid a stone in Zion,
    a tested stone,
    a precious cornerstone,
      a sure foundation;
the one who believes
    will be unshakable.
17 And I will make justice
    the measuring line
and righteousness
    the mason's level."
Hail will sweep away
    the false refuge,
and water will flood
    your hiding place.
18 Your deal with Death
    will be dissolved,
and your agreement with Sheol
    will not last.
When the overwhelming scourge
    passes through,
you will be trampled.
19 Every time it passes through,
    it will carry you away;
it will pass through
    every morning—
every day and every night.
Only terror will cause you
    to understand the message.
20 Indeed, the bed is too short
    to stretch out on,
and its cover too small
    to wrap up in.
21 For the LORD will rise up as He did
    at Mount Perazim.
He will rise in wrath,
    as at the valley of Gibeon,
to do His work, His strange work,
and to perform His task,
    His disturbing task.
22 So now, do not mock,
    or your shackles
    will become stronger.
Indeed, I have heard
    from the Lord GOD of Hosts
a decree of destruction
    for the whole land.

23 Listen and hear my voice.
    Pay attention and hear what I say.
24 Does the plowman plow every day
    to plant seed?
Does he continuously break up
    and cultivate the soil?
25 When he has leveled its surface,

does he not then scatter cumin
    and sow black cumin?
He plants wheat in rows
    and barley in plots,
with spelt as their border.
26 His God teaches him order;
    He instructs him.
27 Certainly black cumin
    is not threshed
with a threshing board,
and a cart wheel is not rolled
    over the cumin.
But black cumin is beaten out
    with a stick,
and cumin with a rod.
28 Bread grain is crushed,
    but is not threshed endlessly.
Though the wheel of the farmer's
    cart rumbles,
his horses do not crush it.
29 This also comes from the LORD
    of Hosts.
He gives wonderful advice;
He gives great wisdom.

29 Woe to Ariel, Ariel,
    the city where David camped!
Continue year after year;
    let the festivals recur.
2 I will oppress Ariel,
    and there will be mourning
    and crying,
and she will be to Me like an Ariel.
3 I will camp in a circle around you;
I will besiege you
    with earth ramps,
and I will set up my siege towers
    against you.
4 You will be brought down;
you will speak from the ground,
and your words will come
    from low in the dust.
Your voice will be like that
    of a spirit from the ground;
your speech will whisper
    from the dust.

5 The multitude of your foes will be
    like fine dust,
and the multitude of the ruthless,
    like blowing chaff.
Then suddenly, in an instant,
6 you will be visited by the LORD of
    Hosts

with thunder, earthquake,
 and loud noise,
storm, tempest, and a flame
 of consuming fire.
7 The multitude of all the nations
 going out to battle against Ariel—
all the attackers, the siege-works
 against her,
and those who oppress her—
will then be like a dream, a vision
 in the night.
8 It will be like a hungry one
 who dreams he is eating,
then wakes and is still hungry;
and like a thirsty one who dreams
 he is drinking,
then wakes and is still thirsty,
 longing for water.
So will be the multitude
 of all the nations
who go to battle
 against Mount Zion.

9 Stop and be astonished;
 blind yourselves and be blind!
They are drunk, but not
 with wine;
they stagger, but not with beer.
10 For the LORD has poured out
 on you
an overwhelming urge to sleep;
He has shut your eyes—
 the prophets,
and covered your heads—
 the seers.

11 For you the entire vision will be like
the words of a sealed document. If it is
given to one who can read and he is
asked to read it, he will say, "I can't read
it, because it is sealed." 12 And if the
document is given to one who cannot
read and he is asked to read it, he will
say, "I can't read."
13 The Lord said:

Because these people
 approach Me
 with their mouths
to honor Me with lip-service —
yet their hearts are far from Me,
and their worship consists of
 man-made rules
 learned by rote—

14 therefore I will again confound
 these people
with wonder after wonder.
The wisdom of their wise men
 will vanish,
and the understanding
 of the perceptive
 will be hidden.

15 Woe to those who go
 to great lengths
to hide their plans from the LORD.
They do their works in darkness,
and say, "Who sees us?
 Who knows us?"
16 You have turned things around,
as if the potter were the same
 as the clay.
How can what is made say
 about its maker,
"He didn't make me"?
How can what is formed
say about the one who formed it,
"He doesn't understand
 what he's doing"?

17 Isn't it true that in just
 a little while
Lebanon will become an orchard,
and the orchard will seem
 like a forest?
18 On that day the deaf will hear
 the words of a document,
and out of a deep darkness
 the eyes of the blind will see.
19 The humble will have joy
 after joy in the LORD,
and the poor people will rejoice
 in the Holy One of Israel.
20 For the ruthless one will vanish,
 the scorner will disappear,
and all those who lie in wait
 with evil intent
 will be killed—
21 those who, with their speech,
 accuse a person of wrongdoing,
who set a trap at the gate
 for the mediator,
and without cause deprive
 the righteous of justice.

22 Therefore, the LORD who redeemed
Abraham says this about the house of
Jacob:

1151

Jacob will no longer be ashamed
and his face will no longer
be pale.
23 For when he sees his children,
the work of My hands
within his nation,
they will honor My name,
they will honor the Holy One
of Jacob
and stand in awe of the God
of Israel.
24 Those who are confused
will gain understanding
and those who grumble
will accept instruction.

PSALM 114:1-8

1 When Israel came out of Egypt—
the house of Jacob from a people
who spoke a foreign language—
2 Judah became His sanctuary,
Israel, His dominion.

3 The sea looked and fled;
the Jordan turned back.
4 The mountains skipped like rams,
the hills, like lambs.
5 Why was it, sea, that you fled?
Jordan, that you turned back?
6 Mountains, that you skipped like
rams?
Hills, like lambs?

7 Tremble, earth, at the presence of
the Lord,
at the presence of the God of
Jacob,
8 who turned the rock into a pool of
water,
the flint into a spring of water.

PROVERBS 23:24-25

24 The father of a righteous son will
rejoice greatly,
and one who fathers a wise son
will delight in him.
25 Let your father and mother have
joy,
and let her who gave birth to you
rejoice.

GALATIANS 4:12-31

12 I beg you, brothers: become like
me, for I also became like you. You have
not wronged me; 13 you know that previously I preached the gospel to you in
physical weakness, 14 and though my
physical condition was a trial for you,
you did not despise or reject me. On the
contrary, you received me as an angel of
God, as Christ Jesus Himself.
15 What happened to this blessedness
of yours? For I testify to you that, if possible, you would have torn out your eyes
and given them to me. 16 Have I now become your enemy by telling you the
truth? 17 They are enthusiastic about you,
but not for any good. Instead, they want
to isolate you so you will be enthusiastic
about them. 18 Now it is always good to
be enthusiastic about good—and not just
when I am with you. 19 My children,
again I am in the pains of childbirth for
you until Christ is formed in you. 20 I'd
like to be with you right now and change
my tone of voice, because I don't know
what to do about you.
21 Tell me, you who want to be under
the law, don't you hear the law? 22 For it
is written that Abraham had two sons,
one by a slave and the other by a free
woman. 23 But the one by the slave was
born according to the flesh, while the
one by the free woman was born as
the result of a promise. 24 These things
are illustrations, for the women represent the two covenants. One is from
Mount Sinai and bears children into
slavery—this is Hagar. 25 Now Hagar is
Mount Sinai in Arabia and corresponds
to the present Jerusalem, for she is in
slavery with her children. 26 But the
Jerusalem above is free, and she is our
mother. 27 For it is written:

Rejoice, O barren woman
who does not give birth.
Break forth and shout,
you who are not in labor,
for the children of the desolate
are many,
more numerous than those
of the woman who has a husband.

²⁸ Now you, brothers, like Isaac, are children of promise. ²⁹ But just as then the child born according to the flesh persecuted the one born according to the Spirit, so also now. ³⁰ But what does the Scripture say?

Throw out the slave and her son, for the son of the slave will never inherit with the son of the free woman.

³¹ Therefore, brothers, we are not children of the slave but of the free woman.

More Than a Recitation

These people approach Me with their mouths
to honor Me with lip-service—
yet their hearts are far from Me.—ISAIAH 29:13

Some Christians think that prayer consists solely of reciting the words of the Lord's Prayer, but, as the great preacher C. H. Spurgeon once said: "To recite the Lord's Prayer and believe that you have then prayed is the height of foolishness." This does not mean, of course, that there is no spiritual value in reciting it, providing we realize that it is not just a prayer to be recited. Personally, I would not want to deprive Christian congregations of the pleasure and joy of reciting together the Lord's Prayer, but I do want to encourage them to view it as a departure point rather than an arrival platform.

If Jesus advised His disciples to avoid "[babbling] like the idolaters" (Mt 6:7), would He then immediately follow it by giving us a prayer to simply recite? Obviously, as I have said, one can derive great spiritual pleasure from repeating the words that Jesus gave us, but if we are to obtain the greatest value from the Lord's Prayer, then we must view it as a skeleton on which we have to put flesh. If we view these words, not merely as something to recite, but as an outline from which we must work our way when praying, no matter what we are praying about, then we will experience a growing confidence that we are praying the way Jesus taught.

You see, it's one thing to recite a prayer; it's another thing to know how to pray.

Prayer

Heavenly Father, I see there can be great value in reciting a prayer, but I want to be able to do more than repeat a prayer—I want to pray. Help me, for without You I can do nothing. For Jesus' sake. Amen.

Further Study

Gl 4:1-11; Mt 23:14, 6:5
What is Paul saying about ritualism?
When does prayer become hypocritical?

SEPTEMBER 30

ISAIAH 30:1–32:10

30 Woe to the rebellious children!
This is the LORD's declaration.
They carry out a plan,
but not Mine,
They make an alliance,
but against My will,
piling sin on top of sin.
² They set out to go down to Egypt
without asking My advice,
in order to seek shelter
under Pharaoh's protection
and take refuge in Egypt's shadow.
³ But Pharaoh's protection
will become your shame,
and refuge in Egypt's shadow
your disgrace.
⁴ For though his princes are at Zoan
and his messengers reach
as far as Hanes,
⁵ everyone will be ashamed
because of a people
who can't help.
They are of no benefit, they are
no help;
they are good for nothing
but shame and reproach.

⁶ An oracle about the animals of the Negev:

Through a land of trouble
and distress,
of lioness and lion,
of viper and flying serpent,
they carry their wealth
on the backs of donkeys
and their treasures on the humps
of camels,
to a people who will not
help them.
⁷ Egypt's help is
completely worthless;
therefore, I call her:
Rahab Who Just Sits.

⁸ Go now, write it on a tablet
in their presence
and inscribe it on a scroll;
it will be for the future,
forever and ever.
⁹ They are a rebellious people,
deceptive children,
children who do not obey
the LORD's instruction.
¹⁰ They say to the seers,
"Do not see,"
and to the prophets,
"Do not prophesy the truth to us.
Tell us flattering things.
Prophesy illusions.
¹¹ Get out of the way!
Leave the pathway.
Rid us of the Holy One of Israel."
¹² Therefore the Holy One
of Israel says:
"Because you have rejected
this message
and have trusted in oppression
and deceit,
and have depended on them,
¹³ this iniquity of yours will be
like a spreading breach,
a bulge in a high wall
whose collapse will come
very suddenly.
¹⁴ Its collapse will be
like the shattering
of a potter's jar,
crushed to pieces,
so that not even a fragment
of pottery
will be found among
its shattered remains—
no fragment large enough
to take fire from a hearth
or scoop water from a cistern."
¹⁵ For the Lord GOD, the Holy One
of Israel, has said:
"You will be delivered
by returning and resting;
your strength will lie
in quiet confidence.

But you are not willing."
¹⁶ You say, "No!
We will escape on horses"—
therefore you will escape!—
and, "We will ride
on fast horses"—
but those who pursue you
will be faster.
¹⁷ One thousand will flee
at the threat of one,
at the threat of five you will flee,
until you alone remain
like a solitary pole
on a mountaintop
or a banner on a hill.

¹⁸ Therefore the LORD is waiting
to show you mercy,
and is rising up
to show you compassion,
for the LORD is a just God.
Happy are all who wait patiently
for Him.

¹⁹ For you people will live on Zion in Jerusalem and will never cry again. He will show favor to you at the sound of your cry; when He hears, He will answer you. ²⁰ The Lord will give you meager bread and water during oppression, but your Teacher will not hide Himself any longer. Your eyes will see your Teacher, ²¹ and whenever you turn to the right or to the left, your ears will hear this command behind you: "This is the way. Walk in it." ²² Then you will defile your silver-plated idols and your gold-plated images. You will throw them away like menstrual cloths, and call them filth.

²³ Then He will send rain for your seed that you have sown in the ground, and the food, the produce of the ground, will be rich and plentiful. On that day your cattle will graze in open pastures. ²⁴ The oxen and donkeys that work the ground will eat salted fodder scattered with winnowing shovel and fork. ²⁵ Streams and watercourses will be on every high mountain and every raised hill on the day of great slaughter when the towers fall. ²⁶ The moonlight will be as bright as the sunlight, and the sunlight will be seven times brighter—like the light of seven days—on the day that the LORD

bandages His people's injuries and heals the wounds He inflicted.

²⁷ Look, Yahweh comes
from far away,
His anger burning and heavy
with smoke.
His lips are full of fury,
and His tongue is
like a consuming fire.
²⁸ His breath is like
an overflowing torrent
that rises to the neck.
He comes to sift the nations
in a sieve of destruction
and to put a bridle on the jaws
of the peoples
to lead them astray.
²⁹ Your singing will be like that
on the night of a holy festival,
And your heart will rejoice
like one who walks to the music
of a flute,
going up to the mountain
of the LORD,
to the Rock of Israel.
³⁰ And the LORD will make
the splendor
of His voice heard
and reveal His arm striking
in angry wrath and a flame
of consuming fire,
in driving rain, a torrent,
and hailstones.
³¹ Assyria will be shattered
by the voice of the LORD.
He will strike with a rod.
³² And every stroke of the appointed
staff
that the LORD brings down on him
will be to the sound
of tambourines and lyres;
He will fight against him
with brandished weapons.
³³ Indeed! Topheth has been ready
for the king for a long time now.
His funeral pyre is deep and wide,
with plenty of fire and wood.
The breath of the LORD,
like a torrent of brimstone,
kindles it.

31 Woe to those who go down
to Egypt for help

and who depend on horses!
They trust in the number
of chariots
and in the great strength
of charioteers.
They do not look to the Holy One
of Israel
and they do not seek
the LORD's help.
² But He also is wise
and brings disaster.
He does not go back on what
He says;
He will rise up against the house
of wicked men
and against the allies of evildoers.
³ Egyptians are men, not God;
their horses are flesh, not spirit.
When the LORD raises His hand
to strike,
the helper will stumble
and the helped will fall;
both will perish together.

⁴ For this is what the LORD said to me:

As a lion or young lion growls
over its prey
when a band of shepherds
is called out against it,
and is not terrified
by their shouting
or subdued by their noise,
so the LORD of Hosts
will come down
to fight on Mount Zion
and on its hill.

⁵ Like hovering birds,
so the LORD of Hosts
will protect Jerusalem—
by protecting it,
He will rescue it,
by sparing it, He will deliver it.

⁶ Return to the One the Israelites
have greatly rebelled against. ⁷ For on
that day, each one will reject the silver
and gold idols that your own hands have
sinfully made.

⁸ Then Assyria will fall,
but not by human sword;
a sword will devour him,

but not one made by man.
He will flee from the sword,
his young men will be put
to forced labor.
⁹ His rock will pass away
because of fear,
and his officers will be afraid
because of the signal flag.

This is the LORD's declaration—whose
fire is in Zion and whose furnace is in
Jerusalem.

32 Indeed, a king
will reign righteously,
and rulers will rule justly.
² Each will be like a shelter
from the wind,
a refuge from the rain,
like streams of water in a dry land
and the shade of a massive rock
in an arid land.
³ Then the eyes of those who see
will not be closed,
and the ears of those who hear
will listen.
⁴ The reckless mind
will gain knowledge,
and the stammering tongue
will speak clearly and fluently.
⁵ A fool will no longer be called
a noble,
nor a scoundrel said
to be important.
⁶ For a fool speaks foolishness
and his mind plots iniquity.
He lives in a godless way
and speaks falsely
about the LORD.
He leaves the hungry empty
and deprives the thirsty of drink.
⁷ The scoundrel's weapons
are destructive;
he hatches plots to destroy
the needy with lies,
and by charging the poor
during a judgment.
⁸ But a noble person plans
noble things;
he stands up for noble causes.
⁹ Stand up, you complacent women;
listen to me.

Pay attention to what I say,
you overconfident daughters.
¹⁰ In a little more than a year
you overconfident ones
will shudder,
for the vintage will fail
and the harvest will not come.

*P*SALM 115:1-8

¹ Not to us, LORD, not to us,
but to Your name give glory
because of Your faithful love,
because of Your truth.
² Why should the nations say,
"Where is their God?"
³ Our God is in heaven
and does whatever He pleases.

⁴ Their idols are silver and gold,
made by human hands.
⁵ They have mouths, but cannot
speak,
eyes, but cannot see.
⁶ They have ears,
but cannot hear,
noses, but cannot smell.
⁷ They have hands,
but cannot feel,
feet, but cannot walk.
They cannot make a sound with
their throats.
⁸ Those who make them are just
like them,
as are all who trust in them.

*P*ROVERBS 23:26-28

²⁶ My son, give me your heart,
and let your eyes observe my
ways.
²⁷ For a prostitute is a deep pit,
and a forbidden woman is a
narrow well;
²⁸ indeed, she sets an ambush like a
robber
and increases those among men
who are unfaithful.

*G*ALATIANS 5:1-18

5 Christ has liberated us into freedom. Therefore stand firm and don't
submit again to a yoke of slavery. ² Take
note! I, Paul, tell you that if you get circumcised, Christ will not benefit you at
all. ³ Again I testify to every man who
gets circumcised that he is obligated to
keep the entire law. ⁴ You who are trying
to be justified by the law are alienated
from Christ; you have fallen from grace!
⁵ For by the Spirit we eagerly wait for
the hope of righteousness from faith.
⁶ For in Christ Jesus neither circumcision nor uncircumcision accomplishes
anything; what matters is faith working
through love.

⁷ You were running well. Who prevented you from obeying the truth?
⁸ This persuasion did not come from
Him who called you. ⁹ A little yeast leav-
ens the whole lump of dough. ¹⁰ In the
Lord I have confidence in you that you
will not accept any other view. But
whoever it is who is troubling you will
pay the penalty. ¹¹ Now brothers, if I
still preach circumcision, why am I still
persecuted? In that case the offense of
the cross has been abolished. ¹² I wish
those who are disturbing you might also
get themselves castrated!

¹³ For you are called to freedom,
brothers; only don't use this freedom as
an opportunity for the flesh, but serve
one another through love. ¹⁴ For the entire law is fulfilled in one statement:
Love your neighbor as yourself. ¹⁵ But
if you bite and devour one another,
watch out, or you will be consumed by
one another.

¹⁶ I say then, walk by the Spirit and
you will not carry out the desire of the
flesh. ¹⁷ For the flesh desires what is
against the Spirit, and the Spirit desires
what is against the flesh; these are opposed to each other, so that you don't
do what you want. ¹⁸ But if you are led
by the Spirit, you are not under the law.

More Than Performance

My son, give me your heart, and let your eyes observe my ways.

—PROVERBS 23:26

Many Christians live on the surface of life and rarely, if ever, look below the waterline. They do have inner longings sometimes to climb higher with God, but their response to these feelings is to focus their attention on what goes on above the waterline—the area of performance and behavior. So they try harder in terms of more Bible reading, more prayer, more giving, more Christian activities.

I would be the last person to view greater obedience as unimportant, but it is not the only, or indeed the final, answer. A great mistake made by many Christians who recognize they are not receiving from God the things they ought to be receiving is to think that the solution lies solely in more spiritual effort, the assumption being that as we do more above the waterline, the problems that lie below the waterline will all come right.

Now sometimes greater obedience and more responsible effort do have this result. I have often found, for example, that when a man who falls out of love with his wife chooses a change in behavior and deliberately sets out to do loving things for her, the loving behavior can trigger loving feelings.

There is more to spiritual change, however, than a change on the surface. It can begin there, but it is not complete until the focus moves from the surface down into the depths. Those who remain above the waterline in their Christian living and resist the invitation to look beneath the surface will soon become legalists—good at performing but bad at being.

Prayer

My Father and my God, I see that if change is to take place in me, then it must take place in all of me. Help me to see even more clearly that while what I do is important, what I am in the depth of my being is even more important. In Jesus' name. Amen.

Further Study

2 Tm 3:1-5; Is 29:1-13
What did Paul say would be a characteristic of the last days?
What was the Lord's complaint against the children of Israel?

OCTOBER 1

ISAIAH 32:11–34:17

¹¹ Shudder, you complacent ones;
tremble, you overconfident ones!
Strip yourselves bare
and put sackcloth
about your waists.
¹² Beat your breasts in mourning
for the delightful fields
and the fruitful vines,
¹³ for the ground of my people
growing thorns and briers,
indeed, for every joyous house
in the joyful city.
¹⁴ For the palace will be forsaken,
the busy city abandoned.
The hill and the watchtower
will become
barren places forever,
the joy of wild asses,
and a pasture for flocks,
¹⁵ until the Spirit from heaven
is poured out on us.
Then the desert will become
an orchard,
and the orchard will seem
like a forest.
¹⁶ Then justice will inhabit
the wilderness,
and righteousness will dwell
in the orchard.
¹⁷ The result of righteousness
will be peace;
the effect of righteousness
will be quiet confidence forever.
¹⁸ Then my people will dwell
in a peaceful place,
and in safe and restful dwellings.
¹⁹ But hail will level the forest,
and the city will sink
into the depths.
²⁰ Happy are you who sow seed
beside abundant waters,
who let ox and donkey range freely.

33 Woe, you destroyer
never destroyed,

you traitor never betrayed!
When you have
finished destroying,
you will be destroyed.
When you have finished betraying,
they will betray you.

² LORD, be gracious to us! We wait
for You.
Be our strength every morning,
and our salvation in time
of trouble.
³ The peoples flee
at the thunderous noise;
the nations scatter when You rise
in Your majesty.
⁴ Your spoil will be gathered
as locusts are gathered;
people will swarm over it
like an infestation of locusts.
⁵ The LORD is exalted, for He dwells
on high;
He has filled Zion with justice
and righteousness.
⁶ There will be times of security
for you—
a storehouse of salvation, wisdom,
and knowledge.
The fear of the LORD is
Zion's treasure.

⁷ Listen! Their warriors cry loudly
in the streets;
the messengers of peace
weep bitterly.
⁸ The highways are deserted;
travel has ceased.
An agreement has been broken,
and cities despised.
and human life disregarded.
⁹ The land mourns and withers;
Lebanon is ashamed and decayed.
Sharon is like a desert;
Bashan and Carmel shake off their
leaves.
¹⁰ "Now I will rise up,"
says the LORD.

"Now I will lift Myself up.
Now I will be exalted.
11 You will conceive chaff;
you will give birth to stubble.
Your breath is fire that will
consume you.
12 The peoples will be burned
to ashes,
like thorns cut down and burned
in a fire.
13 You who are far off, hear what
I have done;
you who are near,
know My strength."

14 The sinners in Zion are afraid;
trembling seizes the ungodly:
"Who among us can dwell
with a consuming fire?
Who among us can dwell
with ever-burning flames?"
15 The one who lives righteously
and speaks rightly,
who refuses gain from extortion,
whose hand never takes a bribe,
who stops his ears from listening
to murderous plots
and shuts his eyes to avoid
endorsing evil—
16 he will dwell on the heights;
his refuge will be
the rocky fortresses,
his food provided, his water assured.

17 Your eyes will see the king
in his beauty;
you will see a vast land.
18 Your mind will meditate
on the past terror:
"Where is the accountant?
Where is the tribute collector?
Where is the one who spied out
our defenses?"
19 You will no longer see
the barbarians,
a people whose speech is difficult
to comprehend—
who stammer in a language that is
not understood.
20 Look at Zion, the city
of our festival times.
Your eyes will see Jerusalem,
a peaceful pasture, a tent
that does not wander;

its tent pegs will not be pulled up
nor will any of its cords
be loosened.
21 For there the majestic One,
the Lord, will be for us,
a place of rivers
and broad streams,
where ships that are rowed
will not go,
and majestic vessels will not pass.
22 For the Lord is our Judge,
the Lord is our lawgiver,
the Lord is our King.
He will save us.
23 Your ropes are slack;
they cannot hold the base
of the mast
or spread out the flag.
Then abundant spoil
will be divided,
the lame will plunder it,
24 and none there will say,
"I am sick."
The people who dwell there
will be forgiven their iniquity.

34 You nations, come here
and listen;
you peoples, pay attention!
Let the earth hear, and all
that fills it,
the world and all that comes
from it.
2 The Lord is angry with all
the nations—
furious with all their armies.
He will set them apart
for destruction,
giving them over to slaughter.
3 Their slain will be thrown out,
and the stench of their corpses
will rise;
the mountains flow
with their blood.
4 All the heavenly bodies
will dissolve.
The skies will roll up like a scroll,
and their stars will all wither
as leaves wither on the vine,
and foliage on the fig tree.
5 When My sword has drunk its fill
in the heavens
it will then come down on Edom

and on the people I have set apart
for destruction.
6 The LORD's sword is covered
with blood.
It drips with fat,
with the blood of lambs and goats,
with the fat of the kidneys of rams.
For the LORD has a sacrifice
in Bozrah,
a great slaughter in the land
of Edom.
7 The wild oxen will be struck down
with them,
and young bulls
with the mighty bulls.
Their land will be soaked with
blood,
and their soil will be saturated
with fat.

8 For the LORD has a day
of vengeance,
a time of paying back Edom
for its hostility against Zion.
9 Edom's streams will be turned
into pitch,
her soil into sulfur;
her land will become
burning pitch.
10 It will never go out—day or night.
Its smoke will go up forever.
It will be desolate,
from generation
to generation;
no one will pass through it forever
and ever.
11 The desert owl and the hedgehog
will possess it,
and the great owl and the raven
will dwell there.
The LORD will stretch out
a measuring line
and a plumb line over her
for her destruction and chaos.
12 No nobles will be left to proclaim
a king,
and all her princes will come
to nothing.
13 Her palaces will be overgrown
with thorns;
her fortified cities, with thistles
and briers.
She will become a dwelling
for jackals,

an abode for ostriches.
14 The wild beasts will meet hyenas,
and one wild goat will call
to another.
Indeed, the screech owl
will stay there
and will find a resting place
for herself.
15 The sand partridge will make
her nest there;
she will lay and hatch her eggs
and will gather her brood
under her shadow.
Indeed, the birds of prey
will gather there,
each with its mate.
16 Search and read the scroll
of the LORD:
Not one of them will be missing,
none will be lacking its mate,
because He has ordered it by my
mouth,
and He will gather them
by His Spirit.
17 He has ordained a lot for them;
His hand allotted their portion
with a measuring line.
They will possess it forever;
they will dwell in it
from generation
to generation.

PSALM 115:9-13

9 Israel, trust in the LORD!
He is their help and shield.
10 House of Aaron, trust in the LORD!
He is their help and shield.
11 You who fear the LORD, trust in
the LORD!
He is their help and shield.
12 The LORD remembers us and will
bless us.
He will bless the house of Israel;
He will bless the house of Aaron;
13 He will bless those who fear the
LORD—
small and great alike.

PROVERBS 23:29-30

29 Who has woe? Who has sorrow?
Who has conflicts? Who has
complaints?

Who has wounds for no reason?
Who has red eyes?
³⁰ Those who linger over wine,
those who go looking for mixed
wine.

GALATIANS 5:19–6:18

¹⁹ Now the works of the flesh are obvious: sexual immorality, moral impurity, promiscuity, ²⁰ idolatry, sorcery, hatreds, strife, jealousy, outbursts of anger, selfish ambitions, dissensions, factions, ²¹ envy, drunkenness, carousing, and anything similar, about which I tell you in advance—as I told you before—that those who practice such things will not inherit the kingdom of God. ²² But the fruit of the Spirit is love, joy, peace, patience, kindness, goodness, faith, ²³ gentleness, self-control. Against such things there is no law. ²⁴ Now those who belong to Christ Jesus have crucified the flesh with its passions and desires. ²⁵ If we live by the Spirit, we must also follow the Spirit. ²⁶ We must not become conceited, provoking one another, envying one another.

6 Brothers, if someone is caught in any wrongdoing, you who are spiritual should restore such a person with a gentle spirit, watching out for yourselves so you won't be tempted also. ² Carry one another's burdens; in this way you will fulfill the law of Christ. ³ For if anyone considers himself to be something when he is nothing, he is deceiving himself. ⁴ But each person should examine his own work, and then he will have a reason for boasting in himself alone, and not in respect to someone else. ⁵ For each person will have to carry his own load.

⁶ The one who is taught the message must share his goods with the teacher. ⁷ Don't be deceived: God is not mocked. For whatever a man sows he will also reap, ⁸ because the one who sows to his flesh will reap corruption from the flesh, but the one who sows to the Spirit will reap eternal life from the Spirit. ⁹ So we must not get tired of doing good, for we will reap at the proper time if we don't give up. ¹⁰ Therefore, as we have opportunity, we must work for the good of all, especially for those who belong to the household of faith.

¹¹ Look at what large letters I have written to you in my own handwriting. ¹² Those who want to make a good showing in the flesh are the ones who would compel you to be circumcised—but only to avoid being persecuted for the cross of Christ. ¹³ For even the circumcised don't keep the law themselves; however, they want you to be circumcised in order to boast about your flesh. ¹⁴ But as for me, I will never boast about anything except the cross of our Lord Jesus Christ, through whom the world has been crucified to me, and I to the world. ¹⁵ For both circumcision and uncircumcision mean nothing; what matters instead is a new creation. ¹⁶ May peace be on all those who follow this standard, and mercy also be on the Israel of God!

¹⁷ From now on, let no one cause me trouble, because I carry the marks of Jesus on my body. ¹⁸ Brothers, the grace of our Lord Jesus Christ be with your spirit. Amen.

Why an Inside Look?

He will dwell on the heights; his refuge will be the rocky fortresses.
—ISAIAH 33:16

Before we can dwell on the heights, we must be prepared to take an honest look at what is going on beneath the surface of our lives. Doing this, of course, can be dangerous unless it is approached in the right attitude. Some Christians use the process of self-examination as a means of avoiding rather than assuming responsibility. They look at what is going on inside themselves and allow what they discover there to develop into a cynical negativism, which hinders rather than helps their Christian life.

Those who do this fail to understand the purpose of godly self-examination: to bring what is discovered to the Lord so that He can deal with it. Many commentators have pointed out, in the incident when the Israelites in the wilderness were bitten by the snakes, that when they looked at themselves and recognized their condition, they were then highly motivated to look to the brass serpent for help (see Nm 21:4-9).

The purpose of taking such an honest look at what is going on beneath the surface of our lives is to promote a deeper dependence on the Lord and thus contribute to our spiritual effectiveness. Recognition of our true condition provides a strong motivation to look away from ourselves and turn in simple faith to the Lord Jesus Christ. As you take this journey into the core of your being, be willing to face yourself in a way that you have never done before. I cannot promise you it will be painless, but I can promise you it will be profitable.

Prayer

Father, give me the courage to overcome the fears that would rise within me saying: "I am not sure that I can face it." Deepen the conviction within me that with You, I can face anything. Amen.

Further Study

1 Co 11:23-33; Lm 3:40; Gl 6:4
How does Paul admonish us?
How does the writer of Lamentations put it?

OCTOBER 2

ISAIAH 35:1–37:20

35 The wilderness and the dry land
will be glad;
the desert will rejoice
and blossom like a rose.
2 It will blossom abundantly
and will also rejoice with joy
and singing.

The glory of Lebanon
will be given to it,
the splendor of Carmel
and Sharon.
They will see the glory
of the LORD,
the splendor of our God.
3 Strengthen the weak hands,
steady the shaking knees!

⁴ Say to the faint-hearted:
"Be strong; do not fear!
Here is your God;
    vengeance is coming.
God's retribution is coming;
    He will save you."
⁵ Then the eyes of the blind
    will be opened,
and the ears of the deaf unstopped.
⁶ Then the lame will leap
    like a deer,
and the tongue of the mute
    will sing for joy,
for water will gush
    in the wilderness,
and streams in the desert;
⁷ the parched ground will become
    a pool of water,
and the thirsty land springs
    of water.
In the haunt of jackals,
    in their lairs,
there will be grass, reeds,
    and papyrus.
⁸ A road will be there and a way;
it will be called the Holy Way.
The unclean will not travel on it,
but it will be for him who walks
    the path.
Even the fool will not go astray.
⁹ There will be no lion there,
and no vicious beast will go up
    on it;
they will not be found there.
But the redeemed will walk on it,
¹⁰ and the ransomed of the LORD
    will return
and come to Zion with singing,
crowned with unending joy.
Joy and gladness
    will overtake them,
and sorrow and sighing will flee.

36 In the fourteenth year of King Hezekiah, Sennacherib king of Assyria advanced against all the fortified cities of Judah and captured them. ² Then the king of Assyria sent the Rabshakeh, along with a massive army, from Lachish to King Hezekiah at Jerusalem. The Assyrian stood near the conduit of the upper pool, by the road to the Fuller's Field. ³ Eliakim son of Hilkiah, who was in charge of the palace, Shebna the scribe, and Joah son of Asaph, the record keeper, came out to him.
⁴ The Rabshakeh said to them, "Tell Hezekiah:

The great king, the king of Assyria, says this: 'What are you basing your confidence on? ⁵ I say that your plans and military preparedness are mere words. Now who are you trusting in that you have rebelled against me? ⁶ Look, you are trusting in Egypt, that splintered reed of a staff, which will enter and pierce the hand of anyone who leans on it. This is how Pharaoh king of Egypt is to all who trust in him. ⁷ Suppose you say to me: We trust in the LORD our God. Isn't He the One whose high places and altars Hezekiah has removed, saying to Judah and Jerusalem: You are to worship at this altar?

⁸ Now make a deal with my master, the king of Assyria. I'll give you 2,000 horses if you can put riders on them! ⁹ How then can you repel the attack of even the weakest of my master's officers, and trust in Egypt for chariots and horsemen? ¹⁰ Have I attacked this land to destroy it without the LORD's approval? The LORD said to me, 'Attack this land and destroy it.' "

¹¹ Then Eliakim, Shebna, and Joah said to the Rabshakeh, "Please speak to your servants in Aramaic, for we understand it; don't speak to us in Hebrew within earshot of the people who are on the wall."
¹² But the Rabshakeh replied, "Has my master sent me to speak these words to your master and to you, and not to the men who sit on the wall, who are destined with you to eat their excrement and drink their urine?"
¹³ Then the Rabshakeh stood and called out loudly in Hebrew:

Listen to the words of the great king, the king of Assyria! ¹⁴ The king says: "Don't let Hezekiah deceive you, for he cannot deliver you. ¹⁵ Don't let Hezekiah persuade you to trust the LORD, saying, 'The LORD will surely deliver us. This city will not be handed over to the king of Assyria.' "

¹⁶ Don't listen to Hezekiah. For the king of Assyria says: "Make peace with me and surrender to me; then every one of you will eat from his own vine and his own fig tree and drink water from his own cistern ¹⁷ until I come and take you away to a land like your land, a land of grain and new wine, a land of bread and vineyards. ¹⁸ Beware that Hezekiah does not mislead you by saying, 'The LORD will deliver us.' Has any one of the gods of the nations delivered his land from the hand of the king of Assyria? ¹⁹ Where are the gods of Hamath and Arpad? Where are the gods of Sepharvaim? Have they delivered Samaria from my hand? ²⁰ Who of all the gods of these lands ever delivered his land from my hand, that the LORD should deliver Jerusalem?"

²¹ But they were silent and did not answer him at all, for the king's command was, "Don't answer him." ²² Then Eliakim son of Hilkiah, who was in charge of the palace, Shebna the scribe, and Joah son of Asaph, the record keeper, came to Hezekiah with their clothes torn, and they reported to him the words of the Rabshakeh.

37 When King Hezekiah heard their report, he tore his clothes, put on sackcloth, and went to the house of the LORD. ² Then he sent Eliakim, who was in charge of the palace, Shebna the scribe, and the older priests, wearing sackcloth, to the prophet Isaiah son of Amoz. ³ They said to him, "Hezekiah says: 'Today is a day of distress, rebuke, and disgrace, as when children come to the point of birth, and there is no strength to deliver them. ⁴ Perhaps the LORD your God will hear the words of the Rabshakeh, whom his master, the

king of Assyria, sent to mock the living God, and will rebuke him for the words that the LORD your God has heard. Therefore offer a prayer for the surviving remnant.' "

⁵ When King Hezekiah's servants came to Isaiah, ⁶ Isaiah said to them, "Say this to your master, 'The LORD says: Don't be afraid because of the words you have heard, which the king of Assyria's attendants have blasphemed Me with. ⁷ Look! I am putting a spirit in him and he will hear a rumor and return to his own land, where I will cause him to fall by the sword.' "

⁸ When the Rabshakeh heard that the king had left Lachish, he returned and discovered that the king of Assyria was fighting against Libnah. ⁹ The king had heard this about Tirhakah, king of Cush: "He has set out to fight against you." So when he heard this, he sent messengers to Hezekiah, saying, ¹⁰ "Say this to Hezekiah king of Judah: 'Don't let your God, whom you trust, deceive you by saying that Jerusalem won't be handed over to the king of Assyria. ¹¹ Look, you have heard what the kings of Assyria have done to all the countries; they destroyed them completely. Will you be rescued? ¹² Did the gods of the nations that my predecessors destroyed rescue them—Gozan, Haran, Rezeph, and the Edenites in Telassar? ¹³ Where is the king of Hamath, the king of Arpad, the king of the city of Sepharvaim, Hena, or Ivvah?' "

¹⁴ Hezekiah took the letter from the messengers, read it, then went up to the LORD's house and spread it out before the LORD. ¹⁵ Hezekiah prayed to the LORD: ¹⁶ "LORD of Hosts, God of Israel, who is enthroned above the cherubim, You are God—You alone—of all the kingdoms of the earth. You made the heavens and the earth. ¹⁷ Listen closely, LORD, and hear; open Your eyes, LORD, and see; hear all the words that Sennacherib has sent to mock the living God. ¹⁸ LORD, it is true that the kings of Assyria have devastated all these countries and their lands ¹⁹ and have thrown their gods into the fire; for they were not gods but made by human hands—

wood and stone. So they have destroyed them. ²⁰ Now, LORD our God, save us from his hand so that all the kingdoms of the earth may know that You are the LORD—You alone."

PSALM 115:14-18

¹⁴ May the LORD add to your
  numbers,
  both yours and your children's.
¹⁵ May you be blessed by the LORD,
  the Maker of heaven and earth.
¹⁶ The heavens are the LORD's,
  but the earth He has given to the
  human race.
¹⁷ It is not the dead who praise the
  LORD,
  nor any of those descending into
  the silence of death.
¹⁸ But we will praise the LORD,
  both now and forever.
  Hallelujah!

PROVERBS 23:31-32

³¹ Don't gaze at wine when it is red,
  when it gleams in the cup
  and goes down smoothly.
³² In the end it bites like a snake
  and stings like a viper.

EPHESIANS 1:1-23

1 Paul, an apostle of Christ Jesus by God's will:
To the saints and believers in Christ Jesus at Ephesus.
² Grace to you and peace from God our Father and the Lord Jesus Christ.
³ Blessed be the God and Father of our Lord Jesus Christ, who has blessed us with every spiritual blessing in the heavens, in Christ; ⁴ for He chose us in Him, before the foundation of the world, to be holy and blameless in His sight. In love ⁵ He predestined us to be adopted through Jesus Christ for Himself, according to His favor and will, ⁶ to the praise of His glorious grace that He favored us with in the Beloved.

⁷ In Him we have redemption through His blood, the forgiveness of our trespasses, according to the riches of His grace ⁸ that He lavished on us with all wisdom and understanding. ⁹ He made known to us the mystery of His will, according to His good pleasure that He planned in Him ¹⁰ for the administration of the days of fulfillment—to bring everything together in the Messiah, both things in heaven and things on earth in Him.

¹¹ In Him we were also made His inheritance, predestined according to the purpose of the One who works out everything in agreement with the decision of His will, ¹² so that we who had already put our hope in the Messiah might bring praise to His glory.

¹³ In Him you also, when you heard the word of truth, the gospel of your salvation—in Him when you believed—were sealed with the promised Holy Spirit. ¹⁴ He is the down payment of our inheritance, for the redemption of the possession, to the praise of His glory.

¹⁵ This is why, since I heard about your faith in the Lord Jesus and your love for all the saints, ¹⁶ I never stop giving thanks for you as I remember you in my prayers. ¹⁷ I pray that the God of our Lord Jesus Christ, the glorious Father, would give you a spirit of wisdom and revelation in the knowledge of Him. ¹⁸ I pray that the eyes of your heart may be enlightened so you may know what is the hope of His calling, what are the glorious riches of His inheritance among the saints, ¹⁹ and what is the immeasurable greatness of His power to us who believe, according to the working of His vast strength.

²⁰ He demonstrated this power in the Messiah by raising Him from the dead and seating Him at His right hand in the heavens— ²¹ far above every ruler and authority, power and dominion, and every title given, not only in this age but also in the one to come. ²² And **He put everything under His feet** and appointed Him as head over everything for the church, ²³ which is His body, the fullness of the One who fills all things in every way.

"We've Won a Holiday"

In Him we have redemption through His blood,
the forgiveness of our trespasses,
according to the riches of His grace.—EPHESIANS 1:7

What is it in the heart of most men and women that rejects the idea of God's free and generous offer of salvation? It is pride, the deadliest of all the deadly sins. Bernard Shaw, an example of a modern-day thinker, said: "Forgiveness is a beggar's refuge. We must pay our debts." But we cannot pay our debts. As our spiritual fathers saw so clearly, the only language we can use in the presence of a God who demands so much and whose demands we are unable to meet is:

> Just as I am without one plea
> But that Thy blood was shed for me,
> And that Thou bidd'st me come to Thee,
> O Lamb of God, I come, I come.

In response to our coming, the free unmerited favor of God flows down to us, cancels our debt, imputes and imparts Christ's righteousness to us. How can Christ's righteousness be imputed and imparted to us? It's His righteousness, not ours.

A simple illustration may help to illuminate this point. A dull little boy came home from school one day and said to his mother: "We've won a holiday." The truth was, another boy had come top of the region in the examinations, and the head teacher decided to give the whole school a holiday. Yet the dull little lad said: "We've won a holiday."

Grace is like that. God permits the righteousness of Jesus to cover us and then—as we open ourselves to it—to enter us. He did it, but we benefit from it. Isn't grace really amazing?

Prayer

O Father, as I contemplate still further the "riches" of Your grace, once again I have to confess it's truly amazing. No wonder men and women use that term to describe Your grace. No other adjective will do! Amen.

Further Study

Php 4:1-19; 1 Tm 1:14; Ti 3:6
What has God promised?
What did Paul testify to Timothy?

OCTOBER 3

*I*SAIAH 37:21–39:8

²¹ Then Isaiah son of Amoz sent a message to Hezekiah: "The LORD, the God of Israel, says: 'Because you prayed to Me about Sennacherib king of Assyria, ²² this is the word the LORD has spoken against him:

The young woman, Daughter Zion,
despises you and scorns you:
Daughter Jerusalem
   shakes her head
behind your back.
²³ Who is it you have mocked
   and blasphemed?
Who have you raised your
   voice against
and lifted your eyes in pride?
Against the Holy One of Israel!
²⁴ You have mocked the LORD
   through your servants.
You have said: With my
   many chariots
I have gone up to the heights
   of the mountains,
to the far recesses of Lebanon.
I cut down its tallest cedars,
its choice cypress trees.
I came to its remotest heights,
its densest forest.
²⁵ I dug wells and drank water.
I dried up all the streams of Egypt
with the soles of my feet.

²⁶ Have you not heard?
I designed it long ago;
I planned it in days gone by.
I have now brought it to pass,
and you have crushed
   fortified cities
into piles of rubble.
²⁷ Their inhabitants have
   become powerless,
dismayed, and ashamed.
They are plants of the field,
tender grass,

grass on the rooftops,
blasted by the east wind.

²⁸ But I know your sitting down,
your going out
   and your coming in,
and your raging against Me.
²⁹ Because your raging against Me
and your arrogance has reached
   My ears,
I will put My hook in your nose
and My bit in your mouth;
I will make you go back
the way you came.

³⁰ " 'This will be the sign for you: This year you will eat what grows on its own, and in the second year what grows from that. But in the third year sow and reap, plant vineyards and eat their fruit. ³¹ The surviving remnant of the house of Judah will again take root downward and bear fruit upward. ³² For a remnant will go out from Jerusalem, and survivors from Mount Zion. The zeal of the LORD of Hosts will accomplish this.'

³³ " 'Therefore, this is what the LORD says about the king of Assyria:

He will not enter this city
or shoot an arrow there
or come before it with a shield
or build up an assault ramp
   against it.
³⁴ He will go back
on the road that he came
and he will not enter this city.
   This is the LORD's declaration.

³⁵ I will defend this city
   and rescue it,
because of Me
and because of
   My servant David.' "

³⁶ Then the angel of the LORD went out and struck down 185,000 in the

camp of the Assyrians. When the people got up the next morning—there were all the dead bodies! ³⁷ So Sennacherib king of Assyria broke camp and left. He returned home and lived in Nineveh.

³⁸ One day, while he was worshiping in the temple of his god Nisroch, his sons Adrammelech and Sharezer struck him down with the sword and escaped to the land of Ararat. Then his son Esarhaddon became king in his place.

38 In those days Hezekiah became terminally ill. The prophet Isaiah son of Amoz came and said to him, "This is what the LORD says: 'Put your affairs in order, for you are about to die; you will not recover.' "

² Then Hezekiah turned his face to the wall and prayed to the LORD. ³ He said, "Please, LORD, remember how I have walked before You faithfully and wholeheartedly, and have done what is good in Your sight." And Hezekiah wept bitterly.

⁴ Then the word of the LORD came to Isaiah: ⁵ "Go and tell Hezekiah that this is what the LORD God of your ancestor David says: I have heard your prayer; I have seen your tears. Look, I am going to add 15 years to your life. ⁶ And I will deliver you and this city from the hand of the king of Assyria; I will defend this city. ⁷ This is the sign to you from the LORD that the LORD will do what He has promised: ⁸ I am going to make the sun's shadow that goes down on Ahaz's stairway return by 10 steps." So the sun's shadow went back the 10 steps it had descended.

⁹ A poem by Hezekiah king of Judah after he had been sick and had recovered from his illness:

¹⁰ I said: In the prime of my life
I must go to the gates of Sheol;
I am deprived of the rest
of my years.
¹¹ I said: I will never see the LORD,
the LORD in the land of the living;
I will not look on humanity
any longer
with the inhabitants of what is
passing away.

¹² My dwelling is plucked up
and removed from me
like a shepherd's tent.
I have rolled up my life
like a weaver;
He cuts me off from the loom.
You make an end of me from day
until night.
¹³ I thought until the morning:
He will break all my bones
like a lion;
You make an end of me
day and night.
¹⁴ I chirp like a swallow or a crane;
I moan like a dove.
My eyes grow weak looking upward.
Lord, I am oppressed; support me.
¹⁵ What can I say?
He has spoken to me,
and He Himself has done it.
I walk along slowly all my years
because of the bitterness
of my soul,
¹⁶ Lord, because of these promises
people live,
and in all of them is the life
of my spirit as well;
You have restored me to health
and let me live.
¹⁷ Indeed, it was for my own
welfare
that I had such great bitterness;
but Your love has delivered me
from the Pit of destruction,
for You have thrown all my sins
behind Your back.
¹⁸ For Sheol cannot thank You;
Death cannot praise You.
Those who go down to the Pit
cannot hope for Your faithfulness.
¹⁹ The living, only the living
can thank You,
as I do today;
a father will make
Your faithfulness known
to children
²⁰ The LORD will save me;
we will play stringed instruments
all the days of our lives
at the house of the LORD.

²¹ Now Isaiah had said, "Let them take a lump of figs and apply it to his infected

skin, so that he may recover." ²² And Hezekiah had asked, "What is the sign that I will go up to the LORD's temple?"

39 At that time Merodach-baladan son of Baladan, king of Babylon, sent letters and a gift to Hezekiah since he heard that he had been sick and had recovered. ² Hezekiah was pleased with them, and showed them his treasure house—the silver, the gold, the spices, and the precious oil—and all his armory, and everything that was found in his treasuries. There was nothing in his palace and in all his realm that Hezekiah did not show them.

³ Then Isaiah the prophet came to King Hezekiah and asked him, "What did these men say? The men who came to you—where were they from?"

Hezekiah replied, "They came to me from a distant country, from Babylon."

⁴ And he asked, "What have they seen in your palace?"

Hezekiah answered, "They have seen everything in my palace. There isn't anything in my storehouses that I didn't show them."

⁵ Then Isaiah said to Hezekiah, "Hear the word of the LORD of Hosts: ⁶ 'The time will certainly come when everything in your palace and all that your fathers have stored up until this day will be carried off to Babylon; nothing will be left,' says the LORD. ⁷ 'Some of your descendants who come from you will be taken away, and they will be eunuchs in the palace of the king of Babylon.'"

⁸ Then Hezekiah said to Isaiah, "The word of the LORD that you have spoken is good." For he thought: There will be peace and security during my lifetime.

PSALM 116:1-7

1 I love the LORD because He has heard
my appeal for mercy.
2 Because He has turned His ear to me,
I will call out to Him as long as I live.

3 The ropes of death were wrapped around me,
and the torments of Sheol overcame me;
I encountered trouble and sorrow.
4 Then I called on the name of the LORD:
"LORD, save me!"

5 The LORD is gracious and righteous;
our God is compassionate.
6 The LORD guards the inexperienced;
I was helpless, and He saved me.
7 Return to your rest, my soul,
for the LORD has been good to you.

PROVERBS 23:33-35

33 Your eyes will see strange things,
and you will say absurd things.
34 You'll be like someone sleeping out at sea
or lying down on the top of a ship's mast.
35 "They struck me, but I feel no pain!
They beat me, but I didn't know it!
When will I wake up?
I'll look for another drink."

EPHESIANS 2:1-22

2 And you were dead in your trespasses and sins ² in which you previously walked according to this worldly age, according to the ruler of the atmospheric domain, the spirit now working in the disobedient. ³ We too all previously lived among them in our fleshly desires, carrying out the inclinations of our flesh and thoughts, and by nature we were children under wrath, as the others were also. ⁴ But God, who is abundant in mercy, because of His great love that He had for us, ⁵ made us alive with the Messiah even though we were dead in trespasses. By grace you are saved! ⁶ He also raised us up with Him and seated us with Him in the heavens, in Christ Jesus, ⁷ so that in the coming ages He might display the immeasurable riches of His grace in His kindness to us in Christ Jesus. ⁸ For by grace you are saved through faith, and this is not from yourselves; it is God's gift— ⁹ not from works, so that no one can boast. ¹⁰ For we are His creation— created in Christ Jesus for good works, which God prepared ahead of time so that we should walk in them.

¹¹ So then, remember that at one time you were Gentiles in the flesh—called "the uncircumcised" by those called "the circumcised," done by hand in the flesh. ¹² At that time you were without the Messiah, excluded from the citizenship of Israel, and foreigners to the covenants of the promise, with no hope and without God in the world. ¹³ But now in Christ Jesus, you who were far away have been brought near by the blood of the Messiah. ¹⁴ For He is our peace, who made both groups one and tore down the dividing wall of hostility. In His flesh, ¹⁵ He did away with the law of the commandments in regulations, so that He might create in Himself one new man from the two, resulting in peace. ¹⁶ He did this so that He might reconcile both to God in one body through the cross and put the hostility to death by it. ¹⁷ When Christ came, He proclaimed the good news of peace to you who were far away and peace to those who were near. ¹⁸ For through Him we both have access by one Spirit to the Father. ¹⁹ So then you are no longer foreigners and strangers, but fellow citizens with the saints, and members of God's household, ²⁰ built on the foundation of the apostles and prophets, with Christ Jesus Himself as the cornerstone. ²¹ The whole building is being fitted together in Him and is growing into a holy sanctuary in the Lord, ²² in whom you also are being built together for God's dwelling in the Spirit.

Sovereign Grace

For by grace you are saved through faith . . . it is God's gift.

—EPHESIANS 2:8

In order to understand grace, we must see it in relation to a Sovereign. As one writer puts it: "Grace is bound to be sovereign since it cannot by its very nature be subject to compulsion." This is why we often refer to it as free grace. There is no reason for grace but grace.

I believe the old definition of grace cannot be improved upon: "Grace is the free, unmerited favor of God." At the heart of all true communion with God there lies this gripping truth: God took the initiative. He is more inclined toward us than we are toward Him. We cannot earn His affection. We have simply to receive it. Always the initiative is from God.

When you originally came to Him, you came because He first drew you. The very faith by which you lay hold of Him is not of yourself; it is, as our text says, "the gift of God." Every step you make on your spiritual pilgrimage is possible because of His grace.

I know this teaching affronts many modern-day men and women because they like to feel that they can "work their passage to heaven," as one preacher puts it. This is like someone in debt for a million pounds trying to get the one to whom he is indebted to accept his resources of a few pence as being sufficient to clear the debt. Listen to the Word of God again and let it sink deep into your soul: "For by grace you are saved through faith . . . it is God's gift." Grace is a gift. You do not have to achieve but simply receive.

Prayer

O Father, once again my heart is moved as I realize it was not my merit but Your mercy, acting in grace, that drew You to me and me to You. All honor and glory be to Your mighty and everlasting name. Amen.

Further Study

Rm 5:1-21; Ti 3:7
How does Paul define grace?
Write out your own definition of grace.

OCTOBER 4

ISAIAH 40:1–41:20

40 "Comfort, comfort My people,"
says your God.
² Speak tenderly to Jerusalem,
and announce to her
that her time of servitude is over,
her iniquity has been pardoned,
and she has received
from the LORD's hand
double for all her sins.

³ A voice of one crying out:

Prepare the way of the LORD
in the wilderness;
make a straight highway
for our God in the desert.
⁴ Every valley will be lifted up,
and every mountain and hill
will be leveled;
the uneven ground
will become smooth,
and the rough places a plain.
⁵ And the glory of the LORD
will appear,
and all humanity will see it
together,

for the mouth of the LORD
has spoken.

⁶ A voice was saying, "Cry out!"
Another said,
"What should I cry out?"
"All humanity is grass,
and all its goodness is
like the flower of the field.
⁷ The grass withers,
the flowers fade
when the breath of the LORD
blows on them;
indeed, the people are grass.
⁸ The grass withers,
the flowers fade,
but the word of our God
remains forever."

⁹ Zion, herald of good news,
go up on a high mountain.
Jerusalem, herald of good news,
raise your voice loudly.
Raise it, do not be afraid!
Say to the cities of Judah,
"Here is your God!"
¹⁰ See, the Lord GOD comes
with strength,
and His power establishes His rule.

His reward is with Him,
and His gifts accompany Him.
11 He protects His flock
like a shepherd;
He gathers the lambs in His arms
and carries them in the fold
of His garment.
He gently leads those
that are nursing.

12 Who has measured the waters
in the hollow of his hand
or marked off the heavens
with the span of his hand?
Who has gathered the dust
of the earth in a measure
or weighed the mountains
in a balance
and the hills in scales?
13 Who has directed the Spirit
of the LORD,
or who gave Him His counsel?
14 Who did He consult with?
Who gave Him understanding
and taught Him the paths
of justice?
Who taught Him knowledge
and showed Him the way
of understanding?
15 Look, the nations are like a drop
in a bucket;
they are considered as a speck
of dust on the scales;
He lifts up the islands
like fine dust.
16 Lebanon is not enough for fuel,
or its animals enough for a
burnt offering.
17 All the nations are as nothing
before Him;
they are considered by Him
as nothingness and emptiness.

18 Who will you compare God with?
What likeness will you
compare Him to?
19 To an idol?—something that
a smelter casts,
and a metalworker plates
with gold
and makes silver welds for it?
20 To one who shapes a pedestal,
choosing wood that does not rot?
He looks for a skilled craftsman

to set up an idol that will not
fall over.

21 Do you not know?
Have you not heard?
Has it not been declared to you
from the beginning?
Have you not considered
the foundations of the earth?
22 God is enthroned above the circle
of the earth;
its inhabitants are
like grasshoppers.
He stretches out the heavens
like thin cloth
and spreads them out like a tent
to live in.
23 He reduces princes to nothing
and makes the judges of the earth
to be irrational.
24 They are barely planted,
barely sown,
their stem hardly takes root
in the ground
when He blows on them
and they wither,
and a whirlwind carries them
away like stubble.

25 "Who will you compare Me to,
or who is My equal?"
asks the Holy One.
26 Look up and see:
who created these?
He brings out the starry host
by number;
He calls all of them by name.
Because of His great power
and strength,
not one of them is missing.

27 Jacob, why do you say,
and Israel, why do you assert:
"My way is hidden from the LORD,
and my claim is ignored
by my God"?
28 Do you not know?
Have you not heard?
Yahweh is the everlasting God,
the Creator of the whole earth.
He never grows faint or weary;
there is no limit
to His understanding.
29 He gives strength to the weary

and strengthens the powerless.
30 Youths may faint and grow weary,
and young men stumble and fall,
31 but those who trust in the LORD
will renew their strength;
they will soar on wings like eagles;
they will run and not grow weary;
they will walk and not faint.

41 "Be silent before Me, islands!
And let peoples renew
their strength.
Let them approach,
then let them testify;
let us come together for the trial.
2 Who has stirred him up
from the east?
He calls righteousness to his feet.
The LORD hands nations over
to him,
and he subdues kings.
He makes them like dust with
his sword,
like wind-driven stubble with
his bow.
3 He pursues them, going on safely,
hardly touching the path
with his feet.
4 Who has performed
and done this,
calling the generations
from the beginning?
I, the LORD, am the first,
and with the last —I am He."

5 The islands see and are afraid,
the ends of the earth tremble.
They approach and arrive.
6 Each one helps the other,
and says to another,
"Take courage!"
7 The craftsman encourages
the metalworker;
the one who flattens
with the hammer
supports the one who strikes
the anvil,
saying of the soldering,
"It is good."
He fastens it with nails so that
it will not fall over.

8 But you, Israel, My servant,
Jacob, whom I have chosen,

descendant of Abraham,
My friend—
9 I brought you from the ends
of the earth
and called you
from its farthest corners.
I said to you: You are My servant;
I have chosen you and not
rejected you.
10 Do not fear, for I am with you;
do not be afraid, for I am your God.
I will strengthen you; I will
help you;
I will hold on to you
with My righteous right hand.

11 Be sure that all who are enraged
against you
will be ashamed and disgraced;
those who contend with you
will become as nothing
and will perish.
12 You will look for those
who contend with you,
but you will not find them.
Those who war against you
will become absolutely nothing.
13 For I, the LORD your God,
hold your right hand
and say to you: Do not fear,
I will help you.
14 Do not fear, you worm Jacob,
you men of Israel:
I will help you—
the LORD's declaration.
Your Redeemer is the Holy One
of Israel.
15 See, I will make you
into a sharp threshing board,
new, with many teeth.
You will thresh mountains
and pulverize them,
and make hills like chaff.
16 You will winnow them
and a wind will carry them away,
and a gale will scatter them.
But you will rejoice in the LORD;
you will boast in the Holy One
of Israel.

17 The poor and the needy
seek water, but there is none;
their tongues are parched with thirst.
I, the LORD, will answer them;

I, the God of Israel, do not
forsake them.
18 I will open rivers
on the barren heights,
and springs in the middle
of the plains.
I will turn the desert into a pool
of water
and dry land into springs of water.
19 I will plant cedars in the desert,
acacias, myrtles, and olive trees.
I will put cypress trees
in the desert,
elms and box trees together,
20 so that all may see and know,
consider and understand,
that the hand of the LORD
has done this,
the Holy One of Israel
has created it.

PSALM 116:8-14

8 For You, LORD, rescued me from
death,
my eyes from tears,
my feet from stumbling.
9 I will walk before the LORD
in the land of the living.
10 I believed, even when I said,
"I am severely afflicted."
11 In my alarm I said,
"Everyone is a liar."

12 How can I repay the LORD
all the good He has done for me?
13 I will take the cup of salvation
and worship the LORD.
14 I will fulfill my vows to the LORD
in the presence of all His people.

PROVERBS 24:1-2

24 Don't envy evil men
or desire to be with them,
2 for their hearts plan violence,
and their words stir up trouble.

EPHESIANS 3:1-21

3 For this reason, I, Paul, the prisoner
of Christ Jesus on behalf of you
Gentiles— 2 you have heard, haven't
you, about the administration of God's
grace that He gave to me for you? 3 The
mystery was made known to me by revelation, as I have briefly written above.
4 By reading this you are able to understand my insight about the mystery
of the Messiah. 5 This was not made
known to people in other generations as
it is now revealed to His holy apostles
and prophets by the Spirit: 6 the Gentiles are co-heirs, members of the same
body, and partners of the promise in
Christ Jesus through the gospel. 7 I was
made a servant of this gospel by the gift
of God's grace that was given to me by
the working of His power.

8 This grace was given to me—the
least of all the saints!—to proclaim to
the Gentiles the incalculable riches of
the Messiah, 9 and to shed light for all
about the administration of the mystery
hidden for ages in God who created all
things. 10 This is so that God's multi-
faceted wisdom may now be made
known through the church to the rulers
and authorities in the heavens. 11 This is
according to the purpose of the ages,
which He made in the Messiah, Jesus
our Lord, 12 in whom we have boldness,
access, and confidence through faith in
Him. 13 So then I ask you not to be discouraged over my afflictions on your behalf, for they are your glory.

14 For this reason I bow my knees before the Father 15 from whom every
family in heaven and on earth is named.
16 I pray that He may grant you, according to the riches of His glory, to be
strengthened with power through His
Spirit in the inner man, 17 and that the
Messiah may dwell in your hearts
through faith. I pray that you, being
rooted and firmly established in love,
18 may be able to comprehend with all
the saints what is the length and width,
height and depth of God's love, 19 and to
know the Messiah's love that surpasses
knowledge, so you may be filled with all
the fullness of God.

20 Now to Him who is able to do above
and beyond all that we ask or think—according to the power that works in
you— 21 to Him be glory in the church
and in Christ Jesus to all generations,
forever and ever. Amen.

"Eccentric" Christians

God is enthroned above the circle of the earth;
its inhabitants are like grasshoppers.—ISAIAH 40:22

The man-centered focus that is creeping into today's church must be resisted at all costs. Such matters as disciplining children, dealing with marital problems, and establishing proper priorities should be addressed also, but we must be careful that "market forces" do not mold our theology.

It could be argued that our problems are so acute because we are deficient in our knowledge of God. The context in which we think and feel is so limited that it is no wonder our souls feel stifled and claustrophobic. One preacher describes our condition in this way: "We are like Peter trying to walk on the water but becoming so engrossed in the winds and the waves that we lose sight of the all-sufficient Christ who is right there beside us. The immediate environment has blotted out the sense of the eternal."

This is why I have chosen today's reading from the magnificent book of Isaiah. The prophet does what a doctor would do upon visiting a patient with a minor sickness and finding the windows shut fast and the room lacking in oxygen. He would throw open the windows and invite the patient to inhale the purer air. "Take a deep breath of the oxygen of the Spirit," Isaiah is saying in effect. "See how great and powerful God is. Set your problems in the context of His omnipotence."

We become like the thing we focus on. If we center on man rather than God, then we ought not be surprised if we finish up off center—eccentric.

Prayer

O God, save me from being an off-center Christian and thus an eccentric Christian—the true meaning of that term. May my primary focus be always on You. Grant it, dear Lord. In Jesus' name I pray. Amen.

Further Study

2 Co 4:13-18; Heb 3:1; 12:2; Ps 141:8
What was Paul's focus?
What is the exhortation of the writer of Hebrews?

OCTOBER 5

ISAIAH 41:21–43:13

21 "Submit your case," says the LORD.
"Present your arguments,"
     says Jacob's King.
22 "Let them come and tell us
what will happen.
Tell us the past events,
so that we may reflect on it
and know the outcome.
Or tell us the future.
23 Tell us the coming events,
then we will know
     that you are gods.
Indeed, do something good or bad,
then we will be in awe
     and perceive.
24 Look, you are nothing
and your work is worthless.
Anyone who chooses you
     is detestable.

25 "I have raised up one
     from the north,
     and he has come,
one from the east who invokes My
     name.
He will march over rulers as if
     they were mud,
like a potter who treads the clay.
26 Who told about this
     from the beginning,
so that we might know,
and from times past,
so that we might say: He is right?
No one announced it,
no one told it,
no one heard your words.
27 I was the first to say to Zion:
Look! Here they are!
and I gave a herald of good news
     to Jerusalem.
28 When I look, there is no one;
there is no counselor
     among them;
when I ask them, they have
     nothing to say.

29 Look, all of them are a delusion;
their works are nonexistent;
their images are wind
     and emptiness.

42 "This is My Servant;
     I strengthen Him,
this is My Chosen One; I delight
     in Him.
I have put My Spirit on Him;
He will bring justice
     to the nations.
2 He will not cry out or shout
or make His voice heard
     in the streets.
3 He will not break a bruised reed,
and He will not put out
     a smoldering wick;
He will faithfully bring justice.
4 He will not grow weak
     or be discouraged
until He has established justice
     on earth.
The islands will wait
     for His instruction."

5 This is what God the LORD says—
who created the heavens
     and stretched them out,
who spread out the earth
     and what comes from it,
who gives breath to the people
     on it
and life to those who walk on it—
6 "I, the LORD, have called you
for a righteous purpose,
and I will hold you by your hand.
I will keep you, and I make you
a covenant for the people
and a light to the nations,
7 in order to open blind eyes,
to bring out prisoners
     from the dungeon,
and those sitting in darkness
     from the prison house.
8 I am Yahweh, that is My name;
I will not give My glory to another,

or My praise to idols.
9 The past events
have indeed happened.
Now I declare new events;
I announce them to you
before they occur."

10 Sing a new song to the LORD;
sing His praise from the ends
of the earth,
you who go down to the sea
with all that fills it,
you islands with your inhabitants.
11 Let the desert and its cities shout,
the settlements
where Kedar dwells cry aloud.
Let the inhabitants of Sela
sing for joy;
let them cry out
from the mountaintops.
12 Let them give glory to the LORD,
and declare His praise
in the islands.
13 The LORD advances like a warrior;
He stirs up His zeal like a soldier.
He shouts, He roars aloud,
He prevails over His enemies.

14 "I have kept silent from ages past;
I have been quiet
and restrained Myself.
But now, I will groan like a woman
in labor,
gasping breathlessly.
15 I will lay waste mountains
and hills,
and dry up all their vegetation.
I will turn rivers into islands,
and dry up marshes.
16 I will lead the blind by a way
they did not know;
I will guide them on paths
they have not known.
I will turn darkness to light
in front of them,
and rough places
into level ground.
This is what I will do for them,
and I will not forsake them.
17 They will be turned back and
utterly ashamed—
those who trust in idols
and say to metal-plated images:
You are our gods!

18 "Listen, you deaf!
Look, you blind, so that
you may see.
19 Who is blind but My servant,
or deaf like My messenger
I am sending?
Who is blind like My
dedicated one,
or blind like the servant
of the LORD?
20 Though seeing many things,
you do not obey.
Though his ears are open,
he does not listen."

21 The LORD was pleased, because of
His righteousness,
to magnify His instruction
and make it glorious.
22 But this is a people plundered
and looted,
all of them trapped in holes
or imprisoned in dungeons.
They have become plunder,
with no one to rescue them,
and loot, with no one saying
"Give it back!"
23 Who among you will pay attention
to this?
Let him listen and obey
in the future.
24 Who gave Jacob to the robber,
and Israel to the plunderers?
Was it not the LORD?
Have we not sinned against Him?
They were not willing to walk
in His ways,
and they would not listen
to His instruction.
25 So He poured out on Jacob
His furious anger
and the power of war.
It surrounded him with fire,
but he did not know it;
it burned him, but he paid
no attention.

43 Now this is what the
LORD says—
the One who created you, Jacob,
and the One who formed
you, Israel—
"Do not fear, for I have
redeemed you;

I have called you by your name;
  you are Mine.
² I will be with you
when you pass
    through the waters,
and when you pass
    through the rivers,
they will not overwhelm you.
You will not be scorched
when you walk through the fire,
and the flame will not burn you.
³ For I the LORD your God,
the Holy One of Israel,
    and your Savior,
give Egypt as a ransom for you,
Cush and Seba in your place.
⁴ Because you are precious
    in My sight
and honored, and I love you,
I will give human beings
    in your place,
and peoples in place of your life.
⁵ Do not fear, for I am with you;
I will bring your descendants
    from the east,
and gather you from the west.
⁶ I will say to the north: Give them
    up!
and to the south:
    Do not hold them back!
Bring My sons from far away,
and My daughters from the ends
    of the earth—
⁷ everyone called by My name
and created for My glory.
I have formed him;
    indeed, I have made him."

⁸ Bring out a people who are blind,
    yet have eyes,
and are deaf, yet have ears.
⁹ All the nations
    are gathered together,
and the peoples are assembled.
Who among them can declare this,
and tell us the former things?
Let them present their witnesses
to vindicate themselves,
so that people may hear and say,
    "It is true."
¹⁰ "You are My witnesses"—
    the LORD's declaration—
"and My servant
    whom I have chosen,

so that you may know
    and believe Me
and understand that I am He.
No god was formed before Me,
and there will be none after Me.
¹¹ I, I am the LORD,
and there is no other Savior
    but Me.
¹² I alone declared, saved,
    and proclaimed—
and not some foreign god
    among you.
So you are My witnesses"—
    the LORD's declaration—
"and I am God.
¹³ Also, from today on
    I am He alone,
and no one can take anything
    from My hand.
I act, and who can reverse it?"

$\mathcal{P}$SALM 116:15-19

¹⁵ The death of His faithful ones
    is valuable in the LORD's sight.
¹⁶ LORD, I am indeed Your servant;
I am Your servant, the son of Your
    female servant.
You have loosened my bonds.

¹⁷ I will offer You a sacrifice of
    thanksgiving
and will worship the LORD.
¹⁸ I will fulfill my vows to the LORD,
in the very presence of all His
    people,
¹⁹ in the courts of the LORD's
    house—
within you, Jerusalem.
Hallelujah!

$\mathcal{P}$ROVERBS 24:3-4

³ A house is built by wisdom,
and it is established by
    understanding;
⁴ by knowledge the rooms are filled
with every precious and beautiful
    treasure.

$\mathcal{E}$PHESIANS 4:1-24

4 I, therefore, the prisoner in the
Lord, urge you to walk worthy of

the calling you have received, ² with all humility and gentleness, with patience, accepting one another in love, ³ diligently keeping the unity of the Spirit with the peace that binds us. ⁴ There is one body and one Spirit, just as you were called to one hope at your calling; ⁵ one Lord, one faith, one baptism, ⁶ one God and Father of all, who is above all and through all and in all.

⁷ Now grace was given to each one of us according to the measure of the Messiah's gift. ⁸ For it says:

When He ascended on high,
He took prisoners
into captivity;
He gave gifts to people.

⁹ But what does "He ascended" mean except that He descended to the lower parts of the earth? ¹⁰ The One who descended is the same as the One who ascended far above all the heavens, that He might fill all things. ¹¹ And He personally gave some to be apostles, some prophets, some evangelists, some pastors and teachers, ¹² for the training of the saints in the work of ministry, to build up the body of Christ, ¹³ until we all reach unity in the faith and in the knowledge of God's Son, growing into a mature man with a stature measured by Christ's fullness. ¹⁴ Then we will no longer be little children, tossed by the waves and blown around by every wind of teaching, by human cunning with cleverness in the techniques of deceit. ¹⁵ But speaking the truth in love, let us grow in every way into Him who is the head—Christ. ¹⁶ From Him the whole body, fitted and knit together by every supporting ligament, promotes the growth of the body for building up itself in love by the proper working of each individual part.

¹⁷ Therefore, I say this and testify in the Lord: You should no longer walk as the Gentiles walk, in the futility of their thoughts. ¹⁸ They are darkened in their understanding, excluded from the life of God, because of the ignorance that is in them and because of the hardness of their hearts. ¹⁹ They became callous and gave themselves over to promiscuity for the practice of every kind of impurity with a desire for more and more.

²⁰ But that is not how you learned about the Messiah, ²¹ assuming you heard Him and were taught by Him, because the truth is in Jesus: ²² you took off your former way of life, the old man that is corrupted by deceitful desires; ²³ you are being renewed in the spirit of your minds; ²⁴ you put on the new man, the one created according to God's likeness in righteousness and purity of the truth.

The Great Creator

The LORD . . . who created the heavens and stretched them out, who spread out the earth and what comes from it.—ISAIAH 42:5

The Bible never argues that there is a God; everywhere it assumes and asserts the fact. Majestically the opening verse of Scripture says: "In the beginning God . . ." Its paramount concern is not to persuade us that God is but to tell us who God is and what He does. This is why the first thing we see Him do in the Scriptures is to act creatively, to show His might and omnipotence.

I love the story about a group of researchers who set out to discover what really happened when the earth was created. They spent months gathering information and feeding data into a computer. Finally they hit the print-out key and waited. Soon a message appeared with these words: "See Genesis 1:1."

Many think the only reference to God's creative act is the one that appears in the first two chapters of Genesis, but this truth is woven inextricably into the very texture of both the Old and New Testaments. One example of this is found in our text for today. We cannot have a right conception of God or contemplate Him correctly unless we think of Him as being all-powerful. He who cannot do what He wills and pleases cannot be God. As God has a will to do good, so He has the necessary power to execute that will. Who can look upward to the midnight sky, behold its wonders, and not exclaim: "Of what were these mighty orbs formed?" A great and powerful God brought them into being simply by saying: "Let them be." This kind of God can have my heart anytime.

Prayer

Father, I sense that the more enlightened my understanding, the more my soul responds to that enlightenment with thanksgiving, adoration, and praise. Enlighten me still more, dear Father. In Jesus' name I pray. Amen.

Further Study

Ac 14:8-15; Neh 9:5-6; Ps 102:25; Heb 11:3
What did Paul and Barnabas declare?
How do we understand that God formed the universe?

OCTOBER 6

*I*SAIAH 43:14–45:10

¹⁴ This is what the LORD, your Redeemer, the Holy One of Israel says:

Because of you, I will send
    to Babylon
and bring all of them as fugitives,
even the Chaldeans in the ships
    in which they rejoice.
¹⁵ I am the LORD, your Holy One,
    the Creator of Israel, your King.

¹⁶ This is what the LORD says—
    who makes a way in the sea,
and a path
    through surging waters,
¹⁷ who brings out the chariot
    and horse,
the army
    and the mighty one together
(they lie down, they do not
    rise again;
they are extinguished,
    quenched like a wick)—
¹⁸ "Do not remember
    the past events,
pay no attention to things of old.
¹⁹ Look, I am about to do
    something new;

even now it is coming.
  Do you not see it?
Indeed, I will make a way
  in the wilderness,
rivers in the desert.
20 The animals of the field
    will honor Me,
  jackals and ostriches,
because I provide water
  in the wilderness,
and rivers in the desert,
  to give drink to My chosen people.
21 The people I formed for Myself
  will declare My praise.

22 "But Jacob, you have not called
    on Me,
  because, Israel, you have
    become weary of Me.
23 You have not brought Me
    your sheep for burnt offerings
  or honored Me
    with your sacrifices.
I have not burdened you
    with offerings
  or wearied you with incense.
24 You have not bought Me
    aromatic cane with silver,
  or satisfied Me with the fat
    of your sacrifices.
But you have burdened Me
    with your sins;
  you have wearied Me
    with your iniquities.

25 "It is I who sweep away
    your transgressions
  for My own sake
and remember your sins no more.
26 Take Me to court; let us argue
    our case together.
  State your case, so that you may
    be vindicated.
27 Your first father sinned,
  and your mediators have rebelled
    against Me.
28 So I defiled the officers
    of the sanctuary,
  and gave Jacob over
    to total destruction
  and Israel to abuse.

44 "And now listen,
    Jacob My servant,

Israel whom I have chosen.
2 This is the word of the LORD
  your Maker who shaped you
    from birth;
He will help you:
  Do not fear; Jacob is My servant;
  I have chosen Jeshurun.
3 For I will pour water
    on the thirsty land,
  and streams on the dry ground;
I will pour out My Spirit
    on your descendants
  and My blessing on your offspring.
4 They will sprout among the grass
  like poplars by the streambeds.
5 This one will say: I am the LORD's;
  another will call himself
    by the name of Jacob;
still another will write
    on his hand: The LORD's,
  and name himself by the name
    of Israel."

6 This is what the LORD, the King of
Israel and its Redeemer, the LORD of
Hosts, says:

  I am the first and I am the last.
  There is no God but Me.
7 Who, like Me, can announce
    the future?
  Let him say so and make a case
    before Me,
  since I have established
    an ancient people.
  Let these gods declare
    the coming things,
  and what will take place.
8 Do not be startled or afraid.
  Have I not told you and declared it
    long ago?
  You are my witnesses!
  Is there any God but Me?
  There is no other Rock;
    I do not know any.

9 All who make idols are nothing,
  and what they treasure
    does not profit.
  Their witnesses do not see
    or know anything,
  so they will be put to shame.
10 Who makes a god or casts
    a metal image

for no profit?

11 Look, all its worshipers will be
        put to shame,
    and the craftsmen are humans.
    They all will assemble and stand;
    they all will be startled
        and put to shame.

12 The ironworker labors
        over the coals,
    shapes the idol with hammers,
    and works it with his strong arm.
    Also he grows hungry
        and his strength fails;
    he doesn't drink water
        and is faint.

13 The woodworker stretches out
        a measuring line,
    he outlines it with a stylus;
    he shapes it with chisels
    and outlines it with a compass.
    He makes it according to
        a human likeness,
    like a beautiful person,
    to dwell in a temple.

14 He cuts down cedars for his use,
    or he takes a cypress or an oak.
    He lets it grow strong
        among the trees of the forest.
    He plants a laurel, and the rain
        makes it grow.

15 It serves as fuel for man.
    He takes some of it
        and warms himself;
    also he kindles a fire
        and bakes bread;
    he even makes it into a god
        and worships it;
    he makes it an idol
        and bows down to it.

16 He burns half of it in a fire,
    and he roasts meat on that half.
    He eats the roast and is satisfied.
    He warms himself and says, "Ah!
    I am warm, I see the blaze."

17 He makes a god or his idol
        with the rest of it.
    He bows down to it and worships;
    He prays to it, "Save me, for you
        are my god."

18 Such people do not comprehend
    and cannot understand,
    for He has shut their eyes
        so they cannot see,

and their minds
    so they cannot understand.

19 No one reflects,
    no one has the perception
        or insight to say,
    "I burned half of it in the fire,
    I also baked bread on its coals,
    I roasted meat and ate.
    I will make something detestable
        with the rest of it,
    and I will bow down to a block
        of wood."

20 He feeds on ashes.
    His deceived mind
        has led him astray,
    and he cannot deliver himself,
    or say, "Isn't there a lie
        in my right hand?"

21 Remember these things, Jacob,
    and Israel, for you are My servant;
    I formed you, you are My servant;
    Israel, you will never be forgotten
        by Me.

22 I have swept away
        your transgressions
        like a cloud,
    and your sins like a mist.
    Return to Me,
    for I have redeemed you.

23 Rejoice, heavens, for the LORD
        has acted;
    shout, depths of the earth.
    Break out into singing, mountains,
    forest, and every tree in it.
    For the LORD has redeemed Jacob,
    and glorifies Himself
        through Israel.

24 This is what the LORD, your
Redeemer who formed you from the
womb, says:

    I am the LORD,
        who made everything;
    who stretched out the heavens
        by Myself;
    who alone spread out the earth;

25 who destroys the omens
        of the false prophets
    and makes fools of diviners;
    who confounds the wise
    and makes
        their knowledge foolishness;

26 who confirms the message
 of His servant
and fulfills the counsel
 of His messengers;
who says to Jerusalem: She will
 be inhabited,
and to the cities of Judah:
 They will be rebuilt,
and I will restore her ruins;
27 who says to the depths of the sea:
 Be dry,
and I will dry up your rivers;
28 who says to Cyrus: My shepherd,
he will fulfill all My pleasure
and say to Jerusalem: She will
 be rebuilt,
and of the temple: Its foundation
 will be laid.

45 The LORD says this to Cyrus,
 His anointed,
whose right hand I have grasped
to subdue nations before him,
to unloose the loins of kings,
to open the doors before him
and the gates will not be shut:
2 "I will go before you
and level the uneven places;
I will shatter the bronze doors
and cut the iron bars in two.
3 I will give you the treasures
 of darkness
and riches from secret places,
so that you may know that I,
 the LORD,
the God of Israel call you
 by your name.
4 I call you by your name,
because of Jacob My servant
and Israel My chosen one.
I give a name to you,
though you do not know Me.
5 I am the LORD, and there is
 no other;
there is no God but Me.
I will strengthen you,
though you do not know Me,
6 so that all may know
 from the rising of the sun
 to its setting
that there is no one but Me.
I am the LORD, and there is
 no other.
7 I form light and create darkness,

I make success
 and create disaster;
I, the LORD, do all these things.

8 "Heavens, sprinkle from above,
and let the skies
 shower righteousness.
Let the earth open up
that salvation sprout
and righteousness spring up
 with it.
I, the LORD, have created it.

9 "Woe to the one who argues
 with his Maker—
one clay pot among many.
Does clay say to the one
 forming it:
What are you making?
Or does your work say:
He has no hands?
10 How absurd is the one who says
 to his father:
What are you fathering?
or to his mother:
What are you giving birth to?"

PSALM 117:1–118:4

1 Praise the LORD, all nations!
 Glorify Him, all peoples!
2 For great is His faithful love to us;
 the LORD's faithfulness endures
 forever.
Hallelujah!

1 Give thanks to the LORD, for He is
 good;
His faithful love endures forever.
2 Let Israel say,
 "His faithful love endures
 forever."
3 Let the house of Aaron say,
 "His faithful love endures
 forever."
4 Let those who fear the LORD say,
 "His faithful love endures
 forever."

PROVERBS 24:5-6

5 A wise warrior is better than a
 strong one,

and a man of knowledge than one of strength;
⁶ for you should wage war with sound guidance—
victory comes with many counselors.

ƐPHESIANS 4:25–5:14

²⁵ Since you put away lying, **Speak the truth, each one to his neighbor,** because we are members of one another. ²⁶ **Be angry and do not sin.** Don't let the sun go down on your anger, ²⁷ and don't give the Devil an opportunity. ²⁸ The thief must no longer steal. Instead, he must do honest work with his own hands, so that he has something to share with anyone in need. ²⁹ No rotten talk should come from your mouth, but only what is good for the building up of someone in need, in order to give grace to those who hear. ³⁰ And don't grieve God's Holy Spirit, who sealed you for the day of redemption. ³¹ All bitterness, anger and wrath, insult and slander must be removed from you, along with all wickedness. ³² And be kind and compassionate to one another, forgiving one another, just as God also forgave you in Christ.

5 Therefore, be imitators of God, as dearly loved children. ² And walk in love, as the Messiah also loved us and gave Himself for us, a sacrificial and fragrant offering to God. ³ But sexual immorality and any impurity or greed should not even be heard of among you, as is proper for saints. ⁴ And coarse and foolish talking or crude joking are not suitable, but rather giving thanks. ⁵ For know and recognize this: no sexually immoral or impure or greedy person, who is an idolater, has an inheritance in the kingdom of the Messiah and of God.

⁶ Let no one deceive you with empty arguments, for because of these things God's wrath is coming on the disobedient. ⁷ Therefore, do not become their partners. ⁸ For you were once darkness, but now you are light in the Lord. Walk as children of light— ⁹ for the fruit of the light results in all goodness, righteousness, and truth— ¹⁰ discerning what is pleasing to the Lord. ¹¹ Don't participate in the fruitless works of darkness, but instead, expose them. ¹² For it is shameful even to mention what is done by them in secret. ¹³ Everything exposed by the light is made clear, ¹⁴ for what makes everything clear is light. Therefore it is said:

Get up, sleeper, and rise up
from the dead,
and the Messiah will shine
on you.

For the Sake of Christ

Be kind and compassionate to one another, forgiving one another, just as God also forgave you in Christ.—EPHESIANS 4:32

We experience divine forgiveness for our sins only as we extend forgiveness to those who have offended us.

This cuts deep.

Perhaps you might be saying at this moment, "But I can't forgive; I have been hurt too deeply." Then, may I say it very tenderly, but very solemnly, you can never, never be forgiven. "But if you don't forgive people," says Jesus, "your Father will not forgive your wrongdoing" (Mt 6:15). In refusing to forgive others you break the bridge over which you yourself must pass.

A man once said to me: "I know I'm a Christian, but someone did such an awful thing to me that I find I can't forgive him." After spending a good deal of time with him, and getting nowhere, I said: "If it is really true that you can't forgive this person, it suggests that you yourself have not been forgiven, and you may be deluding yourself that you are a Christian." He looked at me aghast and went white in the face. My counseling methods are not always as abrupt as that; however, this brought him face to face with reality—and it worked. He got down on his knees, right where he was, and said: "Father, because You have forgiven me, I offer Your forgiveness and my forgiveness to my brother who has offended me, and I absolve him of his offense in Jesus' name." Then what happened? Instantly the joy of the Lord streamed right into the center of his being, and he laughed and laughed, literally, for almost an hour.

Prayer

Lord Jesus, You who forgave those who spat in Your face and nailed You to a cross, help me to open my heart now and forgive all those who have hurt me. I do it in Your strength and power. Thank You, Lord Jesus. Amen.

Further Study

Mt 18:21-35; 5:7; Lk 6:36; Pr 3:3
How does this parable apply to us?
What is the basis of forgiving others?

OCTOBER 7

ISAIAH 45:11–48:11

11 This is what the LORD,
    the Holy One of Israel
    and its Maker, says:
"Ask Me what is to happen to
    My sons,
and instruct Me about the work
    of My hands.
12 I made the earth,
    and created man on it.
It was My hands
    that stretched out
    the heavens,
and I commanded all their host.

13 I have raised him up
    in righteousness,
and will level all roads for him.
He will rebuild My city,
    and set My exiles free,
not for a price or a bribe,"
    says the LORD of Hosts.

14 This is what the LORD says:

The products of Egypt
    and the merchandise of Cush
and the Sabeans, men of stature,
will come over to you
    and will be yours;

they will follow you,
they will come over in chains;
and bow down to you.
They will confess to you:
God is indeed with you,
    and there is no other;
there is no other God.
15 Yes, You are a God
    who hides Himself,
God of Israel, Savior.
16 All of them are put to shame,
    even humiliated;
the makers of idols
    go in humiliation together.
17 Israel will be saved by the LORD
with an everlasting salvation;
you will not be put to shame
    or humiliated
for all eternity.

18 For this is what the LORD says—
God is the Creator of the heavens.
He formed the earth and made it;
He established it;
He did not create it to be empty,
but formed it to be inhabited—
"I am the LORD,
and there is no other.
19 I have not spoken in secret,
somewhere in a land of darkness.
I did not say to the descendants
    of Jacob:
Seek Me in a wasteland.
I, the LORD, speak truthfully;
I say what is right.

20 "Come, gather together,
and draw near, you fugitives
    of the nations.
Those who carry
    their wooden idols,
and pray to a god
    who cannot save,
have no knowledge.
21 Speak up and present
    your case—
yes, let them
    take counsel together.
Who predicted this long ago?
Who announced it
    from ancient times?
Was it not I, the LORD?
There is no other God but Me,
a righteous God and Savior;

there is no one except Me.
22 Turn to Me and be saved,
all the ends of the earth.
For I am God,
and there is no other.
23 By Myself I have sworn;
Truth has gone from My mouth,
a word that will not be revoked:
Every knee will bow to Me,
every tongue will swear allegiance.
24 It will be said to Me:
    Only in the LORD
is righteousness and strength."
All who are incensed against Him
will come to Him and be
    put to shame.
25 All the descendants of Israel
will be justified and find glory
    through the LORD.

46 Bel crouches; Nebo cowers.
Their idols are consigned
    to beasts and cattle.
The images you carry are loaded,
as a burden
    for the weary animal.
2 The gods cower;
    they crouch together;
they are not able to rescue
    the burden,
but they themselves go
    into captivity.

3 "Listen to Me, house of Jacob,
all the remnant of the house
    of Israel,
who have been sustained
    from the womb,
carried along since birth.
4 I will be the same until your
    old age,
and I will bear you up when you
    turn gray.
I have made you,
    and I will carry you;
I will bear and save you.

5 "Who will you compare Me
    or make Me equal to?
Who will you measure Me with,
so that we should be
    like each other?
6 Those who pour out their bags
    of gold

and weigh out silver on scales—
they hire a goldsmith
and he makes it into a god.
Then they kneel and bow down
to it.
7 They lift it to their shoulder
and bear it along;
they set it in its place, and there
it stands;
it does not budge from its place.
They cry out to it
but it doesn't answer;
it saves no one from his trouble.

8 "Remember this and be brave;
take it to heart, you transgressors!
9 Remember what happened
long ago,
for I am God, and there is
no other;
I am God, and no one is like Me.
10 I declare the end
from the beginning,
and from long ago what is
not yet done,
saying: My plan will take place,
and I will do all My will.
11 I call a bird of prey from the east,
a man for My purpose
from a far country.
Yes, I have spoken; so I will also
bring it about.
I have planned it; I will also do it.
12 Listen to me, you hardhearted,
far removed from justice:
13 I am bringing My justice near;
it is not far away,
and My salvation will not delay.
I will put salvation in Zion,
My splendor in Israel.

47 "Go down and sit in the dust,
Virgin Daughter Babylon.
Sit on the ground
without a throne,
Daughter Chaldea!
For you will no longer be called
pampered and spoiled.
2 Take millstones and grind meal;
remove your veil,
strip off your skirt,
bare your thigh,
wade through the streams.
3 Your nakedness will be uncovered,

and your shame will be exposed.
I will take vengeance;
I will spare no one.
4 The Holy One of Israel is
our Redeemer;
the LORD of Hosts is His name.

5 "Daughter Chaldea,
sit in silence and go into darkness.
For you will no longer be called
mistress of kingdoms.
6 I was angry with My people;
I profaned My possession,
and I placed them
under your control.
You showed them no mercy;
you made your yoke very heavy
on the elderly.
7 You said: I will be
the mistress forever.
You did not take these things
to heart
or think about their outcome.

8 "So now hear this, lover of luxury,
who sits securely,
who says to herself:
I, and no one else,
will never be a widow
or know the loss of children.
9 These two things will happen
to you
suddenly, in one day:
loss of children and widowhood.
They will happen to you
in their entirety,
in spite of your many sorceries
and the potency of your spells.
10 You were secure
in your wickedness;
you said: No one sees me.
Your wisdom and knowledge
led you astray.
You said to yourself:
I, and no one else.
11 But disaster will happen to you;
you will not know how to avert it.
And it will fall on you,
but you will be unable to ward
it off.
Devastation will happen
to you suddenly
and unexpectedly.
12 So take your stand with your spells

and your many sorceries,
which you have
wearied yourself with
from your youth.
Perhaps you will be able
to succeed;
perhaps you will inspire terror!
13 You are worn out
with your many consultations.
So let them stand and save you—
the astrologers, who observe
the stars,
who predict monthly
what will happen to you.
14 Look, they are like stubble;
fire burns them up.
They cannot deliver themselves
from the power of the flame.
This is not a coal
for warming themselves,
or a fire to sit beside!
15 This is what they are to you—
those who have wearied you
and have traded with you
from your youth—
each wanders on his own way;
no one can save you.

48 "Listen to this, house of Jacob—
those who are called
by the name Israel
and have descended from Judah,
who swear by the name
of the LORD
and declare the God of Israel,
but not in truth or righteousness.
2 For they are named
after the Holy City,
and lean on the God of Israel;
His name is Yahweh of Hosts.
3 I declared the past events
long ago;
they came out of My mouth;
I proclaimed them.
Suddenly I acted,
and they occurred.
4 Because I know
that you are stubborn,
and your neck is iron
and your forehead bronze,
5 therefore I declared to you
long ago;
I announced it to you
before it occurred,

so you could not claim: My idol
caused them;
my carved image and cast idol
control them.
6 You have heard it. Observe it all.
Will you not acknowledge it?
From now on I will announce
new things to you,
hidden things that
you have not known.
7 They have been created now,
and not long ago;
you have not heard of them
before today,
so you could not claim, "I already
knew them!"
8 You have never heard; you have
never known;
For a long time your ears have not
been open.
For I knew that you
were very treacherous,
and were known as a rebel
from birth.
9 I will delay My anger
for the honor of My name,
and I will restrain Myself
for your benefit and for
My praise,
so that you will not be destroyed.
10 Look, I have refined you, but not
as silver;
I have tested you in the furnace
of affliction.
11 I will act for My own sake,
indeed, My own,
for how can I be defiled?
I will not give My glory
to another.

*P*SALM 118:5-9

5 I called to the LORD in distress;
the LORD answered me and put me
in a spacious place.
6 The LORD is for me; I will not be
afraid.
What can man do to me?
7 With the LORD for me as my
helper,
I will look in triumph on those
who hate me.

8 It is better to take refuge in the
LORD
than to trust in man.
9 It is better to take refuge in the
LORD
than to trust in nobles.

PROVERBS 24:7-9

7 Wisdom is inaccessible to a fool;
he does not open his mouth at the
gate.
8 The one who plots evil
will be called a schemer.
9 A foolish scheme is sin,
and a mocker is detestable to
people.

EPHESIANS 5:15-33

15 Pay careful attention, then, to how you walk—not as unwise people but as wise— 16 making the most of the time, because the days are evil. 17 So don't be foolish, but understand what the Lord's will is. 18 And don't get drunk with wine, which leads to reckless actions, but be filled with the Spirit:

19 speaking to one another in psalms,
hymns, and spiritual songs,
singing and making music
to the Lord in your heart,
20 giving thanks always
for everything
to God the Father in the name
of our Lord Jesus Christ,

21 submitting to one another
in the fear of Christ.

22 Wives, submit to your own husbands as to the Lord, 23 for the husband is head of the wife as also Christ is head of the church. He is the Savior of the body. 24 Now as the church submits to Christ, so wives should submit to their husbands in everything. 25 Husbands, love your wives, just as also Christ loved the church and gave Himself for her, 26 to make her holy, cleansing her in the washing of water by the word. 27 He did this to present the church to Himself in splendor, without spot or wrinkle or any such thing, but holy and blameless. 28 In the same way, husbands should love their wives as their own bodies. He who loves his wife loves himself. 29 For no one ever hates his own flesh, but provides and cares for it, just as Christ does for the church, 30 since we are members of His body.

31 For this reason a man will leave
his father and mother
and be joined to his wife,
and the two will become
one flesh.

32 This mystery is profound, but I am talking about Christ and the church. 33 To sum up, each one of you is to love his wife as himself, and the wife is to respect her husband.

A Command to Be Obeyed

*And don't get drunk with wine . . .
but be filled with the Spirit.*
—EPHESIANS 5:18

In *The Amplified Bible* this text reads: "And do not get drunk with wine . . . but ever be filled and stimulated with the (Holy) Spirit."

However we may view the doctrine of the Holy Spirit, or whatever experience we may have had of Him in the past, if we do not enjoy an ever-present flow of His power in our lives, then we are living below the New Testament standard. This text, as many commentators have pointed out, is a command to be obeyed. If we are not experiencing what the Bible commands, then our lives are not in harmony with God's purposes.

I meet many Christians who are sighing over lost ecstasies, mourning over lost victories, and who are downcast because they have lost touch with God. It is largely because they are living not "the life of the Spirit," but the life of following an ideal with their own resources, stirred by emotion through a special sermon or something they read in a book. They grow tired and are on the point of giving up.

A translator in India, working on an early edition of *Every Day Light* on the Holy Spirit, wrote: "I'd like another subject. I'm tired of working on the Holy Spirit." A lot of Christians have that problem; they grow tired of working on the Holy Spirit, instead of letting the Holy Spirit work on them. Let's stop working on the Spirit, and allow Him to work on us!

Prayer

Blessed Holy Spirit, help me as I thread my way through the maze of thoughts and attitudes about You. Help me to come out with Your thoughts and attitudes. I want to be filled with the Spirit—today and always. For Jesus' sake. Amen.

Further Study

Rm 8:1-17; Ezk 36:27; Jn 14:17; Heb 10:15-16
What is the result of "the Spirit's law of life"?
What is Paul teaching about the Holy Spirit?

OCTOBER 8

ISAIAH 48:12–50:11

12 "Listen to Me, Jacob,
　　and Israel, the one called by Me:
　　I am He; I am the first,
　　I am also the last.
13 My own hand founded the earth,
　　and My right hand spread out
　　　　the heavens;
　　when I summoned them,
　　they stood up together.
14 All of you, assemble and listen!
　　Who among the idols has declared
　　　　these things?

The LORD loves him;
　　he will accomplish His will
　　　　against Babylon,
　　and His arm will be against
　　　　the Chaldeans.
15 I—I have spoken;
　　yes, I have called him;
　　I have brought him,
　　and he will succeed in his mission.
16 Approach Me and listen to this.
　　From the beginning I have not
　　　　spoken in secret;
　　from the time anything existed,
　　　　I was there."

1191

And now the Lord God
has sent me and His Spirit.

¹⁷ This is what the Lord, your
Redeemer, the Holy One of Israel says:

I am the Lord your God,
who teaches you for your benefit,
who leads you in the way
you should go.
¹⁸ If only you had paid attention
to My commands.
Then your peace would have been
like a river,
and your righteousness
like the waves of the sea.
¹⁹ Your descendants
would have been as countless
as the sand,
and the offspring of your body
like its grains;
their name would not be cut off
or eliminated from My presence.

²⁰ Leave Babylon,
flee from the Chaldeans!
Declare with a shout of joy,
proclaim this,
let it go out to the end
of the earth;
announce,
"The Lord has redeemed
His servant Jacob!"
²¹ They did not thirst
when He led them
through the deserts;
He made water flow for them
from the rock;
He split the rock, and water
gushed out.
²² "There is no peace,"
says the Lord,
"for the wicked."

49 Coastlands, listen to me;
distant peoples, pay attention.
The Lord called me
before I was born.
He named me while I was
in my mother's womb.
² He made my words
like a sharp sword;
He hid me in the shadow
of His hand.

He made me
like a sharpened arrow;
He hid me in His quiver.
³ He said to me, "You are
My servant, Israel;
I will be glorified in him."
⁴ But I myself said: I have labored
in vain,
I have spent my strength
for nothing and futility;
yet my vindication is
with the Lord,
and my reward is with my God.
⁵ And now, says the Lord,
who formed me from the womb
to be His servant,
to bring Jacob back to Him
so that Israel might be gathered
to Him;
for I am honored in the sight
of the Lord,
and my God is my strength—
⁶ He says,
"It is not enough for you to be
My servant
raising up the tribes of Jacob
and restoring the protected ones
of Israel.
I will also make you a light
for the nations,
to be My salvation to the ends
of the earth."
⁷ This is what the Lord,
the Redeemer of Israel,
his Holy One says
to one who is despised,
to one abhorred by people,
to a servant of rulers:
"Kings will see and stand up,
and princes will bow down,
because of the Lord,
who is faithful,
the Holy One of Israel—
and He has chosen you."

⁸ This is what the Lord says:

I will answer you in a time
of favor,
and I will help you in the day
of salvation.
I will keep you,
and I will appoint you
to be a covenant for the people,

to restore the land,
to make them possess
the desolate inheritances,
⁹ saying to the prisoners: Come out,
and to those who are in darkness:
Show yourselves.
They will feed along the pathways,
and their pastures will be on all
the barren heights.
¹⁰ They will not hunger or thirst,
the scorching heat or sun will not
strike them;
for their compassionate One
will guide them,
and lead them to springs of water.
¹¹ I will make all My mountains
into a road,
and My highways will be raised up.
¹² See, these will come
from far away,
from the north and from the west,
and from the land of Sinim.

¹³ Shout for joy, you heavens!
Earth, rejoice!
Mountains break
into joyful shouts!
For the LORD has comforted
His people,
and will have compassion
on His afflicted ones.

¹⁴ Zion says, "The LORD
has abandoned me;
The Lord has forgotten me!"
¹⁵ "Can a woman forget
her nursing child,
or lack compassion for the child
of her womb?
Even if these forget,
yet I will not forget you.
¹⁶ Look, I have inscribed you
on the palms of My hands;
your walls are continually
before Me.
¹⁷ Your builders hurry;
those who destroy
and devastate you
will leave you.
¹⁸ Look up, and look around.
They all gather together;
they come to you.
As I live"—
the LORD's declaration—

"you will wear all your children
as jewelry,
and put them on as a bride does.
¹⁹ For your waste
and desolate places
and your land marked by ruins—
will now be indeed too small
for the inhabitants,
and those who swallowed you up
will be far away.
²⁰ The children that you have been
deprived of
will yet say in your hearing:
This place is too small for me;
make room for me so that
I may settle.
²¹ Then you will say within yourself:
Who fathered these for me?
I was deprived of my children
and barren,
exiled and wandering—
but who brought them up?
See, I was left by myself—
but these, where did
they come from?"

²² This is what the Lord GOD says:

Look, I will lift up My hand
to the nations,
and raise My banner
to the peoples.
They will bring your sons
in their arms,
and your daughters will be carried
on their shoulders.
²³ Kings will be your foster fathers,
and their queens
your nursing mothers.
They will bow down to you
with their faces to the ground,
and lick the dust at your feet.
Then you will know that I am
the LORD;
those who put their hope in Me
will not be put to shame.

²⁴ Can the prey be taken
from the mighty,
or the captives of the righteous
be delivered?
²⁵ For this is what the LORD says:
"Even the captives
of a mighty man will be taken,

and the prey of a tyrant
will be delivered;
I will contend with the one
who contends with you,
and I will save your children.
26 I will make your oppressors eat
their own flesh,
and they will be drunk
with their own blood
as with sweet wine.
Then all flesh will know
that I, the LORD, am your Savior,
and your Redeemer,
the Mighty One of Jacob."

50 This is what the LORD says:

Where is
your mother's divorce certificate
that I used to send her away?
Or who were My creditors
that I sold you to?
Look, you were sold
for your iniquities,
and your mother was put away
because of your transgressions.
2 Why was no one there
when I came?
Why was there no one to answer
when I called?
Is My hand too short to redeem?
Or do I have no power to deliver?
Look, I dry up the sea
by My rebuke;
I turn the rivers into a wilderness;
their fish rot because of lack
of water
and die of thirst.
3 I dress the heavens in black
and make sackcloth their clothing.

4 The Lord GOD has given Me
the tongue of those
who are instructed
to know how to sustain the weary
with a word.
He awakens Me each morning;
He awakens My ear to listen
like those being instructed.
5 The Lord GOD has opened My ear,
and I was not rebellious;
I did not turn back.
6 I gave My back to those
who beat Me,

and My cheeks to those
who tore out My beard.
I did not hide My face from scorn
and spitting.
7 The Lord GOD will help Me;
therefore I have not
been humiliated;
therefore I have set My face
like flint,
and I know I will not
be put to shame.
8 The One who justifies Me is near;
who will contend with Me?
Let us confront each other.
Who has a case against Me?
Let him come near Me!
9 In truth, the Lord GOD
will help Me;
who is he who will condemn Me?
Indeed, all of them will wear out
like a garment;
a moth will devour them.
10 Who among you fears the LORD,
listening to the voice
of His servant?
Who among you walks
in darkness,
and has no light?
Let him trust in the name
of the LORD;
let him lean on his God.
11 Look, all you who kindle a fire,
who encircle yourselves with
firebrands;
walk in the light of your fire
and in the firebrands you have lit!
This is what you'll get
from My hand:
you will lie down in a place
of torment.

PSALM 118:10-14

10 All the nations surrounded me;
in the name of the LORD I
destroyed them.
11 They surrounded me, yes, they
surrounded me;
in the name of the LORD I
destroyed them.
12 They surrounded me like bees;
they were extinguished like a fire
among thorns;

in the name of the LORD I
destroyed them.
¹³ You pushed me hard to make me
fall,
but the LORD helped me.
¹⁴ The LORD is my strength and my
song;
He has become my salvation.

PROVERBS 24:10-12

¹⁰ If you do nothing in a difficult
time,
your strength is limited.
¹¹ Rescue those being taken off to
death,
and save those stumbling toward
slaughter.
¹² If you say, "But we didn't know
about this,"
won't He who weighs hearts
consider it?
Won't He who protects your life
know?
Won't He repay a person
according to his work?

EPHESIANS 6:1-24

6 Children, obey your parents in the
Lord, because this is right. ² **Honor
your father and mother**—which is the
first commandment with a promise—
³ **that it may go well with you and that
you may have a long life in the land.**
⁴ And fathers, don't stir up anger in your
children, but bring them up in the training and instruction of the Lord.

⁵ Slaves, obey your human masters
with fear and trembling, in the sincerity
of your heart, as to Christ. ⁶ Don't work
only while being watched, in order to
please men, but as slaves of Christ, do
God's will from your heart. ⁷ Render
service with a good attitude, as to the
Lord and not to men, ⁸ knowing that
whatever good each one does, slave or
free, he will receive this back from the
Lord. ⁹ And masters, treat them the
same way, without threatening them,
because you know that both their and
your Master is in heaven, and there is
no favoritism with Him.

¹⁰ Finally, be strengthened by the
Lord and by His vast strength. ¹¹ Put on
the full armor of God so that you can
stand against the tactics of the Devil.
¹² For our battle is not against flesh and
blood, but against the rulers, against the
authorities, against the world powers of
this darkness, against the spiritual
forces of evil in the heavens. ¹³ This is
why you must take up the full armor of
God, so that you may be able to resist in
the evil day, and having prepared everything, to take your stand. ¹⁴ Stand,
therefore,

with truth like a belt
around your waist,
righteousness like armor
on your chest,
¹⁵ and your feet sandaled
with readiness for the gospel
of peace.
¹⁶ In every situation take the shield
of faith,
and with it you will be able
to extinguish
the flaming arrows of the evil one.
¹⁷ Take the helmet of salvation,
and the sword of the Spirit,
which is God's word.

¹⁸ With every prayer and request, pray
at all times in the Spirit, and stay alert
in this, with all perseverance and intercession for all the saints. ¹⁹ Pray also for
me, that the message may be given to
me when I open my mouth to make
known with boldness the mystery of the
gospel. ²⁰ For this I am an ambassador in
chains. Pray that I might be bold enough
in Him to speak as I should.

²¹ Tychicus, our dearly loved brother
and faithful servant in the Lord, will tell
you everything so that you also may
know how I am and what I'm doing. ²² I
am sending him to you for this very reason, to let you know how we are and to
encourage your hearts.

²³ Peace to the brothers, and love with
faith, from God the Father and the Lord
Jesus Christ. ²⁴ Grace be with all who
have undying love for our Lord Jesus
Christ.

A Call to Arms

For our battle is not against flesh and blood.
——EPHESIANS 6:12

Ephesians 6:10-20 concerns the spiritual protection that is available to every Christian when doing battle with the Devil. All those who have committed their lives to Jesus Christ know (or should know) that the kingdoms of God and the Devil are locked together in mortal combat. And Christians, whether they like it or not, are thrust right onto the cutting edge of that conflict.

Many Christians are pacifists when it comes to the matter of earthly warfare, but no one can be a pacifist when it comes to the matter of spiritual warfare. Once we enlist in the army of God, we are then expected to train in the art of offensive and defensive spiritual warfare. At certain times and occasions in the Christian life, we find ourselves in a battle that demands fierce hand-to-hand combat with the forces of darkness, and unless we know how to handle these trying situations, we shall easily be overthrown.

The Bible shows us that the Devil and his minions are bitter enemies of God, but because they are powerless against the Almighty, they turn their concentrated attention on those who are His followers—you and me. Notice how many times the word "against" appears in Ephesians 6:10-13. It occurs six times in all, showing that when anyone comes over to the side of Jesus Christ, they are immediately identified as being for God and against the Devil. There can be no compromise on this issue, no peaceful coexistence pact. To be for God is to be against the Devil.

Prayer

Gracious and loving Father, help me get my perspectives clear. Train me in the art of spiritual warfare so that I will be able to resist every onslaught of the Devil and come through every conflict victoriously. In Jesus' name. Amen.

Further Study

2 Co 10:1-5; 1 Tm 1:18; 6:12
What does Paul say about our weapons of warfare?
What was Paul's charge to Timothy?

OCTOBER 9

ISAIAH 51:1–54:3

51 Listen to Me, you
who pursue righteousness,
you who seek the LORD:
Look to the rock from which
you were cut,
and to the quarry from which
you were dug.
² Look to Abraham your father,
and to Sarah who gave birth
to you in pain.
When I called him, he was
only one;
I blessed him and made him many.
³ For the LORD will comfort Zion;
He will comfort
all her waste places,
and He will make her wilderness
like Eden,
and her desert like the garden
of the LORD.
Joy and gladness will be found
in her,
thanksgiving and melodious song.

⁴ Pay attention to Me, My people,
and listen to Me, My nation;
for instruction will come from Me,
and My justice for a light
to the nations.
I will bring it about quickly.
⁵ My righteousness is near,
My salvation appears,
and My arms will bring justice
to the nations.
The coastlands will put their hope
in Me,
and they will look to My strength.
⁶ Look up to the heavens,
and look at the earth beneath;
for the heavens will vanish
like smoke,
the earth will wear out
like a garment,
and its inhabitants will die
in like manner.

But My salvation will last forever,
and My righteousness will never
be shattered.

⁷ Listen to Me, you who
know righteousness,
the people in whose heart is
My instruction:
do not fear disgrace by men,
and do not be shattered
by their taunts.
⁸ For the moth will devour them
like a garment,
and the worm will eat them
like wool.
But My righteousness
will last forever,
and My salvation
for all generations.

⁹ Wake up, wake up!
Put on the strength
of the LORD's power.
Wake up as in days past,
as in generations of long ago.
Wasn't it You who hacked Rahab
to pieces,
who pierced the sea monster?
¹⁰ Wasn't it You who dried up
the sea,
the waters of the great deep,
who made the sea-bed into a road
for the redeemed to pass over?
¹¹ And the ransomed of the LORD
will return
and come to Zion with singing,
crowned with unending joy.
Joy and gladness
will overtake them,
and sorrow and sighing will flee.

¹² I—I am the One
who comforts you.
Who are you that you should
fear man who dies,
or a son of man who is given up
like grass?

13 But you have forgotten the LORD,
      your Maker,
   who stretched out the heavens
   and laid the foundations
      of the earth.
   You are in constant dread
      all day long
   because of the fury
      of the oppressor,
   who has set himself to destroy.
   But where is the fury
      of the oppressor?
14 The prisoner is soon to be
      set free;
   he will not die and go to the Pit,
   and his food will not be lacking.
15 For I am the LORD your God
   who stirs up the sea so that
      its waves roar—
   His name is Yahweh of Hosts.
16 I have put My words
      in your mouth,
   and covered you in the shadow
      of My hand,
   in order to plant the heavens,
   to found the earth,
   and to say to Zion, "You are
      My people."

17 Wake yourself, wake yourself up!
   Stand up, Jerusalem,
   you who have drunk the cup
      of His fury
   from the hand of the LORD;
   you who have drunk the goblet
      to the dregs—
   the cup that causes people
      to stagger.
18 There is no one to guide her
   among all the children
      she has raised;
   there is no one to take hold
      of her hand
   among all the offspring
      she has brought up.
19 These two things have happened
      to you:
   devastation and destruction,
   famine and sword.
   Who will grieve for you?
   How can I comfort you?
20 Your children have fainted;
   they lie at the head of every street
   like an antelope in a net.

They are full of the LORD's fury,
the rebuke of your God.
21 So listen to this, afflicted
   and drunken one—but not
      with wine.
22 This is what your Lord says—
   Yahweh, even your God,
   who defends His people—
   "Look, I have removed
   the cup of staggering
      from your hand;
   that goblet, the cup of My fury.
   You will never drink it again.
23 I will put it into the hands
      of your tormenters,
   who said to you:
   Lie down, so we can walk over you.
   You made your back
      like the ground,
   and like a street for those
      who walk on it.

52 "Wake up, wake up;
   put on your strength, Zion!
   Put on your beautiful garments,
   Jerusalem, the Holy City!
   For the uncircumcised
      and the unclean
   will no longer enter you.
2 Stand up, shake the dust
      off yourself!
   Take your seat, Jerusalem.
   Remove the bonds
      from your neck,
   captive Daughter Zion."
3 For this is what the LORD says:
   "You were sold for nothing,
   and you will be redeemed
      without silver."
4 For this is what
      the Lord GOD says:
   "At first My people went down
      to Egypt to live there,
   then Assyria oppressed them
      without cause.
5 So now what have I here"—
            the LORD's declaration—
   "that My people are taken away
      for nothing?
   Its rulers wail"—
            the LORD's declaration—
   "and My name is continually
   blasphemed all day long.

⁶ Therefore My people will know
My name;
therefore they will know
on that day
that I am He who says:
Here I am."

⁷ How beautiful on the mountains
are the feet of the herald,
who proclaims peace,
who brings news of good things,
who proclaims salvation,
who says to Zion,
"Your God reigns!"

⁸ The voices of your watchmen—
they lift up their voices,
shouting for joy together;
for every eye will see
when the LORD returns to Zion.

⁹ Be joyful, rejoice together,
you ruins of Jerusalem!
For the LORD has comforted
His people;
He has redeemed Jerusalem.

¹⁰ The LORD has displayed
His holy arm
in the sight of all the nations;
all the ends of the earth will see
the salvation of our God.

¹¹ Leave, leave, go out from there!
Do not touch anything unclean;
go out from her, purify yourselves,
you who carry the vessels
of the LORD.

¹² For you will not leave in a hurry,
and you will not have
to take flight;
because the LORD is going
before you,
and the God of Israel is
your rear guard.

¹³ See, My servant will act wisely;
He will be raised and lifted up
and greatly exalted.

¹⁴ Just as many were appalled at You —
His appearance was so disfigured
that He did not look like a man,
and His form did not resemble
a human being —

¹⁵ so He will sprinkle many nations.
Kings will shut their mouths
because of Him,

For they will see
what had not been told them,
and they will understand
what they had not heard.

53 Who has believed
what we have heard?
And who has the arm of the LORD
been revealed to?

² He grew up before Him
like a young plant
and like a root out of dry ground.
He had no form or splendor
that we should look at Him,
no appearance that we should
desire Him.

³ He was despised and rejected
by men,
a man of suffering who knew
what sickness was.
He was like one
people turned away from;
He was despised, and we didn't
value Him.

⁴ Yet He Himself bore
our sicknesses,
and He carried our pains;
but we in turn
regarded Him stricken,
struck down by God, and afflicted.

⁵ But He was pierced because of
our transgressions,
crushed because of our iniquities;
punishment for our peace was
on Him,
and we are healed by His wounds.

⁶ We all went astray like sheep;
we all have turned
to our own way;
and the LORD has punished Him
for the iniquity of us all.

⁷ He was oppressed and afflicted,
yet He did not open His mouth.
Like a lamb led to the slaughter
and like a sheep silent
before her shearers,
He did not open His mouth.

⁸ He was taken away because of
oppression and judgment;
and who considered His fate?
For He was cut off from the land
of the living;

He was struck because of
  My people's rebellion.
9 They made His grave
    with the wicked,
and with a rich man at His death,
although He had done no violence
and had not spoken deceitfully.

10 Yet the LORD was pleased
    to crush Him,
and He made Him sick.
When You make Him a
    restitution offering,
He will see His seed,
    He will prolong His days,
and the will of the LORD
    will succeed by His hand.
11 He will see it out of His anguish,
and He will be satisfied
    with His knowledge.
My righteous servant
    will justify many,
and He will carry their iniquities.
12 Therefore I will give Him
    the many as a portion,
and He will receive the mighty
    as spoil,
because He submitted Himself
    to death,
and was counted
    among the rebels;
yet He bore the sin of many
and interceded for the rebels.

54 "Rejoice, barren one,
    who did not give birth;
burst into song and shout,
you who have not been in labor!
For the children of the forsaken one
    will be more
than the children
    of the married woman,"
says the LORD.
2 "Enlarge the site of your tent,
and let your tent curtains
    be stretched out;
do not hold back;
lengthen your ropes,
and drive your pegs deep.
3 For you will spread out
    to the right and to the left,
and your descendants
    will dispossess nations
and inhabit the desolate cities.

PSALM 118:15-21

15 There are shouts of joy and
    victory
in the tents of the righteous:
"The LORD's right hand strikes
    with power!
16 The LORD's right hand is raised!
The LORD's right hand strikes with
    power!"
17 I will not die, but I will live
and proclaim what the LORD has
    done.
18 The LORD disciplined me severely
but did not give me over to death.

19 Open the gates of righteousness
    for me;
I will enter through them and give
    thanks to the LORD.
20 This is the gate of the LORD;
the righteous will enter through it.
21 I will give thanks to You because
    You have answered me
and have become my salvation.

PROVERBS 24:13-14

13 Eat honey, my son, for it is good,
and the honeycomb is sweet to
    your palate;
14 realize that wisdom is the same
    for you.
If you find it, you will have a
    future,
and your hope will never fade.

PHILIPPIANS 1:1-20

1 Paul and Timothy, slaves of Christ
Jesus:
To all the saints in Christ Jesus who
are in Philippi, including the overseers
and deacons.
2 Grace to you and peace from God
our Father and the Lord Jesus Christ.
3 I give thanks to my God for every remembrance of you, 4 always praying
with joy for all of you in my every
prayer, 5 because of your partnership in
the gospel from the first day until now.
6 I am sure of this, that He who started
a good work in you will carry it on to

completion until the day of Christ Jesus. [7] It is right for me to think this way about all of you, because I have you in my heart, and you are all partners with me in grace, both in my imprisonment and in the defense and establishment of the gospel. [8] For God is my witness, how I deeply miss all of you with the affection of Christ Jesus. [9] And I pray this: that your love will keep on growing in knowledge and every kind of discernment, [10] so that you can determine what really matters and can be pure and blameless in the day of Christ, [11] filled with the fruit of righteousness that comes through Jesus Christ, to the glory and praise of God.

[12] Now I want you to know, brothers, that what has happened to me has actually resulted in the advancement of the gospel, [13] so that it has become known throughout the whole imperial guard, and to everyone else, that my imprison-ment is for Christ. [14] Most of the brothers in the Lord have gained confidence from my imprisonment and dare even more to speak the message fearlessly. [15] Some, to be sure, preach Christ out of envy and strife, but others out of good will. [16] These do so out of love, knowing that I am appointed for the defense of the gospel; [17] the others proclaim Christ out of rivalry, not sincerely, seeking to cause me trouble in my imprisonment. [18] What does it matter? Just that in every way, whether out of false motives or true, Christ is proclaimed. And in this I rejoice. Yes, and I will rejoice [19] because I know this will lead to my deliverance through your prayers and help from the Spirit of Jesus Christ. [20] My eager expectation and hope is that I will not be ashamed about anything, but that now as always, with all bold-ness, Christ will be highly honored in my body, whether by life or by death.

Enter at Your Own Risk

My eager expectation and hope is that I will not be ashamed about anything, but that . . . Christ will be highly honored in my body, whether by life or by death.—PHILIPPIANS 1:20

Jesus is the supreme example of living without fear of being disappointed by others: "He emptied Himself by assuming the form of a slave. . . . He humbled Himself by becoming obedient to the point of death—even to death on a cross" (Php 2:7-8).

Disappointed people sometimes find it difficult to move out toward others. After all, people—even Christian people—can be rude, uncouth, obnoxious, and sometimes downright disgusting. I sometimes think it might be helpful if we put a sign outside some churches saying: "Enter here at your own risk." Forgive my cynicism, but I have lived long enough to know that Christians can hurt! What are we supposed to do when we know that to move toward another person in love exposes us to the risk of being disappointed? We move forward in love: easy to say, but more difficult to do. Making ourselves vulnerable to disappointment is frightening, but this has to happen if we are to love as we are loved.

Mature Christians are those who are willing to look fully into the face of disappointment and feel it, knowing that because they do, they will come to a deeper awareness that no one can comfort the heart like Jesus Christ. In the presence of such pain, one more easily sees the uselessness of every attempt to find solace in one's own independent strategies. Facing and feeling the pain of disappointment underlies more than anything else the gripping truth that only in God can we trust.

Prayer

Father, at times Your purposes seem to run diametrically opposite to my interests, but the more I ponder them, the more I see that You always have my highest interests at heart. Help me to trust You more—and myself less. In Jesus' name. Amen.

Further Study

Mt 26; 2 Tm 2:13; Php 2:3
What disappointments must Jesus have felt?
How often do you disappoint Him?

OCTOBER 10

ISAIAH 54:4–57:13

4 "Do not be afraid, for you will not
    be put to shame;
don't be humiliated,
    for you will not be disgraced.
For you will forget the shame
    of your youth,
and you will no longer remember
the disgrace of your widowhood.
5 For your husband is
    your Maker—
His name is Yahweh of Hosts—
and the Holy One of Israel is
    your Redeemer;
He is called the God of all
    the earth.
6 For the LORD has called you,
like a wife deserted and wounded
    in spirit,
a wife of one's youth
    when she is rejected,"
says your God.
7 "I deserted you
    for a brief moment,
but I will take you back
    with great compassion.
8 In a surge of anger

I hid My face from you
    for a moment,
but I will have compassion on you
with everlasting love,"
says the LORD your Redeemer.
9 "For this is like the days of Noah
    to Me:
when I swore that the waters
    of Noah
would never flood the earth again,
so I have sworn that I will not
    be angry with you
or rebuke you.
10 Though the mountains move
and the hills shake,
My love will not be removed
    from you
and My covenant of peace will not
    be shaken,"
says your compassionate LORD.
11 "Poor Jerusalem, storm-tossed,
    and not comforted,
I will set your stones
    in black mortar,
and lay your foundations
    in sapphires.
12 I will make your battlements
    of rubies,

1202

your gates of sparkling stones,
and all your walls
of precious stones.
13 Then all your children
will be taught by the LORD,
their prosperity will be great,
14 and you will be established
on a foundation of righteousness.
You will be far from oppression,
you will certainly not be afraid;
you will be far from terror,
it will certainly not
come near you.
15 If anyone attacks you,
it is not from Me;
whoever attacks you
will fall before you.
16 Look, I have created the craftsman
who blows on the charcoal fire
and produces a weapon suitable
for its task;
and I have created the destroyer
to work havoc.
17 No weapon formed against you
will succeed,
and you will refute any accusation
raised against you in court.
This is the heritage
of the LORD's servants,
and their righteousness is
from Me."
This is the LORD's declaration.

55 "Come, everyone who is thirsty,
come to the waters;
and you without money,
come, buy, and eat!
Come, buy wine and milk
without money and without cost!
2 Why do you spend money on what
is not food,
and your wages on what
does not satisfy?
Listen carefully to Me, and eat
what is good,
and you will enjoy the choicest
of foods.
3 Pay attention and come to Me;
listen, so that you will live.
I will make an everlasting covenant
with you,
the promises assured to David.
4 Since I have made him a witness
to the peoples,

a leader and commander
for the peoples,
5 so you will summon a nation
you do not know,
and nations who do not know you
will run to you.
For the LORD your God,
even the Holy One of Israel,
has glorified you."

6 Seek the LORD
while He may be found;
call to Him while He is near.
7 Let the wicked one abandon
his way,
and the sinful one his thoughts;
let him return to the LORD,
so He may have compassion
on him,
and to our God, for He will
freely forgive.

8 "For My thoughts are not
your thoughts,
and your ways are not My ways."
This is the LORD's declaration.
9 "For as heaven is higher than earth,
so My ways are higher
than your ways,
and My thoughts
than your thoughts.
10 For just as rain and snow fall
from heaven,
and do not return there
without saturating the earth,
and making it germinate
and sprout,
and providing seed to sow
and food to eat,
11 so My word that comes
from My mouth
will not return to Me empty,
but it will accomplish
what I please,
and will prosper in what I send it
to do."

12 You will indeed go out with joy
and be peacefully guided;
the mountains and the hills
will break into singing
before you,
and all the trees of the field
will clap their hands.

¹³ Instead of the thornbush,
  a cypress will come up,
and instead of the brier, a myrtle
  will come up;
it will make a name for the LORD
as an everlasting sign that will not
  be destroyed.

56 This is what the LORD says:

Preserve justice and do
  what is right,
for My salvation is coming soon,
and My righteousness
  will be revealed.
² Happy is the man who does this,
anyone who maintains this,
who keeps the Sabbath
  without desecrating it,
and keeps his hand from doing
  any evil.

³ No foreigner who has converted
  to the LORD
should say,
"The LORD will exclude me
  from His people";
and the eunuch should not say,
"Look, I am a dried-up tree."
⁴ For the LORD says this:
"For the eunuchs who keep
  My Sabbaths,
and choose what pleases Me,
and hold firmly to My covenant,
⁵ I will give them, in My house
  and within My walls,
a memorial and a name
better than sons and daughters.
I will give each of them
  an everlasting name
that will never be cut off.
⁶ And the foreigners who convert
  to the LORD,
minister to Him,
  love the LORD's name,
and are His servants,
all who keep the Sabbath
  without desecrating it,
and who hold firmly
  to My covenant—
⁷ I will bring them
  to My holy mountain
and let them rejoice in My house
  of prayer.

Their burnt offerings
  and sacrifices
will be acceptable on My altar,
for My house will be called
  a house of prayer
for all nations."
   ⁸ This is the declaration
     of the Lord GOD,
who gathers the dispersed
     of Israel:
"I will gather to them still others
besides those already gathered."

⁹ All you animals of the field
  and forest,
  come and eat!
¹⁰ Israel's watchmen are blind,
  all of them,
they know nothing;
all of them are mute dogs,
they cannot bark;
they dream, lie down,
and love to sleep.
¹¹ These dogs have
  fierce appetites;
they never have enough.
And they are shepherds
who have no discernment;
all of them turn to their own way,
every last one for his own gain.
¹² "Come, let me get some wine,
let's guzzle some; beer;
and tomorrow will be like today,
only far better!"

57 The righteous one perishes,
  and no one takes it to heart;
faithful men are swept away,
with no one realizing
that the righteous one
  is swept away
from the presence of evil.
² He will enter into peace—
they will rest on their beds—
everyone who lives uprightly.

³ But come here,
you sons of a sorceress,
offspring of an adulterer
  and a prostitute!
⁴ Who is it you are mocking?
Who is it you are opening
  your mouth
and sticking out your tongue at?

Isn't it you,
you rebellious children,
you race of liars,
5 who burn with lust
among the oaks,
under every flourishing tree,
who slaughter children in the
wadis
below the clefts of the rocks?
6 Your portion is
among the smooth stones
of the wadi;
indeed, they are your lot.
You have even poured out
a drink offering to them;
you have offered a grain offering;
should I be satisfied with these?
7 You have placed your bed
on a high and lofty mountain;
you also went up there
to offer sacrifice.
8 You have set up your memorial
behind the door and doorpost.
For away from Me, you stripped,
went up, and made your bed wide,
and you have made a bargain
for yourself with them.
You have loved their bed;
you have gazed on their genitals.
9 You went to the king with oil
and multiplied your perfumes;
you sent your envoys far away
and sent them down even to
Sheol.
10 You became weary
on your many journeys,
but you did not say, "I give up!"
You found a renewal
of your strength;
therefore you did not grow weak.
11 Who was it you dreaded
and feared,
so that you lied and didn't
remember Me
or take it to heart?
Have I not kept silent for such
a long time
and you do not fear Me?
12 I will expose your righteousness,
and your works—they will not
profit you.
13 When you cry out,
let your collection of idols
deliver you!

The wind will carry
all of them off,
a breath will take them away.
But whoever takes refuge in Me
will inherit the land
and possess My holy mountain.

PSALM 118:22-29

22 The stone that the builders
rejected
has become the cornerstone.
23 This came from the LORD;
it is wonderful in our eyes.
24 This is the day the LORD has made;
let us rejoice and be glad in it.
25 LORD, save us!
LORD, please grant us success!
26 Blessed is he who comes in the
name of the LORD.
From the house of the LORD we
bless you.
27 The LORD is God and has given us
light.
Bind the festival sacrifice with
cords to the horns of the altar.
28 You are my God, and I will give
You thanks.
You are my God; I will exalt You.
29 Give thanks to the LORD, for He is
good;
His faithful love endures forever.

PROVERBS 24:15-16

15 Don't set an ambush, wicked man,
at the camp of the righteous
man;
don't destroy his dwelling.
16 Though a righteous man falls
seven times, he will get up,
but the wicked will stumble into
ruin.

PHILIPPIANS 1:21–2:11

21 For me, living is Christ and dying is
gain. 22 Now if I live on in the flesh, this
means fruitful work for me; and I don't
know which one I should choose. 23 I am
pressured by both. I have the desire to
depart and be with Christ—which is far

better— ²⁴ but to remain in the flesh is more necessary for you. ²⁵ Since I am persuaded of this, I know that I will remain and continue with all of you for your advancement and joy in the faith, ²⁶ so that, because of me, your confidence may grow in Christ Jesus when I come to you again.

²⁷ Just one thing: live your life in a manner worthy of the gospel of Christ. Then, whether I come and see you or am absent, I will hear about you that you are standing firm in one spirit, with one mind, working side by side for the faith of the gospel, ²⁸ not being frightened in any way by your opponents. This is evidence of their destruction, but of your deliverance—and this is from God. ²⁹ For it has been given to you on Christ's behalf not only to believe in Him, but also to suffer for Him, ³⁰ having the same struggle that you saw I had and now hear about me.

2 If then there is any encouragement in Christ, if any consolation of love, if any fellowship with the Spirit, if any affection and mercy, ² fulfill my joy by thinking the same way, having the same love, sharing the same feelings, focusing on one goal. ³ Do nothing out of rivalry or conceit, but in humility consider others as more important than yourselves. ⁴ Everyone should look out not only for his own interests, but also for the interests of others.

⁵ Make your own attitude that of Christ Jesus,

⁶ who, existing in the form of God,
did not consider
equality with God
as something to be used
for His own advantage.
⁷ Instead He emptied Himself
by assuming the form
of a slave,
taking on the likeness of men.
And when He had come as a man
in His external form,
⁸ He humbled Himself
by becoming obedient
to the point of death—
even to death on a cross.
⁹ For this reason God also
highly exalted Him
and gave Him the name that is
above every name,
¹⁰ so that at the name of Jesus
every knee should bow—
of those who are in heaven
and on earth
and under the earth—
¹¹ and every tongue should confess
that Jesus Christ is Lord,
to the glory of God the Father.

The God Who Speaks

*So My ways are higher than your ways,
and My thoughts than your thoughts.*—Isaiah 55:9

Although we know that God is all-powerful, we also know that He is personal. But what does it mean to be a person? What predicates personality?

The best definition of personality I know is the one given to me by the tutor who taught me theology: "To be a person, we have to be able to think, to reason, to feel, to judge, to choose, and to communicate in words that constitute a language." Richard Swinburne, a theologian, observes that people use language not only to communicate and for private thought, but to argue, to raise a consideration, to object to another. Unlike animals that show evidence only of wanting food and drink, people can want not to want something—like a fasting man, for example, wanting not to want food.

Now with that in mind—that one of the constituents of personality is the ability to think and speak—read the first chapter of Genesis. Notice how many times the words appear: "God said." Count them. God is portrayed to us as a speaking God. And because speech is one of the constituent parts of personality, this proves to us that the Deity is a personal Being. We are not long into Genesis before we are brought face-to-face with the fact that there is more to God than mere power; the Almighty is a Person. This means, among other things, that the Almighty cannot be studied from a "safe" distance. Because He is a Person, He is someone who wants and waits to be known.

Prayer

Loving heavenly Father, how thankful I am that You made me like Yourself—to know and be known. May my strongest desire be to know You, not merely to know myself. For it is only when I know You that I can most truly know myself. Amen.

Further Study

Gn 1:1-31; Jb 33:13-14; 1 Kg 19:12; Ezk 43:2
How many times does it say "God said"?
How did Ezekiel describe God's voice?

OCTOBER 11

ISAIAH 57:14–60:16

14 He said,
"Build it up, build it up,
    prepare the way,
remove every obstacle
    from My people's way."
15 For the High and Exalted One
who lives forever, whose name
        is Holy says this:
"I live in a high and holy place,
and with the oppressed and lowly
        of spirit,
to revive the spirit of the lowly
and revive the heart
    of the oppressed.
16 For I will not accuse you forever,

and I will not always be angry;
for then the spirit
        would grow weak before Me,
    even the breath of man,
        which I have made.
17 Because of his sinful greed
        I was angry,
so I struck him; I was angry and hid;
    but he went on turning back
        to the desires of his heart.
18 I have seen his ways,
        but I will heal him;
I will lead him and comfort him
        and his mourners,
19 creating words of praise."
The LORD says,
"Peace, peace to the one
        who is far or near,

and I will heal him.
20 But the wicked are
like the storm-tossed sea,
for it cannot be still,
and its waters churn up mire
and muck.
21 There is no peace for the wicked,"
says my God.

58 "Cry out loudly, don't hold back!
Raise your voice like a trumpet.
Tell My people their transgression,
and the house of Jacob their sins.
2 They seek Me day after day
and delight to know My ways,
like a nation that does
what is right
and does not abandon the justice
of their God.
They ask Me
for righteous judgments;
they delight in the nearness
of God."
3 "Why have we fasted,
but You have not seen?
We have denied ourselves,
but You haven't noticed!"
"Look, you do as you please
on the day of your fast,
and oppress all your workers.
4 You fast with contention and strife
to strike viciously with your fist.
You cannot fast as you do today,
hoping to make your voice heard
on high.
5 Will the fast I choose be like this:
A day for a person
to deny himself,
to bow his head like a reed,
and to spread out sackcloth
and ashes?
Will you call this a fast
and a day acceptable to the LORD?
6 Isn't the fast I choose:
To break the chains of wickedness,
to untie the ropes of the yoke,
to set the oppressed free,
and to tear off every yoke?
7 Is it not to share your bread
with the hungry,
to bring the poor and homeless
into your house,
to clothe the naked
when you see him,

and to not ignore your own flesh
and blood?
8 Then your light will appear
like the dawn,
and your recovery
will come quickly.
Your righteousness will go
before you,
and the LORD's glory will be
your rear guard.
9 At that time, when you call,
the LORD will answer;
when you cry out, He will say:
Here I am.
If you get rid of the yoke
from those around you,
the finger-pointing
and malicious speaking,
10 and if you offer yourself
to the hungry,
and satisfy the afflicted one,
then your light will shine
in the darkness,
and your night will be like noonday.
11 The LORD will always lead you,
satisfy you in a parched land,
and strengthen your bones.
You will be like a watered garden
and like a spring whose waters
never run dry.
12 Some of you will rebuild
the ancient ruins;
you will restore
the foundations laid long ago;
you will be called the repairer
of broken walls,
the restorer of streets
where people live.
13 "If you keep from desecrating
the Sabbath,
from doing whatever you want
on My holy day;
if you call the Sabbath a delight,
and the holy day
of the LORD honorable;
if you honor it, not going
your own ways,
seeking your own pleasure,
or talking too much;
14 then you will delight yourself
in the LORD,
and I will make you ride
over the heights of the land,

and let you enjoy the heritage
of your father Jacob."
For the mouth of the LORD
has spoken.

59 Indeed, the LORD's hand is not
too short to save,
and His ear is not too deaf to hear.
2 But your iniquities
have built barriers
between you and your God,
and your sins have made Him
hide His face from you
so that He does not listen.
3 For your hands are defiled
with blood,
and your fingers with iniquity;
your lips have spoken lies,
and you mutter injustice.
4 No one makes claims justly;
no one pleads honestly.
They trust in empty
and worthless words;
they conceive trouble
and give birth to iniquity.
5 They hatch viper's eggs
and weave spider's webs.
Whoever eats their eggs will die;
crack one open, and a viper
is hatched.
6 Their webs cannot
become clothing,
and they cannot cover themselves
with their works.
Their works are sinful works,
and violent acts are in their hands.
7 Their feet run after evil,
and they rush to shed
innocent blood.
Their thoughts are sinful thoughts;
ruin and wretchedness are
in their paths.
8 They have not known the path
of peace,
and there is no justice
in their ways.
They have made
their roads crooked;
no one who walks on them
will know peace.

9 Therefore justice is far from us,
and righteousness does not
reach us.

We hope for light,
but there is darkness;
for brightness, but we live
in the night.
10 We grope along a wall
like the blind;
we grope like those without eyes.
We stumble at noon as though
it were twilight;
we are like the dead among those
who are healthy.
11 We all growl like bears
and moan like doves.
We hope for justice,
but there is none;
for salvation, but it is far from us.
12 For our transgressions
have multiplied before You,
and our sins testify against us.
For our transgressions are with us,
and we know our iniquities:
13 transgression and deception
against the LORD,
turning away from following
our God,
speaking oppression and revolt,
conceiving and uttering
lying words from the heart.
14 Justice is turned back,
and righteousness stands far off.
For truth has stumbled
in the public square,
and honesty cannot enter.
15 Truth is missing,
and whoever turns from evil
is plundered.

The LORD saw that there was
no justice,
and He was offended.
16 He saw that there was no man—
He was amazed that there was
no one interceding;
so His own arm brought salvation,
and His own righteousness
supported Him.
17 He put on righteousness
like a breastplate,
and a helmet of salvation
on His head;
He put on garments of vengeance
for clothing,
and He wrapped Himself in zeal
as in a cloak.

¹⁸ Thus He will repay according to
their deeds:
fury to His enemies,
retribution to His foes,
and He will repay the coastlands.
¹⁹ They will fear the name
of the LORD in the west,
and His glory in the east;
for He will come
like a rushing stream
driven by the wind of the LORD.
²⁰ The Redeemer will come to Zion,
and to those in Jacob who turn
from transgression.
This is the LORD's declaration.

²¹ "As for Me, this is My covenant
with them," says the LORD: "My Spirit
who is on you, and My words that I have
put in your mouth, will not depart from
your mouth, or from the mouth of your
children, or from the mouth of your
children's children, from now on and
forever," says the LORD.

60 Arise, shine, for your light
has come,
and the glory of the LORD shines
over you.
² For look, darkness covers the earth,
and total darkness the peoples;
but the LORD will shine over you,
and His glory will appear
over you.
³ Nations will come to your light,
and kings to the brightness
of your radiance.
⁴ Raise your eyes and look around:
they all gather and come to you;
your sons will come
from far away,
and your daughters will be carried
on the hip.
⁵ Then you will see and be radiant,
and your heart will tremble
and rejoice,
because the riches of the sea
will become yours,
and the wealth of the nations
will come to you.
⁶ Caravans of camels will cover
your land—
young camels of Midian
and Ephah—

all of them will come from Sheba.
They will carry gold
and frankincense
and proclaim the praises
of the LORD.
⁷ All the flocks of Kedar
will be gathered to you;
the rams of Nebaioth
will serve you
and go up on My altar
as an acceptable sacrifice.
I will glorify My beautiful house.

⁸ Who are these who fly
like a cloud,
like doves to their shelters?
⁹ Yes, the islands will wait for Me
with the ships of Tarshish
in the lead,
to bring your children
from far away,
their silver and gold with them,
for the honor of the LORD
your God,
the Holy One of Israel,
who has glorified you.
¹⁰ Foreigners will build up
your walls,
and their kings will serve you.
Although I struck you
in My wrath,
yet I will show mercy to you
with My favor.
¹¹ Your gates will always be open;
they will never be shut
day or night
so that the wealth of the nations
may be brought into you,
with their kings being led
in procession.
¹² For the nation and the kingdom
that will not serve you will perish;
those nations will be annihilated.
¹³ The glory of Lebanon will come
to you—
its pine, fir, and cypress
together—
to beautify the place
of My sanctuary,
and I will glorify
My dwelling place.
¹⁴ The sons of your oppressors
will come and bow down to you;
all who reviled you

will fall down on their faces
   at your feet.
They will call you the City
   of the LORD,
Zion of the Holy One of Israel.
¹⁵ Instead of your being deserted
   and hated,
   with no one passing through,
   I will make you an object
   of eternal pride,
   a joy from age to age.
¹⁶ You will nurse on the milk
   of nations,
   and nurse at the breast of kings;
   you will know that I, the LORD,
   am your Savior
   and Redeemer, the Mighty One
   of Jacob.

PSALM 119:1-4

¹ How happy are those whose way
   is blameless,
   who live according to the law of
   the LORD!
² Happy are those who keep His
   decrees
   and seek Him with all their heart.
³ They do nothing wrong;
   they follow His ways.
⁴ You have commanded that Your
   precepts
   be diligently kept.

PROVERBS 24:17-18

¹⁷ Don't gloat when your enemy
   falls,
   and don't let your heart rejoice
   when he stumbles,
¹⁸ or the LORD will see, be
   displeased,
   and turn His wrath away from
   him.

PHILIPPIANS 2:12-30

¹² So then, my dear friends, just as
you have always obeyed, not only in my
presence, but now even more in my absence, work out your own salvation
with fear and trembling. ¹³ For it is God
who is working in you, enabling you
both to will and to act for His good purpose. ¹⁴ Do everything without grum-
bling and arguing, ¹⁵ so that you may be
blameless and pure, children of God
who are faultless in a crooked and perverted generation, among whom you
shine like stars in the world. ¹⁶ Hold
firmly the message of life. Then I can
boast in the day of Christ that I didn't
run in vain or labor for nothing. ¹⁷ But
even if I am poured out as a drink offering on the sacrifice and service of your
faith, I am glad and rejoice with all of
you. ¹⁸ In the same way you also should
rejoice and share your joy with me.

¹⁹ Now I hope in the Lord Jesus to
send Timothy to you soon so that I also
may be encouraged when I hear news
about you. ²⁰ For I have no one else likeminded who will genuinely care about
your interests; ²¹ all seek their own interests, not those of Jesus Christ. ²² But
you know his proven character, because
he has served with me in the gospel
ministry like a son with a father.
²³ Therefore, I hope to send him as soon
as I see how things go with me. ²⁴ And I
am convinced in the Lord that I myself
will also come quickly.

²⁵ But I considered it necessary to
send you Epaphroditus—my brother,
co-worker, and fellow soldier, as well as
your messenger and minister to my
need— ²⁶ since he has been longing for
all of you and was distressed because
you heard that he was sick. ²⁷ Indeed, he
was so sick that he nearly died.
However, God had mercy on him, and
not only on him but also on me, so that
I would not have one grief on top of another. ²⁸ For this reason, I am very eager
to send him so that you may rejoice
when you see him again and I may be
less anxious. ²⁹ Therefore, welcome him
in the Lord with all joy and hold men
like him in honor, ³⁰ because he came
close to death for the work of Christ,
risking his life to make up what was
lacking in your ministry to me.

Doing His Will—Now

For it is God who is working in you, enabling you both to will and to act for His good purpose.—PHILIPPIANS 2:13

Theologians are divided about whether the statement of Jesus in the Lord's Prayer should be translated "*in* earth as it is in heaven" or "*on* earth as it is in heaven." We decided to examine both prepositions, and today we look at the words "on earth."

Most commentators believe the phrase has reference to the world of human beings who have their home on this earth. In other words—us. Fantastic as it may sound, a day will dawn when this earth will be peopled with those who will do the will of God, not with resentment or resignation, but with rejoicing. That day may not be as far distant as we may think, so we ought to double our efforts in prayer and joyously become involved in bringing our lives in line with His will. One thing is sure—the more you and I conform to His will, the more quickly can His purposes for this earth be realized. John Wesley famously said: "God does nothing redemptively in this world except by prayer." Can you see what he is saying? The purposes of God for the future will have to cross the bridge of prayer.

This raises the question: how committed are you and I to doing the will of God? Are we hindering or are we promoting the interests of His future kingdom? It is vital that we Christians, both individually and corporately, focus our prayers on this issue with fervency and passion, remembering as we do so that the more abandoned we are to the divine will, the more speedily will His purposes come to pass for the world.

Prayer

O Father, in the light of this challenge today, I feel like praying: "Your will be done, on earth in me as it is done in heaven." Grant it, I pray, for the honor and glory of Your peerless name. Amen.

Further Study

Mt 3; Jn 8:29; 1 Th 4:1; Heb 13:16
What was the pronouncement from heaven?
Could this be said of your life?

OCTOBER 12

ISAIAH 60:17–63:19

17 I will bring gold instead of bronze;
I will bring silver instead of iron,
bronze instead of wood,
and iron instead of stones.
I will appoint peace as your guard
and righteousness as your ruler.
18 Violence will never again
be heard of in your land;
devastation and destruction
will be gone from your borders.
But you will name
your walls salvation,
and your gates praise.
19 The sun will no longer be
your light by day,
and the brightness of the moon
will not shine on you;
but the LORD will be
your everlasting light,
and your God will be
your splendor.
20 Your sun will no longer set,
and your moon will not fade;
for the LORD will be
your everlasting light,
and the days of your sorrow
will be over.
21 Then all your people
will be righteous;
they will possess the land forever;
they are the branch I planted,
the work of My hands,
so that I may be glorified.
22 The least will become a thousand,
the smallest a mighty nation.
I am the LORD;
I will accomplish it quickly
in its time.

61 The Spirit of the Lord GOD is
on Me,
because the LORD has anointed Me
to bring good news to the poor.
He has sent Me to heal
the brokenhearted,

to proclaim liberty to the captives,
and freedom to the prisoners;
2 to proclaim the year
of the LORD's favor,
and the day
of our God's vengeance;
to comfort all who mourn,
3 to provide for those who mourn
in Zion;
to give them a crown of beauty
instead of ashes,
festive oil instead of mourning,
and splendid clothes
instead of despair.
And they will be called
righteous trees,
planted by the LORD,
to glorify Him.

4 They will rebuild
the ancient ruins;
they will restore
the former devastations;
they will renew the ruined cities,
the devastations
of many generations.
5 Strangers will stand and feed
your flocks,
and foreigners will be
your plowmen
and vinedressers.
6 But you will be called
the LORD's priests;
they will speak of you as ministers
of our God;
you will eat the wealth
of the nations,
and you will boast in their riches.
7 Because your shame was double,
and they cried out,
"Disgrace is their portion,"
therefore, they will possess
double in their land,
and eternal joy will be theirs.

8 For I the LORD love justice;
I hate robbery and injustice;

I will faithfully reward them
and make an everlasting covenant
with them.
9 Their descendants will be known
among the nations,
and their posterity
among the peoples.
All who see them will recognize
that they are a people the Lord
has blessed.

10 I greatly rejoice in the Lord,
I exult in my God;
for He has clothed me
with the garments of salvation
and wrapped me in a robe
of righteousness,
as a bridegroom wears a turban
and as a bride adorns herself
with her jewels.
11 For as the earth brings forth
its growth,
and as a garden enables
what is sown to spring up,
so the Lord God
will cause righteousness
and praise
to spring up before all the nations.

62 I will not keep silent
because of Zion,
and I will not keep still
because of Jerusalem
until her righteousness shines
like a bright light,
and her salvation
like a flaming torch.
2 Nations will see
your righteousness,
and all kings your glory.
You will be called by a new name
that the Lord's mouth
will announce.
3 You will be a glorious crown
in the Lord's hand,
and a royal diadem in the palm
of your God.
4 You will no longer
be called Deserted,
and your land will not
be called Desolate;
instead, you will be called
My Delight is in Her,
and your land Married;

for the Lord delights in you,
and your land will be married.
5 For as a young man marries
a virgin,
so your sons will marry you;
and as a bridegroom rejoices
over his bride,
so your God will rejoice over you.

6 Jerusalem,
I have appointed watchmen
on your walls;
they will never be silent,
day or night.
You, who remind the Lord,
no rest for you!
7 Do not give Him rest
until He establishes
and makes her Jerusalem
the praise of the earth.

8 The Lord has sworn
with His right hand
and His strong arm:
I will no longer give your grain
to your enemies for food,
and foreigners will not drink
your new wine
you have labored for.
9 For those who gather grain
will eat it
and praise the Lord,
and those who harvest the grapes
will drink the wine
in My holy courts.

10 Go out, go out through the gates;
prepare a way for the people!
Build it up, build up the highway;
clear away the stones!
Raise a banner for the peoples.
11 Look, the Lord has proclaimed
to the end of the earth,
"Say to Daughter Zion:
Look, your salvation is coming,
His reward is with Him,
and His recompense is
before Him."
12 And they will be called
the Holy People,
the Lord's Redeemed;
and you will be called Cared For,
A City Not Deserted.

63 Who is this coming from Edom
in crimson-stained garments
   from Bozrah—
this One who is splendid
   in His apparel,
rising up proudly
   in His great might?

It is I, proclaiming vindication,
   powerful to save.

2 Why is Your clothing red,
   and Your garments like one
      who treads a winepress?

3 I trampled the winepress alone,
   and no one from the nations was
      with Me.
I trampled them in My anger
   and ground them underfoot
      in My fury;
   their blood spattered My garments,
   and all My clothes were stained.

4 For I planned the day of vengeance,
   and the year of My redemption
      came.

5 I looked, but there was no one
      to help,
   and I was amazed
      that no one assisted;
   so My arm accomplished victory
      for Me,
   and My wrath assisted Me.

6 I crushed nations in My anger;
   I made them drunk
      with My wrath
   and poured out their blood
      on the ground.

7 I will make known
      the LORD's faithful love
   and the LORD's praiseworthy acts,
   because of all the LORD has done
      for us—
   even the many good things
   He has done for the house
      of Israel
   and has done for them based on
      His compassions
   and the abundance of
      His faithful love.

8 He said, "They are indeed
      My people,
   children who will not be disloyal,"

and He became their Savior.

9 In all their suffering, He suffered,
   and the Angel of His Presence
      saved them.
He redeemed them
   because of His love
      and compassion;
He lifted them up
   and carried them
      all the days of the past.

10 But they rebelled,
   and grieved His Holy Spirit.
So He became their enemy
   and fought against them.

11 Then He remembered the days
      of the past,
   the days of Moses
      and his people.
Where is He who
   brought them up
      out of the sea
   with the shepherds of His flock?
Where is He who put
   His Holy Spirit
      among the flock?

12 He sent His glorious arm
   at Moses' right hand,
   divided the waters before them
   to obtain eternal fame for Himself,

13 and led them through the depths
   like a horse in the wilderness,
   so that they did not stumble.

14 Like cattle that go down
      into the valley,
   the Spirit of the LORD gave them
      rest.
You led Your people this way
   to make a glorious name
      for Yourself.

15 Look down from heaven and see
   from Your lofty home—
      holy and beautiful.
Where is Your zeal and Your might?
Your yearning
   and Your compassion
   are withheld from me.

16 Yet You are our Father,
   even though Abraham does not
      know us
   and Israel doesn't recognize us.
You, LORD, are our Father;
   from ancient times,
   Your name is our Redeemer.

¹⁷ Why, LORD, do You make us stray
from Your ways?
You harden our hearts
so we do not fear You.
Return, because of Your servants,
the tribes of Your heritage.
¹⁸ Your holy people had a possession
for a little while,
but our enemies
have trampled down
Your sanctuary.
¹⁹ We have become like those
You never ruled over,
like those not called by Your name.

PSALM 119:5-8

⁵ If only my ways were committed
to keeping Your statutes!
⁶ Then I would not be ashamed
when I think about all Your
commands.
⁷ I will praise You with a sincere
heart
when I learn Your righteous
judgments.
⁸ I will keep Your statutes;
never abandon me.

PROVERBS 24:19-20

¹⁹ Don't worry because of evildoers,
and don't envy the wicked.
²⁰ For the evil have no future;
the lamp of the wicked will be put
out.

PHILIPPIANS 3:1-21

3 Finally, my brothers, rejoice in the
Lord. To write to you again about
this is no trouble for me and is a pro-
tection for you. ² Watch out for "dogs," watch out for
evil workers, watch out for those who
mutilate the flesh. ³ For we are the circumcision, the ones who serve by the
Spirit of God, boast in Christ Jesus, and
do not put confidence in the flesh—
⁴ although I once had confidence in the
flesh too. If anyone else thinks he has
grounds for confidence in the flesh, I
have more: ⁵ circumcised the eighth

day; of the nation of Israel, of the tribe
of Benjamin, a Hebrew born of Hebrews;
as to the law, a Pharisee; ⁶ as to zeal,
persecuting the church; as to the righteousness that is in the law, blameless.
⁷ But everything that was a gain to
me, I have considered to be a loss because of Christ. ⁸ More than that, I also
consider everything to be a loss in view
of the surpassing value of knowing
Christ Jesus my Lord. Because of Him I
have suffered the loss of all things and
consider them filth, so that I may gain
Christ ⁹ and be found in Him, not having
a righteousness of my own from the
law, but one that is through faith in
Christ—the righteousness from God
based on faith. ¹⁰ My goal is to know
Him and the power of His resurrection
and the fellowship of His sufferings, being conformed to His death, ¹¹ assuming
that I will somehow reach the resurrection from among the dead.
¹² Not that I have already reached the
goal or am already fully mature, but I
make every effort to take hold of it because I also have been taken hold of by
Christ Jesus. ¹³ Brothers, I do not consider myself to have taken hold of it. But
one thing I do: forgetting what is behind
and reaching forward to what is ahead,
¹⁴ I pursue as my goal the prize prom-
ised by God's heavenly call in Christ
Jesus. ¹⁵ Therefore, all who are mature
should think this way. And if you think
differently about anything, God will reveal this to you also. ¹⁶ In any case, we
should live up to whatever truth we
have attained. ¹⁷ Join in imitating me,
brothers, and observe those who live according to the example you have in us.
¹⁸ For I have often told you, and now say
again with tears, that many live as enemies of the cross of Christ. ¹⁹ Their end
is destruction; their god is their stomach; their glory is in their shame. They
are focused on earthly things, ²⁰ but our
citizenship is in heaven, from which
we also eagerly wait for a Savior, the
Lord Jesus Christ. ²¹ He will transform
the body of our humble condition into
the likeness of His glorious body, by the
power that enables Him to subject
everything to Himself.

Meeting the Person

My goal is to know Him
and the power of His resurrection.
—PHILIPPIANS 3:10

It must not be assumed that the study of Scripture and the contemplation of the principles that God has built into His Word are unimportant. They most certainly are. But let us be on our guard that we do not fall into the trap of contemplating the principles that God has built into the universe more than God Himself.

I have often seen students of Scripture fall into this trap when, in reading their Bible, the only things that get their attention are the principles that relate to godliness. They underline them in their Bible, mark alongside them other Scriptural references, and think that by doing this they are growing spiritually. The problem, however, is that only the principles of daily personal godliness capture their interest; their heavenly Father does not.

Imagine treating a love letter that way: identifying and underlining the principles, reflecting on the profundity of some of the insights, marveling at the clarity of the language and yet missing the main purpose of the letter—romantic passion and love. Yet this is the way some people approach the Bible. Our aim in studying the nature and character of God must be to know God better (not merely know His Word better), and we must seek to enlarge our acquaintance not simply with the characteristics of His nature, but with the living God whose characteristics they are.

Prayer

O God, help me never to approach the Bible content to know only the written Word. Give me a passion that never remains satisfied until, through the written Word, I discover more of the living Word. In Jesus' name. Amen.

Further Study

Rv 2:1-7; 2 Co 5:14
What was the church in Ephesus commended for?
Why was this insufficient?

OCTOBER 13

ISAIAH 64:1–66:24

64 If only You would tear
the heavens open
and come down,
so that mountains would quake
at Your presence—
2 as fire kindles the brushwood,
and fire causes water to boil—
to make Your name known
to Your enemies,
so that nations will tremble
at Your presence!
3 When You did awesome deeds
that we did not expect,
You came down,
and the mountains quaked
at Your presence.
4 From ancient times no one
has heard,
no one has listened,
no eye has seen any God
except You,
who acts on behalf of the one
who waits for Him.
5 You welcome the one who joyfully
does what is right;
they remember You
in Your ways.
But we have sinned, and You
were angry;
we will remain in Your ways
and be saved.
6 All of us have become
like something unclean,
and all our righteous acts are
like a polluted garment;
all of us wither like a leaf,
and our iniquities carry us away
like the wind.
7 No one calls on Your name,
striving to take hold of You.
For You have hidden Your face
from us
and made us melt because of
our iniquity.

8 Yet LORD, You are our Father;
we are the clay, and You are
our potter;
we all are the work of Your hands.
9 LORD, do not be terribly angry
or remember our
iniquity forever.
Please look—all of us are
Your people!
10 Your holy cities have become
a wilderness;
Zion has become a wilderness,
Jerusalem a desolation.
11 Our holy and beautiful temple,
where our fathers praised You,
has been burned with fire,
and all that was dear to us lies
in ruins.
12 LORD, after all this, will You
restrain Yourself?
Will You keep silent
and afflict severely?

65 "I was sought by those
who did not ask;
I was found by those
who did not seek Me.
I said: Here I am, here I am,
to a nation that was not called by
My name.
2 I spread out My hands all day long
to a rebellious people
who walk in the wrong path,
following their own thoughts.
3 These people
continually provoke Me
to My face,
sacrificing in gardens,
burning incense on bricks,
4 sitting among the graves,
spending nights in secret places,
eating swine's flesh,
and putting polluted broth
in their bowls.
5 They say: Keep to yourself,
don't come near me,
for I am too holy for you!

These practices are smoke
in My nostrils,
a fire that burns all day long.
⁶ It is written before Me:
I will not keep silent,
but I will repay;
I will repay them fully
⁷ for your iniquities
and the iniquities
of your fathers together,"
says the LORD.
"Because they burned incense
on the mountains
and reproached Me on the hills,
I will reward them fully
for their former deeds."

⁸ The LORD says this:

As the new wine is found
in a bunch of grapes,
and one says: Don't destroy it,
for there's some good in it,
so I will act because of
My servants
and not destroy them all.
⁹ I will produce descendants
from Jacob,
and heirs to My mountains
from Judah;
My chosen ones will possess it,
and My servants will dwell there.
¹⁰ Sharon will be a pasture for flocks,
and the Valley of Achor a place
for cattle to lie down,
for My people
who have sought Me.
¹¹ But you who abandon the LORD,
who forget My holy mountain,
who prepare a table for Fortune
and fill bowls of mixed wine
for Destiny,
¹² I will destine you for the sword,
and all of you will kneel down
to be slaughtered,
because I called
and you did not answer,
I spoke and you did not hear;
you did what was evil in My sight
and chose
what I did not delight in.

¹³ Therefore, this is what the Lord
GOD says:

My servants will eat,
but you will be hungry;
My servants will drink,
but you will be thirsty;
My servants will rejoice,
but you will be put to shame.
¹⁴ My servants will shout for joy
from a glad heart,
but you will cry out
from an anguished heart,
and you will lament out of
a broken spirit.
¹⁵ You will leave your name behind
as a curse for My chosen ones,
and the Lord GOD will kill you;
but He will give His servants
another name.
¹⁶ Whoever is blessed in the land
will be blessed by the God
of truth,
and whoever swears in the land
will swear by the God of truth.
For the former troubles
will be forgotten
and hidden from My sight.

¹⁷ "For I will create a new heaven
and a new earth;
the past events will not
be remembered or come
to mind.
¹⁸ Then be glad and rejoice forever
in what I am creating;
for I will create Jerusalem to be
a joy,
and its people to be a delight.
¹⁹ I will rejoice in Jerusalem
and be glad in My people.
The sound of weeping and crying
will no longer be heard in her.
²⁰ In her, a nursing infant
will no longer live
only a few days,
or an old man not live out
his days.
Indeed, the youth will die
at a hundred years,
and the one who misses
a hundred years
will be cursed.
²¹ People will build houses and live
in them;
they will plant vineyards and eat
their fruit.

22 They will not build and others live
in them;
they will not plant and others eat.
For My people's lives will be
like the lifetime of a tree.
My chosen ones will fully enjoy
the work of their hands.
23 They will not labor
without success
or bear children destined
for disaster,
for they will be a people blessed
by the LORD
along with their descendants.
24 Even before they call,
I will answer;
while they are still speaking,
I will hear.
25 The wolf and the lamb
will feed together,
and the lion will eat straw
like the ox,
but the serpent's food
will be dust!
They will not do what is evil
or destroy
on My entire holy mountain,"
says the LORD.

66 This is what the LORD says:

Heaven is My throne,
and earth is My footstool.
What house could you
possibly build for Me?
And what place could be
My home?
2 My hand made all these things,
and so they all came into being.
This is the LORD's declaration.
I will look favorably on this kind
of person:
one who is humble, submissive
in spirit,
and who trembles at My word.
3 One slaughters an ox, one kills
a man;
one sacrifices a lamb, one breaks
a dog's neck;
one offers a grain offering,
one offers swine's blood;
one offers incense, one praises
an idol—
all these have chosen their ways

and delight in their abominations.
4 So I will choose their punishment,
and I will bring on them
what they dread,
because I called
and no one answered;
I spoke and they didn't hear;
they did what is evil in My sight
and chose what I didn't delight in.

5 You who tremble at His word,
hear the word of the LORD:
"Your brothers who hate
and exclude you
because of Me have said:
Let the LORD be glorified,
so that we can see your joy!
But they will be put to shame."

6 A sound of uproar from the city!
A voice from the temple—
the voice of the LORD,
paying back His enemies
what they deserve!

7 Before Zion was in labor,
she gave birth;
before she was in pain,
she delivered a boy.
8 Who has heard of such a thing?
Who has seen such things?
Can a land be born in one day,
or a nation be delivered
in an instant?
Yet as soon as Zion was in labor,
she gave birth to her sons.
9 "Will I bring a baby to the point
of birth
and not deliver it?"
says the LORD;
"or will I who deliver,
close the womb?"
says your God.
10 Be glad for Jerusalem and rejoice
over her,
all who love her.
Rejoice greatly with her,
all who mourn over her—
11 so that you may nurse
and be satisfied
from her comforting breast
and drink deeply
and delight yourselves
from her glorious breasts.

¹² For this is what the LORD says:

I will make peace flow to her
  like a river,
and the wealth of nations
  like a flood;
you will nurse and be carried
  on her hip,
and bounced on her lap.
¹³ As a mother comforts her son,
  so I will comfort you,
and you will be comforted
  in Jerusalem.

¹⁴ You will see, you will rejoice,
  and you will flourish like grass;
then the LORD's power
  will be revealed
  to His servants,
but He will show His wrath
  against His enemies.
¹⁵ Look, the LORD will come
  with fire—
His chariots are
  like the whirlwind—
to execute His anger with fury,
  and His rebuke with flames
  of fire.
¹⁶ For the LORD
  will execute judgment
on all flesh with His fiery sword,
  and many will be slain
  by the LORD.

¹⁷ "Those who dedicate and purify themselves to enter the groves following their leader, eating meat from pigs, vermin, and rats, will perish together." This is the LORD's declaration. ¹⁸ "Knowing their works and their thoughts, I have come to gather all nations and languages; they will come and see My glory. ¹⁹ I will establish a sign among them, and I will send survivors from them to the nations—to Tarshish, Put, Lud (who are archers), Tubal, Javan, and the islands far away—who have not heard of My fame or seen My glory. And they will proclaim My glory among the nations. ²⁰ They will bring all your brothers from all the nations as a gift to the LORD on horses and chariots, in litters, and on mules and camels, to My holy mountain Jerusalem, says the LORD, just as the Israelites bring an offering in a clean vessel to the house of the LORD. ²¹ I will also take some of them as priests and Levites," says the LORD.

²² "For just as the new heavens
  and the new earth,
which I will make,
will endure before Me"—
  the LORD's declaration—
"so will your offspring
  and your name endure.
²³ All mankind will come
  to worship Me,
from one New Moon to another,
  and from one Sabbath to another,"
says the LORD.

²⁴ "As they leave, they will see the dead bodies of the men who have rebelled against Me; for their maggots will never die, their fire will never go out, and they will be a horror to all mankind."

𝒫SALM 119:9-11

⁹ How can a young man keep his
  way pure?
By keeping Your word.
¹⁰ I have sought You with all my
  heart;
don't let me wander from Your
  commands.
¹¹ I have treasured Your word in my
  heart
so that I may not sin against You.

𝒫ROVERBS 24:21-22

²¹ My son, fear the LORD, as well as
  the king,
and don't associate with rebels,
²² for their destruction will come
  suddenly;
who knows what disaster these
  two can bring?

𝒫HILIPPIANS 4:1-23

4 So then, in this way, my dearly loved brothers, my joy and crown, stand firm in the Lord, dear friends. ² I urge

Euodia and I urge Syntyche to agree in the Lord. ³ Yes, I also ask you, true partner, to help these women who have contended for the gospel at my side, along with Clement and the rest of my coworkers whose names are in the book of life. ⁴ Rejoice in the Lord always. I will say it again: Rejoice! ⁵ Let your graciousness be known to everyone. The Lord is near. ⁶ Don't worry about anything, but in everything, through prayer and petition with thanksgiving, let your requests be made known to God. ⁷ And the peace of God, which surpasses every thought, will guard your hearts and your minds in Christ Jesus.

⁸ Finally brothers, whatever is true, whatever is honorable, whatever is just, whatever is pure, whatever is lovely, whatever is commendable—if there is any moral excellence and if there is any praise—dwell on these things. ⁹ Do what you have learned and received and heard and seen in me, and the God of peace will be with you.

¹⁰ I rejoiced in the Lord greatly that now at last you have renewed your care for me. You were, in fact, concerned about me, but lacked the opportunity to show it. ¹¹ I don't say this out of need, for I have learned to be content in whatever circumstances I am. ¹² I know both how to have a little, and I know how to have a lot. In any and all circumstances I have learned the secret of being content—whether well-fed or hungry, whether in abundance or in need. ¹³ I am able to do all things through Him who strengthens me. ¹⁴ Still, you did well by sharing with me in my hardship.

¹⁵ And you, Philippians, know that in the early days of the gospel, when I left Macedonia, no church shared with me in the matter of giving and receiving except you alone. ¹⁶ For even in Thessalonica you sent gifts for my need several times. ¹⁷ Not that I seek the gift, but I seek the fruit that is increasing to your account. ¹⁸ But I have received everything in full, and I have an abundance. I am fully supplied, having received from Epaphroditus what you provided—a fragrant offering, a welcome sacrifice, pleasing to God. ¹⁹ And my God will supply all your needs according to His riches in glory in Christ Jesus. ²⁰ Now to our God and Father be glory forever and ever. Amen.

²¹ Greet every saint in Christ Jesus. Those brothers who are with me greet you. ²² All the saints greet you, but especially those from Caesar's household. ²³ The grace of the Lord Jesus Christ be with your spirit.

We Need to Tell Him

In everything, through prayer and petition with thanksgiving, let your requests be made known to God.—PHILIPPIANS 4:6

One of the reasons Jesus taught us to pray "Give us today our daily bread" was because He wanted to build in us a barrier against ingratitude.

Do you pray daily for your physical needs? Do you ask God daily for things like food, shelter, and the other physical necessities of life? I must confess that when I asked myself this question before writing this page, I had to admit that I did not. Now I have made a decision to apply myself to this part of the Lord's Prayer with greater sincerity.

Of course some people argue that because Jesus said: "Your Father knows the things you need before you ask Him" (Mt 6:8), then it is pointless to inform God of our physical needs because He knows them already. But the central value of prayer is that prayer is not something by which we inform God of our needs and thus influence Him to give things to us. Prayer is designed to influence us; it is we who are in need of this kind of prayer, not God. Of course God knows what we are in need of, but He also knows that unless we come face to face daily with the fact that we are creatures of need, then we can soon develop a spirit of independence and withdraw ourselves from close contact with Him.

Prayer, then, is something we need. God may not need to be told, but we need to tell Him. That's the point. And unless we grasp it, we can miss one of the primary purposes of prayer.

Prayer

O Father, thank You for showing me that prayer is not begging for blessings. It is becoming a blessing—to myself. I pray, not to change Your attitude towards me, but to change my attitude towards You. Thank You, Father. Amen.

Further Study

Mt 6:19-34; Ps 37:5; 118:8; 125:1
What should be our attitude to worldly cares?
What should be our first priority?

OCTOBER 14

JEREMIAH 1:1–2:37

1 The words of Jeremiah, the son of Hilkiah, one of the priests living in Anathoth in the territory of Benjamin. ² The word of the LORD came to him in the thirteenth year of the reign of Josiah son of Amon, king of Judah. ³ It also came throughout the days of Jehoiakim son of Josiah, king of Judah, until the fifth month of the eleventh year of Zedekiah son of Josiah, king of Judah, when the people of Jerusalem went into exile.
⁴ The word of the LORD came to me:

⁵ I chose you before I formed you
in the womb;
I set you apart
before you were born.

I appointed you a prophet
to the nations.

⁶ But I protested, "Oh no, Lord GOD! Look, I don't know how to speak since I am only a youth."
⁷ Then the LORD said to me:

Do not say: I am only a youth,
for you will go to everyone
I send you to
and speak whatever I tell you.
⁸ Do not be afraid of anyone,
for I will be with you
to deliver you.
This is the LORD's declaration.

⁹ Then the LORD reached out His hand, touched my mouth, and told me:

1223

Look, I have filled your mouth
with My words.
10 See, today I have set you
over nations and kingdoms
to uproot and tear down,
to destroy and demolish,
to build and plant.

11 Then the word of the LORD came to
me, asking, "What do you see,
Jeremiah?"

I replied, "I see a branch of an almond tree."

12 The LORD said to me, "You have seen
correctly, for I watch over My word to
accomplish it." 13 Again the word of the
LORD came to me inquiring, "What do
you see?"

And I replied, "I see a boiling pot, its
mouth tilted from the north to the
south."

14 Then the LORD said to me, "Disaster
will be poured out from the north on all
who live in the land. 15 Indeed, I am
about to summon all the clans and kingdoms of the north."

This is the LORD's declaration.

They will come, and each king
will set up his throne
at the entrance
to Jerusalem's gates.
They will attack
all her surrounding walls
and all the other cities of Judah.

16 "I will pronounce My judgments
against them for all the evil they did
when they abandoned Me to burn incense to other gods and to worship the
works of their own hands.

17 "Now, get ready. Stand up and tell
them everything that I command you.
Do not be intimidated by them or I
will cause you to cower before them.
18 Today, I am the One who has made
you a fortified city, an iron pillar, and
bronze walls against the whole land—
against the kings of Judah, its officials,
its priests, and the population. 19 They
will fight against you but never prevail
over you, since I am with you to rescue
you."

This is the LORD's declaration.

2 The word of the LORD came to me:
2 "Go and announce directly to
Jerusalem that this is what the LORD
says:

I remember the loyalty
of your youth,
your love as a bride—
how you followed Me
in the wilderness,
in a land not sown.
3 Israel was holy to the LORD,
the firstfruits of His harvest.
All who ate of it found
themselves guilty;
disaster came on them."
This is the LORD's declaration.

4 Hear the word of the LORD,
house of Jacob
and all families of the house
of Israel.
5 Here is what the LORD says:

What fault did your fathers find
in Me
that they went so far from Me,
followed worthless idols,
and became worthless
themselves?
6 They stopped asking: Where is
the LORD
who brought us from the land
of Egypt,
who led us
through the wilderness,
through a land of deserts
and ravines,
through a land of drought
and darkness,
a land no one traveled through
and where no one lived?
7 I brought you to a fertile land
to eat its fruit and bounty,
but after you entered, you defiled
My land;
you made My inheritance
detestable.
8 The priests quit asking: Where is
the LORD?
The experts in the law no longer
knew Me,
and the rulers rebelled
against Me.

The prophets prophesied by Baal
and followed useless idols.

⁹ Therefore, I will bring a case
　against you again.
　　This is the LORD's declaration.
I will bring a case
　against your children's
　children.
¹⁰ Cross over to Cyprus and take
　a look.
Send someone to Kedar
　and consider carefully;
see if there has ever been
　anything like this:
¹¹ Has a nation ever exchanged
　its gods?
　(but they were not gods!)
Yet My people have exchanged
　their Glory
for useless idols.
¹² Be horrified at this, heavens;
be shocked and utterly appalled.
　　This is the LORD's declaration.

¹³ For My people have committed
　a double evil:
They have abandoned Me,
　the fountain of living water,
and dug cisterns for themselves,
　cracked cisterns that cannot
　hold water.

¹⁴ Is Israel a slave?
Was he born into slavery?
Why else has he become a prey?
¹⁵ The young lions have roared
　at him;
they have roared loudly.
They have laid waste his land.
His cities are in ruins,
　without inhabitants.
¹⁶ The men of Memphis
　and Tahpanhes
have also broken your skull.
¹⁷ Have you not brought this
　on yourself
by abandoning the LORD your God
while He was leading you
　along the way?
¹⁸ Now what will you gain
by traveling along the way
　to Egypt
to drink the waters of the Nile?

What will you gain
by traveling along the way
　to Assyria
to drink the waters
　of the Euphrates?
¹⁹ Your own evil will discipline you;
your own apostasies
　will reprimand you.
Think it over and see how evil
　and bitter it is
for you to abandon the LORD
　your God
and to have no fear of Me.
　　This is the declaration
　　of the Lord GOD of Hosts.

²⁰ For long ago I broke your yoke;
I tore off your fetters.
You insisted: I will not serve!
On every high hill
and under every leafy tree
you lie down like a prostitute.

²¹ I planted you, a choice vine
from the very best seed.
How then could you turn into
a degenerate, foreign vine?

²² Even if you wash with lye
and use a great amount of soap,
the stain of your guilt is still
　in front of Me.
　　This is the Lord GOD's declaration.
²³ How can you protest:
　I am not defiled;
I have not followed the Baals?
Look at your behavior
　in the valley;
acknowledge what you have done.
You are a swift young camel
twisting and turning on her way,
²⁴ a wild donkey at home
　in the wilderness.
She sniffs the wind in the heat
　of her desire.
Who can control her passion?
All who look for her will not
　become tired;
they will find her
　in her mating season.
²⁵ Keep your feet from going bare
and your throat from thirst.
But you say: It's hopeless;
I love strangers,

and I will continue
to follow them.

26 Like the shame of a thief
when he is caught,
so the house of Israel has been
put to shame.
They, their kings, their officials,
their priests, and their prophets
27 say to a tree: You are my father,
and to a stone: You gave birth
to me.
For they have turned their back
to Me
and not their face,
but in their time of disaster
they beg:
Rise up and save us!
28 But where are your gods
you made for yourself?
Let them rise up and save you
in your time of disaster
if they can,
for your gods are as numerous
as your cities, Judah.

29 Why do you bring a case
against Me?
All of you have rebelled
against Me.
This is the LORD's declaration.
30 I have struck down your children
in vain;
they would not accept discipline.
Your own sword has devoured
your prophets
like a ravaging lion.
31 Evil generation,
pay attention to the word
of the LORD!
Have I been a wilderness to Israel
or a land of dense darkness?
Why do My people claim:
We will go where we want;
we will no longer come to You?
32 Can a young woman forget
her jewelry
or a bride her wedding sash?
Yet My people have forgotten Me
for countless days.
33 How skillfully you pursue love;
you also teach evil women
your ways.
34 Moreover, your skirts are stained

with the blood
of the innocent poor.
You did not catch them breaking
and entering.
But in spite of all these things
35 you claim: I am innocent.
His anger is sure to turn away
from me.
But I will certainly judge you
because you have said: I have
not sinned.
36 How unstable you are,
constantly changing your way!
You will be put to shame by Egypt
just as you were put to shame
by Assyria.
37 Moreover, you will be led out
from here
with your hands on your head
since the LORD has rejected
those you trust;
you will not succeed even with
their help.

PSALM 119:12-16

12 LORD, may You be praised;
teach me Your statutes.
13 With my lips I proclaim
all the judgments from Your mouth.
14 I rejoice in the way revealed by
Your decrees
as much as in all riches.
15 I will meditate on Your precepts
and think about Your ways.
16 I will delight in Your statutes;
I will not forget Your word.

PROVERBS 24:23-25

23 These sayings also belong to the
wise:

It is not good to show partiality in
judgment.
24 Whoever says to the guilty, "You
are innocent"—
people will curse him, and tribes
will denounce him;
25 but it will go well with those who
convict the guilty,
and a generous blessing will come
to them.

COLOSSIANS 1:1-20

1 Paul, an apostle of Christ Jesus by God's will, and Timothy our brother:
² To the saints and faithful brothers in Christ in Colossae.

Grace to you and peace from God our Father.

³ We always thank God, the Father of our Lord Jesus Christ, when we pray for you, ⁴ for we have heard of your faith in Christ Jesus and of the love you have for all the saints ⁵ because of the hope reserved for you in heaven. You have already heard about this hope in the message of truth, ⁶ the gospel that has come to you. It is bearing fruit and growing all over the world, just as it has among you since the day you heard it and recognized God's grace in the truth. ⁷ You learned this from Epaphras, our much loved fellow slave. He is a faithful minister of the Messiah on your behalf, ⁸ and he has told us about your love in the Spirit.

⁹ For this reason also, since the day we heard this, we haven't stopped praying for you. We are asking that you may be filled with the knowledge of His will in all wisdom and spiritual understanding, ¹⁰ so that you may walk worthy of the Lord, fully pleasing to Him, bearing fruit in every good work and growing in the knowledge of God. ¹¹ May you be strengthened with all power, according to His glorious might, for all endurance and patience, with joy ¹² giving thanks to the Father, who has enabled you to share in the saints' inheritance in the light. ¹³ He has rescued us from the domain of darkness and transferred us into the kingdom of the Son He loves, ¹⁴ in whom we have redemption, the forgiveness of sins.

¹⁵ He is the image
　of the invisible God,
the firstborn over all creation;
¹⁶ because by Him everything
　was created,
in heaven and on earth, the visible
　and the invisible,
whether thrones or dominions
　or rulers or authorities—
all things have been created
　through Him and for Him.
¹⁷ He is before all things,
　and by Him all things
　hold together.
¹⁸ He is also the head of the body,
　the church;
He is the beginning, the firstborn
　from the dead,
so that He might come to have
　first place in everything.
¹⁹ For God was pleased to have
　all His fullness dwell in Him,
²⁰ and through Him to reconcile
　everything to Himself
by making peace
　through the blood
　of His cross—
whether things on earth or things
　in heaven.

Wrong Places

My people have committed a double evil: They have abandoned Me,
the fountain of living water, and dug . . . cracked cisterns
that cannot hold water.

—JEREMIAH 2:13

One of the major problems with which we are all confronted is that we have at the core of our being a deep thirst for God, which makes us entirely dependent on Him for satisfaction. Our sinful human nature resents this, because it dislikes the feeling of helplessness that such dependence brings; it prefers to have a hand in bringing about its own satisfaction.

This terrible tendency of the human heart to try to satisfy its own thirst independently of God is brought out clearly in the passage before us today. The Prophet Jeremiah indicts Israel—the people of God—for depending on "cracked cisterns" in their efforts to quench their spiritual thirst (cisterns which they themselves made but which can hold no water).

Note the two observations our text for today suggests. First, the people were thirsty, and second, they moved in the wrong direction to satisfy their thirst.

God said it was as if they walked right past the clear waters He provided and chose instead to dig their own well. They wanted to run their own lives and refused to come to God, allowing Him to quench their deep thirst. This stubborn commitment to independence is responsible more than anything else for preventing us from having feet like "hinds' feet."

Prayer

Gracious Father, I see that the problem You had with the nation of Israel is my problem, too. For far too often I try to dig my own well. You are searching deeply into my life. Help me not to evade or avoid any issue. In Jesus' name. Amen.

Further Study

Jdg 17:1-6; 21:25; Pr 28:26; 1 Co 10:12
How does the book of Judges sum up the human heart?
What was Paul's admonition to the Corinthians?

OCTOBER 15

JEREMIAH 3:1–4:31

3 If a man divorces his wife
and she leaves him
to marry another,
can he ever return to her?
Wouldn't such a land become
totally defiled?
But you!
You have played the prostitute
with many partners—
can you return to Me?
This is the LORD's declaration.

2 Look to the barren heights
and see.
Where have you not been immoral?
You sat waiting for them
beside the highways
like a nomad in the desert.
You have defiled the land
with your prostitution
and wickedness.
3 This is why the showers
haven't come—
why there has been
no spring rain.

You have the brazen look
of a prostitute
and refuse to be ashamed.
⁴ Have you not lately called Me:
My Father,
my youthful companion?
⁵ Will He bear a grudge forever?
Will He be endlessly infuriated?
This is what you have spoken
and done,
the evil you are capable of.

⁶ In the days of King Josiah the LORD asked me, "Have you seen what unfaithful Israel has done? She has ascended every high hill and gone under every green tree to prostitute herself there. ⁷ I thought: After she has done all these things, she will return to Me. But she didn't return, and her treacherous sister Judah saw it. ⁸ I observed that it was because unfaithful Israel had committed adultery that I had sent her away and had given her a certificate of divorce. Nevertheless, her treacherous sister Judah was not afraid but also went and prostituted herself. ⁹ Indifferent to her prostitution, she defiled the land and committed adultery with stone and tree. ¹⁰ Yet in spite of all this, her treacherous sister Judah didn't return to Me with all her heart—only in pretense."
This is the LORD's declaration.

¹¹ The LORD announced to me, "Unfaithful Israel has shown herself more righteous than treacherous Judah. ¹² Go, proclaim these words to the north, and say:

Return, unfaithful Israel.
This is the LORD's declaration.
I will not look on you with anger,
for I am unfailing in My love.
This is the LORD's declaration.
I will not be angry forever.
¹³ Only acknowledge your guilt—
you have rebelled against the LORD
your God.
You have scattered your favors
to strangers
under every green tree
and have not obeyed My voice.
This is the LORD's declaration.

¹⁴ "Return, you faithless children"—this is the LORD's declaration—"for I am your master, and I will take you, one from a city and two from a family, and I will bring you to Zion. ¹⁵ I will give you shepherds who are loyal to Me, and they will shepherd you with knowledge and skill. ¹⁶ When you multiply and increase in the land, in those days"—the LORD's declaration—"no one will say any longer: The ark of the LORD's covenant. It will never come to mind, and no one will remember or miss it. It will never again be made. ¹⁷ At that time Jerusalem will be called, The LORD's Throne, and all the nations will be gathered to it, to the name of the LORD in Jerusalem. They will cease to follow the stubbornness of their evil hearts. ¹⁸ In those days the house of Judah will join with the house of Israel, and they will come together from the land of the north to the land I have given your ancestors to inherit."

¹⁹   I thought: How I long to make you
My sons
and give you a desirable land,
the most beautiful inheritance
of all the nations.
I thought: You will call Me,
my Father,
and never turn away from Me.
²⁰   However, as a woman may betray
her lover,
so you have betrayed Me,
house of Israel.
This is the LORD's declaration.

²¹   A sound is heard
on the barren heights,
the children of Israel weeping
and begging for mercy,
for they have perverted their way;
they have forgotten the LORD
their God.
²²   Return, you faithless children.
I will heal your unfaithfulness.
"Here we are, coming to You,
for You are the LORD our God.
²³   Surely, falsehood comes
from the hills,
commotion from the mountains,
but the salvation of Israel

is only in the LORD our God.
²⁴ From the time of our youth
the shameful one has consumed
what our fathers
have worked for—
their flocks and their herds,
their sons and their daughters.
²⁵ Let us lie down in our shame;
let our disgrace cover us.
We have sinned against the LORD
our God,
both we and our fathers,
from the time of our youth
even to this day.
We have not obeyed the voice
of the LORD our God."

4 If you return, Israel—
this is the LORD's declaration—
if you return to Me,
if you remove
your detestable idols
from My presence
and do not waver,
² if you swear, As the LORD lives,
in truth, in justice,
and in righteousness,
then the nations will be blessed
by Him
and will pride themselves in Him.
³ For this is what the LORD says to the men of Judah and Jerusalem:

Break up the unplowed ground;
do not sow among the thorns.
⁴ Circumcise yourselves
to the LORD;
remove the foreskin
of your hearts,
men of Judah and residents
of Jerusalem.
Otherwise, My wrath
will break out like fire
and burn with no one
to extinguish it
because of your evil deeds.

⁵ Declare in Judah, proclaim in Jerusalem, and say:

Blow the ram's horn
throughout the land.
Cry out loudly and say:
Assemble yourselves,

and let's flee
to the fortified cities.
⁶ Lift up a signal flag toward Zion.
Run for cover! Don't stand still!
For I am bringing disaster
from the north—
a great destruction.
⁷ A lion has gone up
from his thicket;
a destroyer of nations has set out.
He has left his lair
to make your land a waste.
Your cities will be reduced
to uninhabited ruins.
⁸ Because of this, put on sackcloth;
mourn and wail,
for the LORD's burning anger
has not turned away from us.

⁹ "On that day"—this is the LORD's declaration—"the king and the officials will lose their courage. The priests will tremble in fear, and the prophets will be scared speechless."

¹⁰ I said, "Oh no, Lord GOD, You have certainly deceived this people and Jerusalem, by announcing, 'You will have peace,' while a sword is at our throats."

¹¹ At that time it will be said to this people and to Jerusalem, "A searing wind blows from the barren heights in the wilderness on the way to My dear people. It comes not to winnow or to sift; ¹² a wind too strong for this comes at My call. Now I will also pronounce judgments against them."

¹³ Look, he advances like clouds;
his chariots are like a storm.
His horses are swifter than eagles.
Woe to us, for we are ruined!
¹⁴ Wash the evil from your heart,
Jerusalem,
so that you will be delivered.
How long will you harbor
malicious thoughts within you?
¹⁵ For a voice announces from Dan,
proclaiming malice
from Mount Ephraim.
¹⁶ Warn the nations: Look!
Proclaim to Jerusalem:
Those who besiege are coming
from a distant land;
they raise their voices

against the cities of Judah.

17 They have her surrounded
like those who guard a field,
because she has rebelled
against Me.
This is the LORD's declaration.

18 Your way of life and your actions
have brought this on you.
This is your punishment. It is
very bitter,
because it has reached your heart!

19 My anguish, my anguish! I writhe
in agony!
Oh, the pain in my heart!
My heart pounds;
I cannot be silent.
For you, my soul,
have heard the sound
of the ram's horn—
the shout of battle.

20 Disaster after disaster is reported,
for the whole land is destroyed.
Suddenly my tents are destroyed,
my tent curtains, in a moment.

21 How long must I see
the signal flag
and hear the sound
of the ram's horn?

22 For My people are fools;
they do not know Me.
They are foolish children,
without understanding.
They are skilled in doing
what is evil,
but they do not know how to do
what is good.

23 I looked at the earth,
and it was formless and empty.
I looked to the heavens,
and their light was gone.

24 I looked at the mountains,
and they were quaking;
all the hills shook.

25 I looked, and no man was left;
all the birds of the sky had fled.

26 I looked, and the fertile field was
a wilderness.
All its cities were torn down
because of the LORD
and His burning anger.

27 For this is what the LORD says:

The whole land will be
a desolation,
but I will not finish it off.

28 Because of this, the earth
will mourn;
the skies above will grow dark.
I have spoken; I have planned,
and I will not relent or turn back
from it.

29 Every city flees
at the sound of the horseman
and the archer.
They enter the thickets
and climb among the rocks.
Every city is abandoned;
no inhabitant is left.

30 And you devastated one, what are
you doing
that you dress yourself in scarlet,
that you adorn yourself
with gold jewelry,
that you enlarge your eyes
with paint?
You beautify yourself for nothing.
Your lovers reject you;
they want to take your life.

31 I hear a cry like a woman in labor,
a cry of anguish like one bearing
her first child.
The cry of Daughter Zion
gasping for breath,
stretching out her hands:
Woe is me, for my life is weary
because of the murderers!

PSALM 119:17-20

17 Deal generously with Your servant
so that I might live;
then I will keep Your word.

18 Open my eyes so that I may see
wonderful things in Your law.

19 I am a stranger on earth;
do not hide Your commands from
me.

20 I am continually overcome
by longing for Your judgments.

PROVERBS 24:26-27

26 He who gives an honest answer
gives a kiss on the lips.

27 Complete your outdoor work, and
 prepare your field;
 afterwards, build your house.

COLOSSIANS 1:21–2:15

21 And you were once alienated and
hostile in mind because of your evil actions. 22 But now He has reconciled you
by His physical body through His death,
to present you holy, faultless, and
blameless before Him— 23 if indeed you
remain grounded and steadfast in the
faith, and are not shifted away from the
hope of the gospel that you heard. This
gospel has been proclaimed in all creation under heaven, and I, Paul, have
become a minister of it.

24 Now I rejoice in my sufferings for
you, and I am completing in my flesh
what is lacking in Christ's afflictions for
His body, that is, the church. 25 I have
become its minister, according to God's
administration that was given to me for
you, to make God's message fully
known, 26 the mystery hidden for ages
and generations but now revealed to His
saints. 27 God wanted to make known to
those among the Gentiles the glorious
wealth of this mystery, which is Christ
in you, the hope of glory. 28 We proclaim
Him, warning and teaching everyone
with all wisdom, so that we may present
everyone mature in Christ. 29 I labor for
this, striving with His strength that
works powerfully in me.

2 For I want you to know how great a
struggle I have for you, for those in
Laodicea, and for all who have not seen
me in person. 2 I want their hearts to be
encouraged and joined together in love,
so that they may have all the riches of

assured understanding, and have the
knowledge of God's mystery—Christ.
3 In Him all the treasures of wisdom and
knowledge are hidden.

4 I am saying this so that no one will
deceive you with persuasive arguments.
5 For I may be absent in body, but I am
with you in spirit, rejoicing to see your
good order and the strength of your
faith in Christ.

6 Therefore as you have received
Christ Jesus the Lord, walk in Him,
7 rooted and built up in Him and established in the faith, just as you were
taught, and overflowing with thankfulness.

8 Be careful that no one takes you captive through philosophy and empty deceit based on human tradition, based on
the elemental forces of the world, and
not based on Christ. 9 For in Him the entire fullness of God's nature dwells
bodily, 10 and you have been filled by
Him, who is the head over every ruler
and authority. 11 In Him you were also
circumcised with a circumcision not
done with hands, by putting off the
body of flesh, in the circumcision of the
Messiah. 12 Having been buried with
Him in baptism, you were also raised
with Him through faith in the working
of God, who raised Him from the dead.
13 And when you were dead in trespasses and in the uncircumcision of your
flesh, He made you alive with Him and
forgave us all our trespasses. 14 He
erased the certificate of debt, with its
obligations, that was against us and opposed to us, and has taken it out of the
way by nailing it to the cross. 15 He dis-
armed the rulers and authorities and
disgraced them publicly; He triumphed
over them by Him.

In the Right Direction

We proclaim Him, warning and teaching everyone with all wisdom,
so that we may present everyone mature in Christ.
—COLOSSIANS 1:28

In the Spirit-controlled life, self is still there, but now it is not self-centered but God-centered, and therefore, rhythmic and harmonious. "Perfect function," said a famous doctor, "is perfect health." The self functions perfectly and is, therefore, perfectly healthy; it is a self you can live with. The sex drive is still there, but now, being God-centered, it functions as God intended it to function. If one is married, then it can be expressed in a physical relationship, but if one is unmarried, then it can be sublimated and channeled into creativity in other directions. The herd instinct is still there, but now it is fastened on the kingdom of God, and one moves with the rest of the church toward the unity of the faith and of the Spirit.

The life of the Spirit is not one of asceticism but one of assertion. We get rid of unacceptable desires in the only way possible, by replacing them with higher desires. We get rid of self-centeredness by God-centeredness, through surrender. We get rid of sex domination by surrendering the drive to God and the controls He places upon it, so that sex serves us and makes us creative in the whole of life—not just within the physical relationship of marriage. We get rid of the herd dominance by surrender to God and, when surrendered, we love people more because we are no longer dominated or intimidated by them. The expulsive power of a new affection casts out "lower loves" by focusing them on higher objectives.

Prayer

Holy Spirit, I am beginning to learn that when You have control, everything is a perfect cosmos; when I have control, it is chaos. As life is for living, I want to live it to the brim. Help me not just to surrender, but to stay surrendered. Amen.

Further Study

Heb 6; Mt 5:48; 2 Co 13:11
What did Paul mean by "perfection"?
What was Paul's desire?

OCTOBER 16

JEREMIAH 5:1–6:21

5 Roam through the streets
of Jerusalem.
Look and take note;
search in her squares.
If you find a single person,
anyone who acts justly,
who seeks to be faithful,
then I will forgive her.
2 When they say,
"As the LORD lives,"
they are swearing falsely.
3 LORD, don't Your eyes look for
faithfulness?
You have struck them,
but they felt no pain.
You finished them off,
but they refused
to accept discipline.
They made their faces harder
than rock,
and they refused to return.

4 Then I thought:

They are just the poor;
they have played the fool.
For they don't understand the way
of the LORD,
the justice of their God.
5 I will go to the powerful
and speak to them.
Surely they know the way
of the LORD,
the justice of their God.
However, these also had broken
the yoke
and torn off the fetters.
6 Therefore, a lion from the forest
will strike them down.
A wolf from an arid plain
will ravage them.
A leopard keeps watch over
their cities.
Anyone who leaves them
will be torn to pieces

because their rebellious acts
are many,
their unfaithful deeds numerous.
7 Why should I forgive you?
Your children have abandoned Me
and sworn by those who are
not gods.
I satisfied their needs, yet they
committed adultery;
they gashed themselves
at the prostitute's house.
8 They are well-fed, eager stallions,
each neighing after
someone else's wife.
9 Should I not punish them
for these things?
This is the LORD's declaration.
Should I not avenge Myself
on such a nation as this?

10 Go up among
her vineyard terraces
and destroy them,
but do not finish them off.
Prune away her shoots,
for they do not belong
to the LORD.
11 They, the house of Israel
and the house of Judah,
have dealt very treacherously
with Me.
This is the LORD's declaration.
12 They have contradicted the LORD
and insisted, "It won't happen.
Harm won't come to us;
we won't see sword or famine."
13 The prophets become only wind,
for the LORD's word is not
in them.
This will in fact happen to them.

14 Therefore, this is what the Lord
GOD of Hosts says:

Because you have spoken
this word,

1234

I am going to make My words
become fire in your mouth.
These people are the wood,
and the fire will consume them.
¹⁵ I am about to bring a nation
from far away against you,
house of Israel.
This is the LORD's declaration.
It is an established nation,
an ancient nation,
a nation whose language
you do not know
and whose speech
you do not understand.
¹⁶ Their quiver is like an open grave;
they are all mighty warriors.
¹⁷ They will consume your harvest
and your food.
They will consume your sons
and your daughters.
They will consume your flocks
and your herds.
They will consume your vines
and your fig trees.
They will destroy with the sword
your fortified cities in which
you trust.

¹⁸ "But even in those days"—this is
the LORD's declaration—"I will not finish
you off. ¹⁹ When people ask: For what offense has the LORD our God done all
these things to us? You will respond to
them: Just as you abandoned Me and
served foreign gods in your land, so will
you serve strangers in a land that is not
yours.
²⁰ "Declare this in the house of Jacob;
proclaim it in Judah, saying:

²¹ Hear this,
you foolish and senseless people.
They have eyes, but they don't see.
They have ears,
but they don't hear.
²² Do you not fear Me?
This is the LORD's declaration.
Do you not tremble before Me,
the One who set the sand
as the boundary of the sea,
an enduring barrier that
it cannot cross?
The waves surge, but they
cannot prevail.

They roar but cannot pass over it.
²³ But these people have stubborn
and rebellious hearts.
They have turned aside
and have gone away.
²⁴ They have not said to themselves:
Let's fear the LORD our God,
who gives the rain, both early
and late, in its season,
who guarantees to us
the fixed weeks
of the harvest.
²⁵ Your guilty acts have diverted
these things from you.
Your sins have withheld My
bounty from you,
²⁶ for wicked men live
among My people.
They watch like fowlers
lying in wait.
They set a trap;
they catch men.
²⁷ Like a cage full of birds,
so their houses are full of deceit.
Therefore they have
grown powerful and rich.
²⁸ They have become fat and sleek.
They have also excelled
in evil matters.
They have not taken up cases,
such as the case of orphans,
so they might prosper,
and they have not defended
the rights of the needy.
²⁹ Should I not punish them
for these things?
This is the LORD's declaration.
Should I not avenge Myself
on such a nation as this?

³⁰ A horrible, terrible thing
has taken place in the land.
³¹ The prophets prophesy falsely,
and the priests rule
by their own authority.
My people love it like this.
But what will you do at the end
of it?

6 Run for cover, Benjaminites,
out of Jerusalem!
Sound the ram's horn in Tekoa;
raise a smoke signal over Beth-
haccherem,

for disaster threatens
    from the north,
even great destruction.
² Though she is beautiful
    and delicate,
I will destroy Daughter Zion.
³ Shepherds and their flocks
    will come against her;
they will pitch their tents
    all around her.
Each will pasture his own portion.
⁴ Set them apart for war against her;
rise up, let's attack at noon.
Woe to us, for the day is passing;
the evening shadows grow long.
⁵ Rise up, let's attack by night.
Let us destroy her fortresses."

⁶ For this is what the LORD of Hosts
says:

Cut down the trees;
raise a siege ramp
    against Jerusalem.
This city must be punished.
There is nothing but oppression
    within her.
⁷ As a well gushes out its water,
so she pours forth her evil.
Violence and destruction resound
    in her.
Sickness and wounds keep coming
    to My attention.
⁸ Be warned, Jerusalem,
or I will be torn away from you;
I will make you a desolation,
a land devoid of inhabitant.

⁹ This is what the LORD of Hosts says:

Glean as thoroughly as a vine
the remnant of Israel.
Pass your hand once more
    like a grape gatherer
over the branches.

¹⁰ Who can I speak to and give
    such a warning
that they will listen?
Look, their ear is uncircumcised,
so they cannot pay attention.
See, the word of the LORD
    has become contemptible
    to them—

they find no pleasure in it.
¹¹ But I am full of the LORD's wrath;
I am tired of holding it back.
Pour it out on the children
    in the street,
on the gang of young men as well.
For both husband and wife
    will be captured,
the old with the very old.
¹² Their houses will be turned over
    to others,
their fields and wives as well,
for I will stretch out My hand
against the residents of the land.
    This is the LORD's declaration.

¹³ For from the least to the greatest
    of them,
everyone is gaining profit unjustly.
From prophet to priest,
everyone deals falsely.
¹⁴ They have treated
    My people's brokenness
    superficially,
claiming: Peace, peace,
when there is no peace.
¹⁵ Were they ashamed
    when they acted
    so abhorrently?
They weren't at all ashamed.
They can no longer
    feel humiliation.
Therefore, they will fall
    among the fallen.
When I punish them,
    they will collapse,
says the LORD.

¹⁶ This is what the LORD says:

Stand by the roadways and look.
Ask about the ancient paths:
Which is the way to what is good?
Then take it
and find rest for yourselves.
But they protested: We won't!
¹⁷ I appointed watchmen over you
and said: Listen for the sound
    of the ram's horn.
But they protested:
    We won't listen!

¹⁸ Therefore listen, you nations
and you witnesses,

learn what the charge is
    against them.
¹⁹ Listen, earth!
I am about to bring disaster
    on these people,
the fruit of their own plotting,
for they have paid no attention
    to My word.
They have rejected My law.
²⁰ What use to Me is frankincense
        from Sheba
or sweet cane from a distant land?
Your burnt offerings
    are not acceptable;
your sacrifices do not please Me.
²¹ Therefore, this is what
        the LORD says:
I am going to place stumbling blocks
    before these people;
fathers and sons together
    will stumble over them;
friends and neighbors will also
    perish.

PSALM 119:21-24

²¹ You rebuke the proud, the accursed,
    who wander from Your commands.
²² Take insult and contempt away
        from me,
    for I have kept Your decrees.
²³ Though princes sit together
        speaking against me,
    Your servant will think about Your
        statutes;
²⁴ Your decrees are my delight
    and my counselors.

PROVERBS 24:28-29

²⁸ Don't testify against your neighbor
        without cause.
    Don't deceive with your lips.
²⁹ Don't say, "I'll do to him what he
        did to me;
    I'll repay the man for what he has
        done."

COLOSSIANS 2:16–3:17

¹⁶ Therefore don't let anyone judge
you in regard to food and drink or in the
matter of a festival or a new moon or

a sabbath day. ¹⁷ These are a shadow
of what was to come; the substance is
the Messiah. ¹⁸ Let no one disqualify
you, insisting on ascetic practices and
the worship of angels, claiming access
to a visionary realm and inflated without cause by his fleshly mind. ¹⁹ He
doesn't hold on to the head, from whom
the whole body, nourished and held together by its ligaments and tendons, develops with growth from God.

²⁰ If you died with Christ to the elemental forces of this world, why do you
live as if you still belonged to the world?
Why do you submit to regulations:
²¹ "Don't handle, don't taste, don't
touch"? ²² All these regulations refer to
what is destroyed by being used up;
they are human commands and doctrines. ²³ Although these have a reputation of wisdom by promoting ascetic
practices, humility, and severe treatment of the body, they are not of any
value against fleshly indulgence.

3 So if you have been raised with
the Messiah, seek what is above,
where the Messiah is, seated at the
right hand of God. ² Set your minds on
what is above, not on what is on the
earth. ³ For you have died, and your life
is hidden with the Messiah in God.
⁴ When the Messiah, who is your life, is
revealed, then you also will be revealed
with Him in glory.

⁵ Therefore, put to death whatever in
you is worldly: sexual immorality, impurity, lust, evil desire, and greed,
which is idolatry. ⁶ Because of these,
God's wrath comes on the disobedient,
⁷ and you once walked in these things
when you were living in them. ⁸ But
now you must also put away all the following: anger, wrath, malice, slander,
and filthy language from your mouth.
⁹ Do not lie to one another, since you
have put off the old man with his practices ¹⁰ and have put on the new man,
who is being renewed in knowledge according to the image of his Creator.
¹¹ Here there is not Greek and Jew, circumcision and uncircumcision, barbar-
ian, Scythian, slave and free; but Christ
is all and in all.

[12] Therefore, God's chosen ones, holy and loved, put on heartfelt compassion, kindness, humility, gentleness, and patience, [13] accepting one another and forgiving one another if anyone has a complaint against another. Just as the Lord has forgiven you, so also you must forgive. [14] Above all, put on love—the perfect bond of unity. [15] And let the peace of the Messiah, to which you were also called in one body, control your hearts. Be thankful. [16] Let the message about the Messiah dwell richly among you, teaching and admonishing one another in all wisdom, and singing psalms, hymns, and spiritual songs, with gratitude in your hearts to God. [17] And whatever you do, in word or in deed, do everything in the name of the Lord Jesus, giving thanks to God the Father through Him.

Patience and Kindness

God's chosen ones . . . put on . . . kindness . . . and patience.

—COLOSSIANS 3:12

The fourth fruit of the Spirit listed by Paul is patience. The King James Version uses the word "longsuffering." Someone has suggested that longsuffering is "love stretched out." It is so elastic and tough that it doesn't break up into impatience. It maintains a patient attitude amidst the flux of human events.

Patience, however, must not be confused with indifference. One group of people in ancient history—the Stoics—made indifference a virtue. Some people in the early centuries of the church tried to Christianize this characteristic, but it couldn't be done. A Christian is someone who cares. Because we care, we suffer, but in the midst of suffering, we discover the Spirit's enabling patience.

A woman, after finding Christ, went through a time of great persecution from her family. She said, "I have never been a patient woman, but since Christ and the Holy Spirit came into my life, He has turned me upside down and inside out. I always had to have the last word, but my last word is silence." Now, whenever she says something, her family listens, because she speaks out of the depth of silence. *The Amplified Bible* presents Galatians 5:22 as, "But the fruit of the . . . Spirit [the work which His presence within accomplishes] is . . . patience."

The next fruit is kindness. This may seem a very ordinary virtue, but yet, without it, the other virtues are incomplete. It is not by chance that this virtue is in the middle of the nine, for it puts flavor in all the others.

Prayer

Father, I want all the other virtues to be flavored with kindness, so that the spirit of kindness pervades everything I do and everything I am. For Jesus' sake. Amen.

Further Study

1 Th 1; Rm 5:3; 12:12; Lk 21:19; Jms 1:4
How did Paul relate patience to tribulation?
In what did Paul rejoice?

OCTOBER 17

JEREMIAH 6:22–8:13

²² This is what the LORD says:

Look, an army is coming
    from a northern land;
a great nation will be awakened
from the remote regions
    of the earth.
²³ They grasp bow and javelin.
They are cruel and show no mercy.
Their voice roars like the sea,
and they ride on horses,
lined up like men
    in battle formation
against you, Daughter Zion.

²⁴ We have heard about it,
and we are discouraged.
Distress has seized us—
pain like a woman in labor.
²⁵ Don't go out to the fields;
don't walk on the road.
For the enemy has a sword;
terror is on every side.

²⁶ My dear people, dress yourselves
    in sackcloth
and roll in the dust.
Mourn as you would for
    an only son,
a bitter lament,
for suddenly the destroyer
    will come on us.

²⁷ I have appointed you to be
    an assayer among My people—

a refiner—
so you may know and assay
    their way of life.
²⁸ All are stubborn rebels
spreading slander.
They are bronze and iron;
all of them are corrupt.
²⁹ The bellows blow,
blasting the lead with fire.
The refining is completely in vain;
the evil ones are not
    separated out.
³⁰ They are called rejected silver,
for the LORD has rejected them.

7 This is the word that came to Jeremiah from the LORD: ² "Stand in the gate of the house of the LORD and there call out this word: Hear the word of the LORD, all you people of Judah who enter through these gates to worship the LORD.

³ "This is what the LORD of Hosts, the God of Israel, says: Correct your ways and your deeds, and I will allow you to live in this place. ⁴ Do not trust deceitful words, chanting: This is the temple of the LORD, the temple of the LORD, the temple of the LORD. ⁵ Instead, if you really change your ways and your actions, if you act justly toward one another, ⁶ if you no longer oppress the alien, the fatherless, and the widow and no longer shed innocent blood in this place or follow other gods, bringing harm on yourselves, ⁷ I will allow you to live in this place, the land I gave to your ancestors

forever and ever. ⁸ But look, you keep trusting in deceitful words that cannot help.

⁹ "Do you steal, murder, commit adultery, swear falsely, burn incense to Baal, and follow other gods that you have not known? ¹⁰ Then do you come and stand before Me in this house called by My name and insist: We are safe? As a result, you are free to continue doing all these detestable acts! ¹¹ Has this house, which is called by My name, become a den of robbers in your view? Yes, I too have seen it."

This is the LORD's declaration.

¹² "But return to My place that was at Shiloh, where I made My name dwell at first. See what I did to it because of the evil of My people Israel. ¹³ Now, because you have done all these things"— this is the LORD's declaration—"and because I have spoken to you time and time again but you wouldn't listen, and I have called to you, but you wouldn't answer, ¹⁴ what I did to Shiloh I will do to the house that is called by My name—the house in which you trust—the place that I gave you and your ancestors. ¹⁵ I will drive you from My presence, just as I drove out all of your brothers, all the descendants of Ephraim.

¹⁶ "As for you, do not pray for these people. Do not offer a cry or a prayer on their behalf, and do not beg Me, for I will not listen to you. ¹⁷ Don't you see how they behave in the cities of Judah and in the streets of Jerusalem? ¹⁸ The sons gather wood, the fathers light the fire, and the women knead dough to make cakes for the queen of heaven, and they pour out drink offerings to other gods so that they provoke Me to anger. ¹⁹ But are they really provoking Me?" This is the LORD's declaration. "Isn't it they themselves being provoked to disgrace?"

²⁰ Therefore, this is what the Lord GOD says: "Look, My anger—My burning wrath—is about to be poured out on this place, on man and beast, on the tree of the field, and on the fruit of the ground. My wrath will burn and not be quenched."

²¹ This is what the LORD of Hosts, the God of Israel, says: "Add your burnt offerings to your other sacrifices, and eat the meat yourselves, ²² for when I brought your ancestors out of the land of Egypt, I did not speak with them or command them concerning burnt offering and sacrifice. ²³ However, I did give them this command: Obey Me, and then I will be your God, and you will be My people. You must walk in every way I command you so that it may go well with you." ²⁴ Yet they didn't listen or pay attention but walked according to their own advice and according to their own stubborn, evil heart. They went backward and not forward. ²⁵ Since the day your ancestors came out of the land of Egypt until this day, I have sent all My servants the prophets to you time and time again. ²⁶ However, they wouldn't listen to Me or pay attention but became obstinate; they did more evil than their ancestors.

²⁷ "When you speak all these things to them, they will not listen to you. When you call to them, they will not answer you. ²⁸ You must therefore declare to them: This is the nation that would not listen to the voice of the LORD their God and would not accept discipline. Truth has perished—it has disappeared from their mouths. ²⁹ Cut off the hair of your sacred vow and throw it away. Raise up a dirge on the barren heights, for the LORD has rejected and abandoned the generation under His wrath.

³⁰ "For the Judeans have done what is evil in My sight." This is the LORD's declaration. "They have set up their detestable things in the house that is called by My name and defiled it. ³¹ They have built the high places of Topheth in the Valley of Hinnom in order to burn their sons and daughters in the fire, a thing I did not command; I never entertained the thought.

³² "Therefore, take note! Days are coming"—the LORD's declaration—"when this place will no longer be called Topheth and the Valley of Hinnom, but the Valley of Slaughter. Topheth will become a cemetery, because there will be no other burial

place. ³³ The corpses of these people will become food for the birds of the sky and for the wild animals of the land, with no one to scare them off. ³⁴ I will remove from the cities of Judah and the streets of Jerusalem the sound of joy and gladness and the voices of the bridegroom and the bride, for the land will become a desolate waste.

8 "At that time"—this is the LORD's declaration—"the bones of the kings of Judah, the bones of her officials, the bones of the priests, the bones of the prophets, and the bones of the residents of Jerusalem will be brought out of their graves. ² They will be exposed to the sun, the moon, and the whole heavenly host, which they have loved, served, followed, pursued, and worshiped. Their bones will not be collected and buried but will become like manure on the surface of the soil. ³ Death will be chosen over life by all the survivors of this evil family, those who remain wherever I have banished them." This is the declaration of the LORD of Hosts.

⁴ You are to say to them: This is what the LORD says:

Do people fall and not
    get up again?
If they turn away, do they
    not return?
⁵ Why have these people
    turned away?
Why is Jerusalem always
    turning away?
They take hold of deceit;
    they refuse to return.
⁶ I have paid careful attention.
They do not speak what is right.
No one regrets his evil,
    asking: What have I done?
Everyone has stayed his course
    like a horse rushing into battle.
⁷ Even the stork in the sky
    knows her seasons.
The turtledove, swallow,
    and crane
are aware of their migration,
but My people do not know
    the requirements of the LORD.

⁸ How can you claim: We are wise;
    the law of the LORD is with us?
In fact, the lying pen of scribes
    has produced falsehood.
⁹ The wise will be put to shame;
    they will be dismayed and snared.
They have rejected the word
    of the LORD,
so what wisdom do they
    really have?
¹⁰ Therefore, I will give their wives
    to other men,
their fields to new occupants,
for from the least to the greatest,
    everyone is gaining profit unjustly.
From prophet to priest,
    everyone deals falsely.
¹¹ They have treated superficially
    the brokenness
of My dear people,
    claiming: Peace, peace,
    when there is no peace.
¹² Were they ashamed
    when they acted
    so abhorrently?
They weren't at all ashamed.
They can no longer
    feel humiliation.
Therefore, they will fall
    among the fallen.
When I punish them,
    they will collapse,
says the LORD.

¹³ I will gather them and bring them
    to an end.
    This is the LORD's declaration.
There will be no grapes
    on the vine,
no figs on the fig tree,
and even the leaf will wither.
Whatever I have given them
    will be lost to them.

....

PSALM 119:25-27

²⁵ My life is down in the dust;
    give me life through Your word.
²⁶ I told You about my life, and You
    listened to me;
    teach me Your statutes.
²⁷ Help me understand the meaning
    of Your precepts

so that I can meditate on Your wonders.

*P*ROVERBS 24:30-34

30 I went by the field of a slacker
and by the vineyard of a man
lacking sense.
31 Thistles had come up everywhere,
weeds covered the ground,
and the stone wall was ruined.
32 I saw, and took it to heart;
I looked, and received instruction:
33 a little sleep, a little slumber,
a little folding of the arms to rest,
34 and your poverty will come like a
robber,
your need, like a bandit.

*C*OLOSSIANS 3:18–4:18

18 Wives, be submissive to your husbands, as is fitting in the Lord.
19 Husbands, love your wives and don't become bitter against them.
20 Children, obey your parents in everything, for this is pleasing in the Lord.
21 Fathers, do not exasperate your children, so they won't become discouraged.
22 Slaves, obey your human masters in everything; don't work only while being watched, in order to please men, but work wholeheartedly, fearing the Lord.
23 Whatever you do, do it enthusiastically, as something done for the Lord and not for men, 24 knowing that you will receive the reward of an inheritance from the Lord— you serve the Lord Christ. 25 For the wrongdoer will be paid back for whatever wrong he has done, and there is no favoritism.

4 Masters, supply your slaves with what is right and fair, since you know that you too have a Master in heaven.
2 Devote yourselves to prayer; stay alert in it with thanksgiving. 3 At the same time, pray also for us that God may open a door to us for the message, to speak the mystery of the Messiah— for which I am in prison— 4 so that I may reveal it as I am required to speak. 5 Walk in wisdom toward outsiders, making the most of the time. 6 Your speech should always be gracious, seasoned with salt, so that you may know how you should answer each person.
7 Tychicus, a loved brother, a faithful servant, and a fellow slave in the Lord, will tell you all the news about me. 8 I have sent him to you for this very purpose, so that you may know how we are, and so that he may encourage your hearts. 9 He is with Onesimus, a faithful and loved brother, who is one of you. They will tell you about everything here.
10 Aristarchus, my fellow prisoner, greets you, as does Mark, Barnabas' cousin (concerning whom you have received instructions: if he comes to you, welcome him), 11 and so does Jesus who is called Justus. These alone of the circumcision are my co-workers for the kingdom of God, and they have been a comfort to me. 12 Epaphras, who is one of you, a slave of Christ Jesus, greets you. He is always contending for you in his prayers, so that you can stand mature and fully assured in everything God wills. 13 For I testify about him that he works hard for you, for those in Laodicea, and for those in Hierapolis. 14 Luke, the loved physician, and Demas greet you. 15 Give my greetings to the brothers in Laodicea, and to Nympha and the church in her house. 16 And when this letter has been read among you, have it read also in the church of the Laodiceans; and see that you also read the letter from Laodicea. 17 And tell Archippus, "Pay attention to the ministry you have received in the Lord, so that you can accomplish it."
18 This greeting is in my own hand— Paul. Remember my imprisonment. Grace be with you.

Various Forms of Prayer

Devote yourselves to prayer; stay alert in it with thanksgiving.

—COLOSSIANS 4:2

Today we ask ourselves: what does it mean to "pray always with all prayer and supplication"? The phrase "praying always" presents no difficulty; quite clearly, this means praying as often as possible, regularly and constantly. But what does it mean to pray "with all prayer and supplication"? Paul means, I believe, that we should pray with all forms or kinds of prayer.

You see, there are many different forms of prayer that are available to us. First, there is verbal prayer when we present our prayer to God in carefully chosen words and phrases. Second, there is silent prayer, when no words cross our lips, but prayer flows directly from our hearts. Third, there is ejaculatory prayer, when we express sounds rather than words, as when we sigh or groan in prayer. Then there is public prayer, common prayer, or "praying together"—or, as some prefer to call it, "praying in concert." So praying with "all prayer" means using every form of prayer available to us, praying in every way and manner we can. We are to be at it always and in endless ways.

But there is a certain form of prayer to which the apostle refers which deserves our closer examination—the prayer of "supplication" or "petition"—when we pray with regard to special requests and needs. We must not overlook this, for it is so easy to be caught up in adoration and praise that we neglect to focus our prayers on the various needs that arise from time to time, not only in our own lives, but also in the lives of others. This, too, is a necessary kind of prayer.

Prayer

Father, help me to see the senselessness of trying to muddle through life in my own strength when You have made Your power and resources available to me through prayer. Help me grow in prayer. In Jesus' name. Amen.

Further Study

Mt 7:1-12; Ac 1:14; 4:24; 12:12; 21:5
What is evident about the early church?
How does Jesus relate fatherhood to prayer?

OCTOBER 18

JEREMIAH 8:14–10:17

14 Why are we just sitting here?
Gather together; let us enter
the fortified cities
and there suffer our fate,
for the LORD our God
has condemned us.
He has given us poisoned water
to drink,
because we have sinned
against the LORD.
15 We hoped for peace,
but there was nothing good;
for a time of healing,
but there was only terror.

16 From Dan is heard
the snorting of horses.
At the sound of the neighing
of mighty steeds,
the whole land quakes.
They come to devour the land
and everything in it,
the city and all its residents.
17 Indeed, I am about to send snakes
among you,
poisonous vipers that cannot
be charmed.
They will bite you.
This is the LORD's declaration.

18 My joy has flown away;
grief has settled on me.
My heart is sick.
19 Listen—the cry of my dear people
from a far away land:
Is the LORD no longer in Zion,
her King not in her midst?
Why have they provoked Me
to anger
with their graven images,
with their worthless foreign idols?
20 Harvest has passed,
summer has ended,
but we have not been saved.
21 I am broken by the brokenness
of my dear people.
I mourn; horror has taken hold
of me.
22 Is there no balm in Gilead?
Is there no physician there?
So why has the healing of my dear
people
not come about?

9 If my head were water,
my eyes a fountain of tears,
I would weep day and night
over the slain of my dear people.
2 If only I had a traveler's
lodging place
in the wilderness,
I would abandon my people
and depart from them,
for they are all adulterers,
a solemn assembly
of treacherous people.

3 They bent their tongues like
their bows;
lies and not faithfulness prevail
in the land,
for they proceed from one evil
to another,
and they do not take Me
into account.
This is the LORD's declaration.

4 Everyone has to be on guard
against his friend.
Don't trust any brother,
for every brother will
certainly deceive,
and every friend spread slander.
5 Each one betrays his friend;
no one tells the truth.
They have taught their tongues
to speak lies;
they wear themselves out
doing wrong.
6 You live in a world of deception.
In their deception they refuse
to know Me.
This is the LORD's declaration.

⁷ Therefore, this is what the LORD of Hosts says:

> I am about to refine them
>   and test them,
> for what else can I do
> because of My dear people?
> ⁸ Their tongues are deadly arrows—
> they speak deception.
> With his mouth
> a man speaks peaceably
>   with his friend,
> but inwardly he sets up an ambush.
> ⁹ Should I not punish them
>   for these things?
> This is the LORD's declaration.
> Should I not take My revenge
> against a nation such as this?

> ¹⁰ I will raise weeping and a lament
> over the mountains,
> a dirge over the wilderness
>   grazing land,
> for they have been so scorched
> that no one passes through.
> The sound of cattle is
>   no longer heard.
> From the birds of the sky
> to the animals,
> everything has fled—they have
>   gone away.
> ¹¹ I will make Jerusalem a heap
>   of rubble,
> a jackals' den.
> I will make the cities of Judah
>   a desolation,
> an uninhabited place.

¹² Who is the man wise enough to understand this? Who has the LORD spoken to, that he may explain it? Why is the land destroyed and scorched like a wilderness, so no one can pass through? ¹³ The LORD said, "It is because they abandoned My law I set in front of them and did not obey My voice or walk according to it. ¹⁴ Instead, they followed the stubbornness of their hearts and the Baals, as their fathers taught them." ¹⁵ Therefore, this is what the LORD of Hosts, the God of Israel, says: "I am about to feed this people wormwood and give them poisonous waters to drink. ¹⁶ I will scatter them among nations that they and their fathers have not known. I will send a sword after them until I have finished them off." ¹⁷ This is what the LORD of Hosts says:

> Consider, and summon
>   the women who mourn;
> send for the skillful women.
> ¹⁸ Let them come quickly to raise
>   a lament over us
> so that our eyes may overflow
>   with tears,
> our eyelids soaked with weeping.
> ¹⁹ For a sound of lamentation
>   is heard from Zion:
> How devastated we are.
> We are greatly ashamed,
> for we have abandoned the land;
> our dwellings have been
>   torn down.

> ²⁰ Now hear the word of the LORD,
>   you women.
> Pay attention to the word
>   of His mouth.
> Teach your daughters a lament
> and one another a dirge,
> ²¹ for Death has climbed
>   through our windows;
> it has entered our fortresses,
> cutting off children
>   from the streets,
> young men from the squares.
> ²² Speak as follows:
> This is what the LORD says:

> Human corpses will fall
> like manure on the surface
>   of the field,
> like newly cut grain
>   after the reaper
> with no one to gather it.
> ²³ This is what the LORD says:

> The wise must not boast
>   in his wisdom;
> the mighty must not boast
>   in his might;
> the rich must not boast
>   in his riches.
> ²⁴ But the one who boasts
>   should boast in this,
> that he understands
>   and knows Me—

that I am the LORD,
showing faithful love,
justice, and righteousness
on the earth,
for I delight in these things.
This is the LORD's declaration.

25 "The days are coming"—the LORD's declaration—"when I will punish all the circumcised yet uncircumcised: 26 Egypt, Judah, Edom, the Ammonites, Moab, all those who clip the hair on their temples and reside in the wilderness. All these nations are uncircumcised, and the whole house of Israel is uncircumcised in heart."

10

Hear the word that the LORD has spoken to you, house of Israel. 2 This is what the LORD says:

Do not learn the way of the nations
or be terrified by signs
in the heavens,
although the nations are terrified
by them,
3 for the customs of the peoples
are worthless.
Someone cuts down a tree
from the forest;
it is worked by the hands
of a craftsman with a chisel.
4 He decorates it with silver
and gold.
It is fastened with hammer
and nails,
so it won't totter.
5 Like scarecrows
in a cucumber patch,
their idols cannot speak.
They must be carried because
they cannot walk.
Do not fear them for they can do
no harm—
and they cannot do any good.

6 LORD, there is no one like You.
You are great;
Your name is great in power.
7 Who should not fear You,
King of the nations?
It is what You deserve.
For among all the wise people
of the nations

and among all their kingdoms,
there is no one like You.
8 They are both senseless
and foolish,
instructed by worthless idols
made of wood!
9 Beaten silver is brought
from Tarshish,
and gold from Uphaz
from the hands of a goldsmith,
the work of a craftsman.
Their clothing is blue and purple,
all the work of skilled artisans.
10 But the LORD is the true God;
He is the living God
and eternal King.
The earth quakes at His wrath,
and the nations cannot endure
His rage.

11 You are to say this to them: The gods that did not make the heavens and the earth will perish from the earth and from under these heavens.

12 He made the earth by His power,
established the world
by His wisdom,
and spread out the heavens
by His understanding.
13 When He thunders,
the waters in the heavens
are in turmoil,
and He causes the clouds to rise
from the ends of the earth.
He makes lightning for the rain
and brings the wind
from His storehouses.

14 Everyone is stupid and ignorant.
Every goldsmith is put to shame
by his carved image,
for his cast images are a lie;
there is no breath in them.
15 They are worthless, a work
to be mocked.
At the time of their punishment
they will be destroyed.
16 Jacob's Portion is not like these
because He is the One
who formed all things.
Israel is the tribe
of His inheritance;
the LORD of Hosts is His name.

¹⁷ Gather up your belongings
from the ground,
you who live under siege.

*P*SALM 119:28-32

²⁸ I am weary from grief;
strengthen me through Your word.
²⁹ Keep me from the way of deceit,
and graciously give me Your
instruction.
³⁰ I have chosen the way of truth;
I have set Your ordinances before
me.
³¹ I cling to Your decrees;
LORD, do not put me to shame.
³² I pursue the way of Your
commands,
for You broaden my
understanding.

*P*ROVERBS 25:1-3

25 These too are proverbs
of Solomon,
which the men of Hezekiah, king
of Judah, copied.

² It is the glory of God to conceal a
matter
and the glory of kings to
investigate a matter.
³ As the heaven is high and the
earth is deep,
so the hearts of kings cannot be
investigated.

1 *T*HESSALONIANS 1:1–2:12

1 Paul, Silvanus, and Timothy:
To the church of the Thessalonians
in God the Father and the Lord Jesus
Christ.
Grace to you and peace.
² We always thank God for all of you,
remembering you constantly in our
prayers. ³ We recall, in the presence of
our God and Father, your work of faith,
labor of love, and endurance of hope in
our Lord Jesus Christ, ⁴ knowing your
election, brothers loved by God. ⁵ For
our gospel did not come to you in word
only, but also in power, in the Holy
Spirit, and with much assurance. You
know what kind of men we were among
you for your benefit, ⁶ and you became
imitators of us and of the Lord when, in
spite of severe persecution, you welcomed the message with the joy from
the Holy Spirit. ⁷ As a result, you became an example to all the believers in
Macedonia and Achaia. ⁸ For the Lord's
message rang out from you, not only in
Macedonia and Achaia, but in every
place that your faith in God has gone
out, so we don't need to say anything.
⁹ For they themselves report about us
what kind of reception we had from
you: how you turned to God from idols
to serve the living and true God, ¹⁰ and
to wait for His Son from heaven, whom
He raised from the dead—Jesus, who
rescues us from the coming wrath.

2 For you yourselves know, brothers,
that our visit with you was not with-
out result. ² On the contrary, after we
had previously suffered and been outrageously treated in Philippi, as you know,
we were emboldened by our God to
speak the gospel of God to you in spite
of great opposition. ³ For our exhortation didn't come from error or impurity
or an intent to deceive. ⁴ Instead, just as
we have been approved by God to be
entrusted with the gospel, so we speak,
not to please men, but rather God, who
examines our hearts. ⁵ For we never
used flattering speech, as you know, or
had greedy motives—God is our wit-
ness— ⁶ and we didn't seek glory from
people, either from you or from others.
⁷ Although we could have been a burden
as Christ's apostles, instead we were
gentle among you, as a nursing mother
nurtures her own children. ⁸ We cared
so much for you that we were pleased
to share with you not only the gospel
of God but also our own lives, because
you had become dear to us. ⁹ For you
remember our labor and hardship,
brothers. Working night and day so that
we would not burden any of you, we
preached God's gospel to you. ¹⁰ You
are witnesses, and so is God, of how
devoutly, righteously, and blamelessly

we conducted ourselves with you be- | aged, comforted, and implored each one
lievers. ¹¹ As you know, like a father | of you to walk worthy of God, who calls
with his own children, ¹² we encour- | you into His own kingdom and glory.

Our Only Hope

*I am the LORD, showing faithful love, justice,
and righteousness on the earth.*

——JEREMIAH 9:24

In today's church, we seem more interested in knowing about ourselves than in knowing God. The result of this is increased anxiety, depression, and a hundred other ills. However, God has revealed Himself through the Scripture in many different ways: as powerful, personal, plural, having holy love, a God of wrath, trustworthy, gracious, all-knowing, and all-wise.

It's interesting, isn't it, as our passage for today shows, that when the Lord talks about Himself in the Scriptures, it is usually in terms of His attributes or character traits: kindness, justice, righteousness, and so on. And there is a clear and definite purpose in this: the more we know of God, the more established our lives will be here on the earth.

I myself am convinced that there is nothing more important than knowing God through contemplation of Him. I am not talking about mere intellectual knowledge. I speak of the knowledge of God that comes through contemplation of Him, the ability to see life from His perspective, through His eyes. It means to look out at life's circumstances through the lens of faith, bearing in mind God's plan, to accept that whatever is happening is allowed by God and that everything comes under His personal surveillance. This kind of God-understanding and God-awareness is our only hope for coping with the problems of our day.

Prayer

Father, I am convinced. I see that if I am to operate in a context of confidence, I can only do so as I look out at life through Your eyes. Help me to do more than glance at You occasionally. Help me to gaze on You continually. Amen.

Further Study

Php 3:1-11; Col 1:9-10
What was Paul's desire?
What did Paul pray for the Colossians?

OCTOBER 19

JEREMIAH 10:18–12:17

¹⁸ For this is what the LORD says:

Look, I am slinging out
the land's residents at this time
and bringing them such distress
that they will feel it.

¹⁹ Woe to me because of
my brokenness—
I am severely wounded!
I exclaimed, "This is
my intense suffering,
but I must bear it."
²⁰ My tent is destroyed;
all my tent cords are snapped.
My sons have departed from me
and are no more.
I have no one to pitch
my tent again
or to hang up my curtains.
²¹ For the shepherds are stupid:
they don't seek the LORD.
Therefore they have not
prospered,
and their whole flock is scattered.
²² Listen! A noise—it is coming—
a great commotion from the land
to the north.
The cities of Judah will be
made desolate,
a jackals' den.

²³ I know, LORD,
that a man's way of life is not
his own;
no one who walks determines
his own steps.
²⁴ Discipline me, LORD,
but with justice—
not in Your anger,
or You will reduce me to nothing.
²⁵ Pour out Your wrath on the nations
that don't recognize You
and on the families
that don't call on Your name,

for they have consumed Jacob;
they have consumed him
and finished him off
and made his homeland desolate.

11 This is the word that came to Jeremiah from the LORD: ² "Listen to the words of this covenant, and tell them to the men of Judah and the residents of Jerusalem. ³ You must tell them: This is what the LORD, the God of Israel, says: Let a curse be on the man who does not obey the words of this covenant, ⁴ which I commanded your ancestors when I brought them out of the land of Egypt, out of the iron furnace. I declared: 'Obey Me, and do everything that I command you, and you will be My people, and I will be your God,' ⁵ in order to establish the oath I swore to your ancestors, to give them a land flowing with milk and honey, as it is today."

I answered, "Amen, LORD."

⁶ The LORD said to me, "Proclaim all these words in the cities of Judah and in the streets of Jerusalem: Obey the words of this covenant and carry them out. ⁷ For I strongly warned your ancestors when I brought them out of the land of Egypt until today, warning them time and time again: Obey My voice. ⁸ Yet they would not obey or pay attention; each one followed the stubbornness of his evil heart. So I brought on them all the curses of this covenant, because they had not done what I commanded them to do."

⁹ The LORD said to me, "A conspiracy has been discovered among the men of Judah and the residents of Jerusalem. ¹⁰ They have returned to the sins of their ancestors who refused to obey My words and have followed other gods to worship them. The house of Israel and the house of Judah broke My covenant I made with their ancestors.

[11] "Therefore, this is what the LORD says: I am about to bring on them disaster that they cannot escape. They will cry out to Me, but I will not hear them. [12] Then the cities of Judah and the residents of Jerusalem will go and cry out to the gods they have been burning incense to, but they certainly will not save them in their time of disaster. [13] Your gods are indeed as numerous as your cities, Judah, and the altars you have set up to Shame—altars to burn incense to Baal—as numerous as the streets of Jerusalem.

[14] "As for you, do not pray for these people. Do not raise up a cry or a prayer on their behalf, for I will not be listening when they call out to Me at the time of their disaster.

[15] What right does My beloved have
to be in My house,
having carried out so many
evil schemes?
Can holy meat prevent
your disaster
so you can rejoice?
[16] The LORD named you
a flourishing olive tree,
beautiful with well-formed fruit.
He has set fire to it,
and its branches are consumed
with a great roaring sound.

[17] "The LORD of Hosts who planted you has decreed disaster against you, because of the harm the house of Israel and the house of Judah brought on themselves, provoking Me to anger by burning incense to Baal."

[18] The LORD informed me, so I knew.
Then You helped me to see
their deeds,
[19] for I was like a docile lamb led
to slaughter.
I didn't know that they had
devised plots against me:
"Let's destroy the tree
with its fruit;
let's cut him off from the land
of the living
so that his name will no longer
be remembered."

[20] But, LORD of Hosts,
who judges righteously,
who tests heart and mind,
let me see Your vengeance
on them,
for I have presented my case
to You.

[21] Therefore, here is what the LORD says concerning the people of Anathoth who want to take your life. They warn, "You must not prophesy in the name of the LORD, or you will certainly die at our hand." [22] Therefore, this is what the LORD of Hosts says: "I am about to punish them. The young men will die by the sword; their sons and daughters will die by famine. [23] They will have no remnant, for I will bring disaster on the people of Anathoth in the year of their punishment."

12 You will be righteous, LORD,
even if I bring a case
against You.
Yet, I wish to contend with You:
Why does the way of the wicked
prosper?
Why do the treacherous live
at ease?
[2] You planted them, and they
have taken root.
They have grown
and produced fruit.
You are ever on their lips,
but far from their conscience.
[3] As for You, You know me, LORD;
You see me.
You test whether my heart is
with You.
Drag the wicked away like sheep
to slaughter,
and set them apart for the day
of killing.
[4] How long will the land mourn
and the grass of every field
wither?
Because of the evil
of its residents,
animals and birds have been
swept away,
for the people have said,
"He cannot see what our end
will be."

5 If you have raced with runners
and they have worn you out,
how can you compete
with horses?
If you stumble in a peaceful land,
what will you do in the thickets
of the Jordan?
6 Even your brothers—
your own father's household—
even they were treacherous
to you;
even they have cried out loudly
after you.
Do not have confidence in them,
though they speak well of you.

7 I have abandoned My house;
I have deserted My inheritance.
I have given the love of My life
into the hand of her enemies.
8 My inheritance has acted
toward Me
like a lion in the forest.
She has roared against Me.
Therefore, I hate her.
9 Is My inheritance like a hyena
to Me?
Are birds of prey circling her?
Go, gather all the wild animals;
bring them to devour her.
10 Many shepherds have destroyed
My vineyard;
they have trampled My plot
of land.
They have turned
My desirable plot
into a desolate wasteland.
11 They have made it a desolation.
It mourns, desolate, before Me.
All the land is desolate,
but no one takes it to heart.
12 Over all the barren heights
in the wilderness
the destroyers have come,
for the LORD has a sword
that devours
from one end of the earth
to the other.
No one has peace.
13 They have sown wheat
but harvested thorns.
They have exhausted themselves
but have no profit.
Be put to shame by your harvests

because of the LORD's
burning anger.

14 This is what the LORD says: "Concerning all My evil neighbors who attack the inheritance that I bequeathed to My people, Israel, I am about to uproot them from their land, and I will uproot the house of Judah from among them. 15 After I have uprooted them, I will once again have compassion on them and return each one to his inheritance and to his land. 16 If they will diligently learn the ways of My people—to swear by My name, 'As the LORD lives,' just as they taught My people to swear by Baal—they will be built up among My people. 17 However, if they will not obey, then I will uproot and destroy that nation."

This is the LORD's declaration.

*P*SALM 119:33-36

33 Teach me, LORD, the meaning of
Your statutes,
and I will always keep them.
34 Help me understand Your
instruction, and I will obey it
and follow it with all my heart.
35 Help me stay on the path of Your
commands,
for I take pleasure in it.
36 Turn my heart to Your decrees
and not to material gain.

*P*ROVERBS 25:4-7

4 Remove impurities from silver,
and a vessel will be produced for a
silversmith.
5 Remove the wicked from the
king's presence,
and his throne will be established
in righteousness.

6 Don't brag about yourself before
the king,
and don't stand in the place of the
great;
7 for it is better for him to say to
you, "Come up here!"
than to demote you in plain view
of a noble.

1 THESSALONIANS 2:13–3:13

[13] Also, this is why we constantly thank God, because when you received the message about God that you heard from us, you welcomed it not as a human message, but as it truly is, the message of God, which also works effectively in you believers. [14] For you, brothers, became imitators of God's churches in Christ Jesus that are in Judea, since you have also suffered the same things from people of your own country, just as they did from the Jews. [15] They killed both the Lord Jesus and the prophets, and persecuted us; they displease God, and are hostile to everyone, [16] hindering us from speaking to the Gentiles so that they may be saved. As a result, they are always adding to the number of their sins, and wrath has overtaken them completely.

[17] But as for us, brothers, after we were forced to leave you for a short time (in person, not in heart), we greatly desired and made every effort to return and see you face to face. [18] So we wanted to come to you—even I, Paul, time and again—but Satan hindered us. [19] For who is our hope, or joy, or crown of boasting in the presence of our Lord Jesus at His coming? Is it not you? [20] For you are our glory and joy!

3 Therefore, when we could no longer stand it, we thought it was better to be left alone in Athens. [2] And we sent Timothy, our brother and God's co-worker in the gospel of Christ, to strengthen and encourage you concerning your faith, [3] so that no one will be shaken by these persecutions. For you yourselves know that we are appointed to this. [4] In fact, when we were with you, we told you previously that we were going to suffer persecution, and as you know, it happened. [5] For this reason, when I could no longer stand it, I also sent to find out about your faith, fearing that the tempter had tempted you and that our labor might be for nothing.

[6] But now Timothy has come to us from you and brought us good news about your faith and love, and that you always have good memories of us, wanting to see us, as we also want to see you. [7] Therefore, brothers, in all our distress and persecution, we were encouraged about you through your faith. [8] For now we live, if you stand firm in the Lord. [9] How can we thank God for you in return for all the joy we experience because of you before our God, [10] as we pray earnestly night and day to see you face to face and to complete what is lacking in your faith?

[11] Now may our God and Father Himself, and our Lord Jesus, direct our way to you. [12] And may the Lord cause you to increase and overflow with love for one another and for everyone, just as we also do for you. [13] May He make your hearts blameless in holiness before our God and Father at the coming of our Lord Jesus with all His saints. Amen.

The Power of Truth

I have chosen the way of truth; I have set Your ordinances before me.

—PSALM 119:30

We cannot do battle with the Devil until we have girded our waists with truth. Girding the waist was always a symbol of readiness to fight. That is why this comes first. The officers in the Roman army wore short skirts, very much like a Scottish kilt. Over this they had a cloak or tunic which was secured at the waist with a girdle. When they were about to enter battle, they would tuck the tunic up under the girdle so as to leave their legs unencumbered for the fight. What does Paul's phrase, "with truth like a belt around your waist," really mean? What significance does it have for us today? The word "truth" can be looked at in two ways: one, objective truth, as it is to be found in Jesus Christ, and two, subjective truth as it is to be found in the qualities of honesty and sincerity. The Puritan, William Gurnall, points out that whether the word implies truth of doctrine or truth of heart, one kind of truth will not do without the other.

I believe that in Ephesians 6, Paul is emphasizing subjective truth—truth that resides in the inner being. When we are deceitful or hypocritical, or when we resort to intrigue and scheming, we are playing the Devil's game. And we will never be able to beat the Devil at his own game!

What Satan despises is transparent truth. He flees from it as quickly as darkness runs from the dawn. Having our waists girded with truth, then, means being possessed with truth, guided by truth, and controlled by truth. Where truth is absent, we have no power over Satan. It is as simple as that.

Prayer

O Father, I see that You have set standards by which I rise or fall. When I fulfill them, I rise—when I break them, I fall. Give me the strength I need to fulfill all Your laws, especially the law of truth. In Jesus' name. Amen.

Further Study

Jn 8:34-45; Col 3:9; Ps 51:6; Pr 12:22
What can protect us from the Devil?
Where should we desire truth?

OCTOBER 20

JEREMIAH 13:1–15:4

13 This is what the LORD said to me: "Go and buy yourself linen underwear and put it on, but don't get it wet." ² So I bought underwear as the LORD instructed me and put it on.

³ Then the word of the LORD came to me a second time: ⁴ "Take the underwear that you bought and are wearing, and go at once to the Euphrates River and hide it in a rocky crevice." ⁵ So I went and hid it by the Euphrates, as the LORD commanded me.

⁶ A long time later the LORD said to me, "Go at once to the Euphrates and get the underwear that I commanded you to hide there." ⁷ So I went to the Euphrates and dug up the underwear and got it from the place where I had hidden it, but it was ruined—of no use whatsoever.

8 Then the word of the LORD came to me: 9 "This is what the LORD says: Just like this I will ruin the great pride of both Judah and Jerusalem. 10 These evil people, who refuse to listen to Me, who walk in the stubbornness of their own hearts, and who have followed other gods to serve and worship—they will be like this underwear, of no use whatsoever. 11 Just as underwear clings to one's waist, so I fastened the whole house of Israel and of Judah to Me"—this is the LORD's declaration—"so that they might be My people for My fame, praise, and glory, but they would not obey.

12 "Say this to them: This is what the LORD, the God of Israel, says: Every jar should be filled with wine. Then they will respond to you: Don't we know that every jar should be filled with wine? 13 And you will say to them, This is what the LORD says: I am about to fill all who live in this land—the kings who reign for David on his throne, the priests, the prophets and all the residents of Jerusalem—with drunkenness. 14 I will smash them against each other, fathers and sons alike"—the LORD's declaration. "I will allow no mercy, pity, or compassion to keep Me from destroying them."

15 Listen and pay attention.
   Do not be proud,
   for the LORD has spoken.
16 Give glory to the LORD your God
   before He brings darkness,
   before your feet stumble
   on the mountains at dusk.
   You wait for light,
   but He brings darkest gloom
   and makes thick darkness.
17 But if you will not listen,
   my innermost being will weep
      in secret
   because of your pride.
   My eyes will overflow with tears,
   for the LORD's flock has been
      taken captive.
18 Say to the king
      and the queen mother:
   Take a humble seat,
   for your glorious crowns

have fallen from your heads.
19 The cities of the Negev are
      under siege;
   no one can help them.
   All of Judah has been taken
      into exile,
   taken completely into exile.
20 Look up and see
   those coming from the north.
   Where is the flock entrusted
      to you,
   the sheep that were your pride?
21 What will you say
      when He appoints
   close friends as leaders over you,
   ones you yourself trained?
   Won't labor pains seize you,
   as they do a woman in labor?
22 And when you ask yourself:
   Why have these things happened
      to me?—
   it is because of your great guilt
   that your skirts have been
      stripped off,
   your body ravished.
23 Can the Cushite change his skin,
   or a leopard his spots?
   If so, you might be able to do
      what is good,
   you who are instructed in evil.
24 I will scatter you like drifting chaff
   before the desert wind.
25 This is your lot,
   what I have decreed for you—
      this is the LORD's declaration—
   because you have forgotten Me
   and trusted in Falsehood.
26 I will pull your skirts up
      over your face
   so that your shame might be seen.
27 Your adulteries and your lustful
      neighings,
   your heinous prostitution
   on the hills, in the fields—
   I have seen your detestable acts.
   Woe to you, Jerusalem!
   You are unclean—
   for how long yet?

14 The word of the LORD that came to Jeremiah concerning the drought:

2 Judah mourns;
her gates languish.
Her people are on the ground
in mourning;
Jerusalem's cry rises up.
3 Their nobles send their servants
for water.
They go to the cisterns;
they find no water;
their containers return empty.
They are ashamed and humiliated;
they cover their heads.
4 The ground is cracked
since no rain has fallen
on the land.
The farmers are ashamed;
they cover their heads.
5 Even the doe in the field
gives birth and abandons
her fawn
since there is no grass.
6 Wild donkeys stand
on the barren heights
panting for air like jackals.
Their eyes fail
because there are no green plants.
7 Though our guilt testifies
against us,
LORD, act for Your name's sake.
Indeed, our rebellions are many;
we have sinned against You.
8 Hope of Israel,
its Savior in time of distress,
why are You like an alien
in the land,
like a traveler stopping only
for the night?
9 Why are You like a helpless man,
like a warrior unable to save?
Yet You are among us, LORD,
and we are called by Your name.
Don't leave us!
10 This is what the LORD says concerning these people:

Truly they love to wander;
they never rest their feet.
So the LORD does not accept them.
Now He will remember their guilt
and punish their sins.

11 Then the LORD said to me, "Do not pray for the well-being of these people. 12 If they fast, I will not hear their cry of despair. If they offer burnt offering and grain offering, I will not accept them. Rather, I will finish them off by sword, famine, and plague."

13 And I replied, "Oh no, Lord GOD! The prophets are telling them, 'You won't see sword or suffer famine. I will certainly give you true peace in this place.' "

14 But the LORD said to me, "These prophets are prophesying a lie in My name. I did not send them, nor did I command them or speak to them. They are prophesying to you a false vision, worthless divination, the deceit of their own minds. 15 "Therefore, this is what the LORD says concerning the prophets who prophesy in My name, though I did not send them, and who say: There will never be sword or famine in this land: By sword and famine these prophets will meet their end. 16 The people they are prophesying to will be thrown into the streets of Jerusalem because of the famine and the sword. There will be no one to bury them—they, their wives, their sons, and their daughters. I will pour out their own evil on them."

17 You are to speak this word
to them:
Let my eyes overflow with tears;
day and night may they not stop,
for the virgin daughter
of my people
has been destroyed
by a great disaster,
an extremely severe wound.
18 If I go out to the field,
look—those slain by the sword!
If I enter the city,
look—those ill from famine!
For both prophet and priest
travel to a land they do not know.

19 Have You completely
rejected Judah?
Do You detest Zion?
Why do You strike us
with no hope of healing for us?
We hoped for peace,
but there was nothing good;
for a time of healing,
but there was only terror.

20 We acknowledge
       our wickedness, LORD,
    the guilt of our fathers;
    indeed, we have sinned
       against You.
21 Because of Your name,
       don't despise us.
    Don't disdain
       Your glorious throne.
    Remember Your covenant with us;
    do not break it.
22 Can any of the worthless idols
       of the nations bring rain?
    Or can the skies alone
       give showers?
    Are You not the LORD our God?
    We therefore put our hope in You,
    for You have done all these things.

15 Then the LORD said to me: "Even
if Moses and Samuel should
stand before Me, My compassions
would not reach out to these people.
Send them from My presence, and let
them go. ²If they ask you: Where will
we go? you must tell them: This is what
the LORD says:

    Those destined for death,
       to death;
    those destined for the sword,
       to the sword.
    Those destined for famine,
       to famine;
    those destined for captivity,
       to captivity.

³ "I will ordain four kinds of judgment
for them"—this is the LORD's declaration—"the sword to kill, the dogs to
drag away, and the birds of the sky
and the wild animals of the land to devour and destroy. ⁴I will make them a
horror to all the kingdoms of the earth
because of Manasseh son of Hezekiah,
the king of Judah, for what he did in
Jerusalem.

PSALM 119:37-40

37 Turn my eyes from looking at
       what is worthless;
    give me life in Your ways.

38 Confirm what You said to Your
       servant,
    for it produces reverence for You.
39 Turn away the disgrace I dread;
    indeed, Your judgments are good.
40 How I long for Your precepts!
    Give me life through Your
       righteousness.

PROVERBS 25:8-10

8 Don't take a matter to court
       hastily.
    Otherwise, what will you do
       afterwards
    if your opponent humiliates you?
9 Make your case with your
       opponent
    without revealing another's
       secret;
10 otherwise, the one who hears will
       disgrace you,
    and you'll never live it down.

I THESSALONIANS 4:1–5:7

4 Finally then, brothers, we ask and
encourage you in the Lord Jesus,
that as you have received from us how
you must walk and please God—as you
are doing—do so even more. ²For
you know what commands we gave you
through the Lord Jesus.

³For this is God's will, your sanctification: that you abstain from sexual immorality, ⁴so that each of you knows
how to possess his own vessel in sanctification and honor, ⁵not with lustful desires, like the Gentiles who don't know
God. ⁶This means one must not transgress against and defraud his brother in
this matter, because the Lord is an
avenger of all these offenses, as we also
previously told and warned you. ⁷For
God has not called us to impurity, but to
sanctification. ⁸Therefore, the person
who rejects this does not reject man,
but God, who also gives you His Holy
Spirit.

⁹About brotherly love: you don't need
me to write you because you yourselves
are taught by God to love one another.

[10] In fact, you are doing this toward all the brothers in the entire region of Macedonia. But we encourage you, brothers, to do so even more, [11] to seek to lead a quiet life, to mind your own business, and to work with your own hands, as we commanded you, [12] so that you may walk properly in the presence of outsiders and not be dependent on anyone.

[13] We do not want you to be uninformed, brothers, concerning those who are asleep, so that you will not grieve like the rest, who have no hope. [14] Since we believe that Jesus died and rose again, in the same way God will bring with Him those who have fallen asleep through Jesus. [15] For we say this to you by a revelation from the Lord: We who are still alive at the Lord's coming will certainly have no advantage over those who have fallen asleep. [16] For the Lord Himself will descend from heaven with a shout, with the archangel's voice, and with the trumpet of God, and the dead in Christ will rise first. [17] Then we who are still alive will be caught up together with them in the clouds to meet the Lord in the air; and so we will always be with the Lord. [18] Therefore encourage one another with these words.

5 About the times and the seasons: brothers, you do not need anything to be written to you. [2] For you yourselves know very well that the Day of the Lord will come just like a thief in the night. [3] When they say, "Peace and security," then sudden destruction comes on them, like labor pains on a pregnant woman, and they will not escape. [4] But you, brothers, are not in the dark, so that this day would overtake you like a thief. [5] For you are all sons of light and sons of the day. We're not of the night or of darkness. [6] So then, we must not sleep, like the rest, but we must stay awake and be sober. [7] For those who sleep, sleep at night, and those who get drunk are drunk at night.

Precise Scripture

This is what the Lord said.—Jeremiah 13:1

Let us focus on what is meant by the phrase—"the sword of the Spirit, which is God's word." The sword is the Word of God—the Bible, the inspired Scriptures.

In Matthew 4:4 and 4:7, we see a perfect illustration of how Jesus used the sword of the Spirit when rebutting the temptations of the Devil when He begins His response, "It is written . . ." and "It is also written . . ." Notice how, prior to the temptation, Jesus was anointed by the Holy Spirit (Mt 3:13-17). Next we are informed that Jesus was "led by the Spirit into the wilderness to be tempted by the Devil" (4:1).

During the temptation our Lord, filled with the Spirit, resisted every one of the Devil's statements by using the precise words of Scripture. Follow me closely, for this is extremely important: Christ did not merely utter a newly formed statement or something that came to Him on the spur of the moment, but quoted a text which had already been given by God and written down. The weapon used by our Lord was the Word of God, the Scriptures.

Can you see the point I am making? Satan is not rebuffed by clever phrases that are made up on the spur of the moment and sound theologically sophisticated and refined. He is defeated only when we quote to him the precise words of Scripture. If this was the strategy Jesus had to use, then how much more you and I.

Nothing defeats Satan more thoroughly and effectively than the sword of the Spirit, which is the Word of God.

Prayer

O God, open my eyes that I might see more clearly than ever the power and authority that lies in Your sacred Word, the Bible. Help me to know it better. For Your own dear name's sake. Amen.

Further Study

1 Pt 1:13-25; Ps 119:89,103; Jr 15:16
What did Jeremiah do with God's Word?
How did the psalmist describe it?

OCTOBER 21

JEREMIAH 15:5–17:18

5 Who will have pity on you,
    Jerusalem?
Who will show sympathy
    toward you?
Who will turn aside
to ask about your welfare?
6 You have left Me.
    This is the LORD's declaration.
You have turned your back,
so I have stretched out My hand
    against you
and destroyed you.
I am tired of showing compassion.
7 I scattered them
    with a winnowing fork
at the gates of the land.
I made them childless; I destroyed
    My people.
They would not turn
    from their ways.
8 I made their widows
    more numerous
than the sand of the seas.
I brought against the mother
    of young men
a destroyer at noon.

I suddenly released on her
    agitation and terrors.
9 The mother of seven grew faint;
she breathed her last breath.
Her sun set while it was still day;
she was ashamed and humiliated.
The rest of them I will give over
    to the sword
in the presence of their enemies."
    This is the LORD's declaration.

10 Woe is me, my mother,
that you gave birth to me,
a man who incites dispute
    and conflict
in all the land.
I did not lend or borrow,
yet everyone curses me.
11 The LORD said:

Assuredly, I will set you free
    and care for you.
Assuredly, I will intercede for you
in a time of trouble,
in your time of distress,
    with the enemy.
12 Can anyone smash iron,
iron from the north, or bronze?
13 Your wealth and your treasures

1258

I will give as plunder, without cost,
for all your sins,
and within all your borders.
¹⁴ Then I will make you serve
your enemies
in a land you do not know,
for My anger will kindle a fire
that will burn against you.

¹⁵ You know, Lord;
remember me and take note
of me.
Avenge me
against my persecutors.
In Your patience,
don't take me away.
Know that I suffer disgrace
for Your honor.
¹⁶ Your words were found,
and I ate them.
Your words became a delight to me
and the joy of my heart,
for I am called by Your name,
Lord God of Hosts.
¹⁷ I never sat with the band
of revelers,
and I did not celebrate
with them.
Because Your hand was on me,
I sat alone,
for You filled me with indignation.
¹⁸ Why has my pain
become unending,
my wound incurable,
refusing to be healed?
You truly have become
like a mirage to me—
water that is not reliable.
¹⁹ Therefore, this is what the Lord says:

If you return, I will restore you;
you will stand in My presence.
And if you speak noble words,
rather than worthless ones,
you will be My spokesman.
It is they who must return to you;
you must not return to them.
²⁰ Then I will make you
a fortified wall of bronze
to this people.
They will fight against you
but will not overcome you,
for I am with you

to save you and deliver you.
This is the Lord's declaration.
²¹ I will deliver you from the power
of evil people
and redeem you from the control
of the ruthless.

16 The word of the Lord came to me: ² "You must not marry or have sons or daughters in this place. ³ For this is what the Lord says concerning sons and daughters born in this place as well as concerning the mothers who bear them and the fathers who father them in this land: ⁴ They will die from deadly diseases. They will not be mourned or buried but will be like manure on the face of the earth. They will be finished off by sword and famine. Their corpses will become food for the birds of the sky and for the wild animals of the land.

⁵ "For this is what the Lord says: Don't enter a house where a mourning feast is taking place. Don't go to lament or sympathize with them, for I have removed My peace from these people"— this is the Lord's declaration—"as well as My faithful love and compassion. ⁶ Both great and small will die in this land without burial. No lament will be made for them, nor will anyone cut himself or shave his head for them. ⁷ Food won't be provided for the mourner to comfort him because of the dead. A cup of consolation won't be given him because of the loss of his father or mother. ⁸ You must not enter the house where feasting is taking place to sit with them to eat and drink. ⁹ For this is what the Lord of Hosts, the God of Israel, says: I am about to eliminate from this place, before your very eyes and in your time, the sound of joy and gladness, the voice of the bridegroom and the bride.

¹⁰ "When you tell these people all these things, they will say to you: Why has the Lord declared all this great disaster against us? What is our guilt? What is our sin that we have committed against the Lord our God? ¹¹ Then you will answer them: Because your fathers abandoned Me"—the Lord's declaration—"and followed other gods, served

them, and worshiped them. Indeed, they abandoned Me and did not keep My law. ¹²You did more evil than your fathers. Look, each one of you was following the stubbornness of his evil heart, not obeying Me. ¹³So I will hurl you from this land into a land that you and your fathers are not familiar with. There you will worship other gods both day and night, for I will not grant you grace. ¹⁴"However, take note! The days are coming"—the LORD's declaration— "when it will no longer be said: As the LORD lives who brought the Israelites from the land of Egypt, ¹⁵but rather: As the LORD lives who brought the Israelites from the land of the north and from all the other lands where He had banished them. For I will return them to their land that I gave to their ancestors.

¹⁶"I am about to send for many fishermen"—the LORD's declaration—"and they will fish for them. Then I will send for many hunters, and they will hunt them down on every mountain and hill and out of the clefts of the rocks, ¹⁷for My gaze takes in all their ways. They are not concealed from Me, and their guilt is not hidden from My sight. ¹⁸I will first repay them double for their guilt and sin because they have polluted My land. They have filled My inheritance with the lifelessness of their detestable and abhorrent idols."

¹⁹ LORD, my strength
   and my stronghold,
 my refuge in a time of distress,
 the nations will come to You
   from the ends of the earth,
   and they will say,
 "Our fathers inherited only lies,
 worthless idols of no benefit
   at all."
²⁰ Can one make gods for himself?
 But they are not gods.
²¹ "Therefore, I am about
   to inform them,
 and this time I will
   make them know
 My power and My might;
 then they will know that My name
   is Yahweh."

17 The sin of Judah is written
   with an iron stylus.
 With a diamond point
 it is engraved on the tablet
   of their hearts
 and on the horns of their altars,
² while their children remember
   their altars
 and their Asherah poles,
   by the green trees
 on the high hills—
³ My mountains in the countryside.
 Your wealth and all your treasures
 I will give up as plunder
 because of the sin of your
   high places
 within all your borders.
⁴ You will, of yourself, relinquish
   your inheritance
 that I gave you.
 I will make you serve
   your enemies
 in a land you do not know,
 for you have set My anger on fire;
 it will burn forever.
⁵ This is what the LORD says:

 Cursed is the man who trusts
   in mankind,
 who makes human flesh
   his strength
 and turns his heart from the LORD.
⁶ He will be like a juniper in the
   Arabah;
 he cannot see when good comes
 but dwells in the parched places
   in the wilderness,
 in a salt land where no one lives.
⁷ Blessed is the man who trusts
   in the LORD,
 whose confidence indeed is
   the LORD.
⁸ He will be like a tree planted
   by water:
 it sends its roots out
   toward a stream,
 it doesn't fear when heat comes,
 and its foliage remains green.
 It will not worry in a year
   of drought
 or cease producing fruit.

⁹ The heart is more deceitful
   than anything else

and desperately sick—
who can understand it?
¹⁰ I, the LORD, examine the mind,
I test the heart
to give to each according to
his way,
according to what
his actions deserve.
¹¹ He who makes a fortune unjustly
is like a partridge
that hatches eggs it didn't lay.
In the middle of his days
his riches will abandon him,
so in the end he will be a fool.

¹² A throne of glory
on high from the beginning
is the place of our sanctuary,
¹³ LORD, the hope of Israel,
all who abandon You
will be put to shame.
All who turn away from Me
will be written in the dirt,
for they have abandoned
the fountain of living water,
the LORD.

¹⁴ Heal me, LORD,
and I will be healed;
save me, and I will be saved,
for You are my praise.
¹⁵ Hear how they keep
challenging me,
"Where is the word of the LORD?
Let it come!"
¹⁶ But I have not run away
from being Your shepherd,
and I have not longed for
the fatal day.
You know my words were spoken
in Your presence.
¹⁷ Don't become a terror to me.
You are my refuge in the day
of disaster.
¹⁸ Let my persecutors be
put to shame,
but don't let me be put to shame.
Let them be terrified, but don't
let me be terrified.
Bring on them the day of disaster;
shatter them with total
destruction.

*P*SALM 119:41-44

⁴¹ Let Your faithful love come to me,
LORD,
Your salvation, as You promised.
⁴² Then I can answer the one who
taunts me,
for I trust in Your word.
⁴³ Never take the word of truth from
my mouth,
for I hope in Your judgments.
⁴⁴ I will always keep Your law,
forever and ever.

*P*ROVERBS 25:11-12

¹¹ A word spoken at the right time
is like golden apples on a silver
tray.
¹² A wise correction to a receptive
ear
is like a gold ring or an ornament
of gold.

1 *T*HESSALONIANS
5:8-28

⁸ But since we are of the day, we must
be sober and put the armor of faith and
love on our chests, and put on a helmet
of the hope of salvation. ⁹ For God did
not appoint us to wrath, but to obtain
salvation through our Lord Jesus Christ,
¹⁰ who died for us, so that whether
we are awake or asleep, we will live together with Him. ¹¹ Therefore encourage one another and build each other up
as you are already doing.
¹² Now we ask you, brothers, to give
recognition to those who labor among
you and lead you in the Lord and admonish you, ¹³ and to esteem them very
highly in love because of their work. Be
at peace among yourselves. ¹⁴ And we
exhort you, brothers: warn those who
are lazy, comfort the discouraged, help
the weak, be patient with everyone.
¹⁵ See to it that no one repays evil for
evil to anyone, but always pursue what
is good for one another and for all.

¹⁶ Rejoice always!
¹⁷ Pray constantly.

18 Give thanks in everything, for this is God's will for you in Christ Jesus.
19 Don't stifle the Spirit.
20 Don't despise prophecies,
21 but test all things. Hold on to what is good.
22 Stay away from every form of evil.
23 Now may the God of peace Himself sanctify you completely. And may your spirit, soul, and body be kept sound and blameless for the coming of our Lord Jesus Christ. 24 He who calls you is faithful, who also will do it. 25 Brothers, pray for us also. 26 Greet all the brothers with a holy kiss. 27 I charge you by the Lord that this letter be read to all the brothers. 28 May the grace of our Lord Jesus Christ be with you!

Don't Dampen the Spirit

Don't stifle the Spirit.

—1 THESSALONIANS 5:19

The sin described in Scripture as "blasphemy against the Spirit" rarely occurs in the life of a Christian. It is rather a conscious resistance, and anyone worrying about it has not committed it. There is, however, a more frequent sin. It is one that almost all Christians have committed and is known as "quenching the Spirit."

How do we "quench" the Holy Spirit? We can do this in many ways, but the chief way is by refusing to let Him have full control of our lives. *The Amplified Bible* says: "Do not quench (suppress or subdue) the (Holy) Spirit." You see, it is possible for you to possess the Holy Spirit without the Holy Spirit possessing you. Dr. Handley Moule, the great Anglican bishop of a past generation, used to say: "The difference between someone who is quenching the Spirit and someone who is allowing the Spirit to have free course in their life, is the difference between a well in which there is a spring of water choked, and a well in which the obstruction is removed so that the water springs up and fills the well." If we are choked by fears, resentments, indecision, self-centeredness, then we are suppressing the Holy Spirit who resides in us in order to free us.

I know that many are afraid to surrender completely to the Spirit, afraid that they will become what some people call "hot-pots." But the danger to the present church is not from "hot-pots" but from "cold fish"! Unless I am greatly mistaken, our churches are more in danger of freezing up than burning up.

Prayer

O God, forgive me, I pray, for not allowing Your Holy Spirit to have full sway in my life and experience. Let Your divine fire burn within me, and help me not to dampen it. For Jesus' sake. Amen.

OCTOBER 22

JEREMIAH 17:19–20:6

¹⁹ This is what the LORD said to me, "Go and stand in the People's Gate, through which the kings of Judah enter and leave, and in all the gates of Jerusalem. ²⁰ Announce to them: Hear the word of the LORD, kings of Judah, all Judah, and all the residents of Jerusalem who enter through these gates. ²¹ This is what the LORD says: Watch yourselves; do not pick up a load and bring it in through the gates of Jerusalem on the Sabbath day. ²² You must not carry a load out of your houses on the Sabbath day or do any work, but you must consecrate the Sabbath day, just as I commanded your ancestors. ²³ They wouldn't listen or pay attention but became obstinate, not listening or accepting discipline.

²⁴ "However, if you listen to Me, says the LORD, and do not bring loads through the gates of this city on the Sabbath day and consecrate the Sabbath day and do no work on it, ²⁵ kings and princes will enter through the gates of this city. They will sit on the throne of David, riding in chariots and on horses with their officials, the men of Judah, and the residents of Jerusalem. This city will be inhabited forever. ²⁶ Then people will come from the cities of Judah and from the area around Jerusalem, from the land of Benjamin and from the Judean foothills, from the hill country

and from the Negev bringing burnt offerings and sacrifice, grain offerings and frankincense, and thank offerings to the house of the LORD. ²⁷ If you do not listen to Me to consecrate the Sabbath day by not carrying a load while entering the gates of Jerusalem on the Sabbath day, I will set fire to its gates, and it will consume the citadels of Jerusalem and not be extinguished."

18 This is the word that came to Jeremiah from the LORD: ² "Go down at once to the potter's house; there I will reveal My words to you." ³ So I went down to the potter's house, and there he was, working away at the wheel. ⁴ But the jar that he was making from the clay became flawed in the potter's hand, so he made it into another jar, as it seemed right for him to do.

⁵ The word of the LORD came to me: ⁶ "House of Israel, can I not treat you as this potter treats his clay?"—this is the LORD's declaration. "Just like clay in the potter's hand, so are you in My hand, house of Israel. ⁷ At one moment I might announce concerning a nation or a kingdom that I will uproot, tear down, and destroy it. ⁸ However, if that nation I have made an announcement about, turns from its evil, I will not bring the disaster on it I had planned. ⁹ At another time I announce that I will build and plant a nation or a kingdom. ¹⁰ However, if it does what is evil in My sight by not listening to My voice, I will

not bring the good I had said I would do to it. ¹¹ So now, say to the men of Judah and to the residents of Jerusalem: This is what the LORD says: I am about to bring harm to you and make plans against you. Turn now, each from your evil way, and correct your ways and your deeds. ¹² But they will say: It's hopeless. We will continue to follow our plans, and each of us will continue to act according to the stubbornness of his evil heart."

¹³ Therefore, this is what the LORD says:

Ask among the nations,
Who has heard things like these?
Virgin Israel has done
a most terrible thing.
¹⁴ Does the snow of Lebanon
ever leave the highland crags?
Or does cold water flowing
from a distance ever fail?
¹⁵ Yet My people have forgotten Me.
They burn incense to false idols
that make them stumble
in their ways—
in the ancient roads—
to walk on new paths,
not the highway.
¹⁶ They have made their land
a horror,
a perpetual object of scorn;
everyone who passes by it
will be horrified
and shake his head.
¹⁷ I will scatter them
before the enemy
like the east wind.
I will show them My back and not
My face
on the day of their calamity.

¹⁸ Then certain ones said, "Come, let's make plans against Jeremiah, for the law will never be lost from the priest, or counsel from the wise, or an oracle from the prophet. Come, let's denounce him and pay no attention to all his words."

¹⁹ Pay attention to me, LORD.
Hear what my opponents are saying!
²⁰ Should good be repaid with evil?
Yet they have dug a pit for me.
Remember how I stood before You

to speak good on their behalf,
to turn Your anger from them.
²¹ Therefore, hand their children
over to famine,
and pour the sword's power
on them.
Let their wives become childless
and widowed,
their husbands slain
by deadly disease,
their young men struck down
by the sword in battle.
²² Let a cry be heard
from their houses
when You suddenly bring raiders
against them,
for they have dug a pit
to capture me
and have hidden snares
for my feet.
²³ But You, LORD, know
all their deadly plots against me.
Do not wipe out their guilt;
do not blot out their sin
before You.
Let them be forced to stumble
before You;
deal with them in the time
of Your anger.

19 This is what the LORD says: "Go, buy a potter's clay jug. Take some of the elders of the people and some of the elders of the priests ² and go out to the Valley of Hinnom near the entrance of the Potsherd Gate. Proclaim there the words I speak to you. ³ Say: Hear the word of the LORD, kings of Judah and residents of Jerusalem. This is what the LORD of Hosts, the God of Israel, says: I am going to bring such disaster on this place that everyone who hears about it will shudder ⁴ because they have abandoned Me and made this a foreign place. They have burned incense in it to other gods that they, their fathers, and the kings of Judah have never known. They have filled this place with the blood of the innocent. ⁵ They have built high places to Baal on which to burn their children in the fire as burnt offerings to Baal, something I have never commanded or mentioned; I never entertained the thought.

⁶ "Therefore, take note! The days are coming"—this is the LORD's declaration—"when this place will no longer be called Topheth and the Valley of Hinnom, but the Valley of Slaughter. ⁷ I will spoil the plans of Judah and Jerusalem in this place. I will make them fall by the sword before their enemies, by the hand of those who want to take their life. I will provide their corpses as food for the birds of the sky and for the wild animals of the land. ⁸ I will make this city desolate, an object of scorn. Everyone who passes by it will be horrified and scoff because of all its wounds. ⁹ I will make them eat the flesh of their sons and their daughters, and they will eat each other's flesh in the siege and distress that their enemies, those who want to take their life, inflict on them.

¹⁰ "Then you are to shatter the jug in the presence of the people traveling with you, ¹¹ and you are to proclaim to them: This is what the LORD of Hosts says: I will shatter these people and this city, like one shatters a potter's jar that can never again be mended. They will bury in Topheth until there is no place left to bury. ¹² I will do so to this place"—this is the declaration of the LORD—"and to its residents, making this city like Topheth. ¹³ The houses of Jerusalem and the houses of the kings of Judah will become impure like that place Topheth—all the houses on whose rooftops they have burned incense to the whole heavenly host and poured out drink offerings to other gods."

¹⁴ Jeremiah came back from Topheth, where the LORD had sent him to prophesy, stood in the courtyard of the LORD's temple, and proclaimed to all the people, ¹⁵ "This is what the LORD of Hosts, the God of Israel, says: 'I am about to bring on this city—and on all its dependent villages—all the disaster that I spoke against it, for they have become obstinate, not obeying My words.' "

20 Pashhur the priest, the son of Immer and chief officer in the house of the LORD, heard Jeremiah prophesying these things. ² So Pashhur had Jeremiah the prophet beaten and put him in the stocks at the Upper Benjamin Gate in the LORD's temple. ³ The next day, when Pashhur released Jeremiah from the stocks, Jeremiah said to him, "The LORD does not call you Pashhur, but Magor-missabib, ⁴ for this is what the LORD says, 'I am about to make you a terror to both yourself and those you love. They will fall by the sword of their enemies before your very eyes. I will hand Judah over to the king of Babylon, and he will deport them to Babylon and put them to the sword. ⁵ I will give away all the wealth of this city, all its products and valuables. Indeed, I will hand all the treasures of the kings of Judah over to their enemies. They will plunder them, seize them, and carry them off to Babylon. ⁶ As for you, Pashhur, and all who live in your house, you will go into captivity. You will go to Babylon. There you will die, and there you will be buried, you and all your friends that you prophesied falsely to.' "

𝒫SALM 119:45-48

⁴⁵ I will walk freely in an open place
   because I seek Your precepts.
⁴⁶ I will speak of Your decrees before
      kings
   and not be ashamed.
⁴⁷ I delight in Your commands,
   which I love.
⁴⁸ I will lift up my hands to Your
      commands, which I love,
   and will meditate on Your statutes.

𝒫ROVERBS 25:13

¹³ To those who send him, a
      trustworthy messenger
   is like the coolness of snow on a
      harvest day;
   he refreshes the life of his masters.

2 𝒯HESSALONIANS 1:1–2:12

1 Paul, Silvanus, and Timothy:
   To the church of the Thessalonians in God our Father and the Lord Jesus Christ.

² Grace to you and peace from God our Father and the Lord Jesus Christ.

³ We must always thank God for you, brothers, which is fitting, since your faith is flourishing, and the love of every one of you for one another is increasing. ⁴ Therefore we ourselves boast about you among God's churches—about your endurance and faith in all the persecutions and afflictions you endure. ⁵ It is a clear evidence of God's righteous judgment that you will be counted worthy of God's kingdom, for which you also are suffering, ⁶ since it is righteous for God to repay with affliction those who afflict you, ⁷ and to reward with rest you who are afflicted, along with us. This will take place at the revelation of the Lord Jesus from heaven with His powerful angels, ⁸ taking vengeance with flaming fire on those who don't know God and on those who don't obey the gospel of our Lord Jesus. ⁹ These will pay the penalty of everlasting destruction, away from the Lord's presence and from His glorious strength, ¹⁰ in that day when He comes to be glorified by His saints and to be admired by all those who have believed, because our testimony among you was believed. ¹¹ And in view of this, we always pray for you that our God will consider you worthy of His calling, and will, by His power, fulfill every desire for goodness and the work of faith, ¹² so that the name of our Lord Jesus will be glorified by you, and you by Him, according to the grace of our God and the Lord Jesus Christ.

2 Now concerning the coming of our Lord Jesus Christ and our being gathered to Him: we ask you, brothers, ² not to be easily upset in mind or troubled, either by a spirit or by a message or by a letter as if from us, alleging that the Day of the Lord has come. ³ Don't let anyone deceive you in any way. For that day will not come unless the apostasy comes first and the man of lawlessness is revealed, the son of destruction. ⁴ He opposes and exalts himself above every so-called god or object of worship, so that he sits in God's sanctuary, publicizing that he himself is God.

⁵ Don't you remember that when I was still with you I told you about this? ⁶ And you know what currently restrains him, so that he will be revealed in his time. ⁷ For the mystery of lawlessness is already at work; but the one now restraining will do so until he is out of the way, ⁸ and then the lawless one will be revealed. The Lord Jesus will destroy him with the breath of His mouth and will bring him to nothing with the brightness of His coming. ⁹ The coming of the lawless one is based on Satan's working, with all kinds of false miracles, signs, and wonders, ¹⁰ and with every unrighteous deception among those who are perishing. They perish because they did not accept the love of the truth in order to be saved. ¹¹ For this reason God sends them a strong delusion so that they will believe what is false, ¹² so that all will be condemned—those who did not believe the truth but enjoyed unrighteousness.

Their Days Are Numbered

The lawless one will be revealed. The Lord Jesus will destroy him with the . . . brightness of His coming.
——2 THESSALONIANS 2:8

Despite all evidences to the contrary, God is in charge of the world's affairs, and the days of rebellious kingdoms on earth are numbered. Our God reigns! The "power and the glory" spoken of in the final words of the Lord's Prayer are talking about kingdom power and glory. The other type of power and glory, that which is measured by earthly standards alone and rejected by Jesus in His temptation in the wilderness, is doomed to dissolution and decay.

Ezekiel the prophet, speaking centuries ago of the impermanence of anything not founded on kingdom values, said, "Doom has gone out. The rod [of wickedness] has blossomed; arrogance has bloomed" (Ezk 7:10). Note the telltale steps: doom appears, sin blossoms, and pride has budded. And the fruit of all this? Dissolution and decay.

When speaking of a prominent figure who will arise in the last days and challenge the authority of God's kingdom, Moffat refers to him in his translation as "the Lawless One, the doomed One" (2 Th 2:3). Those who break the laws of God's kingdom, which are written into the very nature of things, are doomed. Perhaps not today, nor tomorrow, but inevitably, anything that is against God's kingdom is destined to destruction. It carries within itself the seeds of its own dissolution and decay.

Prayer

Gracious Father, I have looked upon the kingdom of the world until my eyes are tired—tired of looking at death. Now lift up my eyes, and let me look at life. Let me look upon You. And I see You, not as a reclining God, but a reigning God. Hallelujah!

Further Study

Eph 6:10-18; Jn 12:30-31; Heb 2:14; 1 Jn 3:8
What is Paul's exhortation?
How can we take dominion?

OCTOBER 23

JEREMIAH 20:7–22:30

7 You deceived me, LORD,
        and I was deceived.
    You seized me and prevailed.
    I am a laughingstock all the time;
        everyone ridicules me.
8 For whenever I speak, I cry out—
        I proclaim: Violence and destruction!

because the word of the LORD
        has become for me
    constant disgrace and derision.
9 If I say: I won't mention Him
        or speak any longer in His name,
    His message becomes
        a fire burning in my heart,
    shut up in my bones.
    I become tired of holding it in,

and I cannot prevail.
10 For I have heard the gossip
      of the multitudes,
   "Terror is on every side!
   Report him; let's report him!"
   Everyone I trusted watches
      for my fall.
   "Perhaps he will be deceived
   so that we might prevail
      against him
   and take our vengeance on him."
11 But the LORD is with me
      like a violent warrior.
   Therefore, my persecutors
      will stumble and not prevail.
   Since they have not succeeded,
      they will be utterly shamed,
   an everlasting humiliation
      that will never be forgotten.
12 LORD of Hosts, testing
      the righteous
   and seeing the heart and mind,
   let me see Your vengeance
      on them,
   for I have presented my case
      to You.
13 Sing to the LORD!
   Praise the LORD,
   for He rescues the life of the needy
   from the hand of evil people.

14 Cursed be the day
      on which I was born.
   The day my mother bore me—
      let it never be blessed.
15 Cursed be the man
      who brought the news
         to my father, saying,
   "A male child is born to you,"
      bringing him great joy.
16 Let that man be like the cities
   the LORD overthrew
      without compassion.
   Let him hear an outcry
      in the morning
   and a war cry at noontime
17 because he didn't kill me
      in the womb
   so that my mother
      might have been my grave,
   her womb eternally pregnant.
18 Why did I come out of the womb
   to see only struggle and sorrow,
   to end my life in shame?

21 This is the word that came to Jeremiah from the LORD when King Zedekiah sent Pashhur son of Malchijah and the priest Zephaniah son of Maaseiah to Jeremiah, asking, ² "Ask the LORD on our behalf, since Nebuchadnezzar king of Babylon is making war against us. Perhaps the LORD will perform for us something like all His past wonderful works so that Nebuchadnezzar will withdraw from us."

³ But Jeremiah answered, "This is what you are to say to Zedekiah: ⁴ 'This is what the LORD, the God of Israel, says: I will repel the weapons of war in your hands, those you are using to fight the king of Babylon and the Chaldeans who are besieging you outside the wall, and I will bring them into the center of this city. ⁵ I will fight against you with an outstretched hand and a mighty arm, with anger, rage, and great wrath. ⁶ I will strike the residents of this city, both man and beast. They will die in a great plague. ⁷ Afterwards'"—this is the LORD's declaration—"'King Zedekiah of Judah, his officers, and the people—those in this city who survive the plague, the sword, and the famine—I will hand over to King Nebuchadnezzar of Babylon, to their enemies, yes, to those who want to take their lives. He will put them to the sword; he won't spare them or show pity or compassion.'

⁸ "But you must say to this people, 'This is what the LORD says: Look, I am presenting to you the way of life and the way of death. ⁹ Whoever stays in this city will die by the sword, famine, and plague, but whoever goes out and surrenders to the Chaldeans who are besieging you will live and will retain his life like the spoils of war. ¹⁰ For I have turned against this city to bring disaster and not good'"—this is the LORD's declaration. "'It will be handed over to the king of Babylon, who will burn it down.'

¹¹ "And to the house of the king of Judah say this: 'Hear the word of the LORD! ¹² House of David, this is what the LORD says:

   Administer justice every morning,
   and rescue the victim of robbery

from the hand of his oppressor,
or My anger will flare up like fire
and burn unquenchably
because of their evil deeds.
13 Beware! I am against you,
you who sit above the valley,
you atop the rocky plateau—
this is the LORD's declaration—
you who say: Who can come down
against us?
Who can enter our hiding places?
14 I will punish you according to
what you have done—
this is the LORD's declaration.
I will kindle a fire in its forest
that will consume everything
around it.' "

22 This is what the LORD says: "Go down to the palace of the king of Judah and announce this word there. ² You are to say: Hear the word of the LORD, king of Judah, you who sit on the throne of David—you, your officers, and your people who enter these gates. ³ This is what the LORD says: Administer justice and righteousness. Rescue the victim of robbery from the hand of his oppressor. Don't exploit or brutalize the alien, the fatherless, or the widow. Don't shed innocent blood in this place. ⁴ For if you conscientiously carry out this word, then kings sitting on David's throne will enter through the gates of this palace riding on chariots and horses—they, their officers, and their people. ⁵ But if you do not obey these words, then I swear by Myself"—this is the LORD's declaration—"that this house will become a ruin."

⁶ For this is what the LORD says concerning the house of the king of Judah:

You are like Gilead to Me,
or the summit of Lebanon,
but I will certainly turn you
into a wilderness,
uninhabited cities.
7 I will appoint destroyers
against you,
each with his weapons.
They will cut down the choicest
of your cedars
and throw them into the fire.

⁸ "Many nations will pass by this city and ask one another: Why did the LORD do such a thing to this great city? ⁹ They will answer: Because they abandoned the covenant of the LORD their God and worshiped and served other gods."

10 Do not weep for the dead;
do not mourn for him.
Weep bitterly for the one
who has gone away,
for he will never return again
and see his native land.

¹¹ For this is what the LORD says concerning Shallum son of Josiah, king of Judah, who succeeded Josiah his father as king: "He has left this place—he will never return here again, ¹² but he will die in the place where they deported him, never seeing this land again."

13 Woe for the one who builds
his palace
through unrighteousness,
his upper rooms through injustice,
who makes his fellow man serve
without pay
and will not give him his wages,
14 who says: I will build myself
a massive palace,
with spacious upper rooms.
He will cut windows in it,
and it will be paneled with cedar
and painted with vermilion.
15 Are you a king because you excel
in cedar?
Your own father, did he not
eat and drink?
He administered justice
and righteousness,
then it went well with him.
16 He took up the case of the poor
and needy,
then it went well.
Is this not what it means
to know Me?
This is the LORD's declaration.
17 But you have eyes and heart
for nothing
except your own unjust gain,
shedding innocent blood
and committing extortion
and oppression.

¹⁸ Therefore, this is what the LORD says concerning Jehoiakim son of Josiah, king of Judah:

They will not mourn
for him, saying,
Woe, my brother! or Woe, my
sister!
They will not mourn
for him, saying,
Woe, lord! Woe, his majesty!
¹⁹ He will be buried like a donkey,
dragged off and thrown
outside the gates of Jerusalem.
²⁰ Go up to Lebanon and cry out;
raise your voice in Bashan;
cry out from Abarim,
for all your lovers
have been crushed.
²¹ I spoke to you when
you were secure.
You said: I will not listen.
This has been your way since youth;
indeed, you have never listened
to Me.
²² The wind will take charge of all
your shepherds,
and your lovers will go
into captivity.
Then you will be ashamed
and humiliated
because of all your evil.
²³ You residents of Lebanon,
nestled among the cedars,
how you will groan
when labor pains come on you,
agony like a woman in labor.

²⁴ "As I live," says the LORD, "though you, Coniah son of Jehoiakim, the king of Judah, were a signet ring on My right hand, I would tear you from it. ²⁵ In fact, I will hand you over to those you dread, who want to take your life, to Nebuchadnezzar king of Babylon and the Chaldeans. ²⁶ I will hurl you and the mother who gave birth to you into another land, where neither of you were born, and there you will both die. ²⁷ They will never return to the land they long to return to."

²⁸ Is this man Coniah
a despised, shattered pot,

a jar no one wants?
Why are he and his descendants
hurled out
and cast into a land
they have not known?
²⁹ Earth, earth, earth,
hear the word of the LORD!
³⁰ This is what the LORD says:

Record this man as childless,
a man who will not be successful
in his lifetime.
None of his descendants
will succeed
in sitting on the throne of David
or ruling again in Judah.

PSALM 119:49-52

⁴⁹ Remember Your word to Your
servant;
You have given me hope through it.
⁵⁰ This is my comfort in my
affliction:
Your promise has given me life.
⁵¹ The arrogant constantly ridicule
me,
but I do not turn away from Your
instruction.
⁵² LORD, I remember Your judgments
from long ago
and find comfort.

PROVERBS 25:14-15

¹⁴ The man who boasts about a gift
that does not exist
is like clouds and wind without
rain.
¹⁵ A ruler can be persuaded through
patience,
and a gentle tongue can break a
bone.

2 THESSALONIANS 2:13–3:18

¹³ But we must always thank God for you, brothers loved by the Lord, because from the beginning God has chosen you for salvation through sanctification by the Spirit and through belief in the

truth. [14] He called you to this through our gospel, so that you might obtain the glory of our Lord Jesus Christ. [15] Therefore, brothers, stand firm and hold to the traditions you were taught, either by our message or by our letter.

[16] May our Lord Jesus Christ Himself and God our Father, who has loved us and given us eternal encouragement and good hope by grace, [17] encourage your hearts and strengthen you in every good work and word.

3 Finally, pray for us, brothers, that the Lord's message may spread rapidly and be honored, just as it was with you, [2] and that we may be delivered from wicked and evil men, for not all have faith. [3] But the Lord is faithful; He will strengthen and guard you from the evil one. [4] We have confidence in the Lord about you, that you are doing and will do what we command. [5] May the Lord direct your hearts to God's love and Christ's endurance.

[6] Now we command you, brothers, in the name of our Lord Jesus Christ, to keep away from every brother who walks irresponsibly and not according to the tradition received from us. [7] For you yourselves know how you must imitate us: we were not irresponsible among you; [8] we did not eat anyone's bread free of charge; instead, we labored and toiled, working night and day, so that we would not be a burden to any of you. [9] It is not that we don't have the right to support, but we did it to make ourselves an example to you so that you would imitate us. [10] In fact, when we were with you, this is what we commanded you: "If anyone isn't willing to work, he should not eat." [11] For we hear that there are some among you who walk irresponsibly, not working at all, but interfering with the work of others. [12] Now we command and exhort such people, by the Lord Jesus Christ, that quietly working, they may eat their own bread. [13] Brothers, do not grow weary in doing good.

[14] And if anyone does not obey our instruction in this letter, take note of that person; don't associate with him, so that he may be ashamed. [15] Yet don't treat him as an enemy, but warn him as a brother.

[16] May the Lord of peace Himself give you peace always in every way. The Lord be with all of you. [17] This greeting is in my own hand—Paul. This is a sign in every letter; this is how I write. [18] The grace of our Lord Jesus Christ be with all of you.

For New Christians

Stand firm and hold to the traditions you were taught.

—2 THESSALONIANS 2:15

Christians need to stand with their feet shod with the preparation of the gospel of peace. The moment we begin to compromise on the Word of God and the great truths of the gospel, we shall not only slide in the understanding of our faith but also in its practice.

Permit me to say a word to those who have been in the Christian life for just a short time. Now that you are a Christian, take your stand unflinchingly on the Lord's side. When you meet your old friends—those you used to hang around with in the days before you came to know the Lord—and they propose that you go on doing the things you used to do that you know are not in harmony with God's Word, then be resolute and refuse. Take a firm stand, and watch that you do not slip toward them. Have your feet shod with the preparation of the gospel of peace.

The first thing that strikes everyone who comes into the Christian life is that it is entirely different from one's former life. You must determine to take your stand with Jesus Christ, and when others tempt you, say: "I cannot betray my Lord. I am bound to Him for all eternity. My feet are shod and I am not moving." You have to know what you believe and be resolute and determined to stand for it—come what may. If I had not done this in the days following my conversion to Christ, then I would have forfeited an adventure that has taken me deeper and deeper into God.

Prayer

O God, how can I have faith in You unless I have faith in the words You have spoken to me in the Bible? Help me stand firm in the faith—today and every day. In Jesus' name. Amen.

Further Study

Gl 5:1-13; Php 1:27; 1 Pt 5:7-11
What did Paul say to the Galatians?
How should we conduct ourselves?

OCTOBER 24

JEREMIAH 23:1–24:10

23 "Woe to the shepherds who destroy and scatter the sheep of My pasture!" This is the LORD's declaration. ² "Therefore, this is what the LORD, the God of Israel, says about the shepherds who shepherd My people: You have scattered My flock, banished them, and have not attended to them. I will attend to you because of your evil acts"—the LORD's declaration. ³ "I will gather the remnant of My flock from all the lands where I have banished them, and I will return them to their grazing land. They will become fruitful and numerous. ⁴ I will raise up shepherds over

them who will shepherd them. They will no longer be afraid or dismayed, nor will any be missing." This is the LORD's declaration.

⁵ "The days are coming"—this is the LORD's declaration—"when I will raise up a righteous Branch of David. He will reign wisely as king and administer justice and righteousness in the land. ⁶ In His days Judah will be saved, and Israel will dwell securely. This is what He will be named: The LORD Is Our Righteousness. ⁷ The days are coming"—the LORD's declaration—"when it will no longer be said: As the LORD lives who brought the Israelites from the land of Egypt, ⁸ but: As the LORD lives, who brought and led the descendants of the

house of Israel from the land of the
north and from all the other countries
where I had banished them. They will
dwell once more in their own land."
⁹ Concerning the prophets:

My heart is broken within me,
and all my bones tremble.
I have become like a drunkard,
like a man overcome by wine,
because of the LORD,
because of His holy words.
¹⁰ For the land is full of adulterers;
the land mourns because
of the curse,
and the grazing lands
in the wilderness
have dried up.
Their way of life has become evil,
and their power is not
rightly used
¹¹ because both prophet and priest
are ungodly,
even in My house I have found
their evil.
This is the LORD's declaration.
¹² Therefore, their way will be
to them
like slippery paths in the gloom.
They will be driven away
and fall down there,
for I will bring disaster on them,
the year of their punishment.
This is the LORD's declaration.

¹³ Among the prophets of Samaria
I saw something disgusting:
They prophesied by Baal
and led My people Israel astray.
¹⁴ Among the prophets
of Jerusalem also
I saw a horrible thing:
They commit adultery and walk
in lies.
They strengthen the hands
of evildoers,
and none turns his back on evil.
They are all like Sodom to Me;
Jerusalem's residents are
like Gomorrah.

¹⁵ Therefore, this is what the LORD of
Hosts says concerning the prophets:

I am about to feed them
wormwood
and give them poisoned water
to drink,
for from the prophets
of Jerusalem
ungodliness has spread
throughout the land.

¹⁶ This is what the LORD of Hosts says:
"Do not listen to the words of the
prophets who prophesy to you. They are
making you worthless. They speak visions from their own minds, not from
the LORD's mouth. ¹⁷ They keep on saying to those who despise Me: The LORD
has said: You will have peace. To everyone who walks in the stubbornness of
his heart they have said, No harm will
come to you."

¹⁸ For who has stood in the council
of the LORD
to see and hear His word?
Who has paid attention
to His word and obeyed?
¹⁹ Look, a storm from the LORD!
Wrath has gone forth,
a whirling storm.
It will whirl about the head
of the wicked.
²⁰ The LORD's anger will not
turn back
until He has completely fulfilled
the purposes of His heart.
In time to come you will
understand it clearly.

²¹ I did not send these prophets,
yet they ran with a message.
I did not speak to them,
yet they prophesied.
²² If they had really stood
in My council,
they would have enabled
My people to hear My words
and would have turned them back
from their evil ways
and their evil deeds.

²³ "Am I a God who is only near"—
this is the LORD's declaration—"and not
a God who is far away? ²⁴ Can a
man hide himself in secret places
where I cannot see him?"—the LORD's

declaration. "Do I not fill the heavens and the earth?"—the LORD's declaration.

²⁵ "I have heard what the prophets who prophesy a lie in My name have said: I had a dream! I had a dream! ²⁶ How long will this continue in the minds of the prophets prophesying lies, prophets of the deceit of their own minds? ²⁷ Through their dreams that they tell one another, they make plans to cause My people to forget My name as their fathers forgot My name through Baal worship. ²⁸ The prophet who has only a dream should recount the dream, but the one who has My word should speak My word truthfully, for what is straw compared to grain?"—the LORD's declaration. ²⁹ "Is not My word like fire"—the LORD's declaration—"and like a sledgehammer that pulverizes rock? ³⁰ Therefore, take note! I am against the prophets"—the LORD's declaration—"who steal My words from each other. ³¹ I am against the prophets"—the LORD's declaration—"who use their own tongues to deliver an oracle. ³² I am against those who prophesy false dreams"—the LORD's declaration—"telling them and leading My people astray with their falsehoods and their boasting. It was not I who sent or commanded them, and they are of no benefit at all to these people"—this is the LORD's declaration.

³³ "Now when these people or a prophet or a priest asks you: What is the burden of the LORD? you will respond to them: What is the burden? I will throw you away"—this is the LORD's declaration. ³⁴ "As for the prophet, priest, or people who say: The burden of the LORD, I will punish that man and his household. ³⁵ This is what each man is to say to his friend and to his brother: What has the LORD answered? or What has the LORD spoken? ³⁶ But no longer refer to the burden of the LORD, for each man's word becomes his burden and you pervert the words of the living God, the LORD of Hosts, our God. ³⁷ You must say to the prophet: What has the LORD answered you? and What has the LORD spoken? ³⁸ But if you say: The burden of

the LORD, then this is what the LORD says: Because you have said, The burden of the LORD, and I specifically told you not to say, The burden of the LORD, ³⁹ I will surely forget you and throw away from My presence both you and the city that I gave you and your fathers. ⁴⁰ I will bring on you everlasting shame and humiliation that will never be forgotten."

24 After Nebuchadnezzar king of Babylon had deported Jeconiah son of Jehoiakim king of Judah, the officials of Judah, and the craftsmen and metalsmiths from Jerusalem and had brought them to Babylon, the LORD showed me two baskets of figs placed before the temple of the LORD. ² One basket contained very good figs, like early figs, but the other basket contained very bad figs, so bad they were inedible. ³ The LORD said to me, "What do you see, Jeremiah?" I said, "Figs! The good figs are very good, but the bad figs are extremely bad, so bad they are inedible."

⁴ The word of the LORD came to me: ⁵ "This is what the LORD, the God of Israel, says: Like these good figs, so I regard as good the exiles from Judah I sent away from this place to the land of the Chaldeans. ⁶ I will keep My eyes on them for their good and will return them to this land. I will build them up and not demolish them; I will plant them and not uproot them. ⁷ I will give them a heart to know Me, that I am the LORD. They will be My people, and I will be their God because they will return to Me with all their heart.

⁸ "But as for the bad figs, so bad they are inedible, this is what the LORD says: in this way I will deal with Zedekiah king of Judah, his officials, and the remnant of Jerusalem—those remaining in this land and those living in the land of Egypt. ⁹ I will make them an object of horror and disaster to all the kingdoms of the earth, a disgrace, an object of scorn, ridicule, and cursing, wherever I have banished them. ¹⁰ I will send the sword, famine, and plague against them until they have perished from the land I gave to them and their ancestors."

PSALM 119:53-56

53 Rage seizes me because of the
wicked
who reject Your instruction.
54 Your statutes are the theme of my
song
during my earthly life.
55 I remember Your name in the
night, LORD,
and I keep Your law.
56 This is my practice:
I obey Your precepts.

PROVERBS 25:16-17

16 If you find honey, eat only what
you need;
otherwise, you'll get sick from it
and vomit.
17 Seldom set foot in your neighbor's
house;
otherwise, he'll get sick of you
and hate you.

1 TIMOTHY 1:1-20

1 Paul, an apostle of Christ Jesus according to the command of God our Savior and of Christ Jesus, our hope: 2 To Timothy, my true child in the faith.

Grace, mercy, and peace from God the Father and Christ Jesus our Lord.

3 As I urged you when I went to Macedonia, remain in Ephesus so that you may command certain people not to teach other doctrine 4 or to pay attention to myths and endless genealogies. These promote empty speculations rather than God's plan, which operates by faith. 5 Now the goal of our instruction is love from a pure heart, a good conscience, and a sincere faith. 6 Some have deviated from these and turned aside to fruitless discussion. 7 They want to be teachers of the law, although

they don't understand what they are saying or what they are insisting on. 8 Now we know that the law is good, provided one uses it legitimately. 9 We know that the law is not meant for a righteous person, but for the lawless and rebellious, for the ungodly and sinful, for the unholy and irreverent, for those who kill their fathers and mothers, for murderers, 10 for the sexually immoral and homosexuals, for kidnappers, liars, perjurers, and for whatever else is contrary to the sound teaching 11 based on the glorious gospel of the blessed God that was entrusted to me.

12 I give thanks to Christ Jesus our Lord, who has strengthened me, because He considered me faithful, appointing me to the ministry— 13 one who was formerly a blasphemer, a persecutor, and an arrogant man. Since it was out of ignorance that I had acted in unbelief, I received mercy, 14 and the grace of our Lord overflowed, along with the faith and love that are in Christ Jesus. 15 This saying is trustworthy and deserving of full acceptance: "Christ Jesus came into the world to save sinners"—and I am the worst of them. 16 But I received mercy because of this, so that in me, the worst of them, Christ Jesus might demonstrate the utmost patience as an example to those who would believe in Him for eternal life. 17 Now to the King eternal, immortal, invisible, the only God, be honor and glory forever and ever. Amen.

18 Timothy, my child, I am giving you this instruction in keeping with the prophecies previously made about you, so that by them you may strongly engage in battle, 19 having faith and a good conscience. Some have rejected these and have suffered the shipwreck of their faith. 20 Hymenaeus and Alexander are among them, and I have delivered them to Satan, so that they may be taught not to blaspheme.

The Burden of Revival

But no longer refer to the burden of the LORD,
for each man's word becomes his burden.—JEREMIAH **23:36**

God loves His children to be involved with Him in bringing about His purposes, and it is not in God's nature to ignore the great principle of prayer which He himself has established in the universe. Although revival begins in the sovereign purposes of God, it comes into the world through the doorway of believing prayer.

John Wallace, principal of the Bible college I attended prior to entering the ministry, used to say: "Before somebody can experience a blessing, somebody has to bear a burden." He used to illustrate the point in this way: "Before deliverance came to the nation of Israel when they were in Egypt, Moses had to bear a burden. Before the great Temple of God could be built in Jerusalem, Solomon was called to bear a burden. Before the sins of the world could be removed Christ had to bear a burden. Before somebody can experience a blessing, somebody has to bear a burden."

This is a principle that can be traced throughout the whole of the Bible—from Genesis to Revelation. It can be seen at work, too, in the history of all religious revivals. Before God comes from heaven to work in extraordinary ways He places the burden of revival on the hearts of His people. And who does He choose to carry this burden? You can be sure that they will be men and women who are drawn to prayer and understand something of its power and potential. Would you, I wonder, be one?

Prayer

Gracious Father, You know how my heart shrinks from such a great challenge as this. All I can say is—I am willing to be made willing. Help me, dear Father. In Jesus' name. Amen.

Further Study

Ps 21:1-13; 38:9; 73:25; Is 26:9; Mk 11:24
What will God grant to us?
How can a desire become a burden?

OCTOBER 25

JEREMIAH 25:1–26:24

25 This is the word that came to Jeremiah concerning all the people of Judah in the fourth year of Jehoiakim son of Josiah, king of Judah (which was the first year of Nebuchadnezzar king of Babylon). ²The prophet Jeremiah spoke concerning all the people of Judah and all the residents of Jerusalem as follows: ³"From the thirteenth year of Josiah son of Amon, king of Judah, until this very day—23 years—the word of the LORD has come to me, and I have spoken to you time and time again, but you have not obeyed. ⁴The LORD sent all His servants the prophets to you time and time again, but you have not obeyed or even paid attention. ⁵He announced, 'Turn, each of you, from your evil way of life and from your evil deeds. Live in the land the LORD gave to you and your ancestors forever and ever. ⁶Do not follow other gods to serve them and to worship them, and do not provoke Me to anger by the work of your hands. Then I will do you no harm.

⁷" 'But you would not obey Me'—this is the LORD's declaration—'in order that you might provoke Me to anger by the work of your hands and bring disaster on yourselves.'

⁸"Therefore, this is what the LORD of Hosts says: 'Because you have not obeyed My words, ⁹I am going to send for all the families of the north'—this is the LORD's declaration—'and send for My servant Nebuchadnezzar king of Babylon, and I will bring them against this land, against its residents, and against all these surrounding nations, and I will completely destroy them and make them a desolation, a derision, and ruins forever. ¹⁰I will eliminate the sound of joy and gladness from them—the voice of the bridegroom and the bride, the sound of the millstones and the light of the lamp. ¹¹This whole land will become a desolate ruin, and these nations will serve the king of Babylon for 70 years. ¹²When the 70 years are completed, I will punish the king of Babylon and that nation'—this is the LORD's declaration—'the land of the Chaldeans, for their guilt, and I will make it a ruin forever. ¹³I will bring on that land all My words I have spoken against it, all that is written in this book that Jeremiah prophesied against all the nations. ¹⁴For many nations and great kings will enslave them, and I will repay them according to their deeds and the work of their hands.' "

¹⁵This is what the LORD, the God of Israel, said to me: "Take this cup of the wine of wrath from My hand and make all the nations I am sending you to drink from it. ¹⁶They will drink, stagger, and go out of their minds because of the sword I am sending among them."

¹⁷So I took the cup from the LORD's hand and made all the nations drink from it, everyone the LORD sent me to. ¹⁸These included:

Jerusalem and the other cities of Judah, its kings and its officials, to make them a desolate ruin, an object of scorn and cursing—as it is today;
¹⁹Pharaoh king of Egypt, his officers, his leaders, all his people, ²⁰and all the mixed peoples;
all the kings of the land of Uz;
all the kings of the land of the Philistines—Ashkelon, Gaza, Ekron, and the remnant of Ashdod;
²¹Edom, Moab, and the Ammonites;
²²all the kings of Tyre,
all the kings of Sidon,
and the kings of the coastlands across the sea;

²³ Dedan, Tema, Buz, and all those who shave their temples; ²⁴ all the kings of Arabia, and all the kings of the mixed peoples who have settled in the desert; ²⁵ all the kings of Zimri, all the kings of Elam, and all the kings of Media; ²⁶ all the kings of the north, both near and far from one another; that is, all the kingdoms of the world which are on the face of the earth. Finally, the king of Sheshach will drink after them.

²⁷ "Then you are to say to them: This is what the LORD of Hosts, the God of Israel, says: Drink, get drunk, and vomit. Fall down and never get up again, as a result of the sword I am sending among you. ²⁸ If they refuse to take the cup from you and drink, you are to say to them: This is what the LORD of Hosts says: You must drink! ²⁹ For I am already bringing disaster on the city that bears My name, so how could you possibly go unpunished? You will not go unpunished, for I am summoning a sword against all the inhabitants of the earth"—this is the declaration of the LORD of Hosts.

³⁰ "As for you, you are to prophesy all these things to them, and say to them:

The LORD roars from on high;
He raises His voice
    from His holy dwelling.
He roars loudly
    over His grazing land;
He calls out with a shout,
    like those who tread grapes,
against all the inhabitants
    of the earth.
³¹ The tumult reaches to the ends
    of the earth
because the LORD brings a case
    against the nations.
He enters into judgment
    with all flesh.
As for the wicked,
He hands them over
    to the sword—
This is the LORD's declaration.

³² "This is what the LORD of Hosts says:

Pay attention! Disaster goes forth
    from nation to nation.
A great storm is stirred up
    from the ends of the earth."

³³ Those slain by the LORD on that day will be spread from one end of the earth to the other. They will not be mourned, gathered, or buried. They will be like manure on the surface of the ground.

³⁴ Wail, you shepherds, and cry out.
Roll in the dust, you leaders
    of the flock.
Because the days of your slaughter
    have come,
you will fall and become shattered
    like a precious vase.
³⁵ Flight will be impossible
    for the shepherds,
and escape, for the leaders
    of the flock.
³⁶ Hear the sound
    of the shepherds' cry,
the wail of the leaders
    of the flock,
for the LORD is destroying
    their pasture.
³⁷ Peaceful grazing land
    will become lifeless
because of
    the LORD's burning anger.
³⁸ He has left His den like a lion,
for their land has become
    a desolation
because of the sword
    of the oppressor,
because of His burning anger.

26 At the beginning of the reign of Jehoiakim son of Josiah, king of Judah, this word came from the LORD: ² "This is what the LORD says: Stand in the courtyard of the LORD's temple and speak all the words I have commanded you to speak to all Judah's cities that are coming to worship there. Do not hold back a word. ³ Perhaps they will listen and return—each from his evil way of life—so that I might relent concerning the disaster that I plan to do to them because of the evil of their deeds. ⁴ You are to say to them: This is what the LORD says: If you do not listen to Me by living according to My law that I set before you ⁵ and by listening to the words of My servants the prophets I have been sending you time and time again, though you did not listen, ⁶ I will make this temple like Shiloh. I will make this city an object of cursing for all the nations of the earth."

⁷ The priests, the prophets, and all the people heard Jeremiah speaking these words in the temple of the LORD. ⁸ He finished the address the LORD had commanded him to deliver to all the people. Then the priests, the prophets, and all the people took hold of him, yelling, "You must surely die! ⁹ How dare you prophesy in the name of the LORD, 'This temple will become like Shiloh and this city will become an uninhabited ruin'!" Then all the people assembled against Jeremiah at the LORD's temple.

¹⁰ When the officials of Judah heard these things, they went up from the king's palace to the LORD's temple and sat at the entrance of the New Gate. ¹¹ Then the priests and prophets said to the officials and all the people, "This man deserves the death sentence because he has prophesied against this city, as you have heard with your own ears."

¹² Then Jeremiah said to all the officials and the people, "The LORD sent me to prophesy all the words that you have heard against this temple and city. ¹³ So now, correct your ways and deeds and obey the voice of the LORD your God so that He might relent concerning the disaster that He warned about. ¹⁴ As for me, here I am in your hands; do to me what you think is good and right. ¹⁵ But know for certain that if you put me to death, you will bring innocent blood on yourselves, on this city, and on its residents, for it is certain the LORD has sent me to speak all these things directly to you."

¹⁶ Then the officials and all the people told the priests and prophets, "This man doesn't deserve the death sentence, for he has spoken to us in the name of the LORD our God!"

¹⁷ Some of the elders of the land stood up and said to all the assembled people, ¹⁸ "Micah the Moreshite prophesied in the days of Hezekiah king of Judah and said to all the people of Judah, 'This is what the LORD of Hosts says:

Zion will be plowed like a field,
Jerusalem will become ruins,
and the temple mount
a forested hill.'

¹⁹ Did Hezekiah king of Judah and all the people of Judah put him to death? Did he not fear the LORD and plead for the LORD's favor, and did not the LORD relent concerning the disaster He had pronounced against them? We are about to bring great harm on ourselves!"

²⁰ Another man was also prophesying in the name of the LORD—Uriah son of Shemaiah from Kiriath-jearim. He prophesied against this city and against this land in words like all those of Jeremiah. ²¹ King Jehoiakim, all his warriors, and all the officials heard his words, and the king tried to put him to death. When Uriah heard, he fled in fear and went to Egypt. ²² But King Jehoiakim sent men to Egypt: Elnathan son of Achbor and certain other men with him went to Egypt. ²³ They brought Uriah out of Egypt and took him to King Jehoiakim, who executed him with the sword and threw his corpse into the burial place of the common people.

²⁴ But Ahikam son of Shaphan supported Jeremiah, so he was not handed over to the people to be put to death.

....

℘SALM 119:57-60

⁵⁷ The LORD is my portion;
   I have promised to keep Your
      words.
⁵⁸ I have sought Your favor with all
      my heart;
   be gracious to me according to
      Your promise.

⁵⁹ I thought about my ways
and turned my steps back to Your
decrees.
⁶⁰ I hurried, not hesitating
to keep Your commands.

PROVERBS 25:18-20

¹⁸ A man giving false testimony
against his neighbor
is like a club, a sword, or a sharp
arrow.
¹⁹ Trusting an unreliable person in a
time of trouble
is like a rotten tooth or a faltering
foot.

²⁰ Singing songs to a troubled heart
is like taking off clothing on a cold
day,
or like pouring vinegar on soda.

1 TIMOTHY 2:1–3:7

2 First of all, then, I urge that petitions, prayers, intercessions, and thanksgivings be made for everyone, ² for kings and all those who are in authority, so that we may lead a tranquil and quiet life in all godliness and dignity. ³ This is good, and it pleases God our Savior, ⁴ who wants everyone to be saved and to come to the knowledge of the truth.

⁵ For there is one God
and one mediator between God
and man,
a man, Christ Jesus,
⁶ who gave Himself—a ransom for
all,
a testimony at the proper time.

⁷ For this I was appointed a herald, an apostle (I am telling the truth; I am not lying), and a teacher of the Gentiles in faith and truth.
⁸ Therefore I want the men in every place to pray, lifting up holy hands without anger or argument. ⁹ Also, the women are to dress themselves in modest clothing, with decency and good sense; not with elaborate hairstyles, gold, pearls, or expensive apparel, ¹⁰ but with good works, as is proper for women who affirm that they worship God. ¹¹ A woman should learn in silence with full submission. ¹² I do not allow a woman to teach or to have authority over a man; instead, she is to be silent. ¹³ For Adam was created first, then Eve. ¹⁴ And Adam was not deceived, but the woman was deceived and transgressed. ¹⁵ But she will be saved through childbearing, if she continues in faith, love, and holiness, with good sense.

3 This saying is trustworthy: "If anyone aspires to be an overseer, he desires a noble work." ² An overseer, therefore, must be above reproach, the husband of one wife, self-controlled, sensible, respectable, hospitable, an able teacher, ³ not addicted to wine, not a bully but gentle, not quarrelsome, not greedy— ⁴ one who manages his own household competently, having his children under control with all dignity. ⁵ (If anyone does not know how to manage his own household, how will he take care of God's church?) ⁶ He must not be a new convert, or he might become conceited and fall into the condemnation of the Devil. ⁷ Furthermore, he must have a good reputation among outsiders, so that he does not fall into disgrace and the Devil's trap.

The First Thing to Do

*I want the men in every place to pray, lifting up holy
hands without anger or argument.*—1 TIMOTHY 2:8

Although doubt can be turned destructively against error, it is also possible for it to be turned destructively against truth. How do we deal with the darker side of doubt? The first thing we must do is to bring every doubt into the open and examine it. Most Christians fail to do this; they do nothing with their doubts and just hope they will go away.

But the way people react to their doubts is an indication of their attitude to doubt itself. Many feel ashamed when they experience doubt and thus push it below the surface of their minds and refuse to recognize it. Some even regard doubt as the unpardonable sin. Others treat it as an unmentionable subject and never refer to any doubts they have for fear they are letting the team down. I myself sometimes struggle with doubt—even after more than fifty years in the Christian life.

In the months following my conversion, I had doubts about the inspiration and inerrancy of the Bible until I decided to accept it by faith. When I did, all my doubts concerning it were immediately dissolved, and from that day to this I have never had one doubt about the reliability of Scripture. But I have doubted other things—particularly in the area of personal guidance. I have learned, however, not to let doubts threaten or intimidate me, and when they come I simply look them in the face and say: "I am going to put you in harness and make you work to bring me closer to God."

Now my doubts get fewer and fewer.

Prayer

Father, how can I sufficiently thank You for showing me how to take the negative things of life and turn them into positives? Nothing need work against me when I have You within. I am so thankful. Amen.

Further Study

1 Jn 2:1-20; 3:24; 1 Co 13:12
What did Paul admit to?
What did John affirm?

OCTOBER 26

JEREMIAH 27:1–29:14

27 At the beginning of the reign of Zedekiah son of Josiah, king of Judah, this word came to Jeremiah from the LORD: ² "This is what the LORD said to me: Make fetters and yoke bars for yourself and put them on your neck. ³ Send word to the king of Edom, the king of Moab, the king of the Ammonites, the king of Tyre, and the king of Sidon through messengers who are coming to Zedekiah king of Judah in Jerusalem. ⁴ Command them to go to their masters, saying: This is what the LORD of Hosts, the God of Israel, says: This is what you must say to your masters: ⁵ By My great strength and outstretched arm, I made the earth, and the people, and animals on the face of the earth. I give it to anyone I please. ⁶ So now I have placed all these lands under the authority of My servant Nebuchadnezzar, king of Babylon. I have even given him the wild animals to serve him. ⁷ All nations will serve him, his son, and his grandson until the time for his own land comes, and then many nations and great kings will enslave him.

⁸ "As for the nation or kingdom that does not serve Nebuchadnezzar king of Babylon and does not place its neck under the yoke of the king of Babylon, that nation I will punish by sword, famine, and plague"—this is the LORD's declaration—"until through him I have destroyed it. ⁹ But as for you, do not listen to your prophets, your diviners, your dreamers, your fortune-tellers, or your sorcerers who say to you: Don't serve the king of Babylon! ¹⁰ for they prophesy a lie to you so that you will be removed from your land. I will banish you, and you will perish. ¹¹ But as for the nation that will put its neck under the yoke of the king of Babylon and serve him, I will

leave it in its own land, and that nation will till it and reside in it." This is the LORD's declaration.

¹² I spoke to Zedekiah king of Judah in the same way: "Put your necks under the yoke of the king of Babylon, serve him and his people, and live! ¹³ Why should you and your people die by the sword, famine, or plague as the LORD has threatened against any nation that does not serve the king of Babylon? ¹⁴ Do not listen to the words of the prophets who are telling you, 'You must not serve the king of Babylon,' for they are prophesying a lie to you. ¹⁵ 'I have not sent them'—this is the LORD's declaration—'and they are prophesying falsely in My name; therefore, I will banish you, and you will perish—you and the prophets who are prophesying to you.' "

¹⁶ Then I spoke to the priests and all these people, saying, "This is what the LORD says, 'Do not listen to the words of your prophets. They are prophesying to you, claiming: Look, very soon now the articles of the LORD's temple will be brought back from Babylon. They are prophesying a lie to you. ¹⁷ Do not listen to them. Serve the king of Babylon and live! Why should this city become a ruin? ¹⁸ If they are indeed prophets and if the word of the LORD is with them, let them intercede with the LORD of Hosts not to let the articles that remain in the LORD's temple, in the palace of the king of Judah, and in Jerusalem go to Babylon.' ¹⁹ For this is what the LORD of Hosts says about the pillars, the sea, the water carts, and the rest of the articles that still remain in this city, ²⁰ those Nebuchadnezzar king of Babylon did not take when he deported Jeconiah son of Jehoiakim, king of Judah, from Jerusalem to Babylon along with all the nobles of Judah and Jerusalem. ²¹ Yes, this is what the LORD of Hosts, the God

of Israel, says about the articles that remain in the temple of the LORD, in the palace of the king of Judah, and in Jerusalem: ²² 'They will be brought to Babylon and will remain there until I attend to them again.' This is the LORD's declaration. 'Then I will bring them up and restore them to this place.' "

28 In that same year, at the beginning of the reign of Zedekiah king of Judah, in the fifth month of the fourth year, the prophet Hananiah son of Azzur from Gibeon said to me in the temple of the LORD in the presence of the priests and all the people, ² "This is what the LORD of Hosts, the God of Israel, says: 'I have broken the yoke of the king of Babylon. ³ Within two years I will restore to this place all the articles of the LORD's temple that Nebuchadnezzar king of Babylon took from here and transported to Babylon. ⁴ And I will restore to this place Jeconiah son of Jehoiakim, king of Judah, and all the exiles from Judah who went to Babylon'— this is the LORD's declaration—'for I will break the yoke of the king of Babylon.' "

⁵ The prophet Jeremiah replied to the prophet Hananiah in the presence of the priests and all the people who were standing in the temple of the LORD. ⁶ The prophet Jeremiah said, "Amen! May the LORD do so. May the LORD make the words you have prophesied come true and may He restore the articles of the LORD's temple and all the exiles from Babylon to this place! ⁷ Only listen to this message I am speaking in your hearing and in the hearing of all the people. ⁸ The prophets who preceded you and me from ancient times prophesied war, disaster, and plague against many lands and great kingdoms. ⁹ As for the prophet who prophesies peace— only when the word of the prophet comes true will the prophet be recognized as one whom the LORD has truly sent."

¹⁰ The prophet Hananiah then took the yoke bar from the neck of Jeremiah the prophet and broke it. ¹¹ In the presence of all the people Hananiah pro-

claimed, "This is what the LORD says: 'In this way, within two years I will break the yoke of Nebuchadnezzar, king of Babylon, from the neck of all the nations.' " Jeremiah the prophet then went on his way.

¹² The word of the LORD came to Jeremiah after Hananiah the prophet had broken the yoke bar from the neck of Jeremiah the prophet: ¹³ "Go say to Hananiah: This is what the LORD says: You broke a wooden yoke bar, but in its place you will make an iron yoke bar. ¹⁴ For this is what the LORD of Hosts, the God of Israel, says: I have put an iron yoke on the neck of all these nations that they might serve Nebuchadnezzar king of Babylon, and they will serve him. I have also put the wild animals under him."

¹⁵ The prophet Jeremiah said to the prophet Hananiah, "Listen, Hananiah! The LORD did not send you, but you have led these people to trust in a lie. ¹⁶ Therefore, this is what the LORD says: 'I am about to send you off the face of the earth. You will die this year because you have spoken rebellion against the LORD.' " ¹⁷ And the prophet Hananiah died that year in the seventh month.

29 This is the text of the letter that Jeremiah the prophet sent from Jerusalem to the rest of the elders of the exiles, the priests, the prophets, and all the people Nebuchadnezzar had deported from Jerusalem to Babylon. ² This was after King Jeconiah, the queen mother, the court officials, the officials of Judah and Jerusalem, the craftsmen, and the metalsmiths had left Jerusalem. ³ The letter was sent by Elasah son of Shaphan and Gemariah son of Hilkiah whom Zedekiah king of Judah had sent to Babylon to Nebuchadnezzar king of Babylon. The letter stated:

⁴ This is what the LORD of Hosts, the God of Israel, says to all the exiles I deported from Jerusalem to Babylon: ⁵ "Build houses and live in them. Plant gardens and eat their produce. ⁶ Take wives and have sons and daughters. Take wives for

your sons and give your daughters to men in marriage so that they may bear sons and daughters. Multiply there; do not decrease. [7] Seek the welfare of the city I have deported you to. Pray to the LORD on its behalf, for when it has prosperity, you will prosper."

[8] For this is what the LORD of Hosts, the God of Israel, says: "Don't let your prophets who are among you and your diviners deceive you, and don't listen to the dreams you elicit from them, [9] for they are prophesying falsely to you in My name. I have not sent them." This is the LORD's declaration.

[10] For this is what the LORD says: "When 70 years for Babylon are complete, I will attend to you and will confirm My promise concerning you to restore you to this place. [11] For I know the plans I have for you"—this is the LORD's declaration—"plans for your welfare, not for disaster, to give you a future and a hope. [12] You will call to Me and come and pray to Me, and I will listen to you. [13] You will seek Me and find Me when you search for Me with all your heart. [14] I will be found by you"—the LORD's declaration—"and I will restore your fortunes and gather you from all the nations and places where I banished you"—the LORD's declaration. "I will restore you to the place I deported you from."

PSALM 119:61-64

[61] Though the ropes of the wicked
were wrapped around me,
I did not forget Your law.
[62] I rise at midnight to thank You
for Your righteous judgments.
[63] I am a friend to all who fear You,
to those who keep Your precepts.
[64] LORD, the earth is filled with Your
faithful love;
teach me Your statutes.

PROVERBS 25:21-22

[21] If your enemy is hungry, give him
food to eat,
and if he is thirsty, give him water
to drink;
[22] for you will heap coals on his
head,
and the LORD will reward you.

1 TIMOTHY 3:8–4:16

[8] Deacons, likewise, should be worthy of respect, not hypocritical, not drinking a lot of wine, not greedy for money, [9] holding the mystery of the faith with a clear conscience. [10] And they must also be tested first; if they prove blameless, then they can serve as deacons. [11] Wives, too, must be worthy of respect, not slanderers, self-controlled, faithful in everything. [12] Deacons must be husbands of one wife, managing their children and their own households competently. [13] For those who have served well as deacons acquire a good standing for themselves, and great boldness in the faith that is in Christ Jesus.

[14] I write these things to you, hoping to come to you soon. [15] But if I should be delayed, I have written so that you will know how people ought to act in God's household, which is the church of the living God, the pillar and foundation of the truth. [16] And most certainly, the mystery of godliness is great:

He was manifested in the flesh,
justified in the Spirit,
seen by angels,
preached among the Gentiles,
believed on in the world,
taken up in glory.

4 Now the Spirit explicitly says that in the latter times some will depart from the faith, paying attention to deceitful spirits and the teachings of demons, [2] through the hypocrisy of liars whose consciences are seared. [3] They forbid marriage and demand abstinence from foods that God created to be received with gratitude by those who be-

lieve and know the truth. ⁴For everything created by God is good, and nothing should be rejected if it is received with thanksgiving, ⁵since it is sanctified by the word of God and by prayer.

⁶If you point these things out to the brothers, you will be a good servant of Christ Jesus, nourished by the words of the faith and of the good teaching that you have followed. ⁷But have nothing to do with irreverent and silly myths. Rather, train yourself in godliness, ⁸for,

the training of the body has a
    limited benefit,
but godliness is beneficial in every
    way,
since it holds promise for the
    present life
and also for the life to come.

⁹This saying is trustworthy and deserves full acceptance. ¹⁰In fact, we labor and strive for this, because we have put our hope in the living God, who is the Savior of everyone, especially of those who believe.

¹¹Command and teach these things. ¹²No one should despise your youth; instead, you should be an example to the believers in speech, in conduct, in love, in faith, in purity. ¹³Until I come, give your attention to public reading, exhortation, and teaching. ¹⁴Do not neglect the gift that is in you; it was given to you through prophecy, with the laying on of hands by the council of elders. ¹⁵Practice these things; be committed to them, so that your progress may be evident to all. ¹⁶Be conscientious about yourself and your teaching; persevere in these things, for by doing this you will save both yourself and your hearers.

Missing by Inches

*You will seek Me and find Me when you search
for Me with all your heart.*

—JEREMIAH 29:13

We are looking today at what I consider one of the greatest truths we can discover about receiving from God: "God does not just answer prayer—He answers you."

The Almighty does not just listen to the words we weave into the air when we pray; He listens also to the attitude of our hearts. If the two are not properly correlated, then we miss out on many of God's blessings. And this missing out is not because God is stingy about the way He dispenses His blessings, but because we short-circuit our own spiritual system and become imperfect receivers. To put it another way: our failure to receive isn't due to the fact that God is not good at giving, but because we are not good at receiving. The fault is always in us, never in Him.

Are you a fully integrated person? When you present your requests to God, are your heart and mind as one? Is what you ask with your lips fully supported by what you are saying in your heart? If not, then when you attempt to climb higher with God, you will not have the precise coordination you need in order to scale the precipitous heights. The awesome fact that has to be faced by all those who want to climb the mountains of God is this—it is possible to miss your step on those steep slopes not by feet, but merely by inches. And it is in those seemingly trivial inches that our spiritual direction is often determined.

Prayer

O Father, I am seeing more and more the perils that come from being inwardly at cross-purposes. Help me, however, to see that although the challenge is great, the power behind me is greater than the challenge in front of me. In Jesus' name. Amen.

Further Study

Jl 2:1-13; Dt 6:5; Ps 119:2
What was God's message through Joel?
When are we blessed?

OCTOBER 27

JEREMIAH 29:15–31:14

¹⁵ You have said, "The LORD has raised up prophets for us in Babylon!" ¹⁶ But this is what the LORD says concerning the king sitting on David's throne and concerning all the people living in this city—that is, concerning your brothers who did not go with you into exile. ¹⁷ This is what the LORD of Hosts says: "I am about to send against them sword, famine, and plague and will make them like rotten figs that are inedible because they are so bad. ¹⁸ I will pursue them with sword, famine, and plague. I will make them a horror to all the kingdoms of the earth—a curse and a desolation, an object of scorn and a disgrace among all the nations where I will have banished them. ¹⁹ I will do this because they have not listened to My words"—this is the LORD's declaration—"that I sent to them with My servants the prophets time and time again. And you too have not listened." This is the LORD's declaration.

²⁰ Hear the word of the LORD, all you exiles I have sent from Jerusalem to Babylon. ²¹ This is what the LORD of Hosts, the God of Israel, says to Ahab son of Kolaiah and to Zedekiah son of Maaseiah, the ones prophesying a lie to you in My name: "I am about to hand them over to Nebuchadnezzar king of Babylon, and he will kill them before your very eyes. ²² Based on what happens to them, all the exiles of Judah who are in Babylon will create a curse that says: May the LORD make you like Zedekiah and Ahab, whom the king of Babylon roasted in the fire! ²³ because they have committed an outrage in Israel by committing adultery with their neighbors' wives and have spoken a lie in My name, which I did not command them. I am He who knows, and I am a witness." This is the LORD's declaration.

²⁴ To Shemaiah the Nehelamite you are to say, ²⁵ "This is what the LORD of Hosts, the God of Israel, says: You

in your own name have sent out letters to all the people of Jerusalem, to the priest Zephaniah son of Maaseiah, and to all the priests, saying: ²⁶ The LORD has appointed you priest in place of Jehoiada the priest to be the chief officer in the temple of the LORD, responsible for every madman who acts like a prophet. You must confine him in stocks and an iron collar. ²⁷ So now, why have you not rebuked Jeremiah of Anathoth who has been acting like a prophet among you? ²⁸ For he has sent word to us in Babylon, claiming: The exile will be long. Build houses and settle down. Plant gardens and eat their produce."

²⁹ Zephaniah the priest read this letter in the hearing of Jeremiah the prophet.

³⁰ Then the word of the LORD came to Jeremiah: ³¹ "Send a message to all the exiles, saying: This is what the LORD says concerning Shemaiah the Nehelamite. Because Shemaiah prophesied to you, though I did not send him, and made you trust a lie, ³² this is what the LORD says: I am about to punish Shemaiah the Nehelamite and his descendants. There will not be even one of his descendants living among these people, nor will any ever see the good that I will bring to My people"—this is the LORD's declaration—"for he has preached rebellion against the LORD."

30 This is the word that came to Jeremiah from the LORD. ² This is what the LORD, the God of Israel, says: "Write down on a scroll all the words that I have spoken to you, ³ for the days are certainly coming"—this is the LORD's declaration—"when I will restore the fortunes of My people Israel and Judah"—the LORD's declaration. "I will restore them to the land I gave to their ancestors and they will possess it."

⁴ These are the words the LORD spoke to Israel and Judah. ⁵ Yes, this is what the LORD says:

We have heard a cry of terror,
of dread—there is no peace.

⁶ Ask and see
whether a male can give birth.
Why then do I see every man
with his hands on his stomach
like a woman in labor
and every face turned pale?
⁷ How awful that day will be!
There will be none like it!
It will be a time of trouble
for Jacob,
but he will be delivered out of it.

⁸ "On that day"—this is the declaration of the LORD of Hosts—"I will break his yoke from your neck and snap your fetters so strangers will never again enslave him. ⁹ They will serve the LORD their God and I will raise up David their king for them."

¹⁰ As for you, My servant Jacob,
do not be afraid—
this is the LORD's declaration—
and do not be dismayed, Israel,
for I will without fail save you
from far away,
your descendants, from the land
of their captivity!
Jacob will return and have calm
and quiet
with no one to frighten him.
¹¹ For I will be with you—
this is the LORD's declaration—
to save you!
I will bring destruction
on all the nations
where I have scattered you;
however, I will not
bring destruction on you.
I will discipline you justly,
but I will by no means
leave you unpunished.

¹² For this is what the LORD says:

Your injury is incurable;
your wound most severe.
¹³ No one takes up the case
for your sores.
You have nothing that can heal you.
¹⁴ All your lovers have forgotten you;
they no longer look for you,
for I have struck you
like an enemy would,

with the discipline
　　of someone cruel,
because of your enormous guilt
　　and your innumerable sins.
¹⁵ Why do you cry out
　　about your injury?
Your pain has no cure!
I have done these things to you
because of your enormous guilt
　　and your innumerable sins.
¹⁶ Nevertheless, all who devoured
　　you will be devoured,
and all your adversaries—
　　all of them—
will go off into exile.
Your despoilers will become spoil,
and all who plunder you
　　will be plundered.

¹⁷ But I will bring you health
　　and will heal you
　　　of your wounds—
　　this is the LORD's declaration—
for they call you The Outcast,
that Zion no one cares about.

¹⁸ This is what the LORD says:

I will certainly restore
　　the fortunes of Jacob's tents
　　and show compassion
　　　on his dwellings.
Every city will be rebuilt
　　on its mound;
every citadel will stand
　　on its proper site.
¹⁹ Thanksgiving will come
　　out of them,
a sound of celebration.
I will multiply them,
　　and they will not decrease;
I will honor them,
　　and they will not
　　be insignificant.
²⁰ His children will be
　　as in past days;
his congregation
　　will be established
　　in My presence.
I will punish all his oppressors.
²¹ Jacob's leader will be one of them;
his ruler will issue from him.
I will invite him to Me,
　　and he will approach Me,

for who would otherwise
　　risk his life to approach Me?
　　This is the LORD's declaration.
²² You will be My people,
　　and I will be your God.

²³ Look, a storm from the LORD!
Wrath has gone forth.
A churning storm,
it will whirl about the head
　　of the wicked.
²⁴ The LORD's burning anger will not
　　turn back
until He has completely fulfilled
　　the purposes of His heart.
In time to come you will
　　understand it.

31 "At that time"—this is the LORD's
declaration—"I will be God of all
the families of Israel, and they will be
My people."
² This is what the LORD says:

They found favor in the wilderness—
　　the people who survived
　　　the sword.
When Israel went to find rest,
³ 　the LORD appeared to him
　　from far away.
I have loved you
　　with an everlasting love;
therefore, I have continued
　　to extend faithful love to you.
⁴ Again I will build you so that
　　you will be rebuilt,
Virgin Israel.
You will take up
　　your tambourines again
and go forth in joyful dancing.
⁵ You will plant vineyards again
　　on the mountains of Samaria;
the planters will plant
　　and will enjoy the fruit.
⁶ For there will be a day
　　when watchmen will call out
in the hill country of Ephraim:
Get up, let's go up to Zion,
to the LORD our God!

⁷ For this is what the LORD says:

Sing with joy for Jacob;
shout for the chief of the nations!

Proclaim, praise, and say:
Lord, save Your people,
the remnant of Israel!
8 Watch! I am going to bring them
from the northern land.
I will gather them
from remote regions
of the earth—
the blind and the lame will be
with them,
along with those who are pregnant
and those about to give birth.
They will return here
as a great assembly!
9 They will come weeping,
but I will bring them back
with consolation.
I will lead them to wadis filled
with water
by a smooth way where
they will not stumble,
for I am Israel's Father,
and Ephraim is My firstborn.
10 Nations, hear the word
of the Lord,
and tell it among the
far off coastlands!
Say: The One who scattered Israel
will gather him.
He will watch over him
as a shepherd guards
his flock,
11 for the Lord has ransomed Jacob
and redeemed him
from the power of one
stronger than he.
12 They will come and shout for joy
on the heights of Zion;
they will be radiant with joy
because of the Lord's goodness,
because of the grain,
the new wine, the fresh oil,
and because of the young
of the flocks and herds.
Their life will be
like an irrigated garden,
and they will no longer grow weak
from hunger.
13 Then the virgin will rejoice
with dancing,
while young and old men rejoice
together.
I will turn their mourning into joy,
give them consolation,

and bring happiness out of grief.
14 I will give the priests their fill
with abundance,
and My people will be satisfied
with My goodness.
This is the Lord's declaration.

PSALM 119:65-68

65 Lord, You have treated Your
servant well,
just as You promised.
66 Teach me good judgment and
discernment,
for I rely on Your commands.
67 Before I was afflicted I went
astray,
but now I keep Your word.
68 You are good, and You do what is
good;
teach me Your statutes.

PROVERBS 25:23-24

23 The north wind produces rain,
and a backbiting tongue, angry
looks.
24 Better to live on the corner of a
roof
than in a house shared with a
nagging wife.

1 TIMOTHY 5:1-25

5 Do not rebuke an older man, but
exhort him as a father, younger men
as brothers, 2 older women as mothers,
and with all propriety, the younger
women as sisters.
3 Support widows who are genuinely
widows. 4 But if any widow has children
or grandchildren, they should learn to
practice their religion toward their own
family first and to repay their parents,
for this pleases God. 5 The real widow,
left all alone, has put her hope in God
and continues night and day in her petitions and prayers; 6 however, she who is
self-indulgent is dead even while she
lives. 7 Command this, so that they won't
be blamed. 8 Now if anyone does not
provide for his own relatives, and especially for his household, he has denied

the faith and is worse than an unbeliever. ⁹ No widow should be placed on the official support list unless she is at least 60 years old, has been the wife of one husband, ¹⁰ and is well known for good works—that is, if she has brought up children, shown hospitality, washed the saints' feet, helped the afflicted, and devoted herself to every good work. ¹¹ But refuse to enroll younger widows; for when they are drawn away from Christ by desire, they want to marry, ¹² and will therefore receive condemnation because they have renounced their original pledge. ¹³ At the same time, they also learn to be idle, going from house to house; they are not only idle, but are also gossips and busybodies, saying things they shouldn't say. ¹⁴ Therefore, I want younger women to marry, have children, manage their households, and give the adversary no opportunity to accuse us. ¹⁵ For some have already turned away to follow Satan. ¹⁶ If any believing woman has widows, she should help them, and the church should not be burdened, so that it can help those who are genuinely widows.

¹⁷ The elders who are good leaders should be considered worthy of an ample honorarium, especially those who work hard at preaching and teaching. ¹⁸ For the Scripture says:

You must **not muzzle an ox that is threshing grain,** and,
The laborer is worthy of his wages.

¹⁹ Don't accept an accusation against an elder unless it is supported by two or three witnesses. ²⁰ Publicly rebuke those who sin, so that the rest will also be afraid. ²¹ I solemnly charge you, before God and Christ Jesus and the elect angels, to observe these things without prejudice, doing nothing out of favoritism. ²² Don't be too quick to lay hands on anyone, and don't share in the sins of others. Keep yourself pure. ²³ Don't continue drinking only water, but use a little wine because of your stomach and your frequent illnesses. ²⁴ Some people's sins are evident, going before them to judgment, but the sins of others follow them. ²⁵ Likewise, good works are obvious, and those that are not obvious cannot remain hidden.

What a Tranquilizer!

I have loved you with an everlasting love.

—JEREMIAH 31:3

"How little real love there is for God," says theologian Arthur W. Pink. He suggests that the low level of spirituality in today's church is caused by our hearts being so little occupied with thoughts of the divine love. "The better we are acquainted with His love—its character, its fullness, its blessedness," he says, "the more will our hearts be drawn out in love to Him."

We focus now on the fact that God's love is eternal.

God being eternal, it follows that His love also is eternal. This means that God loved us before earth and heaven were called into existence, that He has set His heart upon us from all eternity. This is the truth set forth in Ephesians 1:4-5, where we are told that we were chosen in Christ before the foundation of the world. What a tranquilizer this is for our hearts! If God's love for us had no beginning, then it has no ending either. It is from "everlasting to everlasting."

Another thing we need to know about the love of God is that it is a holy love. This means that His love is not regulated by whim or caprice or sentiment, but by principle. Just as His grace reigns not at the expense of righteousness but "through" it (Rm 5:21), so His love never conflicts with His holiness. This is why John says that God is "light" before he says God is "love." And this is why, too, the Almighty never lets us get away with anything. He loves us too much for that. His love is pure, holy, and unmixed with maudlin sentimentality. God will not wink at sin, not even in His own people.

Prayer

O Father, the more I learn about Your love, the more my heart is set on fire. Increase my understanding, for I see that the more I comprehend how much I am loved, the more secure I am in that love. Amen.

Further Study

Rm 8:18-39; 1 Pt 1:17-21
What was Paul convinced of?
How does Peter portray the eternal perspective?

OCTOBER 28

JEREMIAH 31:15–32:25

15 This is what the LORD says:

A voice was heard in Ramah,
a lament with bitter weeping—
Rachel weeping for her children,
refusing to be comforted
for her children
because they are no more.

16 This is what the LORD says:

Keep your voice from weeping
and your eyes from tears,
for the reward for your work
will come—
this is the LORD's declaration—
and your children will return
from the enemy's land.

17 There is hope for your future—
this is the LORD's declaration—
and your children will return
to their own territory.
18 I have heard Ephraim moaning:
You disciplined me,
and I have been disciplined
like an untrained calf.
Restore me, and I will return,
for you, LORD, are my God.
19 After I returned, I repented;
After I was instructed, I struck
my thigh in grief.
I was ashamed and humiliated
because I bore the disgrace
of my youth.
20 Isn't Ephraim a precious son
to Me,
a delightful child?
Whenever I speak against him,

I certainly still think about him.
Therefore, My inner being yearns
for him;
I will truly have compassion on him.
This is the LORD's declaration.

21 Set up road markers for yourself;
establish signposts!
Keep the highway in mind,
the way you have traveled.
Return, Virgin Israel!
Return to these cities of yours.
22 How long will you turn
here and there,
faithless daughter?
For the LORD creates
something new in the land—
a female will shelter a man.

23 This is what the LORD of Hosts, the God of Israel, says: "When I restore their fortunes, they will once again speak this word in the land of Judah and in its cities: May the LORD bless you, righteous settlement, holy mountain. 24 Judah and all its cities will live in it together—also farmers and those who move with the flocks—25 for I satisfy the thirsty person and feed all those who are weak."

26 At this I awoke and looked around. My sleep had been most pleasant to me.

27 "The days are coming"—this is the LORD's declaration—"when I will sow the house of Israel and the house of Judah with the seed of man and the seed of beast. 28 Just as I watched over them to uproot and to tear them down, to demolish and to destroy, and to cause disaster, so will I be attentive to build and to plant them," says the LORD. 29 "In those days, it will never again be said:

The fathers have eaten sour grapes,
and the children's teeth are set
on edge.

30 Rather, each will die for his own wrongdoing. Anyone who eats sour grapes—his own teeth will be set on edge.

31 "Look, the days are coming"—this is the LORD's declaration—"when I will make a new covenant with the house of Israel and with the house of Judah. 32 This one will not be like the covenant I made with their ancestors when I took them by the hand to bring them out of the land of Egypt—a covenant they broke even though I had married them"—the LORD's declaration. 33 "Instead, this is the covenant I will make with the house of Israel after those days"—the LORD's declaration. "I will place My law within them and write it on their hearts. I will be their God, and they will be My people. 34 No longer will one teach his neighbor or his brother, saying: Know the LORD, for they will all know Me, from the least to the greatest of them"—the LORD's declaration. "For I will forgive their wrongdoing and never again remember their sin."

35 This is what the LORD says:

The One who gives the sun
for light by day,
the fixed order of moon and stars
for light by night,
who stirs up the sea and makes
its waves roar—
the LORD of Hosts is His name:
36 If this fixed order departs
from My presence—
this is the LORD's declaration—
then also Israel's descendants
will cease
to be a nation before Me forever.

37 This is what the LORD says:

If the heavens above
can be measured
and the foundations
of the earth below explored,
I will reject all of
Israel's descendants
because of all they have done—
this is the LORD's declaration.

38 "Look, the days are coming"—the LORD's declaration—"when the city from the Tower of Hananel to the Corner Gate will be rebuilt for the LORD. 39 A measuring line will once again stretch out straight to the hill of Gareb and then turn toward Goah. 40 The whole valley—the corpses, the ashes, and all the fields

as far as the Kidron Valley to the corner of the Horse Gate to the east—will be holy to the LORD. It will never be uprooted or demolished again."

32 This is the word that came to Jeremiah from the LORD in the tenth year of Zedekiah king of Judah, which was the eighteenth year of Nebuchadnezzar. ² At that time, the army of the king of Babylon was besieging Jerusalem, and Jeremiah the prophet was imprisoned in the guard's courtyard in the palace of the king of Judah. ³ Zedekiah king of Judah had imprisoned him, saying: "Why are you prophesying, 'This is what the LORD says: Look, I am about to hand this city over to Babylon's king, and he will capture it. ⁴ Zedekiah king of Judah will not escape from the Chaldeans; indeed, he will certainly be handed over to Babylon's king. They will speak face to face and meet eye to eye. ⁵ He will take Zedekiah to Babylon where he will stay until I attend to him'—this is the LORD's declaration. 'You will fight the Chaldeans, but you will not succeed'?"

⁶ Jeremiah replied, "The word of the LORD came to me: ⁷ 'Watch! Hanamel, the son of your uncle Shallum, is coming to you to say: Buy my field in Anathoth for yourself, for you own the right of redemption to buy it.'

⁸ "Then my cousin Hanamel came to the guard's courtyard as the LORD had said and urged me, 'Please buy my field in Anathoth in the land of Benjamin, for you own the right of inheritance and redemption. Buy it for yourself.' Then I knew that this was the word of the LORD. ⁹ So I bought the field in Anathoth from my cousin Hanamel, and I weighed out to him the money—17 shekels of silver. ¹⁰ I recorded it on a scroll, sealed it, called in witnesses, and weighed out the silver on a scale. ¹¹ I took the purchase agreement—the sealed copy with its terms and conditions and the open copy— ¹² and gave the purchase agreement to Baruch son of Neriah, son of Mahseiah. I did this in the sight of my cousin Hanamel, the witnesses who were signing the purchase agreement, and all the Judeans sitting in the guard's courtyard.

¹³ "I instructed Baruch in their sight, ¹⁴ 'This is what the LORD of Hosts, the God of Israel, says: Take these scrolls—this purchase agreement with the sealed copy and this open copy—and put them in an earthen storage jar so they will last a long time. ¹⁵ For this is what the LORD of Hosts, the God of Israel, says: Houses, fields, and vineyards will again be bought in this land.'

¹⁶ "After I had given the purchase agreement to Baruch, son of Neriah, I prayed to the LORD: ¹⁷ Ah, Lord GOD! You Yourself made the heavens and earth by Your great power and with Your outstretched arm. Nothing is too difficult for You! ¹⁸ You show faithful love to thousands but lay the fathers' sins on their sons' laps after them, great and mighty God whose name is the LORD of Hosts, ¹⁹ the One great in counsel and mighty in deed, whose eyes are on all the ways of the sons of men in order to give to each person according to his ways and the result of his deeds. ²⁰ You performed signs and wonders in the land of Egypt and do so to this very day both in Israel and among mankind. You made a name for Yourself, as is the case today. ²¹ You brought Your people Israel out of Egypt with signs and wonders, with a strong hand and an outstretched arm, and with great terror. ²² You gave them this land You swore to give to their ancestors, a land flowing with milk and honey. ²³ They entered and possessed it, but they did not obey Your voice or live according to Your law. They failed to perform all You commanded them to do, and so You have brought all this disaster on them. ²⁴ Look! Siege ramps have come against the city to capture it, and the city, as a result of the sword, famine, and plague, has been handed over to the Chaldeans who are fighting against it. What You have spoken has happened. Look, You can see it! ²⁵ Yet You, Lord GOD, have said to me: Buy the field with silver and call in witnesses—even though the city has been handed over to the Chaldeans!"

PSALM 119:69-72

69 The arrogant have smeared me
   with lies,
   but I obey Your precepts with all
      my heart.
70 Their hearts are hard and
      insensitive,
   but I delight in Your instruction.
71 It was good for me to be afflicted
   so that I could learn Your statutes.
72 Instruction from Your lips is better
      for me
   than thousands of gold and silver
      pieces.

PROVERBS 25:25-26

25 Good news from a distant land
   is like cold water to a parched
      throat.
26 A righteous person who yields to
      the wicked
   is like a muddied spring or a
      polluted well.

1 TIMOTHY 6:1-21

6 All who are under the yoke as slaves
   must regard their own masters to be
worthy of all respect, so that God's
name and His teaching will not be blasphemed. ² And those who have believing masters should not be disrespectful
to them because they are brothers, but
should serve them better, since those
who benefit from their service are believers and dearly loved.

Teach and encourage these things. ³ If
anyone teaches other doctrine and does
not agree with the sound teaching of
our Lord Jesus Christ and with the
teaching that promotes godliness, ⁴ he is
conceited, understanding nothing, but
having a sick interest in disputes and
arguments over words. From these
come envy, quarreling, slanders, evil
suspicions, ⁵ and constant disagreement
among men whose minds are depraved
and deprived of the truth, who imagine
that godliness is a way to material gain.
⁶ But godliness with contentment is a
great gain.

⁷ For we brought nothing into the
world, and we can take nothing out.
⁸ But if we have food and clothing,
we will be content with
these.

⁹ But those who want to be rich fall
into temptation, a trap, and many foolish and harmful desires, which plunge
people into ruin and destruction. ¹⁰ For
the love of money is a root of all kinds
of evil, and by craving it, some have
wandered away from the faith and
pierced themselves with many pains.

¹¹ Now you, man of God, run from
   these things;
   but pursue righteousness,
      godliness, faith,
   love, endurance, and gentleness.
¹² Fight the good fight for the faith;
   take hold of eternal life,
   to which you were called
   and have made a good confession
   before many witnesses.

¹³ In the presence of God, who gives life
to all, and before Christ Jesus, who gave
a good confession before Pontius Pilate,
I charge you ¹⁴ to keep the commandment without spot or blame until the
appearing of our Lord Jesus Christ,
¹⁵ which God will bring about in His
own time. He is

   the blessed and only Sovereign,
   the King of kings,
   and the Lord of lords,
¹⁶ the only One who has immortality,
   dwelling in unapproachable light,
   whom none of mankind has seen
      or can see,
   to whom be honor and eternal
      might.
   Amen.

¹⁷ Instruct those who are rich in the
present age not to be arrogant or to set
their hope on the uncertainty of wealth,
but on God, who richly provides us with
all things to enjoy. ¹⁸ Instruct them to do
good, to be rich in good works, to be
generous, willing to share, ¹⁹ storing up

for themselves a good foundation for the age to come, so that they may take hold of life that is real.

²⁰ Timothy, guard what has been entrusted to you, avoiding irreverent, empty speech and contradictions from the "knowledge" that falsely bears that name. ²¹ By professing it, some people have deviated from the faith.

Grace be with all of you.

The Shield of Faith

Fight the good fight for the faith; take hold of eternal life, to which you were called.—1 TIMOTHY 6:12

The fourth piece of equipment in the Christian soldier's armor is the shield of faith: "In every situation," says the apostle, "take the shield of faith, and with it you will be able to extinguish the flaming arrows of the evil one" (Eph 6:16).

Some take Paul's use of the expression "above all" (as some texts begin this verse) to mean "above everything else in importance," and from this they go on to argue that the last three pieces of armor are more important than the first three. But the phrase really means "in addition to all this." It is a transition phrase designed to introduce us to a section of the armor that has a different purpose.

The six pieces of armor fall clearly into two main groups, the first consisting of the belt of truth, the breastplate of righteousness, and the shoes of the preparation of the gospel of peace. The second group comprises the shield of faith, the helmet of salvation, and the sword of the Spirit. The first three pieces of armor were fixed to the body by a special fastening, and hence, to a certain degree, were immovable. But the shield was not fixed to the body; it was something quite separate. The same applies to the helmet; that, too, was something that could be put on or taken off quite easily. And obviously the same was true of the sword of the Spirit.

The lesson, quite clearly, is this—the first three pieces of equipment should be worn at all times, while the other three are to be taken up when and where necessary.

Prayer

Gracious and loving heavenly Father, I am so thankful for the care and design that have gone into providing for me a sure defense against Satan. I have learned much, yet I see there is still much more to learn. Teach me, my Father. Amen.

Further Study

1 Tm 1:12-20; 6:12; 1 Th 5:8; 1 Jn 5:4
What had some rejected?
What was the result?

OCTOBER 29

JEREMIAH 32:26–34:11

²⁶ Then the word of the LORD came to Jeremiah: ²⁷ "Look, I am the LORD, the God of all flesh. Is anything too difficult for Me? ²⁸ Therefore, this is what the LORD says: I am about to hand this city over to the Chaldeans, to Babylon's king Nebuchadnezzar, and he will capture it. ²⁹ The Chaldeans who are going to fight against this city will come, set this city on fire, and burn it along with the houses where incense has been burned to Baal on their rooftops and where drink offerings have been poured out to other gods to provoke Me to anger. ³⁰ From their youth, the Israelites and Judeans have done nothing but what is evil in My sight! They have done nothing but provoke Me to anger by the work of their hands"—this is the LORD's declaration— ³¹ "for this city has been up against My wrath and fury from the day it was built until now. I will therefore remove it from My presence, ³² because of all the evil the Israelites and Judeans have done to provoke Me to anger— they, their kings, their officials, their priests, and their prophets, the men of Judah, and the residents of Jerusalem. ³³ They have turned their backs to Me and not their faces. Though I taught them time and time again, they do not listen and receive discipline. ³⁴ They have placed their detestable things in the house that is called by My name and have defiled it. ³⁵ They have built the high places of Baal in the Valley of Hinnom to make their sons and daughters pass through the fire to Molech—something I had not commanded them. I had never entertained the thought that they do this detestable act causing Judah to sin!

³⁶ "Now therefore, this is what the LORD, the God of Israel, says to this city about which you said: It has been handed over to Babylon's king through sword, famine, and plague: ³⁷ I am about to gather them from all the lands where I have banished them in My wrath, rage, and great fury, and I will return them to this place and make them live in safety. ³⁸ They will be My people, and I will be their God. ³⁹ I will give them one heart and one way so that for their good and for the good of their descendants after them, they will fear Me always. ⁴⁰ "I will make with them an everlasting covenant: I will never turn away from doing good to them, and I will put fear of Me in their hearts so they will never again turn away from Me. ⁴¹ I will rejoice over them to do what is good to them, and I will plant them faithfully in this land with all My mind and heart.

⁴² "For this is what the LORD says: Just as I have brought all this great disaster on these people, so am I about to bring on them all the good I am promising them. ⁴³ Fields will be bought in this land about which you are saying: It's a desolation without man or beast; it has been handed over to the Chaldeans! ⁴⁴ Fields will be purchased with silver, the transaction written on a scroll and sealed, and witnesses will be called on in the land of Benjamin, in the areas surrounding Jerusalem, and in Judah's cities—the cities of the hill country, the cities of the Judean foothills, and the cities of the Negev— because I will restore their fortunes." This is the LORD's declaration.

33 While he was still confined in the guard's courtyard, the word of the LORD came to Jeremiah a second time: ² "The LORD who made the earth, the LORD who forms it to establish it, the LORD is His name, says this: ³ Call to Me and I will answer you and tell you great and wondrous things you do not know. ⁴ For this is what the LORD, the

God of Israel, says concerning the houses of this city and the palaces of Judah's kings, the ones torn down for defense against the siege ramps and the sword: [5] The people coming to fight the Chaldeans will fill the houses with the corpses of their own men I strike down in My wrath and rage. I have hidden My face from this city because of all their evil. [6] Yet I will certainly bring health and healing to it and will indeed heal them. I will let them experience the abundance of peace and truth. [7] I will restore the fortunes of Judah and of Israel and will rebuild them as in former times. [8] I will purify them from all the wrongs they have committed against Me, and I will forgive all the wrongs they have committed against Me, rebelling against Me. [9] This city will bear on My behalf a name of joy, praise, and glory before all the nations of the earth, who will hear of all the good I will do for them. They will tremble with awe because of all the good and all the peace I will bring about for them.

[10] "This is what the LORD says: In this place which you say is a ruin, without man or beast—that is, in Judah's cities and Jerusalem's streets that are a desolation without man, without inhabitant, and without beast—there will be heard again [11] a sound of joy and gladness, the voice of the bridegroom and the bride, and the voice of those saying,

Praise the LORD of Hosts,
for the LORD is good;
His faithful love endures forever

as they bring thank offerings to the temple of the LORD. For I will restore the fortunes of the land as in former times, says the LORD.

[12] "This is what the LORD of Hosts says: In this desolate place—without man or beast—and in all its cities there will once more be a grazing land where shepherds may rest flocks. [13] The flocks will again pass under the hands of the one who counts them in the cities of the hill country, the cities of the Judean foothills, the cities of the Negev, the land of Benjamin—the cities surrounding Jerusalem and Judah's cities, says the LORD.

[14] "Look, the days are coming"—this is the LORD's declaration—"when I will fulfill the good promises that I have spoken concerning the house of Israel and the house of Judah. [15] In those days and at that time I will cause a Branch of righteousness to sprout up for David, and He will administer justice and righteousness in the land. [16] In those days Judah will be saved, and Jerusalem will dwell securely, and this is what she will be named: The LORD Is Our Righteousness. [17] For this is what the LORD says: David will never fail to have a man sitting on the throne of the house of Israel. [18] The Levitical priests will never fail to have a man always before Me to offer burnt offerings, to burn grain offerings, and to make sacrifices."

[19] The word of the LORD came to Jeremiah: [20] "This is what the LORD says: If you can break My covenant with the day and My covenant with the night so that day and night cease to come at their regular time, [21] then also My covenant with My servant David may be broken so that he will not have a son reigning on his throne, and the Levitical priests will not be My ministers. [22] The hosts of heaven cannot be counted; the sand of the sea cannot be measured. So, too, I will make the descendants of My servant David and the Levites who minister to Me innumerable."

[23] The word of the LORD came to Jeremiah: [24] "Have you not noticed what these people have said? They say: The LORD has rejected the two families He had chosen. My people are treated with contempt and no longer regarded as a nation among them. [25] This is what the LORD says: If I do not keep My covenant with the day and with the night and fail to establish the fixed order of heaven and earth, [26] then I might also reject the seed of Jacob and of My servant David—not taking from his descendants rulers over the descendants of Abraham, Isaac, and Jacob. Instead, I will restore their fortunes and have compassion on them."

34 This is the word that came to Jeremiah from the LORD when Nebuchadnezzar, king of Babylon, all his army, all the earthly kingdoms under his control, and all other nations were fighting against Jerusalem and all its surrounding cities: ² "This is what the LORD, the God of Israel, says: Go, speak to Zedekiah, king of Judah, and tell him: This is what the LORD says: I am about to hand this city over to the king of Babylon, and he will burn it down. ³ As for you, you will not escape from his hand but are certain to be captured and handed over to him. You will meet the king of Babylon eye to eye and speak face to face; you will go to Babylon.

⁴ "Yet hear the LORD's word, Zedekiah, king of Judah. This is what the LORD says concerning you: You will not die by the sword; ⁵ you will die peacefully. There will be a burning ceremony for you just like the burning ceremonies for your fathers, the former kings who preceded you. Alas, lord! will be the lament for you, for I have spoken this word." This is the LORD's declaration.

⁶ So Jeremiah the prophet related all these words to Zedekiah king of Judah in Jerusalem ⁷ while the king of Babylon's army was attacking Jerusalem and all of Judah's remaining cities— against Lachish and Azekah, for only they were left among Judah's fortified cities.

⁸ This is the word that came to Jeremiah from the LORD after King Zedekiah made a covenant with all the people who were in Jerusalem to proclaim freedom to them, ⁹ so each man would free his male and female Hebrew slaves and no one enslave his Judean brother. ¹⁰ All the officials and people who entered into covenant to free their male and female slaves—in order not to enslave them any longer—obeyed and freed them. ¹¹ Afterwards, however, they changed their minds and took back their male and female slaves they had freed and forced them to become slaves again.

PSALM 119:73-77

⁷³ Your hands made me and formed me;
give me understanding so that I can learn Your commands.
⁷⁴ Those who fear You will see me and rejoice,
for I hope in Your word.
⁷⁵ I know, LORD, that Your judgments are just
and that You have afflicted me fairly.
⁷⁶ May Your faithful love comfort me,
as You promised Your servant.
⁷⁷ May Your compassion come to me so that I may live,
for Your instruction is my delight.

PROVERBS 25:27-28

²⁷ It is not good to eat too much honey,
or to seek glory after glory.
²⁸ A man who does not control his temper
is like a city whose wall is broken down.

2 TIMOTHY 1:1-18

1 Paul, an apostle of Christ Jesus by God's will, for the promise of life in Christ Jesus: ² To Timothy, my dearly loved child.

Grace, mercy, and peace from God the Father and Christ Jesus our Lord.

³ I thank God, whom I serve with a clear conscience as my forefathers did, when I constantly remember you in my prayers night and day. ⁴ Remembering your tears, I long to see you so that I may be filled with joy, ⁵ clearly recalling your sincere faith that first lived in your grandmother Lois, then in your mother Eunice, and that I am convinced is in you also.

⁶ Therefore, I remind you to keep ablaze the gift of God that is in you through the laying on of my hands. ⁷ For God has not given us a spirit of fearfulness, but one of power, love, and sound judgment.

⁸ So don't be ashamed of the testimony about our Lord, or of me His prisoner. Instead, share in suffering for the gospel, relying on the power of God,

⁹ who has saved us and called us
with a holy calling,
not according to our works, but
according to His own purpose
and grace,
which was given to us in Christ
Jesus before time began.

¹⁰ This has now been made evident
through the appearing of our
Savior Christ Jesus, who has
abolished death
and has brought life and
immortality to light through
the gospel.

¹¹ For this gospel I was appointed a herald, apostle, and teacher, ¹² and that is why I suffer these things. But I am not ashamed, because I know whom I have believed and am persuaded that He is able to guard what has been entrusted to me until that day. ¹³ Hold on to the pattern of sound teaching that you have heard from me, in the faith and love that are in Christ Jesus. ¹⁴ Guard, through the Holy Spirit who lives in us, that good thing entrusted to you. ¹⁵ This you know: all those in Asia have turned away from me, including Phygelus and Hermogenes. ¹⁶ May the Lord grant mercy to the household of Onesiphorus, because he often refreshed me and was not ashamed of my chains. ¹⁷ On the contrary, when he was in Rome, he diligently searched for me and found me. ¹⁸ May the Lord grant that he obtain mercy from the Lord on that day. And you know how much he ministered at Ephesus.

Handling Confusion

*For God has not given us a spirit of fearfulness,
but one of power, love, and sound judgment.*

—2 TIMOTHY 1:7

A feeling that Satan delights to arouse in a heart unprotected by a spiritual breastplate is the feeling of confusion. None of us likes confusion, because it erodes our sense of competence. Satan, knowing this, steps in whenever he can to take full advantage of it.

Deep in the center of our being is a compulsive demand to be in control. And to satisfy that demand, we have to live in a predictable, understandable world. Confusion presents a serious challenge to our desire for control and is the enemy of those who demand to have clear answers for everything.

Whenever Satan sees that we are not wearing our spiritual breastplate, he comes to us and says something like this: "Look at the great problems that are all around you—earthquakes, famines, violence, cruelty to children. How can you believe in a God of love when these things are going on in the world?" Sometimes he presses home these arguments with such power that you have no clear answers.

There is only one clear answer against such assaults; it is to put on the "breastplate of righteousness." You cannot understand particular happenings; you cannot give any explanation. But you do know that the God who clothed you with His righteousness and saved you from a lost eternity must have your highest interests and those of His universe at heart. When you hold on to that, your heart is protected from despair, even if your mind struggles to comprehend what is happening. You can live in peace even though you do not know all the answers.

Prayer

Father God, I see that I can experience security in my heart even when my mind cannot understand Your ways. Hidden in Christ and His righteousness, I am safe. I am so thankful. Amen.

Further Study

2 Tm 1:1-7; 1 Co 14:33; Is 26:3; Rm 8:39
Where does our peace stem from?
Where does confusion come from?

OCTOBER 30

JEREMIAH 34:12–36:26

¹² Then the word of the LORD came to Jeremiah from the LORD: ¹³ "This is what the LORD, the God of Israel, says: I made a covenant with your ancestors when I brought them out of the land of Egypt, out of the place of slavery, saying: ¹⁴ At the end of seven years, each of you must free his Hebrew brother who sold himself to you. He may serve you six years, but then you must send him out free from you. But your ancestors did not obey Me or pay any attention. ¹⁵ Today you repented and did what pleased Me, each of you proclaiming freedom for his neighbor. You made a covenant before Me at the temple called by My name. ¹⁶ But you have changed your minds and profaned My name. Each has taken back his male and female slaves who had been freed to go wherever they wanted, and you have again subjugated them to be your slaves.

¹⁷ "Therefore, this is what the LORD says: You have not obeyed Me by proclaiming freedom, each man for his brother and for his neighbor. I hereby proclaim freedom for you"—this is the LORD's declaration—"to the sword, to plague, and to famine! I will make you a horror to all the earth's kingdoms. ¹⁸ As for those who disobeyed My covenant, not keeping the terms of the covenant they made before Me, I will treat them like the calf they cut in two in order to pass between its pieces. ¹⁹ The officials of Judah and Jerusalem, the court officials, the priests, and all the people of the land who passed between the pieces of the calf ²⁰ will be handed over to their enemies, to those who want to take their life. Their corpses will become food for the birds of the sky and for the wild animals of the land. ²¹ I will hand Zedekiah king of Judah and his officials over to their enemies, to those who want to take their life, to the king of Babylon's army that is withdrawing. ²² I am about to give the command"—this is the LORD's declaration—"and I will bring them back to this city. They will fight against it, capture it, and burn it down. I will make Judah's cities a desolation, without inhabitant."

35 This is the word that came to Jeremiah from the LORD in the days of Jehoiakim son of Josiah, king of Judah: ² "Go to the house of the Rechabites, speak to them, and bring them to one of the chambers of the temple of the Lord to offer them a drink of wine."

³ So I took Jaazaniah son of Jeremiah, son of Habazziniah, and his brothers and all his sons—the entire house of the Rechabites— ⁴ and I brought them into the temple of the Lord to a chamber occupied by the sons of Hanan son of Igdaliah, a man of God, who had a chamber near the officials' chamber, which was above the chamber of Maaseiah son of Shallum the doorkeeper. ⁵ I set jars filled with wine and some cups before the sons of the house of the Rechabites and said to them, "Drink wine!"

⁶ But they replied, "We do not drink wine, for Jonadab, son of our ancestor Rechab, commanded: 'You and your sons must never drink wine. ⁷ You must not build a house or sow seed or plant a vineyard. Those things are not for you. Rather, you must live in tents your whole life, so you may live a long time on the soil where you stay as a resident alien.' ⁸ We have obeyed the voice of Jonadab, son of our ancestor Rechab, in all he commanded us. So we haven't drunk wine our whole life—we, our wives, our sons, and our daughters. ⁹ We also have not built houses to live in and do not have vineyard, field, or seed. ¹⁰ But we have lived in tents and have obeyed and done as our ancestor Jonadab commanded us. ¹¹ However, when Nebuchadnezzar king of Babylon marched into the land, we said: Come, let's go into Jerusalem to get away from the Chaldean and Aramean armies. So we have been living in Jerusalem."

¹² Then the word of the Lord came to Jeremiah: ¹³ "This is what the Lord of Hosts, the God of Israel, says: Go, say to the men of Judah and the residents of Jerusalem: Will you not accept discipline by listening to My words?"—this is the Lord's declaration. ¹⁴ "The words of Jonadab, son of Rechab, have been carried out. He commanded his sons not to drink wine, and they have not drunk to this very day because they

have obeyed their ancestor's command. But I have spoken to you time and time again, and you have not obeyed Me! ¹⁵ Time and time again I have sent you all My servants the prophets, proclaiming: Turn, each one from his evil way of life, and correct your actions. Stop following other gods to serve them. Live in the land that I gave you and your ancestors. But you would not pay attention or obey Me. ¹⁶ Yes, the sons of Jonadab son of Rechab carried out their ancestor's command he gave them, but these people have not obeyed Me. ¹⁷ Therefore, this is what the Lord, the God of Hosts, the God of Israel, says: I will certainly bring to Judah and to all the residents of Jerusalem all the disaster I have pronounced against them because I have spoken to them, but they have not obeyed, and I have called to them, but they would not answer."

¹⁸ Jeremiah said to the house of the Rechabites: "This is what the Lord of Hosts, the God of Israel, says: 'Because you have obeyed the command of your ancestor Jonadab and have kept all his commands and have done all that he commanded you, ¹⁹ this is what the Lord of Hosts, the God of Israel, says: Jonadab son of Rechab will never fail to have a man to always stand before Me.' "

36 In the fourth year of Jehoiakim son of Josiah, king of Judah, this word came to Jeremiah from the Lord: ² "Take a scroll, and write on it all the words I have spoken to you concerning Israel, Judah, and all the nations from the time I first spoke to you during Josiah's reign until today. ³ Perhaps, when the house of Judah hears about all the disaster I am planning to bring on them, each one of them will turn from his evil way. Then I will forgive their wrongdoing and sin."

⁴ So Jeremiah summoned Baruch son of Neriah. At Jeremiah's dictation, Baruch wrote on a scroll all the words the Lord had spoken to Jeremiah. ⁵ Then Jeremiah commanded Baruch, "I am restricted; I cannot enter the temple of the Lord, ⁶ so you must go and read from the scroll—which you wrote at my

dictation—the words of the LORD in the hearing of the people at the temple of the LORD on a day of fasting. You must also read them in the hearing of all the Judeans who are coming from their cities. [7] Perhaps their petition will come before the LORD, and each one will turn from his evil way, for the anger and fury that the LORD has pronounced against this people are great." [8] So Baruch son of Neriah did everything Jeremiah the prophet had commanded him. At the LORD's temple he read the LORD's words from the scroll.

[9] In the fifth year of Jehoiakim son of Josiah, king of Judah, in the ninth month, all the people of Jerusalem and all those coming in from Judah's cities into Jerusalem proclaimed a fast before the LORD. [10] Then at the LORD's temple, in the chamber of Gemariah son of Shaphan the scribe, in the upper courtyard at the opening of the New Gate of the LORD's temple, in the hearing of all the people, Baruch read Jeremiah's words from the scroll.

[11] When Micaiah son of Gemariah, son of Shaphan, heard all the words of the LORD from the scroll, [12] he went down to the scribe's chamber in the king's palace. All the officials were sitting there—Elishama the scribe, Delaiah son of Shemaiah, Elnathan son of Achbor, Gemariah son of Shaphan, Zedekiah son of Hananiah, and all the other officials. [13] Micaiah reported to them all the words he had heard when Baruch read from the scroll in the hearing of the people. [14] Then all the officials sent word to Baruch through Jehudi son of Nethaniah, son of Shelemiah, son of Cushi, saying, "Bring the scroll that you read in the hearing of the people, and come." So Baruch son of Neriah took the scroll and went to them. [15] They said to him, "Sit down and read it in our hearing." So Baruch read it in their hearing.

[16] When they had heard all the words, they turned to each other in fear and said to Baruch, "We must surely tell the king all these things." [17] Then they asked Baruch, "Tell us—how did you write all these words? At his dictation?" [18] Baruch said to them, "At his dicta-

tion. He recited all these words to me while I was writing on the scroll in ink."

[19] The officials said to Baruch, "You and Jeremiah must hide yourselves and tell no one where you are." [20] Then they came to the king at the courtyard, having deposited the scroll in the chamber of Elishama the scribe, and reported everything in the hearing of the king. [21] The king sent Jehudi to get the scroll, and he took it from the chamber of Elishama the scribe. Jehudi then read it in the hearing of the king and all the officials who were standing by the king. [22] Since it was the ninth month, the king was sitting in his winter quarters with a fire burning in front of him. [23] As soon as Jehudi would read three or four columns, Jehoiakim would cut the scroll with a scribe's knife and throw the columns into the blazing fire until the entire scroll was consumed by the fire in the brazier. [24] As they heard all these words, the king and all of his servants did not become terrified or tear their garments. [25] Even though Elnathan, Delaiah, and Gemariah had urged the king not to burn the scroll, he would not listen to them. [26] Then the king commanded Jerahmeel the king's son, Seraiah son of Azriel, and Shelemiah son of Abdeel to seize Baruch the scribe and Jeremiah the prophet, but the LORD had hidden them.

PSALM 119:78-81

78 Let the arrogant be put to shame
  for slandering me with lies;
  I will meditate on Your precepts.
79 Let those who fear You,
  those who know Your decrees,
  turn to me.
80 May my heart be blameless
  regarding Your statutes
  so that I will not be put to shame.

81 I long for Your salvation;
  I hope in Your word.

PROVERBS 26:1-3

26 Like snow in summer and rain at harvest,

honor is inappropriate for a fool.
² Like a flitting sparrow or a
fluttering swallow,
an undeserved curse goes
nowhere.
³ A whip for the horse, a bridle for
the donkey,
and a rod for the backs of fools.

2 TIMOTHY 2:1-21

2 You, therefore, my child, be strong
in the grace that is in Christ Jesus.
² And what you have heard from me in
the presence of many witnesses, commit to faithful men who will be able to
teach others also. ³ Share in suffering as a good soldier
of Christ Jesus. ⁴ To please the recruiter,
no one serving as a soldier gets entangled in the concerns of everyday life.
⁵ Also, if anyone competes as an athlete,
he is not crowned unless he competes
according to the rules. ⁶ It is the hard-
working farmer who ought to be the
first to get a share of the crops. ⁷ Consider what I say, for the Lord will give
you understanding in everything.
⁸ Keep in mind Jesus Christ, risen
from the dead, descended from David,
according to my gospel. ⁹ For this I suffer, to the point of being bound like a
criminal; but God's message is not
bound. ¹⁰ This is why I endure all things
for the elect: so that they also may obtain salvation, which is in Christ Jesus,
with eternal glory. ¹¹ This saying is trustworthy:

For if we have died with Him, we
will also live with Him;

¹² if we endure, we will also reign
with Him;
if we deny Him, He will also deny
us;
¹³ if we are faithless, He remains
faithful,
for He cannot deny Himself.

¹⁴ Remind them of these things,
charging them before God not to fight
about words; this is in no way profitable
and leads to the ruin of the hearers.
¹⁵ Be diligent to present yourself approved to God, a worker who doesn't
need to be ashamed, correctly teaching
the word of truth. ¹⁶ But avoid irreverent, empty speech, for this will produce
an even greater measure of godlessness.
¹⁷ And their word will spread like gan-
grene, among whom are Hymenaeus
and Philetus. ¹⁸ They have deviated from
the truth, saying that the resurrection
has already taken place, and are overturning the faith of some. ¹⁹ Nevertheless, God's solid foundation stands firm,
having this inscription:

The Lord knows those who are
His, and
Everyone who names the name of
the Lord
must turn away from
unrighteousness.

²⁰ Now in a large house there are not
only gold and silver bowls, but also
those of wood and earthenware, some
for special use, some for ordinary. ²¹ So
if anyone purifies himself from these
things, he will be a special instrument,
set apart, useful to the Master, prepared
for every good work.

Fear and Cold Feet

You, therefore, my child, be strong in the grace that is in Christ Jesus.
—2 TIMOTHY 2:1

When Simon Peter stepped out of the boat and attempted to walk on the water to Jesus, he was afraid. "And beginning to sink he cried out 'Lord, save me!'" (Mt 14:30). Fear makes you sink.

When Jesus healed the paralytic, His first word was, "Have courage, son," and His second, "Your sins are forgiven" (Mt 9:2). When Jesus lifted the guilt, this lifted the fear which, in turn, lifted the paralysis.

When the disciples fell on their faces at the top of the Mount of Transfiguration, terrified because they had heard the voice of God, Jesus said: "Get up; don't be afraid" (Mt 17:7). Fear puts you down; faith lifts you up.

The man who brought back the unused talent said: "I was afraid and went off and hid your talent in the ground" (Mt 25:25). His life investment was in a hole in the ground! Fear did it.

Again, it was said of the disciples that they were gathered "with the doors locked because of their fear of the Jews" (Jn 20:19). Fear always puts you behind closed doors; it causes you to become an ingrown person.

Joseph of Arimathea was "a disciple of Jesus—but secretly because of his fear of the Jews" (Jn 19:38). Fear always drives a person underground.

A man I know says that fear gave him cold feet. Prior to the Lord delivering him from fear, his circulation was so bad that he had to wear socks in bed. "Now," he says, "my circulation is normal. God took away my fear and gave me warm feet."

Prayer

God, I see that fear is indeed costly. It is so costly that I dare not keep it. But I cannot easily get rid of it, for it has put its roots deep within me. Help me tear it up, root and branch. In Jesus' name I pray. Amen.

Further Study

Mk 4:35-41; 5:25-34
What had Jesus said to His disciples?
What had this caused Him to do?

OCTOBER 31

JEREMIAH 36:27–38:28

27 After the king had burned the scroll with the words Baruch had written at Jeremiah's dictation, the word of the LORD came to Jeremiah: 28 "Take another scroll, and once again write on it the very words that were on the original scroll that Jehoiakim king of Judah burned. 29 You are to proclaim concerning Jehoiakim king of Judah: This is what the LORD says: You have burned the scroll, saying: Why have you written on it: The king of Babylon will certainly come and destroy this land and cause it to be without man or beast? 30 There-

fore, this is what the LORD says concerning Jehoiakim king of Judah: He will have no one to sit on David's throne, and his corpse will be thrown out to be exposed to the heat of day and the frost of night. [31] I will punish him, his descendants, and his officers for their wrongdoing. I will bring on them, on the residents of Jerusalem, and on the men of Judah all the disaster, which I warned them about but they did not listen."

[32] Then Jeremiah took another scroll and gave it to Baruch son of Neriah, the scribe, and he wrote on it at Jeremiah's dictation all the words of the scroll that Jehoiakim, Judah's king, had burned in the fire. And many other words like them were added.

37 Zedekiah son of Josiah reigned as king in the land of Judah in place of Jehoiachin son of Jehoiakim, for Nebuchadnezzar king of Babylon made him king. [2] He and his officers and the people of the land did not obey the words of the LORD that He spoke through Jeremiah the prophet.

[3] Nevertheless, King Zedekiah sent Jehucal son of Shelemiah and Zephaniah son of Maaseiah, the priest, to Jeremiah the prophet, requesting, "Please pray to the LORD our God for us!" [4] Jeremiah was going about his daily tasks among the people, for they had not yet put him into the prison. [5] Pharaoh's army had left Egypt, and when the Chaldeans, who were besieging Jerusalem, heard the report, they withdrew from Jerusalem.

[6] The word of the LORD came to Jeremiah the prophet: [7] "This is what the LORD, the God of Israel, says: This is what you will say to Judah's king, who is sending you to inquire of Me: Watch: Pharaoh's army, which has come out to help you, is going to return to its own land of Egypt. [8] The Chaldeans will then return and fight against this city. They will capture it and burn it down. [9] This is what the LORD says: Don't deceive yourselves by saying: The Chaldeans will leave us for good, for they will not leave. [10] Indeed, if you were to strike down the entire Chaldean army that is fighting with you, and there remained among them only the badly wounded men, each in his tent, they would get up and burn this city down."

[11] When the Chaldean army withdrew from Jerusalem because of Pharaoh's army, [12] Jeremiah started to leave Jerusalem to go to the land of Benjamin to claim his portion there among the people. [13] But when he was at the Benjamin Gate, an officer of the guard was there, whose name was Irijah son of Shelemiah, son of Hananiah, and he apprehended Jeremiah the prophet, saying, "You are deserting to the Chaldeans."

[14] "That's a lie," Jeremiah replied. "I am not deserting to the Chaldeans!" Irijah would not listen to him but apprehended Jeremiah and took him to the officials. [15] The officials were angry at Jeremiah and beat him and placed him in jail in the house of Jonathan the scribe, for it had been made into a prison. [16] So Jeremiah went into a cell in the dungeon and stayed there many days.

[17] King Zedekiah later sent for him and received him, and in his house privately asked him, "Is there a word from the LORD?"

"There is," Jeremiah responded, and he continued, "You will be handed over to the king of Babylon." [18] Then Jeremiah said to King Zedekiah, "How have I sinned against you or your servants or these people that you have put me in prison? [19] Where are your prophets who prophesied to you, claiming, 'The king of Babylon will not come against you and this land'? [20] So now please listen, my lord the king. May my petition come before you. Don't send me back to the house of Jonathan the scribe, or I will die there."

[21] So King Zedekiah gave orders, and Jeremiah was placed in the guard's courtyard. He was given a loaf of bread each day from the baker's street until all the bread was gone from the city. So Jeremiah remained in the guard's courtyard.

38 Now Shephatiah son of Mattan, Gedaliah son of Pashhur, Jucal son of Shelemiah, and Pashhur son of Malchijah heard the words Jeremiah was speaking to all the people: ² "This is what the LORD says: 'Whoever stays in this city will die by the sword, famine, and plague, but whoever surrenders to the Chaldeans will live. He will keep his life like the spoils of war and will live.' ³ This is what the LORD says: 'This city will most certainly be handed over to the king of Babylon's army, and he will capture it.' "

⁴ The officials then said to the king, "This man ought to die, because he is weakening the morale of the warriors who remain in this city and of all the people by speaking to them in this way. This man is not seeking the well-being of this people, but disaster."

⁵ King Zedekiah said, "Here he is; he's in your hands since the king can't do anything against you." ⁶ So they took Jeremiah and dropped him into the cistern of Malchiah the king's son, which was in the guard's courtyard, lowering Jeremiah with ropes. There was no water in the cistern, only mud, and Jeremiah sank in the mud.

⁷ But Ebed-melech, a Cushite court official employed in the king's palace, heard Jeremiah had been put into the cistern. While the king was sitting at the Benjamin Gate, ⁸ Ebed-melech went from the king's palace and spoke to the king: ⁹ "My lord king, these men have been evil in all they have done to Jeremiah the prophet. They have dropped him into the cistern where he will die from hunger, because there is no more bread in the city."

¹⁰ So the king commanded Ebed-melech, the Cushite, "Take from here 30 men under your authority and pull Jeremiah the prophet up from the cistern before he dies."

¹¹ So Ebed-melech took the men under his authority and went to the king's palace to a place below the storehouse. From there he took old rags and worn-out clothes and lowered them by ropes to Jeremiah in the cistern. ¹² Ebed-melech the Cushite cried out to Jeremiah, "Place these old rags and clothes between your armpits and the ropes." Jeremiah did so, ¹³ and they pulled him up with the ropes and lifted him out of the cistern, but he continued to stay in the guard's courtyard.

¹⁴ King Zedekiah sent for Jeremiah the prophet and received him at the third entrance of the LORD's temple. The king said to Jeremiah, "I am going to ask you something; don't hide anything from me."

¹⁵ Jeremiah replied to Zedekiah, "If I tell you, you will kill me, won't you? Besides, if I give you advice, you won't listen to me anyway."

¹⁶ King Zedekiah swore to Jeremiah in private, "As the LORD lives, who has given us this life, I will not kill you or hand you over to these men who want to take your life."

¹⁷ Jeremiah therefore said to Zedekiah, "This is what the LORD, the God of Hosts, the God of Israel, says: 'If indeed you surrender to the officials of the king of Babylon, then you will live, this city will not be burned down, and you and your household will survive. ¹⁸ But if you do not surrender to the officials of the king of Babylon, then this city will be handed over to the Chaldeans. They will burn it down, and you yourself will not escape from them.' "

¹⁹ But King Zedekiah said to Jeremiah, "I am worried about the Judeans who have deserted to the Chaldeans. They may hand me over to them to abuse me."

²⁰ "They will not hand you over," Jeremiah replied. "Obey the voice of the LORD in what I am telling you, so it may go well for you and you can live. ²¹ But if you refuse to surrender, this is the verdict that the LORD has shown me: ²² 'All the women who remain in the palace of Judah's king will be brought out to the officials of the king of Babylon and will say:

> Your trusted friends misled you
> and overcame you.
> Your feet sank into the mire,
> and they deserted you.

²³ All your wives and sons will be brought out to the Chaldeans. You your-

self will not escape from them, for you will be seized by the king of Babylon and this city will burn down.' " ²⁴ Then Zedekiah warned Jeremiah, "Don't let anyone know about these things or you will die. ²⁵ If the officials hear that I have spoken with you and come and demand of you, 'Tell us what you said to the king; don't hide anything from us and we won't kill you. Also, what did the king say to you?' ²⁶ then you will tell them, 'I was bringing before the king my petition that he not return me to the house of Jonathan to die there.' " ²⁷ When all the officials came to Jeremiah and questioned him, he reported the exact words to them the king had commanded, and they quit speaking with him because nothing had been heard. ²⁸ Jeremiah remained in the guard's courtyard until the day Jerusalem was captured, and he was there when it happened.

PSALM 119:82-88

⁸² My eyes grow weary looking for
what You have promised;
I ask, "When will You comfort me?"
⁸³ Though I have become like a
wineskin dried by smoke,
I do not forget Your statutes.
⁸⁴ How many days must Your servant
wait?
When will You execute judgment
on my persecutors?
⁸⁵ The arrogant have dug pits for me;
they violate Your instruction.
⁸⁶ All Your commands are true;
people persecute me with lies—
help me!
⁸⁷ They almost ended my life on
earth,
but I did not abandon Your
precepts.
⁸⁸ Give me life in accordance with
Your faithful love,
and I will obey the decree You
have spoken.

PROVERBS 26:4-6

⁴ Don't answer a fool according to
his foolishness,

or you'll be like him yourself.
⁵ Answer a fool according to his
foolishness,
or he'll become wise in his own
eyes.
⁶ The one who sends a message by
a fool's hand
cuts off his own feet and drinks
violence.

2 TIMOTHY 2:22–3:17

²² Flee from youthful passions, and pursue righteousness, faith, love, and peace, along with those who call on the Lord from a pure heart. ²³ But reject foolish and ignorant disputes, knowing that they breed quarrels. ²⁴ The Lord's slave must not quarrel, but must be gentle to everyone, able to teach, and patient, ²⁵ instructing his opponents with gentleness. Perhaps God will grant them repentance to know the truth. ²⁶ Then they may come to their senses and escape the Devil's trap, having been captured by him to do his will.

3 But know this: difficult times will come in the last days. ² For people will be lovers of self, lovers of money, boastful, proud, blasphemers, disobedient to parents, ungrateful, unholy, ³ unloving, irreconcilable, slanderers, without self-control, brutal, without love for what is good, ⁴ traitors, reckless, conceited, lovers of pleasure rather than lovers of God, ⁵ holding to the form of religion but denying its power. Avoid these people!

⁶ For among them are those who worm their way into households and capture idle women burdened down with sins, led along by a variety of passions, ⁷ always learning and never able to come to a knowledge of the truth. ⁸ Just as Jannes and Jambres resisted Moses, so these also resist the truth, men who are corrupt in mind, worthless in regard to the faith. ⁹ But they will not make further progress, for their lack of understanding will be clear to all, as theirs was also.

¹⁰ But you have followed my teaching, conduct, purpose, faith, patience, love,

and endurance, [11] along with the persecutions and sufferings that came to me in Antioch, Iconium, and Lystra. What persecutions I endured! Yet the Lord rescued me from them all. [12] In fact, all those who want to live a godly life in Christ Jesus will be persecuted. [13] Evil people and imposters will become worse, deceiving and being deceived. [14] But as for you, continue in what you have learned and firmly believed, knowing those from whom you learned, [15] and that from childhood you have known the sacred Scriptures, which are able to instruct you for salvation through faith in Christ Jesus. [16] All Scripture is inspired by God and is profitable for teaching, for rebuking, for correcting, for training in righteousness, [17] so that the man of God may be complete, equipped for every good work.

Getting What We Give

Don't answer a fool according to his foolishness, or you'll be like him yourself.—PROVERBS 26:4

Karl Menninger says: "I know from clinical experience that in some women, the degree of discomfort both in pregnancy and parturition (childbirth) has been directly proportional to the intensity of their resentment at having to live through this phase of the female role."

Sometimes resentments and grudges can be unconscious. As one doctor put it: "It is very difficult to get people to see that illness is the price they pay for their unconscious resentments toward the very things they protest they love." A woman of sixty-five gave her heart to Christ and said: "I've lived with a stone in my heart ever since my mother said she hated me for stopping her from going to another man. Now this stone has gone. I'm free—for the first time in almost half a century."

A man gave a golf ball the name of someone he disliked and struck it, but the ball went into the rough. Isn't that instructive? If you bear a grudge against anyone, you can neither see straight nor drive straight. The fact is this—you cannot hurt another person without hurting yourself. As the Chinese put it: "He who spits against the wind spits in his own face." We become the product of the qualities we give out. If we give out evil in return for good, then we become evil; we become the thing we give out. But if we give out good for evil, we become good. So mark this and mark it well—you cannot maintain spiritual freshness while you are bearing a grudge.

Prayer

Heavenly Father, I see that I cannot be an echo of the treatment people give to me. I must echo You and treat people as You treat them. But I cannot do this except by Your grace. I receive that grace now. In Jesus' name I pray. Amen.

Further Study

Rm 12:1-17; Lv 19:18; Pr 20:22
What are we not to do?
What are we not to say?

NOVEMBER 1

JEREMIAH 39:1–41:18

39 In the ninth year of Zedekiah king of Judah, in the tenth month, King Nebuchadnezzar of Babylon advanced against Jerusalem with his entire army and laid siege to it. ² In the fourth month of Zedekiah's eleventh year, on the ninth day of the month, the city was broken into. ³ All the officials of the king of Babylon entered and sat at the Middle Gate: Nergal-sharezer, Samgarnebo, Sarsechim the Rab-saris, Nergalsharezer the Rab-mag, and all the rest of the officials of Babylon's king.

⁴ When he saw them, Zedekiah king of Judah and all the soldiers fled. They left the city at night by way of the king's garden through the gate between the two walls. They left along the route to the Arabah. ⁵ However, the Chaldean army pursued them and overtook Zedekiah in the plains of Jericho, arrested him, and brought him to Nebuchadnezzar, Babylon's king, at Riblah in the land of Hamath. The king passed sentence on him there.

⁶ At Riblah the king of Babylon slaughtered Zedekiah's sons before his eyes, and he also slaughtered all Judah's nobles. ⁷ Then he blinded Zedekiah and put him in bronze chains to take him to Babylon. ⁸ The Chaldeans next burned down the king's palace and the people's houses and tore down the walls of Jerusalem. ⁹ Nebuzaradan, the commander of the guards, deported to Babylon the rest of the people—those who had remained in the city and those deserters who had defected to him along with the rest of the people who had remained. ¹⁰ However, Nebuzaradan, the commander of the guards, left in the land of Judah some of the poor people who owned nothing, and he gave them vineyards and fields at that time.

¹¹ Speaking through Nebuzaradan, captain of the guard, King Nebuchadnezzar of Babylon gave orders concerning Jeremiah, saying: ¹² "Take him, look after him, and don't let any harm come to him; do for him whatever he says." ¹³ Nebuzaradan, captain of the guard, Nebushazban the Rab-saris, Nergalsharezer the Rab-mag, and all the captains of the king of Babylon ¹⁴ had Jeremiah brought from the guard's courtyard and turned him over to Gedaliah son of Ahikam, son of Shaphan, to take him home. So he settled among his own people.

¹⁵ Now the word of the LORD had come to Jeremiah when he was confined in the guard's courtyard: ¹⁶ "Go tell Ebed-melech the Cushite: This is what the LORD of Hosts, the God of Israel, says: I am about to fulfill My words for harm and not for good against this city. They will take place before your eyes on that day. ¹⁷ But I will rescue you on that day"—this is the LORD's declaration—"and you will not be handed over to the men you fear.

¹⁸ Indeed, I will certainly deliver you so that you do not fall by the sword. Because you have trusted in Me, you will keep your life like the spoils of war." This is the LORD's declaration.

40 This is the word that came to Jeremiah from the LORD after Nebuzaradan, captain of the guard, released him at Ramah when he had been bound in chains with all the exiles of Jerusalem and Judah who were being exiled to Babylon. ² The captain of the guard took Jeremiah and said to him, "The LORD your God decreed this disaster on this place, ³ and the LORD has fulfilled it. He has done just what He decreed. Because you people have sinned against the LORD and have not obeyed Him, this thing has happened. ⁴ Now pay attention to what I say. Today I am setting you free from the chains that were on your hands. If it pleases you to come with me to Babylon, come, and I will take care of you. But if it seems wrong to you to come with me to Babylon, go no farther. Look—the whole land is in front of you. Wherever it seems good and right for you to go, go there." ⁵ When Jeremiah had not yet turned to go, Nebuzaradan said to him: "Return to Gedaliah son of Ahikam, son of Shaphan, whom the king of Babylon has appointed over the cities of Judah, and stay with him among the people or go wherever you want to go." So the captain of the guard gave him a ration and a gift and released him. ⁶ Jeremiah therefore went to Gedaliah son of Ahikam at Mizpah, and he stayed with him among the people who remained in the land.

⁷ When all the commanders of the armies in the field—they and their men—heard that the king of Babylon had appointed Gedaliah son of Ahikam over the land and that he had put him in charge of the men, women, and children, the poorest of the land who had not been deported to Babylon, ⁸ they came to Gedaliah at Mizpah. The commanders included; Ishmael son of Nethaniah, Johanan and Jonathan the sons of Kareah, Seraiah son of Tanhu-

meth, the sons of Ephai the Netophathite, and Jezaniah son of the Maacathite—they and their men.

⁹ Gedaliah son of Ahikam, son of Shaphan, swore an oath to them and their men, assuring them, "Don't be afraid to serve the Chaldeans. Live in the land and serve the king of Babylon, and it will go well for you. ¹⁰ As for me, I am going to live in Mizpah to represent you before the Chaldeans who come to us. As for you, gather wine, summer fruit, and oil, place them in your storage jars, and live in the cities you have captured."

¹¹ When all the Judeans in Moab and among the Ammonites and in Edom and in all the other lands also heard that the king of Babylon had left a remnant in Judah and had appointed Gedaliah son of Ahikam, son of Shaphan, over them, ¹² they all returned from all the places where they had been banished and came to the land of Judah, to Gedaliah at Mizpah, and harvested a great amount of wine and summer fruit.

¹³ Meanwhile, Johanan son of Kareah and all the commanders of the armies in the field came to Gedaliah at Mizpah ¹⁴ and warned him, "Don't you realize that Baalis, king of the Ammonites, has sent Ishmael son of Nethaniah to strike you down?" But Gedaliah son of Ahikam would not believe them. ¹⁵ Then Johanan son of Kareah suggested to Gedaliah in private at Mizpah, "Let me go kill Ishmael son of Nethaniah. No one will know it. Why should he strike you down and scatter all of Judah that has gathered to you so that the remnant of Judah would perish?"

¹⁶ But Gedaliah son of Ahikam responded to Johanan son of Kareah, "Don't do that! What you're saying about Ishmael is a lie."

41 In the seventh month, Ishmael son of Nethaniah, son of Elishama, of the royal family and one of the king's chief officers, came with 10 men to Gedaliah son of Ahikam at Mizpah. They ate a meal together there in Mizpah, ² but then Ishmael son of Nethaniah and the 10 men who were with him got up and struck down Gedaliah son of Ahikam, son of Shaphan, with the sword; he killed the one the king of Babylon had appointed in the land. ³ Ishmael also struck down all the Judeans who were with Gedaliah at Mizpah, as well as the Chaldean soldiers who were there.

⁴ On the second day after he had killed Gedaliah, when no one knew yet, ⁵ 80 men came from Shechem, Shiloh, and Samaria who had shaved their beards, torn their garments, and gashed themselves, and who were carrying grain and incense offerings to bring to the temple of the LORD. ⁶ Ishmael son of Nethaniah came out of Mizpah to meet them, weeping as he came. When he encountered them, he said: "Come to Gedaliah son of Ahikam!" ⁷ But when they came into the city, Ishmael son of Nethaniah and the men with him slaughtered them and threw them into a cistern.

⁸ However, there were 10 men among them who said to Ishmael, "Don't kill us, for we have hidden treasure in the field—wheat, barley, oil, and honey!" So he stopped and did not kill them along with their companions. ⁹ Now the cistern where Ishmael had thrown all the corpses of the men he had struck down was a large one that King Asa had made in the encounter with Baasha king of Israel. Ishmael son of Nethaniah filled it with the slain.

¹⁰ Then Ishmael took captive all the remnant of the people of Mizpah including the daughters of the king—all those who remained in Mizpah over whom Nebuzaradan, captain of the guard, had appointed Gedaliah son of Ahikam. Ishmael son of Nethaniah took them captive and set off to cross over to the Ammonites.

¹¹ When Johanan son of Kareah and all the commanders of the armies with him heard of all the evil that Ishmael son of Nethaniah had done, ¹² they took all their men and went to fight with Ishmael son of Nethaniah and found him by the great pool in Gibeon. ¹³ When all the people with Ishmael saw Johanan son of Kareah and all the commanders

of the army with him, they rejoiced, ¹⁴ and all the people whom Ishmael had taken captive from Mizpah turned around and rejoined Johanan son of Kareah. ¹⁵ But Ishmael son of Nethaniah escaped from Johanan with eight men and went to the Ammonites. ¹⁶ Johanan son of Kareah and all the commanders of the armies with him then took from Mizpah all the remnant of the people whom he had recovered from Ishmael son of Nethaniah after Ishmael had killed Gedaliah son of Ahikam—men, soldiers, women, children, and court officials whom he brought back from Gibeon. ¹⁷ They left, stopping in Geruth Chimham, which is near Bethlehem, in order to make their way into Egypt ¹⁸ away from the Chaldeans. For they feared them because Ishmael son of Nethaniah had struck down Gedaliah son of Ahikam, whom the king of Babylon had appointed in the land.

PSALM 119:89-95

⁸⁹ LORD, Your word is forever;
   it is firmly fixed in heaven.
⁹⁰ Your faithfulness is for all
      generations;
   You established the earth, and it
      stands firm.
⁹¹ They stand today in accordance
      with Your judgments,
   for all things are Your servants.
⁹² If Your instruction had not been
      my delight,
   I would have died in my affliction.
⁹³ I will never forget Your precepts,
   for You have given me life through
      them.
⁹⁴ I am Yours; save me,
   for I have sought Your precepts.
⁹⁵ The wicked hope to destroy me,
   but I contemplate Your decrees.

PROVERBS 26:7-9

⁷ A proverb in the mouth of a fool
   is like lame legs that hang limp.
⁸ Giving honor to a fool
   is like binding a stone in a sling.
⁹ A proverb in the mouth of a fool

is like a stick with thorns,
   brandished by the hand of a
   drunkard.

2 TIMOTHY 4:1-22

4 Before God and Christ Jesus, who is going to judge the living and the dead, and by His appearing and His kingdom, I solemnly charge you: ² proclaim the message; persist in it whether convenient or not; rebuke, correct, and encourage with great patience and teaching. ³ For the time will come when they will not tolerate sound doctrine, but according to their own desires, will accumulate teachers for themselves because they have an itch to hear something new. ⁴ They will turn away from hearing the truth and will turn aside to myths. ⁵ But as for you, keep a clear head about everything, endure hardship, do the work of an evangelist, fulfill your ministry.

⁶ For I am already being poured out as a drink offering, and the time for my departure is close. ⁷ I have fought the good fight, I have finished the race, I have kept the faith. ⁸ In the future, there is reserved for me the crown of righteousness, which the Lord, the righteous Judge, will give me on that day, and not only to me, but to all those who have loved His appearing.

⁹ Make every effort to come to me soon, ¹⁰ for Demas has deserted me, because he loved this present world, and has gone to Thessalonica. Crescens has gone to Galatia, Titus to Dalmatia. ¹¹ Only Luke is with me. Bring Mark with you, for he is useful to me in the ministry. ¹² I have sent Tychicus to Ephesus. ¹³ When you come, bring the cloak I left in Troas with Carpus, as well as the scrolls, especially the parchments. ¹⁴ Alexander the coppersmith did great harm to me. The Lord will repay him according to his works. ¹⁵ Watch out for him yourself, because he strongly opposed our words.

¹⁶ At my first defense, no one came to my assistance, but everyone deserted me. May it not be counted against them. ¹⁷ But the Lord stood with me and strengthened me, so that the proclamation might be fully made through me, and all the Gentiles might hear. So I was rescued from the lion's mouth. ¹⁸ The Lord will rescue me from every evil work and will bring me safely into His heavenly kingdom. To Him be the glory forever and ever! Amen.

¹⁹ Greet Prisca and Aquila, and the household of Onesiphorus. ²⁰ Erastus has remained at Corinth; Trophimus I left sick at Miletus. ²¹ Make every effort to come before winter. Eubulus greets you, as do Pudens, Linus, Claudia, and all the brothers.

²² The Lord be with your spirit. Grace be with you!

"Flaming Arrows"

The Lord stood with me and strengthened me . . . So I was rescued from the lion's mouth.—2 TIMOTHY 4:17

The main purpose of the Roman shield was to protect soldiers from the fiery darts thrown at them by the enemy. These darts, made either of wood or metal, were covered with inflammable material and set alight immediately before being thrown. Enemies would throw these at each other in great numbers and from all directions so as to produce confusion. When thus attacked, a soldier would hold up the shield in front of him, allowing the fiery darts to land on the fireproof metal surface, from which they would drop away harmlessly.

The apostle says that we Christians need a "shield of faith"—in order "to extinguish the flaming arrows of the evil one." An understanding of what these "flaming arrows" are is essential if we are to stand firm against the adversary. Have you ever gone to bed at night feeling perfectly happy, only to wake in a sad mood? If there was no obvious physical or psychological reason for this, the chances are that you have experienced one of Satan's "flaming arrows."

Sometimes they come as evil thoughts that intrude suddenly into our thinking, often at the most incongruous times. We may be reading the Bible, we may be praying, when all of a sudden some filthy thought flashes into our mind. It is a "flaming arrow" from the Devil. These do not come from inside us but from outside us. They strike us. Some thoughts do arise from within our carnal nature, but these of which I am speaking come from without—from Satan. And we are foolish if we do not recognize this and deal with them in this light.

Prayer

O Father, help me to be alert and able to recognize the "flaming arrows" of Satan when they are hurled at me. For I see that it is only when I recognize them that I can deal effectively with them. Give me insight and understanding. In Jesus' name. Amen.

Further Study

Jms 1:1-22; 1 Co 10:13; 2 Co 11:3
What is the progression in temptation?
What was Paul's concern?

NOVEMBER 2

JEREMIAH 42:1–44:14

42 Then all the commanders of the armies, along with Johanan son of Kareah, Jazaniah son of Hoshaiah, and all the people from the least to the greatest, approached ² Jeremiah the prophet and said, "May our petition come before you; pray to the LORD your God on our behalf, on behalf of this entire remnant (for few of us remain out of the many, as you can see with your own eyes), ³ that the LORD your God may tell us the way we should walk and the thing we should do."

⁴ So Jeremiah the prophet said to them, "I have heard. I will now pray to the LORD your God according to your words, and every word that the LORD answers you I will tell you; I won't withhold a word from you."

⁵ And they said to Jeremiah, "As for every word the LORD your God sends you to tell us, if we don't act accordingly, may the LORD be a true and faithful witness against us. ⁶ Whether it is pleasant or unpleasant, we will obey the voice of the LORD our God to whom we are sending you so that it may go well with us. We will certainly obey the voice of the LORD our God!"

⁷ Now at the end of 10 days, the word of the LORD came to Jeremiah, ⁸ and he summoned Johanan son of Kareah, all the commanders of the armies who were with him, and all the people from the least to the greatest.

⁹ He said to them, "This is what the LORD says, the God of Israel to whom you sent me to bring your petition before Him: ¹⁰ 'If you will indeed stay in this land, then I will rebuild and not demolish you, and I will plant and not uproot you, because I relent concerning the disaster that I have brought on you. ¹¹ Don't be afraid of the king of Babylon whom you now fear; don't be afraid of him'—this is the LORD's declaration—'because I am with you to save you and deliver you from him. ¹² I will grant you compassion, and he will have compassion on you and allow you to return to your own soil. ¹³ But if you say: We will not stay in this land, so as not to obey the voice of the LORD your God, ¹⁴ and if you say: No, instead we'll go to the land of Egypt where we will not see war or hear the sound of the ram's horn or hunger for food, and we'll live there, ¹⁵ then hear the word of the LORD, remnant of Judah! This is what the LORD of Hosts, the God of Israel, says: If you are firmly resolved to go to Egypt and live there for a while, ¹⁶ then the sword you fear will overtake you there in the land of Egypt, and the famine you are worried about will follow on your heels there to Egypt, and you will die there. ¹⁷ All who resolve to go to Egypt to live there for a while will die by the sword, famine, and plague. They will have no survivor or escapee from the disaster I will bring on them.'

¹⁸ "For this is what the LORD of Hosts, the God of Israel, says: 'Just as My anger and fury were poured out on Jerusalem's residents, so will My fury pour out on you if you go to Egypt. You will become an object of execration, scorn, cursing, and disgrace, and you will never see this place again.' ¹⁹ The LORD has spoken concerning you, remnant of Judah: 'Don't go to Egypt.' Know for certain that I have warned you today! ²⁰ You have led your own selves astray because you are the ones who sent me to the LORD your God, saying, 'Pray to the LORD our God on our behalf, and as for all that the LORD our God says, tell it to us, and we'll act accordingly.' ²¹ For I have told you today, but you have not obeyed the voice of the LORD your God in everything He has sent me to tell you. ²² Now therefore, know for certain that by the sword, famine, and plague you will die in the place where you desired to go to live for a while."

43 When Jeremiah had finished speaking to all the people all the words of the LORD their God—all these words the LORD their God had sent him to give them— ² then Azariah son of Hoshaiah, Johanan son of Kareah, and all the other arrogant men responded to Jeremiah, "You are speaking a lie! The LORD our God has not sent you to say, 'You must not go to Egypt to live there for a while!' ³ Rather, Baruch son of Neriah is inciting you against us to hand us over to the Chaldeans to put us to death or to deport us to Babylon!"

⁴ So Johanan son of Kareah and all the commanders of the armies did not obey the voice of the LORD to stay in the land of Judah. ⁵ Instead, Johanan son of Kareah and all the commanders of the armies took the whole remnant of Judah, those who had returned from all the nations where they had been banished to live in the land of Judah for a while— ⁶ the men, women, children, king's daughters, and everyone whom Nebuzaradan, captain of the guard, had allowed to remain with Gedaliah son of Ahikam son of Shaphan, along with Jeremiah the prophet and Baruch son of Neriah— ⁷ and they went to the land of Egypt because they did not obey the voice of the LORD. They went as far as Tahpanhes.

⁸ Then the word of the LORD came to Jeremiah at Tahpanhes: ⁹ "Pick up some large stones and set them in the mortar of the brick pavement that is at the opening of Pharaoh's palace at Tahpanhes. Do this in the sight of the Judean men ¹⁰ and tell them: This is what the

LORD of Hosts, the God of Israel, says: I will send for My servant Nebuchadnezzar king of Babylon, and I will place his throne on these stones that I have embedded, and he will pitch his pavilion over them. ¹¹ He will come and strike down the land of Egypt—those destined for death, to death; those destined for captivity, to captivity; and those destined for the sword, to the sword. ¹² I will kindle a fire in the temples of Egypt's gods, and he will burn them and take them prisoner. He will clean the land of Egypt as a shepherd picks lice off his garment, and he will leave there unscathed. ¹³ He will smash the sacred pillars of the sun temple in the land of Egypt and burn down the temples of the Egyptian gods."

44 This is the word that came to Jeremiah for all the Jews living in the land of Egypt—at Migdol, Tahpanhes, Memphis, and in the land of Pathros: ² "This is what the LORD of Hosts, the God of Israel, says: You have seen all the disaster I brought against Jerusalem and all Judah's cities; look, they are a ruin today without an inhabitant in them ³ because of their evil ways that provoked Me to anger, going and burning incense to serve other gods they, you, and your fathers did not know. ⁴ So I sent you all My servants the prophets time and time again, saying, Don't do this detestable thing that I hate. ⁵ But they did not listen or pay attention; they did not turn from their evil or stop burning incense to other gods. ⁶ So My fierce wrath poured forth and burned in Judah's cities and Jerusalem's streets so that they became the desolate ruin they are today.

⁷ "So now, this is what the LORD, the God of Hosts, the God of Israel, says: Why are you doing such great harm to yourselves? You are cutting off man and woman, child and infant from Judah, leaving yourselves without a remnant. ⁸ You are provoking Me to anger by the work of your hands. You are burning incense to other gods in the land of Egypt where you have gone to live for a while. As a result, you will be cut off and be-come an object of cursing and insult among all the nations of earth. ⁹ Have you forgotten the evils of your fathers, the evils of Judah's kings, the evils of their wives, your own evils, and the evils of your wives that were committed in the land of Judah and in the streets of Jerusalem? ¹⁰ They have not become humble to this day, and they have not feared or walked by My law or My statutes that I set before you and your ancestors.

¹¹ "Therefore, this is what the LORD of Hosts, the God of Israel, says: I am about to turn against you to bring disaster, to cut off all Judah. ¹² And I will take away the remnant of Judah, those who have resolved to go to the land of Egypt to live there for a while; they will meet their end. All of them in the land of Egypt will fall by the sword; they will meet their end by famine. From the least to the greatest, they will die by the sword and by famine. Then they will be-come an object of execration, of scorn, of cursing, and of disgrace. ¹³ I will punish those living in the land of Egypt just as I punished Jerusalem by sword, famine, and plague. ¹⁴ Then the remnant of Judah—those going to live for a while there in the land of Egypt—will have no fugitive or survivor to return to the land of Judah where they are longing to re-turn to live, for they will not return ex-cept for a few fugitives."

....

PSALM 119:96-100

⁹⁶ I have seen a limit to all
      perfection,
   but Your command is without
      limit.

⁹⁷ How I love Your teaching!
   It is my meditation all day long.
⁹⁸ Your command makes me wiser
      than my enemies,
   for it is always with me.
⁹⁹ I have more insight than all my
      teachers
   because Your decrees are my
      meditation.
¹⁰⁰ I understand more than the elders
   because I obey Your precepts.

PROVERBS 26:10-12

10 The one who hires a fool, or who
hires those passing by,
is like an archer who wounds
everyone.
11 As a dog returns to its vomit,
so a fool repeats his foolishness.
12 Do you see a man who is wise in
his own eyes?
There is more hope for a fool than
for him.

TITUS 1:1–2:8

1 Paul, a slave of God, and an apostle of Jesus Christ for the faith of God's elect and the knowledge of the truth that leads to godliness, ² in the hope of eternal life that God, who cannot lie, promised before time began, ³ and has in His own time revealed His message in the proclamation that I was entrusted with by the command of God our Savior:

⁴ To Titus, my true child in our common faith.

Grace and peace from God the Father and Christ Jesus our Savior.

⁵ The reason I left you in Crete was to set right what was left undone and, as I directed you, to appoint elders in every town: ⁶ someone who is blameless, the husband of one wife, having faithful children not accused of wildness or rebellion. ⁷ For an overseer, as God's manager, must be blameless, not arrogant, not quick tempered, not addicted to wine, not a bully, not greedy for money, ⁸ but hospitable, loving what is good, sensible, righteous, holy, self-controlled, ⁹ holding to the faithful message as taught, so that he will be able both to encourage with sound teaching and to refute those who contradict it.

¹⁰ For there are also many rebellious people, idle talkers and deceivers, especially those from Judaism. ¹¹ It is necessary to silence them; they overthrow whole households by teaching for dishonest gain what they should not. ¹² One of their very own prophets said,

Cretans are always liars, evil
beasts, lazy gluttons.

¹³ This testimony is true. So, rebuke them sharply, that they may be sound in the faith ¹⁴ and may not pay attention to Jewish myths and the commandments of men who reject the truth.

¹⁵ To the pure, everything is pure, but to those who are defiled and unbelieving nothing is pure; in fact, both their mind and conscience are defiled. ¹⁶ They profess to know God, but they deny Him by their works. They are detestable, disobedient, and disqualified for any good work.

2 But you must speak what is consistent with sound teaching. ² Older men are to be self-controlled, worthy of respect, sensible, and sound in faith, love, and endurance. ³ In the same way, older women are to be reverent in behavior, not slanderers, not addicted to much wine. They are to teach what is good, ⁴ so that they may encourage the young women to love their husbands and children, ⁵ to be sensible, pure, good homemakers, and submissive to their husbands, so that God's message will not be slandered.

⁶ Likewise, encourage the young men to be sensible ⁷ about everything. Set an example of good works yourself, with integrity and dignity in your teaching. ⁸ Your message is to be sound beyond reproach, so that the opponent will be ashamed, having nothing bad to say about us.

Spiritual Digestion

How I love Your teaching! It is my meditation all day long. . . .
I have more insight than all my teachers because
Your decrees are my meditation.—PSALM 119:97, 99

One of the highest priorities in order to stay spiritually fresh is to cultivate the art of Scripture meditation.

For some reason, Bible meditation has become a lost art in our day. A survey conducted among Christians in the United States showed that only one in ten thousand knew how to meditate on the Scriptures.

What, then, is the art of Scripture meditation? Is it reading parts of the Bible as slowly as possible so that every word sinks in? No. Is it studying a passage with the aid of a commentary so that one understands exactly what the Scripture is saying? No. Is it memorizing certain texts and recalling them to mind whenever one has a spare moment? No. You can do all of these things and still not know how to meditate.

Andrew Murray describes it as "holding the word of God in your heart and mind until it has affected every area of your life." My own definition is this: meditation is the process by which we place the Word of God into the digestive system of the soul, where it is transformed into faith and spiritual energy.

Psalm 1:2-3 paints a picture of amazing freshness and vitality: "His delight is in the LORD's instruction, and he meditates on it day and night. He is like a tree planted beside streams of water that bears its fruit in season and whose leaf does not wither." What is the secret of this amazing freshness? It is simple—meditation. To draw from Scripture the inspiration and power we need to stay spiritually fresh, we must do more than read it, study it, or even memorize it—we must meditate on it.

Prayer

O Father, I want so much to learn the art of meditation. Quicken my desire to hide Your Word in my heart so that it becomes the hidden springs of action and determines my character and my conduct. In Jesus' name. Amen.

Further Study

Jos 1:1-9; 24:31
What was God's promise to Joshua?
What was the condition—and the result?

NOVEMBER 3

JEREMIAH 44:15–47:7

¹⁵ However, all the men who knew that their wives were burning incense to other gods, all the women standing by—a great assembly—and all the people who were living in the land of Egypt at Pathros answered Jeremiah, ¹⁶ "As for the word you spoke to us in the name of the LORD, we are not going to listen to you! ¹⁷ Instead, we will do everything we said we would: burn incense to the queen of heaven and offer drink offerings to her just as we, our fathers, our kings, and our officials did in Judah's cities and in Jerusalem's streets. Then we had enough food and good things and saw no disaster, ¹⁸ but from the time we ceased to burn incense to the queen of heaven and to offer her drink offerings, we have lacked everything, and through sword and famine we have met our end."

¹⁹ And the women said, "When we burned incense to the queen of heaven and poured out drink offerings to her, was it apart from our husbands' knowledge that we made sacrificial cakes in her image and poured out drink offerings to her?"

²⁰ But Jeremiah responded to all the people—the men, women, and all the people who were answering him—saying, ²¹ "As for the incense you burned in Judah's cities and in Jerusalem's streets—you, your fathers, your kings, your officials, and the people of the land—did the LORD not remember them? He brought this to mind. ²² The LORD can no longer bear your evil deeds and the detestable acts you have committed, so your land has become a waste, a desolation, and an object of cursing, without inhabitant, as you see today. ²³ Because you burned incense and sinned against the LORD and didn't obey the LORD's voice and didn't walk in His law, His statutes, and His testimonies, this disaster has come to you, as you see today."

²⁴ Then Jeremiah said to all the people, including all the women, "Hear the word of the LORD, all Judah who are in the land of Egypt. ²⁵ This is what the LORD of Hosts, the God of Israel, says: 'As for you and your wives, you women have spoken with your mouths, and you men fulfilled it by your deeds, saying: We will keep our vows we have made to burn incense to the queen of heaven and to pour out drink offerings for her. Go ahead, confirm your vows! Pay your vows!'

²⁶ "Therefore, hear the word of the LORD, all you Judeans who live in the land of Egypt: 'I have sworn by My great name, says the LORD, that My name will never again be invoked by anyone of Judah in all the land of Egypt, saying, As the Lord GOD lives. ²⁷ I am watching over them for disaster and not for good, and every man of Judah who is in the land of Egypt will meet his end by sword or famine until they are finished off. ²⁸ Those who escape the sword will return from the land of Egypt to the land of Judah only few in number, and the whole remnant of Judah, the ones going to the land of Egypt to live there for a while, will know whose word stands, Mine or theirs! ²⁹ This will be a sign to you'—this is the LORD's declaration—'that I am about to punish you in this place, so you may know that My words of disaster concerning you will certainly come to pass. ³⁰ This is what the LORD says: I am about to hand over Pharaoh Hophra, Egypt's king, to his enemies, to those who want to take his life, just as I handed over Judah's King Zedekiah to Babylon's King Nebuchadnezzar, who was his enemy, the one who wanted to take his life.' "

45 This is the word that Jeremiah the prophet spoke to Baruch son of Neriah when he wrote these words on a scroll at Jeremiah's dictation in the fourth year of Jehoiakim son of Josiah, king of Judah: ² "This is what the LORD, the God of Israel, says to you, Baruch: ³ 'You have said, Woe is me, because the LORD has added misery to my pain! I am worn out with groaning and have found no rest.

⁴ " 'This is what you are to say to him: This is what the LORD says: What I have built I am about to demolish, and what I have planted I am about to uproot— the whole land! ⁵ But as for you, do you seek great things for yourself? Stop seeking! For I am about to bring disaster on every living creature'—this is the LORD's declaration—'but I will grant you your life like the spoils of war wherever you go.' "

46 The word of the LORD that came to Jeremiah the prophet about the nations:

² About Egypt and the army of Pharaoh Neco, Egypt's king, which was defeated at Carchemish on the Euphrates River by Nebuchadnezzar king of Babylon in the fourth year of Judah's King Jehoiakim son of Josiah:

³ Deploy small shields and large;
    draw near for battle!
⁴ Harness the horses;
    mount the steeds;
    take your positions
        with helmets on!
    Polish the lances;
    put on armor!
⁵ Why have I seen this?
    They are terrified,
    they are retreating,
    their warriors are crushed,
    they flee headlong,
    they never look back,
    terror is on every side!
        This is the LORD's declaration.
⁶ The swift cannot flee,
    and the warrior cannot escape!
    In the north by the bank
        of the Euphrates River,
    they stumble and fall.

⁷ Who is this, rising like the Nile,
    like rivers whose waters churn?
⁸ Egypt rises like the Nile,
    and its waters churn like rivers.
    He boasts: I will go up,
        I will cover the earth;
    I will destroy cities
        with their residents.
⁹ Rise up, you cavalry!
    Race furiously, you chariots!
    Let the warriors go forth—
    Cush and Put,
    who are able to handle shields,
    and the Ludim,
    who are able to handle and string
        the bow.
¹⁰ That day belongs to the Lord,
        the GOD of Hosts,
    a day of vengeance
        to avenge Himself
    against His adversaries.
    The sword will devour
        and be satisfied;
    it will drink its fill of their blood,
    because it will be a sacrifice
        to the Lord, the GOD of Hosts,
    in the northern land
        by the Euphrates River.

¹¹ Go up to Gilead and get balm,
    Virgin Daughter Egypt!
    You have multiplied remedies
        in vain;
    there is no healing for you.
¹² The nations have heard
        of your dishonor,
    and your outcry fills the earth,
    because warrior stumbles
        against warrior
    and together both of them
        have fallen.

¹³ This is the word the LORD spoke to Jeremiah the prophet about the coming of Nebuchadnezzar king of Babylon to defeat the land of Egypt:

¹⁴ Announce it in Egypt,
        and proclaim it in Migdol!
    Proclaim it in Memphis
        and in Tahpanhes!
    Say: Take positions!
        Prepare yourself,
    for the sword devours
        all around you.

¹⁵ Why have your strong ones
been swept away?
Each has not stood,
for the LORD has thrust him down.
¹⁶ He continues to stumble.
Indeed, each falls over the other.
They say: Get up! Let's return
to our people
and to the land of our birth,
away from the sword
that oppresses.
¹⁷ There they will cry out:
Pharaoh king of Egypt
was all noise;
he let the opportune moment pass.

¹⁸ As I live—
this is the King's declaration;
the LORD of Hosts is His name.
He will come like Tabor
among the mountains
and like Carmel by the sea.
¹⁹ Pack your bags for exile,
inhabitant of Daughter Egypt!
For Memphis will become
a desolation,
uninhabited ruins.

²⁰ Egypt is a beautiful young cow,
but a horsefly from the north
is coming against her.
²¹ Even her mercenaries among her
are like stall-fed calves.
They too will turn back;
together they will flee;
they will not take their stand,
for the day of their calamity
is coming on them,
the time of their punishment.
²² Egypt will hiss
like a slithering snake,
for the enemy will come
with an army;
with axes they will come against her
like those who cut trees.
²³ They will cut down her forest—
this is the LORD's declaration—
though it is dense,
for they are more numerous
than locusts;
they cannot be counted.
²⁴ Daughter Egypt will be
put to shame,
handed over to a northern people.

²⁵ The LORD of Hosts, the God of Israel, says: "I am about to punish Amon,
god of Thebes, along with Pharaoh,
Egypt, her gods, and her kings—Pharaoh
and those trusting in him. ²⁶ I will hand
them over to those who want to take
their lives—to Nebuchadnezzar king of
Babylon and his officers. But after this, it
will be inhabited again as in ancient
times."
This is the LORD's declaration.

²⁷ But you, My servant Jacob,
do not be afraid,
and do not be discouraged, Israel,
for without fail I will save you
from far away
and your descendants,
from the land of their captivity!
Jacob will return and have calm
and quiet
with no one to frighten him.
²⁸ And you, My servant Jacob,
do not be afraid—
this is the LORD's declaration—
for I will be with you.
I will bring destruction
on all the nations
where I have banished you,
but I will not bring destruction
on you.
I will discipline you with justice,
but I will by no means
leave you unpunished.

47 This is the word of the LORD that
came to Jeremiah the prophet
about the Philistines before Pharaoh defeated Gaza. ² This is what the LORD
says:

Look, waters are rising
from the north
and becoming an overflowing wadi.
They will overflow the land
and everything in it,
the cities and their inhabitants.
The people will cry out,
and every inhabitant of the land
will wail.
³ At the sound
of the stomping hooves
of his stallions,
the rumbling of his chariots,

and the clatter of their wheels,
fathers will not turn back
     for their sons,
because they will be utterly helpless
⁴ on account of the day that is coming
     to destroy all the Philistines,
to cut off from Tyre and Sidon
     every remaining ally.
Indeed, the LORD is about to destroy
     the Philistines,
the remnant of the islands
     of Caphtor.
⁵ Baldness is coming to Gaza.
Ashkelon will become silent,
     a remnant of their valley.
How long will you gash yourself?

⁶ Ah, sword of the LORD!
How long will you be restless?
Go back to your scabbard;
     be still; be silent!
⁷ How can it rest
     when the LORD has given it
          a command?
He has assigned it
against Ashkelon and the shore
     of the sea.

PSALM 119:101-104

¹⁰¹ I have kept my feet from every
          evil path
     to follow Your word.
¹⁰² I have not turned from Your
          judgments,
     for You Yourself have instructed me.
¹⁰³ How sweet Your word is to my
          taste—
     sweeter than honey to my mouth.
¹⁰⁴ I gain understanding from Your
          precepts;
     therefore I hate every false way.

PROVERBS 26:13-16

¹³ The slacker says, "There's a lion in
          the road—
     a lion in the public square!"
¹⁴ A door turns on its hinge,
     and a slacker, on his bed.
¹⁵ The slacker buries his hand in the
          bowl;
     he is too weary to bring it to his
          mouth.

¹⁶ In his own eyes, a slacker is wiser
     than seven men who can answer
          sensibly.

TITUS 2:9–3:15

⁹ Slaves are to be submissive to their
masters in everything, and to be well-
pleasing, not talking back ¹⁰ or stealing,
but demonstrating utter faithfulness, so
that they may adorn the teaching of God
our Savior in everything.
¹¹ For the grace of God has appeared,
with salvation for all people, ¹² instructing us to deny godlessness and worldly
lusts and to live in a sensible, righteous,
and godly way in the present age,
¹³ while we wait for the blessed hope and
the appearing of the glory of our great
God and Savior, Jesus Christ. ¹⁴ He gave
Himself for us to redeem us from all lawlessness and to cleanse for Himself a
special people, eager to do good works.
¹⁵ Say these things, and encourage
and rebuke with all authority. Let no
one disregard you.

3 Remind them to be submissive to
rulers and authorities, to obey, to be
ready for every good work, ² to slander
no one, to avoid fighting, and to be kind,
always showing gentleness to all people.
³ For we too were once foolish, disobedient, deceived, captives of various passions and pleasures, living in malice and
envy, hateful, detesting one another.

⁴ But when the goodness and love
          for man
     appeared from God our Savior,
⁵ He saved us—
     not by works of righteousness that
          we had done,
     but according to His mercy,
     through the washing of
          regeneration
     and renewal by the Holy Spirit.
⁶ This Spirit He poured out on us
          abundantly
     through Jesus Christ our Savior,
⁷ so that having been justified by
          His grace,
     we may become heirs with the
          hope of eternal life.

⁸ This saying is trustworthy. I want you to insist on these things, so that those who have believed God might be careful to devote themselves to good works. These are good and profitable for everyone. ⁹ But avoid foolish debates, genealogies, quarrels, and disputes about the law, for they are unprofitable and worthless. ¹⁰ Reject a divisive person after a first and second warning, ¹¹ knowing that such a person is perverted and sins, being self-condemned.

¹² When I send Artemas to you, or Tychicus, make every effort to come to me in Nicopolis, for I have decided to spend the winter there. ¹³ Diligently help Zenas the lawyer and Apollos on their journey, so that they will lack nothing.

¹⁴ And our people must also learn to devote themselves to good works for cases of urgent need, so that they will not be unfruitful. ¹⁵ All those who are with me greet you. Greet those who love us in the faith. Grace be with all of you.

What If?

Say these things, and encourage and rebuke with all authority.
—Titus 2:15

A little boy, when asked what the Holy Spirit meant, replied: "I suppose it is what puts the 'oomph' into Christianity." He was on the right track but failed to use the correct pronoun—not "it" but "He." The Holy Spirit is not an influence but a Person. This is why Scripture, when referring to Him, uses personal pronouns such as "He," "who," and "whom."

Suppose there had been no Holy Spirit? Then we would have been faced with a religion in which there was little "oomph." We would have the four Gospels without the upper room—distinctive, but not dynamic.

Take Mark's Gospel, for example. If there had been no day of Pentecost, if the promised Holy Spirit had not been poured out upon God's people, the message of Christ would have ended with these words: "So they went out and started running from the tomb, because trembling and astonishment overwhelmed them. And they said nothing to anyone, since they were afraid" (Mk 16:8).

What a sad plight we would all be in if the message of Christ had ended there. The Resurrection had taken place, the whole of the redemptive process was complete, the gladdest news that had ever burst upon human ears was in the possession of the disciples—but "they said nothing to anyone, since they were afraid." If Christianity had ended there, it would not have been a gospel that conquered the world. No amount of good information could have transformed those early disciples. Something else was needed—the Holy Spirit.

Prayer

O God, help me not to live in the twilight zone between Resurrection and Pentecost. I want to know all the fullness of the upper room in my life. Turn me from a flickering torch into a flaming torch. In Jesus' name. Amen.

Further Study

Jn 16:1-16; 14:26; 15:26-27; Ac 1:8
What did Jesus say of the Holy Spirit?
What is another title of the Holy Spirit?

NOVEMBER 4

JEREMIAH 48:1–49:6

48 About Moab, this is what the LORD of Hosts, the God of Israel, says:

Woe to Nebo, because it is
    about to be destroyed;
Kiriathaim will be put to shame;
    it will be taken captive.
The fortress will be put to shame
    and dismayed!
2 There is no longer praise for Moab;
they plan harm against her
    in Heshbon:
Come, let's cut her off
    from nationhood.
You madmen will also be silenced;
the sword will pursue you.
3 A voice cries out from Horonaim:
devastation and great disaster!
4 Moab will be shattered;
her little ones will cry out.
5 For on the ascent to Luhith
they will be weeping continually,
and on the descent to Horonaim
will be heard cries of distress
    over the destruction:
6 Flee! Save your lives!
Be like a juniper bush
    in the wilderness.
7 Because you trust in your works
    and treasures,
you will be captured also.
Chemosh will go into exile
with his priests and officials.
8 The destroyer will move
    against every town;

not one town will escape.
The valley will perish,
and the plain will be annihilated,
as the LORD has said.
9 Make Moab a salt marsh,
for she will run away;
her towns will become
    a desolation,
without inhabitant.

10 Cursed is the one
who does
    the LORD's business deceitfully,
and cursed is the one
who withholds his sword
    from bloodshed.

11 Moab has been left quiet
    since his youth,
settled like wine on its dregs.
He hasn't been poured
    from one container to another
or gone into exile.
So his taste has remained
    the same,
and his aroma hasn't changed.
12 Therefore look, the days
    are coming—
this is the LORD's declaration—
when I will send those to him,
    who will pour him out.
They will empty his containers
and smash his jars.
13 Moab will be put to shame
    because of Chemosh,
just as the house of Israel was
    put to shame

1323

because of Bethel
    that they trusted in.

14 How can you say,
    We are warriors—
mighty men ready for battle?
15 The destroyer of Moab
    and its towns
has come up,
and the best of its young men
have gone down to slaughter.
    This is the King's declaration;
    the LORD of Hosts is His name.
16 Moab's calamity is near at hand;
his disaster is rushing swiftly.
17 Mourn for him,
    all you surrounding nations,
everyone who knows his name.
Say: How the mighty scepter
    is shattered,
the glorious staff!

18 Come down from glory;
    sit on parched ground,
resident of the daughter of Dibon,
for the destroyer of Moab
    has come against you;
he has destroyed your fortresses.
19 Stand by the highway and look,
resident of Aroer!
Ask him who is fleeing or her
    who is escaping,
What happened?
20 Moab is put to shame,
    indeed dismayed.
Wail and cry out!
Declare by the Arnon
that Moab is destroyed.

21 "Judgment has come to the land of the plateau—to Holon, Jahzah, Mephaath, 22 Dibon, Nebo, Beth-diblathaim, 23 Kiriathaim, Beth-gamul, Beth-meon, 24 Kerioth, Bozrah, and all the towns of the land of Moab, those far and near. 25 Moab's horn is chopped off; his arm is shattered."

    This is the LORD's declaration.
26 "Make him drunk, because he has exalted himself against the LORD. Moab will wallow in his own vomit, and he will also become a laughingstock. 27 Wasn't Israel a laughingstock to you? Was he ever found among thieves? For

whenever you speak of him you shake your head."

28 Abandon the towns!
    Live in the cliffs,
residents of Moab!
Be like a dove
    that nests inside the mouth
    of a cave.

29 We have heard of Moab's pride,
great pride, indeed—
his insolence, arrogance, pride,
and haughty heart.
30 I know his outburst.
    This is the LORD's declaration.
It is empty.
His boast is empty.
31 Therefore, I will wail over Moab.
I will cry out for Moab, all of it;
he will moan for the men
    of Kir-heres.
32 I will weep for you, vine of Sibmah,
with more than the weeping
    for Jazer.
Your tendrils have extended
    to the sea;
they have reached to the sea
    and to Jazer.
The destroyer has fallen
    on your summer fruit
    and grape harvest.
33 Joy and celebration are taken
    from the fertile field
and from the land of Moab.
I have stopped the flow of wine
    from the winepresses;
no one will tread with shouts
    of joy.
The shouting is not a shout of joy.

34 "There is a cry from Heshbon to Elealeh; they raise their voices as far as Jahaz—from Zoar to Horonaim and Eglath-shelishiyah—because even the waters of Nimrim have become desolate. 35 In Moab, I will stop"—this is the LORD's declaration—"the one who offers sacrifices on the high place and burns incense to his gods. 36 Therefore, My heart moans like flutes for Moab, and My heart moans like flutes for the people of Kir-heres. And therefore, the wealth he has gained has perished.

³⁷ Indeed, every head is bald and every beard clipped; on every hand is a gash and sackcloth around the waist. ³⁸ On all the rooftops of Moab and in her public squares, everyone is mourning because I have shattered Moab like a jar no one wants." This is the LORD's declaration. ³⁹ "How broken it is! They wail! How Moab has turned his back! He is ashamed. Moab will become a laughing-stock and a shock to all those around him."

⁴⁰ For this is what the LORD says:

He will swoop down like an eagle
and spread his wings against Moab.
⁴¹ The towns have been captured,
and the strongholds seized.
In that day the heart
of Moab's warriors
will be like the heart of a woman
with contractions.
⁴² Moab will be destroyed as a people
because he has exalted himself
against the LORD.
⁴³ Panic, pit, and trap
await you, resident of Moab.
This is the LORD's declaration.
⁴⁴ He who flees from the panic
will fall in the pit,
and he who climbs from the pit
will be captured in the trap,
for I will bring against Moab
the year of their punishment.
This is the LORD's declaration.

⁴⁵ Those who flee will stand exhausted
in Heshbon's shadow
because fire has come out
from Heshbon
and a flame from within Sihon.
It will devour Moab's forehead
and the skull of the noisemakers.
⁴⁶ Woe to you, Moab!
The people of Chemosh
have perished
because your sons have been
taken captive
and your daughters have gone
into captivity.
⁴⁷ Yet, I will restore the fortunes
of Moab in the last days.
This is the LORD's declaration.
The judgment on Moab ends here.

49

About the Ammonites, this is what the LORD says:

Does Israel have no sons?
Is he without an heir?
Why then has Milcom
dispossessed Gad
and his people settled in their cities?
² Therefore look, the days
are coming—
this is the LORD's declaration—
when I will make the shout
of battle heard
against Rabbah of the Ammonites.
It will become a desolate mound,
and its villages will be
burned down.
Israel will dispossess
their dispossessors,
says the LORD.
³ Wail, Heshbon, for Ai is devastated;
cry out, daughters of Rabbah!
Clothe yourselves with sackcloth,
and lament;
run back and forth
within your walls,
because Milcom will go into exile
together with his priests
and officials.
⁴ Why do you brag
about your valleys,
your flowing valley,
you faithless daughter?
You who trust in your treasures
and boast: Who can attack me?
⁵ Look, I am about to bring terror
on you—
this is the declaration of the Lord,
the GOD of Hosts—
from all those around you.
You will be banished,
each man headlong,
with no one to gather up
the fugitives.
⁶ But after that, I will restore
the fortunes
of the Ammonites.
This is the LORD's declaration.

PSALM 119:105-108

¹⁰⁵ Your word is a lamp for my feet
and a light on my path.

106 I have solemnly sworn
to keep Your righteous judgments.
107 I am severely afflicted;
LORD, give me life through Your
word.
108 LORD, please accept my willing
offerings of praise,
and teach me Your judgments.

PROVERBS 26:17-19

17 A passer-by who meddles in a
quarrel that's not his
is like one who grabs a dog by the
ears.
18 Like a madman who throws
flaming darts and deadly
arrows,
19 so is the man who deceives his
neighbor
and says, "I was only joking!"

PHILEMON 1-25

Paul, a prisoner of Christ Jesus, and
Timothy, our brother:

To Philemon, our dear friend and co-
worker, 2 to Apphia our sister, to Archippus our fellow soldier, and to the
church that meets in your house.
3 Grace to you and peace from God
our Father and the Lord Jesus Christ.
4 I always thank my God when I mention you in my prayers, 5 because I hear
of your love and faith toward the Lord
Jesus and for all the saints. 6 I pray that
your participation in the faith may become effective through knowing every
good thing that is in us for the glory of
Christ. 7 For I have great joy and encouragement from your love, because
the hearts of the saints have been refreshed through you, brother.
8 For this reason, although I have
great boldness in Christ to command
you to do what is right, 9 I appeal, instead, on the basis of love. I, Paul, as an
elderly man and now also as a prisoner
of Christ Jesus, 10 appeal to you for my
child, whom I fathered while in
chains—Onesimus. 11 Once he was useless to you, but now he is useful to both
you and me. 12 I am sending him—a part
of myself—back to you. 13 I wanted to
keep him with me, so that in my imprisonment for the gospel he might serve
me in your place. 14 But I didn't want to
do anything without your consent, so
that your good deed might not be out of
obligation, but of your own free will.
15 For perhaps this is why he was separated from you for a brief time, so that
you might get him back permanently,
16 no longer as a slave, but more than a
slave—as a dearly loved brother. This is
especially so to me, but even more to
you, both in the flesh and in the Lord.
17 So if you consider me a partner, accept him as you would me. 18 And if he
has wronged you in any way, or owes
you anything, charge that to my account. 19 I, Paul, write this with my own
hand: I will repay it—not to mention to
you that you owe me even your own
self. 20 Yes, brother, may I have joy from
you in the Lord; refresh my heart in
Christ. 21 Since I am confident of your
obedience, I am writing to you, knowing that you will do even more than I
say. 22 But meanwhile, also prepare a
guest room for me, for I hope that
through your prayers I will be restored
to you.
23 Epaphras, my fellow prisoner in
Christ Jesus, greets you, and so do
24 Mark, Aristarchus, Demas, and Luke,
my co-workers.
25 The grace of the Lord Jesus Christ
be with your spirit.

Don't Miss the Point

Your word is a lamp for my feet and a light on my path.
——PSALM 119:105

There are some who claim that having our "feet sandaled with readiness for the gospel of peace" means that we should always be ready to carry the gospel to others. That interpretation certainly fits in with Romans 10:15: "How welcome are the feet of those who announce the gospel of good things!" but this is not, in my opinion, what Paul had in mind when he wrote the words of Ephesians 6:15.

In Ephesians 6 the apostle is dealing with one thing only—the Christian's engagement with the Devil. He said: "Our battle is not against flesh and blood, but against . . . the spiritual forces of evil" (v. 12). His purpose is to show us how to stand against the "tactics" of the Devil. Although Paul was an evangelist with a strong evangelistic spirit, he was not thinking here of evangelizing, vital though it is. He was rather picturing a Christian who is under attack by Satan, warning us that unless our feet are firmly shod, we can easily be knocked down and disabled.

Those who claim that the phrase the "readiness for the gospel of peace" relates to evangelism miss the point of his exposition. No one would deny the importance of always being ready to share Christ with others, but the readiness to which Paul is referring here is the readiness to stand firm on the truths of the gospel. In other words, he is saying: don't get into a fight with the Devil in your bare feet. Make sure you are well shod, for if you are not, he will most certainly get the better of you.

Prayer

O Father, I am so grateful that You breathed into Your servant Paul to write these illuminating words. They are inspired, for they inspire me. Continue to teach me, dear Lord. I am hungry for more and more of Your truth. Amen.

Further Study

Ps 119:97-105; Is 40:8; 1 Pt 1:23-25; 2 Tm 2:15
How did the psalmist view God's Word?
Why is God's Word a sure foundation?

NOVEMBER 5

JEREMIAH 49:7–50:23

⁷ About Edom, this is what the LORD of Hosts says:

Is there no longer wisdom in Teman?
Has counsel perished
   from the prudent?
Has their wisdom rotted away?
⁸ Run! Turn back! Lie low,
   residents of Dedan,
for I will bring Esau's calamity
   on him
at the time I punish him.
⁹ If grape harvesters came to you,
   wouldn't they leave
      some gleanings?
Were thieves to come in the night,
   they would destroy only
      what they wanted.
¹⁰ But I will strip Esau bare;
   I will uncover his secret places.
He will try to hide himself,
   but he will be unable.
His descendants will be destroyed
   along with his relatives
      and neighbors.
He will exist no longer.
¹¹ Abandon your orphans;
      I will preserve them;
   let your widows trust in Me.

¹² "For this is what the LORD says: If those who do not deserve to drink the cup must drink it, can you possibly remain unpunished? You will not remain unpunished, for you must drink it too. ¹³ For by Myself I have sworn"—the LORD's declaration—"Bozrah will become a desolation, a disgrace, a ruin, and a curse, and all her cities will become ruins forever."

¹⁴ I have heard a message
      from the LORD;
   an envoy has been sent
      among the nations:

Assemble yourselves to come
   against her.
Rise up for war!

¹⁵ Look, I will certainly make you
      insignificant
   among the nations,
   despised among humanity.
¹⁶ As to the terror you cause,
   your presumptuous heart
      has deceived you.
You who live in the clefts
      of the rock,
   you who occupy
      the mountain summit,
though you elevate your nest
      like the eagle,
   even from there I will bring
      you down.
      This is the LORD's declaration.

¹⁷ "Edom will become a desolation. Everyone who passes by her will be horrified and scoff because of all her wounds. ¹⁸ As when Sodom and Gomorrah were overthrown along with their neighbors," says the LORD, "no one will live there; no human being will even stay in it as a resident alien.

¹⁹ "Look, it will be like a lion coming up from the thickets of the Jordan to the perennially watered grazing land. Indeed, I will chase Edom away from her land in a flash. I will appoint whoever is chosen for her. For who is like Me? Who will summon Me? Who is the shepherd who can stand against Me?"

²⁰ Therefore, hear the plans that the LORD has drawn up against Edom and the strategies He has devised against the people of Teman: The flock's little lambs will certainly be dragged away, and their grazing land will be made desolate because of them. ²¹ At the sound of their fall the earth will quake; the sound of her cry will be heard at the Red Sea. ²² Look! It will be like an eagle

soaring upward, then swooping down and spreading its wings over Bozrah. In that day the hearts of Edom's warriors will be like the heart of a woman with contractions.

²³ About Damascus:

Hamath and Arpad are
put to shame,
for they have heard a bad report
and are agitated;
in the sea there is anxiety
that cannot be calmed.
²⁴ Damascus has become weak;
she has turned to run;
panic has gripped her.
Distress and labor pains
have seized her
like a woman in labor.
²⁵ How can the city of praise
not be abandoned,
the town that brings Me joy?
²⁶ Therefore, her young men will fall
in her public squares;
all the warriors will be silenced
in that day.
This is the declaration of
the LORD of Hosts.
²⁷ I will set fire to the wall
of Damascus;
it will devour Ben-hadad's citadels.

²⁸ About Kedar and the kingdoms of Hazor, which Nebuchadnezzar, Babylon's king, defeated, this is what the LORD says:

Rise up, go against Kedar,
and destroy the people
of the east!
²⁹ They will take their tents
and their flocks
along with their tent curtains
and all their equipment.
They will take their camels
for themselves.
They will call out to them:
Terror is on every side!
³⁰ Run! Escape quickly! Lie low,
residents of Hazor—
this is the LORD's declaration—
for Nebuchadnezzar
king of Babylon
has drawn up a plan against you;

he has devised a strategy
against you.
³¹ Rise up, go up against a nation
at ease,
one living in security.
This is the LORD's declaration.
They have no doors, not even
a gate bar;
they live alone.
³² Their camels will become plunder,
and their massive herds of cattle
will become spoil.
I will scatter them to the wind
in every direction,
those who shave their temples;
I will bring calamity on them
across all their borders.
This is the LORD's declaration.
³³ Hazor will become a jackals' den,
a desolation forever.
No one will live there;
no human being will even stay
in it as a resident alien.

³⁴ This is the word of the LORD that came to Jeremiah the prophet about Elam at the beginning of the reign of Zedekiah king of Judah. ³⁵ This is what the LORD of Hosts says:

I am about to shatter Elam's bow,
the source of their might.
³⁶ I will bring the four winds
against Elam
from the four corners
of the heavens,
and I will scatter them
to all these winds.
There will not be a nation
to which Elam's banished ones
will not go.
³⁷ I will devastate Elam
before their enemies,
before those who want to take
their lives.
I will bring disaster on them,
My burning anger.
This is the LORD's declaration.
I will send the sword after them
until I finish them off.
³⁸ I will set My throne in Elam,
and I will destroy the king
and officials from there.
This is the LORD's declaration.

39 In the last days,
   I will restore the fortunes of Elam.
     This is the LORD's declaration.

50 The word the LORD spoke about Babylon, the land of the Chaldeans, through Jeremiah the prophet:

2 Announce to the nations;
   proclaim and raise up a signal flag;
   proclaim, and hide nothing.
   Say: Babylon is captured;
   Bel is put to shame;
   Marduk is devastated;
   her idols are put to shame;
   her false gods, devastated.
3 For a nation from the north
    will come against her;
   it will make her land desolate.
   No one will be living in it—
   both man and beast will escape.
4 In those days and at that time—
    this is the LORD's declaration—
   the Israelites and Judeans
    will come together,
   weeping as they come,
   and will seek the LORD their God.
5 They will ask about Zion,
   turning their faces to this road.
   They will come
    and join themselves
    to the LORD
   in an everlasting covenant
    that will never be forgotten.

6 My people are lost sheep;
   their shepherds have
    led them astray,
   guiding them the wrong way
    in the mountains.
   They have wandered
    from mountain to hill;
   they have forgotten
    their resting place.
7 All who found them
    devoured them.
   Their adversaries said:
    We're not guilty;
   instead, they have sinned
    against the LORD,
   their righteous grazing land,
   the hope of their ancestors,
   the LORD.

8 Escape from Babylon;
   depart from the Chaldeans' land.
   Be like the rams that lead the flock.
9 For I will soon stir up and bring
    against Babylon
   an assembly of great nations
    from the north country.
   They will line up
    in battle formation against her;
   from there she will be captured.
   Their arrows will be like those
    of a skilled warrior
   who does not
    return empty-handed.
10 The Chaldeans will
    become plunder;
   all her plunderers will be
    fully satisfied.
     This is the LORD's declaration.
11 Because you rejoice,
   because you sing in triumph—
   you who plundered
    My inheritance—
   because you frolic like a young cow
    treading grain
   and neigh like stallions,
12 your mother will be
    utterly humiliated;
   she who bore you will be
    put to shame.
   Look! She will lag behind all
    the nations—
   a dry land, a wilderness, an
    Arabah.
13 Because of the LORD's wrath,
   she will not be inhabited;
   she will become a desolation,
    every bit of her.
   Everyone who passes
    through Babylon
   will be horrified
   and scoff because of
    all her wounds.
14 Line up in battle formation
    around Babylon,
   all you archers!
   Shoot at her! Do not spare
    an arrow,
   for she has sinned against the LORD.
15 Raise a war cry against her
    on every side!
   She has thrown up her hands
    in surrender;
   her defense towers have fallen;

her walls are demolished.
Since this is the LORD's vengeance,
take out your vengeance on her;
as she has done, do the same to her.

¹⁶ Cut off the sower from Babylon
as well as him who wields
the sickle at harvest time.
Because of the oppressor's sword,
each will turn to his own people,
each will flee to his own land.

¹⁷ Israel is a stray lamb,
chased by lions.
The first who devoured him was
the king of Assyria;
this last who has crunched his bones
was Nebuchadnezzar
king of Babylon.

¹⁸ Therefore, this is what the LORD of Hosts, the God of Israel, says: "I am about to punish the king of Babylon and his land just as I punished the king of Assyria.

¹⁹ I will return Israel
to his grazing land,
and he will feed on Carmel
and Bashan;
he will be satisfied
in the hill country of Ephraim
and of Gilead.

²⁰ In those days and at that time—
this is the LORD's declaration—
one will search for Israel's guilt,
but there will be none,
and for Judah's sins,
but they will not be found,
for I will forgive those I leave
as a remnant.

²¹ Go against the land of Merathaim,
and against those living in Pekod.
Put them to the sword;
completely destroy them—
this is the LORD's declaration—
do everything I have
commanded you.

²² The sound of war is in the land—
a great destruction.

²³ How the hammer of the whole earth
is cut down and smashed!
What a horror Babylon has become
among the nations!

ᴾSALM 119:109-112

¹⁰⁹ My life is constantly in danger,
yet I do not forget Your instruction.

¹¹⁰ The wicked have set a trap for me,
but I have not wandered from
Your precepts.

¹¹¹ I have Your decrees as a heritage
forever;
indeed, they are the joy of my
heart.

¹¹² I am resolved to obey Your statutes
to the very end.

ᴾROVERBS 26:20-23

²⁰ Without wood, fire goes out;
without a gossip, conflict dies
down.

²¹ As charcoal for embers and wood
for fire,
so is a quarrelsome man for
kindling strife.

²² A gossip's words are like choice
food
that goes down to one's innermost
being.

²³ Smooth lips with an evil heart
are like glaze on an earthen
vessel.

ᴴEBREWS 1:1–2:9

1 Long ago God spoke to the fathers by the prophets at different times and in different ways. ² In these last days, He has spoken to us by His Son, whom He has appointed heir of all things and through whom He made the universe. ³ He is the radiance of His glory, the exact expression of His nature, and He sustains all things by His powerful word. After making purification for sins, He sat down at the right hand of the Majesty on high. ⁴ So He became higher in rank than the angels, just as the name He inherited is superior to theirs.

⁵ For to which of the angels did He ever say, **You are My Son; today I have become Your Father,** or again, **I will be His Father, and He will be My Son?**

[6] When He again brings His firstborn into the world, He says, **And all God's angels must worship Him.** [7] And about the angels He says:

He makes His angels winds,
and His servants a fiery flame;

[8] but about the Son:

Your throne, O God, is forever
and ever,
and the scepter of Your kingdom
is a scepter of justice.
[9] You have loved righteousness
and hated lawlessness;
this is why God, Your God, has
anointed You,
rather than Your companions,
with the oil of joy.

[10] And:

In the beginning, Lord, You
established the earth,
and the heavens are the works
of Your hands;
[11] they will perish, but You remain.
They will all wear out like
clothing;
[12] You will roll them up like a cloak,
and they will be changed like a
robe.
But You are the same,
and Your years will never end.

[13] Now to which of the angels has He ever said:

Sit at My right hand
until I make Your enemies Your
footstool?

[14] Are they not all ministering spirits sent out to serve those who are going to inherit salvation?

2 We must therefore pay even more attention to what we have heard, so that we will not drift away. [2] For if the message spoken through angels was legally binding, and every transgression and disobedience received a just punishment, [3] how will we escape if we neglect such a great salvation? It was first spoken by the Lord and was confirmed to us by those who heard Him. [4] At the same time, God also testified by signs and wonders, various miracles, and distributions of gifts from the Holy Spirit according to His will.

[5] For He has not subjected to angels the world to come that we are talking about. [6] But one has somewhere testified:

What is man, that You remember
him,
or the son of man, that You care
for him?
[7] You made him lower than the
angels for a short time;
You crowned him with glory and
honor
[8] and subjected everything under
his feet.

For in **subjecting everything** to him, He left nothing not subject to him. As it is, we do not yet see **everything subjected** to him. [9] But we do see Jesus— **made lower than the angels for a short time** so that by God's grace He might taste death for everyone—crowned with glory and honor because of the suffering of death.

We See Jesus

*We do not yet see everything subjected to him.
But we do see Jesus.*—HEBREWS 2:8-9

Are you troubled as you look out at the situation in the world? Well, according to the Bible, things are going to get worse. As Jesus said: "People will faint from fear and expectation of the things that are coming on the world" (Lk 21:26). How are Christians going to stand when the darkness deepens and things get very much worse? What will we do when international tension increases?

Christians have a glorious hope—the hope of salvation. It is this, and this alone, that enables believers to live out their lives free from mental distress. I am sure you have already discovered that after reading the morning newspaper, you move into the day feeling somewhat depressed. Why is this? It is because almost daily, our newspapers are filled with murder, rape, violence, economic distress, child abuse. And our conscience, which through conversion has been sensitized to the moral laws of God, begins to reverberate as it comes up against the reports of things we know are contrary to the divine principles.

Satan, seeing our concern, attempts to exploit it to his own ends. "Things are getting worse, aren't they?" he says. "Why don't you just admit that God has lost control of His world?" If we did not have the helmet of salvation to put on at such a moment, we would finish up with the same attitude as H. G. Wells, who, after the Second World War, wrote: "The spectacle of evil in the world has come near to breaking my spirit." Again I say, there is no protection in the world for the mind.

Prayer

My Father and my God, where would I be if I could not cling to a text such as that in my reading for today? My spirit, too, would be near to breaking. I am so thankful that in You there is hope—hope with a capital H.

Further Study

Jn 17; Rm 8:35-37; 1 Jn 5:4
What did Jesus pray for His disciples?
What was Paul's conviction?

NOVEMBER 6

JEREMIAH 50:24–51:32

24 Babylon, I laid a trap for you,
and you were caught,
but you did not even know it.
You were found and captured
because you fought
against the LORD.

25 The LORD opened His armory
and brought out His weapons
of wrath,
because it is a task
of the Lord GOD of Hosts
in the land of the Chaldeans.
26 Come against her
from the most distant places.

Open her granaries;
pile her up like mounds of grain
and completely destroy her.
Leave her no survivors.
²⁷ Put all her young bulls to the sword;
let them go down to the slaughter.
Woe to them, because their day
has come,
the time of their punishment.

²⁸ There is a voice of fugitives
and escapees
from the land of Babylon
announcing in Zion the vengeance
of the LORD our God,
the vengeance for His temple.
²⁹ Summon the archers to Babylon,
all who string the bow;
camp all around her;
let none escape.
Repay her according to her deeds;
just as she has done, do the same
to her,
for she has acted arrogantly
against the LORD,
against the Holy One of Israel.
³⁰ Therefore, her young men will fall
in her public squares;
all the warriors will be silenced
in that day.
This is the LORD's declaration.
³¹ Look, I am against you,
you arrogant one—
this is the declaration of
the Lord GOD of Hosts—
because your day has come,
the time when I will punish you.
³² The arrogant will stumble and fall
with no one to pick him up.
I will set fire to his cities,
and it will consume everything
around him."

³³ This is what the LORD of Hosts says:

Israelites and Judeans alike
have been oppressed.
All their captors hold them fast;
they refuse to release them.
³⁴ Their Redeemer is strong;
the LORD of Hosts is His name.
He will fervently plead their case
so that He might bring rest
to the earth

but turmoil to those who live
in Babylon.
³⁵ A sword is over the Chaldeans—
this is the LORD's declaration—
against those who live in Babylon,
against her officials, and against
her sages.
³⁶ A sword is against the diviners,
and they will act foolishly.
A sword is
against her heroic warriors,
and they will be terrified.
³⁷ A sword is against his horses
and chariots
and against all the foreigners
among them,
and they will be like women.
A sword is against her treasuries,
and they will be plundered.
³⁸ A drought will come
on her waters,
and they will be dried up.
For it is a land of carved images,
and they go mad because of
terrifying things.

³⁹ Therefore, desert creatures
will live with jackals,
and ostriches will also live in her.
It will never again be inhabited
or lived in through all generations.
⁴⁰ Just as when God overthrew Sodom
and Gomorrah
and their neighboring towns—
this is the LORD's declaration—
so no one will live there;
no human being will even stay in it
as a resident alien.

⁴¹ Look! A people comes
from the north.
A great nation and many kings
will be stirred up
from the remote regions
of the earth.
⁴² They grasp bow and javelin.
They are cruel and show no mercy.
Their voice roars like the sea,
and they ride on horses,
lined up like men
in battle formation
against you, Daughter of Babylon.
⁴³ The king of Babylon has heard
reports about them,

and his hands fall helpless.
Distress has seized him—
pain, like a woman in labor.

⁴⁴ "Look, it will be like a lion coming up from the thickets of the Jordan to the perennially watered grazing land. Indeed, I will chase Babylon away from her land in a flash. I will appoint whoever is chosen for her. For who is like Me? Who will summon Me? Who is the shepherd who can stand against Me?" ⁴⁵ Therefore, hear the plans that the LORD has drawn up against Babylon and the strategies He has devised against the land of the Chaldeans: Certainly the flock's little lambs will be dragged away; certainly the grazing land will be made desolate because of them. ⁴⁶ At the sound of Babylon's conquest the earth will quake; a cry will be heard among the nations.

51

This is what the LORD says:

I am about to stir up
a destructive wind
against Babylon
and against the population
of Leb-qamai.
² I will send strangers to Babylon
who will scatter her and strip
her land bare,
for they will come against her
from every side in the day
of disaster.
³ Don't let the archer string his bow;
don't let him put on his armor.
Don't spare her young men;
completely destroy
her entire army!
⁴ Those who were slain will fall
in the land of the Chaldeans,
those who were pierced through,
in her streets.
⁵ For Israel and Judah are not
left widowed
by their God, the LORD of Hosts,
though their land is full of guilt
against the Holy One of Israel.

⁶ Leave Babylon;
save your lives, each of you!
Don't be silenced by her guilt.

For this is the time
of the LORD's vengeance—
He will pay her what she deserves.
⁷ Babylon was a golden cup
in the LORD's hand
making the whole earth drunk.
The nations drank her wine;
therefore, the nations go mad.
⁸ Suddenly Babylon fell
and was shattered.
Wail for her;
get balm for her wound—
perhaps she can be healed.

⁹ We tried to heal Babylon,
but she could not be healed.
Abandon her!
Let each of us go to his own land,
for her judgment extends
to the sky
and reaches as far as the clouds.

¹⁰ The LORD has brought about
our vindication;
come, let's tell in Zion
what the LORD our God
has accomplished.

¹¹ Sharpen the arrows!
Fill the quivers!
The LORD has put it into the mind
of the kings of the Medes
because His plan is aimed
at Babylon
to destroy her,
for it is the LORD's vengeance,
vengeance for His temple.
¹² Raise up a signal flag
against the walls of Babylon;
fortify the watch post;
set the watchmen in place;
prepare the ambush.
For the LORD has both planned
and accomplished
what He has threatened
against those who live in Babylon.
¹³ You who reside by many waters,
rich in treasures,
your end has come,
your life thread is cut.

¹⁴ The LORD of Hosts has sworn by
Himself:

I will fill you up with men
as with locusts,
and they will sing the victory song
over you.

15 He made the earth by His power,
established the world
by His wisdom,
and spread out the heavens
by His understanding.
16 When He thunders,
the waters in the heavens are
in turmoil,
and He causes the clouds
to rise from the ends of the earth.
He makes lightning for the rain
and brings the wind
from His storehouses.

17 Everyone is stupid and ignorant.
Every goldsmith is put to shame
by his carved image,
for his cast images are a lie;
there is no breath in them.
18 They are worthless, a work
to be mocked.
At the time of their punishment
they will be destroyed.
19 Jacob's Portion is not like these
because He is the One
who formed all things.
Israel is the tribe
of His inheritance;
the LORD of Hosts is His name.

20 You are My battle club,
My weapons of war.
With you I will smash nations;
with you I will bring kingdoms
to ruin.
21 With you I will smash the horse
and its rider;
with you I will smash the chariot
and its rider.
22 With you I will smash man
and woman;
with you I will smash the old man
and the youth;
with you I will smash
the young man and the virgin.
23 With you I will smash
the shepherd and his flock;
with you I will smash the farmer
and his ox-team.

With you I will smash governors
and officials.

24 "I will repay Babylon and all the residents of Chaldea for all their evil they have done in Zion before your very eyes."
This is the LORD's declaration.

25 Look, I am against you,
devastating mountain—
this is the LORD's declaration—
you devastate the whole earth.
I will stretch out My hand
against you,
roll you down from the cliffs,
and turn you into
a burned-out mountain.
26 No one will be able to retrieve
a cornerstone
or a foundation stone from you,
because you will become
desolate forever.
This is the LORD's declaration.

27 Raise a signal flag in the land;
blow a ram's horn
among the nations;
set apart the nations against her.
Summon kingdoms against her—
Ararat, Minni, and Ashkenaz.
Appoint a marshal against her;
bring up horses like a swarm
of locusts.
28 Set apart the nations for battle
against her—
the kings of Media,
her governors and all her officials,
and all the lands they rule.
29 The earth quakes and trembles,
because the LORD's purposes
against Babylon stand:
to make the land of Babylon
an uninhabited desolation.
30 Babylon's warriors have
stopped fighting;
they sit in their strongholds.
Their might is exhausted;
they have become like women.
Babylon's homes have been
set ablaze,
her gate bars are shattered.
31 Messenger races
to meet messenger,

and herald to meet herald,
to announce to the king of Babylon
that his city has been captured
from end to end.
³² The fords have been seized,
the marshes set on fire,
and the soldiers are terrified.

PSALM 119:113-120

¹¹³ I hate the double-minded,
but I love Your instruction.
¹¹⁴ You are my shelter and my shield;
I hope in Your word.
¹¹⁵ Depart from me, you evil ones,
so that I may obey my God's
commands.
¹¹⁶ Sustain me as You promised, and I
will live;
do not let me be ashamed of my
hope.
¹¹⁷ Sustain me so that I can be safe
and be concerned with Your
statutes continually.
¹¹⁸ You reject all who stray from Your
statutes,
for their deceit is a lie.
¹¹⁹ You remove all the wicked on
earth as if they were dross;
therefore, I love Your decrees.
¹²⁰ I tremble in awe of You;
I fear Your judgments.

PROVERBS 26:24-26

²⁴ A hateful person disguises himself
with his speech
and harbors deceit within.
²⁵ When he speaks graciously, don't
believe him,
for there are seven abominations
in his heart.
²⁶ Though his hatred is concealed by
deception,
his evil will be revealed in the
assembly.

HEBREWS 2:10–3:11

¹⁰ For it was fitting, in bringing many
sons to glory, that He, for whom and
through whom all things exist, should
make the source of their salvation perfect through sufferings. ¹¹ For the One

who sanctifies and those who are sanctified all have one Father. That is why
He is not ashamed to call them brothers, ¹² saying:

I will proclaim Your name to My
brothers;
I will sing hymns to You in the
congregation.

¹³ Again, I will trust in Him. And again,
Here I am with the children God gave
Me.
¹⁴ Now since the children have flesh
and blood in common, He also shared in
these, so that through His death He
might destroy the one holding the power of death—that is, the Devil— ¹⁵ and
free those who were held in slavery all
their lives by the fear of death. ¹⁶ For it
is clear that He does not reach out to
help angels, but to help Abraham's offspring. ¹⁷ Therefore He had to be like
His brothers in every way, so that He
could become a merciful and faithful
high priest in service to God, to make
propitiation for the sins of the people.
¹⁸ For since He Himself was tested and
has suffered, He is able to help those
who are tested.

3 Therefore, holy brothers and companions in a heavenly calling, consider Jesus, the apostle and high priest
of our confession; ² He was faithful to
the One who appointed Him, just as
Moses was in all God's household. ³ For
Jesus is considered worthy of more
glory than Moses, just as the builder
has more honor than the house. ⁴ Now
every house is built by someone, but
the One who built everything is God.
⁵ Moses was faithful as a servant in all
God's household, as a testimony to what
would be said in the future. ⁶ But Christ
was faithful as a Son over His household, whose household we are if we
hold on to the courage and the confidence of our hope.
⁷ Therefore, as the Holy Spirit says:

Today, if you hear His voice,
⁸ do not harden your hearts as in
the rebellion,

on the day of testing in the desert,
9   where your fathers tested Me,
        tried Me,
    and saw My works ¹⁰ for 40 years.
    Therefore I was provoked with
        this generation

and said, "They always go astray
        in their hearts,
    and they have not known My
        ways."
¹¹ So I swore in My anger,
    "They will not enter My rest."

Two Basic Fears

*And free those who were held in slavery all their lives
by the fear of death.*—HEBREWS 2:15

Psychologists are at pains to point out that fear is different from anxiety. Fear has a specific object, whereas anxiety is a vague and unspecified apprehension.

What, I wonder, is your biggest fear? Benjamin Rank, a social scientist, says that there are basically two forms of fear: the fear of life and the fear of death. The fear of life is the fear of having to live as an isolated individual. The fear of death is the fear of losing individuality. He says: "Between these two fear possibilities, these poles of fear, the individual is thrown back and forth all his life."

The first fear—the fear of life—is vividly illustrated by a small boy's comment: "I suppose the reason for twins is because little children don't like to come into the world alone." The fear of life makes many retreat into illness. It is a refuge from responsibility. Freud found the cause of neurosis in the past—in childhood; Jung, a disciple of Freud, found it in the present. He said: "I ask, what is the necessary task which the patient will not accomplish?" Backing out of life's responsibilities through fear of life is a major cause of problems.

But with many, it is the fear of death that paralyzes them. Our verse today reads, in speaking of Jesus, that He is able to "free those who were held in slavery all their lives by the fear of death" (Heb 2:15). Is it necessary to live under such servitude? Of course not. When Christ has all of you, then fear can have no part of you. It is as simple as that!

Prayer

Father, I am so thankful that You have made it possible for me not to be enslaved by fear. I can be free, gloriously free—and free now. Touch me in the deepest parts of my being this day and set me free from all and every fear. In Jesus' name. Amen.

Further Study

1 Co 15; 2 Co 5:1; Jn 11:25-26
What is the hope of every believer?
Is this your hope?

NOVEMBER 7

JEREMIAH 51:33–52:16

³³ For this is what the LORD of Hosts, the God of Israel, says:

The daughter of Babylon is
    like a threshing floor
at the time it is trampled.
In just a little while
    her harvest time will come.

³⁴ "Nebuchadnezzar of Babylon
        has devoured me;
    he has crushed me.
He has set me aside
        like an empty dish;
    he has swallowed me
        like a sea monster;
    he filled his belly
        with my delicacies;
    he has vomited me out,"
³⁵   says the inhabitant of Zion;
    "Let the violence done to me
        and my family be done
        to Babylon.
Let my blood be on the inhabitants
        of Chaldea,"
    says Jerusalem.

³⁶ Therefore, this is what the LORD says:

I am about to plead your case
    and take vengeance on your behalf;
I will dry up her sea
    and make her fountain run dry.
³⁷ Babylon will become a heap
        of rubble,
    a jackals' den,
    a desolation and an object
        of scorn,
    without inhabitant.
³⁸ They will roar together
        like young lions;
    they will growl like lion cubs.
³⁹ While they are flushed with heat,
    I will serve them a feast,

and I will make them drunk
    so that they revel.
Then they will fall asleep forever
    and never wake up.
    This is the LORD's declaration.
⁴⁰ I will bring them down like lambs
        to the slaughter,
    like rams together with male goats.

⁴¹ How Sheshach has been captured,
    the praise of the whole earth seized.
What a horror Babylon
        has become
    among the nations!
⁴² The sea has risen over Babylon;
    she is covered
        with its turbulent waves.
⁴³ Her cities have become
        a desolation,
    a dry and arid land,
    a land where no one lives,
    where no human being
        passes through.
⁴⁴ I will punish Bel in Babylon.
    I will make him vomit
        what he swallowed.
    The nations will no longer stream
        to him;
    even Babylon's wall will fall.

⁴⁵ Come out from among her,
        My people!
Save your lives, each of you,
    from the LORD's burning anger.
⁴⁶ May you not become faint-hearted
        and fearful
    when the report is proclaimed
        in the land,
    for the report will come one year,
    and then another the next year.
There will be violence in the land
    with ruler against ruler.
⁴⁷ Therefore, look, the days
        are coming
    when I will punish
        Babylon's carved images.
    Her entire land will suffer shame,

and all her slain will lie fallen
within her.
48 Heaven and earth and everything
in them
will shout for joy over Babylon
because the destroyers
from the north
will come against her.
This is the LORD's declaration.

49 Babylon must fall because of
the slain of Israel,
even as the slain of all the earth fell
because of Babylon.
50 You who have escaped the sword,
go and do not stand still!
Remember the LORD from far away,
and let Jerusalem come
to your mind.

51 We are ashamed
because we have heard insults.
Humiliation covers our faces
because foreigners have entered
the holy places of the LORD's temple.

52 Therefore, look, the days
are coming—
this is the LORD's declaration—
when I will punish
her carved images,
and the wounded will groan
throughout her land.
53 Even if Babylon should ascend
to the heavens
and fortify her tall fortresses,
destroyers will come against her
from Me.
This is the LORD's declaration.

54 The sound of a cry from Babylon!
The sound of great destruction
from the land of the Chaldeans!
55 For the LORD is going
to devastate Babylon;
He will silence her mighty voice.
Their waves roar
like abundant waters;
the tumult
of their voice resounds,
56 for a destroyer is coming
against her,
against Babylon.
Her warriors will be captured,

their bows shattered,
for the LORD is a God of retribution;
He will certainly repay.
57 I will make her princes
and sages drunk,
along with her governors, officials,
and warriors.
Then they will fall asleep forever
and never wake up.
This is the King's declaration;
the LORD of Hosts is His name.

58 This is what the LORD of Hosts says:

Babylon's thick walls will be
totally demolished,
and her high gates consumed
by fire.
The peoples will have labored
for nothing;
the nations will exhaust themselves
only to feed the fire.

59 This is what Jeremiah the prophet commanded Seraiah son of Neriah son of Mahseiah, the quartermaster, when he went to Babylon with Zedekiah king of Judah in the fourth year of Zedekiah's reign. 60 Jeremiah wrote on one scroll about all the disaster that would come to Babylon; all these words were written against Babylon.
61 Jeremiah told Seraiah, "When you get to Babylon, see that you read all these words aloud. 62 You must say, 'LORD, You have threatened to cut off this place so that no one will live in it— man or beast. Indeed, it will remain desolate forever.' 63 When you have finished reading this scroll, tie a stone to it and throw it into the middle of the Euphrates River. 64 Then say, 'In the same way, Babylon will sink and never rise again because of the disaster I am bringing on her. They will grow weary.' "
The words of Jeremiah end here.

52 Zedekiah was 21 years old when he became king; he reigned 11 years in Jerusalem. His mother's name was Hamutal daughter of Jeremiah; she was from Libnah. 2 Zedekiah did what was evil in the LORD's sight just as

Jehoiakim had done. ³ Because of the LORD's anger, it came to the point in Jerusalem and Judah that He finally banished them from His presence. Nevertheless, Zedekiah rebelled against the king of Babylon.

⁴ In the ninth year of Zedekiah's reign, on the tenth day of the tenth month, King Nebuchadnezzar of Babylon advanced against Jerusalem with his entire army. They laid siege to the city and built a siege wall all around it. ⁵ The city was under siege until King Zedekiah's eleventh year.

⁶ By the ninth day of the fourth month the famine was so severe in the city that the people of the land had no food. ⁷ Then the city was broken into, and all the warriors fled. They left the city by night by way of the gate between the two walls near the king's garden, though the Chaldeans surrounded the city. They made their way along the route to the Arabah. ⁸ The Chaldean army pursued the king and overtook Zedekiah in the plains of Jericho. Zedekiah's entire army was scattered from him. ⁹ The Chaldeans seized the king and brought him to the king of Babylon at Riblah in the land of Hamath, and he passed sentence on him.

¹⁰ At Riblah the king of Babylon slaughtered Zedekiah's sons before his eyes and also slaughtered the Judean commanders. ¹¹ Then he blinded Zedekiah and bound him with bronze chains. The king of Babylon brought Zedekiah to Babylon, where he kept him in custody until his dying day.

¹² On the tenth day of the fifth month—which was the nineteenth year of King Nebuchadnezzar, king of Babylon—Nebuzaradan, the commander of the guards, entered Jerusalem as the representative of the king of Babylon. ¹³ He burned the LORD's temple, the king's palace, all the houses of Jerusalem, and all the houses of the nobles. ¹⁴ The whole Chaldean army with the commander of the guards tore down all the walls surrounding Jerusalem. ¹⁵ Nebuzaradan, the commander of the guards, deported some of the poorest of the people, as well as the rest of the people who were left in the city, the deserters who had defected to the king of Babylon, and the rest of the craftsmen. ¹⁶ But some of the poor people of the land Nebuzaradan, the commander of the guards, left to be vinedressers and farmers.

PSALM 119:121-128

121 I have done what is just and right;
do not leave me to my oppressors.
122 Guarantee Your servant's well-being;
do not let the arrogant oppress me.
123 My eyes grow weary looking for
Your salvation
and for Your righteous promise.
124 Deal with Your servant based on
Your faithful love;
teach me Your statutes.
125 I am Your servant; give me
understanding
so that I may know Your decrees.
126 It is time for the LORD to act,
for they have broken Your law.
127 Since I love Your commandments
more than gold, even the purest
gold,
128 I carefully follow all Your precepts
and hate every false way.

PROVERBS 26:27-28

27 The one who digs a pit will fall
into it,
and whoever rolls a stone—it will
come back on him.
28 A lying tongue hates those it
crushes,
and a flattering mouth causes ruin.

HEBREWS 3:12–4:13

¹² Watch out, brothers, so that there won't be in any of you an evil, unbelieving heart that departs from the living God. ¹³ But encourage each other daily, while it is still called **today**, so that none of you is hardened by sin's deception. ¹⁴ For we have become companions of the Messiah if we hold firmly until the end the reality that we had at the start. ¹⁵ As it is said:

Today, if you hear His voice,
do not harden your hearts as in
the rebellion.

[16] For who heard and rebelled? Wasn't it really all who came out of Egypt under Moses? [17] And with whom was He "provoked for 40 years"? Was it not with those who sinned, whose bodies fell in the desert? [18] And to whom did He "swear that they would not enter His rest," if not those who disobeyed? [19] So we see that they were unable to enter because of unbelief.

4 Therefore, while the promise remains of entering His rest, let us fear so that none of you should miss it. [2] For we also have received the good news just as they did; but the message they heard did not benefit them, since they were not united with those who heard it in faith [3] (for we who have believed enter the rest), in keeping with what He has said:

So I swore in My anger,
they will not enter My rest.

And yet His works have been finished since the foundation of the world, [4] for somewhere He has spoken about the seventh day in this way:

And on the seventh day
God rested from all His works.

[5] Again, in that passage He says, **They will never enter My rest.** [6] Since it remains for some to enter it, and those who formerly received the good news did not enter because of disobedience, [7] again, He specifies a certain day—today—speaking through David after such a long time, as previously stated:

Today if you hear His voice,
do not harden your hearts.

[8] For if Joshua had given them rest, He would not have spoken later about another day. [9] A Sabbath rest remains, therefore, for God's people. [10] For the person who has entered His rest has rested from his own works, just as God did from His. [11] Let us then make every effort to enter that rest, so that no one will fall into the same pattern of disobedience.

[12] For the word of God is living and effective and sharper than any two-edged sword, penetrating as far as to divide soul, spirit, joints, and marrow; it is a judge of the ideas and thoughts of the heart. [13] No creature is hidden from Him, but all things are naked and exposed to the eyes of Him to whom we must give an account.

Talk to Yourself

For the word of God is living and effective . . . it is a judge of the ideas and thoughts of the heart.—HEBREWS 4:12

Whatever we do, we must not let any lurking doubts go unchallenged. Pascal said: "Doubt is an unhappy state, but there is an indispensable duty to seek when we are in doubt, and thus anyone who doubts and does not seek is at once unhappy and in the wrong."

How do we go about resolving doubts? One way is to bring them to the Lord in prayer and ask Him to help us overcome them. If prayer does not dissolve them, apply the tactic which Nehemiah adopted: "So we prayed to our God and stationed a guard" (Neh 4:9). Take a verse of Scripture that is the opposite of your doubt and hold it in the center of your mind, repeating it to yourself many times throughout the day. Dr. Martin Lloyd-Jones once said: "Have you realized that most of your unhappiness in life is due to the fact that you are listening to yourself instead of talking to yourself? We must talk to ourselves instead of allowing ourselves to talk to us!"

In listening to our doubts instead of talking to them, we fall prey to the same temptation that caught Adam and Eve off guard in the garden of Eden. The order of creation was stood on its head when the first human pair allowed themselves to be dictated to by the animal world (in the form of the serpent), when, in fact, they had been put in a position to dictate to it.

Don't let your doubts dictate to you. Turn the tables and dictate to them. Talk to them with words from the Word of God.

Prayer

Father, help me never to be nonplussed, for in You there are ways to overcome every problem. Drive the truth I have learned today deeply into my spirit so that I may apply it whenever I am faced with doubt. In Jesus' name. Amen.

Further Study

Gn 3; Ps 53:5; Jms 1:6
What was Satan's strategy?
What did Adam confess?

NOVEMBER 8

JEREMIAH 52:17-34

¹⁷ Now the Chaldeans broke into pieces the bronze pillars for the LORD's temple and the water carts and the bronze reservoir that were in the LORD's temple, and carried all the bronze to Babylon. ¹⁸ They took the pots, the shovels, the wick trimmers, the sprinkling basins, the dishes, and all the bronze articles used in temple service. ¹⁹ The commander of the guards took away the bowls, the firepans, the sprinkling basins, the pots, the lampstands, the pans, and the drink offering bowls—whatever was gold or silver.

²⁰ As for the two pillars, the one reservoir, and the 12 bronze bulls under the water carts that King Solomon had made for the LORD's temple, the weight of the bronze of all these articles was beyond measure. ²¹ One pillar was 27 feet tall, had a circumference of 18 feet, was hollow—four fingers thick—²² and had a bronze capital on top of it. One capital, encircled by bronze latticework and pomegranates, stood seven and a half feet high. The second pillar was the same, with pomegranates. ²³ Each capital had 96 pomegranates all around it. All the pomegranates around the latticework numbered 100.

²⁴ The commander of the guards also took away Seraiah the chief priest, Zephaniah the priest of the second rank, and the three doorkeepers. ²⁵ From the city he took a court official who had been appointed over the warriors; seven trusted royal aides found in the city; the secretary of the commander of the army, who enlisted the people of the land for military duty; and 60 men from the common people who were found within the city. ²⁶ Nebuzaradan, the commander of the guards, took them and brought them to the king of Babylon at Riblah. ²⁷ The king of Babylon put them to death at Riblah in the land of Hamath. Thus Judah went into exile from its land.

²⁸ These are the people Nebuchadnezzar deported: in the seventh year, 3,023 Jews; ²⁹ in his eighteenth year, 832 people from Jerusalem; ³⁰ in Nebuchadnezzar's twenty-third year, Nebuzaradan, the commander of the guards, deported 745 Jews. All together 4,600 people were deported.

³¹ On the twenty-fifth day of the twelfth month of the thirty-seventh year of the exile of Judah's King Jehoiachin, Evil-merodach king of Babylon, in the first year of his reign, pardoned King Jehoiachin of Judah and released him from the prison. ³² He spoke kindly to him and set his throne above the thrones of the kings who were with him in Babylon. ³³ So Jehoiachin changed his prison clothes, and he dined regularly in the presence of the king of Babylon for the rest of his life. ³⁴ As for his allowance, a regular allowance was given to him by the king of Babylon, a portion for each day until the day of his death, for the rest of his life.

𝒫SALM 119:129-136

¹²⁹ Your decrees are wonderful;
      therefore I obey them.
¹³⁰ The revelation of Your words
      brings light
      and gives understanding to the
      inexperienced.
¹³¹ I pant with open mouth

because I long for Your commands.
¹³² Turn to me and be gracious to me,
      as is Your practice toward those
      who love Your name.
¹³³ Make my steps steady through
      Your promise;
      don't let sin dominate me.
¹³⁴ Redeem me from human
      oppression,
      and I will keep Your precepts.
¹³⁵ Show favor to Your servant,
      and teach me Your statutes.
¹³⁶ My eyes pour out streams of tears
      because people do not follow Your
      instruction.

𝒫ROVERBS 27:1-2

27 Don't boast about tomorrow,
      for you don't know what a day
      might bring.

² Let another praise you, and not
      your own mouth—
      a stranger, and not your own lips.

ℋEBREWS 4:14—6:8

¹⁴ Therefore since we have a great high priest who has passed through the heavens—Jesus the Son of God—let us hold fast to the confession. ¹⁵ For we do not have a high priest who is unable to sympathize with our weaknesses, but One who has been tested in every way as we are, yet without sin. ¹⁶ Therefore let us approach the throne of grace with boldness, so that we may receive mercy and find grace to help us at the proper time.

5 For every high priest taken from men is appointed in service to God for the people, to offer both gifts and sacrifices for sins. ² He is able to deal gently with those who are ignorant and are going astray, since he himself is also subject to weakness. ³ Because of this, he must make a sin offering for himself as well as for the people. ⁴ No one takes this honor on himself; instead, a person is called by God, just as Aaron was. ⁵ In the same way, the Messiah did not exalt

Himself to become a high priest, but the One who said to Him, **You are My Son; today I have become Your Father,** ⁶ also said in another passage, **You are a priest forever in the order of Melchizedek.**

⁷ During His earthly life, He offered prayers and appeals, with loud cries and tears, to the One who was able to save Him from death, and He was heard because of His reverence. ⁸ Though a Son, He learned obedience through what He suffered. ⁹ After He was perfected, He became the source of eternal salvation to all who obey Him, ¹⁰ and He was declared by God a high priest "in the order of Melchizedek."

¹¹ We have a great deal to say about this, and it's difficult to explain, since you have become slow to understand. ¹² For though by this time you ought to be teachers, you need someone to teach you again the basic principles of God's revelation. You need milk, not solid food. ¹³ Now everyone who lives on milk is inexperienced with the message about righteousness, because he is an infant. ¹⁴ But solid food is for the mature—for those whose senses have been trained to distinguish between good and evil.

6 Therefore, leaving the elementary message about the Messiah, let us go on to maturity, not laying again the foundation of repentance from dead works, faith in God, ² teaching about ritual washings, laying on of hands, the resurrection of the dead, and eternal judgment. ³ And we will do this if God permits.

⁴ For it is impossible to renew to repentance those who were once enlightened, who tasted the heavenly gift, became companions with the Holy Spirit, ⁵ tasted God's good word and the powers of the coming age, ⁶ and who have fallen away, because, to their own harm, they are recrucifying the Son of God and holding Him up to contempt. ⁷ For ground that has drunk the rain that has often fallen on it, and that produces vegetation useful to those it is cultivated for, receives a blessing from God. ⁸ But if it produces thorns and thistles, it is worthless and about to be cursed, and will be burned at the end.

Love with a "Stoop"

Therefore let us approach the throne of grace with boldness.
—HEBREWS 4:16

Grace is more than a synonym for love; it is a characteristic of the Deity which is quite close to love (and mercy) but yet deserves to be seen as different and distinctive. I heard an old Welsh preacher say: "Grace is a word with a 'stoop' in it; love reaches out on the same level, but grace always has to stoop to pick one up." It was probably this same thought that an anonymous writer had in mind when he said: "Grace is love at its loveliest, falling on the unlovable and making it lovely."

But it is to the great Puritan preacher Thomas Goodwin we must turn for the best clarification of the difference between love and grace: "Grace is more than mercy and love. It superadds to them. It denotes not simply love but love of a sovereign, transcendentally superior One that may do what He will, that may freely choose whether He will love or no. There may be love between equals, and an inferior may love a superior, but love in a Superior—and so superior that He may do what He will—in such a One love is called grace. Grace is attributed to princes; they are said to be 'gracious' to their subjects, whereas subjects cannot be gracious to princes."

Grace then is God's kindness bestowed upon the undeserving; benevolence handed down to those who have no merit; a hand reaching down to those who have fallen into a pit. The Bible bids us believe that on the throne of the universe there is a God like that.

Prayer

Loving and gracious God, help me understand more deeply than ever what it means to be a recipient of Your grace. I have some idea, but I long to realize it even more. Help me, my Father. In Jesus' name. Amen.

Further Study

Dn 9:1-18; Dt 9:5; 1 Pt 5:5
Is grace the result of righteousness?
Who does God give grace to?

NOVEMBER 9

ℒAMENTATIONS
1:1–3:12

1 How she sits alone,
the city once crowded
   with people!
She who was great
   among the nations
has become like a widow.
The princess among the provinces
has become a slave.

² She weeps aloud during the night,
with tears on her cheeks.
There is no one to offer her comfort,
not one from all her lovers.
All her friends have betrayed her;
they have become her enemies.

³ Judah has gone into exile
following affliction
   and harsh slavery;

she lives among the nations
but finds no place to rest.
All her pursuers
   have overtaken her
in narrow places.

⁴ The roads to Zion mourn,
for no one comes
   to the appointed festivals.
All her gates are deserted;
her priests groan,
her young women grieve,
and she herself is bitter.

⁵ Her adversaries have become her
   masters;
her enemies are at ease,
for the LORD has made her suffer
because of her
   many transgressions.
Her children have gone away
as captives before the adversary.

6 All her splendor has vanished
from Daughter Zion.
Her leaders are like stags
that find no pasture;
they walk away exhausted
before the hunter.

7 During the days of her affliction
and homelessness
Jerusalem remembers all
her precious belongings
that were hers in days of old.
When her people fell
into the adversary's hand,
she had no one to help.
The adversaries looked at her,
laughing over her downfall.

8 Jerusalem has sinned grievously;
therefore, she has become
an object of scorn.
All who honored her now
despise her,
for they have seen her nakedness.
She herself groans and turns away.

9 Her uncleanness stains her skirts.
She never considered her end.
Her downfall was astonishing;
there was no one to comfort her.
LORD, look on my affliction,
for the enemy triumphs!

10 The adversary has seized
all her precious belongings.
She has even seen the nations
enter her sanctuary—
those You had forbidden
to enter Your assembly.

11 All her people groan
while they search for bread.
They have traded
their precious belongings
for food
in order to stay alive.
LORD, look and see
how I have become despised.

12 Is this nothing to you, all you
who pass by?
Look and see!
Is there any pain like mine,
which was dealt out to me,

which the LORD made me suffer
on the day of His burning anger?

13 He sent fire from on high
into my bones;
He made it descend.
He spread a net for my feet
and turned me back.
He made me desolate,
sick all day long.

14 My transgressions
have been formed into a yoke,
fastened together by His hand;
they have been placed on my neck,
and the Lord has broken
my strength.
He has handed me over
to those I cannot withstand.

15 The Lord has rejected
all the mighty men within me.
He has summoned an army
against me
to crush my young warriors.
The Lord has trampled
Virgin Daughter Judah
like grapes in a winepress.

16 I weep because of these things;
my eyes flow with tears.
For there is no one nearby
to comfort me,
no one to keep me alive.
My children are desolate
because the enemy has prevailed.

17 Zion stretches out her hands;
there is no one to comfort her.
The LORD has issued a decree
against Jacob
that his neighbors should be
his adversaries.
Jerusalem has become
something impure among them.

18 The LORD is in the right,
for I have rebelled
against His command.
Listen, all you people;
look at my pain.
My young men and women
have gone into captivity.

19 I called to my lovers,
but they betrayed me.
My priests and elders
perished in the city
while searching for food
to keep themselves alive.

20 LORD, see how I am in distress.
I am churning within;
my heart is broken,
for I have been very rebellious.
Outside, the sword takes
the children;
inside, there is death.

21 People have heard me groaning,
but there is no one to comfort me.
All my enemies have heard
of my misfortune;
they are glad that
You have caused it.
Bring on the day
You have announced,
so that they may become like me.

22 Let all their wickedness come
before You,
and deal with them
as You have dealt with me
because of all my transgressions.
For my groans are many,
and I am sick at heart.

2 How the Lord has overshadowed
Daughter Zion with His anger!
He has thrown down Israel's glory
from heaven to earth.
He has abandoned His footstool
in the day of His anger.

2 Without compassion the Lord
has swallowed up
all the dwellings of Jacob.
In His wrath He has demolished
the fortified cities
of Daughter Judah.
He brought them to the ground
and defiled the kingdom
and its leaders.

3 He has cut off every horn of Israel
in His burning anger
and withdrawn His right hand
in the presence of the enemy.

He has blazed against Jacob
like a flaming fire
that consumes everything
in its path.

4 Like an enemy He has bent
His bow;
His right hand is positioned
like an adversary.
He has killed everyone
who was loved,
pouring out His wrath like fire
on the tent of Daughter Zion.

5 The Lord is like an enemy;
He has swallowed up Israel.
He swallowed up all its palaces
and destroyed its fortified cities.
He has multiplied mourning
and lamentation
within Daughter Judah.

6 He has done violence to His temple
as if it were a garden booth,
destroying His place of meeting.
The LORD has abolished
appointed festivals and Sabbaths
in Zion.
He has despised king and priest
in His fierce anger.

7 The Lord has rejected His altar,
repudiated His sanctuary;
He has handed the walls
of her palaces
over to the enemy.
They have raised a shout
in the house of the LORD
as on the day
of an appointed festival.

8 The LORD determined to destroy
the wall of Daughter Zion.
He stretched out a measuring line
and did not restrain Himself
from destroying.
He made the ramparts
and walls grieve;
together they waste away.

9 Zion's gates have fallen
to the ground;
He has destroyed and shattered
the bars on her gates.

Her king and her leaders live
    among the nations,
instruction is no more,
and even her prophets receive
    no vision from the LORD.

¹⁰ The elders of Daughter Zion
    sit on the ground in silence.
They have thrown dust
    on their heads
    and put on sackcloth.
The young women of Jerusalem
    have bowed their heads
        to the ground.

¹¹ My eyes are worn out
    from weeping;
I am churning within.
My heart is poured out in grief
    because of the destruction
        of my dear people,
because children and infants faint
    in the streets of the city.

¹² They cry out to their mothers:
    Where is the grain and wine?
as they faint like the wounded
    in the streets of the city,
as their lives fade away
    in the arms of their mothers.

¹³ What can I say on your behalf?
    To what can I compare you,
        Daughter Jerusalem?
What can I liken you to,
    so that I may console you,
        Virgin Daughter Zion?
For your ruin is as vast as the sea.
Who can heal you?

¹⁴ Your prophets saw visions for you
    that were empty and deceptive;
they did not reveal your guilt
    and so restore your fortunes.
They saw oracles for you
    that were empty and misleading.

¹⁵ All who pass by
    scornfully clap their hands at you.
They hiss and shake their heads
    at Daughter Jerusalem:
Is this the city that was called
    the perfection of beauty,
    the joy of the whole earth?

¹⁶ All your enemies
    open their mouths against you.
They hiss and gnash their teeth,
    saying, "We have swallowed
        her up.
This is the day
    we have waited for!
We have lived to see it."

¹⁷ The LORD has done
    what He planned;
He has accomplished His decree,
    which He ordained in days of old.
He has demolished
    without compassion,
letting the enemy gloat over you
and exalting the horn
    of your adversaries.

¹⁸ The hearts of the people cry out
    to the Lord.
Wall of Daughter Zion,
let your tears run down
    like a river
day and night.
Give yourself no relief
and your eyes no rest.

¹⁹ Arise, cry out in the night,
    from the first watch of the night.
Pour out your heart like water
    before the Lord's presence.
Lift up your hands to Him
    for the lives of your children
who are fainting from hunger
    on the corner of every street.

²⁰ LORD, look and consider
    who You have done this to.
Should women eat
    their own children,
the infants they have nurtured?
Should priests and prophets
    be killed in the Lord's sanctuary?

²¹ Both young and old
    are lying on the ground
        in the streets.
My young men and women
    have fallen by the sword.
You have killed them in the day
    of Your anger,
slaughtering without compassion.

²² You summoned my attackers
　　on every side,
　　as if for an appointed
　　　festival day;
on the day of the LORD's anger
　no one escaped or survived.
My enemy has destroyed
　those I nurtured and reared.

3 I am the man
who has seen affliction
　under the rod of God's wrath.
² He has driven me away
　　and forced me to walk
in darkness instead of light.
³ Yes, He repeatedly turns His hand
　against me all day long.

⁴ He has worn away my flesh
　　and skin;
He has shattered my bones.
⁵ He has laid siege against me,
　encircling me with bitterness
　　and hardship.
⁶ He has made me dwell
　　in darkness
like those who have been dead
　　for ages.

⁷ He has walled me in
　　so I cannot escape;
He has weighed me down
　　with chains.
⁸ Even when I cry out and plead
　　for help,
He rejects my prayer.
⁹ He has walled in my ways
　　with cut stones;
He has made my paths crooked.

¹⁰ He is a bear waiting in ambush,
　a lion in hiding;
¹¹ He forced me off my way
　　and tore me to pieces;
He left me desolate.
¹² He bent His bow
　and set me as the target
　　for His arrow.

PSALM 119:137-140

¹³⁷ You are righteous, LORD,
　and Your judgments are just.

¹³⁸ The decrees You issue are
　　righteous
and altogether trustworthy.
¹³⁹ My anger overwhelms me
　because my foes forget Your
　　words.
¹⁴⁰ Your word is completely pure,
　and Your servant loves it.

PROVERBS 27:3-4

³ A stone is heavy and sand, a
　　burden,
but aggravation from a fool
　outweighs them both.

⁴ Fury is cruel, and anger is a flood,
　but who can withstand jealousy?

HEBREWS 6:9–7:10

⁹ Even though we are speaking this way, dear friends, in your case we are confident of the better things connected with salvation. ¹⁰ For God is not unjust; He will not forget your work and the love you showed for His name when you served the saints—and you continue to serve them. ¹¹ Now we want each of you to demonstrate the same diligence for the final realization of your hope, ¹² so that you won't become lazy, but imitators of those who inherit the promises through faith and perseverance.

¹³ For when God made a promise to Abraham, since He had no one greater to swear by, He swore by Himself:

¹⁴ **I will most certainly bless you,
　and I will greatly multiply you.**

¹⁵ And so, after waiting patiently, Abraham obtained the promise. ¹⁶ For men swear by something greater than themselves, and for them a confirming oath ends every dispute. ¹⁷ Because God wanted to show His unchangeable purpose even more clearly to the heirs of the promise, He guaranteed it with an oath, ¹⁸ so that through two unchangeable things, in which it is impossible for God to lie, we who have fled for refuge

might have strong encouragement to seize the hope set before us. [19] We have this hope—like a sure and firm anchor of the soul—that enters the inner sanctuary behind the curtain. [20] Jesus has entered there on our behalf as a forerunner, because He has become a "high priest forever in the order of Melchizedek."

7 For this Melchizedek—

King of Salem, priest of the Most High God,
who met Abraham and blessed him as he returned from defeating the kings,
[2] and Abraham gave him a tenth of everything;
first, his name means "king of righteousness,"
then also, "king of Salem," meaning "king of peace";
[3] without father, mother, or genealogy,

having neither beginning of days nor end of life,
but resembling the Son of God—

remains a priest forever.
[4] Now consider how great this man was, to whom even Abraham the patriarch gave a tenth of the plunder! [5] The sons of Levi who receive the priestly office have a commandment according to the law to collect a tenth from the people—that is, from their brothers—though they have also descended from Abraham. [6] But one without this lineage collected tithes from Abraham and blessed the one who had the promises. [7] Without a doubt, the inferior is blessed by the superior. [8] In the one case, men who will die receive tithes; but in the other case, Scripture testifies that he lives. [9] And in a sense Levi himself, who receives tithes, has paid tithes through Abraham, [10] for he was still within his forefather when Melchizedek met him.

Christ—Our Precursor

Jesus has entered there on our behalf as a forerunner.—HEBREWS 6:20

Out of all the aspects of truth that surround the fact of our Lord's ascension, one of the greatest is surely this—Christ is our Precursor. A precursor is really a forerunner—an advance runner—and that is precisely the term which our text for today applies to the climactic ministry of our ascended Lord.

The NIV translates the word *prodromos* (forerunner) thus: "who went before us." That translation, in my opinion, is not nearly as appealing as that found in other versions, where the word "forerunner" is actually used. "Forerunner" brings to mind a picture of our Lord as a celestial outrider "bringing many sons to glory" (Heb 2:10) and reminds us of a petition in the great high priestly prayer: "Father, I desire those You have given Me to be with Me where I am. Then they will see My glory." (Jn 17:24).

Henry Longfellow, in his *Golden Legend*, put it like this:

When Christ ascended
Triumphantly, from start to star,
He left the gates of heaven ajar!

Much as I like Longfellow, I have to disagree. Our Lord left the gates of heaven not just "ajar" but wide open. One of the creeds expresses it more effectively: "When Thou hadst overcome the sharpness of death, Thou didst open the kingdom of heaven to all believers." Whatever the future holds for us, we who are Christ's can be sure of this: our Lord has ascended into heaven. And so, too, shall we.

Prayer

O Father, I see that not only was there an ascension in the life of Your Son, but there is to be one in mine too. According to Your Word, I am to be "caught up in the clouds" and to be with You forever. Lord Jesus, come quickly. Amen.

Further Study

Jn 17:1-26; 1:12; Gl 4:7; 1 Co 15:39-44
What does being sons make us?
What do we enter into through death?

NOVEMBER 10

LAMENTATIONS 3:13-66

13 He pierced my kidneys
    with His arrows.
14 I am a laughingstock
        to all my people,
    mocked by their songs all day long.
15 He filled me with bitterness,
    sated me with wormwood.

16 He ground my teeth on gravel
    and made me cower in the dust.
17 My soul has been deprived
        of peace;
    I have forgotten what happiness is.
18 Then I thought: My future is lost,
    as well as my hope from the LORD.

19 Remember my affliction
        and my homelessness,
    the wormwood and the poison.
20 I continually remember them
    and have become depressed.
21 Yet I call this to mind,
    and therefore I have hope:

22 Because of the LORD's
        faithful love

we do not perish,
    for His mercies never end.
23 They are new every morning;
    great is Your faithfulness!
24 I say: The LORD is my portion,
    therefore I will put my hope
        in Him.

25 The LORD is good to those
        who wait for Him,
    to the person who seeks Him.
26 It is good to wait quietly
    for deliverance from the LORD.
27 It is good for a man to bear
        the yoke
    while he is still young.

28 Let him sit alone and be silent,
    for God has disciplined him.
29 Let him put his mouth
        in the dust—
    perhaps there is still hope.
30 Let him offer his cheek
    to the one who would strike him;
    let him be filled with shame.

31 For the Lord
    will not reject us forever.
32 Even if He causes suffering,

He will show compassion
according to His abundant,
faithful love.
³³ For He does not enjoy
bringing affliction
or suffering on mankind.

³⁴ Crushing all the prisoners
of the land
beneath one's feet,
³⁵ denying justice to a man
in the presence of the Most High,
³⁶ or suppressing
a person's lawsuit—
the Lord does not approve
of these things.

³⁷ Who is there who speaks
and it happens,
unless the Lord has ordained it?
³⁸ Do not both adversity and good
come from the mouth
of the Most High?
³⁹ Why should any living
person complain,
any man, because
of the punishment for his sins?

⁴⁰ Let us search out and examine
our ways,
and turn back to the LORD.
⁴¹ Let us lift up our hearts and our
hands
to God in heaven:
⁴² We have sinned and rebelled;
You have not forgiven.

⁴³ You have covered Yourself in anger
and pursued us;
You have killed
without compassion.
⁴⁴ You have covered Yourself
with a cloud
so that no prayer can pass through.
⁴⁵ You have made us disgusting filth
among the peoples.

⁴⁶ All our enemies
open their mouths against us.
⁴⁷ We have experienced panic
and pitfall,
devastation and destruction.
⁴⁸ My eyes flow with streams
of tears

because of the destruction
of my dear people.
⁴⁹ My eyes overflow unceasingly,
without end,
⁵⁰ until the LORD looks down
from heaven and sees.
⁵¹ My eyes bring me grief
because of the fate of
all the women in my city.

⁵² For no apparent reason,
my enemies
hunted me like a bird.
⁵³ They dropped me alive into a pit
and threw stones at me.
⁵⁴ Water flooded over my head,
and I thought: I'm going to die!

⁵⁵ I called on Your name, Yahweh,
from the depths of the Pit.
⁵⁶ You hear my plea:
Do not ignore my cry for relief.
⁵⁷ You come near when I call on You;
You say: "Do not be afraid."

⁵⁸ You defend my cause, Lord;
You redeem my life.
⁵⁹ LORD, You see the wrong
done to me;
judge my case.
⁶⁰ You see all their malice,
all their plots against me.

⁶¹ LORD, You hear their insults,
all their plots against me.
⁶² The slander and murmuring
of my opponents
attack me all day long.
⁶³ When they sit and when
they rise, look,
I am mocked by their songs.

⁶⁴ You will pay them back
what they deserve, LORD,
according to the work
of their hands.
⁶⁵ You will give them a heart
filled with anguish.
May Your curse be on them!
⁶⁶ You will pursue them in anger
and destroy them
under Your heavens.

PSALM 119:141-144

141 I am insignificant and despised,
but I do not forget Your precepts.

142 Your righteousness is an
everlasting righteousness,
and Your instruction is true.

143 Trouble and distress have
overtaken me,
but Your commands are my
delight.

144 Your decrees are righteous forever.
Give me understanding, and I will
live.

PROVERBS 27:5-6

5 Better an open reprimand
than concealed love.

6 The wounds of a friend are
trustworthy,
but the kisses of an enemy are
excessive.

HEBREWS 7:11–8:6

11 If, then, perfection came through the Levitical priesthood (for under it the people received the law), what further need was there for another priest to arise in the order of Melchizedek, and not to be described as being in the order of Aaron? 12 For when there is a change of the priesthood, there must be a change of law as well. 13 For the One about whom these things are said belonged to a different tribe, from which no one has served at the altar. 14 Now it is evident that our Lord came from Judah, and about that tribe Moses said nothing concerning priests. 15 And this becomes clearer if another priest like Melchizedek arises, 16 who doesn't become a priest based on a legal command concerning physical descent but based on the power of an indestructible life. 17 For it has been testified:

**You are a priest forever in the
order of Melchizedek.**

18 So the previous commandment is annulled because it was weak and unprofitable 19 (for the law perfected nothing), but a better hope is introduced, through which we draw near to God. 20 None of this happened without an oath. For others became priests without an oath, 21 but He with an oath made by the One who said to Him:

**The Lord has sworn, and He will
not change His mind,
You are a priest forever.**

22 So Jesus has also become the guarantee of a better covenant. 23 Now many have become Levitical priests, since they are prevented by death from remaining in office. 24 But because He remains forever, He holds His priesthood permanently. 25 Therefore He is always able to save those who come to God through Him, since He always lives to intercede for them. 26 For this is the kind of high priest we need: holy, innocent, undefiled, separated from sinners, and exalted above the heavens. 27 He doesn't need to offer sacrifices every day, as high priests do—first for their own sins, then for those of the people. He did this once for all when He offered Himself. 28 For the law appoints as high priests men who are weak, but the promise of the oath, which came after the law, appoints a Son, who has been perfected forever.

8 Now the main point of what is being said is this: we have this kind of high priest, who sat down at the right hand of the throne of the Majesty in the heavens, 2 a minister of the sanctuary and the true tabernacle, which the Lord set up, and not man. 3 For every high priest is appointed to offer gifts and sacrifices; therefore it was necessary for this priest also to have something to offer. 4 Now if He were on earth, He wouldn't be a priest, since there are those offering the gifts prescribed by the law. 5 These serve as a copy and shadow of the heavenly things, as Moses was warned when he was about to complete the tabernacle. For He said,

Be careful that you make everything according to the pattern that was shown to you on the mountain. ⁶ But Jesus has now obtained a superior ministry, and to that degree He is the mediator of a better covenant, which has been legally enacted on better promises.

"I Know I'm Saved"

[Jesus] is always able to save those who come to God through Him.—HEBREWS 7:25

Is it possible to know without any shadow of doubt that one is saved and ready to meet God? This question, says one writer, goes right to the roots of religious experience. Christianity says "yes." Other religions are not sure. Without exception they will tell you that it savors of presumption to say one is certain that one is saved.

I know some Christians have difficulty here also. They contend that we can hope to be saved, or claim we are being saved, but that no one can state with any degree of assurance that they *are* saved. It is gross self-centeredness, they maintain, and a sign of self-absorption to claim here and now on this earth, "I am saved." Yet John Wesley declared it. On May 24, 1738, he walked into a room in Aldersgate Street, London, where he heard someone read the Preface to Luther's commentary on Romans, and as he listened there was given him "an assurance" that God had taken away his sins and saved him from the law of sin and death.

Millions all over the world can say as Wesley did that they have an assurance they are saved and know that when they die they will go to heaven. It is not presumption to say you are saved providing, of course, you have entered into a personal relationship with Jesus Christ. Indeed, it is offensive for anyone who has given himself or herself to Christ not to say they are saved. As we see from our text today, Christ promises to save and save *completely*. I know I'm saved. How about you?

Prayer

O Father, thank You that not only do You save me from my sins and draw me to Yourself but You give me the assurance that I am Yours forever. How can I thank You enough for such wondrous grace? With my stammering tongue, however, I will try. Amen.

Further Study

2 Tm 1:1-12; 1 Jn 3:14; Jb 19:25
What was Paul able to write to Timothy?
What was Job able to say?

NOVEMBER 11

*L*AMENTATIONS
4:1–5:22

4 How the gold has become tarnished,
the fine gold become dull!
The stones of the temple
lie scattered
at the corner of every street.

2 Zion's precious people—
once worth their weight
in pure gold —
how they are regarded as clay jars,
the work of a potter's hands!

3 Even jackals offer their breasts
to nurse their young,
but my dear people
have become cruel
like ostriches in the wilderness.

4 The nursing infant's tongue
clings to the roof of his mouth
from thirst.
Little children beg for bread,
but no one gives them any.

5 Those who used to eat delicacies
are destitute in the streets;
those who were reared
in purple garments
huddle in garbage heaps.

6 The punishment
of my dear people
is greater than that of Sodom,
which was overthrown
in an instant
without a hand laid on it.

7 Her dignitaries were brighter
than snow,
whiter than milk;
their bodies were more ruddy
than coral,
their appearance like sapphire.

8 Now they appear darker
than soot;
they are not recognized
in the streets.
Their skin has shriveled
on their bones;
it has become dry like wood.

9 Those slain by the sword are
better off
than those slain by hunger,
who waste away,
pierced with pain
because the fields lack produce.

10 The hands
of compassionate women
have cooked their own children;
they became their food
during the destruction
of my dear people.

11 The LORD has exhausted
His wrath,
poured out His burning anger;
He has ignited a fire in Zion,
and it has consumed
her foundations.

12 The kings of the earth
and all the world's inhabitants
did not believe
that an enemy or adversary
could enter Jerusalem's gates.

13 Yet it happened because of
the sins of her prophets
and the guilt of her priests,
who shed the blood of the righteous
within her.

14 Blind, they stumbled
in the streets,
defiled by this blood,
so that no one dared
to touch their garments.

¹⁵ "Stay away! Unclean!"
    people shouted at them.
"Away, away! Don't touch us!"
So they wandered aimlessly.
It was said among the nations,
"They can stay here no longer."

¹⁶ The LORD Himself
    has scattered them;
He regards them no more.
The priests are not respected;
the elders find no favor.

¹⁷ All the while our eyes were failing
as we looked in vain for assistance;
we watched from our towers
for a nation that refused to help.

¹⁸ Our steps were closely followed,
so that we could not walk
    in our streets.
Our end drew near; our time
    ran out.
Our end had come!

¹⁹ Those who chased us were swifter
than eagles in the sky;
they relentlessly pursued us
    over the mountains
and ambushed us
    in the wilderness.

²⁰ The LORD's anointed, the breath
    of our life,
was captured in their traps;
we had said about him:
We will live under his protection
    among the nations.

²¹ So rejoice and be glad,
    Daughter Edom,
you resident of the land of Uz!
Yet the cup will pass to you
    as well;
you will get drunk
    and expose yourself.

²² Daughter Zion, your punishment
    is complete;
He will not lengthen your exile.
But He will punish your iniquity,
    Daughter Edom,
and will expose your sins.

5 Yahweh, remember
    what has happened to us.
Look, and see our disgrace!
² Our inheritance
    has been turned over
    to strangers,
our houses to foreigners.
³ We have become
    orphans, fatherless;
our mothers are widows.
⁴ We must pay for the water
    we drink;
our wood comes at a price.
⁵ We are closely pursued;
we are tired, and no one
    offers us rest.
⁶ We made a treaty with Egypt
and with Assyria,
    to get enough food.
⁷ Our fathers sinned;
    they no longer exist,
but we bear their punishment.
⁸ Slaves rule over us;
no one rescues us
    from their hands.
⁹ We secure our food at the risk
    of our lives
because of the sword
    in the wilderness.
¹⁰ Our skin is as hot as an oven
from the ravages of hunger.
¹¹ Women are raped in Zion,
virgins in the cities of Judah.
¹² Princes are hung up
    by their hands;
elders are shown no respect.
¹³ Young men labor at millstones;
boys stumble under loads of
    wood.
¹⁴ The elders have left the city gate,
the young men, their music.
¹⁵ Joy has left our hearts;
our dancing has turned
    to mourning.
¹⁶ The crown has fallen
    from our head.
Woe to us, for we have sinned.
¹⁷ Because of this, our heart is sick;
because of these, our eyes
    grow dim:
¹⁸ because of Mount Zion,
    which lies desolate
and has jackals prowling in it.
¹⁹ You, LORD, are enthroned forever;

Your throne endures
from generation to generation.
20 Why have You
forgotten us forever,
abandoned us for our entire lives?
21 LORD, restore us to Yourself, so we
may return;
renew our days as in former times,
22 unless You have completely
rejected us
and are intensely angry with us.

PSALM 119:145-152

145 I call with all my heart; answer
me, LORD.
I will obey Your statutes.
146 I call to You; save me,
and I will keep Your decrees.
147 I rise before dawn and cry out for
help;
I hope in Your word.
148 I am awake through each watch of
the night
to meditate on Your promise.
149 In keeping with Your faithful love,
hear my voice.
LORD, give me life, in keeping with
Your justice.
150 Those who pursue evil plans come
near;
they are far from Your instruction.
151 You are near, LORD,
and all Your commands are true.
152 Long ago I learned from Your
decrees
that You have established them
forever.

PROVERBS 27:7-8

7 A person who is full tramples on a
honeycomb,
but to a hungry person, any bitter
thing is sweet.

8 A man wandering from his home
is like a bird wandering from its
nest.

HEBREWS 8:7–9:14

7 For if that first covenant had been
faultless, no opportunity would have

been sought for a second one. 8 But finding fault with His people, He says:

"Look, the days are coming,"
says the Lord,
"when I will make a new
covenant
with the house of Israel
and with the house of Judah—
9 not like the covenant
that I made with their fathers
on the day I took them by their
hand
to lead them out of the land of
Egypt.
Because they did not continue in
My covenant,
I disregarded them," says the
Lord.
10 "But this is the covenant that I
will make with the house of
Israel
after those days," says the Lord:
"I will put My laws into their
minds,
and I will write them on their
hearts,
and I will be their God,
and they will be My people.
11 And each person will not teach
his fellow citizen,
and each his brother, saying,
'Know the Lord,'
because they will all know Me,
from the least to the greatest of
them.
12 For I will be merciful to their
wrongdoing,
and I will never again remember
their sins."

13 By saying, **a new covenant**, He has
declared that the first is old. And what
is old and aging is about to disappear.

9 Now the first covenant also had regulations for ministry and an earthly
sanctuary. 2 For a tabernacle was set up;
and in the first room, which is called
"the holy place," were the lampstand,
the table, and the presentation loaves.
3 Behind the second curtain, the tabernacle was called "the holy of holies." 4 It
contained the gold altar of incense and

the ark of the covenant, covered with gold on all sides, in which there was a gold jar containing the manna, Aaron's rod that budded, and the tablets of the covenant. 5 The cherubim of glory were above it overshadowing the mercy seat. It is not possible to speak about these things in detail right now.

6 These things having been set up this way, the priests enter the first room repeatedly, performing their ministry. 7 But the high priest alone enters the second room, and that only once a year, and never without blood, which he offers for himself and for the sins of the people committed in ignorance. 8 The Holy Spirit was making it clear that the way into the holy of holies had not yet been disclosed while the first tabernacle was still standing. 9 This is a symbol for the present time, during which gifts and sacrifices are offered that cannot perfect the worshiper's conscience. 10 They are physical regulations and only deal with food, drink, and various washings imposed until the time of restoration.

11 Now the Messiah has appeared, high priest of the good things that have come. In the greater and more perfect tabernacle not made with hands (that is, not of this creation), 12 He entered the holy of holies once for all, not by the blood of goats and calves, but by His own blood, having obtained eternal redemption. 13 For if the blood of goats and bulls and the ashes of a heifer sprinkling those who are defiled, sanctify for the purification of the flesh, 14 how much more will the blood of the Messiah, who through the eternal Spirit offered Himself without blemish to God, cleanse our consciences from dead works to serve the living God?

The Belt of Truth

You are near, LORD, and all Your commands are true.
—PSALM 119:151

Paul, in listing the six main pieces of a soldier's equipment, illustrated the six main ways by which we can defend ourselves against the power of Satan—truth, righteousness, steadfastness, faith, salvation, and the Word of God.

Most commentators believe that the reason why Paul chose these six pieces of armor to describe the Christian's protective system against satanic attack was because he was chained to a soldier as he wrote the letter (Eph 6:20). Although it is probably unlikely that the soldier standing guard in prison would have worn the full armor of an infantryman on the battlefield, the sight of him would have kindled Paul's imagination.

The list begins with the belt of truth. Why, we ask ourselves, does the apostle start with such a seemingly insignificant item? Why did he not begin with one of the bigger and more important pieces of equipment, such as the breastplate, the shield, or the sword of the Spirit? The order in which these pieces are given to us is an inspired order, and if we change the order we make our position extremely perilous. For example, the reason why many Christians fail to wield the sword of the Spirit effectively is because they have not first girded their waist with truth. If we reverse the order, we succeed only in weakening our spiritual defense.

It is very important that we grasp this. Girding our waist with truth is always the place to start whenever we are under satanic attack. If we don't start right, then we will not finish right. We cannot do battle with the Devil until we first gird our waists with truth.

Prayer

Gracious and loving Father, help me to absorb this thought into my inner being this day so that it will stay with me for the rest of my life: I cannot do battle with the Devil until I first gird my waist with truth. Amen.

Further Study

2 Pt 1:1-12; Pr 23:23; 3 Jn 1-4
In what are we to be established?
In what did John rejoice?

NOVEMBER 12

EZEKIEL 1:1–3:15

1 In the thirtieth year, in the fourth month, on the fifth day of the month, while I was among the exiles by the Chebar Canal, the heavens opened and I saw visions of God. ² On the fifth day of the month—it was the fifth year of King Jehoiachin's exile— ³ the word of the LORD came directly to Ezekiel the priest, the son of Buzi, in the land of the Chaldeans by the Chebar Canal. And the LORD's hand was on him there.

⁴ I looked and there was a whirlwind coming from the north, a great cloud with fire flashing back and forth and brilliant light all around it. In the center of the fire, there was a gleam like amber. ⁵ The form of four living creatures came from it. And this was their appearance: They had human form, ⁶ but each of them had four faces and four wings. ⁷ Their legs were straight, and the soles of their feet were like the hooves of a calf, sparkling like the gleam of polished bronze. ⁸ They had human hands under their wings on their four sides. All four of them had faces and

wings. ⁹ Their wings were touching. The creatures did not turn as they moved; each one went straight ahead. ¹⁰ The form of each of their faces was that of a man, and each of the four had the face of a lion on the right, the face of an ox on the left, and the face of an eagle. ¹¹ That is what their faces were like. Their wings were spread upward; each had two wings touching that of another and two wings covering its body. ¹² Each creature went straight ahead. Wherever the Spirit wanted to go, they went without turning as they moved.

¹³ The form of the living creatures was like the appearance of burning coals of fire and torches. Fire was moving back and forth between the living creatures; it was bright, with lightning coming out of it. ¹⁴ The creatures were darting back and forth like flashes of lightning.

¹⁵ When I looked at the living creatures, there was one wheel on the ground beside each creature that had four faces. ¹⁶ The appearance of the wheels and their craftsmanship was like the gleam of beryl, and all four had the same form. Their appearance and craftsmanship

was like a wheel within a wheel. [17] When they moved, they went in any of the four directions, without pivoting as they moved. [18] Their rims were large and frightening. Each of their four rims were full of eyes all around. [19] So when the living creatures moved, the wheels moved beside them, and when the creatures rose from the earth, the wheels also rose. [20] Wherever the Spirit wanted to go, the creatures went in the direction the Spirit was moving. The wheels rose alongside them, for the spirit of the living creatures was in the wheels. [21] When the creatures moved, the wheels moved; when the creatures stood still, the wheels stood still; and when the creatures rose from the earth, the wheels rose alongside them, for the spirit of the living creatures was in the wheels.

[22] The shape of an expanse, with a gleam like awe-inspiring crystal, was spread out over the heads of the living creatures. [23] And under the expanse their wings extended one toward another. Each of them also had two wings covering their bodies. [24] When they moved, I heard the sound of their wings like the roar of mighty waters, like the voice of the Almighty, and a sound of commotion like the noise of an army. When they stood still, they lowered their wings.

[25] A voice came from above the expanse over their heads; when they stood still, they lowered their wings. [26] The shape of a throne with the appearance of sapphire stone was above the expanse. There was a form with the appearance of a human on the throne high above. [27] From what seemed to be His waist up, I saw a gleam like amber, with what looked like fire enclosing it all around. From what seemed to be His waist down, I also saw what looked like fire. There was a brilliant light all around Him. [28] The appearance of the brilliant light all around was like that of a rainbow in a cloud on a rainy day. This was the appearance of the form of the LORD's glory. When I saw it, I fell facedown and heard a voice speaking.

2 He said to me, "Son of man, stand up on your feet and I will speak with you." [2] As He spoke to me, the Spirit entered me and set me on my feet, and I listened to the One who was speaking to me. [3] He said to me: "Son of man, I am sending you to the Israelites and to the rebellious nations who have rebelled against Me. The Israelites and their ancestors have transgressed against Me to this day. [4] The children are obstinate and hardhearted. I am sending you to them, and you must say to them: This is what the Lord GOD says. [5] Whether they listen or refuse to listen—for they are a rebellious house—they will know that a prophet has been among them.

[6] "But you, son of man, do not be afraid of them or their words, though briers and thorns are beside you and you live among scorpions. Don't be afraid of their words or be discouraged by the look on their faces, for they are a rebellious house. [7] But speak My words to them whether they listen or refuse to listen, for they are rebellious.

[8] "And you, son of man, listen to what I tell you: Do not be rebellious like that rebellious house. Open your mouth and eat what I am giving you." [9] So I looked and saw a hand reaching out to me, and there was a written scroll in it. [10] When He unrolled it before me, it was written on the front and back; words of lamentation, mourning, and woe were written on it.

3 He said to me: "Son of man, eat what you find here. Eat this scroll, then go and speak to the house of Israel." [2] So I opened my mouth, and He fed me the scroll. [3] "Son of man," he said to me, "eat and fill your stomach with this scroll I am giving you." So I ate it, and it was as sweet as honey in my mouth.

[4] Then He said to me: "Son of man, go to the house of Israel and speak My words to them. [5] For you are not being sent to a people of unintelligible speech or difficult language but to the house of Israel. [6] You are not being sent to many peoples of unintelligible speech or difficult language, whose words you cannot

understand. No doubt, if I sent you to them, they would listen to you. [7] But the house of Israel will not want to listen to you because they do not want to listen to Me. For the whole house of Israel is hardheaded and hardhearted. [8] Look, I have made your face as hard as their faces and your forehead as hard as their foreheads. [9] I have made your forehead like a diamond, harder than flint. Don't be afraid of them or discouraged by the look on their faces, even though they are a rebellious house."

[10] Next He said to me: "Son of man, listen carefully to all My words that I speak to you and take them to heart. [11] Go to your people, the exiles, and speak to them. Tell them: This is what the Lord God says, whether they listen or refuse to listen."

[12] The Spirit then lifted me up, and I heard a great rumbling sound behind me—praise the glory of the Lord in His place! — [13] with the sound of the living creatures' wings brushing against each other and the sound of the wheels beside them, a great rumbling sound. [14] So the Spirit lifted me up and took me away. I left in bitterness and in an angry spirit, and the Lord's hand was on me powerfully. [15] I came to the exiles at Tel-abib, who were living by the Chebar Canal, and I sat there stunned for seven days.

PSALM 119:153-160

[153] Consider my affliction and
   rescue me,
   for I have not forgotten Your
   instruction.
[154] Defend my cause, and redeem me;
   give me life, as You promised.
[155] Salvation is far from the wicked
   because they do not seek Your
   statutes.
[156] Your compassions are many, Lord;
   give me life, according to Your
   judgments.
[157] My persecutors and foes are
   many.
   I have not turned from Your
   decrees.

[158] I have seen the disloyal and feel
   disgust
   because they do not keep Your
   word.
[159] Consider how I love Your precepts;
   Lord, give me life, according to
   Your faithful love.
[160] The entirety of Your word is truth,
   and all Your righteous judgments
   endure forever.

PROVERBS 27:9-10

[9] Oil and incense bring joy to the
   heart,
   and the sweetness of a friend is
   better than self-counsel.

[10] Don't abandon your friend or your
   father's friend,
   and don't go to your brother's
   house in your time of
   calamity;
   better a neighbor nearby than a
   brother far away.

HEBREWS 9:15–10:10

[15] Therefore He is the mediator of a new covenant, so that those who are called might receive the promise of the eternal inheritance, because a death has taken place for redemption from the transgressions committed under the first covenant. [16] Where a will exists, the death of the testator must be established. [17] For a will is valid only when people die, since it is never in force while the testator is living. [18] That is why even the first covenant was inaugurated with blood. [19] For when every commandment had been proclaimed by Moses to all the people according to the law, he took the blood of calves and goats, along with water, scarlet wool, and hyssop, and sprinkled the scroll itself and all the people, [20] saying, **This is the blood of the covenant that God has commanded for you.** [21] In the same way, he sprinkled the tabernacle and all the vessels of worship with blood. [22] According to the law almost everything is purified with blood, and with-

out the shedding of blood there is no forgiveness.

23 Therefore it was necessary for the copies of the things in the heavens to be purified with these sacrifices, but the heavenly things themselves to be purified with better sacrifices than these. 24 For the Messiah did not enter a sanctuary made with hands (only a model of the true one) but into heaven itself, that He might now appear in the presence of God for us. 25 He did not do this to offer Himself many times, as the high priest enters the sanctuary yearly with the blood of another. 26 Otherwise, He would have had to suffer many times since the foundation of the world. But now He has appeared one time, at the end of the ages, for the removal of sin by the sacrifice of Himself. 27 And just as it is appointed for people to die once—and after this, judgment— 28 so also the Messiah, having been offered once to bear the sins of many, will appear a second time, not to bear sin, but to bring salvation to those who are waiting for Him.

10 Since the law has only a shadow of the good things to come, and not the actual form of those realities, it can never perfect the worshipers by the same sacrifices they continually offer year after year. 2 Otherwise, wouldn't they have stopped being offered, since the worshipers, once purified, would no longer have any consciousness of sins? 3 But in the sacrifices there is a reminder of sins every year. 4 For it is impossible for the blood of bulls and goats to take away sins.

5 Therefore, as He was coming into the world, He said:

> You did not want sacrifice and offering,
> but You prepared a body for Me.
> 6 You did not delight
> in whole burnt offerings and sin offerings.
> 7 Then I said, "See, I have come—
> it is written about Me
> in the volume of the scroll—
> to do Your will, O God!"

8 After He says above, You did not desire or delight in sacrifices and offerings, whole burnt offerings and sin offerings, (which are offered according to the law), 9 He then says, See, I have come to do Your will. He takes away the first to establish the second. 10 By this will, we have been sanctified through the offering of the body of Jesus Christ once and for all.

A Temple, Not a Trap

You prepared a body for Me.—HEBREWS 10:5

We continue to meditate on things we must do if we are to stay spiritually fresh. My next suggestion may come as a surprise: keep your body in good physical shape.

One of the most disastrous divorces that ever took place in Christendom was that between the physical and the spiritual. In the early days of Christianity, the two were one. When the disciples wanted men to look after the physical nourishment of those who were in need in the early church, the first of those they selected was Stephen, "a man full of faith and the Holy Spirit" (Ac 6:5). This combination of faith and the Holy Spirit was to be carried into the satisfying of physical needs, for the early church regarded the physical as being important as well as the spiritual. Not supremely important, of course, but important nevertheless.

In more recent centuries, the physical has been looked upon with greater suspicion in the church. In my youth I heard thundering sermons on the text, "our vile body" (Php 3:21, KJV), in which preachers propounded the idea that the body was the enemy of the soul. The suggestion was that the body must be ignored until the day when it is finally discarded and we are given a new resurrection body. These preachers failed to understand that the phrase "vile body" in the King James Version really means "the body of our humble condition" (HCSB) and not something to be treated with contempt. Let's be done with this morbid idea concerning the body that still lingers in parts of the Christian church. Our bodies are not to be seen as traps, but as temples of the Holy Spirit.

Prayer

Blessed Lord Jesus, help me see my body in the way You saw Yours—not as something to be avoided but as something to be used. Show me the steps I need to take to be healthy in soul and in body. For Your own dear name's sake. Amen.

Further Study

Rm 12:1-8; 6:13; 2 Co 6:16
What are we to offer God?
What are we to honor God with?

NOVEMBER 13

EZEKIEL 3:16–6:14

¹⁶ Now at the end of seven days the word of the LORD came to me: ¹⁷ "Son of man, I have made you a watchman over the house of Israel. When you hear a word from My mouth, give them a warning from Me. ¹⁸ If I say to the wicked person: You will surely die, but you do not warn him—you don't speak out to warn him about his wicked way in order to save his life—that wicked person will die for his iniquity. Yet I will hold you responsible for his blood. ¹⁹ But if you warn a wicked person and he does not turn from his wickedness or his wicked way, he will die for his iniq-

uity, but you will have saved your life. ²⁰ Now if a righteous person turns from his righteousness and practices iniquity, and I put a stumbling block in front of him, he will die. If you did not warn him, he will die because of his sin and the righteous acts he did will not be remembered. Yet I will hold you responsible for his blood. ²¹ But if you warn the righteous person that he should not sin, and he does not sin, he will indeed live because he listened to your warning, and you will have saved your life."

²² Then the hand of the LORD was on me there, and He said to me, "Get up, go out to the plain, and I will speak with you there." ²³ So I got up and went out to the plain. The LORD's glory was pres-

ent there, like the glory I had seen by the Chebar Canal, and I fell facedown. ²⁴ The Spirit entered me and set me on my feet. He spoke with me and said: "Go, shut yourself inside your house. ²⁵ And you, son of man, they will put ropes on you and bind you with them so you cannot go out among them. ²⁶ I will make your tongue stick to the roof of your mouth, and you will be mute and unable to rebuke them, for they are a rebellious house. ²⁷ But when I speak with you, I will open your mouth, and you will say to them: This is what the Lord GOD says. Let the one who listens, listen, and let the one who refuses, refuse—for they are a rebellious house.

4 "Now you, son of man, take a brick, set it in front of you, and draw the city of Jerusalem on it. ² Then lay siege against it: construct a siege wall, build a ramp, pitch military camps, and place battering rams against it on all sides. ³ Take an iron plate and set it up as an iron wall between yourself and the city. Turn your face toward it so that it is under siege, and besiege it. This will be a sign for the house of Israel.

⁴ "Then lie down on your left side and place the iniquity of the house of Israel on it. You will bear their iniquity for the number of days you lie on your side. ⁵ For I have assigned you the years of their iniquity according to the number of days you lie down, 390 days; so you will bear the iniquity of the house of Israel. ⁶ When you have completed these days, lie down again, but on your right side, and bear the iniquity of the house of Judah. I have assigned you 40 days, a day for each year. ⁷ You must turn your face toward the siege of Jerusalem with your arm bared, and prophesy against it. ⁸ Be aware that I will put cords on you so you cannot turn from side to side until you have finished the days of your siege.

⁹ "Also take wheat, barley, beans, lentils, millet, and spelt. Put them in a single container and make them into bread for yourself. You are to eat it during the number of days you lie on your side, 390 days. ¹⁰ The food you eat each day will be eight ounces by weight; you will eat it from time to time. ¹¹ You are also to drink water by measure, one-sixth of a gallon, which you will drink from time to time. ¹² You will eat it as you would a barley cake and bake it over dried human excrement in their sight." ¹³ The LORD said, "This is how the Israelites will eat their bread—ceremonially unclean—among the nations where I will banish them."

¹⁴ But I said, "Ah, Lord GOD, I have never been defiled. From my youth until now I have not eaten anything that died naturally or was mauled by wild beasts. And impure meat has never entered my mouth."

¹⁵ He replied to me, "Look, I will let you use cow dung instead of human excrement, and you can make your bread over that." ¹⁶ Then He said to me, "Son of man, I am going to cut off the supply of bread in Jerusalem. They will anxiously eat bread rationed by weight and in dread drink water by measure. ¹⁷ So they will lack bread and water; everyone will be devastated and waste away because of their iniquity.

5 "Now you, son of man, take a sharp sword, use it as you would a barber's razor, and shave your head and beard. Then take a pair of scales and divide the hair. ² You are to burn up one third of it in the city when the days of the siege have ended; you are to take one third and slash it with the sword all around the city; and you are to scatter one third to the wind, for I will draw a sword to chase after them. ³ But you are to take a few strands from the hair and secure them in the folds of your robe. ⁴ Take some more of them, throw them into the fire, and burn them in it. A fire will spread from it to the whole house of Israel.

⁵ "This is what the Lord GOD says: I have set this Jerusalem in the center of the nations, with countries all around her. ⁶ But she has rebelled against My ordinances with more wickedness than the nations, and against My statutes more than the countries that surround her. For her people have rejected My

ordinances and have not walked in My statutes.

7 "Therefore, this is what the Lord GOD says: Because you have been more insubordinate than the nations around you—you have not walked in My statutes or kept My ordinances; you have not even kept the ordinances of the nations around you—⁸ therefore, this is what the Lord GOD says: See, I am against you, Jerusalem, and I will execute judgments within you in the sight of the nations. ⁹ Because of all your abominations, I will do to you what I have never done before and what I will never do again. ¹⁰ As a result, fathers will eat their sons within Jerusalem, and sons will eat their fathers. I will execute judgments against you and scatter all your survivors to every direction of the wind.

¹¹ "Therefore, as I live"—this is the declaration of the Lord GOD—"I am going to cut you off and show you no pity, because you have defiled My sanctuary with all your detestable practices and abominations. Yes, I will not spare you. ¹² One third of your people will die by plague and be consumed by famine within you; one third will fall by the sword all around you; and I will scatter one third to every direction of the wind, and I will draw a sword to chase after them. ¹³ When My anger is spent and I have vented My wrath on them, I will be appeased. Then, after I have spent My wrath on them, they will know that I, the LORD, have spoken in My jealousy.

¹⁴ "I will make you a ruin and a disgrace among the nations around you, in the sight of everyone who passes by. ¹⁵ So you will be a disgrace and a taunt, a warning and a horror, to the nations around you when I execute judgments against you in anger, wrath, and furious rebukes. I, the LORD, have spoken. ¹⁶ When I shoot deadly arrows of famine at them, arrows for destruction that I will send to destroy you, inhabitants of Jerusalem, I will intensify the famine against you and cut off your supply of bread. ¹⁷ I will send famine and dangerous animals against you. They will leave

you childless, Jerusalem. Plague and bloodshed will sweep through you, and I will bring a sword against you. I, the LORD, have spoken."

6 The word of the LORD came to me: ² "Son of man, turn your face toward the mountains of Israel and prophesy against them. ³ You are to say: Mountains of Israel, hear the word of the Lord GOD! This is what the Lord GOD says to the mountains and the hills, to the ravines and the valleys: I am about to bring a sword against you, and I will destroy your high places. ⁴ Your altars will be desolated and your incense altars smashed. I will throw down your slain in front of your idols. ⁵ I will lay the corpses of the Israelites in front of their idols and scatter your bones around your altars. ⁶ Wherever you live the cities will be in ruins and the high places will be desolate, so that your altars will lie in ruins and be desecrated, your idols smashed and obliterated, your incense altars cut down, and your works wiped out. ⁷ The slain will fall among you, and you will know that I am the LORD.

⁸ "Yet I will leave a remnant when you are scattered among the nations, for throughout the countries there will be some of you who will escape the sword. ⁹ Then your survivors will remember Me among the nations where they are taken captive, how I was crushed by their promiscuous hearts that turned away from Me and by their eyes that lusted after their idols. They will loathe themselves because of the evil things they did, their abominations of every kind. ¹⁰ And they will know that I am the LORD; I did not threaten to bring this disaster on them without a reason.

¹¹ "This is what the Lord GOD says: Clap your hands, stamp your feet, and cry out over all the evil abominations of the house of Israel, who will fall by the sword, famine, and plague. ¹² The one who is far off will die by plague; the one who is near will fall by the sword; and the one who remains and is spared will die of famine. In this way I will exhaust My wrath on them. ¹³ You will all know

that I am the LORD when their slain lie among their idols around their altars, on every high hill, on all the mountaintops, and under every green tree and every leafy oak—the places where they offered pleasing aromas to all their idols. [14] I will stretch out My hand against them, and wherever they live I will make the land a desolate waste, from the wilderness to Diblah. Then they will know that I am Yahweh."

PSALM 119:161-168

[161] Princes have persecuted me
without cause,
but my heart fears only Your word.
[162] I rejoice over Your promise
like one who finds vast treasure.
[163] I hate and abhor falsehood,
but I love Your instruction.
[164] I praise You seven times a day
for Your righteous judgments.
[165] Abundant peace belongs to those
who love Your instruction;
nothing makes them stumble.
[166] LORD, I hope for Your salvation
and carry out Your commands.
[167] I obey Your decrees
and love them greatly.
[168] I obey Your precepts and decrees,
for all my ways are before You.

PROVERBS 27:11-13

[11] Be wise, my son, and bring my
heart joy,
so that I can answer anyone who
taunts me.

[12] The sensible see danger and take
cover;
the foolish keep going and are
punished.

[13] Take his garment, for he has put
up security for a stranger;
get collateral if it is for foreigners.

HEBREWS 10:11-31

[11] Now every priest stands day after day ministering and offering time after

time the same sacrifices, which can never take away sins. [12] But this man, after offering one sacrifice for sins forever, sat down at the right hand of God. [13] He is now waiting until His enemies are made His footstool. [14] For by one offering He has perfected forever those who are sanctified. [15] The Holy Spirit also testifies to us about this. For after He had said:

[16] This is the covenant that I will
make with them
after those days, says the Lord:
I will put My laws on their
hearts,
and I will write them on their
minds,

[17] He adds:

I will never again remember
their sins and their lawless acts.

[18] Now where there is forgiveness of these, there is no longer an offering for sin.
[19] Therefore, brothers, since we have boldness to enter the sanctuary through the blood of Jesus, [20] by the new and living way that He has inaugurated for us, through the curtain (that is, His flesh); [21] and since we have a great high priest over the house of God, [22] let us draw near with a true heart in full assurance of faith, our hearts sprinkled clean from an evil conscience and our bodies washed in pure water. [23] Let us hold on to the confession of our hope without wavering, for He who promised is faithful. [24] And let us be concerned about one another in order to promote love and good works, [25] not staying away from our meetings, as some habitually do, but encouraging each other, and all the more as you see the day drawing near.
[26] For if we deliberately sin after receiving the knowledge of the truth, there no longer remains a sacrifice for sins, [27] but a terrifying expectation of judgment, and the fury of a fire about to consume the adversaries. [28] If anyone disregards Moses' law, he dies without

mercy, based on the testimony of two or three witnesses. ²⁹ How much worse punishment, do you think one will deserve who has trampled on the Son of God, regarded as profane the blood of the covenant by which he was sancti-fied, and insulted the Spirit of grace? ³⁰ For we know the One who has said, **Vengeance belongs to Me, I will repay,** and again, **The Lord will judge His people.** ³¹ It is a terrifying thing to fall into the hands of the living God!

The Spirit—Outraged

How much worse punishment, do you think one will deserve who has . . . insulted the Spirit?—HEBREWS 10:29

One of the devices Satan uses to keep some Christians from experiencing all the fullness of the Spirit is to persuade them that the obsessive or unclean thoughts they might have in connection with the Holy Spirit are direct "blasphemy" against the Spirit. Such thoughts are usually due to deep emotional and psychological problems and not deliberate disobedience against the Holy Spirit. They can be forgiven.

Another verse that seems to cause problems for some Christians is the one before us today. In the days of the early church, there were some Jews who, after embracing Christianity, decided to abandon it and return to their old religion: Judaism. Before being readmitted to the faith of their fathers, they were required to renounce the Christian gospel by figuratively trampling on the blood of Christ, at the same time saying words to this effect: "I renounce the blood of Jesus as unworthy and ineffectual."

In the religion of the Jews, trampling on the blood was a sign of contempt. What greater insolence, then, to the Christian faith than to tread under foot the blood of the Son of God, and openly state that it was ineffectual and unworthy. Such an act, said the writer to the Hebrews, not only insulted the Holy Spirit, but outraged Him (Heb 10:29). Such an action is seldom committed in modern times. Take it from me, most upsets in connection with the Holy Spirit are caused by the Spirit of grace calling us to repentance and forgiveness.

Prayer

O Father, release me, I pray, from all Satan's attempts to influence my thinking, and enable me to enjoy, from this day forward, the freedom of "life in the Spirit." For Jesus' sake. Amen.

Further Study

Heb 9; Mt 26:28; Rm 5:9; 1 Pt 1:18-19
Why is Christ's shed blood so precious?
How does it apply to accusing thoughts?

NOVEMBER 14

EZEKIEL 7:1–9:11

7 And the word of the LORD came to me: ² "Son of man, this is what the Lord GOD says to the land of Israel:

An end! The end has come
on the four corners of the land.
³ The end is now on you;
I will send My anger against you
and judge you according to
your ways.
I will punish you for all
your abominations.
⁴ I will not look on you with pity
or spare you,
but I will punish you for your ways
and for your abominations
within you.
Then you will know that I am
the LORD."

⁵ This is what the Lord GOD says:

Look, one disaster after another
is coming!
⁶ An end has come; the end
has come!
It has awakened against you.
Look, it is coming!
⁷ Doom has come on you,
inhabitants of the land.
The time has come; the day is near.
There will be panic
on the mountains
and not celebration.
⁸ I will pour out My wrath on you
very soon;
I will exhaust My anger against you
and judge you
according to your ways.
I will punish you for all
your abominations.
⁹ I will not look on you with pity
or spare you.
I will punish you for your ways

and for your abominations
within you.
Then you will know
that it is I, the LORD, who strikes.

¹⁰ Look, the day is coming!
Doom has gone out.
The rod has blossomed;
arrogance has bloomed.
¹¹ Violence has grown into a rod
of wickedness;
none of them will remain:
none of their multitude,
none of their wealth,
and none of the eminent
among them.

¹² The time has come; the day
has arrived.
Let the buyer not rejoice
and the seller not mourn,
for wrath is on all her multitude.
¹³ The seller will certainly not return
to what was sold
as long as he and the buyer
remain alive.
For the vision concerning
all its people
will not be revoked,
and none of them will preserve
his life because of his iniquity.

¹⁴ They have blown the trumpet
and prepared everything,
but no one goes to war,
for My wrath is on all
her multitude.
¹⁵ The sword is on the outside;
plague and famine are
on the inside.
Whoever is in the field will die
by the sword,
and famine and plague will devour
whoever is in the city.

¹⁶ The survivors among them
will escape

and live on the mountains
like doves of the valley,
all of them moaning,
each over his own iniquity.
¹⁷ All their hands will become weak,
and all their knees will turn
to water.
¹⁸ They will put on sackcloth,
and horror will overwhelm them.
Shame will cover all their faces,
and all their heads will be bald.

¹⁹ They will throw their silver
into the streets,
and their gold will seem like
something filthy.
Their silver and gold
will be unable to save them
in the day of the LORD's wrath.
They will not satisfy their appetites
or fill their stomachs,
for these were
the stumbling blocks
that brought about their iniquity.

²⁰ He appointed
His beautiful ornaments
for majesty,
but they made
their abhorrent images
from them,
their detestable things.
Therefore, I have made these
into something filthy for them.
²¹ I will hand these things over
to foreigners as plunder
and to the wicked of the earth
as spoil,
and they will profane them.
²² I will turn My face from the wicked
as they profane
My treasured place.
Violent men will enter it
and profane it.
²³ Forge the chain,
for the land is filled with crimes
of bloodshed,
and the city is filled with violence.
²⁴ So I will bring the most evil
of nations
to take possession of their houses.
I will put an end to the pride
of the strong,

and their sacred places
will be profaned.
²⁵ Anguish is coming!
They will seek peace,
but there will be none.
²⁶ Disaster after disaster will come,
and there will be rumor
after rumor.
Then they will seek a vision
from a prophet,
but instruction will perish
from the priests
and counsel from the elders.
²⁷ The king will mourn;
the prince will be clothed in grief;
and the hands of the people
of the land will tremble.
I will deal with them according to
their own conduct,
and I will judge them
by their own standards.
Then they will know that I am
the LORD.

8 In the sixth year, in the sixth month, on the fifth day of the month, I was sitting in my house and the elders of Judah were sitting in front of me, and there the hand of the Lord GOD came down on me. ² I looked, and there was a form that had the appearance of a man. From what seemed to be His waist down was fire, and from His waist up was something that looked bright, like the gleam of amber. ³ He stretched out what appeared to be a hand and took me by the hair of my head. Then the Spirit lifted me up between earth and heaven and carried me in visions of God to Jerusalem, to the entrance of the inner gate that faces north, where the offensive statue that provokes jealousy was located. ⁴ I saw the glory of the God of Israel there, like the vision I had seen in the plain.

⁵ The LORD said to me, "Son of man, look toward the north." I looked to the north, and there was this offensive statue north of the altar gate, at the entrance. ⁶ He said to me, "Son of man, do you see what they are doing, the great abominations that the house of Israel is committing here, so that I must depart

from My sanctuary? You will see even greater abominations."

⁷ Then He brought me to the entrance of the court, and when I looked there was a hole in the wall. ⁸ He said to me, "Son of man, dig through the wall." So I dug through the wall, and there was a doorway. ⁹ He said to me, "Go in and see the terrible abominations they are committing here." ¹⁰ I went in and looked, and there engraved all around the wall was every form of detestable thing, crawling creatures and beasts, as well as all the idols of the house of Israel.

¹¹ Seventy elders from the house of Israel were standing before them, with Jaazaniah son of Shaphan standing among them. Each had an incense burner in his hand, and a fragrant cloud of incense was rising up. ¹² Then He said to me, "Son of man, do you see what the elders of the house of Israel are doing in the darkness, each at the shrine of his idol? For they are saying: The LORD does not see us. The LORD has abandoned the land." ¹³ Again He said to me, "You will see even greater abominations, which they are committing."

¹⁴ So He brought me to the entrance of the north gate of the LORD's house, and I saw women sitting there weeping for Tammuz. ¹⁵ And He said to me, "Do you see this, son of man? You will see even greater abominations than these."

¹⁶ So He brought me to the inner court of the LORD's house, and there were about 25 men at the entrance of the LORD's temple, between the portico and the altar, with their backs to the LORD's temple and their faces turned to the east. They were bowing to the east in worship of the sun. ¹⁷ And He said to me, "Do you see this, son of man? Is it not enough for the house of Judah to commit the abominations they are practicing here, that they must also fill the land with violence and repeatedly provoke Me to anger, even putting the branch to their nose? ¹⁸ Therefore I will respond with wrath. I will not show pity or spare them. Though they cry out in My ears with a loud voice, I will not listen to them."

9 Then He called to me directly with a loud voice, "Come near, executioners of the city, each of you with a destructive weapon in his hand." ² And I saw six men coming from the direction of the Upper Gate, which faces north, each with a war club in his hand. There was another man among them, clothed in linen, with writing equipment at his side. They came and stood beside the bronze altar.

³ Then the glory of the God of Israel rose from above the cherubim where it had been, to the threshold of the temple. He called to the man clothed in linen with the writing equipment at his side. ⁴ "Pass throughout the city of Jerusalem," the LORD said to him, "and put a mark on the foreheads of the men who sigh and groan over all the abominations committed in it."

⁵ To the others He said in my hearing, "Pass through the city after him and start killing; do not show pity or spare them! ⁶ Slaughter the old men, the young men and women, as well as the older women and little children, but do not come near anyone who has the mark. Now begin at My sanctuary." So they began with the elders who were in front of the temple. ⁷ Then He said to them, "Defile the temple and fill the courts with the slain. Go!" So they went out killing people in the city.

⁸ While they were killing, I was left alone. And I fell facedown and cried out, "Ah, Lord GOD! Are You going to destroy the entire remnant of Israel when You pour out Your wrath on Jerusalem?"

⁹ He answered me: "The iniquity of the house of Israel and Judah is extremely great; the land is full of bloodshed, and the city full of perversity. For they say: The LORD has abandoned the land; He does not see. ¹⁰ But as for Me, I will not show pity or spare them. I will bring their actions down on their own heads." ¹¹ Then the man clothed in linen with the writing equipment at his side reported back, "I have done as You commanded me."

PSALM 119:169-176

169 Let my cry reach You, LORD;
give me understanding according
to Your word.
170 Let my plea reach You;
rescue me according to Your
promise.
171 My lips pour out praise,
for You teach me Your statutes.
172 My tongue sings about Your
promise,
for all Your commandments are
righteous.
173 May Your hand be ready to help me,
for I have chosen Your precepts.
174 I long for Your salvation, LORD,
and Your instruction is my delight.
175 Let me live, and I will praise You;
may Your judgments help me.
176 I wander like a lost sheep;
seek Your servant,
for I do not forget Your commands.

PROVERBS 27:14-16

14 If one blesses his neighbor with a
loud voice early in the
morning,
it will be counted as a curse to him.
15 An endless dripping on a rainy day
and a nagging wife are alike.
16 The one who controls her controls
the wind
and grasps oil with his right hand.

HEBREWS 10:32–11:12

32 Remember the earlier days when,
after you had been enlightened, you endured a hard struggle with sufferings.
33 Sometimes you were publicly exposed
to taunts and afflictions, and at other
times you were companions of those
who were treated that way. 34 For you
sympathized with the prisoners and accepted with joy the confiscation of your
possessions, knowing that you yourselves have a better and enduring possession. 35 So don't throw away your
confidence, which has a great reward.
36 For you need endurance, so that after
you have done God's will, you may receive what was promised.

37 For in yet **a very little while,
the Coming One will come and
not delay.**
38 **But My righteous one will live
by faith;
and if he draws back,
My soul has no pleasure in him.**

39 But we are not those who draw back
and are destroyed, but those who have
faith and obtain life.

11 Now faith is the reality of what is
hoped for, the proof of what is
not seen. 2 For by it our ancestors were
approved.
3 By faith we understand that the universe was created by the word of God,
so that what is seen has been made
from things that are not visible.
4 By faith Abel offered to God a better
sacrifice than Cain did. By this he was
approved as a righteous man, because
God approved his gifts, and even though
he is dead, he still speaks through this.
5 By faith, Enoch was taken away so
that he did not experience death, and
**he was not to be found because God
took him away.** For prior to his transformation he was approved, having
pleased God. 6 Now without faith it is
impossible to please God, for the one
who draws near to Him must believe
that He exists and rewards those who
seek Him.
7 By faith Noah, after being warned
about what was not yet seen, in reverence built an ark to deliver his family.
By this he condemned the world and became an heir of the righteousness that
comes by faith.
8 By faith Abraham, when he was
called, obeyed and went out to a place
he was going to receive as an inheritance; he went out, not knowing where
he was going. 9 By faith he stayed as a
foreigner in the land of promise, living
in tents with Isaac and Jacob, co-heirs of
the same promise. 10 For he was looking
forward to the city that has foundations,
whose architect and builder is God.

¹¹ By faith even Sarah herself, when she was barren, received power to conceive offspring, even though she was past the age, since she considered that the One who had promised was faithful.

¹² And therefore from one man—in fact, from one as good as dead—came offspring as numerous as the stars of heaven and as innumerable as the grains of sand by the seashore.

Faith, Not Demandingness

Now faith is the reality of what is hoped for, the proof of what is not seen.——HEBREWS 11:1

I am frequently asked: "Doesn't what you say about demandingness destroy the faith we ought to have when we approach God in prayer? Isn't powerful praying the ability to insist on God giving us the things we know we ought to be receiving?"

There is a world of difference between "praying in faith" and demandingness. When we "pray in faith," we have the assurance in our hearts that God wants to bring about a certain purpose for His own glory, whereupon faith reaches into heaven and pulls down the answer through fervent, believing prayer. Demandingness is another thing entirely—it insists on getting the answers that are in accord with its own desires rather than God's purposes. It is an attempt to bring God in line with our will rather than bringing our wills in line with His will.

Dr. Francis Schaeffer, when advised that he was suffering from a terminal illness, became assured that his work on earth was finished and that soon he would leave this world and go to his heavenly home. Thousands of people prayed for his healing, and when he himself was asked why he did not claim the Bible's promises concerning health and wholeness, he replied: "When I am in the presence of God, it seems uniquely unbecoming to demand anything."

Some have interpreted these words as a lack of faith, but I think I understand what he meant. It is one thing to plead and pray with passion for something very personal; it is another to demand that the will of the Almighty be one with our own.

Prayer

Father, I see that the line between demandingness and faith is so fine that I can easily cross from one to the other without knowing it. Tune my spirit so that I will always be able to discern the difference between these two things. In Jesus' name. Amen.

Further Study

Ps 143:1-10; Mt 12:50; Jms 4:1-15
What was the desire of the psalmist?
How does James put it?

NOVEMBER 15

EZEKIEL 10:1–12:7

10 Then I looked, and there above the expanse over the heads of the cherubim was something like sapphire stone resembling the shape of a throne that appeared above them. ² The LORD spoke to the man clothed in linen and said, "Go inside the wheelwork beneath the cherubim. Fill your hands with hot coals from among the cherubim and scatter them over the city." So he went in as I watched.

³ Now the cherubim were standing to the south of the temple when the man went in, and the cloud filled the inner court. ⁴ Then the glory of the LORD rose from above the cherubim to the threshold of the temple. The temple was filled with the cloud, and the court was filled with the brightness of the LORD's glory. ⁵ The sound of the cherubim's wings could be heard as far as the outer court; it was like the voice of God Almighty when He speaks.

⁶ After the LORD commanded the man clothed in linen, saying, "Take fire from inside the wheelwork, from among the cherubim," the man went in and stood beside a wheel. ⁷ Then one of the cherubim reached out his hand to the fire that was among them. He took some, and put it into the hands of the man clothed in linen, who took it and went out. ⁸ The cherubim appeared to have the form of human hands under their wings.

⁹ I looked, and there were four wheels beside the cherubim, one wheel beside each cherub. The luster of the wheels was like the gleam of beryl. ¹⁰ In appearance, all four had the same form, like a wheel within a wheel. ¹¹ When they moved, they would go in any of the four directions, without pivoting as they moved. But wherever the head faced, they would go in that direction, without pivoting as they went. ¹² Their entire bodies, including their backs, hands, wings, and the wheels that the four of them had, were full of eyes all around. ¹³ As I listened the wheels were called "the wheelwork." ¹⁴ Each one had four faces: the first face was that of a cherub, the second that of a man, the third that of a lion, and the fourth that of an eagle.

¹⁵ The cherubim ascended; these were the living creatures I had seen by the Chebar Canal. ¹⁶ When the cherubim moved, the wheels moved beside them, and when they lifted their wings to rise from the earth, even then the wheels did not veer away from them. ¹⁷ When the cherubim stood still, the wheels stood still, and when they ascended, the wheels ascended with them, for the spirit of the living creatures was in them.

¹⁸ Then the glory of the LORD moved away from the threshold of the temple and stood above the cherubim. ¹⁹ The cherubim lifted their wings and ascended from the earth right before my eyes; the wheels were beside them as they went. The glory of the God of Israel was above them, and it stood at the entrance to the eastern gate of the LORD's house.

²⁰ These were the living creatures I had seen beneath the God of Israel by the Chebar Canal, and I recognized that they were cherubim. ²¹ Each had four faces and each had four wings, with the form of human hands under their wings. ²² Their faces looked like the same faces I had seen by the Chebar Canal. Each creature went straight ahead.

11 The Spirit then lifted me up and brought me to the eastern gate of the LORD's house, which faces east, and at the gate's entrance were 25 men. Among them I saw Jaazaniah son of

Azzur, and Pelatiah son of Benaiah, leaders of the people. [2] The LORD said to me, "Son of man, these are the men who plan evil and give wicked advice in this city. [3] They are saying: Isn't the time near to build houses? The city is the pot, and we are the meat. [4] Therefore, prophesy against them. Prophesy, son of man!"

[5] Then the Spirit of the LORD came on me, and He told me, "You are to say: This is what the LORD says: That is what you are thinking, house of Israel; and I know the thoughts that arise in your mind. [6] You have multiplied your slain in this city, filling its streets with the dead.

[7] "Therefore, this is what the Lord GOD says: The slain you have put within it are the meat, and the city is the pot, but I will remove you from it. [8] You fear the sword, so I will bring the sword against you." This is the declaration of the Lord GOD. [9] "I will bring you out of the city and hand you over to foreigners; I will execute judgments against you. [10] You will fall by the sword, and I will judge you at the border of Israel. Then you will know that I am the LORD. [11] The city will not be a pot for you, and you will not be the meat within it. I will judge you at the border of Israel, [12] so you will know that I am the LORD, whose statutes you have not followed and whose ordinances you have not practiced. Instead, you have acted according to the ordinances of the nations around you."

[13] Now while I was prophesying, Pelatiah son of Benaiah died. Then I fell facedown and cried out with a loud voice: "Ah, Lord GOD! Will You bring to an end the remnant of Israel?"

[14] The word of the LORD came to me again: [15] "Son of man, your own relatives, those who have the right to redeem you, and the entire house of Israel, all of them, are those the residents of Jerusalem have said this to: Stay away from the LORD; this land has been given to us as a possession.

[16] "Therefore say: This is what the Lord GOD says: Though I sent them far away among the nations and scattered them among the countries, yet for a little while I have been a sanctuary for them in the countries where they have gone.

[17] "Therefore say: This is what the Lord GOD says: I will gather you from the peoples and assemble you from the countries where you have been scattered, and I will give you the land of Israel.

[18] "When they arrive there, they will remove all its detestable things and all its abominations from it. [19] And I will give them one heart and put a new spirit within them; I will remove their heart of stone from their bodies and give them a heart of flesh, [20] so they may follow My statutes, keep My ordinances, and practice them. Then they will be My people, and I will be their God. [21] But as for those whose hearts pursue their desire for detestable things and abominations, I will bring their actions down on their own heads." This is the declaration of the Lord GOD.

[22] Then the cherubim, with the wheels beside them, lifted their wings, and the glory of the God of Israel was above them. [23] The glory of the LORD rose up from within the city and stood on the mountain east of the city. [24] The Spirit lifted me up and brought me to Chaldea and to the exiles in a vision from the Spirit of God. After the vision I had seen left me, [25] I spoke to the exiles about all the things the LORD had shown me.

12 The word of the LORD came to me: [2] "Son of man, you are living among a rebellious house. They have eyes to see but do not see, and ears to hear but do not hear, for they are a rebellious house.

[3] "Son of man, pack your bags for exile and go into exile in their sight during the day. You will go into exile from your place to another place while they watch; perhaps they will understand, though they are a rebellious house. [4] During the day, bring out your bags like an exile's bags while they look on. Then in the evening go out in their sight like those going into exile. [5] As they watch, dig through the wall and take the

bags out through it. ⁶ And while they look on, lift the bags to your shoulder and take them out in the dark; cover your face so that you cannot see the land. For I have made you a sign to the house of Israel."

⁷ So I did just as I was commanded. I brought out my bags like an exile's bags in the daytime. In the evening I dug through the wall by hand; I took them out in the dark, carrying them on my shoulder in their sight.

PSALM 120:1-7

¹ In my distress I called to the LORD,
   and He answered me:
² "LORD, deliver me from lying lips
   and a deceitful tongue."

³ What will He give you,
   and what will He do to you,
   you deceitful tongue?
⁴ A warrior's sharp arrows,
   with burning charcoal!

⁵ What misery that I have stayed in
   Meshech,
   that I have lived among the tents
   of Kedar!
⁶ I have lived too long
   with those who hate peace.
⁷ I am for peace; but when I speak,
   they are for war.

PROVERBS 27:17-18

¹⁷ Iron sharpens iron,
   and one man sharpens another.

¹⁸ Whoever tends a fig tree will eat
   its fruit,
   and whoever looks after his
   master will be honored.

HEBREWS 11:13-31

¹³ These all died in faith without having received the promises, but they saw them from a distance, greeted them, and confessed that they were foreigners and temporary residents on the earth. ¹⁴ Now those who say such things make

it clear that they are seeking a homeland. ¹⁵ If they had been remembering that land they came from, they would have had opportunity to return. ¹⁶ But they now aspire to a better land—a heavenly one. Therefore God is not ashamed to be called their God, for He has prepared a city for them.

¹⁷ By faith Abraham, when he was tested, offered up Isaac; he who had received the promises was offering up his unique son, ¹⁸ about whom it had been said, **In Isaac your seed will be called.** ¹⁹ He considered God to be able even to raise someone from the dead, from which he also got him back as an illustration.

²⁰ By faith Isaac blessed Jacob and Esau concerning things to come. ²¹ By faith Jacob, when he was dying, blessed each of the sons of Joseph, and, **he worshiped, leaning on the top of his staff.** ²² By faith Joseph, as he was nearing the end of his life, mentioned the exodus of the sons of Israel and gave instructions concerning his bones.

²³ By faith Moses, after he was born, was hidden by his parents for three months, because they saw that the child was beautiful, and they didn't fear the king's edict. ²⁴ By faith Moses, when he had grown up, refused to be called the son of Pharaoh's daughter ²⁵ and chose to suffer with the people of God rather than to enjoy the short-lived pleasure of sin. ²⁶ For he considered reproach for the sake of the Messiah to be greater wealth than the treasures of Egypt, since his attention was on the reward.

²⁷ By faith he left Egypt behind, not being afraid of the king's anger, for he persevered, as one who sees Him who is invisible. ²⁸ By faith he instituted the Passover and the sprinkling of the blood, so that the destroyer of the first-born might not touch them. ²⁹ By faith they crossed the Red Sea as though they were on dry land. When the Egyptians attempted to do this, they were drowned.

³⁰ By faith the walls of Jericho fell down after being encircled for seven days. ³¹ By faith Rahab the prostitute received the spies in peace and didn't perish with those who disobeyed.

Seeing the Invisible

He persevered, as one who sees Him who is invisible.
——HEBREWS 11:27

What is it that prompts some people to take more interest in the principles of godliness than in God Himself? I think one reason could be that we are more comfortable dealing in the realm of the visible than the invisible. We prefer to work with things we can touch, handle, and apply so that we feel an immediate impact rather than to launch out into the unseen and to simply trust.

I often saw people come up against this problem in the days when much of my time was spent in personal counseling. I would bring people to a place where they could accept that the roots of their problem lay in a deficient relationship with God. However, when a movement of simple basic trust toward Him was called for, terror would appear for a moment in their eyes, and they would say: "Give me some steps I can take to deal with my problem, some principles I can follow that will act as a ladder on which I can climb out of this pit."

We all find it easier to do than to be; we prefer a plan to follow rather than a Person to trust. What our carnal nature hates to be faced with is the challenge of throwing ourselves in utter dependency on a God who is invisible and intangible. Yet this is what a relationship with God entails. The thing that marks Moses out as outstanding in the chapter before us today is not his works but his faith. He persevered because he saw Him who is invisible. It is possible to see the invisible, but it is possible only to the eye of faith.

Prayer

My Father and my God, help me recognize this terrible tendency in myself to be more comfortable with working than trusting. Let Your Word reach deep into my heart today. Teach me how to be. In Jesus' name I pray. Amen.

Further Study

Rm 1:16-23; Heb 11:1-2; 1 Tm 1:17
Why are men without excuse?
What is the essence of faith?

NOVEMBER 16

EZEKIEL 12:8–14:11

⁸ Then the word of the LORD came to me in the morning: ⁹ "Son of man, hasn't the house of Israel, that rebellious house, asked you: What are you doing? ¹⁰ Say to them: This is what the Lord GOD says: This oracle is about the prince in Jerusalem and all the house of Israel who are living there. ¹¹ You are to say: I am a sign for you. Just as I have done, so it will be done to them; they will go into exile, into captivity. ¹² The prince who is among them will lift his bags to his shoulder in the dark and go out. They will dig through the wall to bring him out through it. He will cover his face so he cannot see the land with his eyes. ¹³ But I will spread My net over him, and he will be caught in My snare. I will bring him to Babylon, the land of the Chaldeans, yet he will not see it, and he will die there. ¹⁴ I will also scatter all the attendants who surround him and all his troops to every direction of the wind, and I will draw a sword to chase after them. ¹⁵ They will know that I am the LORD when I disperse them among the nations and scatter them among the countries. ¹⁶ But I will spare a few of them from the sword, famine, and plague so they can tell about all their abominations among the nations where they go. Then they will know that I am the LORD."

¹⁷ The word of the LORD came to me: ¹⁸ "Son of man, eat your bread with trembling and drink your water with shaking and anxiety. ¹⁹ Then say to the people of the land: This is what the Lord GOD says about the residents of Jerusalem in the land of Israel: They will eat their bread with anxiety and drink their water in dread, for their land will be stripped of everything in it because of the violence of all who live there. ²⁰ The inhabited cities will be destroyed, and the land will become a desolation. Then you will know that I am the LORD."

²¹ Again the word of the LORD came to me: ²² "Son of man, what is this proverb you people have about the land of Israel, which goes:

The days keep passing by,
and every vision fails?

²³ Therefore say to them: This is what the Lord GOD says: I will put a stop to this proverb, and they will not use it again in Israel. But say to them: The days draw near, as well as the fulfillment of every vision. ²⁴ For there will no longer be any false vision or flattering divination within the house of Israel. ²⁵ But I, the LORD, will speak whatever message I will speak, and it will be done. It will no longer be delayed. For in your days, rebellious house, I will speak a message and bring it to pass." This is the declaration of the Lord GOD.

²⁶ The word of the LORD came to me: ²⁷ "Son of man, notice that the house of Israel is saying: The vision that he sees concerns many years from now; he prophesies about distant times. ²⁸ Therefore say to them: This is what the Lord GOD says: None of My words will be delayed any longer. The message I speak will be fulfilled." This is the declaration of the Lord GOD.

13 The word of the LORD came to me: ² "Son of man, prophesy against the prophets of Israel who are prophesying. Say to those who prophesy out of their own imagination: Hear the word of the LORD! ³ This is what the Lord GOD says: Woe to the foolish prophets who follow their own spirit and have seen nothing. ⁴ Your prophets, Israel, are like jackals among ruins. ⁵ You did not go up to the gaps or restore the wall around the house of Israel so that it might stand in battle on the day of the LORD. ⁶ They see false visions and speak lying divinations. They claim: This is the LORD's declaration, when the LORD did not send them, yet they wait for the fulfillment of their message. ⁷ Didn't you see a false vision and speak a lying divination when you proclaimed: This is the LORD's declaration, even though I had not spoken?

⁸ "Therefore, this is what the Lord GOD says: I am against you because you have spoken falsely and had lying visions." This is the declaration of the Lord GOD. ⁹ "My hand will be against the prophets who see false visions and speak lying divinations. They will not be present in the fellowship of My people or be recorded in the register of the house of Israel, and they will not enter the land of Israel. Then you will know that I am the Lord GOD.

¹⁰ "Since they have led My people astray saying: Peace, when there is no peace, for when someone builds a wall they plaster it with whitewash, ¹¹ therefore, tell those who plaster it that it will fall. Torrential rain will come, and I will send hailstones plunging down, and a windstorm will be released. ¹² Now when the wall has fallen, will you not be asked: Where is the coat of whitewash that you put on it?

¹³ "So this is what the Lord GOD says: I will release a windstorm in My wrath. Torrential rain will come in My anger, and hailstones will fall in destructive fury. ¹⁴ I will tear down the wall you plastered with whitewash and knock it to the ground so that its foundation is exposed. The city will fall, and you will be destroyed within it. Then you will know that I am the LORD. ¹⁵ After I exhaust My wrath against the wall and against those who plaster it with whitewash, I will say to you: The wall is no more and neither are those who plastered it— ¹⁶ those prophets of Israel who prophesied to Jerusalem and saw a vision of peace for her when there was no peace." This is the declaration of the Lord GOD.

¹⁷ "Now, son of man, turn toward the women of your people who prophesy out of their own imagination. Prophesy against them ¹⁸ and say: This is what the Lord GOD says: Woe to the women who sew magic bands on the wrist of every hand and who make veils for the heads of people of every height in order to ensnare lives. Will you ensnare the lives of My people but preserve your own? ¹⁹ You profane Me in front of My people for handfuls of barley and scraps of bread; you kill those who should not die and spare those who should not live, when you lie to My people, who listen to lies.

²⁰ "Therefore, this is what the Lord GOD says: I am against your magic bands that you ensnare people with like birds, and I will tear them from your arms. I will free the people you have ensnared like birds. ²¹ I will also tear off your veils and deliver My people from your hands, so that they will no longer be prey in your hands. Then you will know that I am the LORD. ²² Because you have disheartened the righteous person with lies, even though I have not caused him grief, and because you have encouraged the wicked person not to turn from his evil way to save his life, ²³ therefore you will no longer see false visions or practice divination. I will deliver My people from your hands. Then you will know that I am the LORD."

14 Some of the elders of Israel came to me and sat down in front of me. ² Then the word of the LORD came to me: ³ "Son of man, these men have set up idols in their hearts and have put sinful stumbling blocks before their faces. Should I be consulted by them at all?

⁴ "Therefore, speak to them and tell them: This is what the Lord GOD says: When anyone from the house of Israel sets up idols in his heart, puts a sinful stumbling block before his face, and then comes to the prophet, I, the LORD, will answer him appropriately. I will answer him according to his many idols, ⁵ so that I may take hold of the house of Israel by their hearts, because they are all estranged from Me by their idols.

⁶ "Therefore, say to the house of Israel: This is what the Lord GOD says: Repent and turn away from your idols; turn your faces away from all your abominations. ⁷ For when anyone from the house of Israel or from the foreigners who reside in Israel separates himself from Me, setting up idols in his heart and putting a sinful stumbling block before his face, and then comes to the prophet to inquire of Me, I, the LORD, will answer him Myself. ⁸ I will turn against that one and make him a sign and a proverb; I will cut him off from among My people. Then you will know that I am the LORD.

⁹ "But if the prophet is deceived and speaks a message, it was I, the LORD, who deceived that prophet. I will stretch out My hand against him and destroy him from among My people Israel. ¹⁰ They will bear their punishment—the punishment of the one who inquires will be the same as that of the prophet— ¹¹ in order that the house of Israel may no longer stray from following Me and no longer defile themselves with all their transgressions. Then they will be My people and I will be their God." This is the declaration of the Lord GOD.

PSALM 121:1-8

¹ I raise my eyes toward the
   mountains.
Where will my help come from?
² My help comes from the LORD,
   the Maker of heaven and earth.

³ He will not allow your foot to slip;
   your Protector will not slumber.
⁴ Indeed, the Protector of Israel
   does not slumber or sleep.

⁵ The LORD protects you;
   the LORD is a shelter right by your
   side.
⁶ The sun will not strike you by day,
   or the moon by night.

⁷ The LORD will protect you from all
   harm;

He will protect your life.
⁸ The LORD will protect your coming
   and going
both now and forever.

PROVERBS 27:19-20

¹⁹ As the water reflects the face,
   so the heart reflects the person.

²⁰ Sheol and Abaddon are never
   satisfied,
and people's eyes are never
   satisfied.

HEBREWS 11:32–12:11

³² And what more can I say? Time is too short for me to tell about Gideon, Barak, Samson, Jephthah, of David and Samuel and the prophets, ³³ who by faith conquered kingdoms, administered justice, obtained promises, shut the mouths of lions, ³⁴ quenched the raging of fire, escaped the edge of the sword, gained strength after being weak, became mighty in battle, and put foreign armies to flight. ³⁵ Women received their dead raised to life again. Some men were tortured, not accepting release, so that they might gain a better resurrection, ³⁶ and others experienced mockings and scourgings, as well as bonds and imprisonment. ³⁷ They were stoned, they were sawed in two, they died by the sword, they wandered about in sheepskins, in goatskins, destitute, afflicted, and mistreated. ³⁸ The world was not worthy of them. They wandered in deserts, mountains, caves, and holes in the ground.

³⁹ All these were approved through their faith, but they did not receive what was promised, ⁴⁰ since God had provided something better for us, so that they would not be made perfect without us.

12 Therefore since we also have such a large cloud of witnesses surrounding us, let us lay aside every weight and the sin that so easily ensnares us, and run with endurance the race that lies before us, ²keeping our eyes on Jesus, the source and perfecter of our faith, who for the joy that lay before Him endured a cross and despised the shame, and has sat down at the right hand of God's throne.

³ For consider Him who endured such hostility from sinners against Himself, so that you won't grow weary and lose heart. ⁴ In struggling against sin, you have not yet resisted to the point of shedding your blood. ⁵ And you have forgotten the exhortation that addresses you as sons:

> My son, do not take the Lord's discipline lightly,
> or faint when you are reproved by Him;
> ⁶ for the Lord disciplines the one He loves,

and punishes every son whom He receives.

⁷ Endure it as discipline: God is dealing with you as sons. For what son is there whom a father does not discipline? ⁸ But if you are without discipline—which all receive—then you are illegitimate children and not sons. ⁹ Furthermore, we had natural fathers discipline us, and we respected them. Shouldn't we submit even more to the Father of spirits and live? ¹⁰ For they disciplined us for a short time based on what seemed good to them, but He does it for our benefit, so that we can share His holiness. ¹¹ No discipline seems enjoyable at the time, but painful. Later on, however, it yields the fruit of peace and righteousness to those who have been trained by it.

Gaze on His Face

Let us . . . run with endurance the race that lies before us, keeping our eyes on Jesus, the source and perfecter of our faith.—HEBREWS 12:1-2

In order to stay spiritually fresh you must keep your eyes fully focused on Jesus.

Our Lord was the most alert and alive person the world has ever seen. Never once do we read that He experienced spiritual staleness or had to confess to being out of touch with heaven. He was always confident, always assured, always in the right place, always doing the right thing at the right time. Even after a period of prolonged fasting in the wilderness when He faced the fiercest of temptations, He turned—not exhausted and limp as a wet rag—but "in the power of the Spirit." Here was spiritual freshness to the nth degree.

Our text today tells us that one of the ways by which we can become more and more like Christ is to stand with unveiled faces and continually gaze upon Him. It is a breathtaking concept—and so simple. Yet how profound. Look beyond yourself to Another, and thus free yourself from self-preoccupation. Have you noticed how many of the religious cults get their followers to concentrate on the divinity within them? Then what happens? They finish up preoccupied with their own states of mind and emotion. As someone put it: "If I worship the divinity within me, I will probably end up worshiping myself."

2 Corinthians 3:18 gets our gaze in the right place—on the face of Christ: "We all, with unveiled faces, are reflecting the glory of the Lord and are being transformed into the same image from glory to glory." The attention we give to this is important, for whatever gets our attention gets us. Therefore, when Christ gets our attention, He also gets us. Our gaze must be person-centered, not problem-centered. And that Person must be Jesus Christ.

Prayer

Blessed Lord Jesus, when I look at myself I feel unworthy and inadequate. But when I look at You, I feel anything is possible. Help me not just to glance at You, but gaze at You—continuously. Amen.

Further Study

Rm 8:29-39; Jn 1:36; Col 2:2-3
What is God's plan for us?
What was John's declaration?

NOVEMBER 17

EZEKIEL 14:12–16:34

¹² The word of the LORD came to me: ¹³ "Son of man, if a land sins against Me by acting faithlessly, and I stretch out My hand against it to cut off its supply of bread, to send famine through it, and to wipe out both man and animal from it, ¹⁴ even if these three men—Noah, Daniel, and Job—were in it, they would deliver only themselves by their righteousness." This is the declaration of the Lord GOD.

¹⁵ "If I allow dangerous animals to pass through the land and depopulate it so that it becomes desolate, with no one passing through it for fear of the animals, ¹⁶ even if these three men were in it, as I live"—the declaration of the Lord GOD—"they could not deliver their sons or daughters. They alone would be delivered, but the land would be desolate.

¹⁷ "Or if I bring a sword against that land and say: Let a sword pass through it, so that I wipe out both man and animal from it, ¹⁸ even if these three men were in it, as I live"—the declaration of the Lord GOD—"they could not deliver their sons or daughters, but they alone would be delivered.

¹⁹ "Or if I send a plague into that land and pour out My wrath on it with bloodshed to wipe out both man and animal from it, ²⁰ even if Noah, Daniel, and Job were in it, as I live"—the declaration of the Lord GOD—"they could not deliver their son or daughter. They would deliver only themselves by their righteousness.

²¹ "For this is what the Lord GOD says: How much worse will it be when I send My four devastating judgments against Jerusalem—sword, famine, dangerous animals, and plague—in order to wipe out both man and animal from it! ²² Even so, there will be survivors left in it, sons and daughters who will be brought out. Indeed, they will come out to you, and you will observe their conduct and actions. Then you will be consoled about the devastation I have brought on Jerusalem, about all I have brought on it. ²³ They will bring you consolation when you see their conduct and actions, and you will know that it was not without cause that I have done

what I did to it." This is the declaration of the Lord GOD.

15 Then the word of the LORD came to me: ² "Son of man, how does the wood of the vine, that branch among the trees of the forest, compare to any other wood? ³ Can wood be taken from it to make something useful? Or can anyone make a peg from it to hang things on? ⁴ In fact, it is put into the fire as fuel. The fire devours both of its ends, and the middle is charred. Can it be useful for anything? ⁵ Even when it was whole it could not be made into a useful object. How much less can it ever be made into anything useful when the fire has devoured it and it is charred!

⁶ "Therefore, this is what the Lord GOD says: Like the wood of the vine among the trees of the forest, which I have given to the fire as fuel, so I will give up the residents of Jerusalem. ⁷ I will turn against them. They may have escaped from the fire, but it will still consume them. And you will know that I am the LORD when I turn against them. ⁸ I will make the land desolate because they have acted unfaithfully." This is the declaration of the Lord GOD.

16 The word of the LORD came to me again: ² "Son of man, explain Jerusalem's abominations to her. ³ You are to say: This is what the Lord GOD says to Jerusalem: Your origin and your birth were in the land of the Canaanites. Your father was an Amorite and your mother a Hittite. ⁴ As for your birth, your umbilical cord wasn't cut on the day you were born, and you weren't washed clean with water. You were not rubbed with salt or wrapped in cloths. ⁵ No one cared enough about you to do even one of these things out of compassion for you. But you were thrown out into the open field because you were despised on the day you were born.

⁶ "I passed by you and saw you lying in your blood, and I said to you as you lay in your blood: Live! Yes, I said to you as you lay in your blood: Live! ⁷ I made you thrive like plants of the field. You grew up and matured and became very beautiful. Your breasts were formed and your hair grew, but you were stark naked.

⁸ "Then I passed by you and saw you, and you were indeed at the age for love. So I spread the edge of My garment over you and covered your nakedness. I pledged Myself to you, entered into a covenant with you, and you became Mine." This is the declaration of the Lord GOD. ⁹ "I washed you with water, rinsed off your blood, and anointed you with oil. ¹⁰ I clothed you in embroidered cloth and provided you with leather sandals. I also wrapped you in fine linen and covered you with silk. ¹¹ I adorned you with jewelry, putting bracelets on your wrists and a chain around your neck. ¹² I put a ring in your nose, earrings on your ears, and a beautiful tiara on your head. ¹³ So you were adorned with gold and silver, and your clothing was made of fine linen, silk, and embroidered cloth. You ate fine flour, honey, and oil. You became extremely beautiful and attained royalty. ¹⁴ Your fame spread among the nations because of your beauty, for it was perfect through My splendor, which I had bestowed on you." This is the declaration of the Lord GOD.

¹⁵ "But you were confident in your beauty and acted like a prostitute because of your fame. You lavished your sexual favors on everyone who passed by. Your beauty became his. ¹⁶ You took some of your garments and made colorful high places for yourself, and you engaged in prostitution on them. These places should not have been built, and this should never have happened! ¹⁷ You also took your beautiful jewelry made from the gold and silver I had given you, and you made male images so that you could engage in prostitution with them. ¹⁸ Then you took your embroidered garments to cover them, and set My oil and incense before them. ¹⁹ You also set before them as a pleasing aroma the food I gave you—the fine flour, oil, and honey that I fed you. That is what happened." This is the declaration of the Lord GOD.

²⁰ "You even took your sons and

daughters you bore to Me and sacrificed them to these images as food. Wasn't your prostitution enough? ²¹ You slaughtered My children and gave them up when you passed them through the fire to the images. ²² In all your abominations and acts of prostitution, you did not remember the days of your youth when you were stark naked and lying in your blood.

²³ "Then after all your evil—Woe, woe to you!"—the declaration of the Lord GOD— ²⁴ "you built yourself a mound and made yourself an elevated place in every square. ²⁵ You built your elevated place at the head of every street and turned your beauty into an abomination. You spread your legs to everyone who passed by and increased your prostitution. ²⁶ You engaged in promiscuous acts with Egyptian men, your well-endowed neighbors, and increased your prostitution to provoke Me to anger.

²⁷ "Therefore, I stretched out My hand against you and reduced your provisions. I gave you over to the desire of those who hate you, the Philistine women, who were embarrassed by your indecent behavior. ²⁸ Then you engaged in prostitution with the Assyrian men because you were not satisfied. Even though you did this with them, you were still not satisfied. ²⁹ So you extended your prostitution to Chaldea, the land of merchants, but you were not even satisfied with this!

³⁰ "How your heart was inflamed with lust"—the declaration of the Lord GOD—"when you did all these things, the acts of a brazen prostitute, ³¹ building your mound at the head of every street and making your elevated place in every square. But you were unlike a prostitute because you scorned payment. ³² You adulterous wife, who receives strangers instead of her husband! ³³ Men give gifts to all prostitutes, but you gave gifts to all your lovers. You bribed them to come to you from all around for your sexual favors. ³⁴ So you were the opposite of other women in your acts of prostitution; no one solicited you. When you paid a fee instead of one being paid to you, you were the opposite.

PSALM 122:1–123:4

1 I rejoiced with those who said to me,
"Let us go to the house of the LORD."
2 Our feet are standing within your gates, Jerusalem—
3 Jerusalem, built as a city should be, solidly joined together,
4 where the tribes, the tribes of the LORD, go up
to give thanks to the name of the LORD.
(This is an ordinance for Israel.)
5 There, thrones for judgment are placed,
thrones of the house of David.

6 Pray for the peace of Jerusalem:
"May those who love you prosper;
7 may there be peace within your walls,
prosperity within your fortresses."
8 Because of my brothers and friends, I will say, "Peace be with you."
9 Because of the house of the LORD our God,
I will seek your good.

1 I lift my eyes to You,
the One enthroned in heaven.
2 Like a servant's eyes on His master's hand,
like a servant girl's eyes on her mistress's hand,
so our eyes are on the LORD our God
until He shows us favor.

3 Show us favor, LORD, show us favor,
for we've had more than enough contempt.
4 We've had more than enough scorn from the arrogant
and contempt from the proud.

PROVERBS 27:21-22

21 Silver is tested in a crucible, gold in a smelter,

and a man, by the praise he receives.

22 Though you grind a fool in a mortar with a pestle along with grain,
you will not separate his foolishness from him.

*H*EBREWS 12:12-29

12 Therefore strengthen your tired hands and weakened knees, 13 and make straight paths for your feet, so that what is lame may not be dislocated, but healed instead.

14 Pursue peace with everyone, and holiness—without it no one will see the Lord. 15 See to it that no one falls short of the grace of God and that no root of bitterness springs up, causing trouble and by it, defiling many. 16 And see that there isn't any immoral or irreverent person like Esau, who sold his birthright in exchange for one meal. 17 For you know that later, when he wanted to inherit the blessing, he was rejected because he didn't find any opportunity for repentance, though he sought it with tears.

18 For you have not come to what could be touched, to a blazing fire, to darkness, gloom, and storm, 19 to the blast of a trumpet, and the sound of words. (Those who heard it begged that not another word be spoken to them, 20 for they could not bear what was commanded: **And if even an animal touches the mountain, it must be stoned!** 21 And the appearance was so terrifying that Moses said, **I am terrified and trembling.**) 22 Instead, you have come to Mount Zion, to the city of the living God (the heavenly Jerusalem), to myriads of angels in festive gathering, 23 to the assembly of the firstborn whose names have been written in heaven, to God who is the judge of all, to the spirits of righteous people made perfect, 24 to Jesus (mediator of a new covenant), and to the sprinkled blood, which says better things than the blood of Abel.

25 See that you do not reject the One who speaks; for if they did not escape when they rejected Him who warned them on earth, even less will we if we turn away from Him who warns us from heaven. 26 His voice shook the earth at that time, but now He has promised, **Yet once more I will shake not only the earth but also heaven.** 27 Now this expression, "Yet once more," indicates the removal of what can be shaken—that is, created things—so that what is not shaken might remain. 28 Therefore, since we are receiving a kingdom that cannot be shaken, let us hold on to grace. By it, we may serve God acceptably, with reverence and awe; 29 for our God is a consuming fire.

The Consuming Fire

Our God is a consuming fire.
—HEBREWS 12:29

George MacDonald writes: "Nothing is inexorable but love, for love loves unto purity. Love has ever in view the absolute loveliness of that which it beholds. Where loveliness is incomplete, and love cannot love its fill of loving, it spends itself to make more lovely, that it may love more; it strives for perfection even that itself may be perfected—not in itself but in the object. Therefore all that is not beautiful in the beloved, all that comes between and is not of love's kind, must be destroyed. Our God is a consuming fire."

Powerful words.

The nature of God is so terribly pure that it destroys everything that is not as pure as fire.

God desires us to worship Him in "the splendor of His holiness" (Ps 29:2). This means that He wants the purity in us to match the purity in Him. We cannot arrive at this purity by self-effort, of course, but the more we draw nigh to Him, the more the fire of His purity will burn out the dross within us.

"It is not the fire that will burn us up if we do not worship," said George MacDonald, "but the fire will burn us up until we worship." And the fire will go on burning within us after everything that is foreign to it has been consumed, no longer with pain and a sense of something unwanted being consumed, but as the highest consciousness of life.

God is a consuming fire. He always was, and always will be—world without end.

Prayer

O God, I long with all my heart that my worship might be all You want it to be. May Your consuming fire burn out all the dross within me until everything that is foreign to Your nature is part of me no more. In Jesus' name I ask it. Amen.

Further Study

Ps 97:1-5; Is 66:15; 1 Co 3:12-14
What does the psalmist say about fire?
What will the fire do?

NOVEMBER 18

EZEKIEL 16:35–17:24

35 "Therefore, you prostitute, hear the word of the LORD! 36 This is what the Lord GOD says: Because your lust was poured out and your nakedness exposed by your acts of prostitution with your lovers, and because of all your detestable idols and the blood of your children that you gave to them, 37 I am therefore going to gather all the lovers you pleased—all those you loved as well as all those you hated. I will gather them against you from all around and expose your nakedness to them so they see you completely naked. 38 I will judge you the way adulteresses and those who shed blood are judged. Then I will bring about your bloodshed in wrath and jealousy. 39 I will hand you over to them, and they will level your mounds and tear down your elevated places. They will strip off your clothes, take your beautiful jewelry, and leave you stark naked. 40 They will bring a mob against you to stone you and cut you to pieces with their swords. 41 Then they will burn down your houses and execute judgments against you in the sight of many women. I will stop you from being

a prostitute, and you will never again pay fees for lovers. ⁴² So I will satisfy My wrath against you, and My jealousy will turn away from you. Then I will be silent and no longer angry. ⁴³ Because you did not remember the days of your youth but enraged Me with all these things, I will also bring your actions down on your own head." This is the declaration of the Lord GOD. "Haven't you committed immoral acts in addition to all your abominations?

⁴⁴ "Look, everyone who uses proverbs will say this proverb about you:

Like mother, like daughter.

⁴⁵ You are the daughter of your mother, who despised her husband and children. You are the sister of your sisters, who despised their husbands and children. Your mother was a Hittite and your father an Amorite. ⁴⁶ Your older sister was Samaria, who lived with her daughters to the north of you, and your younger sister was Sodom, who lived with her daughters to the south of you. ⁴⁷ Didn't you walk in their ways and practice their abominations? It was only a short time before you behaved more corruptly than they did.

⁴⁸ "As I live"—the declaration of the Lord GOD—"your sister Sodom and her daughters have not behaved as you and your daughters have. ⁴⁹ Now this was the iniquity of your sister Sodom: she and her daughters had pride, plenty of food, and comfortable security, but didn't support the poor and needy. ⁵⁰ They were haughty and did detestable things before Me, so I removed them when I saw this. ⁵¹ But Samaria did not commit even half your sins. You have multiplied your abominations beyond theirs and made your sisters appear righteous by all the abominations you have committed. ⁵² You must also bear your disgrace, since you have been an advocate for your sisters. For they appear more righteous than you because of your sins, which you committed more abhorrently than they did. So you also, be ashamed and bear your disgrace, since you have made your sisters appear righteous.

⁵³ "I will restore their fortunes, the fortunes of Sodom and her daughters and those of Samaria and her daughters. I will also restore your fortunes among them, ⁵⁴ so you will bear your disgrace and be ashamed of all you did when you comforted them. ⁵⁵ As for your sisters, Sodom and her daughters and Samaria and her daughters will return to their former state. You and your daughters will also return to your former state. ⁵⁶ Didn't you treat your sister Sodom as an object of scorn when you were proud, ⁵⁷ before your wickedness was exposed? It was like the time you were scorned by the daughters of Aram and all those around her, and by the daughters of the Philistines—those who treated you with contempt from every side. ⁵⁸ You yourself must bear the consequences of your indecency and abominations"—the LORD's declaration.

⁵⁹ "For this is what the Lord GOD says: I will deal with you according to what you have done, since you have despised the oath by breaking the covenant. ⁶⁰ But I will remember the covenant I made with you in the days of your youth, and I will establish an everlasting covenant with you. ⁶¹ Then you will remember your ways and be ashamed when you receive your older and younger sisters. I will give them to you as daughters, but not because of your covenant. ⁶² I will establish My covenant with you, and you will know that I am the LORD, ⁶³ so that when I make atonement for all you have done, you will remember and be ashamed, and never open your mouth again because of your disgrace." This is the declaration of the Lord GOD.

17 The word of the LORD came to me: ² "Son of man, pose a riddle and speak a parable to the house of Israel. ³ You are to say: This is what the Lord GOD says:

A great eagle with great wings,
    long pinions,
and full plumage of many colors
    came to Lebanon and took the top
    of the cedar.

⁴ He plucked off its topmost shoot,
    brought it to the land of merchants,
    and set it in a city of traders.
⁵ Then he took some
        of the land's seed
    and put it in a fertile field;
    he set it like a willow,
    a plant by abundant waters.
⁶ It sprouted and became
        a spreading vine,
    low in height with its branches
        turned toward him,
    yet its roots stayed under it.
    So it became a vine,
    produced branches,
        and sent forth shoots.

⁷ But there was another great eagle
    with great wings
        and thick plumage.
    And this vine bent its roots
        toward him!
    It stretched out its branches to him
    from its planting bed,
    so that he might water it.
⁸ It had been planted
    in a good field by abundant waters
    in order to produce branches,
    bear fruit, and become
        a splendid vine.

⁹ You are to say: This is what the Lord GOD says:

    Will it flourish?
    Will he not tear out its roots
    and strip off its fruit
    so that it shrivels?
    All its fresh leaves will wither!
    Great strength and many people
    will not be needed to pull it
        from its roots.
¹⁰   Even though it is planted,
        will it flourish?
    Won't it completely wither
    when the east wind strikes it?
    It will wither on the bed
        where it sprouted."

¹¹ The word of the LORD came to me:
¹² "Now say to that rebellious house: Don't you know what these things mean? Tell them: The king of Babylon came to Jerusalem, took its king and of-

ficials, and brought them back with him to Babylon. ¹³ He took one of the royal family and made a covenant with him, putting him under oath. Then he took away the leading men of the land, ¹⁴ so the kingdom might be humble and not exalt itself but might keep his covenant in order to endure. ¹⁵ However, this king revolted against him by sending his ambassadors to Egypt so they might give him horses and a large army. Will he flourish? Will the one who does such things escape? Can he break a covenant and still escape?

¹⁶ "As I live"—this is the declaration of the Lord GOD—"he will die in Babylon, in the land of the king who put him on the throne, whose oath he despised and whose covenant he broke. ¹⁷ Pharaoh will not help him with his great army and vast horde in battle, when ramps are built and siege walls constructed to destroy many lives. ¹⁸ He despised the oath by breaking the covenant. He did all these things even though he gave his hand in pledge. He will not escape!"

¹⁹ Therefore, this is what the Lord GOD says: "As I live, I will bring down on his head My oath that he despised and My covenant that he broke. ²⁰ I will spread My net over him, and he will be captured in My snare. I will bring him to Babylon and execute judgment on him there for the treachery he committed against Me. ²¹ All the fugitives among his troops will fall by the sword, and those who survive will be scattered to every direction of the wind. Then you will know that I, Yahweh, have spoken."

²² This is what the Lord GOD says:

    I will take a sprig
    from the lofty top of the cedar
        and plant it.
    I will pluck a tender sprig
    from its topmost shoots,
    and I will plant it
    on a high towering mountain.
²³   I will plant it on Israel's
        high mountain
    so that it may bear branches,
        produce fruit,

and become a majestic cedar.
Birds of every kind will nest
    under it,
taking shelter in the shade
    of its branches.
²⁴ Then all the trees of the field
    will know
that I am the LORD.
I bring down the tall tree,
and make the low tree tall.
I cause the green tree to wither
and make
    the withered tree thrive.
I, Yahweh, have spoken
and I will do it.

PSALM 124:1-8

¹ If the LORD had not been on our
    side—
    let Israel say—
² If the LORD had not been on our
    side
    when men attacked us,
³ then they would have swallowed
    us alive
    in their burning anger against us.
⁴ Then the waters would have
    engulfed us;
    the torrent would have swept
    over us;
⁵ the raging waters would have
    swept over us.

⁶ Praise the LORD,
    who has not let us be ripped apart
    by their teeth.
⁷ We have escaped like a bird from
    the hunter's net;
    the net is torn, and we have
    escaped.
⁸ Our help is in the name of the
    LORD,
    the Maker of heaven and earth.

PROVERBS 27:23-24

²³ Know well the condition of your
    flock,
    and pay attention to your herds,
²⁴ for wealth is not forever;
    not even a crown lasts for all time.

HEBREWS 13:1-25

13 Let brotherly love continue. ² Don't
neglect to show hospitality, for
by doing this some have welcomed
angels as guests without knowing it.
³ Remember the prisoners, as though
you were in prison with them, and the
mistreated, as though you yourselves
were suffering bodily. ⁴ Marriage must
be respected by all, and the marriage
bed kept undefiled, because God will
judge immoral people and adulterers.
⁵ Your life should be free from the love
of money. Be satisfied with what you
have, for He Himself has said, **I will
never leave you or forsake you.**
⁶ Therefore, we may boldly say:

**The Lord is my helper;
I will not be afraid.
What can man do to me?**

⁷ Remember your leaders who have
spoken God's word to you. As you carefully observe the outcome of their lives,
imitate their faith. ⁸ Jesus Christ is the
same yesterday, today, and forever.
⁹ Don't be led astray by various kinds of
strange teachings; for it is good for the
heart to be established by grace and not
by foods, since those involved in them
have not benefited. ¹⁰ We have an altar
from which those who serve the tabernacle do not have a right to eat. ¹¹ For
the bodies of those animals whose
blood is brought into the holy of holies
by the high priest as a sin offering are
burned outside the camp. ¹² Therefore
Jesus also suffered outside the gate, so
that He might sanctify the people by His
own blood. ¹³ Let us then go to Him outside the camp, bearing His disgrace.
¹⁴ For here we do not have an enduring
city; instead, we seek the one to come.
¹⁵ Therefore, through Him let us continually offer up to God a sacrifice of
praise, that is, the fruit of our lips that
confess His name. ¹⁶ Don't neglect to do
good and to share, for God is pleased
with such sacrifices. ¹⁷ Obey your leaders and submit to them, for they keep
watch over your souls as those who will

give an account, so that they can do this with joy and not with grief, for that would be unprofitable for you. ¹⁸ Pray for us; for we are convinced that we have a clear conscience, wanting to conduct ourselves honorably in everything. ¹⁹ And I especially urge you to pray that I may be restored to you very soon.

²⁰ Now may the God of peace, who brought up from the dead our Lord Jesus—the great Shepherd of the sheep—with the blood of the everlasting covenant, ²¹ equip you with all that is good to do His will, working in us what is pleasing in His sight, through Jesus Christ, to whom be glory forever and ever. Amen.

²² Brothers, I urge you to receive this word of exhortation, for I have written to you in few words. ²³ Be aware that our brother Timothy has been released. If he comes soon enough, he will be with me when I see you. ²⁴ Greet all your leaders and all the saints. Those who are from Italy greet you. ²⁵ Grace be with all of you.

Pray for Me That . . .

Pray for us; for we are convinced that we have a clear conscience, wanting to conduct ourselves honorably in everything. And I especially urge you to pray that I may be restored to you very soon.—HEBREWS 13:18-19

The apostle ends his discussion of spiritual warfare (Eph 6:10-20) on the following personal note: "Pray also for me, that the message may be given to me when I open my mouth to make known with boldness the mystery of the gospel . . . that I might be bold enough in Him to speak as I should" (vv. 19-20).

Paul was wise enough to know his own need of supernatural strength in being able to stand against the enemy, and he was humble enough to ask his brothers and sisters to pray for him in this matter.

Imagine this great apostle, probably the most powerful and effective disciple of Christ the world has ever seen, asking his friends to pray for him. Truly, the greater a Christian is, the more he realizes his dependence on the prayers of others. Paul knew full well the power that was against him, and he did not hesitate to ask for the prayers of the church in Ephesus.

Notice also that his request for prayer was clear and specific. When you ask someone to pray for you, be equally specific. Don't just say, "Pray for me," but "Pray for me that . . ." Paul's request was not that he might be delivered from prison, but that through his testimony in prison the gospel of Christ might be advanced. He knew that the most important thing was not to triumph over prison but to triumph in it. He knew he was where God wanted him for that time, and he would allow no self-interest to interfere with the divine schedule.

Prayer

O Father, teach me, as You taught Your servant Paul, to know Your will and purpose so clearly that I might know just how and what to pray for. I ask this in and through the strong and mighty name of Jesus. Amen.

Further Study

2 Th 3; 1 Th 5:25; Rm 12:2
What was Paul's request?
Whom are you praying for regularly?

NOVEMBER 19

EZEKIEL 18:1–19:14

18 The word of the LORD came to me: [2] "What do you mean by using this proverb concerning the land of Israel:

The fathers eat sour grapes,
and the children's teeth are set
on edge?

[3] As I live"—this is the declaration of the Lord GOD—"you will no longer use this proverb in Israel. [4] Look, every life belongs to Me. The life of the father is like the life of the son—both belong to Me. The person who sins is the one who will die.

[5] "Now suppose a man is righteous and does what is just and right: [6] He does not eat at the mountain shrines or raise his eyes to the idols of the house of Israel. He does not defile his neighbor's wife or come near a woman during her menstrual impurity. [7] He doesn't oppress anyone but returns his collateral to the debtor. He does not commit robbery, but gives his bread to the hungry and covers the naked with clothing. [8] He doesn't lend at interest or for profit but keeps his hand from wrongdoing and carries out true justice between men. [9] He follows My statutes and keeps My ordinances, acting faithfully. Such a person is righteous; he will certainly live." This is the declaration of the Lord GOD.

[10] "Now suppose the man has a violent son, who sheds blood and does any of these things, [11] though the father has done none of them. Indeed, when the son eats at the mountain shrines and defiles his neighbor's wife, [12] and when he oppresses the poor and needy, commits robbery, and does not return collateral, and when he raises his eyes to the idols, commits abominations, [13] and lends at interest or for profit, will he live? He will not live! Since he has committed all these abominations, he will certainly die. His blood will be on him.

[14] "Now suppose he has a son who sees all the sins his father has committed, and though he sees them, he does not do likewise. [15] He does not eat at the mountain shrines or raise his eyes to the idols of the house of Israel. He does not defile his neighbor's wife. [16] He doesn't oppress anyone, hold collateral, or commit robbery. He gives his bread to the hungry and covers the naked with clothing. [17] He keeps his hand from harming the poor, not taking interest or profit on a loan. He practices My ordinances and follows My statutes. Such a person will not die for his father's iniquity. He will certainly live.

[18] "As for his father, he will die for his own iniquity because he practiced fraud, robbed his brother, and did what was wrong among his people. [19] But you may ask: Why doesn't the son suffer punishment for the father's iniquity?

1391

Since the son has done what is just and right, carefully observing all My statutes, he will certainly live. ²⁰ The person who sins is the one who will die. A son won't suffer punishment for the father's iniquity, and a father won't suffer punishment for the son's iniquity. The righteousness of the righteous person will be on him, and the wickedness of the wicked person will be on him.

²¹ "Now if the wicked person turns from all the sins he has committed, keeps all My statutes, and does what is just and right, he will certainly live; he will not die. ²² None of the transgressions he has committed will be held against him. He will live because of the righteousness he has practiced. ²³ Do I take any pleasure in the death of the wicked?" This is the declaration of the Lord GOD. "Instead, don't I take pleasure when he turns from his ways and lives? ²⁴ But when a righteous person turns from his righteousness and practices iniquity, committing the same abominations that the wicked do, will he live? None of the righteous acts he did will be remembered. He will die because of the treachery he has engaged in and the sin he has committed.

²⁵ "But you say: The Lord's way isn't fair. Now listen, house of Israel: Is it My way that is unfair? Instead, isn't it your ways that are unfair? ²⁶ When a righteous person turns from his righteousness and practices iniquity, he will die for this. He will die because of the iniquity he has practiced. ²⁷ But if a wicked person turns from the wickedness he has committed and does what is just and right, he will preserve his life. ²⁸ He will certainly live because he thought it over and turned from all the transgressions he had committed; he will not die. ²⁹ But the house of Israel says: The Lord's way isn't fair. Is it My ways that are unfair, house of Israel? Instead, isn't it your ways that are unfair?

³⁰ "Therefore, house of Israel, I will judge each one of you according to his ways." This is the declaration of the Lord GOD. "Repent and turn from all your transgressions, so they will not be a stumbling block that causes your pun-

ishment. ³¹ Throw off all the transgressions you have committed, and make yourselves a new heart and a new spirit. Why should you die, house of Israel? ³² For I take no pleasure in anyone's death." This is the declaration of the Lord GOD. "So repent and live!

19 "Now, lament for the princes of Israel ² and say:

What was your mother? A lioness!
She lay down among the lions;
she reared her cubs
    among the young lions.
³ She brought up one of her cubs,
and he became a young lion.
After he learned to tear prey,
he devoured people.
⁴ When the nations
    heard about him,
he was caught in their pit.
Then they led him away
    with hooks
to the land of Egypt.

⁵ When she saw that she waited
    in vain,
that her hope was lost,
she took another of her cubs
and made him a young lion.
⁶ He prowled among the lions,
and he became a young lion.
After he learned to tear prey,
he devoured people.
⁷ He devastated their strongholds
and destroyed their cities.
The land and everything
    in it shuddered
at the sound of his roaring.
⁸ Then the nations from
    the surrounding provinces
set out against him.
They spread their net over him;
he was caught in their pit.
⁹ They put a wooden yoke on him
    with hooks
and led him away to the king
    of Babylon.
They brought him into the
    fortresses
so his roar could no longer
    be heard
on the mountains of Israel.

¹⁰ Your mother was like a vine
    in your vineyard,
planted by the water;
    it was fruitful and full of branches
    because of plentiful waters.
¹¹ It had strong branches, fit for
    the scepters of rulers;
its height towered
    among the clouds.
So it was conspicuous
    for its height
as well as its many branches.
¹² But it was uprooted in fury,
    thrown to the ground,
and the east wind dried up its fruit.
Its strong branches were torn off
    and dried up;
fire consumed them.
¹³ Now it is planted
    in the wilderness,
in a dry and thirsty land.
¹⁴ Fire has gone out from its
    main branch
and has devoured its fruit,
so that it no longer has
    a strong branch,
a scepter for ruling.

This is a lament and should be used as a lament."

*P*SALM 125:1-5

¹ Those who trust in the LORD are
    like Mount Zion.
It cannot be shaken; it remains
    forever.
² Jerusalem—the mountains
    surround her.
And the LORD surrounds His
    people,
both now and forever.

³ The scepter of the wicked will not
    remain
over the land allotted to the
    righteous,
so that the righteous will not
    apply their hands to injustice.
⁴ Do good, LORD, to the good,
    to those whose hearts are upright.
⁵ But as for those who turn aside to
    crooked ways,

the LORD will banish them with
    the evildoers.

Peace be with Israel.

*P*ROVERBS 27:25-27

²⁵ When hay is removed and new
    growth appears
and the grain from the hills is
    gathered in,
²⁶ lambs will provide your clothing,
    and goats, the price of a field;
²⁷ there will be enough goat's milk
    for your food—
food for your household and
    nourishment for your
    servants.

*J*AMES 1:1-21

1 James, a slave of God and of the
  Lord Jesus Christ:
To the 12 tribes in the Dispersion.
Greetings.
² Consider it a great joy, my brothers, whenever you experience various trials, ³ knowing that the testing of your faith produces endurance. ⁴ But endurance must do its complete work, so that you may be mature and complete, lacking nothing.
⁵ Now if any of you lacks wisdom, he should ask God, who gives to all generously and without criticizing, and it will be given to him. ⁶ But let him ask in faith without doubting. For the doubter is like the surging sea, driven and tossed by the wind. ⁷ That person should not expect to receive anything from the Lord. ⁸ An indecisive man is unstable in all his ways.
⁹ The brother of humble circumstances should boast in his exaltation; ¹⁰ but the one who is rich should boast in his humiliation, because he will pass away like a flower of the field. ¹¹ For the sun rises with its scorching heat and dries up the grass; its flower falls off, and its beautiful appearance is destroyed. In the same way, the rich man will wither away while pursuing his activities.

¹² Blessed is a man who endures trials, because when he passes the test he will receive the crown of life that He has promised to those who love Him. ¹³ No one undergoing a trial should say, "I am being tempted by God." For God is not tempted by evil, and He Himself doesn't tempt anyone. ¹⁴ But each person is tempted when he is drawn away and enticed by his own evil desires. ¹⁵ Then after desire has conceived, it gives birth to sin, and when sin is fully grown, it gives birth to death. ¹⁶ Don't be deceived, my dearly loved brothers. ¹⁷ Every generous act and every perfect gift is from above, coming down from the Father of lights; with Him there is no variation or shadow cast by turning. ¹⁸ By His own choice, He gave us a new birth by the message of truth so that we would be the firstfruits of His creatures.

¹⁹ My dearly loved brothers, understand this: everyone must be quick to hear, slow to speak, and slow to anger, ²⁰ for man's anger does not accomplish God's righteousness. ²¹ Therefore, ridding yourselves of all moral filth and evil excess, humbly receive the implanted word, which is able to save you.

"Some Extra Practice"

Consider it a great joy, my brothers, whenever you experience various trials.—JAMES 1:2

The Bible is replete with instances of God's wisdom moving men and women through the most difficult times to the most wonderful ends. Take Abraham, for example. Although he is known in Scripture as the "the friend of God," he was capable of some shabby behavior. On one occasion he actually compromised his wife's chastity (Gn 12:10-20), and later, submitting to her pressure, fathered a child by Hagar, their maid (Gn 16:1-16). Then, seeking to avoid Sarah's hysterical recriminations, he allowed her to drive Hagar away from their household (Gn 21:8-21). Clearly, Abraham was not a man of strong principle, and there were great flaws in his character. But God in wisdom dealt with this man and brought him through some great trials until he was changed from a man of the world to a true man of God.

The same wisdom that ordered the path Abraham trod orders our lives. We should never be taken aback when unexpected and upsetting things happen to us. We should recognize that no matter how hard the trial, God's power will be there to get us through, and God's wisdom will ensure that the trial will be worth more than it costs.

I like the way Jim Packer describes what may be God's design when He permits us to go through trials: "Perhaps he means to strengthen us in patience, good humor, compassion, humility, or meekness by giving us some extra practice in exercising these graces under specially difficult situations." "Some extra practice." Some of us, myself included, sorely need it.

Prayer

Father, help me grasp this truth once and for all, that Your wisdom ensures the trials I go through are worth far more than they cost. You are more committed to making me like Jesus than I am myself. It hurts sometimes, but deep down I am grateful.

Further Study

Is 48:1-10; Ps 66:10; Mal 3:3; 1 Pt 1:7
What process is God's testing likened to?
What is the end result?

NOVEMBER 20

*E*ZEKIEL 20:1–21:7

20 In the seventh year, in the fifth month, on the tenth day of the month, some of Israel's elders came to consult the LORD, and they sat down in front of me. ² Then the word of the LORD came to me: ³ "Son of man, speak with the elders of Israel and tell them: This is what the Lord GOD says: Are you coming to consult Me? As I live, I will not be consulted by you." This is the declaration of the Lord GOD.

⁴ "Will you pass judgment against them, will you pass judgment, son of man? Explain to them the abominations of their fathers. ⁵ Say to them: This is what the Lord GOD says: On the day I chose Israel, I swore an oath to the descendants of Jacob's house and made Myself known to them in the land of Egypt. I swore to them, saying: I am the LORD your God. ⁶ On that day I swore to them that I would bring them out of the land of Egypt into a land I had searched out for them, a land flowing with milk and honey, the most beautiful of all lands. ⁷ I also said to them: Each of you must throw away the detestable things that are before your eyes and not defile yourselves with the idols of Egypt. I am the LORD your God.

⁸ "But they rebelled against Me and were unwilling to listen to Me. None of them threw away the detestable things that were before their eyes, and they did not forsake the idols of Egypt. So I considered pouring out My wrath on them, exhausting My anger against them within the land of Egypt. ⁹ But I acted for the sake of My name, so that it would not be profaned in the eyes of the nations they were living among, in whose sight I had made Myself known to Israel by bringing them out of Egypt.

¹⁰ "So I brought them out of the land of Egypt and led them into the wilderness. ¹¹ Then I gave them My statutes and explained My ordinances to them— the person who does them will live by them. ¹² I also gave them My Sabbaths to serve as a sign between Me and them, so they will know that I am the LORD who sets them apart as holy.

¹³ "But the house of Israel rebelled against Me in the wilderness. They did not follow My statutes and they rejected My ordinances—the person who does them will live by them. They also completely profaned My Sabbaths. So I considered pouring out My wrath on them in the wilderness to put an end to them. ¹⁴ But I acted because of My name, so that it would not be profaned in the eyes of the nations in whose sight I had brought them out. ¹⁵ However, I swore to them in the wilderness that I would not bring them into the land I had given them—the most beautiful of all lands, flowing with milk and honey— ¹⁶ because they rejected My ordinances, profaned My Sabbaths, and did not follow My statutes. For their hearts went after their idols. ¹⁷ But I spared

them from destruction and did not bring them to an end in the wilderness. ¹⁸ "Then I said to their children in the wilderness: Don't follow the statutes of your fathers, defile yourselves with their idols, or keep their ordinances. ¹⁹ I am the LORD your God. Follow My statutes, keep My ordinances, and practice them. ²⁰ Keep My Sabbaths holy, and they will be a sign between Me and you, so you may know that I am the LORD your God.

²¹ "But the children rebelled against Me. They did not follow My statutes or carefully keep My ordinances—the person who does them will live by them. They also profaned My Sabbaths. So I considered pouring out My wrath on them and exhausting My anger against them in the wilderness. ²² But I withheld My hand and acted because of My name, so that it would not be profaned in the eyes of the nations in whose sight I brought them out. ²³ However, I swore to them in the wilderness that I would disperse them among the nations and scatter them among the countries. ²⁴ For they did not practice My ordinances but rejected My statutes and profaned My Sabbaths, and their eyes were fixed on their fathers' idols. ²⁵ I also gave them statutes that were not good and ordinances that did not bring them life. ²⁶ When they made every firstborn pass through the fire, I defiled them through their gifts in order to devastate them so they would know that I am the LORD.

²⁷ "Therefore, son of man, speak to the house of Israel, and tell them: This is what the Lord GOD says: In this way also your fathers blasphemed Me by committing treachery against Me: ²⁸ When I brought them into the land that I swore to give them and they saw any high hill or leafy tree, they offered their sacrifices and presented their offensive offerings there. They also sent up their pleasing aromas and poured out their drink offerings there. ²⁹ So I asked them: What is this high place you are going to? And it is called High Place to this day.

³⁰ "Therefore say to the house of Israel: This is what the Lord GOD says: Are you defiling yourselves the way your fathers did, and prostituting yourselves with their detestable things? ³¹ When you offer your gifts, making your children pass through the fire, you continue to defile yourselves with all your idols to this day. So should I be consulted by you, house of Israel? As I live"—this is the declaration of the Lord GOD—"I will not be consulted by you!

³² "When you say: Let us be like the nations, like the peoples of other countries, worshiping wood and stone, what you have in mind will never happen. ³³ As I live"—the declaration of the Lord GOD—"I will rule over you with a strong hand, an outstretched arm, and outpoured wrath. ³⁴ I will bring you from the peoples and gather you from the countries where you were scattered, with a strong hand, an outstretched arm, and outpoured wrath. ³⁵ I will lead you into the wilderness of the peoples and enter into judgment with you there face to face. ³⁶ Just as I entered into judgment with your fathers in the wilderness of the land of Egypt, so I will enter into judgment with you." This is the declaration of the Lord GOD. ³⁷ "I will make you pass under the rod and will bring you into the bond of the covenant. ³⁸ And I will also purge you of those who rebel and transgress against Me. I will bring them out of the land where they live as foreign residents, but they will not enter the land of Israel. Then you will know that I am the LORD.

³⁹ "As for you, house of Israel, this is what the Lord GOD says: Go and serve your idols, each of you. But afterwards you will surely listen to Me, and you will no longer defile My holy name with your gifts and idols. ⁴⁰ For on My holy mountain, Israel's high mountain"—the declaration of the Lord GOD—"there the entire house of Israel, all of them, will serve Me in the land. There I will accept them and will require your contributions and choicest gifts, all your holy offerings. ⁴¹ When I bring you from the peoples and gather you from the countries where you have been scat-

tered, I will accept you as a pleasing aroma. And I will demonstrate My holiness through you in the sight of the nations. ⁴²When I lead you into the land of Israel, the land I swore to give your fathers, you will know that I am the LORD. ⁴³There you will remember your ways and all your deeds you have defiled yourselves with, and you will loathe yourselves for all the evil things you have done. ⁴⁴You will know that I am the LORD, house of Israel, when I have dealt with you because of My name rather than according to your evil ways and corrupt acts." This is the declaration of the Lord GOD.

⁴⁵The word of the LORD came to me: ⁴⁶"Son of man, face the south and preach against it. Prophesy against the forest land in the Negev, ⁴⁷and say to the forest there: Hear the word of the LORD! This is what the Lord GOD says: I am about to ignite a fire in you, and it will devour every green tree and every dry tree in you. The blazing flame will not be extinguished, and every face from the south to the north will be scorched by it. ⁴⁸Then all people will see that I, Yahweh, have kindled it. It will not be extinguished."

⁴⁹Then I said, "Ah, Lord GOD, they are saying of me: Isn't he just posing riddles?"

21 The word of the LORD came to me again: ²"Son of man, turn your face toward Jerusalem and preach against the sanctuaries. Prophesy against the land of Israel, ³and say to it: This is what the LORD says: I am against you. I will draw My sword from its sheath and cut off both the righteous and the wicked from you. ⁴Since I will cut off both the righteous and the wicked, My sword will therefore come out of its sheath against everyone from the south to the north. ⁵So all the people will know that I, the LORD, have taken My sword from its sheath—it will not be sheathed again.

⁶"But you, son of man, groan! Groan bitterly with a broken heart right before their eyes. ⁷And when they ask you: Why are you groaning? then say:

Because of the news that is coming. Every heart will melt, and every hand will become weak. Every spirit will be discouraged, and every knee will turn to water. Yes, it is coming and it will happen." This is the declaration of the Lord GOD.

𝒫SALM 126:1-6

¹ When the LORD restored the
    fortunes of Zion,
  we were like those who dream.
² Our mouths were filled with
    laughter then,
  and our tongues with shouts of joy.
  Then they said among the nations,
  "The LORD has done great things
    for them."
³ The LORD had done great things
    for us;
  we were joyful.

⁴ Restore our fortunes, LORD,
  like watercourses in the Negev.
⁵ Those who sow in tears
  will reap with shouts of joy.
⁶ Though one goes along weeping,
  carrying the bag of seed,
  he will surely come back with
    shouts of joy,
  carrying his sheaves.

𝒫ROVERBS 28:1-3

28 The wicked flee when no one is
    pursuing them,
  but the righteous are as bold as a
    lion.

² When a land is in rebellion, it has
    many rulers,
  but with a discerning and
    knowledgeable person, it
    endures.

³ A destitute leader who oppresses
    the poor
  is like a driving rain that leaves no
    food.

JAMES 1:22–2:17

²² But be doers of the word and not hearers only, deceiving yourselves. ²³ Because if anyone is a hearer of the word and not a doer, he is like a man looking at his own face in a mirror; ²⁴ for he looks at himself, goes away, and right away forgets what kind of man he was. ²⁵ But the one who looks intently into the perfect law of freedom and perseveres in it, and is not a forgetful hearer but a doer who acts—this person will be blessed in what he does.

²⁶ If anyone thinks he is religious, without controlling his tongue but deceiving his heart, his religion is useless. ²⁷ Pure and undefiled religion before our God and Father is this: to look after orphans and widows in their distress and to keep oneself unstained by the world.

2 My brothers, hold your faith in our glorious Lord Jesus Christ without showing favoritism. ² For suppose a man comes into your meeting wearing a gold ring, dressed in fine clothes, and a poor man dressed in dirty clothes also comes in. ³ If you look with favor on the man wearing the fine clothes so that you say, "Sit here in a good place," and yet you say to the poor man, "Stand over there," or, "Sit here on the floor by my footstool," ⁴ haven't you discriminated among yourselves and become judges with evil thoughts?

⁵ Listen, my dear brothers: Didn't God choose the poor in this world to be rich in faith and heirs of the kingdom that He has promised to those who love Him? ⁶ Yet you dishonored that poor man. Don't the rich oppress you and drag you into the courts? ⁷ Don't they blaspheme the noble name that you bear?

⁸ If you really carry out the royal law prescribed in Scripture, **Love your neighbor as yourself**, you are doing well. ⁹ But if you show favoritism, you commit sin and are convicted by the law as transgressors. ¹⁰ For whoever keeps the entire law, yet fails in one point, is guilty of breaking it all. ¹¹ For He who said, **Do not commit adultery,** also said, **Do not murder.** So if you do not commit adultery, but you do murder, you are a lawbreaker.

¹² Speak and act as those who will be judged by the law of freedom. ¹³ For judgment is without mercy to the one who hasn't shown mercy. Mercy triumphs over judgment.

¹⁴ What good is it, my brothers, if someone says he has faith, but does not have works? Can his faith save him? ¹⁵ If a brother or sister is without clothes and lacks daily food, ¹⁶ and one of you says to them, "Go in peace, keep warm, and eat well," but you don't give them what the body needs, what good is it? ¹⁷ In the same way faith, if it doesn't have works, is dead by itself.

The Glory

Hold your faith in our glorious Lord Jesus Christ.

—JAMES 2:1

Can you think of anything that could occupy our attention more profitably than considering how to become more like Jesus? The central condition of this is the "unveiled face." As the Scripture says, "We all, with unveiled faces, are reflecting the glory of the Lord and are being transformed into the same image from glory to glory" (2 Co 3:18).

Notice, however, that we must lift the veils if we are to be transformed. When Jesus was crucified, the veil of the temple was rent in two, symbolizing the fact that the heart of the universe was laid bare as redemptive love. Since God has unveiled Himself in Jesus, so we in response ought to unveil our faces, drop our masks, gaze in wonder—and in the gazing, be made like Him. It may be that there will be many veils that you will have to lift—veils of dishonesty, hypocrisy, legalism, pride—but I assure you that when they go, He comes.

Just think—we who are born of the dust of the earth are being gradually transformed into the most beautiful image this planet has ever seen: the image of Christ. What a destiny! The wonder of that transformation can only be explained by one word—"glory." The drabness, staleness, and dullness of life is replaced by living that has freshness in it. Can we live continuously like that? Yes—in His strength. "Grace" and "glory" are often connected in the New Testament. Take the grace, and you get the glory. What a way to live. Glory! Glory! Glory!

Prayer

Father, help me to lift every veil in my life so that the light of Your countenance may shine through. You are Light and You want to make me light. Let Your radiance steal into every darkened corner of my being now and forever. Amen.

Further Study

Jn 1:10-14; Col 1:6; 2 Pt 3:18
What were the characteristics of Christ's glory?
Make them the characteristics of your own life.

NOVEMBER 21

*E*ZEKIEL 21:8–22:31

⁸ The word of the LORD came to me: ⁹ "Son of man, prophesy: This is what the Lord says! You are to proclaim:

A sword! A sword is sharpened
and also polished.
¹⁰ It is sharpened for slaughter,
polished to flash like lightning!
Should we rejoice?
The scepter of My son,
the sword despises every tree.
¹¹ The sword is given to be polished,

to be grasped in the hand.
It is sharpened, and it is polished,
to be put in the hand of the slayer.
¹² Cry out and wail, son of man,
for it is against My people.
It is against all the princes
of Israel!
They are given over to the sword
with My people.
Therefore strike your thigh
in grief.
¹³ Surely it will be a trial!
And what if the sword despises
even the scepter?

The scepter will not continue.
This is the declaration
of the Lord GOD.

14 Therefore, son of man, prophesy
and clap your hands together.
Let the sword strike two times,
even three.
It is a sword for massacre,
a sword for great massacre—
it surrounds them!
15 I have appointed a sword
for slaughter
at all their gates,
so that their hearts may melt
and many may stumble.
Alas! It is ready to flash
like lightning;
it is drawn for slaughter.
16 Slash to the right;
turn to the left—
wherever your blade is directed.
17 I also will clap My hands together,
and I will satisfy My wrath.
I, the LORD, have spoken."

18 Then the word of the LORD came to me: 19 "Now you, son of man, mark out two roads that the sword of Babylon's king can take. Both of them should originate from the same land. And make a signpost at the fork in the road to each city. 20 Mark out a road that the sword can take to Rabbah of the Ammonites and to Judah into fortified Jerusalem. 21 For the king of Babylon stands at the split in the road, at the fork of the two roads, to practice divination: he shakes the arrows, consults the idols, and observes the liver. 22 The answer marked Jerusalem appears in his right hand, indicating that he should set up battering rams, give the order to slaughter, raise a battle cry, set battering rams against the gates, build a ramp, and construct a siege wall. 23 It will seem like false divination in the eyes of those who have sworn an oath to the Babylonians, but it will draw attention to their guilt so that they will be captured.

24 "Therefore, this is what the Lord GOD says: Because you have drawn attention to your guilt, exposing your transgressions, so that your sins are re-

vealed in all your actions, since you have done this, you will be captured by them.

25 And you, profane
and wicked prince of Israel,
the day has come
for your punishment."
26 This is what the Lord GOD says:

Remove the turban, and take off
the crown.
Things will not remain as they are;
exalt the lowly and bring down
the exalted.
27 A ruin, a ruin,
I will make it a ruin!
Yet this will not happen
until He comes;
I have given the judgment to Him.

28 "Now prophesy, son of man, and say: This is what the Lord GOD says concerning the Ammonites and their contempt. You are to proclaim:

Sword, sword!
You are drawn for slaughter,
polished to consume, to flash
like lightning.
29 While they offer false visions
and lying divinations about you,
the time has come to put you
to the necks of the profane
wicked ones;
the day has come
for your punishment.

30 Return it to its sheath!

I will judge you
in the place
where you were created,
in the land of your origin.
31 I will pour out My indignation
on you;
I will blow the fire of My fury
on you.
I will hand you over
to brutal men,
skilled at destruction.
32 You will be fuel for the fire.
Your blood will be spilled
in the land.

You will not be remembered, for I, the LORD, have spoken."

22 The word of the LORD came to me: ² "Now, son of man, will you pass judgment? Will you pass judgment against the city of blood? Then explain all her abominations to her. ³ You are to say: This is what the Lord GOD says: A city that sheds blood within her walls so that her time of judgment has come and who makes idols for herself so that she is defiled! ⁴ You are guilty of the blood you have shed, and you are defiled from the idols you have made. You have brought your judgment days near and have come to your years of punishment. Therefore, I have made you a disgrace to the nations and a mockery to all the lands. ⁵ Those who are near and those far away from you will mock you, you infamous one full of turmoil.

⁶ "Look, every prince of Israel within you has used his strength to shed blood. ⁷ Father and mother are treated with contempt, and the foreign resident is exploited within you. The fatherless and widow are oppressed in you. ⁸ You despise My holy things and profane My Sabbaths. ⁹ There are men within you who slander in order to shed blood. People who live in you eat at the mountain shrines; they commit immoral acts within you. ¹⁰ Men within you have sexual intercourse with their father's wife, and violate women during their menstrual impurity. ¹¹ One man within you commits an abomination with his neighbor's wife; another wickedly defiles his daughter-in-law; and yet another violates his sister, his father's daughter. ¹² People who live in you accept bribes in order to shed blood. You take interest and profit on a loan and brutally extort your neighbors. You have forgotten Me." This is the declaration of the Lord GOD.

¹³ "Now look, I clap My hands together against the unjust gain you have made and against the blood shed among you. ¹⁴ Will your courage endure or your hands be strong in the days when I deal with you? I, the LORD, have spoken, and I will act. ¹⁵ I will disperse you among the nations and scatter you among the countries; I will purge your uncleanness. ¹⁶ You will be profaned in the sight of the nations. Then you will know that I am the LORD."

¹⁷ The word of the LORD came to me: ¹⁸ "Son of man, the house of Israel has become dross to Me. All of them are copper, tin, iron, and lead inside the furnace; they are the dross of silver. ¹⁹ Therefore, this is what the Lord GOD says: Because all of you have become dross, I am about to gather you into Jerusalem. ²⁰ Just as one gathers silver, copper, iron, lead, and tin into the furnace to blow fire on them and melt them, so I will gather you in My anger and wrath, put you inside, and melt you. ²¹ Yes, I will gather you together and blow on you with the fire of My fury, and you will be melted within the city. ²² As silver is melted inside a furnace, so you will be melted inside the city. Then you will know that I, the LORD, have poured out My wrath on you."

²³ The word of the LORD came to me: ²⁴ "Son of man, say to her: You are a land that has not been cleansed, that has not received rain in the day of indignation. ²⁵ The conspiracy of her prophets within her is like a roaring lion tearing its prey: they devour people, seize wealth and valuables, and multiply the widows within her. ²⁶ Her priests do violence to My law and profane My holy things. They make no distinction between the holy and the common, and they do not explain the difference between the clean and the unclean. They disregard My Sabbaths, and I am profaned among them.

²⁷ "Her officials within her are like wolves tearing their prey, shedding blood, and destroying lives in order to get unjust gain. ²⁸ Her prophets plaster with whitewash for them by seeing false visions and lying divinations, and they say: This is what the Lord GOD says, when the LORD has not spoken. ²⁹ The people of the land have practiced extortion and committed robbery. They have oppressed the poor and needy and unlawfully exploited the foreign resident.

³⁰ I searched for a man among them who would repair the wall and stand in the gap before Me on behalf of the land so that I might not destroy it, but I found no one. ³¹ So I have poured out My indignation on them and consumed them with the fire of My fury. I have brought their actions down on their own heads." This is the declaration of the Lord GOD.

PSALM 127:1-5

¹ Unless the LORD builds a house,
  its builders labor over it in vain;
  unless the LORD watches over a
    city,
  the watchman stays alert in vain.
² In vain you get up early and stay
    up late,
  eating food earned by hard work;
  certainly He gives sleep to the one
    He loves.

³ Sons are indeed a heritage from
    the LORD,
  children, a reward.
⁴ Like arrows in the hand of a
    warrior
  are the sons born in one's youth.
⁵ Happy is the man who has filled
    his quiver with them.
  Such men will never be put to
    shame
  when they speak with their
    enemies at the city gate.

PROVERBS 28:4-5

⁴ Those who reject the law praise
    the wicked,
  but those who keep the law battle
    against them.

⁵ Evil men do not understand
    justice,
  but those who seek the LORD
    understand everything.

JAMES 2:18–3:12

¹⁸ But someone will say, "You have faith, and I have works." Show me your faith without works, and I will show you faith from my works. ¹⁹ You believe that God is one; you do well. The demons also believe—and they shudder. ²⁰ Foolish man! Are you willing to learn that faith without works is useless? ²¹ Wasn't Abraham our father justified by works when he offered Isaac his son on the altar? ²² You see that faith was active together with his works, and by works, faith was perfected. ²³ So the Scripture was fulfilled that says, **Abraham believed God, and it was credited to him for righteousness**, and he was called God's friend. ²⁴ You see that a man is justified by works and not by faith alone. ²⁵ And in the same way, wasn't Rahab the prostitute also justified by works when she received the messengers and sent them out by a different route? ²⁶ For just as the body without the spirit is dead, so also faith without works is dead.

3 Not many should become teachers, my brothers, knowing that we will receive a stricter judgment; ² for we all stumble in many ways. If anyone does not stumble in what he says, he is a mature man who is also able to control his whole body.

³ Now when we put bits into the mouths of horses to make them obey us, we also guide the whole animal. ⁴ And consider ships: though very large and driven by fierce winds, they are guided by a very small rudder wherever the will of the pilot directs. ⁵ So too, though the tongue is a small part of the body, it boasts great things. Consider how large a forest a small fire ignites. ⁶ And the tongue is a fire. The tongue, a world of unrighteousness, is placed among the parts of our bodies; it pollutes the whole body, sets the course of life on fire, and is set on fire by hell.

⁷ For every creature—animal or bird, reptile or fish—is tamed and has been tamed by man, ⁸ but no man can tame the tongue. It is a restless evil, full of deadly poison. ⁹ With it we bless our Lord and Father, and with it we curse men who are made in God's likeness. ¹⁰ Out of the same mouth come blessing and cursing. My brothers, these things

should not be this way. ¹¹ Does a spring pour out sweet and bitter water from the same opening? ¹² Can a fig tree pro- duce olives, my brothers, or a grapevine produce figs? Neither can a saltwater spring yield fresh water.

This God Is Your God

Will your courage endure or your hands be strong in the days when I deal with you?—Ezekiel 22:14

God is powerful in judgment. When He smites, none can resist Him. The flood of Noah's day is one such example, when the entire race—with the exception of eight people—was swept away (Gn 6:1–9:18). When a shower of fire and brimstone fell from heaven on Sodom and Gomorrah, all the cities of the plain were destroyed (Gn 19:1-29). Pharaoh and his hosts found themselves impotent when God blew upon them at the Red Sea (Ex 14:1-31).

What does the contemplation of God's power do for us?

First, it causes us to tremble before Him. The trouble with many modern men and women is that they do not tremble before God. To treat with impudence the One who can crush us more easily than we can a tiny ant is, as someone put it, "a suicidal policy." "Pay homage to the Son," said the psalmist, "or He will be angry, and you will perish . . . for His anger may ignite at any moment" (Ps 2:12).

Second, contemplating God's great power causes us to adore Him. Who can consider the might of this awesome God without wanting to worship Him? The rebellious heart will resist this, but the heart cleansed by the blood of Christ will bow in homage and say: "Who is like You, glorious in holiness, revered with praises, performing wonders?" (Ex 15:11). No prayer is too hard for Him to answer, no need too great for Him to supply, no predicament too great for Him to solve. Lay hold on this great and gripping truth: this God is your God.

Prayer

O Father, I see that contemplation of You tilts my soul in Your direction. I realize that without You I am nothing. May I tremble before You until my trembling turns to adoration and ever-increasing trust. Amen.

Further Study

Ps 114:1-8; 1 Ch 16:30-31; Is 66:1-3
What can the presence of the Lord do?
Who does the Lord esteem?

NOVEMBER 22

*E*ZEKIEL 23:1–24:5

23 The word of the LORD came to me again: [2] Son of man, there were two women, daughters of the same mother, [3] who acted like prostitutes in Egypt, behaving promiscuously in their youth. Their breasts were fondled there, and their virgin nipples caressed. [4] The older one was named Oholah, and her sister was Oholibah. They became Mine and gave birth to sons and daughters. As for their names, Oholah represents Samaria and Oholibah represents Jerusalem.

[5] "Oholah acted like a prostitute even though she was Mine. She lusted after her lovers, the Assyrians: warriors [6] dressed in blue, governors and prefects, all of them desirable young men, horsemen riding on steeds. [7] She offered her sexual favors to them; all of them were the elite of Assyria. She defiled herself with all those she lusted after and with all their idols. [8] She didn't give up her promiscuity that began in Egypt, when men slept with her in her youth, caressed her virgin nipples, and poured out their lust on her. [9] Therefore, I handed her over to her lovers, the Assyrians she lusted for. [10] They exposed her nakedness, seized her sons and daughters, and killed her with the sword. Since they executed judgment against her, she became notorious among women.

[11] "Now her sister Oholibah saw this, but she was even more depraved in her lust than Oholah, and made her promiscuous acts worse than those of her sister. [12] She lusted after the Assyrians: governors and prefects, warriors splendidly dressed, horsemen riding on steeds, all of them desirable young men. [13] And I saw that she had defiled herself; both of them had taken the same path. [14] But she increased her promiscuity when she saw male figures carved on the wall, images of the Chaldeans, engraved in vermilion, [15] wearing belts on their waists and flowing turbans on their heads; all of them looked like officers, a depiction of the Babylonians in Chaldea, the land of their birth. [16] At the sight of them she lusted after them and sent messengers to them in Chaldea. [17] Then the Babylonians came to her, to the bed of love, and defiled her with their lust. But after she was defiled by them, she turned away from them in disgust. [18] When she flaunted her promiscuity and exposed her nakedness, I turned away from her in disgust just as I turned away from her sister. [19] Yet she multiplied her acts of promiscuity, remembering the days of her youth when she acted like a prostitute in the land of Egypt [20] and lusted after their lovers, whose sexual members were like those of donkeys and whose emission was like that of stallions. [21] So you revisited the indecency of your youth, when the Egyptians caressed your nipples to enjoy your youthful breasts.

[22] "Therefore Oholibah, this is what the Lord GOD says: I am going to incite your lovers against you, those you turned away from in disgust. I will bring them against you from every side: [23] the Babylonians and all the Chaldeans; Pekod, Shoa, and Koa; and all the Assyrians with them—desirable young men, all of them governors and prefects, officers and administrators, all of them riding on horses. [24] They will come against you with an alliance of nations and with weapons, chariots, and wagons. They will set themselves against you on every side with shields, bucklers, and helmets. I will delegate judgment to them, and they will judge you by their own standards. [25] When I vent My jealous rage on you, they will deal with you in wrath. They will cut off

your nose and ears, and your descendants will fall by the sword. They will seize your sons and daughters, and your descendants will be consumed by fire. ²⁶ They will strip off your clothes and take your beautiful jewelry. ²⁷ So I will put an end to your indecency and sexual immorality, which began in the land of Egypt, and you will not look longingly at them or remember Egypt any more.

²⁸ "For this is what the Lord GOD says: I am going to hand you over to those you hate, to those you turned away from in disgust. ²⁹ They will treat you with hatred, take all you have worked for, and leave you stark naked, so that the shame of your debauchery will be exposed, both your indecency and promiscuity. ³⁰ These things will be done to you because you acted like a prostitute with the nations, defiling yourself with their idols. ³¹ You have followed the path of your sister, so I will put her cup in your hand."

³² This is what the Lord GOD says:

You will drink your sister's cup,
which is deep and wide.
You will be an object of ridicule
and scorn,
for it holds so much.
³³ You will be filled
with drunkenness and grief,
with a cup of devastation
and desolation,
the cup of your sister Samaria.
³⁴ You will drink it and drain it;
then you will gnaw
its broken pieces,
and tear your breasts.
For I have spoken.
This is the declaration
of the Lord GOD.

³⁵ Therefore, this is what the Lord GOD says: "Because you have forgotten Me and cast Me behind your back, you must bear the consequences of your indecency and promiscuity."

³⁶ Then the LORD said to me: "Son of man, will you pass judgment against Oholah and Oholibah? Then declare their abominations to them. ³⁷ For they have committed adultery, and blood is on their hands; they have committed adultery with their idols. They have even made the children they bore to Me pass through the fire as food for the idols. ³⁸ They also did this to Me: they defiled My sanctuary on that same day and profaned My Sabbaths. ³⁹ On the same day they slaughtered their children for their idols, they entered My sanctuary to profane it. Yes, that is what they did inside My house.

⁴⁰ "In addition, they sent for men who came from far away when a messenger was dispatched to them. And look how they came! You bathed, painted your eyes, and adorned yourself with jewelry for them. ⁴¹ You sat on a luxurious couch with a table spread before it, on which you had set My incense and oil. ⁴² The sound of a carefree crowd was there. Drunkards from the desert were brought in, along with common men. They put bracelets on the women's hands and beautiful crowns on their heads. ⁴³ Then I said concerning this woman worn out by adultery: Will they now have illicit sex with her, even her? ⁴⁴ Yet they had sex with her as one does with a prostitute. This is how they had sex with Oholah and Oholibah, those obscene women. ⁴⁵ But righteous men will judge them the way adulteresses and those who shed blood are judged, for they are adulteresses and blood is on their hands.

⁴⁶ "This is what the Lord GOD says: Summon an assembly against them and consign them to terror and plunder. ⁴⁷ The assembly will stone them and cut them down with their swords. They will kill their sons and daughters and burn their houses with fire. ⁴⁸ So I will put an end to indecency in the land, and all the women will be admonished not to imitate your indecent behavior. ⁴⁹ They will repay you for your indecency, and you will bear the consequences for your sins of idolatry. Then you will know that I am the Lord GOD."

24 The word of the LORD came to me in the ninth year, in the tenth month, on the tenth day of the month: ² "Son of man, write down today's date, this very day. The king of

Babylon has laid siege to Jerusalem this very day. ³ Now speak a parable to the rebellious house. Tell them: This is what the Lord GOD says:

Put the pot on the fire—
put it on,
and then pour water into it!
⁴ Place the pieces of meat in it,
every good piece—
thigh and shoulder.
Fill it with choice bones.
⁵ Take the choicest of the flock
and also pile up the fuel under it.
Bring it to a boil
and cook the bones in it."

PSALM 128:1-6

¹ How happy is everyone who fears
the LORD,
who walks in His ways!
² You will surely eat what your
hands have worked for.
You will be happy, and it will go
well for you.
³ Your wife will be like a fruitful
vine within your house,
your sons, like young olive trees
around your table.
⁴ In this very way the man who
fears the LORD
will be blessed.

⁵ May the LORD bless you from Zion,
so that you will see the prosperity
of Jerusalem
all the days of your life,
⁶ and will see your children's
children!

Peace be with Israel.

PROVERBS 28:6-8

⁶ Better a poor man who lives with
integrity
than a rich man who distorts right
and wrong.

⁷ A discerning son keeps the law,
but a companion of gluttons
humiliates his father.

⁸ Whoever increases his wealth
through excessive interest
collects it for one who is kind to
the poor.

JAMES 3:13–4:17

¹³ Who is wise and understanding among you? He should show his works by good conduct with wisdom's gentleness. ¹⁴ But if you have bitter envy and selfish ambition in your heart, don't brag and lie in defiance of the truth. ¹⁵ Such wisdom does not come down from above, but is earthly, sensual, demonic. ¹⁶ For where envy and selfish ambition exist, there is disorder and every kind of evil. ¹⁷ But the wisdom from above is first pure, then peace-loving, gentle, compliant, full of mercy and good fruits, without favoritism and hypocrisy. ¹⁸ And the fruit of righteousness is sown in peace by those who make peace.

4 What is the source of the wars and the fights among you? Don't they come from the cravings that are at war within you? ² You desire and do not have. You murder and covet and cannot obtain. You fight and war. You do not have because you do not ask. ³ You ask and don't receive because you ask wrongly, so that you may spend it on your desires for pleasure.

⁴ Adulteresses! Do you not know that friendship with the world is hostility toward God? So whoever wants to be the world's friend becomes God's enemy. ⁵ Or do you think it's without reason the Scripture says that the Spirit He has caused to live in us yearns jealously? ⁶ But He gives greater grace. Therefore He says:

God resists the proud,
but gives grace to the humble.

⁷ Therefore, submit to God. But resist the Devil, and he will flee from you. ⁸ Draw near to God, and He will draw near to you. Cleanse your hands, sinners, and purify your hearts, double-

minded people! ⁹ Be miserable and mourn and weep. Your laughter must change to mourning and your joy to sorrow. ¹⁰ Humble yourselves before the Lord, and He will exalt you.

¹¹ Don't criticize one another, brothers. He who criticizes a brother or judges his brother criticizes the law and judges the law. But if you judge the law, you are not a doer of the law but a judge. ¹² There is one lawgiver and judge who is able to save and to destroy. But who are you to judge your neighbor?

¹³ Come now, you who say, "Today or tomorrow we will travel to such and such a city and spend a year there and do business and make a profit." ¹⁴ You don't even know what tomorrow will bring—what your life will be! For you are a bit of smoke that appears for a little while, then vanishes.

¹⁵ Instead, you should say, "If the Lord wills, we will live and do this or that." ¹⁶ But as it is, you boast in your arrogance. All such boasting is evil. ¹⁷ So, for the person who knows to do good and doesn't do it, it is a sin.

"Nearer My God to Thee"

Draw near to God, and He will draw near to you.

—JAMES 4:8

The final two verses of Psalm 73 form a conclusion and a resolution. Listen to them here: "Those far from You will certainly perish; You destroy all who are unfaithful to You. But as for me, God's presence is my good. I have made the Lord GOD my refuge, so I can tell about all You do" (vv. 27-28). The psalmist has finished his review of the past and is now hammering out a philosophy with which to face the future. He is resolved that no matter what anyone else may do, he is going to live in close companionship with God. He helps us to see the importance of this resolution by putting it in the form of a contrast: "Those far from You will certainly perish . . . but as for me, God's presence is my good."

Really, when it comes down to it, there are only two positions in life—close to God or far away from Him. I wonder, as the psalmist penned these words, was something like this going through his mind: "What caused me so much trouble in recent days and accounted for all my difficulties was the fact that I did not keep close to God. I erroneously believed that the cause of my problems was the prosperity of the ungodly, but having entered into the sanctuary of God I see that this was not he cause of my problems at all. My problems came because I had chosen not to remain close to Him. For me there is now only one thing that matters—staying close to God."

How are things with you at this moment? Do you feel close to God? If you don't, then let me put what I want to say in the words of a wayside pulpit that arrested my attention some years ago: "If you feel that God is far away, guess who moved?"

Prayer

Father, I am grateful for the promise of Your Word to me today that when I draw near to You, You will draw near to me. Help me put those words to the test by moving closer to You than I have ever done before. In Jesus' name. Amen.

Further Study

Ps 46:1-11; 2 Sm 22:3; Ps 9:9; Ps 62:1-12
What does the psalmist affirm?
What does the psalmist exhort the people?

NOVEMBER 23

*E*ZEKIEL 24:6–26:6

⁶ Therefore, this is what the Lord GOD says:

Woe to the city of bloodshed,
the pot that has rust inside it,
and whose rust will not come off!
Empty it piece by piece;
lots should not be cast
for its contents.
⁷ For the blood she shed is
in her midst.
She put it out on the bare rock;
she didn't pour it on the ground
to cover it with dust.
⁸ In order to stir up wrath
and take vengeance,
I have put her blood
on the bare rock,
so that it would not be covered.

⁹ Therefore, this is what the Lord GOD says:

Woe to the city of bloodshed!
I Myself will make the pile
of kindling large.
¹⁰ Pile on the logs and kindle the fire!
Cook the meat well
and mix in the spices!
Let the bones be burned!
¹¹ Set the empty pot on its coals
so that it becomes hot
and its copper glows.
Then its impurity will melt
inside it;

its rust will be consumed.
¹² It has frustrated every effort;
its thick rust will not come off.
Into the fire with its rust!
¹³ Because of the indecency
of your uncleanness—
since I tried to purify you,
but you would not be purified
from your uncleanness—
you will not be pure again
until I have satisfied My wrath
on you.
¹⁴ I, the LORD, have spoken.
It is coming, and I will do it!
I will not refrain, I will not show pity,
and I will not relent.
I will judge you
according to your ways and deeds.
This is the declaration
of the Lord GOD.

¹⁵ Then the word of the LORD came to me: ¹⁶ "Son of man, I am about to take the delight of your eyes away from you with a fatal blow. But you must not lament or weep or let your tears flow. ¹⁷ Groan quietly; do not observe mourning rites for the dead. Put on your turban and strap your sandals on your feet; do not cover your mustache or eat the bread of mourners." ¹⁸ I spoke to the people in the morning, and my wife died in the evening. The next morning I did just as I was commanded. ¹⁹ Then the people asked me, "Won't you tell us what these things you are doing mean for us?"

²⁰ So I answered them: "The word of the LORD came to me: ²¹ 'Say to the house of Israel: This is what the Lord GOD says: I am about to desecrate My sanctuary, the pride of your power, the delight of your eyes, and the desire of your heart. Also, the sons and daughters you left behind will fall by the sword. ²² Then you will do just as I have done: You will not cover your mustache or eat the bread of mourners. ²³ Your turbans will remain on your heads and your sandals on your feet. You will not lament or weep but will waste away because of your sins and will groan to one another. ²⁴ Now Ezekiel will be a sign for you. You will do everything that he has done. When this happens, you will know that I am the Lord GOD.

²⁵ " 'Son of man, know that on the day I take their stronghold from them, their pride and joy, the delight of their eyes and the longing of their hearts, as well as their sons and daughters, ²⁶ on that day a fugitive will come to you and report the news. ²⁷ On that day your mouth will be opened to talk with him; you will speak and no longer be mute. So you will be a sign for them, and they will know that I am the LORD.' "

25 Then the word of the LORD came to me: ² "Son of man, turn your face toward the Ammonites and prophesy against them. ³ Say to the Ammonites: Hear the word of the Lord GOD: This is what the Lord GOD says: Because you said: Good! about My sanctuary when it was desecrated, about the land of Israel when it was laid waste, and about the house of Judah when they went into exile, ⁴ therefore I am about to give you to the people of the east as a possession. They will set up their encampments and pitch their tents among you. They will eat your fruit and drink your milk. ⁵ I will make Rabbah a pasture for camels and Ammon a sheepfold. Then you will know that I am the LORD."

⁶ For this is what the Lord GOD says: "Because you clapped your hands, stamped your feet, and rejoiced over the land of Israel with wholehearted contempt, ⁷ therefore I am about to stretch out My hand against you and give you as plunder to the nations. I will cut you off from the peoples and eliminate you from the countries. I will destroy you, and you will know that I am the LORD."

⁸ This is what the Lord GOD says: "Because Moab and Seir said: Look, the house of Judah is like all the other nations, ⁹ therefore I am about to expose Moab's flank beginning with its frontier cities, the pride of the land: Beth-jeshimoth, Baal-meon, and Kiriathaim. ¹⁰ I will give it along with Ammon to the people of the east as a possession, so that Ammon will not be remembered among the nations. ¹¹ So I will execute judgments against Moab, and they will know that I am the LORD."

¹² This is what the Lord GOD says: "Because Edom acted vengefully against the house of Judah and incurred grievous guilt by taking revenge on them, ¹³ therefore this is what the Lord GOD says: I will stretch out My hand against Edom and cut off both man and animal from it. I will make it a wasteland; they will fall by the sword from Teman to Dedan. ¹⁴ I will take My vengeance on Edom through My people Israel, and they will deal with Edom according to My anger and wrath. So they will know My vengeance." This is the declaration of the Lord GOD.

¹⁵ This is what the Lord GOD says: "Because the Philistines acted in vengeance and took revenge with deep contempt, destroying because of their ancient hatred, ¹⁶ therefore this is what the Lord GOD says: I am about to stretch out My hand against the Philistines, cutting off the Cherethites and wiping out what remains of the coastal peoples. ¹⁷ I will execute great vengeance against them with furious rebukes. They will know that I am the LORD when I take My vengeance on them."

26 In the eleventh year, on the first day of the month, the word of the LORD came to me: ² "Son of man, because Tyre said about Jerusalem: Good! The gateway to the peoples is shattered.

She has been turned over to me. I will be filled now that she lies in ruins, ³ therefore this is what the Lord GOD says: See, I am against you, Tyre! I will raise up many nations against you, just as the sea raises its waves. ⁴ They will destroy the walls of Tyre and demolish her towers. I will scrape the soil from her and turn her into a bare rock. ⁵ She will become a place in the sea to spread nets, for I have spoken." This is the declaration of the Lord GOD. "She will become plunder for the nations, ⁶ and her villages on the mainland will be slaughtered by the sword. Then they will know that I am the LORD."

PSALM 129:1-8

¹ Since my youth they have often
   attacked me—
   let Israel say—
² Since my youth they have often
   attacked me,
   but they have not prevailed
   against me.
³ Plowmen plowed over my back;
   they made their furrows long.
⁴ The LORD is righteous;
   He has cut the ropes of the wicked.

⁵ Let all who hate Zion
   be driven back in disgrace.
⁶ Let them be like grass on the
   rooftops,
   which withers before it grows up
⁷ and can't even fill the hands of
   the reaper
   or the arms of the one who binds
   sheaves.
⁸ Then none who pass by will say,
   "May the LORD's blessing be on
   you."

   We bless you in the name of the
   LORD.

PROVERBS 28:9-11

⁹ Anyone who turns his ear away
   from hearing the law—
   even his prayer is detestable.

¹⁰ The one who leads the upright
    into an evil way
    will fall into his own pit,
    but the blameless will inherit
    what is good.

¹¹ A rich man is wise in his own
    eyes,
    but a poor man who has
    discernment sees through him.

JAMES 5:1-20

5 Come now, you rich people! Weep and wail over the miseries that are coming on you. ² Your wealth is ruined: your clothes are moth-eaten; ³ your silver and gold are corroded, and their corrosion will be a witness against you and will eat your flesh like fire. You stored up treasure in the last days! ⁴ Look! The pay that you withheld from the workers who reaped your fields cries out, and the outcry of the harvesters has reached the ears of the Lord of Hosts. ⁵ You have lived luxuriously on the land and have indulged yourselves. You have fattened your hearts for the day of slaughter. ⁶ You have condemned—you have murdered—the righteous man; he does not resist you.

⁷ Therefore, brothers, be patient until the Lord's coming. See how the farmer waits for the precious fruit of the earth and is patient with it until it receives the early and the late rains. ⁸ You also must be patient. Strengthen your hearts, because the Lord's coming is near.

⁹ Brothers, do not complain about one another, so that you will not be judged. Look, the judge stands at the door! ¹⁰ Brothers, take the prophets who spoke in the Lord's name as an example of suffering and patience. ¹¹ See, we count as blessed those who have endured. You have heard of Job's endurance and have seen the outcome from the Lord: the Lord is very compassionate and merciful.

¹² Now above all, my brothers, do not swear, either by heaven or by earth or with any other oath. Your "yes" must be

"yes," and your "no" must be "no," so that you won't fall under judgment. [13] Is anyone among you suffering? He should pray. Is anyone cheerful? He should sing praises. [14] Is anyone among you sick? He should call for the elders of the church, and they should pray over him after anointing him with olive oil in the name of the Lord. [15] The prayer of faith will save the sick person, and the Lord will raise him up; and if he has committed sins, he will be forgiven. [16] Therefore, confess your sins to one another and pray for one another, so

that you may be healed. The intense prayer of the righteous is very powerful. [17] Elijah was a man with a nature like ours; yet he prayed earnestly that it would not rain, and for three years and six months it did not rain on the land. [18] Then he prayed again, and the sky gave rain and the land produced its fruit.

[19] My brothers, if any among you strays from the truth, and someone turns him back, [20] he should know that whoever turns a sinner from the error of his way will save his life from death and cover a multitude of sins.

Down, but Not Out

Since my youth they have often attacked me, but they have not prevailed against me.—PSALM 129:2

The opening verses of this psalm spell out the simple but powerful message that though the world has always harassed the people of God, the world will never win. "Since my youth they have often attacked me," says the psalmist, "but they have not prevailed against me." The man or woman who clings closely to God outlasts all oppressors. He or she is provided with an inner fortitude that is enduring. Perseverance, patience, stickablity—this then is the message of Psalm 129.

There is no better way of seeing the persistency of faith than by setting it in the context of history. God's people have been ostracized, ridiculed, humiliated, scorned, persecuted, and beaten, but in the midst of the most horrific trials they have continued to serve God. If the persistence that flows from faith was merely a fad, then we would not be talking about it now.

Faith—persistent faith, that is—is not a fad; it is a fact. It runs like a thread throughout all history and is shared by the men and women of every generation. Those who think of the Christian faith as a plant that flourishes only in good weather ought to take a look at history.

Faith is hardy perennial that survives all weather conditions—drought, storm, even floods. J. B. Phillips, in his brilliant paraphrase of the New Testament, sums it up admirably: "We may be knocked down but we are never knocked out!" (2 Co 4:9). A preacher friend of mine puts it equally well when he says: "We may be floored but we are not flattened."

Prayer

Gracious Father, help me see that my perseverance is not so much a matter of my persevering but Your persevering in me. I supply the willingness; You supply the power. Together we will make it, You and I. All glory be to Your wonderful name. Amen.

Further study

Jms 1:1-27; 5:1-11; Gl 6:9; Heb 12:1
What is Paul's exhortation?
What will enable us to persevere?

NOVEMBER 24

EZEKIEL 26:7–27:36

7 For this is what the Lord GOD says: "See, I am about to bring King Nebuchadnezzar of Babylon, king of kings, against Tyre from the north with horses, chariots, cavalry, and a vast company of troops. 8 He will slaughter your villages on the mainland with the sword. He will set up siege works against you, and will build a ramp and raise a wall of shields against you. 9 He will direct the blows of his battering rams against your walls and tear down your towers with his iron tools. 10 His horses will be so numerous that their dust will cover you. When he enters your gates as an army entering a breached city, your walls will shake from the noise of cavalry, wagons, and chariots. 11 He will trample all your streets with the hooves of his horses. He will slaughter your people with the sword, and your mighty pillars will fall to the ground. 12 They will take your wealth as spoil and plunder your merchandise. They will also demolish your walls and tear down your beautiful homes. Then they will throw your stones, timber, and soil into the water. 13 I will put an end to the noise of your songs, and the sound of your lyres will no longer be heard. 14 I will turn you into a bare rock, and you will be a place to spread nets. You will never be rebuilt, for I, the LORD, have spoken." This is the declaration of the Lord GOD.

15 This is what the Lord GOD says to Tyre: "Won't the coasts and islands quake at the sound of your downfall, when the wounded groan and slaughter occurs within you? 16 All the princes of the sea will descend from their thrones, remove their robes, and strip off their embroidered garments. They will clothe themselves with trembling; they will sit on the ground, tremble continually, and be appalled at you. 17 Then they will lament for you and say of you:

How you have perished,
    city of renown,
you who were populated
    from the seas!
She who was powerful on the sea,
she and all of her inhabitants
inflicted their terror.
18 Now the coastlands tremble
    on the day of your downfall;
    the islands in the sea
    are alarmed by your demise."

19 For this is what the Lord GOD says: "When I make you a ruined city like other deserted cities, when I raise up the deep against you so that the mighty waters cover you, 20 then I will bring you down to be with those who descend to the Pit, to the people of antiquity. I will make you dwell in the underworld like the ancient ruins, with those who descend to the Pit, so that you will no longer be inhabited or display your splendor in the land of the living. 21 I will make you an object of

horror, and you will no longer exist. You will be sought but will never be found again." This is the declaration of the Lord GOD.

27 The word of the LORD came to me: ² "Now, son of man, lament for Tyre. ³ Say to Tyre, who is located at the entrance of the sea, merchant of the peoples to many coasts and islands: This is what the Lord GOD says:

Tyre, you declared:
I am perfect in beauty.
⁴ Your realm was in the heart
    of the sea;
your builders perfected
    your beauty.
⁵ They constructed all your planking
    with pine trees from Senir.
They took a cedar from Lebanon
to make a mast for you.
⁶ They made your oars of oaks
    from Bashan.
They made your deck
    of cypress wood
from the coasts of Cyprus,
inlaid with ivory.
⁷ Your sail was made of
fine embroidered linen from Egypt,
and served as your banner.
Your awning was of blue
    and purple fabric
from the coasts of Elishah.
⁸ The inhabitants of Sidon
    and Arvad
were your rowers.
Your wise men were
    within you, Tyre;
they were your helmsmen.
⁹ The elders of Gebal and its
    wise men
were within you,
    repairing your leaks.

All the ships of the sea
    and their sailors
came to you to barter
    for your goods.
¹⁰ Men of Persia, Lud, and Put
were in your army, serving
    as your warriors.
They hung shields and helmets
    in you;

they gave you splendor.
¹¹ Men of Arvad and Helech
were stationed on your walls
    all around,
and Gamadites were
    in your towers.
They hung their shields all around
    your walls;
they perfected your beauty.

¹² "Tarshish was your trading partner because of your great wealth of every kind. They exchanged silver, iron, tin, and lead for your merchandise. ¹³ Javan, Tubal, and Meshech were your merchants. They exchanged slaves and bronze utensils for your goods. ¹⁴ Those from Beth-togarmah exchanged horses, war horses, and mules for your merchandise. ¹⁵ Men of Dedan were also your merchants; many coasts and islands were your regular markets. They brought back ivory tusks and ebony as your payment. ¹⁶ Aram was your trading partner because of your numerous products. They exchanged turquoise, purple and embroidered cloth, fine linen, coral, and rubies for your merchandise. ¹⁷ Judah and the land of Israel were your merchants. They exchanged wheat from Minnith, meal, honey, oil, and balm for your goods. ¹⁸ Damascus was also your trading partner because of your numerous products and your great wealth of every kind, trading in wine from Helbon and white wool. ¹⁹ Vedan and Javan from Uzal dealt in your merchandise; wrought iron, cassia, and aromatic cane were exchanged for your goods. ²⁰ Dedan was your merchant in saddlecloths for riding. ²¹ Arabia and all the princes of Kedar were your business partners, trading with you in lambs, rams, and goats. ²² The merchants of Sheba and Raamah traded with you. They exchanged gold, the best of all spices, and all kinds of precious stones for your merchandise. ²³ Haran, Canneh, Eden, the merchants of Sheba, Asshur, and Chilmad traded with you. ²⁴ They were your merchants in choice garments, cloaks of blue and embroidered materials, and multicolored carpets, which were bound and secured with

cords in your marketplace. ²⁵ Ships of Tarshish were the carriers for your goods.

> So you became full
> and heavily loaded
> in the heart of the sea.
> ²⁶ Your rowers have brought you
> onto the high seas,
> but the east wind
> has shattered you
> in the heart of the sea.
> ²⁷ Your wealth, merchandise,
> and goods,
> your sailors and helmsmen,
> those who repair your leaks,
> those who barter for your goods,
> and all the warriors within you,
> with all the other people
> on board,
> sink into the heart of the sea
> on the day of your downfall.

²⁸ The countryside shakes
at the sound of your sailors' cries.
²⁹ All those who handle an oar
disembark from their ships.
The sailors and all the helmsmen
of the sea
stand on the shore.
³⁰ They raise their voices over you
and cry out bitterly.
They throw dust on their heads;
they roll in ashes.
³¹ They shave their heads
because of you
and wrap themselves in sackcloth.
They weep over you
with deep anguish
and bitter mourning.

³² In their wailing they lament
for you,
mourning over you:
Who was like Tyre,
silenced in the middle of the sea?
³³ When your merchandise
was unloaded from the seas,
you satisfied many peoples.
You enriched the kings
of the earth
with your abundant wealth
and goods.
³⁴ Now you are shattered by the sea

in the depths of the waters;
your goods and the people
within you
have gone down.
³⁵ All the inhabitants of the coasts
and islands
are appalled at you.
Their kings shudder with fear;
their faces are contorted.
³⁶ Those who trade
among the peoples
hiss at you;
you have become an object
of horror
and will never exist again."

PSALM 130:1-8

¹ Out of the depths I call to You,
LORD!
² Lord, listen to my voice;
let Your ears be attentive
to my cry for help.

³ LORD, if You considered sins,
Lord, who could stand?
⁴ But with You there is forgiveness,
so that You may be revered.

⁵ I wait for the LORD; I wait,
and put my hope in His word.
⁶ I wait for the Lord
more than watchmen for the
morning—
more than watchmen for the
morning.

⁷ Israel, hope in the LORD.
For there is faithful love with the
LORD,
and with Him is redemption in
abundance.
⁸ And He will redeem Israel
from all its sins.

PROVERBS 28:12-14

¹² When the righteous triumph,
there is great rejoicing,
but when the wicked come to
power, people hide
themselves.

13 The one who conceals his sins will
   not prosper,
   but whoever confesses and
   renounces them will find
   mercy.

14 Happy is the one who is always
   reverent,
   but one who hardens his heart
   falls into trouble.

....

I *P*ETER I:1-21

1 Peter, an apostle of Jesus Christ:
   To the temporary residents of the
Dispersion in the provinces of Pontus,
Galatia, Cappadocia, Asia, and Bithynia,
chosen 2 according to the foreknowledge of God the Father and set apart by
the Spirit for obedience and for the
sprinkling with the blood of Jesus
Christ.
   May grace and peace be multiplied to
you.
   3 Blessed be the God and Father of
our Lord Jesus Christ. According to His
great mercy, He has given us a new
birth into a living hope through the resurrection of Jesus Christ from the dead,
4 and into an inheritance that is imperishable, uncorrupted, and unfading,
kept in heaven for you, 5 who are being
protected by God's power through faith
for a salvation that is ready to be revealed in the last time. 6 You rejoice in
this, though now for a short time you
have had to be distressed by various trials 7 so that the genuineness of your
faith—more valuable than gold, which
perishes though refined by fire—may
result in praise, glory, and honor at the
revelation of Jesus Christ. 8 You love
Him, though you have not seen Him.
And though not seeing Him now, you
believe in Him and rejoice with inex-

pressible and glorious joy, 9 because you
are receiving the goal of your faith, the
salvation of your souls.
   10 Concerning this salvation, the
prophets who prophesied about the
grace that would come to you searched
and carefully investigated. 11 They inquired into what time or what circumstances the Spirit of Christ within them
was indicating when He testified in advance to the messianic sufferings and
the glories that would follow. 12 It was
revealed to them that they were not
serving themselves but you concerning
things that have now been announced
to you through those who preached the
gospel to you by the Holy Spirit sent
from heaven. Angels desire to look into
these things.
   13 Therefore, get your minds ready
for action, being self-disciplined, and
set your hope completely on the grace
to be brought to you at the revelation of
Jesus Christ. 14 As obedient children, do
not be conformed to the desires of your
former ignorance 15 but, as the One who
called you is holy, you also are to be
holy in all your conduct; 16 for it is written, **Be holy, because I am holy.**
   17 And if you address as Father the
One who judges impartially based on
each one's work, you are to conduct
yourselves in reverence during this time
of temporary residence. 18 For you know
that you were redeemed from your
empty way of life inherited from the fathers, not with perishable things, like
silver or gold, 19 but with the precious
blood of Christ, like that of a lamb without defect or blemish. 20 He was destined before the foundation of the
world, but was revealed at the end of
the times for you 21 who through Him
are believers in God, who raised Him
from the dead and gave Him glory, so
that your faith and hope are in God.

Organizing a Quiet Time

I wait, and put my hope in His word.
I wait for the Lord more than watchmen for the morning.

—PSALM 130:5-6

Someone has described the morning quiet time as "turning the dial until we tune in to God's wavelength—then we get the message." But how do we gain the best results from our quiet time?

First, decide on the amount of time you want to invest in waiting before God. Next, take your Bible and read a portion slowly. Let it soak in. If some words or verses strike you, focus on them in meditation. They will yield up new meanings to you. Write these down.

After the reading, let go, relax, and say to Him: "Father, have You anything to say to me?" Learn to listen. All those who hear God's voice on a regular basis say that it is something they have had to develop over time and by experience. They pause, they wait, and they learn after a while to disentangle their own thoughts from what God is saying.

Then speak to God in prayer. And finally, thank Him for the answer. He always answers—whether it is "yes," "no," or "wait." His "no" is just as much an answer as His "yes"—sometimes even a better answer.

Not far from my home is the River Thames. Sometimes I walk along the riverbank and watch small boats entering the locks from the adjoining rivers. To get into the Thames, these boats must enter the lock and wait there to be lifted up to a higher level. Our quiet time does that. It shuts us in with God. But then infinite resources begin to bubble up from below, and we are lifted silently and without strain onto a higher level. The lifting is the result of being shut in with God.

Prayer

O Father, help me resolve to spend a quiet time with You every day. May my quiet time at this moment be the open door through which I glide out onto a higher level of life. In Jesus' name. Amen.

Further Study

Ps 130:1-8; 27:14; 37:7; 62:5; Is 30:18
What do we often find the hardest thing to do?
Take time out today to do this.

NOVEMBER 25

*E*ZEKIEL 28:1–30:8

28 The word of the LORD came to me:
² "Son of man, say to the ruler of Tyre: This is what the Lord GOD says:

> Your heart is proud,
> and you have said: I am a god;
> I sit in the seat of gods
> in the heart of the sea.
> Yet you are a man and not a god,
> though you have regarded
> your heart
> as that of a god.
> ³ Yes, you are wiser than Daniel;
> no secret is hidden from you!
> ⁴ By your wisdom
> and understanding
> you have acquired wealth
> for yourself.
> You have acquired gold and silver
> for your treasuries.
> ⁵ By your great skill in trading
> you have increased your wealth,
> but your heart has become proud
> because of your wealth."

⁶ Therefore this is what the Lord GOD says:

> Because you regard your heart
> as that of a god,
> ⁷ I am about to bring strangers
> against you,
> ruthless men from the nations.
> They will draw their swords
> against your magnificent wisdom
> and will defile your splendor.
> ⁸ They will bring you down to the
> Pit,
> and you will die a violent death
> in the heart of the sea.
> ⁹ Will you still say: I am a god,
> in the presence of those who kill
> you?
> Yet you will be shown to be
> a man, not a god,

> in the hands of those
> who kill you.
> ¹⁰ You will die the death
> of the uncircumcised
> at the hands of strangers.
> For I have spoken.
>> This is the declaration
>> of the Lord GOD.

¹¹ The word of the LORD came to me:
¹² "Son of man, lament for the king of Tyre and say to him: This is what the Lord GOD says:

> You were the seal of perfection,
> full of wisdom and perfect
> in beauty.
> ¹³ You were in Eden, the garden
> of God.
> Every kind of precious stone
> covered you:
> carnelian, topaz, and diamond,
> beryl, onyx, and jasper,
> sapphire, turquoise and emerald.
> Your mountings and settings
> were crafted in gold;
> they were prepared on the day
> you were created.
> ¹⁴ You were an anointed
> guardian cherub,
> for I had appointed you.
> You were on the holy mountain
> of God;
> you walked among
> the fiery stones.
> ¹⁵ From the day you were created
> you were blameless in your ways
> until wickedness was found in you.
> ¹⁶ Through the abundance
> of your trade,
> you were filled with violence,
> and you sinned.
> So I expelled you in disgrace
> from the mountain of God,
> and banished you,
> guardian cherub,
> from among the fiery stones.

17 Your heart became proud
     because of your beauty;
For the sake of your splendor
     you corrupted your wisdom.
So I threw you down to the earth;
     I made a spectacle of you
          before kings.
18 You profaned your sanctuaries
     by the magnitude
          of your iniquities
     in your dishonest trade.
So I sent out fire from within you,
     and it consumed you.
I reduced you to ashes
     on the ground
     in the sight of everyone
          watching you.
19 All those who know you
     among the nations
     are appalled at you.
You have become an object
     of horror
and will never exist again."

20 The word of the LORD came to me:
21 "Son of man, turn your face toward
Sidon and prophesy against it. 22 You are
to say: This is what the Lord GOD says:

     Look! I am against you, Sidon,
     and I will display My glory
          within you.
     They will know that I am the LORD
     when I execute judgments
          against her
     and demonstrate My holiness
          through her.
23 I will send a plague against her
     and bloodshed in her streets;
     the slain will fall within her,
     while the sword is against her
          on every side.
     Then they will know that
          I am the LORD.

24 "The house of Israel will no longer
be hurt by prickling briers or painful
thorns from all their neighbors who
treat them with contempt. Then they
will know that I am the Lord GOD.
25 "This is what the Lord GOD says:
When I gather the house of Israel from
the peoples where they are scattered
and demonstrate My holiness through

them in the sight of the nations, then
they will live in their own land, which I
gave to My servant Jacob. 26 They will
live there securely, build houses, and
plant vineyards. They will live securely
when I execute judgments against all
their neighbors who treat them with
contempt. Then they will know that I
am the LORD their God."

29 In the tenth year, in the tenth
month on the twelfth day of the
month, the word of the LORD came to
me: 2 "Son of man, turn your face toward Pharaoh king of Egypt and prophesy against him and against all of Egypt.
3 Speak to him and say: This is what the
Lord GOD says:

     Look, I am against you, Pharaoh
          king of Egypt,
     the great monster lying
          in the middle of his Nile,
     who says: My Nile is my own;
     I made it for myself.
4   I will put hooks in your jaws
     and make the fish of your streams
          cling to your scales.
     I will haul you up
     from the middle of your Nile,
     and all the fish of your streams
          will cling to your scales.
5   I will leave you in the desert,
     you and all the fish
          of your streams.
     You will fall on the open ground
     and will not be taken away
          or gathered for burial.
     I have given you
     to the beasts of the earth
     and the birds of the sky as food.

6   Then all the inhabitants of Egypt
     will know that I am the LORD,
     for they have been a staff made
          of reed
     to the house of Israel.
7   When Israel grasped you
          by the hand,
     you splintered, tearing all
          their shoulders;
     when they leaned on you,
     you shattered and made all
          their hips unsteady.

8 "Therefore this is what the Lord GOD says: I am going to bring a sword against you and wipe out man and animal from you. 9 The land of Egypt will be a desolate ruin. Then they will know that I am the LORD. Because you said: The Nile is my own; I made it, 10 therefore, I am against you and your Nile. I will turn the land of Egypt into ruins, a desolate waste from Migdol to Syene, as far as the border of Cush. 11 No human foot will pass through it, and no animal foot will pass through it. It will be uninhabited for 40 years. 12 I will make the land of Egypt a desolation among desolate lands, and its cities will be a desolation among ruined cities for 40 years. I will disperse the Egyptians among the nations and scatter them across the countries.

13 "For this is what the Lord GOD says: At the end of 40 years I will gather the Egyptians from the nations where they were dispersed. 14 I will restore the fortunes of Egypt and bring them back to the land of Pathros, the land of their origin. There they will be a lowly kingdom. 15 Egypt will be the lowliest of kingdoms and will never again exalt itself over the nations. I will make them so small they cannot rule over the nations. 16 It will never again be an object of trust for the house of Israel, drawing attention to their sin of turning to the Egyptians. Then they will know that I am the Lord GOD."

17 In the twenty-seventh year in the first month, on the first day of the month, the word of the LORD came to me: 18 "Son of man, Nebuchadnezzar king of Babylon made his army labor strenuously against Tyre. Every head was made bald and every shoulder chafed, but he and his army received no compensation from Tyre for the labor he expended against it. 19 Therefore this is what the Lord GOD says: I am going to give the land of Egypt to Nebuchadnezzar king of Babylon, who will carry off its wealth, seizing its spoil and taking its plunder. This will be his army's compensation. 20 I have given him the land of Egypt as the pay he labored for, since they worked for Me." This is the

declaration of the Lord GOD. 21 "In that day I will cause a horn to sprout for the house of Israel, and I will enable you to speak out among them. Then they will know that I am the LORD."

30 The word of the LORD came to me: 2 "Son of man, prophesy and say: This is what the Lord GOD says:

Wail: Alas for the day!
3 For a day is near;
a day belonging to the LORD is near.
It will be a day of clouds,
a time of doom for the nations.
4 A sword will come against Egypt,
and there will be anguish in Cush
when the slain fall in Egypt,
and its wealth is taken away,
and its foundations are torn down.
5 Cush, Put, and Lud,
and all the various foreign troops,
plus Libya and the men
of the covenant land
will fall by the sword
along with them.
6 This is what the LORD says:
Those who support Egypt will fall,
and its proud strength will collapse.
From Migdol to Syene
they will fall within it
by the sword.
This is the declaration
of the Lord GOD.
7 They will be desolate
among desolate lands,
and their cities will lie
among ruined cities.
8 They will know that I am the LORD
when I set fire to Egypt
and all its allies are shattered.

ℙSALM 131:1–132:5

1 LORD, my heart is not proud; my
eyes are not haughty.
I do not get involved with things
too great or too difficult
for me.
2 Instead, I have calmed and
quieted myself
like a little weaned child with its
mother;

I am like a little child.

3 Israel, hope in the LORD,
both now and forever.

1 LORD, remember David
and all the hardships he endured,
2 and how he swore an oath to the
LORD,
making a vow to the Mighty One
of Jacob:
3 "I will not enter my house
or get into my bed,
4 I will not allow my eyes to sleep
or my eyelids to slumber
5 until I find a place for the LORD,
a dwelling for the Mighty One of
Jacob."

PROVERBS 28:15-18

15 A wicked ruler over a helpless
people
is like a roaring lion or a charging
bear.

16 A leader who lacks understanding
is very oppressive,
but one who hates unjust gain
prolongs his life.

17 A man burdened by bloodguilt
will be a fugitive until death.
Let no one help him.

18 The one who lives with integrity
will be helped,
but one who distorts right and
wrong will suddenly fall.

1 PETER 1:22–2:17

22 By obedience to the truth, having
purified yourselves for sincere love of
the brothers, love one another earnestly from a pure heart, 23 since you have
been born again—not of perishable
seed but of imperishable—through the
living and enduring word of God. 24 For

All flesh is like grass,
and all its glory like a flower of
the grass.

The grass withers, and the
flower drops off,
25 but the word of the Lord
endures forever.

And this is the word that was preached
as the gospel to you.

2 So rid yourselves of all wickedness,
all deceit, hypocrisy, envy, and all
slander. 2 Like newborn infants, desire
the unadulterated spiritual milk, so that
you may grow by it in your salvation,
3 since you have tasted that the Lord is
good. 4 Coming to Him, a living stone—
rejected by men but chosen and valuable to God— 5 you yourselves, as living
stones, are being built into a spiritual
house for a holy priesthood to offer spiritual sacrifices acceptable to God through
Jesus Christ. 6 For it stands in Scripture:

Look! I lay a stone in Zion,
a chosen and valuable
cornerstone,
and the one who believes in Him
will never be put to shame!

7 So the honor is for you who believe;
but for the unbelieving,

The stone that the builders
rejected—
this One has become the
cornerstone,

and

8 A stone that causes men to
stumble,
and a rock that trips them up.

They stumble by disobeying the message; they were destined for this.

9 But you are a chosen race,
a royal priesthood,
a holy nation, a people for His
possession,
so that you may proclaim the
praises
of the One who called you out of
darkness
into His marvelous light.

¹⁰ Once you were not a people,
but now you are God's people;
you had not received mercy,
but now you have received
mercy.

¹¹ Dear friends, I urge you as aliens and temporary residents to abstain from fleshly desires that war against you. ¹² Conduct yourselves honorably among the Gentiles, so that in a case where they speak against you as those who do evil, they may, by observing your good works, glorify God in a day of visitation. ¹³ Submit to every human institution because of the Lord, whether to the Emperor as the supreme authority, ¹⁴ or to governors as those sent out by him to punish those who do evil and to praise those who do good. ¹⁵ For it is God's will that you, by doing good, silence the ignorance of foolish people. ¹⁶ As God's slaves, live as free people, but don't use your freedom as a way to conceal evil. ¹⁷ Honor everyone. Love the brotherhood. Fear God. Honor the Emperor.

The Devil's Cleft Foot

*You were the seal of perfection, full of wisdom and perfect in beauty. . . .
From the day you were created you were blameless in your ways.*
—EZEKIEL 28:12,15

New Christians often ask: just who is the Devil, and where did he come from? The seventeenth century poet John Donne wrote that there were two things he could not fathom: "Where all the past years are, and who cleft the Devil's foot." The origin, existence, and activities of the Devil have always been among man's most puzzling problems. The books of Isaiah and Ezekiel give us a very clear picture, however, of what someone has called "The Rise and Fall of the Satanic Empire."

Jesus said one day to His disciples: "I watched Satan fall from heaven like a lightning flash" (Lk 10:18). Before he was known as the Devil, Satan was called Lucifer and was created as a perfect angelic being. The passages before us today show him to have been a beautiful and morally perfect being. "You were the seal of perfection, full of wisdom and perfect in beauty. . . . From the day you were created you were blameless in your ways" (Ezk 28:12,15).

Upright, beautiful, brilliant, and with an enormous capacity for achievement, the angel Lucifer was entrusted by God with the highest of all the offices in the interstellar universe: "You were an anointed guardian cherub . . . You were on the holy mountain of God" (Ezk 28:14). In his heart, however, arose a rebellious thought: "I will make myself like the Most High" (Is 14:14). Five times that phrase "I will" is used in this passage. Those two little words— "I will"—reveal what lies behind the awful blight of sin—a created will coming into conflict with the will of the Creator.

Prayer

O Father, now that I see the real issue that lies behind sin—a created will colliding with the will of the Creator—help me constantly to align my will with Your will. In Jesus' name I ask it. Amen.

Further Study

Pr 16:1-18; 26:12; 3:7
What comes before a fall?
What attitude should we guard against?

NOVEMBER 26

*E*ZEKIEL 30:9–32:16

⁹ On that day, messengers will go out from Me in ships to terrify confident Cush. Anguish will come over them on the day of Egypt's doom. For indeed it is coming."

¹⁰ This is what the Lord GOD says:

I will put an end to the hordes
   of Egypt
by the hand of Nebuchadnezzar
   king of Babylon.
¹¹ He along with his people,
   ruthless men from the nations,
will be brought in to destroy
   the land.
They will draw their swords
   against Egypt
and fill the land with the slain.
¹² I will make the streams dry
and sell the land into the hands
   of evil men.
I will bring desolation
on the land and everything in it
by the hands of foreigners.
I, the LORD, have spoken.

¹³ This is what the Lord GOD says:

I will destroy the idols and put
   an end
to the false gods in Memphis.
There will no longer be
a prince from the land of Egypt.
So I will instill fear in that land.
¹⁴ I will make Pathros desolate,

set fire to Zoan,
and execute judgments on Thebes.
¹⁵ I will pour out My wrath
   on Pelusium,
the stronghold of Egypt,
and will wipe out the crowds
   of Thebes.
¹⁶ I will set fire to Egypt;
Pelusium will writhe in anguish,
Thebes will be breached,
and Memphis will face foes
   in broad daylight.
¹⁷ The young men of On
   and Pi-beseth
will fall by the sword,
and those cities will go
   into captivity.
¹⁸ The day will be dark
   in Tehaphnehes,
when I break the yoke
   of Egypt there
and its proud strength
comes to an end in the city.
A cloud will cover Tehaphnehes,
and its villages will go
   into captivity.
¹⁹ So I will execute judgments
   against Egypt,
and they will know that
   I am the LORD.

²⁰ In the eleventh year, in the first month, on the seventh day of the month, the word of the LORD came to me: ²¹ "Son of man, I have broken the arm of Pharaoh king of Egypt. Look, it has not been bandaged—no medicine

has been applied and no splint put on to bandage it so that it can grow strong enough to handle a sword. ²² Therefore this is what the Lord GOD says: Look! I am against Pharaoh king of Egypt. I will break his arms, both the strong one and the one already broken, and will make the sword fall from his hand. ²³ I will disperse the Egyptians among the nations and scatter them among the countries. ²⁴ I will strengthen the arms of Babylon's king and place My sword in his hand. But I will break the arms of Pharaoh, and he will groan before him as a mortally wounded man. ²⁵ I will strengthen the arms of Babylon's king, but Pharaoh's arms will fall. They will know that I am the LORD when I place My sword in the hand of Babylon's king and he wields it against the land of Egypt. ²⁶ When I disperse the Egyptians among the nations and scatter them among the countries, they will know that I am the LORD."

31 In the eleventh year, in the third month, on the first day of the month, the word of the LORD came to me: ² "Son of man, say to Pharaoh king of Egypt and to his hordes:

Who are you like in your greatness?
³ Think of Assyria, a cedar
    in Lebanon,
with beautiful branches
    and shady foliage,
and of lofty height.
Its top was among the clouds.
⁴ The waters caused it to grow;
the underground springs
    made it tall,
directing their rivers all around
the place where the tree
    was planted
and sending their channels
to all the trees of the field.
⁵ Therefore the cedar
    became greater in height
than all the trees of the field.
Its branches multiplied,
and its boughs grew long
as it spread them out
because of the plentiful water.
⁶ All the birds of the sky

nested in its branches,
and all the animals of the field
gave birth beneath its boughs;
all the great nations lived
    in its shade.
⁷ It was beautiful in its greatness,
in the length of its limbs,
for its roots extended
    to abundant water.
⁸ The cedars in God's garden
    could not rival it;
the pine trees couldn't compare
    with its branches,
nor could the plane trees match
    its boughs.
No tree in the garden of God
could compare with it in beauty.
⁹ I made it beautiful with its
    many limbs,
and all the trees of Eden,
which were in God's garden,
    envied it.

¹⁰ "Therefore this is what the Lord GOD says: Since it became great in height and set its top among the clouds, and it grew proud on account of its height, ¹¹ I determined to hand it over to a ruler of nations; he would surely deal with it. I banished it because of its wickedness. ¹² Foreigners, ruthless men from the nations, cut it down and left it lying. Its limbs fell on the mountains and in every valley; its boughs lay broken in all the earth's ravines. All the peoples of the earth left its shade and abandoned it. ¹³ All the birds of the sky nested on its fallen trunk, and all the animals of the field were among its boughs. ¹⁴ This happened so that no trees planted beside water would become great in height and set their tops among the clouds, and so that no other well-watered trees would reach them in height. For they have all been consigned to death, to the underworld, among the people who descend to the Pit.

¹⁵ "This is what the Lord GOD says: I caused grieving on the day the cedar went down to Sheol. I closed off the underground deep because of it: I held back the rivers of the deep, and its abundant waters were restrained. I made Lebanon mourn on account of it,

and all the trees of the field fainted because of it. ¹⁶ I made the nations quake at the sound of its downfall, when I threw it down to Sheol to be with those who descend to the Pit. Then all the trees of Eden, all the well-watered trees, the choice and best of Lebanon, were comforted in the underworld. ¹⁷ They too descended with it to Sheol, to those slain by the sword. As its allies they had lived in its shade among the nations.

¹⁸ "Who then are you like in glory and greatness among Eden's trees? You also will be brought down to the underworld to be with the trees of Eden. You will lie among the uncircumcised with those slain by the sword. This is Pharaoh and all his hordes"—the declaration of the Lord GOD.

32

In the twelfth year, in the twelfth month, on the first day of the month, the word of the LORD came to me: ² "Son of man, lament for Pharaoh king of Egypt and say to him:

You compare yourself to a lion
of the nations,
but you are like a monster
in the seas.
You thrash about in your rivers,
churn up the waters
with your feet,
and muddy the rivers."

³ This is what the Lord GOD says:

I will spread My net over you
with an assembly of many peoples,
and they will haul you up
in My net.
⁴ I will abandon you on the land
and hurl you on the open field.
I will cause all the birds of the sky
to settle on you
and let the beasts
of the entire earth
eat their fill of you.
⁵ I will put your flesh
on the mountains
and fill the valleys
with your carcass.
⁶ I will drench the land

with the flow of your blood,
even to the mountains;
the ravines will be filled
with your gore.
⁷ When I snuff you out,
I will cover the heavens
and darken their stars.
I will cover the sun with a cloud,
and the moon will not give
its light.
⁸ I will darken all the shining lights
in the heavens over you,
and will bring darkness
on your land.
This is the declaration
of the Lord GOD.
⁹ I will trouble the hearts
of many peoples,
when I bring about
your destruction
among the nations,
in countries you do not know.
¹⁰ I will cause many nations
to be appalled at you,
and their kings will shudder
with fear because of you
when I brandish My sword
in front of them.
On the day of your downfall
each of them will tremble
every moment for his life.

¹¹ For this is what the Lord GOD says:

The sword of Babylon's king
will come against you!
¹² I will make your hordes fall
by the swords of warriors,
all of them ruthless men
from the nations.
They will ravage Egypt's pride,
and all its hordes
will be destroyed.
¹³ I will slaughter all its cattle
that are beside many waters.
No human foot
will churn them again,
and no cattle hooves
will disturb them.
¹⁴ Then I will let their waters settle
and will make their rivers flow
like oil.

This is the declaration of the Lord GOD.
15 When I make the land of Egypt
a desolation,
so that it is emptied of everything in it,
when I strike down all
who live there,
then they will know that
I am the LORD.

16 "This is a lament that will be chanted; the women of the nations will chant it. They will chant it over Egypt and all its hordes." This is the declaration of the Lord GOD.

PSALM 132:6-12

6 We heard of the ark in Ephrathah;
we found it in the fields of Jaar.
7 Let us go to His dwelling place;
let us worship at His footstool.
8 Arise, LORD, come to Your resting place,
You and the ark that shows Your strength.
9 May Your priests be clothed with righteousness,
and may Your godly people shout for joy.
10 Because of Your servant David,
do not reject Your anointed one.

11 The LORD swore an oath to David,
a promise He will not abandon:
"I will set one of your
descendants on your throne.
12 If your sons keep My covenant
and My decrees that I will teach them,
their sons will also sit on your throne, forever."

PROVERBS 28:19-22

19 The one who works his land will
have plenty of food,
but whoever chases fantasies will
have his fill of poverty.

20 A faithful man will have many blessings,
but one in a hurry to get rich will not go unpunished.

21 It is not good to show partiality—
yet a man may sin for a piece of bread.

22 A greedy man is in a hurry for wealth;
he doesn't know that poverty will come to him.

I PETER 2:18–3:12

18 Household slaves, submit yourselves to your masters with all respect, not only to the good and gentle but also to the cruel. 19 For it brings favor if, because of conscience toward God, someone endures grief from suffering unjustly. 20 For what credit is there if you endure when you sin and are beaten? But when you do good and suffer, if you endure, it brings favor with God.

21 For you were called to this,
because Christ also suffered for you,
leaving you an example,
so that you should follow in His steps.
22 He did not commit sin,
and no deceit was found in His mouth;
23 when reviled, He did not revile in return;
when suffering, He did not threaten,
but committed Himself to the One who judges justly.
24 He Himself bore our sins
in His body on the tree,
so that, having died to sins,
we might live for righteousness;
by His wounding you have been healed.
25 For you were like sheep going astray,
but you have now returned
to the shepherd and guardian of your souls.

3 Wives, in the same way, submit yourselves to your own husbands so that, even if some disobey the Christian message, they may be won over without a message by the way their wives live, ² when they observe your pure, reverent lives. ³ Your beauty should not consist of outward things like elaborate hairstyles and the wearing of gold ornaments or fine clothes; ⁴ instead, it should consist of the hidden person of the heart with the imperishable quality of a gentle and quiet spirit, which is very valuable in God's eyes. ⁵ For in the past, the holy women who hoped in God also beautified themselves in this way, submitting to their own husbands, ⁶ just as Sarah obeyed Abraham, calling him lord. You have become her children when you do good and aren't frightened by anything alarming.

⁷ Husbands, in the same way, live with your wives with understanding of their weaker nature yet showing them honor as co-heirs of the grace of life, so that your prayers will not be hindered.

⁸ Now finally, all of you should be likeminded and sympathetic, should love believers, and be compassionate and humble, ⁹ not paying back evil for evil or insult for insult but, on the contrary, giving a blessing, since you were called for this, so that you can inherit a blessing.

¹⁰ For the one who wants to love life
and to see good days
must keep his tongue from evil
and his lips from speaking deceit,
¹¹ and he must turn away from evil
and do good.
He must seek peace and pursue it,
¹² because the eyes of the Lord
are on the righteous
and His ears are open
to their request.
But the face of the Lord is
against those who do evil.

The Breastplate

May Your priests be clothed with righteousness, and may Your godly people shout for joy.—PSALM 132:9

The second piece of armor with which we are to defend ourselves against the tactics of the Devil is the breastplate of righteousness.

A soldier's breastplate generally extended from the base of the neck to the upper part of the thighs so it would cover many important parts of the body, in particular the heart. Some commentators think that the word breastplate suggests that this piece of equipment covered only the front of the chest and thus gave no protection for the back. They deduce from this that a Christian should face the Devil and never turn his back on him, or else he will expose a part that is unguarded. It is an interesting idea, but it must not be given too much credence, for the soldier's breastplate often covered his back as well as his front.

What spiritual lesson can we draw from the "breastplate of righteousness"? Most commentators believe that because the soldier's breastplate primarily covered his heart, the spiritual application of this is that in Christ we have all the protection we need against negative or desolating feelings—the heart being seen as the focal point of the emotions.

What an exciting thought: by putting on the breastplate of righteousness, we have the spiritual resources to deal with all those debilitating feelings that tend to bring us down into despair—unworthiness, inadequacy, fear, and so on. When I mentioned this to a friend who asked me what I thought the breastplate of righteousness was for, he said: "It sounds too good to be true." I replied: "It's too good not to be true."

NOVEMBER 27

*E*ZEKIEL 32:17–33:33

¹⁷ In the twelfth year, on the fifteenth day of the month, the word of the LORD came to me: ¹⁸ "Son of man, wail over the hordes of Egypt and bring Egypt and the daughters of mighty nations down to the underworld, to be with those who descend to the Pit:

¹⁹ Whom do you surpass in loveliness?
Go down and be laid to rest
with the uncircumcised!
²⁰ They will fall among those slain
by the sword.
A sword is appointed!
They drag her and all
her hordes away.
²¹ Warrior leaders will speak
from the middle of Sheol
about him and his allies:
They have come down;
the uncircumcised lie
slain by the sword.

²² Assyria is there with all
her company;
her graves are all around her.

All of them are slain, fallen
by the sword.
²³ Her graves are set
in the deepest regions
of the Pit,
and her company is all around
her burial place.
All of them are slain, fallen
by the sword—
they who once spread terror
in the land of the living.

²⁴ Elam is there
with all her hordes
around her grave.
All of them are slain, fallen
by the sword—
they who went down
to the underworld
uncircumcised,
who once spread their terror
in the land of the living.
They bear their disgrace
with those who descend
to the Pit.
²⁵ Among the slain
they prepare a resting place
for Elam
with all her hordes.

Her graves are all around her.
All of them are uncircumcised,
slain by the sword,
although their terror was once
spread
in the land of the living.
They bear their disgrace
with those who descend
to the Pit.
They are placed among the slain.

26 Meshech and Tubal are there,
with all their hordes.
Their graves are all around them.
All of them are uncircumcised,
slain by the sword,
although their terror was once
spread
in the land of the living.
27 They do not lie down
with the fallen warriors
of the uncircumcised,
who went down to Sheol
with their weapons of war,
whose swords were placed
under their heads.
The punishment for their sins
rested on their bones,
although the terror of these
warriors
was once in the land
of the living.
28 But you will be shattered
and will lie down
among the uncircumcised,
with those slain by the sword.

29 Edom is there, her kings and all
her princes,
who, despite their strength,
have been placed
among those slain by the sword.
They lie down
with the uncircumcised,
with those who descend
to the Pit.
30 All the leaders of the north
and all the Sidonians are there.
They went down in shame
with the slain,
despite the terror
their strength inspired.
They lie down uncircumcised
with those slain by the sword.

They bear their disgrace
with those who descend to the Pit.

31 Pharaoh will see them
and be comforted over all
his hordes—
Pharaoh and all his army,
slain by the sword.
This is the declaration
of the Lord GOD.

32 For I will spread My terror
in the land of the living,
so Pharaoh and all his hordes
will be laid to rest
among the uncircumcised,
with those slain by the sword."
This is the declaration
of the Lord GOD.

33 The word of the LORD came to me: 2 "Son of man, speak to your people and tell them: Suppose I bring the sword against a land, and the people of that land select a man from among them, appointing him as their watchman, 3 and he sees the sword coming against the land and blows his trumpet to warn the people. 4 Then, if anyone hears the sound of the trumpet but ignores the warning, and the sword comes and takes him away, his blood will be on his own head. 5 Since he heard the sound of the trumpet but ignored the warning, his blood is on his own hands. If he had taken warning, he would have saved his life. 6 However, if the watchman sees the sword coming but doesn't blow the trumpet, so that the people aren't warned, and the sword comes and takes away their lives, then they have been taken away because of their iniquity, but I will hold the watchman accountable for their blood.

7 "As for you, son of man, I have made you a watchman for the house of Israel. When you hear a word from My mouth, give them a warning from Me. 8 If I say to the wicked: Wicked one, you will surely die, but you do not speak out to warn him about his way, that wicked person will die for his iniquity, yet I will hold you responsible for his blood. 9 But if you warn a wicked person to turn

from his way and he doesn't turn from it, he will die for his iniquity, but you will have saved your life.

¹⁰ "Now as for you, son of man, say to the house of Israel: You have said this: Our transgressions and our sins are heavy on us, and we are wasting away because of them! How then can we survive? ¹¹ Tell them: As I live"—the declaration of the Lord GOD—"I take no pleasure in the death of the wicked, but rather that the wicked person should turn from his way and live. Repent, repent of your evil ways! Why will you die, house of Israel?

¹² "Now, son of man, say to your people: The righteousness of the righteous person will not save him on the day of his transgression; neither will the wickedness of the wicked person cause him to stumble on the day he turns from his wickedness. The righteous person won't be able to survive by his righteousness on the day he sins. ¹³ When I tell the righteous person that he will surely live, but he trusts in his righteousness and commits iniquity, then none of his righteousness will be remembered, and he will die because of the iniquity he has committed.

¹⁴ "So when I tell the wicked person: You will surely die, but he repents of his sin and does what is just and right— ¹⁵ he returns collateral, makes restitution for what he has stolen, and walks in the statutes of life without practicing iniquity—he will certainly live; he will not die. ¹⁶ None of the sins he committed will be held against him. He has done what is just and right; he will certainly live.

¹⁷ "But your people say: The Lord's way isn't fair, even though it is their own way that isn't fair. ¹⁸ When a righteous person turns from his righteousness and commits iniquity, he will die on account of this. ¹⁹ But when a wicked person turns from his wickedness and does what is just and right, he will live because of this. ²⁰ Yet you say: The Lord's way isn't fair. I will judge each of you according to his ways, house of Israel."

²¹ In the twelfth year of our exile, in the tenth month, on the fifth day of the month, a fugitive from Jerusalem came to me and reported, "The city has been taken!" ²² Now the hand of the LORD had been on me the evening before the fugitive arrived, and He opened my mouth before the man came to me in the morning. So my mouth was opened and I was no longer mute.

²³ Then the word of the LORD came to me: ²⁴ "Son of man, those who live in the ruins in the land of Israel are saying: Abraham was only one person, yet he received possession of the land. But we are many; the land has been given to us as a possession. ²⁵ Therefore say to them: This is what the Lord GOD says: You eat meat with blood in it, raise your eyes to your idols, and shed blood. Should you then receive possession of the land? ²⁶ You have relied on your swords, you have committed abominations, and each of you has defiled his neighbor's wife. Should you then receive possession of the land?

²⁷ "Tell them this: This is what the Lord GOD says: As surely as I live, those who are in the ruins will fall by the sword, those in the open field I have given to wild animals to be devoured, and those in the strongholds and caves will die by plague. ²⁸ I will make the land a desolate waste, and its proud strength will come to an end. The mountains of Israel will become desolate, with no one passing through. ²⁹ They will know that I am the LORD when I make the land a desolate waste because of all the abominations they have committed.

³⁰ "Now, son of man, your people are talking about you near the city walls and in the doorways of their houses. One person speaks to another, each saying to his brother: Come and hear what the message is that comes from the LORD! ³¹ So My people come to you in crowds, sit in front of you, and hear your words, but they don't obey them. Although they express love with their mouths, their hearts pursue unjust gain. ³² Yes, to them you are like a singer of love songs who has a beautiful voice and plays skillfully on an instrument. They hear your words, but they don't obey

them. ³³ Yet when it comes—and it will definitely come—then they will know that a prophet has been among them."

PSALM 132:13-18

¹³ For the LORD has chosen Zion;
He has desired it for His home:
¹⁴ "This is My resting place forever;
I will make My home here
because I have desired it.
¹⁵ I will abundantly bless its food;
I will satisfy its needy with bread.
¹⁶ I will clothe its priests with
salvation,
and its godly people will shout for
joy.
¹⁷ There I will make a horn grow for
David;
I have prepared a lamp for My
anointed one.
¹⁸ I will clothe his enemies with
shame,
but the crown he wears will be
glorious."

PROVERBS 28:23-25

²³ One who rebukes a person will
later find more favor
than one who flatters with his
tongue.

²⁴ The one who robs his father or
mother and says, "That's no
sin,"
is a companion to a man who
destroys.

²⁵ A greedy person provokes conflict,
but whoever trusts in the LORD
will prosper.

1 PETER 3:13–4:11

¹³ And who will harm you if you are passionate for what is good? ¹⁴ But even if you should suffer for righteousness, you are blessed. **Do not fear what they fear or be disturbed,** ¹⁵ but set apart the Messiah as Lord in your hearts, and always be ready to give a defense to anyone who asks you for a reason for the hope that is in you. ¹⁶ However, do this with gentleness and respect, keeping your conscience clear, so that when you are accused, those who denounce your Christian life will be put to shame. ¹⁷ For it is better to suffer for doing good, if that should be God's will, than for doing evil.

¹⁸ For Christ also suffered for sins
once for all,
the righteous for the unrighteous,
that He might bring you to God,
after being put to death in the
fleshly realm
but made alive in the spiritual
realm.

¹⁹ In that state He also went and made a proclamation to the spirits in prison ²⁰ who in the past were disobedient, when God patiently waited in the days of Noah while an ark was being prepared; in it, a few—that is, eight people —were saved through water. ²¹ Baptism, which corresponds to this, now saves you (not the removal of the filth of the flesh, but the pledge of a good conscience toward God) through the resurrection of Jesus Christ. ²² Now that He has gone into heaven, He is at God's right hand, with angels, authorities, and powers subjected to Him.

4 Therefore, since Christ suffered in the flesh, arm yourselves also with the same resolve—because the One who suffered in the flesh has finished with sin— ² in order to live the remaining time in the flesh, no longer for human desires, but for God's will. ³ For there has already been enough time spent in doing the will of the pagans: carrying on in unrestrained behavior, evil desires, drunkenness, orgies, carousing, and lawless idolatry. ⁴ In regard to this, they are surprised that you don't plunge with them into the same flood of dissipation—and they slander you. ⁵ They will give an account to the One who stands ready to judge the living and the dead. ⁶ For this reason the gospel was also preached to those who are now dead, so that, although they might

be judged by men in the fleshly realm, they might live by God in the spiritual realm.

⁷ Now the end of all things is near; therefore, be clear-headed and disciplined for prayer. ⁸ Above all, keep your love for one another at full strength, since love covers a multitude of sins. ⁹ Be hospitable to one another without complaining. ¹⁰ Based on the gift they have received, everyone should use it to serve others, as good managers of the varied grace of God. ¹¹ If anyone speaks, his speech should be like the oracles of God; if anyone serves, his service should be from the strength God provides, so that in everything God may be glorified through Jesus Christ. To Him belong the glory and the power forever and ever. Amen.

The Dividing Line

After being put to death in the fleshly realm but made alive in the spiritual realm.—1 PETER 3:18

It was the Holy Spirit who transformed the early disciples from timid and disconsolate men into ones who were ablaze and invincible.

If you draw a line through the pages of the New Testament, you will find on one side a good deal of spiritual staleness while on the other an abundance of spiritual freshness. That line runs straight through an upper room where a group of people waited in simple confidence for the promise their Master had made to them to be fulfilled. We read in Acts 2:4: "They were all filled with the Holy Spirit." That filling was the dividing line in the moral and spiritual development of humanity. It marked a new era—the era of the Holy Spirit.

On the other side of that dividing line, prior to Pentecost, the disciples were spasmodic in their allegiance and achievements. Sometimes they could rejoice that evil spirits were subject to them, and sometimes they had to ask, "Why could we not cast it out?" Sometimes they appeared ready to go to death with Jesus, and sometimes they quarreled over who should have first place in His kingdom. Simon Peter could whip out a sword and cut off the ear of the high priest's servant and then quail before the gaze of a serving maid.

Then came Pentecost. A divine reinforcement took place. They were new men doing new work—no longer spasmodic, but stable. On which side of that dividing line are you? Are you a pre-Pentecost Christian, spasmodic and intermittent, or a post-Pentecost Christian—dynamic and different?

Prayer

O God, forgive me that so often I am crouching behind closed doors instead of being out on the open road. Make me a post-Pentecost Christian. In Jesus' name. Amen.

Further Study

2 Co 3:1-6; Jn 6:63; Rm 8:11
What does the letter of the law do?
What changes this?

NOVEMBER 28

EZEKIEL 34:1–36:12

34 The word of the LORD came to me: ² "Son of man, prophesy against the shepherds of Israel. Prophesy, and say to them: This is what the Lord GOD says to the shepherds: Woe to the shepherds of Israel, who have been feeding themselves! Shouldn't the shepherds feed their flock? ³ You eat the fat, wear the wool, and butcher the fatlings, but you do not tend the flock. ⁴ You have not strengthened the weak, healed the sick, bandaged the injured, brought back the strays, or sought the lost. Instead, you have ruled them with violence and cruelty. ⁵ They were scattered for lack of a shepherd; they became food for all the wild animals when they were scattered. ⁶ My flock went astray on all the mountains and every high hill. They were scattered over the whole face of the earth, and there was no one searching or seeking for them.

⁷ "Therefore, you shepherds, hear the word of the LORD. ⁸ As I live"—the declaration of the Lord GOD—"because My flock has become prey and food for every wild animal since they lack a shepherd, for My shepherds do not search for My flock, and because the shepherds feed themselves rather than My flock, ⁹ therefore, you shepherds, hear the word of the LORD!

¹⁰ "This is what the Lord GOD says: Look, I am against the shepherds. I will demand My flock from them and prevent them from shepherding the flock. The shepherds will no longer feed themselves, for I will rescue My flock from their mouths so that they will not be food for them.

¹¹ "For this is what the Lord GOD says: See, I Myself will search for My flock and look for them. ¹² As a shepherd looks for his sheep on the day he is among his scattered flock, so I will look for My flock. I will rescue them from all the places where they have been scattered on a cloudy and dark day. ¹³ I will bring them out from the peoples, gather them from the countries, and bring them into their own land. I will shepherd them on the mountains of Israel, in the ravines, and in all the inhabited places of the land. ¹⁴ I will tend them with good pasture, and their grazing place will be on Israel's lofty mountains. There they will lie down in a good grazing place; they will feed in rich pasture on the mountains of Israel. ¹⁵ I will tend My flock and let them lie down." This is the declaration of the Lord GOD. ¹⁶ "I will seek the lost, bring back the strays, bandage the injured, and strengthen the weak, but I will destroy the fat and the strong. I will shepherd them with justice.

¹⁷ "The Lord GOD says to you, My flock: I am going to judge between one sheep and another, between the rams and male goats. ¹⁸ Isn't it enough for you to feed on the good pasture? Must you also trample the rest of the pasture with

your feet? Or isn't it enough that you drink the clear water? Must you also muddy the rest with your feet? ¹⁹ Yet My flock has to feed on what your feet have trampled, and drink what your feet have muddied.

²⁰ "Therefore, this is what the Lord GOD says to them: See, I Myself will judge between the fat sheep and the lean sheep. ²¹ Since you have pushed with flank and shoulder and butted all the weak ones with your horns until you scattered them all over, ²² I will save My flock, and they will no longer be prey for you. I will judge between one sheep and another. ²³ I will appoint over them a single shepherd, My servant David, and he will shepherd them. He will tend them himself and will be their shepherd. ²⁴ I, the LORD, will be their God, and My servant David will be a prince among them. I, the LORD, have spoken.

²⁵ "I will make a covenant of peace with them and eliminate dangerous animals in the land, so that they may live securely in the wilderness and sleep in the forest. ²⁶ I will make them and the area around My hill a blessing: I will send down showers in their season— showers of blessing. ²⁷ The trees of the field will give their fruit, and the land will yield its produce; My flock will be secure in their land. They will know that I am the LORD when I break the bars of their yoke and rescue them from the hands of those who enslave them. ²⁸ They will no longer be prey for the nations, and the wild animals of the land will not consume them. They will live securely, and no one will frighten them. ²⁹ I will establish for them a place renowned for its agriculture, and they will no longer be victims of famine in the land. They will no longer endure the insults of the nations. ³⁰ Then they will know that I, the LORD their God, am with them, and that they, the house of Israel, are My people." This is the declaration of the Lord GOD. ³¹ "You are My flock, the human flock of My pasture, and I am your God." This is the declaration of the Lord GOD.

35 The word of the LORD came to me: ² "Son of man, turn your face toward Mount Seir and prophesy against it. ³ Say to it: This is what the Lord GOD says:

Look! I am against you, Mount Seir.
I will stretch out My hand
    against you
and make you a desolate waste.
⁴ I will turn your cities into ruins,
and you will become a desolation.
Then you will know that
    I am the LORD.

⁵ "Because you maintained an ancient hatred and handed over the Israelites to the power of the sword in the time of their disaster, the time of final punishment, ⁶ therefore, as I live"—this is the declaration of the Lord GOD—"I will destine you for bloodshed, and it will pursue you. Since you did not hate bloodshed, it will pursue you. ⁷ I will make Mount Seir a desolate waste and will cut off from it those who come and go. ⁸ I will fill its mountains with the slain; those slain by the sword will fall on your hills, in your valleys, and in all your ravines. ⁹ I will make you a perpetual desolation; your cities will not be inhabited. Then you will know that I am the LORD.

¹⁰ "Because you said: These two nations and two lands will be mine, and we will possess them—though the LORD was there— ¹¹ therefore, as I live"—the declaration of the Lord GOD—"I will treat you according to the anger and jealousy you showed in your hatred of them. I will make Myself known among them when I judge you. ¹² Then you will know that I, the LORD, have heard all the blasphemies you uttered against the mountains of Israel, saying: They are desolate. They have been given to us to devour! ¹³ You boasted against Me with your mouth, and spoke many words against Me. I heard it Myself!

¹⁴ "This is what the Lord GOD says: While the whole world rejoices, I will make you a desolation. ¹⁵ Just as you rejoiced over the inheritance of the house of Israel because it became a desolation,

so I will deal with you: you will become a desolation, Mount Seir, and so will all Edom in its entirety. Then they will know that I am the LORD.

36 "Son of man, prophesy to the mountains of Israel and say: Mountains of Israel, hear the word of the LORD. ² This is what the Lord GOD says: Because the enemy has said about you, 'Good! The ancient heights have become our possession,' ³ therefore, prophesy and say: This is what the Lord GOD says: Because they have made you desolate and have trampled you from every side, so that you became a possession for the rest of the nations and an object of people's gossip and slander, ⁴ therefore, mountains of Israel, hear the word of the Lord GOD. This is what the Lord GOD says to the mountains and hills, to the ravines and valleys, to the desolate ruins and abandoned cities, which have become plunder and a mockery to the rest of the nations all around.

⁵ "This is what the Lord GOD says: Certainly in My burning zeal I speak against the rest of the nations and all of Edom, who took My land as their own possession with wholehearted rejoicing and utter contempt, so that its pastureland became plunder. ⁶ Therefore, prophesy concerning the land of Israel and say to the mountains and hills, to the ravines and valleys: This is what the Lord GOD says: Look, I speak in My burning zeal because you have endured the insults of the nations. ⁷ Therefore this is what the Lord GOD says: I swear that the nations all around you will endure their own insults.

⁸ "You, mountains of Israel, will put forth your branches and bear your fruit for My people Israel, since their arrival is near. ⁹ Look! I am on your side; I will turn toward you, and you will be tilled and sown. ¹⁰ I will fill you with people, with the whole house of Israel in its entirety. The cities will be inhabited and the ruins rebuilt. ¹¹ I will fill you with people and animals, and they will increase and be fruitful. I will make you inhabited as you once were and make

you better off than you were before. Then you will know that I am the LORD. ¹² I will cause people, My people Israel, to walk on you; they will possess you, and you will be their inheritance. You will no longer deprive them of their children.

PSALM 133:1–134:3

¹ How good and pleasant it is
when brothers can live together!
² It is like fine oil on the head,
running down on the beard,
running down Aaron's beard,
on his robes.
³ It is like the dew of Hermon
falling on the mountains of Zion.
For there the LORD has appointed
the blessing—
life forevermore.

¹ Now praise the LORD, all you
servants of the LORD
who stand in the LORD's house at
night!
² Lift up your hands in the holy
place,
and praise the LORD!

³ May the LORD, Maker of heaven
and earth,
bless you from Zion.

PROVERBS 28:26-28

²⁶ The one who trusts in himself is a
fool,
but one who walks in wisdom will
be safe.

²⁷ The one who gives to the poor
will not be in need,
but one who turns his eyes away
will receive many curses.

²⁸ When the wicked come to power,
people hide,
but when they are destroyed, the
righteous flourish.

I PETER 4:12–5:14

¹² Dear friends, when the fiery ordeal arises among you to test you, don't be surprised by it, as if something unusual were happening to you. ¹³ Instead, as you share in the sufferings of the Messiah rejoice, so that you may also rejoice with great joy at the revelation of His glory. ¹⁴ If you are ridiculed for the name of Christ, you are blessed, because the Spirit of glory and of God rests on you. ¹⁵ None of you, however, should suffer as a murderer, a thief, an evildoer, or as a meddler. ¹⁶ But if anyone suffers as a Christian, he should not be ashamed, but should glorify God with that name. ¹⁷ For the time has come for judgment to begin with God's household; and if it begins with us, what will the outcome be for those who disobey the gospel of God?

¹⁸   And if the righteous is saved
        with difficulty,
    what will become of the ungodly
        and the sinner?

¹⁹ So those who suffer according to God's will should, in doing good, entrust themselves to a faithful Creator.

5 Therefore, as a fellow elder and witness to the sufferings of the Messiah, and also a participant in the glory about to be revealed, I exhort the elders among you: ² shepherd God's flock among you, not overseeing out of compulsion but freely, according to God's will; not for the money but eagerly; ³ not lording it over those entrusted to you, but being examples to the flock. ⁴ And when the chief Shepherd appears, you will receive the unfading crown of glory.

⁵ Likewise, you younger men, be subject to the elders. And all of you clothe yourselves with humility toward one another, because

**God resists the proud,
but gives grace to the humble.**

⁶ Humble yourselves therefore under the mighty hand of God, so that He may exalt you in due time, ⁷ casting all your care upon Him, because He cares about you.

⁸ Be sober! Be on the alert! Your adversary the Devil is prowling around like a roaring lion, looking for anyone he can devour. ⁹ Resist him, firm in the faith, knowing that the same sufferings are being experienced by your brothers in the world.

¹⁰ Now the God of all grace, who called you to His eternal glory in Christ Jesus, will personally restore, establish, strengthen, and support you after you have suffered a little. ¹¹ To Him be the dominion forever. Amen.

¹² Through Silvanus, whom I consider a faithful brother, I have written briefly, encouraging you and testifying that this is the true grace of God. Take your stand in it! ¹³ She who is in Babylon, also chosen, sends you greetings, as does Mark, my son. ¹⁴ Greet one another with a kiss of love. Peace to all of you who are in Christ.

Danger—the Devil at Work

Your adversary the Devil is prowling around like a roaring lion, looking for anyone he can devour.—1 PETER 5:8

A woman said to me once: "I think you are giving too much credit to the Devil. He is such an insignificant person compared to God that we ought not even mention his name." In one way I can sympathize with this view, for when you listen to some Christians talk, you get the impression that they have a small God and a big devil.

It would be unrealistic to think, however, that we can go through life without coming into direct contact with Satan and his forces. What is even more unrealistic is to think that many (though certainly not all) of the problems which confront us day by day have no devilish strategy behind them.

Satan is responsible for more of our individual woes and international wars, our crime and violence, our human sorrow, sickness, and death than we may believe. The late Dr. Martyn Lloyd-Jones said: "I am certain that one of the main causes of the ill state of the church today is the fact that the Devil is being forgotten. . . . We are ignorant of this great objective fact—the being, the existence of the Devil, the adversary, the accuser, and his fiery darts."

Does the thought of doing battle with the Devil frighten you? Then heed the words of Corrie ten Boom, who said: "The fear of the Devil is most likely from the Devil himself." God has given us all the protection we need to defend ourselves against the attacks of Satan, and when we know how to avail ourselves of this protection, we will no longer be afraid of the Devil. Rather, he will be afraid of us.

Prayer

O God, as I go deeper into this subject, I am becoming increasingly aware of the intensity of the spiritual battle in which I am engaged. Dispel every fear that may arise in me, and show me the way to power and victory. In Jesus' name. Amen.

Further Study

2 Co 2:1-11; 11:3; 2 Th 2:9
What did Paul say about his knowledge of the Devil?
What was his reason?

NOVEMBER 29

EZEKIEL 36:13–37:28

13 "This is what the Lord GOD says: Because people are saying to you: You devour men and deprive your nation of children, 14 therefore, you will no longer devour men and deprive your nation of children." This is the declaration of the Lord GOD. 15 "I will no longer allow the insults of the nations to be heard against you, and you will not have to endure the reproach of the peoples any more; you will no longer cause your nation to stumble." This is the declaration of the Lord GOD.

16 The word of the LORD came to me: 17 "Son of man, while the house of Israel lived in their land, they defiled it

with their conduct and actions. Their behavior before Me was like menstrual impurity. ¹⁸ So I poured out My wrath on them because of the blood they had shed on the land, and because they had defiled it with their idols. ¹⁹ I dispersed them among the nations, and they were scattered among the countries. I judged them according to their conduct and actions. ²⁰ When they came to the nations where they went, they profaned My holy name, because it was said about them: These are the people of the Lord, yet they had to leave His land in exile. ²¹ Then I had concern for My holy name, which the house of Israel profaned among the nations where they went.

²² "Therefore, say to the house of Israel: This is what the Lord GOD says: It is not for your sake that I will act, house of Israel, but for My holy name, which you profaned among the nations where you went. ²³ I will honor the holiness of My great name, which has been profaned among the nations—the name you have profaned among them. The nations will know that I am Yahweh"—the declaration of the Lord GOD—"when I demonstrate My holiness through you in their sight.

²⁴ "For I will take you from the nations and gather you from all the countries, and will bring you into your own land. ²⁵ I will also sprinkle clean water on you, and you will be clean. I will cleanse you from all your impurities and all your idols. ²⁶ I will give you a new heart and put a new spirit within you; I will remove your heart of stone and give you a heart of flesh. ²⁷ I will place My Spirit within you and cause you to follow My statutes and carefully observe My ordinances. ²⁸ Then you will live in the land that I gave your fathers; you will be My people, and I will be your God. ²⁹ I will save you from all your uncleanness. I will summon the grain and make it plentiful, and will not bring famine on you. ³⁰ I will also make the fruit of the trees and the produce of the field plentiful, so that you will no longer experience reproach among the nations on account of famine.

³¹ "Then you will remember your evil ways and your deeds that were not good, and you will loathe yourselves for your iniquities and abominations. ³² It is not for your sake that I will act"—the declaration of the Lord GOD—"let this be known to you. Be ashamed and humiliated because of your ways, house of Israel!

³³ "This is what the Lord GOD says: On the day I cleanse you from all your iniquities, I will cause the cities to be inhabited, and the ruins will be rebuilt. ³⁴ The desolate land will be cultivated instead of lying desolate in the sight of everyone who passes by. ³⁵ Then they will say: This land that was desolate has become like the garden of Eden. The cities that were once ruined, desolate, and destroyed are now fortified and inhabited. ³⁶ Then the nations that remain around you will know that I, the Lord, have rebuilt what was destroyed and have replanted what was desolate. I, the Lord, have spoken and I will do it.

³⁷ "This is what the Lord GOD says: I will respond to the house of Israel and do this for them: I will multiply them in number like a flock. ³⁸ So the ruined cities will be filled with a flock of people, just as the flock of sheep for sacrifice is filled in Jerusalem during its appointed festivals. Then they will know that I am the Lord."

37 The hand of the Lord was on me, and He brought me out by His Spirit and set me down in the middle of the valley; it was full of bones. ² He led me all around them. There were a great many of them on the surface of the valley, and they were very dry. ³ Then He said to me, "Son of man, can these bones live?"

I replied, "Lord GOD, only You know."

⁴ He said to me, "Prophesy concerning these bones and say to them: Dry bones, hear the word of the Lord! ⁵ This is what the Lord GOD says to these bones: I will cause breath to enter you, and you will live. ⁶ I will put tendons on you, make flesh grow on you, and cover you with skin. I will put breath in you so

that you come to life. Then you will know that I am the LORD."

⁷ So I prophesied as I had been commanded. While I was prophesying, there was a noise, a rattling sound, and the bones came together, bone to bone. ⁸ As I looked, tendons appeared on them, flesh grew, and skin covered them, but there was no breath in them. ⁹ He said to me, "Prophesy to the breath, prophesy, son of man. Say to it: This is what the Lord GOD says: Breath, come from the four winds and breathe into these slain so that they may live!" ¹⁰ So I prophesied as He commanded me; the breath entered them, and they came to life and stood on their feet, a vast army.

¹¹ Then He said to me, "Son of man, these bones are the whole house of Israel. Look how they say: Our bones are dried up, and our hope has perished; we are cut off. ¹² Therefore, prophesy and say to them: This is what the Lord GOD says: I am going to open your graves and bring you up from them, My people, and lead you into the land of Israel. ¹³ You will know that I am the LORD, My people, when I open your graves and bring you up from them. ¹⁴ I will put My Spirit in you, and you will live, and I will settle you in your own land. Then you will know that I am the LORD. I have spoken, and I will do it." This is the declaration of the LORD.

¹⁵ The word of the LORD came to me: ¹⁶ "Son of man, take a single stick and write on it: Belonging to Judah and the Israelites associated with him. Then take another stick and write on it: Belonging to Joseph—the stick of Ephraim—and all the house of Israel associated with him. ¹⁷ Then join them together into a single stick so that they become one in your hand. ¹⁸ When your people ask you: Won't you explain to us what you mean by these things?— ¹⁹ tell them: This is what the Lord GOD says: I am going to take the stick of Joseph—which is in the hand of Ephraim—and the tribes of Israel associated with him, and put them together with the stick of Judah. I will make them into a single

stick so that they become one in My hand. ²⁰ "When the sticks you have written on are in your hand and in full view of the people, ²¹ tell them: This is what the Lord GOD says: I am going to take the Israelites out of the nations where they have gone. I will gather them from all around and bring them into their own land. ²² I will make them one nation in the land, on the mountains of Israel, and one king will rule over all of them. They will no longer be two nations and will no longer be divided into two kingdoms. ²³ They will not defile themselves any more with their idols, their detestable things, and all their transgressions. I will save them from all their apostasies by which they sinned, and I will cleanse them. Then they will be My people, and I will be their God. ²⁴ My servant David will be king over them, and there will be one shepherd for all of them. They will follow My ordinances, and keep My statutes and obey them.

²⁵ "They will live in the land that I gave to My servant Jacob, where your fathers lived. They will live in it forever with their children and grandchildren, and My servant David will be their prince forever. ²⁶ I will make a covenant of peace with them; it will be an everlasting covenant with them. I will establish and multiply them, and will set My sanctuary among them forever. ²⁷ My dwelling place will be with them; I will be their God, and they will be My people. ²⁸ When My sanctuary is among them forever, the nations will know that I, the LORD, sanctify Israel."

PSALM 135:1-7

1   Hallelujah!
    Praise the name of the LORD.
    Give praise, you servants of the
        LORD
2   who stand in the house of the
        LORD,
    in the courts of the house of our
        God.
3   Praise the LORD, for the LORD is
        good;

sing praise to His name, for it is
   delightful.
⁴ For the LORD has chosen Jacob for
   Himself,
   Israel as His treasured possession.

⁵ For I know that the LORD is great;
   our Lord is greater than all gods.
⁶ The LORD does whatever He
   pleases
in heaven and on earth,
in the seas and all the depths.
⁷ He causes the clouds to rise from
   the ends of the earth.
He makes lightning for the rain
and brings the wind from His
   storehouses.

PROVERBS 29:1-3

29 One who becomes stiff-necked
      after many reprimands
will be broken suddenly—and
   without a remedy.

² When the righteous flourish, the
   people rejoice,
but when the wicked rule, people
   groan.

³ A man who loves wisdom brings
   joy to his father,
but one who consorts with
   prostitutes destroys his
   wealth.

2 PETER 1:1-21

1 Simeon Peter, a slave and an apostle
   of Jesus Christ:
To those who have obtained a faith of
equal privilege with ours through the
righteousness of our God and Savior
Jesus Christ.
² May grace and peace be multiplied
to you through the knowledge of God
and of Jesus our Lord.
³ For His divine power has given us
everything required for life and godliness, through the knowledge of Him
who called us by His own glory and
goodness. ⁴ By these He has given us
very great and precious promises, so

that through them you may share in the
divine nature, escaping the corruption
that is in the world because of evil desires. ⁵ For this very reason, make every
effort to supplement your faith with
goodness, goodness with knowledge,
⁶ knowledge with self-control, self-
control with endurance, endurance
with godliness, ⁷ godliness with brotherly affection, and brotherly affection
with love. ⁸ For if these qualities are
yours and are increasing, they will keep
you from being useless or unfruitful in
the knowledge of our Lord Jesus Christ.
⁹ The person who lacks these things is
blind and shortsighted, and has forgotten the cleansing from his past sins.
¹⁰ Therefore, brothers, make every effort to confirm your calling and election, because if you do these things you
will never stumble. ¹¹ For in this way,
entry into the eternal kingdom of our
Lord and Savior Jesus Christ will be
richly supplied to you.
¹² Therefore I will always remind you
about these things, even though you
know them and are established in the
truth you have. ¹³ I consider it right, as
long as I am in this tent, to wake you up
with a reminder, ¹⁴ knowing that I will
soon lay aside my tent, as our Lord Jesus
Christ has also shown me. ¹⁵ And I will
also make every effort that after my departure you may be able to recall these
things at any time.
¹⁶ For we did not follow cleverly con-
trived myths when we made known to
you the power and coming of our Lord
Jesus Christ; instead, we were eyewitnesses of His majesty. ¹⁷ For when He
received honor and glory from God the
Father, a voice came to Him from the
Majestic Glory:

This is My beloved Son.
I take delight in Him!

¹⁸ And we heard this voice when it came
from heaven while we were with Him
on the holy mountain. ¹⁹ So we have the
prophetic word strongly confirmed. You
will do well to pay attention to it, as to
a lamp shining in a dismal place, until
the day dawns and the morning star

arises in your hearts. ²⁰ First of all, you should know this: no prophecy of Scripture comes from one's own inter-

pretation, ²¹ because no prophecy ever came by the will of man; instead, moved by the Holy Spirit, men spoke from God.

Standing on Promises

He has given us very great and precious promises.
—2 PETER 1:4

It is one thing to accept the faithfulness of God as a clear biblical truth; it is quite another to act upon it. God has given us many great and precious promises, as our text for today puts it, but do we actually count on them being fulfilled?

We have to be careful that we do not hold God to promises He has not given. I have seen a good deal of heartache suffered by Christians because someone encouraged them to take a statement from the Word of God, turn it into a "promise," and believe for it to come to pass. Then when nothing happened, they became deeply discouraged.

One woman told me that many years ago she had taken the words found in Acts 16:31, "Believe on the Lord Jesus, and you will be saved—you and your household," and claimed them as a promise. When her husband and son died unrepentant, she was devastated. I pointed out to her that even God cannot save those who don't want to be saved, and that the promise given by Paul and Silas was for the Philippian jailer, not anyone else.

There are hundreds of promises that God has given in His Word that we can claim without equivocation. Someone who has counted all God's promises in the Bible numbers them as being over 3,000. That ought to be enough to keep you going if you lived to be a hundred. Be careful, however, that it is a general promise you are banking on, not a specific one.

Prayer

Father, I have Your promise that You will guide me into all truth, so my trust is in You that You will give me the wisdom to discern between a promise which is general and one that is specific. In Jesus' name. Amen.

Further Study

Heb 1:1-12; 13:8; 2 Co 4:18
Why is Jesus so dependable?
Where do we fix our eyes?

NOVEMBER 30

EZEKIEL 38:1–39:29

38 The word of the LORD came to me: ² "Son of man, turn your face toward Gog, of the land of Magog, the chief prince of Meshech and Tubal. Prophesy against him ³ and say: This is what the Lord GOD says: Look, I am against you, Gog, chief prince of Meshech and Tubal. ⁴ I will turn you around, put hooks in your jaws, and bring you out with all your army, including horses and riders, who are all splendidly dressed, a huge company armed with shields and bucklers, all of them brandishing swords. ⁵ Persia, Cush, and Put are with them, all of them with shields and helmets; ⁶ Gomer with all its troops; and Beth-togarmah from the remotest parts of the north along with all its troops—many peoples are with you.

⁷ "Be prepared and get yourself ready, you and all your company who have been mobilized around you; you will be their guard. ⁸ After a long time you will be summoned. In the last years you will enter a land that has been restored from war and regathered from many peoples to the mountains of Israel, which had long been a ruin. They were brought out from the peoples, and all of them now live securely. ⁹ You, all of your troops, and many peoples with you will advance, coming like a thunderstorm; you will be like a cloud covering the land.

¹⁰ "This is what the Lord GOD says: On that day, thoughts will arise in your mind, and you will devise an evil plan. ¹¹ You will say: I will go up against a land of open villages; I will come against a tranquil people who are living securely, all of them living without walls and without bars or gates— ¹² in order to seize spoil and carry off plunder, to turn your hand against ruins now inhabited and against a people gathered from the nations, who have been acquiring cattle and possessions and who live at the center of the world. ¹³ Sheba and Dedan and the merchants of Tarshish with all its rulers will ask you: Have you come to seize spoil? Have you assembled your hordes to carry off plunder, to make off with silver and gold, to take cattle and possessions, to seize great spoil?

¹⁴ "Therefore prophesy, son of man, and say to Gog: This is what the Lord GOD says: On that day when My people Israel are dwelling securely, will you not know this ¹⁵ and come from your place in the remotest parts of the north—you and many peoples with you, who are all riding horses—a mighty horde, a huge army? ¹⁶ You will advance against My people Israel like a cloud covering the land. It will happen in the last days, Gog, that I will bring you against My land so that the nations may know Me, when I show Myself holy through you in their sight.

¹⁷ "This is what the Lord GOD says: Are you the one I spoke about in former times through My servants, the prophets of Israel, who for years prophesied in those times that I would bring you against them? ¹⁸ Now on that day, the day when Gog comes against the land of Israel"—this is the declaration of the Lord GOD—"My wrath will flare up. ¹⁹ I swear in My zeal and fiery rage: On that day there will be a great earthquake in the land of Israel. ²⁰ The fish of the sea, the birds of the sky, the animals of the field, every creature that crawls on the ground, and every human being on the face of the earth will tremble before Me. The mountains will be thrown down, the cliffs will collapse, and every wall will fall to the ground. ²¹ I will call for a sword against him on all My mountains"—the declaration of the Lord GOD—"and every man's sword will be

against his brother. ²²I will execute judgment on him with plague and bloodshed. I will pour out torrential rain, hailstones, fire, and brimstone on him, as well as his troops and the many peoples who are with him. ²³I will display My greatness and holiness, and will reveal Myself in the sight of many nations. Then they will know that I am the LORD.

39 "As for you, son of man, prophesy against Gog and say: This is what the Lord GOD says: Look, I am against you, Gog, chief prince of Meshech and Tubal. ²I will turn you around, drive you on, and lead you up from the remotest parts of the north. I will bring you against the mountains of Israel. ³Then I will knock your bow from your left hand and make your arrows drop from your right hand. ⁴You, all your troops, and the peoples who are with you will fall on the mountains of Israel. I will give you as food to every kind of predatory bird and to the wild animals. ⁵You will fall on the open field, for I have spoken." This is the declaration of the Lord GOD.

⁶"I will send fire against Magog and those who live securely on the coasts and islands. Then they will know that I am the LORD. ⁷So I will make My holy name known among My people Israel and will no longer allow it to be profaned. Then the nations will know that I am the LORD, the Holy One in Israel. ⁸Yes, it is coming, and it will happen." This is the declaration of the Lord GOD. "This is the day I have spoken about.

⁹"Then the inhabitants of Israel's cities will go out, kindle fires, and burn the weapons—the bucklers and shields, the bows and arrows, the clubs and spears. For seven years they will use them to make fires. ¹⁰They will not gather wood from the countryside or cut it down from the forests, for they will use the weapons to make fires. They will take the loot from those who looted them and plunder those who plundered them." This is the declaration of the Lord GOD.

¹¹"Now on that day I will give Gog a burial place there in Israel—the Valley of the Travelers east of the Sea. It will block those who travel through, for Gog and all his hordes will be buried there. So it will be called the Valley of Hamongog. ¹²The house of Israel will spend seven months burying them in order to cleanse the land. ¹³All the people of the land will bury them and their fame will spread on the day I display My glory." This is the declaration of the Lord GOD.

¹⁴"They will appoint men on a full-time basis to pass through the land and bury the invaders who remain on the surface of the ground, in order to cleanse it. They will make their search at the end of the seven months. ¹⁵When they pass through the land and one of them sees a human bone, he will erect a marker next to it until the buriers have buried it in the Valley of Hamongog. ¹⁶There will even be a city named Hamonah there. So they will cleanse the land.

¹⁷"Son of man, this is what the Lord GOD says: Tell every kind of bird and all the wild animals: Assemble and come! Gather from all around to My sacrificial feast that I am slaughtering for you, a great feast on the mountains of Israel; you will eat flesh and drink blood. ¹⁸You will eat the flesh of mighty men and drink the blood of the earth's princes: rams, lambs, male goats, and bulls, all of them fatlings of Bashan. ¹⁹You will eat fat until you are satisfied and drink blood until you are drunk, at My sacrificial feast that I have prepared for you. ²⁰At My table you will eat your fill of horses and riders, of mighty men and all the warriors." This is the declaration of the Lord GOD.

²¹"I will display My glory among the nations, and all the nations will see the judgment I have executed and the hand I have laid on them. ²²From that day forward the house of Israel will know that I am the LORD their God. ²³And the nations will know that the house of Israel went into exile on account of their iniquity, because they dealt unfaithfully with Me. Therefore, I hid My face from them and handed them over to their en-

emies, so that they all fell by the sword. ²⁴ I dealt with them according to their uncleanness and transgressions, and I hid My face from them.

²⁵ "So this is what the Lord GOD says: Now I will restore the fortunes of Jacob and have compassion on the whole house of Israel, and I will be jealous for My holy name. ²⁶ They will feel remorse for their disgrace and all the unfaithfulness they committed against Me, when they live securely in their land with no one to frighten them. ²⁷ When I bring them back from the peoples and gather them from the countries of their enemies, I will demonstrate My holiness through them in the sight of many nations. ²⁸ They will know that I am the LORD their God when I regather them to their own land after having exiled them among the nations. I will leave none of them behind. ²⁹ I will no longer hide My face from them, for I will pour out My Spirit on the house of Israel." This is the declaration of the Lord GOD.

*P*SALM 135:8-12

⁸ He struck down the firstborn of Egypt,
both people and animals.
⁹ He sent signs and wonders against you, Egypt,
against Pharaoh and all his officials.
¹⁰ He struck down many nations and slaughtered mighty kings:
¹¹ Sihon king of the Amorites,
Og king of Bashan,
and all the kings of Canaan.
¹² He gave their land as an inheritance,
an inheritance to His people Israel.

*P*ROVERBS 29:4-6

⁴ By justice a king brings stability to a land,
but a man who demands "contributions" demolishes it.

⁵ A man who flatters his neighbor spreads a net for his feet.

⁶ An evil man is caught by sin,
but the righteous one sings and rejoices.

2 *P*ETER 2:1-22

2 But there were also false prophets among the people, just as there will be false teachers among you. They will secretly bring in destructive heresies, even denying the Master who bought them, and will bring swift destruction on themselves. ² Many will follow their unrestrained ways, and because of them the way of truth will be blasphemed. ³ In their greed they will exploit you with deceptive words. Their condemnation, pronounced long ago, is not idle, and their destruction does not sleep.

⁴ For if God didn't spare the angels who sinned, but threw them down into Tartarus and delivered them to be kept in chains of darkness until judgment; ⁵ and if He didn't spare the ancient world, but protected Noah, a preacher of righteousness, and seven others, when He brought a flood on the world of the ungodly; ⁶ and if He reduced the cities of Sodom and Gomorrah to ashes and condemned them to ruin, making them an example to those who were going to be ungodly; ⁷ and if He rescued righteous Lot, distressed by the unrestrained behavior of the immoral ⁸ (for as he lived among them, that righteous man tormented himself day by day with the lawless deeds he saw and heard)— ⁹ then the Lord knows how to rescue the godly from trials and to keep the unrighteous under punishment until the day of judgment, ¹⁰ especially those who follow the polluting desires of the flesh and despise authority.

Bold, arrogant people! They do not tremble when they blaspheme the glorious ones; ¹¹ however, angels, who are greater in might and power, do not bring a slanderous charge against them before the Lord. ¹² But these people, like irrational animals—creatures of instinct born to be caught and destroyed—speak blasphemies about things they don't understand, and in their destruction they too will be destroyed, [13] suffering harm as the payment for unrighteousness. They consider it a pleasure to carouse in the daytime. They are blots and blemishes, delighting in their deceptions as they feast with you, [14] having eyes full of adultery and always looking for sin, seducing unstable people, and with hearts trained in greed. Accursed children! [15] By abandoning the straight path, they have gone astray and have followed the path of Balaam, the son of Bosor, who loved the wages of unrighteousness, [16] but received a rebuke for his transgression: a speechless donkey spoke with a human voice and restrained the prophet's madness.

[17] These people are springs without water, mists driven by a whirlwind. The gloom of darkness has been reserved for them. [18] For uttering bombastic, empty words, they seduce, by fleshly desires and debauchery, people who have barely escaped from those who live in error. [19] They promise them freedom, but they themselves are slaves of corruption, since people are enslaved to whatever defeats them. [20] For if, having escaped the world's impurity through the knowledge of our Lord and Savior Jesus Christ, they are again entangled in these things and defeated, the last state is worse for them than the first. [21] For it would have been better for them not to have known the way of righteousness than, after knowing it, to turn back from the holy commandment delivered to them. [22] It has happened to them according to the true proverb: **A dog returns to its own vomit,** and, "a sow, after washing itself, wallows in the mud."

The Upper Room

I will pour out My Spirit on the house of Israel.
——Ezekiel 39:29

The upper room has been described as "the birthplace of the church." Certainly it was there that power was loosed which changed the world. Some commentators believe that the upper room was part of someone's home—someone sympathetic to Jesus and His ministry. Why did the Holy Spirit come upon the disciples in a home and not in a sacred place such as the temple? If the Holy Spirit had come upon them in the temple, then His coming would have been associated with a sacred place, sacred services, or sacred occasions. The Holy Spirit came in the most common of all places—a home—as if He was saying, "I am here not just for 'sacred' occasions, but for all occasions, for all of life."

One writer said in commenting on the ordinariness of the upper room, "The Holy Spirit is not a spiritual luxury to be imported into the unusual, but a spiritual necessity for the usual." He is to be the pulse-beat of all we do—the usual as well as the unusual, the ordinary as well as the extraordinary. In the coming of the Holy Spirit, the ordinary and seemingly insignificant things of life are touched with divine significance: every bush is aflame with the glory of God, every moment is packed with eternity, and every contact we make is part of His perfect purposes.

Prayer

O God, I am so thankful that I don't have to wander from sacred place to sacred place in search of Your power and Your glory. You come to me just where I am until my heart glows with Your shekinah glory. Amen.

Further Study

Jl 2:18-32; Is 32:15; 59:21
What did God say would follow the coming of the Spirit?
What is the Lord exhorting the Israelites to do?

DECEMBER I

*E*ZEKIEL 40:1–41:7

40 In the twenty-fifth year of our exile, at the beginning of the year, on the tenth day of the month in the fourteenth year after Jerusalem had been captured, on that very day the LORD's hand was on me, and He brought me there. ² In visions of God He took me to the land of Israel and set me down on a very high mountain. On its southern slope was a structure resembling a city. ³ He brought me there, and I saw a man whose appearance was like bronze, with a linen cord and a measuring rod in his hand. He was standing by the gate. ⁴ He spoke to me: "Son of man, look with your eyes, listen with your ears, and pay attention to everything I am going to show you, for you have been brought here so that I might show it to you. Report everything you see to the house of Israel."

⁵ Now there was a wall surrounding the outside of the temple. The measuring rod in the man's hand was six units of 21 inches; each unit was the standard length plus three inches. He measured

the thickness of the wall structure; it was about 10 feet, and its height was the same. ⁶ Then he came to the gate that faced east and climbed its steps. He measured the threshold of the gate; it was 10 feet deep—the first threshold was 10 feet deep. ⁷ Each recess was about 10 feet long and 10 feet deep, and there was a space of; eight and three-quarter feet between the recesses. The inner threshold of the gate on the temple side next to the gate's portico was about 10 feet. ⁸ Next he measured the portico of the gate; ⁹ it was 14 feet, and its pilasters were three and a half feet. The portico of the gate was on the temple side.

¹⁰ There were three recesses on each side of the east gate, each with the same measurements, and the pilasters on either side also had the same measurements. ¹¹ Then he measured the width of the gate's entrance; it was 17 and a half feet, while the width of the gateway was 22 and three-quarter feet. ¹² There was a barrier of 21 inches in front of the recesses on both sides, and the recesses on each side were 10 and a half feet square. ¹³ Then he measured

the gateway from the roof of one recess to the roof of the opposite one; the distance was 43 and three-quarter feet. The openings of the recesses faced each other. ¹⁴ Next, he measured the pilasters—105 feet. The gate extended around to the pilaster of the court. ¹⁵ The distance from the front of the gate at the entrance to the front of the gate's portico on the inside was 87 and a half feet. ¹⁶ The recesses and their pilasters had beveled windows all around the inside of the gateway. The porticos also had windows all around on the inside. Each pilaster was decorated with palm trees.

¹⁷ Then he brought me into the outer court, and there were chambers and a paved surface laid out all around the court. Thirty chambers faced the pavement, ¹⁸ which flanked the gates and corresponded to the length of the gates; this was the lower pavement. ¹⁹ Then he measured the distance from the front of the lower gate to the exterior front of the inner court; it was 175 feet. This was the east; next the north is described

²⁰ He measured the gate of the outer court facing north, both its length and width. ²¹ Its three recesses on each side, its pilasters, and its portico had the same measurements as the first gate: 87 and a half feet long and 43 and three-quarter feet wide. ²² Its windows, portico, and palm trees had the same measurements as those of the gate that faced east. Seven steps led up to the gate, and its portico was ahead of them. ²³ The inner court had a gate facing the north gate, like the one on the east. He measured the distance from gate to gate; it was 175 feet.

²⁴ He brought me to the south side, and there was also a gate on the south. He measured its pilasters and portico; they had the same measurements as the others. ²⁵ Both the gate and its portico had windows all around, like the other windows. It was 87 and a half feet long and 43 and three-quarter feet wide. ²⁶ Its stairway had seven steps, and its portico was ahead of them. It had palm trees on its pilasters, one on each side.

²⁷ The inner court had a gate on the south. He measured from gate to gate on the south; it was 175 feet.

²⁸ Then he brought me to the inner court through the south gate. When he measured the south gate, it had the same measurements as the others. ²⁹ Its recesses, pilasters, and portico had the same measurements as the others. Both it and its portico had windows all around. It was 87 and a half feet long and 43 and three-quarter feet wide. ³⁰ (There were porticoes all around, 43 and three-quarter feet long and eight and three-quarter feet wide.) ³¹ Its portico faced the outer court, and its pilasters were decorated with palm trees. Its stairway had eight steps.

³² Then he brought me to the inner court on the east side. When he measured the gate, it had the same measurements as the others. ³³ Its recesses, pilasters, and portico had the same measurements as the others. Both it and its portico had windows all around. It was 87 and a half feet long and 43 and three-quarter feet wide. ³⁴ Its portico faced the outer court, and its pilasters were decorated with palm trees on each side. Its stairway had eight steps.

³⁵ Then he brought me to the north gate. When he measured it, it had the same measurements as the others, ³⁶ as did its recesses, pilasters, and portico. It also had windows all around. It was 87 and a half feet long and 43 and three-quarter feet wide. ³⁷ Its portico faced the outer court, and its pilasters were decorated with palm trees on each side. Its stairway had eight steps.

³⁸ There was a chamber whose door opened into the portico of the gate. The burnt offering was to be washed there. ³⁹ Inside the portico of the gate there were two tables on each side, on which to slaughter the burnt offering, sin offering, and restitution offering. ⁴⁰ Outside, as one approaches the entrance of the north gate, there were two tables on one side and two more tables on the other side of the gate's portico. ⁴¹ So there were four tables inside the gate and four outside, eight tables in all on which the slaughtering was to be done.

⁴²There were also four tables of cut stone for the burnt offering, each 31 and a half inches long, 31 and a half inches wide, and 21 inches high. The utensils used to slaughter the burnt offerings and other sacrifices were placed on them. ⁴³There were three-inch hooks fastened all around the inside of the room, and the flesh of the offering was to be laid on the tables.

⁴⁴Outside the inner gate, within the inner court, there were chambers for the singers: one beside the north gate, facing south, and another beside the south gate, facing north. ⁴⁵Then the man said to me: "This chamber that faces south is for the priests who keep charge of the temple. ⁴⁶The chamber that faces north is for the priests who keep charge of the altar. These are the sons of Zadok, the ones from the sons of Levi who may approach the LORD to serve Him." ⁴⁷Next he measured the court. It was square, 175 feet long and 175 feet wide. The altar was in front of the temple.

⁴⁸Then he brought me to the portico of the temple and measured the pilasters of the portico; they were eight and three-quarter feet thick on each side. The width of the gateway was 24 and a half feet, and the sidewalls of the gate were five and a quarter feet wide on each side. ⁴⁹The portico was 35 feet across and 21 feet deep, and 10 steps led up to it. There were pillars by the pilasters, one on each side.

41 Next he brought me into the great hall and measured the pilasters; on each side the width of the pilaster was 10 and a half feet. ²The width of the entrance was 17 and a half feet, and the sidewalls of the entrance were eight and three-quarter feet wide on each side. He also measured the length of the great hall, 70 feet, and the width, 35 feet. ³He went inside the next room and measured the pilasters at the entrance; they were three and a half feet wide. The entrance was 10 and a half feet wide, and the width of the entrance's sidewalls on each side was 12 and a quarter feet. ⁴He then measured the length of the room adjacent to the great hall, 35 feet, and the width, 35 feet. And he said to me, "This is the most holy place."

⁵Then he measured the wall of the temple; it was 10 and a half feet thick. The width of the side rooms all around the temple was seven feet. ⁶The side rooms were arranged one above another in three stories of 30 rooms each. There were ledges on the wall of the temple all around to serve as supports for the side rooms, so that the supports would not be in the temple wall itself. ⁷The side rooms surrounding the temple widened at each successive story, for the structure surrounding the temple went up by stages. This was the reason for the temple's broadness as it rose. And so, one would go up from the lowest story to the highest by means of the middle one.

𝒫SALM 135:13-21

¹³ LORD, Your name endures forever,
   Your reputation, LORD, through all
      generations.
¹⁴ For the LORD will judge His people
   and have compassion on His
      servants.

¹⁵ The idols of the nations are of
      silver and gold,
   made by human hands.
¹⁶ They have mouths, but cannot
      speak,
   eyes, but cannot see.
¹⁷ They have ears, but cannot hear;
   indeed, there is no breath in their
      mouths.
¹⁸ Those who make them are just
      like them,
   as are all who trust in them.

¹⁹ House of Israel, praise the LORD!
   House of Aaron, praise the LORD!
²⁰ House of Levi, praise the LORD!
   You who revere the LORD, praise
      the LORD!
²¹ May the LORD be praised from
      Zion;
   He dwells in Jerusalem.
   Hallelujah!

PROVERBS 29:7-9

7 The righteous person knows the
rights of the poor,
but the wicked one does not
understand these concerns.

8 Mockers inflame a city,
but the wise turn away anger.

9 If a wise man goes to court with a
fool,
there will be ranting and raving
but no resolution.

2 PETER 3:1-18

3 Dear friends, this is now the second
letter I've written you; in both, I
awaken your pure understanding with a
reminder, ² so that you can remember
the words previously spoken by the holy
prophets, and the commandment of our
Lord and Savior given through your
apostles. ³ First, be aware of this: scoffers will come in the last days to scoff,
following their own lusts, ⁴ saying,
"Where is the promise of His coming?
For ever since the fathers fell asleep, all
things continue as they have been since
the beginning of creation." ⁵ They willfully ignore this: long ago the heavens
and the earth existed out of water and
through water by the word of God.
⁶ Through these the world of that time
perished when it was flooded by water.
⁷ But by the same word the present
heavens and earth are held in store for
fire, being kept until the day of judgment and destruction of ungodly men.

⁸ Dear friends, don't let this one thing
escape you: with the Lord one day is
like 1,000 years, and 1,000 years like

one day. ⁹ The Lord does not delay His
promise, as some understand delay, but
is patient with you, not wanting any to
perish, but all to come to repentance.
¹⁰ But the Day of the Lord will come
like a thief; on that day the heavens will
pass away with a loud noise, the elements will burn and be dissolved, and
the earth and the works on it will be disclosed. ¹¹ Since all these things are to be
destroyed in this way, it is clear what
sort of people you should be in holy
conduct and godliness ¹² as you wait for
and earnestly desire the coming of the
day of God, because of which the heavens will be on fire and be dissolved, and
the elements will melt with the heat.
¹³ But based on His promise, we wait for
new heavens and a new earth, where
righteousness will dwell.

¹⁴ Therefore, dear friends, while you
wait for these things, make every effort
to be found in peace without spot or
blemish before Him. ¹⁵ Also, regard the
patience of our Lord as an opportunity
for salvation, just as our dear brother
Paul, according to the wisdom given to
him, has written to you. ¹⁶ He speaks
about these things in all his letters, in
which there are some matters that are
hard to understand. The untaught and
unstable twist them to their own destruction, as they also do with the rest
of the Scriptures.

¹⁷ Therefore, dear friends, since you
have been forewarned, be on your
guard, so that you are not led away by
the error of the immoral and fall from
your own stability. ¹⁸ But grow in the
grace and knowledge of our Lord and
Savior Jesus Christ. To Him be the glory
both now and to the day of eternity.
Amen.

Slow Growth—Good Growth

*But grow in the grace and knowledge of our Lord
and Savior Jesus Christ.*—2 PETER 3:18

Resentment poisons the one who holds it. Think how free of resentment our Lord was. His "first word" from the cross shows how He dealt with any possible temptation to be resentful. I believe that He was as free to walk away from Calvary as he was to walk away from the cliff-edge above Nazareth. He accepted death. Sin and love were in decisive battle. Had He drawn back, sin would have won. And He who lives in us can love in us—if we let Him.

We must allow time for change. Change is more often than not a process. I want to emphasize this because many, when once they see the way out of their dilemma, want change to take place too quickly. Some changes in our lives take place quickly. The night I surrendered my life to Jesus Christ, a lot of my sinful habits left me. But some didn't, and the process of change was long and tedious. Deep healing and supernatural change can take place in a moment, but often it takes months of struggle, trial and error, learning and unlearning.

All of us have different timetables when it comes to growing, and no one should judge another's timetable. There is an assumption that when God is involved, then all change will be instantaneous. It can happen that way, but be prepared also for it to take place over a period of time. A gardener friend of mine says: "Slow growth is good growth." It is the same in the garden of the soul.

Prayer

Father, help me to be content with Your timetable for my spiritual growth. Sometimes I want to grow more quickly than is good for me. Help me be patient with Your patience. In Jesus' name. Amen.

Further Study

2 Pt 1:2-8; Ps 1:1-3; Jr 17:7-8; Ezk 31:3-9
What do we grow in?
Compare spiritual growth to a tree's growing.

DECEMBER 2

*E*ZEKIEL 41:8–43:12

8 I saw that the temple had a raised platform surrounding it; this foundation for the side rooms was 10 and a half feet high. 9 The thickness of the outer wall of the side rooms was eight and three-quarter feet. The free space between the side rooms of the temple 10 and the outer chambers was 35 feet wide all around the temple. 11 The side rooms opened into the free space, one entrance toward the north and another to the south. The area of free space was

eight and three-quarter feet wide all around.

¹²Now the building that faced the temple yard toward the west was 122 and a half feet wide. The wall of the building was eight and three-quarter feet thick on all sides, and the building's length was 157 and a half feet. ¹³Then the man measured the temple; it was 175 feet long. In addition, the temple yard and the building, including its walls, were 175 feet long. ¹⁴The width of the front of the temple along with the temple yard to the east was 175 feet. ¹⁵Next he measured the length of the building facing the temple yard to the west, with its galleries on each side; it was 175 feet.

The interior of the great hall and the porticoes of the court— ¹⁶the thresholds, the beveled windows, and the balconies all around with their three levels opposite the threshold—were overlaid with wood on all sides. They were paneled from the ground to the windows (but the windows were covered), ¹⁷reaching to the top of the entrance, and as far as the inner temple and on the outside. On every wall all around, on the inside and outside, was a pattern ¹⁸carved with cherubim and palm trees. There was a palm tree between each pair of cherubim. Each cherub had two faces: ¹⁹a human face turned toward the palm tree on one side, and a lion's face turned toward it on the other. They were carved throughout the temple on all sides. ²⁰Cherubim and palm trees were carved from the ground to the top of the entrance and on the wall of the great hall.

²¹The doorposts of the great hall were square, and the front of the sanctuary had the same appearance. ²²The altar was made of wood, five and a quarter feet high and three and a half feet long. It had corners, and its length and sides were of wood. The man told me, "This is the table that stands before the LORD."

²³The great hall and the sanctuary each had a double door, ²⁴and each of the doors had two swinging panels. There were two panels for one door and two for the other. ²⁵Cherubim and palm trees were carved on the doors of the great hall like those carved on the walls. There was a wooden canopy outside, in front of the portico. ²⁶There were beveled windows and palm trees on both sides, on the sidewalls of the portico, the side rooms of the temple, and the canopies.

42 Then the man led me out by way of the north gate into the outer court. He brought me to the group of chambers opposite the temple yard and opposite the building to the north. ²Along the length of the chambers, which was 175 feet, there was an entrance on the north; the width was 87 and a half feet. ³Opposite the 35 foot space belonging to the inner court and opposite the paved surface belonging to the outer court, the structure rose gallery by gallery in three tiers. ⁴In front of the chambers was a walkway toward the inside, 17 and a half feet wide and 175 feet long, and their entrances were on the north. ⁵The upper chambers were narrower because the galleries took away more space from them than from the lower and middle stories of the building. ⁶For they were arranged in three stories and had no pillars like the pillars of the courts; therefore the upper chambers were set back from the ground more than the lower and middle stories. ⁷A wall on the outside ran in front of the chambers, parallel to them, toward the outer court; it was 87 and a half feet long. ⁸For the chambers on the outer court were 87 and a half feet long, while those facing the great hall were 175 feet long. ⁹At the base of these chambers there was an entryway on the east side as one enters them from the outer court.

¹⁰In the thickness of the wall of the court toward the south, there were chambers facing the temple yard and the western building, ¹¹with a passageway in front of them, just like the chambers that faced north. Their length and width, as well as all their exits, measurements, and entrances, were identi-

cal. ¹²The entrance at the beginning of the passageway, the way in front of the corresponding wall as one enters on the east side, was similar to the entrances of the chambers that were on the south side.

¹³Then the man said to me, "The northern and southern chambers that face the temple yard are the holy chambers where the priests who approach the LORD will eat the most holy offerings. There they will deposit the most holy offerings—the grain offerings, sin offerings, and restitution offerings—for the place is holy. ¹⁴Once the priests have entered, they must not go out from the holy area to the outer court until they have removed the clothes they minister in, for these are holy. They are to put on other clothes before they approach the public area."

¹⁵When he finished measuring inside the temple complex, he led me out by way of the gate that faced east and measured all around the complex.

¹⁶He measured the east side with
a measuring rod;
it was 875 feet by the measuring
rod.
¹⁷He measured the north side;
it was 875 feet by the measuring
rod.
¹⁸He measured the south side;
it was 875 feet by the measuring
rod.
¹⁹Then he turned to the west side
and measured 875 feet by the
measuring rod.

²⁰He measured the temple complex on all four sides. It had a wall all around it, 875 feet long and 875 feet wide, to separate the holy from the common.

43 He led me to the gate, the one that faces east, ²and I saw the glory of the God of Israel coming from the east. His voice sounded like the roar of mighty waters, and the earth shone with His glory. ³The vision I saw was like the one I had seen when He came to destroy the city, and like the ones I had seen by the Chebar Canal. I fell

facedown. ⁴The glory of the LORD entered the temple by way of the gate that faced east. ⁵Then the Spirit lifted me up and brought me to the inner court, and the glory of the LORD filled the temple.

⁶While the man was standing beside me, I heard someone speaking to me from the temple. ⁷He said to me: "Son of man, this is the place of My throne and the place for the soles of My feet, where I will dwell among the Israelites forever. The house of Israel and their kings will no longer defile My holy name by their religious prostitution and by the corpses of their kings at their high places. ⁸Whenever they placed their threshold next to My threshold and their doorposts beside My doorposts, with only a wall between Me and them, they were defiling My holy name by the abominations they committed. So I destroyed them in My anger. ⁹Now let them remove their prostitution and the corpses of their kings far from Me, and I will dwell among them forever.

¹⁰"As for you, son of man, describe the temple to the house of Israel, so that they may be ashamed of their iniquities. Let them measure its pattern, ¹¹and they will be ashamed of all that they have done. Reveal the design of the temple to them—its layout with its exits and entrances—its complete design along with all its statutes, design specifications, and laws. Write it down in their sight so that they may observe its complete design and all its statutes and may carry them out. ¹²This is the law of the temple: all its surrounding territory on top of the mountain will be especially holy. Yes, this is the law of the temple.

𝒫SALM 136:1-9

¹ Give thanks to the LORD, for He is
good.
His love is eternal.
² Give thanks to the God of gods.
His love is eternal.
³ Give thanks to the Lord of lords.
His love is eternal.
⁴ He alone does great wonders.
His love is eternal.

5 He made the heavens skillfully.
His love is eternal.
6 He spread the land on the waters.
His love is eternal.
7 He made the great lights:
His love is eternal.
8 the sun to rule by day,
His love is eternal.
9 the moon and stars to rule by
night.
His love is eternal.

PROVERBS 29:10-12

10 Bloodthirsty men hate an honest
person,
but the upright care about him.

11 A fool gives full vent to his anger,
but a wise man holds it in check.

12 If a ruler listens to lies,
all his servants will be wicked.

I JOHN 1:1–2:11

1 What was from the beginning,
what we have heard,
what we have seen with our eyes,
what we have observed,
and have touched with our hands,
concerning the Word of life—
2 that life was revealed,
and we have seen it
and we testify and declare to you
the eternal life that was with the
Father
and was revealed to us—
3 what we have seen and heard
we also declare to you,
so that you may have fellowship
along with us;
and indeed our fellowship is with
the Father
and with His Son Jesus Christ.
4 We are writing these things
so that our joy may be complete.
5 Now this is the message we have
heard from Him and declare to you: God
is light, and there is absolutely no darkness in Him. 6 If we say, "We have fellowship with Him," and walk in darkness,
we are lying and are not practicing the
truth. 7 But if we walk in the light as He
Himself is in the light, we have fellowship with one another, and the blood of
Jesus His Son cleanses us from all sin.
8 If we say, "We have no sin," we are deceiving ourselves, and the truth is not in
us. 9 If we confess our sins, He is faithful and righteous to forgive us our sins
and to cleanse us from all unrighteousness. 10 If we say, "We have not sinned,"
we make Him a liar, and His word is not
in us.

2 My little children, I am writing you
these things so that you may not sin.
But if anyone does sin, we have an advocate with the Father—Jesus Christ
the righteous One. 2 He Himself is the
propitiation for our sins, and not only
for ours, but also for those of the whole
world.
3 This is how we are sure that we have
come to know Him: by keeping His commands. 4 The one who says, "I have
come to know Him," without keeping
His commands, is a liar, and the truth is
not in him. 5 But whoever keeps His
word, truly in him the love of God is
perfected. This is how we know we are
in Him: 6 the one who says he remains
in Him should walk just as He walked.
7 Dear friends, I am not writing you a
new command, but an old command
that you have had from the beginning.
The old command is the message you
have heard. 8 Yet I am writing you a new
command, which is true in Him and in
you, because the darkness is passing
away and the true light is already shining.
9 The one who says he is in the light
but hates his brother is in the darkness
until now. 10 The one who loves his
brother remains in the light, and there
is no cause for stumbling in him. 11 But
the one who hates his brother is in the
darkness, walks in the darkness, and
doesn't know where he's going, because
the darkness has blinded his eyes.

Logically Necessary

Give thanks to the God of gods. His love is eternal.
—PSALM 136:2

The Trinity is implicit in the whole Bible from the beginning, though it might not be evident to someone unfamiliar with the Book who started reading at Genesis until they had reached the books of the New Testament.

Ian Macpherson, in his book *The Faith Once Delivered*, says that when the island now known as Trinidad was discovered by Columbus, he thought at first it was three islands, as all he could see were three hills silhouetted against the sky. When he got closer, however, he found that what he had seen was not three islands at all but just one island. From a distance it looked like three, but close up it was only one. Hence he named the island "Trinidad"—Spanish for "Trinity."

That is the kind of experience you get when reading the Bible. At first it seems to be talking about three Gods, but as you go deeper into the Scriptures you discover there are not three Gods but one—one God in three Persons.

It must be noted, though, that it is not only in isolated texts that one encounters the doctrine of the Trinity. The very concept of God's love presupposes plurality in the Godhead. Love, to be love, must have an object. Self-love is love's opposite. Since God is eternal love, He must have had objects of eternal affection. The objects of His affection were the Son and the Spirit. The doctrine of the Trinity, therefore, is not only theologically but logically necessary to an understanding of the nature of the Deity.

Prayer

Father, help me understand that a being fully comprehended could not be God. In Your unfathomable depths all my thoughts are drowned. Symbolically I remove my shoes, for I sense I stand on holy ground. Amen.

Further Study

Eph 4:1-6; Dt 4:35; Ps 83:18; 1 Co 8:4
What did Paul confirm to the Ephesians and Corinthians?
What was the psalmist's conviction?

DECEMBER 3

EZEKIEL 43:13–44:31

13 "These are the measurements of the altar in units of length (each unit being the standard length plus three inches): the gutter is 21 inches deep and 21 inches wide, with a rim of nine inches around its edge. This is the base of the altar. 14 The distance from the gutter on the ground to the lower ledge is three and a half feet, and the width of the ledge is 21 inches. There are seven feet from the small ledge to the large ledge, whose width is also 21 inches. 15 The altar hearth is seven feet high, and four horns project upward from the hearth. 16 The hearth is square, 21 feet long by 21 feet wide. 17 The ledge is 24 and a half feet long by 24 and a half feet wide, with four equal sides. The rim all around it is 10 and a half inches, and its gutter is 21 inches all around it. The altar's steps face east."

18 Then He said to me: "Son of man, this is what the Lord GOD says: These are the statutes for the altar on the day it is constructed, so that burnt offerings may be sacrificed on it and blood may be sprinkled on it: 19 You are to give a bull from the herd as a sin offering to the Levitical priests who are from the offspring of Zadok, who approach Me in order to serve Me." This is the declaration of the Lord GOD. 20 "You must take some of its blood and apply it to the four horns of the altar, the four corners of the ledge, and all around the rim. In this way you will purify the altar and make atonement for it. 21 Then you must take away the bull for the sin offering, and it must be burned outside the sanctuary in the place appointed for the temple.

22 "On the second day you are to present an unblemished male goat as a sin offering. They will purify the altar just as they did with the bull. 23 When you have finished the purification, you are to present a young, unblemished bull and an unblemished ram from the flock. 24 You must present them before the LORD; the priests will throw salt on them and sacrifice them as a burnt offering to the LORD. 25 You will offer a goat for a sin offering each day for seven days. A young bull and a ram from the flock, both unblemished, must also be offered. 26 For seven days the priests are to make atonement for the altar and cleanse it. In this way they will consecrate it 27 and complete the days of purification. Then on the eighth day and afterwards, the priests will offer your burnt offerings and fellowship offerings on the altar, and I will accept you." This is the declaration of the Lord GOD.

44 The man then brought me back toward the sanctuary's outer gate that faced east, and it was closed. 2 The LORD said to me: "This gate will remain closed. It will not be opened, and no one will enter through it, because the LORD, the God of Israel, has entered through it. Therefore it will remain closed. 3 The prince himself will sit in the gateway to eat a meal before the LORD. He must enter by way of the portico of the gate and go out the same way."

4 Then the man brought me by way of the north gate to the front of the temple. I looked, and the glory of the LORD filled His temple. And I fell facedown. 5 The LORD said to me: "Son of man, pay attention; look with your eyes and listen with your ears to everything I tell you about all the statutes and laws of the LORD's temple. Take careful note of the entrance of the temple along with all the exits of the sanctuary.

6 "Say to the rebellious people, the house of Israel: This is what the Lord GOD says: I have had enough of all your

abominations, house of Israel. [7] When you brought in foreigners, uncircumcised in both heart and flesh, to occupy My sanctuary, you defiled My temple while you offered My food—the fat and the blood. You broke My covenant with all your abominations. [8] You have not kept charge of My holy things but have appointed others to keep charge of My sanctuary for you.

[9] "This is what the Lord GOD says: No foreigner, uncircumcised in heart and flesh, may enter My sanctuary, not even a foreigner who is among the Israelites. [10] Surely the Levites who wandered away from Me when Israel went astray, and who strayed from Me after their idols, will bear the consequences of their sin. [11] Yet they will occupy My sanctuary, serving as guards at the temple gates and ministering at the temple. They will slaughter the burnt offerings and other sacrifices for the people and will stand before them to serve them. [12] Because they ministered to the house of Israel before their idols and became a sinful stumbling block to them, therefore I swore an oath against them"—this is the declaration of the Lord GOD—"that they would bear the consequences of their sin. [13] They must not approach Me to serve Me as priests or come near any of My holy things or the most holy things. They will bear their disgrace and the consequences of the abominations they committed. [14] Yet I will make them responsible for the duties of the temple—for all its work and everything done in it.

[15] "But the Levitical priests descended from Zadok, who kept charge of My sanctuary when the Israelites went astray from Me, will approach Me to serve Me. They will stand before Me to offer Me fat and blood." This is the declaration of the Lord GOD. [16] "They are the ones who may enter My sanctuary and draw near to My table to serve Me. They will keep My mandate. [17] When they enter the gates of the inner court they must wear linen garments; they must not have on them anything made of wool when they minister at the gates of the inner court and within it. [18] They must wear linen turbans on their heads and linen undergarments around their waists. They are not to put on anything that makes them sweat. [19] Before they go out to the outer court, to the people, they must take off the clothes they have been ministering in, leave them in the holy chambers, and dress in other clothes so that they do not transmit holiness to the people through their clothes.

[20] "They may not shave their heads or let their hair grow long, but must carefully trim their hair. [21] No priest may drink wine before he enters the inner court. [22] He is not to marry a widow or a divorced woman, but must marry a virgin from the offspring of the house of Israel, or a widow who is the widow of a priest. [23] They must teach My people the difference between the holy and the common, and explain to them the difference between the clean and the unclean.

[24] "In a dispute, they will officiate as judges and decide the case according to My ordinances. They must observe My laws and statutes regarding all My appointed festivals, and keep My Sabbaths holy. [25] A priest may not come near a dead person so that he becomes defiled. However, he may defile himself for a father, a mother, a son, a daughter, a brother, or an unmarried sister. [26] After he is cleansed, he is to count off seven days for himself. [27] On the day he goes into the sanctuary, into the inner court to minister in the sanctuary, he must present his sin offering." This is the declaration of the Lord GOD.

[28] "This will be their inheritance: I am their inheritance. You are to give them no possession in Israel: I am their possession. [29] They will eat the grain offering, the sin offering, and the restitution offering. Everything in Israel that is permanently dedicated to the LORD will belong to them. [30] The best of all the firstfruits of every kind and contribution of every kind from all your gifts will belong to the priests. You are to give your first batch of dough to the priest so that a blessing may rest on your homes. [31] The priests may not eat

any bird or animal that died naturally or was mauled by wild beasts.

PSALM 136:10-16

¹⁰ He struck the firstborn of the
Egyptians
His love is eternal.
¹¹ and brought Israel out from
among them
His love is eternal.
¹² with a strong hand and
outstretched arm.
His love is eternal.
¹³ He divided the Red Sea
His love is eternal.
¹⁴ and led Israel through,
His love is eternal.
¹⁵ but hurled Pharaoh and his army
into the Red Sea.
His love is eternal.
¹⁶ He led His people in the wilderness.
His love is eternal.

PROVERBS 29:13-14

¹³ The poor and the oppressor have
this in common:
the LORD gives light to the eyes of
both.

¹⁴ A king who judges the poor with
fairness—
his throne will be established
forever.

1 JOHN 2:12-29

¹² I am writing to you, little children,
because your sins have been
forgiven on account of His
name.
¹³ I am writing to you, fathers,
because you have come to know
the One who is from the
beginning.
I am writing to you, young men,
because you have had victory over
the evil one.
¹⁴ I have written to you, children,
because you have come to know
the Father.
I have written to you, fathers,

because you have come to know
the One who is from the
beginning.
I have written to you, young
men,
because you are strong,
God's word remains in you,
and you have had victory over the
evil one.

¹⁵ Do not love the world or the things that belong to the world. If anyone loves the world, love for the Father is not in him. Because everything that belongs to the world— ¹⁶ the lust of the flesh, the lust of the eyes, and the pride in one's lifestyle—is not from the Father, but is from the world. ¹⁷ And the world with its lust is passing away, but the one who does God's will remains forever.

¹⁸ Children, it is the last hour. And as you have heard, "Antichrist is coming," even now many antichrists have come. We know from this that it is the last hour. ¹⁹ They went out from us, but they did not belong to us; for if they had belonged to us, they would have remained with us. However, they went out so that it might be made clear that none of them belongs to us.

²⁰ But you have an anointing from the Holy One, and you all have knowledge. ²¹ I have not written to you because you don't know the truth, but because you do know it, and because no lie comes from the truth. ²² Who is the liar, if not the one who denies that Jesus is the Messiah? He is the antichrist, the one who denies the Father and the Son. ²³ No one who denies the Son can have the Father; he who confesses the Son has the Father as well.

²⁴ What you have heard from the beginning must remain in you. If what you have heard from the beginning remains in you, then you will remain in the Son and in the Father. ²⁵ And this is the promise that He Himself made to us: eternal life. ²⁶ I have written these things to you about those who are trying to deceive you.

²⁷ The anointing you received from Him remains in you, and you don't need anyone to teach you. Instead, His

anointing teaches you about all things, and is true and is not a lie; just as it has taught you, remain in Him.

²⁸ So now, little children, remain in Him, so that when He appears we may have boldness and not be ashamed before Him at His coming. ²⁹ If you know that He is righteous, you know this as well: everyone who does what is right has been born of Him.

God Is a Father

I am writing to you, fathers, because you have come to know the One who is from the beginning.—1 JOHN 2:13

God is a Father in the creative sense and the familial sense. So, for whom was the Lord's Prayer designed—for everyone or only for God's redeemed children? There is no doubt in my mind that it was intended for Christ's true disciples. Obviously many people outside the Christian church find the words of the Lord's Prayer greatly appealing, but much of the appeal is sentimental rather than spiritual.

To understand the Lord's Prayer and apply its principles in the way our Lord intended, one needs to have experienced a genuine conversion. Then, and only then, does its meaning become apparent. Jesus shows us in the first sentence of His prayer pattern that true prayer must begin with a concept of God as Father. Someone has pointed out that the term "Father" answers all the philosophical questions about the nature of God. A father is a person; therefore God is not an impersonal being, aloof from all our troubles and trials. And, above all, a father is predisposed, by reason of his familial relationship, to give careful attention to what his child says.

When we pray, then, to the Father, we must hold in our minds the picture of our eternal Creator as a being who has a father's heart, a father's love, and a father's strength. This, then, must be the second note we strike when praying—God is a Father, and we must come to Him with all the trust and frankness of a child. Otherwise it is not a prayer.

Prayer

O God, I am so grateful that in the word "Father" I discover the greatest truth about You. My heart pillows itself on that glorious and wonderful fact. Thank You—Father. Amen.

Further Study

Jn 5:17-47; 1:12; 2 Co 6:17-18; Gl 4:5-6
How did Jesus speak of His Father?
What is God's promise to those who believe?

DECEMBER 4

*E*ZEKIEL 45:1–47:5

45 "When you divide the land by lot as an inheritance, you must set aside a donation to the LORD, a holy portion of the land, eight and one-third miles long and six and two-thirds miles wide. This entire tract of land will be holy. ² In this area there will be a square section for the sanctuary, 875 by 875 feet, with 87 and a half feet of open space all around it. ³ From this holy portion, you will measure off an area eight and one-third miles long and three and one-third miles wide, in which the sanctuary, the most holy place, will stand. ⁴ It will be a holy area of the land to be used by the priests who minister in the sanctuary, who draw near to serve the LORD. It will be a place for their houses, as well as a holy area for the sanctuary. ⁵ There will be another area eight and one-third miles long and three and one-third miles wide for the Levites who minister in the temple; it will be their possession for towns to live in.

⁶ "As the property of the city, you must set aside an area one and two-thirds of a mile wide and eight and one-third miles long, adjacent to the holy donation of land. It will be for the whole house of Israel. ⁷ And the prince will have the area on each side of the holy donation of land and the city's property, adjacent to the holy donation and the city's property, stretching to the west on the west side and to the east on the east side. Its length will correspond to one of the tribal portions from the western boundary to the eastern boundary. ⁸ This will be his land as a possession in Israel. My princes will no longer oppress My people but give the rest of the land to the house of Israel according to their tribes.

⁹ "This is what the Lord GOD says: You have gone too far, princes of Israel! Put away violence and oppression and do what is just and right. Put an end to your evictions of My people." This is the declaration of the Lord GOD. ¹⁰ "You must have honest balances, an honest dry measure, and an honest liquid measure. ¹¹ The dry measure and the liquid measure will be uniform, with the liquid measure containing five and a half gallons and the dry measure holding half a bushel. Their measurement will be one-tenth of the standard larger capacity measure. ¹² The shekel will weigh 20 gerahs. Your mina will equal 60 shekels.

¹³ "This is the contribution you are to offer: Three quarts from five bushels of wheat and three quarts from five bushels of barley. ¹⁴ The quota of oil in liquid measures will be one percent of every cor. The cor equals 10 liquid measures or one standard larger capacity measure, since 10 liquid measures equal one standard larger capacity measure. ¹⁵ And the quota from the flock is one animal out of every 200 from the well-watered pastures of Israel. These are for the grain offerings, burnt offerings, and fellowship offerings, to make atonement for the people." This is the declaration of the Lord GOD. ¹⁶ "All the people of the land must take part in this contribution for the prince in Israel. ¹⁷ Then the burnt offerings, grain offerings, and drink offerings for the festivals, New Moons, and Sabbaths—for all the appointed times of the house of Israel—will be the prince's responsibility. He will provide the sin offerings, grain offerings, burnt offerings, and fellowship offerings to make atonement on behalf of the house of Israel.

¹⁸ "This is what the Lord GOD says: In the first month, on the first day of the month, you are to take a young, unblemished bull and purify the sanctu-

ary. ¹⁹ The priest must take some of the blood from the sin offering and apply it to the temple doorposts, the four corners of the altar's ledge, and the doorposts of the gate to the inner court. ²⁰ You must do the same thing on the seventh day of the month for everyone who sins unintentionally or through ignorance. In this way you will make atonement for the temple.

²¹ "In the first month, on the fourteenth day of the month, you are to celebrate the Passover, a festival of seven days during which unleavened bread will be eaten. ²² On that day the prince will provide a bull as a sin offering on behalf of himself and all the people of the land. ²³ During the seven days of the festival, he will provide seven bulls and seven rams without blemish as a burnt offering to the LORD on each of the seven days, along with a male goat each day for a sin offering. ²⁴ He will also provide a grain offering of half a bushel per bull and half a bushel per ram, along with a gallon of oil for every half bushel. ²⁵ At the festival that begins on the fifteenth day of the seventh month, he will provide the same things for seven days— the same sin offerings, burnt offerings, grain offerings, and oil.

46 "This is what the Lord GOD says: The gate of the inner court that faces east must be closed during the six days of work, but it will be opened on the Sabbath day and opened on the day of the New Moon. ² The prince should enter from the outside by way of the gate's portico and stand at the doorpost of the gate while the priests sacrifice his burnt offerings and fellowship offerings. He will bow in worship at the threshold of the gate and then depart, but the gate must not be closed until evening. ³ The people of the land will also bow in worship before the LORD at the entrance of that gate on the Sabbaths and New Moons.

⁴ "The burnt offering that the prince presents to the LORD on the Sabbath day is to be six unblemished lambs and an unblemished ram. ⁵ The grain offering will be half a bushel with the ram, and

the grain offering with the lambs will be whatever he wants to give, as well as a gallon of oil for every half bushel. ⁶ On the day of the New Moon, the burnt offering is to be a young, unblemished bull, as well as six lambs and a ram without blemish. ⁷ He will provide a grain offering of half a bushel with the bull, half a bushel with the ram, and whatever he can afford with the lambs, together with a gallon of oil for every half bushel. ⁸ When the prince enters, he must go in by way of the gate's portico and go out the same way.

⁹ "When the people of the land come before the LORD at the appointed times, whoever enters by way of the north gate to worship must go out by way of the south gate, and whoever enters by way of the south gate must go out by way of the north gate. No one must return through the gate by which he entered, but must go out by the opposite gate. ¹⁰ When the people enter, the prince will enter with them, and when they leave, he will leave. ¹¹ At the festivals and appointed times, the grain offering will be half a bushel with the bull, half a bushel with the ram, and whatever he wants to give with the lambs, along with a gallon of oil for every half bushel.

¹² "When the prince makes a freewill offering, whether a burnt offering or a fellowship offering as a freewill offering to the LORD, the gate that faces east must be opened for him. He is to offer his burnt offering or fellowship offering just as he does on the Sabbath day. Then he will go out, and the gate must be closed after he leaves.

¹³ "You must offer an unblemished year-old male lamb as a daily burnt offering to the LORD; you will offer it every morning. ¹⁴ You must also prepare a grain offering every morning along with it: three quarts, with one-third of a gallon of oil to moisten the fine flour— a grain offering to the LORD. This is a permanent statute to be observed regularly. ¹⁵ They will offer the lamb, the grain offering, and the oil every morning as a regular burnt offering.

¹⁶ "This is what the Lord GOD says: If the prince gives a gift to each of his sons

as their inheritance, it will belong to his sons. It will become their property by inheritance. ¹⁷ But if he gives a gift from his inheritance to one of his servants, it will belong to that servant until the year of freedom, when it will revert to the prince. His inheritance belongs only to his sons; it is theirs. ¹⁸ The prince must not take any of the people's inheritance, evicting them from their property. He is to provide an inheritance for his sons from his own property, so that none of My people will be displaced from his own property."

¹⁹ Then he brought me through the entrance that was at the side of the gate, into the priests' holy chambers, which faced north. I saw a place there at the far western end. ²⁰ He said to me, "This is the place where the priests will boil the restitution offering and the sin offering, and where they will bake the grain offering, so that they do not bring them into the outer court and transmit holiness to the people." ²¹ Next he brought me into the outer court and led me past its four corners. There was a separate court in each of its corners. ²² In the four corners of the outer court there were enclosed courts, 70 feet long by 52 and a half feet wide. All four corner areas had the same dimensions. ²³ There was a stone wall around the inside of them, around the four of them, with ovens built at the base of the walls on all sides. ²⁴ He said to me: "These are the kitchens where those who minister at the temple will cook the people's sacrifices."

47 Then he brought me back to the entrance of the temple and there was water flowing from under the threshold of the temple toward the east, for the temple faced east. The water was coming down from under the south side of the threshold of the temple, south of the altar. ² Next he brought me out by way of the north gate and led me around to the outside to the outer gate that faced east; there the water was trickling from the south side. ³ As the man went out east with a measuring line in his hand, he measured off a third

of a mile and led me through the water. It came up to my ankles. ⁴ Then he measured off a third of a mile and led me through the water. It came up to my knees. He measured off another third of a mile and led me through the water. It came up to my waist. ⁵ Again he measured off a third of a mile, and it was a river that I could not cross on foot. For the water had risen; it was deep enough to swim in, a river that could not be crossed on foot.

PSALM 136:17-26

¹⁷ He struck down great kings
His love is eternal.
¹⁸ and slaughtered famous kings—
His love is eternal.
¹⁹ Sihon king of the Amorites
His love is eternal.
²⁰ and Og king of Bashan—
His love is eternal.
²¹ and gave their land as an inheritance,
His love is eternal.
²² an inheritance to Israel His servant.
His love is eternal.
²³ He remembered us in our humiliation
His love is eternal.
²⁴ and rescued us from our foes.
His love is eternal.
²⁵ He gives food to every creature.
His love is eternal.
²⁶ Give thanks to the God of heaven!
His love is eternal.

PROVERBS 29:15-17

¹⁵ A rod of correction imparts wisdom,
but a youth left to himself is a disgrace to his mother.

¹⁶ When the wicked increase, rebellion increases,
but the righteous will see their downfall.

¹⁷ Discipline your son, and he will give you comfort;
he will also give you delight.

1 JOHN 3:1-24

3 ¹ Look at how great a love the Father has given us, that we should be called God's children. And we are! The reason the world does not know us is that it didn't know Him. ² Dear friends, we are God's children now, and what we will be has not yet been revealed. We know that when He appears, we will be like Him, because we will see Him as He is. ³ And everyone who has this hope in Him purifies himself just as He is pure.

⁴ Everyone who commits sin also breaks the law; sin is the breaking of law. ⁵ You know that He was revealed so that He might take away sins, and there is no sin in Him. ⁶ Everyone who remains in Him does not sin; everyone who sins has not seen Him or known Him.

⁷ Little children, let no one deceive you! The one who does what is right is righteous, just as He is righteous. ⁸ The one who commits sin is of the Devil, for the Devil has sinned from the beginning. The Son of God was revealed for this purpose: to destroy the Devil's works. ⁹ Everyone who has been born of God does not sin, because His seed remains in him; he is not able to sin, because he has been born of God. ¹⁰ This is how God's children—and the Devil's children—are made evident.

Whoever does not do what is right is not of God, especially the one who does not love his brother. ¹¹ For this is the message you have heard from the beginning: we should love one another,

¹² unlike Cain, who was of the evil one and murdered his brother. And why did he murder him? Because his works were evil, and his brother's were righteous. ¹³ Do not be surprised, brothers, if the world hates you. ¹⁴ We know that we have passed from death to life because we love our brothers. The one who does not love remains in death. ¹⁵ Everyone who hates his brother is a murderer, and you know that no murderer has eternal life residing in him.

¹⁶ This is how we have come to know love: He laid down His life for us. We should also lay down our lives for our brothers. ¹⁷ If anyone has this world's goods and sees his brother in need but shuts off his compassion from him—how can God's love reside in him?

¹⁸ Little children, we must not love in word or speech, but in deed and truth; ¹⁹ that is how we will know we are of the truth, and will convince our hearts in His presence, ²⁰ because if our hearts condemn us, God is greater than our hearts and knows all things.

²¹ Dear friends, if our hearts do not condemn us we have confidence before God, ²² and can receive whatever we ask from Him because we keep His commands and do what is pleasing in His sight. ²³ Now this is His command: that we believe in the name of His Son Jesus Christ, and love one another as He commanded us. ²⁴ The one who keeps His commands remains in Him, and He in him. And the way we know that He remains in us is from the Spirit He has given us.

Self-Protection

Now this is His command: that we believe in the name of His Son Jesus Christ, and love one another.—1 JOHN 3:23

An advantage of being willing to feel disappointment is that it enables us to come in touch with another hidden sin of the heart—self-protection.

Whenever we are disappointed, we naturally feel hurt and experience inner pain. Some people are so affected by this that a pool of pain builds up inside them, and they say to themselves:

"People are a source of hurt. Stay away from them, and don't get too closely involved." They see noninvolvement as the best way to avoid the pain of possible disappointment.

But this attitude is a violation of the law of love. Lawrence Crabb, a Christian psychologist, says: "Deficient love is always central to our problems." Behind most of our problems is a failure to love others as we love ourselves. If we refuse to move towards someone in the spirit of love for fear they may disappoint us, then we are more interested in protecting ourselves from pain than we are in loving—and that is sin.

Did you ever think of self-protection as a sin? Well, it is, and in my estimation it is one of the most subtle of all. Many of our relationships are ruined by this—particularly marriage relationships. A man who shouts angrily at his wife early in his marriage is setting up a self-protective system that says: "Disappoint me, and you will have to suffer the consequences." What is he doing? He is protecting himself more than he is loving his wife. And that, no matter how one might attempt to rationalize it, is sin.

Prayer

Father, Your challenges are sometimes more than I can bear, yet I see the sense and wisdom that lies behind them. Reveal to me my own self-protective devices, and help me be willing to give them up in favor of loving as I have been loved. Amen.

Further Study

Lk 10:25-37; Rm 13:10; Jms 1:27
What did the priest and Levite display?
What did the Samaritan display?

DECEMBER 5

*E*ZEKIEL 47:6–48:35

⁶ He asked me, "Do you see this, son of man?" Then he led me back to the bank of the river. ⁷ When I had returned, I saw a very large number of trees along both sides of the riverbank. ⁸ He said to me, "This water flows out to the eastern region and goes down to the Arabah. When it enters the sea, the sea of foul water, the water of the sea becomes fresh. ⁹ Every kind of living creature that swarms will live wherever the river flows, and there will be a huge number of fish because this water goes there. Since the water will become fresh, there will be life everywhere the river goes. ¹⁰ Fishermen will stand beside it from En-gedi to En-eglaim. These will become places where nets are spread out to dry.

Their fish will consist of many different kinds, like the fish of the Mediterranean Sea. [11] Yet its swamps and marshes will not be healed; they will be left for salt. [12] All kinds of trees providing food will grow along both banks of the river. Their leaves will not wither, and their fruit will not fail. Each month they will bear fresh fruit because the water comes from the sanctuary. Their fruit will be used for food and their leaves for medicine."

[13] This is what the Lord GOD says: "This is the border you will use to divide the land as an inheritance for the 12 tribes of Israel. Joseph will receive two shares. [14] You will inherit it in equal portions, since I swore to give it to your ancestors. So this land will fall to you as an inheritance.

[15] "This is to be the border of the land:

On the north side it will extend from the Mediterranean Sea by way of Hethlon and Lebo-hamath to Zedad, [16] Berothah, and Sibraim (which is between the border of Damascus and the border of Hamath), as far as Hazer-hatticon, which is on the border of Hauran. [17] So the border will run from the sea to Hazar-enon at the border of Damascus, with the territory of Hamath to the north. This will be the northern side.

[18] On the east side it will run between Hauran and Damascus, along the Jordan between Gilead and the land of Israel; you will measure from the northern border to the eastern sea. This will be the eastern side.

[19] On the south side it will run from Tamar to the waters of Meribath-kadesh, and on to the Brook of Egypt as far as the Mediterranean Sea. This will be the southern side.

[20] On the west side the Mediterranean Sea will be the border, from the southern border up to a point

opposite Lebo-hamath. This will be the western side.

[21] "You are to divide this land among yourselves according to the tribes of Israel. [22] You will allot it as an inheritance for yourselves and for the foreigners living among you, who have fathered children among you. You will treat them like native-born Israelites; along with you, they will be allotted an inheritance among the tribes of Israel. [23] In whatever tribe the foreigner lives, you will assign his inheritance there." This is the declaration of the Lord GOD.

48

"Now these are the names of the tribes:

From the northern end, along the road of Hethlon, to Lebo-hamath as far as Hazar-enon, at the northern border of Damascus, alongside Hamath and extending from the eastern side to the sea, will be Dan—one portion.
[2] Next to the territory of Dan, from the east side to the west, will be Asher—one portion.
[3] Next to the territory of Asher, from the east side to the west, will be Naphtali—one portion.
[4] Next to the territory of Naphtali, from the east side to the west, will be Manasseh—one portion.
[5] Next to the territory of Manasseh, from the east side to the west, will be Ephraim—one portion.
[6] Next to the territory of Ephraim, from the east side to the west, will be Reuben—one portion.
[7] Next to the territory of Reuben, from the east side to the west, will be Judah—one portion.

[8] "Next to the territory of Judah, from the east side to the west, will be the portion you donate to the LORD, eight and one-third miles wide, and as long as one of the tribal portions from the east side to the west. The sanctuary will be in the middle of it.
[9] "The special portion you donate to

the LORD will be eight and one-third miles long and three and one-third miles wide. [10] This holy donation will be set apart for the priests alone. It will be eight and one-third miles long on the northern side, three and one-third miles wide on the western side, three and one-third miles wide on the eastern side, and eight and one-third miles long on the southern side. The LORD's sanctuary will be in the middle of it. [11] It is for the consecrated priests, the sons of Zadok, who kept My charge and did not go astray as the Levites did when the Israelites went astray. [12] It will be a special donation for them out of the holy donation of the land, a most holy place adjacent to the territory of the Levites.

[13] "Next to the territory of the priests, the Levites will have an area eight and one-third miles long and three and one-third miles wide. The total length will be eight and one-third miles and the width three and one-third miles. [14] They must not sell or exchange any of it, and they must not transfer this choice part of the land, for it is holy to the LORD.

[15] "The remaining area, one and two-thirds of a mile wide and eight and one-third miles long, will be for common use by the city, for both residential and open space. The city will be in the middle of it. [16] These are the city's measurements:

one and a half miles on the north side;
one and a half miles on the south side;
one and a half miles on the east side;
and one and a half miles on the west side.

[17] The city's open space will extend:

425 feet to the north,
425 feet to the south,
425 feet to the east,
and 425 feet to the west.

[18] "The remainder of the length alongside the holy donation will be three and one-third miles to the east and three and one-third miles to the west. It will run alongside the holy donation. Its produce will be food for the workers of the city. [19] The city's workers from all the tribes of Israel will cultivate it. [20] The entire donation will be eight and one-third miles by eight and one-third miles; you are to set apart the holy donation along with the city property as a square area.

[21] "The remaining area on both sides of the holy donation and the city property will belong to the prince. He will own the land adjacent to the tribal portions, next to the eight and one-third miles of the donation as far as the eastern border and next to the eight and one-third miles of the donation as far as the western border. The holy donation and the sanctuary of the temple will be in the middle of it. [22] Except for the Levitical property and the city property in the middle of the area belonging to the prince, the area between the territory of Judah and that of Benjamin will belong to the prince.

[23] "As for the rest of the tribes:

From the east side to the west,
will be Benjamin—one portion.
[24] Next to the territory of
Benjamin, from the east side to
the west, will be Simeon—one
portion.
[25] Next to the territory of Simeon,
from the east side to the west,
will be Issachar—one portion.
[26] Next to the territory of Issachar,
from the east side to the west,
will be Zebulun—one portion.
[27] Next to the territory of Zebulun,
from the east side to the west,
will be Gad—one portion.

[28] Next to the territory of Gad toward the south side, the border will run from Tamar to the waters of Meribath-kadesh, to the Brook of Egypt, and out to the Mediterranean Sea. [29] This is the land you are to allot as an inheritance to Israel's tribes, and these will be their portions." This is the declaration of the Lord GOD.

[30] "These are the exits of the city:

On the north side, which measures one and a half miles, ³¹ there will be three gates facing north, the gates of the city being named for the tribes of Israel: one, the gate of Reuben; one, the gate of Judah; and one, the gate of Levi. ³² On the east side, which is one and a half miles, there will be three gates: one, the gate of Joseph; one, the gate of Benjamin; and one, the gate of Dan. ³³ On the south side, which measures one and a half miles, there will be three gates: one, the gate of Simeon; one, the gate of Issachar; and one, the gate of Zebulun. ³⁴ On the west side, which is one and a half miles, there will be three gates: one, the gate of Gad; one, the gate of Asher; and one, the gate of Naphtali.

³⁵ The perimeter of the city will be six miles, and the name of the city from that day on will be: Yahweh Is There."

*P*SALM 137:1-6

¹ By the rivers of Babylon—
   there we sat down and wept
   when we remembered Zion.
² There we hung up our lyres
   on the poplar trees,
³ for our captors there asked us for
      songs,
   and our tormentors, for rejoicing:
   "Sing us one of the songs of Zion."

⁴ How can we sing the LORD's song
   on foreign soil?
⁵ If I forget you, Jerusalem,
   may my right hand forget its skill.
⁶ May my tongue stick to the roof
      of my mouth
   if I do not remember you,
   if I do not exalt Jerusalem as my
      greatest joy!

*P*ROVERBS 29:18-21

¹⁸ Without revelation people run
      wild,

but one who keeps the law will be
   happy.

¹⁹ A servant cannot be disciplined by
      words;
   though he understands, he doesn't
      respond.

²⁰ Do you see a man who speaks too
      soon?
   There is more hope for a fool than
      for him.

²¹ A slave pampered from his youth
   will become arrogant later on.

I *J*OHN 4:1-21

4 Dear friends, do not believe every spirit, but test the spirits to determine if they are from God, because many false prophets have gone out into the world. ² This is how you know the Spirit of God: Every spirit who confesses that Jesus Christ has come in the flesh is from God. ³ But every spirit who does not confess Jesus is not from God. This is the spirit of the antichrist; you have heard that he is coming, and he is already in the world now.

⁴ You are from God, little children, and you have conquered them, because the One who is in you is greater than the one who is in the world. ⁵ They are from the world. Therefore what they say is from the world, and the world listens to them. ⁶ We are from God. Anyone who knows God listens to us; anyone who is not from God does not listen to us. From this we know the Spirit of truth and the spirit of deception.

⁷ Dear friends, let us love one another, because love is from God, and everyone who loves has been born of God and knows God. ⁸ The one who does not love does not know God, because God is love. ⁹ God's love was revealed among us in this way: God sent His One and Only Son into the world so that we might live through Him. ¹⁰ Love consists in this: not that we loved God, but that He loved us and sent His Son to be the

propitiation for our sins. ¹¹ Dear friends, if God loved us in this way, we also must love one another. ¹² No one has ever seen God. If we love one another, God remains in us and His love is perfected in us.

¹³ This is how we know that we remain in Him and He in us: He has given to us from His Spirit. ¹⁴ And we have seen and we testify that the Father has sent the Son as Savior of the world. ¹⁵ Whoever confesses that Jesus is the Son of God—God remains in him and he in God. ¹⁶ And we have come to know and to believe the love that God has for us. God is love, and the one who remains in love re-mains in God, and God remains in him. ¹⁷ In this, love is perfected with us so that we may have confidence in the day of judgment; for we are as He is in this world. ¹⁸ There is no fear in love; instead, perfect love drives out fear, because fear involves punishment. So the one who fears has not reached perfection in love. ¹⁹ We love because He first loved us.

²⁰ If anyone says, "I love God," yet hates his brother, he is a liar. For the person who does not love his brother whom he has seen cannot love God whom he has not seen. ²¹ And we have this command from Him: the one who loves God must also love his brother.

God—the Aggressive Lover

Love consists in this: not that we loved God, but that He loved us.—1 JOHN 4:10

When we perceive how much God loves us, an amazing effect is produced in our personalities—we begin to love like Him. We cannot help it. Love—*agape* love—is not the fruit of labor; it is a response. When we stand at the foot of Calvary, the place where the love of God is fully focused and caught up, the scales drop from our eyes, and our own love flames in response. We love Him because He first loved us.

Teresa of Avila tells how one day, going into her private room, she noticed a picture of our Lord being scourged before His crucifixion. She must have seen it hundreds of times, but in that moment of revelation she saw it as she had never seen it before. She saw God suffering—suffering for love and suffering for her. The revelation sent her to her knees sobbing in pain and wonder, and when she arose, she was a changed woman. The revelation of Calvary's love was the great divide in her life. She said that she arose with a sense of "unpayable debt" and went out to share God's realized love with others.

Don't try to manufacture love. Linger in the shadow of the Cross. The love of God finds its most burning expression there. Meditate on it. Contemplate it. Remember that heaven knows no higher strategy for begetting love in mortal hearts than by granting us a vision of how much we are loved, a vision strong enough to evoke a response in our hearts—and by that answering love begotten in us by the Holy Spirit, we are freed and purged and saved.

Prayer

Gracious Father, I see that before I can love, I must comprehend how much I am loved. Help me be aware that in my heart I have the most aggressive Lover in the universe. I am eternally grateful. Amen.

Further Study

Rm 5:1-8; Jr 31:3; Eph 2:4-5; 1 Jn 3:1
How has God demonstrated His love for us?
What kind of love is God's love?

DECEMBER 6

DANIEL 1:1–2:35

1 In the third year of the reign of Jehoiakim king of Judah, Nebuchadnezzar king of Babylon came to Jerusalem and laid siege to it. ² The Lord handed Jehoiakim king of Judah over to him, along with some of the vessels from the house of God. Nebuchadnezzar carried them to the land of Babylon, to the house of his god, and put the vessels in the treasury of his god.

³ The king ordered Ashpenaz, the chief of his court officials, to bring some of the Israelites from the royal family and from the nobility— ⁴ young men without any physical defect, good-looking, suitable for instruction in all wisdom, knowledgeable, perceptive, and capable of serving in the king's palace—and to teach them the Chaldean language and literature. ⁵ The king assigned them daily provisions from the royal food and from the wine that he drank. They were to be trained for three years, and at the end of that time they were to serve in the king's court. ⁶ Among them, from the descendants of Judah, were Daniel, Hananiah, Mishael, and Azariah. ⁷ The chief official gave them different names: to Daniel, he gave the name Belteshazzar; to Hananiah, Shadrach; to Mishael, Meshach; and to Azariah, Abednego.

⁸ Daniel determined that he would not defile himself with the king's food or with the wine he drank. So he asked permission from the chief official not to defile himself. ⁹ God had granted Daniel favor and compassion from the chief official, ¹⁰ yet he said to Daniel, "My lord the king assigned your food and drink. I'm afraid of what would happen if he saw your faces looking thinner than those of the other young men your age. You would endanger my life with the king."

¹¹ So Daniel said to the guard whom the chief official had assigned to Daniel, Hananiah, Mishael, and Azariah, ¹² "Please test your servants for 10 days. Let us be given vegetables to eat and water to drink. ¹³ Then examine our appearance and the appearance of the young men who are eating the king's food, and deal with your servants based on what you see." ¹⁴ He agreed with them in this matter and tested them for 10 days. ¹⁵ At the end of 10 days they looked better and healthier than all the young men who were eating the king's food. ¹⁶ So the guard continued to remove their food and the wine they were to drink and gave them vegetables.

¹⁷ God gave these four young men knowledge and understanding in every kind of literature and wisdom. Daniel also understood visions and dreams of every kind. ¹⁸ At the end of the time that the king had said to present them, the chief official presented them to Nebuchadnezzar. ¹⁹ The king interviewed them, and among all of them, no one was found equal to Daniel, Hananiah,

Mishael, and Azariah. So they began to serve in the king's court. ²⁰ In every matter of wisdom and understanding that the king consulted them about, he found them 10 times better than all the diviner-priests and mediums in his entire kingdom. ²¹ Daniel remained there until the first year of King Cyrus.

2 In the second year of his reign, Nebuchadnezzar had dreams that troubled him, and sleep deserted him. ² So the king gave orders to summon the diviner-priests, mediums, sorcerers, and Chaldeans to tell the king his dreams. When they came and stood before the king, ³ he said to them, "I have had a dream and am anxious to understand it."

⁴ The Chaldeans spoke to the king: "May the king live forever. Tell your servants the dream, and we will give the interpretation."

⁵ The king replied to the Chaldeans, "My word is final: If you don't tell me the dream and its interpretation, you will be torn limb from limb, and your houses will be made a garbage dump. ⁶ But if you make the dream and its interpretation known to me, you'll receive gifts, a reward, and great honor from me. So make the dream and its interpretation known to me."

⁷ They answered a second time, "May the king tell the dream to his servants, and we will give the interpretation."

⁸ The king replied, "I know for certain you are trying to gain some time, because you see that my word is final. ⁹ If you don't tell me the dream, there is one decree for you. You have conspired to tell me something false or fraudulent until the situation changes. So tell me the dream and I will know you can give me its interpretation."

¹⁰ The Chaldeans answered the king, "No one on earth can make known what the king requests. Consequently, no king, however great and powerful, has ever asked anything like this of any diviner-priest, medium, or Chaldean. ¹¹ What the king is asking is so difficult that no one can make it known to him except the gods, whose dwelling is not with mortals." ¹² Because of this, the

king became violently angry and gave orders to destroy all the wise men of Babylon. ¹³ The decree was issued that the wise men were to be executed, and they searched for Daniel and his friends, to execute them.

¹⁴ Then Daniel responded with tact and discretion to Arioch, the commander of the king's guard, who had gone out to execute the wise men of Babylon. ¹⁵ He asked Arioch, the king's officer, "Why is the decree from the king so harsh?" Then Arioch explained the situation to Daniel. ¹⁶ So Daniel went and asked the king to give him some time, so that he could give the king the interpretation.

¹⁷ Then Daniel went to his house and told his friends Hananiah, Mishael, and Azariah about the matter, ¹⁸ urging them to ask the God of heaven for mercy concerning this mystery, so Daniel and his friends would not be killed with the rest of Babylon's wise men. ¹⁹ The mystery was then revealed to Daniel in a vision at night, and Daniel praised the God of heaven ²⁰ and declared:

May the name of God
be praised forever and ever,
for wisdom and power belong
    to Him.
²¹ He changes the times and seasons;
He removes kings
    and establishes kings.
He gives wisdom to the wise
and knowledge to those
who have understanding.
²² He reveals the deep
    and hidden things;
He knows what is in the darkness,
and light dwells with Him.
²³ I offer thanks and praise to You,
God of my fathers,
because You have given me
wisdom and power.
And now You have let me know
what we asked of You,
for You have let us know
the king's mystery.

²⁴ Therefore Daniel went to Arioch, whom the king had assigned to destroy the wise men of Babylon. He came and

said to him, "Don't kill the wise men of Babylon! Bring me before the king, and I will give him the interpretation."

²⁵ Then Arioch quickly brought Daniel before the king and said to him, "I have found a man among the Judean exiles who can let the king know the interpretation."

²⁶ The king said in reply to Daniel, whose name was Belteshazzar, "Are you able to tell me the dream I had and its interpretation?"

²⁷ Daniel answered the king: "No wise man, medium, diviner-priest, or astrologer is able to make known to the king the mystery he asked about. ²⁸ But there is a God in heaven who reveals mysteries, and He has let King Nebuchadnezzar know what will happen in the last days. Your dream and the visions that came into your mind as you lay in bed were these: ²⁹ Your Majesty, while you were in your bed, thoughts came to your mind about what will happen in the future. The revealer of mysteries has let you know what will happen. ³⁰ As for me, this mystery has been revealed to me, not because I have more wisdom than anyone living, but in order that the interpretation might be made known to the king, and that you may understand the thoughts of your mind.

³¹ "My king, as you were watching, a colossal statue appeared. That statue, tall and dazzling, was standing in front of you, and its appearance was terrifying. ³² The head of the statue was pure gold, its chest and arms were silver, its stomach and thighs were bronze, ³³ its legs were iron, and its feet were partly iron and partly fired clay. ³⁴ As you were watching, a stone broke off without a hand touching it, struck the statue on its feet of iron and fired clay, and crushed them. ³⁵ Then the iron, the fired clay, the bronze, the silver, and the gold were shattered and became like chaff from the summer threshing floors. The wind carried them away, and not a trace of them could be found. But the stone that struck the statue became a great mountain and filled the whole earth.

PSALM 137:7–138:3

⁷ Remember, LORD, what the
  Edomites said
that day at Jerusalem:
"Destroy it! Destroy it
down to its foundations!"
⁸ Daughter Babylon, doomed to
  destruction,
happy is the one who pays you
  back
what you have done to us.
⁹ Happy is he who takes your little
  ones
and dashes them against the rocks.

¹ I will give You thanks with all my
  heart;
I will sing Your praise before the
  heavenly beings.
² I will bow down toward Your holy
  temple
and give thanks to Your name
for Your constant love and
  faithfulness.
You have exalted Your name and
  Your promise above
  everything else.
³ On the day I called, You answered
  me;
You increased strength within me.

PROVERBS 29:22-23

²² An angry man stirs up conflict,
  and a hot-tempered man increases
  rebellion.

²³ A person's pride will humble him,
  but a humble spirit will gain
  honor.

1 JOHN 5:1-21

5 Everyone who believes that Jesus is the Messiah has been born of God, and everyone who loves the parent also loves his child. ² This is how we know that we love God's children when we love God and obey His commands. ³ For this is what love for God is: to keep His commands. Now His commands are not a burden, ⁴ because whatever has been

born of God conquers the world. This is the victory that has conquered the world: our faith. ⁵ And who is the one who conquers the world but the one who believes that Jesus is the Son of God?

⁶ Jesus Christ—He is the One who came by water and blood; not by water only, but by water and by blood. And the Spirit is the One who testifies, because the Spirit is the truth. ⁷ For there are three that testify: ⁸ the Spirit, the water, and the blood—and these three are in agreement. ⁹ If we accept the testimony of men, God's testimony is greater, because it is God's testimony that He has given about His Son. ¹⁰ (The one who believes in the Son of God has the testimony in himself. The one who does not believe God has made Him a liar, because he has not believed in the testimony that God has given about His Son.) ¹¹ And this is the testimony: God has given us eternal life, and this life is in His Son.

¹² The one who has the Son has life. The one who doesn't have the Son of God does not have life. ¹³ I have written these things to you who believe in the name of the Son of God, so that you may know that you have eternal life.

¹⁴ Now this is the confidence we have before Him: whenever we ask anything according to His will, He hears us. ¹⁵ And if we know that He hears whatever we ask, we know that we have what we have asked Him for.

¹⁶ If anyone sees his brother committing a sin that does not bring death, he should ask, and God will give life to him—to those who commit sin that doesn't bring death. There is sin that brings death. I am not saying he should pray about that. ¹⁷ All unrighteousness is sin, and there is sin that does not bring death.

¹⁸ We know that everyone who has been born of God does not sin, but the One who is born of God keeps him, and the evil one does not touch him. ¹⁹ We know that we are of God, and the whole world is under the sway of the evil one. ²⁰ And we know that the Son of God has come and has given us understanding so that we may know the true One. We are in the true One—that is, in His Son Jesus Christ. He is the true God and eternal life.

²¹ Little children, guard yourselves from idols.

Truth in a Nutshell

On the day I called, You answered me;
You increased strength within me.—Psalm 138:3

What are the benefits of keeping our gaze continually focused on God? I can think of at least three.

First, the more we study Him, the more we will want to become like Him. The most natural thing in the world, when there is a good relationship between parents and their children, is for that child to want to become like them. That is the way it is also with God our Father. The more we discover of His love, His holiness, His purity, His trustworthiness, His strength, His patience, the more we want to emulate Him.

Second, the more we study God, the better we will know ourselves. When Isaiah stepped into the Temple and had a vision of God, he also saw the truth about himself. Things that were hidden deep within him came to light in the presence of the Eternal.

Third, the more we study Him, the clearer will be our perspective on the world. When you see that God is in charge, then you won't panic every time you open the newspaper. You can only know God, of course, through Christ, and because You have Him, instead of saying, "Look what the world has come to," you will be able to say, "Look what has come to the world."

The people who know their God will firmly resist the Adversary, says Daniel. He writes, "The people who know their God will be strong and take action" (Dn 11:32). I can do no more than to say—there you have it in a nutshell. The more you know God, the stronger you will be.

Prayer

My Father and my God, now I set my course for the wide seas. With Your truth as my compass and Your Word as my chart, I set sail on this great adventure to know You better. I can count on You, but can I count on me? With Christ's help I can. Amen.

Further Study

2 Tm 1:1-12; Jn 17:3; Jb 19:25
What did Jesus pray?
What was the key to Job's facing his difficult circumstances?

DECEMBER 7

DANIEL 2:36–3:30

³⁶ "This was the dream; now we will tell the king its interpretation. ³⁷ Your Majesty, you are king of kings. The God of heaven has given you sovereignty, power, strength, and glory. ³⁸ Wherever people live—or wild animals, or birds of the air—He has handed them over to you and made you ruler over them all. You are the head of gold.

³⁹ "After you, there will arise another kingdom, inferior to yours, and then another, a third kingdom, of bronze, which will rule the whole earth. ⁴⁰ A fourth kingdom will be as strong as iron; for iron crushes and shatters everything, and like iron that smashes, it will crush and smash all the others. ⁴¹ You saw the feet and toes, partly of a pot-ter's fired clay and partly of iron—it will be a divided kingdom, though some of the strength of iron will be in it. You saw the iron mixed with clay, ⁴² and that the toes of the feet were part iron and part fired clay—part of the kingdom will be strong, and part will be brittle. ⁴³ You saw the iron mixed with clay—the peoples will mix with one another but will not hold together, just as iron does not mix with fired clay.

⁴⁴ "In the days of those kings, the God of heaven will set up a kingdom that will never be destroyed, and this kingdom will not be left to another people. It will crush all these kingdoms and bring them to an end, but will itself endure forever. ⁴⁵ You saw a stone break off from the mountain without a hand touching it, and it crushed the iron,

bronze, fired clay, silver, and gold. The great God has told the king what will happen in the future. The dream is true, and its interpretation certain."

⁴⁶ Then King Nebuchadnezzar fell down, paid homage to Daniel, and gave orders to present an offering and incense to him. ⁴⁷ The king said to Daniel, "Your God is indeed God of gods, Lord of kings, and a revealer of mysteries, since you were able to reveal this mystery." ⁴⁸ Then the king promoted Daniel and gave him many generous gifts. He made him ruler over the entire province of Babylon and chief governor over all the wise men of Babylon. ⁴⁹ At Daniel's request, the king appointed Shadrach, Meshach, and Abednego to manage the province of Babylon. But Daniel remained at the king's court.

3 King Nebuchadnezzar made a gold statue, 90 feet high and nine feet wide. He set it up on the plain of Dura in the province of Babylon. ² King Nebuchadnezzar sent word to assemble the satraps, prefects, governors, advisers, treasurers, judges, magistrates, and all the rulers of the provinces to attend the dedication of the statue King Nebuchadnezzar had set up. ³ So the satraps, prefects, governors, advisers, treasurers, judges, magistrates, and all the rulers of the provinces assembled for the dedication of the statue the king had set up. Then they stood before the statue Nebuchadnezzar had set up.

⁴ A herald loudly proclaimed, "People of every nation and language, you are commanded: ⁵ When you hear the sound of the horn, flute, zither, lyre, harp, drum, and every kind of music, you are to fall down and worship the gold statue that King Nebuchadnezzar has set up. ⁶ But whoever does not fall down and worship will immediately be thrown into a furnace of blazing fire."

⁷ Therefore, when all the people heard the sound of the horn, flute, zither, lyre, harp, and every kind of music, people of every nation and language fell down and worshiped the gold statue that King Nebuchadnezzar had set up.

⁸ Some Chaldeans took this occasion

to come forward and maliciously accuse the Jews. ⁹ They said to King Nebuchadnezzar, "May the king live forever. ¹⁰ You as king have issued a decree that everyone who hears the sound of the horn, flute, zither, lyre, harp, drum, and every kind of music must fall down and worship the gold statue. ¹¹ Whoever does not fall down and worship will be thrown into a furnace of blazing fire. ¹² There are some Jews you have appointed to manage the province of Babylon: Shadrach, Meshach, and Abednego. These men have ignored you, the king; they do not serve your gods or worship the gold statue you have set up."

¹³ Then in a furious rage Nebuchadnezzar gave orders to bring in Shadrach, Meshach, and Abednego. So these men were brought before the king. ¹⁴ Nebuchadnezzar asked them, "Shadrach, Meshach, and Abednego, is it true that you don't serve my gods or worship the gold statue I have set up? ¹⁵ Now if you're ready, when you hear the sound of the horn, flute, zither, lyre, harp, drum, and every kind of music, fall down and worship the statue I made. But if you don't worship it, you will immediately be thrown into a furnace of blazing fire—and who is the god who can rescue you from my power?"

¹⁶ Shadrach, Meshach, and Abednego replied to the king, "Nebuchadnezzar, we don't need to give you an answer to this question. ¹⁷ If the God we serve exists, then He can rescue us from the furnace of blazing fire, and He can rescue us from the power of you, the king. ¹⁸ But even if He does not rescue us, we want you as king to know that we will not serve your gods or worship the gold statue you set up."

¹⁹ Then Nebuchadnezzar was filled with rage, and the expression on his face changed toward Shadrach, Meshach, and Abednego. He gave orders to heat the furnace seven times more than was customary, ²⁰ and he commanded some of the strongest soldiers in his army to tie up Shadrach, Meshach, and Abednego and throw them into the furnace of blazing fire. ²¹ So these men, in their trousers, robes, head coverings,

and other clothes, were tied up and thrown into the furnace of blazing fire. ²² Since the king's command was so urgent and the furnace extremely hot, the raging flames killed those men who carried Shadrach, Meshach, and Abednego up. ²³ And these three men, Shadrach, Meshach, and Abednego fell, bound, into the furnace of blazing fire. ²⁴ Then King Nebuchadnezzar jumped up in alarm. He said to his advisers, "Didn't we throw three men, bound, into the fire?"

"Yes, of course, Your Majesty," they replied to the king.

²⁵ He exclaimed, "Look! I see four men, not tied, walking around in the fire unharmed; and the fourth looks like a son of the gods."

²⁶ Nebuchadnezzar then approached the door of the furnace of blazing fire and called: "Shadrach, Meshach, and Abednego, you servants of the Most High God—come out!" So Shadrach, Meshach, and Abednego came out of the fire. ²⁷ When the satraps, prefects, governors, and the king's advisers gathered around, they saw that the fire had no effect on the bodies of these men: not a hair of their heads was singed, their robes were unaffected, and there was no smell of fire on them. ²⁸ Nebuchadnezzar exclaimed, "Praise to the God of Shadrach, Meshach, and Abednego! He sent His angel and rescued His servants who trusted in Him. They violated the king's command and risked their lives rather than serve or worship any god except their own God. ²⁹ Therefore I issue a decree that anyone of any people, nation, or language who says anything offensive against the God of Shadrach, Meshach, and Abednego will be torn limb from limb and his house made a garbage dump. For there is no other god who is able to deliver like this." ³⁰ Then the king rewarded Shadrach, Meshach, and Abednego in the province of Babylon.

PSALM 138:4-8

⁴ All the kings on earth will give
   You thanks, LORD,

when they hear what You have
   promised.
⁵ They will sing of the LORD's ways,
   for the LORD's glory is great.
⁶ Though the LORD is exalted,
   He takes note of the humble;
   but He knows the haughty from
      afar.

⁷ If I walk in the thick of danger,
   You will preserve my life from the
      anger of my enemies.
   You will extend Your hand;
   Your right hand will save me.
⁸ The LORD will fulfill His purpose
      for me.
   LORD, Your love is eternal;
   do not abandon the work of Your
      hands.

PROVERBS 29:24-25

²⁴ To be a thief's partner is to hate
      oneself;
   he hears the curse but will not
      testify.

²⁵ The fear of man is a snare,
   but the one who trusts in the
      LORD is protected.

2 JOHN 1-13

The Elder:
To the elect lady and her children, whom I love in truth—and not only I, but also all who have come to know the truth— ² because of the truth that remains in us and will be with us forever.

³ Grace, mercy, and peace will be with us from God the Father and from Jesus Christ, the Son of the Father, in truth and love.

⁴ I was very glad to find some of your children walking in truth, in keeping with a command we have received from the Father. ⁵ So now I urge you, lady—not as if I were writing you a new command, but one we have had from the beginning—that we love one another. ⁶ And this is love: that we walk according to His commands. This is the command

as you have heard it from the beginning: you must walk in love.

⁷ Many deceivers have gone out into the world; they do not confess the coming of Jesus Christ in the flesh. This is the deceiver and the antichrist. ⁸ Watch yourselves so that you don't lose what we have worked for, but you may receive a full reward. ⁹ Anyone who does not remain in the teaching about Christ, but goes beyond it, does not have God. The one who remains in that teaching, this one has both the Father and the Son. ¹⁰ If anyone comes to you and does not bring this teaching, do not receive him into your home, and don't say, "Welcome," to him; ¹¹ for the one who says, "Welcome," to him shares in his evil works.

¹² Though I have many things to write to you, I don't want to do so with paper and ink. Instead, I hope to be with you and talk face to face so that our joy may be complete.

¹³ The children of your elect sister send you greetings.

Demandingness in Action

We want you as king to know that we will not serve your gods or worship the gold statue you set up.

—DANIEL 3:18

How does demandingness manifest itself? One way is by an insistence that God answer our prayers in the way we think He should. I talked with a woman whose husband had abandoned her and their three small children. As she talked, I grew uncomfortable, for she told me: "I know God is going to bring him back. If He doesn't, then He is not as faithful as He says He is. That can't be, so my husband will come back."

Can you hear the spirit of demandingness in these words? I sympathized with her hurt to such a degree that it was painful for me to have to explain this: that faith is one thing but demandingness is another. Her "faith" in God was based not on unconditional confidence in His character and sovereign purposes, but rather in the hope that He would relieve her suffering in the way she thought best.

Deep hurt is a most suitable environment in which we can wrongfully nourish a demanding spirit. Nothing convinces us more that God must answer our prayers in the way we think He should than when we are experiencing continued heartache. And the line between legitimate desiring and illegitimate demanding is a thin one which is easily crossed.

How can we be sure our desiring does not turn into demanding? When we are willing to say: "If God does not grant what I desire, then I can still go on because I know that He will never abandon me, and in His love I have all the strength I need to handle whatever comes."

Prayer

O God, save me from an insistent and demanding spirit. You who are always reaching out to me in love and awakening me, help me to recognize the difference between a desire and a demand. In Jesus' name. Amen.

Further Study

Mt 26:36-46; Ps 40:8; Eph 6:6; Php 1:1
How did Jesus express desire without demandingness?
How did Paul express it?

DECEMBER 8

*D*ANIEL 4:1–5:31

4 King Nebuchadnezzar,

To those of every people, nation, and language, who live in all the earth:

May your prosperity increase. ² I am pleased to tell you about the miracles and wonders the Most High God has done for me.

³ How great are His miracles,
and how mighty His wonders!
His kingdom is an eternal kingdom,
and His dominion is
    from generation to generation.

⁴ I, Nebuchadnezzar, was at ease in my house and flourishing in my palace. ⁵ I had a dream, and it frightened me; while in my bed, the images and visions in my mind alarmed me. ⁶ So I issued a decree to bring all the wise men of Babylon to me in order that they might make the dream's interpretation known to me. ⁷ When the diviner-priests, mediums, Chaldeans, and astrologers came in, I told them the dream, but they could not make its interpretation known to me. ⁸ Finally Daniel, named Belteshazzar after the name of my god—and the spirit of the holy gods is in him—came before me. I told him the dream: ⁹ Belteshazzar, head of the diviners, because I know that you have a spirit of the holy

gods and that no mystery puzzles you, explain to me the visions of my dream that I saw, and its interpretation. ¹⁰ In the visions of my mind as I was lying in bed, I saw this:

There was a tree in the middle
    of the earth,
and its height was great.
¹¹ The tree grew large and strong;
its top reached to the sky,
and it was visible to the ends
    of the earth.
¹² Its leaves were beautiful, its fruit
    was abundant,
and on it was food for all.
Wild animals found shelter under it,
the birds of the air lived
    in its branches,
and every creature was fed from it.

¹³ As I was lying in my bed, I also saw in the visions of my mind an observer, a holy one, coming down from heaven. ¹⁴ He called out loudly:

Cut down the tree and chop off
    its branches;
strip off its leaves and scatter
    its fruit.
Let the animals flee from under it,
and the birds from its branches.
¹⁵ But leave the stump with its roots
    in the ground,
and with a band of iron
    and bronze around it,
in the tender grass of the field.

1475

Let him be drenched with dew
　　from the sky
and share the plants of the earth
　　with the animals.
¹⁶ Let his mind be changed from that
　　of a man,
and let him be given the mind
　　of an animal
for seven periods of time.
¹⁷ This word is by decree
　　of the observers;
the matter is a command
　　from the holy ones.
This is so the living will know
that the Most High is ruler
over the kingdom of men.
He gives it to anyone He wants
and sets over it the lowliest
　　of men.

¹⁸ This is the dream that I, King Nebuchadnezzar, had. Now, Belteshazzar, tell me the interpretation, because none of the wise men of my kingdom can make the interpretation known to me. But you can, because you have the spirit of the holy gods.

¹⁹ Then Daniel, whose name is Belteshazzar, was stunned for a moment, and his thoughts alarmed him. The king said, "Belteshazzar, don't let the dream or its interpretation alarm you."

Belteshazzar answered, "My lord, may the dream apply to those who hate you, and its interpretation to your enemies! ²⁰ The tree you saw, which grew large and strong, whose top reached to the sky and was visible to all the earth, ²¹ whose leaves were beautiful and its fruit abundant—and on it was food for all, under it the wild animals lived, and in its branches the birds of the air lived— ²² that tree is you, the king. For you have become great and strong: your greatness has grown and even reaches the sky, and your dominion extends to the ends of the earth.

²³ "The king saw an observer, a holy one, coming down from heaven and saying, 'Cut down the tree and destroy it, but leave the stump with its roots in the ground and with a band of iron and bronze around it, in the tender grass of the field. Let him be drenched with dew

from the sky, and share food with the wild animals for seven periods of time.' ²⁴ This is the interpretation, Your Majesty, and this is the sentence of the Most High that has been passed against my lord the king: ²⁵ You will be driven away from people to live with the wild animals. You will feed on grass like cattle and be drenched with dew from the sky for seven periods of time, until you acknowledge that the Most High is ruler over the kingdom of men, and He gives it to anyone He wants. ²⁶ As for the command to leave the tree's stump with its roots, your kingdom will be restored to you as soon as you acknowledge that Heaven rules. ²⁷ Therefore, may my advice seem good to you my king. Separate yourself from your sins by doing what is right, and from your injustices by showing mercy to the needy. Perhaps there will be an extension of your prosperity."

²⁸ All this happened to King Nebuchadnezzar. ²⁹ At the end of 12 months, as he was walking on the roof of the royal palace in Babylon, ³⁰ the king exclaimed, "Is this not Babylon the Great that I have built by my vast power to be a royal residence and to display my majestic glory?"

³¹ While the words were still in the king's mouth, a voice came from heaven: "King Nebuchadnezzar, to you it is declared that the kingdom has departed from you. ³² You will be driven away from people to live with the wild animals, and you will feed on grass like cattle for seven periods of time, until you acknowledge that the Most High is ruler over the kingdom of men, and He gives it to anyone He wants."

³³ At that moment the sentence against Nebuchadnezzar was executed. He was driven away from people. He ate grass like cattle, and his body was drenched with dew from the sky, until his hair grew like eagles' feathers and his nails like birds' claws.

³⁴ But at the end of those days, I, Nebuchadnezzar, looked up to heaven, and my sanity returned to me. Then I praised the Most High and honored and glorified Him who lives forever:

For His dominion is
    an everlasting dominion,
    and His kingdom is
    from generation to generation.
³⁵ All the inhabitants of the earth
    are counted as nothing,
    and He does what He wants
    with the army of heaven
    and the inhabitants of the earth.
There is no one
    who can hold back His hand
or say to Him,
    "What have You done?"

³⁶ At that time my sanity returned to me, and my majesty and splendor returned to me for the glory of my kingdom. My advisers and my nobles sought me out, I was reestablished over my kingdom, and even more greatness came to me. ³⁷ Now I, Nebuchadnezzar, praise, exalt, and glorify the King of heaven, because all His works are true and His ways are just. And He is able to humble those who walk in pride.

5 King Belshazzar held a great feast for 1,000 of his nobles and drank wine in their presence. ² Under the influence of the wine, Belshazzar gave orders to bring in the gold and silver vessels that his predecessor Nebuchadnezzar had taken from the temple in Jerusalem, so that the king and his nobles, wives, and concubines could drink from them. ³ So they brought in the gold vessels that had been taken from the temple, the house of God in Jerusalem, and the king and his nobles, wives, and concubines drank from them. ⁴ They drank the wine and praised their gods made of gold and silver, bronze, iron, wood, and stone.
⁵ At that moment the fingers of a man's hand appeared and began writing on the plaster of the king's palace wall next to the lampstand. As the king watched the hand that was writing, ⁶ his face turned pale, and his thoughts so terrified him that his hip joints shook and his knees knocked together. ⁷ The king called out to bring in the mediums, Chaldeans, and astrologers. He said to these wise men of Babylon, "Whoever

reads this inscription and gives me its interpretation will be clothed in purple, have a gold chain around his neck, and have the third highest position in the kingdom." ⁸ So all the king's wise men came in, but none could read the inscription or make known its interpretation to him. ⁹ Then King Belshazzar became even more terrified, his face turned pale, and his nobles were bewildered.
¹⁰ Because of the outcry of the king and his nobles, the queen came to the banquet hall. "May the king live forever," she said. "Don't let your thoughts terrify you or your face be pale. ¹¹ There is a man in your kingdom who has the spirit of the holy gods in him. In the days of your predecessor he was found to have insight, intelligence, and wisdom like the wisdom of the gods. Your predecessor, King Nebuchadnezzar, appointed him chief of the diviners, mediums, Chaldeans, and astrologers. Your own predecessor, the king, ¹² did this because Daniel, the one the king named Belteshazzar, was found to have an extraordinary spirit, knowledge and perception, and the ability to interpret dreams, explain riddles, and solve problems. Therefore, summon Daniel, and he will give the interpretation."
¹³ Then Daniel was brought before the king. The king said to him, "Are you Daniel, one of the Judean exiles that my predecessor the king brought from Judah? ¹⁴ I've heard that you have the spirit of the gods in you, and that you have insight, intelligence, and extraordinary wisdom. ¹⁵ Now the wise men and mediums were brought before me to read this inscription and make its interpretation known to me, but they could not give its interpretation. ¹⁶ However, I have heard about you that you can give interpretations and solve problems. Therefore, if you can read this inscription and give me its interpretation, you will be clothed in purple, have a gold chain around your neck, and have the third highest position in the kingdom."
¹⁷ Then Daniel answered the king, "You may keep your gifts, and give your rewards to someone else; however, I

will read the inscription for the king and make the interpretation known to him. ¹⁸ Your Majesty, the Most High God gave sovereignty, greatness, glory, and majesty to your predecessor Nebuchadnezzar. ¹⁹ Because of the greatness He gave him, all peoples, nations, and languages were terrified and fearful of him. He killed anyone he wanted and kept alive anyone he wanted; he exalted anyone he wanted and humbled anyone he wanted. ²⁰ But when his heart was exalted and his spirit became arrogant, he was deposed from his royal throne and his glory was taken from him. ²¹ He was driven away from people, his mind was like an animal's, he lived with the wild donkeys, he was fed grass like cattle, and his body was drenched with dew from the sky until he acknowledged that the Most High God is ruler over the kingdom of men and sets anyone He wants over it.

²² "But you his successor, Belshazzar, have not humbled your heart, even though you knew all this. ²³ Instead, you have exalted yourself against the Lord of heaven. The vessels from His house were brought to you, and as you and your nobles, wives, and concubines drank wine from them, you praised the gods made of silver and gold, bronze, iron, wood, and stone, which do not see or hear or understand. But you have not glorified the God who holds your life-breath in His hand and who controls the whole course of your life. ²⁴ Therefore, He sent the hand, and this writing was inscribed. ²⁵ "This is the writing that was inscribed:

MENE, MENE, TEKEL, PARSIN

²⁶ This is the interpretation of the message:

MENE means that God has numbered the days of your kingdom and brought it to an end. ²⁷ TEKEL means that you have been weighed in the balance and found deficient.

²⁸ PERES means that your kingdom has been divided and given to the Medes and Persians."

²⁹ Then Belshazzar gave an order, and they clothed Daniel in purple, placed a gold chain around his neck, and issued a proclamation concerning him that he should be the third ruler in the kingdom.

³⁰ That very night Belshazzar the king of the Chaldeans was killed, ³¹ and Darius the Mede received the kingdom at the age of 62.

ΡSALM 139:1-6

¹ LORD, You have searched me and known me.
² You know when I sit down and when I stand up;
You understand my thoughts from far away.
³ You observe my travels and my rest;
You are aware of all my ways.
⁴ Before a word is on my tongue, You know all about it, LORD.
⁵ You have encircled me;
You have placed Your hand on me.
⁶ This extraordinary knowledge is beyond me.
It is lofty; I am unable to reach it.

ΡROVERBS 29:26-27

²⁶ Many seek a ruler's favor,
but a man receives justice from the LORD.

²⁷ An unjust man is detestable to the righteous,
and one whose way is upright is detestable to the wicked.

3 JOHN 1-14

The Elder:
To my dear friend Gaius, whom I love in truth.
² Dear friend, I pray that you may prosper in every way and be in good health, just as your soul prospers. ³ For I

was very glad when some brothers came and testified to your faithfulness to the truth—how you are walking in the truth. [4] I have no greater joy than this: to hear that my children are walking in the truth.

[5] Dear friend, you are showing your faith by whatever you do for the brothers, and this you are doing for strangers; [6] they have testified to your love before the church. You will do well to send them on their journey in a manner worthy of God, [7] since they set out for the sake of the name, accepting nothing from pagans. [8] Therefore, we ought to support such men, so that we can be coworkers with the truth.

[9] I wrote something to the church, but Diotrephes, who loves to have first place among them, does not receive us. [10] This is why, if I come, I will remind him of the works he is doing, slandering us with malicious words. And he is not satisfied with that! He not only refuses to welcome the brothers himself, but he even stops those who want to do so and expels them from the church.

[11] Dear friend, do not imitate what is evil, but what is good. The one who does good is of God; the one who does evil has not seen God. [12] Demetrius has a good testimony from everyone, and from the truth itself. And we also testify for him, and you know that our testimony is true.

[13] I have many things to write you, but I don't want to write to you with pen and ink. [14] I hope to see you soon, and we will talk face to face.

Peace be with you. The friends send you greetings. Greet the friends by name.

"Do It Yourself"

You have not glorified the God who holds your life-breath in His hand and who controls the whole course of your life.—DANIEL 5:23

Most Christians do not pant after God in the way the psalmist described in Psalm 42:1. Now I must attempt to make clear what I mean.

First, let me pull into focus the major problem with which we all struggle as soon as we are born. When God created us in the beginning, He designed us to have a relationship with Him. This means that deep within our being is a thirst for God which will not go away. It can be ignored, disguised, misunderstood, wrongly labeled, or submerged underneath a wealth of activity, but it will not disappear. And for good reason. We were designed to enjoy something better than this world can give us, particularly in the sphere of relationships. No human relationship can satisfy in the way that a relationship with God does.

This deep thirst for God that resides within us makes us dependent on God for satisfaction, and that is something our sinful human nature deeply resents. You see, due to Adam and Eve's sin in the garden of Eden, we have all been left a legacy called "Do It Yourself." There is something within every single one of us that wants to take charge and have a hand in bringing about our own salvation. So here is the problem: facing the fact realistically that we inwardly thirst after God puts us in touch with a level of helplessness from which our sinful human nature shrinks. It reinforces the conviction that we are dependent on someone outside of ourselves for satisfaction. And that is something we don't care to acknowledge.

Prayer

O Father, I recognize this elemental drive in my nature which causes me to resist standing in utter helplessness before You. But I sense that there can be no breakthrough in my life until I face this issue and deal with it. Help me, Father. In Jesus' name. Amen.

Further Study

Ps 143:1-6; 42:2; 63:1
What did the psalmist recognize?
What does it mean to "thirst"?

DECEMBER 9

DANIEL 6:1–7:28

6 Darius decided to appoint 120 satraps over the kingdom, stationed throughout the realm, ² and over them three administrators, including Daniel. These satraps would be accountable to them so that the king would not be defrauded. ³ Daniel distinguished himself above the administrators and satraps because he had an extraordinary spirit, so the king planned to set him over the whole realm. ⁴ The administrators and satraps, therefore, kept trying to find a charge against Daniel regarding the kingdom. But they could find no charge or corruption, for he was trustworthy, and no negligence or corruption was found in him. ⁵ Then these men said, "We will never find any charge against this Daniel unless we find something against him concerning the law of his God."

⁶ So the administrators and satraps went together to the king and said to him, "May King Darius live forever. ⁷ All the administrators of the kingdom, the prefects, satraps, advisers, and gover-

nors have agreed that the king should establish an ordinance and enforce an edict that for 30 days, anyone who petitions any god or man except you, the king, will be thrown into the lions' den. ⁸ Therefore, Your Majesty, establish the edict and sign the document so that, as a law of the Medes and Persians, it is irrevocable and cannot be changed." ⁹ So King Darius signed the document.

¹⁰ When Daniel learned that the document had been signed, he went into his house. The windows in its upper room opened toward Jerusalem, and three times a day he got down on his knees, prayed, and gave thanks to his God, just as he had done before. ¹¹ Then these men went as a group and found Daniel petitioning and imploring his God. ¹² So they approached the king and asked about his edict: "Didn't you sign an edict that for 30 days any man who petitions any god or man except you, the king, will be thrown into the lions' den?"

The king answered, "As a law of the Medes and Persians, the order stands and is irrevocable."

¹³ Then they replied to the king, "Daniel, one of the Judean exiles, has ignored you, the king, and the edict you signed, for he prays three times a day." ¹⁴ As soon as the king heard this, he was very displeased; he set his mind on rescuing Daniel and made every effort until sundown to deliver him.

¹⁵ Then these men went to the king and said to him, "You as king know it is a law of the Medes and Persians that no edict or ordinance the king establishes can be changed."

¹⁶ So the king gave the order, and they brought Daniel and threw him into the lions' den. The king said to Daniel, "May your God, whom you serve continually, rescue you!" ¹⁷ A stone was brought and placed over the mouth of the den. The king sealed it with his own signet ring and with the signet rings of his nobles, so that nothing in regard to Daniel could be changed. ¹⁸ Then the king went to his palace and spent the night fasting. No diversions were brought to him, and he could not sleep.

¹⁹ At the first light of dawn the king got up and hurried to the lions' den. ²⁰ When he reached the den, he cried out in anguish to Daniel. "Daniel, servant of the living God," the king said, "has your God whom you serve continually been able to rescue you from the lions?"

²¹ Then Daniel spoke with the king: "May the king live forever. ²² My God sent His angel and shut the lions' mouths. They haven't hurt me, for I was found innocent before Him. Also, I have not committed a crime against you my king."

²³ The king was overjoyed and gave orders to take Daniel out of the den. So Daniel was taken out of the den, uninjured, for he trusted in his God. ²⁴ The king then gave the command, and those men who had maliciously accused Daniel were brought and thrown into the lions' den—they, their children, and their wives. They had not reached the bottom of the den before the lions overpowered them and crushed all their bones.

²⁵ Then King Darius wrote to those of every people, nation, and language who live in all the earth: "May your prosperity abound. ²⁶ I issue a decree that in all my royal dominion, people must tremble in fear before the God of Daniel:

For He is the living God,
and He endures forever;
His kingdom will never
    be destroyed,
and His dominion has no end.
²⁷ He rescues and delivers;
He performs signs and wonders
in the heavens and on the earth,
for He has rescued Daniel
from the power of the lions."

²⁸ So Daniel prospered during the reign of Darius and the reign of Cyrus the Persian.

7 In the first year of Belshazzar king of Babylon, Daniel had a dream with visions in his mind as he was lying in his bed. He wrote down the dream, and here is the summary of his account. ² Daniel said, "In my vision at night I was watching, and suddenly the four winds of heaven stirred up the great sea. ³ Four huge beasts came up from the sea, each different from the other.

⁴ "The first was like a lion but had eagle's wings. I continued watching until its wings were torn off. It was lifted up from the ground, set on its feet like a man, and given a human mind.

⁵ "Suddenly, another beast appeared, a second one, that looked like a bear. It was raised up on one side, with three ribs in its mouth between its teeth. It was told, 'Get up! Gorge yourself on flesh.'

⁶ "While I was watching, another beast appeared. It was like a leopard with four wings of a bird on its back. It had four heads and was given authority to rule.

⁷ "While I was watching in the night visions, a fourth beast appeared, frightening and dreadful, and incredibly strong, with large iron teeth. It devoured and crushed, and it trampled with its feet whatever was left. It was different from all the beasts before it, and it had 10 horns.

8 "While I was considering the horns, suddenly another horn, a little one, came up among them, and three of the first horns were uprooted before it. There were eyes in this horn like a man's, and it had a mouth that spoke arrogantly.

9 "As I kept watching,

> thrones were set in place,
> and the Ancient of Days
> took His seat.
> His clothing was white like snow,
> and the hair of His head
> like whitest wool.
> His throne was flaming fire;
> its wheels were blazing fire.

10 A river of fire was flowing,
> coming out from His presence.
> Thousands upon thousands
> served Him;
> ten thousand times ten thousand
> stood before Him.
> The court was convened,
> and the books were opened.

11 "I watched, then, because of the sound of the arrogant words the horn was speaking. As I continued watching, the beast was killed and its body destroyed and given over to the burning fire. 12 As for the rest of the beasts, their authority to rule was removed, but an extension of life was granted to them for a certain period of time. 13 I continued watching in the night visions,

> and I saw One like a son of man
> coming with the clouds of heaven.
> He approached the Ancient of Days
> and was escorted before Him.

14 He was given authority to rule,
> and glory, and a kingdom;
> so that those of every people,
> nation, and language
> should serve Him.
> His dominion is
> an everlasting dominion
> that will not pass away,
> and His kingdom is one
> that will not be destroyed.

15 "As for me, Daniel, my spirit was deeply distressed within me, and the

visions in my mind terrified me. 16 I approached one of those who were standing by and asked him the true meaning of all this. So he let me know the interpretation of these things: 17 'These huge beasts, four in number, are four kings who will rise from the earth. 18 But the holy ones of the Most High will receive the kingdom and possess it forever, yes, forever and ever.'

19 "Then I wanted to know the true meaning of the fourth beast, the one different from all the others, extremely terrifying, with iron teeth and bronze claws, devouring, crushing, and trampling with its feet whatever was left. 20 I also wanted to know about the 10 horns on its head and about the other horn that came up, before which three fell— the horn that had eyes, and a mouth that spoke arrogantly, and that was more visible than the others. 21 As I was watching, this horn made war with the holy ones and was prevailing over them 22 until the Ancient of Days arrived and a judgment was given in favor of the holy ones of the Most High, for the time had come, and the holy ones took possession of the kingdom.

23 "This is what he said: 'The fourth beast will be a fourth kingdom on the earth, different from all the other kingdoms. It will devour the whole earth, trample it down, and crush it. 24 The 10 horns are 10 kings who will rise from this kingdom. Another, different from the previous ones, will rise after them and subdue three kings. 25 He will speak words against the Most High and oppress the holy ones of the Most High. He will intend to change religious festivals and laws, and the holy ones will be handed over to him for a time, times, and half a time. 26 But the court will convene, and his dominion will be taken away, to be completely destroyed forever. 27 The kingdom, dominion, and greatness of the kingdoms under all of heaven will be given to the people, the holy ones of the Most High. His kingdom will be an everlasting kingdom, and all rulers will serve and obey Him.'

28 "This is the end of the interpretation. As for me, Daniel, my thoughts ter-

rified me greatly, and my face turned pale, but I kept the matter to myself."

𝒫SALM 139:7-12

7 Where can I go to escape Your Spirit?
Where can I flee from Your presence?
8 If I go up to heaven, You are there;
if I make my bed in Sheol, You are there.
9 If I live at the eastern horizon or settle at the western limits,
10 even there Your hand will lead me; Your right hand will hold on to me.
11 If I say, "Surely the darkness will hide me,
and the light around me will become night"—
12 even the darkness is not dark to You.
The night shines like the day; darkness and light are alike to You.

𝒫ROVERBS 30:1-2

30 The words of Agur son of Jakeh. The oracle.

The man's oration to Ithiel, to Ithiel and Ucal:

2 I am the least intelligent of men, and I lack man's ability to understand.

𝒥UDE 1-13

Jude, a slave of Jesus Christ, and a brother of James:
To those who are the called, loved by God the Father and kept by Jesus Christ. 2 May mercy, peace, and love be multiplied to you.
3 Dear friends, although I was eager to write you about our common salvation, I found it necessary to write and exhort you to contend for the faith that was delivered to the saints once for all. 4 For certain men, who were designated for this judgment long ago, have come in by stealth; they are ungodly, turning the grace of our God into promiscuity and denying our only Master and Lord, Jesus Christ.

5 Now I want to remind you, though you know all these things: the Lord, having first of all saved a people out of Egypt, later destroyed those who did not believe; 6 and He has kept, with eternal chains in darkness for the judgment of the great day, angels who did not keep their own position but deserted their proper dwelling. 7 In the same way, Sodom and Gomorrah and the cities around them committed sexual immorality and practiced perversions, just as they did, and serve as an example by undergoing the punishment of eternal fire.

8 Nevertheless, these dreamers likewise defile their flesh, despise authority, and blaspheme glorious beings. 9 Yet Michael the archangel, when he was disputing with the Devil in a debate about Moses' body, did not dare bring an abusive condemnation against him, but said, "The Lord rebuke you!" 10 But these people blaspheme anything they don't understand, and what they know by instinct, like unreasoning animals— they destroy themselves with these things. 11 Woe to them! For they have traveled in the way of Cain, have abandoned themselves to the error of Balaam for profit, and have perished in Korah's rebellion.

12 These are the ones who are like dangerous reefs at your love feasts. They feast with you, nurturing only themselves without fear. They are waterless clouds carried along by winds; trees in late autumn—fruitless, twice dead, pulled out by the roots; 13 wild waves of the sea, foaming up their shameful deeds; wandering stars for whom is reserved the blackness of darkness forever!

Satanic Forces

*He has kept, with eternal chains in darkness for the judgment
of the great day, angels who did not keep their own position
but deserted their proper dwelling.*—Jude 6

The Devil was created as a wise and morally perfect being (then known as Lucifer) who aspired to take over the throne of God and thus usurp the position of his Creator. Once that happened, Lucifer was expelled from heaven, together with the other angels who had sensed and shared his rebellious attitude. This is the fall from heaven that Jesus told His disciples He had witnessed.

Since his fall from heaven, Satan, apparently losing little of his administrative skill, has marshaled these fallen angels (now known as demons) into a hostile force to work against God and His creation. We do not know just how many angels fell with Satan, but doubtless it must have been a colossal number. When Jesus once asked a demoniac: "What is your name?" (Luke 8:30), the demons answered: "Legion." If they were telling the truth, the man was controlled by thousands of demons. A Roman legion contained six thousand men!

It is little wonder, then, that the Apostle Paul warned the Ephesians that they were involved in a tremendous spiritual conflict: "For our battle is not against flesh and blood, but against the rulers, against the authorities, against the world powers of this darkness, against the spiritual forces of evil in the heavens" (Eph 6:12).

One of America's founding fathers said: "If men will not be governed by God, then they will be ruled by tyrants." How sad that people actually choose to be governed by Satan rather than by God.

Prayer

O God my Father, I am so thankful that I have left the tyranny and rule of Satan to come under the sway of Your eternal and everlasting kingdom. May I come more and more under its sway hour by hour and day by day. In Jesus' name I pray. Amen.

Further Study

Lk 10:1-19; Ps 44:5; Rm 8:31
What event did Jesus witness?
What power did He give to His disciples?

DECEMBER 10

DANIEL 8:1–9:27

8 In the third year of King Belshazzar's reign, a vision appeared to me, Daniel, after the one that had appeared to me earlier. [2] I saw the vision, and as I watched, I was in the fortress city of Susa, in the province of Elam. I saw in the vision that I was beside the Ulai Canal. [3] I looked up, and there was a ram standing beside the canal. He had two horns. The two horns were long, but one was longer than the other, and the longer one came up last. [4] I saw the ram charging to the west, the north, and the south. No animal could stand against him, and there was no rescue from his power. He did whatever he wanted and became great.

[5] As I was observing, a male goat appeared, coming from the west across the surface of the entire earth without touching the ground. The goat had a conspicuous horn between his eyes. [6] He came toward the two-horned ram I had seen standing beside the canal and rushed at him with savage fury. [7] I saw him approaching the ram, and infuriated with him, he struck the ram, shattering his two horns, and the ram was not strong enough to stand against him. The goat threw him to the ground and trampled him, and there was no one to rescue the ram from his power. [8] Then the male goat became very great, but when he became powerful, the large horn was shattered. Four conspicuous horns came up in its place, pointing toward the four winds of heaven.

[9] From one of them a little horn emerged and grew extensively toward the south and the east and toward the beautiful land. [10] It grew as high as the heavenly host, made some of the stars and some of the host fall to the earth, and trampled them. [11] It made itself great, even up to the Prince of the host;

it removed His daily sacrifice and overthrew the place of His sanctuary. [12] Because of rebellion, a host, together with the daily sacrifice, will be given over. The horn will throw truth to the ground and will be successful in whatever it does.

[13] Then I heard a holy one speaking, and another holy one said to the speaker, "How long will the events of this vision last—the daily sacrifice, the rebellion that makes desolate, and the giving over of the sanctuary and of the host to be trampled?"

[14] He said to me, "For 2,300 evenings and mornings; then the sanctuary will be restored."

[15] While I, Daniel, was watching the vision and trying to understand it, there stood before me someone who appeared to be a man. [16] I heard a human voice calling from the middle of the Ulai: "Gabriel, explain the vision to this man."

[17] So he approached where I was standing; when he came near, I was terrified and fell facedown. "Son of man," he said to me, "understand that the vision refers to the time of the end." [18] While he was speaking to me, I fell into a deep sleep, with my face to the ground. Then he touched me, made me stand up, [19] and said, "I am here to tell you what will happen at the conclusion of the time of wrath, because it refers to the appointed time of the end. [20] The two-horned ram that you saw represents the kings of Media and Persia. [21] The shaggy goat represents the king of Greece, and the large horn between his eyes represents the first king. [22] The four horns that took the place of the shattered horn represent four kingdoms. They will rise from that nation, but without its power.

[23] Near the end of their kingdoms, when the rebels have reached

the full measure of their sin,
an insolent king, skilled in intrigue,
will come to the throne.
²⁴ His power will be great,
but it will not be his own.
He will cause terrible destruction
and succeed in whatever he does.
He will destroy the powerful
along with the holy people.
²⁵ He will cause deceit to prosper
through his cunning
and by his influence,
and in his own mind he will
make himself great.
In a time of peace,
he will destroy many;
he will even stand
against the Prince of princes.
But he will be shattered,
not by human hands.
²⁶ The vision of the evenings
and the mornings
that has been told is true.
Now you must seal up the vision
because it refers to many days
in the future."

²⁷ I, Daniel, was overcome and lay sick for days. Then I got up and went about the king's business. I was greatly disturbed by the vision and could not understand it.

9 In the first year of Darius, who was the son of Ahasuerus, was a Mede by birth, and was ruler over the kingdom of the Chaldeans— ² in the first year of his reign, I, Daniel, understood from the books according to the word of the LORD to Jeremiah the prophet that the number of years for the desolation of Jerusalem would be 70. ³ So I turned my attention to the Lord God to seek Him by prayer and petitions, with fasting, sackcloth, and ashes.
⁴ I prayed to the LORD my God and confessed:

Ah, Lord—the great and awe-inspiring God who keeps His gracious covenant with those who love Him and keep His commandments— ⁵ we have sinned, done wrong, acted wickedly, rebelled,

and turned away from Your commandments and ordinances. ⁶ We have not listened to Your servants the prophets, who spoke in Your name to our kings, leaders, fathers, and all the people of the land.

⁷ Lord, righteousness belongs to You, but this day public shame belongs to us: the men of Judah, the residents of Jerusalem, and all Israel—those who are near and those who are far, in all the countries where You have dispersed them because of the disloyalty they have shown toward You. ⁸ LORD, public shame belongs to us, our kings, our leaders, and our fathers, because we have sinned against You. ⁹ Compassion and forgiveness belong to the Lord our God, though we have rebelled against Him ¹⁰ and have not obeyed the voice of the LORD our God by following His instructions that He set before us through His servants the prophets.

¹¹ All Israel has broken Your law and turned away, refusing to obey You. The promised curse written in the law of Moses, the servant of God, has been poured out on us because we have sinned against Him. ¹² He has carried out His words that He spoke against us and against our rulers by bringing on us so great a disaster that nothing like what has been done to Jerusalem has ever been done under all of heaven. ¹³ Just as it is written in the law of Moses, all this disaster has come on us, yet we have not appeased the LORD our God by turning from our injustice and paying attention to Your truth. ¹⁴ So the LORD kept the disaster in mind and brought it on us, for the LORD our God is righteous in all He has done. But we have not obeyed Him.

¹⁵ Now, Lord our God, who brought Your people out of the land of Egypt with a mighty hand and made Your name renowned as it is this

day, we have sinned, we have acted wickedly. [16] Lord, in keeping with all Your righteous acts, may Your anger and wrath turn away from Your city Jerusalem, Your holy mountain; for because of our sins and the injustices of our fathers, Jerusalem and Your people have become an object of ridicule to all those around us.

[17] Therefore, our God, hear the prayer and the petitions of Your servant. Show Your favor to Your desolate sanctuary for the Lord's sake. [18] Listen, my God, and hear. Open Your eyes and see our desolations and the city called by Your name. For we are not presenting our petitions before You based on our righteous acts, but based on Your abundant compassion. [19] Lord, hear! Lord, forgive! Lord, listen and act! My God, for Your own sake, do not delay, because Your city and Your people are called by Your name.

[20] While I was speaking, praying, confessing my sin and the sin of my people Israel, and presenting my petition before Yahweh my God concerning the holy mountain of my God— [21] while I was praying, Gabriel, the man I had seen in the first vision, came to me in my extreme weariness, about the time of the evening offering. [22] He gave me this explanation: "Daniel, I've come now to give you understanding. [23] At the beginning of your petitions an answer went out, and I have come to give it, for you are treasured by God. So consider the message and understand the vision:

[24] Seventy weeks are decreed
about your people
and your holy city—
to bring the rebellion to an end,
to put a stop to sin,
to wipe away injustice,
to bring in everlasting righteousness,
to seal up vision and prophecy,
and to anoint the most holy place.
[25] Know and understand this:

From the issuing of the decree
to restore and rebuild Jerusalem
until Messiah the Prince
will be seven weeks and 62 weeks.
It will be rebuilt with a plaza
and a moat,
but in difficult times.
[26] After those 62 weeks
the Messiah will be cut off
and will have nothing.
The people of the coming prince
will destroy the city
and the sanctuary.
The end will come with a flood,
and until the end there will be war;
desolations are decreed.
[27] He will make a firm covenant
with many for one week,
but in the middle of the week
he will put a stop to sacrifice
and offering.
And the abomination of desolation
will be on a wing of the temple
until the decreed destruction
is poured out on the desolator."

PSALM 139:13-18

[13] For it was You who created my
inward parts;
You knit me together in my
mother's womb.
[14] I will praise You,
because I am unique in
remarkable ways.
Your works are wonderful,
and I know this very well.
[15] My bones were not hidden from
You
when I was made in secret,
when I was formed in the depths
of the earth.
[16] Your eyes saw me when I was
formless;
all my days were written in Your
book and planned
before a single one of them began.

[17] God, how difficult Your thoughts
are for me to comprehend
how vast their sum is!
[18] If I counted them, they would
outnumber the grains of sand;

when I wake up, I am still with
You.

PROVERBS 30:3-4

3 I have not gained wisdom,
and I have no knowledge of the
Holy One.
4 Who has gone up to heaven and
come down?
Who has gathered the wind in His
hands?
Who has bound up the waters in a
cloak?
Who has established all the ends
of the earth?
What is His name, and what is the
name of His Son—
if you know?

JUDE 14-25

14 And Enoch, in the seventh generation from Adam, prophesied about
them:

Look! The Lord comes with
thousands of His holy ones
15 to execute judgment on all, and to
convict them
of all their ungodly deeds that
they have done in an ungodly
way,

and of all the harsh things ungodly
sinners
have said against Him.

16 These people are discontented grum-
blers, walking according to their desires;
their mouths utter arrogant words, flattering people for their own advantage.
17 But you, dear friends, remember
the words foretold by the apostles of
our Lord Jesus Christ; 18 they told you,
"In the end time there will be scoffers
walking according to their own ungodly
desires." 19 These people create divisions and are merely natural, not having
the Spirit.
20 But you, dear friends, building yourselves up in your most holy faith and
praying in the Holy Spirit, 21 keep yourselves in the love of God, expecting the
mercy of our Lord Jesus Christ for eternal life. 22 Have mercy on some who
doubt; 23 save others by snatching them
from the fire; on others have mercy in
fear, hating even the garment defiled by
the flesh.
24 Now to Him who is able to protect
you from stumbling and to make you
stand in the presence of His glory,
blameless and with great joy, 25 to the
only God our Savior, through Jesus
Christ our Lord, be glory, majesty,
power, and authority before all time,
now, and forever. Amen.

"Plenty of Time for You"

*God, how difficult Your thoughts are for me to comprehend;
how vast their sum is!*—PSALM **139:17**

The constituent parts of personality are predicted of God on almost every page of the Bible.
"I will raise up a faithful priest for Myself. He will do whatever is in My heart and mind," said
the Lord to Eli in 1 Samuel 2:35. This shows (if it needs showing) that God has a mind with
which He thinks.

God has emotions also—another aspect of personality. Some modern-day theologians
claim that God is unable to feel, but clearly this is not supported by Scripture. God can be angry
(Ps 2:12), jealous (Zch 1:14-15), merciful (Ps 78:38), and joyful (Dt 30:9). These are just a few of
the emotions which Scripture talks about, but there are many more. Again, God chooses and
decides. "The LORD regretted that He had made man on the earth . . . Then the LORD said, 'I will

wipe off the face of the earth: man . . . together with the animals, creatures that crawl, and birds of the sky'" (Gn 6:6-7).

While the majority of people believe in some kind of God, many view Him as being so great that He cannot possibly take a personal interest in such insignificant creatures as ourselves. Dr. Henry Norris Russell, one of the great astronomers of this century and a Christian, once gave a talk on the vastness of the universe. Afterwards, someone asked him this question: "How is it possible for such a great and infinite God to have time for me?" This was his reply: "An infinite God can dispatch the affairs of this universe in the twinkling of an eye, thus giving Him plenty of time for you."

Prayer

O Father, help me in the midst of every trial and difficulty to drop my anchor in this reassuring and encouraging revelation: no matter what my problem, You always have plenty of time to give to me. I am so deeply, deeply thankful. Amen.

Further Study

Heb 4:12-16; Ps 2:12; Zch 1:14-15; Ps 78:38; Dt 30:9
Can you think of other Scriptures showing God's emotions?
What is God able to do through Christ?

DECEMBER 11

DANIEL 10:1–11:45

10 In the third year of Cyrus king of Persia, a message was revealed to Daniel, who was named Belteshazzar. The message was true and was about a great conflict. He understood the message and had understanding of the vision.

² In those days I, Daniel, was mourning for three full weeks. ³ I didn't eat any rich food, no meat or wine entered my mouth, and I didn't put any oil on my body until the three weeks were over. ⁴ On the twenty-fourth day of the first month, as I was standing on the bank of the great river, the Tigris, ⁵ I looked up, and there was a man dressed in linen, with a belt of gold from Uphaz around his waist. ⁶ His body was like topaz, his face like the brilliance of lightning, his eyes like flaming torches, his arms and feet like the gleam of polished bronze, and the sound of his words like the sound of a multitude.

⁷ Only I, Daniel, saw the vision. The men who were with me did not see it, but a great terror fell on them, and they ran and hid. ⁸ I was left alone, looking at this great vision. No strength was left in me; my face grew deathly pale, and I was powerless. ⁹ I heard the words he said, and when I heard them I fell into a

deep sleep, with my face to the ground.
¹⁰ Suddenly, a hand touched me and raised me to my hands and knees. ¹¹ He said to me, "Daniel, you are a man treasured by God. Understand the words that I'm saying to you. Stand on your feet, for I have now been sent to you." After he said this to me, I stood trembling.

¹² "Don't be afraid, Daniel," he said to me, "for from the first day that you purposed to understand and to humble yourself before your God, your prayers were heard. I have come because of your prayers. ¹³ But the prince of the kingdom of Persia opposed me for 21 days. Then Michael, one of the chief princes, came to help me after I had been left there with the kings of Persia. ¹⁴ Now I have come to help you understand what will happen to your people in the last days, for the vision refers to those days."

¹⁵ While he was saying these words to me, I turned my face toward the ground and was speechless. ¹⁶ Suddenly one with human likeness touched my lips. I opened my mouth and said to the one standing in front of me, "My lord, because of the vision, I am overwhelmed and powerless. ¹⁷ How can someone like me, your servant, speak with someone like you, my lord? Now I have no strength, and there is no breath in me."

¹⁸ Then the one with human likeness touched me again and strengthened me. ¹⁹ He said, "Don't be afraid, you who are treasured by God. Peace to you; be very strong!"

As he spoke to me, I was strengthened and said, "Let my lord speak, for you have strengthened me."

²⁰ He said, "Do you know why I've come to you? I must return at once to fight against the prince of Persia, and when I leave, the prince of Greece will come. ²¹ No one has the courage to support me against them except Michael, your prince. However, I will tell you what is recorded in the book of truth.

11 ¹ In the first year of Darius the Mede, I stood up to strengthen and protect him. ² Now I will tell you the truth.

"Three more kings will arise in Persia, and the fourth will be far richer than the others. By the power he gains through his riches, he will stir up everyone against the kingdom of Greece. ³ Then a warrior king will arise; he will rule a vast realm and do whatever he wants. ⁴ But as soon as he is established, his kingdom will be broken up and divided to the four winds of heaven, but not to his descendants; it will not be the same kingdom that he ruled, because his kingdom will be uprooted and will go to others besides them.

⁵ "The king of the South will grow powerful, but one of his commanders will grow more powerful and will rule a kingdom greater than his. ⁶ After some years they will form an alliance, and the daughter of the king of the South will go to the king of the North to seal the agreement. She will not retain power, and his strength will not endure. She will be given up, together with her entourage, her father, and the one who supported her during those times. ⁷ In the place of the king of the South, one from her family will rise up, come against the army, and enter the fortress of the king of the North. He will take action against them and triumph. ⁸ He will take even their gods captive to Egypt, with their metal images and their precious articles of silver and gold. For some years he will stay away from the king of the North, ⁹ who will enter the kingdom of the king of the South and then return to his own land.

¹⁰ "His sons will mobilize for war and assemble a large number of armed forces. They will advance, sweeping through like a flood, and will again wage war as far as his fortress. ¹¹ Infuriated, the king of the South will march out to fight with the king of the North, who will raise a great multitude, but the multitude will be handed over to his enemy. ¹² When the multitude is carried off, he will become arrogant and cause tens of thousands to fall, but he will not triumph. ¹³ The king of the North will again raise a multitude larger than the first. After some years he will advance with a great army and many supplies.

¹⁴ "In those times many will rise up against the king of the South. Violent ones among your own people will assert themselves to fulfill a vision, but they will fail. ¹⁵ Then the king of the North will come, build up an assault ramp, and capture a well-fortified city. The forces of the South will not stand; even their select troops will not be able to resist. ¹⁶ The king of the North who comes against him will do whatever he wants, and no one can oppose him. He will establish himself in the beautiful land with total destruction in his hand. ¹⁷ He will resolve to come with the force of his whole kingdom and will reach an agreement with him. He will give him a daughter in marriage to destroy it, but she will not stand with him or support him. ¹⁸ Then he will turn his attention to the coasts and islands and capture many. But a commander will put an end to his taunting; instead, he will turn his taunts against him. ¹⁹ He will turn his attention back to the fortresses of his own land, but he will stumble, fall, and be no more.

²⁰ "In his place one will arise who will send out a tax collector for the glory of the kingdom; but within a few days he will be shattered, though not in anger or in battle.

²¹ "In his place a despised person will arise; royal honors will not be given to him, but he will come during a time of peace and seize the kingdom by intrigue. ²² A flood of forces will be swept away before him; they will be shattered, as well as the covenant prince. ²³ After an alliance is made with him, he will act deceitfully. He will rise to power with a small nation. ²⁴ During a time of peace, he will come into the richest parts of the province and do what his fathers and predecessors never did. He will lavish plunder, loot, and wealth on his followers, and he will make plans against fortified cities, but only for a time.

²⁵ "With a large army he will stir up his power and his courage against the king of the South. The king of the South will prepare for battle with an extremely large and powerful army, but he will not succeed, because plots will be made against him. ²⁶ Those who eat his provisions will destroy him; his army will be swept away, and many will fall slain. ²⁷ The two kings, whose hearts are bent on evil, will speak lies at the same table but to no avail, for still the end will come at the appointed time. ²⁸ The king of the North will return to his land with great wealth, but his heart will be set against the holy covenant; he will take action, then return to his own land.

²⁹ "At the appointed time he will come again to the South, but this time will not be like the first. ³⁰ Ships of Kittim will come against him, and being intimidated, he will withdraw. Then he will rage against the holy covenant and take action. On his return, he will favor those who abandon the holy covenant. ³¹ His forces will rise up and desecrate the temple fortress. They will abolish the daily sacrifice and set up the abomination of desolation. ³² With flattery he will corrupt those who act wickedly toward the covenant, but the people who know their God will be strong and take action. ³³ Those who are wise among the people will give understanding to many, yet they will die by sword and flame, and be captured and plundered for a time. ³⁴ When defeated, they will be helped by some, but many others will join them insincerely. ³⁵ Some of the wise will fall so that they may be refined, purified, and cleansed until the time of the end, for it will still come at the appointed time.

³⁶ "Then the king will do whatever he wants. He will exalt and magnify himself above every god, and he will say outrageous things against the God of gods. He will be successful until the time of wrath is completed, because what has been decreed will be accomplished. ³⁷ He will not show regard for the gods of his fathers, the god longed for by women, or for any other god, because he will magnify himself above all. ³⁸ Instead, he will honor a god of fortresses—a god his fathers did not know—with gold, silver, precious stones, and riches. ³⁹ He will deal with the strongest fortresses with the help of a foreign god. He will greatly honor those who

acknowledge him, making them rulers over many and distributing land as a reward.

⁴⁰ "At the time of the end, the king of the South will engage him in battle, but the king of the North will storm against him with chariots, horsemen, and many ships. He will invade countries and sweep through them like a flood. ⁴¹ He will also invade the beautiful land, and many will fall. But these will escape from his power: Edom, Moab, and the prominent people of the Ammonites. ⁴² He will extend his power against the countries, and not even the land of Egypt will escape. ⁴³ He will get control over the hidden treasures of gold and silver and over all the riches of Egypt. The Libyans and Cushites will also be in submission. ⁴⁴ But reports from the east and the north will terrify him, and he will go out with great fury to destroy and annihilate many. ⁴⁵ He will pitch his royal tents between the sea and the beautiful holy mountain, but he will meet his end with no one to help him.

PSALM 139:19-24

¹⁹ God, if only You would kill the wicked—
   you bloodthirsty men, stay away from me—
²⁰ who invoke You deceitfully.
   Your enemies swear by You falsely.
²¹ LORD, don't I hate those who hate You,
   and detest those who rebel against You?
²² I hate them with extreme hatred;
   I consider them my enemies.

²³ Search me, God, and know my heart;
   test me and know my concerns.
²⁴ See if there is any offensive way in me;
   lead me in the everlasting way.

PROVERBS 30:5-6

⁵ Every word of God is pure;
   He is a shield to those who take refuge in Him.

⁶ Don't add to His words,
   or He will rebuke you, and you will be proved a liar.

REVELATION 1:1-20

1 The revelation of Jesus Christ that God gave Him to show His slaves what must quickly take place. He sent it and signified it through His angel to His slave John, ² who testified to God's word and to the testimony about Jesus Christ, in all he saw. ³ Blessed is the one who reads and blessed are those who hear the words of this prophecy and keep what is written in it, because the time is near!

⁴ John:

To the seven churches in the province of Asia.

Grace and peace to you from the One who is, who was, and who is coming; from the seven spirits before His throne; ⁵ and from Jesus Christ, the faithful witness, the firstborn from the dead and the ruler of the kings of the earth.

To Him who loves us and has set us free from our sins by His blood, ⁶ and made us a kingdom, priests to His God and Father—to Him be the glory and dominion forever and ever. Amen.

⁷ Look! He is coming
     with the clouds,
   and every eye will see Him,
   including those who pierced Him.
   And all the families of the earth
   will mourn over Him.
   This is certain. Amen.

⁸ "I am the Alpha and the Omega," says the Lord God, "the One who is, who was, and who is coming, the Almighty."

⁹ I, John, your brother and partner in the tribulation, kingdom, and perseverance in Jesus, was on the island called Patmos because of God's word and the testimony about Jesus. ¹⁰ I was in the Spirit on the Lord's day, and I heard behind me a loud voice like a trumpet ¹¹ saying, "Write on a scroll what you see and send it to the seven churches: Ephesus, Smyrna, Pergamum, Thyatira, Sardis, Philadelphia, and Laodicea."

¹²I turned to see the voice that was speaking to me. When I turned I saw seven gold lampstands, ¹³and among the lampstands was One like the Son of Man, dressed in a long robe, and with a gold sash wrapped around His chest. ¹⁴His head and hair were white like wool—white as snow, His eyes like a fiery flame, ¹⁵His feet like fine bronze fired in a furnace, and His voice like the sound of cascading waters. ¹⁶In His right hand He had seven stars; from His mouth came a sharp two-edged sword; and His face was shining like the sun at midday.

¹⁷When I saw Him, I fell at His feet like a dead man. He laid His right hand on me, and said, "Don't be afraid! I am the First and the Last, ¹⁸and the Living One. I was dead, but look—I am alive forever and ever, and I hold the keys of death and Hades. ¹⁹Therefore write what you have seen, what is, and what will take place after this. ²⁰The secret of the seven stars you saw in My right hand, and of the seven gold lampstands, is this: the seven stars are the angels of the seven churches, and the seven lampstands are the seven churches.

The Searchlight of Truth

Search me, God, and know my heart;
test me and know my concerns.—PSALM 139:23

To have "truth like a belt around [our] waist" means to be possessed by truth. If we are to defend ourselves effectively against the attacks of Satan, then truth and honesty are vital necessities.

The mental health experts tell us that being willing to face the truth about ourselves is an important part of our growth toward maturity. The same is true in the realm of the spiritual. How easy it is to hide from the truth and imagine ourselves to be truthful when really we are not.

Whatever his personal idiosyncrasies and his rebellious attitude toward Christianity, Sigmund Freud made an interesting contribution to our understanding of human personality when he documented with true genius the incredibly subtle ways in which we lie to ourselves. Psychologists call them "defense mechanisms," but a more biblical view of them would be "lying mechanisms." We would all much prefer to be called defensive than dishonest. But whenever we allow ourselves to be self-deceived, we not only impede our spiritual growth—we also lower our defenses against Satan. He thrives on deception, and if he can push us toward self-deception, he maintains a definite advantage over us.

Many of us might react with horror to the suggestion that we are being dishonest, for we would not dream of doing or saying anything that was not according to the truth. Yet it is possible to be open and honest on the outside and yet hide from truth on the inside. All of us, even mature and experienced Christians, are capable of hiding from truth.

Prayer

O Father, I see that if I am to overcome Satan, then I must know truth inwardly as well as outwardly. Search my heart today, dear Lord, and bring to the surface the things within me that are untrue. In Jesus' name I ask it. Amen.

Further Study

2 Ch 7:1-14; Is 44:20; Jms 1:22
What are God's people to turn from?
What does James warn against?

DECEMBER 12

DANIEL 12:1–HOSEA 3:5

12 At that time
Michael the great prince
who stands watch
over your people will rise up.
There will be a time of distress
such as never has occurred
since nations came into being
until that time.
But at that time all your people
who are found written in the book
will escape.
2 Many of those who sleep in the dust
of the earth will awake,
some to eternal life,
and some to shame
and eternal contempt.
3 Those who are wise will shine
like the bright expanse
of the heavens,
and those who lead many
to righteousness,
like the stars forever and ever.

4 "But you, Daniel, keep these words
secret and seal the book until the time
of the end. Many will roam about, and
knowledge will increase."
5 Then I, Daniel, looked, and two others were standing there, one on this
bank of the river and one on the other.
6 One said to the man dressed in linen,
who was above the waters of the river,
"How long until the end of these extraordinary things?" 7 Then I heard the
man dressed in linen, who was above
the waters of the river. He raised both
his hands toward heaven and swore by
Him who lives eternally that it would
be for a time, times, and half a time.
When the power of the holy people is
shattered, all these things will be completed.
8 I heard but did not understand. So I
asked, "My lord, what will be the outcome of these things?"
9 He said, "Go on your way, Daniel,
for the words are secret and sealed until the time of the end. 10 Many will be
purified, cleansed, and refined, but the
wicked will act wickedly; none of the
wicked will understand, but the wise
will understand. 11 From the time the
daily sacrifice is abolished and the abomination of desolation is set up, there will
be 1,290 days. 12 Blessed is the one who
waits for and reaches 1,335 days. 13 But
as for you, go on your way to the end;
you will rest, then rise to your destiny at
the end of the days."

1 The word of the LORD that came to
Hosea son of Beeri during the reigns
of Uzziah, Jotham, Ahaz, and Hezekiah,
kings of Judah, and of Jeroboam son of
Joash, king of Israel.
2 When the LORD first spoke to Hosea,
He said this to him:

Go and marry a promiscuous wife
and have children of promiscuity,

for the whole land has been
promiscuous
by abandoning the LORD.

³ So he went and married Gomer
daughter of Diblaim, and she conceived
and bore him a son. ⁴ Then the LORD said
to him:

Name him Jezreel, for in a little
while
I will avenge the bloodshed of
Jezreel
on the house of Jehu
and put an end to the kingdom of
the house of Israel.
⁵ On that day I will break the bow
of Israel
in the valley of Jezreel.

⁶ She conceived again and gave birth
to a daughter, and the LORD said to him:

Name her No Compassion,
for I will no longer have
compassion
on the house of Israel.
I will certainly take them away.
⁷ But I will have compassion on the
house of Judah,
and I will deliver them by the
LORD their God.
I will not deliver them by bow,
sword, or war,
or by horses and cavalry.

⁸ After Gomer had weaned No Compassion, she conceived and gave birth to
a son. ⁹ Then the LORD said:

Name him Not My People,
for you are not My people,
and I will not be your God.
¹⁰ Yet the number of the Israelites
will be like the sand of the sea,
which cannot be measured or
counted.
And in the place where they were
told:
You are not My people,
they will be called: Sons of the
living God.
¹¹ And the Judeans and the Israelites
will be gathered together.

They will appoint for themselves a
single ruler,
and go up from the land.
For the day of Jezreel will be great.
2 Call your brothers: My People
and your sisters: Compassion.

² Rebuke your mother; rebuke her.
For she is not My wife and I am
not her husband.
Let her remove the promiscuous
look from her face
and her adultery from between
her breasts.
³ Otherwise, I will strip her naked
and expose her as she was on the
day of her birth.
I will make her like a desert
and like a parched land,
and I will let her die of thirst.
⁴ I will have no compassion on her
children
because they are the children of
promiscuity.
⁵ For their mother is promiscuous;
she conceived them and acted
shamefully.
For she thought: I will go after my
lovers,
the men who give me my food and
water,
my wool and flax, my oil and drink.
⁶ Therefore, this is what I will do:
I will block her way with thorns;
I will enclose her with a wall,
so that she cannot find her paths.
⁷ She will pursue her lovers but not
catch them;
she will seek them but not find
them.
Then she will think:
I will go back to my former husband,
for then it was better for me than
now.
⁸ She does not recognize
that it is I who gave her the grain,
the new wine, and the oil.
I lavished silver and gold on her,
which they used for Baal.
⁹ Therefore, I will take back My
grain in its time
and My new wine in its season;
I will take away My wool and
linen,

which were to cover her
  nakedness.
10 Now I will expose her shame
    in the sight of her lovers,
    and no one will rescue her from
    My hands.
11 I will put an end to all her
    celebrations:
    her feasts, New Moons, and
    Sabbaths—
    all her festivals.
12 I will devastate her vines and fig
    trees.
    She thinks that these are her
    wages
    that her lovers have given her.
    I will turn them into a thicket,
    and the wild animals will eat
    them.
13 And I will punish her for the days
    of the Baals
    when she burned incense to them,
    put on her rings and jewelry,
    and went after her lovers,
    but forgot Me.
          This is the Lord's declaration.

14 Therefore, I am going to persuade
    her,
    lead her to the wilderness,
    and speak tenderly to her.
15 There I will give her vineyards
    back to her
    and make the Valley of Achor
    into a gateway of hope.
    There she will respond as she did
    in the days of her youth,
    as in the day she came out of the
    land of Egypt.
16 In that day—
          the Lord's declaration—
    you will call Me: My husband,
    and no longer call Me: My Baal.
17 For I will remove the names of the
    Baals
    from her mouth;
    they will no longer be
    remembered by their names.
18 On that day I will make a
    covenant for them
    with the wild animals, the birds of
    the sky,
    and the creatures that crawl on
    the ground.

    I will shatter bow, sword,
    and weapons of war in the land
    and will enable the people to rest
    securely.
19 I will take you to be My wife
    forever.
    I will take you to be My wife in
    righteousness,
    justice, love, and compassion.
20 I will take you to be My wife in
    faithfulness,
    and you will know the LORD.
21 On that day I will respond—
          the LORD's declaration.
    I will respond to the sky,
    and it will respond to the earth.
22 The earth will respond to the
    grain,
    the new wine, and the oil,
    and they will respond to Jezreel.
23 I will sow her in the land for
    Myself,
    and I will have compassion
    on No Compassion;
    I will say to Not My People:
    You are My people,
    and he will say: You are My God.

3 Then the LORD said to me, "Go
  again; show love to a woman who is
loved by another man and is an adulteress, just as the LORD loves the Israelites
though they turn to other gods and love
raisin cakes." [2] So I bought her for 15 shekels of silver and five bushels of barley. [3] I said to
her, "You must live with me many days.
Don't be promiscuous or belong to any
man, and I will act the same way toward
you."
[4] For the Israelites must live many
days without king or prince, without
sacrifice or sacred pillar, and without
ephod or household idols. [5] Afterwards,
the people of Israel will return and seek
the LORD their God and David their
king. They will come with awe to the
LORD and to His goodness in the last days.

*P*SALM 140:1-5

1 Rescue me, LORD, from evil men.
  Keep me safe from violent men

² who plan evil in their hearts.
  They stir up wars all day long.
³ They make their tongues as sharp
    as a snake's bite;
  viper's venom is under their lips.
                              Selah

⁴ Protect me, LORD, from the
    clutches of the wicked.
  Keep me safe from violent men
  who plan to make me stumble.
⁵ The proud hide a trap with ropes
    for me;
  they spread a net along the path
  and set snares for me.   *Selah*

PROVERBS 30:7-9

⁷ Two things I ask of You;
  don't deny them to me before I die:
⁸ Keep falsehood and deceitful
    words far from me.
  Give me neither poverty nor
    wealth;
  feed me with the food I need.
⁹ Otherwise, I might have too
    much
  and deny You, saying, "Who is the
    LORD?"
  or I might have nothing and steal,
  profaning the name of my God.

REVELATION 2:1-17

2 "To the angel of the church in
  Ephesus write:
"The One who holds the seven stars
in His right hand and who walks among
the seven gold lampstands says: ² I know
your works, your labor, and your endurance, and that you cannot tolerate
evil. You have tested those who call
themselves apostles and are not, and
you have found them to be liars. ³ You
also possess endurance and have tolerated many things because of My name,
and have not grown weary. ⁴ But I have
this against you: you have abandoned
the love you had at first. ⁵ Remember
then how far you have fallen; repent,
and do the works you did at first.
Otherwise, I will come to you and remove your lampstand from its place—

unless you repent. ⁶ Yet you do have
this: you hate the practices of the
Nicolaitans, which I also hate.
⁷ "Anyone who has an ear should listen to what the Spirit says to the
churches. I will give the victor the right
to eat from the tree of life, which is in
the paradise of God.
⁸ "To the angel of the church in
Smyrna write:
"The First and the Last, the One who
was dead and came to life, says: ⁹ I know
your tribulation and poverty, yet you are
rich. I know the slander of those who
say they are Jews and are not, but are a
synagogue of Satan. ¹⁰ Don't be afraid of
what you are about to suffer. Look, the
Devil is about to throw some of you into
prison to test you, and you will have
tribulation for 10 days. Be faithful until
death, and I will give you the crown of
life.
¹¹ "Anyone who has an ear should listen to what the Spirit says to the
churches. The victor will never be
harmed by the second death.
¹² "To the angel of the church in
Pergamum write:
"The One who has the sharp, two-
edged sword says: ¹³ I know where you
live—where Satan's throne is! And you
are holding on to My name and did not
deny your faith in Me, even in the days
of Antipas, My faithful witness, who
was killed among you, where Satan
lives. ¹⁴ But I have a few things against
you. You have some there who hold to
the teaching of Balaam, who taught
Balak to place a stumbling block in front
of the sons of Israel: to eat meat sacrificed to idols and to commit sexual immorality. ¹⁵ In the same way, you also
have those who hold to the teaching of
the Nicolaitans. ¹⁶ Therefore repent!
Otherwise, I will come to you quickly
and fight against them with the sword
of My mouth.
¹⁷ "Anyone who has an ear should listen to what the Spirit says to the
churches. I will give the victor some of
the hidden manna. I will also give him a
white stone, and on the stone a new
name is inscribed that no one knows except the one who receives it.

God Is Not Father of All

Where they were told: You are not My people,
they will be called: Sons of the living God.—HOSEA 1:10

Jim Packer said: "You sum up the whole of New Testament teaching in a single phrase if you speak of it as a revelation of the Fatherhood of the Holy Creator. In the same way you sum up the whole of the New Testament religion if you describe it as the knowledge of God as one's Holy Father. Father is the Christian name for God."

There are those who claim that the teaching given in the Old Testament is quite different. There, they say, God is viewed as being the Father of all. But is He? Consider this: "Israel is My firstborn son . . . 'Let My son go'" (Ex 4:22-23). There are many such passages. The Old Testament as well and the New shows God as the Father, not of all men and women but of His own people, Abraham's descendants. Galatians 3:26 tells us that God is not the Father of all, but only of those who know themselves to be sinners and have accepted His Son into their hearts. When we have done this, Paul says, we belong to Christ and are ourselves Abraham's offspring.

Divine sonship is not ours because we have been born into this world; it is ours because we have been born again into another realm—the kingdom of God. Sonship is a gift, a gift of grace. It is not a natural sonship but an adoptive sonship. God takes those who receive His Son and makes them His adopted children, to see and share His glory into which His one and only Son has already come.

Prayer

O Father, once again I want to record my deepest thanks that because of Your Son I am an heir of God and a joint heir with Christ. How wonderful. How truly wonderful. All honor and glory be to Your precious name. Amen.

Further Study

Rm 9:4-12; Jr 31:9; Hs 11:1; 2 Co 6:18
What makes people children of God?
What does "Abraham's children" mean?

DECEMBER 13

HOSEA 4:1–7:16

4 Hear the word of the LORD,
   people of Israel,
for the LORD has a case
against the inhabitants of the land:
There is no truth, no faithful love,
and no knowledge of God in the
   land!
² Cursing, lying, murder, stealing,
   and adultery are rampant;
one act of bloodshed follows
   another.
³ For this reason the land mourns,
and everyone who lives in it
   languishes,
along with the wild animals and
   the birds of the sky;
even the fish of the sea disappear.
⁴ But let no one dispute; let no one
   argue,
for My case is against you priests.
⁵ You will stumble by day;
the prophet will also stumble with
   you by night.
And I will destroy your mother.
⁶ My people are destroyed for lack
   of knowledge.
Because you have rejected
   knowledge,
I will reject you from serving as
   My priest.
Since you have forgotten the law
   of your God,
I will also forget your sons.

⁷ The more they multiplied,
the more they sinned against Me.
I will change their honor into
   disgrace.
⁸ They feed on the sin of My people;
they have an appetite for their
   transgressions.
⁹ The same judgment will happen
   to both people and priests.
I will punish them for their ways
and repay them for their deeds.

¹⁰ They will eat but not be satisfied;
they will be promiscuous but not
   multiply;
for they have abandoned their
   devotion to the LORD.
¹¹ Promiscuity, wine, and new wine
take away one's understanding.

¹² My people consult their wooden
   idols,
and their divining rods inform
   them.
For a spirit of promiscuity leads
   them astray;
they act promiscuously
in disobedience to their God.
¹³ They sacrifice on the
   mountaintops,
and they burn offerings on the
   hills,
and under oaks, poplars, and
   terebinths,
because their shade is pleasant.
And so your daughters act
   promiscuously
and your daughters-in-law commit
   adultery.
¹⁴ I will not punish your daughters
when they act promiscuously
or your daughters-in-law
when they commit adultery,
for the men themselves go off
   with prostitutes
and make sacrifices with cult
   prostitutes.
People without discernment are
   doomed.

¹⁵ Israel, if you act promiscuously,
don't let Judah become guilty!
Do not go to Gilgal
or make a pilgrimage to Beth-aven,
and do not swear an oath: As the
   LORD lives!
¹⁶ For Israel is as obstinate as a
   stubborn cow.
Can the LORD now shepherd them

like a lamb in an open meadow?
17 Ephraim is attached to idols;
leave him alone!
18 When their drinking is over,
they turn to promiscuity.
Israel's leaders fervently love
disgrace.
19 A wind with its wings will carry
them off,
and they will be ashamed of their
sacrifices.

5 Hear this, priests!
Pay attention, house of Israel!
Listen, royal house!
For the judgment applies to you
because you have been a snare at
Mizpah
and a net spread out on Tabor.
2 Rebels are deeply involved in
slaughter;
I will be a punishment for all of
them.
3 I know Ephraim,
and Israel is not hidden from Me.
For now, Ephraim,
you have acted promiscuously;
Israel is defiled.
4 Their actions do not allow them
to return to their God,
for a spirit of promiscuity is
among them,
and they do not know the LORD.
5 Israel's arrogance testifies against
them.
Both Israel and Ephraim stumble
because of their wickedness;
even Judah will stumble with
them.
6 They go with their flocks and herds
to seek the LORD
but do not find Him;
He has withdrawn from them.
7 They betrayed the LORD;
indeed, they gave birth to
illegitimate children.
Now the New Moon will devour
them
along with their fields.

8 Blow the horn in Gibeah,
the trumpet in Ramah;
raise the war cry in Beth-aven:
After you, Benjamin!

9 Ephraim will become a desolation
on the day of punishment;
I announce what is certain
among the tribes of Israel.
10 The princes of Judah are like those
who move boundary markers;
I will pour out My fury on them
like water.
11 Ephraim is oppressed, crushed in
judgment,
for he is determined to follow
what is worthless.
12 So I am like rot to Ephraim
and like decay to the house of
Judah.
13 When Ephraim saw his sickness
and Judah his wound,
Ephraim went to Assyria
and sent a delegation to the great
king.
But he cannot cure you or heal
your wound.
14 For I am like a lion to Ephraim
and like a young lion to the house
of Judah.
Yes, I will tear them to pieces and
depart.
I will carry them off,
and no one can rescue them.
15 I will depart and return to My
place
until they recognize their guilt
and seek My face;
they will search for Me in their
distress.

6 Come, let us return to the LORD.
For He has torn us,
and He will heal us;
He has wounded us,
and He will bind up our wounds.
2 He will revive us after two days,
and on the third day He will raise
us up
so we can live in His presence.
3 Let us strive to know the LORD.
His appearance is as sure as the
dawn.
He will come to us like the rain,
like the spring showers that water
the land.

4 What am I going to do with you,
Ephraim?

What am I going to do with you,
Judah?
Your loyalty is like the morning
mist
and like the early dew that
vanishes.
⁵ This is why I have used the
prophets
to cut them down;
I have killed them with the words
of My mouth.
My judgment strikes like lightning.
⁶ For I desire loyalty and not
sacrifice,
the knowledge of God rather than
burnt offerings.

⁷ But they, like Adam, have violated
the covenant;
there they have betrayed Me.
⁸ Gilead is a city of evildoers,
tracked with bloody footprints.
⁹ Like robbers who wait in ambush
for someone,
a band of priests murders on the
road to Shechem.
They commit atrocities.
¹⁰ I have seen something horrible in
the house of Israel:
Ephraim's promiscuity is there;
Israel is defiled.
¹¹ A harvest is also appointed for
you, Judah.

When I return My people from
captivity,
7 ¹ when I heal Israel,
the sins of Ephraim and the crimes
of Samaria
will be exposed.
For they practice fraud;
a thief breaks in;
a gang pillages outside.
² But they never consider that I
remember all their evil.
Now their sins are all around them;
they are right in front of My face.

³ They please the king with their
evil,
the princes with their lies.
⁴ All of them commit adultery;
they are like an oven heated by a
baker

who stops stirring the fire
from the kneading of the dough
until it is leavened.
⁵ On the day of our king,
the princes are sick with the heat
of wine—
there is a conspiracy with traitors.
⁶ For they—their hearts like an
oven—
draw him into their oven.
Their anger smolders all night;
in the morning it blazes like a
flaming fire.
⁷ All of them are as hot as an oven,
and they consume their rulers.
All their kings fall;
not one of them calls on Me.

⁸ Ephraim has allowed himself to
get mixed up with the
nations.
Ephraim is unturned bread, baked
on a griddle.
⁹ Foreigners consume his strength,
but he does not notice.
Even his hair is streaked with gray,
but he does not notice.
¹⁰ Israel's arrogance testifies against
them,
yet they do not return to the LORD
their God,
and for all this, they do not seek
Him.

¹¹ So Ephraim has become like a
silly, senseless dove;
they call to Egypt, and they go to
Assyria.
¹² As they are going, I will spread
My net over them;
I will bring them down like birds
of the sky.
I will discipline them in accordance
with the news that reaches their
assembly.

¹³ Woe to them, for they fled from
Me;
destruction to them, for they
rebelled against Me!
Though I want to redeem them,
they speak lies against Me.
¹⁴ They do not cry to Me from their
hearts;

rather, they wail on their beds.
They slash themselves for grain
and wine;
they turn away from Me.
15 I trained and strengthened their
arms,
but they plot evil against Me.
16 They turn, but not to what is
above;
they are like a faulty bow.
Their leaders will fall by the
sword
because of the cursing of their
tongue.
They will be ridiculed for this in
the land of Egypt.

PSALM 140:6-13

6 I say to the LORD, "You are my
God."
Listen, LORD, to my cry for help.
7 Lord GOD, my strong Savior,
You shield my head on the day of
battle.
8 LORD, do not grant the desires of
the wicked;
do not let them achieve their
goals.
Otherwise, they will become
proud.   *Selah*

9 As for the heads of those who
surround me,
let the trouble their lips cause
overwhelm them.
10 Let hot coals fall on them.
Let them be thrown into the fire,
into the abyss, never again to rise.
11 Do not let a slanderer stay in the
land.
Let evil relentlessly hunt down a
violent man.

12 I know that the LORD upholds the
just cause of the poor,
justice for the needy.
13 Surely the righteous will praise
Your name;
the upright will live in Your
presence.

PROVERBS 30:10-12

10 Don't slander a servant to his
master,
or he will curse you, and you will
become guilty.

11 There is a generation that curses
its father
and does not bless its mother.
12 There is a generation that is pure
in its own eyes,
yet is not washed from its filth.

REVELATION 2:18–3:6

18 "To the angel of the church in
Thyatira write:
"The Son of God, the One whose
eyes are like a fiery flame, and whose
feet are like fine bronze says: 19 I know
your works—your love, faithfulness,
service, and endurance. Your last works
are greater than the first. 20 But I have
this against you: you tolerate the
woman Jezebel, who calls herself a
prophetess, and teaches and deceives
My slaves to commit sexual immorality
and to eat meat sacrificed to idols. 21 I
gave her time to repent, but she does
not want to repent of her sexual immorality. 22 Look! I will throw her into a
sickbed, and those who commit adultery with her into great tribulation, unless they repent of her practices. 23 I will
kill her children with the plague. Then
all the churches will know that I am the
One who examines minds and hearts,
and I will give to each of you according
to your works. 24 I say to the rest of you
in Thyatira, who do not hold this teaching, who haven't known the deep things
of Satan—as they say—I do not put any
other burden on you. 25 But hold on to
what you have until I come. 26 The victor and the one who keeps My works to
the end: I will give him authority over
the nations—

27 and He will shepherd them
with an iron scepter;
He will shatter them
like pottery—

just as I have received this from My Father. [28] I will also give him the morning star.

[29] "Anyone who has an ear should listen to what the Spirit says to the churches.

3 "To the angel of the church in Sardis write:

"The One who has the seven spirits of God and the seven stars says: I know your works; you have a reputation for being alive, but you are dead. [2] Be alert and strengthen what remains, which is about to die, for I have not found your works complete before My God. [3] Re-

member therefore what you have received and heard; keep it, and repent. But if you are not alert, I will come like a thief, and you have no idea at what hour I will come against you. [4] But you have a few people in Sardis who have not defiled their clothes, and they will walk with Me in white, because they are worthy. [5] In the same way, the victor will be dressed in white clothes, and I will never erase his name from the book of life, but will acknowledge his name before My Father and before His angels.

[6] "Anyone who has an ear should listen to what the Spirit says to the churches.

"Nutty" Is the Word

Your loyalty is like the morning mist and like the early dew that vanishes.—HOSEA 6:4

A danger that we must acquaint ourselves with as we discuss the need to contemplate God more deeply is that of becoming more interested in godliness than in God Himself. Theologian Jim Packer puts the point effectively when he says that "moving in evangelical circles as I do, I am often troubled by what I find. While my fellow believers are constantly seeking to advance in godliness, they show little direct interest in God Himself. When they study Scripture, only the principles of personal godliness get their attention; their heavenly Father does not. It is as if they should concentrate on the ethics of marriage and fail to spend time with their spouse!" He goes on to say: "There is something narcissistic, and, to tell the truth, nutty in being more concerned with godliness than about God."

I think "nutty" is the right word.

I knew a man who went to every seminar he could find on the subject of marriage, and whenever he came upon a new idea or a deep insight, he would reflect for hours on its wonder and profundity. The only trouble was he never got past the reflecting stage, and while he indulged himself in new and profound ideas, his wife was left languishing at home.

How sad that a man can take more interest in the principles that undergird his marriage than in the partner whom he has pledged to love, honor, and cherish. Let's be watchful that we don't care more for the principles of godliness than the God we are called to praise and please every day of our lives.

Prayer

Gracious and loving heavenly Father, forgive me, I pray, if I have been caught up more in the mechanics of my faith than in the dynamics of it. May nothing ever become more important to me than my relationship with You. Amen.

DECEMBER 14

HOSEA 8:1–10:15

8 Put the horn to your mouth!
One like an eagle comes
against the house of the LORD,
because they transgress My
covenant
and rebel against My law.
² Israel cries out to Me:
My God, we know You!
³ Israel has rejected what is good;
an enemy will pursue him.

⁴ They have installed kings,
but not through Me.
They have appointed leaders,
but without My approval.
They make their silver and gold
into idols for themselves
for their own destruction.
⁵ Your calf-idol is rejected, Samaria.
My anger burns against them.
How long will they be incapable of
innocence?
⁶ For this thing is from Israel—
a craftsman made it, and it is not
God.
The calf of Samaria will be
smashed to bits!

⁷ Indeed, they sow the wind
and reap the whirlwind.
There is no standing grain;
what sprouts fails to yield flour.
Even if they did,
foreigners would swallow it up.
⁸ Israel is swallowed up!

Now they are among the nations
like discarded pottery.
⁹ For they have gone up to Assyria
like a wild donkey going off on its
own.
Ephraim has paid for love.
¹⁰ Even though they hire lovers
among the nations,
I will now round them up,
and they will begin to decrease in
number
under the burden of the king and
leaders.

¹¹ When Ephraim multiplied his
altars for sin,
they became his altars for sinning.
¹² Though I were to write out for
him
ten thousand points of My law,
they would be regarded as
something alien.
¹³ Though they offer sacrificial gifts
and eat the flesh,
the LORD does not accept them.
Now He will remember their
guilt
and punish their sins;
they will return to Egypt.
¹⁴ Israel has forgotten his Maker and
built palaces;
Judah has also multiplied fortified
cities.
I will send fire on their cities,
and it will consume their citadels.

9 Israel, do not rejoice jubilantly
    as the nations do,
  for you have acted promiscuously,
    leaving your God.
  You have loved the wages of a
    prostitute
  on every grain-threshing floor.
2 Threshing floor and wine vat will
    not sustain them,
  and the new wine will fail them.
3 They will not stay in the land of
    the LORD.
  Instead, Ephraim will return to
    Egypt,
  and they will eat unclean food in
    Assyria.

4 They will not pour out
    their wine offerings to the LORD,
  and their sacrifices will not please
    Him.
  Their food will be like the bread
    of mourners;
  all who eat it become defiled.
  For their bread will be for their
    appetites alone;
  it will not enter the house of the
    LORD.
5 What will you do on a festival day,
  on the day of the LORD's feast?
6 For even if they flee from
    devastation,
  Egypt will gather them, and
    Memphis will bury them.
  Thistles will take possession of
    their precious silver;
  thorns will invade their tents.

7 The days of punishment have
    come;
  the days of retribution have come.
  Let Israel recognize it!
  The prophet is a fool,
  and the inspired man is insane,
  because of the magnitude
  of your guilt and hostility.
8 Ephraim's watchman is with my
    God.
  The prophet encounters a fowler's
    snare
  on all his ways.
  Hostility is in the house of his God!
9 They have deeply corrupted
    themselves

as in the days of Gibeah.
He will remember their guilt;
He will punish their sins.

10 I discovered Israel
  like grapes in the wilderness.
  I saw your fathers
  like the first fruit of the fig tree in
    its first season.
  But they went to Baal-peor,
  consecrated themselves to Shame,
  and became detestable,
  like the thing they loved.
11 Ephraim's glory will fly away like a
    bird:
  no birth, no gestation, no
    conception.
12 Even if they raise children,
  I will bereave them of each one.
  Yes, woe to them when I depart
    from them!
13 I have seen Ephraim like Tyre,
  planted in a meadow,
  so Ephraim will bring out his
    children
  to the executioner.
14 Give them, LORD—
  What should You give?
  Give them a womb that miscarries
  and breasts that are dry!

15 All their evil appears at Gilgal,
  for there I came to hate them.
  I will drive them from My house
  because of their evil, wicked
    actions.
  I will no longer love them;
  all their leaders are rebellious.
16 Ephraim is blighted;
  their roots are withered;
  they cannot bear fruit.
  Even if they bear children,
  I will kill the precious offspring of
    their wombs.
17 My God will reject them
  because they have not listened to
    Him;
  they will become wanderers
    among the nations.

10 Israel is a lush vine;
    it yields fruit for itself.
  The more his fruit increased,
  the more he increased the altars.

The better his land produced,
the better they made the sacred
pillars.

2 Their hearts are devious;
now they must bear their guilt.
The LORD will break down their
altars
and demolish their sacred pillars.

3 In fact, they are now saying:
"We have no king!
For we do not fear the LORD.
What can a king do for us?"

4 They speak mere words,
taking false oaths while making
covenants.
So lawsuits break out
like poisonous weeds in the
furrows of a field.

5 The residents of Samaria will have
anxiety
over the calf of Beth-aven.
Indeed, its idolatrous priests
rejoiced over it;
the people will mourn over it,
over its glory.
It will certainly depart from them.

6 The calf itself will be taken to
Assyria
as an offering to the great king.
Ephraim will experience shame;
Israel will be ashamed of its
counsel.

7 Samaria's king will disappear
like foam on the surface of the
water.

8 The high places of Aven, the sin of
Israel,
will be destroyed;
thorns and thistles will grow over
their altars.
They will say to the mountains,
"Cover us!"
and to the hills, "Fall on us!"

9 Israel, you have sinned
since the days of Gibeah;
they have taken their stand there.
Will not war against the unjust
overtake them in Gibeah?

10 I will discipline them at my
discretion;
nations will be gathered against
them

to put them in bondage
for their two crimes.

11 Ephraim is a well-trained young
cow
that loves to thresh,
but I will place a yoke on her fine
neck.
I will harness Ephraim;
Judah will plow;
Jacob will do the final plowing.

12 Sow righteousness for yourselves
and reap faithful love;
break up your untilled ground.
It is time to seek the LORD
until He comes and sends
righteousness
on you like the rain.

13 You have plowed wickedness and
reaped injustice;
you have eaten the fruit of lies.
Because you have trusted in your
own way
and in your large number of
soldiers,

14 the roar of battle will rise against
your people,
and all your fortifications will be
demolished
in a day of war,
like Shalman's destruction of
Beth-arbel.
Mothers will be dashed to pieces
along with their children.

15 So it will be done to you, Bethel,
because of your extreme evil.
At dawn the king of Israel will be
totally destroyed.

PSALM 141:1-6

1 LORD, I call on You; hurry to help
me.
Listen to my voice when I call on
You.

2 May my prayer be set before You
as incense,
the raising of my hands as the
evening offering.

3 LORD, set up a guard for my
mouth;

keep watch at the door of my lips.
4 Do not let my heart turn to any
    evil thing
or wickedly perform reckless acts
    with men who commit sin.
Do not let me feast on their
    delicacies.
5 Let the righteous one strike me—
    it is an act of faithful love;
let him rebuke me—it is oil for
    my head;
let me not refuse it.
Even now my prayer is against the
    evil acts of the wicked.
6 When their rulers will be thrown
    off the sides of a cliff,
the people will listen to my
    words, for they are pleasing.

PROVERBS 30:13-14

13 There is a generation—how
    haughty its eyes
and pretentious its looks.
14 There is a generation whose teeth
    are swords,
whose fangs are knives,
devouring the oppressed from the
    land
and the needy from among
    mankind.

REVELATION 3:7-22

7 "To the angel of the church in
Philadelphia write:
"The Holy One, the True One, the
One who has the key of David, who
opens and no one will close, and closes
and no one opens says: 8 I know your
works. Because you have limited
strength, have kept My word, and have
not denied My name, look, I have
placed before you an open door that no
one is able to close. 9 Take note! I will
make those from the synagogue of
Satan, who claim to be Jews and are
not, but are lying—note this—I will
make them come and bow down at your
feet, and they will know that I have
loved you. 10 Because you have kept My
command to endure, I will also keep
you from the hour of testing that is going to come over the whole world to
test those who live on the earth. 11 I am
coming quickly. Hold on to what you
have, so that no one takes your crown.
12 The victor: I will make him a pillar in
the sanctuary of My God, and he will
never go out again. I will write on him
the name of My God, and the name of
the city of My God—the new Jerusalem, which comes down out of heav-
en from My God—and My new name.
13 "Anyone who has an ear should listen to what the Spirit says to the
churches.
14 "To the angel of the church in
Laodicea write:
"The Amen, the faithful and true
Witness, the Originator of God's creation says: 15 I know your works, that
you are neither cold nor hot. I wish that
you were cold or hot. 16 So, because you
are lukewarm, and neither hot nor cold,
I am going to vomit you out of My
mouth. 17 Because you say, 'I'm rich; I
have become wealthy, and need nothing,' and you don't know that you are
wretched, pitiful, poor, blind, and
naked, 18 I advise you to buy from Me
gold refined in the fire so that you may
be rich, and white clothes so that you
may be dressed and your shameful
nakedness not be exposed, and ointment to spread on your eyes so that you
may see. 19 As many as I love, I rebuke
and discipline. So be committed and repent. 20 Listen! I stand at the door and
knock. If anyone hears My voice and
opens the door, I will come in to him
and have dinner with him, and he with
Me. 21 The victor: I will give him the
right to sit with Me on My throne, just
as I also won the victory and sat down
with My Father on His throne.
22 "Anyone who has an ear should listen to what the Spirit says to the
churches."

A Disciplined Tongue

LORD, set up a guard for my mouth;
keep watch at the door of my lips.—PSALM 141:3

Proverbs 10:19 states, "The one who controls his lips is wise." I'm glad God included in the Psalms and Proverbs the words that are before us today about controlling our speech. It's important to talk, but talking too much is as bad as not talking at all. Proverbs extols rationing our words.

Once, when Thomas Edison the inventor was at a reception, the toastmaster stood up and complimented him on his many inventions, especially the talking machine. After the toastmaster sat down, the aged inventor rose to his feet and said, "Thank you for those remarks, but I must correct one thing. It was God who invented the talking machine. I only invented the first one that can be shut off."

A doctor told me that once, while writing out a prescription, he asked a woman to put out her tongue. When he had finished, she said to him, "But doctor, you never even looked at my tongue." The doctor replied, "It wasn't necessary, I just wanted you to keep quiet while I wrote the prescription." Amidst the humor of today's notes, don't miss the point—words are important, but don't overdo them. I like the advice of an anonymous poet who wrote:

> If your lips would keep from slips
> Five things observe with care:
> Of whom you speak, to whom you speak,
> And how and when and where.

A wise person has a disciplined tongue. Many need to learn this, for, like the tongue in old shoes, our tongue is often the last thing to be worn out. If a disciplined tongue is your need, ask God to help you, for an undisciplined tongue is an unloving tongue.

Prayer

Father, I realize that oftentimes my tongue is the most difficult thing to bring under control. Yet I have the promise of Your help even in this. I give you my tongue to be bridled—take over the reins. In Jesus' name I pray. Amen.

Further Study

Mt 12:30-37; Ti 1:1-10; Jb 11:3
What did Jesus say we will have to account for?
What did Paul mean by "idle talkers" (Ti 1:10)?

DECEMBER 15

HOSEA 11:1–14:9

11 When Israel was a child, I loved him,
and out of Egypt I called My son.
2 The more they called them,
the more they departed from Me.
They kept sacrificing to the Baals
and burning offerings to idols.
3 It was I who taught Ephraim to walk,
taking them in My arms,
but they never knew that I healed them.
4 I led them with human cords,
with ropes of kindness.
To them I was like one
who eases the yoke from their jaws;
I bent down to give them food.
5 Israel will not return to the land of Egypt
and Assyria will be his king,
because they refused to repent.
6 A sword will whirl through his cities;
it will destroy and devour the bars of his gates,
because of their schemes.
7 My people are bent on turning from Me.
Though they call to Him on high,
He will not exalt them at all.

8 How can I give you up, Ephraim?
How can I surrender you, Israel?
How can I make you like Admah?
How can I treat you like Zeboiim?
I have had a change of heart;
My compassion is stirred!
9 I will not vent the full fury of My anger;
I will not turn back to destroy Ephraim.
For I am God and not man,
the Holy One among you;
I will not come in rage.
10 They will follow the LORD;

He will roar like a lion.
When He roars,
His children will come trembling from the west.
11 They will be roused like birds from Egypt
and like doves from the land of Assyria.
Then I will settle them in their homes.
This is the Lord's declaration.

12 Ephraim surrounds me with lies,
the house of Israel, with deceit.
Judah still wanders with El
and is faithful to holy ones.

12 Ephraim chases the wind
and pursues the east wind.
He continually multiplies lies and violence.
He makes a covenant with Assyria,
and olive oil is carried to Egypt.

2 The LORD also has a dispute with Judah.
He is about to punish Jacob according to his ways;
He will repay him based on his actions.
3 In the womb he grasped his brother's heel,
and as an adult he wrestled with God.
4 Jacob struggled with the Angel and prevailed;
he wept and sought His favor.
He found him at Bethel,
and there He spoke with him.
5 Yahweh is the God of Hosts;
Yahweh is His name.
6 But you must return to your God.
Maintain love and justice,
and always put your hope in God.

7 A merchant loves to extort
with dishonest scales in his hands.

8 But Ephraim says:
"How rich I have become;
I made it all myself.
In all my earnings,
no one can find any crime in me
that I can be punished for!"

9 I have been the LORD your God
ever since the land of Egypt.
I will make you live in tents again,
as in the festival days.
10 I spoke through the prophets
and granted many visions;
I gave parables through the
prophets.
11 Since Gilead is full of evil,
they will certainly come to
nothing.
They sacrifice bulls in Gilgal;
even their altars will be like heaps
of rocks
on the furrows of a field.

12 Jacob fled to the land of Aram.
Israel worked to earn a wife;
he tended flocks for a wife.
13 The LORD brought Israel from
Egypt by a prophet,
and Israel was tended by a
prophet.

14 Ephraim has provoked bitter
anger,
so his Lord will leave his
bloodguilt on him
and repay him for his contempt.

13 When Ephraim spoke, there was
trembling;
he was exalted in Israel.
But he incurred guilt through Baal
and died.

2 Now they continue to sin
and make themselves a cast image,
idols skillfully made from their
silver,
all of them the work of craftsmen.
People say about them,
"Let the men who sacrifice kiss
the calves."
3 Therefore, they will be like the
morning mist,
like the early dew that vanishes,

like chaff blown from a threshing
floor,
or like smoke from a window.

4 I have been the LORD your God
ever since the land of Egypt;
you know no God but Me,
and no Savior exists besides Me.
5 I knew you in the wilderness,
in the land of drought.
6 When they had pasture,
they became satisfied;
they were satisfied,
and their hearts became proud.
Therefore they forgot Me.
7 So I will be like a lion to them;
I will lurk like a leopard on the
path.
8 I will attack them
like a bear robbed of her cubs
and tear open the rib cage over
their hearts.
I will devour them there like a
lioness,
like a wild beast that would rip
them open.
9 I will destroy you, Israel;
you have no help but Me.

10 Where now is your king,
that he may save you in all your
cities,
and the rulers you demanded,
saying:
Give me a king and leaders?
11 I give you a king in My anger
and take away a king in My
wrath.
12 Ephraim's guilt is preserved;
his sin is stored up.
13 Labor pains come on him.
He is not a wise son.
When the time comes,
he will have no success in giving
birth.

14 I will ransom them from the
power of Sheol.
I will redeem them from death.
Death, where are your barbs?
Sheol, where is your sting?
Compassion is hidden from My
eyes.

15 Although he flourishes among his
  brothers,
an east wind will come,
a wind from the LORD rising up
  from the desert.
His water source will fail,
and his spring will run dry.
The wind will plunder the
  treasury
of every precious item.

16 Samaria will bear her guilt
because she has rebelled against
  her God.
They will fall by the sword;
their little ones will be dashed to
  pieces,
and their pregnant women ripped
  open.

14 Israel, return to the LORD your
  God,
for you have stumbled in your sin.
2 Take words of repentance with
  you
and return to the LORD.
Say to Him: "Forgive all our sin
and accept what is good,
so that we may repay You
with praise from our lips.
3 Assyria will not save us,
we will not ride on horses,
and we will no longer proclaim:
  Our gods!
to the work of our hands.
For the fatherless receives
  compassion in You."

4 I will heal their apostasy;
I will freely love them,
for My anger will have turned
  from him.
5 I will be like the dew to Israel;
he will blossom like the lily
and take root like the cedars of
  Lebanon.
6 His new branches will spread,
and his splendor will be like the
  olive tree,
his fragrance, like the forest of
  Lebanon.
7 The people will return and live
  beneath his shade.
They will grow grain

and blossom like the vine.
His renown will be like the wine
  of Lebanon.

8 Ephraim, why should I have
  anything more
to do with idols?
It is I who answer and watch over
  him.
I am like a flourishing pine tree;
your fruit comes from Me.

9 Let whoever is wise understand
  these things,
and whoever is insightful
  recognize them.
For the ways of the LORD are right,
and the righteous walk in them,
but the rebellious stumble in
  them.

PSALM 141:7-10

7 As when one plows and breaks up
  the soil, turning up rocks,
so our bones have been scattered
  at the mouth of Sheol.

8 But my eyes look to You, Lord
  GOD.
I seek refuge in You; do not let me
  die.
9 Protect me from the trap they
  have set for me,
and from the snares of evildoers.
10 Let the wicked fall into their own
  nets,
while I pass safely by.

PROVERBS 30:15-17

15 The leech has two daughters:
  Give, Give.
Three things are never satisfied;
four never say, "Enough!":
16 Sheol; a barren womb;
earth, which is never satisfied
  with water;
and fire, which never says,
  "Enough!"

17 As for the eye that ridicules a
  father

and despises obedience to a
mother,
may ravens of the valley pluck it
out
and young vultures eat it.

REVELATION 4:1–5:14

4 After this I looked, and there in heaven was an open door. The first voice that I had heard speaking to me like a trumpet said, "Come up here, and I will show you what must take place after this."
² Immediately I was in the Spirit, and there in heaven a throne was set. One was seated on the throne, ³ and the One seated looked like jasper and carnelian stone. A rainbow that looked like an emerald surrounded the throne. ⁴ Around that throne were 24 thrones, and on the thrones sat 24 elders dressed in white clothes, with gold crowns on their heads. ⁵ From the throne came flashes of lightning, rumblings, and thunder. Burning before the throne were seven fiery torches, which are the seven spirits of God. ⁶ Also before the throne was something like a sea of glass, similar to crystal. In the middle and around the throne were four living creatures covered with eyes in front and in back. ⁷ The first living creature was like a lion; the second living creature was like a calf; the third living creature had a face like a man; and the fourth living creature was like a flying eagle. ⁸ Each of the four living creatures had six wings; they were covered with eyes around and inside. Day and night they never stop, saying:

Holy, holy, holy,
Lord God, the Almighty,
who was, who is,
and who is coming.

⁹ Whenever the living creatures give glory, honor, and thanks to the One seated on the throne, the One who lives forever and ever, ¹⁰ the 24 elders fall down before the One seated on the throne, worship the One who lives forever and ever, cast their crowns before the throne, and say:

¹¹ Our Lord and God,
You are worthy to receive
glory and honor and power,
because You have created
all things,
and because of Your will
they exist and were created.

5 Then I saw in the right hand of the One seated on the throne a scroll with writing on the inside and on the back, sealed with seven seals. ² I also saw a mighty angel proclaiming in a loud voice, "Who is worthy to open the scroll and break its seals?" ³ But no one in heaven or on earth or under the earth was able to open the scroll or even to look in it. ⁴ And I cried and cried because no one was found worthy to open the scroll or even to look in it.
⁵ Then one of the elders said to me, "Stop crying. Look! The Lion from the tribe of Judah, the Root of David, has been victorious so that He may open the scroll and its seven seals." ⁶ Then I saw one like a slaughtered lamb standing between the throne and the four living creatures and among the elders. He had seven horns and seven eyes, which are the seven spirits of God sent into all the earth. ⁷ He came and took the scroll out of the right hand of the One seated on the throne.
⁸ When He took the scroll, the four living creatures and the 24 elders fell down before the Lamb. Each one had a harp and gold bowls filled with incense, which are the prayers of the saints. ⁹ And they sang a new song:

You are worthy to take the scroll
and to open its seals;
because You were slaughtered,
and You redeemed people for God
by Your blood
from every tribe and language
and people and nation.
¹⁰ You made them a kingdom
and priests to our God,
and they will reign on the earth.

¹¹ Then I looked, and heard the voice of many angels around the throne, and also of the living creatures, and of the elders. Their number was countless thousands, plus thousands of thousands. ¹² They said with a loud voice:

The Lamb who was slaughtered
is worthy
to receive power and riches
and wisdom and strength
and honor and glory and blessing!

¹³ I heard every creature in heaven, on earth, under the earth, on the sea, and everything in them say:

Blessing and honor and glory
and dominion
to the One seated on the throne,
and to the Lamb, forever
and ever!

¹⁴ The four living creatures said, "Amen," and the elders fell down and worshiped.

The Only Cure

Take words of repentance with you and return to the LORD.
—HOSEA 14:2

How do we deal with demandingness? We must repent of it. Our passage today tells us how.

First: "Return to the LORD." The key to ridding ourselves of anything that is spiritually injurious is to return to God. The pursuit of God involves a shift away from dependence on one's own resources to dependence on God. Doing good and correcting wrong behavior does not automatically make us good people. Obedience is extremely important, but it must be accompanied by deep, heart repentance.

Second, the passage says: "Take words of repentance with you." This phrase means that we must put into words a clear description of what we are repenting of. If we are not clear about what is going on inside us, how can we repent of it?

Next: "Forgive all our sin." Repentance puts us in touch with God's forgiveness. We can work to bring about change also, but the greatest catalyst for change is humbly positioning ourselves before God and asking for His forgiveness.

Then: "Accept what is good, so that we may repay You with praise from our lips." The thought here is: "Receive us that we may worship You more effectively." The purpose of all restoration is to worship God. We will be drawn into true worship when we give up insisting on our own way and learn to trust God for our own happiness. When repentance moves us from a spirit of demandingness to absolute trust in God, then we are in the place where God is able to make our feet like "hinds' feet" and equip us with the ability to ascend into the heights with Him.

Prayer

Tender and skillful Invader of my heart, I yield my stricken being to You for healing. "Be of sin the double cure." Drain every drop of demandingness from my being. For I want not only to be better but to be whole. In Jesus' name. Amen.

Further Study

Jl 2:12-18; Is 55:7; Ps 34:18; 51:17
What does God not despise?
What does it mean to "rend your heart"?

DECEMBER 16

JOEL 1:1–2:32

1 The word of the LORD that came to Joel son of Pethuel:

2 Hear this, you elders;
listen, all you inhabitants of the land.
Has anything like this ever happened in your days
or in the days of your ancestors?
3 Tell your children about it,
and let your children tell their children,
and their children the next generation.
4 What the devouring locust has left,
the swarming locust has eaten;
what the swarming locust has left,
the young locust has eaten;
and what the young locust has left,
the destroying locust has eaten.

5 Wake up, you drunkards, and weep;
wail, all you wine drinkers,
because of the sweet wine,
for it has been taken from your mouth.
6 For a nation has invaded My land,
powerful and without number;
its teeth are the teeth of a lion,
and it has the fangs of a lioness.
7 It has devastated My grapevine
and splintered My fig tree.
It has stripped off its bark and thrown it away;
its branches have turned white.

8 Grieve like a young woman
dressed in sackcloth,
mourning for the husband of her youth.
9 Grain and drink offerings have been cut off
from the house of the LORD;
the priests, who are ministers of the LORD, mourn.
10 The fields are destroyed;
the land grieves;
indeed, the grain is destroyed;
the new wine is dried up;
and the olive oil fails.
11 Be ashamed, you farmers,
wail, you vinedressers,
over the wheat and the barley,
because the harvest of the field has perished.
12 The grapevine is dried up,
and the fig tree is withered;
the pomegranate, the date palm, and the apple—
all the trees of the orchard—have withered.
Indeed, human joy has dried up.

13 Dress in sackcloth and lament, you priests;
wail, you ministers of the altar.
Come and spend the night in sackcloth,
you ministers of my God,
because grain and drink offerings are withheld from the house of your God.
14 Announce a sacred fast;

proclaim an assembly!
Gather the elders
and all the residents of the land
at the house of the LORD your God,
and cry out to the LORD.

¹⁵ Woe because of that day!
For the Day of the LORD is near
and will come as devastation from
the Almighty.
¹⁶ Hasn't the food been cut off
before our eyes,
joy and gladness
from the house of our God?
¹⁷ The seeds lie shriveled in their
casings.
The storehouses are in ruin,
and the granaries are broken
down,
because the grain has withered
away.
¹⁸ How the animals groan!
The herds of cattle wander in
confusion
since they have no pasture.
Even the flocks of sheep suffer
punishment.
¹⁹ I call to You, LORD,
for fire has consumed
the pastures of the wilderness,
and flames have devoured
all the trees of the countryside.
²⁰ Even the wild animals cry out to
You,
for the river beds are dried up,
and fire has consumed
the pastures of the wilderness.

2 Blow the horn in Zion;
sound the alarm on My holy
mountain!
Let all the residents of the land
tremble,
for the Day of the LORD is coming;
in fact, it is near—
² a day of darkness and gloom,
a day of clouds and dense overcast,
like the dawn spreading over the
mountains;
a great and strong people appears,
such as never existed in ages past
and never will again
in all the generations to come.

³ A fire destroys in front of them,
and behind them a flame devours.
The land in front of them
is like the Garden of Eden,
but behind them,
it is like a desert wasteland;
there is no escape from them.
⁴ Their appearance is like that of
horses,
and they gallop like war horses.
⁵ They bound on the tops of the
mountains.
Their sound is like the sound of
chariots,
like the sound of fiery flames
consuming stubble,
like a mighty army deployed for
war.
⁶ Nations writhe in horror before
them;
all faces turn pale.
⁷ They attack as warriors attack;
they scale walls as men of war do.
Each goes on his own path,
and they do not change their
course.
⁸ They do not push each other;
each man proceeds on his own
path.
They dodge the missiles, never
stopping.
⁹ They storm the city;
they run on the wall;
they climb into the houses;
they enter through the windows
like thieves.

¹⁰ The earth quakes before them;
the sky shakes.
The sun and moon grow dark,
and the stars cease their shining.
¹¹ The LORD raises His voice
in the presence of His army.
His camp is very large;
Those who carry out His
command are powerful.
Indeed, the Day of the LORD is
terrible and dreadful—
who can endure it?

¹² Even now—
this is the LORD's declaration—
turn to Me with all your heart,

with fasting, weeping, and
mourning.
13 Tear your hearts,
not just your clothes,
and return to the LORD your God.
For He is gracious and
compassionate,
slow to anger, rich in faithful love,
and He relents from sending
disaster.
14 Who knows? He may turn and
relent
and leave a blessing behind Him,
so you can offer grain and wine
to the LORD your God.

15 Blow the horn in Zion!
Announce a sacred fast;
proclaim an assembly.
16 Gather the people;
sanctify the congregation;
assemble the aged;
gather the children,
even those nursing at the breast.
Let the bridegroom leave his
bedroom,
and the bride her honeymoon
chamber.
17 Let the priests, the LORD's
ministers,
weep between the portico and the
altar.
Let them say:
"Have pity on Your people, LORD,
and do not make Your inheritance
a disgrace,
an object of scorn among the
nations.
Why should it be said among the
peoples,
'Where is their God?' "

18 Then the LORD became jealous for
His land and spared His people. 19 The
LORD answered His people:

Look, I am about to send you
grain, new wine, and olive oil.
You will be satiated with them,
and I will no longer make you
a disgrace among the nations.

20 I will drive the northerner far
from you

and banish him to a dry and
desolate land,
his front ranks into the Dead Sea,
and his rear guard into the
Mediterranean Sea.
His stench will rise;
yes, his rotten smell will rise,
for he has done catastrophic
things.

21 Don't be afraid, land;
rejoice and be glad,
for the LORD has done great things.
22 Don't be afraid, wild animals,
for the wilderness pastures have
turned green,
the trees bear their fruit,
and the fig tree and grapevine
yield their riches.
23 Children of Zion, rejoice and be
glad
in the LORD your God,
because He gives you the autumn
rain
for your vindication.
He sends showers for you,
both autumn and spring rain as
before.
24 The threshing floors will be full of
grain,
and the vats will overflow
with new wine and olive oil.

25 I will repay you for the years
that the swarming locust ate,
the young locust, the destroying
locust,
and the devouring locust—
My great army that I sent against
you.
26 You will have plenty to eat and be
satisfied.
You will praise the name of
Yahweh your God,
who has dealt wondrously with
you.
My people will never again be put
to shame.
27 You will know that I am present in
Israel
and that I am the LORD your God,
and there is no other.
My people will never again be put
to shame.

28 After this
I will pour out My Spirit on all
humanity;
then your sons and your daughters
will prophesy,
your old men will have dreams,
and your young men will see
visions.
29 I will even pour out My Spirit
on the male and female slaves in
those days.
30 I will display wonders
in the heavens and on the earth:
blood, fire, and columns of
smoke.
31 The sun will be turned to
darkness
and the moon to blood
before the great and awe-inspiring
Day of the LORD comes.
32 Then everyone who calls
on the name of Yahweh will be
saved,
for there will be an escape
for those on Mount Zion and in
Jerusalem,
as the LORD promised,
among the survivors the LORD
calls.

PSALM 142:1-7

1 I cry aloud to the LORD;
I plead aloud to the LORD for
mercy.
2 I pour out my complaint before
Him;
I reveal my trouble to Him.
3 Although my spirit is weak
within me,
You know my way.

Along this path I travel
they have hidden a trap for me.
4 Look to the right and see:
no one stands up for me;
there is no refuge for me;
no one cares about me.

5 I cry to You, LORD;
I say, "You are my shelter,
my portion in the land of the
living."

6 Listen to my cry,
for I am very weak.
Rescue me from those who
pursue me,
for they are too strong for me.
7 Free me from prison
so that I can praise Your name.
The righteous will gather
around me
because You deal generously
with me.

PROVERBS 30:18-20

18 Three things are beyond me;
four I can't understand:
19 the way of an eagle in the sky,
the way of a snake on a rock,
the way of a ship at sea,
and the way of a man with a
young woman.

20 This is the way of an
adulteress:
she eats and wipes her mouth
and says, "I've done nothing
wrong."

REVELATION 6:1-17

6 Then I saw the Lamb open one of
the seven seals, and I heard one of
the four living creatures say with a voice
like thunder, "Come!" 2 I looked, and
there was a white horse. The horseman
on it had a bow; a crown was given to
him, and he went out as a victor to conquer.

3 When He opened the second seal, I
heard the second living creature say,
"Come!" 4 Then another horse went
out, a fiery red one, and its horseman
was empowered to take peace from the
earth, so that people would slaughter
one another. And a large sword was
given to him.

5 When He opened the third seal, I
heard the third living creature say,
"Come!" And I looked, and there was a
black horse. The horseman on it had a
balance scale in his hand. 6 Then I heard
something like a voice among the four
living creatures say, "A quart of wheat

for a denarius, and three quarts of barley for a denarius—but do not harm the olive oil and the wine."

[7] When He opened the fourth seal, I heard the voice of the fourth living creature say, "Come!" [8] And I looked, and there was a pale green horse. The horseman on it was named Death, and Hades was following after him. Authority was given to them over a fourth of the earth, to kill by the sword, by famine, by plague, and by the wild animals of the earth.

[9] When He opened the fifth seal, I saw under the altar the souls of those slaughtered because of God's word and the testimony they had. [10] They cried out with a loud voice: "O Lord, holy and true, how long until You judge and avenge our blood from those who live on the earth?" [11] So a white robe was given to each of them, and they were told to rest a little while longer until the number of their fellow slaves and their

brothers, who were going to be killed just as they had been, would be completed.

[12] Then I saw Him open the sixth seal. A violent earthquake occurred; the sun turned black like sackcloth made of goat hair; the entire moon became like blood; [13] the stars of heaven fell to the earth as a fig tree drops its unripe figs when shaken by a high wind; [14] the sky separated like a scroll being rolled up; and every mountain and island was moved from its place.

[15] Then the kings of the earth, the nobles, the military commanders, the rich, the powerful, and every slave and free person hid in the caves and among the rocks of the mountains. [16] And they said to the mountains and to the rocks, "Fall on us and hide us from the face of the One seated on the throne and from the wrath of the Lamb, [17] because the great day of Their wrath has come! And who is able to stand?"

Under the Surface

I will pour out My Spirit on all humanity.
—JOEL 2:28

What are some evidences of the Spirit-filled life? How do we know when we are fully indwelt by the divine Paraclete?

I am not going to begin where you might expect, in the area of spiritual gifts, but in a realm I believe to be equally important yet seldom mentioned. I refer to the area of the subconscious.

The longer I live, the more I feel the church has missed its way here. We have talked much about the works of the Spirit on the conscious level but little of His work at a subconscious level. We have failed to see, generally speaking, that part of the work of the Holy Spirit in the life of a Christian is to project His power and presence into the depths of the personality—even the subconscious.

We are told that about one-tenth of the mind is conscious and the other nine-tenths subconscious. Like the iceberg, which is nine-tenths submerged, life is largely lived in the submerged part of our being. Now, if this is so, then it becomes evident at once that if the submerged nine-tenths is not working with the conscious purposes of the one-tenth, then there is going to be a serious division, and a division this serious becomes divisive. Whatever controls the nine-tenths greatly influences the one-tenth. The Holy Spirit wants to project Himself into that submerged part of our being in order to harness those untamed forces and make them work for us and not against us. Then the subconscious is no longer an enemy but a friend.

Prayer

O God, my Father, I am grateful that You have provided for my deepest need—the need of unifying and controlling the depths within me. My heart tingles at the thought that I can be unified—on the inside. Thank You, Father. Amen.

Further Study

Jl 2:18-32; Rm 12:2; 1 Co 14:3; 2 Tm 1:7; Mt 12:25
What did Joel prophesy?
What is the difference between dreams and visions?

DECEMBER 17

JOEL 3:1–AMOS 2:16

3 Yes, in those days and at that time, when I restore the fortunes of Judah and Jerusalem,
2 I will gather all the nations
and take them to the Valley of Jehoshaphat.
I will enter into judgment with them there
because of My people, My inheritance Israel.
The nations have scattered the Israelites
in foreign countries
and divided up My land.
3 They cast lots for My people;
they bartered a boy for a prostitute
and sold a girl for wine to drink.

4 And also: Tyre, Sidon, and all the territories of Philistia—what are you to Me? Are you paying Me back or trying to get even with Me? I will quickly bring retribution on your heads. 5 For you took My silver and gold and carried My finest treasures to your temples. 6 You sold the people of Judah and Jerusalem to the Greeks to remove them far from their own territory. 7 Look, I am about to rouse them up from the place where you sold them; I will bring retribution on your heads. 8 I will sell your sons and daughters into the hands of the people of Judah, and they will sell them to the Sabeans, to a distant nation, for the LORD has spoken.

9 Proclaim this among the nations:
Prepare for holy war;
rouse the warriors;
let all the men of war advance and attack!
10 Hammer your plowshares into swords
and your pruning knives into spears.
Let even the weakling say: I am a warrior.
11 Come quickly, all you surrounding nations;
gather yourselves.
Bring down Your warriors there, LORD.

12 Let the nations be roused
and come to the Valley of
Jehoshaphat,
for there I will sit down
to judge all the surrounding
nations.
13 Swing the sickle
because the harvest is ripe.
Come and trample the grapes
because the winepress is full;
the wine vats overflow
because the wickedness of the
nations is great.

14 Multitudes, multitudes
in the valley of decision!
For the Day of the LORD is near
in the valley of decision.
15 The sun and moon will grow dark,
and the stars will cease their
shining.
16 The LORD will roar from Zion
and raise His voice from Jerusalem;
heaven and earth will shake.
But the LORD will be a refuge for
His people,
a stronghold for the Israelites.

17 Then you will know
that I am the LORD your God,
who dwells in Zion, My holy
mountain.
Jerusalem will be holy,
and foreigners will never overrun
it again.
18 In that day
the mountains will drip with
sweet wine,
and the hills will flow with milk.
All the streams of Judah will flow
with water,
and a spring will issue from the
LORD's house,
watering the Valley of Acacias.
19 Egypt will become desolate,
and Edom a desert wasteland,
because of the violence done to
the people of Judah
in whose land they shed innocent
blood.
20 But Judah will be inhabited forever,
and Jerusalem from generation to
generation.
21 I will pardon their bloodguilt,

which I have not pardoned,
for the LORD dwells in Zion.

1 The words of Amos, who was one of
the sheep breeders from Tekoa—
what he saw regarding Israel in the days
of Uzziah, king of Judah, and Jeroboam
son of Joash, king of Israel, two years
before the earthquake. 2 He said:

The LORD roars from Zion
and raises His voice from Jerusalem;
the pastures of the shepherds
mourn,
and the summit of Carmel withers.

3 The LORD says:

I will not relent from punishing
Damascus
for three crimes, even four,
because they threshed Gilead with
iron sledges.
4 Therefore, I will send fire against
Hazael's palace,
and it will consume Ben-hadad's
citadels.
5 I will break down the gates of
Damascus.
I will cut off the ruler from the
Valley of Aven,
and the one who wields the
scepter from Beth-eden.
The people of Aram will be exiled
to Kir.
The LORD has spoken.

6 The LORD says:

I will not relent from punishing
Gaza
for three crimes, even four,
because they exiled a whole
community,
handing them over to Edom.
7 Therefore, I will send fire against
the walls of Gaza,
and it will consume its citadels.
8 I will cut off the ruler from
Ashdod,
and the one who wields the
scepter from Ashkelon.
I will also turn My hand against
Ekron,

and the remainder of the
Philistines will perish.
The Lord GOD has spoken.

⁹ The LORD says:

I will not relent from punishing
Tyre
for three crimes, even four,
because they handed over
a whole community of exiles to
Edom
and broke a treaty of brotherhood.

¹⁰ Therefore, I will send fire against
the walls of Tyre,
and it will consume its citadels.

¹¹ The LORD says:

I will not relent from punishing
Edom
for three crimes, even four,
because he pursued his brother
with the sword.
He stifled his compassion,
his anger tore at them
continually,
and he harbored his rage
incessantly.

¹² Therefore, I will send fire against
Teman,
and it will consume the citadels of
Bozrah.

¹³ The LORD says:

I will not relent from punishing
the Ammonites
for three crimes, even four,
because they ripped open
the pregnant women of Gilead
in order to enlarge their territory.

¹⁴ Therefore, I will set fire to the
walls of Rabbah,
and it will consume its citadels.
There will be shouting on the day
of battle
and a violent wind on the day of
the storm.

¹⁵ Their king and his princes
will go into exile together.
The LORD has spoken.

2 The LORD says:

I will not relent from punishing
Moab
for three crimes, even four,
because he burned to lime
the bones of the king of Edom.

² Therefore, I will send fire against
Moab,
and it will consume the citadels of
Kerioth.
Moab will die with a tumult,
with shouting and the sound of
the ram's horn.

³ I will cut off the judge from the
land
and kill all its officials with him.
The LORD has spoken.

⁴ The LORD says:

I will not relent from punishing
Judah
for three crimes, even four,
because they have rejected the
law of the LORD
and have not kept His statutes.
The lies that their ancestors
followed
have led them astray.

⁵ Therefore, I will send fire against
Judah,
and it will consume the citadels of
Jerusalem.

⁶ The LORD says:

I will not relent from punishing
Israel
for three crimes, even four,
because they sell a righteous
person for silver
and a needy person for a pair of
sandals.

⁷ They trample the heads of the poor
on the dust of the ground
and block the path of the needy.
A man and his father have sexual
relations
with the same girl,
profaning My holy name.

⁸ They stretch out beside every
altar
on garments taken as collateral,

and they drink in the house of
their God
wine obtained through fines.

9 Yet I destroyed the Amorite as
Israel advanced;
his height was like the cedars
and he was as sturdy as the oaks;
I destroyed his fruit above and his
roots beneath.
10 And I brought you from the land
of Egypt
and led you 40 years in the
wilderness
in order to possess the land of the
Amorite.
11 I raised up some of your sons as
prophets
and some of your young men as
Nazirites.
Is this not the case, Israelites?
This is the LORD's declaration.

12 But you made the Nazirites drink
wine
and commanded the prophets:
Do not prophesy.
13 Look, I am about to crush you in
your place
as a wagon full of sheaves crushes
grain.
14 Escape will fail the swift,
the strong one will not prevail by
his strength,
and the brave will not save his life.
15 The archer will not stand his
ground,
the one who is swift of foot
will not save himself,
and the one riding a horse will not
save his life.
16 Even the most courageous of the
warriors
will flee naked on that day—
the LORD's declaration.

PSALM 143:1-6

1 LORD, hear my prayer.
In Your faithfulness listen to my
plea,
and in Your righteousness answer
me.

2 Do not bring Your servant into
judgment,
for no one alive is righteous in
Your sight.
3 For the enemy has pursued me,
crushing me to the ground,
making me live in darkness
like those long dead.
4 My spirit is weak within me;
my heart is overcome with
dismay.

5 I remember the days of old;
I meditate on all You have done;
I reflect on the work of Your
hands.
6 I spread out my hands to You;
I am like parched land before You.
Selah

PROVERBS 30:21-23

21 The earth trembles under three
things;
it cannot bear up under four:
22 a servant when he becomes king,
a fool when he is stuffed with
food,
23 an unloved woman when she
marries,
and a serving girl when she ousts
her lady.

REVELATION 7:1-17

7 After this I saw four angels standing
at the four corners of the earth, restraining the four winds of the earth so
that no wind could blow on the earth or
on the sea or on any tree. 2 Then I saw
another angel rise up from the east,
who had the seal of the living God. He
cried out in a loud voice to the four
angels who were empowered to harm
the earth and the sea: 3 "Don't harm the
earth or the sea or the trees until we
seal the slaves of our God on their foreheads." 4 And I heard the number of
those who were sealed:

144,000 sealed from every tribe
of the sons of Israel:

5 12,000 sealed from the tribe
of Judah,
12,000 from the tribe of Reuben,
12,000 from the tribe of Gad,
6 12,000 from the tribe of Asher,
12,000 from the tribe of Naphtali,
12,000 from the tribe
of Manasseh,
7 12,000 from the tribe of Simeon,
12,000 from the tribe of Levi,
12,000 from the tribe of Issachar,
8 12,000 from the tribe of Zebulun,
12,000 from the tribe of Joseph,
12,000 sealed from the tribe
of Benjamin.

9 After this I looked, and there was a vast multitude from every nation, tribe, people, and language, which no one could number, standing before the throne and before the Lamb. They were robed in white with palm branches in their hands. 10 And they cried out in a loud voice:

Salvation belongs to our God,
who is seated on the throne,
and to the Lamb!

11 All the angels stood around the throne, the elders, and the four living creatures, and they fell on their faces before the throne and worshiped God, 12 saying:

Amen! Blessing and glory
and wisdom
and thanksgiving and honor
and power and strength,
be to our God forever and ever.
Amen.

13 Then one of the elders asked me, "Who are these people robed in white, and where did they come from?"
14 I said to him, "Sir, you know."
Then he told me:

These are the ones coming out
of the great tribulation.
They washed their robes
and made them white
in the blood of the Lamb.
15 For this reason they are
before the throne of God,
and they serve Him day and night
in His sanctuary.
The One seated on the throne
will shelter them:
16 no longer will they hunger;
no longer will they thirst;
no longer will the sun strike them,
or any heat.
17 Because the Lamb who is
at the center of the throne
will shepherd them;
He will guide them to springs
of living waters,
and God will wipe away every tear
from their eyes.

Fresh Water

*The Lamb . . . will guide them to springs of living waters,
and God will wipe away every tear from their eyes.*
——REVELATIONS 7:17

The idea for the theme of "staying spiritually fresh" arose out of a letter I received some time ago which said: "Over the past year or so, my Christian life has become stale—insufferably so. I have lost the freshness and spontaneity I once knew. Can you say something that will help bring back the sparkle into my Christian experience? What is the remedy?"

But can we expect always to live in a state of spiritual alertness and freshness? Isn't that being unrealistically optimistic? Well, what does Scripture say? It shows us that the people of God are meant to be beautiful gardens in the midst of a dry desert. The prophet Isaiah puts it like this: "You will be like a watered garden and like a spring whose waters never run dry" (Is 58:11).

In Ezekiel 47:8, Ezekiel says that the river flows into the sea and "the sea becomes fresh." How thrilling! The river of God flowing into our dead seas turns them fresh. Whatever reasons there are for our lives becoming spiritually stale, it is quite clear from Scripture that they need not be so. God offers to exchange His strength daily for our weakness, His freshness for our staleness.

Prayer

My Father and my God, I come at the beginning of these meditations to ask that You will make my life like a watered garden. Let Your fresh rivers run into my dead seas so that my whole being is revived—day after day after day. Amen.

Further Study

Jn 4:1-29; 7:37-38; Rv 7:17
What is the quality of the water that Christ gives?
How did Jesus describe it to the woman?

DECEMBER 18

*A*MOS 3:1–5:27

3 Hear this word that the LORD has spoken against you, Israelites, against the entire clan that I brought from the land of Egypt:

2 I have known only you
out of all the clans of the earth;
therefore, I will punish you for all
your iniquities.
3 Can two walk together
without agreeing to meet?
4 Does a lion roar in the forest
when it has no prey?

Does a young lion growl from its lair
unless it has captured something?
5 Does a bird land in a trap on the ground
if there is no bait for it?
Does a trap spring from the ground
when it has caught nothing?
6 If a ram's horn is blown in a city,
aren't people afraid?
If a disaster occurs in a city,
hasn't the LORD done it?
7 For the Lord GOD does nothing
without revealing His counsel
to His servants the prophets.

⁸ A lion has roared;
who will not fear?
The Lord GOD has spoken;
who will not prophesy?

⁹ Proclaim on the citadels in Ashdod
and on the citadels in the land of
Egypt:
Assemble on the mountains of
Samaria
and see the great turmoil in the
city
and the acts of oppression within it.
¹⁰ The people are incapable of doing
right—
the LORD's declaration—
those who store up violence and
destruction
in their citadels.

¹¹ Therefore, the Lord GOD says:

An enemy will surround the land;
he will destroy your strongholds
and plunder your citadels.

¹² The LORD says:

As the shepherd snatches two legs
or a piece of an ear
from the lion's mouth,
so the Israelites who live in
Samaria
will be rescued
with only the corner of a bed
or the cushion of a couch.

¹³ Listen and testify against the
house of Jacob—
this is the declaration
of the Lord GOD, the God of Hosts.
¹⁴ I will punish the altars of Bethel
on the day I punish Israel for its
crimes;
the horns of the altar will be cut
off
and fall to the ground.
¹⁵ I will demolish the winter house
and the summer house;
the houses inlaid with ivory will
be destroyed,
and the great houses will come to
an end—
the LORD's declaration.

4 Listen to this message, you cows
of Bashan
who are on the hill of Samaria,
women who oppress the poor
and crush the needy,
who say to their husbands,
"Bring us something to drink."

² The Lord GOD has sworn by His holiness:

Look, the days are coming
when you will be taken away with
hooks,
every last one of you with
fishhooks.
³ You will go through breaches in
the wall,
each woman straight ahead,
and you will be driven along
toward Harmon.
This is the LORD's declaration.

⁴ Come to Bethel and rebel;
rebel even more at Gilgal!
Bring your sacrifices every
morning,
your tenths every three days.
⁵ Offer leavened bread as a thank
offering,
and loudly proclaim your freewill
offerings,
for that is what you Israelites love
to do!
This is the LORD's declaration.

⁶ I gave you absolutely nothing to eat
in all your cities,
a shortage of food in all your
communities,
yet you did not return to Me—
the LORD's declaration.

⁷ I also withheld the rain from you
while there were still three
months until harvest.
I sent rain on one city
but no rain on another.
One field received rain
while a field with no rain
withered.
⁸ Two or three cities staggered
to another city to drink water
but were not satisfied,

yet you did not return to Me—
the LORD's declaration.

9 I struck you with blight and mildew;
the locust devoured
your many gardens and vineyards,
your fig trees and olive trees,
yet you did not return to Me—
the LORD's declaration.

10 I sent plagues like those of Egypt;
I killed your young men with the
sword,
along with your captured horses.
I caused the stench of your camp
to fill your nostrils,
yet you did not return to Me—
the LORD's declaration.

11 I overthrew some of you
as I overthrew Sodom and
Gomorrah,
and you were like a burning stick
snatched from a fire,
yet you did not return to Me—
the LORD's declaration.

12 Therefore, Israel, that is what I
will do to you,
and since I will do that to you,
Israel, prepare to meet your God!
13 He is here:
the One who forms the mountains,
creates the wind,
and reveals His thoughts to man,
the One who makes the dawn out
of darkness,
and strides on the heights of the
earth.
Yahweh, the God of Hosts, is His
name.

5 Hear this message that I am singing
for you, a lament, house of Israel:

2 She has fallen;
Virgin Israel will never rise again.
She lies abandoned on her land,
with no one to raise her up.

3 For the Lord GOD says:

The city that marches out a
thousand strong

will have only a hundred left,
and the one that marches out a
hundred strong
will have only ten left in the
house of Israel.

4 For the LORD says to the house of
Israel:

Seek Me and live!
5 Do not seek Bethel
or go to Gilgal
or journey to Beer-sheba,
for Gilgal will certainly go into
exile,
and Bethel will come to nothing.
6 Seek the LORD and live,
or He will spread like fire
throughout the house of Joseph;
it will consume everything,
with no one at Bethel to
extinguish it.
7 Those who turn justice into
wormwood
throw righteousness to the ground.

8 The One who made the Pleiades
and Orion,
who turns darkness into dawn
and darkens day into night,
who summons the waters of the
sea
and pours them out over the face
of the earth—
Yahweh is His name.
9 He brings destruction on the
strong
and it falls on the stronghold.
10 They hate the one who convicts
the guilty
at the city gate
and despise the one who speaks
with integrity.
11 Therefore, because you trample
on the poor
and exact a grain tax from him,
you will never live in the houses
of cut stone
you have built;
you will never drink the wine
from the lush vineyards
you have planted.
12 For I know your crimes are many

and your sins innumerable.
They oppress the righteous, take a
bribe,
and deprive the poor of justice at
the gates.
13 Therefore, the wise person will
keep silent
at such a time,
for the days are evil.

14 Seek good and not evil
so that you may live,
and the LORD, the God of Hosts,
will be with you,
as you have claimed.
15 Hate evil and love good;
establish justice in the gate.
Perhaps the LORD, the God of
Hosts, will be gracious
to the remnant of Joseph.

16 Therefore Yahweh, the God of
Hosts, the Lord, says:

There will be wailing in all the
public squares;
they will cry out in anguish in all
the streets.
The farmer will be called on to
mourn,
and professional mourners to wail.
17 There will be wailing in all the
vineyards,
for I will pass among you.
The LORD has spoken.

18 Woe to you who long for the Day
of the LORD!
What will the Day of the LORD be
for you?
It will be darkness and not light.
19 It will be like a man who flees
from a lion
only to have a bear confront him.
He goes home and rests his hand
against the wall
only to have a snake bite him.
20 Won't the Day of the LORD
be darkness rather than light,
even gloom without any
brightness in it?
21 I hate, I despise your feasts!
I can't stand the stench

of your solemn assemblies.
22 Even if you offer Me
your burnt offerings and grain
offerings,
I will not accept them;
I will have no regard
for your fellowship offerings of
fattened cattle.
23 Take away from Me the noise of
your songs!
I will not listen to the music of
your harps.
24 But let justice flow like water,
and righteousness, like an
unfailing stream.

25 "House of Israel, was it sacrifices
and grain offerings that you presented
to Me during the 40 years in the
wilderness? 26 But you have taken up
Sakkuth your king and Kaiwan your
star god, images you have made for
yourselves. 27 So I will send you into exile beyond Damascus." Yahweh, the God
of Hosts, is His name. He has spoken.

PSALM 143:7-12

7 Answer me quickly, LORD;
my spirit fails.
Don't hide Your face from me,
or I will be like those going down
to the Pit.
8 Let me experience Your faithful
love in the morning,
for I trust in You.
Reveal to me the way I should go,
because I long for You.
9 Rescue me from my enemies, LORD;
I come to You for protection.
10 Teach me to do Your will, for You
are my God.
May Your gracious Spirit lead me
on level ground.

11 Because of Your name, LORD, let
me live.
In Your righteousness deliver me
from trouble,
12 and in Your faithful love destroy
my enemies.
Wipe out all those who attack me,
for I am Your servant.

PROVERBS 30:24-28

24 Four things on earth are small,
yet they are extremely wise:
25 the ants are not a strong people,
yet they store up their food in the
summer;
26 hyraxes are not a mighty people,
yet they make their homes in the
cliffs;
27 locusts have no king,
yet all of them march in ranks;
28 a lizard can be caught in your hands,
yet it lives in kings' palaces.

REVELATION 8:1–9:12

8 When He opened the seventh seal, there was silence in heaven for about half an hour. ² Then I saw the seven angels who stand in the presence of God; seven trumpets were given to them. ³ Another angel, with a gold incense burner, came and stood at the altar. He was given a large amount of incense to offer with the prayers of all the saints on the gold altar in front of the throne. ⁴ The smoke of the incense, with the prayers of the saints, went up in the presence of God from the angel's hand. ⁵ The angel took the incense burner, filled it with fire from the altar, and hurled it to the earth; there were thunders, rumblings, lightnings, and an earthquake. ⁶ And the seven angels who had the seven trumpets prepared to blow them.

⁷ The first angel blew his trumpet, and hail and fire, mixed with blood, were hurled to the earth. So a third of the earth was burned up, a third of the trees were burned up, and all the green grass was burned up.

⁸ The second angel blew his trumpet, and something like a great mountain ablaze with fire was hurled into the sea. So a third of the sea became blood, ⁹ a third of the living creatures in the sea died, and a third of the ships were destroyed.

¹⁰ The third angel blew his trumpet, and a great star, blazing like a torch, fell from heaven. It fell on a third of the rivers and springs of water. ¹¹ The name of the star is Wormwood, and a third of the waters became wormwood. So, many of the people died from the waters, because they had been made bitter.

¹² The fourth angel blew his trumpet, and a third of the sun was struck, a third of the moon, and a third of the stars, so that a third of them were darkened. A third of the day was without light, and the night as well.

¹³ I looked, and I heard an eagle, flying in mid-heaven, saying in a loud voice, "Woe! Woe! Woe to those who live on the earth, because of the remaining trumpet blasts that the three angels are about to sound!"

9 The fifth angel blew his trumpet, and I saw a star that had fallen from heaven to earth. The key to the shaft of the abyss was given to him. ² He opened the shaft of the abyss, and smoke came up out of the shaft like smoke from a great furnace so that the sun and the air were darkened by the smoke from the shaft. ³ Then out of the smoke locusts came to the earth, and power was given to them like the power that scorpions have on the earth. ⁴ They were told not to harm the grass of the earth, or any green plant, or any tree, but only people who do not have God's seal on their foreheads. ⁵ They were not permitted to kill them, but were to torment them for five months; their torment is like the torment caused by a scorpion when it strikes a man. ⁶ In those days people will seek death and will not find it; they will long to die, but death will flee from them.

⁷ The appearance of the locusts was like horses equipped for battle. On their heads were something like gold crowns; their faces were like men's faces; ⁸ they had hair like women's hair; their teeth were like lions' teeth; ⁹ they had chests like iron breastplates; the sound of their wings was like the sound of chariots with many horses rushing into battle; ¹⁰ and they had tails with stingers, like scorpions, so that with their tails they had the power to harm people for five

months. [11] They had as their king the angel of the abyss; his name in Hebrew is Abaddon, and in Greek he has the name Apollyon. [12] The first woe has passed. There are still two more woes to come after this.

The Standard Note

Let me experience Your faithful love in the morning, for I trust in You.
—Psalm 143:8

Jesus felt the need for three simple habits in His earthly life: (1) He stood up to read; (2) He went up a mountain to pray; (3) He taught people the Scriptures—all "as usual" (Lk 4:16).

These three habits—reading the Scriptures, exposing oneself to God in prayer, and passing on to others what one has found—are basic to the spiritual life. If Jesus Himself couldn't get along without them, how can we?

I am often asked by interviewers how I maintain my spiritual life. I usually reply that it centers on a daily quiet time with God. There are some days when a morning quiet time is not possible, but most of my mornings begin with a time closeted with God in prayer.

Someone sent me a brochure once, telling me of a home that had opened, which they described as "a place in the country where those who have lost their spiritual freshness may come to tone up and be invigorated." My quiet time is such a "place."

A sheep rancher in Australia found that his violin was out of tune, and being unable to find another musical instrument to provide him with a standard note, he wrote to a radio station asking them to strike that note. They did just that—stopped a program and struck the note. The sheep rancher caught it, and the violin was in tune again. Your daily quiet time will help you hear God's "standard notes." Then you can tune your flattened notes to His.

Prayer

O God, I know there is nothing better than what I have found in You—except more of what I have found in You. Help me today to catch Your "standard note" and tune every part of my life to it. In Christ's name I ask it. Amen.

Further Study

Ac 10:1-8; Lk 6:12; 2 Ch 29:2
What is recorded of Cornelius?
What is said about Hezekiah?

DECEMBER 19

AMOS 6:1–8:14

6 Woe to those who are at ease
in Zion
and to those who feel secure on
the hill of Samaria—
the notable people in this first of
the nations,
those the house of Israel comes to.
2 Cross over to Calneh and see;
go from there to great Hamath;
then go down to Gath of the
Philistines.
Are you better than these
kingdoms?
Is their territory larger than yours?
3 You dismiss any thought of the
evil day
and bring in a reign of violence.

4 They lie on beds inlaid with
ivory,
sprawled out on their couches,
and dine on lambs from the flock
and calves from the stall.
5 They improvise songs to the sound
of the harp
and invent their own musical
instruments like David.
6 They drink wine by the bowlful
and anoint themselves with the
finest oils,
but do not grieve over the ruin of
Joseph.
7 Therefore, they will now go into
exile
as the first of the captives,
and the feasting of those who
sprawl out
will come to an end.

8 The Lord GOD has sworn by Himself—
the declaration of Yahweh, the God of
Hosts:

I loathe Jacob's pride
and hate his citadels,

so I will hand over the city and
everything in it.

9 And if there are 10 men left in one
house, they will die. 10 A close relative
and a burner, will remove his corpse
from the house. He will call to someone
in the inner recesses of the house, "Any
more with you?"
That person will reply, "None."
Then he will say, "Silence, because
Yahweh's name must not be invoked."
11 For the LORD commands:

The large house will be smashed
to pieces,
and the small house to rubble.

12 Do horses run on rock,
or does someone plow it with
oxen?
Yet you have turned justice into
poison
and the fruit of righteousness into
wormwood—
13 you who rejoice over Lo-debar
and say, "Didn't we capture
Karnaim
for ourselves by our own
strength?"
14 But look, I am raising up
a nation
against you, house of Israel—
this is the declaration of the Lord,
the GOD of Hosts—
and they will oppress you
from the entrance of Hamath
to the Brook of the Arabah.

7 The Lord GOD showed me this: He
was forming a swarm of locusts at
the time the spring crop first began to
sprout—after the cutting of the king's
hay. 2 When the locusts finished eating
the vegetation of the land, I said, "Lord
GOD, please forgive! How will Jacob survive since he is so small?"

³ The Lord relented concerning this. "It will not happen," He said.

⁴ The Lord God showed me this: The Lord God was calling for a judgment by fire. It consumed the great deep and devoured the land. ⁵ Then I said, "Lord God, please stop! How will Jacob survive since he is so small?"

⁶ The Lord relented concerning this. "This will not happen either," said the Lord God.

⁷ He showed me this: The Lord was standing there by a vertical wall with a plumb line in His hand. ⁸ The Lord asked me, "What do you see, Amos?"

I replied, "A plumb line."

Then the Lord said, "I am setting a plumb line among My people Israel; I will no longer spare them:

⁹ Isaac's high places will be deserted,
  and Israel's sanctuaries will be in
    ruins;
  I will rise up against the house of
    Jeroboam
  with a sword."

¹⁰ Amaziah the priest of Bethel sent word to Jeroboam king of Israel, saying, "Amos has conspired against you right here in the house of Israel. The land cannot endure all his words, ¹¹ for Amos has said this: 'Jeroboam will die by the sword, and Israel will certainly go into exile from its homeland.' "

¹² Then Amaziah said to Amos, "Go away, you seer! Flee to the land of Judah. Earn your living and give your prophecies there, ¹³ but don't ever prophesy at Bethel again, for it is the king's sanctuary and a royal temple."

¹⁴ So Amos answered Amaziah, "I was not a prophet or the son of a prophet; rather, I was a herdsman, and I took care of sycamore figs. ¹⁵ But the Lord took me from following the flock and said to me, 'Go, prophesy to My people Israel.' "

¹⁶ Now hear the word of the Lord. You say:

Do not prophesy against Israel;
  do not preach against the house of
    Isaac.

¹⁷ Therefore, this is what the Lord says:

Your wife will be a prostitute in
  the city,
your sons and daughters will fall
  by the sword,
and your land will be divided up
  with a measuring line.
You yourself will die on pagan soil,
  and Israel will certainly go into
    exile
  from its homeland.

8 The Lord God showed me this: A basket of summer fruit. ² He asked me, "What do you see, Amos?"

I replied, "A basket of summer fruit."

The Lord said to me, "The end has come for My people Israel; I will no longer spare them. ³ In that day the temple songs will become wailing"—the Lord God's declaration. "Many dead bodies, thrown everywhere! Silence!"

⁴ Hear this, you who trample on the
    needy
  and do away with the poor of the
    land,
⁵ asking, "When will the New Moon
    be over
  so we may sell grain,
  and the Sabbath,
  so we may market wheat?
We can reduce the measure
  while increasing the price,
  and cheat with dishonest scales.
⁶ We can buy the poor with silver
  and the needy for a pair of
    sandals,
  and even sell the wheat husks!"

⁷ The Lord has sworn by the Pride of Jacob:

I will never forget all their deeds.
⁸ Because of this, won't the land
    quake
  and all who dwell in it mourn?
All of it will rise like the Nile;
  it will surge and then subside
  like the Nile in Egypt.

9 And in that day—
      this is the declaration
         of the Lord GOD—
I will make the sun go down at
      noon;
I will darken the land in the
      daytime.
10 I will turn your feasts into
      mourning
and all your songs into
      lamentation;
I will cause everyone to wear
      sackcloth
and every head to be shaved.
I will make that grief
like mourning for an only son
and its outcome like a bitter day.

11 Hear this! The days are coming—
      this is the declaration
         of the Lord GOD—
when I will send a famine through
      the land:
not a famine of bread or a thirst
      for water,
but of hearing the words of the
      LORD.
12 People will stagger from sea to sea
and roam from north to east,
seeking the word of the LORD,
but they will not find it.
13 In that day the beautiful young
      women,
the young men also, will faint
      from thirst.
14 Those who swear by the guilt of
      Samaria
and say, "As your god lives, Dan,"
or "As the way of Beer-sheba
      lives"—
they will fall, never to rise again.

PSALM 144:1-8

1 May the LORD my rock be praised,
who trains my hands for battle
and my fingers for warfare.
2 He is my faithful love and my
      fortress,
my stronghold and my deliverer.
He is my shield, and I take refuge
      in Him;
He subdues my people under me.

3 LORD, what is man, that You care
      for him,
the son of man, that You think of
      him?
4 Man is like a breath;
his days are like a passing shadow.

5 LORD, part Your heavens and come
      down.
Touch the mountains, and they
      will smoke.
6 Flash Your lightning and scatter
      the foe;
shoot Your arrows and rout them.
7 Reach down from on high;
rescue me from deep water, and
      set me free
from the grasp of foreigners
8 whose mouths speak lies,
whose right hands are deceptive.

PROVERBS 30:29-33

29 Three things are stately in their
      stride,
even four are stately in their walk:
30 a lion, which is mightiest among
      beasts
and doesn't retreat before
      anything,
31 a strutting rooster, a goat,
and a king at the head of his army.

32 If you have been foolish by
      exalting yourself,
or if you've been scheming, put
      your hand over your mouth.
33 For the churning of milk produces
      butter,
and twisting a nose draws blood,
and stirring up anger produces
      strife.

REVELATION 9:13–10:11

13 The sixth angel blew his trumpet. From the four horns of the gold altar that is before God, I heard a voice 14 say to the sixth angel who had the trumpet, "Release the four angels bound at the great river Euphrates." 15 So the four angels who were prepared for the hour,

day, month, and year were released to kill a third of the human race. [16] The number of mounted troops was 200 million; I heard their number. [17] This is how I saw the horses in my vision: The horsemen had breastplates that were fiery red, hyacinth blue, and sulfur yellow. The heads of the horses were like lions' heads, and from their mouths came fire, smoke, and sulfur. [18] A third of the human race was killed by these three plagues—by the fire, the smoke, and the sulfur that came from their mouths. [19] For the power of the horses is in their mouths and in their tails, because their tails, like snakes, have heads, and they inflict injury with them.

[20] The rest of the people, who were not killed by these plagues, did not repent of the works of their hands to stop worshiping demons and idols of gold, silver, bronze, stone, and wood, which are not able to see, hear, or walk. [21] And they did not repent of their murders, their sorceries, their sexual immorality, or their thefts.

10 Then I saw another mighty angel coming down from heaven, surrounded by a cloud, with a rainbow over his head. His face was like the sun, his legs were like fiery pillars, [2] and he had a little scroll opened in his hand. He put his right foot on the sea, his left on the land, [3] and he cried out with a loud voice like a roaring lion. When he cried

out, the seven thunders spoke with their voices. [4] And when the seven thunders spoke, I was about to write. Then I heard a voice from heaven, saying, "Seal up what the seven thunders said, and do not write it down!"

[5] Then the angel that I had seen standing on the sea and on the land raised his right hand to heaven. [6] He swore an oath by the One who lives forever and ever, who created heaven and what is in it, the earth and what is in it, and the sea and what is in it: "There will no longer be an interval of time, [7] but in the days of the sound of the seventh angel, when he will blow his trumpet, then God's hidden plan will be completed, as He announced to His servants the prophets."

[8] Now the voice that I heard from heaven spoke to me again and said, "Go, take the scroll that lies open in the hand of the angel who is standing on the sea and on the land."

[9] So I went to the angel and asked him to give me the little scroll. He said to me, "Take and eat it; it will be bitter in your stomach, but it will be as sweet as honey in your mouth."

[10] Then I took the little scroll from the angel's hand and ate it. It was as sweet as honey in my mouth, but when I ate it, my stomach became bitter. [11] And I was told, "You must prophesy again about many peoples, nations, languages, and kings."

How to Forgive

Twisting a nose draws blood,
and stirring up anger produces strife.
——PROVERBS 30:33

If difficulties concerning basic trust on a natural level can hinder our ability to trust at a spiritual level, how do we as Christians overcome this? The first thing we must do is demonstrate a willingness to forgive those who hurt us. "That's hard," you might say. My reply is: "Yes, in the case of those who have been badly let down, it is hard—but not impossible."

Here's how you do it. Focus first on how much you have been forgiven. The key to forgiving others is to enter into a realized awareness of how much God has forgiven you. When people say to me during a counseling session, "My problem is that I can't forgive," I usually respond by saying, "No, that's not your problem. Your problem is that you don't know how much you have been forgiven." It may be difficult for some to see this, especially those who have gone through deep hurt, but nothing others have done to you is as awful as what you have done to God.

If you have difficulty with the last statement, it is because you do not understand the nature of sin. Sin is taking the Creator of the universe and relegating Him to irrelevance; it is saying to the One who made us—"I can run my life on my own terms." Sin is insanity—and you and I have been guilty of that. Yet in Christ God has forgiven us, pardoned us, and bestowed upon us His royal favor. Having been given such forgiveness, can we, dare we, withhold it from anyone who has betrayed our trust, no matter how horrifying that hurt has been?

Prayer

Father, Your Word is frank and open—help me to respond to it in the same way. Take from me every biting hesitancy, every fear and apprehension, every refusal to accept responsibility. In Jesus' name I pray. Amen.

Further Study

Col 3:1-14; Mk 11:25; Lk 17:4; Eph 4:32
How are we to forgive?
Do you need to forgive someone today?

DECEMBER 20

AMOS 9:1– OBADIAH 21

9 I saw the LORD standing beside the altar, and He said:

Strike the capitals of the pillars
so that the thresholds shake;
knock them down on the heads of
all the people.
Then I will kill the rest of them
with the sword.
None of those who flee will get away;

none of their fugitives will escape.
2 If they dig down to Sheol,
from there My hand will take
them;
if they climb up to heaven,
from there I will bring them
down.
3 If they hide themselves
on the top of Carmel,
from there I will track them down
and seize them;
if they conceal themselves
from My sight on the sea floor,
from there I will command

the sea serpent to bite them.
4 And if they are driven
by their enemies into captivity,
from there I will command
the sword to kill them.
I will fix My eyes on them
for harm and not for good.

5 The Lord, the GOD of Hosts—
He touches the earth;
it melts, and all who dwell on it
mourn;
all of it rises like the Nile
and subsides like the Nile of Egypt.
6 He builds His upper chambers
in the heavens
and lays the foundation of His
vault
on the earth.
He summons the waters of the sea
and pours them out on the face of
the earth.
Yahweh is His name.

7 Israelites, are you not like the
Cushites to Me?
This is the LORD's declaration.
Didn't I bring Israel from the land
of Egypt,
the Philistines from Caphtor,
and the Arameans from Kir?
8 Look, the eyes of the Lord GOD
are on the sinful kingdom,
and I will destroy it
from the face of the earth.
However, I will not totally destroy
the house of Jacob—
the LORD's declaration—
9 for I am about to give the
command,
and I will shake the house of Israel
among all the nations,
as one shakes a sieve,
but not a pebble will fall to the
ground.
10 All the sinners among My people,
who say: Disaster will never
overtake
or confront us,
will die by the sword.

11 In that day
I will restore the fallen booth of
David:

I will repair its gaps,
restore its ruins,
and rebuild it as in the days of old,
12 so that they may possess
the remnant of Edom
and all the nations
that are called by My name—
this is the LORD's declaration—

He will do this.

13 Hear this! The days are coming—
the LORD's declaration—
when the plowman will overtake
the reaper
and the one who treads grapes,
the sower of seed.
The mountains will drip with
sweet wine,
and all the hills will flow with it.
14 I will restore the fortunes of My
people Israel.
They will rebuild and occupy
ruined cities,
plant vineyards and drink their
wine,
make gardens and eat their
produce.
15 I will plant them on their land,
and they will never again be
uprooted
from the land I have given them.
Yahweh your God has spoken.

1 The vision of Obadiah.
This is what the Lord GOD has said
about Edom:

We have heard a message
from the LORD;
an envoy has been sent
among the nations:
Rise up, and let us go to war
against her.
2 Look, I will make you insignificant
among the nations;
you will be deeply despised.
3 Your presumptuous heart
has deceived you,
you who live in clefts of the rock
in your home on the heights,
who say to yourself:
Who can bring me down
to the ground?

⁴ Though you seem to soar
    like an eagle
and make your nest
    among the stars,
even from there I will
    bring you down.
      This is the LORD's declaration.

⁵ If thieves came to you,
if marauders by night—
how ravaged you will be!—
    wouldn't they steal only
      what they wanted?
If grape pickers came to you,
wouldn't they leave some grapes?
⁶ How Esau will be pillaged,
his hidden treasures
    searched out!
⁷ Everyone who has a treaty
    with you
will drive you to the border;
everyone at peace with you
will deceive and conquer you.
Those who eat your bread
will set a trap for you.
He will be unaware of it.
⁸ In that day—
      the LORD's declaration—
will I not eliminate the wise ones
    of Edom
and those who understand
from the hill country of Esau?
⁹ Teman, your warriors
    will be terrified
so that everyone
    from the hill country of Esau
will be destroyed by slaughter.

¹⁰ You will be covered with shame
and destroyed forever
because of violence done
    to your brother Jacob.
¹¹ On the day you stood aloof,
on the day strangers captured
    his wealth,
while foreigners entered his gate
and cast lots for Jerusalem,
you were just like one of them.
¹² Do not gloat over your brother
in the day of his calamity;
do not rejoice over the people
    of Judah
in the day of their destruction;
do not boastfully mock

in the day of distress.
¹³ Do not enter the gate
    of My people
in the day of their disaster.
Yes, you—do not gloat
    over their misery
in the day of their disaster
and do not appropriate
    their possessions
in the day of their disaster.
¹⁴ Do not stand at the crossroads
to cut off their fugitives,
and do not hand over their survivors
in the day of distress.

¹⁵ For the Day of the LORD is near,
against all the nations.
As you have done, so it will be
    done to you;
what you deserve will return
    on your own head.
¹⁶ For as you have drunk
    on My holy mountain,
so all the nations will drink
    continually.
They will drink and gulp down
and be as though they had
    never been.
¹⁷ But there will be a deliverance
    on Mount Zion,
and it will be holy;
the house of Jacob will dispossess
those who dispossessed them.
¹⁸ Then the house of Jacob will be
    a blazing fire,
and the house of Joseph a burning
    flame,
but the house of Esau
    will be stubble;
they will set them on fire
    and consume them.
Therefore no survivor will remain
of the house of Esau,
for the LORD has spoken.

¹⁹ People from the Negev
    will possess
the hill country of Esau;
those from the Judean foothills
    will possess
the land of the Philistines.
They will possess
    the territories of Ephraim
    and Samaria,

while Benjamin
will possess Gilead.

20 The exiles of the Israelites
who are in Halah
who are among the Canaanites
as far as Zarephath
and the exiles of Jerusalem
who are in Sepharad
will possess the cities
of the Negev.

21 Saviors will ascend Mount Zion
to rule over the hill country
of Esau,
but the kingdom will be
the LORD's.

PSALM 144:9-15

9 God, I will sing a new song to You;
I will play on a ten-stringed harp
for You—

10 the One who gives victory to
kings,
who frees His servant David from
the deadly sword.

11 Set me free and rescue me from
the grasp of foreigners
whose mouths speak lies,
whose right hands are deceptive.

12 Then our sons will be like plants
nurtured in their youth,
our daughters, like corner pillars
that are carved in the palace
style.

13 Our storehouses will be full,
supplying all kinds of
produce;
our flocks will increase by
thousands
and tens of thousands in our open
fields.

14 Our cattle will be well fed.
There will be no breach in the
walls, no going into captivity,
and no cry of lament in our public
squares.

15 Happy are the people with such
blessings.
Happy are the people whose God
is the LORD.

PROVERBS 31:1-3

31 The words of King Lemuel,
an oracle that his mother taught
him:

2 What should I say, my son?
What, son of my womb?
What, son of my vows?

3 Don't spend your energy on
women
or your efforts on those who
destroy kings.

REVELATION 11:1-19

11 Then I was given a measuring
reed like a rod, with these
words: "Go and measure God's sanctuary and the altar, and count those who
worship there. ² But exclude the courtyard outside the sanctuary. Don't measure it, because it is given to the
nations, and they will trample the holy
city for 42 months. ³ I will empower my
two witnesses, and they will prophesy
for 1,260 days, dressed in sackcloth."
⁴ These are the two olive trees and the
two lampstands that stand before the
Lord of the earth. ⁵ If anyone wants to
harm them, fire comes from their
mouths and consumes their enemies; if
anyone wants to harm them, he must be
killed in this way. ⁶ These men have the
power to close the sky so that it does
not rain during the days of their
prophecy. They also have power over
the waters to turn them into blood, and
to strike the earth with any plague
whenever they want.
⁷ When they finish their testimony,
the beast that comes up out of the abyss
will make war with them, conquer
them, and kill them. ⁸ Their dead bodies
will lie in the public square of the great
city, which is called, prophetically,
Sodom and Egypt, where also their Lord
was crucified. ⁹ And representatives
from the peoples, tribes, languages, and
nations will view their bodies for three
and a half days and not permit their
bodies to be put into a tomb. ¹⁰ Those
who live on the earth will gloat over

them and celebrate and send gifts to one another, because these two prophets tormented those who live on the earth.

[11] But after the three and a half days, the breath of life from God entered them, and they stood on their feet. So great fear fell on those who saw them. [12] Then they heard a loud voice from heaven saying to them, "Come up here." They went up to heaven in a cloud, while their enemies watched them. [13] At that moment a violent earthquake took place, a tenth of the city fell, and 7,000 people were killed in the earthquake. The survivors were terrified and gave glory to the God of heaven. [14] The second woe has passed. Take note: the third woe is coming quickly!

[15] The seventh angel blew his trumpet, and there were loud voices in heaven saying:

> The kingdom of the world has become the kingdom
> of our Lord and of His Messiah,
> and He will reign forever
> and ever!

[16] The 24 elders, who were seated before God on their thrones, fell on their faces and worshiped God, [17] saying:

> We thank You, Lord God,
>   the Almighty, who is
>   and who was,
> because You have taken
>   Your great power
>   and have begun to reign.
>
> [18] The nations were angry,
>   but Your wrath has come.
> The time has come for the dead
>   to be judged,
> and to give the reward
>   to Your servants the prophets,
> to the saints, and to those
>   who fear Your name,
>   both small and great,
> and the time has come to destroy
>   those who destroy the earth.

[19] God's sanctuary in heaven was opened, and the ark of His covenant appeared in His sanctuary. There were lightnings, rumblings, thunders, an earthquake, and severe hail.

The Doxology

The kingdom of the world has become the kingdom of our Lord and of His Messiah.——REVELATION 11:15

The end of the Lord's Prayer—"For Yours is the kingdom and the power and the glory forever. Amen"—is a doxology so beautiful that it somehow seems almost irreverent to try to dissect it. Some believe that Jesus did not actually say these words. They claim that they were added by someone else at a later date, which is why they are not included in some versions of the Bible. Some manuscripts have it, and some do not. I have looked long at the evidence for and against their inclusion in the sacred Scriptures, and I am perfectly satisfied myself that they were part of Jesus' original pattern of prayer.

The prayer ends as it begins, with an assertion of God's majesty and glory: "Yours is the kingdom." I believe that the emphasis here should be placed on the word "is," to read, "Yours *is* the kingdom"—now.

Despite all appearances to the contrary, God has never abdicated His position as ruler of the universe. What a heartening thought this can be in these days, a thought to fill the soul with song and flood the heart with hope and gladness. It is true that there are many things in the world that militate against His authority—war, poverty, unemployment, drink, gambling, social impurity, and so on. All these seem a flat and final refutation of the phrase "Yours is the kingdom," but their days are numbered. The hour will come when the kingdoms of this world will signal their final surrender and pledge allegiance to their rightful Lord.

Prayer

O Father, help me to see, despite all the situations and circumstances which might deny Your eternal Kingship, that You are reigning over the world now. Yours is the final control. I am so thankful. Amen.

Further Study

Mt 4:1-11; Ob 21; Heb 12:28; 2 Pt 1:11
Why was Satan's temptation foolish?
How did Jesus respond?

DECEMBER 21

JONAH 1:1–4:11

1 The word of the LORD came to Jonah son of Amittai: ² "Get up! Go to the great city of Nineveh and preach against it, because their wickedness has confronted Me." ³ However, Jonah got up to flee to Tarshish from the LORD's presence. He went down to Joppa and found a ship going to Tarshish. He paid the fare and went down into it to go with them to Tarshish, from the LORD's presence.

⁴ Then the LORD hurled a violent wind on the sea, and such a violent storm arose on the sea that the ship threatened to break apart. ⁵ The sailors were afraid, and each cried out to his god. They threw the ship's cargo into the sea to lighten the load. Meanwhile, Jonah had gone down to the lowest part of the vessel and had stretched out and fallen into a deep sleep.

⁶ The captain approached him and said, "What are you doing sound asleep? Get up! Call to your god. Maybe this god will consider us, and we won't perish."

⁷ "Come on!" the sailors said to each other. "Let's cast lots. Then we will know who is to blame for this trouble we're in." So they cast lots, and the lot singled out Jonah. ⁸ Then they said to him, "Tell us who is to blame for this trouble we're in. What is your business and where are you from? What is your country and what people are you from?"

⁹ He answered them, "I am a Hebrew. I worship Yahweh, the God of the heavens, who made the sea and the dry land."

¹⁰ Then the men were even more afraid and said to him, "What is this you've done?" For the men knew he was fleeing from the LORD's presence,

because he had told them. ¹¹ So they said to him, "What should we do to you to calm this sea that's against us?" For the sea was getting worse and worse.

¹² He answered them, "Pick me up and throw me into the sea so it may quiet down for you, for I know that I'm to blame for this violent storm that is against you." ¹³ Nevertheless, the men rowed hard to get back to dry land, but they could not because the sea was raging against them more and more.

¹⁴ So they called out to the LORD: "Please, Yahweh, don't let us perish because of this man's life, and don't charge us with innocent blood! For You, Yahweh, have done just as You pleased." ¹⁵ Then they picked up Jonah and threw him into the sea, and the sea stopped its raging. ¹⁶ The men feared the LORD even more, and they offered a sacrifice to the LORD and made vows. ¹⁷ Then the LORD appointed a great fish to swallow Jonah, and Jonah was in the fish three days and three nights.

2 Jonah prayed to the LORD his God from inside the fish:

² I called to the LORD in my distress,
    and He answered me.
  I cried out for help in the belly of
    Sheol;
  You heard my voice.
³ You threw me into the depths,
    into the heart of the seas,
    and the current overcame me.
  All Your breakers and Your billows
    swept over me.
⁴ But I said: I have been banished
    from Your sight,
  yet I will look once more
    toward Your holy temple.
⁵ The waters engulfed me up to the
    neck;
  the watery depths overcame me;
  seaweed was wrapped around my
    head.
⁶ I sank to the foundations of the
    mountains;
  the earth with its prison bars
    closed behind me forever!
  But You raised my life from the
    Pit, LORD my God!

⁷ As my life was fading away,
    I remembered the LORD.
  My prayer came to You,
    to Your holy temple.
⁸ Those who cling to worthless idols
    forsake faithful love,
⁹ but as for me, I will sacrifice to
    You
  with a voice of thanksgiving.
  I will fulfill what I have vowed.
  Salvation is from the LORD!

¹⁰ Then the LORD commanded the fish, and it vomited Jonah onto dry land.

3 Then the word of the LORD came to Jonah a second time: ² "Get up! Go to the great city of Nineveh and preach the message that I tell you." ³ So Jonah got up and went to Nineveh according to the LORD's command.

Now Nineveh was an extremely large city, a three-day walk. ⁴ Jonah set out on the first day of his walk in the city and proclaimed, "In 40 days Nineveh will be overthrown!" ⁵ The men of Nineveh believed in God. They proclaimed a fast and dressed in sackcloth—from the greatest of them to the least.

⁶ When word reached the king of Nineveh, he got up from his throne, took off his royal robe, put on sackcloth, and sat in ashes. ⁷ Then he issued a decree in Nineveh:

By order of the king and his nobles: No man or beast, herd or flock, is to taste anything at all. They must not eat or drink water. ⁸ Furthermore, both man and beast must be covered with sackcloth, and everyone must call out earnestly to God. Each must turn from his evil ways and from the violence he is doing. ⁹ Who knows? God may turn and relent; He may turn from His burning anger so that we will not perish.

¹⁰ Then God saw their actions—that they had turned from their evil ways—so God relented from the disaster He had threatened to do to them. And He did not do it.

4 But Jonah was greatly displeased and became furious. ² He prayed to the LORD: "Please, LORD, isn't this what I said while I was still in my own country? That's why I fled toward Tarshish in the first place. I knew that You are a merciful and compassionate God, slow to become angry, rich in faithful love, and One who relents from sending disaster. ³ And now, LORD, please take my life from me, for it is better for me to die than to live."

⁴ The LORD asked, "Is it right for you to be angry?"

⁵ Jonah left the city and sat down east of it. He made himself a shelter there and sat in its shade to see what would happen to the city. ⁶ Then the LORD God appointed a plant, and it grew up to provide shade over Jonah's head to ease his discomfort. Jonah was greatly pleased with the plant. ⁷ When dawn came the next day, God appointed a worm that attacked the plant, and it withered.

⁸ As the sun was rising, God appointed a scorching east wind. The sun beat down on Jonah's head so that he almost fainted, and he wanted to die. He said, "It's better for me to die than to live."

⁹ Then God asked Jonah, "Is it right for you to be angry about the plant?"

"Yes, " he replied. " It is right. I'm angry enough to die!"

¹⁰ So the LORD said, "You cared about the plant, which you did not labor over and did not grow. It appeared in a night and perished in a night. ¹¹ Should I not care about the great city of Nineveh, which has more than 120,000 people who cannot distinguish between their right and their left, as well as many animals?"

PSALM 145:1-7

¹ I exalt You, my God the King,
and praise Your name forever and ever.
² I will praise You every day;
I will honor Your name forever and ever.
³ The LORD is great and is highly praised;
His greatness is unsearchable.
⁴ One generation will declare Your works to the next
and will proclaim Your mighty acts.
⁵ I will speak of Your glorious splendor
and Your wonderful works.
⁶ They will proclaim the power of Your awesome works,
and I will declare Your greatness.
⁷ They will give a testimony of Your great goodness
and will joyfully sing of Your righteousness.

PROVERBS 31:4-7

⁴ It is not for kings, Lemuel,
it is not for kings to drink wine
or for rulers to desire beer.
⁵ Otherwise, they will drink, forget what is decreed,
and pervert justice for all the oppressed.
⁶ Give beer to one who is dying,
and wine to one whose life is bitter.
⁷ Let him drink so that he can forget his poverty
and remember his trouble no more.

REVELATION 12:1-18

12 A great sign appeared in heaven: a woman clothed with the sun, with the moon under her feet, and a crown of 12 stars on her head. ² She was pregnant and cried out in labor and agony to give birth. ³ Then another sign appeared in heaven: There was a great fiery red dragon having seven heads and 10 horns, and on his heads were seven diadems. ⁴ His tail swept away a third of the stars in heaven and hurled them to the earth. And the dragon stood in front of the woman who was about to give birth, so that when she did give birth he might devour her child. ⁵ But she gave birth to a Son—a male who is going to shepherd all nations with an iron scepter—and her child was caught up to God and to His throne. ⁶ The woman fled into the wilderness, where she had a place prepared by God, to be fed there for 1,260 days.

⁷ Then war broke out in heaven: Michael and his angels fought against the dragon. The dragon and his angels also fought, ⁸ but he could not prevail, and there was no place for them in heaven any longer. ⁹ So the great dragon was thrown out—the ancient serpent, who is called the Devil and Satan, the one who deceives the whole world. He was thrown to earth, and his angels with him.

¹⁰ Then I heard a loud voice in heaven say:

The salvation and the power
    and the kingdom of our God
and the authority of His Messiah
    have now come,
because the accuser of our brothers
    has been thrown out:
the one who accuses them
    before our God day and night.
¹¹ They conquered him by the blood
    of the Lamb
and by the word of their testimony,

for they did not love their lives
    in the face of death.
¹² Therefore rejoice, O heavens,
    and you who dwell in them!
Woe to the earth and the sea,
for the Devil has come down
    to you with great fury,
because he knows he has
    a short time.

¹³ When the dragon saw that he had been thrown to earth, he persecuted the woman who gave birth to the male. ¹⁴ The woman was given two wings of a great eagle, so that she could fly from the serpent's presence to her place in the wilderness, where she was fed for a time, times, and half a time. ¹⁵ From his mouth the serpent spewed water like a river after the woman, to sweep her away in a torrent. ¹⁶ But the earth helped the woman: the earth opened its mouth and swallowed up the river that the dragon had spewed from his mouth. ¹⁷ So the dragon was furious with the woman and left to wage war against the rest of her offspring—those who keep the commandments of God and have the testimony about Jesus. ¹⁸ He stood on the sand of the sea.

Reflect on Perfection

I will speak of Your glorious splendor and Your wonderful works.—Psalm 145:5

The fact that God knows everything ought to strengthen our faith and cause us to bow down in adoration before Him. Yet how little do we reflect on this divine perfection! Those who are inclined to rebel against God hate this aspect of His being and would do away with it if they could. They wish there might be no Witness to their sin, no Searcher of their hearts, no Judge of their deeds. How very solemn are the words of the psalmist recorded in Psalm 90:8: "You have set our unjust ways before You, our secret sins in the light of Your presence."

To the believer, however, the truth of God's omniscience (His all-knowledge) ought to be one of tremendous comfort and security. In times of perplexity we ought to say like Job: "He knows the way I have taken; when He has tested me, I will emerge as pure gold" (Jb 23:10). Whatever might be going on in our lives that is profoundly mysterious to us and quite incomprehensible to those who are around us, we must never lose sight of the fact that "He knows the way [we] have taken." The psalmist, when seeking to stir his soul to confidence and hope, reminded himself in the midst of his weakness and weariness: "He knows what we are made of, remembering that we are dust" (Ps 103:14). And Simon Peter, when his failure brought him almost to the point of despair and the searching question came "Do you love me?" said: "Lord, you know everything! You know that I love you" (Jn 21:17). Such knowledge should ever cause us to worship.

Prayer

Father, help me reflect on this fact that You know everything, for I see that the more I understand it, the more secure I will feel in my soul. Teach me still more, dear Lord. In Jesus' name. Amen.

Further Study

Is 55:1-9; Heb 4:12-13; 1 Jn 3:20
What statement did God make?
What did the writer to the Hebrews confirm?

DECEMBER 22

MICAH 1:1–4:13

1 The word of the LORD that came to Micah the Moreshite—what he saw regarding Samaria and Jerusalem in the days of Jotham, Ahaz, and Hezekiah, kings of Judah.

2 Listen, all you peoples;
pay attention, earth and everyone in it!
The Lord GOD will be a witness against you,
the Lord, from His holy temple.
3 Look, the LORD is leaving His place and coming down to trample the heights of the earth.
4 The mountains will melt beneath Him,
and the valleys will split apart,
like wax near a fire,
like water cascading down a mountainside.
5 All this will happen because of Jacob's rebellion
and the sins of the house of Israel.
What is the rebellion of Jacob?
Isn't it Samaria?
And what is the high place of Judah?
Isn't it Jerusalem?
6 Therefore, I will make Samaria a heap of ruins in the countryside,
a planting area for a vineyard.
I will roll her stones into the valley
and expose her foundations.
7 All her carved images will be smashed to pieces,
all her wages will be burned in the fire,

and I will destroy all her idols.
Since she collected the wages of a
prostitute,
they will be used again for a
prostitute.

8 Because of this I will lament and
wail;
I will walk barefoot and naked.
I will howl like the jackals
and mourn like ostriches.
9 For her wound is incurable
and has reached even Judah;
it has approached the gate of my
people,
as far as Jerusalem.

10 Don't announce it in Gath,
don't weep at all.
In Beth-leaphrah roll in the dust.
11 Depart in shameful nakedness,
you residents of Shaphir;
the residents of Zaanan will not
come out.
Beth-ezel is lamenting;
its support is taken from you.
12 Though the residents of Maroth
anxiously wait for something good,
calamity has come from the LORD
to the gate of Jerusalem.
13 Harness the horses to the chariot,
you residents of Lachish.
This was the beginning of sin for
Daughter Zion,
because Israel's acts of rebellion
can be traced to you.
14 Therefore, send farewell gifts to
Moresheth-gath;
the houses of Achzib are a
deception
to the kings of Israel.
15 I will again bring a conqueror
against you who live in Mareshah.
The nobility of Israel will come to
Adullam.
16 Shave yourselves bald and cut off
your hair
in sorrow for your precious
children;
make yourselves as bald as an
eagle,
for they have been taken from you
into exile.

2 Woe to those who dream up
wickedness
and prepare evil plans on their
beds!
At morning light they accomplish it
because the power is in their
hands.
2 They covet fields and seize them;
they also take houses.
They deprive a man of his home,
a person of his inheritance.

3 Therefore, the LORD says:

I am now planning a disaster
against this nation;
you cannot free your necks from it.
Then you will not walk so proudly
because it will be an evil time.
4 In that day one will take up a
taunt against you,
and lament mournfully, saying:
We are totally ruined!
He measures out the allotted land
of my people.
How He removes it from me!
He allots our fields to traitors.
5 Therefore, there will be no one
in the assembly of the LORD
to divide the land by casting lots.

6 "Stop your preaching," they
preach.
"They should not preach these
things;
shame will not overtake us."
7 House of Jacob, should it be asked:
"Is the Spirit of the LORD
impatient?
Are these the things He does?"
Don't My words bring good
to the one who walks uprightly?
8 But recently My people have risen
up
like an enemy:
You strip off the splendid robe
from those who are
passing through confidently,
like those returning from war.
9 You force the women of My
people
out of their comfortable homes,
and you take My blessing
from their children forever.

¹⁰ Get up and leave,
    for this is not your place of rest,
    because defilement brings
       destruction—
    a grievous destruction!
¹¹ If a man of spirit comes
    and invents lies:
    "I will preach to you about wine
      and beer,"
    he would be just the preacher for
    this people!

¹² I will indeed gather all of you,
    Jacob;
    I will collect the remnant of Israel.
    I will bring them together like
      sheep in a pen,
    like a flock in the middle of its
      fold.
    It will be noisy with people.
¹³ One who breaks open the way
    will advance before them;
    they will break out, pass through
      the gate,
    and leave by it.
    Their King will pass through
      before them,
    the LORD as their leader.

3 Then I said: "Now listen,
    leaders of Jacob,
    you rulers of the house of Israel.
    Aren't you supposed to know what
      is just?
² You hate good and love evil.
    You tear off the skin of people
    and strip their flesh from their
      bones.
³ You eat the flesh of my people
    after you strip their skin from them
    and break their bones.
    You chop them up
    like flesh for the cooking pot,
    like meat in a caldron."
⁴ Then they will cry out to the LORD,
    but He will not answer them.
    He will hide His face from them at
      that time
    because of the crimes they have
      committed.

⁵ This is what the LORD says
    concerning the prophets
    who lead my people astray,

    who proclaim peace
    when they have food to sink their
      teeth into
    but declare war against the one
    who puts nothing in their mouths.
⁶ Therefore, it will be night for
      you—
    without visions;
    it will grow dark for you—
    without divination.
    The sun will set on these prophets,
    and the daylight will turn black
      over them.
⁷ Then the seers will be ashamed
    and the diviners disappointed.
    They will all cover their mouths
    because there will be no answer
      from God.

⁸ But as for me, I am filled with
      power
    by the Spirit of the LORD,
    with justice and courage,
    to proclaim to Jacob his rebellion
    and to Israel his sin.

⁹ Listen to this, leaders of the house
      of Jacob,
    you rulers of the house of Israel,
    who abhor justice
    and pervert everything that is
      right,
¹⁰ who build Zion with bloodshed
    and Jerusalem with injustice.
¹¹ Her leaders issue rulings for a
      bribe,
    her priests teach for payment,
    and her prophets practice
      divination for money.
    Yet they lean on the LORD, saying,
    "Isn't the LORD among us?
    No calamity will overtake us."
¹² Therefore, because of you,
    Zion will be plowed like a field,
    Jerusalem will become ruins,
    and the hill of the temple mount
    will be a thicket.

4 In the last days
    the mountain of the LORD's house
    will be established
    at the top of the mountains
    and will be raised above the hills.
    Peoples will stream to it,

2 and many nations will come and say,
"Come, let us go up to the
mountain of the LORD,
to the house of the God of Jacob.
He will teach us about His ways
so we may walk in His paths."
For instruction will go out of Zion
and the word of the LORD from
Jerusalem.
3 He will settle disputes among
many peoples
and provide arbitration for strong
nations
that are far away.
They will beat their swords into
plows,
and their spears into pruning
knives.
Nation will not take up the sword
against nation,
and they will never again train for
war.
4 But each man will sit under his
grapevine
and under his fig tree
with no one to frighten him.
For the mouth of the LORD of Hosts
has promised this.
5 Though all the peoples each walk
in the name of their gods,
we will walk in the name of
Yahweh our God
forever and ever.

6 On that day—
this is the LORD's declaration—
I will assemble the lame
and gather the scattered,
those I have injured.
7 I will make the lame into a
remnant,
those far removed into a strong
nation.
Then the LORD will rule over them
in Mount Zion
from this time on and forever.
8 And you, watchtower for the flock,
fortified hill of Daughter Zion,
the former rule will come to you,
sovereignty will come to Daughter
Jerusalem.

9 Now, why are you shouting loudly?
Is there no king with you?

Has your counselor perished,
so that anguish grips you like a
woman in labor?
10 Writhe and cry out, Daughter
Zion,
like a woman in labor.
For now you will leave the city
and camp in the open fields.
You will go to Babylon;
there you will be rescued;
there the LORD will redeem you
from the power of your enemies!
11 Many nations have now assembled
against you;
they say, "Let her be defiled,
and let us feast our eyes on Zion."
12 But they do not know the LORD's
intentions
or understand His plan,
that He has gathered them
like sheaves to the threshing floor.
13 Rise and thresh, Daughter Zion,
for I will make your horns iron
and your hooves bronze,
so you can crush many peoples.
Then you will devote
what they plundered to the LORD,
their wealth to the Lord of all the
earth.

PSALM 145:8-13

8 The LORD is gracious and
compassionate,
slow to anger and great in faithful
love.
9 The LORD is good to everyone;
His compassion rests on all He has
made.
10 All You have made will praise You,
LORD;
the godly will bless You.
11 They will speak of the glory of
Your kingdom
and will declare Your might,
12 informing all people of Your
mighty acts
and of the glorious splendor of
Your kingdom.
13 Your kingdom is an everlasting
kingdom;
Your rule is for all generations.

PROVERBS 31:8-9

8 Speak up for those who have no
voice,
for the justice of all who are
dispossessed.
9 Speak up, judge righteously,
and defend the cause of the
oppressed and needy.

REVELATION 13:1-18

13 And I saw a beast coming up out of the sea. He had 10 horns and seven heads. On his horns were 10 diadems, and on his heads were blasphemous names. ²The beast I saw was like a leopard, his feet were like a bear's, and his mouth was like a lion's mouth. The dragon gave him his power, his throne, and great authority. ³One of his heads appeared to be fatally wounded, but his fatal wound was healed. The whole earth was amazed and followed the beast. ⁴They worshiped the dragon because he gave authority to the beast. And they worshiped the beast, saying, "Who is like the beast? Who is able to wage war against him?"

⁵A mouth was given to him to speak boasts and blasphemies. He was also given authority to act for 42 months. ⁶He began to speak blasphemies against God: to blaspheme His name and His dwelling—those who dwell in heaven. ⁷And he was permitted to wage war against the saints and to conquer them. He was also given authority over every tribe, people, language, and nation. ⁸All those who live on the earth will worship him, everyone whose name was not written from the foundation of the world in the book of life of the Lamb who was slaughtered.

⁹If anyone has an ear, he should listen:

10 If anyone is destined for captivity,
into captivity he goes.
If anyone is to be killed
with a sword,
with a sword he will be killed.

Here is the endurance and the faith of the saints.

¹¹Then I saw another beast coming up out of the earth; he had two horns like a lamb, but he sounded like a dragon. ¹²He exercises all the authority of the first beast on his behalf and compels the earth and those who live on it to worship the first beast, whose fatal wound was healed. ¹³He also performs great signs, even causing fire to come down from heaven to earth before people. ¹⁴He deceives those who live on the earth because of the signs that he is permitted to perform on behalf of the beast, telling those who live on the earth to make an image of the beast who had the sword wound yet lived. ¹⁵He was permitted to give a spirit to the image of the beast, so that the image of the beast could both speak and cause whoever would not worship the image of the beast to be killed. ¹⁶And he requires everyone—small and great, rich and poor, free and slave—to be given a mark on his right hand or on his forehead, ¹⁷so that no one can buy or sell unless he has the mark: the beast's name or the number of his name.

¹⁸Here is wisdom: The one who has understanding must calculate the number of the beast, because it is the number of a man. His number is 666.

We Are All Charismatics

They will speak of the glory of Your kingdom and will declare Your might, informing all people of Your mighty acts.—PSALM 145:11-12

A friend of mine shared with his weekly Bible study group that he believed their church lacked visible evidence of the Holy Spirit's supernatural power. One of the group remonstrated with him and said, "Don't use that word 'supernatural' here—it frightens me and upsets me." Isn't it sad that a Christian (and there are many others who share his dislike) can be afraid of one of the most valid and needed ministries in the church today—supernatural power.

The word "supernatural" means "beyond the powers of nature, or miraculous." How much of that which goes on in today's church can be explained by this word? If you are saying to yourself, "Selwyn seems to be strongly supporting the charismatic movement," then let me make clear my views on that subject. I believe every Christian is a charismatic, for the word charisma simply means "gifts of grace," and every Christian has at least one basic gift—hence every Christian is a charismatic.

The reason why the charismatic movement came into prominence was because of the reluctance of many to face up to the fact that supernatural signs and wonders are part of God's program for His church in this present day. I know the movement has caused divisions, and there are signs that the emphasis is now diminishing, but whether it diminishes or not, one thing remains sure—God wants His people to demonstrate to the world that the signs, wonders, and miracles the early church experienced are still part of His purposes for today.

Prayer

O Father, help me to think this through, and take away any fears I might have of the supernatural. Show me that a church that can be explained only in natural terms is a million miles from the mark. In Jesus' name I ask it. Amen.

Further Study

Rm 15; Mk 16:17-20; Ac 4:29-30, 33
What was Paul's testimony?
What is recorded of the early disciples?

DECEMBER 23

MICAH 5:1–7:20

5 Now daughter who is under attack,
you slash yourself in grief;
a siege is set against us!
They are striking the judge of Israel

on the cheek with a rod.
2 Bethlehem Ephrathah,
you are small among the clans of Judah;
One will come from you
to be ruler over Israel for Me.
His origin is from antiquity,
from eternity.

3 Therefore, He will abandon them
  until the time
when she who is in labor has
  given birth;
then the rest of His brothers will
  return
to the people of Israel.
4 He will stand and shepherd them
in the strength of Yahweh,
in the majestic name of Yahweh
  His God.
They will live securely,
for then His greatness will extend
to the ends of the earth.
5 There will be peace.
When Assyria invades our land,
when it marches against our
  fortresses,
we will raise against it seven
  shepherds,
even eight leaders of men.
6 They will shepherd the land of
  Assyria with the sword,
the land of Nimrod with a drawn
  blade.
So He will rescue us from Assyria
when it invades our land,
when it marches against our
  territory.

7 Then the remnant of Jacob
will be among many peoples
like dew from the LORD,
like showers on the grass,
which do not wait for anyone
or linger for mankind.
8 Then the remnant of Jacob
will be among the nations, among
  many peoples,
like a lion among animals of the
  forest,
like a young lion among flocks of
  sheep,
which tramples and tears as it
  passes through,
and there is no one to rescue
  them.
9 Your hand will be lifted up against
  your adversaries,
and all your enemies will be
  destroyed.

10 In that day—
          the LORD's declaration—

I will remove your horses from you
and wreck your chariots.
11 I will remove the cities of your
  land
and tear down all your fortresses.
12 I will remove sorceries from your
  hands,
and you will not have any more
  fortune-tellers.
13 I will remove your carved images
and sacred pillars from you,
so that you will not bow down
  again
to the work of your hands.
14 I will pull up the Asherah poles
  from among you
and demolish your cities.
15 I will take vengeance in anger and
  wrath
against the nations that have not
  obeyed Me.

6 Now listen to what the LORD is saying:

Rise, plead your case before the
  mountains,
and let the hills hear your voice.
2 Listen to the LORD's lawsuit,
you mountains and enduring
  foundations of the earth,
because the LORD has a case
  against His people,
and He will argue it against Israel.
3 My people, what have I done to
  you,
or how have I wearied you?
Testify against Me!
4 Indeed, I brought you up from the
  land of Egypt
and redeemed you from that place
  of slavery.
I sent Moses, Aaron, and Miriam
  ahead of you.
5 My people,
remember what Balak king of
  Moab proposed,
what Balaam son of Beor
  answered him,
and what happened from Acacia
  Grove to Gilgal,
so that you may acknowledge
the LORD's righteous acts.

⁶ What should I bring before the
LORD
when I come to bow before God
on high?
Should I come before Him with
burnt offerings,
with year-old calves?
⁷ Would the LORD be pleased with
thousands of rams,
or with ten thousand streams of
oil?
Should I give my firstborn for my
transgression,
the child of my body for my own
sin?

⁸ He has told you men what is good
and what it is the LORD requires of
you:
Only to act justly,
to love faithfulness,
and to walk humbly with your God.

⁹ The voice of the LORD calls out to
the city
(and it is wise to fear Your name):
"Pay attention to the rod
and the One who ordained it.
¹⁰ Are there still the treasures of
wickedness
and the accursed short measure
in the house of the wicked?
¹¹ Can I excuse wicked scales
or bags of deceptive weights?
¹² For the wealthy of the city are full
of violence,
and its residents speak lies;
the tongues in their mouths are
deceitful.

¹³ "As a result, I have begun to strike
you severely,
bringing desolation because of
your sins.
¹⁴ You will eat but not be satisfied,
for there will be hunger within
you.
What you acquire, you cannot save,
and what you do save,
I will give to the sword.
¹⁵ You will sow but not reap;
you will press olives
but not anoint yourself with oil;
and you will tread grapes

but not drink the wine.
¹⁶ The statutes of Omri
and all the practices of Ahab's
house
have been observed;
you have followed their policies.
Therefore, I will make you a
desolate place
and the city's residents an object
of contempt;
you will bear the scorn of My
people."

7 How sad for me!
For I am like one who—
when the summer fruit has been
gathered
after the gleaning of the grape
harvest—
finds no grape cluster to eat,
no early fig, which I crave.
² Godly people have vanished from
the land;
there is no one upright among the
people.
All of them wait in ambush to
shed blood;
they hunt each other with a net.
³ Both hands are good at
accomplishing evil:
the official and the judge demand
a bribe;
when the powerful man
communicates his evil desire,
they plot it together.
⁴ The best of them is like a brier;
the most upright is worse than a
hedge of thorns.
The day of your watchmen,
the day of your punishment, is
coming;
at this time their panic is here.
⁵ Do not rely on a friend;
don't trust in a close companion.
Seal your mouth
from the woman who lies in your
arms.
⁶ For a son considers his father a
fool,
a daughter opposes her mother,
and a daughter-in-law is against
her mother-in-law;
a person's enemies are the people
in his own home.

7 But as for me, I will look to the
   LORD;
   I will wait for the God of my
      salvation.
   My God will hear me.

8 Do not rejoice over me, my enemy!
   Though I have fallen, I will stand
      up;
   though I sit in darkness,
   the LORD will be my light.

9 Because I have sinned against Him,
   I must endure the LORD's rage
   until He argues my case
   and establishes justice for me.
   He will bring me into the light;
   I will see His salvation.

10 Then my enemy will see,
   and she will be covered with
      shame,
   the one who said to me,
   "Where is the LORD your God?"
   My eyes will look at her in
      triumph;
   at that time she will be trampled
   like mud in the streets.

11 A day will come for rebuilding
      your walls;
   on that day your boundary will be
      extended.

12 On that day people will come to
      you
   from Assyria and the cities of
      Egypt,
   even from Egypt to the Euphrates
      River
   and from sea to sea
   and mountain to mountain.

13 Then the earth will become a
      wasteland
   because of its inhabitants,
   and as a result of their actions.

14 Shepherd Your people with Your
      staff,
   the flock that is Your possession.
   They live alone in a scrubland,
   surrounded by pastures.
   Let them graze in Bashan and
      Gilead
   as in ancient times.

15 I will show them wondrous deeds

as in the days of your exodus
from the land of Egypt.

16 Nations will see and be ashamed
of all their power.
They will put their hands over
   their mouths,
and their ears will become deaf.

17 They will lick the dust like a
   snake;
they will come trembling out of
   their hiding places
like reptiles slithering on the
   ground.
They will tremble before the LORD
   our God;
they will stand in awe of You.

18 Who is a God like You,
removing iniquity and passing
   over rebellion
for the remnant of His
   inheritance?
He does not hold on to His anger
   forever,
because He delights in faithful
   love.

19 He will again have compassion on
   us;
He will vanquish our iniquities.
You will cast all our sins
into the depths of the sea.

20 You will show loyalty to Jacob
and faithful love to Abraham,
as You swore to our fathers
from days long ago.

PSALM 145:14-21

14 The LORD helps all who fall;
He raises up all who are
   oppressed.

15 All eyes look to You,
and You give them their food in
   due time.

16 You open Your hand
and satisfy the desire of every
   living thing.

17 The LORD is righteous in all His
   ways
and gracious in all His acts.

18 The LORD is near all who call out
to Him,

all who call out to Him with
integrity.
19 He fulfills the desires of those
who fear Him;
He hears their cry for help and
saves them.
20 The LORD guards all those who
love Him,
but He destroys all the wicked.
21 My mouth will declare the LORD's
praise;
let every living thing praise His
holy name forever and ever.

PROVERBS 31:10-12

10 Who can find a capable wife?
She is far more precious than
jewels.
11 The heart of her husband trusts in
her,
and he will not lack anything good.
12 She rewards him with good, not
evil,
all the days of her life.

REVELATION 14:1-20

14 Then I looked, and there on
Mount Zion stood the Lamb, and
with Him were 144,000 who had His
name and His Father's name written on
their foreheads. 2 I heard a sound from
heaven like the sound of cascading waters and like the rumbling of loud thunder. The sound I heard was also like
harpists playing on their harps. 3 They
sang a new song before the throne and
before the four living creatures and the
elders, but no one could learn the song
except the 144,000 who had been redeemed from the earth. 4 These are the
ones not defiled with women, for they
have kept their virginity. These are the
ones who follow the Lamb wherever He
goes. They were redeemed from the human race as the firstfruits for God and
the Lamb. 5 No lie was found in their
mouths; they are blameless.
6 Then I saw another angel flying in
mid-heaven, having the eternal gospel
to announce to the inhabitants of the
earth—to every nation, tribe, language,

and people. 7 He spoke with a loud
voice: "Fear God and give Him glory, because the hour of His judgment has
come. Worship the Maker of heaven and
earth, the sea and springs of water."
8 A second angel followed, saying: "It
has fallen, Babylon the Great has fallen,
who made all nations drink the wine of
her sexual immorality, which brings
wrath."
9 And a third angel followed them and
spoke with a loud voice: "If anyone worships the beast and his image and receives a mark on his forehead or on
his hand, 10 he will also drink the wine
of God's wrath, which is mixed full
strength in the cup of His anger. He will
be tormented with fire and sulfur in the
sight of the holy angels and in the sight
of the Lamb, 11 and the smoke of their
torment will go up forever and ever.
There is no rest day or night for those
who worship the beast and his image, or
anyone who receives the mark of his
name. 12 Here is the endurance of the
saints, who keep the commandments of
God and the faith in Jesus."
13 Then I heard a voice from heaven
saying, "Write: Blessed are the dead
who die in the Lord from now on."
"Yes," says the Spirit, "let them rest
from their labors, for their works follow
them!"
14 Then I looked, and there was a
white cloud, and One like the Son of
Man was seated on the cloud, with a
gold crown on His head and a sharp
sickle in His hand. 15 Another angel
came out of the sanctuary, crying out in
a loud voice to the One who was seated
on the cloud, "Use your sickle and reap,
for the time to reap has come, since
the harvest of the earth is ripe." 16 So
the One seated on the cloud swung His
sickle over the earth, and the earth was
harvested.
17 Then another angel who also had a
sharp sickle came out of the sanctuary
in heaven. 18 Yet another angel, who had
authority over fire, came from the altar,
and he called with a loud voice to the
one who had the sharp sickle, "Use your
sharp sickle and gather the clusters of
grapes from earth's vineyard, because

its grapes have ripened." [19] So the angel swung his sickle toward earth and gathered the grapes from earth's vineyard, and he threw them into the great winepress of God's wrath. [20] Then the press was trampled outside the city, and blood flowed out of the press up to the horses' bridles for about 180 miles.

Familiar with Failure

*The LORD is near all who call out to Him,
all who call out to Him with integrity.*—PSALM 145:18

Many years ago, a young man came to see me and said: "I am not making a success of my life spiritually. I want with all my heart to become a successful Christian, but I seem to be failing in everything I do." At that time I was not as aware of the subtleties of the human heart as I am today, and I encouraged him to keep trying. I said, "Responsible effort and dogged obedience will bring you what you need; keep going no matter what." The advice I gave him was good, but it was not complete.

About a year later, after God had allowed me to see the subtleties and deceptions of my own heart, and after putting some personal things right before Him myself, I sat down once again with the young man and asked him how things were going. "A little better," he said, "but even though I keep asking God to help me become a successful Christian, I am still failing."

I took a deep breath and tentatively suggested that perhaps, deep down in his heart, he preferred failure to success. He looked at me in amazement and after a few seconds said, "Say some more about that. I feel you are touching something very vulnerable inside me."

We talked for hours, and he told me how all his life he had lived with failure, and it soon became obvious that he preferred the familiar feelings of failure to the unfamiliar feelings of success—even spiritual success. This one insight was all he needed to open up the whole of his being to God.

Prayer

Father, if I too need something to trigger off a deeper openness and self-awareness in my heart, then give it to me today. I want nothing more than to be an honest person, not only on the surface but also at the depths. Help me—in Jesus' name. Amen.

Further Study

Ex 16:1-3; Nm 11:1-6; 13:17-33
What was the problem of the children of Israel?
Why were they not prepared to move forward?

DECEMBER 24

NAHUM 1:1–3:19

1 The oracle concerning Nineveh. The book of the vision of Nahum the Elkoshite.

2 The LORD is a jealous and avenging God;
the LORD takes vengeance
and is fierce in wrath.
The LORD takes vengeance against His foes;
He is furious with His enemies.
3 The LORD is slow to anger but great in power;
the LORD will never leave the guilty unpunished.
His path is in the whirlwind and storm,
and clouds are the dust beneath His feet.
4 He rebukes the sea so that it dries up,
and He makes all the rivers run dry.
Bashan and Carmel wither;
even the flower of Lebanon withers.
5 The mountains quake before Him,
and the hills melt;
the earth trembles at His presence—
the world and all who live in it.
6 Who can withstand His indignation?
Who can endure His burning anger?
His wrath is poured out like fire,
even rocks are shattered before Him.

7 The LORD is good,
a stronghold in a day of distress;
He cares for those who take refuge in Him.
8 But He will completely destroy Nineveh

with an overwhelming flood,
and He will chase His enemies into darkness.

9 Whatever you plot against the LORD,
He will bring it to complete destruction;
oppression will not rise up a second time.
10 For they will be consumed
like entangled thorns,
like a drunkard's drink,
and like straw that is fully dry.
11 One has gone out from Nineveh,
who plots evil against the LORD,
and is a wicked counselor.

12 This is what the LORD says:

Though they are strong and numerous,
they will still be mowed down,
and he will pass away.
Though I have afflicted you,
I will afflict you no longer.
13 For I will now break off his yoke from you
and tear off your shackles.

14 The LORD has issued an order concerning you:

There will be no offspring
to carry on your name.
I will eliminate the carved idol
and cast image
from the house of your gods;
I will prepare your grave,
for you are contemptible.

15 Look to the mountains—
the feet of one bringing good news
and proclaiming peace!
Celebrate your festivals, Judah;
fulfill your vows.
For the wicked one will never again

march through you;
he will be entirely wiped out.

2 One who scatters is coming up
against you.
Man the fortifications!
Watch the road!
Brace yourself!
Summon all your strength!

2 For the LORD will restore the
majesty of Jacob,
yes, the majesty of Israel,
though ravagers have ravaged
them
and ruined their vine branches.

3 The shields of his warriors are
dyed red;
the valiant men are dressed in
scarlet.
The fittings of the chariot flash
like fire
on the day of its battle
preparations,
and the spears are brandished.

4 The chariots dash madly through
the streets;
they rush around in the plazas.
They look like torches;
they dart back and forth like
lightning.

5 He gives orders to his officers;
they stumble as they advance.
They race to its wall;
the protective shield is set in
place.

6 The river gates are opened,
and the palace erodes away.

7 Beauty is stripped,
she is carried away;
her ladies-in-waiting moan
like the sound of doves,
and beat their breasts.

8 Nineveh has been like a pool of
water
from her first days,
but they are fleeing.
"Stop! Stop!" they cry,
but no one turns back.

9 "Plunder the silver! Plunder the
gold!"
There is no end to the treasure,

an abundance of every precious
thing.

10 Desolation, decimation,
devastation!
Hearts melt,
knees tremble,
loins shake,
every face grows pale!

11 Where is the lions' lair,
or the feeding ground of the
young lions,
where the lion and lioness
prowled,
and the lion's cub,
with nothing to frighten them
away?

12 The lion mauled whatever its cubs
needed
and strangled prey for its
lionesses.
It filled up its dens with the kill,
and its lairs with mauled prey.

13 Beware, I am against you—
the declaration
of the Lord of Hosts.
I will make your chariots go up in
smoke
and the sword will devour your
young lions.
I will cut off your prey from the
earth,
and the sound of your messengers
will never be heard again.

3 Woe to the city of blood,
totally deceitful,
full of plunder,
never without prey.

2 The crack of the whip
and rumble of the wheel,
galloping horse
and jolting chariot!

3 Charging horseman,
flashing sword,
shining spear;
heaps of slain,
mounds of corpses,
dead bodies without end—
they stumble over their dead.

4 Because of the continual
prostitution
of the prostitute,
the attractive mistress of sorcery,

who betrays nations by her
        prostitution
and clans by her witchcraft,
5 I am against you —
                the declaration
        of the Lord of Hosts.
I will lift your skirts over your
        face
and display your nakedness to
        nations,
your shame to kingdoms.
6 I will throw filth on you
and treat you with contempt;
I will make a spectacle of you.
7 Then all who see you will recoil
        from you, saying:
Nineveh is devastated;
who will show sympathy to her?
Where can I find anyone to
        comfort you?

8 Are you better than Thebes
that sat along the Nile
with water surrounding her,
whose rampart was the sea,
the river her wall?
9 Cush and Egypt were her endless
        source of strength;
Put and Libya were among her
        allies.
10 Yet she became an exile;
she went into captivity.
Her children were also dashed to
        pieces
at the head of every street.
They cast lots for her dignitaries,
and all her nobles were bound in
        chains.
11 You also will become drunk;
you will hide yourself.
You also will seek refuge from the
        enemy.

12 All your fortresses are fig trees
with figs that ripened first;
when shaken, they fall—
right into the mouth of the eater!

13 Look, your troops are women
        among you;
the gates of your land
are wide open to your enemies.
Fire will devour the bars of your
        gates.

14 Draw water for the siege;
strengthen your fortresses.
Step into the clay and tread the
        mortar;
take hold of the brick-mold!
15 The fire will devour you there;
the sword will cut you down.
It will devour you like the young
        locust.
Multiply yourselves like the young
        locust,
multiply like the swarming locust!
16 You have made your merchants
more numerous than the stars of
        the sky.
The young locust strips the land
and flies away.
17 Your court officials are like the
        swarming locust,
and your scribes like clouds of
        locusts,
which settle on the walls on a
        cold day;
when the sun rises, they take off,
and no one knows where they are.

18 King of Assyria, your shepherds
        slumber;
your officers sleep.
Your people are scattered across
        the mountains
with no one to gather them
        together.
19 There is no remedy for your injury;
your wound is severe.
All who hear the news about you
will clap their hands because of
        you,
for who has not experienced
your constant cruelty?

PSALM 146:1-10

1 Hallelujah!
My soul, praise the LORD.
2 I will praise the LORD all my life;
I will sing to the LORD as long as I
        live.

3 Do not trust in nobles,
in man, who cannot save.
4 When his breath leaves him,
        he returns to the ground;
on that day his plans die.

⁵ Happy is the one whose help is
the God of Jacob,
whose hope is in the Lᴏʀᴅ his God,
⁶ the Maker of heaven and earth,
the sea and everything in them.
He remains faithful forever,
⁷ executing justice for the exploited
and giving food to the hungry.
The Lᴏʀᴅ frees prisoners.
⁸ The Lᴏʀᴅ opens the eyes of the
blind.
The Lᴏʀᴅ raises up those who are
oppressed.
The Lᴏʀᴅ loves the righteous.
⁹ The Lᴏʀᴅ protects foreigners
and helps the fatherless and the
widow,
but He frustrates the ways of the
wicked.

¹⁰ The Lᴏʀᴅ reigns forever;
Zion, your God reigns for all
generations.
Hallelujah!

𝒫ROVERBS 31:13-14

¹³ She selects wool and flax
and works with willing hands.
¹⁴ She is like the merchant ships,
bringing her food from far away.

𝓡EVELATION 15:1–16:11

15 Then I saw another great and awe-inspiring sign in heaven: seven angels with the seven last plagues, for with them, God's wrath will be completed. ² I also saw something like a sea of glass mixed with fire, and those who had won the victory from the beast, his image, and the number of his name, were standing on the sea of glass with harps from God. ³ They sang the song of God's servant Moses, and the song of the Lamb:

Great and awe-inspiring are
Your works, Lord God,
the Almighty;
righteous and true are Your ways,
King of the Nations.

⁴ Lord, who will not fear and glorify
Your name?
Because You alone are holy,
because all the nations will come
and worship before You,
because Your righteous acts
have been revealed.

⁵ After this I looked, and the heavenly sanctuary—the tabernacle of testimony—was opened. ⁶ Out of the sanctuary came the seven angels with the seven plagues, dressed in clean, bright linen, with gold sashes wrapped around their chests. ⁷ One of the four living creatures gave the seven angels seven gold bowls filled with the wrath of God who lives forever and ever. ⁸ Then the sanctuary was filled with smoke from God's glory and from His power, and no one could enter the sanctuary until the seven plagues of the seven angels were completed.

16 Then I heard a loud voice from the sanctuary saying to the seven angels, "Go and pour out the seven bowls of God's wrath on the earth." ² The first went and poured out his bowl on the earth, and severely painful sores broke out on the people who had the mark of the beast and who worshiped his image.
³ The second poured out his bowl into the sea. It turned to blood like a dead man's, and all life in the sea died.
⁴ The third poured out his bowl into the rivers and the springs of water, and they became blood. ⁵ I heard the angel of the waters say:

You are righteous, who is
and who was, the Holy One,
for You have decided these things.
⁶ Because they poured out
the blood of the saints
and the prophets,
You also gave them blood to drink;
they deserve it!

⁷ Then I heard someone from the altar say:

Yes, Lord God, the Almighty,
true and righteous are
Your judgments.

⁸The fourth poured out his bowl on the sun. He was given the power to burn people with fire, ⁹and people were burned by the intense heat. So they blasphemed the name of God who had the power over these plagues, and they did not repent and give Him glory.

¹⁰The fifth poured out his bowl on the throne of the beast, and his kingdom was plunged into darkness. People gnawed their tongues from pain ¹¹and blasphemed the God of heaven because of their pains and their sores, yet they did not repent of their actions.

Climbing Higher

Look to the mountains—the feet of one bringing good news and proclaiming peace!
—NAHUM 1:15

There are numerous references in Scripture where the pursuit of God is likened to a deer climbing steadily, sure-footedly toward the high mountain peaks, and the more we consider the simile, the more rich and rewarding are the truths that flow out of it.

Why does God liken the pursuit of Himself to a deer making its way upward to the high places? And why does He focus so much attention upon the deer's feet? Well, the deer has an amazing ability, when climbing a steep mountain slope, of ensuring that its back feet alight on the exact spot where its front feet were positioned. This perfect correlation between its front and back feet enables the deer to avoid the dangers that would befall a less coordinated animal.

The Bible writers, in drawing attention to the sure-footedness of the deer, are attempting to show (so I believe) that what the deer experiences in the natural realm, we can experience in the spiritual realm. Do you really want to climb higher with God than you have ever gone before? Is there a deep longing in your heart to ascend, like the prophets and seers of old, into the mountain of the Lord? Then take heart—you can. This can be the greatest time of spiritual advance you have ever known. If you supply the willingness, then I promise you—God will supply the power.

Prayer

O Father, my prayer is—make this the greatest time of my life. I long more than anything to ascend into the mountain peaks with You. I am willing—now send the power. In Jesus' name. Amen.

Further Study

Is 55; Pss 42:2; 63:1; 143:6
What did the psalmist express continually?
What does God promise?

DECEMBER 25

*H*ABAKKUK 1:1–3:19

1 The oracle that Habakkuk the prophet saw.

2 How long, LORD, must I call for
    help
and You do not listen,
or cry out to You about violence
and You do not save?
3 Why do You force me to look at
    injustice?
Why do You tolerate wrongdoing?
Oppression and violence are right
    in front of me.
Strife is ongoing, and conflict
    escalates.
4 This is why the law is ineffective
and justice never emerges.
For the wicked restrict the
    righteous;
therefore, justice comes out
    perverted.

5 Look at the nations and observe—
be utterly astounded!
For something is taking place in
    your days
that you will not believe
when you hear about it.
6 Look! I am raising up the
    Chaldeans,
that bitter, impetuous nation
that marches across the earth's
    open spaces
to seize territories not its own.
7 They are fierce and terrifying;
their views of justice and
    sovereignty
stem from themselves.
8 Their horses are swifter than
    leopards
and more fierce than wolves of
    the night.
Their horsemen charge ahead;
their horsemen come from distant
    lands.

They fly like an eagle, swooping to
    devour.
9 All of them come to do violence;
their faces are set in
    determination.
They gather prisoners like sand.
10 They mock kings,
and rulers are a joke to them.
They laugh at every fortress
and build siege ramps to capture
    it.
11 Then they sweep by like the wind
and pass through.
They are guilty; their strength is
    their god.

12 Are You not from eternity, Yahweh
    my God?
My Holy One, You will not die.
LORD, You appointed them to
    execute judgment;
my Rock, You destined them to
    punish us.
13 Your eyes are too pure to look on
    evil,
and You cannot tolerate
    wrongdoing.
So why do You tolerate those who
    are treacherous?
Why are You silent
while one who is wicked swallows
    up
one who is more righteous than
    himself?
14 You have made mankind
like the fish of the sea,
like marine creatures that have no
    ruler.
15 The Chaldeans pull them all up
    with a hook,
catch them in their dragnet,
and gather them in their fishing
    net;
that is why they are glad and
    rejoice.
16 That is why they sacrifice to their
    dragnet

and burn incense to their fishing
net,
for by these things their portion is
rich
and their food plentiful.
¹⁷ Will they therefore empty their net
and continually slaughter nations
without mercy?

2 I will stand at my guard post
and station myself on the lookout
tower.
I will watch to see what He will
say to me
and what I should reply about my
complaint.

² The LORD answered me:

Write down this vision;
clearly inscribe it on tablets
so one may easily read it.
³ For the vision is yet for the
appointed time;
it testifies about the end and will
not lie.
Though it delays, wait for it,
since it will certainly come and
not be late.
⁴ Look, his ego is inflated;
he is without integrity.
But the righteous one will live by
his faith.
⁵ Moreover, wine betrays;
an arrogant man is never at rest.
He enlarges his appetite like Sheol,
and like Death he is never
satisfied.
He gathers all the nations to
himself;
he collects all the peoples for
himself.

⁶ Won't all of these take up a taunt
against him,
with mockery and riddles about
him?
They will say:

Woe to him who amasses what is
not his—
how much longer?—
and loads himself with goods
taken in pledge.

⁷ Won't your creditors suddenly
arise,
and those who disturb you wake up?
Then you will become spoil for
them.
⁸ Since you have plundered many
nations,
all the peoples who remain will
plunder you—
because of human bloodshed
and violence against lands, cities,
and all who live in them.

⁹ Woe to him who unjustly gains
wealth for his house
to place his nest on high,
to escape from the reach of
disaster!
¹⁰ You have planned shame for your
house
by wiping out many peoples
and sinning against your own self.
¹¹ For the stones will cry out from
the wall,
and the rafters will answer them
from the woodwork.

¹² Woe to him who builds a city with
bloodshed
and founds a town with injustice!
¹³ Is it not from the LORD of Hosts,
that the peoples labor only to fuel
the fire
and countries exhaust themselves
for nothing?
¹⁴ For the earth will be filled
with the knowledge of the LORD's
glory,
as the waters cover the sea.

¹⁵ Woe to him who gives his
neighbors drink,
pouring out your wrath
and even making them drunk,
in order to look at their
nakedness!
¹⁶ You will be filled with disgrace
instead of glory.
You also—drink,
and expose your uncircumcision!
The cup in the LORD's right hand
will come around to you,
and utter disgrace will cover your
glory.

¹⁷ For your violence against
     Lebanon
will overwhelm you;
   the destruction of animals will
     terrify you,
because of your human bloodshed
     and violence
against lands, cities, and all who
     live in them.

¹⁸ What use is a carved idol
after its craftsman carves it?
It is only a cast image, a teacher of
     lies.
For the one who crafts its shape
     trusts in it
and makes idols that cannot speak.
¹⁹ Woe to him who says to wood:
     Wake up!
or to mute stone: Come alive!
Can it teach?
Look! It may be plated with gold
     and silver,
yet there is no breath in it at all.

²⁰ But the LORD is in His holy temple;
let everyone on earth
be silent in His presence.

3 A prayer of Habakkuk the prophet.
According to Shigionoth.

² LORD, I have heard the report
     about You;
LORD, I stand in awe of Your
     deeds.
Revive Your work in these years;
make it known in these years.
In Your wrath remember mercy!

³ God comes from Teman,
the Holy One from Mount Paran.
               Selah
His splendor covers the heavens,
and the earth is full of His praise.
⁴ His brilliance is like light;
rays are flashing from His hand.
This is where His power is hidden.
⁵ Plague goes before Him,
and pestilence follows in His steps.
⁶ He stands and shakes the earth;
He looks and startles the nations.
The age-old mountains break apart;
the ancient hills sink down.

His pathways are ancient.
⁷ I see the tents of Cushan in
     distress;
the tent curtains of the land of
     Midian tremble.
⁸ Are You angry at the rivers, LORD?
Is Your wrath against the rivers?
Or is Your rage against the sea
when You ride on Your horses,
Your victorious chariot?
⁹ You took the sheath from Your
     bow;
the arrows are ready to be used
   with an oath.   *Selah*
You split the earth with rivers.
¹⁰ The mountains see You and
     shudder;
a downpour of water sweeps by.
The deep roars with its voice
and lifts its waves high.
¹¹ Sun and moon stand still in their
     lofty residence,
at the flash of Your flying arrows,
at the brightness of Your shining
     spear.
¹² You march across the earth with
     indignation;
You trample down the nations in
     wrath.
¹³ You come out to save Your people,
to save Your anointed.
You crush the leader of the house
     of the wicked
and strip him from foot to neck.
               Selah
¹⁴ You pierce his head
with his own spears;
his warriors storm out to scatter
     us,
gloating as if ready to secretly
     devour the weak.
¹⁵ You tread the sea with Your horses,
stirring up the great waters.

¹⁶ I heard, and I trembled within;
my lips quivered at the sound.
Rottenness entered my bones;
I trembled where I stood.
Now I must quietly wait for the
     day of distress
to come against the people
     invading us.
¹⁷ Though the fig tree does not bud
and there is no fruit on the vines,

though the olive crop fails
and the fields produce no food,
though there are no sheep in the
    pen
and no cattle in the stalls,
¹⁸ yet I will triumph in the LORD;
I will rejoice in the God of my
    salvation!
¹⁹ Yahweh my Lord is my strength;
He makes my feet like those of a
    deer
and enables me to walk on
    mountain heights!
For the choir director: on stringed instruments.

PSALM 147:1-6

¹ Hallelujah!
How good it is to sing to our God,
for praise is pleasant and lovely.

² The LORD rebuilds Jerusalem;
He gathers Israel's exiled people.
³ He heals the brokenhearted
and binds up their wounds.
⁴ He counts the number of the stars;
He gives names to all of them.
⁵ Our Lord is great, vast in power;
His understanding is infinite.
⁶ The LORD helps the afflicted
but brings the wicked to the
    ground.

PROVERBS 31:15-17

¹⁵ She rises while it is still night
and provides food for her
    household
and portions for her servants.
¹⁶ She evaluates a field and buys it;
she plants a vineyard with her
    earnings.
¹⁷ She draws on her strength
and reveals that her arms are
    strong.

REVELATION 16:12–17:8

¹² The sixth poured out his bowl on
the great river Euphrates, and its water
was dried up to prepare the way for the
kings from the east. ¹³ Then I saw three
unclean spirits like frogs coming from
the dragon's mouth, from the beast's
mouth, and from the mouth of the false
prophet. ¹⁴ For they are spirits of demons performing signs, who travel to
the kings of the whole world to assemble them for the battle of the great day
of God, the Almighty.
¹⁵ "Look, I am coming like a thief.
Blessed is the one who is alert and remains clothed so that he may not go
naked, and they see his shame."
¹⁶ So they assembled them at the
place called in Hebrew Armagedon.
¹⁷ Then the seventh poured out his
bowl into the air, and a loud voice came
out of the sanctuary, from the throne,
saying, "It is done!" ¹⁸ There were lightnings, rumblings, and thunders. And a
severe earthquake occurred like no other
since man has been on the earth—so
great was the quake. ¹⁹ The great city
split into three parts, and the cities of
the nations fell. Babylon the Great was
remembered in God's presence; He
gave her the cup filled with the wine of
His fierce anger. ²⁰ Every island fled,
and the mountains disappeared. ²¹ Enormous hailstones, each weighing about
100 pounds, fell from heaven on the
people, and they blasphemed God for
the plague of hail because that plague
was extremely severe.

17 Then one of the seven angels
who had the seven bowls came
and spoke with me: "Come, I will show
you the judgment of the notorious prostitute who sits on many waters. ² The
kings of the earth committed sexual immorality with her, and those who live on
the earth became drunk on the wine of
her sexual immorality." ³ So he carried
me away in the Spirit to a desert. I saw
a woman sitting on a scarlet beast that
was covered with blasphemous names,
having seven heads and 10 horns. ⁴ The
woman was dressed in purple and scar-
let, adorned with gold, precious stones,
and pearls. She had a gold cup in her
hand filled with everything vile and
with the impurities of her prostitution.

⁵ On her forehead a cryptic name was written:

> BABYLON THE GREAT
> THE MOTHER OF PROSTITUTES
> AND OF THE VILE THINGS OF
> THE EARTH

⁶ Then I saw that the woman was drunk on the blood of the saints and on the blood of the witnesses to Jesus. When I saw her, I was utterly astounded.

⁷ Then the angel said to me, "Why are you astounded? I will tell you the secret meaning of the woman and of the beast, with the seven heads and the 10 horns, that carries her. ⁸ The beast that you saw was, and is not, and is about to come up from the abyss and go to destruction. Those who live on the earth whose names were not written in the book of life from the foundation of the world will be astounded when they see the beast that was, and is not, and will be present again.

God Knows All

Our Lord is great, vast in power;
His understanding is infinite.—PSALM 147:5

Two aspects of God's nature which cannot be examined separately are His knowledge and His wisdom. I link these two characteristics together because really it is almost impossible to consider one without considering the other.

The difference between knowledge and wisdom has been described like this: "Knowledge is what we know; wisdom is the right application of what we know." God, of course, knows everything: everything possible, everything actual. He is perfectly acquainted with every detail in the life of every being in heaven, in earth, and in hell. Daniel said of Him: "He knows what is in the darkness, and light dwells with Him" (Dn 2:22). Nothing escapes His notice, nothing can be hidden from Him, and nothing can be forgotten by Him.

Many Christians, when referring to their conversion, say that God has forgotten their sins, but strictly speaking that is not so. God never forgets anything. What He promises to do with our sins is "never again remember" (Jr 31:34). There is a great difference between forgetting something and deciding not to remember it. Realizing, then, as we do, that God knows everything ought to strengthen our faith and cause us to bow in adoration before Him. The hymnist put it effectively when he wrote these words:

> The knowledge of this life is small,
> The eye of faith is dim,
> But 'tis enough that God knows all
> And I shall be with Him.

Prayer

O Father, how consoling it is to know that You know everything. Nothing ever escapes Your attention. This means I can relax, for what I don't know You know. And because You know it, then what I don't know can't hurt me. Amen.

Further Study

Jb 31:1-4; 34:21-25; Ps 147:5; Ezk 11:5
What was Job's question?
What was Elihu's response?

DECEMBER 26

ZEPHANIAH 1:1–3:20

1 The word of the LORD that came to Zephaniah son of Cushi, son of Gedaliah, son of Amariah, son of Hezekiah, in the days of Josiah son of Amon, king of Judah.

2 I will completely sweep away everything
from the face of the earth —
this is the LORD's declaration.
3 I will sweep away man and animal;
I will sweep away the birds of the sky
and the fish of the sea,
and the ruins along with the wicked.
I will cut off mankind
from the face of the earth—
the LORD's declaration.

4 I will stretch out My hand against Judah
and against all the residents of Jerusalem.
I will cut off from this place
every vestige of Baal,
the names of the pagan priests along with the priests;
5 those who bow in worship on the rooftops
to the heavenly host;
those who bow and pledge loyalty to the LORD

but also pledge loyalty to Milcom;
6 and those who turn back from following the LORD,
who do not seek the LORD or inquire of Him.
7 Be silent in the presence of the Lord GOD,
for the Day of the LORD is near.
Indeed, the LORD has prepared a sacrifice;
He has consecrated His guests.

8 On the day of the LORD's sacrifice
I will punish the officials, the king's sons,
and all who are dressed in foreign clothing.
9 On that day I will punish
all who skip over the threshold,
who fill their master's house
with violence and deceit.

10 On that day—
the LORD's declaration—
there will be an outcry from the Fish Gate,
a wailing from the Second District,
and a loud crashing from the hills.
11 Wail, you residents of the Hollow,
for all the merchants will be silenced;
all those loaded with silver will be cut off.

12 And at that time I will search Jerusalem with lamps

and punish the men who settle
down comfortably,
who say to themselves:
The LORD will not do good or evil.
13 Their wealth will become plunder
and their houses a ruin.
They will build houses but never
live in them,
plant vineyards but never drink
their wine.

14 The great Day of the LORD is near,
near and rapidly approaching.
Listen, the Day of the LORD—
there the warrior's cry is bitter.
15 That day is a day of wrath,
a day of trouble and distress,
a day of destruction and
desolation,
a day of darkness and gloom,
a day of clouds and blackness,
16 a day of trumpet blast and battle
cry
against the fortified cities,
and against the high corner towers.
17 I will bring distress on mankind,
and they will walk like the blind
because they have sinned against
the LORD.
Their blood will be poured out
like dust
and their flesh like dung.
18 Their silver and their gold
will not be able to rescue them
on the day of the LORD's wrath.
The whole earth will be consumed
by the fire of His jealousy.
For He will make a complete,
yes, a horrifying end
of all the inhabitants of the earth.

2 Gather yourselves together;
gather together, undesirable nation,
2 before the decree takes effect
and the day passes like chaff,
before the burning of the LORD's
anger overtakes you,
before the day of the LORD's anger
overtakes you.
3 Seek the LORD, all you humble of
the earth,
who carry out what He
commands.
Seek righteousness, seek humility;

perhaps you will be concealed
on the day of the LORD's anger.

4 For Gaza will be abandoned,
and Ashkelon will become a ruin.
Ashdod will be driven out at noon,
and Ekron will be uprooted.
5 Woe, inhabitants of the seacoast,
nation of the Cherethites!
The word of the LORD is against
you,
Canaan, land of the Philistines:
I will destroy you until there is no
one left.
6 The seacoast will become
pasturelands
with caves for shepherds and folds
for sheep.
7 The coastland will belong
to the remnant of the house of
Judah;
they will find pasture there.
They will lie down in the evening
among the houses of Ashkelon,
for the LORD their God will return
to them
and restore their fortunes.

8 I have heard the taunting of Moab
and the insults of the Ammonites,
who have taunted My people
and threatened their territory.
9 Therefore, as I live—
the declaration
of the LORD of Hosts,
the God of Israel—
Moab will be like Sodom
and the Ammonites like
Gomorrah—
a place overgrown with weeds,
a salt pit, and a perpetual
wasteland.
The remnant of My people will
plunder them;
the remainder of My nation will
dispossess them.
10 This is what they get for their
pride,
because they have taunted and
acted arrogantly
against the people of the LORD of
Hosts.
11 The LORD will be terrifying to
them

when He starves all the gods of
   the earth.
Then all the distant coastlands of
   the nations
will bow in worship to Him,
each in its own place.

12 You Cushites will also be slain by
   My sword.

13 He will also stretch out His hand
   against the north
and destroy Assyria;
He will make Nineveh a desolate
   ruin,
dry as the desert.
14 Herds will lie down in the middle
   of it,
every kind of wild animal.
Both the desert owl and the
   screech owl
will roost in the capitals of its
   pillars.
Their calls will sound from the
   window,
but devastation will be on the
   threshold,
for He will expose the cedar work.
15 This is the self-assured city
that lives in security,
that thinks to herself:
I am, and there is no one besides
   me.
What a desolation she has become,
a place for wild animals to lie
   down!
Everyone who passes by her
jeers and shakes his fist.

3 Woe to the city that is rebellious
      and defiled,
   the oppressive city!
2 She has not obeyed;
   she has not accepted discipline.
   She has not trusted in the LORD;
   she has not drawn near to her God.
3 The princes within her are roaring
      lions;
   her judges are wolves of the night,
   which leave nothing for the
      morning.
4 Her prophets are reckless—
   treacherous men.
   Her priests profane the sanctuary;

they do violence to instruction.
5 The righteous LORD is in her;
He does no wrong.
He applies His justice morning by
   morning;
He does not fail at dawn,
yet the one who does wrong
   knows no shame.

6 I have cut off nations;
their corner towers are destroyed.
I have laid waste their streets,
with no one to pass through.
Their cities lie devastated,
without a person, without an
   inhabitant.
7 I thought: You will certainly fear
   Me
and accept correction.
Then her dwelling place
would not be cut off
based on all that I had allocated to
   her.
However, they became more
   corrupt
in all their actions.
8 Therefore, wait for Me—
         the LORD's declaration—
until the day I rise up for plunder.
For My decision is to gather
   nations,
to assemble kingdoms,
in order to pour out My
   indignation on them,
all My burning anger;
for the whole earth will be
   consumed
by the fire of My jealousy.

9 For I will then restore
pure speech to the peoples
so that all of them may call
on the name of Yahweh
and serve Him with a single
   purpose.
10 From beyond the rivers of Cush
My supplicants, My dispersed
   people,
will bring an offering to Me.
11 On that day you will not be put to
   shame
because of everything you have
   done
in rebelling against Me.

For then I will remove
your boastful braggarts from
among you,
and you will never again be
haughty
on My holy mountain.
12 I will leave
a meek and humble people among
you,
and they will trust in the name of
Yahweh.
13 The remnant of Israel will no
longer
do wrong or tell lies;
a deceitful tongue will not be
found
in their mouths.
But they will pasture and lie down,
with nothing to make them afraid.

14 Sing for joy, Daughter Zion;
shout loudly, Israel!
Be glad and rejoice with all your
heart,
Daughter Jerusalem!
15 The LORD has removed your
punishment;
He has turned back your enemy.
The King of Israel, the LORD, is
among you;
you need no longer fear harm.
16 On that day it will be said to
Jerusalem:
"Do not fear;
Zion, do not let your hands grow
weak.
17 The LORD your God is among you,
a warrior who saves.
He will rejoice over you with
gladness.
He will bring you quietness with
His love.
He will delight in you with shouts
of joy."

18 I will gather those who have been
driven
from the appointed festivals;
They will be a tribute from you,
and reproach on her.
19 Yes, at that time
I will deal with all who afflict you.
I will save the lame and gather the
scattered;

I will make those who were
disgraced
throughout the earth
receive praise and fame.
20 At that time I will bring you back,
yes, at the time I will gather you.
I will make you famous and
praiseworthy
among all the peoples of the earth,
when I restore your fortunes
before your eyes.
Yahweh has spoken.

PSALM 147:7-14

7 Sing to the LORD with thanksgiving;
play the lyre to our God,
8 who covers the sky with clouds,
prepares rain for the earth,
and causes grass to grow on the
hills.
9 He provides the animals with their
food,
and the young ravens, what they
cry for.

10 He is not impressed by the
strength of a horse;
He does not value the power of a
man.
11 The LORD values those who fear
Him,
those who hope in His faithful
love.

12 Exalt the LORD, Jerusalem;
praise your God, Zion!
13 For He strengthens the bars of
your gates
and blesses your children within
you.
14 He endows your territory with
prosperity;
He satisfies you with the finest
wheat.

PROVERBS 31:18-19

18 She sees that her profits are good,
and her lamp never goes out at
night.
19 She extends her hands to the
spinning staff,
and her hands hold the spindle.

REVELATION 17:9–18:8

9 "Here is the mind with wisdom: the seven heads are seven mountains on which the woman is seated. 10 They are also seven kings: five have fallen, one is, the other has not yet come, and when he comes, he must remain for a little while. 11 The beast that was and is not, is himself the eighth, yet is of the seven and goes to destruction. 12 The 10 horns you saw are 10 kings who have not yet received a kingdom, but they will receive authority as kings with the beast for one hour. 13 These have one purpose, and they give their power and authority to the beast. 14 These will make war against the Lamb, but the Lamb will conquer them because He is Lord of lords and King of kings. Those with Him are called and elect and faithful."

15 He also said to me, "The waters you saw, where the prostitute was seated, are peoples, multitudes, nations, and languages. 16 The 10 horns you saw, and the beast, will hate the prostitute. They will make her desolate and naked, devour her flesh, and burn her up with fire. 17 For God has put it into their hearts to carry out His plan by having one purpose, and to give their kingdom to the beast until God's words are accomplished. 18 And the woman you saw is the great city that has an empire over the kings of the earth."

18 After this I saw another angel with great authority coming down from heaven, and the earth was illuminated by his splendor. 2 He cried in a mighty voice:

> It has fallen, Babylon the Great
> has fallen!

> She has become a dwelling
> for demons,
> a haunt for every unclean spirit,
> a haunt for every unclean bird,
> and a haunt for every unclean
> and despicable beast.
> 3 For all the nations have drunk
> the wine of her sexual immorality,
> which brings wrath.
> The kings of the earth
> have committed
> sexual immorality with her,
> and the merchants of the earth
> have grown wealthy
> from her excessive luxury.

4 Then I heard another voice from heaven:

> Come out of her, My people,
> so that you will not share
> in her sins,
> or receive any of her plagues.
> 5 For her sins are piled up
> to heaven,
> and God has remembered
> her crimes.
> 6 Pay her back the way she also paid,
> and double it
> according to her works.
> In the cup in which she mixed,
> mix a double portion for her.
> 7 As much as she glorified herself
> and lived luxuriously,
> give her that much torment
> and grief.
> Because she says in her heart,
> 'I sit as queen;
> I am not a widow,
> and I will never see grief,'
> 8 therefore her plagues will come
> in one day—
> death, and grief, and famine.
> She will be burned up with fire,
> because the Lord God
> who judges her is mighty.

Staying Close to the Shepherd

*The King of Israel, the LORD, is among you;
you need no longer fear harm.*
—ZEPHANIAH 3:15

A classic example of the way in which the divine Shepherd ministers to His children is seen in Luke 22:24-32. Jesus tells Simon Peter that Satan has sought to tempt him and sift him like wheat but that He has prayed that Peter's faith might not fail in that moment of overwhelming testing. Where would I have been, where would you have been, but for that blessed ministry of the divine Shepherd—going before us, anticipating our circumstances, and supportively working and praying for us, so that we might not be overtaken by the enemy of our souls? If He did not minister to us in this way . . . where should we be?

This does not mean, of course, that the responsibility for our safety and security rest entirely on our divine Shepherd. We, too, have a responsibility—a responsibility to make sure that we keep as close to Him as we possibly can. This is the one sure place of safety. "It is always the distant sheep, the roamers, the wanderers," says one shepherd, "which are picked off by predators in an unsuspecting moment. Sometimes the sheep is so overtaken by fear that it is too frightened to even cry out. It might give a plaintive bleat before its blood is spilled." The divine Shepherd wants to forestall every calamity that would come our way and strives to keep our lives free from serious dangers and hazards. And, of course, our lives will be danger-free if we stay close to Him, where He can provide for us and protect us.

Prayer

My Father and my God, thank You for reminding me that although You make Yourself responsible for my safety and security, I also have a responsibility—to stay as close as I possibly can to You. Help me to do just that—today and every day. For Jesus' sake. Amen.

Further Study

Heb 2; 7:25; 1 Co 10:13; Jms 4:7; Rm 16:20
What does Christ do in our times of temptation?
What should we do?

DECEMBER 27

HAGGAI 1:1–ZECHARIAH 1:21

1 In the second year of King Darius, on the first day of the sixth month, the word of the LORD came through Haggai the prophet to Zerubbabel son of Shealtiel, the governor of Judah, and to Joshua son of Jehozadak, the high priest: ² "The LORD of Hosts says this: These people say: The time has not come for the house of the LORD to be rebuilt."

³ The word of the LORD came through Haggai the prophet: ⁴ "Is it a time for you yourselves to live in your paneled houses, while this house lies in ruins?" ⁵ Now, the LORD of Hosts says this: "Think carefully about your ways:

⁶ You have planted much
but harvested little.
You eat
but never have enough to be
satisfied.
You drink
but never have enough to become
drunk.
You put on clothes
but never have enough to get
warm.
The wage earner puts his wages
into a bag with a hole in it."

⁷ The LORD of Hosts says this: "Think carefully about your ways. ⁸ Go up into the hills, bring down lumber, and build the house. Then I will be pleased with it and be glorified," says the LORD. ⁹ "You expected much, but then it amounted to little. When you brought the harvest to your house, I ruined it. Why?" This is the declaration of the LORD of Hosts. "Because My house still lies in ruins, while each of you is busy with his own house.

¹⁰ So on your account,
the skies have withheld the dew
and the land its crops.
¹¹ I have summoned a drought
on the fields and the hills,
on the grain, new wine, olive oil,
and whatever the ground yields,
on the people and animals,
and on all that your hands
produce."

¹² Then Zerubbabel son of Shealtiel, the high priest Joshua son of Jehozadak, and the entire remnant of the people obeyed the voice of the LORD their God and the words of the prophet Haggai, because the LORD their God had sent him. So the people feared the LORD. ¹³ Haggai, the LORD's messenger, delivered the LORD's message to the people, "I am with you"—the LORD's declaration. ¹⁴ The LORD stirred up the spirit of Zerubbabel son of Shealtiel, governor of Judah, the spirit of the high priest Joshua son of Jehozadak, and the spirit of all the remnant of the people. They began work on the house of Yahweh of Hosts, their God, ¹⁵ on the twenty-fourth day of the sixth month, in the second year of King Darius.

2 On the twenty-first day of the seventh month, the word of the LORD came through Haggai the prophet: ² "Speak to Zerubbabel son of Shealtiel, governor of Judah, to the high priest Joshua son of Jehozadak, and to the remnant of the people: ³ Who is left among you who saw this house in its former glory? How does it look to you now? Doesn't it seem like nothing to you? ⁴ Even so, be strong, Zerubbabel"—the LORD's declaration. "Be strong, Joshua son of Jehozadak, high priest. Be strong, all you people of the land"—the LORD's declaration. "Work!

For I am with you"—the declaration of the LORD of Hosts. ⁵ "This is the promise I made to you when you came out of Egypt, and My Spirit is present among you; don't be afraid."

⁶ For the LORD of Hosts says this: "Once more, in a little while, I am going to shake the heavens and the earth, the sea and the dry land. ⁷ I will shake all the nations so that the treasures of all the nations will come, and I will fill this house with glory," says the LORD of Hosts. ⁸ "The silver and gold belong to Me"—the declaration of the LORD of Hosts. ⁹ "The final glory of this house will be greater than the first," says the LORD of Hosts. "I will provide peace in this place"—the declaration of the LORD of Hosts.

¹⁰ On the twenty-fourth day of the ninth month, in the second year of Darius, the word of the LORD came to Haggai the prophet: ¹¹ "This is what the LORD of Hosts says: Ask the priests for a ruling. ¹² If a man is carrying consecrated meat in the fold of his garment, and with his fold touches bread, stew, wine, oil, or any other food, does it become holy?"

The priests answered, "No."

¹³ Then Haggai asked, "If someone defiled by contact with a corpse touches any of these, does it become defiled?"

The priests answered, "It becomes defiled."

¹⁴ Then Haggai replied, "So is this people, and so is this nation before Me"—the LORD's declaration. "And so is every work of their hands; even what they offer there is defiled.

¹⁵ "Now, reflect back from this day: Before one stone was placed on another in the LORD's temple, ¹⁶ what state were you in? When someone came to a grain heap of 20 measures, it only amounted to 10; when one came to the winepress to dip 50 measures from the vat, it only amounted to 20. ¹⁷ I struck you—all the work of your hands—with blight, mildew, and hail, but you didn't turn to Me"—the LORD's declaration. ¹⁸ "Consider carefully from this day forward; from the twenty-fourth day of the ninth month, from the day the foundation of

the LORD's temple was laid; consider it carefully. ¹⁹ Is there still seed left in the granary? The vine, the fig, the pomegranate, and the olive tree have not yet produced. But from this day on I will bless you."

²⁰ The word of the LORD came to Haggai a second time on the twenty-fourth day of the month: ²¹ "Speak to Zerubbabel, governor of Judah: I am going to shake the heavens and the earth. ²² I will overturn royal thrones and destroy the power of the Gentile kingdoms. I will overturn chariots and their riders. Horses and their riders will fall, each by his brother's sword. ²³ On that day"—the declaration of the LORD of Hosts—"I will take you, Zerubbabel son of Shealtiel, My servant"—the LORD's declaration—"and make you like My signet ring, for I have chosen you." This is the declaration of the LORD of Hosts.

1 In the eighth month, in the second year of Darius, the word of the LORD came to the prophet Zechariah son of Berechiah, son of Iddo: ² "The LORD was extremely angry with your ancestors. ³ So tell the people: This is what the LORD of Hosts says: Return to Me"—this is the declaration of the LORD of Hosts—"and I will return to you, says the LORD of Hosts. ⁴ Do not be like your ancestors; the earlier prophets proclaimed to them: This is what the LORD of Hosts says: Turn from your evil ways and your evil deeds. But they did not listen or pay attention to Me"—the LORD's declaration. ⁵ "Where are your ancestors now? And do the prophets live forever? ⁶ But didn't My words and My statutes that I commanded My servants the prophets overtake your ancestors? They repented and said: As the LORD of Hosts purposed to deal with us for our ways and deeds, so He has dealt with us."

⁷ On the twenty-fourth day of the eleventh month, which is the month of Shebat, in the second year of Darius, the word of the LORD came to the prophet Zechariah son of Berechiah, son of Iddo:

⁸ I looked out in the night and saw a man riding on a red horse. He was

standing among the myrtle trees in the valley. Behind him were red, sorrel, and white horses. ⁹ I asked, "What are these, my lord?"

The angel who was talking to me replied, "I will show you what they are."

¹⁰ Then the man standing among the myrtle trees explained, "They are the ones the LORD has sent to patrol the earth."

¹¹ They reported to the Angel of the LORD standing among the myrtle trees, "We have patrolled the earth, and right now the whole earth is calm and quiet."

¹² Then the Angel of the LORD responded, "How long, LORD of Hosts, will You withhold mercy from Jerusalem and the cities of Judah that You have been angry with these 70 years?" ¹³ The LORD replied with kind and comforting words to the angel who was speaking with me.

¹⁴ So the angel who was speaking with me said, "Proclaim: The LORD of Hosts says: I am extremely jealous for Jerusalem and Zion. ¹⁵ I am fiercely angry with the nations that are at ease, for I was a little angry, but they made it worse. ¹⁶ Therefore, this is what the LORD says: I have graciously returned to Jerusalem; My house will be rebuilt within it"—the declaration of the LORD of Hosts—"and a measuring line will be stretched out over Jerusalem.

¹⁷ "Proclaim further: This is what the LORD of Hosts says: My cities will again overflow with prosperity; the LORD will once more comfort Zion and again choose Jerusalem."

¹⁸ Then I looked up and saw four horns. ¹⁹ So I asked the angel who was speaking with me, "What are these?"

And he said to me, "These are the horns that scattered Judah, Israel, and Jerusalem."

²⁰ Then the LORD showed me four craftsmen. ²¹ I asked, "What are they coming to do?"

He replied, "These are the horns that scattered Judah so no one could raise his head. These craftsmen have come to terrify them, to cut off the horns of the nations that raised their horns against the land of Judah to scatter it."

PSALM 147:15-20

15 He sends His command
   throughout the earth;
   His word runs swiftly.
16 He spreads snow like wool;
   He scatters frost like ashes;
17 He throws His hailstones like
   crumbs.
   Who can withstand His cold?
18 He sends His word and melts
   them;
   He unleashes His winds, and the
   waters flow.

19 He declares His word to Jacob,
   His statutes and judgments to
   Israel.
20 He has not done this for any
   nation;
   they do not know His judgments.
   Hallelujah!

PROVERBS 31:20-22

20 Her hands reach out to the poor,
   and she extends her hands to the
   needy.
21 She is not afraid for her
   household when it snows,
   for all in her household are doubly
   clothed.
22 She makes her own bed coverings;
   her clothing is fine linen and
   purple.

REVELATION 18:9-24

⁹ The kings of the earth who have committed sexual immorality and lived luxuriously with her will weep and mourn over her when they see the smoke of her burning. ¹⁰ They stand far off in fear of her torment, saying:

Woe, woe, the great city,
Babylon, the mighty city!
For in a single hour
your judgment has come.

¹¹ The merchants of the earth will also weep and mourn over her, because no one buys their merchandise any longer—

[12] merchandise of gold, silver, precious stones, and pearls; fine fabrics of linen, purple, silk, and scarlet; all kinds of fragrant wood products; objects of ivory; objects of expensive wood, brass, iron, and marble; [13] cinnamon, spice, incense, myrrh, and frankincense; wine, olive oil, fine wheat flour, and grain; cattle and sheep; horses and carriages; and human bodies and souls.

[14] The fruit you craved has left you.
All your splendid
and glamorous things
are gone;
they will never find them again.

[15] The merchants of these things, who became rich from her, will stand far off in fear of her torment, weeping and mourning, [16] saying:

Woe, woe, the great city,
clothed in fine linen, purple,
and scarlet,
adorned with gold,
precious stones, and pearls;
[17] because in a single hour
such fabulous wealth
was destroyed!

And every shipmaster, seafarer, the sailors, and all who do business by sea, stood far off [18] as they watched the smoke from her burning and kept crying out: "Who is like the great city?" [19] They threw dust on their heads and kept crying out, weeping, and mourning:

Woe, woe, the great city,
where all those who have ships
on the sea
became rich from her wealth;
because in a single hour
she was destroyed.
[20] Rejoice over her, heaven, and you
saints, apostles, and prophets,
because God has executed
your judgment on her!

[21] Then a mighty angel picked up a stone like a large millstone and threw it into the sea, saying:

In this way, Babylon the great city
will be thrown down violently
and never be found again.
[22] The sound of harpists, musicians,
flutists, and trumpeters
will never be heard in you again;
no craftsman of any trade
will ever be found in you again;
the sound of a mill
will never be heard in you again;
[23] the light of a lamp
will never shine in you again;
and the voice of a groom
and bride
will never be heard in you again.
All this will happen
because your merchants
were the nobility of the earth,
because all the nations
were deceived
by your sorcery,
[24] and the blood of prophets
and saints,
and all those slaughtered on earth,
was found in you.

The Divine Design

His word runs swiftly.—PSALM 147:15

When we come to God's Word, laying aside all preconceived ideas and depending entirely on the Holy Spirit to reveal its truth to us, we put ourselves in a position where the Holy Spirit can impress the truth of the Scriptures into our innermost being. There it takes root within us, and whenever we stand in need of a word with which to rebut the Devil, the Holy Spirit brings it to our remembrance.

And here's the most wonderful thing—the Word of God on our lips will have the same effect upon the Devil as if he were hearing it from the lips of Jesus Himself! Every time we open the Bible, we must be careful to pray for the illumination of the Spirit so that we don't finish up making the Bible say what we want it to say. When we receive that help, we are following the divine design—letting the Spirit bring home to our hearts the truth and meaning of His own Word.

This attitude of humility and receptivity gives the Holy Spirit the opportunity He needs to build the truth of the Word of God into our spirits. Approaching the Bible in this way, said the late J. B. Phillips, "is like rewiring a house where the electricity has not been turned off." As we read the Scriptures, we are touching something that has a current of power flowing through its pages—a power not put there by any man. The Holy Spirit has gone into it, so is it any wonder that the Holy Spirit comes out of it?

Prayer

My Father and my God, I know the Spirit dwells in Your Word. I come to ask that He might dwell also in me, to open up my whole being to the truth and power that lies in its inspired pages. In Jesus' name I ask it. Amen.

Further Study

Jn 14:26; 15:18-27; Lk 12:11-12; Rm 8:14
What did Jesus declare about the Holy Spirit's ministry?
What promise did Jesus give to His disciples?

DECEMBER 28

ZECHARIAH 2:1–6:15

2 I looked up and saw a man with a measuring line in his hand. ² I asked, "Where are you going?"

He answered me, "To measure Jerusalem to determine its width and length."

³ Then the angel who was speaking with me went out, and another angel went out to meet him. ⁴ He said to him, "Run and tell this young man: Jerusalem will be inhabited without walls because of the number of people and livestock in it." ⁵ The declaration of the LORD: "I will be a wall of fire around it, and I will be the glory within it."

⁶ "Get up! Leave the land of the north"—the LORD's declaration—"for I have scattered you like the four winds

of heaven"—the LORD's declaration. [7] "Go, Zion! Escape, you who are living with Daughter Babylon." [8] For the LORD of Hosts says this: "He has sent Me for His glory against the nations who are plundering you, for anyone who touches you touches the pupil of His eye. [9] I will move against them with My power, and they will become plunder for their own servants. Then you will know that the LORD of Hosts has sent Me.

[10] "Daughter Zion, shout for joy and be glad, for I am coming to dwell among you"—the LORD's declaration. [11] "Many nations will join themselves to the LORD on that day and become My people. I will dwell among you, and you will know that the LORD of Hosts has sent Me to you. [12] The LORD will take possession of Judah as His portion in the Holy Land, and He will once again choose Jerusalem. [13] Let all people be silent before the LORD, for He is coming from His holy dwelling."

3 Then he showed me Joshua the high priest standing before the Angel of the LORD, with Satan standing at his right side to accuse him. [2] The LORD said to Satan: "The LORD rebuke you, Satan! May the LORD who has chosen Jerusalem rebuke you! Isn't this man a burning stick snatched from the fire?"

[3] Now Joshua was dressed with filthy clothes as he stood before the Angel. [4] So He spoke to those standing before Him, "Take off his filthy clothes!" Then He said to him, "See, I have removed your guilt from you, and I will clothe you with splendid robes."

[5] Then I said, "Let them put a clean turban on his head." So a clean turban was placed on his head, and they clothed him in garments while the Angel of the LORD was standing nearby.

[6] Then the Angel of the LORD charged Joshua: [7] "This is what the LORD of Hosts says: If you walk in My ways and keep My instructions, you will both rule My house and take care of My courts; I will also grant you access among these who are standing here.

[8] "Listen, Joshua the high priest, you and your colleagues sitting before you;

indeed, these men are a sign that I am about to bring My servant, the Branch. [9] Notice the stone I have set before Joshua; on that one stone are seven eyes. I will engrave an inscription on it"—the declaration of the LORD of Hosts—"and I will take away the guilt of this land in a single day. [10] On that day, each of you will invite his neighbor to sit under his vine and fig tree." This is the declaration of the LORD of Hosts.

4 The angel who was speaking with me then returned and roused me as one awakened out of sleep. [2] He asked me, "What do you see?"

I replied, "I see a solid gold lampstand there with a bowl on its top. It has seven lamps on it and seven channels for each of the lamps on its top. [3] There are also two olive trees beside it, one on the right of the bowl and the other on its left."

[4] Then I asked the angel who was speaking with me, "What are these, my lord?"

[5] "Don't you know what they are?" replied the angel who was speaking with me.

I said, "No, my lord."

[6] So he answered me, "This is the word of the LORD to Zerubbabel: 'Not by strength or by might, but by My Spirit,' says the LORD of Hosts. [7] 'What are you, great mountain? Before Zerubbabel you will become a plain. And he will bring out the capstone accompanied by shouts of: Grace, grace to it!' "

[8] Then the word of the LORD came to me: [9] "Zerubbabel's hands have laid the foundation of this house, and his hands will complete it. Then you will know that the LORD of Hosts has sent me to you. [10] For who scorns the day of small things? These seven eyes of the LORD, which scan throughout the whole earth, will rejoice when they see the plumb line in Zerubbabel's hand."

[11] I asked him, "What are the two olive trees on the right and left of the lampstand?" [12] And I questioned him further, "What are the two olive branches beside the two gold conduits, from which golden oil pours out?"

¹³ Then he inquired of me, "Don't you know what these are?"

"No, my lord," I replied.

¹⁴ "These are the two anointed ones," he said, "who stand by the Lord of the whole earth."

5 I looked up again and saw a flying scroll. ² "What do you see?" he asked me.

"I see a flying scroll," I replied, "30 feet long and 15 feet wide."

³ Then he said to me, "This is the curse that is going out over the whole land, for every thief will be removed according to what is written on one side, and everyone who swears falsely will be removed according to what is written on the other side. ⁴ I will send it out,"— the declaration of the LORD of Hosts— "and it will enter the house of the thief and the house of the one who swears falsely by My name. It will stay inside his house and destroy it along with its timbers and stones."

⁵ Then the angel who was speaking with me came forward and told me, "Look up and see what this is that is approaching."

⁶ So I asked, "What is it?"

He responded, "It's a measuring basket that is approaching." And he continued, "This is their iniquity in all the land." ⁷ Then a lead cover was lifted, and there was a woman sitting inside the basket. ⁸ "This is Wickedness," he said. He shoved her down into the basket and pushed the lead weight over its opening. ⁹ Then I looked up and saw two women approaching with the wind in their wings. Their wings were like those of a stork, and they lifted up the basket between earth and sky.

¹⁰ So I asked the angel who was speaking with me, "Where are they taking the basket?"

¹¹ "To build a shrine for it in the land of Shinar," he told me. "When that is ready, the basket will be placed there on its pedestal."

6 Then I looked up again and saw four chariots coming from between two mountains. And the mountains were made of bronze. ² The first chariot had red horses, the second chariot black horses, ³ the third chariot white horses, and the fourth chariot dappled horses— all strong horses. ⁴ So I inquired of the angel who was speaking with me, "What are these, my lord?"

⁵ The angel told me, "These are the four spirits of heaven going out after presenting themselves to the Lord of the whole earth. ⁶ The one with the black horses is going to the land of the north, the white horses are going after them, but the dappled horses are going to the land of the south." ⁷ As the strong horses went out, they wanted to go patrol the earth, and the LORD said, "Go, patrol the earth." So they patrolled the earth. ⁸ Then He summoned me saying, "See, those going to the land of the north have pacified My Spirit in the northern land."

⁹ The word of the LORD came to me: ¹⁰ "Take an offering from the exiles, from Heldai, Tobijah, and Jedaiah, who have arrived from Babylon, and go that same day to the house of Josiah son of Zephaniah. ¹¹ Take silver and gold, make crowns and place them on the head of Joshua son of Jehozadak, the high priest. ¹² You are to tell him: This is what the LORD of Hosts says: Here is a man whose name is Branch; He will branch out from His place and build the LORD's temple. ¹³ Yes, He will build the LORD's temple; He will be clothed in splendor and will sit on His throne and rule. There will also be a priest on His throne, and there will be peaceful counsel between the two of them. ¹⁴ The crown will reside in the LORD's temple as a memorial to Heldai, Tobijah, Jedaiah, and Hen son of Zephaniah. ¹⁵ People who are far off will come and build the LORD's temple, and you will know that the LORD of Hosts has sent Me to you. This will happen when you fully obey the LORD your God."

PSALM 148:1-6

¹ Hallelujah!
Praise the LORD from the heavens;

praise Him in the heights.
2 Praise Him, all His angels;
praise Him, all His hosts.
3 Praise Him, sun and moon;
praise Him, all you shining stars.
4 Praise Him, highest heavens,
and you waters above the heavens.
5 Let them praise the name of the
LORD,
for He commanded, and they were
created.
6 He set them in position forever
and ever;
He gave an order that will never
pass away.

PROVERBS 31:23-25

23 Her husband is known at the city
gates,
where he sits among the elders of
the land.
24 She makes and sells linen garments;
she delivers belts to the merchants.
25 Strength and honor are her
clothing,
and she can laugh at the time to
come.

REVELATION 19:1-21

19 After this I heard something like
the loud voice of a vast multitude
in heaven, saying:

Hallelujah!
Salvation, glory, and power belong
to our God,
2 because His judgments are true
and righteous,
because He has judged
the notorious prostitute
who corrupted the earth
with her sexual immorality;
and He has avenged the blood
of His servants that was
on her hands.

3 A second time they said:

Hallelujah!
Her smoke ascends forever
and ever!

4 Then the 24 elders and the four living creatures fell down and worshiped God, who is seated on the throne, saying:

Amen! Hallelujah!

5 A voice came from the throne, saying:

Praise our God,
all you His servants,
you who fear Him,
both small and great!

6 Then I heard something like the voice of a vast multitude, like the sound of cascading waters, and like the rumbling of loud thunder, saying:

Hallelujah—because
our Lord God, the Almighty,
has begun to reign!
7 Let us be glad, rejoice,
and give Him glory,
because the marriage of the Lamb
has come,
and His wife has prepared herself.
8 She was permitted to wear
fine linen, bright and pure.

For the fine linen represents the righteous acts of the saints.
9 Then he said to me, "Write: Blessed are those invited to the marriage feast of the Lamb!" He also said to me, "These words of God are true." 10 Then I fell at his feet to worship him, but he said to me, "Don't do that! I am a fellow slave with you and your brothers who have the testimony about Jesus. Worship God, because the testimony about Jesus is the spirit of prophecy."
11 Then I saw heaven opened, and there was a white horse! Its rider is called Faithful and True, and in righteousness He judges and makes war. 12 His eyes were like a fiery flame, and on His head were many crowns. He had a name written that no one knows except Himself. 13 He wore a robe stained with blood, and His name is called the Word of God. 14 The armies that were in heaven followed Him on white horses,

wearing pure white linen. ¹⁵ From His mouth came a sharp sword, so that with it He might strike the nations. He will shepherd them with an iron scepter. He will also trample the winepress of the fierce anger of God, the Almighty. ¹⁶ And on His robe and on His thigh He has a name written:

> **KING OF KINGS**
> **AND LORD OF LORDS**

¹⁷ Then I saw an angel standing in the sun, and he cried out in a loud voice, saying to all the birds flying in mid-heaven, "Come, gather together for the great supper of God, ¹⁸ so that you may eat the flesh of kings, the flesh of commanders, the flesh of mighty men, the flesh of horses and of their riders, and the flesh of everyone, both free and slave, small and great."

¹⁹ Then I saw the beast, the kings of the earth, and their armies gathered together to wage war against the rider on the horse and against His army. ²⁰ But the beast was taken prisoner, and along with him the false prophet, who had performed signs on his authority, by which he deceived those who accepted the mark of the beast and those who worshiped his image. Both of them were thrown alive into the lake of fire that burns with sulfur. ²¹ The rest were killed with the sword that came from the mouth of the rider on the horse, and all the birds were filled with their flesh.

Is There a Personal Devil?

> *Then I saw the beast, the kings of the earth,*
> *and their armies gathered together*
> *to wage war against the rider on the horse*
> *and against His army.*—REVELATION **19:19**

Surprising as it may sound, some Christians do not believe in a personal devil. A modern-day theologian writes: "Let us put to sleep this idea of a personal devil who walks about with a pitchfork seeking to tumble people into hell. Evil is not a personality but an influence—it is just the darkness where the light ought to be."

While I agree that the picture of a personal devil walking about with a pitchfork and with horns and a tail is not to be found anywhere in Scripture, the concept of a personal devil is found everywhere in Scripture. One evidence of this is the fact that many of the names given to him denote his personality: Satan, deceiver, liar, murderer, accuser, tempter, prince of the power of the air, and so on. Listen to what someone has written on this subject:

Men don't believe in the Devil now, as their fathers used to do.
They reject one creed because it's old, for another because it's new.
But who dogs the steps of the toiling saint,
   who spreads the net for his feet?
Who sows the tares in the world's broad fields
   where the Savior sows His wheat?
They may say the Devil has never lived;
   they may say the Devil has gone,
But simple people would like to know—
   who carries his business on?

Take it from me, whether or not you believe in the Devil, he most certainly believes in you.

Prayer

Father, help me see that it is to Satan's advantage for me not to believe in him. Then he can do his evil work unresisted. Over these coming weeks, unfold to me the strategies I need to overcome him. In Christ's name I ask it. Amen.

Further Study

2 Co 11:1-14; 1 Th 3:5; 1 Pt 5:8; Rv 12:10; Jn 8:44
What are some of the guises in which Satan comes to us?
How does Peter describe him?

DECEMBER 29

ZECHARIAH 7:1–10:12

7 In the fourth year of King Darius, the word of the LORD came to Zechariah on the fourth day of the ninth month, which is Chislev. ² Now the people of Bethel had sent Sharezer, Regem-melech, and their men to plead for the LORD's favor ³ by asking the priests who were at the house of the LORD of Hosts as well as the prophets, "Should we mourn and fast in the fifth month as we have done these many years?"

⁴ Then the word of the LORD of Hosts came to me: ⁵ "Ask all the people of the land and the priests: When you fasted and lamented in the fifth and in the seventh months for these 70 years, did you really fast for Me? ⁶ When you eat and drink, don't you eat and drink simply for yourselves? ⁷ Aren't these the words that the LORD proclaimed through the earlier prophets when Jerusalem was inhabited and secure, along with its surrounding cities, and when the southern region and the Judean foothills were inhabited?"

⁸ The word of the LORD came to Zechariah: ⁹ "The LORD of Hosts says this: Render true justice. Show faithful love and compassion to one another. ¹⁰ Do not oppress the widow or the fatherless, the stranger or the poor, and do not plot evil in your hearts against one another. ¹¹ But they refused to pay attention and turned a stubborn shoulder; they closed their ears so they could not hear. ¹² They made their hearts like a rock so as not to obey the law and the words that the LORD of Hosts had sent by His Spirit through the earlier prophets. Therefore great anger came from the LORD of Hosts. ¹³ Just as He had called, and they would not listen, so when they called, I would not listen," says the LORD of Hosts. ¹⁴ "I scattered them with a windstorm over all the nations that had not known them, and the land was left desolate behind them, with no one coming or going. They turned a pleasant land into a desolation."

8 The word of the LORD of Hosts came: ² "The LORD of Hosts says

this: I am extremely jealous for Zion; I am jealous for her with great wrath." ³ The LORD says this: "I will return to Zion and live in Jerusalem. Then Jerusalem will be called the Faithful City, the mountain of the LORD of Hosts, and the Holy Mountain." ⁴ The LORD of Hosts says this: "Old men and women will again sit along the streets of Jerusalem, each with a staff in hand because of advanced age. ⁵ The streets of the city will be filled with boys and girls playing in them." ⁶ The LORD of Hosts says this: "Though it may seem incredible to the remnant of this people in those days, should it also seem incredible to Me?"—the declaration of the LORD of Hosts. ⁷ The LORD of Hosts says this: "I will save My people from the land of the east and the land of the west. ⁸ I will bring them back to live in Jerusalem. They will be My people, and I will be their faithful and righteous God."

⁹ The LORD of Hosts says this: "Let your hands be strong, you who now hear these words that the prophets spoke when the foundations were laid for the rebuilding of the temple, the house of the LORD of Hosts. ¹⁰ For prior to those days neither man nor beast had wages. There was no safety from the enemy for anyone who came or went, for I turned everyone against his neighbor. ¹¹ But now, I will not treat the remnant of this people as in the former days"—the declaration of the LORD of Hosts. ¹² "For they will sow in peace: the vine will yield its fruit, the land will yield its produce, and the skies will yield their dew. I will give the remnant of this people all these things as an inheritance. ¹³ As you have been a curse among the nations, house of Judah and house of Israel, so I will save you, and you will be a blessing. Don't be afraid; let your hands be strong." ¹⁴ For the LORD of Hosts says this: "As I resolved to treat you badly when your fathers provoked Me to anger, and would not relent," says the LORD of Hosts, ¹⁵ "so I have resolved again in these days to do what is good to Jerusalem and the house of Judah. Don't be afraid. ¹⁶ These

are the things you must do: Speak truth to one another; render honest and peaceful judgments in your gates. ¹⁷ Do not plot evil in your hearts against your neighbor, and do not love perjury, for I hate all this"— the LORD's declaration.

¹⁸ Then the word of the LORD of Hosts came to me: ¹⁹ "The LORD of Hosts says this: The fast of the fourth month, the fast of the fifth, the fast of the seventh, and the fast of the tenth will become times of joy, gladness, and cheerful festivals for the house of Judah. Therefore, love truth and peace." ²⁰ The LORD of Hosts says this: "Peoples will yet come, the residents of many cities; ²¹ the residents of one city will go to another, saying: Let's go at once to plead for the LORD's favor and to seek the LORD of Hosts. I am also going. ²² Many peoples and strong nations will come to seek the LORD of Hosts in Jerusalem and to plead for the LORD's favor." ²³ The LORD of Hosts says this: "In those days, 10 men from nations of every language will grab the robe of a Jewish man tightly, urging: Let us go with you, for we have heard that God is with you."

9   An Oracle

The word of the LORD
is against the land of Hadrach,
and Damascus is its resting
    place—
for the eyes of men
and all the tribes of Israel
are on the LORD—
² and also against Hamath, which
    borders it,
as well as Tyre and Sidon,
though they are very shrewd.
³ Tyre has built herself a fortress;
she has heaped up silver like dust
and gold like the dirt of the
    streets.
⁴ Listen! The Lord will impoverish
    her
and cast her wealth into the sea;
she herself will be consumed by
    fire.
⁵ Ashkelon will see it and be afraid;
Gaza too, and will writhe in great
    pain,

as will Ekron, for her hope will
   fail.
There will cease to be a king in
   Gaza,
and Ashkelon will become
   uninhabited.
⁶ A mongrel people will live in
   Ashdod,
and I will destroy the pride of the
   Philistines.
⁷ I will remove the blood from their
   mouths
and the detestable things
from between their teeth.
Then they too will become a
   remnant for our God;
they will become like a clan in
   Judah
and Ekron like the Jebusites.
⁸ I will set up camp at My house
   against an army,
against those who march back and
   forth,
and no oppressor will march
   against them again,
for now I have seen with My own
   eyes.

⁹ Rejoice greatly, Daughter Zion!
Shout in triumph, Daughter
   Jerusalem!
See, your King is coming to you;
He is righteous and victorious,
humble and riding on a donkey,
on a colt, the foal of a donkey.
¹⁰ I will cut off the chariot from
   Ephraim
and the horse from Jerusalem.
The bow of war will be removed,
and He will proclaim peace to the
   nations.
His dominion will extend from sea
   to sea,
from the Euphrates River
to the ends of the earth.
¹¹ As for you,
because of the blood of your
   covenant,
I will release your prisoners
from the waterless cistern.
¹² Return to a stronghold,
you prisoners who have hope;
today I declare that I will restore
   double to you.

¹³ For I will bend Judah as My bow;
I will fill that bow with Ephraim.
I will rouse your sons, Zion,
against your sons, Greece.
I will make you like a warrior's
   sword.
¹⁴ Then the LORD will appear over
   them,
and His arrow will fly like
   lightning.
The Lord GOD will sound the
   trumpet
and advance with the southern
   storms.
¹⁵ The LORD of Hosts will defend
   them.
They will consume and conquer
   with slingstones;
they will drink and be rowdy as if
   with wine.
They will be as full as the
   sprinkling basin,
like those at the corners of the
   altar.
¹⁶ The LORD their God will save them
   on that day
as the flock of His people;
for they are like jewels in a crown,
sparkling over His land.
¹⁷ How lovely and beautiful they will
   be!
Grain will make the young men
   flourish,
and new wine, the young women.

10 Ask the LORD for rain
   in the season of spring rain.
The LORD makes the rain clouds,
and He will give them showers of
   rain
and crops in the field for everyone.
² For the idols speak falsehood,
and the diviners see illusions;
they relate empty dreams
and offer empty comfort.
Therefore the people wander like
   sheep;
they suffer affliction because
   there is no shepherd.
³ My anger burns against the
   shepherds,
so I will punish the leaders.
For the LORD of Hosts has tended
   His flock,

the house of Judah;
He will make them like His
majestic steed in battle.
4 From them will come the
cornerstone,
from them the tent peg,
from them the battle bow,
from them every ruler.
Together ⁵they will be like
warriors in battle
trampling down the mud of the
streets.
They will fight because the LORD
is with them,
and they will put horsemen to
shame.
6 I will strengthen the house of
Judah
and deliver the house of Joseph.
I will restore them
because I have compassion on
them,
and they will be
as though I had never rejected
them.
For I am the LORD their God,
and I will answer them.
7 Ephraim will be like a warrior,
and their hearts will be glad as if
with wine.
Their children will see it and be
glad;
their hearts will rejoice in the LORD.

8 I will whistle and gather them
because I have redeemed them;
they will be as numerous as they
once were.
9 Though I sow them among the
nations,
they will remember Me in the
distant lands;
they and their children will live
and return.
10 I will bring them back from the
land of Egypt
and gather them from Assyria.
I will bring them to the land of
Gilead
and to Lebanon,
but it will not be enough for
them.
11 He will pass through the sea of
distress

and strike the waves of the sea;
all the depths of the Nile will
dry up.
The pride of Assyria will be
brought down,
and the scepter of Egypt will come
to an end.
12 I will strengthen them in the LORD,
and they will march in His
name—
this is Yahweh's declaration.

PSALM 148:7-14

7 Praise the LORD from the earth,
all sea monsters and ocean depths,
8 lightning and hail, snow and
cloud,
powerful wind that executes His
command,
9 mountains and all hills,
fruit trees and all cedars,
10 wild animals and all cattle,
creatures that crawl and flying
birds,
11 kings of the earth and all peoples,
princes and all judges of the earth,
12 young men as well as young
women,
old and young together.
13 Let them praise the name of the
LORD,
for His name alone is exalted.
His majesty covers heaven and
earth.
14 He has raised up a horn for His
people,
praise from all His godly ones,
from the Israelites, the people
close to Him.
Hallelujah!

PROVERBS 31:26-27

26 She opens her mouth with
wisdom,
and loving instruction is on her
tongue.
27 She watches over the activities of
her household
and is never idle.

REVELATION 20:1–21:4

20 Then I saw an angel coming down from heaven with the key to the abyss and a great chain in his hand. ² He seized the dragon, that ancient serpent who is the Devil and Satan, and bound him for 1,000 years. ³ He threw him into the abyss, closed it, and put a seal on it so that he would no longer deceive the nations until the 1,000 years were completed. After that, he must be released for a short time.

⁴ Then I saw thrones, and people seated on them who were given authority to judge. I also saw the souls of those who had been beheaded because of their testimony about Jesus and because of God's word, who had not worshiped the beast or his image, and who had not accepted the mark on their foreheads or their hands. They came to life and reigned with the Messiah for 1,000 years. ⁵ The rest of the dead did not come to life until the 1,000 years were completed. This is the first resurrection. ⁶ Blessed and holy is the one who shares in the first resurrection! The second death has no power over these, but they will be priests of God and the Messiah, and they will reign with Him for 1,000 years.

⁷ When the 1,000 years are completed, Satan will be released from his prison ⁸ and will go out to deceive the nations at the four corners of the earth, Gog and Magog, to gather them for battle. Their number is like the sand of the sea. ⁹ They came up over the surface of the earth and surrounded the encampment of the saints, the beloved city. Then fire came down from heaven and consumed them. ¹⁰ The Devil who deceived them was thrown into the lake of fire and sulfur where the beast and the false prophet are, and they will be tormented day and night forever and ever.

¹¹ Then I saw a great white throne and One seated on it. Earth and heaven fled from His presence, and no place was found for them. ¹² I also saw the dead, the great and the small, standing before the throne, and books were opened. Another book was opened, which is the book of life, and the dead were judged according to their works by what was written in the books.

¹³ Then the sea gave up its dead, and Death and Hades gave up their dead; all were judged according to their works. ¹⁴ Death and Hades were thrown into the lake of fire. This is the second death, the lake of fire. ¹⁵ And anyone not found written in the book of life was thrown into the lake of fire.

21 Then I saw a new heaven and a new earth, for the first heaven and the first earth had passed away, and the sea existed no longer. ² I also saw the Holy City, new Jerusalem, coming down out of heaven from God, prepared like a bride adorned for her husband.

³ Then I heard a loud voice from the throne:

> Look! God's dwelling is with men,
> and He will live with them.
> They will be His people,
> and God Himself will be
>   with them and be their God.
> ⁴ He will wipe away every tear
>   from their eyes.
> Death will exist no longer;
> grief, crying, and pain will exist
>   no longer,
> because the previous things
>   have passed away.

Kindness and Generosity

She opens her mouth with wisdom,
and loving instruction is on her tongue.—Proverbs 31:26

The fifth fruit of the Spirit is kindness. In the unforgettable description of a model wife in Proverbs 31, there is this statement: "She opens her mouth with wisdom, and loving instruction is on her tongue" (v. 26). Note the use of the word "loving." A model wife passes an inner law in the legislature of her personality that everything she says and does will be loving. Kindness is not something set in her emotions—it is set in her will and thus becomes a life attitude. May we, on bended knee, this day pass the same law in the legislature of our own hearts and so come under its sway forever.

The sixth fruit of the Spirit is goodness. The Greek word *agathosune* means, according to the experts, "kindness at work." This is why the word is best understood as it is sometimes translated: "generosity." This leads us to an interesting statement which Jesus once made: "If your Eye is generous, the whole of your body will be illumined" (Mt 6:22, Moffatt). If your "Eye" (your outlook on life, your whole way of looking at things) is generous, then your whole personality will be illuminated or lit up.

Jesus was generous toward everyone—the poor, the meek, the sinful and the unlovely—and His whole personality was full of light. By the ministry of the Holy Spirit, this characteristic of Jesus is generated in us—if we let it. And when we do, then we begin to see everyone with "the generous Eye."

Prayer

Lord Jesus, your generous Eye saw in me something that wasn't there—and then it was there! Help me to thus create what I see in others. For Your own dear name's sake. Amen.

Further Study

2 Pt 1; Rm 12:10; 1 Co 13:4; Eph 4:32; Col 3:12
From what does kindness flow out?
How can you show kindness today?

DECEMBER 30

ZECHARIAH 11:1–14:21

11 Open your gates, Lebanon, and fire will consume your cedars.

² Wail, cypress, for the cedar has fallen;
the glorious trees are destroyed!
Wail, oaks of Bashan,
for the stately forest has fallen!

³ Listen to the wail of the shepherds,
for their glory is destroyed.
Listen to the roar of young lions,
for the thickets of the Jordan are
destroyed.

⁴ The LORD my God says this: "Shepherd the flock intended for slaughter. ⁵ Those who buy them slaughter them but are not punished. Those who sell them say: Praise the LORD because I have become rich! Even their own shepherds have no compassion for them. ⁶ Indeed, I will no longer have compassion on the inhabitants of the land"— the LORD's declaration. "Instead, I will turn everyone over to his neighbor and his king. They will devastate the land, and I will not deliver it from them."

⁷ So I shepherded the flock intended for slaughter, the afflicted of the flock. I took two staffs, calling one Favor and the other Union, and I shepherded the flock. ⁸ In one month I got rid of three shepherds. I became impatient with them, and they also detested me. ⁹ Then I said, "I will no longer shepherd you. Let what is dying die, and let what is going astray go astray; let the rest devour each other's flesh." ¹⁰ Next I took my staff called Favor and cut it in two, annulling the covenant I had made with all the peoples. ¹¹ It was annulled on that day, and so the afflicted of the flock who were watching me knew that it was the word of the LORD. ¹² Then I said to them, "If it seems right to you, give me

my wages; but if not, keep them." So they weighed my wages, 30 pieces of silver.

¹³ "Throw it to the potter," the LORD said to me—this magnificent price I was valued by them. So I took the 30 pieces of silver and threw it into the house of the LORD, to the potter. ¹⁴ Then I cut in two my second staff, Union, annulling the brotherhood between Judah and Israel.

¹⁵ The LORD also said to me: "Take the equipment of a foolish shepherd. ¹⁶ I am about to raise up a shepherd in the land who will not care for those who are going astray, and he will not seek the lost or heal the broken. He will not sustain the healthy, but he will devour the flesh of the fat sheep and tear off their hooves.

¹⁷ Woe to the worthless shepherd
who deserts the flock!
May a sword strike his arm
and his right eye!
May his arm wither away
and his right eye go completely
blind!"

12 An Oracle

The word of the LORD concerning
Israel.
A declaration of the LORD,
who stretched out the heavens,
laid the foundation of the earth,
and formed the spirit of man
within him.

² "Look, I will make Jerusalem a cup that causes staggering for the peoples who surround the city. The siege against Jerusalem will also involve Judah. ³ On that day I will make Jerusalem a heavy stone for all the peoples; all who try to lift it will injure themselves severely when all the

nations of the earth gather against her. [4] On that day"—the LORD's declaration—"I will strike every horse with panic and its rider with madness. I will keep a watchful eye on the house of Judah but strike all the horses of the nations with blindness. [5] Then each of the leaders of Judah will think to himself: The residents of Jerusalem are my strength through the LORD of Hosts, their God. [6] On that day I will make the leaders of Judah like a firepot in a woodpile, like a flaming torch among sheaves; they will consume all the peoples around them on the right and the left, while Jerusalem continues to be inhabited on its site, in Jerusalem. [7] The LORD will save the tents of Judah first, so that the glory of David's house and the glory of Jerusalem's residents may not be greater than that of Judah. [8] On that day the LORD will defend the inhabitants of Jerusalem, so that the one who is weakest among them will be like David on that day, and the house of David will be like God, like the Angel of the LORD, before them. [9] On that day I will set out to destroy all the nations that come against Jerusalem.

[10] "Then I will pour out a spirit of grace and prayer on the house of David and the residents of Jerusalem, and they will look at Me whom they pierced. They will mourn for Him as one mourns for an only child and weep bitterly for Him as one weeps for a firstborn. [11] On that day the mourning in Jerusalem will be as great as the mourning of Hadad-rimmon in the plain of Megiddo. [12] The land will mourn, every family by itself: the family of David's house by itself and their women by themselves; the family of Nathan's house by itself and their women by themselves; [13] the family of Levi's house by itself and their women by themselves; the family of Shimei by itself and their women by themselves; [14] all the remaining families, every family by itself, and their women by themselves.

13 "On that day a fountain will be opened for the house of David and for the residents of Jerusalem, to wash away sin and impurity. [2] On that day"—the declaration of the LORD of Hosts—"I will erase the names of the idols from the land, and they will no longer be remembered. I will remove the prophets and the unclean spirit from the land. [3] If a man still prophesies, his father and his mother who bore him will say to him: You cannot remain alive because you have spoken falsely in the name of the LORD. When he prophesies, his father and his mother who bore him will pierce him through. [4] On that day every prophet will be ashamed of his vision when he prophesies; they will not put on a hairy cloak in order to deceive. [5] He will say: I am not a prophet; I am a tiller of the soil, for a man purchased me as a servant since my youth. [6] If someone asks him: What are these wounds on your chest?—then he will answer: The wounds I received in the house of my friends.

[7] Sword, awake against My
          shepherd,
    against the man who is My
          associate—
    the declaration of the LORD of Hosts.
    Strike the shepherd, and the
          sheep will be scattered;
    I will also turn My hand against
          the little ones.
[8] In the whole land—
          the LORD's declaration—
    two-thirds will be cut off and die,
    but a third will be left in it.
[9] I will put this third through the
          fire;
    I will refine them as silver is
          refined
    and test them as gold is tested.
    They will call on My name,
    and I will answer them.
    I will say: They are My people,
    and they will say: The LORD is our
          God."

14 A day of the LORD is coming when your plunder will be divided in your presence. [2] I will gather all the nations against Jerusalem for battle. The city will be captured, the houses looted, and the women raped. Half the city will go into exile, but the rest of the people will not be removed from the city.

³ Then the LORD will go out to fight against those nations as He fights on a day of battle. ⁴ On that day His feet will stand on the Mount of Olives, which faces Jerusalem on the east. The Mount of Olives will be split in half from east to west, forming a huge valley, so that half the mountain will move to the north and half to the south. ⁵ You will flee by My mountain valley, for the valley of the mountains will extend to Azal. You will flee as you fled from the earthquake in the days of Uzziah king of Judah. Then the LORD my God will come and all the holy ones with Him.

⁶ On that day there will be no light; the sunlight and moonlight will diminish. ⁷ It will be a day known only to Yahweh, without day or night, but there will be light at evening.

⁸ On that day living water will flow out from Jerusalem, half of it toward the eastern sea and the other half toward the western sea, in summer and winter alike. ⁹ On that day Yahweh will become king over all the earth—Yahweh alone, and His name alone. ¹⁰ All the land from Geba to Rimmon south of Jerusalem will be changed into a plain. But Jerusalem will be raised up and will remain on its site from the Benjamin Gate to the place of the First Gate, to the Corner Gate, and from the Tower of Hananel to the royal winepresses. ¹¹ People will live there, and never again will there be a curse of destruction. So Jerusalem will dwell in security.

¹² This will be the plague the LORD strikes all the peoples with, who have warred against Jerusalem: their flesh will rot while they stand on their feet, their eyes will rot in their sockets, and their tongues will rot in their mouths. ¹³ On that day a great panic from the LORD will be among them, so that each will seize the hand of another, and the hand of one will rise against the other. ¹⁴ Judah will also fight at Jerusalem, and the wealth of all the surrounding nations will be collected: gold, silver, and

clothing in great abundance. ¹⁵ The same plague as the previous one will strike the horses, mules, camels, donkeys, and all the animals that are in those camps.

¹⁶ Then all the survivors from the nations that came against Jerusalem will go up year after year to worship the King, the LORD of Hosts, and to celebrate the Festival of Booths. ¹⁷ Should any of the families of the earth not go up to Jerusalem to worship the King, the LORD of Hosts, rain will not fall on them. ¹⁸ And if the people of Egypt will not go up and enter, then rain will not fall on them; this will be the plague the LORD inflicts on the nations who do not go up to celebrate the Festival of Booths. ¹⁹ This will be the punishment of Egypt and all the nations that do not go up to celebrate the Festival of Booths.

²⁰ On that day, the words

> **HOLY TO THE LORD**

will be on the bells of the horses. The pots in the house of the LORD will be like the sprinkling basins before the altar. ²¹ Every pot in Jerusalem and in Judah will be holy to the LORD of Hosts. Everyone who sacrifices will come and take some of the pots to cook in. And on that day there will no longer be a Canaanite in the house of the LORD of Hosts.

𝒫SALM 149:1-9

¹ Hallelujah!
   Sing to the LORD a new song,
   His praise in the assembly of the
      godly.
² Let Israel celebrate its Maker;
   let the children of Zion rejoice in
      their King.
³ Let them praise His name with
      dancing
   and make music to Him with
      tambourine and lyre.
⁴ For the LORD takes pleasure in His
      people;

He adorns the humble with
salvation.
5 Let the godly celebrate in
triumphal glory;
let them shout for joy on their beds.

6 Let the exaltation of God be in
their mouths
and a two-edged sword in their
hands,
7 inflicting vengeance on the
nations
and punishment on the peoples,
8 binding their kings with chains
and their dignitaries with iron
shackles,
9 carrying out the judgment
decreed against them.
This honor is for all His godly
people.
Hallelujah!

PROVERBS 31:28-29

28 Her sons rise up and call her
blessed.
Her husband also praises her:
29 "Many women are capable,
but you surpass them all!"

REVELATION 21:5-27

5 Then the One seated on the throne
said, "Look! I am making everything
new." He also said, "Write, because
these words are faithful and true." 6 And
He said to me, "It is done! I am the
Alpha and the Omega, the Beginning
and the End. I will give to the thirsty
from the spring of living water as a gift.
7 The victor will inherit these things,
and I will be his God, and he will be My
son. 8 But the cowards, unbelievers,
vile, murderers, sexually immoral, sorcerers, idolaters, and all liars—their
share will be in the lake that burns with
fire and sulfur, which is the second
death."

9 Then one of the seven angels, who
had held the seven bowls filled with the
seven last plagues, came and spoke with
me: "Come, I will show you the bride,
the wife of the Lamb." 10 He then car-

ried me away in the Spirit to a great and
high mountain and showed me the holy
city, Jerusalem, coming down out of
heaven from God, 11 arrayed with God's
glory. Her radiance was like a very precious stone, like a jasper stone, bright as
crystal. 12 The city had a massive high
wall, with 12 gates. Twelve angels were
at the gates; on the gates, names were
inscribed, the names of the 12 tribes of
the sons of Israel. 13 There were three
gates on the east, three gates on the
north, three gates on the south, and
three gates on the west. 14 The city wall
had 12 foundations, and on them were
the 12 names of the Lamb's 12 apostles.

15 The one who spoke with me had a
gold measuring rod to measure the city,
its gates, and its wall. 16 The city is laid
out in a square; its length and width are
the same. He measured the city with
the rod at 12,000 stadia. Its length,
width, and height are equal. 17 Then he
measured its wall, 144 cubits according
to human measurement, which the angel used. 18 The building material of its
wall was jasper, and the city was pure
gold like clear glass.

19 The foundations of the city wall
were adorned with every kind of precious stone:

the first foundation jasper,
the second sapphire,
the third chalcedony,
the fourth emerald,
20 the fifth sardonyx,
the sixth carnelian,
the seventh chrysolite,
the eighth beryl,
the ninth topaz,
the tenth chrysoprase,
the eleventh jacinth,
the twelfth amethyst.

21 The 12 gates are 12 pearls; each individual gate was made of a single pearl.
The broad street of the city was pure
gold, like transparent glass.

22 I did not see a sanctuary in it, because the Lord God the Almighty and
the Lamb are its sanctuary. 23 The city
does not need the sun or the moon to
shine on it, because God's glory illumi-

nates it, and its lamp is the Lamb. ²⁴ The nations will walk in its light, and the kings of the earth will bring their glory into it. ²⁵ Each day its gates will never close because it will never be night there. ²⁶ They will bring the glory and honor of the nations into it. ²⁷ Nothing profane will ever enter it: no one who does what is vile or false, but only those written in the Lamb's book of life.

Subdued Puppies?

For the LORD takes pleasure in His people;
He adorns the humble with salvation.
—PSALM 149:4

Part of Christ's prescription for happiness is "Blessed are the meek, for they shall inherit the earth" (Mt 5:5, KJV). How we have shied away from that word "meek." We have thought of meekness as a weakness and thus have a totally wrong concept of what Jesus meant. *The Amplified Bible* translates it thus: "Blessed are the meek (the mild, patient, long-suffering), for they shall inherit the earth." The dictionary defines "meek" as "humble, compliant, and submissive". Does this mean that Jesus expects the children of the kingdom to be like subdued puppies who crawl into their master's presence and cower at his feet? Or to become the type of people who lack inner fortitude and gumption, who can be easily pushed around and manipulated?

The truly meek person—in the biblical sense of the word—is not timid, shy, hesitant, and unassuming, but trusting, confident, and secure. The root meaning of the word "meekness" is that of yieldedness or surrender—a characteristic without which no real progress can be made in the Christian life. What happens, for example, to the scientist who approaches the mysteries of the universe in a spirit of meekness? He finds its richest secrets unfolding themselves to him, and he is able to harness the mighty forces around him to advantage. The Christian who approaches life in the same spirit—the spirit of meekness and submission—discovers the true meaning of his existence and the purpose of God in all his affairs.

Prayer

Gracious Father, help me to understand clearly the difference between meekness and weakness. And show me how to apply this principle in all I say and in all I do. This I ask in Christ's powerful and precious name. Amen.

Further Study

Jms 1:12-21; Zph 2:3; Gl 5:22-23; 1 Pt 3:4
What are we to receive with meekness?
Does the biblical definition of meekness fit you?

DECEMBER 31

MALACHI 1:1–4:6

1 An oracle: The word of the LORD to Israel through Malachi.

² "I have loved you," says the LORD.

But you ask: "How have You loved us?"

"Wasn't Esau Jacob's brother?" This is the LORD's declaration. "Even so, I loved Jacob, ³ but I hated Esau. I turned his mountains into a wasteland, and gave his inheritance to the desert jackals."

⁴ Though Edom says: "We have been devastated, but we will rebuild the ruins," the LORD of Hosts says this: "They may build, but I will demolish. They will be called a wicked country and the people the LORD has cursed forever. ⁵ Your own eyes will see this, and you yourselves will say: The LORD is great, even beyond the borders of Israel.

⁶ "A son honors his father, and a servant his master. But if I am a father, where is My honor? And if I am a master, where is your fear of Me? says the LORD of Hosts to you priests, who despise My name."

Yet you ask: "How have we despised Your name?"

⁷ "By presenting defiled food on My altar."

You ask: "How have we defiled You?"

When you say: "The LORD's table is contemptible."

⁸ "When you present a blind animal for sacrifice, is it not wrong? And when you present a lame or sick animal, is it not wrong? Bring it to your governor! Would he be pleased with you or show you favor?" asks the LORD of Hosts. ⁹ "And now ask for God's favor. Will He be gracious to us? Since this has come from your hands, will He show any of you favor?" asks the LORD of Hosts. ¹⁰ "I wish one of you would shut the temple doors, so you would no longer kindle a useless fire on My altar! I am not pleased with you," says the LORD of Hosts, "and I will accept no offering from your hands.

¹¹ "For My name will be great among the nations, from the rising of the sun to its setting. Incense and pure offerings will be presented in My name in every place because My name will be great among the nations," says the LORD of Hosts.

¹² But you are profaning it when you say: "The Lord's table is defiled, and its product, its food, is contemptible." ¹³ You also say: "Look, what a nuisance!" "And you scorn it," says the LORD of Hosts. "You bring stolen, lame, or sick animals. You bring this as an offering! Am I to accept that from your hands?" asks the LORD.

¹⁴ "The deceiver is cursed who has an acceptable male in his flock and makes a vow but sacrifices a defective animal to the Lord. For I am a great King," says the LORD of Hosts, "and My name will be feared among the nations.

2 "Therefore, this decree is for you priests: ² If you don't listen, and if you don't take it to heart to honor My name," says the LORD of Hosts, "I will send a curse among you, and I will curse your blessings. In fact, I have already begun to curse them because you are not taking it to heart.

³ "Look, I am going to rebuke your descendants, and I will spread animal waste over your faces, the waste from your festival sacrifices, and you will be taken away with it. ⁴ Then you will know that I sent you this decree so My covenant with Levi may continue," says the LORD of Hosts. ⁵ "My covenant with him was one of life and peace, and I gave these to him; it called for reverence, and he revered Me and stood in awe of My name. ⁶ True instruction was

in his mouth, and nothing wrong was found on his lips. He walked with Me in peace and fairness and turned many from sin. [7] For the lips of a priest should guard knowledge, and people should seek instruction from his mouth, because he is the messenger of the LORD of Hosts.

[8] "You, on the other hand, have turned from the way. You have caused many to stumble by your instruction. You have violated the covenant of Levi," says the LORD of Hosts. [9] "So I in turn have made you despised and humiliated before all the people because you are not keeping My ways but are showing partiality in your instruction."

[10] Don't all of us have one Father? Didn't one God create us? Why then do we act treacherously against one another, profaning the covenant of our fathers? [11] Judah has acted treacherously, and a detestable thing has been done in Israel and in Jerusalem. For Judah has profaned the LORD's sanctuary, which He loves, and has married the daughter of a foreign god. [12] To the man who does this, may the LORD cut off any descendants from the tents of Jacob, even if they present an offering to the LORD of Hosts.

[13] And this is another thing you do: you cover the LORD's altar with tears, with weeping and groaning, because He no longer respects your offerings or receives them gladly from your hands. [14] Yet you ask, "For what reason?" Because the LORD has been a witness between you and the wife of your youth. You have acted treacherously against her, though she was your marriage partner and your wife by covenant. [15] Didn't the one God make us with a remnant of His life-breath? And what does the One seek? A godly offspring. So watch yourselves carefully, and do not act treacherously against the wife of your youth.

[16] "If he hates and divorces his wife," says the LORD God of Israel, "he covers his garment with injustice," says the LORD of Hosts. Therefore, watch yourselves carefully, and do not act treacherously.

[17] You have wearied the LORD with your words.

Yet you ask, "How have we wearied Him?"

When you say, "Everyone who does evil is good in the LORD's sight, and He is pleased with them," or "Where is the God of justice?"

3 "See, I am going to send My messenger, and he will clear the way before Me. Then the Lord you seek will suddenly come to His temple, the Messenger of the covenant you desire—see, He is coming," says the LORD of Hosts. [2] But who can endure the day of His coming? And who will be able to stand when He appears? For He will be like a refiner's fire and like cleansing lye. [3] He will be like a refiner and purifier of silver; He will purify the sons of Levi and refine them like gold and silver. Then they will present offerings to the LORD in righteousness. [4] And the offerings of Judah and Jerusalem will please the LORD as in days of old and years gone by.

[5] "I will come to you in judgment, and I will be ready to witness against sorcerers and adulterers; against those who swear falsely; against those who oppress the widow and the fatherless, and cheat the wage earner; and against those who deny justice to the foreigner. They do not fear Me," says the LORD of Hosts. [6] "Because I, Yahweh, have not changed, you descendants of Jacob have not been destroyed.

[7] "Since the days of your fathers, you have turned from My statutes; you have not kept them. Return to Me, and I will return to you," says the LORD of Hosts.

But you ask: "How can we return?"

[8] "Will a man rob God? Yet you are robbing Me!"

You ask: "How do we rob You?"

"By not making the payments of 10 percent and the contributions. [9] You are suffering under a curse, yet you—the whole nation—are still robbing Me. [10] Bring the full 10 percent into the storehouse so that there may be food in My house. Test Me in this way," says the LORD of Hosts. "See if I will not open the floodgates of heaven and pour out a blessing for you without measure. ¹¹ I will rebuke the devourer for you, so that it will not ruin the produce of your ground, and your vine in your field will not be barren," says the LORD of Hosts. ¹² "Then all the nations will consider you fortunate, for you will be a delightful land," says the LORD of Hosts.

¹³ "Your words against Me are harsh," says the LORD.

Yet you ask: "What have we spoken against You?"

¹⁴ You have said: "It is useless to serve God. What have we gained by keeping His requirements and walking mournfully before the LORD of Hosts? ¹⁵ So now we consider the arrogant to be fortunate. Not only do those who commit wickedness prosper, they even test God and escape."

¹⁶ At that time those who feared the LORD spoke to one another. The LORD took notice and listened. So a book of remembrance was written before Him for those who feared Yahweh and had high regard for His name. ¹⁷ "They will be Mine," says the LORD of Hosts, "a special possession on the day I am preparing. I will have compassion on them as a man has compassion on his son who serves him. ¹⁸ So you will again see the difference between the righteous and the wicked, between one who serves God and one who does not serve Him.

4 "For indeed, the day is coming, burning like a furnace, when all the arrogant and everyone who commits wickedness will become stubble. The coming day will consume them," says the LORD of Hosts, "not leaving them root or branches. ² But for you who fear My name, the sun of righteousness will rise with healing in its wings, and you will go out and playfully jump like calves from the stall. ³ You will trample the wicked, for they will be ashes under the soles of your feet on the day I am preparing," says the LORD of Hosts.

⁴ "Remember the instruction of Moses My servant, the statutes and ordinances I commanded him at Horeb for all Israel. ⁵ Look, I am going to send you

Elijah the prophet before the great and awesome Day of the LORD comes. ⁶ And he will turn the hearts of fathers to their children and the hearts of children to their fathers. Otherwise, I will come and strike the land with a curse."

PSALM 150:1-6

¹ Hallelujah!
Praise God in His sanctuary.
Praise Him in His mighty heavens.
² Praise Him for His powerful acts;
praise Him for His abundant greatness.

³ Praise Him with trumpet blast;
praise Him with harp and lyre.
⁴ Praise Him with tambourine and dance;
praise Him with flute and strings.
⁵ Praise Him with resounding cymbals;
praise Him with clashing cymbals.

⁶ Let everything that breathes praise the LORD.
Hallelujah!

PROVERBS 31:30-31

³⁰ Charm is deceptive and beauty is fleeting,
but a woman who fears the LORD will be praised.
³¹ Give her the reward of her labor,
and let her works praise her at the city gates.

REVELATION 22:1-21

22 Then he showed me the river of living water, sparkling like crystal, flowing from the throne of God and of the Lamb ² down the middle of the broad street of the city. On both sides of the river was the tree of life bearing 12 kinds of fruit, producing its fruit every month. The leaves of the tree are for healing the nations, ³ and there will no longer be any curse. The throne of God and of the Lamb will be in the city, and His servants will serve Him. ⁴ They will

see His face, and His name will be on their foreheads. ⁵ Night will no longer exist, and people will not need lamplight or sunlight, because the Lord God will give them light. And they will reign forever and ever.

⁶ Then he said to me, "These words are faithful and true. And the Lord, the God of the spirits of the prophets, has sent His angel to show His servants what must quickly take place."

⁷ "Look, I am coming quickly! Blessed is the one who keeps the prophetic words of this book."

⁸ I, John, am the one who heard and saw these things. When I heard and saw them, I fell down to worship at the feet of the angel who had shown them to me. ⁹ But he said to me, "Don't do that! I am a fellow slave with you, your brothers the prophets, and those who keep the words of this book. Worship God." ¹⁰ He also said to me, "Don't seal the prophetic words of this book, because the time is near. ¹¹ Let the unrighteous go on in unrighteousness; let the filthy go on being made filthy; let the righteous go on in righteousness; and let the holy go on being made holy."

¹² "Look! I am coming quickly, and My reward is with Me to repay each person according to what he has done. ¹³ I am the Alpha and the Omega, the First and the Last, the Beginning and the End.

¹⁴ "Blessed are those who wash their robes, so that they may have the right to the tree of life and may enter the city by the gates. ¹⁵ Outside are the dogs, the sorcerers, the sexually immoral, the murderers, the idolaters, and everyone who loves and practices lying.

¹⁶ "I, Jesus, have sent My angel to attest these things to you for the churches. I am the Root and the Offspring of David, the Bright Morning Star."

¹⁷ Both the Spirit and the bride say, "Come!" Anyone who hears should say, "Come!" And the one who is thirsty should come. Whoever desires should take the living water as a gift.

¹⁸ I testify to everyone who hears the prophetic words of this book: If anyone adds to them, God will add to him the plagues that are written in this book. ¹⁹ And if anyone takes away from the words of this prophetic book, God will take away his share of the tree of life and the holy city, written in this book.

²⁰ He who testifies about these things says, "Yes, I am coming quickly." Amen! Come, Lord Jesus!

²¹ The grace of the Lord Jesus be with all the saints. Amen.

Commending Our Savior

At that time those who feared the LORD spoke to one another.
—MALACHI 3:16

It is vital to share Christ with others: experience and expression are the alternate beats of the Christian heart. And if these two things are not in operation, the Christian heart ceases to beat. Then what happens? We settle down to dead forms, dead attitudes, and dead prayers.

This matter of sharing, however, must not be limited only to evangelism. It applies also to sharing with other Christians the things God has shared with us.

If God has shown you something today from His Word, then it is imperative that you share it with another Christian. As we have been saying, nothing is really ours until we share it— the expression will deepen the impression. So in seeking to stay spiritually fresh, discipline yourself to share appropriate issues with your Christian and non-Christian friends. Many do not do this. They are disciplined in their quiet time or their study of the Scriptures, but they have never disciplined themselves to share. Someone has defined a Christian as one who says by word or deed: "Let me commend my Savior to you." There is no better definition.

I saw a cartoon in a newspaper which showed a woman putting a garment around the shivering body of a little girl. Behind the woman stood Christ throwing a cloak around her shoulders. The title of the cartoon was this: "A proven assembly line." It is indeed. Give out to others, and it will be given to you—pressed down and running over. Especially running over.

Prayer

Father, I reach up to You with one hand and reach out to those in need with the other. Give me some word or message to pass on to a non-Christian or one of my Christian brothers or sisters this day. In Jesus' name. Amen.

Further Study

Jr 20:1-9; Ac 4:20; 2 Co 4:13
What was Jeremiah's confession?
What does believing produce?

TITLES BY
SELWYN HUGHES

Selwyn Hughes is founder of **Crusade for World Revival**, an international publishing and training ministry designed to apply God's Word to everyday life and relationships. *Every Day with Jesus* has been the banner of his daily devotional writings for 40 years, enjoyed by over 750,000 people around the world daily.

THE SEVEN LAWS OF
SPIRITUAL SUCCESS

Having spent a lifetime in Christian ministry, Selwyn Hughes has discovered there are key elements in the Chrisitan life that are more than just principles —they are laws. *The Seven Laws of Spiritual Success* draws parallels between the laws of nature and those laws essential for a successful Chrisitan life.

The seven laws are:
First Things First
Count Your Blessings
Keep on Keeping On
Remember to Forget
Give Yourself to Others
Stay Close to God
Cultivate Your Soul

This book is a refined presentation of Selwyn Hughes' most powerful Biblical observations.

Available Summer 2005

EVERY DAY
WITH
JESUS®
~
Devotional Collection

His devotional writings have resonated with readers for 40 years. They come from a well that's being constantly nourished and replenished by the truths of God's Word. These vital truths, arranged in thematic groupings, never tire but continue to satisfy.

And now we're making Hughes' classic expressions of God's love and provision more readily available than ever, presented in two-month samplings of style and substance that are a daily treat to enjoy and a true blessing to share.

~

THE ARMOR OF GOD
0-8054-3079-2 $3.99

STAYING SPIRITUALLY
FRESH
0-8054-3080-6 $3.99

THE CHARACTER
OF GOD
0-8054-2737-6 $3.99

HIND'S FEET,
HIGH PLACES
0-8054-3088-1 $3.99

THE LORD'S PRAYER
0-8054-2735-X $3.99

THE SPIRIT-FILLED LIFE
0-8054-2736-8 $3.99

EVERY DAY LIGHT
DEVOTIONALS

Selwyn Hughes joins forces with renown painters Thomas Kinkade and Larry Dyke for the popular and endearing *Every Day Light* series of daily devotionals. Powerful, inspirational, and moving paintings, and Hughes' tender, wise and insightful commentaries lead readers on a daily walk with their Creator.

EVERY DAY LIGHT
WITH PAINTINGS BY
THOMAS KINKADE
0-8054-0188-1
$19.99

EVERY DAY LIGHT
DEVOTIONAL JOURNAL
0-8054-3309-0
$14.99

WATER FOR THE SOUL
WITH PAINTINGS BY THOMAS KINKADE
0-8054-1774-5 $19.99

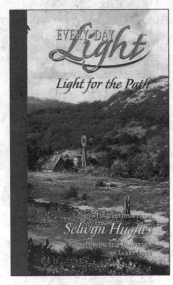

LIGHT FOR THE PATH
WITH PAINTINGS
BY LARRY DYKE
0-8054-2143-2 $19.99

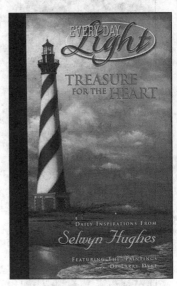

TREASURE FOR THE HEART
WITH PAINTINGS
BY LARRY DYKE
0-8054-2428-8 $19.99

SELWYN HUGHES
SIGNATURE SERIES

~

The Selwyn Hughes Signature Series is based on Hughes' popular *"Every Day with Jesus"* devotionals. His daily inspirations help believers establish meaningful relationships with people, both inside and outside the church, and instill the courage and strength needed to freely care for all people. The readings in each volume include devotionals, a pertinent Bible passage, Selwyn Hughes' own notes and commentary, and a prayer for daily meditation.

BORN TO PRAISE
0-8054-2091-6 $14.99

GOD—THE ENOUGH
0-8054-2372-9 $14.99

DISCOVERING LIFE'S
GREATEST PURPOSE
0-8054-2323-0 $14.99

PRAYER—
THE GREATEST POWER
0-8054-2349-4 $14.99

HOPE ETERNAL
ENCOURAGING WORDS FOR DISCOURAGING TIMES

Designed as a 40-day devotional guide, readers are treated not only to the encouraging words of renowned author Selwyn Hughes but also encouraged to journal their own thoughts. *Hope Eternal* also offers suggestions for incorporating quiet time in a busy life, ways to enrich quiet time, a 52-week guide for reading through the Bible and a section on how to experience new life in Christ.

0-8054-1767-2 $14.99

~

JESUS
THE LIGHT OF THE WORLD
WITH PAINTINGS BY LARRY DIKE

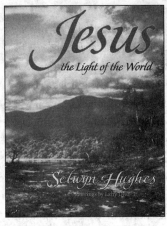

Larry Dyke's vibrant paintings and Selwyn Hughes' wise, reassuring words converge in this spiritually enriching book that brings the gentle yet all-powerful presence of Jesus Christ into high relief. The nature of God, the meaning of life, the mysteries of death, the reason for pain and suffering – Hughes addresses the five most-often questioned issues that touch us most deeply, and offers comforting words of encouragement. Dyke's magnificent paintings give each concept new dimension and emotional impact.

0-8054-2089-4 $14.99

CHRIST EMPOWERED LIVING
CELEBRATING YOUR SIGNIFICANCE IN GOD

A culmination of his life's work, Selwyn Hughes' *Christ Empowered Living* delves into the fundamental questions of human personality to reveal the reverberating havoc sin has reeked on humankind since Eden. But from the mire of human sinfulness, God's perfect plan of redemption has always been at work, and the power found in the wisdom of God's ways can serve as a spiritual road map when life is veering off course.

0-8054-2450-4 $17.99

WHY REVIVAL WAITS

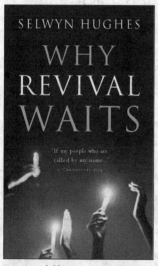

Available Summer 2005

Why does revivial not come when we want it? What is true revival? Can we help usher in revival?

"*...and My people who are called by My name humble themselves, pray and seek My face, and turn from their evil ways, then I will hear from heaven, forgive their sin, and heal their land.*"—II Chronicles 7:14

Why Revival Waits looks at what revival really is. Using "God's final and finished formula on the subject," the text of II Chronicles 7:14, Selwyn helps us discover what part we play in facing up to this challenge. Selwyn Hughes believes passionately that there is no greater issue facing the church of Jesus Christ at this time than the subject of Holy Spirit revival.

A DIARY OF REVIVAL
A CENTENARY CELEBRATION OF THE 1904 WELSH AWAKENING

by Kevin Adams
foreword by Selwyn Hughes

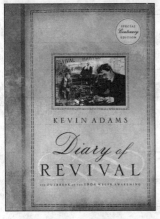

Using biography, newspaper accounts, and eyewitness testimonies to place the events in context, *A Diary of Revival* takes extracts from young evangelist Evan Robert's diary between September and November 1904 to paint a picture of the struggles and victories in the great Welsh Awakening.

0-8054-3195-0 $14.99

A PICTORIAL HISTORY OF REVIVAL
A CENTENARY CELEBRATION OF THE 1904 WELSH AWAKENING

by Kevin Adams and Emyr Jones; foreword by Selwyn Hughes

A Pictorial History of Revival is a companion volume to *A Diary of Revival* bringing a visual dimension and additional insights into this exciting movement of God.

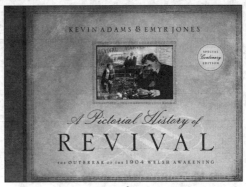

0-8054-3194-2 $24.99

NOTES

NOTES

NOTES

NOTES

NOTES

NOTES

NOTES

NOTES

NOTES

NOTES

NOTES

NOTES

NOTES

NOTES

NOTES

NOTES

NOTES